MAZDA

MAZDA 1987-92 REPAIR MANUAL

CHILTON'S

CHILTON BOOK COMPANY

ONE OF THE ***DIVERSIFIED PUBLISHING COMPANIES,*** *A PART OF* ***CAPITAL CITIES/ABC, INC.***

Manufactured in USA

Chilton Way Radnor, Pa. 19089
ISBN 0-8019-8264-2
Library of Congress Catalog Card No. 91-058871

4567890123 4321098765

Contents

Contents

SAFETY NOTICE

Proper service and repair procedures are vital to the safe, reliable operation of all motor vehicles, as well as the personal safety of those performing repairs. This manual outlines procedures for servicing and repairing vehicles using safe, effective methods. The procedures contain many NOTES, CAUTIONS and WARNINGS which should be followed along with standard safety procedures to eliminate the possibility of personal injury or improper service which could damage the vehicle or compromise its safety.

It is important to note that the repair procedures and techniques, tools and parts for servicing motor vehicles, as well as the skill and experience of the individual performing the work vary widely. It is not possible to anticipate all of the conceivable ways or conditions under which vehicles may be serviced, or to provide cautions as to all of the possible hazards that may result. Standard and accepted safety precautions and equipment should be used when handling toxic or flammable fluids, and safety goggles or other protection should be used during cutting, grinding, chiseling, prying, or any other process that can cause material removal or projectiles.

Some procedures require the use of tools specially designed for a specific purpose. Before substituting another tool or procedure, you must be completely satisfied that neither your personal safety, nor the performance of the vehicle will be endangered.

Although information in this manual is based on industry sources and is complete as possible at the time of publication, the possibility exists that some car manufacturers made later changes which could not be included here. While striving for total accuracy, Chilton Book Company cannot assume responsibility for any errors, changes or omissions that may occur in the compilation of this data.

PART NUMBERS

Part numbers listed in this reference are not recommendations by Chilton for any product by brand name. They are references that can be used with interchange manuals and aftermarket supplier catalogs to locate each brand supplier's discrete part number.

SPECIAL TOOLS

Special tools are recommended by the vehicle manufacturer to perform their specific job. Use has been kept to a minimum, but where absolutely necessary, they are referred to in the text by the part number of the tool manufacturer. These tools can be purchased, under the appropriate part number, from your Mazda dealer or regional distributor, or an equivalent tool can be purchased locally from a tool supplier or parts outlet. Before substituting any tool for the one recommended, read the SAFETY NOTICE at the top of this page.

ACKNOWLEDGMENTS

The Chilton Book Company expresses appreciation to Mazda Motors of America (East), Inc., Jacksonville, FL and Toyo Kogyo Co., Ltd., Hiroshima, Japan for their generous assistance.

1 GENERAL INFORMATION AND MAINTENANCE

HOW TO USE THIS BOOK

Chilton's Total Car Care for Mazda Pickups, Navajo and MPV is intended to help you learn more about the inner workings of your truck and save you money on its upkeep and operation.

The first two Sections will be the most used, since they contain maintenance and tune-up information and procedures. Studies have shown that a properly tuned and maintained truck can get at least 10% better gas mileage (which translates into lower operating costs) and periodic maintenance will catch minor problems before they turn into major repair bills. The other Sections deal with the more complex systems of your truck. Operating systems from engine through brakes are covered to the extent that the average do-it-yourselfer becomes mechanically involved. This book will give you the detailed instructions to help you change your own brake pads and shoes, tune-up the engine, replace spark plugs and filters, and do many more repair operations that will save you money, give you personal satisfaction and help you avoid expensive problems.

A secondary purpose of this book is a reference guide for owners who want to understand their truck and/or their mechanics better. In this case, no tools at all are required. Knowing just what a particular repair job requires in parts and labor effort will allow you to evaluate whether or not you're getting a fair price quote and help decipher itemized bills from a repair shop.

Before attempting any repairs or service on your truck, read through the entire procedure outlined in the appropriate section. This will give you the overall view of what tools and supplies will be required. There is nothing more frustrating than having to walk to the bus stop on Monday morning because you were short one gasket on Sunday afternoon. So read ahead and plan ahead. Each operation should be approached logically and all procedures thoroughly understood before attempting any work. Some special tools that may be required can often be rented from local automotive jobbers or places specializing in renting tools and equipment. Check the yellow pages of your phone book.

All sections contain adjustments, maintenance, removal and installation procedures, and overhaul procedures. When overhaul is not considered practical, we tell you how to remove the failed part and then how to install the new or rebuilt replacement. In this way, you at least save the labor costs. Backyard overhaul of some components (such as the alternator or water pump) is just not practical, but the removal and installation procedure is often simple and well within the capabilities of the average truck owner.

Two basic mechanic's rules should be mentioned here. First, whenever the LEFT side of the truck or engine is referred to, it is meant to specify the DRIVER'S side of the truck. Conversely, the RIGHT side of the truck means the PASSENGER'S side. Second, all screws and bolts are removed by turning counterclockwise, and tightened by turning clockwise.

Safety is always the most important rule. Constantly be aware of the dangers involved in working on or around an automobile and take proper precautions to avoid the risk of personal injury, or damage to the vehicle. See the page(s) in this section "Servicing Your Vehicle Safely" and the SAFETY NOTICE on the acknowledgment page before attempting any service procedures and pay attention to the instructions provided. There are 3 common mistakes in mechanical work:

1. Incorrect order of assembly, disassembly or adjustment. When taking something apart or putting it together, doing things in the wrong order usually just costs you extra time; however it CAN break something. Read the entire procedure before beginning disassembly. Do everything in the order in which the instructions say you should do it, even if you can't immediately see a reason for it. When you're taking apart something that is very intricate (for example a carburetor), you might want to draw a picture of how it looks when assembled at one point in order to make sure you get everything back in its proper position. We will supply exploded views whenever possible, but sometimes the job requires more attention to detail than an illustration provides. When making adjustments (especially tune-up adjustments), do them in order. One adjustment often affects another and you cannot expect satisfactory results unless each adjustment is made only when it cannot be changed by any other.

2. Overtorquing (or undertorquing) nuts and bolts. While it is more common for overtorquing to cause damage, undertorquing can cause a fastener to vibrate loose and cause serious damage, especially when dealing with aluminum parts. Pay attention to torque specifications and utilize a torque wrench in assembly. If a torque figure is not available remember that, if you are using the right tool to do the job, you will probably not have to strain yourself to get a fastener tight enough. The pitch of most threads is so slight that the tension you put on the wrench will be multiplied many times in actual force on what you are tightening. A good example of how critical torque is can be seen in the case of spark plug installation, especially where you are putting the plug into an aluminum cylinder head. Too little torque can fail to crush the gasket, causing leakage of combustion gases and consequent overheating of the plug and engine parts. Too much torque can damage the threads or distort the plug, which changes the spark gap at the electrode. Since more and more manufacturers are using aluminum in their engine and chassis parts to save weight, a torque wrench should be in any serious do-it-yourselfer's tool box.

There are many commercial chemical products available for ensuring that fasteners won't come loose, even if they are not torqued just right (a very common brand is Loctite®). If you're worried about getting something together tight enough to hold, but loose enough to avoid mechanical damage during assembly, one of these products might offer substantial insurance. Read the label on the package and make sure the product is compatible with the materials, fluids, etc. involved before choosing one.

3. Crossthreading. This occurs when a part such as a bolt is screwed into a nut or casting at the wrong angle and forced, causing the threads to become damaged. Crossthreading is more likely to occur if access is difficult. It helps to clean and lubricate fasteners, and to start threading with the part to be installed going straight in, using your fingers. If you encounter resistance, unscrew the part and start over again at a different angle until it can be inserted and turned several times without much effort. Keep in mind that many parts, especially spark plugs, use tapered threads so that gentle turning will automatically bring the part you're threading to the proper angle if you don't force it or resist a change in angle. Don't put a wrench on the part until it's been turned in a couple of times by hand. If you suddenly encounter resistance and the part has not seated fully, don't force it. Remove it and make sure it's clean and threading properly.

Always take your time and be patient; once you have some experience, working on your truck will become an enjoyable hobby.

TOOLS AND EQUIPMENT

➧ SEE FIGS. 1-5

Naturally, without the proper tools and equipment it is impossible to properly service your vehicle. It would be impossible to catalog each tool that you would need to perform each or every operation in this book. It would also be unwise for the amateur to rush out and buy an expensive set of tools an the theory that he may need one or more of them at sometime.

The best approach is to proceed slowly, gathering together a good quality set of those tools that are used most frequently. Don't be misled by the low cost of bargain tools. It is far better to spend a little more for better quality. Forged wrenches, 6- or 12-point sockets and fine tooth ratchets are by far preferable to their less expensive counterparts. As any good mechanic can tell you, there are few worse experiences than trying to work on a truck with bad tools. Your monetary savings will be far outweighed by frustration and mangled knuckles.

Begin accumulating those tools that are used most frequently; those associated with routine maintenance and tune-up.

In addition to the normal assortment of screwdrivers and pliers you should have the following tools for routine maintenance jobs (your Mazda, depending on the model year, uses both SAE and metric fasteners):

1. SAE and Metric wrenches, sockets and combination open end/box end wrenches in sizes from $^1/_8$ in. (3mm) to $^3/_4$ in. (19mm); and the correct size spark plug socket ($^5/_8$ in. or $^{13}/_{16}$ in.). If possible, buy various length socket drive extensions. One break in this department is that the metric sockets available in the U.S. will all fit the ratchet handles and extensions you may already have ($^1/_4$ in., $^3/_8$ in., and $^1/_2$ in. drive).
2. Jackstands for support
3. Oil filter wrench
4. Oil filter spout for pouring oil
5. Grease gun for chassis lubrication
6. Hydrometer for checking the battery
7. A container for draining oil
8. Many rags for wiping up the inevitable mess.

In addition to the above items there are several others that are not absolutely necessary, but handy to have around. These include oil-dry, a transmission funnel and the usual supply of lubricants, antifreeze and fluids, although these can be purchased as needed. This is a basic list for routine maintenance, but only your personal needs and desires can accurately determine your list of necessary tools.

The second list of tools is for tune-ups. While the tools involved here are slightly more sophisticated, they need not be outrageously expensive. There are several inexpensive tachometers on the market that are every bit as good for the average mechanic as a "professional" model. Just be sure that it works on 4-, 6- and 8-cylinder engines. A basic list of tune-up equipment could include:

1. Tachometer
2. Spark plug wrench
3. Timing light with induction pick-up that is powered by the truck's battery is best.
4. Wire spark plug gauge/adjusting tools
5. Set of feeler blades.

In addition to these basic tools, there are several other tools and gauges you may find useful. These include:

1. A compression gauge. The screw-in type is slower to use, but eliminates the possibility of a faulty reading due to escaping pressure
2. A manifold vacuum gauge
3. A test light
4. An induction meter. This is used for determining whether or not there is current in a wire. These are handy for use if a wire is broken somewhere in a wiring harness.

As a final note, you will probably find a torque wrench necessary for all but the most basic work. The beam type models are perfectly adequate, although the newer click (breakaway) type are more precise, and you don't have to crane your neck to see a torque reading in awkward situations. The breakaway torque wrenches are more expensive and should be recalibrated periodically.

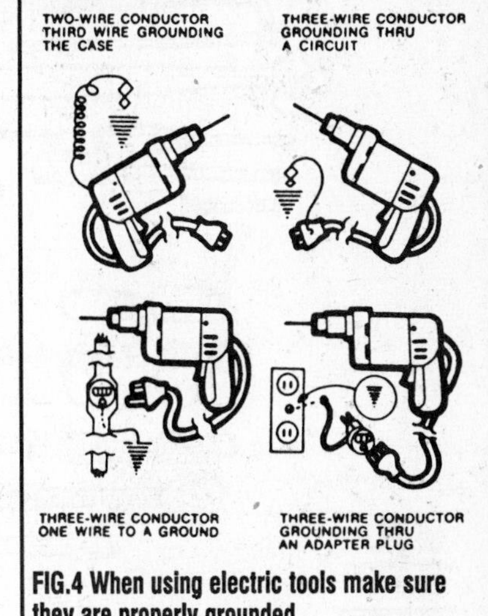

FIG.4 When using electric tools make sure they are properly grounded

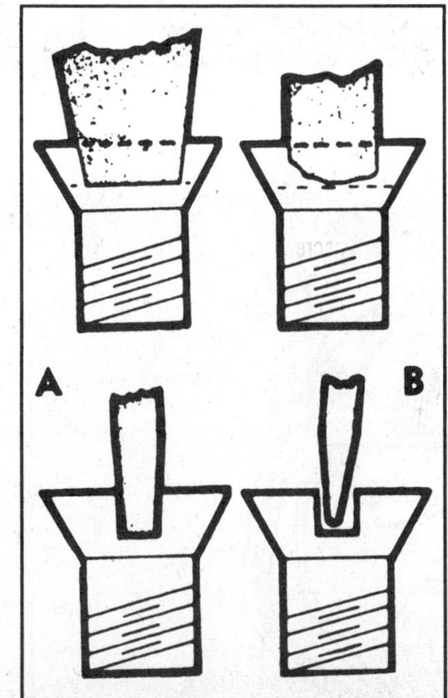

FIG.2 Keep screwdriver tips in good shape. They should fit the slot as shown in "A". If they look like those in "B", they need grinding or replacing

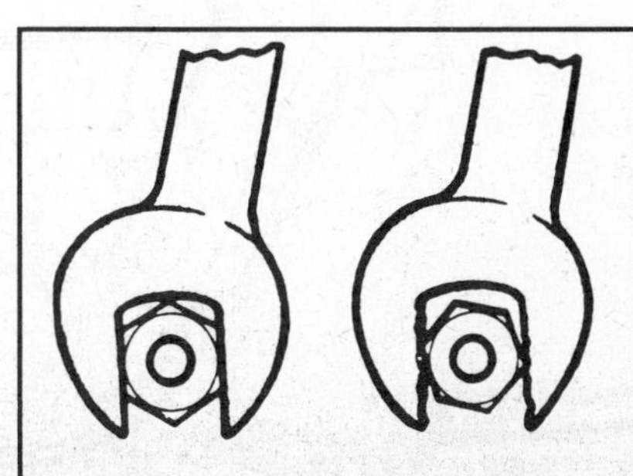

FIG.3 When you're using an open end wrench, use the correct size and position it properly on the flats of the nut or bolt

FIG.5 Always use jackstands when working under your vehicle

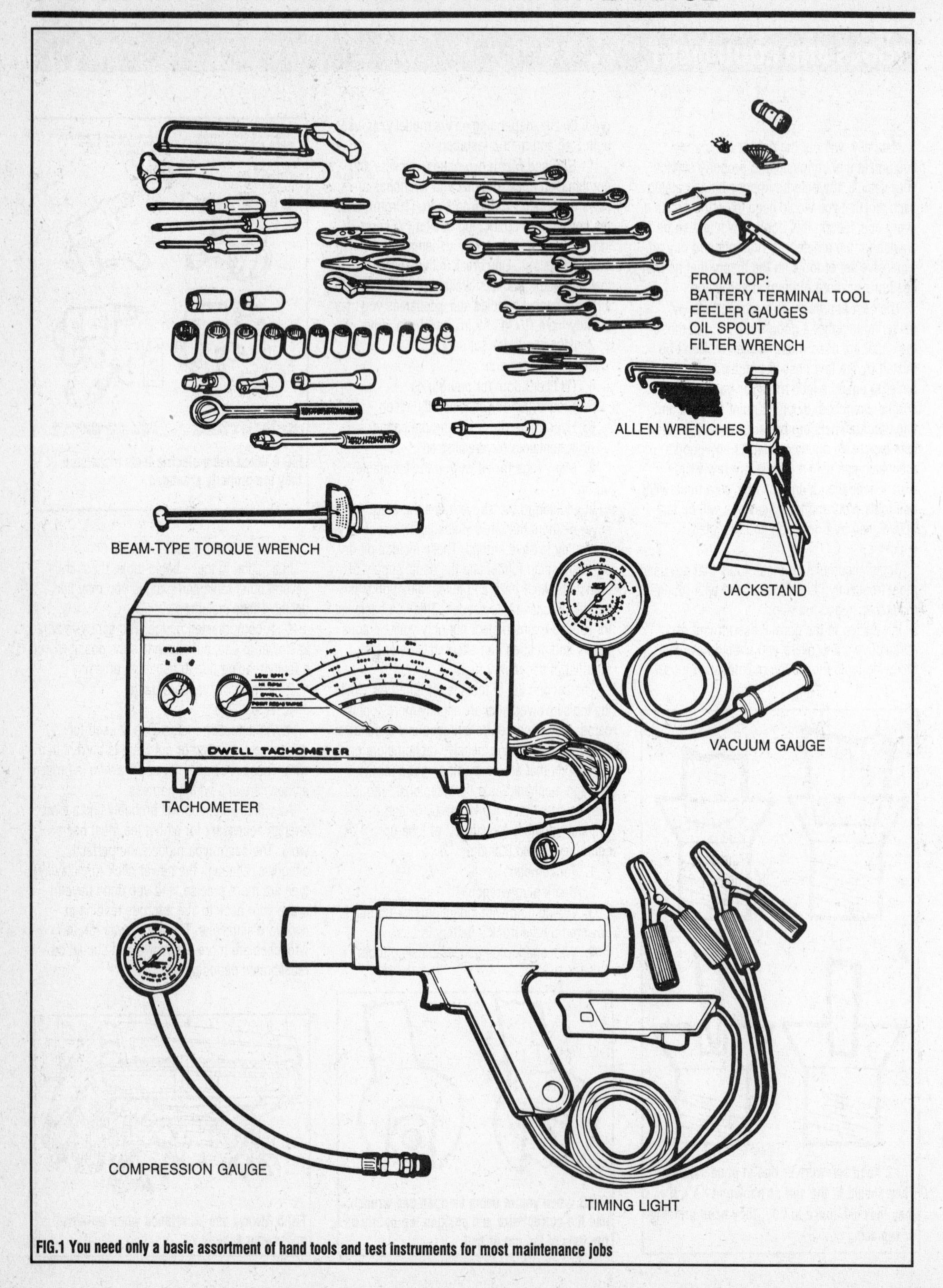

FIG.1 You need only a basic assortment of hand tools and test instruments for most maintenance jobs

Torque specification for each fastener will be given in the procedure in any case that a specific torque value is required. If no torque specifications are given, use the following values as a guide, based upon fastener size:

Bolts marked 6T

6mm bolt/nut — 5-7 ft. lbs.
8mm bolt/nut — 12-17 ft. lbs.
10mm bolt/nut — 23-34 ft. lbs.
12mm bolt/nut — 41-59 ft. lbs.
14mm bolt/nut — 56-76 ft. lbs.

Bolts marked 8T

6mm bolt/nut — 6-9 ft. lbs.
8mm bolt/nut — 13-20 ft. lbs.
10mm bolt/nut — 27-40 ft. lbs.
12mm bolt/nut — 46-69 ft. lbs.
14mm bolt/nut — 75-101 ft. lbs.

Special Tools

Normally, the use of special factory tools is avoided for repair procedures, since these are not readily available for the do-it-yourself mechanic. When it is possible to perform the job with more commonly available tools, it will be pointed out, but occasionally, a special tool was designed to perform a specific function and should be used. Before substituting another tool, you should be convinced that neither your safety nor the performance of the vehicle will be compromised.

Some special tools are available commercially from major tool manufacturers. Others can be purchased from your car dealer. In most cases where a tool is designed for a particular job on a particular car model and therefore made available through the dealer network, you can also purchase a similar tool at an automotive parts store or elsewhere. You might want to give the factory part number to not only your dealer but to other sources and shop competitively for the item you need.

➡ **Special tools are occasionally necessary to perform a specific job or are recommended to make a job easier. Their use has been kept to a minimum. When a special tool is indicated, it will be referred to by manufacturer's part number, and, where possible, an illustration of the tool will be provided so that an equivalent tool may be used.**

SERVICING YOUR VEHICLE SAFELY

It is virtually impossible to anticipate all of the hazards involved with automotive maintenance and service, but care and common sense will prevent most accidents.

The rules of safety for mechanics range from "don't smoke around gasoline," to "use the proper tool for the job." The trick to avoiding injuries is to develop safe work habits and take every possible precaution.

Dos

- Do keep a fire extinguisher and first aid kit within easy reach.
- Do wear safety glasses or goggles when cutting, drilling or prying, even if you have 20–20 vision. If you wear glasses for the sake of vision, they should be made of hardened glass that can also serve as safety glasses, or wear safety goggles over your regular glasses.
- Do shield your eyes whenever you work around the battery. Batteries contain sulphuric acid; in case of contact with the eyes or skin, flush the area with water or a mixture of water and baking soda and get medical attention immediately.
- Do use safety stands for any undertruck service. Jacks are for raising vehicles; safety stands are for making sure the vehicle stays raised until you want it to come down. Whenever the vehicle is raised, block the wheels remaining on the ground and set the parking brake.
- Do use adequate ventilation when working with any chemicals. Like carbon monoxide, the asbestos dust resulting from brake lining wear can be poisonous in sufficient quantities.
- Do disconnect the negative battery cable when working on the electrical system. The primary ignition system can contain up to 40,000 volts.
- Do follow manufacturer's directions whenever working with potentially hazardous materials. Both brake fluid and antifreeze are poisonous if taken internally.
- Do properly maintain your tools. Loose hammerheads, mushroomed punches and chisels, frayed or poorly grounded electrical cords, excessively worn screwdrivers, spread wrenches (open end), cracked sockets, slipping ratchets, or faulty droplight sockets can cause accidents.
- Do use the proper size and type of tool for the job being done.
- Do when possible, pull on a wrench handle rather than push on it, and adjust your stance to prevent a fall.
- Do be sure that adjustable wrenches are tightly adjusted on the nut or bolt and pulled so that the face is on the side of the fixed jaw.
- Do select a wrench or socket that fits the nut or bolt. The wrench or socket should sit straight, not cocked.
- Do strike squarely with a hammer — avoid glancing blows.
- Do set the parking brake and block the drive wheels if the work requires that the engine be running.

Don'ts

- Don't run an engine in a garage or anywhere else without proper ventilation — EVER! Carbon monoxide is poisonous; it takes a long time to leave the human body and you can build up a deadly supply of it in your system by simply breathing in a little every day. You may not realize you are slowly poisoning yourself. Always use power vents, windows, fans or open the garage doors.
- Don't work around moving parts while wearing a necktie or other loose clothing. Short sleeves are much safer than long, loose sleeves and hard-toed shoes with neoprene soles protect your toes and give a better grip on slippery surfaces. Jewelry such as watches, fancy belt buckles, beads or body adornment of any kind is not safe working around a truck. Long hair should be hidden under a hat or cap.
- Don't use pockets for toolboxes. A fall or bump can drive a screwdriver deep into you body. Even a wiping cloth hanging from the back pocket can wrap around a spinning shaft or fan.
- Don't smoke when working around gasoline, cleaning solvent or other flammable material.
- Don't smoke when working around the battery. When the battery is being charged, it gives off explosive hydrogen gas.

• Don't use gasoline to wash your hands; there are excellent soaps available. Gasoline may contain lead, and lead can enter the body through a cut, accumulating in the body until you are very ill. Gasoline also removes all the natural oils from the skin so that bone dry hands will suck up oil and grease.

• Don't service the air conditioning system unless you are equipped with the necessary tools and training. The refrigerant, R-12, is extremely cold and when exposed to the air, will instantly freeze any surface it comes in contact with, including your eyes. Although the refrigerant is normally non-toxic, R-12 becomes a deadly poisonous gas in the presence of an open flame. One good whiff of the vapors from burning refrigerant can be fatal.

SERIAL NUMBER IDENTIFICATION

➧ SEE FIGS. 6-9

Vehicle/Chassis Number

Pickups

The chassis number is stamped on the front of the right frame member, visible from the engine compartment.

MPV

The serial number is stamped on a plate located on the driver's side windshield pillar and is visible through the glass.

Navajo

A 17 digit combination of numbers and letters forms the vehicle identification number (VIN). The VIN is stamped on a metal tab that is riveted to the instrument panel close to the windshield. The VIN plate is visible by looking through the windshield on the driver's side. The VIN number is also found on the Safety Compliance Certification Label which is described below.

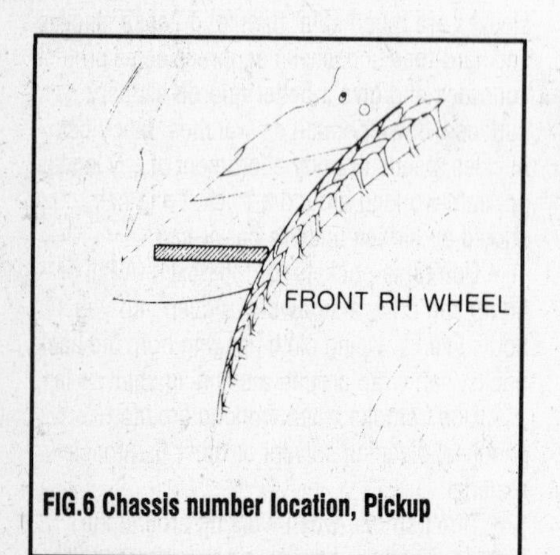

FIG.6 Chassis number location, Pickup

Engine Number

Pickup

The engine number is located on a machined pad on the left front of the block, just behind the distributor.

MPV

The engine number is located on a machined pad extending from the cylinder block just below No. 1 spark plug.

Navajo

The engine identification code is a letter located in the eighth digit of the Vehicle Identification Number stamped on a metal tab that is riveted to the instrument panel close to the windshield. Specific engine data is located on a label attached to the timing cover.

Model Plate

The model plate, containing the truck model, engine model, engine displacement and chassis number is riveted to the right rear corner of the engine compartment on the firewall.

Motor Vehicle Safety Certification Label

This label is attached to the left door lock pillar and proclaims the fact that the truck conforms to all necessary safety regulations in effect at the time of manufacture.

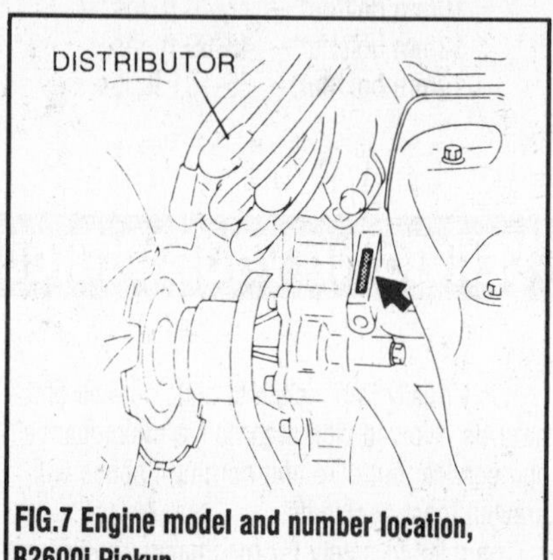

FIG.7 Engine model and number location, B2600i Pickup

Emission Control Certification Label

This label is found attached to the right hand panel of the engine compartment, and states that the truck conforms to the emission regulations for the country of destination.

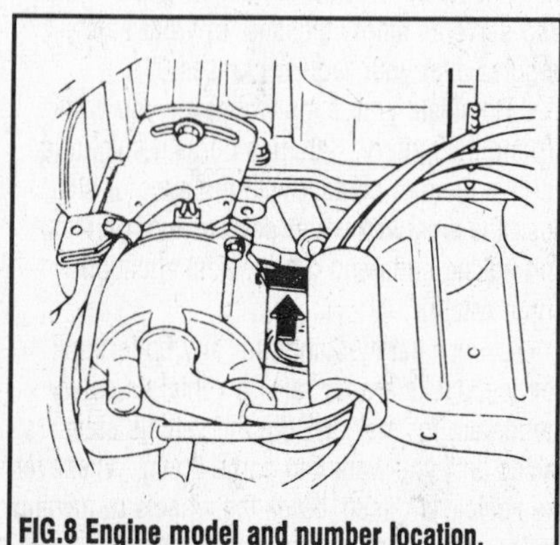

FIG.8 Engine model and number location, B2200 Pickup

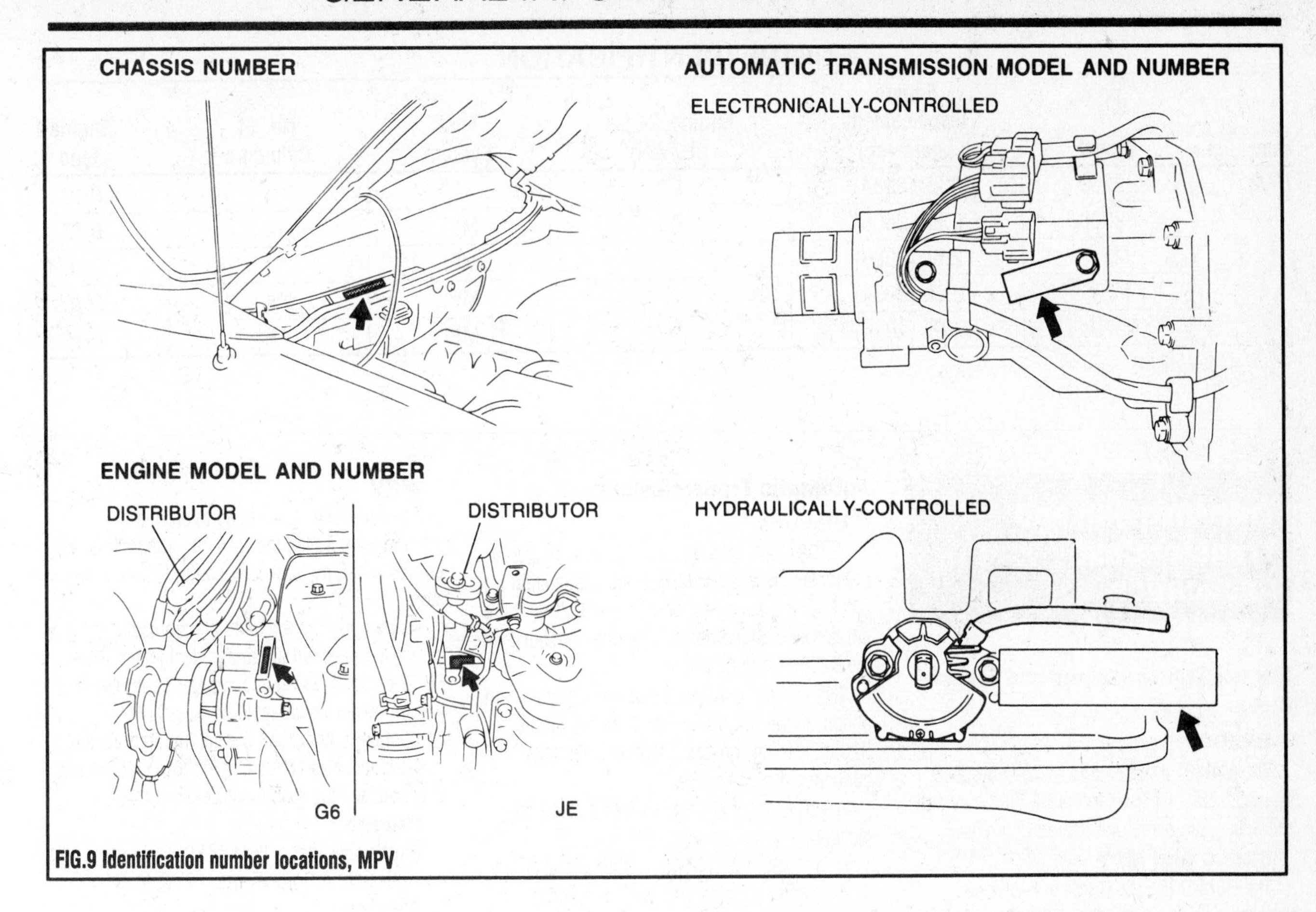

FIG.9 Identification number locations, MPV

ENGINE IDENTIFICATION

Year	Model	Engine Displacement Liters (cc)	Engine Series (ID/VIN)	Fuel System	No. of Cylinders	Engine Type
1987	B2200	2.2L (2184)	F2	2 bbl	4	OHC
	B2600	2.6L (2555)	G54B	2 bbl	4	OHC
1988	B2200	2.2L (2184)	F2	2 bbl	4	OHC
	B2600	2.6L (2555)	G54B	2 bbl	4	OHC
1989	B2200	2.2L (2184)	F2	2 bbl	4	OHC
	B2600i	2.6L (2555)	G6	MPI	4	OHC
	MPV	2.6L (2606)	G6	MPI	4	OHC
	MPV	3.0L (2954)	JE	MPI	6	OHC
1990	B2200	2.2L (2184)	F2	①	4	OHC
	B2600i	2.6L (2606)	G6	MPI	4	OHC
	MPV	2.6L (2606)	G6	MPI	4	OHC
	MPV	3.0L (2954)	JE	MPI	6	OHC
1991	B2200	2.2L (2184)	F2	①	4	OHC
	B2600i	2.6L (2606)	G6	MPI	4	OHC
	MPV	2.6L (2606)	G6	MPI	4	OHC
	MPV	3.0L (2954)	JE	MPI	6	OHC
	Navajo	4.0L (4016)	X	MPI	6	OHV

ENGINE IDENTIFICATION

Year	Model	Engine Displacement Liters (cc)	Engine Series (ID/VIN)	Fuel System	No. of Cylinders	Engine Type
1992	B2200	2.2L (2184)	F2	①	4	OHC
	B2600i	2.6L (2606)	G6	MPI	4	OHC
	MPV	2.6L (2606)	G6	MPI	4	OHC
	MPV	3.0L (2954)	JE	MPI	6	OHC
	Navajo	4.0L (4016)	X	MPI	6	OHV

① Except CA.—2 bbl
CA.—MPI

Transmission and Transfer Case Application

Manual Transmissions and Transfer Cases

B2200

The M4M-D 4-speed and M5M-D 5-speed transmissions are used in the B2200. They are essentially the same unit geared differently.

B2600 and MPV

The R5M-D (R5MX-D w/4×4) 5-speed transmission are used in the B2600 and MPV. A transfer case is attached to the five speed unit on 4×4 models

Navajo

The Navajo uses the M50D 5-speed transmission. A Borg-Warner 13-54 transfer case is used.

Automatic Transmissions

Pickups

In 1987, a 3-speed lock-up torque converter transmission was introduced. Its designation is L3N71B. It was offered only on the B2200. There are no band adjustments. This unit continued on the B2200 through 1988.

Also in 1987 a 4-speed unit was offered as an option on the B2200 and as standard on the B2600. It is designated L4N71B. This unit continues through 1988.

In 1989, only the L4N71B was offered on pickups.

From 1990, the N4A-HL 4-speed is used on all 4-cylinder pickups and 2WD 6-cylinder pickups. 4WD 6-cylinder pickups use the electronically controlled R4AX-EL 4-speed.

MPV

The MPV uses a 4-speed overdrive transmission called the N4A-HL. This unit is a conventional, hydraulically controlled transmission.

As an option, there is an electronically controlled 4-speed automatic designated R4A-EL. The transmission is computer controlled and has no owner serviceable or adjustable components other than the neutral start switch.

4-Wheel Drive MPVs use the R4AX-EL, which is essentially the same unit as the R4A-EL.

Navajo

The Navajo uses a Ford A4LD 4-speed transmission. A Borg-Warner 13-54 transfer case is used.

ROUTINE MAINTENANCE

Routine, or preventive maintenance is exactly as it implies; maintenance that is performed at suggested intervals that keeps small problems from becoming large ones. For example, it is much easier (and cheaper in the long run) to check the engine oil regularly than to have the engine run low on oil and damage the bearings (a major overhaul job). Read this section carefully and follow its recommendations closely for as close to optimum performance as possible.

Air Cleaner

➧ SEE FIGS. 10-13

The air cleaner uses a disposable paper element on carbureted and fuel injected engines. The air filter should be replaced at least every two years or 24,000–30,000 miles. If the car is driven in a dry and dusty climate, clean or replace the air filter twice as often. Inspect the air cleaner element for accumulations of dirt and oil and wipe the air cleaner housing with a cleaner. Replace the element as necessary.

If the engine is equipped with a carburetor, the air may be cleaned by directing low pressure air from the inside of the filter out.

FIG.10 Air cleaner and element, carburetor equipped

CAUTION

On fuel injection equipped engines, do not attempt to clean the air filter with low pressure air.

➡ In severe service, such as off-road use or in extremely dusty areas, the maintenance interval should be cut in half.

REMOVAL & INSTALLATION

Replacing the air cleaner element is a simple, routine maintenance operation. You should be careful, however, to keep dust and dirt out of the air cleaner housing, as they accelerate engine wear. If the outside of the air cleaner housing is dusty, wipe it with a clean rag before beginning work.

Carbureted Pickups

1. Remove the wing nut at the center of the housing and then unclip the retaining clips situated around the sides.
2. Pull the top cover off and remove the air cleaner element.
3. When installing the new element, make sure it seats squarely around the bulge in the center of the lower air cleaner housing. Install the housing top, turning it until the wing nut mounting stud lines up with the hole in the top (it's usually off center). Note that the top cover should seat tightly all around. Install the wing nut and reclip the clips.

Fuel Injected Pickups and MPV

1. Loosen the clamp on the air intake hose and pull the hose off the housing.
2. Disconnect the airflow sensor electrical connector.
3. Unbolt and remove the housing. Note the direction in which the element is installed and install the new element in the same way (it may be marked **TOP**). Install the top of the housing and connect the other components.

Navajo

1. Loosen the clamps that secure the hose assembly to the air cleaner.
2. Remove the screws that attach the air cleaner to the bracket.
3. Disconnect the hose and inlet tube from the air cleaner.
4. Remove the screws attaching the air cleaner cover.

FIG.11 On fuel injected models, remove the screws that hold down the top of the air cleaner

FIG.12 On fuel injected models, lift the cover from on top of the filter element

FIG.13 On fuel injected models, remove/install the air cleaner element

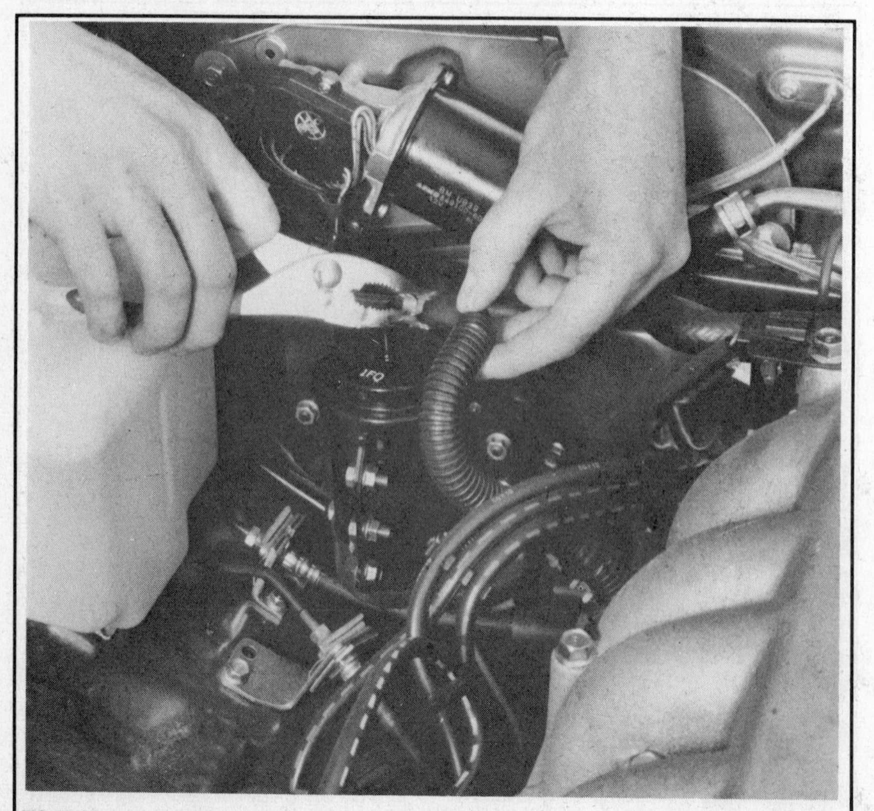

FIG.15 After releasing fuel system pressure, disconnect the fuel lines on models equipped with fuel injection, B2600i shown

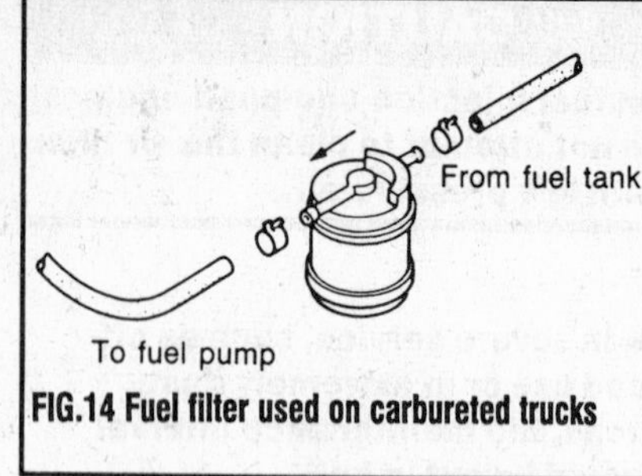

FIG.14 Fuel filter used on carbureted trucks

5. Remove the air filter and tubes.
6. Install the new element. Place the cover into position and install the retaining screws. Connect the other components. Don't overtighten the hose clamps! A torque of 12–15 inch lbs. is sufficient.

Fuel Filter

➧ SEE FIGS. 14-16

LOCATION

On the B2200 and 1987 B2600 models, it is located in the engine compartment, on the intake manifold side, next to the carbon canister.

On the 1988–92 B2600 and the Navajo, it is located on the right rear frame member, near the fuel tank.

On the MPV, it is located on the right fender well just below the battery.

REMOVAL & INSTALLATION

Carbureted Engines

To replace the filter, loosen the clamps at both ends of the filter and pull off the hoses. Pop the filter from its clamp.

Fuel Injected Engines

✱✱ CAUTION

RELIEVE THE FUEL SYSTEM PRESSURE BEFORE SERVICING ANY PART OF THE FUEL SYSTEM.

PICKUPS AND MPV

1. Relieve the pressure from the fuel system as described in "Relieving Fuel System Pressure" located in this section.
2. Disconnect the battery negative cable.
3. Slide the fuel line clamps back off the connections on the filter. Then, slowly pull one connection off just until fuel begins to seep out. Place a small plastic container or stuff a couple of rags under the filter to absorb any excess fuel.
4. Pull both fuel hoses off the connectors. Remove the filter from the clamp. On some models, it will be necessary to unbolt the fuel filter from the mounting bracket.
5. Place the new filter in the clamp or attach to the bracket if so equipped.
6. Connect the hoses to the filter connections and secure the hoses with the clamps.
7. Connect the negative battery cable.
8. Start the engine and check the fuel filter connections for leaks.

NAVAJO

1. Relieve the fuel system pressure as described below.
2. Raise and support the vehicle safely.
3. Remove the push connect fittings at both ends of fuel filter. Install new retainer clips in each push connect fitting.
4. Remove the filter from the bracket by loosening the filter retaining clamp enough to allow the filter to pass through.

➡ **The flow arrow direction should be positioned as installed in the bracket to ensure proper flow of fuel through the replacement filter.**

5. Install the filter in the bracket, ensuring proper direction of flow as noted by arrow. Tighten clamp to 15–25 inch lbs.
6. Install the push connect fittings at both ends of the filter.
7. Lower the vehicle.
8. Start the engine and check for leaks.

Clean all dirt and/or grease from the fuel filter fittings. "Quick Connect" fittings are used on models equipped with a pressurized fuel system. These fittings must be disconnected using the proper procedure or the fittings may be damaged. The fuel filter uses a "hairpin" clip retainer. Spread the two hairpin clip legs about 1/8 in. (3mm) each to disengage it from the fitting, then pull the clip outward. Use finger pressure only; do not use any tools. Push the quick connect fittings onto the filter ends. Mazda recommends that the retaining clips be replaced whenever removed. The fuel tubes used on these fuel systems are manufactured in 5/16 in. (8mm) and 3/8 in. (9.5mm) diameters. Each fuel tube takes a different size hairpin clip, so keep this in mind when purchasing new clips. A click will be heard when the hairpin clip snaps into its proper position. Pull on the lines with moderate pressure to ensure proper connection. Start the engine and check for fuel leaks. If the inertia switch (reset switch) was disconnected to relieve the fuel system pressure, cycle the ignition switch from the **OFF** to **ON** position several times to re-charge the fuel system before attempting to start the engine.

FIG.16 Removing the mounting bracket and filter, fuel injected models, B2600i shown

RELIEVING FUEL SYSTEM PRESSURE

All Fuel Injected Engines

Any time the fuel system is opened for maintenance, the fuel system pressure must be relieved first. On fuel injected engines, there is pressure in the fuel lines even when the engine is not running.

Pickups and MPV

1. Start the engine.
2. While the engine is running, disconnect the fuel pump or circuit opening relay connector(s).
3. Allow the engine to run until it stalls.
4. Reconnect the fuel pump or circuit opening relay connector(s).
5. Proceed with the fuel system repairs.

Whenever a connection is loosened, use rags to prevent fuel leakage. If a line or connection is to left open for an extended period of time, plug or cover it.

Navajo

Disconnect the electrical connector from the inertia switch (located under the instrument panel to the right of the transmission hump on the toe board) and crank the engine for about 15–30 seconds until it runs out of fuel and dies.

PCV Valve

The Positive Crankcase Ventilation (PCV) valve should be inspected for blockage periodically. It is located in the valve cover, connected to the intake manifold by a vacuum hose.

TESTING THE PCV VALVE

1. Warm the up the engine and allow it run at idle speed.
2. Disconnect the PCV valve with the ventilator hose from the valve cover.
3. Cover the valve opening with your finger and listen for a change in the idle speed.
4. If the idle speed drops, the valve is working properly. If the idle speed does not change, replace the valve.

REMOVAL & INSTALLATION

Simply pull the PCV valve from the grommet in the valve cover and remove the hose clamp. Then, pull it from the hose. Install the new valve and install the clamp.

➡ **If your engine exhibits lower than normal gas mileage and poor idle characteristics for no apparent reason, suspect the PCV valve. It is probably blocked and should be replaced.**

Evaporator Canister

REMOVAL & INSTALLATION

The evaporative canister is located under the hood in the engine compartment and is designed to store fuel vapors and prevent their escaping into the atmosphere. On early models, when the engine is not running, fuel that has evaporated into the condenser tank is returned to the fuel tank as the ambient temperatures rise and the vapors are condensed. Later models do not have a condenser tank. During periods when the engine is running, fuel vapor that has not condensed in the condenser tank moves to the carbon canister. The stored vapors are removed by fresh air through the bottom of the inlet hole and passed through the air cleaner to the combustion chamber. Because of the design of the system, the only maintenance associated with the canister is to replace it periodically as indicted in the Maintenance Interval charts.

Battery

➧ SEE FIGS. 17-22

Loose, dirty, or corroded battery terminals are a major cause of "no-start." Every 3 months or so, remove the battery terminals and clean them, giving them a light coating of petroleum jelly when you are finished. This will help to retard corrosion.

Check the battery cables for signs of wear or chafing and replace any cable or terminal that looks marginal. Battery terminals can be easily cleaned and inexpensive terminal cleaning tools are an excellent investment that will pay for themselves many times over. They can usually be purchased from any well equipped auto store or parts department. Side terminal batteries require a different tool to clean the threads in the battery case. The accumulated white powder and corrosion can be cleaned from the top of the battery with an old toothbrush and a solution of baking soda and water.

Unless you have a maintenance free battery, check the electrolyte level (see Battery under Fluid Level Checks in this section) and check the specific gravity of each cell. Be sure that the vent holes in each cell cap are not blocked by grease or dirt. The vent holes allow hydrogen gas, formed by the chemical reaction in the battery, to escape safely.

REPLACEMENT BATTERIES

The cold power rating of a battery measures battery starting performance and provides an approximate relationship between battery size and engine size. The cold power rating of a replacement battery should match or exceed your engine size in cubic inches.

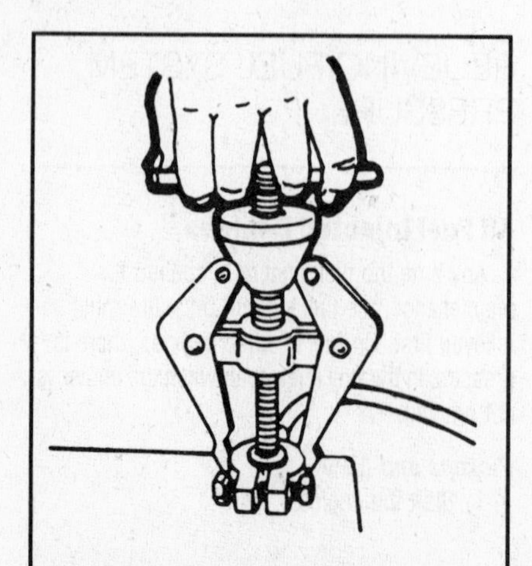

FIG.17 Top terminal battery cables can be removed with this inexpensive tool

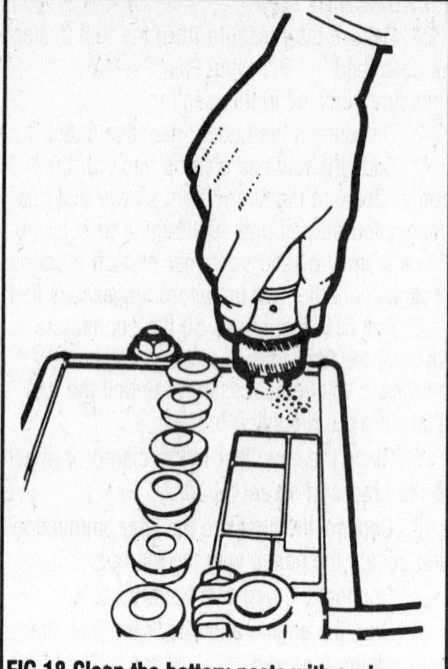

FIG.18 Clean the battery posts with a wire terminal cleaner

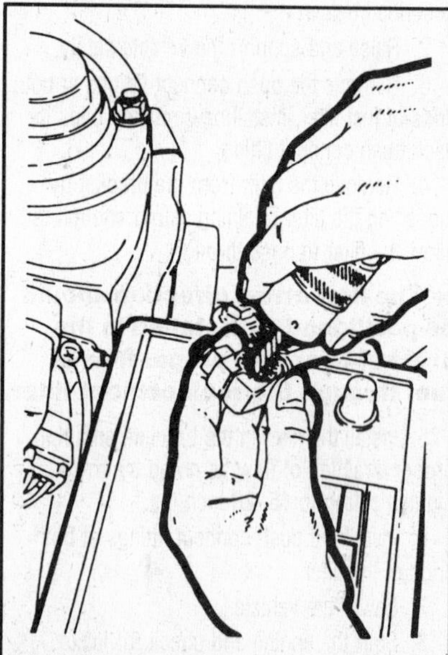

FIG.19 Clean the cable ends with a stiff wire cleaning tool

FLUID LEVEL EXCEPT MAINTENANCE FREE BATTERIES

Check the battery electrolyte level at least once a month, or more often in hot weather or during periods of extended truck operation. The level can be checked through the case on translucent polypropylene batteries; the cell caps must be removed on other models. The electrolyte level in each cell should be kept filled to the split ring inside, or the line marked on the outside of the case.

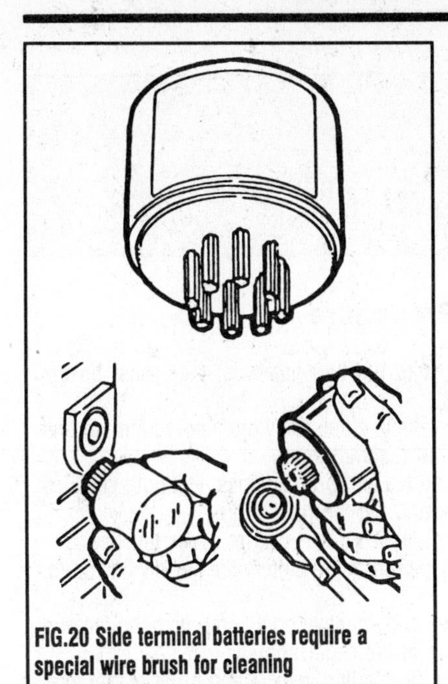
FIG.20 Side terminal batteries require a special wire brush for cleaning

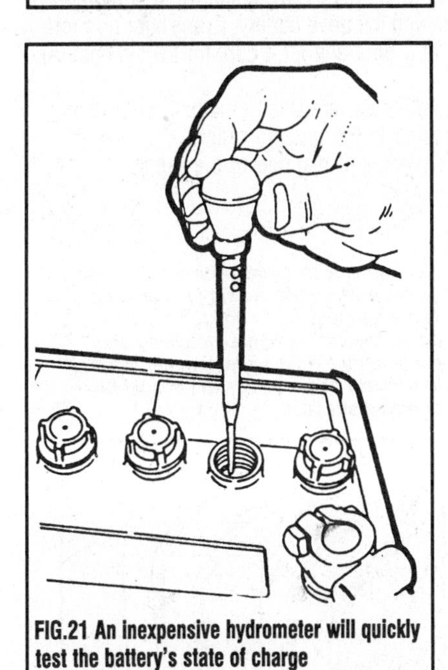
FIG.21 An inexpensive hydrometer will quickly test the battery's state of charge

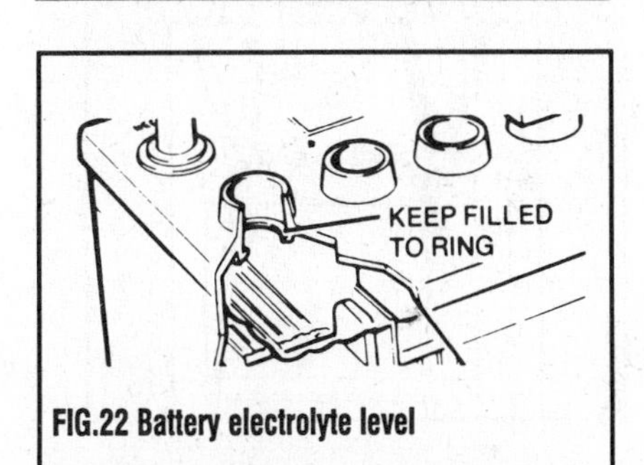

FIG.22 Battery electrolyte level

If the level is low, add only distilled water, or colorless, odorless drinking water, through the opening until the level is correct. Each cell is completely separate from the others, so each must be checked and filled individually.

If water is added in freezing weather, the truck should be driven several miles to allow the water to mix with the electrolyte. Otherwise, the battery could freeze.

SPECIFIC GRAVITY EXCEPT MAINTENANCE FREE BATTERIES

At least once a year, check the specific gravity of the battery. It should be between 1.20 in.Hg and 1.26 in.Hg at room temperature.

The specific gravity can be check with the use of an hydrometer, an inexpensive instrument available from many sources, including auto parts stores. The hydrometer has a squeeze bulb at one end and a nozzle at the other. Battery electrolyte is sucked into the hydrometer until the float is lifted from its seat. The specific gravity is then read by noting the position of the float. Generally, if after charging, the specific gravity between any two cells varies more than 50 points (0.50), the battery is bad and should be replaced.

It is not possible to check the specific gravity in this manner on sealed (maintenance free) batteries. Instead, the indicator built into the top of the case must be relied on to display any signs of battery deterioration. If the indicator is dark, the battery can be assumed to be OK. If the indicator is light, the specific gravity is low, and the battery should be charged or replaced.

CABLES AND CLAMPS

Once a year, the battery terminals and the cable clamps should be cleaned. Loosen the clamps and remove the cables, negative cable first. On batteries with posts on top, the use of a puller specially made for the purpose is recommended. These are inexpensive, and available in auto parts stores. Side terminal battery cables are secured with a bolt.

Clean the cable lamps and the battery terminal with a wire brush, until all corrosion, grease, etc., is removed and the metal is shiny. It is especially important to clean the inside of the clamp thoroughly, since a small deposit of foreign material or oxidation there will prevent a sound electrical connection and inhibit either starting or charging. Special tools are available for cleaning these parts, one type for conventional batteries and another type for side terminal batteries.

Before installing the cables, loosen the battery holddown clamp or strap, remove the battery and check the battery tray. Clear it of any debris, and check it for soundness. Rust should be wire brushed away, and the metal given a coat of anti-rust paint. Replace the battery and tighten the holddown clamp or strap securely, but be careful not to overtighten, which will crack the battery case.

After the clamps and terminals are clean, reinstall the cables, negative cable last; do not hammer on the clamps to install. Tighten the clamps securely, but do not distort them. Give the clamps and terminals a thin external coat of grease after installation, to retard corrosion.

Check the cables at the same time that the terminals are cleaned. If the cable insulation is cracked or broken, or if the ends are frayed, the cable should be replaced with a new cable of the same length and gauge.

CAUTION

Keep flame or sparks away from the battery; it gives off explosive hydrogen gas. Battery electrolyte contains sulphuric acid. If you should splash any on your skin or in your eyes, flush the affected area with plenty of clear water. If it lands in your eyes, get medical help immediately.

Drive Belts

➧ SEE FIGS. 23-35

INSPECTION

Check the condition of the drive belt(s) and the belt tension at least every 15,000 miles (24,000 km).

JUMP STARTING A DEAD BATTERY

The chemical reaction in a battery produces explosive hydrogen gas. This is the safe way to jump start a dead battery, reducing the chances of an accidental spark that could cause an explosion.

Jump Starting Precautions

1. Be sure both batteries are of the same voltage.
2. Be sure both batteries are of the same polarity (have the same grounded terminal).
3. Be sure the vehicles are not touching.
4. Be sure the vent cap holes are not obstructed.
5. Do not smoke or allow sparks around the battery.
6. In cold weather, check for frozen electrolyte in the battery. Do not jump start a frozen battery.
7. Do not allow electrolyte on your skin or clothing.
8. Be sure the electrolyte is not frozen.

CAUTION: Make certin that the ignition key, in the vehicle with the dead battery, is in the OFF position. Connecting cables to vehicles with on-board computers will result in computer destruction if the key is not in the OFF position.

Jump Starting Procedure

1. Determine voltages of the two batteries; they must be the same.
2. Bring the starting vehicle close (they must not touch) so that the batteries can be reached easily.
3. Turn off all accessories and both engines. Put both vehicles in Neutral or Park and set the handbrake.
4. Cover the cell caps with a rag—do not cover terminals.
5. If the terminals on the run-down battery are heavily corroded, clean them.
6. Identify the positive and negative posts on both batteries and connect the cables in the order shown.
7. Start the engine of the starting vehicle and run it at fast idle. Try to start the car with the dead battery. Crank it for no more than 10 seconds at a time and let it cool for 20 seconds in between tries.
8. If it doesn't start in 3 tries, there is something else wrong.
9. Disconnect the cables in the reverse order.
10. Replace the cell covers and dispose of the rags.

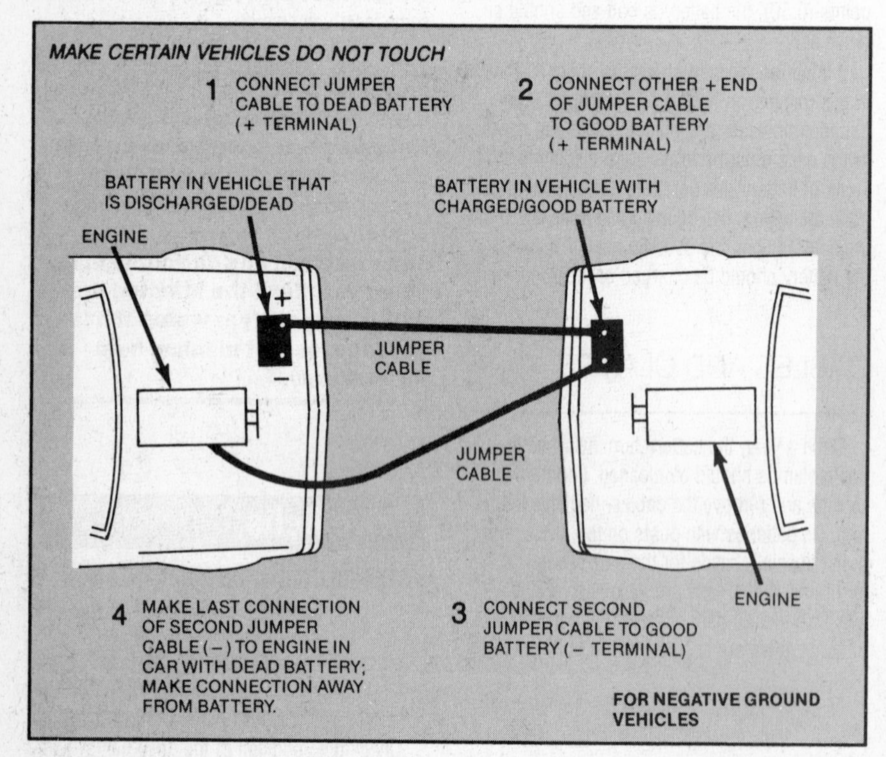
MAKE CERTAIN VEHICLES DO NOT TOUCH
1 CONNECT JUMPER CABLE TO DEAD BATTERY (+ TERMINAL)
2 CONNECT OTHER + END OF JUMPER CABLE TO GOOD BATTERY (+ TERMINAL)
BATTERY IN VEHICLE THAT IS DISCHARGED/DEAD
BATTERY IN VEHICLE WITH CHARGED/GOOD BATTERY
ENGINE
+
−
JUMPER CABLE
JUMPER CABLE
ENGINE
4 MAKE LAST CONNECTION OF SECOND JUMPER CABLE (−) TO ENGINE IN CAR WITH DEAD BATTERY; MAKE CONNECTION AWAY FROM BATTERY.
3 CONNECT SECOND JUMPER CABLE TO GOOD BATTERY (− TERMINAL)
FOR NEGATIVE GROUND VEHICLES

Side terminal batteries occasionally pose a problem when connecting jumper cables. There frequently isn't enough room to clamp the cables without touching sheet metal. Side terminal adaptors are available to alleviate this problem and should be removed after use

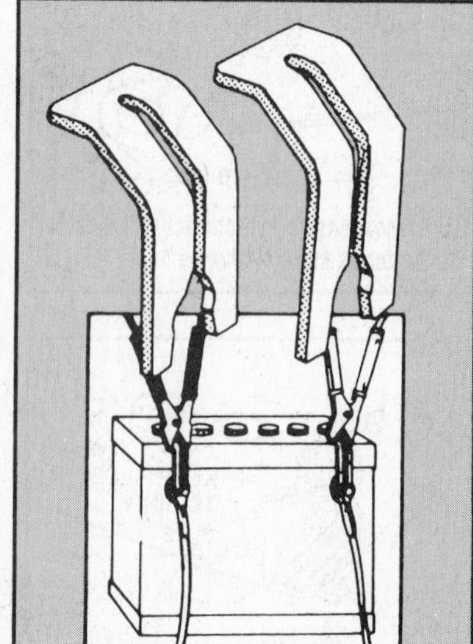

Inspect the belts for signs of glazing or cracking. A glazed belt will be perfectly smooth from slippage, while a good belt will have a slight texture of fabric visible. Cracks will generally start at the inner edge of the belt and run outward. Replace the belt at the first sign of cracking or if the glazing is severe.

TENSION CHECKING AND ADJUSTING

The drive belts should be checked for wear and tension as indicted in the Maintenance Interval charts. If the belt is worn, cracked or frayed, replace it with a new one. To check the belt tension:

Some models may use an adjusting bolt on either the idler pulley (a pulley which is not directly associated with any of the accessories) or on the power steering pump itself. This bolt makes adjustment much easier because you don't have to hold the accessory under a great deal of tension while tightening mounting bolts.

On models where the idler pulley has a lockbolt at its center, simply loosen the lockbolt and then turn the adjusting bolt clockwise to increase belt tension or counterclockwise to decrease it or remove the belt. Just don't forget to retighten the lockbolt when tension is correct, or vibration may cause it be lost. Recheck the tension with the lockbolt tightened and readjust if necessary.

On models with the 4 ridge or 5 ridge ribbed type V-belt driving both the air conditioner and power steering pump, belt tension is much greater. With a used belt, deflection should only be about 1/4 in. (6mm).

V-Belts

1. Apply thumb pressure (about 22 lbs.) to the fan belt midway between the pulleys and check the deflection. I should be approximately 3/8 in. (10mm) for new belts and 1/2 in. (13mm) for used belts.

2. To adjust the tension, loosen the alternator mounting bolt and adjusting bolt.

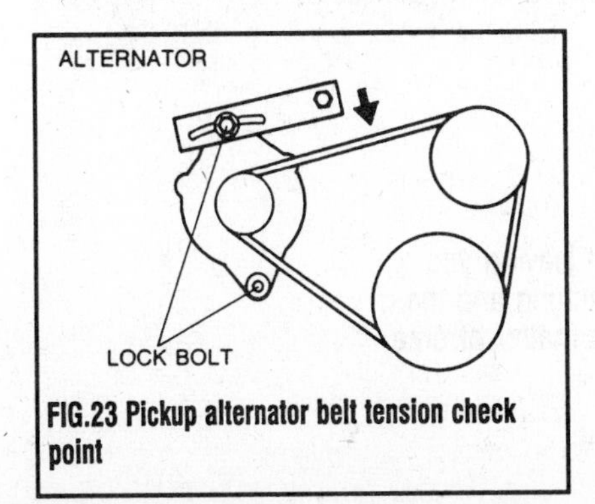

FIG.23 Pickup alternator belt tension check point

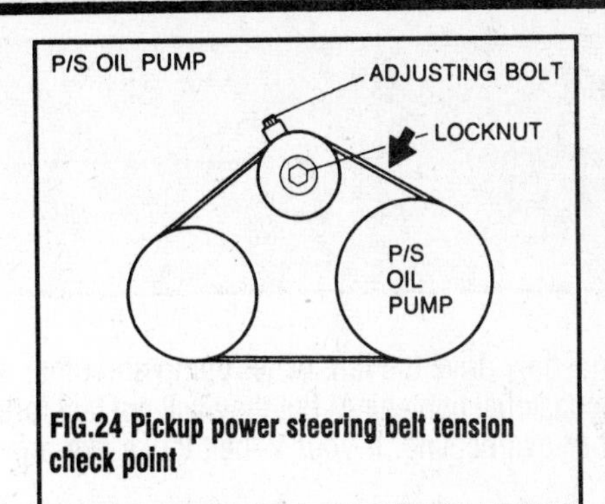

FIG.24 Pickup power steering belt tension check point

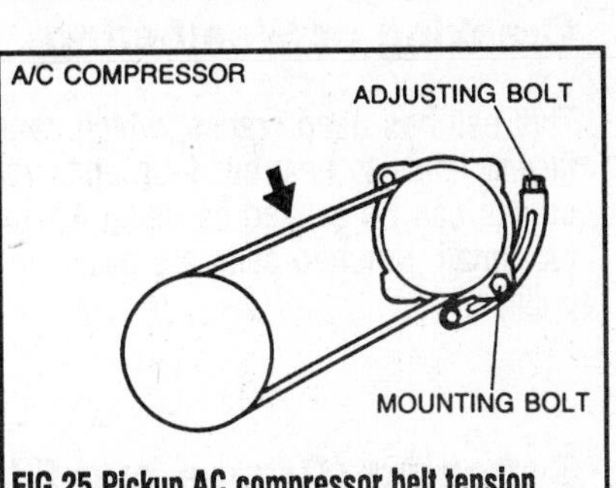

FIG.25 Pickup AC compressor belt tension check point

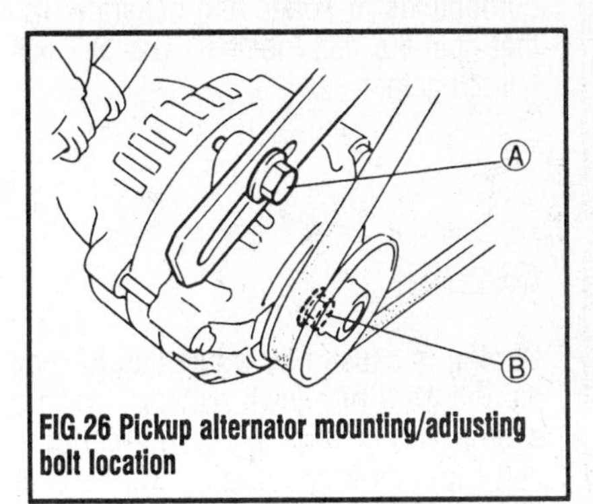

FIG.26 Pickup alternator mounting/adjusting bolt location

3. Move the alternator in the direction necessary to loosen or tighten the tension.

4. Tighten the mounting and adjusting bolts and recheck the tension.

Navajo

The Navajo uses a single accessory drive belt that is tensioned by a spring loaded tensioner, no adjustment is necessary. While there is no adjusting with the automatic tensioner and Poly-V belt used, it may be necessary to check the belt tension if squealing or excessive belt wear is noticed. If deflection is greater than 1/4 in. (6mm), the belt probably should be replaced. Before replacement, however, check the accessory component mountings for looseness and check the condition of the automatic tensioner. Repair or replace parts as necessary.

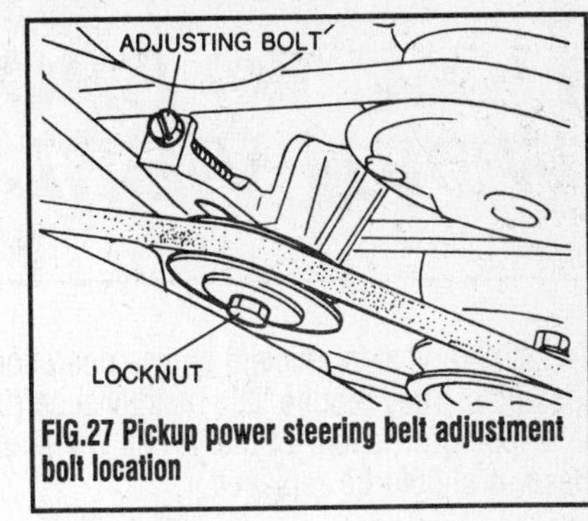

FIG.27 Pickup power steering belt adjustment bolt location

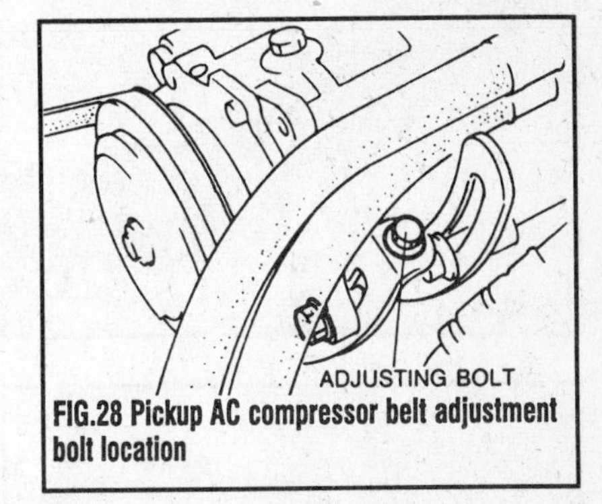

FIG.28 Pickup AC compressor belt adjustment bolt location

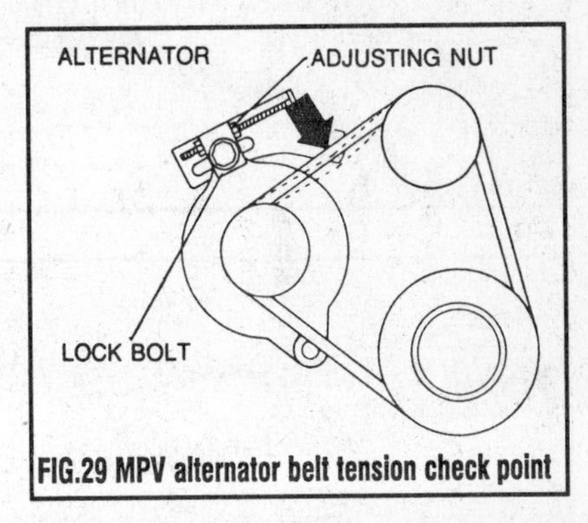

FIG.29 MPV alternator belt tension check point

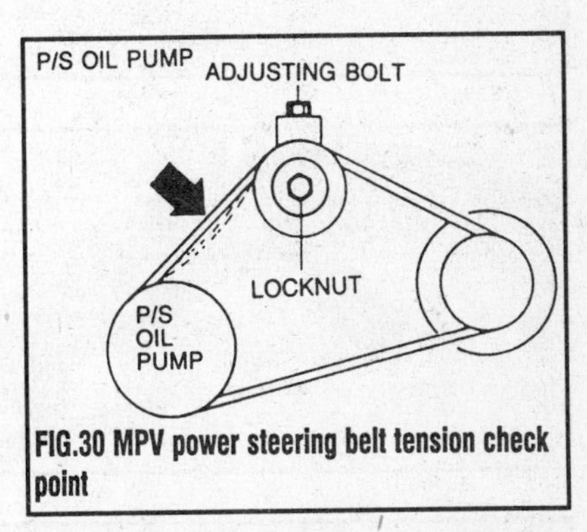

FIG.30 MPV power steering belt tension check point

REMOVAL & INSTALLATION

Refer to the previous "Tension Checking and Adjustment" procedure. Release the tension on the belt being replaced and the belts that are in front of it. Remove the belt(s). Position the replacement belt in the pulleys and apply the

HOW TO SPOT WORN V-BELTS

V–Belts are vital to efficient engine operation – they drive the fan, water pump and other accessories. They require little maintenance (occasional tightening) but they will not last forever. Slipping or failure of the V–belt will lead to overheating. If your V–belt looks like any of these, it should be replaced.

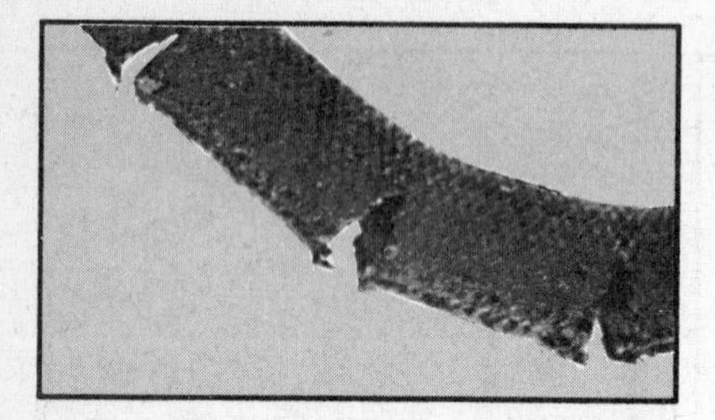

Cracking or Weathering

This belt has deep cracks, which cause it to flex. Too much flexing leads to heat build–up and premature failure. These cracks can be caused by using the belt on a pulley that is too small. Notched belts are available for small diameter pulleys.

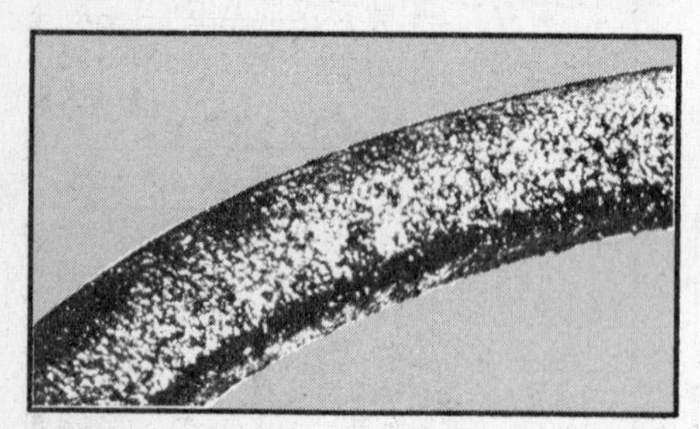

Softening (Grease and Oil)

Oil and grease on a belt can cause the belt's rubber compounds to soften and separate from the reinforcing cords that hold the belt together. The belt will first slip, then finally fail altogether.

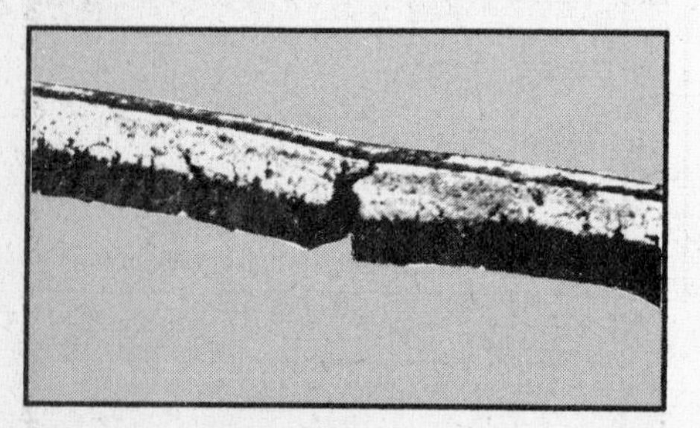

Glazing

Glazing is caused by a belt that is slipping. A slipping belt can cause a run-down battery, erratic power steering, overheating or poor accessory performance. The more the belt slips, the more glazing will be built up on the surface of the belt. The more the belt is glazed, the more it will slip. If the glazing is light, tighten the belt.

Worn Cover

The cover of this belt is worn off and is peeling away. The reinforcing cords will begin to wear and the belt will shortly break. When the belt cover wears in spots or has a rough jagged appearance, check the pulley grooves for roughness.

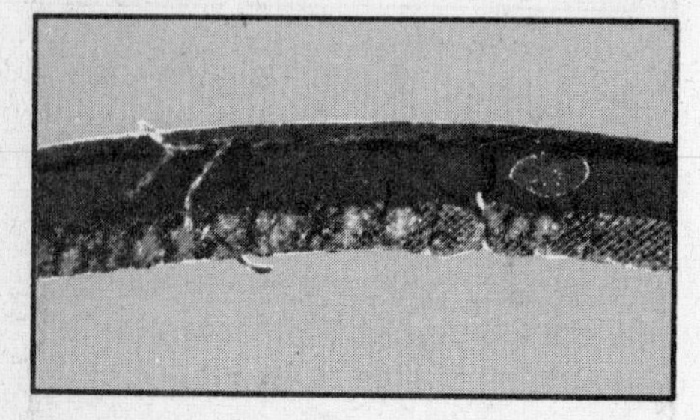

Separation

This belt is on the verge of breaking and leaving you stranded. The layers of the belt are separating and the reinforcing cords are exposed. It's just a matter of time before it breaks completely.

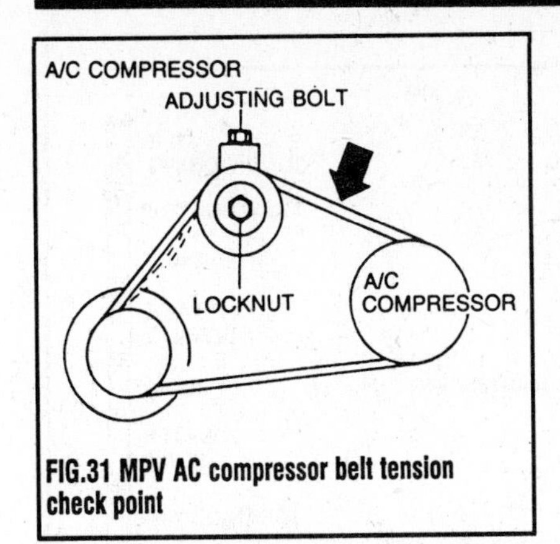

FIG.31 MPV AC compressor belt tension check point

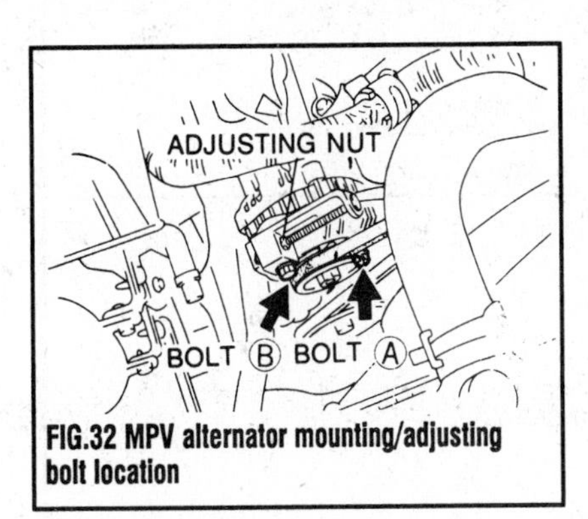

FIG.32 MPV alternator mounting/adjusting bolt location

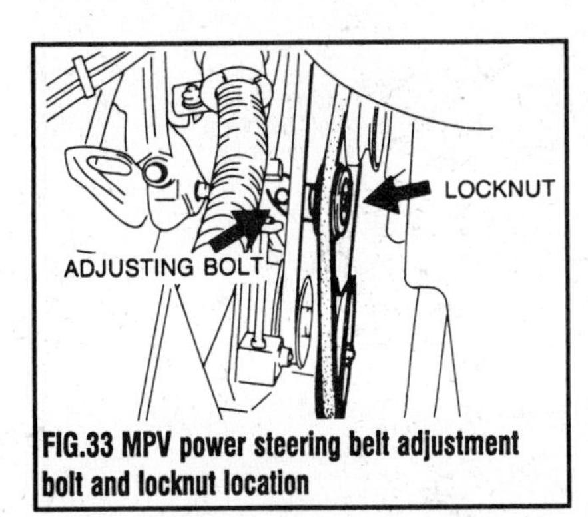

FIG.33 MPV power steering belt adjustment bolt and locknut location

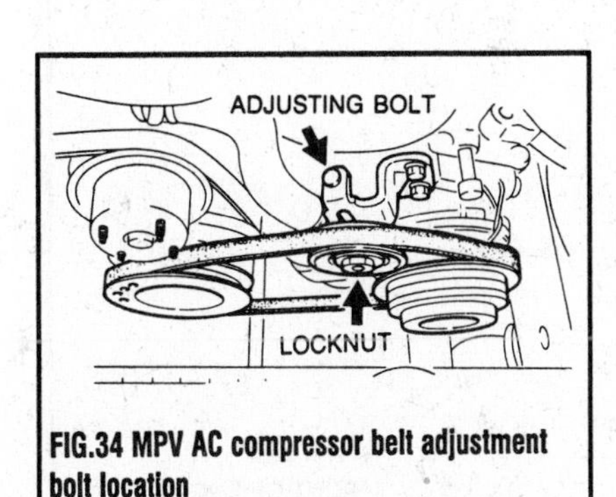

FIG.34 MPV AC compressor belt adjustment bolt location

correct tension. Secure the adjustment pulley, or mounting and adjustment bolts.

Navajo

The Navajo's belt is replaced as follows:

1. Lift the tensioner while rotating counterclockwise and remove the old belt.
2. Install the new belt over the pulleys. Make sure that all V-grooves make proper contact with the pulleys.
3. Lift the tensioner and slide the belt under the tensioner pulley. Release the tensioner slowly until it rests on the belt.

Hoses

REMOVAL & INSTALLATION

1. Drain the existing antifreeze and coolant. Open the radiator and engine drain petcocks, or disconnect the bottom radiator hose, at the radiator outlet.

CAUTION

When draining the coolant, keep in mind that cats and dogs are attracted by the ethylene glycol antifreeze, and are quite likely to drink any that is left in an uncovered container or in puddles on the ground. This will prove fatal in sufficient quantity. Always drain the coolant into a sealable container. Coolant should be reused unless it is contaminated or several years old.

➡ Before opening the radiator petcock, spray it with some penetrating lubricant.

2. Loosen the clamp on each end of the hose to be removed.
3. Slide the hose off the connections.
4. Position the clamps on each end of the new hose.
5. Slide the hose onto the connections, then tighten the clamps. If the connections have a bead around the edges, make sure the clamps are located beyond the beads.
6. Refill the cooling system with coolant. Run the engine for several minutes, then check the hose connections for leaks.

Air Conditioning

➧ SEE FIGS. 36 and 37

GENERAL SERVICING PROCEDURES

The most important aspect of air conditioning service is the maintenance of pure and adequate charge of refrigerant in the system. A refrigeration system cannot function properly if a significant percentage of the charge is lost. Leaks are common because the severe vibration encountered in an automobile can easily cause a sufficient cracking or loosening of the air conditioning fittings. As a result, the extreme operating pressures of the system force refrigerant out.

The problem can be understood by considering what happens to the system as it is operated with a continuous leak. Because the expansion valve regulates the flow of refrigerant to the evaporator, the level of refrigerant there is fairly constant. The receiver/drier stores any excess of refrigerant, and so a loss will first appear there as a reduction in the level of liquid. As this level nears the bottom of the vessel, some refrigerant vapor bubbles will begin 40;appear in the stream of liquid supplied to the expansion valve. This vapor decreases the capacity of the expansion valve very little as the valve opens to compensate for its presence. As the quantity of liquid in the condenser decreases, the operating pressure will drop there and throughout the high side of the system. As the R-12 continues to be expelled, the pressure available to force the liquid through the expansion valve will continue to decrease, and, eventually, the valve's orifice will prove to be too much of a restriction for adequate flow even with the needle fully withdrawn.

At this point, low side pressure will start to drop, and severe reduction in cooling capacity, marked by freeze-up of the evaporator coil, will result. Eventually, the operating pressure of the evaporator will be lower than the pressure of the atmosphere surrounding it, and air will be drawn into the system wherever there are leaks in the low side.

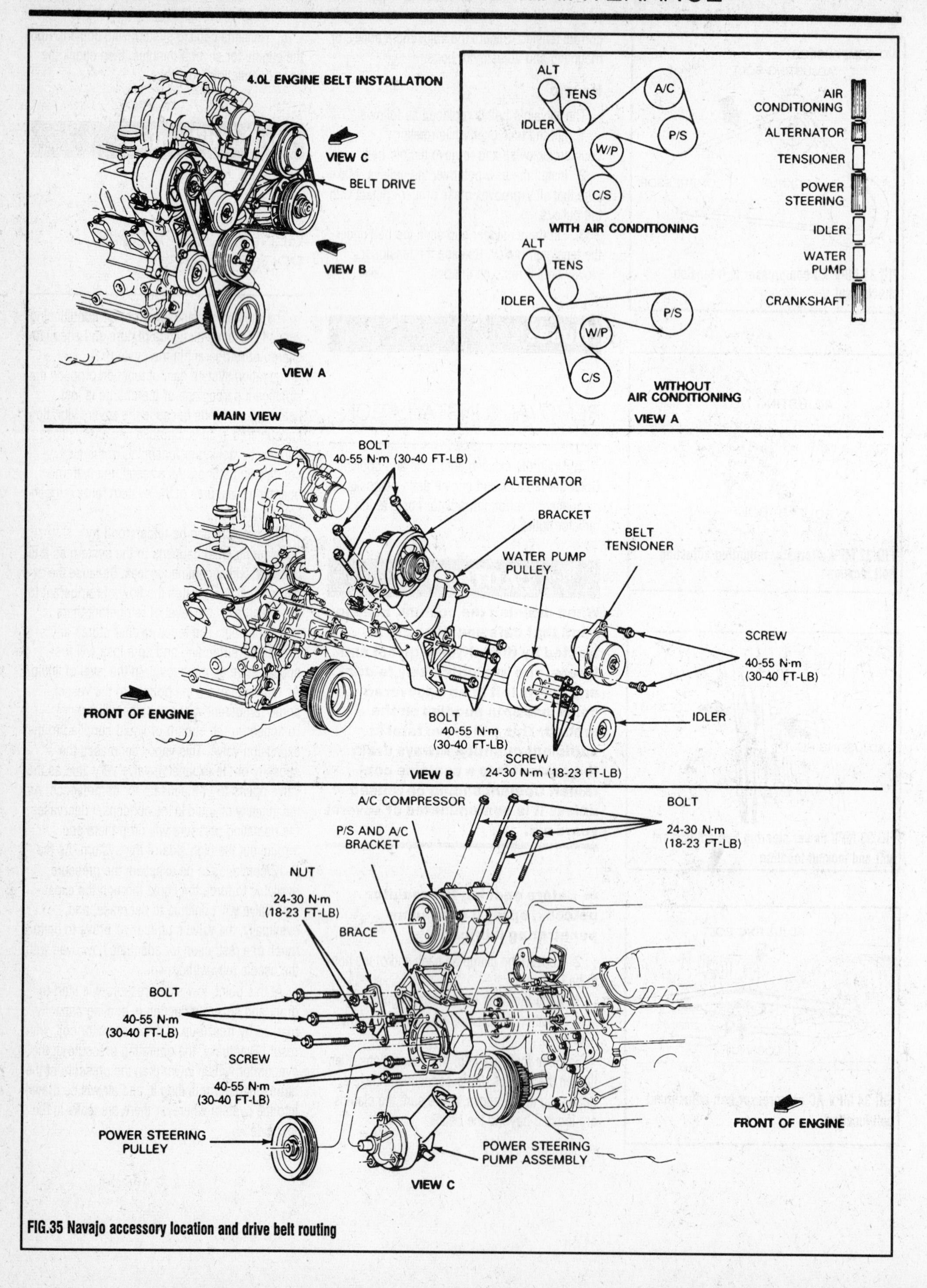

FIG.35 Navajo accessory location and drive belt routing

HOW TO SPOT BAD HOSES

Both the upper and lower radiator hoses are called upon to perform difficult jobs in an inhospitable environment. They are subject to nearly 18 psi at under hood temperatures often over 280°F, and must circulate nearly 7500 gallons of coolant an hour—3 good reasons to have good hoses.

Swollen Hose

A good test for any hose is to feel it for soft or spongy spots. Frequently these will appear as swollen areas of the hose. The most likely cause is oil soaking. This hose could burst at any time, when hot or under pressure.

Cracked Hose

Cracked hoses can usually be seen but feel the hoses to be sure they have not hardened; a prime cause of cracking. This hose has cracked down to the reinforcing cords and could split at any of the cracks.

Frayed Hose End (Due to Weak Clamp)

Weakened clamps frequently are the cause of hose and cooling system failure. The connection between the pipe and hose has deteriorated enough to allow coolant to escape when the engine is hot.

Debris In Cooling System

Debris, rust and scale in the cooling system can cause the inside of a hose to weaken. This can usually be felt on the outside of the hose as soft or thinner areas.

Because all atmospheric air contains at least some moisture, water will enter the system and mix with the R-12 and the oil. Trace amounts of moisture will cause sludging of the oil, and corrosion of the system. Saturation and clogging of the filter/drier, and freezing of the expansion valve orifice will eventually result. As air fills the system to a greater and greater extend, it will interfere more and more with the normal flows of refrigerant and heat.

A list of general precautions that should be observed while doing this follows:

1. Keep all tools as clean and dry as possible.
2. Thoroughly purge the service gauges and hoses of air and moisture before connecting them to the system. Keep them capped when not in use.
3. Thoroughly clean any refrigerant fitting before disconnecting it, in order to minimize the entrance of dirt into the system.
4. Plan any operation that requires opening the system beforehand in order to minimize the length of time it will be exposed to open air. Cap or seal the open ends to minimize the entrance of foreign material.
5. When adding oil, pour it through an extremely clean and dry tube or funnel. Keep the oil capped whenever possible. Do not use oil that has not been kept tightly sealed.
6. Use only refrigerant 12. Purchase refrigerant intended for use in only automotive air conditioning system. Avoid the use of refrigerant 12 that may be packaged for another use, such as cleaning, or powering a horn, as it is impure.
7. Completely evacuate any system that has been opened to replace a component, other than when isolating the compressor, or that has leaked sufficiently to draw in moisture and air. This requires evacuating air and moisture with a good vacuum pump for at least one hour.

If a system has been open for a considerable length of time it may be advisable to evacuate the system for up to 12 hours (overnight).

8. Use a wrench on both halves of a fitting that is to be disconnected, so as to avoid placing torque on any of the refrigerant lines.

ADDITIONAL PREVENTIVE MAINTENANCE CHECKS

Antifreeze

In order to prevent heater core freeze-up during A/C operation, it is necessary to maintain permanent type antifreeze protection of +15°F (-9°C) or lower. A reading of -15°F (-26°C) is ideal since this protection also supplies sufficient corrosion inhibitors for the protection of the engine cooling system.

WARNING

Do not use antifreeze longer than specified by the manufacturer.

Radiator Cap

For efficient operation of an air conditioned truck's cooling system, the radiator cap should have a holding pressure which meets manufacturer's specifications. A cap which fails to hold these pressure should be replaced.

Condenser

Any obstruction of or damage to the condenser configuration will restrict the air flow which is essential to its efficient operation. It is therefore, a good rule to keep this unit clean and in proper physical shape.

➡ Bug screens are regarded as obstructions.

Condensation Drain Tube

This single molded drain tube expels the condensation, which accumulates on the bottom of the evaporator housing, into the engine compartment.

If this tube is obstructed, the air conditioning performance can be restricted and condensation buildup can spill over onto the vehicle's floor.

SAFETY PRECAUTIONS

Because of the importance of the necessary safety precautions that must be exercised when working with air conditioning systems and R-12 refrigerant, a recap of the safety precautions is outlined.

1. Avoid contact with a charged refrigeration system, even when working on another part of the air conditioning system or vehicle. If a heavy tool comes into contact with a section of copper tubing or a heat exchanger, it can easily cause the relatively soft material to rupture.
2. When it is necessary to apply force to a fitting which contains refrigerant, as when checking that all system couplings are securely tightened, use a wrench on both parts of the fitting involved, if possible. This will avoid putting torque on the refrigerant tubing. (It is advisable, when possible, to use tube or line wrenches when tightening these flare nut fittings.)
3. Do not attempt to discharge the system by merely loosening a fitting, or removing the service valve caps and cracking these valves. Precise control is possibly only when using the service gauges. Place a rag under the open end of the center charging hose while discharging the system to catch any drops of liquid that might escape. Wear protective gloves when connecting or disconnecting service gauge hoses.
4. Discharge the system only into a sealed container made for capturing refrigerant and do so only in a well ventilated area, as high concentrations of the gas can exclude oxygen and act as an anesthetic. When leak testing or soldering this is particularly important, as toxic gas is formed when R-12 contacts any flame.
5. Never start a system without first verifying that both service valves are back-seated, if equipped, and that all fittings throughout the system are snugly connected.
6. Avoid applying heat to any refrigerant line or storage vessel. Charging may be aided by using water heated to less than 125°F (52°C) to warm the refrigerant container. Never allow a refrigerant storage container to sit out in the sun, or near any other source of heat, such as a radiator.
7. Always wear goggles when working on a system to protect the eyes. If refrigerant contacts the eye, it is advisable in all cases to see a physician as soon as possible.
8. Frostbite from liquid refrigerant should be treated by first gradually warming the area with cool water, and then gently applying petroleum jelly. A physician should be consulted.
9. Always keep refrigerant can fittings capped when not in use. Avoid sudden shock to the can which might occur from dropping it, or from banging a heavy tool against it. Never carry a refrigerant can in the passenger compartment of a truck.
10. Always completely discharge the system before painting the vehicle (if the paint is to be baked on), or before welding anywhere near the refrigerant lines.

TEST GAUGES

Most of the service work performed in air conditioning requires the use of a set of two gauges, one for the high (head) pressure side of the system, the other for the low (suction) side.

The low side gauge records both pressure and vacuum. Vacuum readings are calibrated from 0 to 30 inches Hg and the pressure graduations read from 0 to no less than 60 psi (413.7 kpa).

The high side gauge measures pressure from 0 to at last 600 psi (4137 kpa).

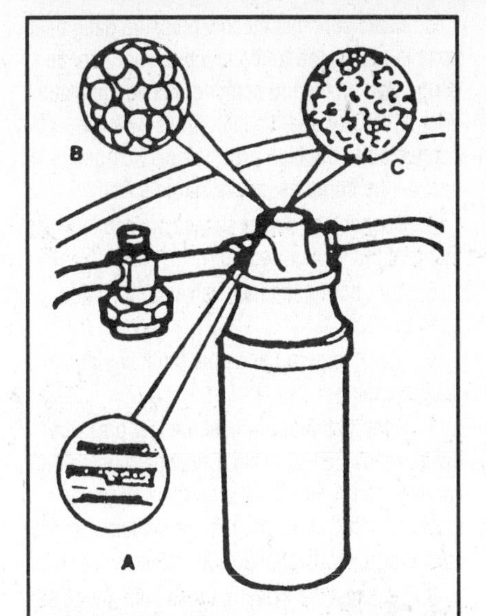

FIG.36 Oil streaks (A), constant bubbles (B), or foam (C) indicate that there is not enough refrigerant in the system. Occasional bubbles during initial operation are normal. A clear sight glass indicates a proper charge of refrigerant or no charge at all, which can be determined by the presence of cold air at the vents. If the glass is clouded with a milky white substance, the receiver/dryer should be checked

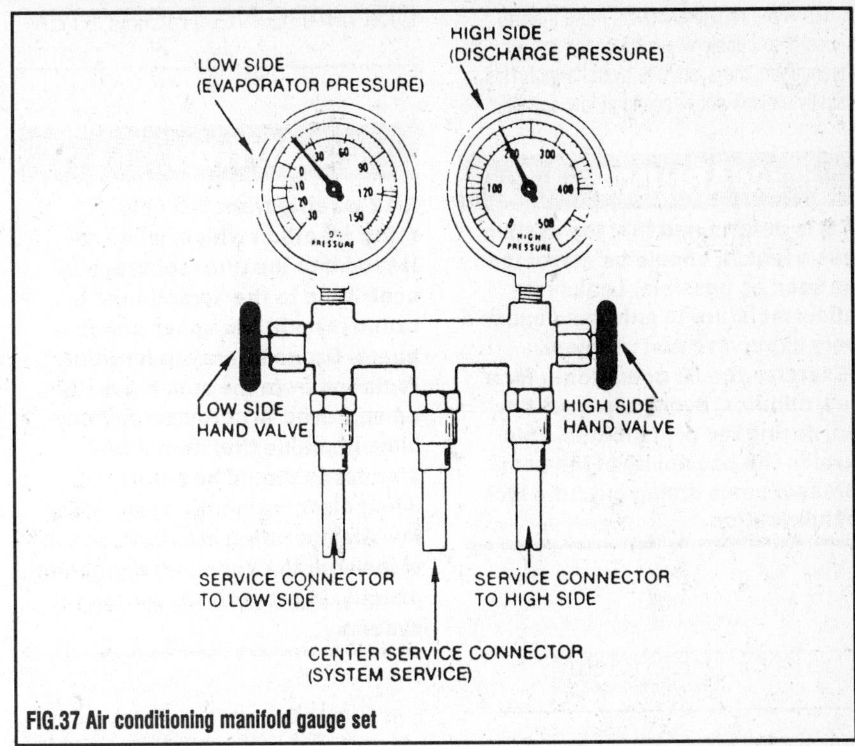

FIG.37 Air conditioning manifold gauge set

Both gauges are threaded into a manifold that contains two hand shut-off valves. Proper manipulation of these valves and the use of the attached test hoses allow the user to perform the following services:

1. Test high and low side pressures.
2. Remove air, moisture, and contaminated refrigerant.
3. Purge the system (of refrigerant).
4. Charge the system (with refrigerant).

The manifold valves are designed so that they have no direct effect on gauge readings, but serve only to provide for, or cut off, flow of refrigerant through the manifold. During all testing and hook-up operations, the valves are kept in a close position to avoid disturbing the refrigeration system. The valves are opened only to purge the system or refrigerant or to charge it.

INSPECTION

CAUTION

The compressed refrigerant used in the air conditioning system expands into the atmosphere at a temperature of -21.7°F (-30°C) or lower. This will freeze any surface, including your eyes, that it contacts. In addition, the refrigerant decomposes into a poisonous gas in the presence of a flame. Do not open or disconnect any part of the air conditioning system.

Sight Glass Check

You can safely make a few simple checks to determine if your air conditioning system needs service. The tests work best if the temperature is warm (about 70°F [21.1°C]).

➡ **If your vehicle is equipped with an aftermarket air conditioner, the following system checks may not apply. You should contact the manufacturer of the unit for instructions on systems checks.**

1. Place the automatic transmission in Park or the manual transmission in Neutral. Set the parking brake.
2. Run the engine at a fast idle (about 1,500 rpm) either with the help of a friend or by temporarily readjusting the idle speed screw.
3. Set the controls for maximum cold with the blower on High.
4. Locate the sight glass in one of the system lines. Usually it is on the left alongside the top of the radiator.
5. If you see bubbles, the system must be recharged. Very likely there is a leak at some point.
6. If there are no bubbles, there is either no refrigerant at all or the system is fully charged. Feel the two hoses going to the belt driven compressor. If they are both at the same temperature, the system is empty and must be recharged.
7. If one hose (high pressure) is warm and the other (low pressure) is cold, the system may be all right. However, you are probably making these tests because you think there is something wrong, so proceed to the next step.
8. Have an assistant in the truck turn the fan control on and off to operate the compressor clutch. Watch the sight glass.
9. If bubbles appear when the clutch is disengaged and disappear when it is engaged, the system is properly charged.

10. If the refrigerant takes more than 45 seconds to bubble when the clutch is disengaged, the system is overcharged. This usually causes poor cooling at low speeds.

⁂ WARNING

If it is determined that the system has a leak, it should be corrected as soon as possible. Leaks may allow moisture to enter and cause a very expensive rust problem.

Exercise the air conditioner for a few minutes, every two weeks or so, during the cold months. This avoids the possibility of the compressor seals drying out from lack of lubrication.

TESTING THE SYSTEM

1. Connect a gauge set.
2. Close (clockwise) both gauge set valves.
4. Park the truck in the shade, at least 5 feet from any walls. Start the engine, set the parking brake, place the transmission in NEUTRAL and establish an idle of 1,100–1,300 rpm.
5. Run the air conditioning system for full cooling, in the MAX or COLD mode.
6. The low pressure gauge should read 5–20 psi (34.5–138 kpa); the high pressure gauge should indicate 120–180 psi (827.4–1241 kpa).

⁂ WARNING

These pressures are the norm for an ambient temperature of 70–80°F (21–27°C). Higher air temperatures along with high humidity will cause higher system pressures. At idle speed and an ambient temperature of 110°F (43°C), the high pressure reading can exceed 300 psi (2068.5 kpa). Under these extreme conditions, you can keep the pressures down by directing a large electric floor fan through the condenser.

DISCHARGING THE SYSTEM

⁂ CAUTION

R-12 is refrigerant is a chlorofluorocarbon which, when released into the atmosphere, can contribute to the depletion of the ozone layer in the upper atmosphere. Ozone filters out harmful radiation from the sun. If possible, an approved R-12 Recovery/Recycling machine that meets SAE standards should be employed when discharging the system. Follow the operating instructions provided with the approved equipment, exactly, to properly discharge the system.

1. Remove the caps from the high and low pressure charging valves in the high and low pressure lines.
2. Turn both manifold gauge set hand valves to the fully closed (clockwise) position.
3. Connect the manifold gauge set.
4. If the gauge set hoses do not have the gauge port actuating pins, install fitting adapters on the manifold gauge set hoses. If the truck does not have a service access gauge port valve, connect the gauge set low pressure hose to the evaporator service access gauge port valve. A special adapter is required to attach the manifold gauge set to the high pressure service access gauge port valve.
5. Connect the end of the center hose to the recycling apparatus.
6. Open the low pressure gauge valve slightly and allow the system pressure to bleed off.
7. When the system is just about empty, open the high pressure valve very slowly to avoid losing an excessive amount of refrigerant oil. Allow any remaining refrigerant to escape.

EVACUATING THE SYSTEM

➡ This procedure requires the use of a vacuum pump.

1. Connect the manifold gauge set.
2. Discharge the system.
3. Make sure that the low pressure gauge set hose is connected to the low pressure service gauge port on the top center of the accumulator/drier assembly and the high pressure hose connected to the high pressure service gauge port on the compressor discharge line.
4. Connect the center service hose to the inlet fitting of the vacuum pump.
5. Turn both gauge set valves to the wide open position.
6. Start the pump and note the low side gauge reading.
7. Operate the pump until the low pressure gauge reads 25–30 in.Hg. Continue running the vacuum pump for 10 minutes more. If you've replaced some component in the system, run the pump for an additional 20–30 minutes.
8. Leak test the system. Close both gauge set valves. Turn off the pump. The needle should remain stationary at the point at which the pump was turned off. If the needle drops to zero rapidly, there is a leak in the system which must be repaired.

CHARGING THE SYSTEM

⁂ CAUTION

NEVER OPEN THE HIGH PRESSURE SIDE WITH A CAN OF REFRIGERANT CONNECTED TO THE SYSTEM! OPENING THE HIGH PRESSURE SIDE WILL OVER PRESSURIZE THE CAN, CAUSING IT TO EXPLODE!

1. Connect the gauge set.
2. Close (clockwise) both gauge set valves.
3. Connect the center hose to the refrigerant can opener valve.
4. Make sure the can opener valve is closed, that is, the needle is raised, and connect the valve to the can. Open the valve, puncturing the can with the needle.
5. Loosen the center hose fitting at the pressure gauge, allowing refrigerant to purge the hose of air. When the air is bled, tighten the fitting.

⁂ CAUTION

IF THE LOW PRESSURE GAUGE SET HOSE IS NOT CONNECTED TO THE ACCUMULATOR/DRIER, KEEP THE CAN IN AN UPRIGHT POSITION!

6. Disconnect the wire harness snap-lock connector from the clutch cycling pressure switch and install a jumper wire across the two terminals of the connector.

7. Open the low side gauge set valve and the can valve.

8. Allow refrigerant to be drawn into the system.

9. When no more refrigerant is drawn into the system, start the engine and run it at about 1,500 rpm. Turn on the system and operate it at the full high position. The compressor will operate and pull refrigerant gas into the system.

➡ To help speed the process, the can may be placed, upright, in a pan of warm water, not exceeding 125°F (52°C).

10. If more than one can of refrigerant is needed, close the can valve and gauge set low side valve when the can is empty and connect a new can to the opener. Repeat the charging process until the sight glass indicates a full charge. The frost line on the outside of the can will indicate what portion of the can has been used.

✻✻ CAUTION

NEVER ALLOW THE HIGH PRESSURE SIDE READING TO EXCEED 240 psi (1654.8 kpa).

11. When the charging process has been completed, close the gauge set valve and can valve. Remove the jumper wire and reconnect the cycling clutch wire. Run the system for at least five minutes to allow it to normalize. Low pressure side reading should be 4–25 psi (27.6–172.4 kpa); high pressure reading should be 120–210 psi (827.4–1448 kpa) at an ambient temperature of 70–90 °F (21–32°C).

12. Loosen both service hoses at the gauges to allow any refrigerant to escape. Remove the gauge set and install the dust caps on the service valves.

➡ Multi-can dispensers are available which allow a simultaneous hook-up of up to four 1 lb. (0.45 kg) cans of R-12.

LEAK TESTING

Some leak tests can be performed with a soapy water solution. There must be at least a 1/2 lb. (0.23 kg) charge in the system for a leak to be detected. The most extensive leak tests are performed with either a Halide flame type leak tester or the more preferable electronic leak tester.

In either case, the equipment is expensive, and, the use of a Halide detector can be **extremely** hazardous!

WINDSHIELD WIPERS

➧ SEE FIG 38

Windshield Washer Adjustment

The washer spray direction can be adjusted by inserting a pin into the nozzle and turning it to the desired position.

Windshield Wipers

Intense heat from the sun, snow and ice, road oils and the chemicals used in windshield washer solvents combine to deteriorate the rubber wiper refills. The refills should be replaced about twice a year or whenever the blades begin to streak or chatter.

WIPER REFILL REPLACEMENT

Normally, if the wipers are not cleaning the windshield properly, only the refill has to be replaced. The blade and arm usually require replacement only in the event of damage. It is not necessary (except on new Tridon® refills) to remove the arm or the blade to replace the refill (rubber part), though you may have to position the arm higher on the glass. You can do this turning the ignition switch on and operating the wipers. When they are positioned where they are accessible, turn the ignition switch off.

There are several types of refills and your vehicle could have any kind, since aftermarket blades and arms may not use exactly the same refill as the original equipment.

Most Anco® styles use a release button that is pushed down to allow the refill to slide out of the yoke jaws. The new refills slide in and locks in place. Some Anco® refills are removed by locating where the metal backing strip or the refill is wider. Insert a small screwdriver blade between the frame and metal backing strip. Press down to release the refill from the retaining tab.

The Trico® style is unlocked at one end by squeezing 2 metal tabs, and the refill is slid out of the frame jaws. When the new refill is installed, the tabs will click into place, locking the refill.

The polycarbonate type is held in place by a locking lever that is pushed downward out of the groove in the arm to free the refill. When the new refill is installed, it will lock in place automatically.

The Tridon® refill has a plastic backing strip with a notch about 1 in. (25mm) from the end. Hold the blade (frame) on a hard surface so that the frame is tightly bowed. Grip the tip of the backing strip and pull up while twisting counterclockwise. The backing strip will snap out of the retaining tab. Do this for the remaining tabs until the refill is free of the arm. The length of these refills is molded into the end and they should be replaced with identical types.

No matter which type of refill you use, be sure that all of the frame claws engage the refill. Before operating the wipers, be sure that no part of the metal frame is contacting the windshield.

WIPER ARM REPLACEMENT

To remove the arm and blade assembly, raise the blade end of the arm off of the windshield and move the slide latch away from the pivot shaft. The wiper arm can now be removed from the shaft without the use of any tools.

To install, push the main head over the pivot shaft. Be sure the wipers are in the pared position, and the blade assembly is in its correct position. Hold the main arm head onto the pivot shaft while raising the blade end of the wiper arm and push the slide latch into the lock under the pivot shaft head. Then, lower the blade to the windshield. If the blade does not lower to the windshield, the slide latch is not completely in place.

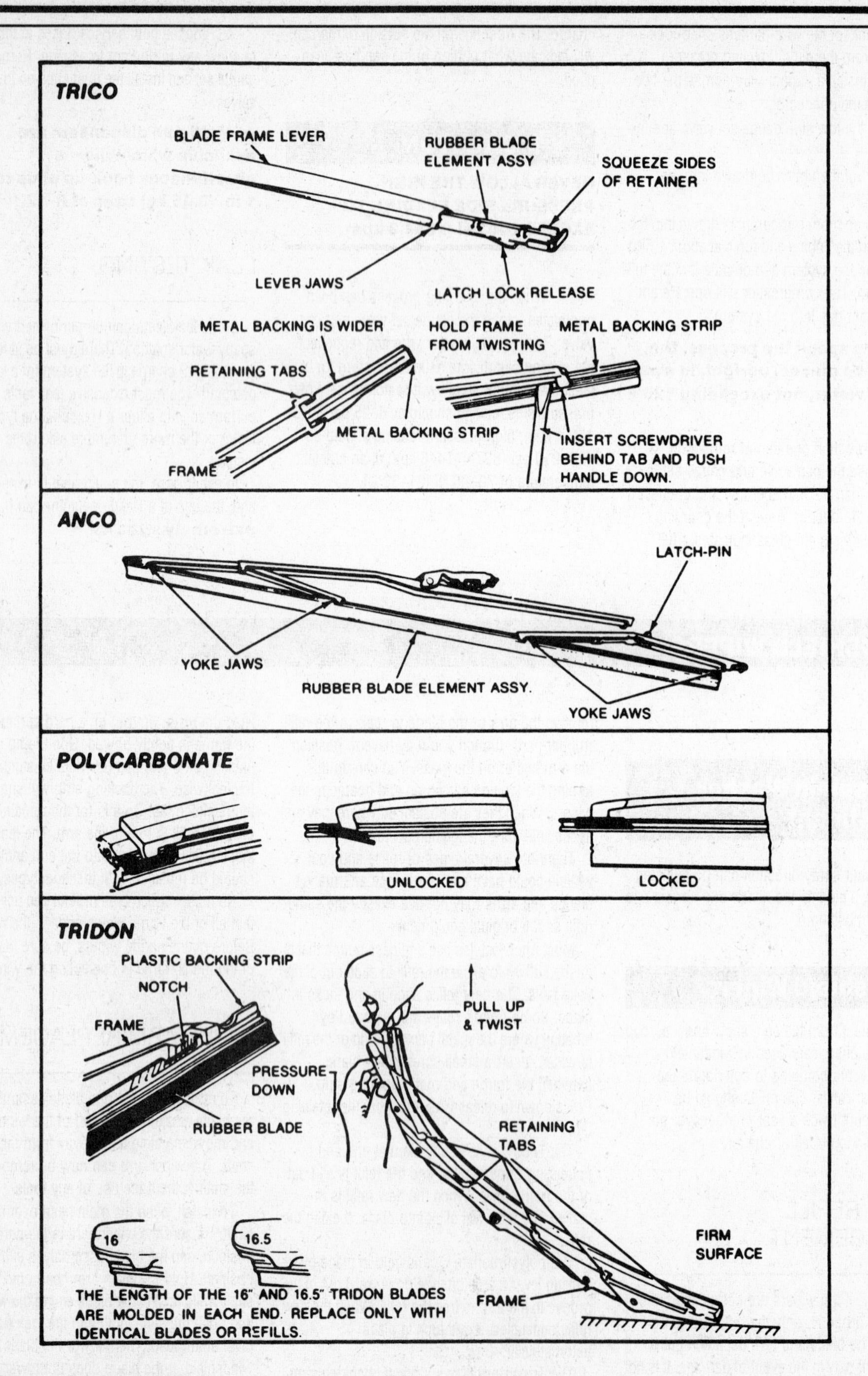

FIG.38 Popular styles of wiper refills

TIRES AND WHEELS

SEE FIGS. 39–43

The tires should be rotated as specified in the Maintenance Intervals Chart. Refer to the accompanying illustrations for the recommended rotation patterns.

The tires on your truck should have built-in tread wear indicators, which appear as $^1/_2$ in. (12.7mm) bands when the tread depth gets as low as $^1/_{16}$ in. (1.6mm). When the indicators appear in 2 or more adjacent grooves, it's time for new tires.

For optimum tire life, you should keep the tires properly inflated, rotate them often and have the wheel alignment checked periodically.

Pressures should be checked before driving, since pressure can increase as much as 6 psi (41.4 kpa) due to heat. It is a good idea to have an accurate gauge and to check pressures weekly. Not all gauges on service station air pumps are to be trusted. In general, truck type tires require higher pressures and flotation type tires, lower pressures.

TIRE ROTATION

It is recommended that you have the tires rotated and the balance checked every 6,000 miles. There is no way to give a tire rotation diagram for every combination of tires and vehicles, but the accompanying diagrams are a general rule to follow. Radial tires should not be cross-switched; they last longer if their direction of rotation is not changed. Some truck tires and some high-performance tires sometimes have directional tread, indicated by arrows on the sidewalls; the arrow shows the direction of rotation. They will wear very rapidly if reversed. Studded snow tires will lose their studs if their direction of rotation is reversed.

Mark the wheel position or direction of rotation on radial tires or studded snow tires before removing them.

If your truck is equipped with tires having different load ratings on the front and the rear, the tires should not be rotated front to rear. Rotating these tires could affect tire life (the tires with the lower rating will wear faster, and could become overloaded), and upset the handling of the truck.

TIRE USAGE

The tires on your truck were selected to provide the best all around performance for normal operation when inflated as specified. Oversize tires will not increase the maximum carrying capacity of the vehicle, although they will provide an extra margin of tread life. Be sure to check overall height before using larger size tires which may cause interference with suspension components or wheel wells. When replacing conventional tire sizes with other tire size designations, be sure to check the manufacturer's recommendations. Interchangeability is not always possible because of differences in load ratings, tire dimensions, wheel well clearances, and rim size. Also due to differences in handling characteristics, 70 Series and 60 Series tires should be used only in pairs on the same axle; radial tires should be used only in sets of four.

Many states have vehicle height restrictions; some states prohibit the lifting of vehicles beyond their design limits.

The wheels must be the correct width for the tire. Tire dealers have charts of tire and rim compatibility. A mismatch can cause sloppy handling and rapid tread wear. The old rule of thumb is that the tread width should match the rim width (inside bead to inside bead) within an inch. For radial tires, the rim width should be 80% or less of the tire (not tread) width.

The height (mounted diameter) of the new tires can greatly change speedometer accuracy, engine speed at a given road speed, fuel mileage, acceleration, and ground clearance. Tire manufacturers furnish full measurement specifications. Speedometer drive gears are available for correction.

Dimensions of tires marked the same size may vary significantly, even among tires from the same manufacturer.

The spare tire should be of the same size, construction and design as the tires on the vehicle. It's not a good idea to carry a spare of a different construction.

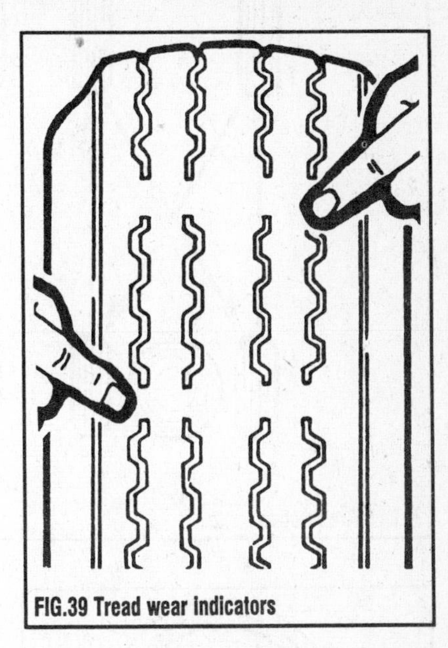

FIG.39 Tread wear indicators

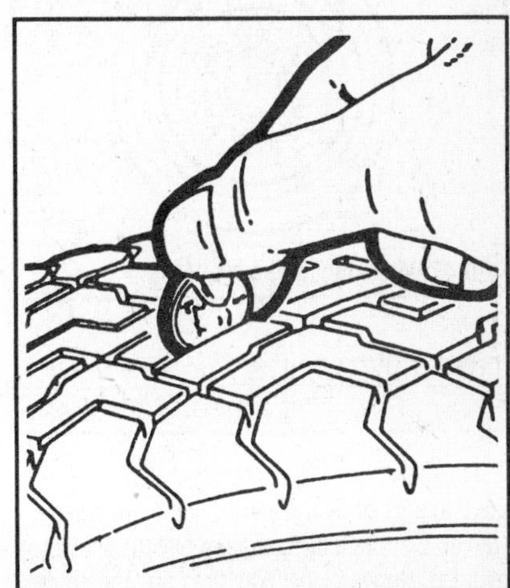

FIG.40 Tread depth can be checked with a penny; when the top of Lincoln's head is visible, it's time for new tires

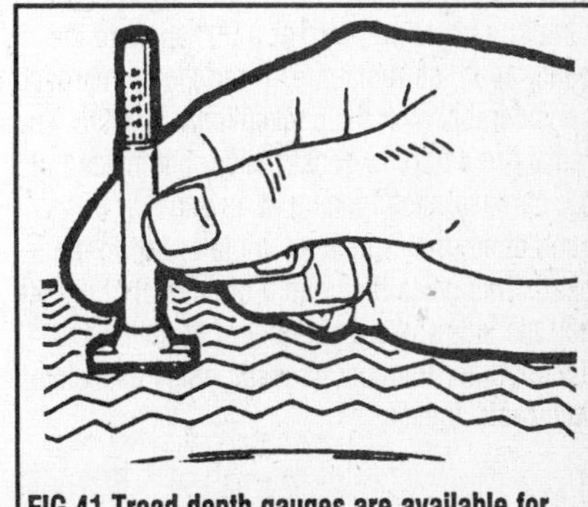

FIG.41 Tread depth gauges are available for precise wear measurements

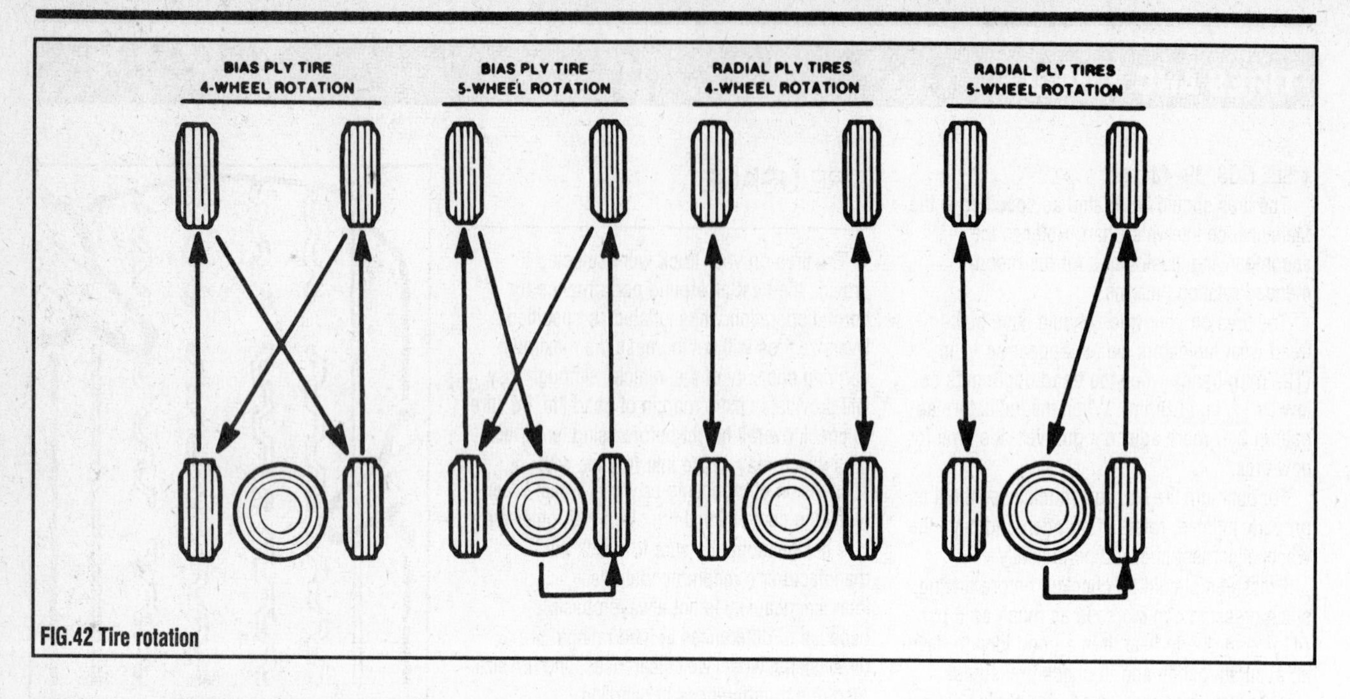

FIG.42 Tire rotation

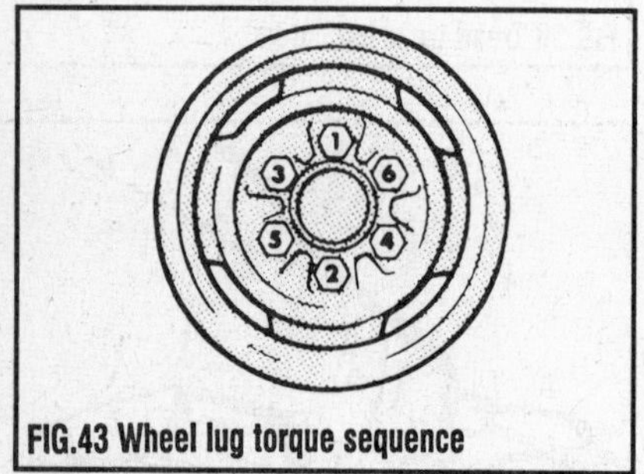

FIG.43 Wheel lug torque sequence

TIRE DESIGN

For maximum satisfaction, tires should be used in sets of five. Mixing or different types (radial, bias-belted, fiberglass belted) should be avoided. Conventional bias tires are constructed so that the cords run bead-to-bead at an angle. Alternate plies run at an opposite angle. This type of construction gives rigidity to both tread and sidewall. Bias-belted tires are similar in construction to conventional bias ply tires. Belts run at an angle and also at a 90° angle to the bead, as in the radial tire. Tread life is improved considerably over the conventional bias tire. The radial tire differs in construction, but instead of the carcass plies running at an angle of 90° to each other, they run at an angle of 90° to the bead. This gives the tread a great deal of rigidity and the sidewall a great deal of flexibility and accounts for the characteristic bulge associated with radial tires.

When radial tires are used, tire sizes and wheel diameters should be selected to maintain ground clearance and tire load capacity equivalent to the minimum specified tire. Radial tires should always be used in sets of five, but in an emergency, radial tires can be used with caution on the rear axle only. If this is done, both tires on the rear should be of radial design.

WARNING

Radial tires should never be used on only the front axle!

STORAGE

Store the tires at the proper inflation pressure if they are mounted on wheels. Keep them in a cool dry place, laid on their sides. If the tires are stored in the garage or basement, do not let them stand on a concrete floor; set them on strips of wood or stack of newspapers.

CARE OF SPECIAL WHEELS

If you have invested money in special sport wheels, special precautions should be taken to make your investment is not wasted and that your special wheels look good for the lifetime of the vehicle.

Special wheels are easily scratched and/or damaged. Occasionally check the rims for cracking, impact damage or air leaks, if any of these are found, replace the wheel.

Use extra care not to damage the wheels during removal, installation, balancing, etc. After removing the wheels, place them in a safe location away from the work area. If they are to be stored, never stand them upright; the tread will develop flat spots.

While driving, avoid obstacles, holes and sharp objects.

When washing, use a mild detergent and water. Avoid cleanser with abrasives or the use of hard brushes. There are many cleaners and polishes for special wheels – use them.

If possible, remove the special wheels from the vehicle during winter months. Salt and sand used for snow removal can severely damage the finish. Never install snow chains over special wheels; severe damage to the wheels may occur.

Make sure the recommended lug nut torque is never exceeded or the wheel may crack. Always hand tighten the lugs, to the proper torque, in a criss-cross pattern.

FLUIDS AND LUBRICANTS

Oil and Fuel Recommendations

FUEL

All vehicles covered in this book use unleaded fuel. Leaded fuel may not be used in these models, because they are equipped with a catalytic converter for emission control purposes. Leaded fuel will render the converter useless, raising the emission content of the exhaust to illegal and environmentally unacceptable levels. It will also block the converter passages, increasing exhaust back pressure; in extreme cases, exhaust blockage will be raised to the point where the engine will not run.

Fuels of the same octane rating have varying anti-knock qualities. Thus if your engine knocks or pings, try switching brands of gasoline before trying a more expensive higher octane fuel. If you must use unleaded fuel, this may be your only alternative.

Your engine's fuel requirements can change with time, due to carbon buildup which changes the compression ratio. If switching brands or grades of gas doesn't work, check the ignition timing. If it is necessary to retard timing from specifications, don't change it more than about 4°. Retard timing will reduce power output and fuel mileage and increase engine temperature.

ENGINE OIL

➧ SEE FIGS. 44-50

The SAE grade number indicates the viscosity of the engine oil, or its ability to lubricate under a given temperature. The lower the SAE grade number, the lighter the oil; the lower the viscosity, the easier it is to crank the engine in cold weather.

The API (American Petroleum Institute) designation indicates the classification of engine oil for use under given operating conditions. Only oils designated for Service SF/SG, or just SG, should be used to provide maximum engine protection. Both the SAE grade number and the API designation can be found on the container.

➡ **Non-detergent or straight mineral oils should not be used.**

Oil viscosities should be chosen from those oils recommended for the lowest anticipated temperatures during the oil change interval.

OIL LEVEL CHECK

When checking the oil level, it is best that the oil be at operating temperature, although checking the level immediately after stopping will give a false reading because all of the oil will not have drained back into the crankcase. Be sure that the truck is on a level surface, allowing tine for all of the oil to drain back into the crankcase.

1. Open the hood and locate the engine oil dipstick.
2. Remove the dipstick and wipe it clean with a rag.
3. Insert the dipstick fully into the tube and remove it again. Hold the dipstick horizontal and read the level on the dipstick. The level should be between the **F** (Full) and **L** (Low) marks. If the oil level is at or below the **L** mark, sufficient oil should be added to restore the level to the proper place. Oil is added through the capped opening in the top of the valve cover. See the section on "Oil and Fuel Recommendations" for the proper viscosity and oil to use.
4. Replace the dipstick and check the level after adding oil. Be careful not to overfill the crankcase.

OIL AND FILTER CHANGE

CAUTION

The EPA warns that prolonged contact with used engine oil may cause a number of skin disorders, including cancer! You should make every effort to minimize your exposure to used engine oil. Protective gloves should be worn when changing the oil. Wash your hands and any other exposed skin areas as soon as possible after exposure to used engine oil. Soap and water, or waterless hand cleaner should be used.

The engine oil and filter should always be changed together. To skip an oil filter change is to leave a quart of contaminated oil in the engine. Engine oil and filter should be changed according to the schedule in the Maintenance Intervals chart.

Under the following conditions, the oil change and filter replacement interval should be cut in half:

- Driving in dusty conditions
- Continuous trailer pulling or RV use
- Extensive or prolonged idling
- Extensive short trip operation in freezing temperatures (when the engine is not thoroughly warmed up)
- Frequent long runs at high speeds and high ambient temperatures
- Stop-and-go service, such as delivery trucks

Operation of the engine in severe conditions, such as a dust storm, may require an immediate oil and filter change.

To change the engine oil and filter, the truck should be parked on a level surface and the engine should be at operating temperature. This is to ensure that foreign matter will be drained away with the oil and not left behind in the engine to form sludge, which will happen if the engine is drained cold. Oil that is slightly brownish when drained is a good sign that the contaminants are being drained away. You should have available a container that will hold at least five quarts, a wrench to fit the oil drain plug, a spout for pouring in new oil and some rags to clean up the inevitable mess. If the filter is being replaced, you will also need a band wrench to fit the filter.

1. Position the truck on a level surface and set the parking brake or block the wheels. Slide a drain pan under the oil drain plug.
2. From under the truck, loosen, but do not remove the oil drain plug. Cover your hand with a heavy rag or glove and slowly unscrew the drain plug. Push the plug against the threads to prevent oil from leaking past the threads.

CAUTION

The engine oil will be hot. Keep your arms, face and hands away from the oil as it drains out.

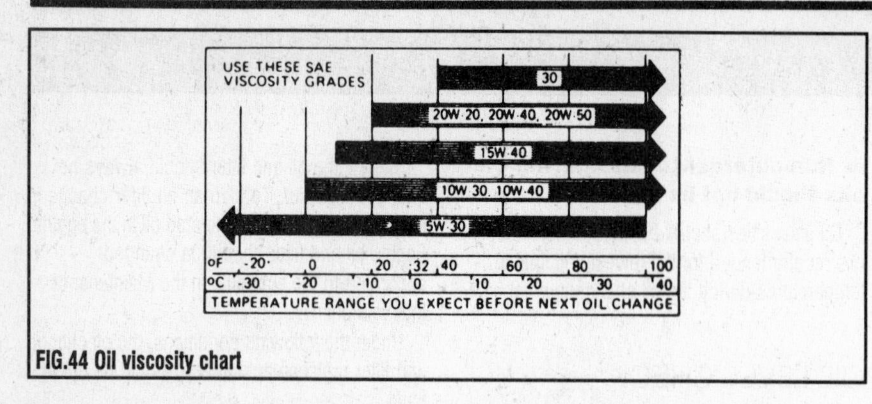

FIG.44 Oil viscosity chart

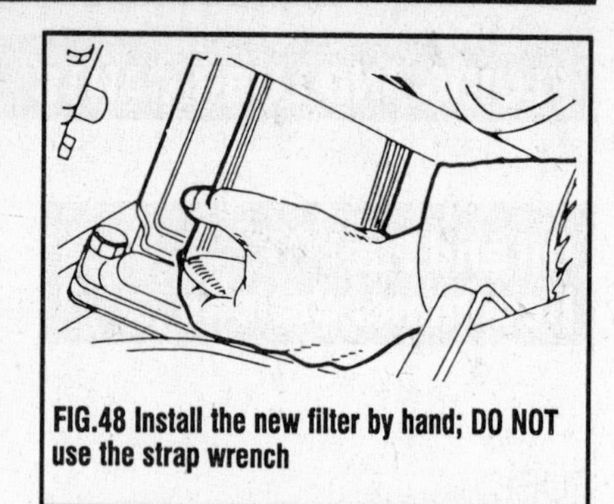

FIG.48 Install the new filter by hand; DO NOT use the strap wrench

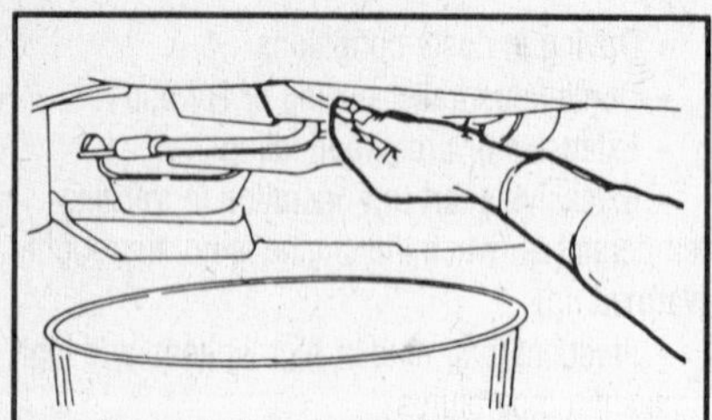

FIG.45 Keep an inward pressure on the plug as you unscrew it, so the oil won't escape until you pull the plug away

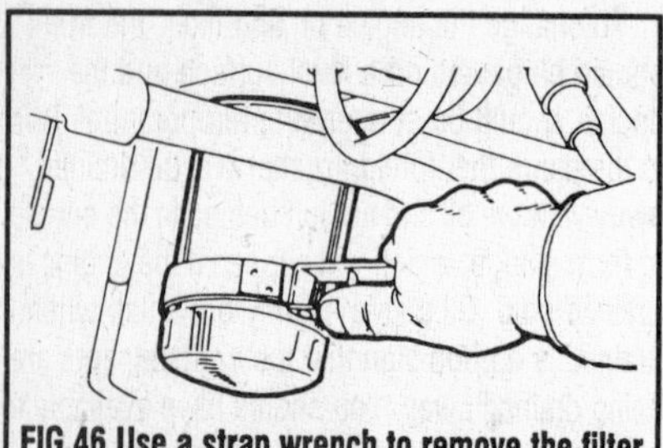

FIG.46 Use a strap wrench to remove the filter

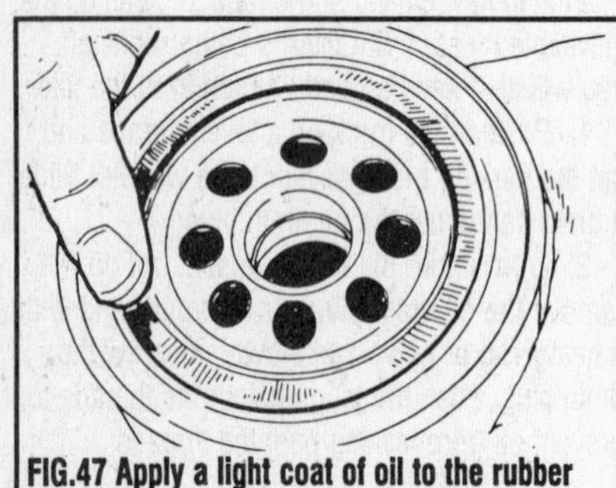

FIG.47 Apply a light coat of oil to the rubber gasket on the oil filter before installing it

3. As the plug comes to the end of the threads, whisk it away from the hole, letting the oil drain into the pan, which hopefully is still under the drain plug. This method usually avoids the messy task of reaching into a tub full of hot, dirty oil to retrieve a usually elusive drain plug. Crawl out from under the truck and wait for the oil to drain.

4. When the oil is drained, install the drain plug.

5. Change the engine oil filter as necessary or desired. Loosen the filter with a band wrench and spin the filter off by hand. Be careful of the one quart of hot, dirty oil that inevitably overflows the filter.

6. Coat the rubber gasket on a new filter with engine oil and install the filter. Screw the filter onto the mounting stud and tighten according to the directions on the filter.

7. Refill the engine with the specified amount of clean engine oil. Be sure to use the proper viscosity. Pour the oil in through the capped opening.

8. Run the engine for several minutes, checking for oil pressure and leaks. Check the level of the oil and add if necessary.

➡ **Take the drained oil, in a suitable container, to your local service station, or a special designated oil recycling station for disposal.**

Manual Transmission

FLUID RECOMMENDATION

API GL-4 or GL-5 80W-90 or 75W-90 gear lube is recommended.

LEVEL CHECK

➧ SEE FIGS. 51-53

1. Clean the dirt away from the area of the filler plug.

2. Jack the truck if necessary and support it on jackstands, make sure the vehicle is level.

3. Remove the filler plug from the case. The filler plug is the one on the side of the case. Do not remove the plug from the bottom of the case unless you wish to drain the transmission.

4. If lubricant flows from the area of the filler plug as it is removed, the level is satisfactory. If lubricant does not flow from the filler hole when the plug is removed, add enough of the specified lubricant to bring the level to the bottom of the filler hole with the truck in a level position.

FLUID CHANGE

Pickups and MPV

The same procedure is used for both 4-speed and 5-speed transmission, but note that the 5-speed transmissions have two filler plugs and two drain plugs. Thus, to drain the 5-speed, both drain plugs must be removed, and to fill it, both filler plugs must be removed. The truck should be parked on a level surface, and the transmission should be at normal operating temperature (oil hot).

1. With the truck parked on a level surface (parking brake applied), place a pan of at least four quarts capacity under the transmission drain plug(s).

2. Remove the filler plug(s) to provide a vent; this will speed the draining process.

3. On the pickup, remove the drain plug(s) and allow the old oil to drain into the pan. On the MPV, remove plugs labeled "A", "B" and "C" in the illustration. Apply upward pressure on the drain plug until you can pull it out and direct the fluid into the drain pan.

4. Clean the drain plug(s) thoroughly and replace. On the pickup, tighten to 15–20 ft. lbs. if you have a torque wrench handy; otherwise, just snug the plug or plugs in. Overtightening will strip the aluminum threads in the case. On the MPV, coat all plug threads with sealant and install them. Torque plug "A" to 29–43 ft. lbs., plug "B" and "D" to 18–29 ft. lbs.

FIG.49 Remove the engine oil dipstick, B2600i shown

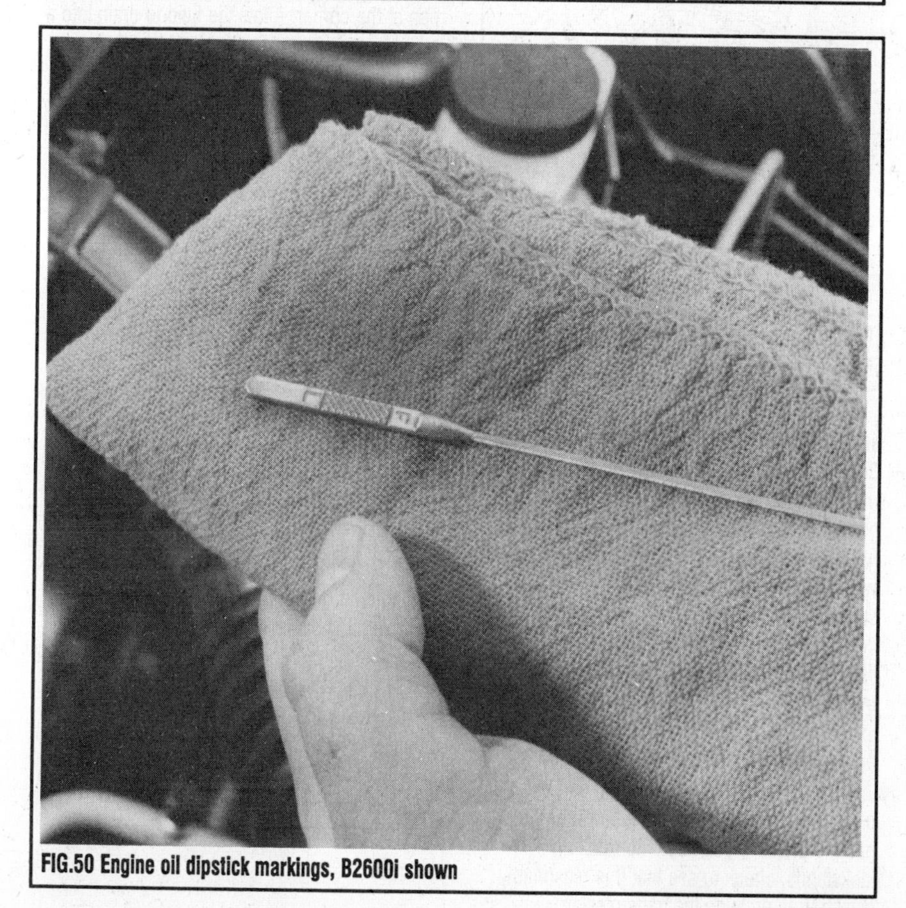

FIG.50 Engine oil dipstick markings, B2600i shown

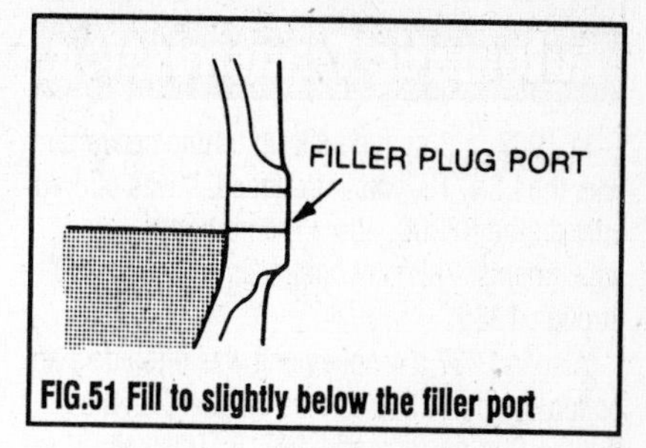

FIG.51 Fill to slightly below the filler port

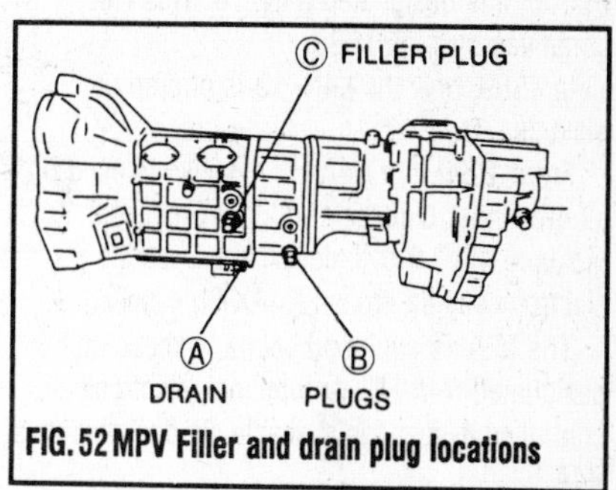

FIG.52 MPV Filler and drain plug locations

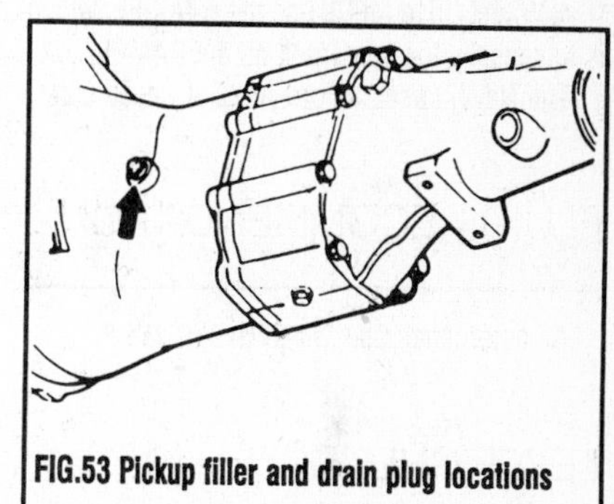

FIG.53 Pickup filler and drain plug locations

5. Add lubricant through the filler plug(s) until it comes right up to the edge of the filler hole. Use the recommended gear oil. It usually comes in a squeeze bottle with a nozzle attached to the cap, but you can use a squeeze bulb or suction gun for additions.

6. Install the filler plug(s). Tightening torque is 15–20 ft. lbs. for pickups; 18–29 ft. lbs. for MPV. Check for leaks after the truck has been driven for a few miles.

Navajo

Drain and refill the transmission daily if the vehicle has been operating in water. All you have to do is remove the drain plug which is located at the bottom of the transmission. Allow all the lubricant to run out before replacing the plug. Replace with the recommended gear oil. If you are experiencing hard shifting and the weather is very cold, use a lighter weight fluid in the transmission. If you don't have a pressure gun to install the oil, use a suction gun.

Automatic Transmission

In 1987, a 3-speed lock-up torque converter unit, the L3N71B, was introduced. It was offered only on the B2200. There are no band adjustments. This unit continues on the B2200 through 1988.

Also in 1987 a 4-speed unit was offered as an option on the B2200 and as standard on the B2600. It is designated L4N71B. This unit continues through 1988.

In 1989, only the L4N71B is offered on pickups.

From 1990, the N4A-HL 4-speed is used on all 4-cylinder pickups and 2WD 6-cylinder pickups. 4WD 6-cylinder pickups use the electronically controlled R4AX-EL 4-speed.

The MPV is equipped with a 4-speed unit designated N4A-HL. An optional, electronically controlled 4-speed is available. Its designation is R4A-EL.

4-Wheel Drive MPVs use the R4AX-EL, which is essentially the same unit as the R4A-EL.

The Navajo uses a Ford A4LD 4-speed unit.

FIG.54 Automatic transmission dipstick location

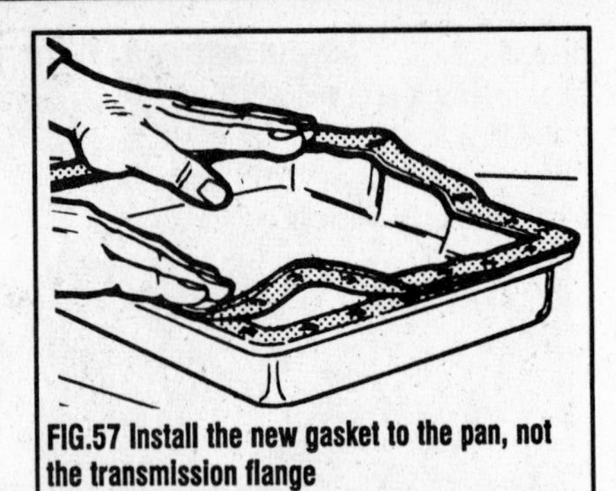

FIG.57 Install the new gasket to the pan, not the transmission flange

FIG.58 Transmission fluid is added through the dipstick tube

FLUID RECOMMENDATION

All automatics use **Dexron®II ATF**.

LEVEL CHECK

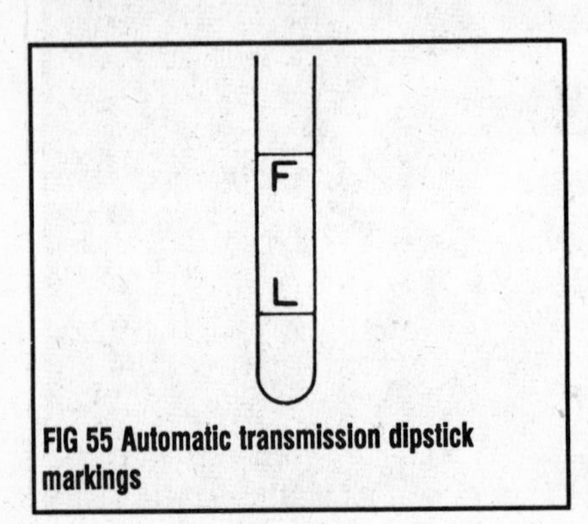

FIG 55 Automatic transmission dipstick markings

➧ SEE FIGS. 54 and 55

1. Drive the vehicle for several miles to bring the fluid level to operating temperature.
2. Park the truck on a level surface.
3. Put the automatic transmission in PARK. Leave the engine running.
4. Remove the dipstick from the tube and wipe it clean.
5. Reinsert the dipstick so that it is fully seated.
6. Remove the dipstick and note the reading. If the fluid is at or below the **Add** mark, add sufficient fluid to bring the level to the **Full** mark. Do not overfill the transmission. Overfilling will lead to fluid aeration.

DRAIN AND REFILL

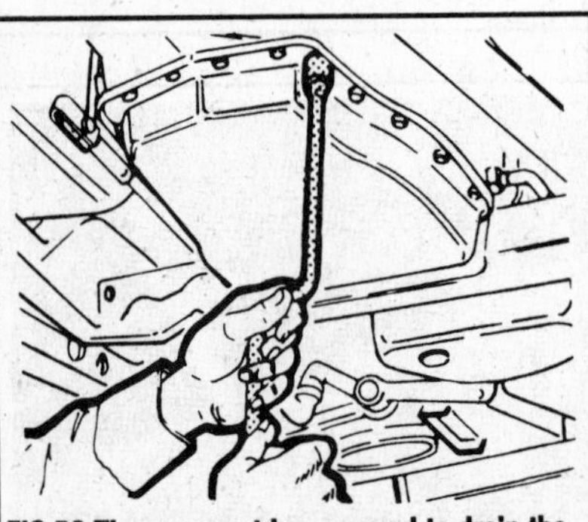

FIG.56 The pan must be removed to drain the automatic transmission

➧ SEE FIGS. 56-58

The automatic transmission fluid is a long lasting type, and Mazda does not specify that it need ever be changed. However, if you have brought the truck used, driven it in water deep enough to reach the transmission, or used the truck for trailer pulling or delivery service, you may want to change the fluid and filter. It is a good idea to measure the amount of fluid drained from the transmission, and to use this as a guide when refilling. Some parts of the transmission, such as the torque converter, will not drain completely, and using the dry refill capacity listed in the Capacities Chart may lead to overfilling.

1. Drive the truck until it is at normal operating temperature.
2. If a hoist is not being used, park the truck on a level surface, block the wheels, and set the parking brake. If you raise the truck on jackstands, check to see that it is reasonably level before draining the transmission.
3. There is no drain plug, so the transmission pan must be removed to drain the fluid. Carefully remove the screws from the pan and lower the pan at the corner. Allow the fluid to drain into a suitable container. After the fluid has drained, remove the pan.
4. The filter is bolted to the lower valve body. Remove the filter attaching bolts and remove. Clean it thoroughly in solvent, if it is a screen type, allow it to air dry completely, and replace it. Tightening torque for the attaching bolts is only 24–36 inch lbs., so be careful not to overtighten them.
5. Remove the old gasket and install a new one. The pan may be cleaned with solvent, if desired. After cleaning, allow the pan to air dry thoroughly. Do not use a rag to dry it, or you risk leaving bits of lint in the pan that will clog the transmission fluid passages. When the pan is completely dry, replace it, and tighten the bolts in a circular pattern, working from the center outward. Tighten gently to 40–60 inch lbs.
6. Refill the transmission. Fluid is added through the dipstick tube. This process is considerably easier if you have a funnel and a long tube to pour through. Add three quarts (2.8 liters) of fluid initially.
7. After adding fluid, start the engine and allow it to idle. Shift through all gear positions slowly to allow the fluid to fill all the hydraulic passages, and return the shift lever to Park. Do not race the engine.

8. Run the engine at fast idle to allow the fluid to reach operating temperature. Place the selector lever at **N** or **P** and check the fluid level. It should be above the **L** mark on the hot side of the dipstick. If necessary, add enough fluid to bring the level between the **L** and **F** marks. Do not overfill the transmission. Overfilling will cause foaming, fluid loss, and plate slippage.

9. After a few days of running, check the pan bolts. They will, probably have loosened as the gasket has shrunk. Retorque them.

Transfer Case

FLUID RECOMMENDATION

Pickups and MPV

Use API GL-5, SAE 75W-80 gear oil for year-round use when refilling or adding fluid to the transfer case.

Navajo

Use Dexron®II automatic transmission fluid when refilling or adding fluid to the transfer case.

LEVEL CHECK

Position the vehicle on level ground. Remove the transfer case fill plug (the upper plug) located on the rear of the transfer case. The fluid level should be up to the fill hole. If lubricant doesn't run out when the plug is removed, add lubricant until it does run out and then replace the fill plug.

DRAIN AND REFILL

The transfer case is serviced at the same time and in the same manner as the transmission. Clean the area around the filler and drain plugs and remove the filler plug on the side of the transfer case. Remove the drain plug on the bottom of the transfer case and allow the lubricant to drain completely. Clean and install the drain plug. Add the proper lubricant.

Front and Rear Drive Axle

FLUID RECOMMENDATIONS

API GL-4 or GL-5 80W-90 or 75W-90 gear lube is recommended.

LEVEL CHECK

The drive axle fluid level is checked from underneath the truck.

1. Clean the dirt and grease away from the area of the filler (top) plug.
2. Remove the filler plug. The lubricant level should be even with the bottom of the filler plug hole.
3. If lubricant is required, use only the specified type. It will probably have to be pumped in through the filler hole. Hypoid SAE 90 lubricant usually does not pour very well.

➡ **On Navajo models with the front locking differential, add 2 oz. of an approved friction modifier. On Navajo models with the rear locking differential, use only locking differential fluid, and add 4 oz. of friction modifier.**

DRAIN AND REFILL

Pickups and MPV

These models use a removable carrier axle which has a drain and fill plug.

1. Jack the front and/or rear of the vehicle and support it with jackstands.
2. Position a suitable container under the axle drain plug. Remove the fill plug to provide a vent.
3. Remove the drain plug and allow the lubricant to drain out.

➡ **Do not confuse the drain and fill plugs. The drain lug is magnetic to attract fine particles of metal which are inevitably present.**

4. Clean the magnetic drain plug.
5. Install the drain plug.
6. Fill the rear axle with the specified amount and type of fluid. Install the filler plug.
7. Lower the truck to the ground and drive the truck, checking for leaks after the fluid is warm.

Navajo

Remove the filler plug. Remove the oil with a suction gun. Refill the axle housings with the SAE 80W/90 gear oil. Be sure and clean the area around the drain plug before removing the plug.

Cooling System

➧ SEE FIGS. 59-61

CAUTION

Never remove the radiator cap under any conditions while the engine is running! Failure to follow these instructions could result in damage to the cooling system or engine and/or personal injury. To avoid having scalding hot coolant or steam blow out of the radiator, use extreme care when removing the radiator cap from a hot radiator. Wait until the engine has cooled, then wrap a thick cloth around the radiator cap and turn it slowly to the first stop. Step back while the pressure is released from the cooling system. When you are sure the pressure has been released, press down on the radiator cap (still have the cloth in position) turn and remove the radiator cap.

At least once every 2 years, the engine cooling system should be inspected, flushed, and refilled with fresh coolant. If the coolant is left in the system too long, it loses its ability to prevent rust and corrosion. If the coolant has too much water, it won't protect against freezing.

The pressure cap should be looked at for signs of age or deterioration. Fan belt and other drive belts should be inspected and adjusted to the proper tension. (See checking belt tension).

Hose clamps should be tightened, and soft or cracked hoses replaced. Damp spots, or accumulations of rust or dye near hoses, water pump or other areas, indicate possible leakage, which must be corrected before filling the system with fresh coolant.

FLUID RECOMMENDATIONS

A 50/50 mixture of ethylene glycol and water for year round use. Use a good quality antifreeze that is safe for use with aluminum components.

LEVEL CHECK

Most vehicles are equipped with a coolant reservoir tank (expansion tank) connected to the radiator by a small hose. When the engine is cold, look through the plastic tank; the fluid level should be between the FULL and Low lines. If the level is too low, remove the reservoir fill cover and add the proper mix of coolant until it reaches the FULL mark.

CHECK THE RADIATOR CAP

While you are checking the coolant level, check the radiator cap for a worn or cracked gasket. It the cap doesn't seal properly, fluid will be lost and the engine will overheat.

Worn caps should be replaced with a new one.

CLEAN RADIATOR OF DEBRIS

Periodically clean any debris — leaves, paper, insects, etc. — from the radiator fins. Pick the large pieces off by hand. The smaller pieces can be washed away with water pressure from a hose.

Carefully straighten any bent radiator fins with a pair of needle nose pliers. Be careful — the fins are very soft. Don't wiggle the fins back and forth too much. Straighten them once and try not to move them again.

DRAIN, REFILL AND FLUSHING

Completely draining and refilling the cooling system every two years at least will remove accumulated rust, scale and other deposits. Coolant in late model trucks is a 50/50 mixture of ethylene glycol (make sure it is safe for aluminum components) and water for year round use. Use a good quality antifreeze with water pump lubricants, rust inhibitors and other corrosion inhibitors along with acid neutralizers.

1. Drain the existing antifreeze and coolant. It may be necessary to remove a splash shield, on some models, to gain access to the drain at the bottom of the radiator. Open the radiator and engine drain petcocks, or disconnect the bottom radiator hose, at the radiator outlet.

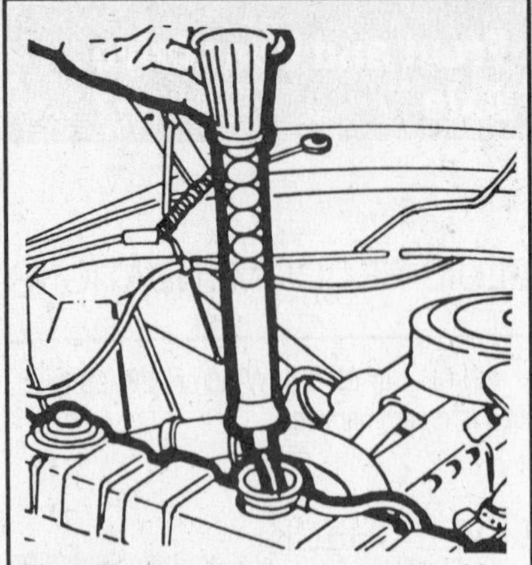

FIG.59 Check the anti-freeze protection with an inexpensive tester

CAUTION

When draining the coolant, keep in mind that cats and dogs are attracted by the ethylene glycol antifreeze, and are quite likely to drink any that is left in an uncovered container or in puddles on the ground. This will prove fatal in sufficient quantity. Always drain the coolant into a sealable container. Coolant should be reused unless it is contaminated or several years old.

➡ Before opening the radiator petcock, spray it with some penetrating lubricant.

2. Close the petcock or reconnect the lower hose and fill the system with water.
3. Add a can of quality radiator flush.
4. Idle the engine until the upper radiator hose gets hot.
5. Drain the system again.
6. Repeat this process until the drained water is clear and free of scale.
7. Close all petcocks and connect all the hoses.
8. If equipped with a coolant recovery system, flush the reservoir with water and leave empty.
9. Determine the capacity of your coolant system (see capacities specifications). Add a 50/50 mix of quality antifreeze (ethylene glycol) and water to provide the desired protection to the level of the radiator filler port. Fill the coolant reservoir to the correct level. Install the radiator cap.

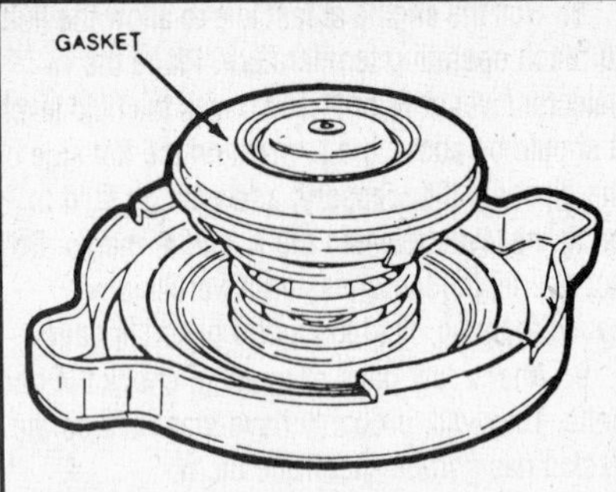

FIG.60 Check the radiator cap gasket for wear or cracks

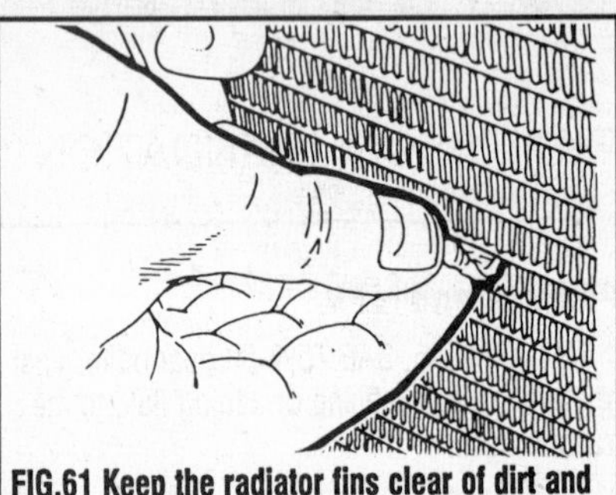

FIG.61 Keep the radiator fins clear of dirt and bugs for maximum cooling

10. Run the engine to operating temperature.
11. Stop the engine. Allow the engine to cool and check the coolant level in the radiator. Add more coolant if necessary to the radiator.
12. Check the level of protection with an antifreeze tester, replace the cap and check for leaks.

Brake Master Cylinder

➧ SEE FIG 62

FLUID RECOMMENDATIONS

Use only a good quality brake fluid meeting specifications DOT-3 or DOT-4.

LEVEL CHECK

Check the level of the fluid in the brake master cylinder at the specified interval or more often.

1. Park the truck on a level surface.
2. If the vehicle is not equipped with a see through reservoir, clean all dirt from the area of the master cylinder reservoir cover.

3. Remove the top from the master cylinder reservoir. Be careful when doing this. Brake fluid that is dripped on painted surfaces will quickly destroy the paint.

4. The level should be maintained approximately 1/4–1/2 in. (6–13mm) below the top of the reservoir. On see-through reservoirs, the fluid level should be level with the FULL mark.

5. If brake fluid is needed, use only a good quality brake fluid meeting specifications DOT-3 or DOT-4.

6. If necessary, add fluid to maintain the proper level and replace the top on the master cylinder reservoir securely.

➡ **If the fluid level is constantly low, it would be a good idea to look into the matter. This is a good indication of problems elsewhere in the system.**

Clutch Master Cylinder

➧ SEE FIG 63

The clutch master cylinder is located at the left rear corner of the engine compartment. Check the level in the clutch master cylinder in the same manner as the brake master cylinder. The level should be kept approximately 1/4 in. (6mm) from the top of the cylinder. Use brake fluid in the clutch system. Be sure that the truck is on a level surface.

Manual Steering Gear

LEVEL CHECK

1. Clean the area around the plug and remove the plug from the top of the gear housing.

2. The oil level should just reach the plug hole.

3. If necessary, add 80W-90 gear oil until the fluid is at the proper level.

4. Install the plug.

FIG.62 Brake master cylinder reservoir High/Low fluid level markings

FIG.63 Clutch master cylinder reservoir High/Low fluid level markings

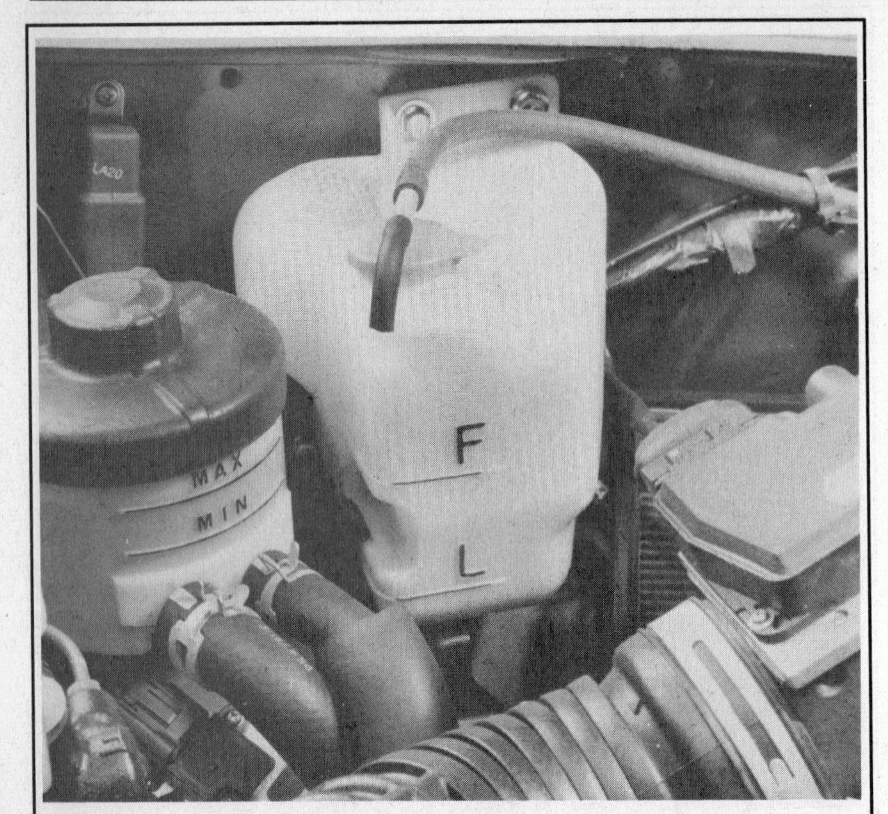

FIG.64 Power steering reservoir showing the Max/Min fluid level markings. Also shown is the coolant expansion reservoir

Power Steering Pump

➧ SEE FIG 64

LEVEL CHECK

The power steering reservoir is usually located on the left side of the engine. A dipstick is part of the cap. With the fluid hot — 10 minutes of driving — the level should be between the **F** and **L** or **Max/Min** marks. Use Dexron®II automatic transmission fluid.

Chassis Maintenance

Complete chassis maintenance should include an inspection of all rubber suspension bushings, lubrication of all body hinges, as well inspection of the front suspension components and steering linkage.

Body Lubrication and Maintenance

LOCK CYLINDERS

Apply graphite lubricant sparingly thought the key slot. Insert the key and operate the lock several times to be sure that the lubricant is worked into the lock cylinder.

DOOR HINGES AND HINGE CHECKS

Spray a silicone lubricant on the hinge pivot points to eliminate any binding conditions. Open and close the door several times to be sure that the lubricant is evenly and thoroughly distributed.

TAILGATE

Spray a silicone lubricant on all of the pivot and friction surfaces to eliminate any squeaks or binds. Work the tailgate to distribute the lubricant evenly.

BODY DRAIN HOLES

Be sure that the drain holes in the doors and rocker panels are cleared of obstruction. A small screwdriver can be used to clear them of any debris.

Front Wheel Bearings

2-Wheel Drive Vehicles

➧ SEE FIGS. 65-74

**** CAUTION**

Brake shoes contain asbestos, which has been determined to be a cancer causing agent. Never clean the brake surfaces with compressed air! Avoid inhaling any dust from any brake surface! When cleaning brake surfaces, use a commercially available brake cleaning fluid.

FRONT WHEEL BEARING LOOSENESS TEST

MPV

The MPV has integral hub/bearing assemblies. No service, other than replacement, is possible.

1. Raise the front of the car and support it with jack stands.
2. Grasp the wheel at the 1 o'clock and 7 o'clock positions and shake it sideways.
3. Rotate the tire and make sure that it turns smoothly and that the bearings are not noisy.
4. Remove the front wheel.
5. Remove the caliper assembly and suspend it with a rope from the strut (see section 9, Caliper, Removal and Installation).

6. Mount a dial indicator so that the stylus of the dial is positioned on the face of the wheel hub cap. Zero the indicator.
7. Grasp the rotor disc by hand and try to move in the axial direction (in and out). Measure the endplay on the dial indicator. The maximum allowable endplay is 0.002 in. (0.05mm). If the endplay exceeds that amount, replace the wheel bearing.
8. Install the brake caliper assembly and torque the caliper retaining bolts to 58–86 ft. lbs.
9. Install the wheel and torque the wheel lug nuts to 65–87 ft. lbs.
10. Repeat the procedure for the remaining front wheel.

To replace the hub/bearing assembly:

1. Raise and support the front end on jackstands.
2. Remove the wheel.
3. Remove the hub locknut.
4. Remove the hub. Do not reuse the lug bolts. Buy new ones. Drive the lug bolts into the new hub.
5. Install the hub on the spindle.
6. Install a new locknut and tighten it to 130–174 ft. lbs. Check the endplay with a dial indicator. If the play exceeds 0.002 in. (0.05mm), loosen the hub nut and retighten it to 174 ft. lbs. Stake the locknut in the groove in the spindle.
7. Recheck the endplay. If the endplay is still excessive, the hub and bearing assembly is either defective or was installed incorrectly.

ADJUSTMENT

Pickups

1. Raise and support the front end on jackstands. Check both the bearing axial play and the ease and smoothness of rotation. Axial play should be 0; the wheel should rotate smoothly, with no perceptible bearing noise.
2. Remove the wheel. Remove the brake drum or disc brake caliper. Suspend the caliper out of the way. Don't disconnect the brake line.
3. Attach a spring scale to a wheel lug.
4. Pull the scale horizontally and check the force needed to start the wheel turning. The force should be 1.3–2.4 lbs. (0.6–1.1 kg). If the reading is not correct, proceed.
5. Remove the grease cap and cotter pin.
6. Tighten or loosen the hub nut until the correct pull rating is obtained.
7. Align the cotter pin holes and insert a new cotter pin. Replace the grease cap and wheel.

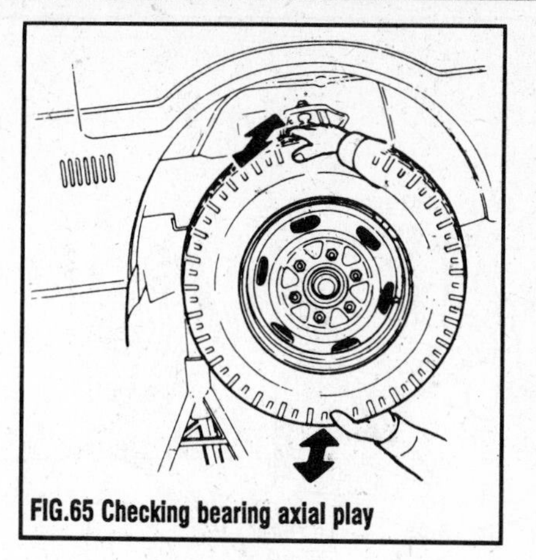
FIG.65 Checking bearing axial play

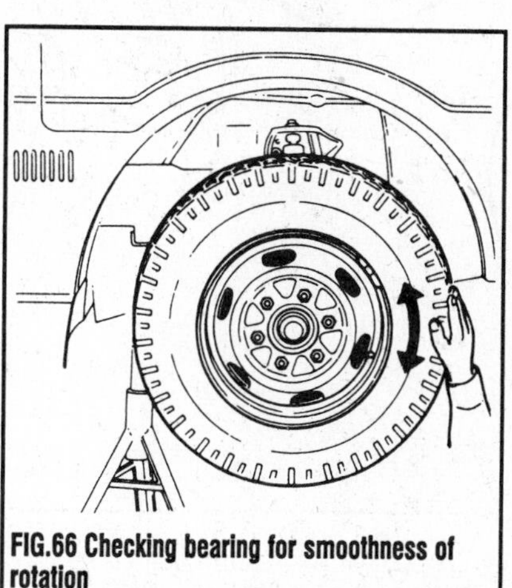
FIG.66 Checking bearing for smoothness of rotation

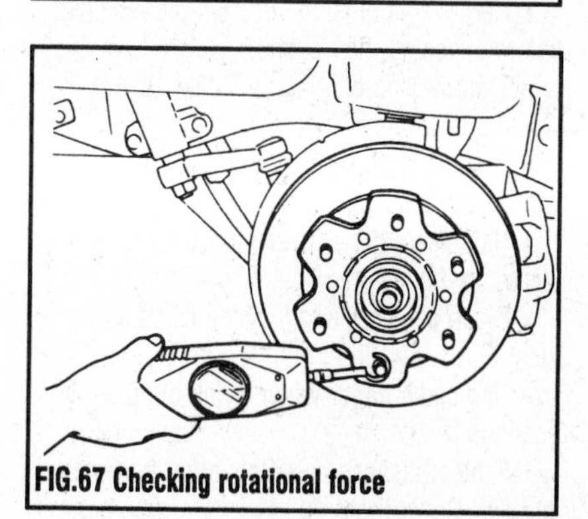
FIG.67 Checking rotational force

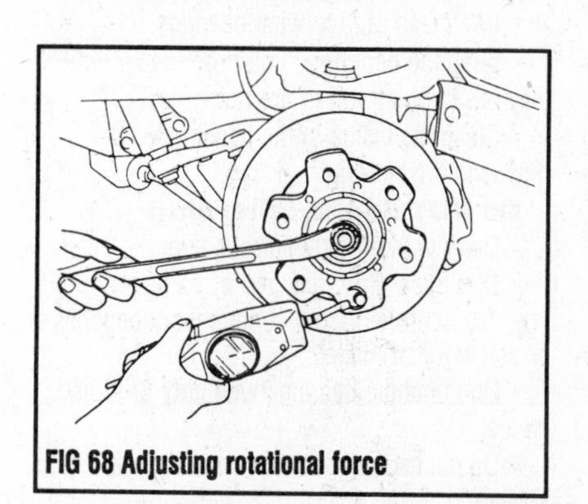
FIG 68 Adjusting rotational force

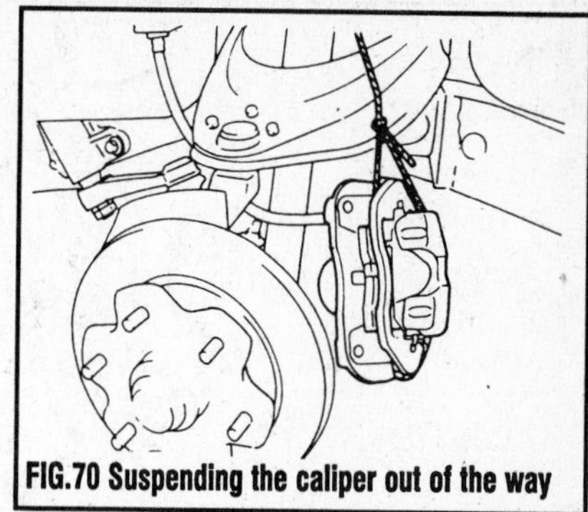
FIG.70 Suspending the caliper out of the way

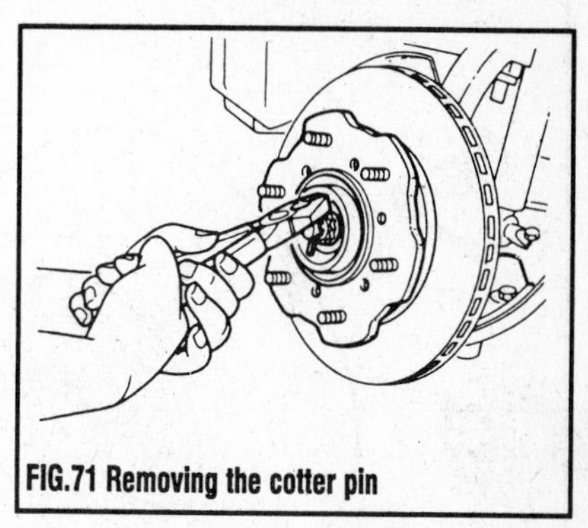
FIG.71 Removing the cotter pin

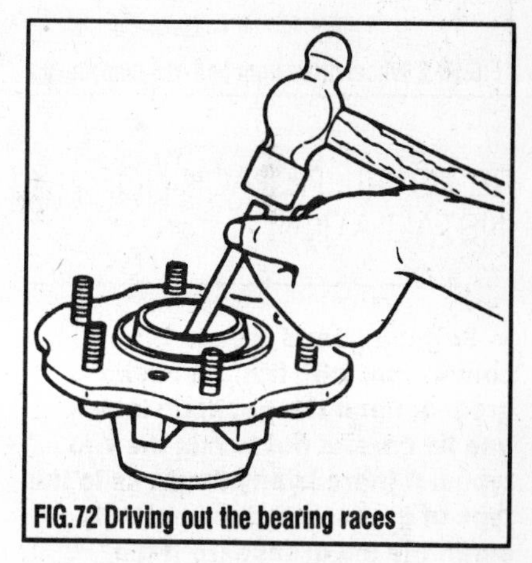
FIG.72 Driving out the bearing races

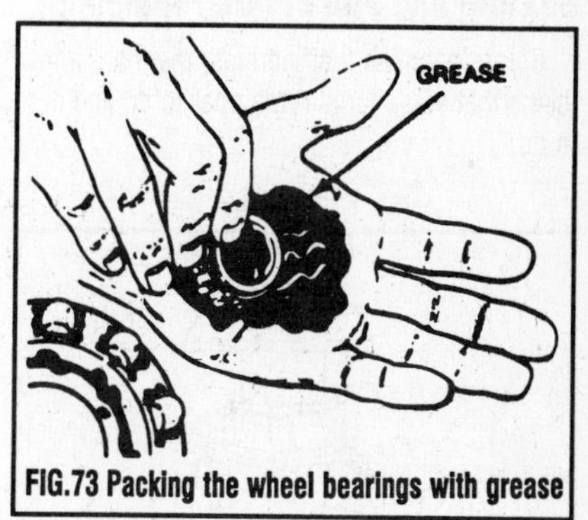

FIG.73 Packing the wheel bearings with grease

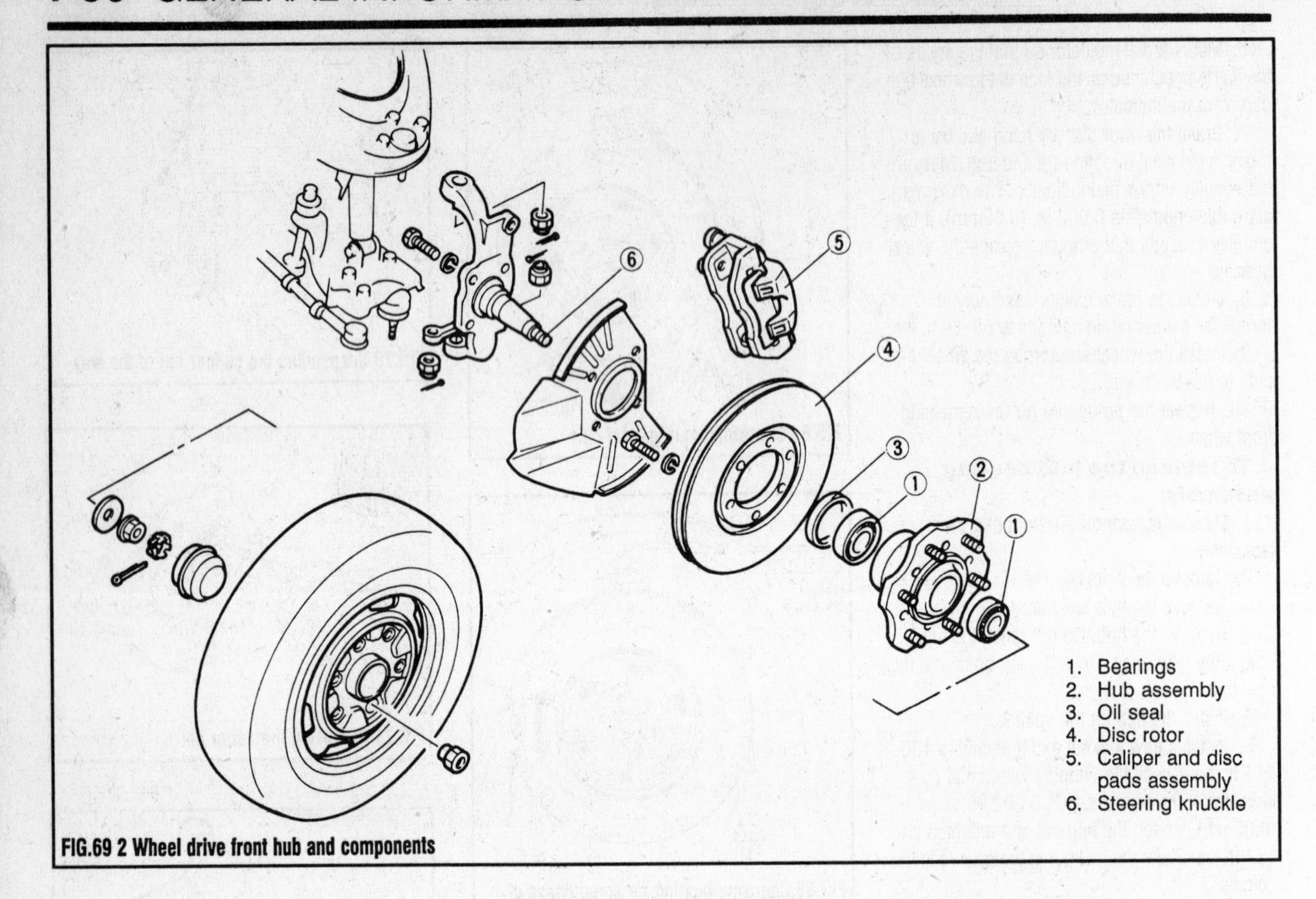

FIG.69 2 Wheel drive front hub and components

REMOVAL, REPACKING, INSTALLATION

➡ Sodium-based grease is not compatible with lithium-based grease. Read the package labels and be careful not to mix the two types. If there is any doubt as to the type of grease used, completely clean the old grease from the bearing and hub before replacing.

Before handling the bearings, there are a few things that you should remember to do and not to do.

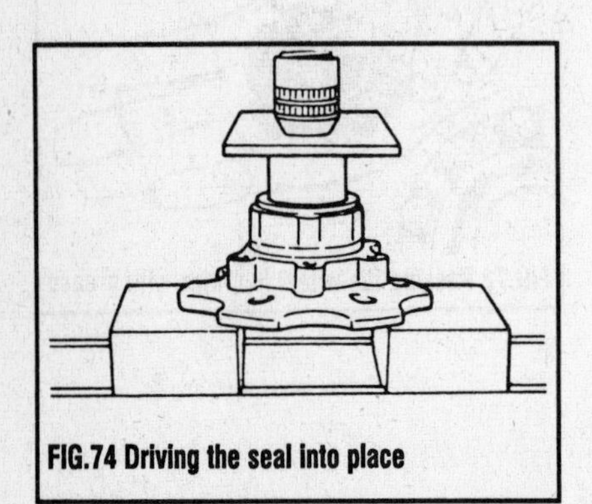
FIG.74 Driving the seal into place

Remember to DO the following:

- Remove all outside dirt from the housing before exposing the bearing.
- Treat a used bearing as gently as you would a new one.
- Work with clean tools in clean surroundings.
- Use clean, dry canvas gloves, or at least clean, dry hands.
- Clean solvents and flushing fluids are a must.
- Use clean paper when laying out the bearings to dry.
- Protect disassembled bearings from rust and dirt. Cover them up.
- Use clean rags to wipe bearings.
- Keep the bearings in oil-proof paper when they are to be stored or are not in use.
- Clean the inside of the housing before replacing the bearing.

Do NOT do the following:

- Don't work in dirty surroundings.
- Don't use dirty, chipped or damaged tools.
- Try not to work on wooden work benches or use wooden mallets.
- Don't handle bearings with dirty or moist hands.
- Do not use gasoline for cleaning; use a safe solvent.
- Do not spin-dry bearings with compressed air. They will be damaged.
- Do not spin dirty bearings.
- Avoid using cotton waste or dirty cloths to wipe bearings.
- Try not to scratch or nick bearing surfaces.
- Do not allow the bearing to come in contact with dirt or rust at any time.

1. Raise and support the front end on jackstands.
2. Remove the wheel.
3. Remove the grease cap, cotter pin, hub nut and flat washer.
4. On trucks with disc brakes, remove the caliper and suspend it out of the way without disconnecting the brake line. Slowly pull the hub from the spindle, positioning your hand to catch the outer bearing.
5. Remove the spacer, inner seal and inner bearing. Discard the seal.
6. Thoroughly clean the bearings and inside of the hub with a nonflammable solvent. Allow them to air dry.
7. Inspect the bearings for wear, damage, heat discoloration or other signs of fatigue. If they are at all suspect, replace them. When replacing bearings, it is a good idea to replace the bearing races as a set, as bearings do wear the races in a definite pattern which may not be compatible with new bearings.

8. To replace the races, carefully drive them out of the hub with a drift.

9. Coat the outside of the new races with clean wheel bearing grease and drive them into place until they bottom in their bore. Make certain that they are completely bottomed! A drift can be used as a driver, if you hammer evenly around the rim of the race and are very careful not to slip and scratch the surface of the race. A driver made for the purpose is much easier to use.

10. Pack the inside of the hub with clean wheel bearing grease until it is flush packed.

11. Pack each bearing with clean grease, making sure that it is thoroughly packed. Special devices are sold for packing bearings. They are inexpensive and readily available. If you don't have one, just make certain that the bearing is as full of grease as possible by working it in with your fingers.

12. Install the inner bearing and seal. Drive the seal into place carefully until it is seated.

13. Install the spacer and the hub on the spindle.

14. Install the outer bearing, flat washer and hub nut.

15. Adjust the bearing as explained above.

16. Install the nut cap, cotter pin and grease cap. Install the wheel.

Front Wheel Bearings 4-Wheel Drive

➧ SEE FIGS. 75-79

➡ For front locking hub removal and service, see Section 7.

ADJUSTMENT

Pickups

1. Raise and support the front end on jackstands.
2. Remove the wheels.
3. Grasp the brake rotor and check for noticeable bearing play. There should be no (0) play. If play is detected, proceed.
4. Remove the caliper and suspend it out of the way.
5. Remove the locking hub. See Section 7.
6. Remove the snapring and spacer.
7. Remove the set bolts and bearing set plate.
8. Tighten the locknut and turn the hub 2 or 3 complete turns to seat the bearings.
9. Loosen the locknut until it can be turned by hand.
10. Attach a pull scale to a wheel lug and check the bearing rotational effort. Rotational effort should be 1.3–2.6 lb. (0.6–1.1 kg). If not, tighten the locknut until the effort is within specifications.
11. Install the set bolts and set plate.
12. Install the snapring and spacer.
13. Install the locking hub.
14. Install the caliper.
15. Install the wheels.

Navajo

1. Raise the vehicle and install jackstands.
2. Remove the wheel and tire assembly.
3. Remove the retainer washers from the lug nut studs and remove the locking hub assembly from the spindle.
4. Remove the snapring from the end of the spindle shaft.

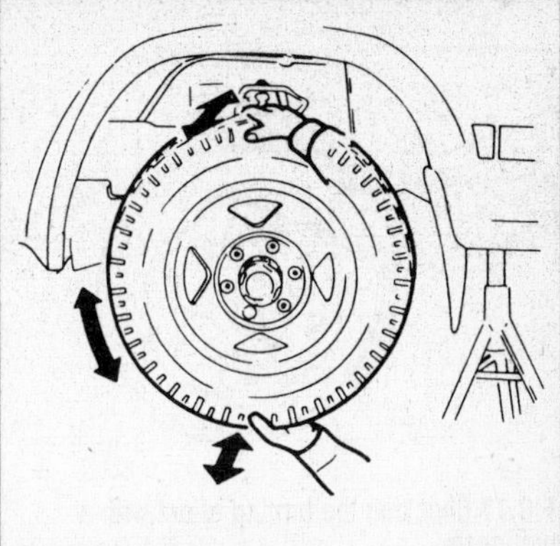

FIG.76 Checking the wheel bearing play on models with 4 wheel drive

5. Remove the axle shaft spacer, needle thrust bearing and the bearing spacer.
6. Remove the outer wheel bearing locknut from the spindle using a 4 prong spindle nut spanner wrench. Make sure the tabs on the tool engage the slots in the locknut.
7. Remove the locknut washer from the spindle.
8. Loosen the inner wheel bearing locknut using a 4 prong spindle nut spanner wrench. Make sure that the tabs on the tool engage the slots in the locknut and that the slot in the tool is over the pin on the locknut.
9. Tighten the inner locknut to 35 ft. lbs. to seat the bearings.
10. Spin the rotor and back off the inner locknut 1/4 turn. Install the lockwasher on the spindle. Retighten the inner locknut to 16 inch lbs. It may be necessary to turn the inner locknut slightly so that the pin on the locknut aligns with the closest hole in the lockwasher.

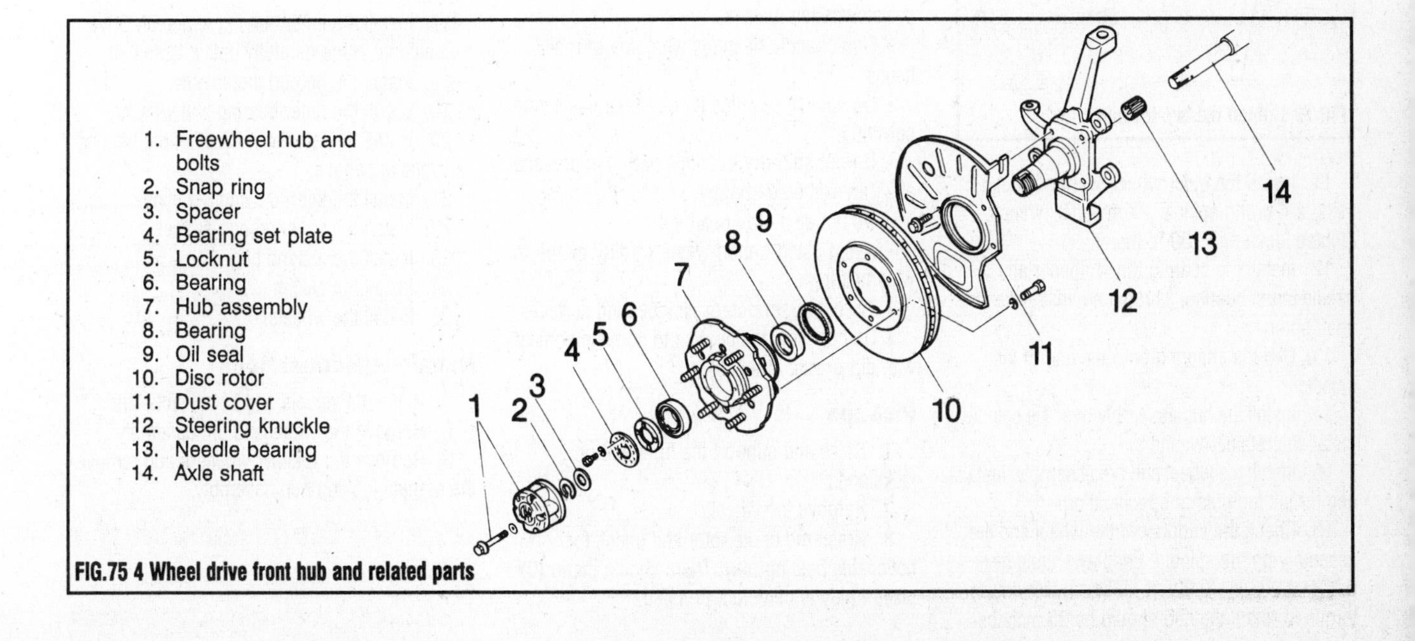

FIG.75 4 Wheel drive front hub and related parts

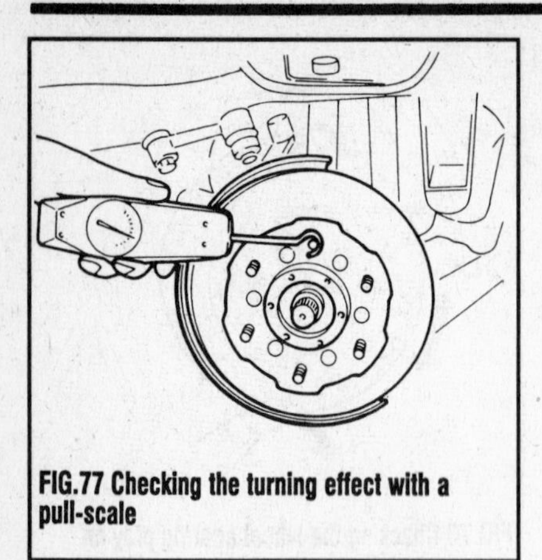
FIG.77 Checking the turning effect with a pull-scale

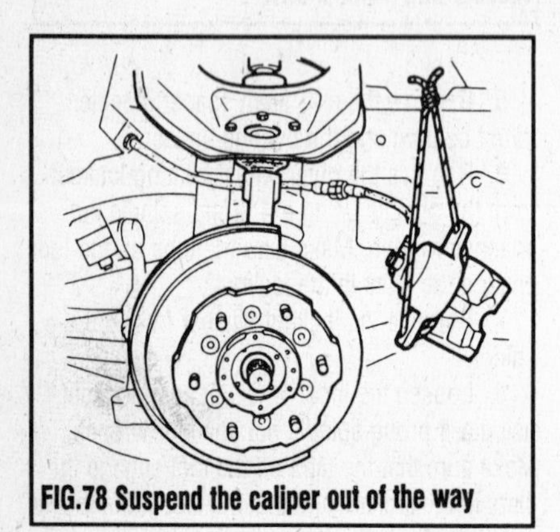
FIG.78 Suspend the caliper out of the way

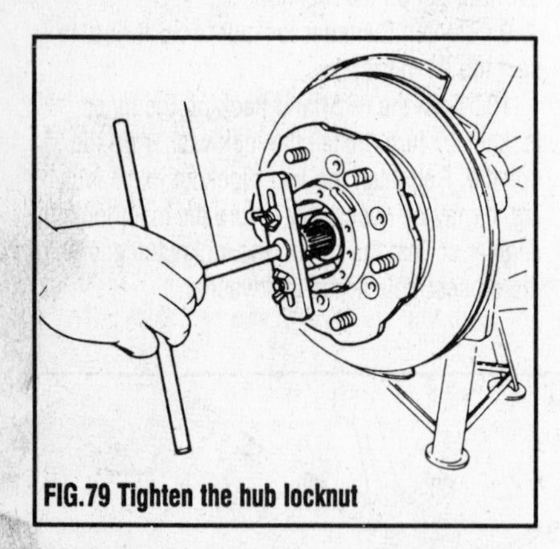
FIG.79 Tighten the hub locknut

11. Install the outer wheel bearing locknut using a 4 prong spindle nut spanner wrench. Tighten locknut to 150 ft. lbs.
12. Install the bearing thrust spacer and needle thrust bearing, as required. Install the axle shaft spacer.
13. Clip the snapring onto the end of the spindle.
14. Install the hub assembly over the spindle. Install the retainer washers.
15. Install the wheel and tire assembly. Install and torque lug nuts to specification.
16. Check the endplay of the wheel and tire assembly on the spindle. Endplay should be 0.001–0.003 in. (0.025–0.076mm). Maximum torque to rotate the hub should be 25 inch lbs.

REMOVAL, PACKING AND INSTALLATION

➡ Sodium-based grease is not compatible with lithium-based grease. Read the package labels and be careful not to mix the two types. If there is any doubt as to the type of grease used, completely clean the old grease from the bearing and hub before replacing.

Before handling the bearings, there are a few things that you should remember to do and not to do.

Remember to DO the following:

- Remove all outside dirt from the housing before exposing the bearing.
- Treat a used bearing as gently as you would a new one.
- Work with clean tools in clean surroundings.
- Use clean, dry canvas gloves, or at least clean, dry hands.
- Clean solvents and flushing fluids are a must.
- Use clean paper when laying out the bearings to dry.
- Protect disassembled bearings from rust and dirt. Cover them up.
- Use clean rags to wipe bearings.
- Keep the bearings in oil-proof paper when they are to be stored or are not in use.
- Clean the inside of the housing before replacing the bearing.

Do NOT do the following:

- Don't work in dirty surroundings.
- Don't use dirty, chipped or damaged tools.
- Try not to work on wooden work benches or use wooden mallets.
- Don't handle bearings with dirty or moist hands.
- Do not use gasoline for cleaning; use a safe solvent.
- Do not spin-dry bearings with compressed air. They will be damaged.
- Do not spin dirty bearings.
- Avoid using cotton waste or dirty cloths to wipe bearings.
- Try not to scratch or nick bearing surfaces.
- Do not allow the bearing to come in contact with dirt or rust at any time.

Pickups

1. Raise and support the front end on jackstands.
2. Remove the wheels.
3. Grasp the brake rotor and check for noticeable bearing play. There should be no (0) play. If play is detected, proceed.
4. Remove the caliper and suspend it out of the way.
5. Remove the locking hub. See Section 7.
6. Remove the snapring and spacer.
7. Remove the set bolts and bearing set plate.
8. Remove the locknut.
9. Pull of the hub and plate, taking care to catch the washer and bearing.
10. Using a wood driver, such as a hammer handle, drive out the inner bearing and oil seal.
11. Thoroughly clean the bearings and inside of the hub with a nonflammable solvent. Allow them to air dry.
12. Inspect the bearings for wear, damage, heat discoloration or other signs of fatigue. If they are at all suspect, replace them. When replacing bearings, it is a good idea to replace the bearing races as a set, as bearings do wear the races in a definite pattern which may not be compatible with new bearings.
13. To replace the races, carefully drive them out of the hub with a drift.
14. Coat the outside of the new races with clean wheel bearing grease and drive them into place until they bottom in their bore. Make certain that they are completely bottomed! A drift can be used as a driver, if you hammer evenly around the rim of the race and are very careful not to slip and scratch the surface of the race. A driver made for the purpose is much easier to use.
15. Pack the inside of the hub with clean wheel bearing grease until it is flush packed.
16. Pack each bearing with clean grease, making sure that it is thoroughly packed. Special devices are sold for packing bearings. They are inexpensive and readily available. If you don't have one, just make certain that the bearing is as full of grease as possible by working it in with your fingers.
17. Install the inner bearing and seal. Drive the seal into place carefully until it is seated.
18. Install the hub on the spindle.
19. Install the outer bearing and washer.
20. Install the locknut and adjust the bearing as explained above.
21. Install the set bolts and set plate.
22. Install the snapring and spacer.
23. Install the locking hub.
24. Install the caliper.
25. Install the wheels.

Navajo w/Manual Hubs

1. Raise the vehicle and install jackstands.
2. Remove the wheel and tire assembly.
3. Remove the retainer washers and remove the manual locking hub assembly.

4. Remove the caliper and wire it to the side using mechanics wire.
5. Remove the snapring from the end of the spindle shaft.
6. Remove the axle shaft spacer, needle thrust bearing and the bearing spacer.
7. Remove the outer wheel bearing locknut from the spindle using 4 prong spindle nut spanner wrench, T86T-1197-A or equivalent. Make sure the tabs on the tool engage the slots in the locknut.
8. Remove the locknut washer from the spindle.
9. Remove the inner wheel bearing adjusting nut using 4 prong spindle nut spanner wrench, Ford tool T86T-1197-A or equivalent. Make sure that the tabs on the tool engage the slots in the locknut and that the slot in the tool is over the pin on the locknut.
10. Remove the disc brake rotor and the hub assembly. Remove the outer wheel bearing cone assembly.
11. Remove the grease seal from the rotor with seal remover tool 1175-AC and slide hammer 750T-100-A or equivalent. Discard seal and replace with a new one upon assembly.
12. Remove the inner wheel bearing.
13. Inspect the bearing cups for pits or cracks. If necessary, remove them with internal puller tool D80L-943-A and slide hammer 750T-100-A. or equivalent.

➡ **If new cups are installed, install new cone and roller assemblies.**

To install:

14. Lubricate the bearings with disc brake wheel bearing grease. Clean all old grease from the hub. Pack the cones and rollers. If a bearing packer is not available, work as much lubricant as possible between the rollers and the cages.
15. If bearing cups are to be installed, position cups in rotor and drive in place with bearing cup tool T73T-4222-B and driver handle T80T-4000-W.
16. Position the inner bearing in the inner cup in the rotor. Install the grease seal by driving in place with hub seal replacer tool T83T-1175-B and Driver Handle T80T-4000-W.
17. Carefully install the rotor onto the spindle. Install the outer wheel bearing in the rotor.
18. Install the inner adjusting nut with the pin facing out. Tighten the inner adjusting nut to 35 ft. lbs. to seat the bearings.
19. Spin the rotor and back off the inner nut 1/4 turn. Retighten the inner nut to 16 inch lbs. Install the locking washer. It may be necessary to turn the inner nut slightly so that the pin on the nut aligns with the closest hole in the lock-washer.
20. Install the outer wheel bearing locknut using 4 prong spindle nut spanner wrench. Tighten locknut to 150 ft. lbs.
21. Install the bearing thrust spacer and needle thrust bearing, as required. Install the axle shaft spacer.
22. Clip the snapring onto the end of the spindle.
23. Install the caliper. Install the locking hub assembly.
24. Install the wheel assembly. Lower the vehicle.

Navajo w/Automatic Hubs

1. Raise the vehicle and install jackstands.
2. Remove the wheel and tire assembly.
3. Remove the retainer washers and remove the automatic locking hub assembly.
4. Remove the caliper and wire it to the side using mechanics wire.
5. Remove the snapring from the end of the spindle shaft.
6. Remove the axle shaft spacer, needle thrust bearing and the bearing spacer.
7. Remove the outer wheel bearing locknut from the spindle using 4 prong spindle nut spanner wrench, T86T-1197-A or equivalent. Make sure the tabs on the tool engage the slots in the locknut.
8. Remove the locknut washer from the spindle.
9. Remove the inner wheel bearing adjusting nut using 4 prong spindle nut spanner wrench, tool T83T-1197-A for 1987-89 vehicles and tool T86T-1197-A for 1990-91 vehicles or equivalent. Make sure that the tabs on the tool engage the slots in the locknut and that the slot in the tool is over the pin on the locknut.
10. Remove the disc brake rotor and the hub assembly. Remove the outer wheel bearing cone assembly.
11. Remove the grease seal from the rotor with seal remover tool 1175-AC and slide hammer 750T-100-A or equivalent. Discard seal and replace with a new one upon assembly.
12. Remove the inner wheel bearing.
13. Inspect the bearing cups for pits or cracks. If necessary, remove them with internal puller tool D80L-943-A and slide hammer 750T-100-A. or equivalent.

➡ **If new cups are installed, install new cone and roller assemblies.**

To install:

14. Lubricate the bearings with disc brake wheel bearing grease. Clean all old grease from the hub. Pack the cones and rollers. If a bearing packer is not available, work as much lubricant as possible between the rollers and the cages.
15. If bearing cups are to be installed, position cups in rotor and drive in place with bearing cup tool T73T-4222-B and driver handle T80T-4000-W.
16. Position the inner bearing in the inner cup in the rotor. Install the grease seal by driving in place with hub seal replacer tool T83T-1175-B and Driver Handle T80T-4000-W.
17. Carefully install the rotor onto the spindle. Install the outer wheel bearing in the rotor.
18. Install the inner adjusting nut, with the pin facing out. Tighten the inner locknut to 35 ft. lbs. to seat the bearings.
19. Spin the rotor and back off the inner locknut 1/4 turn (90°). Retighten the inner locknut to 16 inch lbs. Install the locking washer. It may be necessary to turn the inner locknut slightly so that the pin on the locknut aligns with the closest hole in the lockwasher.
20. Install the outer wheel bearing locknut using 4 prong spindle nut spanner wrench, tool T83T-1197-A for 1987-89 vehicles and tool T86T-1197-A for 1990-91 vehicles or equivalent. Tighten locknut to 150 ft. lbs.
21. Install the bearing thrust spacer and needle thrust bearing, as required. Install the axle shaft spacer.
22. Clip the snapring onto the end of the spindle.
23. Install the caliper. Install the locking hub assembly.
24. Install the wheel. Lower the vehicle.

TRAILER TOWING

Factory trailer towing packages are available on most trucks. However, if you are installing a trailer hitch and wiring on your truck, there are a few thing that you ought to know.

Trailer Weight

Trailer weight is the first, and most important, factor in determining whether or not your vehicle is suitable for towing the trailer you have in mind. The horsepower-to-weight ratio should be calculated. The basic standard is a ratio of 35:1. That is, 35 pounds of GVW for every horsepower.

To calculate this ratio, multiply you engine's rated horsepower by 35, then subtract the weight of the vehicle, including passengers and luggage. The resulting figure is the ideal maximum trailer weight that you can tow. One point to consider: a numerically higher axle ratio can offset what appears to be a low trailer weight. If the weight of the trailer that you have in mind is somewhat higher than the weight you just calculated, you might consider changing your rear axle ratio to compensate.

Hitch Weight

There are three kinds of hitches: bumper mounted, frame mounted, and load equalizing.

Bumper mounted hitches are those which attach solely to the vehicle's bumper. Many states prohibit towing with this type of hitch, when it attaches to the vehicle's stock bumper, since it subjects the bumper to stresses for which it was not designed. Aftermarket rear step bumpers, designed for trailer towing, are acceptable for use with bumper mounted hitches.

Frame mounted hitches can be of the type which bolts to two or more points on the frame, plus the bumper, or just to several points on the frame. Frame mounted hitches can also be of the tongue type, for Class I towing, or, of the receiver type, for Classes II and III.

Load equalizing hitches are usually used for large trailers. Most equalizing hitches are welded in place and use equalizing bars and chains to level the vehicle after the trailer is hooked up.

The bolt-on hitches are the most common, since they are relatively easy to install.

Check the gross weight rating of your trailer. Tongue weight is usually figured as 10% of gross trailer weight. Therefore, a trailer with a maximum gross weight of 2,000 lb. (907 kg) will have a maximum tongue weight of 200 lb. (90.7 kg). Class I trailers fall into this category. Class II trailers are those with a gross weight rating of 2,000–3,500 lb. (907–1588 kg), while Class III trailers fall into the 3,500–6,000 lb. (1588–2722 kg) category. Class IV trailers are those over 6,000 lb. (2722 kg) and are for use with fifth wheel trucks, only.

When you've determined the hitch that you'll need, follow the manufacturer's installation instructions, exactly, especially when it comes to fastener torques. The hitch will subjected to a lot of stress and good hitches come with hardened bolts. Never substitute an inferior bolt for a hardened bolt.

Wiring

Wiring the truck for towing is fairly easy. There are a number of good wiring kits available and these should be used, rather than trying to design your own. All trailers will need brake lights and turn signals as well as tail lights and side marker lights. Most states require extra marker lights for overly wide trailers. Also, most states have recently required back-up lights for trailers, and most trailer manufacturers have been building trailers with back-up lights for several years.

Additionally, some Class I, most Class II and just about all Class III trailers will have electric brakes.

Add to this number an accessories wire, to operate trailer internal equipment or to charge the trailer's battery, and you can have as many as seven wires in the harness.

Determine the equipment on your trailer and buy the wiring kit necessary. The kit will contain all the wires needed, plus a plug adapter set which included the female plug, mounted on the bumper or hitch, and the male plug, wired into, or plugged into the trailer harness.

When installing the kit, follow the manufacturer's instructions. The color coding of the wires is standard throughout the industry.

One point to note, some domestic vehicles, and most imported vehicles, have separate turn signals. On most domestic vehicles, the brake lights and rear turn signals operate with the same bulb. For those vehicles with separate turn signals, you can purchase an isolation unit so that the brake lights won't blink whenever the turn signals are operated, or, you can go to your local electronics supply house and buy four diodes to wire in series with the brake and turn signal bulbs. Diodes will isolate the brake and turn signals. The choice is yours. The isolation units are simple and quick to install, but far more expensive than the diodes. The diodes, however, require more work to install properly, since they require the cutting of each bulb's wire and soldering in place of the diode.

One final point, the best kits are those with a spring loaded cover on the vehicle mounted socket. This cover prevents dirt and moisture from corroding the terminals. Never let the vehicle socket hang loosely. Always mount it securely to the bumper or hitch.

Cooling

ENGINE

One of the most common, if not THE most common, problem associated with trailer towing is engine overheating.

With factory installed trailer towing packages, a heavy duty cooling system is usually included. Heavy duty cooling systems are available as optional equipment on most trucks, with or without a trailer package. If you have one of these extra-capacity systems, you shouldn't have any overheating problems.

If you have a standard cooling system, without an expansion tank, you'll definitely need to get an aftermarket expansion tank kit, preferably one with at least a 2 quart capacity. These kits are easily installed on the radiator's overflow hose, and come with a pressure cap designed for expansion tanks.

Another helpful accessory is a Flex Fan. These fan are large diameter units are designed to provide more airflow at low speeds, with blades that have deeply cupped surfaces. The blades then flex, or flatten out, at high speed, when less cooling air is needed. These fans are far lighter in weight than stock fans, requiring less horsepower to drive them. Also, they are far quieter than stock fans.

If you do decide to replace your stock fan with a flex fan, note that if your truck has a fan clutch, a spacer between the flex fan and water pump hub will be needed.

Aftermarket engine oil coolers are helpful for prolonging engine oil life and reducing overall engine temperatures. Both of these factors increase engine life.

While not absolutely necessary in towing Class I and some Class II trailers, they are recommended for heavier Class II and all Class III towing.

Engine oil cooler systems consist of an adapter, screwed on in place of the oil filter, a remote filter mounting and a multi-tube, finned heat exchanger, which is mounted in front of the radiator or air conditioning condenser.

TRANSMISSION

An automatic transmission is usually recommended for trailer towing. Modern automatics have proven reliable and, of course, easy to operate, in trailer towing.

The increased load of a trailer, however, causes an increase in the temperature of the automatic transmission fluid. Heat is the worst enemy of an automatic transmission. As the temperature of the fluid increases, the life of the fluid decreases.

It is essential, therefore, that you install an automatic transmission cooler.

The cooler, which consists of a multi-tube, finned heat exchanger, is usually installed in front of the radiator or air conditioning compressor, and hooked inline with the transmission cooler tank inlet line. Follow the cooler manufacturer's installation instructions.

Select a cooler of at least adequate capacity, based upon the combined gross weights of the truck and trailer.

Cooler manufacturers recommend that you use an aftermarket cooler in addition to, and not instead of, the present cooling tank in your truck's radiator. If you do want to use it in place of the radiator cooling tank, get a cooler at least two sizes larger than normally necessary.

➡ **A transmission cooler can, sometimes, cause slow or harsh shifting in the transmission during cold weather, until the fluid has a chance to come up to normal operating temperature. Some coolers can be purchased with or retrofitted with a temperature bypass valve which will allow fluid flow through the cooler only when the fluid has reached operating temperature, or above.**

PUSHING AND TOWING

Pushing

Mazda trucks with manual transmissions can be push started, but this is not recommended if you value the appearance of your truck. Mazda trucks with automatic transmission cannot be pushed started.

To push start trucks with manual transmissions, make sure that both bumpers are in reasonable alignment and protected with old blankets or something similar. Be careful in judging the alignment of bumpers as bent sheet metal and inflamed tempers are both predictable results of misaligned bumpers. Turn the ignition key to ON and engine High gear. Turn off all accessories. Depress the clutch pedal. When a speed of about 10 mph is reached, lightly depress the gas pedal and slowly release the clutch pedal. Do not attempt to engage the clutch while both vehicles are in contact.

CAUTION

Never get a starting assist by having your truck towed!

Towing

MANUAL TRANSMISSION

If the transmission and rear axle are not damaged, the vehicle may be towed from the front. Otherwise it should be lifted and towed from the rear. Be sure that the parking brake is OFF and the transmission is in Neutral.

AUTOMATIC TRANSMISSION

With the automatic transmission, the rear wheels must be lifted off the ground or the driveshaft must be disconnected. If this is not done, the transmission may be damaged.

MANUAL OR AUTOMATIC TRANSMISSION

Do not attach chains to the bumpers or bracketing. All attachments should be made to structural members. Safety chains should also be used. If you are flat towing, remember that the power steering and power brake assists will not work with the engine OFF.

JACKING

➧ SEE FIG 80

The jack supplied with your truck was meant for changing tires. It was not meant to support the truck while you work under it. Whenever it is necessary to get under your truck to perform service operations, be sure that it is adequately supported on jackstands.

Do not lift the truck by the front bumper. Be careful when lifting the truck on a two-post hoist. Damage to the suspension may occur if care is not exercised in positioning the hoist adapters.

➡ To support your Mazda with the jack supplied with the truck, refer to the accompanying illustrations.

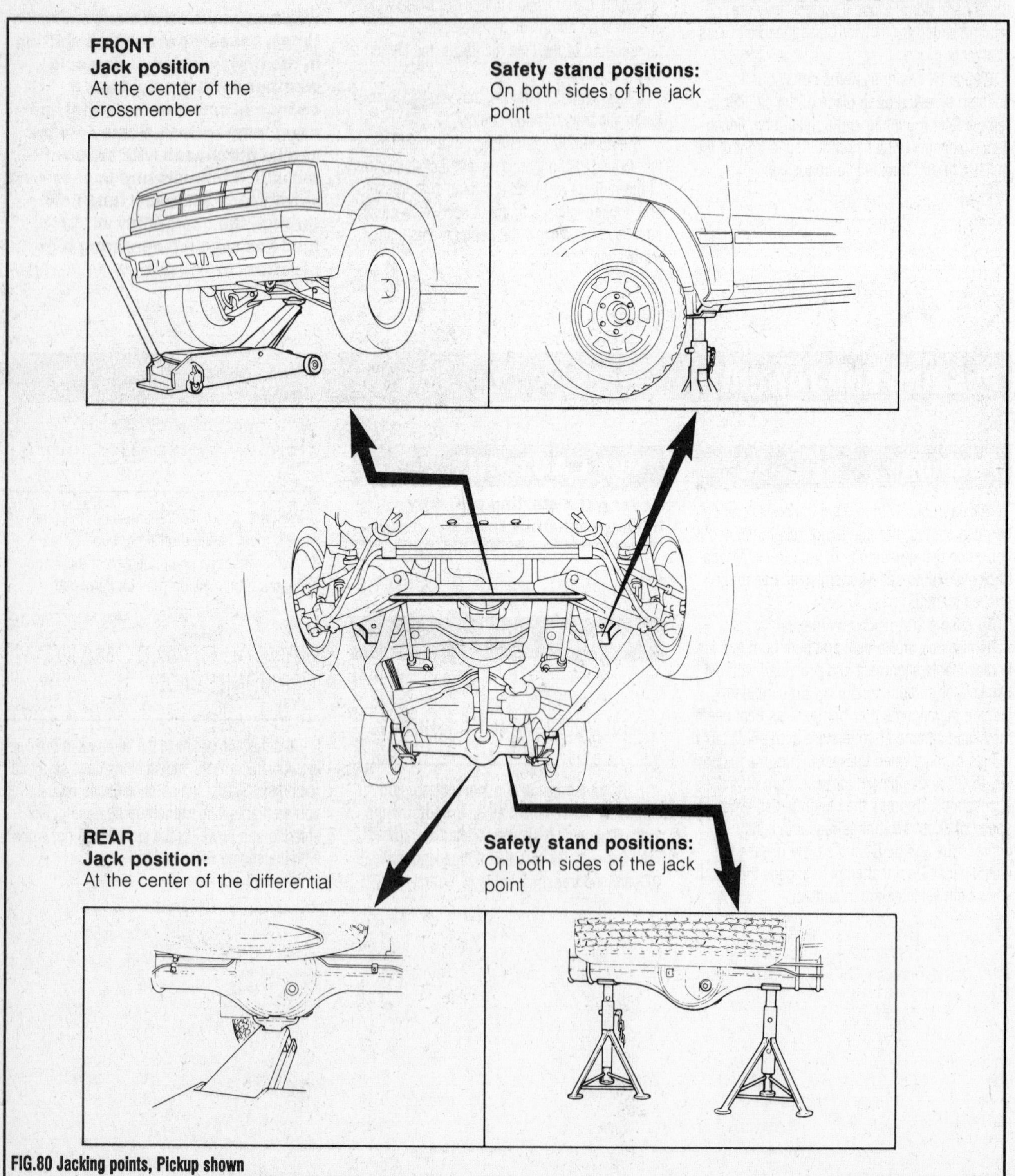

FIG.80 Jacking points, Pickup shown

CAPACITIES

Year	Model	Engine ID/VIN	Engine Displacement Liters (cc)	Engine Crankcase with Filter	Transmission (pts.)			Transfer case (pts.)	Drive Axle		Fuel Tank (gal.)	Cooling System (qts.)
					4-Spd	5-Spd	Auto.		Front (pts.)	Rear (pts.)		
1987	B2200	F2	2.2 (2184)	4.4	3.6	4.2	15.8	—	—	2.6	①	②
	B2600	G54B	2.6 (2555)	③	—	⑤	15.8	4	2.6	3.6	①	⑥
1988	B2200	F2	2.2 (2184)	4.4	3.6	4.2	15.8	—	—	2.6	①	②
	B2600	G54B	2.6 (2555)	③	—	⑤	15.8	4	2.6	3.6	①	⑥
1989	B2200	F2	2.2 (2184)	4.3	3.6	4.2	15.8	—	—	2.6	①	⑥
	B2600i	G6	2.6 (2606)	5.0	—	6.8	15.8	4.2	3.2	3.6	14.8	7.2
	MPV	G6	2.6 (2606)	5.0	—	5.2	18.2	3.2	3.6	3.2	15.9	⑨
	MPV	JE	3.0 (2954)	5.0	—	5.2	18.2	3.2	3.6	3.2	19.6	⑧
1990	B2200	F2	2.2 (2184)	4.3	3.6	4.2	15.8	—	—	2.6	①	⑥
	B2600i	G6	2.6 (2606)	5.0	—	⑨	⑩	4.2	3.2	3.6	14.8	7.2
	MPV	G6	2.6 (2606)	5.0	—	5.2	⑩	3.2	3.6	3.2	15.9	⑦
	MPV	JE	3.0 (2954)	5.0	—	5.2	⑩	3.2	3.6	3.2	19.6	⑧
1991	B2200	F2	2.2 (2184)	4.3	3.6	4.2	15.8	—	—	2.6	①	②
	B2600i	G6	2.6 (2606)	5.0	—	⑨	⑩	4.2	3.2	3.6	14.8	②
	MPV	G6	2.6 (2606)	5.0	—	⑪	⑩	4.2	3.6	3.2	15.9	⑦
	MPV	JE	3.0 (2954)	5.0	—	⑪	⑩	4.2	3.6	3.2	19.6	⑧
	Navajo	X	4.0 (4016)	5.0	—	5.6	⑫	2.5	3.5	5.3	19.3	⑬
1992	B2200	F2	2.2 (2184)	4.3	—	4.2	15.8	—	—	2.6	①	②
	B2600i	G6	2.6 (2606)	5.0	—	⑨	⑩	4.2	3.2	3.6	14.8	②
	MPV	G6	2.6 (2606)	5.0	—	6.0	⑩	4.2	3.6	3.2	15.9	⑦
	MPV	JE	3.0 (2954)	5.0	—	6.0	⑩	4.2	3.6	3.2	19.6	⑧
	Navajo	X	4.0 (4016)	5.0	—	5.6	⑫	2.5	3.5	5.3	19.3	⑬

① Short bed, Cab plus—14.8
Long bed—17.4
② With heater—7.9
Without heater—7.3
③ 2WD—4.4
4WD—5.2
④ 2WD—4.0
4WD—4.8
⑤ 2WD—6.0
4WD—6.8
⑥ With heater—7.9
Without heater—7.4
⑦ With manual transmission—7.2
With automatic transmission—7.6
⑧ With manual transmission—10.1
With automatic transmission—10.3
⑨ 2WD—6.0
4WD—6.8
⑩ Hydraulically controlled—15.8
Electronically controlled—17.2
⑪ 2WD—5.2
4WD—6.0
⑫ 2WD—19.4
4WD—20.0
⑬ Standard cooling system, all transmission and manual air conditioning—8.1
Super cooling with automatic transmission and air conditioning—8.5

TORQUE SPECIFICATIONS

Component	U.S.	Metric
4WD Wheel Bearing:		
Inner Nut:	16 inch lbs.	1.8 Nm
Outer Locknut:	150 ft. lbs.	204 Nm
Plug "A":	29-43 ft. lbs.	39–58 Nm
Plug "B" and "D":	18-29 ft. lbs.	24–39 Nm
Air Cleaner Cover Screws:	12-15 inch lbs.	1.3–1.7 Nm
Auto Transmission Oil Pan Bolts:	40-60 inch lbs.	4.5–6.7 Nm
Drain and Filler Plugs Manual Transmission (exc. MPV):	15-20 ft. lbs.	20–27 Nm
Filler Plugs MPV Manual Transmission:	18-29 ft. lbs.	24–39 Nm
Inline Fuel Filter Hose Clamps:	15-25 inch lbs.	1.7–2.8 Nm
MPV Front Axle Locknut:	130-174 ft. lbs.	177–237 Nm
Pickup 2wd Caliper Retaining Bolts:	58-86 ft. lbs.	79–117 Nm
Pickup 2WD Wheel Lug Nuts:	65-87 ft. lbs.	88–118 Nm
Screen Type Filter Mounting Screw, Automatic Transmission:	24-36 inch lbs.	2.7–4.0 Nm

MAINTENANCE INTERVALS

Component	Serivice	Interval
	Intervals are for every: miles/Km or miles/months/Km	
	Under heavy duty operating conditions, the maintenance intervals should be halved. Service even more frequently if continuous severe operation is experienced.	
	B2200 (2.2L) 1987-92	
Engine		
Engine Oil and Oil Filter (1)	replace	7,500/7.5/12,000
Choke System (Carb only)	clean	15,000/15/24,000
Idle Switch (Carb only)	inspect	15,000/15/24,000
Drive Belts (1987-88)	inspect	15,000/15/24,000
Drive Belts (1989-92)	inspect	30,000/30/48,000
Air Cleaner Element (2)	replace	30,000/30/48,000
Timing Belt	replace	30,000/48,000
Oxygen Sensor	replace	80,000/128,000
EGR Control Valve	replace	60,000/60/96,000
PCV Valve	inspect	60,000/60/96,000
Emission Hoses & Tubes	replace	60,000/60/96,000
HAC Air Filter	replace	60,000/60/96,000
Ignition System		
Spark Plugs	replace	30,000/30/48,000
Ignition Timing	inspect	60,000/60/96,000
Fuel System		
Idle Speed	inspect	15,000/15/24,000
Fuel Lines	inspect	30,000/30/48,000
Fuel Filter	replace	30,000/30/48,000
Cooling System		
Cooling System	inspect	15,000/15/24,000
Engine Coolant	replace	30,000/30/48,000
Chassis and Body		
Brake Lines & Connections	inspect	30,000/30/48,000
Brake Fluid Level	replace	30,000/30/48,000
Drum Brakes (Rear)	inspect	30,000/30/48,000
Disc Brakes (Front)	inspect	30,000/30/48,000
Manual Steering Gear Oil	inspect	30,000/30/48,000
Steering Operations & Gear Housing	inspect	30,000/30/48,000
Steering Linkage, Tie Rod Ends & arms	inspect	30,000/30/48,000
Suspension Ball Joints (Front)	inspect	30,000/30/48,000
Upper Arm Shafts	lube	30,000/30/48,000
Front Wheel Bearings	lube	30,000/30/48,000
Manual Transmission Oil	replace	60,000/60/96,000
Rear Axle Oil	replace	60,000/60/96,000
Body & Chassis Nuts and Bolts	Tighten	30,000/30/48,000
Exhaust System Heat Shield	inspect	30,000/30/48,000
Air Conditioning System		
Refrigerant	inspect	annually
Compressor	operation	annually

(1) We recommend that the oil filter be replaced with each oil change.

(2) Replace as required under heavy duty driving conditions.

MAINTENANCE INTERVALS

Component	Serivice	Interval
	Intervals are for every: miles/Km or miles/months/Km	
	Under heavy duty operating conditions, the maintenance intervals should be halved. Service even more frequently if continuous severe operation is experienced.	
	B2600 (2.6L) 1987-88	
Engine		
Engine Oil and Oil Filter (1)	replace	7,500/7.5/12,000
Choke System	clean	30,000/30/48,000
Jet Valve Clearance	Adjust	15,000/15/24,000
Drive Belts	inspect	15,000/15/24,000
Air Cleaner Element (2)	replace	30,000/30/48,000
Oxygen Sensor	replace	50,000/50/80,000
EGR Control Valve	replace	60,000/60/96,000
PCV Valve	inspect	50,000/50/80,000
Emission Hoses & Tubes	replace	60,000/60/96,000
HAC Air Filter	replace	60,000/60/96,000
Intake Temperature Control System	inspect	50,000/50/80,000
Secondary Air System	inspect	50,000/50/80,000
Vacuum Control System Air Filters	replace	50,000/50/80,000
Throttle Position System	inspect	15,000/15/24,000
Ignition System		
Spark Plugs	replace	30,000/30/48,000
Ignition Timing	inspect	50,000/50/80,000
Ignition Cables	replace	50,000/50/80,000
Distributor Spark Advance System	inspect	50,000/50/80,000
Fuel System		
Idle Speed	inspect	15,000/15/24,000
Fuel Lines	inspect	30,000/30/48,000
Fuel Filter	replace	30,000/30/48,000
Cooling System		
Cooling System	inspect	15,000/15/24,000
Engine Coolant	replace	30,000/30/48,000
Chassis and Body		
Brake Lines & Connections	inspect	15,000/15/24,000
Brake Fluid Level	replace	30,000/30/48,000
Clutch Pedal	inspect	15,000/15/24,000
Drum Brakes (Rear)	inspect	30,000/30/48,000
Disc Brakes (Front)	inspect	15,000/15/24,000
Manual Steering Gear Oil	inspect	15,000/15/24,000
Steering Operations & Gear Housing	inspect	30,000/30/48,000
Steering Linkage, Tie Rod Ends & Arms	inspect	15,000/15/24,000
Suspension Ball Joints (Front)	inspect	30,000/30/48,000
Upper Arm Shafts	lube	30,000/30/48,000
Front Wheel Bearings	lube	30,000/30/48,000
Manual Transmission Oil	replace	30,000/30/48,000
Front and/or Rear Axle Oil	replace	30,000/30/48,000
Body & Chassis Nuts and Bolts	Tighten	15,000/15/24,000
Exhaust System Heat Shield	inspect	30,000/30/48,000
Drive Shaft Dust Boots	inspect	30,000/30/48,000
Propeller Shaft Joints	lube	30,000/30/48,000
Automatic Transmission Fluid	replace	30,000/30/48,000
Transfer Case Oil	replace	30,000/30/48,000
Air Conditioning System		
Refrigerant	inspect	annually
Compressor	operation	annually

(1) We recommend that the oil filter be replaced with each oil change.

(2) Replace as required under heavy duty driving conditions.

MAINTENANCE INTERVALS

Component	Serivice	Interval
	Intervals are for every: miles/Km or miles/months/Km	
	Under heavy duty operating conditions, the maintenance intervals should be halved. Service even more frequently if continuous severe operation is experienced.	
	B2600i (2.6L) 1989-92	
Engine		
Engine Oil and Oil Filter (1)	replace	7,500/7.5/12,000
Drive Belts	inspect	30,000/30/48,000
Air Cleaner Element	replace	30,000/30/48,000
Oxygen Sensor	replace	80,000/80/128,000
PCV Valve	inspect	50,000/50/80,000
Emission Hoses & Tubes	replace	60,000/60/96,000
Ignition System		
Spark Plugs	replace	30,000/30/48,000
Ignition Timing	inspect	60,000/60/96,000
Fuel System		
Idle Speed	inspect	15,000/15/24,000
Fuel Lines	inspect	30,000/30/48,000
Fuel Filter	replace	60,000/60/96,000
Cooling System		
Cooling System	inspect	15,000/15/24,000
Engine Coolant	replace	30,000/30/48,000
Chassis and Body		
Brake Lines & Connections	inspect	30,000/30/48,000
Brake Fluid Level	replace	30,000/30/48,000
Drum Brakes (Rear)	inspect	60,000/60/96,000
Disc Brakes (Front)	inspect	30,000/30/48,000
Steering Operations & Gear Housing	inspect	30,000/30/48,000
Steering Linkage, Tie Rod Ends & Arms	inspect	30,000/30/48,000
Suspension Ball Joints (Front)	inspect	30,000/30/48,000
Upper Arm Shafts	lube	30,000/30/48,000
Front Wheel Bearings	lube	30,000/30/48,000
Manual Transmission Oil	replace	60,000/60/96,000
Transfer Oil	replace	52,000/52/84,000
Driveshaft Dust Bolts	inspect	30,000/30/48,000
Propeller Shaft Joints	lube	15,000/15/24,000
Rear Axle Oil, Front Axle Oil	replace	60,000/60/96,000
Bolts and Nuts on Chassis and Body	Tighten	30,000/30/48,000
Exhaust System Heat Shield	inspect	30,000/30/48,000
Air Conditioning System		
Refrigerant	inspect	annually
Compressor	operation	annually

(1) We recommend that the oil filter be replaced with each oil change.

(2) Replace as required under heavy duty driving conditions.

MAINTENANCE INTERVALS

Component	Serivice	Interval
	Intervals are for every: miles/Km or miles/months/Km	
	Under heavy duty operating conditions, the maintenance intervals should be halved. Service even more frequently if continuous severe operation is experienced.	
	MPV (2.6L) 1989-92	
Engine		
Engine Oil and Oil Filter (1)	replace	7,500/7.5/12,000
Drive Belts	inspect	30,000/30/48,000
Air Cleaner Element	replace	30,000/30/48,000
Oxygen Sensor	replace	80,000/80/128,000
PCV Valve	inspect	50,000/50/80,000
Emission Hoses & Tubes	replace	80,000/128,000
Ignition System		
Spark Plugs	replace	30,000/30/48,000
Ignition Timing	inspect	60,000/60/96,000
Fuel System		
Idle Speed	inspect	15,000/15/24,000
Fuel Lines	inspect	30,000/30/48,000
Fuel Filter	replace	60,000/60/96,000
Cooling System		
Cooling System	inspect	15,000/15/24,000
Engine Coolant	replace	30,000/30/48,000
Chassis and Body		
Brake Lines & Connections	inspect	30,000/30/48,000
Brake Fluid Level	replace	30,000/30/48,000
Drum Brakes (Rear)	inspect	30,000/30/48,000
Steering Operations & Gear Housing	inspect	30,000/30/48,000
Front Suspension Ball Joints	inspect	30,000/30,48,000
Front Axle Oil (2WD) Rear Axle Oil (4WD, 2WD)	replace	60,000/60/96,000
Manual Transmission Oil	replace	60,000/60,96,000
Transfer Case Oil (4WD)	replace	60,000/60/96,000
Driveshaft Dust Boots (4WD)	inspect	30,000/30/48,000
Propeller Shaft Bolts (4WD)	lube	15,000/15/24,000
Bolts and Nuts on Chassis and Body	Tighten	30,000/30/48,000
Exhaust System Heat Shield	inspect	30,000/30/48,000
All Locks and Hinges	lube	7,500/7/12,000
Air Conditioning System		
Refrigerant	inspect	annually
Compressor	operation	annually

(1) We recommend that the oil filter be replaced with each oil change.

(2) Replace as required under heavy duty driving conditions.

MAINTENANCE INTERVALS

Component	Serivice	Interval
	Intervals are for every: miles/Km or miles/months/Km	
	Under heavy duty operating conditions, the maintenance intervals should be halved. Service even more frequently if continuous severe operation is experienced.	
	MPV (3.0L) 1989-92	
Engine		
Engine Oil and Oil Filter (1)	replace	7,500/7.5/12,000
Drive Belts	inspect	30,000/30/48,000
Air Cleaner Element	replace	30,000/30/48,000
Oxygen Sensor	replace	80,000/80/128,000
Engine Timing Belt	replace	60,000/96,000
PCV Valve	inspect	50,000/50/80,000
Emission Hoses & Tubes	replace	60,000/60/96,000
Ignition System		
Spark Plugs	replace	30,000/30/48,000
Ignition Timing	inspect	60,000/60/96,000
Fuel System		
Idle Speed	inspect	15,000/15/24,000
Fuel Lines	inspect	30,000/30/48,000
Fuel Filter	replace	60,000/60/96,000
Cooling System		
Cooling System	inspect	15,000/15/24,000
Engine Coolant	replace	30,000/30/48,000
Chassis and Body		
Brake Lines & Connections	inspect	30,000/30/48,000
Brake Fluid Level	replace	30,000/30/48,000
Drum Brakes (Rear)	inspect	60,000/60/96,000
Disc Brakes (Front)	inspect	30,000/30/48,000
Front Suspension Ball Joints	inspect	30,000/30,48,000
Front Axle Oil (2WD) Rear Axle Oil (4WD, 2WD)	replace	60,000/60/96,000
Manual Transmission Oil	replace	60,000/60,96,000
Transfer Case Oil (4WD)	replace	60,000/60/96,000
Driveshaft Dust Boots (4WD)	inspect	30,000/30/48,000
Propeller Shaft Bolts (4WD)	lube	15,000/15/24,000
Bolts and Nuts on Chassis and Body	Tighten	30,000/30/48,000
Exhaust System Heat Shield	inspect	30,000/30/48,000
All Locks and Hinges	lube	7,500/7/12,000
Air Conditioning System		
Refrigerant	inspect	annually
Compressor	operation	annually

(1) We recommend that the oil filter be replaced with each oil change.

(2) Replace as required under heavy duty driving conditions.

MAINTENANCE INTERVALS

Component	Serivice	Interval
	Intervals are for every: miles/Km or miles/months/Km Under heavy duty operating conditions, the maintenance intervals should be halved. Service even more frequently if continuous severe operation is experienced.	
	Navajo (4.0L) 1991-92	
Engine & Emission Control Systems		
Engine Oil and Oil Filter (1)	replace	7,500/12,000
Drive Belts	inspect	30,000/48,000
Air Cleaner Element	replace	30,000/48,000
PCV Valve	replace	60,000/96,000
Ignition System		
Spark Plugs	replace	30,000/48,000
Ignition Wires	replace	60,000/96,000
Cooling System		
Cooling System	inspect	annually
Engine Coolant	replace	30,000/36/48,000
Chassis, Body and Other Systems		
Warning Lights & Gauges	inspect	15,000/24,000
Wheel Lug Nut Torque	inspect	7,500/12,000
Rotate Tires	perform	15,000/24,000
Clutch Reservoir Fluid Level	inspect	7,500/12,000
Shift Linkage Cable (AT)	inspect & lube	7,500/12,000
Front Wheel Bearings	inspect & lube	30,000/48,000
Disc Brake System & Caliper Slide Rails	inspect & lube	15,000/24,000
Drum Brake Linings, Lines and Hoses	inspect	30,000/48,000
Exhaust System	inspect	30,000/48,000
Driveshafts w/Fittings	lube	7,500/12,000
Throttle and Kickdown Linkage	lube	30,000/48,000
Rear Prop Shaft Cardan Joint Centering Ball	lube	7,500/12,000
RH Front Axle Slip Joint (4WD)	lube	30,000/48,000
Front Spindle Bearings & Thrust Bearings	inspect & lube	30,000/48,000
Hub Locks (Inspect) 4WD	lube	30,000/48,000
Transfer Case Oil	replace	60,000/96,000
Steering Linkage (w/Fittings)	lube	7,500/12,000
Air Conditioning System		
Refrigerant	inspect	annually
Compressor	operation	annually

(1) We recommend that the oil filter be replaced with each oil change.

(2) Replace as required under heavy duty driving conditions.

Troubleshooting Basic Air Conditioning Problems

Problem	Cause	Solution
There's little or no air coming from the vents (and you're sure it's on)	• The A/C fuse is blown • Broken or loose wires or connections • The on/off switch is defective	• Check and/or replace fuse • Check and/or repair connections • Replace switch
The air coming from the vents is not cool enough	• Windows and air vent wings open • The compressor belt is slipping • Heater is on • Condenser is clogged with debris • Refrigerant has escaped through a leak in the system • Receiver/drier is plugged	• Close windows and vent wings • Tighten or replace compressor belt • Shut heater off • Clean the condenser • Check system • Service system
The air has an odor	• Vacuum system is disrupted • Odor producing substances on the evaporator case • Condensation has collected in the bottom of the evaporator housing	• Have the system checked/repaired • Clean the evaporator case • Clean the evaporator housing drains
System is noisy or vibrating	• Compressor belt or mountings loose • Air in the system	• Tighten or replace belt; tighten mounting bolts • Have the system serviced
Sight glass condition		
Constant bubbles, foam or oil streaks	• Undercharged system	• Charge the system
Clear sight glass, but no cold air	• No refrigerant at all	• Check and charge the system
Clear sight glass, but air is cold	• System is OK	
Clouded with milky fluid	• Receiver drier is leaking dessicant	• Have system checked
Large difference in temperature of lines	• System undercharged	• Charge and leak test the system
Compressor noise	• Broken valves • Overcharged • Incorrect oil level • Piston slap • Broken rings • Drive belt pulley bolts are loose	• Replace the valve plate • Discharge, evacuate and install the correct charge • Isolate the compressor and check the oil level. Correct as necessary. • Replace the compressor • Replace the compressor • Tighten with the correct torque specification
Excessive vibration	• Incorrect belt tension • Clutch loose • Overcharged • Pulley is misaligned	• Adjust the belt tension • Tighten the clutch • Discharge, evacuate and install the correct charge • Align the pulley
Condensation dripping in the passenger compartment	• Drain hose plugged or improperly positioned • Insulation removed or improperly installed	• Clean the drain hose and check for proper installation • Replace the insulation on the expansion valve and hoses

Troubleshooting Basic Air Conditioning Problems (cont.)

Problem	Cause	Solution
Frozen evaporator coil	• Faulty thermostat • Thermostat capillary tube improperly installed • Thermostat not adjusted properly	• Replace the thermostat • Install the capillary tube correctly • Adjust the thermostat
Low side low—high side low	• System refrigerant is low • Expansion valve is restricted	• Evacuate, leak test and charge the system • Replace the expansion valve
Low side high—high side low	• Internal leak in the compressor—worn	• Remove the compressor cylinder head and inspect the compressor. Replace the valve plate assembly if necessary. If the compressor pistons, rings or
Low side high—high side low (cont.)	 • Cylinder head gasket is leaking • Expansion valve is defective • Drive belt slipping	cylinders are excessively worn or scored replace the compressor • Install a replacement cylinder head gasket • Replace the expansion valve • Adjust the belt tension
Low side high—high side high	• Condenser fins obstructed • Air in the system • Expansion valve is defective • Loose or worn fan belts	• Clean the condenser fins • Evacuate, leak test and charge the system • Replace the expansion valve • Adjust or replace the belts as necessary
Low side low—high side high	• Expansion valve is defective • Restriction in the refrigerant hose	• Replace the expansion valve • Check the hose for kinks—replace if necessary
Low side low—high side high	• Restriction in the receiver/drier • Restriction in the condenser	• Replace the receiver/drier • Replace the condenser
Low side and high normal (inadequate cooling)	**• Air in the system** **• Moisture in the system**	**• Evacuate, leak test and charge the system** **• Evacuate, leak test and charge the system**

Troubleshooting Basic Wheel Problems

Problem	Cause	Solution
The car's front end vibrates at high speed	• The wheels are out of balance • Wheels are out of alignment	• Have wheels balanced • Have wheel alignment checked/adjusted
Car pulls to either side	• Wheels are out of alignment • Unequal tire pressure • Different size tires or wheels	• Have wheel alignment checked/adjusted • Check/adjust tire pressure • Change tires or wheels to same size
The car's wheel(s) wobbles	• Loose wheel lug nuts • Wheels out of balance • Damaged wheel • Wheels are out of alignment • Worn or damaged ball joint • Excessive play in the steering linkage (usually due to worn parts) • Defective shock absorber	• Tighten wheel lug nuts • Have tires balanced • Raise car and spin the wheel. If the wheel is bent, it should be replaced • Have wheel alignment checked/adjusted • Check ball joints • Check steering linkage • Check shock absorbers
Tires wear unevenly or prematurely	• Incorrect wheel size • Wheels are out of balance • Wheels are out of alignment	• Check if wheel and tire size are compatible • Have wheels balanced • Have wheel alignment checked/adjusted

Troubleshooting Basic Tire Problems

Problem	Cause	Solution
The car's front end vibrates at high speeds and the steering wheel shakes	• Wheels out of balance • Front end needs aligning	• Have wheels balanced • Have front end alignment checked
The car pulls to one side while cruising	• Unequal tire pressure (car will usually pull to the low side) • Mismatched tires • Front end needs aligning	• Check/adjust tire pressure • Be sure tires are of the same type and size • Have front end alignment checked
Abnormal, excessive or uneven tire wear See "How to Read Tire Wear"	• Infrequent tire rotation • Improper tire pressure • Sudden stops/starts or high speed on curves	• Rotate tires more frequently to equalize wear • Check/adjust pressure • Correct driving habits
Tire squeals	• Improper tire pressure • Front end needs aligning	• Check/adjust tire pressure • Have front end alignment checked

2

ENGINE PERFORMANCE AND TUNE-UP

GASOLINE ENGINE TUNE-UP SPECIFICATIONS

Year	Engine ID/VIN	Engine Displacement Liters (cc)	Spark Plugs Gap (in.)	Ignition Timing (deg.)		Fuel Pump (psi)	Idle Speed (rpm)		Valve Clearance	
				MT	AT		MT	AT	In.	Ex.
1987	F2	2.2L (2184)	0.030	6B	6B	①	825	825	Hyd.	Hyd.
	G54B	2.6L (2555)	0.041	7B	7B	2.8–3.6	825	825	Hyd.	Hyd.
1988	F2	2.2L (2184)	0.030	6B	6B	①	325	825	Hyd.	Hyd.
	G54B	2.6L (2555)	0.041	7B	7B	2.8–3.6	825	825	Hyd.	Hyd.
1989	F2	2.2L (2184)	0.030	6B②	6B②	①	825	825	Hyd.	Hyd.
	G6	2.6L (2606)	0.041	5B②	5B②	64–85	750②	750②	Hyd.	Hyd.
	G6	2.6L (2606)	0.041	5B②	5B②	64–85	750②	750②	Hyd.	Hyd.
	JE	3.0L (2954)	0.041	11B②	11B②	64–85	800②	800②	Hyd.	Hyd.
1990	F2	2.2L (2184)	④	6B②	6B②	①	⑤ ②	⑥ ②	Hyd.	Hyd.
	G6	2.6L (2606)	0.041	5B②	5B②	64–85	750②	750②	Hyd.	Hyd.
	G6	2.6L (2606)	0.041	5B②	5B②	64–85	750②	750②	Hyd.	Hyd.
	JE	3.0L (2954)	0.041	11B②	11B②	64–85	800②	800②	Hyd.	Hyd.
1991	F2	2.2L (2184)	④	6B②	6B②	①	⑤ ②	⑥ ②	Hyd.	Hyd.
	G6	2.6L (2606)	0.041	5B②	5B②	64–85	750②	750②	Hyd.	Hyd.
	G6	2.6L (2606)	0.041	5B②	5B②	64–85	750②	750②	Hyd.	Hyd.
	JE	3.0L (2954)	0.041	11B②	11B②	64–85	800②	800②	Hyd.	Hyd.
	X	4.0L (4016)	0.054	10B	10B	35–45	⑦	⑦	Hyd.	Hyd.
1992	F2	2.2L (2184)	④	6B②	6B②	①	⑤ ②	⑥ ②	Hyd.	Hyd.
	G6	2.6L (2606)	0.041	5B②	5B②	64–85	750②	750②	Hyd.	Hyd.
	G6	2.6L (2606)	0.041	5B②	5B②	64–85	750②	750②	Hyd.	Hyd.
	JE	3.0L (2954)	0.041	11B②	11B②	64–85	800②	800②	Hyd.	Hyd.
	X	4.0L (4016)	0.054	10B	10B	35–45	⑦	⑦	Hyd.	Hyd.

NOTE: The lowest cylinder pressure should be within 75% of the highest cylinder pressure reading. For example, if the highest cylinder is 134 psi, the lowest should be 101. Engine should be at normal operating temperature with throttle valve in the wide open position.

The underhood specifications sticker often reflects tune-up specification changes in production. Sticker figures must be used if they disagree with those in this chart.

① Carbureted engine
Manual transmission—mechanical pump: 3.7–4.7
Automatic transmission—electric pump: 2.8–3.6
Fuel injection engine: 64–85

② With test connector grounded

③ Carbureted engine: BPR5ES
Fuel injected engine: BPR5ES-11

④ Carbureted engine: 0.030
Fuel injected engine: 0.041

⑤ Carbureted engine: 800
Fuel injected engine: 750

⑥ Carbureted engine: 800
Fuel injected engine: 770

⑦ See underhood emissions information label

TUNE-UP PROCEDURES

Neither tune-up nor troubleshooting can be considered independently since each has direct bearing on the other.

An engine tune-up is a service designed to restore the maximum capability of power, performance, economy and reliability in an engine, and, at the same time, assure the owner of a complete check and more lasting results in efficiency and trouble-free performance. Engine tune-up becomes increasingly important each year, to ensure that pollutant levels are in compliance with federal emissions standards.

A complete tune-up should be performed every 12,000 to 15,000 miles or twelve to fifteen months, whichever comes first. This interval should be halved if the vehicle is operated under severe conditions, such as trailer towing, prolonged idling, continual stop and start driving, or if starting or running problems are noticed. It is assumed that the routine maintenance described in Section 1 has been kept up, as this will have a decided effect on the results of a tune-up. All of the applicable steps of a tune-up should be followed in order, as the result is a cumulative one.

If the specifications on the tune-up sticker in the engine compartment disagree with the Tune-Up Specifications Chart in this Section, the figures on the sticker must be used. The sticker often reflects changes made during the production run.

It is advisable to follow a definite and thorough tune-up procedure. Tune-up consists of three separate steps: Analysis, the process of determining whether normal wear is responsible for performance loss, and whether parts require replacement or service; Parts Replacement or Service; and Adjustment, where engine adjustments are returned to the original factory specifications.

The extent of an engine tune-up is usually determined by the length of time since the previous service, although the type of driving and the general mechanical condition of the engine must be considered. Specific maintenance should also be performed at regular intervals, depending on operating conditions.

It is advisable to read the entire Section before beginning a tune-up, although those who are more familiar with tune-up procedures may wish to go directly to the instructions.

Tune up time is also a good time to look around the engine compartment for potential problems, such as fuel and oil leaks, cracking or hard radiator or heater hoses, loose or frayed belts, loose wire connections, etc.

**** CAUTION**

When working around a running engine, always be certain there is plenty of ventilation. Make sure the transmission is in Neutral, on manual transmission equipped vehicles; or in Park, on automatic transmission equipped vehicles (unless otherwise specified) and the parking brake is fully applied. Always keep hands, hair, and clothing away from the fan, hot manifolds and radiator. Remove any jewelry or neckties. When the engine is running, do not grasp the ignition wires, distributor cap or coil wire, as a shock in excess of 20,000 volts may result. Whenever working around the distributor, even if the engine is not running, make sure that the ignition is switched off. Removing or disturbing the distributor cap on an electronic ignition system with the ignition switch "on" can often cause the system to fire.

Spark Plugs

➧ SEE FIGS. 1-7

A typical spark plug consists of a metal shell surrounding a ceramic insulator. A metal electrode extends downward through the center of the insulator and protrudes a small distance. Located at the end of the plug and attached to the side of the outer metal shell is the side electrode. The side electrode bends in at a 90° angle so that its tip is even with, and parallel to, the tip of the center electrode. The distance between these two electrodes (measured in thousandths of an inch or hundreths of a millimeter) is called the spark plug gap. The spark plug in no way produces a spark but merely provides a gap across which the current can arc. The coil produces anywhere from 20,000 to 40,000 volts which travels to the distributor where it is distributed through the spark plug wires to the spark plugs. The current passes along the center electrode and jumps the gap to the side electrode, and, in do doing, ignites the air/fuel mixture in the combustion chamber.

Spark plugs ignite the air and fuel mixture in the cylinder as the piston reaches the top of the compression stroke. The controlled explosion that results forces the piston down, turning the crankshaft and the rest of the drive train.

The average life of a spark plug is dependent on a number of factors: the mechanical condition of the engine; the type of engine; the type of fuel; driving conditions; and the driver.

Spark plugs should be checked frequently (approximately 5,000 miles) depending on use. All the recommendations are based on the ambient conditions as well as driving conditions. If you drive at high speeds constantly, the plugs will probably not need as much attention to those used for constant stop-and-start driving.

The electrode end of the plug (the end with the threads) is a good indicator of the internal condition of your engine. If a spark plug has fouled and caused the engine to misfire, the problem will have to be found and corrected. Often, reading the color and type of deposits on the spark plug insulator, electrode and surrounding area can help you determine engine condition. Spark plug conditions and probable causes follow:

Brown to grayish-tan deposits with slight electrode wear shows normal engine conditions. The plug can be cleaned, gapped and install in the engine.

Dry, fluffy black carbon deposits indicate poor ignition output. Check distributor to coil connections and spark plug wires.

Wet, oily deposits with very little electrode wear. Can be related to the "break-in" of a new or recently overhauled engine. Will most of relate to excessive valve stem to guide clearance or worn intake valve stem oil seals. The plugs can usually be clean and installed. Refer to Section 3 for engine problem corrections. Replace the valve stem oil seals.

Red, brown, yellow and white colored coatings on the insulator. Engine misses intermittently under severe operating conditions. These are a by-product of combustion. Clean, gap and install the plugs. If heavily coated, replace the spark plugs.

Colored coatings heavily deposited on the portion of the plug projecting into the chamber and the side facing the intake valve. If only in one or two cylinders, could be caused by leaking valve stem oil seals. Check the seals, replace them as required. Clean, gap and install the plugs.

Shiny yellow glaze coating the insulator. Result of melted by-products of combustion. Avoid sudden acceleration with wide-open throttle after long periods of low speed driving. Replace the spark plugs.

Burned or blistered insulator tips and badly eroded electrodes. Caused by overheating. Check the cooling system. Check for a lean air/fuel mixture. Check the heat range of the spark plugs, they may be to hot a plug for the engine. Check the ignition timing, may be over-advanced. Check the torque valve of the plugs to ensure good plug to engine seat contact.

Broken or cracked insulator tips. Caused by heat shock from sudden rise in tip temperature under severe operating conditions or improper gapping of the plugs. Replace the plugs. Gap the plugs correctly.

It is a good idea to pull the plugs once in a while just to get an idea of the internal condition of your engine.

➡ A small amount of light tan colored deposits on the electrode end of the spark plug is quite normal. These plugs need not be replaced unless they are severely worn.

The gap between the center electrode and the side or ground electrode can be expected to increase not more than 0.001 in. (0.025mm) every 1,000 miles 1609 km) under normal conditions.

When a spark plug is functioning normally or, more accurately, when the plug is installed in an engine that is functioning properly, the plugs can be taken out, cleaned, gapped, and reinstalled in the engine without doing the engine any harm.

When, and if, a plug fouls and beings to misfire, you will have to investigate, correct the cause of the fouling, and either clean or replace the plug.

SPARK PLUG HEAT RANGE

Spark plug heat range is the ability of the plug to dissipate heat. The longer the insulator (or the farther it extends into the engine), the hotter the plug will operate; the shorter the insulator the cooler it will operate. A plug that absorbs little heat and remains too cool will quickly accumulate deposits of oil and carbon since it is not hot enough to burn them off. This leads to plug fouling and consequently to misfiring. A plug that absorbs too much heat will have no deposits, but, due to the excessive heat, the electrodes will burn away quickly and in some instances, preignition may result. Preignition takes place when plug tips get so hot that they glow sufficiently to ignite the fuel/air mixture before the actual spark occurs. This early ignition will usually cause a pinging during low speeds and heavy loads.

The general rule of thumb for choosing the correct heat range when picking a spark plug is: if most of your driving is long distance, high speed travel, use a colder plug; if most of your driving is stop and to, use a hotter plug. Original equipment plugs are compromise plugs, but most people never have occasion to change their plugs from the factory-recommended heat range.

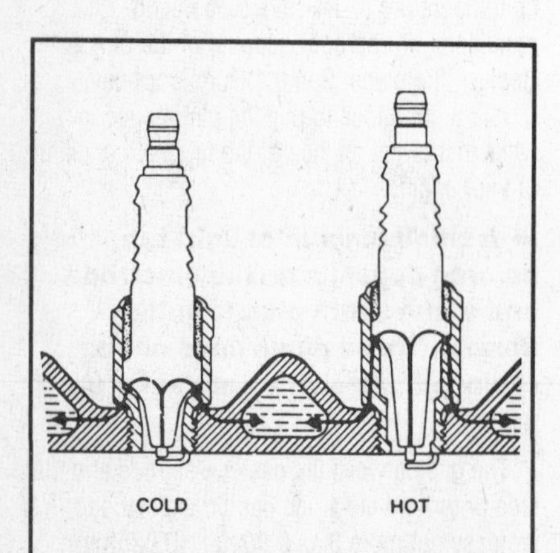

FIG.1 The plug with the higher heat range is on the right; it has a longer heat flow path and thus operates at a higher tip temperature. It should be used for slower driving and light load conditions which promote carbon accumulation

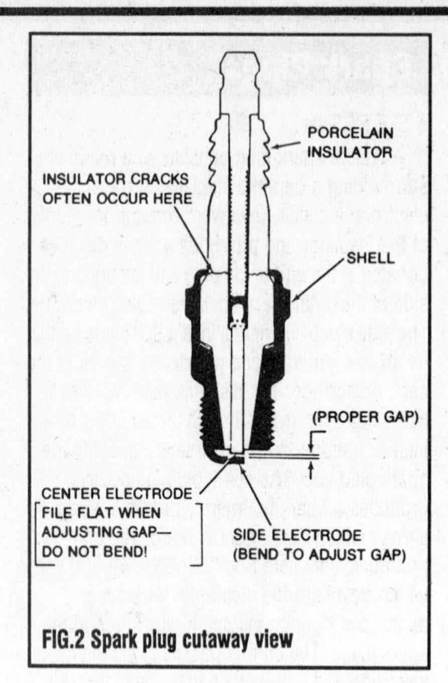

FIG.2 Spark plug cutaway view

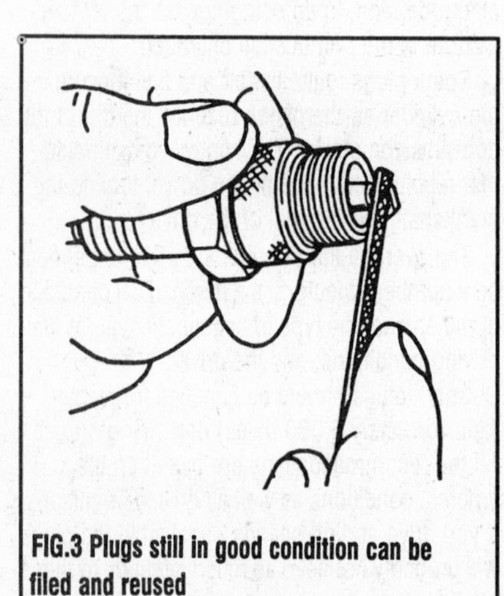

FIG.3 Plugs still in good condition can be filed and reused

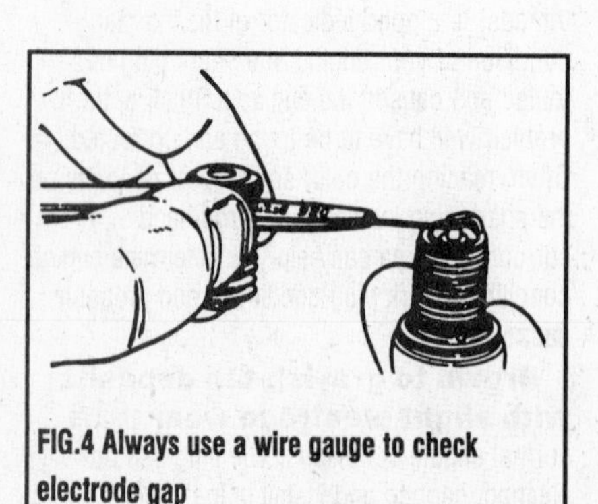

FIG.4 Always use a wire gauge to check electrode gap

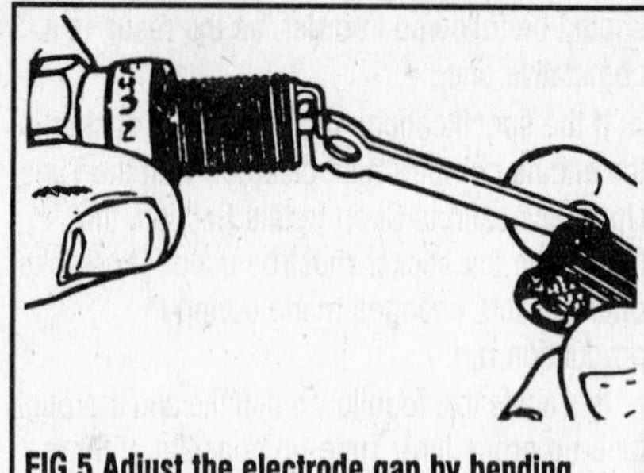

FIG.5 Adjust the electrode gap by bending the side electrode with the special tool shown

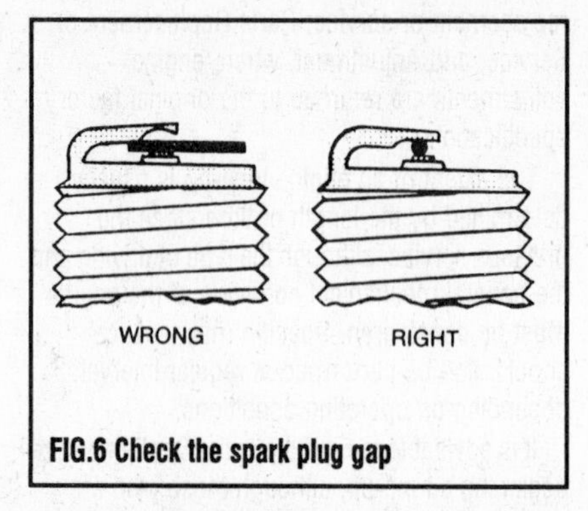

FIG.6 Check the spark plug gap

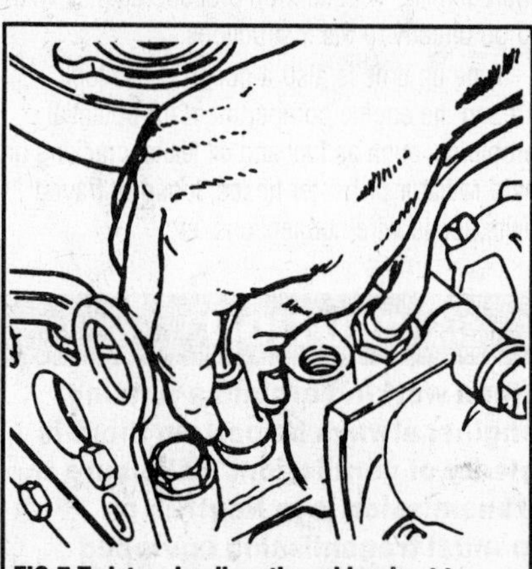

FIG.7 Twist and pull on the rubber boot to remove the spark plug wire; never pull on the wire itself

REMOVAL

1. Raise the hood and locate all the spark plugs.
2. If the spark plug wires are not numbered, mark each one with a small piece of masking tape. Print the number of the cylinder on the piece of tape.
3. Disconnect the wire from the plug by grasping, twisting and pulling the molded cap from the plug. Do not simply yank the wire from the plug as the connection inside the cap can become damaged.

4. Using a spark plug socket, loosen the plug a few turns.
5. If compressed air is available, blow out the area around the base of the spark plug to remove foreign matter.
6. Remove the plug the rest of the way and inspect them. It is a good idea to inspect the plugs whether or not they are going to be reused.

INSPECTION

1. "Read" the deposit color and condition of the spark plugs as described in the previous paragraphs. It should be remembered that any type of deposit will decrease the efficiency of the plug. If the plugs are not to be replaced, they should be thoroughly cleaned before installation. If the electrode ends of the plugs are worn or damaged and if they are to be reused, wipe of the porcelain insulator on each plug and check for cracks or breaks. If either condition exists, the plug must be replaced.
2. If the plugs are judged reusable, have them cleaned on a plug cleaning machine (found in most service stations) or remove the deposits with a stiff wire brush.
3. Check the plug gap on both new and used plugs before installing them in the engine. The ground electrode must be parallel to the center electrode and the specified size wire gauge should pass through the opening with a slight drag. If the center or ground electrode has worn unevenly, level them off with a file. If the air gap between the two electrodes is not correct, open or close the ground electrode, with the proper tool, to bring it to specifications. Such a tool is usually provided with a gap gauge.

INSTALLATION

1. Coat the threads of new plugs with an anti-seize compound. Insert the plugs into the engine and tighten them finger tightly.
2. Be sure that the plugs are not crossthreaded. If the plugs use metal gaskets, new gaskets should be installed each time the plugs are removed and installed.
3. Tighten the spark plugs to 11–15 ft. lbs.
4. Install the spark plug wires on their respective plugs. Be sure that each wire is firmly connected.
5. While you are checking the spark plugs, the spark plug wires should also be checked. Any wires that are cracked or brittle should be replaced.

➡ On the Navajo, whenever a high tension wire is removed for any reason from a spark plug, coil or distributor terminal housing, silicone grease must be applied to the boot before it is reconnected. Using a small clean tool, coat the entire interior surface of the boot with silicone grease.

Spark Plug Wires

TESTING

Spark plug and coil wires are those which carry electricity between the center tower of the distributor cap and the center tower of the coil, and those that carry electricity between the distributor cap and the spark plugs.

These may be tested visually by gently bending them and inspecting the bends for signs of cracking. If cracks are found, replace the wires. It's a good idea to replace the wires in sets, rather than individually.

The wires should also be tested for resistance with an ohmmeter. Resistance should be:

- Pickups and MPV — 16kΩ per 3.28 feet (1m) of wire
- Navajo — 7kΩ per foot (30cm) of wire

➡ On the Navajo, whenever a high tension wire is removed for any reason from a spark plug, coil or distributor terminal housing, silicone grease must be applied to the boot before it is reconnected. Using a small clean tool, coat the entire interior surface of the boot with Ford silicone grease D7AZ 19A331-A or equivalent.

FIRING ORDERS

➧ SEE FIGS. 8-11

➡ To avoid confusion, remove and tag the wires one at a time, for replacement.

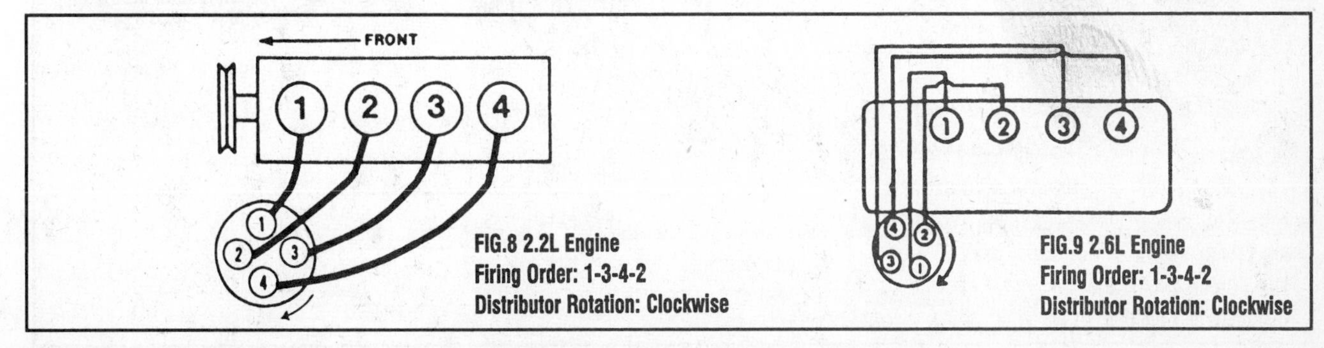

FIG.8 2.2L Engine
Firing Order: 1-3-4-2
Distributor Rotation: Clockwise

FIG.9 2.6L Engine
Firing Order: 1-3-4-2
Distributor Rotation: Clockwise

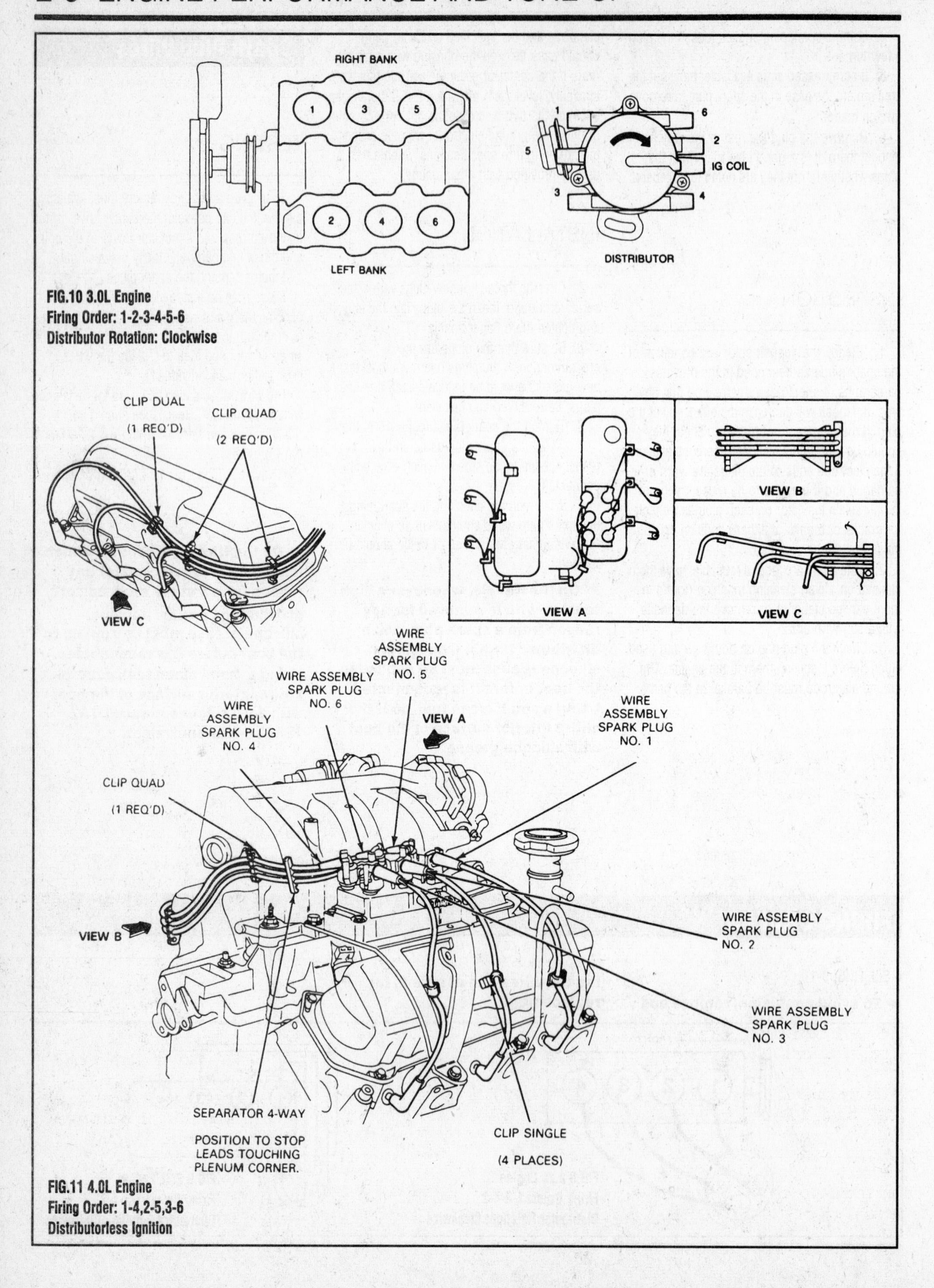

FIG.10 3.0L Engine
Firing Order: 1-2-3-4-5-6
Distributor Rotation: Clockwise

FIG.11 4.0L Engine
Firing Order: 1-4,2-5,3-6
Distributorless Ignition

ELECTRONIC IGNITION

Description and Operation

Electronic ignition systems offer many advantages over the old conventional breaker point type ignition system. By eliminating the points, maintenance requirements are greatly reduced. An electronic ignition system is capable of producing much higher voltage which in turn aids in starting, reduces spark plug fouling and provides better emission control.

A basic electronic ignition system consists of a distributor with a signal generator, and ignition coil and an electronic igniter. The "signal generator" is used to activate the electronic components of the igniter. It is located in the distributor and consists of three main components; the signal rotor, sometimes call a reluctor (do not confuse with the normal rotor located under the cap), the pickup coil, and the permanent magnet (breaker). The signal rotor revolves with the distributor shaft, while the pickup and the permanent magnet are stationary. As the signal rotor spins, the teeth on it pass a projection leading from the pickup coil. When this happens, voltage is allowed to flow through the system, firing the spark plugs. There is no physical contact and no electrical arcing, hence no need to replace burnt or worn parts.

Fuel injected versions of the Pickup, from 1990, and 2.6L MPV models use a distributor mounted crank angle sensor in place of the usual distributor mounted electronic components.

The most commonly replaced parts are the rotor and cap, which are still routine maintenance items. Other items, such as the pickup coil and signal rotor, are replaced when they fail. An air gap adjustment is possible only on the 1987–88 2.6L. Adjustments are not possible on later models.

An Electronic Distributorless Ignition System (EDIS) is used on Navajo models. The system consists of a crankshaft timing sensor (VRS), EDIS ignition module, ignition coil pack, the part of the main computer (ECU) that deals with spark angle and related wiring.

The crankshaft timing sensor, used on the Navajo, is a variable reluctance-type sensor, triggered by a trigger wheel machined into the rear of the front crankshaft damper. The signal generated by this sensor is called a Variable Reluctance Sensor signal (VRS). The VRS signal provides the timing information to the EDIS module.

The EDIS Module receives the VRS signal from the crankshaft timing sensor. The module processes the VRS signal into Profile Ignition Pickup (PIP) information and transmits it to the ECU (Engine Control Unit). The ECU processes the PIP signal along with signals received from other engine sensors according to a spark advance map programmed into the ECU. Using this information, the ECU produces a Spark Angle Word (SAW) signal which it sends back to the EDIS module. Using the SAW and VRS information, the EDIS switches primary current to the ignition coils like the contact points in an breaker point type ignition system, except that it sequences the spark among the three coils and provides the optimum amount of spark advance and dwell. The EDIS module also sends back to the ECU and Ignition Diagnostic Monitor signal (IDM) which the ECU uses to indicate a failure mode and which is also used to provide an rpm signal to the instrument panel tachometer.

The ignition coil pack contains three separate ignition coils which are controlled by the EDIS module through three coil leads. Each ignition coil fires two spark plugs simultaneously; one plug on the compression stroke and one on the exhaust stroke. The spark plug fired on the exhaust stroke uses very little of the coil's stored energy. The majority of the energy is used by the spark plug on the compression stroke.

During some EDIS faults, the failure mode effects management (FMEM) portion of the EDIS ignition module will maintain vehicle operation. If the EDIS module does not receive the SAW input, it will result in a fixed spark timing of 10° BTDC (before top dead center). If the EDIS module does not receive the VRS input, synchronization cannot be achieved, and the engine will not start.

Diagnosis and Testing

➧ SEE FIGS. 12-34

You will need an accurate ohmmeter, a jumper wire and a test light. Before proceeding with troubleshooting, make sure that all connections are tight and all wiring is intact.

1. Check for spark at the coil high tension lead by removing the lead from the distributor cap and holding it about 1/4 in. (6mm) from the engine block or other good ground. Use a heavy rubber glove or non-conductive clamp, such as a fuse puller or clothes pin, to hold the wire. Crank the engine and check for spark. If a good spark is noted, check the cap and rotor; if the spark is weak or nonexistent, replace the high tension lead, clean and tighten the connections and retest. If a weak spark is still noted, proceed to Step 2.

2. Check the coil primary resistance. Connect an ohmmeter across the coil primary terminals and check resistance on the low scale. Resistance (@ 68°F; 20°C) should be:

Pickups

1987–92 B2200 w/carb: 1.0–1.3Ω
1990–92 B2200 w/inj: 0.81–0.99Ω
1987–88 B2600: 1.0–1.3Ω
1989 B2600i Point 1: 0.77–0.95Ω
Point 2: 0.9–1.1kΩ
1990–92 B2600i: 0.81–0.99Ω

MPV

1989–92 2.6L Point 1: 0.77–0.95Ω
Point 2: 0.9–1.1kΩ
1989–91 3.0L; 0.81–0.99Ω
1992 3.0L; 0.72–0.88Ω

If the resistance is not correct, replace the coil.

3. Check the coil secondary resistance. Connect an ohmmeter across the distributor side of the coil and the coil center tower. Read resistance on the high scale. Resistance (@ 68°F; 20°C) should be:

Pickups

1987–88 B2200: 6–30kΩ
1987–88 B2600: 10–20kΩ
1989–82 B2200 and B2600i: 6–30kΩ

MPV

1989–92 2.6L Point 1: 0.77–0.95Ω
Point 2: 0.9–1.1kΩ
1989–91 3.0L; 0.81–0.99Ω
1992 3.0L; 0.72–0.88Ω

If resistance is much higher, replace the coil.

4. Next, remove the distributor cap and rotor. Crank the engine until a spoke on the rotor is aligned with the pickup coil contact. Use a flat feeler gauge to check the gap. Gap should be 0.20–0.60mm. The gap is not adjustable (procedure for 1987–1988 B2600 air gap adjustment in following paragraph). On these models, gap is corrected by parts replacement.

5. On B2200 carbureted models, check the pickup coil resistance. If resistance is not correct, replace the pickup coil.

6. Finally, test the ignition module. The only way to test the module is to substitute a known good module in its place.

Pickup Coil Resistance

Unplug the primary ignition wire connector and connect an ohmmeter across the two prongs of the pickup coil connector. Resistance, at 68°F (20°C), should be 900–1,200Ω.

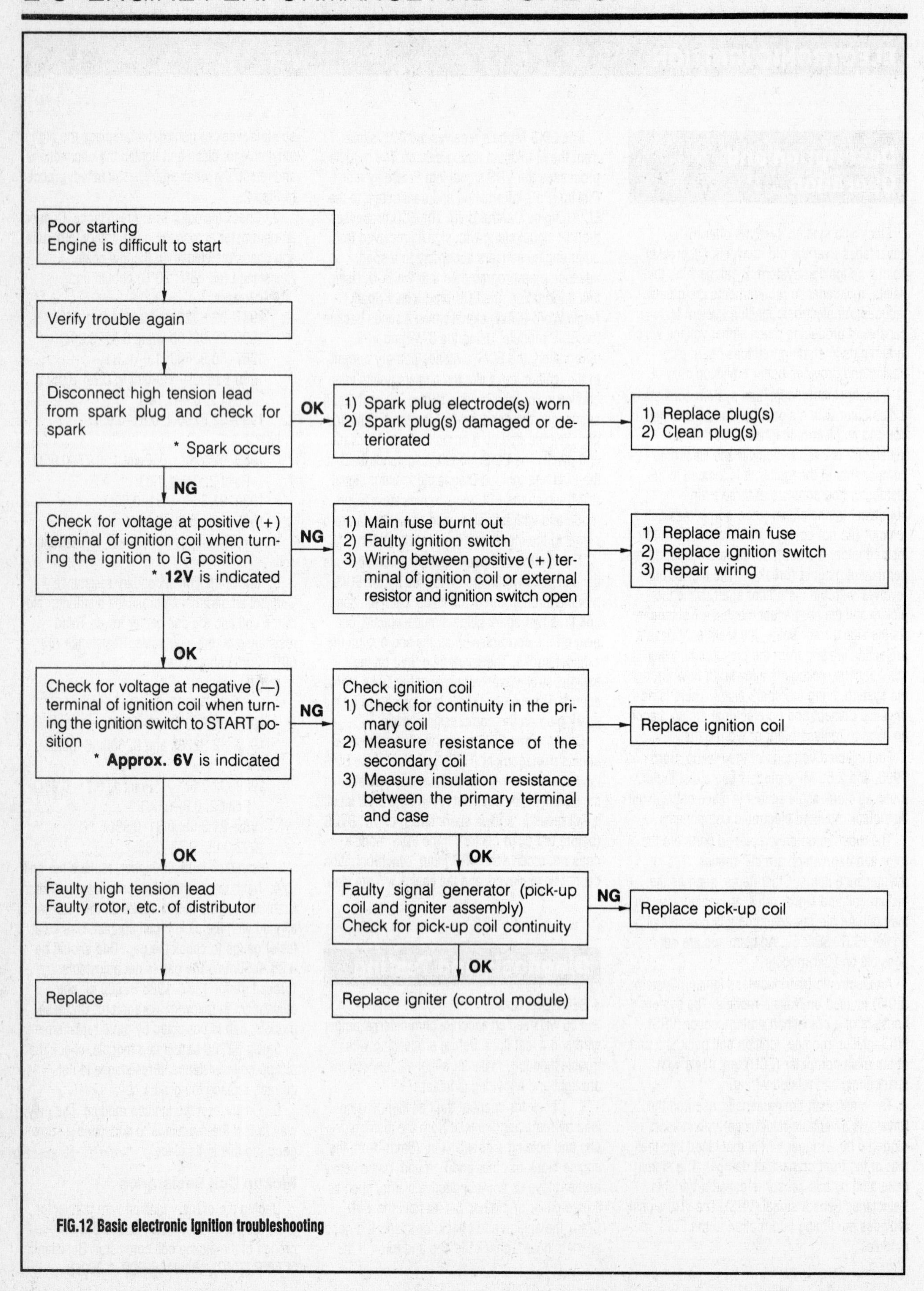

FIG.12 Basic electronic ignition troubleshooting

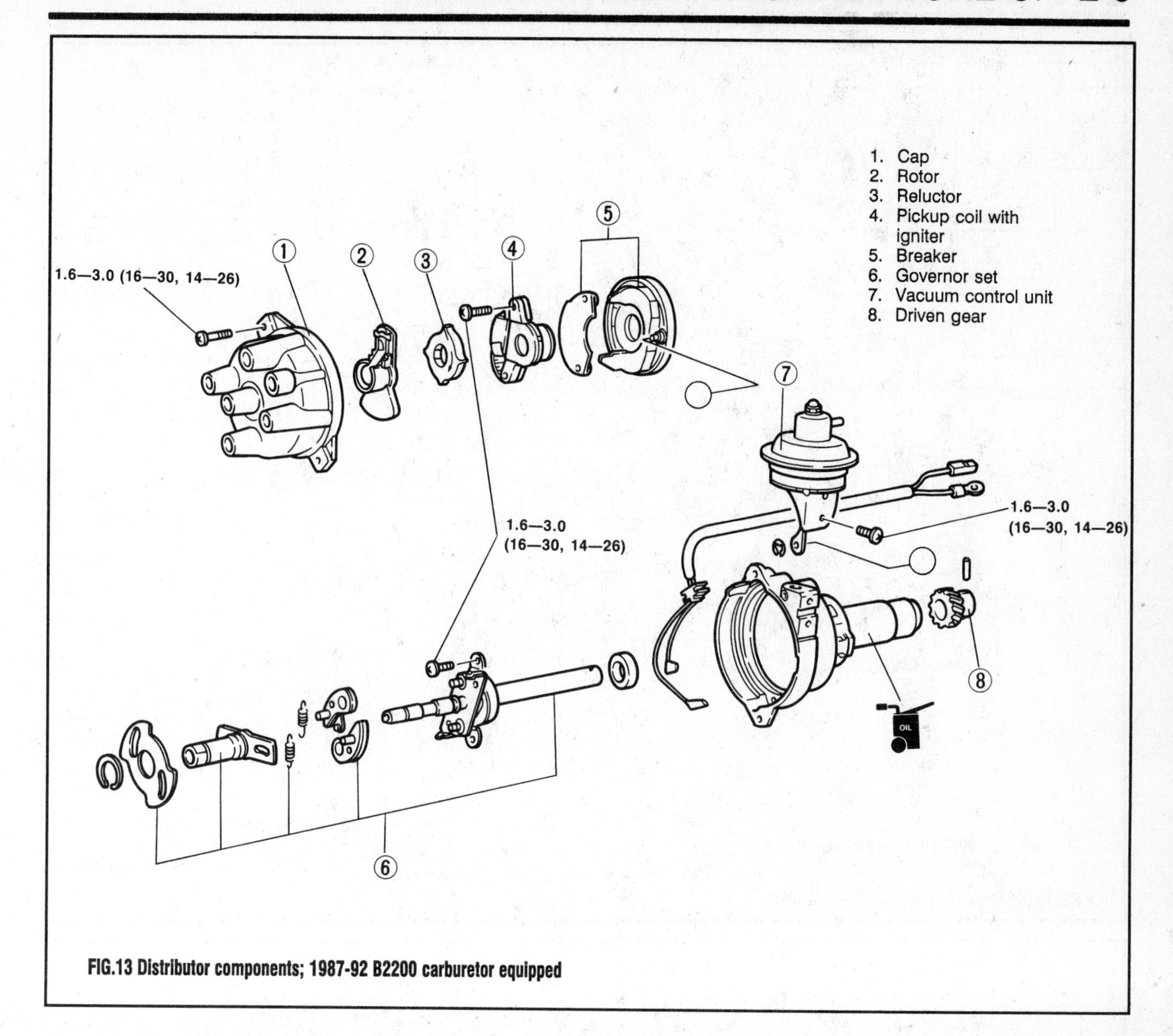

FIG.13 Distributor components; 1987-92 B2200 carburetor equipped

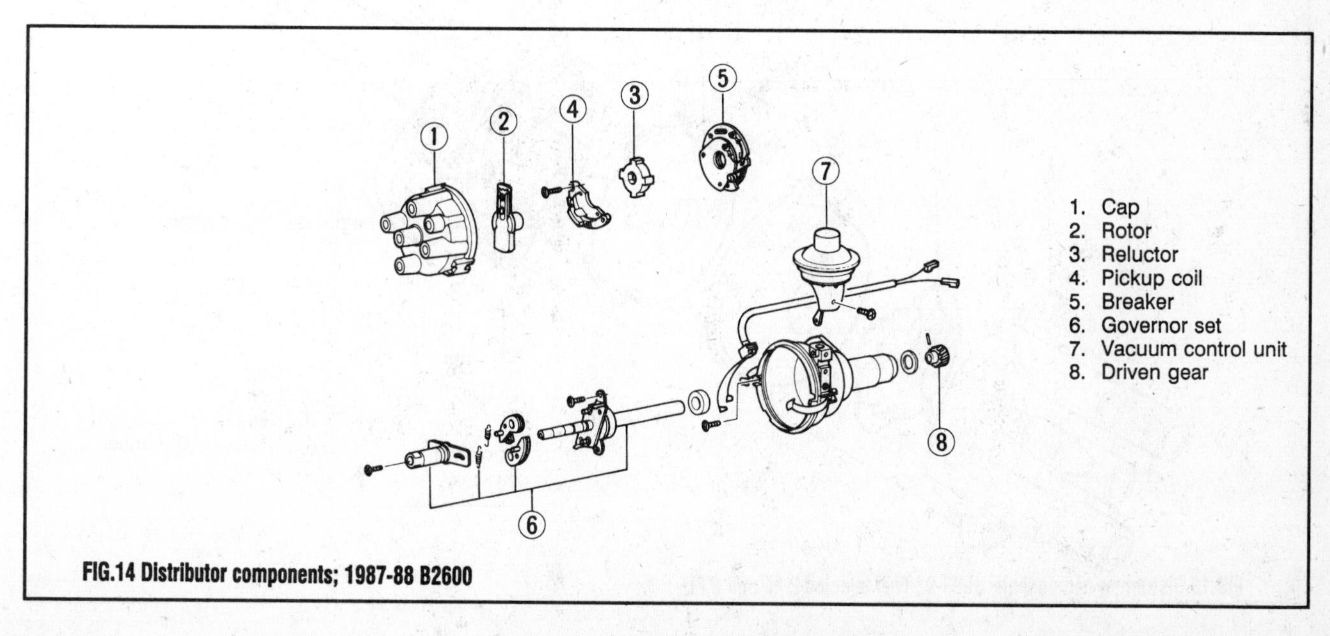

FIG.14 Distributor components; 1987-88 B2600

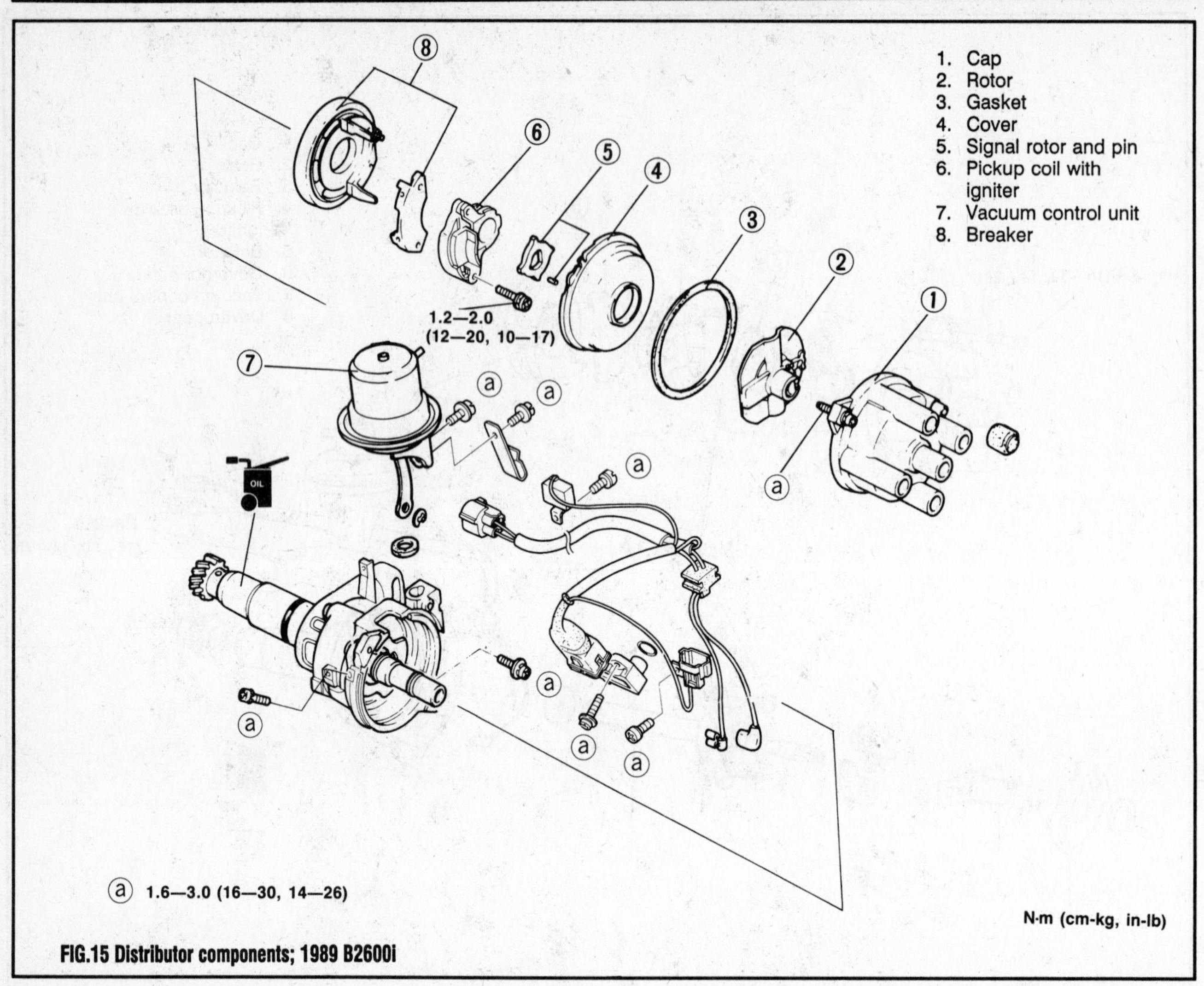

FIG.15 Distributor components; 1989 B2600i

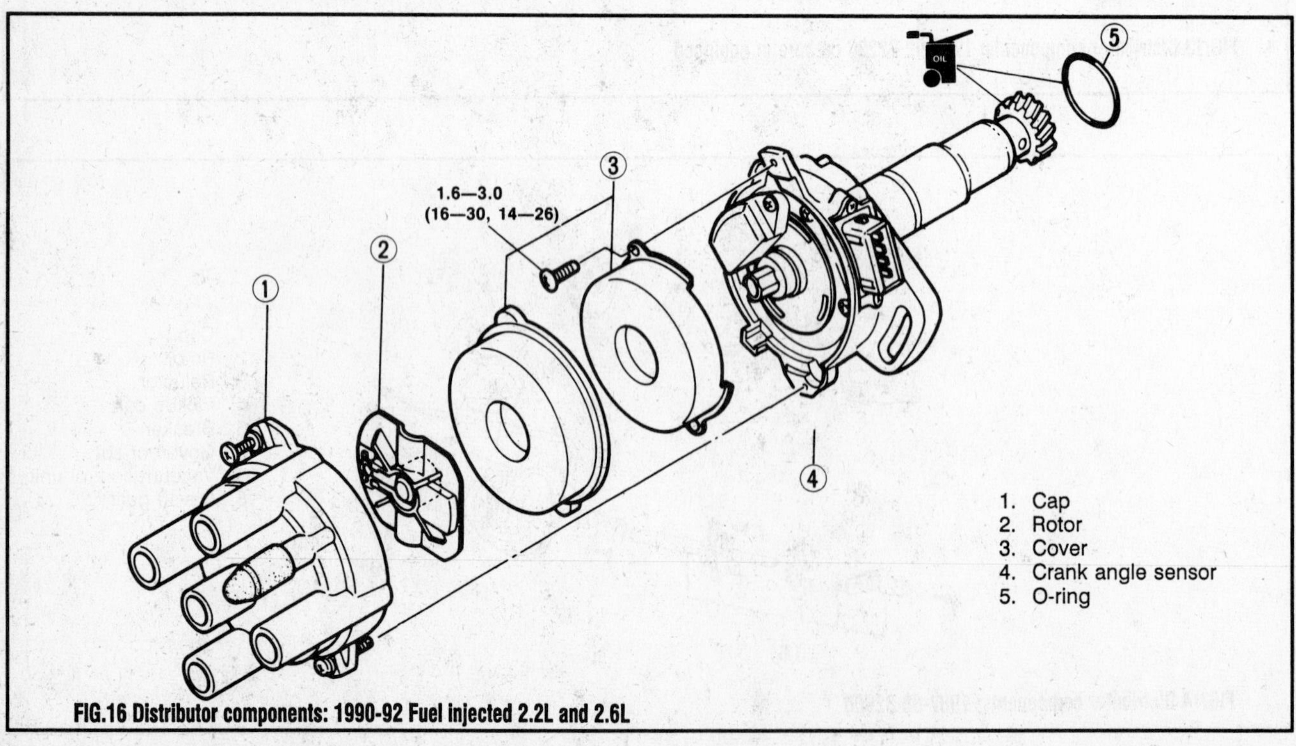

FIG.16 Distributor components: 1990-92 Fuel injected 2.2L and 2.6L

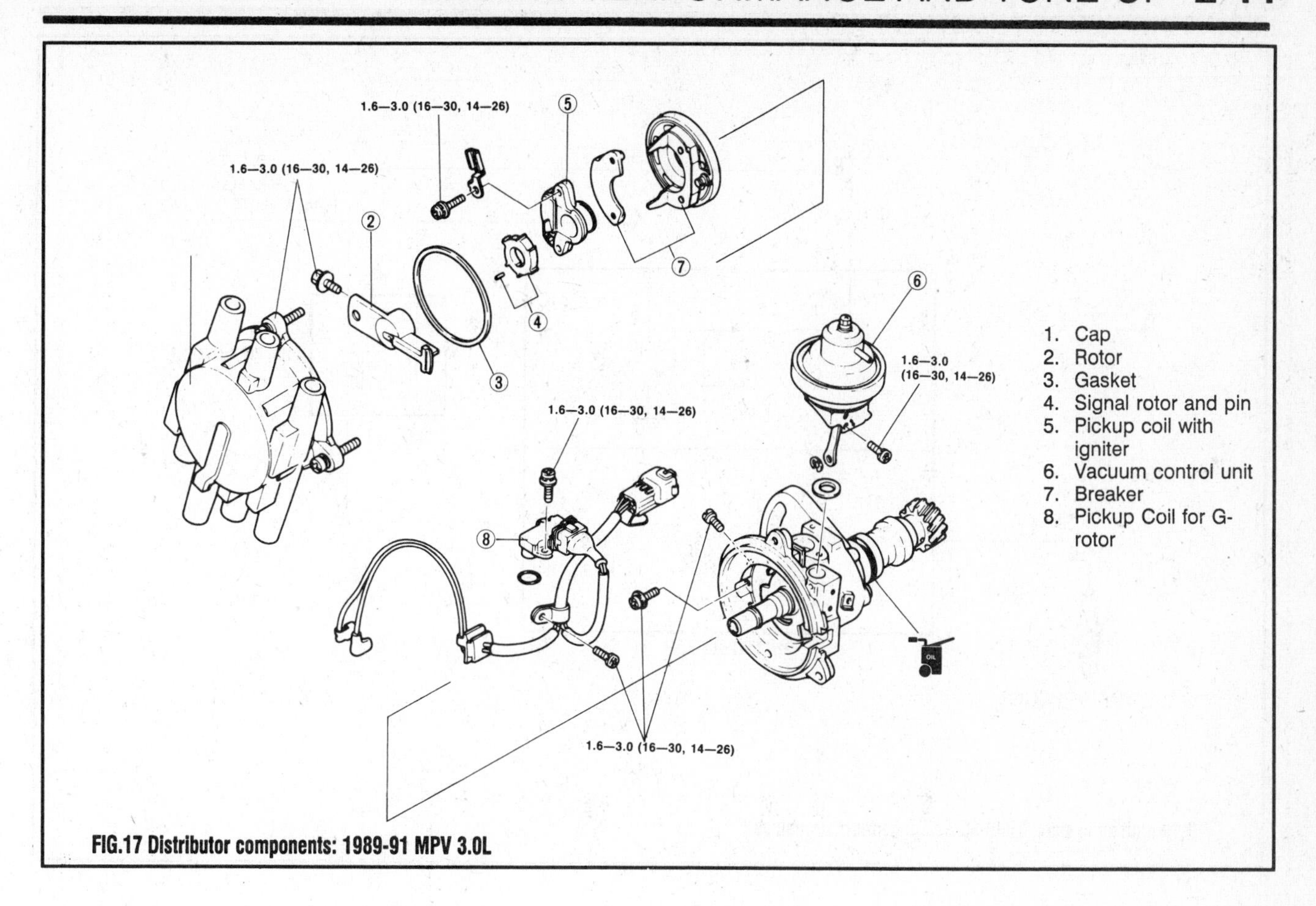

FIG.17 Distributor components: 1989-91 MPV 3.0L

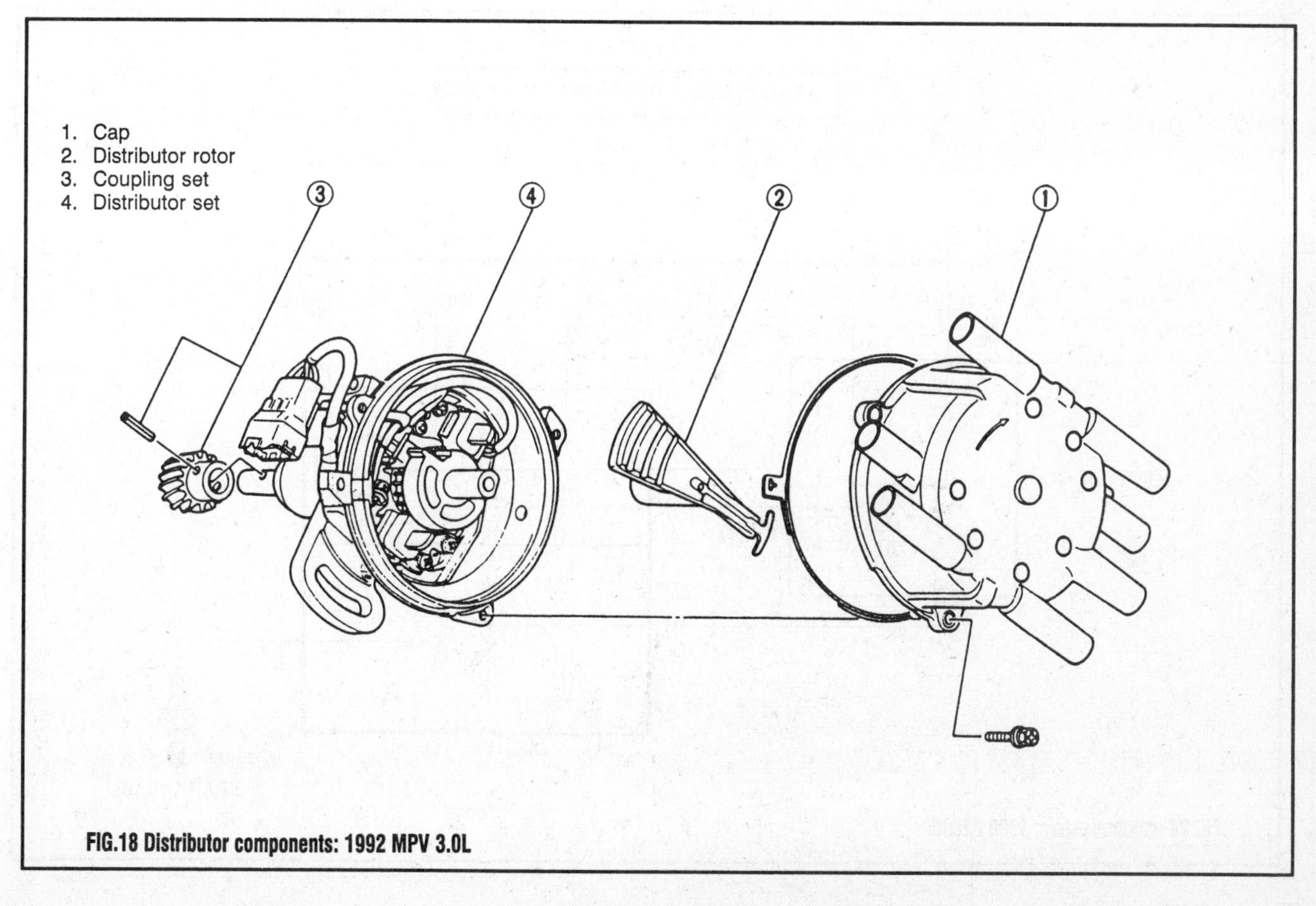

FIG.18 Distributor components: 1992 MPV 3.0L

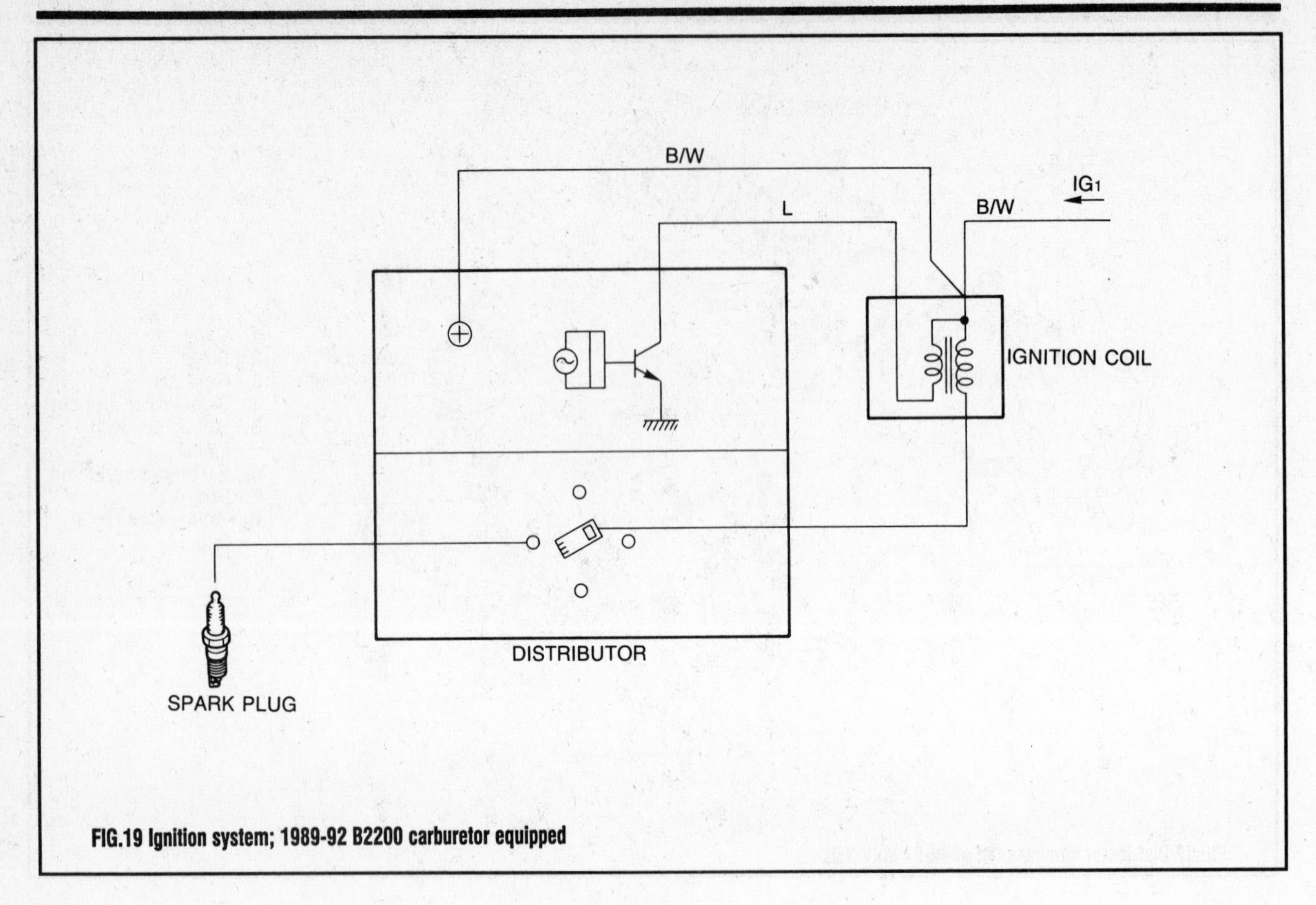

FIG.19 Ignition system; 1989-92 B2200 carburetor equipped

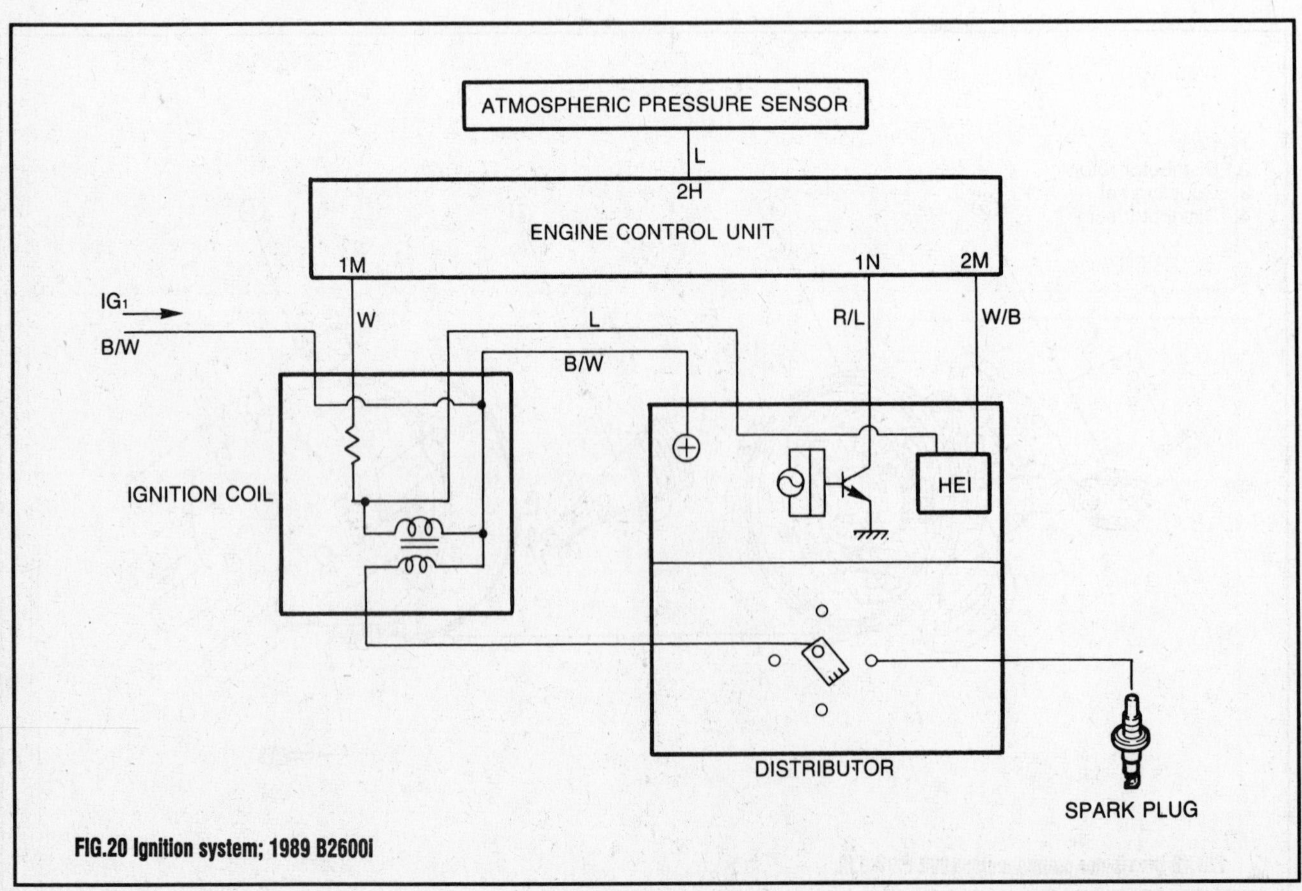

FIG.20 Ignition system; 1989 B2600i

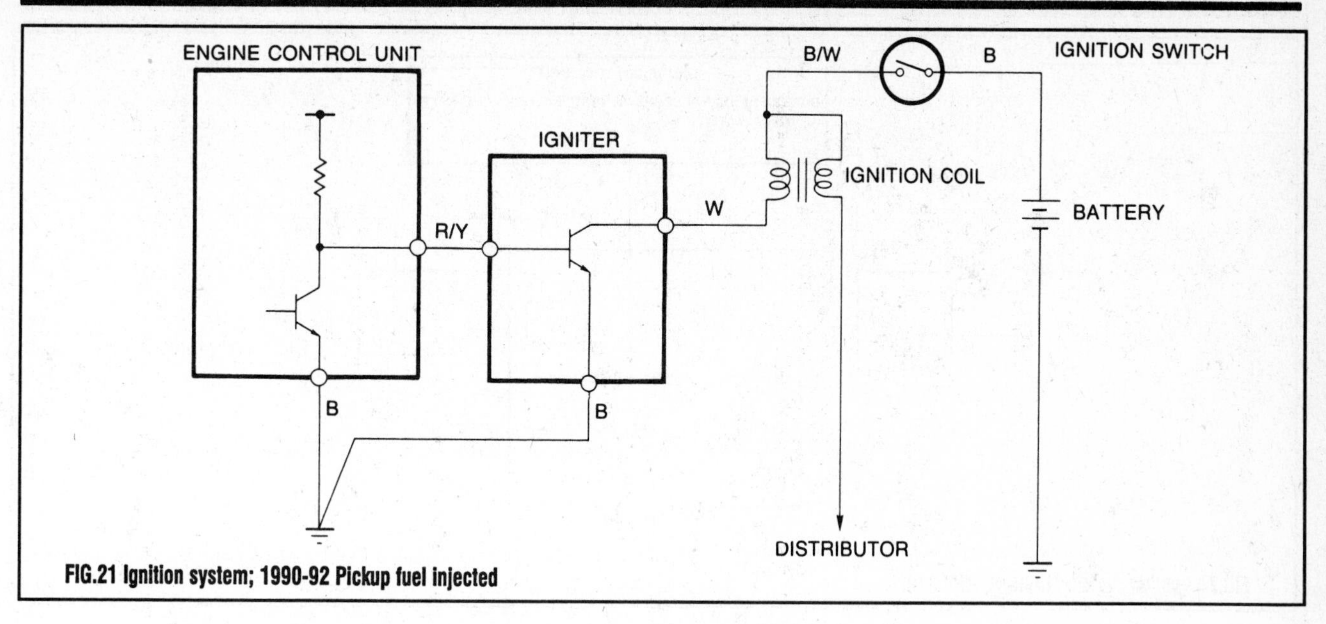

FIG.21 Ignition system; 1990-92 Pickup fuel injected

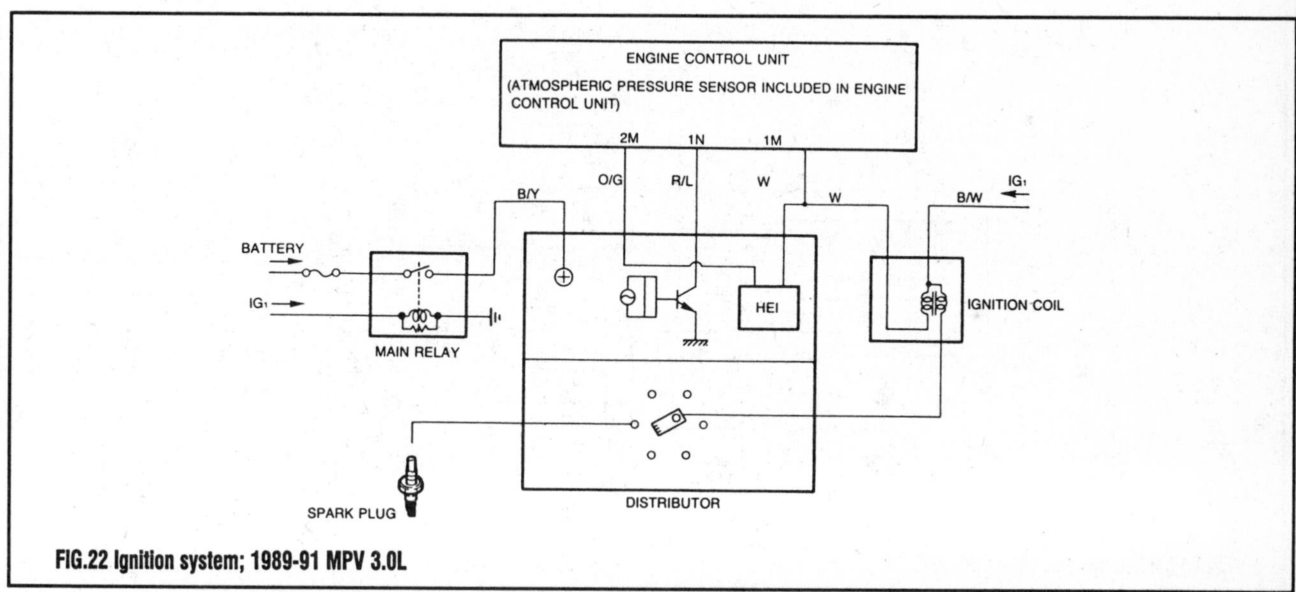

FIG.22 Ignition system; 1989-91 MPV 3.0L

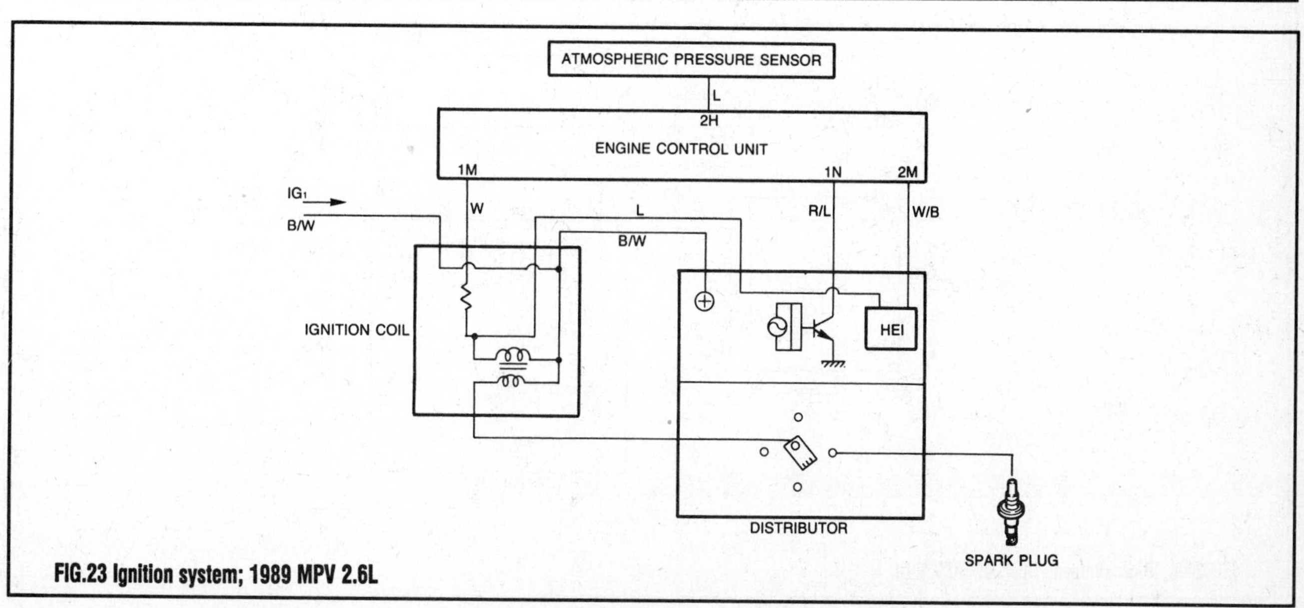

FIG.23 Ignition system; 1989 MPV 2.6L

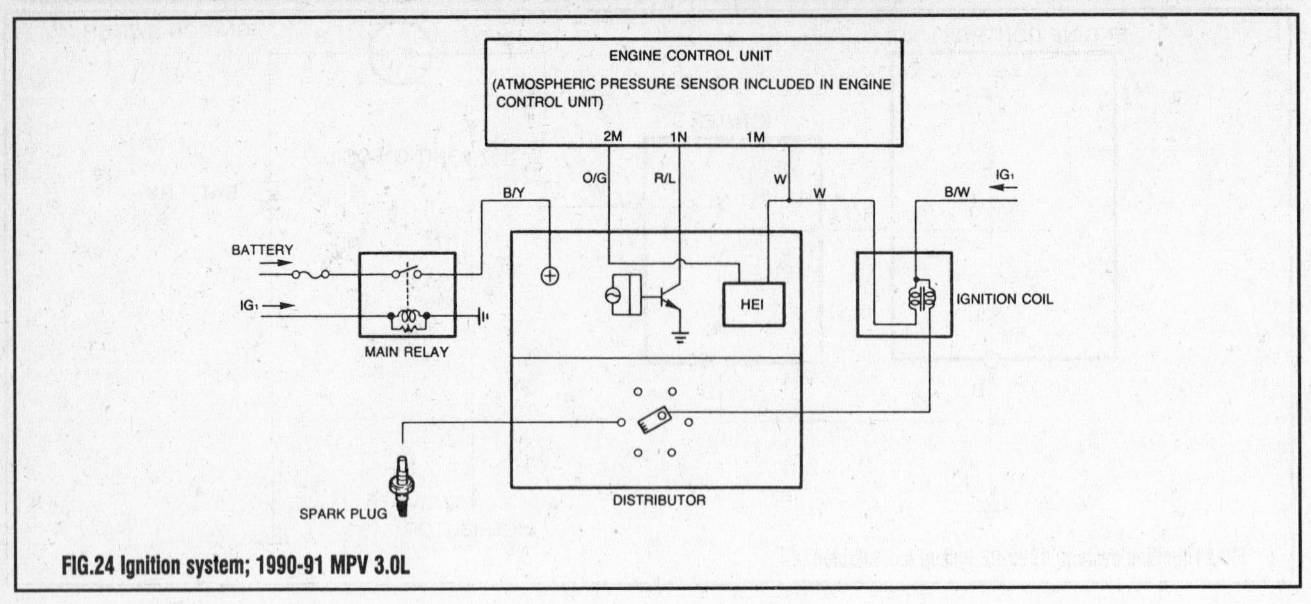

FIG.24 Ignition system; 1990-91 MPV 3.0L

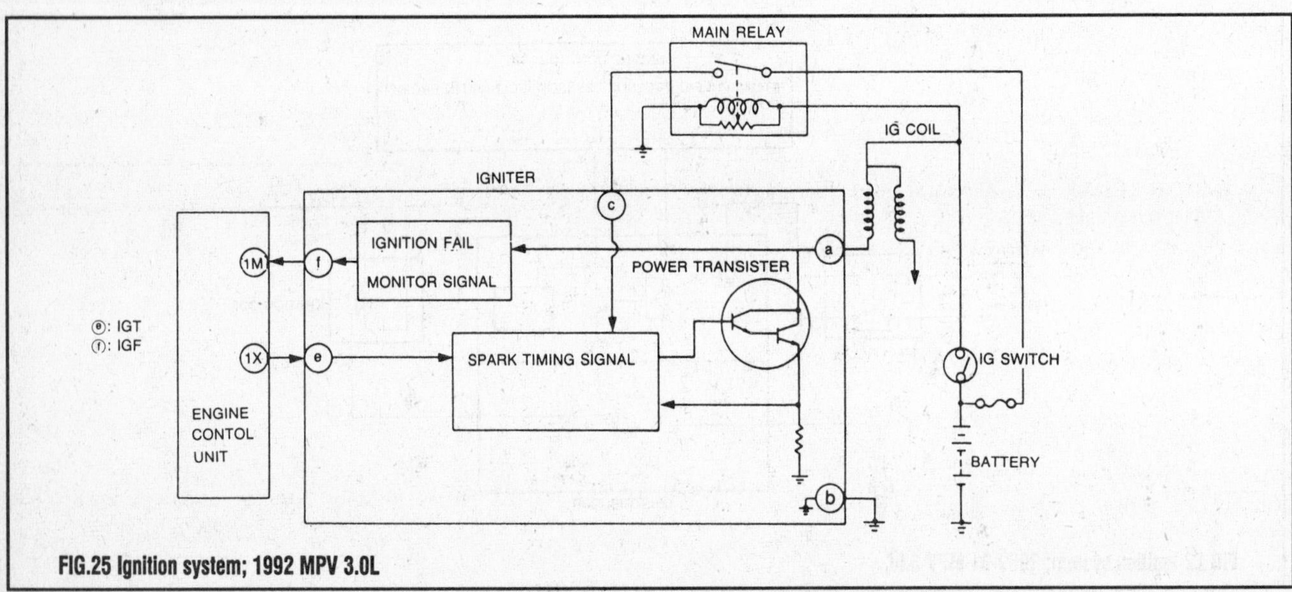

FIG.25 Ignition system; 1992 MPV 3.0L

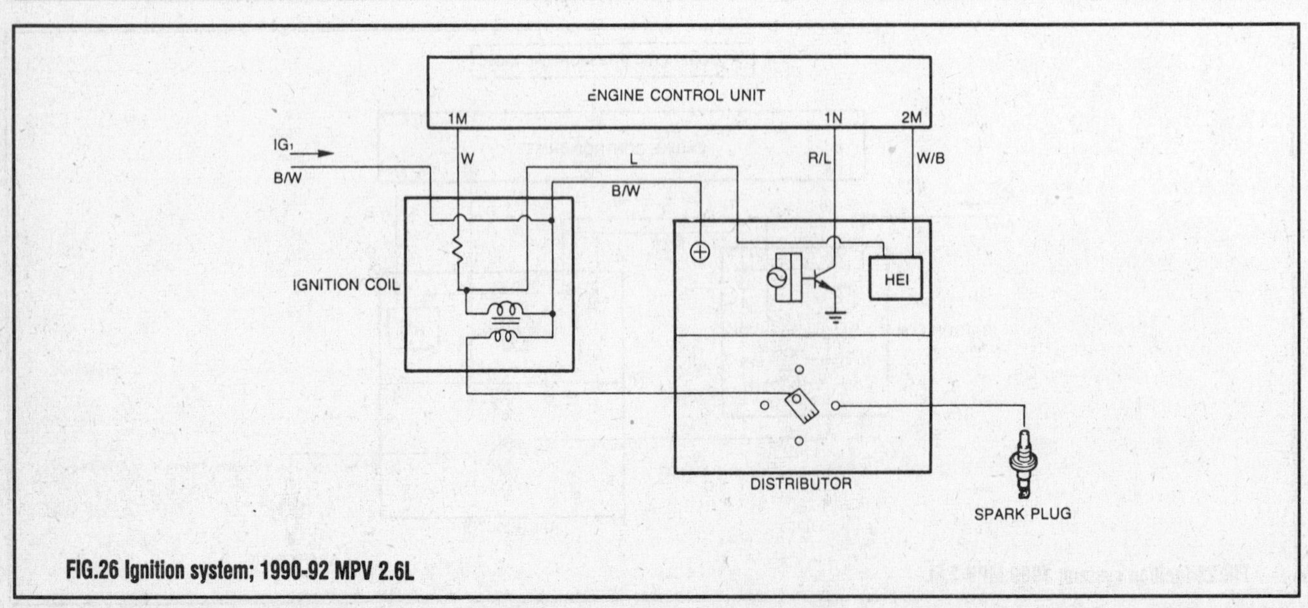

FIG.26 Ignition system; 1990-92 MPV 2.6L

External Resistor

1987–1988 B2600 models are equipped with an external resister. Measure the resistance at the two end contacts on the resistor. Resistance should be 1.0–1.5Ω.

Inspection of Components

1. The distributor cap on all engines, except the 1987–88 2.6L is held on by two screws. On the 1987–88 2.6L, the cap is held on by 2 spring clips. Remove the screws or unsnap the clips and lift the cap straight up with the wires still attached. Inspect the cap for cracks, carbon tracking and worn contacts. Replace it, if necessary, transferring the spark plug wires one at a time to avoid miswiring.
2. Pull the rotor straight up to remove it. Replace the rotor if it appears worn, burned or pitted.
3. Inspect the spark plug wires for cracks or brittleness. Replace them, one at a time, if they appear at all suspect. Avoid bending the wires sharply, or kinking them, as the carbon cores are subject to such damage.

Spark Advance Control

Distributors not equipped with a crank angle sensor are equipped with two methods of spark advance. They are, an internal centrifugal advance consisting of governor weights and springs; and an external advance controlled by engine vacuum. Models equipped with fuel injection are equipped with an electronic advance device.

To test the internal advance: Connect a timing light to the engine. Warm up the engine to normal operating temperature. Check that the idle speed and ignition timing are correct. Disconnect and plug the vacuum lines at the vacuum advance. Gradually increase the engine speed while checking the timing mark with the timing light. If the mark move to what seems like an excessive amount of advance, the cause could be a weak governor spring. If the mark moves slowly and seems like an insufficient amount of advance, the cause could be a governor weight or advance cam malfunction.

To test the vacuum advance: Warm the engine to normal operating temperature. Check that the idle speed and ignition timing are correct. Disconnect the vacuum lines from the vacuum control and plug them. Connect a vacuum hand pump to the vacuum control, slowly apply vacuum and check the advance with a timing light. If the spark advance seems sluggish or not operating, replace the vacuum control.

To test fuel injected models equipped with an electronic advance, connect a timing light and verify that the timing advances with engine acceleration.

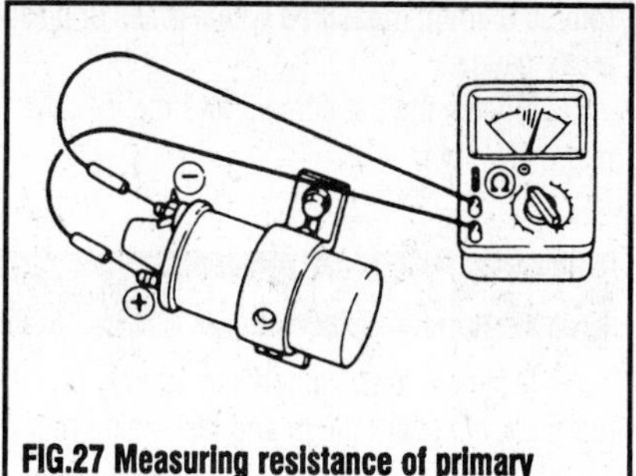

FIG.27 Measuring resistance of primary coil

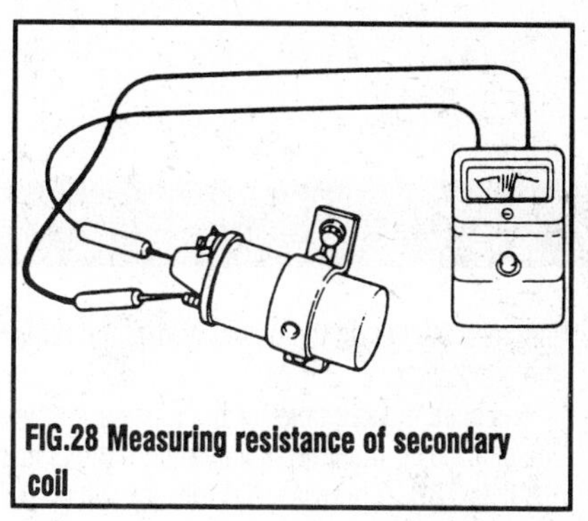

FIG.28 Measuring resistance of secondary coil

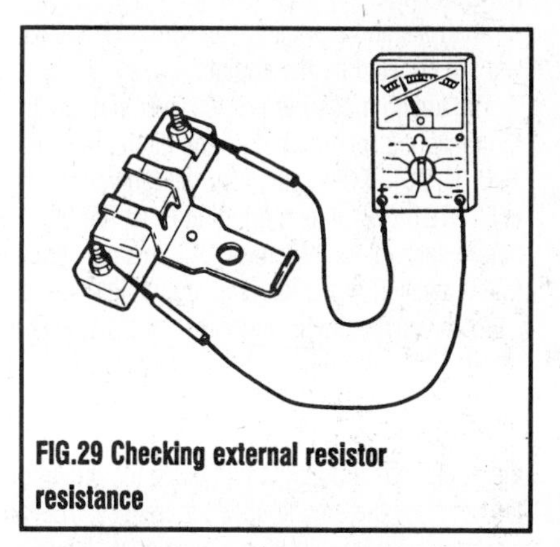

FIG.29 Checking external resistor resistance

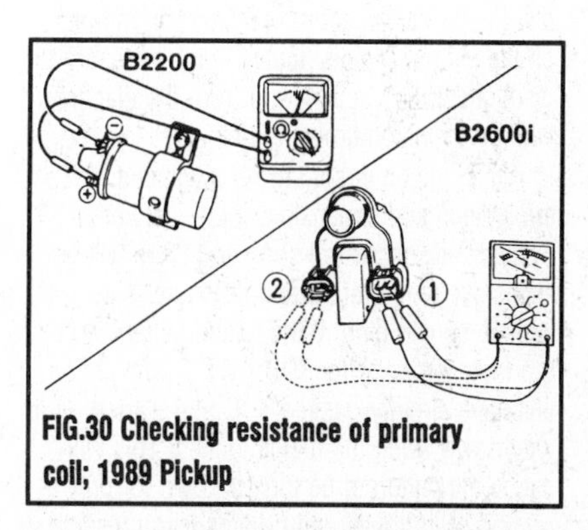

FIG.30 Checking resistance of primary coil; 1989 Pickup

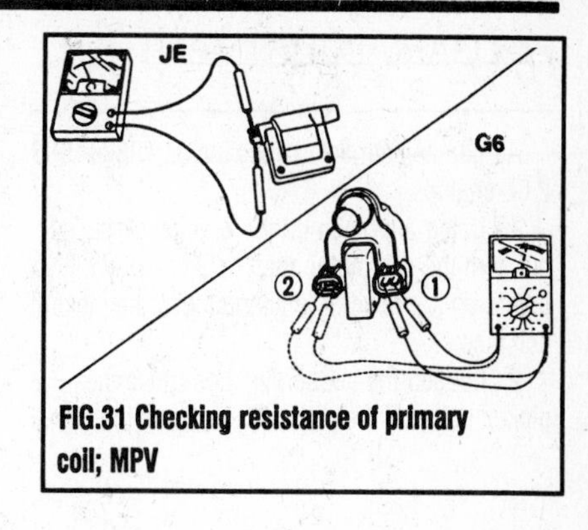

FIG.31 Checking resistance of primary coil; MPV

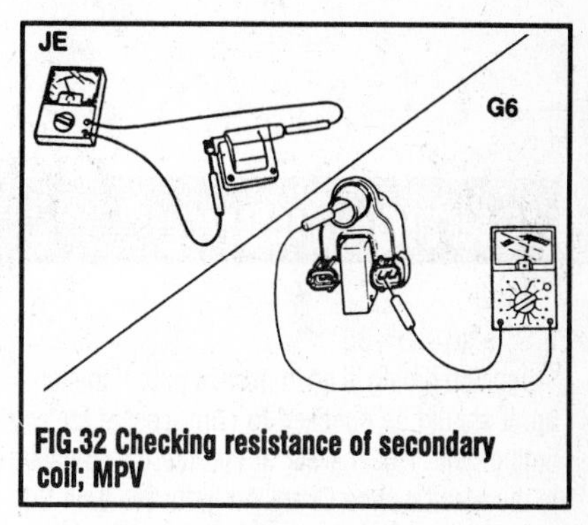

FIG.32 Checking resistance of secondary coil; MPV

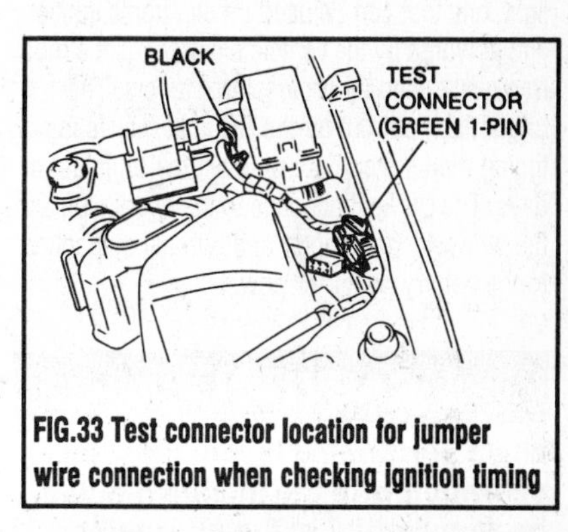

FIG.33 Test connector location for jumper wire connection when checking ignition timing

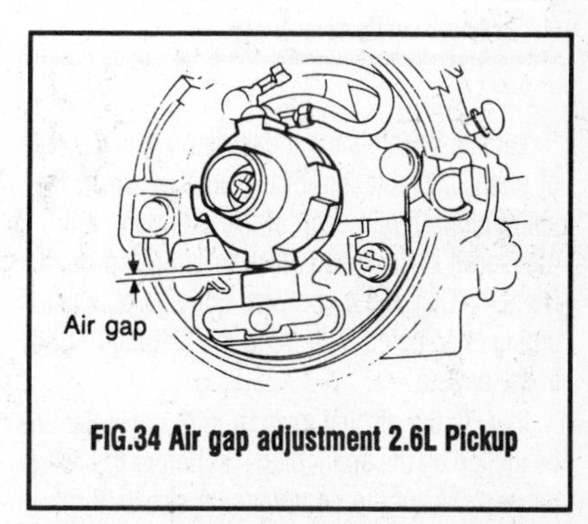

FIG.34 Air gap adjustment 2.6L Pickup

The Navajo has a fixed timing at 10° BTDC (before top dead center). It is not adjustable and timing is controlled by the ECU.

Adjustments

The only adjustments on distributor components are as follows:

AIR GAP ADJUSTMENT

Air gap adjustment is possible on 1987–1988 2.6L engines.

1. Using a wrench on the crankshaft pulley nut, turn the distributor shaft until one of the high points on the reluctor is aligned with the pickup coil face.
2. Loosen the set screws and move the pickup coil until the gap between it and the signal rotor is 0.8mm, measured with a brass or plastic feeler gauge.
3. Tighten the set screws and recheck the gap.

Parts Replacement

An electrical tune-up consists mostly of replacing the spark plugs and inspecting or replacing the distributor and distributor rotor. The wires' resistance should be checked, but only replaced if necessary. These parts are not expensive and can prevent many embarrassing failures. Retailers and auto departments run sales which can save you more money. Refer to the included distributor illustrations, if further distributor servicing is necessary, parts are disassembled in the callout numerical order shown.

IGNITION TIMING

➧ SEE FIGS. 35-36

Ignition timing is an important part of the tune-up. It should be checked to compensate for timing belt or gear wear at the interval specified in the Maintenance Chart. An inductive type DC light, one that can be used on electronic ignition, and powered by the vehicle's battery, is the most frequently used by professional tuners. The bright flash put out by the DC light makes the timing marks stand out on even the brightest of days. The DC light attaches to the spark plug and the wire with an adapter and two clips attached to the battery posts for power.

⁂ CAUTION

When performing this or any other operation with the engine running, be very careful of the alternator belt and pulleys. Make sure that your timing light wires don't interfere with the belt.

Ignition timing is the measurement, in degrees of crankshaft rotation, of the point at which the spark plugs fire in each of the cylinders. It is measured in degrees before or after Top Dead Center (TDC) of the compression stroke. Ignition timing is adjusted by turning the distributor body in the engine.

Ideally, the air/fuel mixture in the cylinder will be ignited by the spark plug just before the piston passes TDC of the compression stroke. If this happens, the piston will be beginning its downward motion of the power stroke just as the compressed and ignited air/fuel mixture begins to develop a considerable amount of pressure. The expansion of the air/fuel mixture then forces the piston down on the power stroke and turns the crankshaft.

Because it takes time for the mixture to burn, the spark plug must fire a little before the piston reaches TDC. Otherwise, the mixture will not be burned completely early enough in the downstroke and the full power of the explosion will not be used by the engine.

The timing measurement is given in degrees of crankshaft rotation before the piston reaches TDC (BTDC). If the setting for the ignition timing is 5° BTDC (5B), the spark plug must fire 5° before each piston reaches TDC. This only holds true, however, when the engine is at idle speed.

As the engine speed increases, the pistons go faster. The spark plugs have to ignite the fuel even sooner if it is to be completely ignited when the piston reaches TDC. To do this, the distributor has a means to advance the timing of the spark as the engine speed increases. This is accomplished by centrifugal weights within the distributor and a vacuum diaphragm, mounted on the side of the distributor. It is necessary to disconnect the vacuum line from the diaphragm when the ignition timing is being set.

If the ignition is set too far advanced (BTDC), the ignition and expansion of the fuel in the cylinder will occur too soon and there will be excessive temperature and pressure. This causes engine ping. If the ignition spark is set too far retarded, after TDC (ATDC), the piston will have already passed TDC and started on its way down when the fuel is ignited. This will cause the piston to be forced down for only a portion of its travel and creates less pressure in the cylinder, resulting in poor engine performance and lack of power.

The timing is best checked with a timing light. This device is connected in series (or through induction) with the No. 1 spark plug. The current which fires the spark plug also causes the timing light to flash.

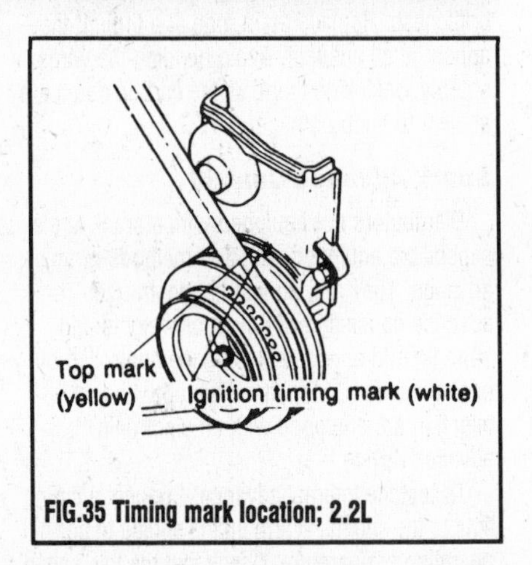

FIG.35 Timing mark location; 2.2L

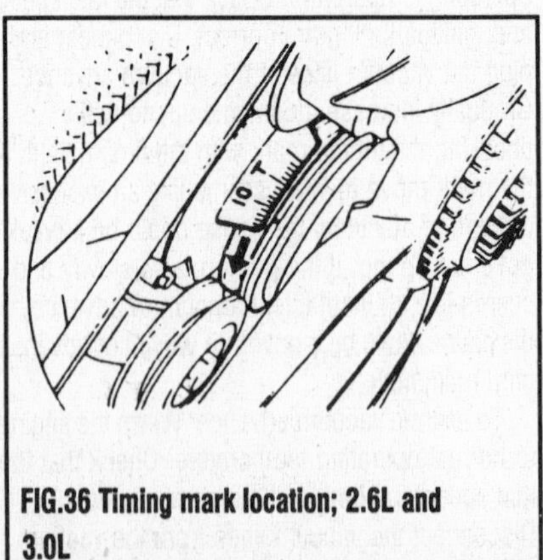

FIG.36 Timing mark location; 2.6L and 3.0L

The timing marks are located at the front crankshaft pulley and consist of a notch on the crankshaft pulley and a scale of degrees of crankshaft rotation attached to the front cover.

When the engine is running, the timing light is aimed at the marks on the flywheel pulley and the pointer.

ADJUSTMENT

Through 1988

1. Raise the hood and clean and mark the timing marks. Chalk or fluorescent paint makes a good, visible mark.
2. Disconnect the vacuum line to the distributor and plug the disconnected line. Disconnect the line at the vacuum source, not at the distributor.
3. Connect a timing light to the front (no.1) cylinder, a power source and ground. Follow the manufacturer's instructions.
4. Connect a tachometer to the engine.
5. Start the engine and reduce the idle to 700–750 rpm to be sure that the centrifugal advance mechanism is not working.
6. With the engine running, shine the timing light at the timing pointer and observe the position of the pointer in relation to the timing mark on the crankshaft pulley. All models have two notches on the pulley. Looking straight down on the marks, the one on the left is TDC, the one on the right is BTDC
7. If the timing is not as specified, adjust the timing by loosening the distributor holddown bolt and rotating the distributor in the proper direction. When the proper ignition timing is obtained, tighten the holddown bolt on the distributor.
8. Check the centrifugal advance mechanism by accelerating the engine to about 2,000 rpm. If the ignition timing advances, the mechanism is working properly.
9. Stop the engine and remove the timing light.
10. Reset the idle to specifications.
11. Remove the tachometer.

1989–92 Pickup and MPV

1. Run the engine to normal operating temperature.
2. Turn all electrical accessories OFF.
3. Disconnect the vacuum hoses from the vacuum control and plug it.
4. On fuel injected models, connect a jumper wire between the green, 1-pin test connector and ground.
5. Check the idle speed, and, if necessary, adjust it.
6. Mark the correct timing mark with white paint.
7. Connect a timing light according to the manufacturer's instructions.
8. With the engine running at idle, aim the timing light at the timing marks. If the correct timing is not indicated, loosen the distributor locknut and turn the distributor as needed to align the marks.
9. Tighten the locknut and recheck the timing.
10. Reconnect the vacuum hose and remove the jumper wire.

Navajo

With the EEC-IV EDIS systems no ignition timing adjustment is possible (preset at the factory to 10° BTDC and is computer controlled) and none should be attempted.

VALVE LASH

Valve adjustment determines how far the valves enter the cylinder and how long they stay open and closed.

If the valve clearance is too large, part of the lift of the camshaft will be used in removing the excessive clearance. Consequently, the valve will not be opening as far as it should, it will start to open too late and will close too early. This condition has two effects: the valve train components will emit a tapping sound as they take up the excessive clearance and as the valves slam shut, and the engine will preform poorly because the valves don't open fully and allow the proper amount of gases to flow into and out of the engine.

If the valve clearance is too small, the intake valves and the exhaust valves will open too far and they will not fully seat on the cylinder head when they close. When a valve seats itself on the cylinder head, it does two things: it seals the combustion chamber so that none of the gasses in the cylinder escape and it cools itself by transferring some of the heat it absorbs from the combustion in the cylinder to the cylinder head and to the engine's cooling system. If the valve clearance is too small, the engine will run poorly because of the gases escaping from the combustion chamber. The valves will also become overheated and will warp, since they cannot transfer heat unless they are touching the valve seat in the cylinder head.

➡ While all valve adjustments must be made as accurately as possible, it is better to have the valve adjustment slightly loose than slightly tight, as a burned valve may result from overly tight adjustments.
This holds true for valve adjustments on most engines.

ADJUSTMENT

➧ SEE FIG. 37

1987–88 Engines

These engines use hydraulic lash adjusters for the intake and exhaust valves, which require no routine adjustment.

However, these engines also incorporate a 3rd valve per cylinder called the jet valve which should be periodically checked and adjusted.

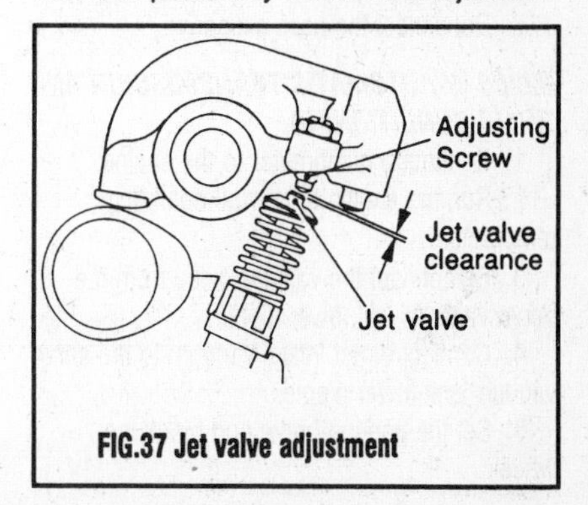

FIG.37 Jet valve adjustment

1. Run the engine to normal operating temperature. Then, shut it off.
2. Remove the valve cover.
3. Rotate the engine by hand until the No.1 cylinder is at TDC compression. Both the intake and exhaust valves will feel loose and the timing mark for 0 will be aligned with the pointer.
4. Check the jet valve clearance with a flat feeler gauge. Clearance for all engines should be 0.25mm. If not, loosen the locknut on the rocker arm and turn the adjusting screw until a slight drag is felt on the feeler gauge. The jet valve spring is relatively weak, so don't press down on the valve stem or you'll get an erroneous reading.
5. Turn the engine by hand, in the normal direction of rotation, until each cylinder in the firing order reaches TDC of its compression stroke and adjust each jet valve in turn.
6. Install the valve cover.

1989-91 Engines

No routine adjustment is necessary or possible.

IDLE SPEED AND MIXTURE ADJUSTMENTS

➧ SEE FIGS 38-43

Idle Speed

1987 Engines

EXCEPT B2200 W/AUTOMATIC TRANSMISSION

1. Connect a tachometer to the engine.
2. Run the engine to normal operating temperature.
3. Check the idle speed in NEUTRAL or PARK. If it is not 800–850 rpm, turn the Throttle Adjusting Screw until it is.

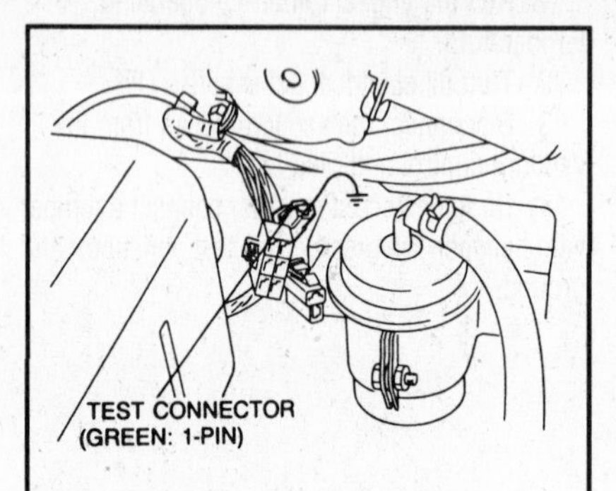

FIG.38 Idle speed adjustment, connect a jumper wire between the test connector Green 1-pin and a ground. Injected Pickups

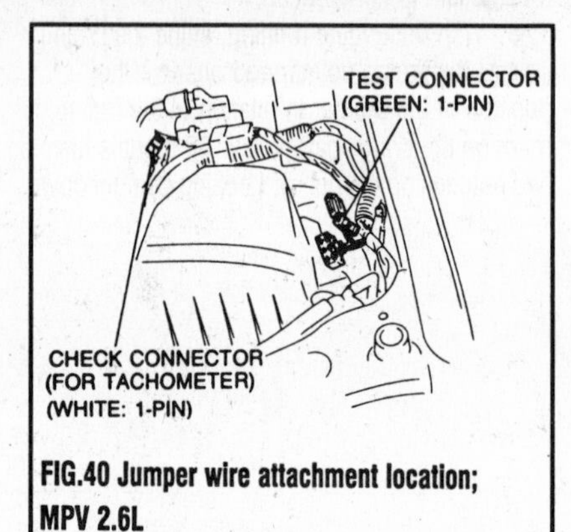

FIG.40 Jumper wire attachment location; MPV 2.6L

B2200 W/AUTOMATIC TRANSMISSION AND WO/AIR CONDITIONING

1. Connect a tachometer to the engine.
2. Run the engine to normal operating temperature.
3. Disconnect the vacuum hose from the servo vacuum unit.
4. Connect direct intake vacuum to the servo vacuum unit.
5. Set the parking brake and block the wheels.
6. Check the idle speed in DRIVE. If it is not 920–970 rpm, turn the Throttle Adjusting Screw until it is.
7. Reconnect the hose properly.

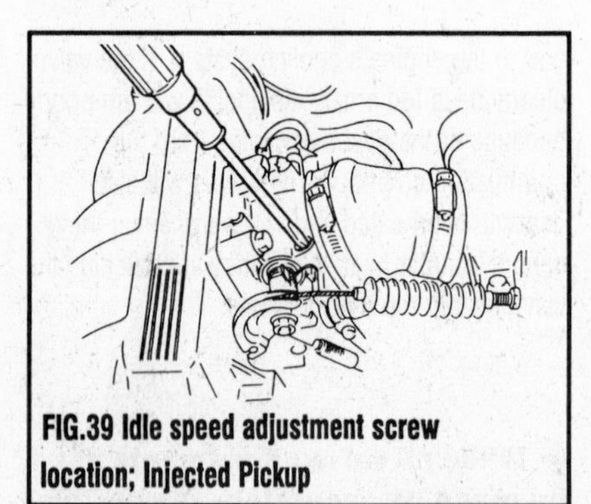
FIG.39 Idle speed adjustment screw location; Injected Pickup

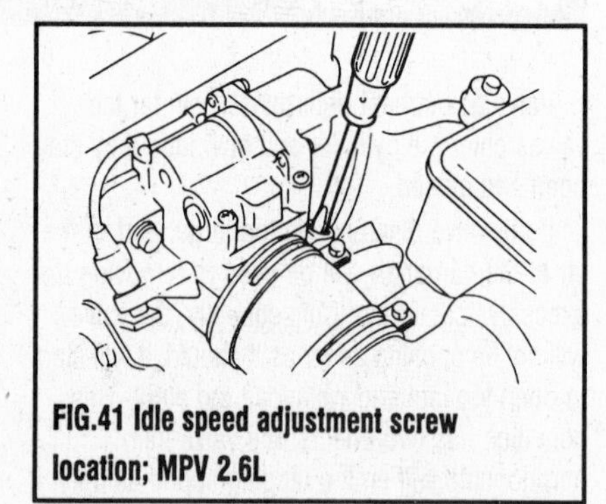
FIG.41 Idle speed adjustment screw location; MPV 2.6L

B2200 W/AUTOMATIC TRANSMISSION AND W/AIR CONDITIONING

1. Connect a tachometer to the engine.
2. Run the engine to normal operating temperature.
3. Disconnect the vacuum hose from the servo vacuum unit lower nipple.
4. Connect direct intake vacuum to the servo vacuum unit lower nipple.
5. Set the parking brake and block the wheels.
6. Check the idle speed in DRIVE. If it is not 1,300–1,500 rpm, turn the Throttle Adjusting Screw until it is.
7. Reconnect the hose properly.

1988-92 Carbureted Engines

1. Connect a tachometer to the engine.
2. Run the engine to normal operating temperature, make sure the choke is fully opened. The cooling fan motor must not be operating during this operation.

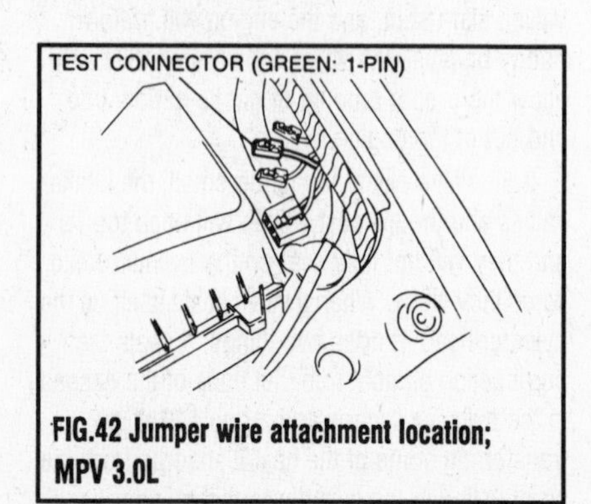

FIG.42 Jumper wire attachment location; MPV 3.0L

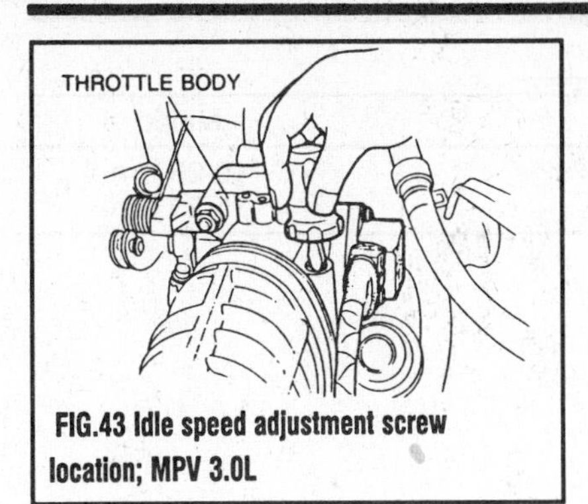

FIG.43 Idle speed adjustment screw location; MPV 3.0L

3. Check the idle speed in NEUTRAL or PARK. If it is not 800–850 rpm, turn the Throttle Adjusting Screw until it is.

1989-92 Fuel Injected Engines

EXCEPT NAVAJO

1. Place manual transmission in neutral or automatic transmission in park.
2. Make sure all accessories are Off.
3. Connect a tachometer and timing light to the engine.
4. Warm up the engine to normal operating temperature.
5. Check the ignition timing and adjust, if necessary.
6. Ground the green 1-pin test connector to the body with a jumper wire.
7. Check the idle speed. Specifications are as follows: 2.2L and 2.6L engines — Manual transmission: 730–770 rpm. Automatic transmission: 750–790 rpm.

3.0L engine — Manual and automatic transmission: 780–820 rpm.

8. If the idle speed is not within specification, adjust by turning the air adjusting screw.
9. After adjustment, disconnect the jumper wire from the test connector. Recheck the ignition timing.

NAVAJO

1. Place manual transmission in neutral or automatic transmission in Park. Apply the parking brake.
2. Make sure the heater and accessories are Off.
3. Start the engine and bring to normal operating temperature. Make sure the throttle lever is resting on the throttle plate stop screw.
4. Check the ignition timing and adjust, if necessary.
5. Shut off the engine and disconnect the negative battery cable for 5 minutes minimum. Reconnect the negative battery cable.
6. Start the engine and let it stabilize for 2 minutes. Rev the engine and let it return to idle, lightly depress and release the accelerator and let the engine idle.
7. If the engine does not idle properly, shut off the engine and disconnect the idle speed control-air bypass solenoid.
8. Run the engine at 2500 rpm for 30 seconds, then let it idle for 2 minutes.
9. Check/adjust the idle rpm to 675 rpm by turning the throttle plate stop screw.

➡ If the screw must be turned in, shut the engine off and make the estimated adjustment, then start the engine and repeat Steps 8 and 9.

10. Shut the engine off and repeat Steps 8 and 9.
11. Shut the engine off and disconnect the negative battery cable for 5 minutes minimum.
12. With the engine off, reconnect the idle speed control-air bypass solenoid. Make sure the throttle is not stuck in the bore and the linkage is not preventing the throttle from closing.
13. Start the engine and let it stabilize for 2 minutes. Rev the engine and let it return to idle, lightly depress and release the accelerator and let the engine idle.

➡ A condition may occur where the engine rpm will oscillate. This can be caused by the throttle plates being open enough to allow purge flow. To make sure of this condition, disconnect the carbon canister purge line and plug it. If purge is present, the throttle plates must be closed until the purge flow induced idle oscillations stop.

Mixture Adjustment

1987-88 Engines

➡ You'll need a dwell meter with a 90° scale.

1. Run the engine to normal operating temperature.

2a. On the 1987–88 2.6L engine, connect the dwell meter (+) positive lead to the yellow/green wire in the check connector, located near the No.3 air control valve and reed case assembly. Connect the (–) lead to ground.

2b. On the 2.2L engine, connect the dwell meter (+) positive lead to the brown/yellow wire in the check connector, located near the No.3 air control valve and reed case assembly. Connect the (–) lead to ground.

3. With the engine at the normal idle speed the dwell meter should read 27–45° for the 1987–88 2.6L engine, or 20–70° for the 2.2L engine.
4. If not, check the oxygen sensor, the wiring between the oxygen sensor and the feedback control unit, and the control unit itself. See Section 5 for procedures. If all components check out satisfactorily, adjust the mixture with the adjusting screw.

1989-91 Engines

The idle mixture is controlled by the Electronic Control Unit (ECU) and is not adjustable.

TORQUE SPECIFICATIONS

Component	U.S.	Metric
Distributor holddown bolt:	14-19 ft. lbs.	19-25 Nm
Spark plugs:	11-17 ft. lbs.	15-23 Nm

3 ENGINE AND ENGINE OVERHAUL

ENGINE ELECTRICAL

Understanding the Engine Electrical System

The engine electrical system can be broken down into three separate and distinct systems:

1. The starting system.
2. The charging system.
3. The ignition system.

BATTERY AND STARTING SYSTEM

Basic Operating Principles

The battery is the first link in the chain of mechanisms which work together to provide cranking of the automobile engine. In most modern cars, the battery is a lead/acid electrochemical device consisting of six 2v subsections connected in series so the unit is capable of producing approximately 12v of electrical pressure. Each subsection, or cell, consists of a series of positive and negative plates held a short distance apart in a solution of sulfuric acid and water. The two types of plates are of dissimilar metals. This causes a chemical reaction to be set up, and it is this reaction which produces current flow from the battery when its positive and negative terminals are connected to an electrical appliance such as a lamp or motor. The continued transfer of electrons would eventually convert the sulfuric acid in the electrolyte to water, and make the two plates identical in chemical composition. As electrical energy is removed from the battery, its voltage output tends to drop. Thus, measuring battery voltage and battery electrolyte composition are two ways of checking the ability of the unit to supply power. During the starting of the engine, electrical energy is removed from the battery. However, if the charging circuit is in good condition and the operating conditions are normal, the power removed from the battery will be replaced by the generator (or alternator) which will force electrons back through the battery, reversing the normal flow, and restoring the battery to its original chemical state.

The battery and starting motor are linked by very heavy electrical cables designed to minimize resistance to the flow of current. Generally, the major power supply cable that leaves the battery goes directly to the starter, while other electrical system needs are supplied by a smaller cable. During starter operation, power flows from the battery to the starter and is grounded through the car's frame and the battery's negative ground strap.

The starting motor is a specially designed, direct current electric motor capable of producing a very great amount of power for its size. One thing that allows the motor to produce a great deal of power is its tremendous rotating speed. It drives the engine through a tiny pinion gear (attached to the starter's armature), which drives the very large flywheel ring gear at a greatly reduced speed. Another factor allowing it to produce so much power is that only intermittent operation is required of it. This, little allowance for air circulation is required, and the windings can be built into a very small space.

The starter solenoid is a magnetic device which employs the small current supplied by the starting switch circuit of the ignition switch. This magnetic action moves a plunger which mechanically engages the starter and electrically closes the heavy switch which connects it to the battery. The starting switch circuit consists of the starting switch contained within the ignition switch, a transmission neutral safety switch or clutch pedal switch, and the wiring necessary to connect these in series with the starter solenoid or relay.

A pinion, which is a small gear, is mounted to a one-way drive clutch. This clutch is splined to the starter armature shaft. When the ignition switch is moved to the **start** position, the solenoid plunger slides the pinion toward the flywheel ring gear via a collar and spring. If the teeth on the pinion and flywheel match properly, the pinion will engage the flywheel immediately. If the gear teeth butt one another, the spring will be compressed and will force the gears to mesh as soon as the starter turns far enough to allow them to do so. As the solenoid plunger reaches the end of its travel, it closes the contacts that connect the battery and starter and then the engine is cranked.

As soon as the engine starts, the flywheel ring gear begins turning fast enough to drive the pinion at an extremely high rate of speed. At this point, the one-way clutch begins allowing the pinion to spin faster than the starter shaft so that the starter will not operate at excessive speed. When the ignition switch is released from the starter position, the solenoid is de-energized, and a spring contained within the solenoid assembly pulls the gear out of mesh and interrupts the current flow to the starter.

Some starter employ a separate relay, mounted away from the starter, to switch the motor and solenoid current on and off. The relay thus replaces the solenoid electrical switch, buy does not eliminate the need for a solenoid mounted on the starter used to mechanically engage the starter drive gears. The relay is used to reduce the amount of current the starting switch must carry.

THE CHARGING SYSTEM

Basic Operating Principles

The automobile charging system provides electrical power for operation of the vehicle's ignition and starting systems and all the electrical accessories. The battery services as an electrical surge or storage tank, storing (in chemical form) the energy originally produced by the engine driven generator. The system also provides a means of regulating generator output to protect the battery from being overcharged and to avoid excessive voltage to the accessories.

The storage battery is a chemical device incorporating parallel lead plates in a tank containing a sulfuric acid/water solution. Adjacent plates are slightly dissimilar, and the chemical reaction of the two dissimilar plates produces electrical energy when the battery is connected to a load such as the starter motor. The chemical reaction is reversible, so that when the generator is producing a voltage (electrical pressure) greater than that produced by the battery, electricity is forced into the battery, and the battery is returned to its fully charged state.

The vehicle's generator is driven mechanically, through V-belts, by the engine crankshaft. It consists of two coils of fine wire, one stationary (the stator), and one movable (the rotor). The rotor may also be known as the armature, and consists of fine wire wrapped around an iron core which is mounted on a shaft. The electricity which flows through the two coils of wire (provided initially by the battery in some cases) creates an intense magnetic field around both rotor and stator, and the interaction between the two fields creates voltage, allowing the generator to power the accessories and charge the battery.

There are two types of generators: the earlier is the direct current (DC) type. The current produced by the DC generator is generated in the armature and carried off the spinning armature by stationary brushes contacting the commutator. The commutator is a series of smooth metal contact plates on the end of the armature. The commutator is a series of smooth metal contact plates on the end of the armature. The commutator plates, which are separated from one another by a very short gap, are connected to the armature circuits so that current will flow in one directions only in the wires carrying the generator output. The generator stator consists of two stationary coils of wire which draw some of the output current of the generator to form a powerful magnetic field and create the interaction of fields which generates the voltage. The generator field is wired in series with the regulator.

Today's vehicles use alternating current generators or alternators, because they are more efficient, can be rotated at higher speeds, and have fewer brush problems. In an alternator, the field rotates while all the current produced passes only through the stator winding. The brushes bear against continuous slip rings rather than a commutator. This causes the current produced to periodically reverse the direction of its flow. Diodes (electrical one-way switches) block the flow of current from traveling in the wrong direction. A series of diodes is wired together to permit the alternating flow of the stator to be converted to a pulsating, but unidirectional flow at the alternator output. The alternator's field is wired in series with the voltage regulator.

The regulator consists of several circuits. Each circuit has a core, or magnetic coil of wire, which operates a switch. Each switch is connected to ground through one or more resistors. The coil of wire responds directly to system voltage. When the voltage reaches the required level, the magnetic field created by the winding of wire closes the switch and inserts a resistance into the generator field circuit, thus reducing the output. The contacts of the switch cycle open and close many times each second to precisely control voltage.

While alternators are self-limiting as far as maximum current is concerned, DC generators employ a current regulating circuit which responds directly to the total amount of current flowing through the generator circuit rather than to the output voltage. The current regulator is similar to the voltage regulator except that all system current must flow through the energizing coil on its way to the various accessories.

MPV

- 1989–1992 2.6L: Point 1 — 0.77–0.95Ω; Point 2 — 0.9–1.1kΩ
- 1989–1991 3.0L: 0.81–0.99Ω
- 1992 3.0L: 0.72–0.88Ω

3. You can also check for bad coil insulation by measuring the resistance between the coil (–) primary connection and the metal body (case) of the coil. If resistance is less then 10mΩ, replace the coil. This test may not be entirely satisfactory unless you have a megaohm tester that records 500 volts. If the tests below do not reveal the problem and, especially, if operating the engine at night may produce some bluish sparks around the coil, you may want to remove the coil and have it tested at a diagnostic center.

4. If the coil resistances are not as specified, replace the coil.

If the coil tests out ok, replace the igniter and pickup coil. However, you should make sure before doing this work that there are no basic maintenance problems in the secondary circuit of the system, since it is often impossible to return electrical parts. We suggest that before you replace the igniter and pickup coil, you carefully inspect the cap and rotor for carbon tracks or cracks and disconnect the wires and measure their resistance with an ohmmeter. Resistance should be 16,000Ω per length of 100cm. Also, check for cracks in the insulation. Replace secondary parts as inspection/testing deems necessary before replacing the igniter and pickup coil.

REMOVAL & INSTALLATION

1. Disconnect the negative battery cable and make sure the ignition switch is off. Remove any protective boots from the top of the coil, if necessary by sliding them back the coil-to-distributor wire.

2. Carefully pull the high tension wire out of the coil, twisting it gently as near as possible to the tower to get it started.

3. Note the routing and colors of the primary wires, and then remove nuts and lockwashers, retaining all parts for installation. On models equipped with plug-in connections, carefully pull the connecter from the coil assembly. Clean the primary terminals, if necessary, to ensure a clean connection. Then, loosen the through bolt or bolts which clamp the coil in place and slide the coil out of its mount. If the mounting bracket is part of the coil, remove the mounting bolts and the coil.

4. Install the new coil in exact reverse order, making sure the primary connections are tight. Ensure also that the coil-to-distributor wire is fully seated in the tower and that the protective boot is fully installed on the outside of the tower.

Ignition Coil

TESTING

Refer to Section 2 for hookup and measuring point illustrations.

1. Connect an ohmmeter set to the X1 scale to the + and – primary connectors of the coil, as shown. The coil should have good continuity. That is, resistance should be approximately:

Pickups

- 1987–1989 B2200 carbureted: 1.0–1.3Ω
- 1990–1992 B2200 injected: 0.81–0.99Ω
- 1987–1988 B2600: 1.0–1.3Ω
- 1989 B2600i: Point 1 — 0.77–0.95Ω; Point 2 — 0.9–1.1kΩ
- 1990–1992 B2600i: 0.81–0.99Ω

MPV

- 1989–1992 2.6L: Point 1: — 0.77–0.95Ω; Point 2 — 0.9–1.1kΩ
- 1989–1991 3.0L: 0.81–0.99Ω
- 1992 3.0L: 0.72–0.88Ω

If resistance is much higher, replace the coil.

2. Disconnect the high tension wire and move the connector leading to the minus terminal over to the metallic connector inside the coil tower. Set the ohmmeter to the X1000 scale. Resistance must be:

Pickups

- 1987–1988 B2200: 6–30kΩ
- 1987–1988 B2600: 10–20kΩ
- 1989–1982 B2200 and B2600i: 6–30kΩ

Ignition Igniter (External)

REMOVAL & INSTALLATION

1. Disconnect the harness connector from the top of the igniter.
2. Remove the two attaching screws and remove the igniter.
3. Install the new igniter and secure it with the two attaching screws.
4. Connect the harness connector.

Distributor

➧ SEE FIGS. 1-3.

The Navajo has no distributor. See Section 2.

REMOVAL

1. Disconnect the negative battery cable.
2. Remove the distributor cap from the distributor, leaving the spark plug wires attached. If spark plug wire removal is necessary to remove the distributor cap, tag the wires prior to removal so they can be reinstalled in the correct position.
3. Disconnect the electrical connectors and vacuum hose(s), if equipped, from the distributor.
4. Mark the position of the rotor in relation to the distributor housing and the position of the distributor housing on the cylinder head.
5. Remove the distributor hold-down bolt(s) and remove the distributor.
6. Check the distributor O-ring for cuts or other damage and replace, if necessary.

INSTALLATION

Timing Not Disturbed

1. Lubricate the distributor O-ring with clean engine oil.
2. Install the distributor with the hold-down bolt(s), aligning the marks that were made during removal. Tighten the hold-down bolt(s) to 14–19 ft. lbs. (19–25 Nm).
3. Connect the electrical connectors and vacuum hose(s), if equipped.

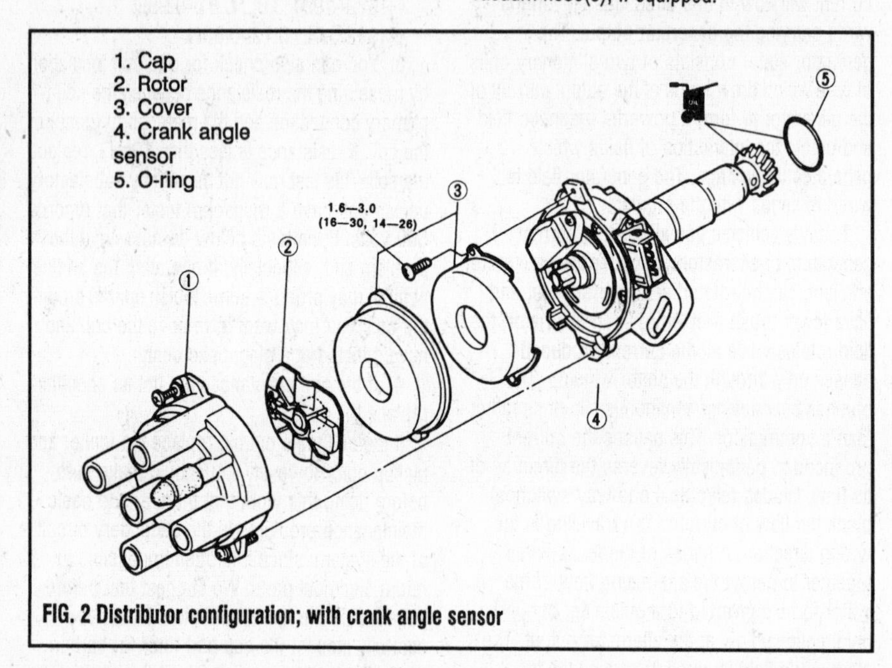

FIG. 2 Distributor configuration; with crank angle sensor

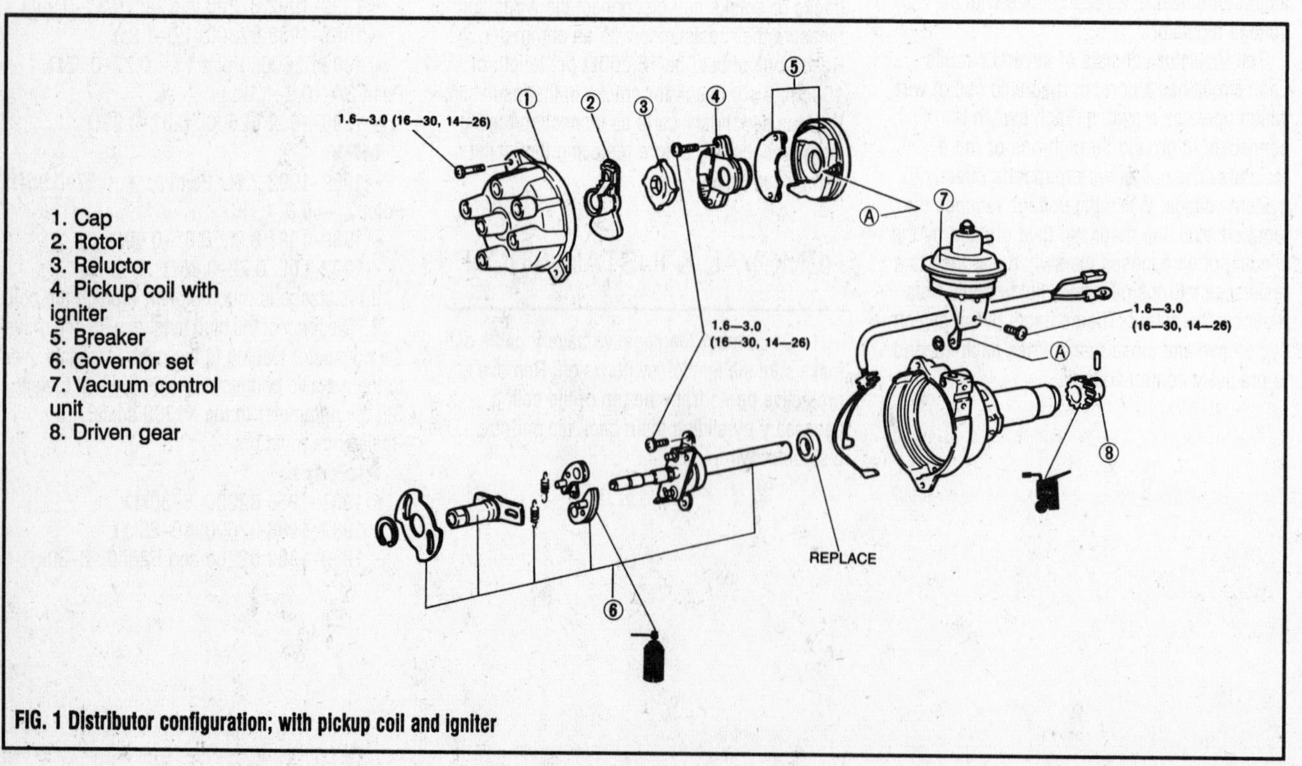

FIG. 1 Distributor configuration; with pickup coil and igniter

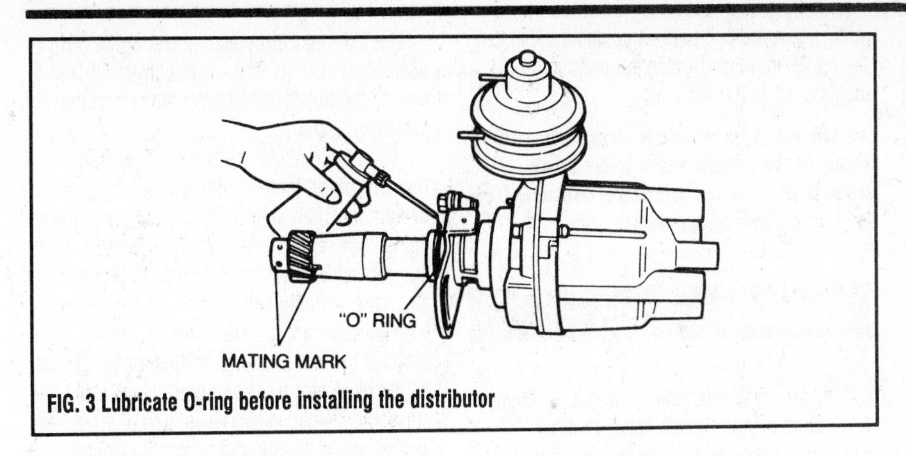

FIG. 3 Lubricate O-ring before installing the distributor

4. Install the distributor cap on the distributor. Connect the spark plug wires, if removed.
5. Connect the negative battery cable. Start the engine and check the ignition timing.

Timing Disturbed

1. Disconnect the spark plug wire from the No. 1 cylinder spark plug and remove the spark plug. Make sure the engine is cool enough to touch, place a finger over the spark plug hole.
2. Turn the crankshaft in the normal direction of rotation until compression is felt at the spark plug hole.
3. Align the mark on the crankshaft pulley with the TDC mark on the timing belt cover.
4. Lubricate the distributor O-ring with clean engine oil.
5. Turn the distributor shaft until the rotor points to the No. 1 spark plug tower on the distributor cap and install the distributor. Install the distributor hold-down bolt(s) and align the distributor housing with the mark made on the cylinder head during removal. Snug the bolt(s).
6. Connect the electrical connectors and vacuum hose(s), if equipped.
7. Install the distributor cap on the distributor. Connect the spark plug wires, if removed.
8. Install the spark plug in the No. 1 cylinder and connect the spark plug wire.
9. Connect the negative battery cable. Start the engine and adjust the ignition timing. Tighten the distributor hold-down bolt(s) to 14–19 ft. lbs. (19–25 Nm) after the timing has been set.

Distributorless Ignition Navajo

REMOVAL & INSTALLATION

➧ SEE FIGS. 4-7

Crankshaft Position Sensor

1. Disconnect the negative battery cable.
2. Disconnect the sensor electrical connector from the wiring harness.
3. Remove the crankshaft sensor mounting bolts and remove the sensor.
4. Place the sensor in position and secure it with the retaining bolts. Tighten the bolts to 75–106 inch lbs. (8.5–12 Nm).

Ignition Module

1. Disconnect the battery cables and remove the battery.
2. Disconnect the electrical connector at the module.
3. Remove the module retaining bolt and remove the module.
4. Position the rivet on the module into the teardrop shaped mounting hole on the fender apron. Push the module into position and secure it with the mounting bolt. Tighten the mounting bolt to 22–31 inch lbs. (2.5–3.5 Nm).

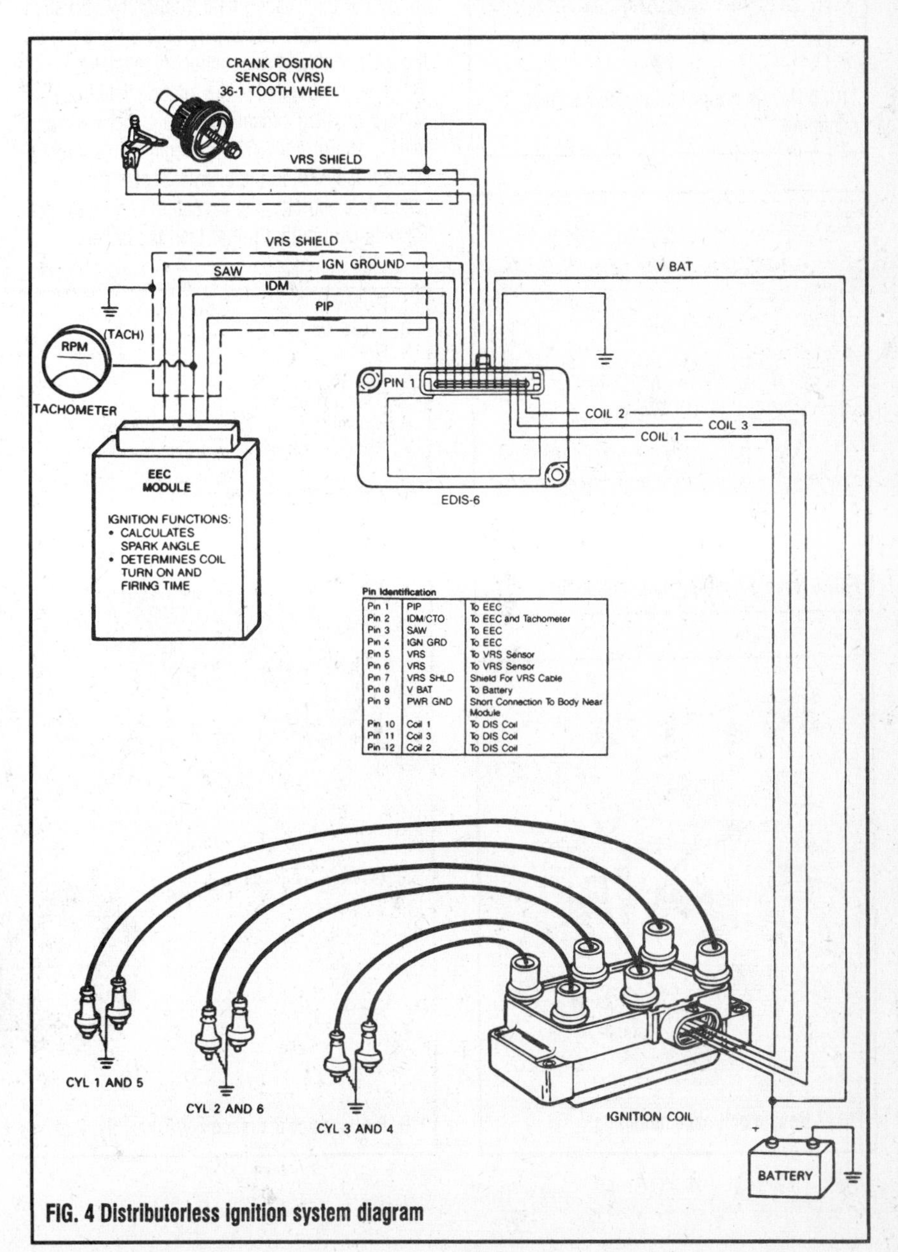

Pin Identification

Pin 1	PIP	To EEC
Pin 2	IDM/CTO	To EEC and Tachometer
Pin 3	SAW	To EEC
Pin 4	IGN GRD	To EEC
Pin 5	VRS	To VRS Sensor
Pin 6	VRS	To VRS Sensor
Pin 7	VRS SHLD	Shield For VRS Cable
Pin 8	V BAT	To Battery
Pin 9	PWR GND	Short Connection To Body Near Module
Pin 10	Coil 1	To DIS Coil
Pin 11	Coil 3	To DIS Coil
Pin 12	Coil 2	To DIS Coil

FIG. 4 Distributorless ignition system diagram

Ignition Coil Pack

1. Disconnect the negative battery cable.
2. Disconnect the electrical harness connector from the coil pack.
3. Remove the spark plug wires by squeezing the locking tabs to release the coil boot retainers.
4. Remove the coil pack retaining bolts and remove the coil pack.
5. Place the coil pack in position and install the retaining bolts. Tighten the bolts to 40–62 inch lbs. (4.5–7.0 Nm).

➡ **Be sure to place some silicone dielectric compound into each spark plug boot prior to installation of the spark plug wire.**

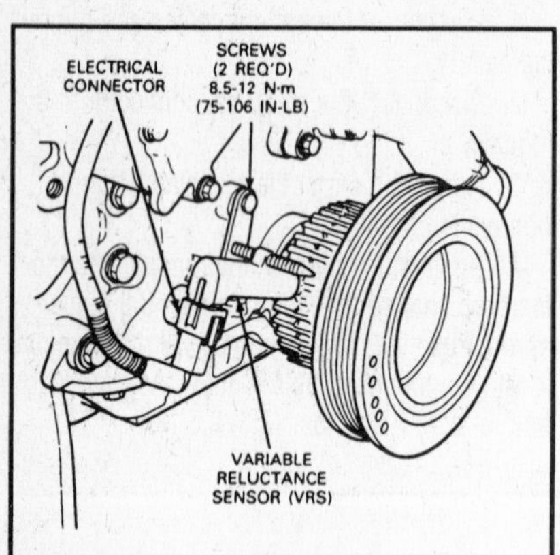

FIG. 5 Navajo crankshaft position sensor mounting

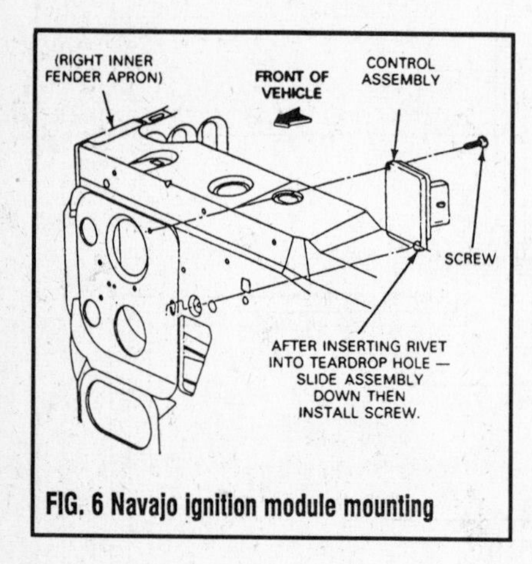

FIG. 6 Navajo ignition module mounting

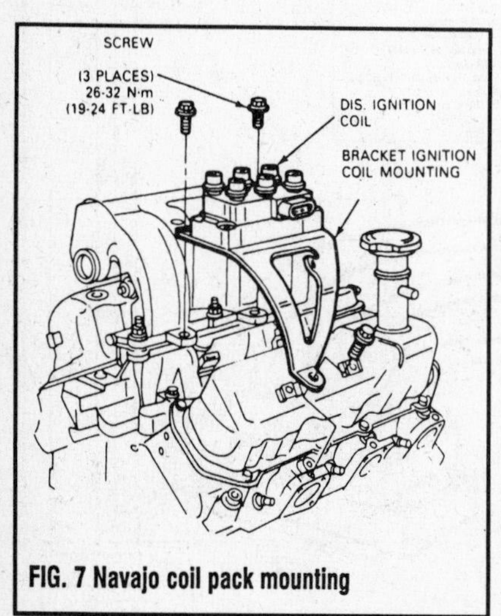

FIG. 7 Navajo coil pack mounting

Alternator

➧ SEE FIGS. 8-9

The alternator charging system is a negative (–) ground system which consists of an alternator, a regulator, a charge indicator, a storage battery and wiring connecting the components, and fuse link wire.

The alternator is belt-driven from the engine. Energy is supplied from the alternator/regulator system to the rotating field through two brushes to two slip-rings. The slip-rings are mounted on the rotor shaft and are connected to the field coil. This energy supplied to the rotating field from the battery is called excitation current and is used to initially energize the field to begin the generation of electricity. Once the alternator starts to generate electricity, the excitation current comes from its own output rather than the battery.

The alternator produces power in the form of alternating current. The direct current is used to charge the battery and power the rest of the electrical system.

When the ignition key is turned on, current flows from the battery, through the charging system indicator light on the instrument panel, to the voltage regulator, and to the alternator. Since the alternator is not producing any current, the alternator warning light comes on. When the engine is started, the alternator begins to produce current and turns the alternator light off. As the alternator turns and produces current, the current is divided in two ways: part to the battery to charge the battery and power the electrical components of the vehicle, and part is returned

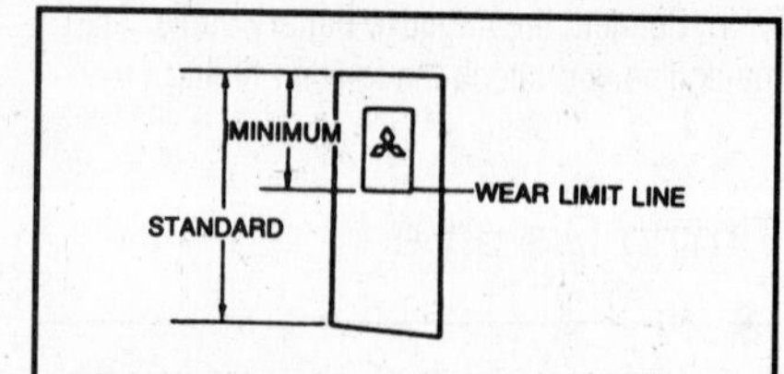

FIG. 9 Alternator brush wear; Standard size: 21.5mm (0.846 in.) Minimum size: 8.0mm (0.315 in.)

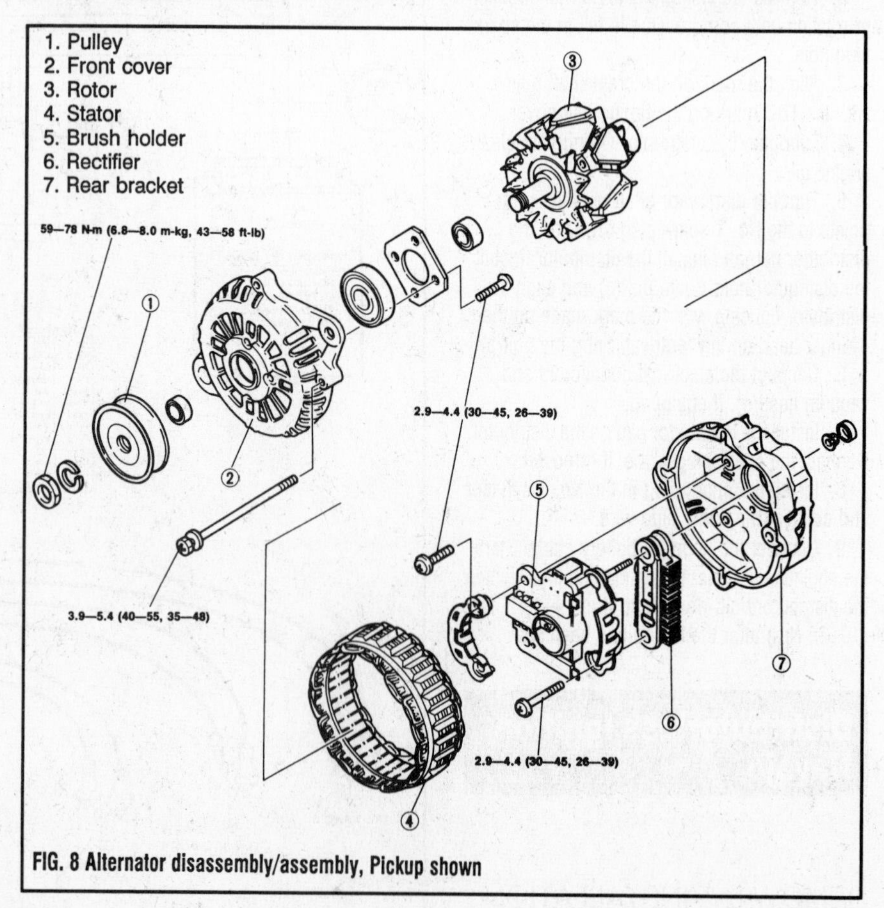

FIG. 8 Alternator disassembly/assembly, Pickup shown

to the alternator to enable it to increase its output. In this situation, the alternator is receiving current from the battery and from itself. A voltage regulator is wired into the current supply to the alternator to prevent it from receiving too much current which would cause it to put out too much current. Conversely, if the voltage regulator does not allow the alternator to receive enough current, the battery will not be fully charged and will eventually go dead.

The battery is connected to the alternator at all times, whether the ignition key is turned on or not. If the battery were shorted to ground, the alternator would also be shorted. This would damage the alternator. To prevent this, a fuse link is installed in the wiring between the battery and the alternator. If the battery is shorted, the fuse link is melted, protecting the alternator.

ALTERNATOR PRECAUTIONS

To prevent damage to the alternator and regulator, the following precautionary measures must be taken when working with the electrical system.

- If the battery is removed for any reason, make sure it is reconnected with the correct polarity. Reversing the battery connections may result in damage to the one-way rectifiers.
- When utilizing a booster battery as a starting aid, always connect the positive to positive terminals and the negative terminal from the booster battery to a good engine ground on the vehicle being started.
- Never use a fast charger as a booster to start vehicles.
- Disconnect the battery cables when charging the battery with a fast charger.
- Never attempt to polarize the alternator.
- Do not use test lights of more than 12V when checking diode continuity.
- Do not short across or ground any of the alternator terminals.
- The polarity of the battery, alternator and regulator must be matched and considered before making any electrical connections within the system.
- Never separate the alternator on an open circuit. Make sure all connections within the circuit are clean and tight.
- Disconnect the battery ground terminal when performing any service on electrical components.
- Disconnect the battery if arc welding is to be done on the vehicle.

REMOVAL & INSTALLATION

Refer to Section 1 for drive belt tensions and mounting instructions.

Pickups w/2.2L

1. Disconnect the negative (ground) cable. On some models, it may be necessary to remove the battery.
2. Remove the nut holding the alternator wire to the terminal at the rear of the alternator.
3. Pull the multiple connector from the rear of the alternator.
4. Remove the alternator adjusting arm bolt. Swing the alternator in and disengage the fan belt.
5. Remove the alternator pivot bolt and remove the alternator from the truck.
6. Place the alternator in position and install the pivot bolt hand tight. Install the adjusting arm bolt. Place the drive belt in position and tension it properly. Secure the adjusting and pivot bolts. Be sure to adjust the drive belt tension and to connect the battery properly.

Pickups w/2.6L (1987-88)

1. Disconnect the negative battery cable.
2. Disconnect the wiring and label for easy installation.
3. Remove the adjusting strap mounting bolt.
4. Remove the drive belts.
5. Remove the support mounting bolt and nut.
6. Remove the alternator assembly.
7. Position the alternator assembly against the engine and install the support bolt.
8. Install the adjusting strap mounting bolt.
9. Install the alternator belts and adjust to specification.
10. Tighten all the support bolts and nuts.
11. Connect all alternator terminals.
12. Connect the negative battery cable.

Pickups w/2.6L (1989-92)

1. Disconnect the negative battery cable.
2. Disconnect the wiring and label for easy installation.
3. Remove the power steering pump pulley, if it interferes with alternator removal (1992 models).
4. Remove the drive belts.
5. Remove the support mounting bolt and nut.
6. Remove the alternator assembly.
7. Position the alternator assembly against the engine and install the support bolt.
8. Install the adjusting strap mounting bolt.
9. Install the alternator belts and adjust to specification.
10. Install the power steering pump pulley.
11. Tighten all the support bolts and nuts.
12. Connect all alternator terminals.
13. Connect the negative battery cable.

MPV w/2.6L

1. Disconnect the negative battery cable.
2. Disconnect the wiring and label for easy installation.
3. Remove the power steering pump pulley.
4. Remove the drive belts.
5. Remove the support mounting bolt and nut.
6. Remove the alternator assembly.
7. Position the alternator assembly against the engine and install the support bolt.
8. Install the adjusting strap mounting bolt.
9. Install the alternator belts and adjust to specification.
10. Install the power steering pump pulley.
11. Tighten all the support bolts and nuts.
12. Connect all alternator terminals.
13. Connect the negative battery cable.

MPV w/3.0L

1. Disconnect the negative battery cable.
2. Disconnect the wiring and label for easy installation.
3. Remove the mounting and adjusting bolts.
4. Remove the drive belts.
6. Remove the alternator assembly.
7. Position the alternator assembly against the engine and install the support bolt.
8. Install the adjusting strap mounting bolt.
9. Install the alternator belts and adjust to specification.
10. Tighten all the support bolts and nuts.
11. Connect all alternator terminals.
12. Connect the negative battery cable.

Navajo

1. Disconnect the battery ground cable.
2. Disconnect the wire harness connector from the alternator. Remove the wiring connector bracket.
3. Remove the drive belt.
4. Remove the mounting bolts and the alternator.
5. Position the alternator and install the mounting bolts. Install the drive belt. Secure the wiring connector bracket to the alternator and connect the wiring harness. Connect the battery ground cable.

BRUSH REPLACEMENT

The alternator used on the Navajo is serviced as an assembly. If the alternator requires service, it must be replaced as an assembly.

➡ **All of the following procedures may not be necessary to perform the service required. Perform only those steps that apply.**

1. Remove the alternator from the vehicle.
2. Scribe a line across the end housing and stator frame for alignment reference during assembly.
3. Remove the housing through bolts.
4. Separate the front housing and rotor assembly from the stator and rear housing assembly. It may be necessary to tap the front housing with a plastic tipped hammer to loosen the front housing from the stator frame.
5. When the alternator assembly halves are separated, the brush springs will usually push the brushes, and themselves, from the brush holder. Remove the springs from the brush holder, if necessary.
6. Depending on what components require servicing, remove the nut(s), washer(s) and insulator(s) on the back and/or side of the rear housing. If just brush replacement is required, remove only the brush holder terminal attachments (models equipped). Note the color and location of the insulators for assembly reference. Replacement brushes may be sold as brushes only, or come as a brush holder assembly, depending on the vehicle being serviced.
7. If only brush replacement is necessary, remove the screws retaining the brush holder and remove it. If other components require servicing, remove the stator, brush holder and rectifier assembly from the rear housing; or the stator, rectifier and brush holder, depending on the year, model, and engine or style of the alternator used.
8. If service to the front bearing or rotor are necessary, clamp the front housing in a vise that has soft jaws. Remove the front pulley nut and washer. Use a suitable puller and remove the pulley and fan assembly from the rotor.
9. Carefully pull the rotor from the front housing. Remove the front housing from the vise.
10. Service the front and rear bearings, if required. Remove the front bearing cover retainer mounting screws and the retainer. Both the front and rear bearings are pressed into their respective housings. A suitable arbor type press will be required to service them.
11. Wipe the rotor, stator and bearing with a clean cloth. Do not clean these parts with solvent.

To install:

12. If components other than the brushes were serviced, assemble and install the components in the order of their removal. Install the brushes and springs into the brush holder. Hold the brushes against the spring pressure and install a piece of stiff wire through the hole provided in the brush holder (models equipped). This will keep the brushes up in the brush holder and ease alternator assembly. Place the brush holder assembly in position and secure the mounting screws, and connector terminal (models equipped). Make sure that the brush retaining wire sticks through the rear of the housing so that it can be removed once the alternator is assembled.
13. Align the scribed reference mark and assemble the rear housing to the front. Install and secure the through bolts. Remove the wire holding the brushes up. Install the alternator.

Regulator

All trucks use an integral regulator, built into the alternator. No adjustments are possible.

Battery

REMOVAL & INSTALLATION

1. Disconnect the two battery cables.
2. Remove the holddown clamps.
3. Using a lifting strap, lift the battery from its platform.

⁂ CAUTION

Don't tilt the battery. It contains sulfuric acid!

4. While wearing goggles, thoroughly clean the cables and clamps and buff them with a wire brush until clean and shiny.
5. Using a baking soda and warm water solution, neutralize the acid residue in the battery platform area. Flush the area with clean water.
6. Install the battery on the platform.
7. Install the cables and tighten the clamp bolts.
8. Install the holddown clamps.

Starter

➧ SEE FIGS. 10-11

Engine cranking occurs when the starter solenoid (usually mounted on the starter) is energized through the ignition switch. The solenoid shifts the starter pinion into mesh with the flywheel ring gear. At the same time, the main contacts of the solenoid are closed and the battery current is directed to the starter causing the armature to rotate. After the engine starts, the starter is disengaged when the ignition switch is returned to the RUN position. This opens the circuit to the starter solenoid and the solenoid return spring causes the shift lever to disengage the starter drive from the flywheel ring gear.

DIAGNOSIS

Starter Won't Crank The Engine

1. Dead battery.
2. Open starter circuit, such as:
   a. Broken or loose battery cables.
   b. Inoperative starter motor solenoid.
   c. Broken or loose wire from ignition switch to solenoid.
   d. Poor solenoid or starter ground.
   e. Bad ignition switch.
3. Defective starter internal circuit, such as:
   a. Dirty or burnt commutator.
   b. Stuck, worn or broken brushes.
   c. Open or shorted armature.
   d. Open or grounded fields.
4. Starter motor mechanical faults, such as:
   a. Jammed armature end bearings.
   b. Bad bearings, allowing armature to rub fields.
   c. Bent shaft.
   d. Broken starter housing.
   e. Bad starter drive mechanism.
   f. Bad starter drive or flywheel-driven gear.
5. Engine hard or impossible to crank, such as:
   a. Hydrostatic lock, water in combustion chamber.
   b. Crankshaft seizing in bearings.
   c. Piston or ring seizing.
   d. Bent or broken connecting rod.
   e. Seizing of connecting rod bearings.
   f. Flywheel jammed or broken.

Starter Spins Freely, Won't Engage

1. Sticking or broken drive mechanism.
2. Damaged ring gear.

REMOVAL & INSTALLATION

Except 4WD MPV

1. Disconnect the negative battery cable. Raise and safely support the vehicle.
2. Disconnect the electrical connectors from the starter.

3. Remove the starter mounting bolts and remove the starter.

4. Place the starter in position, after cleaning the mounting flange surfaces. Install and tighten the mounting bolts. Tighten the starter mounting bolts to:

- 1987-88 — 24–33 ft. lbs. (32–46 Nm)
- 1989-92 exc. 4.0L — 27–38 ft. lbs. (37–52 Nm) 4.0L — 15–20 ft. lbs. (21–27 Nm)

5. Connect all wiring connectors. Connect the negative battery cable.

4WD MPV

1. Disconnect the negative battery cable.
2. Remove the drive belts. Remove the power steering pump pulley. Remove the alternator.
3. Raise and safely support the vehicle. Remove the splash shields.
4. Remove the power steering pump mounting bolts and position the pump aside, without disconnecting the power steering hoses.
5. Remove the automatic transmission cooler line brackets.
6. Mark the position of the driveshaft on the axle flange and remove the front driveshaft.
7. Remove the wiring harness bracket and the automatic transmission cooler line bracket that is next to the starter.
8. Disconnect the electrical connectors from the starter.
9. Remove the fuel and brake line shield.
10. Remove the starter mounting bolts and remove the starter.
11. Clean the mounting surface flanges. Place the starter motor into position and install the mounting bolts. Tighten the starter mounting bolts to 27–38 ft. lbs. (37–52 Nm).
12. Install the fuel and brake line shield. Connect the starter motor wiring. Install the wiring harness bracket.
13. Connect the driveshaft. Install the transmission cooler line brackets. Install the power steering pump and the splash shields.
14. Lower the vehicle. Install the alternator. Install the power steering pump pulley. Install and tension the drive belts. Connect the negative battery cable.

BRUSH REPLACEMENT

1. Remove the starter. Remove the two screws attaching the brush end bearing cover and remove the bearing cover. (Models equipped).
2. Remove the through-bolts.
3. Remove the C-washer, washer and spring from the brush end of the armature shaft.
4. Pull the brush end cover from the starter frame.

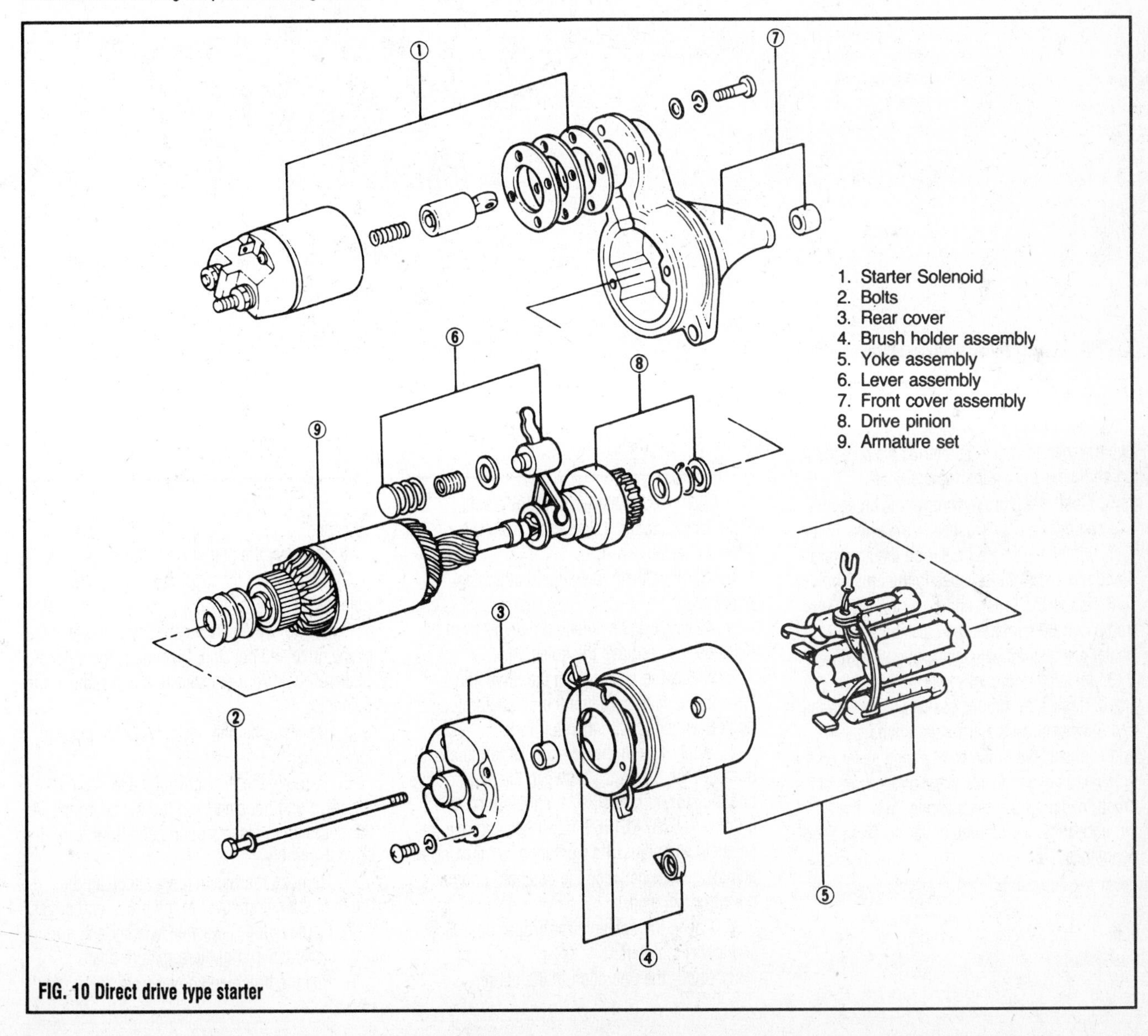

FIG. 10 Direct drive type starter

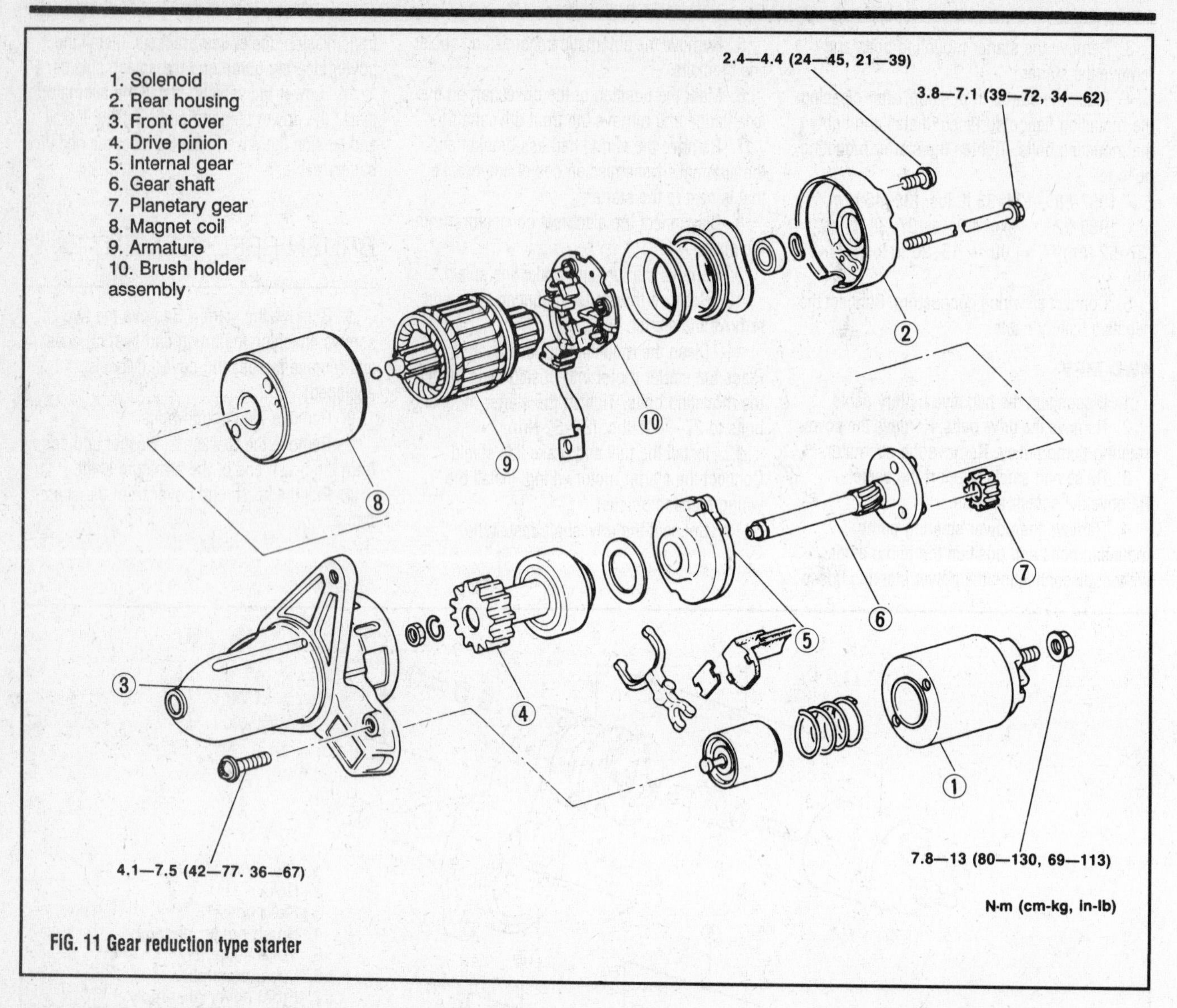

FIG. 11 Gear reduction type starter

5. Depending on starter design: Unsolder the two brushes from the field terminals an slide the brush holder from the armature shaft.

6. Cut the two brush wires at the brush holder and solder two new brushes to the brush holder.

7. Install the brush holder on the armature shaft and install the brushes in the brush holder.

8. Install the brush end cover on the starter frame and be sure that the ear tabs of the brush holder are aligned with the through-bolt holes.

9. Install the through-bolts.

10. Install the rubber gasket, spring, washer and C-washer on the armature shaft.

11. Install the brush end bearing cover on the brush end cover and install the two screws. If the brush holder tabs are not aligned with the through-bolts, the bearing cover screws cannot be installed.

SOLENOID REPLACEMENT

1. Remove the starter from the truck.

2. Disconnect the field strap from the solenoid terminal.

3. Remove the two solenoid attaching screws.

4. Disengage the solenoid plunger from the shift fork and remove the solenoid.

5. Install the solenoid on the drive end housing, making sure that the solenoid plunger hook is engaged with the shift fork.

6. Apply 12v to the solenoid **S** terminal and measure the clearance between the starter drive and the stop-ring retainer. It should be 2.0-5.0mm (0.0787-0.1969 in.). If not, remove the solenoid and adjust the clearance by inserting an adjusting shim between the solenoid body and drive end housing.

7. Check the solenoid for proper operation and install the starter.

8. Check the operation of the starter.

STARTER OVERHAUL

2.2L

1. Remove the starter from the truck.

2. Disconnect the field strap from the solenoid.

3. Remove the screws attaching the solenoid to the drive end housing. Disengage the solenoid plunger hook from the shift fork and remove the solenoid.

4. Remove the shift fork pivot bolt, nut and lockwasher.

5. Remove the through-bolts and separate the drive end housing from the starter frame. At the same time, disengage the shift fork from the drive assembly.

6. Remove the two screws attaching the brush end bearing cover to the brush end cover.

7. Remove the C-washer, washer and spring from the brush end of the armature shaft.

8. Pull the brush end cover from the starter frame.

9. Slide the armature from the starter frame and brushes.

10. Slide the drive stop-ring retainer toward the armature and remove the stop-ring. Slide the retainer and drive assembly off the armature shaft.

11. Remove the field brushes from the brush holder and separate the brush holder from the starter frame.

12. Position the drive assembly on the armature shaft.

13. Position the drive stop-ring retainer on the armature shaft and install the drive stop-ring. Slide the stop-ring retainer over the stop-ring to secure the stop-ring on the shaft.

14. Position the armature in the starter frame. Install the brush holder on the armature and starter frame. Install the brushes in the brush holder.

15. Install the drive end housing on the armature shaft and starter housing. Engage the shift fork with the starter drive assembly as you move the drive end housing toward the starter frame.

16. Install the brush end cover on the starter frame making sure that the rear tabs of the brush holder are aligned wit the through-bolt holes.

17. Install the through-bolts.

18. Install the rubber washer, spring, washer and C-washer on the armature shaft at the brush end. Install the brush end bearing cover on the brush end cover and install the attaching screws. If the brush end cover is not properly positioned, the bearing cover screws cannot be installed.

19. Align the shift fork with the pivot bolt hole and install the pivot bolt, lockwasher and nut. Tighten the nut securely.

20. Position the solenoid on the drive end housing. Be sure that the solenoid plunger hook is engaged with the shift fork.

21. Install the two solenoid retaining screws and washers.

22. Apply 12v to the solenoid S terminal (ground the M terminal) and check the clearance between the starter drive and the stop-ring retainer. The clearance should be 2.0-5.0mm (0.0787-0.1969 in.). If not, the solenoid plunger is not properly adjusted. The clearance can be adjusted by inserting an adjusting shim between the solenoid body and drive end housing.

23. Install the field strap and tighten the nut.

24. Install the starter. Check the operation of the starter.

Except 2.2L

DIRECT DRIVE STARTER

➡ **Starter removed from car.**

1. Remove the wire connecting the starter solenoid to the starter.

2. Remove the two screws holding starter solenoid on the starter drive housing and remove the solenoid.

3. Remove the two long through bolts at the rear of the starter and separate the armature yoke from the armature.

4. Carefully remove the armature and the starter drive engagement lever from the front bracket, after making a mental note of the way they are positioned along with the attendant spring and spring retainer.

5. Loosen the two screws and remove the rear bracket.

6. Tap the stopper ring at the end of the drive gear engagement shaft in towards the drive gear to expose the snap ring. Remove the snap ring.

7. Pull the stopper, drive gear and overrunning clutch from the end of the shaft. Inspect the pinion and spline teeth for wear or damage. If the engagement teeth are damaged, visually check the flywheel ring gear through the starter hole to insure that it is not damaged. It will be necessary to turn the engine over by hand to completely inspect the ring gear. Check the brushes for wear. Their service limit length is 11.5mm (0.4528 in.). Replace if necessary.

8. Assembly is performed in the following manner.

9. Install the spring retainer and spring on the armature shaft.

10. Install the overrunning clutch assembly on the armature shaft.

11. Fit the stopper ring with its open side facing out on the shaft.

12. Install a new snap ring and, using a gear puller, pull the stopper ring into place over the snap ring.

13. Fit the small washer on the front end of the armature shaft.

14. Fit the engagement lever into the overrunning clutch and refit the armature into the front housing.

15. Fit the engagement lever spring and spring retainer into place and slide the armature yoke over the armature. Make sure you position the yoke with the spring retainer cutout space in line with the spring retainer.

➡ **Make sure the brushes are seated on the commutator.**

16. Replace the rear bracket and two retainer screws.

17. Install the two through bolts in the end of the yoke.

18. Refit the starter solenoid, making sure you fit the plunger over the engagement lever. Install the screws and connect the wire running from the starter yoke to the starter solenoid.

GEAR REDUCTION TYPE

➡ **Starter removed from car.**

1. Remove the wire connecting the starter solenoid to the starter.

2. Remove the two screws holding the solenoid and, pulling out, unhook it from the engagement lever.

3. Remove the two through bolts in the end of the starter and remove the two bracket screws.Pull off the rear bracket.

➡ **Since the conical spring washer is contained in the rear bracket, be sure to take it out.**

4. Remove the yoke and brush holder assembly while pulling the brush upward.

5. Pull the armature assembly out of the mounting bracket.

6. On the side of the armature mounting bracket there is a small dust shield held on by two screws, remove the shield. Remove the snap ring and washer located under the shield.

7. Remove the remaining bolts in the mounting bracket and separate the reduction case.

➡ **Several washers will come out of the reduction case when you separate it. These adjust the armature end play: do not lose them!**

8. Remove the reduction gear, lever and lever spring from the front bracket.

9. Use a brass drift or a deep socket to knock the stopper ring on the end of the shaft in toward the pinion. Remove the snap ring. Remove the stopper, pinion and pinion shaft assembly.

10. Remove the ball bearings at both ends of the armature.

➡ **The ball bearings are pressed into the front bracket and are not replaceable. Replace them together with the bracket. Inspect the pinion and spline teeth for wear or damage. If the pinion drive teeth are damaged, visually check the engine flywheel ring gear. Check the flywheel ring gear by looking through the starter motor mounting hole. It will be necessary to turn the engine over by hand to completely inspect the ring gear. Check the starter brushes for wear. Their service limit length is 11.5mm (0.4528 in.). Replace if necessary.**

11. Be sure to replace all the adjusting and thrust washers that you removed. When replacing the rear bracket, fit the conical spring pinion washer with its convex side facing out. Make sure that the brushes seat themselves on the commutator. Assemble the starter.

Navajo

➡ **Starter removed from vehicle.**

1. Disconnect the brush connector strap from the front of the starter mounted solenoid. Remove the solenoid retaining screws and remove the solenoid from the starter motor.
2. Remove the through bolts and separate the drive end housing from the motor frame. Remove the housing seal assembly from the drive. Remove the drive and gear assembly from the housing.
3. Remove the drive lever from the drive housing. Remove the stop ring and retainer from the driveshaft, then remove the drive assembly from the shaft. Push the retaining "E" ring off of the driveshaft and remove the gear assembly.
4. Remove the brush plate screws and brush plate from the motor frame. Remove the brush assembly and push the armature out of the frame.
5. Clean the components, but do not wash the starter drive because solvent will wash out the lubricant causing the drive to slip. Use a brush or compressed air to clean the drive, armature, brush, and gear assemblies, drive end housing, pole pieces and planet gears. Wash all other parts in solvent and dry them. Inspect all parts, replace any that show excessive wear.
6. Inspect the armature windings for broken or burned insulation and unwelded or opened connections. Have the armature checked for opened circuits, shorts and grounds. Check for armature rubbing. Have the armature checked for runout. If the commutator is rough, or shows excessive wear, or has .005 ins. runout, have the commutator machined or replace the armature.
7. Install the armature into the motor frame. Apply a thin coating of Molybdenun grease on both ends of the armature shaft and spline. Install the brush assembly, making sure the brushes fit correctly over the commutator. Apply grease to the bore in the brush end plate. Push the grommet onto the frame and attach the brush end cover with the mounting screws. Tighten the brush end plate to 20-30 inch lbs. (2.3-3.4 Nm).
8. Apply grease to the driveshaft spline and place the stationary gear assembly over the driveshaft. Install the armature thrust washer and push the "E" ring onto the driveshaft. Place the drive assembly onto the driveshaft and install the stop ring and retainer. Attach the drive lever to the drive assembly.
9. Grease and install the planet gears. Apply grease into the drive housing bearing bore. Install the drive gear assembly into the housing, making sure the bolt holes in the gear assembly line up with the gear housing. Place the gear retainer over the gear assembly. Install the housing seal assembly into the drive end housing.
10. Position the motor frame to the drive gear housing and install the through bolts. Tighten the through bolts to 45-84 inch lbs. (5.0-9.5 Nm).
11. Correctly position the solenoid to the housing making sure the solenoid plunger is attached through the drive lever. Tighten the solenoid mounting bolts to 45-85 inch lbs. (5.1-9.6 Nm).
12. Attach the brush strap to the solenoid. Install the starter motor.

Sending Units and Sensors

REMOVAL & INSTALLATION

Coolant Temperature

1. Disconnect the negative battery cable.
2. Drain the cooling system until the coolant level is below the coolant sensor.
3. Disconnect the electrical connector from the sensor.
4. Remove the sensor from the engine. On some applications, the coolant sensor is located in the thermostat housing.
5. Install in the reverse order of removal. Fill and bleed the cooling system.

Oil Pressure Switch

1. Disconnect the negative battery cable.
2. Disconnect the electrical connector from the oil pressure switch.
3. Remove the oil pressure switch from the engine.
4. Install in the reverse order of removal.

ENGINE MECHANICAL

Engine Overhaul Tips

Most engine overhaul procedures are fairly standard. In addition to specific parts replacement procedures and complete specifications for your individual engine, this Section also is a guide to accepted rebuilding procedures. Examples of standard rebuilding practice are shown and should be used along with specific details concerning your particular engine.

Competent and accurate machine shop services will ensure maximum performance, reliability and engine life.

In most instances it is more profitable for the do-it-yourself mechanic to remove, clean and inspect the component, buy the necessary parts and deliver these to a shop for actual machine work.

On the other hand, much of the rebuilding work (crankshaft, block, bearings, piston rods, and other components) is well within the scope of the do-it-yourself mechanic.

TOOLS

The tools required for an engine overhaul or parts replacement will depend on the depth of your involvement. With a few exceptions, they will be the tools found in a mechanic's tool kit (see Section 1). More in-depth work will require any or all of the following:

- a dial indicator (reading in thousandths) mounted on a universal base
- micrometers and telescope gauges
- jaw and screw-type pullers
- scraper
- valve spring compressor
- ring groove cleaner
- piston ring expander and compressor
- ridge reamer
- cylinder hone or glaze breaker
- Plastigage®
- engine stand

The use of most of these tools is illustrated in this Section. Many can be rented for a one-time use from a local parts jobber or tool supply house specializing in automotive work.

Occasionally, the use of special tools is called for. See the information on Special Tools and Safety Notice in the front of this book before substituting another tool.

INSPECTION TECHNIQUES

Procedures and specifications are given in this Section for inspecting, cleaning and assessing the wear limits of most major components. Other procedures such as Magnaflux® and Zyglo® can be used to locate material flaws and stress cracks. Magnaflux® is a magnetic process applicable only to ferrous materials. The Zyglo® process coats the material with a fluorescent dye penetrant and can be used on any material Check for suspected surface cracks can be more readily made using spot check dye. The dye is sprayed onto the suspected area, wiped off and the area sprayed with a developer. Cracks will show up brightly.

TIPS

Aluminum has become extremely popular for use in engines, due to its low weight. Observe the following precautions when handling aluminum parts:

- Never hot tank aluminum parts (the caustic hot tank solution will eat the aluminum.
- Remove all aluminum parts (identification tag, etc.) from engine parts prior to the tanking.
- Always coat threads lightly with engine oil or anti-seize compounds before installation, to prevent seizure.
- Never over-torque bolts or spark plugs especially in aluminum threads.

Stripped threads in any component can be repaired using any of several commercial repair kits (Heli-Coil®, Microdot®, Keenserts®, etc.).

When assembling the engine, any parts that will be frictional contact must be prelubed to provide lubrication at initial start-up. Any product specifically formulated for this purpose can be used, but engine oil is not recommended as a prelube.

When semi-permanent (locked, but removable) installation of bolts or nuts is desired, threads should be cleaned and coated with Loctite® or other similar, commercial non-hardening sealant.

REPAIRING DAMAGED THREADS

➧ SEE FIGS. 12-16

Several methods of repairing damaged threads are available. Heli-Coil® (shown here), Keenserts® and Microdot® are among the most widely used. All involve basically the same principle–drilling out stripped threads, tapping the hole and installing a prewound insert–making welding, plugging and oversize fasteners unnecessary.

Two types of thread repair inserts are usually supplied–a standard type for most Inch Coarse, Inch Fine, Metric Coarse and Metric Fine thread sizes and a spark lug type to fit most spark plug port sizes. Consult the individual manufacturer's catalog to determine exact applications. Typical thread repair kits will contain a selection of prewound threaded inserts, a tap (corresponding to the outside diameter threads of the insert) and an installation tool. Spark plug inserts usually differ because they require a tap equipped with pilot threads and a combined reamer/tap. Most manufacturers also supply blister-packed thread

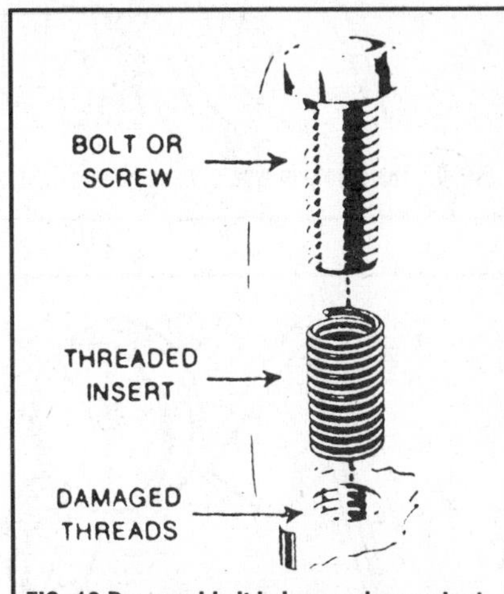

FIG. 12 Damaged bolt holes can be repaired with thread coil repair inserts

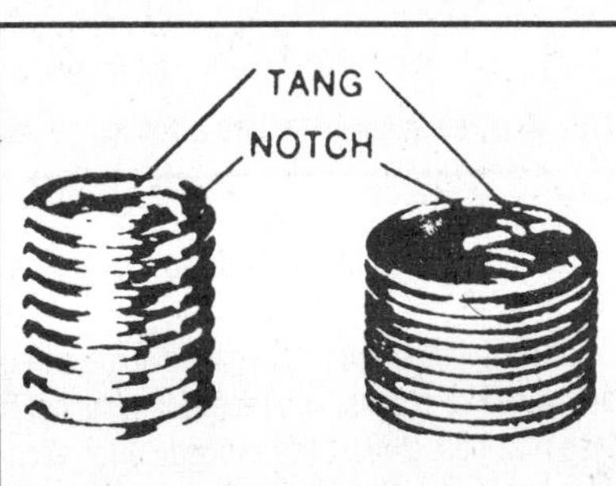

FIG. 13 Standard thread repair insert (left) and spark plug thread insert (right)

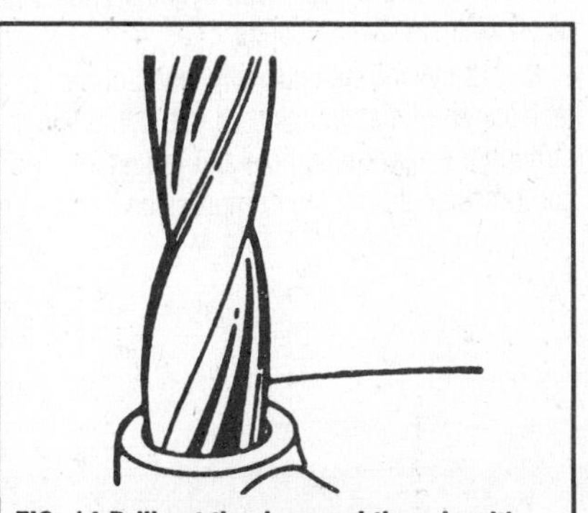
FIG. 14 Drill out the damaged threads with specified drill Drill completely through the hole or to the bottom of a blind hole

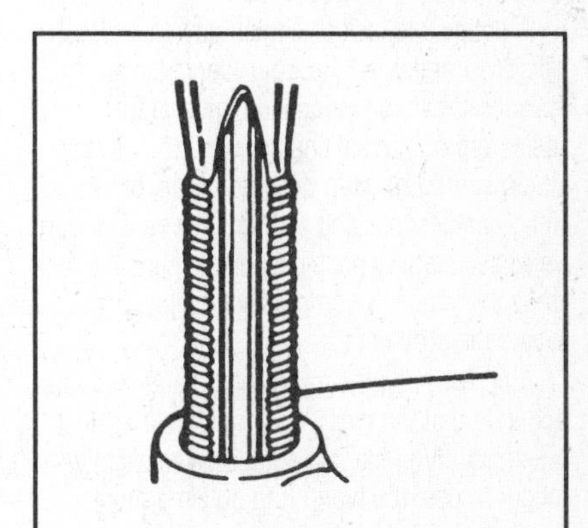
FIG. 15 With the tap supplied, tap the hole to receive the thread insert. Keep the tap well oiled and back it out frequently to avoid clogging the threads

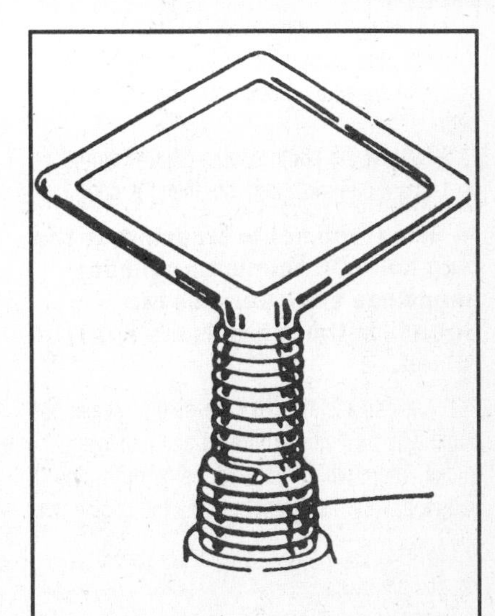
FIG. 16 Screw the threaded insert onto the installation tool until the tang engages the slot. Screw the insert into the tapped hole until it is $^1/_4$–$^1/_2$ turn below the top surface. After installation, break off the tang with a hammer and punch

repair inserts separately in addition to a master kit containing a variety of taps and inserts plus installation tools.

Before effecting a repair to a threaded hole, remove any snapped, broken or damaged bolts or studs. Penetrating oil can be used to free frozen threads; the offending item can be removed with locking pliers or with a screw or stud extractor. After the hole is clear, the thread can be repaired, as follows:

Checking Engine Compression

➧ SEE FIGS. 17 and 18

A noticeable lack of engine power, excessive oil consumption and/or poor fuel mileage measured over an extended period are all indicators of internal engine war. Worn piston rings, scored or worn cylinder bores, blown head gaskets, sticking or burnt valves and worn valve seats are all possible culprits here. A check of each cylinder's compression will help you locate the problems.

A screw-in type compression gauge is more accurate that the type you simply hold against the spark plug hole, although it takes slightly longer to use. It's worth it to obtain a more accurate reading. Follow the procedures below.

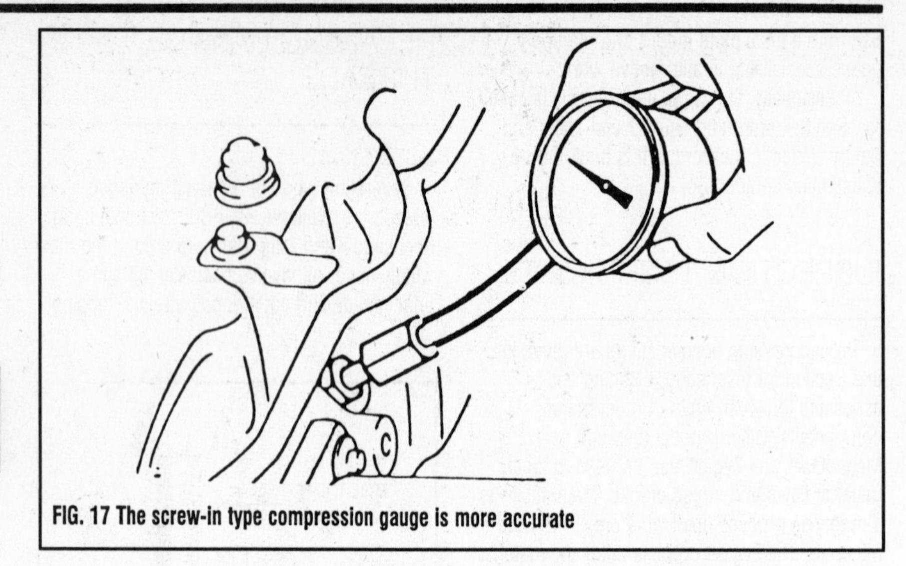

FIG. 17 The screw-in type compression gauge is more accurate

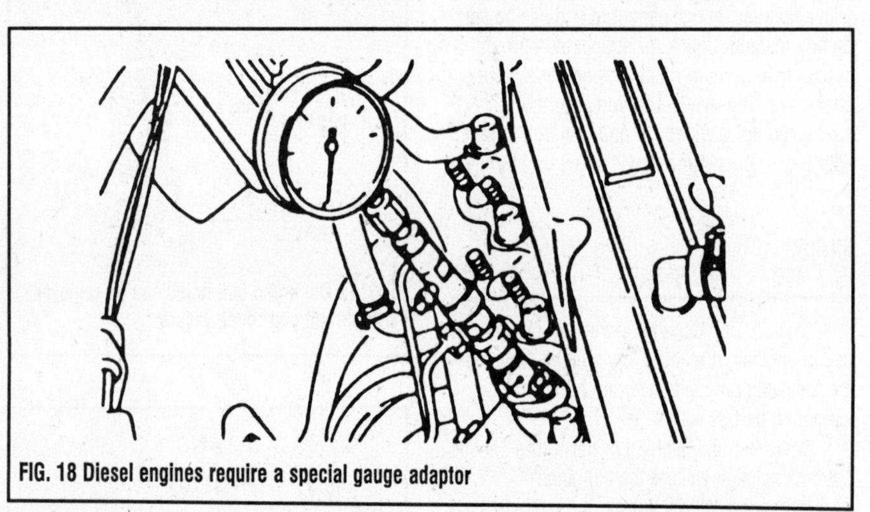

FIG. 18 Diesel engines require a special gauge adaptor

1. Warm up the engine to normal operating temperature.
2. Remove all spark plugs.
3. Disconnect the high tension lead from the ignition coil.
4. On fully open the throttle either by operating the carburetor throttle linkage by hand or by having an assistant floor the accelerator pedal.
5. Screw the compression gauge into the no.1 spark plug hole until the fitting is snug.

➡ Be careful not to crossthread the plug hole. On aluminum cylinder heads use extra care, as the threads in these heads are easily ruined.

6. Ask an assistant to depress the accelerator pedal fully on both carbureted and fuel injected trucks. Then, while you read the compression gauge, ask the assistant to crank the engine two or three times in short bursts using the ignition switch.
7. Read the compression gauge at the end of each series of cranks, and record the highest of these readings. Repeat this procedure for each of the engine's cylinders.

A cylinder's compression pressure is usually acceptable if it is not less than 80% of maximum. The difference between each cylinder should be no more than 12-14 pounds.

8. If a cylinder is unusually low, pour a tablespoon of clean engine oil into the cylinder through the spark plug hole and repeat the compression test. If the compression comes up after adding the oil, it appears that the cylinder's piston rings or bore are damaged or worn. If the pressure remains low, the valves may not be seating properly (a valve job is needed), or the head gasket may be blown near that cylinder. If compression in any two adjacent cylinders is low, and if the addition of oil doesn't help the compression, there is leakage past the head gasket. Oil and coolant water in the combustion chamber can result from this problem. There may be evidence of water droplets on the engine dipstick when a head gasket has blown.

GENERAL ENGINE SPECIFICATIONS

Year	Engine ID/VIN	Engine Displacement Liters (cc)	Fuel System Type	Net Horsepower @ rpm	Net Torque @ rpm (ft. lbs.)	Bore × Stroke (in.)	Com-pression Ratio	Oil Pressure @ rpm
1987	F2	2.2L (2184)	2 bbl	85 @ 4500	118 @ 2500	3.395 × 3.700	8:6.1	60 @ 2000
	G54B	2.6L (2555)	2 bbl	105 @ 5000	139 @ 2500	3.586 × 3.858	8.7:1	57 @ 2000
1988	F2	2.2L (2184)	2 bbl	85 @ 4500	118 @ 2500	3.395 × 3.700	8:6.1	43–57 @ 3000
	G54B	2.6L (2555)	2 bbl	105 @ 5000	139 @ 2500	3.586 × 3.858	8.7:1	78 @ 3000
1989	F2	2.2L (2184)	2 bbl	85 @ 4500	118 @ 2500	3.395 × 3.700	8:6.1	43–57 @ 3000
	G6	2.6L (2606)	MPI	121 @ 4600	149 @ 3500	3.622 × 3.858	8.4:1	44–58 @ 3000
	JE	3.0L (2954)	MPI	150 @ 5000	165 @ 4000	3.540 × 3.050	8.5:1	53–75 @ 3000
1990	F2	2.2L (2184)	①	②	③	3.395 × 3.700	8:6.1	43–57 @ 3000
	G6	2.6L (2606)	MPI	121 @ 4600	149 @ 3500	3.622 × 3.858	8.4:1	44–58 @ 3000
	JE	3.0L (2954)	MPI	150 @ 5000	165 @ 4000	3.540 × 3.050	8.5:1	53–75 @ 3000
1991	F2	2.2L (2184)	①	②	③	3.395 × 3.700	8:6.1	43–57 @ 3000
	G6	2.6L (2606)	MPI	121 @ 4600	149 @ 3500	3.622 × 3.858	8.4:1	44–58 @ 3000
	JE	3.0L (2954)	MPI	150 @ 5000	165 @ 4000	3.540 × 3.050	8.5:1	53–75 @ 3000
	X	4.0L (4016)	MPI	155 @ 4200	220 @ 2400	3.950 × 3.320	9.0:1	40–60 @ 2000
1992	F2	2.2L (2184)	①	②	③	3.395 × 3.700	8:6.1	43–57 @ 3000
	G6	2.6L (2606)	MPI	121 @ 4600	149 @ 3500	3.622 × 3.858	8.4:1	44–58 @ 3000
	JE	3.0L (2954)	MPI	150 @ 5000	165 @ 4000	3.540 × 3.050	8.5:1	53–75 @ 3000
	X	4.0L (4016)	MPI	155 @ 4200	220 @ 2400	3.950 × 3.320	9.0:1	40–60 @ 2000

NOTE: Horsepower and torque are SAE net figures. They are measured at the rear of the transmission with all accessories installed and operating. Since the figures vary when a given engine is installed in different models, some are representative rather than exact.

① Except CA.—2 bbl
CA—MPI

② Except CA.—85 @ 4500
CA—91 @ 4500

③ Except CA.—188 @ 2500
CA—118 @ 2000

VALVE SPECIFICATIONS

Year	Engine ID/VIN	Engine Displacement Liters (cc)	Seat Angle (deg.)	Face Angle (deg.)	Spring Test Pressure (lbs. @ in.)	Spring Installed Height (in.)	Stem-to-Guide Clearance (in.)		Stem Diameter (in.)	
							Intake	Exhaust	Intake	Exhaust
1987	F2	2.2L (2184)	45	45	NA	NA	0.0010–0.0024	0.0012–0.0026	0.3161–0.3167	0.3159–0.3165
	G54B	2.6L (2555)	45	45	NA	NA	0.0010–0.0023	0.0020–0.0035	0.3130–0.3140	0.3120–0.3130
1988	F2	2.2L (2184)	45	45	NA	NA	0.0010–0.0024	0.0012–0.0026	0.3161–0.3167	0.3159–0.3165
	G54B	2.6L (2555)	45	45	NA	NA	0.0010–0.0023	0.0020–0.0035	0.3130–0.3140	0.3120–0.3130
1989	F2	2.2L (2184)	45	45	①	NA	0.0010–0.0024	0.0012–0.0026	0.3161–0.3167	0.3159–0.3165
	G6	2.6L (2606)	45	45	43.8–49.7 @ 1.693 in.	NA	0.0010–0.0024	0.0012–0.0026	0.2744–0.2750	0.2742–0.2748
	JE	3.0L (2954)	45	45	②	NA	0.0010–0.0024	0.0012–0.0026	0.2744–0.2750	0.3159–0.3165

VALVE SPECIFICATIONS

Year	Engine ID/VIN	Engine Displacement Liters (cc)	Seat Angle (deg.)	Face Angle (deg.)	Spring Test Pressure (lbs. @ in.)	Spring Installed Height (in.)	Stem-to-Guide Clearance (in.) Intake	Stem-to-Guide Clearance (in.) Exhaust	Stem Diameter (in.) Intake	Stem Diameter (in.) Exhaust
1990	F2	2.2L (2184)	45	45	①	NA	0.0010–0.0024	0.0012–0.0026	0.3161–0.3167	0.3159–0.3165
	G6	2.6L (2606)	45	45	43.8–49.7 @ 1.693 in.	NA	0.0010–0.0024	0.0012–0.0026	0.2744–0.2750	0.2742–0.2748
	JE	3.0L (2954)	45	45	③	NA	0.0010–0.0024	0.0012–0.0026	0.2744–0.2750	0.3159–0.3165
1991	F2	2.2L (2184)	45	45	①	NA	0.0010–0.0024	0.0012–0.0026	0.3161–0.3167	0.3159–0.3165
	G6	2.6L (2606)	45	45	43.8–49.7 @ 1.693 in.	NA	0.0010–0.0024	0.0012–0.0026	0.2744–0.2750	0.2742–0.2748
	JE	3.0L (2954)	45	45	③	NA	0.0010–0.0024	0.0012–0.0026	0.2744–0.2750	0.3159–0.3165
	X	4.0L (4016)	45	44	138–149 @ 1.22 in.	1.58–1.61	0.0008–0.0025	0.0018–0.0035	0.3159–0.3167	0.3149–0.3156
1992	F2	2.2L (2184)	45	45	①	NA	0.0010–0.0024	0.0012–0.0026	0.3161–0.3167	0.3159–0.3165
	G6	2.6L (2606)	45	45	43.8–49.7 @ 1.693 in.	NA	0.0010–0.0024	0.0012–0.0026	0.2744–0.2750	0.2742–0.2748
	JE	3.0L (2954)	45	45	②	NA	0.0010–0.0024	0.0012–0.0026	0.2744–0.2750	0.3159–0.3165
	X	4.0L (4016)	45	44	138–149 @ 1.22 in.	1.58–1.61	0.0008–0.0025	0.0018–0.0035	0.3159–0.3167	0.3149–0.3156

① Outer spring—94.6 @ 1.22 in.
Inner spring—66.0 @ 1.04 in.

② Intake
Outer—29.3–33.2 @ 1.732 in.
Inner—19.6–22.2 @ 1.555 in.
Exhaust
Outer—51.9–58.7 @ 1.772 in.
Inner—33.2–37.4 in.

③ Intake
Outer—31–33 @ 1.969 in.
Inner—21–22 @ 1.555 in.
Exhaust
Outer—51.9–58.7 @ 1.386 in.
Inner—27.5–37.4 @ 1.496 in.

CAMSHAFT SPECIFICATIONS

All measurements given in inches.

Year	Engine ID/VIN	Engine Displacement Liters (cc)	Journal Diameter 1	2	3	4	5	Elevation In.	Ex.	Bearing Clearance	Camshaft End Play
1987	F2	2.2L (2184)	1.2575–1.2584	1.2563–1.2573	1.2563–1.2573	1.2563–1.2573	1.2575–1.2584	1.497–1.499	1.497–1.499	①	0.0030–0.0060
	G54B	2.6L (2555)	1.3360–1.3366	1.3360–1.3366	1.3360–1.3366	1.3360–1.3366	1.3360–1.3366	1.669	1.669	0.0020–0.0040	0.0008–0.0070
1988	F2	2.2L (2184)	1.2575–1.2584	1.2563–1.2573	1.2563–1.2573	1.2563–1.2573	1.2575–1.2584	1.497–1.499	1.497–1.499	①	0.0030–0.0060
	G54B	2.6L (2555)	1.3360–1.3366	1.3360–1.3366	1.3360–1.3366	1.3360–1.3366	1.3360–1.3366	1.669	1.669	0.0020–0.0040	0.0008–0.0070
1989	F2	2.2L (2184)	1.2575–1.2584	1.2563–1.2573	1.2563–1.2573	1.2563–1.2573	1.2575–1.2584	1.4984	1.4984	①	0.0031–0.0063
	G6	2.6L (2606)	1.1727–1.1797	1.1776–1.1785	1.1776–1.1785	1.1776–1.1785	1.1787–1.1797	1.6423	1.6344	①	0.0008–0.0059
	JE	3.0L (2954)	1.9268–1.9274	1.9258–1.9266	1.9258–1.9266	1.9267–1.9274	—	1.6163	1.6257	②	0.0020–0.0071
1990	F2	2.2L (2184)	1.2575–1.2584	1.2563–1.2573	1.2563–1.2573	1.2563–1.2573	1.2575–1.2584	1.4984	1.4984	①	0.0031–0.0063
	G6	2.6L (2606)	1.1727–1.1797	1.1776–1.1785	1.1776–1.1785	1.1776–1.1785	1.1787–1.1797	1.6423	1.6344	①	0.0008–0.0059
	JE	3.0L (2954)	1.9268–1.9274	1.9258–1.9266	1.9258–1.9266	1.9267–1.9274	—	1.6163	1.6257	②	0.0020–0.0071
1991	F2	2.2L (2184)	1.2575–1.2584	1.2563–1.2573	1.2563–1.2573	1.2563–1.2573	1.2575–1.2584	1.4984	1.4984	①	0.0031–0.0063
	G6	2.6L (2606)	1.1727–1.1797	1.1776–1.1785	1.1776–1.1785	1.1776–1.1785	1.1787–1.1797	1.6423	1.6344	①	0.0008–0.0059
	JE	3.0L (2954)	1.9268–1.9274	1.9258–1.9266	1.9258–1.9266	1.9267–1.9274	—	1.6163	1.6257	②	0.0020–0.0071
	X	4.0L (4016)	1.9510–1.9520	1.9370–1.9380	1.9220–1.9230	1.9070–1.9080	—	NA	NA	0.0010–0.0026	0.0008–0.0040
1992	F2	2.2L (2184)	1.2575–1.2584	1.2563–1.2573	1.2563–1.2573	1.2563–1.2573	1.2575–1.2584	1.4984	1.4984	①	0.0031–0.0063
	G6	2.6L (2606)	1.1727–1.1797	1.1776–1.1785	1.1776–1.1785	1.1776–1.1785	1.1787–1.1797	1.6423	1.6344	①	0.0008–0.0059
	JE	3.0L (2954)	1.9268–1.9274	1.9258–1.9266	1.9258–1.9266	1.9267–1.9274	—	1.6163	1.6257	③	0.0020–0.0071
	X	4.0L (4016)	1.9510–1.9520	1.9370–1.9380	1.9220–1.9230	1.9070–1.9080	—	NA	NA	0.0010–0.0026	0.0008–0.0040

NA—Not available
① No. 1 and No. 5: 0.0014–0.0033
No. 2 and No. 4: 0.0026–0.0045
② No. 1 and No. 4: 0.0024–0.0035
No. 2 and No. 3: 0.0031–0.0045
③ No. 1 and No. 4: 0.0031–0.0044
No. 2 and No. 3: 0.0031–0.0047

CRANKSHAFT AND CONNECTING ROD SPECIFICATIONS

All measurements are given in inches.

Year	Engine ID/VIN	Engine Displacement Liters (cc)	Crankshaft Main Brg. Journal Dia.	Crankshaft Main Brg. Oil Clearance	Crankshaft Shaft End-play	Crankshaft Thrust on No.	Connecting Rod Journal Diameter	Connecting Rod Oil Clearance	Connecting Rod Side Clearance
1987	F2	2.2L (2184)	2.3597–2.3605	0.0012–0.0019	0.0031–0.0071	3	2.0055–2.0061	0.0011–0.0026	0.0040–0.0100
	G54B	2.6L (2555)	2.3614–2.3622	0.0008–0.0020	0.0020–0.0071	3	2.0855–2.0866	0.0008–0.0024	0.0040–0.0100
1988	F2	2.2L (2184)	2.3597–2.3605	0.0012–0.0019	0.0031–0.0071	3	2.0055–2.0061	0.0011–0.0026	0.0040–0.0100
	G54B	2.6L (2555)	2.3614–2.3622	0.0008–0.0020	0.0020–0.0071	3	2.0855–2.0866	0.0008–0.0024	0.0040–0.0100
1989	F2	2.2L (2184)	2.3597–2.3604	①	0.0031–0.0071	3	2.0055–2.0061	0.0011–0.0026	0.0043–0.0103
	G6	2.6L (2606)	2.3697–2.3604	0.0010–0.0017	0.0031–0.0071	4	2.0055–2.0061	0.0011–0.0026	0.0043–0.0103
	JE	3.0L (2954)	2.4385–2.4392	0.0010–0.0015	0.0031–0.0111	4	2.0842–2.0848	0.0009–0.0025	0.0070–0.0130
1990	F2	2.2L (2184)	2.3597–2.3604	①	0.0031–0.0071	3	2.0055–2.0061	0.0011–0.0026	0.0043–0.0103
	G6	2.6L (2606)	2.3697–2.3604	0.0010–0.0017	0.0031–0.0071	4	2.0055–2.0061	0.0011–0.0026	0.0043–0.0103
	JE	3.0L (2954)	2.4385–2.4392	0.0010–0.0015	0.0031–0.0111	4	2.0842–2.0848	0.0009–0.0025	0.0070–0.0130
1991	F2	2.2L (2184)	2.3597–2.3604	①	0.0031–0.0071	3	2.0055–2.0061	0.0011–0.0026	0.0043–0.0103
	G6	2.6L (2606)	2.3697–2.3604	0.0010–0.0017	0.0031–0.0071	4	2.0055–2.0061	0.0011–0.0026	0.0043–0.0103
	JE	3.0L (2954)	2.4385–2.4392	0.0010–0.0015	0.0031–0.0111	4	2.0842–2.0848	0.0009–0.0025	0.0070–0.0130
	X	4.0L (4016)	2.2433–2.2441	0.0005–0.0019	—	3	2.1252–2.1260	0.0005–0.0022	—
1992	F2	2.2L (2184)	2.3597–2.3604	①	0.0031–0.0071	3	2.0055–2.0061	0.0011–0.0026	0.0043–0.0103
	G6	2.6L (2606)	2.3697–2.3604	0.0010–0.0017	0.0031–0.0071	4	2.0055–2.0061	0.0011–0.0026	0.0043–0.0103
	JE	3.0L (2954)	2.4385–2.4392	0.0010–0.0015	0.0031–0.0111	4	2.0842–2.0848	0.0009–0.0025	0.0070–0.0130
	X	4.0L (4016)	2.2433–2.2441	0.0005–0.0019	—	3	2.1252–2.1260	0.0005–0.0022	—

① No. 1, 2, 4, and 5: 0.0010–0.0017
No. 3: 0.0012–0.0019

PISTON AND RING SPECIFICATIONS

All measurements are given in inches.

Year	Engine ID/VIN	Engine Displacement Liters (cc)	Piston Clearance	Ring Gap			Ring Side Clearance		
				Top Compression	Bottom Compression	Oil Control	Top Compression	Bottom Compression	Oil Control
1987	F2	2.2L (2184)	0.0014–0.0030	0.008–0.014	0.006–0.012	0.012–0.035	0.0012–0.0028	0.0012–0.0028	Snug
	G54B	2.6L (2555)	0.0008–0.0160	0.012–0.018	0.010–0.016	0.012–0.024	0.0020–0.0035	0.0008–0.0024	Snug
1988	F2	2.2L (2184)	0.0014–0.0030	0.008–0.014	0.006–0.012	0.012–0.035	0.0012–0.0028	0.0012–0.0028	Snug
	G54B	2.6L (2555)	0.0008–0.0160	0.012–0.018	0.010–0.016	0.012–0.024	0.0020–0.0035	0.0008–0.0024	Snug
1989	F2	2.2L (2184)	0.0014–0.0030	0.008–0.014	0.006–0.012	0.008–0.028	0.0012–0.0028	0.0012–0.0028	Snug
	G6	2.6L (2606)	0.0023–0.0029	0.008–0.014	0.010–0.016	0.008–0.028	0.0012–0.0028	0.0012–0.0028	Snug
	JE	3.0L (2954)	0.0019–0.0026	0.008–0.014	0.006–0.012	0.008–0.028	0.0012–0.0028	0.0012–0.0028	Snug
1990	F2	2.2L (2184)	0.0014–0.0030	0.008–0.014	0.006–0.012	0.008–0.028	0.0012–0.0028	0.0012–0.0028	Snug
	G6	2.6L (2606)	0.0023–0.0029	0.008–0.014	0.010–0.016	0.008–0.028	0.0012–0.0028	0.0012–0.0028	Snug
	JE	3.0L (2954)	0.0019–0.0026	0.008–0.014	0.006–0.012	0.008–0.028	0.0012–0.0028	0.0012–0.0028	Snug
1991	F2	2.2L (2184)	0.0014–0.0030	0.008–0.014	0.006–0.012	0.008–0.028	0.0012–0.0028	0.0012–0.0028	Snug
	G6	2.6L (2606)	0.0023–0.0029	0.008–0.014	0.010–0.016	0.008–0.028	0.0012–0.0028	0.0012–0.0028	Snug
	JE	3.0L (2954)	0.0019–0.0026	0.008–0.014	0.006–0.012	0.008–0.028	0.0012–0.0028	0.0012–0.0028	Snug
	X	4.0L (4016)	0.0008–0.0019	0.015–0.023	0.015–0.023	0.015–0.055	0.0020–0.0033	0.0020–0.0033	Snug
1992	F2	2.2L (2184)	0.0014–0.0030	0.008–0.014	0.006–0.012	0.008–0.028	0.0012–0.0028	0.0012–0.0028	Snug
	G6	2.6L (2606)	0.0023–0.0029	0.008–0.014	0.010–0.016	0.008–0.028	0.0012–0.0028	0.0012–0.0028	Snug
	JE	3.0L (2954)	0.0019–0.0026	0.008–0.014	0.006–0.012	0.008–0.028	0.0012–0.0028	0.0012–0.0028	Snug
	X	4.0L (4016)	0.0008–0.0019	0.015–0.023	0.015–0.023	0.015–0.055	0.0020–0.0033	0.0020–0.0033	Snug

TORQUE SPECIFICATIONS

All readings in ft. lbs.

Year	Engine ID/VIN	Engine Displacement Liters (cc)	Cylinder Head Bolts	Main Bearing Bolts	Rod Bearing Bolts	Crankshaft Damper Bolts	Flywheel Bolts	Manifold Intake	Manifold Exhaust	Spark Plugs	Lug Nut
1987	F2	2.2L (2184)	59-64	61-65	48-51	9-13	71-76	14-19	19	11-15	⑧
	G54B	2.6L (2555)	①	54-61	33-35	80-94	94-101	11-14	19	11-15	⑧
1988	F2	2.2L (2184)	59-64	61-65	48-51	9-13	71-76	14-19	19	11-15	⑧
	G54B	2.6L (2555)	①	54-61	33-35	80-94	94-101	11-14	19	11-15	⑧
1989	F2	2.2L (2184)	59-64	61-65	48-51	9-13	71-76	14-19	19	11-15	⑧
	G6	2.6L (2606)	59-64	61-65	48-51	130-145	67-72	14-19	19	11-15	⑧
	JE	3.0L (2954)	②	③	④	116-123	76-81	14-19	19	11-15	65-87
1990	F2	2.2L (2184)	59-64	61-65	48-51	9-13	71-76	14-19	19	11-15	⑧
	G6	2.6L (2606)	59-64	61-65	48-51	130-145	67-72	14-19	19	11-15	⑧
	JE	3.0L (2954)	②	③	④	116-123	76-81	14-19	19	11-15	65-87
1991	F2	2.2L (2184)	59-64	61-65	48-51	9-13	71-76	14-19	19	11-15	⑧
	G6	2.6L (2606)	59-64	61-65	48-51	130-145	67-72	14-19	19	11-15	⑧
	JE	3.0L (2954)	②	③	④	116-123	76-81	14-19	19	11-15	65-87
	X	4.0L (4016)	⑤	66-77	19-24	⑥	59	⑦	19	11-15	100
1992	F2	2.2L (2184)	59-64	61-65	48-51	9-13	71-76	14-19	19	11-15	⑧
	G6	2.6L (2606)	59-64	61-65	48-51	130-145	67-72	14-19	19	11-15	⑧
	JE	3.0L (2954)	②	③	④	116-123	76-81	14-19	19	11-15	65-87
	X	4.0L (4016)	⑤	66-77	19-24	⑥	59	⑦	19	11-15	100

① Bolts 1-10: 65-72
Bolts 11-12: 11-16

② Tighten in 3 steps:
Step 1: 14 ft. lbs.
Step 2: +90 degree turn
Step 3: +90 degree turn

③ Tighten in 3 steps:
Step 1: 14 ft. lbs.
Step 2: +90 degree turn
Step 3: +45 degree turn

④ Tighten in 2 steps:
Step 1: 22 ft. lbs.
Step 2: +90 degree turn

⑤ Tighten in 7 steps:
Step 1: Tighten cyl. head bolts to 44 ft. lbs.
Step 2: Tighten intake man. bolts to 3-6 ft. lbs.
Step 3: Tighten cyl. head bolts to 59 ft. lbs.
Step 4: Tighten intake man. bolts to 6-11 ft. lbs.
Step 5: Tighten cyl. head bolts + 85 degree turn
Step 6: Tighten intake man. bolts to 11-15 ft. lbs.
Step 7: Tighten intake man. bolts to 15-18 ft. lbs.

⑥ Tighten in 2 steps:
Step 1: 30-37 ft. lbs.
Step 2: +90 degree turn

⑦ Tighten in 4 steps:
Step 1: 3-6 ft. lbs.
Step 2: 6-11 ft. lbs.
Step 3: 11-15 ft. lbs.
Step 4: 15-18 ft. lbs.

⑧ Design wheels 65-87
Stylad wheels 87-108

Engine

➧ SEE FIGS. 19-27

REMOVAL & INSTALLATION

B Series Pickup

1. Relieve the fuel system pressure on fuel injected models. Disconnect the battery cables and remove the battery.
2. Raise and safely support the vehicle. Drain the engine oil and coolant. Remove the splash shields, as necessary.
3. Remove the starter and the transmission.

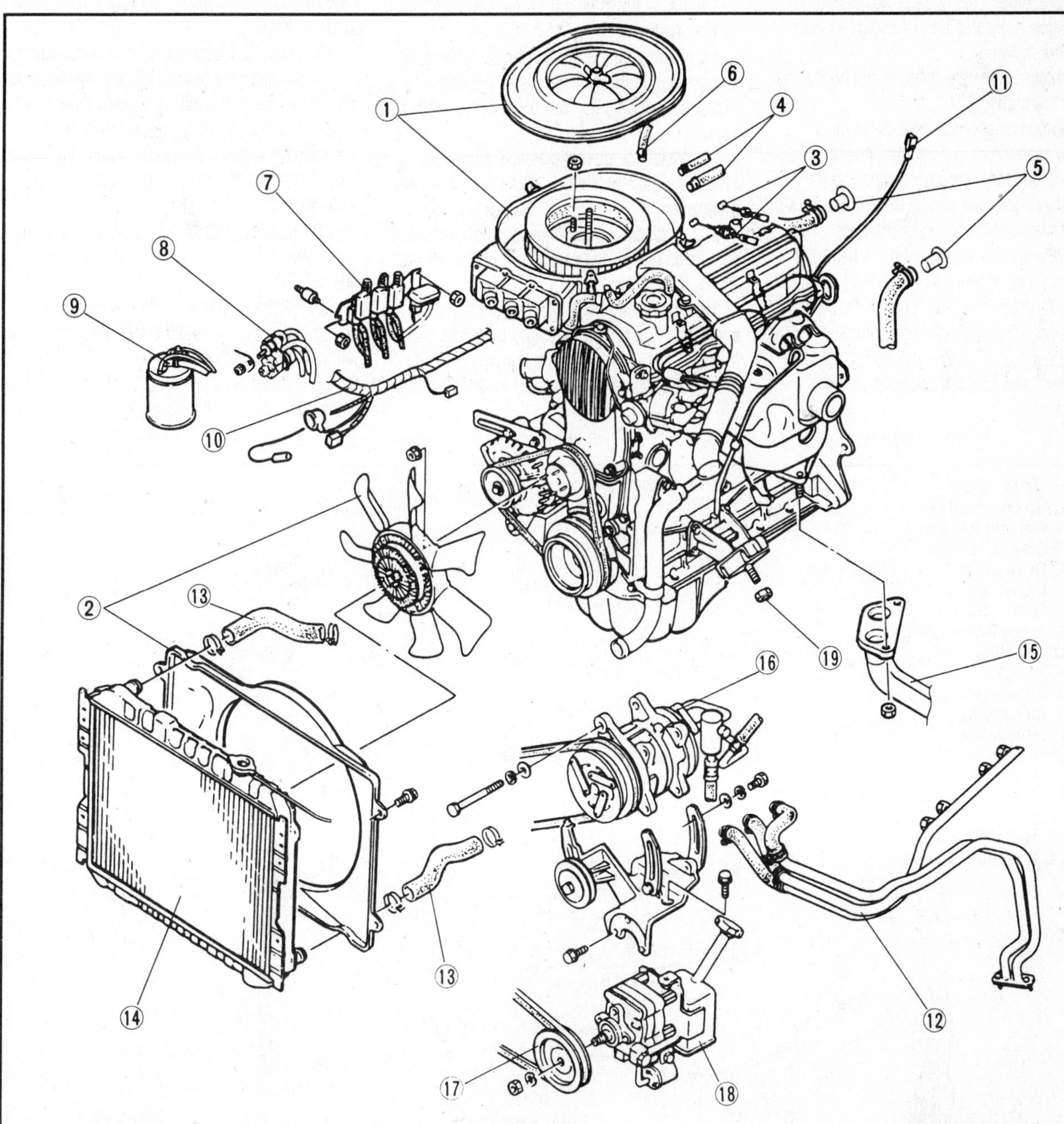

1. Air cleaner assembly
2. Cooling fan and radiator cowling
3. Accelerator cable
4. Fuel hoses
5. Heater hoses
6. Brake vacuum hose
7. Three-way solenoid valve assembly
8. Vacuum solenoid valve assembly
9. Canister hoses
10. Engine harness
11. Engine ground
12. Secondary air pipe (carbureted)
13. Radiator hoses
14. Radiator
15. Exhaust pipe
16. AC compressor
17. Power steering pump pulley
18. Power steering pump
19. Engine mount nuts

FIG. 19 B2200 engine removal; Remove the listed components in numerical order

4. Disconnect the exhaust system from the exhaust manifold. Lower the vehicle.

5. Remove the air cleaner assembly, if carburetor equipped. Disconnect the accelerator cable.

6. Remove the cooling fan and the radiator shroud. Disconnect the radiator hoses and transmission oil cooler lines, if equipped and remove the radiator.

7. Disconnect the fuel lines, heater hoses and brake vacuum hose.

8. Tag and disconnect the necessary electrical connectors and vacuum hoses.

9. If carburetor equipped, disconnect the secondary air pipe assembly. On 1989–92 2.6L engine, remove the resonance chamber.

10. Remove the accessory drive belt(s). If equipped, remove the power steering pump pulley and the power steering pump. Position the pump aside, leaving the hoses connected.

11. If equipped, remove the air conditioning compressor and position aside, leaving the hoses attached.

12. Remove the gusset plates, if equipped. Remove the transmission oil cooler line retainers, if equipped.

13. Attach suitable engine lifting equipment to the engine. Remove the engine mount nuts and remove the engine from the vehicle.

14. Install the engine on a workstand.

To install:

15. Remove the engine from the workstand and position in the vehicle. Install the engine mount nuts and tighten to 30–36 ft. lbs. (40–49 Nm).

16. Install the gusset plates, if equipped. Attach the transmission oil cooler line retainers, if equipped.

17. Install the air conditioning compressor, if equipped. Tighten the mounting bolts to 29–40 ft. lbs. (39–54 Nm).

18. Install the power steering pump, if equipped. Tighten the mounting bolts to 23–34 ft. lbs. (31–46 Nm). Install the power steering pump pulley and tighten the nut to 36–43 ft. lbs. (49–59 Nm).

19. Install the secondary air pipe, if equipped. Install the resonance chamber, if equipped.

20. Connect all vacuum lines and electrical connectors. Connect the brake vacuum hose, heater hoses and fuel lines.

21. Install the accessory drive belt(s) and cooling fan. Install the fan shroud, radiator and radiator hoses.

22. Adjust the accessory drive belt tension.

23. Connect the accelerator cable. Install the air cleaner assembly on carbureted engine.

24. Raise and safely support the vehicle. Connect the exhaust pipe to the exhaust manifold and tighten the attaching nuts to 30–36 ft. lbs. (40–49 Nm).

25. Install the starter and the transmission assembly. Install the splash shields and lower the vehicle.

26. Fill the crankcase with the proper type and quantity of engine oil. Install the battery and connect the battery cables.

27. Fill and bleed the cooling system. Run the engine and check for leaks and proper operation.

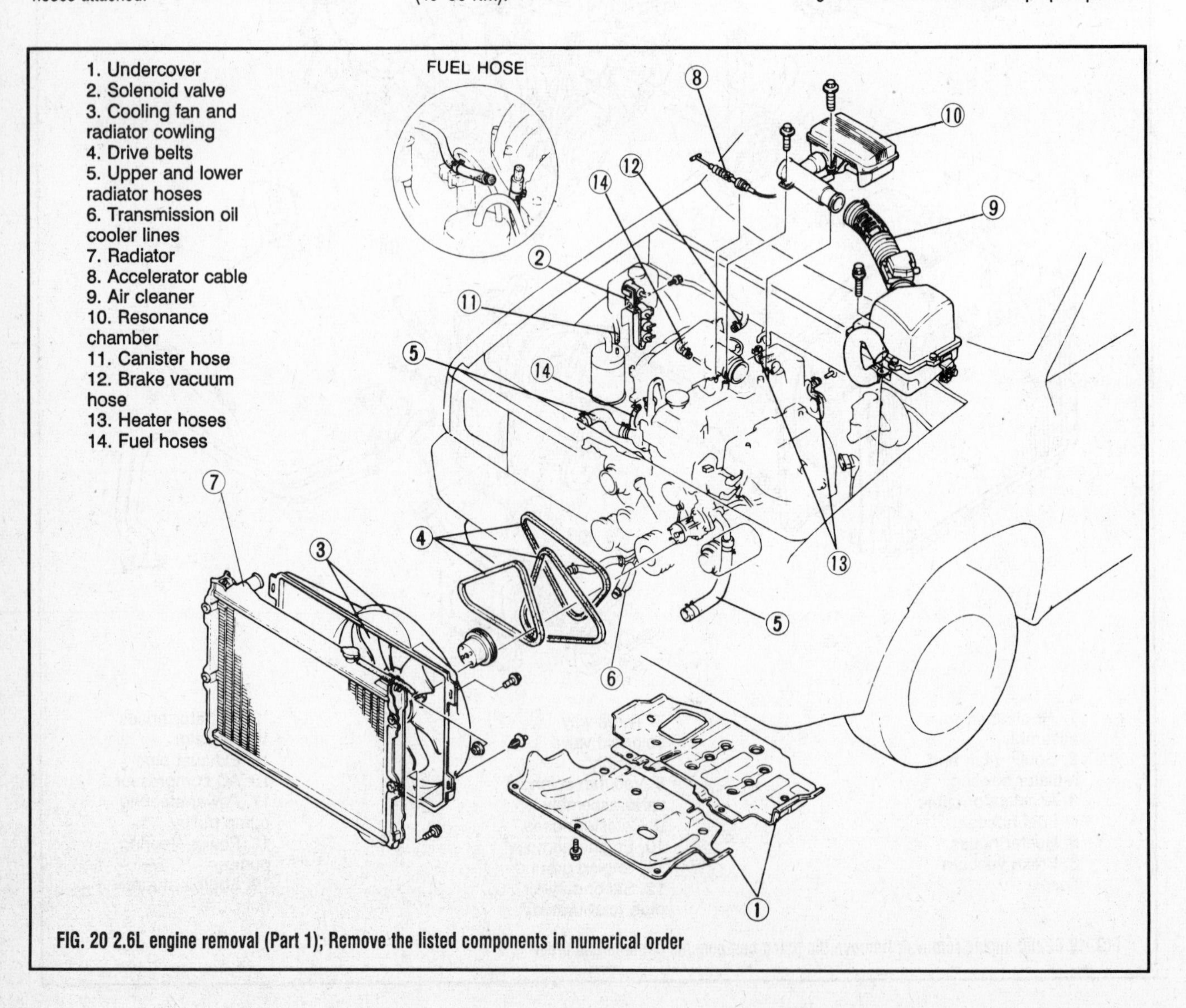

FIG. 20 2.6L engine removal (Part 1); Remove the listed components in numerical order

MPV

1. Relieve the fuel system pressure, disconnect the battery cables and remove the battery.

2. Raise and safely support the vehicle. Drain the engine oil and coolant. Remove the splash shield.

3. Remove the starter and the transmission.

4. Disconnect the exhaust pipes from the exhaust manifolds and lower the vehicle.

5. Remove the fresh air duct and the radiator hoses. Disconnect the transmission oil cooler lines from the radiator, if equipped.

6. Remove the radiator, fan shroud and cooling fan. Remove the accessory drive belts.

7. Tag and disconnect the necessary electrical connectors and vacuum lines. Disconnect the brake vacuum hose,heater hoses and fuel lines.

8. On 2.6L engine, disconnect the accelerator cable and remove the resonance chamber and air cleaner. On 3.0L engine, disconnect the accelerator cable and remove the air cleaner and airflow meter.

9. Remove the shroud upper panel and the air conditioning pipe bracket. On 3.0L engine, remove the protector cover from the front of the engine.

10. If equipped, remove the power steering pump and position aside, leaving the hoses attached. It is necessary to remove the power steering pulley prior to removing the pump.

11. If equipped, remove the air conditioning compressor and position aside, leaving the hoses attached.

12. Remove the lower grille and radiator grille. Remove the shroud upper plate and the additional condenser fan, if equipped.

13. Attach suitable engine lifting equipment to the engine. Remove the engine mount nuts and remove the engine from the vehicle.

14. Install the engine on a workstand.

To Install:

15. Remove the engine from the workstand. Lower the engine into the vehicle, being careful not to damage the piping.

➡ **Lean the air conditioning condenser forward to ease engine installation.**

16. Install the engine mount nuts and tighten to 25–36 ft. lbs. (34–49 Nm). Install the additional condenser fan, if equipped.

17. Apply a bead of sealer to each side of the front support, then install the shroud upper plate. Tighten the mounting bolts to 61–87 inch lbs. (6.9–9.8 Nm).

18. Install the radiator grille and lower grille.

19. Install the air conditioning compressor, if equipped. Tighten the mounting bolts to 13–20

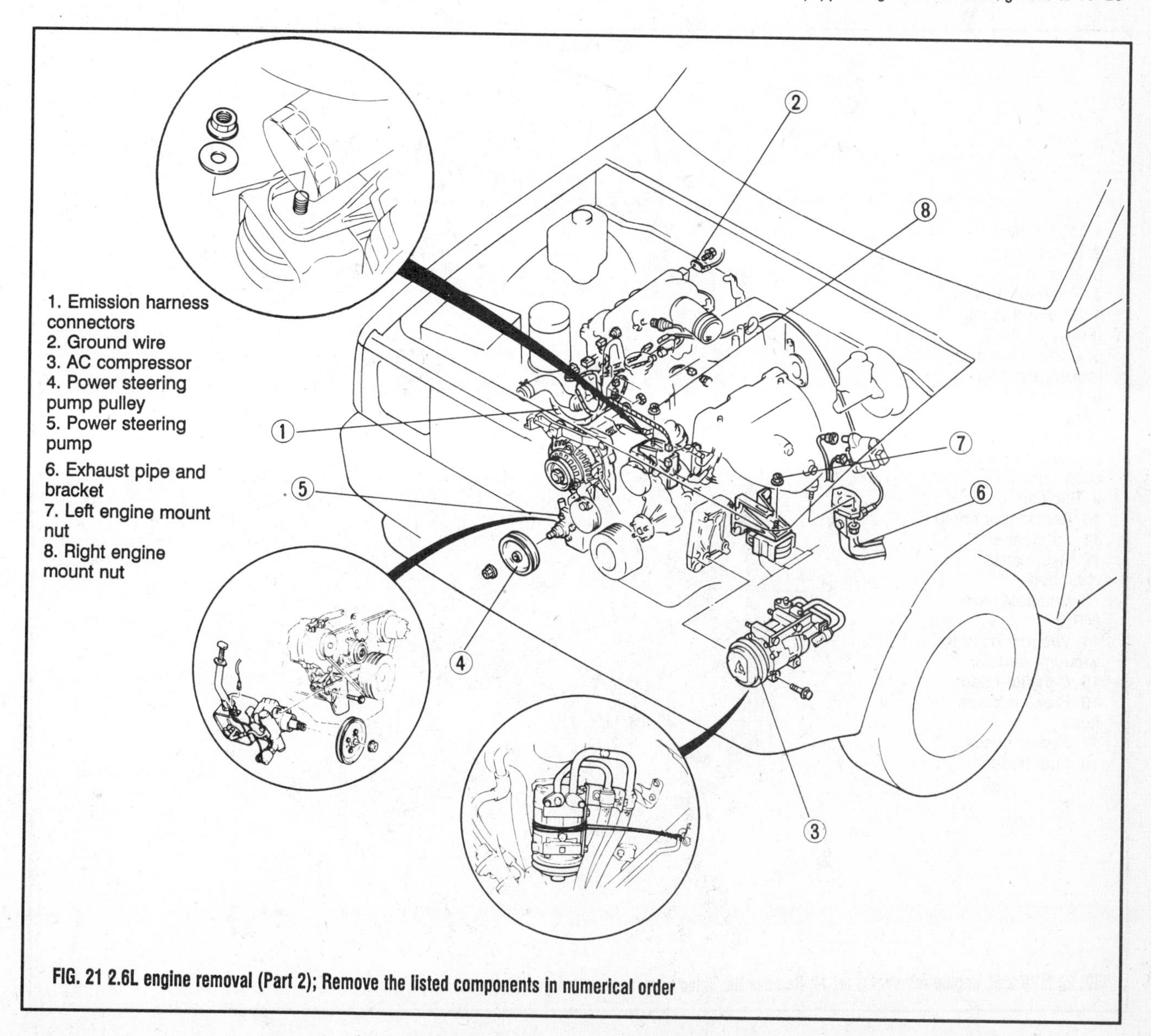

FIG. 21 2.6L engine removal (Part 2); Remove the listed components in numerical order

ft. lbs. (18–26 Nm). Install the air conditioner pipe bracket and tighten the mounting nuts to 61–87 inch lbs. (6.9–9.8 Nm).

20. Install the power steering pump, if equipped. Tighten the mounting bolts to 23–34 ft. lbs. (31–46 Nm). Install the pump pulley and tighten the nut to 29–43 ft. lbs. (39–59 Nm).

21. Install the shroud upper panel and tighten the bolts to 69–95 inch lbs. (7.8–11.0 Nm).

22. Connect the accelerator cable. On 2.6L engine, install the resonance chamber and air filter. On 3.0L engine, install the air cleaner and airflow meter.

23. Connect all electrical connectors and vacuum hoses.

24. Connect the brake vacuum hose, heater hoses and fuel lines.

25. Install the accessory drive belts and the cooling fan. Install the fan shroud and the radiator. Adjust the drive belt tension.

26. Install the radiator hoses and fresh air duct. If equipped, connect the transmission oil cooler lines.

27. Raise and safely support the vehicle. Connect the exhaust pipes to the exhaust manifolds. Tighten the nuts to 25–36 ft. lbs. (34–49 Nm).

28. Install the starter and transmission assembly. Install the splash shield and lower the vehicle.

29. Install the battery and connect the negative battery cables. Fill the crankcase with the proper type and quantity of engine oil.

30. Fill and bleed the cooling system. Run the engine and check for leaks and proper operation.

Navajo

1. Disconnect the negative battery cable and relieve the fuel system pressure. Drain the cooling system.

2. Mark the position of the hood on the hinges and remove the hood. Remove the air cleaner intake hose.

3. Disconnect the radiator hoses at the radiator. Disconnect the fan shroud and position it over the fan. Remove the radiator, then the shroud.

4. Remove the alternator and bracket and position the alternator aside. Disconnect the alternator ground wire from the cylinder block.

5. Remove the air conditioning compressor and power steering pump and position aside, if equipped.

6. Disconnect the heater hoses at the intake manifold and water pump. Remove the ground wires from the cylinder block.

7. Disconnect the fuel lines from the fuel supply manifold. Disconnect the throttle cable shield and linkage at the throttle body and intake manifold.

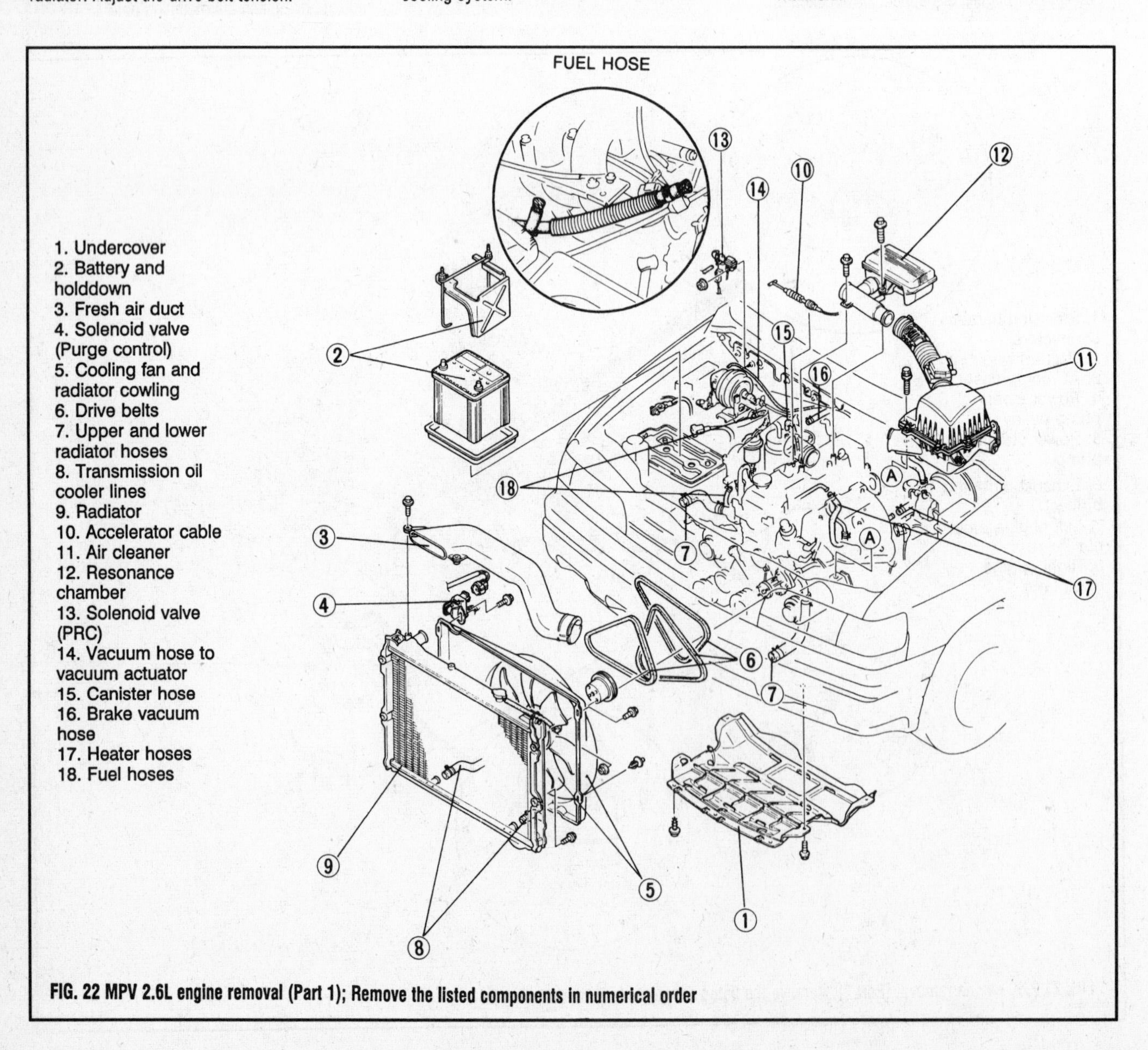

FIG. 22 MPV 2.6L engine removal (Part 1); Remove the listed components in numerical order

8. Tag and disconnect the vacuum connections at the rear vacuum fitting in the upper intake manifold.

9. Disconnect the wiring from the ignition coil and oil pressure and engine coolant temperature senders. Disconnect the injector harness, air charge temperature sensor and throttle position sensor. Disconnect the brake booster vacuum hose.

10. Raise and safely support the vehicle. Disconnect the exhaust pipes at the manifolds. Disconnect the starter cable and remove the starter.

11. Remove the engine front mount-to-crossmember attaching nuts or through bolts.

12. Remove the converter inspection cover and disconnect the converter from the flywheel. Remove the cable.

13. Remove the converter housing-to-engine block bolts and the adapter plate-to-converter housing bolt. Lower the vehicle.

14. Position a jack under the transmission and install suitable engine lifting equipment.

15. Raise the engine slightly and carefully pull it from the transmission. Carefully lift the engine out of the engine compartment so the rear cover plate is not bent or components damaged. Install the engine on a workstand.

To install:

16. Remove the engine from the workstand and carefully lower it into the engine compartment. Make sure the exhaust manifolds are aligned with the exhaust pipes.

17. At the transmission, start the converter pilot into the crankshaft. Install the converter housing upper bolts, making sure the dowels in the cylinder block engage the flywheel housing. Tighten the bolts to 33–45 ft. lbs. (45–61 Nm).

18. Remove the jack from under the transmission and the engine lifting equipment.

19. Position the kickdown rod on the transmission and engine. Raise and safely support the vehicle.

20. Position the transmission linkage bracket and install the remaining converter housing bolts. Install the adapter plate-to-converter housing bolt. Install the converter-to-flywheel nuts and install the inspection cover. Connect the kickdown rod on the transmission.

21. Install the starter and connect the cable. Connect the exhaust pipes at the manifolds.

22. Install the engine front mount nuts and washers or through bolts. Lower the vehicle.

23. Install the ground wires to the engine block. Connect the ignition coil wiring, then

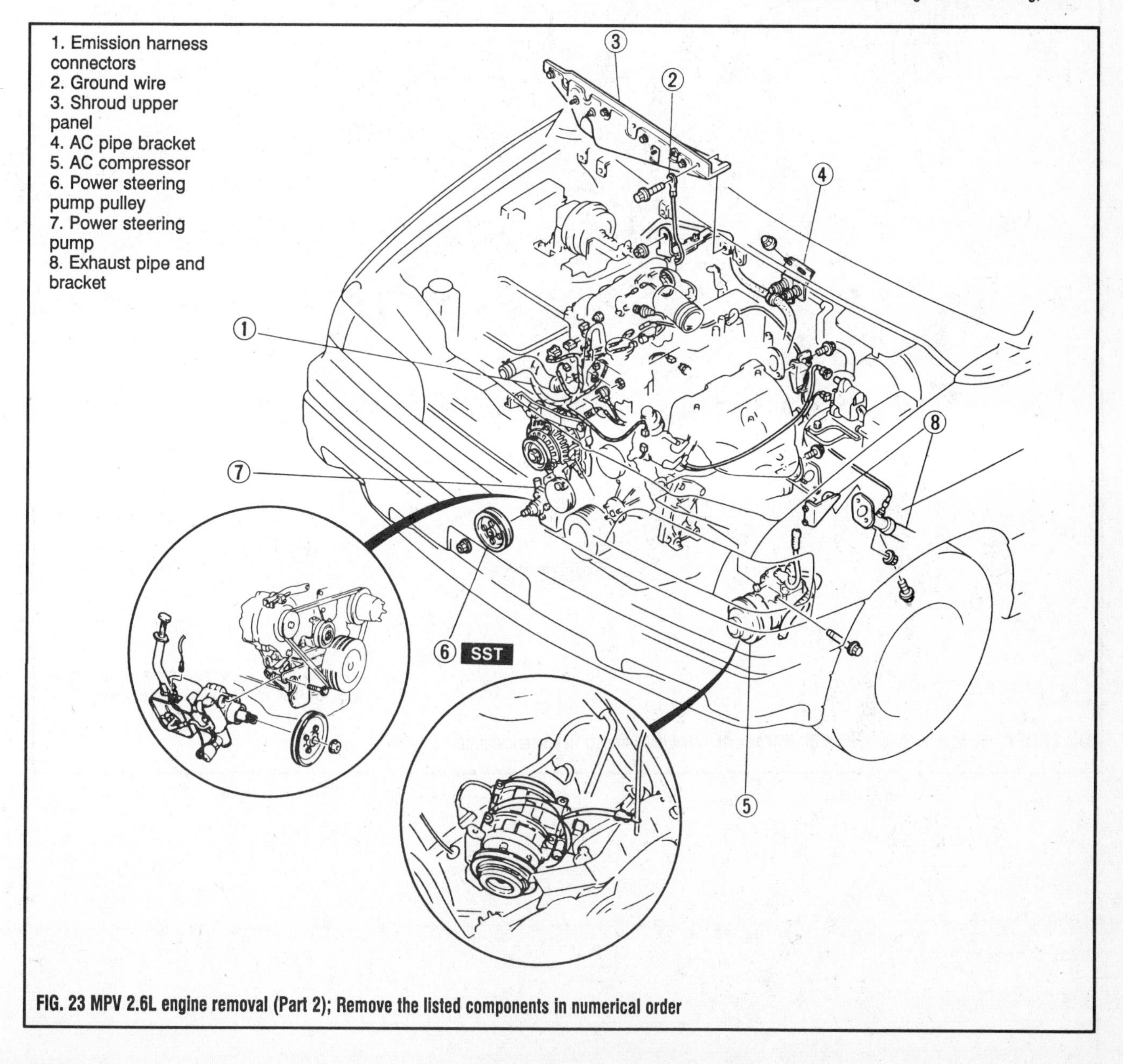

FIG. 23 MPV 2.6L engine removal (Part 2); Remove the listed components in numerical order

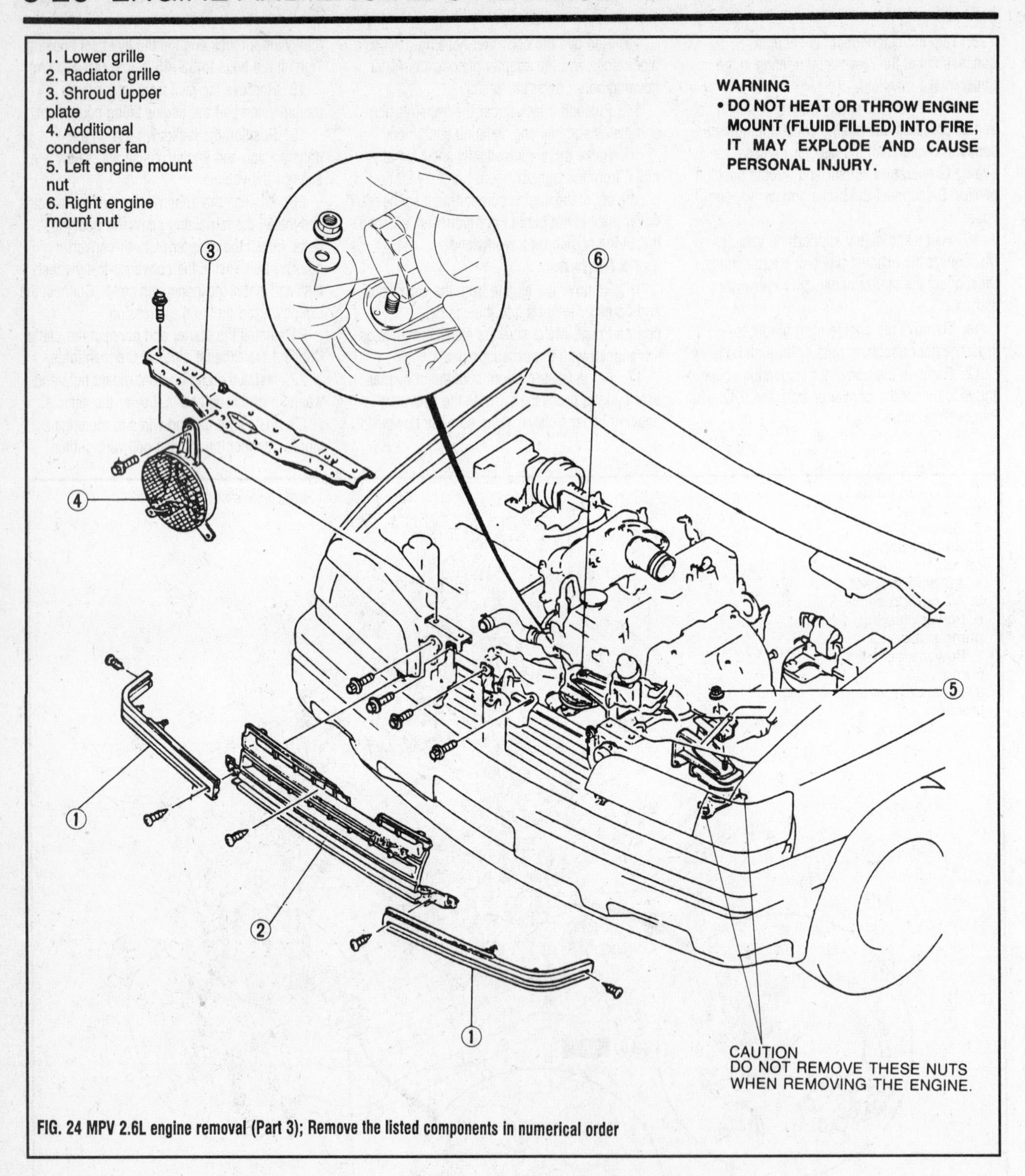
1. Lower grille
2. Radiator grille
3. Shroud upper plate
4. Additional condenser fan
5. Left engine mount nut
6. Right engine mount nut
WARNING
• DO NOT HEAT OR THROW ENGINE MOUNT (FLUID FILLED) INTO FIRE, IT MAY EXPLODE AND CAUSE PERSONAL INJURY.
CAUTION
DO NOT REMOVE THESE NUTS WHEN REMOVING THE ENGINE.

FIG. 24 MPV 2.6L engine removal (Part 3); Remove the listed components in numerical order

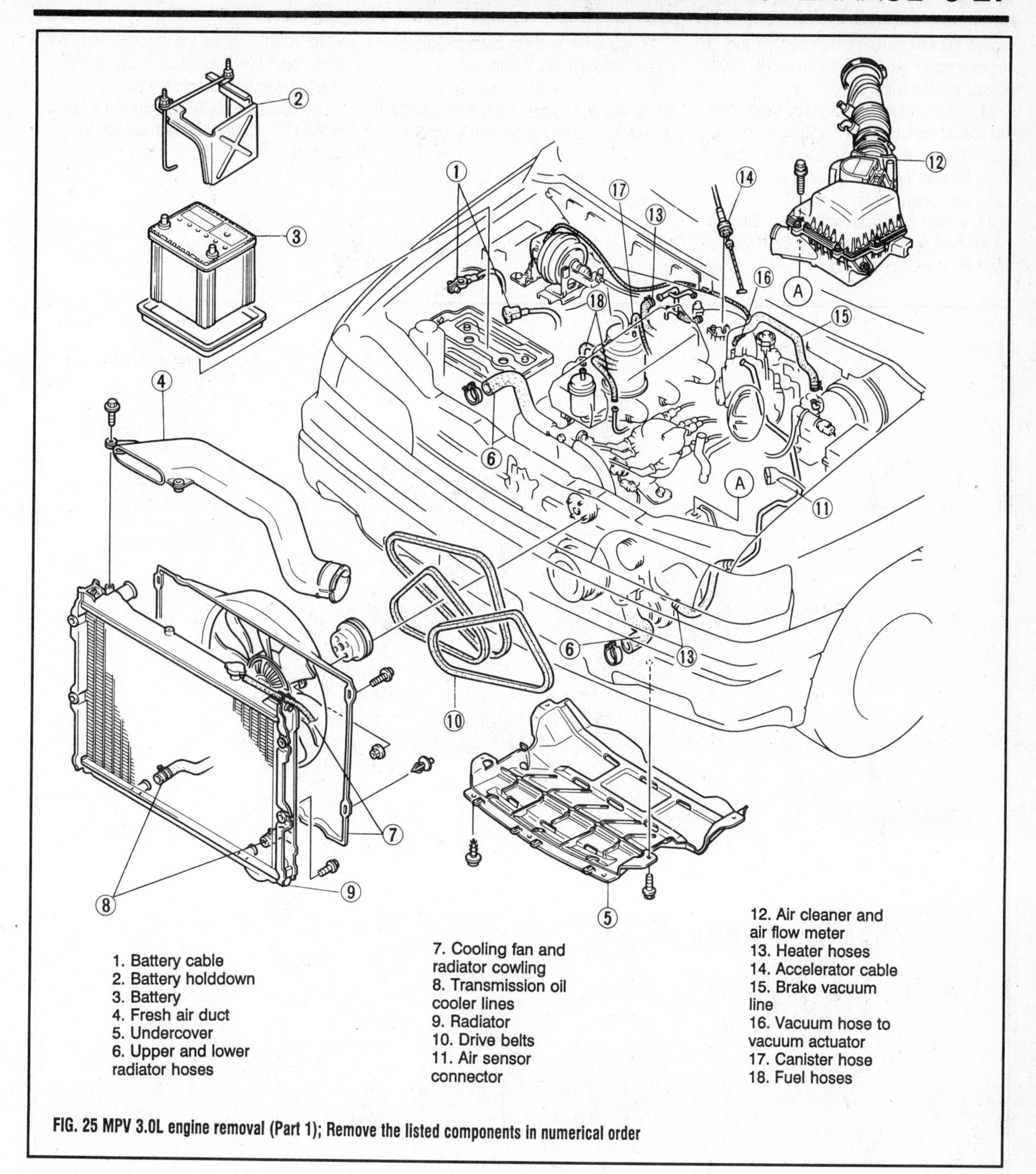

FIG. 25 MPV 3.0L engine removal (Part 1); Remove the listed components in numerical order

connect the coolant temperature sending unit and oil pressure sending unit. Connect the brake booster vacuum hose.

24. Install the throttle linkage and connect the fuel lines at the fuel supply manifold.

25. Connect the ground cable at the engine block. Connect the heater hoses to the water pump and cylinder block.

26. Install the alternator and bracket. Connect the alternator ground wire to the engine block. Install the accessory drive belt.

27. Install the air conditioner compressor and power steering pump, if equipped.

28. Position the shroud over the fan. Install the radiator and connect the radiator upper and lower hoses. Install the fan shroud attaching bolts.

29. Connect the negative battery cable. Fill and bleed the cooling system.

30. Run the engine and check for leaks and proper operation. If equipped, evacuate and charge the air conditioning system.

31. Install the intake hose. Install the hood, aligning the marks that were made during removal.

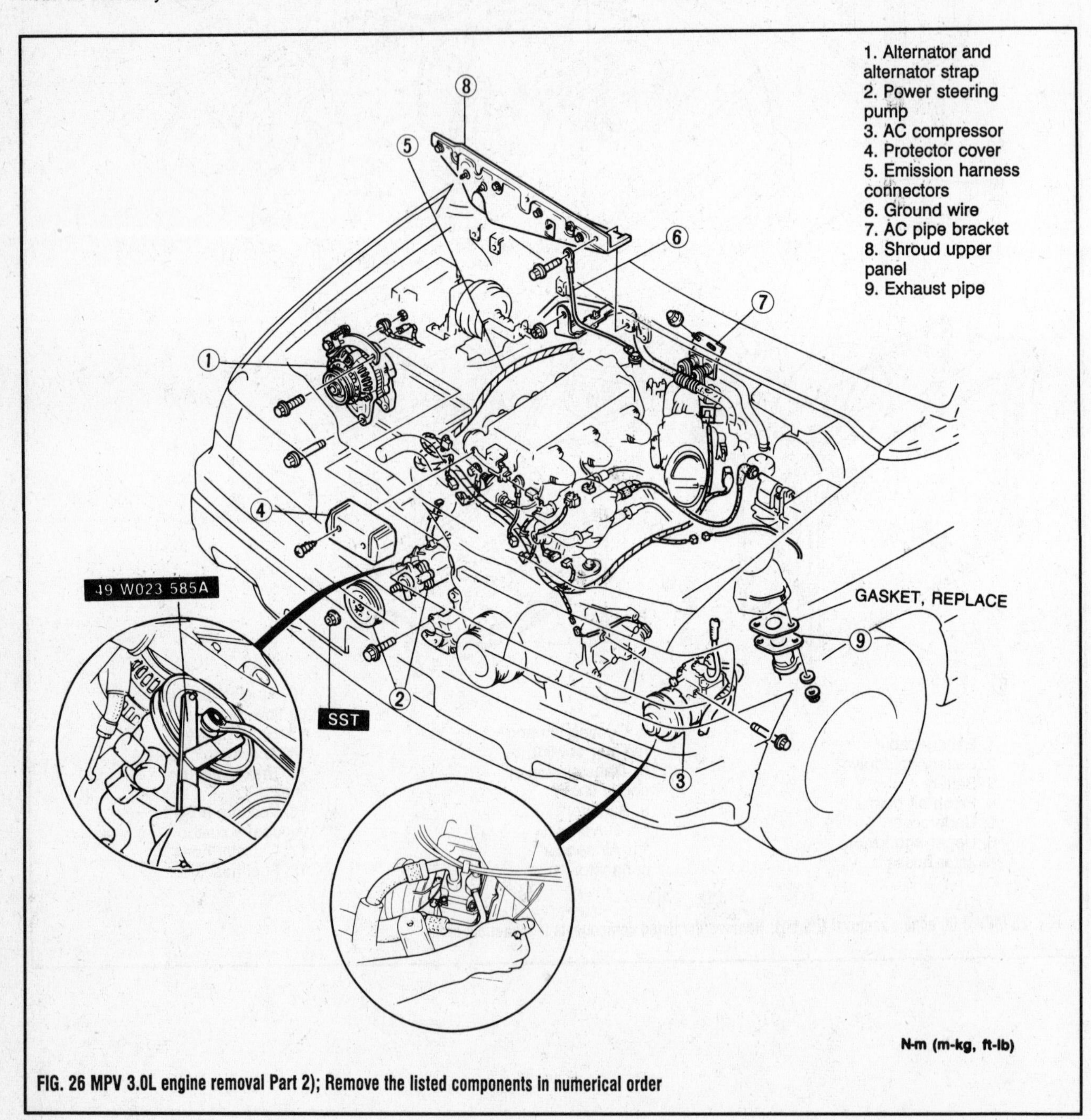

FIG. 26 MPV 3.0L engine removal Part 2); Remove the listed components in numerical order

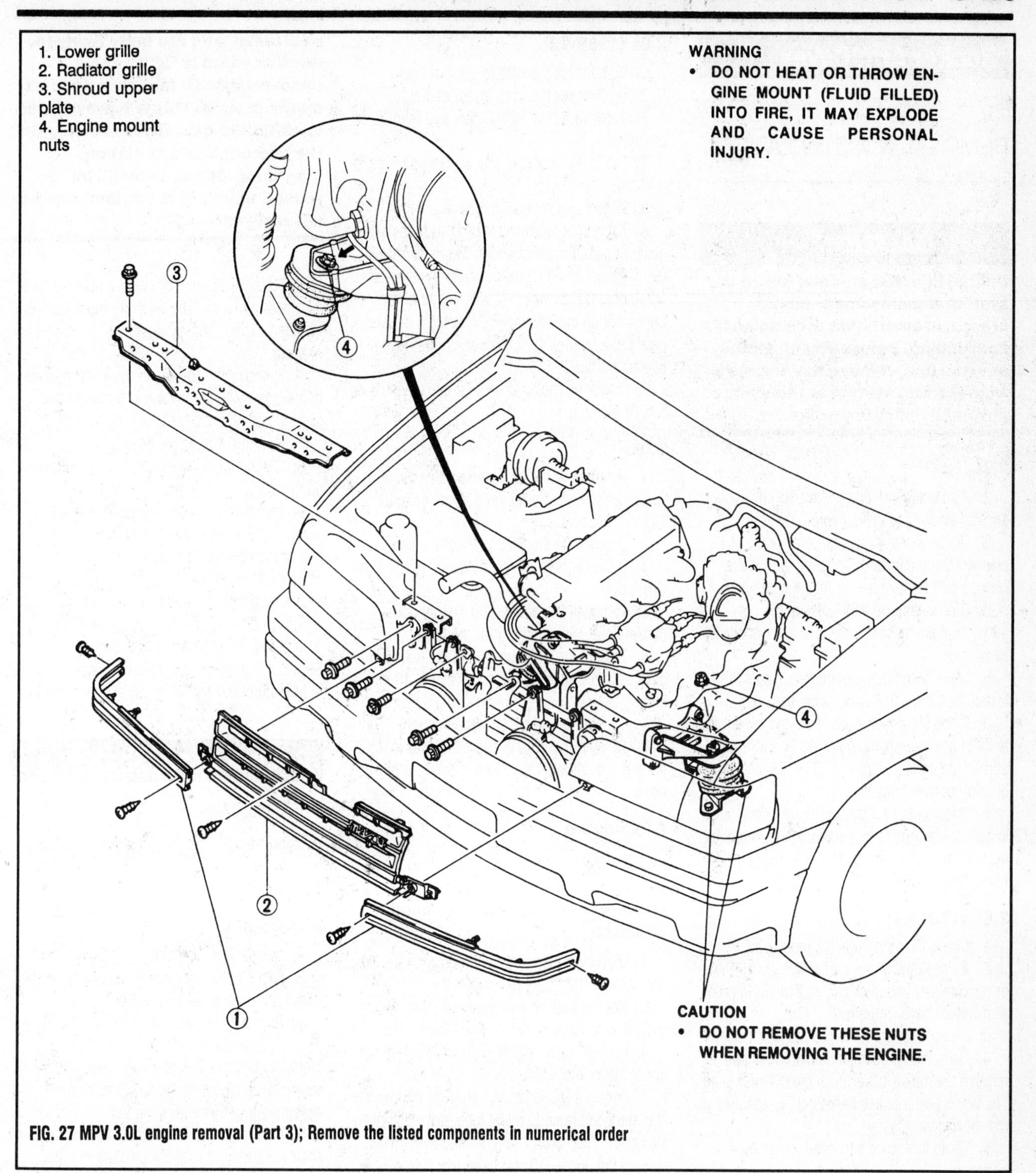
1. Lower grille
2. Radiator grille
3. Shroud upper plate
4. Engine mount nuts
WARNING
• DO NOT HEAT OR THROW ENGINE MOUNT (FLUID FILLED) INTO FIRE, IT MAY EXPLODE AND CAUSE PERSONAL INJURY.
3
4
4
2
1
CAUTION
• DO NOT REMOVE THESE NUTS WHEN REMOVING THE ENGINE.

FIG. 27 MPV 3.0L engine removal (Part 3); Remove the listed components in numerical order

Rocker Arm Cover

REMOVAL & INSTALLATION

CAUTION

On fuel injected models, fuel in the system remains under high pressure, even when the engine is not running. Before disconnecting any fuel line, release the pressure from the fuel system to reduce the possibility of injury or fire.

2.2L

1. If so equipped, disconnect the choke cable and the air bypass valve cable.
2. On carbureted models, remove the air cleaner. On fuel injected models, loosen the clamps and remove the air intake crossover.
3. Disconnect the PCV valve at the cover.
4. Remove the retaining bolts and remove the cam cover.
5. Clean all gasket mounting surfaces. To install the cover, first install new gaskets.
6. Place the cover in position and tighten the bolts in several stages, going back and forth across the cover, (tighten to 26 – 35 inch lbs.) but do not over tighten.
7. Once all the associated components are installed, start the engine and allow it to reach normal operating temperature. Retighten the bolts. Check for leaks.

2.6L (1987-88)

1. Disconnect the negative battery cable.
2. Remove the air cleaner assembly. Remove or relocate any hoses or cables that will interfere with rocker cover removal.
3. Disconnect the hoses to the PCV tube.
4. Remove the cover mounting bolts and remove the rocker cover from the cylinder head. The water pump pulley belt shield is attached at rear of rocker cover.
5. Clean the cover and head mounting surfaces.
6. Apply RTV sealant to the top of the rubber cam seal and install the rocker cover.
7. With rocker cover installed, apply RTV sealant to top of semi-circular packing.
8. Tighten screws to 55 inch lbs..
9. Install the vacuum hoses and spark plug wires.
10. Install the air cleaner assembly.
11. Connect the battery cable.

2.6L (1989-92)

1. Disconnect the battery ground cable.
2. Disconnect the accelerator cable.
3. Remove the air intake pipe and resonance chamber.
4. Tag and disconnect any wires and hoses in the way.
5. Unbolt and remove the cover.
6. Thoroughly clean all mating surfaces of old gasket material and/or sealer. The cover may use a gasket or RTV gasket sealer. If a gasket is used, coat the new gasket with sealer and position it on the head. If RTV material is used, squeeze a 1/8 inch (3mm) bead on the head sealing surface.
7. Install the rocker cover. Torque the bolts to 52–78 inch lbs.

3.0L

1. Disconnect the air bypass valve cable.
2. Loosen the clamps and remove the air intake crossover.
3. Disconnect the PCV valve at the cover.
4. Remove the retaining bolts and remove the cam cover.
5. To install the cover, first supply new gaskets and seal washers for the bolts.
6. Tighten the bolts in several stages, going back and forth across the cover to 30–40 inch lbs.
7. Once all the associated components are installed, start the engine and allow it to reach normal operating temperature. Check for oil leaks.

4.0L Engine

➡ Failure to install new rocker cover gaskets and rocker cover reinforcement pieces will result in oil leaks.

1. Disconnect the negative battery cable. Tag and remove the spark plug wires.
2. Relieve fuel system pressure. Disconnect and remove the fuel supply and return lines.
3. For left rocker cover removal, remove the upper intake manifold.
4. For right rocker cover removal, remove air inlet duct and hose to oil fill tube, drive belt from alternator, alternator. Drain cooling system remove the upper radiator hose from the engine. Remove the EDIS ignition coil and bracket assembly. Remove the A/C low pressure hose bracket if so equipped. Remove the PCV valve hose and breather.

CAUTION

When draining the coolant, keep in mind that cats and dogs are attracted by the ethylene glycol antifreeze, and are quite likely to drink any that is left in an uncovered container or in puddles on the ground. This will prove fatal in sufficient quantity. Always drain the coolant into a sealable container. Coolant should be reused unless it is contaminated or several years old.

5. Remove the rocker cover bolts and load distribution pieces. The washers must be installed in their original positions, so keep track of them.
6. Remove the rocker cover. It will probably be necessary to tap the cover loose with a plastic or rubber mallet.
7. Remove the rocker covers.
8. Clean all gasket material from the cover and head.
9. Installation is the reverse of removal. Always use a new gasket coated with sealer. If any of the RTV silicone gasket material was removed from the mating area of the head(s) and intake manifold, replace it. Torque the bolts to 3–5 ft. lbs.
10. Reconnect the negative battery cable. Start the engine and run to normal operating temperature and check for oil and fuel leaks.

Rocker Arms/Shafts

➧ SEE FIGS. 28-34

REMOVAL & INSTALLATION

2.2L Engine

1. Disconnect the negative battery cable.
2. Remove the air cleaner assembly or air intake hose, as required.
3. Remove the rocker arm cover.
4. Loosen the rocker arm/shaft assembly mounting bolts in 2–3 steps in the proper sequence. Remove the rocker arm/shaft assembly together with the bolts.
5. If necessary, disassemble the rocker arm/shaft assembly, noting the position of each component to ease reassembly.
6. Check for wear or damage to the contact surfaces of the shafts and rocker arms; replace as necessary.
7. Measure the rocker arm inner diameter, it should be 0.6300–0.6310 in. (16.000–16.027mm). Measure the rocker arm shaft diameter, it should be 0.6286–0.6293 in. (15.966–15.984mm).
8. Subtract the shaft diameter from the rocker arm diameter to get the oil clearance. The oil

clearance should be 0.0006–0.0024 in. (0.016–0.061mm) and should not exceed 0.004 in. (0.10mm). Replace parts, as necessary, if the oil clearance is not within specification.

To install:

9. Apply clean engine oil to the rocker arm shafts and rocker arms and assemble the rocker arm/shaft assembly in the reverse order of disassembly. Make sure the rocker arm shaft oil holes in the center camshaft cap face each other.

➡ Use the mounting bolts for alignment.

10. Apply silicone sealant to the cylinder head on the front and rear camshaft cap mounting surface. Apply clean engine oil to the camshaft journals and valve stem tips.

11. Install the rocker arm/shaft assembly and tighten the bolts, in sequence, in 2–3 steps to a maximum torque of 13–20 ft. lbs. (18–26 Nm).

12. Apply silicone sealant to each side of the front and rear camshaft cap and the cylinder head in the area where the caps meet the cylinder head.

13. Install the rocker arm cover and tighten the mounting bolts to 26–35 inch lbs. (2.9–3.9 Nm).

14. Install the air cleaner assembly or air intake tube. Connect the negative battery cable, start the engine and check for leaks and proper operation.

2.6L Engine 1987-88

1. Disconnect the negative battery cable.
2. Remove the air cleaner assembly.
3. Remove the rocker arm cover.
4. Install hydraulic lash adjuster holder tool 49 U012 001 or equivalent, over the ends of each rocker arm to keep the hydraulic lash adjuster from falling out when the rocker arm/shaft assembly is removed.
5. Loosen the rocker arm/shaft assembly mounting bolts and remove the assembly. Leave the mounting bolts in place in the shaft to keep the assembly together, if there will be no further disassembly.
6. If necessary, disassemble the rocker arm/shaft assembly, noting the position of each component to ease reassembly.
7. Check for wear or damage to the contact surfaces of the shafts and rocker arms; replace as necessary.
8. Measure the rocker arm inner diameter, it should be 0.7445–0.7452 in. (18.910–18.928mm). Measure the rocker arm shaft diameter, it should be 0.7435–0.7440 in. (18.885–18.898mm).
9. Subtract the shaft diameter from the rocker arm diameter to get the oil clearance. The oil clearance should be 0.0005–0.0017 in. (0.012–0.043mm) and should not exceed 0.004 in. (0.10mm). Replace parts, as necessary, if the oil clearance is not within specification.

To install:

10. Apply clean engine oil to the rocker arm shafts and rocker arms and assemble the rocker arm/shaft assembly in the reverse order of disassembly. Be sure to align the mating mark on the front of the shaft with the mating mark on the front camshaft cap.
11. Apply clean engine oil to the camshaft journals and valve stem tips.
12. Install the rocker arm/shaft assembly and tighten the mounting bolts, in sequence, in 2–3 steps to a maximum torque of 14–15 ft. lbs. (19–20 Nm).
13. Remove the hydraulic lash adjuster holder tools. Adjust the jet valve lash.
14. Install the rocker arm cover and tighten to 43–61 inch lbs. (5–7 Nm). Install the air cleaner assembly.
15. Connect the negative battery cable, start the engine and bring to normal operating temperature. Check for leaks and proper operation. With the engine warm, readjust the jet valve clearance.

2.6L Engine 1989-92

1. Disconnect the negative battery cable.
2. Remove the air intake hose.
3. Remove the rocker arm cover.
4. Loosen the rocker arm/shaft assembly mounting bolts in 2–3 steps in the proper sequence. Remove the rocker arm/shaft assembly together with the bolts.
5. If necessary, disassemble the rocker arm/shaft assembly, noting the position of each component to ease reassembly.
6. Check for wear or damage to the contact surfaces of the shafts and rocker arms; replace as necessary.
7. Measure the rocker arm inner diameter, it should be 0.8268–0.8281 in. (21.000–21.033mm). Measure the rocker arm shaft diameter, it should be 0.8252–0.8260 in. (20.959–20.980mm).
8. Subtract the shaft diameter from the rocker arm diameter to get the oil clearance. The oil clearance should be 0.0008–0.0029 in. (0.020–0.074mm) and should not exceed 0.004 in. (0.10mm). Replace parts, as necessary, if the oil clearance is not within specification.

To install:

9. Apply clean engine oil to the rocker arm shafts and rocker arms and assemble the rocker arm/shaft assembly in the reverse order of disassembly, noting the following:
   a. The intake side shaft has twice as many oil holes as the exhaust side shaft.
   b. The No. 4 camshaft cap has an oil hole from the cylinder head; make sure it is installed correctly.
10. Apply clean engine oil to the camshaft journals and valve stem tips.
11. Install the rocker arm/shaft assembly and tighten the mounting bolts, in sequence, in 2–3 steps to a maximum torque of 14–19 ft. lbs. (19–25 Nm).
12. Coat a new gasket with silicone sealer and install on the rocker arm cover. Apply sealer to the cylinder head in the area of the half circle seals and install the rocker arm cover. Install the mounting bolts and tighten to 52–78 inch lbs. (5.9–8.8 Nm).
13. Install the air intake hose. Connect the negative battery cable, start the engine and check for leaks and proper operation.

3.0L Engine

1. Disconnect the negative battery cable.
2. If removing the driver's side rocker arm/shaft assembly, proceed as follows:
   a. Remove the air inlet tube.
   b. Disconnect the necessary electrical connectors and vacuum hoses from the throttle body and intake air pipe.
   c. Disconnect the throttle cable.
   d. Remove the throttle body and intake air pipe.
3. Remove the rocker arm cover.
4. Loosen the rocker arm/shaft assembly mounting bolts in sequence, in 2–3 steps. Remove the assembly with the bolts.
5. If necessary, disassemble the rocker arm/shaft assembly, noting the position of each component to ease reassembly.
6. Check for wear or damage to the contact surfaces of the shafts and rocker arms; replace as necessary.
7. Measure the rocker arm inner diameter, it should be 0.7480–0.7493 in. (19.000–19.033mm). Measure the rocker arm shaft diameter, it should be 0.7464–0.7472 in. (18.959–18.980mm).
8. Subtract the shaft diameter from the rocker arm diameter to get the oil clearance. The oil clearance should be 0.0008–0.0029 in. (0.020–0.074mm) and should not exceed 0.004 in. (0.10mm). Replace parts, as necessary, if the oil clearance is not within specification.

To install:

9. Apply clean engine oil to the rocker arm shafts and rocker arms and assemble the rocker arm/shaft assembly in the reverse order of disassembly, noting the following. The intake side shaft has twice as many oil holes as the exhaust side shaft.
10. Apply clean engine oil to the camshaft journals and valve stem tips.
11. Install the rocker arm/shaft assembly and tighten the mounting bolts, in sequence, in

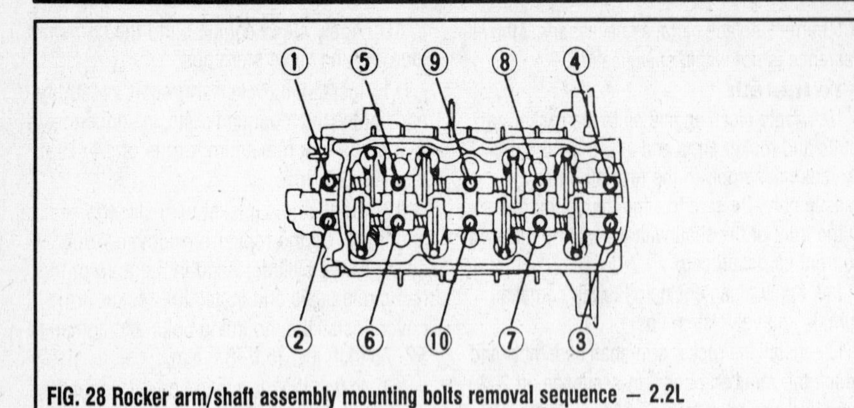

FIG. 28 Rocker arm/shaft assembly mounting bolts removal sequence — 2.2L

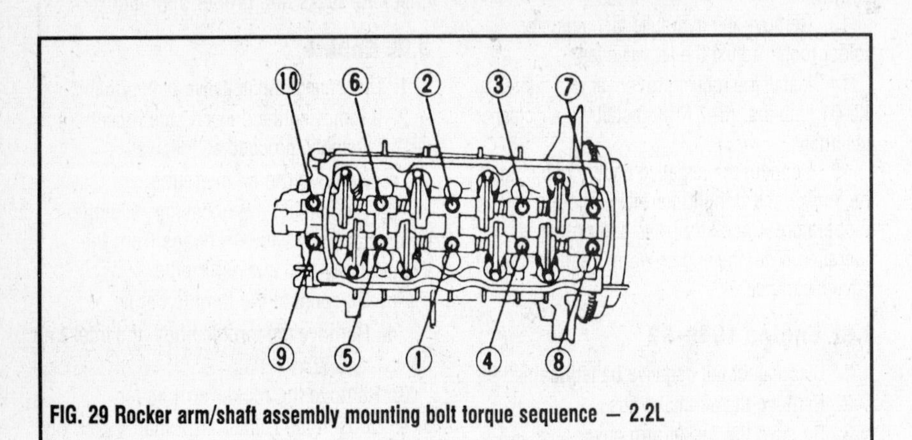

FIG. 29 Rocker arm/shaft assembly mounting bolt torque sequence — 2.2L

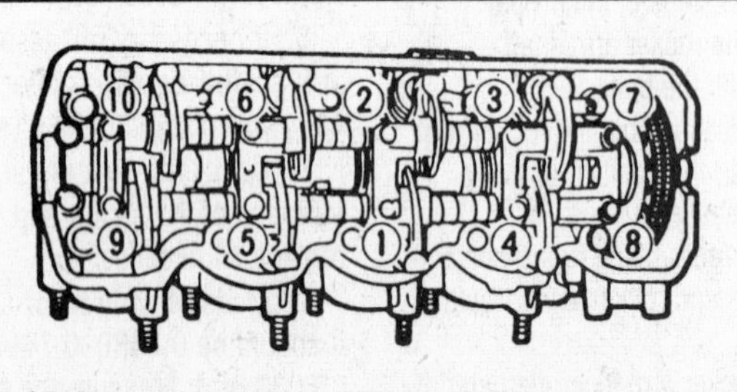

FIG. 30 Rocker arm/shaft assembly mounting bolts torque sequence — 1987–88 2.6L

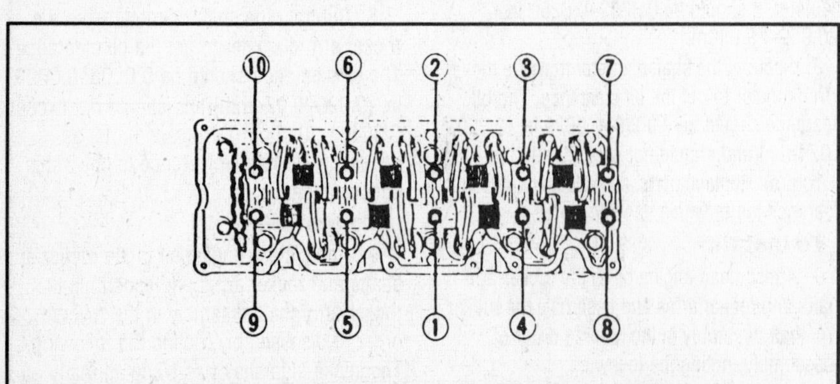

FIG. 31 Rocker arm/shaft assembly mounting bolts removal sequence — 1989–92 2.6L

2–3 steps to a maximum torque of 14–19 ft. lbs. (19–25 Nm).

➡ **Be careful that the rocker arm shaft spring does not get caught between the shaft and mounting boss during installation.**

12. Coat a new gasket with silicone sealant and install on the rocker arm cover. Install the rocker arm cover with new seal washers and tighten the bolts to 30–39 inch lbs. (3.4–4.4 Nm).

13. Install the intake air pipe, throttle body and air intake tube, if removed. Connect the throttle cable and the necessary electrical connectors and vacuum hoses.

14. Connect the negative battery cable, start the engine and check for leaks and proper operation.

4.0L Engine

1. Disconnect the negative battery cable. Remove the intake shield and air intake tube.
2. If removing the right rocker arm/shaft assembly, proceed as follows:
   a. Remove the alternator and the coil pack.
   b. Remove the retaining bolt from the air conditioning pipe over the upper intake manifold.
   c. Remove the spark plug wires from the clips on the valve cover.
   d. Remove the 2 wiring harnesses from the right rocker arm cover.
   e. Disconnect the vacuum hose at the coupling over the rocker arm cover.
   f. Remove the engine wiring harness clip from the rocker arm cover-to-intake manifold stud. Do not pull on the harness but rather lift up on the clip.
   g. Remove the right rocker arm cover bolts, reinforcement plate and the cover.
3. If removing the right rocker arm/shaft assembly, proceed as follows:
   a. Remove the bolt from the air conditioning pipe over the upper intake manifold, if not already done.
   b. Disconnect the air conditioning compressor clutch connector and remove the wiring harness from the back of the compressor.
   c. Remove the air conditioning compressor bolts, pull up the tube that goes around the back of the engine and reposition the compressor and tube aside.
   d. Tag and disconnect the power brake vacuum hose and other hoses from the vacuum tee on the plenum.
   e. Remove the PCV hose and valve. Remove the wiring harness from the valve cover and position aside.

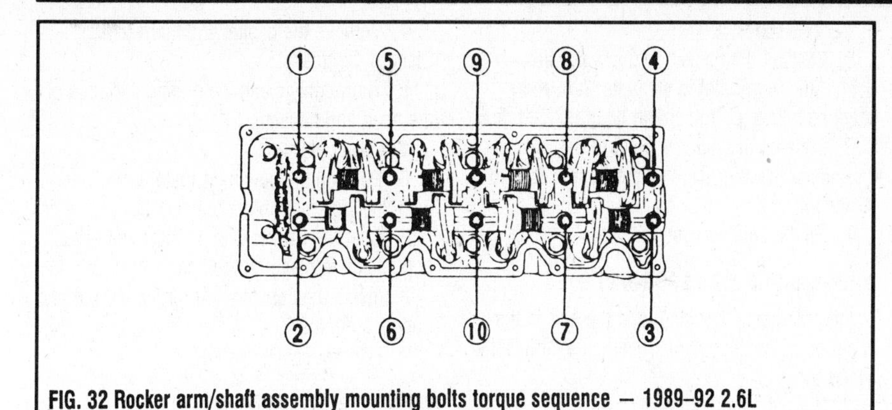

FIG. 32 Rocker arm/shaft assembly mounting bolts torque sequence — 1989–92 2.6L

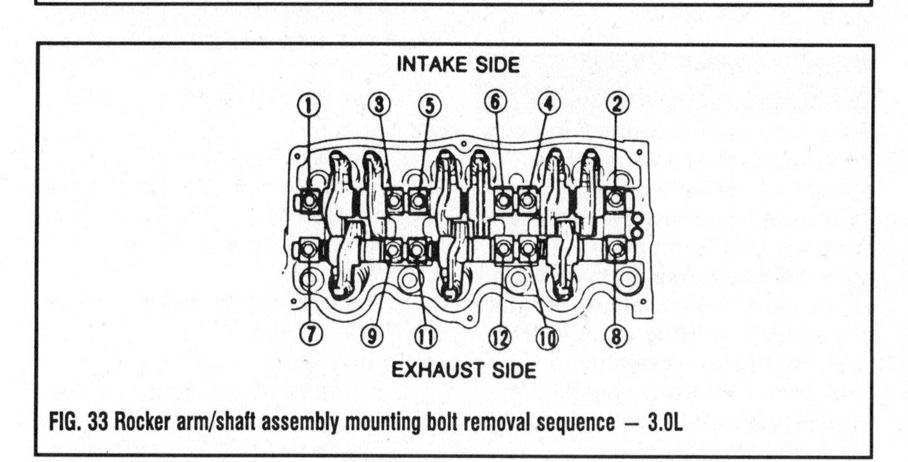

FIG. 33 Rocker arm/shaft assembly mounting bolt removal sequence — 3.0L

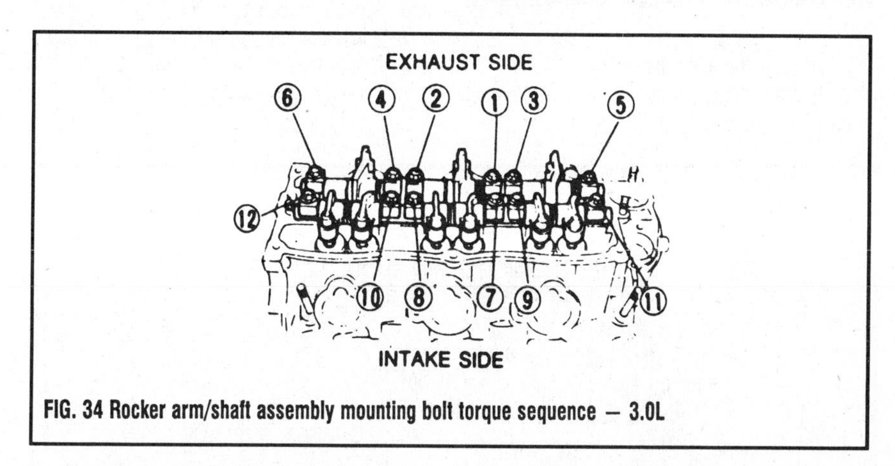

FIG. 34 Rocker arm/shaft assembly mounting bolt torque sequence — 3.0L

f. Tag and disconnect the spark plug wires from the spark plugs and clips on the rocker arm cover.

g. Remove the engine wiring harness clip from the rocker arm cover-to-intake manifold stud. Do not pull on the harness but rather lift up on the clip.

h. Remove the retaining bolt from the fuel hose clip to the front of the engine to allow the fuel hoses to be moved enough to gain access to the upper front rocker arm cover bolt.

i. Remove the bolts, reinforcement plates and left rocker arm cover.

4. Remove the rocker arm shafts by loosening the support bolts 2 turns at a time until the shaft can be removed.

5. If necessary, disassemble the rocker arm/shaft assembly by removing the spring washer and pin from each end of the shaft and sliding the rocker arms, springs and rocker arm shaft supports off the shaft. Note the position of each component to ease reassembly.

6. Inspect all components for wear and replace, as necessary.

To install:

7. Coat the rocker arms and shafts with clean engine oil and reassemble. The oil holes in the shaft must point down when the shaft is installed. This position can be recognized by a notch on the front face of the shaft.

8. Lubricate the pushrod ends and valve stem tips.

9. Install the rocker arm/shaft assembly and draw the shaft support bolts down evenly, 2 turns at a time, until the rocker arm/shaft assembly is fully down. Tighten the shaft support bolts to 46–52 ft. lbs. (62–70 Nm).

10. Clean all gasket mating surfaces.

11. Apply silicone sealant to the intake manifold-to-cylinder head parting seam and an $^{1}/_{8}$ in. (3mm) ball of sealer to the rocker arm cover bolt holes on the exhaust side.

12. Install a new gasket on the rocker arm cover and install the cover, reinforcing plates and bolts. Tighten the bolts to 53–70 inch lbs. (6–8 Nm) working in a criss-cross pattern and starting at the center bolts.

13. Install the remaining components. Connect the negative battery cable, start the engine and check for leaks and proper operation.

Thermostat

➧ SEE FIGS. 35 and 36

REMOVAL & INSTALLATION

➡ If the replacement thermostat is equipped with a "jiggle pin", the pin must be install facing upwards toward the top of the engine (12 o'clock), and should be on the side facing the water outlet. When installing the thermostat gasket, the seal print side should face the cylinder head.

Pickups w/2.2L

1. Drain enough coolant to bring the coolant level down below the thermostat housing. the thermostat housing is located on the left front side of the cylinder block.

CAUTION

When draining the coolant, keep in mind that cats and dogs are attracted by the ethylene glycol antifreeze, and are quite likely to drink any that is left in an uncovered container or in puddles on the ground. This will prove fatal in sufficient quantity. Always drain the coolant into a sealable container. Coolant should be

reused unless it is contaminated or several years old.

2. Disconnect the temperature sending unit wire.
3. Remove the coolant outlet elbow.
4. If so equipped, position the vacuum control valve out of the way. The vacuum control valve is not used on California trucks.
5. Disconnect the coolant by-pass hose from the thermostat housing.
6. Remove the thermostat and housing from the engine.
7. Note the position of the jiggle pin and remove the thermostat from the housing.
8. Remove all gasket material from the parts.

To install:

9. Position the thermostat in the housing with the jiggle pin up. Coat a new gasket with sealer and install it on the thermostat housing.
10. Install the thermostat housing using a new gasket with water resistant sealer. Torque the bolts to 20 ft. lbs.
11. Install the coolant outlet elbow and vacuum control valve (if equipped).
12. Connect the by-pass and radiator hoses.
13. Connect the temperature sending unit wire.
14. Fill the cooling system with the proper coolant. Operate the engine and check the coolant lever. Check for leaks.

Pickups w/2.6L (1987-88) Engine

The thermostat is located in a water box at the timing belt end of the intake manifold.

1. Drain the cooling system to a level below the thermostat.

CAUTION

When draining the coolant, keep in mind that cats and dogs are attracted by the ethylene glycol antifreeze, and are quite likely to drink any that is left in an uncovered container or in puddles on the ground. This will prove fatal in sufficient quantity. Always drain the coolant into a sealable container. Coolant should be reused unless it is contaminated or several years old.

2. Remove the hoses from the thermostat housing.
3. Remove the thermostat housing.
4. Remove the thermostat and discard the gasket. Clean the gasket surfaces thoroughly.

To install:

5. Position the gasket on the water box. Center the thermostat in the water box and attached housing. Tighten the bolts to 15 ft. lbs.
6. Connect the radiator hose to the thermostat housing. Tighten the hose clamp to 35 inch lbs.
7. Fill the cooling system.

Pickups w/2.6L (1989-92)

The thermostat housing is at the end of the upper hose, on the cylinder head side, above the alternator.

1. Drain the cooling system to a point below the housing.

CAUTION

When draining the coolant, keep in mind that cats and dogs are attracted by the ethylene glycol antifreeze, and are quite likely to drink any that is left in an uncovered container or in puddles on the ground. This will prove fatal in sufficient quantity. Always drain the coolant into a sealable container. Coolant should be reused unless it is contaminated or several years old.

2. Remove the upper hose.
3. Remove the upper nut and lower bolt and remove the housing.
4. Remove the gasket and thermostat. Discard the gasket.
5. Thoroughly clean the mating surfaces of the head and housing.

To install:

6. Position the new thermostat in the head with the jiggle pin on the upper side.
7. Coat the gasket with an adhesive sealer and stick it in place on the head.
8. Install the housing and torque the nut and bolt to 19 ft. lbs.
9. Fill the cooling system.

MPV w/2.6L (1989-92)

The thermostat housing is at the end of the upper hose, on the cylinder head side, above the alternator.

1. Drain the cooling system to a point below the housing.
2. Remove the upper hose.
3. Remove the upper nut and lower bolt and remove the housing.
4. Remove the gasket and thermostat. Discard the gasket.
5. Thoroughly clean the mating surfaces of the head and housing.

To install:

6. Position the new thermostat in the head with the jiggle pin on the upper side.
7. Coat the gasket with an adhesive sealer and stick it in place on the head.
8. Install the housing and torque the nut and bolt to 19 ft. lbs.
9. Fill the cooling system.

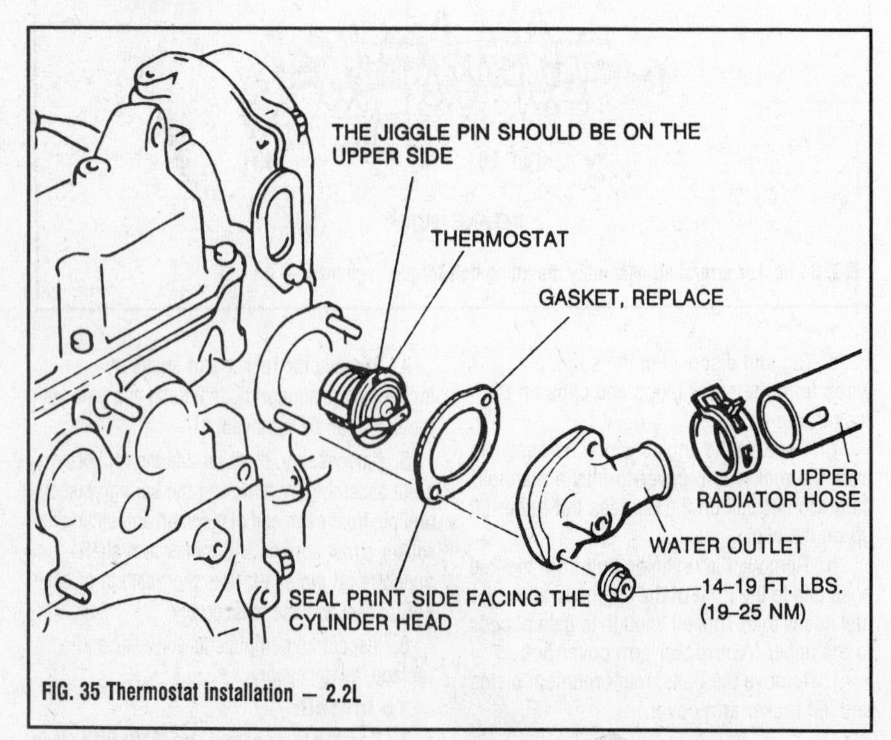

FIG. 35 Thermostat installation — 2.2L

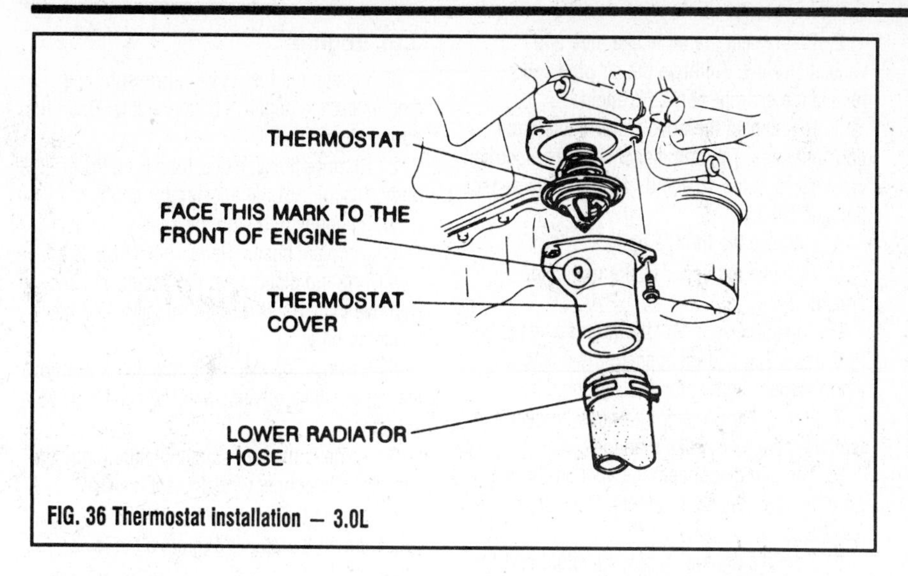

FIG. 36 Thermostat installation — 3.0L

MPV w/3.0L

The thermostat housing is located at the engine end of the lower radiator hose.

1. Raise and support the front end on jackstands.
2. Drain the cooling system.
3. Remove the lower hose.
4. Unbolt and remove the housing and thermostat.

➡ Some engines have a housing which incorporates an O-ring, eliminating the need for a gasket. On these engines, use no sealer when replacing the housing. On engines which incorporate a gasket, thoroughly clean the mating surfaces and use a new gasket coated with adhesive sealer.

5. Install a new thermostat in the housing and position the housing on the engine. Some housings are equipped with a location mark on the side, the mark should face the front of the engine when the housing is installed. Torque the bolts to 19 ft. lbs.
6. Install the lower hose.
7. Fill the cooling system.

4.0L Engines

1. Drain the cooling system.

⁂ CAUTION

When draining the coolant, keep in mind that cats and dogs are attracted by the ethylene glycol antifreeze, and are quite likely to drink any that is left in an uncovered container or in puddles on the ground. This will prove fatal in sufficient quantity. Always drain the coolant into a sealable container. Coolant should be reused unless it is contaminated or several years old.

2. Disconnect the battery ground.
3. Remove the air cleaner duct assembly.
4. Remove the upper radiator hose.
5. Remove the 3 thermostat housing attaching bolts.
6. Remove the thermostat housing. You may have to tap it loose with a plastic mallet or your hand.

To install:

7. Clean all mating surfaces thoroughly. Don't use a sharp metal tool! The housing and engine are aluminum.
8. Make sure that the sealing ring is properly installed on the thermostat rim. Position the thermostat in the housing making sure that the air release valve is in the **up** (12 o'clock) position.
9. Coat the mating surfaces of the housing and engine with an adhesive type sealer. Position the new gasket on the housing and place the housing on the engine. Torque the bolts to 7–10 ft. lbs.

Cooling System Bleeding

Except Navajo

Use the following steps to remove air from the system and ensure a complete fill.

1. Close the radiator draincock and install the cylinder block drain plug, if removed.
2. Slowly pour a 50/50 mixture of water and antifreeze into the radiator up to the coolant filler port.
3. Fill the coolant reservoir with the same mixture up to the FULL level.
4. Install the radiator cap securely and start the engine.
5. Run the engine at idle speed until it reaches normal operating temperature.

➡ If the temperature increases beyond normal, there is excessive air in the system. Stop the engine, allow it to cool and repeat Steps 2-4.

6. Run the engine up to 2200–2800 rpm for 5 seconds and return to idle. Repeat several times.
7. Stop the engine and wait until the system has cooled down. Remove the radiator cap and check the coolant level. If the coolant level has dropped, repeat the procedure from Step 2.

Navajo

Use the following steps to remove air from the system and ensure a complete fill.

1. Close the radiator draincock and install the cylinder block drain plug, if removed.
2. Fill the cooling system with a 50/50 mixture of water and antifreeze. Allow several minutes for trapped air to escape and for coolant mixture to flow through the radiator.
3. Install the radiator cap to the fully installed position, then back off to the first stop.
4. Slide the heater temperature and mode selection levers to maximum heat position.
5. Start the engine and operate at approximately 2000 rpm for 3–4 minutes.
6. Shut the engine off. Wrap the radiator cap with a thick cloth and carefully remove the cap.
7. Add coolant mixture to bring the coolant level up to the filler neck seat.

⁂ CAUTION

Use caution when adding coolant to the radiator to avoid hot coolant or steam blowing out from the radiator and possibly causing personal injury.

8. Install the radiator cap to the fully installed position, then back off to the first stop.
9. Run the engine at fast idle until the upper radiator hose is warm, indicating the thermostat is open.
10. Shut the engine off. Wrap the radiator cap with a thick cloth and carefully remove the cap. Add coolant, if necessary and reinstall the cap to the fully installed position.

11. Remove the coolant reservoir cap and add 1.1 qts. of coolant mixture to the reservoir. Install the cap.

Intake Manifold

➧ SEE FIGS. 37-40

REMOVAL & INSTALLATION

✻✻ CAUTION

On fuel injected models, fuel in the system remains under high pressure, even when the engine is not running. Before disconnecting any fuel line, release the pressure from the fuel system to reduce the possibility of injury or fire.

Never smoke when working around gasoline! Avoid all sources of sparks or ignition. Gasoline vapors are EXTREMELY volatile!

2.2L and 2.6L Engines

CARBURETED

1. Disconnect the negative battery cable. Drain the cooling system.
2. Remove the air cleaner assembly.
3. Disconnect the accelerator cable. Tag and disconnect the necessary electrical connectors and vacuum hoses.
4. Disconnect the coolant hoses and fuel line.
5. Remove the intake manifold mounting nuts and remove the intake manifold.

To install:

6. Clean all gasket mating surfaces.
7. Position a new intake manifold gasket on the cylinder head and install the intake manifold.
8. Install the intake manifold mounting nuts and tighten, in 2–3 steps, to 14–19 ft. lbs. (19–25 Nm) on 2.2L engine or 11–14 ft. lbs. (15–19 Nm) on 2.6L engine. Tighten the nuts at the center of the manifold first and work towards the ends.
9. Connect the fuel line and the coolant hoses.
10. Connect the electrical connectors and vacuum hoses. Connect the accelerator cable.
11. Install the air cleaner assembly and connect the negative battery cable.
12. Fill and bleed the cooling system. Run the engine and check for leaks.

FUEL INJECTED

1. Relieve the fuel system pressure and disconnect the negative battery cable. Drain the cooling system.
2. Disconnect the air intake tube and ventilation hose. Remove the air pipe and resonance chamber on 2.6L engine.
3. Disconnect the accelerator cable and coolant hoses. Tag and disconnect the electrical connectors to the solenoid valve, throttle sensor and idle switch.
4. Remove the throttle body.
5. Remove the upper intake manifold brackets.
6. Tag and disconnect the vacuum hoses and PCV hose. Tag and disconnect the intake air thermosensor connector and ground wire.
7. Remove the injector harness bracket and remove the upper intake manifold.
8. Tag and disconnect the vacuum hoses from the lower intake manifold. Disconnect the fuel lines.
9. Remove the fuel supply manifold and the injectors. Remove the injector harness and bracket.
10. Remove the pulsation damper and the intake manifold bracket. Remove the attaching nuts and remove the lower intake manifold.

To install:

11. Clean all gasket mating surfaces.
12. Position a new intake manifold-to-cylinder head gasket and install the lower intake manifold. Tighten the nuts to 14–19 ft. lbs. (19–25 Nm).
13. Install the intake manifold bracket and pulsation damper. Install the injector harness and bracket. Tighten the pulsation damper and injector harness bracket bolts to 69–95 inch lbs. (7.8–11.0 Nm).
14. Install the injectors and the fuel supply manifold. Tighten the fuel supply manifold attaching bolts and tighten to 14–19 ft. lbs. (19–25 Nm).
15. Connect the fuel lines. Connect the vacuum hoses to the lower intake manifold.
16. Position a new gasket and install the upper intake manifold. Tighten the attaching bolts/nuts to 14–19 ft. lbs. (19–25 Nm).
17. Install the injector harness bracket. Connect the ground wire and air thermosensor electrical connector. Connect the PCV hose and the vacuum hoses to the upper intake manifold.
18. Install the upper intake manifold brackets.
19. Position a new gasket and install the throttle body. Tighten the mounting nuts to 14–19 ft. lbs. (19–25 Nm).
20. Connect the electrical connectors at the idle switch, throttle sensor and solenoid valve.
21. Connect the coolant hoses and the accelerator cable. On 2.6L engine, install the air pipe and resonance chamber.
22. Connect the ventilation hose and air intake hose. Connect the negative battery cable.
23. Fill and bleed the cooling system. Run the engine and check for leaks and proper operation.

3.0L Engine

1. Relieve the fuel system pressure and disconnect the negative battery cable. Drain the cooling system.
2. Remove the air intake tube from the throttle body. Disconnect the accelerator cable.
3. Disconnect the throttle sensor connector and the coolant hoses. Remove the throttle body.
4. Tag and disconnect the vacuum hoses. Remove the bypass air control valve and the intake air pipe.
5. Remove the extension manifolds. Remove the upper intake plenum with the shutter valve actuator.
6. Remove the fuel supply manifold and the injectors. Disconnect the coolant hoses.
7. Loosen the lower intake manifold nuts, in sequence, in 2 steps and remove the lower intake manifold.

To install:

8. Clean all gasket mating surfaces.
9. Position new lower intake manifold-to-cylinder head gaskets and install the lower intake manifold.
10. Install the intake manifold washers with the white paint mark upward. Install the nuts and tighten, in sequence, in 2 steps to a maximum torque of 14–19 ft. lbs. (19–25 Nm).
11. Install the injectors and the fuel supply manifold. Tighten the attaching bolts to 14–19 ft. lbs. (19–25 Nm).
12. Connect the coolant hoses.
13. Install a new O-ring on the lower intake manifold and install the upper intake plenum. Apply clean engine oil to new O-rings and install on the extension manifolds. Position new gaskets and install the extension manifolds. Tighten the attaching nuts to 14–19 ft. lbs. (19–25 Nm).
14. Position a new gasket and install the intake air pipe. Install the bypass air control valve. Tighten the attaching bolts/nuts to 14–19 ft. lbs. (19–25 Nm).
15. Position a new gasket and install the throttle body. Tighten the attaching nuts to 14–19 ft. lbs. (19–25 Nm).
16. Connect the coolant and vacuum hoses. Connect the throttle sensor connector and accelerator cable.
17. Adjust the accelerator cable deflection to 0.039–0.118 inch (1–3mm).
18. Connect the air intake tube and the negative battery cable.
19. Fill and bleed the cooling system. Run the engine and check for leaks and proper operation.

4.0L Engine

1. Disconnect the negative battery cable and relieve the fuel system pressure.
2. Remove the air cleaner air intake duct from the throttle body.

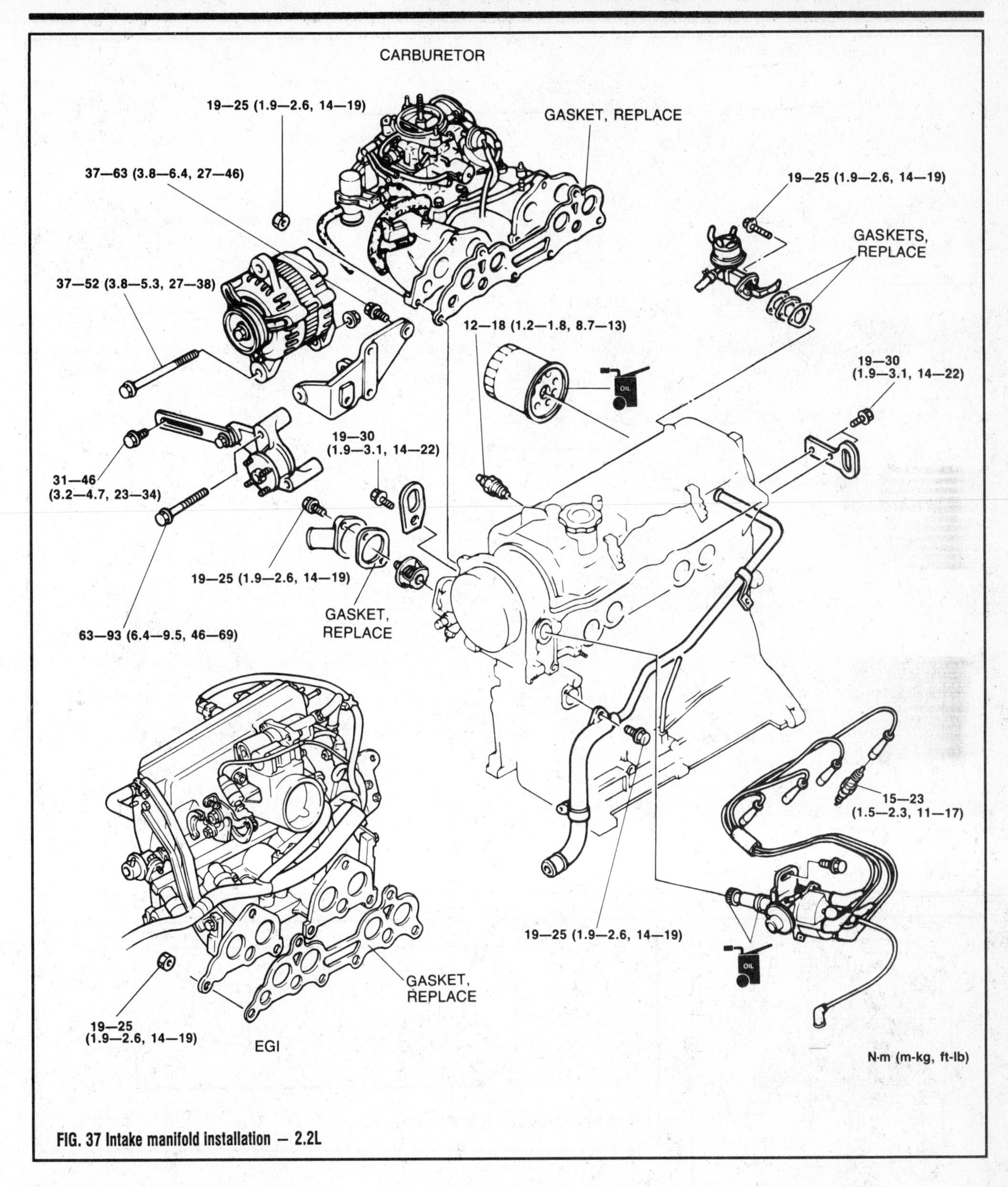

FIG. 37 Intake manifold installation — 2.2L

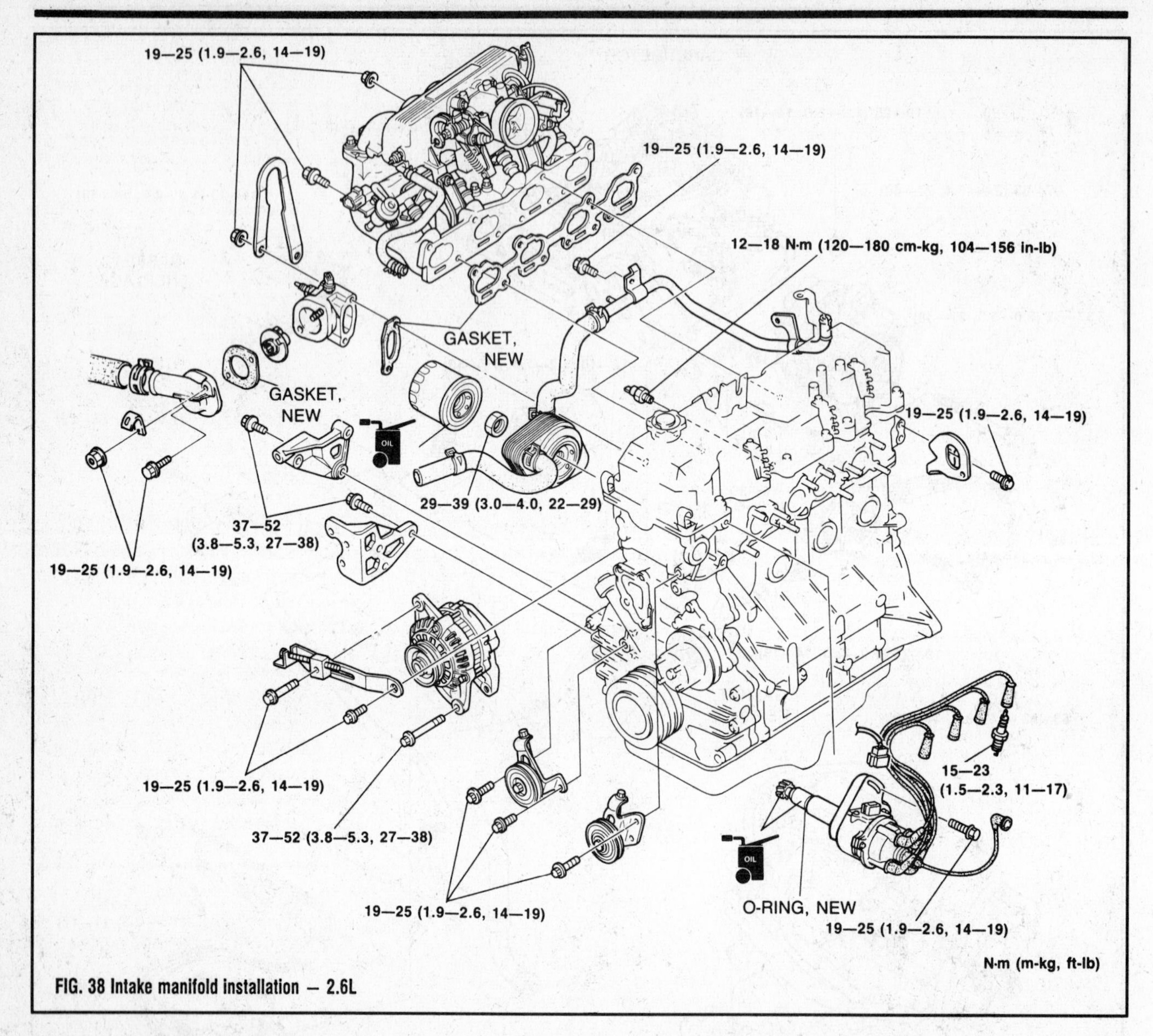

FIG. 38 Intake manifold installation — 2.6L

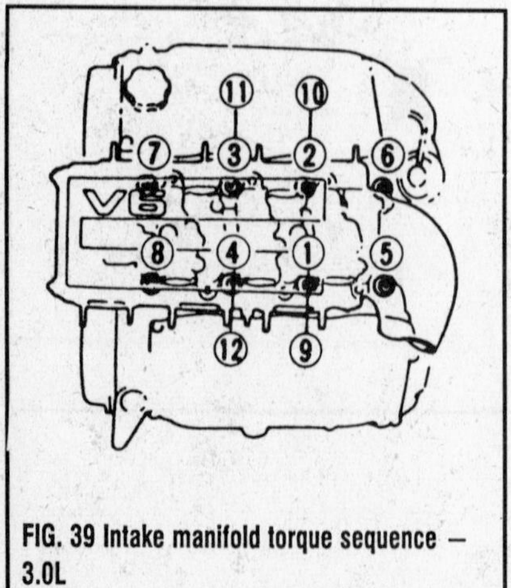

FIG. 39 Intake manifold torque sequence — 3.0L

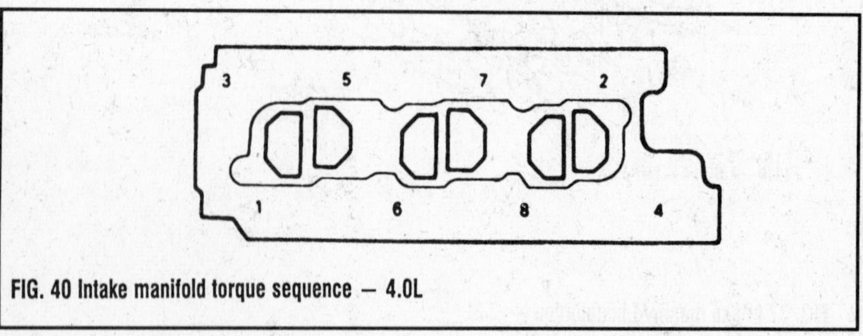

FIG. 40 Intake manifold torque sequence — 4.0L

3. Remove the snow/ice shield and disconnect the throttle cable and bracket assembly.
4. Tag and disconnect the vacuum hoses from the fittings on the upper intake manifold.
5. Tag and disconnect the electrical connectors at the throttle body, upper intake manifold, lower intake manifold and injectors.
6. Disconnect the fuel lines from the fuel supply manifold.
7. Remove the ignition coil and bracket assembly.
8. Remove the mounting nuts and remove the upper intake manifold.
9. Remove the rocker arm covers.
10. Remove the intake manifold attaching bolts and nuts. Tap the manifold lightly with a plastic mallet to break the gasket seal and remove the manifold.

To install:

11. Clean all gasket mating surfaces.
12. Apply silicone sealer to the block and cylinder head mating surfaces at the 4 corners of the lifter valley opening. Install the intake manifold gaskets and again apply sealer to the same locations.
13. Position the intake manifold on the 2 guide studs and install the nuts and bolts hand tight. Tighten the bolts, in sequence, in 4 steps, first to 3–6 ft. lbs. (4–8 Nm), then to 6–11 ft. lbs. (8–15 Nm), then to 11–15 ft. lbs. (15–21 Nm) and finally to 15–18 ft. lbs. (21–25 Nm).
14. Apply silicone sealer to the 4 locations where the intake manifold and the cylinder heads meet. Install the rocker arm covers with new gaskets and tighten evenly to 3–5 ft. lbs. (4–7 Nm). Wait 2 minutes and tighten the bolts again to the same specification.
15. Install the upper intake manifold and tighten the nuts to 15–18 ft. lbs. (20–25 Nm).
16. Install the ignition coil and bracket assembly. Connect the fuel lines to the fuel supply manifold.
17. Connect the electrical connectors at the throttle body, upper intake manifold, lower intake manifold and injectors.
18. Connect the vacuum hoses to the fittings on the upper intake manifold.
19. Install the throttle cable and bracket assembly and the snow/ice shield to the throttle body.
20. Connect the air cleaner air intake duct to the throttle body.
21. Connect the negative battery cable. Fill and bleed the cooling system. Run the engine and check for leaks.

Exhaust Manifold

REMOVAL & INSTALLATION

Pickups w/2.2L

1. Raise and support the truck.
2. Remove the two attaching nuts from the exhaust pipe at the manifold.
3. Remove the manifold attaching nuts.
4. Remove the manifold.
5. Apply a light film of graphite grease to the exhaust manifold mating surfaces before installation.
6. Install the manifold on the studs and install the attaching nuts. Torque the attaching nuts to specifications.
7. Install a new exhaust pipe gasket. Connect the exhaust pipe gasket. Connect the exhaust pipe and torque the nuts to 16–21 ft. lbs.

Pickups w/2.6L (1987-88)

1. Disconnect the negative battery cable.
2. Remove the air cleaner assembly.
3. Remove the belt from the power steering pump.
4. Raise the vehicle and make sure it is supported safely.
5. Remove the exhaust pipe from the manifold.
6. Disconnect the air injection tube assembly from the exhaust manifold and lower the vehicle.
7. Remove the power steering pump assembly and move to one side.
8. Remove the heat cowl from the exhaust manifold.
9. Remove the exhaust manifold retaining nuts and remove the assembly from the vehicle.
10. Remove the carburetor air heater from the manifold.
11. Separate the exhaust manifold from the catalytic converter by removing the retaining screws.
12. Clean gasket material from cylinder head and exhaust manifold gasket surfaces. Check mating surfaces for cracks or distortion.

To install:

13. Install a new gasket between the exhaust manifold and catalytic converter. Install mounting screws and tighten to 24 ft. lbs. (32 N.m).
14. Install the carburetor air heater on manifold and tighten to 80 inch lbs.
15. Lightly coat the new exhaust manifold gasket with sealant (P/N 3419115) or equivalent on cylinder head side.
16. Install the exhaust manifold and mounting nuts. Tighten to 16–21 ft. lbs.
17. Install the heat cowl to manifold and tighten screws to 80 inch lbs.
18. Install the air cleaner support bracket.
19. Install the power steering pump assembly.
20. Install the air injection tube assembly to air pump.
21. Raise the vehicle and install air injection tube assembly to exhaust manifold.
22. Install the exhaust pipe to manifold.
23. Lower the vehicle and install power steering belt.
24. Fill the cooling system.
25. Install the air cleaner assembly.
26. Connect the negative battery cable.

Pickups w/2.6L (1989-92)

1. Disconnect the battery ground.
2. Drain the cooling system.

✻✻ CAUTION

When draining the coolant, keep in mind that cats and dogs are attracted by the ethylene glycol antifreeze, and are quite likely to drink any that is left in an uncovered container or in puddles on the ground. This will prove fatal in sufficient quantity. Always drain the coolant into a sealable container. Coolant should be reused unless it is contaminated or several years old.

3. Remove the oil dipstick tube.
4. It may make the job easier to remove the coolant bypass pipe.
5. Disconnect the exhaust pipe from the manifold.
6. Remove the heat shield.
7. Unbolt and remove the manifold. Discard the gasket.
8. Clean all mating surfaces. Place a new gasket and exhaust manifold in position and loosely install the mounting bolts. After all of the manifold bolts and attached components are loosely installed, secure all mounting bolts. Torque the bolts to 18 ft. lbs.

MPV

1. Disconnect the negative battery cable. Raise and safely support the vehicle.
2. Disconnect the exhaust pipe from the exhaust manifold. If necessary, disconnect the electrical connector from the oxygen sensor.
3. Lower the vehicle.
4. Remove the exhaust manifold insulator, if equipped.
5. If necessary, remove the engine oil dipstick and the dipstick tube.

6. On models with the 3.0L engine, disconnect or remove the exhaust manifold crossover.
7. Remove the exhaust manifold attaching bolts/nuts and remove the exhaust manifold.
8. Clean all mating surfaces. Place a new gasket and exhaust manifold in position and loosely install the mounting bolts. After all of the manifold bolts and attached components are loosely installed, secure all mounting bolts. Tighten the exhaust manifold attaching bolts/nuts to 19 ft. lbs. (25 Nm).

Navajo 4.0L Engine

LEFT SIDE

1. Disconnect the negative battery cable. Remove the oil level indicator tube bracket.
2. Remove the power steering pump hoses, if necessary for working clearance.
3. Remove the exhaust pipe-to-manifold bolts.
4. Unbolt and remove the manifold.
5. Clean and lightly oil all fastener threads.
6. Clean the mating surfaces of the manifold and cylinder head. Position the manifold on the cylinder head and install the fasteners, replace all gaskets, if equipped. Install the remaining removed components. Torque the manifold bolts to 19 ft. lbs.; the exhaust pipe nuts to 20 ft. lbs. TIGHTEN BOTH EXHAUST PIPE RETAINING NUTS IN EQUAL AMOUNTS TO CORRECTLY SEAT INLET PIPE FLANGE.

RIGHT SIDE

1. Drain the cooling system.

⁂ CAUTION

When draining the coolant, keep in mind that cats and dogs are attracted by the ethylene glycol antifreeze, and are quite likely to drink any that is left in an uncovered container or in puddles on the ground. This will prove fatal in sufficient quantity. Always drain the coolant into a sealable container. Coolant should be reused unless it is contaminated or several years old.

2. Remove the heater hose support bracket.
3. Disconnect the heater hoses.
4. Remove the exhaust pipe-to-manifold nuts.
5. Unbolt and remove the manifold.
6. Clean the mating surfaces of the manifold and cylinder head. Position the manifold on the cylinder head and install the fasteners, replace all gaskets, if equipped. Install the remaining removed components. Torque the manifold bolts to 19 ft. lbs.; the exhaust pipe nuts to 20 ft. lbs. TIGHTEN BOTH EXHAUST PIPE RETAINING NUTS IN EQUAL AMOUNTS TO CORRECTLY SEAT INLET PIPE FLANGE.

Radiator

➧ SEE FIGS. 41-49

REMOVAL & INSTALLATION

Pickups

1. Drain the cooling system.

⁂ CAUTION

When draining the coolant, keep in mind that cats and dogs are attracted by the ethelyne glycol antifreeze, and are quite likely to drink any that is left in an uncovered container or in puddles on the ground. This will prove fatal in sufficient quantity. Always drain the coolant into a sealable container. Coolant should be reused unless it is contaminated or several years old.

2. If equipped, remove the fan shroud.
3. Remove the fan. Don't lay the fan, if equipped with a fan clutch, on its side. Fluid will be lost and the fan clutch will have to be replaced.
4. Disconnect the upper and lower radiator hoses.
5. Disconnect the coolant reservoir hose.
6. On trucks with automatic transmission, disconnect the cooler lines.
7. Unbolt and remove the radiator.
8. Install the radiator against the supports and tighten the mounting bolts.
9. Install the hoses on the radiator. Tighten the clamps.
10. Install the fan.
11. If equipped, install the fan shroud.
12. Refill the cooling system with the specified amount and type of coolant. Run the engine and check for leaks.

MPV

1. Drain the cooling system.
2. Remove the fresh air duct.
3. Disconnect the upper and lower radiator hoses.
4. Disconnect the coolant reservoir hose.
5. On trucks with automatic transmission, disconnect the cooler lines.
6. Remove the fan shroud.
7. Remove the fan. Don't lay the fan, if equipped with a fan clutch, on its side. Fluid will be lost and the fan clutch will have to be replaced.
8. Unbolt and remove the radiator.
9. Install the radiator against the supports and tighten the mounting bolts.
10. Install the hoses and cooler lines on the radiator. Tighten the clamps.
11. Install the fan.
12. Install the fan shroud.
13. Refill the cooling system with the specified amount and type of coolant. Run the engine and check for leaks.

Navajo

1. Drain the cooling system. Remove the overflow tube from the coolant recovery bottle and from the radiator.

⁂ CAUTION

When draining the coolant, keep in mind that cats and dogs are attracted by the ethylene glycol antifreeze, and are quite likely to drink any that is left in an uncovered container or in puddles on the ground. This will prove fatal in sufficient quantity. Always drain the coolant into a sealable container. Coolant should be reused unless it is contaminated or several years old.

2. Disconnect the transmission cooling lines from the bottom of the radiator, if so equipped.
3. Remove the retaining bolts at the top of the shroud, and position the shroud over the fan, clear of the radiator.
4. Disconnect the upper and lower hoses from the radiator.
5. Remove the radiator retaining bolts or the upper supports and lift the radiator from the vehicle.
6. Install the radiator in the reverse order of removal. Fill the cooling system and check for leaks.

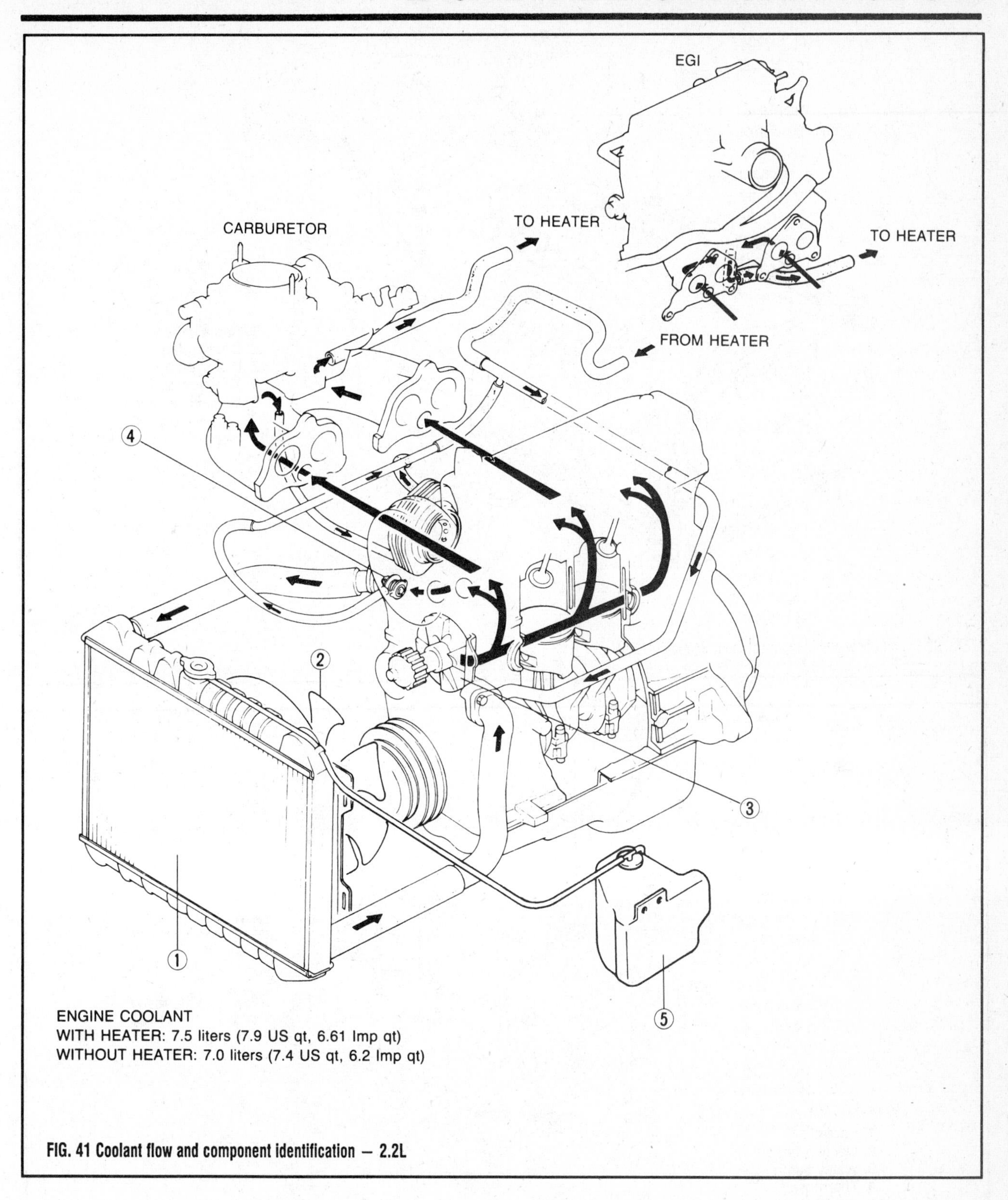

FIG. 41 Coolant flow and component identification – 2.2L

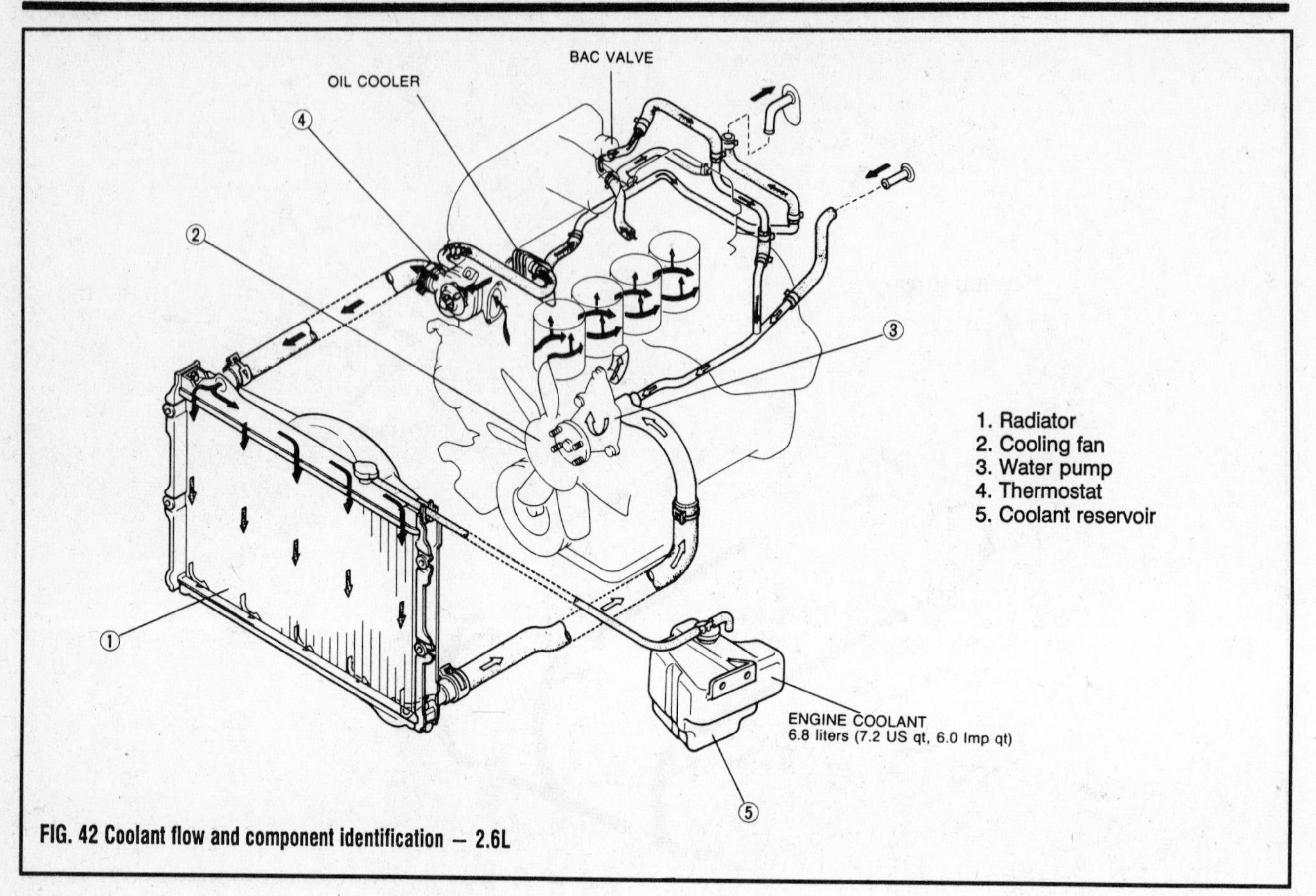

FIG. 42 Coolant flow and component identification – 2.6L

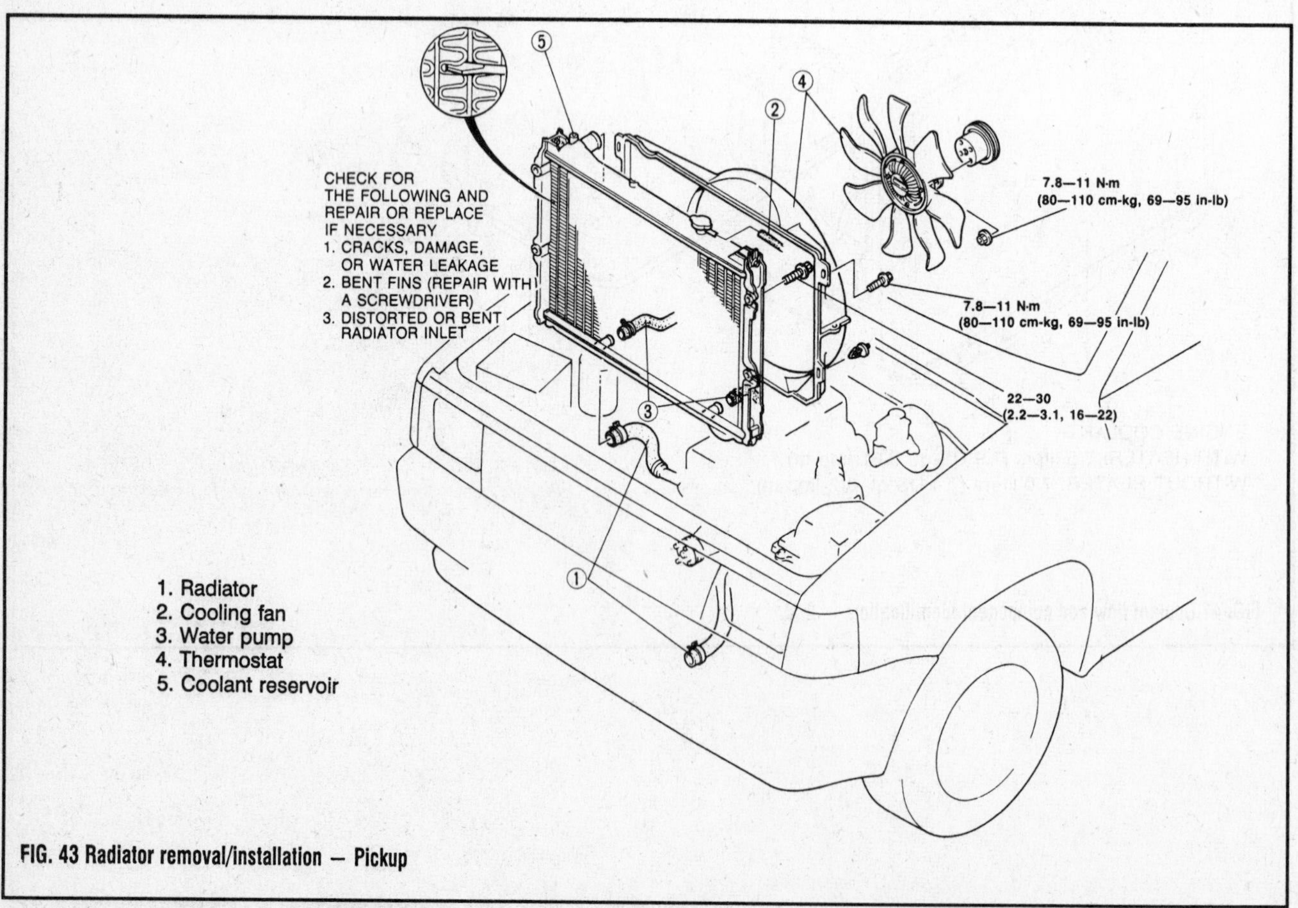

FIG. 43 Radiator removal/installation – Pickup

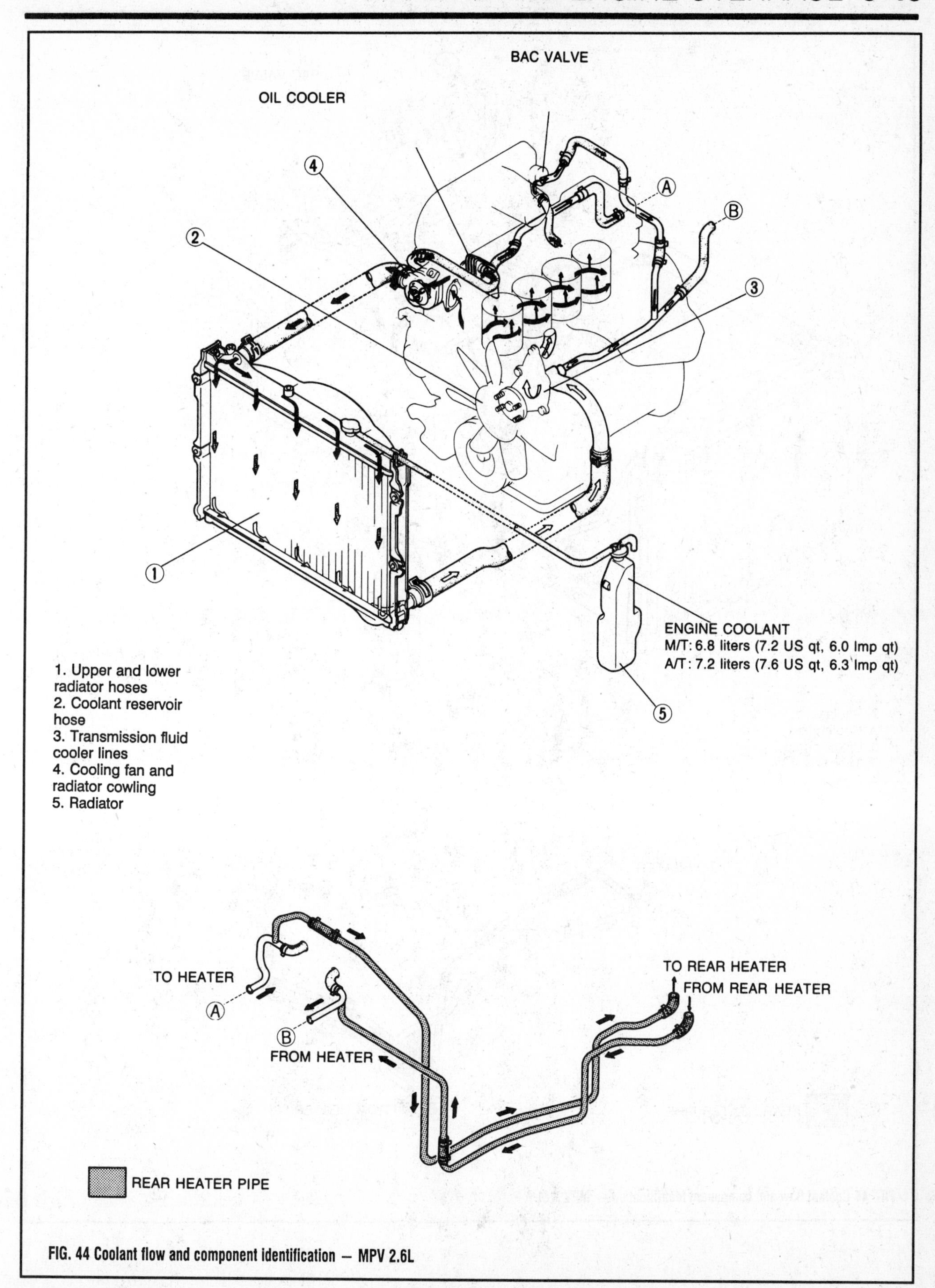

FIG. 44 Coolant flow and component identification – MPV 2.6L

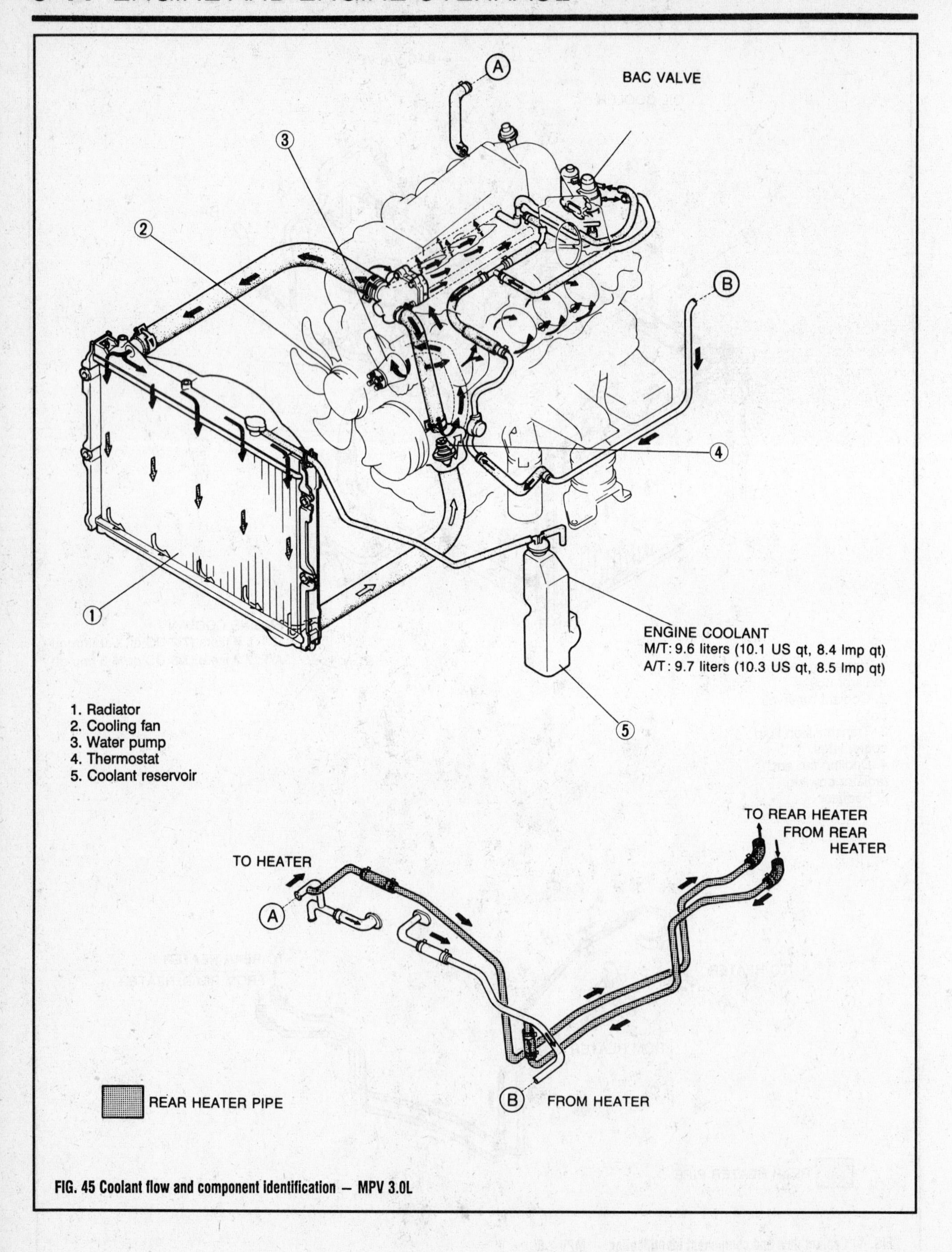

FIG. 45 Coolant flow and component identification — MPV 3.0L

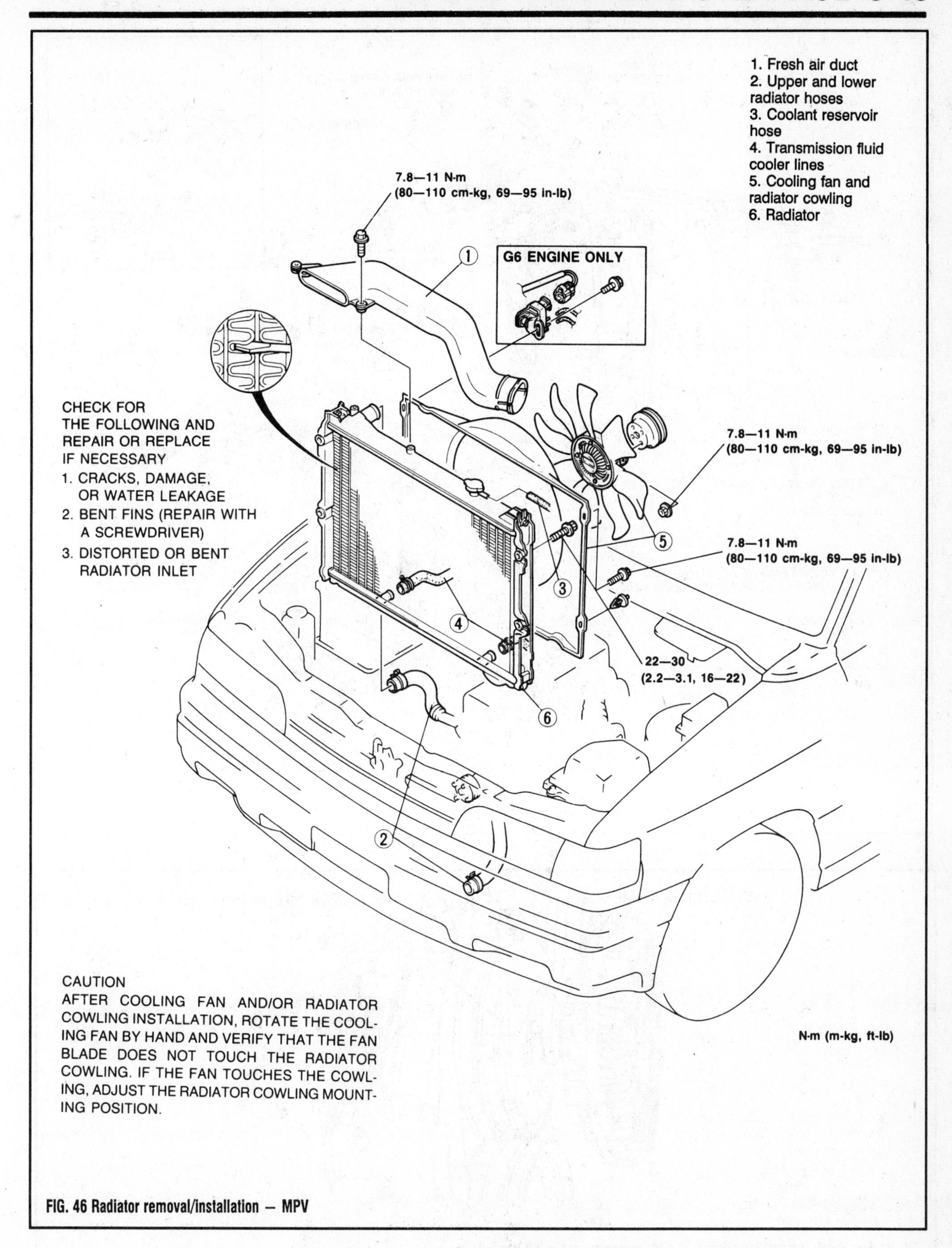
1. Fresh air duct
2. Upper and lower radiator hoses
3. Coolant reservoir hose
4. Transmission fluid cooler lines
5. Cooling fan and radiator cowling
6. Radiator
7.8—11 N·m (80—110 cm-kg, 69—95 in-lb)
G6 ENGINE ONLY
CHECK FOR THE FOLLOWING AND REPAIR OR REPLACE IF NECESSARY
1. CRACKS, DAMAGE, OR WATER LEAKAGE
2. BENT FINS (REPAIR WITH A SCREWDRIVER)
3. DISTORTED OR BENT RADIATOR INLET
7.8—11 N·m (80—110 cm-kg, 69—95 in-lb)
7.8—11 N·m (80—110 cm-kg, 69—95 in-lb)
22—30 (2.2—3.1, 16—22)
CAUTION
AFTER COOLING FAN AND/OR RADIATOR COWLING INSTALLATION, ROTATE THE COOLING FAN BY HAND AND VERIFY THAT THE FAN BLADE DOES NOT TOUCH THE RADIATOR COWLING. IF THE FAN TOUCHES THE COWLING, ADJUST THE RADIATOR COWLING MOUNTING POSITION.
N·m (m-kg, ft-lb)

FIG. 46 Radiator removal/installation — MPV

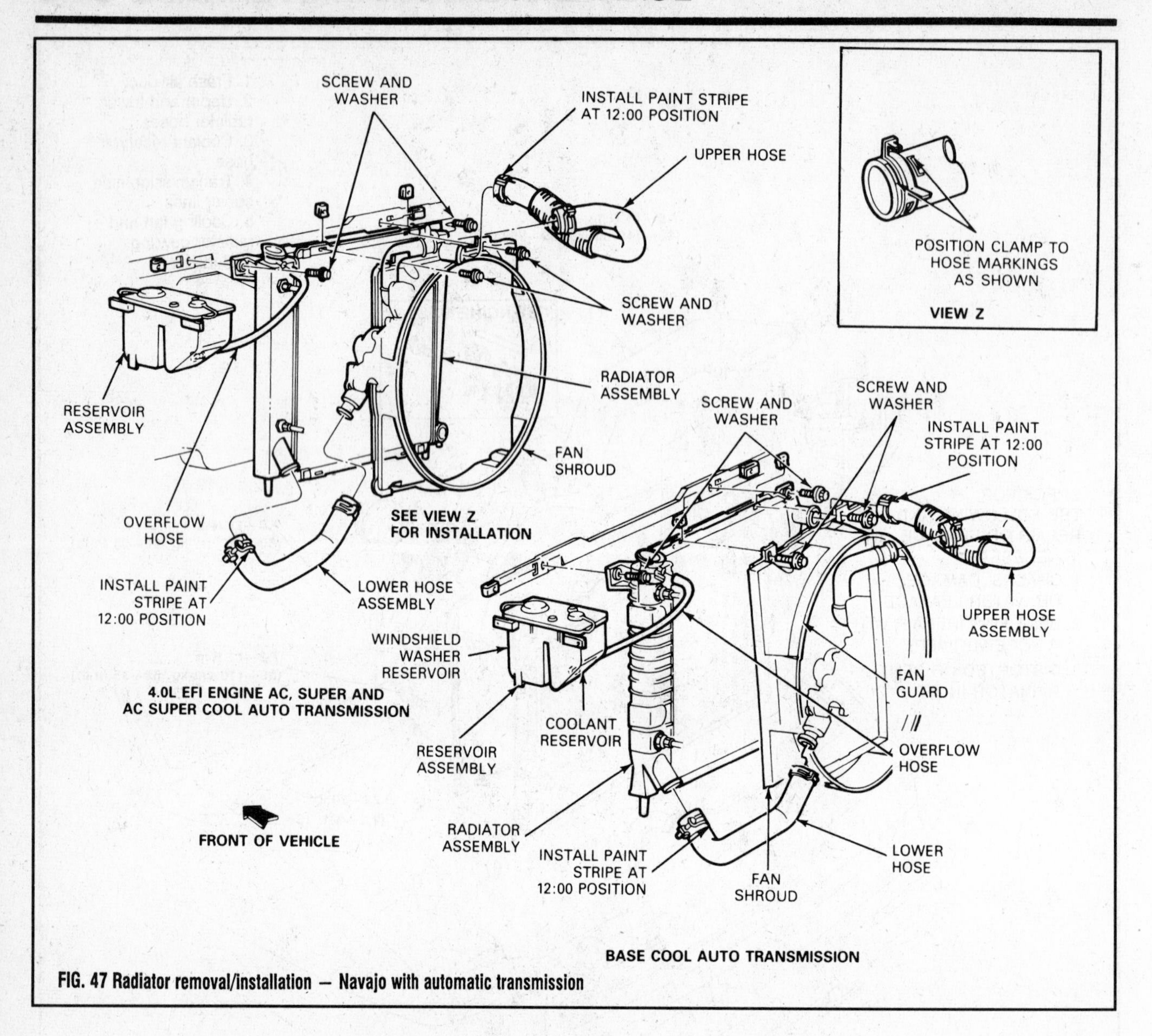

FIG. 47 Radiator removal/installation — Navajo with automatic transmission

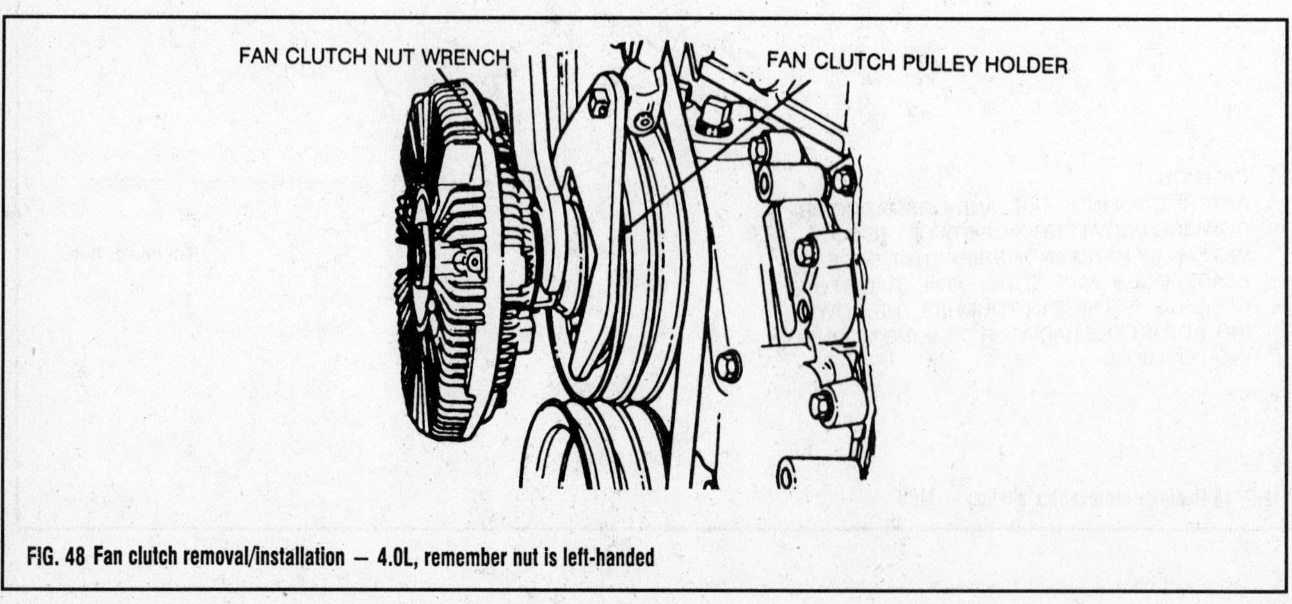

FIG. 48 Fan clutch removal/installation — 4.0L, remember nut is left-handed

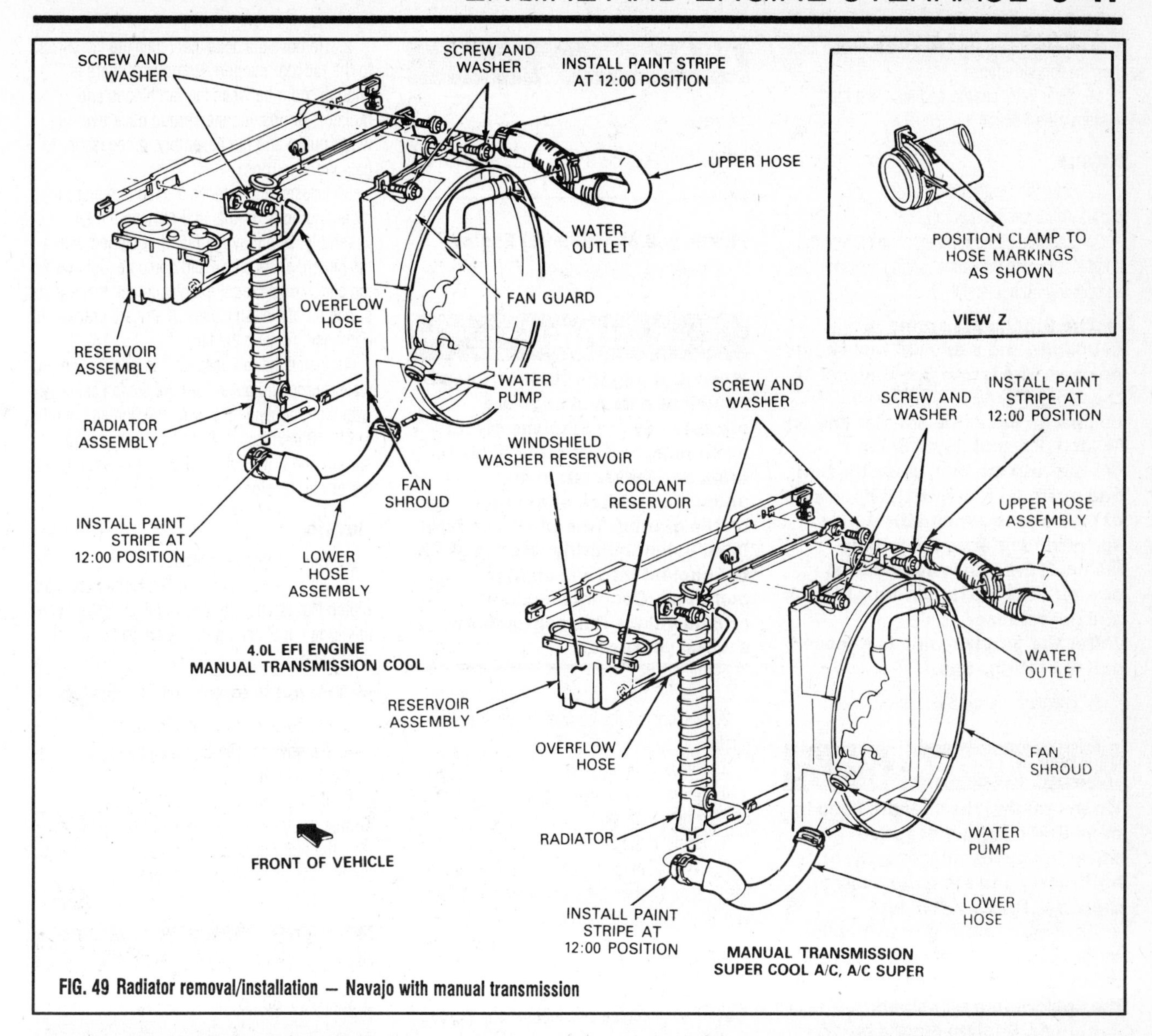

FIG. 49 Radiator removal/installation — Navajo with manual transmission

Air Conditioning Condenser

REMOVAL & INSTALLATION

Pickups

1. Disconnect the negative battery cable. Safely discharge the refrigerant system. See Section 1.
2. Remove the air cleaner assembly.
3. As required, remove the front grille, air seal cover and side lamps. Remove the clamps and the hood lock brace, if installed.
4. Disconnect and plug the condenser inlet, outlet and liquid lines to prevent the entry of moisture and dirt.
5. Remove the necessary components (such as the cooling fan) in order to gain access to the condenser mounting bolts.
6. Remove the condenser mounting bolts. Remove the condenser from the vehicle.

To install:

7. Lower the condenser into the vehicle and secure it with the mounting bolts. Reinstall all other parts.
8. Connect the suction, discharge and liquid lines to the condenser.
9. Install the hood lock brace and the clamps, if removed. Install the air seal and the front grille and side lamps.

➡ **If a new condenser was installed, add approximately 30cc of clean compressor oil to the unit.**

10. Install the air cleaner assembly. Connect the negative battery cable.
11. Evacuate, charge and test the system as described in Section 1.

MPV

1. Disconnect the battery ground cable.
2. Discharge the refrigerant system. See Section 1.
3. Remove the lower grille and radiator grille.
4. Remove the hood lock.
5. Disconnect the condenser fan wires.
6. Unbolt and remove the fan(s).
7. Using a back-up wrench, disconnect the refrigerant lines at the condenser. Cap all openings at once!
8. Unbolt and remove the condenser.
9. Installation is the reverse of removal. Add 30cc of refrigerant oil to a new condenser. Torque the line connections to 16 ft. lbs., using a back-up wrench. On models with the 2.6L (1989-92) engine and automatic transmission,

install the right side fan first, then the hood lock, then the left side fan.

10. Evacuate, charge and leak-test the system. See Section 1.

Navajo

1. Have the system discharged by a professional service person.
2. Disconnect the refrigerant lines from the condenser using the proper spring lock tool. Cap all opening immediately!

➡ The fittings are spring-lock couplings and a special tool should be used. The larger opening end of the tool is for 1/2 inch (12.7mm) discharge lines; the smaller end for 3/8 inch (9.5mm) liquid lines.
To operate the tool, close the tool and push the tool into the open side of the cage to expand the garter spring and release the female fitting. If the tool is not inserted straight, the garter spring will cock and not release.
After the garter spring is released, pull the fittings apart.

3. Drain the cooling system.

✲✲ CAUTION

When draining the coolant, keep in mind that cats and dogs are attracted by the ethylene glycol antifreeze, and are quite likely to drink any that is left in an uncovered container or in puddles on the ground. This will prove fatal in sufficient quantity. Always drain the coolant into a sealable container. Coolant should be reused unless it is contaminated or several years old.

4. Disconnect the upper radiator hose.
5. Remove the bolts retaining the ends of the radiator upper support to the side supports.
6. Carefully pull the top edge of the radiator rearward and remove the condenser upper support.
7. Lift out the condenser.
8. If a new condenser is being installed, add 1 fluid oz. of new refrigerant oil to the new condenser. Installation is the reverse of removal. Always use new O-rings coated with clean refrigerant oil on the line fittings. Charge and leak test the system. See Section 1.

Oil Cooler

REMOVAL & INSTALLATION

Pickup w/2.6L (1989-92) Engine

1. Drain the cooling system.

✲✲ CAUTION

When draining the coolant, keep in mind that cats and dogs are attracted by the ethelyne glycol antifreeze, and are quite likely to drink any that is left in an uncovered container or in puddles on the ground. This will prove fatal in sufficient quantity. Always drain the coolant into a sealable container. Coolant should be reused unless it is contaminated or several years old.

2. Disconnect the coolant hoses at the oil cooler.
3. Remove the oil filter.
4. Remove the nut securing the cooler to the oil filter mounting stud.
5. Remove the cooler.
6. Installation is the reverse of removal. Coat the O-rings on the filter and cooler with clean engine oil prior to installation.

MPV w/2.6L (1989-92)

1. Drain the cooling system.
2. Disconnect the coolant hoses at the oil cooler.
3. Remove the oil filter.
4. Remove the nut securing the cooler to the oil filter mounting stud.
5. Remove the cooler.
6. Installation is the reverse of removal. Coat the O-rings on the filter and cooler with clean engine oil prior to installation.

Engine Fan

REMOVAL & INSTALLATION

Except Navajo

1. Loosen and remove the drive belts.
2. Remove the bolts that retain the fan shroud to the radiator support. Remove (if there is enough room between the fan blades and radiator) or position the shroud back over the water pump and fan assembly, if necessary to gain working room.
3. Loosen and remove the fan to water pump mounting bolts or nuts and remove the fan assembly. Don't lay the fan, if equipped with a fan clutch, on its side. Fluid could be lost and the fan clutch might require replacement. Inspect the condition of the fan blades, if any are cracked or damaged, replace the fan.
4. Install the fan assembly in position on the water pump and pulley. Secure the fan assembly with the mounting nuts or bolts. Tighten the nuts to 69–70 inch lbs. (7.8 – 11 Nm). Install the shroud and drive belts. Adjust the drive belts to the proper tension.

Navajo

1. Remove the fan shroud.
2. Using a Fan Clutch Pulley Holder and Fan Clutch Nut Wrench, or their equivalents, loosen the large nut attaching the clutch to the water pump hub.

➡ The nut is loosened clockwise.

3. Remove the fan/clutch assembly.
4. Remove the fan-to-clutch bolts.

To install:

5. Installation is the reverse of removal. Torque the fan-to-clutch bolts to 55–70 inch lbs.; the hub nut to 50–100 ft. lbs. Don't forget, the hub is tightened counterclockwise.

Water Pump

➧ SEE FIGS. 50-53

REMOVAL & INSTALLATION

Pickup w/2.2L

➡ Use special tool No. 49E301060 or equivalent on the engine flywheel gear to stop the engine from rotating during removal and installation of the crankshaft pulley.

1. Drain the cooling system.

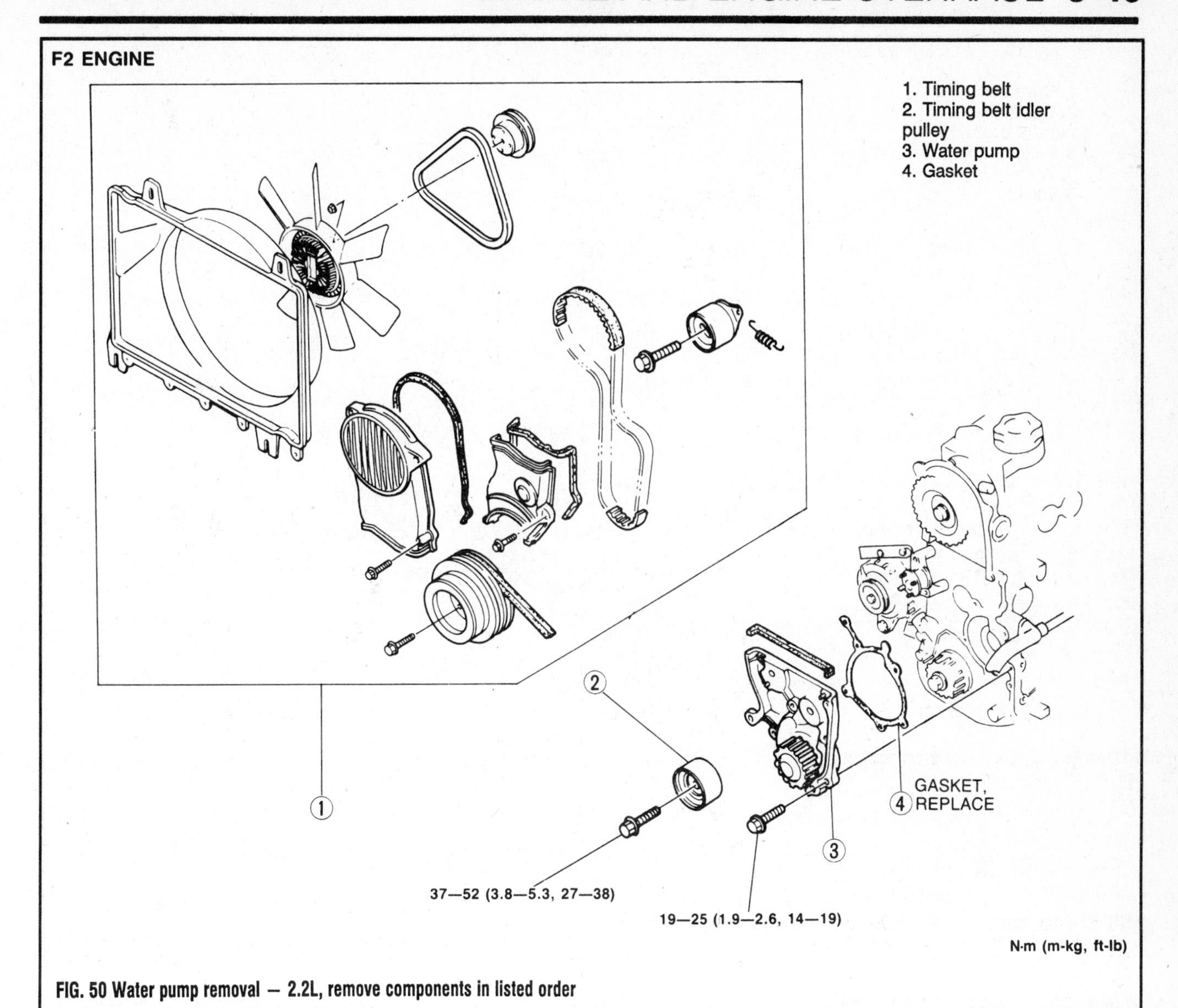

FIG. 50 Water pump removal — 2.2L, remove components in listed order

CAUTION

When draining the coolant, keep in mind that cats and dogs are attracted by the ethylene glycol antifreeze, and are quite likely to drink any that is left in an uncovered container or in puddles on the ground. This will prove fatal in sufficient quantity. Always drain the coolant into a sealable container. Coolant should be reused unless it is contaminated or several years old.

2. Disconnect the negative battery cable.
3. Remove the alternator belt.
4. Remove the power steering pump belt.
5. Remove the upper and the lower timing belt covers.
6. Turn the crankshaft to position the **A** mark on the camshaft pulley with the mark on the housing.
7. Remove the crankshaft pulley mounting bolts and the pulley.
8. Remove the tensioner pulley lock bolt, the pulley and the spring.
9. Remove the water inlet pipe from the water pump.
10. Remove the water pump retaining bolts. Remove the water pump from its mounting.
11. Thoroughly clean the mounting surfaces of the pump and engine.
12. Install the components in the reverse order. Install the timing belt and be sure the timing mark on the timing belt pulley is aligned with the matching mark. Make sure that the mark (A) of the camshaft pulley is aligned with the timing mark. If it is not, turn the camshaft to align it.
13. Install the timing belt tensioner and spring. Temporarily secure it as the spring is fully extended.
14. Loosen the tensioner lock bolt. Turn the crankshaft twice in the direction of rotation. Align the timing marks. Tighten the timing belt tensioner lock bolt to 28–38 ft. lbs. Check the timing belt tension. The timing belt deflection should be 11-13mm (0.43-0.51 inch) at 22 lbs.
15. Use new O-rings and gaskets when installing the pump. Use a new O-ring and 3 rubber seals. Fill the cooling system and check the timing.

Pickup w/2.6L (1987-88)

1. Drain the cooling system.

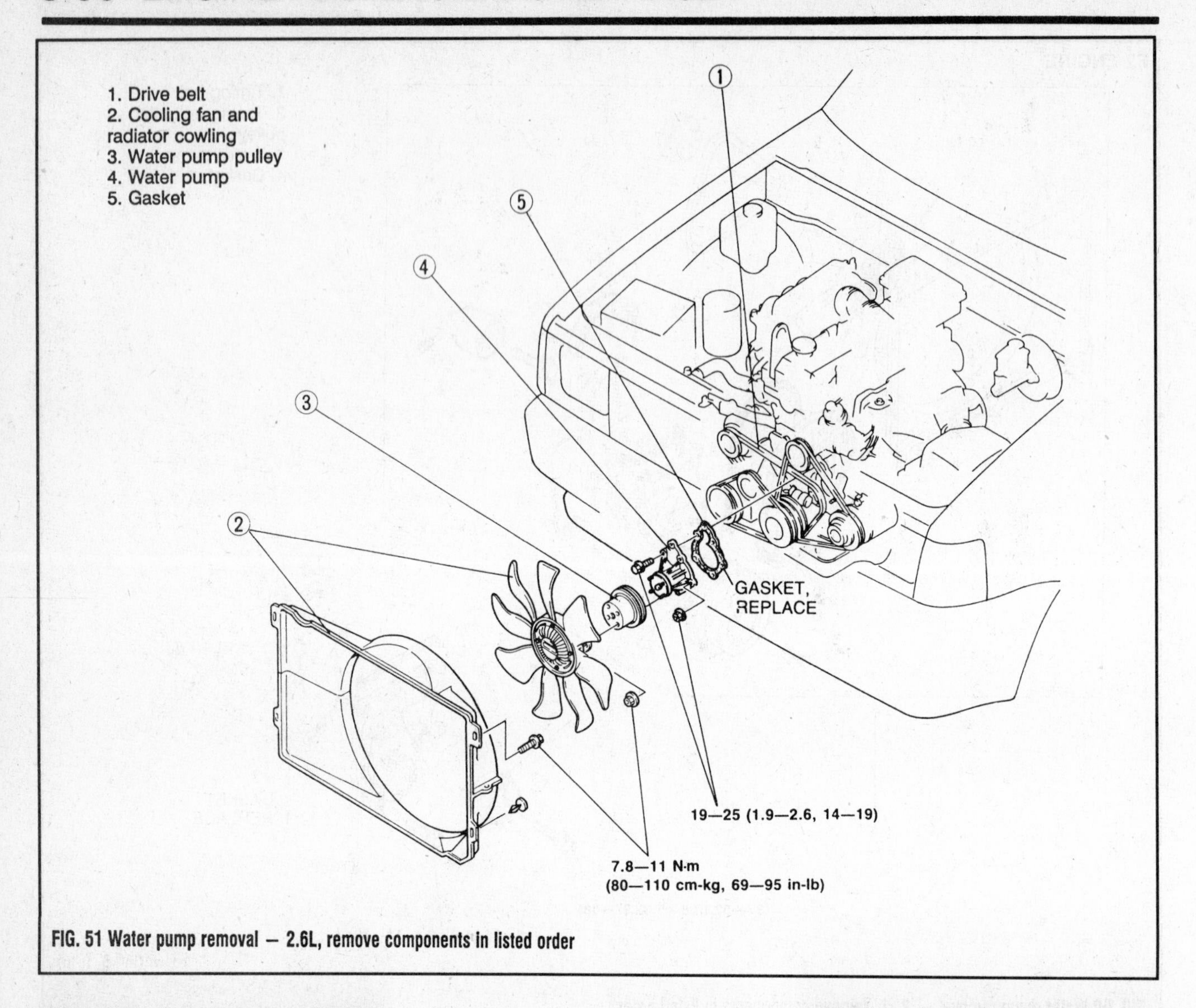

FIG. 51 Water pump removal — 2.6L, remove components in listed order

CAUTION

When draining the coolant, keep in mind that cats and dogs are attracted by the ethylene glycol antifreeze, and are quite likely to drink any that is left in an uncovered container or in puddles on the ground. This will prove fatal in sufficient quantity. Always drain the coolant into a sealable container. Coolant should be reused unless it is contaminated or several years old.

2. Remove the radiator hose, by-pass hose and heater hose from the water pump.
3. Remove the drive pulley shield.
4. Remove the locking screw and pivot screws.
5. Remove the drive belt and water pump from the engine.
6. Install a new O-ring gasket in O-ring groove of pump body assembly to cylinder block.
7. Position the water pump assembly against the engine and install pivot screws and locking screw finger tight.
8. Install the water pump drive belt and adjust to specification. New belt 8mm (0.3 inch) deflection, used belt 9mm (0.35 inch) deflection.
9. Install drive belt pulley cover.
10. Install the radiator hose, by-pass hose and heater hose.
11. Fill the cooling system.

Pickup w/2.6L (1989-92)

1. Disconnect the battery ground.
2. Drain the cooling system.

CAUTION

When draining the coolant, keep in mind that cats and dogs are attracted by the ethylene glycol antifreeze, and are quite likely to drink any that is left in an uncovered container or in puddles on the ground. This will prove fatal in sufficient quantity. Always drain the coolant into a sealable container. Coolant should be reused unless it is contaminated or several years old.

3. Remove the accessory drive belts.
4. Remove the fan and shroud.
5. Remove the water pump pulley.
6. Unbolt and remove the water pump.
7. Thoroughly clean the gasket mounting surfaces.

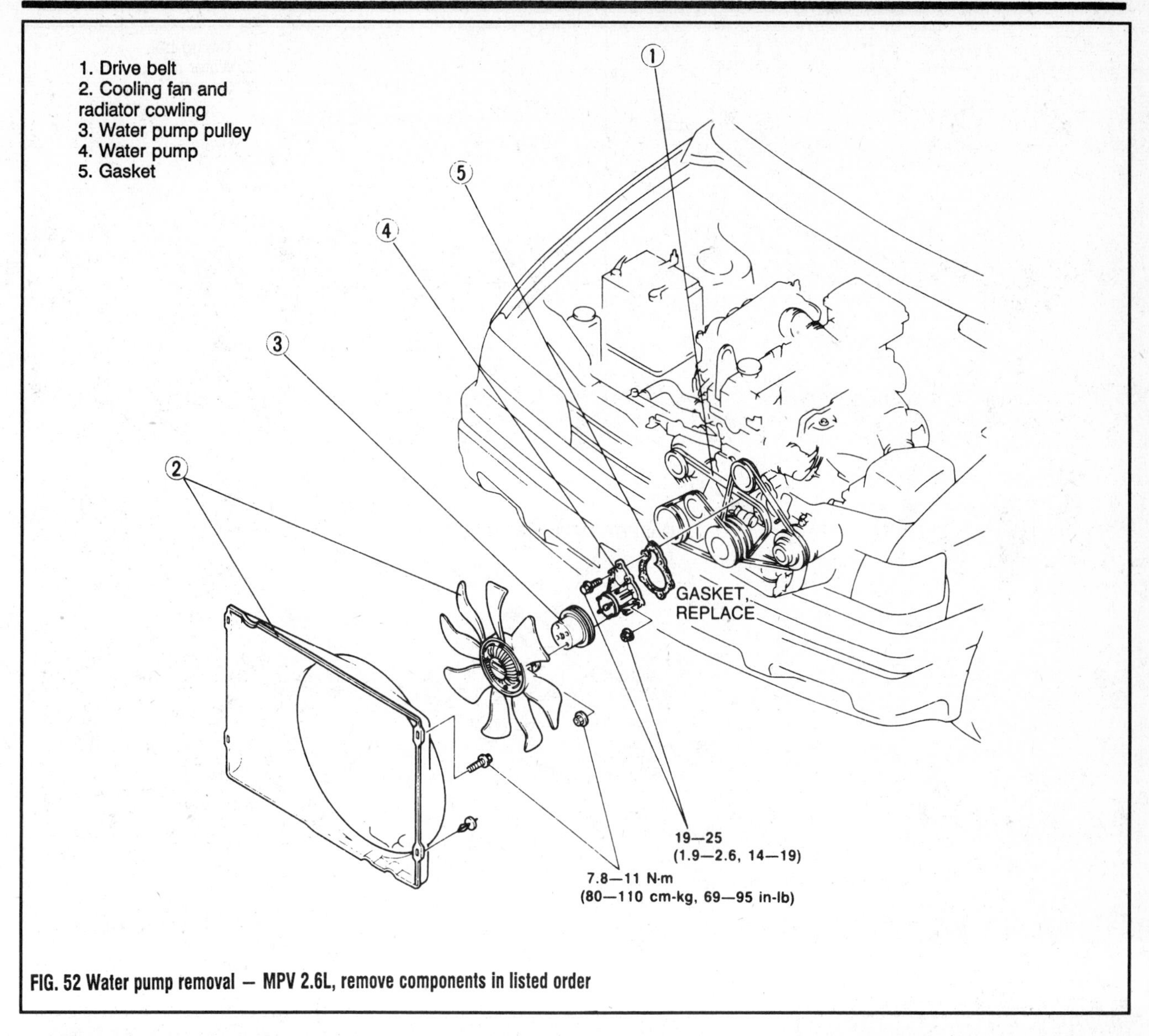

FIG. 52 Water pump removal — MPV 2.6L, remove components in listed order

8. Using a new gasket coated with sealer, position the water pump on the engine. Tighten the bolts to 19 ft. lbs.
9. Install all the remaining parts.
10. Fill the cooling system.
11. Run the engine and check for leaks.

MPV w/2.6L (1989-92)

1. Disconnect the battery ground.
2. Drain the cooling system.
3. Remove the accessory drive belts.
4. Remove the fan and shroud.
5. Remove the water pump pulley.
6. Unbolt and remove the water pump.
7. Thoroughly clean the gasket mounting surfaces.
8. Using a new gasket coated with sealer, position the water pump on the engine. Tighten the bolts to 19 ft. lbs.
9. Install all the remaining parts.
10. Fill the cooling system.
11. Run the engine and check for leaks.

MPV w/3.0L

1. Position the engine at TDC on the compression stroke.
2. Properly relieve the fuel system pressure.
3. Disconnect the negative battery cable.
4. Remove the air cleaner assembly.
5. Drain the cooling system.
6. Remove the spark plug wires.
7. Remove the fresh air duct assembly.
8. Remove the cooling fan and radiator cowling.
9. Remove the drive belts.
10. Remove the air conditioning compressor idler pulley. If necessary, remove the compressor and position it to the side.
11. Remove the crankshaft pulley and baffle plate.
12. Remove the coolant bypass hose.
13. Remove the upper radiator hose.
14. Remove the timing belt cover assembly retaining bolts.
15. Remove the timing belt cover assembly and gasket.
16. Turn the crankshaft to align the mating marks of the pulleys.
17. Remove the upper idler pulley.
18. Remove the timing belt. If reusing the belt be sure to mark the direction of rotation.
19. Remove the timing belt auto tensioner.
20. Unbolt and remove the water pump. Discard the gasket.
21. Thoroughly clean the mating surfaces of the pump and engine.

To install:

22. Position the pump and a new gasket, coated with sealer, on the engine. Torque the bolts to 19 ft. lbs.
23. Refer to "Timing Belt Installation" procedures later in this Section. To install the

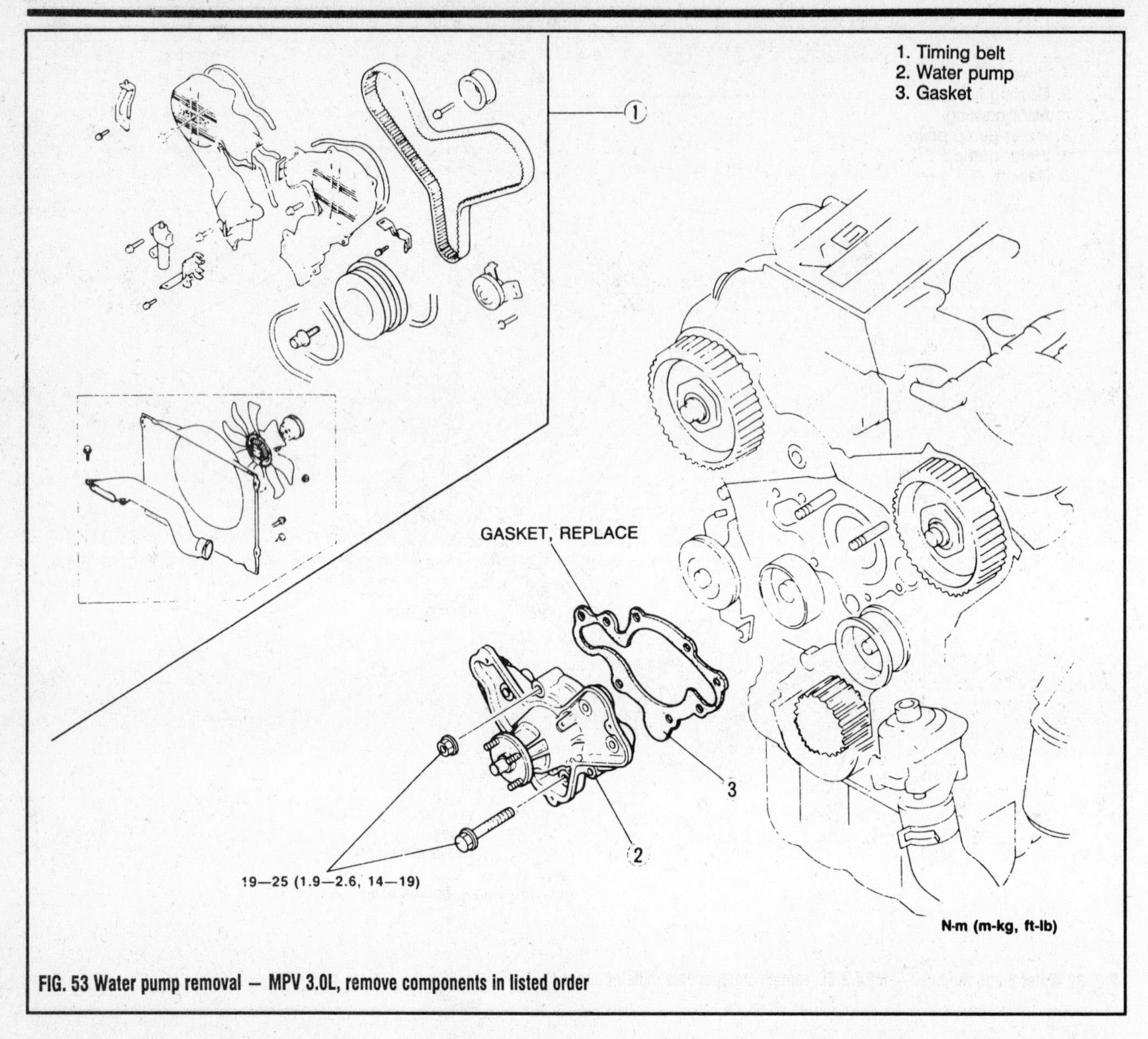

FIG. 53 Water pump removal – MPV 3.0L, remove components in listed order

timing belt, first the automatic tensioner must be loaded. To load the tensioner, place a flat washer on the bottom of the tensioner body to prevent damage to the body and position the unit on an arbor press. Press the rod into the tensioner body. Do not use more than 2,000 lbs of pressure. Once the rod is fully inserted into the body, insert a suitable L-shaped pin or a small Allen wrench through the body and the rod to hold the rod in place. Remove the unit from the press and install onto the block and torque the mounting bolt to 14–19 ft. lbs. Leave the pin in place, it will be removed later.

24. Make sure that all the timing marks are aligned properly. With the upper idler pulley removed, hang the timing belt on each pulley in the proper order. Install the upper idler pulley and torque the mounting bolt to 27–38 ft. lbs. Rotate the crankshaft twice in the normal direction of rotation to align all the timing marks.

25. Make sure all the marks are aligned correctly. If not, repeat Step 24.

26. Remove the pin from the auto tensioner. Again turn the crankshaft twice in the normal direction of rotation and make sure that all the timing marks are aligned properly.

27. Check the timing belt deflection by applying 22 lbs. of force. If the deflection is not 0.20–0.28 inch (5.0-7.0mm), repeat the adjustment procedure.

➡ Excessive belt deflection is caused by auto tensioner failure or an excessively stretched timing belt.

28. Install the timing belt cover assembly and new gasket.

29. Install the timing belt cover assembly retaining bolts.

30. Install the upper radiator hose.

31. Install the coolant bypass hose.

32. Install the crankshaft pulley and baffle plate.

33. Install the compressor.

34. Install the air conditioning compressor idler pulley.

35. Install and adjust the drive belts.

36. Install the cooling fan and radiator cowling.

37. Install the fresh air duct assembly.

38. Install the spark plug wires.

39. Fill the cooling system.

40. Install the air cleaner assembly.

41. Connect the negative battery cable.

4.0L Engine

1. Drain the cooling system.

CAUTION

When draining the coolant, keep in mind that cats and dogs are attracted by the ethylene glycol antifreeze, and are quite likely to drink any that is left in an uncovered container or in puddles on the ground. This will prove fatal in sufficient quantity. Always drain the coolant into a sealable container. Coolant should be reused unless it is contaminated or several years old.

2. Remove the lower radiator hose.
3. Disconnect the heater hose at the pump.
4. Remove the fan and fan clutch assembly. You'll have to hold the pulley while loosening the fan clutch nut. There is a tool made for this purpose which will make the job easier.

➡ The nut has left-hand threads. It is removed by turning it clockwise.

5. Loosen the alternator mounting bolts and remove the belt. On vehicles with air conditioning, remove the alternator and bracket.
6. Remove the water pump pulley.
7. Remove the attaching bolts and remove the water pump.

To Install:

8. Clean the mounting surfaces of the pump and front cover thoroughly. Remove all traces of gasket material.
9. Apply adhesive gasket sealer to both sides of a new gasket and place the gasket on the pump.
10. Position the pump on the cover and install the bolts finger-tight. When all bolts are in place, torque them to 72–108 inch lbs. (6–9 ft. lbs.).
11. Install the pulley.
12. On vehicles with air conditioning, install the alternator and bracket.
13. Install and adjust the drive belt.
14. Connect the hoses and tighten the clamps.
15. Install the fan and clutch assembly. Tighten the nut to 50–100 ft. lbs.

➡ The nut is tightened counterclockwise.

16. Fill and bleed the cooling system. Start the engine and check for leaks.

Cylinder Head

➧ SEE FIGS. 54-63

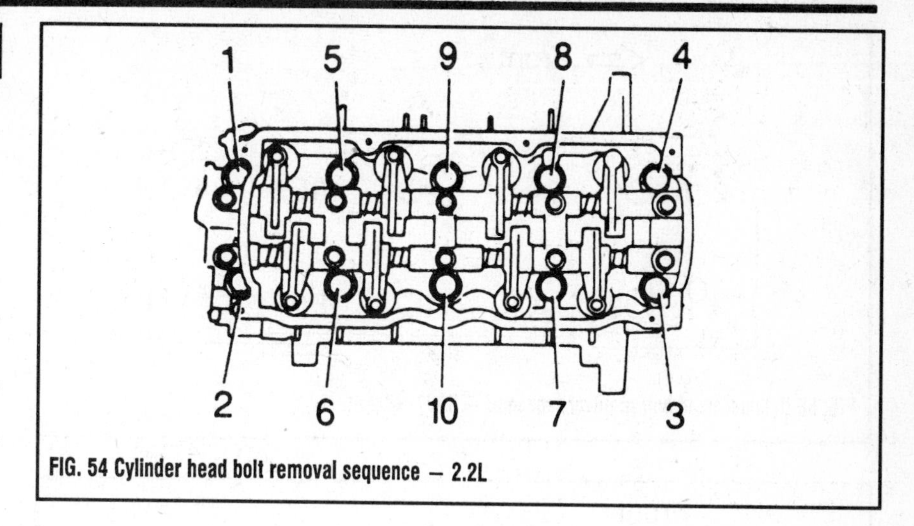

FIG. 54 Cylinder head bolt removal sequence — 2.2L

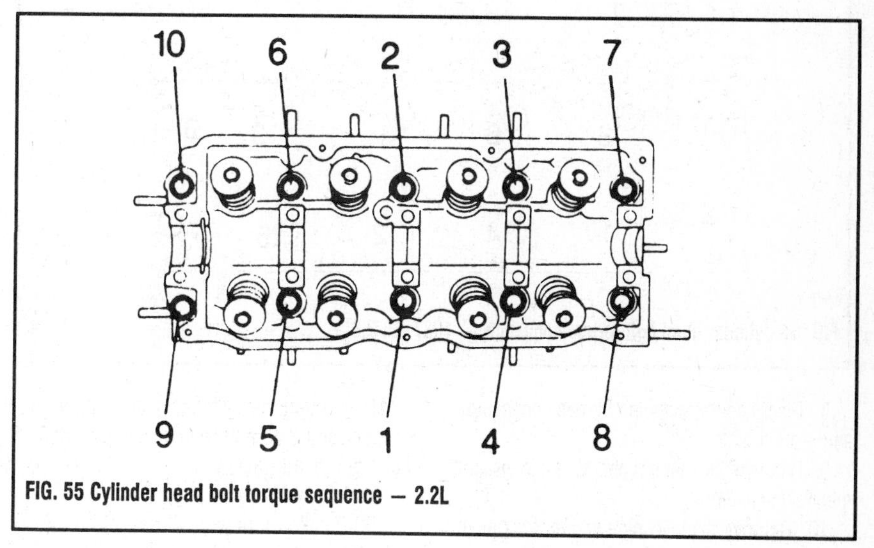

FIG. 55 Cylinder head bolt torque sequence — 2.2L

REMOVAL & INSTALLATION

Pickup w/2.2L

1. Relieve the fuel system pressure if an injected model. Disconnect the negative battery cable and drain the cooling system.

CAUTION

When draining the coolant, keep in mind that cats and dogs are attracted by the ethylene glycol antifreeze, and are quite likely to drink any that is left in an uncovered container or in puddles on the ground. This will prove fatal in sufficient quantity. Always drain the coolant into a sealable container. Coolant should be reused unless it is contaminated or several years old.

2. Disconnect the spark plug wires and remove the spark plugs.
3. Disconnect the accelerator cable. If equipped with automatic transmission, disconnect the throttle cable.
4. Remove the air intake pipe.
5. Remove the air cleaner and fuel hose. Cover the fuel hose to prevent leakage, if equipped with a carburetor. If injected, remove the air intake hose. If equipped with a carburetor, remove the fuel pump.

CAUTION

Never smoke when working around gasoline! Avoid all sources of sparks or ignition. Gasoline vapors are EXTREMELY volatile!

6. Remove the upper radiator hose, water by-pass hose, heater hose, and brake vacuum hose.
7. Remove the 3-way and EGR solenoid valve assemblies.

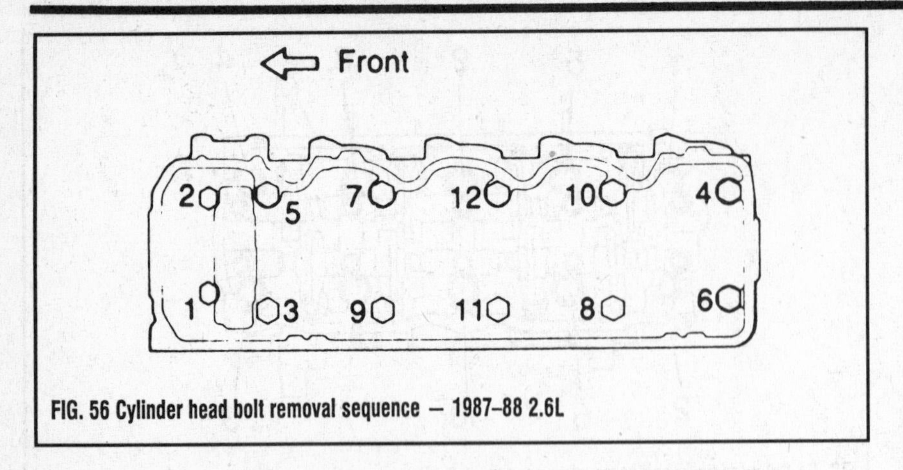

FIG. 56 Cylinder head bolt removal sequence — 1987–88 2.6L

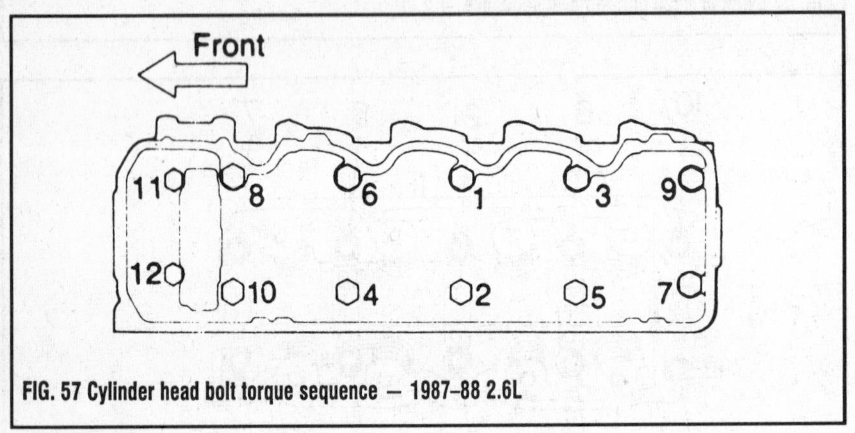

FIG. 57 Cylinder head bolt torque sequence — 1987–88 2.6L

8. Disconnect the engine harness connector and ground wire.
9. Remove the vacuum chamber and exhaust manifold insulator.
10. Remove the EGR pipe and exhaust pipe.
11. Remove the exhaust manifold.
12. Remove the intake manifold bracket and the intake manifold.
13. Remove the distributor.
14. Loosen the air conditioning compressor and bracket, position it off to the side and tie it out of the way. Do not disconnect the refrigerant lines!
15. Remove the upper timing belt cover and the timing belt tensioner spring.
16. To remove the timing belt, perform the following:
a. Rotate the crankshaft so that the **1** on the camshaft pulley is aligned with the timing mark on the front housing.
b. When timing marks are aligned, loosen the timing belt tensioner lock bolt. Pull the tensioner as far out as will go and then temporarily tighten the lock bolt to hold it there.
c. Lift the timing belt from the camshaft pulley and position it out of the way.
17. Remove the cylinder head cover and cover gasket.
18. Loosen the cylinder head bolts in the proper sequence and remove the cylinder head and head gasket.

To install:

19. Position a new head gasket on the cylinder block and install the cylinder head. Apply oil to the threads and seat faces of the cylinder head bolts and install.
20. Tighten the cylinder head bolts in 2–3 steps in the proper sequence. The final torque specification is 59–64 ft. lbs. (80–86 Nm).
21. Apply silicone sealer to each side of the front and rear camshaft bearing caps where the cap meets the cylinder head. Install the rocker arm cover and tighten the bolts to 26–35 inch lbs. (2.9–3.9 Nm).
22. Install the timing belt and tensioner. Install the timing belt front cover.
23. Install the intake and exhaust manifolds.
24. Install the upper radiator and water by-pass hoses. If carburetor equipped, install the secondary air pipe.
25. Install the distributor. Install the spark plugs and connect the spark plug wires.
26. Connect all vacuum hoses and electrical connectors. Connect the heater hoses and the brake vacuum hose.
27. If equipped, install the fuel pump. Connect the fuel lines.
28. Install the cooling fan and shroud.
29. Connect the accelerator cable. Install the air cleaner or air intake hose.
30. Install the splash shield. Connect the negative battery cable.
31. Fill and bleed the cooling system. Run the engine and check for leaks.
32. Check and adjust the ignition timing.

Pickup w/2.6L (1987-88)

1. Relieve fuel system pressure, if injected. Disconnect the negative battery cable. Drain the cooling system.

✽✽ CAUTION

When draining the coolant, keep in mind that cats and dogs are attracted by the ethylene glycol antifreeze, and are quite likely to drink any that is left in an uncovered container or in puddles on the ground. This will prove fatal in sufficient quantity. Always drain the coolant into a sealable container. Coolant should be reused unless it is contaminated or several years old.

2. Remove the air cleaner assembly.
3. Remove the bracket from the exhaust side of the cylinder head and remove the exhaust manifold.
4. Remove the water by-pass pipe. Disconnect all necessary vacuum hoses and electrical connectors. Disconnect the fuel lines.

✽✽ CAUTION

Never smoke when working around gasoline! Avoid all sources of sparks or ignition. Gasoline vapors are EXTREMELY volatile!

5. Remove the carburetor and intake manifold. Remove the distributor.
6. Remove the rocker arm cover. Remove the rocker arm and shaft assembly, leaving the bolts in place in the shaft to keep the assembly together. Install hydraulic lash adjuster holder tools 49 U012 001 or equivalent to keep the adjusters from falling.
7. Hold the crankshaft pulley bolt with a wrench to keep it from turning, then remove the camshaft sprocket bolt. Remove the camshaft. With the camshaft sprocket and timing chain meshed together, place the sprocket on the sprocket holder.

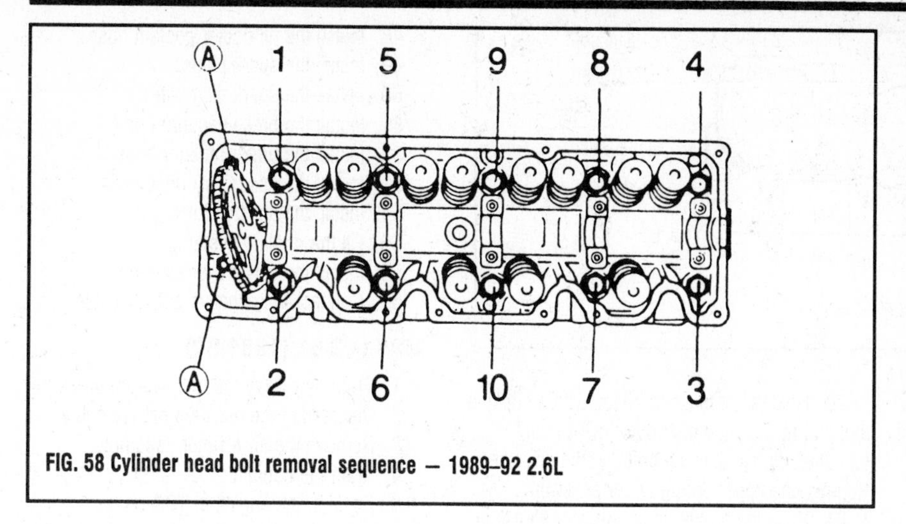

FIG. 58 Cylinder head bolt removal sequence — 1989–92 2.6L

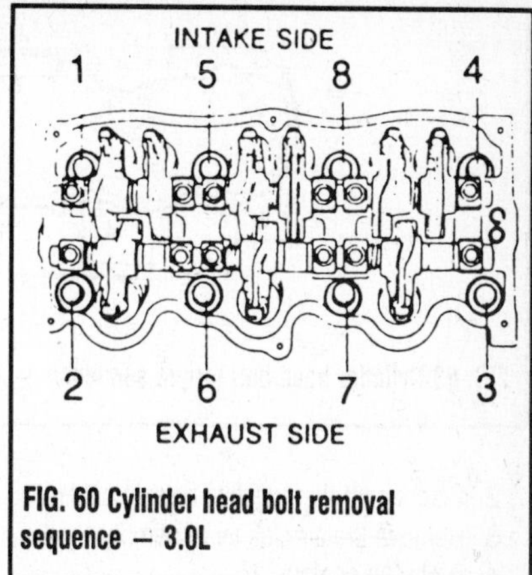

FIG. 60 Cylinder head bolt removal sequence — 3.0L

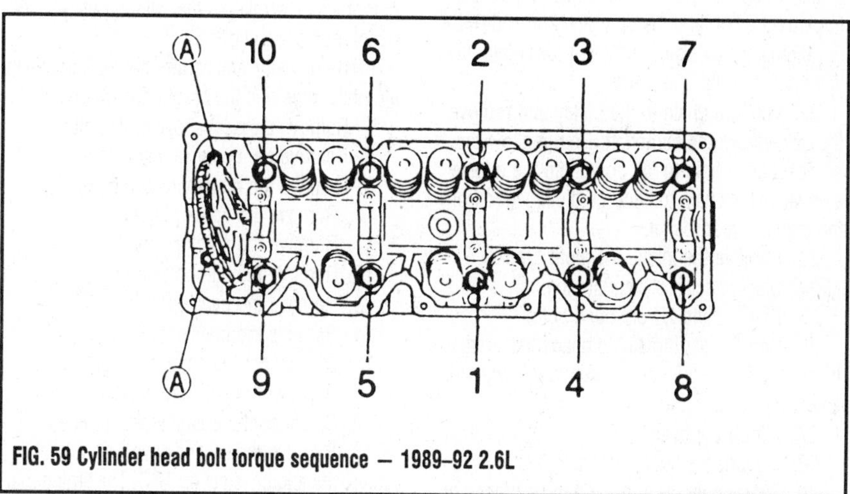

FIG. 59 Cylinder head bolt torque sequence — 1989–92 2.6L

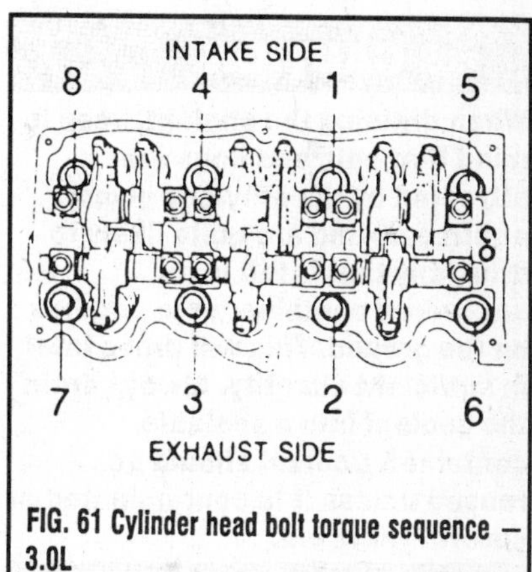

FIG. 61 Cylinder head bolt torque sequence — 3.0L

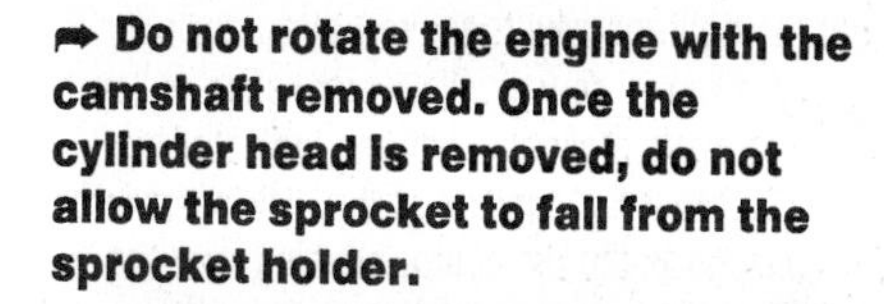

➡ Do not rotate the engine with the camshaft removed. Once the cylinder head is removed, do not allow the sprocket to fall from the sprocket holder.

8. Remove the cylinder head-to-timing chain case bolts.

9. Loosen the cylinder head bolts in 2–3 steps in the proper sequence. Remove the bolts and remove the cylinder head.

10. Clean all gasket mating surfaces. Measure the cylinder head for distortion in 6 directions using a straightedge. The maximum allowable distortion is 0.008 in. (0.20mm).

11. If distortion is excessive, resurface or replace the cylinder head. If resurfacing, do not remove more than 0.008 in. (0.20mm). The cylinder head height should be 3.539–3.547 in. (89.9–90.1mm).

To install:

12. Apply a thin coat of sealer to the cylinder block and timing chain cover contact surfaces, install a new head gasket and the cylinder head. Do not apply sealer to the cylinder head gasket.

13. Apply oil to the threads and seat faces of the cylinder head bolts and install. With the engine cold, tighten the cylinder head bolts, in sequence in 2–3 steps. Final torque on bolts 1–10 should be 65–72 ft. lbs. (88–98 Nm) and on bolts 11 and 12, 11–16 ft. lbs. (15–22 Nm).

14. Apply engine oil to the camshaft journals and install the camshaft, aligning the dowel pin with the camshaft sprocket. Install the distributor drive gear and the lock bolt. Tighten the lock bolt by hand only at this time.

15. Coat the circular packing with sealant and install in the rear of the cylinder head. Install the rocker arms/shafts assembly and tighten the mounting bolts, in sequence, to 14–15 ft. lbs. (19–20 Nm) except for the No. 5 bearing cap rear bolt, which should be tightened to 15–20 ft. lbs. (20–26 Nm).

16. Tighten the distributor drive gear/camshaft sprocket lock bolt to 36–43 ft. lbs. (49–58 Nm).

17. Remove the hydraulic lash adjuster holders. Adjust the jet valve clearance.

18. Install the half-circle packing in the front of the cylinder head and apply sealer across the top of the packing and on both sides of the packing on the cylinder head. Install the rocker arm cover and tighten the bolts to 43–61 inch lbs. (5.0–6.8 Nm).

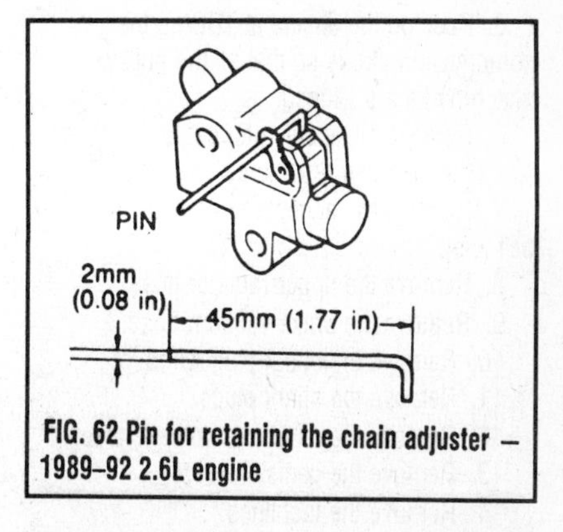

FIG. 62 Pin for retaining the chain adjuster — 1989–92 2.6L engine

19. Install the remaining components. Fill and bleed the cooling system. Run the engine and check for leaks. Check and adjust the ignition timing.

Pickup w/2.6L (1989-92)

1. Properly relieve the fuel system pressure.

CAUTION

Never smoke when working around gasoline! Avoid all sources of sparks or ignition. Gasoline vapors are EXTREMELY volatile!

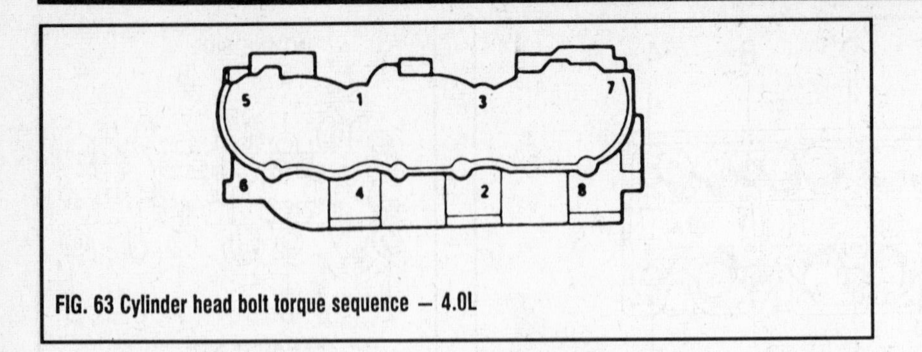

FIG. 63 Cylinder head bolt torque sequence — 4.0L

2. Disconnect the negative battery cable.
3. Remove the air cleaner assembly.
4. Drain the coolant.

CAUTION

When draining the coolant, keep in mind that cats and dogs are attracted by the ethylene glycol antifreeze, and are quite likely to drink any that is left in an uncovered container or in puddles on the ground. This will prove fatal in sufficient quantity. Always drain the coolant into a sealable container. Coolant should be reused unless it is contaminated or several years old.

5. Position the engine at TDC on the compression stroke so that all the pulley matchmarks are aligned.
6. Remove the accelerator cable. Remove the air intake pipe and resonance chamber.
7. Remove the accessory drive belts and AC belt idler.
8. Remove the upper radiator hose.
9. Remove the brake vacuum hose.
10. Remove the spark plug wires.
11. Remove the spark plugs.
12. Remove the oil cooler coolant hose.
13. Remove the canister hose.
14. Remove the fuel lines.
15. Disconnect the oxygen sensor.
16. Remove the solenoid valves.
17. Disconnect the emissions harness.
18. Remove the rocker cover. Check to ensure the engine is set on TDC. The timing mark on the camshaft sprocket should be 90 degrees to the right, parallel to the top of the cylinder head. Make sure the yellow crankshaft pulley timing mark is aligned with the indicator pin.
19. Mark the position of the distributor rotor in relation to the distributor housing, and the distributor housing in relation to the cylinder head. Remove the distributor. Do not rotate the engine after distributor removal.
20. Hold the crankshaft pulley with a suitable tool and remove the distributor drive gear/camshaft pulley retaining bolt and the drive gear. Remove the upper timing cover assembly.
21. Push the timing chain adjuster sleeve in towards the left, and insert a pin (2mm [0.0787 in.] diameter by 45mm [1.77 in.] long) into the lever hole to hold it in place.
22. Wire the chain to the pulley and remove the pulley from the camshaft. Do not allow the sprocket and chain to fall down into the engine and cause the chain to become disengaged from the crankshaft sprocket.
23. Remove the intake manifold bracket.
24. Disconnect the exhaust pipe.
25. Remove the 2 front head bolts.
26. Remove the remaining head bolts starting from the middle and working outward toward the ends of the head.
27. Lift off the head.
28. Discard the head gasket.
29. Thoroughly clean the mating surfaces of the head and block.
30. Check the head and block for flatness with a straightedge.

To install:

31. Apply RTV sealer to the top front of the block as shown.
32. Place a new head gasket on the block.
33. Position the head on the block.
34. Clean the head bolts and apply oil to the threads.
35. Tighten the head bolts, in 2 even steps, to 64 ft. lbs.
36. Torque the two front bolts, to 17 ft. lbs.
37. Place the camshaft pulley on the camshaft and tighten the bolt to 95 inch lbs.; the nut to 87 inch lbs.
38. Connect the exhaust pipe.
39. Install the intake manifold bracket.
40. Install the upper timing cover assembly.
41. Install the distributor.
42. Install the rocker cover.
43. Connect the emissions harness.
44. Install the solenoid valves.
45. Connect the oxygen sensor.
46. Install the fuel lines.
47. Install the canister hose.
48. Install the oil cooler coolant hose.
49. Install the spark plugs.
50. Install the spark plug wires.
51. Install the brake vacuum hose.
52. Install the upper radiator hose.
53. Install the accessory drive belts.
54. Install the accelerator cable.
55. Fill the cooling system.
56. Install the air cleaner assembly.
57. Connect the negative battery cable.

MPV w/2.6L (1989-92)

1. Properly relieve the fuel system pressure.
2. Disconnect the negative battery cable.
3. Remove the air cleaner assembly.
4. Drain the coolant.
5. Position the engine at TDC on the compression stroke so that all the pulley matchmarks are aligned.
6. Remove the accelerator cable. Remove the air intake pipe and the resonance chamber.
7. Remove the accessory drive belts.
8. Remove the upper radiator hose.
9. Remove the brake vacuum hose.
10. Remove the spark plug wires.
11. Remove the spark plugs.
12. Remove the oil cooler coolant hose.
13. Remove the canister hose.
14. Remove the fuel lines.
15. Disconnect the oxygen sensor.
16. Remove the solenoid valves.
17. Disconnect the emissions harness.
18. Remove the rocker cover. Check to ensure the engine is set on TDC. The timing mark on the camshaft sprocket should be 90 degrees to the right, parallel to the top of the cylinder head. Make sure the yellow crankshaft pulley timing mark is aligned with the indicator pin.
19. Mark the position of the distributor rotor in relation to the distributor housing, and the distributor housing in relation to the cylinder head. Remove the distributor. Do not rotate the engine after distributor removal.
20. Hold the crankshaft pulley with a suitable tool and remove the distributor drive gear/camshaft pulley retaining bolt and the drive gear. Remove the upper timing cover assembly.
21. Push the timing chain adjuster sleeve in towards the left, and insert a pin (2mm diameter by 45mm long) into the lever hole to hold it in place.
22. Wire the chain to the pulley and remove the pulley from the camshaft. Do not allow the sprocket and chain to fall down into the engine and cause the chain to become disengaged from the crankshaft sprocket.
23. Remove the intake manifold bracket.
24. Disconnect the exhaust pipe.
25. Remove the 2 front head bolts.

26. Remove the remaining head bolts, working from the middle of the head outward toward the ends.
27. Lift off the head.
28. Discard the head gasket.
29. Thoroughly clean the mating surfaces of the head and block.
30. Check the head and block for flatness with a straightedge.

To install:

31. Apply RTV sealer to the top front of the block as shown.
32. Place a new head gasket on the block.
33. Position the head on the block.
34. Clean the head bolts and apply oil to the threads.
35. Tighten the large head bolts, in 2 even steps, in proper sequence, to 64 ft. lbs.
36. Torque the remaining 2 bolts, to 17 ft. lbs.
37. Place the camshaft pulley on the camshaft and tighten the bolt to 95 inch lbs.; the nut to 87 inch lbs.
38. Connect the exhaust pipe.
39. Install the intake manifold bracket.
40. Install the upper timing cover assembly.
41. Install the distributor.
42. Install the rocker cover.
43. Connect the emissions harness.
44. Install the solenoid valves.
45. Connect the oxygen sensor.
46. Install the fuel lines.
47. Install the canister hose.
48. Install the oil cooler coolant hose.
49. Install the spark plugs.
50. Install the spark plug wires.
51. Install the brake vacuum hose.
52. Install the upper radiator hose.
53. Install the accessory drive belts.
54. Install the accelerator cable.
55. Fill the cooling system.
56. Install the air cleaner assembly.
57. Connect the negative battery cable.

MPV w/3.0L

1. Position the engine at TDC on the compression stroke.
2. Properly relieve the fuel system pressure.
3. Disconnect the negative battery cable.
4. Remove the air cleaner assembly.
5. Drain the cooling system.
6. Remove the spark plug wires.
7. Remove the fresh air duct assembly.
8. Remove the cooling fan and radiator cowling.
9. Remove the drive belts.
10. Remove the air conditioning compressor idler pulley. If necessary, remove the compressor and position it to the side.
11. Remove the crankshaft pulley and baffle plate.
12. Remove the coolant bypass hose.
13. Remove the upper radiator hose.
14. Remove the timing belt cover assembly retaining bolts. Remove the timing belt cover assembly and gasket.
15. Turn the crankshaft to align the mating marks of the pulleys.
16. Remove the upper idler pulley.
17. Remove the timing belt. If reusing the belt be sure to mark the direction of rotation.
18. Disconnect and plug canister, brake vacuum and fuel hoses. If equipped with automatic transmission, disconnect the automatic transmission vacuum hose.
19. Remove the 3-way solenoid valve assembly and disconnect all engine harness connector and grounds.
20. If equipped with automatic transmission, remove the dipstick. Disconnect the required vacuum hoses. Disconnect the accelerator linkage.
21. Remove the distributor and the EGR pipe.
22. Remove the six extension manifolds. Remove the O-rings from the extension manifolds and purchase new ones. Remove the intake manifold by loosening the retaining bolts in the proper sequence.
23. Remove the cylinder head cover, gasket and seal washers.
24. Remove the center exhaust pipe insulator and pipe. Disconnect the exhaust manifold retaining bolts. Remove the exhaust manifold with insulator.
25. Remove the seal plate.
26. Remove the cylinder head retaining bolts in the proper sequence in 2 or 3 stages. Remove the cylinder head from the vehicle.
27. Thoroughly clean the cylinder head and cylinder block contact surfaces to remove any dirt or oil. Check the cylinder head for warpage and cracks. The maximum allowable warpage is 0.10mm. Inspect the cylinder head bolts for damaged threads and make sure they are free from grease and dirt. After the bolts are cleaned, measure the length of each bolt and replace out of specifications bolts as required.

Length

Intake: 108mm
Exhaust: 138mm

Maximum

Intake: 109mm
Exhaust: 139mm

28. Check the oil control plug projection at the cylinder block. Projection should be 0.53–0.57mm. If correct, apply clean engine oil to a new O-ring and position it on the control plug.

To install:

29. Place the new cylinder head gasket on the left bank with the **L** mark facing up. Place the new cylinder head gasket on the right bank with the **R** mark facing up. Install the cylinder onto the block. Tighten the head bolts in the following manner:
   a. Coat the threads and the seating faces of the head bolts with clean engine oil.
   b. Torque the bolts in the proper sequence to 14 ft. lbs.
   c. Paint a mark on the head of each bolt.
   d. Using this mark as a reference, tighten the bolts in the proper sequence an additional 90°.
   e. Repeat Step d.
30. Install the seal plate.
31. Install the exhaust manifold with insulator.
32. Connect the exhaust manifold retaining bolts.
33. Install the center exhaust pipe insulator and pipe.
34. Install the cylinder head cover, gasket and seal washers.
35. Install the intake manifold by loosening the retaining bolts in the proper sequence.
36. Install the O-rings from the extension manifolds.
37. Install the six extension manifolds.
38. Install the distributor and the EGR pipe.
39. If equipped with automatic transmission, install the dipstick. Connect the required vacuum hoses. Connect the accelerator linkage.
40. Install the 3-way solenoid valve assembly and connect all engine harness connector and grounds.
41. Connect the canister, brake vacuum and fuel hoses. If equipped with automatic transmission, connect the automatic transmission vacuum hose.
42. To install the timing belt, first the automatic tensioner must be loaded. To load the tensioner:
   a. Place a flat washer on the bottom of the tensioner body to prevent damage to the body and position the unit on an arbor press.
   b. Press the rod into the tensioner body. Do not use more than 2,000 lbs of pressure.
   c. Once the rod is fully inserted into the body, insert a suitable L-shaped pin or a small Allen wrench through the body and the rod to hold the rod in place.
   d. Remove the unit from the press and install onto the block and torque the mounting bolt to 14–19 ft. lbs.
   e. Leave the pin in place, it will be removed later.
43. Make sure that all the timing marks are aligned properly. With the upper idler pulley removed, hang the timing belt on each pulley in the order shown in the illustration.
44. Install the upper idler pulley and torque the mounting bolt to 27–38 ft. lbs.

45. Rotate the crankshaft twice in the normal direction of rotation to align all the timing marks.

46. Make sure all the marks are aligned correctly. If not, repeat Step 22.

47. Remove the pin from the auto tensioner. Again turn the crankshaft twice in the normal direction of rotation and make sure that all the timing marks are aligned properly.

48. Check the timing belt deflection by applying 22 lbs. of force. If the deflection is not 5-7mm, repeat the adjustment procedure.

➡ **Excessive belt deflection is caused by auto tensioner failure or an excessively stretched timing belt.**

49. Install the upper idler pulley.

50. Install the timing belt cover assembly and new gasket.

51. Install the upper radiator hose.

52. Install the coolant bypass hose.

53. Install the crankshaft pulley and baffle plate.

54. Install the compressor.

55. Install the air conditioning compressor idler pulley.

56. Install the accessory drive belts.

57. Install the cooling fan and radiator cowling.

58. Install the fresh air duct assembly.

59. Install the spark plug wires.

60. Fill the cooling system.

61. Install the air cleaner assembly.

62. Connect the negative battery cable.

4.0L Engine

1. Relieve fuel system pressure. Disconnect the negative battery cable. Drain the cooling system (engine cold) into a clean container and save the coolant for reuse.

CAUTION

When draining the coolant, keep in mind that cats and dogs are attracted by the ethylene glycol antifreeze, and are quite likely to drink any that is left in an uncovered container or in puddles on the ground. This will prove fatal in sufficient quantity. Always drain the coolant into a sealable container. Coolant should be reused unless it is contaminated or several years old.

2. Disconnect the battery ground cable.

3. Remove the air cleaner.

4. Remove the upper and lower intake manifolds as described earlier.

5. If the left cylinder head is being removed:

a. Remove the accessory drive belt.

b. Remove the air conditioning compressor.

c. Remove the power steering pump and bracket assembly. DO NOT disconnect the hoses. Tie the assembly out of the way.

d. Remove the spark plugs.

6. If the right head is being removed:

a. Remove the accessory drive belt.

b. Remove the alternator and bracket.

c. Remove the EDIS ignition coil and bracket.

d. Remove the spark plugs.

7. Remove the exhaust manifold(s).

8. Remove the rocker arm covers as previously described.

9. Remove the rocker shaft assembly.

10. Remove the pushrods, keeping them in order so they may be installed in their original locations.

11. Loosen the cylinder head attaching bolts in reverse of the torque sequence, then remove the bolts and discard them. They cannot be re-used.

12. Lift off the cylinder head(s).

13. Remove and discard the old cylinder head gasket(s).

To install:

14. Clean the cylinder heads, intake manifolds, valve rocker arm cover and cylinder block gasket surfaces of all traces of old gasket material and/or sealer. Refer to the following overhaul procedures for cylinder head component removal, valve replacement, resurfacing, etc.

15. Lightly oil all bolt and stud bolt threads except those specifying special sealant. Position the new head gasket(s) on the cylinder block, using the dowels for alignment. The dowels should be replaced if damaged.

➡ **The cylinder head(s) and intake manifold are torqued alternately and in sequence, to assure a correct fit and gasket crush.**

16. Position the cylinder head(s) on the block.

17. Apply a bead of RTV silicone gasket material to the mating joints of the head and block at the 4 corners. Install the intake manifold gasket and again apply the sealer.

➡ **This sealer sets within 15 minutes, so work quickly!**

18. Install the lower intake manifold and install the bolts and nuts for the manifold and head(s). Tighten all fasteners finger-tight.

19. Tighten the intake manifold fasteners, in sequence, to 36–72 inch lbs.

WARNING

Do not re-use the old head bolts. ALWAYS use new head bolts!

20. Torque the head bolts, in sequence, to 59 ft. lbs.

21. Tighten the intake manifold fasteners, in sequence, to 6–11 ft. lbs.

22. Tighten the head bolts, in sequence, an additional 80–85 DEGREES tighter. 85 degrees is a little less than $^1/_4$ turn. $^1/_4$ turn would equal 90 degrees.

23. Torque the intake manifold fasteners, in sequence, to 11–15 ft. lbs.; then, in sequence, to 15–18 ft. lbs.

24. Dip each pushrod in heavy engine oil then install the pushrods in their original locations.

25. Install the rocker shaft assembly(ies) and tighten the bolts to 46–52 ft. lbs., front to rear, in several equal stages.

26. Apply another bead of RTV sealer at the 4 corners where the intake manifold and heads meet.

27. Install the rocker covers, using new gaskets coated with sealer. Torque the bolts to 36–60 inch lbs. After 2 minutes, re-torque the cover bolts.

28. Install the upper intake manifold. Torque the nuts to 15–18 ft. lbs.

29. Install the exhaust manifold(s).

30. Install the spark plugs and wires.

31. If the left head was removed, install the power steering pump, compressor and drive belt.

32. If the right head was removed, install the EDIS coil and bracket, alternator and bracket, and the drive belt.

33. Install the air cleaner.

34. Fill the cooling system. See Section 1.

➡ **At this point, it's a good idea to change the engine oil. Coolant contamination of the engine oil often occurs during cylinder head removal.**

35. Connect the battery ground cable.

36. Start the engine and check for leaks.

CLEANING AND INSPECTION

1. With the valves installed to protect the valve seats, remove deposits from the combustion chambers and valve heads with a scraper and a wire brush. Be careful not to damage the cylinder head gasket surface. After the valves are removed, clean the valve guide bores with a valve guide cleaning tool. Using cleaning solvent to remove dirt, grease and other

deposits, clean all bolts holes; be sure the oil passage is clean (V6 engines).

2. Remove all deposits from the valves with a fine wire brush or buffing wheel.

3. Inspect the cylinder heads for cracks or excessively burned areas in the exhaust outlet ports.

4. Check the cylinder head for cracks and inspect the gasket surface for burrs and nicks. Replace the head if it is cracked.

5. On cylinder heads that incorporate valve seat inserts, check the inserts for excessive wear, cracks, or looseness.

RESURFACING

SEE FIGS. 64-65

Cylinder Head Flatness

When the cylinder head is removed, check the flatness of the cylinder head gasket surfaces.

1. Place a straightedge across the gasket surface of the cylinder head. Using feeler gauges, determine the clearance at the center of the straightedge.

2. If warpage exceeds 0.08mm (0.0031 in.) in a 152mm (5.98 in.) span over the total length, the cylinder head must be resurfaced.

3. If necessary to refinish the cylinder head gasket surface, do not plane or grind off more than 0.25mm (0.0098 in.) from the original gasket surface.

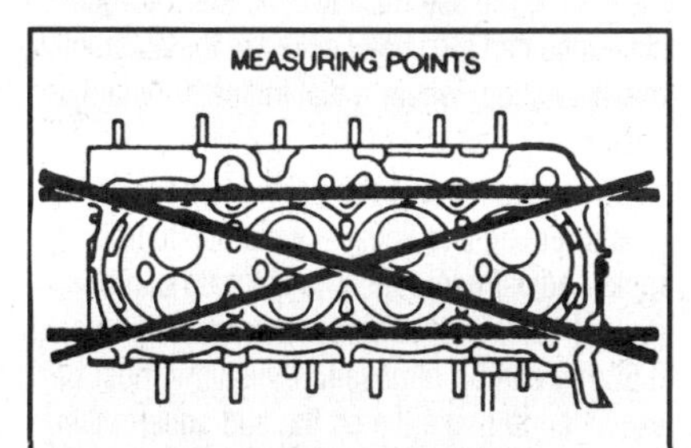

FIG. 64 Use a straightedge to measure cylinder head flatness at these points

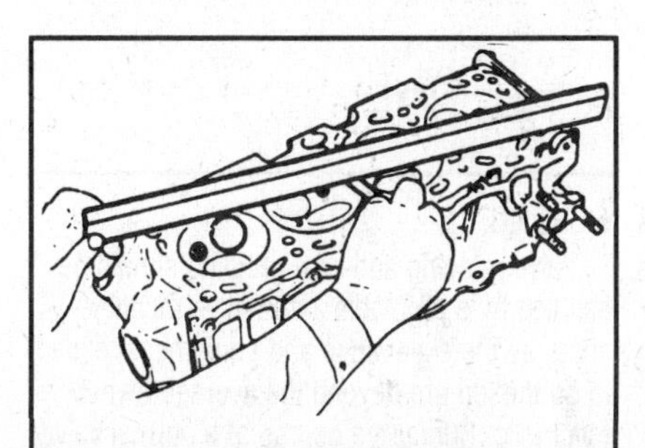

FIG. 65 Check the cylinder head flatness and warpage with a straightedge and feeler gauge. Warpage should not exceed 0.004 inch

When milling the cylinder heads of V6 engines, the intake manifold mounting position is altered, and must be corrected by milling the manifold flange a proportionate amount. Consult an experienced machinist about this.

Valves and Valve Springs

SEE FIG. 66

REMOVAL & INSTALLATION

A valve spring compressor is needed to remove the valves and springs; these are available at most auto parts and auto tool shops. A small magnet is very helpful for removing keepers and spring seats (if equipped).

Set the cylinder head on its side on the work bench. Install the spring compressor so that the fixed side of the tool is flat against the valve head in the combustion chamber, and the screw side is against the retainer. Slowly turn the screw in towards the head, compressing the spring. As the spring compresses, the keepers will be revealed; pick them off the valve stem with the magnet as they are easily fumbled and lost. When the keepers are removed, back the screw out and remove the retainers and springs. Remove the compressor and pull the valves out of the head. Remove the valve seals from the valve guides, and remove the spring seats, if equipped.

Since it is very important that each valve and its spring, retainer, spring seat and keepers is reassembled in its original location, you must keep these parts in order. The best way to do this is to cut either eight (for four cylinder) or twelve (for six cylinder) holes in a piece of cardboard or wood. Label each hole with the cylinder number and either IN or EX, corresponding to the location of each valve, intake or exhaust, in the head. As you remove each valve, insert it into the holder. Place the spring seats, springs, keepers and retainers in a labeled egg carton or similar compartmentized container. This way each valve and its attendant parts are keep together, and can be put back into the head in their proper locations. Of course, if new parts are to be installed there is no wear and the replacements can be installed in any cylinder location.

After the cylinder head valve seats and valves are refaced, or serviced as required, and the valves are lapped (see Valve Lapping), oil each valve stem, and install each valve into the head. Install the valve spring seats, if equipped. Install new valve stem oil seals. Place the valve spring and retainer on the valve stem.

Install the spring compressor, and compress the valve spring with the retainer in position. Compress the spring enough to expose the keeper groove on the valve stem. Coat the groove with a wipe of grease (to hold the keepers in position when the spring tension is released) and install both keepers, wide end up. Slowly back the screw of the compressor out until the spring retainer covers the keepers. Remove the compressor. Lightly tap the end of each valve stem with a plastic or soft hammer to ensure proper fit of the retainer and keepers.

INSPECTION

SEE FIGS. 67-70

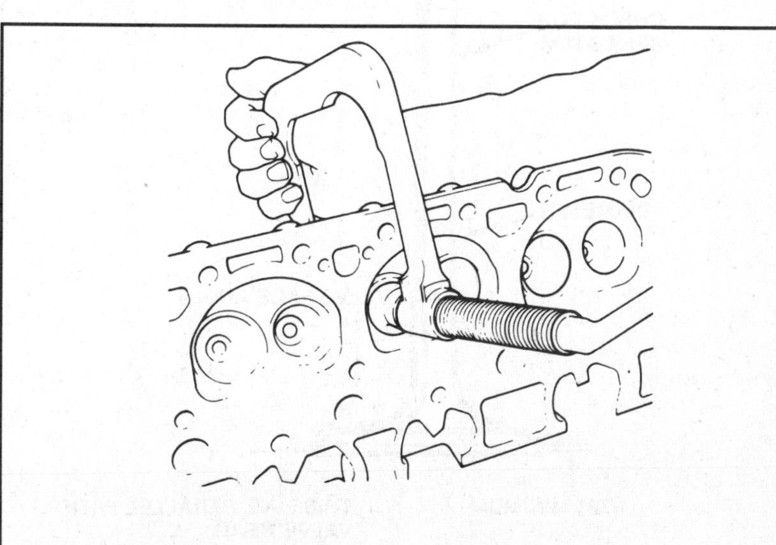

FIG. 66 Compressing the valve spring using a clamp type compressor

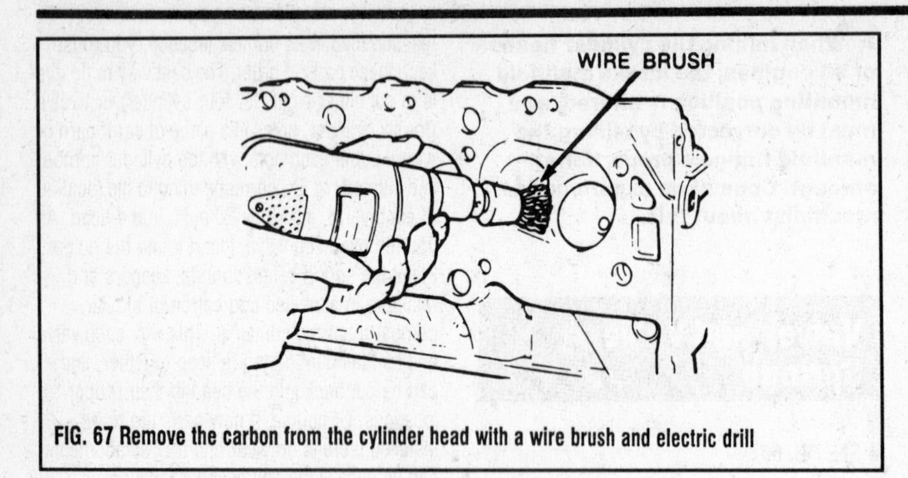

FIG. 67 Remove the carbon from the cylinder head with a wire brush and electric drill

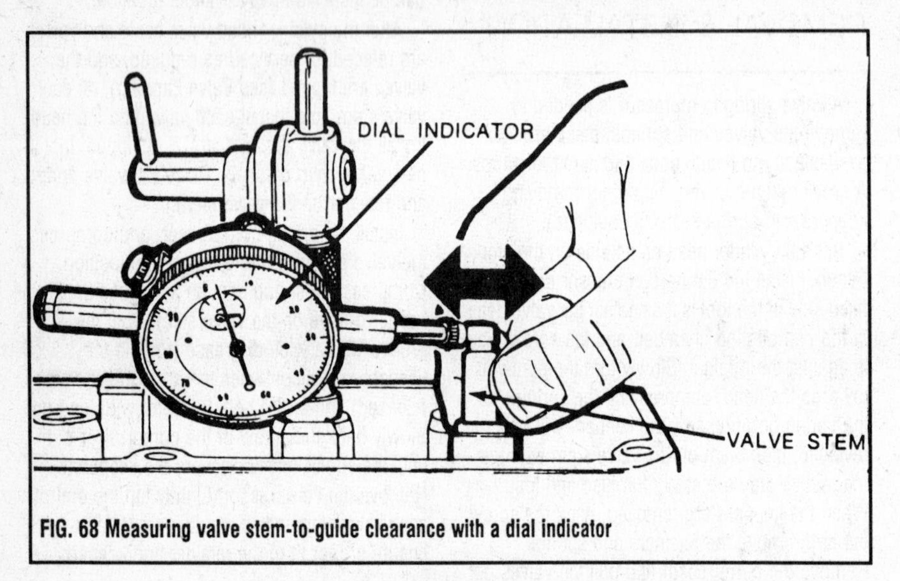

FIG. 68 Measuring valve stem-to-guide clearance with a dial indicator

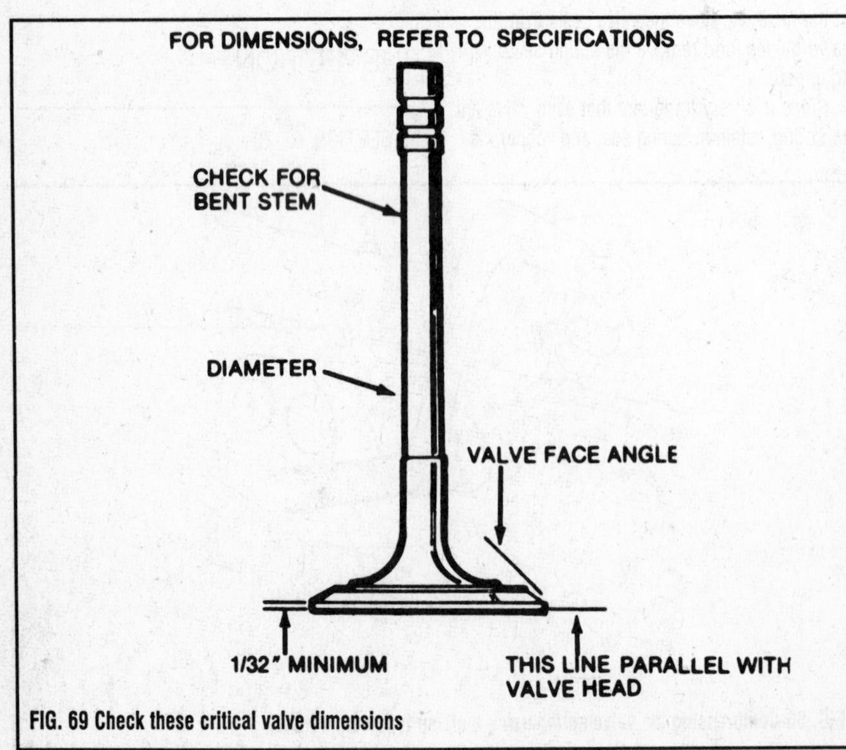

FIG. 69 Check these critical valve dimensions

Before the valves can be properly inspected, the stem, lower end of the stem and the entire valve face and head must be cleaned. An old valve works well for chipping carbon from the valve head, and a wire brush, gasket scrapper or putty knife can be used for cleaning the valve face and the area between the face and the lower stem. Do not scratch the face of the valve during cleaning. Clean the entire stem with a rag soaked in safe solvent to remove all varnish and gum.

Thorough inspection of the valves requires the use of a micrometer, and a dial indicator is needed to measure the inside diameter of the valve guides. If these instruments are not available to you, the valves and the head can be taken to a reputable automotive machine shop for inspection.

If the above instruments are at your disposal, measure the diameter of each valve stem at the top, middle and bottom of the stem. Measure in two dimensions (when viewed from the top of the stem). This is six measurements per valve: jot these measurements down in order for each valve.

Using the dial indicator, measure the inside diameter of the valve guides at their bottom, middle and top. Again, measure in two dimensions, Six measurements per guide, jot these measurements down also.

Subtract the valve stem measurement from the valve guide inside measurement; if the clearances exceed that listed in the specifications chart under Stem-to-Guide Clearance, replace the valve(s). Stem-to-guide clearance can also be checked at the automotive machine shop, where a dial indicator would be used.

Check the top of each valve stem for pitting, mushrooming and unusual wear due to improper rocker adjustment, etc. The stem tip can be ground flat if it is worn, but no more than 0.50mm can be removed. If this limit must be exceeded to make the tip flat and square, then the valve must be replaced. Most automotive machine shops are equipped to do this job for you.

REFACING

➧ SEE FIG. 71

Valve refacing and seat grinding should be handled by a reputable automotive machine shop, as the experience and equipment needed to do the job are beyond the average owner/ mechanic. During the course of a normal valve job, refacing is necessary when simply lapping the valves into their seats will not correct the seat and face wear. When the valves are reground (refaced), the valve seats must be recut, again

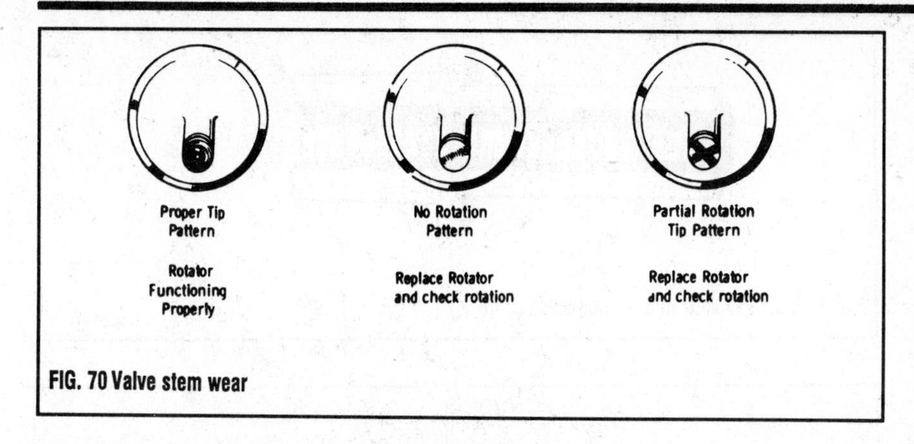

FIG. 70 Valve stem wear

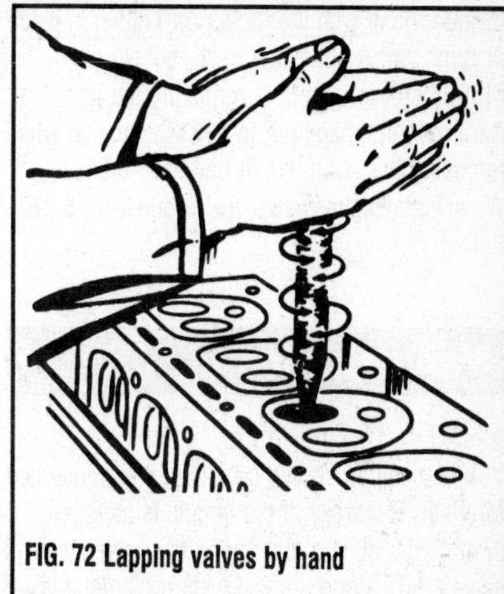

FIG. 72 Lapping valves by hand

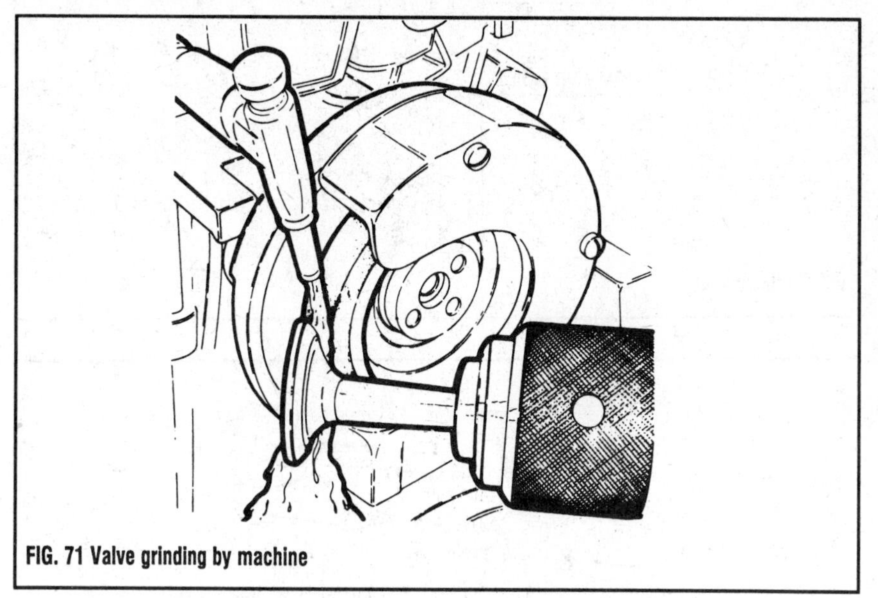

FIG. 71 Valve grinding by machine

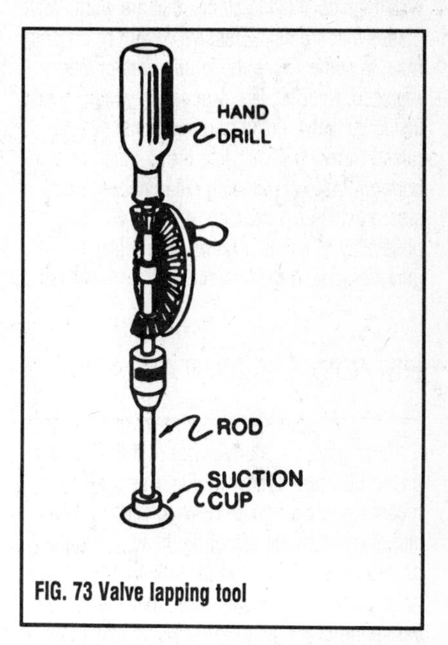

FIG. 73 Valve lapping tool

requiring special equipment and experience. The valve seats cannot be accurately ground if excessive valve guide wear is present. If the guides are worn beyond specifications, replacement or repair is required.

When refacing the valves with a refacing tool, following the instructions of the tool manufacturer. Only enough metal to clean up faces and seats should be removed.

If the valve and/or valve seat has been refaced, it will be necessary to check the clearance between the rocker arm pad and the valve stem tip with the valve train assembly installed in the engine.

VALVE LAPPING

➧ SEE FIGS. 72-73

This procedure should be performed after the valves and seats have been machined, to insure that each valve mates to each seat precisely.

1. Invert the cylinder head, lightly lubricate the valve stems, and install the valves in the head as numbered.
2. Coat valve seats with fine grinding compound, and attach the lapping tool suction cup to a valve head.

➡ **Moisten the suction cup.**

3. Rotate the tool between your palms, changing position and lifting the tool often to prevent grooving.
4. Lap the valve until a smooth, polished seat is evident.
5. Remove the valve and tool, and rinse away all traces of grinding compound.

VALVE STEM OIL SEALS

Positive valves seals are used. The seal fits over to top of the valve guide. Always install new valve stem seals when reassembling the cylinder head.

VALVE SPRING TESTING

Place the spring on a flat surface next to a square. Measure the height of the spring, and rotate it against the edge of the square to measure distortion. If spring height varies (by comparison) by more than 1.5mm (0.059 in.) or if distortion exceeds 1.5mm (0.059 in.), replace the spring.

In addition to evaluating the spring as above, test the spring pressure at the installed and compressed (installed height minus valve lift) height using a valve spring tester. Spring pressure should be ± 1 lb. of all other springs in either position.

Jet Valves

REMOVAL & INSTALLATION

The jet valve can be removed from the

cylinder head with the rocker arm either in place or removed. A special socket, tool No. MD998310, is helpful in removing the jet valve. Care must be taken not to twist the socket while removing the valve, it can be easily broken. When installing the valve, the torque is 13.5-15.5 ft. lbs.

Valve Guides

➧ SEE FIG. 74-76

Valve guides should be cleaned and checked for wear. Generally, if the engine is using oil through the guides (assuming the valve stem oil seals are OK) and the valve stem diameter is within specs, it is the guides that are worn. Valve guides that are not excessively worn or distorted may, in some cases, be knurled rather than replaced. Knurling is a process in which metal inside the valve guide bore is displaced and raised (forming a very fine cross-hatch or spiral pattern), thereby reducing clearance. Knurling also provides for excellent oil control. The possibility of knurling rather than replacing the guides should be discussed with a machinist.

REMOVAL & INSTALLATION

Valve guides are driven out of the head from the combustion chamber side. Use a driver meant for this purpose. New guides are driven into place from the top of the head, using the proper driver. Check the protrusion of the valve guide above the head surface, measuring from the spring seat upward. Protrusion should be: 2.2L engine; 0.752–0.772 inch (19.1–19.6mm). 2.6L engine; 0.925–0,953 inch (23.5–24.2mm). 3.0L engine; intake 0.520–0.543 inch (13.2–13.8mm); exhaust 0.772–0.795 inch (19.6–20.2mm). Some replacement guides are equipped with spring clips, if so carefully drive the guide into the head until the clip just touches the head surface, check the installed height.

➡ On the 3.0L engines, intake and exhaust valve guides originally used are different shapes, but you should use exhaust type guides for replacement on both sides.

Valve Seats

➧ SEE FIG. 77

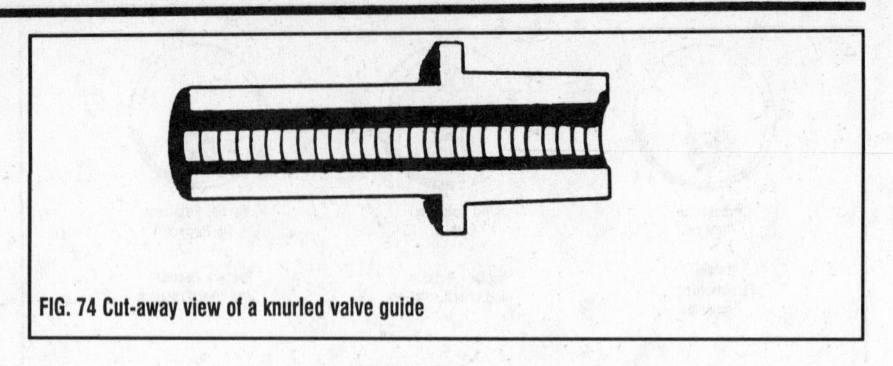

FIG. 74 Cut-away view of a knurled valve guide

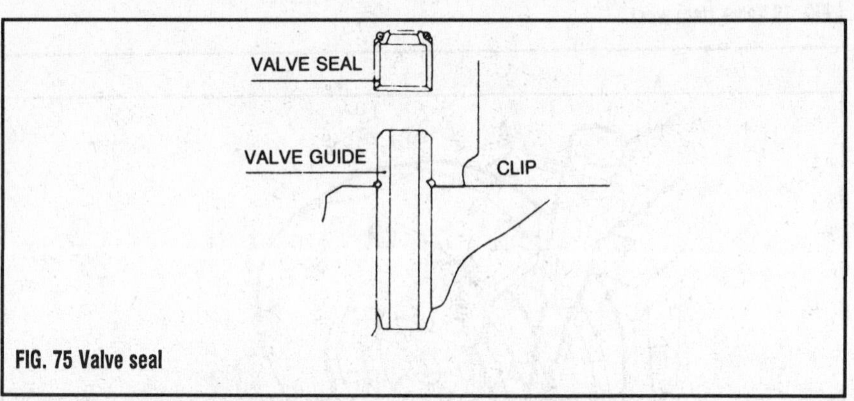

FIG. 75 Valve seal

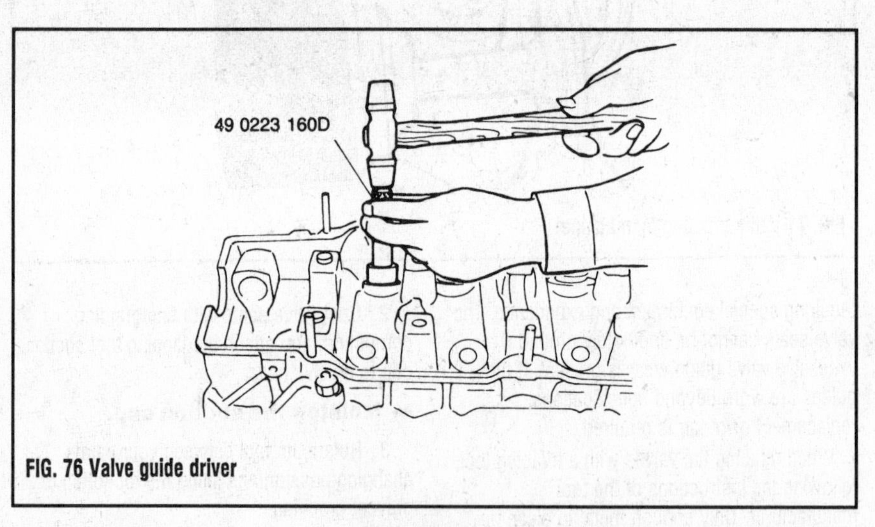

FIG. 76 Valve guide driver

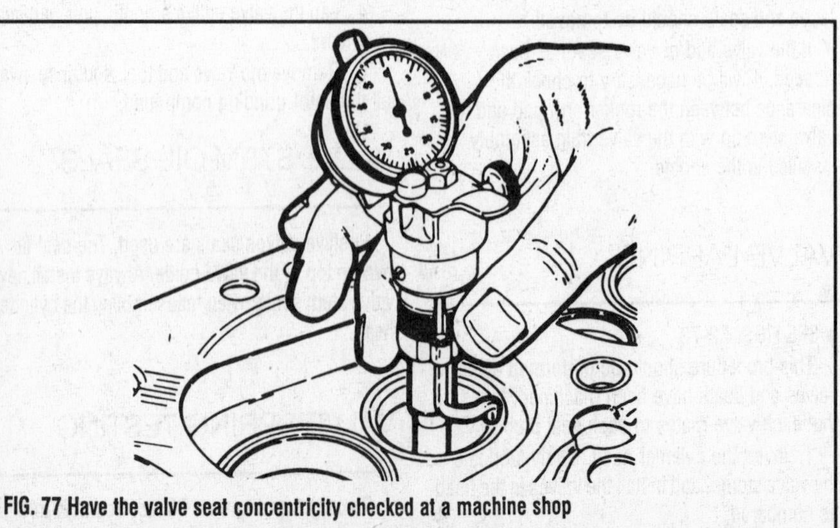

FIG. 77 Have the valve seat concentricity checked at a machine shop

REMOVAL & INSTALLATION

2.6L (1987-88) Engines

The valve seat inserts are replaceable on the 2.6L (1987-88) engines.

1. With the valve removed, check the seat for wear, cracks, damage or uneven contact with the valve. If the damage or contact problem is slight, the valve may be refaced with a lapping compound and lapping tool. The compound is spread on the seat face and the valve inserted. The valve is then ground against the seat with the lapping tool, removing a small amount of metal and creating a polished surface.
2. If the damage or contact problem cannot be rectified by lapping, the insert can be cut with a special seat cutter which will remove the damaged material and cut the correct angle.
3. If the seat insert is cracked, too thin, or burnt,it must be replaced. An automotive machine shop can handle the job for you.

Except 2.6L (1987-88) Engines

These valve seats are not replaceable. If valve seats have cracks, burrs, or ridges, or angles and dimensions are not correct, remove the minimum amount of metal that will correct them with a valve seat grinder. Note that seat grinding must be done after valve guide replacement, where it is required. Contact of valve and seat must be checked by applying Prussian Blue dye to seat, seating valve, and then repeatedly reseating the valve while rotating it. If the dye marking on the valve is uneven, the valve must be lapped in.

When valve/seat machining has been performed, it is necessary to check the distance between the valve spring seat on the cylinder head and the top of the valve stem so that adequate spring tension is assured. Check the dimension using Vernier calipers or a steel scale. This will give you the assembled height.

The finished valve seat should contact the approximate center of the valve face. It is good practice to determine where the valve seat contacts the valve face. To do this, coat the seat with Prussian blue and set the valve in place. Rotate the valve with light pressure. If the blue is transferred to the top edge of the valve face, lower the valve seat. If the blue is transferred to the bottom edge of the valve face, raise the valve seat.

Valve Lifter (Tappets)

All engines, except the 4.0L, are equipped with hydraulic lash adjusters located in the rocker arms. The hydraulic lash adjusters can be removed by hand or with suitable pliers after the rocker arm/shaft assembly has been removed.

REMOVAL & INSTALLATION

4.0L Engine

1. Remove the upper and lower intake manifolds.
2. Remove the rocker covers.
3. Remove the rocker shaft assembly.
4. Remove and mark the pushrods for installation.
5. Remove the tappets with a magnet. If they are to be re-used, identify them.

➡ If the tappets are stuck in their bores, you'll need a claw-type removal tool.

6. Coat the new tappets with clean engine oil and insert them in their bores.
7. Coat the pushrods with heavy engine oil and insert them into the bores from which they came.
8. Install the rocker shaft assembly.
9. Install the rocker covers.
10. Install the upper and lower manifold.

Oil Pan

➧ SEE FIGS. 78-85

REMOVAL & INSTALLATION

✻✻ CAUTION

The EPA warns that prolonged contact with used engine oil may cause a number of skin disorders, including cancer! You should make every effort to minimize your exposure to used engine oil. Protective gloves should be worn when changing the oil. Wash your hands and any other exposed skin areas as soon as possible after exposure to used engine oil. Soap and water, or waterless hand cleaner should be used.

B Series Pickup

1. Disconnect the negative battery cable.
2. Raise and support the vehicle safely.
3. Remove the necessary splash shields.
4. Position a drain pan under the oil pan. Remove the drain plug and drain the engine oil.
5. On the 1987 and 1988 2.6L engine, remove the rear subframe.
6. If equipped with 4WD, remove the front differential.
7. Remove the necessary steering linkage.
8. Remove the gusset plates and the clutch housing cover, if equipped.
9. Remove the oil pan mounting bolts and remove the oil pan. If necessary, insert a scraper or other suitable tool between the oil pan and block to separate them. Be careful not to bend the pan.

To install:

10. Clean all gasket mating surfaces and the oil pan.
11. Apply sealant to the cylinder block and install a new gasket.
12. Install the oil pan with the attaching bolts. Tighten the bolts to 61–104 inch lbs. (6.9–12.0 Nm) on 2.2L engine, 52–61 inch lbs. (6–7 Nm) on 1988 2.6L engine or 69–95 inch lbs. (7.8–11.0 Nm) on 1989–92 2.6L engine.

➡ Apply Loctite® to the bolt threads on 1989-92 2.6L engine before installation.

13. Install the remaining components in the reverse order of removal. Lower the vehicle and connect the negative battery cable.
14. Fill the crankcase with the proper type and quantity of engine oil. Run the engine and check for leaks.

MPV

2.6L Engine

1. Disconnect the negative battery cable. Remove the fan shroud.
2. Install engine support tool 49 G017 5A0 or equivalent. Remove the engine mount nuts and lift the engine slightly to gain removal clearance.
3. Raise and safely support the vehicle. Support the transmission with a transmission jack and remove the transmission lower mount.
4. Remove the splash shield.
5. Position a drain pan under the oil pan. Remove the drain plug and drain the engine oil.

✻✻ CAUTION

The EPA warns that prolonged contact with used engine oil may cause a number of skin disorders, including cancer! You should make every effort to minimize your exposure to used engine oil. Protective gloves should be worn when changing the oil. Wash your hands and any other exposed skin areas as soon as possible after exposure to used engine oil. Soap and water, or waterless hand cleaner should be used.

6. Remove the gusset plates and stabilizer bar brackets.

7. Remove the oil pan mounting bolts and remove the oil pan. If necessary, insert a scraper or other suitable tool between the oil pan and block to separate them. Be careful not to bend the pan.

To install:

8. Clean all gasket mating surfaces and the oil pan.

9. Apply sealant to the cylinder block and install a new gasket.

10. Install the oil pan with the attaching bolts. Tighten the bolts to 69–95 inch lbs. (7.8–11.0 Nm). Apply Loctite® to the bolt threads before installation.

11. Install the remaining components in the reverse order of removal. Lower the vehicle and remove the engine support tool. Install the engine mount nuts.

12. Connect the negative battery cable. Fill the crankcase with the proper type and quantity of engine oil. Run the engine and check for leaks.

3.0L Engine — 2WD

1. Disconnect the negative battery cable.
2. Raise and safely support the vehicle.
3. Remove the splash shield.
4. Position a drain pan under the oil pan. Remove the drain plug and drain the engine oil.

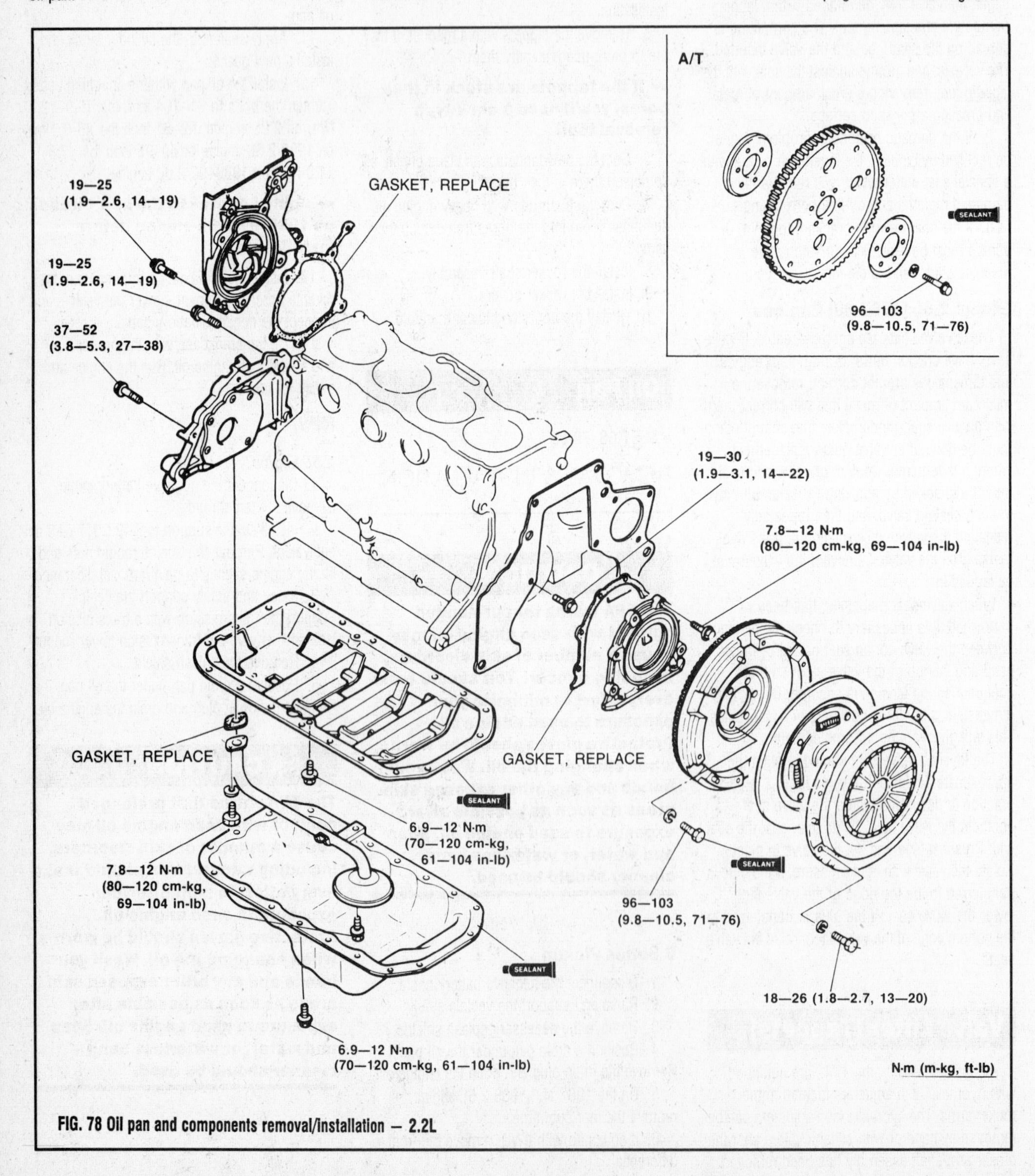

FIG. 78 Oil pan and components removal/installation — 2.2L

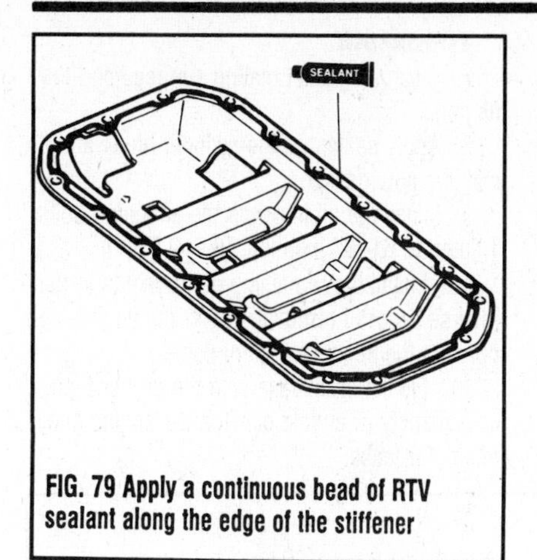

FIG. 79 Apply a continuous bead of RTV sealant along the edge of the stiffener

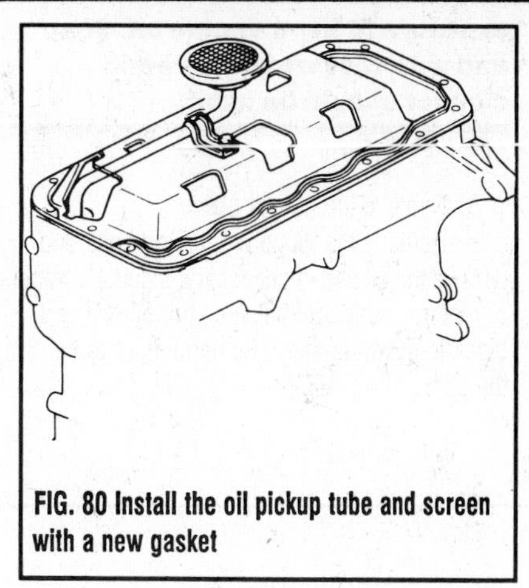

FIG. 80 Install the oil pickup tube and screen with a new gasket

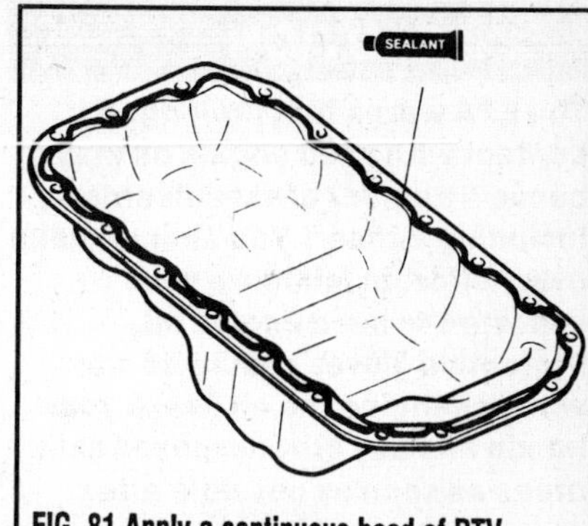

FIG. 81 Apply a continuous bead of RTV sealant to the oil pan around the insides of the mounting holes and overlap the ends

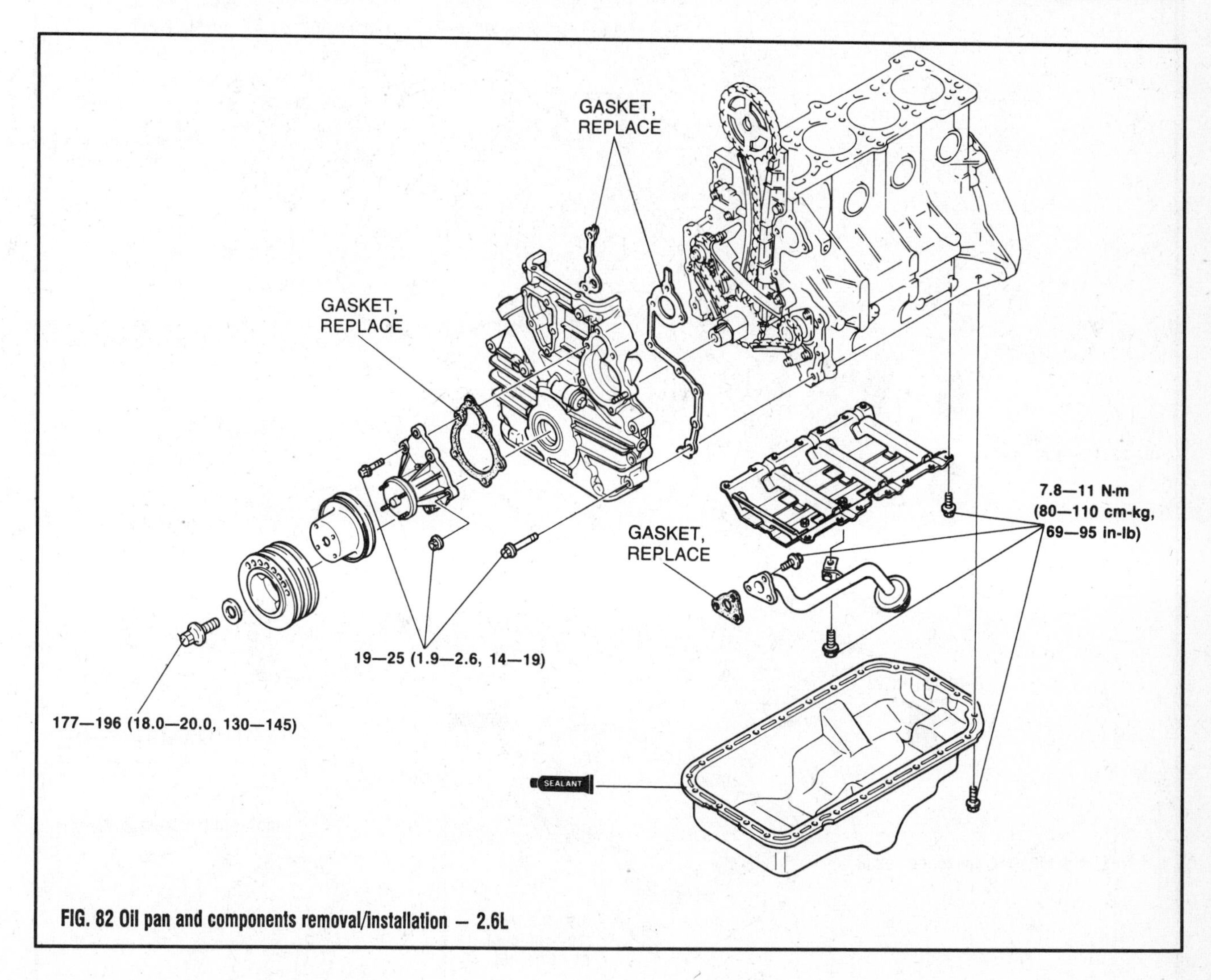

FIG. 82 Oil pan and components removal/installation — 2.6L

⁂ CAUTION

The EPA warns that prolonged contact with used engine oil may cause a number of skin disorders, including cancer! You should make every effort to minimize your exposure to used engine oil. Protective gloves should be worn when changing the oil. Wash your hands and any other exposed skin areas as soon as possible after exposure to used engine oil. Soap and water, or waterless hand cleaner should be used.

5. Remove the gusset plates.
6. Remove the oil pan mounting bolts and remove the oil pan. If necessary, insert a scraper or other suitable tool between the oil pan and block to separate them. Be careful not to bend the pan.

To install:

7. Clean all gasket mating surfaces and the oil pan.
8. Apply sealant to the cylinder block and install a new gasket.
9. Install the oil pan with the attaching bolts. Tighten to 61–87 inch lbs. (6.9–9.8 Nm).
10. Install the remaining components in the reverse order of removal. Lower the vehicle and connect the negative battery cable.
11. Fill the crankcase with the proper type and quantity of engine oil. Run the engine and check for leaks.

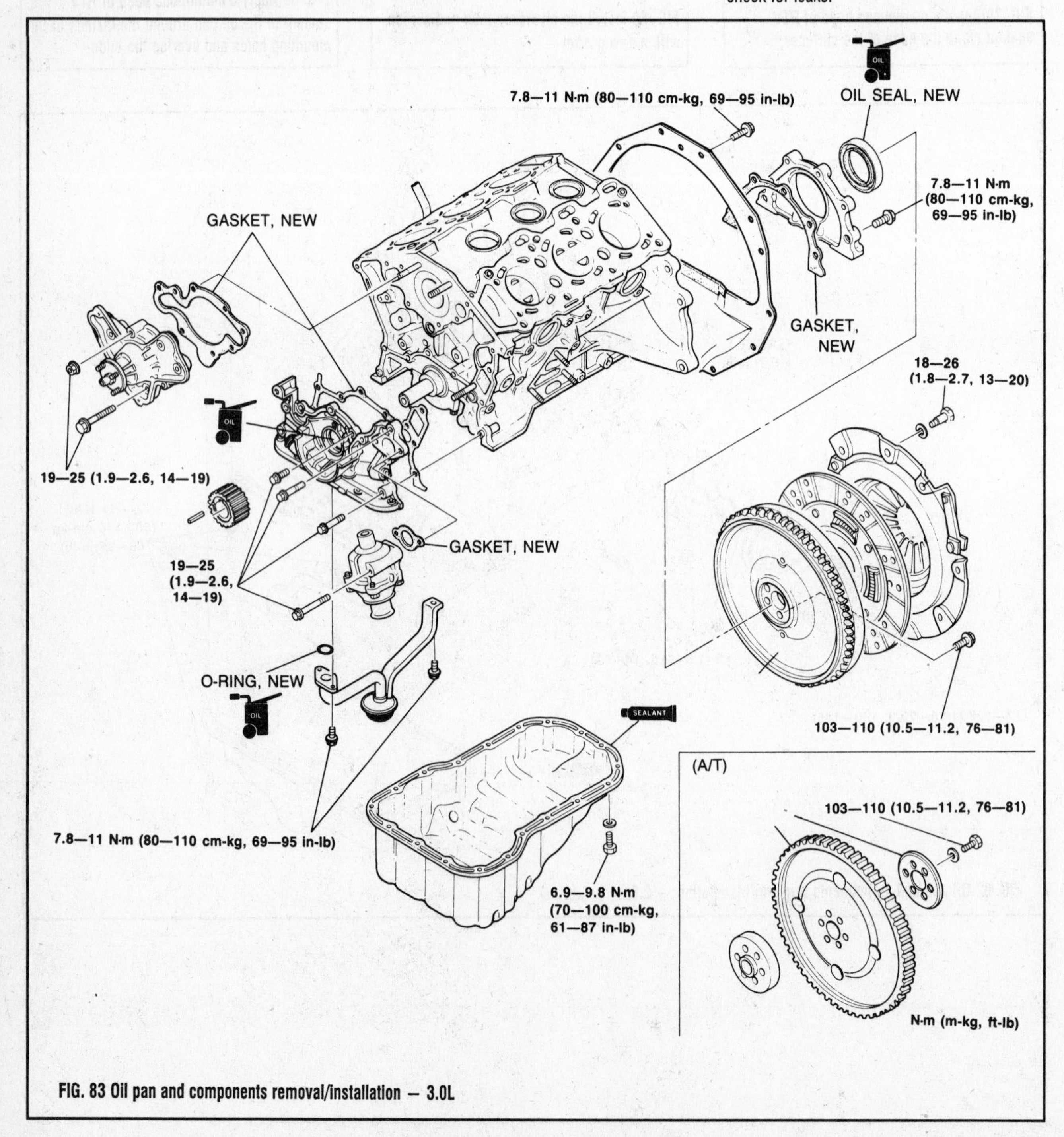

FIG. 83 Oil pan and components removal/installation – 3.0L

3.0L Engine — 4WD

1. Disconnect the negative battery cable. Remove the fresh air duct and fan shroud.
2. Install engine support tool 49 G017 5A0 or equivalent. Remove the engine mount nuts and lift the engine slightly to gain removal clearance.
3. Raise and safely support the vehicle. Support the transmission with a transmission jack and remove the transmission lower mount.
4. Remove the splash shields.
5. Position a drain pan under the oil pan. Remove the drain plug and drain the engine oil.

CAUTION

The EPA warns that prolonged contact with used engine oil may cause a number of skin disorders, including cancer! You should make every effort to minimize your exposure to used engine oil. Protective gloves should be worn when changing the oil. Wash your hands and any other exposed skin areas as soon as possible after exposure to used engine oil. Soap and water, or waterless hand cleaner should be used.

6. If equipped with automatic transmission, disconnect and reposition the oil cooler hose and tube.
7. Remove the stabilizer bar.
8. Remove the oil pan mounting bolts and remove the oil pan. If necessary, insert a scraper or other suitable tool between the oil pan and block to separate them. Be careful not to bend the pan.

To install:

9. Clean all gasket mating surfaces and the oil pan.
10. Apply sealant to the cylinder block and install a new gasket.
11. Install the oil pan with the attaching bolts. Tighten to 61–87 inch lbs. (6.9–9.8 Nm).

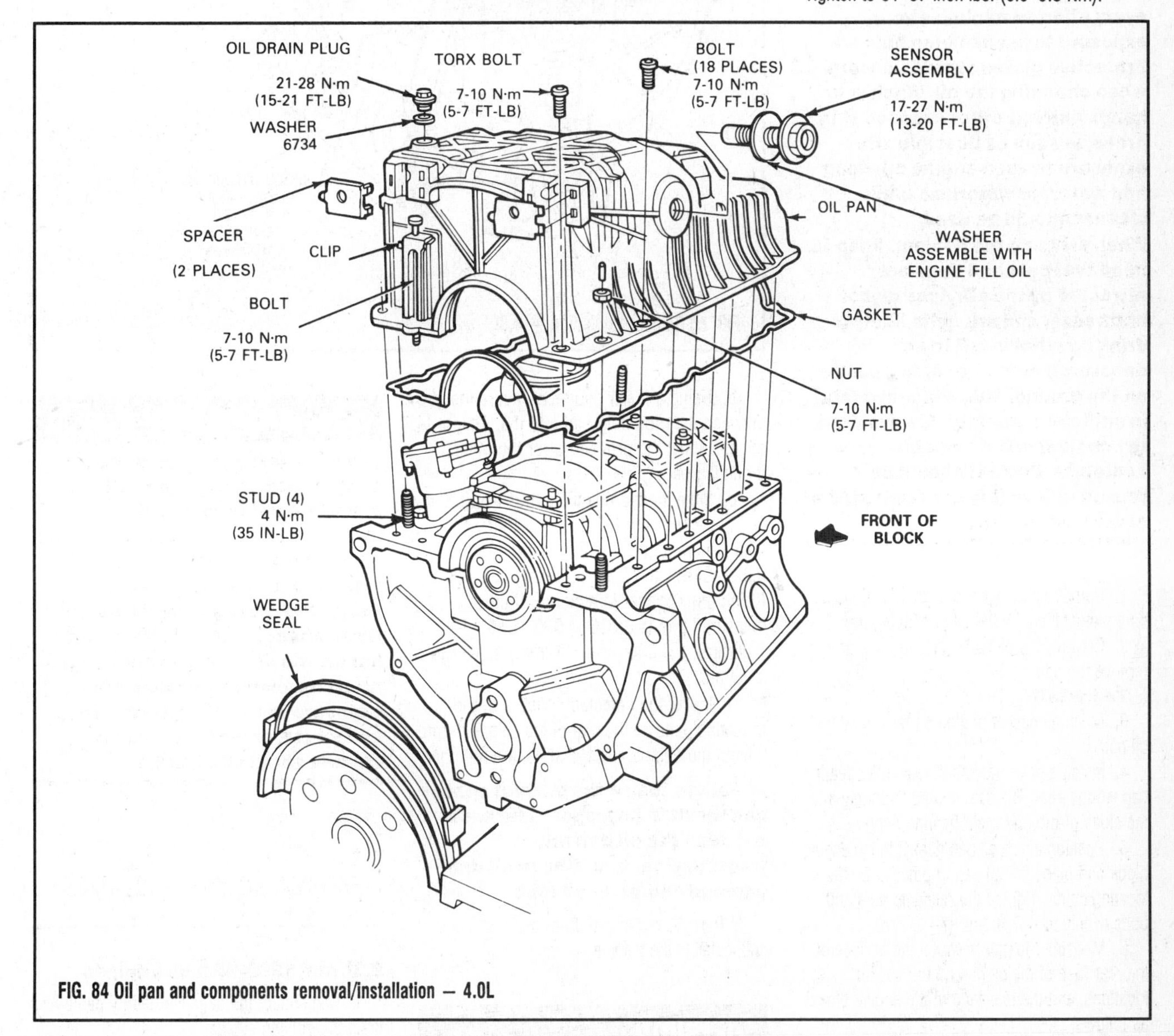

FIG. 84 Oil pan and components removal/installation — 4.0L

12. Install the remaining components in the reverse order of removal. Lower the vehicle and remove the engine support tool. Install the engine mount nuts.

13. Connect the negative battery cable. Fill the crankcase with the proper type and quantity of engine oil. Run the engine and check for leaks.

Navajo

**** CAUTION**

The EPA warns that prolonged contact with used engine oil may cause a number of skin disorders, including cancer! You should make every effort to minimize your exposure to used engine oil. Protective gloves should be worn when changing the oil. Wash your hands and any other exposed skin areas as soon as possible after exposure to used engine oil. Soap and water, or waterless hand cleaner should be used.
When draining the coolant, keep in mind that cats and dogs are attracted by the ethylene glycol antifreeze, and are quite likely to drink any that is left in an uncovered container or in puddles on the ground. This will prove fatal in sufficient quantity. Always drain the coolant into a sealable container. Coolant should be reused unless it is contaminated or several years old.

1. Remove the engine assembly and install on a workstand with the oil pan facing up.

2. Remove the oil pan retaining bolts and remove the pan.

To install:

3. Clean all gasket mating surfaces and the oil pan.

4. Install a new crankshaft rear main bearing cap wedge seal. The seal should fit snugly into the sides of the rear main bearing cap.

5. Position a new oil pan gasket to the engine block and place the oil pan in position on the 4 locating studs. Tighten the retaining nuts and bolts evenly to 5–7 ft. lbs. (7–10 Nm).

6. Measure the gap between the surface of the rear face of the oil pan, at the spacer locations, and the rear face of the engine block as follows:

a. With the oil pan installed on the engine, position a straight edge flat on the rear of the engine block so it extends over 1 of the oil pan/transmission bolt mounting pads.

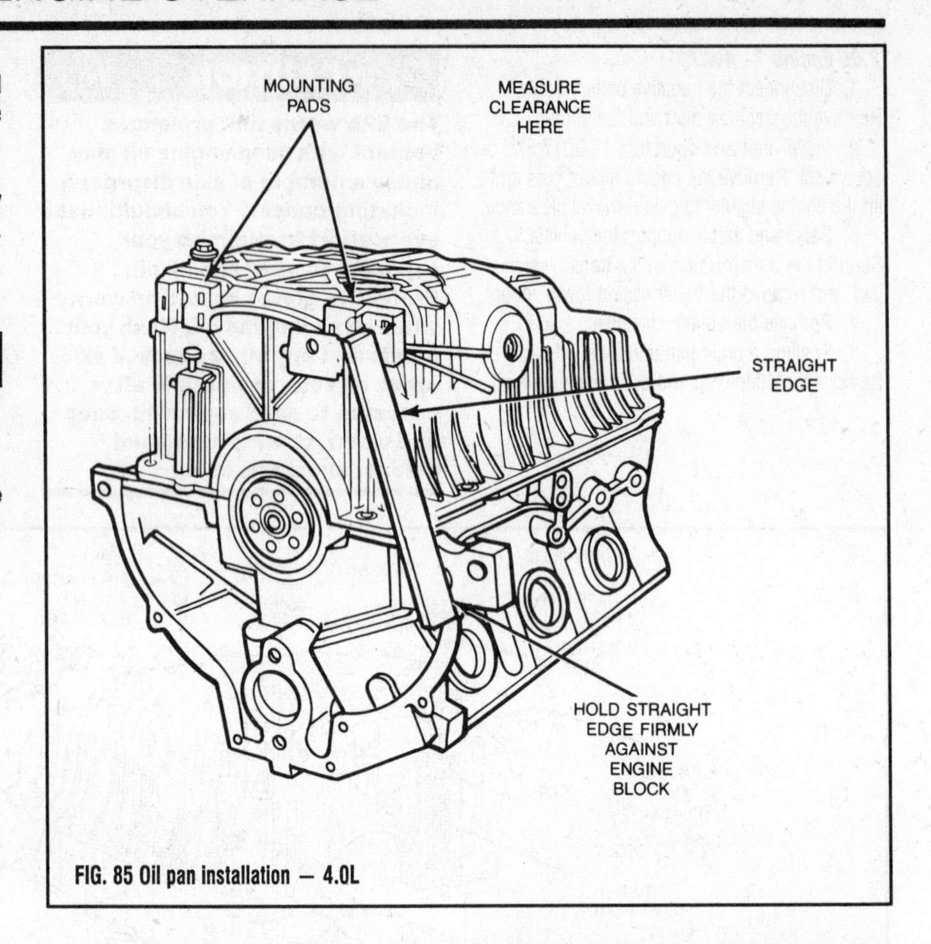

FIG. 85 Oil pan installation — 4.0L

b. Using a feeler gauge, measure the gap between the mounting pad and the straight edge. Repeat the procedure for the other mounting pad.

c. If the measured gap is 0.011–0.020 in. (0.27–0.51mm), a 0.010 in. (0.254mm) spacer is required. If the measured gap is 0.021–0.029 in. (0.52–0.76mm), a 0.020 in. (0.508mm) spacer is required. If the measured gap is 0.030–0.039 in. (0.77–1.00mm), a 0.030 in. (0.762mm) spacer is required.

d. Install the selected spacers to the mounting pads on the rear of the oil pan before bolting the engine and transmission together.

➡ Failure to use the correct spacer can result in improper clearance between the oil pan and transmission, resulting in oil pan damage and/or an oil leak.

7. Remove the engine from the workstand and install in the vehicle.

Oil Pump

➧ SEE FIGS. 86-95

**** CAUTION**

The EPA warns that prolonged contact with used engine oil may cause a number of skin disorders, including cancer! You should make every effort to minimize your exposure to used engine oil. Protective gloves should be worn when changing the oil. Wash your hands and any other exposed skin areas as soon as possible after exposure to used engine oil. Soap and water, or waterless hand cleaner should be used.

REMOVAL & INSTALLATION

2.2L and 1989-93 2.6L Engines

1. Disconnect the negative battery cable and drain the cooling system.

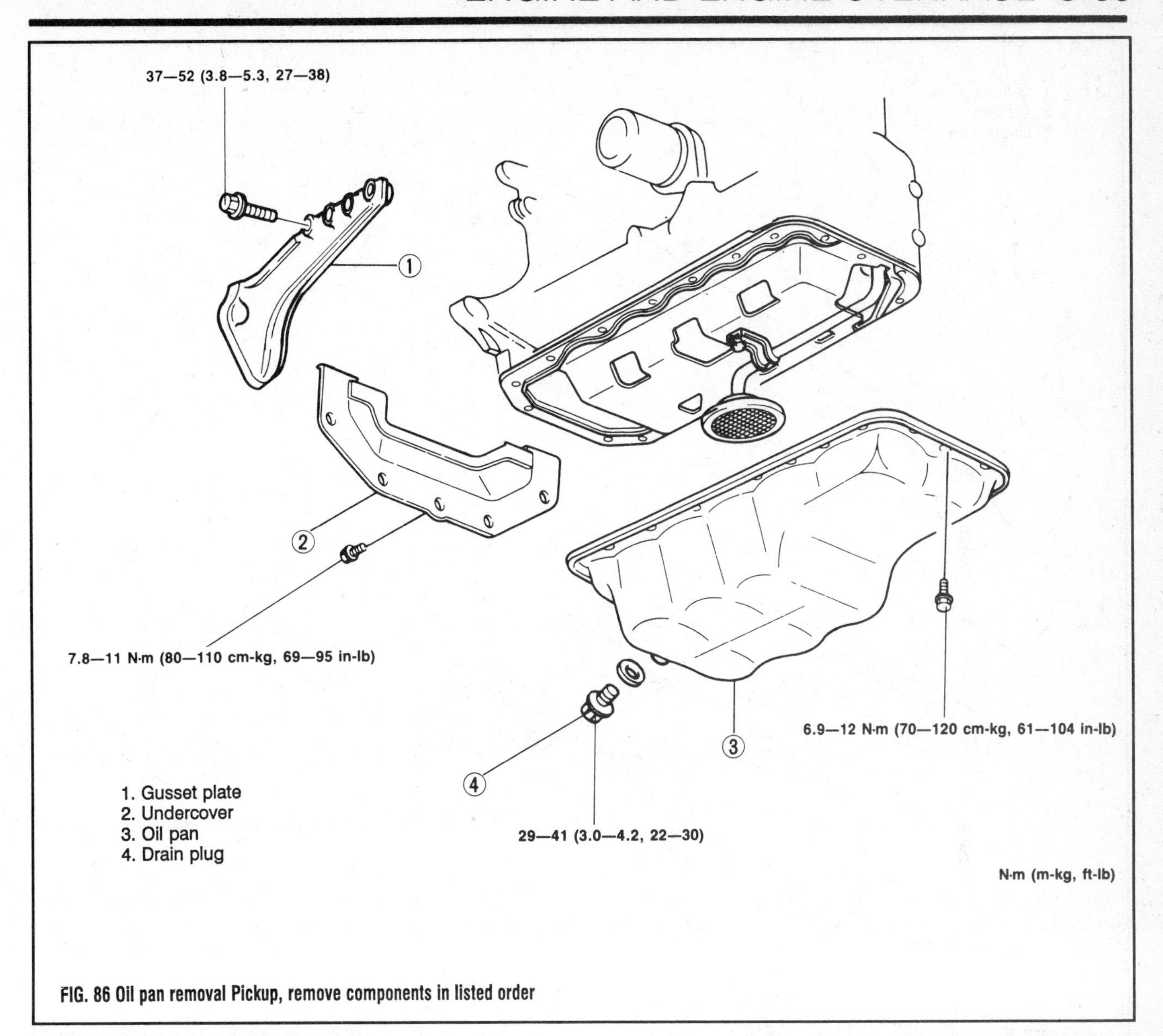

FIG. 86 Oil pan removal Pickup, remove components in listed order

CAUTION

When draining the coolant, keep in mind that cats and dogs are attracted by the ethylene glycol antifreeze, and are quite likely to drink any that is left in an uncovered container or in puddles on the ground. This will prove fatal in sufficient quantity. Always drain the coolant into a sealable container. Coolant should be reused unless it is contaminated or several years old.

2. Raise and safely support the vehicle. Remove the splash shield and drain the engine oil.
3. Remove the oil pan, stiffener and oil pump pickup.
4. Lower the vehicle.
5. On 2.2L engine, remove the timing belt cover, timing belt and crankshaft sprocket. Remove the oil pump mounting bolts and remove the oil pump.
6. On 2.6L engine, remove the cylinder head and the timing chain cover. The oil pump is part of the timing chain cover.
7. If necessary, disassemble the oil pump and check for wear and/or damage. Replace parts as necessary.
8. Pry out the crankshaft oil seal, being careful not to damage the seal housing.

To install:

9. Clean all gasket material.
10. Apply clean engine oil to the lip of a new seal and press the seal into the pump, using a seal installer.
11. On 2.2L engine, proceed as follows:
    a. Apply a continuous bead of silicone sealant to the contact surface of the oil pump. Do not allow sealant to get into the oil hole.
    b. Lubricate a new O-ring and install into the pump body.
    c. Install the oil pump and tighten the three upper, smaller bolts to 14–19 ft. lbs. (19–25 Nm) and the three lower, larger bolts to 27–38 ft. lbs. (37–52 Nm).
    d. Install the crankshaft sprocket, timing belt and timing belt cover.
12. On 2.6L engine, install the timing chain cover and cylinder head.
13. Raise and safely support the vehicle.
14. Install the stiffener. Install a new gasket and the oil pump pickup. Tighten the bolts to 69–95 inch lbs. (7.8–11.0 Nm).
15. Install the oil pan and the splash shield.

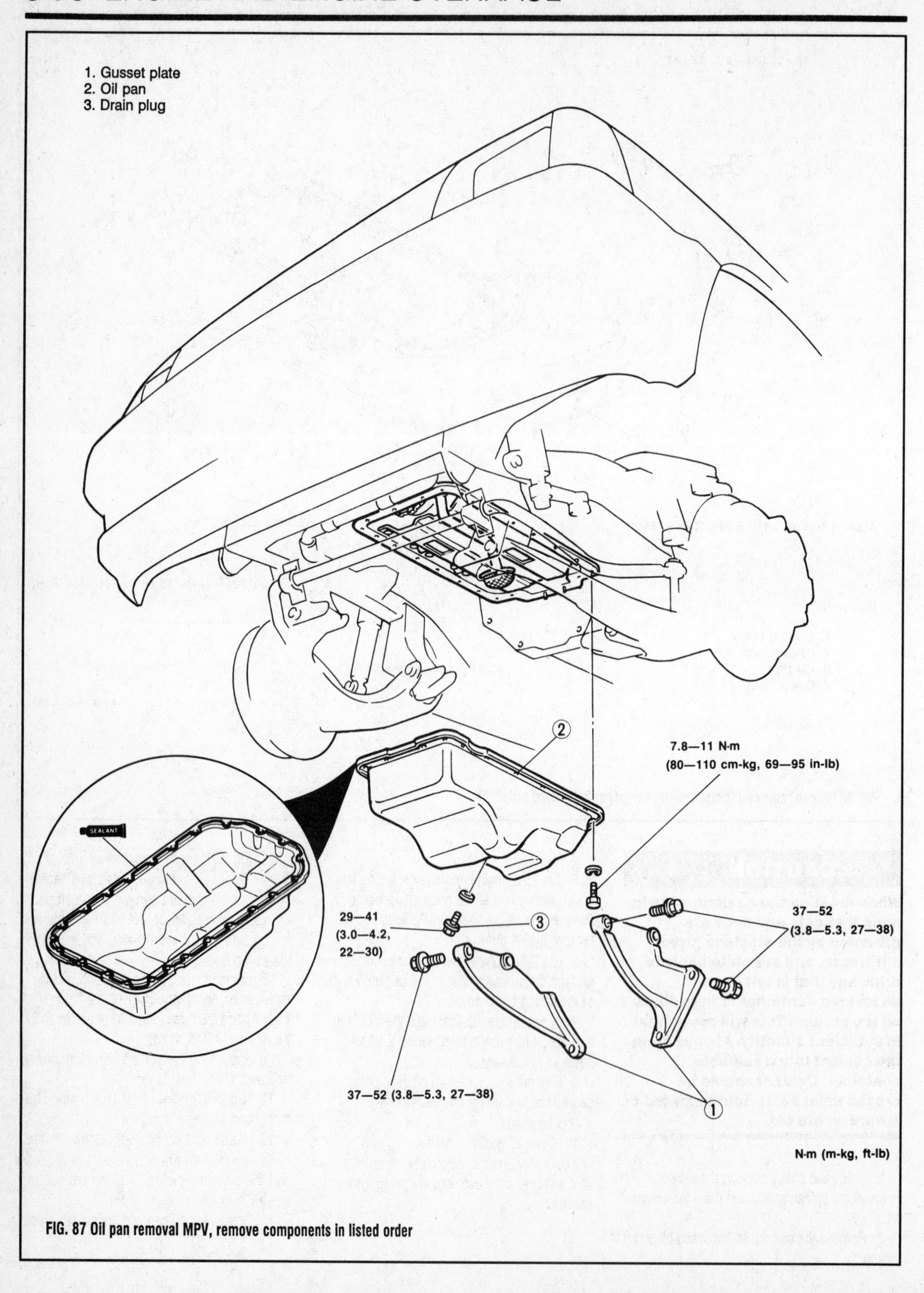

FIG. 87 Oil pan removal MPV, remove components in listed order

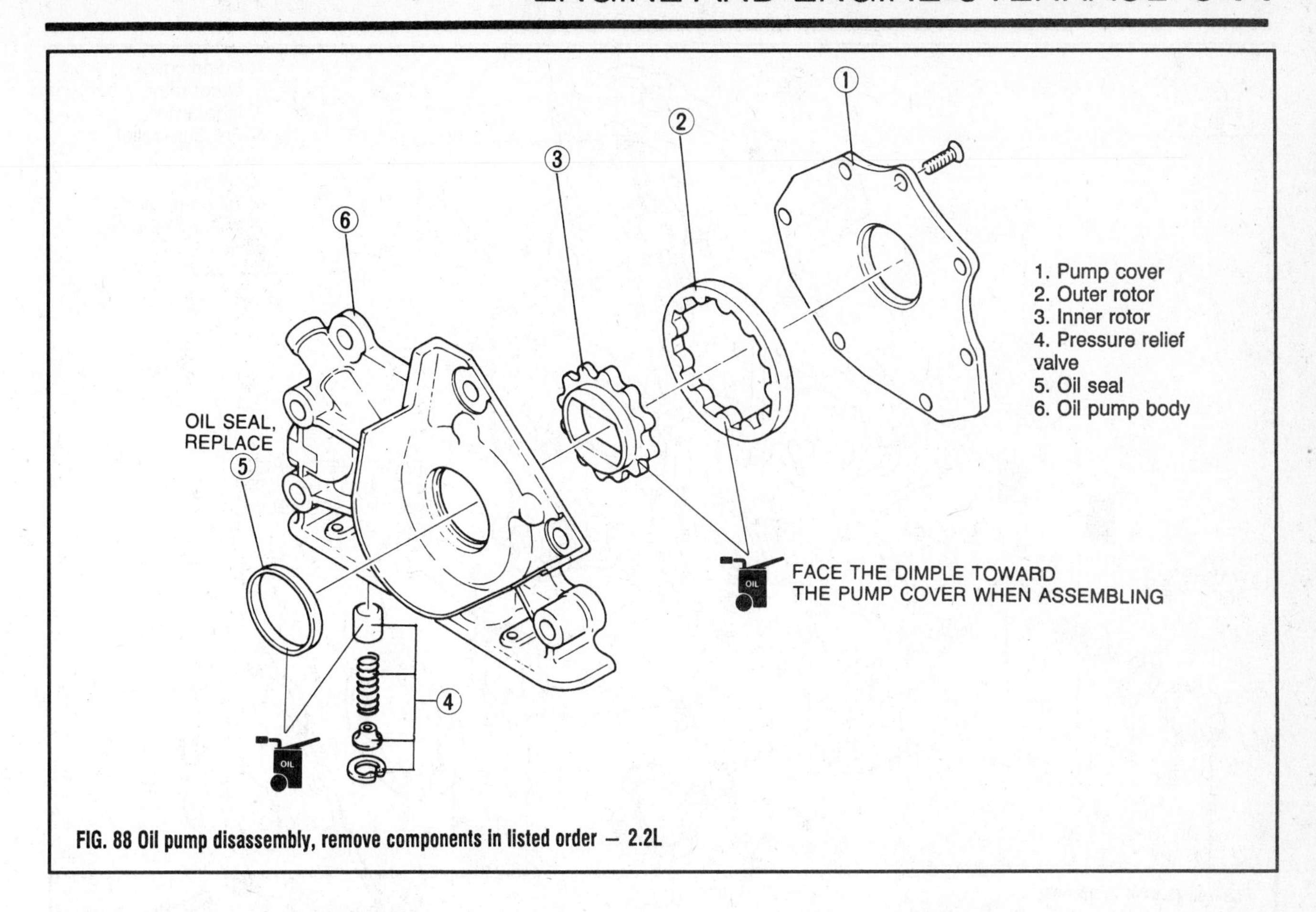

FIG. 88 Oil pump disassembly, remove components in listed order — 2.2L

16. Lower the vehicle and connect the negative battery cable. Fill the engine with the proper type and quantity of engine oil.
17. Run the engine and check for leaks and proper operation.

1987-88 2.6L Engine

1. Relieve the fuel system pressure and disconnect the negative battery cable. Drain the cooling system.

CAUTION

When draining the coolant, keep in mind that cats and dogs are attracted by the ethylene glycol antifreeze, and are quite likely to drink any that is left in an uncovered container or in puddles on the ground. This will prove fatal in sufficient quantity. Always drain the coolant into a sealable container. Coolant should be reused unless it is contaminated or several years old.

2. Raise and safely support the vehicle. Remove the splash shield and drain the engine oil. Remove the oil pan.
3. Lower the vehicle.
4. Remove the cylinder head and timing chain cover.
5. Remove the left and right balancer shaft sprocket bolts and the oil pump drive sprocket bolt.
6. Remove the balancer shaft chain guides.
7. Remove the oil pump and balancer shaft sprockets and chain.
8. Remove the oil pump assembly.
9. If necessary, disassemble the pump and remove the chain tensioner oil pump cover and gears. Inspect all components for wear and/or damage and replace, if necessary.

To install:

10. Clean all gasket mating surfaces.
11. Assemble the oil pump gears, aligning the matching marks and install in the pump with the pump cover.
12. Before installing the pump, put approximately 10cc of clean engine oil in the delivery port.
13. Install the pump with a new gasket and tighten the bolts to 69–78 inch lbs. (8–9 Nm).
14. Install the balancer shaft drive sprocket on the crankshaft. Assemble the balancer shaft sprockets to the balancer shaft chain, making sure the timing marks on the sprockets are aligned with the polished links on the chain.

➡ Be careful not to confuse the right and left sprockets as they are installed in opposite directions.

15. While holding the assembled sprockets and chain, align the timing mark on the crankshaft sprocket with the chain and install the balancer shaft sprockets. Temporarily tighten the bolts by hand.
16. Temporarily install chain guides A, B and C. Set chain guide C to the fully downward position and tighten chain guides A and C to 43–69 inch lbs. (4.9–7.8 Nm).
17. Tighten the balancer shaft sprocket bolt to 43–50 ft. lbs. (59–68 Nm) and the oil pump sprocket bolt to 22–29 ft. lbs. (29–39 Nm).
18. Rotate both balancer shaft sprockets slightly to position the chain slack at the center between the left balancer shaft sprocket and the oil pump sprocket.
19. Adjust the position of chain guide B so that when the chain is pulled away from the guide with the fingertips, the clearance between chain guide B and the chain links is 0.008–0.031 in. (0.2–0.8mm), then tighten the bolts. Tighten the upper bolt to 69–78 inch lbs. (8–9 Nm) and the lower bolt to 11–15 ft. lbs. (15–21 Nm).
20. Carefully install the remaining components.
21. Fill the crankcase with the proper type and quantity of engine oil. Fill and bleed the

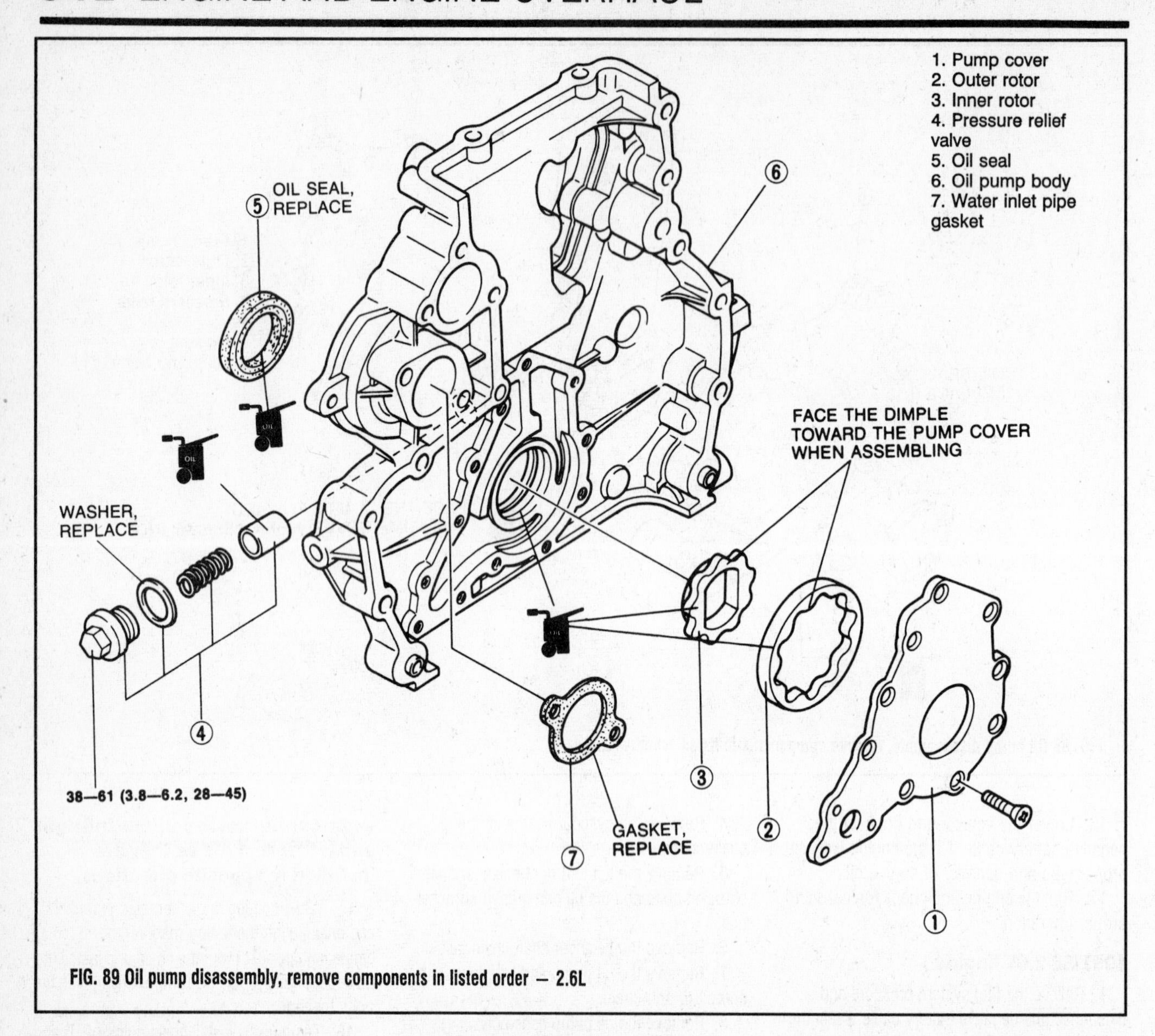

FIG. 89 Oil pump disassembly, remove components in listed order — 2.6L

cooling system. Run the engine and check for leaks and proper operation.

22. Check the idle speed and ignition timing and adjust, if necessary.

3.0L Engine

1. Disconnect the negative battery cable and drain the cooling system.

CAUTION

When draining the coolant, keep in mind that cats and dogs are attracted by the ethylene glycol antifreeze, and are quite likely to drink any that is left in an uncovered container or in puddles on the ground. This will prove fatal in sufficient quantity. Always drain the coolant into a sealable container. Coolant should be reused unless it is contaminated or several years old.

2. Raise and safely support the vehicle. Remove the splash shield and drain the engine oil. Remove the oil pan and oil pump pickup.
3. Lower the vehicle.
4. Remove the timing belt cover, timing belt and crankshaft sprocket.
5. Remove the thermostat assembly.
6. Remove the attaching bolts and remove the oil pump. Disassemble the pump, if necessary and inspect all components for wear and/or damage. Replace components, as necessary.
7. Pry out the crankshaft seal from the pump, being careful not to damage the seal housing.

To install:

8. Clean all gasket mating surfaces.
9. Apply clean engine oil to a new crankshaft seal and install in the pump, using a seal installer.
10. Install a new gasket and the oil pump. Tighten the mounting bolts to 14–19 ft. lbs. (19–25 Nm).
11. Install a new gasket and the thermostat housing. Tighten the mounting bolts to 14–19 ft. lbs. (19–25 Nm).
12. Install the crankshaft sprocket, timing belt and timing belt cover.
13. Raise and safely support the vehicle.
14. Lubricate and install a new O-ring and the oil pump pickup. Tighten the mounting bolts to 69–95 inch lbs. (7.8–11.0 Nm).
15. Install the oil pan and the splash shield. Lower the vehicle.
16. Fill the crankcase with the proper type and quantity of engine oil. Connect the negative battery cable.

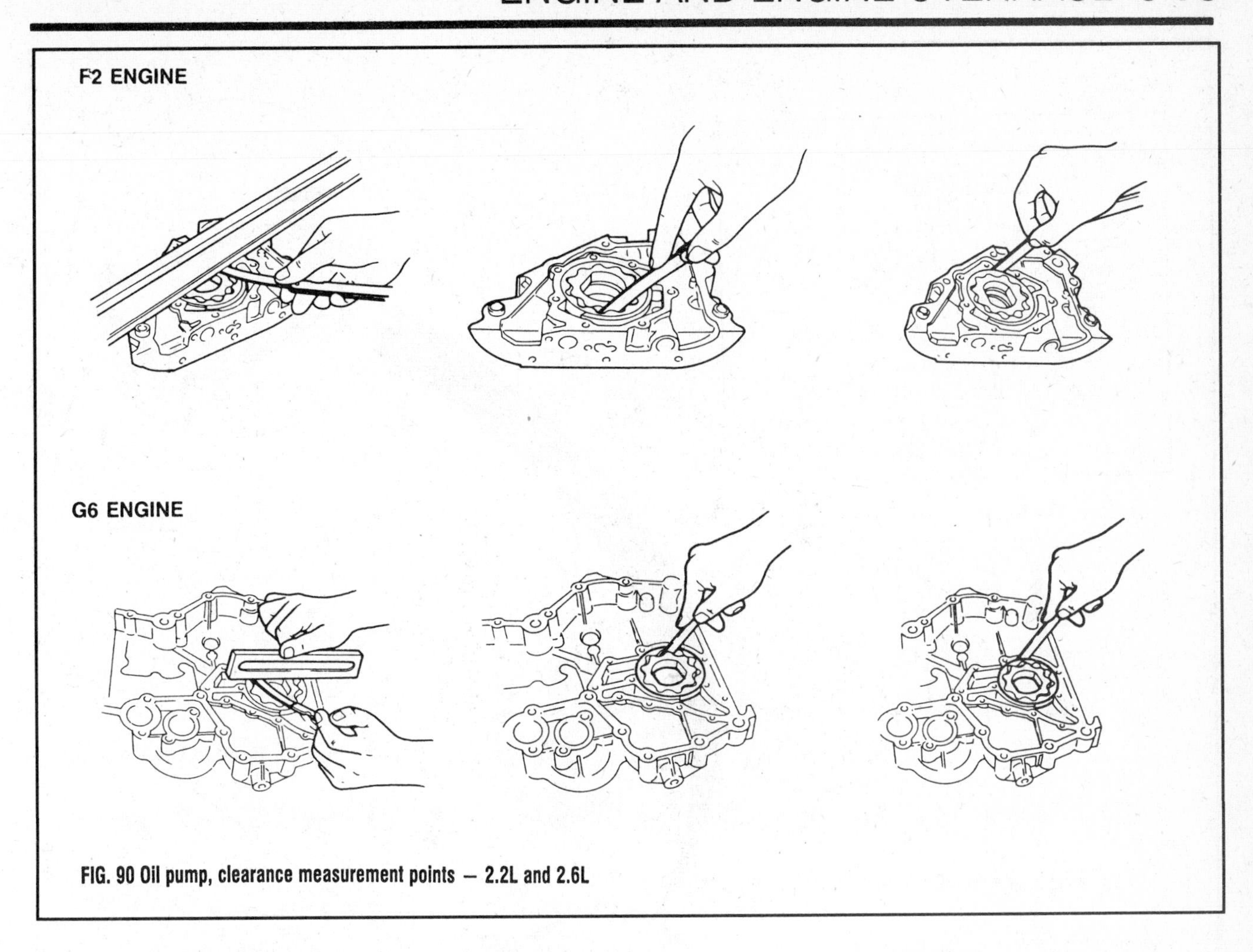

FIG. 90 Oil pump, clearance measurement points — 2.2L and 2.6L

17. Fill and bleed the cooling system. Run the engine and check for leaks and proper operation.

4.0L Engine

1. Remove the engine assembly.
2. Remove the oil pan.
3. Remove the oil pump attaching bolts and withdraw the oil pump driveshaft.

To install:

4. Prime the oil pump by filling either the inlet or outlet port with clean engine oil. Rotate the pump shaft to distribute the oil within the pump body.
5. Insert the oil pump driveshaft into the block with the pointed end facing inward. The pointed end is closest to the pressed-on flange. Position the pump with a new gasket and install the attaching bolts. Tighten to 13–15 ft. lbs. (17–21 Nm).
6. Clean and install the oil pump pickup with a new gasket. Tighten the bolts to 7–10 ft. lbs. (9–13 Nm).
7. Install the oil pan and install the engine assembly.
8. Fill the crankcase with the proper type and quantity of engine oil. Run the engine and check for leaks.

INSPECTION AND OVERHAUL

Except 4.0L Engine and 1987-88 2.6L Engine

1. Remove the pump and disassemble. Clean all parts in solvent and allow to dry.
2. Check for a distorted or damaged oil pump body or cover.
3. Check the relief valve plunger for wear or damage. Check for a weak or broken plunger spring. The spring free length should be 1.827 in. (46.4mm).
4. Check the rotor side clearance as follows: Lay a straightedge across the pump body and, using a feeler gauge, measure between the gear faces and the straightedge. If the clearance exceeds 0.0039 in. (0.10mm) on 2.2L and 1989–93 2.6L engines or 0.0051 in. (0.13mm) on 3.0L engine, replace the pump.
5. Check the rotor tooth tip clearance as follows: Insert a feeler gauge between the gears at the gear tip. If the clearance exceeds 0.0071 in. (0.18mm) on 2.2L and 1989–92 2.6L engines or 0.0094 in. (0.24mm) on 3.0L engine, replace the gears or pump.
6. Check the outer rotor-to-pump body clearance as follows: Insert a feeler gauge between the outer gear and the pump body. If the clearance exceeds 0.0078 in. (0.20mm) on 2.2L and 1989–92 2.6L engine or 0.0091 in. (0.23mm) on 3.0L engine, replace the pump.
7. Apply clean engine oil to the pump components and reassemble. Apply oil to the lip of a new seal and install in the pump, using a seal installer.

4.0L Engine

1. Remove the pump and disassemble. Thoroughly clean all parts in solvent and dry with compressed air.
2. Check the inside of the pump housing and the inner and outer gears for damage or excessive wear. Check the mating surfaces of the pump cover for wear. Minor scuff marks are normal, but if the cover, gears or housing surfaces are excessively worn, scored or grooved, replace the entire pump.
3. Measure the inner to outer rotor tip clearance. With the rotor assembly removed from the pump and resting on a flat surface, the inner and outer rotor tip clearance must not exceed 0.012 in. (0.30mm) with a feeler gauge inserted 1/2 in. (13mm) minimum.

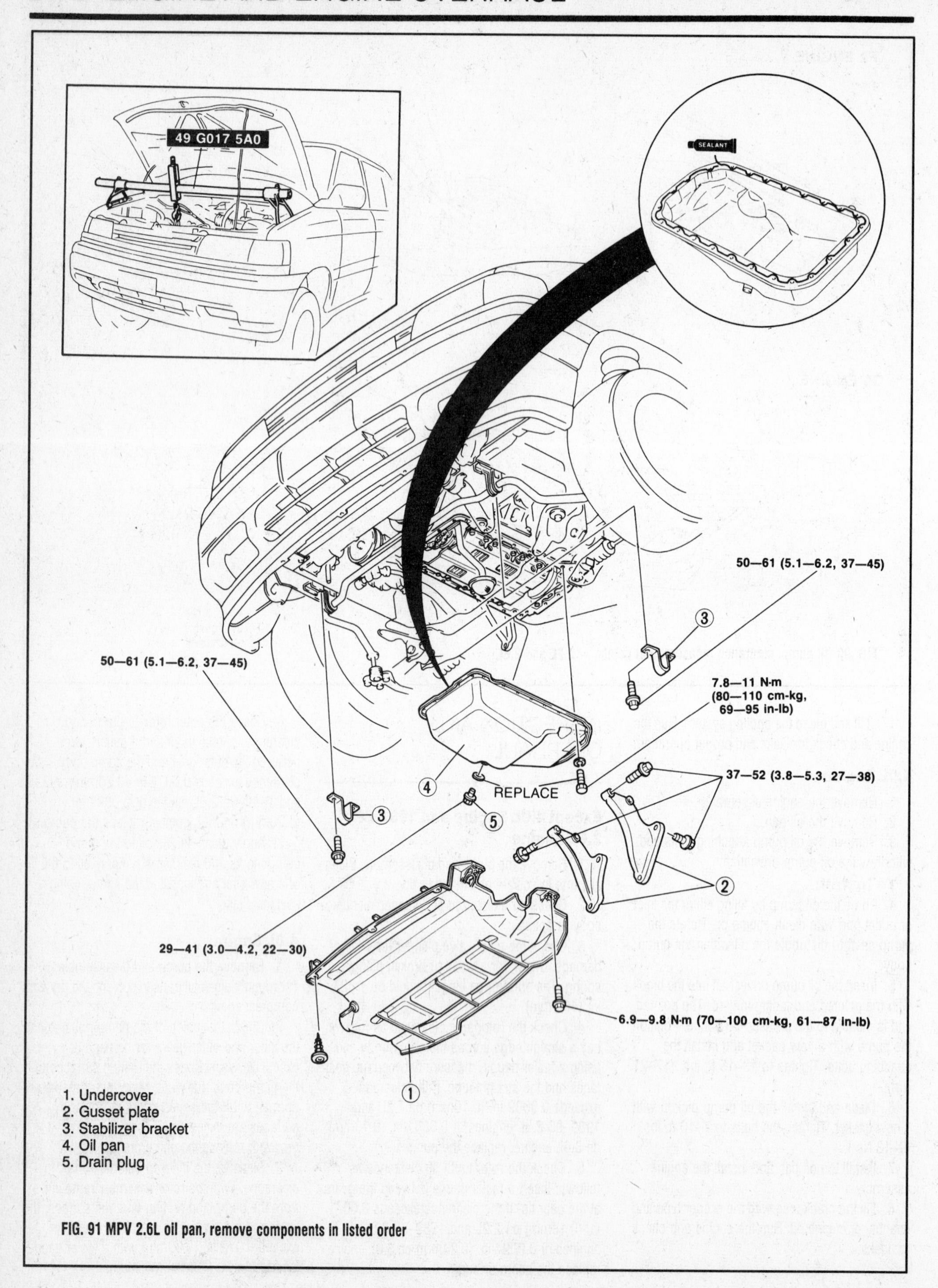

FIG. 91 MPV 2.6L oil pan, remove components in listed order

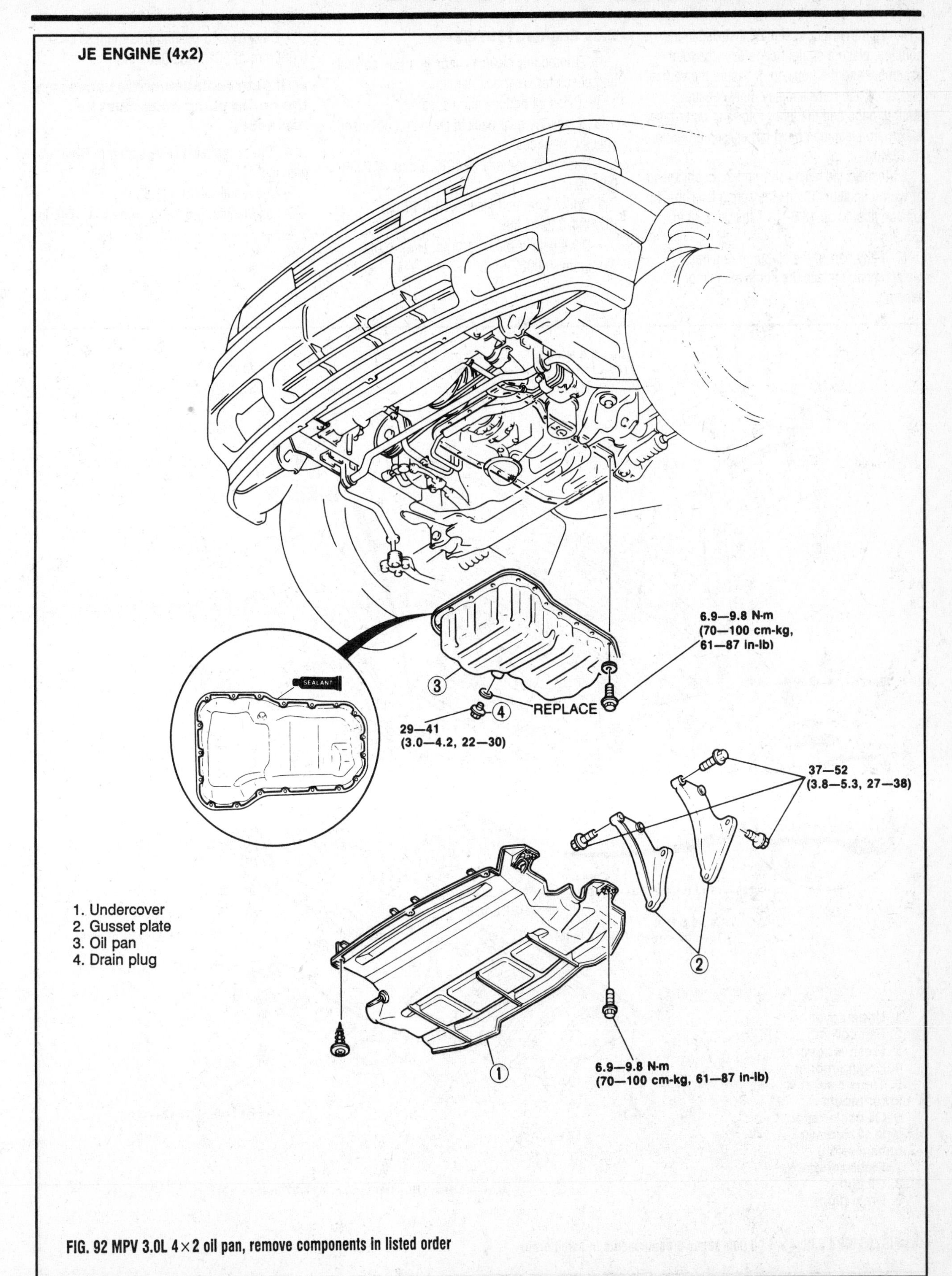

FIG. 92 MPV 3.0L 4×2 oil pan, remove components in listed order

4. With the rotor assembly installed in the housing, place a straight edge over the rotor assembly and the housing. Measure the vertical clearance, the rotor endplay, between the straight edge and the inner rotor and outer race. Maximum clearance must not exceed 0.005 in. (0.13mm).

5. Inspect the relief valve spring for collapsed or worn condition. Check the spring tension. The tension should be 13.6–14.7 lbs. at 1.39 in. (35.3mm).

6. If any part of the oil pump requires replacement, replace the complete pump assembly.

2.6L Engine (1987-88)

1. Thoroughly clean all parts in a safe solvent and check for wear and damage.

2. Clean all orifices and passages.

3. Place the gear back in the pump body and check clearances.

- Gear teeth-to-body: 0.10-0.15mm (0.0039-0.0059 in.)
- Driven gear end play: 0.06-0.12mm (0.0024-0.0047 in.)
- Drive gear-to-bearing (front end): 0.020-0.045mm (0.00079-0.00177 in.)
- Drive gear-to-bearing (rear end): 0.043-0.066mm (0.00169-0.00259 in.)

➡ If gear replacement is necessary, the entire pump body must be replaced.

4. Check the relief valve spring for wear or damage.

- Free length: 47mm (1.85 in.)
- Load/length: 9.5 lb. @ 40mm (1.5748 in.)

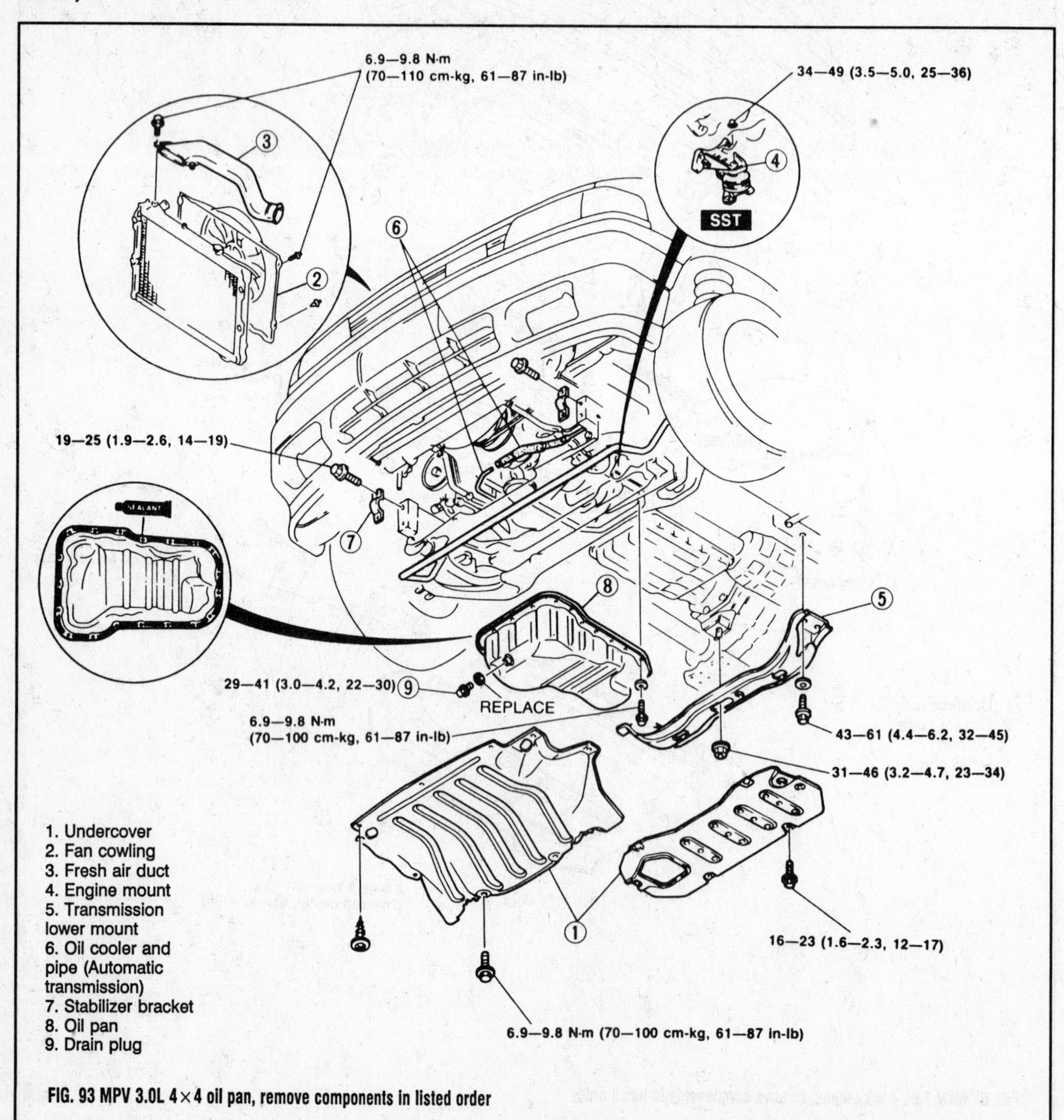

FIG. 93 MPV 3.0L 4×4 oil pan, remove components in listed order

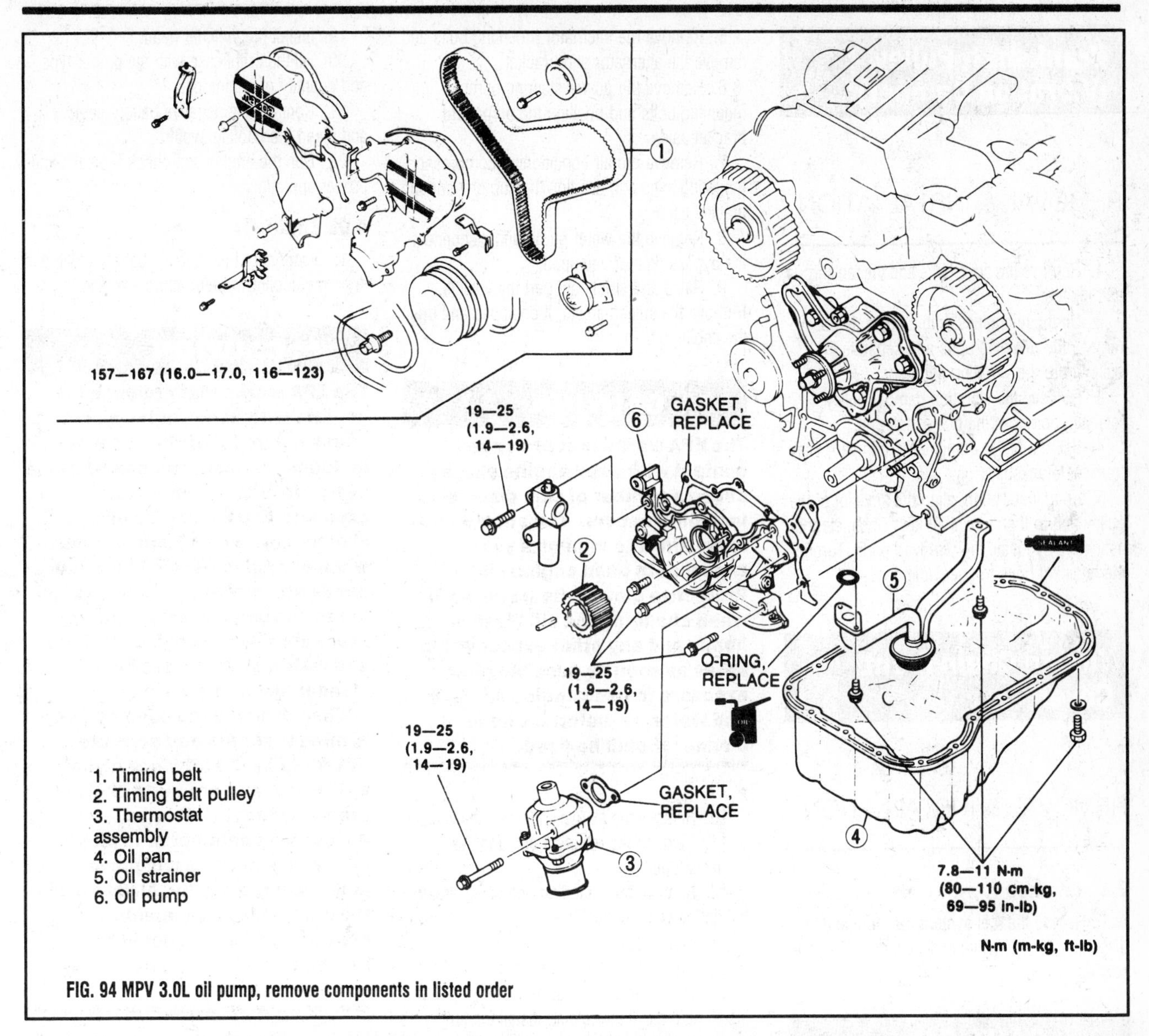

FIG. 94 MPV 3.0L oil pump, remove components in listed order

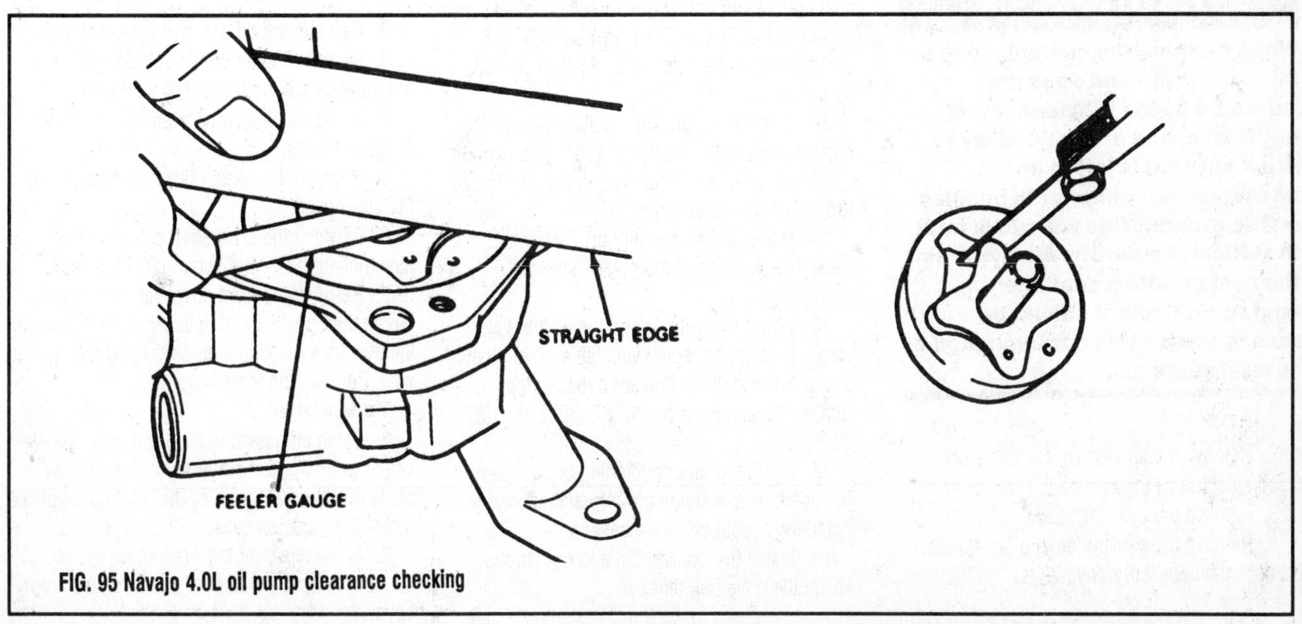

FIG. 95 Navajo 4.0L oil pump clearance checking

Crankshaft Pulley (Vibration Damper)

REMOVAL & INSTALLATION

1. Remove the drive belts and the fan shroud, as required.
2. On those engines with a separate pulley, remove the retaining bolts and separate the pulley from the vibration damper.
3. Remove the vibration damper/pulley retaining bolt from the crankshaft end.
4. Using a puller, remove the damper/pulley from the crankshaft.
5. Upon installation, align the key slot of the pulley hub to the crankshaft key. Complete the assembly by install the removed parts. Torque the retaining bolts to specifications.

Timing Chain Front Cover

REMOVAL & INSTALLATION

2.6L Engines

1. Relieve the fuel system pressure and disconnect the negative battery cable. Drain the cooling system.

**** CAUTION**

When draining the coolant, keep in mind that cats and dogs are attracted by the ethylene glycol antifreeze, and are quite likely to drink any that is left in an uncovered container or in puddles on the ground. This will prove fatal in sufficient quantity. Always drain the coolant into a sealable container. Coolant should be reused unless it is contaminated or several years old.

2. Remove the air cleaner assembly or disconnect the air intake tube.
3. Remove the cylinder head.
4. Remove the cooling fan and fan shroud. Remove the accessory drive belts.
5. Remove the alternator mounting bolts and remove the alternator and bracket.
6. Remove the power steering pump mounting bolts and position the pump and bracket aside.
7. Remove the air conditioning compressor mounting bolts and position the compressor and bracket aside.
8. Remove the water pump and disconnect the bypass pipe, if equipped.
9. Raise and safely support the vehicle. Remove the splash shield, if equipped and drain the engine oil.

**** CAUTION**

The EPA warns that prolonged contact with used engine oil may cause a number of skin disorders, including cancer! You should make every effort to minimize your exposure to used engine oil. Protective gloves should be worn when changing the oil. Wash your hands and any other exposed skin areas as soon as possible after exposure to used engine oil. Soap and water, or waterless hand cleaner should be used.

10. Remove the oil pan and lower the vehicle.
11. Remove the retaining bolt and the crankshaft pulley.
12. Remove the attaching bolts and remove the timing chain cover.

To install:

13. Clean all gasket mating surfaces. Coat new timing chain cover gaskets with sealer and install on the cylinder block. Install the timing chain cover and tighten the mounting bolts to 104–122 inch lbs. (12–14 Nm) on 1987–88 vehicles or 14–19 ft. lbs. (19–25 Nm) on 1989–92 vehicles.
14. Install the crankshaft pulley. Tighten the retaining bolt to 80–94 ft. lbs. (108–128 Nm) on 1987–88 vehicles or 130–145 ft. lbs. (177–196 Nm) on 1989–92 vehicles.
15. Raise and safely support the vehicle. Install the oil pan and the splash shield, if equipped.
16. Lower the vehicle and install the water pump. If equipped, apply vegetable oil to a new O-ring and install the coolant bypass pipe. Tighten the attaching bolt to 27–38 ft. lbs. (37–52 Nm).
17. Install the air conditioning compressor, if equipped, power steering pump and alternator. Install the accessory drive belts.
18. Install the cooling fan and fan shroud. Adjust the drive belt tension.
19. Install the cylinder head.
20. Fill the crankcase with the proper type and quantity of engine oil.
21. Connect the negative battery cable. Fill and bleed the cooling system.
22. Run the engine and check for leaks and proper operation.

4.0L Engine

1. Disconnect the negative battery cable and drain the cooling system and crankcase.

**** CAUTION**

The EPA warns that prolonged contact with used engine oil may cause a number of skin disorders, including cancer! You should make every effort to minimize your exposure to used engine oil. Protective gloves should be worn when changing the oil. Wash your hands and any other exposed skin areas as soon as possible after exposure to used engine oil. Soap and water, or waterless hand cleaner should be used.

When draining the coolant, keep in mind that cats and dogs are attracted by the ethylene glycol antifreeze, and are quite likely to drink any that is left in an uncovered container or in puddles on the ground. This will prove fatal in sufficient quantity. Always drain the coolant into a sealable container. Coolant should be reused unless it is contaminated or several years old.

2. Remove the oil pan and the radiator.
3. Remove the air conditioning compressor and power steering bracket, if equipped.
4. Remove the alternator and drive belt(s). Remove the fan.
5. Remove the water pump and heater and radiator hoses.
6. Remove the crankshaft pulley/damper assembly and the crankshaft timing sensor.
7. Remove the front cover retaining bolts, noting their positions. If necessary, tap the cover lightly with a plastic hammer to break the gasket seal. Remove the front cover.

To install:

8. Clean all gasket mating surfaces. Apply sealer to the gasket surfaces on the cylinder block and the back side of the front cover plate. Install the guide sleeves.
9. Apply sealer to the front cover gasket surface and position a new gasket on the front cover.

10. Install the front cover with the retaining screws. Note the different bolt lengths. Tighten the bolts to 13–15 ft. lbs. (17–21 Nm).

11. Install the crankshaft timing sensor.

12. Install the crankshaft pulley/damper assembly. Tighten the attaching bolt to 30–37 ft. lbs. (40–50 Nm), then tighten an additional 80–90 degrees.

13. Install the remaining components in the reverse order of their removal. Fill and bleed the cooling system. Run the engine and check for leaks.

Front Cover Oil Seal

REMOVAL & INSTALLATION

1. Disconnect the negative battery cable and drain the cooling system.
2. Remove the cooling fan and fan shroud.
3. Disconnect the upper and lower radiator hoses and remove the radiator, if necessary to provide access.

CAUTION

When draining the coolant, keep in mind that cats and dogs are attracted by the ethylene glycol antifreeze, and are quite likely to drink any that is left in an uncovered container or in puddles on the ground. This will prove fatal in sufficient quantity. Always drain the coolant into a sealable container. Coolant should be reused unless it is contaminated or several years old.

4. Remove the accessory drive belt(s).
5. Remove the crankshaft pulley.
6. Pry the seal from the front cover, using a suitable prybar. Be careful not to damage the seal housing.
7. Clean the pulley and seal area. Inspect the crankshaft pulley surface for grooving or other damage. Repair or replace, as necessary.

To install:

8. Install a new seal into the cover using a seal installer. The seal must be flush with the edge of the timing chain cover.
9. Apply clean engine oil to the seal lip and the crankshaft pulley. Install the crankshaft pulley and tighten the retaining bolt to:
   - 1987-88 2.6L — 80–94 ft. lbs. (108–128 Nm)
   - 1989-92 2.6L — 130–145 ft. lbs. (177–196 Nm)
   - 4.0L — 30–37 ft. lbs. (40–50 Nm), plus an additional 80–90 degrees
10. Install the accessory drive belt(s). Install the radiator, if removed.
11. Install the cooling fan and fan shroud. Adjust the drive belt tension.
12. Connect the negative battery cable, start the engine and check for leaks.

Timing Chain and Sprockets

➧ SEE FIGS. 96-102

REMOVAL & INSTALLATION

1987-88 2.6L Engine

CONVENTIONAL METHOD

1. Relieve the fuel system pressure, if injected and disconnect the negative battery cable. Drain the cooling system and engine oil.

CAUTION

The EPA warns that prolonged contact with used engine oil may cause a number of skin disorders, including cancer! You should make every effort to minimize your exposure to used engine oil. Protective gloves should be worn when changing the oil. Wash your hands and any other exposed skin areas as soon as possible after exposure to used engine oil. Soap and water, or waterless hand cleaner should be used.

When draining the coolant, keep in mind that cats and dogs are attracted by the ethylene glycol antifreeze, and are quite likely to drink any that is left in an uncovered container or in puddles on the ground. This will prove fatal in sufficient quantity. Always drain the coolant into a sealable container. Coolant should be reused unless it is contaminated or several years old.

2. Remove the cylinder head, oil pan and timing chain cover.
3. Loosen the balancer shaft sprocket bolts, then remove the balancer shaft chain guides. Remove the balancer shaft sprockets and chain assembly.
4. Push in and hold the chain tensioner head, then remove the timing chain and sprockets. If necessary, remove the timing chain guides.
5. Inspect the chain, sprockets and guides for damage and/or wear. Replace, as necessary.

To install:

6. Install the timing chain guides and tighten to 7.2–8.7 ft. lbs. (10–12 Nm).
7. Align the plated links of the timing chain with the timing marks on the sprockets as the chain and sprockets are assembled.
8. Hold the chain tensioner head in, then slide the crankshaft sprocket onto the crankshaft and place the camshaft sprocket on the sprocket holder.
9. Install the balancer shaft drive sprocket on the crankshaft. Assemble the balancer shaft sprockets to the balancer shaft chain, making sure the timing marks on the sprockets are aligned with the polished links on the chain.

➡ **Be careful not to confuse the right and left sprockets as they are installed in opposite directions.**

10. While holding the assembled sprockets and chain, align the timing mark on the crankshaft sprocket with the chain and install the balancer shaft sprockets. Temporarily tighten the bolts by hand.
11. Temporarily install chain guides A, B and C. Set chain guide C to the fully downward position and tighten chain guides A and C to 43–69 inch lbs. (4.9–7.8 Nm).
12. Tighten the balancer shaft sprocket bolt to 43–50 ft. lbs. (59–68 Nm) and the oil pump sprocket bolt to 22–29 ft. lbs. (29–39 Nm).

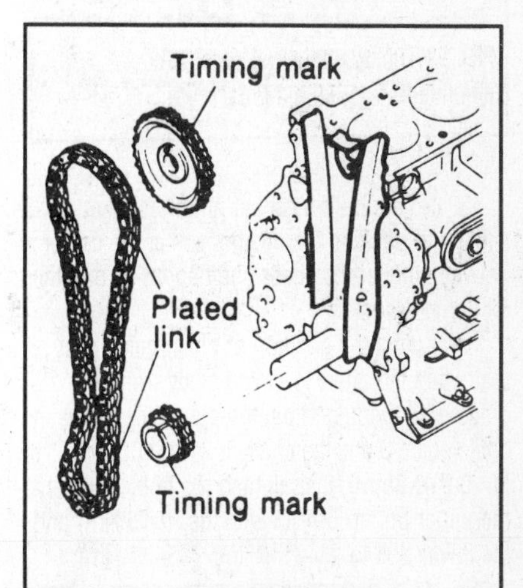

FIG. 96 Timing chain and sprocket alignment — 1987–88 2.6L

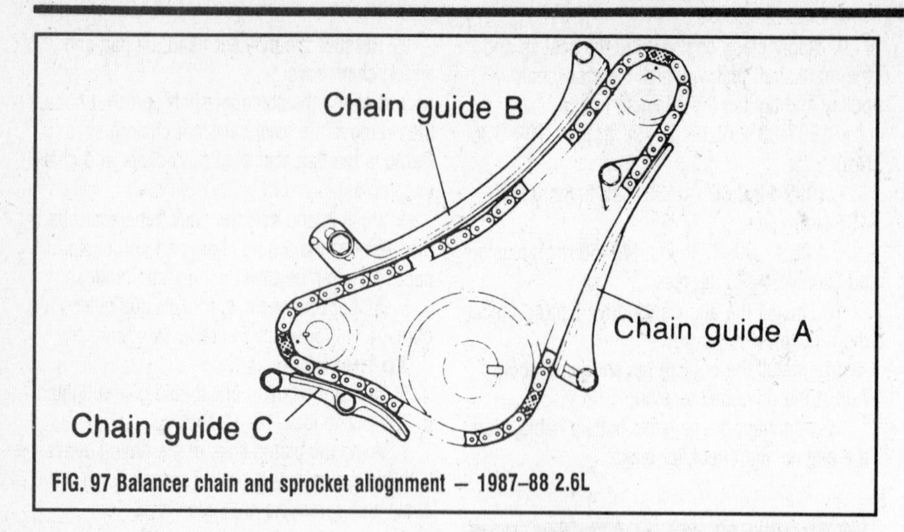

FIG. 97 Balancer chain and sprocket aliognment — 1987–88 2.6L

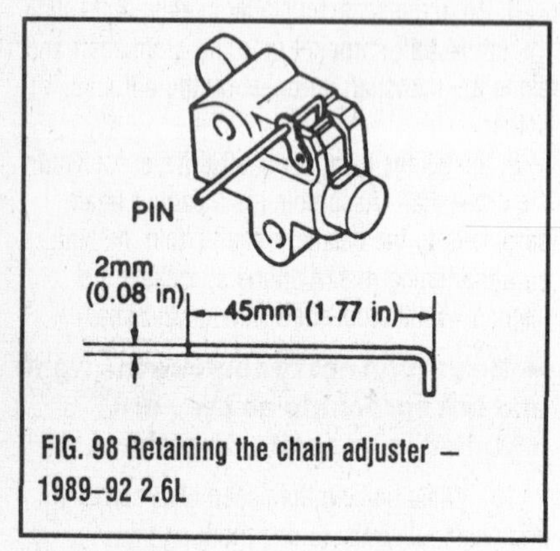

FIG. 98 Retaining the chain adjuster — 1989–92 2.6L

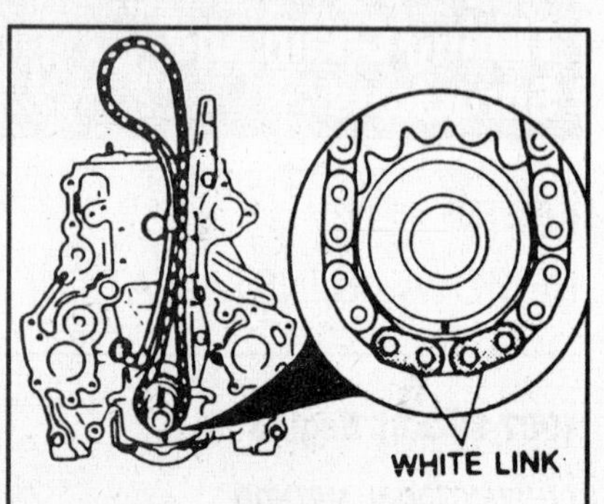

FIG. 100 Timing chain and sprocket alignment — 1989–92 2.6L

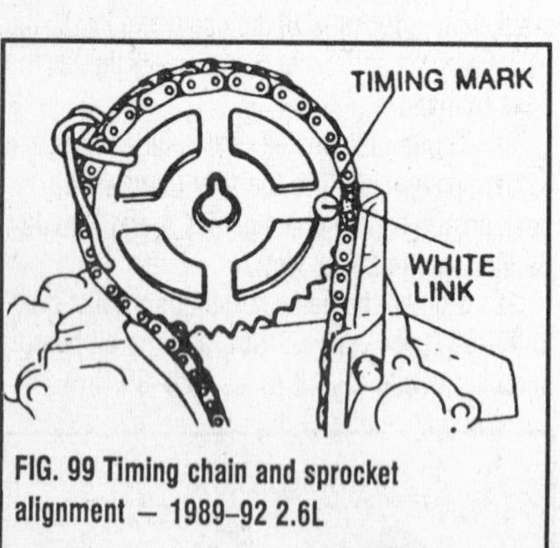

FIG. 99 Timing chain and sprocket alignment — 1989–92 2.6L

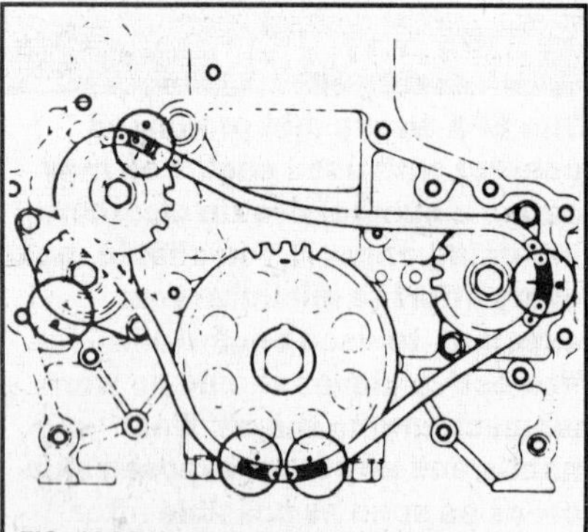
FIG. 101 Balancer chain and sprocket alignment — 1989–92 2.6L

13. Rotate both balancer shaft sprockets slightly to position the chain slack at the center between the left balancer shaft sprocket and the oil pump sprocket.
14. Adjust the position of chain guide B so that when the chain is pulled away from the guide with the fingertips, the clearance between chain guide B and the chain links is 0.008–0.031 in. (0.2–0.8mm), then tighten the bolts. Tighten the upper bolt to 69–78 inch lbs. (8–9 Nm) and the lower bolt to 11–15 ft. lbs. (15–21 Nm).
15. Install the remaining components in the reverse order of removal.
16. Fill the crankcase with the proper type and quantity of engine oil. Fill and bleed the cooling system. Run the engine and check for leaks and proper operation.
17. Check the idle speed and ignition timing and adjust, if necessary.

ALTERNATE METHOD

The following procedure can be used to replace the timing chain without removing the cylinder head or timing chain cover.

1. Disconnect the negative battery cable and remove the air cleaner.
2. Remove the spark plugs and the rocker arm cover.
3. Turn the crankshaft until the polished link is at the top of the camshaft sprocket.

➡ **Stuff rags between the camshaft sprocket and cylinder head to prevent objects from falling into the engine.**

4. Remove the polished link by using chain link remover tool 49 4120 110 or equivalent.
5. Connect the new timing chain to the used chain as follows:
   a. Pass the joint link through the end of the used chain and the end of the new chain.
   b. Attach the polished link and secure it with the clip.
6. Insert suitable wooden wedges between the timing chain and the cylinder head to ensure the chain stays in contact with the sprocket.
7. Turn the crankshaft slowly to engage the new timing chain onto the camshaft sprocket. When the new chain is completely engaged, remove the old chain.
8. Connect the new timing chain as follows:
   a. Insert the intermediate link plate in the center of the chain.
   b. Align the holes and pass the joint link through them.
   c. Attach the polished link and secure with the clip. The open part of the clip must face the passenger's side of the vehicle.
9. Install the rocker arm cover and spark plugs. Install the air cleaner and connect the negative battery cable.
10. Run the engine and check for proper operation. Check the idle speed and the ignition timing.

1989–92 2.6L Engine

1. Relieve the fuel system pressure and disconnect the negative battery cable. Drain the cooling system and engine oil.

✲✲ CAUTION

The EPA warns that prolonged contact with used engine oil may cause a number of skin disorders, including cancer! You should make every effort to minimize your exposure to used engine oil. Protective gloves should be worn when changing the oil. Wash your hands and any other exposed skin areas as soon as possible after exposure to used engine oil. Soap and water, or waterless hand cleaner should be used.

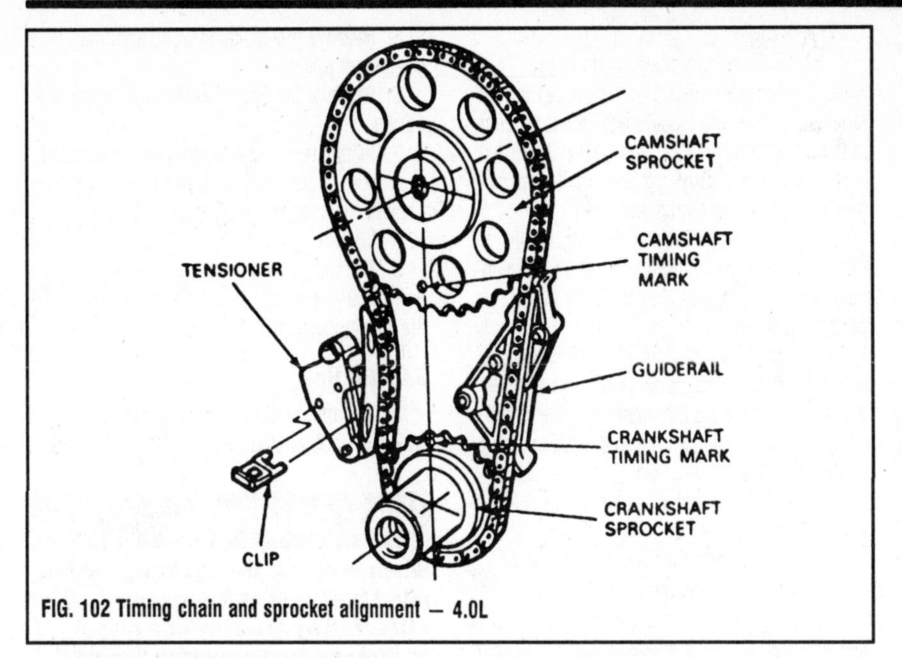

FIG. 102 Timing chain and sprocket alignment — 4.0L

When draining the coolant, keep in mind that cats and dogs are attracted by the ethylene glycol antifreeze, and are quite likely to drink any that is left in an uncovered container or in puddles on the ground. This will prove fatal in sufficient quantity. Always drain the coolant into a sealable container. Coolant should be reused unless it is contaminated or several years old.

2. Remove the cylinder head, oil pan and timing chain cover.
3. Before replacing any further components, check the following:
   a. Check the timing chain tension; if the adjuster sleeve protrudes 13 notches or more, replace the timing chain.
   b. Push the chain lever towards the driver's side of the vehicle. If there is excessive movement, there will be a chain adjuster malfunction or worn chain lever, chain guide, camshaft sprocket or crankshaft sprocket. Inspect and replace as necessary.
   c. Push the chain adjuster sleeve towards the passenger's side of the vehicle. If it moves back, the chain adjuster ratchet will be faulty and the chain adjuster must be replaced.
4. Remove the crankshaft spacer.
5. Loosen the idler sprocket lock bolt, then remove the balancer shaft chain guides.
6. Remove the idler sprocket assembly, crankshaft balancer chain sprocket and balancer chain.
7. Remove the timing chain adjuster.
8. Remove the camshaft sprocket, timing chain and crankshaft sprocket. Remove the key from the crankshaft.
9. Remove the timing chain lever and chain guide.
10. Inspect all components for damage and/or wear and replace as necessary.

To install:

11. Install the chain guide and tighten the mounting bolts to 61–78 inch lbs. (6.9–8.8 Nm).
12. Install the chain lever and check that it moves smoothly from right to left. Tighten the mounting bolt to 69–95 inch lbs. (7.8–11.0 Nm).
13. Push the chain adjuster sleeve in toward the left and insert a 1.77 in. (45mm) long by 0.08 in. (2mm) diameter pin into the lever hole to hold it in position. Install the chain adjuster and tighten the mounting bolts to 69–95 inch lbs. (7.8–11.0 Nm).
14. Install the key into the crankshaft keyway. Install the crankshaft sprocket.
15. Install the timing chain on the crankshaft sprocket, aligning the 2 white links with the crankshaft sprocket timing mark.
16. Install the camshaft sprocket so the timing mark on the sprocket aligns with the single white link of the timing chain. Secure the timing chain to the sprocket with wire and temporarily rest it between the chain lever and guide.
17. Install the crankshaft balancer sprocket.
18. Set the balancer chain on the idler sprocket assembly so the timing mark on the idler sprocket assembly and the brown link of the balancer chain align.
19. Install the balancer chain so the 5 alignment marks on the chain, sprocket and block align and attach the idler sprocket assembly to the cylinder block. Loosely tighten the idler sprocket assembly lock bolt.
20. Install the right and left lower balancer chain guides and tighten the mounting bolts to 69–95 inch lbs. (7.8–11.0 Nm).
21. Install the upper chain guide and loosely tighten the mounting and adjusting bolts.
22. Tighten the idler sprocket assembly lock bolt to 27–38 ft. lbs. (37–52 Nm) and install the spacer.
23. On 1989 B Series pickup and all MPV, adjust the balancer chain tension as follows:
   a. Loosen the upper chain guide adjusting bolt.
   b. Push on the chain guide just above the adjusting slot with a force of approximately 11 lbs., then pull back the guide 0.14 ± 0.012 in. (3.5 ± 0.3mm) and tighten the bolt to 69–95 inch lbs. (7.8–11.0 Nm). Tighten the guide pivot bolt to the same specification.
   c. The chain slack at the notch in the guide should be 0.12 in. (3mm) when the guide is properly adjusted.
24. On 1990–91 B Series pickup with manual transmission, adjust the balancer chain tension as follows:
   a. Tighten the upper chain guide pivot bolt to 69–95 inch lbs. (7.8–11.0 Nm).
   b. Loosen the upper chain guide adjusting bolt.
   c. Push on the chain guide just above the adjusting slot with a force of approximately 11 lbs., then pull back the guide 0.24 ± 0.012 in. (6.0 ± 0.3mm) and tighten the bolt to 69–95 inch lbs. (7.8–11.0 Nm).
   d. The chain slack at the notch in the guide should be 0.23 in. (5.8mm) when the guide is properly adjusted.
25. On all 1992 and 1990–91 B Series pickup with automatic transmission, adjust the balancer chain tension as follows:
   a. Fabricate a piece of wood, 0.118–0.138 in. (3.0–3.5mm) thick and 0.335–0.374 in. (8.5–9.5mm) wide.
   b. Insert the piece of wood in the notch in the upper chain guide.
   c. Push on the chain guide just above the adjusting slot with a force of 2.9–3.7 lbs. and tighten the adjusting and pivot bolts to 69–95 inch lbs. (7.8–11.0 Nm).
   d. Remove the wood from between the chain and chain guide, making sure no wood shavings are left.
   e. Measure the chain slack. It should be 0.039–0.059 in. (1.0–1.5mm) at the notch in the guide.

➡ **If the upper chain guide bottoms on the adjusting bolt during the adjustment procedure, the balancer chain must be replaced.**

26. Install the remaining components in the reverse order of removal.

➡ **Be sure to remove the pin from the timing chain adjuster before installing the service cover.**

27. Fill the crankcase with the proper type and quantity of oil. Fill and bleed the cooling system.
28. Run the engine and check for leaks and proper operation. Check the idle speed and ignition timing.

4.0L Engine

1. Disconnect the negative battery cable and drain the cooling system and crankcase.

✻✻ CAUTION

The EPA warns that prolonged contact with used engine oil may cause a number of skin disorders, including cancer! You should make every effort to minimize your exposure to used engine oil. Protective gloves should be worn when changing the oil. Wash your hands and any other exposed skin areas as soon as possible after exposure to used engine oil. Soap and water, or waterless hand cleaner should be used.

When draining the coolant, keep in mind that cats and dogs are attracted by the ethylene glycol antifreeze, and are quite likely to drink any that is left in an uncovered container or in puddles on the ground. This will prove fatal in sufficient quantity. Always drain the coolant into a sealable container. Coolant should be reused unless it is contaminated or several years old.

2. Remove the oil pan and radiator. Remove the accessory drive belt and crankshaft damper.
3. Remove the water pump and timing chain front cover.
4. Remove the camshaft sprocket retaining bolt and the crankshaft sprocket key.
5. Push the timing chain tensioner into the retracted position and install the retaining clip.
6. Remove the crankshaft and camshaft sprockets with the timing chain. Remove the tensioner and guide, as required.

To install:

7. Install the timing chain guide to the cylinder block with the pin of the guide inserted into the oil hole in the block. Install the 2 retaining bolts and tighten to 7–9 ft. lbs. (10–12 Nm).
8. Position the camshaft and crankshaft so the sprocket timing marks will align.
9. Install the sprockets and timing chain together. Install the timing chain tensioner with the clip in place to lock the tensioner in the retracted position.
10. Install the crankshaft key and check the timing marks on the sprockets for correct alignment. Make sure the tensioner side of the timing chain is held inward and the guide side of the chain is straight and tight.
11. Install the camshaft sprocket retaining bolt and tighten to 44–50 ft. lbs. (60–68 Nm). Remove the clip from the tensioner assembly.
12. Install the timing chain front cover and the remaining components in the reverse order of their removal. Fill the crankcase with the proper type and quantity of engine oil. Fill and bleed the cooling system. Run the engine and check for leaks.

Timing Belt Front Cover

➧ SEE FIGS. 103-104

REMOVAL & INSTALLATION

2.2L Engine

1. Disconnect the negative battery cable and drain the cooling system.

✻✻ CAUTION

When draining the coolant, keep in mind that cats and dogs are attracted by the ethylene glycol antifreeze, and are quite likely to drink any that is left in an uncovered container or in puddles on the ground. This will prove fatal in sufficient quantity. Always drain the coolant into a sealable container. Coolant should be reused unless it is contaminated or several years old.

2. Remove the cooling fan and fan shroud.
3. Remove the accessory drive belt(s) and the cooling fan pulley and bracket.
4. If carburetor equipped, remove the secondary air pipe assembly.
5. Remove the retaining bolts and the crankshaft pulley.
6. Remove the upper and lower timing belt covers.
7. Installation is the reverse of the removal procedure. Install the timing belt covers with new gaskets. Tighten the bolts to 61–87 inch lbs. (6.9–9.8 Nm).
8. Tighten the crankshaft pulley retaining bolts to 9–13 ft. lbs. (12–17 Nm). Fill and bleed the cooling system.

3.0L Engine

1. Disconnect the negative battery cable and drain the cooling system.

✻✻ CAUTION

When draining the coolant, keep in mind that cats and dogs are attracted by the ethylene glycol antifreeze, and are quite likely to drink any that is left in an uncovered container or in puddles on the ground. This will prove fatal in sufficient quantity. Always drain the coolant into a sealable container. Coolant should be reused unless it is contaminated or several years old.

2. Tag and disconnect the spark plug wires from the spark plugs. Remove the spark plugs.
3. Remove the fresh air duct, cooling fan and fan shroud.
4. Remove the accessory drive belt(s) and the air conditioning compressor idler pulley.
5. Remove the retaining bolt and remove the crankshaft pulley.
6. Remove the coolant bypass hose and upper radiator hose.
7. Remove the timing belt covers and gaskets.
8. Installation is the reverse of the removal procedure. Install the timing belt covers with new gaskets. Tighten the 6mm bolts to 69–95 inch lbs. (7.8–11.0 Nm) and the 10mm bolt to 27–38 ft. lbs. (37–52 Nm).
9. Tighten the crankshaft pulley bolt to 116–123 ft. lbs. (157–167 Nm).

OIL SEAL REPLACEMENT

2.2L Engine

CRANKSHAFT SEAL

1. Disconnect the negative battery cable and drain the engine oil.

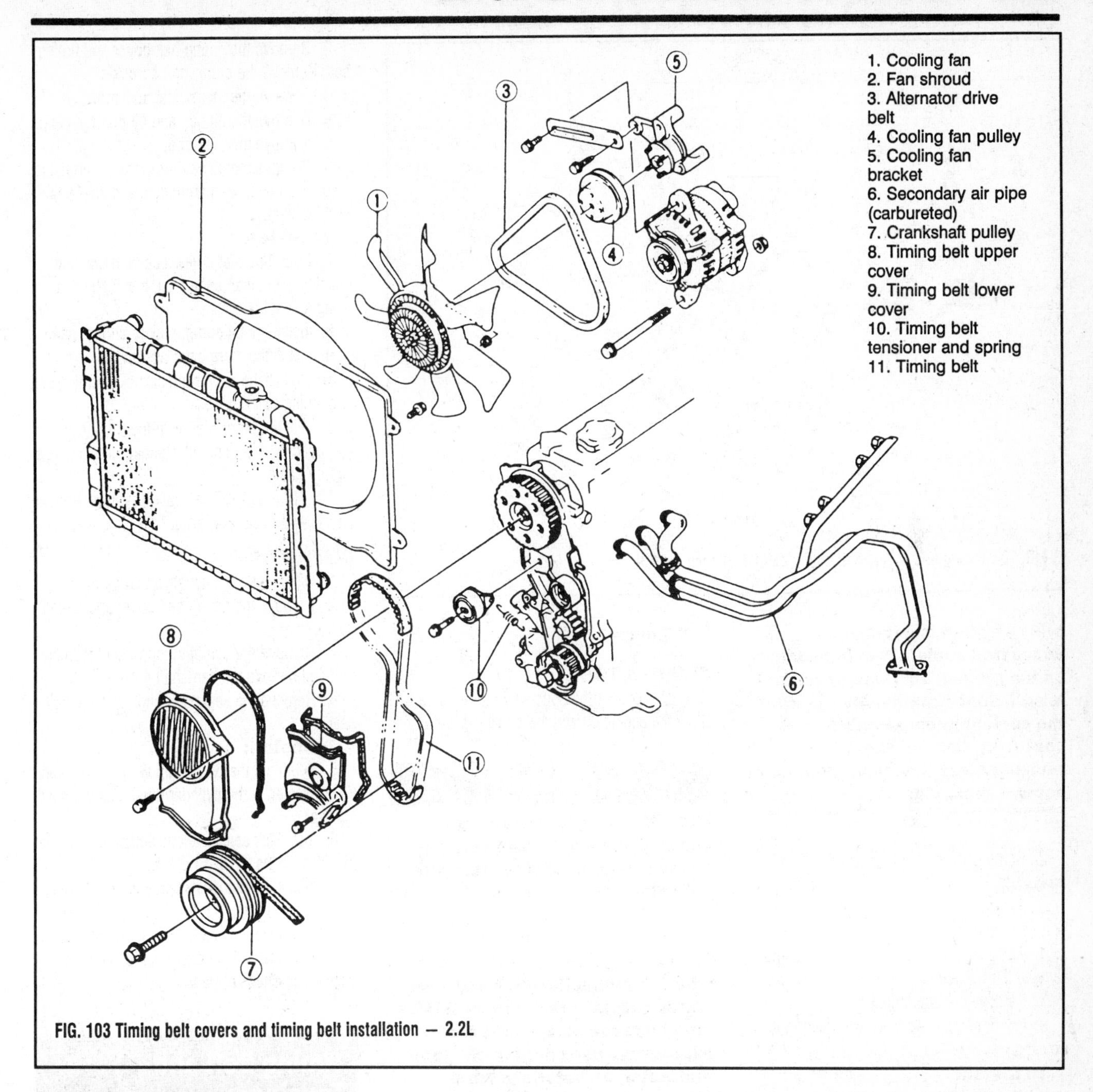

FIG. 103 Timing belt covers and timing belt installation — 2.2L

CAUTION

The EPA warns that prolonged contact with used engine oil may cause a number of skin disorders, including cancer! You should make every effort to minimize your exposure to used engine oil. Protective gloves should be worn when changing the oil. Wash your hands and any other exposed skin areas as soon as possible after exposure to used engine oil. Soap and water, or waterless hand cleaner should be used.

2. Remove the timing belt cover and timing belt.
3. Remove the crankshaft sprocket retaining bolt and the crankshaft sprocket.
4. Remove the oil seal using a small prybar. Be careful not to damage the seal housing.

To install:

5. Apply clean engine oil to the lip of a new seal and fit the seal into the oil pump body.
6. Tap the seal in place using a seal installer until the seal is flush with the edge of the pump body.
7. Install the crankshaft sprocket and tighten the retaining bolt to 116–123 ft. lbs. (157–167 Nm).
8. Install the timing belt and timing belt cover. Connect the negative battery cable.
9. Fill the engine with the proper type and quantity of engine oil. Run the engine and check for leaks.

CAMSHAFT SEAL

1. Disconnect the negative battery cable and drain the cooling system.

CAUTION

When draining the coolant, keep in mind that cats and dogs are attracted by the ethylene glycol antifreeze, and are quite likely to

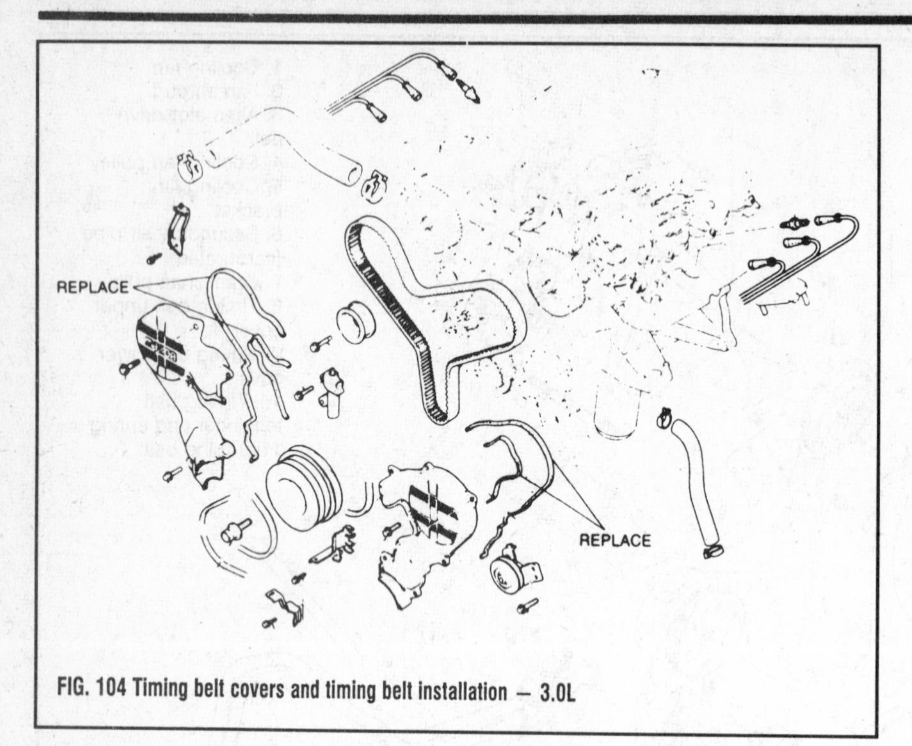

FIG. 104 Timing belt covers and timing belt installation — 3.0L

drink any that is left in an uncovered container or in puddles on the ground. This will prove fatal in sufficient quantity. Always drain the coolant into a sealable container. Coolant should be reused unless it is contaminated or several years old.

2. Remove the timing belt cover and the timing belt.
3. Remove the camshaft sprocket retaining bolt and remove the sprocket.
4. Disconnect the upper radiator hose and remove the distributor.
5. Remove the front housing.
6. Pry or press the oil seal from the front housing.

To install:

7. Clean all gasket mating surfaces.
8. Apply engine oil to the front housing and a new oil seal. Press the seal into the front housing.
9. Apply engine oil to the seal lip and install the front housing with a new gasket. Tighten the mounting bolts to 14–19 ft. lbs. (19–25 Nm).
10. Connect the upper radiator hose and install the distributor.
11. Install the camshaft sprocket and tighten the retaining bolt to 35–48 ft. lbs. (47–65 Nm).
12. Install the timing belt and the timing belt cover. Connect the negative battery cable.
13. Fill and bleed the cooling system. Run the engine and check for leaks. Check the ignition timing.

3.0L Engine

CRANKSHAFT SEAL

1. Disconnect the negative battery cable. Drain the engine oil and the cooling system.

⁂ CAUTION

The EPA warns that prolonged contact with used engine oil may cause a number of skin disorders, including cancer! You should make every effort to minimize your exposure to used engine oil. Protective gloves should be worn when changing the oil. Wash your hands and any other exposed skin areas as soon as possible after exposure to used engine oil. Soap and water, or waterless hand cleaner should be used.

⁂ CAUTION

When draining the coolant, keep in mind that cats and dogs are attracted by the ethylene glycol antifreeze, and are quite likely to drink any that is left in an uncovered container or in puddles on the ground. This will prove fatal in sufficient quantity. Always drain the coolant into a sealable container. Coolant should be reused unless it is contaminated or several years old.

2. Remove the timing belt cover and timing belt. Remove the crankshaft sprocket.
3. Remove the thermostat assembly.
4. Remove the oil pan and oil pump pickup.
5. Remove the oil pump.
6. Remove the oil seal from the pump using a suitable driver. Be careful not to damage the seal housing.

To install:

7. Coat the lip of a new seal and the seal housing with clean engine oil. Install the seal using a seal installer.
8. Install the oil pump, pickup and oil pan.
9. Install the thermostat assembly.
10. Install the crankshaft sprocket, timing belt and timing belt covers.
11. Fill the crankcase with the proper type and quantity of engine oil. Connect the negative battery cable.
12. Fill and bleed the cooling system. Run the engine and check for leaks.

CAMSHAFT SEAL

1. Disconnect the negative battery cable.
2. Remove the timing belt cover and timing belt.
3. Remove the camshaft sprocket retaining bolt and remove the camshaft sprocket.
4. Remove the seal plate and the camshaft seal.

To install:

5. Lubricate the oil seal lip with clean engine oil and install in the cylinder head, using a seal installer.
6. Install the seal plate and tighten the bolts to 69–95 inch lbs. (7.8–11.0 Nm).
7. Install the camshaft sprocket and tighten the retaining bolt to 52–59 ft. lbs. (71–80 Nm).
8. Install the timing belt and timing belt cover. Connect the negative battery cable, start the engine and check for leaks.

Timing Belt and Tensioner

➧ SEE FIGS. 105-114

REMOVAL & INSTALLATION

2.2L Engine

1. Disconnect the negative battery cable and drain the cooling system.

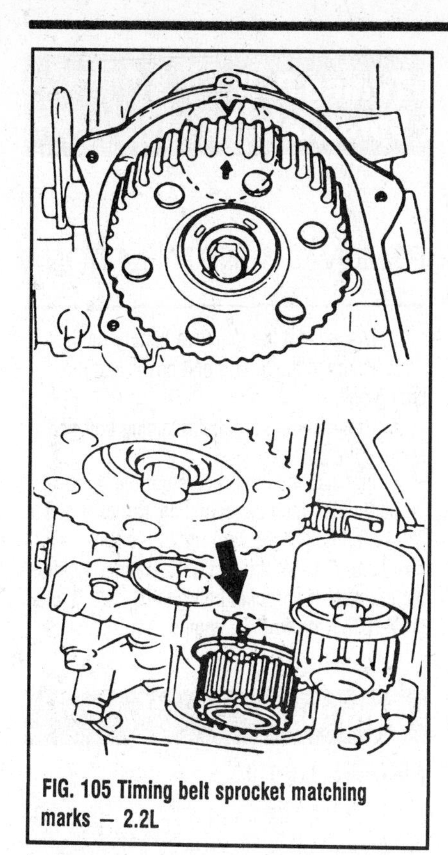

FIG. 105 Timing belt sprocket matching marks — 2.2L

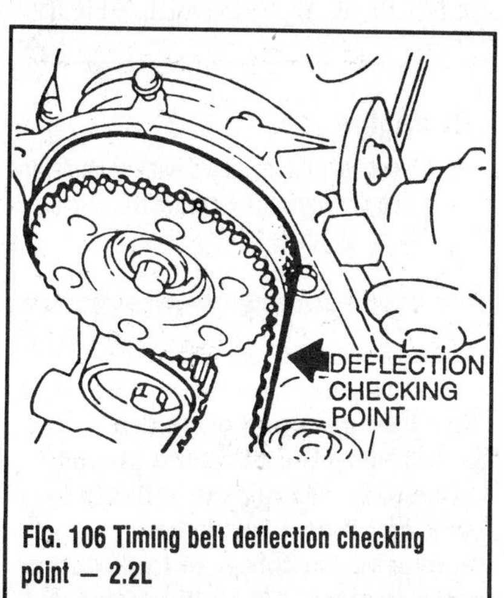

FIG. 106 Timing belt deflection checking point — 2.2L

⁂ CAUTION

When draining the coolant, keep in mind that cats and dogs are attracted by the ethylene glycol antifreeze, and are quite likely to drink any that is left in an uncovered container or in puddles on the ground. This will prove fatal in sufficient quantity. Always drain the coolant into a sealable container. Coolant should be reused unless it is contaminated or several years old.

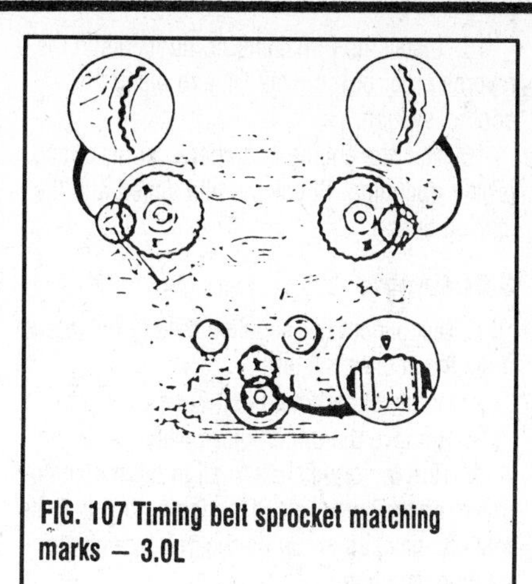

FIG. 107 Timing belt sprocket matching marks — 3.0L

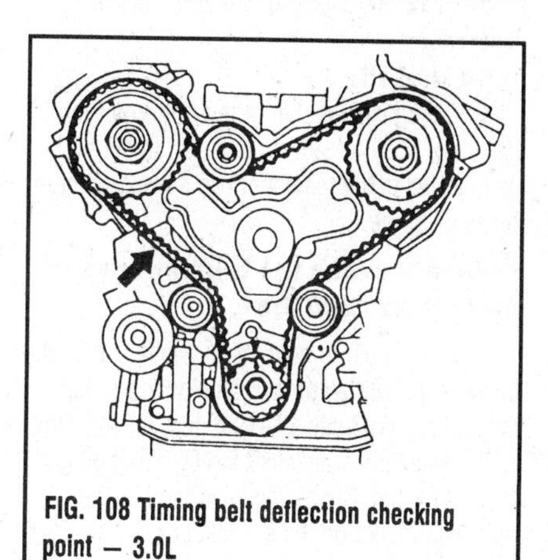

FIG. 108 Timing belt deflection checking point — 3.0L

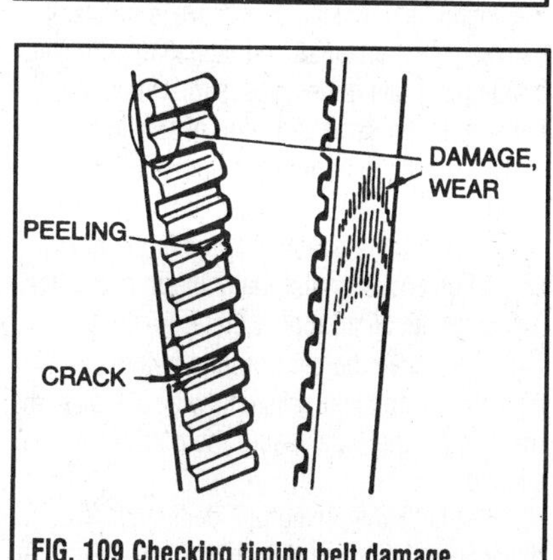

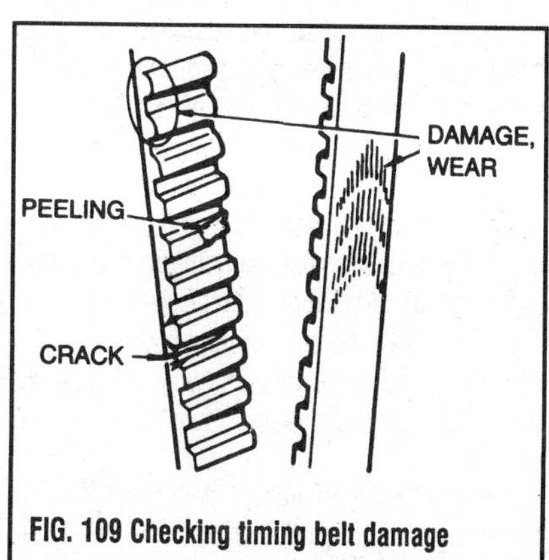

FIG. 109 Checking timing belt damage

2. Remove the timing belt cover.
3. Turn the crankshaft to align the ›1 mark of the camshaft sprocket with the front housing matching mark.
4. Remove the tensioner and spring. Mark the timing belt direction of rotation if it is to be reused.
5. Remove the timing belt.

To install:

6. Make sure the mark on the crankshaft sprocket is aligned with the matching mark on the oil pump body.

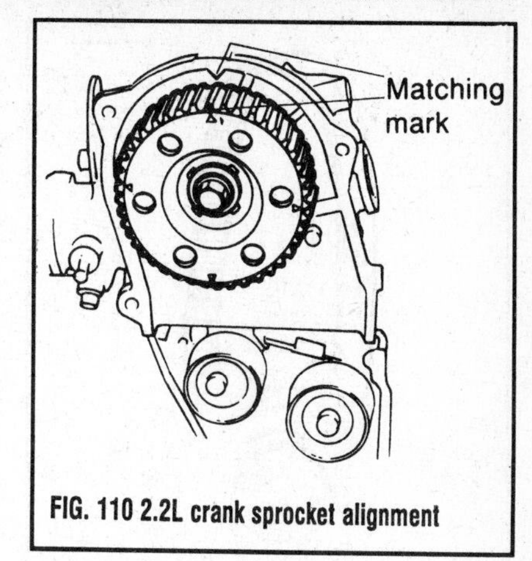

FIG. 110 2.2L crank sprocket alignment

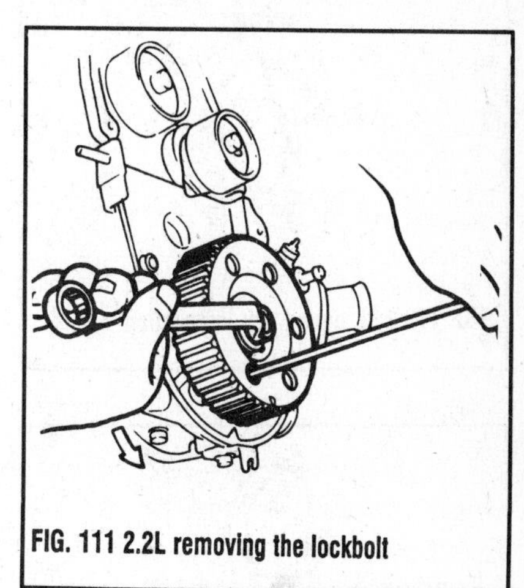

FIG. 111 2.2L removing the lockbolt

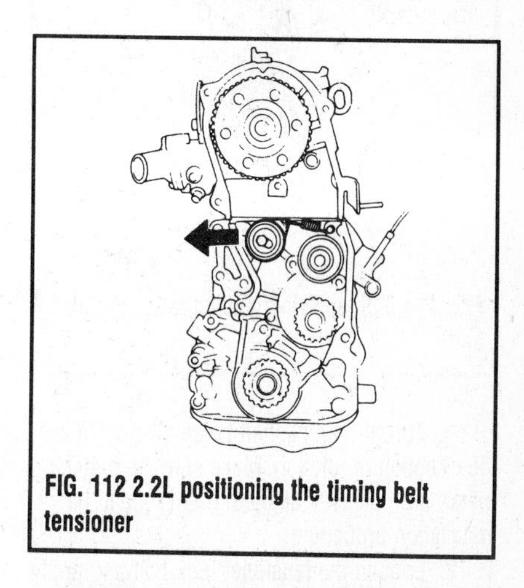

FIG. 112 2.2L positioning the timing belt tensioner

7. Make sure the **›1** mark on the camshaft sprocket is aligned with the matching mark on the front housing.
8. Install the timing belt tensioner and spring. Temporarily secure it with the spring fully extended.
9. Install the timing belt so there is no looseness at the water pump pulley and idler pulley side. If the timing belt is being reused, it must be installed in the same direction of rotation.
10. Remove the spark plugs to make engine rotation easier.

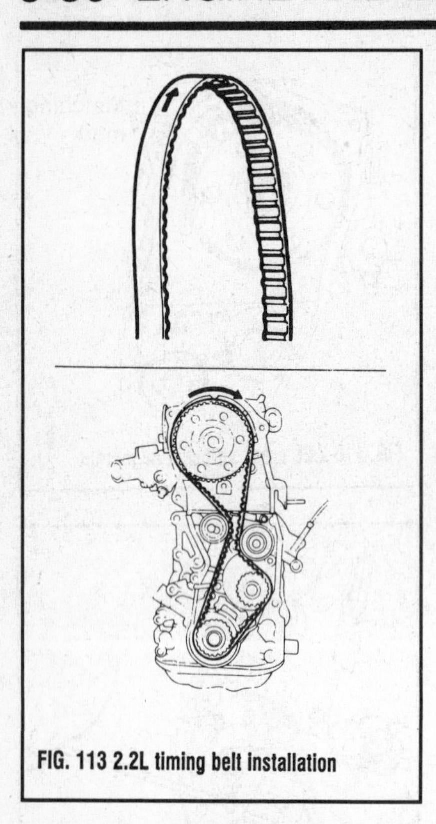

FIG. 113 2.2L timing belt installation

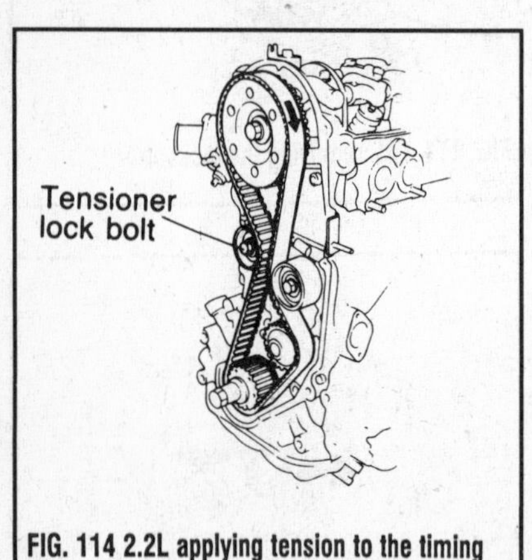

FIG. 114 2.2L applying tension to the timing belt

11. Turn the crankshaft twice clockwise in the direction of rotation. Make sure the matching marks are correctly aligned; if not repeat the installation procedure.

12. Loosen the tensioner lock bolt and apply tension to the belt. Tighten the tensioner lock bolt to 27–38 ft. lbs. (37–52 Nm).

13. Turn the crankshaft twice clockwise in the direction of rotation and align the matching marks. Check the timing belt deflection. The deflection should be 0.31–0.35 in. (8–9mm) on a new belt or 0.35–0.39 in. (9–10mm) on a used belt. Do not apply tension other than that of the tensioner spring.

14. If the deflection is not correct, repeat Steps 11–13.

15. Install the remaining components in the reverse order of removal. Fill and bleed the cooling system.

16. Run the engine and check for leaks and proper operation. Check the idle speed and the ignition timing.

3.0L Engine

1. Disconnect the negative battery cable and drain the cooling system.
2. Remove the timing belt cover.
3. Remove the upper idler pulley.
4. Turn the crankshaft to align the matching marks on the sprockets. If the timing belt is to be reused, make an arrow on the belt to indicate rotation direction.
5. Remove the timing belt and automatic tensioner.

To install:

6. Set a plain washer at the bottom of the tensioner body to prevent damage to the body plug. Press in the tensioner rod slowly, using a press or a vise.

➡ Do not press the tensioner rod more than 2200 lbs.

7. Insert a pin to hold the tensioner rod in the body. Install the automatic tensioner and tighten the mounting bolts to 14–19 ft. lbs. (19–25 Nm).
8. Install the crankshaft pulley lock bolt and loosely tighten. Check the alignment of the matching marks on the sprockets.
9. With the upper idler pulley removed, install the timing belt, making sure there is no slack between the crankshaft and camshaft sprockets. If the timing belt is being reused, it must be installed in the same direction of rotation.
10. Install the upper idler pulley and tighten the attaching bolt to 27–38 ft. lbs. (37–52 Nm).
11. Turn the crankshaft twice in the direction of rotation and align the matching marks. If the marks do not align, repeat Steps 8–11.
12. Remove the pin from the automatic tensioner. Turn the crankshaft twice and align the matching marks. Make sure the marks are aligned.
13. Check the timing belt deflection. The deflection should be 0.20–0.28 in. (5–7mm). Do not apply tension other than that of the automatic tensioner.
14. If the deflection is not correct, repeat Steps 10–13.
15. Remove the crankshaft pulley lock bolt.
16. Install the remaining components in the reverse order of removal. Fill and bleed the cooling system.
17. Run the engine and check for leaks and proper operation. Check the idle speed and the ignition timing.

Timing Belt Sprockets

REMOVAL & INSTALLATION

1. Disconnect the negative battery cable.
2. Remove the timing belt cover and the timing belt.
3. Remove the sprocket retaining bolt and remove the sprocket.
4. Installation is the reverse of the removal procedure. Tighten the camshaft sprocket bolt to 35–48 ft. lbs. (47–65 Nm) on 2.2L engine or 52–59 ft. lbs. (71–80 Nm) on 3.0L engine. Tighten the crankshaft sprocket bolt to 116–123 ft. lbs. (157–167 Nm) on 2.2L engine.

Camshaft

➧ SEE FIGS. 115-119

REMOVAL & INSTALLATION

2.2L Engine

1. Disconnect the negative battery cable and drain the cooling system. Remove the air cleaner assembly or air intake tube.

**** CAUTION**

When draining the coolant, keep in mind that cats and dogs are attracted by the ethylene glycol antifreeze, and are quite likely to drink any that is left in an uncovered container or in puddles on the ground. This will prove fatal in sufficient quantity. Always drain the coolant into a sealable container. Coolant should be reused unless it is contaminated or several years old.

2. Remove the timing belt cover and the timing belt. Remove the camshaft sprocket.
3. Remove the rocker arm cover and rocker arm/shaft assembly.
4. Disconnect the upper radiator hose from the thermostat housing.
5. Remove the distributor.
6. Remove the front housing.
7. Remove the seal cap from the rear of the cylinder head and remove the camshaft.

8. Check the camshaft for wear and/or damage and replace, as necessary.

To install:

9. Clean all gasket mating surfaces.
10. Apply clean engine oil to the camshaft journals, lobes and bearings. Install the camshaft with the dowel pin facing straight up.
11. Apply silicone sealer to the cylinder head on the front and rear camshaft bearing cap mating surface. Install the rocker arm/shaft assembly and tighten the bolts in sequence, in 2–3 steps to 13–20 ft. lbs. (18–26 Nm).
12. Install a new camshaft seal in the front housing. Apply clean engine oil to the seal lip and install the housing using a new gasket. Tighten the bolts to 14–19 ft. lbs.
13. Apply silicone sealer to the cylinder head and both sides of the front and rear camshaft bearing caps where the caps meet the cylinder head. Install the rocker arm cover and tighten the bolts to 26–35 inch lbs. (2.9–3.9 Nm).
14. Install the camshaft sprocket and tighten the retaining bolt to 35–48 ft. lbs. (47–65 Nm).
15. Install the timing belt and timing belt cover.
16. Install the distributor.
17. Connect the upper radiator hose.
18. Install the remaining components in the reverse order of removal. Fill and bleed the cooling system.
19. Run the engine and check for leaks and proper operation. Check the idle speed and the ignition timing.

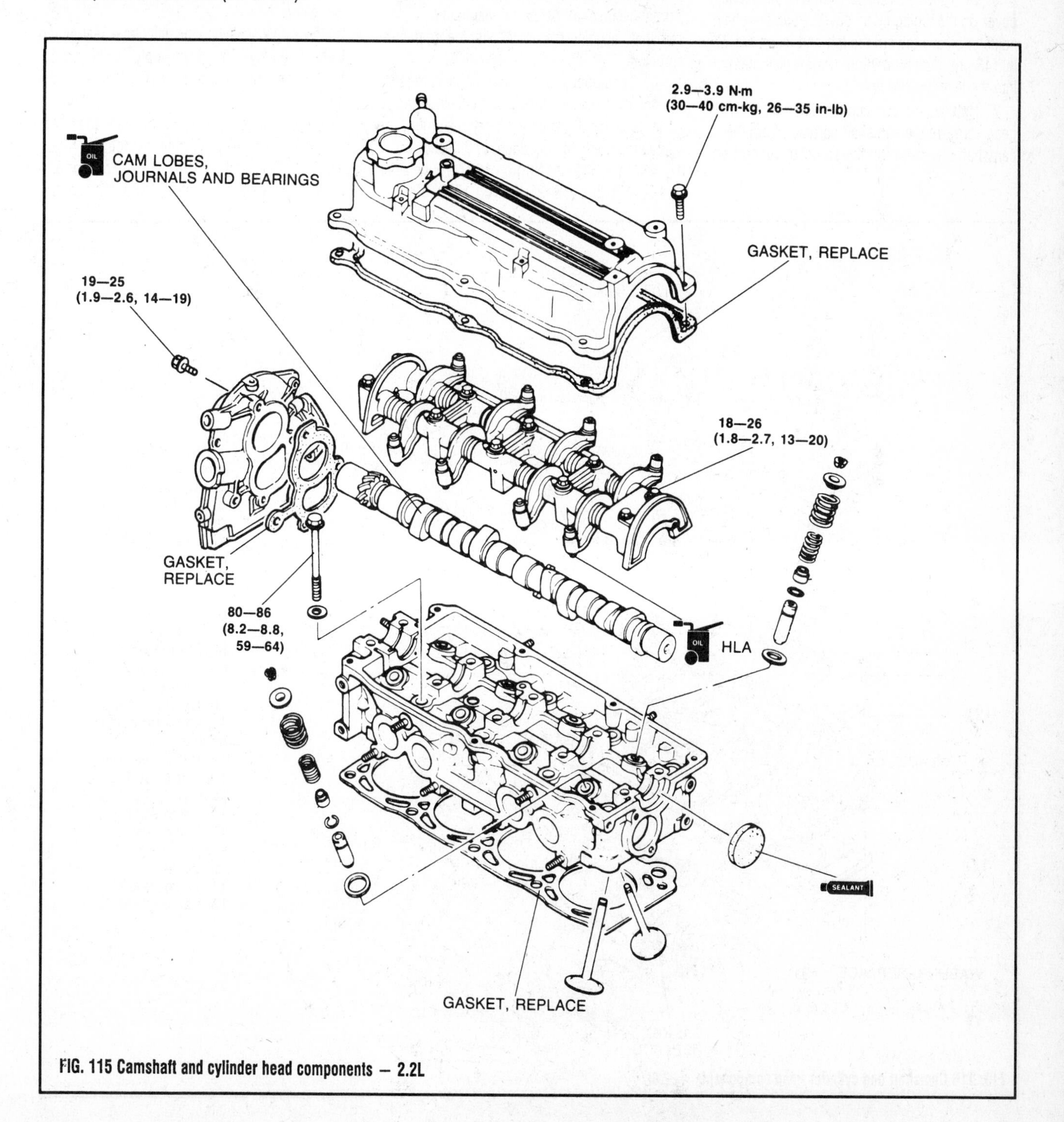

FIG. 115 Camshaft and cylinder head components – 2.2L

2.6L Engines

1. Disconnect the negative battery cable.
2. Remove the air cleaner assembly or air intake tube.
3. Remove the rocker arm cover.
4. Remove the distributor.
5. Remove the rocker arm/shaft assembly. On 1987–88 vehicles, install hydraulic lash adjuster holder tools 49 U012 001 or equivalent, over the ends of the rocker arms prior to removal.
6. On 1989–92 vehicles, remove the service cover on the timing chain cover. Push the chain adjuster sleeve toward the left and insert a 1.77 in. (45mm) long by 0.08 in. (2mm) diameter pin into the lever hole to hold it.
7. Remove the bolt and the distributor drive gear. Remove the camshaft sprocket from the camshaft and rest it on the sprocket support on 1988 vehicles or hold it in position with mechanic's wire on 1989–92 vehicles.

➡ Do not allow the timing chain to become disconnected from the camshaft sprocket or engine timing will be disturbed.

8. Remove the camshaft. Inspect the camshaft for wear or damage and replace, if necessary.

To install:

9. Apply clean engine oil to the camshaft journals, lobes and bearings. Install the camshaft, aligning the dowel with the camshaft sprocket.
10. If equipped, coat the circular packing with sealant and install in the end of the cylinder head.
11. Install the rocker arm/shaft assembly and tighten the bolts, in sequence, in 2–3 steps to 14–15 ft. lbs. (19–20 Nm) on 1987–88 vehicles or 14–19 ft. lbs. (19–25 Nm) on 1989–92 vehicles. Remove the hydraulic lash adjuster holder tools on 1987–88 vehicles.
12. Install the camshaft sprocket to the camshaft. Install the distributor drive gear and lock bolt. Tighten the lock bolt to 36–43 ft. lbs. (49–58 Nm).
13. On 1989–92 vehicles, remove the chain adjuster sleeve retaining pin and install the service cover with a new gasket. Tighten the bolts to 69–95 inch lbs. (7.8–11.0 Nm) and the nuts to 61–87 inch lbs. (6.9–9.8 Nm).
14. On 1987–88 vehicles, adjust the jet valve clearance.
15. Apply sealant to the half circle seal(s) and install in the cylinder head. Apply sealer to the tops of the seals and to the cylinder head in the seal area.
16. Coat a new gasket with sealant and install the rocker arm cover. Tighten the bolts to 43–61 inch lbs. (5–7 Nm) on 1987–88 vehicles or 52–78 inch lbs. (5.9–8.8 Nm) on 1989–92 vehicles.

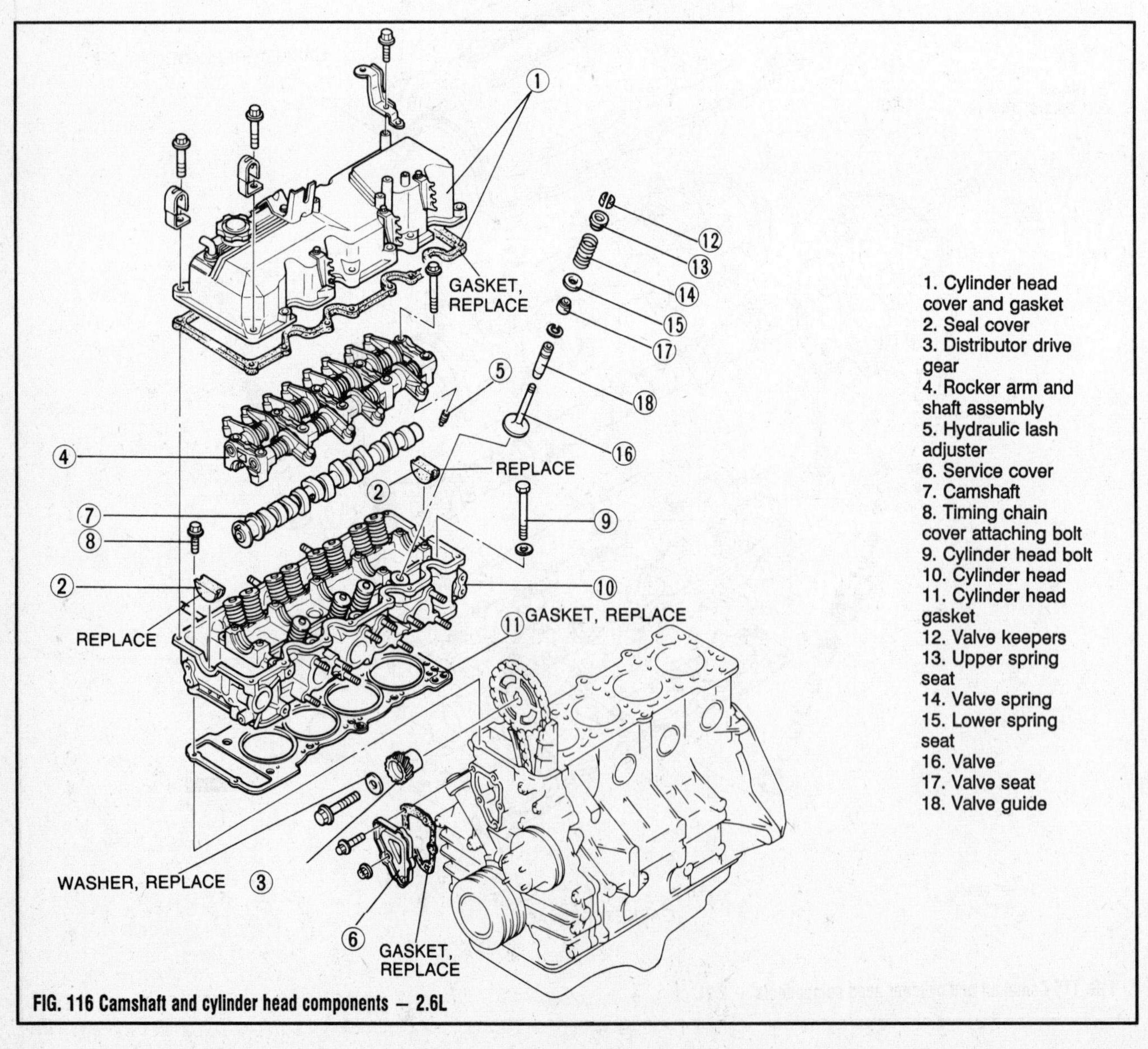

FIG. 116 Camshaft and cylinder head components — 2.6L

17. Install the distributor.

18. Install the air cleaner assembly or air intake tube. Connect the negative battery cable.

19. Run the engine and check for leaks and proper operation. Check the idle speed and ignition timing. On 1987–88 vehicles, readjust the jet valves when the engine is warm.

3.0L Engine

1. Disconnect the negative battery cable and drain the cooling system.

**** CAUTION**

When draining the coolant, keep in mind that cats and dogs are attracted by the ethylene glycol antifreeze, and are quite likely to drink any that is left in an uncovered container or in puddles on the ground. This will prove fatal in sufficient quantity. Always drain the coolant into a sealable container. Coolant should be reused unless it is contaminated or several years old.

2. Remove the timing belt covers and timing belt.

3. Remove the rocker arm cover.

4. If removing the driver's side camshaft, remove the distributor and the distributor spacer.

5. Remove the bolt and the camshaft sprocket.

6. Remove the seal plate. Pry out the camshaft seal, being careful not to damage the seal housing.

7. Remove the rocker arm/shaft assembly.

8. Remove the thrust plate bolts and remove the thrust plate. Slide the camshaft out of the cylinder head. If removing the driver's side camshaft, remove the distributor drive gear.

➡ Components such as the radiator, radiator support and air conditioning condenser may have to be removed to allow camshaft removal. It may be necessary to remove the cylinder head to remove the camshaft.

9. Inspect the camshaft for wear and/or damage and replace if necessary.

To install:

10. If installing the driver's side camshaft, remove all old sealer from the distributor drive gear and apply sealer to the gear face, then seat the gear fully on the camshaft.

11. Apply clean engine oil to the camshaft journals, lobes and bearings. Install the camshaft and the thrust plate. Tighten the thrust plate to 69–95 inch lbs. (7.8–11.0 Nm).

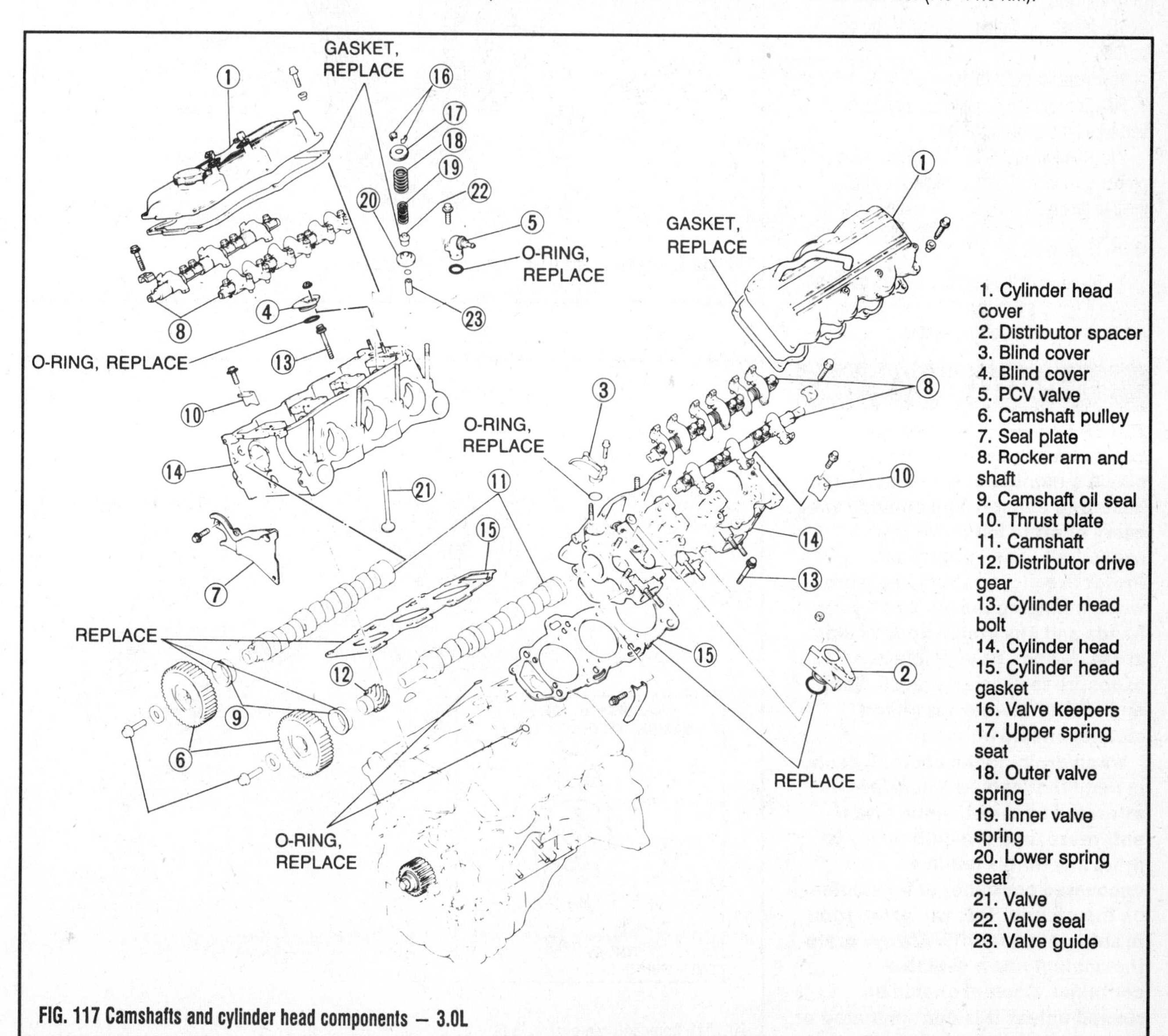

FIG. 117 Camshafts and cylinder head components — 3.0L

12. Apply clean engine oil to a new camshaft seal lip and press the seal into the cylinder head, using a seal installer.
13. Install the rocker arm/shaft assembly and tighten the bolts, in sequence, in 2–3 steps to 14–19 ft. lbs. (19–25 Nm). Make sure the rocker arm shaft spring does not get caught between the shaft and mounting boss during installation.
14. Install the seal plates and tighten the bolts to 69–95 inch lbs. (7.8–11.0 Nm).
15. Install the camshaft sprocket and tighten the bolt to 52–59 ft. lbs. (71–80 Nm).
16. If installing the driver's side camshaft, apply clean engine oil to a new O-ring and install on the distributor spacer. Install the spacer and tighten the nuts to 69–95 inch lbs. (7.8–11.0 Nm).
17. Coat a new gasket with silicone sealant and install on the rocker arm cover. Install the cover and tighten the bolts to 30–39 inch lbs. (3.4–4.4 Nm).
18. Install the timing belt and timing belt covers.
19. Install the distributor.
20. Connect the negative battery cable. Fill and bleed the cooling system.
21. Run the engine and check for leaks and proper operation. Check the idle speed and ignition timing.

4.0L Engine

1. Disconnect the negative battery cable and relieve the fuel system pressure. Drain the crankcase and the cooling system.

✻✻ CAUTION

The EPA warns that prolonged contact with used engine oil may cause a number of skin disorders, including cancer! You should make every effort to minimize your exposure to used engine oil. Protective gloves should be worn when changing the oil. Wash your hands and any other exposed skin areas as soon as possible after exposure to used engine oil. Soap and water, or waterless hand cleaner should be used.

When draining the coolant, keep in mind that cats and dogs are attracted by the ethylene glycol antifreeze, and are quite likely to drink any that is left in an uncovered container or in puddles on the ground. This will prove fatal in sufficient quantity. Always drain the coolant into a sealable container. Coolant should be reused unless it is contaminated or several years old.

2. Remove the rocker arm covers, rocker arm shaft assemblies and pushrods. Note the position of each component so it can be reinstalled in the same place.
3. Remove the intake manifold.
4. Remove the lifters. Identify each lifter so it can be reinstalled in the original position.
5. Remove the front timing chain cover and the timing chain and sprockets.
6. Remove the thrust plate bolts and remove the thrust plate. Carefully remove the camshaft, being careful not to damage the journals, lobes or bearings.

To install:

7. Coat the camshaft lobes with grease and the journals with heavy engine oil. Carefully install the camshaft, being careful not to damage the journals, lobes or bearings.

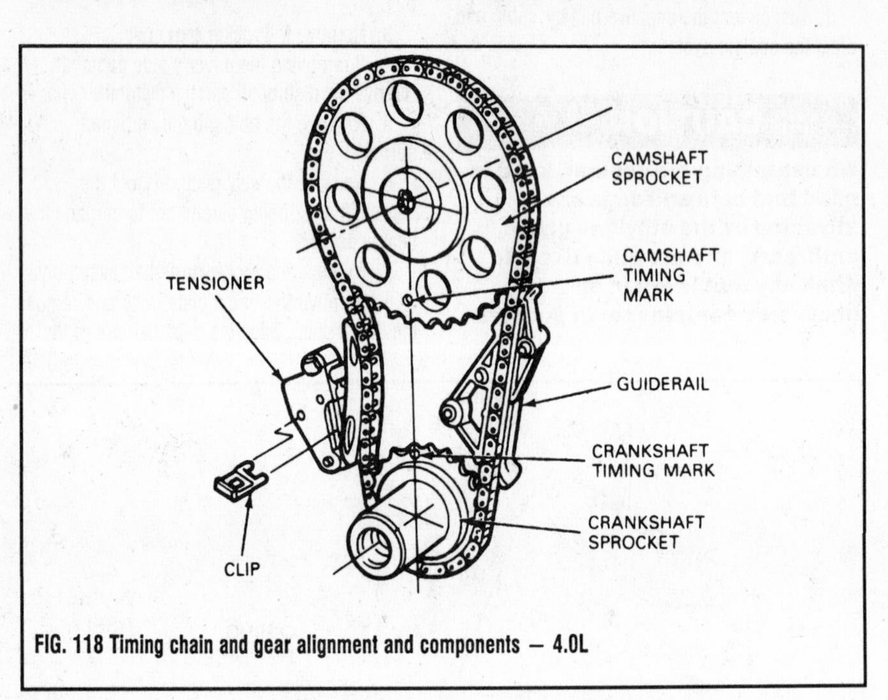

FIG. 118 Timing chain and gear alignment and components — 4.0L

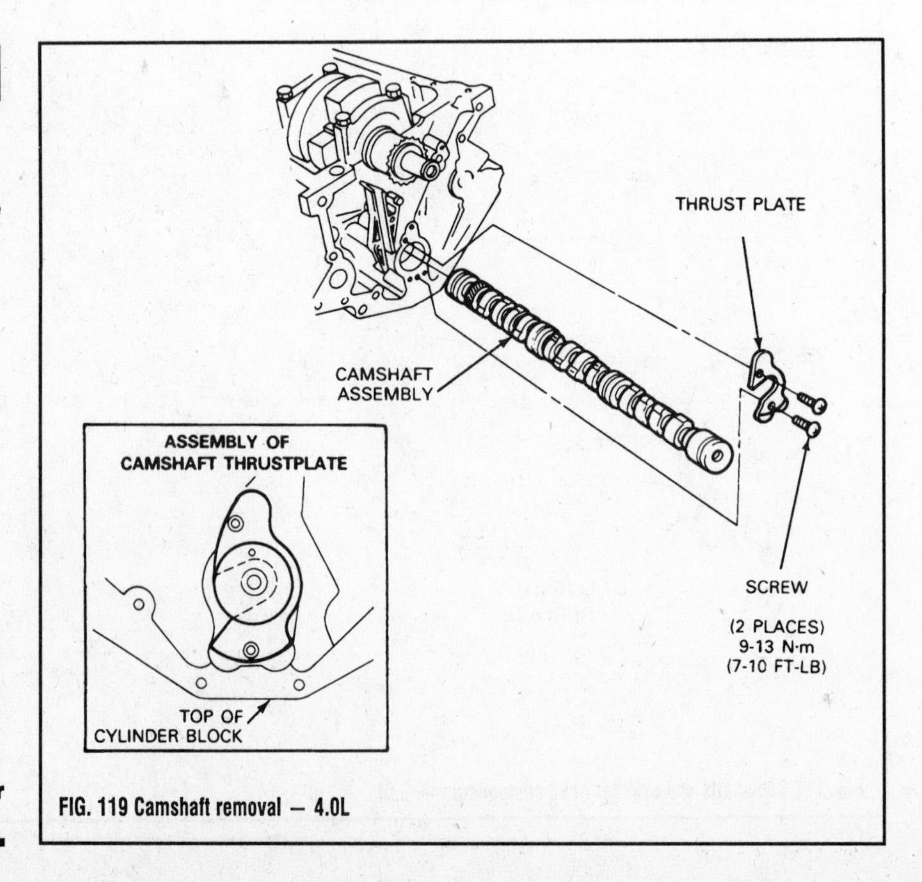

FIG. 119 Camshaft removal — 4.0L

8. Install the thrust plate and the thrust plate retaining bolts. Tighten the bolts to 7–10 ft. lbs. (10–13 Nm).

9. Check the camshaft endplay using a dial indicator. The endplay should be 0.0008–0.004 in. (0.002-0.010mm).

10. Install the remaining components in the reverse order of their removal. Fill the crankcase with the proper type and quantity of engine oil. Fill and bleed the cooling system. Run the engine and check for leaks.

CHECKING CAMSHAFT

➧ SEE FIGS. 120 & 121

Camshaft Lobe Lift

ALL EXCEPT 4.0L

Check the lift of each lobe in consecutive order and make a note of the reading.

1. Remove the fresh air inlet tube and the air cleaner. Remove the heater hose and crankcase ventilation hoses. Remove valve rocker arm cover(s).

2. Remove the rocker arm stud nut or fulcrum bolts, fulcrum seat and rocker arm.

3. Make sure the pushrod is in the valve tappet socket. Install a dial indicator so that the actuating point of the indicator is in the pushrod socket (or the indicator ball socket adaptor is on the end of the pushrod) and in the same plane as the push rod movement.

4. Install an auxiliary starter switch Crank the engine with the ignition switch off. Turn the crankshaft over until the tappet is on the base circle of the camshaft lobe. At this position, the pushrod will be in its lowest position.

5. Zero the dial indicator. Continue to rotate the crankshaft slowly until the pushrod is in the fully raised position.

6. Compare the total lift recorded on the dial indicator with the specification shown on the Camshaft Specification chart.

To check the accuracy of the original indicator reading, continue to rotate the crankshaft until the indicator reads zero. If the left on any lobe is below specified wear limits listed, the camshaft and the valve tappet operating on the worn lobe(s) must be replaced.

7. Install the dial indicator and auxiliary starter switch.

8. Install the rocker arm, fulcrum seat and stud nut or fulcrum bolts. Check the valve clearance. Adjust if required (refer to procedure in this section).

9. Install the valve rocker arm cover(s) and the air cleaner.

4.0L

Check the lift of each lobe in consecutive order and make a note of the reading. Camshaft assembly specifications are sometimes modify by the manufacturer after production. Refer to a local reputable machine shop as necessary.

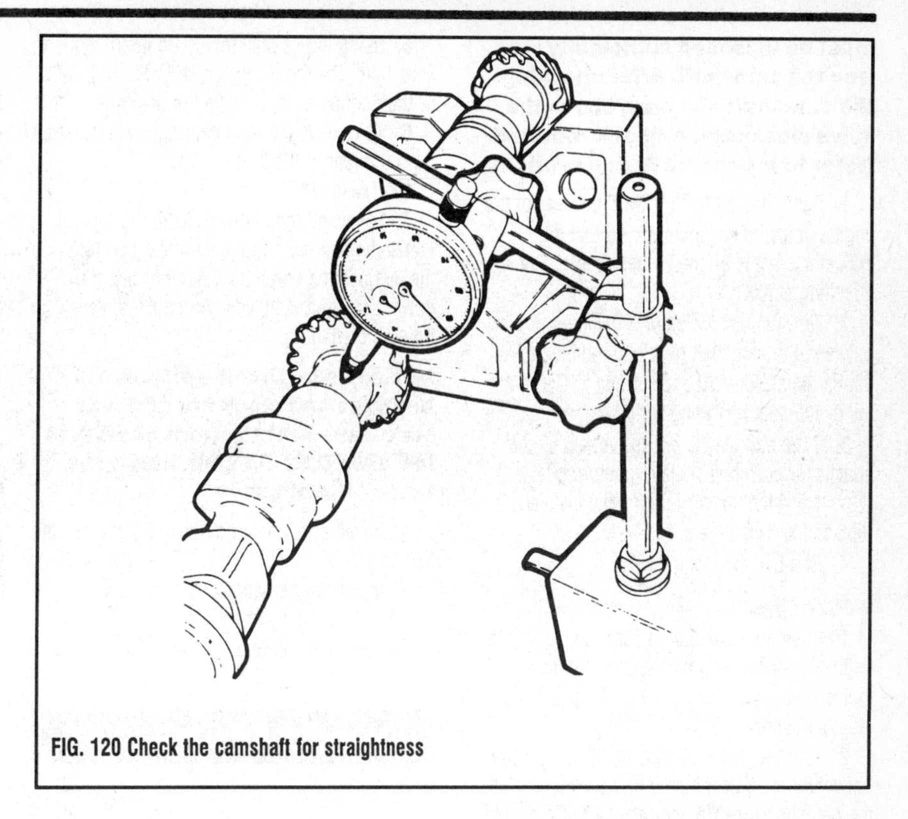

FIG. 120 Check the camshaft for straightness

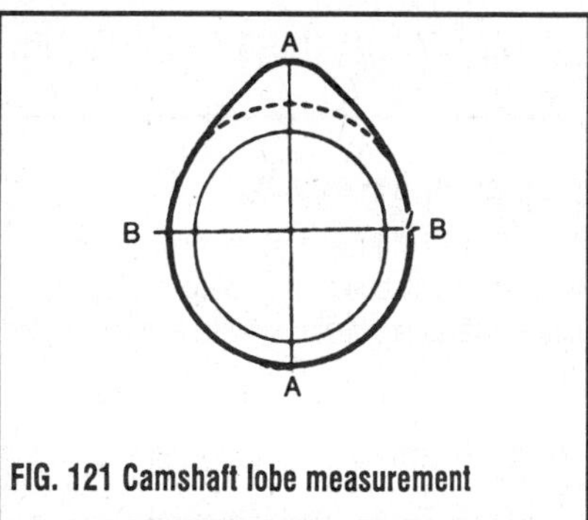

FIG. 121 Camshaft lobe measurement

1. Remove the fresh air inlet tube and the air cleaner. Remove the heater hose and crankcase ventilation hoses. Remove valve rocker arm cover(s).

2. Remove the rocker arm stud nut or fulcrum bolts, fulcrum seat and rocker arm.

3. Make sure the push rod is in the valve tappet socket. Install a dial indicator D78P–4201–B (or equivalent) so that the actuating point of the indicator is in the push rod socket (or the indicator ball socket adapter Tool 6565–AB is on the end of the push rod) and in the same plane as the push rod movement.

4. Disconnect the I terminal and the S terminal at the starter relay. Install an auxiliary starter switch between the battery and S terminals of the starter relay. Crank the engine with the ignition switch off. Turn the crankshaft over until the tappet is on the base circle of the camshaft lobe. At this position, the push rod will be in its lowest position.

5. Zero the dial indicator. Continue to rotate the crankshaft slowly until the push rod is in the fully raised position.

6. Compare the total lift recorded on the dial indicator with the specification. To check the accuracy of the original indicator reading, continue to rotate the crankshaft until the indicator reads zero. If the lift on any lobe is below specified wear limits, the camshaft and the valve tappet operating on the worn lobe(s) must be replaced.

7. Remove the dial indicator and auxiliary starter switch.

8. Install the rocker arm, fulcrum seat and stud nut or fulcrum bolts. Check the valve clearance. Adjust if required.

9. Install the valve rocker arm covers and the air cleaner.

Camshaft End Play

ALL EXCEPT 4.0L

➡ On engines with an aluminum or nylon camshaft sprocket, prying against the sprocket, with the valve train load on the camshaft, can break or damage the sprocket. Therefore, the rocker arm adjusting nuts must be backed off, or the rocker arm and shaft assembly

must be loosened sufficiently to free the camshaft. After checking the camshaft end play, check the valve clearance. Adjust if required (refer to procedure in this section).

1. Push the camshaft toward the rear of the engine. Install a dial indicator so that the indicator point is on the camshaft sprocket attaching screw.
2. Zero the dial indicator. Position a prybar between the camshaft gear and the block. Pull the camshaft forward and release it. Compare the dial indicator reading with the specifications.
3. If the end play is excessive, check the spacer for correct installation before it is removed. If the spacer is correctly installed, replace the thrust plate.
4. Remove the dial indicator.

4.0L ENGINES

1. Push the camshaft toward the rear of the engine. Install a dial indicator so that the indicator point is on the camshaft sprocket attaching screw.
2. Zero the dial indicator. Position a prybar between the camshaft gear and the block. Pull the camshaft forward and release it. Compare the dial indicator reading with the specification. The camshaft endplay specification is 0.0008–0.004 inch (0.020-0.100mm) and the service limit is 0.009 inch (0.228mm). Camshaft specifications are sometimes modified by the manufacturer after production.
3. If the end play is excessive, check the spacer for correct installation before it is removed. If the spacer is correctly installed, replace the thrust plate.

➡ The spacer ring and thrust plate are available in two thicknesses to permit adjusting the end play.

4. Remove the dial indicator.

Camshaft Bearings

On engines, except the 4.0L, excessive oil clearance between the cylinder head and bearing caps to camshaft bearing surfaces, indicates that cylinder head replacement is required.

REMOVAL & INSTALLATION

4.0L Engines

1. Remove the engine and place it on a work stand.
2. Remove the flywheel.
3. Remove the camshaft.
4. Using a sharp punch and hammer, drive a hole in the rear bearing bore plug and pry it out.
5. Using the special tools and instructions in Ford Cam Bearing Replacer Kit T65L–6250–A, or their equivalents, remove the bearings.
6. To remove the front bearing, install the tool from the rear of the block.

To install:

7. Following the instructions in the tool kit, install the bearings. Make sure that you follow the instructions carefully. Failure to use the correct expanding collets can cause severe bearing damage!

➡ Make sure that the oil holes in the bearings and block are aligned! Make sure that the front bearing is installed 0.51–0.89mm below the face of the block.

8. Install a new bearing bore plug coated with sealer.
9. Install the camshaft.
10. Install the flywheel.
11. Install the engine.

Balancer Shafts

REMOVAL & INSTALLATION

2.6L Engine (1987–88)

1. Relieve the fuel system pressure, if injected and disconnect the negative battery cable. Drain the cooling system and the engine oil.

⁂ CAUTION

The EPA warns that prolonged contact with used engine oil may cause a number of skin disorders, including cancer! You should make every effort to minimize your exposure to used engine oil. Protective gloves should be worn when changing the oil. Wash your hands and any other exposed skin areas as soon as possible after exposure to used engine oil. Soap and water, or waterless hand cleaner should be used.

When draining the coolant, keep in mind that cats and dogs are attracted by the ethylene glycol antifreeze, and are quite likely to drink any that is left in an uncovered container or in puddles on the ground. This will prove fatal in sufficient quantity. Always drain the coolant into a sealable container. Coolant should be reused unless it is contaminated or several years old.

2. Remove the cylinder head, oil pan and timing chain cover.
3. Remove the balancer shaft chain and timing chain.
4. Remove the bolts, then push in and hold the chain tensioner head and remove the oil pump and passenger's side balancer shaft assembly.
5. Install 8mm bolts into the threaded holes of the flange and turn the bolts equally to remove the thrust plate. Remove the driver's side balancer shaft.
6. Inspect the balancer shaft for wear and/or damage. Make sure the oil passages are not clogged.

To install:

7. Install the timing chain guides, if removed. Install the timing chain on the sprockets, slide the crankshaft sprocket onto the crankshaft and place the camshaft sprocket on the sprocket holder.
8. Apply clean engine oil to the journals of the driver's side balancer shaft and install the shaft in the cylinder block, being careful not to damage the bearings.

➡ The driver's side and passenger's side balancer shafts are different and not interchangeable.

9. Install a new O-ring into the groove of the thrust plate and apply clean engine oil around the O-ring.
10. Install two 6mm × 50mm guides into the threaded holes for mounting the thrust plate.

➡ The guides must be used to install the thrust plate because damage to the O-ring may result if the plate is not properly aligned.

11. Remove the guides and install the thrust plate mounting bolts. Tighten to 87–95 inch lbs. (10–11 Nm).
12. Install the oil pump gears in the oil pump body, if removed and align the timing mark.

➡ The timing marks must be aligned correctly or the balancer shaft will be out of phase and engine vibration will result.

13. Install the oil pump cover on the body and tighten the screw. After installing the pump cover, put approximately 10cc of clean engine oil in the delivery port.
14. Install the balancer shaft into the oil pump driven gear and tighten to 43–50 ft. lbs. (59–68 Nm).

15. Apply clean engine oil to the journals of the balancer shaft and install the shaft, oil pump and adjuster assembly into the block. Push in the chain adjuster head and hold it during installation. Be careful not to damage the bearings.

16. Tighten the oil pump mounting bolts to 69–78 inch lbs. (8–9 Nm).

17. Install the balancer shaft drive sprocket on the crankshaft. Assemble the balancer shaft sprockets to the balancer shaft chain, making sure the timing marks on the sprockets are aligned with the polished links on the chain.

➡ Be careful not to confuse the right and left sprockets as they are installed in opposite directions.

18. While holding the assembled sprockets and chain, align the timing mark on the crankshaft sprocket with the chain and install the balancer shaft sprockets. Temporarily tighten the bolts by hand.

19. Temporarily install chain guides A, B and C. Set chain guide C to the fully downward position and tighten chain guides A and C to 43–69 inch lbs. (4.9–7.8 Nm).

20. Tighten the balancer shaft sprocket bolt to 43–50 ft. lbs. (59–68 Nm) and the oil pump sprocket bolt to 22–29 ft. lbs. (29–39 Nm).

21. Rotate both balancer shaft sprockets slightly to position the chain slack at the center between the left balancer shaft sprocket and the oil pump sprocket.

22. Adjust the position of chain guide B so that when the chain is pulled away from the guide with the fingertips, the clearance between chain guide B and the chain links is 0.008–0.031 in. (0.2–0.8mm), then tighten the bolts. Tighten the upper bolt to 69–78 inch lbs. (8–9 Nm) and the lower bolt to 11–15 ft. lbs. (15–21 Nm).

23. Install the remaining components in the reverse order of removal.

24. Fill the crankcase with the proper type and quantity of engine oil. Fill and bleed the cooling system. Run the engine and check for leaks and proper operation.

25. Check the idle speed and ignition timing and adjust, if necessary.

2.6L Engine (1989-92)

1. Relieve the fuel system pressure and disconnect the negative battery cable. Drain the engine oil and the cooling system.

⁂ CAUTION

The EPA warns that prolonged contact with used engine oil may cause a number of skin disorders, including cancer! You should make every effort to minimize your exposure to used engine oil. Protective gloves should be worn when changing the oil. Wash your hands and any other exposed skin areas as soon as possible after exposure to used engine oil. Soap and water, or waterless hand cleaner should be used.

When draining the coolant, keep in mind that cats and dogs are attracted by the ethylene glycol antifreeze, and are quite likely to drink any that is left in an uncovered container or in puddles on the ground. This will prove fatal in sufficient quantity. Always drain the coolant into a sealable container. Coolant should be reused unless it is contaminated or several years old.

2. Remove the cylinder head, oil pan and timing chain cover.

3. Remove the balancer shaft chain.

4. Remove the thrust plate lock bolts and remove the balancer shaft(s). Be careful not to damage the balancer shaft journals and bushing during removal.

5. Check the balancer shaft(s) and bushings for wear and/or damage and replace as necessary.

To install:

6. Apply clean engine oil to the balancer shaft journals and install in the cylinder block, being careful not to damage the bushings and journals.

7. Loosely tighten the thrust plate lock bolts and make sure the balancer shaft(s) rotate smoothly. Tighten the lock bolts to 69–95 inch lbs. (7.8–11.0 Nm).

8. Install the crankshaft balancer sprocket.

9. Set the balancer chain on the idler sprocket assembly so the timing mark on the idler sprocket assembly and the brown link of the balancer chain align.

10. Install the balancer chain so the 5 alignment marks on the chain, sprocket and block align and attach the idler sprocket assembly to the cylinder block. Loosely tighten the idler sprocket assembly lock bolt.

11. Install the right and left lower balancer chain guides and tighten the mounting bolts to 69–95 inch lbs. (7.8–11.0 Nm).

12. Install the upper chain guide and loosely tighten the mounting and adjusting bolts.

13. Tighten the idler sprocket assembly lock bolt to 27–38 ft. lbs. (37–52 Nm) and install the spacer.

14. On 1989 B Series pickup and all MPV, adjust the balancer chain tension as follows:

a. Loosen the upper chain guide adjusting bolt.

b. Push on the chain guide just above the adjusting slot with a force of approximately 11 lbs., then pull back the guide 0.14 ± 0.012 in. (3.5 ± 0.3mm) and tighten the bolt to 69–95 inch lbs. (7.8–11.0 Nm). Tighten the guide pivot bolt to the same specification.

c. The chain slack at the notch in the guide should be 0.12 in. (3mm) when the guide is properly adjusted.

15. On 1990–91 B Series pickup with manual transmission, adjust the balancer chain tension as follows:

a. Tighten the upper chain guide pivot bolt to 69–95 inch lbs. (7.8–11.0 Nm).

b. Loosen the upper chain guide adjusting bolt.

c. Push on the chain guide just above the adjusting slot with a force of approximately 11 lbs., then pull back the guide 0.24 ± 0.012 in. (6.0 ± 0.3mm) and tighten the bolt to 69–95 inch lbs. (7.8–11.0 Nm).

d. The chain slack at the notch in the guide should be 0.23 in. (5.8mm) when the guide is properly adjusted.

16. On all 1992 and 1990–91 B Series pickup with automatic transmission, adjust the balancer chain tension as follows:

a. Fabricate a piece of wood, 0.118–0.138 in. (3.0–3.5mm) thick and 0.335–0.374 in. (8.5–9.5mm) wide.

b. Insert the piece of wood in the notch in the upper chain guide.

c. Push on the chain guide just above the adjusting slot with a force of 2.9–3.7 lbs. and tighten the adjusting and pivot bolts to 69–95 inch lbs. (7.8–11.0 Nm).

d. Remove the wood from between the chain and chain guide, making sure no wood shavings are left.

e. Measure the chain slack. It should be 0.039–0.059 in. (1.0–1.5mm) at the notch in the guide.

➡ If the upper chain guide bottoms on the adjusting bolt during the adjustment procedure, the balancer chain must be replaced.

17. Install the remaining components in the reverse order of removal.

➡ Be sure to remove the pin from the timing chain adjuster before installing the service cover.

18. Fill the crankcase with the proper type and quantity of oil. Fill and bleed the cooling system.

19. Run the engine and check for leaks and proper operation. Check the idle speed and ignition timing.

Pistons and Connecting Rods

➧ SEE FIGS. 122-145

REMOVAL

✲✲ CAUTION

The EPA warns that prolonged contact with used engine oil may cause a number of skin disorders, including cancer! You should make every effort to minimize your exposure to used engine oil. Protective gloves should be worn when changing the oil. Wash your hands and any other exposed skin areas as soon as possible after exposure to used engine oil. Soap and water, or waterless hand cleaner should be used.

When draining the coolant, keep in mind that cats and dogs are attracted by the ethylene glycol antifreeze, and are quite likely to drink any that is left in an uncovered container or in puddles on the ground. This will prove fatal in sufficient quantity. Always drain the coolant into a sealable container. Coolant should be reused unless it is contaminated or several years old.

1. Remove the engine assembly from the truck, see Engine Removal and Installation.
2. Remove the intake manifold and cylinder head.
3. Remove the oil pan.
4. Remove the oil pump assembly.
5. Stamp the cylinder number on the machine surfaces of the bolt bosses of the connecting rod and cap for identification when reinstalling. If the pistons are to be removed from the connecting rod, mark the cylinder number on the piston with a silver pencil or quick drying paint for proper cylinder identification and cap-to-rod location.

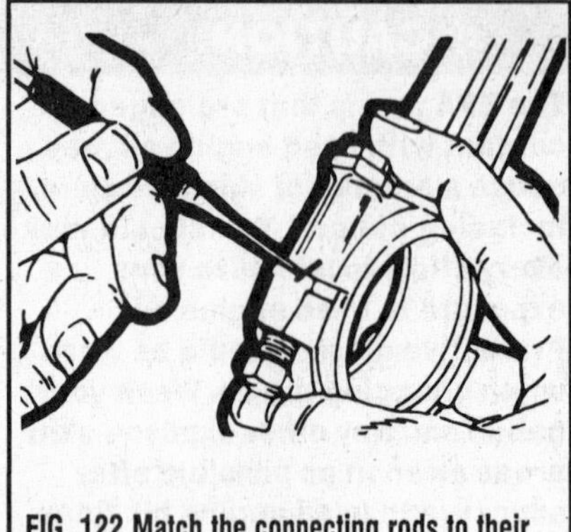

FIG. 122 Match the connecting rods to their caps with a scribe line

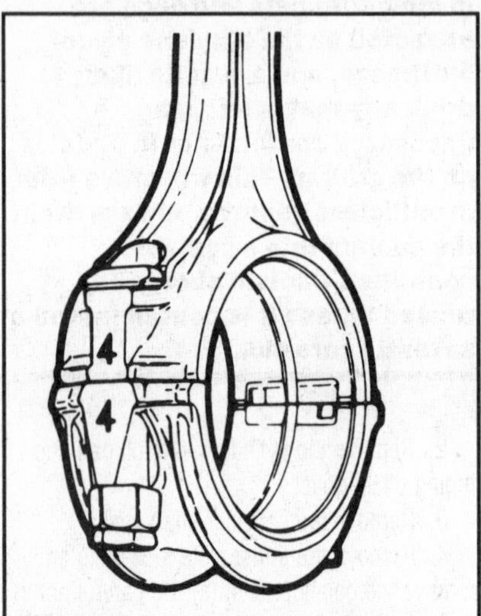

FIG. 123 Match the connecting rods to their cylinders with a number stamp

6. Examine the cylinder bore above the ring travel. If a ridge exists, remove the ridge with a ridge reamer before attempting to remove the piston and rod assembly. Never cut into the ring travel area in excess of 0.8mm (0.0315 in.) when removing the ridges.
7. Remove the rod bearing cap and bearing.
8. Install a guide hose over threads of rod bolts. This is to prevent damage to bearing journal and rod bolt threads.
9. Remove the rod and piston assembly through the top of the cylinder bore.
10. Remove the other rod and piston assemblies in the same manner.

PISTON PIN REMOVAL AND INSTALLATION

Use care at all times when handling and servicing connecting rods and pistons. To

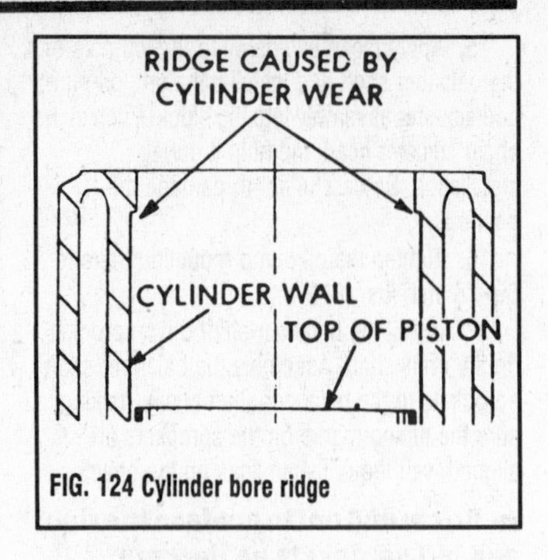

FIG. 124 Cylinder bore ridge

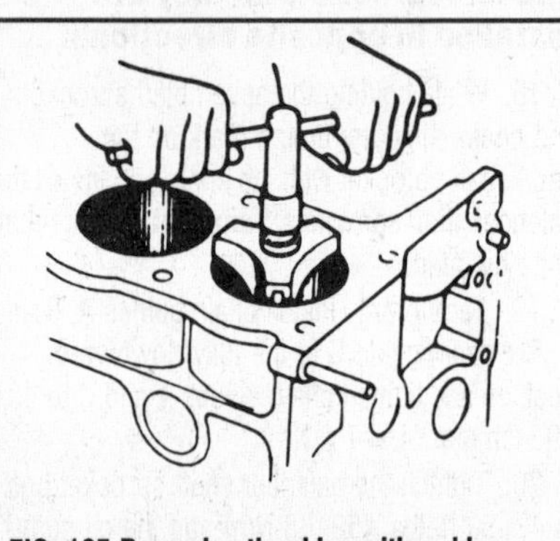

FIG. 125 Removing the ridge with a ridge reamer

prevent possible damage to these units, do not clamp the rod or piston in a vise since they may become distorted. Do not allow the pistons to strike against one another, against hard objects or bench surfaces, since distortion of the piston contour or nicks in the soft aluminum material may result.

All Except 4.0L

1. Remove the piston rings using a suitable piston ring remover.
2. Remove the piston pin lockring, if used. Install the guide bushing of the Then, on all engines, press the piston pin out of the piston with tools designed for this purpose. On the 3.0L V6, if the pressure required to press the pin from the piston exceeds 1,100 lbs., replace the piston pin or the connecting rod. For these engines, it best that a press with adjustable pressure be used or the pistons be sent out to a machine shop so equipped.
3. Install the piston and connecting rod assembly on a support, and place the assembly in an arbor press. Press the pin out of the connecting rod, using the appropriate piston pin tool.
4. Assembly is the reverse of disassembly. Use new lockrings where needed.

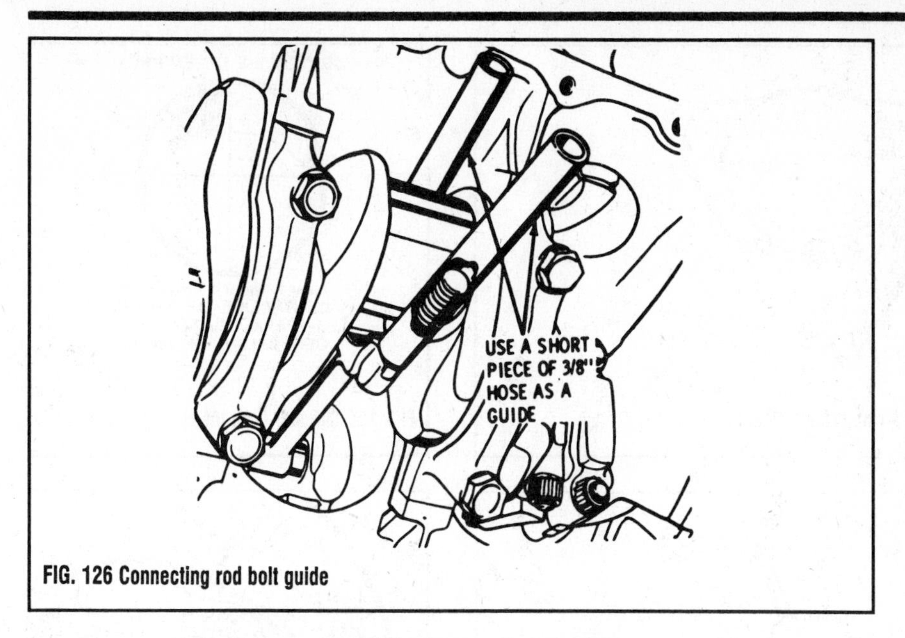
USE A SHORT
PIECE OF 3/8"
HOSE AS A
GUIDE
FIG. 126 Connecting rod bolt guide

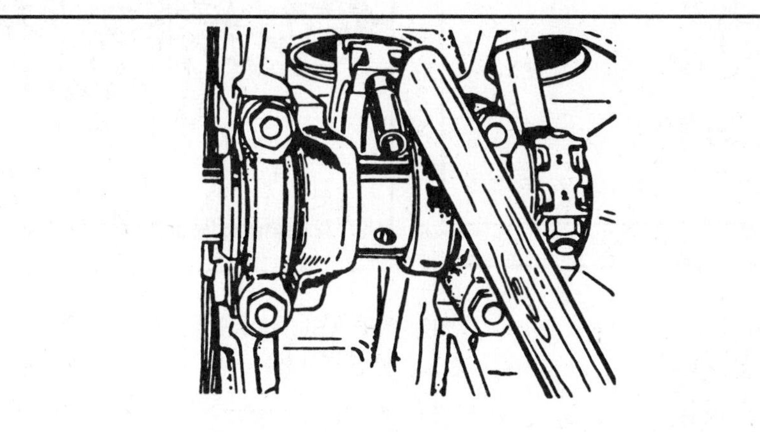
FIG. 127 Push the piston and rod out with a hammer handle

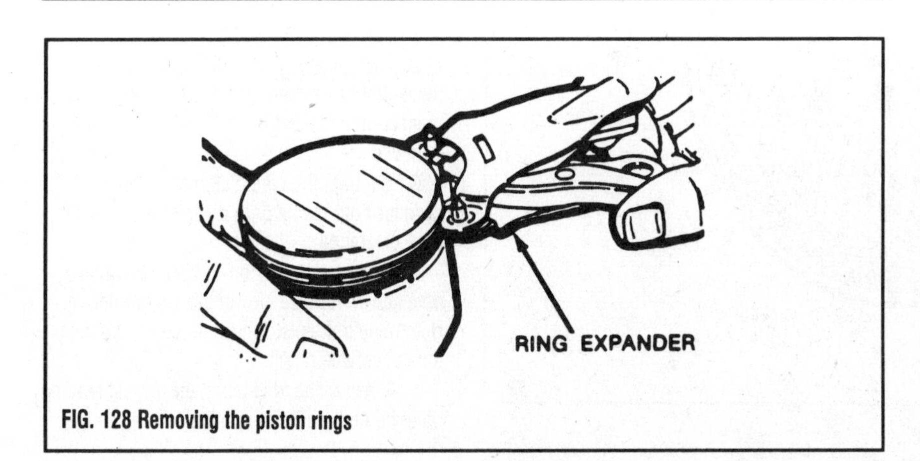
RING EXPANDER
FIG. 128 Removing the piston rings

4.0L Engines

1. Remove the bearing inserts from the connecting rod and cap.
2. Mark the pistons to assure assembly with the same rod, rod position and installation in the same cylinders from which they were removed.
3. Using an Arbor press and adapter, press the piston pin from the piston and connecting rod. Remove the piston rings if they are to be replaced.

➡ Check the fit of a new piston in the cylinder bore before assembling the piston and piston pin to the connecting rod.

4. Apply a light coat of engine oil to all parts. Assemble the piston to the connecting rod with the indentation or notch in the original position.
5. Start the piston pin in the connecting rod (this may require a very light tap with a mallet). Using an Arbor press and adapter, press the piston pin through the piston and connecting rod until the pin is centered in the piston.
6. install the piston rings using a piston ring installation tool of the proper size (refer to Piston Ring Replacement in this section).
7. Be sure the bearing inserts and the bearing bore in the connect rod and cap are clean. Foreign material under the inserts will distort the bearing and cause it to fail.

CLEANING AND INSPECTION

Connecting Rods

Wash connecting rods in cleaning solvent and dry with compressed air. Check for twisted or bent rods and inspect for nicks or cracks. Replace connecting rods that are damaged.

Pistons

Clean varnish from piston skirts and pins with a cleaning solvent. DO NOT WIRE BRUSH ANY PART OF THE PISTON. Clean the ring grooves with a groove cleaner and make sure oil ring holes and slots are clean.

Inspect the piston for cracked ring lands, skirts or pin bosses, wavy or worn ring lands, scuffed or damaged skirts, eroded areas at the top of the piston. Replace pistons that are damaged or show signs of excessive wear. Inspect the grooves for nicks or burrs that might cause the rings to hang up.

Measure piston skirt (across center line of piston pin) and check piston clearance.

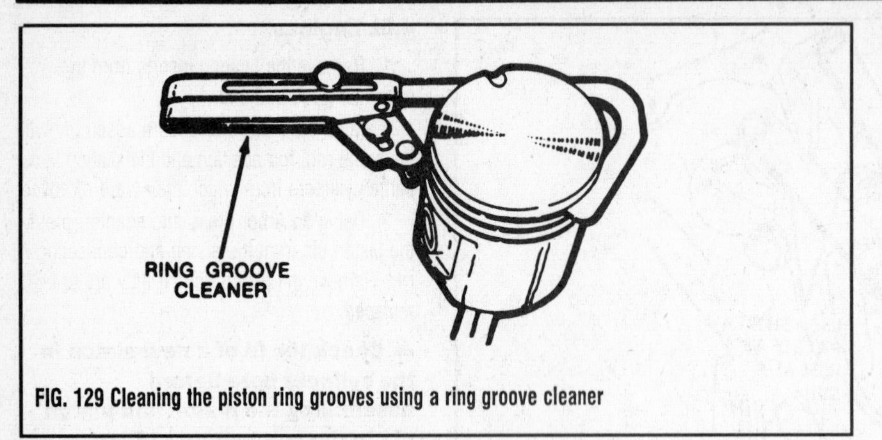

FIG. 129 Cleaning the piston ring grooves using a ring groove cleaner

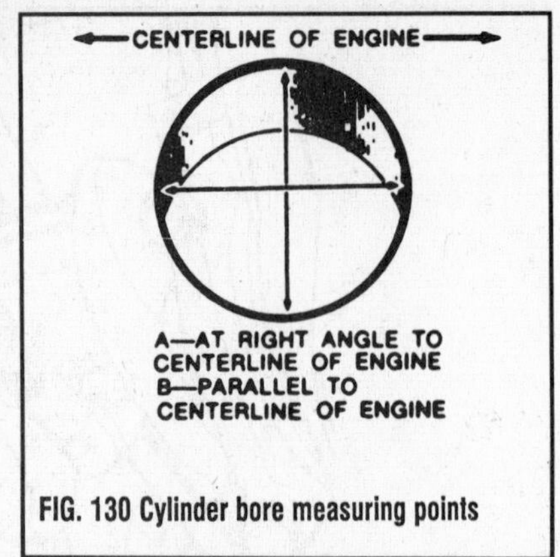

FIG. 130 Cylinder bore measuring points

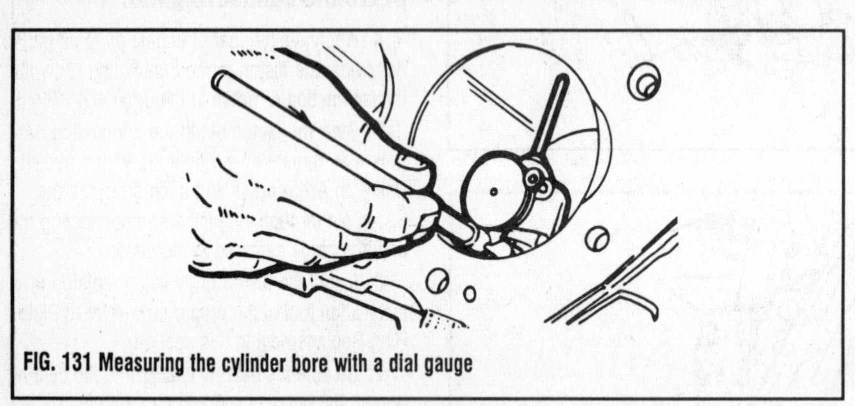

FIG. 131 Measuring the cylinder bore with a dial gauge

FIG. 132 Measuring the piston prior to fitting

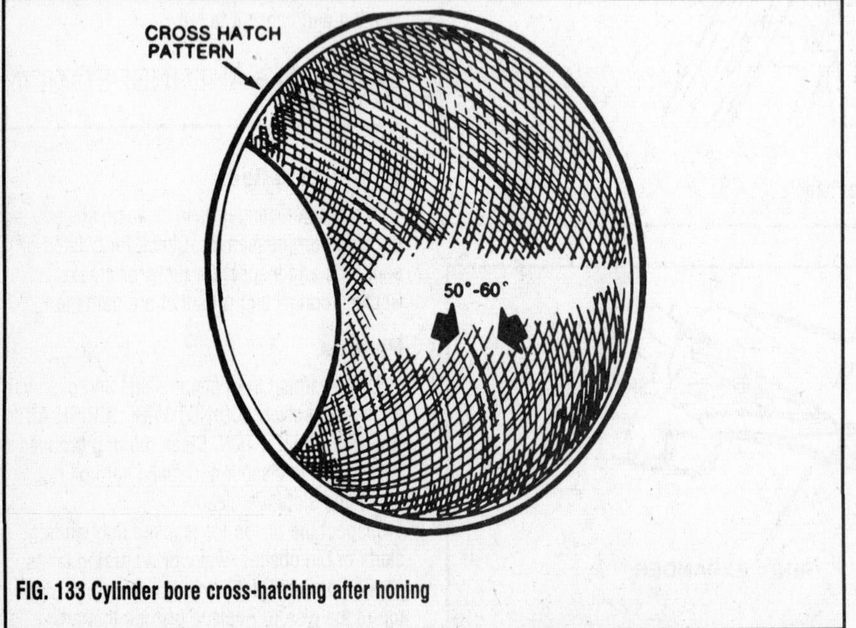

FIG. 133 Cylinder bore cross-hatching after honing

MEASURING THE OLD PISTONS

Check used piston-to-cylinder bore clearance as follows:

1. Measure the cylinder bore diameter with a telescope gauge.
2. Measure the piston diameter. When measuring the pistons for size or taper, measurements must be made with the piston pin removed.
3. Subtract the piston diameter from the cylinder bore diameter to determine piston-to-bore clearance.
4. Compare the piston-to-bore clearances obtained with those clearances recommended. Determine if the piston-to-bore clearance is in the acceptable range.
5. When measuring taper, the largest reading must be at the bottom of the skirt.

SELECTING NEW PISTONS

1. If the used piston is not acceptable, check the service piston size and determine if a new piston can be selected. Service pistons are available in standard, and oversizes of 0.25mm and 0.50mm.

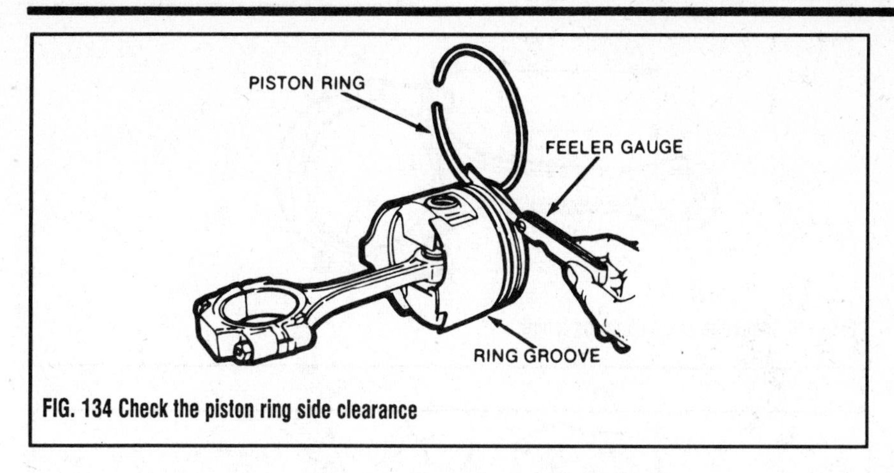

FIG. 134 Check the piston ring side clearance

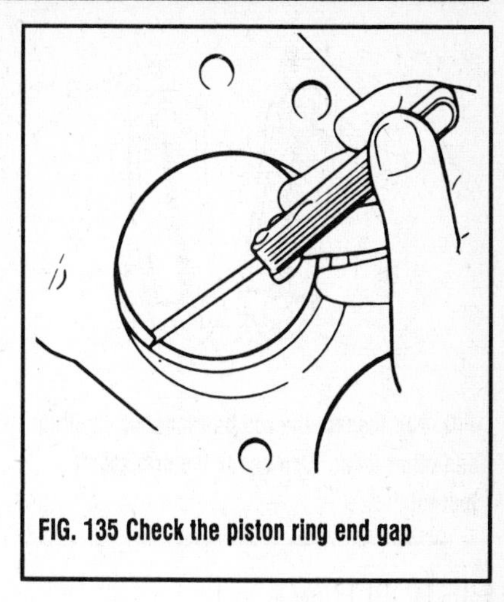
FIG. 135 Check the piston ring end gap

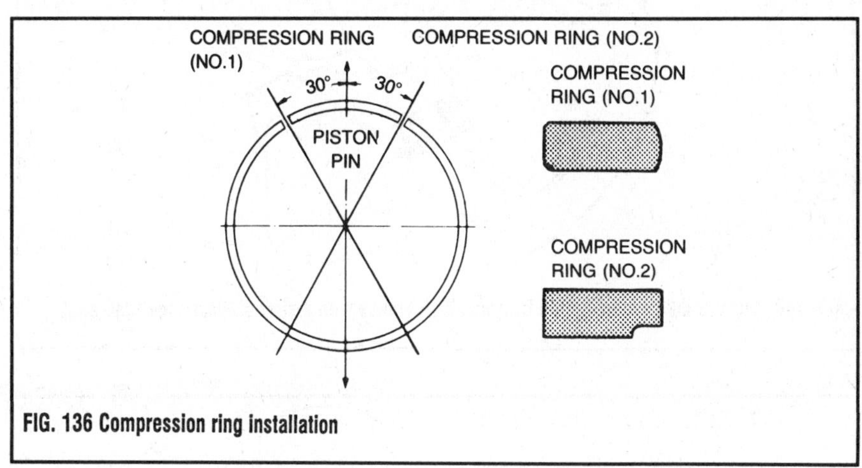

FIG. 136 Compression ring installation

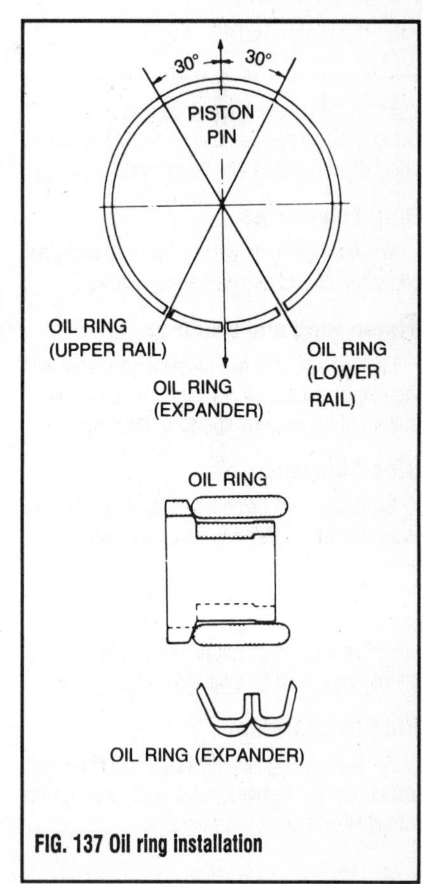

FIG. 137 Oil ring installation

2. If the cylinder bore must be reconditioned, measure the new piston diameter, then hone the cylinder bore to obtain the preferred clearance.

3. Select a new piston and mark the piston to identify the cylinder for which it was fitted.

CYLINDER HONING

1. When cylinders are being honed, follow the manufacturer's recommendations for the use of the hone.

2. Occasionally during the honing operation, the cylinder bore should be thoroughly cleaned and the selected piston checked for correct fit.

3. When finish-honing a cylinder bore, the hone should be moved up and down at a sufficient speed to obtain a very fine uniform surface finish in a cross-hatch pattern of approximately 45-65° included angle. The finish marks should be clean but not sharp, free from embedded particles and torn or folded metal.

4. Permanently mark the piston for the cylinder to which it has been fitted and proceed to hone the remaining cylinders.

➡ **Handle pistons with care. Do not attempt to force pistons through cylinders until the cylinders have been honed to correct size. Pistons can be distorted through careless handling.**

5. Thoroughly clean the bores with hot water and detergent. Scrub well with a stiff bristle brush and rinse thoroughly with hot water. It is extremely essential that a good cleaning operation be performed. If any of the abrasive material is allowed to remain in the cylinder bores, it will rapidly wear the new rings and cylinder bores. The bores should be swabbed several times with light engine oil and a clean cloth and then wiped with a clean dry cloth. CYLINDERS SHOULD NOT BE CLEANED WITH KEROSENE OR GASOLINE! Clean the remainder of the cylinder block to remove the excess material spread during the honing operation.

CHECKING CYLINDER BORE

Cylinder bore size can be measured with inside micrometers or a cylinder gauge. The most wear will occur at the top of the ring travel.

Reconditioned cylinder bores should be held to not more than 0.025mm (0.00098 in.) taper.

If the cylinder bores are smooth, the cylinder walls should not be deglazed. If the cylinder walls are scored, the walls may have to be honed before installing new rings. It is important that reconditioned cylinder bores be thoroughly washed with a soap and water solution to remove all traces of abrasive material to eliminate premature wear.

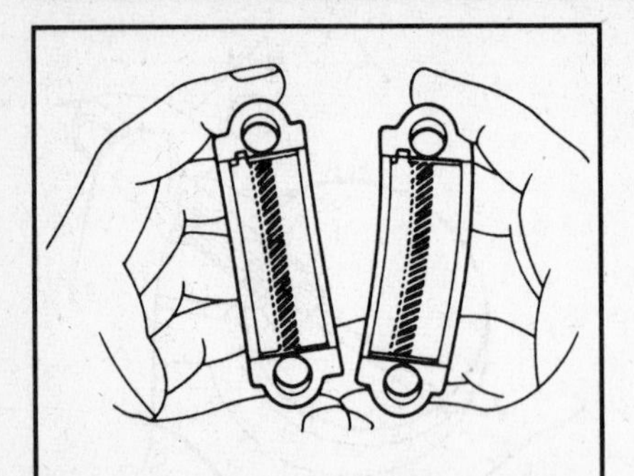

FIG. 138 Inspect the rod bearings for scuffing and other wear. Also check the crankshaft journal

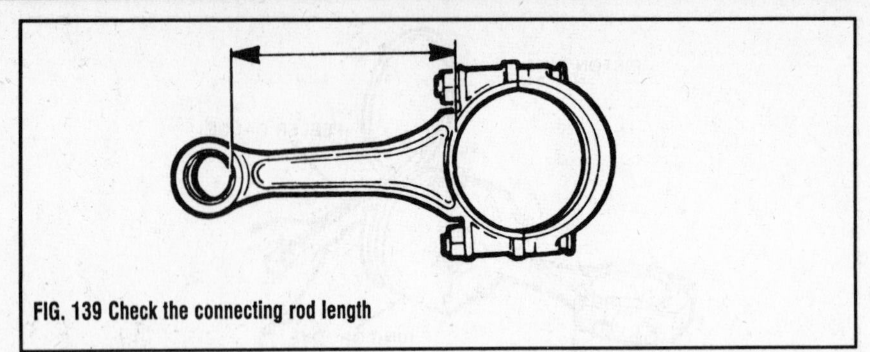

FIG. 139 Check the connecting rod length

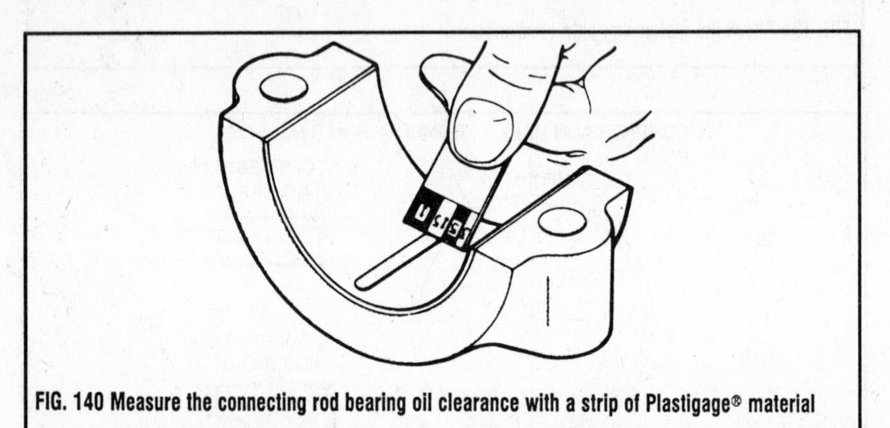

FIG. 140 Measure the connecting rod bearing oil clearance with a strip of Plastigage® material

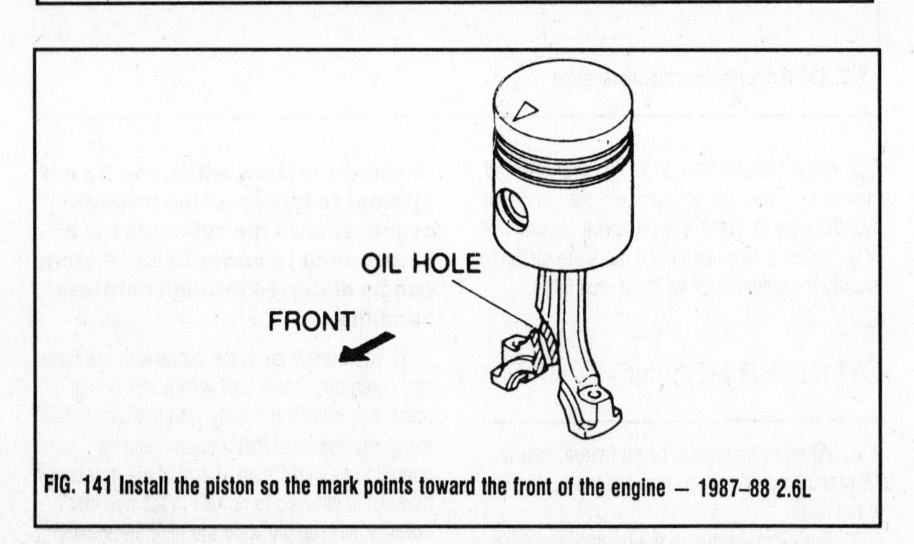

FIG. 141 Install the piston so the mark points toward the front of the engine – 1987–88 2.6L

PISTON RING REPLACEMENT

The pistons have three rings (two compression rings and one oil ring). The oil ring consists of two rails and an expander.

Ring Tolerances

When installing new rings, ring gap and side clearance should be checked as follows:

Piston Ring and Rail Gap

Each ring and rail gap must be measured with the ring or rail positioned squarely and at the bottom of the ring-travel area of the bore.

Side Clearance

Each ring must be checked for side clearance in its respective piston groove by inserting a feeler gauge between the ring and its upper land. The piston grooves must be cleaned before checking the ring for side clearance specifications. To check oil ring side clearance, the oil rings must be installed on the piston.

Ring Installation

For service ring specifications and detailed installation productions, refer to the instructions furnished with the parts package.

ROD BEARING REPLACEMENT

If you have already removed the connecting rod and piston assemblies from the engine, follow only Steps 3-7 of the following procedure.

Removal, Inspection, Installation

ALL EXCEPT 4.0L

The connecting rod bearings are designed to have a slight projection above the rod and cap faces to insure a positive contact. The bearings can be replaced without removing the rod and piston assemblies from the engine.

1. Remove the oil pan. See the Oil Pan procedures.
2. With the connecting rod journal at the bottom, stamp the cylinder number on the machined surfaces of the connecting rod and cap for identification when installing, then remove the caps.
3. Inspect journals for roughness and wear. Slight roughness may be removed with a fine grit polishing cloth saturated with engine oil. Burrs may be removed with a fine oil stone by moving the stone on the journal circumference. Do not move the stone back and forth across the journal. If the journals are scored or ridged, the crankshaft must be replaced.
4. The connecting rod journals should be checked for out-of-round and correct size with a micrometer.

➡ **Crankshaft rod journals will normally be standard size. If any undersized bearings are used, all will be 0.25mm undersize and 0.25mm will be stamped on the number 4 counterweight.**

If plastic gauging material is to be used:

5. Clean oil from the journal bearing cap, connecting rod and outer and inner surfaces of

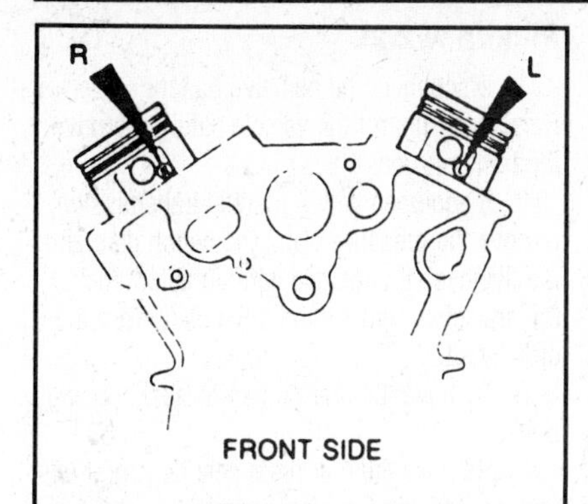

FIG. 142 Install the pistons with the L mark (left bank) and the R mark (right bank) facing the front of the engine — 3.0L

the bearing inserts. Position the insert so that the tang is properly aligned with the notch in the rod and cap.

6. Place a piece of plastic gauging material in the center of lower bearing shell.

7. Remove the bearing cap and determine the bearing clearances by comparing the width of the flattened plastic gauging material at its widest point with the graduation on the container. The number within the graduation on the envelope indicates the clearance in thousandths of an inch or millimeters. If this clearance is excessive, replace the bearing and recheck the clearance with the plastic gauging material. Undersized bearings are available in sizes of 0.25mm, 0.50mm and 0.75mm. Lubricate the bearing with engine oil before installation. Repeat Steps 2-7 on the remaining connecting rod bearings. All rods must be connected to their journals when rotating the crankshaft, to prevent engine damage.

4.0L

1. Drain the crankcase. Remove the oil level dipstick. Remove the oil pan and related parts, following the procedure under Oil Pan removal and installation in this section.

✲✲ CAUTION

The EPA warns that prolonged contact with used engine oil may cause a number of skin disorders, including cancer! You should make every effort to minimize your exposure to used engine oil. Protective gloves should be worn when changing the oil. Wash your hands and any other exposed skin areas as soon as possible after exposure to used engine oil. Soap and water, or waterless hand cleaner should be used.

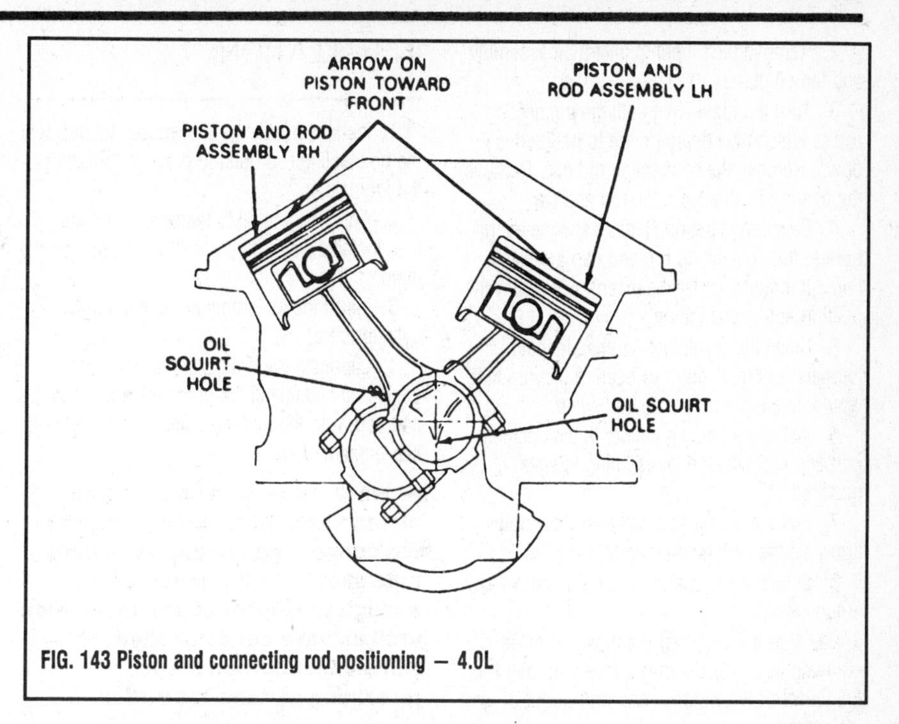

FIG. 143 Piston and connecting rod positioning — 4.0L

FIG. 144 Install the piston with the F mark facing the front of the engine — 2.2L and 1989–92 2.6L

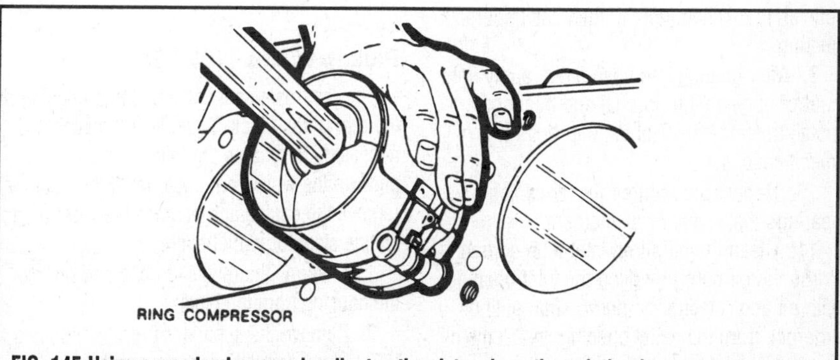

FIG. 145 Using a wooden hammer handle, tap the piston down through the ring compressor and into the cylinder

2. Remove the oil pump inlet tube assembly and the oil pump.

3. Turn the crankshaft until the connecting rod to which new bearings are to be fitted is down. Remove the connecting rod cap. Remove the bearing inserts from the rod and cap.

4. Be sure the bearing inserts and the bearing bore in the connecting rod and cap are clean. Foreign material under the inserts will distort the bearing and cause failure.

5. Clean the crankshaft journal. Inspect journals for nicks, burrs or bearing pick-up that would cause premature bearing wear.

6. Install the bearing inserts in the connect god and cap with the tangs fitting in slots provided.

7. Pull the connecting rod assembly down firmly on the crankshaft journal.

8. Select fit the bearing using the following procedures:

a. Place a piece of Plastigage® or its equivalent, or the bearing surface across the full width of the bearing cap and about 6mm off center.

b. Install cap and tighten bolts to specifications. Do not turn crankshaft while Plastigage® is in place.

c. Remove cap. Using Plastigage® scale, check width of Plastigage® at widest point to get minimum clearance. Check at narrowest point to get maximum clearance. Difference between readings is taper of journal.

d. If clearance exceeds specified limits, try a 0.001 in. (0.025mm) or 0.002 in. (0.50mm) undersize bearing in combination with the standard bearing. Bearing clearance must be within specified limits. If standard and 0.002 in. (0.50mm) undersize bearing does not bring clearance within desired limits, refinish crankshaft journal, then use undersize bearings.

9. After bearing has been fitted, apply light coat of engine oil to journal and bearings. Install bearing cap. Tighten cap bolts to specifications.

10. Repeat procedures for remaining bearings that require replacement.

11. Clean the oil pump inlet tube screen. Prime the oil pump by filing the inlet opening with oil and rotating the pump shaft until oil emerges from the outlet opening. Install the oil pump and inlet tube assembly.

12. Install the oil pan and related parts, following the procedure under Oil Pan removal and installation in this section. Install the oil level dipstick.

13. Fill the crankcase with engine oil. Start the engine and check for oil pressure. Operate the engine at fast idle and check for oil leaks.

INSTALLATION

1. Install some lengths of rubber tubing over the connecting rod bolts to prevent damage to the journals.

2. Apply engine oil to the rings and piston, then install a piston ring compressing tool on the piston.

3. Install the assembly in its respective cylinder bore.

4. Lubricate the crankshaft journal with engine oil and install the connecting rod bearing and cap, with the bearing index tang in rod and cap on same side.

➡ When more than one rod and piston assembly is being installed, the connecting rod cap attaching nuts should be tightened only enough to keep each rod in position until all have been installed. This will aid installation of the remaining piston assemblies.

5. Torque the rod bolt nuts to specification. Using a feeler gauge and small prybar, check connecting rod side clearance.

6. Install all other parts in reverse order of removal.

7. Install the engine in the truck. See Engine Removal and Installation.

Rear Main Oil Seal

➧ SEE FIGS. 146-147

REPLACEMENT

Pickup w/2.6L (1987-88)

The rear main seal is located in a housing on the rear of the block. To replace the seal, it is necessary to remove the transmission and perform the work from underneath the truck or remove the engine and perform the work on an engine stand or work bench.

1. Unscrew the retaining bolts and remove the housing from the block.

2. Remove the separator from the housing.

3. Using a small pry bar, pry out the old seal.

4. Clean the housing and the separator.

5. Lightly oil the replacement seal. Tap the seal into housing using a canister top or other circular piece of metal. The oil seal should be installed so that the seal plate fits into the inner contact surface of the seal case.

6. Install the separator into the housing so that the oil hole faces down.

7. Oil the lips of the seal and install the housing on the rear of the engine block.

Pickup w/2.2L

1. Disconnect the negative battery cable. Raise and support the vehicle safely. Remove the transmission.

2. If equipped with a manual transmission, remove the pressure plate, the clutch disc and the flywheel. If equipped with an automatic transmission, remove the drive plate from the crankshaft.

3. Remove the rear oil pan-to-seal housing bolts.

4. Remove the rear main seal housing bolts and the housing from the engine.

5. Remove the oil seal from the rear main housing.

6. Clean the gasket mounting surfaces.

7. To install, use a new seal, coat the seal and the housing with oil. Drive the seal into the housing, using a seal driver.

8. To complete the installation, use new gaskets, apply sealant to the oil pan mounting surface and reverse the removal procedure. Torque the rear seal housing to 6–8 ft. lbs.

Pickup w/2.6L (1989-92)

1. Disconnect the negative battery cable. Raise and support the vehicle safely. Remove the transmission.

2. If equipped with a manual transmission, remove the pressure plate, the clutch disc and the flywheel. If equipped with an automatic transmission, remove the drive plate from the crankshaft.

3. Remove the rear oil pan-to-seal housing bolts.

4. Remove the rear main seal housing bolts and the housing from the engine.

5. Remove the oil seal from the rear main housing.

6. Clean the gasket mounting surfaces.

7. To install, use a new seal, coat the seal and the housing with RTV silicone sealer. Drive the seal into the housing, using a seal driver.

8. To complete the installation, use new gaskets, apply sealant to the oil pan mounting surface and reverse the removal procedure. Torque the rear seal housing to 95 inch lbs.

MPV w/3.0L Engine

1. Raise and support the vehicle safely. Remove the transmission from the vehicle.

2. If equipped with manual transmission, remove the clutch pressure plate and flywheel.

3. If equipped with automatic transmission, remove the flywheel assembly.

4. Drain the engine oil. Remove the engine oil pan.

5. Remove the rear main seal cover retaining bolts. Remove the rear main seal cover. Remove the seal from the rear cover.

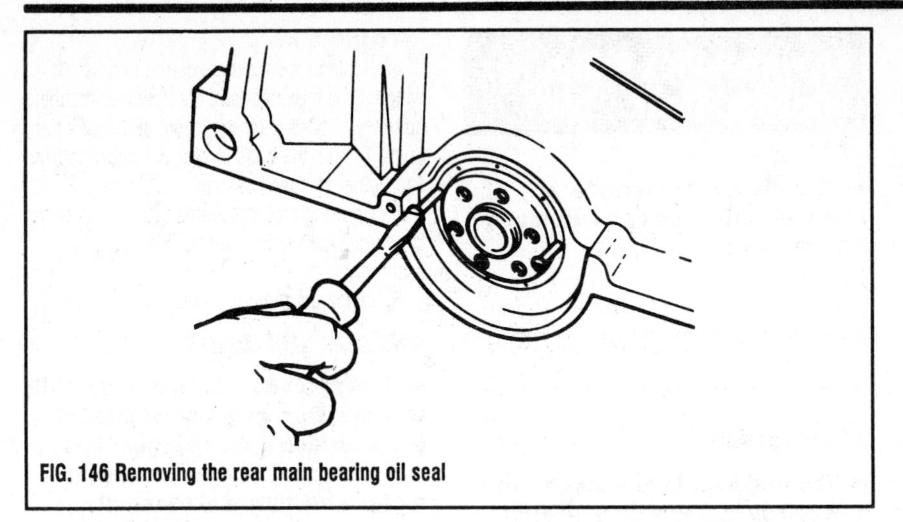

FIG. 146 Removing the rear main bearing oil seal

6. Installation is the reverse of the removal procedure. Apply clean engine oil to the seal before pressing it into the cover.

7. After installing the rear cover cut away the portion of the gasket that projects out toward the oil pan side.

MPV w/2.6L (1989-92)

1. Disconnect the negative battery cable. Raise and support the vehicle safely. Remove the transmission.

2. If equipped with a manual transmission, remove the pressure plate, the clutch disc and the flywheel. If equipped with an automatic transmission, remove the drive plate from the crankshaft.

3. Remove the rear oil pan-to-seal housing bolts.

4. Remove the rear main seal housing bolts and the housing from the engine.

5. Remove the oil seal from the rear main housing.

6. Clean the gasket mounting surfaces.

7. To install, use a new seal, coat the seal and the housing with RTV silicone sealer. Drive the seal into the housing, using a seal driver.

8. To complete the installation, use new gaskets, apply sealant to the oil pan mounting surface and reverse the removal procedure. Torque the rear seal housing to 95 inch lbs.

4.0L Engine

If the crankshaft rear oil seal replacement is the only operation being performed, it can be done in the vehicle as detailed in the following procedure. If the oil seal is being replaced in conjunction with a rear main bearing replacement, the engine must be removed from the vehicle and installed on a work stand.

1. Remove the starter.

2. Remove the transmission from the vehicle.

3. On a manual shift transmission, remove the pressure plate and cover assembly and the clutch disc.

4. Remove the flywheel attaching bolts and remove the flywheel and engine rear cover plate.

5. Use an awl to punch two holes in the crankshaft rear oil seal. Punch the holes on opposite sides of the crankshaft and just above the bearing cap to cylinder block split line. Install a sheet metal screw in each hole. Use two large screwdrivers or small pry bars and pry against both screws at the same time to remove the crankshaft rear oil seal. It may be necessary to place small blocks of wood against the cylinder block to provide a fulcrum point for the pry bars. Use caution throughout this procedure to avoid scratching or otherwise damaging the crankshaft oil seal surface.

To install:

6. Clean the oil seal recess in the cylinder block and main bearing cap.

7. Clean, inspect and polish the rear oil seal rubbing surface on the crankshaft. Coat a new oil seal and the crankshaft with a light film of engine oil. Start the seal in the recess with the seal lip facing forward and install it with a seal driver. Keep the tool straight with the centerline of the crankshaft and install the seal until the tool contacts the cylinder block surface. Remove the

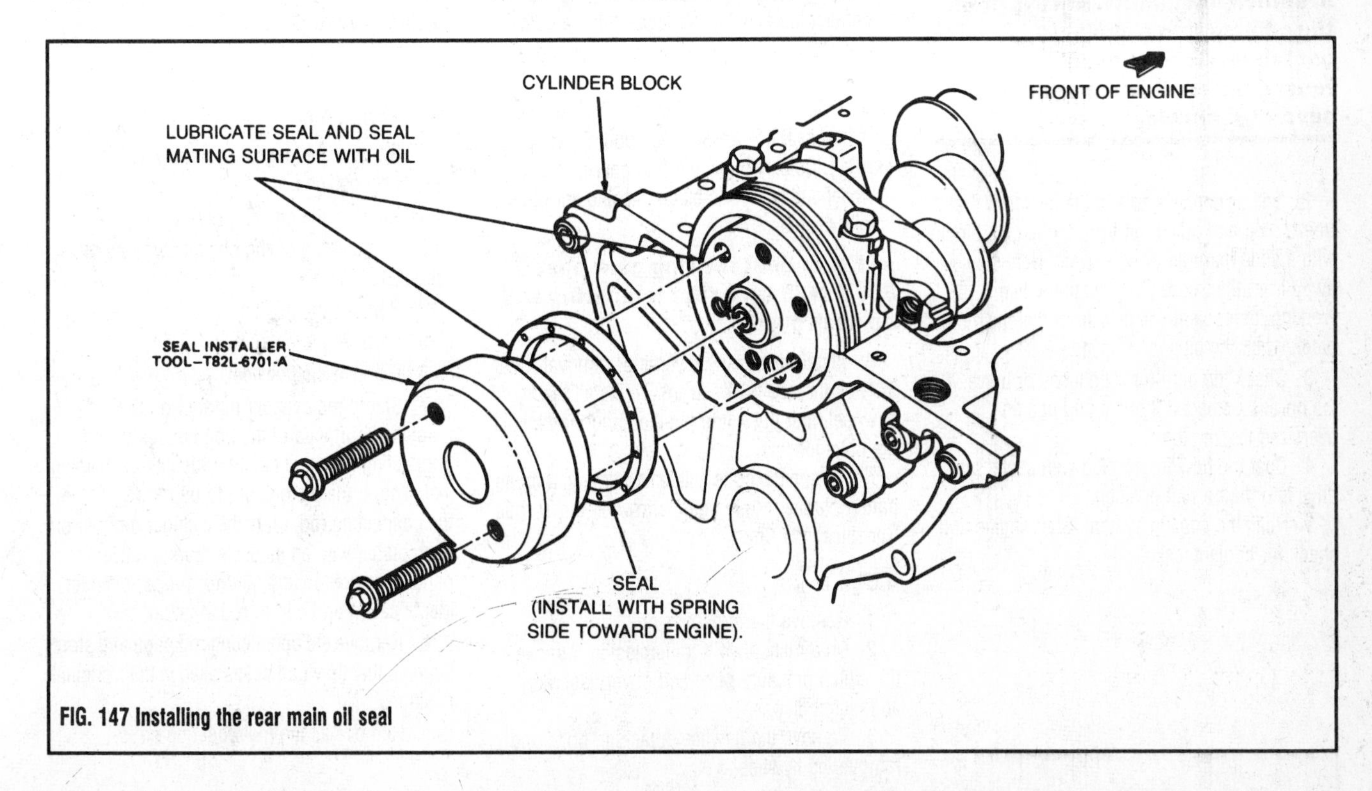

FIG. 147 Installing the rear main oil seal

tool and inspect the seal to be sure it was not damaged during installation.

8. Install the engine rear cover plate. Position the flywheel on the crankshaft flange. Coat the threads of the flywheel attaching bolts with oil-resistant sealer and install the bolts. Tighten the bolts in sequence across from each other to the specifications listed in the Torque Specifications Chart.

9. On a manual shift transmission, install the clutch disc and the pressure plate assembly.

10. Install the transmission.

Freeze (Core) Plugs

REMOVAL & INSTALLATION

All Engines

1. Drain the complete cooling system and engine block.

CAUTION

When draining the coolant, keep in mind that cats and dogs are attracted by the ethylene glycol antifreeze, and are quite likely to drink any that is left in an uncovered container or in puddles on the ground. This will prove fatal in sufficient quantity. Always drain the coolant into a sealable container. Coolant should be reused unless it is contaminated or several years old.

2. Drill or punch a hole in the center of the freeze plug and pull it out from the engine block with a slide hammer or equivalent. Note stay away from the freeze plug location when working, as coolant will flow from the engine block when the plug is removed.

3. Check the bore for roughness or burrs. If the bore is damaged, hone it and use an oversized freeze plug.

4. Coat the new freeze plug with sealer and drive into the correct position.

5. Refill the cooling system. Start engine and check for coolant leaks.

Flywheel/Flex Plate and Ring Gear

➡ **Flex plate is the term for a flywheel mated with an automatic transmission.**

REMOVAL & INSTALLATION

All Except 4.0L

➡ **The ring gear is replaceable only on engines mated with a manual transmission. Engine with automatic transmissions have ring gears which are welded to the flex plate.**

1. Remove the transmission and, on 4WD, the transfer case.

2. Remove the clutch, if equipped, or torque converter from the flywheel. The flywheel bolts should be loosened a little at a time in a cross pattern to avoid warping the flywheel. On trucks with manual transmission, replace the pilot bearing in the end of the crankshaft if removing the flywheel.

3. The flywheel should be checked for cracks and glazing. It can be resurfaced by a machine shop.

4. If the ring gear is to be replaced, drill a hole in the gear between two teeth, being careful not to contact the flywheel surface. Using a cold chisel at this point, crack the ring gear and remove it.

5. Polish the inner surface of the new ring gear and heat it in an oven to about 600°F (315°C). Quickly place the ring gear on the flywheel and tap it into place, making sure that it is fully seated.

➡ **Never heat the ring gear past 800°F (426°C), or the tempering will be destroyed.**

6. Installation is the reverse of removal. Coat the bolt threads with sealant. To install the flywheel, first put it into position and then install the bolts loosely.

7. Torque the bolts a little at a time in a cross pattern, to the torque figure shown in the Torque Specifications Chart.

4.0L

1. Remove the transmission.

2. On a manual shift transmission, remove the clutch pressure plate and cover assembly and clutch disc.

3. Remove the flywheel attaching bolts and remove the flywheel.

To install:

4. Position the flywheel on the crankshaft flange. Coat the threads of the flywheel attaching bolts with Loctite® or equivalent and install the bolts. Tighten the bolts in sequence across from each other to specifications.

5. On a manual shift transmission, install the clutch disc and pressure plate and cover assembly.

6. Install the transmission.

RING GEAR REPLACEMENT

➡ **This procedure is for manual shift transmission only. On automatic transmission if the ring gear has worn, chipped or cracked teeth, replace the flywheel assembly.**

1. Heat the ring gear with a propane torch on the engine side of the gear, and knock it off the flywheel. Do not hit the flywheel when removing the ring gear.

2. Heat the new ring gear evenly until the gear expands enough to slip onto the flywheel. Make sure the gear is properly seated against the shoulder. Do not heat any part of the gear more than 500 degrees F. If this limit is exceeded, the hardness will be removed from the ring gear teeth.

Crankshaft

➧ SEE FIGS. 148-158

REMOVAL

All Except 4.0L

1. Remove the engine assembly as previously outlined.

2. Remove the engine front cover.

3. Remove the timing chain/belt/gears and sprockets.

4. Remove the oil pan.

5. Remove the oil pump.

6. Remove the flywheel.

7. Stamp the cylinder number on the machined surfaces of the bolt bosses of the connecting rods and caps for identification when installing. If the pistons are to be removed from the connecting rod, mark the cylinder number on each piston with an indelible marker, silver pencil or quick drying paint for proper cylinder identification and cap to rod location.

8. Remove the connecting rod caps and store them so that they can be installed in their original positions.

9. Remove all the main bearing caps.

10. Note the position of the keyway in the crankshaft so it can be installed in the same position.

11. Lift the crankshaft out of the block. The rods will pivot to the center of the engine when the crankshaft is removed.

12. Remove the rear main oil seal.

4.0L

1. Remove the engine from the vehicle as previously described, then place it on a work stand.

2. Remove the transmission (if attached), bell housing, flywheel or flex plate and rear plate.

3. Drain the crankcase and remove the oil pan with the engine in a normal upright position.

***** CAUTION**

The EPA warns that prolonged contact with used engine oil may cause a number of skin disorders, including cancer! You should make every effort to minimize your exposure to used engine oil. Protective gloves should be worn when changing the oil. Wash your hands and any other exposed skin areas as soon as possible after exposure to used engine oil. Soap and water, or waterless hand cleaner should be used.

4. Remove the components from the front of the engine and the front cover.

5. Invert the engine and remove the oil pump, pickup tube and baffle, if equipped.

6. Make sure all main and connecting rod bearing caps are marked so they can be installed in their original locations.

7. Remove the connecting rod nuts and lift off the cap with its bearing insert. Install short pieces of rubber hose over the connecting rod studs to protect the crankshaft journals, then carefully push the piston and rod assemblies down into the cylinder bores.

8. Remove the main bearing caps with their bearing inserts.

INSPECTION AND INSTALLATION

All Except 4.0L

1. Using a dial indicator, check the crankshaft journal runout. Measure the crankshaft journals with a micrometer to determine the correct size rod and main bearings to be used. Whenever a

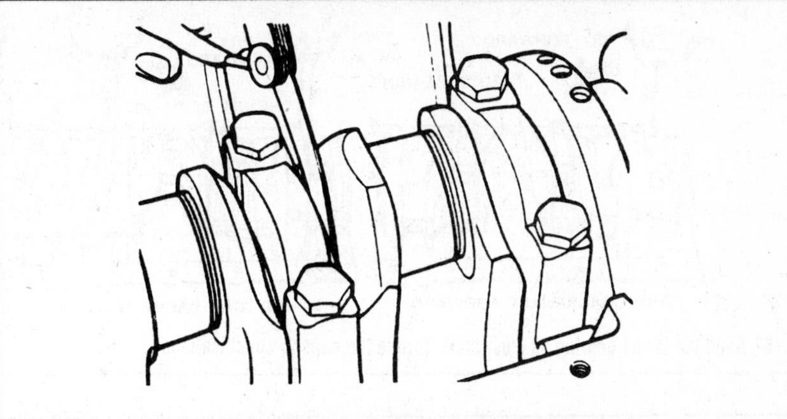

FIG. 148 Use a feeler gauge to check the crankshaft endplay during assembly

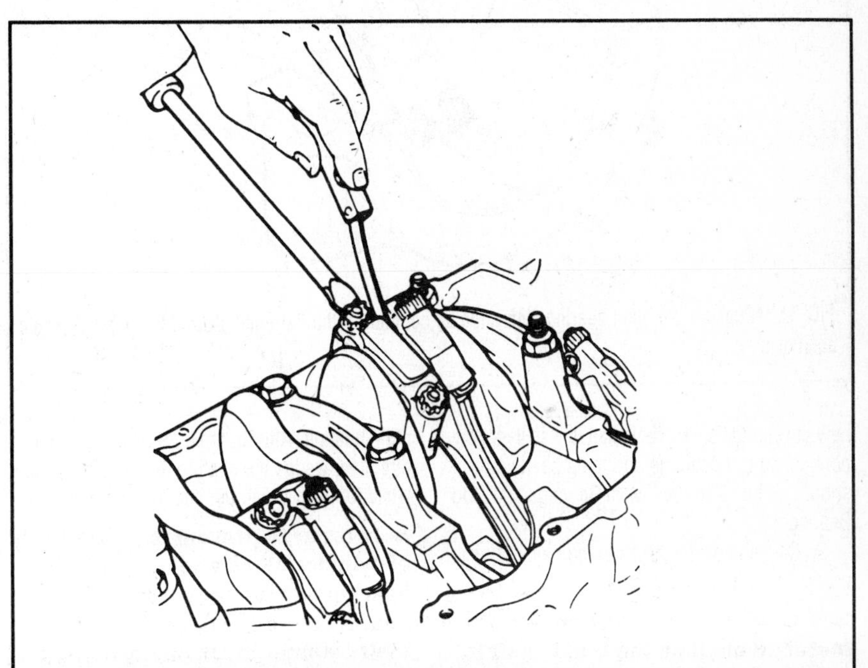

FIG. 149 Check the connecting rod side clearance with a feeler gauge. Use a small pry bar to carefully spread the rods to specified clearance

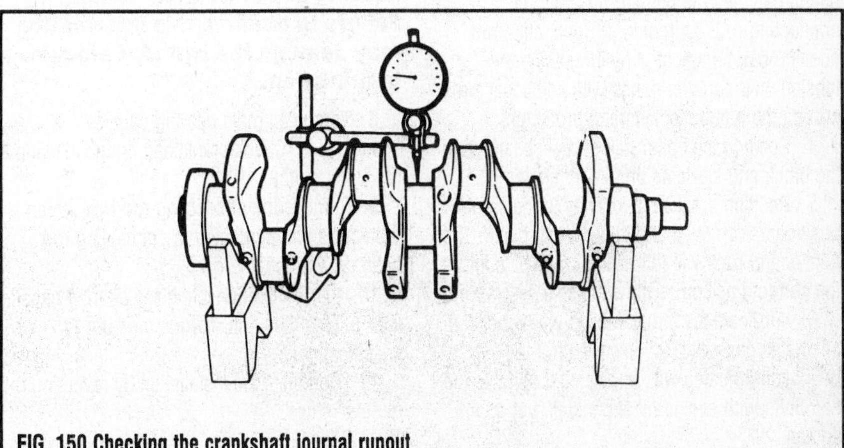

FIG. 150 Checking the crankshaft journal runout

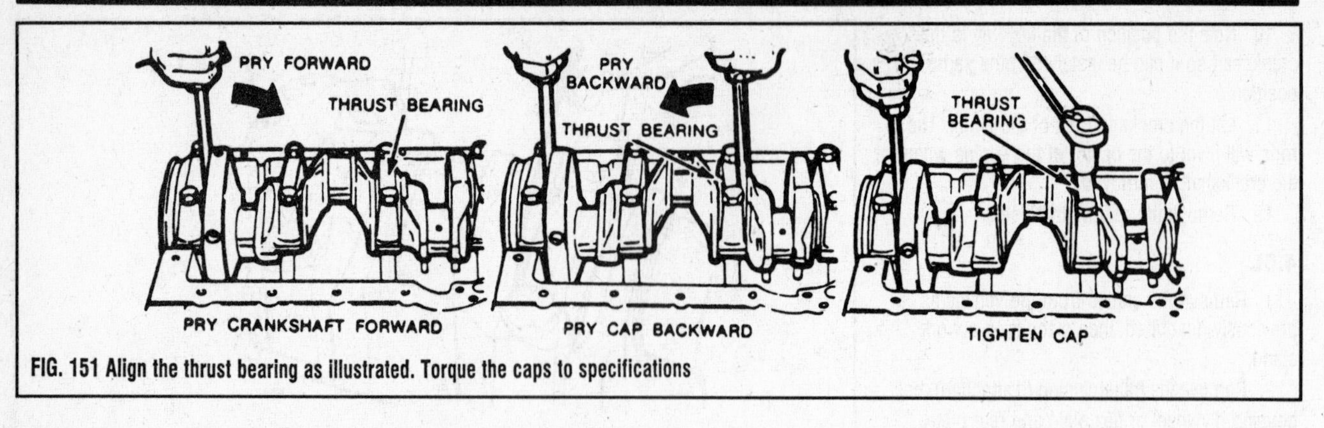

FIG. 151 Align the thrust bearing as illustrated. Torque the caps to specifications

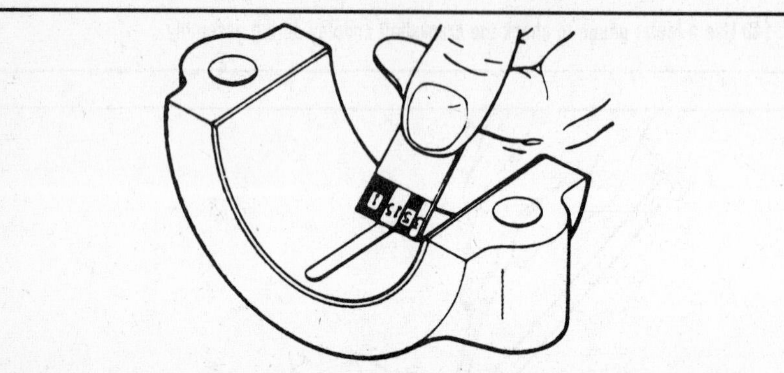

FIG. 152 Measure the main bearing clearance by comparing the flattened strip of Plastigage® scale as shown

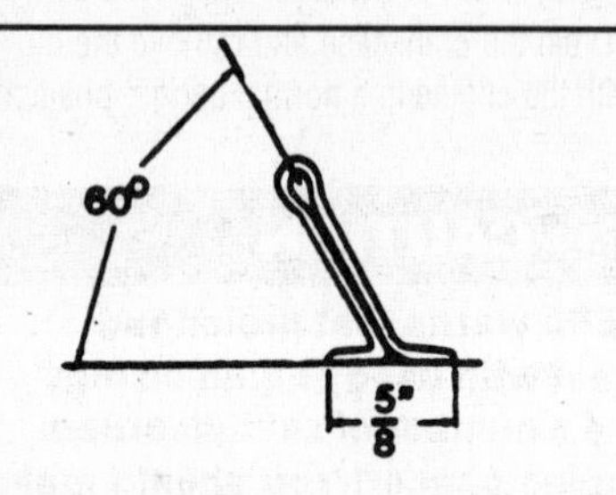

FIG. 153 Fabricate a roll-out pin as illustrated, if necessary

new or reconditioned crankshaft is installed, new connecting rod bearings and main bearings should be installed. See Main Bearings and Rod Bearings.

2. Clean all oil passages in the block (and crankshaft if it is being reused).

➡ **A new rear main seal should be installed anytime the crankshaft is removed or replaced.**

3. Install sufficient oil pan bolts in the block to align with the connecting rod bolts. Use rubber bands between the bolts to position the connecting rods as required. Connecting rod position can be adjusted by increasing the tension on the rubber bands with additional turns around the pan bolts or thread protectors.

4. Position the upper half of main bearings in the block and lubricate them with engine oil.

5. Position crankshaft keyway in the same position as removed and lower it into block. The connecting rods will follow the crank pins into the correct position as the crankshaft is lowered.

6. Lubricate the thrust flanges with rebuilding oil. Install caps with the lower half of the bearings lubricated with engine oil. Lubricate the cap bolts with engine oil and install, but do not tighten.

7. With a block of wood, bump the shaft in each direction to align the thrust flanges of the main bearing. After bumping the shaft in each direction, wedge the shaft to the front and hold it while torquing the thrust bearing cap bolts.

➡ **In order to prevent the possibility of cylinder block and/or main bearing cap damage, the main bearing caps are to be tapped into their cylinder block cavity using a wood or rubber mallet before the bolts are installed. Do not use attaching bolts to pull the main bearing caps into their seats. Failure to observe this information may damage the cylinder block or a bearing cap.**

8. Torque all main bearing caps to specification. Check crankshaft endplay, using a flat feeler gauge.

9. Remove the connecting rod bolt thread protectors and lubricate the connecting rod bearings with engine oil.

10. Install the connecting rod bearing caps in their original position. Torque the nuts to specification.

11. Complete the installation by reversing the removal steps.

4.0L

1. Inspect the crankshaft journals for nicks, burrs or bearing pickup that would cause premature bearing wear. When replacing standard bearings with new bearings, it is good practice to fit the bearing to minimum specified clearance. If the desired clearance cannot be obtained with a standard bearing, try one half of a 0.001 in. (0.025mm) or 0.002 in. (0.050mm) undersize in combination with a standard bearing to obtain the proper clearance.

2. Place a piece of Plastigage® on the bearing surface across the full width of the bearing cap, about 1/4 in. (6mm) off center. Install the cap and tighten the bolts to the specified torque given in the General Engine Specifications Chart. Do not rotate the crankshaft with the Plastigage® in place. Remove the cap and use the scale provided with the kit to check the Plastigage width at its widest and narrowest points. Widest point is minimum clearance, narrowest point is maximum clearance; the difference between the two is the taper reading of the journal.

3. Bearing clearance must be within specified limits. If standard 0.002 in. (0.050mm) undersize bearings do not bring the clearance within desired limits, the crankshaft will have to be refinished or replaced. Remove the remaining main bearing caps and lift out the crankshaft, being careful not to damage the thrust bearing surfaces. Discard the rear main oil seal. The crankshaft should be refinished at a machine shop to give the proper clearance with the next

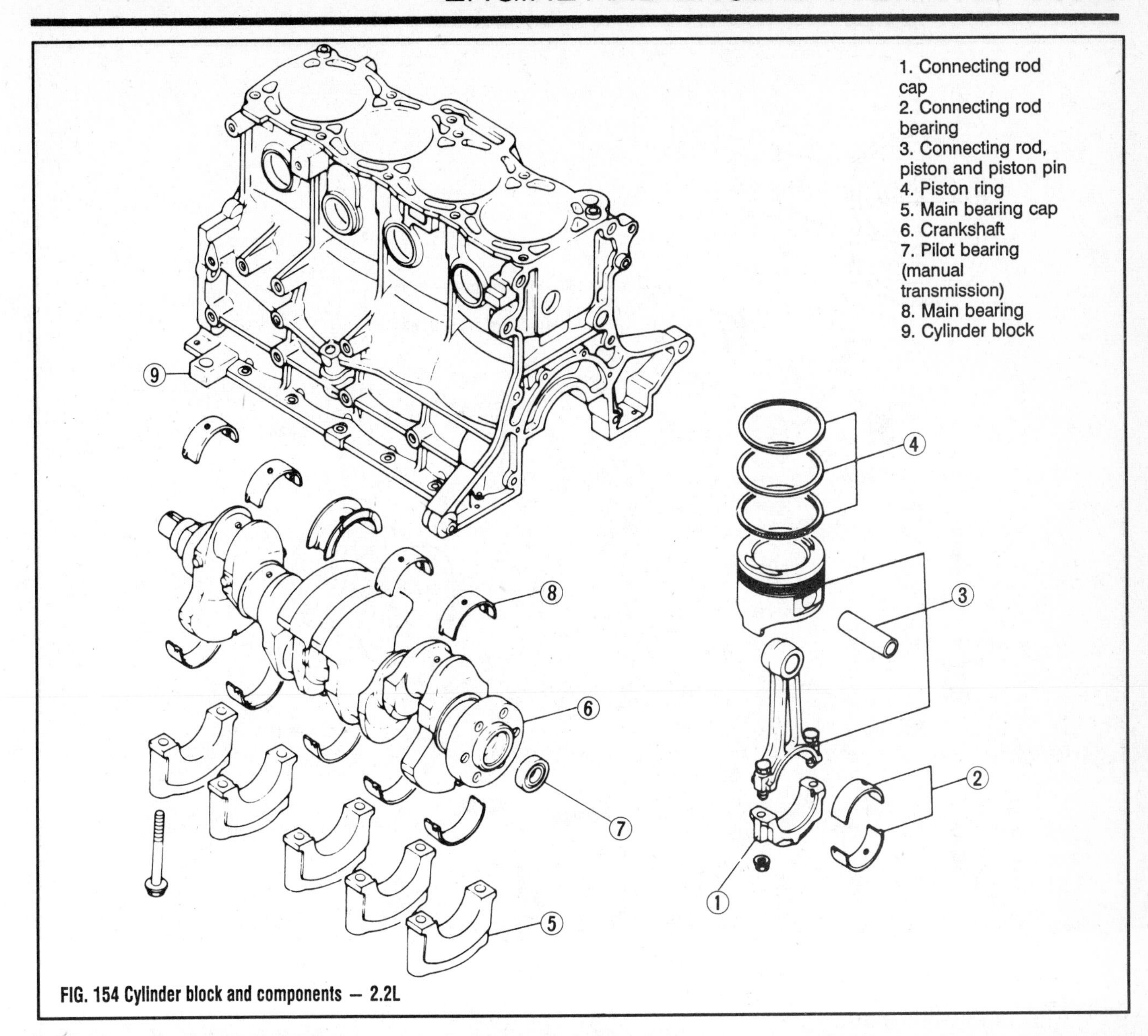

FIG. 154 Cylinder block and components — 2.2L

undersize bearing. If the journal will not clean up to the maximum undersize bearing, the crankshaft will have to be replaced.

4. Clean the bearing bores in the block and caps. Foreign material under the inserts or on the bearing surfaces may distort the insert and cause bearing failure.

5. Assemble the main bearing inserts in their correct location in the bearing caps and cylinder block. Check the oil hole alignment between the bearing inserts and block. Apply a liberal coating of clean heavy SG engine oil to the bearing surfaces, then carefully lower the crankshaft into position.

6. Insert the remaining bearing shells into the main bearing caps and coat the bearings with clean heavy SG engine oil, then install the caps with the arrows pointing toward the front of the engine. Apply a thin even coating of sealing compound to the rear sealing surface of the rear main bearing cap before installing. Install and tighten all main bearing cap bolts finger tight after lightly oiling the threads.

7. Tighten all bearing cap bolts, except for the thrust bearing cap, to the specifications given in the Torque Specifications Chart.

8. Align the thrust bearing surfaces by forcing the crankshaft forward and the thrust bearing cap rearward. While holding in this position, tighten the thrust bearing cap to specifications.

9. Install a new rear main oil seal as previously described.

10. On some engines, use a flat tool such as a large blunt end screwdriver to push the two wedge shaped seals between the cylinder block and rear main bearing cap. Position the seals with the round side facing the main bearing cap.

11. Pull the connecting rods up one at a time and install rod caps after applying a liberal coating of heavy SG engine oil to the bearings. Tighten all bearing caps to specifications. Check the connecting rod side clearance as previously described. Check the crankshaft end play with a dial indicator.

12. Install the oil pump, pickup tube and baffle, if equipped. Prime the oil pump before installation as described under Oil Pump Removal and Installation.

13. Install the front cover and timing chain, belt or gears. Replace the front cover oil seal.

14. Install the rear cover plate (if equipped) and the flywheel or flex plate. Tighten the mounting bolts to specifications.

15. Install the clutch disc, pressure plate and bell housing on manual transmission models.

16. Install the oil pan and tighten the bolts to specifications. See Oil Pan Removal and Installation for gasket and sealer placement.

17. Invert the engine to its normal, upright position and fill the crankcase with the specified amount and type of engine oil. Replace the oil filter.

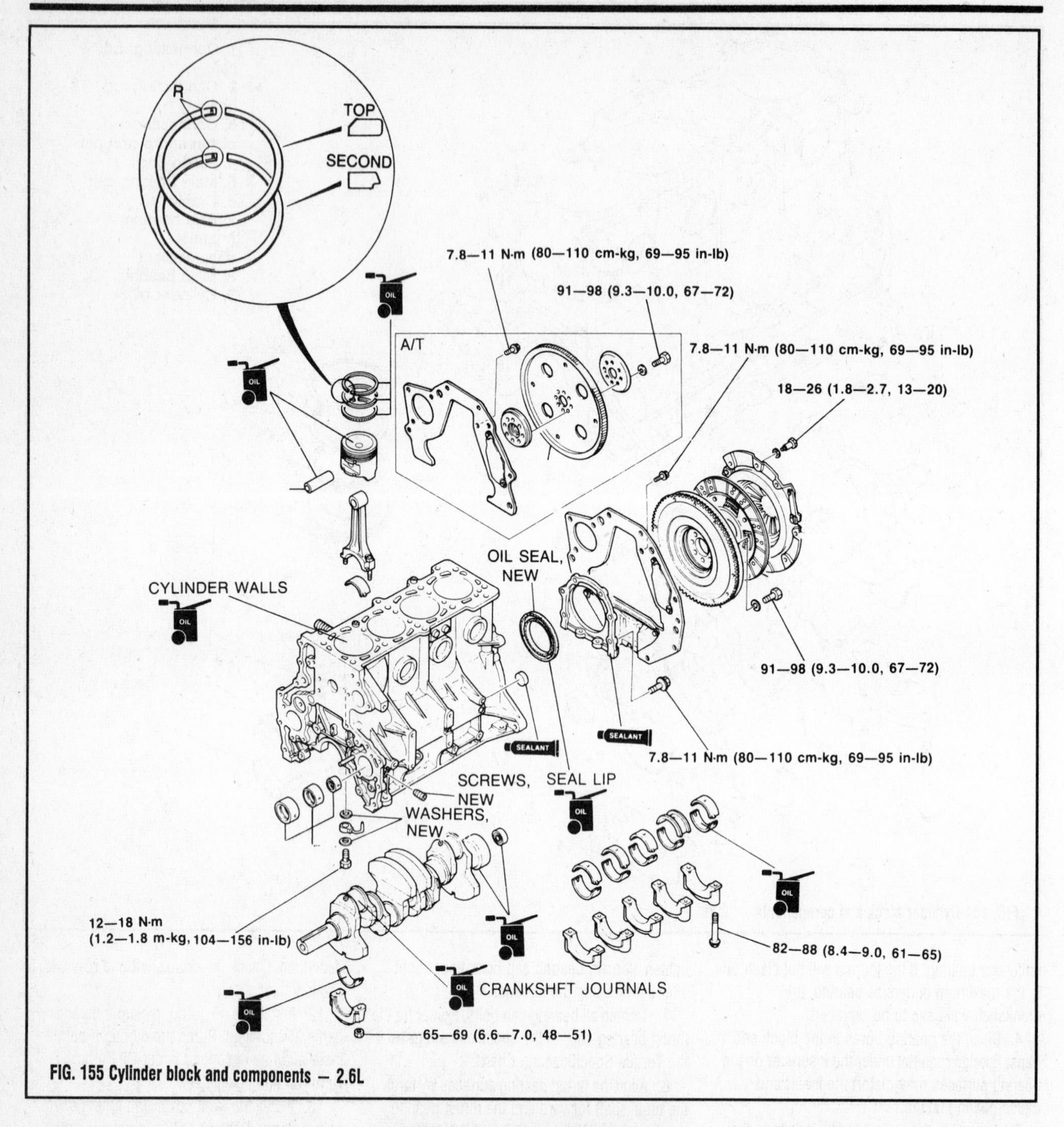

FIG. 155 Cylinder block and components – 2.6L

18. Install the transmission, if removed with the engine.

19. Install the engine in the vehicle as previously described. Roadtest the vehicle for proper operation.

Main Bearings

CHECKING BEARING CLEARANCE

1. Remove the bearing cap and wipe the oil from the crankshaft journal and the outer and inner surfaces of the bearing shell.

2. Place a piece of plastic gauging material in the center of the bearing.

3. Use a floor jack or other means to hold the crankshaft against the upper bearing shell. This is necessary to obtain accurate clearance readings when using plastic gauging material.

4. Install the bearing cap and bearing. Place engine oil on the cap bolts and install. Torque the bolts to specification. On the 3.0L, the main bearing cap bolts should be torqued in proper sequence to the proper torque specification, then an additional 90 degrees and an additional 45 degrees after that. Paint reference marks on each bolt to assist with the angular torque.

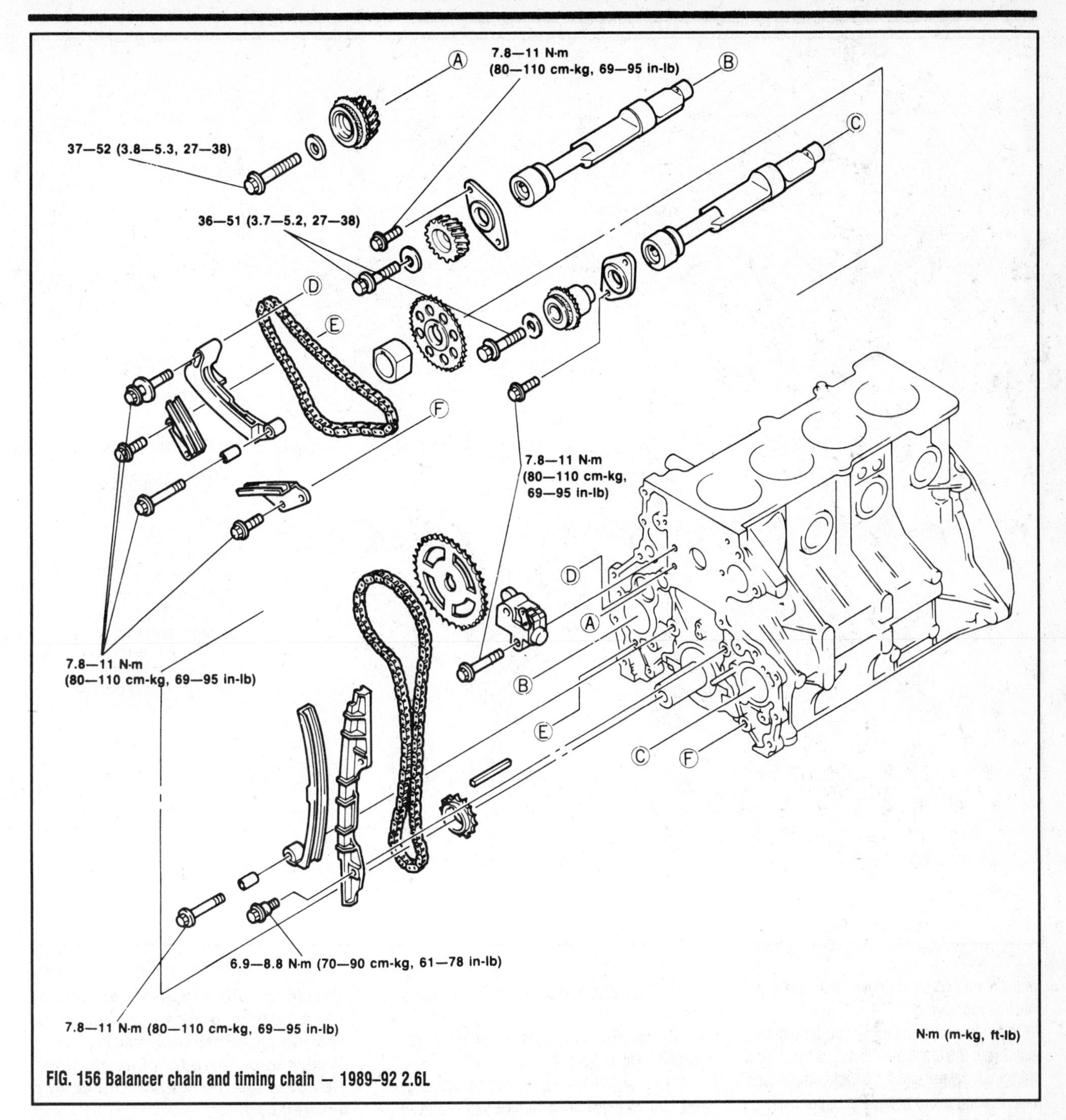

FIG. 156 Balancer chain and timing chain — 1989–92 2.6L

5. Remove the bearing cap and determine the bearing clearance by comparing the width of the flattened plastic gauging material at its widest point with the graduations on the gauging material container. The number within the graduation on the envelope indicates the clearance in millimeters or thousandths of an inch. If the clearance is greater than allowed, REPLACE BOTH BEARING SHELLS AS A SET. Recheck the clearance after replacing the shells. (Refer to Main Bearing Replacement).

REPLACEMENT

Main bearing clearances must be corrected by the use of selective upper and lower shells. Undersized bearings are available in sizes of 0.25mm, 0.50mm and 0.75mm. UNDER NO CIRCUMSTANCES should the use of shims behind the shells to compensate for wear be attempted. To install the main bearing shells, proceed as follows:

1. Remove the oil pan as outlined below. On some models, the oil pump may also have to be removed.
2. Loosen all main bearing caps.
3. Remove the bearing cap and remove the lower shell.
4. Insert a flattened cotter pin or roll pin in the oil passage hole in the crankshaft, then rotate the crankshaft in the direction opposite to cranking rotation. The pin will contact the upper shell and roll it out.
5. The main bearing journals should be checked for roughness and wear. Slight roughness may be removed with a fine grit polishing cloth saturated with engine oil. Burrs may be removed with a fine oil stone. If the

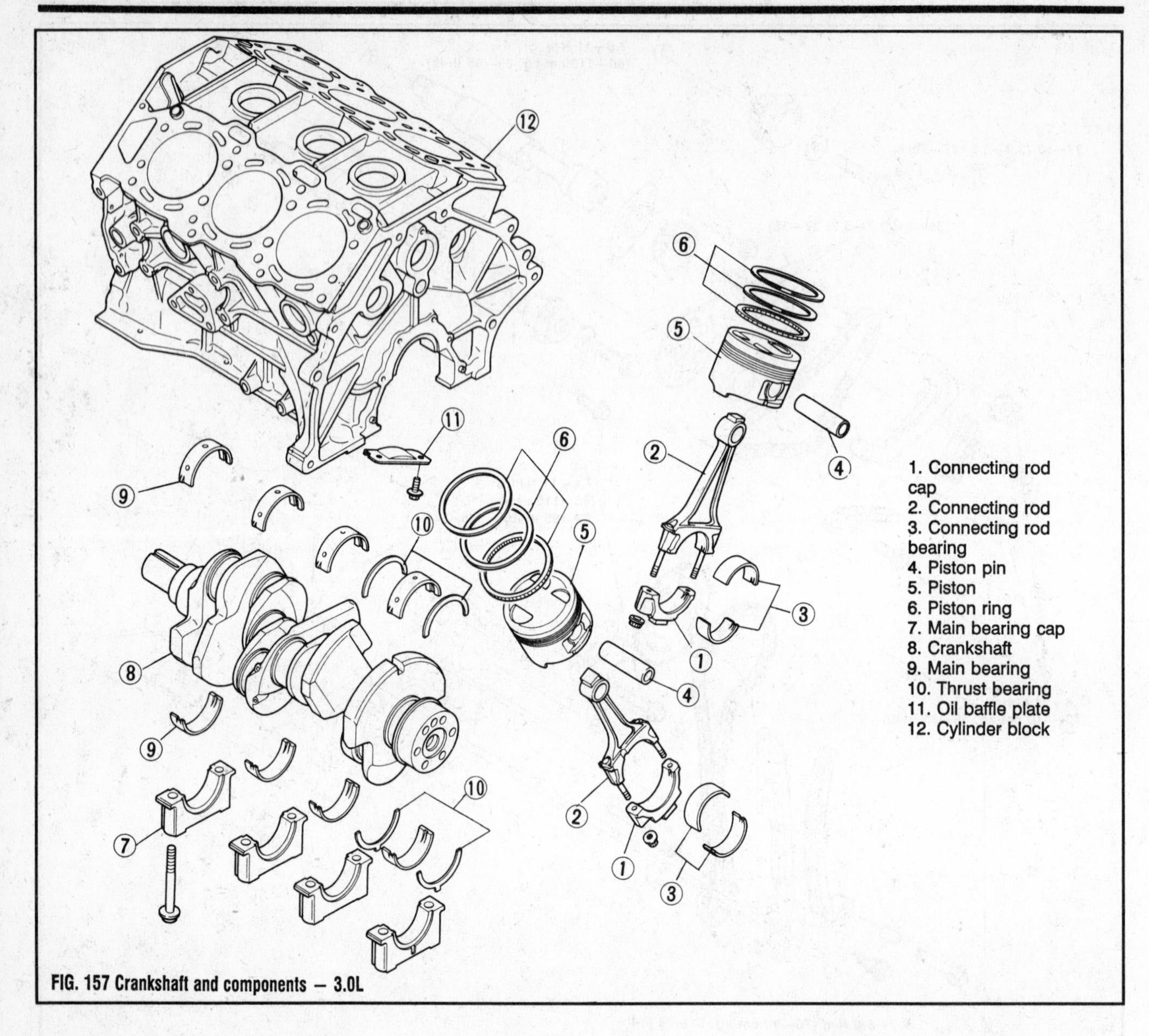

FIG. 157 Crankshaft and components — 3.0L

journals are scored or ridged, the crankshaft must be replaced.

The journals can be measured for out-of-round with the crankshaft installed by using a crankshaft caliper and inside micrometer or a main bearing micrometer. The upper bearing shell must be removed when measuring the crankshaft journals. Maximum out-of-round of the crankshaft journals must not exceed 0.050mm (0.00197 in.).

6. Clean the crankshaft journals and bearing caps thoroughly for installing new main bearings.

7. Apply clean engine oil or rebuilding oil, to the thrust flanges of bearing shells.

8. Place a new upper shell on the crankshaft journal with locating tang in the correct position and rotate the shaft to turn it into place using a cotter pin or roll pin as during removal.

9. Place a new bearing shell in the bearing cap.

10. Install a new oil seal in the rear main bearing cap and block.

11. Lubricate the main bearings with engine oil. Lubricate the thrust surface with lubricant rebuilding oil.

12. Lubricate the main bearing cap bolts with engine oil. On the 3.0L, measure the length of each main bearing bolt prior to the final installation. The bolts are acceptable if they are 3.35–3.37 in. (85–85.5mm) If the bolt length exceeds 3.37 in. (85.5mm), replace the bolt.

➡ In order to prevent the possibility of cylinder block and/or main bearing cap damage, the main bearing caps are to be tapped into their cylinder block cavity using a wood or rubber mallet before the attaching bolts are installed. Do not use attaching bolts to pull the main bearing caps into their seats. Failure to observe this information may damage the cylinder block or a bearing cap.

13. Torque the main bearing cap bolts as specified.

REGRINDING JOURNALS

1. Dress minor scores with an oil stone. If the journals are severely marred or exceed the for the next undersize bearing.

2. Regrind the journals to give the proper clearance with the next undersize bearing. If the journal will not clean up to maximum undersize bearing available, replace the crankshaft.

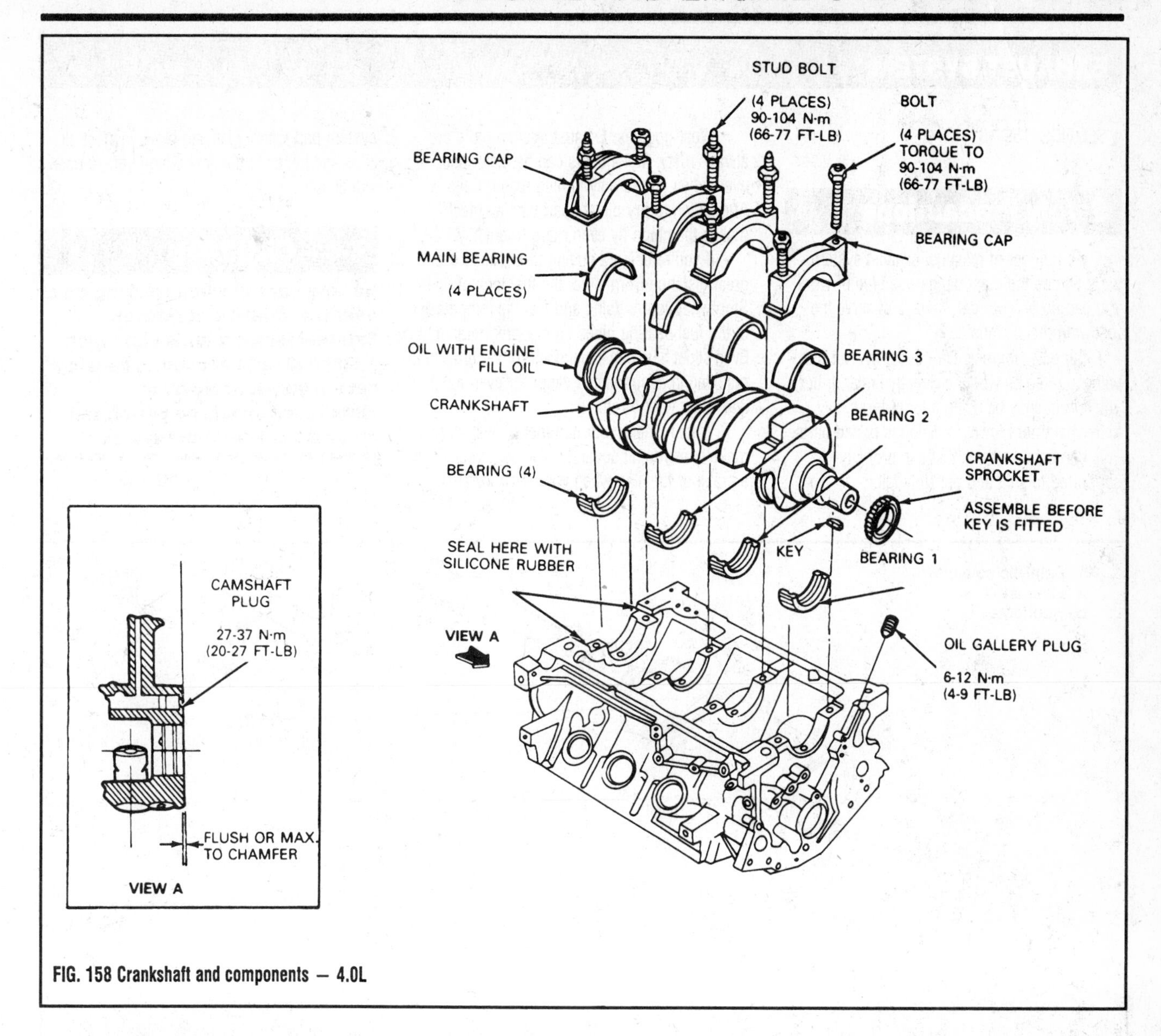

FIG. 158 Crankshaft and components — 4.0L

3. Always reproduce the same journal shoulder radius that existed originally. Too small a radius will result in fatigue failure of the crankshaft. Too large a radius will result in bearing failure due to radius ride of the bearing.

4. After regrinding the journals, chamfer the oil holes; then polish the journals with a No. 320 grit polishing cloth and engine oil. Crocus cloth may also be used as a polishing agent.

EXHAUST SYSTEM

➧ SEE FIGS. 159-161

Safety Precautions

For a number of reasons, exhaust system work can be the most dangerous type of work you can do on your car. Always observe the following precautions:

- Support the truck extra securely. Not only will you often be working directly under it, but you'll frequently be using a lot of force, say, heavy hammer blows, to dislodge rusted parts. This can cause a truck that's improperly supported to shift and possibly fall.
- Wear goggles. Exhaust system parts are always rusty. Metal chips can be dislodged, even when you're only turning rusted bolts. Attempting to pry pipes apart with a chisel makes the chips fly even more frequently.
- If you're using a cutting torch, keep it a great distance from either the fuel tank or lines. Stop what you're doing and feel the temperature of the fuel bearing pipes on the tank frequently. Even slight heat can expand and/or vaporize fuel, resulting in accumulated vapor, or even a liquid leak, near your torch.
- Watch where your hammer blows fall and make sure you hit squarely. You could easily tap a brake or fuel line when you hit an exhaust system part with a glancing blow. Inspect all lines and hoses in the area where you've been working.

CAUTION

Be very careful when working on or near the catalytic converter. External temperatures can reach 1,500°F (816°C) and more, causing severe burns. Removal or installation should be performed only on a cold exhaust system.

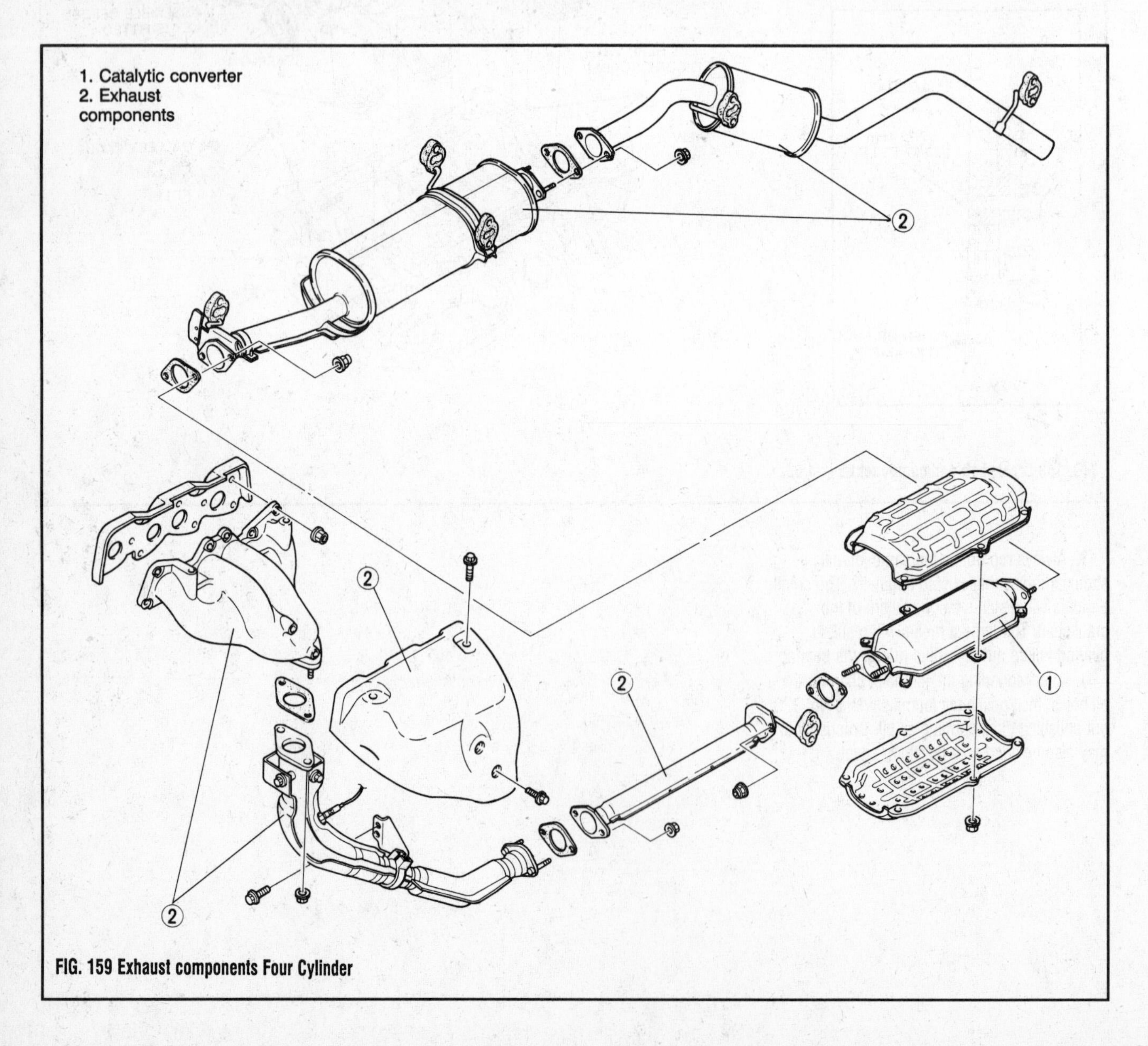

FIG. 159 Exhaust components Four Cylinder

Special Tools

A number of special exhaust system tools can be rented from auto supply houses or local stores that rent special equipment. A common one is a tail pipe expander, designed to enable you to join pipes of identical diameter.

It may also be quite helpful to use solvents designed to loosen rusted bolts or flanges. Soaking rusted parts the night before you do the job can speed the work of freeing rusted parts considerably. Remember that these solvents are often flammable. Apply only to parts after they are cool!

Exhaust Downpipe

REMOVAL & INSTALLATION

1. Raise and safely support the truck on jackstands.
2. Saturate all bolts and nuts with penetrating lubricant.
3. Disconnect the downpipe from the manifold(s) and discard the seal.
4. Support the catalytic converter and disconnect the downpipe. Discard the gasket, if used.
5. Install in reverse order. Use new gaskets and seals. Tighten all fasteners to 23 ft. lbs. Make sure that there is sufficient clearance around all parts.

Catalytic Converter

REMOVAL & INSTALLATION

1. Raise and safely support the truck on jackstands.
2. Saturate all bolts and nuts with penetrating lubricant.
3. Remove the converter-to-downpipe bolts.
4. Remove the converter-to-muffler inlet pipe bolts.
5. Install in reverse order. Use new gaskets. Torque the connections to 23 ft. lbs.

Muffler

REMOVAL & INSTALLATION

1. Raise and safely support the truck on jackstands.
2. Saturate all bolts and nuts with penetrating lubricant.
3. Remove the converter-to-muffler pipe bolts.
4. Remove the muffler-to-silencer pipe bolts.
5. Remove all muffler hangers and lower the muffler from the truck.
6. Installation is the reverse of removal. Use new gaskets. Torque the bolts to 23 ft. lbs.

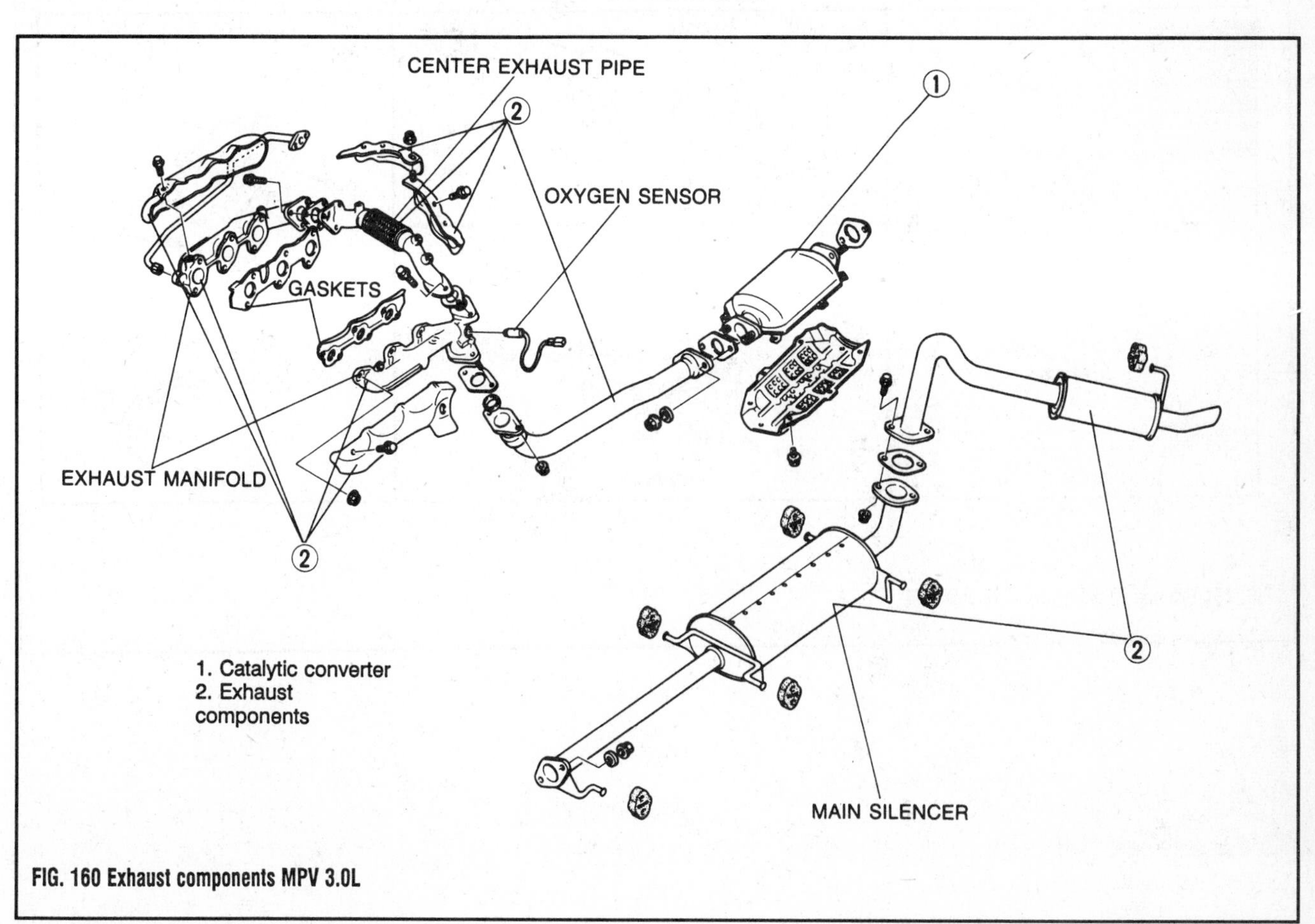

FIG. 160 Exhaust components MPV 3.0L

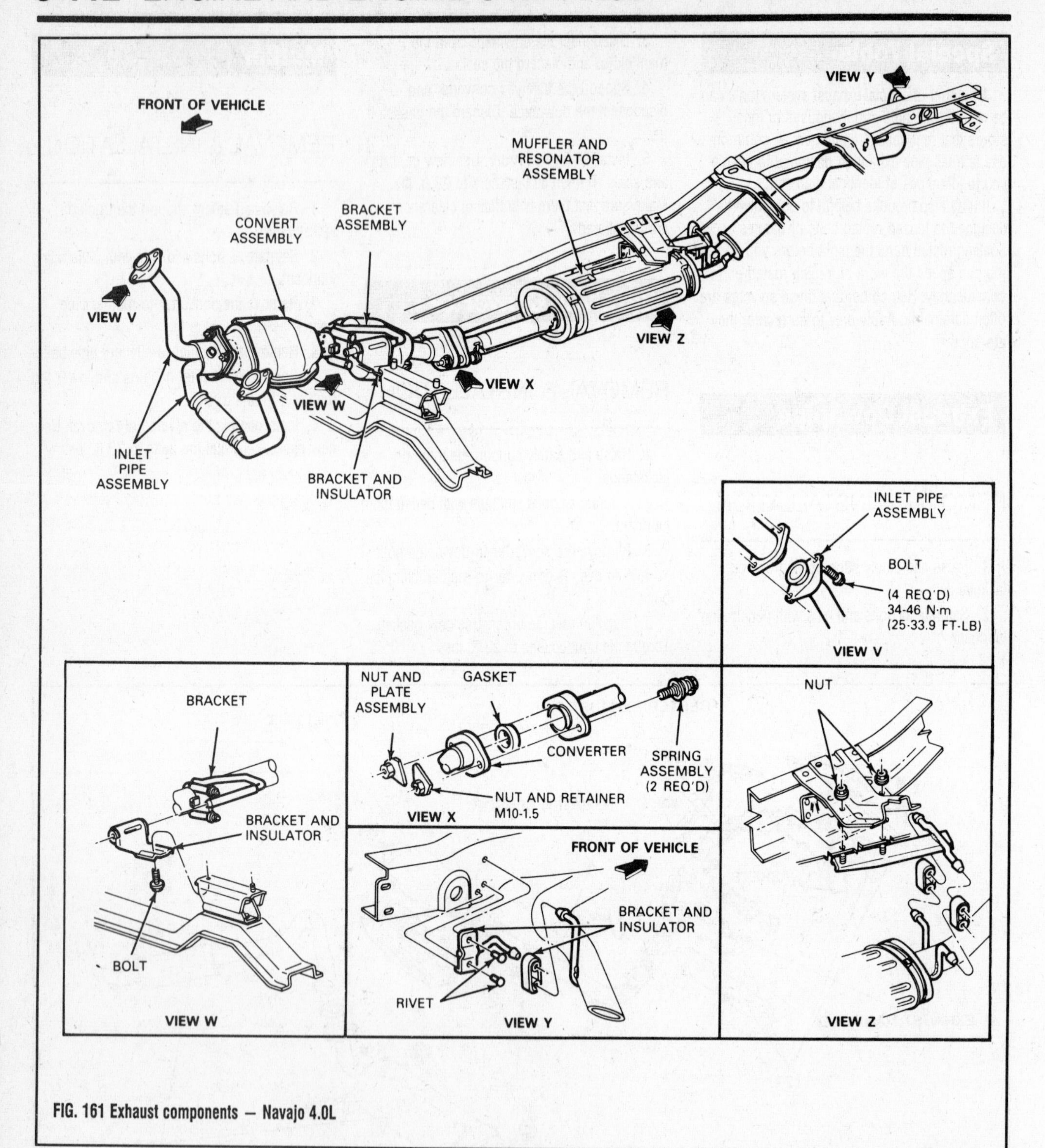

FIG. 161 Exhaust components — Navajo 4.0L

Silencer and Tailpipe

REMOVAL & INSTALLATION

1. Raise and safely support the truck on jackstands.
2. Saturate all bolts and nuts with penetrating lubricant.
3. Remove the muffler-to-silencer pipe bolts.
4. Remove all silencer hangers and lower the silencer from the truck.
5. Installation is the reverse of removal. Use new gaskets. Torque the bolts to 23 ft. lbs.

Muffler, Catalytic Converter, Inlet and Outlet Pipes

REMOVAL & INSTALLATION

Navajo

➡ **The following applies to exhaust systems using clamped joints. Some models, use welded joints at the muffler. These joints will, of course, have to be cut.**

1. Raise and safely support the truck on jackstands.
2. Remove the U-clamps securing the muffler and outlet pipe.
3. Disconnect the muffler and outlet pipe bracket and insulator assemblies.
4. Remove the muffler and outlet pipe assembly. It may be necessary to heat the joints to get the parts to come off. Special tools are available to aid in breaking loose the joints.
5. Remove the extension pipe.
6. Disconnect the catalytic converter bracket and insulator assembly.

➡ **For rod and insulator type hangers, apply a soap solution to the insulator surface and rod ends to allow easier removal of the insulator from the rod end. Don't use oil-based or silicone-based solutions since they will allow the insulator to slip back off once it's installed.**

7. Remove the catalytic converter.
8. On models with Managed Thermactor Air, disconnect the MTA tube assembly.
9. Remove the inlet pipe assembly.
10. Install the components making sure that all the components in the system are properly aligned before tightening any fasteners. Make sure all tabs are indexed and all parts are clear of surrounding body panels.

2.2L ENGINE MECHANICAL SPECIFICATIONS

Component	U.S.	Metric
Bore x stroke	3.39 x 3.70 in.	86.0 x 94.0 mm
Total piston displacement	133.2 cu in.	2,184 cc
Compression pressure		
Standard	173 psi	1,197 KPa
Minimum	121 psi	838 KPa
Maximum difference between cylinders	28 psi	196 KPa
Valve timing		
Intake	Opens 13° BTDC	Closes 57° ABDC
Exhaust	Opens 58° BBDC	Closes 12° ATDC
Valve clearance		
Intake	0	
Exhaust	0	
Cylinder Head		
Height	3.620-3.624 in.	91.95-92.05 mm
Distortion	0.006 in. max.	0.15 mm max.
Grinding	0.008 in. max.	0.20 mm max.
Valve head diameter		
Intake	1.728-1.736 in.	43.9-44.1 mm
Exhaust	1.413-1.421 in.	35.9-36.1 mm
Valve head margin thickness		
Intake	0.031-0.047 in.	0.8-1.2 mm
Exhaust	0.051-0.067 in.	1.3-1.7 mm
Valve face angle		
Intake	45°	
Exhaust	45°	

2.2L ENGINE MECHANICAL SPECIFICATIONS

Component	U.S.	Metric
Valve length		
Intake		
Standard	4.4051 in.	111.89 mm
Minimum	4.3894 in.	111.49 mm
Exhaust		
Standard	4.3972 in.	111.69 mm
Minimum	4.3815 in.	111.29 mm
Valve stem diameter		
Intake	0.3161-0.3167 in.	8.030-8.045 mm
Exhaust	0.3159-0.3165 in.	8.025-8.040 mm
Valve guide inner diameter		
Intake	0.3177-0.3185 in.	8.07-8.09 mm
Exhaust	0.3177-0.3185 in.	8.07-8.09 mm
Valve stem-to-guide clearance		
Intake	0.0010-0.0024 in.	0.025-0.060 mm
Exhaust	0.0012-0.0026 in.	0.030-0.065 mm
Maximum	0.008 in.	0.20 mm
Valve guide projection (Height "A")	0.752-0.772 in.	19.1-19.6 mm
Valve Seat		
Intake	45°	
Exhaust	45°	
Valve seat contact width		
Intake	0.047-0.063 in.	1.2-1.6 mm
Exhaust	0.047-0.063 in.	1.2-1.6 mm
Valve seat sinking (measure valve protruding length)		
Intake		
Standard	1.831 in.	46.5 mm
Maximum	1.890 in.	48.0 mm
Exhaust		
Standard	1.831 in.	46.5 mm
Maximum	1.890 in.	48.0 mm
Valve spring		
Free length		
Intake		
Outer		
Standard	2.047 in.	52.0 mm
Minimum	1.984 in.	50.4 mm
Inner		
Standard	1.732 in.	44.0 mm
Minimum	1.681 in.	42.7 mm
Exhaust		
Outer		
Standard	2.047 in.	52.0 mm
Minimum	1.984 in.	50.4 mm
Inner		
Standard	1.732 in.	44.0 mm
Minimum	1.681 in.	42.7 mm
Out-of-square		
Intake		
Outer	0.07 in. max.	1.8 mm max.
Inner	0.06 in. max.	1.5 mm max.
Exhaust		
Outer	0.07 in. max.	1.8 mm max.
Inner	0.06 in. max.	1.5 mm max.
Setting load height		
Intake		
Outer	94.6 lbs./1.22 in.	421.8 N/31.0mm
Inner	66.0 lbs./1.04 in.	294.3 N/26.5mm
Exhaust		
Outer	94.6 lbs./1.22 in.	421.8 N/31.0mm
Inner	66.0 lbs./1.04 in.	294.3 N/26.5mm

2.2L ENGINE MECHANICAL SPECIFICATIONS

Component	U.S.	Metric
Camshaft		
Cam lobe height		
Intake		
Standard	1.4984 in.	38.059 mm
Minimum	1.4905 in.	37.859 mm
Exhaust		
Standard	1.4984 in.	38.059 mm
Minimum	1.4905 in.	37.859 mm
Journal diameter		
Front and rear (No.1,5)	1.2575-1.2584 in.	31.940-31.965 mm
Center (No.2,3,4)	1.2563-1.2573 in.	31.910-31.935 mm
Out-of-round max.	0.0020 in.	0.05 mm
Camshaft bearing oil clearance		
Front and rear (No.1,5)	0.0014-0.0033 in.	0.035-0.085 mm
Center (No.2,3,4)	0.0026-0.0045 in.	0.065-0.115 mm
Maximum	0.006 in.	0.15 mm
Camshaft runout	0.0012 in. max.	0.03 mm max.
Camshaft end play		
Standard	0.0031-0.0063 in.	0.08-0.16 mm
Maximum	0.008 in.	0.20 mm
Rocker Arms		
Rocker arm inner diameter	0.6300-0.6310 in.	16.000-16.027 mm
Rocker arm shaft diameter	0.6286-0.6293 in.	15.966-15.984 mm
Rocker arm-to-clearance		
Standard	0.0006-0.0024 in.	0.016-0.061 mm
Maximum	0.004 in.	0.10 mm
Cylinder block		
Height	11.87 in.	301.5 mm
Distortion	0.006 in. max.	0.15 mm max.
Grinding	0.008 in. max.	0.20 mm max.
Cylinder bore diameter		
Standard size	3.3858-3.3866 in.	86.000-86.019 mm
0.010 in. oversize (0.25 mm)	3.3957-3.3964 in.	86.250-86-269 mm
0.020 in. oversize (0.50 mm)	3.4055-3.4063 in.	86.500-86.519 mm
Cylinder bore taper	0.0007 in. max.	0.019 mm max.
Cylinder bore out-of-round	0.0004 in. max.	0.010 mm max.
Piston and Rings		
Piston diameter (Measured at 90° to pin bore axis and 0.709 in. (18.0mm) below oil ring groove)		
Standard size	3.3836-3.3844 in.	85.944-85.964 mm
Oversize 0.010 in. (0.25 mm)	3.3935-3.3942 in.	86.194-86.214 mm
Oversize 0.020 in. (0.50 mm)	3.4033-3.4041 in.	86.444-86.464 mm
Piston-to-cylinder clearance		
Standard	0.0017-0.0024 in.	0.043-0.062 mm
Maximum	0.006 in.	0.15 mm
Piston ring		
Thickness	0.058-0.059 in.	1.47-1.49 mm
End gap measured in cylinder		
Top	0.008-0.014 in.	0.20-0.35 mm
Second	0.006-0.012 in.	0.15-0.30 mm
Oil (rail)	0.008-0.028 in.	0.20-0.70 mm
Maximum	0.039 in.	1.0 mm
Ring groove width in piston		
Top	0.0598-0.0606 in.	1.52-1.54 mm
Second	0.0598-0.0606 in.	1.52-1.54 mm
Oil	0.1583-0.1591 in.	4.02-4.04 mm
Piston ring-to-ring land clearance		
Top	0.0012-0.0028 in.	0.03-0.07 mm
Second	0.0012-0.0028 in.	0.03-0.07 mm
Maximum	0.006 in.	0.15 mm

2.2L ENGINE MECHANICAL SPECIFICATIONS

Component	U.S.	Metric
Piston pin		
Diameter	0.8651-0.8654 in.	21.974-21.980 mm
Interference in connecting rod	0.0005-0.0015 in.	0.013-0.037 mm
Piston-to-piston pin clearance	0.0003-0.0009 in.	0.008-0.024 mm
Pressure force	1,100-3,300 lbs.	4,905-14,715 N
Connecting rod		
Length (Center to center)	6.2382-6.2421 in.	158.45-158.55 mm
Bend	0.0094 in. max.	0.24 mm max.
Small end bore	0.8640-0.8646 in.	21.943-21.961 mm
Big end bore	2.1261-2.1266 in.	54.002-54.017 mm
Big end width	1.0566-1.0587 in.	26.838-26.890 mm
Connecting rod side clearance		
Standard	0.0043-0.0103 in.	0.110-0.262 mm
Maximum	0.012 in.	0.30 mm
Crankshaft		
Crankshaft runout	0.0012 in. max.	0.03 mm max.
Main journal diameter		
Standard	2.3597-2.3604 in.	59.937-59.955 mm
0.010 in. undersize (0.25 mm)		
No.1,2,4,5	2.3501-2.3508 in.	59.693-59.711 mm
No.3	2.3499-2.3506 in.	59.687-59.705 mm
0.020 in. undersize (0.50 mm)		
No.1,2,4,5	2.3403-2.3410 in.	59.443-59.461 mm
No.3	2.3400-2.3407 in.	59.437-59.455 mm
0.030 in. undersize (0.75 mm)		
No.1,2,4,5	2.3304-2.3311 in.	59.193-59.211 mm
No.3	2.3302-2.3309 in.	59.187-59.205 mm
Main journal taper	0.002 in. max.	0.05 mm max.
Main journal out-of-round	0.00012 in.	0.003 mm
Crankpin journal diameter		
Standard	2.0055-2.0061 in.	50.940-50.955 mm
0.010 in undersize (0.25 mm)	1.9957-1.9963 in.	50.690-50.705 mm
0.020 in undersize (0.50 mm)	1.9858-1.9864 in.	50.440-50.455 mm
0.030 in undersize (0.75 mm)	1.9760-1.9766 in.	50.190-50.205 mm
Crankpin taper	0.0020 in. max.	0.05 mm max.
Crankpin out-of-round	0.00012 in.	0.003 mm
Main bearing		
Main journal bearing oil clearance		
Standard		
No.1,2,4,5	0.0010-0.0017 in.	0.025-0.043 mm
No.3	0.0012-0.0019 in.	0.031-0.049 mm
Maximum	0.0031 in.	0.08 mm
Available undersize bearing	0.010, 0.020, 0.030 in.	0.25, 0.50, 0.75 mm
Crankpin bearing		
Crankpin bearing oil clearance		
Standard	0.0011-0.0026 in.	0.027-0.067 mm
Maximum	0.004 in.	0.10 mm
Available undersize bearing	0.010, 0.020, 0.030 in.	0.25, 0.50, 0.75 mm
Crankshaft end play		
Standard	0.0031-0.0071 in.	0.08-0.18 mm
Maximum	0.0118 in.	0.30 mm
Thrust Bearing width		
Standard	1.100-1.102 in.	27.94-27.99 mm
0.010 undersize (0.25 mm)	1.104-1.106 in.	28.04-28.09 mm
0.020 undersize (0.50 mm)	1.107-1.109 in.	28.12-28.17 mm
0.030 undersize (0.75 mm)	1.110-1.112 in.	28.20-28.25 mm
Timing belt		
Belt deflection		
New	0.31-0.35 in.	8.0-9.0 mm
Used	0.35-0.39 in.	9.0-10.0 mm

1987-88 2.6L ENGINE MECHANICAL SPECIFICATIONS

Component	U.S.	Metric
Bore x stroke	3.59 x 3.86 in.	91.1 x 98.0 mm
Valve timing		
Intake valve		
Opens	25° BTDC	
Closes	59° ABDC	
Exhaust valve		
Opens	64° BBDC	
Closes	20° ATDC	
Compression pressure @ 250 rpm		
Standard	171 psi	1179 KPa
Minimum	119 psi	820 KPa
Limit of difference between cylinders	28 psi	196 KPa
Valve clearance (Under hot engine condition)		
Jet valve	0.010 in.	0.25 mm
Cylinder head		
Height	3.539-3.547 in.	89.9-90.1mm
Distortion limit	0.008 in.	0.20 mm
Grinding limit	0.008 in.	0.20 mm
Valve seat		
Seat sinking (Dimension "L")		
Standard		
Intake	1.691 in.	42.96 mm
Exhaust	1.691 in.	42.96 mm
Seat angle		
Intake	45°	
Exhaust	45°	
Seat width		
Intake	0.035-0.051 in.	0.9-1.3 mm
Exhaust	0.047-0.063 in.	1.2-1.6 mm
Valve guide, valve and valve spring		
Valve stem to guide clearance		
Standard		
Intake	0.0010-0.0023 in.	0.025-0.058 mm
Exhaust	0.0020-0.0035 in.	0.050-0.088 mm
Maximum	0.0079 in.	0.20 mm
Guide inner diameter	0.3150-0.3157 in.	8.000-8.018 mm
Valve stem diameter		
Standard		
Intake	0.313-0.314 in.	7.960-7.975 mm
Exhaust	0.312-0.313 in.	7.930-7.950 mm
Valve head diameter		
Intake	1.811 in.	46 mm
Exhaust	1.496 in.	38 mm
Valve face angle		
Intake	45°	
Exhaust	45°	
Valve head thickness (margin)		
Intake	0.047 in.	1.2 mm
Exhaust	0.079 in.	2.0 mm
Valve spring angle limit	0.067 in.	1.7 mm
Free length of valve spring		
Standard	1.961 in.	49.8 mm
Rocker arm and rocker arm shaft		
Rocker arm inner diameter	0.7445-0.7452 in.	18.910-19.928 mm
Rocker arm shaft diameter	0.7435-0.7440 in.	18.885-18.898 mm
Clearance in rocker arm		
Standard	0.0005-0.0017 in.	0.012-0.043 mm

1987-88 2.6L ENGINE MECHANICAL SPECIFICATIONS

Component	U.S.	Metric
Camshaft		
Camshaft run-out	0.0008 in. max.	0.02 mm max.
Camshaft end play		
Standard	0.0008-0.0070 in.	0.02-0.18 mm
Wear limit	0.008 in.	0.20 mm
Journal dimeter	1.3360-1.3366 in.	33.935-33.950 mm
Wear limit of journal	0.002 in.	0.05 mm
Camshaft bearing oil clearance		
Standard	0.002-0.004 in.	0.05-0.09 mm
Maximum	0.0059 in.	0.15 mm
Cam height		
Standard	1.669 in.	42.4 mm
Minimum	1.650 in.	41.9 mm
Connecting rod and connecting rod bearing		
Length (center to center)	6.536 in.	166 mm
Maximum allowable twist and bend		
Less than	0.006 in.	0.16 mm
Small end bore	0.8651-0.8655 in.	21.974-21.985 mm
Connecting rod side clearance		
Standard	0.004-0.010 in.	0.10-0.25 mm
Maximum	0.0157 in.	0.40 mm
Crankpin bearing oil clearance	0.0008-0.0024 in.	0.02-0.06 mm
Available undersize bearing	0.010,0.020,0.030 in.	0.25,0.50,0.75 mm
Crankshaft and main bearing		
Crankshaft run-out	0.0012 in. max.	0.03 mm max.
Crankpin diameter		
Standard	2.0855-2.0866 in.	52.973-53.000 mm
Wear limit	0.0012 in.	0.03 mm
Grinding limit	0.030 in.	0.75 mm
Main journal diameter		
Standard	2.3614-2.3622 in.	59.980-60.000 mm
Wear limit	0.0012 in.	0.03 mm
Grinding limit	0.030 in.	0.75 mm
Main journal bearing clearance		
Standard	0.0008-0.0020 in.	0.02-0.05 mm
Available undersize bearing	0.010, 0.020, 0.030 in.	0.25, 0.50, 0.75 mm
Crankshaft end play		
Standard	0.0020-0.0071 in.	0.05-0.18 mm
Maximum	0.010 in.	0.25 mm
Available undersize thrust bearing	0.010, 0.020, 0.030 in.	0.25, 0.50, 0.75 mm
Cylinder block		
Limit of distortion of block	0.0039 in.	0.10 mm
Cylinder bore diameter	3.5874-3.5882 in.	91.12-91.14 mm
Boring size	0.010, 0.020, 0.030, 0.040 in.	0.25, 0.50, 0.75, 1.00mm
Piston and Ring		
Piston diameter (diameter measured at 90° to pin bore axis and 1.65 in. (42 mm) from bottom piston	3.586-3.587 in.	91.08-91.10 mm
Piston and cylinder clearance	0.0008-0.016 in.	0.02-0.04 mm
Available oversize piston	0.010, 0.020, 0.030, 0.040 in.	0.25, 0.50, 0.75, 1.00mm
Clearance between piston ring and ring groove		
Top	0.0020-0.0035 in.	0.05-0.09 mm
Second	0.0018-0.0024 in.	0.02-0.06 mm
Maximum	0.010 in.	0.25 mm
Piston ring end gap		
Top	0.012-0.018 in.	0.30-0.45 mm
Second	0.010-0.016 in.	0.25-0.40 mm
Oil	0.012-0.024 in.	0.30-0.60 mm
Maximum	0.039 in.	1.0 mm

1987-88 2.6L ENGINE MECHANICAL SPECIFICATIONS

Component	U.S.	Metric
Piston and Ring		
Available oversize piston ring	0.010, 0.020, 0.030, 0.40 in.	0.25, 0.50, 0.75, 1.00mm
Piston pin		
Diameter	0.8662-0.8664 in.	22.001-22.007 mm
Interference in piston	0.0006-0.0013 in.	0.016-0.033 mm
Press-in load	1,650-3,850 lbs.	750-1,750 kg
Balance shaft		
Right		
Rear journal diameter	1.693 in.	43 mm
Oil clearance	0.0024-0.0039 in.	0.06-0.10 mm
Left		
Front journal diameter	0.906 in.	23 mm
Rear journal diameter	1.693 in.	43 mm
Oil clearance		
Front	0.0008-0.0024 in.	0.020-0.06 mm
Rear	0.0024-0.0039 in.	0.06-0.10 mm

1989-92 2.6L ENGINE MECHANICAL SPECIFICATIONS

Component	U.S.	Metric
Bore x Stroke	3.62 x 3.86 in.	92.0 x 98.0 mm
Total piston displacement	158.97 cu. in.	2,606 cc
Compresstion pressure @ 270 rpm		
Standard	182 psi	1,255 KPa
Minimum	142 psi	981 KPa
Maximum difference between cylinders	28 psi	196 KPa
Valve timing		
Intake	Opens 10° BTDC	Closes 50° ABDC
Exhaust	Opens 55° BBDC	Closes 15° ATDC
Valve clearance		
Intake	0	
Exhaust	0	
Cylinder head		
Height	3.541-3.545 in.	89.95-90.05 mm
Distortion	0.006 in. max.	0.15 mm max.
Grinding	0.008 in. max.	0.20 mm max.
Valve and valve guide		
Valve head diameter		
Intake	1.307-1.315 in.	89.95-90.05 mm
Exhaust	1.413-1.421 in.	35.9-36.1 mm
Valve head margin thickness		
Intake	0.039 in.	1.0 mm
Exhaust	0.059 in.	1.5 mm
Valve face angle		
Intake	45°	
Exhaust	45°	
Valve length		
Intake		
Standard	4.4367 in.	112.69 mm
Minimum	4.4209 in.	112.29 mm
Exhaust		
Standard	4.4812 in.	113.82 mm
Minimum	4.4654 in.	113.42 mm

1989-92 2.6L ENGINE MECHANICAL SPECIFICATIONS

Component	U.S.	Metric
Valve and valve guide		
Valve stem diameter		
Intake	0.2744-0.2750 in.	6.970-6.985 mm
Exhaust	0.2742-0.2748 in.	6.965-6.980 mm
Guide inner diameter		
Intake	0.2760-0.2768 in.	7.01-7.03 mm
Exhaust	0.2760-0.2768 in.	7.01-7.03 mm
Valve stem-to-guide clearance		
Intake	0.0010-0.0024 in.	0.025-0.060 mm
Exhaust	0.0012-0.0026 in.	0.030-0.065 mm
Maximum	0.008 in.	0.20 mm
Guide projection (Height "A")	0.925-0.953 in.	23.5-24.2 mm
Valve seat		
Seat angle		
Intake	45°	
Exhaust	45°	
Seat contact width		
Intake	0.047-0.063 in.	1.2-1.6 mm
Exhaust	0.047-0.063 in.	1.2-1.6 mm
Seat sinking (Measure valve protruding length)		
Intake		
Standard	1.929 in.	49.0 mm
Maximum	1.949 in.	49.5 mm
Exhaust		
Standard	1.929 in.	49.0 mm
Maximum	1.949 in.	49.5 mm
Valve spring		
Free length		
Intake		
Standard	1.970 in.	50.05 mm
Minimum	1.963 in.	49.85 mm
Exhaust		
Standard	1.970 in.	50.05 mm
Minimum	1.963 in.	49.85 mm
Out-of-square	0.069 in. max.	1.75 mm max.
Setting load/height		
Intake	43.9-49.7 lbs./1.693 in.	195-222 N/43mm
Exhaust	43.8-49.7 lbs./1.693 in.	195-222 N/43mm
Camshaft		
Cam lobe height		
Intake		
Standard	1.6423 in.	41.714 mm
Minimum	1.6344 in.	41.514 mm
Exhaust		
Standard	1.6531 in.	41.988 mm
Minimum	1.6452 in.	41,788 mm
Journal diameter		
Front and rear (No.1,5)	1.1788-1.1797 in.	29.940-29.965 mm
Center (No.2,3,4)	1.1776-1.1786 in.	29.910-29.935 mm
Out-of-round	0.002 in. max.	0.05 mm max.
Camshaft bearing oil clearance		
Front and rear (No.1,5)	0.0014-0.0033 in.	0.035-0.085 mm
Center (No.2,3,4)	0.0026-0.0045 in.	0.065-0.115 mm
Maximum	0.006 in.	0.15 mm
Camshaft runout		
Maximum	0.0012 in.	0.03 mm
Camshaft end play		
Standard	0.0008-0.0059 in.	0.02-0.15 mm
Maximum	0.008 in.	0.20 mm

1989-92 2.6L ENGINE MECHANICAL SPECIFICATIONS

Component	U.S.	Metric
Rocker arm and rocker arm shaft		
Rocker arm inner diameter	0.8268-0.8281 in.	21.000-21.033 mm
Rocker arm shaft diameter	0.8252-0.8260 in.	20.959-20.980 mm
Rocker arm to shaft clearance		
Standard	0.0008-0.0029 in.	0.020-0.074 mm
Maximum	0.004 in.	0.10 mm
Cylinder block		
Height	12.46 in.	316.5 mm
Distortion	0.006 in. max.	0.15 mm max.
Grinding	0.008 in. max.	0.20 mm max.
Cylinder bore diameter		
Standard	3.6220-3.6230 in.	92.000-92.022 mm
0.010 in. oversize (0.25 mm)	3.6320-3.6330 in.	92.250-92.272 mm
0.020 in. oversize (0.50 mm)	3.6420-3.6430 in.	92.500-92.522 mm
Cylinder bore taper and out-of-round	0.0007 in. max.	0.019 mm max.
Piston		
Piston diameter measured at 90° to pin bore axis and 0.709 in. (18.0 mm) below oil ring groove		
Standard	3.6194-3.6202 in.	91.935-91.955 mm
0.010 in. oversize (0.25 mm)	3.6293-3.6301 in.	92.185-92.205 mm
0.020 in. oversize (0.50 mm)	3.6391-3.6400 in.	92.435-92.455 mm
Piston-to-cylinder clearance		
Standard	0.0023-0.0029 in.	0.058-0.074 mm
Maximum	0.006 in.	0.15 mm
Piston ring		
Tickness		
Top	0.058-0.059 in.	1.47-1.49 mm
Second	0.058-0.059 in.	1.47-1.49 mm
End gap measured in cylinder		
Top	0.008-0.014 in.	0.20-0.35 mm
Second	0.010-0.016 in.	0.25-0.40 mm
Oil (rail)	0.008-0.028 in.	0.20-0.70 mm
Maximum	0.039 in.	1.0 mm
Ring groove width in piston		
Top	0.0598-0.0606 in.	1.52-1.54 mm
Second	0.0598-0.0606 in.	1.52-1.54 mm
Oil	0.1583-0.1591 in.	4.02-4.04 mm
Piston ring-to-ring land clearance		
Top	0.0012-0.0028 in.	0.03-0.07 mm
Second	0.0012-0.0028 in.	0.03-0.07 mm
Maximum	0.006 in.	0.15 mm
Piston pin		
Diameter	0.9045-0.9047 in.	22.974-22.980 mm
Interference in connecting rod	0.0005-0.0015 in.	0.013-0.037 mm
Piston to piston pin clearance	0.0003-0.0010 in.	0.008-0.026 mm
Installation force	1,100-3,300 lbs.	500-1,360 kg
Connecting rod and connecting rod bearing		
Length (center to center)	6,553-6.557 in.	166.45-166.55 mm
Bend	0.0098 in. max.	0.249 mm max.
Small end bore	0.9033-0.9040 in.	22.943-22.961 mm
Big end bore	2.1261-2.1266 in.	54.002-54.017 mm
Big end width	1.0094-1.0114 in.	25.638-25.690 mm
Connecting rod side clearance		
Standard	0.0043-0.0103 in.	0.110-0.262 mm
Maximum	0.012 in.	0.30 mm

1989-92 2.6L ENGINE MECHANICAL SPECIFICATIONS

Component	U.S.	Metric
Crankshaft		
Crankshaft runout	0.0012 in. max.	0.03 mm max.
Main journal diameter		
Standard size	2.3597-2.3604 in.	59.937-59.955 mm
0.010 in. undersize (0.25mm)	2.3499-2.3506 in.	59.687-59.705 mm
0.020 in. undersize (0.50mm)	2.3400-2.3407 in.	59.437-59.455 mm
0.030 in. undersize (0.75mm)	2.3302-2.3309 in.	59.187-59.205 mm
Main journal taper and out-of-round	0.0020 in. max.	0.05 mm. max.
Crankpin journal diameter		
Standard	2.0055-2.0061 in.	50.940-50.955 mm
0.010 in. undersize (0.25mm)	1.9957-1.9963 in.	50.690-50.705 mm
0.020 in. undersize (0.50mm)	1.9858-1.9864 in.	50.440-50.455 mm
0.030 in. undersize (0.75mm)	1.9760-1.9766 in.	50.190-50.205 mm
Crankpin taper and out-of-round	0.0020 in. max.	0.05 mm max.
Main bearing		
Main journal bearing oil clearance		
Standard	0.0010-0.0017 in.	0.025-0.044 mm
Maximum	0.0031 in.	0.08 mm
Available undersize bearing	0.010,0.020,0.030 in.	0.25,0.50,0.75 mm
Crankpin bearing		
Crankpin bearing oil clearance		
Standard	0.0011-0.0026 in.	0.027-0.067 mm
Maximum	0.0039 in.	0.10 mm
Available undersize bearing	0.010,0.020,0.030 in.	0.25,0.50,0.75 mm
Thrust bearing (center main bearing)		
Crankshaft end play		
Standard	0.0031-0.0071 in.	0.08-0.18 mm
Maximum	0.0118 in.	0.30 mm
Bearing width		
Standard	1.021-1.023 in.	25.94-25.99 mm
0.010 in. oversize (0.25 mm)	1.025-1.027 in.	26.04-26.09 mm
0.020 in. oversize (0.50 mm)	1.028-1.030 in.	26.12-26.17 mm
0.030 in. oversize (0.75 mm)	1.031-1.033 in.	26.20-26.25 mm
Balance shaft		
Front journal diameter	1.6514-1.6520 in.	41.945-41.960 mm
Center journal diameter	1.5727-1.5732 in.	39.945-39.960 mm
Rear journal diameter	0.8247-0.8251 in.	20.945-20.960 mm
Oil clearance		
Front	0.0020-0.0045 in.	0.050-0.115 mm
Center	0.0031-0.0057 in.	0.080-0.145 mm
Rear	0.0031-0.0057 in.	0.080-0.145 mm

3.0L ENGINE MECHANICAL SPECIFICATIONS

Component	U.S.	Metric
Bore x stroke	3.54 x 3.05 in.	90.0 x 77.4 mm
Total piston displacement	180.2 cu in.	2,954 cc
Compression pressure @ 300 rpm		
Standard	164 psi	1,128 KPa
Minimum	121 psi	834 KPa
Maximum difference between cylinders	28 psi	196 KPa
Valve timing		
Intake	Opens 9° BTDC	Closes 53° ABDC
Exhaust	Opens 51° BBDC	Closes 11° ATDC
Valve clearance		
Intake	0	
Exhaust	0	
Cylinder head		
Height	4.931-4.935 in.	125.25-125.35 mm
Distortion	0.004 in. max.	0.10 mm max.
Grinding	0.006 in. max.	0.15 mm max.
Valve and valve guide		
Valve head diameter		
Intake	1.295-1.303 in.	32.9-33.1 mm
Exhaust	1.492-1.500 in.	37.9-38.1 mm
Valve head margin thickness		
Intake	0.030-0.049 in.	0.75-1.25 mm
Exhaust	0.047-0.071 in.	1.2-1.8 mm
Valve face angle		
Intake	45°	
Exhaust	45°	
Valve length		
Intake		
Standard	4.7760 in.	121.31 mm
Minimum	4.7602 in.	120.91 mm
Exhaust		
Standard	4.8279 in.	122.63 mm
Minimum	4.8122 in.	122.23 mm
Valve stem diameter		
Intake	0.2744-0.2750 in.	6.970-6.985 mm
Exhaust	0.3159-0.3165 in.	8.025-8.040 mm
Guide inner diameter		
Intake	0.2760-0.2768 in.	7.01-7.03 mm
Exhaust	0.3177-0.3185 in.	8.07-8.09 mm
Valve stem-to-guide clearance		
Intake	0.0010-0.0024 in.	0.025-0.060 mm
Exhaust	0.0012-0.0026 in.	0.030-0.065 mm
Maximum	0.008 in.	0.20 mm
Guide projection (Height "A")		
Intake	0.520-0.543 in.	13.2-13.8 mm
Exhaust	0.772-0.795 in.	19.6-20.2 mm
Valve seat		
Seat angle		
Intake	45°	
Exhaust	45°	
Seat contact width		
Intake	0.047-0.063 in.	1.2-1.6 mm
Exhaust	0.047-0.063 in.	1.2-1.6 mm
Seat sinking (measure valve protruding length)		
Intake		
Standard	1.988 in.	50.5 mm
Maximum	2.047 in.	52.0 mm
Exhaust		
Standard	1.949 in.	49.5 mm
Maximum	2.008 in.	51.0 mm

3.0L ENGINE MECHANICAL SPECIFICATIONS

Component	U.S.	Metric
Valve spring		
Free length		
Intake		
Outer		
Standard	2.005 in.	50.9 mm
Minimum	1.73 in.	44.0 mm
Inner		
Standard	1.840 in.	46.73 mm
Minimum	1.56 in.	39.5 mm
Exhaust		
Outer		
Standard	2.296 in.	58.33 mm
Minimum	1.77 in.	45.0 mm
Inner		
Standard	2.092 in.	53.14 mm
Minimum	1.59 in.	40.5 mm
Out-of-square		
Intake		
Outer	0.071 in. max.	1.8 mm max.
Inner	0.063 in. max.	1.6 mm max.
Exhaust		
Outer	0.080 in. max.	2.04 mm max.
Inner	0.073 in. max.	1.86 mm max.
Setting load/height		
Intake		
Outer	31-33 lbs./1.733 in.	137-148 N/44.0mm
Inner	21-22 lbs./1.555 in.	92-99 N/39.5mm
Exhaust		
Outer	51.9-58.7 lbs./1.772 in.	232-262 N/45.0mm
Inner	33.0-37.4 lbs./1.594 in.	148-167 N/40.5mm
Camshaft		
Cam lobe height		
Intake		
Standard	1.6163 in.	41.054 mm
Minimum	1.6084 in.	40.854 mm
Exhaust		
Standard	1.6257 in.	41.293 mm
Minimum	1.6178 in.	41.093 mm
Journal diameter		
Front and rear (No.1,4)	1.9261-1.9267 in.	48.923-48.938 mm
Center (No.2,3)	1.9258-1.9266 in.	48.915-48.935 mm
Out-of-round max.	0.0012 in.	0.03 mm
Camshaft bearing bore diameter		
Front and rear (No.1,4)	1.9297-1.9305 in.	49.015-49.035 mm
Center (No.2,3)	1.9297-1.9305 in.	49.015-49.035 mm
Camshaft bearing oil clearance		
Front and rear (No.1,4)	0.0031-0.0044 in.	0.077-0.112 mm
Center (No.2,3)	0.0031-0.0047 in.	0.080-0.120 mm
Maximum	0.006 in.	0.15 mm
Camshaft runout	0.0012 in. max.	0.03 mm max.
Camshaft end play		
Standard	0.0020-0.0071 in.	0.05-0.18 mm
Maximum	0.008 in.	0.20 mm
Rocker arm and rocker arm shaft		
Rocker arm inner diameter	0.7480-0.7493 in.	19.000-19.033 mm
Rocker arm shaft diameter	0.7464-0.7472 in.	18.959-19.980 mm
Rocker arm-to-shaft clearance		
Standard	0.0008-0.0029 in.	0.020-0.074 mm
Maximum	0.004 in.	0.10 mm

3.0L ENGINE MECHANICAL SPECIFICATIONS

Component	U.S.	Metric
Cylinder block		
Heigth	8.66 in.	220.0 mm
Distortion	0.006 in. max.	0.15 mm max.
Grinding	0.008 in. max.	0.20 mm max.
Cylinder bore diameter		
Standard size	3.5433-3.5442 in.	90.000-90.022 mm
0.010 in. oversize (0.25mm)	3.5531-3.5540 in.	90.250-90.272 mm
0.020 in. oversize (0.50mm)	3.5630-3.5639 in.	90.500-90.522 mm
Cylinder bore taper and out-of-round	0.0007 in. max.	0.019 mm max.
Piston		
Piston diameter (measured at 90° to pin bore axis and 0.866 in. (22.0 mm) below oil ring groove)		
Standard size	3.5417-3.5429 in.	89.958-89.990 mm
0.010 in. oversize (0.25mm)	3.5515-3.5527 in.	90.208-90.240 mm
0.020 in. oversize (0.50mm)	3.5614-3.5626 in.	90.458-90.490 mm
Piston-to-cylinder clearance		
Standard	0.0009-0.0022 in.	0.023-0.051 mm
Maximum	0.006 in.	0.15 mm
Piston ring		
Thickness	0.058-0.059 in.	1.47-1.49 mm
End gap measured in cylinder		
Top	0.008-0.014 in.	0.20-0.35 mm
Second	0.006-0.012 in.	0.15-0.35 mm
Oil (rail)	0.008-0.028 in.	0.20-0.70 mm
Maximum	0.039 in.	1.0 mm
Ring groove with piston		
Top	0.0598-0.0606 in.	1.52-1.54 mm
Second	0.0598-0.0606 in.	1.52-1.54 mm
Oil	0.1583-0.1591 in.	4.02-4.04 mm
Piston ring-to-ring land clearance		
Top	0.0012-0.0028 in.	0.03-0.07 mm
Second	0.0012-0.0028 in.	0.03-0.07 mm
Maximum	0.006 in.	0.15 mm
Piston pin		
Diameter	0.9045-0.9047 in.	22.974-22.980 mm
Interference in connecting rod	0.0005-0.0015 in.	0.013-0.037 mm
Piston-to-piston pin clearance	0.0003-0.0010 in.	0.008-0.026 mm
Pressure force	1,100-3,300 lb.	4,905-14,715 N
Conection rod		
Length (center to center)	5.758-5.762 in.	146.25-146.35 mm
Bend	0.0092 in. max.	0.234 mm max.
Small end bore	0.9033-0.9040 in.	22.943-22.961 mm
Big end bore	2.2047-2.2053 in.	56.000-56.015 mm
Big end width	0.8374-0.8394 in.	21.270-21.322 mm
Connecting rod side clearance		
Standard	0.0070-0.0130 in.	0.178-0.330 mm
Maximum	0.016 in.	0.40 mm
Crankshaft		
Crankshaft runout	0.0012 in. max.	0.03 mm max.
Main journal diameter		
Standard size	2.4385-2.5492 in.	61.937-61.955 mm
0.010 in. undersize (0.25mm)	2.4286-2.4293 in.	61.687-61.705 mm
Main journal taper and out-of-round	0.0020 in. max.	0.05 mm max.
Crankpin journal diameter		
Standard size	2.0842-2.0848 in.	52.940-52.955 mm
0.010 in. undersize (0.25mm)	2.0744-2.0750 in.	52.690-52.705 mm
Crankpin taper and out-of-round	0.0020 in. max.	0.05 mm max.

3.0L ENGINE MECHANICAL SPECIFICATIONS

Component	U.S.	Metric
Main bearing		
Main journal bearing oil clearance		
Standard	0.0010-0.0015 in.	0.025-0.037 mm
Maximum	0.0031 in.	0.08 mm
Available undersize bearing	0.010 in.	0.25 mm
Crankpin bearing		
Crankpin bearing oil clearance		
Standard	0.0009-0.0025 in.	0.023-0.064 mm]
Maximum	0.004 in.	0.10 mm
Thrust bearing		
Crankshaft end play		
Standard	0.0031-0.0111 in.	0.080-0.282 mm
Maximum	0.0118 in.	0.30 mm
Bearing width		
Standard	0.0787-0.0807 in.	2.000-2.050 mm
0.010 in. oversize (0.25mm)	0.0837-0.0856 in.	2.125-2.175 mm
0.020 in. oversize (0.25mm)	0.0886-0.0906 in.	2.250-2.300 mm
Timing belt		
Belt deflection	0.20-0.28 in.	5-7 mm

4.0L ENGINE MECHANICAL SPECIFICATIONS

Component	U.S.	Metric
Displacement	242.1 cu. in.	3,958.4 cc
Bore x stroke	3.94 x 3.31 in.	100 x 84 mm
Oil pressure (hot @ 2000 RPM)	40-60 psi	276-414 KPa
Comustion chamber volume	3.49-3.61 cu. in.	57.2-59.2 cc
Valves		
Valve guide bore diameter	0.3174-0.3184 in.	8.062-8.087mm
Valve seats		
Width		
Intake	0.060-0.079 in.	1.50-2.00mm
Exhaust	0.060-0.079 in.	1.50-2.00mm
Angle	45 degrees	
Runout limit (TIR Max.)	0.0015 in.	0.038mm
Valve stem-to-guide clearance		
Intake	0.0008-0.0025 in.	0.020-0.064mm
Exhaust	0.0018-0.0035 in.	0.046-0.089mm
Service clearance	0.0055 in.	0.14mm
Valve head diameter		
Standard		
Intake	0.3159-0.3167 in.	8.024-8.044mm
Exhaust	0.3149-0.3156 in.	8.000-8.016mm
0.008 in. (0.20mm) oversize		
Intake	0.3239-0.3245 in.	8.227-8.242mm
Exhaust	0.3228-0.3235 in.	8.200-8.217mm
0.016 in. (0.40mm) oversize		
Intake	0.3318-0.3324 in.	8.428-8.443mm
Exhaust	0.3307-0.3314 in.	8.400-8.418mm
Valve springs		
Compression pressure	60-68 lbs./1.585 in.	138-149 N/1.222mm
Free length (approx.)	1.91 in.	48.5mm
Assembled height	$1^{37}/_{64}$-$1^{39}/_{64}$ in.	40.0-41.0mm

4.0L ENGINE MECHANICAL SPECIFICATIONS

Component	U.S.	Metric
Rocker arm		
Shaft diameter	0.7799-0.7811 in.	20.81-20.84mm
Bore diameter	0.7830-0.7842 in.	20.89-20.92mm
Valve roller tappet		
Diameter (Std.)	0.8742-0.8755 in.	22.20-22.24mm
Clearance to bore	0.0005-0.0022 in.	0.013-0.056mm
Service limit	0.005 in.	0.13mm
Camshaft		
Lobe lift		
Allowable lobe lift loss	0.005 in.	0.13mm
Theoretical valve lift @ zero lash		
Intake	0.4024 in.	10.22mm
Exhaust	0.4024 in.	10.22mm
End play	0.0008-0.004 in.	0.02-0.10mm
Service limit	0.009 in.	0.23mm
Thrust plate thickness	0.158-0.159 in.	4.00-4.04mm
Journal-to-bearing clearance	0.001-0.0026 in.	0.025-0.066mm
Service limit	0.006 in.	0.15mm
Bearing outside diameter	0.158-0.159 in.	4.00-4.04mm
#1	1.951-1.952 in.	49.57-49.59 mm
#2	1.937-1.938 in.	49.21-49.23 mm
#3	1.922-1.923 in.	48.83-48.85 mm
#4	1.907-1.908 in.	48.44-48.46 mm
Runout	0.005 in.	0.127 mm
Out-of-round	0.0003 in.	0.0076 mm
Bearing inside diameter		
#1	1.954-1.955 in.	49.635-49.655 mm
#2	1.939-1.940 in.	49.255-49.275 mm
#3	1.919-1.920 in.	48.750-48.768 mm
#4	1.924-1.925 in.	48.875-48.895 mm
Front bearing location	0.040-0.060 in.	1.00-1.50mm
Cylinder block		
Head gasket surface flatness	0.006 in.	0.15mm
Finish	60-150 RMS	
Crankshaft to rear face of block runout		
T.I.R. Max.	0.005 in.	0.13mm
Taper bore diameter	0.8750-0.8760 in.	22.22-22.25mm
Main bearing bore diameter	2.3866-2.3874 in.	60.62-60.64mm
Cylinder bore diameter		
Diameter	3.9527-3.9543 in.	100.40-100.45mm
Surface finish	18.38 RMS	
Out-of-round	0.0015 in.	0.038mm
Out-of-round service limit	0.005 in.	0.13mm
Taper service limit	0.010 in.	0.25mm
Piston		
Height	0.0015-0.0205 in.	0.038-0.52mm
Diameter		
Standard	3.9524-3.9531 in.	100.40-100.41mm
Piston-to-bore clearance	0.0008-0.0019 in.	0.020-0.050mm
Pin bore diameter	0.9450-0.9452 in.	24.00-24.24mm
Ring groove width		
Compression (Top)	0.0803-0.0811 in.	2.40-2.06mm
Compression (Bottom)	0.1197-0.1205 in.	3.04-3.06mm
Oil	0.1579-0.1587 in.	4.00-4.03mm
Piston pin		
Length	2.835-2.866 in.	72.00-72.80mm
Diameter		
Red	0.9446-0.9448 in.	23.993-23.998mm
Blue	0.9448-0.9449 in.	23.998-24.000mm
Pin-to-piston clearance	0.0003-0.0006 in.	0.0076-0.0152mm
Pin-to-rod clearance	interference fit	

4.0L ENGINE MECHANICAL SPECIFICATIONS

Component	U.S.	Metric
Piston rings		
Ring width		
Compression (top)	0.0778-0.0783 in.	1.976-1.988mm
Compression (bottom)	0.1172-0.1177 in.	2.977-2.989mm
Side clearance		
Compression (top)	0.0020-0.0033 in.	0.05-0.84mm
Compression (bottom)	0.0020-0.0033 in.	0.05-0.84mm
Oil ring	Snug fit	
Service limit	0.006 in.	0.15mm
Ring gap		
Compression (top)	0.015-0.023 in.	0.38-0.58mm
Compression (bottom)	0.015-0.023 in.	0.38-0.58mm
Oil ring (steel rail)	0.015-0.055 in.	0.38-1.40mm
Crankshaft and flywheel		
Main bearing journal diameter	2.2433-2.2441 in.	56.98-57.00mm
Out-of-round	0.0006 in.	0.015mm
Taper limit	0.0006 per in.	0.015mm
Journal runout	0.002 in. max.	0.05mm
Surface finish	12 RMS	
Runout service limit	0.005 in.	0.13mm
Thrust bearing journal		
Length	1.039-1.041 in.	26.39-26.44mm
Connecting rod journal		
Diameter	2.1252-2.1260 in.	53.98-54.00mm
Out-of-round	0.0006 in.	0.015mm
Taper limit	0.0006 per in.	0.015mm
Surface finish	12 RMS max.	
Main bearing thrust face		
Surface finish	20 RMS max.	
Runout (T.I.R)	0.001 max. 0.025mm	
Flywheel clutch face runout	0.005 in.	0.13mm
Flywheel ring gear lateral runout (T.I.R.)		
Standard transmission	0.025 in.	0.635mm
Automatic transmission	0.060 in.	1.524mm
Crankshaft free end play	0.0016-0.0126 in.	0.04-0.32mm
Service limit	0.012 in.	0.30mm
Connecting rod bearings		
Clearance to crankshaft	0.0003-0.0024 in.	0.008-0.060mm
Allowable	0.0005-0.0022 in.	0.013-0.056mm
Bearing wall thickness		
Red	0.0548-0.0552 in.	1.392-1.400mm
Blue	0.0552-0.0556 in.	1.400-1.412mm
Main bearing		
Clearance to crankshaft	0.0008-0.0015 in.	0.020-0.038mm
Allowable	0.0005-0.0019 in.	0.013-0.048mm
Bearing wall thickness		
Red	0.0707-0.0711 in.	1.795-1.800mm
Blue	0.0711-0.0714 in.	1.800-1.814mm
Connecting rod		
Connecting rod		
Piston pin bore diameter	0.9432-0.9439 in.	23.957-23.975mm
Crankshaft bearing bore diameter	2.2370-2.2378 in.	56.82-56.84mm
Out-of-round	0.0004 in.	0.010mm
Taper	0.0004 in.	0.010mm
Length (center-to-center)	5.1386-5.1413 in.	130.5-130.6mm
Alignment (Bore-to-bore max. diff.)		
Twist	0.006 in.	0.15mm
Bend	0.002 in.	0.05mm
Side clearance (assembled to crank)		
Standard	0.0002-0.0025 in.	0.005-0.064mm
Service limit	0.014 in.	0.35mm

4.0L ENGINE MECHANICAL SPECIFICATIONS

Component	U.S.	Metric
Lubricating system		
Oil pump		
Relief valve spring tension	13.60-14.7 lbs./1.39 in.	6 kg/35.3mm
Drive shaft-to-housing bearing clearance	0.0015-0.0030 in.	0.038-0.076mm
Relief valve-to-bore clearance	0.0015-0.0030 in.	0.038-0.076mm
Rotor assembly end clearance	0.004 in. max.	0.10mm max.
Outer race-to-housing clearance	0.001-0.013 in.	0.025-0.33mm

TORQUE SPECIFICATIONS

Component	U.S.	Metric
Air conditioning compressor bolts		
B Series	29-40 ft. lbs.	39-54 Nm
MPV	13-20 ft. lbs.	18-27 Nm
Air conditioning pipe bracket nuts		
MPV	61-87 inch lbs.	7-10 Nm
Automatic tensioner bolts		
2.2L	27-38 ft. lbs.	37-52 Nm
3.0L	14-19 ft. lbs.	19-26 Nm
Balancer shaft sprocket bolt		
2.6L (1987-88)	43-50 ft. lbs.	58-68 Nm
Bypass air control valve bolts/nuts		
fuel injected 3.0L	14-19 ft. lbs.	19-26 Nm
Cam cover		
2.2L	26-35 inch lbs.	3-4 Nm
3.0L	30-40 inch lbs.	3.3-4.5 Nm
Camshaft seal plate bolts		
3.0L	69-95 inch lbs.	8-11 Nm
Camshaft pulley		
2.2L & 2.6L (1989-92)		
bolt	95 inch lbs.	11 Nm
nut	87 inch lbs.	10 Nm
Camshaft sprocket bolt		
2.2L	35-48 ft. lbs.	48-65 Nm
2.6L (1987-88)	40 ft. lbs.	54 Nm
2.6L (1989-92)	45 ft. lbs.	61 Nm
3.0L	52-59 ft. lbs.	71-80 Nm
4.0L	44-50 ft. lbs.	60-68 Nm
Camshaft thrust plate		
2.6L (1989-92)	95 inch lbs.	11 Nm
3.0L	6-8 ft. lbs.	8-11 Nm
4.0L	96 inch lbs.	11 Nm
Catalytic converter connections		
pickups	23 ft. lbs.	31 Nm
Coil Pack		
Navajo	40-62 inch lbs.	4.5-20Nm
Converter housing upper bolts		
Navajo	33-45 ft. lbs.	45-61 Nm
Coolant bypass pipe bolts		
2.6L	27-38 ft. lbs.	27-52 Nm
Crankshaft position sensor		
Navajo	75-106 inch lbs.	8.5-12Nm
Crankshaft pulley/damper assembly bolts		
4.0L	30-37 ft. lbs.	30-50 Nm

TORQUE SPECIFICATIONS

Component	U.S.	Metric
Crankshaft pulley bolt		
2.2L	9-13 ft. lbs.	12-18 Nm
2.6L (1987-88)	80-94 ft. lbs.	109-128 Nm
2.6L (1989-92)	145 ft. lbs.	197 Nm
3.0L	116-123 ft. lbs.	158-167 Nm
Crankshaft sprocket bolt		
2.2L	116-123 ft. lbs.	158-167 Nm
Cylinder head bolts		
2.2L	59-64 ft. lbs.	80-87 Nm
2.6L (1987-88)		
bolts 1-10	65-72 ft. lbs.	88-98 Nm
bolts 11, 12	11-16 ft. lbs.	15-22 Nm
2.6L (1989-92)		
Large bolts	64 ft. lbs.	87 Nm
Remaining two head bolts	17 ft. lbs.	23 Nm
3.0L	14 ft. lbs.	19 Nm
4.0L	59 ft. lbs.	80 Nm
Distributor holddown bolt	14-19 ft. lbs.	19-25 Nm
Distributor drive rear/camshaft sprocket lock bolt		
2.6L (1987-88)	36-43 ft. lbs.	49-58 Nm
Distributor drive gear lock bolt		
2.6L (1989-92)	45 ft. lbs.	61 Nm
Engine mount nuts		
B Series	30-36 ft. lbs.	41-49 Nm
MPV	25-36 ft. lbs.	34-49 Nm
Exhaust pipe nuts		
2.2L	16-21 ft. lbs.	22-29 Nm
Exhaust manifold bolts/nuts		
2.6L (1987-88)	24 ft. lbs.	33 Nm
2.6L (1989-92)	18 ft. lbs.	24 Nm
3.0L	19 ft. lbs.	26 Nm
4.0L	19 ft. lbs.	26 Nm
Exhaust pipe to exhaust manifold nuts		
B Series	30-36 ft. lbs.	41-49 Nm
MPV	25-36 ft. lbs.	34-49 Nm
Fan assembly nuts/bolts		
except Navajo	70 inch lbs.	8 Nm
Navajo	55-70 inch lbs.	6-8 Nm
Fan and clutch assembly nut		
4.0L	50-100 ft. lbs.	68-136 Nm
Front housing bolts		
2.2L	14-19 ft. lbs.	19-25 Nm
Fuel supply manifold bolts		
fuel injected 2.2L, 2.6L & 3.0L	14-19 ft. lbs.	19-25 Nm
Heat cowl screws		
2.6L (1987-88)	80 inch lbs.	9 Nm
Idler sprocket assembly lock bolt		
2.6L (1989-92)	27-38 ft. lbs.	37-52 Nm
Ignition Module		
Navajo	22-31 inch lbs.	2.5-3.5Nm
Intake manifold mounting nuts		
carbureted 2.2L	14-19 ft. lbs.	19-25 Nm
carbureted 2.6L	11-14 ft. lbs.	11-19 Nm
fuel injected 3.0L	14-19 ft. lbs.	19-25 Nm
fuel injected 4.0L	see text	
Jet valves	13.5-15.5 ft. lbs.	18-21 Nm

TORQUE SPECIFICATIONS

Component	U.S.	Metric
Oil pan bolts		
2.2L	61-104 inch lbs.	7-12 Nm
1987-88 2.6L	52-61 inch lbs.	6-7 Nm
1989-92 2.6L	69-95 inch lbs.	8-11 Nm
3.0L	61-87 inch lbs.	7-10 Nm
4.0L	5-7 ft. lbs.	7-10 Nm
Oil pick-up brace bolt		
2.2L, 2.6L & 3.0L	69-95 inch lbs.	8-11 Nm
4.0L	7-10 ft. lbs.	10-14 Nm
Oil pump		
2.2L		
A bolts	14-19 ft. lbs.	19-25 Nm
B bolts	27-38 ft. lbs.	37-49 Nm
2.6L (1987-88)	6-7 ft. lbs.	8-10 Nm
3.0L	14-19 ft. lbs.	19-25 Nm
4.0L	13-15 ft. lbs.	18-20 Nm
Oil pump sprocket bolt		
2.6L (1987-88)	22-29 ft. lbs.	30-39 Nm
Power steering pump mounting bolts	23-34 ft. lbs.	31-46 Nm
Power steering pump pulley nut		
B Series	36-43 ft. lbs.	49-58 Nm
MPV	29-43 ft. lbs.	39-58 Nm
Pulsation damper & injector harness bracket bolts		
fuel injected 2.2L & 2.6L	69-95 inch lbs.	8-11 Nm
Radiator hose clamp	35 inch lbs.	4 Nm
Rear seal housing bolt		
2.2L	6-8 ft. lbs.	8-11 Nm
2.6L (1989-92)	95 inch lbs.	11 Nm
Rocker arm/shaft assembly bolts		
2.2L	13-20 ft. lbs.	18-27 Nm
2.6L (1987-88)	14-15 ft. lbs.	19-20 Nm
2.6L (1989-92)	14-19 ft. lbs.	19-25 Nm
3.0L	14-19 ft. lbs.	19-25 Nm
4.0L	46-52 ft. lbs.	63-71 Nm
Rocker cover bolts		
2.2L	26-35 inch lbs.	3-4 Nm
2.6L (1987-88)	55 inch lbs.	6 Nm
2.6L (1989-92)	52-78 inch lbs.	6-9 Nm
3.0L	30-39 inch lbs.	3-4 Nm
4.0L	53-70 inch lbs.	6-8 Nm
Solenoid mounting bolts	45-85 inch lbs.	5.1-9.6 Nm
Starter Mounting Bolts		
1987-88	24-33 ft. lbs.	33-45 Nm
1989-92 except 4.0L	27-38 ft. lbs.	37-52 Nm
4.0L	15-20 ft. lbs.	21-27 Nm
Starter through bolts	45-84 inch lbs.	5.0-9.5 Nm
Tensioner spring bolt		
2.2L	28-38 ft. lbs.	38-52 Nm
Tensioner body		
3.0L	14-19 ft. lbs.	19-25 Nm
Thermostat housing bolts		
2.2L	20 ft. lbs.	27 Nm
2.6L (1987-88)	15 ft. lbs.	18 Nm
2.6L (1989-92)	19 ft. lbs.	25 Nm
3.0L	19 ft. lbs.	25 Nm
4.0L	7-10 ft. lbs.	10-14 Nm
Throttle body nuts	14-19 ft. lbs.	19-25 Nm

TORQUE SPECIFICATIONS

Component	U.S.	Metric
Timing belt cover bolts		
2.2L	61-87 inch lbs.	7-10 Nm
3.0L		
6mm bolts	69-95 inch lbs.	8-11 Nm
10mm bolts	27-38 ft. lbs.	37-52 Nm
Timing belt tensioner lock bolt		
2.2L	28-38 ft. lbs.	38-52 Nm
Timing chain cover bolts		
1988 2.6L	104-122 inch lbs.	12-14 Nm
1989-92	130-145 inch lbs.	15-16 Nm
Timing chain adjuster bolts		
2.6L (1989-92)	95 inch lbs.	11 Nm
Timing chain cover bolts		
2.6L (1989-92)	19 ft. lbs.	25 Nm
Timing chain guide bolts		
2.6L (1987-88) A & C	43-69 inch lbs.	5-8 Nm
2.6L (1987-88)		
upper bolt	69-78 inch lbs.	8-9 Nm
lower bolt	11-15 ft. lbs.	15-18 Nm
2.6L (1989-92)	78 inch lbs.	9 Nm
4.0L	7-9 ft. lbs.	10-13 Nm
Timing chain lever bolts		
2.6L (1989-92)	69-95 inch lbs.	8-11 Nm
Upper idler pulley bolt		
3.0L	27-38 ft. lbs.	38-52 Nm
Upper intake manifold nuts/bolts		
fuel injected 2.2L & 2.6L	14-19 ft. lbs.	19-25 Nm
4.0L	15-18 ft. lbs.	18-24 Nm
Valve cover bolts		
2.6L (1989-92)	78 inch lbs.	9 Nm
Water pump bolts		
2.6L (1989-92)	19 ft. lbs.	25 Nm
3.0L	19 ft. lbs.	25 Nm
4.0L	72-108 inch lbs.	8-12 Nm

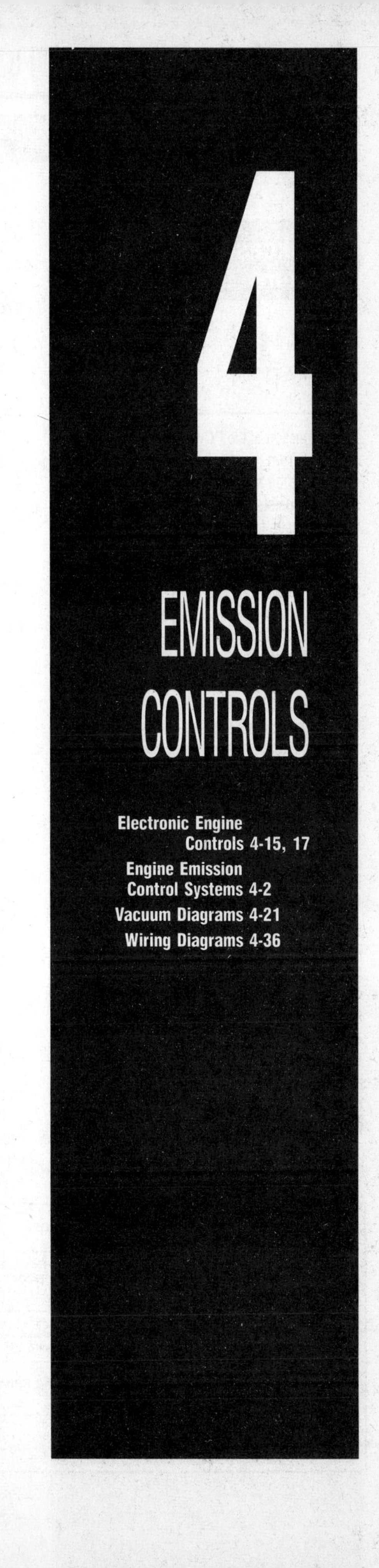
4
EMISSION
CONTROLS

EMISSION CONTROLS

Crankcase Ventilation System

➧SEE FIGS. 1-2

OPERATION

The function of the PCV valve is to divert blow-by gases from the crankcase to the intake manifold to be burned in the cylinders. The system consists of a PCV valve, an oil separator and the hoses necessary to connect the components.

Ventilating air is routed into the rocker cover from the air cleaner. The air is then moved to the oil separator and from the separator to the PCV valve. The PCV valve is operated by differences in air pressure between the intake manifold and the rocker cover.

The most critical component of the system is the PCV valve. This vacuum-controlled valve regulates the amount of gases which are recycled into combustion chamber. At low engine speeds the valve is partially closed, limiting the flow of gases into the intake manifold. As engine speed increases, the valve opens to admit greater quantities of the gasses into the intake manifold. If the valve should become blocked or plugged, the gases will bee prevented from escaping the crankcase by the normal route. Since these gases are under pressure, they will find their own way out of the crankcase. This alternate route is usually a weak oil seal or gasket in the engine. As the gas escapes by the gasket, it also creates an oil leak. Besides causing oil leaks, a clogged PCV valve also allows these gases to remain in the crankcase for an extended period of time, promoting the formation of sludge in the engine.

SERVICE

Testing the System

STANDARD TEST

1. Remove the hose from the PCV valve.
2. Start the engine and run it at approximately 700-1,000 rpm.
3. Cover the end of the PCV valve with a finger. A distinct vacuum should be felt. If no vacuum is felt, replace the valve.

ALTERNATE TEST

Remove the valve from its fitting. Shake the valve. If a rattle is heard, the valve is probably functioning normally. If no rattle is heard, the valve is probably stuck (open or shut) and should be replaced.

REMOVAL & INSTALLATION

1. Disconnect the hose from the PCV valve.
2. Remove the valve from the mounting fitting.
3. Install the valve in the fitting.
4. Connect the hose to the valve.

Evaporative Emission Control System

➧SEE FIGS. 3-16

OPERATION

The evaporative emission control system is designed to control the emission of gasoline vapors into the atmosphere. On carbureted engines, the vapors rising from the gasoline in the fuel tank are vented into a separate condensing tank which is located above the fuel tank. There they condense and return to the fuel tank in liquid form when the engine is not running.

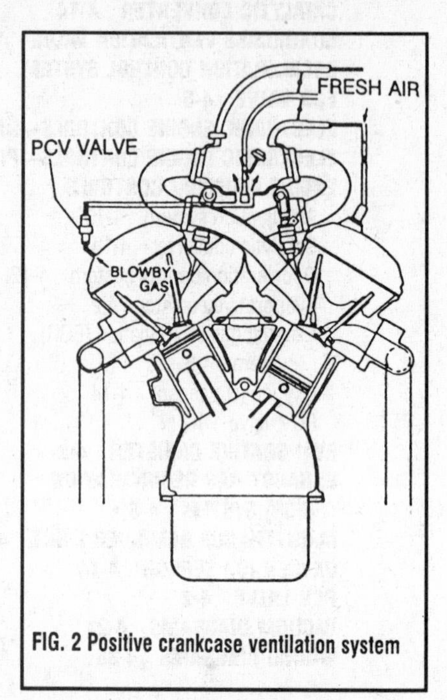

FIG. 2 Positive crankcase ventilation system

When the engine is running, the fuel vapors are sucked directly into the engine through the PCV valve and are burned along with the air/fuel mixture.

Any additional fuel vapors which are not handled by the condensing tank are stored in a charcoal canister. When the engine is running, the charcoal is purged of its stored fuel vapor. On some models, a check valve vents the fuel vapor into the atmosphere if pressure becomes too excessive in the fuel tank.

The system on the carbureted models consists of a charcoal canister, check and cut valve, purge control valves, evaporator shutter valve in air cleaner.

On the pickup and MPV with fuel injection, the system takes fuel vapor that is generated in the fuel tank and stores it in the charcoal canister when the engine is not running. This fuel vapor remains in the canister until the engine is started at which time the fuel vapor is drawn into the dynamic chamber and burned. The system on these models is made up of the charcoal canister, purge control solenoid valves, a three-way check valve, vacuum switch control valve and an electronic control unit.

REMOTE AIR CLEANER OR AIR OUTLET TUBE
CLOSURE HOSE
THROTTLE BODY
PCV VALVE
INT. MAN.
ROCKER COVER
AIR PATH
ENGINE CRANKCASE

FIG. 1 4.0L engine PCV system

On the Navajo, the Evaporative Emission Control System provides a sealed fuel system with the capability to store and condense fuel vapors. The system has three parts: a fill control vent system; a vapor vent and storage system; and a pressure and vacuum relief system (special fill cap). The fill control vent system is a modification to the fuel tank. It uses an air space within the tank which is 10–12% of the tank's volume. The air space is sufficient to provide for the thermal expansion of the fuel. The space also serves as part of the in-tank vapor vent system. The in-tank vent system consists of the air space previously described and a vapor separator assembly. The separator assembly is mounted to the top of the fuel tank and is secured by a cam-lockring, similar to the one which secures the fuel sending unit. Foam material fills the vapor separator assembly. The foam material separates raw fuel and vapors, thus retarding the entrance of fuel into the vapor line.

SERVICE

There are several things to check is a malfunction of the evaporative emission control system is suspected.

Leaks may be traced by using an infrared hydrocarbon tester. Run the test probe along the lines an connections. The meter will indicate the presence of a leak by a high hydrocarbon (HC) reading. This method is much more accurate than a visual inspection which would indicate only the presence of a leak large enough to pass liquid.

Leaks may be caused by any of the following, so always check these areas when looking for them:

a. Defective or worn lines.
b. Disconnected or pinched lines.
c. Improperly routed lines.
d. A defective check valve.

➡ If it becomes necessary to replace any of the lines used in the evaporative emission control system, use only those hoses which are fuel resistant or are marked EVAP.

If the fuel tank has collapsed, it may be the fault of clogged or pinched vent lines, a defective vapor separator, or a plugged or incorrect check valve.

Carbureted Engines

The EEC system consists of a canister No. 3 purge control valve, water thermo valve, check-and-cut valve, purge solenoid valve and an air vent solenoid valve.

The water thermo valve opens the vacuum passage to the No. 1 and No. 3 purge control valves. The canister incorporates the No. 2 purge control valve (2 way check valve), and the No. 1 purge control valve, which opens the fuel vapor passage between the canister and the intake manifold. The No. 3 purge control valve opens the fuel vapor passage between the canister and the intake manifold when the purge solenoid valve is ON.

Port vacuum is applied to the No. 1 purge control valve while the engine is running and to the No. 3 purge control valve during running or heavy load driving.

The check-and-cut valve vents the vapors to the atmosphere if the evaporative hoses become clogged. It also prevents fuel leakage if the vehicle overturns.

1. Check the vacuum hose routing. Repair or replace if necessary.
2. Start the engine and allow it to reach normal operating temperature.
3. Disconnect the vacuum hose from the No. 1 purge control valve. Connect a suitable vacuum gauge to the hose.
4. Increase the engine speed to 2500 rpm and check that the vacuum gauge reads more than 5.9 in. Hg. If the required vacuum is not reached, check the thermo valve. Reconnect the vacuum hose to the control valve.
5. Disconnect the vacuum line from the canister. Connect a vacuum gauge to the hose. Check that vacuum is present when engine speed exceeds 1400 rpm.
6. If no vacuum exists, check the purge solenoid valve, No. 3 purge control valve and the 1V terminal on the emission control unit. Reconnect the vacuum hose to the canister.
7. Disconnect the evaporation hose from the evaporation pipe, then connect a suitable hand operated vacuum pump to the evaporation pipe. Operate the hand pump and check that no vacuum is held in the system. If so, examine the check-and-cut valve and the evaporation pipe for clogging.

AIR VENT SOLENOID VALVE

1. Remove the air cleaner assembly.
2. Touch the air vent solenoid on the carburetor.
3. Verify that when the ignition switch is turned ON and OFF, the solenoid clicking is felt and heard.
4. If not click is heard or felt, check for voltage at the solenoid or replace the solenoid.

CHECK AND CUT VALVE

1. Remove the valve from its location just before the gas tank. Hold the valve in the horizontal position, otherwise the weight of the valve will cause it to move out of position and close the passage.
2. Connect a vacuum gauge in line to the passage which normally connects to the fuel tank — port **A**.
3. Blow air into port **A** and verify that the valve opens at a pressure of 0.78-1.00 psi (5.38-6.89kpa).
4. Remove the vacuum gauge and connect it to the passage to atmosphere — port **B**.
5. Blow air into port **B** and verify that the valve opens at a pressure of 0.14-0.71 psi (0.97-4.89kpa).
6. If not as specified, replace the valve.

WATER THERMO VALVE

1. Remove the water thermo valve and immerse the valve in a container of water.
2. Heat the water gradually and observe the temperature. Remember, you are working with hot metal and hot water, take steps to prevent burning yourself. Blow through the valve. If air passes through the valve at 130°F (54°C) or higher, the valve is operating correctly.

SLOW FUEL CUT SOLENOID VALVE

1. Run the engine at idle speed and disconnect the slow fuel cut solenoid valve connector.
2. If the engine stalls, the solenoid valve is operating properly. If the engine does not stall, replace the solenoid valve.

NO. 1 PURGE CONTROL VALVE

1. Disconnect the vacuum lines from the canister.
2. Blow through port **A** and verify that the air does not flow.
3. Connect a vacuum pump to the purge control valve.
4. Apply 4.3 in. Hg of vacuum to the purge control valve.
5. Blow air through port **B** and verify that air does not flow.
6. If not as specified, replace the purge control valve.

NO. 2 PURGE CONTROL VALVE

1. Disconnect the vacuum hose from the fuel tank to the canister at the canister.
2. Blow air into the canister.
3. Verify that the air flows freely and there are no restrictions.
4. If not as specified, replace the canister.

NO. 3 PURGE CONTROL VALVE

1. Remove the No. 3 purge control valve.
2. Connect a hand vacuum pump to the thermosensor side of the valve.
3. Blow air through the valve from port **A** while applying 3-4 in. Hg of vacuum to the valve.
4. Verify that air flows through the valve from port **A** to port **B**.

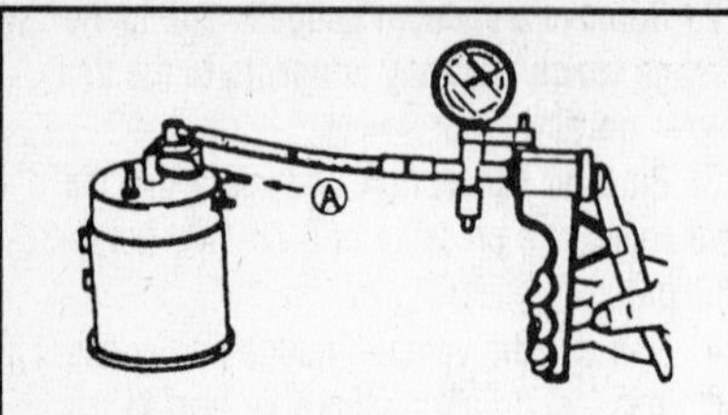

FIG. 3 B2200 carbureted engine, No 1 purge control valve testing

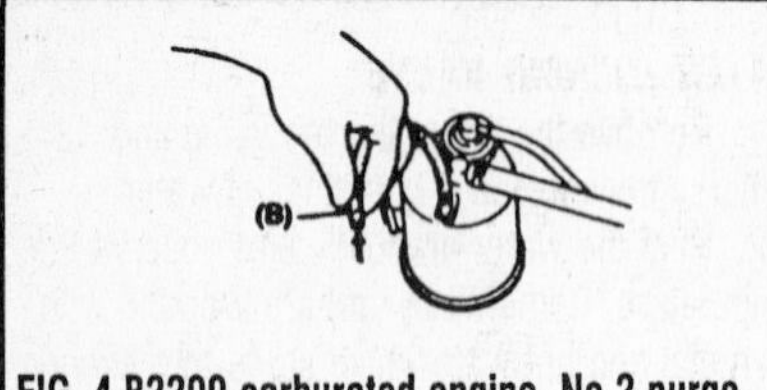

FIG. 4 B2200 carbureted engine, No 2 purge control valve testing

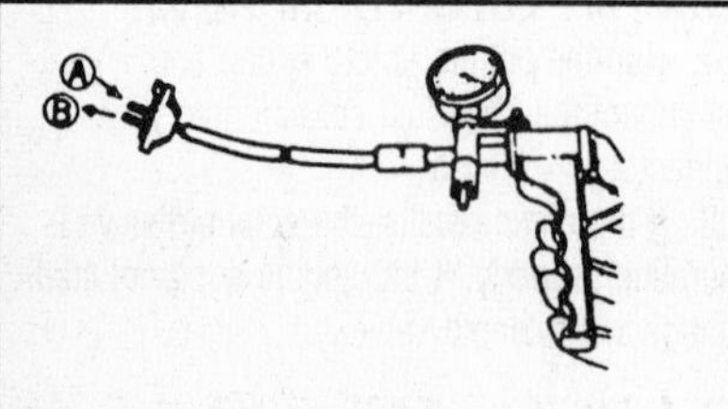

FIG. 5 B2200 carbureted engine, No 3 purge control valve testing

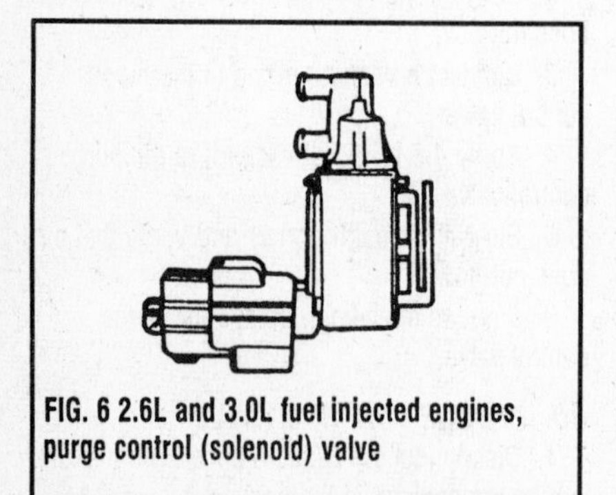

FIG. 6 2.6L and 3.0L fuel injected engines, purge control (solenoid) valve

5. If not as specified, replace the No. 3 purge control valve.

CANISTER

The charcoal canister is non-serviceable and requires not maintenance. Visually check the canister for damage and replace it if necessary.

Pickup and MPV with Fuel Injection

The EEC system consists of a fuel separator, a fuel vapor valve, a check-and-cut valve, a 2 way check valve, a purge control solenoid valve, the engine control unit and input devices.

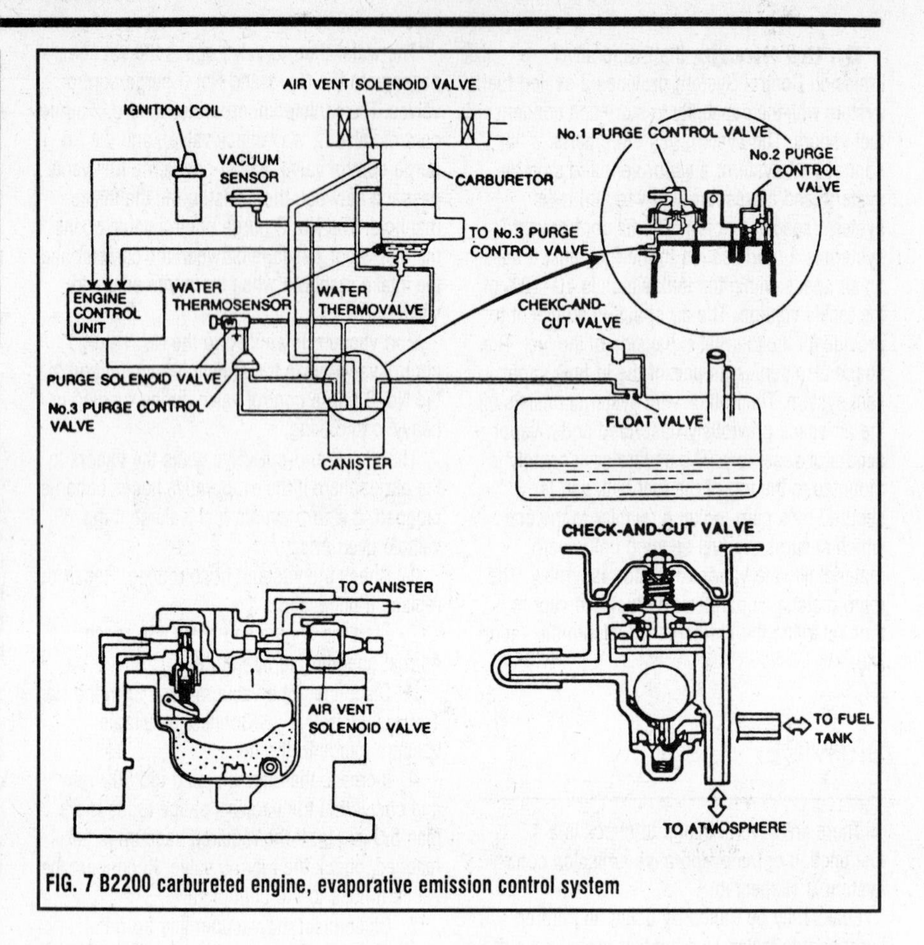

FIG. 7 B2200 carbureted engine, evaporative emission control system

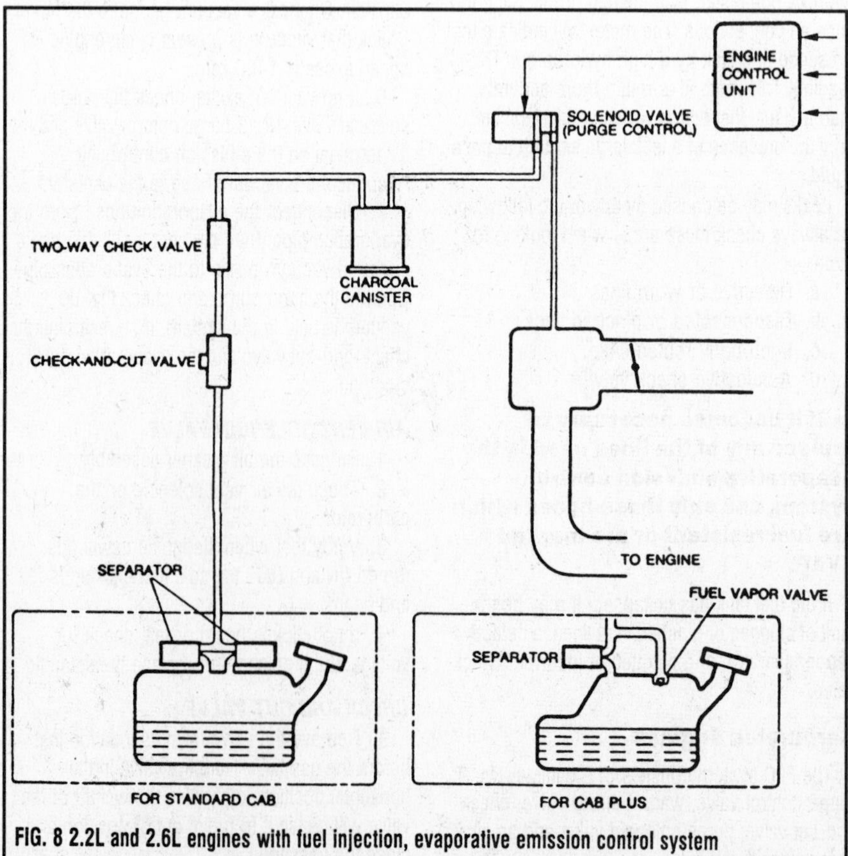

FIG. 8 2.2L and 2.6L engines with fuel injection, evaporative emission control system

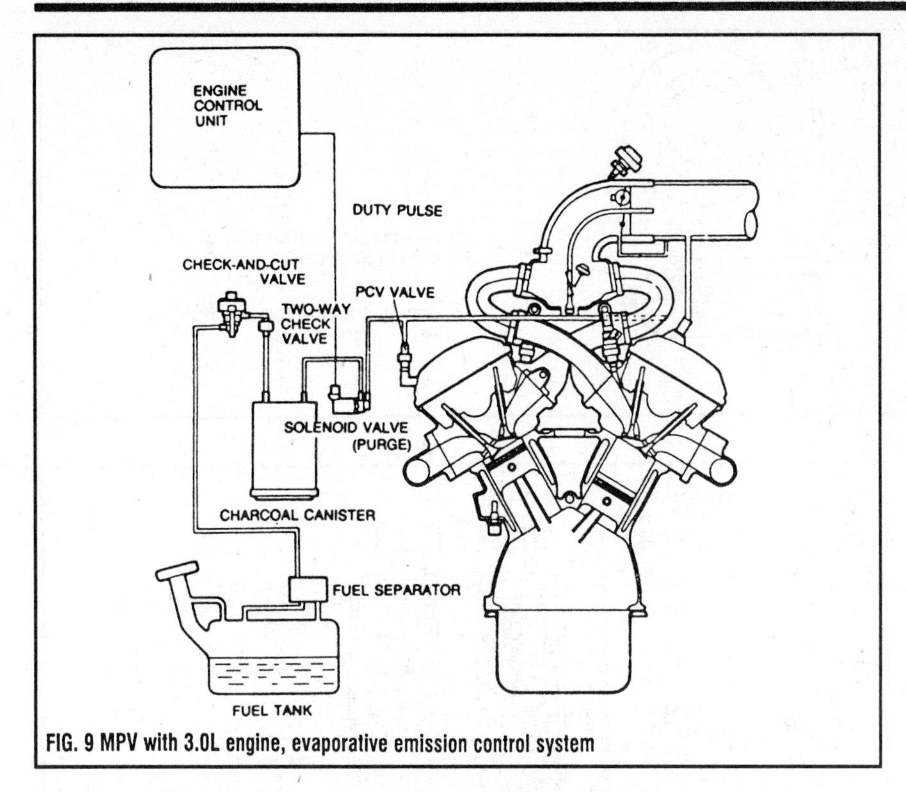

FIG. 9 MPV with 3.0L engine, evaporative emission control system

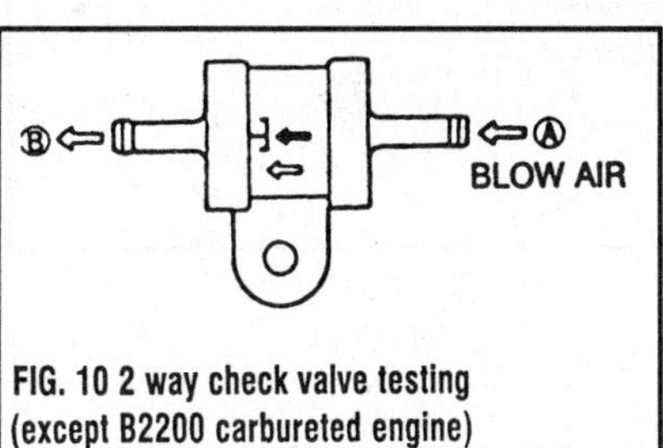

FIG. 10 2 way check valve testing (except B2200 carbureted engine)

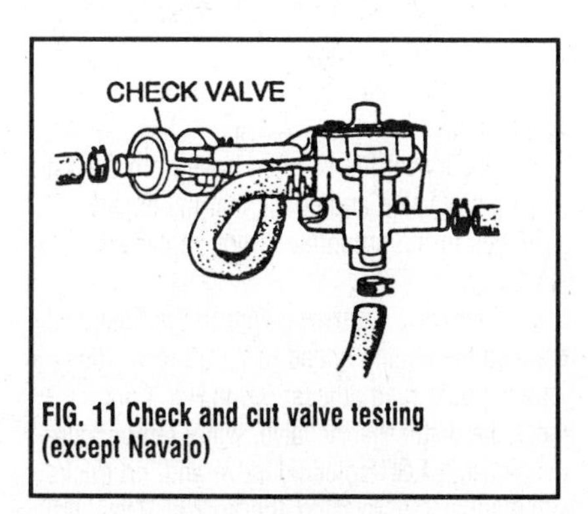

FIG. 11 Check and cut valve testing (except Navajo)

The amount of evaporative fumes introduced into and burned by the engine is controlled by the solenoid valve and control unit to correspond to the engine's operating conditions.

PURGE CONTROL SOLENOID VALVE

1. Start the vehicle and warm the engine.
2. Disconnect the vacuum hose (usually white) closest to the wire connector from the solenoid valve.
3. Verify there is no vacuum at the solenoid valve at idle speed.
4. If there is vacuum at the solenoid valve, turn the engine OFF.
5. Disconnect the other vacuum hose and apply air pressure. Verify that no air flows through the valve.
6. Next, supply 12 volts to the terminals of the solenoid. Apply air pressure and verify that air does flow through the valve.
7. If not as specified, replace the solenoid valve.

FUEL SEPARATOR

The fuel separator is not serviceable and should be checked periodically for damage or leaking. Replace the separator if damage or leaking is evident. The separator is located on the right rear wheelhouse on MPVs, and above the fuel tank on pickup models.

CHECK AND CUT VALVE

1. Remove the valve from its location just before the gas tank. Hold the valve in the horizontal position, otherwise the weight of the valve will cause it to move out of position and close the passage.
2. Connect a vacuum gauge in line to the passage which normally connects to the fuel tank — port **A**.
3. Blow air into port **A** and verify that the valve opens at a pressure of 0.78-1.00 psi (5.38-6.89kpa).
4. Remove the vacuum gauge and connect it to the passage to atmosphere — port **B**.
5. Blow air into port **B** and verify that the valve opens at a pressure of 0.14-0.71 psi (0.96-4.89kpa).
6. If not as specified, replace the valve.

2 WAY CHECK VALVE

The 2 way check valve is not serviceable and should be replaced if damage or leaking is evident.

1. Remove the valve and blow through from port **A** and check that air flows.
2. Blow through from the opposite side port and check that air does not flow through. Replace the valve as required.

CANISTER

The charcoal canister is non-serviceable and requires not maintenance. Visually check the canister for damage and replace it if necessary.

Navajo

Other than a visual check to determine that none of the vapor lines are broken, there is no test for this equipment.

The only maintenance on the evaporative system is to periodically check all hoses and connections for leaks and deterioration. Replace any hoses which are found to be damaged in any way. Under normal circumstances, the charcoal

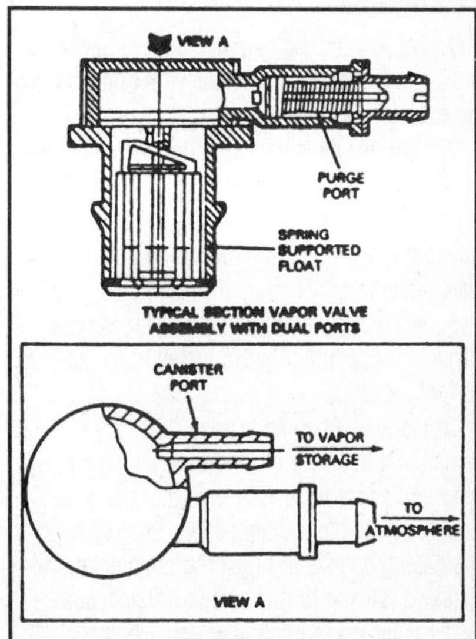

FIG. 12 Vapor valve-orifice rollover valve assembly on the Navajo

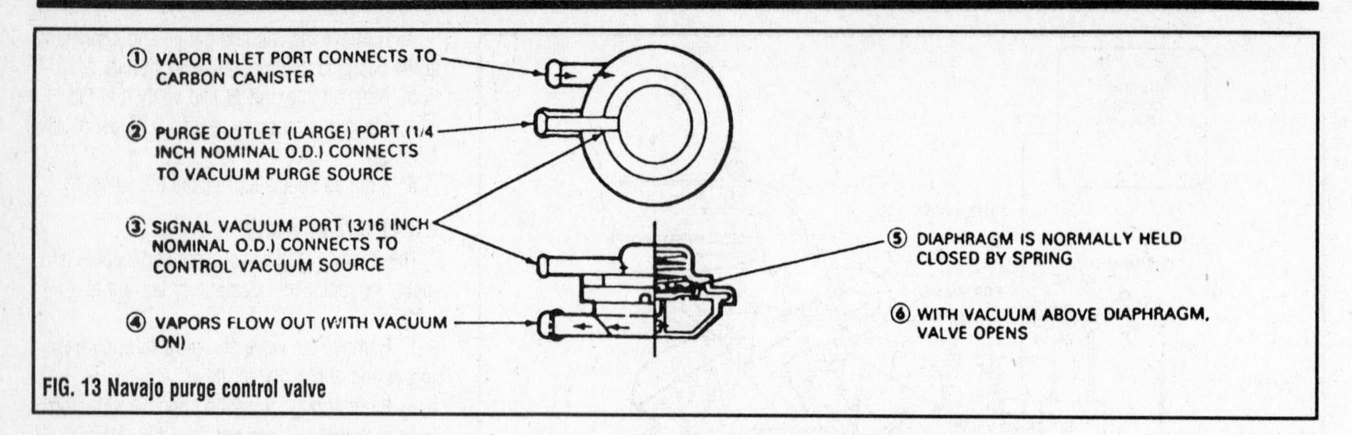
① VAPOR INLET PORT CONNECTS TO CARBON CANISTER
② PURGE OUTLET (LARGE) PORT (1/4 INCH NOMINAL O.D.) CONNECTS TO VACUUM PURGE SOURCE
③ SIGNAL VACUUM PORT (3/16 INCH NOMINAL O.D.) CONNECTS TO CONTROL VACUUM SOURCE
④ VAPORS FLOW OUT (WITH VACUUM ON)
⑤ DIAPHRAGM IS NORMALLY HELD CLOSED BY SPRING
⑥ WITH VACUUM ABOVE DIAPHRAGM, VALVE OPENS

FIG. 13 Navajo purge control valve

canister is expected to last the life of the vehicle, but it should be periodically inspected for any damage or contamination by raw gasoline. Replace any gasoline soaked canister found. Refer to the illustrations for canister mounting and evaporative hose routing on the various engines. Filler cap damage or contamination that clogs the pressure/vacuum valve may result in deformation of the fuel tank.

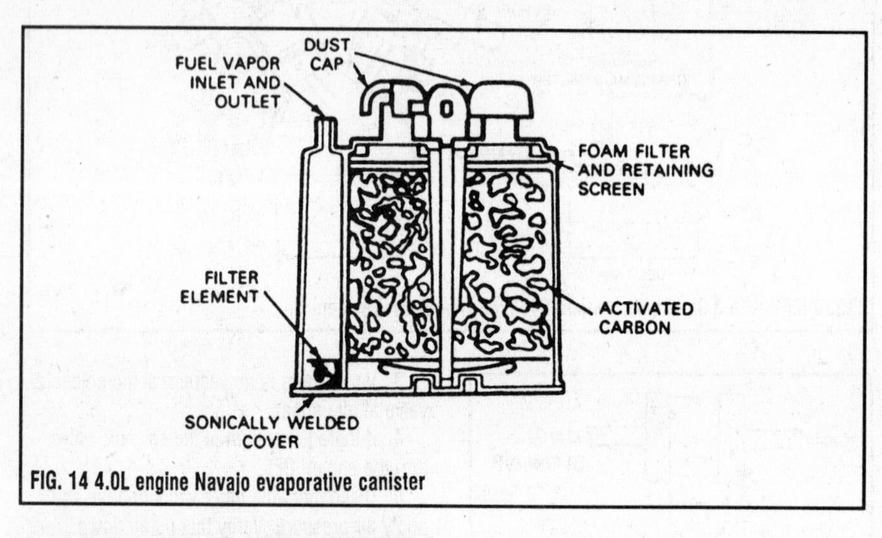
DUST CAP
FUEL VAPOR INLET AND OUTLET
FOAM FILTER AND RETAINING SCREEN
FILTER ELEMENT
ACTIVATED CARBON
SONICALLY WELDED COVER

FIG. 14 4.0L engine Navajo evaporative canister

CARBON CANISTER/VAPOR HOSES REMOVAL & INSTALLATION

All Engines

1. Disconnect the negative battery cable.
2. Mark and disconnect the vapor hoses from the canister assembly.
3. Remove the screw securing the canister to the bracket or fender apron.
4. Lift up on the canister assembly to disengage the tab on the back side and remove the canister.
5. Installation is the reverse of the service removal procedure. Always install vapor hose in correct location.

To disconnect a vapor hose from any component securely grip component with one hand and vapor hose with the other hand as close as possible to connection. Sharply twist hose along its axis to break the connection. No adhesive is used to make hose connections during vehicle assembly, but aging of the connections causes a temporary bond to exist.

If the connection is stubborn and the above method does not work, grip the hose with a pair of small pliers directly over the joint and twist again. Remove the vapor hose from the component.

Exhaust Gas Recirculation System

➧SEE FIGS. 17-21

OPERATION

The function of the EGR system is to reduce Oxides of Nitrogen (NOx) in the exhaust gas, which are the result of high combustion chamber temperatures. The combustion chamber temperature is reduced by directing a portion of the spent exhaust gases into the combustion chamber along with the incoming air/fuel mixture. The lower temperature in the combustion chamber results in reduced amounts of NOx.

The EGR system consists of the EGR valve and various sensors and solenoids which regulate the induction of exhaust gas.

SERVICE

1. Check all vacuum hose to make sure they are tight and not leaking.
2. Run the engine to normal operating temperature.
3. Disconnect the vacuum hose from the 1st EGR control valve and check that the engine continues to run smoothly. If not, replace the valve.
4. Connect a vacuum gauge to the hose and increase the engine speed to 2,500 rpm. The gauge should read at least 5.9 in.Hg. If not, check the water thermovalve, water temperature switch, No.1 EGR solenoid valve and, on trucks with manual transmission, the No.2 EGR vacuum switch.
5. Disconnect the vacuum hose from the 2nd EGR control valve and see that the engine continues to run smoothly. If not, replace the valve.

Canister Purge (CANP) — Pinpoint Test KD

TEST STEP	RESULT ▶	ACTION TO TAKE
KD1 ENTER OUTPUT STATE CHECK (REFER TO QUICK TEST APPENDIX) **NOTE: Do not use SUPER STAR II tester for this step, use VOM/DVOM.** • Key off, wait 10 seconds. • Disconnect electrical connector on the speed control servo; if equipped. • Voltmeter on 20 volt scale. • Connect VOM negative test lead to STO circuit at Self-Test connector and positive test lead to battery positive. • Jumper STI circuit to SIG RTN at the Self-Test connector. • Perform Key On Engine Off Self-Test until the completion of the Continuous Test Codes. • VOM will indicate less than 1.0 volt when test is completed. • Depress and release the throttle. • **Does voltage increase?**	Yes ▶	REMAIN in Output State Check. GO to KD2.
	No ▶	DEPRESS throttle to WOT and release. If STO voltage does not go high, leave equipment hooked up and GO to Pinpoint Test Step QC1
KD2 CHECK CANISTER PURGE (CANP) SOLENOID ELECTRICAL OPERATION • Key on, engine off. • Disconnect CANP solenoid. • Connect voltmeter positive test lead to VPWR circuit and negative test lead to CANP circuit at the CANP solenoid vehicle harness connector. • Voltmeter on 20 volt scale. • While observing VOM depress and release the throttle several times to cycle output. • **Does CANP circuit cycle 0.5 volts or greater?**	Yes ▶	GO to KD3.
	No ▶	REMOVE jumper. GO to KD6.
KD3 CHECK CANP SOLENOID FOR VACUUM LEAKS • Key on, engine off. • CANP solenoid disconnected. • Disconnect vacuum hose at CANP solenoid on manifold vacuum side of CANP solenoid. • Apply 16 In-Hg (54 kPa) of vacuum to manifold vacuum side of CANP solenoid. • **Does CANP solenoid hold vacuum for 20 seconds?**	Yes ▶	REMAIN in Output State Check. Leave vacuum pump setup in place. GO to KD4.
	No ▶	REPLACE CANP solenoid. RERUN Quick Test. If symptom is still present, Evaporative Emission Systems diagnosis.

FIG. 15 4.0L engine Navajo canister purge testing

Canister Purge (CANP) — Pinpoint Test KD

TEST STEP	RESULT ▶	ACTION TO TAKE
KD4 CHECK CANP SOLENOID FOR MECHANICAL OPERATION • While remaining in output state check, reconnect CANP solenoid. • Apply 16 in-Hg (53 kPa) of vacuum to manifold vacuum side of CANP solenoid. • Depress and release throttle. • **Is vacuum released?**	Yes ▶	CHECK hose from CANP solenoid to canister for cracks, leaks, etc. If OK, REMOVE Jumper from STI to SIGNAL RETURN. GO to KD5.
	No ▶	CHECK hose from CANP solenoid to canister for blockage or kinks. If OK, REPLACE CANP solenoid. RERUN Quick Test.
KD5 CHECK FOR VACUUM TO CANP SOLENOID • Disconnect vacuum hose at CANP solenoid at manifold vacuum side. • Start engine. • **Is vacuum present at engine vacuum hose?**	Yes ▶	EEC system OK. If a symptom is still present, Evaporative Emission System diagnosis.
	No ▶	CHECK vacuum line for proper routing, kinks, leak or blockage. If OK,

Canister Purge (CANP) — Pinpoint Test KD

TEST STEP	RESULT ▶	ACTION TO TAKE
KD6 MEASURE CANP SOLENOID RESISTANCE		
Service Code 85/565 indicates a failure in the Canister Purge solenoid (CANP) circuit. Possible causes are: — Faulty CANP solenoid — Open harness — Shorted (Power or Ground) harness — Faulty ECU. • Key off, wait 10 seconds. • Disconnect CANP solenoid. • Ohmmeter on 200 ohm scale. • Measure CANP solenoid resistance. • **Is resistance between 40 and 90 ohms?**	Yes ▶ No ▶	GO to KD7. REPLACE CANP solenoid. RERUN Quick Test.
KD7 CHECK VOLTAGE OF VPWR CIRCUIT		
• Key on, engine off. • CANP solenoid disconnected. • Voltmeter on 20 volt scale. • Measure voltage between VPWR at the CANP solenoid vehicle harness connector and battery ground. • **Is voltage greater than 10.5 volts?**	Yes ▶ No ▶	GO to KD8. SERVICE open harness circuit. RECONNECT CANP solenoid. RERUN Quick Test.
KD8 CHECK CONTINUITY OF CANP CIRCUIT		
• Key off, wait 10 seconds. • CANP solenoid disconnected. • Disconnect ECU 60 pin connectors. Inspect for damaged or pushed out pins, corrosion, loose wires, etc. Service as necessary. • Install breakout box, leave ECU disconnected. • Ohmmeter on 200 ohm scale. • Measure resistance between Test Pin 31 at the breakout box and CANP circuit at the CANP solenoid vehicle harness connector. • **Is resistance less than 5 ohms?**	Yes ▶ No ▶	GO to KD9. SERVICE open circuit. REMOVE breakout box. RECONNECT all components. RERUN Quick Test.

FIG. 16 4.0L engine Navajo canister purge testing

Canister Purge (CANP) — Pinpoint Test KD

TEST STEP	RESULT ▶	ACTION TO TAKE
KD9 CHECK CANP CIRCUIT FOR SHORT TO GROUND		
• Key off, wait 10 seconds. • CANP solenoid disconnected. • Breakout box installed, ECU disconnected. • Ohmmeter on 200,000 ohm scale. • Measure resistance between Test Pin 31 and Test Pins 40, 46 and 60 at the breakout box. • **Is each resistance greater than 10,000 ohms?**	Yes ▶ No ▶	GO to KD10. SERVICE short to ground. REMOVE breakout box. RECONNECT all components. RERUN Quick Test.
KD10 CHECK CANP CIRCUIT FOR SHORT TO POWER		
• Key off, wait 10 seconds. • CANP solenoid disconnected. • Breakout box installed, ECU disconnected. • Ohmmeter on 200,000 ohm scale. • Measure resistance between Test Pin 31 and Test Pins 37 and 57 at the breakout box. • **Is each resistance greater than 10,000 ohms?**	Yes ▶ No ▶	REPLACE ECU. RECONNECT CANP solenoid. REMOVE breakout box. RERUN Quick Test. SERVICE short to power. REMOVE breakout box. RECONNECT all components. REPEAT Quick Test. If code is repeated, REPLACE ECU. RERUN Quick Test.

6. Connect a vacuum gauge to the hose and increase the engine speed to 2,500 rpm. The gauge should read at least 5.9 in.Hg. If not, check the No.2 EGR solenoid valve and the No.1 EGR vacuum switch.

7. Disconnect the hose from the EGR modulator valve and plug it.

8. Connect a length of hose to the port of the EGR modulator valve.

9. Increase the engine speed to 2,500 rpm and blow into the hose. See if the vacuum reading increases. If not, replace the valve.

10. Reconnect all hoses.

Checking 1st EGR Control Valve

PICKUPS

1. Start the engine and run it at idle speed. Apply vacuum to the valve. Check that the engine runs rough or stalls when 1.58 in.Hg of vacuum is applied to the valve.

2. If the engine does not behave as described with the specified amount of vacuum applied, replace the control valve.

Checking 2nd EGR Control Valve

PICKUPS

1. Start the engine and run it at idle speed. Apply vacuum to the valve. Check that the engine runs rough or stalls when 2.76 in.Hg of vacuum is applied to the valve.

2. If the engine does not behave as described with the specified amount of vacuum applied, replace the control valve.

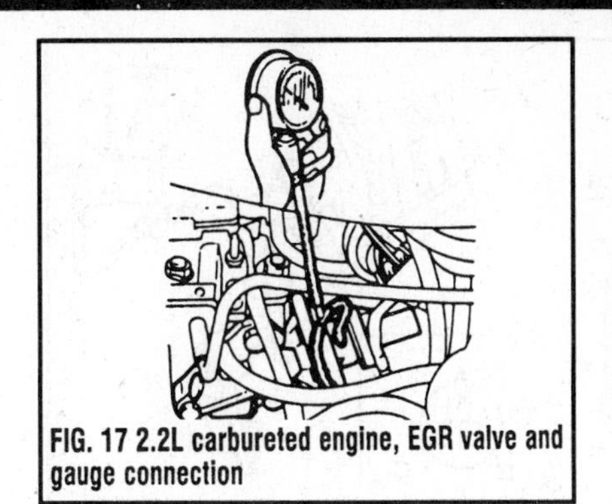

FIG. 17 2.2L carbureted engine, EGR valve and gauge connection

Checking the EGR Position Sensor

PICKUPS

1. The sensor is located on top of the EGR valve. Remove the rubber boot from the connector at the EGR valve.

2. Disconnect the vacuum hose from the EGR valve and connect a hand vacuum pump.

3. Turn the ignition switch ON. Using a voltmeter, check the voltage at each terminal in the harness side of the connector.

4. With no vacuum applied:

- Terminal **A** (B/L) — 0.7 volts
- Terminal **B** (B/LG) — less than 1.5 volts
- Terminal **C** (G/Y) — 4.5-5.5 volts

5. With vacuum applied:

- Terminal **A** (B/L) — 4.7 volts
- Terminal **B** (B/LG) — less than 1.5 volts
- Terminal **C** (G/Y) — 4.5-5.5 volts

6. If the voltage is incorrect for terminals **B** and **C**, check the wiring harness and ECU terminals **1D**, **1F** and **1G**.

7. If incorrect at terminal **A**. check the resistance of the sensor, then the wiring harness and then the ECU.

8. Check the resistance between the terminals while applying 0-5.9 in. Hg of vacuum to the EGR valve:

- Terminals **B** and **C** — 5 kΩ
- Terminals **A** and **C** — 0.0-5.5 kΩ
- Terminals **A** and **B** — 0.7-6.0 kΩ

Checking Duty Solenoid Valve

PICKUPS

1. Disconnect the vacuum hoses from the solenoid valve. Label the hoses for reinstallation.

2. Blow air through the vent hose and air should flow.

3. Disconnect the solenoid valve connector.

4. Connect 12 volts to one terminal of the solenoid valve and ground the other.

5. Blow air through the solenoid valve and verify that air does not flow.

6. Replace the duty solenoid valve if it does not perform as specified.

7. Blow air through the vacuum hose and verify that the air does not flow.

8. Connect 12 volts to one terminal of the solenoid and ground the other.

9. Blow air through the vacuum hose and verify that the air flows through. If not as specified, replace the valve.

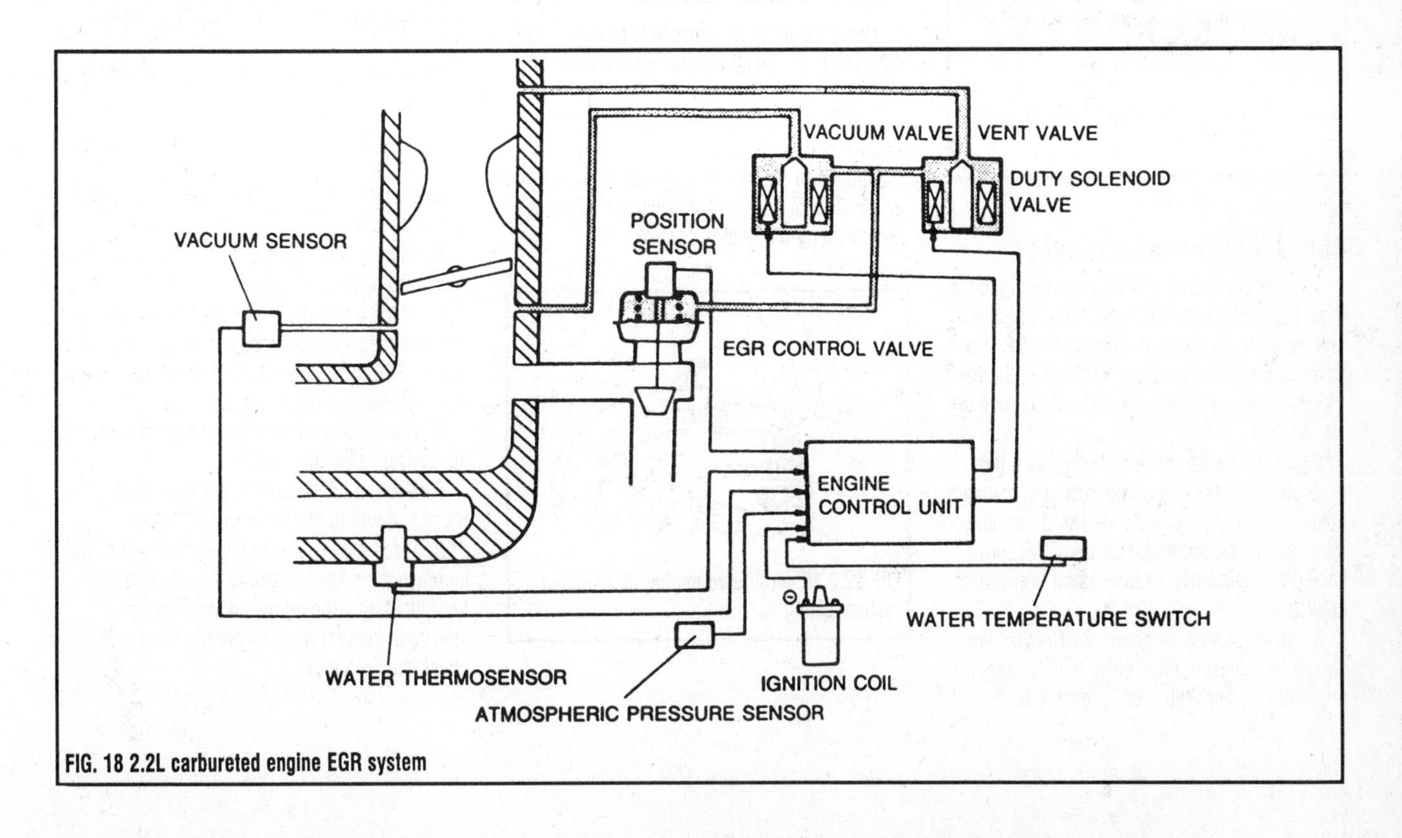

FIG. 18 2.2L carbureted engine EGR system

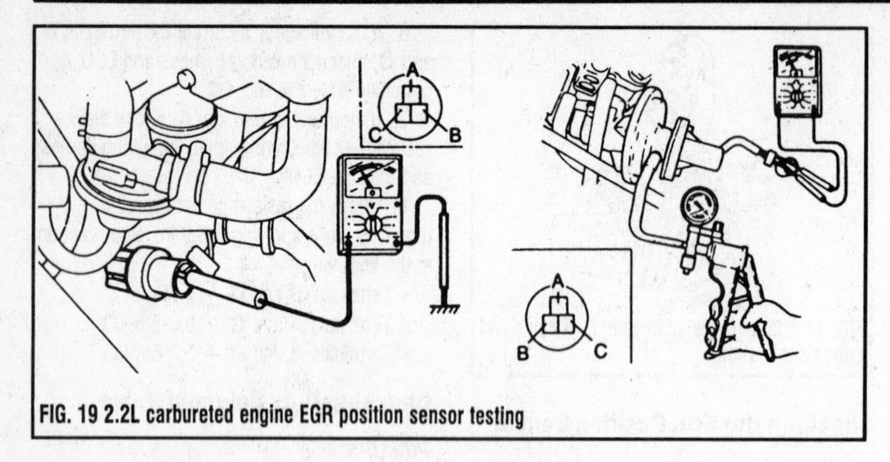

FIG. 19 2.2L carbureted engine EGR position sensor testing

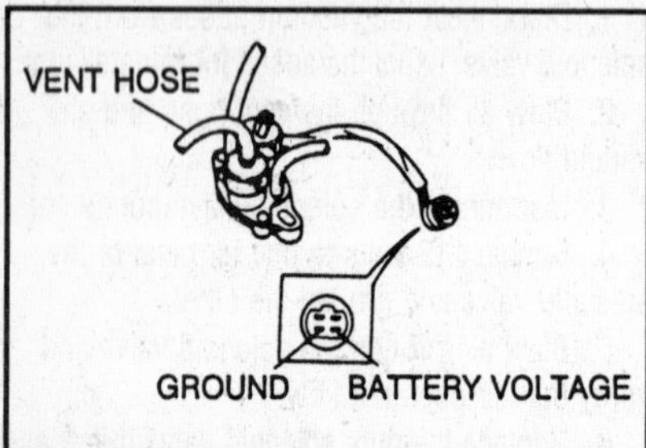

FIG. 20 2.2L carbureted engine duty solenoid vent valve testing

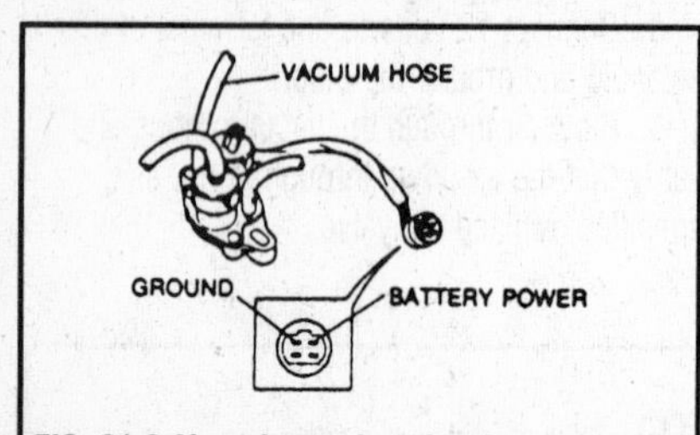

FIG. 21 2.2L carbureted engine duty solenoid vacuum valve testing

EGR Modulator Valve Testing

1. Note the routing of all hoses leading to the modulator valve, especially the hose which is connected to the exhaust side of the EGR valve. Remove the EGR Modulator valve. Plug the No. 1 port and then attach a source of vacuum to the No. 3 port.
2. Attach a clean hose to the exhaust gas port. Blow into the end of the hose and maintain pressure. Apply vacuum to the No. 3 port and then seal off the source of vacuum. Vacuum should be maintained as long as air pressure is applied.
3. Stop applying air pressure. The vacuum should be released. If the valve fails to respond properly in either Step 2 or 3, replace it.

REMOVAL & INSTALLATION

EGR Control Valve

PICKUPS

1. Tag and disconnect the hoses at the valve.
2. Unbolt and remove the valve.
3. Installation is the reverse of removal.

Air Injection System

➧SEE FIGS. 22-29

OPERATION

The function of this system is to burn more completely the spent exhaust gases while they are still in the exhaust system. This is accomplished by injecting fresh air into the exhaust port or main converter. the system is comprised of reed valves, air control valves and an Air Control Valve (ACV) solenoid which is controlled by the engine control unit.

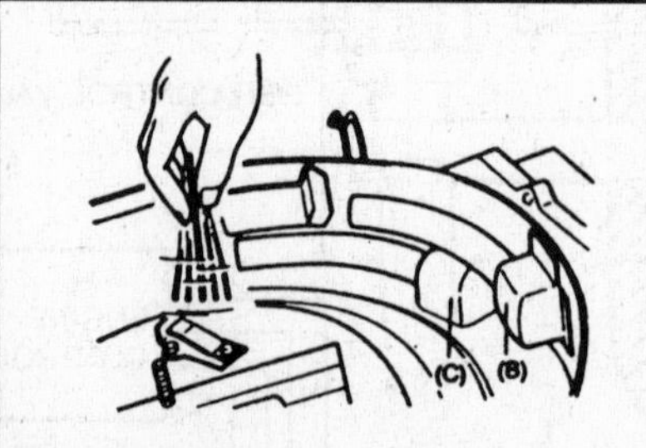

FIG. 22 2.2L carbureted engine air injection system testing

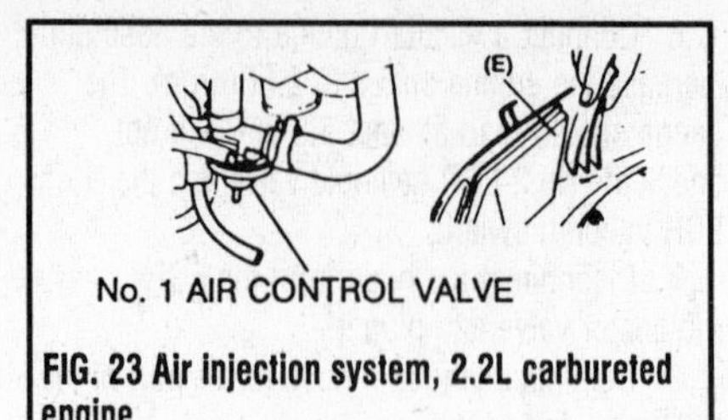

FIG. 23 Air injection system, 2.2L carbureted engine

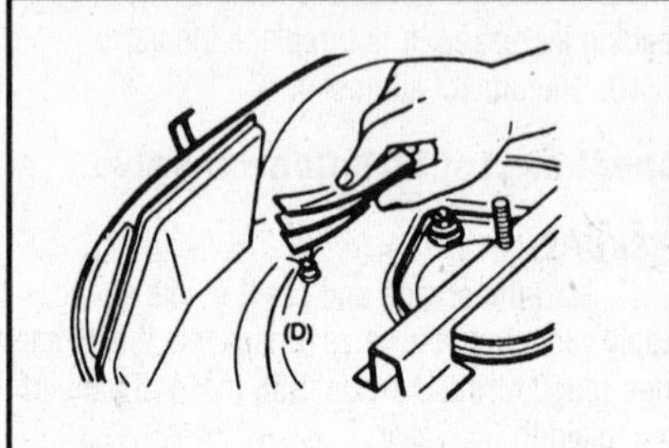

FIG. 24 2.2L carbureted engine air injection system testing

SERVICE

Checking the Reed Valve

1. Run the engine until normal operating temperature is reached. Shut off the engine. Remove the air cleaner cover and filter element.
2. Start and run engine at idle speed. Place a piece of paper over the intake ports **B** and **C** of the reed valve. Air should be sucked into the valve.
3. Increase speed to 1,500 rpm to verify that air is being sucked in.
4. Increase the engine speed to about 3000 rpm and verify that no exhaust gas is leaking from the air inlet port. Replace the reed valve if not as specified.
5. Disconnect the vacuum line from the No.2 air control valve and plug it.
6. Place a thin piece of paper over inlet port **D** of the reed valve. Increase the engine speed to about 1500 rpm and verify that air is being pulled in. If not, inspect No. 1 control valve.
7. Disconnect the vacuum line from the No.1 air control valve and plug it.
8. Using a hand vacuum pump apply 3.54 in Hg of vacuum to the No. 2 control valve.
9. Place a thin piece of paper over port **E** and increase the engine speed to about 1500 rpm. Verify that air is being pulled in. If not as specified, inspect No.2 air control valve and check the reed valve.

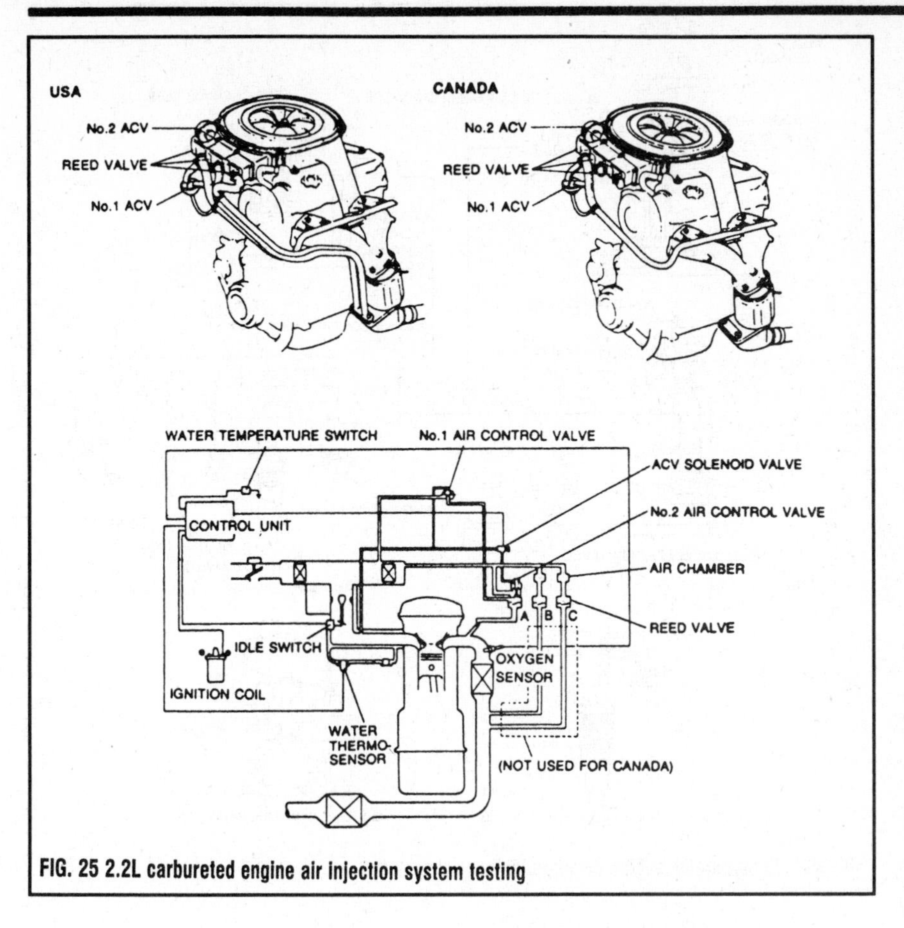

FIG. 25 2.2L carbureted engine air injection system testing

2. Blow air through the solenoid inlet closest to the wire connector and verify that air comes out of the valve air filter.

3. Disconnect the solenoid wire connector and apply battery voltage across the terminals.

4. Blow air through the solenoid inlet closest to the wire connector and verify the air comes out the other vacuum port.

5. If the valve does not operate as specified, replace it.

Checking No.1 Air Control Valve

1. Remove the valve. Connect a vacuum pump to the valve.

2. Blow air into port **A** and verify that the air does not come out port **B**.

3. Apply 15.7 in. Hg of vacuum to the valve.

4. Blow air into port **A** and verify that air does come out port **B**.

5. If not as specified, replace the valve.

Checking No.2 Air Control Valve

1. Remove the valve. Connect a vacuum pump to the valve.

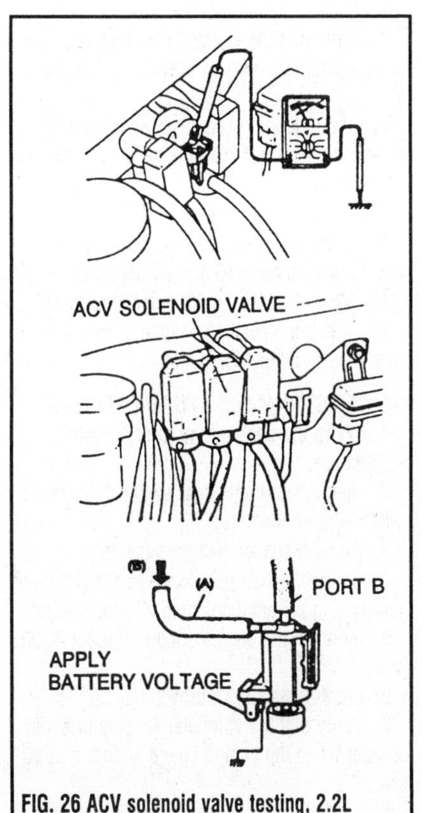

FIG. 26 ACV solenoid valve testing, 2.2L carbureted engine

10. Turn the ignition switch OFF and disconnect the water temperature switch connector. Start the engine and verify that there is no vacuum at the No. 2 air control vacuum valve hose. Increase the engine speed to 1500 rpm and verify that vacuum is present at the hose.

11. If not as specified, ACV solenoid valve operation should be suspect..

Checking the Air Control Valve Solenoid

1. Disconnect the vacuum hoses from solenoid after labeling them for installation reference.

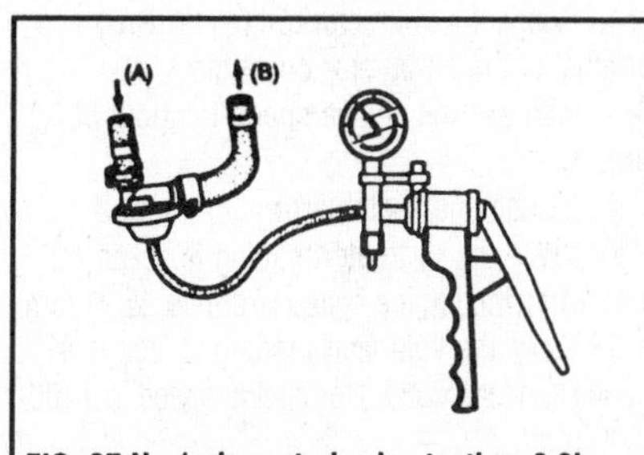

FIG. 27 No 1 air control valve testing, 2.2L carbureted engine

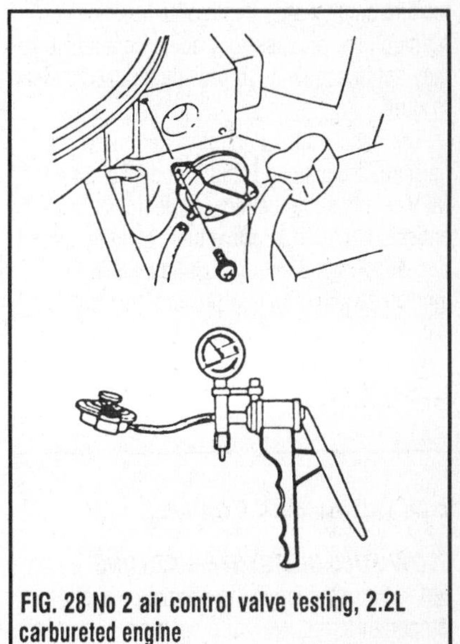
FIG. 28 No 2 air control valve testing, 2.2L carbureted engine

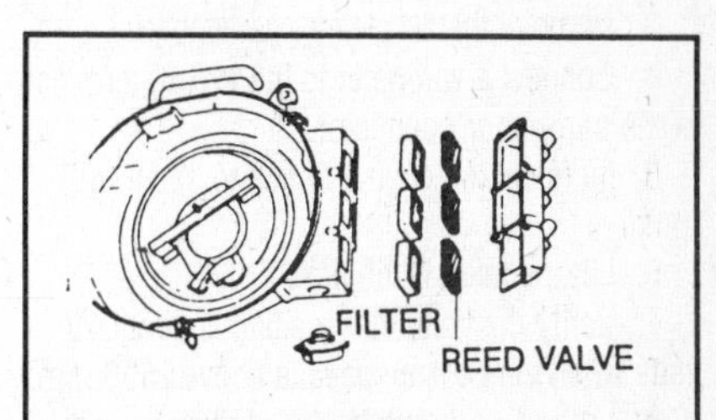

FIG. 29 Reed valve assembly, 2.2L carbureted engine

2. Apply vacuum gradually and verify that the stem of the valve starts to move at approximately 1.97 in. Hg of vacuum and stops at about 3.54 in. Hg vacuum.

3. If not as specified, replace the valve.

Deceleration Control System

SEE FIGS.30-36

OPERATION

The deceleration control system on B2200 carburetor equipped Pickups is designed to maintain a balance air/fuel mixture during periods of engine deceleration. Although the components used vary in some years, the basic theory remains the same: To more thoroughly burn or dilute the initial rich mixture formed when throttle is suddenly closed, and to smooth out the transition to a lean mixture by enriching the mixture slightly after the throttle has closed. Although the process may seem contradictory, they act in sequence to provide an overall ideal mixture.

The deceleration control system used on carburetor equipped B2600 models and on the MPV reduces the fuel flow to decrease HC emissions and to improve fuel economy during deceleration and cut the fuel flow when the ignition switch is OFF to prevent "run-on".

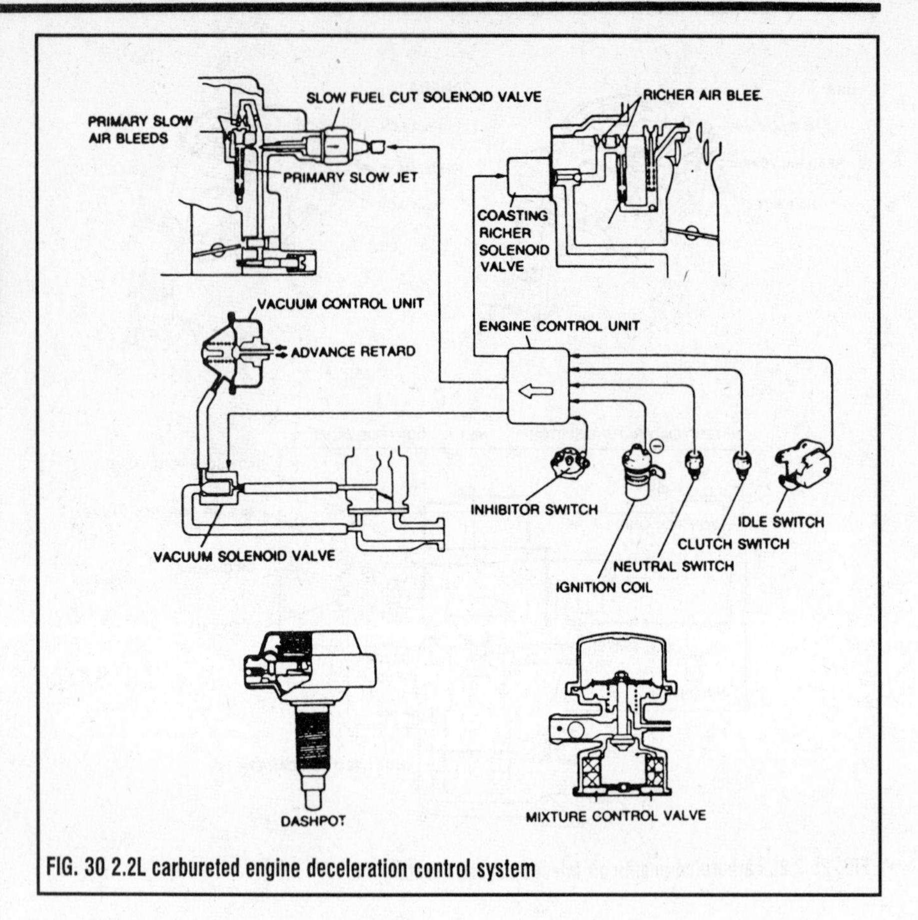

FIG. 30 2.2L carbureted engine deceleration control system

SERVICE

2.2L Carbureted Engine

SLOW FUEL CUT SYSTEM TESTING

1. Warm the engine to normal operating temperature.

2. Disconnect the neutral switch or inhibitor switch wire connectors.

3. Remove the air cleaner assembly.

4. Connect a voltmeter to the **F** (LG) terminal of the carburetor connector.

5. Increase the engine speed to about 300 rpm.

6. Lift the idle switch arm.

7. Verify the voltmeter reading is about 12 volts when the engine speed is above 2500 rpm.

8. Verify that the voltmeter reading is less than 1.5 volts when the engine speed is less than 2500 rpm.

9. If not as specified, check the 2D terminal of the emission control unit and the slow cut solenoid valve.

10. Start the engine and run at idle.

11. Disconnect the carburetor wire connector.

12. Verify that the engine stops running.

13. If not as specified, inspect the carburetor ports or replace the solenoid valve.

COASTING RICHER SYSTEM TESTING

1. Warm the engine to normal operating temperature.

2. Disconnect the neutral switch or inhibitor switch wire connectors.

3. Remove the air cleaner assembly.

4. Connect a voltmeter to the H (BR/B) terminal of the carburetor connector.

5. Increase the engine speed to about 3000 rpm.

6. Lift the idle switch arm.

7. Verify the voltmeter reading is about 12 volts when the engine speed is above 2500 rpm.

8. Verify the voltmeter reading is less than 1.5 volts, one second after engine speed is 1400-2500 rpm.

9. Verify that the voltmeter reading is about 12 volts when the engine speed is below 1400 rpm.

10. If not as specified, inspect terminal 2H of the emission control unit and the coasting richer solenoid valve.

11. Start the engine and run at idle.

12. Ground the H (BR/B) terminal of the carburetor connector with a jumper wire.

13. Verify that the engine speed increases.

14. If not as specified, inspect the carburetor ports or replace the solenoid valve.

COASTING ADVANCE SYSTEM TESTING

1. Warm the engine to normal operating temperature.

2. Disconnect the neutral switch or inhibitor switch wire connectors.

3. Remove the air cleaner assembly.

4. Connect a voltmeter to the W/G terminal of the coasting advance solenoid wire connector.

5. Increase the engine speed to about 3000 rpm.

6. Lift the idle switch arm.

7. Verify that the voltmeter reading is about 12 volts when the engine speed is above 2500 rpm.

8. Verify that the voltmeter reading is less than 1.5 volts when the engine speed is 1700-2500 rpm.

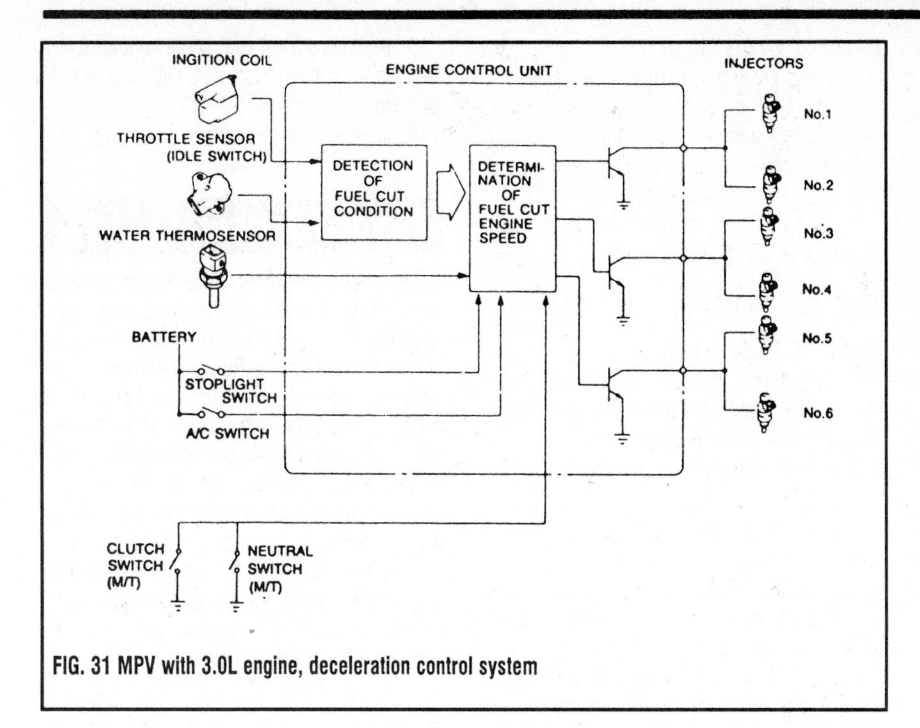

FIG. 31 MPV with 3.0L engine, deceleration control system

9. Verify the voltmeter reading is about 12 volts when the engine speed is below 1700 rpm.
10. If not as specified, inspect terminal 1S of the emission control unit and the vacuum solenoid valve.
11. Remove the vacuum solenoid valve.
12. Connect vacuum hoses to the valve.
13. Blow air through the port closest to the solenoid wire connector.
14. Verify that air comes out of the valve air filter.
15. Apply battery voltage to the terminals of the solenoid valve.
16. Blow air through the solenoid port closest to the wire connector and verify that air comes out the opposite vacuum port.
17. If not as specified, replace the vacuum solenoid valve.

MIXTURE CONTROL VALVE TESTING

1. Start the engine.
2. Block the intake port of the mixture control valve and verify that engine rpm does not increase.
3. Increase the engine speed and quickly decelerate.

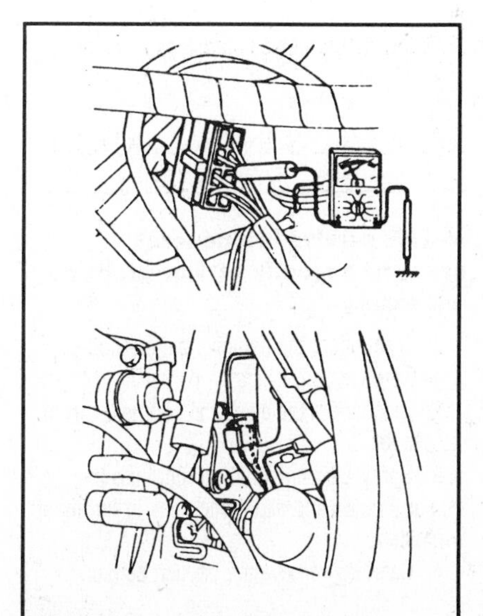

FIG. 32 2.2L engine slow fuel cut system testing

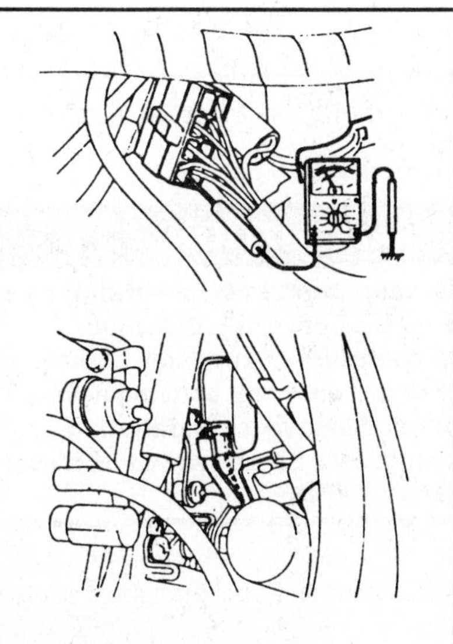

FIG. 33 2.2L engine coasting richer system testing

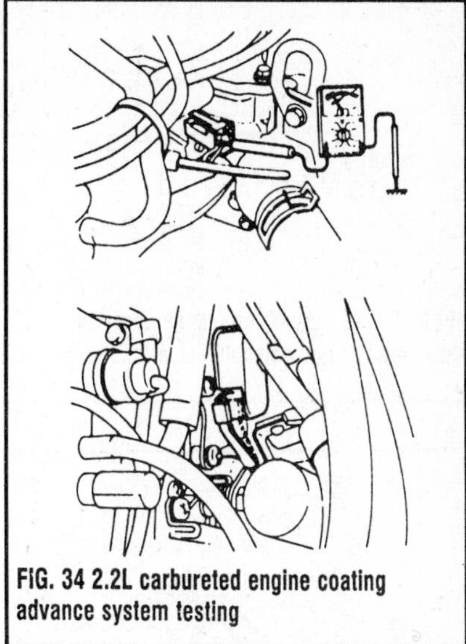

FIG. 34 2.2L carbureted engine coating advance system testing

4. Verify that air is pulled into the intake port of the mixture control valve for about one to two seconds after the accelerator is released.
5. If not as specified, replace the mixture control valve.

DASHPOT TESTING

1. Push the dashpot rod in, making sure the rod goes into the dashpot slowly.
2. Release the rod and make sure it comes out quickly.
3. Replace the dashpot if it does not perform as specified.

DASHPOT ADJUSTMENT

1. Run the engine until normal operating temperature is reached.
2. Connect a suitable tachometer to the engine.
3. Raise the engine speed to above 3500 rpm.
4. Slowly decrease the engine speed making sure the dashpot arm touches the lever at about 2700-2900 rpm.
5. Adjust the dashpot as required, for correct curb idle speed, by loosening the locknut and turning the dashpot in or out as necessary. Tighten the locknut after adjustment.

B2600

SLOW FUEL CUT SYSTEM TESTING

1. Warm the engine to normal operating temperature.
2. Connect a tachometer to the engine.
3. Connect a voltmeter to the solenoid valve connector (e) terminal (YL).
4. Check the voltage at the following conditions. At idle 0-0.6 volts. Accelerate to 4000 rpm and decelerate quickly, momentary voltage should be 13-15 volts.

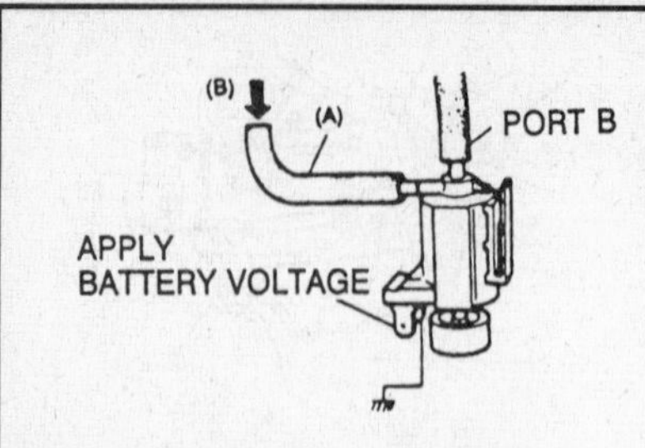

FIG. 35 2.2L carbureted engine coasting advance vacuum solenoid valve testing

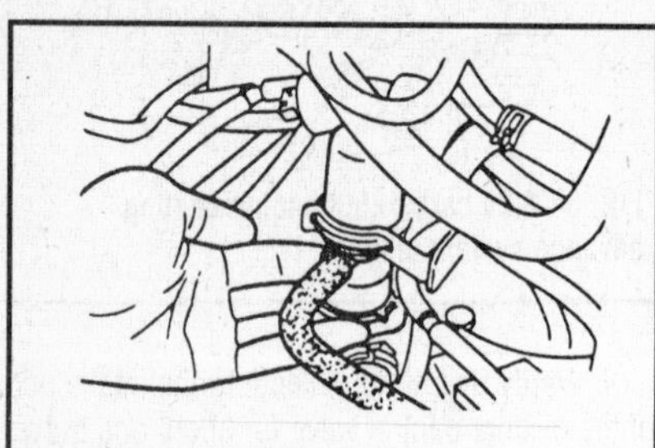
FIG. 36 2.2L carbureted engine mixture control valve testing

5. If not to specifications, check the deceleration vacuum switch, feedback control unit and wiring of the slow fuel cut system.

SLOW FUEL CUT SOLENOID VALVE TEST

1. Run the engine at idle.
2. Disconnect the connector for the solenoid valves.
3. Check that the engine stops.

DECELERATION VACUUM SWITCH TESTING

1. Turn the ignition ON.
2. Connect a hand vacuum pump to the deceleration vacuum switch.
3. Apply 10.2-11.- in. Hg vacuum to the switch and check the voltage at (e) terminal (GB).
4. Voltages should be: with vacuum applied 0 volts. Vacuum not applied 12 volts.
5. If the voltages are not correct check the deceleration vacuum switch.
6. Turn the ignition OFF.
7. Connect the vacuum pump to the deceleration vacuum switch.
8. Disconnect the vacuum switch connector. Apply 10.2-11.- in. Hg of vacuum and check continuity between (e) and (f) terminals (GB) and (B). There should be continuity when vacuum is applied. If not correct, replace the deceleration vacuum switch.

DASHPOT TESTING

Move the throttle lever to the full throttle position, then release the throttle lever and check that the dashpot rod extends slowly.

DASHPOT ADJUSTMENT

1. Warm the engine to normal operating temperature.
2. Connect a tachometer to the engine.
3. Push the dashpot pushrod up into the pot.
4. Loosen the dashpot adjust screw.
5. Turn the adjust screw clockwise and set the curb idle speed to specification.

MPV 3.0L Engine

DASHPOT ADJUSTMENT

1. The dashpot is located at the throttle body. Run the engine until it reaches normal operating temperature and then let it idle.
2. Connect a suitable tachometer to the engine.
3. Raise the engine speed to above 4000 rpm.
4. Slowly decrease the engine speed making sure the dashpot rod touches the lever at about 3200-3800 rpm.
5. To adjust, loosen the locknut and turn the dashpot. Secure the locknut when adjustment is finished.

Catalytic Converter

The catalytic converter is a muffler-shaped device located between the exhaust manifold and the muffler. It is filled with beads containing platinum and palladium which, through catalytic action, enables the HC and CO gases to be converted into water vapor and carbon dioxide.

The converter should be inspected periodically for cracks, corrosion, and any signs of external burning, and replaced as required.

REMOVAL & INSTALLATION

1. Raise the truck and support it on safety stands.

CAUTION

Be very careful when working on or near the converter. External temperatures can reach 1,500°F (815°C) and more, causing severe burns. Removal or installation should only be performed on a cold exhaust system.

2. Remove the front and rear flange attaching nuts.
3. Remove the nut and rubber support which secures the converter bracket, and remove the converter.
4. Installation is the reverse of removal.

Oxygen Sensor

The oxygen sensor monitors the density of the oxygen in the exhaust gas. The sensor consists of a closed-end tube made of ceramic zirconia and other components. Porous platinum electrodes cover the tubes inner and outer surfaces. The tubes outer surface is exposed to the exhaust gases in the exhaust manifold, while its inner surface is exposed to normal air.

The oxygen sensor is usually mounted in the exhaust manifold. The output signal from this sensor, which varies with the oxygen content of the exhaust gas, is provided to the control unit for use in controlling the closed loop compensation of fuel delivery.

TESTING

1. Warm the engine until normal operating temperature is reached. Shut OFF the engine.
2. Disconnect the oxygen sensor and connect a voltmeter between the sensor connector and ground.
3. Start the engine and increase the engine speed to about 4000 rpm until the voltmeter indicates around 0.7 volts.
4. Increase and decrease the engine speed suddenly several times. Check to see when the engine speed increases, the meter reads between 0.5-1.0 volts. When the speed is decreased, the meter should read between 0.0-0.4 volts. If not, replace the oxygen sensor.

REMOVAL & INSTALLATION

➡ This service is a general procedure modify service steps as necessary.

1. Disconnect the negative battery cable. Locate the oxygen sensor.
2. Disconnect the electrical connector from the sensor.
3. Spray a commercial solvent onto the sensor threads and allow it to soak in for about 5 minutes.
4. Carefully remove the oxygen sensor.

To Install:

5. First coat the new sensor's threads with anti-seize compound made for this purpose only. This is NOT a conventional anti-seize paste. The use of a regular compound may electrically insulate the sensor, rendering it inoperative. You must coat ONLY the threads with an electrically conductive anti-seize compound.

6. Install the sensor (installation torque is about 30 ft. lbs. most vehicles) reconnect the electrical connector. Be careful not to damage the electrical connector.

Emission Maintenance Warning Light

The emission maintenance warning light system consists of an instrument panel mounted amber lens that is electrically connected to a sensor module located under the instrument panel. The purpose of the system is to alert the driver that emission system maintenance is required.

The system actually measures accumulated vehicle ignition key on-time and is designed to continuously close an electrical circuit to the amber lens after 2000 hours of vehicle operation. Assuming an average vehicle speed of 30 mph (48 kph), the 2000 hours equates to approximately 60,000 miles (96,500 km) of vehicle operation. Actual vehicle mileage intervals will vary considerably as individual driving habits vary.

Every time the ignition is switched on, the warning light will glow for 2–5 seconds as a bulb check and to verify that the system is operating properly. When approximately 60,000 miles (96,500 km) is reached, the warning light will remain on continuously to indicate that service is required. After the required maintenance is performed, the sensor must be reset for another 60,000 mile (96,500 km) period. The sensor module is located above the right front corner of the glove box assembly.

EMISSION WARNING LIGHT RESET PROCEDURE

1987-88 Models

1. Make sure the ignition key is OFF.
2. Locate the sensor (above the right front corner of the glove box), and lightly push a Phillips screwdriver or small rod tool through the 0.2 in. (5mm) diameter hole with the sticker labeled "RESET" and lightly press down and hold.
3. While lightly holding the screwdriver or tool down, turn the ignition switch to the RUN position. The emission warning light will then light and should remain on for as long as the screwdriver is held down. Hold the screwdriver down for approximately 5 seconds.
4. Remove the screwdriver or tool. The lamp should go out within 2–5 seconds, indicating that a reset has occurred. If the light remains on, begin again at Step 1. If the light goes out, turn the ignition off and go to the next Step.
5. Turn the ignition to the RUN position. The warning light should illuminate for 2–5 seconds and then go out. This verifies that a proper reset of the module has been accomplished. If the light remains on, repeat the reset procedure.

1989-92 Models

B SERIES PICKUP

On Federal and Canadian vehicles, the Malfunction Indicator Light (MIL) will come on at 60,000-80,000 mile (96,500-128,700 km) intervals to indicate the need for scheduled maintenance of the emission control system.

On California vehicles, the MIL will come on any time an engine management input device malfunctions, indicating that service is necessary.

After the required service or maintenance has been performed, the MIL can be reset by changing the connector connections.

MPV

Federal and Canadian vehicles are equipped with a mileage sensor which is linked to the odometer. At every 80,000 miles (128,744 km), the mileage sensor will cause the Malfunction Indicator Light (MIL) to illuminate, indicating that the oxygen sensor must be replaced.

After replacing the oxygen sensor, remove the instrument cluster and reset the MIL by reversing the position of the MIL set screw.

NAVAJO

All vehicles are equipped with a "CHECK ENGINE" or warning light located on the instrument cluster. This light should come on briefly when the ignition key is turned **ON**, but should turn off when the engine starts. If the light does not come ON when the ignition key is turned **ON** or if it comes ON and stays ON when the engine is running, there is a malfunction in the electronic engine control system. After the malfunction has been remedied, using the proper procedures, the "CHECK ENGINE" light will go out.

ELECTRONIC ENGINE CONTROLS

PICKUPS AND MPV

➧SEE FIGS. 37-41

Self Diagnostic System

ENGINE CONTROL UNIT (ECU)

The ECU, through various signals, monitors voltage, engine rpm, amount of air intake, cranking signal, intake temperature, coolant temperature, oxygen concentration in the exhaust gases, throttle opening, atmospheric pressure, gearshift position, clutch engagement, braking, power steering operation and air conditioner compressor operation.

The ECU controls the fuel injection system, idle-up system, evaporative emissions system and ignition timing. The ECU has a built in fail-safe mechanism. If a fault occurs while driving, the ECU will substitute pre-programmed values. Driving performance will be affected, but the vehicle will still be mobile.

➡ On vehicles equipped with Audio Anti-Theft system, before performing any repairs, the owner's Personal Code Number must be obtained and programmed.

SERVICE PRECAUTIONS

- Before connecting or disconnecting control unit ECU harness connectors, make sure the ignition is OFF and the negative battery cable is disconnected to avoid the possibility of damage to the control unit.

• When performing ECU input/output signal diagnosis, remove the terminal retainer from the connectors to make it easier to insert tester probes into the connector.

• When connecting or disconnecting pin connectors from the ECU, take care not to bend or break any pin terminals. Check that there are no bends or breaks on the ECU pin terminals before attempting any connections.

Before replacing any ECU, perform the ECU input/output signal diagnosis to make sure the ECU is functioning properly or not.

• After checking through EFI troubleshooting, perform the EFI self-diagnosos and driving test.

• When measuring supply voltage of ECU controlled components with a circuit tester, separate one tester probe from another. If two tester probes accidentally make contact with the other during measurement, a short circuit will result and could damage the ECU.

READING CODES

Self Diagnosis Checker

A self-diagnosis checker (such as 49-H018-9A1) is used to retrieve code numbers of malfunctions which have happened and were memorized or are continuing. The malfunction is indicated by a code number.

If there is more than one malfunction, the code numbers will display on the self-diagnosis checker one by one in numerical order. In the case of malfunctions, 09, 19, 01, the code numbers are displayed in order of 01, 09 and then 13.

The memory of malfunctions is canceled by disconnecting the negative battery cable.

The ECU had a fail-safe mechanism for the main input sensors. If a malfunction occurs, the emission control unit will substitute values. This will slightly affect the driving performance, but the vehicle may still be driven.

The ECU continuously checks for malfunctions of the input devices during operation. But, the ECU checks for malfunctions of the output devices within three seconds after turning the ignition switch to the ON position and the test connector is grounded.

The malfunction indicator light (MIL) indicates a pattern the same as a self-diagnosis checker when the self-diagnosis check connector is grounded. When the self-diagnosis check connector is not grounded, the lamp illuminates steady while malfunction of the main input sensor occurs and goes out if the malfunction recovers. However the malfunction code is memorized in the emission control unit.

Testing Procedure

SELF-DIAGNOSIS CHECKER

1. Connect the Self-Diagnosis Checker to the check connector. The check connector is usually located above the right side wheel housing.
2. Set the selector switch on the tester to the A position.
3. Ground the green test connector using a suitable jumper wire.
4. Turn the ignition switch to the ON position. Check that number "88" flashes on the digital display and the buzzer sounds for three seconds after turning the ignition switch ON.
5. If the number "88" does not flash, check the main power relay, power supply circuit and check the connector wiring.
6. If the number "88" flashes and the buzzer sounds continuously for more than 20 seconds, replace the ECU and perform steps 3 and 4 again.
7. Note the code numbers and check the causes. Repair as necessary. Be sure to recheck for code numbers after repairing.

MALFUNCTION LIGHT (MIL)

1. During the self-test a service code is reported by the malfunction indicator light. It will represent itself as a flash on the CHECK ENGINE or SERVICE ENGINE SOON light on the dash panel. A single digit number of 3 will be reported by 3 flashes. However, if a service code is represented by a 3-digit number such as 111, the code will appear on the MIL light as three flashes, then after a two second pause, the light will flash three times.
2. Start the engine and allow it to reach normal operating temperatures.
3. Turn the engine off. Connect a jumper wire from the STI to the SIG RTN at the self test connectors and then turn the ignition switch to the ON position. Service codes will be flashed on the MIL light.

Clearing Codes

1. Cancel the memory of malfunctions by disconnecting the negative battery cable and depressing the brake pedal for at least twenty seconds. Reconnect the negative battery cable.
2. Connect the Self-Diagnosis Checker at the check connector. Ground the green one pin test connector using a suitable jumper wire.
3. Turn the ignition switch to the ON position, but do not start the engine for at least six seconds.
4. Start the engine and allow it to reach normal operating temperatures. Run the engine at 2000 rpm for two minutes. Check that no codes are displayed.

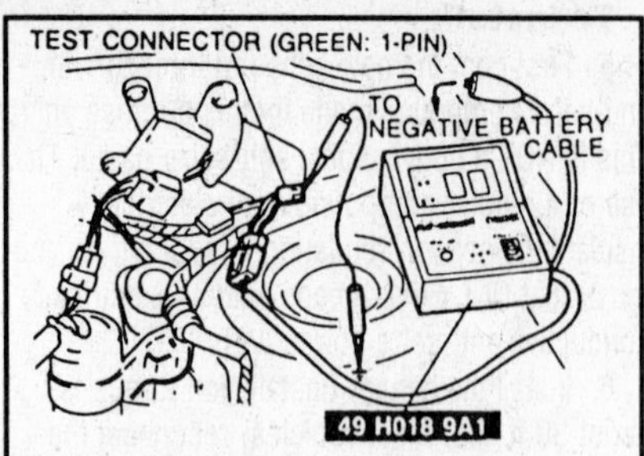

FIG. 37 Connecting the self-diagnosis checker to vehicles without the diagnostic port

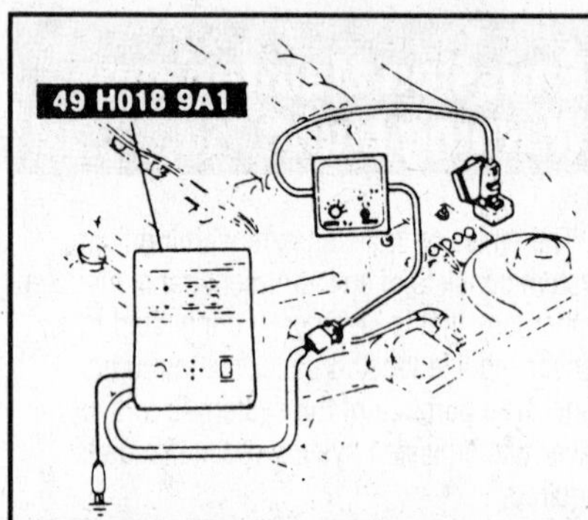

FIG. 38 Connecting the self-diagnosis checker and system selector to vehicles with a diagnostic port

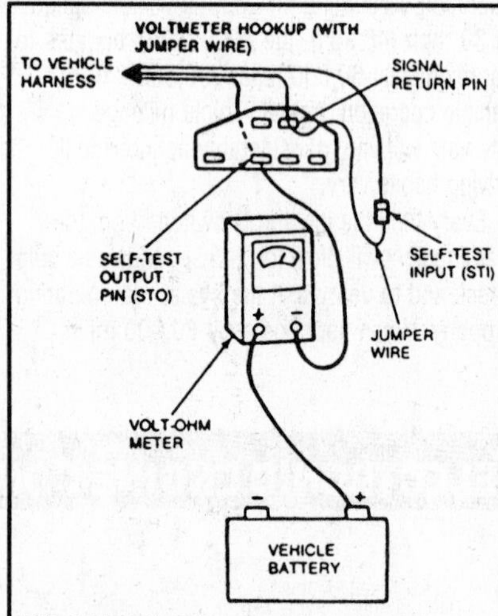

FIG. 39 Retrieving codes with an analog voltmeter (Navajo shown)

Engine Codes

EXCEPT FEEDBACK CARBURETED MODELS

- Code 1-Ignition Pulse
- Code 2-Crank Angle Sensor
- Code 6-Vehicle Speed Sensor
- Code 8-Air Flow Meter
- Code 9-Water Temperature Sensor
- Code 10-Intake Air Temperature at Airflow Meter

- Code 11-Intake Air Temperature at Dynamic Chamber
- Code 12-Throttle Sensor
- Code 14-ECA Atmospheric Pressure Sensor
- Code 15-Oxygen Sensor or Circuit
- Code 16-EGR Position Sensor
- Code 17-Oxygen Sensor Feedback System
- Code 23-Right Side Oxygen Sensor
- Code 24-Right Side Oxygen Sensor Feedback System
- Code 25-Pressure Regulator Solenoid Valve
- Code 26-Purge Control Solenoid Valve
- Code 28-EGR Vacuum Solenoid Valve
- Code 29-EGR Vent Solenoid Valve
- Code 30-Cold Start Injector Relay
- Code 34-Idle Speed Control Valve
- Code 55-Pulse Generator

FEEDBACK CARBURETED MODELS

- Code 1-Ignition Pulse
- Code 9-Water Temperature Sensor
- Code 13-Vacuum Sensor
- Code 14-Atmospheric Pressure Sensor
- Code 15-Oxygen Sensor Open or Short

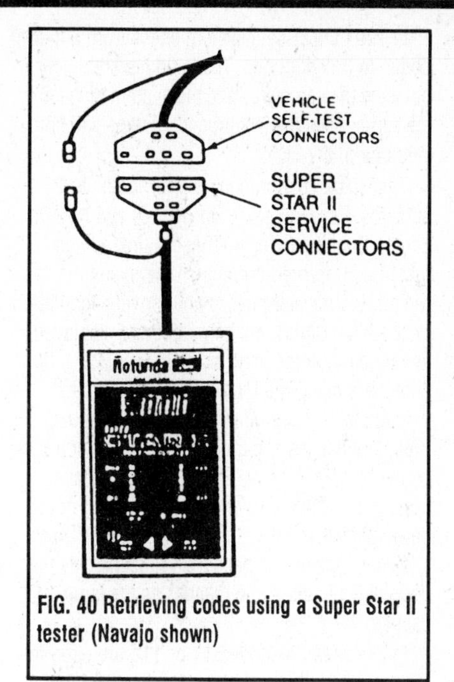

FIG. 40 Retrieving codes using a Super Star II tester (Navajo shown)

TO VEHICLE HARNESS
SELF-TEST CONNECTOR
JUMPER WIRE
"CHECK ENGINE" LIGHT (WITH JUMPER WIRE)
SELF-TEST INPUT (STI)

FIG. 41 Retrieving codes using the instrument panel light

- Code 17-Oxygen Sensor Feedback System
- Code 18-Air/Fuel Solenoid Valve
- Code 22-Slow Fuel Cut Solenoid Valve
- Code 23-Coasting Richer Solenoid Valve
- Code 26-Purge Solenoid Valve
- Code 28-Duty Solenoid Vacuum Valve
- Code 29-Duty Solenoid Vent Valve
- Code 30-Air Control Valve Solenoid
- Code 34-Idle-Up Solenoid Valve for AC
- Code 35-Idle-Up Solenoid Valve for AT
- Code 45-Vacuum Solenoid Valve

ELECTRONIC ENGINE CONTROLS NAVAJO

Self-Diagnostic Systems

EEC-IV ENGINE CONTROL SYSTEM

The EEC-IV engine control system heart is a microcomputer called an Electronic Control Assembly (ECA). This ECC-IV system is the same ECC-IV system used by Ford Motor Company, testing and servicing this system is identical. The ECA receives data (system inputs) for sensors, switches, relays, and other electronic components and issues command signals (system outputs) to various devices in order to control engine operations under a variety of loads and ambient conditions. The ECA is calibrated according to the powertain, axle ratio, and gross vehicle weigh (GVM) to optimize fuel economy and driveability while minimizing harmful emissions.

The EEC-IV system electronically controls the fuel injectors to maintain a 14.7:1 air/fuel ratio under all driving conditions. This 14.7:1 air/fuel mixture allows the 3-way catalytic converter to operate at peak efficiency while getting the most performance and economy from the engine. Ignition spark timing, deceleration fuel cut-off, curb, and fast idle speed, evaporative emissions purge, air conditioning cut-off during wider open throttle, cold engine start and enrichment, electric fuel pump and self-test engine diagnostics are also controlled by the ECA to maintain consistent driveability across a wide range of operating conditions, temperatures, and altitudes. The EEC-IV system is self-adjusting for operation at high altitude elevations (over 4000 feet above sea level) and can actually compensate for engine component wear (a worn timing chain, for example).

The ECA in the EEC-IV system contains the calibration module with the ECA assembly. The harness connectors are edge-card type contacts which provide a more positive connection. The ECA is mounted behind the right front (passenger) kick panel.

Limited Operation Strategy (LOS)

In this operation, the ECA provides the necessary output signals to allow the vehicle to "limp home" when an electronic malfunction occurs, sometimes referred to as limp-in mode. The air bypass valve goes to a fixed voltage, timing is locked at the fixed timing (depends on calibration), and the injector pulse width is constant.

Self-Diagnostic System

➡ **On vehicles equipped with Audio Anti-Theft system, before performing and repairs, the owner's Personal Code Number (P.C.N.) must be obtained and programmed.**

Service Precautions

- Do not operate the fuel pump when the fuel lines are empty.
- Do not reuse fuel hose clamps.
- Make sure all ECA harness connectors are fastened securely. A poor connection can cause an extremely high surge voltage in the coil and condenser and result in damage to integrated circuits.

• Keep the EGI harness at least 4 in. away from the adjacent harnesses to prevent an EGI system malfunction due to external electron "noise."

• Keep all ECA related parts and harnesses dry during service.

• Before attempting to remove any parts, turn off the ignition switch and disconnect the battery ground cable.

• Always use a 12 volt battery as a power source.

• Do not attempt to disconnect the battery cables with the engine running.

• Do not attempt to disassemble the ECA control unit under any circumstances.

• If installing a 2-way or CB radio, keep the antenna as far as possible from the electronic control unit. Keep the antenna feeder line at least 8 in. away from the EGI harness and do not let the 2 run parallel for a long distance. Be sure to ground the radio to the vehicle body.

• Do not apply battery power directly to injectors.

• Handle air flow meter carefully to avoid damage.

• Do not disassemble air flow meter or clean meter with any type of detergent.

➡ If the battery cable(s) is disconnected for longer than 5 minutes, the adaptive fuel factor will be lost. After repair it will be necessary to drive the vehicle at least 10 miles (16 km) to allow the processor to relearn the correct factors. The driving period should include steady-throttle open road driving if possible. During the drive, the vehicle may exhibit driveability symptoms not noticed before. These symptoms should clear as the ECA computes the correction factor. The ECA may also store code indicating loss of power to the controller.

Reading Codes

The EEC-IV system may be interrogated for stored codes using the Quick Test procedures. These tests will reveal faults immediately present during the test as well as any intermittent codes set within the previous 80 warm up cycles. If a code was set before a problem self-corrected (such as momentarily loose connector), the code will be erased if the problem does not reoccur within 80 warm-up cycles.

In 1991 the EEC-VI system check from 2 digit codes to 3 digit codes. These codes are obtained the same way and the system functions the same. All of the test procedures apply to both versions of the ECA.

The Quick Test procedure is divided into 2 sections, Key On Engine Off (KOEO) and Key On Engine Running (KOER). These 2 procedures must be performed correctly if the system is to run the internal self-checks and provide accurate fault codes. Codes will be output and displayed as numbers on the hand scan tool, i.e. 23. If the codes are being read through the dashboard warning lamp, the codes will be displayed as groups of flashes separated by pauses. Code 23 would be shown as two flashes, a pause and three more flashes. A longer pause would occur between codes. If the codes are being read on an analog voltmeter, the needle sweeps indicate the code digits in the same manner as the lamp flashes.

In all cases, the codes 11 or 111 are used to indicate PASS during testing. Note that the PASS code may appear, followed by other stored codes. These are codes from the continuous memory and may indicate intermittent faults, even though the system does not presently contain the fault. The PASS designation only indicates the system passes all internal tests at the moment.

⁂ CAUTION

To prevent injury and/or property damage, always block the drive wheels, firmly apply the parking brake, place the transmission in P or N and turn all the electrical loads off before performing the Quick Test procedures.

TESTING

Super Star II Tester

KEY ON ENGINE OFF (KOEO)

1. Specific instructions for the use of the tester are included with the tester.
2. Plug the tester connectors into the vehicle self-test connectors.
3. Set the switches on the tester to the appropriate settings for type of EEC system and for fast or slow mode. The same information is contained in fast or slow mode, but the fast mode is 100 times faster than the slow and is for use with the Super Star Tester.
4. Turn on the tester power and depress the test button. Turn ON the vehicle ignition key.
5. The tester will read the codes as they exist.

KEY ON ENGINE RUNNING (KOER)

1. Connect the tester as in the KOEO test and start and warm the engine to normal operating temperature.
2. Turn the engine off and depress the test button so it stays in the test position.
3. Restart the engine and the tester will read any existing codes. The tester will display an engine I.D. code, then on some vehicles a Dynamic Response code. The final display will be the service codes.

Analog Voltmeter

KEY ON ENGINE OFF (KOEO) AND CONTINUOUS CODES

1. Turn the vehicle ignition switch to OFF. Set the range of the analog voltmeter to 0-15 volts.
2. Connect the positive lead of an analog voltmeter to the positive of the battery.
3. Connect the negative lead of the voltmeter to the Self-Test Output pin of the Self-Test connector.
4. Connect a jumper wire between the Self-Test Input connector and the Signal Return pin of the Self-Test connector.
5. The needle will sweep 3 times for a code digit of 3, for example. If the code is 123, the needle will sweep once, pause for 2 seconds, sweep twice, pause for 2 seconds, then sweep three times. There will be a 4 second pause between codes. The method of readout of 2 digit codes is similar to the three digit code readout, but only 2 sets of sweeps will occur.
4. The continuous memory codes will be displayed first, then there will be a 6 second pause, a single sweep, anther 6 second pause then the KOEO codes will be displayed.

With Malfunction Indicator or Check Engine Light

KEY ON ENGINE OFF (KOEO) AND CONTINUOUS CODES

1. Connect a jumper wire between the Self-Test Input (STI) connector and the Signal Return pin of the Self-Test connector.
2. This will output the codes to the MIL or Check Engine light on the instrument panel.
3. The light will flash 3 times for a code digit of 3, for example. If the code is 123, the light will flash once, pause for 2 seconds, flash twice, pause for 2 seconds, then flash three times. There will be a 4 second pause between codes. The method of readout for 2 digit code is similar to the three digit code readout, but only 2 sets of sweeps will occur.

4. The continuous memory codes will be displayed first, then there will be a 6 second pause, a single flash, another 6 second pause, then the KOEO codes will be displayed.

Other Test Modes

CONTINUOUS MONITOR OR WIGGLE TEST MODE

Once entered, this mode allows the technician to attempt to recreate the intermittent faults by wiggling or tapping components, wiring or connectors. The test may by performed during either KOEO or KOER procedures. The test requires the use of either an analog voltmeter or a hard scan tool.

To enter the continuous monitor mode during KOEO testing, turn the ignition switch ON. Activate the test, wait 10 seconds, then deactivate and reactivate the test; the system will enter the continuous monitor mode. Tap, move, or wiggle the harness, component, or connector suspected of causing the problem; if a fault is detected, the code will store in the memory. When the fault occurs, the dash warning lamp will illuminate, the STAR tester will light a red indicator (and possible beep) and the analog monitor needle will sweep once.

To enter this mode in the KOER test:

1. Start the engine and run it at 2000 rpm for two minutes. This action warms up the oxygen sensor.
2. Turn the ignition switch to OFF for 10 seconds.
3. Start the engine.
4. Activate the test, wait 10 seconds, then deactivate and reactivate the test; the system will enter the continuous monitor mode.
5. Tap, move, or wiggle the harness, component, or connector suspected of causing the problem; if a fault is detected, the code will store in the memory.
6. When the fault occurs, the dash warning lamp will illuminate, the STAR tester will light the red indicator (and possibly beep) and the analog meter needle will sweep once.

OUTPUT STATE CHECK

This testing mode allows the operator to energize the de-energize most of the outputs controlled by the EEC-IV system. Many of the outputs may be checked at the component by listening for a click or feeling the item move or engage by a hand placed on the case. To enter this check:

1. Enter the KOEO test mode.
2. When all codes have been transmitted, depress the accelerator all the way to the floor and release it.
3. The output actuators are now all ON. Depressing the throttle pedal to the floor again switches all the actuator outputs OFF.
4. This test may be performed as often as necessary, switching between ON and OFF by depressing the throttle.
5. Exit the test by turning the ignition switch OFF, disconnecting the jumper at the diagnostic connector or releasing the test button on the scan tool.

Clearing Codes

CONTINUOUS CODES

1. Run the Self-Test for the output system being used: Super Star II, analog voltmeter, or dash light.
2. When the service codes start to be displayed the codes will be cleared when the Test button is unlatched on the Super Star II tester. For the other retrieval methods the codes will be cleared when the jumper is removed between the Self-Test Input connector and the Signal Return pin of the Self-Test connector.
3. Disconnect the Super Star II tester or voltmeter.

KEEP MEMORY ALIVE

The Keep Alive Memory will be erased when the negative battery cable is disconnected. Keep the cable off for a minimum of 5 minutes. When the cable is connected and the vehicle driven, it may exhibit some drivability problems for the first 10 miles (16 km) or so. This is due to the relearning process where the ECA memorizes values needed for optimum drivability.

CODES AND DESCRIPTION

Navajo 2 Digit Codes

- Code 11-System pass
- Code 12-Cannot control rpm during high rpm check
- Code 13-Cannot control rpm during low rpm check
- Code 14-PIP circuit failure
- Code 15-ECA keep alive only memory (KAM) test failed
- Code 15-ECA read only memory (ROM) test failed
- Code 16-IDM signal not received
- Code 18-Loss of IDM input or SAW circuit open
- Code 19-Failure in ECA internal voltage
- Code 21-ECT out of range
- Code 22-Barometric Pressure (BP) sensor
- Code 23-TP sensor out of self-test range
- Code 24-ACT sensor out of self-test range
- Code 26-MAF out of self-test range
- Code 29-Insufficient input from VSS
- Code 41-Fuel system adaptive limits, no HEGO switch
- Code 41-Lack of HEGO switches, indicates lean
- Code 42-Lack of HEGO switches, indicates rich
- Code 45-Coil 1, 2, or 3 failure
- Code 51-ECT indicated - 40°F (4.4°C) open circuit
- Code 53-TP sensor circuit above maximum voltage
- Code 54-ACT indicated - 40°F (4.4°C) open circuit
- Code 56-MAF circuit above maximum voltage
- Code 61-ECT indicated 254°F (123°C) grounded circuit
- Code 63-TP sensor voltage below minimum voltage
- Code 64-ACT indicated 254°F (123°C) grounded circuit
- Code 66-MAF below minimum voltage
- Code 67-Clutch switch circuit failure
- Code 67-Vehicle not in Park during KOEO
- Code 72-Insufficient MAF change during test
- Code 73-Insufficient TP change dynamic response test
- Code 74-BOO circuit failure/not actuated during self-test
- Code 77-Operator error during test
- Code 79-A/C ON/ Defroster ON/ during self-test
- Code 86-Shift solenoid circuit failure
- Code 87-Primary fuel pump circuit failure
- Code 89-Clutch Converter Override (CCO) circuit failure
- Code 95-Fuel pump circuit open - ECA to motor ground
- Code 96-Fuel pump circuit open - ECA to battery
- Code 98-Hard fault present
- Code not listed

Navajo 3 digit codes

- Code 111-System pass
- Code 112-ACT indicated 254°F (123°C) grounded circuit
- Code 113-ACT indicated - 40°F (4.4°C) open circuit
- Code 114-ACT sensor out of self-test range
- Code 116-ECT out of range
- Code 117-ECT indicated 254°F (123°C) grounded circuit
- Code 118-ECT indicated - 40°F (4.4°C) open circuit
- Code 121-TP sensor out of self-test range
- Code 122-TP sensor circuit below minimum voltage

- Code 123-TP sensor circuit above maximum voltage
- Code 126-Barometric Pressure (BP) sensor
- Code 128-Barometric Pressure (BP) sensor
- Code 129-Insufficient MAF change during test
- Code 136-Fuel control
- Code 137-Fuel control
- Code 139-Fuel control
- Code 144-Fuel control
- Code 157-MAF below minimum voltage
- Code 158-MAF circuit above maximum voltage
- Code 159-MAF out of self-test range
- Code 167-Insufficient TP change dynamic response test
- Code 171-Fuel system at adaptive limits, no HEGO switch
- Code 172-Lack of HEGO switches, indicates lean
- Code 173-Lack of HEGO switches, indicates rich
- Code 174-Fuel control
- Code 175-Fuel control
- Code 176-Fuel control
- Code 177-Fuel control
- Code 178-Fuel control
- Code 179-Lean adaptive limit at part throttle, system rich
- Code 181-Rich adaptive limit at part throttle, system lean
- Code 182-Fuel control
- Code 183-Fuel control
- Code 188-Fuel control
- Code 189-Fuel control
- Code 191-Fuel control
- Code 192-Fuel control
- Code 194-Fuel control
- Code 195-Fuel control
- Code 211-PIP circuit failure
- Code 212-Loss of IDM input or SAW circuit grounded
- Code 213-SAW circuit open
- Code 215-Ignition system
- Code 216-Ignition system
- Code 217-Ignition system
- Code 218-Ignition system
- Code 222-Ignition system
- Code 223-IDM signal not received
- Code 224-IDM signal not received
- Code 226-IDM signal
- Code 232-Coil 1, 2, or 3 failure
- Code 238-Ignition system
- Code 338-Temperature sensor
- Code 339-Temperature sensor
- Code 341-Octane adjust circuit open
- Code 411-Cannot control rpm during low rpm check
- Code 412-Cannot control rpm during high rpm check
- Code 452-Insufficient input from VSS
- Code 511-ECA read only memory (ROM) test failed
- Code 512-ECA keep alive only memory (KAM) test failed
- Code 513-Failure in ECA internal voltage
- Code 522-Vehicle not in P or N during KOEO
- Code 525-Vehicle not in P or N durung KOEO
- Code 528-Clutch switch circuit failure
- Code 529-Check Engine light
- Code 533-Check Engine light
- Code 536-BOO circuit failure/not actuated during self-test
- Code 538-Operator error during test
- Code 539-A/C ON/ Defroster ON/ during self-test
- Code 542-Fuel pump circuit open - ECA to motor guard
- Code 542-Fuel pump circuit open - ECA to battery
- Code 556-Primary fuel pump circuit failure
- Code 565-Canister purge (CANP) circuit failure
- Code 566-Shift solenoid circuit failure
- Code 569-Canister purge (CANP) circuit failure
- Code 629-Clutch Converter Override (CCO) circuit failure
- Code 998-Hard fault present
- Code not listed
- 600 series codes are transmission codes

EMISSION COMPONENT LOCATION AND VACUUM CIRCUIT CHARTS

➧SEE FIGS. 42-77

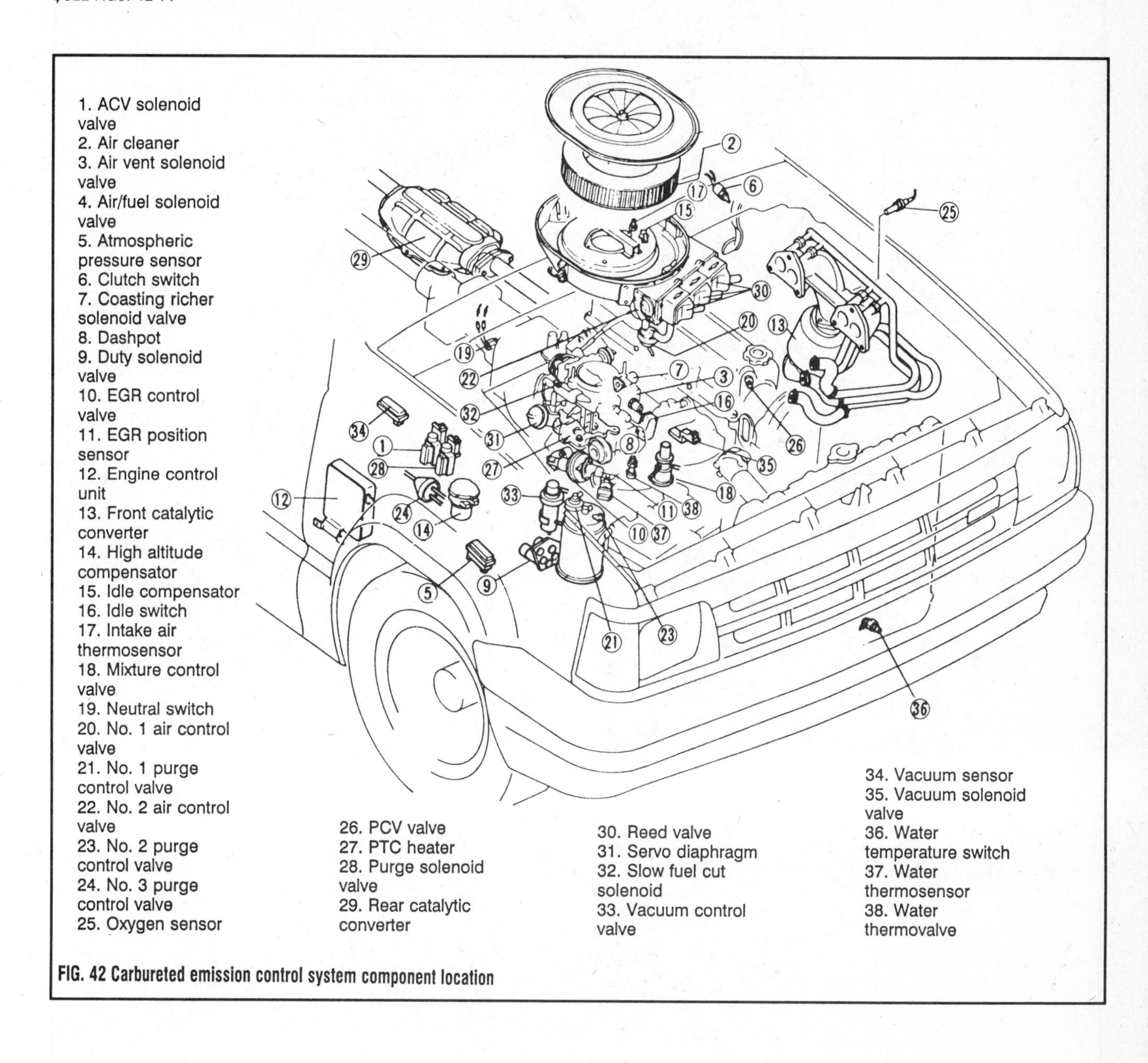

FIG. 42 Carbureted emission control system component location

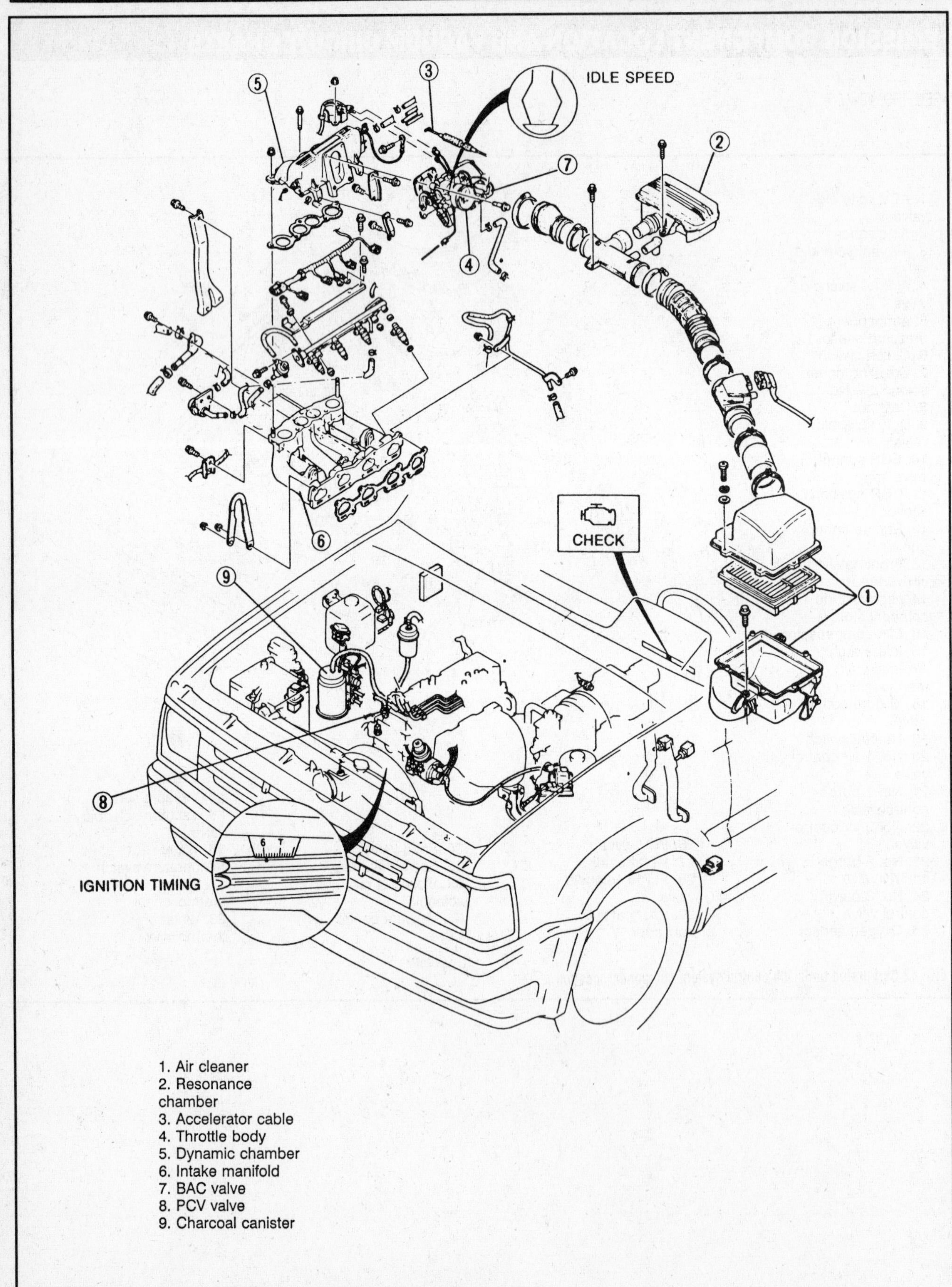

FIG. 43 Pickup fuel injected emission control component location (B2600i shown)

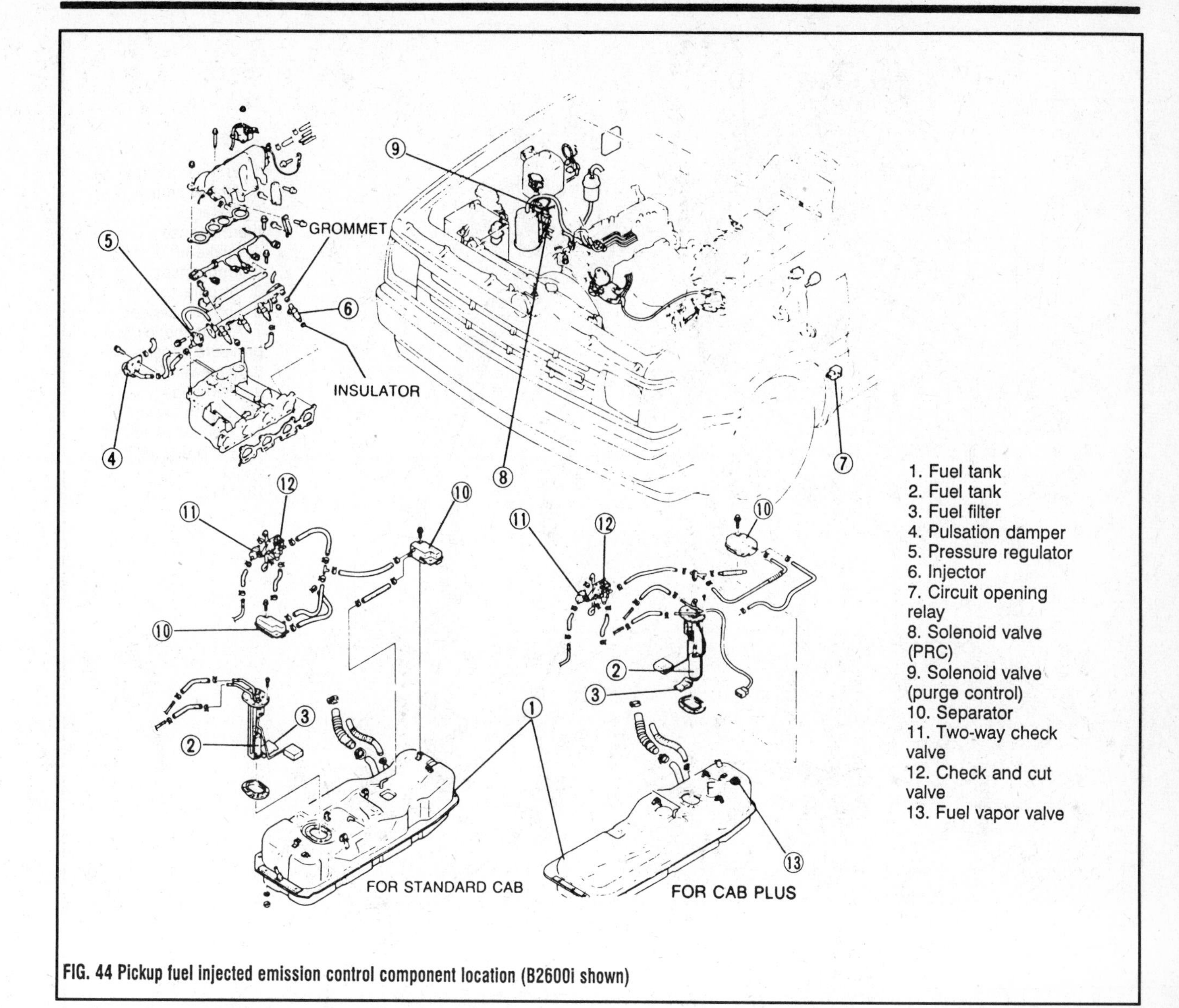

FIG. 44 Pickup fuel injected emission control component location (B2600i shown)

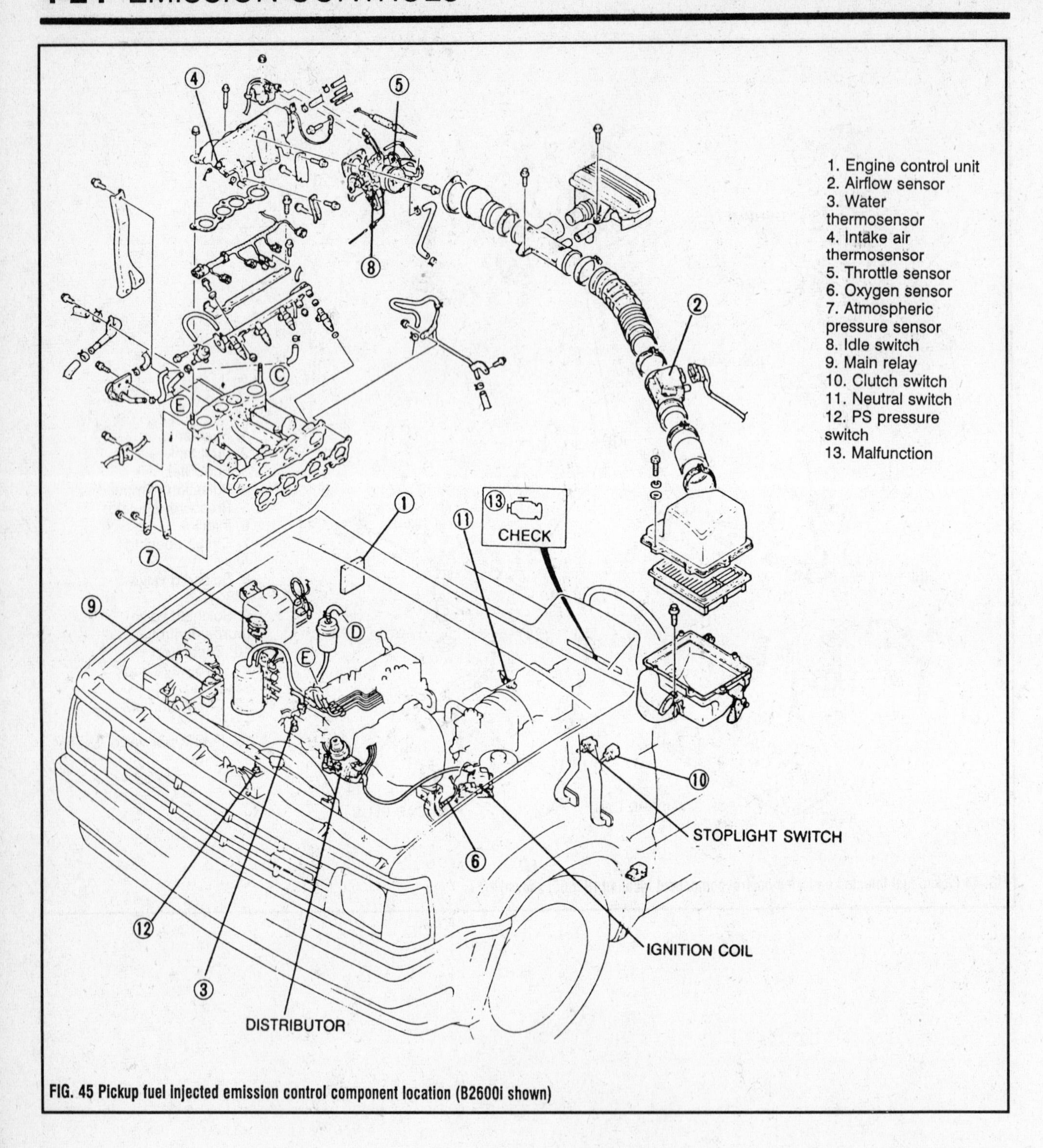

FIG. 45 Pickup fuel injected emission control component location (B2600i shown)

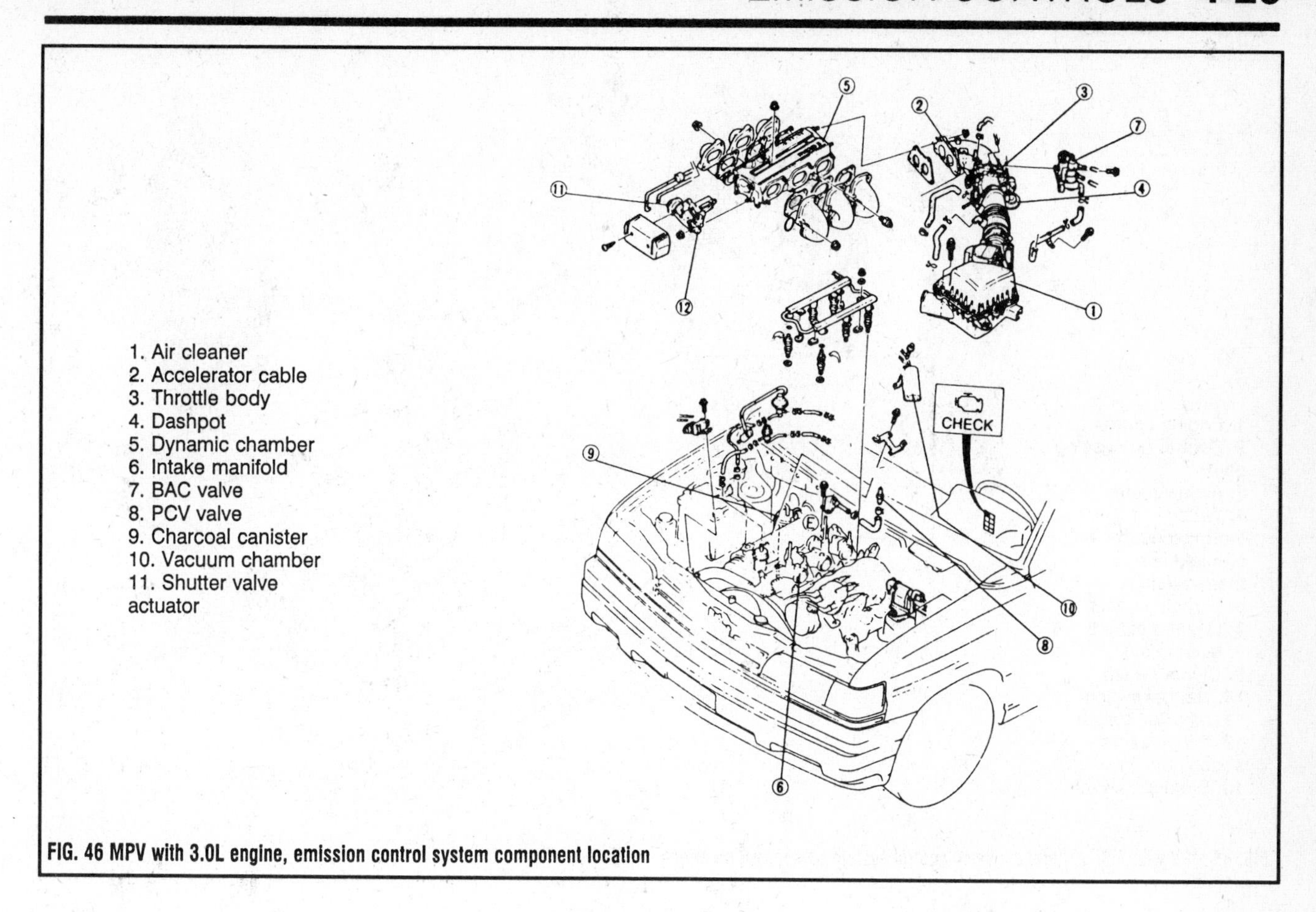

FIG. 46 MPV with 3.0L engine, emission control system component location

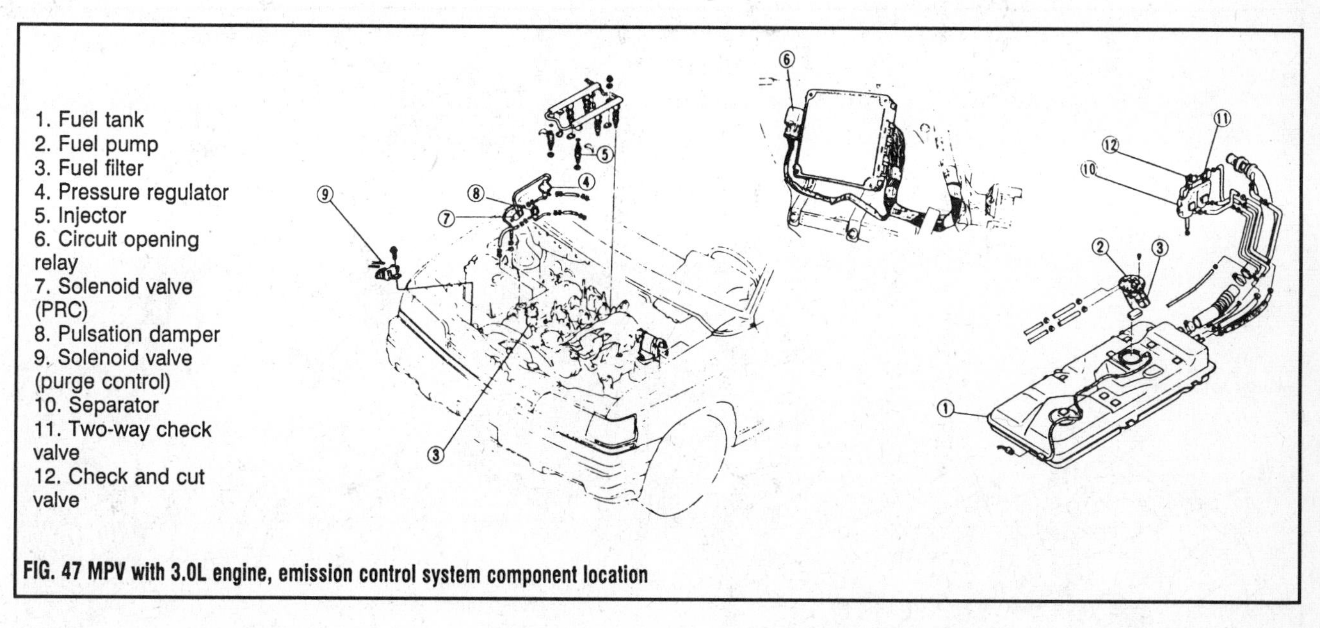

FIG. 47 MPV with 3.0L engine, emission control system component location

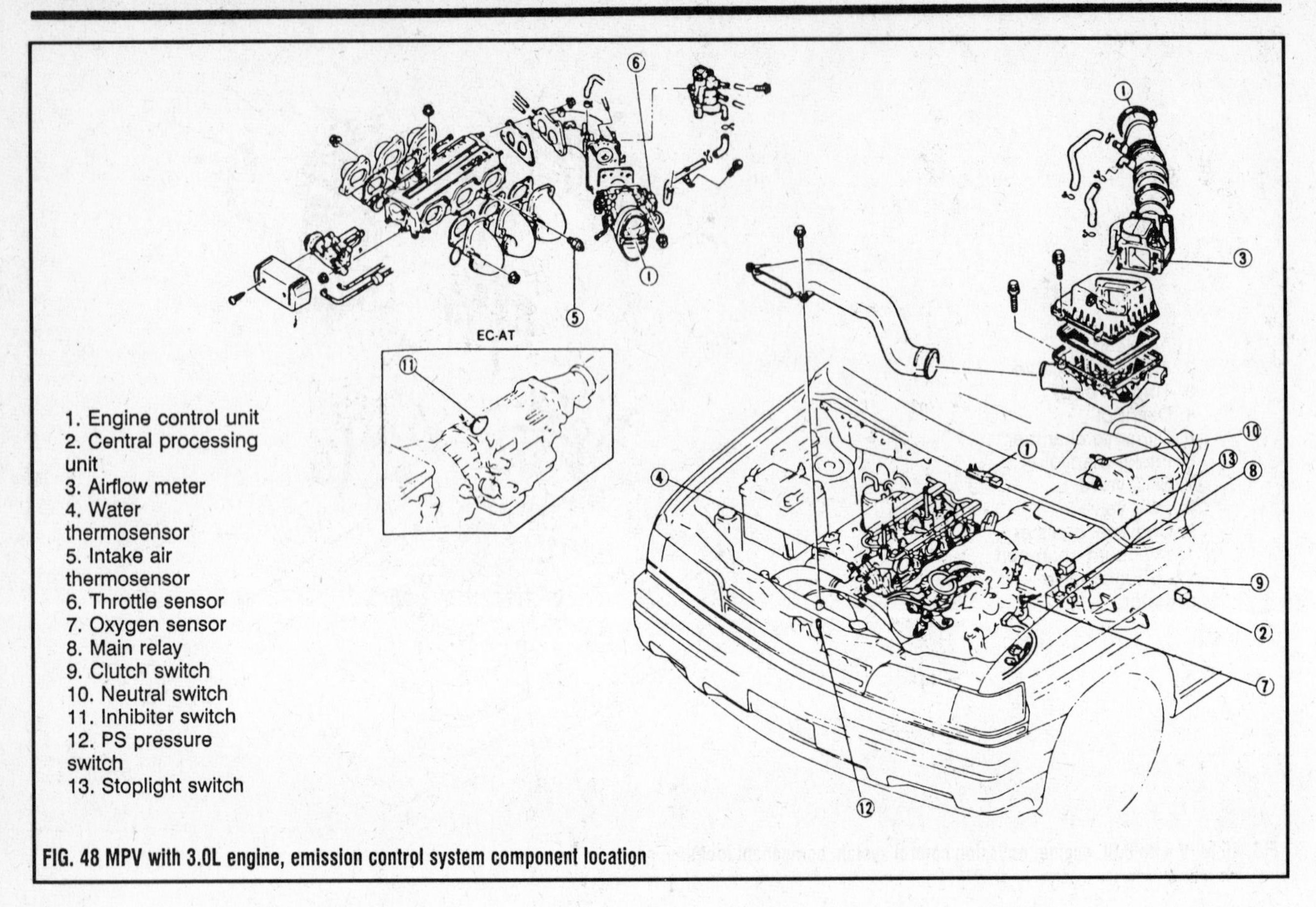

FIG. 48 MPV with 3.0L engine, emission control system component location

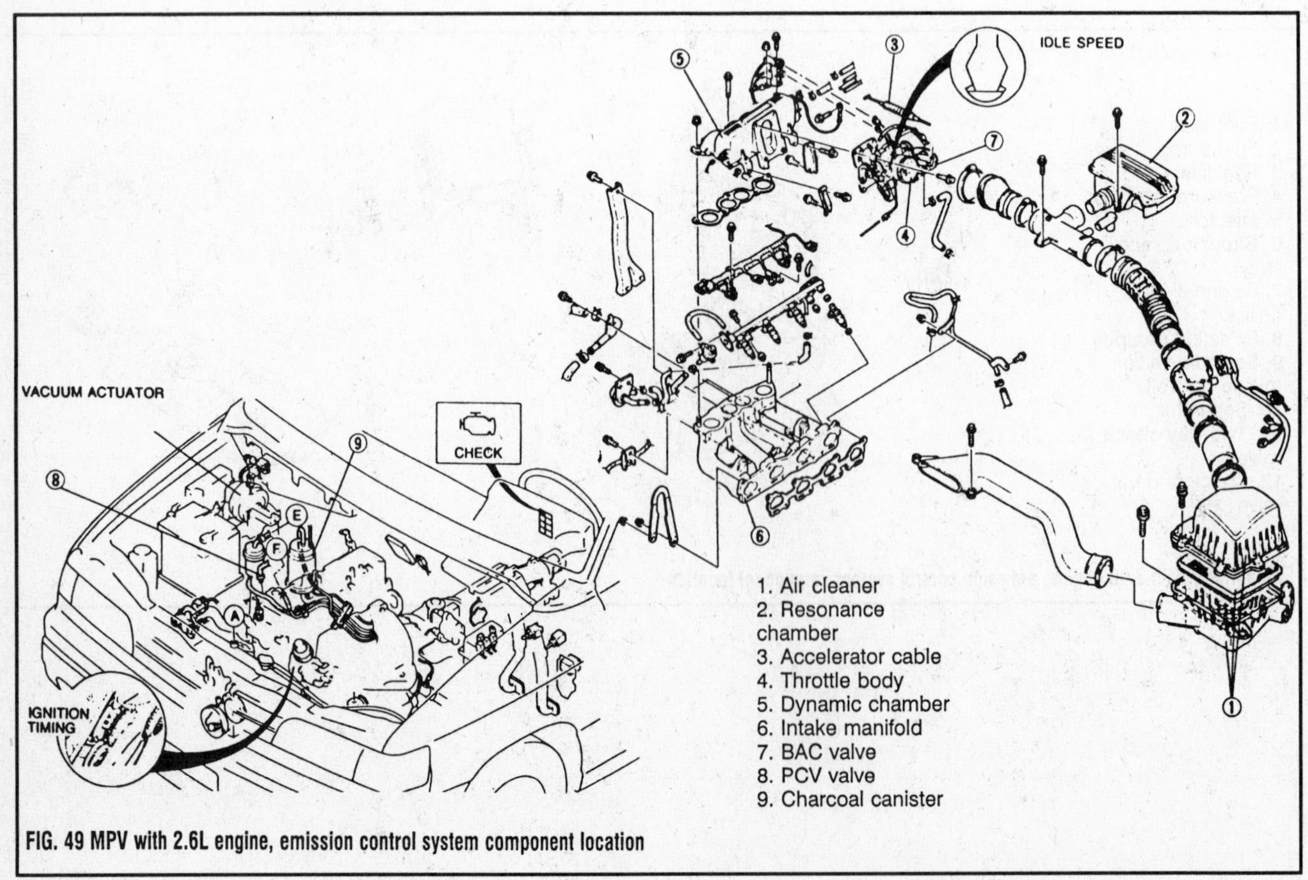

FIG. 49 MPV with 2.6L engine, emission control system component location

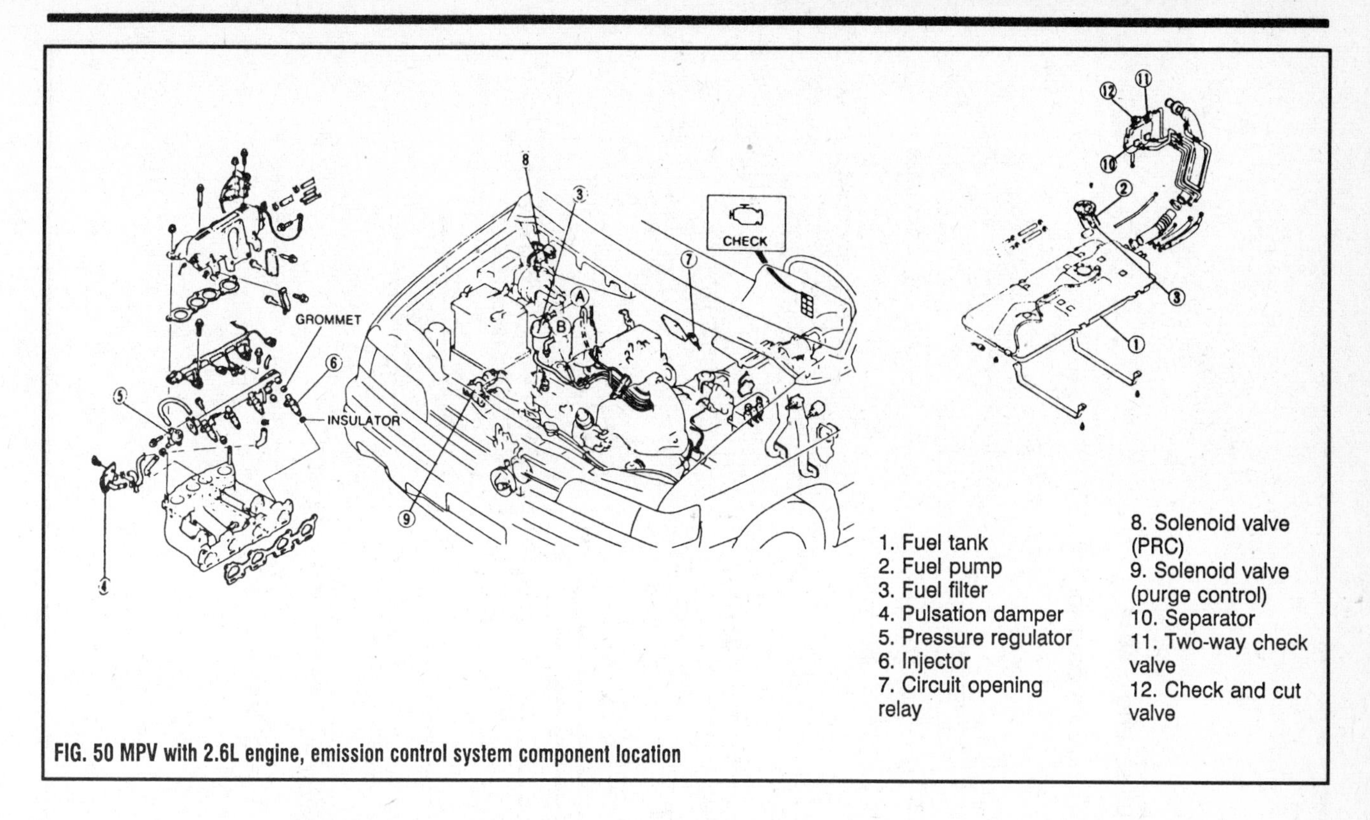

FIG. 50 MPV with 2.6L engine, emission control system component location

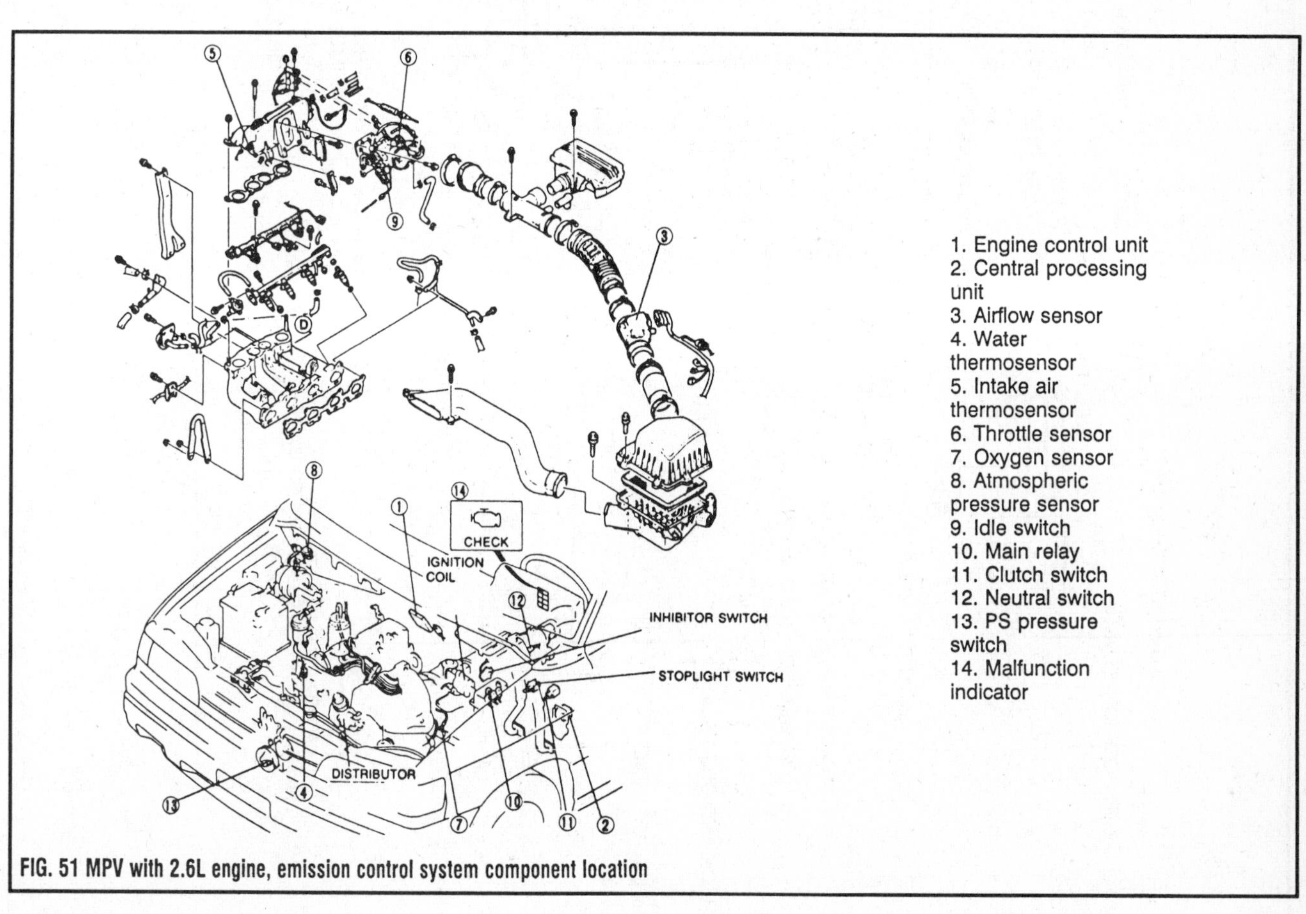

FIG. 51 MPV with 2.6L engine, emission control system component location

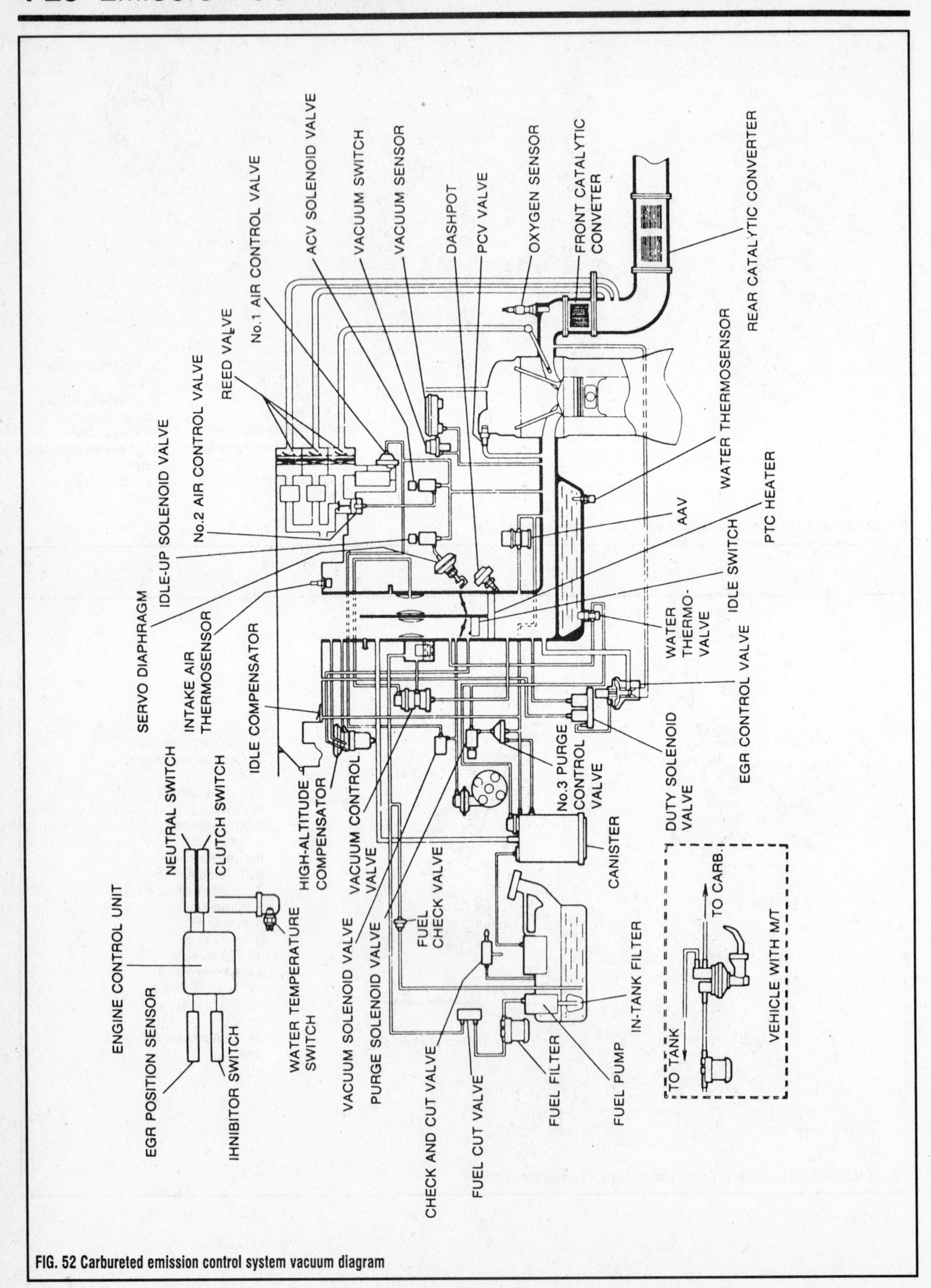
ENGINE CONTROL UNIT
EGR POSITION SENSOR
INHIBITOR SWITCH
NEUTRAL SWITCH
CLUTCH SWITCH
WATER TEMPERATURE SWITCH
SERVO DIAPHRAGM
INTAKE AIR THERMOSENSOR
IDLE COMPENSATOR
HIGH-ALTITUDE COMPENSATOR
VACUUM SOLENOID VALVE
PURGE SOLENOID VALVE
VACUUM CONTROL VALVE
CHECK AND CUT VALVE
FUEL CUT VALVE
FUEL CHECK VALVE
FUEL FILTER
FUEL PUMP
IN-TANK FILTER
CANISTER
No.3 PURGE CONTROL VALVE
DUTY SOLENOID VALVE
EGR CONTROL VALVE
WATER THERMO-VALVE
IDLE SWITCH
PTC HEATER
AAV
WATER THERMOSENSOR
IDLE-UP SOLENOID VALVE
No.2 AIR CONTROL VALVE
REED VALVE
No.1 AIR CONTROL VALVE
ACV SOLENOID VALVE
VACUUM SWITCH
VACUUM SENSOR
DASHPOT
PCV VALVE
OXYGEN SENSOR
FRONT CATALYTIC CONVETER
REAR CATALYTIC CONVERTER
TO TANK
TO CARB.
VEHICLE WITH M/T

FIG. 52 Carbureted emission control system vacuum diagram

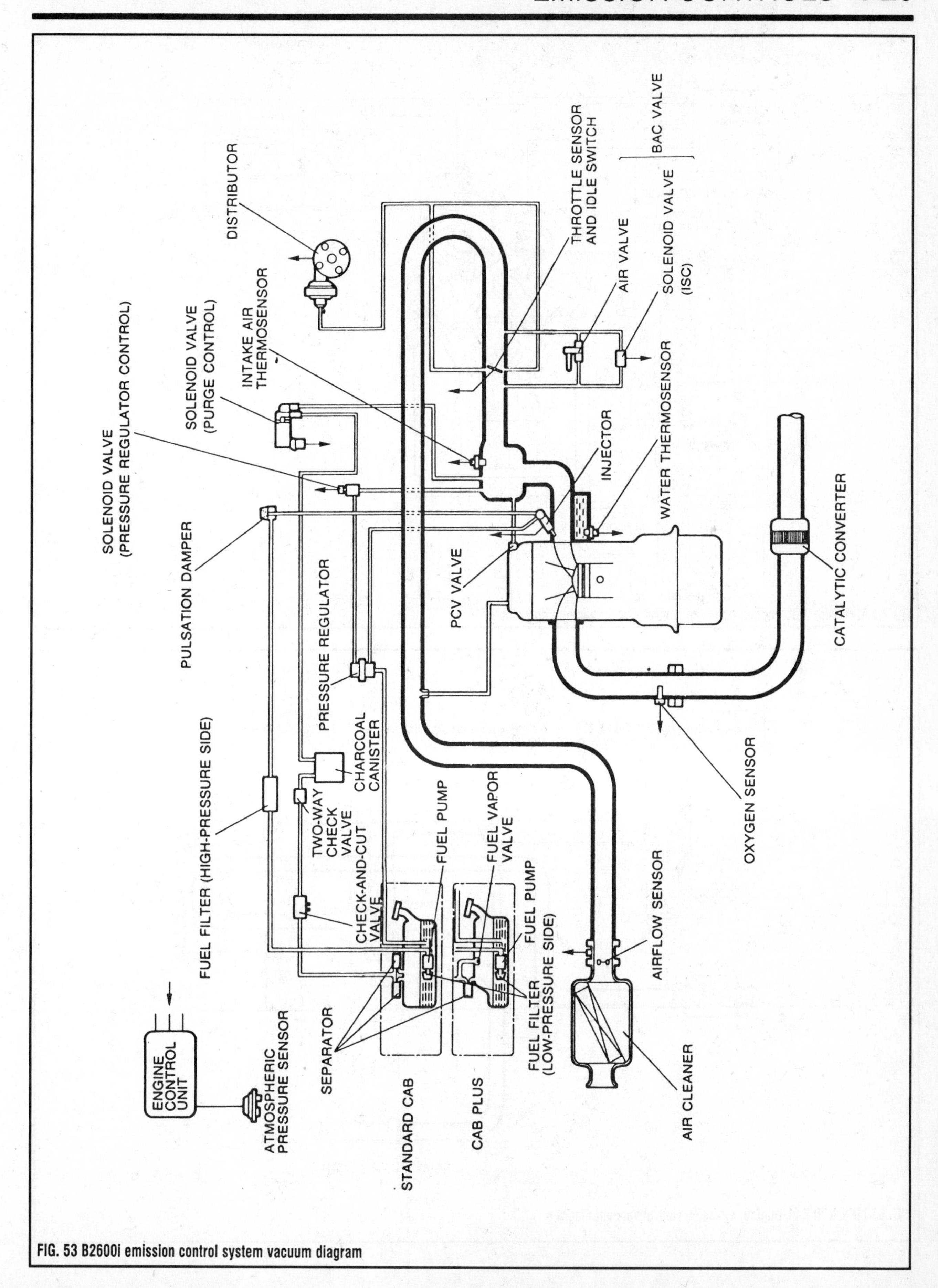
DISTRIBUTOR
THROTTLE SENSOR AND IDLE SWITCH
BAC VALVE
AIR VALVE
SOLENOID VALVE (ISC)
SOLENOID VALVE (PRESSURE REGULATOR CONTROL)
SOLENOID VALVE (PURGE CONTROL)
INTAKE AIR THERMOSENSOR
WATER THERMOSENSOR
INJECTOR
PULSATION DAMPER
PRESSURE REGULATOR
PCV VALVE
CATALYTIC CONVERTER
CHARCOAL CANISTER
FUEL FILTER (HIGH-PRESSURE SIDE)
TWO-WAY CHECK VALVE
FUEL PUMP
FUEL VAPOR VALVE
OXYGEN SENSOR
CHECK-AND-CUT VALVE
FUEL PUMP
AIRFLOW SENSOR
ENGINE CONTROL UNIT
ATMOSPHERIC PRESSURE SENSOR
SEPARATOR
FUEL FILTER (LOW-PRESSURE SIDE)
AIR CLEANER
STANDARD CAB
CAB PLUS

FIG. 53 B2600i emission control system vacuum diagram

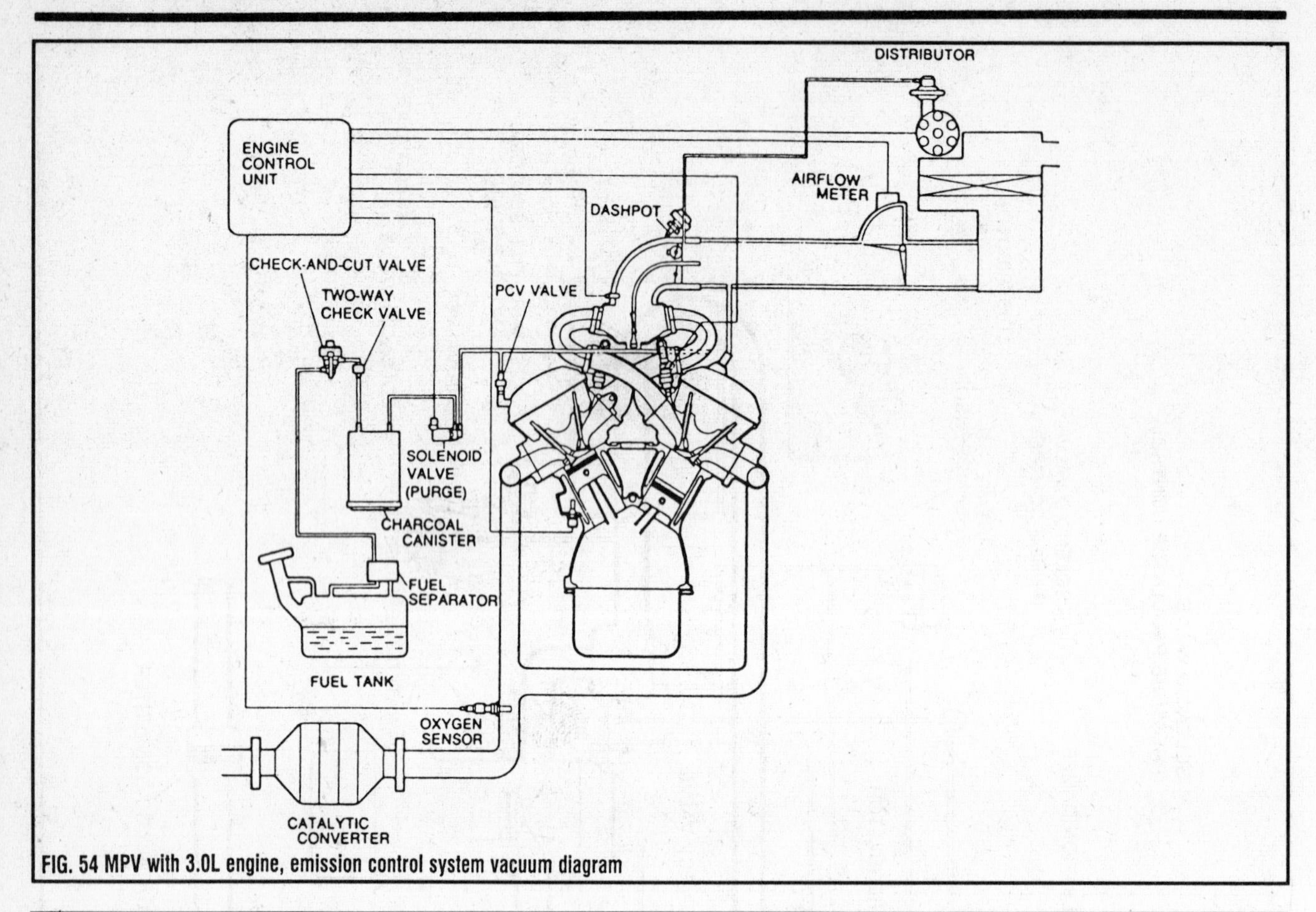

FIG. 54 MPV with 3.0L engine, emission control system vacuum diagram

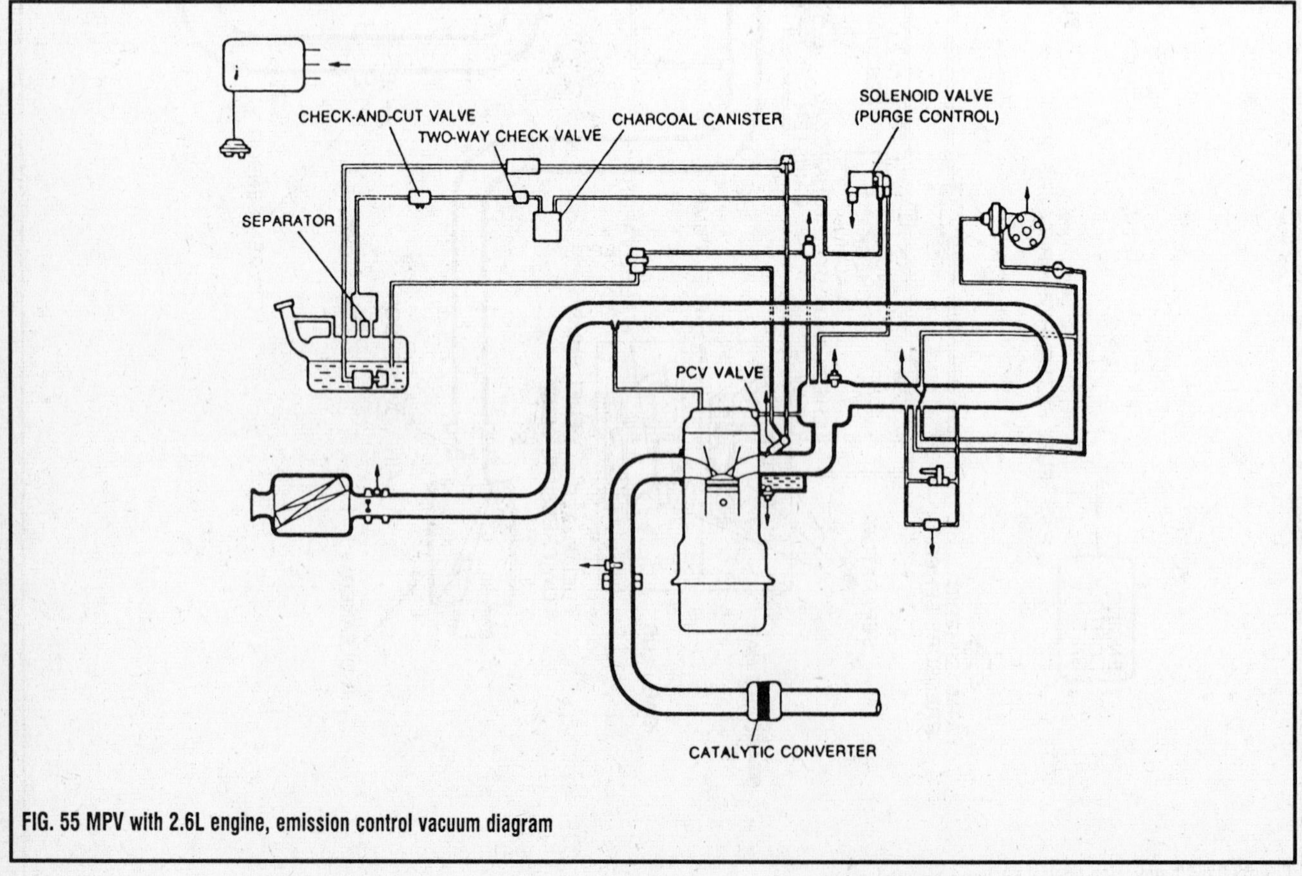

FIG. 55 MPV with 2.6L engine, emission control vacuum diagram

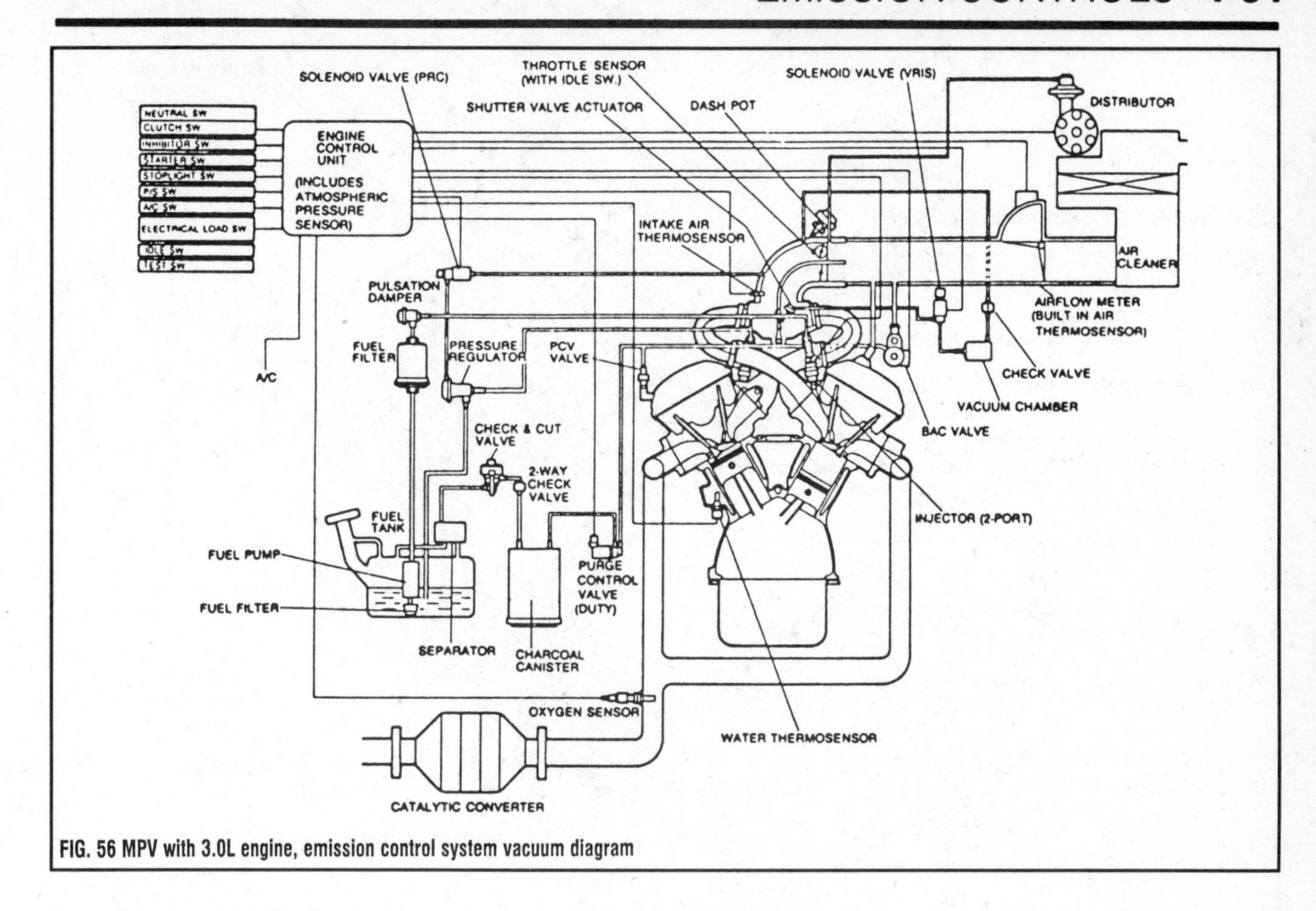

FIG. 56 MPV with 3.0L engine, emission control system vacuum diagram

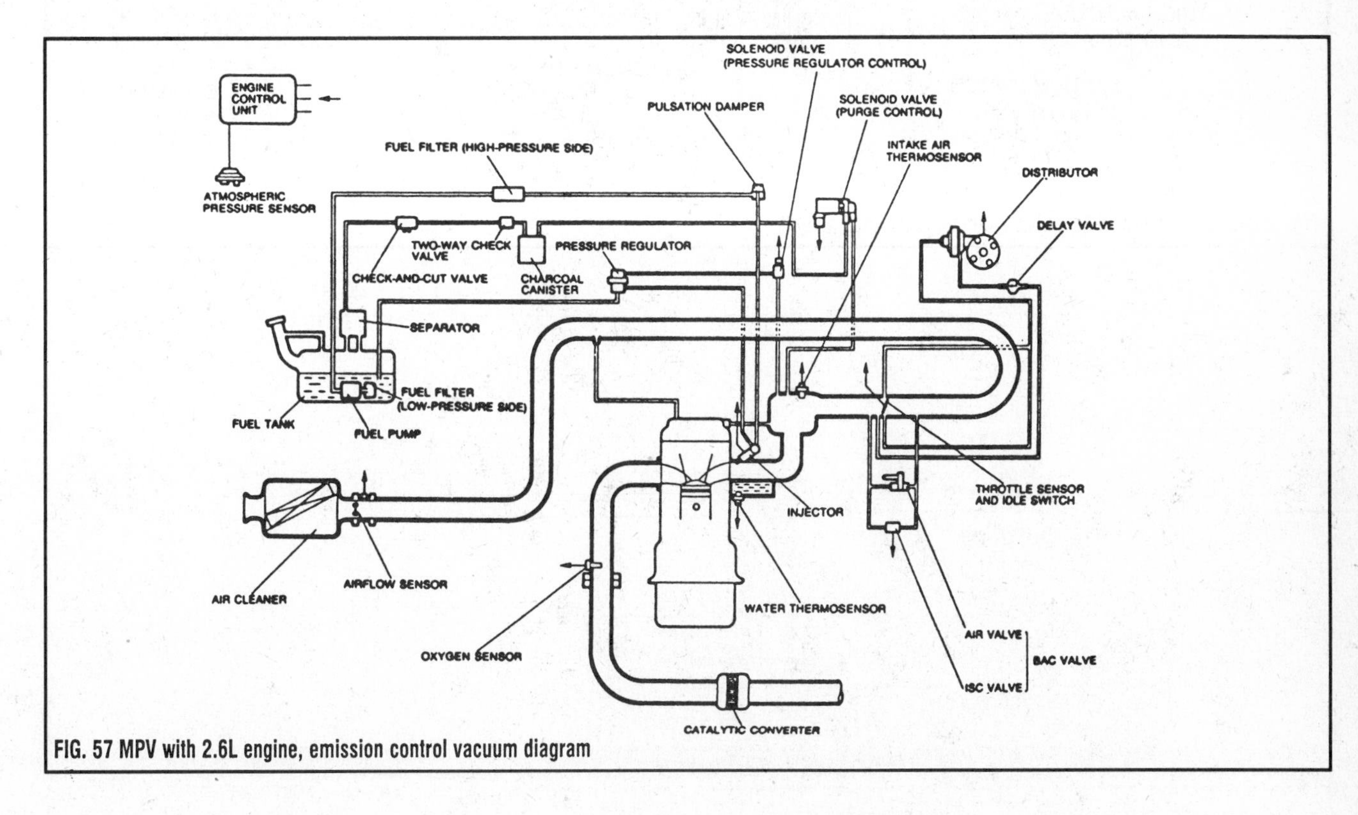

FIG. 57 MPV with 2.6L engine, emission control vacuum diagram

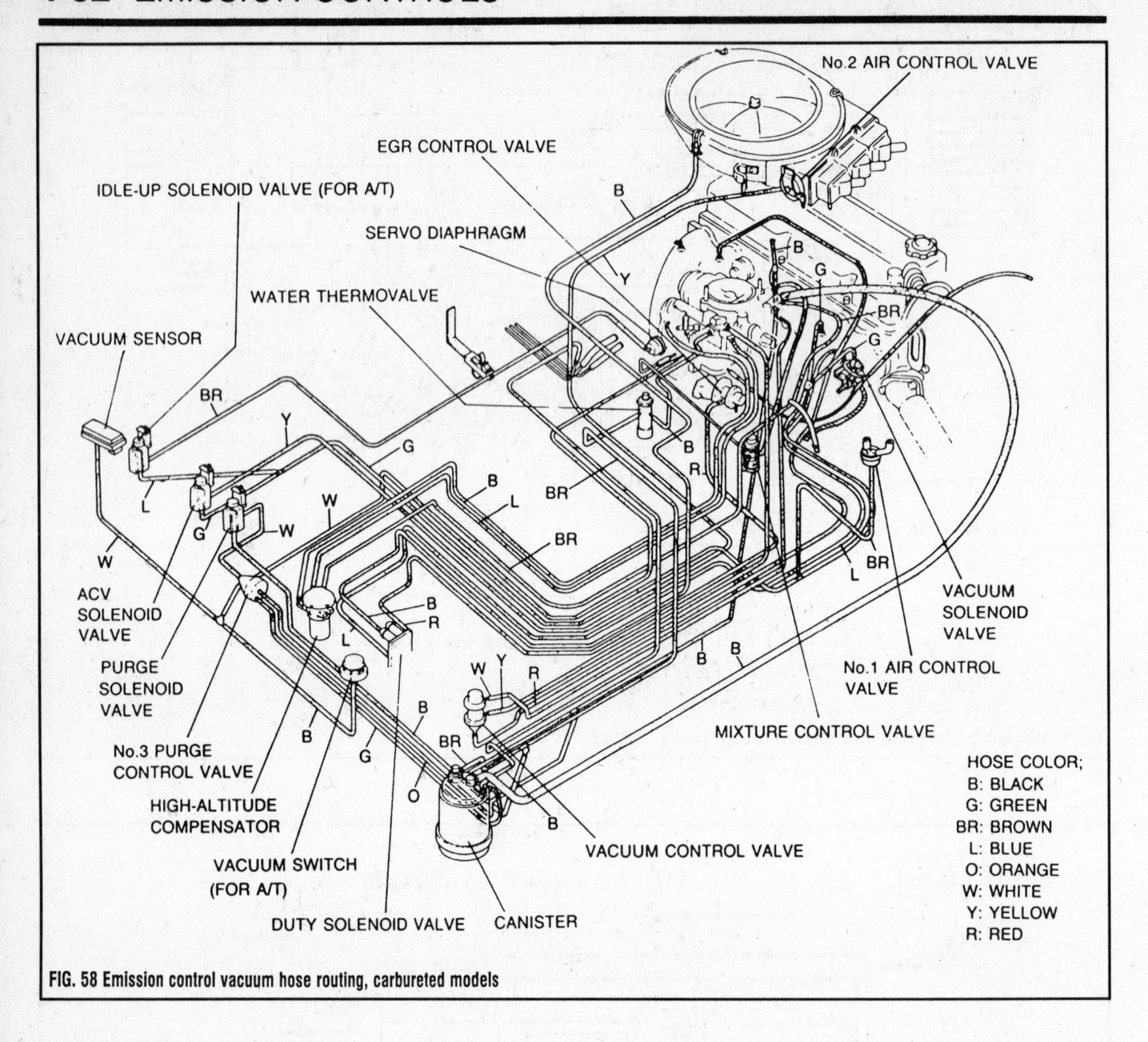

FIG. 58 Emission control vacuum hose routing, carbureted models

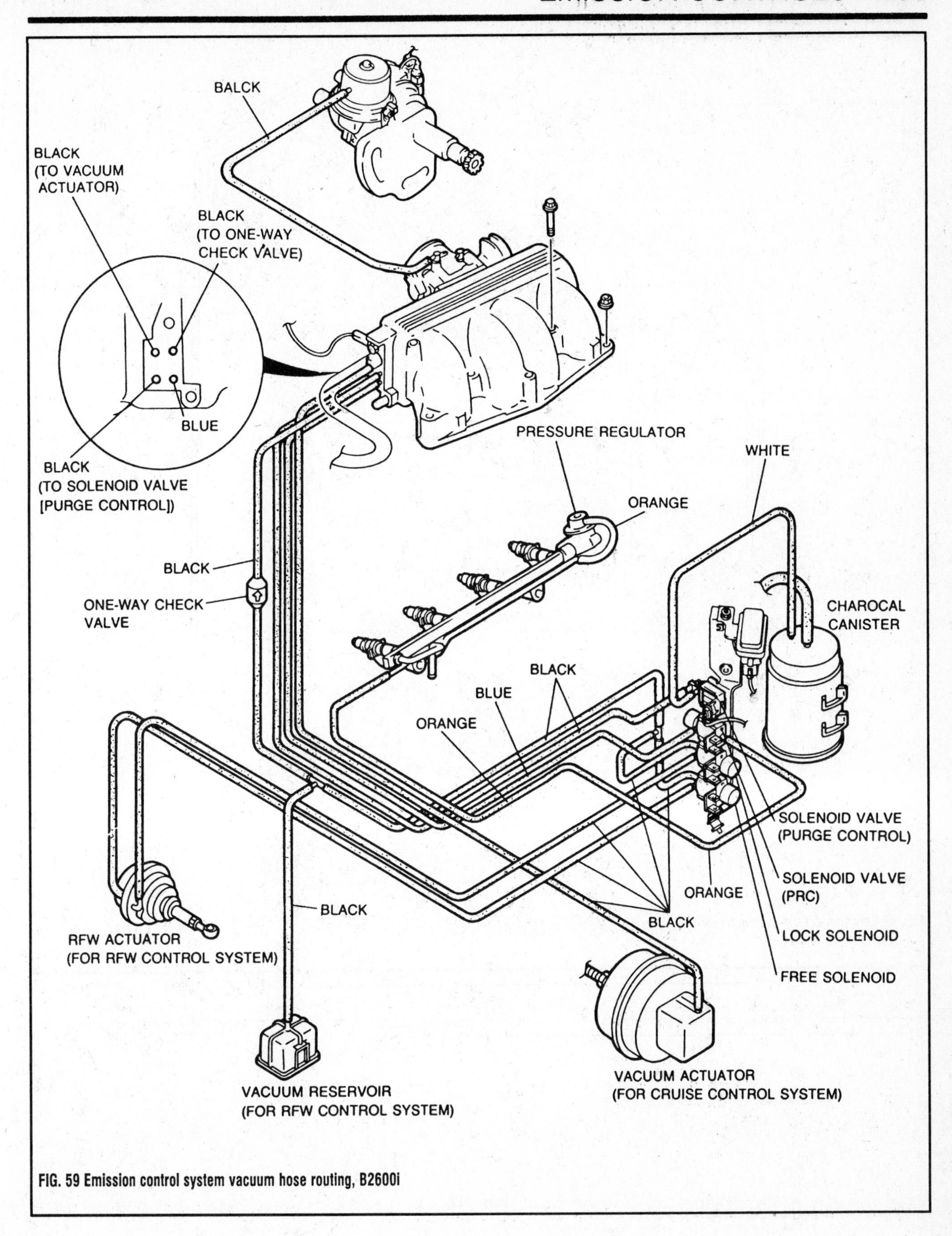

FIG. 59 Emission control system vacuum hose routing, B2600i

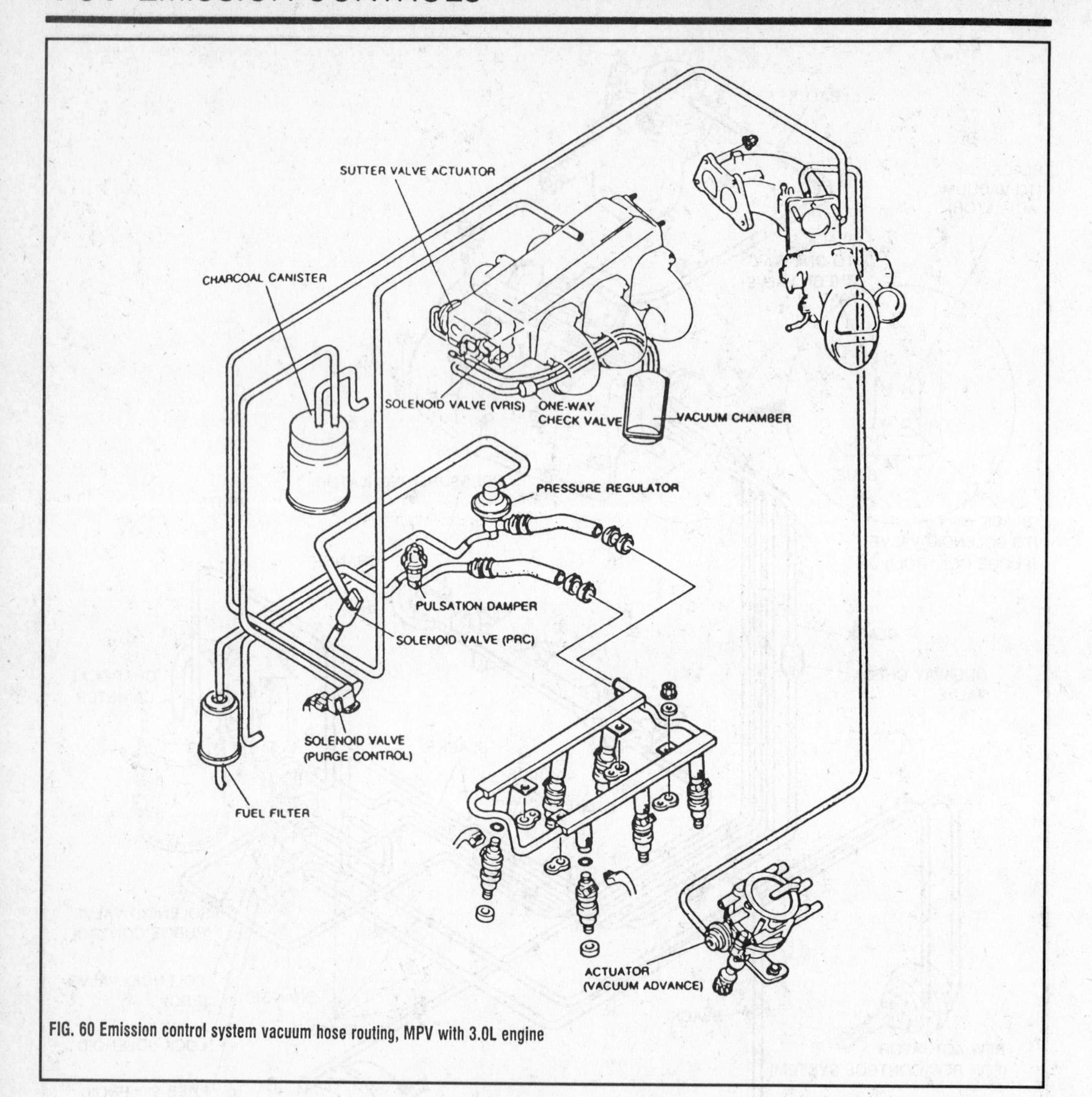

FIG. 60 Emission control system vacuum hose routing, MPV with 3.0L engine

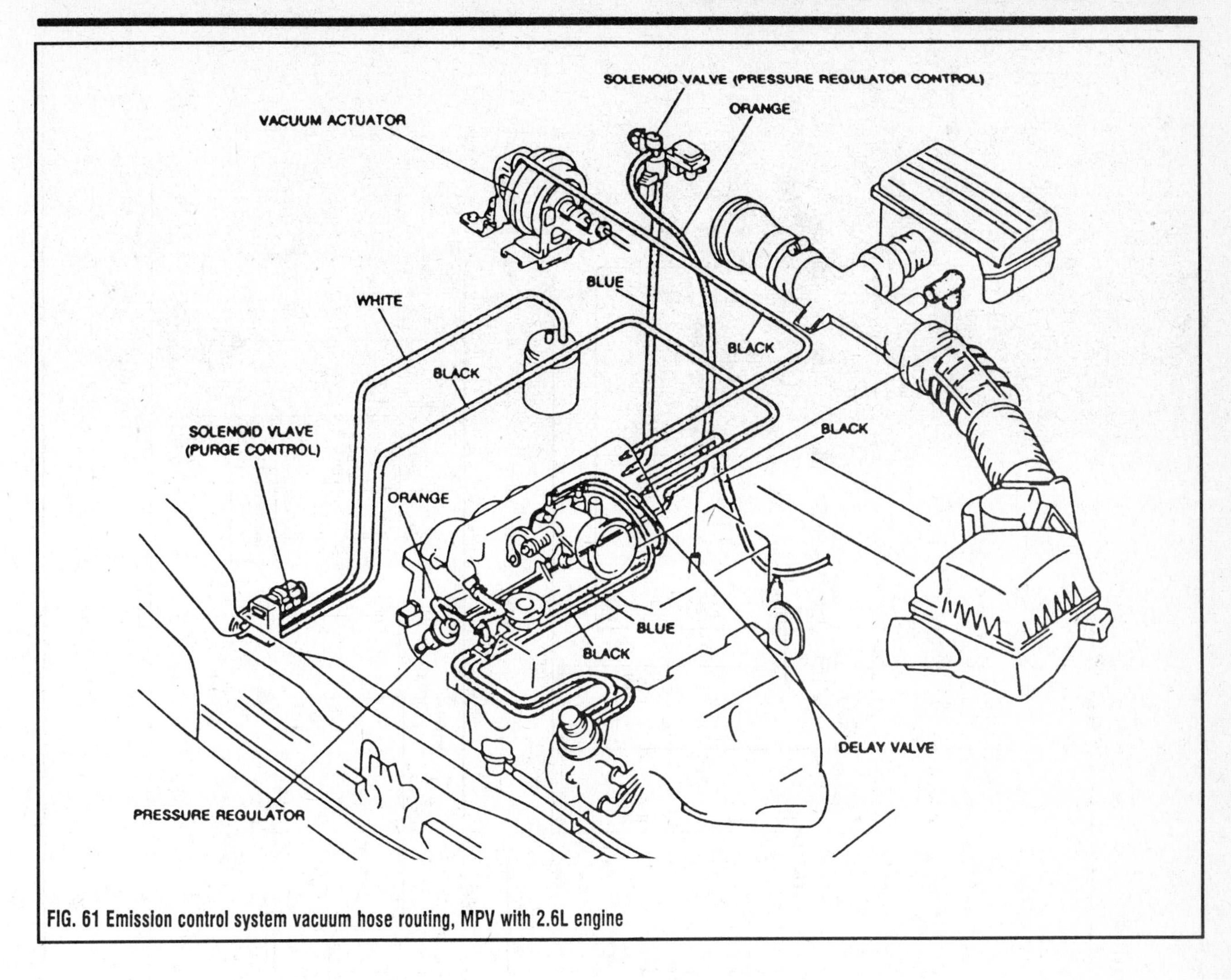

FIG. 61 Emission control system vacuum hose routing, MPV with 2.6L engine

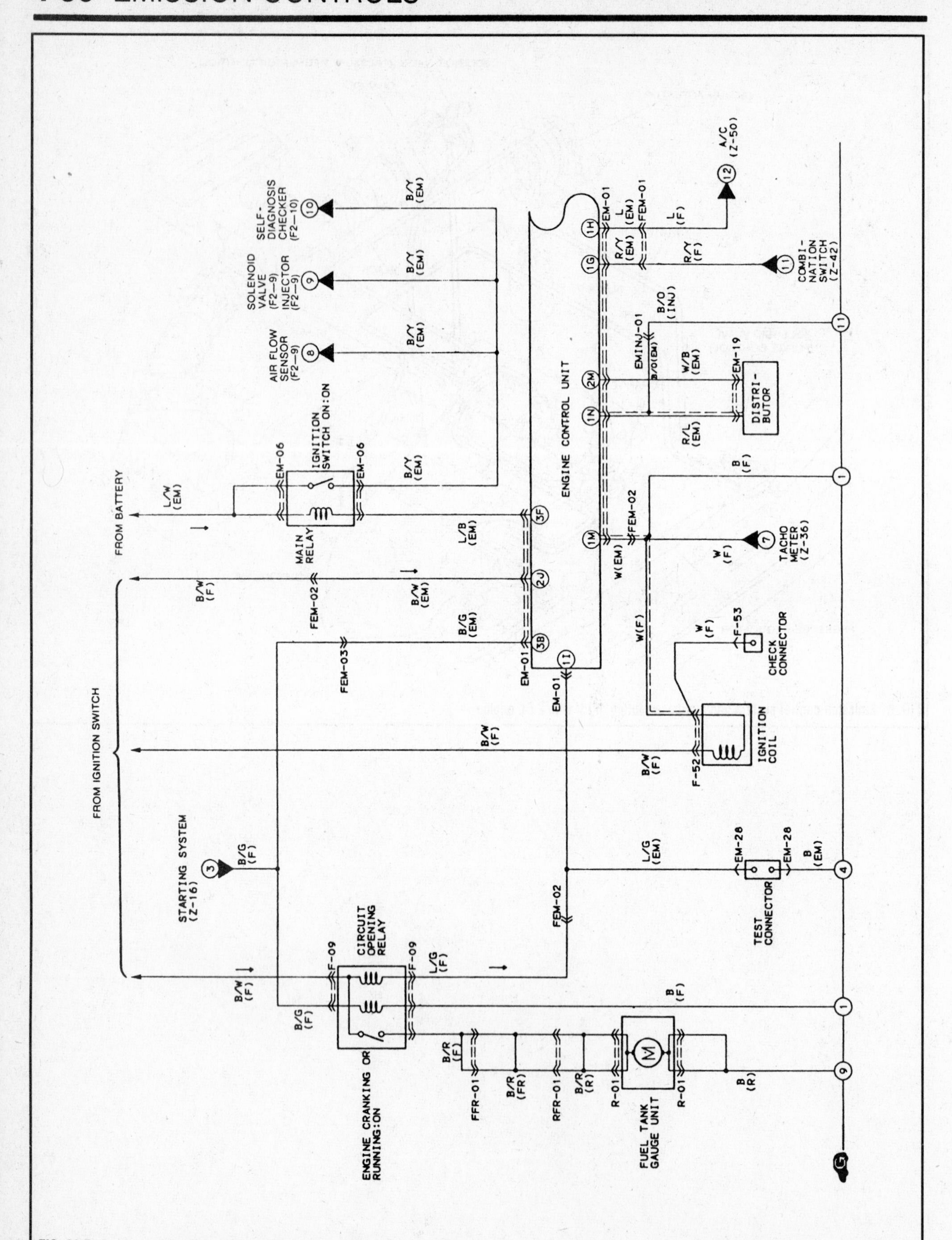

FIG. 62 Emission control system electrical circuit, B2600i

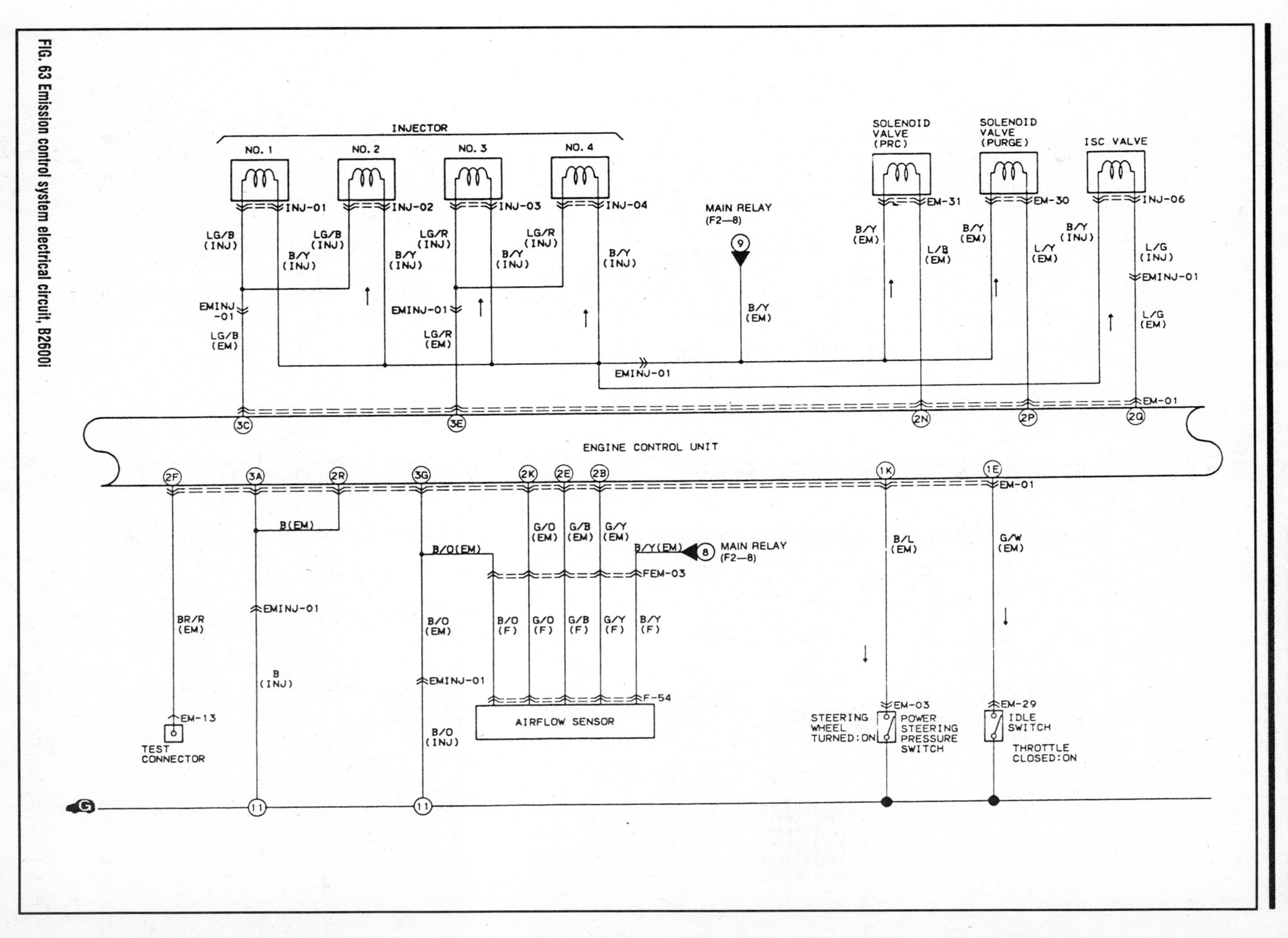

FIG. 63 Emission control system electrical circuit, B2600i

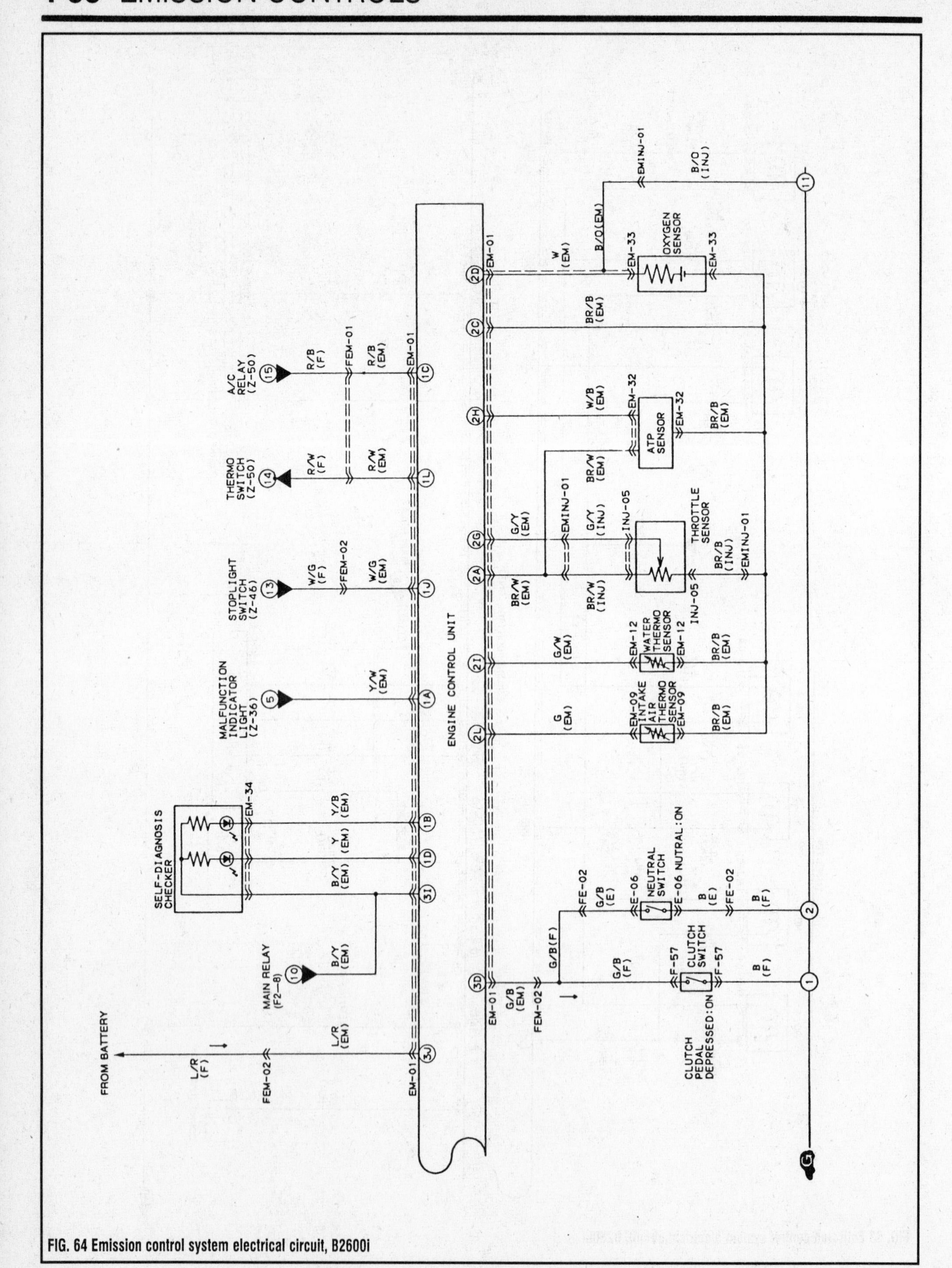

FIG. 64 Emission control system electrical circuit, B2600i

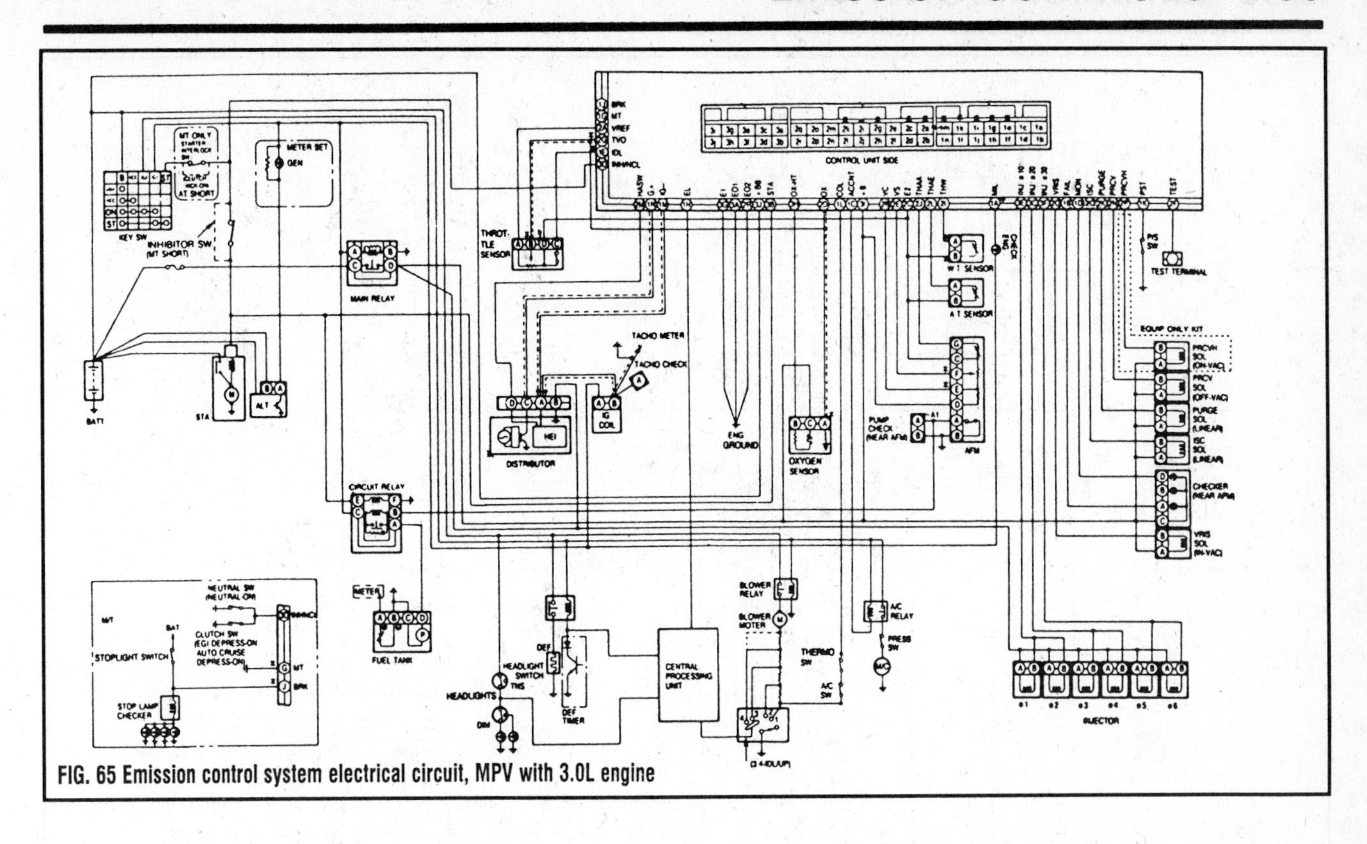

FIG. 65 Emission control system electrical circuit, MPV with 3.0L engine

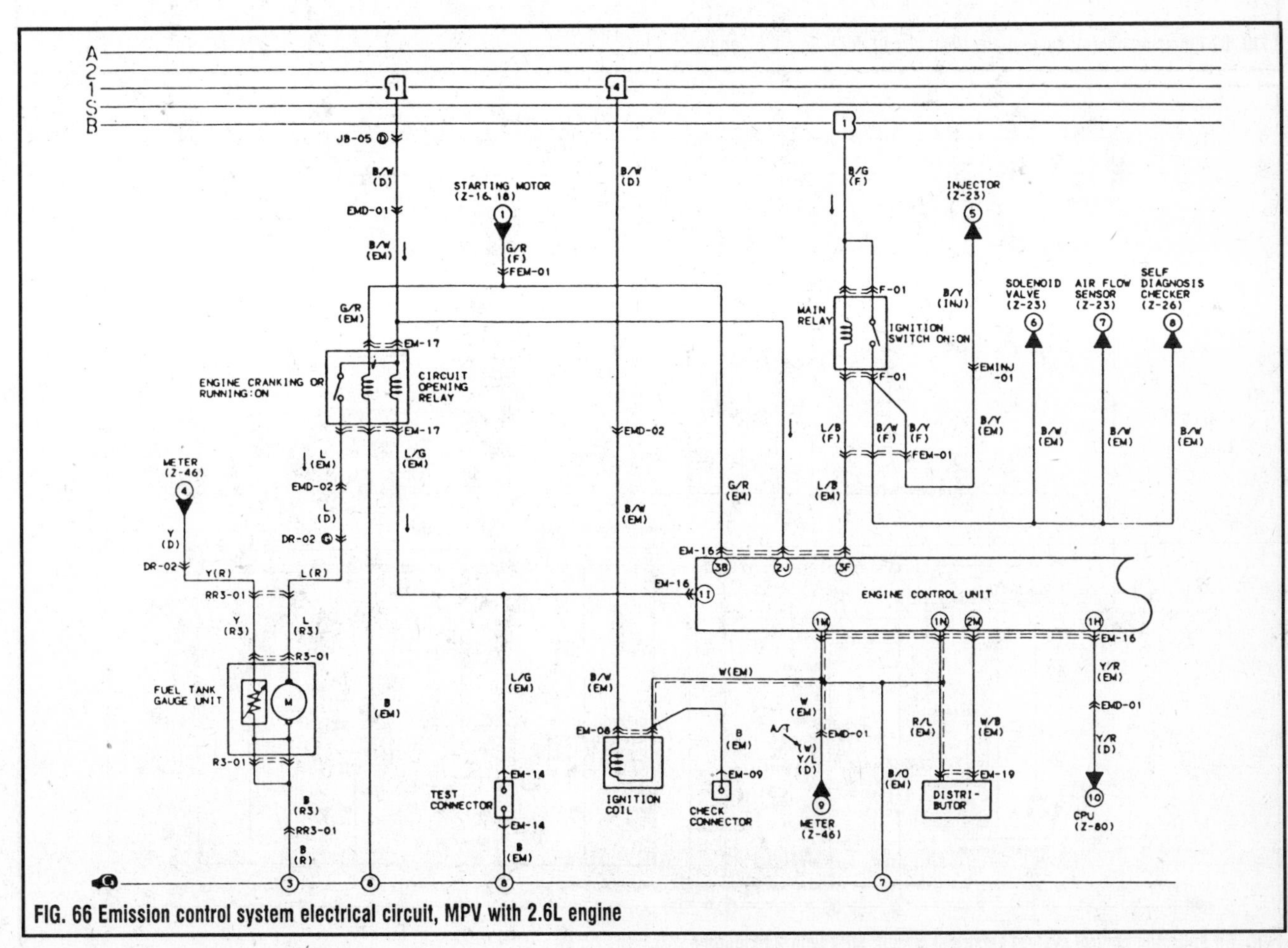

FIG. 66 Emission control system electrical circuit, MPV with 2.6L engine

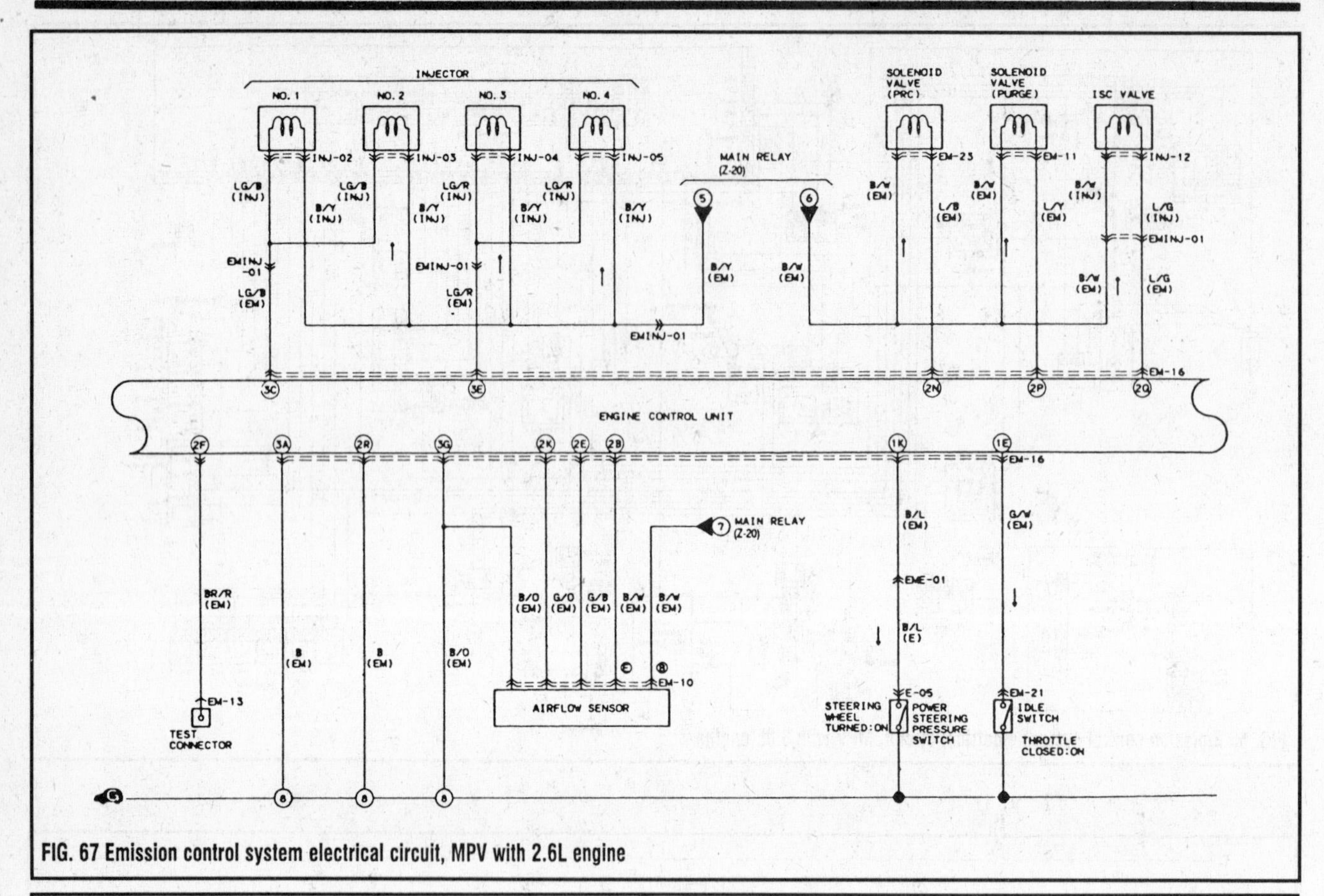
FIG. 67 Emission control system electrical circuit, MPV with 2.6L engine

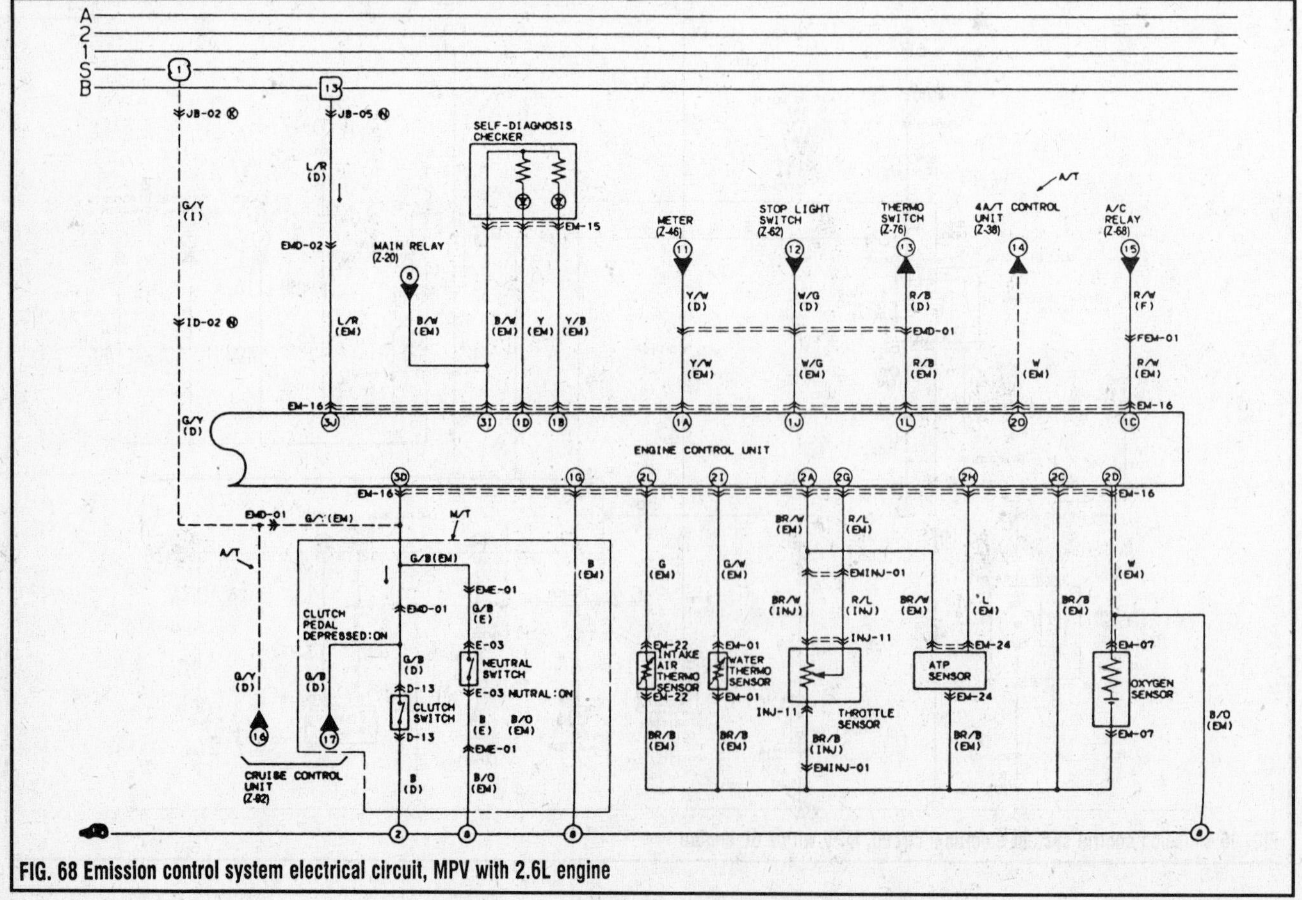
FIG. 68 Emission control system electrical circuit, MPV with 2.6L engine

IMPORTANT VEHICLE INFORMATION — mazda Mazda Motor Corporation — RENSEIGNEMENTS IMPORTANTS SUR LE VÉHICULE

Catalyst / Catalyseur

This vehicle is equipped with EEC, EFI and DIS systems. Engine idle speed, idle mixture, and ignition timing are not adjustable. See Engine/Emissions Diagnosis Shop Manual for additional information.

To check engine timing set parking brake and block wheels. Engine must be at normal operating temperature, transmission in neutral, and accessories off.

(1) Turn off engine.
(2) Disconnect the in-line Spout Connector (=▯◁).
(3) Re-start previously warmed-up engine.
(4) Verify that the ignition timing is 10° BTDC. If not see shop manual.
(5) Turn engine off and restore electrical connection.

Use SAE 5W-30 Oil API Service SG - Energy Conserving II.

Ce véhicule est équipé des systèmes EEC*, EFI* et DIS*. Le régime de ralenti, le mélange de ralenti et le calage de l'allumage ne sont pas réglables. Pour plus de détails, voir le Manuel de diagnostic du moteur et des disp. antipollution.

Pour vérifier l'allumage, serrer le frein de stationnement et bloquer les roues. Le moteur doit être normalement chaud, la BV au point mort et les accessoires hors circuit.

(1) Arrêter le moteur.
(2) Débrancher le connecteur (=▯◁) intercalé dans le circuit de déclenchement de l'étincelle.
(3) Redémarrer le moteur préalablement réchauffé.
(4) Confirmer un calage de 10° avant PMH. Si non conforme, voir le manuel de réparation.
(5) Arrêter le moteur et rebrancher le connecteur.

* EEC=Commande électronique du moteur
EFI=Injection électronique
DIS=Allumage sans distributeur

Huile préconisée: SAE 5W-30, SG, - Économie d'énergie II -.

F2AE-9C485- HHF	4.0L	Spark Plug / *Bougies:* ZZL0-18-110	Gap / *Électrodes:* .052-.056

VACUUM HOSE ROUTING — *SCHÉMA DE DÉPRESSION*

TO BRAKE BOOSTER; MAN VAC; PCV; MAN VAC; A/CL BI MET; FPR; THROTTLE BODY; A/CL DV; MV; TO FUEL TANK; CPRV; CAN; FRONT OF VEHICLE

FIG. 69 Vacuum hose routing and calibration label 2-57B-R00, Navajo 4.0L

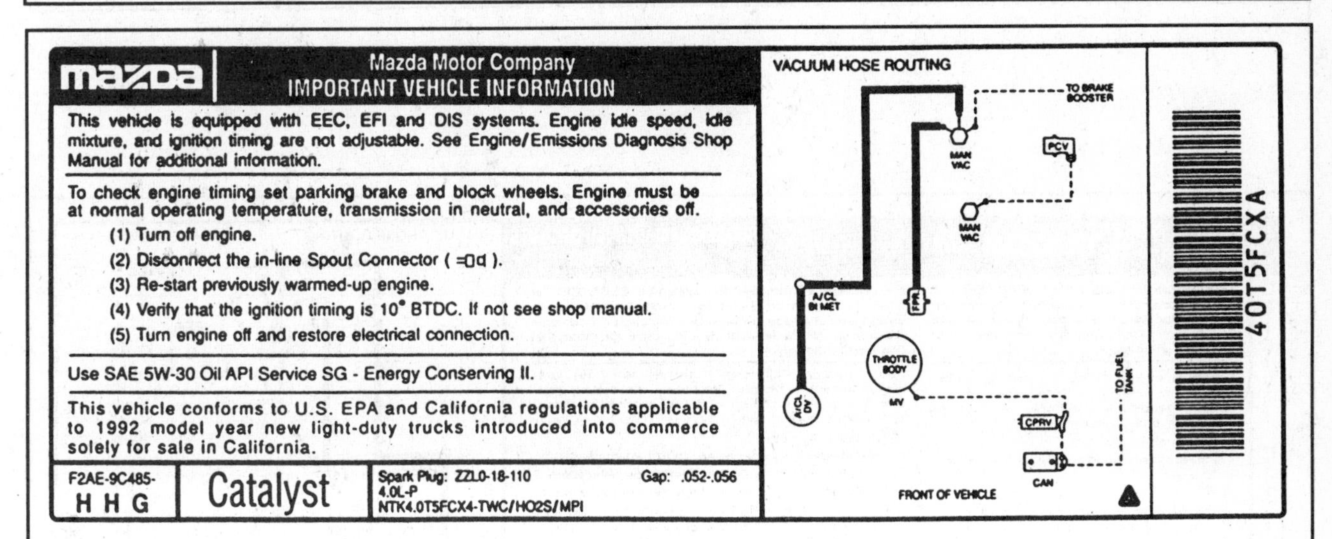
mazda | Mazda Motor Company — IMPORTANT VEHICLE INFORMATION

This vehicle is equipped with EEC, EFI and DIS systems. Engine idle speed, idle mixture, and ignition timing are not adjustable. See Engine/Emissions Diagnosis Shop Manual for additional information.

To check engine timing set parking brake and block wheels. Engine must be at normal operating temperature, transmission in neutral, and accessories off.

(1) Turn off engine.
(2) Disconnect the in-line Spout Connector (=▯◁).
(3) Re-start previously warmed-up engine.
(4) Verify that the ignition timing is 10° BTDC. If not see shop manual.
(5) Turn engine off and restore electrical connection.

Use SAE 5W-30 Oil API Service SG - Energy Conserving II.

This vehicle conforms to U.S. EPA and California regulations applicable to 1992 model year new light-duty trucks introduced into commerce solely for sale in California.

F2AE-9C485- HHG	Catalyst	Spark Plug: ZZL0-18-110 4.0L-P NTK4.0T5FCX4-TWC/HO2S/MPI	Gap: .052-.056

FIG. 70 Vacuum hose routing and calibration label 2-57B-R00, Navajo 4.0L

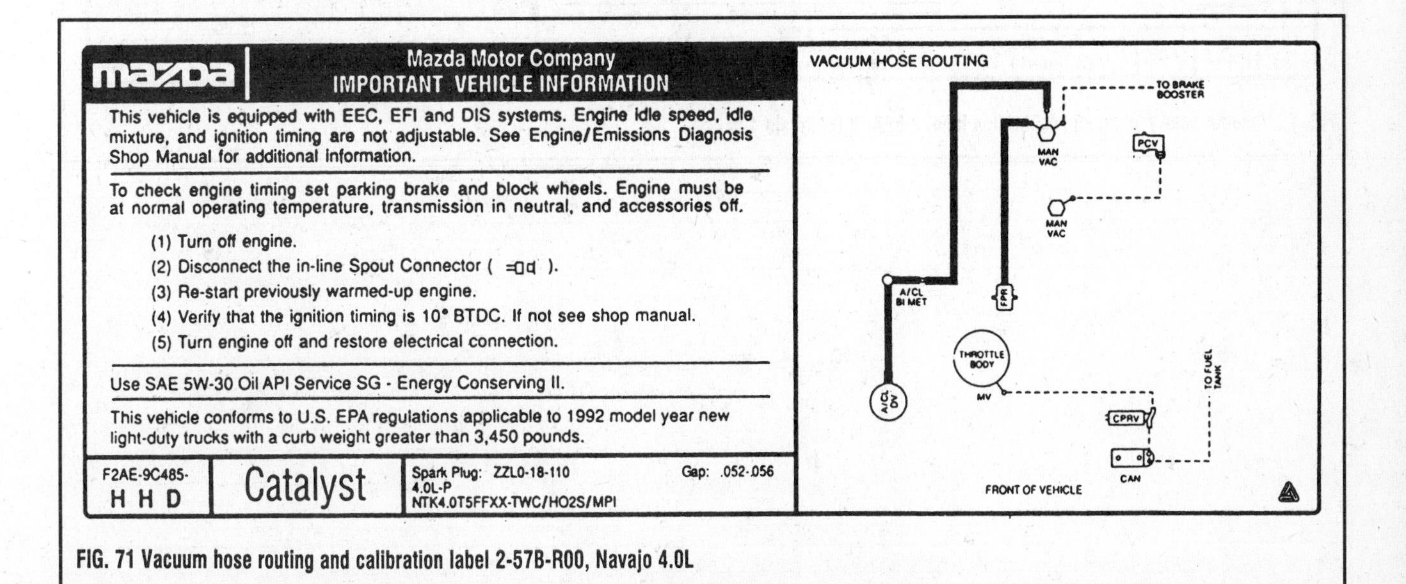
mazda | Mazda Motor Company — IMPORTANT VEHICLE INFORMATION

This vehicle is equipped with EEC, EFI and DIS systems. Engine idle speed, idle mixture, and ignition timing are not adjustable. See Engine/Emissions Diagnosis Shop Manual for additional information.

To check engine timing set parking brake and block wheels. Engine must be at normal operating temperature, transmission in neutral, and accessories off.

(1) Turn off engine.
(2) Disconnect the in-line Spout Connector (=▯◁).
(3) Re-start previously warmed-up engine.
(4) Verify that the ignition timing is 10° BTDC. If not see shop manual.
(5) Turn engine off and restore electrical connection.

Use SAE 5W-30 Oil API Service SG - Energy Conserving II.

This vehicle conforms to U.S. EPA regulations applicable to 1992 model year new light-duty trucks with a curb weight greater than 3,450 pounds.

F2AE-9C485- HHD	Catalyst	Spark Plug: ZZL0-18-110 4.0L-P NTK4.0T5FFXX-TWC/HO2S/MPI	Gap: .052-.056

FIG. 71 Vacuum hose routing and calibration label 2-57B-R00, Navajo 4.0L

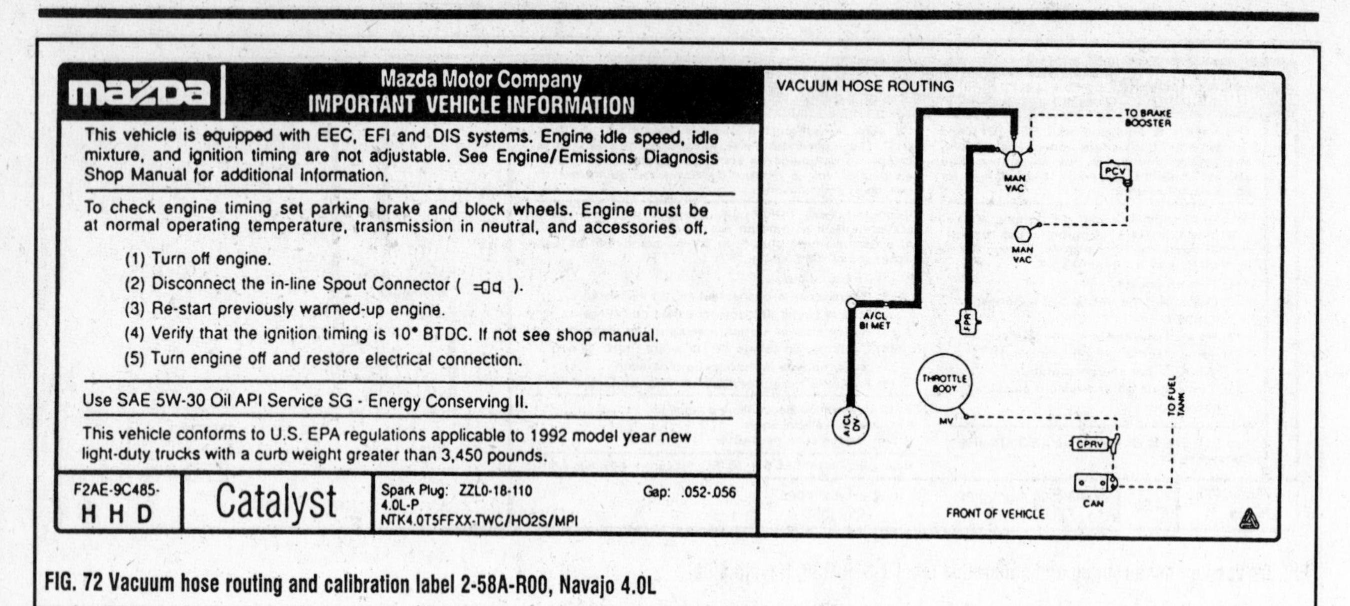

mazda | Mazda Motor Company
IMPORTANT VEHICLE INFORMATION

This vehicle is equipped with EEC, EFI and DIS systems. Engine idle speed, idle mixture, and ignition timing are not adjustable. See Engine/Emissions Diagnosis Shop Manual for additional information.

To check engine timing set parking brake and block wheels. Engine must be at normal operating temperature, transmission in neutral, and accessories off.

(1) Turn off engine.
(2) Disconnect the in-line Spout Connector (=▯◁).
(3) Re-start previously warmed-up engine.
(4) Verify that the ignition timing is 10° BTDC. If not see shop manual.
(5) Turn engine off and restore electrical connection.

Use SAE 5W-30 Oil API Service SG - Energy Conserving II.

This vehicle conforms to U.S. EPA regulations applicable to 1992 model year new light-duty trucks with a curb weight greater than 3,450 pounds.

F2AE-9C485- HHD	Catalyst	Spark Plug: ZZL0-18-110 4.0L-P NTK4.0T5FFXX-TWC/HO2S/MPI	Gap: .052-.056

FIG. 72 Vacuum hose routing and calibration label 2-58A-R00, Navajo 4.0L

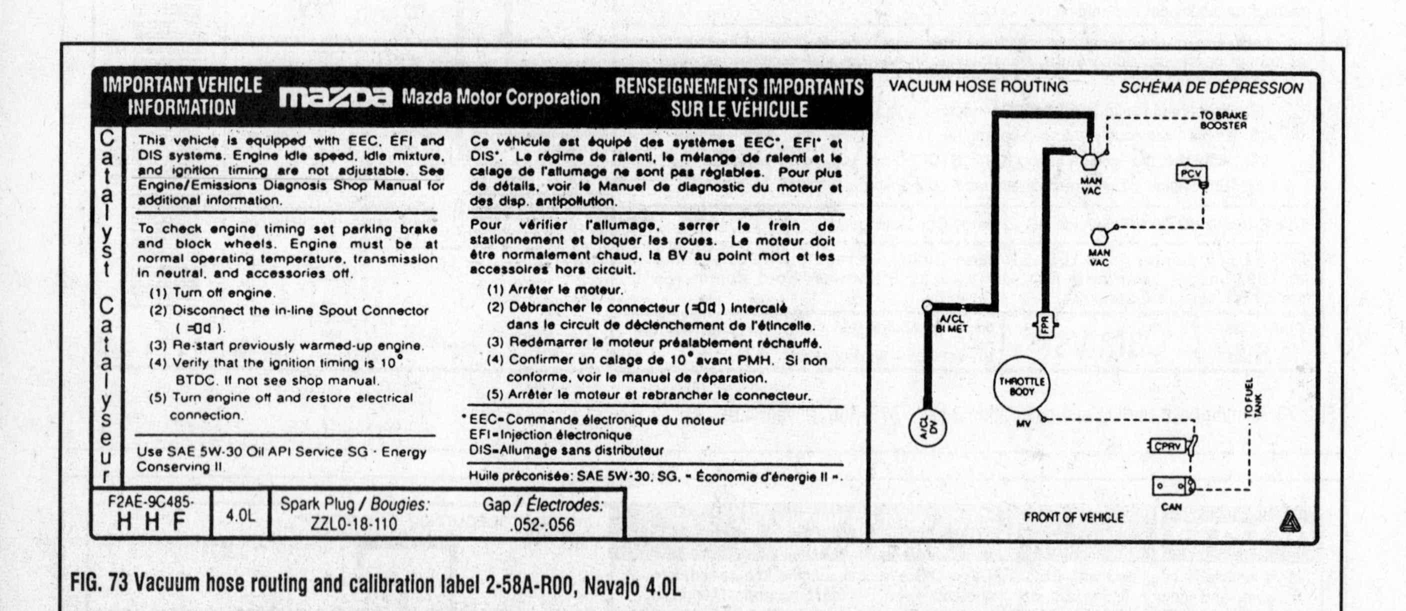

IMPORTANT VEHICLE INFORMATION | mazda Mazda Motor Corporation | RENSEIGNEMENTS IMPORTANTS SUR LE VÉHICULE

Catalyst Catalyseur

This vehicle is equipped with EEC, EFI and DIS systems. Engine idle speed, idle mixture, and ignition timing are not adjustable. See Engine/Emissions Diagnosis Shop Manual for additional information.

To check engine timing set parking brake and block wheels. Engine must be at normal operating temperature, transmission in neutral, and accessories off.

(1) Turn off engine.
(2) Disconnect the in-line Spout Connector (=▯◁).
(3) Re-start previously warmed-up engine.
(4) Verify that the ignition timing is 10° BTDC. If not see shop manual.
(5) Turn engine off and restore electrical connection.

Use SAE 5W-30 Oil API Service SG - Energy Conserving II.

Ce véhicule est équipé des systèmes EEC*, EFI* et DIS*. Le régime de ralenti, le mélange de ralenti et le calage de l'allumage ne sont pas réglables. Pour plus de détails, voir le Manuel de diagnostic du moteur et des disp. antipollution.

Pour vérifier l'allumage, serrer le frein de stationnement et bloquer les roues. Le moteur doit être normalement chaud, la BV au point mort et les accessoires hors circuit.

(1) Arrêter le moteur.
(2) Débrancher le connecteur (=▯◁) intercalé dans le circuit de déclenchement de l'étincelle.
(3) Redémarrer le moteur préalablement réchauffé.
(4) Confirmer un calage de 10° avant PMH. Si non conforme, voir le manuel de réparation.
(5) Arrêter le moteur et rebrancher le connecteur.

* EEC=Commande électronique du moteur
EFI=Injection électronique
DIS=Allumage sans distributeur

Huile préconisée: SAE 5W-30, SG, - Économie d'énergie II -.

F2AE-9C485- HHF	4.0L	Spark Plug / Bougies: ZZL0-18-110	Gap / Électrodes: .052-.056

FIG. 73 Vacuum hose routing and calibration label 2-58A-R00, Navajo 4.0L

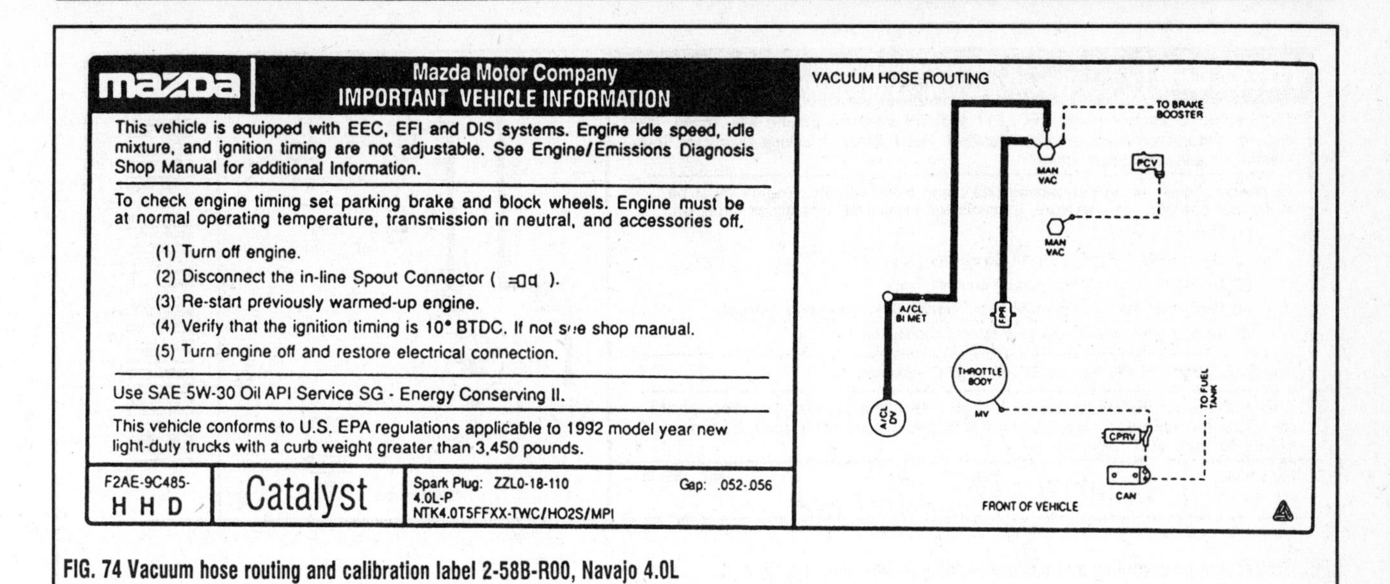

mazda | Mazda Motor Company
IMPORTANT VEHICLE INFORMATION

This vehicle is equipped with EEC, EFI and DIS systems. Engine idle speed, idle mixture, and ignition timing are not adjustable. See Engine/Emissions Diagnosis Shop Manual for additional Information.

To check engine timing set parking brake and block wheels. Engine must be at normal operating temperature, transmission in neutral, and accessories off.

(1) Turn off engine.
(2) Disconnect the in-line Spout Connector (=0d).
(3) Re-start previously warmed-up engine.
(4) Verify that the ignition timing is 10° BTDC. If not see shop manual.
(5) Turn engine off and restore electrical connection.

Use SAE 5W-30 Oil API Service SG - Energy Conserving II.

This vehicle conforms to U.S. EPA regulations applicable to 1992 model year new light-duty trucks with a curb weight greater than 3,450 pounds.

F2AE-9C485-
H H D

Catalyst

Spark Plug: ZZL0-18-110
4.0L-P
NTK4.0T5FFXX-TWC/HO2S/MPI

Gap: .052-.056

FIG. 74 Vacuum hose routing and calibration label 2-58B-R00, Navajo 4.0L

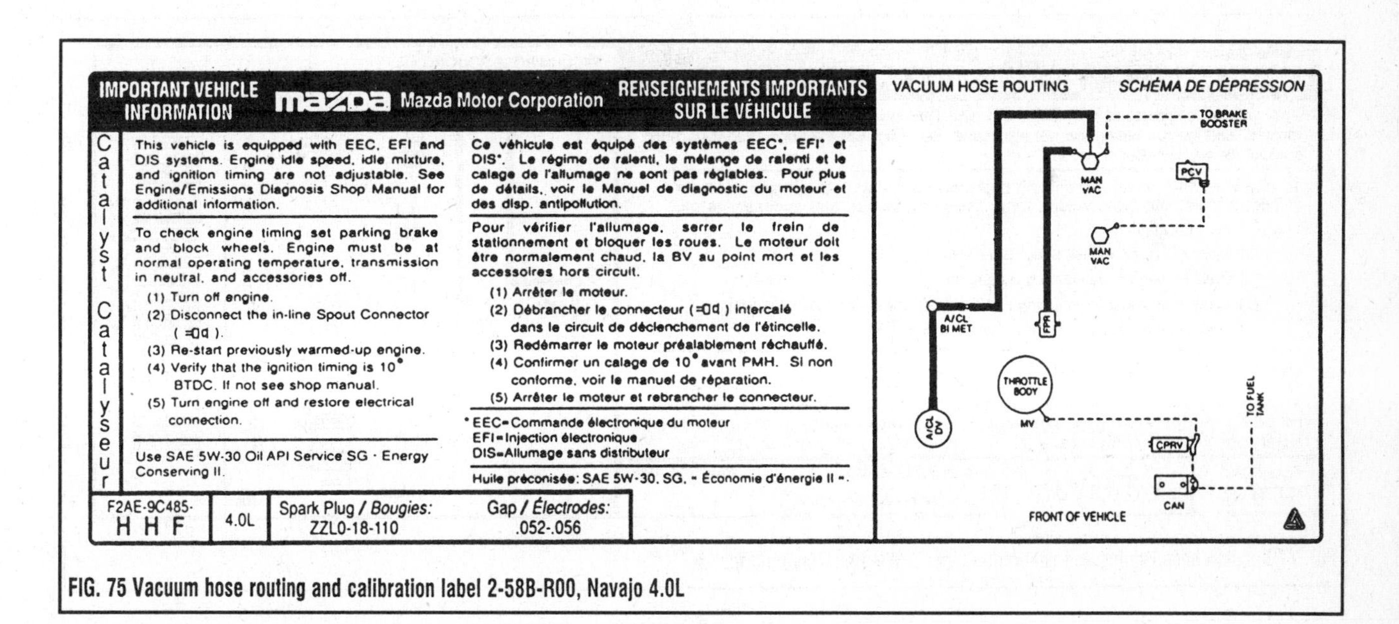

IMPORTANT VEHICLE INFORMATION | mazda Mazda Motor Corporation | RENSEIGNEMENTS IMPORTANTS SUR LE VÉHICULE

Catalyst Catalyseur

This vehicle is equipped with EEC, EFI and DIS systems. Engine idle speed, idle mixture, and ignition timing are not adjustable. See Engine/Emissions Diagnosis Shop Manual for additional information.

To check engine timing set parking brake and block wheels. Engine must be at normal operating temperature, transmission in neutral, and accessories off.

(1) Turn off engine.
(2) Disconnect the in-line Spout Connector (=0d).
(3) Re-start previously warmed-up engine.
(4) Verify that the ignition timing is 10° BTDC. If not see shop manual.
(5) Turn engine off and restore electrical connection.

Use SAE 5W-30 Oil API Service SG - Energy Conserving II.

Ce véhicule est équipé des systèmes EEC*, EFI* et DIS*. Le régime de ralenti, le mélange de ralenti et le calage de l'allumage ne sont pas réglables. Pour plus de détails, voir le Manuel de diagnostic du moteur et des disp. antipollution.

Pour vérifier l'allumage, serrer le frein de stationnement et bloquer les roues. Le moteur doit être normalement chaud, la BV au point mort et les accessoires hors circuit.

(1) Arrêter le moteur.
(2) Débrancher le connecteur (=0d) intercalé dans le circuit de déclenchement de l'étincelle.
(3) Redémarrer le moteur préalablement réchauffé.
(4) Confirmer un calage de 10° avant PMH. Si non conforme, voir le manuel de réparation.
(5) Arrêter le moteur et rebrancher le connecteur.

* EEC=Commande électronique du moteur
EFI=Injection électronique
DIS=Allumage sans distributeur

Huile préconisée: SAE 5W-30, SG, « Économie d'énergie II ».

F2AE-9C485-
H H F

4.0L

Spark Plug / *Bougies:*
ZZL0-18-110

Gap / *Électrodes:*
.052-.056

FIG. 75 Vacuum hose routing and calibration label 2-58B-R00, Navajo 4.0L

mazda | Mazda Motor Company
IMPORTANT VEHICLE INFORMATION

This vehicle is equipped with EEC, EFI and DIS systems. Engine idle speed, idle mixture, and ignition timing are not adjustable. See Engine/Emissions Diagnosis Shop Manual for additional information.

To check engine timing set parking brake and block wheels. Engine must be at normal operating temperature, transmission in neutral, and accessories off.

(1) Turn off engine.
(2) Disconnect the in-line Spout Connector (=▯d).
(3) Re-start previously warmed-up engine.
(4) Verify that the ignition timing is 10° BTDC. If not see shop manual.
(5) Turn engine off and restore electrical connection.

Use SAE 5W-30 Oil API Service SG - Energy Conserving II.

This vehicle conforms to U.S. EPA and California regulations applicable to 1992 model year new light-duty trucks introduced into commerce solely for sale in California.

F2AE-9C485- H H G | Catalyst | Spark Plug: ZZL0-18-110 Gap: .052-.056 4.0L-P NTK4.0T5FCX4-TWC/HO2S/MPI

VACUUM HOSE ROUTING

TO BRAKE BOOSTER
PCV
MAN VAC
MAN VAC
A/CL BI MET
FPR
THROTTLE BODY
MV
TO FUEL TANK
A/CL DV
CPRV
CAN
FRONT OF VEHICLE

40T5FCXA

FIG. 76 Vacuum hose routing and calibration label 2-58P-R00, Navajo 4.0L

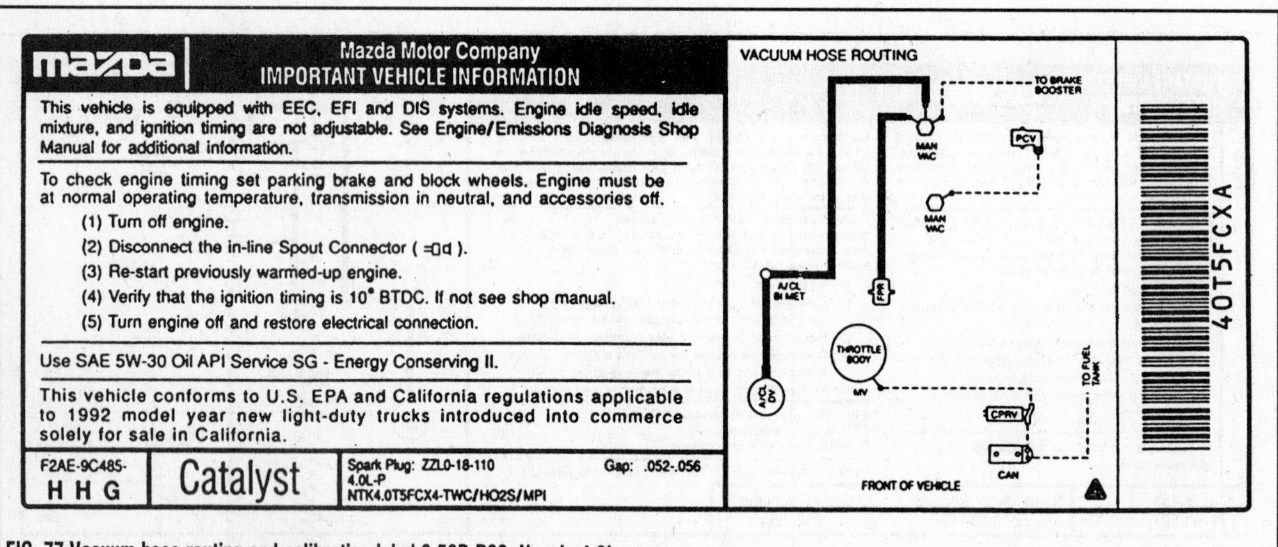

FIG. 77 Vacuum hose routing and calibration label 2-58P-R00, Navajo 4.0L

5

FUEL SYSTEM

SERVICE PRECAUTIONS

Safety is the most important factor when performing not only fuel system maintenance but any type of maintenance. Failure to conduct maintenance and repairs in a safe manner may result in serious personal injury or death. Maintenance and testing of the vehicle's fuel system components can be accomplished safely and effectively by adhering to the following rules and guidelines.

- To avoid the possibility of fire and personal injury, always disconnect the negative battery cable unless the repair or test procedure requires that battery voltage be applied.
- Always relieve the fuel system pressure prior to disconnecting any fuel system component (injector, fuel rail, pressure regulator, etc.), fitting or fuel line connection. Exercise extreme caution whenever relieving fuel system pressure to avoid exposing skin, face and eyes to fuel spray. Please be advised that fuel under pressure may penetrate the skin or any part of the body that it contacts.
- Always place a shop towel or cloth around the fitting or connection prior to loosening to absorb any excess fuel due to spillage. Ensure that all fuel spillage (should it occur) is quickly removed from engine surfaces. Ensure that all fuel soaked cloths or towels are deposited into a suitable waste container.
- Always keep a dry chemical (Class B) fire extinguisher near the work area.
- Do not allow fuel spray or fuel vapors to come into contact with a spark or open flame.
- Always use a backup wrench when loosening and tightening fuel line connection fittings. This will prevent unnecessary stress and torsion to fuel line piping. Always follow the proper torque specifications.
- Always replace worn fuel fitting O-rings with new. Do not substitute fuel hose or equivalent where fuel pipe is installed.

CARBURETED FUEL SYSTEM

➧ SEE FIG. 1

Mechanical Fuel Pump

1987-88 2.2L engine with manual transmission use a mechanically driven fuel pump, mounted on the right side of the cylinder head, driven by the camshaft.

TESTING

1. Disconnect the negative battery cable.
2. Disconnect the fuel line from the carburetor.
3. Connect a fuel pressure gauge to the fuel line.
4. Disconnect the fuel return hose from the fuel pump and plug the fuel pump return outlet.
5. Connect the negative battery cable and start the engine.
6. Check the fuel pressure while the engine is idling. The fuel pressure should be 3.7–4.7 psi.
7. Replace the pump if the pressure is not as specified.
8. Shut off the engine and disconnect the negative battery cable. Remove the fuel pressure gauge and reconnect the fuel lines.
9. Connect the negative battery cable.

REMOVAL & INSTALLATION

1. Disconnect the negative battery cable.
2. Disconnect and plug the inlet, outlet and return hoses at the fuel pump.
3. Remove the fuel pump mounting bolts and remove the fuel pump, insulator and gaskets.

To install:

4. Clean all gasket mating surfaces.
5. Install new gaskets and the insulator and fuel pump. Install the mounting bolts and tighten to 14–19 ft. lbs. (19–25 Nm).
6. Unplug and connect the fuel lines.
7. Connect the negative battery cable, start the engine and check for leaks.

Electric Fuel Pump

TESTING

1. Turn the ignition switch **OFF** and disconnect the negative battery cable.
2. Disconnect the main fuel hose and connect a pressure gauge to it.
3. Connect the negative battery cable. Connect a jumper wire between the **B** and **D** terminals of the fuel pump control unit.
4. Turn the ignition switch **ON** and check the fuel pressure. It should be 2.8–3.6 psi.
5. If the fuel pressure is not as specified, replace the fuel pump.
6. Turn the ignition switch **OFF** and disconnect the negative battery cable.
7. Remove the fuel pressure gauge and reconnect the main fuel hose. Remove the jumper wire from the fuel pump control unit.
8. Connect the negative battery cable.

➡ The fuel pump is located inside the fuel tank, attached to the tank sending unit assembly.

REMOVAL & INSTALLATION

Pickup Models

1. Disconnect the negative battery cable.
2. Remove the fuel tank.
3. Remove any dirt that has accumulated around the sending unit/fuel pump assembly so it will not enter the fuel tank during removal and installation.
4. Remove the attaching screws and remove the sending unit/fuel pump assembly.
5. If necessary, disconnect the electrical connectors and the fuel hose and remove the pump from the sending unit assembly.

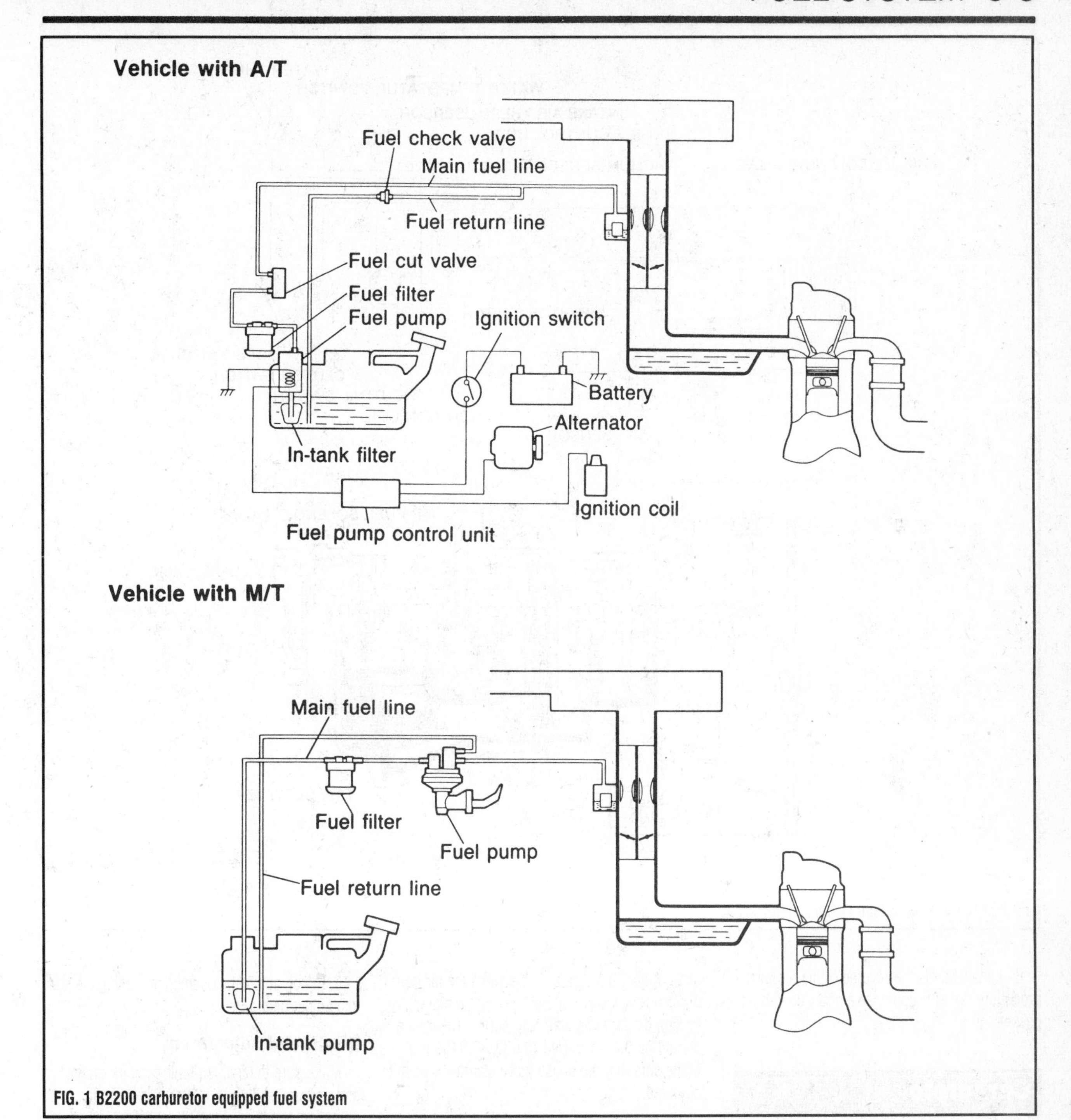

FIG. 1 B2200 carburetor equipped fuel system

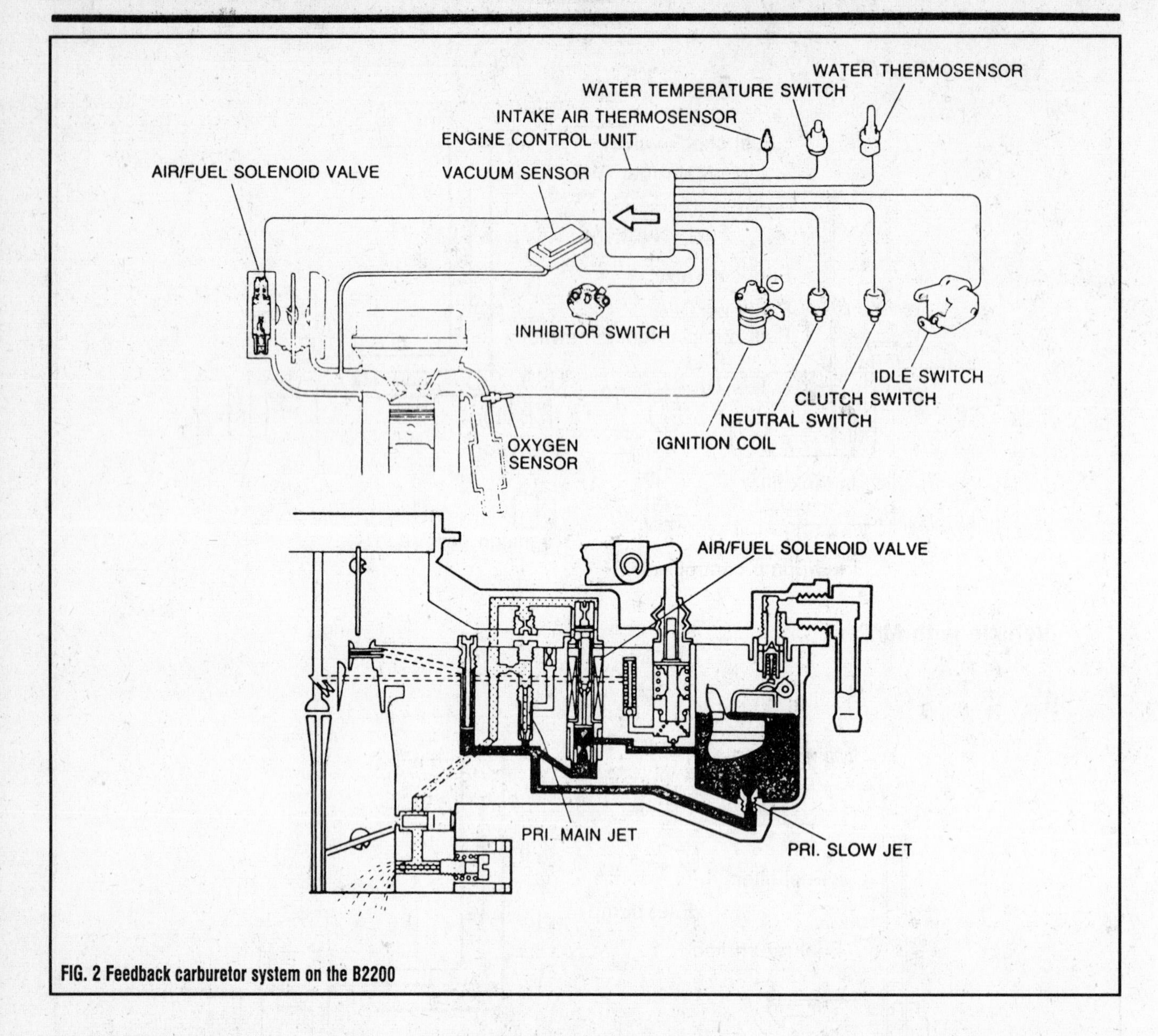

FIG. 2 Feedback carburetor system on the B2200

6. Installation is the reverse of the removal procedure. Be sure to install a new seal rubber gasket.

Carburetor

➧ SEE FIGS. 3-47

ADJUSTMENTS

Fast Idle

2.2L ENGINE

1. Set the fast idle cam so that the fast idle lever rests on the second step of the cam.
2. Adjust the clearance between the air horn wall and the lower edge of the throttle plates, by turning the fast idle adjusting screw. Clearance should be 0.84-1.04mm (0.0331-0.0409 in.). Make sure that the choke valve clearance hasn't changed.

2.6L ENGINE

➡ Before making the adjustment, the carburetor should be at 73°F (23°C) for at least 1 hour.

1. With the carburetor off the engine, invert it and check the opening between the throttle plate and the air horn wall. The clearance should be 0.71mm (0.0279 in.) for trucks with manual transmission; 0.80mm (0.0315 in.) for trucks with automatic transmission.
2. If not, adjust the opening by turning the fast idle adjustment screw.

Idle Speed Adjustment

Make sure the ignition timing, spark plugs, and carburetor float level are all in normal operating condition. Turn off all lights and other unnecessary electrical loads.

1. Connect a tachometer to the engine.
2. Start the engine and allow it to reach normal operating temperature. Make sure the choke valve has fully opened.
3. Check the idle speed. If necessary, adjust it to specification by turning the throttle adjusting screw. The idle speed should be 800–850 rpm with manual transmission in neutral or automatic transmission in **P**.

Idle Mixture Adjustment

2.2L ENGINE

1. Start the engine and allow it to reach normal operating temperature. Let the engine run at idle.
2. Connect a dwellmeter (90°, 4-cylinder) to the air/fuel check connector (Br/Y).
3. Check the idle mixture at the specified idle speed. The idle mixture should be 20–70°. If the idle mixture is not as specified, adjust as follows:
   a. Remove the carburetor and knock out the spring pin. Reinstall the carburetor.
   b. Install the air cleaner and make sure the idle compensator is closed. Make sure all vacuum hoses are properly connected.
   c. Connect a tachometer to the engine.
   d. Warm up the engine and run it at idle. Make sure the idle speed is correct.
   e. Reconnect the dwell meter to the air/fuel check connector.
   f. Adjust the idle mixture to 27–45° by turning the mixture adjust screw.
   g. Tap in the spring pin.

2.6L ENGINE

1. Start the engine and allow it to reach normal operating temperature. Let the engine run at idle.
2. Connect a dwellmeter (90°, 4-cylinder) to the jet mixture solenoid valve connector (YG) wire. The check connector is located near the No. 3 ACV and reed valve case assembly.
3. Check the idle mixture at the specified idle speed. The idle mixture should be 27–45°. If the idle mixture is not as specified, check the oxygen sensor, feedback control unit and the wiring between the sensor and control unit.
4. If the oxygen sensor, feedback control unit and wiring are okay, adjust the idle mixture as follows:
   a. Remove the carburetor and mount it in a vise with the mixture adjust screws facing up. Protect the gasket surface from the vise jaws.
   b. Drill a 0.079 in. (2mm) pilot hole in the casting toward the mixture adjust screw, then redrill the hole to 0.118 in. (3mm).
   c. Insert a blunt punch into the hole and drive out the antitamper plug. Reinstall the carburetor.
   d. Connect a tachometer to the engine. Start the engine and allow it to reach normal operating temperature. Let the engine run at idle. Make sure the idle speed is correct.
   e. Reconnect the dwell meter to the jet mixture solenoid valve connector. Adjust the idle mixture to 36° ± 9° by turning the mixture adjust screw.
   f. Press in a new antitamper plug.

Float and Fuel Level Adjustment

2.2L ENGINE

1. Remove the air horn from the carburetor.
2. Turn the air horn upside down on a level surface. Allow the float to hang under its own weight.
3. Measure the clearance between the float and the air horn gasket surface. The gap should be 11.6-12.6mm (0.4567-0.4960 in.) for trucks with manual transmission; 10.7-11.7mm (0.4212-0.4606 in.) for trucks with automatic transmission. If not, bend the float seat lip to obtain the correct gap.
4. Turn the air horn right side up and allow the float to hang under its own weight.
5. Measure the gap between the BOTTOM of the float and the air horn gasket surface. The gap should be 46.0-47.0mm (1.811-1.850 in.). If not, bend the float stopper until it is.

2.6L ENGINE

1. Remove air horn from carburetor main body.
2. Remove air horn gasket and invert air horn.
3. Using a gauge measure the distance from bottom of float to air horn surface. The distance should be 20mm ± 1mm (0.787 in. ± 0.0394 in.). If distance is not within specification, the shim under the needle and seat must be changed. A shim pack is available which has three shims: 0.2mm, 0.3mm, or 0.5mm. Adding or removing one shim will change the float level three times its thickness.

Accelerator Linkage Adjustment

1. Check the cable deflection at the carburetor. Deflection should be 1.0-3.0mm (0.0394-0.1181 in.). If not, adjust it by turning the adjusting nut at the bracket near the carburetor.
2. Depress the accelerator pedal to the floor. The throttle plates should be vertical. If not, adjust their position by turning the adjusting nut on the accelerator pedal bracket.

Secondary Throttle Valve

The clearance between the primary throttle valve and the air horn wall, when the secondary throttle valve just starts to open should be 7.35-8.25mm (0.2894-0.3249 in.). If not, bend the tab.

Choke

2.2L ENGINE

Three choke related adjustments are performed on these units.

CHOKE DIAPHRAGM

1. Disconnect the vacuum line from the choke diaphragm unit.
2. Using a vacuum pump, apply 15.7 in.Hg to the diaphragm.
3. Using light finger pressure, close the choke valve. Check the clearance at the upper edge of the choke valve. Clearance should be 1.70-2.16mm (0.067-0.085 in.).
4. If not, bend the tab on the choke lever to adjust it.

CHOKE VALVE CLEARANCE

1. Position the fast idle lever on the second step of the fast idle cam.
2. The leading edge of the choke valve should be 0.60-1.14mm (0.024-0.045 in.) from fully closed. If not, bend either the tab on the cam or the choke rod to adjust. The tab will give smaller adjustment increments.

CHOKE UNLOADER

1. Open the primary throttle valve all the way and hold it in this position.
2. The leading edge of the choke valve should be 2.80-3.62mm (0.110-0.143 in.) from fully closed. If not, bend the tab on the throttle lever.

Idle Switch

1. The idle switch adjustment is not necessary unless it has been replaced or tampered with.
2. Start the engine and allow it to reach normal operating temperature. Stop the engine and connect a suitable tachometer.
3. Connect a voltmeter to the idle switch terminal (LgR).
4. Start the engine and increase the speed to above 2000 rpm and decelerate gradually.
5. Take a reading on the voltmeter. At idle, there should be approximately 12 volts and above 100-1200 rpm it should be below 1.5 volts.
6. If the readings do not agree with these specifications, turn the adjusting screw to obtain the correct reading.

REMOVAL & INSTALLATION

1. Remove the air cleaner and duct.
2. Disconnect the accelerator shaft from the throttle lever.
3. Disconnect and plug the fuel supply and fuel return lines and plug these.
4. Disconnect the leads from the throttle solenoid and deceleration valve at the quick-disconnects.
5. Disconnect the carburetor-do-distributor vacuum line.
6. Disconnect the throttle return spring.
7. Disconnect the choke cable, and, if equipped, the cruise control cable.

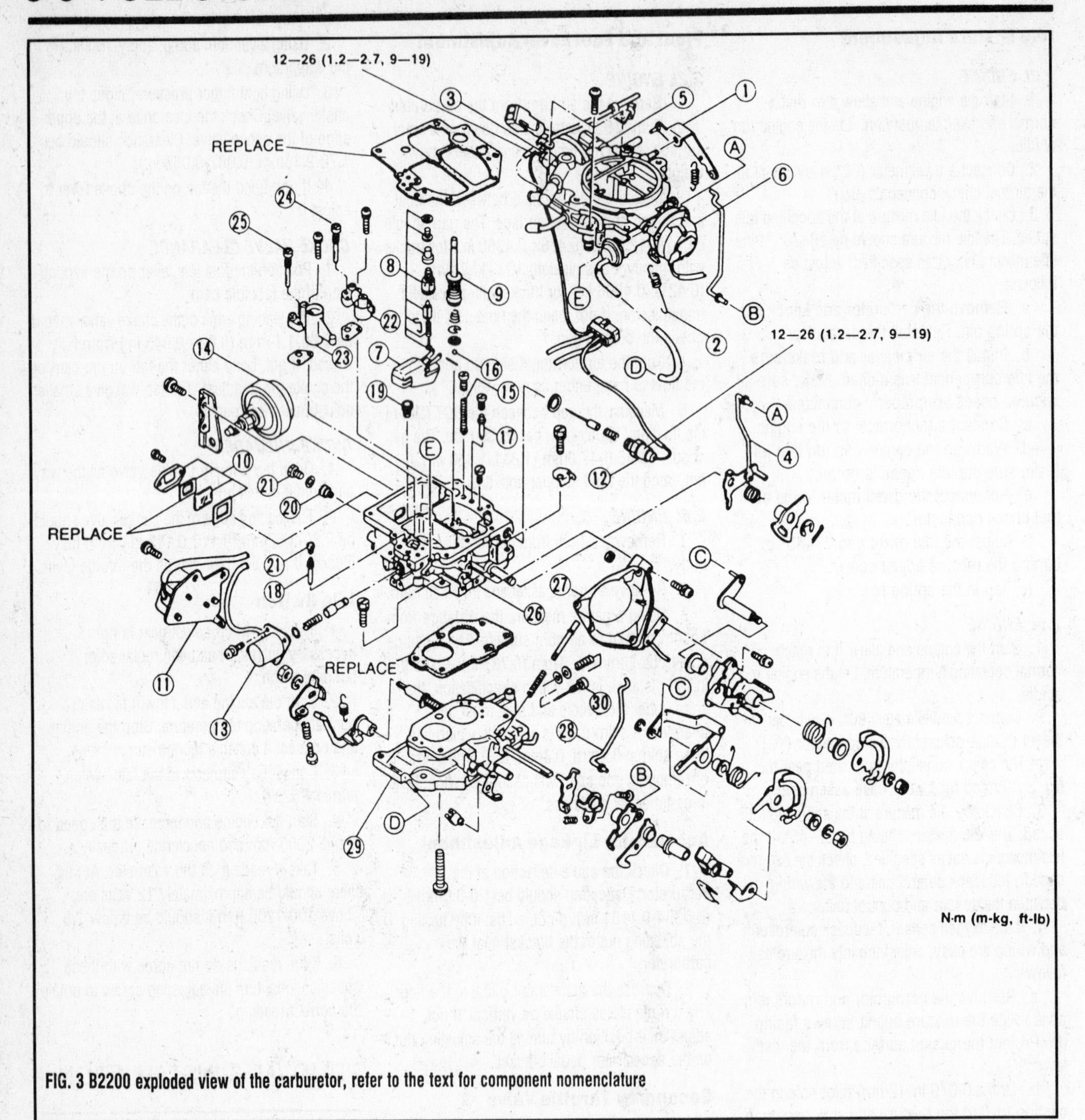

FIG. 3 B2200 exploded view of the carburetor, refer to the text for component nomenclature

8. Remove the carburetor attaching nuts from the intake manifold studs and remove the carburetor. The attaching nuts are tucked underneath the carburetor body and are difficult to reach; a small socket with an "L" shaped hex drive, or a short, thin wrench sold for work on ignition systems will make removal easier.
9. Install a new carburetor gasket on the manifold.
10. Install the carburetor and tighten the carburetor attaching nuts.
11. Connect the throttle return spring.
12. Connect the accelerator shaft to the throttle shaft.
13. Connect the electrical leads to the throttle solenoid and deceleration valve.
14. Connect the distributor vacuum line.
15. Connect the fuel supply and fuel return lines.
16. Connect and adjust the choke cable and, if equipped, the cruise control cable.
17. Install the air cleaner and duct.
18. Start the engine and check for fuel leaks.

OVERHAUL

The following instructions are general overhaul procedures. Most good carburetor rebuilding kits come replete with exploded views and specific instructions.

Efficient operation depends greatly on careful cleaning and inspection during overhaul, since dirt, gum, water, or varnish in or on the carburetor parts are often responsible for poor performance.

Overhaul your carburetor in a clean, dust-free area. Carefully disassemble the carburetor, referring often to the exploded views. Keep all similar and look alike parts segregated during disassembly and cleaning to avoid accidental interchange during assembly. Make a not of all jet sizes.

When the carburetor is disassembled, wash all parts (except diaphragms, electric choke units, pump plunger, and any other plastic, leather, fiber or rubber parts) in clean carburetor solvent. Do not leave parts in the solvent any longer than is necessary to sufficiently loosen the deposits. Excessive cleaning may remove the special finish from the float bowl and choke valve bodies, leaving these parts unfit for service. Rinse all parts in clean solvent and blow them dry with compressed air or allow them to air dry. Wipe clean all cork, plastic, leather, and fiber parts with a clean, lint-free cloth.

Blow out all passages and jets with compressed air and be sure that there are no restrictions or blockages. Never use wire or similar tools to clean jets, fuel passages, or air bleeds. Clean all jets and valves separately to avoid accidental interchange.

Check all parts for wear or damage. If wear or damage is found, replace the defective parts. Especially check the following:

1. Check the float needle and seat for wear. If wear is found, replace the complete assembly.
2. Check the float hinge pin for wear and the float(s) for dents or distortion. Replace the float if fuel has leaked into it.
3. Check the throttle and choke shaft bores for wear or an out-of-round condition. Damage or wear to the throttle arm, shaft, or shaft bore will often require replacement of the throttle body. These parts require a close tolerance of fit; wear may allow air leakage, which could affect starting and idling.

➡ Throttle shafts and bushings are not included in overhaul kits. They can be purchased separately.

4. Inspect the idle moisture adjusting needles for burrs or grooves. Any such condition requires replacement of the needle, since you will not be able to obtain a satisfactory idle.
5. Test the accelerator pump check valves. They should pass air one way but not the other. Test for proper seating by blowing and sucking on the valve. Replace the valve if necessary. If the valve is satisfactory, wash the valve again to remove breath moisture.
6. Check the bowl cover for warped surfaces with a straight edge.
7. Closely inspect the valves and seats for wear or damage, replacing as necessary.
8. After the carburetor is assembled, check the choke valve for freedom of operation.

Carburetor overhaul kits are recommended for each overhaul. These kits contain all gaskets and new parts to replace those that deteriorate most rapidly. Failure to replace all parts supplied with the kit (especially gaskets) can result in poor performance later.

Some carburetor manufacturers supply overhaul kits of three basic types: minor repair; major repair; and gasket kits. Basically, they contain the following:

Minor Repair Kits:

- All gaskets
- Float needle valve
- Volume control screw
- All diaphragms
- Spring for the pump diaphragm

Major Repair Kits:

- All jet and gaskets
- All diaphragms
- Float needle valve
- Volume control screw
- Pump ball valve
- Main jet carrier
- Float
- Complete intermediate rod
- Intermediate pump lever
- Complete injector tube
- Some cover hold-down screws and washers

Gasket Kits:

- All gaskets

After cleaning and checking all components, reassemble the carburetor, using new parts and referring to the exploded view. When reassembling, make sure that all screws and jets are tight in their seats, but do not overtighten as the tips will be distorted. Tighten all screws gradually, in rotation. Do not tighten needle valves into their seats; uneven jetting will result. Always use new gaskets. Be sure to adjust the float lever when reassembling.

B2200 Carburetor

DISASSEMBLY

After removing the carburetor, disassemble the carburetor in the numbered order (refer to the exploded view illustrated in this section) as follows:

1. Accelerator pump connecting rod.
2. Connect spring.
3. Air vent solenoid valve.
4. Choke rod.
5. Air horn.
6. Automatic choke assembly.
7. Float.
8. Needle valve assembly.
9. Accelerator pump.

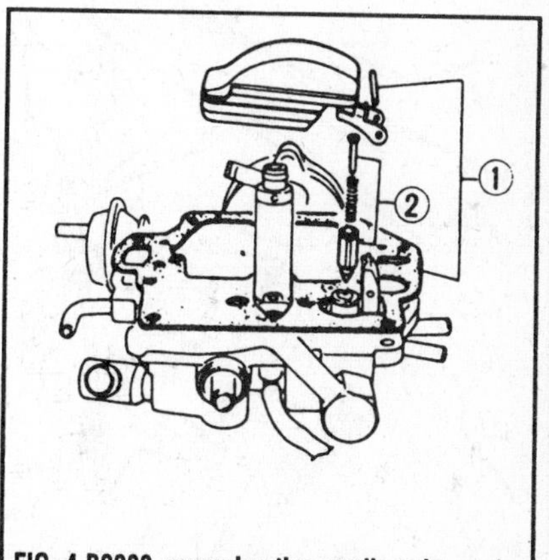

FIG. 4 B2200, removing the needle valve and float

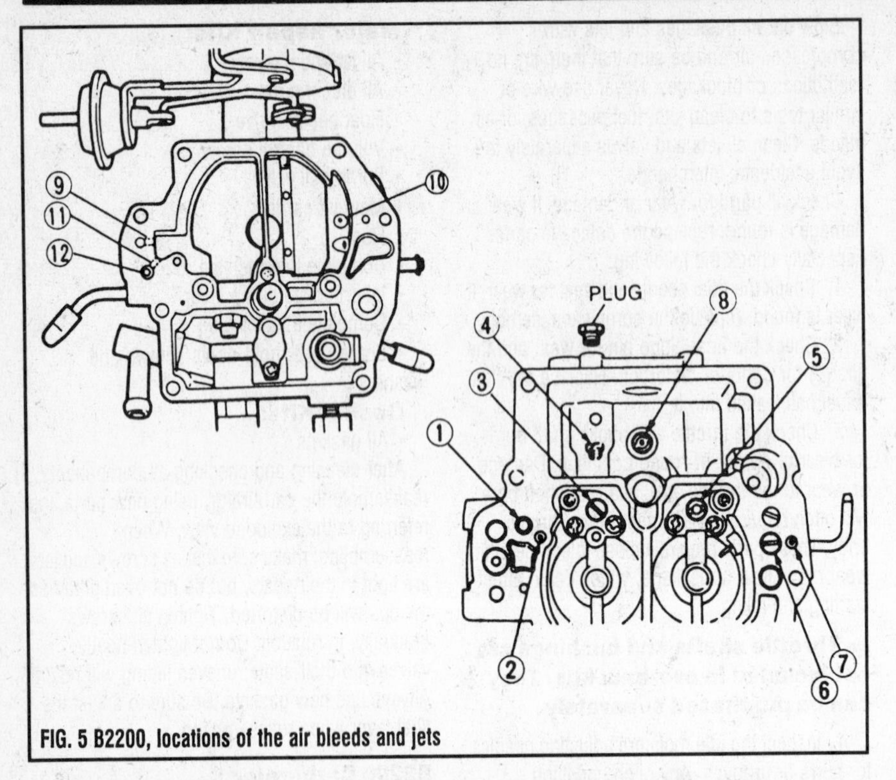

FIG. 5 B2200, locations of the air bleeds and jets

10. Fuel bowl sight glass.
11. Idle switch.
12. Slow cut fuel solenoid valve.
13. Coasting richer solenoid valve.
14. Dashpot.
15. Accelerator pump outlet check ball.
16. Accelerator pump inlet check ball.
17. Primary slow jet.
18. Secondary main jet.
19. Primary main jet.
20. Secondary main jet.
21. Plug.
22. Primary venturi and nozzle.
23. Secondary venturi and nozzle.
24. Primary main air bleed.
25. Secondary main air bleed.
26. Main body.
27. Vacuum diaphragm.
28. Throttle link.
29. Throttle body.
30. Mixture adjusting screw.

➡ Further detailed disassembly procedure for component units follows.

AIR HORN AND AUTOMATIC CHOKE DISASSEMBLY

1. Vacuum hose.
2. Accelerator pump connecting rod, spring and lever.
3. Connect spring.
4. Air vent solenoid valve (separate from connector).
5. Choke rod (disconnect).
6. Air horn and automatic choke (separate from the main body).
7. Air vent solenoid valve, spring and gasket, if necessary.

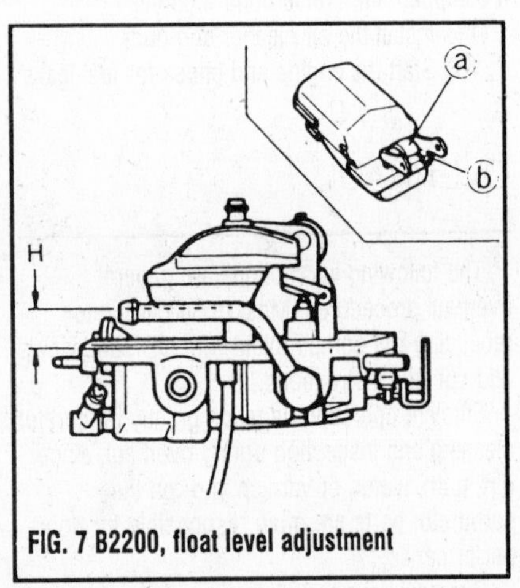

FIG. 7 B2200, float level adjustment

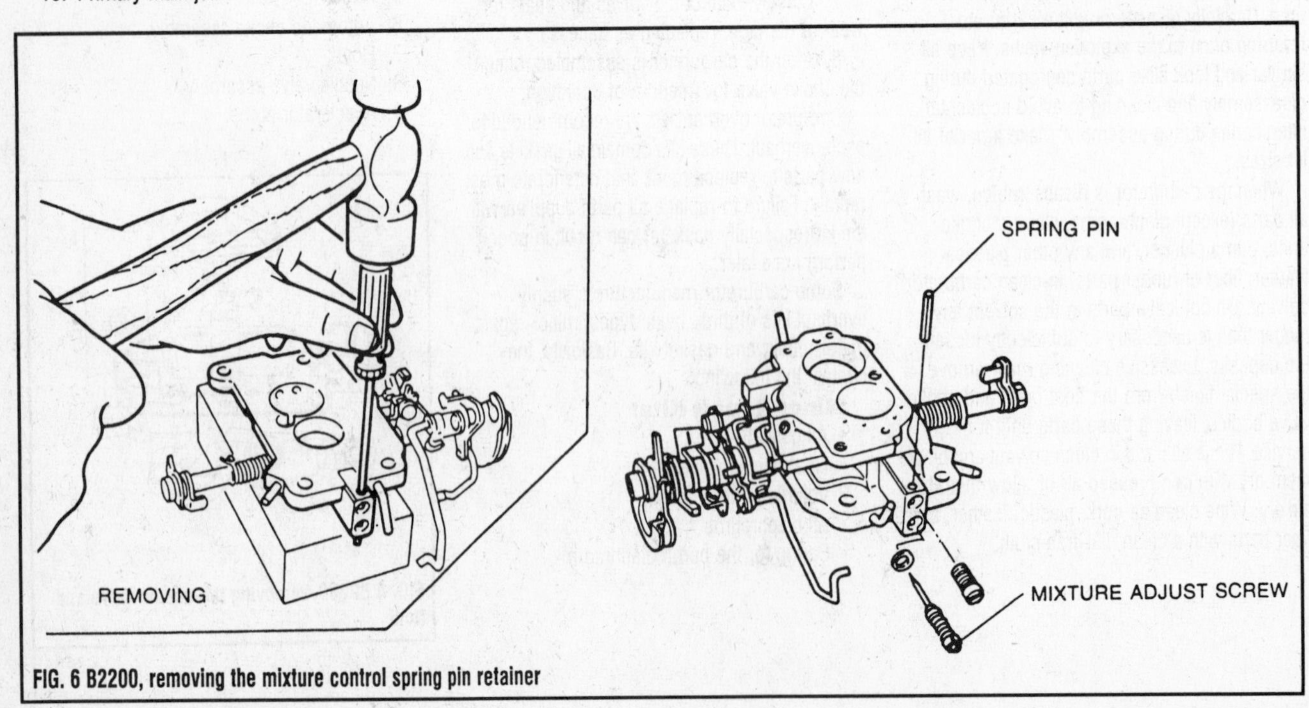

FIG. 6 B2200, removing the mixture control spring pin retainer

NEEDLE VALVE AND FLOAT

1. Float, pin and gasket.
2. Needle valve assembly.
3. Fuel bowl sight glass mounting screws.
4. Cover, gasket, glass and rubber gasket.

AIR BLEED AND JETS

1. Secondary slow jet.
2. Secondary slow air bleed (No.1).
3. Secondary main air bleed.
4. Secondary main jet.
5. Primary main air bleed.
6. Slow jet and plug.
7. Primary slow air bleed (No.1).
8. Primary main jet.
9. Richer air bleed (No.2).
10. Primary slow air bleed (No.2).
11. Richer air bleed (No.1).
12. Richer jet.
13. NOTE THE SIZE OF ALL JETS AND AIR BLEEDS SO THAT THEY ARE REASSEMBLED IN THE CORRECT POSITION.

MAIN BODY

1. Coasting richer solenoid valve and O ring.
2. Idle switch and spring. After installing the idle switch be sure to adjust it.
3. Slow cut solenoid valve, needle valve, spring and gasket.
4. Dashpot bracket and dashpot.
5. Accelerator pump plunger assembly and spring.
6. Retaining clip.
7. Strainer and accelerator pump inlet check ball.
8. Check valve plug.
9. Accelerator pump outlet check ball and spring.
10. Throttle link (disconnect).
11. Vacuum diaphragm connecting rod (disconnect).
12. Throttle return spring (disconnect).
13. Throttle body (separate from the main body). One of the bolts is inside the throttle body.
14. Diaphragm assembly and gasket.
15. Diaphragm cover mounting screws and cover.
16. Spring and diaphragm.
17. Throttle lever hanger mounting screws.

THROTTLE BODY

When removing the mixture adjusting screw, tap out the spring pin as shown in the illustration provided in this section. Do not remove the throttle valve and shaft, the venturi, the choke valve and shaft.

INSPECTION

Before inspection, wash all parts in carburetor cleaner and blow compressed air into the fuel passages to remove any dirt. Never use wire to clean the jets.

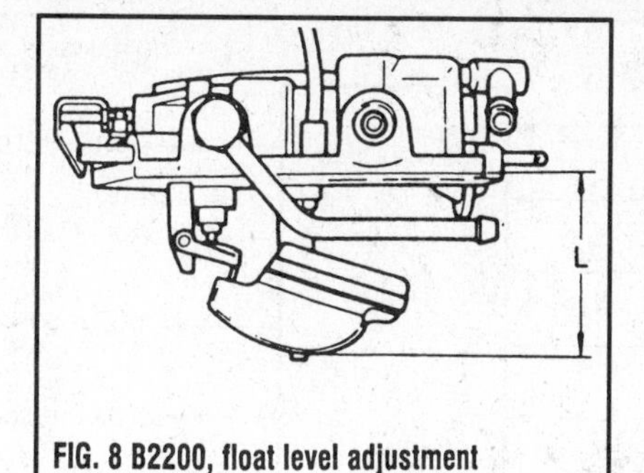

FIG. 8 B2200, float level adjustment

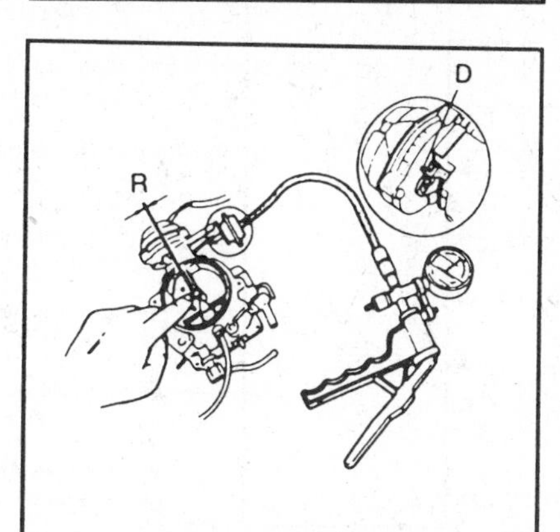

FIG. 9 B2200, adjusting the choke diaphragm

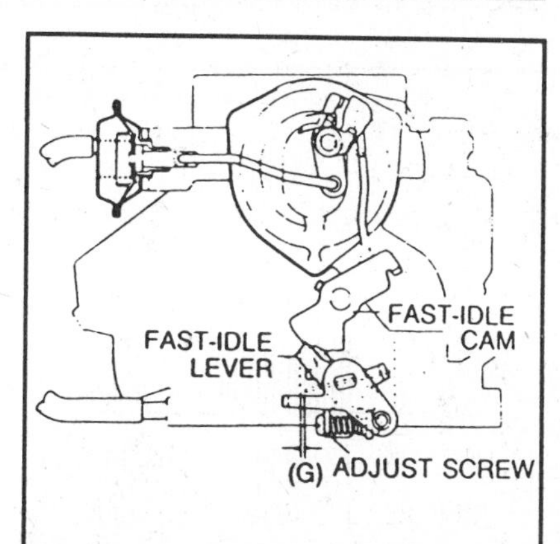

FIG. 10 B2200, fast idle cam adjustment

1. Inspect the air horn, the main body and the throttle body for cracks or breakage.
2. Inspect the choke shaft and throttle shaft for wear. A worn throttle shaft will allow air to enter the combustion chamber and the air/fuel mixture will become lean at low driving speeds.
3. Check the needle and seat for wear and rust. It is a good policy to always replace the needle and seat when cleaning/rebuilding the carburetor.
4. Check the float for damage.
5. Examine all jets and air bleeds for clogging and blow out with compressed air if necessary.

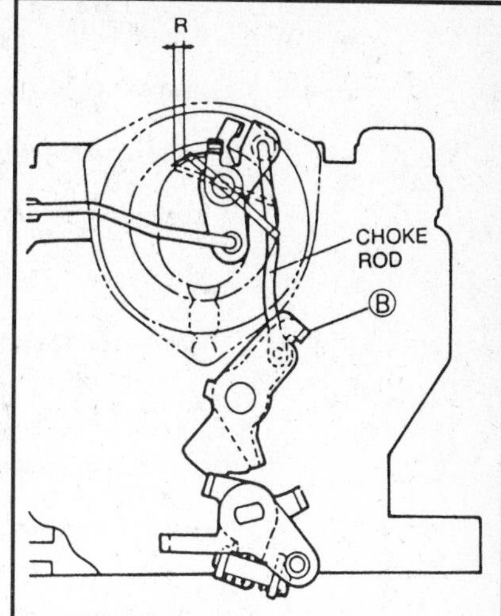

FIG. 11 B2200, adjusting the choke valve clearance

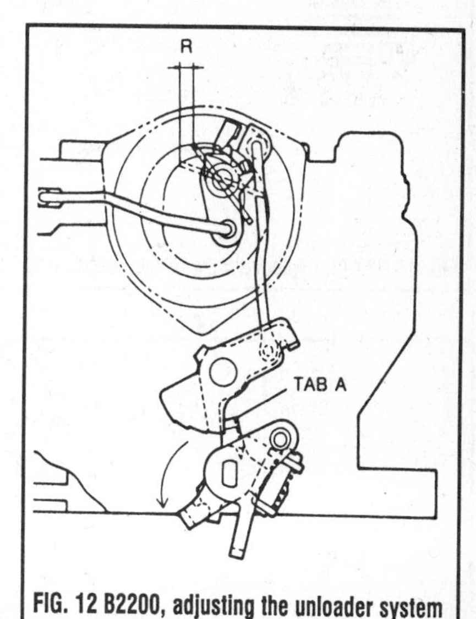

FIG. 12 B2200, adjusting the unloader system

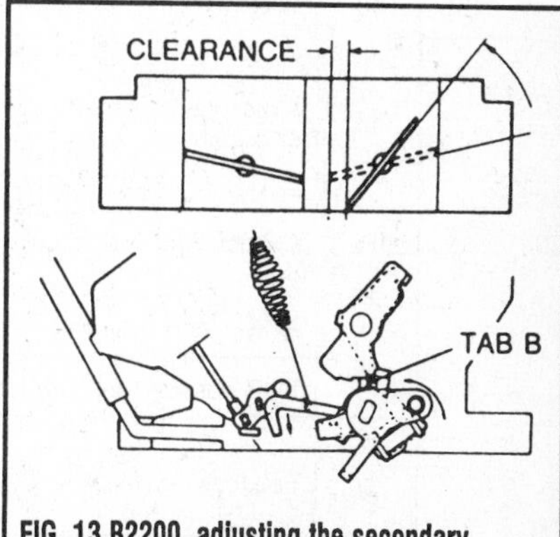

FIG. 13 B2200, adjusting the secondary throttle valve clearance

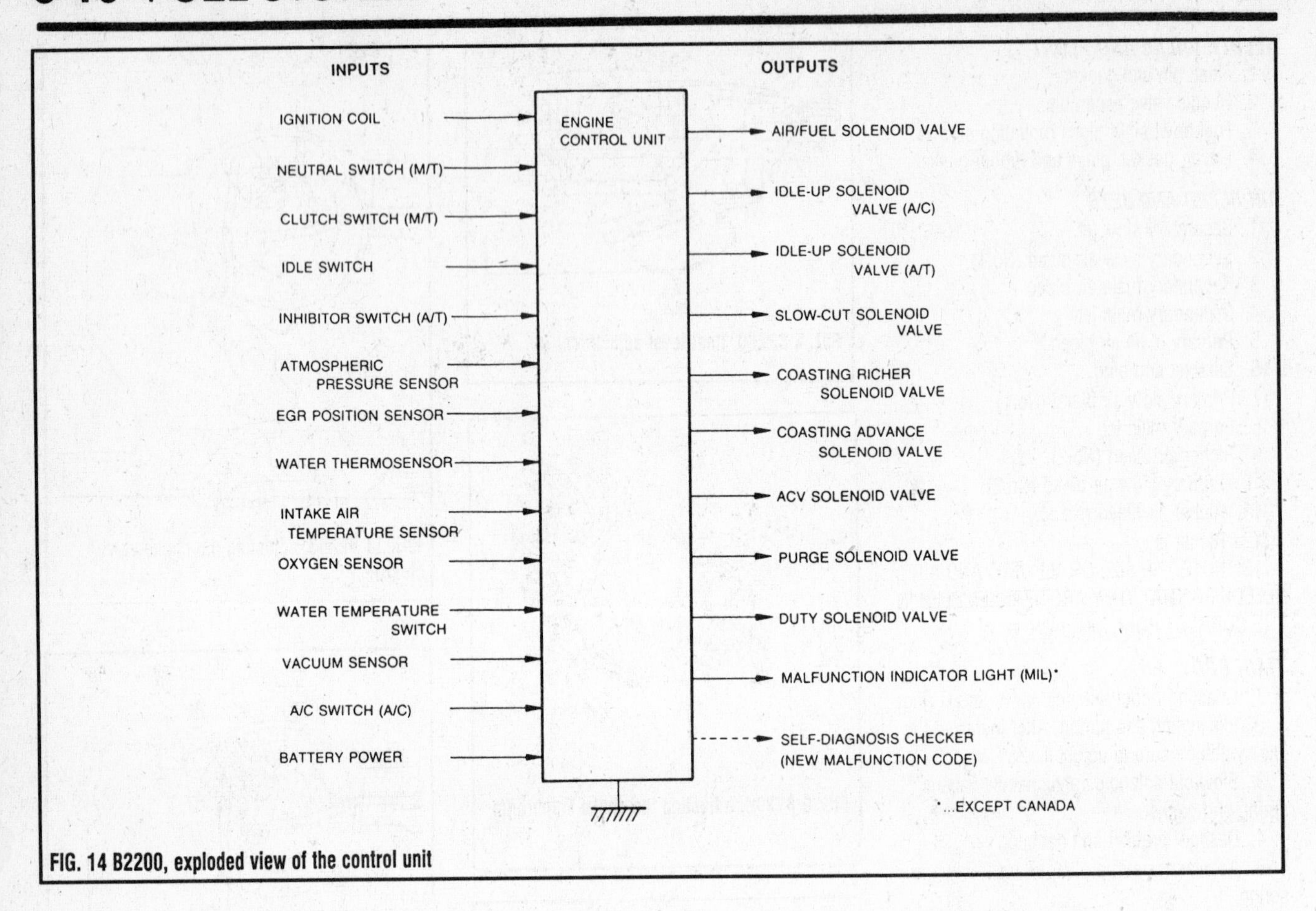

FIG. 14 B2200, exploded view of the control unit

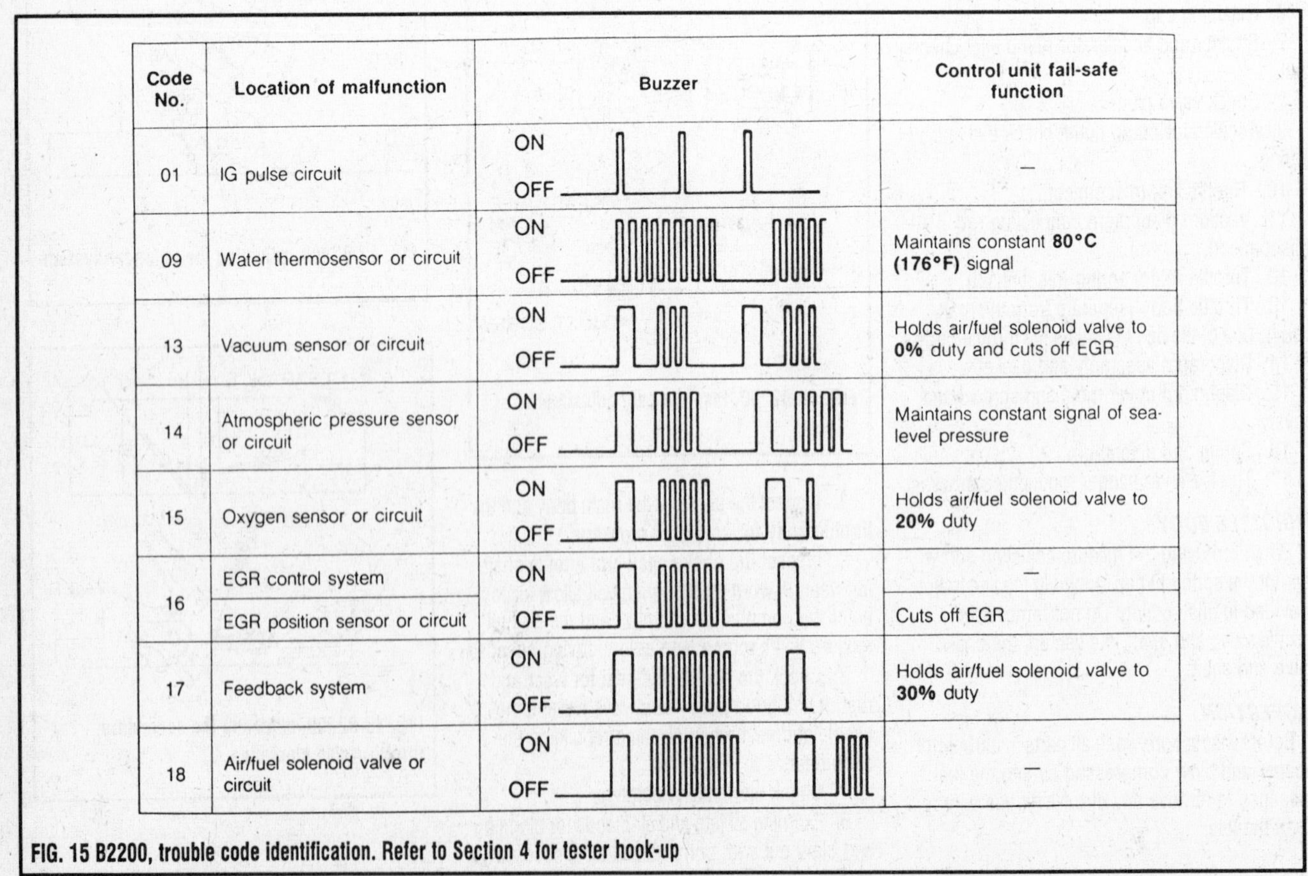

Code No.	Location of malfunction	Buzzer	Control unit fail-safe function
01	IG pulse circuit	ON / OFF	—
09	Water thermosensor or circuit	ON / OFF	Maintains constant **80°C (176°F)** signal
13	Vacuum sensor or circuit	ON / OFF	Holds air/fuel solenoid valve to **0%** duty and cuts off EGR
14	Atmospheric pressure sensor or circuit	ON / OFF	Maintains constant signal of sea-level pressure
15	Oxygen sensor or circuit	ON / OFF	Holds air/fuel solenoid valve to **20%** duty
16	EGR control system	ON / OFF	—
	EGR position sensor or circuit		Cuts off EGR
17	Feedback system	ON / OFF	Holds air/fuel solenoid valve to **30%** duty
18	Air/fuel solenoid valve or circuit	ON / OFF	—

FIG. 15 B2200, trouble code identification. Refer to Section 4 for tester hook-up

6. Inspect the accelerator pump plunger cup. Replace the plunger if it is worn or damaged. It is a good policy to replace the accelerator pump when cleaning or rebuilding the carburetor.

7. Check the diaphragm for damage.

8. Inspect the mixture adjuster for burrs or ridges.

9. Check the operation of the solenoids. To check, connect the solenoid terminal, with jumper wires, to the positive terminal of the battery and ground the solenoid body. When current is applied to the solenoid, the valve stem should be drawn into the valve body. If the valve does not operate properly, replace the solenoid.

10. Use and ohmmeter and check for continuity between the coupler and the choke heater ground. If there is no continuity, replace the choke heater.

11. To check the A/F solenoid valve, connect the terminal to the positive terminal of the battery, and ground the other terminal. Make sure the valve is operating properly by blowing air through it. When current is applied, no air should pass through. When no current is applied, air should pass through. The A/F solenoid cannot be replaced, if it is not operating properly, the air horn assembly must be replaced.

ASSEMBLY

Assemble the components by following the steps in reverse order. After components cleaned and assembled combine them. Always use new gaskets and O rings. Make sure all parts are in good condition and clean. Both the primary and secondary venturi have their respective components which are the same shape. During reassembly be careful not to mix up the parts. Do not install the mixture spring pin until the idle adjustment has been completed. Be sure to make a float level adjustment when assembling the carburetor.

Install the carburetor.

1. Start the engine and check for leaks.

2. With the engine operating, check the fuel level. The fuel level should be at the specified mark on the sight glass.

3. Make the idle adjustment.

4. After the idle adjustment is made, press in the spring pin.

5. Adjust the dashpot. (see Section 4)

6. Adjust the idle switch.

7. After the idle adjustment is completed, check the fast idle speed as follows:

8. Start the engine and allow it to reach normal operating temperature.

9. Stop the engine and remove the air cleaner.

10. Plug the hoses to the idle compensator and the reed valves.

11. While holding the throttle valve slightly opened, push the choke to the fully close it, and then release the choke valve after releasing the throttle valve.

12. Start the engine, but do not touch the accelerator pedal.

13. Check to see that the engine speed increases to 2500-3000 rpm. If the engine speed is not as specified for fast idle, turn the fast idle screw until the correct rpm is obtained.

14. Connect the reed valve and idle compensator hoses. Install the air cleaner.

B2600 Carburetor

DISASSEMBLY

After removing the carburetor, disassemble the carburetor in the numbered order (refer to the exploded view illustrated in this section) as follows:

1. Water hose.
2. Throttle return spring.
3. Choke cover.
4. Throttle sensor.
5. Dashpot.
6. Jet mixture solenoid valve.
7. Enrichment solenoid valve.
8. Slow fuel cut solenoid valve.
9. Air vent solenoid valve.
10. Choke breaker.
11. Secondary diaphragm.
12. Choke rod.
13. Float chamber cover.
14. Float.
15. Needle valve.
16. Main jet.
17. Jet block.
18. Secondary slow jet.
19. Primary slow jet.
20. Jet mixture jet.
21. Outlet check weight and ball.
22. Inlet check ball.
23. Steel ball.
24. Accelerator pump.
25. Mixture adjustment screw.

INSPECTION

Clean all parts with carburetor cleaner and dry with compressed air. Check for the following, replace the part if a problem is found.

1. Damaged float chamber, mixing body, or throttle body.
2. Improper operation of the choke valve or throttle valve.
3. Damaged float.
4. Needle valve abrasion or improper seating.
5. Clogged or damaged jets or air bleeds.
6. Damaged diaphragm on the accelerator pump.
7. Weak or broken spring on the accelerator pump.
8. Damaged diaphragms.
9. Improper solenoid operation.

ASSEMBLY

The carburetor is equipped with a tamper proof choke. To remove the choke cover, grind off the heads of the choke cover lock screws. When installing the cover use new lock screws. After carburetor assembly (in reverse order of the above listed steps), float level adjustment and choke adjustment will be necessary.

1. To adjust the choke; with the cover removed, remove the two lock screws and remove the choke pinion assembly.

2. Fit the strangler spring to the choke lever. Assemble, aligning the inscribed line or black painted line on the tooth of the choke pinion with the inscribed line on the cam lever.

3. Loosely tighten the new lock screws. Set the choke valve by moving the pinion arm up or down, align the punch mark on the float chamber cover with the center of the three inscribed lines, secure the pinion arm with the lock screws.

Inspect the operation of the various solenoid valves. Apply battery power to the valve (positive battery terminal jumper to solenoid terminal and ground solenoid body with another jumper) and check for operational sound from each valve, replace as necessary. Install the carburetor and adjust the idle and fast idle speeds.

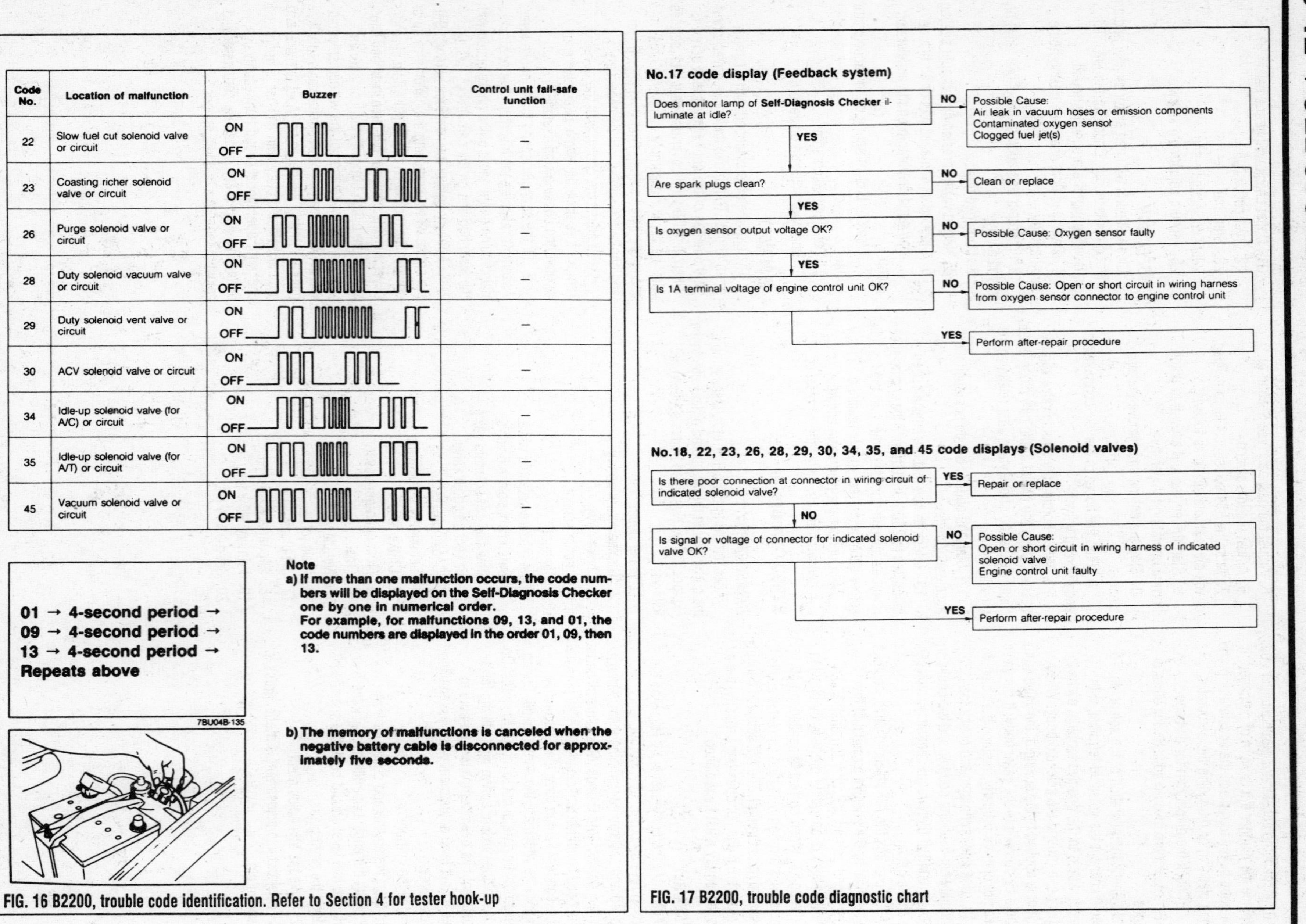

Code No.	Location of malfunction	Buzzer	Control unit fail-safe function
22	Slow fuel cut solenoid valve or circuit	ON / OFF	—
23	Coasting richer solenoid valve or circuit	ON / OFF	—
26	Purge solenoid valve or circuit	ON / OFF	—
28	Duty solenoid vacuum valve or circuit	ON / OFF	—
29	Duty solenoid vent valve or circuit	ON / OFF	—
30	ACV solenoid valve or circuit	ON / OFF	—
34	Idle-up solenoid valve (for A/C) or circuit	ON / OFF	—
35	Idle-up solenoid valve (for A/T) or circuit	ON / OFF	—
45	Vacuum solenoid valve or circuit	ON / OFF	—

01 → 4-second period →
09 → 4-second period →
13 → 4-second period →
Repeats above
7BU04B-135

Note

a) If more than one malfunction occurs, the code numbers will be displayed on the Self-Diagnosis Checker one by one in numerical order.
For example, for malfunctions 09, 13, and 01, the code numbers are displayed in the order 01, 09, then 13.

b) The memory of malfunctions is canceled when the negative battery cable is disconnected for approximately five seconds.

FIG. 16 B2200, trouble code identification. Refer to Section 4 for tester hook-up

No.17 code display (Feedback system)
Does monitor lamp of Self-Diagnosis Checker illuminate at idle?
NO
Possible Cause:
Air leak in vacuum hoses or emission components
Contaminated oxygen sensor
Clogged fuel jet(s)
YES
Are spark plugs clean?
NO
Clean or replace
YES
Is oxygen sensor output voltage OK?
NO
Possible Cause: Oxygen sensor faulty
YES
Is 1A terminal voltage of engine control unit OK?
NO
Possible Cause: Open or short circuit in wiring harness from oxygen sensor connector to engine control unit
YES
Perform after-repair procedure
No.18, 22, 23, 26, 28, 29, 30, 34, 35, and 45 code displays (Solenoid valves)
Is there poor connection at connector in wiring circuit of indicated solenoid valve?
YES
Repair or replace
NO
Is signal or voltage of connector for indicated solenoid valve OK?
NO
Possible Cause:
Open or short circuit in wiring harness of indicated solenoid valve
Engine control unit faulty
YES
Perform after-repair procedure

FIG. 17 B2200, trouble code diagnostic chart

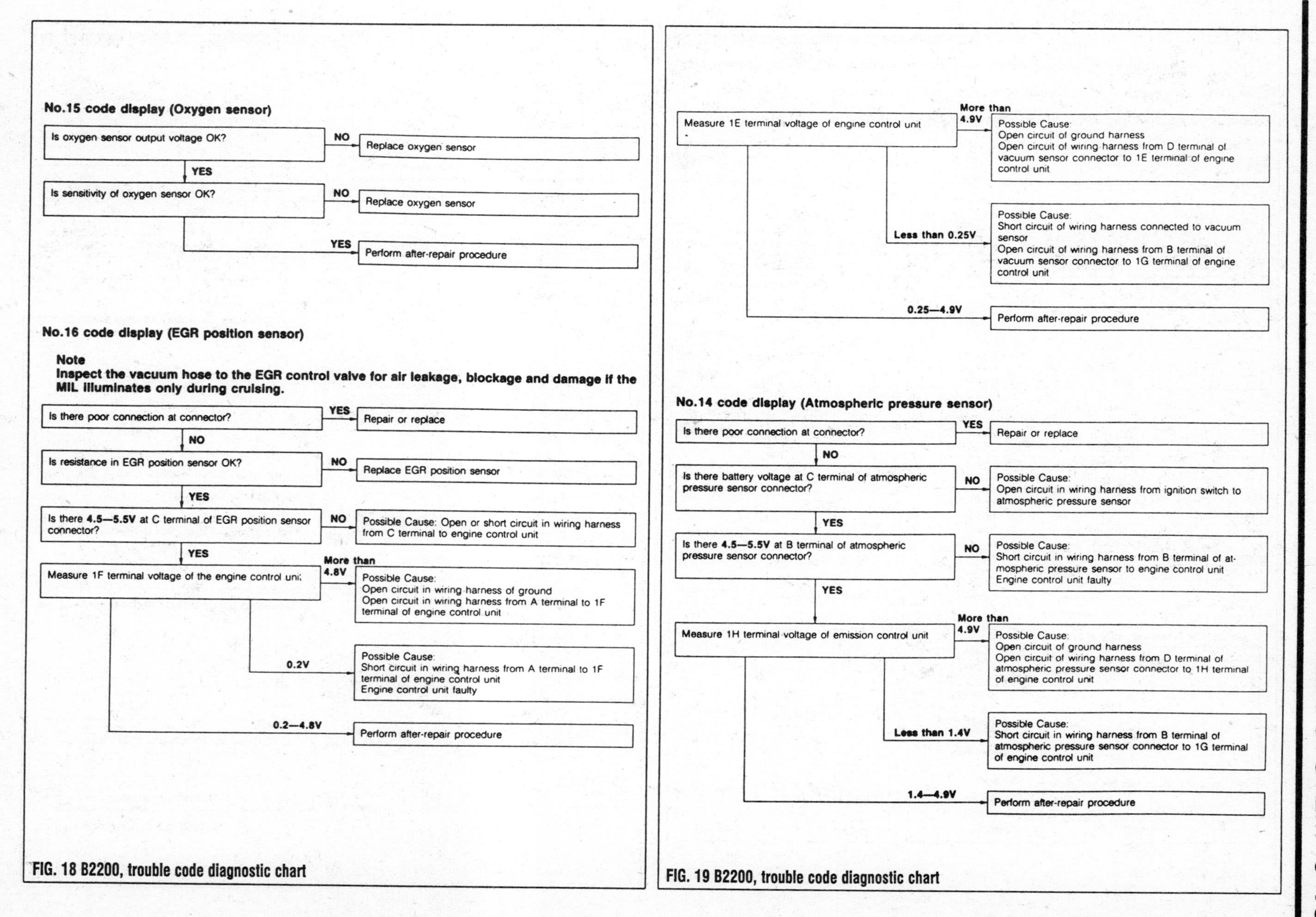
No.15 code display (Oxygen sensor)
Is oxygen sensor output voltage OK?
NO
Replace oxygen sensor
YES
Is sensitivity of oxygen sensor OK?
NO
Replace oxygen sensor
YES
Perform after-repair procedure
No.16 code display (EGR position sensor)
Note
Inspect the vacuum hose to the EGR control valve for air leakage, blockage and damage if the MIL illuminates only during cruising.
Is there poor connection at connector?
YES
Repair or replace
NO
Is resistance in EGR position sensor OK?
NO
Replace EGR position sensor
YES
Is there 4.5—5.5V at C terminal of EGR position sensor connector?
NO
Possible Cause: Open or short circuit in wiring harness from C terminal to engine control unit
YES
Measure 1F terminal voltage of the engine control unit
More than 4.8V
Possible Cause:
Open circuit in wiring harness of ground
Open circuit in wiring harness from A terminal to 1F terminal of engine control unit
0.2V
Possible Cause:
Short circuit in wiring harness from A terminal to 1F terminal of engine control unit
Engine control unit faulty
0.2—4.8V
Perform after-repair procedure
Measure 1E terminal voltage of engine control unit
More than 4.9V
Possible Cause:
Open circuit of ground harness
Open circuit of wiring harness from D terminal of vacuum sensor connector to 1E terminal of engine control unit
Less than 0.25V
Possible Cause:
Short circuit of wiring harness connected to vacuum sensor
Open circuit of wiring harness from B terminal of vacuum sensor connector to 1G terminal of engine control unit
0.25—4.9V
Perform after-repair procedure
No.14 code display (Atmospheric pressure sensor)
Is there poor connection at connector?
YES
Repair or replace
NO
Is there battery voltage at C terminal of atmospheric pressure sensor connector?
NO
Possible Cause:
Open circuit in wiring harness from ignition switch to atmospheric pressure sensor
YES
Is there 4.5—5.5V at B terminal of atmospheric pressure sensor connector?
NO
Possible Cause:
Short circuit in wiring harness from B terminal of atmospheric pressure sensor to engine control unit
Engine control unit faulty
YES
Measure 1H terminal voltage of emission control unit
More than 4.9V
Possible Cause:
Open circuit of ground harness
Open circuit of wiring harness from D terminal of atmospheric pressure sensor connector to 1H terminal of engine control unit
Less than 1.4V
Possible Cause:
Short circuit in wiring harness from B terminal of atmospheric pressure sensor connector to 1G terminal of engine control unit
1.4—4.9V
Perform after-repair procedure

FIG. 18 B2200, trouble code diagnostic chart

FIG. 19 B2200, trouble code diagnostic chart

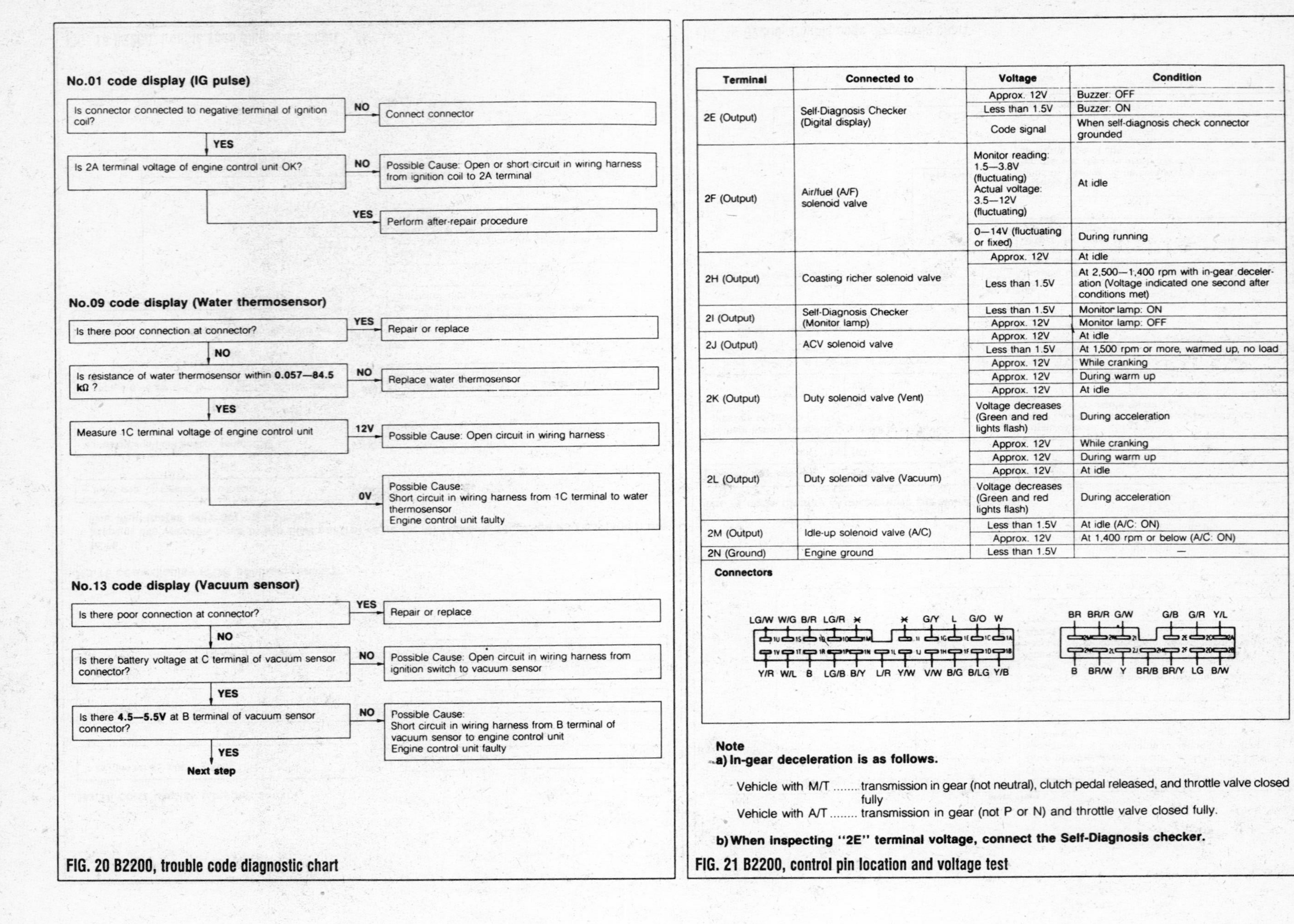
No.01 code display (IG pulse)
Is connector connected to negative terminal of ignition coil?
NO
Connect connector
YES
Is 2A terminal voltage of engine control unit OK?
NO
Possible Cause: Open or short circuit in wiring harness from ignition coil to 2A terminal
YES
Perform after-repair procedure
No.09 code display (Water thermosensor)
Is there poor connection at connector?
YES
Repair or replace
NO
Is resistance of water thermosensor within 0.057—84.5 kΩ ?
NO
Replace water thermosensor
YES
Measure 1C terminal voltage of engine control unit
12V
Possible Cause: Open circuit in wiring harness
0V
Possible Cause:
Short circuit in wiring harness from 1C terminal to water thermosensor
Engine control unit faulty
No.13 code display (Vacuum sensor)
Is there poor connection at connector?
YES
Repair or replace
NO
Is there battery voltage at C terminal of vacuum sensor connector?
NO
Possible Cause: Open circuit in wiring harness from ignition switch to vacuum sensor
YES
Is there 4.5—5.5V at B terminal of vacuum sensor connector?
NO
Possible Cause:
Short circuit in wiring harness from B terminal of vacuum sensor to engine control unit
Engine control unit faulty
YES
Next step

FIG. 20 B2200, trouble code diagnostic chart

Terminal	Connected to	Voltage	Condition
2E (Output)	Self-Diagnosis Checker (Digital display)	Approx. 12V	Buzzer: OFF
		Less than 1.5V	Buzzer: ON
		Code signal	When self-diagnosis check connector grounded
2F (Output)	Air/fuel (A/F) solenoid valve	Monitor reading: 1.5—3.8V (fluctuating) Actual voltage: 3.5—12V (fluctuating)	At idle
		0—14V (fluctuating or fixed)	During running
2H (Output)	Coasting richer solenoid valve	Approx. 12V	At idle
		Less than 1.5V	At 2,500—1,400 rpm with in-gear deceleration (Voltage indicated one second after conditions met)
2I (Output)	Self-Diagnosis Checker (Monitor lamp)	Less than 1.5V	Monitor lamp: ON
		Approx. 12V	Monitor lamp: OFF
2J (Output)	ACV solenoid valve	Approx. 12V	At idle
		Less than 1.5V	At 1,500 rpm or more, warmed up, no load
2K (Output)	Duty solenoid valve (Vent)	Approx. 12V	While cranking
		Approx. 12V	During warm up
		Approx. 12V	At idle
		Voltage decreases (Green and red lights flash)	During acceleration
2L (Output)	Duty solenoid valve (Vacuum)	Approx. 12V	While cranking
		Approx. 12V	During warm up
		Approx. 12V	At idle
		Voltage decreases (Green and red lights flash)	During acceleration
2M (Output)	Idle-up solenoid valve (A/C)	Less than 1.5V	At idle (A/C: ON)
		Approx. 12V	At 1,400 rpm or below (A/C: ON)
2N (Ground)	Engine ground	Less than 1.5V	—

Connectors
LG/W W/G B/R LG/R ✳ ✳ G/Y L G/O W
Y/R W/L B LG/B B/Y L/R Y/W V/W B/G B/LG Y/B
BR BR/R G/W G/B G/R Y/L
B BR/W Y BR/B BR/Y LG B/W

Note

a) In-gear deceleration is as follows.

Vehicle with M/T .... transmission in gear (not neutral), clutch pedal released, and throttle valve closed fully

Vehicle with A/T .... transmission in gear (not P or N) and throttle valve closed fully.

b) When inspecting "2E" terminal voltage, connect the Self-Diagnosis checker.

FIG. 21 B2200, control pin location and voltage test

Terminal	Connected to	Voltage	Condition
1A (Input)	Oxygen sensor	0.3—0.7V	At idle
		More than 0.45V	During acceleration
		Less than 0.45V	During deceleration
1B (Input)	Self-diagnosis check connector	Approx. 12V	Check connector; Not grounded
		0V	Check connector; Grounded
1C (Input)	Water thermosensor	Approx. 0.5V	Warmed-up engine (Thermostat: Open)
1D (Ground)	Water thermosensor, EGR position sensor, Vacuum sensor, Atmospheric pressure sensor, Intake air thermosensor	Less than 1.5V	—
1E (Input)	Vacuum sensor	Approx. 1.3V	At idle
		Approx. 4.0V	Engine stopped (Atmospheric pressure)
1F (Input)	EGR position sensor	Approx. 0.7V	At idle
		0.7—4.7V	During driving
1G (Power supply)	EGR position sensor, Vacuum sensor, Atmospheric pressure sensor	4.5—5.5V	—
1H (Input)	Atmospheric pressure sensor	Approx. 4V	Sea level
1J (Input)	Intake air thermosensor	Approx. 4.1V	At 20°C (68°F)
1L (Memory power)	Battery	Approx. 12V	—
1N (Input)	Neutral and clutch switch	Approx. 12V	In gear
		Less than 1.5V	In neutral or depress clutch pedal
	Inhibitor switch	Less than 1.5V	In N or P range
		Approx. 12V	In other ranges
1O (Input)	Idle switch	Approx. 12V	At idle
		Less than 1.5V	At more than 1,200 rpm with no load
1P (Ground)	Idle switch	Less than 1.5V	—
1Q (Input)	Water temperature switch	Approx. 12V	Radiator coolant temp.: above 17°C (63°F)
		Less than 1.5V	Radiator coolant temp.: below 17°C (63°F)
1R (Ground)	Engine ground	Less than 1.5V	—
1S (Output)	Coasting advance solenoid valve	Approx. 12V	At idle
		Less than 1.5V	At 1,700—2,500 rpm during in-gear deceleration
1T (Output)	Idle-up solenoid valve (A/T)	Less than 1.5V	At less than 1,000 rpm in R, D, 2, or 1 range
		Approx. 12V	In N or P range or more than 1,100 rpm without A/C switch: ON
1U (Output)	Malfunction indicator light	Approx. 12V	light: OFF
		Less than 1.5V	light: ON
1V (Output)	Purge solenoid valve	Approx. 12V	At idle
		Less than 1.5V	At 1,400 rpm with warmed-up engine
2A (Input)	Ignition coil negative terminal	Approx. 12V	—
2B (Battery power)	Ignition switch (ON)	Approx. 12V	Ignition switch: ON
		0V	Ignition switch: OFF
2C (Input)	Air-conditioner magnetic clutch circuit	Approx. 12V	Air conditioner: ON
		0V	Air conditioner: OFF
2D (Output)	Slow fuel cut solenoid valve	Less than 15.V	Ignition switch: ON
		Less than 1.5V	At idle
		Approx. 12V	At 2,500 rpm or more during in-gear deceleration

FIG. 22 B2200, control pin location and voltage test

Item	Transmission type		Unit	Manual	Automatic
Fuel tank capacity	Short bed		Liter (US gal, Imp gal)	56 (14.8, 12.3)	
	Long bed		Liter (US gal, Imp gal)	66 (17.4, 14.5)	
Fuel filter	Type			Filter paper, with magnet	
Fuel pump	Type			Mechanical	Electrical
	Fuel pressure		kPa (kg/cm², psi)	26—32 (0.26—0.33, 3.7—4.7)	20—25 (0.20—0.25, 2.8—3.6)
	Flow rate		cc (cu in)/min	860 (52.5)	1,150 (70.2)
Carburetor	Type			Downdraft (2-barrel, 2-stage, auto-choke)	
	Throat diameter	Pri.	mm (in)	30 (1.181)	
		Sec.	mm (in)	34 (1.339)	
	Venturi diameter	Pri.	mm (in)	24.5 x 15 x 8 (0.965 x 0.591 x 0.315)	
		Sec.	mm (in)	31 x 10 (1.220 x 0.394)	
	Main jet	Pri.	mm (in)	1.04 (0.0409)	
		Sec.	mm (in)	1.50 (0.0591)	
	Main air bleed	Pri.	mm (in)	0.60 (0.0236)	
		Sec.	mm (in)	0.50 (0.0197)	
	Slow jet	Pri.	mm (in)	0.52 (0.0205)	
		Sec.	mm (in)	0.85 (0.0335)	
	Slow air bleed	Pri: No.1	mm (in)	0.80 (0.0315)	
		Pri: No.2	mm (in)	1.10 (0.0433)	
		Sec: No.1	mm (in)	0.80 (0.0315)	
		Sec: No.2	mm (in)	0.50 (0.0197)	
	Coasting richer jet		mm (in)	0.42 (0.0165)	
	Coasting richer air bleed	No.1	mm (in)	1.60 (0.0630)	
		No.2	mm (in)	2.60 (0.1024)	
	High-speed richer jet		mm (in)	1.80 (0.0709)	
	High-speed richer air bleed		mm (in)	1.00 (0.0394)	
	Solenoid controlled fuel jet		mm (in)	0.85 (0.0335)	
	Solenoid controlled air bleed		mm (in)	1.50 (0.0591)	
	Float level	High	mm (in)	11.6—12.6 (0.457—0.496)	10.7—11.7 (0.421—0.461)
		Low	mm (in)	46.0—47.0 (1.811—1.850)	
	Fast idle adjustment	Throttle valve clearance	mm (in)	0.84—1.04 (0.033—0.041)	
		Choke valve clearance	mm (in)	0.60—1.14 (0.024—0.045)	
	Secondary throttle valve adjustment	Throttle valve clearance	mm (in)	7.35—8.25 (0.289—0.325)	
	Unloader system adjustment	Choke valve clearance	mm (in)	2.80—3.62 (0.110—0.143)	
	Choke diaphragm adjustment	Choke valve clearance	mm (in)	1.70—2.16 (0.067—0.085)	
Air cleaner	Fresh-Hot			Bimetal, automatic	
	Element type			Wet	
Accelerator cable	Deflection		mm (in)	1—3 (0.04—0.12)	
Idle speed			rpm (in neutral or P range)	800 $^{+50}_{0}$	

FIG. 23 B2200, feedback carburetor specifications

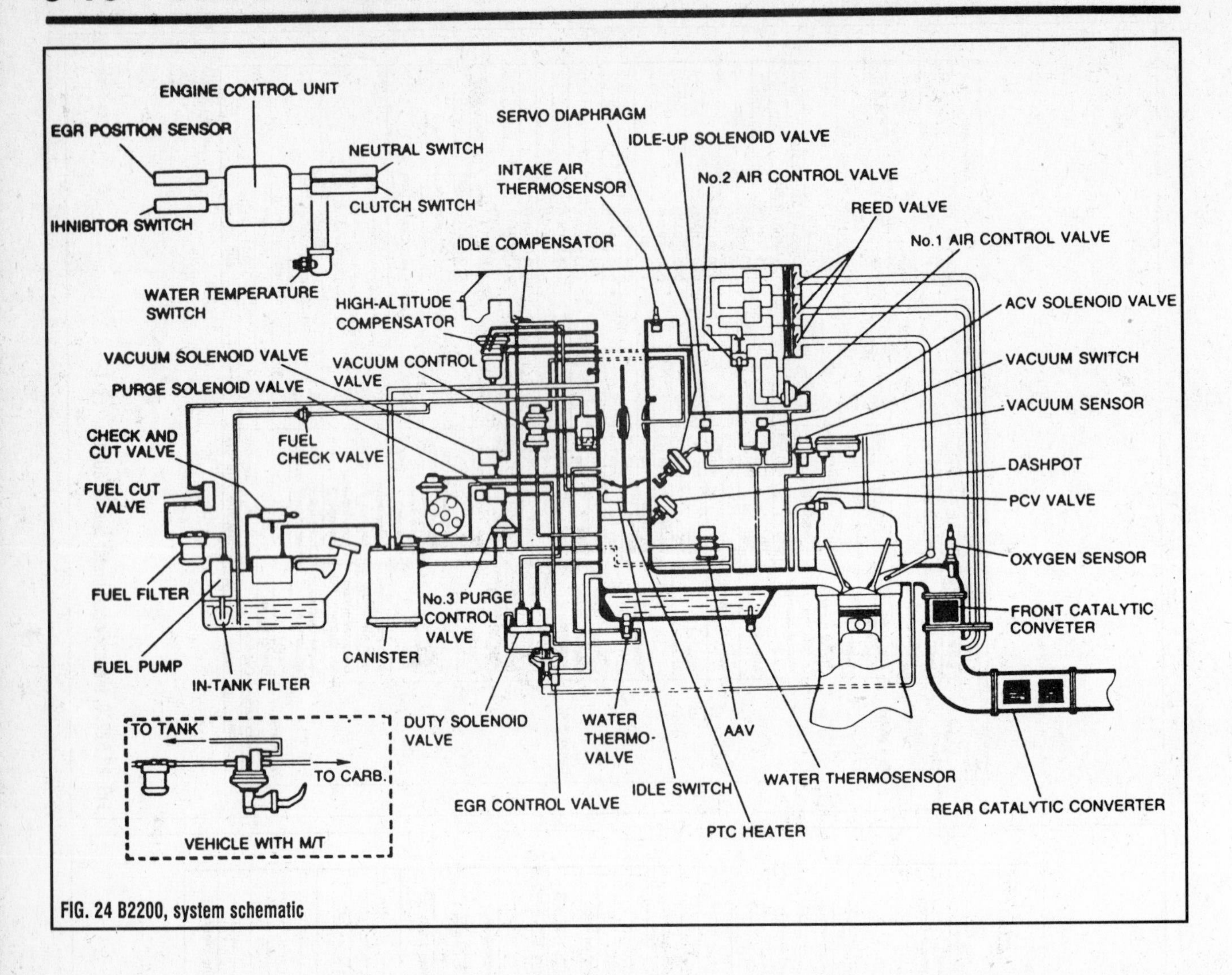

FIG. 24 B2200, system schematic

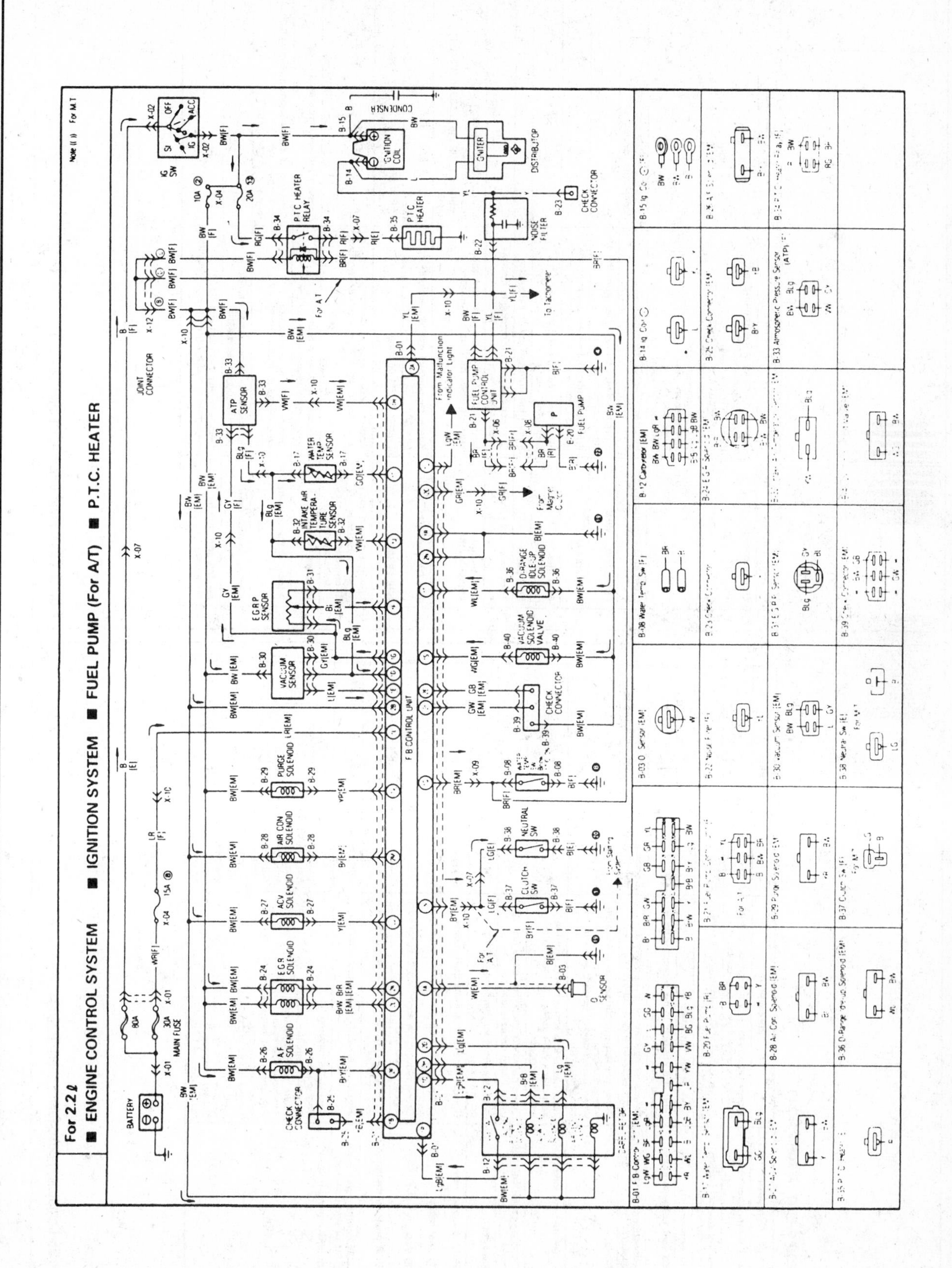

FIG. 25 Engine control, ignition and fuel system schematic, B2200

COMPONENT DESCRIPTIONS

Component	Function	Remarks
ACV solenoid valve	Applies vacuum to No.2 air control valve according to signal from engine control unit	
Air/fuel solenoid valve (in carburetor)	Controls air/fuel mixture according to signal from engine control unit	
Air cleaner	Filters air into carburetor	
Air vent solenoid valve	Vents float chamber to the canister while engine stopped	
Atmospheric pressure sensor	Detects atmospheric pressure (altitude); sends signal to engine control unit	Decreases amount of EGR at high altitude **(higher than 1,000 m, 3,280 ft)**
Canister	Stores gas tank and carburetor fumes while engine stopped When engine started, fumes drawn into intake manifold	
Check-and-cut valve	Vents fuel tank to atmosphere if vent line from check valve to No.2 purge control valve is clogged	
Coasting richer solenoid valve	Opens carburetor secondary stage fuel circuit during deceleration	
Dashpot	Gradually allows throttle closing during deceleration	
Duty solenoid valve **1) Vent valve** **2) Vacuum valve**	Controls vacuum to activate EGR control valve Opens vent according to signal from engine control unit Opens vacuum line according to signal from engine control unit	
EGR position sensor	Detects EGR control valve lift; sends signal to control unit	
EGR control valve (with EGR position sensor)	Introduces exhaust gas to intake manifold	Operates during acceleration and constant speed driving
Engine control unit	Detects the following: Engine speed Engine coolant temperature Intake manifold vacuum Atmospheric pressure Radiator coolant temperature Intake air temperature Oxygen concentration EGR valve lift Throttle opening In-gear condition Air conditioner ON/OFF	 Ignition coil negative (—) terminal Water thermosensor Vacuum sensor Atmospheric pressure sensor Water temperature switch Intake air thermosensor Oxygen sensor EGR position sensor Idle switch Neutral and clutch switch or inhibitor switch Air conditioner

FIG. 26 Component description chart, B2200

Component	Function	Remarks
Engine control unit	Controls operation of the following: Air/fuel (A/F) solenoid valve Idle-up solenoid valves Slow fuel cut solenoid valve Coasting richer solenoid valve Vacuum solenoid valve ACV solenoid valve Purge solenoid valve Duty solenoid valve	
Front catalytic converter	Reduces HC & CO by oxidation Reduces NOx	Converts into CO_2 and H_2O Honeycomb construction
Fuel check valve	Prevents leakage through fuel return line if vehicle turns over	
Fuel cut valve	Prevents leakage from main fuel line if the vehicle turns over	
Fuel filter	Filters fuel entering fuel pump and carburetor	
Fuel pump	Pumps fuel from fuel tank to carburetor	
Fuel pump cut relay	Operates fuel pump according to ignition pulse or alternator operation	
High-altitude compensator	Maintains air/fuel mixture when atmospheric pressure drops because of elevation	Adds air to air bleeds in carburetor and intake manifold Operates at altitude of 500 m (1,640 ft) or higher
Idle compensator	Keeps idle constant with temperature change	
Idle switch	Detects throttle opening	OFF at idle ON at 1,000—1,200 rpm
Idle-up solenoid valve **1) air conditioner** **2) automatic transmission**	Applies vacuum to servo diaphragm according to signal from engine control unit	
Inhibitor switch	Detects select lever position; sends signal to engine control unit	Senses transmission operating range
Intake air thermosensor	Detects intake air temperature; sends signal to engine control unit	Fixes duty of air/fuel solenoid valve at high air temperature (higher than 67°C, 153°C)
Mixture control valve	Supplies fresh air into intake manifold at first period of sudden deceleration	
Neutral and clutch switches	Detects in-gear operation and clutch engagement; sends signal to engine control unit	

FIG. 27 Component description chart, B2200

Component	Function	Remarks
No.1 air control valve	Supplies secondary air to reed valve A according to intake manifold vacuum	
No.1 purge control valve	Purges fuel vapor (stored in canister) into intake manifold during running	
No.2 air control valve	Supplies secondary air to reed valve A when ACV solenoid valve is ON	
No.2 purge control valve	Pressure and vacuum valves operate in accordance with fuel tank pressure	
No.3 purge control valve	Purges fuel vapor (stored in canister) into intake manifold when purge solenoid valve is ON	
Oxygen sensor	Detects exhaust oxygen concentration; sends signal to control unit	
PTC heater	Heats throttle body of carburetor and prevents icing	
Purge solenoid valve	Applies vacuum to No.3 purge control valve according to signal from engine control unit	
Rear catalytic converter (except for Canada)	Reduces HC & CO by oxidation	Converts into CO_2 and H_2O Honeycomb construction
Reed valves **Reed valve A** **Reed valves B and C**	Supplies secondary air to exhaust manifold (valve A) Supplies secondary air to exhaust pipe just behind front catalytic converter (valves B and C)	One-way valve on air cleaner
Servo diaphragm	Opens throttle valve by vacuum from idle-up solenoid valve (for A/C and A/T)	
Slow fuel cut solenoid valve	Cuts off primary slow fuel during deceleration or when ignition switch is OFF	Improves fuel consumption and prevents run-on
Vacuum control valve	Vents float chamber to intake manifold during heavy-load driving	
Vacuum sensor	Detects intake manifold vacuum; sends signal to engine control unit	
Vacuum solenoid valve	Applies intake manifold vacuum to vacuum control unit; advances ignition timing during deceleration	
Water temperature switch	Detects radiator coolant temperature; sends signal to engine control unit	ON at **15—19°C (59—66.2°F)** or lower
Water thermosensor	Detects intake manifold coolant temperature; sends signal to engine control unit	Thermistor
Water thermovalve	Opens and closes depending on engine coolant temperature	Opens at **46—54°C (114.8—129.2°F)** or higher

FIG. 28 Component description chart, B2200

Component	Color	Connected to:
ACV solenoid valve	Yellow Green	No.2 air control valve Intake manifold
Canister	Green Black Brown Black	No.3 purge control valve Intake manifold Water thermovalve Evaporative pipe
Distributor	Black	Intake manifold
Duty solenoid valve	Red Blue Black	EGR control valve Intake manifold Air cleaner
High-altitude compensator	Blue Black Brown	Carburetor (Primary main) Carburetor (Intake manifold) Carburetor (Secondary main)
Idle compensator	Black	Intake manifold
No.1 air control valve	Brown to green	Intake manifold
No.3 purge control valve	White Orange to black Green	Purge solenoid valve Intake manifold Canister
Purge solenoid valve	White Black to brown	No.3 purge control valve Intake manifold
Vacuum control valve	Red White Yellow	Intake manifold Secondary venturi (in carburetor) Float chamber (in carburetor)
Vacuum sensor	White	Intake manifold
Vacuum solenoid valve	Green Black	Intake manifold Distributor

FIG. 29 Vacuum hose color code and ID chart, B2200

Hard start or won't start (Cranks OK)

STEP	QUICK INSPECTION		ACTION		POSSIBLE CAUSE
1	(If trouble occurs only when engine is cold) Check if choke valve is fully closed when engine is cold	Yes	Go to Next Step		
		No	Replace automatic choke assembly		
2	Check if indicator atop battery is blue	Yes	Go to Next Step		
		No	Check if electrolyte level of battery is between upper and lower lines	Yes	Recharge battery
				No	Add distilled water
3	Check if fuel level is at specified mark on carburetor sight glass	Yes	Go to Next Step		
		No	(Higher than specified) Disassemble carburetor and check points shown		Check needle and seat for wear or rust
					Check float for damage
					Set float level
			(Lower than specified) M/T vehicle: Check for specified fuel pressure **Fuel pressure: 26—32 kPa (0.26—0.33 kg/cm², 3.7—4.7 psi)**	Yes	Set float level
				No	Replace fuel pump
			(Lower than specified) A/T vehicle: Check for fuel pump operation sound at fuel filler port [Ign ON, fuel pump control unit terminal-wire (B/R) and (B/W) jumped]	Yes	Check fuel pressure
					Set float level
				No	Check fuel pump control unit
					Replace fuel pump
4	Check for spark at disconnected high-tension lead while cranking	Yes	Go to Next Step		
		No	Check ignition system		
5	Check if spark plug condition is OK	Yes	Go to Next Step		
		No	Repair or replace spark plug(s)		
6	Check for air leakage by listening for sucking noise (Engine running)	Yes	Check points shown		Intake air system component damaged
					Vacuum hose disconnected or damaged
					Bolts or nuts loose
					Gasket damaged
		No	Go to Next Step		
7	Check for correct vacuum hose routing	Yes	Go to Next Step		
		No	Repair		

FIG. 30 B2200, feedback carburetor troubleshooting chart

Hard start or won't start (Cranks OK) (Cont'd)

STEP	QUICK INSPECTION		ACTION		POSSIBLE CAUSE
8	Check if air cleaner element is clean	Yes	Go to Next Step		
		No	Replace		
9	Pinch PCV hose and check if condition improves	Yes	Replace PCV valve		
		No	Go to Next Step		
10	Start engine	Yes	Replace mixture control valve		
	Block intake port of mixture control valve and check if engine speed drops	No	Increase engine speed and quickly decelerate Check that air is pulled into intake port for **1—2 sec** after accelerator is released	Yes	Go to Next Step
				No	Replace mixture control valve
11	Check for malfunction code with SST [Ign ON, test connector (Green: 1-pin) grounded]	Yes	Check for cause by referring to specified check sequence		
		No	Go to Next Step		
12	Disconnect and plug vacuum hose to EGR control valve and check if condition improves	Yes	Check ECU (2K), (2L) terminal voltage with SST **Voltage: 2K—Approx.12V 2L—Approx. 12V (While cranking)**	Yes	Check duty solenoid valve
				No	Check ECU (1C), (1Q) and (2A) terminal voltage with SST
		No	Check EGR control valve for operation	Yes	Go to Next Step
				No	Replace EGR control valve
13	(Only for "won't start" problem) Check if "clicking" is heard from slow fuel cut solenoid valve when ignition switch is turned OFF → ON	Yes	Go to Next Step		
		No	Check ECU (2D) Terminal voltage with SST **Voltage: . Less than 1.5V (Ign ON)**	Yes	Check slow fuel cut solenoid valve
				No	Check ECU (2B) terminal voltage with SST
14	Check carburetor		Check points shown		Check jet(s) for clogging
					Check nozzle for clogging
15	Check engine condition		Check points shown		Camshaft timing
					Compression

FIG. 31 B2200, feedback carburetor troubleshooting chart

Engine stalls during warm up

STEP	QUICK INSPECTION		ACTION		POSSIBLE CAUSE
1	Check if choke valve is slightly open just after starting	Yes	Check for correct choke diaphragm adjustment	Yes	Go to Next Step
				No	Adjust
		No	Check points shown		Check choke diaphragm for damage
					Check choke diaphragm vacuum hose for disconnection or damage
2	Check if choke valve opens as engine warms up	Yes	Go to Next Step		
		No	Check voltage at choke heater (Y/L) wire **Voltage: 6—8V (At idle)**	Yes	Replace automatic choke assembly
				No	Repair or replace wiring harness
3	Check if engine stalls when throttle valve is opened slightly	Yes	Go to Next Step		
		No	Check points shown		Mixture adjustment screw adjustment
					Slow jet clogged
4	Check for air leakage by listening for sucking noise	Yes	Check points shown		Intake air system components damaged
					Vacuum hose disconnected or damaged
					Bolts or nuts loose
					Gasket damaged
		No	Go to Next Step		
5	Check for correct vacuum hose routing	Yes	Go to Next Step		
		No	Repair		
6	Pinch PCV hose and check if condition improves	Yes	Replace PCV valve		
		No	Go to Next Step		
7	Disconnect air hoses (B), (L), and (BR) from carburetor Check high-altitude compensator by blowing through each hose **500 m (1,640 ft) or higher: Air flows** **Less than 500 m (1,640 ft): Air does not flows**	Yes	Go to Next Step		
		No	Replace high-altitude compensator		

FIG. 32 B2200, feedback carburetor troubleshooting chart

Engine stalls during warm up (Cont'd)

STEP	QUICK INSPECTION		ACTION		POSSIBLE CAUSE
8	Move control valve (for air intake temperature control system) inside air cleaner Verify that it moves freely and that spring force is felt	Yes	Go to Next Step		
		No	Replace air cleaner		
9	Check for malfunction code with SST [Ign ON, test connector (Green: 1-pin) grounded]	Yes	Check for cause by referring to specified check sequence		
		No	Go to Next Step		
10	Check switches for correct operation with SST monitor lamp [Ign ON, test connector (Green: 1-pin) grounded]	Yes	Go to Next Step		
		No	Check for cause by referring to specified check sequence		
11	Disconnect and plug vacuum hose to EGR control valve and check if condition improves	Yes	Check ECU (2K) and (2L) terminal voltage with SST **Voltage:** **2K—approx. 12V** **2L—approx. 12V** **(During warm up)**	Yes	Check duty solenoid valve
				No	Check ECU (1C), (1Q), and (2A) terminal voltage with SST
		No	Check EGR control valve for operation	Yes	Go to Next Step
				No	Replace EGR control valve
12	Check carburetor		Check points shown		Check main jet for clogging
					Check main nozzle for clogging

FIG. 33 B2200, feedback carburetor troubleshooting chart

Hard restarting when hot

STEP	QUICK INSPECTION		ACTION		POSSIBLE CAUSE
1	Check if choke valve is fully open when engine is hot	Yes	Go to Next Step		
		No	Check voltage at choke heater (Y/L) wire **Voltage: 6—8V (At idle)**	Yes	Replace automatic choke assembly
				No	Repair or replace wiring harness
2	Check if fuel level is at specified mark on carburetor sight glass	Yes	Go to Next Step		
		No	(Higher than specified) Disassemble carburetor and check points shown		Check needle and seat for wear or rust
					Check float for damage
					Set float level
			(Lower than specified) M/T vehicle: Check for specified fuel pressure **Fuel pressure: 26—32 kPa (0.26—0.33 kg/cm², 3.7—4.7 psi)**	Yes	Set float level
				No	Replace fuel pump
			(Lower than specified) A/T vehicle: Check for fuel pump operation sound at fuel filler port [Ign ON, fuel pump control unit terminal-wire (B/R) and (B/W) jumped]	Yes	Check fuel pressure
					Set float level
				No	Check fuel pump control unit
					Replace fuel pump
3	Pinch PCV hose and check if condition improves	Yes	Replace PCV valve		
		No	Go to Next Step		
4	Check for malfunction code with SST [Ign ON, test connector (Green: 1-pin) grounded]	Yes	Check for cause by referring to specified check sequence		
		No	Go to Next Step		
5	Check switches for correct operation with SST monitor lamp [Ign ON, test connector (Green: 1-pin) grounded]	Yes	Go to Next Step		
		No	Check for cause by referring to specified check sequence		

FIG. 34 B2200, feedback carburetor troubleshooting chart

Hard restarting when hot (Cont'd)

STEP	QUICK INSPECTION		ACTION		POSSIBLE CAUSE
6	Check if "clicking" is heard from slow fuel cut solenoid valve when ignition switch is turned OFF → ON	Yes	Go to Next Step		
		No	Check ECU (2D) terminal voltage with SST **Voltage: Less than 1.5V (Ign ON)**	Yes	Check slow fuel cut solenoid valve
				No	Check ECU (2B) terminal voltage with SST
7	Check if "clicking" is heard from air vent solenoid valve when ignition switch is turned OFF → ON	Yes	Go to Next Step		
		No	Check for solenoid valve operation	Yes	Check wiring harness
				No	Replace solenoid valve
8	Check if idle compensator is in closed position when bimetal temperature is less than specified **Opening temperature: 63°—71°C (145°—160°F)**	Yes	Go to Next Step		
		No	Replace idle compensator		
9	Disconnect and plug vacuum hose (B) from charcoal canister and check if condition improves	Yes	Check vacuum hose routing		
		No	Go to Next Step		
10	Warm up engine and run it at idle Connect dwellmeter to check connector (White: 1-pin) and check if reading is **within 20°—70°**	Yes	Go to Next Step		
		No	**(Fixed at 0°)** Check points shown		ECU (2A) terminal voltage
					ECU (1E) terminal voltage
					ECU (1O) terminal voltage
			(Fixed at 27°) Check points shown		ECU (1J) terminal voltage
					Vacuum hose routing
					ECU (1A) terminal voltage
					Oxygen sensor sensitivity
			(Fixed at 36°) Check points shown		ECU (1C) terminal voltage
			(Fluctuating out of 20°—70° range) Check points shown		Vacuum hose routing
					ECU (1A) terminal voltage
					Oxygen sensor sensitivity
					ECU (2F) terminal voltage
					Air/fuel solenoid valve operation
					Clogged jets and air bleeds in carburetor
					Idle mixture adjustment
11	Check carburetor		Check point shown		Loose jet(s)

Note: High RVP (winter) fuel can cause vapor lock in warm weather if used.

FIG. 35 B2200, feedback carburetor troubleshooting chart

High idle speed after warm up

STEP	QUICK INSPECTION		ACTION		POSSIBLE CAUSE
1	Check if choke valve is fully open when engine is hot	Yes	Go to Next Step		
		No	Check voltage at choke heater (Y/L) wire **Voltage: 6—8V (At idle)**	Yes	Replace automatic choke assembly
				No	Repair or replace wiring harness
2	Check for correct accelerator cable free play **Free play: 1—3mm (0.039—0.188 in)**	Yes	Go to Next Step		
		No	Adjust		
3	Check if idle speed can be adjusted by turning TAS	Yes	Adjust idle speed		
		No	Go to Next Step		
4	Check for correct ignition timing (Vacuum hose disconnected)	Yes	Go to Next Step		
		No	Adjust ignition timing		
5	Check for malfunction code with SST [Ign ON, test connector (Green: 1-pin) grounded]	Yes	Check for cause by referring to specified check sequence		
		No	Go to Next Step		
6	Disconnect vacuum hose(s) from servo diaphragm and check if condition improves	Yes	Check ECU terminal voltage (1T), (2M) with SST **Voltage:** **1T—Less than 1.5V (At less than 1,000 rpm in R, D, 2 or 1 range) Approx. 12V (In N or P range or more than 1,100 rpm without A/C switch: ON)** **2M—Less than 1.5V [At idle (A/C: ON)] Approx. 12V [At 1,400 rpm or below (A/C: ON)]**	Yes	Check idle-up solenoid valve
				No	Check ECU terminal voltage (IN) and (2C) with SST
		No	Go to Next Step		
7	Check if throttle lever separates from dashpot rod **at approx. 1,900—2,100 rpm**	Yes	Go to Next Step		
		No	Adjust		
8	Check carburetor		Check point shown		Carburetor linkage

FIG. 36 B2200, feedback carburetor troubleshooting chart

Engine idles roughly or stalls

STEP	QUICK INSPECTION		ACTION		POSSIBLE CAUSE
1	Check for air leakage by listening for sucking noise	Yes	Check points shown		Intake air system component damaged
					Vacuum hose disconnected or damaged
					Bolts or nuts loose
					Gasket damaged
		No	Go to Next Step		
2	Check if fuel level is at specified mark on carburetor sight glass	Yes	Go to Next Step		
		No	(Higher than specified) Disassemble carburtor and check points shown		Check needle and seat for wear or rust
					Check float for damage
					Set float level
			(Lower than specified) M/T vehicle: Check for specified fuel pressure **Fuel pressure: 26—32 kPa (0.26—0.33 kg/cm² 3.7—4.7 psi)**	Yes	Set float level
				No	Replace fuel pump
			(Lower than specified) A/T vehicle: Check for fuel pump operation sound at fuel filler port [Ign ON, fuel pump control unit terminal-wire (B/R) and (B/W) jumped]	Yes	Check fuel pressure
					Set float level
				No	Check fuel pump control unit
					Replace fuel pump
3	Disconnect high-tension lead from individual cylinders and check if condition changes	Yes	Go to Next Step		
		No	Check ignition system		Spark plug
					High-tension lead
					Distributor cap, rotor
4	Check for correct ignition timing **Ignition timing: 6° ± 1° BTDC**	Yes	Go to Next Step		
		No	Adjust ignition timing		
5	Turn throttle adjustment screw counterclockwise and check if condition improves	Yes	Adjust idle speed		
		No	Go to Next Step		
6	Pinch PCV hose and check if condition improves	Yes	Replace PCV valve		
		No	Go to Next Step		
7	Check for malfunction code with SST [Ign ON, test connector (Green: 1-pin) grounded]	Yes	Check for cause by referring to specified check sequence		
		No	Go to Next Step		
8	Check switches for correct operation with SST monitor lamp [Ign ON, test connector (Green: 1-pin) grounded]	Yes	Go to Next Step		
		No	Check for cause by referring to specified check sequence		

FIG. 37 B2200, feedback carburetor troubleshooting chart

Engine idles roughly or stalls (Cont'd)

STEP	QUICK INSPECTION		ACTION		POSSIBLE CAUSE
9	Check for correct EGR system vacuum hose routing	Yes	Go to Next Step		
		No	Repair or replace vacuum hose		
10	Disconnect and plug vacuum hose to EGR control valve and check if condition improves	Yes	Check ECU (2K) and (2L) terminal voltage with SST **Voltage:** **2K—Approx. 12V** **2L—Approx. 12V** **(At idle)**	Yes	Check duty solenoid valve
				No	Check ECU (1C), (1Q), and (2A) terminal voltage with SST
		No	Check EGR control valve for operation	Yes	Go to Next Step
				No	Replace EGR control valve
11	Check if "clicking" is heard from slow fuel cut solenoid valve when ignition switch is turned OFF → ON	Yes	Go to Next Step		
		No	Check ECU (2D) terminal voltage with SST **Voltage:** **Less than 1.5V** **(Ign ON)**	Yes	Check slow fuel cut solenoid valve
				No	Check ECU (2B) terminal voltage with SST
12	Check if idle compensator is closed when bimetal temperture is **below 63°—71°C (145°—160°F)**	Yes	Go to Next Step		
		No	Replace idle compensator		
13	Disconnect air hoses (B), (L) and (BR) from carburetor Check high-altitude compensator by blowing through each hose **500 m (1,640 ft) or higher: Airflows** **Less than 500 m (1,640 ft): Air does not flow**	Yes	Go to Next Step		
		No	Replace high-altitude compensator		
14	Check vacuum control valve				
15	Check carburetor		Check points shown		Check jet(s) for clogging
					Check carburetor fuel line for clogging
16	Check engine condition		Check point shown		Compression

FIG. 38 B2200, feedback carburetor troubleshooting chart

Hesitation on acceleration or start-up

STEP	QUICK INSPECTION		ACTION		POSSIBLE CAUSE
1	Check if fuel level is at specified mark on sight glass	Yes	Go to Next Step		
		No	(Higher than specified) Disassemble carburetor and check points shown		Check needle and seat for wear or rust
					Check float for damage
					Set float level
			(Lower than specified) M/T vehicle: Check for specified fuel pressure **Fuel pressure:** **26—32 kPa (0.26—0.33 kg/cm², 3.7—4.7 psi)**	Yes	Set float level
				No	Replace fuel pump
			(Lower than specified) A/T vehicle: Check for fuel pump operation sound at fuel filler port [Ign ON, fuel pump control unit terminal-wire (B/R) and (B/W) jumped]	Yes	Check fuel pressure
					Set float level
				No	Check fuel pump control unit
					Replace fuel pump
2	Check if fuel is discharged from accelerator pump nozzle when opening throttle valve	Yes	Go to Next Step		
		No	Check if accelerator pump is damaged	Yes	Replace accelerator pump
				No	Clean carburetor fuel passages
3	Check for correct ignition timing **Ignition timing** **6° ± 1° BTDC**	Yes	Go to Next Step		
		No	Adjust ignition timing		
4	Check for correct idle speed **Idle speed** **800^{+50}_{-0} rpm (A/T: P range)**	Yes	Go to Next Step		
		No	Adjust idle speed		
5	Check for air leakage with throttle valve opened	Yes	Repair		
		No	Go to Next Step		
6	Check for malfunction code with SST [Ign ON, test connector (Green: 1-pin) grounded]	Yes	Check for cause by referring to specified check sequence		
		No	Go to Next Step		
7	Check switches for correct operation with SST monitor lamp [Ign ON, test connector (Green: 1-pin) grounded]	Yes	Go to Next Step		
		No	Check for cause by referring to specified check sequence		

FIG. 39 B2200, feedback carburetor troubleshooting chart

Hesitation on acceleration or start-up (Cont'd)

STEP	QUICK INSPECTION		ACTION		POSSIBLE CAUSE
8	Warm up engine and run it at idle	Yes	Go to Next Step		
	Connect dwellmeter to check connector (White: 1-pin) and check if dwellmeter reading is **within 20°—70°**	No	**(Fixed at 0°)** Check points shown		ECU (2A) terminal voltage
					ECU (1E) terminal voltage
					ECU (1O) terminal voltage
			(Fixed at 27°) Check points shown		ECU (1J) terminal voltage
					Vacuum hose routing
					ECU (1A) terminal voltage
					Oxygen sensor sensitivity
			(Fixed at 36°) Check points shown		ECU (1C) terminal voltage
			(Fluctuating out of 20°—70° range) Check points shown		Vacuum hose routing
					ECU (1A) terminal voltage
					Oxygen sensor sensitivity
					ECU (2F) terminal voltage
					Air/fuel solenoid valve operation
					Clogged jets and air bleeds in carburetor
					Idle mixture adjustment
9	Increase engine speed to **4,500 rpm** and check if dwellmeter indicates a **fixed 0°**	Yes	Go to Next Step		
		No	Replace Engine control unit		
10	Check for correct ignition timing advance	Yes	Go to Next Step		
		No	Insufficient centrifugal advance: Distributor malfunction		
			Insufficient vacuum advance: Check for vacuum routing	Yes	Distributor malfunction
				No	Vacuum hose
11	Disconnect and plug vacuum hose to EGR control valve and check if condition improves	Yes	Check ECU (2K) and (2L) terminal voltage with SST **Voltage: Drops from 12V and green and red lights flash (While accelerating)**	Yes	Check duty solenoid valve
				No	Check ECU (1C), (1Q), and (2A) terminal voltage with SST
		No	Check EGR control valve	Yes	Go to Next Step
				No	Replace EGR control valve
12	Check carburetor		Check point shown		Clogged primary main jet or nozzle

FIG. 40 B2200, feedback carburetor troubleshooting chart

Lack of power

STEP	QUICK INSPECTION		ACTION		POSSIBLE CAUSE
1	Check if air cleaner element is clean	Yes	Go to Next Step		
		No	Replace air cleaner element		
2	Check if fuel level is at specified mark on carburetor sight glass	Yes	Go to Next Step		
		No	(Higher than specified) Disassemble carburetor and check points shown		Check needle and seat for wear or rust
					Check float for damage
					Set float level
			(Lower than specified) M/T vehicle: Check for specified fuel pressure **Fuel pressure: 26—32 kPa (0.26—0.33 kg/cm², 3.7—4.7 psi)**	Yes	Set float level
				No	Replace fuel pump
			(Lower than specified) A/T vehicle: Check for sound at fuel pump operation fuel filler port [Ign ON, fuel pump control unit terminal-wire (B/R) and (B/W) jumped]	Yes	Check fuel pressure
					Set float level
				No	Check fuel pump control unit
					Replace fuel pump
3	Check ignition timing **Ignition timing: 6° ± 1° BTDC**	Yes	Go to Next Step		
		No	Adjust ignition timing		
4	Check for correct ignition timing advance	Yes	Go to Next Step		
		No	Insufficient centrifugal advance: Distributor malfunction		
			Insufficient vacuum advance: Check for correct vacuum hose routing	Yes	Distributor malfunction
				No	Repair vacuum hose
5	Check if spark plug condition is OK	Yes	Go to Next Step		
		No	Repair or replace spark plug(s)		
6	Check for malfunction code with SST [Ign ON, test connector (Green: 1-pin) grounded]	Yes	Check for cause by referring to specified check sequence		
		No	Go to Next Step		

FIG. 41 B2200, feedback carburetor troubleshooting chart

Lack of power (Cont'd)

STEP	QUICK INSPECTION		ACTION		POSSIBLE CAUSE
6	Check switches for correct operation with SST monitor lamp [Ign ON, SST connector (Green: 1-pin) grounded]	Yes	Go to Next Step		
		No	Check for cause by referring to specified check sequence		
7	Disconnect and plug vacuum hose to EGR control valve and check if condition improves	Yes	Check ECU (2K) and (2L) terminal voltage with SST **Voltage: Drops from 12V and green and red lights flash (While acceleration)**	Yes	Check duty solenoid valve
				No	Check ECU (1C), (1O), and (2A) terminal voltage with SST
		No	Check EGR control valve for operation	Yes	Go to Next Step
				No	Replace EGR control valve
8	Warm up engine and run it at idle Connect dwellmeter to check connector (White: 1-pin) and check if reading is **within 20°—70°**	Yes	Go to Next Step		
		No	**(Fixed at 0°)** Check points shown		ECU (2A) terminal voltage
					ECU (1E) terminal voltage
					ECU (1O) terminal voltage
			(Fixed at 27°) Check points shown		ECU (1J) terminal voltage
					Vacuum hose routing
					ECU (1A) terminal voltage
					Oxygen sensor sensitivity
			(Fixed at 36°) Check points shown		ECU (1C) terminal voltage
			(Fluctuating out of 20°—70° range) Check points shown		Vacuum hose routing
					ECU (1A) terminal voltage
					Oxygen sensor sensitivity
					ECU (2F) terminal voltage
					Air/fuel solenoid valve operation
					Clogged jets and air bleeds in carburetor
					Idle mixture adjustment
9	Check engine condition		Check compression		
10	Check carburetor		Check point shown		• Clogged primary main jet or nozzle • Clogged secondary main jet or nozzle • Secondary throttle valve opening
11	Check exhaust system for clogging				

FIG. 42 B2200, feedback carburetor troubleshooting chart

Afterburn on deceleration

STEP	QUICK INSPECTION		ACTION		POSSIBLE CAUSE
1	Check for correct ignition timing **Ignition timing: 6° ± 1° BTDC**	Yes	Go to Next Step		
		No	Adjust ignition timing		
2	Check for correct ignition timing advance	Yes	Go to Next Step		
		No	Insufficient centrifugal advance: Distributor malfunction		
			Insufficient Vacuum advance: Check for vacuum routing	Yes	Distributor malfunction
				No	Repair vacuum hose
3	Check if air cleaner element is clean	Yes	Go to Next Step		
		No	Replace		
4	Check for malfunction code with SST [Ign ON, test connector (Green: 1-pin) grounded]	Yes	Check for cause by referring to specified check sequence		
		No	Go to Next Step		
5	Check switches for correct operation with SST monitor lamp [IGN ON, Test connector (Green: 1-pin) grounded]	Yes	Go to Next Step		
		No	Check for cause by referring to specified check sequence		

FIG. 43 B2200, feedback carburetor troubleshooting chart

Afterburn on deceleration (Cont'd)

STEP	QUICK INSPECTION		ACTION		POSSIBLE CAUSE
6	Disconnect neutral switch (M/T) or inhibitor switch (A/T) connector	Yes	Go to Next Step		
	Decelerate engine from **3,000 rpm** and check if "clicking" sound is heard from slow fuel cut solenid valve	No	Check ECU (2D) terminal voltage with SST **At idle: Less than 1.5V Above 2,500 rpm during deceleration: Approx. 12V**	Yes	Check slow fuel cut solenoid valve
				No	Check ECU (1N), (2A), (1O), and (1P) terminal voltage with SST
7	Disconnect neutral switch (M/T) or inhibitor switch (A/T) connector	Yes	Go to Next Step		
	Decelerate engine from **3,000 rpm** and check if "clicking" sound is heard from coasting richer solenoid valve	No	Check ECU (2H) terminal voltage with SST **At idle: Approx. 12V At 2,500—1,400 rpm during deceleration: Less than 1.5V**	Yes	Check coasting richer solenoid valve
				No	Check ECU (1N), (2A), (1O), and (1P) terminal voltage with SST
8	Disconnect neutral switch (M/T) or inhibitor switch (A/T) connector	Yes	Go to Next Step		
	Decelerate engine from **3,000 rpm** and check if "clicking" is heard from coasting advance solenoid valve	No	Check ECU (1S) terminal voltage with SST **At idle: Approx. 12V At 2,500—1,700 rpm during deceleration: Below 1.5V**	Yes	Check coasting advance solenoid valve
				No	Check ECU (1N), (2A), (1O), and (1P) terminal voltage with SST
9	Start engine	Yes	Replace mixture control valve		
	Block intake port of mixture control valve and check if engine speed drops	No	Increase engine speed and quickly decelerate Verify that air is pulled into intake port for **1—2 sec** after accelerator is released	Yes	Go to Next Step
				No	Replace mixture control valve
10	Check if throttle lever separates from dashpot rod **at 1,900—2,100 rpm**	Yes	Go to Next Step		
		No	Adjust dashpot		

FIG. 44 B2200, feedback carburetor troubleshooting chart

Afterburn on deceleration (Cont'd)

STEP	QUICK INSPECTION		ACTION		POSSIBLE CAUSE
11	Place a thin paper over inlet port of reed valves (B) and (C) Increase engine speed to **1,500 rpm** and check if air is pulled in	Yes	Increase engine speed to **3,000 rpm** and check if exhaust gas leaks from air inlet port	Yes	Replace reed valve(s)
				No	Go to Next Step
		No			Replace reed valve(s)
12	Disconnect and plug vacuum hose (Y) to No.2 air control valve	Yes	Go to Next Step		
	Place a thin paper over inlet port of reed valve (D) and increase engine speed to **1,500 rpm** and check if air is pulled in	No	Check No.1 air control valve for operation	Yes	Replace reed valve
				No	Replace No.1 air control valve
13	Disconnect and plug vacuum hose to No.1 air control valve	Yes	Go to Next Step		
	Apply **90 mmHg (3.54 inHg)** of vacuum to No.2 air control valve Place a thin paper over inlet port (E) of reed valve and increase engine speed to **1,500 rpm** and check if air is pulled in	No	Check No.2 air control valve for operation	Yes	Check reed valve
				No	Replace No.2 air control valve
14	Disconnect water temperature switch connector and check that no vacuum exists at No.2 air control valve vacuum hose (Y)	Yes	Increase engine speed to **1,500 rpm** and check if vacuum is felt at vacuum hose	Yes	Go to Next Step
				No	Check ACV solenoid valve
		No	Check ACV solenoid valve		
15	Check engine condition		Check points shown		Check compression
					Check valve timing

FIG. 45 B2200, feedback carburetor troubleshooting chart

High fuel consumption

STEP	QUICK INSPECTION		ACTION	POSSIBLE CAUSE
1	Check other systems for proper operation • Brake • Clutch • A/T	Yes	Go to Next Step	
		No		Brake dragging
				Clutch slipping
				A/T shifting
2	Check for correct idle speed **Idle speed: 800^{+50}_{-0} rpm (A/T: P range)**	Yes	Go to next Step	
		No	Adjust	
3	Check for correct ignition timing **Ignition timing: 6° ± 1° BTDC**	Yes	Go to Next Step	
		No	Adjust	
4	Check for correct ignition timing advance	Yes	Go to Next Step	
		No	Insufficient centrifugal advance: Distributor malfunction	
			Insufficient vacuum advance: Check vacuum hose routing — Yes	Distributor malfunction
			Insufficient vacuum advance: Check vacuum hose routing — No	Repair or replace vacuum hose
5	Check if air cleaner element is clean	Yes	Go to Next Step	
		No	Replace	
6	Check if fuel level is at specified mark on carburetor sight glass	Yes	Go to Next Step	
		No	Adjust float level setting	
7	Check if choke valve fully opens after warm up	Yes	Go to Next Step	
		No	Replace automatic choke assembly	

FIG. 46 B2200, feedback carburetor troubleshooting chart

High fuel consumption (Cont'd)

STEP	QUICK INSPECTION		ACTION	POSSIBLE CAUSE
8	Check if spark plug condition is OK	Yes	Go to Next Step	
		No	Repair or replace	
9	Check for malfunction code with SST [Ign ON, test connector (Green: 1-pin) grounded]	Yes	Check for cause by referring to specified check sequence	
		No	Go to Next Step	
10	Check switches for correct operation with SST monitor lamp [IGN ON, test connector (Green: 1-pin) grounded]	Yes	Go to Next Step	
		No	Check for cause by referring to specified check sequence	
11	Warm up engine and run it at idle Connect dwellmeter to check connector (White: 1-pin) and check if reading is **within 20°—70°**	Yes	Go to Next Step	
		No	**(Fixed at 0°)** Check points shown	ECU (2A) terminal voltage
				ECU (1E) terminal voltage
				ECU (1C) terminal voltage
			(Fixed at 27°) Check points shown	ECU (1J) terminal voltage
				ECU (1A) terminal voltage
				Oxygen sensor sensitivity
				Vacuum hose routing
			(Fixed at 36°) Check points shown	ECU (1C) terminal voltage
			(Fluctuating out of 20°—70° range) Check points shown	ECU (1A) terminal voltage
				ECU (2F) terminal voltage
				Oxygen sensor sensitivity
				Air/fuel solenoid valve operation
				Vacuum hose routing
				Idle mixture adjustment
				Clogged jet(s) and air bleed(s) in carburetor
12	Check carburetor		Check point shown	Clogged or loose jet(s) and air bleed(s)

Note: Some loss of fuel economy is expected with alchol blended fuels.

FIG. 47 B2200, feedback carburetor troubleshooting chart

FUEL INJECTION GENERAL SERVICE

System Description

The fuel injection system supplies the fuel necessary for combustion to the injectors at a constant pressure. Fuel is metered and injected into the intake manifold according to the injection control signals from the Engine Control Unit (ECU) or Engine Control Assembly (ECA). Most fuel injection systems consist of the following components: a fuel filter, distribution pipe, pulsation dampener, pressure regulator, injectors, fuel pump switch located in the airflow meter or mass airflow sensor for Navajo and the electric fuel pump usually located in the fuel tank in order to keep operating noise to a minimum.

The ECU or ECA, through various input sensors, monitors battery voltage, engine rpm, amount of air intake, cranking signals, intake temperature, coolant temperature, oxygen concentration in the exhaust gases, throttle opening, atmospheric or barometric pressure, gearshift position, clutch engagement, braking, power steering operation and air conditioner compressor operation.

The ECU or ECA controls operation of the fuel injection system, idle up system, fuel evaporation system and ignition timing. The control assembly has a built in fail safe mechanism. If a fault occurs while driving, the control assembly will substitute pre-programmed values. Driving performance will be affected but the vehicle will still, in most cases be drivable.

Fuel System Service Precautions

Safety is the most important factor when performing not only fuel system maintenance but any type of maintenance. Failure to conduct maintenance and repairs in a safe manner may result in serious personal injury or death. Maintenance and testing of the vehicle's fuel system components can be accomplished safely and effectively by adhering to the following rules and guidelines.

- To avoid the possibility of fire and personal injury, always disconnect the negative battery cable unless the repair or test procedure requires that battery voltage be applied.
- Always relieve the fuel system pressure prior to disconnecting any fuel system component (injector, fuel rail, pressure regulator, etc.), fitting or fuel line connection. Exercise extreme caution whenever relieving fuel system pressure to avoid exposing skin, face and eyes to fuel spray. Please be advised that fuel under pressure may penetrate the skin or any part of the body that it contacts.
- Always place a shop towel or cloth around the fitting or connection prior to loosening to absorb any excess fuel due to spillage. Ensure that all fuel spillage (should it occur) is quickly removed from engine surfaces. Ensure that all fuel soaked cloths or towels are deposited into a suitable waste container.
- Always keep a dry chemical (Class B) fire extinguisher near the work area.
- Do not allow fuel spray or fuel vapors to come into contact with a spark or open flame.
- Always use a backup wrench when loosening and tightening fuel line connection fittings. This will prevent unnecessary stress and torsion to fuel line piping. Always follow the proper torque specifications.
- Always replace worn fuel fitting O-rings with new. Do not substitute fuel hose or equivalent where fuel pipe is installed.

Relieving Fuel System Pressure

Fuel lines on fuel injected vehicles will remain pressurized after the engine is shut off. This residual pressure must be relieved before any fuel lines or components are disconnected.

Except Navajo

1. Start the engine.
2. Disconnect the circuit opening relay connector, airflow meter connector or fuel pump connector.
3. After the engine stalls, turn **OFF** the ignition switch.
4. Reconnect the electrical connector.

➡ After releasing fuel system pressure, the system must be primed before starting the engine to avoid excessive cranking. To prime the system, connect the terminals of the yellow 2-pin test connector with a jumper wire and turn the ignition switch ON for approximately 10 seconds. Check for fuel leaks, then turn the ignition switch OFF and remove the jumper wire.

Navajo

1. Disconnect the negative battery cable and remove the fuel filler cap.
2. Remove the cap from the pressure relief valve on the fuel supply manifold. Install pressure gauge 49 UN01 010 or equivalent, to the pressure relief valve.
3. Direct the gauge drain hose into a suitable container and depress the pressure relief button.
4. Remove the gauge and replace the cap on the pressure relief valve.

➡ As an alternate method, disconnect the inertia switch and crank the engine for 15–20 seconds until the pressure is relieved.

Electric Fuel Pump

➧ SEE FIGS. 48-57

TESTING

Except Navajo

1. Relieve the fuel system pressure and disconnect the negative battery cable.
2. Disconnect the fuel line from the fuel filter outlet. Connect a fuel pressure gauge to the fuel filter outlet.
3. Connect the negative battery cable. Connect the terminals of the yellow 2-pin test connector with a jumper wire.
4. Turn the ignition switch **ON** to operate the fuel pump and check the fuel pressure. It should be 64–85 psi.
5. If the fuel pressure is not as specified, replace the fuel pump.
6. Turn the ignition switch **OFF** and disconnect the negative battery cable. Remove the jumper wire from the test connector.
7. Remove the fuel pressure gauge and reconnect the fuel line to the fuel filter outlet.
8. Connect the negative battery cable.

Navajo

1. Make sure there is an adequate fuel supply.
2. Relieve the fuel system pressure.
3. Turn the ignition key **OFF**.
4. Connect a suitable fuel pressure gauge to the Schrader valve on the fuel rail.

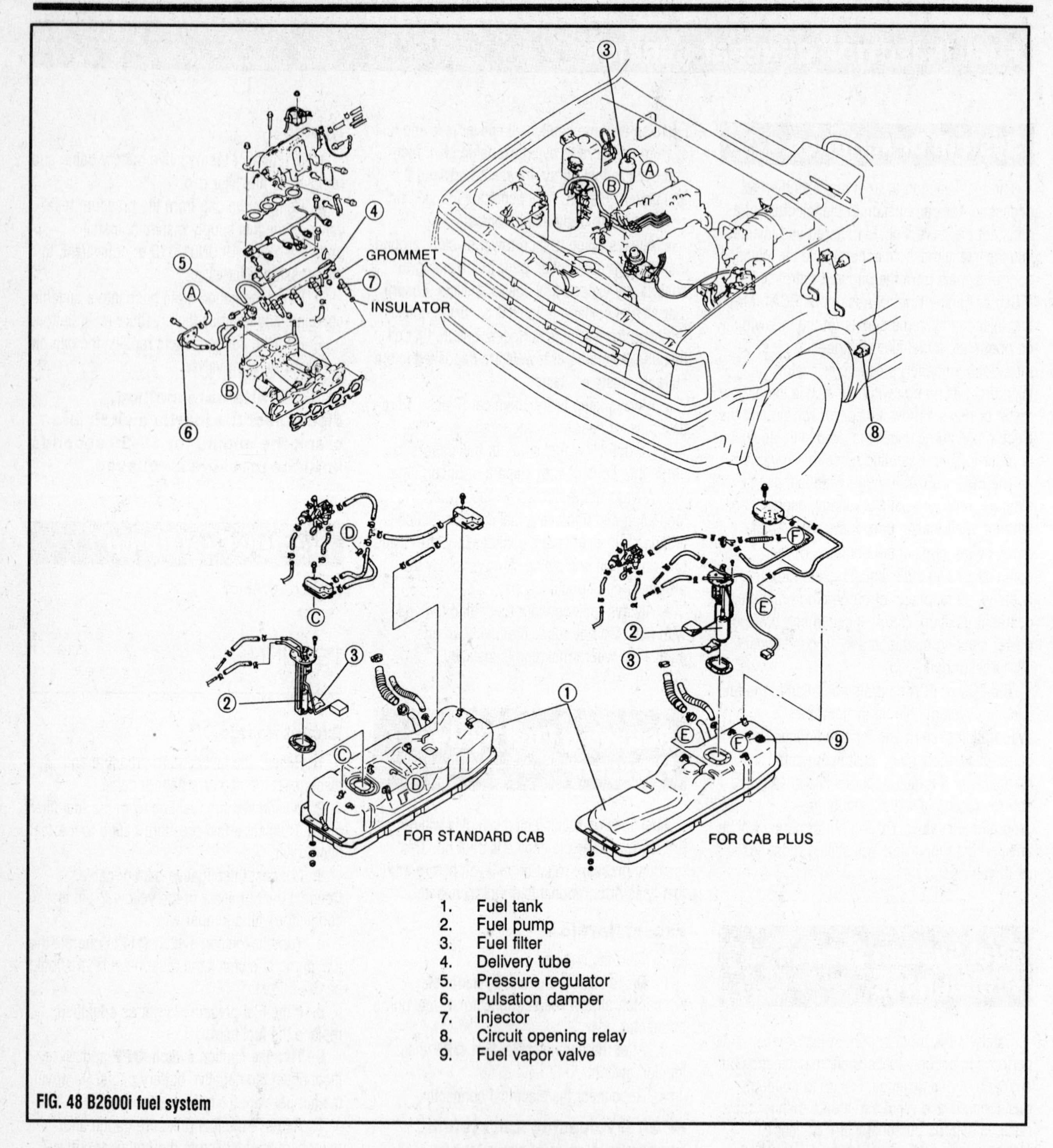

FIG. 48 B2600i fuel system

5. Install a test lead to the **FP** terminal on the VIP test connector.

6. Turn the ignition key to the **RUN** position, then ground the test lead to run the fuel pump.

7. Observe the fuel pressure reading on the pressure gauge. The fuel pressure should be 35–45 psi.

8. Relieve the fuel system pressure and turn the ignition key **OFF**. Remove the fuel pressure gauge and the test lead.

REMOVAL & INSTALLATION

➡ **The fuel pump is located inside the fuel tank, attached to the tank sending unit assembly.**

Pickups Models

1. Relieve the fuel system pressure and disconnect the negative battery cable.

2. Remove the fuel tank.

3. Remove any dirt that has accumulated around the sending unit/fuel pump assembly so it will not enter the fuel tank during removal and installation.

4. Remove the attaching screws and remove the sending unit/fuel pump assembly.

5. If necessary, disconnect the electrical connectors and the fuel hose and remove the pump from the sending unit assembly.

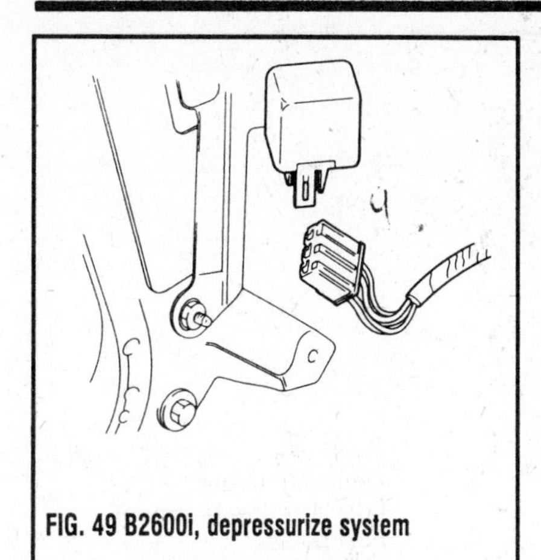

FIG. 49 B2600i, depressurize system

FIG. 50 B2600i, connect fuel pressure gauge

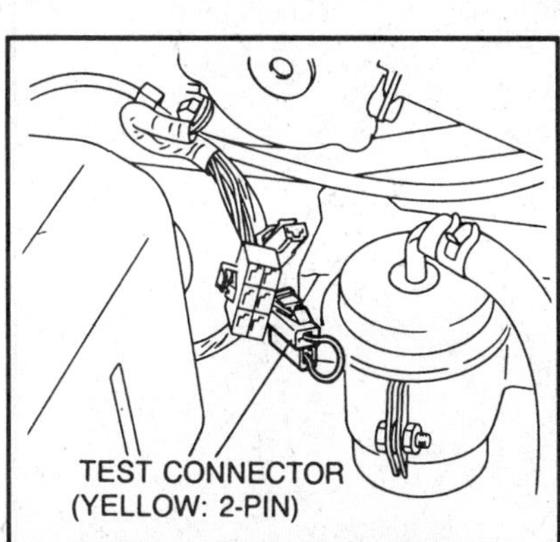

FIG. 51 B2600i, connect the terminals of the test connector (yellow 2 pin) with a jumper wire. Turn the ignition switch ON for 10 seconds to operate the fuel pump. Turn switch OFF and observe the fuel pressure after 5 minutes

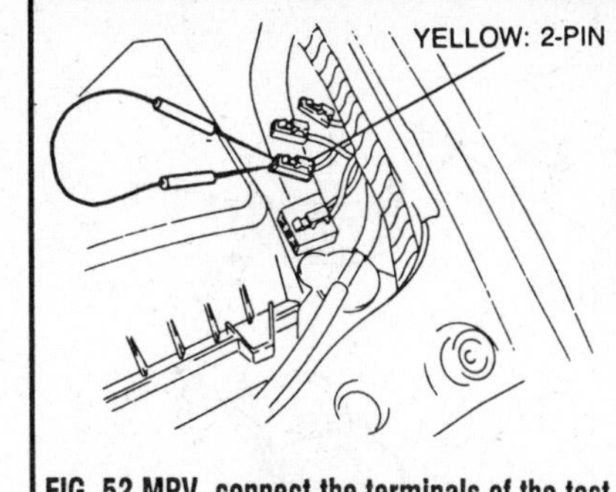

FIG. 52 MPV, connect the terminals of the test connector (yellow 2 pin) with a jumper wire. Turn the ignition switch ON to operate the fuel pump. Pressure should be 64-85 psi.

6. Installation is the reverse of the removal procedure. Be sure to install a new seal rubber gasket.

MPV

1. Relieve the fuel system pressure and disconnect the negative battery cable.
2. Remove the rear seat and lift up the rear floormat. Remove the fuel pump cover.
3. Disconnect the sending unit/fuel pump assembly electrical connector and the fuel lines.
4. Remove any dirt that has accumulated around the sending unit/fuel pump assembly so it will not enter the fuel tank during removal and installation.
5. Remove the attaching screws and remove the sending unit/fuel pump assembly.
6. If necessary, disconnect the electrical connectors and the fuel hose and remove the pump from the sending unit assembly.
7. Installation is the reverse of the removal procedure. Be sure to install a new seal rubber gasket.

Navajo

1. Disconnect the negative battery cable and relieve the fuel system pressure.
2. Raise and safely support the vehicle.
3. Remove the fuel tank.
4. Remove any dirt that has accumulated around the fuel pump attaching flange so it will not enter the fuel tank during removal and installation.
5. Turn the fuel pump locking ring counterclockwise using a suitable tool. Remove the locking ring.
6. Remove the fuel pump and discard the seal ring. Separate the fuel pump from the sending unit, if required.

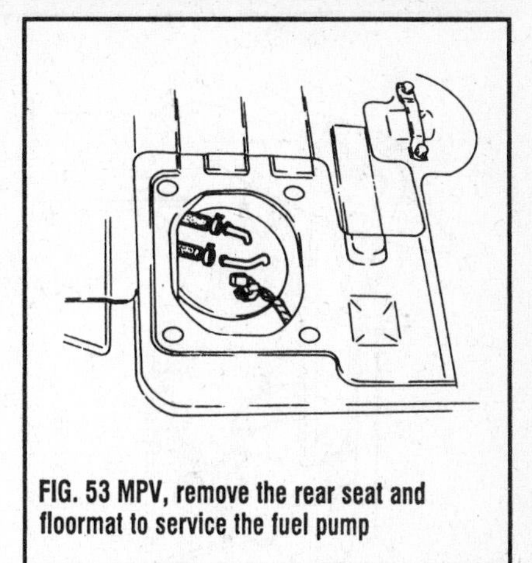

FIG. 53 MPV, remove the rear seat and floormat to service the fuel pump

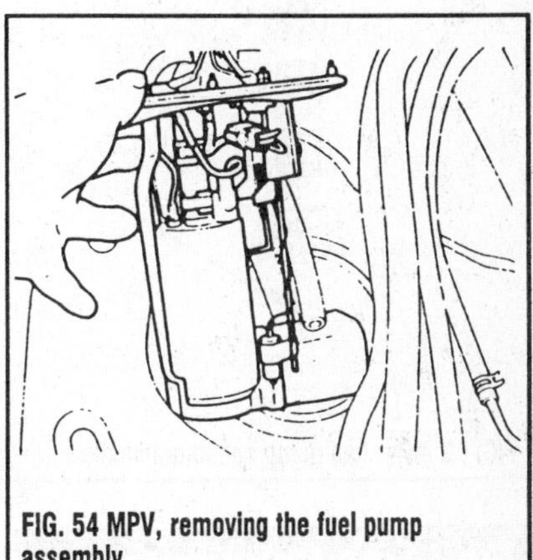

FIG. 54 MPV, removing the fuel pump assembly

To install:

7. Clean the fuel pump mounting flange and tank mounting surface and seal ring groove.
8. Apply a light coating of Molybdenum grease on a new seal ring and install it in the groove.
9. Install the fuel pump to the sending unit, if removed. Install the fuel pump assembly in the tank, making sure the locating keys are in the keyways and the seal ring is in place.
10. Hold the fuel pump assembly and the seal ring in place and install the locking ring. Rotate the ring clockwise using a suitable tool. Tighten the locking ring to 40–45 ft. lbs. (54–61 Nm).
11. Install the fuel tank in the vehicle.
12. Lower the vehicle and fill the fuel tank with at least 10 gallons of fuel. Connect the negative battery cable. Turn the ignition key to **RUN** for 3 seconds repeatedly, 5–10 times, to pressurize the system. Check for leaks.
13. Start the engine and check for leaks.

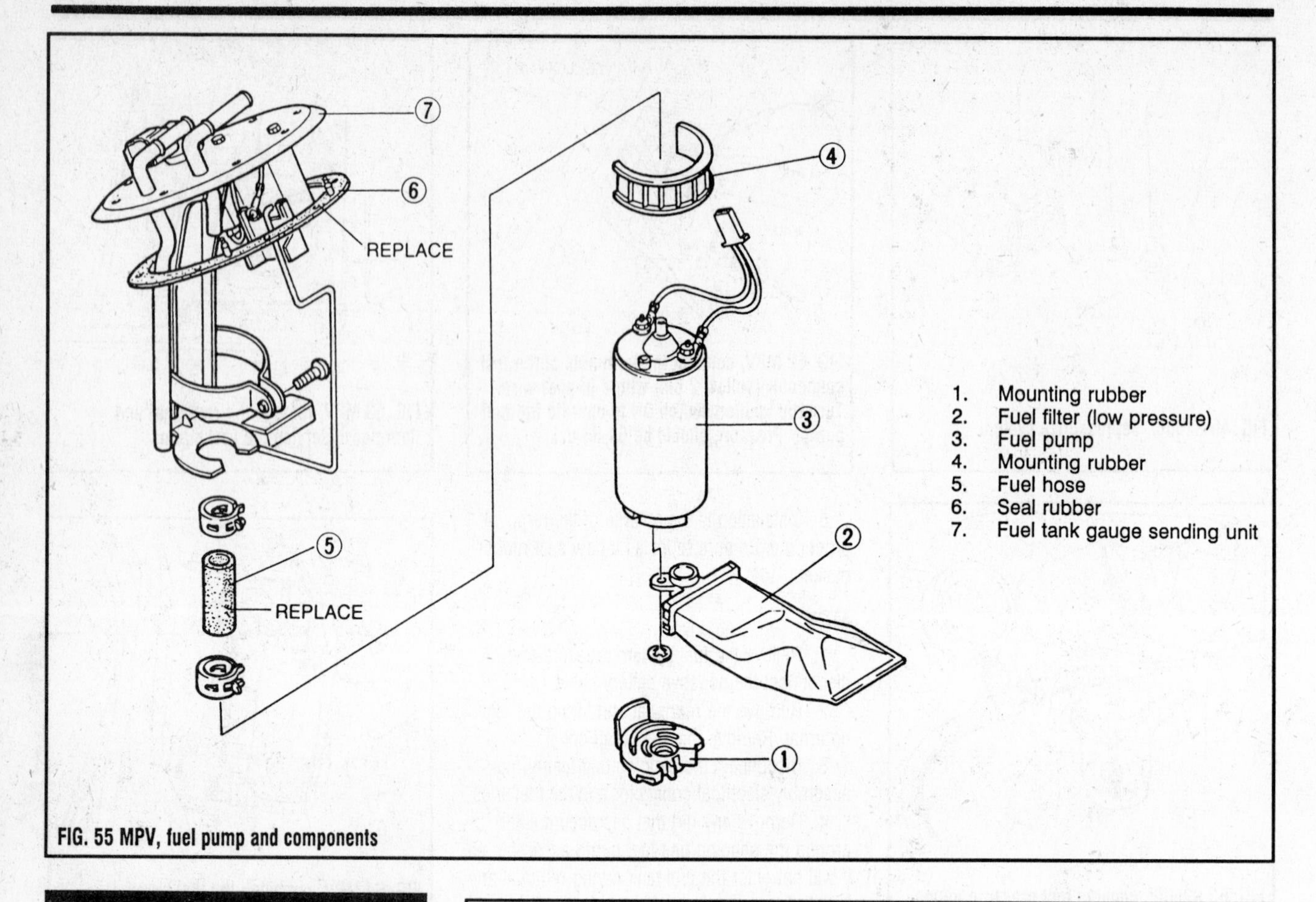

FIG. 55 MPV, fuel pump and components

Fuel Line Couplings

REMOVAL & INSTALLATION

Navajo

There are 2 methods in use to connect the fuel lines and fuel system components on Navajo, the hairpin clip push connect fitting and the spring lock coupling. Each requires a different procedure to disconnect and connect.

HAIRPIN CLIP PUSH CONNECT FITTING

1. Inspect the visible internal portion of the fitting for dirt accumulation. If more than a light coating of dust is present, clean the fitting before disassembly.
2. Some adhesion between the seals in the fitting and the tubing will occur with time. To separate, twist the fitting on the tube, then push and pull the fitting until it moves freely on the tube.
3. Remove the hairpin clip from the fitting by first bending and breaking the shipping tab. Next, spread the 2 clip legs by hand about $^1/_8$ in. each to disengage the body and push the legs into the fitting. Lightly pull the triangular end of the clip and work it clear of the tube and fitting.

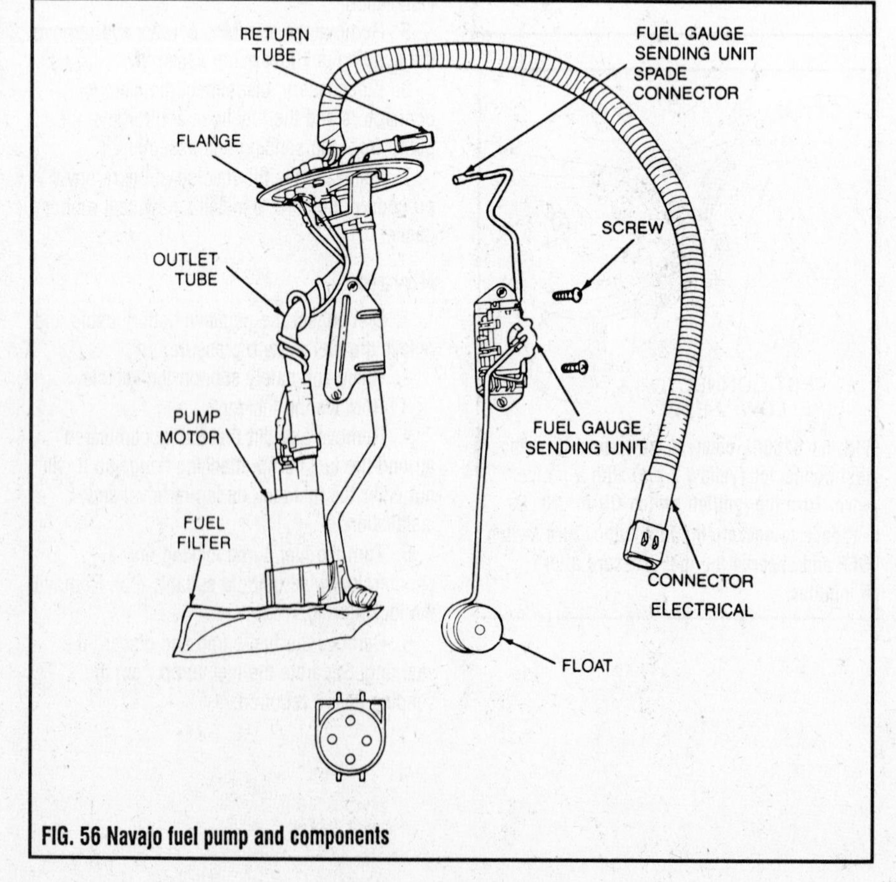

FIG. 56 Navajo fuel pump and components

➡ **Do not use hand tools to complete this operation.**

4. Grasp the fitting and pull in an axial direction to remove the fitting from the tube. Be careful on 90° elbow connectors, as excessive side loading could break the connector body.

5. After disassembly, inspect and clean the tube end sealing surfaces. The tube end should be free of scratches and corrosion that could provide leak paths. Inspect the inside of the fitting for any internal parts such as O-rings and spacers that may have been dislodged from the fitting. Replace any damaged connector.

To Install:

6. Install a new connector if damage was found. Insert a new clip into any 2 adjacent openings with the triangular portion pointing away from the fitting opening. Install the clip until the legs of the clip are locked on the outside of the body. Piloting with an index finger is necessary.

7. Before installing the fitting on the tube, wipe the tube end with a clean cloth. Inspect the inside of the fitting to make sure it is free of dirt and/or obstructions.

8. Apply a light coating of engine oil to the tube end. Align the fitting and tube axially and push the fitting onto the tube end. When the fitting is engaged, a definite click will be heard. Pull on the fitting to make sure it is fully engaged.

SPRING LOCK COUPLING

The spring lock coupling is a fuel line coupling held together by a garter spring inside a circular cage. When the coupling is connected together, the flared end of the female fitting slips behind the garter spring inside the cage of the male fitting. The garter spring and cage then prevent the flared end of the female fitting from pulling out of the cage. As an additional locking feature, most couplings have a horseshoe shaped retaining clip that improves the retaining reliability of the spring lock coupling.

Idle Speed Adjustment

Except Navajo

1. Place manual transmission in neutral or automatic transmission in **P**.
2. Make sure all accessories are **OFF**.
3. Connect a tachometer and timing light to the engine.
4. Warm up the engine to normal operating temperature.
5. Check the ignition timing and adjust, if necessary.
6. Ground the green 1-pin test connector to the body with a jumper wire.
7. Check the idle speed. Specifications are as follows:

- 2.2L and 2.6L engines—Manual transmission: 730–770 rpm. Automatic transmission: 750–790 rpm.

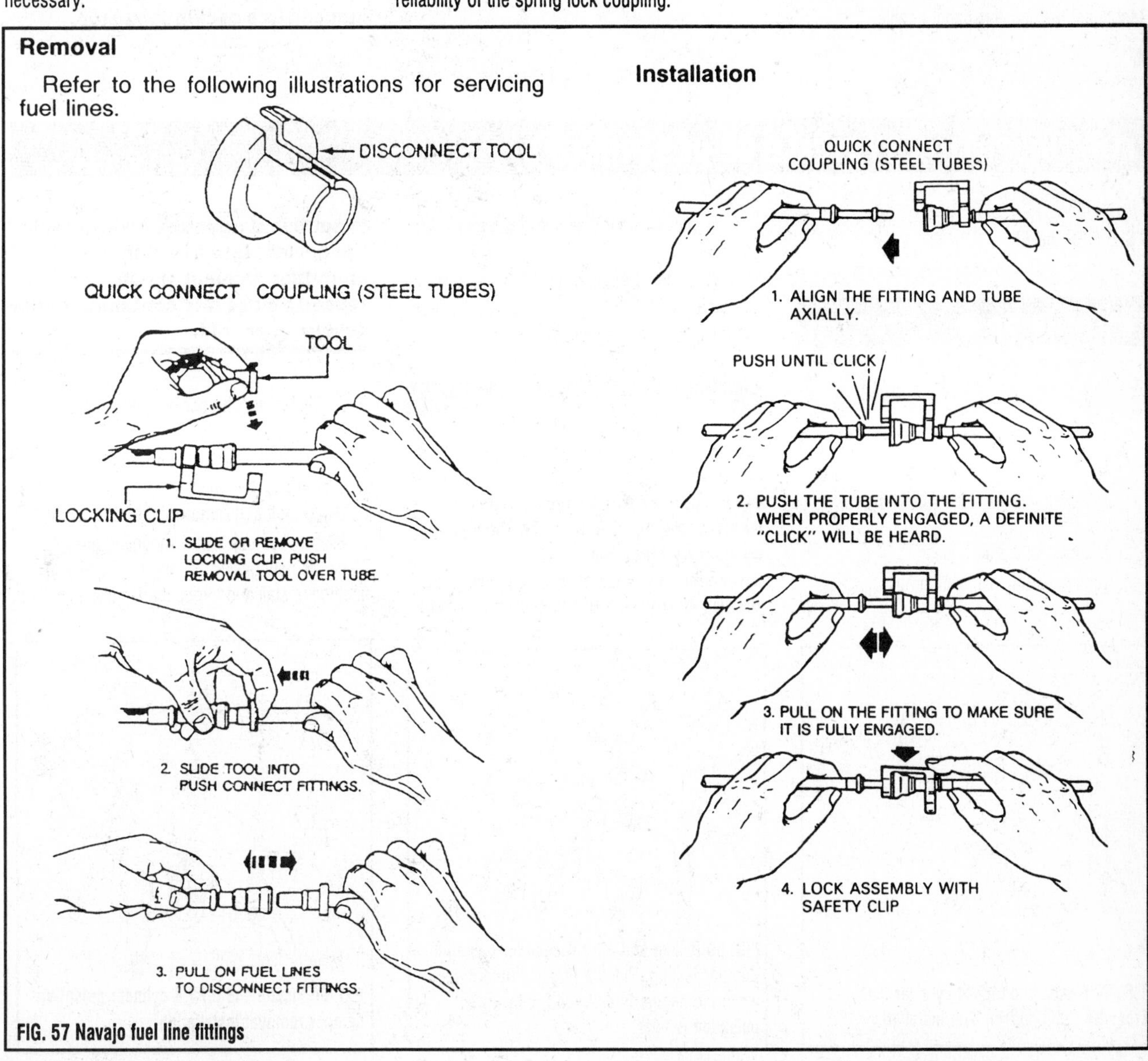
Removal
Refer to the following illustrations for servicing fuel lines.
DISCONNECT TOOL
QUICK CONNECT COUPLING (STEEL TUBES)
TOOL
LOCKING CLIP
1. SLIDE OR REMOVE LOCKING CLIP. PUSH REMOVAL TOOL OVER TUBE.
2. SLIDE TOOL INTO PUSH CONNECT FITTINGS.
3. PULL ON FUEL LINES TO DISCONNECT FITTINGS.
Installation
QUICK CONNECT COUPLING (STEEL TUBES)
1. ALIGN THE FITTING AND TUBE AXIALLY.
PUSH UNTIL CLICK
2. PUSH THE TUBE INTO THE FITTING. WHEN PROPERLY ENGAGED, A DEFINITE "CLICK" WILL BE HEARD.
3. PULL ON THE FITTING TO MAKE SURE IT IS FULLY ENGAGED.
4. LOCK ASSEMBLY WITH SAFETY CLIP

FIG. 57 Navajo fuel line fittings

• 3.0L engine—Manual and automatic transmission: 780–820 rpm.

8. If the idle speed is not within specification, adjust by turning the air adjusting screw.

9. After adjustment, disconnect the jumper wire from the test connector. Recheck the ignition timing.

Navajo

1. Place manual transmission in neutral or automatic transmission in **P**. Apply the parking brake.

2. Make sure the heater and accessories are **OFF**.

3. Start the engine and bring to normal operating temperature. Make sure the throttle lever is resting on the throttle plate stop screw.

4. Check the ignition timing and adjust, if necessary.

5. Shut off the engine and disconnect the negative battery cable for 5 minutes minimum. Reconnect the negative battery cable.

6. Start the engine and let it stabilize for 2 minutes. Rev the engine and let it return to idle, lightly depress and release the accelerator and let the engine idle.

7. If the engine does not idle properly, shut off the engine and disconnect the idle speed control-air bypass solenoid.

8. Run the engine at 2500 rpm for 30 seconds, then let it idle for 2 minutes.

9. Check/adjust the idle rpm to 675 rpm by turning the throttle plate stop screw.

➡ If the screw must be turned in, shut the engine off and make the estimated adjustment, then start the engine and repeat Steps 8 and 9.

10. Shut the engine off and repeat Steps 8 and 9.

11. Shut the engine off and disconnect the negative battery cable for 5 minutes minimum.

12. With the engine off, reconnect the idle speed control-air bypass solenoid. Make sure the throttle is not stuck in the bore and the linkage is not preventing the throttle from closing.

13. Start the engine and let it stabilize for 2 minutes. Rev the engine and let it return to idle, lightly depress and release the accelerator and let the engine idle.

➡ A condition may occur where the engine rpm will oscillate. This can be caused by the throttle plates being open enough to allow purge flow. To make sure of this condition, disconnect the carbon canister purge line and plug it. If purge is present, the throttle plates must be closed until the purge flow induced idle oscillations stop.

FUEL INJECTION SYSTEM B SERIES PICKUPS

➧ SEE FIGS. 58-65

Throttle Body

REMOVAL & INSTALLATION

1. Disconnect the negative battery ground cable.

2. Disconnect the air hose.

3. Disconnect the ventilation hose.

4. Remove the air pipe and resonance chamber.

5. Disconnect the accelerator cable from the throttle lever.

6. Drain the engine coolant.

✲✲ CAUTION

When draining the coolant, keep in mind that cats and dogs are attracted by the ethylene glycol antifreeze, and are quite likely to drink any that is left in an uncovered container or in puddles on the ground. This will prove fatal in sufficient quantity. Always drain the coolant into a sealable container. Coolant should be reused unless it is contaminated or several years old.

7. Disconnect the coolant lines at the manifold.

8. Tag and disconnect all vacuum hoses.

9. Tag and disconnect all wiring.

10. Unbolt and remove the throttle body.

11. Always use a new mounting gasket. Place the new gasket and throttle body in position. Install and torque the fasteners to 15 ft.

FIG. 58 Pickup and MPV 4 cylinder fuel pressure regulator removal/installation

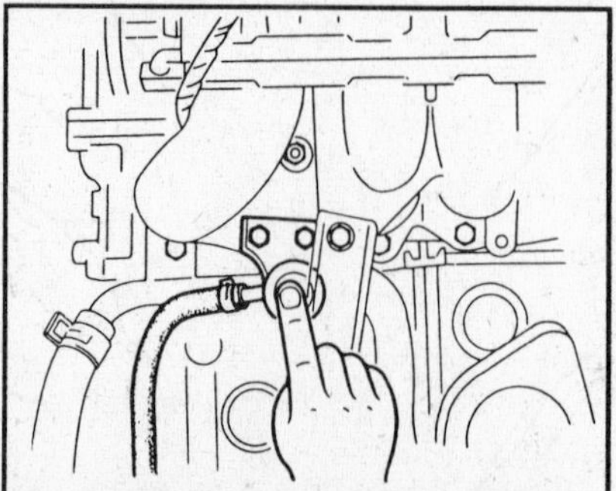

FIG. 59 Pickup and MPV 4 cylinder pulsation damper testing. Place a finger on the damper when the engine is operating, check that pulsation is felt

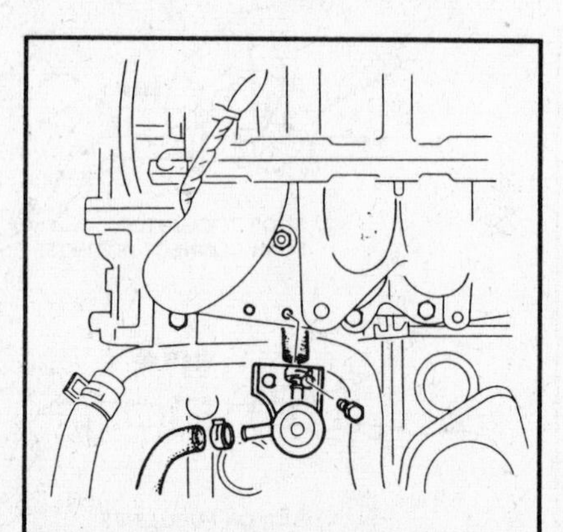

FIG. 60 Pickup and MPV 4 cylinder pulsation damper removal/installation

lbs. Connect the vacuum lines, hoses and intake system components. Fill the cooling system.

Air Chamber

REMOVAL & INSTALLATION

1. Remove the throttle body.
2. Remove the chamber-to-bracket bolts.
3. Tag and disconnect all wiring and hoses.
4. Remove the injector harness bracket.
5. Lift off the air chamber.
6. Install in the reverse order. Always use a new gasket. Torque the chamber-to-bracket bolts to 15 ft. lbs.

Fuel Pressure Regulator

REMOVAL & INSTALLATION

1. Relieve the fuel system pressure.
2. Disconnect the vacuum hose.
3. Disconnect the fuel return hose.
4. Unbolt and remove the unit.
5. Install in the reverse order. Tighten the bolts to 95 inch lbs.

Pulsation Damper

REMOVAL & INSTALLATION

1. Relieve the fuel system pressure.
2. Disconnect the fuel lines.
3. Unbolt and remove the damper.
4. Install in the reverse order. Torque the bolt to 95 inch lbs.

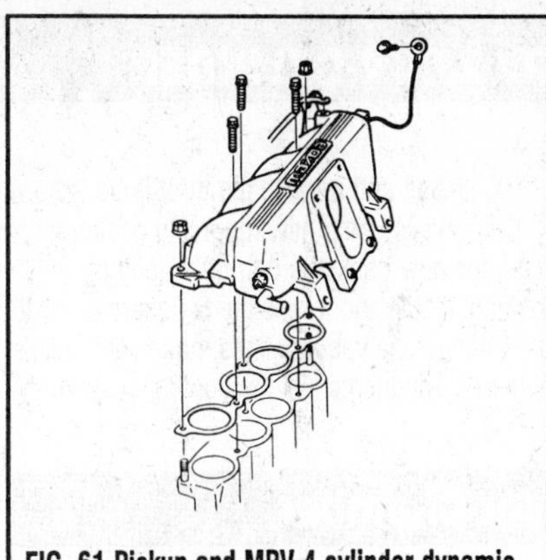

FIG. 61 Pickup and MPV 4 cylinder dynamic chamber removal/installation

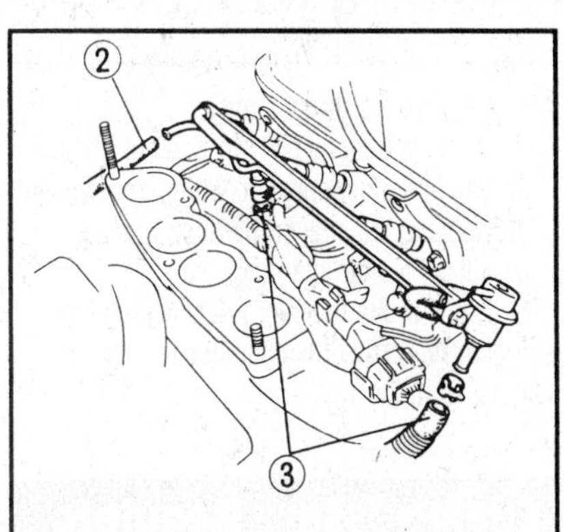

FIG. 62 Pickup and MPV 4 cylinder. Injector removal, disconnect the vacuum lines (2) and fuel lines (3)

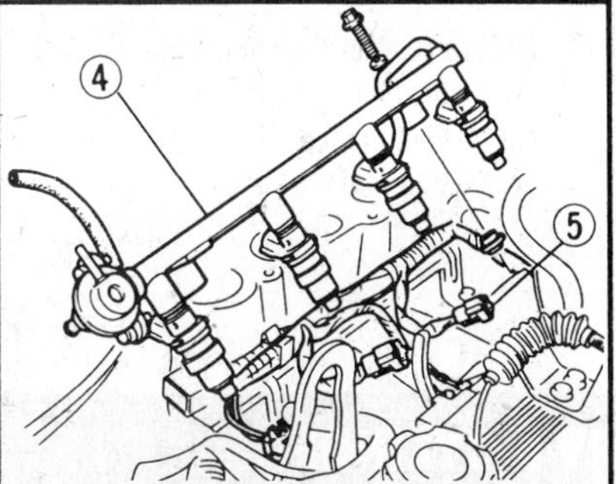

FIG. 63 Pickup and MPV 4 cylinder. Remove the delivery pipe (4) with the pressure regulator (5). Disconnect the injector connections

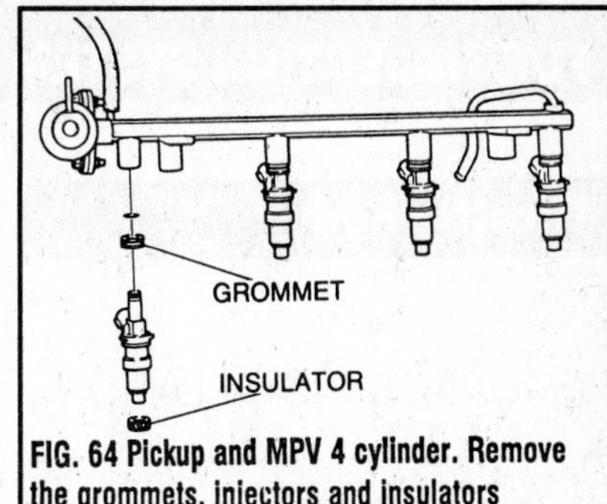

FIG. 64 Pickup and MPV 4 cylinder. Remove the grommets, injectors and insulators

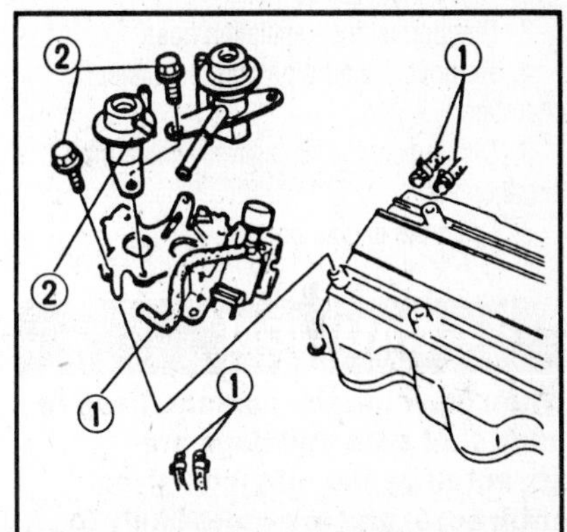

FIG. 65 MPV V6, disconnect the vacuum and fuel hoses (1) remove the pressure regulator and/or pulsation damper (2)

Fuel Injector

REMOVAL & INSTALLATION

1. Relieve the fuel system pressure.
2. Remove the air chamber.
3. Disconnect the vacuum hose.
4. Disconnect the fuel lines.
5. Remove the pressure regulator and delivery pipe.
6. Disconnect the injector wiring.
7. Pull off the injectors. Discard the grommets and O-rings.
8. Installation is the reverse of removal. Torque the delivery pipe bolts to 15 ft. lbs. Always use new O-rings coated with clean engine oil.

FUEL INJECTION SYSTEM MPV 2.6L 4-CYLINDER

Throttle Body

REMOVAL & INSTALLATION

1. Disconnect the battery ground.
2. Disconnect the air hose.
3. Disconnect the ventilation hose.
4. Remove the air pipe and resonance chamber.
5. Disconnect the accelerator cable from the throttle lever.
6. Drain the engine coolant.

CAUTION

When draining the coolant, keep in mind that cats and dogs are attracted by the ethylene glycol antifreeze, and are quite likely to drink any that is left in an uncovered container or in puddles on the ground. This will prove fatal in sufficient quantity. Always drain the coolant into a sealable container. Coolant should be reused unless it is contaminated or several years old.

7. Disconnect the coolant lines at the manifold.
8. Tag and disconnect all vacuum hoses.
9. Tag and disconnect all wiring.
10. Unbolt and remove the throttle body.
11. Always use a new mounting gasket. Place the new gasket and throttle body in position. Install and torque the fasteners to 15 ft. lbs. Connect the vacuum lines, hoses and intake system components. Fill the cooling system.

Air Chamber

REMOVAL & INSTALLATION

1. Remove the throttle body.
2. Remove the chamber-to-bracket bolts.
3. Tag and disconnect all wiring and hoses.
4. Remove the injector harness bracket.
5. Lift off the air chamber.
6. Install in the reverse order. Always use a new gasket. Torque the chamber-to-bracket bolts to 15 ft. lbs.

Fuel Pressure Regulator

REMOVAL & INSTALLATION

1. Relieve the fuel system pressure.
2. Disconnect the vacuum hose.
3. Disconnect the fuel return hose.
4. Unbolt and remove the unit.
5. Install in the reverse order. Tighten the bolts to 95 inch lbs.

Pulsation Damper

REMOVAL & INSTALLATION

1. Relieve the fuel system pressure.
2. Disconnect the fuel lines.
3. Unbolt and remove the damper.
4. Install in the reverse order. Torque the bolt to 95 inch lbs.

Fuel Injector

REMOVAL & INSTALLATION

1. Relieve the fuel system pressure.
2. Remove the air chamber.
3. Disconnect the vacuum hose.
4. Disconnect the fuel lines. Remove the pressure regulator and delivery pipe.
5. Disconnect the injector wiring. Pull off the injectors. Discard the grommets and O-rings.
6. Install in the reverse order. Torque the delivery pipe bolts to 15 ft. lbs. Always use new O-rings coated with clean engine oil.

FUEL INJECTION SYSTEM MPV 6-CYLINDER

➧ SEE FIGS. 66-68

Throttle Body

The throttle body is located at the left end of the air intake plenum. The throttle body contains the throttle position sensor and the automatic idle speed motor.

REMOVAL & INSTALLATION

1. Disconnect battery negative cable.
2. Loosen air cleaner to throttle body hose clamps and remove hose.
3. Remove accelerator cable and transaxle kickdown linkage.
4. Remove harness connector from throttle position sensor (TPS), and automatic idle speed (AIS) motor.
5. Label and remove vacuum hoses necessary.
6. Remove throttle body mounting nuts and remove throttle body and gasket.
7. Install throttle body using a new gasket on air intake plenum. Secure with mounting nuts.
8. Reconnect vacuum hoses, TPS and ASI electrical connectors.
9. Reconnect accelerator cable and transaxle linkage.
10. Install air cleaner to throttle body hose and tighten clamps.
11. Reconnect battery negative cable.

Fuel Injectors

The system uses six fuel injectors retained in a fuel rail by lock rings. Each injector is an electrical solenoid controlled by the Single Module Engine Controller (SMEC). Based on various sensor inputs, the SMEC determines when and how long the fuel injectors should operate. Fuel is supplied to the injectors at a regulated pressure of 48 psi. Unused fuel is redirected to the fuel tank through the fuel return line.

REMOVAL

Removal of the injectors requires removal of the fuel injector rail assembly. Refer to Fuel Injector Rail Removal procedure in this section.

1. Disconnect injector harness from injectors.
2. Invert fuel injector rail assembly.
3. Remove lock rings securing injectors to fuel rail receiver cups. Pull injectors upward from receiver cups.
4. If injectors are to be reused, place a protective cap on injector nozzle to prevent dirt or other damage.
5. Lubricate the new O-ring of each injectors with a clean drop of engine oil prior to installation.
6. Assemble each injectors into fuel rail receiver cups. Be careful not to damage O-rings.
7. Install lock ring between receiver cup ridge and injector slot.

Fuel Injector Rail

REMOVAL

1. Perform fuel system pressure release procedure. Refer to fuel system pressure release procedure in this section.
2. Disconnect the negative battery cable.
3. Loosen clamps securing air cleaner to throttle body hose and remove hose.
4. Remove the throttle cable and transaxle kickdown linkage.
5. Remove harness connector from throttle position sensor (TPS), and automatic idle speed (AIS) motor.

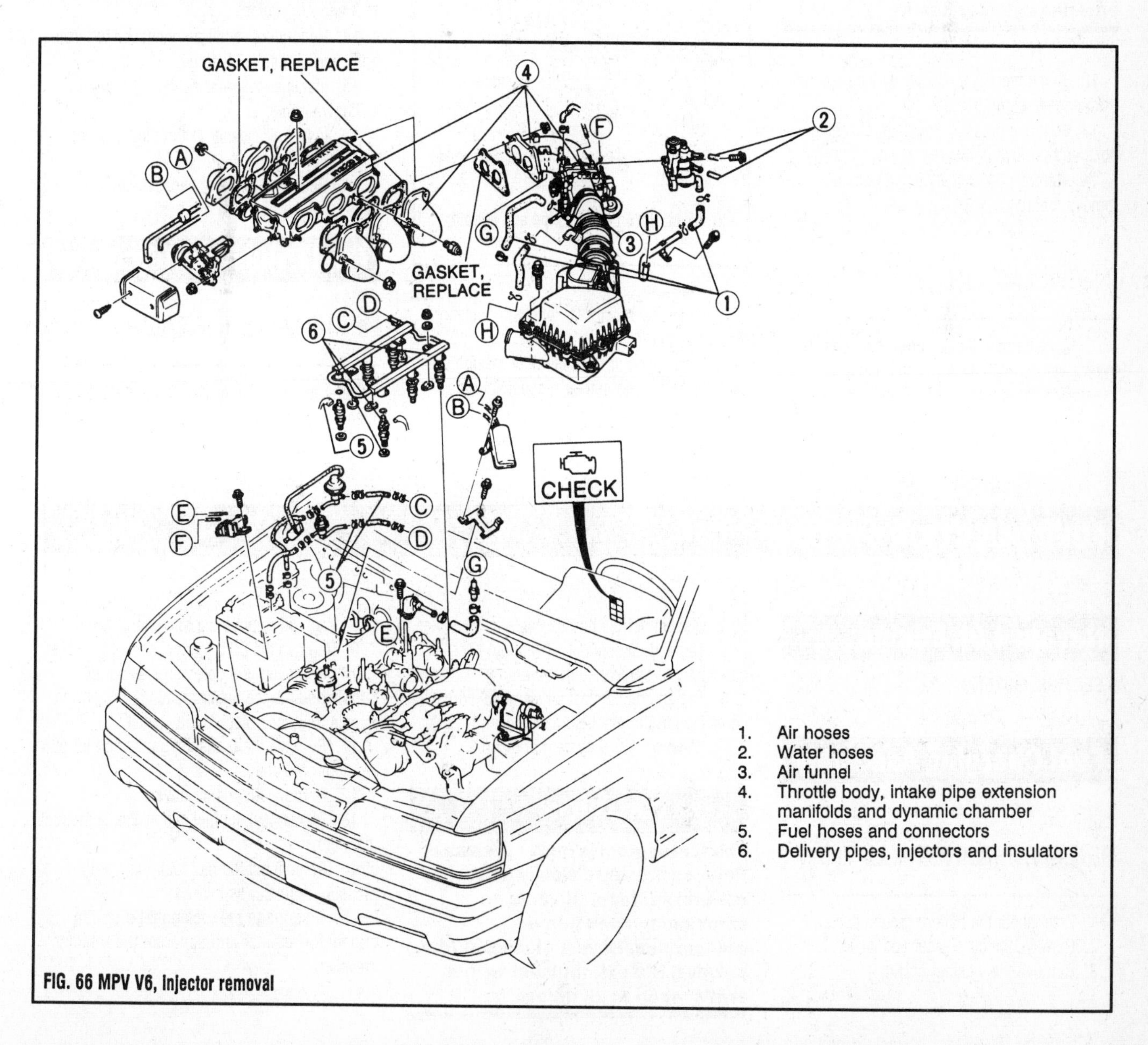

FIG. 66 MPV V6, Injector removal

6. Label and remove vacuum hoses from throttle body. Remove PCV and brake booster hoses from air intake plenum.
7. Remove EGR tube to intake plenum.
8. Remove electrical connection from charge temperature and coolant temperature sensor.
9. Remove vacuum connection from pressure regulator and air intake connection from manifold.
10. Remove fuel hoses to fuel rail connection.
11. Remove air intake plenum to manifold bolts (8) and remove air intake plenum and gaskets.

WARNING

Whenever air intake plenum is remove, cover intake manifold properly to avoid objects from entering cylinder head.

12. Disconnect fuel injector wiring harness from engine wiring harness.
13. Remove pressure regulator attaching bolts and remove pressure regulator from rail.
14. Remove fuel rail attaching bolts and remove fuel rail.

INSTALLATION

1. Make certain injector are properly seated in receiver cup with lock rings in place and injector discharge holes are clean.

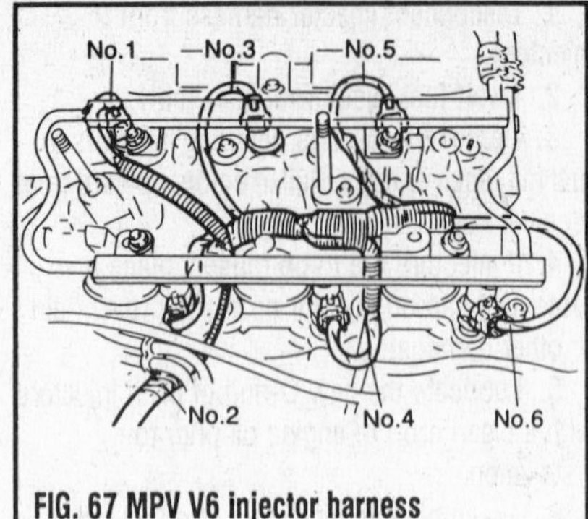

FIG. 67 MPV V6 injector harness

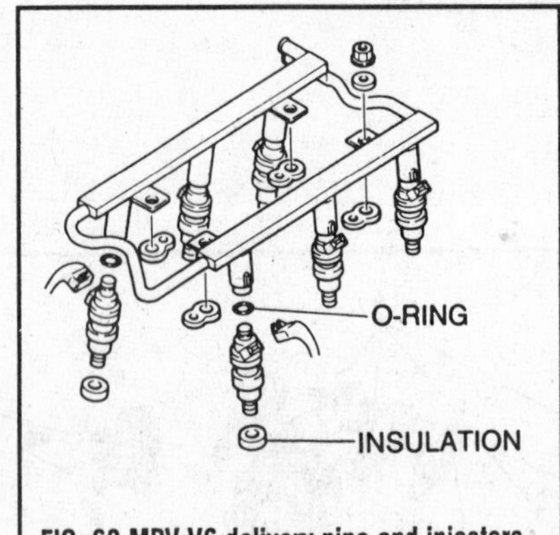

FIG. 68 MPV V6 delivery pipe and injectors

2. Lubricate injector O-rings with a clean drop of engine oil.
3. Install injector rail assembly making sure each injector seats in their respective ports. Torque fuel rail attaching bolts to 115 inch lbs.
4. Lubricate pressure regulator O-ring with a drop of clean engine oil and install regulator to fuel rail. Torque nuts to 77 inch lbs.
5. Install hold down bolts on fuel supply and return tube, and vacuum crossover tube.
6. Install and torque pressure regulator hose clamps to 10 inch lbs.
7. Reconnect injector wiring harness.
8. Reconnect vacuum hoses to fuel pressure regulator and fuel rail.
9. Set the air intake plenum gasket in place with beaded sealer in the **up** position.
10. Install air intake plenum and tighten (8) attaching screws to 115 inch lbs.
11. Reconnect fuel line to fuel rail and tighten clamps to 10 inch lbs.
12. Reconnect EGR tube to intake plenum and torque nuts to 200 inch lbs.
13. Reconnect electrical wiring to charge temperature sensor, coolant temperature sensor, TPS and AIS motor.
14. Reconnect vacuum connection to throttle body and air intake plenum.
15. Install accelerator cable and transaxle kickdown cable.
16. Install air cleaner to throttle body hose and tighten clamps.
17. Reconnect battery negative cable.

Fuel Pressure Regulator

REMOVAL & INSTALLATION

Refer to Fuel Injector Rail Removal and Installation procedure above.

FUEL INJECTION SYSTEM

Navajo 4.0L Engine

SEE FIGS. 69-75

Fuel Charging Assembly

REMOVAL & INSTALLATION

1. Disconnect the battery ground cable.
2. Remove the air cleaner and intake duct.
3. Remove the weather shield.
4. Disconnect the throttle cable and bracket.
5. Tag and disconnect all vacuum lines connected to the manifold.
6. Tag and disconnect all electrical wires connected to the manifold assemblies.
7. Relieve the fuel system pressure.

CAUTION

The fuel system is under pressure. Release pressure slowly and contain spillage. Observe no smoking/no open flame precautions. Have a Class B-C (dry powder) fire extinguisher within arm's reach at all times.

8. Tag and remove the spark plug wires.
9. Remove the EDIS ignition coil and bracket.
10. Remove the 4 screws retaining the throttle body to the upper manifold. Lift off the throttle body and discard the gasket.
11. Remove the 6 attaching nuts and lift off the upper manifold.
12. Remove the rocker covers.
13. Disconnect the fuel supply line at the fuel manifold.
14. Disconnect the fuel return line at the pressure regulator as follows:
    a. Disengage the locking tabs on the connector retainer and separate the retainer halves.

b. Check the visible, internal portion of the fitting for dirt. Clean the fitting thoroughly.

c. Push the fitting towards the regulator, insert the fingers on Fuel Line Coupling Key T90P–9550–A, or equivalent, into the slots in the coupling. Using the tool, pull the fitting from the regulator. The fitting should slide off easily, if properly disconnected.

15. Remove the 6 Torx® head stud bolts retaining the manifold and remove the manifold.

16. Remove the electrical harness connector from each injector.

17. Remove the retaining clip from each injector.

18. Grasp the injector body and pull upward while gently rocking the injector from side-to-side.

19. Remove the lower intake manifold bolts. Tap the manifold lightly with a plastic mallet and remove it.

20. Clean all surfaces of old gasket material.

To install:

21. Apply RTV silicone gasket material at the junction points of the heads and manifold.

➡ This material will set within 15 minutes, so work quickly!

22. Install new manifold gaskets and again apply the RTV material.

23. Position the manifold and install the nuts hand tight. Torque the nuts, in 4 stages, in the sequence shown, to 18 ft. lbs.

24. Once again, apply RTV material to the manifold/head joints.

25. Install the rocker covers.

26. Inspect the O-rings for each injector. There should be 2 for each. Replace them as required.

27. Inspect, and if necessary, replace the plastic cap covering the injector pintle. If there is no plastic cap, it may have fallen into the manifold.

28. Coat the O-rings with 5W engine oil and push/twist each injector into the fuel manifold.

29. Install the retainers and electrical harness connectors.

30. Position the fuel supply manifold and press it down firmly until the injectors are fully seated in the fuel supply manifold and lower intake manifold.

31. Install the 6 Torx® head bolts and tighten them to 7–10 ft. lbs.

32. Install the fuel supply line and tighten the fitting to 15–18 ft. lbs.

33. Install the fuel return line on the regulator by pushing it onto the fuel pressure regulator line of to the shoulder.

WARNING

The connector should grip the line securely!

34. Install the connector retainer and snap the two halves of the retainer together.

35. Install the upper manifold. Tighten the nuts to 18 ft. lbs.

36. Install the EDIS coil.

37. Connect the fuel and return lines.

38. Ensure that the mating surfaces of the throttle body and upper manifold are clean and free of gasket material.

39. Install a new gasket on the manifold and position the throttle body on the manifold. Tighten the bolts to 76–106 inch lbs.

40. Connect all wires.

41. Connect all vacuum lines.

42. Connect the throttle linkage.

43. Install the weather shield.

44. Install the air cleaner and duct.

45. Fill and bleed the cooling system.

46. Connect the battery ground.

47. Run the engine and check for leaks.

Air Throttle Body

REMOVAL & INSTALLATION

1. Disconnect the negative battery cable. Remove the air cleaner inlet tube.

2. Remove the snow shield.

3. Disconnect the throttle cable at the ball stud.

4. Disconnect the canister purge hose from under the throttle body.

5. Disconnect the wiring harness at the throttle position sensor.

6. Remove the 4 retaining bolts and lift the throttle body assembly off the upper intake manifold.

7. Remove and discard the gasket.

To install:

8. Clean and inspect the mounting faces of the throttle body assembly and the upper intake manifold. Both surfaces must be clean and flat.

9. Install a new gasket on the manifold.

10. Install the air throttle body assembly on the intake manifold.

11. Install the bolts finger tight, then tighten them evenly to 76–106 inch lbs.

12. Connect the wiring harness to the throttle position sensor.

13. Install the canister purge hose.

14. Install the snow shield and air cleaner outlet tube. Reconnect the battery cable. Start engine, check for proper operation.

Air Bypass Valve

REMOVAL & INSTALLATION

1. Disconnect the air bypass valve connector.

2. Remove the air bypass valve retaining screws.

3. Remove the air bypass valve and gasket from the air intake/throttle body assembly. If scraping is necessary to remove old gasket material, be careful not to damage the air bypass valve or throttle body gasket mounting surfaces. Do not allow any foreign material to drop into the throttle body during service.

4. Installation is the reverse of removal procedure. Tighten the mounting bolts to 6–8 ft. lbs.

Fuel Supply Manifold Assembly

REMOVAL & INSTALLATION

1. Disconnect the battery ground cable.

2. Remove the air cleaner and intake duct.

3. Remove the weather shield.

4. Disconnect the throttle cable and bracket.

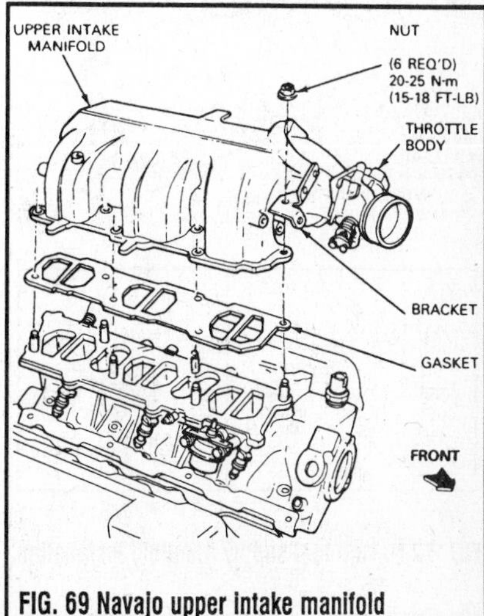

FIG. 69 Navajo upper intake manifold

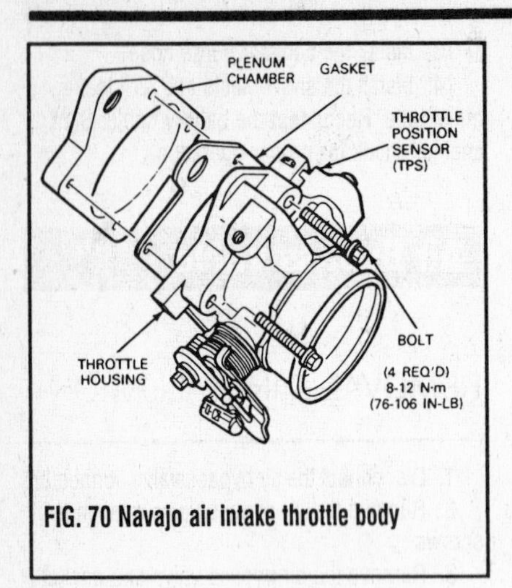

FIG. 70 Navajo air intake throttle body

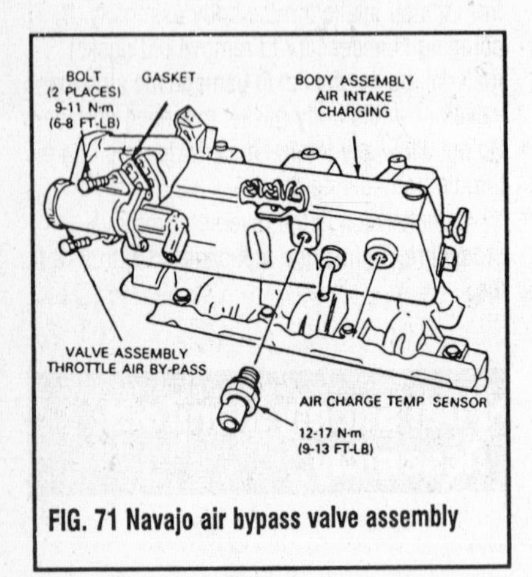

FIG. 71 Navajo air bypass valve assembly

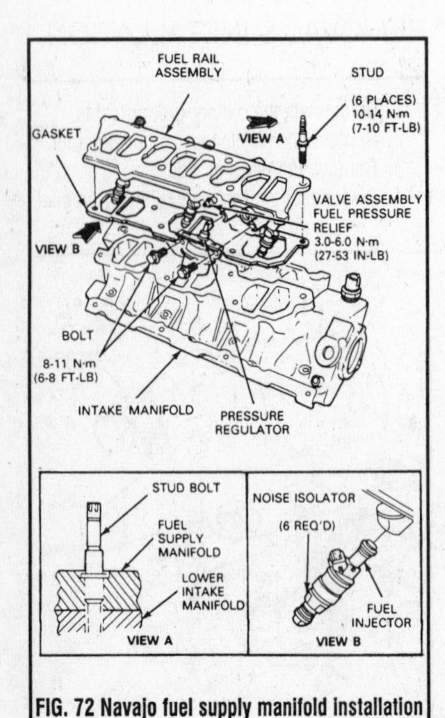

FIG. 72 Navajo fuel supply manifold installation

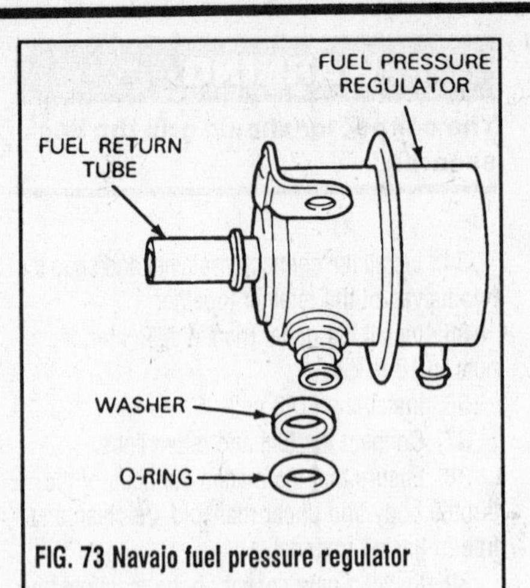

FIG. 73 Navajo fuel pressure regulator

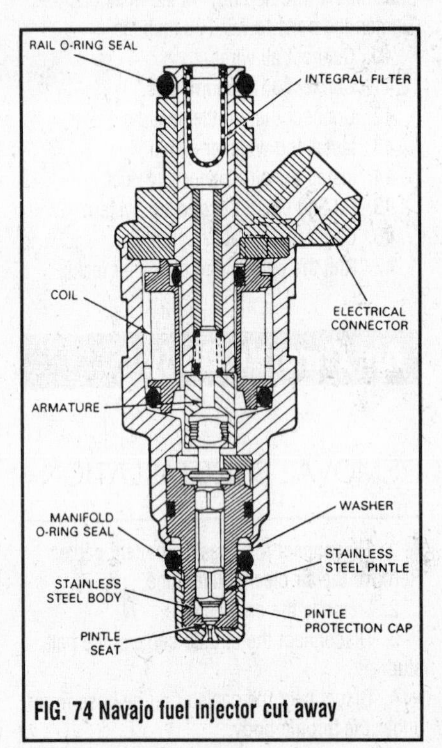

FIG. 74 Navajo fuel injector cut away

5. Tag and disconnect all vacuum lines connected to the manifold.
6. Tag and disconnect all electrical wires connected to the manifold assemblies.
7. Relieve the fuel system pressure.

✲✲ CAUTION

The fuel system is under pressure. Release pressure slowly and contain spillage. Observe no smoking/no open flame precautions. Have a Class B-C (dry powder) fire extinguisher within arm's reach at all times.

8. Tag and remove the spark plug wires.
9. Remove the EDIS ignition coil and bracket.
10. Remove the 4 screws retaining the throttle body to the upper manifold. Lift off the throttle body and discard the gasket.
11. Remove the 6 attaching nuts and lift off the upper manifold.
12. Disconnect the fuel supply line at the fuel manifold.
13. Disconnect the fuel return line at the pressure regulator as follows:
    a. Disengage the locking tabs on the connector retainer and separate the retainer halves.
    b. Check the visible, internal portion of the fitting for dirt. Clean the fitting thoroughly.
    c. Push the fitting towards the regulator, insert the fingers on Fuel Line Coupling Key T90P-9550-A, or equivalent, into the slots in the coupling. Using the tool, pull the fitting from the regulator. The fitting should slide off easily, if properly disconnected.
14. Remove the 6 Torx® head stud bolts retaining the manifold and remove the manifold.

To install:

15. Position the fuel supply manifold and press it down firmly until the injectors are fully seated in the fuel supply manifold and lower intake manifold.
16. Install the 6 Torx® head bolts and tighten them to 7-10 ft. lbs.
17. Install the fuel supply line and tighten the fitting to 15-18 ft. lbs.
18. Install the fuel return line on the regulator by pushing it onto the fuel pressure regulator line of to the shoulder.

✲✲ WARNING

The connector should grip the line securely!

19. Install the connector retainer and snap the two halves of the retainer together.
20. Install the upper manifold. Tighten the nuts to 18 ft. lbs.
21. Install the EDIS coil.
22. Connect the fuel and return lines.
23. Ensure that the mating surfaces of the throttle body and upper manifold are clean and free of gasket material.
24. Install a new gasket on the manifold and position the throttle body on the manifold. Tighten the bolts to 76-106 inch lbs.
25. Connect all wires.
26. Connect all vacuum lines.
27. Connect the throttle linkage.

28. Install the weather shield.
29. Install the air cleaner and duct.
30. Fill and bleed the cooling system.
31. Connect the battery ground.
32. Run the engine and check for leaks.

Fuel Pressure Regulator

REMOVAL & INSTALLATION

1. Depressurize the fuel system.

CAUTION

The fuel system is under pressure. Release pressure slowly and contain spillage. Observe no smoking/no open flame precautions. Have a Class B-C (dry powder) fire extinguisher within arm's reach at all times.

2. Remove the vacuum and fuel lines at the pressure regulator.
3. Remove the 2 or 3 Allen retaining screws from the regulator housing.
4. Remove the pressure regulator assembly, gasket and O-ring. Discard the gasket and check the O-ring for signs of cracks or deterioration.

To install:

5. Clean the gasket mating surfaces. If scraping is necessary, be careful not to damage the fuel pressure regulator or supply line gasket mating surfaces.
6. Lubricate the pressure regulator O-ring with light engine oil. Do not use silicone grease; it will clog the injectors.
7. Install the O-ring and a new gasket on the pressure regulator.
8. Install the pressure regulator on the fuel manifold and tighten the retaining screws to 6–8 ft. lbs.
9. Install the vacuum and fuel lines at the pressure regulator. Build up fuel pressure by turning the ignition switch ON and OFF at least 6 times, leaving the ignition on for at least 5 seconds each time. Check for fuel leaks.

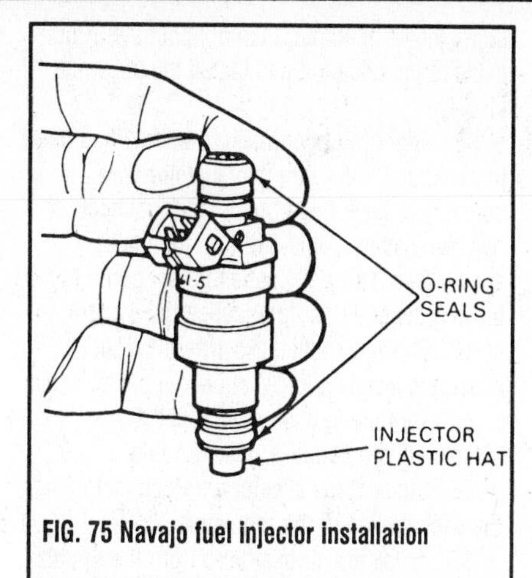

FIG. 75 Navajo fuel injector installation

Fuel Injector

REMOVAL & INSTALLATION

1. Disconnect the negative battery cable and relieve the fuel system pressure.
2. Disconnect the electrical connectors at the air bypass valve, TPS and ACT sensor.
3. Remove the snow/ice shield to expose the throttle linkage. Remove the throttle cable bracket and disconnect the cable from the ball stud on the throttle body.
4. Remove the air inlet tube from the air cleaner to the throttle body.
5. Disconnect the PCV valve from the valve cover.
6. Disconnect the spark plug wires from the comb at the rear of the manifold.
7. Remove the canister purge line from the fitting in the throttle housing.
8. Remove the bolt that retains the air conditioner line at the upper rear of the upper manifold.
9. Remove the 6 upper intake manifold retaining nuts and remove the upper intake and throttle body assembly.
10. Disconnect the fuel supply line fitting at the fuel manifold.
11. Disconnect the fuel return line from the fuel pressure regulator as follows:
    a. Disengage the locking tabs on the connector retainer and separate the retainer halves.
    b. Inspect the visible internal portion of the fitting for dirt accumulation. Clean the fitting before disassembly.
    c. To disengage the fitting from the regulator, push the fitting toward the regulator, insert the fingers on fuel line coupling key 49 UN01 006 or equivalent, into the slots in the coupling.
    d. Using the tool, pull the fitting from the regulator.

➡ If the fitting has been properly disengaged, the fitting should slide off the regulator with minimum effort.

12. Disconnect the electrical connectors from the fuel injectors.
13. Remove the 6 bolts retaining the fuel supply manifold and remove the manifold.
14. Remove the injector retaining clips and remove the injectors from the manifold by grasping the injector body and pulling up while rocking the injector from side-to-side.
15. Remove and discard the injector O-rings.
16. Inspect the injector plastic pintle protection cap and washer for signs of deterioration. Replace the complete injector as required. If the plastic pintle protection cap is missing, look for it in the intake manifold.

➡ The plastic pintle protection cap is not available as a separate part.

To install:

17. Lubricate new O-rings with clean light grade oil and install 2 on each injector.

➡ Never use silicone grease at it will clog the injectors.

18. Install the injectors, using a light, twisting, pushing motion.
19. Install the fuel supply manifold, pushing down to make sure all the fuel injector O-rings are fully seated in the fuel supply manifold cups and intake manifold.
20. Install the 6 retaining bolts and tighten to 7–10 ft. lbs. (10–14 Nm). Install the retainer clips.
21. Install the fuel supply line and tighten the fitting to 15–18 ft. lbs. (20–24 Nm).
22. Install the fuel return line to the fuel pressure regulator by pushing it onto the fuel pressure regulator line up to the shoulder on the regulator line.

➡ The connector should grip the regulator line securely.

23. Install the connector retainer and snap the 2 halves of the retainer together.
24. Clean and inspect the mounting faces of the fuel manifold and upper intake manifold.

25. Position a new gasket on the mounting studs and install the upper intake manifold on the studs.

26. Install the 6 upper intake manifold retaining nuts and tighten to 15–18 ft. lbs. (20–25 Nm).

27. Connect the spark plug wires to the retainer comb at the rear of the intake manifold.

28. Attach the air conditioner line retainer and automatic transmission vacuum line retainer at the upper intake manifold.

29. Install the canister purge line on the throttle body fitting.

30. Connect the vacuum lines to the vacuum tree. Connect the electrical connectors at the air bypass valve, TPS and ACT sensor.

31. Install the PCV valve in the grommet at the rear of the right valve cover.

32. Attach the throttle cable bracket to the upper intake manifold, then connect the throttle cable to the ball stud and install the snow/ice shield.

33. After the upper intake manifold has been installed and before the fuel injector wire connectors have been connected, connect the negative battery cable and turn the ignition switch **ON**. This will cause the fuel pump to run for 2–3 seconds and pressurize the system.

34. Check for fuel leaks where the fuel injector is installed into the fuel supply manifold.

35. Turn the ignition switch **OFF** and disconnect the negative battery cable.

36. Connect the injector wire connectors and the vacuum line to the regulator.

37. Install the air inlet tube from the throttle body to the air cleaner.

38. Connect the negative battery cable, start the engine and let it idle for 2 minutes.

39. Turn the engine **OFF** and check for fuel leaks.

Inertia Switch

This switch shuts off fuel to the engine in event of collision. Once the switch has shut off fuel to the engine it must be manually reset to start the engine. The switch is located on the toe-board to the right of the transmission hump.

To reset the switch; turn the ignition OFF. Check for leaking fuel in the engine compartment, fuel lines and tank. If no fuel leak is apparant, reset the switch by pushing the reset button on the top of the switch. Turn the ignition to START for a few seconds, then to OFF. Once again check for fuel leaks. If the vehicle is in a no start condition, check and reset this switch.

FUEL TANK

REMOVAL & INSTALLATION

Pickup Models

1. Relieve the fuel system pressure and disconnect the negative battery cable.

2. Remove the fuel filler cap. Raise and safely support the vehicle.

3. Position a suitable container under the fuel tank. Remove the drain plug and drain the tank.

4. Disconnect the electrical connector from the sending unit or sending unit/fuel pump assembly.

5. Disconnect the fuel filler hose, evaporative hoses, breather hose and fuel lines.

6. Position a jack under the fuel tank and remove the tank attaching nuts. Lower the tank from the vehicle.

To install:

7. Raise the tank into position and install the attaching nuts. Remove the jack.

8. Connect the fuel lines and evaporative hoses, making sure they are pushed onto the fuel tank fittings at least 1 in. (25mm). Connect the breather hose.

9. Connect the fuel filler hose, making sure the hose is pushed onto the fuel tank pipe and filler pipe at least 1.4 in. (35mm).

10. Connect the electrical connector to the sending unit or sending unit/fuel pump assembly.

11. Install the drain plug and lower the vehicle.

12. Fill the fuel tank and install the filler cap. Check for leaks.

13. Start the engine and check for leaks.

MPV

1. Relieve the fuel system pressure and disconnect the negative battery cable.

2. Remove the fuel filler cap. Raise and safely support the vehicle.

3. Position a suitable container under the fuel tank. Remove the drain plug and drain the tank.

4. Disconnect the fuel pump electrical connector.

5. Disconnect the fuel lines, evaporative hoses, breather hose and fuel filler hose.

6. Support the tank with a jack. Remove the retaining bolts and the fuel tank straps.

7. Lower the fuel tank from the vehicle.

To install:

8. Raise the fuel tank into position and install the straps and retaining bolts. Tighten to 32–44 ft. lbs. (43–61 Nm). Remove the jack.

9. Connect the fuel lines and evaporative hoses, making sure they are pushed onto the fuel tank fittings at least 1 in. (25mm). Connect the breather hose.

10. Connect the fuel filler hose, making sure the hose is pushed onto the fuel tank pipe and filler pipe at least 1.4 in. (35mm).

11. Connect the fuel pump electrical connector.

12. Install the drain plug and lower the vehicle.

13. Fill the fuel tank and install the filler cap. Check for leaks.

14. Start the engine and check for leaks.

Navajo

1. Disconnect the negative battery cable and relieve the fuel system pressure.

2. Raise and safely support the vehicle.

3. Drain the fuel from the fuel tank.

4. Remove the shield, skid plate and fuel tank front strap.

5. Support the tank with a jack and remove the bolt from the fuel tank rear strap.

6. Disconnect the filler pipe and vent pipe and lower the tank. Disconnect the vapor hose, fuel lines and electrical connector.

7. Lower the tank from the vehicle.

To install:

8. Raise the fuel tank and connect the electrical connector, fuel lines and vapor hose.

9. Connect the filler pipe and vent pipe. Attach the rear fuel tank strap.

10. Install the shield, skid plate and front strap.

11. Remove the jack and lower the vehicle.

12. Fill the fuel tank and check for leaks. Connect the negative battery cable.

SENDING UNIT REPLACEMENT

To replace the fuel level sending unit on models equipped with an electric fuel pump that is internally mounted in the fuel tank, follow the fuel pump replacement procedures.

On models that are equipped with a mechanical fuel pump, or externally mounted electric fuel pump, follow the fuel tank removal procedures:

1. Relieve fuel system pressure. Disconnect the negative battery cable.
2. Remove the fuel tank, or remove the floor access cover (depending on model).
3. Remove the fuel lines from the tank connectors and remove the connectors and gauge sending unit from the tank. Install in the reverse order.

Fuel Filter

REMOVAL & INSTALLATION

Pickup Models

The fuel filter is located in the engine compartment on all except 1987-88 B2600 and all B2200 with automatic transmission. On 1987-88 B2600 and all B2200 with automatic transmission, the fuel filter is located under the rear of the vehicle, near the fuel tank.

1. Relieve the fuel system pressure. Disconnect the negative battery cable.
2. Raise and safely support the vehicle, if necessary.
3. Disconnect the fuel lines from the fuel filter.
4. Remove the fuel filter or, if equipped, remove the fuel filter and bracket assembly.
5. Installation is the reverse of the removal procedure. Make sure the flow arrow on the fuel filter is facing in the proper direction of fuel flow.

MPV

The fuel filter is located in the engine compartment, next to the pulsation damper.

1. Relieve the fuel system pressure. Disconnect the negative battery cable.
2. Disconnect the fuel lines from the filter.
3. Remove the filter bracket bolts and remove the filter and bracket assembly.
4. Remove the fuel filter from the mounting bracket, if necessary.
5. Installation is the reverse of the removal procedure. Make sure the flow arrow on the fuel filter is facing in the proper direction of fuel flow.

Navajo

The fuel filter is located on the underside of the vehicle, attached to the frame rail.

1. Disconnect the negative battery cable and relieve the fuel system pressure.
2. Raise and support the vehicle safely.
3. Disconnect the fuel lines from the fuel filter.
4. Remove the fuel filter from the bracket. Note the direction of the flow arrow so the replacement filter can be installed correctly.
5. Installation is the reverse of the removal procedure. Start the engine and check for leaks.
6. Lower the vehicle.

TROUBLESHOOTING FUEL INJECTED ENGINES

➧ SEE FIGS. 76-213

➡ Refer to Section 4 for diagnostic tester use and the dash Malfunction Light activation.

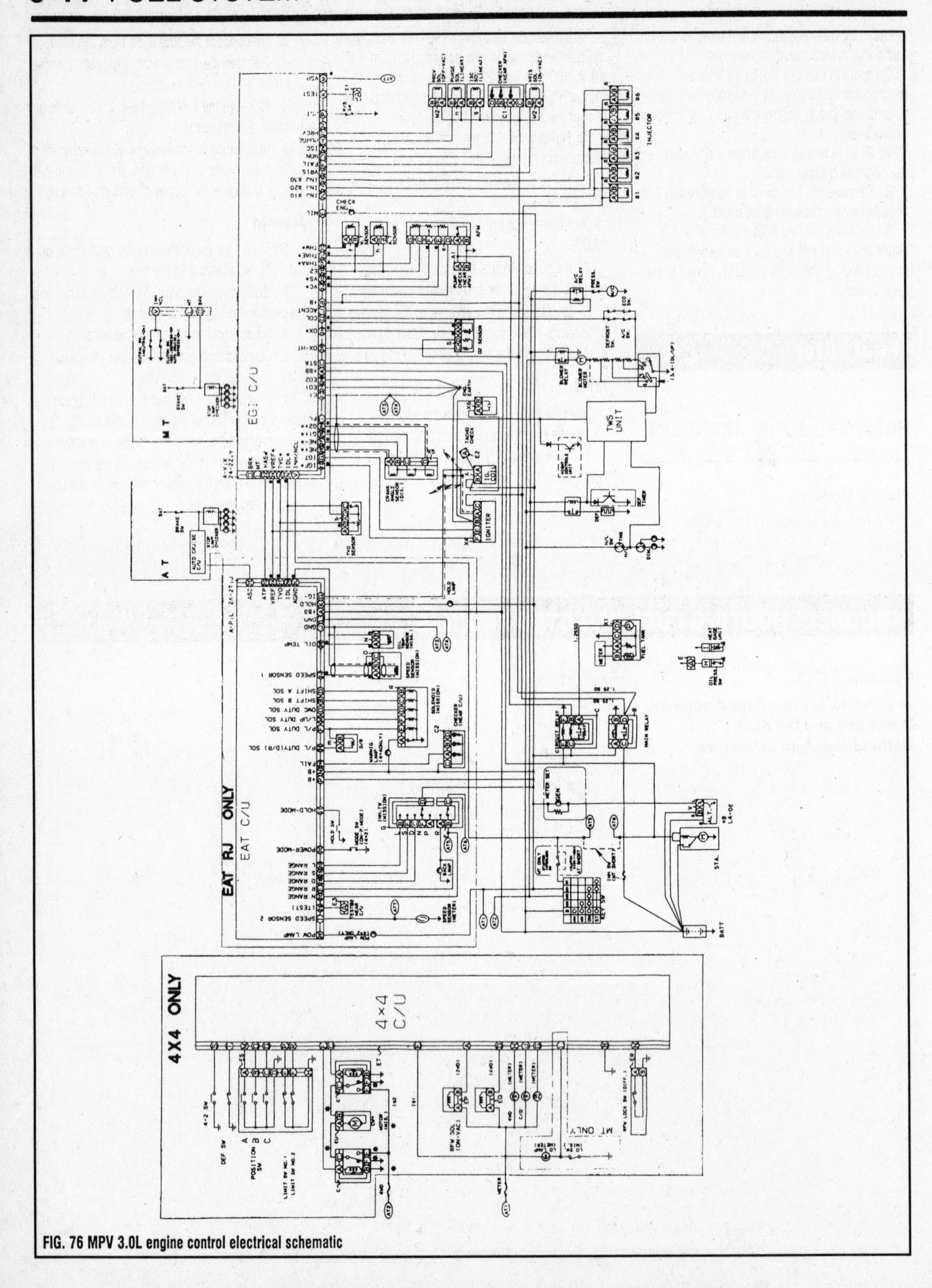

FIG. 76 MPV 3.0L engine control electrical schematic

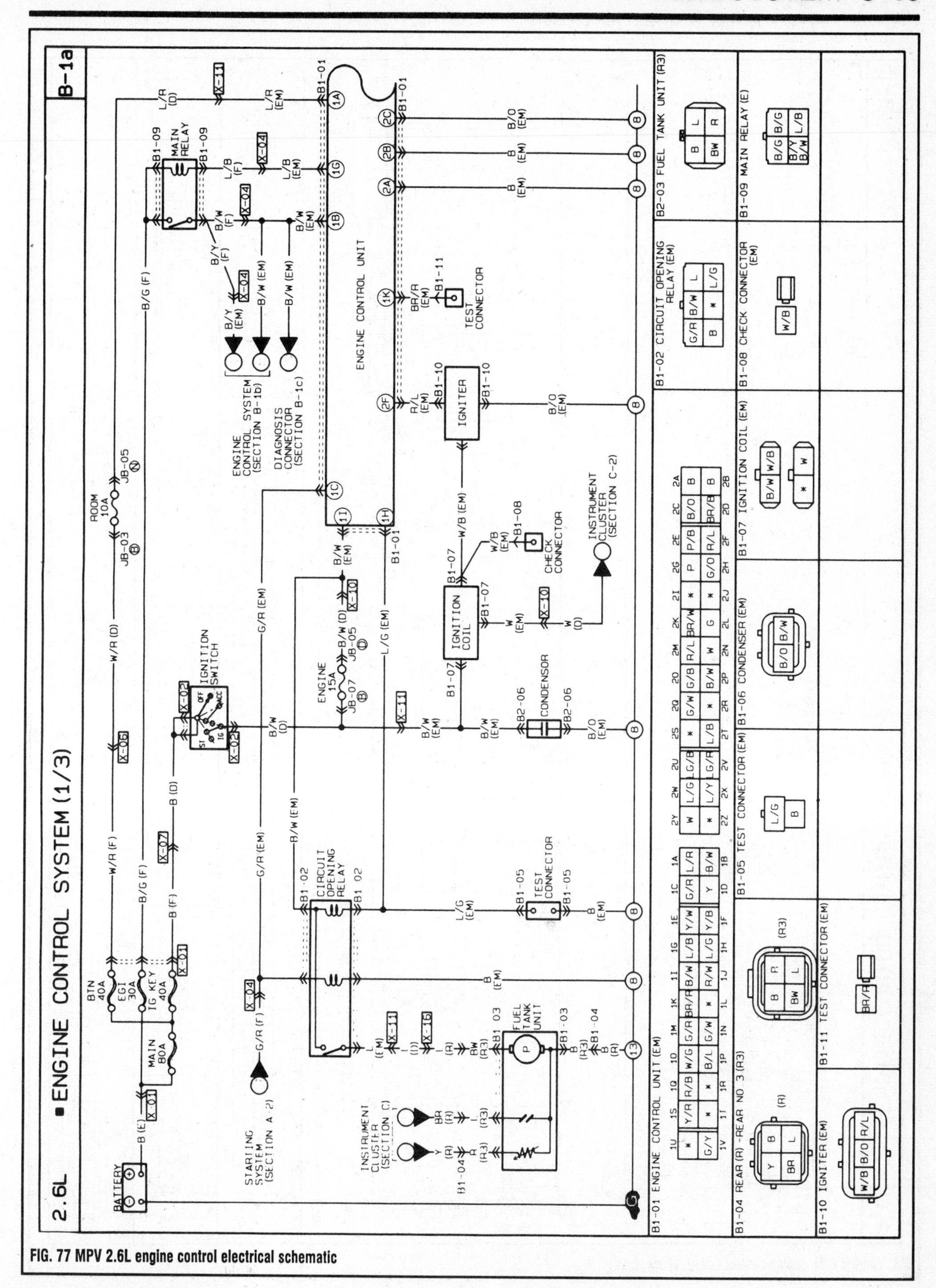

FIG. 77 MPV 2.6L engine control electrical schematic

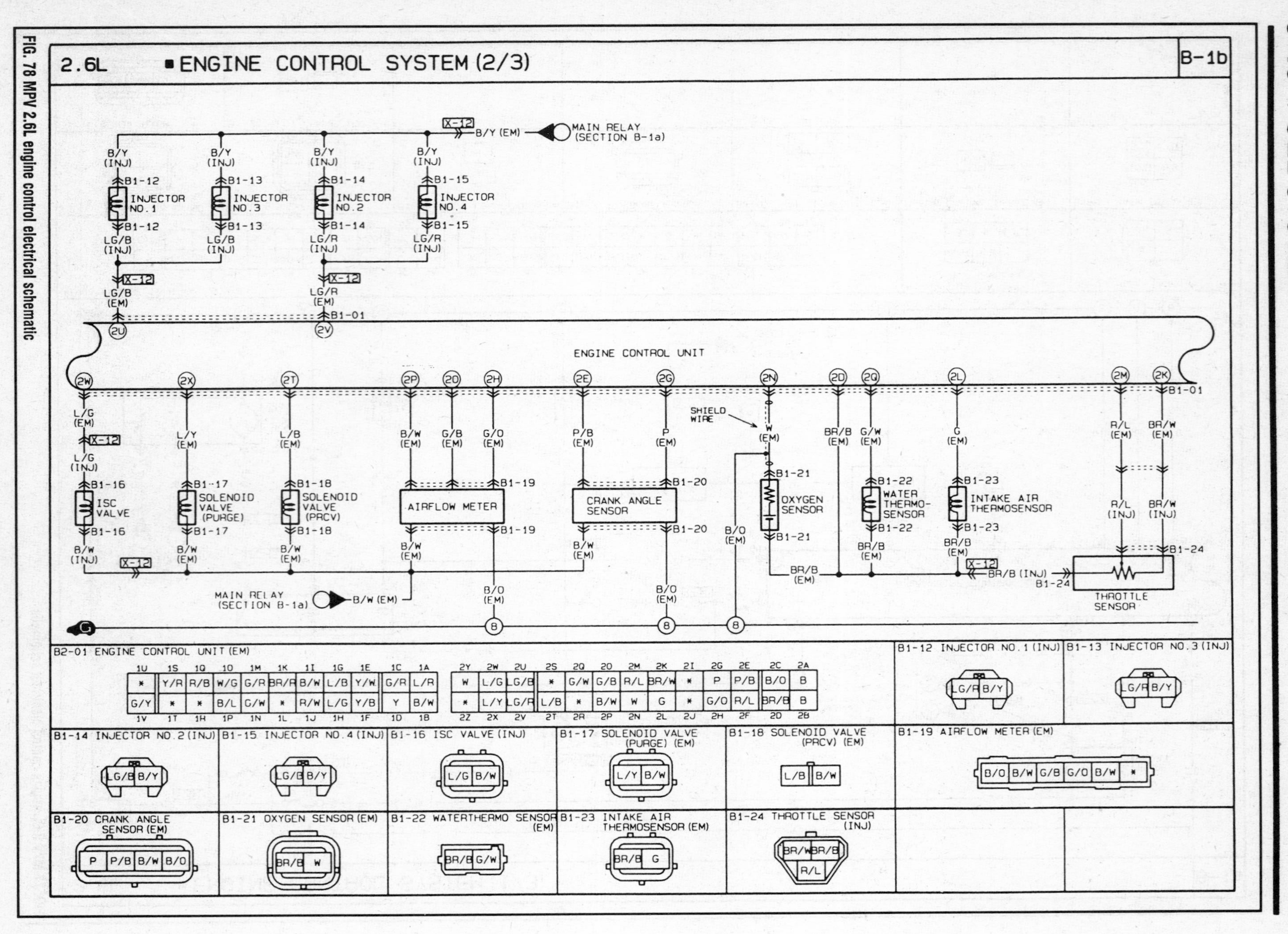

FIG. 78 MPV 2.6L engine control electrical schematic

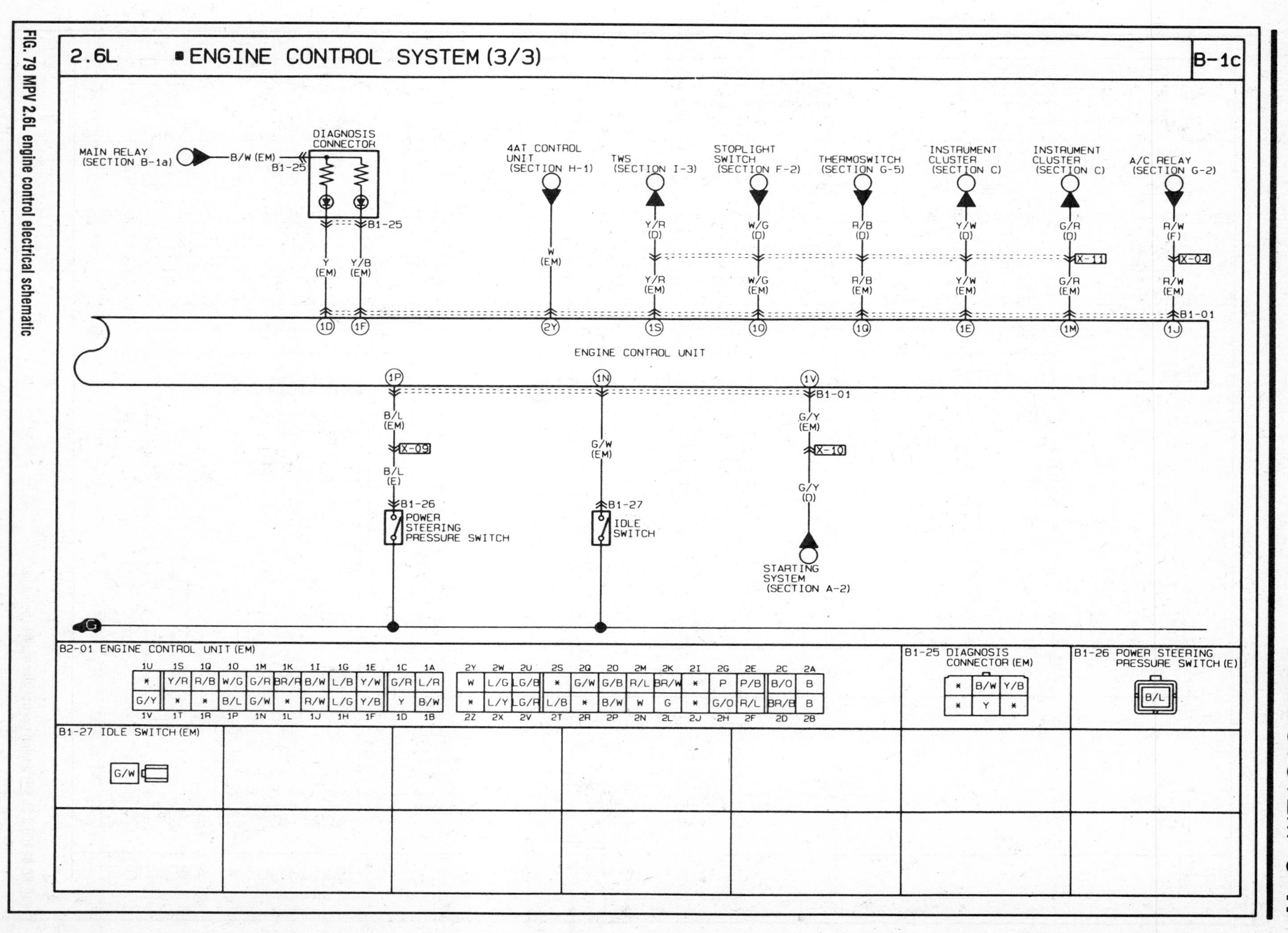

FIG. 79 MPV 2.6L engine control electrical schematic

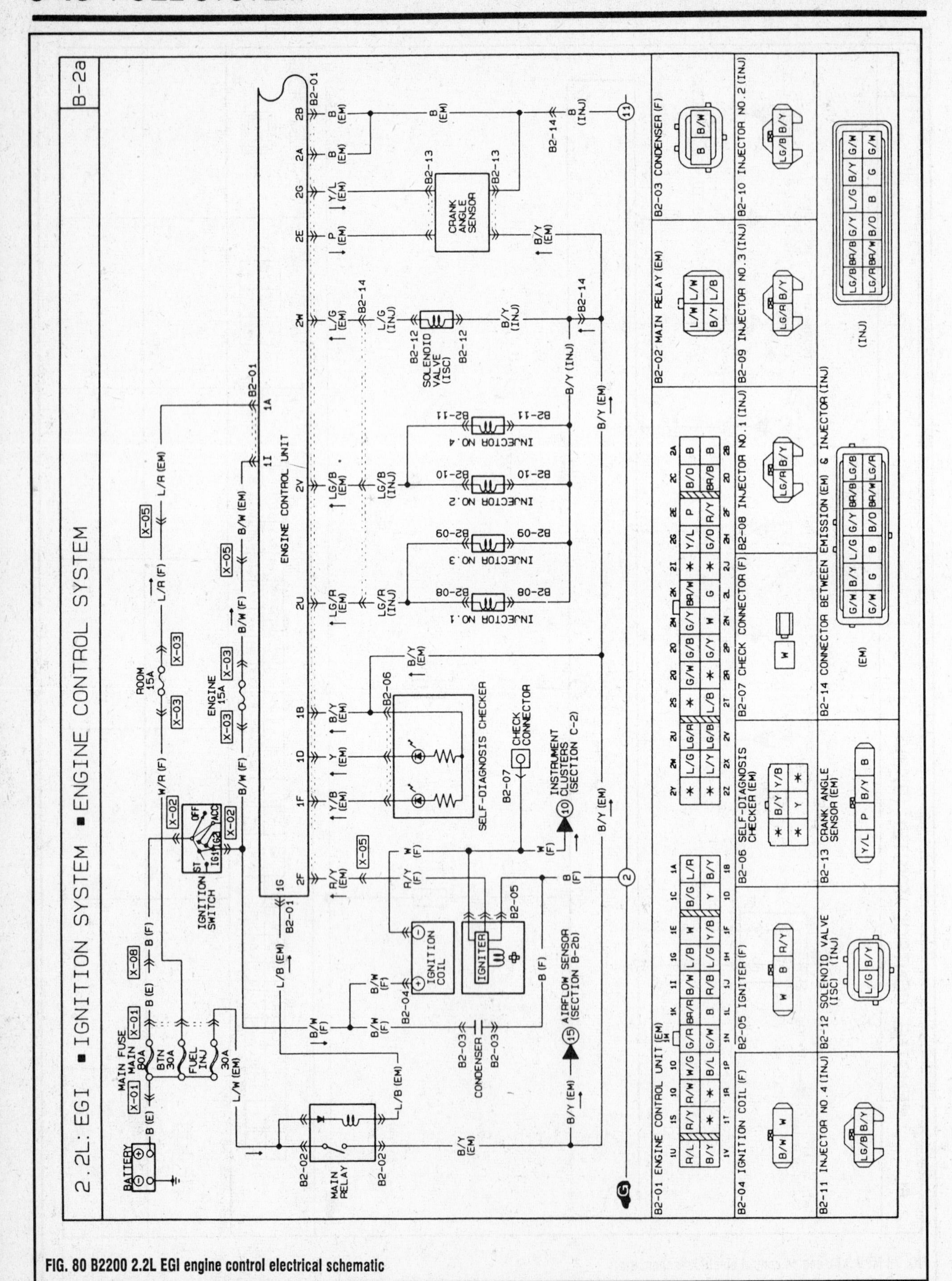

FIG. 80 B2200 2.2L EGI engine control electrical schematic

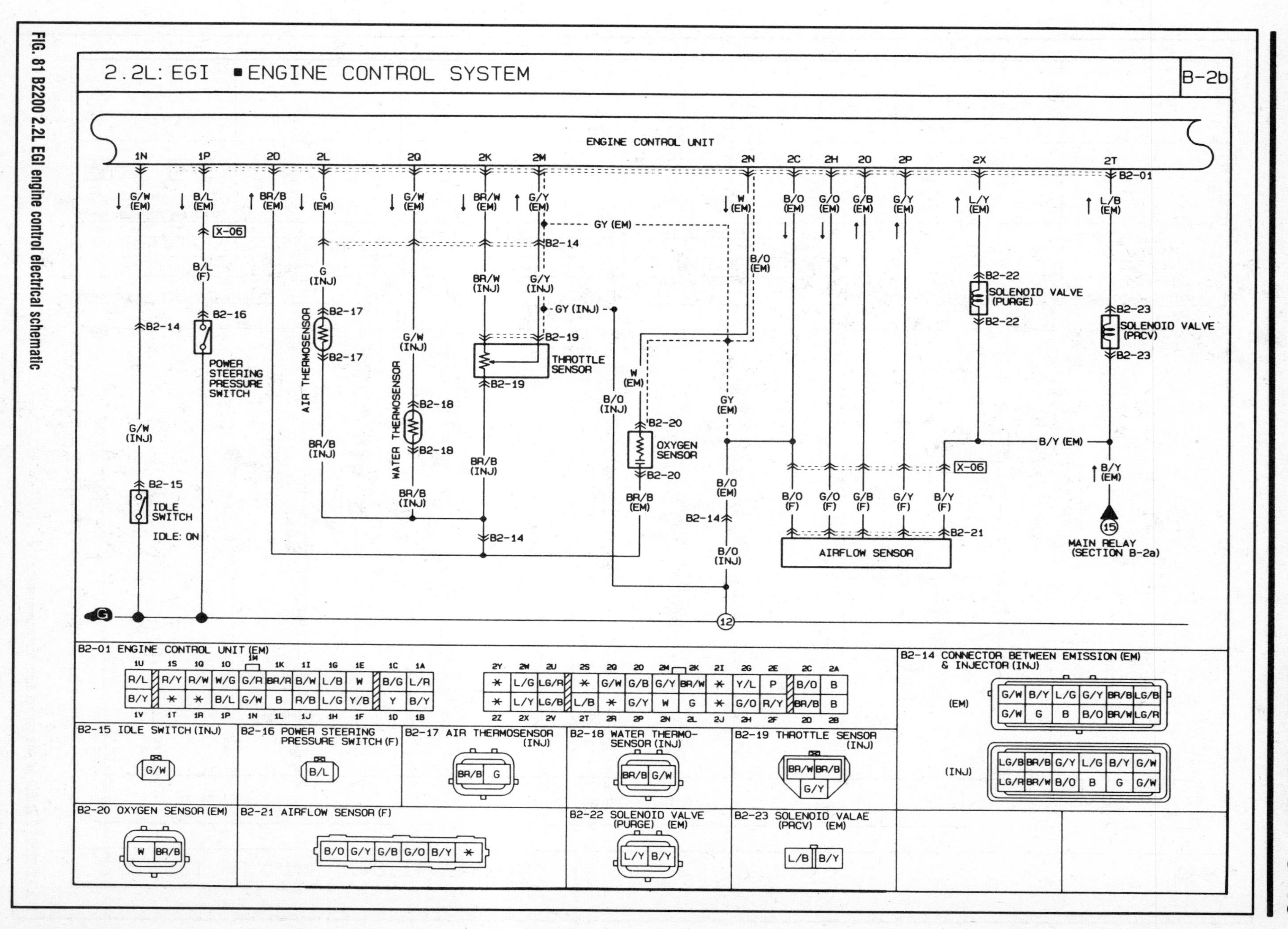

FIG. 81 B2200 2.2L EGI engine control electrical schematic

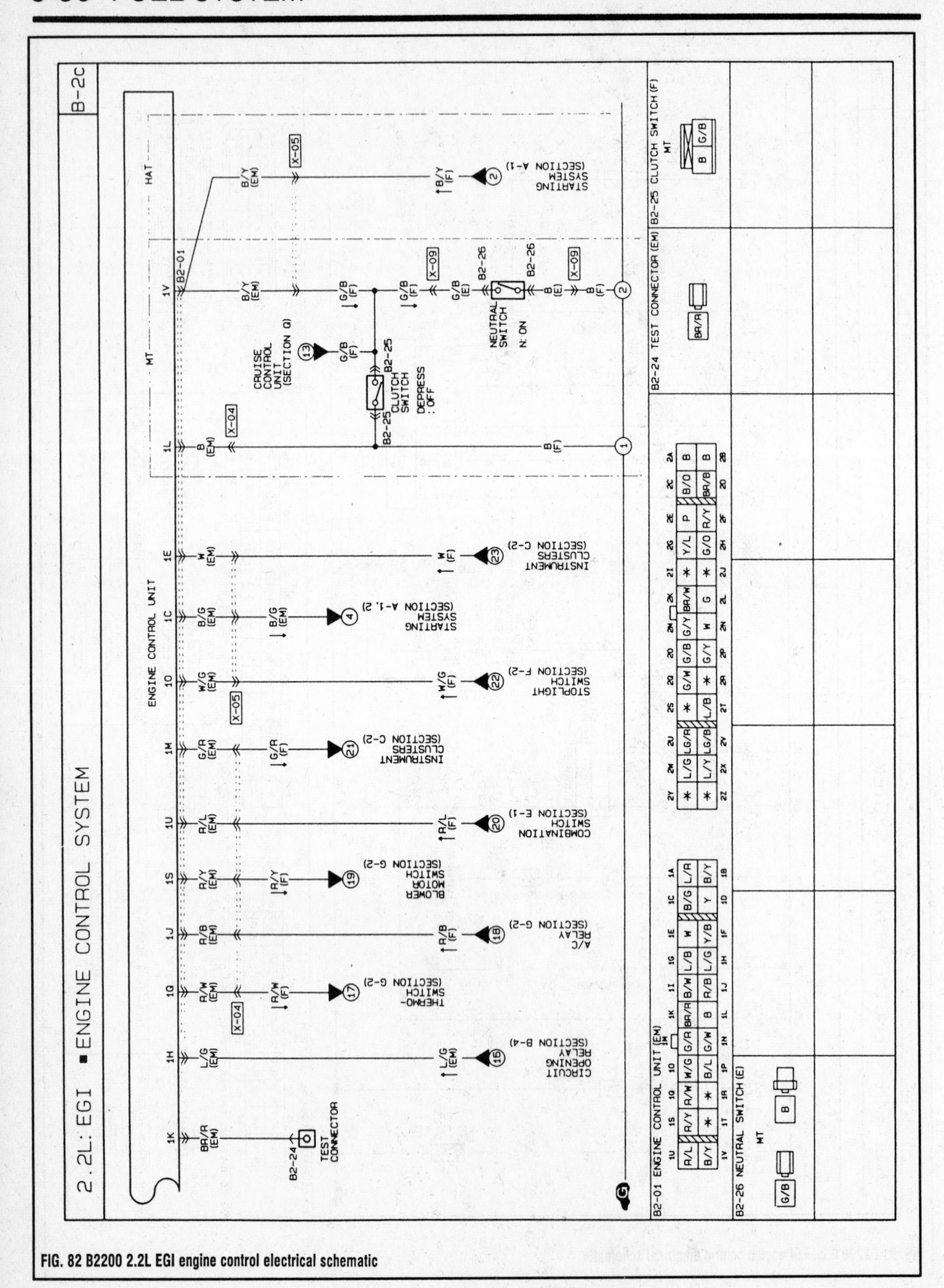

FIG. 82 B2200 2.2L EGI engine control electrical schematic

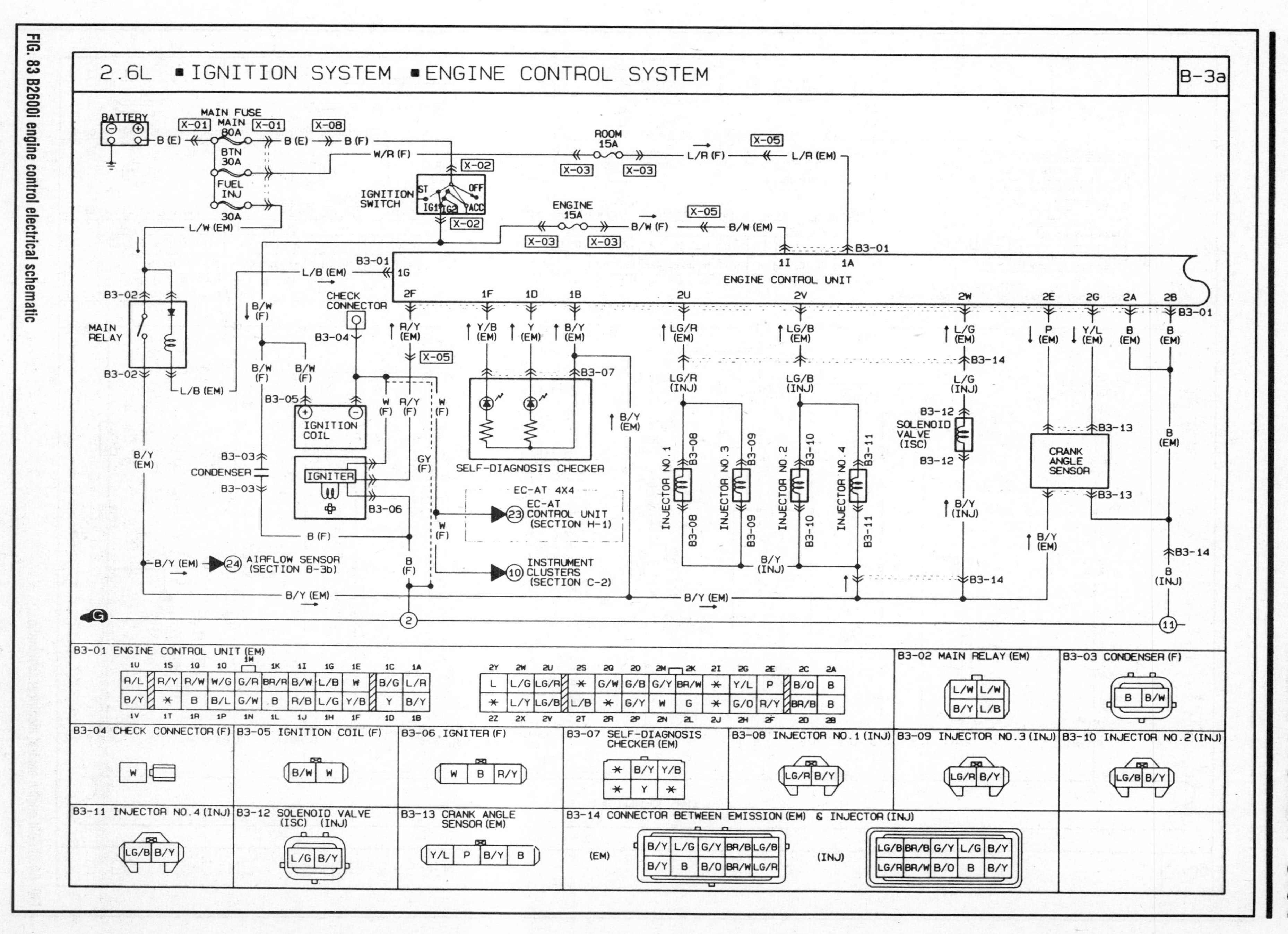

FIG. 83 B2600i engine control electrical schematic

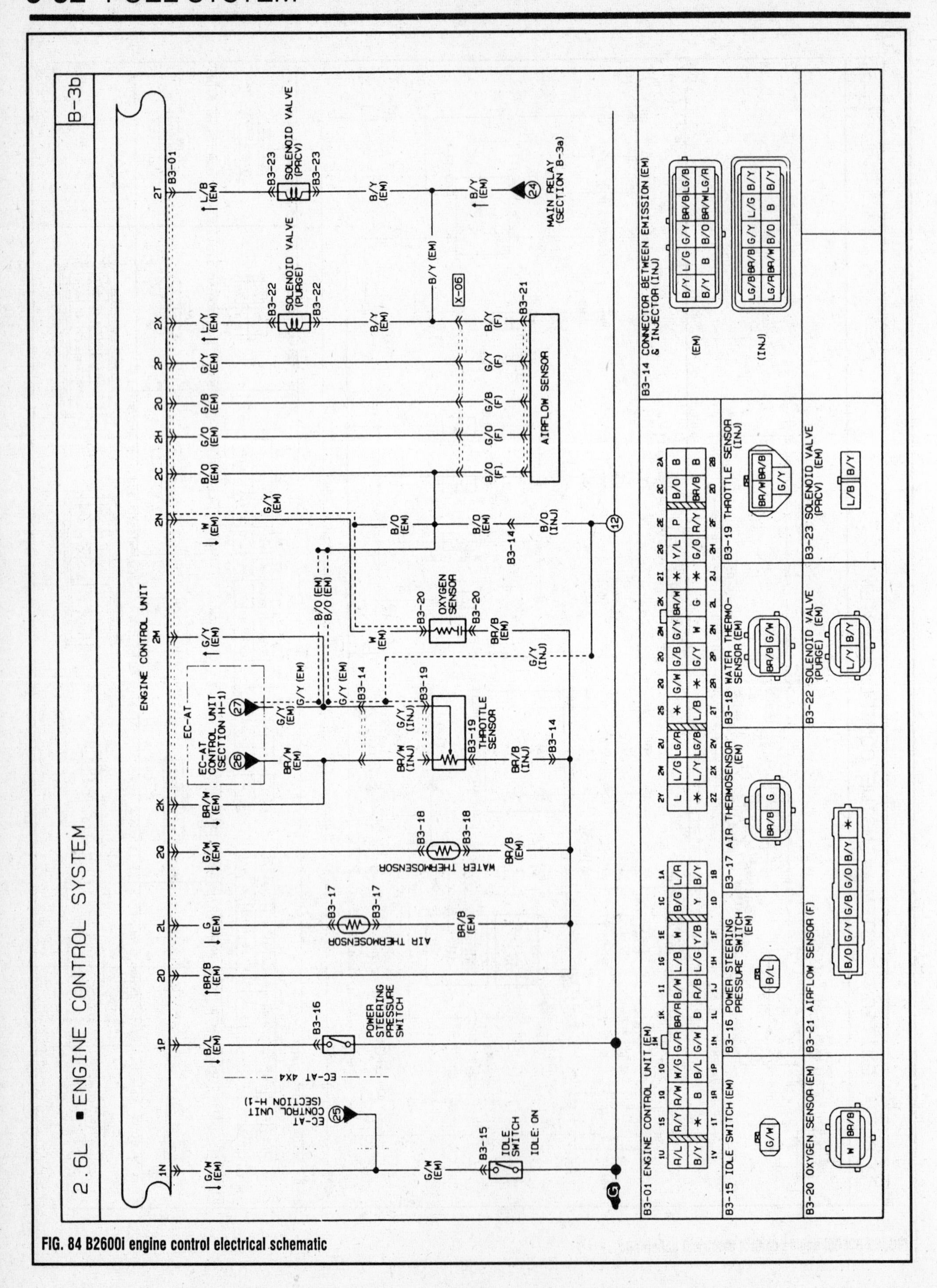

FIG. 84 B2600i engine control electrical schematic

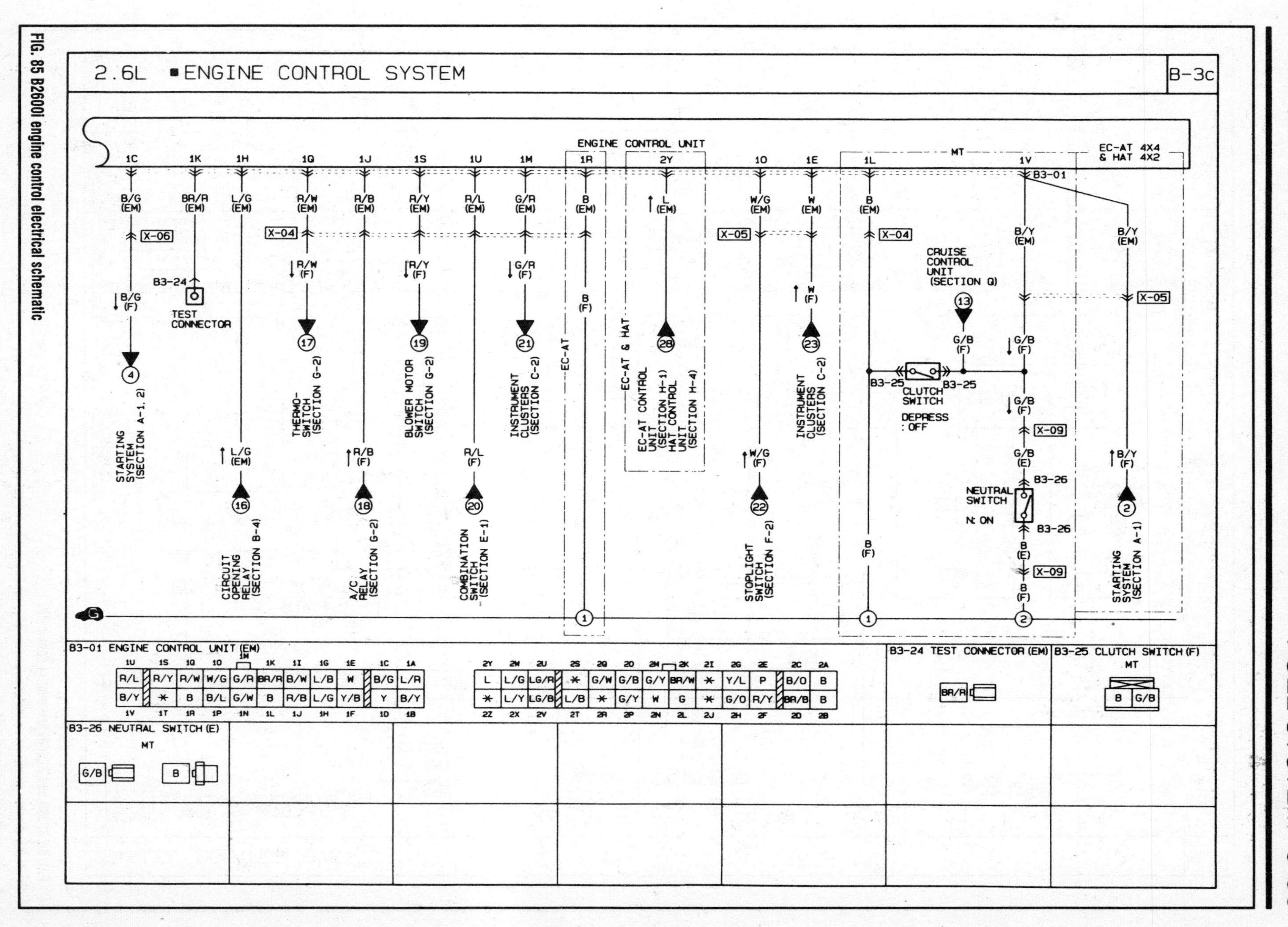

FIG. 85 B2600i engine control electrical schematic

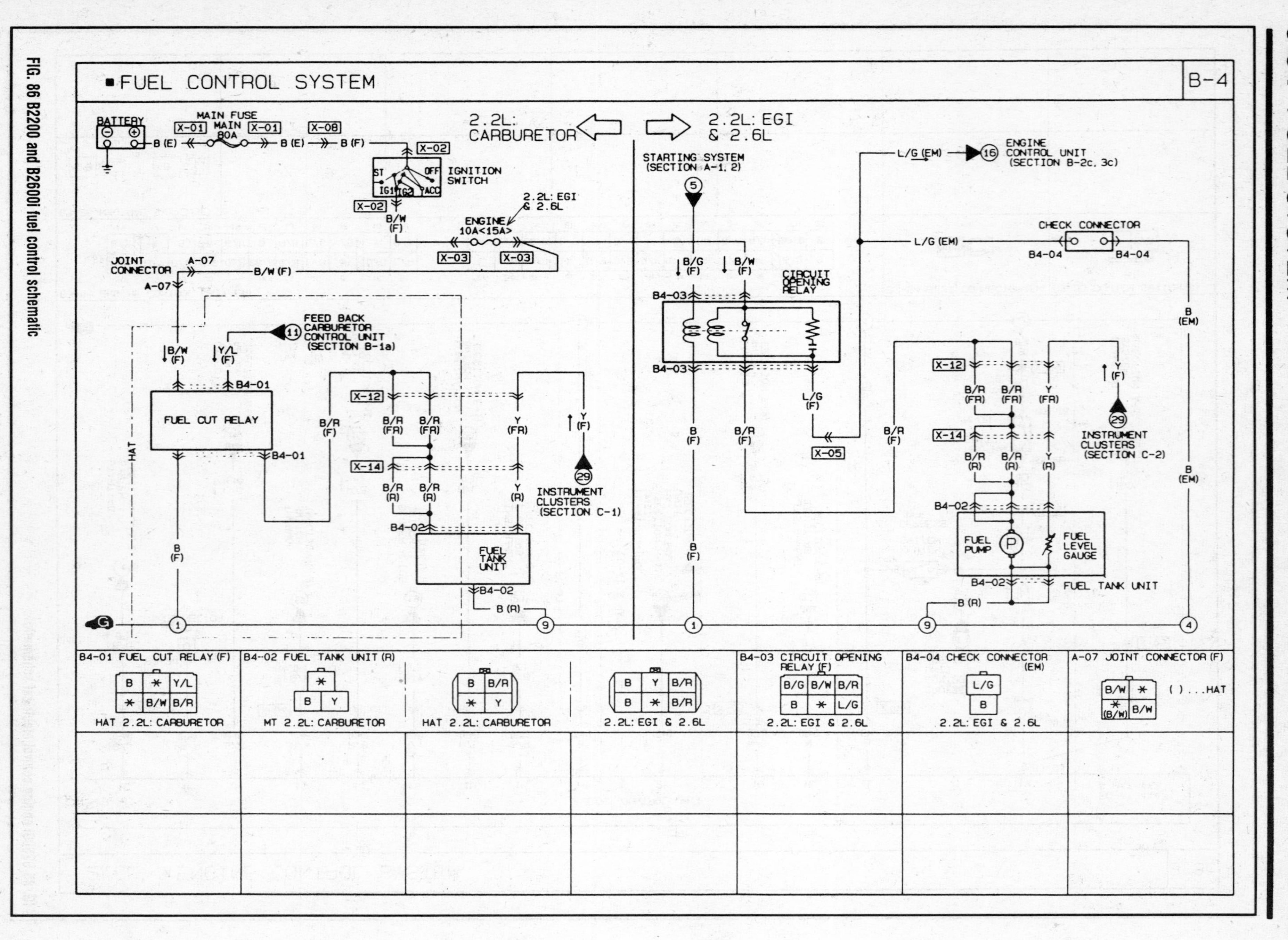

FIG. 86 B2200 and B2600i fuel control schematic

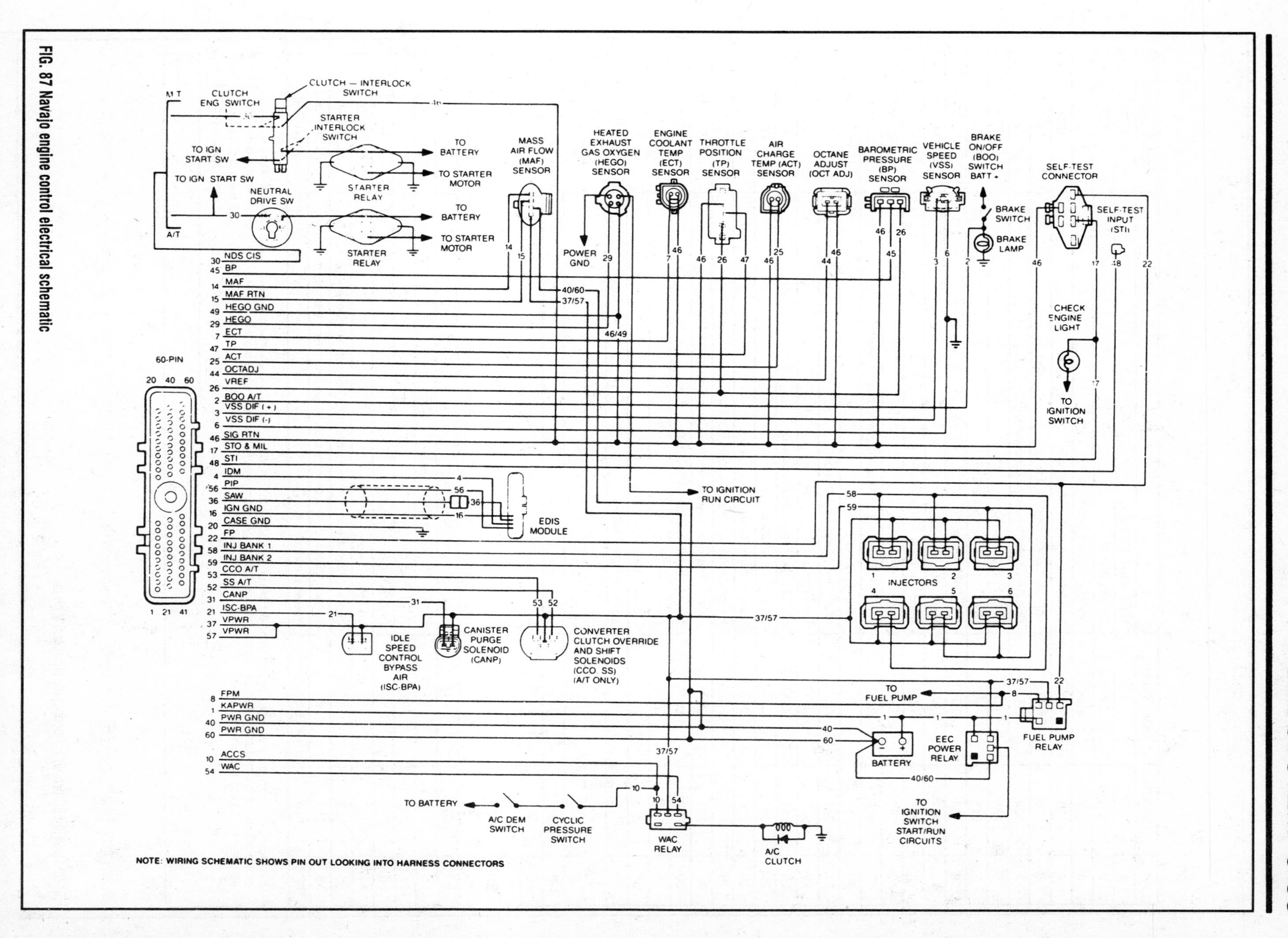

FIG. 87 Navajo engine control electrical schematic

Pin	Circuit	Wire Color	Application	Abbreviations
1	37	Y	Keep Alive Power	KAPWR
2	511	LG	Brake On/Off	BOO
3	679	DG/W	Vehicle Speed Sensor (+)	VSS (+)
4	11	T/Y	Ignition Diagnostic Monitor	IDM
6	676	BK/Y	Vehicle Speed Sensor (−)	VSS (−)
7	354	LG/R	Engine Coolant Temperature Sensor	ECT
8	238	P/B	Fuel Pump Monitor	FPM
9	915	B/O	Data Communications Link (−)	DATA (−)
10	198	DG/O	A/C Cycling Switch	ACCS
14	967	LB/R	Mass Air Flow Sensor	MAF
15	968	T/LB	Mass Air Flow Return	MAF RTN
16	259	O/R	Ignition Ground	IGN GND
17	658	P/LG	Self-Test Output and Malfunction Indicator Light	STO and MIL
20	57	B	Case Ground	CASE GND
21	264	W/LB	Idle Speed Control Solenoid	ISC
22	926	LB/O	Fuel Pump	FP
25	743	GY	Air Charge Temperature Sensor	ACT
26	351	BR/W	Reference Voltage	VREF
28	914	T/O	Data Communications Link (+)	DATA (+)
29	74	GY/LB	Heated Exhaust Gas Oxygen Sensor	HEGO
30	199	LB/Y	Clutch Interlock Switch Neutral Gear Switch (M/T Only)	CIS/NGS
30	199	LB/Y	Neutral Drive Switch (A/T Only)	NDS
31	101	GY/Y	Canister Purge	CANP
34	305	LB/P	Data Output Link	DOL
36	929	P	Spark Angle Width	SAW
37	361	R	Vehicle Power	VPWR
40	570	B/W	Power Ground	PWR GND
44	242	DG	Octane Adjust	OCT ADJ
46	359	GY/R	Signal Return	SIG RTN
47	355	GY/W	Throttle Position Sensor	TP
48	209	W/P	Self-Test Input	STI
49	89	O	Heated Exhaust Gas Oxygen Sensor Ground	HEGO GND
52	237	O/Y	Shift Solenoid (A/T Only)	SS
53	480	P/Y	Clutch Converter Override (A/T Only)	CCO
54	331	P/Y	WOT A/C Cut-Off	WAC
56	395	GY/O	Profile Ignition Pick-Up	PIP
57	361	R	Vehicle Power	VPWR
58	555	T	Injector (Bank 1 — Controls Engine Cylinder Numbers 1, 2, and 3)	INJ BANK 1
59	556	W	Injector (Bank 2 — Controls Engine Cylinder Numbers 4, 5, and 6)	INJ BANK 2
60	570	B/LG	Power Ground	PWR GND

Pin locations given for reference only. Probing 60 pin connector with DVOM probe will result in permanent damage to the pin connectors. Always probe as directed, using the Breakout Box.

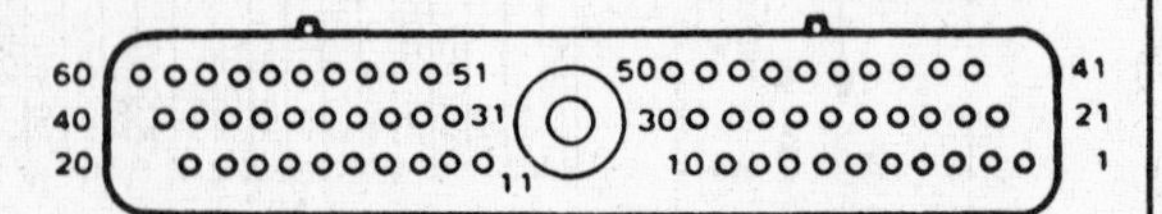

FIG. 88 Navajo EEC processor connector pin identification

CODE NUMBERS

Code No.	Malfunction display: Pattern of output signal (Self-Diagnosis Checker or MIL (California only))	Sensor or subsystem	Self-diagnosis	Fail-safe
02	ON / OFF	Ne signal	No Ne signal	—
03	ON / OFF	G signal	No G signal	Cancels 2-group injection
08	ON / OFF	Airflow sensor	Open or short circuit	Basic fuel injection amount fixed as for two driving modes (1) Idle switch: ON (2) Idle switch: OFF
09	ON / OFF	Water thermosensor	Open or short circuit	Maintains constant 20°(68°F) command
11	ON / OFF	Intake air thermosensor (dynamic chamber)	Open or short circuit	Maintains constant 20°C (68°F) command
12	ON / OFF	Throttle sensor	Open or short circuit	Maintains constant command of throttle valve fully open
14	ON / OFF	Atmospheric pressure sensor	Open or short circuit	Maintains constant command of sea level pressure
15	ON / OFF	Oxygen sensor (Inactivation)	Sensor output continues less than 0.45V 180 sec. after engine exceeds 1,500 rpm	Cancels engine feedback operation
17	ON / OFF	Oxygen sensor (Inversion)	Sensor output not changed 20 sec. after engine exceeds 1,500 rpm	Cancels engine feedback operation
25	ON / OFF	Solenoid valve (pressure regulator control)	Open or short circuit	—
26	ON / OFF	Solenoid valve (purge control)		—
34	ON / OFF	Solenoid valve (idle speed control)		—

Caution

a) If there is more than one failure present, the lowest number malfunction code is displayed first, the remaining codes are displayed in order.

b) After repairing all failures, turn off the ignition switch, disconnect the negative battery cable for more than 20 seconds to erase the memory of a malfunction code from the engine control unit.

FIG. 89 2.2L and 2.6L EFI diagnostic code chart

Code No.02 (Distributor Ne-signal) — **PC: Possible Cause**

- Check distributor circuit for poor connection
  - YES → Repair or replace connector
  - NO ↓
- Check terminal-wire (B) for continuity
  - NO → Repair or replace
  - YES ↓
- Check if battery voltage exists at distributor terminal-wire (B/Y)
  - NO → Check for open circuit in wiring from distributor to main relay (FUEL INJ relay)
  - YES ↓
- Check terminal-wire (P) between distributor and ECU terminal 2E for continuity
  - NO → Repair or replace
  - YES ↓
- Check if ECU terminal 2E voltage is OK (Refer to page F2-177)
  - YES → Replace ECU
  - NO ↓
- Check if approx. 0V or approx. 5V exists at distributor terminal-wire (P)
  - YES → Remove the distributor from the engine and reconnect the distributor wiring. Check if ECU terminal 2E Voltage alternates from approx. 0V to 5V when the distributor shaft is rotated by hand
    - YES → Replace ECU
    - NO → Check for short circuit in wiring from distributor to ECU
  - NO ↓
- Check if approx. 5V exists at ECU terminal 2E (With distributor connector disconnected)
  - YES → Check for short circuit in wiring from distributor to ECU
    - NO → Replace distributor
  - NO → Replace ECU

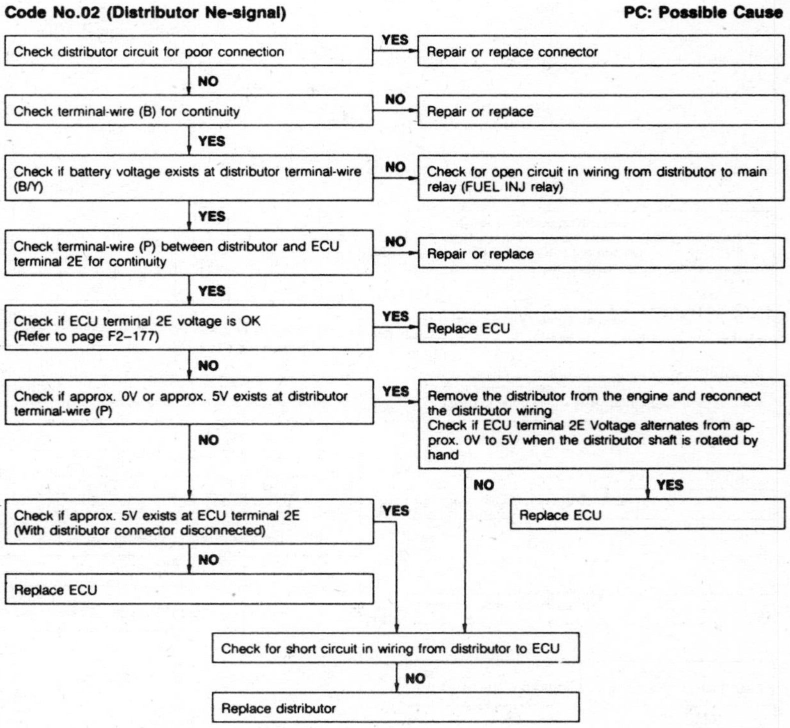

FIG. 90 2.2L and 2.6L EFI diagnostic code chart

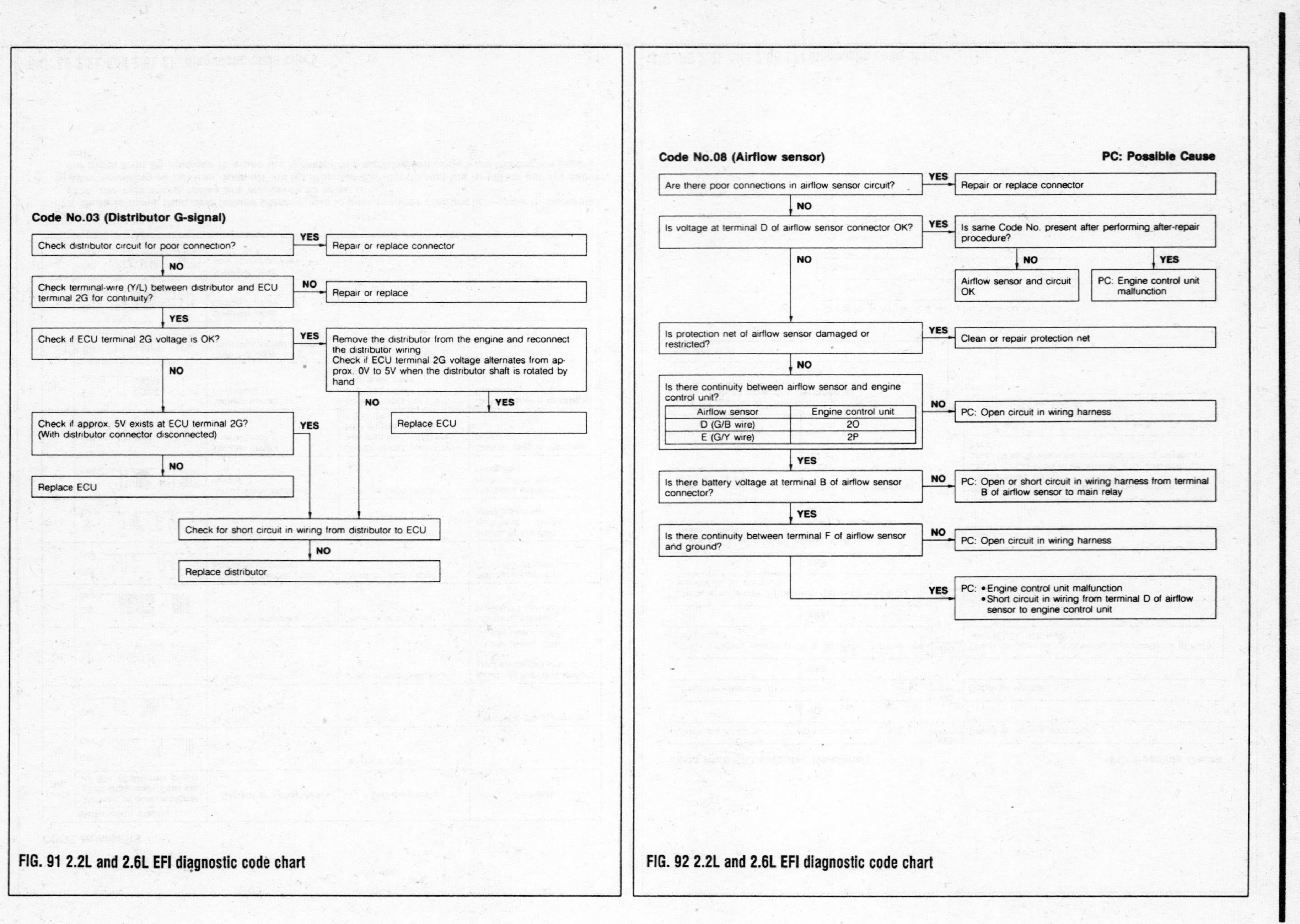
Code No.03 (Distributor G-signal)
Check distributor circuit for poor connection?
YES
Repair or replace connector
NO
Check terminal-wire (Y/L) between distributor and ECU terminal 2G for continuity?
NO
Repair or replace
YES
Check if ECU terminal 2G voltage is OK?
YES
Remove the distributor from the engine and reconnect the distributor wiring
Check if ECU terminal 2G voltage alternates from approx. 0V to 5V when the distributor shaft is rotated by hand
NO
YES
Replace ECU
NO
Check if approx. 5V exists at ECU terminal 2G? (With distributor connector disconnected)
YES
NO
Replace ECU
Check for short circuit in wiring from distributor to ECU
NO
Replace distributor
Code No.08 (Airflow sensor)
PC: Possible Cause
Are there poor connections in airflow sensor circuit?
YES
Repair or replace connector
NO
Is voltage at terminal D of airflow sensor connector OK?
YES
Is same Code No. present after performing after-repair procedure?
NO
YES
Airflow sensor and circuit OK
PC: Engine control unit malfunction
NO
Is protection net of airflow sensor damaged or restricted?
YES
Clean or repair protection net
NO
Is there continuity between airflow sensor and engine control unit?
Airflow sensor
Engine control unit
D (G/B wire)
2O
E (G/Y wire)
2P
NO
PC: Open circuit in wiring harness
YES
Is there battery voltage at terminal B of airflow sensor connector?
NO
PC: Open or short circuit in wiring harness from terminal B of airflow sensor to main relay
YES
Is there continuity between terminal F of airflow sensor and ground?
NO
PC: Open circuit in wiring harness
YES
PC: • Engine control unit malfunction
• Short circuit in wiring from terminal D of airflow sensor to engine control unit

FIG. 91 2.2L and 2.6L EFI diagnostic code chart

FIG. 92 2.2L and 2.6L EFI diagnostic code chart

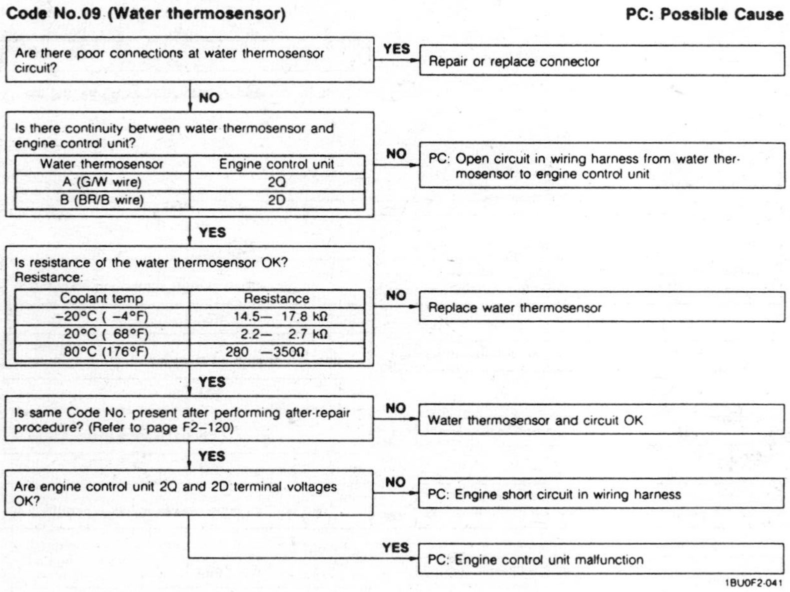

Code No.09 (Water thermosensor)

PC: Possible Cause

Are there poor connections at water thermosensor circuit?
- YES → Repair or replace connector
- NO ↓

Is there continuity between water thermosensor and engine control unit?

Water thermosensor	Engine control unit
A (G/W wire)	2Q
B (BR/B wire)	2D

- NO → PC: Open circuit in wiring harness from water thermosensor to engine control unit
- YES ↓

Is resistance of the water thermosensor OK?
Resistance:

Coolant temp	Resistance
−20°C (−4°F)	14.5— 17.8 kΩ
20°C (68°F)	2.2— 2.7 kΩ
80°C (176°F)	280 —350Ω

- NO → Replace water thermosensor
- YES ↓

Is same Code No. present after performing after-repair procedure? (Refer to page F2–120)
- NO → Water thermosensor and circuit OK
- YES ↓

Are engine control unit 2Q and 2D terminal voltages OK?
- NO → PC: Engine short circuit in wiring harness
- YES → PC: Engine control unit malfunction

1BU0F2-041

FIG. 93 2.2L and 2.6L EFI diagnostic code chart

No.11 Code (Intake air thermosensor)

PC: Possible Cause

Are there poor connections at intake air thermosensor connectors?
- YES → Repair or replace connector
- NO ↓

Is there continuity between intake air thermosensor (dynamic chamber) and engine control unit?

Intake air thermosensor (dynamic chamber)	Engine control unit
A (G wire)	2L
B (BR/B wire)	2D

- NO → PC: Open circuit in wiring harness
- YES ↓

Is resistance of intake air thermosensor (dynamic chamber) OK?
Resistance:

Temperature	Resistance
25°C (77°F)	29.7—36.3 kΩ
85°C (185°F)	3.3—3.7 kΩ

- NO → Replace intake air thermosensor (dynamic chamber)
- YES ↓

Is same Code No. present after performing after-repair procedure?
- No → Intake air thermosensor and circuit OK
- YES ↓

Are engine control unit 2L and 2D terminal voltages OK?
- NO → PC: Short circuit in wiring harness
- YES → PC: Engine control unit malfunction

1BU0F2-042

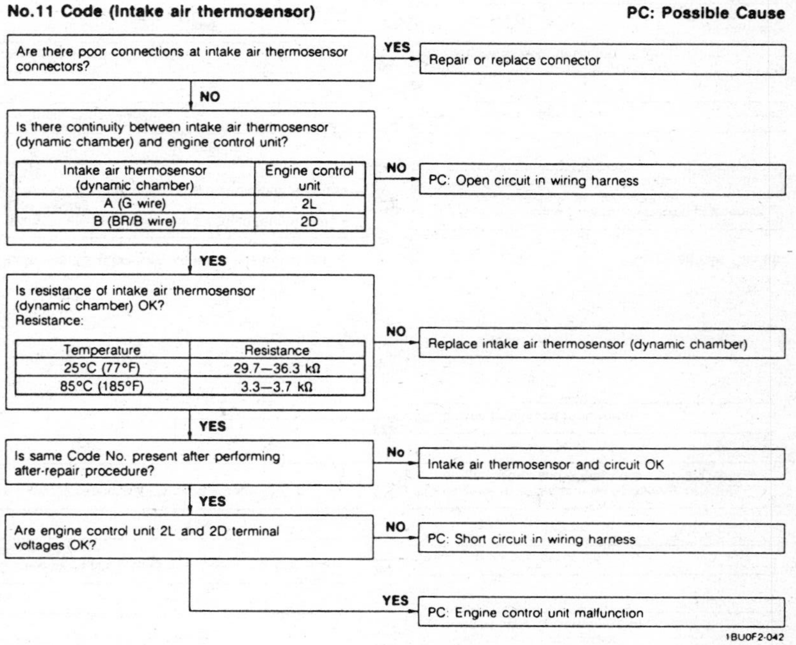

FIG. 94 2.2L and 2.6L EFI diagnostic code chart

Code No.12 (Throttle sensor)

PC: Possible cause

Are there poor connections in throttle sensor circuit?	YES	Repair or replace connector terminal
↓ NO		
Is there 4.5—5.5 V at A terminal of throttle sensor connector?	NO	PC: • Open or short circuit in wiring harness from A terminal of throttle sensor to 2K terminal of engine control unit • Engine control unit malfunction
↓ YES		
Is C terminal of throttle sensor connector grounded?	NO	PC: Open circuit in wiring harness from C terminal of throttle sensor to ground
↓ YES		
Is throttle sensor adjusted correctly?	NO	Adjust throttle sensor (Refer to page F2–181)
↓ YES		
Is same Code No. present after performing after-repair procedure?	NO	Throttle sensor and circuit OK
↓ YES		
Is engine control unit 2M terminal voltage OK?	NO	PC: Open or short circuit in wiring harness from B terminal of throttle sensor to 2M terminal of engine control unit
	YES	PC: Engine control unit malfunction

Code No.14 (Atmospheric pressure sensor in ECU)

Replace ECU

FIG. 95 2.2L and 2.6L EFI diagnostic code chart

Code No.15 (Oxygen sensor—Inactivation)

PC: Possible Cause

Note
When Codes No.15 and 17 are present at the same time, first perform the checking procedure for Code No.17.

Are there poor connections in oxygen sensor circuit?	YES	Repair or replace connector
↓ NO		
Is oxygen sensor output voltage OK?	NO	Replace oxygen sensor
↓ YES		
Is sensitivity of oxygen sensor OK?	NO	PC: • Oxygen sensor malfunction • Engine control unit malfunction
↓ YES		
Is same Code No. present after performing after-repair procedure?	NO	Oxygen sensor and circuit OK
↓ YES		
Is engine control unit 2N terminal voltage OK?	NO	PC: Open or short circuit in wiring harness between oxygen sensor and engine control unit 2N terminal
	YES	PC: Engine control unit malfunction

Code No.17 (Oxygen sensor—Inversion)

PC: Possible Cause

Warm up engine and run it at 2,500—3,000 rpm for three minutes Does monitor lamp of Self-Diagnosis Checker illuminate at idle?	NO	PC: • Air leak in vacuum hoses or emission component • Contaminated oxygen sensor • Insufficient fuel injection
↓ YES		
Are spark plugs clean?	NO	Clean or replace spark plugs
↓ YES		
Is oxygen sensor voltage OK?	NO	PC: Oxygen sensor malfunction
↓ YES		
Is same Code No. present after performing after-repair procedure?	NO	Feedback system OK
↓ YES		
Is engine control unit 2N terminal voltage OK?	NO	PC: Open or short circuit in wiring harness between oxygen sensor and engine control unit 2N terminal
	YES	PC: Engine control unit malfunction

FIG. 96 2.2L and 2.6L EFI diagnostic code chart

Code No.25 (Solenoid valve—Pressure regulator control)

PC: Possible Cause

- Are there poor connections in solenoid valve circuit?
  - YES → Repair or replace connector
  - NO → next step
- Is there continuity of solenoid valve?
  - NO → Replace solenoid valve
  - YES → next step
- Is there battery voltage at (B/Y) wire of solenoid valve connector?
  - NO → PC: Open circuit in wiring harness from (B/Y) wire to main relay
  - YES → next step
- Is there continuity between solenoid valve and engine control unit?

Solenoid valve	Engine control unit
B (L/B wire)	2T

  - NO → PC: Open circuit in wiring harness from solenoid valve to engine control unit
  - YES → PC: • Short circuit in wiring harness • Engine control unit malfunction

Code No.26 (Solenoid valve—Purge control)

- Are there poor connections in solenoid valve circuit?
  - YES → Repair or replace connector
  - NO → next step
- Is there continuity of solenoid valve?
  - NO → Replace solenoid valve
  - YES → next step
- Is there battery voltage at (B/Y) wire of solenoid valve circuit?
  - NO → PC: Open circuit in wiring harness from (B/Y) wire to main relay
  - YES → next step
- Is there continuity between solenoid valve and engine control unit?

Solenoid valve	Engine control unit
B (L/Y wire)	2X

  - NO → PC: Open circuit in wiring harness from solenoid valve to engine control unit
  - YES → PC: • Short circuit in wiring harness • Engine control unit malfunction

Code No.34 (Solenoid valve—Idle speed control (ISC))

PC: Possible Cause

- Are there poor connections in solenoid valve circuit?
  - YES → Repair or replace connector
  - NO → next step
- Is resistance of solenoid valve OK? Resistance: 7.7—9.3Ω
  - NO → Replace BAC valve
  - YES → next step
- Is there battery voltage at (B/Y) wire of solenoid valve connector?
  - NO → PC: Open or short circuit in wiring harness from (B/Y) wire to main relay
  - YES → next step
- Is there continuity between solenoid valve and engine control unit?

Solenoid valve	Engine control unit
B (L/G wire)	2W

  - NO → PC: Open circuit in wiring harness from solenoid valve to engine control unit
  - YES → PC: • Short circuit in wiring harness • Engine control unit malfunction

FIG. 97 2.2L and 2.6L EFI diagnostic code chart

CODE NUMBER
Input Devices

Malfunction Code No.	Input devices	Malfunction	Fail-safe function	Pattern of output signals (Self-Diagnosis Checker or MIL)
01	Ignition pulse (Igniter, Ignition coil)	Broken wire, short circuit	—	
02	Distributor (Ne signal)	Ne signal not input for 1.5 sec. during cranking	—	
03	Distributor (G1 signal)	Broken wire, short circuit	—	
04	Distributor (G2 signal)	Broken wire, short circuit	—	
08	Airflow meter	Broken wire, short circuit	Basic fuel injection amount fixed as for 2 driving modes 1) Idle switch: ON 2) Idle switch: OFF	
09	Water thermosensor	Broken wire, short circuit	Coolant temp. input fixed at 80°C (176°F)	
10	Intake air thermosensor (Airflow meter)	Broken wire, short circuit	Intake air temp. input fixed at 20°C (68°F)	
11	Intake air thermosensor (Dynamic chamber)	Broken wire, short circuit	Intake air temp. input fixed at 20°C (68°F)	
12	Throttle sensor	Broken wire, short circuit	Throttle valve opening angle signal input fixed at fully open	
14	Atmospheric pressure sensor	ECU	Atmospheric pressure input fixed at 760 mmHg (29.9 in Hg)	
15	Oxygen sensor	Oxygen sensor output below 0.55V 120 sec. after engine at 1,500 rpm	Feedback system canceled (for EGI)	
17	Feedback system	Oxygen sensor output does not change from 0.55V 60 sec. after engine at 1,500 rpm	Feedback system canceled (for EGI)	

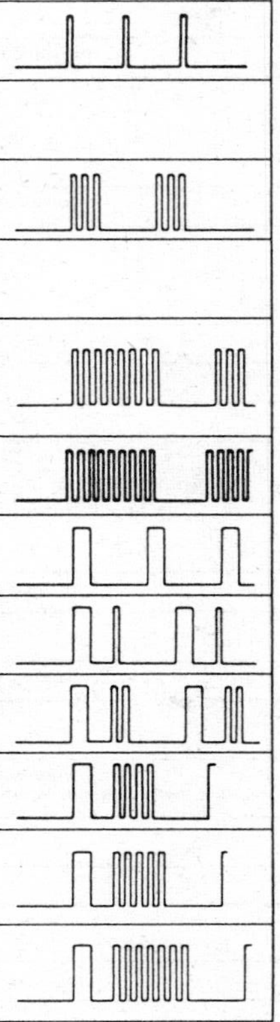

FIG. 98 3.0L diagnostic code chart

Output Devices

Code No.	Output devices	Output signal pattern (Self-Diagnosis Checker or MIL)
25	Solenoid valve (Pressure regulator control)	
26	Solenoid valve (Purge control)	
34	Idle speed control valve (BAC valve)	
36	Oxygen sensor heater	
41	Solenoid valve (Variable resonance induction system)	

Caution
- **If there is more than one failure present, the lowest number malfunction code is displayed first, the subsequent malfunction codes appear in order.**
- **After repairing all failures, turn the ignition switch OFF, disconnect the negative battery cable, for approx. 20 seconds to erase the malfunction code memory.**

FIG. 99 3.0L diagnostic code chart

If a malfunction code number is illuminated on the **SST**, check the following chart along with the wiring diagram.

PC: Possible Cause

No.01 Code

- Are there poor connections at ignition coil connectors? — YES → Repair or replace connector
- NO ↓
- Is resistance of ignition coil OK ? Resistance: Primary 0.72—0.88Ω, Secondary 10—30 kΩ — NO → Replace ignition coil
- YES ↓
- Is operation of igniter OK ? (Refer to Section G) — NO → Replace igniter
- YES ↓
- Is there continuity between IGf terminal of igniter connector (wiring harness side) and engine control unit (1G) terminal ? — NO → PC: Open circuit in wiring harness from igniter to engine control unit (1G) terminal
- YES ↓
- Is engine control unit (1M) terminal voltage OK? — NO → PC: Short circuit wiring harness
- YES → Replace engine control unit

No.02 Code

- Are there poor connections at distributor connectors? — YES → Repair or replace connector
- NO ↓
- Is resistance of distributor OK? (Refer to Section G) — NO → Replace distributor
- YES ↓
- Is there continuity between distributor connector (wiring harness side) and engine control unit? — NO → PC: Open circuit in wiring harness

Distributor	Engine control unit
Ne ① W	2E
COM ② G	2F

- YES ↓
- Are engine control unit (2E) and (2F) terminal voltages OK? — NO → PC: Short circuit in wiring harness
- YES → Replace engine control unit

FIG. 100 3.0L diagnostic code chart

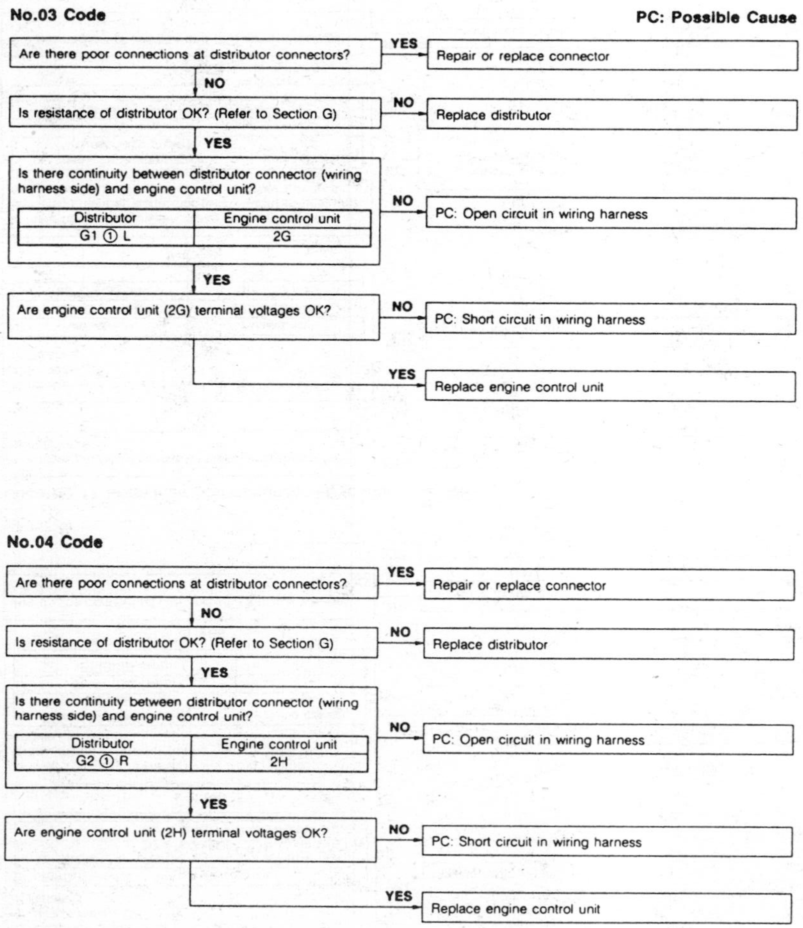

No.03 Code

PC: Possible Cause

- Are there poor connections at distributor connectors?
  - YES → Repair or replace connector
  - NO ↓
- Is resistance of distributor OK? (Refer to Section G)
  - NO → Replace distributor
  - YES ↓
- Is there continuity between distributor connector (wiring harness side) and engine control unit?

Distributor	Engine control unit
G1 ① L	2G

  - NO → PC: Open circuit in wiring harness
  - YES ↓
- Are engine control unit (2G) terminal voltages OK?
  - NO → PC: Short circuit in wiring harness
  - YES → Replace engine control unit

No.04 Code

- Are there poor connections at distributor connectors?
  - YES → Repair or replace connector
  - NO ↓
- Is resistance of distributor OK? (Refer to Section G)
  - NO → Replace distributor
  - YES ↓
- Is there continuity between distributor connector (wiring harness side) and engine control unit?

Distributor	Engine control unit
G2 ① R	2H

  - NO → PC: Open circuit in wiring harness
  - YES ↓
- Are engine control unit (2H) terminal voltages OK?
  - NO → PC: Short circuit in wiring harness
  - YES → Replace engine control unit

FIG. 101 3.0L diagnostic code chart

Code No.08 (Airflow meter)

PC: Possible Cause

- Are there poor connections at airflow meter connectors?
  - YES → Repair or replace connector
  - NO ↓
- Is resistance of airflow meter OK?
  Resistance:

Terminal	Fully closed (Ω)	Fully open (Ω)
E_2 ↔ Vs	20—400	20—1,000
E_2 ↔ Vc	100—300	
E_2 ↔ V_B	200—400	

  - NO → Repair airflow meter
  - YES ↓
- Is there continuity between airflow meter connector (wiring harness side) and engine control unit?

Airflow meter	Control unit
V_B (B/W wire)	3I
Vc (B/W wire)	2B
Vs (G/B wire)	2E
E_2 (BR/B wire)	2C

  - NO → PC: Open circuit in wiring harness from airflow meter to engine control unit
  - YES ↓
- Are engine control unit terminal voltages OK?
  Check terminals 2B, 2C, 2E, 3I
  - NO → PC: Short circuit in wiring harness
  - YES → Replace engine control unit

Code No.09 (Water thermosensor)

- Are there poor connections at water thermosensor connectors?
  - YES → Repair or replace connectors
  - NO ↓
- Is resistance of water thermosensor OK?
  Resistance:

Coolant temp	Resistance
−20°C (−4°F)	14.5—17.8 kΩ
20°C (68°F)	2.2— 2.7 kΩ
40°C (104°F)	1.0— 1.3 kΩ
60°C (140°F)	0.5— 0.7 kΩ
80°C (176°F)	0.28— 0.35 kΩ

  - NO → Replace water thermosensor
  - YES ↓
- Is there continuity between water thermosensor connector (wiring harness side) and engine control unit?

Water thermosensor	Engine control unit
(G/W wire)	2I

  - NO → PC: Open circuit in wiring harness from water thermosensor to engine control unit
  - YES ↓
- Are engine control unit (2I) terminal voltages OK?
  - NO → PC: Short circuit in wiring harness
  - YES → Replace engine control unit

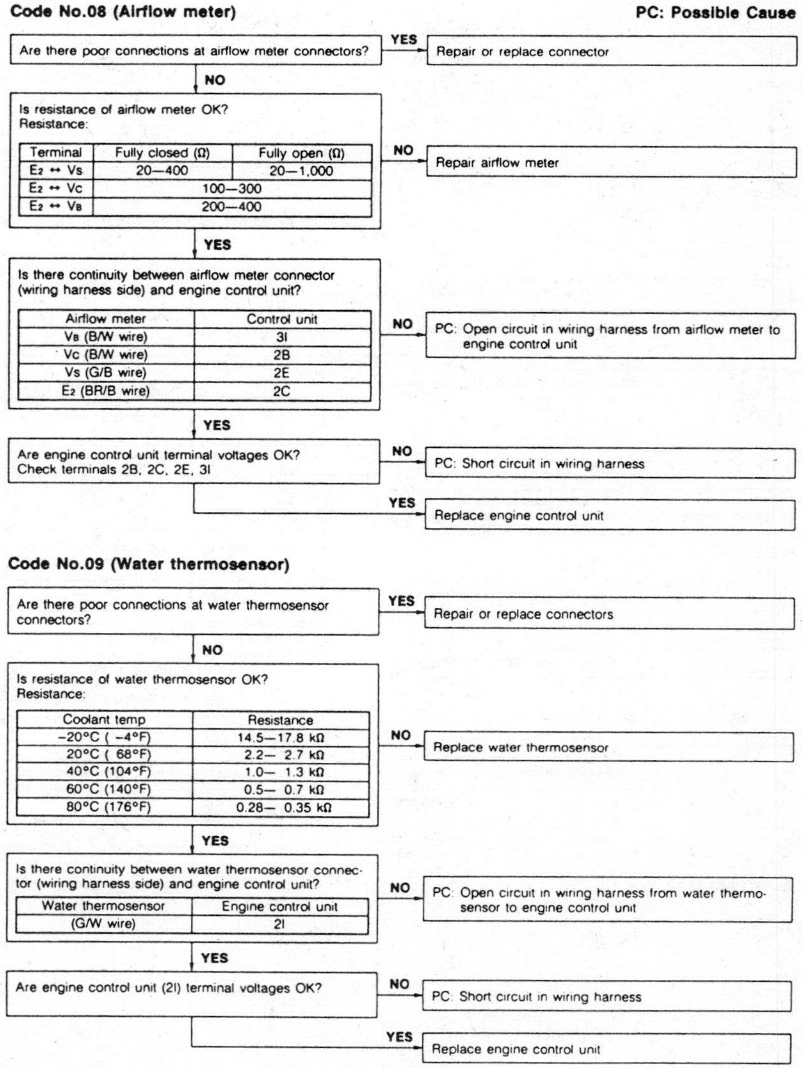

FIG. 102 3.0L diagnostic code chart

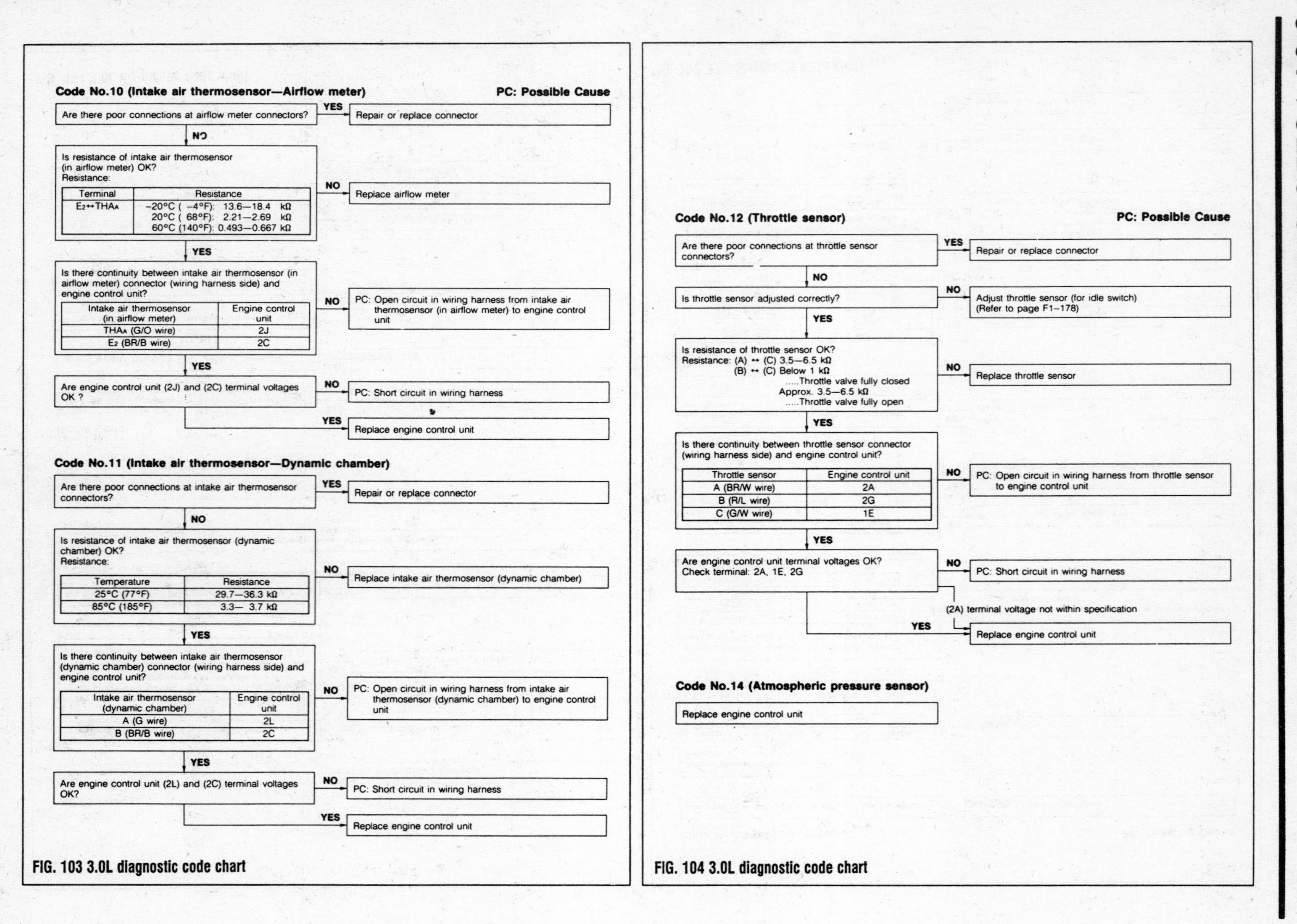

Code No.10 (Intake air thermosensor—Airflow meter)
PC: Possible Cause
Are there poor connections at airflow meter connectors?
YES
Repair or replace connector
NO
Is resistance of intake air thermosensor (in airflow meter) OK?
Resistance:
Terminal
Resistance
E2↔THAA
−20°C (−4°F): 13.6—18.4 kΩ
20°C (68°F): 2.21—2.69 kΩ
60°C (140°F): 0.493—0.667 kΩ
NO
Replace airflow meter
YES
Is there continuity between intake air thermosensor (in airflow meter) connector (wiring harness side) and engine control unit?
Intake air thermosensor (in airflow meter)
Engine control unit
THAA (G/O wire)
2J
E2 (BR/B wire)
2C
NO
PC: Open circuit in wiring harness from intake air thermosensor (in airflow meter) to engine control unit
YES
Are engine control unit (2J) and (2C) terminal voltages OK ?
NO
PC: Short circuit in wiring harness
YES
Replace engine control unit
Code No.11 (Intake air thermosensor—Dynamic chamber)
Are there poor connections at intake air thermosensor connectors?
YES
Repair or replace connector
NO
Is resistance of intake air thermosensor (dynamic chamber) OK?
Resistance:
Temperature
Resistance
25°C (77°F)
29.7—36.3 kΩ
85°C (185°F)
3.3— 3.7 kΩ
NO
Replace intake air thermosensor (dynamic chamber)
YES
Is there continuity between intake air thermosensor (dynamic chamber) connector (wiring harness side) and engine control unit?
Intake air thermosensor (dynamic chamber)
Engine control unit
A (G wire)
2L
B (BR/B wire)
2C
NO
PC: Open circuit in wiring harness from intake air thermosensor (dynamic chamber) to engine control unit
YES
Are engine control unit (2L) and (2C) terminal voltages OK?
NO
PC: Short circuit in wiring harness
YES
Replace engine control unit
Code No.12 (Throttle sensor)
PC: Possible Cause
Are there poor connections at throttle sensor connectors?
YES
Repair or replace connector
NO
Is throttle sensor adjusted correctly?
NO
Adjust throttle sensor (for idle switch) (Refer to page F1-178)
YES
Is resistance of throttle sensor OK?
Resistance: (A) ↔ (C) 3.5—6.5 kΩ
(B) ↔ (C) Below 1 kΩ
.....Throttle valve fully closed
Approx. 3.5—6.5 kΩ
.....Throttle valve fully open
NO
Replace throttle sensor
YES
Is there continuity between throttle sensor connector (wiring harness side) and engine control unit?
Throttle sensor
Engine control unit
A (BR/W wire)
2A
B (R/L wire)
2G
C (G/W wire)
1E
NO
PC: Open circuit in wiring harness from throttle sensor to engine control unit
YES
Are engine control unit terminal voltages OK?
Check terminal: 2A, 1E, 2G
NO
PC: Short circuit in wiring harness
(2A) terminal voltage not within specification
YES
Replace engine control unit
Code No.14 (Atmospheric pressure sensor)
Replace engine control unit

FIG. 103 3.0L diagnostic code chart

FIG. 104 3.0L diagnostic code chart

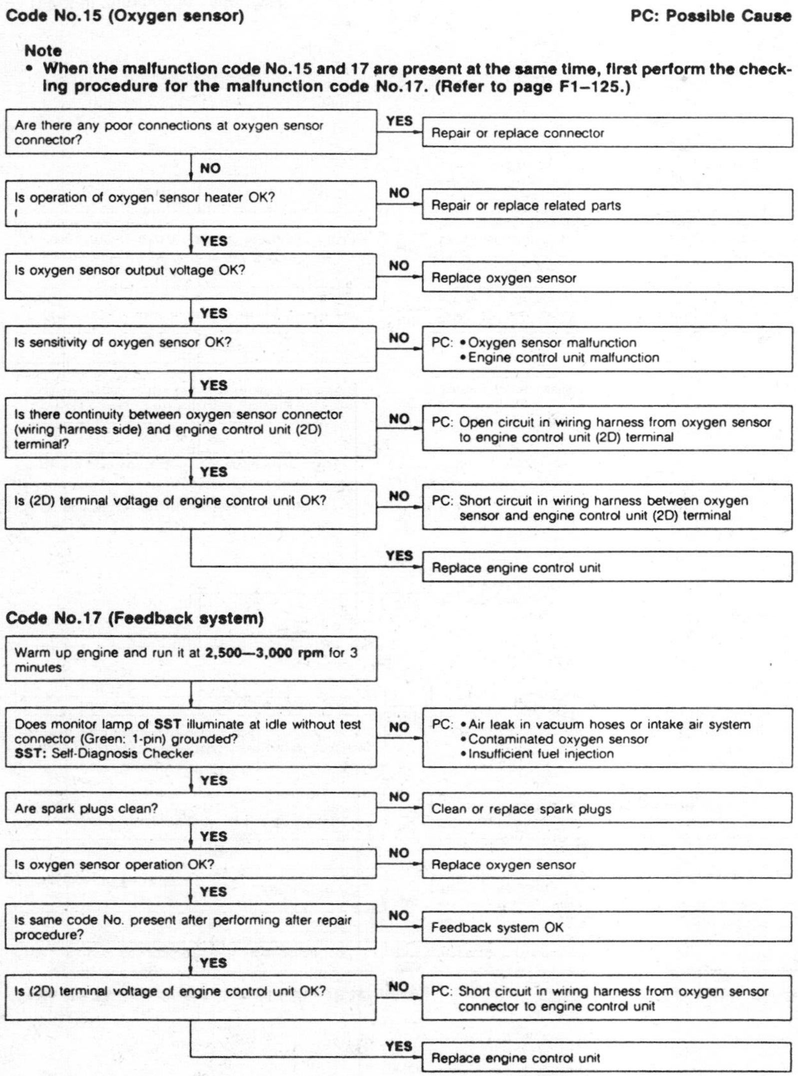

Code No.15 (Oxygen sensor)

PC: Possible Cause

Note
- **When the malfunction code No.15 and 17 are present at the same time, first perform the checking procedure for the malfunction code No.17. (Refer to page F1–125.)**

1. Are there any poor connections at oxygen sensor connector?
   - YES → Repair or replace connector
   - NO ↓
2. Is operation of oxygen sensor heater OK?
   - NO → Repair or replace related parts
   - YES ↓
3. Is oxygen sensor output voltage OK?
   - NO → Replace oxygen sensor
   - YES ↓
4. Is sensitivity of oxygen sensor OK?
   - NO → PC: • Oxygen sensor malfunction • Engine control unit malfunction
   - YES ↓
5. Is there continuity between oxygen sensor connector (wiring harness side) and engine control unit (2D) terminal?
   - NO → PC: Open circuit in wiring harness from oxygen sensor to engine control unit (2D) terminal
   - YES ↓
6. Is (2D) terminal voltage of engine control unit OK?
   - NO → PC: Short circuit in wiring harness between oxygen sensor and engine control unit (2D) terminal
   - YES → Replace engine control unit

Code No.17 (Feedback system)

1. Warm up engine and run it at **2,500—3,000 rpm** for 3 minutes
   ↓
2. Does monitor lamp of **SST** illuminate at idle without test connector (Green: 1-pin) grounded?
   SST: Self-Diagnosis Checker
   - NO → PC: • Air leak in vacuum hoses or intake air system • Contaminated oxygen sensor • Insufficient fuel injection
   - YES ↓
3. Are spark plugs clean?
   - NO → Clean or replace spark plugs
   - YES ↓
4. Is oxygen sensor operation OK?
   - NO → Replace oxygen sensor
   - YES ↓
5. Is same code No. present after performing after repair procedure?
   - NO → Feedback system OK
   - YES ↓
6. Is (2D) terminal voltage of engine control unit OK?
   - NO → PC: Short circuit in wiring harness from oxygen sensor connector to engine control unit
   - YES → Replace engine control unit

FIG. 105 3.0L diagnostic code chart

Code No.25 (Solenoid valve (Pressure regulator control))

PC: Possible Cause

1. Are there poor connections at solenoid valve (PRC) connectors?
   - YES → Repair or replace connector
   - NO ↓
2. Is there continuity of solenoid valve (PRC)?
   - NO → Replace solenoid valve
   - YES ↓
3. Is there battery voltage at (B/W) wire of solenoid valve (PRC) connector?
   - NO → PC: Open or short circuit in wiring harness from (B/W) wire to main relay (for engine control unit)
   - YES ↓
4. Is there continuity between solenoid valve (PRC) connector (wiring harness side) and engine control unit?

Solenoid valve (PRC)	Engine control unit
L/B wire	2N

   - NO → PC: Open circuit in wiring harness from solenoid valve (PRC) to engine control unit
   - YES → PC: • Engine control unit malfunction • Short circuit in wiring harness

Code No.26 (Solenoid valve (Purge control))

1. Are there poor connections at solenoid valve (purge control) connectors?
   - YES → Repair or replace connector
   - NO ↓
2. Is there continuity of solenoid valve (purge control)?
   - NO → Replace solenoid valve
   - YES ↓
3. Is there battery voltage at (B/W) wire of solenoid valve (purge control) connector?
   - NO → PC: Open or short circuit in wiring harness from (B/W) wire to main relay (for engine control unit)
   - YES ↓
4. Is there continuity between solenoid valve (purge control) connector (wiring harness side) and engine control unit?

Solenoid valve	Engine control unit
L/O wire	2K

   - NO → PC: Open circuit in wiring harness from solenoid valve (purge control) to engine control unit
   - YES → PC: • Engine control unit malfunction • Short circuit in wiring harness

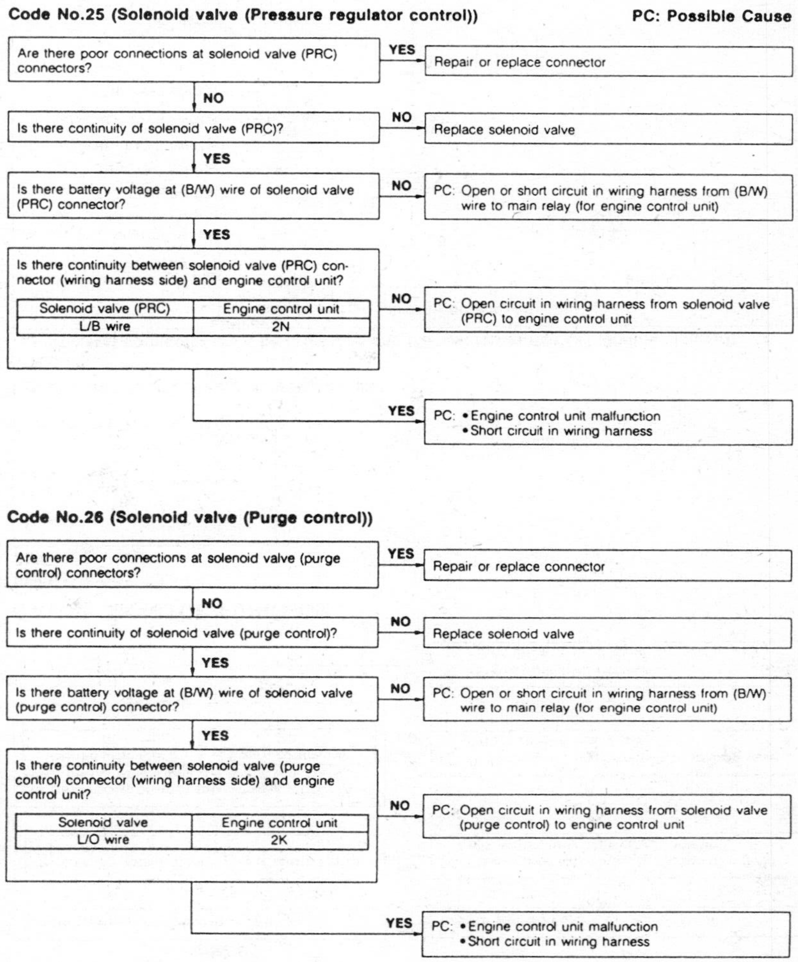

FIG. 106 3.0L diagnostic code chart

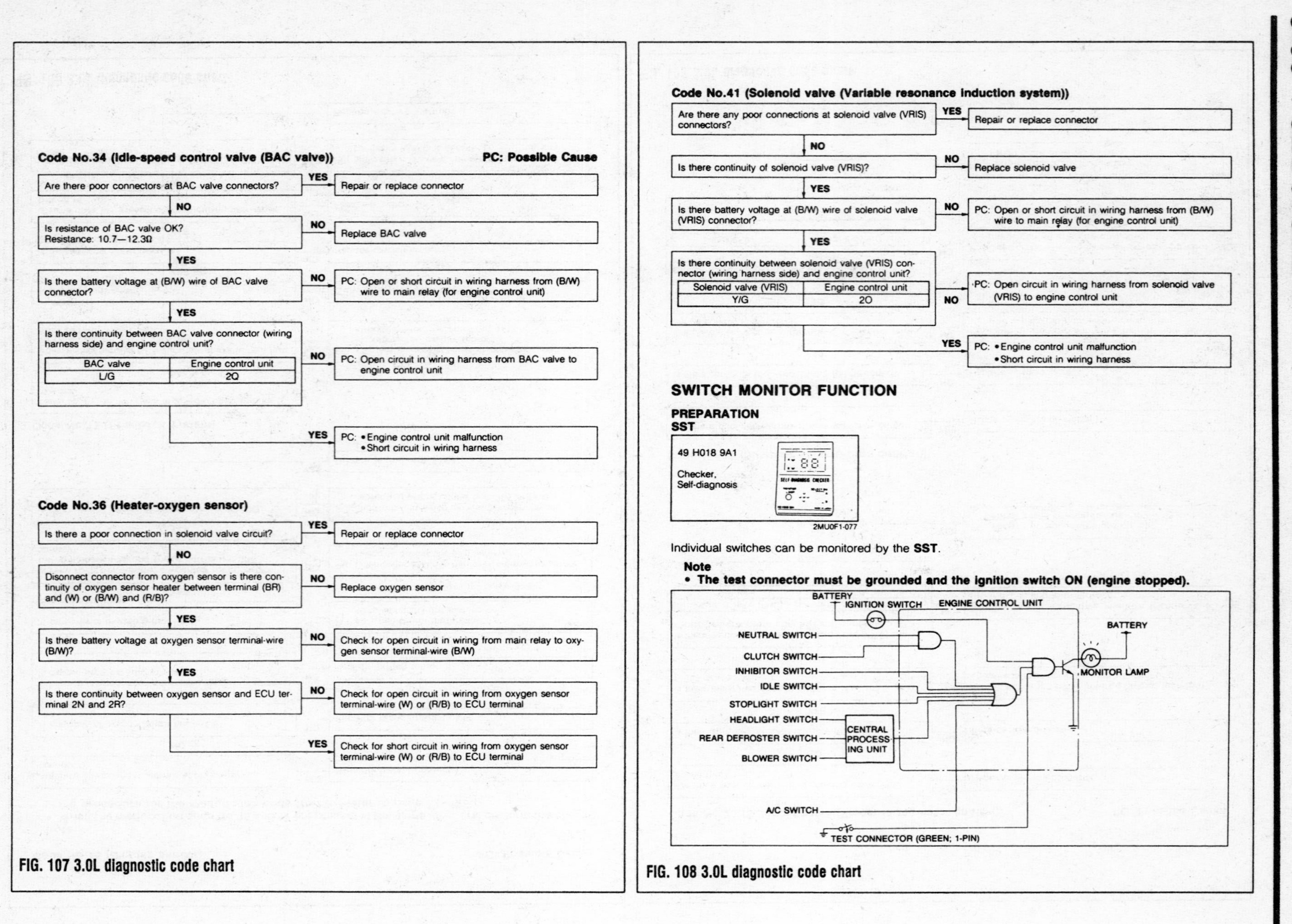
Code No.34 (Idle-speed control valve (BAC valve))
PC: Possible Cause
Are there poor connectors at BAC valve connectors?
YES
Repair or replace connector
NO
Is resistance of BAC valve OK? Resistance: 10.7—12.3Ω
NO
Replace BAC valve
YES
Is there battery voltage at (B/W) wire of BAC valve connector?
NO
PC: Open or short circuit in wiring harness from (B/W) wire to main relay (for engine control unit)
YES
Is there continuity between BAC valve connector (wiring harness side) and engine control unit?
BAC valve | Engine control unit
L/G | 2Q
NO
PC: Open circuit in wiring harness from BAC valve to engine control unit
YES
PC: •Engine control unit malfunction •Short circuit in wiring harness
Code No.36 (Heater-oxygen sensor)
Is there a poor connection in solenoid valve circuit?
YES
Repair or replace connector
NO
Disonnect connector from oxygen sensor is there continuity of oxygen sensor heater between terminal (BR) and (W) or (B/W) and (R/B)?
NO
Replace oxygen sensor
YES
Is there battery voltage at oxygen sensor terminal-wire (B/W)?
NO
Check for open circuit in wiring from main relay to oxygen sensor terminal-wire (B/W)
YES
Is there continuity between oxygen sensor and ECU terminal 2N and 2R?
NO
Check for open circuit in wiring from oxygen sensor terminal-wire (W) or (R/B) to ECU terminal
YES
Check for short circuit in wiring from oxygen sensor terminal-wire (W) or (R/B) to ECU terminal

FIG. 107 3.0L diagnostic code chart

Code No.41 (Solenoid valve (Variable resonance induction system))
Are there any poor connections at solenoid valve (VRIS) connectors?
YES
Repair or replace connector
NO
Is there continuity of solenoid valve (VRIS)?
NO
Replace solenoid valve
YES
Is there battery voltage at (B/W) wire of solenoid valve (VRIS) connector?
NO
PC: Open or short circuit in wiring harness from (B/W) wire to main relay (for engine control unit)
YES
Is there continuity between solenoid valve (VRIS) connector (wiring harness side) and engine control unit?
Solenoid valve (VRIS) | Engine control unit
Y/G | 2O
NO
PC: Open circuit in wiring harness from solenoid valve (VRIS) to engine control unit
YES
PC: •Engine control unit malfunction •Short circuit in wiring harness

SWITCH MONITOR FUNCTION

PREPARATION

SST

49 H018 9A1
Checker, Self-diagnosis
2MU0F1-077

Individual switches can be monitored by the **SST**.

Note
- **The test connector must be grounded and the ignition switch ON (engine stopped).**

BATTERY
IGNITION SWITCH
ENGINE CONTROL UNIT
BATTERY
NEUTRAL SWITCH
CLUTCH SWITCH
INHIBITOR SWITCH
IDLE SWITCH
STOPLIGHT SWITCH
HEADLIGHT SWITCH
REAR DEFROSTER SWITCH
BLOWER SWITCH
CENTRAL PROCESSING UNIT
MONITOR LAMP
A/C SWITCH
TEST CONNECTOR (GREEN; 1-PIN)

FIG. 108 3.0L diagnostic code chart

EEC Quick Test — Procedures and Appendix

TEST STEP	RESULT ▶	ACTION TO TAKE
1.0 VISUAL CHECK		
• Check vacuum hoses for damage and proper connection. • Check EEC system wiring harness for proper connections. **NOTE: If additional information is required on Visual Checks, refer to Quick Test Appendix.** • Are all visual checks OK?	Yes ▶ No ▶	GO to Quick Test Step [2.0]. SERVICE as necessary.
2.0 VEHICLE PREPARATION AND EQUIPMENT HOOKUP		
• Apply parking brake. • Place shift lever firmly in PARK (NEUTRAL for manual transmissions). • Block drive wheels. • Turn off all electrical loads. • Connect appropriate test equipment to the Self-Test connector in order to run Self-Test. **NOTE: If additional information is required for Vehicle Preparation and Equipment Hookup, refer to Quick Test Appendix.** • Is vehicle prepared to run Self-Test?	Yes ▶ No ▶	GO to Quick Test Step [3.0]. REPEAT this test step.

FIG. 109 4.0L diagnostic code chart

EEC Quick Test — Procedures and Appendix

TEST STEP	RESULT ▶	ACTION TO TAKE
3.0 PERFORM KOEO SELF-TEST		
• Start engine and idle until vehicle is at operating temperature. **NOTE: If engine does not start or stalls after starting, continue to perform KOEO Self-Test.** • Key off, wait 10 seconds. • Activate Self-Test. • Key on, engine off. **NOTE: If additional information is required for KOEO Self-Test, refer to Quick Test Appendix.** • Record all KOEO and Continuous Memory Codes received. • **Is a PASS code "11" or "111" present in KOEO? (11, 111-10-any code)** **NOTE: The first two are PASS codes from KOEO. The "10" is considered the separator code between KOEO and Continuous Memory.**	Yes ▶	**If "CHECK ENGINE" light is on:** GO to Three-Digit Service Code Charts [6.0], before addressing any other symptoms. If engine runs rough or idles rough: GO to Quick Test Step [3.1]. If engine is a no start: GO to Pinpoint Test Step [AA1]. If these symptoms are not present: GO to Quick Test Step [4.0].
	No ▶	**If KOEO service codes are received:** GO to Three-Digit Service Code Charts [6.0]. **If no service codes are received:** GO to Pinpoint Test Step [QA1].

FIG. 110 4.0L diagnostic code chart

EEC Quick Test — Procedures and Appendix

TEST STEP	RESULT ▶	ACTION TO TAKE
3.1 CHECK FOR CONTINUOUS MEMORY SERVICE CODES 45, 46, 48, 215, 216, 217, 232 or 238		
• Was Continuous Memory service code 45, 46, 48, 215, 216, 217, 232 or 238 received during KOEO Self-Test?	Yes ▶	GO to Pinpoint Test Step [N15].
	No ▶	GO to Pinpoint Test Step [S2].
4.0 CHECK BASE TIMING		
• Key off, wait 10 seconds. • Activate Engine Running Self-Test. • Start engine. **NOTE: If additional information is required for Engine Running Self-Test, refer to Quick Test Appendix.** **If engine starts but stalls or stalls during Self-Test, GO to Pinpoint Test Step [S1].** **Engine Running Service Code 98 indicates vehicle is in Failure Mode Effects Management (FMEM) and DID NOT PASS KOEO On-Demand/Continuous Memory Self-Test. Engine Running Self-Test cannot be performed while in FMEM. Go to Continuous Memory code charts, Quick Test Step [8.0].** • Check computed timing after the last service code has been displayed. The timing will remain fixed for two minutes, unless Self-Test is deactivated. **NOTE: Computed timing is equal to base timing plus 20 degrees BTDC with 3 degrees tolerance. See vehicle decal for correct base timing.** • Is computed timing within specs?	Yes ▶ No ▶	Go to Quick Test Step [5.0]. GO to Pinpoint Test Step [P2].

FIG. 111 4.0L diagnostic code chart

EEC Quick Test — Procedures and Appendix

TEST STEP	RESULT ▶	ACTION TO TAKE
5.0 PERFORM ENGINE RUNNING SELF-TEST		
• Deactivate Self-Test. • Start engine and idle until vehicle is at operating temperature. • Activate Engine Running Self-Test. • Turn engine off. • Start engine. **NOTE: If additional information is required for Engine Running Self-Test, refer to Quick Test Appendix.** • Record all service codes displayed. **NOTE: Engine Running Service Code 98/998 indicates vehicle is in Failure Mode Effects Management (FMEM) and DID NOT PASS KOEO On-Demand/Continuous Memory Self-Test. Engine Running Self-Test cannot be performed while in FMEM.** • **Is a PASS Code (11 or 111) received during Engine Running Self-Test?** • Rerun KOEO Self-Test Quick Test Step [3.0].	Yes ▶	**If any Continuous Memory service codes were received in Quick Test Step [3.0]:** GO to Three-Digit Service Code Charts [6.0]. **If a Continuous Memory PASS code (11 or 111) was received in Quick Test Step [3.0] and no symptoms are present:** EEC diagnostic testing is complete. **If a Continuous Memory PASS Code (11 or 111) was received in Quick Test Step [3.0] and symptoms are present:** GO to Diagnosis By Symptom chart Quick Test Step [9.0].
	No ▶	**If Engine Running service codes are received:** GO to Three-Digit Service Code Charts [6.0]. **If no service codes are received:** GO to Pinpoint Test Step [QA1].

FIG. 112 4.0L diagnostic code chart

QUICK TEST STEP: Three-Digit Service Code Charts

6.0

Service Code	Pinpoint Test Step Go to Direction		
	KOEO	ER	Cont
No Codes	QA1	QA1	QA1
111	Pass	Pass	Pass
112	DA20	—	DA90
113	DA10	—	DA90
114	DA1	DA1	—
116	DA1	DA1	—
117	DA20	—	DA90
118	DA10	—	DA90
121	DH2	DH1	—
122	DH10	—	DH94
123	DH3	—	DH90
126	DF1	DF1	DF90
128	—	—	DF11
129	—	DC10	—
136	—	H1	—
137	—	H1	—
139	—	—	H1
144	—	—	H1
157	—	—	DC10
158	DC20	—	DC20
159	DC1	DC1	—
167	—	DH20	—
171	—	—	H1
172	—	H1	H1
173	—	H1	H1
174	—	—	H1
175	—	—	H1
176	—	—	H1
177	—	—	H1
178	—	—	H1
179	—	—	HA15
181	—	—	HA1
182	—	—	HA15
183	—	—	HA1
188	—	—	HA15
189	—	—	HA1
191	—	—	HA15
192	—	—	HA1
194	—	—	H5
195	—	—	H5
211	—	—	NC1
212	—	—	NC3
213	—	PC1	—
215	—	—	Section F-15
216	—	—	Section F-15

(Continued)

FIG. 113 4.0L EEC quick test code chart

QUICK TEST STEP: Three-Digit Service Code Charts

6.0

Service Code	Pinpoint Test Step Go to Direction		
	KOEO	ER	Cont
217	—	—	Section F-15
218	—	—	Section F-15
222	—	—	Section F-15
223	—	—	Section F-15
224	—	—	Section F-15
225	—	DG1	—
226	NC2	—	—
232	—	—	Section F-15
238	—	—	Section F-15
338	—	—	DA100
339	—	—	DA101
341	KP1	—	—
411	—	KE15	—
412	—	KE1	—
452	—	—	DP1
511	Replace Processor		
512	—	—	QB1
513	Replace Processor		
522	TA1	—	—
525	TA1	—	TA1
528	—	—	TA1
529	—	—	ML25
533	—	—	ML25
536	—	FD1	FD90
538	—	M1	—
539	KM40	—	—
543	J30	—	J93
556	J7	—	J95
565	KD6	—	—
566	TC10	—	—
569	KD6	—	—
617	—	—	TG90
618	—	—	TG90
619	—	—	TG90
621	TC1	—	—
622	TC1	—	—
624	TC10	—	TG90
625	TC10	—	TG90
626	TC1	—	—
627	TC1	—	—
628	—	—	TG90
629	TC10	—	—
631	TB1	—	—
632	—	TB1	—
633	TB1	—	—

(Continued)

FIG. 114 4.0L EEC quick test code chart

QUICK TEST STEP: Three-Digit Service Code Charts — 6.0

Service Code	Pinpoint Test Step Go to Direction: KOEO	ER	Cont
634	TD1	—	TG90
636	TE1	TE1	—
637	TE10	—	TG91
638	TE20	—	TG91
639	—	TF1	TF90
641	TC1	—	—
643	TC20	—	TC30
645	—	—	TG90
646	—	—	TG90
647	—	—	TG90
648	—	—	TG90
649	—	—	TG90
651	—	—	TG90
652	TC1	—	—
654	TD1	—	—
656	—	—	TG95
998	TC10	Quick Test Step 3.0	
Codes Not Listed	QA1	QA1	QA1

FIG. 115 4.0L EEC quick test code chart

EEC No Start (EDIS) — Pinpoint Test AA

WARNING

STOP THIS TEST AT THE FIRST SIGN OF A FUEL LEAK AND SERVICE AS REQUIRED.

CAUTION

No open flame — No smoking during fuel delivery checks.

TEST STEP	RESULT ▶	ACTION TO TAKE
AA1 ATTEMPT TO CRANK ENGINE		
NOTE: Verify fuel pump inertia switch is set (button pushed in). Refer to Owner's Guide for location. • **Does engine crank?**	Yes ▶ No ▶	GO to AA2.
AA2 CHECK FOR VREF AT THROTTLE POSITION SENSOR		
• Key off, wait 10 seconds. • Voltmeter on 20 volt scale. • Disconnect TP sensor. • Key on, engine off. • Measure voltage between VREF circuit and SIG RTN circuit at the TP sensor vehicle harness connector. • **Is voltage between 4.0 volts and 6.0 volts?**	Yes ▶ No ▶	RECONNECT TP sensor. GO to AA3. GO to Pinpoint Test Step C1.
AA3 CHECK FOR SPARK AT PLUGS		
• Disconnect the spark plug wire to any accessible cylinder. • Connect spark tester between spark plug wire and engine ground. • Crank engine and check for spark. • Reconnect the spark plug wire to the spark plug. • **Was spark present and consistent?**	Yes ▶ No ▶	GO to AA4. for EDIS diagnosis.

FIG. 116 4.0L EEC pinpoint test

EEC No Start (EDIS) | **Pinpoint Test** | **AA**

TEST STEP	RESULT ▶	ACTION TO TAKE
AA4 CHECK CONTINUITY OF IGNITION GROUND CIRCUIT		
• Key off, wait 10 seconds. • Disconnect ECU 60 pin connector. Inspect for damaged or pushed out pins, corrosion, loose wires, etc. Service as necessary. • Install breakout box, leave ECU disconnected. • Ohmmeter on 200 ohm scale. • Disconnect EDIS module. • Measure resistance between Test Pin 16 at the breakout box and IGN GND circuit at the EDIS module vehicle harness connector. • **Is resistance less than 5.0 ohms?**	Yes ▶ No ▶	GO to AA5. SERVICE open circuit. REMOVE breakout box. RECONNECT all components. RERUN Quick Test.
AA5 CHECK PIP CIRCUIT FOR SHORT TO POWER		
• Key off, wait 10 seconds. • Breakout box installed, ECU disconnected. • EDIS module disconnected. • Ohmmeter on 200,000 ohm scale. • Measure resistance between Test Pin 56 (PIP) at the breakout box and battery negative post. • **Is voltage greater than 7.0 volts?**	Yes ▶ No ▶	GO to AA6. SERVICE short circuit. REMOVE breakout box. RECONNECT all components. RERUN Quick Test.
AA6 CHECK PIP CIRCUIT CONTINUITY		
• Key off. • Breakout box installed, ECU disconnected. • EDIS module disconnected. • Measure resistance between Test Pin 56 at the breakout box and PIP circuit at the EDIS module vehicle harness connector. • **Is resistance less than 5.0 ohms?**	Yes ▶ No ▶	GO to AA7. SERVICE open circuit. REMOVE breakout box. RECONNECT all components. RERUN Quick Test.
AA7 CHECK PIP SIGNAL CIRCUIT FOR SHORTS TO GROUND		
• Key off. • Breakout box installed, ECU disconnected. • EDIS module disconnected. • Measure resistance between Test Pin 56 (PIP) and Test Pins 16, 40, 46, 60 (short to GROUND). • **Is each resistance greater than 10,000 ohms?**	Yes ▶ No ▶	GO to AA8. SERVICE short circuit. REMOVE breakout box. RECONNECT all components. RERUN Quick Test. If vehicle does not start. GO to AA8.

FIG. 117 4.0L EEC pinpoint test

EEC No Start (EDIS) | **Pinpoint Test** | **AA**

TEST STEP	RESULT ▶	ACTION TO TAKE
AA8 ISOLATE SHORT(S) IN PROCESSOR		
• Key off, wait 10 seconds. • Breakout box installed. • Reconnect ECU to breakout box. • EDIS module disconnected. • Ohmmeter on 200,000 ohm scale. • Measure resistance between Test Pin 56 (PIP) and Test Pins 37, 57 (short to POWER), 40, and 60 (short to GROUND) at the breakout box. • **Is each resistance between 20,000 and 150,000 ohms?**	Yes ▶ No ▶	RECONNECT all components. GO to AA9. REPLACE ECU. REMOVE breakout box. RECONNECT all components. RERUN Quick Test.
AA9 CHECK PIP SIGNAL		
• Key off. • Breakout box installed, ECU connected. • Voltmeter to 20 volt scale. • Reconnect EDIS module. • Measure voltage between Test Pin 56 and Test Pin 16 at the breakout box. • Crank engine, record reading. • **Is voltage between 3.0 and 7.0 volts?**	Yes ▶ No ▶	GO to AA10. GO to AA6.
AA10 CHECK FUEL PUMP		
• **No smoking nearby.** • Connect fuel pressure gauge. • Note initial pressure reading. • Observe pressure gauge as you pressurize fuel system. (Turn key to RUN for 1 second, then turn key to OFF. Wait 10 seconds. Repeat 5 times.) • **Does fuel pressure increase?** **WARNING: If fuel starts leaking, turn key off immediately. No smoking.**	Yes ▶ No ▶	GO to Pinpoint Test Step S1. check for mechanical problems in fuel system.

FIG. 118 4.0L EEC pinpoint test

Vehicle Battery — Pinpoint Test B

TEST STEP	RESULT ▶	ACTION TO TAKE
B1 CHECK BATTERY VOLTAGE • Key on, engine off. • Voltmeter on 20 volt scale. • Measure voltage across battery terminals. • **Is voltage greater than 10.5 volts?**	Yes ▶ No ▶	GO to B2. SERVICE discharged battery
B2 CHECK PWR GND CIRCUIT CONTINUITY • Key off, wait 10 seconds. • Disconnect ECU 60 pin connector. Inspect for damaged or pushed out pins, corrosion, loose wires, etc. Service as necessary. • Install breakout box and connect ECU to breakout box. • Ohmmeter on 200 ohm scale. • Measure resistance between battery negative post and Test Pins 40 and 60 at the breakout box. • **Is each resistance less than 5 ohms?**	Yes ▶ No ▶	GO to B3. SERVICE open in PWR GND circuit. REMOVE breakout box. RECONNECT ECU. RERUN Quick Test.
B3 CHECK FOR OPEN BETWEEN SIG RTN AND PWR GND CIRCUITS AT PROCESSOR • Key off, wait 10 seconds. • Breakout box installed, ECU connected. • Ohmmeter on 200 ohm scale. • Measure resistance between Test Pin 46 and Test Pins 40 and 60 at the breakout box. • **Is each resistance less than 5 ohms?**	Yes ▶ No ▶	GO to B4. REPLACE ECU. REMOVE breakout box. RERUN Quick Test.

FIG. 119 4.0L EEC pinpoint test

Vehicle Battery — Pinpoint Test B

TEST STEP	RESULT ▶	ACTION TO TAKE
B4 CHECK SIG RTN CIRCUIT CONTINUITY • Key off, wait 10 seconds. • Breakout box installed, ECU connected. • Ohmmeter on 200 ohm scale. • Measure resistance between Test Pin 46 at the breakout box and SIG RTN circuit in the Self-Test connector. • **Is resistance less than 5.0 ohms?**	Yes ▶ No ▶	REMOVE breakout box. RECONNECT ECU. GO to B5. SERVICE open in SIG RTN circuit. REMOVE breakout box. RECONNECT ECU. RERUN Quick Test.
B5 CHECK KAPWR CIRCUIT VOLTAGE AT EEC POWER RELAY • Key off. • Disconnect EEC power relay. • Key on, engine off. • Voltmeter on 20 volt scale. • Measure voltage between KAPWR circuit at the EEC power relay connector and battery negative post. • **Is voltage greater than 10.5 volts?**	Yes ▶ No ▶	GO to B6. SERVICE open in KAPWR circuit between EEC power relay and battery positive post. RECONNECT all components. RERUN Quick Test.
B6 CHECK IGNITION CIRCUIT VOLTAGE AT EEC POWER RELAY • Key on, engine off. • Disconnect EEC power relay. • Voltmeter on 20 volt scale. • Measure voltage between the battery negative post and ignition switch circuit at the EEC power relay connector. • **Is voltage greater than 10.5 volts?**	Yes ▶ No ▶	GO to B7. SERVICE open in ignition switch circuits. RECONNECT all components. RERUN Quick Test.

FIG. 120 4.0L EEC pinpoint test

Vehicle Battery — Pinpoint Test B

TEST STEP	RESULT ▶	ACTION TO TAKE
B7 CHECK PWR GND CIRCUIT CONTINUITY • Key off, wait 10 seconds. • Disconnect ECU. • Ohmmeter on 200 ohm scale. • Measure resistance between PWR GND circuit at the EEC power relay connector and battery negative post. • **Is the resistance less than 10 ohms?**	Yes ▶ No ▶	GO to B8. SERVICE open circuit. RECONNECT ECU. RERUN Quick Test.
B8 CHECK VPWR CIRCUIT CONTINUITY • Key off. • Breakout box installed, ECU connected. • EEC power relay removed. • Measure resistance between test pins 37/57 at the breakout box and the VPWR terminal of the EEC power relay connector. • Is resistance less than 5 ohms?	Yes ▶ No ▶	GO to B9. SERVICE open in VPWR circuit between EEC power relay connector and ECU. Remove breakout box. RECONNECT all components. RERUN Quick Test.
B9 CHECK VPWR CIRCUIT VOLTAGE AT EEC POWER RELAY • Key off. • Breakout box installed, ECU connected, EEC power relay connected. • Key on, engine off. • Voltmeter on 20 volt scale. • Measure voltage between test pin 37/57 and test pins 40/60 at the breakout box. • **Is voltage greater than 10.5 volts?**	Yes ▶ No ▶	SERVICE open or short to ground in VPWR circuit between ECU and EEC power relay. REMOVE breakout box. RERUN Quick Test. REPLACE EEC power relay. REMOVE breakout box. RERUN Quick Test.

FIG. 121 4.0L EEC pinpoint test

Reference Voltage — Pinpoint Test C

TEST STEP	RESULT ▶	ACTION TO TAKE
C1 CHECK VEHICLE BATTERY POWER CIRCUIT • Key off, wait 10 seconds. • Disconnect 60 pin connector. Inspect for damaged or pushed out pins, corrosion, loose wires, etc. Service as necessary. • Install breakout box and connect ECU to breakout box. • Voltmeter on 20 volt scale. • Key on, engine off. • Measure voltage between Test Pin 37 at the breakout box and SIG RTN/PWR GND circuit in the Self-Test connector. • **Are both voltages greater than 10.5 volts, and are both voltages within 1.0 volts of each other?**	Yes ▶ No ▶	GO to C2. RECONNECT sensor (if applicable). GO to B1.
C2 CHECK VREF VOLTAGE • Key on, engine off. • Breakout box installed, ECU connected. • Voltmeter on 20 volt scale. • Measure voltage between Test Pin 26 and Test Pin 46 at the breakout box. • **What is the voltage?**	Greater than 6.0 volts ▶ Less than 4.0 volts ▶ Between 4.0 volts and 6.0 volts ▶	GO to C4. GO to C5. GO to C3.
C3 CHECK VREF AND SIG RTN CIRCUITS FOR CONTINUITY • Key off. • Sensor that sent you here disconnected. • Breakout box installed. • Disconnect ECU. • Ohmmeter on 200 ohm scale. • Measure resistance between Test Pin 26 at breakout box and VREF circuit at vehicle harness connector of the sensor that sent you here. • Measure resistance between Test Pin 46 at breakout box and SIG RTN circuit at vehicle harness connector of the sensor that sent you here. • **Is each resistance less than 5.0 ohms?**	Yes ▶ No ▶	Reference voltage OK. REMOVE breakout box. RECONNECT sensor. RERUN Quick Test. SERVICE open in VREF or SIG RTN circuits. REMOVE breakout box. RECONNECT all components. RERUN Quick Test.

FIG. 122 4.0L EEC pinpoint test

Reference Voltage — Pinpoint Test C

TEST STEP	RESULT	ACTION TO TAKE
C4 CHECK FOR EXCESS VOLTAGE ON VREF CIRCUIT		
• Key off, wait 10 seconds. • Breakout box installed. • Disconnect ECU. • Disconnect SUPER STAR II Tester (if applicable.) **NOTE: For proper results of this test, the SUPER STAR II must be disconnected. Due to the circuitry of the SUPER STAR II Tester and the vehicle, voltage can be fed to the VREF circuit giving the false indication of a short to power.** • Key on, engine off. • Voltmeter on 20 volt scale. • Measure voltage between Test Pin 26 at the breakout box and battery ground. • **Is voltage less than 0.5 volts?**	Yes ▶	REPLACE ECU. REMOVE breakout box RECONNECT sensor. RERUN Quick Test.
	No ▶	SERVICE short to battery power in vehicle harness. REMOVE breakout box. RECONNECT ECU and sensor. RERUN Quick Test. If condition persists, REPLACE ECU.
C5 CHECK FOR SHORTED THROTTLE POSITION SENSOR		
• Key off, wait 10 seconds. • Breakout box installed, ECU connected. • Disconnect Throttle Position (TP) sensor from vehicle harness. • Key on, engine off. • Voltmeter on 20 volt scale. • Measure voltage between Test Pin 26 and Test Pin 46 at the breakout box. • **Is voltage less than 4.0 volts?**	Yes ▶	Key off. RECONNECT TP sensor. GO to C7 .
	No ▶	REPLACE TP sensor. REMOVE breakout box. RECONNECT all components. RERUN Quick Test.

FIG. 123 4.0L EEC pinpoint test

Reference Voltage — Pinpoint Test C

TEST STEP	RESULT	ACTION TO TAKE
C7 CHECK FOR SHORTED BP SENSOR		
• Key off, wait 10 seconds. • Breakout box installed, ECU connected. • Disconnect BP sensor. • Key on, engine off. • Voltmeter on 20 volt scale. • Measure voltage between Test Pin 26 and Test Pin 46 at the breakout box. • **Is voltage less than 4.0 volts?**	Yes ▶	Key off. RECONNECT BP sensor. GO to C10 .
	No ▶	REPLACE BP sensor. REMOVE breakout box. RECONNECT ECU and sensor(s). RERUN Quick Test.
C10 CHECK FOR SHORT TO GROUND IN VREF		
• Key off, wait 10 seconds. • Breakout box installed. • Disconnect ECU. • TP sensor disconnected. • BP sensor disconnected. • Ohmmeter on 200 ohm scale. • Measure resistance between Test Pin 26 and Test Pins 20, 40, 46 and 60 at the breakout box. • **Is any resistance less than 5 ohms?**	Yes ▶	SERVICE short to ground. REMOVE breakout box. RECONNECT all components. CONNECT all sensors. RERUN Quick Test. If original condition still exists, REPLACE ECU.
	No ▶	REPLACE ECU. REMOVE breakout box. RECONNECT all components. RERUN Quick Test.

FIG. 124 4.0L EEC pinpoint test

Temperature Sensor Test ACT and ECT — Pinpoint Test DA

TEST STEP	RESULT ▶	ACTION TO TAKE
DA1 SERVICE CODE 21/116 OR 24/114: CHECK OPERATION, INSTALLATION OF TEMPERATURE SENSOR		
Service Code 21/116 (ECT) or 24/114 (ACT) indicates that the corresponding sensor is out of Self-Test range. Correct range of measure is 0.3 to 3.7 volts. Possible causes: — Low coolant level (ECT). — Ambient temperature below 50°F (ACT). — Faulty harness connector. — Faulty sensor. • Run engine for 2 minutes at 2000 rpm. — **For NO STARTS:** GO to [DA3]. — **For vehicle STALLS:** GO to [S1]. • Check that upper radiator hose is hot and pressurized. • Rerun Quick Test. • **Are codes 21, 24, 114 or 116 present?**	Yes ▶ No ▶	GO to [DA2]. SERVICE other codes as necessary.
DA2 CHECK VREF CIRCUIT VOLTAGE AT THROTTLE POSITION SENSOR		
• Refer to schematic in Pinpoint Test [DH]. • Key off, wait 10 seconds. • Disconnect TP sensor. • Voltmeter on 20 volt scale. • Key on, engine off. • Measure voltage between VREF circuit and SIG RTN circuit at the TP sensor vehicle harness connector. • **Is voltage between 4.0 volts and 6.0 volts?**	Yes ▶ No ▶	RECONNECT TP sensor. GO to [DA3]. GO to Pinpoint Test Step [C1].

FIG. 125 4.0L EEC pinpoint test

Temperature Sensor Test ACT and ECT — Pinpoint Test DA

TEST STEP	RESULT ▶	ACTION TO TAKE
DA3 CHECK RESISTANCE OF TEMPERATURE SENSOR WITH ENGINE OFF		
• Key off, wait 10 seconds. • Disconnect suspect temperature sensor. • Ohmmeter on 200,000 ohm scale. • Measure resistance between sensor signal circuit and SIG RTN circuit at the temperature sensor. Refer to the corresponding chart at the beginning of this Pinpoint Test for resistance specifications. • **Is resistance within specifications?**	Yes ▶ No ▶	GO to [DA4]. **For ECT sensor with a NO START:** Do not Service Code 21/116 at this time, GO to [A1]. REPLACE suspect sensor. RECONNECT vehicle harness. RERUN Quick Test.

FIG. 126 4.0L EEC pinpoint test

Temperature Sensor Test ACT and ECT — Pinpoint Test DA

TEST STEP	RESULT ▶	ACTION TO TAKE
DA4 CHECK RESISTANCE OF TEMPERATURE SENSOR WITH ENGINE RUNNING		
NOTE: Engine may have cooled down. Always warm engine before taking ECT sensor resistance measurements. Check for open thermostat. • Key off, wait 10 seconds. • Suspect temperature sensor disconnected. • Ohmmeter on 200,000 ohm scale. • Run engine for 2 minutes at 2000 rpm. • Measure resistance between sensor signal circuit and SIG RTN circuit at the temperature sensor. Refer to the corresponding chart at the beginning of this Pinpoint Test for resistance specifications. • **Is resistance within specification?**	Yes ▶	REPLACE ECU. RECONNECT vehicle harness. RERUN Quick Test.
	No ▶	REPLACE suspect sensor. RECONNECT vehicle harness. RERUN Quick Test.
DA10 SERVICE CODE 51/118 OR 54/113 INDUCE OPPOSITE CODE 61/117 OR 64/112		
Service Codes 51/118 (ECT) and 54/113 (ACT) indicate that the corresponding sensor signal is greater than the Self-Test maximum. The maximum for ECT and ACT sensors is 4.6 volts. Possible causes: — Open in harness (ACT or ECT). — Faulty connection. — Faulty sensor. — Faulty ECU. • Key off, wait 10 seconds. • Disconnect suspect temperature sensor. • Connect a jumper wire between the sensor signal circuit and SIG RTN circuit at the temperature sensor vehicle harness connector. • Run Key On Engine Off Self-Test. • **Is Code 61, 64, 112 or 117 present?**	Yes ▶	REPLACE suspect sensor. REMOVE jumper wire. RECONNECT vehicle harness. RERUN Quick Test.
	No ▶	REMOVE jumper wire. GO to DA11.

FIG. 127 4.0L EEC pinpoint test

Temperature Sensor Test ACT and ECT — Pinpoint Test DA

TEST STEP	RESULT ▶	ACTION TO TAKE
DA11 CHECK CONTINUITY OF SENSOR SIGNAL AND SIG RTN CIRCUITS		
• Key off, wait 10 seconds. • Suspect temperature sensor disconnected. • Disconnect ECU 60 Pin connector. Inspect for damaged or pushed out pins, corrosion, loose wires, etc. Service as necessary. • Install breakout box, leave ECU disconnected. • Ohmmeter on 200 ohm scale. • Measure resistance between sensor signal circuit at the temperature sensor vehicle harness connector and Test Pin 7 (ECT) or 25 (ACT) at the breakout box. • Measure resistance between SIG RTN circuit at the temperature sensor vehicle harness connector and Test Pin 46 at the breakout box. • **Is each resistance less than 5 ohms?**	Yes ▶	REPLACE ECU. REMOVE breakout box. RECONNECT all components. RERUN Quick Test.
	No ▶	SERVICE open circuits. REMOVE breakout box. RECONNECT all components. RERUN Quick Test.
DA20 SERVICE CODE 61/117 OR 64/112: INDUCE OPPOSITE CODE 51/118 OR 54/113		
Service Codes 61/117 (ECT) or 64/112 (ACT) indicate that the corresponding sensor's signal is less than the Self-Test minimum. The ACT and ECT sensor minimum is 0.2 volts. Possible causes: — Grounded circuit in harness. — Faulty sensor. — Faulty ECU. — Faulty connection. • Key off, wait 10 seconds. • Disconnect vehicle harness from suspect sensor. Inspect for damaged, corroded, pushed out pins of loose wires, etc. Service as necessary. • Run Key On Engine Off Self-Test. • **Is Code 51, 54, 113 or 118 present?**	Yes ▶	REPLACE sensor. RECONNECT harness. RERUN Quick Test.
	No ▶	GO to DA21.

FIG. 128 4.0L EEC pinpoint test

Temperature Sensor Test ACT and ECT — Pinpoint Test DA

TEST STEP	RESULT	ACTION TO TAKE
DA21 CHECK VREF CIRCUIT VOLTAGE AT THROTTLE POSITION SENSOR		
• Refer to schematic in Pinpoint Test DH. • Key off, wait 10 seconds. • Suspect temperature sensor disconnected. • Disconnect TP sensor. • Voltmeter on 20 volt scale. • Key on, engine off. • Measure voltage between VREF circuit and SIG RTN circuit at the TP sensor vehicle sensor connector. • **Is voltage between 4.0 volts and 6.0 volts?**	Yes ▶ No ▶	RECONNECT TP sensor, GO to DA22. GO to Pinpoint Test Step C1.
DA22 CHECK TEMPERATURE SENSOR SIGNAL CIRCUIT FOR SHORT TO GROUND		
• Key off, wait 10 seconds. • Suspect temperature sensor disconnected. • Disconnect ECU 60 Pin connector. Inspect for damaged or pushed out pins, corrosion, loose wires, etc. Service as necessary. • Install breakout box, leave ECU disconnected. • Ohmmeter on 200,000 ohm scale. • Measure resistance between Test Pin 7 (ECT) or 25 (ACT) and Test Pins 40, 46 and 60 at the breakout box. • **Is each resistance greater than 10,000 ohms?**	Yes ▶ No ▶	REPLACE ECU. REMOVE breakout box. RECONNECT all components. RERUN Quick Test. SERVICE short circuit. REMOVE breakout box. RECONNECT all components. RERUN Quick Test.

FIG. 129 4.0L EEC pinpoint test

Temperature Sensor Test ACT and ECT — Pinpoint Test DA

TEST STEP	RESULT	ACTION TO TAKE
DA90 CONTINUOUS MEMORY CODE 51/118, 54/113, 61/117 OR 64/112: CHECK SENSOR		
Continuous Memory Codes 51/118 and 54/113 indicate that the sensor signal was greater than the Self-Test maximum of 4.6 volts. The code was generated under normal driving conditions. Continuous Memory Codes 61/117 and 64/112, indicate that the sensor signal was less than the Self-Test minimum of 0.2 volts. The code was generated under normal driving conditions. (see table below) Possible causes: — Faulty sensor. — Open circuit in harness. — Grounded circuit in harness. — Faulty ECU. • Enter Key On Engine Off continuous monitor mode. Refer to Quick Test Appendix. • Observe Voltmeter or SUPER STAR II for indication of a fault while performing the following: — Tap on the sensor to simulate road shock. — Wiggle the sensor connector. • **Is a fault indicated?**	Yes ▶ No ▶	DISCONNECT and inspect connectors. If OK, REPLACE the sensor. CLEAR Continuous Memory RERUN Quick Test. GO to DA91.

Sensors	Continuous Memory Codes
ACT	54/113 and 64/112
ECT	51/118 and 61/117

POWER OR VREF CIRCUIT
SIGNAL
SIG RTN
ECU
HARNESS
ACT SENSOR

FIG. 130 4.0L EEC pinpoint test

Temperature Sensor Test ACT and ECT — Pinpoint Test DA

TEST STEP	RESULT ▶	ACTION TO TAKE
DA91 CHECK EEC VEHICLE HARNESS		
• Still in Key On Engine Off continuous monitor mode. • Observe Voltmeter or SUPER STAR II for fault indication while performing the following: — Refer to the illustration in Step DA90. Grasp the vehicle harness close to the sensor connector. Wiggle, shake, or bend a small section of the EEC system vehicle harness while working your way to the dash panel. Also wiggle, shake, or bend the EEC system vehicle harness from the dash panel to the ECU. • **Is a fault indicated?**	Yes ▶	ISOLATE fault and SERVICE as necessary. CLEAR Continuous Memory, RERUN Quick Test.
	No ▶	GO to DA92.
DA92 CHECK ECU AND VEHICLE HARNESS CONNECTORS		
• Key off, wait 10 seconds. • Disconnect ECU 60 Pin connector. Disconnect sensor connector. Inspect for damage, loose or pushed out pins, loose or poorly crimped wires. • **Are connectors and terminals OK?**	Yes ▶	CLEAR Continuous Memory RERUN Quick Test.
	No ▶	SERVICE as necessary. CLEAR Continuous Memory RERUN Quick Test.
DA100 CONTINUOUS MEMORY CODE 338		
Service Code 338 indicates the engine had not reached the normal operating temperature or the system is not heating. The cooling system is not properly controlling the engine temperature. Possible causes: — Thermostat stuck open. — Water outlet gasket leak. — Water pump gasket leak. — Head gasket leak. — Heater hose leak.		

FIG. 131 4.0L EEC pinpoint test

Temperature Sensor Test ACT and ECT — Pinpoint Test DA

TEST STEP	RESULT ▶	ACTION TO TAKE
DA101 CONTINUOUS MEMORY CODE 339		
Service Code 339 indicates the engine had exceeded the high temperature limit. The cooling system is not properly controlling the engine temperature. Possible causes: — Thermostat stuck closed. — Water passages clogged. — Faulty water pump. — Faulty cooling fan. — Low coolant level. — Faulty radiator cap. — Radiator fins clogged. — Coolant leakage.		

FIG. 132 4.0L EEC pinpoint test

Barometric Pressure (BP) Sensor — Pinpoint Test — DF

TEST STEP	RESULT ▶	ACTION TO TAKE
DF1 SERVICE CODE 22/126: CHECK FOR POWER TO BP SENSOR		
Service Code 22/126 indicates that the Barometric Pressure (BP) sensor is out of Self-Test range. Correct BP tester range of measurement is typically from 1.4 to 1.6 volts. Possible causes: — BP SIG circuit open between sensor vehicle harness connector and processor. — BP SIG circuit shorted to VREF, SIG RTN, or GND. Faulty BP sensor. — Vacuum trapped at BP sensor. — High atmospheric pressure. — Damaged ECU. — VREF circuit open at BP sensor. — SIG RTN circuit open at BP sensor. • Key off. • Disconnect the BP sensor from the vehicle harness. • Connect the BP tester between the vehicle harness connector and the BP sensor. • Insert BP banana plugs into Voltmeter. • Set Voltmeter to 20 volt scale. **NOTE: Green light on tester indicates VREF is OK (4-6v). Red light (or no light) indicates VREF is either too low or too high.** • Key on. • **Is green light on?**	Yes ▶ No ▶	GO to DF3. GO to DF2.
DF2 CHECK FOR POWER AT SENSOR VEHICLE HARNESS CONNECTOR		
NOTE: Green light reaffirms that VREF is OK (4-6v). Red light (or no light) indicates VREF is either too low or too high. • Key on. • BP tester connected. • Voltmeter connected to BP tester. • Disconnect Bp sensor. • **Is green light on?**	Yes ▶ No ▶	REPLACE BP sensor. RERUN Quick Test. REMOVE BP tester. RECONNECT the BP sensor. GO to Pinpoint Test Step C1.

FIG. 133 4.0L EEC pinpoint test

Barometric Pressure (BP) Sensor — Pinpoint Test — DF

TEST STEP	RESULT ▶	ACTION TO TAKE
DF3 CHECK BP SENSOR OUTPUT		
NOTE: Measure several known good BP sensors on available vehicles. The measured voltage will be typical for your location on the day of testing. • Key on. • BP tester connected. • Voltmeter connected to BP tester. • Measure BP sensor voltage on customer vehicle. • **Is voltage in range for your altitude?**	Yes ▶ No ▶	REMOVE BP tester. GO to DF4. REMOVE BP tester. GO to DF5.

Approximate Altitude (Ft.)	Voltage Output (+/ − .04 Volts)
0	1.59
1000	1.56
2000	1.53
3000	1.50
4000	1.47
5000	1.44
6000	1.41
7000	1.39

TEST STEP	RESULT ▶	ACTION TO TAKE
DF4 CHECK CONTINUITY OF BP SIG CIRCUIT		
• Key off, wait 10 seconds. • BP sensor disconnected. • Disconnect ECU 60 pin connector. Inspect for damaged or pushed out pins, corrosion, loose wires, etc. Service as necessary. • Install breakout box, leave processor disconnected. • Ohmmeter on 200 ohm scale • Measure resistance between BP SIG circuit at the BP sensor vehicle harness connector and Test Pin 45 at the breakout box. • **Is resistance less than 5.0 ohms?**	Yes ▶ No ▶	REPLACE ECU. REMOVE breakout box. RECONNECT BP sensor. RERUN Quick Test. SERVICE open circuit. REMOVE breakout box. RECONNECT all components. RERUN Quick Test.

FIG. 134 4.0L EEC pinpoint test

Barometric Pressure (BP) Sensor — Pinpoint Test DF

TEST STEP	RESULT ▶	ACTION TO TAKE
DF5 CHECK BP SIG CIRCUIT FOR SHORTS TO VREF, SIG RTN AND GROUND		
• Key off, wait 10 seconds. • BP sensor disconnected. • Disconnect ECU 60 pin connector. Inspect for damaged or pushed out pins, corrosion, loose wires, etc. Service as necessary. • Install breakout box, leave ECU disconnected. • Ohmmeter on 200,000 ohm scale. • Measure resistance between Test Pin 45 and Test Pins 26, 46, 40 and 60 at the breakout box. • **Is each resistance greater than 10,000 ohms?**	Yes ▶	REPLACE BP sensor. REMOVE breakout box. RECONNECT ECU. RERUN Quick Test.
	No ▶	SERVICE short circuit. REMOVE breakout box. RECONNECT all components. RERUN Quick Test.

FIG. 135 4.0L EEC pinpoint test

Barometric Pressure (BP) Sensor — Pinpoint Test DF

TEST STEP	RESULT ▶	ACTION TO TAKE
DF90 CONTINUOUS MEMORY CODE 22/126: EXERCISE BP SENSOR		
Continuous Memory Service Code 22/126 indicates the Barometric Pressure (BP) sensor was out of self-test range. The code was set during normal driving conditions. Correct range of measurement is typically from 1.4 to 1.6 volts. Possible causes: — Faulty BP sensor. — Faulty EEC vehicle harness. — Faulty BP sensor vehicle harness connectors and/or terminals. — Unusually high/low barometric pressure. • Using Key On, Engine Off Continuous Monitor Mode, observe Voltmeter or SUPER STAR II for indication of a fault while performing the following: — Connect a vacuum pump to the BP sensor. — Slowly apply 84 kPa (25 in-Hg) vacuum to the BP sensor. — Slowly bleed vacuum off the BP sensor. — Lightly tap on BP sensor (simulate road shock). — Wiggle BP connector. • **Is fault indicated?**	Yes ▶	DISCONNECT and INSPECT connectors. If connector and terminals are good, REPLACE BP sensor, RERUN Quick Test.
	No ▶	GO to DF91.

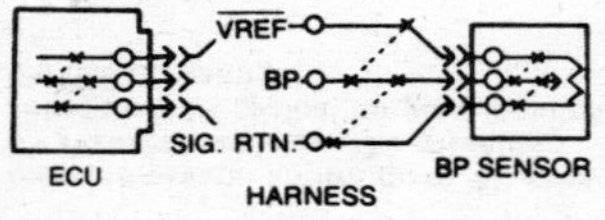

FIG. 136 4.0L EEC pinpoint test

Barometric Pressure (BP) Sensor — Pinpoint Test DF

TEST STEP	RESULT ▶	ACTION TO TAKE
DF91 CHECK EEC VEHICLE HARNESS		
• Remain in Key On, Engine Off Continuous Monitor Mode. • **Observe Voltmeter or SUPER STAR II for a fault indication while performing the following:** — **Referring to the illustration in Step DF90, grasp the vehicle harness close to the sensor connector. Wiggle, shake or bend a small section of the EEC system vehicle harness while working your way to the dash panel. Also wiggle, shake or bend the EEC vehicle harness from the dash panel to the ECU.** • **Is a fault indicated?**	Yes ▶ No ▶	ISOLATE fault and SERVICE as necessary. CLEAR Continuous Memory Code RERUN Quick Test. GO to DF10.
DF92 CHECK ECU AND VEHICLE HARNESS CONNECTORS		
• Key off, wait 10 seconds. • Disconnect ECU 60 pin connector. • Inspect connectors and connector terminals for obvious damage or faults. • **Are connectors and terminals OK?**	No ▶ Yes ▶	SERVICE as necessary. RERUN Quick Test. CLEAR Continuous Memory RERUN Quick Test.

FIG. 137 4.0L EEC pinpoint test

Vehicle Speed Sensor (VSS) — Pinpoint Test DP

VEHICLE SPEED SENSOR (VSS) DRIVE CYCLE

- Record and clear EEC Continuous Memory Codes.
- Warm engine to operating temperature.
- Perform the drive cycle below as appropriate for the vehicle being tested.

Automatic Transmission

Place the gear selector in DRIVE range and heavily accelerate to 35 mph, then coast down to an idle and stop the vehicle. Shut engine off.

Run Key On Engine Off Self-Test and record Continuous Memory Codes.

Manual Transmission

Starting in first gear, shift to second gear and moderately accelerate to 40 mph, then coast down to an idle and stop vehicle. Shut engine off.

Run Key On Engine Off Self-Test and record Continuous Memory Codes.

TEST STEP	RESULT ▶	ACTION TO TAKE
DP1 CONTINUOUS MEMORY CODE 29/452: COMPLETE VSS DRIVE CYCLE: VERIFY CODE OR DRIVE COMPLAINT		
Continuous Memory Code 29/452 indicates that sometime during the last 40 to 80 warm-up cycles, the processor detected an error in the VSS output signal. Possible causes are: — Faulty VSS. — Open or shorted circuit(s). — Faulty ECU. • Perform Vehicle Speed Sensor Drive Cycle at least three times as outlined below. • **VEHICLE SPEED SENSOR (VSS) DRIVE CYCLE:** — Record and clear continuous memory codes. — Warm engine to operating temperature. **AUTOMATIC TRANSMISSIONS:** — Place gear selector in DRIVE range. — Obey all local traffic laws. Accelerate heavily to 35 mph. — Coast down to an idle and stop the vehicle. — Shut the engine off. — After the drive cycle is completed, run Key On Engine Off Self-Test and record the continuous memory service codes displayed. **MANUAL TRANSMISSIONS:** — From first gear, shift to second. — Obey all local traffic laws. Accelerate moderately to 40 mph. — Coast down to an idle and stop the vehicle. — Shut the engine off. — After the drive cycle is completed, run Key On Engine Off Self-Test and record the continuous memory service codes displayed. • **Did Continuous Memory Code 29 or 452 repeat?**	Yes ▶ No ▶	GO to DP2. CLEAR Continuous Memory

FIG. 138 4.0L EEC pinpoint test

Vehicle Speed Sensor (VSS) — Pinpoint Test DP

TEST STEP	RESULT ▶	ACTION TO TAKE
DP2 CHECK CONTINUITY OF VEHICLE SPEED SENSOR HARNESS CIRCUITS		
• Key off. • Disconnect ECU 60 pin connector. Inspect for damaged or pushed out pins, corrosion, loose wires, etc. Service as necessary. • Install breakout box, ECU disconnected. • Disconnect vehicle speed sensor. • Measure resistance between Test Pin 3 at the Breakout Box and VSSDIF (+) circuit at the vehicle speed sensor vehicle harness connector. • Measure resistance between Test Pin 6 at the breakout box and VSSDIF (−) circuit at the vehicle speed sensor vehicle harness connector. • **Is each resistance less than 5.0 ohms?**	Yes ▶	GO to DP3.
	No ▶	SERVICE open circuit. REMOVE breakout box. RECONNECT all components. REPEAT Test Step DP1 to verify elimination of code or drive complaint.
DP3 CHECK VEHICLE SPEED SENSOR SIGNAL HARNESS CIRCUITS FOR SHORTS TO POWER OR GROUND		
• Key off. • Vehicle speed sensor disconnected. • Breakout box installed, ECU disconnected. • Measure resistance between Test Pin 3 and Test Pins 6, 37 and 40 at the breakout box. • **Is each resistance greater than 500 ohms?**	Yes ▶	RECONNECT the ECU. GO to DP4.
	No ▶	SERVICE short circuit. REMOVE breakout box. RECONNECT all components. REPEAT Test Step DP1 to verify elimination of code or drive complaint.
DP4 CHECK VEHICLE SPEED SENSOR RESISTANCE		
• Key off. • Vehicle speed sensor disconnected. • Measure the resistance of the vehicle speed sensor. • **Is resistance between 190 and 250 ohms?**	Yes ▶	REMOVE breakout box. REPLACE ECU. RECONNECT the vehicle speed sensor. REPEAT Test Step DP1 to verify elimination of code or drive complaint.
	No ▶	REPLACE the vehicle speed sensor. REMOVE breakout box. REPEAT Test Step DP1 to verify elimination of code or drive complaint.

FIG. 139 4.0L EEC pinpoint test

Neutral Drive Input — Pinpoint Test FA

TEST STEP	RESULT ▶	ACTION TO TAKE
FA1 CODE 67/522, 525 or 528 SYSTEM IDENTIFICATION		
A Code 67/522, 525 or 528 resulted from voltage being high at either: — Pin 10 = A/C input — Pin 30 = Neutral drive while cranking the engine or during KOEO test. Possible causes are: — A/C circuit shorted to power — Clutch engage/interlock circuits open — Neutral drive/gear switch open — Damaged ECU — Starter relay disconnected during Self-Test.	▶	GO to FA8.

FIG. 140 4.0L EEC pinpoint test

Neutral Drive Input — Pinpoint Test FA

TEST STEP	RESULT ▶	ACTION TO TAKE
FA8 CHECK NEUTRAL DRIVE INPUT		
• Key off, wait 10 seconds. • Verify A/C control is in OFF position, if so equipped. • Verify transmission is in NEUTRAL or PARK. • Disconnect ECU 60 pin connector. Inspect for damaged or pushed out pins, corrosion, loose wires, etc. Service as necessary. • Install breakout box, leave ECU connected. • Key on, engine off. • Voltmeter on 20 volt scale. • Measure voltage between Test Pin 30 at the breakout box and chassis ground. • **Is voltage less than 1.0 volt?**	Yes ▶	**For vehicles with A/C:** Perform Pinpoint Test FA10. **For all others:** REPLACE ECU.
	No ▶	GO to FA9.

FIG. 141 4.0L EEC pinpoint test

Neutral Drive Input — Pinpoint Test FA

TEST STEP	RESULT ▶	ACTION TO TAKE
FA9 CHECK NEUTRAL DRIVE SWITCH		
• Key off, wait 10 seconds. • Breakout box installed, ECU disconnected. • Ohmmeter on 200 ohm scale. • Locate the Neutral Drive switch. • Disconnect vehicle harness from the Neutral Drive switch and measure resistance across the switch. • **Is resistance less than 5 ohms?**	Yes ▶	SERVICE open in vehicle harness Neutral Drive circuit. REMOVE breakout box. RECONNECT all components. RERUN Quick Test.
	No ▶	REPLACE Neutral Drive switch. REMOVE breakout box. RECONNECT all components. RERUN Quick Test.
FA10 CHECK A/C INPUT		
NOTE: Before entering this test, verify A/C selector is off. If A/C was on, rerun Quick Test. If code 67/522, 525 or 528, or 79 is present, continue with this test. • Disconnect ECU 60 pin connector. Inspect for damaged or pushed out pins, corrosion, loose wires, etc. Service as necesary. • Install breakout box, leave ECU disconnected. • Key on, engine off. • Voltmeter on 20 volt scale. • Measure voltage between Test Pin 10 at the breakout box and chassis ground. • **Is voltage greater than 1.0 volt?**	Yes ▶	SERVICE short to power in A/C circuit. REMOVE breakout box. RECONNECT all components. RERUN Quick Test.
	No ▶	REPLACE ECU. REMOVE breakout box. RECONNECT all components. RERUN Quick Test.

FIG. 142 4.0L EEC pinpoint test

Neutral Drive Input — Pinpoint Test FA

TEST STEP	RESULT ▶	ACTION TO TAKE
FA11 CHECK A/C INPUT CIRCUIT		
NOTE: A low idle with A/C on could be the result of the ECU not receiving, or recognizing the A/C input on Pin 10. • Key off, wait 10 seconds. • Disconnect ECU 60 pin connector. Inspect for damaged or pushed out pins, corrosion, loose wires, etc. Service as necessary. • Install breakout box, leave ECU disconnected. • Voltmeter on 20 volt scale. • Key on, engine off. • A/C on. • Measure voltage between Test Pin 10 and Test Pin 40. • **Is voltage greater than 10.5 volts?**	Yes ▶	REPLACE ECU. REMOVE breakout box. RECONNECT all components. RERUN Quick Test.
	No ▶	SERVICE open in A/C circuit. REMOVE breakout box. RECONNECT all components. RERUN Quick Test.

FIG. 143 4.0L EEC pinpoint test

Brake On/Off (BOO) — Pinpoint Test FD

*** TEST PINS LOCATED ON BREAKOUT BOX. ALL HARNESS CONNECTORS VIEWED INTO MATING SURFACES.**

TEST STEP	RESULT ▶	ACTION TO TAKE
FD1 SERVICE CODE 74/536 VERIFY BRAKE WAS PRESSED		
Service Code 74/536 indicates that when the brake pedal was depressed and released during the Engine Running Self-Test, the BOO signal did not cycle high and low. Possible causes: — Brake pedal not depressed and released during the Engine Running Self-Test. — Brake pedal depressed during entire Engine Running Self-Test. — Open BOO/stoplamp circuit. — Short to GROUND or POWER. — Damaged brake switch. — Damaged processor. • **Did you press brake during the Engine Running Self-Test?** **NOTE: On some vehicles it is necessary to depress and release the brake after the Dynamic Response Code 1(0) but before the brief WOT.**	Yes ▶	GO to FD2.
	No ▶	RERUN Engine Running Self-Test. PRESS brake once during test.
FD2 CHECK OPERATION OF STOPLAMPS		
• Key on. • Check stoplamp operation.	Stoplamps operate normally ▶	GO to FD3.
	Stoplamps never on ▶	GO to FD4.
	Stoplamps always on ▶	GO to FD5.
FD3 CHECK FOR BOO CIRCUIT CYCLING		
• Key off. • Disconnect ECU 60 pin connector. Inspect for damaged or pushed out pins, corrosion, loose wires, etc. Service as necessary. • Install breakout box, leave ECU disconnected. • DVOM on 20 volt scale. • Measure voltage between BOO Test Pin (refer to chart on FD cover page) and Test Pin 40 at the breakout box while depressing and releasing brake. • **Does the voltage cycle?**	Yes ▶	REPLACE ECU. REMOVE breakout box. RERUN Quick Test.
	No ▶	SERVICE open in BOO circuit between ECU and BOO connection to stoplamp circuit. RERUN Quick Test.

FIG. 144 4.0L EEC pinpoint test

Brake On/Off (BOO) — Pinpoint Test FD

TEST STEP	RESULT ▶	ACTION TO TAKE
FD4 CHECK FOR POWER TO BRAKE SWITCH		
NOTE: Verify integrity of related fuses in fuse panel and condition of stoplamp bulbs. • Key off. • Disconnect brake switch (located on brake pedal). • Measure voltage between BATT (+) input to brake switch and chassis ground. • **Is voltage greater than 10 volts?**	Yes ▶	VERIFY operation of brake switch. If OK, SERVICE open circuit between brake switch and stoplamp ground. RECONNECT brake switch connector. RERUN Quick Test.
	No ▶	SERVICE open BATT (+) circuit to brake switch. RECONNECT brake switch connector. RERUN Quick Test.
FD5 VERIFY BRAKE SWITCH IS NOT ALWAYS CLOSED		
• Key off. • Disconnect brake switch (located on brake pedal). • Key on, engine off. • **Are stoplamps still on?**	Yes ▶	GO to FD6.
	No ▶	VERIFY proper installation of brake switch. If OK, REPLACE brake switch. RECONNECT harness connector. RERUN Quick Test.
FD6 CHECK FOR SHORT TO POWER IN ECU		
• Key off. • Brake switch disconnected. • Disconnect ECU. • Key on, engine off. • **Are stoplamps still on?**	Yes ▶	SERVICE short to power in BOO/Stoplamp circuit. RECONNECT all components. RERUN Quick Test.
	No ▶	REPLACE ECU. RECONNECT brake switch. RERUN Quick Test.

FIG. 145 4.0L EEC pinpoint test

Brake On/Off (BOO) — Pinpoint Test FD

TEST STEP	RESULT ▶	ACTION TO TAKE
FD10 SERVICE CODE 75/531: CHECK OPERATION OF BRAKE LAMPS		
Service Code 75/531 indicates that while the brake pedal was released during the Engine Running Self-Test, the BOO signal was high. Possible causes: — Brake pedal depressed during entire Engine Running Self-Test. — Open BOO/stoplamp circuit (between ECU and stoplamp ground). — Short to POWER. — Damaged brake switch. — Damaged processor. • Key on. • Check stoplamp operation.	Stoplamps operate normally ▶	GO to FD11.
	Stoplamps always on ▶	GO to FD5.
	Stoplamps never on ▶	VERIFY condition of stoplamp bulbs. If OK, SERVICE open circuit between BOO connection to stoplamp circuit and stoplamp ground. RERUN Quick Test.
FD11 CHECK BOO CIRCUIT CONTINUITY		
• Key off. • Disconnect ECU 60 pin connector. Inspect for damaged or pushed out pins, corrosion, loose wires, etc. Service as necessary. • Install breakout box, leave ECU disconnected. • Disconnect brake switch (located on brake pedal). • Measure resistance between Test Pin 2 at the breakout box and circuit to stoplamps pin at the brake switch vehicle harness connector. • **Is resistance less than 5.0 ohms?**	Yes ▶	REPLACE ECU. RECONNECT brake switch. REMOVE breakout box. RERUN Quick Test.
	No ▶	SERVICE open BOO circuit between ECU and BOO connection to stoplamp circuit. REMOVE Breakout Box. RECONNECT ECU and brake switch. RERUN Quick Test.

FIG. 146 4.0L EEC pinpoint test

Brake On/Off (BOO) — Pinpoint Test — FD

TEST STEP	RESULT ▶	ACTION TO TAKE
FD90 CONTINUOUS MEMORY CODE 536: CHECK FOR PROPER STOPLAMP SWITCH INSTALLATION		
Continuous Memory Code 536 indicates a BOO circuit failure. If the BOO input does not cycle after a predetermined number of transitions from 0 mph to a specific speed, the BOO input is assumed to be damaged and Continuous Memory Code 536 is set. Possible causes: — Stoplamp switch improperly installed. — Open stoplamp/BOO circuit. — Stoplamp/BOO circuit. — Stoplamp/BOO circuit shorted to power. — Damaged stoplamp switch. — Damaged stoplamp ground connection. • Check stoplamp switch for proper installation (alignment with pedal), corrosion, frayed wires, etc. • **Is stoplamp switch in good condition and properly installed?**	Yes ▶ No ▶	GO to FD91. SERVICE as necessary. CLEAR Continuous Memory RERUN Quick Test.
FD91 CHECK STOPLAMP GROUND		
• Check stoplamp ground connection for corrosion or other damage. • Check stoplamp connector and wires for corrosion or other damage. • **Are stoplamp wires, connector, and ground connection OK?**	Yes ▶ No ▶	GO to FD92. SERVICE as necessary. CLEAR Continuous Memory RERUN Quick Test.
FD92 CHECK STOPLAMP/BOO CIRCUITS FOR SHORT TO POWER		
• Key on, engine off. • Brake pedal NOT depressed. • Wiggle stoplamp/BOO circuit wires and connectors while observing stoplamps. • **Do stoplamps flash on while wiggling?**	Yes ▶ No ▶	ISOLATE short to power and SERVICE as necessary. CLEAR Continuous Memory RERUN Quick Test. GO to FD93.

FIG. 147 4.0L EEC pinpoint test

Brake On/Off (BOO) — Pinpoint Test — FD

TEST STEP	RESULT ▶	ACTION TO TAKE
FD93 CHECK STOPLAMP CIRCUIT CONTINUITY		
• Key off. • Depress brake pedal and hold. • Wiggle stoplamp circuit wires and connectors while observing stoplamps. • Lightly tap stoplamp switch (simulate road shock) while observing stoplamps. • **Do stoplamps ever go off?**	Yes ▶ No ▶	ISOLATE open in stoplamp circuit and SERVICE as necessary. CLEAR Continuous Memory RERUN Quick Test. GO to FD94.
FD94 CHECK BOO CIRCUIT CONTINUITY		
• Key off. • Release brake pedal. • Disconnect ECU 60 pin connector. Inspect for damaged or pushed out pins, corrosion, loose wires, etc. Service as necessary. • Install breakout box, leave ECU disconnected. • Connect DVOM between BOO Test Pin (refer to schematic) at the breakout box and stoplamp circuit at the stoplamp switch. • DVOM on 200 ohm scale. • Wiggle BOO circuit wires and connectors while observing DVOM. • **Is resistance ever greater than 5.0 ohms while wiggling?**	Yes ▶ No ▶	ISOLATE open in BOO circuit and SERVICE as necessary. REMOVE breakout box. RECONNECT ECU. RERUN Quick Test. GO to FD99.

FIG. 148 4.0L EEC pinpoint test

Fuel Control — Pinpoint Test H

TEST STEP	RESULT ▶	ACTION TO TAKE
H1 CHECK FUEL PRESSURE HEGO Engine Running code 41/172 indicates the system is always lean. HEGO Engine running code 42/173 indicates the system is always rich. • Key off, wait 10 seconds. • Install fuel pressure gauge. • Verify that manifold vacuum is connected to the fuel pressure regulator if applicable. • Start and run engine at idle. • Is fuel pressure within specification for the engine being tested? **For No Starts:** • If engine will not run, cycle the key off to on several times. • **Is fuel pressure within specification for the engine being tested?** **ENGINE RUNNING**: 30-45 PSI, 210-310 kPa **KEY ON ENGINE OFF**: 35-45 PSI, 240-310 kPa **NOTE: Maximum fuel pressure is obtainable at WOT or with the vacuum hose removed from the fuel pressure regulator.** INJECTOR BANK RESISTANCE SPECIFICATION 4.0 TO 5.5 ohms SINGLE INJECTOR RESISTANCE SPECIFICATION 13.0 to 16.0 ohms	Yes ▶	GO to H2 .
	No ▶	GO to Electric Fuel pump and fuel pressure regulator checks.

FIG. 149 4.0L EEC pinpoint test

Fuel Control — Pinpoint Test H

TEST STEP	RESULT ▶	ACTION TO TAKE
H2 CHECK SYSTEM'S ABILITY TO HOLD FUEL PRESSURE • Key on, engine off. • **Does fuel pressure remain at specification for 60 seconds?**	Yes ▶	**For No Starts:** GO to H3 . **For Runs Rough, Misses or Fuel Service Code (41, 42):** REMOVE fuel pressure gauge. GO to H4 .
	No ▶	GO to H6 .
H3 FUEL DELIVERY TEST **NOTE: Verify fuel quality; air and/or water will also pressurize and look like acceptable fuel delivery.** • Key off. • Fuel pressure gauge installed. • Pressurize fuel system per step H1 . • Locate and disconnect the inertia switch. • Crank engine for 5 seconds. • **Does pressure drop greater than 5 psi. (34 kPa.) by the end of the 5 second crank cycle?**	Yes ▶	The EEC system is not the cause of the No Start. REMOVE the fuel pressure gauge. RECONNECT the inertia switch.
	No ▶	REMOVE fuel pressure gauge. RECONNECT inertia switch. GO to H4 .

FIG. 150 4.0L EEC pinpoint test

Fuel Control | **Pinpoint Test** | **H**

TEST STEP	RESULT ▶	ACTION TO TAKE
H4 CHECK RESISTANCE OF INJECTOR(S) AND HARNESS		
• Key off, wait 10 seconds. • Disconnect ECU 60 pin connector. Inspect for damaged or pushed out pins, corrosion, loose wires, etc. Service as necessary. • Install breakout box, leave ECU disconnected. • Ohmmeter on 200 ohm scale. • Measure resistance of INJECTOR BANK 1 between Test Pin 37 and Test Pin 58 at the breakout box. Record resistance. • Measure resistance of INJECTOR BANK 2 between Test Pin 37 and Test Pin 59 at the breakout box. Record resistance. • **Is each resistance within specifications?**	Yes ▶ No ▶	GO to H6 . GO to H5 . **For NO START:** SERVICE open in VPWR circuit.

FIG. 151 4.0L EEC pinpoint test

Fuel Control | **Pinpoint Test** | **H**

TEST STEP	RESULT ▶	ACTION TO TAKE
H5 ISOLATE FAULTY INJECTOR CIRCUIT		
• Key off. • Breakout box installed, ECU disconnected. • Disconnect all injectors on suspect bank. • Ohmmeter on 200 ohm scale. • Connect one injector and measure resistance between Test Pin 37 and either Test Pin 58 or 59 as appropriate. • Disconnect that injector and repeat process for each of the remaining injectors. • **Is each resistance within 13-16 ohms?**	Yes ▶ No ▶	GO to H6 . SERVICE open or short in VPWR or injector circuit of the suspect injector(s). If OK, REPLACE injector. REMOVE breakout box. RECONNECT ECU and injectors. DRIVE vehicle five miles at 55 mph. RERUN Quick Test.
H6 CHECK INJECTOR DRIVER SIGNAL		
Requires standard non-powered 12 volt test lamp. • Key off. • Connect ECU to breakout box • Connect test lamp between Test Pin 37 and Test Pin 58 at the breakout box. • Connect test lamp between Test Pin 37 and 59 at the breakout box. • Crank or start engine. **NOTE: Properly operating systems will show a dim glow on the lamp.** • **Is glow on lamp dim?**	Yes ▶ No ▶	GO To H7 . **No light:** VERIFY 12 volt at Test Pins 37 and 57. **Bright light:** CHECK injector circuit for shorts to ground. If system checks OK, REPLACE ECU. REMOVE breakout box. RERUN Quick Test.

FIG. 152 4.0L EEC pinpoint test

Fuel Control | **Pinpoint Test** | **H**

TEST STEP	RESULT ▶	ACTION TO TAKE
H7 CHECK EXTERNAL SOURCE FOR FUEL PRESSURE PROBLEM		
• Key off. • Pressurize fuel system per Test Step [H1]. — Visually look for fuel leaking at fuel injector O-rings, fuel pressure regulator, and fuel rails. • **Is there a visible leak?**	Yes ▶	REMOVE pressure gauge. SERVICE as necessary. After servicing leak, RERUN Quick Test.
	No ▶	GO to [H8].
H8 INJECTOR BALANCE TEST		
• Connect tachometer to engine. Run engine at idle. • Disconnect and reconnect the injectors one at a time: Note rpm drop for each injector. • **Does each injector produce at least a 100 rpm momentary drop?** **NOTE: ISC will attempt to re-establish rpm.**	Yes ▶	Fuel delivery OK. Problem is in an area common to all cylinders i.e. air/vacuum leak, fuel contamination. SERVICE as necessary.
	No ▶	GO to injector testing and cleaning instructions. After any servicing, RERUN Quick Test.

FIG. 153 4.0L EEC pinpoint test

Fuel Control | **Pinpoint Test** | **H**

TEST STEP	RESULT ▶	ACTION TO TAKE
H11 SERVICE CODE 41/172 FUEL CONTROL ALWAYS LEAN		
HEGO Engine Running code 41 indicates the system is always lean. • Run engine at 2000 rpm for 2 minutes. • Key off, wait 10 seconds. • Rerun Engine Running Self-Test. • **Is Code 41 or 172 present?**	Yes ▶	GO to [H14].
	No ▶	GO to [H20].

FIG. 154 4.0L EEC pinpoint test

Fuel Control — Pinpoint Test H

TEST STEP	RESULT ▶	ACTION TO TAKE
H14 CHECK HEGO SENSOR		
NOTE: The purpose of this test is to verify the HEGO sensor can generate greater than 0.5 volts during Engine Running Self-Test. Any Vacuum/air leaks in non-EEC areas could also cause Code 41/172 or 91/136. Check for: — Leaking vacuum actuator (e.g. A/C control motor). — Engine sealing. — PCV system. — Unmetered air leak between Mass Air Flow sensor and throttle body. — Lead contaminated HEGO sensor. • Key off. • Disconnect appropriate HEGO sensor from vehicle harness. • Connect voltmeter to HEGO SIGNAL and HEGO GND at the HEGO sensor connector. • Voltmeter on 20 volt scale. • Run engine at approximately 2000 rpm for two minutes. • Rerun Engine Running Self-Test and monitor HEGO sensor voltage. • **Is the voltage greater than 0.5 volts at the end of Self-Test?**	Yes ▶ No ▶	GO to H15. REPLACE HEGO sensor. RERUN Quick Test.

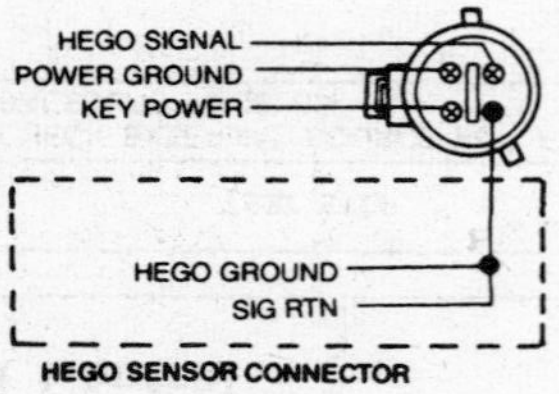

FIG. 155 4.0L EEC pinpoint test

Fuel Control — Pinpoint Test H

TEST STEP	RESULT ▶	ACTION TO TAKE
H15 CHECK CONTINUITY OF HEGO SIGNAL AND HEGO GROUND CIRCUITS		
• Key off. • Disconnect ECU 60 pin connector. Inspect for damaged or pushed out pins, corrosion, loose wires, etc. Service as necessary. • Install breakout box, leave ECU disconnected. • HEGO disconnected. • Ohmmeter on 200 ohm scale. • Measure resistance between Test Pin 49 and Test Pin 46 at the breakout box and HEGO GND at the HEGO vehicle harness connector. • **Is each resistance less than 5.0 ohms?**	Yes ▶ No ▶	GO to H16. SERVICE open circuit. REMOVE breakout box. RECONNECT ECU, HEGO sensor, and any other components that are disconnected or removed. RERUN Quick Test.

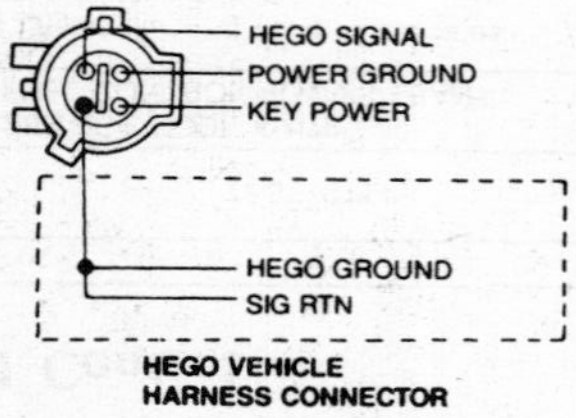

FIG. 156 4.0L EEC pinpoint test

Fuel Control — Pinpoint Test H

TEST STEP	RESULT ▶	ACTION TO TAKE
H16 CHECK HEGO CIRCUIT FOR SHORT TO GROUND		
• Key off. • Breakout box installed, ECU disconnected. • HEGO disconnected. • Ohmmeter on 200,000 ohm scale. • Measure resistance between Test Pin 29 and Test Pins 40 and 49 at the breakout box. • Measure resistance between Test Pin 29 and Test Pins 40 and 46 at the breakout box. • **Is each resistance greater than 10,000 ohms?**	Yes ▶	GO to H17 .
	No ▶	SERVICE short circuit. RECONNECT ECU and HEGO sensor. RERUN Quick Test.
H17 CHECK HEGO SENSOR FOR SHORT TO GROUND		
• Key off. • Breakout box installed, ECU disconnected. • HEGO disconnected. • Ohmmeter on 200,000 ohm scale. • Measure resistance between PWR GND and HEGO SIGNAL at the HEGO sensor connector. • Measure resistance between HEGO GND and SIG RTN at the HEGO sensor connector. • **Is resistance greater than 10,000 ohms?**	Yes ▶	REMOVE breakout box. RECONNECT HEGO sensor. REPLACE ECU. RERUN Quick Test.
	No ▶	REPLACE HEGO sensor. RECONNECT ECU. RERUN Quick Test.

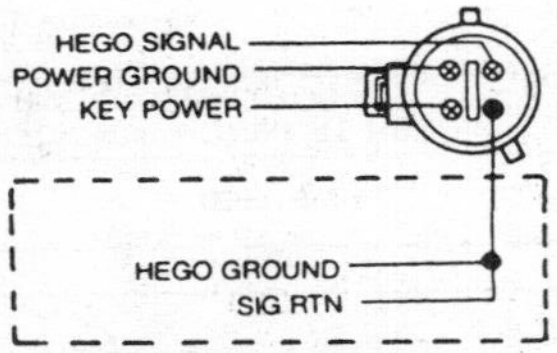

FIG. 157 4.0L EEC pinpoint test

Fuel Control — Pinpoint Test H

TEST STEP	RESULT ▶	ACTION TO TAKE
H20 CHECK RESISTANCE OF HEATER ELEMENT ON HEGO		
• Key off. • Disconnect HEGO. • Ohmmeter on 200 ohm scale. • Measure resistance between KPWR circuit and PWR GND circuit at HEGO sensor connector. • Hot to warm resistance specification is 5.0 to 30.0 ohms. • Room temperature resistance specification is 2.0 to 5.0 ohms. • **Is resistance within specification?**	Yes ▶	GO to H21 .
	No ▶	REPLACE HEGO sensor. RERUN Quick Test.

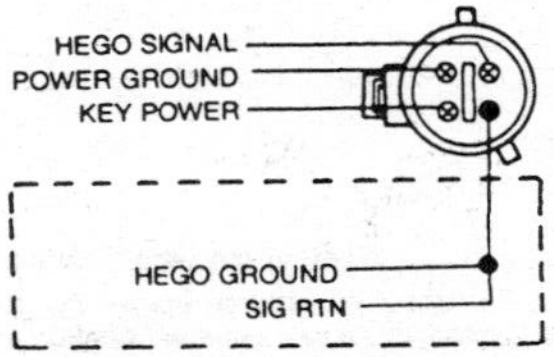

FIG. 158 4.0L EEC pinpoint test

Fuel Control | **Pinpoint Test** | **H**

TEST STEP	RESULT ▶	ACTION TO TAKE
H21 CHECK FOR POWER AT HEGO HARNESS CONNECTOR		
• Key on, engine off. • HEGO disconnected. • Voltmeter on 20 volt scale. • Measure voltage between KEY POWER circuit and PWR GND circuit at the HEGO vehicle harness connector. • **Is voltage greater than 10.5 volts?**	Yes ▶	RECONNECT HEGO sensor. HEGO sensor system OK. GO to H1.
	No ▶	GO to H22.
H22 CHECK CONTINUITY OF POWER GROUND CIRCUIT		
• Key off, wait 10 seconds. • HEGO disconnected. • Ohmmeter on 200 ohm scale. • Measure resistance between PWR GND circuit at the HEGO vehicle harness connector and battery negative post. • **Is resistance less than 5.0 ohms?**	Yes ▶	SERVICE open in KEY POWER circuit. RECONNECT HEGO sensor. RERUN Quick Test.
	No ▶	SERVICE open in PWR GND circuit. RECONNECT HEGO sensor. RERUN Quick Test.

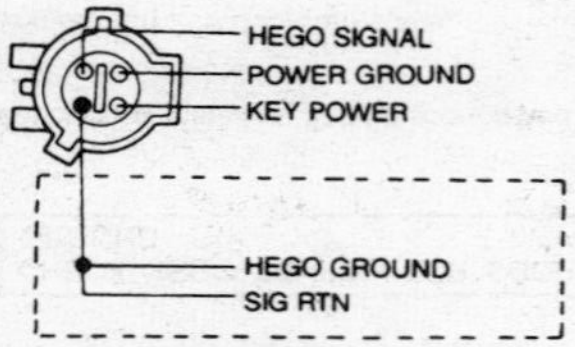

FIG. 159 4.0L EEC pinpoint test

Fuel Control | **Pinpoint Test** | **H**

TEST STEP	RESULT ▶	ACTION TO TAKE
H23 SERVICE CODE 42/173, 92/137, 177: FUEL CONTROL ALWAYS RICH; CHECK HEGO SIGNAL FOR SHORT TO POWER		
With dual HEGO, code 42/173 refers to right or rear HEGO, code 92/137 or 177 refers to left or front HEGO. HEGO Engine Running Code 42/173 indicates the system is always rich. • Key off, wait 10 seconds. • Disconnect the appropriate HEGO sensor for Code 42/173 or 92/137 or 177. • Voltmeter on 20 volt scale. • Key on, engine off. • Measure voltage between HEGO SIG and PWR GND at the HEGO vehicle harness connector. • **Is voltage less than 0.5 volts?**	Yes ▶	GO to H24.
	No ▶	SERVICE HEGO circuit short to power. RECONNECT HEGO sensor. RERUN Quick Test.

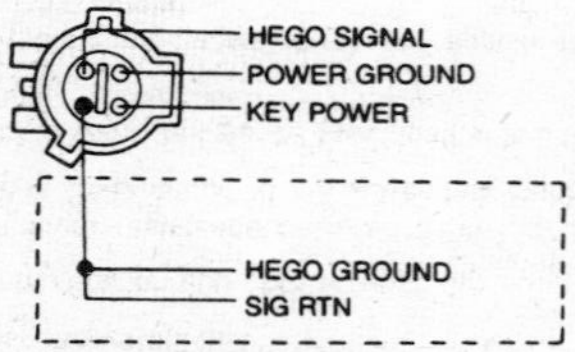

FIG. 160 4.0L EEC pinpoint test

Fuel Control | **Pinpoint Test** | **H**

TEST STEP	RESULT ▶	ACTION TO TAKE
H24 CHECK HEGO SENSOR FOR SHORT TO IGNITION RUN CIRCUIT • Key off. • HEGO disconnected. • Ohmmeter on 200,000 ohm scale. • Measure resistance between KPWR circuit and HEGO SIG circuit at the HEGO sensor connector. • **Is resistance greater than 10,000 ohms?** HEGO SIGNAL / POWER GROUND / KEY POWER / HEGO GROUND / SIG RTN / HEGO SENSOR CONNECTOR	Yes ▶	GO to H25.
	No ▶	REPLACE HEGO sensor. RERUN Quick Test.
H25 ATTEMPT TO GENERATE CODE 41/172, 91/136 or 176 Non-EEC areas could cause a Service Code 42/92. Check for: — Fuel contaminated engine oil — Ignition caused misfire (fouled spark plug) — CANP problems • Key off, wait 10 seconds. • HEGO disconnected. • Jumper HEGO SIG circuit at the HEGO vehicle harness connector to battery negative post. • Rerun Engine Running Self-Test. • **Is Code 41/172, 91/136 or 176 present?**	Yes ▶	REMOVE jumper. GO to H28.
	No ▶	REMOVE jumper. RECONNECT HEGO sensor. DISCONNECT ECU 60 pin connector. Inspect for damaged or pushed out pins, corrosion, loose wires, etc. SERVICE as necessary. If OK REPLACE ECU. RERUN Quick Test.

FIG. 161 4.0L EEC pinpoint test

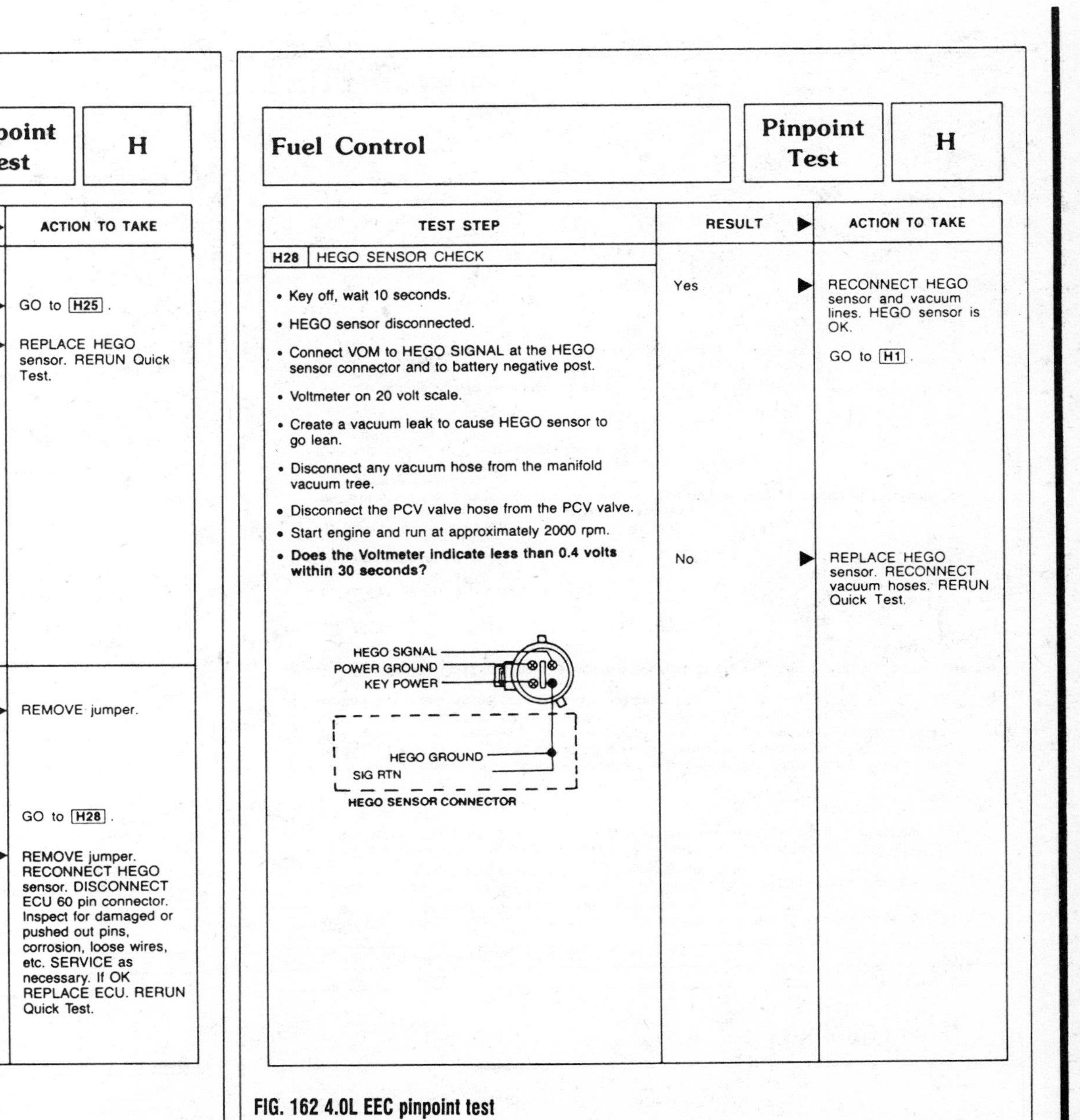

Fuel Control | **Pinpoint Test** | **H**

TEST STEP	RESULT ▶	ACTION TO TAKE
H28 HEGO SENSOR CHECK • Key off, wait 10 seconds. • HEGO sensor disconnected. • Connect VOM to HEGO SIGNAL at the HEGO sensor connector and to battery negative post. • Voltmeter on 20 volt scale. • Create a vacuum leak to cause HEGO sensor to go lean. • Disconnect any vacuum hose from the manifold vacuum tree. • Disconnect the PCV valve hose from the PCV valve. • Start engine and run at approximately 2000 rpm. • **Does the Voltmeter indicate less than 0.4 volts within 30 seconds?** HEGO SIGNAL / POWER GROUND / KEY POWER / HEGO GROUND / SIG RTN / HEGO SENSOR CONNECTOR	Yes ▶	RECONNECT HEGO sensor and vacuum lines. HEGO sensor is OK. GO to H1.
	No ▶	REPLACE HEGO sensor. RECONNECT vacuum hoses. RERUN Quick Test.

FIG. 162 4.0L EEC pinpoint test

Fuel Control	Pinpoint Test	H

H29 CONTINUOUS MEMORY CODE 41/172 EXHAUST ODOR, SMOKE:

CODE 41/172 — Indicates that a HEGO circuit has not switched during closed loop fuel control.

CONTINUOUS MEMORY CODE 41/172 EXHAUST ODOR, SMOKE:

NOTE: In this situation, Code 41/172 does not necessarily indicate a lean condition.

Before attempting to service a Continuous Memory Code 41/172, DIAGNOSE all other driveability complaints first (e.g. rough idle, misses, etc.) using Diagnosis by Symptom.

Exhaust odor, smoke is possible to appear without code 41/172, it is an intermittent fault and could be due to loose HEGO SIG or HEGO GND connection or poor HEGO harness insulation near the exhaust manifold. The ECU thinks the system is lean and therefore leads to an over-rich fuel condition.

Some areas to check are:

- HEGO SIG and GND connections.
- HEGO harness insulation near the exhaust manifold.
- Unmetered Air (vacuum leaks/intake air leaks):
  - — Canister purge system.
  - — PCV system.
  - — Engine sealing.
  - — Crimped fuel lines.
  - — Plugged fuel filter.
  - — Fouled fuel injectors.
  - — Air leaks between mass air flow sensor and air outlet tube to throttle body.
- HEGO Fuel Fouled:

  Whenever an over-rich fuel condition has been experienced (fuel fouled spark plugs), make a thorough check of the ignition system. If a HEGO sensor is suspected of being fuel fouled (low output or slow response), run the vehicle at sustained high speed (within legal limits) followed by a few hard accels. This will burn off the HEGO contamination and restore proper HEGO operation.
- Ignition System:

  If engine is always in DEFAULT spark (base timing) refer to Quick Test Step [4.0].
- Improper Fueling:

  Lead fouled HEGO sensor.
- Fuel Pressure:

  Perform Pinpoint Test Steps [H1] and [H2].
- TP Sensor:

  Turn key to RUN position. While moving throttle slowly toward wide-open position, measure voltage between Test Pins 47 and 46 at the breakout box. If the voltage does not increase with the increase of throttle opening, replace TP sensor or linkage as necessary.
- If at this point the driveability concern is still present, perform Pinpoint Test Steps [H3] through [H6].

FIG. 163 4.0L EEC pinpoint test

Fuel Control	Pinpoint Test	H

H30 CONTINUOUS MEMORY CODE 41 or 42:

Code 41/172 — HEGO indicated the fuel system was lean for more than 15 seconds when the fuel system should have been in closed loop fuel control.

Code 42/173 — HEGO indicated the fuel system was rich for more than 15 seconds when the fuel system should have been in closed loop fuel control.

- Before attempting to service a Continuous Memory Code 41/172 or 42/173 DIAGNOSE all other driveability complaints first. Examples: rough idle, misses, etc. using Diagnosis By Symptom.
- Whenever an over-rich fuel condition has been experienced (fuel fouled spark plugs), make a thorough check of the ignition system. If a HEGO sensor is suspected of being fuel fouled (low output or slow response), after the vehicle service, run the vehicle at sustained high speed (within legal limits) followed by a few hard accels. This will burn off the HEGO contamination and restore proper HEGO operation.
- The fuel Service Code may help to isolate the cause of the fuel control problem. Some areas to check are:

For Code 41/172:

- Intermittent HEGO circuit (SIG or GND).
- Low fuel pressure at WOT.
  - — Low-pressure fuel pump.
  - — Restricted fuel supply (crimped fuel lines or plugged fuel filter or screen at the Fuel Pressure Regulator).
- Low fuel flow at WOT with correct fuel pressure.
  - — Clogged fuel injectors.
  - — Low battery voltage less than 11 volts.

FIG. 164 4.0L EEC pinpoint test

Fuel Control — Pinpoint Test H

H30 (CONTINUED)

For Code 42/173:

- Intermittent HEGO circuit (SIGNAL or GROUND).
- Excessive fuel pressure. Check for fuel pressure regulator vacuum line disconnected or kinked fuel return line.
- Excessive fuel flow. Check for damaged or stuck open fuel injector(s).

For Both Codes 41/172 and 42/173:

- Intermittent HEGO circuit (SIGNAL or GROUND).
- Contaminated HEGO sensor (lead or silicone fouled).
- Improper fuel pressure. Check fuel pump and fuel pressure regulator.

FIG. 165 4.0L EEC pinpoint test

Fuel Pump Circuit — Pinpoint Test J

TEST STEP	RESULT ▶	ACTION TO TAKE
J1 NO FUEL PUMP PRESSURE: CHECK FOR FUEL PUMP ELECTRICAL OPERATION		
• To check if fuel pump runs, turn key from Off to Run position, repeat several times. (Do not turn to start position.)	Yes ▶	
• **Does fuel pump run briefly each time the key is turned to RUN position?**	No ▶	GO to J2 .
J2 CHECK FOR VPWR TO ECU		
• Key off. • Breakout box installed, ECU connected. • Voltmeter on 20 volt scale. • Key on, engine off.	Yes ▶	GO to J5 .
• Measure voltage between Test Pin 37 and Test Pin 40 at the breakout box and between Test Pin 57 and Test Pin 60 at the breakout box. • **Are both voltages greater than 10.5 volts?**	No ▶	GO to B1 .
J5 CHECK FOR VOLTAGE TO POWER-TO-PUMP CIRCUIT		
• Key on, engine off. • Breakout box installed, ECU connected. • Voltmeter on 20 volt scale. • Measure voltage between chassis ground and Power-To-Pump circuit at fuel pump relay while cranking engine.	Yes ▶	GO to Section 11 for open in Power-To-Pump circuit, Fuel pump GND, open in pump, etc. Also REFER to Section F-02.
• **Is voltage greater than 8.0 volts during crank?**	No ▶	GO to J6 .
J6 CHECK FOR BATT+ TO FUEL PUMP RELAY		
• Key on, engine off. • Breakout box installed (if applicable), ECU connected.	Yes ▶	GO to J11 .
• Voltmeter on 20 volt scale. • Measure voltage between chassis ground and BATT(+) at the fuel pump relay. • **Is voltage greater than 10.5 volts?**	No ▶	SERVICE open in BATT (+) between fuel pump relay and battery positive post (for relay block applications, between fuel pump relay and EEC power relay). REMOVE breakout box. RECONNECT ECU. RERUN Quick Test.

FIG. 166 4.0L EEC pinpoint test

Fuel Pump Circuit — Pinpoint Test J

TEST STEP	RESULT ▶	ACTION TO TAKE
J11 CHECK FOR VOLTAGE AT POWER-TO-PUMP CIRCUIT		
• Key off. • Breakout box installed, ECU disconnected. • Connect jumper wire from Test Pin 22 to Test Pin 40 or 60 at the breakout box. • Voltmeter on 20 volt scale. • Key on, engine off. • Measure voltage between chassis ground and Power-To-Pump circuit at fuel pump relay. • **Is voltage greater than 10.5 volts?**	Yes ▶	REPLACE ECU. REMOVE breakout box.. RERUN Quick Test.
	No ▶	REPLACE fuel pump relay. REMOVE breakout box. RECONNECT ECU. RERUN Quick Test.
J20 SERVICE CODE 95/542: DOES ENGINE START		
Service Code 95/542 indicates that one of the following has occurred: No Start: — Inertia switch not reset or electrically open (if in secondary circuit). — Open circuit in or between the fuel pump and FPM circuit connection to the Power-To-Pump circuit. — Poor fuel pump ground Vehicle Starts: — Fuel pump secondary circuit short to power. — Fuel pump relay contacts always closed. — Open in FPM circuit between ECU and connection to the Power-To-Pump circuit. — Faulty ECU. • **Does the engine start?**	Yes ▶	GO to J21.
	No ▶	GO to J25.
J21 VERIFY THAT FUEL PUMP IS OFF		
• Key on. Wait five seconds. • Listen for motor noise from fuel pump. • **Is fuel pump off?**	Yes ▶	GO to J23.
	No ▶	GO to J22.

FIG. 167 4.0L EEC pinpoint test

Fuel Pump Circuit — Pinpoint Test J

TEST STEP	RESULT ▶	ACTION TO TAKE
J22 CHECK FOR FUEL PUMP RELAY ALWAYS CLOSED		
• Key off. • Locate and disconnect fuel pump relay. • Key on. • **Does fuel pump shut off when relay is disconnected?**	Yes ▶	REPLACE fuel pump relay. RERUN Quick Test.
	No ▶	SERVICE short to power in POWER-TO-PUMP/ FPM circuit. RECONNECT fuel pump relay. RERUN Quick Test.
J23 CHECK FPM CIRCUIT CONTINUITY		
• Key off. • Disconnect ECU 60 pin connector. Inspect for damaged or pushed out pins, corrosion, loose wires, etc. Service as necessary. • Install breakout box, leave ECU disconnected. • Disconnect fuel pump relay. • Ohmmeter on 200 ohm scale. • Measure resistance between Test Pin 8 at the breakout box and Power-To-Pump circuit at the fuel pump relay vehicle harness connector. • **Is resistance less than 5.0 ohms?**	Yes ▶	REPLACE ECU. REMOVE breakout box. RECONNECT fuel pump relay. RERUN Quick Test.
	No ▶	SERVICE open circuit. REMOVE breakout box. RECONNECT all components. RERUN Quick Test.

FUEL PUMP RELAY VEHICLE HARNESS CONNECTOR (USE APPLICABLE DRAWING)

FIG. 168 4.0L EEC pinpoint test

Fuel Pump Circuit — Pinpoint Test J

TEST STEP	RESULT ▶	ACTION TO TAKE
J24 CHECK FUEL PUMP PRIMARY CIRCUIT FOR SHORT TO GROUND • Key off. • Breakout box installed, ECU disconnected. • Fuel pump relay disconnected. • Ohmmeter on 200,000 ohm scale. • Measure resistance between Test Pin 22 and Test Pin 40 at the breakout box. • **Is resistance greater than 10,000 ohms?**	Yes ▶	REPLACE ECU. REMOVE breakout box. RECONNECT fuel pump relay. RERUN Quick Test.
	No ▶	SERVICE short circuit. REMOVE breakout box. RECONNECT all components. RERUN Quick Test.
J25 CHECK INERTIA SWITCH • Key off, wait 10 seconds. • Locate and disconnect fuel pump inertia switch (verify that switch is reset). • Ohmmeter on 200 ohm scale. • Measure resistance of the fuel pump inertia switch. • **Is resistance less than 5.0 ohms?**	Yes ▶	RECONNECT inertia switch. GO to J26 .
	No ▶	REPLACE or RESET inertia switch. RERUN Quick Test.

FIG. 169 4.0L EEC pinpoint test

Fuel Pump Circuit — Pinpoint Test J

TEST STEP	RESULT ▶	ACTION TO TAKE
J26 CHECK FOR CONTINUITY BETWEEN FPM CIRCUIT AND GROUND • Key off. • Breakout box installed, ECU disconnected. • Fuel pump relay disconnected. • Ohmmeter on 200 ohm scale. • Measure resistance between Test Pin 8 at the breakout box and battery negative post. • **Is resistance less than 10.0 ohms?**	Yes ▶	REPLACE ECU. REMOVE breakout box. RECONNECT fuel pump relay. RERUN Quick Test.
	No ▶	REMOVE breakout box. RECONNECT all components. GO to Electric Fuel Pump, for open in Power-To-Pump circuit, poor fuel pump ground, open in fuel pump, etc.
J30 SERVICE CODE 96/543: DOES ENGINE START? Service Code 96/543 indicates a fuel pump secondary circuit failure between the BATT(+) supply and the FPM connection to the Power-To-Pump circuit. Possible causes are: — Open circuit. — Faulty fuel pump relay. — Faulty ECU. • Key off, wait 10 seconds. • Locate fuel pump relay. • Voltmeter on 20 volt scale. • Measure voltage between BATT(+) circuit at the fuel pump relay and battery negative post. • **Is voltage greater than 10.5 volts?** POWER -TO- PUMP / BATT (+) / BATT (+) / POWER -TO- PUMP FUEL PUMP RELAY VEHICLE HARNESS CONNECTOR (USE APPLICABLE DRAWING)	Yes ▶	GO to J31 .
	No ▶	SERVICE open in BATT(+) circuit. RERUN Quick Test.

FIG. 170 4.0L EEC pinpoint test

Fuel Pump Circuit — Pinpoint Test J

<table>
<tr><th>TEST STEP</th><th>RESULT ▶</th><th>ACTION TO TAKE</th></tr>
<tr><td colspan="3">J90 CONTINUOUS MEMORY CODE 95/542: CHECK EEC HARNESS</td></tr>
<tr><td rowspan="2">A Continuous Memory Code 95/542 indicates that one of the following intermittent conditions has occurred:
— Fuel pump circuit activated when ECU expected circuit to be off (i.e., fuel system test or prime procedure).
— Open circuit in or between the fuel pump and FPM circuit at the ECU (refer to schematic).
— Poor fuel pump ground.
— FPM or Power-To-Pump circuit short to power.
— Fuel pump relay contacts stuck closed.
— Left front HEGO circuit short to power.
• Start engine.
• Check for engine stall/stumble while performing the following (also, if possible, listen for fuel pump turning off.)
— Shake, wiggle, bend the Power-To-Pump circuit between the Power-To-Pump pin at the fuel pump relay and the fuel pump.
— Shake, wiggle, bend the fuel pump ground circuit from the fuel pump to ground.
— Lightly tap the fuel pump to simulate road shock.
— For vehicles with the inertia switch in the Power-To-Pump circuit (refer to schematic), lightly tap inertia switch to simulate road shock.
• Key off.
• Inspect the fuel pump vehicle harness connector and the fuel pump ground for corrosion, damaged pins, etc.
• Is fault indicated/found?</td><td>Yes ▶</td><td>ISOLATE fault and SERVICE as necessary. CLEAR Continuous Memory

RERUN Quick Test.</td></tr>
<tr><td>No ▶</td><td>GO to J91.</td></tr>
<tr><td colspan="3">J31 CHECK FOR VOLTAGE AT POWER-TO-PUMP CIRCUIT TO VERIFY FUEL PUMP RELAY OPERATION</td></tr>
<tr><td rowspan="2">• Key off.
• Fuel pump relay connected.
• Voltmeter on 20 volt scale.
• Connect Voltmeter between Power-To-Pump circuit at the fuel pump relay and battery negative post.
• Observe Voltmeter as you activate fuel pump relay (turn key to run for 1 second, then to off for 10 seconds. Repeat 5 times.)
• Does voltage measure greater than 10.5 volts for about 1 second after key is turned to RUN position during test?</td><td>Yes ▶</td><td>REPLACE ECU. RERUN Quick Test.</td></tr>
<tr><td>No ▶</td><td>REPLACE fuel pump relay. RERUN Quick Test.</td></tr>
</table>

FIG. 171 4.0L EEC pinpoint test

Fuel Pump Circuit — Pinpoint Test J

<table>
<tr><th>TEST STEP</th><th>RESULT ▶</th><th>ACTION TO TAKE</th></tr>
<tr><td colspan="3">J91 CHECK FPM CIRCUIT</td></tr>
<tr><td rowspan="2">• Key off.
• Disconnect ECU 60 pin connector. Inspect for damaged or pushed out pins, corrosion, loose wires, etc. Service as necessary.
• Install breakout box, leave ECU disconnected.
• Key on, engine off.
• Connect a TEST LAMP between Test Pin 8 and Test Pin 37 at the breakout box.
• Observe test lamp for an indication of a fault while performing the following (The light will go out when a fault is found, indicating an open):
— Shake, wiggle, bend the fuel pump monitor circuit between the fuel pump relay (or splice if applicable, see schematic) and the processor.
• Is fault indicated?</td><td>Yes ▶</td><td>ISOLATE fault and SERVICE as necessary. REMOVE breakout box. CLEAR Continuous Memory

RERUN Quick Test.</td></tr>
<tr><td>No ▶</td><td>GO to J92.</td></tr>
<tr><td colspan="3">J92 CHECK FOR SHORTS TO POWER</td></tr>
<tr><td rowspan="2">• Key on, engine off.
• Breakout box installed, ECU disconnected.
• Connect a TEST LAMP between Test Pin 8 and Test Pin 40.
• Observe test lamp for an indication of a fault while performing the following (The light will turn on when a fault is detected, indicating a short to power. Also, if possible, listen for fuel pump turning on.):
— Shake, wiggle, bend the fuel pump monitor circuit and Power-To-Pump circuit, especially where they may be in the vicinity of a power circuit.
• Lightly tap the fuel pump relay (to simulate road shock).
• Is fault indicated?</td><td>Yes ▶</td><td>ISOLATE fault and SERVICE as necessary. REMOVE breakout box. RECONNECT ECU. CLEAR Continuous Memory

RERUN Quick Test.</td></tr>
<tr><td>No ▶</td><td>CLEAR Continuous Memory

RERUN Quick Test.</td></tr>
</table>

FIG. 172 4.0L EEC pinpoint test

Fuel Pump Circuit — Pinpoint Test J

TEST STEP	RESULT ▶	ACTION TO TAKE
J93 CONTINUOUS MEMORY CODE 96/543: CHECK FOR CONTINUOUS MEMORY CODE 87/556		
• **Is Continuous Memory Code 87 or 556 also present?**	Yes ▶	GO to J95 .
	No ▶	GO to J94 .
J94 CHECK EEC HARNESS		
A Continuous Memory Code 96/543, without the presence of a Continuous Memory Code 87/556, indicates that during vehicle operation, one of the following has occurred: — Open in the BATT(+) circuit between BATT(+) and the fuel pump relay. — Fuel pump relay contacts opened. — Open in the Power-To-Pump circuit from the fuel pump relay to the FPM splice, if applicable (see schematic). • Start engine. • Check for engine stall/stumble while performing the following (also, if possible, listen for fuel pump turning off): — Shake, wiggle, bend the BATT(+) circuit from BATT(+) to the fuel pump relay. — Lightly tap the fuel pump relay (to simulate road shock). — Shake, wiggle, bend the Power-To-Pump circuit from the fuel pump relay to the FPM splice, if applicable (See schematic). • Key off. • Inspect the fuel pump relay connectors and BATT(+) connector terminal for corrosion, damaged pins, etc. • **Is fault indicated/found?**	Yes ▶	ISOLATE fault and SERVICE as necessary. CLEAR Continuous Memory RERUN Quick Test.
	No ▶	CLEAR Continuous Memory RERUN Quick Test.

FIG. 173 4.0L EEC pinpoint test

Fuel Pump Circuit — Pinpoint Test J

TEST STEP	RESULT ▶	ACTION TO TAKE
J95 CONTINUOUS MEMORY CODE 87/556: CHECK EEC HARNESS		
A Continuous Memory Code 87/556 indicates that a fuel pump primary circuit failure has occurred during vehicle operation. Possible causes are: — Open in VPWR circuit between the EEC power relay and the fuel pump relay. — Open coil in fuel pump relay. — Open in fuel pump circuit (Pin 22). — Damaged inertia switch. • Start engine. • Check for engine stall/stumble while performing the following (also, if possible, listen for fuel pump turning off): — Shake, wiggle, bend the VPWR circuit between the EEC power relay and the fuel pump relay. For vehicles with the inertia switch in the VPWR circuit (refer to schematic), lightly tap the inertia switch to simulate road shock. — Shake, wiggle, bend the EEC vehicle harness fuel pump circuit (Test Pin 22) between the ECU and the fuel pump relay. — Lightly tap the fuel pump relay to simulate road shock. • Key off. • Inspect the ECU 60 pin connector and the fuel pump relay connectors for corrosion, damaged pins, etc. damaged pins, etc. • **Is fault indicated/found?**	Yes ▶	ISOLATE fault and SERVICE as necessary. CLEAR Continuous Memory
	No ▶	CLEAR Continuous Memory RERUN Quick Test.

FIG. 174 4.0L EEC pinpoint test

Idle Speed Control (Bypass Air) — Pinpoint Test KE

TEST STEP	RESULT	ACTION TO TAKE
KE1 SERVICE CODE 12/412, 16: CHECK FOR RPM DROP		
Service Code 12/412 indicates that during Engine Running Self-Test, engine rpm could not be controlled within the Self-Test upper limit band. Service Code 16 indicates that during Engine Running Self-Test, engine rpm was too low to perform the HEGO Test. Possible causes are: — Open or shorted circuit — Throttle linkage binding — Improper idle airflow set — Throttle body/ISC solenoid contamination — Items external to Idle Speed Control system that could affect engine rpm. — Faulty ISC solenoid — Faulty ECU • Key off. • Connect engine tachometer. • Start engine. • Disconnect ISC harness connector. • **Does rpm drop or stall?**	Yes ▶ No ▶	GO to KE3. GO to KE4.

FIG. 175 4.0L EEC pinpoint test

Idle Speed Control (Bypass Air) — Pinpoint Test KE

TEST STEP	RESULT	ACTION TO TAKE
KE3 CHECK FOR OTHER EEC CODES		
• **Are Service Codes 22/126, 41/172, 42/173, 91/136 or 92/137 present?**	Yes ▶ No ▶	RECONNECT ISC solenoid. GO to Quick Test Step 7.0 for appropriate Pinpoint Test. GO to KE4.
KE4 MEASURE ISC SOLENOID RESISTANCE		
• Key off. • ISC solenoid disconnected. • Ohmmeter on 200 ohm scale. • Measure solenoid resistance. **NOTE: Due to diode in solenoid, place voltmeter (+) lead on VPWR pin and (−) lead on ISC pin** • **Is resistance between 6.0 and 13.0 ohms?** ISC VPWR ISC SOLENOID CONNECTOR	Yes ▶ No ▶	GO to KE5. REPLACE ISC solenoid. RERUN Quick Test.
KE5 CHECK FOR INTERNAL SHORT TO ISC SOLENOID CASE		
• Key off. • ISC solenoid disconnected. • Ohmmeter on 200,000 ohm scale. • Measure resistance from either ISC solenoid pin to ISC housing. • **Is resistance greater than 10,000 ohms?**	Yes ▶ No ▶	GO to KE6. REPLACE ISC solenoid. RERUN Quick Test.

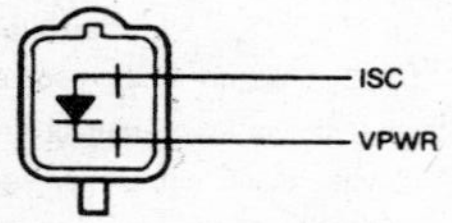

FIG. 176 4.0L EEC pinpoint test

Idle Speed Control (Bypass Air) — Pinpoint Test KE

TEST STEP	RESULT ▶	ACTION TO TAKE
KE6 CHECK VPWR CIRCUIT VOLTAGE		
• Key on, engine off. • ISC solenoid disconnected. • Voltmeter on 20 volt scale. • Measure voltage between VPWR circuit at the ISC solenoid vehicle harness connector and battery ground. • **Is voltage greater than 10.5 volts?**	Yes ▶ No ▶	GO to KE7. SERVICE open circuit. RERUN Quick Test.
KE7 CHECK ISC CIRCUIT CONTINUITY		
• Key off. • ISC solenoid disconnected. • Disconnect ECU and inspect both 60 pin connectors for damaged or pushed out pins, corrosion, loose wires, etc. Service as necessary. • Install breakout box, leave ECU disconnected. • Ohmmeter on 200 ohm scale. • Measure resistance between Test Pin 21 at the breakout box and ISC circuit at ISC solenoid vehicle harness connector. • **Is resistance less than 5 ohms?**	Yes ▶ No ▶	GO to KE8. SERVICE open circuit. REMOVE breakout box. RECONNECT all components. RERUN Quick Test.
KE8 CHECK ISC CIRCUIT FOR SHORT TO GROUND		
• Key off. • Breakout box installed, ECU disconnected. • ISC solenoid disconnected. • Ohmmeter on 200,000 ohm scale. • Measure resistance between Test Pin 21 and Test Pins 40, 46 and 60 at the breakout box. • **Is each resistance greater than 10,000 ohms?**	Yes ▶ No ▶	GO to KE9. SERVICE short circuit. REMOVE breakout box. RECONNECT all components. RERUN Quick Test.
KE9 CHECK ISC CIRCUIT FOR SHORT TO POWER		
• Key off. • Breakout box installed, ECU disconnected. • ISC solenoid disconnected. • Key on. • Measure voltage between breakout box and chassis ground. • **Is voltage less than 1.0 volt?**	Yes ▶ No ▶	GO to KE10. SERVICE short circuit. REMOVE breakout box. RECONNECT all components. RERUN Quick Test. If code or symptom is still present, REPLACE ECU.

FIG. 177 4.0L EEC pinpoint test

Idle Speed Control (Bypass Air) — Pinpoint Test KE

TEST STEP	RESULT ▶	ACTION TO TAKE
KE10 CHECK FOR ISC SIGNAL FROM THE ECU		
• Key off. • Breakout box installed. • Reconnect ECU to breakout box. • Reconnect ISC solenoid. • Voltmeter on 20 volt scale. • Connect voltmeter between Test Pin 21 and Test Pin 40. • Start engine. • Slowly increase rpm to 3000 rpm then release. • **Does voltage vary?**	Yes ▶ No ▶	GO to KE11. REMOVE ISC solenoid and verify that it is not stuck open. If OK REPLACE ECU. REMOVE breakout box. RERUN Quick Test.
KE11 CHECK IDLE		
• **Is idle speed within specification?**	Yes ▶	Remove ISC solenoid and INSPECT for contamination. If contamination is present, determine if solenoid is type that can be cleaned. **No contamination or solenoid cannot be cleaned** — REPLACE ISC solenoid. RERUN Quick Test. **Solenoid is contaminated or can be cleaned** — CLEAN as necessary RERUN Quick Test. If code/ symptom is still present, REPLACE ISC solenoid.
	No ▶	RESET idle to specification. procedure. RERUN Quick Test. If UNABLE to RESET idle to specification, GO to KE12.

FIG. 178 4.0L EEC pinpoint test

Idle Speed Control (Bypass Air) — Pinpoint Test — KE

TEST STEP	RESULT ▶	ACTION TO TAKE
KE12 CHECK FOR PROBLEMS AFFECTING PROPER ENGINE SPEED		
• Check throttle linkage and/or speed control linkage for binding. • Inspect throttle body for contamination. • Check engine vacuum hoses. Refer to VECI decal. • Check for leaks around ISC solenoid (e.g. mounting gasket, etc.). • **Are all the above checks OK?**	Yes ▶	Remove ISC solenoid and INSPECT for contamination. If contamination is present, determine if solenoid is type that can be cleaned. **No contamination or solenoid cannot be cleaned** — REPLACE ISC solenoid. RERUN Quick Test. **Solenoid is contaminated or can be cleaned** — CLEAN as necessary RERUN Quick Test. If code/symptom is still present, REPLACE ISC solenoid.
	No ▶	SERVICE as necessary. REMOVE breakout box. RECONNECT processor. RERUN Quick Test.

FIG. 179 4.0L EEC pinpoint test

Idle Speed Control (Bypass Air) — Pinpoint Test — KE

TEST STEP	RESULT ▶	ACTION TO TAKE
KE15 SERVICE CODE 13/411: VERIFY IDLE SPEED IS WITHIN SPECIFICATION		
Service Code 13/411 indicates that during Engine Running Self-Test, engine rpm could not be controlled within the Self-Test lower limit band. Possible causes are: — Improper idle airflow set. — Vacuum leaks. — Throttle linkage binding. — Throttle plates open. — Throttle body/ISC solenoid contamination. — ISC circuit short to ground. — Damaged ISC solenoid. • **Is idle speed within specification?**	Yes ▶	Remove ISC solenoid and INSPECT for contamination. If contamination is present, to determine if solenoid is type that can be cleaned. **No contamination or solenoid cannot be cleaned** — REPLACE ISC solenoid. RERUN Quick Test. **Solenoid is contaminated or can be cleaned** — CLEAN as necessary RERUN Quick Test. If code/symptom is still present, REPLACE ISC solenoid.
	No ▶	RESET idle airflow to specification. idle airflow set adjust procedure. If UNABLE to RESET idle to specification, GO to KE16.

FIG. 180 4.0L EEC pinpoint test

Idle Speed Control (Bypass Air) — Pinpoint Test KE

TEST STEP	RESULT ▶	ACTION TO TAKE
KE16 CHECK FOR CONDITIONS AFFECTING IDLE • Check engine vacuum hoses for leaks. Refer to VECI decal. • Check throttle linkage and/or speed control linkage for binding. • Check that throttle plates are closed. • Check for induction system leaks. (e.g. ISC solenoid to throttle body gasket, loose ISC, etc.) • Check throttle body for contamination. • Check that CANP solenoid is not stuck open. • **Are all the above checks OK?**	Yes ▶	GO to KE17.
	No ▶	SERVICE as necessary. RERUN Quick Test.
KE17 CHECK FOR INTERNAL SHORT TO ISC SOLENOID CASE • Key off. • Disconnect ISC solenoid. • Ohmmeter on 200,000 ohm scale. • Measure resistance from either ISC solenoid pin to ISC housing. • **Is resistance greater than 10,000 ohms?**	Yes ▶	GO to KE18.
	No ▶	REPLACE ISC solenoid. RERUN Quick Test.
KE18 CHECK ISC CIRCUIT FOR SHORT TO GROUND • Key off. • ISC solenoid disconnected. • Disconnect the ECU 60 pin connector. Inspect for damaged or pushed out pins, corrosion, loose wires, etc. Service as necessary. • Install breakout box, leave ECU disconnected. • Ohmmeter on 200,000 ohm scale. • Measure resistance between Test Pin 21 and Test Pins 40, 46 and 60 at the breakout box. • **Are all resistances greater than 10,000 ohms?**	Yes ▶	GO to KE19.
	No ▶	SERVICE short circuit. REMOVE breakout box. RECONNECT all components. RERUN Quick Test.

FIG. 181 4.0L EEC pinpoint test

Idle Speed Control (Bypass Air) — Pinpoint Test KE

TEST STEP	RESULT ▶	ACTION TO TAKE
KE19 CHECK ECU OUTPUT • Key off. • Breakout box installed. • Reconnect ECU to breakout box. • Reconnect ISC solenoid. • Voltmeter on 20 volt scale. • Connect Voltmeter between Test Pin 21 and Test Pin 40. • Start engine. • Slowly increase rpm to 3000. • **Is voltage between 3.0 and 11.5 volts?**	Yes ▶	Remove ISC solenoid and INSPECT for contamination. If contamination is present, to determine if solenoid is type that can be cleaned. **No contamination or solenoid cannot be cleaned** — REPLACE ISC solenoid. RERUN Quick Test. **Solenoid is contaminated or can be cleaned** — CLEAN as necessary RERUN Quick Test. If code/symptom is still present, REPLACE ISC solenoid.
	No ▶	REPLACE ECU. REMOVE breakout box. RERUN Quick Test.

FIG. 182 4.0L EEC pinpoint test

Idle Speed Control (Bypass Air) — Pinpoint Test — KE

TEST STEP	RESULT ▶	ACTION TO TAKE
KE22 SERVICE CODE 16: HIGH ISC RPM		
Service Code 16 indicates that with the ISC off, engine rpm was above a Self-Test limit. Possible causes are: — Improper idle set — Purge solenoid — Air/vacuum leaks • **Is Code 48 present?**	Yes ▶	RESET throttle plate. VECI decal for curb idle set procedure. RERUN Quick Test. If Code 48 is still present, GO to KE21 .
	No ▶	GO to KD15 .
KE25 SERVICE CODE 19: LOW ISC RPM		
Service Code 19 indicates that with the ISC off, engine rpm dropped below a Self-Test limit (usually around 600 rpm). Possible causes are: — Engine not at operating temperature. — Throttle body/air inlet contamination. — Improper idle set. • Key off. • Deactivate Self-Test. • Run engine at 2000 rpm for 2 minutes or until inlet radiator hose is hot and pressurized. • Key off. • Rerun Engine Running Self-Test. • **Does engine stumble and/or is code 19 still present?**	Yes ▶	INSPECT throttle body and air inlet for contamination. SERVICE as necessary. If OK, ADJUST base idle RERUN Quick Test.
	No ▶	SERVICE other codes as necessary.

FIG. 183 4.0L EEC pinpoint test

WOT A/C Cutout (WAC) A/C Demand — Pinpoint Test — KM

TEST STEP	RESULT ▶	ACTION TO TAKE
KM1 NO A/C: CHECK FOR VOLTAGE AT A/C CLUTCH		
NOTE: Before proceeding with "NO A/C" diagnostics, verify integrity of related fuses in fuse panel. • Key off. • Disconnect A/C clutch. • A/C demand switch to A/C. • Voltmeter on 20 volt scale. • Start engine, wait 10 seconds. • Measure voltage between the power side of the A/C clutch vehicle harness connector and battery negative post (allow time for normal on/off cycling of the ACC/S or L P switch). • **Is voltage greater than 10.5 volts?**	Yes ▶	EEC system OK. check for poor ground, open circuit in clutch, mechanical problems, etc.
	No ▶	GO to KM2 .
KM2 CHECK POWER-TO-CLUTCH CIRCUIT CONTINUITY		
• Key off. • A/C clutch disconnected. • Disconnect WAC relay. • Ohmmeter on 200 ohm scale. • Measure resistance between power side of the A/C clutch vehicle harness connector and POWER-TO-CLUTCH pin at the WAC relay vehicle harness connector. • **Is resistance less than 5.0 ohms?**	Yes ▶	RECONNECT A/C clutch. GO to KM3 .
	No ▶	SERVICE open circuit. RECONNECT all components. RE-EVALUATE symptom.

FIG. 184 4.0L EEC pinpoint test

WOT A/C Cutout (WAC) A/C Demand — Pinpoint Test KM

TEST STEP	RESULT ▶	ACTION TO TAKE
KM3 CHECK FOR POWER ON A/C DEMAND CIRCUIT		
• Key on, engine off. • WAC relay disconnected. • A/C demand switch to A/C. • Voltmeter on 20 volt scale. • Measure voltage between A/C demand input pin at WAC relay vehicle harness connector and chassis ground. • **Is voltage greater than 10.5 volts?**	Yes ▶	GO to KM6 .
	No ▶	VERIFY operation of A/C clutch cyclic pressure switch and A/C demand switch. If OK, SERVICE open circuit. RECONNECT all components. RE-EVALUATE symptom.
KM6 CHECK WAC CIRCUIT FOR SHORT TO GROUND		
• Key off. • WAC relay disconnected. • Disconnect ECU 60 pin connector. Inspect for damaged or pushed out pins, corrosion, loose wires, etc. Service as necessary. Leave processor disconnected. • Ohmmeter on 200,000 ohm scale. • Measure resistance between WAC circuit at the WAC relay or A/C fan controller harness connector and chassis ground. • **Is resistance greater than 10,000 ohms?**	Yes ▶	GO to KM9 .
	No ▶	SERVICE short circuit. RECONNECT all components. RE-EVALUATE symptom.

FIG. 185 4.0L EEC pinpoint test

WOT A/C Cutout (WAC) A/C Demand — Pinpoint Test KM

TEST STEP	RESULT ▶	ACTION TO TAKE
KM9 CHECK WAC RELAY		
• Key off. • ECU disconnected. • Reconnect WAC relay • Disconnect A/C clutch. • Voltmeter on 20 volt scale. • Key on, engine off. • A/C demand switch to A/C. • Measure voltage between the power side of the A/C clutch vehicle harness connector and the battery negative post. • **Is voltage greater than 10.5 volts?**	Yes ▶	REPLACE ECU. RECONNECT A/C clutch. RE-EVALUATE symptom.
	No ▶	REPLACE WAC relay. RECONNECT all components. RE-EVALUATE symptom.

FIG. 186 4.0L EEC pinpoint test

WOT A/C Cutout (WAC) A/C Demand — Pinpoint Test KM

TEST STEP	RESULT ▶	ACTION TO TAKE
KM15 NO A/C CUTOUT AT WOT: ENTER OUTPUT STATE CHECK (REFER TO QUICK TEST APPENDIX)		
NOTE: Do not use SUPER STAR II tester for this Step, use Voltmeter. • Key off, wait 10 seconds. • Voltmeter on 20 volt scale. • Disconnect electrical connector on the Speed Control servo; if equipped. • Connect Voltmeter negative test lead to STO at the Self-Test connector and positive test lead to battery positive post. • Jumper STI to SIGNAL RETURN at the Self-Test connector. • Perform Key On Engine Off Self-Test until the completion of the Continuous Memory Codes. • Voltmeter will indicate less than 1.0 volt when test complete. • Depress and release the throttle. • **Does voltage increase to greater than 10.5 volts?**	Yes ▶	REMAIN in Output State Check. GO to KM17.
	No ▶	DEPRESS throttle to WOT and RELEASE. If STO voltage does not go high, leave equipment hooked up and GO to Pinpoint Test Step QC2.
KM17 CHECK FOR VPWR TO RELAY		
• Still in Output State Check. • Disconnect harness from WAC relay. • Voltmeter on 20 volt scale. • Measure voltage between VPWR circuit at the WAC relay vehicle harness connector and chassis ground. • **Is voltage greater than 10.5 volts?**	Yes ▶	GO to KM18.
	No ▶	SERVICE open in VPWR circuit between power relay and WAC relay. RECONNECT all components and REMOVE jumper. RE-EVALUATE symptom.

FIG. 187 4.0L EEC pinpoint test

WOT A/C Cutout (WAC) A/C Demand — Pinpoint Test KM

TEST STEP	RESULT ▶	ACTION TO TAKE
KM18 CHECK FOR WAC CYCLING		
• Still in Output State Check. • WAC relay disconnected. • Voltmeter on 20 volt scale. • Connect Voltmeter positive test lead to the VPWR circuit and the negative test lead to the WAC circuit at the WAC relay vehicle harness connector. • While observing Voltmeter, depress and release throttle several times (to cycle output on and off). • **Does voltage cycle high and low?**	Yes ▶	REPLACE WAC relay. REMOVE jumper. RE-EVALUATE symptom.
	No ▶	REMOVE jumper. RECONNECT Speed Control servo. GO to KM19.
KM19 CHECK WAC CIRCUIT CONTINUITY		
• Key off. • Disconnect ECU 60 pin connector. Inspect for damaged or pushed out pins, corrosion, loose wires, etc. Service as necessary. • Install breakout box, leave ECU disconnected. • Disconnect WAC relay. • Measure resistance between Test Pin 54 at the breakout box and WAC circuit at the WAC relay vehicle harness connector. • **Is resistance less than 5.0 ohms?**	Yes ▶	GO to KM20.
	No ▶	SERVICE open circuit. REMOVE breakout box. RECONNECT all components. RE-EVALUATE symptom.
KM20 CHECK WAC CIRCUIT FOR SHORT TO POWER		
• Key off. • Breakout box installed, ECU disconnected. • WAC relay disconnected. • Key on, engine off. • Measure voltage between Test Pin 54 and chassis ground. • **Is voltage less than 1.0 volt?**	Yes ▶	REPLACE ECU. RECONNECT WAC relay. RE-EVALUATE symptom.
	No ▶	SERVICE short circuit. REMOVE breakout box. RECONNECT all components. RE-EVALUATE symptom. If symptom is still present, REPLACE ECU.

FIG. 188 4.0L EEC pinpoint test

WOT A/C Cutout (WAC) A/C Demand — Pinpoint Test KM

TEST STEP	RESULT ▶	ACTION TO TAKE
KM30 CYCLE A/C DEMAND SWITCH • Key off, wait 10 seconds. • Disconnect ECU 60 pin connector. Inspect for damaged or pushed out pins, corrosion, loose wires, etc. Service as necessary. • Install breakout box, leave ECU disconnected. • Voltmeter on 20 volt scale. • Key on, engine off. • Connect Voltmeter positive test lead to Test Pin 43 and negative test lead to Test Pin 40. • **Does voltage cycle high and low when A/C demand switch is cycled?**	Yes ▶ No ▶	REPLACE ECU. REMOVE breakout box. RERUN Quick Test. GO to KM31.
KM31 CHECK ACD CIRCUIT CONTINUITY • Key off, wait 10 seconds. • Breakout box installed, ECU disconnected. • Ohmmeter on 200 ohm scale. • Measure resistance between Test Pin 43 at the breakout box and A/C demand switch. • **Is resistance greater than 5 ohms?**	Yes ▶ No ▶	SERVICE open in ACD circuit. REMOVE breakout box. RECONNECT ECU. RERUN Quick Test. EEC system OK. REMOVE breakout box. RECONNECT ECU.
KM35 CHECK ACD CIRCUIT FOR SHORT TO POWER • Key off. • Disconnect ECU 60 pin connector. Inspect for damaged or pushed out pins, corrosion, loose wires, etc. Service as necessary. • Install breakout box, leave ECU disconnected. • Disconnect WAC relay (TRK). • A/C demand switch "OFF". • Voltmeter on 20 volt scale. • Key on, engine off. • Measure voltage between Test Pin 43 at the breakout box and chassis ground. • **Is voltage less than 1.0 volt?**	Yes ▶ No ▶	EEC system OK. REMOVE breakout box. RECONNECT all components. VERIFY operation of A/C demand switch. IF OK, SERVICE short circuit. REMOVE breakout box. RECONNECT all components. RE-EVALUATE symptom.

FIG. 189 4.0L EEC pinpoint test

WOT A/C Cutout (WAC) A/C Demand — Pinpoint Test KM

TEST STEP	RESULT ▶	ACTION TO TAKE
KM50 ATTEMPT TO GENERATE CODE 539 • Key off. • A/C demand switch to A/C. • Perform KOEO Self-Test. • **Is Code 539 present during Self-Test?**	Yes ▶ No ▶	GO to KM51. GO to KM60.
KM51 CHECK FOR VOLTAGE TO A/C RELAY • Key off. • Disconnect A/C relay. • Key on. • Measure voltage between IGN RUN circuit at A/C relay vehicle harness connector and chassis ground. • Measure voltage between BATT(+) circuit at A/C relay vehicle harness connector and chassis ground. • **Are both voltages greater than 10.5 volts?** 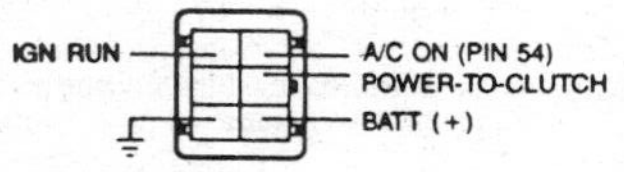 A/C RELAY VEHICLE HARNESS CONNECTOR	Yes ▶ No ▶	GO to KM52. SERVICE open circuit. RECONNECT all components. RE-EVALUATE symptom.
KM52 CHECK POWER-TO-CLUTCH CIRCUIT CONTINUITY • Key off. • A/C relay disconnected. • A/C clutch disconnected. • Measure resistance between power side of A/C clutch vehicle harness connector and Power-To-Clutch circuit at A/C relay vehicle harness connector. • **Is resistance less than 5.0 ohms?**	Yes ▶ No ▶	GO to KM53. SERVICE open circuit. RECONNECT all components. RE-EVALUATE symptom.

FIG. 190 4.0L EEC pinpoint test

WOT A/C Cutout (WAC) A/C Demand — Pinpoint Test KM

TEST STEP	RESULT ▶	ACTION TO TAKE
KM53 CHECK A/C RELAY		
• Key off. • A/C clutch disconnected. • Reconnect A/C relay. • Jumper A/C ON circuit at A/C relay vehicle harness connector to battery ground. • Key on. • Measure voltage between power side of A/C clutch vehicle harness connector and chassis ground. • **Is voltage greater than 10.5 volts?**	Yes ▶ No ▶	Key off. REMOVE jumper. GO to KM54. REPLACE A/C relay. RECONNECT all components. RE-EVALUATE symptom.
KM54 CHECK A/C ON CIRCUIT CONTINUITY		
• Key off. • Disconnect ECU 60 pin connector. Inspect for damaged or pushed out pins, corrosion, loose wires, etc. Service as necessary. • Install breakout box, leave ECU disconnected. • Disconnect A/C relay. • Measure resistance between Test Pin 54 at breakout box and A/C ON circuit at A/C relay vehicle harness connector. • **Is resistance less than 5.0 ohms?**	Yes ▶ No ▶	REPLACE ECU. REMOVE breakout box. RECONNECT all components. RE-EVALUATE symptom. SERVICE open circuit. RECONNECT all components. RE-EVALUATE symptom.
KM60 CHECK ACD CIRCUIT CONTINUITY TO LOW PRESSURE (LP) SWITCH		
• Key off. • A/C demand switch to A/C • Disconnect LP switch. • Measure resistance between A/C demand switch side of LP switch vehicle harness connector and chassis ground. • **Is resistance less than 5.0 ohms?**	Yes ▶ No ▶	GO to KM61. VERIFY operation of A/C demand switch. If OK, SERVICE open circuit. RECONNECT all components. RE-EVALUATE symptom.

FIG. 191 4.0L EEC pinpoint test

WOT A/C Cutout (WAC) A/C Demand — Pinpoint Test KM

TEST STEP	RESULT ▶	ACTION TO TAKE
KM61 MEASURE RESISTANCE OF LP SWITCH		
• Key off. • LP switch disconnected. • Measure resistance of LP switch. • **Is resistance less than 5.0 ohms?**	Yes ▶ No ▶	GO to KM62. RECONNECT all components. RE-EVALUATE symptom.
KM62 CHECK ACD CIRCUIT CONTINUITY FROM LP SWITCH TO PROCESSOR		
• Key off. • LP switch disconnected. • Disconnect ECU 60 pin connector. Inspect for damaged or pushed out pins, corrosion, loose wires, etc. Service as necessary. • Install breakout box, leave ECU disconnected. • Measure resistance between Test Pin 23 at breakout box and ECU side of LP switch vehicle harness connector. • **Is resistance less than 5.0 ohms?**	Yes ▶ No ▶	REPLACE ECU. REMOVE breakout box. RECONNECT all components. RE-EVALUATE SYMPTOM. SERVICE open circuit. RECONNECT all components. RE-EVALUATE symptom.
KM70 SERVICE CODE 539: CHECK A/C INPUT		
Service Code 539 indicates that the A/C demand input to the ECU was low (A/C on) during Self-Test. **NOTE: Before entering this test, verify A/C selector is off. If A/C was on, rerun Quick Test. If Code 539 is present, continue with this test.** • Key off. • A/C off. • Disconnect LP switch. • Measure resistance between A/C demand switch side of LP switch vehicle harness connector and chassis ground. • **Is resistance greater than 10,000 ohms?**	Yes ▶ No ▶	GO to KM71. VERIFY operation of A/C demand switch. If OK, SERVICE short to ground. RECONNECT all components. RERUN Quick Test.
KM71 CHECK LOW PRESSURE (LP) SWITCH		
• Key off. • LP switch disconnected. • Measure resistance between chassis ground and both pins of LP switch. • **Are both resistances greater than 10,000 ohms?**	Yes ▶ No ▶	GO to KM72. REPLACE LP switch. RECONNECT all components. RERUN Quick Test.

FIG. 192 4.0L EEC pinpoint test

WOT A/C Cutout (WAC) A/C Demand — Pinpoint Test KM

TEST STEP	RESULT ▶	ACTION TO TAKE
KM72 CHECK ACD CIRCUIT TO ECU FOR SHORT TO GROUND		
• Key off. • LP switch disconnected. • Disconnect ECU 60 pin connector. Inspect for damaged or pushed out pins, corrosion, loose wires, etc. Service as necessary. • Measure resistance between ECU side of LP switch vehicle harness connector and chassis ground. • **Is resistance greater than 10,000 ohms?**	Yes ▶	REPLACE ECU. RECONNECT all components. RERUN Quick Test.
	No ▶	SERVICE short to ground. RECONNECT all components. RERUN Quick Test.
KM80 A/C ALWAYS ON: CHECK POWER-TO-CLUTCH CIRCUIT FOR SHORT TO POWER		
NOTE: **Before entering this test, verify Code 539 was not received during Self-Test. If Code 539 is present, refer to Section F-16 for proper Pinpoint Test direction.** • Key off. • Disconnect A/C relay. • Disconnect A/C clutch. • Key on. • Measure voltage between power side of A/C clutch vehicle harness connector and battery negative post. • **Is voltage less than 1.0 volt?**	Yes ▶	GO to KM81.
	No ▶	SERVICE short to power. RECONNECT all components. RE-EVALUATE symptom.
KM81 CHECK A/C RELAY		
• Key off. • A/C relay disconnected. • Measure resistance between Power-To-Clutch Pin and both the IGN RUN and BATT(+) Pins at the A/C relay. • Measure resistance between A/C ON Pin and GROUND Pin at A/C relay. • **Are all resistances greater than 10,000 ohms?**	Yes ▶	GO to KM82.
	No ▶	REPLACE A/C relay. RECONNECT all components. RE-EVALUATE symptom.

FIG. 193 4.0L EEC pinpoint test

WOT A/C Cutout (WAC) A/C Demand — Pinpoint Test KM

TEST STEP	RESULT ▶	ACTION TO TAKE
KM82 CHECK A/C ON CIRCUIT FOR SHORT TO GROUND		
• Key off. • A/C relay disconnected. • Disconnect ECU 60 pin connector. Inspect for damaged or pushed out pins, corrosion, loose wires, etc. Service as necessary. • Measure resistance between A/C ON circuit at A/C relay vehicle harness connector and chassis ground. • **Is resistance greater than 10,000 ohms?**	Yes ▶	REPLACE ECU. RECONNECT all components. RE-EVALUATE symptom.
	No ▶	SERVICE short to ground. RECONNECT all components. RE-EVALUATE symptom.

FIG. 194 4.0L EEC pinpoint test

Fuel Pressure Regulator Control (FPRC) Solenoid — Pinpoint Test KN

TEST STEP	RESULT	ACTION TO TAKE
KN1 KOEO SERVICE CODE 554: ENTER OUTPUT STATE CHECK (REFER TO QUICK TEST APPENDIX)		
Service Code 554 indicates a failure in the Fuel Pressure Regulator Control (FPRC) solenoid circuit. Possible causes: — FPRC solenoid — Damaged vacuum hose(s) — Open in harness — Short (to power or ground) in harness — Faulty ECU. **NOTE: Do not use STAR tester for this step. Use a VOM/DVOM.** • Key off. • Disconnect electrical connector on the speed control servo, if equipped. • DVOM on 20 volt scale. • Connect DVOM negative test lead to STO circuit at Self-Test Connector and positive test lead to battery positive. • Jumper STI circuit to SIG RTN at Self-Test connector. • Perform Key On Engine Off Self-Test until completion of Continuous Test codes. • DVOM will indicate less than 1.0 volt when test is completed. • Depress and release throttle. • **Does voltage increase?**	Yes ▶	REMAIN in Output State Check. GO to KN2 .
	No ▶	DEPRESS throttle to WOT and release. If STO voltage does not go high leave equipment hooked up and PERFORM Pinpoint Test QC .
KN2 CHECK FUEL PRESSURE REGULATOR CONTROL SOLENOID ELECTRICAL OPERATION		
• Key on, engine off. • Disconnect FPRC solenoid. • Connect DVOM positive test lead to VPWR pin and negative test lead to FPRC signal circuit at the FPRC solenoid vehicle harness connector. • DVOM on 20 volt scale. • While observing DVOM depress and release throttle several times to cycle solenoid output. • **Does FPRC solenoid output voltage change greater than 1.0 volt?**	Yes ▶	RECONNECT FPRC solenoid. REMOVE jumper. GO to KN3 .
	No ▶	REMOVE jumper. GO to KN5 .

FIG. 195 4.0L EEC pinpoint test

Fuel Pressure Regulator Control (FPRC) Solenoid — Pinpoint Test KN

TEST STEP	RESULT	ACTION TO TAKE
KN3 CHECK VACUUM SIGNAL BETWEEN FUEL PRESSURE REGULATOR AND FPRC SOLENOID		
• Key off. • Disconnect and inspect vacuum hose between fuel pressure regulator and FPRC solenoid for blockage, kinks, etc. Service as necessary. • Start and idle engine for about five minutes to allow it to reach normal operating temperatures. • Key off. • Tee in a standard vacuum gauge between fuel pressure regulator and FPRC solenoid. • Start and idle engine while observing vacuum gauge needle. Observe vacuum gauge needle for about five minutes. • **Did vacuum signal appear after about two minutes of engine idle?**	Yes ▶	REMOVE vacuum gauge.
	No ▶	REMOVE vacuum gauge. GO to KN4 .
KN4 CHECK VACUUM SIGNAL BETWEEN FPRC SOLENOID AND MANIFOLD VACUUM SOURCE		
• Key off. • Tee in a standard vacuum gauge between the FPRC solenoid and manifold vacuum source. • Start and idle engine while observing the vacuum gauge needle. • **Was any vacuum signal present.**	Yes ▶	REPLACE FPRC solenoid. REMOVE vacuum gauge. RERUN Quick Test and/or verify elimination of drive symptom.
	No ▶	REPLACE vacuum hose between FPRC solenoid and source vacuum. REMOVE vacuum gauge. RERUN Quick Test and/or verify elimination of drive symptom.
KN5 CHECK FPRC SOLENOID VPWR		
• Key off. • FPRC solenoid disconnected. • Key on, engine off. • Measure voltage between VPWR at FPRC solenoid vehicle harness connector and battery ground. • **Is voltage greater than 10.5 volts?**	Yes ▶	GO to KN6 .
	No ▶	SERVICE open in VPWR harness circuit. RECONNECT FPRC solenoid. RERUN Quick Test and/or verify elimination of drive symptom.

FIG. 196 4.0L EEC pinpoint test

Fuel Pressure Regulator Control (FPRC) Solenoid — Pinpoint Test KN

TEST STEP	RESULT	ACTION TO TAKE
KN6 CHECK FPRC CIRCUIT CONTINUITY • Key off. • FPRC solenoid disconnected • Disconnect ECU 60 pin connector. Inspect for damaged or pushed out pins, corrosion, loose wires, etc. Service as necessary. • Install breakout box, leave ECU disconnected. • Measure resistance between Test Pin 13 at breakout box and FPRC circuit at solenoid vehicle harness connector. • **Is resistance less than 5.0 ohms?**	Yes ▶	GO to KN7.
	No ▶	SERVICE open circuit. REMOVE breakout box. RECONNECT all components. RERUN Quick Test and/or verify elimination of drive symptom.
KN7 CHECK FPRC CIRCUIT FOR SHORT TO POWER AND GROUND • Key off. • FPRC solenoid disconnected. • Breakout box installed, ECU disconnected. • Measure resistance betwen Test Pin 13 and Test Pins 37 and 57 at Breakout Box. • Measure resistance between Test Pin 13 and Test Pins 40, 46 and 60 at breakout box. • **Is each resistance greater than 10,000 ohms?**	Yes ▶	REPLACE ECU. REMOVE breakout box. RECONNECT all components. RERUN Quick Test and/or verify elimination of drive symptom.
	No ▶	SERVICE short circuit. REMOVE breakout box. RECONNECT all components. RERUN Quick Test and/or verify elimination of drive symptom.

FIG. 197 4.0L EEC pinpoint test

Dynamic Response Test — Pinpoint Test M

TEST STEP	RESULT	ACTION TO TAKE
M1 SERVICE CODE 77/538 SYSTEM FAILED TO RECOGNIZE BRIEF WOT **NOTE: A brief snap of the throttle may not be sufficient to pass this test. Be sure to go to WOT and return.** • Rerun Engine Running Self-Test. Be sure operator is familiar with the Engine Running format which proceeds as follows: — Start engine. — Activate Self-Test. — ID Code 2 (0); start of test. — Dynamic Response code 1 (0); perform brief WOT. — Testing over. — Service code output begins. • **Is Code 77 or 538 still present?**	Yes ▶	GO to M2.
	No ▶	Dynamic Response Test passed. SERVICE any other service code(s) received as necessary.
M2 DID ENGINE ACHIEVE GREATER THAN 2000 RPM? • **During the WOT in the Dynamic response test, did the engine achieve greater than 2000 rpm?**	Yes ▶	REPLACE ECU RERUN Quick Test.
	No ▶	CHECK for conditions that would present engine from achieving greater than 2000 rpm (binding throttle linkage, etc).

FIG. 198 4.0L EEC pinpoint test

Mass Air Flow (MAF) Sensor — Pinpoint Test — DC

TEST STEP	RESULT ▶	ACTION TO TAKE
DC1 SERVICE CODE 26/159: CHECK VPWR CIRCUIT VOLTAGE		
Service Code 26/159 indicates that the Mass Air Flow (MAF) sensor is out of Self-Test range. Key On Engine Off Service Code 26/159 indicates that the MAF Signal was greater than .70 volts during Key On, Engine Off Self-Test. Key On Engine Running Service Code 26/159 indicates that the MAF Signal was not between .20 and 1.50 volts during Key On Engine Running Self-Test. **NOTE: Service Code 26/159 could be generated by the garage exhaust ventilation system. Remove ventilation system and properly vent to outside atmosphere before rerunning Self-Test.** Possible causes: — Faulty MAF sensor. — Faulty ECU. • Key off. • Disconnect MAF sensor. • Voltmeter on 20 volt scale. • Key on, engine off. • Measure voltage between VPWR circuit at the MAF sensor vehicle harness connector and battery negative post. • **Is voltage greater than 10.5 volts?**	Yes ▶ No ▶	GO to DC2 . SERVICE open in VPWR circuit. RERUN Quick Test.
DC2 CHECK MAF SENSOR GROUND		
• Key on, engine off. • MAF sensor disconnected. • Voltmeter on 20 volt scale. • Measure voltage between VPWR circuit and PWR GND circuit at the MAF sensor vehicle harness connector. • **Is voltage greater than 10.5 volts?**	Yes ▶ No ▶	GO to DC10 . SERVICE open PWR GND circuit. RECONNECT MAF sensor. RERUN Quick Test.

FIG. 199 4.0L EEC pinpoint test

Mass Air Flow (MAF) Sensor — Pinpoint Test — DC

TEST STEP	RESULT ▶	ACTION TO TAKE
DC10 SERVICE CODE 66/157 OR 72/129: CHECK CONTINUITY OF MAF AND VPWR CIRCUITS		
Service Code 66/157 indicates that the Mass Air Flow (MAF) sensor signal went below .40 volts sometime during last 80 warm-up cycles. Engine Running Service Code 72/129 indicates insufficient MAF change during Dynamic Response Test. Possible causes: — Open MAF circuit. — Open VPWR circuit to MAF sensor. — Open PWR GND circuit to MAF sensor. — Open MAF RTN circuit to MAF sensor. — MAF circuit shorted to ground. — Faulty ECU. — Faulty MAF sensor. — Air leak before or after MAF sensor. — MAF sensor disconnected. • Key off. • Disconnect MAF sensor. • Disconnect ECU 60 Pin connector. Inspect for damaged or pushed out pins, corrosion, loose wires, etc. Service as necessary. • Install breakout box, leave ECU disconnected. • Ohmmeter on 200 ohm scale. • Measure resistance between VPWR circuit at the MAF sensor vehicle harness connector and Test Pins 37 and 57 at the breakout box. • Measure resistance between MAF circuit at the MAF sensor vehicle harness connector and Test Pin 14 at the breakout box. • **Is each resistance less than 5 ohms?**	Yes ▶ No ▶	GO to DC11 . SERVICE open circuit. REMOVE breakout box. RECONNECT all components. RERUN Quick Test.

FIG. 200 4.0L EEC pinpoint test

Mass Air Flow (MAF) Sensor — Pinpoint Test — DC

TEST STEP	RESULT ▶	ACTION TO TAKE
DC11 CHECK MAF CIRCUIT FOR SHORTS TO GROUND AND MAF RTN CIRCUIT • Key off. • MAF sensor disconnected. • Breakout box installed, ECU disconnected. • Ohmmeter on 200,000 ohm scale. • Measure resistance between Test Pin 14 and Test Pins 15, 40 and 60 at the breakout box. • **Is each resistance greater than 10,000 ohms?**	Yes ▶ No ▶	GO to DC12. SERVICE short circuit(s). REMOVE breakout box. RECONNECT all components. RERUN Quick Test.
DC12 CHECK CONTINUITY OF PWR GND CIRCUIT • Key off. • MAF sensor disconnected. • Breakout box installed, ECU disconnected. • Ohmmeter on 200 ohm scale. • Measure resistance between PWR GND circuit at the MAF sensor vehicle harness connector and battery negative post. • **Is resistance less than 10 ohms?**	Yes ▶ No ▶	GO to DC13. SERVICE open circuit. REMOVE breakout box. RECONNECT all components. RERUN Quick Test.
DC13 CHECK CONTINUITY OF MAF RTN CIRCUIT • Key off. • MAF sensor disconnected. • Breakout box installed, ECU disconnected. • Ohmmeter on 200 ohm scale. • Measure resistance between MAF RTN circuit at the MAF sensor vehicle harness connector and Test Pin 15 at the breakout box. • **Is resistance less than 5 ohms?**	Yes ▶ No ▶	GO to DC14. SERVICE open circuit. REMOVE breakout box. RECONNECT all components. RERUN Quick Test.

FIG. 201 4.0L EEC pinpoint test

Mass Air Flow (MAF) Sensor — Pinpoint Test — DC

TEST STEP	RESULT ▶	ACTION TO TAKE
DC14 CHECK MAF CIRCUIT FOR SHORT TO GROUND • Key off. • MAF sensor disconnected. • Breakout box installed. • Connect ECU to breakout box. • Ohmmeter on 200,000 ohm scale. • Measure resistance between Test Pin 14 and Test Pins 15, 40 and 60 at the breakout box. • **Is each resistance greater than 10,000 ohms?**	Yes ▶ No ▶	GO to DC15. REPLACE ECU. REMOVE breakout box. RECONNECT MAF sensor. RERUN Quick Test.
DC15 CHECK MAF CIRCUIT OUTPUT • Key off. • Reconnect MAF sensor. • Breakout box installed, ECU connected. • Voltmeter on 20 volt scale. • Key on, engine running. • Measure voltage between Test Pin 14 at the breakout box and battery negative post. • **Is voltage between .36 and 1.50 volts?**	Yes ▶ No ▶	REPLACE ECU. REMOVE breakout box. RERUN Quick Test. REPLACE MAF sensor. REMOVE breakout box. RECONNECT ECU. RERUN Quick Test.
DC16 CHECK MAF CIRCUIT OUTPUT • Key off. • Reconnect MAF sensor. • Breakout box installed, ECU connected. • Key on, engine running. • Measure voltage between Test Pin 14 and Test Pin 15 at the breakout box. • **Is voltage between .36 and 1.50 volts?**	Yes ▶ No ▶	REPLACE ECU. REMOVE breakout box. RERUN Quick Test. REPLACE MAF sensor. REMOVE breakout box. RECONNECT ECU. RERUN Quick Test.

FIG. 202 4.0L EEC pinpoint test

Mass Air Flow (MAF) Sensor — Pinpoint Test DC

TEST STEP	RESULT ▶	ACTION TO TAKE
DC20 SERVICE CODE 56/158: RERUN SELF-TEST WITH MAF SENSOR DISCONNECTED		
Service Code 56/158 indicates that the Mass Air Flow (MAF) sensor signal went above 4.5 volts during normal engine operation (continuous) or during Self-Test. • Key off. • Disconnect MAF sensor. • Start engine, idle one minute. • Key off. • Rerun Key On Engine Off Self-Test. • **Is Service Code 66 or 157 present?**	Yes ▶ No ▶	REPLACE MAF sensor. RERUN Quick Test. GO to DC21.
DC21 CHECK MAF CIRCUIT FOR SHORT TO VPWR		
• Key off. • MAF sensor disconnected. • Disconnect ECU 60 Pin connector. Inspect for damaged or pushed out pins, corrosion, loose wires, etc. Service as necessary. • Install breakout box, leave ECU disconnected. • Ohmmeter on 200,000 ohm scale. • Measure resistance between MAF circuit and VPWR circuit at the MAF sensor vehicle harness connector. • **Is resistance greater than 10,000 ohms?**	Yes ▶ No ▶	REPLACE ECU. REMOVE breakout box. RECONNECT MAF sensor. RERUN Quick Test. SERVICE short circuit. REMOVE breakout box. RECONNECT all components. RERUN Quick Test.

FIG. 203 4.0L EEC pinpoint test

Throttle Position (TP) Sensor — Pinpoint Test DH

TEST STEP	RESULT ▶	ACTION TO TAKE
DH1 ENGINE RUNNING SERVICE CODE 23/121: CHECK FOR OTHER SERVICE CODES		
Service Code 23/121 indicates that the Throttle Position (TP) sensor's rotational setting may be out of Self-Test range. Possible causes are: — Binding throttle linkage. — TP sensor may not be seated properly (tightened down). — Faulty TP sensor. — Faulty ECU. • Check for Codes 31/327 in Key On Engine Running Self-Test. • **Are either of the above codes present with Code 23 or 121?**	Yes ▶ No ▶	RETURN to the Key On Engine Running Service Code chart and PROCEED as directed with Code 31/327. GO to DH2.
DC2 SERVICE CODE 23/121: CHECK FOR STUCK THROTTLE PLATE		
Service Code 23/121 indicates that the Throttle Position (TP) sensor's rotational setting may be out of Self-Test range. Possible causes are: — Binding throttle linkage. — TP sensor may not be seated properly (tightened down). — Faulty TP sensor. — Faulty ECU. • Visually inspect throttle body and throttle linkage for binding or sticking. • Verify the throttle linkage is at mechanical/closed throttle. Check for: binding throttle linkage, speed control linkage, vacuum line/electrical harness interference, etc. • **Does throttle move freely and return to closed throttle position?**	Yes ▶ No ▶	GO to DH3. SERVICE as necessary. RERUN Quick Test.

FIG. 204 4.0L EEC pinpoint test

Throttle Position (TP) Sensor — Pinpoint Test DH

TEST STEP	RESULT ▶	ACTION TO TAKE
DH3 SERVICE CODE 53/123: ATTEMPT TO GENERATE CODE 63/122 Service Code 53/153 indicates that the Throttle Position (TP) sensor signal is greater than the Self-Test maximum value. Possible causes are: — TP sensor may not be seated properly (tightened down). — Faulty TP sensor. — Short to power in harness. — Faulty ECU. • Key off, wait 10 seconds. • Disconnect TP sensor. Inspect for damaged or pushed out pins, corrosion, loose wires, etc. Service as necessary. • Rerun Key On Engine Off Self-Test. • **Is Code 63 or 122 present (ignore all other codes)?**	Yes ▶ No ▶	GO to DH4. GO to DH6.
DH4 CHECK VREF CIRCUIT VOLTAGE • Key off, wait 10 seconds. • TP sensor disconnected. • Voltmeter on 20 volt scale. • Key on, engine off. • Measure voltage between VREF circuit and SIG RTN circuit at the TP sensor vehicle harness connector. • **Is voltage between 4.0 and 6.0 volts?**	Yes ▶ No ▶	REPLACE TP sensor. RERUN Quick Test. RECONNECT TP sensor. GO to Pinpoint Test Step C1.

FIG. 205 4.0L EEC pinpoint test

Throttle Position (TP) Sensor — Pinpoint Test DH

TEST STEP	RESULT ▶	ACTION TO TAKE
DH6 CHECK TP CIRCUIT FOR SHORTS TO POWER • Key off, wait 10 seconds. • TP sensor disconnected. • Disconnect ECU 60 pin connector. Inspect for damaged or pushed out pins, corrosion, loose wires, etc. Service as necessary. • Install breakout box, leave ECU disconnected. • Ohmmeter on 200,000 ohm scale. • Measure resistance between Test Pin 47 and Test Pins 26 and 57 at the breakout box. • **Is each resistance greater than 10,000 ohms?**	Yes ▶ No ▶	REPLACE ECU. REMOVE breakout box. RECONNECT TP sensor. RERUN Quick Test. SERVICE short circuit. REMOVE breakout box. RECONNECT all components. RERUN Quick Test.

FIG. 206 4.0L EEC pinpoint test

Throttle Position (TP) Sensor — Pinpoint Test DH

TEST STEP	RESULT ▶	ACTION TO TAKE
DH10 SERVICE CODE 63/122: ATTEMPT TO GENERATE CODE 53/123 OR 23/121		
Service Code 63/122 indicates that the Throttle Position (TP) sensor signal is less than the Self-Test minimum value. Possible causes are: — TP sensor may not be seated properly (tightened down). — Faulty TP sensor. — Open harness. — Grounded harness. — Faulty ECU. • Key off, wait 10 seconds. • Disconnect TP sensor. Inspect for damaged or pushed out pins, corrosion, loose wires, etc. Service as necessary. • Jumper VREF circuit to TP circuit at TP sensor vehicle harness connector. • Perform Key On Engine Off Self-Test. **NOTE: If no codes are generated, immediately remove jumper and go directly to DH14.** • **Is Code 53/123 or 23/121 present (ignore all other codes)?**	Yes ▶ No ▶	REPLACE TP sensor. REMOVE jumper. RERUN Quick Test. REMOVE jumper. GO to DH11.
DH11 CHECK VREF CIRCUIT VOLTAGE		
• Key off, wait 10 seconds. • TP sensor disconnected. • Voltmeter on 20 volt scale. • Key on engine off. • Measure voltage between VREF circuit and SIG RTN circuit at the TP sensor vehicle harness connector. • **Is voltage between 4.0 and 6.0 volts?**	Yes ▶ No ▶	GO to DH12. RECONNECT all components. GO to Pinpoint Test Step C1.

FIG. 207 4.0L EEC pinpoint test

Throttle Position (TP) Sensor — Pinpoint Test DH

TEST STEP	RESULT ▶	ACTION TO TAKE
DH12 CHECK TP CIRCUIT CONTINUITY		
• Key off, wait 10 seconds. • TP sensor disconnected. • Disconnect ECU 60 pin connector. Inspect for damaged or pushed out pins, corrosion, loose wires, etc. Service as necessary. • Install breakout box, and leave ECU disconnected. • Ohmmeter on 200 ohm scale. • Measure resistance between TP circuit at the TP sensor vehicle harness connector and Test Pin 47 at the breakout box. • **Is the resistance less than 5.0 ohms?**	Yes ▶ No ▶	GO to DH14. SERVICE open circuit. REMOVE breakout box. RECONNECT all components. RERUN Quick Test.
DH14 CHECK TP CIRCUIT FOR SHORTS TO GROUND		
• Key off, wait 10 seconds. • TP sensor disconnected. • Disconnect ECU 60 pin connector. Inspect for damaged or pushed out pins, corrosion, loose wires, etc. Service as necessary. • Install breakout box, leave ECU disconnected. • Ohmmeter on 200,000 ohm scale. • Measure resistance between Test Pin 47 and Test Pins 40, 46, and 60 at the breakout box. • **Is each resistance greater than 10,000 ohms?**	Yes ▶ No ▶	REPLACE ECU. REMOVE breakout box. RECONNECT all components. RERUN Quick Test. SERVICE short circuit. REMOVE breakout box. RECONNECT all components. RERUN Quick Test.

FIG. 208 4.0L EEC pinpoint test

Throttle Position (TP) Sensor — Pinpoint Test — DH

TEST STEP	RESULT ▶	ACTION TO TAKE
DH20 ENGINE RUNNING SERVICE CODE 73/167: PERFORM PROPER DYNAMIC RESPONSE TEST AT WIDE OPEN THROTTLE		
NOTE: Engine Running Service Code 73/167 indicates the TP sensor did not exceed 25 percent of its rotation during the Dynamic Reponse Test. A complete wide open throttle must be performed during the Dynamic Response portion of the test. • Run Key On Engine Running Self-Test. Be sure a complete WOT is performed during the Dynamic Response portion of the test. • **Is Code 73 or 167 still present?**	Yes ▶ No ▶	GO to DH21. Unable to duplicate Code 73/167 at this time. Running Codes. Otherwise, testing completed.
DH21 CHECK TP SENSOR MOVEMENT DURING DYNAMIC RESPONSE TEST		
• Key off. • Disconnect ECU 60 pin connector. Inspect for damaged or pushed out pins, corrosion, loose wires, etc. Service as necessary. • Install breakout box and connect ECU to breakout box. • Voltmeter on 20 volt scale. • Connect Voltmeter to Test Pin 47 and Test Pin 46 at the breakout box. • Rerun Engine Running Self-Test with a proper WOT Dynamic Response portion of the test. • **Does voltage increase to greater than 3.5 volts during the Dynamic Response Test?**	Yes ▶ No ▶	REPLACE ECU. REMOVE breakout box. RERUN Quick Test. VERIFY TP sensor is properly installed to throttle body. If OK, REPLACE TP sensor. RERUN Quick Test.

FIG. 209 4.0L EEC pinpoint test

Throttle Position (TP) Sensor — Pinpoint Test — DH

TEST STEP	RESULT ▶	ACTION TO TAKE
DH90 CONTINUOUS MEMORY CODE 53/123: MONITOR TP CIRCUIT UNDER SIMULATED ROAD SHOCK		
• Enter Key On Engine Off Continuous Monitor mode. Refer to Quick Test Appendix. • Observe Voltmeter or SUPER STAR II for indication of a fault while performing the following: — Move throttle slowly to WOT position. — Release throttle slowly to closed position and lightly tap on TP sensor (simulate road shock). — Wiggle TP harness connector. • **Does Voltmeter or SUPER STAR II indicate a fault?** POWER OR VREF CIRCUIT VREF TP SIG SIG. RTN ECU HARNESS TP SENSOR	Yes ▶ No ▶	GO to DH91. GO to DH92.
DH91 MEASURE THROTTLE POSITION SIGNAL VOLTAGE WHILE EXERCISING TP SENSOR		
• Key off, wait 10 seconds. • Disconnect ECU 60 pin connector. Inspect for damaged or pushed out pins, corrosion, loose wires, etc. Service as necessary. • Install breakout box and connect ECU to breakout box. • Voltmeter or SUPER STAR II still connected to STO as in previous step. • Connect a VOM from Test Pin 47 to Test Pin 46 at the breakout box. • Voltmeter on 20 volt scale. • Key on, engine off. • While observing VOM, repeat step DH90. • **Does the fault occur below 4.25 volts?**	Yes ▶ No ▶	DISCONNECT and INSPECT connectors. If connector and terminals are good, REPLACE TP sensor, CLEAR Continuous Memory (REFER to Quick Test Appendix). RERUN Quick Test. Throttle position sensor overtravel may have caused the Continuous Memory Code 53/123. VERIFY vehicle harness integrity, GO to DH92.

FIG. 210 4.0L EEC pinpoint test

Throttle Position (TP) Sensor — Pinpoint Test DH

TEST STEP	RESULT ▶	ACTION TO TAKE
DH92 CHECK EEC VEHICLE HARNESS • Still in Key On Engine Off Continuous Monitor mode. • Observe Voltmeter or SUPER STAR II for a fault indication while performing the following: — Referring to the illustration in Step DH90, grasp the vehicle harness close to the sensor connector. Wiggle, shake or bend a small section of the EEC system vehicle harness while working your way to the dash panel. Also wiggle, shake or bend the EEC vehicle harness from the dash panel to the ECU. • **Does Voltmeter or SUPER STAR II indicate a fault?**	Yes ▶ No ▶	ISOLATE fault. SERVICE as necessary. REFER to appropriate figure. CLEAR Continuous Memory RERUN Quick Test. GO to DH93.
DH93 CHECK ECU AND HARNESS CONNECTORS • Key off, wait 10 seconds. • Disconnect ECU 60 pin connector. Inspect for damaged or pushed out pins, corrosion, loose wires, etc. Service as necessary. • **Are connectors and terminals OK?**	No ▶ Yes ▶	SERVICE as necessary. CLEAR Continuous Memory RERUN Quick Test. CLEAR Continuous Memory RERUN Quick Test.

FIG. 211 4.0L EEC pinpoint test

Throttle Position (TP) Sensor — Pinpoint Test DH

TEST STEP	RESULT ▶	ACTION TO TAKE
DH94 CONTINUOUS MEMORY CODE 63/122: MONITOR TP CIRCUIT UNDER SIMULATED ROAD SHOCK • Enter Key On Engine Off Continuous Monitor mode. Refer to Quick Test Appendix. • **Observe Voltmeter or SUPER STAR II for indication of a fault while performing the following:** — Move throttle slowly to WOT position. — Release throttle slowly to closed position. — Lightly tap on TP sensor (simulate road shock). — Wiggle TP harness connector. • **Does Voltmeter or SUPER STAR II indicate a fault?** [Diagram labels: TO GROUND, VREF, TP SIG, SIG. RTN, ECU, HARNESS, TP SENSOR]	Yes ▶ No ▶	**INSPECT connectors. If connectors and terminals are good, REPLACE TP sensor, CLEAR Continuous Memory RERUN Quick Test.** GO to DH95.
DH95 CHECK EEC VEHICLE HARNESS • Still in Key On Engine Off Continuous Monitor mode. • Observe Voltmeter or SUPER STAR II for a fault indication while performing the following: — Referring to the illustration in Step DH94, grasp the vehicle harness close to the sensor connector. Wiggle, shake or bend a small section of the EEC system vehicle harness while working your way to the dash panel. Also wiggle, shake or bend the EEC vehicle harness from the dash panel to the ECU. • **Does Voltmeter or SUPER STAR II indicate a fault?**	Yes ▶ No ▶	ISOLATE fault. SERVICE as necessary. REFER to appropriate figure. CLEAR Continuous Memory RERUN Quick Test. GO to DH96.

FIG. 212 4.0L EEC pinpoint test

Throttle Position (TP) Sensor	Pinpoint Test	DH

TEST STEP	RESULT ▶	ACTION TO TAKE
DH96 CHECK ECU AND HARNESS CONNECTORS		
• Key off, wait 10 seconds. • Disconnect ECU 60 pin connector. Inspect for damaged or pushed out pins, corrosion, loose wires, etc. • **Are connectors and terminals OK?**	No ▶	SERVICE as necessary. CLEAR Continuous Memory. RERUN Quick Test.
	Yes ▶	CLEAR Continuous Memory RERUN Quick Test.

FIG. 213 4.0L EEC pinpoint test

TORQUE SPECIFICATIONS

Component	U.S.	Metric
Air bypass valve bolts		
Navajo	6-8 ft. lbs.	8.16-10.88 Nm
Air chamber-to-bracket bolts		
MPV w/4-cylinders	15 ft. lbs.	20.4 Nm
Pickups	15 ft. lbs.	20.4 Nm
Air intake plenum screws		
MPV w/6-cylinder	115 inch lbs.	12.88 Nm
Air throttle body bolts		
Navajo	76-106 inch lbs.	8.512-11.872 Nm
Delivery pipe bolts		
MPV w/4-cylinders	15 ft. lbs.	20.4 Nm
Pickups	15 ft. lbs.	20.4 Nm
EGR tube nuts		
MPV w/6-cylinders	200 inch lbs.	22.4 Nm
Fuel injector O-ring bolts		
Navajo	7-10 ft. lbs.	10-14 Nm
Fuel line to fuel rail clamps		
MPV w/6-cylinders	10 inch lbs.	1.12 Nm
Fuel pressure regulator bolts		
Pickups	95 inch lbs.	10.64 Nm
MPV w/4-cylinder	95 inch lbs.	10.64 Nm
Fuel pump locking ring		
Navajo	40-45 ft. lbs.	54-61 Nm
Fuel pump mounting bolts		
B2200	14-19 ft. lbs.	19-25 Nm
Fuel rail attaching bolts		
MPV w/6-cylinder	115 inch lbs.	12.88 Nm
Fuel supply line fitting		
Navajo	15-18 ft. lbs.	20.4-24.48 Nm
Fuel tank bolts		
MPV	32-44 ft. lbs.	43-61 Nm
Pressure regulator O-ring nuts		
MPV w/6-cylinder	77 inch lbs.	8.624 Nm
Pressure regulator hose clamps		
MPV w/6-cylinders	10 inch lbs.	1.12 Nm
Pressure regulator screws		
Navajo	6-8 ft. lbs.	8.16-10.88 Nm
Pulsation damper bolt		
MPV w/4-cylinders	95 inch lbs.	10.64 Nm
Pickups	95 inch lbs.	10.64 Nm
Throttle body nuts/bolts		
MPV w/4-cylinders	15 ft. lbs.	20.4 Nm
Navajo	76-106 inch lbs.	8.512-11.872 Nm
Pickups	15 ft. lbs.	20.4 Nm
Upper intake manifold nuts		
Navajo	15-18 ft. lbs.	20-24 Nm
Upper manifold nuts		
Navajo	18 ft. lbs.	24.48 Nm

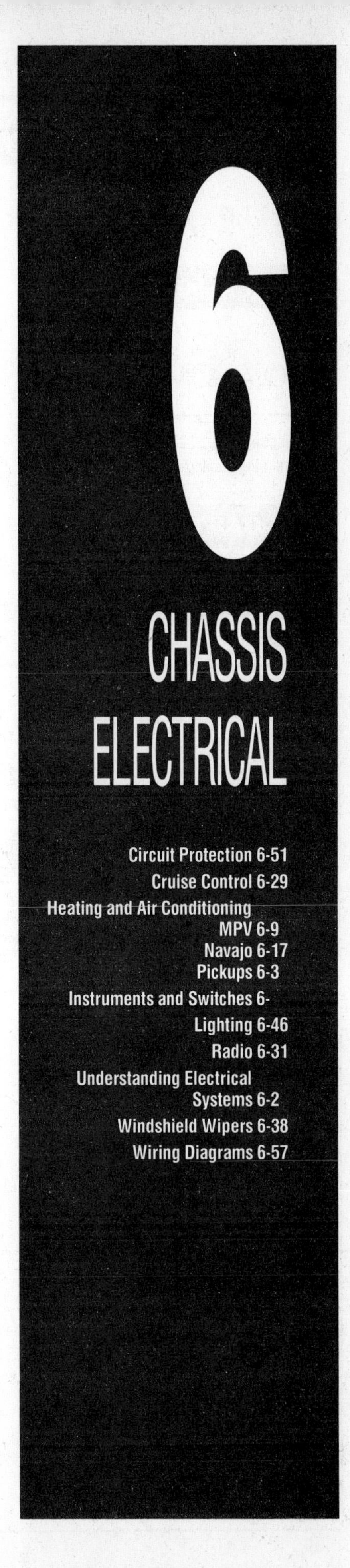
6
CHASSIS
ELECTRICAL
Circuit Protection 6-51
Cruise Control 6-29
Heating and Air Conditioning
MPV 6-9
Navajo 6-17
Pickups 6-3
Instruments and Switches 6-
Lighting 6-46
Radio 6-31
Understanding Electrical
Systems 6-2
Windshield Wipers 6-38
Wiring Diagrams 6-57

PICKUP HEATING AND AIR CONDITIONING

➧ SEE FIGS. 1-12

Heater Assembly

REMOVAL & INSTALLATION

1. Disconnect the battery ground cable.
2. Drain the cooling system.

✲✲ CAUTION

When draining the coolant, keep in mind that cats and dogs are attracted by the ethelyne glycol antifreeze, and are quite likely to drink any that is left in an uncovered container or in puddles on the ground. This will prove fatal in sufficient quantity. Always drain the coolant into a sealable container. Coolant should be reused unless it is contaminated or several years old.

3. Remove the water valve shield at the left side of the heater.
4. Disconnect the two hoses from the left side of the heater.
5. At the heat-defroster door, the water valve and the outside recirculation door, disengage the control cable housing from the mounting clip on the heater. Disconnect each of the three cable wires from the crank arms.
6. Disconnect the fan motor electrical lead.
7. Remove the glove compartment for clearance.
8. Working inside the engine compartment, remove the two retaining nuts and the single bolt and washer which hold the heater to the firewall. Later models also have a retaining bolt inside the passenger compartment which must be removed.
9. Disconnect the two defroster ducts from the heater and remove the heater.
10. Install the heater on the dash so that the heater duct indexes with the air intake duct and the two mounting studs enter their respective holes.
11. From the engine side of the firewall, install the nuts on the mounting studs. While an assistant holds the heater in position, install the mounting bolt.

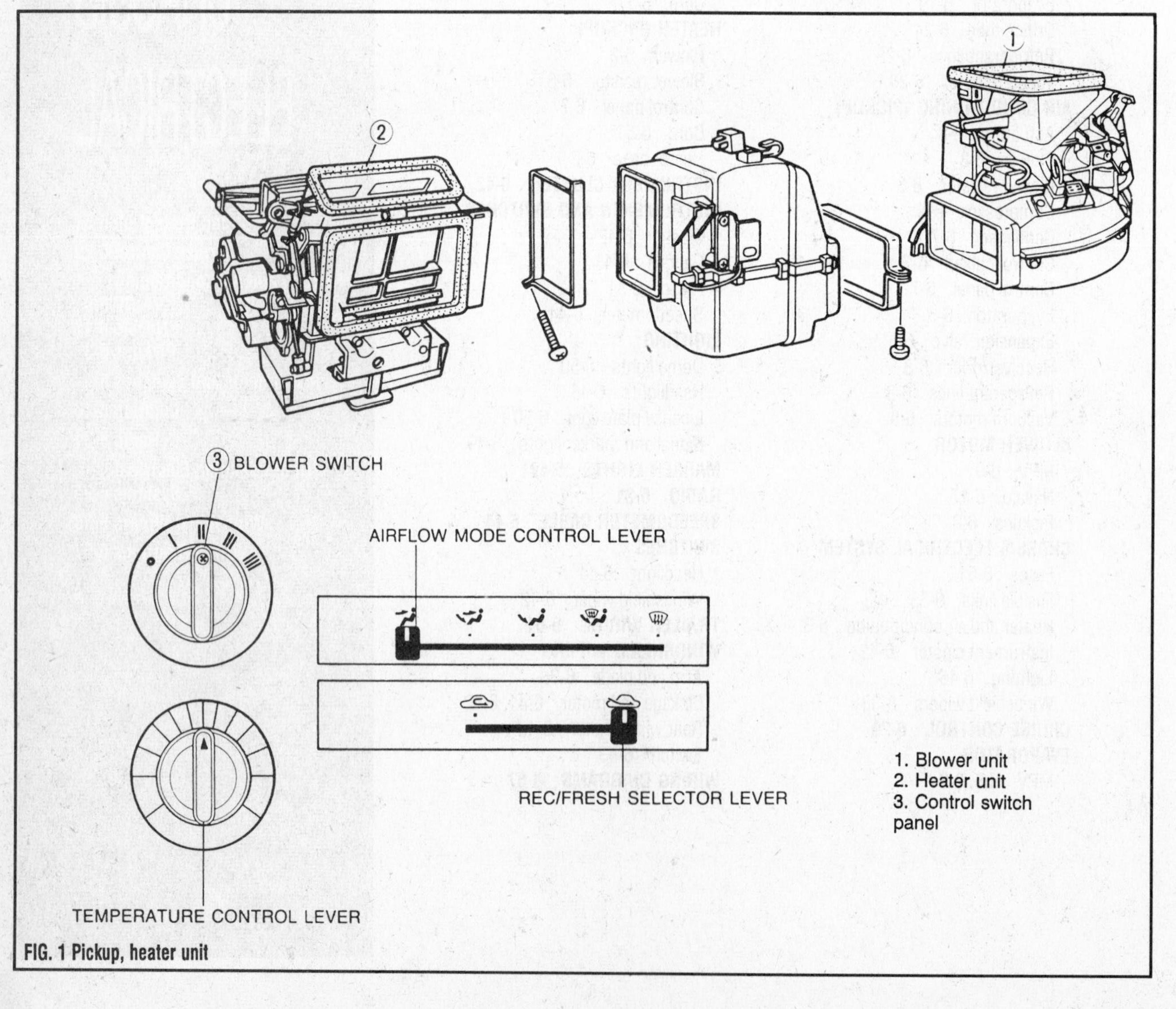

FIG. 1 Pickup, heater unit

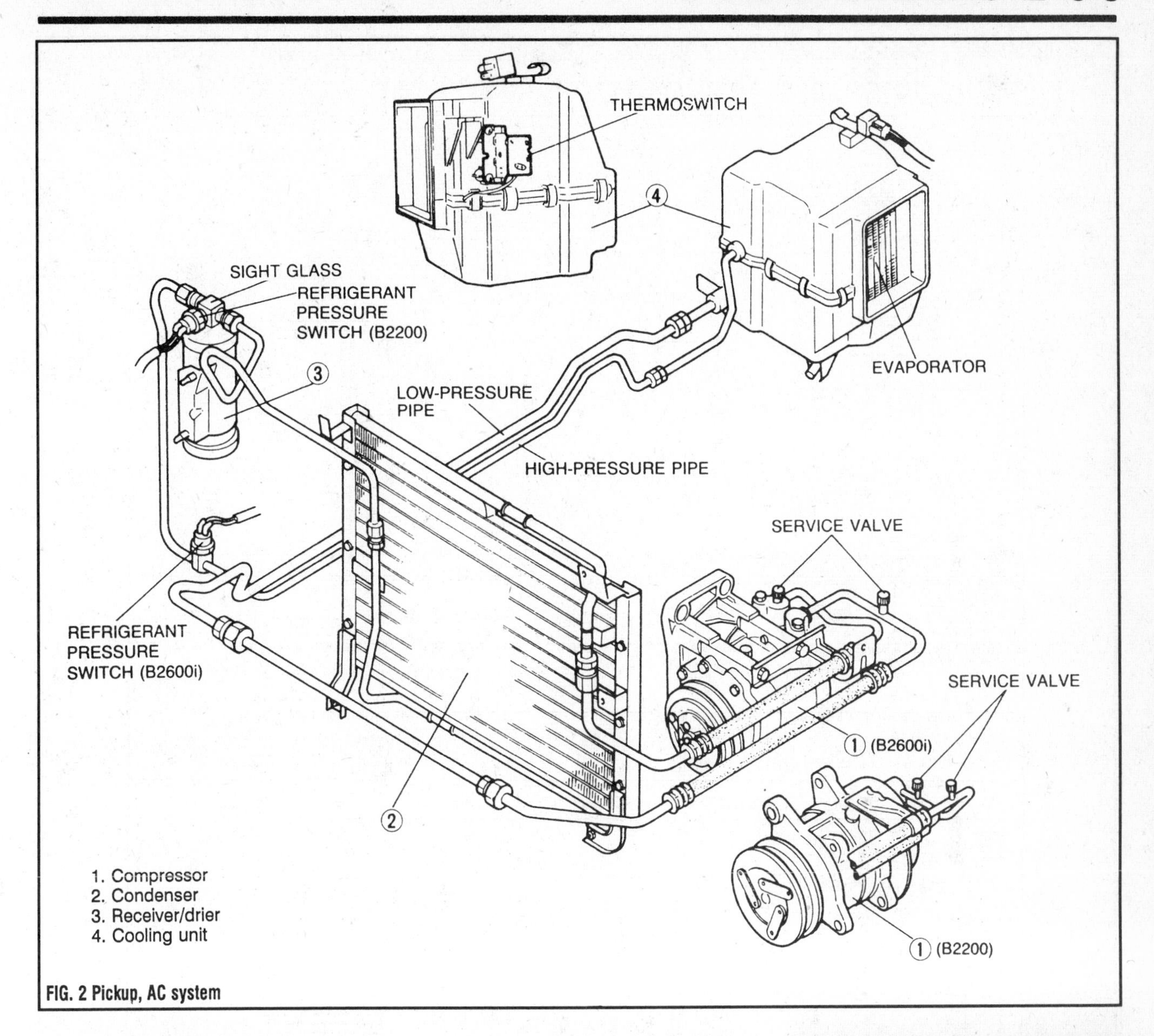

FIG. 2 Pickup, AC system

12. Connect the defroster ducts.
13. Connect the heat-defrost door control cable to the door crank arm. Set the control lever (upper) in the HEAT position and turn the crank arm toward the mounting clip as far as it will go. Engage the cable housing in the clip and install the screw in the clip.
14. Connect the water valve control cable wire to the crank arm on the water valve lever. Locate the cable housing in the mounting clip. Set the control lever in the HOT position and pull the valve plunger and lever to the full outward position. This will move the lever crank arm toward the cable mounting clip as far as it will go. Tighten the clip and screw.
15. Insert the outside recirculation door control cable into the hole in the door crank arm. Bend the wire over and tighten the screw Set the center control lever in the REC position and turn the door crank arm toward the mounting clip as far as it will go. Engage the cable housing in the clip and install the screw in the clip.
16. Connect the fan motor electrical lead.
17. Connect the two hoses to the heater core tubes, at the left side of the heater, and tighten the clamp.
18. Install the water valve shield and tighten the three screws (left side of the heater).
19. Refill the cooling system and connect the battery ground cable.
20. Run the engine and check for leaks. Check the operation of the heater.
21. Replace the glove compartment.

Heater Motor and Blower Fan

REMOVAL & INSTALLATION

1. Remove the heater assembly.
2. Remove the five screws and separate the halves of the heater assembly.
3. Loosen the fan retaining nut. Lightly tap on the nut to loosen the fan. Remove the fan and nut from the motor shaft.
4. Remove the three motor-to-case retaining screws and disconnect the bullet connector to the resistor and ground screw.

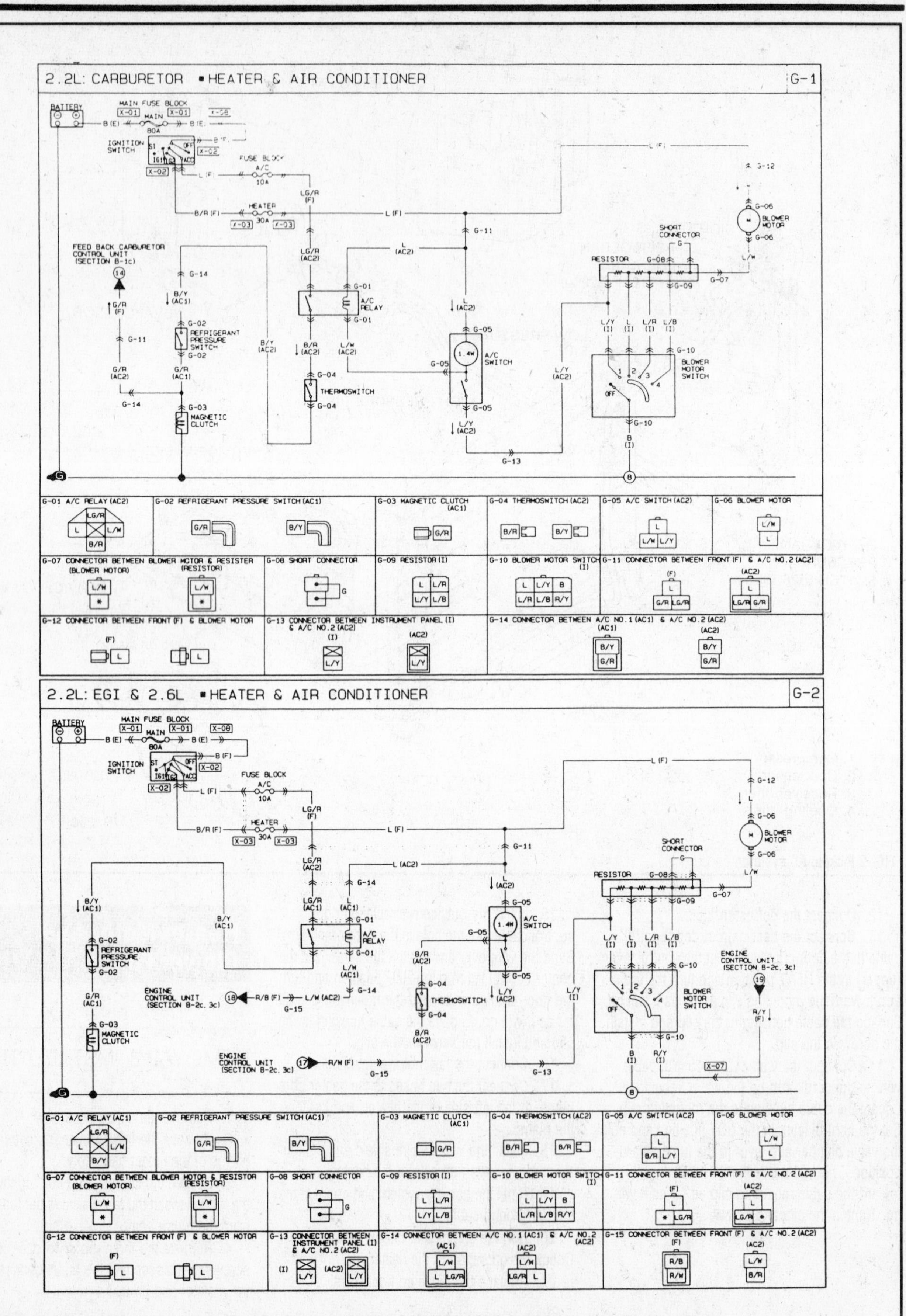

FIG. 3 Pickup, 2.2L carburetor heater and air conditioning circuits, and, 2.2L EGI and 2.6L heater and air conditioning circuits

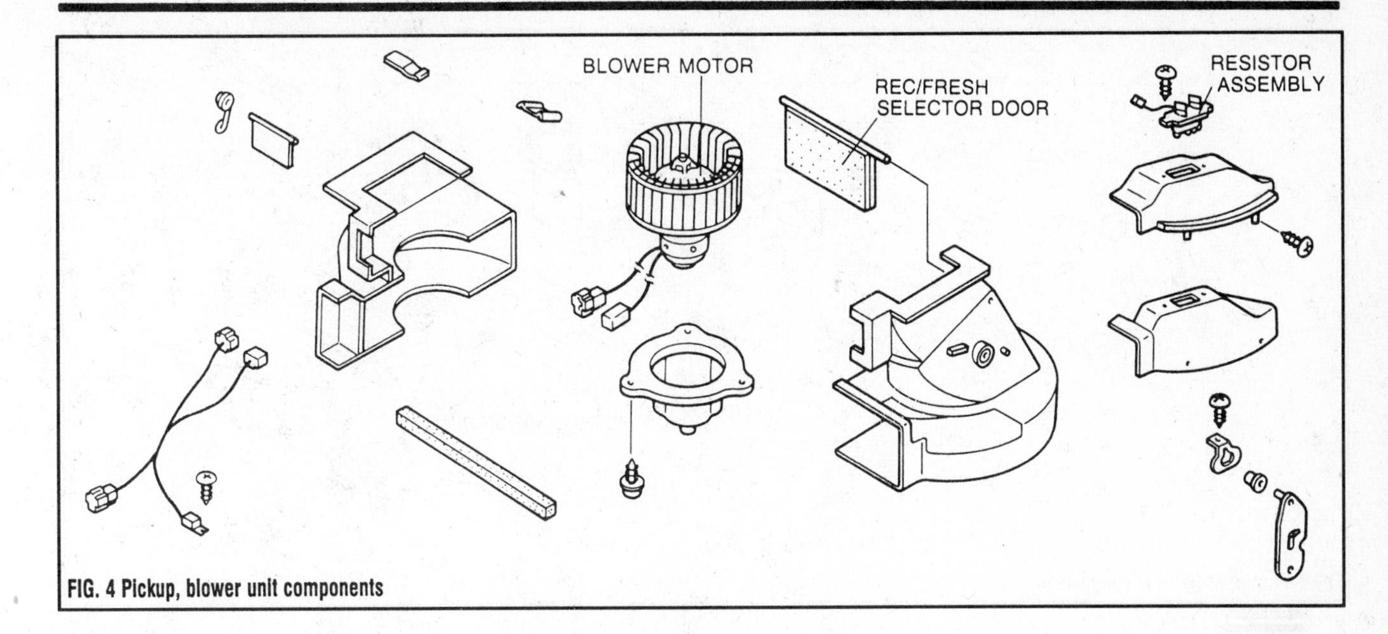

FIG. 4 Pickup, blower unit components

5. Rotate the motor and remove it from the case.
6. Install the motor in the case, rotating it slightly.
7. Install the retaining screws and connect the bullet connector and ground wire.
8. Install the fan on the shaft and install the nut.
9. Assemble the halves together and install the five retaining screws.
10. Install the heater in the trucks. Check the operation of the heater.

Heater Core

REMOVAL & INSTALLATION

1. Remove the heater from the truck.
2. Remove the five screws and separate the halves of the case.
3. Loosen the hose clamps and slide the heater core from the case.
4. Slide the replacement core into the case. at the same time, connect the core tube to the water valve tube with the short hose and clamps.
5. Assemble the halves of the heater and install the five screws.
6. Install the heater in the truck. Check the operation of the heater.

Evaporator Core

REMOVAL & INSTALLATION

1. Discharge the refrigerant system. See Section 1.
2. Disconnect the battery ground cable.
3. Drain the cooling system.

**** CAUTION**

When draining the coolant, keep in mind that cats and dogs are attracted by the ethelyne glycol antifreeze, and are quite likely to drink any that is left in an uncovered container or in puddles on the ground. This will prove fatal in sufficient quantity. Always drain the coolant into a sealable container. Coolant should be reused unless it is contaminated or several years old.

4. Remove the water valve shield at the left side of the heater.
5. Disconnect the two hoses from the left side of the heater.
6. Using a back-up wrench, disconnect the refrigerant lines at the core connectors. Plug all openings at once!
7. At the heat-defroster door, the water valve and the outside recirculation door, disengage the control cable housing from the mounting clip on the heater. Disconnect each of the three cable wires from the crank arms.
8. Disconnect the fan motor electrical lead.
9. Remove the glove compartment for clearance.
10. Working inside the engine compartment, remove the fasteners which hold the heater/evaporator case to the firewall. Later models also have a retaining bolt inside the passenger compartment which must be removed.
11. Disconnect the defroster ducts from the heater/evaporator case and remove the unit.

To Install:

12. Install the unit on the firewall so that the heater duct indexes with the air intake duct and the two mounting studs enter their respective holes.
13. From the engine side of the firewall, install the fasteners. While an assistant holds the unit in position, install the mounting bolts.
14. Connect the defroster ducts.
15. Connect the heat-defrost door control cable to the door crank arm. Set the control lever (upper) in the HEAT position and turn the crank arm toward the mounting clip as far as it will go. Engage the cable housing in the clip and install the screw in the clip.
16. Connect the water valve control cable wire to the crank arm on the water valve lever. Locate the cable housing in the mounting clip.

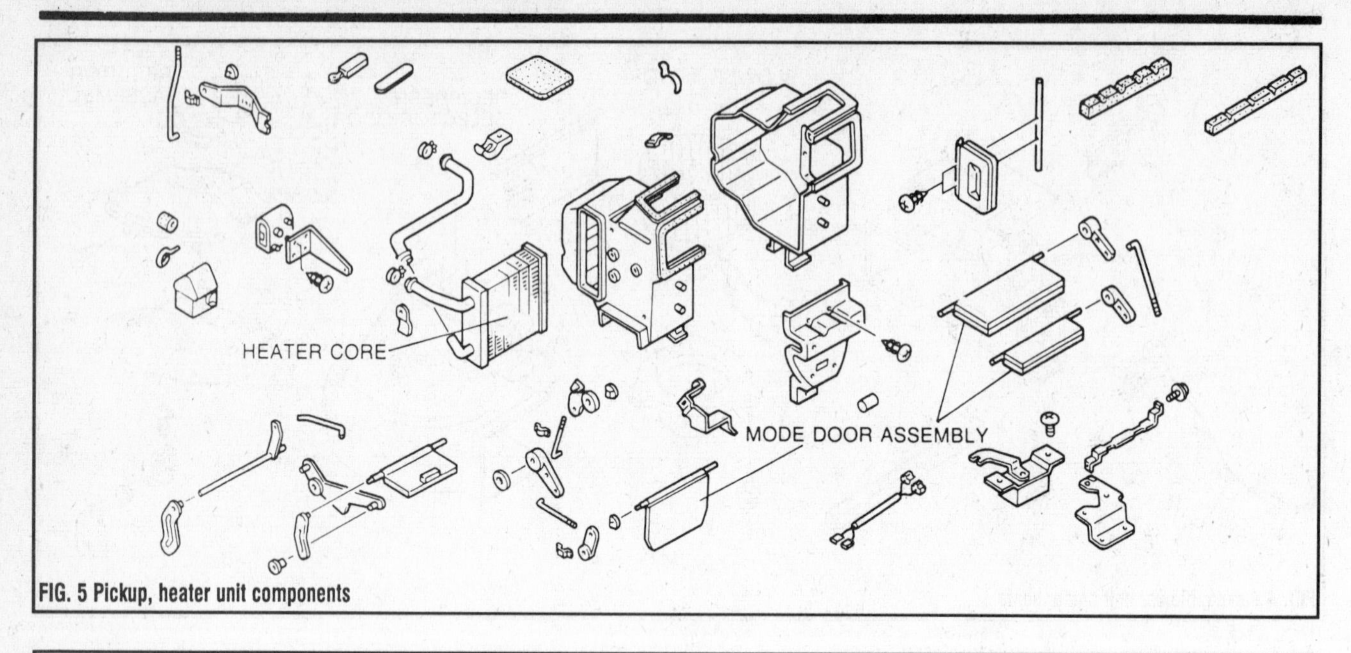

FIG. 5 Pickup, heater unit components

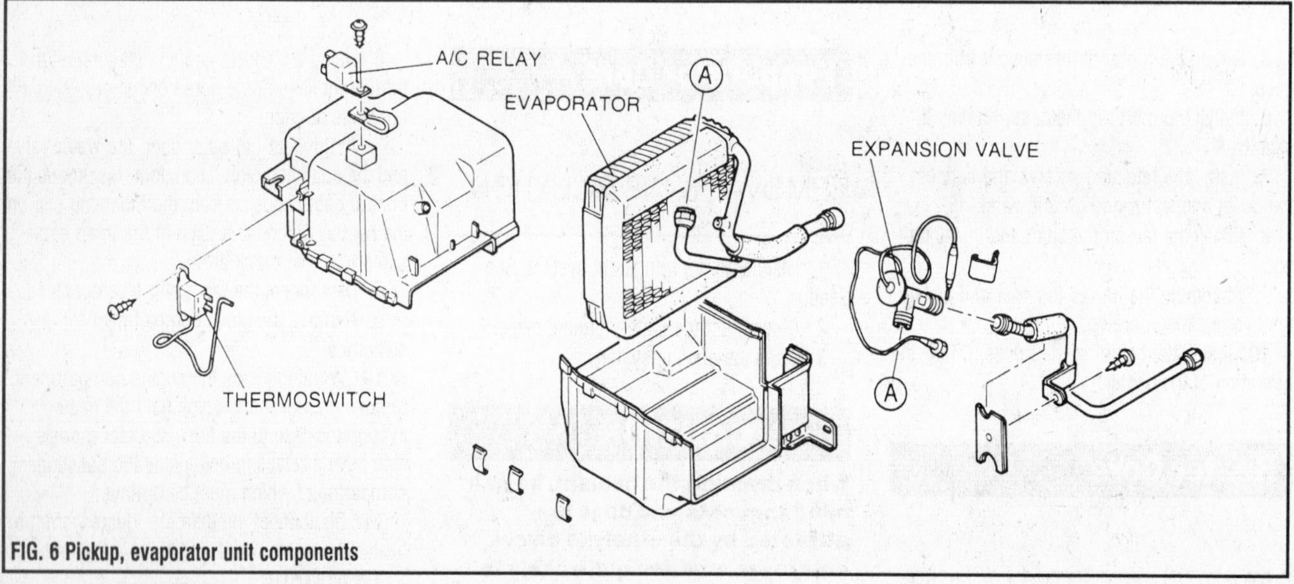

FIG. 6 Pickup, evaporator unit components

Set the control lever in the HOT position and pull the valve plunger and lever to the full outward position. This will move the lever crank arm toward the cable mounting clip as far as it will go. Tighten the clip and screw.

17. Insert the outside recirculation door control cable into the hole in the door crank arm. Bend the wire over and tighten the screw Set the center control lever in the REC position and turn the door crank arm toward the mounting clip as far as it will go. Engage the cable housing in the clip and install the screw in the clip.

18. Connect the fan motor electrical lead.

19. Using a back-up wrench and new O-rings coated with clean refrigerant oil, connect the refrigerant lines to the core tubes.

20. Connect the two hoses to the heater core tubes, at the left side of the heater, and tighten the clamp.

21. Install the water valve shield and tighten the three screws (left side of the heater).

22. Refill the cooling system and connect the battery ground cable.

23. Evacuate, charge and leak-test the refrigerant system. See Section 1.

24. Run the engine and check for leaks. Check the operation of the heater.

25. Replace the glove compartment.

Blower Motor Resistor

REMOVAL & INSTALLATION

1. Disconnect the negative battery cable.
2. Remove the glove box and lower panel, if required.
3. Disconnect the blower motor resistor wire connector.
4. Remove the attaching screw and remove the resistor.
5. Install in reverse order.

AC Compressor

REMOVAL & INSTALLATION

1. Disconnect the negative battery cable.
2. Properly discharge the AC system. See Section 1.

3. Disconnect the wiring harness to the compressor clutch.
4. Loosen the locknut and adjusting bolts and remove the drive belt.
5. Disconnect and plug the refrigerant line at the compressor. Remove the mounting bolts and the compressor.
6. Place the compressor in position and install the mounting bolts. Attach the components in reverse order of removal. Install and properly adjust the drive belt.
7. Evacuate, recharge and test the system.

Condenser

REMOVAL & INSTALLATION

1. Disconnect the negative battery cable.
2. Properly discharge the AC system. See Section 1.
3. Remove the radiator grille and front parking lights.
4. Remove the lower refrigerant line bracket. Disconnect the lower refrigerant line and remove it. Cap all openings immediately to minimize contamination.
5. Remove the hood lock brace and center support bracket.
6. Disconnect the high and low side refrigerant lines. Cap all openings.
7. Remove the condenser attaching nuts and remove the condenser.
8. Install in reverse order. Use new O-rings on all fittings. If a new condenser is installed, add 1.5 to 1.8 oz. of new oil to the compressor during charging.
9. Evacuate, recharge and test the system.

Control Panel

REMOVAL & INSTALLATION

1. Disconnect the negative battery cable.
2. Remove the instrument panel meter hood.
3. Remove the attaching screw, knobs and nuts. Disconnect the AC and cigarette lighter connector.
4. Remove the center panel. Remove the glove compartment. Remove the attaching screws and disconnect the control head wire connectors.
5. Remove the control head assembly. Disconnect the control cables.

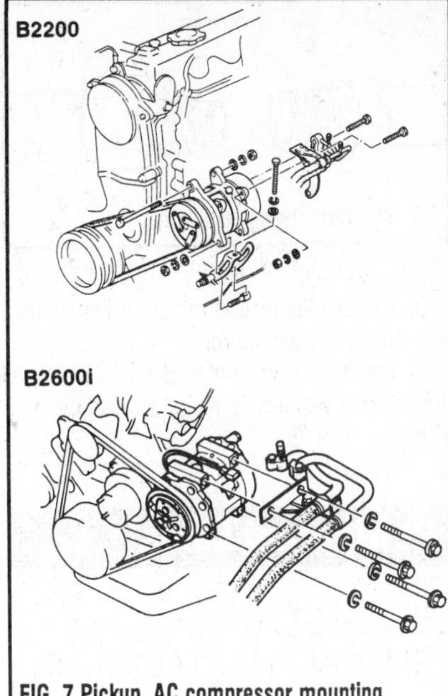

FIG. 7 Pickup, AC compressor mounting

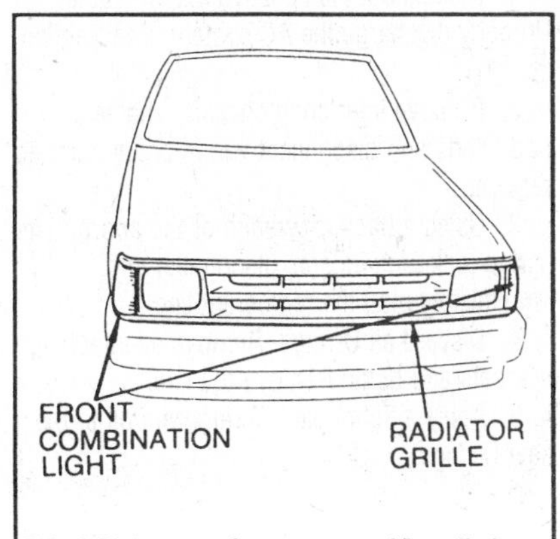

FIG. 8 Pickup, condenser removal/installation

6. Install in reverse order. Connect the negative battery cable.

Control Cables

ADJUSTMENT

1. To adjust the airflow mode cable: Set the airflow mode control lever to the DEFROST position. Install the airflow mode cable with the shutter lever on the heater unit pushed fully forward. Attach the securing clip. Turn the blower switch to position 4 and make sure there are no air leaks from the center and floor outlets.

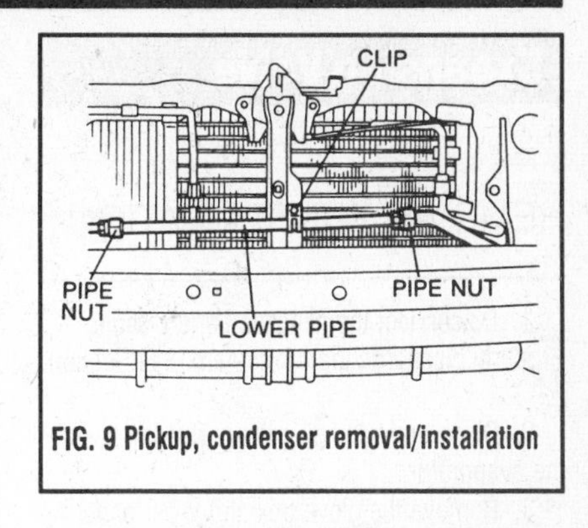

FIG. 9 Pickup, condenser removal/installation

2. To adjust the temperature control cable: Set the temperature control lever to the COLD position. Install the temperature control cable with the shutter lever on the heater unit pushed fully upward. Attach the securing clip. Make sure the temperature control lever move fully from the COLD to HOT position.
3. To adjust the rec/fresh control cable: Set the rec/fresh selector lever to the RECIRCULATE position. Install the rec/fresh cable with the shutter lever on the blower unit pushed fully upward. Attach the securing clip. Make sure the rec/fresh selector move fully from the RECIRCULATE to the FRESH position.

REMOVAL & INSTALLATION

See the preceding Control Head procedure.

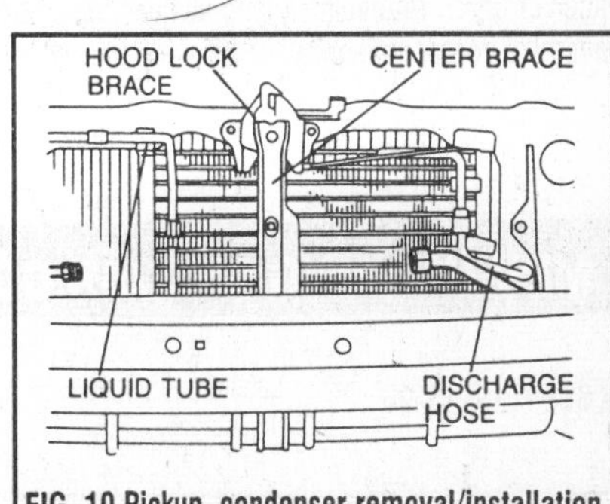

FIG. 10 Pickup, condenser removal/installation

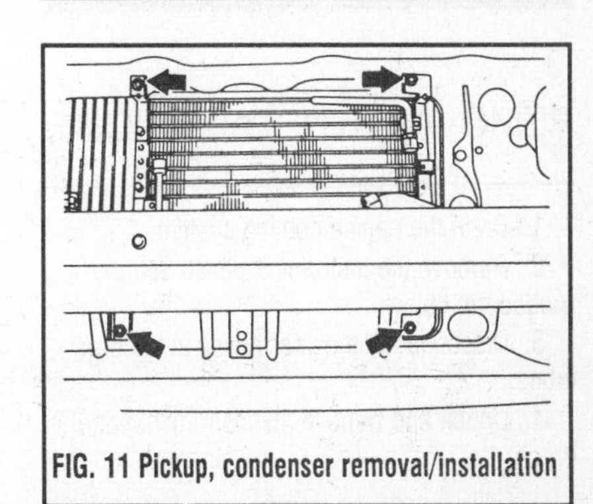
FIG. 11 Pickup, condenser removal/installation

Expansion Valve

REMOVAL & INSTALLATION

1. Disconnect the negative battery cable. Properly discharge the AC system. See Section 1.
2. Disconnect and plug the refrigerant lines at the evaporator.
3. Remove the glove box and lower panel. Remove the air ducts, if required.
4. Remove the evaporator unit seal plates and remove the unit. Remove the evaporator securing clips. Disassemble the unit.
5. Remove the thermo switch. Remove the capillary tube from the outlet pipe. Remove the expansion valve.
6. Install in reverse order. Use new O-rings at the fittings. Evacuate, recharge and test system.

Receiver/Dryer

REMOVAL & INSTALLATION

1. Disconnect the negative battery cable. Properly discharge the AC system. See Section 1.
2. Disconnect the refrigerant lines at the receiver/dryer. Immediately cap all lines to minimize contamination.

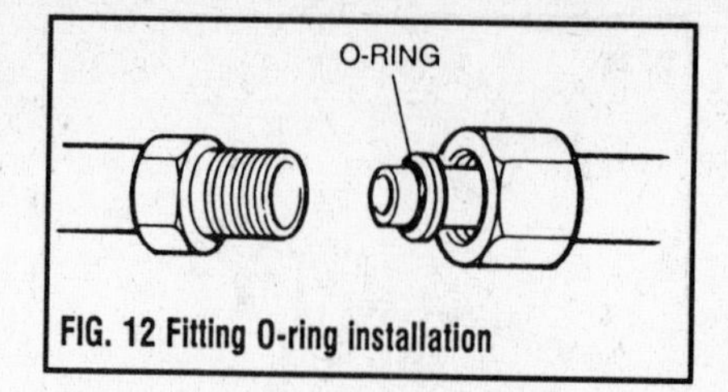

FIG. 12 Fitting O-ring installation

3. Remove the receiver/dryer attaching nuts and remove the receiver/dryer.
4. Install in reverse order. Use new O-ring at the fittings. Evacuate, recharge and test the system.

Refrigerant Lines

REMOVAL & INSTALLATION

1. Disconnect the negative battery cable. Properly discharge the AC system. See Section 1.
2. Remove interfering chassis, engine or body parts and disconnect wiring connectors as required.
3. Using a backup wrench or the appropriate spring lock tool, loosen, disconnect and immediately plug the refrigerant line.
4. Discard all O-rings. Remove all attaching brackets and bolts. Remove the line.
5. Apply a light coat of refrigerant oil to the new O-rings.
6. Connect the line, use the original routing and secure the line with attaching brackets and bolts.
7. Evacuate, recharge and test the system.

Actuators

REMOVAL & INSTALLATION

1. Disconnect the negative battery cable. Locate the actuator.
2. Remove the passenger or drivers side panel, if required.
3. Disconnect the actuator wire connector. Remove the actuator mounting screws. Remove the actuator.
4. Install in reverse order.

Vacuum Motors

REMOVAL & INSTALLATION

1. Disconnect the negative battery cable.
2. Remove the glove box assembly. Disconnect the vacuum hose.
3. Remove the screws attaching the vacuum motor to the plenum. Remove the vacuum motor.
4. Install in reverse order.

MPV HEATING AND AIR CONDITIONING

➧ SEE FIGS. 13-26

Front Heater Case

REMOVAL & INSTALLATION

1. Drain the engine cooling system.
2. Remove the instrument panel. See the procedure, below.
3. Disconnect the heater hoses at the core tubes.
4. Unbolt and remove the instrument panel brace.
5. Support the heater case and remove the mounting nuts.
6. Carefully lift off the case and remove it from the van. Be Careful! There will be a substantial amount of coolant left in the core.
7. Installation is the reverse of removal. Use new sealer around the case. Refill the cooling system. Check for leaks.

Front Heater Core

REMOVAL & INSTALLATION

1. Drain the engine cooling system.
2. Remove the instrument panel. See the procedure, below.
3. Disconnect the heater hoses at the core tubes.
4. Unbolt and remove the instrument panel brace.
5. Support the heater case and remove the mounting nuts.
6. Carefully lift off the case and remove it from the van. Be Careful! There will be a substantial amount of coolant left in the core.
7. Lift out the heater core.
8. Installation is the reverse of removal. Use new sealer around the case and core. Refill the cooling system. Check for leaks.

Front Blower Motor

REMOVAL & INSTALLATION

1. Remove the passenger's side lower panel and lower cover.
2. Disconnect the wiring at the motor connector.
3. Remove the mounting nuts and lift out the blower motor.
4. Installation is the reverse of removal.

Rear Heater Case

REMOVAL & INSTALLATION

1. Disconnect the battery ground.
2. Set the rear heater temperature control knob to WARM.
3. Drain the engine coolant.
4. Remove the driver's seat.
5. Disconnect the heater hoses at the core tubes.
6. Disconnect the wiring at the connector.
7. Remove the mounting bolts and lift out the heater case.
8. Installation is the reverse of removal. Replace any damaged sealer.

Rear Heater Core

REMOVAL & INSTALLATION

1. Disconnect the battery ground.
2. Set the rear heater temperature control knob to WARM.
3. Drain the engine coolant.
4. Remove the driver's seat.
5. Disconnect the heater hoses at the core tubes.
6. Disconnect the wiring at the connector.
7. Remove the mounting bolts and lift out the heater case.
8. Separate the case halves and lift out the core.
9. Installation is the reverse of removal. Replace any damaged sealer.

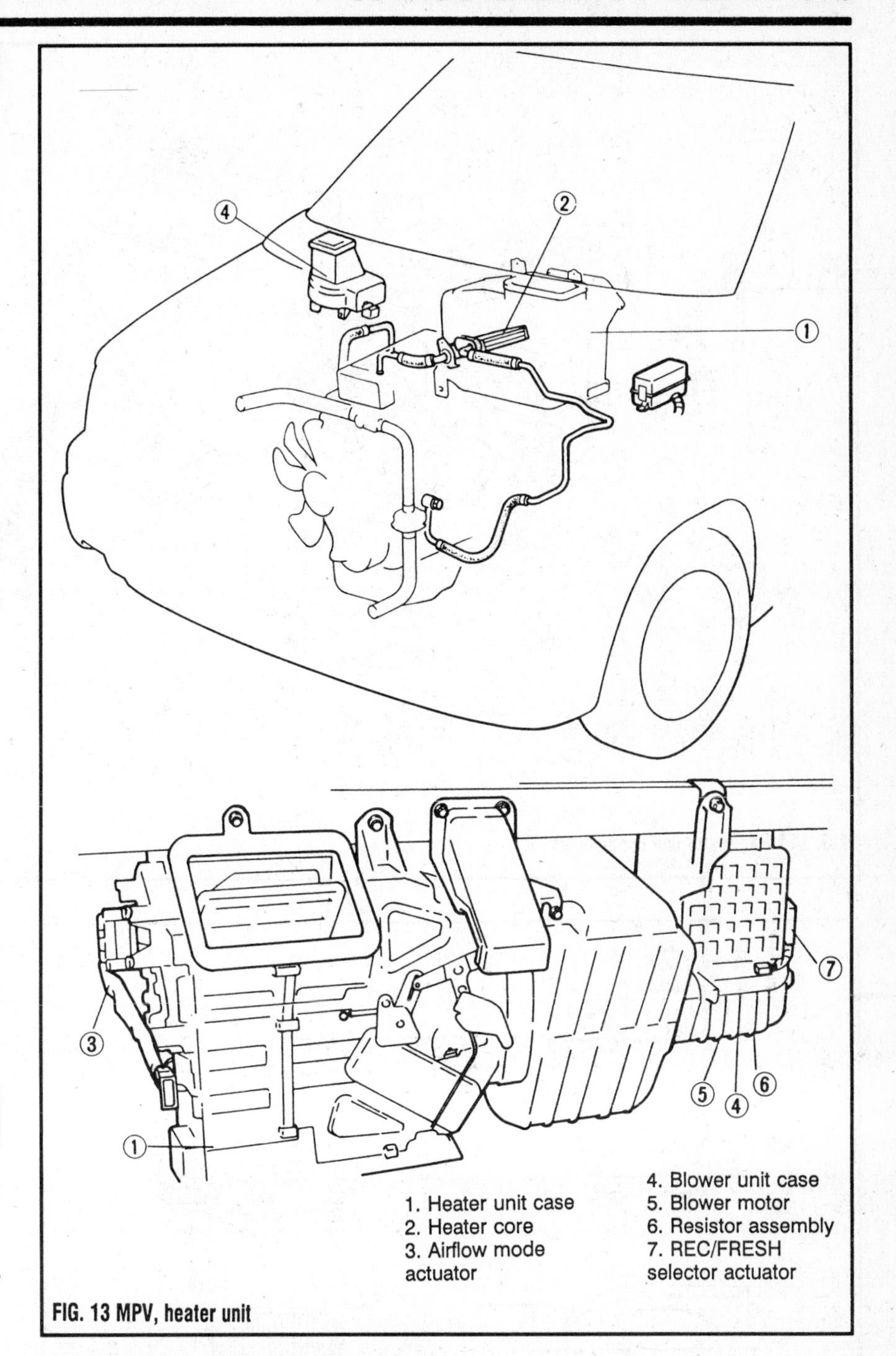

FIG. 13 MPV, heater unit

Rear Heater Blower Motor

REMOVAL & INSTALLATION

1. Disconnect the battery ground.
2. Set the rear heater temperature control knob to WARM.
3. Drain the engine coolant.
4. Remove the driver's seat.
5. Disconnect the heater hoses at the core tubes.
6. Disconnect the wiring at the connector.
7. Remove the mounting bolts and lift out the heater case.
8. Remove the mounting screws and lift out the blower motor.
9. Installation is the reverse of removal. Replace any damaged sealer.

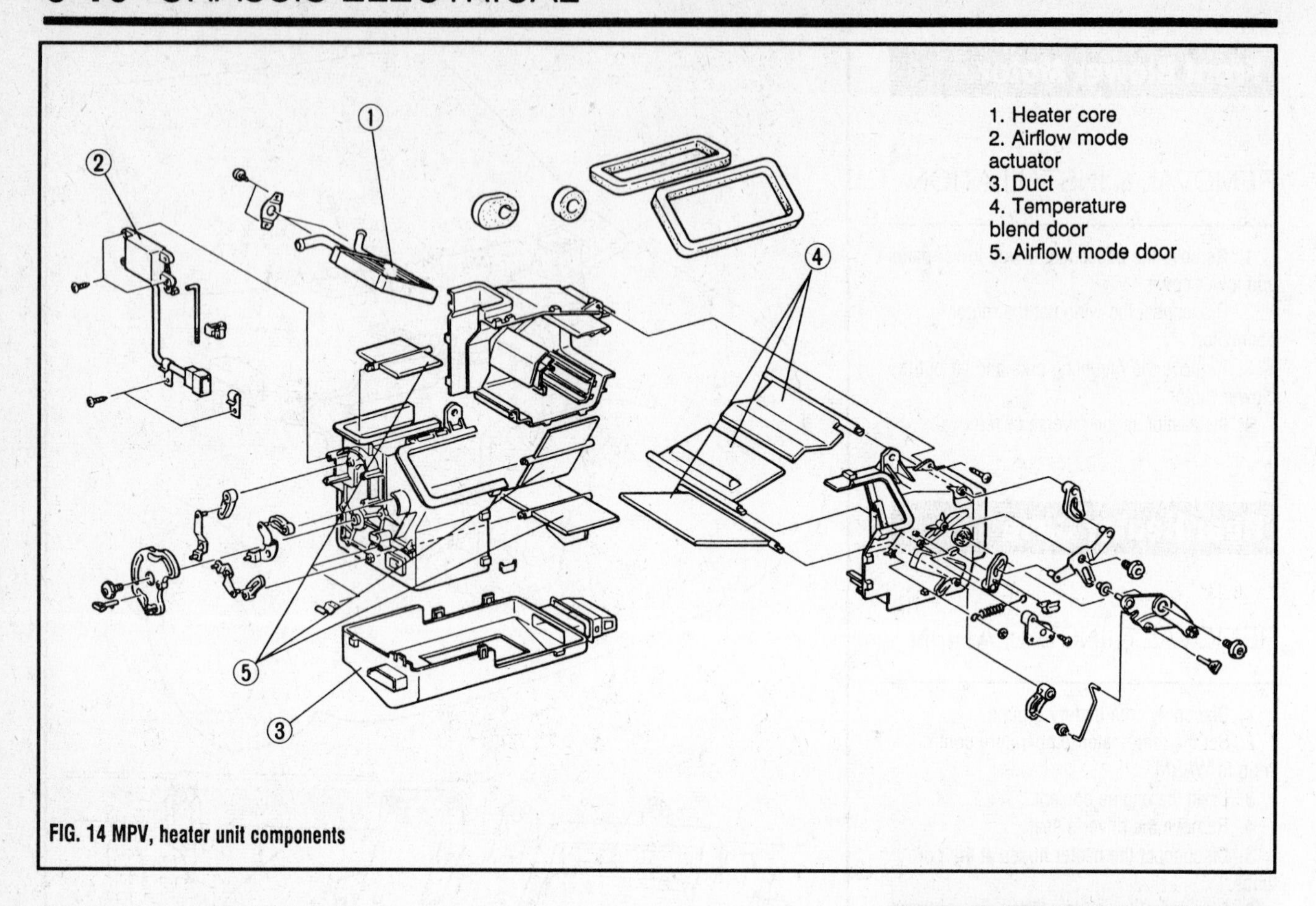

FIG. 14 MPV, heater unit components

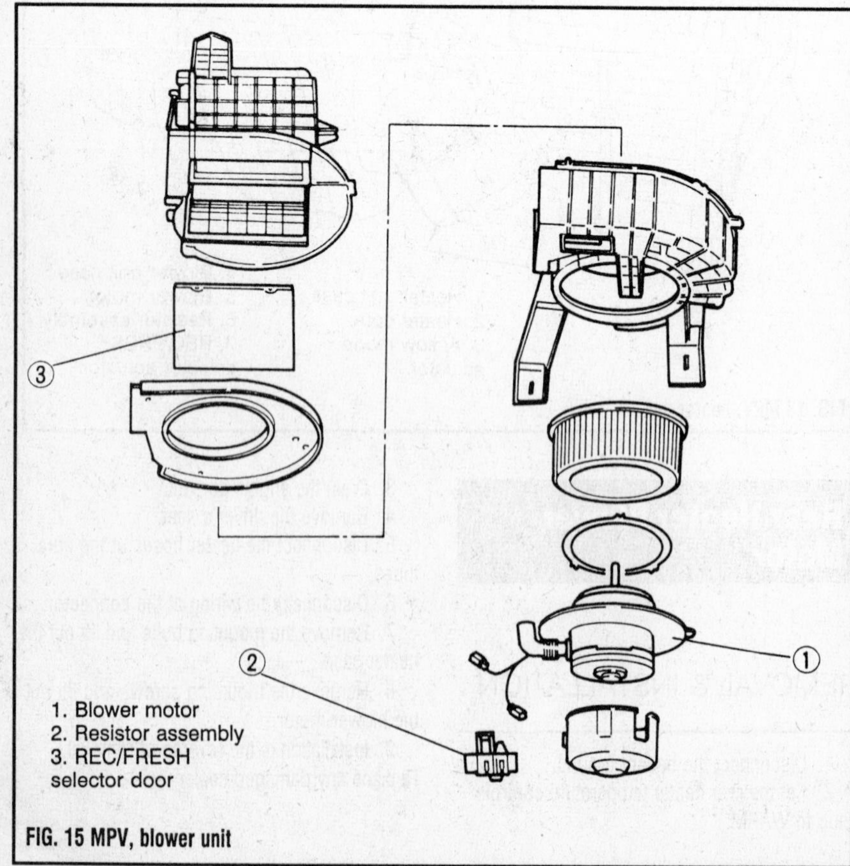

FIG. 15 MPV, blower unit

Front Evaporator Core

REMOVAL & INSTALLATION

1. Disconnect the battery ground cable.
2. Discharge the refrigerant system. See Section 1.
3. Using a back-up wrench, disconnect the refrigerant lines at the core tubes. Cap all openings at once!
4. Remove the grommets around the lines.
5. Remove the glove box and lower instrument panel cover.
6. Disconnect the wiring at the unit.
7. Support the case and remove the mounting nuts. Lift out the case.
8. Separate the case halves and lift out the core.
9. Installation is the reverse of removal. Note the following:
   a. Make sure the case mates properly with the heater case and ducts.
   b. Always use new O-rings coated with clean refrigerant oil at the core tube connections.

c. Always use a back-up wrench when connecting the refrigerant lines.

d. If a new core is being installed, add 50cc of refrigerant oil to the compressor when charging the system

e. Tighten the discharge lines to 10 ft. lbs.; the suction line to 25 ft. lbs.

f. Evacuate, charge and leak-test the system. See Section 1.

Rear Evaporator Core

REMOVAL & INSTALLATION

1. Disconnect the battery ground cable.
2. Discharge the refrigerant system. See Section 1.
3. Remove the left side rear trim panel.
4. Using a back-up wrench, disconnect the refrigerant lines at the core tubes. Cap all openings at once!
5. Disconnect the wiring at the connectors near the rear case.
6. Remove the rear case mounting fasteners and lift out the case.
7. Separate the case halves and lift out the core.
8. Installation is the reverse of removal. Note the following:

a. Always use new O-rings coated with clean refrigerant oil at the core tube connections.

b. Always use a back-up wrench when connecting the refrigerant lines.

c. If a new core is being installed, add 50cc of refrigerant oil to the compressor when charging the system.

d. Tighten the discharge lines to 10 ft. lbs.; the suction line to 25 ft. lbs.

e. Evacuate, charge and leak-test the system. See Section 1.

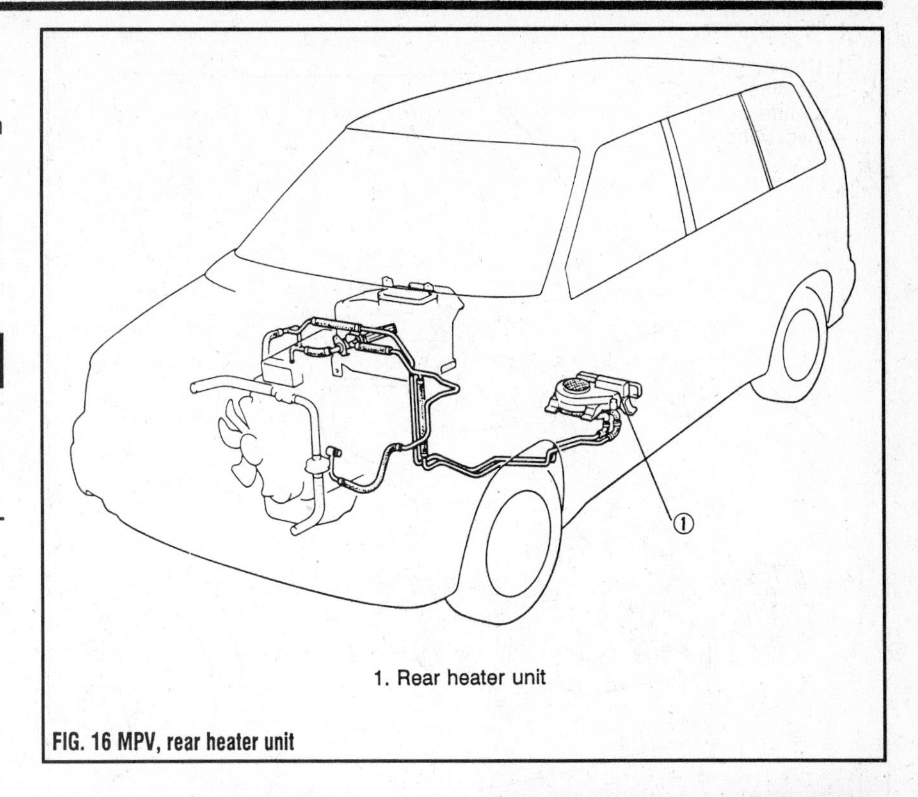

FIG. 16 MPV, rear heater unit

Condenser Fan

REMOVAL & INSTALLATION

1. Disconnect the negative battery cable.
2. Remove the lower grille and the radiator grille.

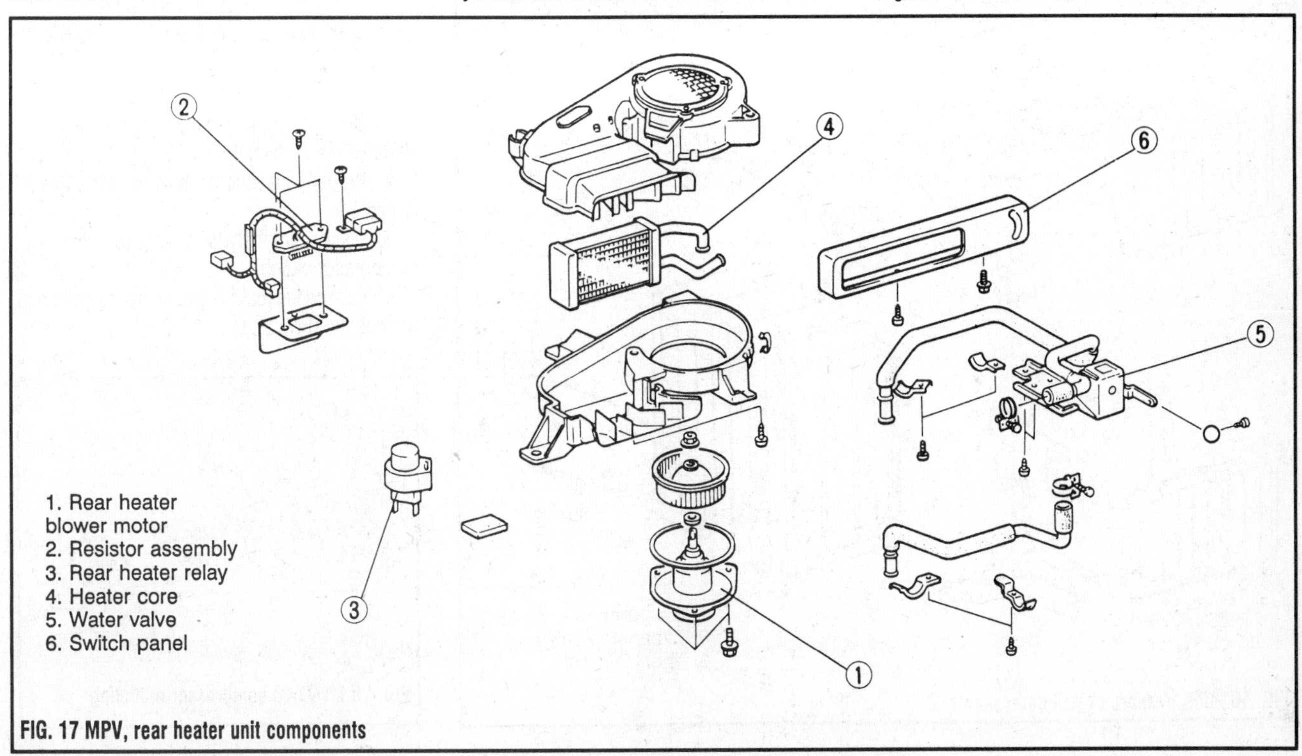

FIG. 17 MPV, rear heater unit components

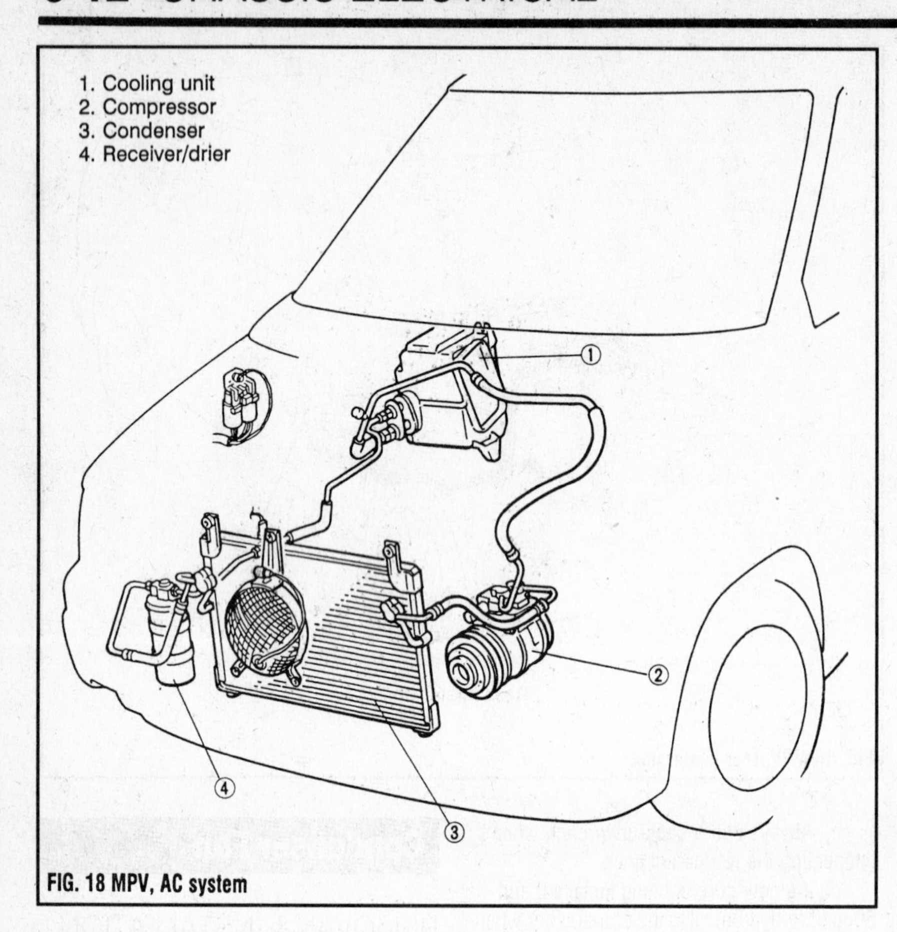

FIG. 18 MPV, AC system

3. Remove the hood lock assembly.
4. Disconnect the condenser fan wiring connector. Remove the fan mounting bolts and remove the fan.
5. Install in reverse order.

Condenser

REMOVAL & INSTALLATION

1. Disconnect the negative battery cable. Properly discharge the AC system. See Section 1.
2. Remove the lower grille and the radiator grille.
3. Remove the hood lock assembly. Remove the condenser fan assembly.
4. Disconnect the refrigerant high and low side pressure lines. Cap all line openings.
5. Remove the condenser mounting nuts and remove the condenser.
6. Install in reverse order. Use new O-rings on the fittings. If a new condenser is being installed, add 1.0 oz. of new refrigerant oil to the compressor when charging. Evacuate, recharge and test system.

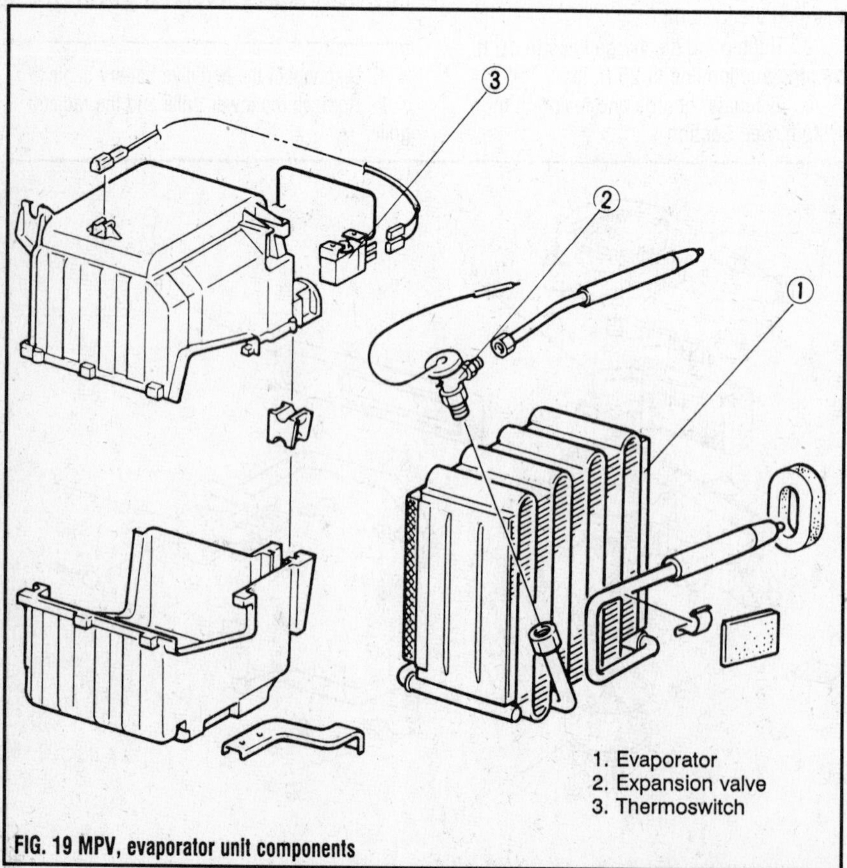

FIG. 19 MPV, evaporator unit components

AC Compressor

REMOVAL & INSTALLATION

1. Disconnect the negative battery cable. Remove the air funnel.
2. Properly discharge the AC system. See Section 1.
3. Disconnect the wiring harness to the compressor clutch.
4. Loosen the locknut and adjusting bolts and remove the drive belt.

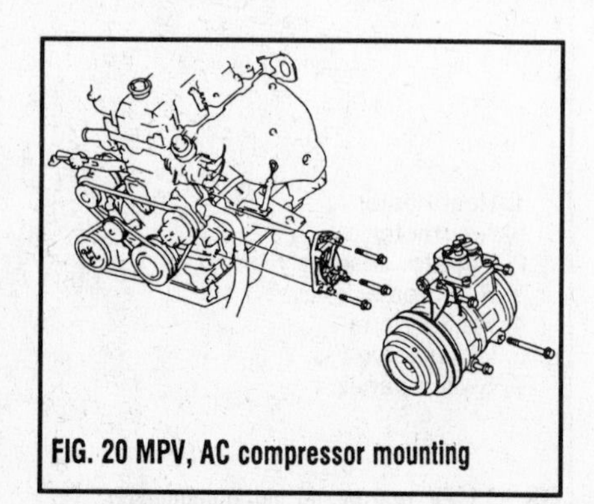
FIG. 20 MPV, AC compressor mounting

5. Disconnect and plug the refrigerant line at the compressor. Remove the mounting bolts and the compressor.

6. Place the compressor in position and install the mounting bolts. Attach the components in reverse order of removal. Install and properly adjust the drive belt.

7. Evacuate, recharge and test the system.

Expansion Valve

REMOVAL & INSTALLATION

1. Disconnect the negative battery cable. Properly discharge the AC system. See Section 1.

2. Disconnect and plug the refrigerant lines at the evaporator.

3. Remove the glove box and lower panel. Remove the air ducts, if required.

4. Remove the evaporator unit seal plates and remove the unit. Remove the evaporator securing clips. Disassemble the unit.

5. Remove the thermo switch. Remove the capillary tube from the outlet pipe. Remove the expansion valve.

6. Install in reverse order. Use new O-rings at the fittings. Evacuate, recharge and test system.

Receiver/Dryer

REMOVAL & INSTALLATION

1. Disconnect the negative battery cable. Properly discharge the AC system. See Section 1.

2. Remove the lower grille and radiator grille. Remove the right side parking lamp and headlight. Disconnect the refrigerant lines at the receiver/dryer. Immediately cap all lines to minimize contamination.

3. Remove the receiver/dryer attaching nuts and remove the receiver/dryer.

4. Install in reverse order. Use new O-ring at the fittings. Evacuate, recharge and test the system.

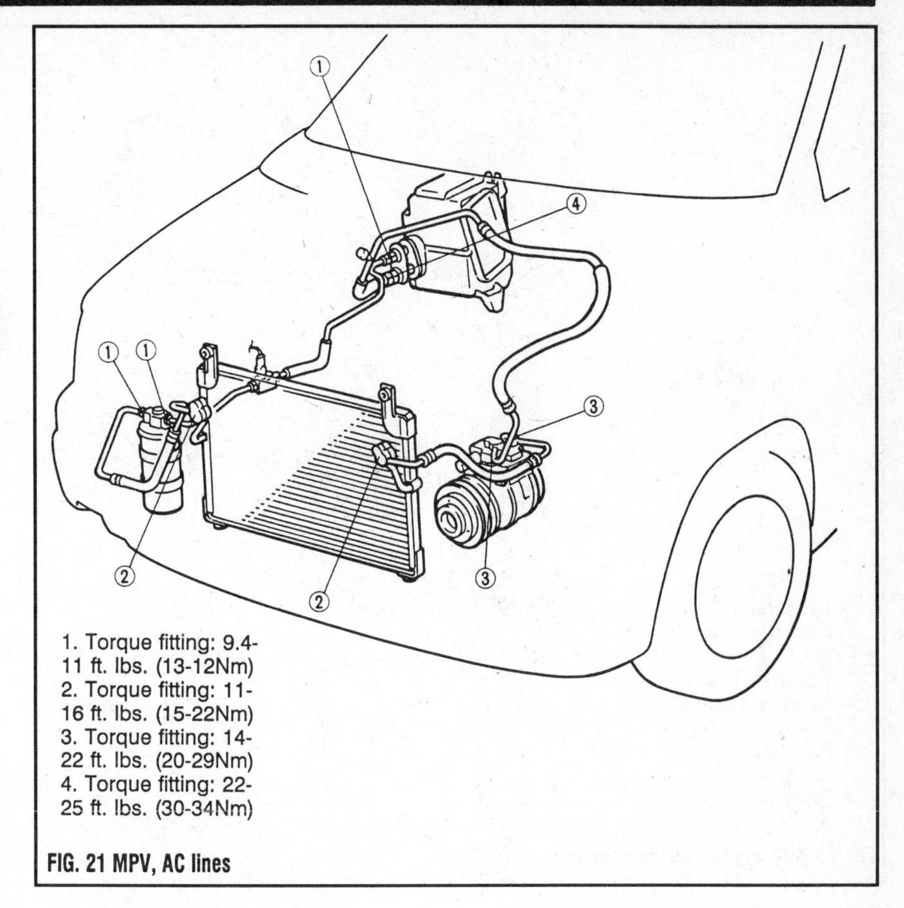

FIG. 21 MPV, AC lines

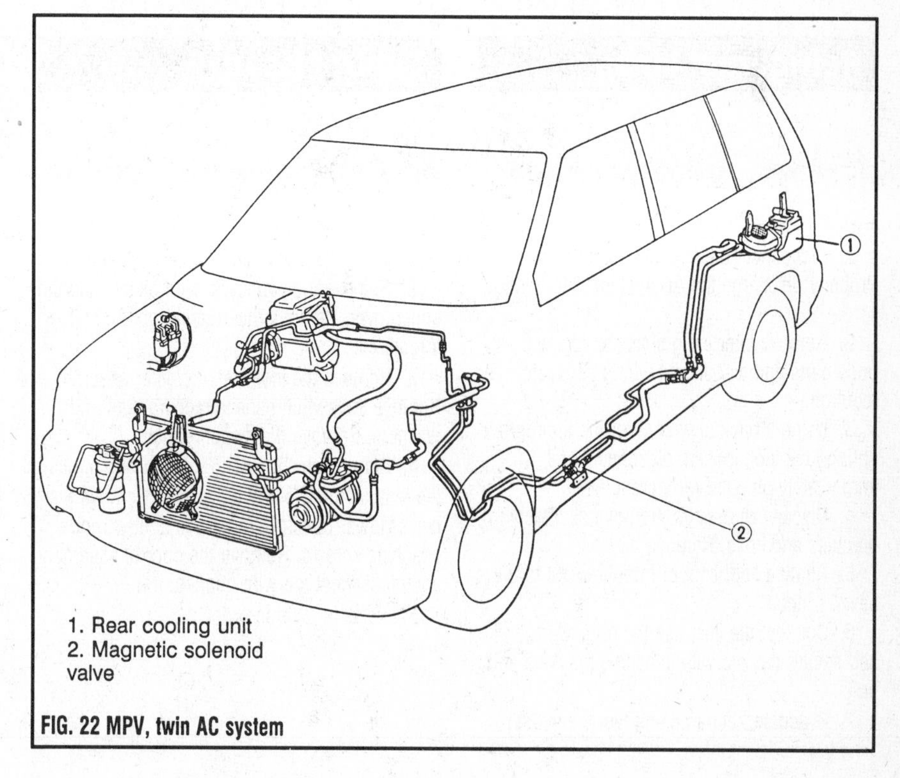

FIG. 22 MPV, twin AC system

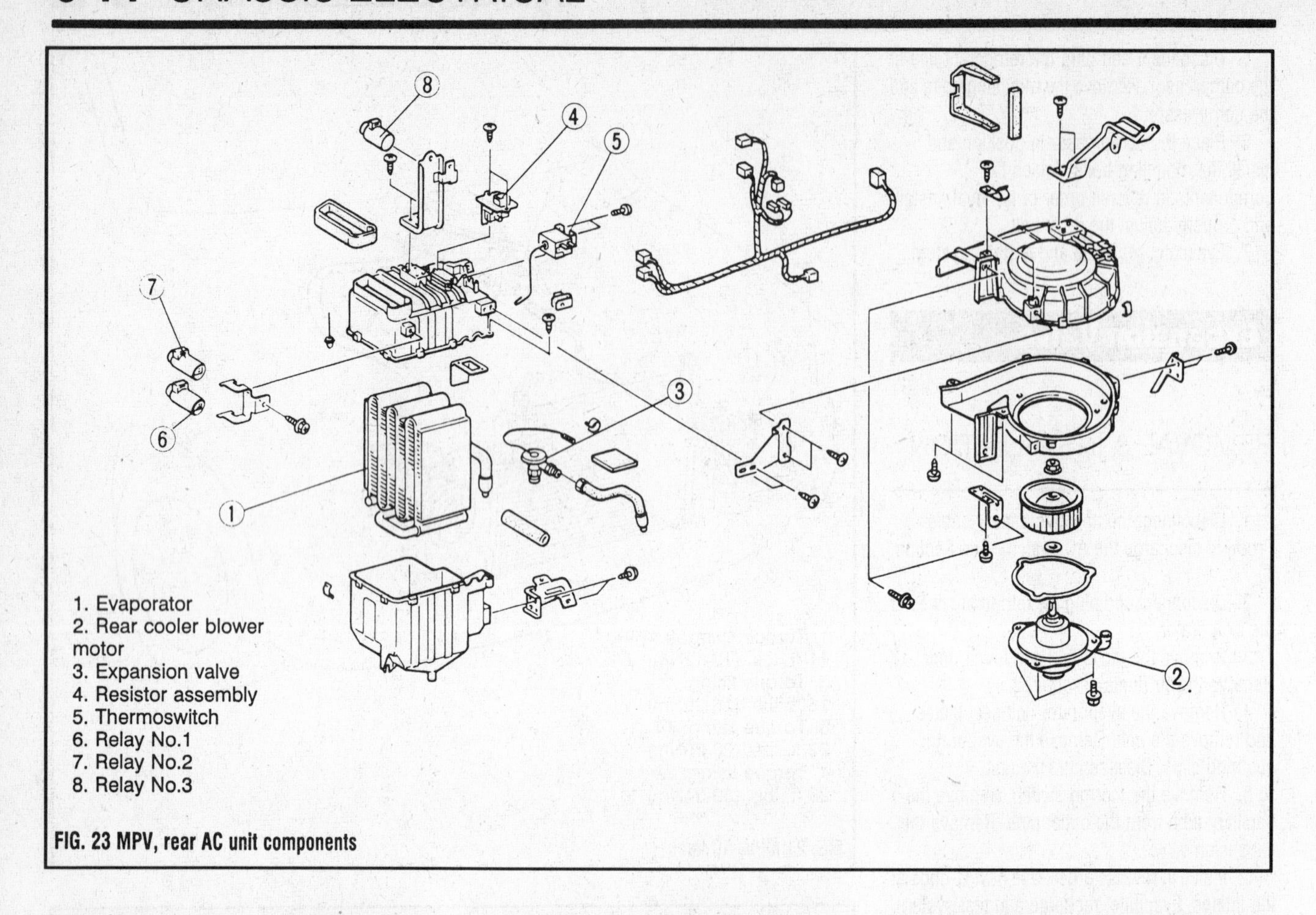

FIG. 23 MPV, rear AC unit components

Refrigerant Lines

REMOVAL & INSTALLATION

1. Disconnect the negative battery cable. Properly discharge the AC system. See Section 1.
2. Remove interfering chassis, engine or body parts and disconnect wiring connectors as required.
3. Using a backup wrench or the appropriate spring lock tool, loosen, disconnect and immediately plug the refrigerant line.
4. Discard all O-rings. Remove all attaching brackets and bolts. Remove the line.
5. Apply a light coat of refrigerant oil to the new O-rings.
6. Connect the line, use the original routing and secure the line with attaching brackets and bolts.
7. Evacuate, recharge and test the system.

Control Head

REMOVAL & INSTALLATION

1. Disconnect the negative battery cable.
2. Remove the two lower side panels and the undercover. Remove the steering column cover, if required.
3. Remove the instrument cluster assembly. Remove the switch panel attaching nuts and washers. Remove the switch panel.
4. Remove the attaching screws and remove the temperature control assembly. Remove the center lower panel. Remove the airflow mode attaching screws. Remove the control assembly and disconnect the wire connectors.
5. Install in reverse order.

Control Cables

ADJUSTMENT

1. To adjust the temperature control cable: Set the temperature control lever to the MAX-HOT position. Install the cable and secure the attaching clip with the heater unit shutter lever all the way to the right. Make sure the temperature control lever moves easily from the HOT to COLD position.
2. To adjust the airflow cable: Set the airflow mode control lever to the DEFROST position. Install the cable and attaching clip with the heater unit shutter lever at its closest point. Make sure the control lever moves easily between the DEFROST and VENT positions.
3. To adjust the rec/fresh control cable: Set the rec/fresh lever to the RECIRCULATE position. Install the cable and attaching clip with the blower unit shutter lever at its closest point. Make sure the control lever moves easily from the RECIRCULATE to the FRESH position.

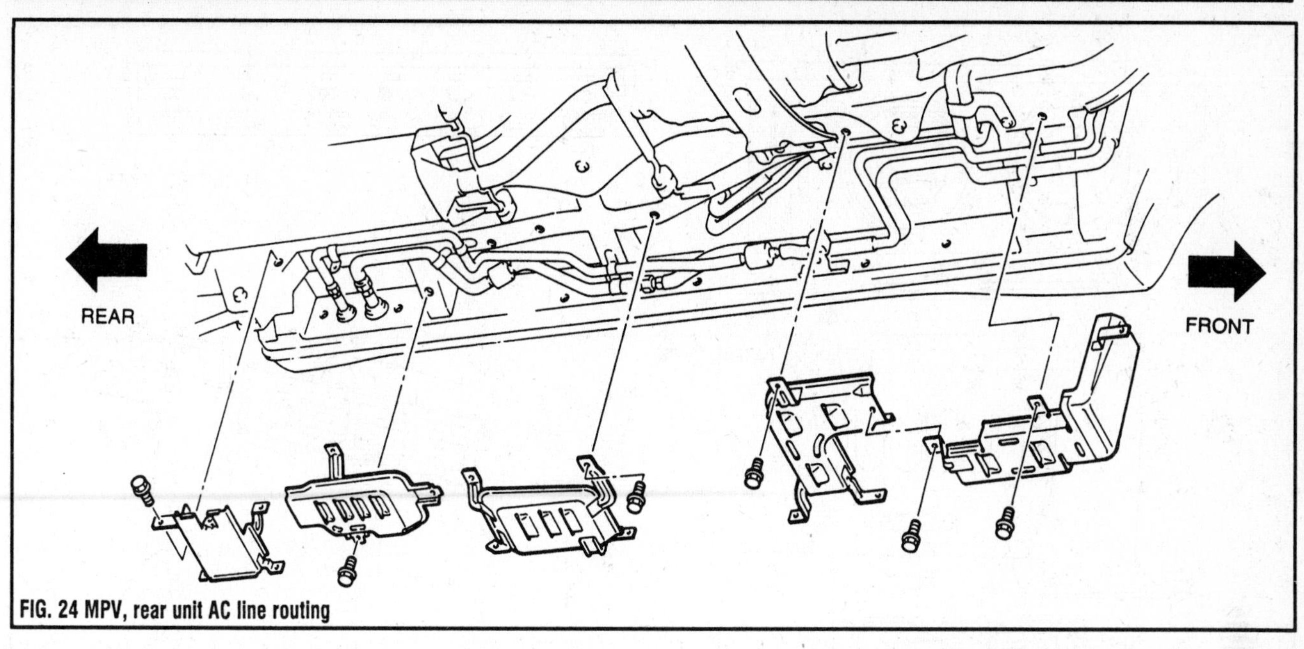

FIG. 24 MPV, rear unit AC line routing

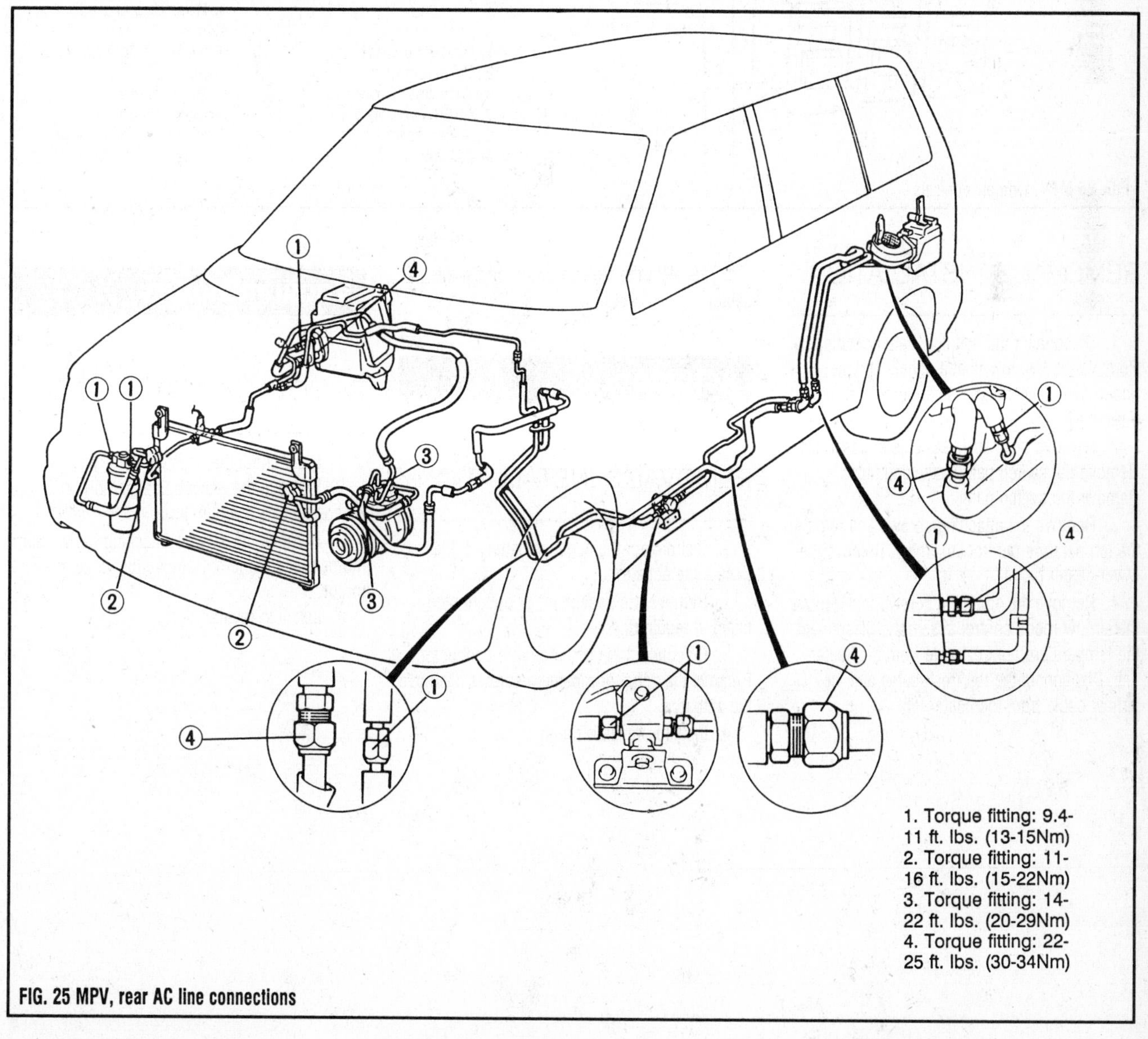

FIG. 25 MPV, rear AC line connections

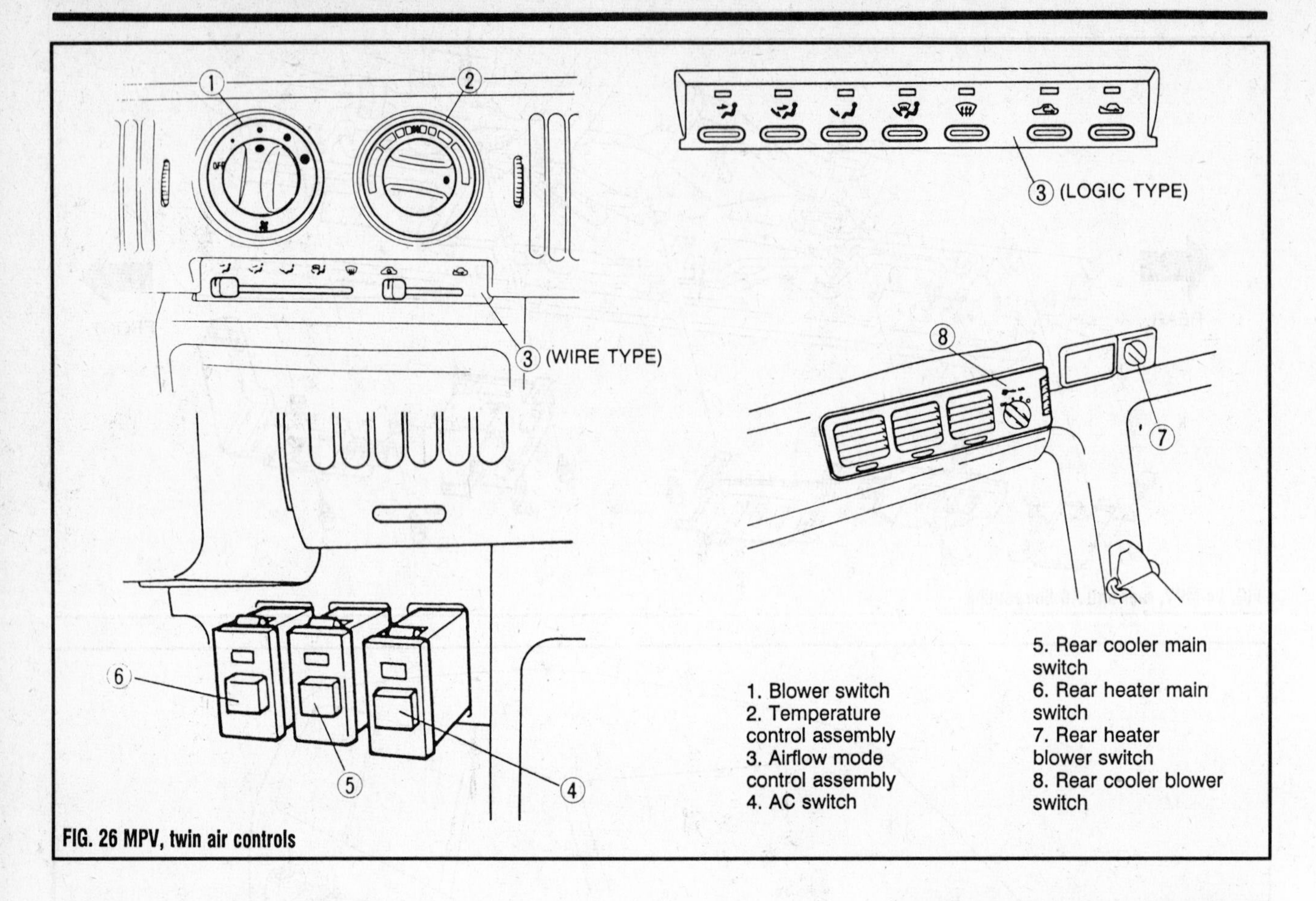

FIG. 26 MPV, twin air controls

REMOVAL & INSTALLATION

1. Disconnect the negative battery cable. Remove the two lower side panels and the undercover. Remove the steering column cover, if required.
2. Remove the instrument cluster assembly. Remove the switch panel attaching nuts. Remove the switch panel.
3. Remove the attaching screws and remove the temperature control assembly. Remove the lower center panel.
4. Remove the attaching screws and remove the airflow mode control assembly. Disconnect the temperature control cable from the heater unit. Disconnect the rec/fresh cable and the airflow cable from the heater unit.
5. Install in the reverse order. Adjust the cables.

Actuators

REMOVAL & INSTALLATION

1. Disconnect the negative battery cable. Locate the actuator.
2. Remove the passenger or drivers side panel, if required.
3. Disconnect the actuator wire connector. Remove the actuator mounting screws. Remove the actuator.
4. Install in reverse order.

Vacuum Motors

REMOVAL & INSTALLATION

1. Disconnect the negative battery cable.
2. Remove the glove box assembly. Disconnect the vacuum hose.
3. Remove the screws attaching the vacuum motor to the plenum. Remove the vacuum motor.
4. Install in reverse order.

NAVAJO HEATING AND AIR CONDITIONING

➧ SEE FIGS. 27-46

➡ **When the negative battery cable is disconnected and reconnected, some abnormal drivability symptoms may occur on restart. About 10 driving miles are needed for the ECU to re-establish the computer settings.**

Blower Motor

REMOVAL & INSTALLATION

Without Air Conditioning

1. Disconnect the negative battery cable.
2. Remove the air cleaner or air inlet duct, as necessary.
3. Remove the 2 screws attaching the vacuum reservoir to the blower assembly and remove the reservoir.
4. Disconnect the wire harness connector from the blower motor by pushing down on the connector tabs and pulling the connector off of the motor.
5. Disconnect the blower motor cooling tube at the blower motor.
6. Remove the 3 screws attaching the blower motor and wheel to the heater blower assembly.
7. Holding the cooling tube aside, pull the blower motor and wheel from the heater blower assembly and remove it from the vehicle.
8. Remove the blower wheel push-nut or clamp from the motor shaft and pull the blower wheel from the motor shaft.

To install:

9. Install the blower wheel on the blower motor shaft.
10. Install the hub clamp or push-nut.
11. Holding the cooling tube aside, position the blower motor and wheel on the heater blower assembly and install the 3 attaching screws.
12. Connect the blower motor cooling tube and the wire harness connector.
13. Install the vacuum reservoir on the hoses with the 2 screws.
14. Install the air cleaner or air inlet duct, as necessary.
15. Connect the negative battery cable and check the system for proper operation.

With Air Conditioning

1. Disconnect the negative battery cable.
2. In the engine compartment, disconnect the wire harness from the motor by pushing down on the tab while pulling the connection off at the motor.
3. Remove the air cleaner or air inlet duct, as necessary.
4. Remove the solenoid box cover retaining bolts and the solenoid box cover, if equipped.
5. Disconnect the blower motor cooling tube from the blower motor.
6. Remove the 3 blower motor mounting plate attaching screws and remove the motor and wheel assembly from the evaporator assembly blower motor housing.
7. Remove the blower motor hub clamp from the motor shaft and pull the blower wheel from the shaft.

To install:

8. Install the blower motor wheel on the blower motor shaft and install a new hub clamp.
9. Install a new motor mounting seal on the blower housing before installing the blower motor.
10. Position the blower motor and wheel assembly in the blower housing and install the 3 attaching screws.
11. Connect the blower motor cooling tube.
12. Connect the electrical wire harness hardshell connector to the blower motor by pushing into place.
13. Position the solenoid box cover, if equipped, into place and install the 3 retaining screws.
14. Install the air cleaner or air inlet duct, as necessary.
15. Connect the negative battery cable and check the blower motor in all speeds for proper operation.

Heater Core

REMOVAL & INSTALLATION

1. Disconnect the negative battery cable. Allow the engine to cool down. Drain the cooling system.

✽✽ CAUTION

When draining the coolant, keep in mind that cats and dogs are attracted by the ethylene glycol antifreeze, and are quite likely to drink any that is left in an uncovered container or in puddles on the ground. This will prove fatal in sufficient quantity. Always drain the coolant into a sealable container. Coolant should be reused unless it is contaminated or several years old.

2. Disconnect the heater hoses from the heater core tubes and plug hoses.
3. In the passenger compartment, remove the five screws attaching the heater core access cover to the plenum assembly and remove the access cover.
4. Pull the heater core rearward and down, removing it from the plenum assembly.

To install:

5. Position the heater core and seal in the plenum assembly.
6. Install the heater core access cover to the plenum assembly and secure with five screws.
7. Install the heater hoses to the heater core tubes at the dash panel in the engine compartment. Do not over-tighten hose clamps.
8. Check the coolant level and add coolant as required. Connect the negative battery cable.
9. Start the engine and check the system for coolant leaks.

Control Head

REMOVAL & INSTALLATION

1. Disconnect the negative battery cable.
2. Open the ash tray and remove the 2 screws that hold the ash tray drawer slide to the instrument panel. Remove the ash tray and drawer slide bracket from the instrument panel.

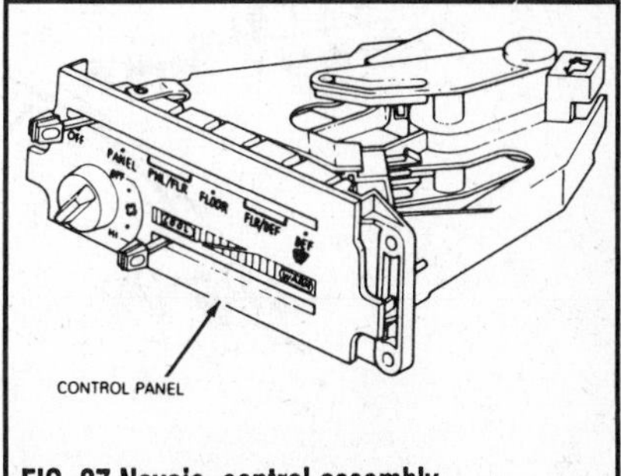

FIG. 27 Navajo, control assembly

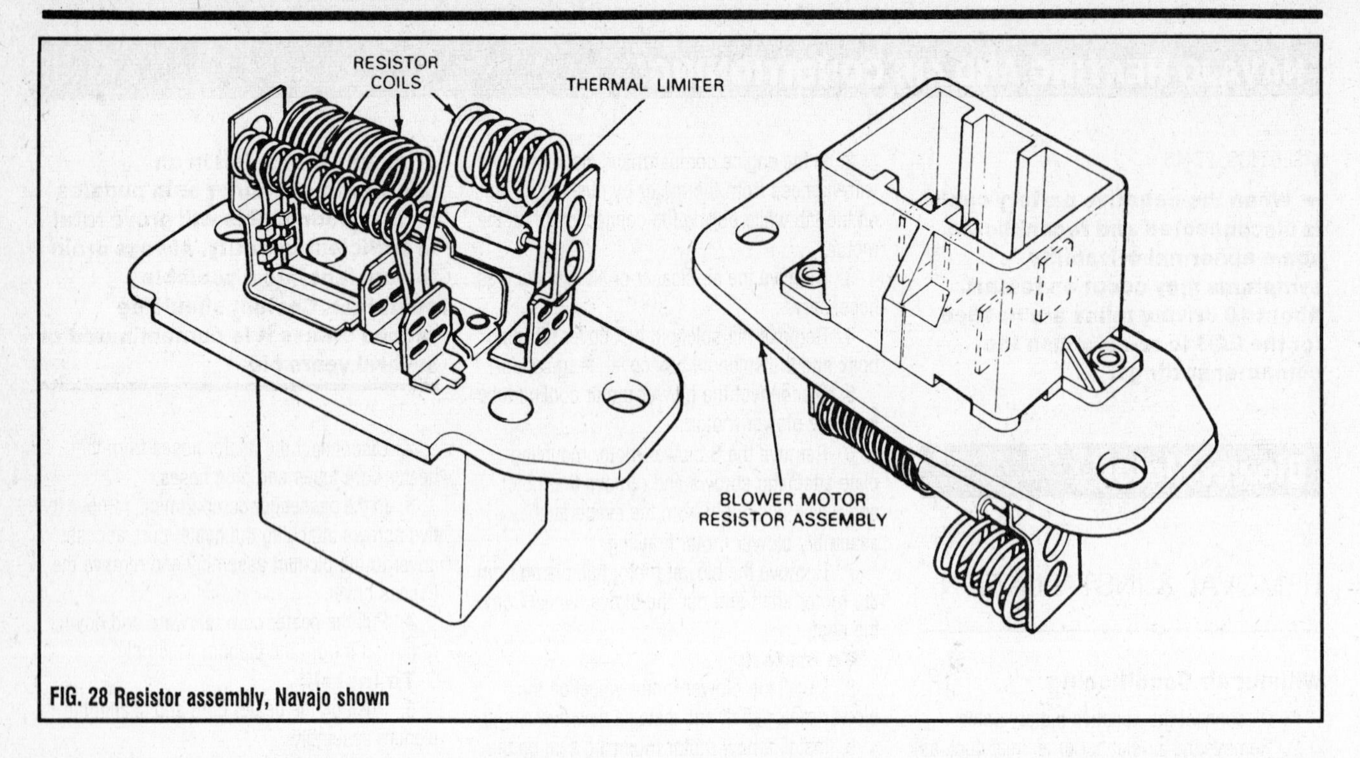

FIG. 28 Resistor assembly, Navajo shown

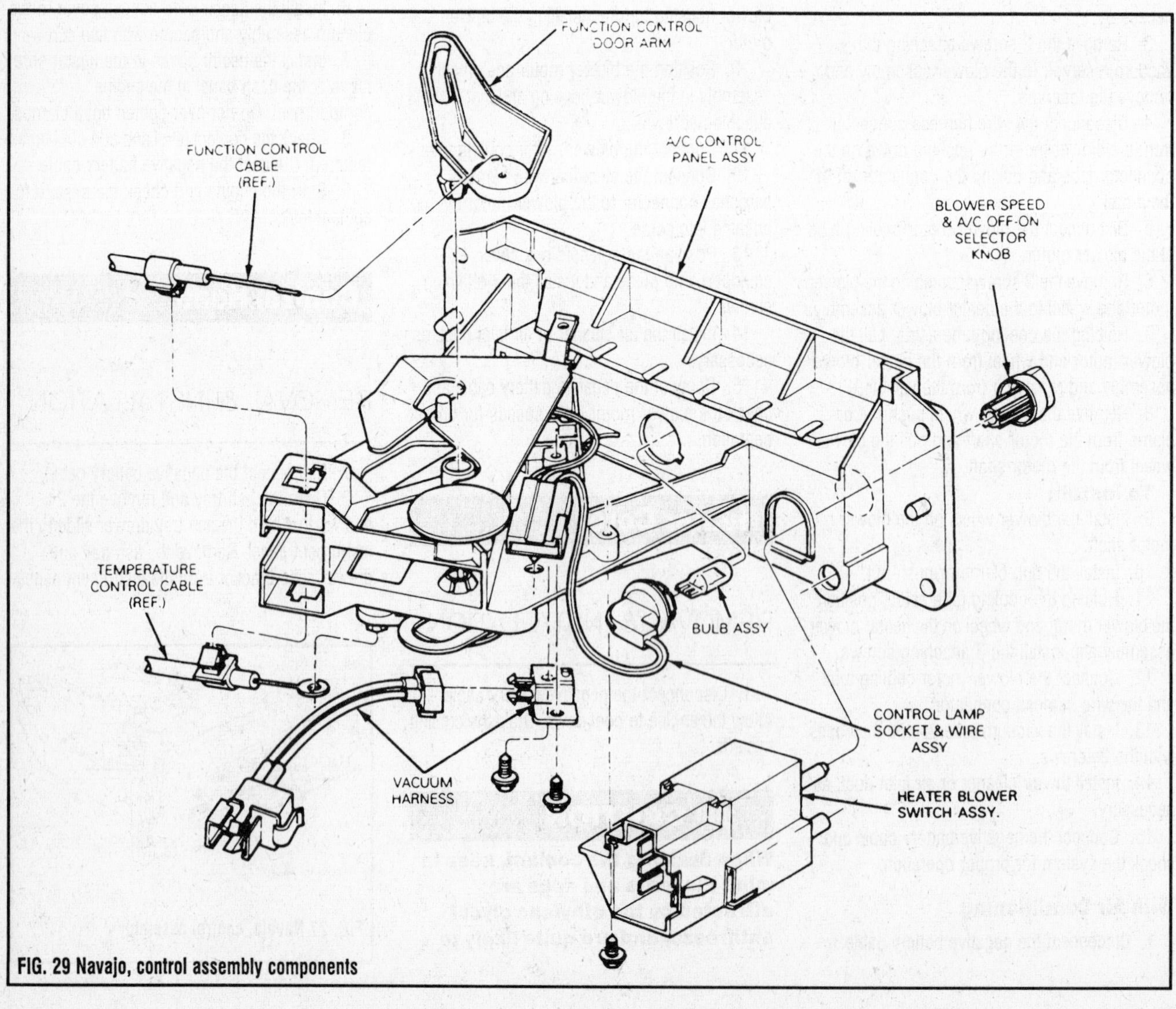

FIG. 29 Navajo, control assembly components

3. Gently pull the finish panel away from the instrument panel and the cluster. The finish panel pops straight back for approximately 1 in., then up to remove. Be careful not to trap the finish panel around the steering column.

➡ If equipped with the electronic 4×4 shift-on-the-fly module, disconnect the wire from the rear of the 4×4 transfer switch before trying to remove the finish panel from the instrument panel.

4. Remove the 4 screws attaching the control assembly to the instrument panel.
5. Pull the control through the instrument panel opening far enough to allow removal of the electrical connections from the blower switch and control assembly illumination lamp. Using a suitable tool, remove the 2 hose vacuum harness from the vacuum switch on the side of the control.
6. At the rear of the control, using a suitable tool, release the temperature and function cable snap-in flags from the white control bracket.
7. On the bottom side of the control, remove the temperature cable from the control by rotating the cable until the T-pin releases the cable. The temperature cable is black with a blue snap-in flag.
8. Pull enough cable through the instrument panel opening until the function cable can be held vertical to the control, then remove the control cable from the function lever. The function cable is white with a black snap-in flag.
9. Remove the control assembly from the instrument panel.

To install:

10. Pull the control cables through the control assembly opening in the instrument panel for a distance of approximately 8 in. (203mm).
11. Hold the control assembly up to the instrument panel with it's face directed toward the floor of the vehicle. This will locate the face of the control in a position that is 90° out of it's installed position.
12. Carefully bend and attach the function cable that has a white color code and a black snap-in terminal to the white plastic lever on the control assembly. Rotate the control assembly back to it's normal position for installation, then snap the black cable flag into the control assembly bracket.
13. On the opposite side of the control assembly, attach the black temperature control cable with the blue plastic snap-in flag to the blue plastic lever on the control. Make sure the end of the cable is seated securely with the T-top pin on the control. Rotate the cable to it's operating position and snap the blue cable flag into the control assembly bracket.

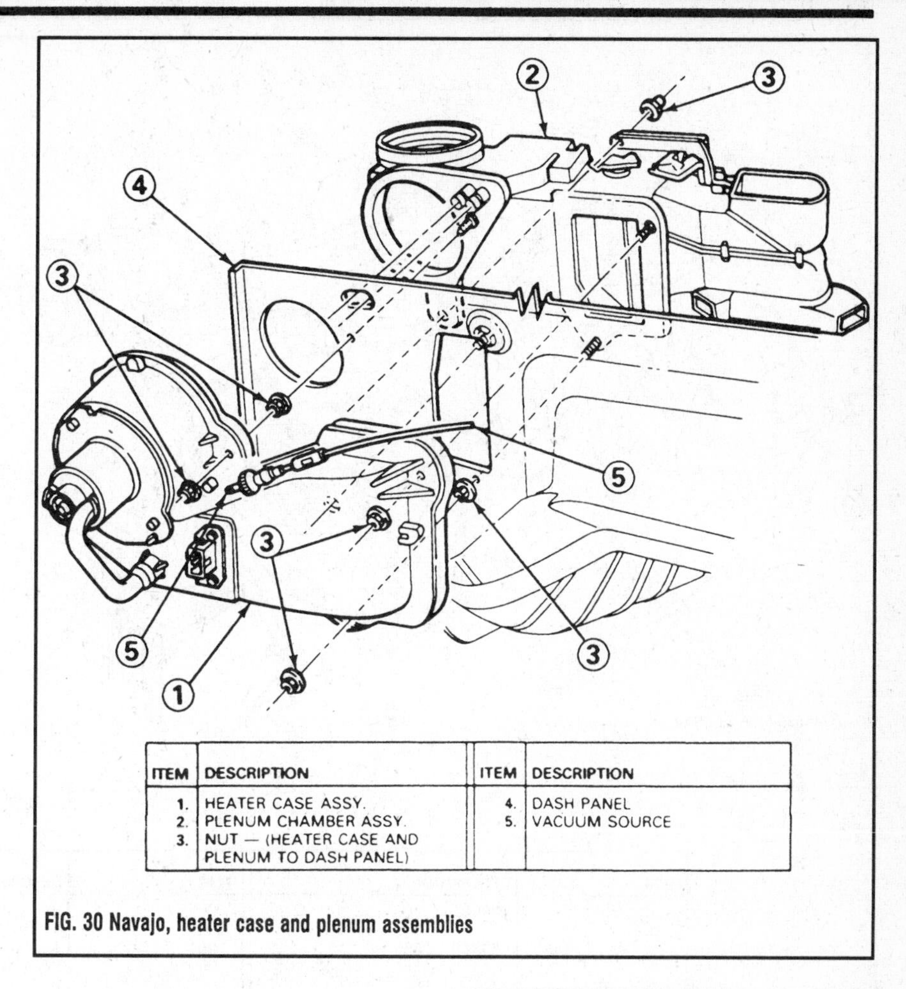

ITEM	DESCRIPTION	ITEM	DESCRIPTION
1.	HEATER CASE ASSY.	4.	DASH PANEL
2.	PLENUM CHAMBER ASSY.	5.	VACUUM SOURCE
3.	NUT — (HEATER CASE AND PLENUM TO DASH PANEL)		

FIG. 30 Navajo, heater case and plenum assemblies

14. Connect the wiring harness to the blower switch and the illumination lamp to it's receptacle on the control assembly. Connect the dual terminal on the vacuum hose to the vacuum switch on the control assembly.
15. Position the control assembly into the instrument panel opening and install the 4 mounting screws.
16. If equipped, reconnect the 4×4 electric shift harness on the rear of the cluster finish panel.
17. Install the cluster finish panel with integral push-pins. Make sure that all pins are fully seated around the rim of the panel.
18. Reinsert the ash tray slide bracket and reconnect the illumination connection circuit. Reinstall the 2 screws that retain the ash tray retainer bracket and the finish panel.
19. Replace the ash tray and reconnect the cigarette lighter.
20. Connect the negative battery cable and check the heater system for proper control assembly operation.

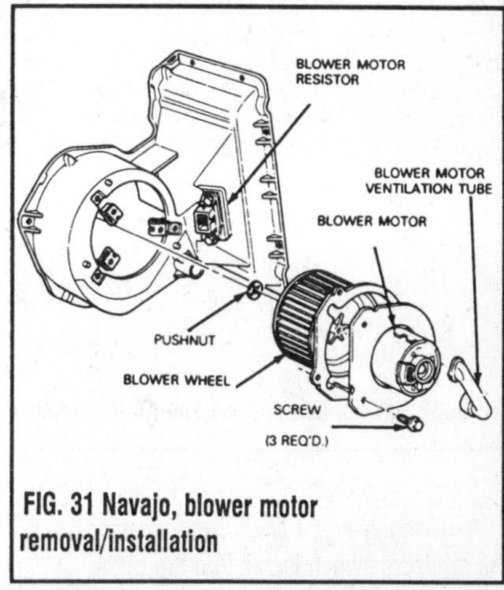

FIG. 31 Navajo, blower motor removal/installation

Evaporator Core

REMOVAL & INSTALLATION

1. Disconnect the negative battery cable.
2. Discharge the refrigerant from the air conditioning system according to the proper procedure. See Section 1, for the procedure.

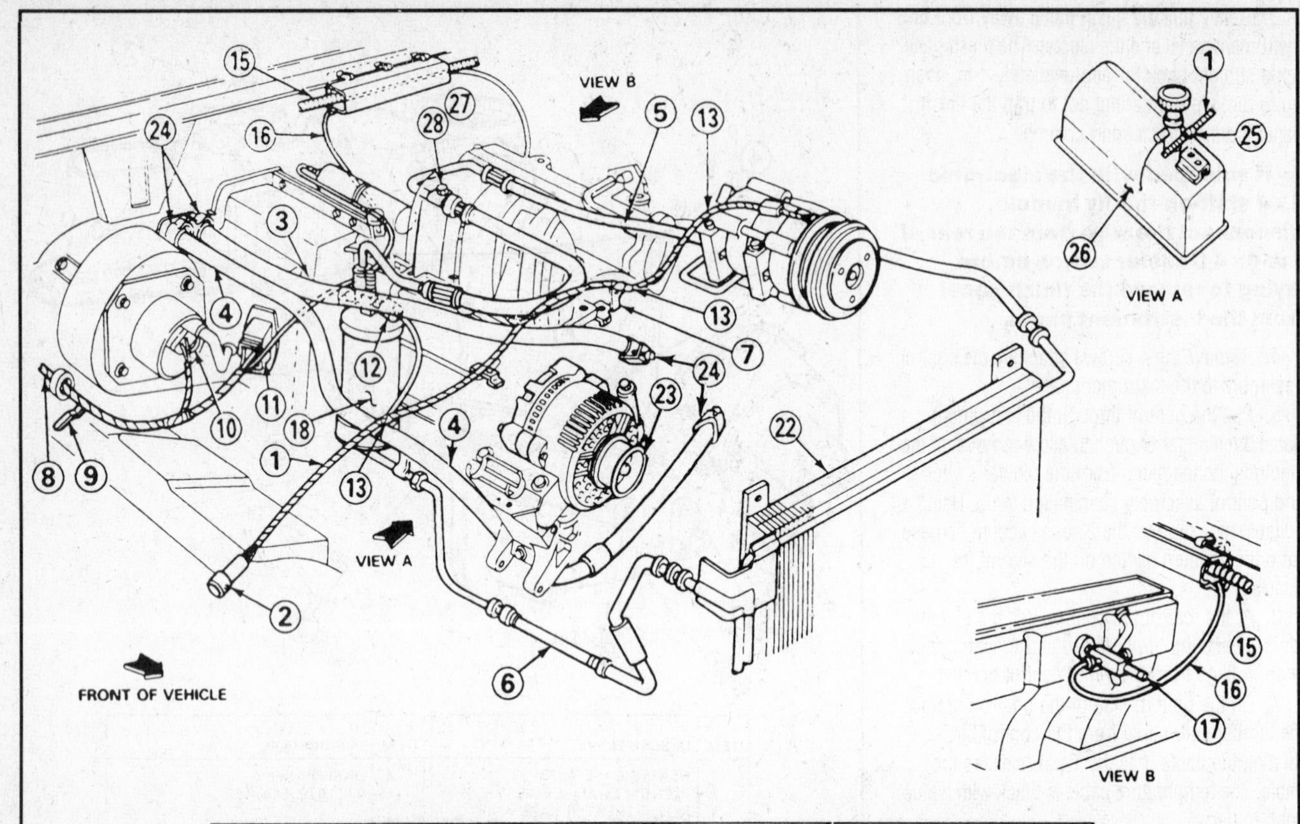

ITEM	DESCRIPTION	ITEM	DESCRIPTION
1.	WIRING ASSY.	17.	VACUUM SOURCE,
2.			PART OF ENGINE (P.I.A.)
3.	HEATER HOSE	18.	ACCUMULATOR
4.	HEATER HOSE	19.	RELAY ASSY.
5.	A/C TUBE ASSY.		(WOT-A/C CUT-OUT)
6.	HOSE ASSY.		
7.	INTAKE BRACKET	20.	WIRING ASSY.
8.	WIRING ASSY.	21.	WIRING ASSY.
9.	LOCATOR, PART OF 19D605		
	WIRING ASSY., INSTALL IN HOLE	22.	CONDENSER ASSY.
	PROVIDED	23.	ALTERNATOR
10.	BLOWER MOTOR ASSY.	24.	CLAMP (4 REQ'D.)
11.	BLOWER RESISTOR ASSY.	25.	POSITION LOCATOR ONTO
12.	A/C PRESSURE SWITCH		ROCKER COVER MOUNTING
13.	INSTALL LOCATOR IN HOLE		PLATE AS SHOWN
	PROVIDED	26.	VALVE COVER
14.	POWER INTWORK BOX	27.	BOLT
15.	WIRING ASSY.	28.	CLIP
16.	VACUUM HOSE	29.	NUT & WASHER ASSY.
		30.	EXISTING SCREW

FIG. 32 Navajo, heater hose and AC line routing

3. Disconnect the electrical connector from the pressure switch located on top of the accumulator/drier. Remove the pressure switch.

4. Disconnect the suction hose from the accumulator/drier using the spring-lock coupling disconnect procedure. Cap the openings to prevent the entrance of dirt and moisture.

5. Disconnect the liquid line from the evaporator core inlet tube using a backup wrench to loosen the fitting. Cap the openings to prevent the entrance of dirt and moisture.

6. Remove the screws holding the evaporator case service cover and vacuum reservoir to the evaporator case assembly.

7. Store the vacuum reservoir in a secure position to avoid vacuum line damage.

8. Remove the 2 dash panel mounting nuts.

9. Remove the evaporator case service cover from the evaporator case assembly.

10. Remove the evaporator core and accumulator/drier assembly from the vehicle.

To Install:

➡ Add 3 oz. (90ml) of clean refrigerant oil to a new replacement evaporator core to maintain the total system oil charge.

11. Position the evaporator core and accumulator/drier assembly into the evaporator case out-board half.

12. Position the evaporator case service cover into place on the evaporator case assembly.

*ALSO SUPPLIED IN KIT WITH GARTER SPRINGS
†ALSO SUPPLIED IN KIT

O RINGS
GARTER SPRING
FEMALE FITTING
MALE FITTING
CAGE

SPRING LOCK COUPLING DISCONNECTED

TO CONNECT COUPLING

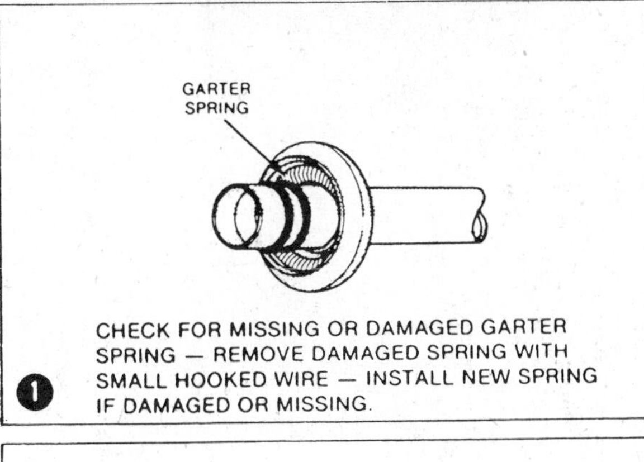
GARTER
SPRING

1 CHECK FOR MISSING OR DAMAGED GARTER SPRING — REMOVE DAMAGED SPRING WITH SMALL HOOKED WIRE — INSTALL NEW SPRING IF DAMAGED OR MISSING.

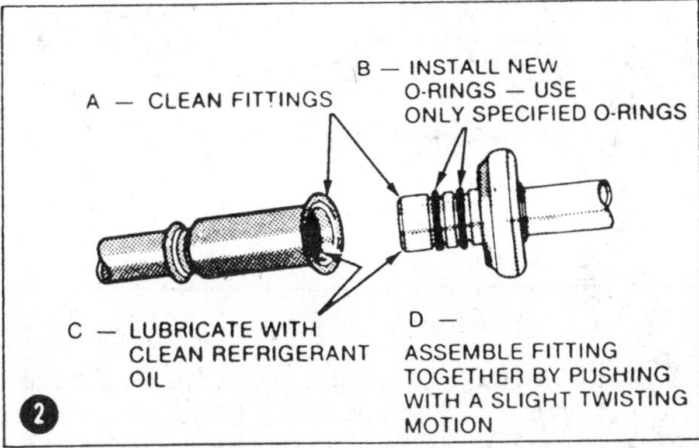
A — CLEAN FITTINGS
B — INSTALL NEW
O-RINGS — USE
ONLY SPECIFIED O-RINGS
C — LUBRICATE WITH
CLEAN REFRIGERANT
OIL
D —
ASSEMBLE FITTING
TOGETHER BY PUSHING
WITH A SLIGHT TWISTING
MOTION

2

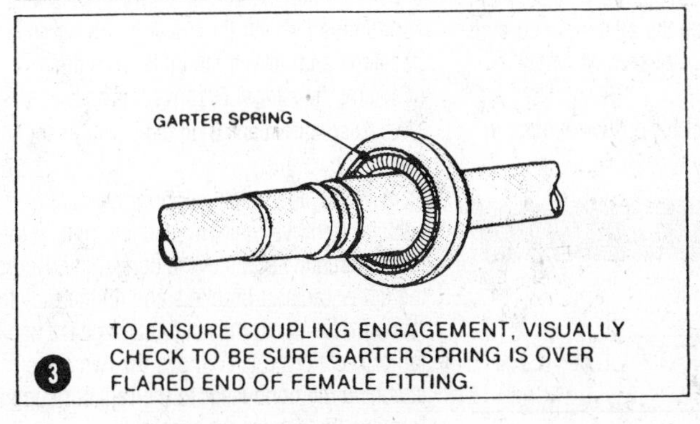
GARTER SPRING

3 TO ENSURE COUPLING ENGAGEMENT, VISUALLY CHECK TO BE SURE GARTER SPRING IS OVER FLARED END OF FEMALE FITTING.

TO DISCONNECT COUPLING

CAUTION — DISCHARGE SYSTEM BEFORE DISCONNECTING COUPLING

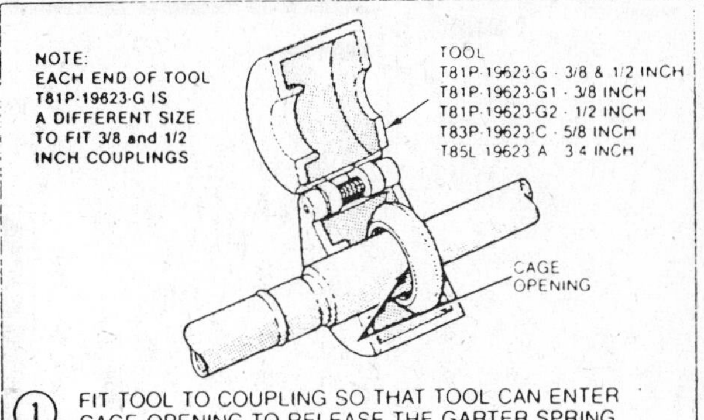
NOTE:
EACH END OF TOOL
T81P-19623-G IS
A DIFFERENT SIZE
TO FIT 3/8 and 1/2
INCH COUPLINGS
TOOL
T81P-19623-G - 3/8 & 1/2 INCH
T81P-19623-G1 - 3/8 INCH
T81P-19623-G2 - 1/2 INCH
T83P-19623-C - 5/8 INCH
T85L-19623-A - 3/4 INCH
CAGE
OPENING

(1) FIT TOOL TO COUPLING SO THAT TOOL CAN ENTER CAGE OPENING TO RELEASE THE GARTER SPRING.

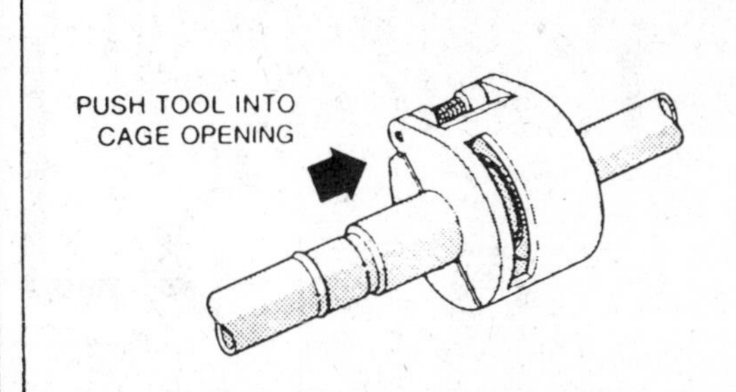
PUSH TOOL INTO
CAGE OPENING

(2) PUSH THE TOOL INTO THE CAGE OPENING TO RELEASE THE FEMALE FITTING FROM THE GARTER SPRING.

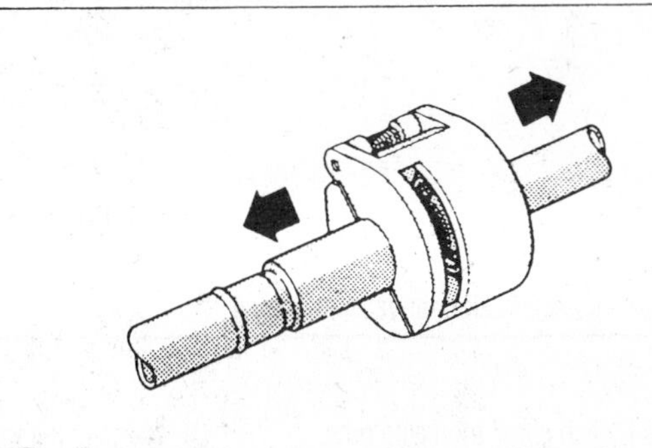

(3) PULL THE COUPLING MALE AND FEMALE FITTINGS APART.

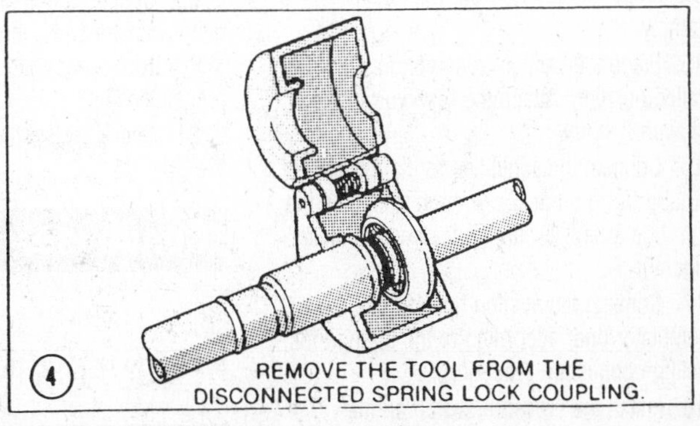

(4) REMOVE THE TOOL FROM THE DISCONNECTED SPRING LOCK COUPLING.

FIG. 33 AC line fitting tools, removal/installation

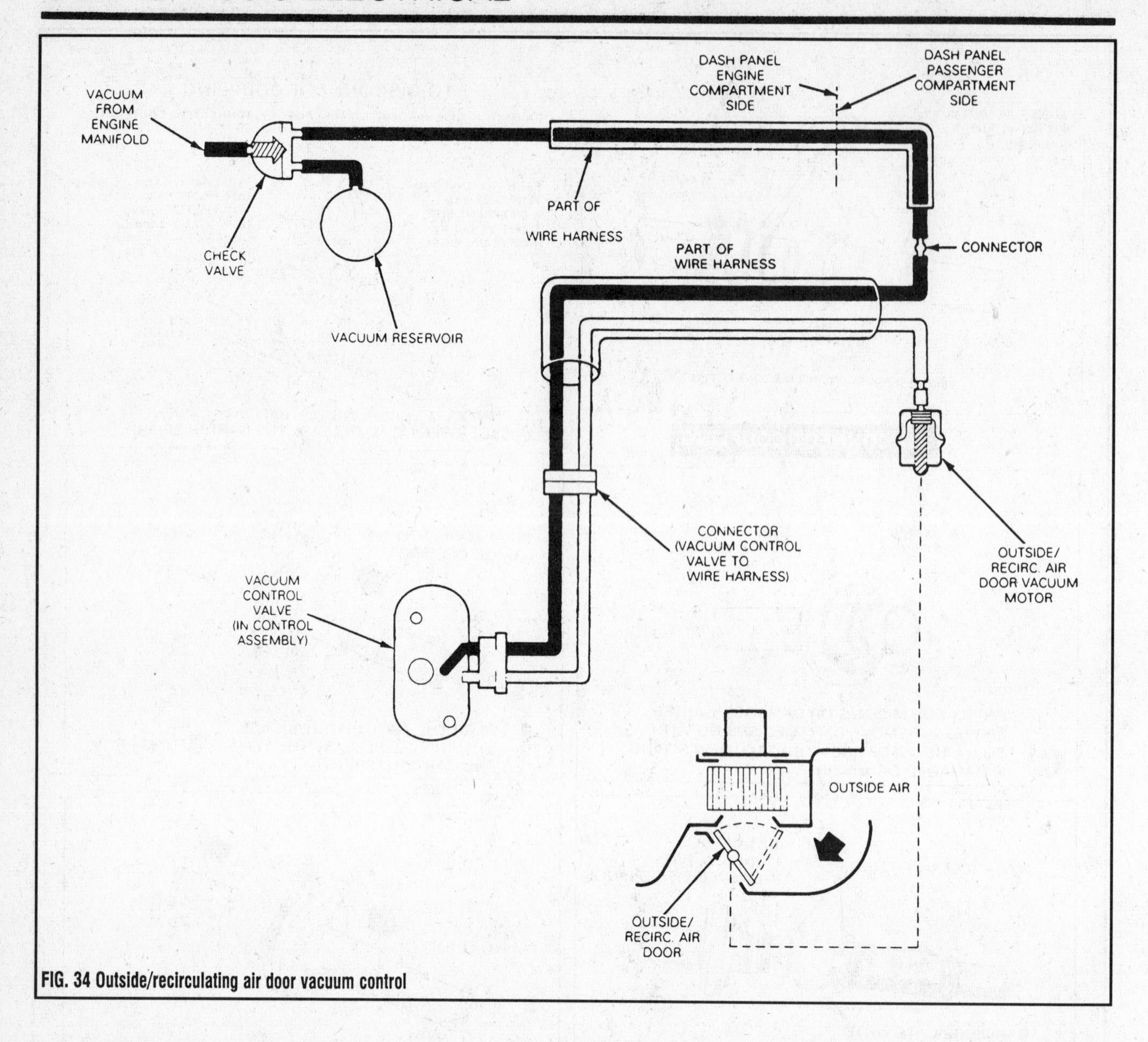

FIG. 34 Outside/recirculating air door vacuum control

13. Install the 2 dash panel mounting nuts.
14. Install the screws holding the evaporator service case half to the evaporator case assembly.
15. Place the vacuum reservoir in it's installed position. Attach the reservoir to the case with 2 screws.
16. Connect the liquid line to the evaporator inlet tube using a backup wrench to tighten the fitting. Use a new O-ring lubricated with clean refrigerant oil.
17. Connect the suction hose to the accumulator/drier according to the spring-lock coupling connection procedure.
18. Install the pressure switch on the accumulator/drier and tighten finger-tight.

➡ **Do not use a wrench to tighten the pressure switch.**

19. Connect the electrical connector to the pressure switch.
20. Connect the negative battery cable. Leak test, evacuate and charge the system according to the proper procedure. Observe all safety precautions.
21. Check the system for proper operation.

Condenser

REMOVAL & INSTALLATION

1. Disconnect the negative battery cable. Properly discharge the AC system. See Section 1.
2. Remove the five plastic retainers on top of the grille. Remove the two screws attaching the grille to the headlamp housing. Depress the spring tabs through the lower outboard grille openings and detach the grille from the headlamp housings. Remove the grille.
3. Disconnect and plug the compressor lines. Cap all openings.
4. Raise and safely support the front of the vehicle. Remove the two attaching nuts at the lower mounting studs of the condenser. Remove the upper radiator brackets and tilt the radiator rearward being careful not to damage the cooling fan or radiator core. Remove the two bolts attaching the condenser to the radiator support. Remove the condenser assembly.
5. Install in reverse order. Evacuate, recharge and test the system.

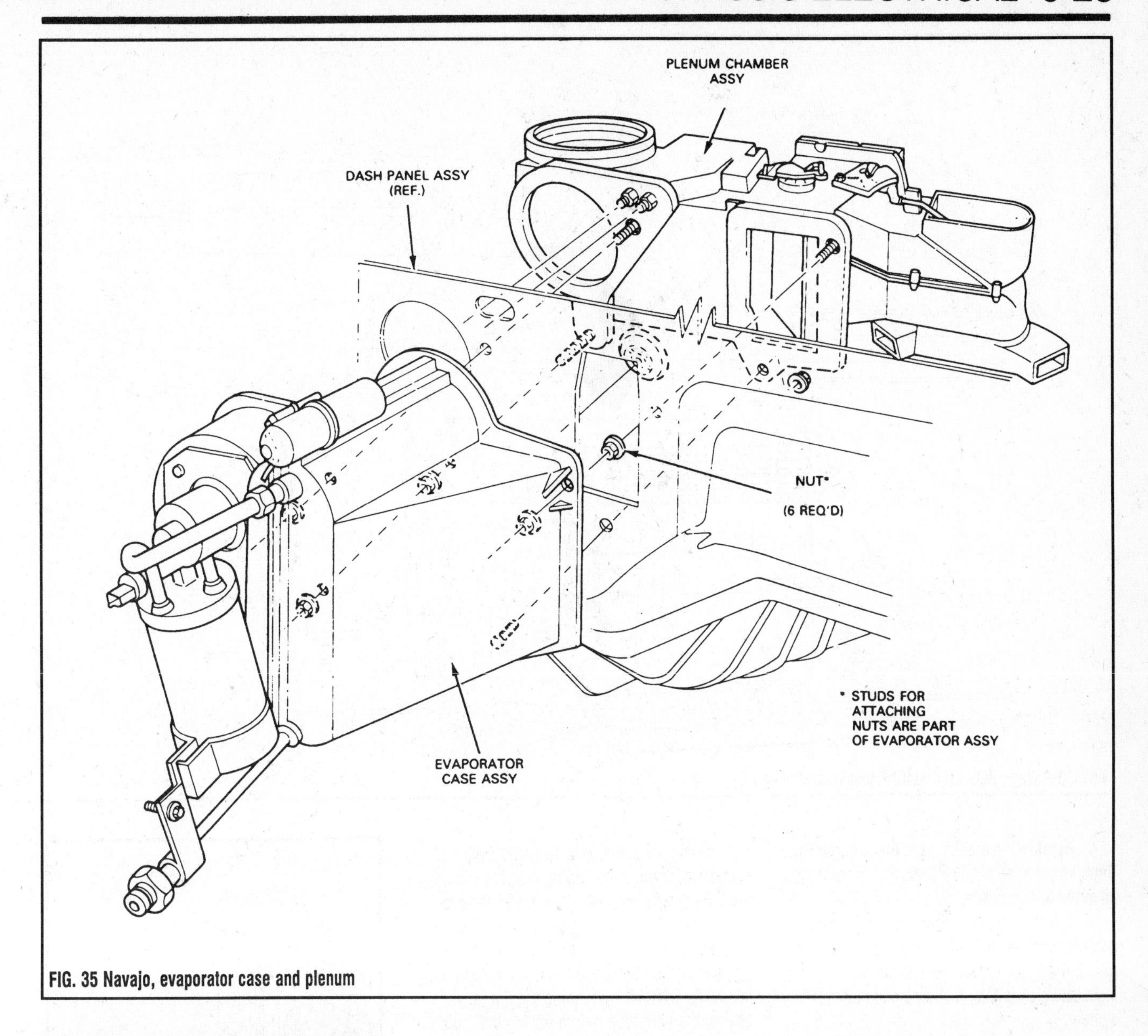

FIG. 35 Navajo, evaporator case and plenum

AC Compressor

REMOVAL & INSTALLATION

1. Disconnect the negative battery cable. Remove the air funnel.
2. Properly discharge the AC system. See Section 1.
3. Disconnect the wiring harness to the compressor clutch.
4. Loosen the locknut and adjusting bolts and remove the drive belt.
5. Disconnect and plug the refrigerant line at the compressor. Remove the mounting bolts and the compressor.
6. Place the compressor in position and install the mounting bolts. Attach the components in reverse order of removal. Install and properly adjust the drive belt.
7. Evacuate, recharge and test the system.

Accumulator

REMOVAL & INSTALLATION

➡ The accumulator should be replaced whenever a major component of the AC system requires replacement.

1. Disconnect the negative battery cable. Properly discharge the AC system. See Section 1.
2. Disconnect the wire connector from the pressure switch at the accumulator. Remove the pressure switch, if required. Disconnect and plug the refrigerant low pressure line using the appropriate spring lock coupling tool. Using a backup wrench, loosen the accumulator to evaporator low pressure line.
3. Loosen the attaching screws holding the flanges of the case to the bracket and the evaporator inlet to the accumulator together. Disconnect and plug the accumulator to evaporator line.

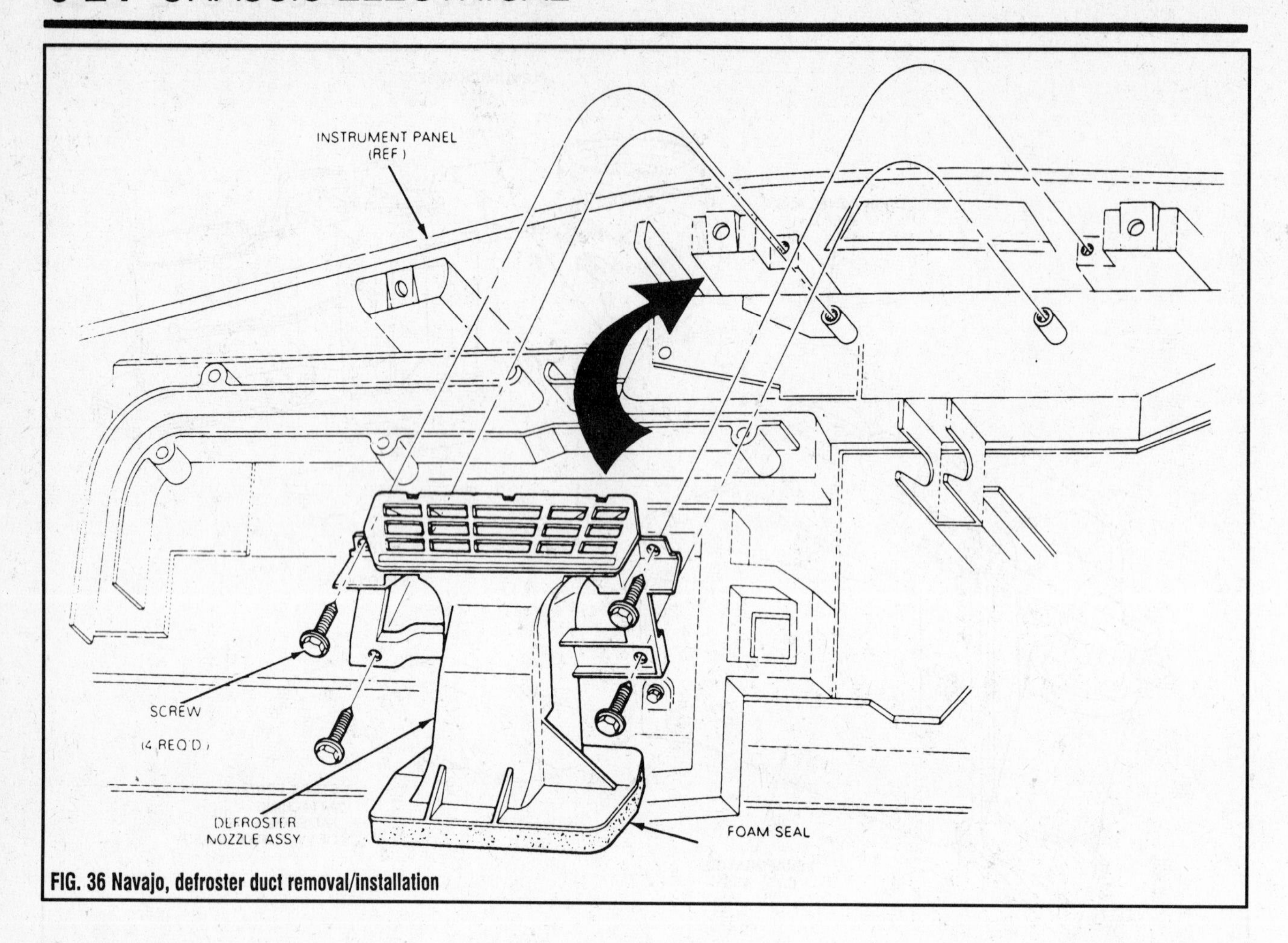

FIG. 36 Navajo, defroster duct removal/installation

4. Remove the bracket from the accumulator. Remove the accumulator. Drain and measure the oil in the accumulator.

5. Install in reverse order. Add the same amount of oil as drained from the accumulator, plus 2.0 oz. to the accumulator during installation. Evacuate, recharge and test the system.

Fixed Orifice Tube

REMOVAL & INSTALLATION

1. Disconnect the negative battery cable. Properly discharge the AC system. See Section 1.

2. Disconnect and plug the lower evaporator inlet line. Apply a small amount of refrigerant oil to the evaporator inlet to lubricate the orifice tube during removal.

3. Using a suitable tool 49 UN01 060, or equivalent, engage the two tabs on the orifice tube. Be careful not to twist or rotate the tube which might cause the tube to break off in the evaporator line. Pull the tube directly out. On some extraction tools, a nut is used to secure the handle for removal by running the nut down against the core tube before pulling the orifice tube out.

4. If the tube breaks during removal, use a special extractor tool 49 UN01 061, or equivalent, to remove the remaining pieces.

5. Install in reverse order. Liberally apply clean refrigerant oil to the evaporator tube before installing the new orifice tube up to its stop. Use new O-rings. Evacuate, recharge and test the system.

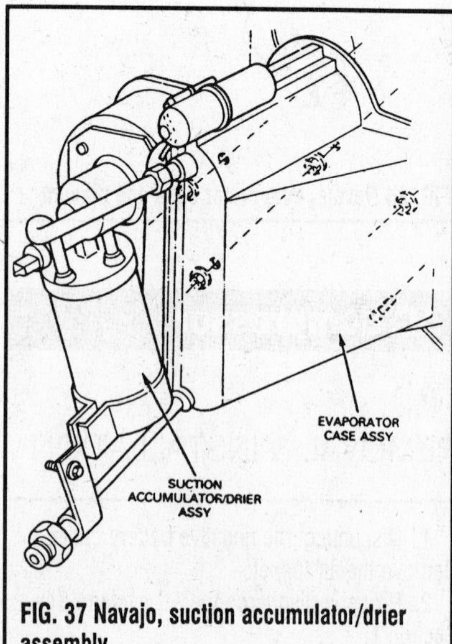

FIG. 37 Navajo, suction accumulator/drier assembly

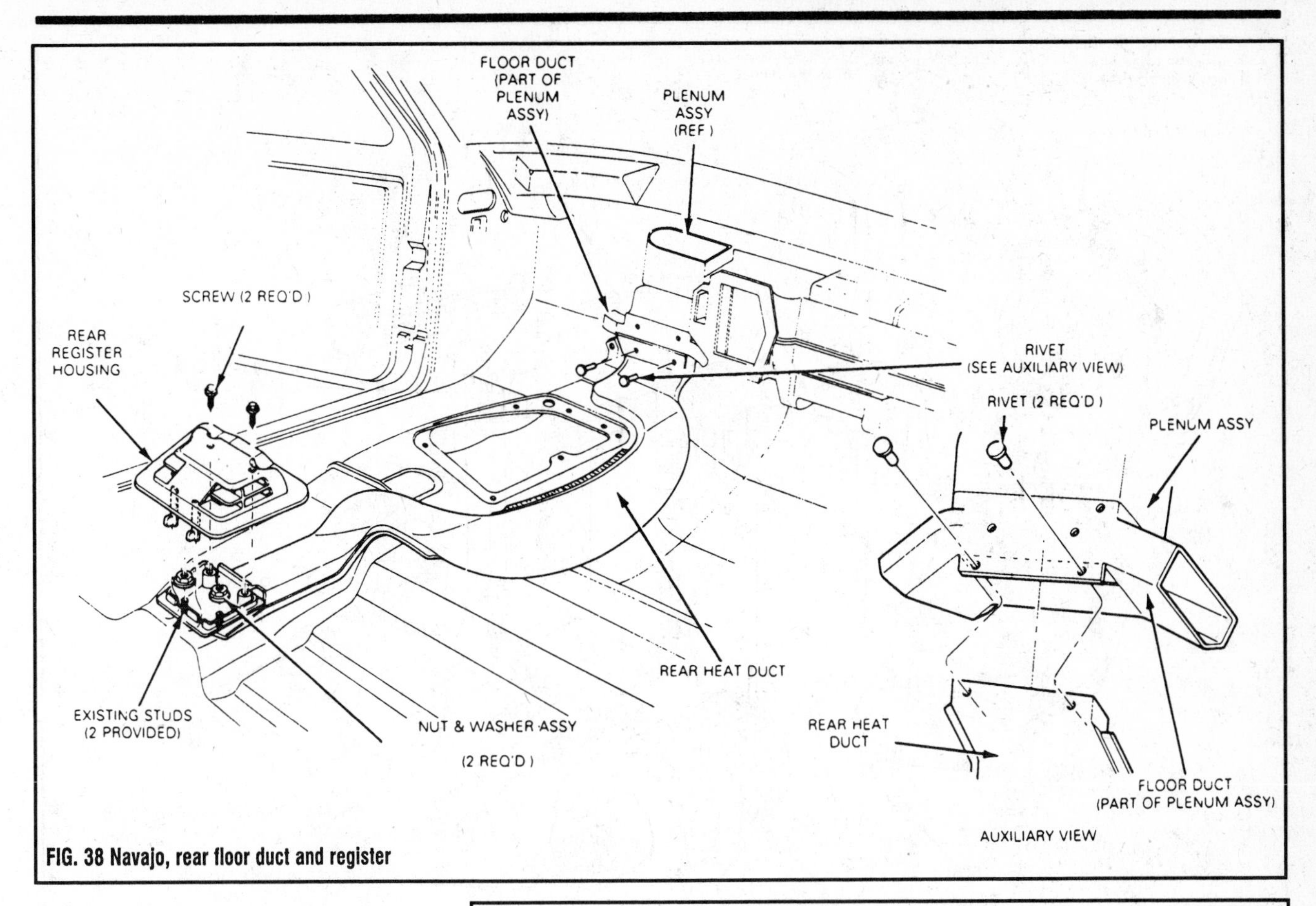

FIG. 38 Navajo, rear floor duct and register

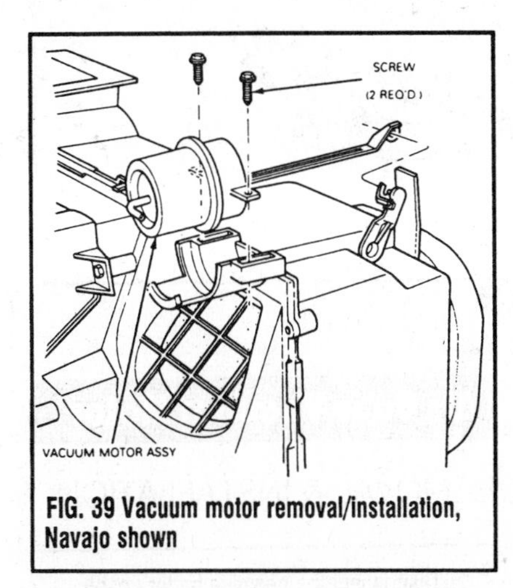

FIG. 39 Vacuum motor removal/installation, Navajo shown

Refrigerant Lines

REMOVAL & INSTALLATION

1. Disconnect the negative battery cable. Properly discharge the AC system. See Section 1.

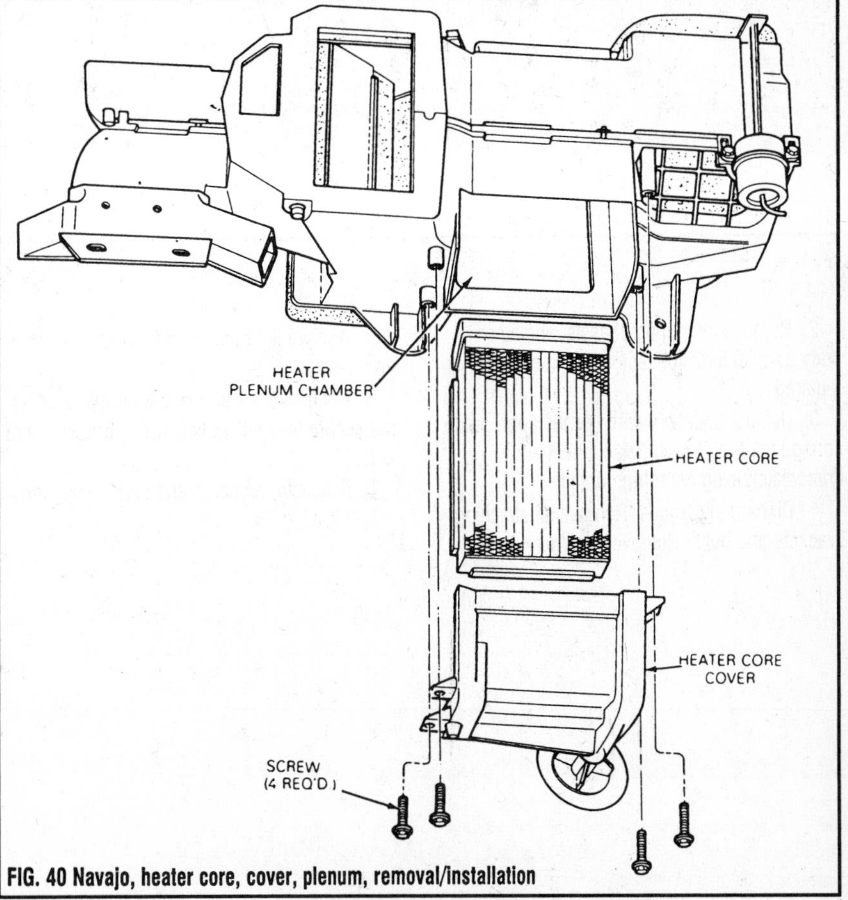

FIG. 40 Navajo, heater core, cover, plenum, removal/installation

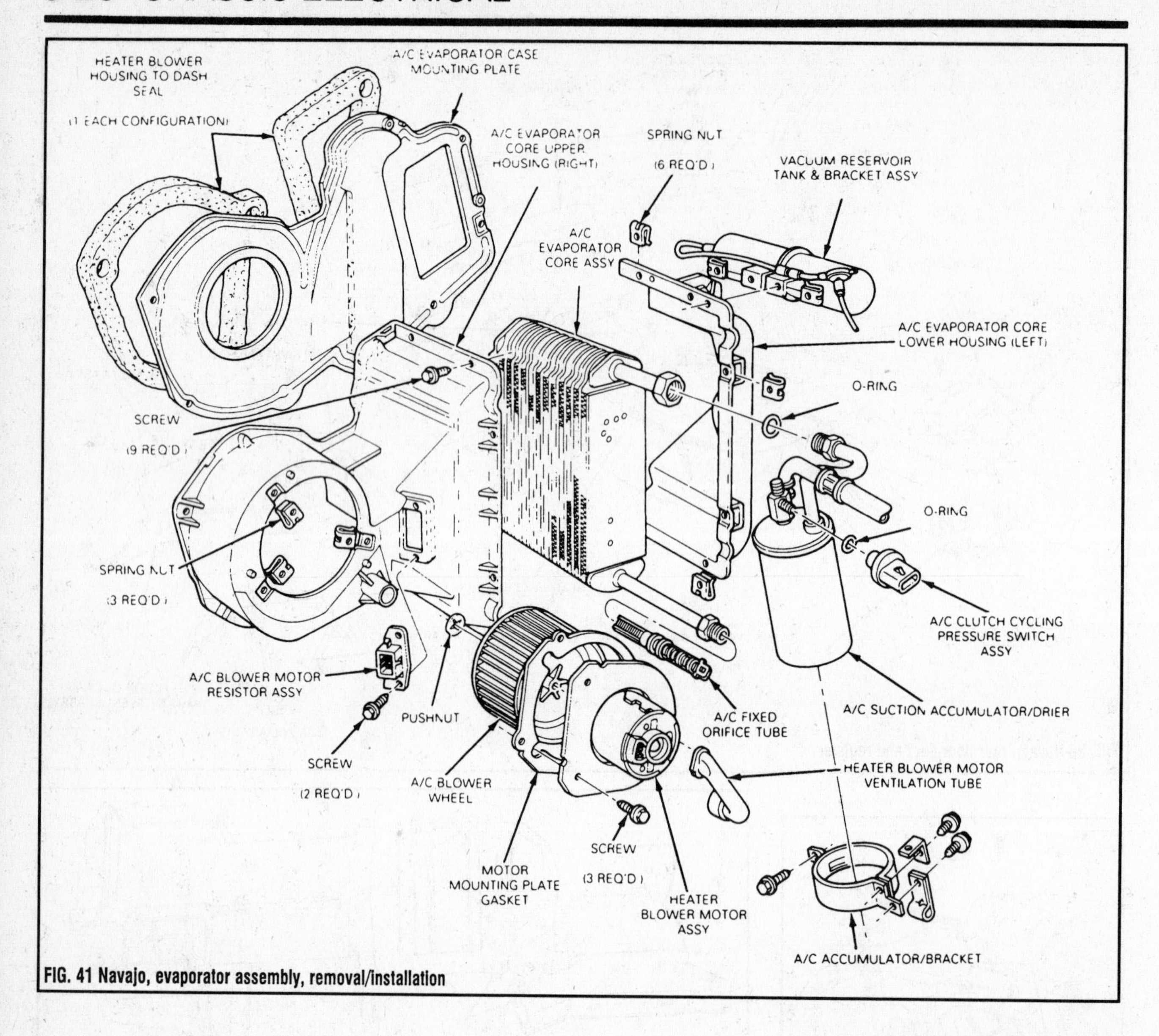

FIG. 41 Navajo, evaporator assembly, removal/installation

2. Remove interfering chassis, engine or body parts and disconnect wiring connectors as required.
3. Using a backup wrench or the appropriate spring lock tool, loosen, disconnect and immediately plug the refrigerant line.
4. Discard all O-rings. Remove all attaching brackets and bolts. Remove the line.
5. Apply a light coat of refrigerant oil to the new O-rings.
6. Connect the line, use the original routing and secure the line with attaching brackets and bolts.
7. Evacuate, recharge and test the system.

Air Door Vacuum Motor

REMOVAL & INSTALLATION

1. Disconnect the negative battery cable.
2. Remove the glove box. Disconnect the vacuum connection.
3. Remove the motor to plenum mounting screws and remove the motor.
4. Install in reverse order.

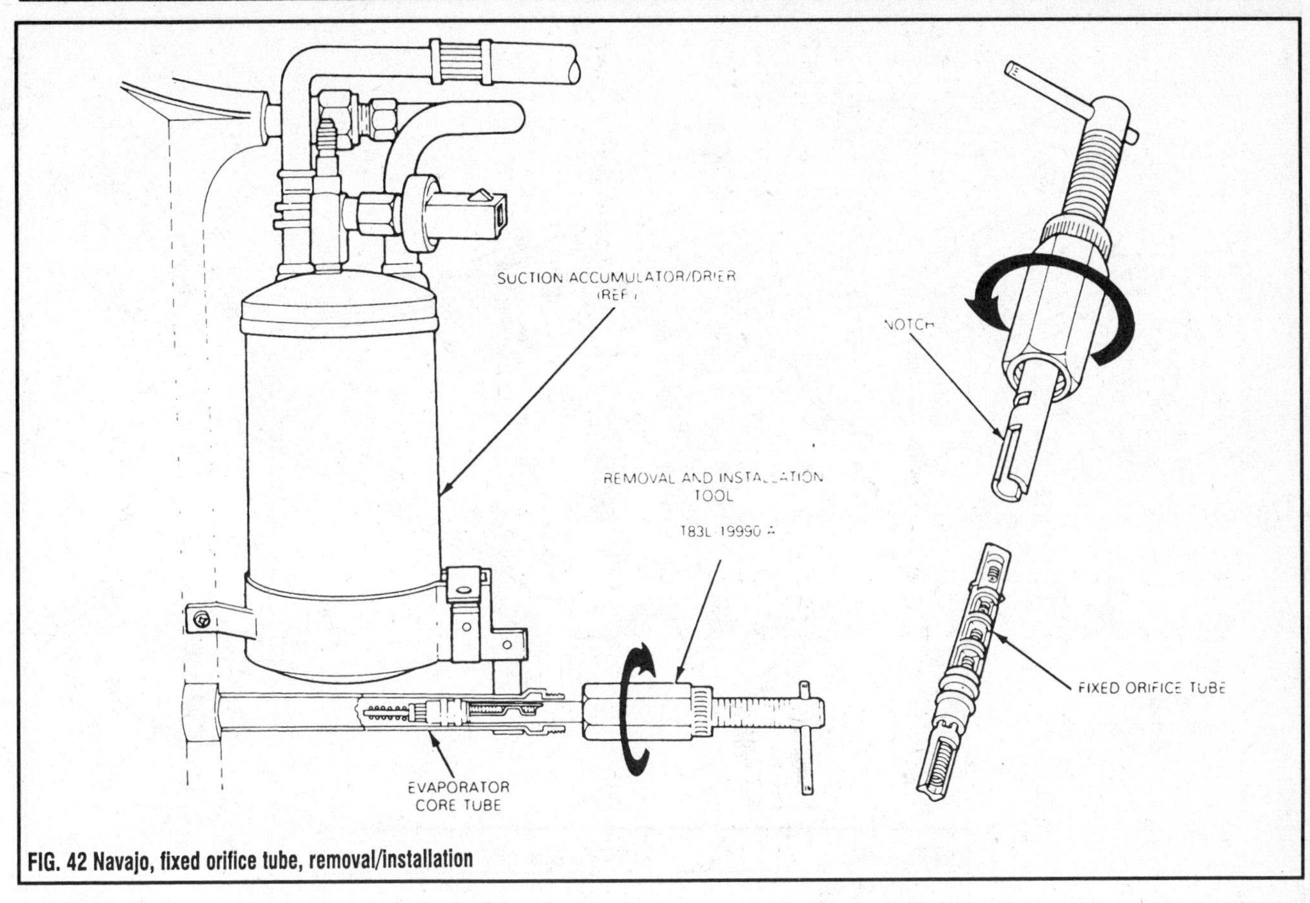

FIG. 42 Navajo, fixed orifice tube, removal/installation

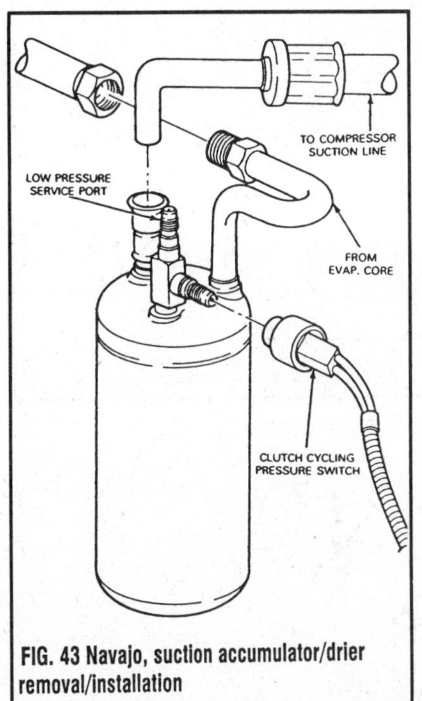

FIG. 43 Navajo, suction accumulator/drier removal/installation

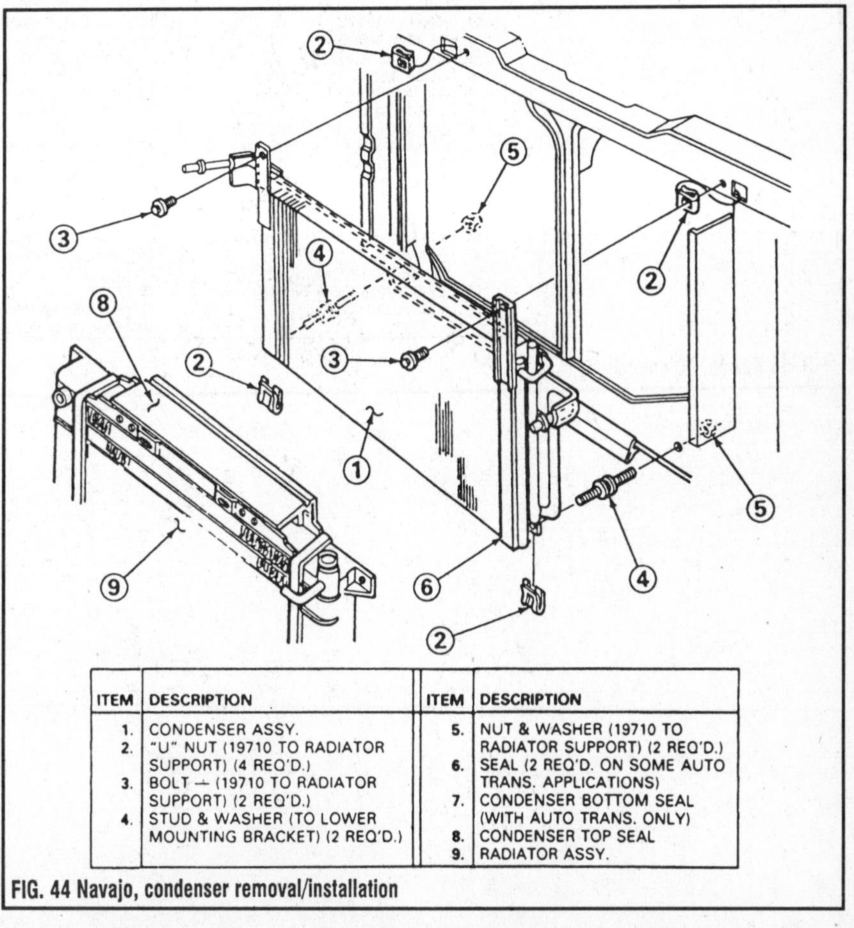

ITEM	DESCRIPTION	ITEM	DESCRIPTION
1.	CONDENSER ASSY.	5.	NUT & WASHER (19710 TO RADIATOR SUPPORT) (2 REQ'D.)
2.	"U" NUT (19710 TO RADIATOR SUPPORT) (4 REQ'D.)	6.	SEAL (2 REQ'D. ON SOME AUTO TRANS. APPLICATIONS)
3.	BOLT — (19710 TO RADIATOR SUPPORT) (2 REQ'D.)	7.	CONDENSER BOTTOM SEAL (WITH AUTO TRANS. ONLY)
4.	STUD & WASHER (TO LOWER MOUNTING BRACKET) (2 REQ'D.)	8.	CONDENSER TOP SEAL
		9.	RADIATOR ASSY.

FIG. 44 Navajo, condenser removal/installation

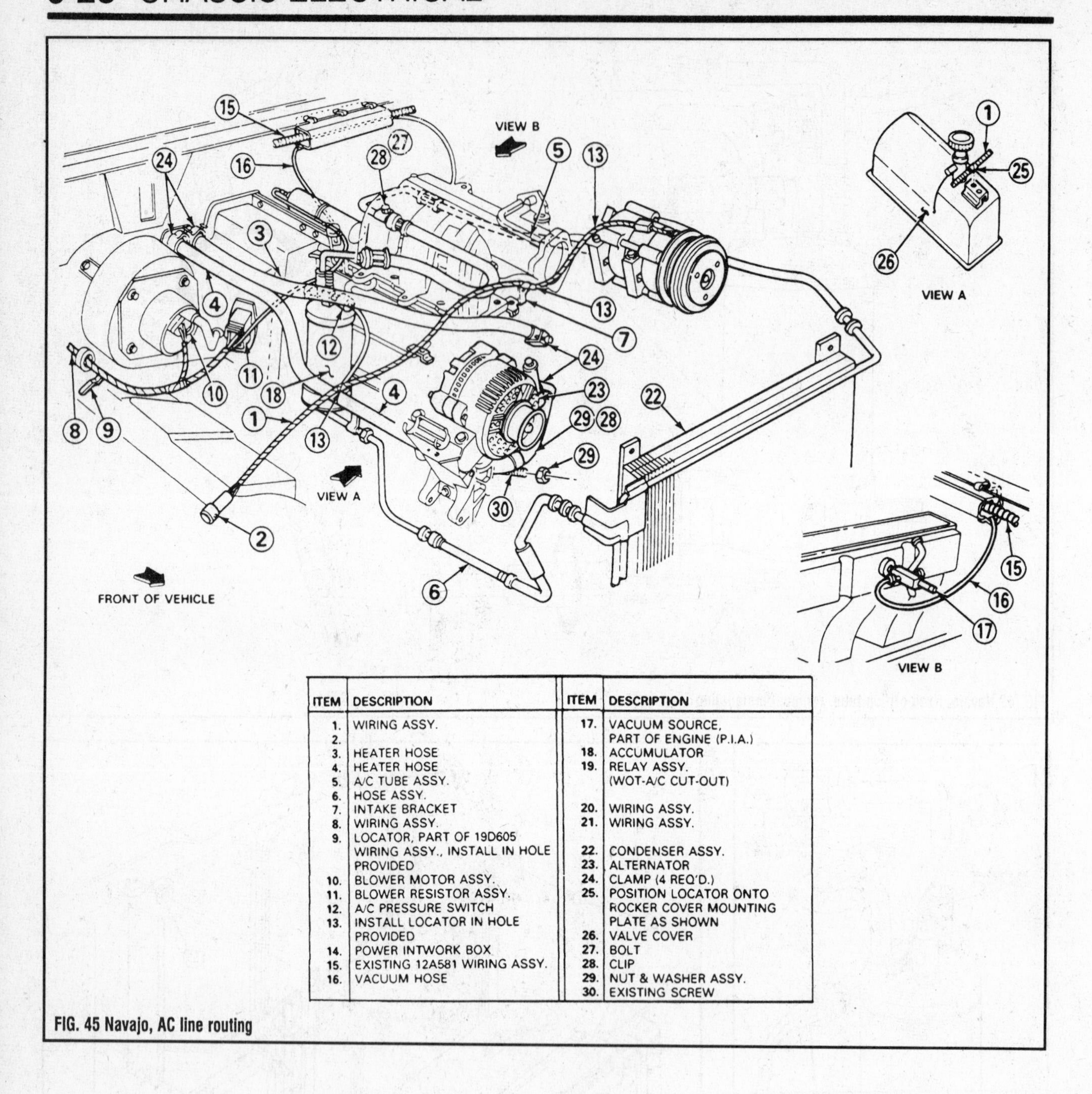

ITEM	DESCRIPTION	ITEM	DESCRIPTION
1.	WIRING ASSY.	17.	VACUUM SOURCE, PART OF ENGINE (P.I.A.)
2.		18.	ACCUMULATOR
3.	HEATER HOSE	19.	RELAY ASSY. (WOT-A/C CUT-OUT)
4.	HEATER HOSE	20.	WIRING ASSY.
5.	A/C TUBE ASSY.	21.	WIRING ASSY.
6.	HOSE ASSY.	22.	CONDENSER ASSY.
7.	INTAKE BRACKET	23.	ALTERNATOR
8.	WIRING ASSY.	24.	CLAMP (4 REQ'D.)
9.	LOCATOR, PART OF 19D605 WIRING ASSY., INSTALL IN HOLE PROVIDED	25.	POSITION LOCATOR ONTO ROCKER COVER MOUNTING PLATE AS SHOWN
10.	BLOWER MOTOR ASSY.	26.	VALVE COVER
11.	BLOWER RESISTOR ASSY.	27.	BOLT
12.	A/C PRESSURE SWITCH	28.	CLIP
13.	INSTALL LOCATOR IN HOLE PROVIDED	29.	NUT & WASHER ASSY.
14.	POWER INTWORK BOX	30.	EXISTING SCREW
15.	EXISTING 12A581 WIRING ASSY.		
16.	VACUUM HOSE		

FIG. 45 Navajo, AC line routing

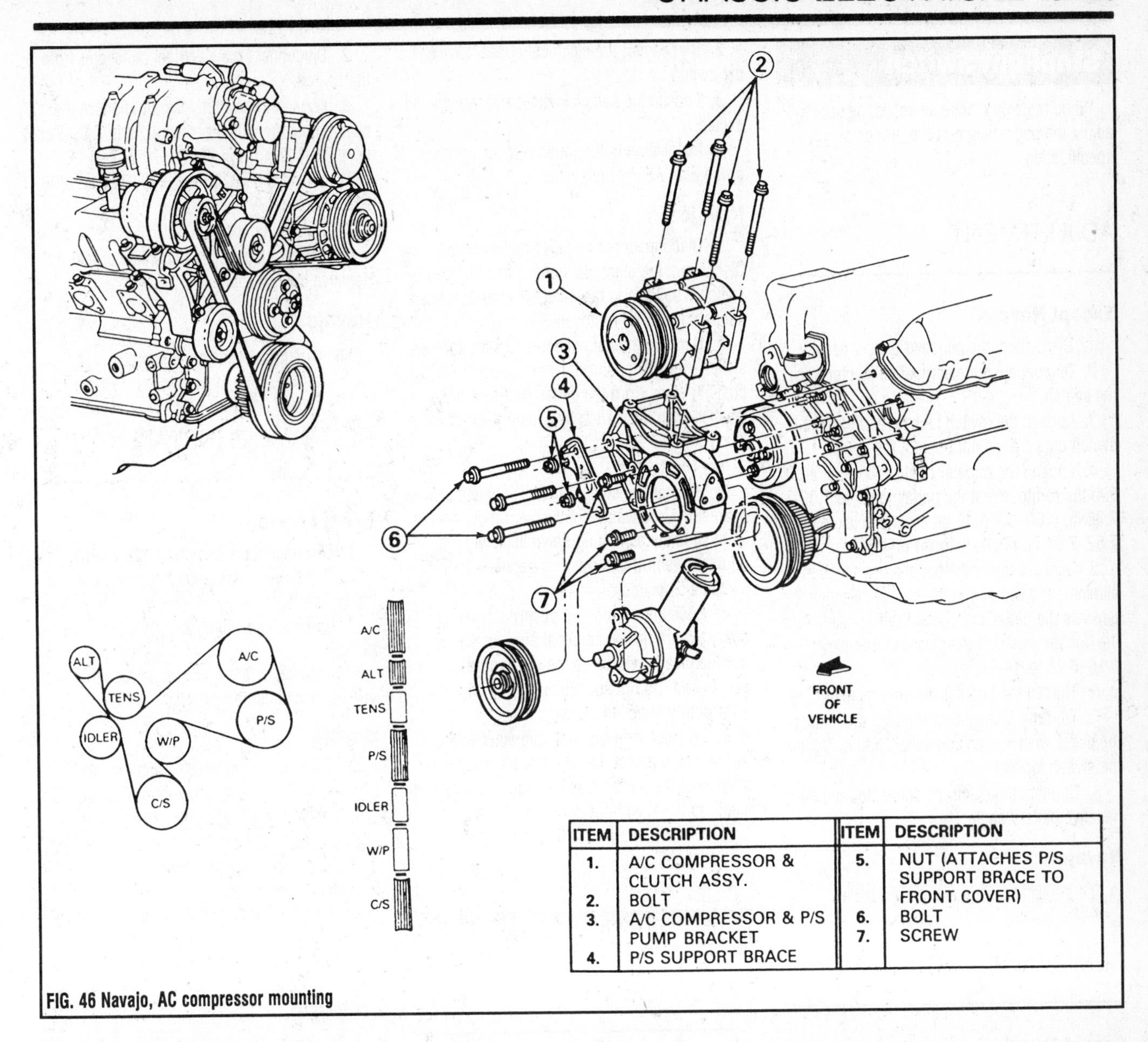

ITEM	DESCRIPTION	ITEM	DESCRIPTION
1.	A/C COMPRESSOR & CLUTCH ASSY.	5.	NUT (ATTACHES P/S SUPPORT BRACE TO FRONT COVER)
2.	BOLT	6.	BOLT
3.	A/C COMPRESSOR & P/S PUMP BRACKET	7.	SCREW
4.	P/S SUPPORT BRACE		

FIG. 46 Navajo, AC compressor mounting

CRUISE CONTROL

Actuator Cable

ADJUSTMENT

Except Navajo

1. Remove the clamp.
2. Adjust the nut so the actuator cable free-play is 0.04–0.12 in. (1–3mm) when the cable is pressed lightly.
3. Reinstall the clamp.

Navajo

1. Remove the cable retaining clip.
2. Disengage the throttle positioner.
3. Set the engine at hot idle.
4. Pull on the actuator cable to take up any slack. Maintain a light tension on the cable.
5. While holding the cable, insert the cable retaining clip and snap securely.

Vacuum Dump Valve

ADJUSTMENT

Navajo

1. Firmly hold the brake pedal in the up, released, position.
2. Push in the dump valve until the valve bottoms against the pad on the brake pedal.

Stoplight Switch

When replacing these switches, be sure to adjust the pedal height to the proper specification.

ADJUSTMENT

Except Navajo

1. Disconnect the negative battery cable.
2. Disconnect the electrical connector from the switch.
3. Loosen the switch locknut and turn the switch until it does not contact the pedal.
4. Loosen the booster pushrod locknut and turn the rod to adjust the pedal height to 7.09–7.28 in. (180–185mm) on B series pickup or 7.52–7.91 in. (191–201mm) on MPV.
5. Depress the brake pedal a few times to eliminate the vacuum in the system. Gently depress the pedal and check the free-play. Turn the booster pushrod to adjust the free-play to 0.16–0.28 in. (4–7mm).
6. Tighten the booster pushrod locknut.
7. Turn the stoplight switch until it contacts the pedal, then turn an additional 1/2 turn. Tighten the switch locknut.
8. Connect the electrical connector and the negative battery cable.

Navajo

The stoplight switch is not adjustable.

REMOVAL & INSTALLATION

Except Navajo

1. Disconnect the negative battery cable.
2. Disconnect the electrical connector from the switch.
3. Loosen the switch locknut and remove the switch.
4. Installation is the reverse of the removal procedure. Adjust the switch.

Navajo

1. Disconnect the negative battery cable. Disconnect the electrical connector from the switch. The locking tab must be lifted before the connector can be removed.
2. Remove the hairpin clip and slide the switch, booster pushrod, nylon washer and bushing away from the pedal. Remove the washer, then the switch by sliding the switch up or down.

To Install:

3. Position the switch so the U-shaped side is nearest the pedal and directly over/under the pin. Then slide the switch up/down installing the booster pushrod and bushing between the switch side plates.
4. Push the switch and pushrod assembly firmly toward the brake pedal arm. Install the outside plastic washer to the pin and install the hairpin clip. Do not substitute for this clip. Use only factory supplied hairpin clips.
5. Connect the electrical connector to the switch and connect the negative battery cable. Make sure the switch wire harness has sufficient length to travel with the switch during the full stroke of the brake pedal. Check the switch for proper operation.

Clutch Switch

ADJUSTMENT

Except Navajo

1. Disconnect the negative battery cable.
2. Disconnect the electrical connector from the switch.
3. Loosen the switch locknut and turn the switch until the clutch pedal height is 7.13–7.52 in. (181–191mm) on B2200, 7.52–7.91 in. (191–201mm) on B2600 or 8.19–8.58 in. (208–218mm) on MPV.
4. Tighten the locknut.
5. Connect the electrical connector and the negative battery cable.

Navajo

The clutch switch is not adjustable.

REMOVAL & INSTALLATION

Except Navajo

1. Disconnect the negative battery cable.
2. Disconnect the electrical connector from the switch.
3. Loosen the switch locknut and remove the switch.
4. Installation is the reverse of the removal procedure. Adjust the switch.

Navajo

1. Disconnect the negative battery cable. Disconnect the wiring harness from the switch.
2. Pull the orientation clip away from the switch to separate it from the pin on the switch.
3. Rotate the switch to expose the plastic retainer.
4. Push the tabs together to allow the retainer to slide rearward and separate from the switch.
5. Remove the switch from the pushrod.
6. Installation is the reverse of the removal procedure.

AUDIO SYSTEMS

➧ SEE FIGS. 47-54

For best FM reception, adjust the antenna to a height of 31 inches. For best AM reception, extend the antenna to its full height.

⁂ WARNING

Never operate the radio with the speaker lead or antenna disconnected! Operation of the radio without a load will damage the amplifier's output transistors. If a replacement speaker is installed, be sure it is of the same impedance (resistance in ohms) as the original.

REMOVAL & INSTALLATION

Pickups

1. Disconnect the battery ground.
2. Disconnect the antenna lead, wiring and speaker connectors behind the radio.
3. Remove the radio pod mounting screws and lift out the unit.
4. Installation is the reverse of removal.

MPV

1. Disconnect the battery ground.
2. Remove the radio trim panel.
3. Remove the radio mounting screws and pull the radio out slowly until you can reach the wiring connectors. Disconnect the wiring and unplug the antenna.
4. Installation is the reverse of removal.

Navajo

KNOB TYPE RADIO

1. Disconnect the battery ground cable.
2. Remove the knobs and discs from the radio control shafts.
3. Remove the two steering column shroud-to-panel retaining screws and remove the shroud.
4. Detach the cluster trim cover or appliques from the instrument panel by removing the eight screws.
5. Remove the four screws securing the mounting plate assembly to the instrument panel and remove the radio with the mounting plate and rear bracket.

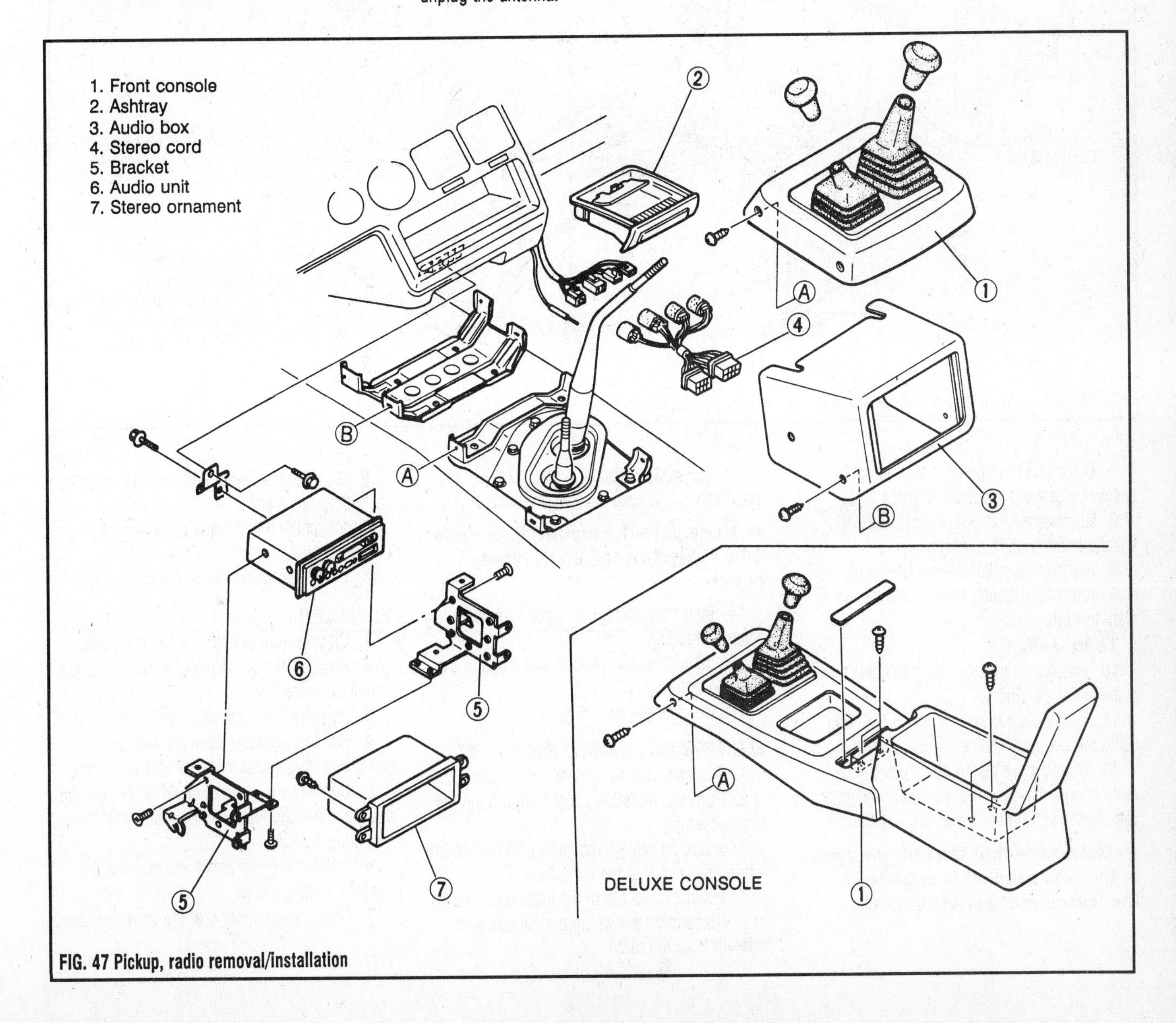

FIG. 47 Pickup, radio removal/installation

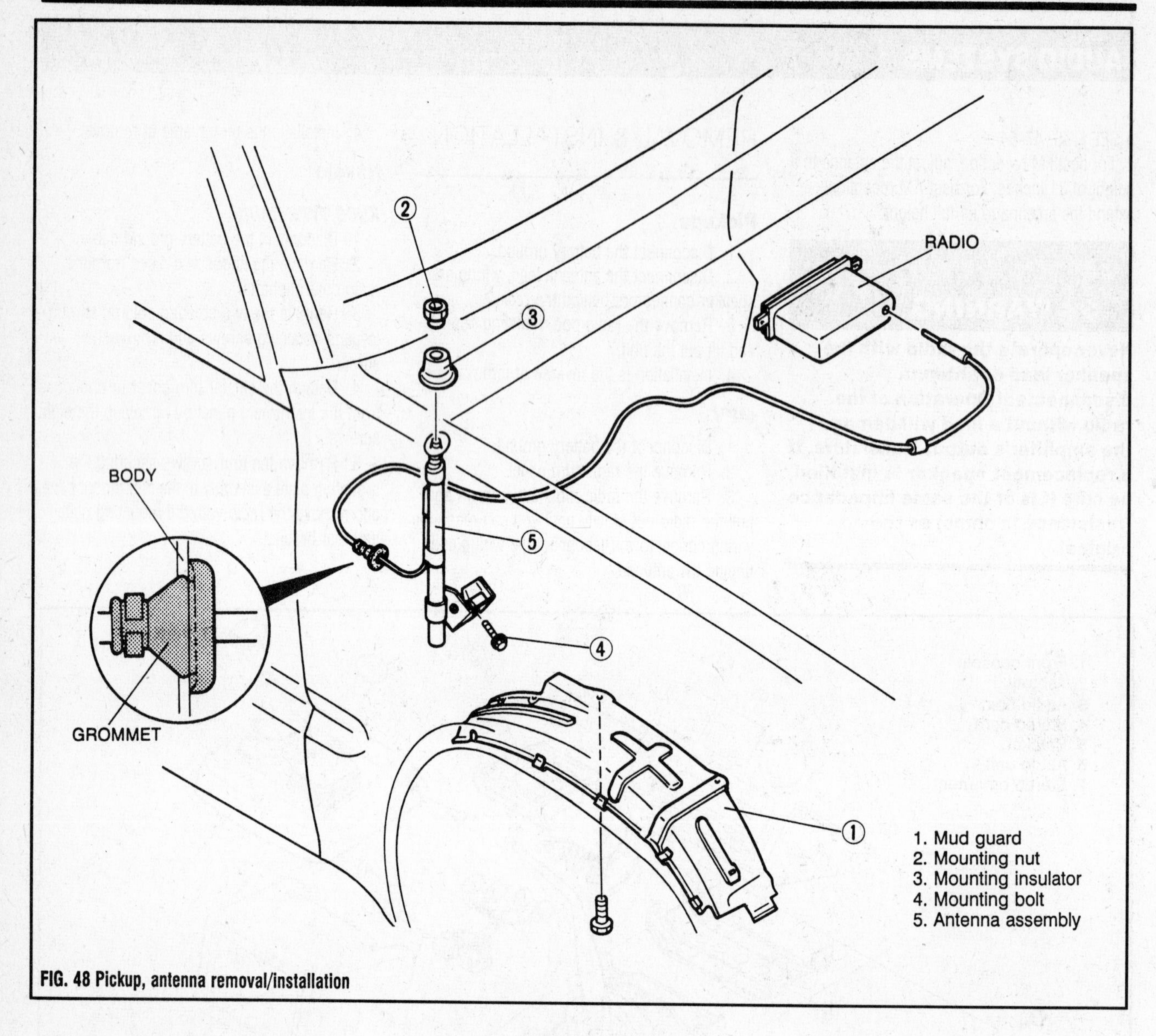

FIG. 48 Pickup, antenna removal/installation

7. Disconnect the antenna lead-in cable, speaker wires and the radio (power) wire.
8. Remove the nut and washer assembly attaching the radio rear support.
9. Remove the nuts and washers from the radio control shafts and remove the mounting plate from the radio.

To install:

10. Install the radio rear support using the nut and washer assembly.
11. Install the mounting plate to the radio using the two lock washers and two nuts.
12. Connect the wiring connectors to the radio and position the radio with the mounting plate to the instrument panel.

➡ Make sure that the hair pin area of the rear bracket is engaged to the instrument panel support.

13. Secure the mounting plate to the instrument panel with the four screws.

➡ Make sure the mounting plate is fully seated on the instrument panel.

14. Install the panel trim covers and steering column shroud.
15. Install the panel knobs and discs to the radio control shafts.
16. Connect the battery ground cable.

ELECTRONICALLY TUNED RADIO (ETR)

1. Disconnect the negative battery cable.
2. Remove the finish panel from around the radio assembly.
3. Insert the radio removal tool T87P-19061-A or equivalent, into the radio face.
4. Pull the radio out of the instrument panel.
5. Disconnect the wiring connectors and antenna from the radio.
6. Connect the wiring and slide the radio into the instrument panel.
7. Install the finish panel and connect the battery cable.
8. Check the operation of the radio.

EQUALIZER

1. Disconnect the negative battery cable.
2. Remove the finish panel from around the equalizer assembly.
3. Remove the 4 equalizer mounting screws.
4. Pull the equalizer from the instrument panel and disconnect the electrical connector.
5. Connect the electrical lead and install the equalizer into the instrument panel. Install the mounting screws.
6. Install the finish panel and connect the negative battery cable.
7. Check the operation of the stereo system.

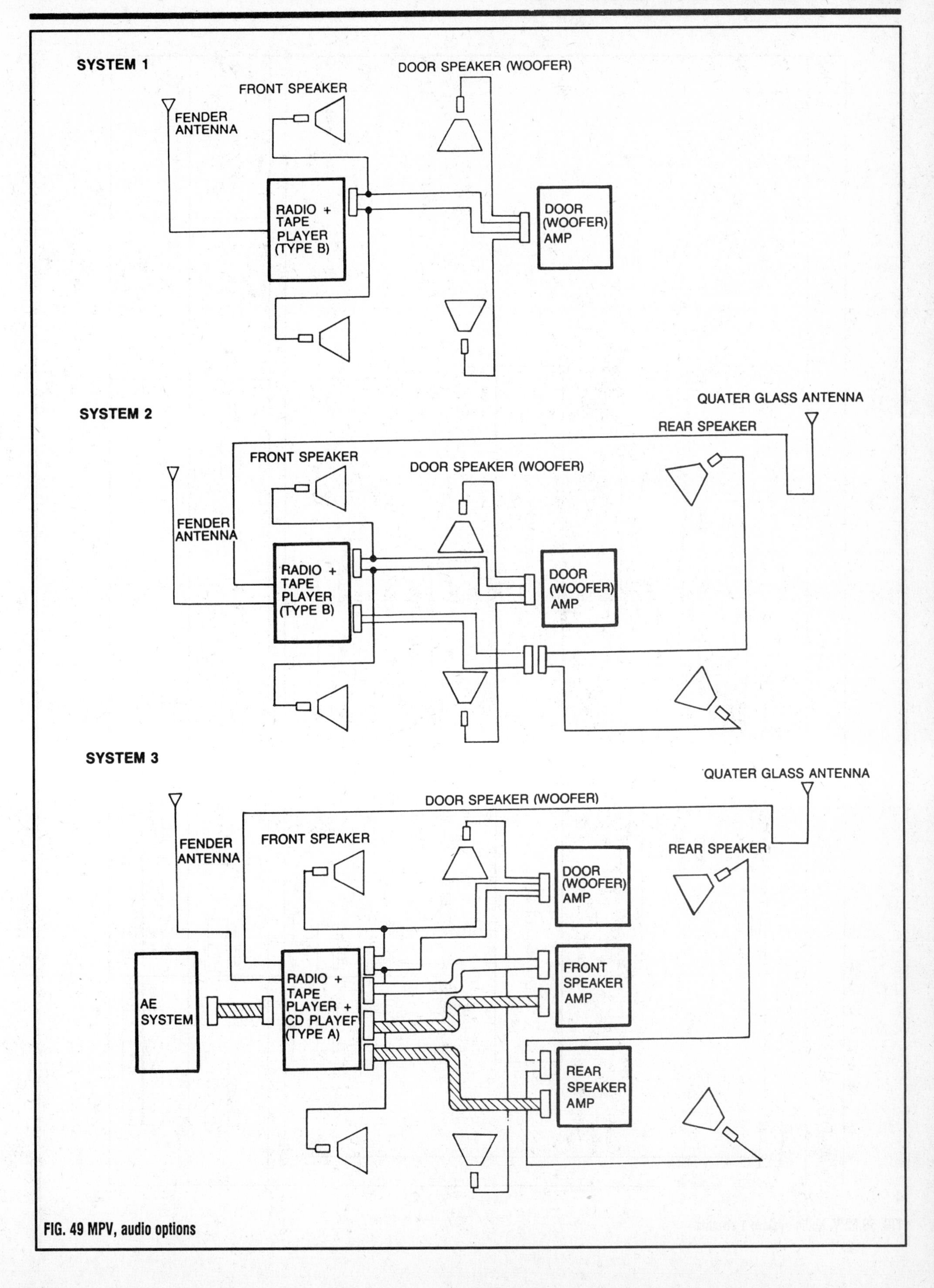

FIG. 49 MPV, audio options

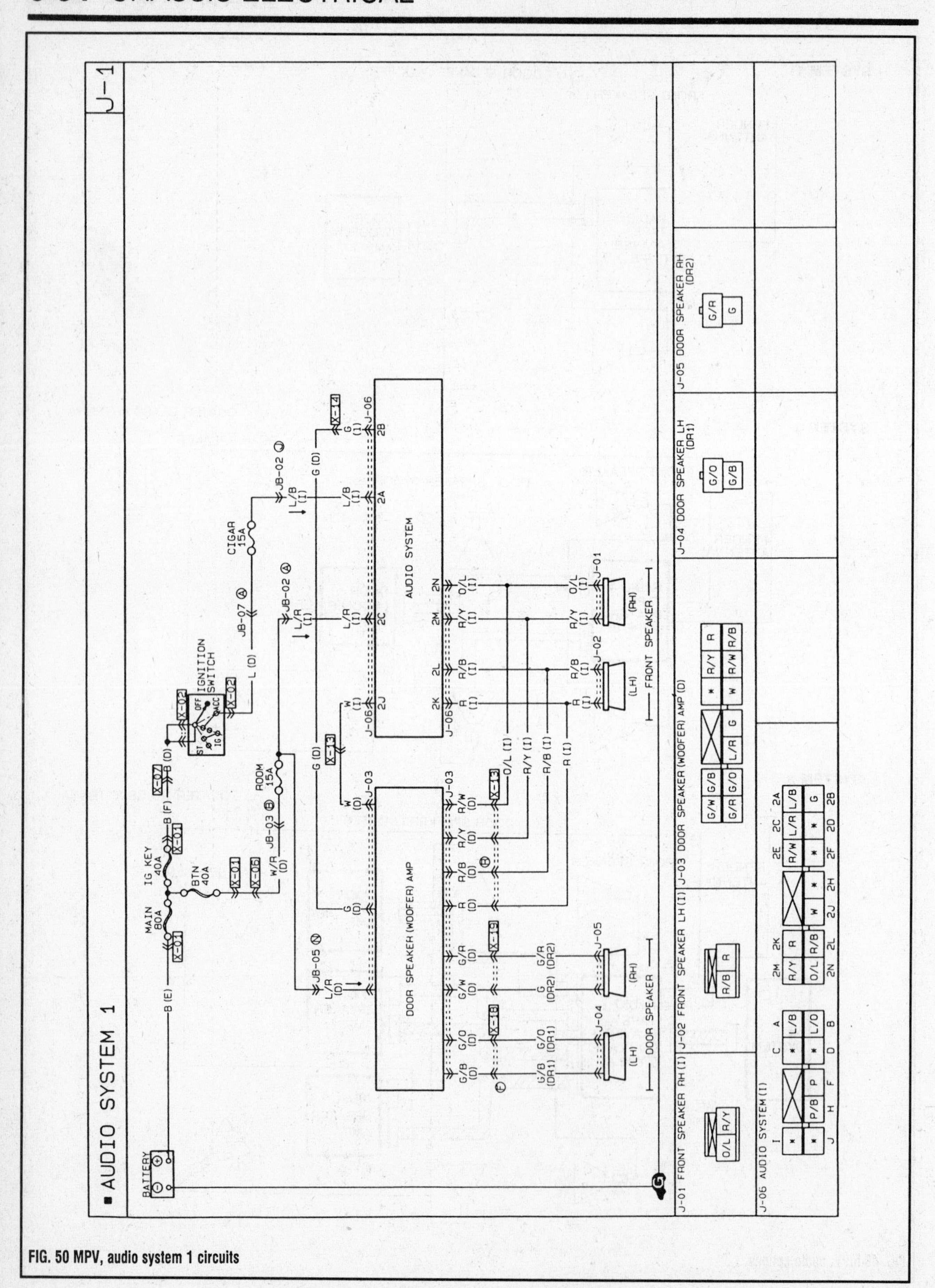

FIG. 50 MPV, audio system 1 circuits

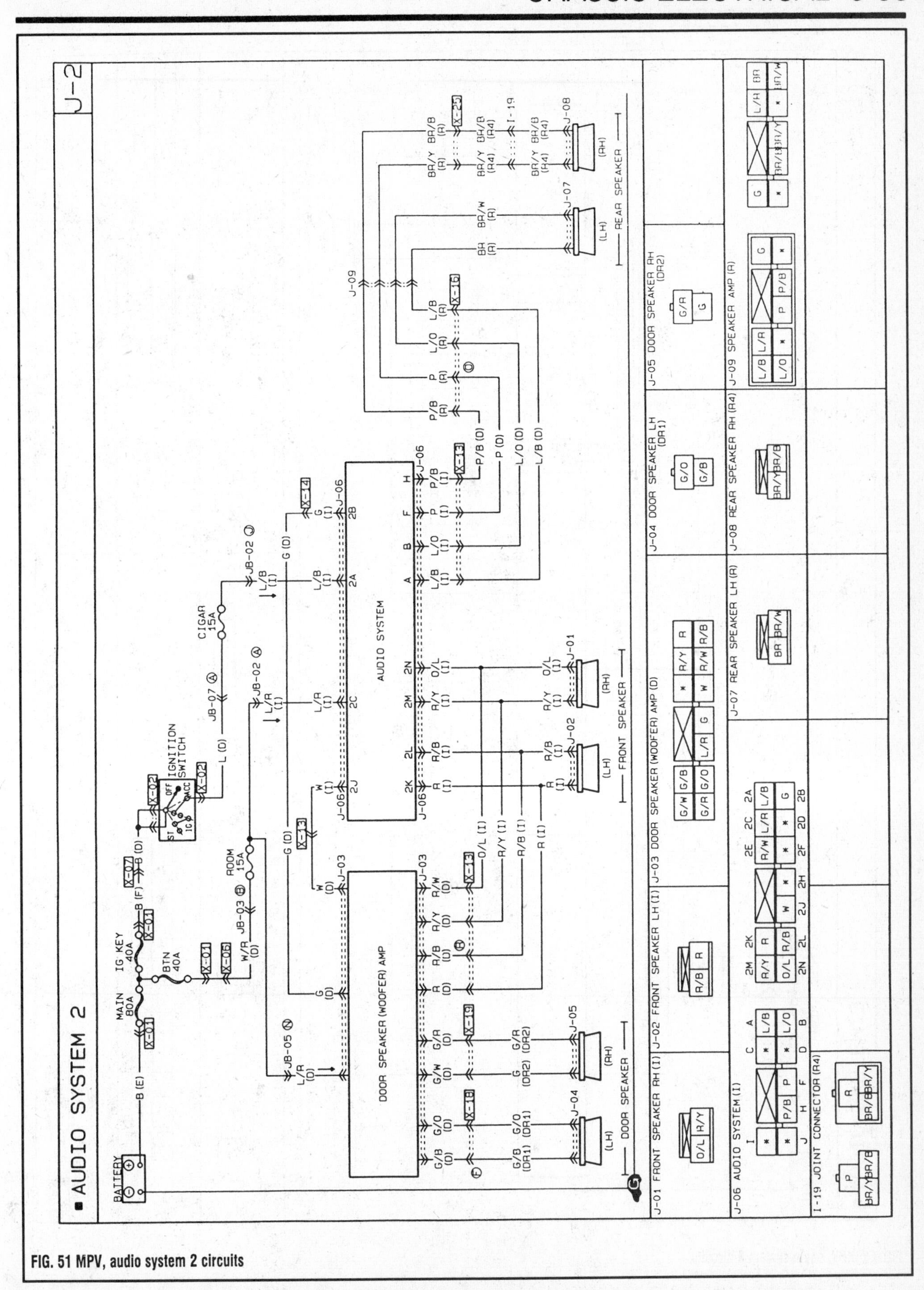

FIG. 51 MPV, audio system 2 circuits

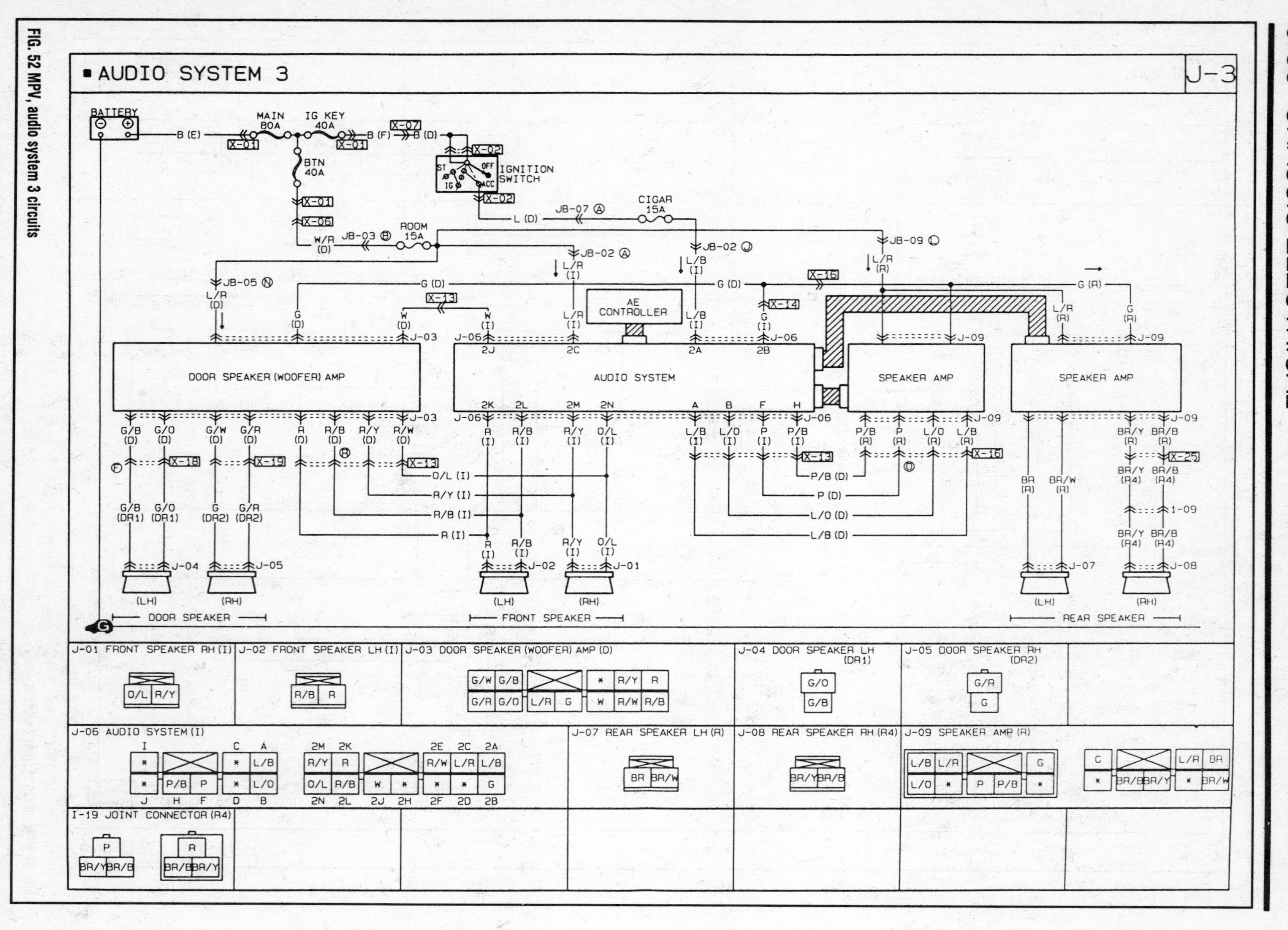

FIG. 52 MPV, audio system 3 circuits

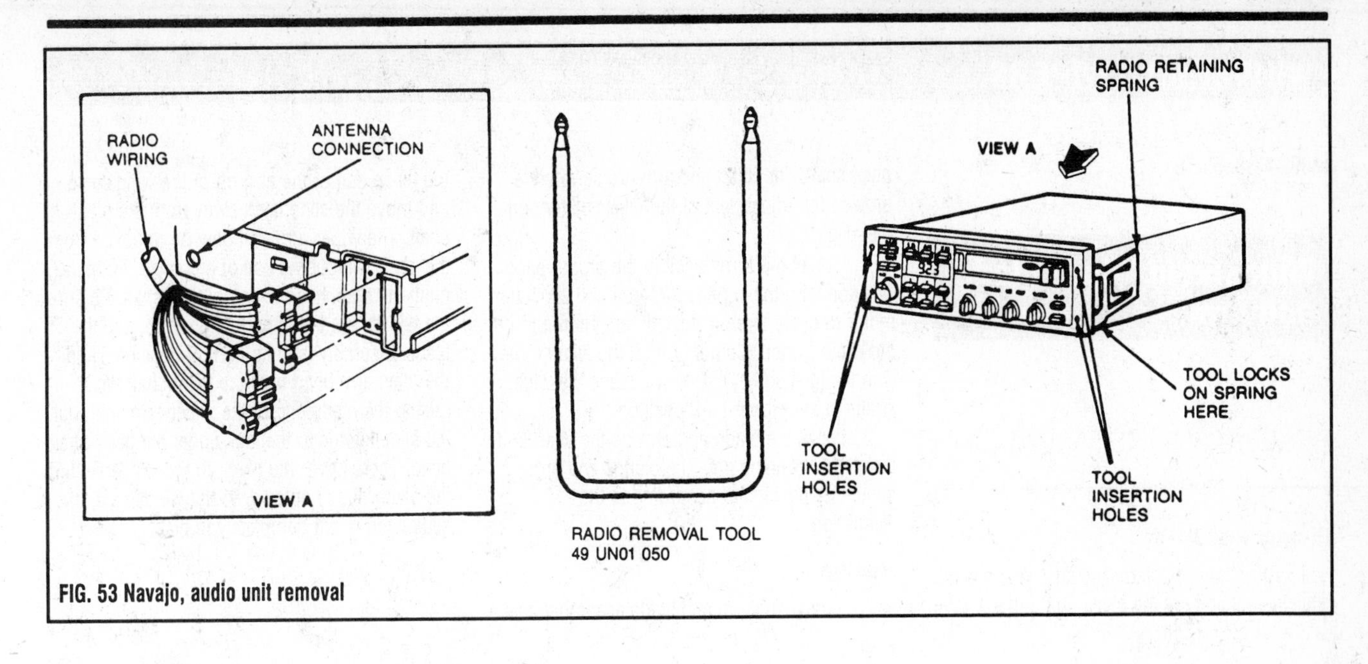

FIG. 53 Navajo, audio unit removal

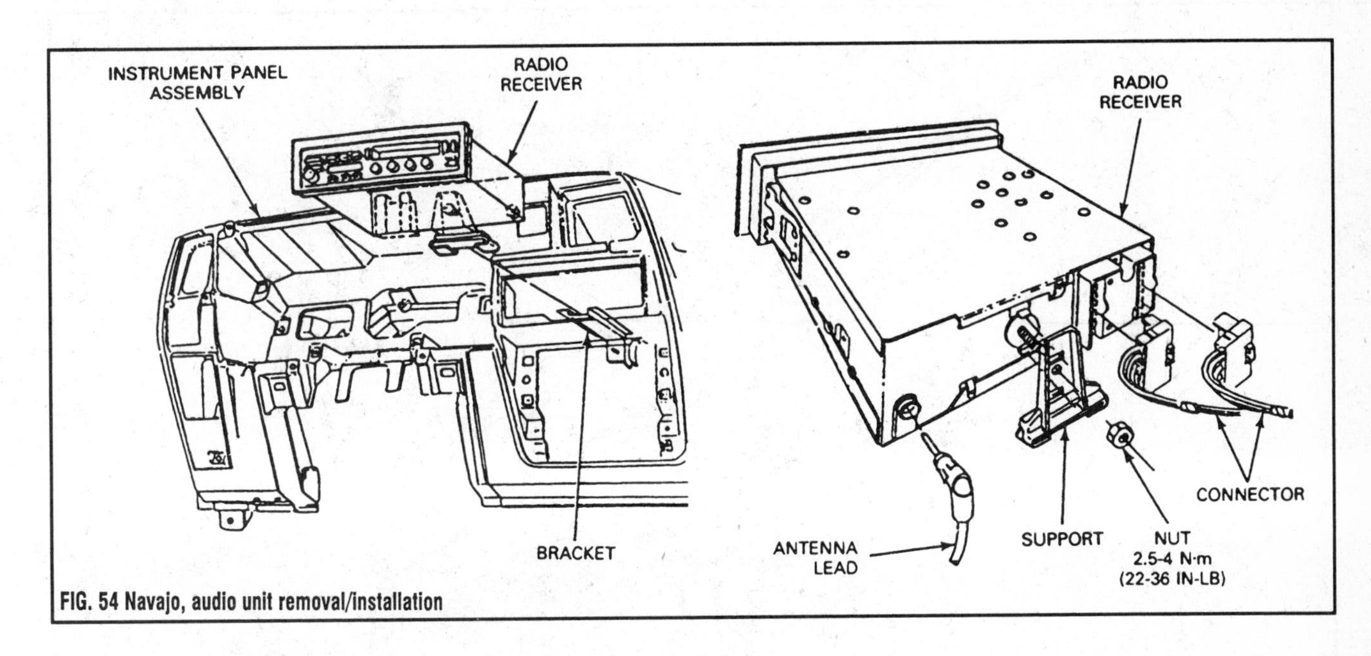

FIG. 54 Navajo, audio unit removal/installation

WINDSHIELD WIPERS

➧ SEE FIGS. 55-59

Windshield Wiper Blade and Arm

REMOVAL & INSTALLATION

Pickup and MPV

1. To remove the blade and arm, unscrew the retaining nut and pry the blade and arm from the pivot shaft. The shaft and arm are serrated to provide for adjustment of the wiper pattern on the glass.

2. To set the arms back in the proper park position, turn the wiper switch on and allow the motor to cycle three or four times. Then turn off the wiper switch (do not turn off the wiper motor with the ignition key). This will place the wiper shafts in the proper park position.

3. Install the blade and arm on the shaft and install the retaining nut. The blades and arms should be positioned according to the illustration.

Navajo

To remove the arm and blade assembly, raise the blade end of the arm off of the windshield and move the slide latch away from the pivot shaft. The wiper arm can now be removed from the shaft without the use of any tools. To install, push the main head over the pivot shaft. Be sure the wipers are in the parked position, and the blade assembly is in its correct position. Hold the main arm head onto the pivot shaft while raising the blade end of the wiper arm and push the slide latch into the lock under the pivot shaft head. Then, lower the blade to the windshield. If the blade does not lower to the windshield, the slide latch is not completely in place.

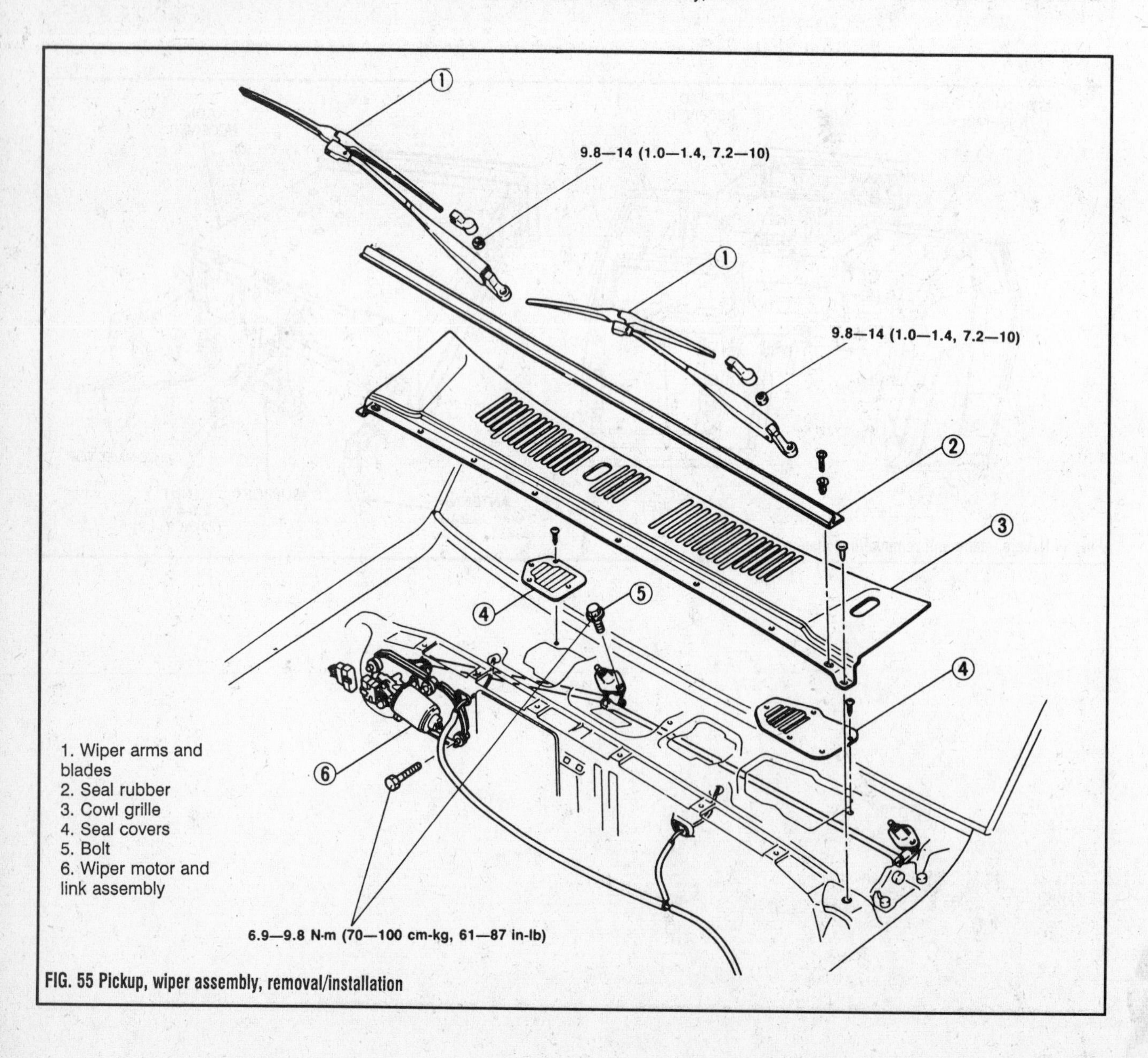

FIG. 55 Pickup, wiper assembly, removal/installation

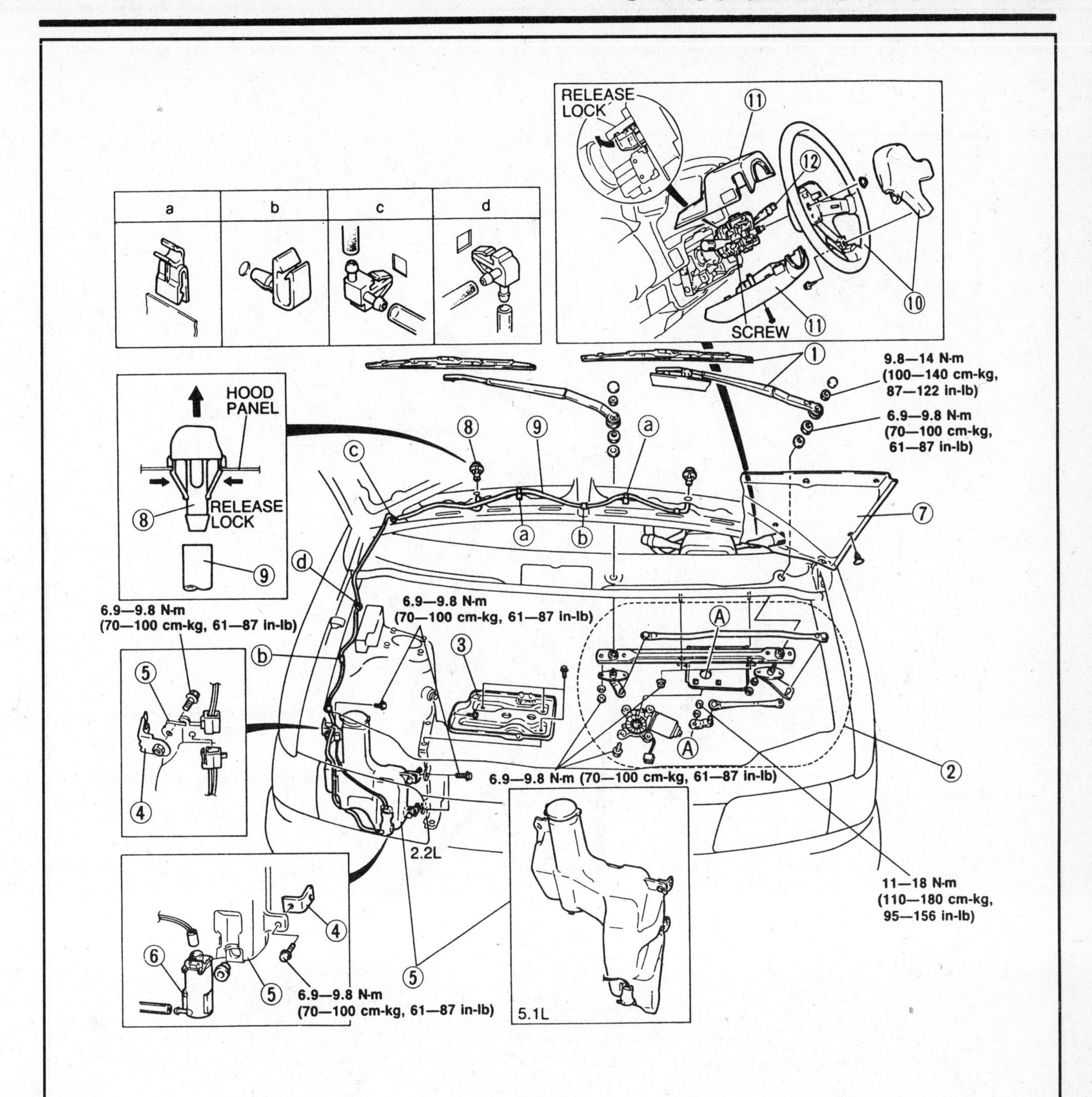

1. Wiper arm and blade
2. Wiper motor and link
Washer tank and motor
3. Battery tray
4. Tank bracket
5. Washer tank assembly
6. Washer motor
Washer pipe and nozzle
7. Hood insulator
8. Washer nozzle
9. Washer pipe
Wiper and washer switch
10. Steering column
11. Column cover
12. Wiper and washer switch (in combination switch)

FIG. 56 MPV, windshield wiper and components, removal/installation

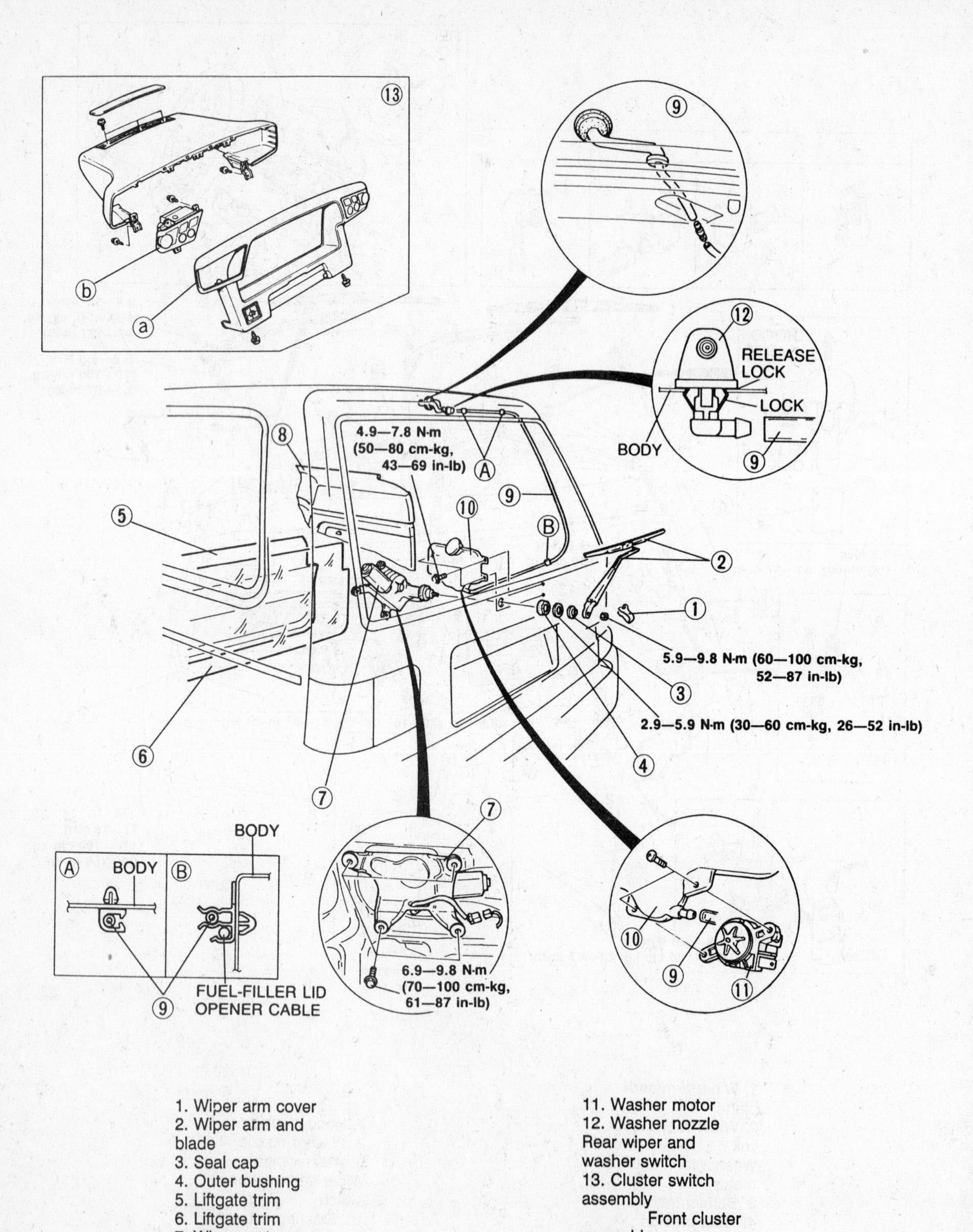

1. Wiper arm cover
2. Wiper arm and blade
3. Seal cap
4. Outer bushing
5. Liftgate trim
6. Liftgate trim
7. Wiper motor
Washer
8. Side trim
9. Washer pipe
10. Washer tank
11. Washer motor
12. Washer nozzle
Rear wiper and washer switch
13. Cluster switch assembly
Front cluster assembly
Rear wiper and washer switch (in left cluster)

FIG. 57 MPV, rear window wiper and components, removal/installation

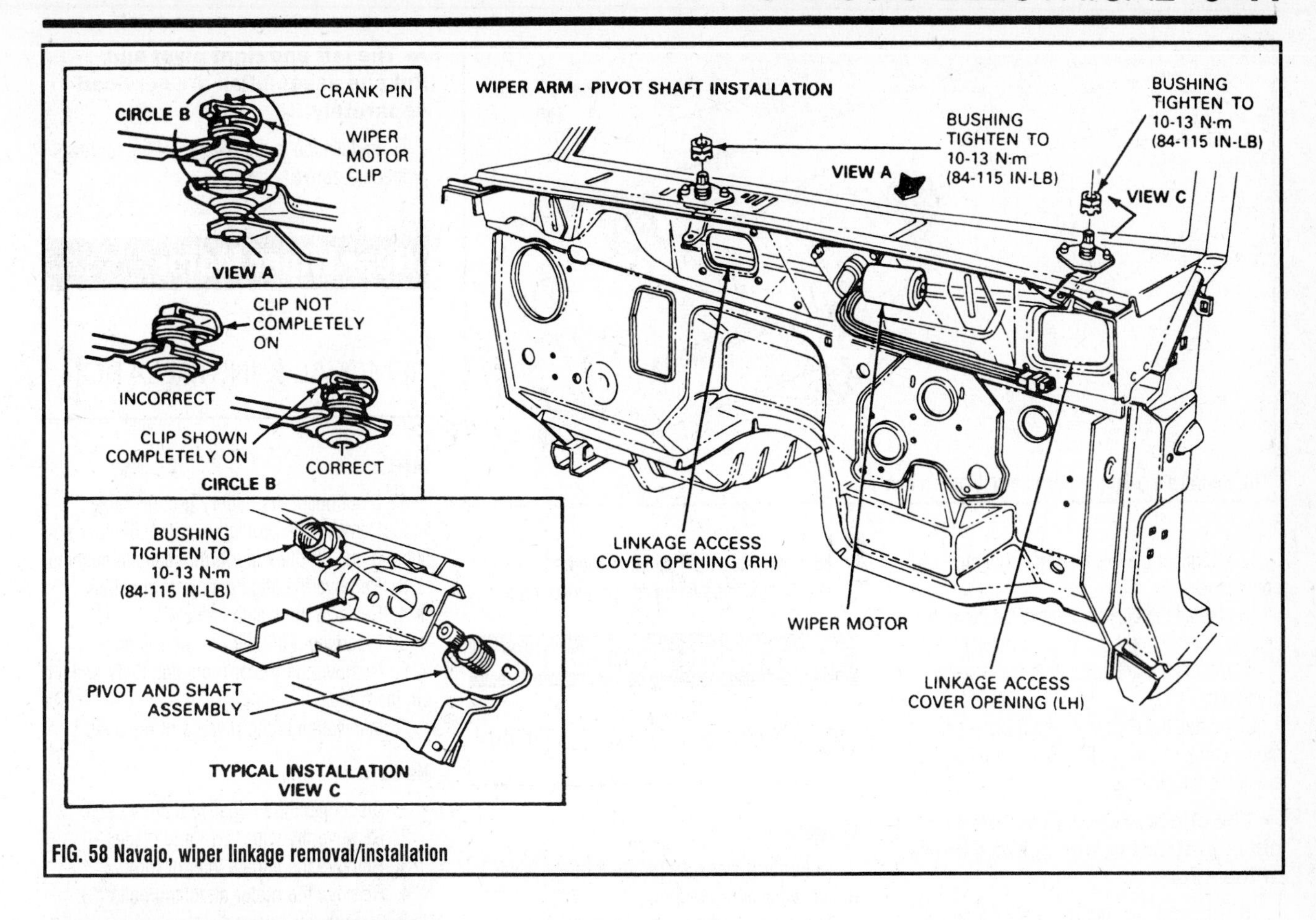

FIG. 58 Navajo, wiper linkage removal/installation

Windshield Wiper Motor, Linkage and Bracket

REMOVAL & INSTALLATION

Pickup

1. Remove the wiper arm/blade assembly. Note that the arms are different. Don't confuse them.
2. Remove the rubber seal from the leading edge of the cowl.
3. Unbolt and remove the cowl.
4. Remove the access hole covers.
5. Remove the bolts holding the wiper shaft drives.
6. Matchmark the position of the wiper crank arm in relation to the face of the wiper motor. Disconnect the wiper linkage from the wiper motor crank arm.
7. Remove the wiper linkage.
8. Unbolt and remove the wiper motor. Disconnect the wiring harness.
9. Installation is the reverse of removal. Make sure that the parked height of the wiper arms, measured from the blade tips to the windshield molding is 20mm (0.787 in.). Torque the arm retaining nuts to 8–10 ft. lbs.

Windshield Wiper Motor

REMOVAL & INSTALLATION

MPV

1. Remove the wiper arms.
2. Remove the drive link nuts from the top of the cowl.
3. Working under the hood, disconnect the battery ground cable.
4. Remove the motor and linkage mounting bolts and lift out the assembly.
5. After removal, you can separate the linkage from the motor. If you don't have to, don't remove the motor arm from the motor. The position of the arm on the motor shaft controls the automatic park position.
6. Installation is the reverse of removal. When installing the wiper arms, make sure that the at-rest position gives a gap of 30mm between the blade tips and the lower windshield molding.

Navajo

1. Turn the wiper switch on. Turn the ignition switch on until the blades are straight up and then turn ignition off to keep them there.
2. Remove the right wiper arm and blade.
3. Remove the negative battery cable.
4. Remove the right pivot nut and allow the linkage to drop into the cowl.
5. Remove the linkage access cover, located on the right side of the dash panel near the wiper motor.
6. Reach through the access cover opening and unsnap the wiper motor clip.
7. Push the clip away from the linkage until it clears the nib on the crank pin. Then, push the clip off the linkage.
8. Remove the wiper linkage from motor crank pin.
9. Disconnect the wiper motor's wiring connector.
10. Remove the wiper motor's three attaching screws and remove the motor.

To install:

11. Install the motor and attach the three attaching screws. Tighten to 60-65 inch lbs. (6.7-7.3 Nm).

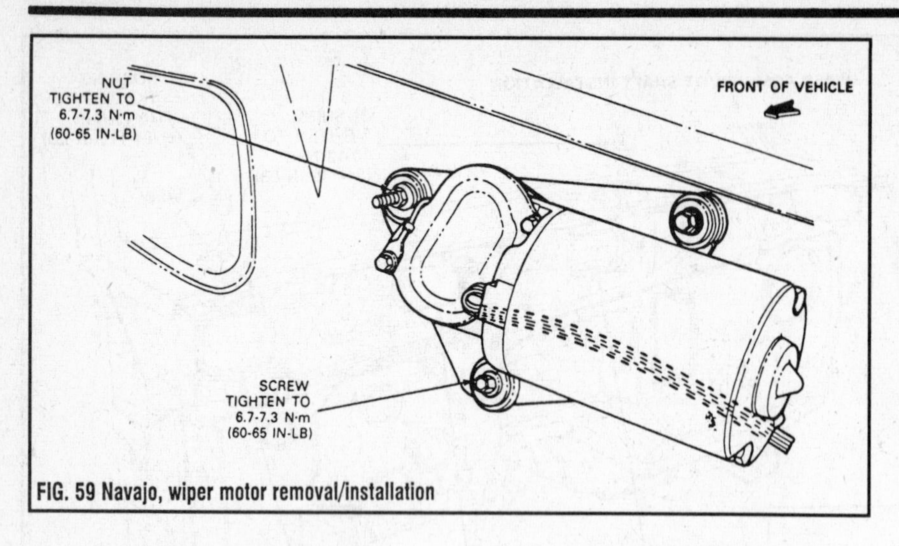

FIG. 59 Navajo, wiper motor removal/installation

12. Connect the wiper motor's wiring connector.
13. Install the clip completely on the right linkage. Make sure the clip is completely on.
14. Install the left linkage on the wiper motor crank pin.
15. Install the right linkage on the wiper motor crank pin and pull the linkage on to the crank pin until it snaps.

➡ **The clip is properly installed if the nib is protruding through the center of the clip.**

16. Reinstall the right wiper pivot shaft and nut.
17. Reconnect the battery and turn the ignition **ON**. Turn the wiper switch off so the wiper motor will park, then turn the ignition **OFF**. Replace the right linkage access cover.
18. Install the right wiper blade and arm.
19. Check the system for proper operation.

Pivot Shaft and Linkage

REMOVAL & INSTALLATION

Navajo

1. Perform steps 1 through 8 of the wiper motor removal procedure.
2. Slide the right pivot shaft and linkage assembly out through the R.H. access opening.
3. If the left linkage is to be serviced, remove the L.H. wiper arm and blade assembly.
4. Remove the left linkage access cover.
5. Remove the left pivot nut, lower the linkage and slide it out through the L.H. access opening.

➡ **The left and right pivot and linkage assemblies are serviced separately.**

6. Installation is the reverse of the removal procedure above.

Rear Wiper Motor

REMOVAL & INSTALLATION

MPV

1. Disconnect the battery ground cable.
2. Remove the protective cap and wiper arm nut and pull off the wiper arm, seal and bushing.
3. Remove the liftgate inner trim panels.
4. Remove the weathershield.
5. Disconnect the wiper motor wiring.
6. Remove the motor mounting bolts and lift out the motor.
7. Installation is the reverse of removal.

Navajo

1. Disconnect the negative battery cable.
2. Remove the wiper arm and blade.
3. Remove the liftgate interior trim.
4. Remove the motor attaching bolts (3). Disconnect the electrical leads.
5. Remove the wiper motor from the vehicle.
6. Install the wiper motor in position and connect the electrical leads.
7. Install the liftgate trim. Connect the negative battery cable.

INSTRUMENTS AND SWITCHES

Instrument Cluster

➧ SEE FIGS. 60-65

REMOVAL & INSTALLATION

Pickup

1. Disconnect the battery ground cable.
2. Reach behind the cluster and disconnect the speedometer cable.
3. Remove the screws attaching the cluster hood and carefully lift the hood off.
4. Remove the screw attaching the cluster pod to the dash panel and pull the pod out toward you, gradually. Reach behind the pod and disconnect the wiring connectors.
5. Remove the trip meter knob, and, on clusters w/tachometer, the clock adjust knob.
6. Remove the screws retaining the lens cover and lift off the cover.
7. Remove the screws retaining the cluster bezel and lift off the bezel.
8. Lift out the warning light plate.
9. On clusters wo/tachometer, remove, in order:
   - fuel gauge
   - speedometer
   - temperature gauge
   - printed circuit board
10. On cluster w/tachometer, remove, in order:
   - speedometer
   - digital clock
   - tachometer
   - fuel gauge
   - temperature gauge
   - printed circuit board
11. Installation is the reverse of removal.

MPV

1. Disconnect the battery ground.

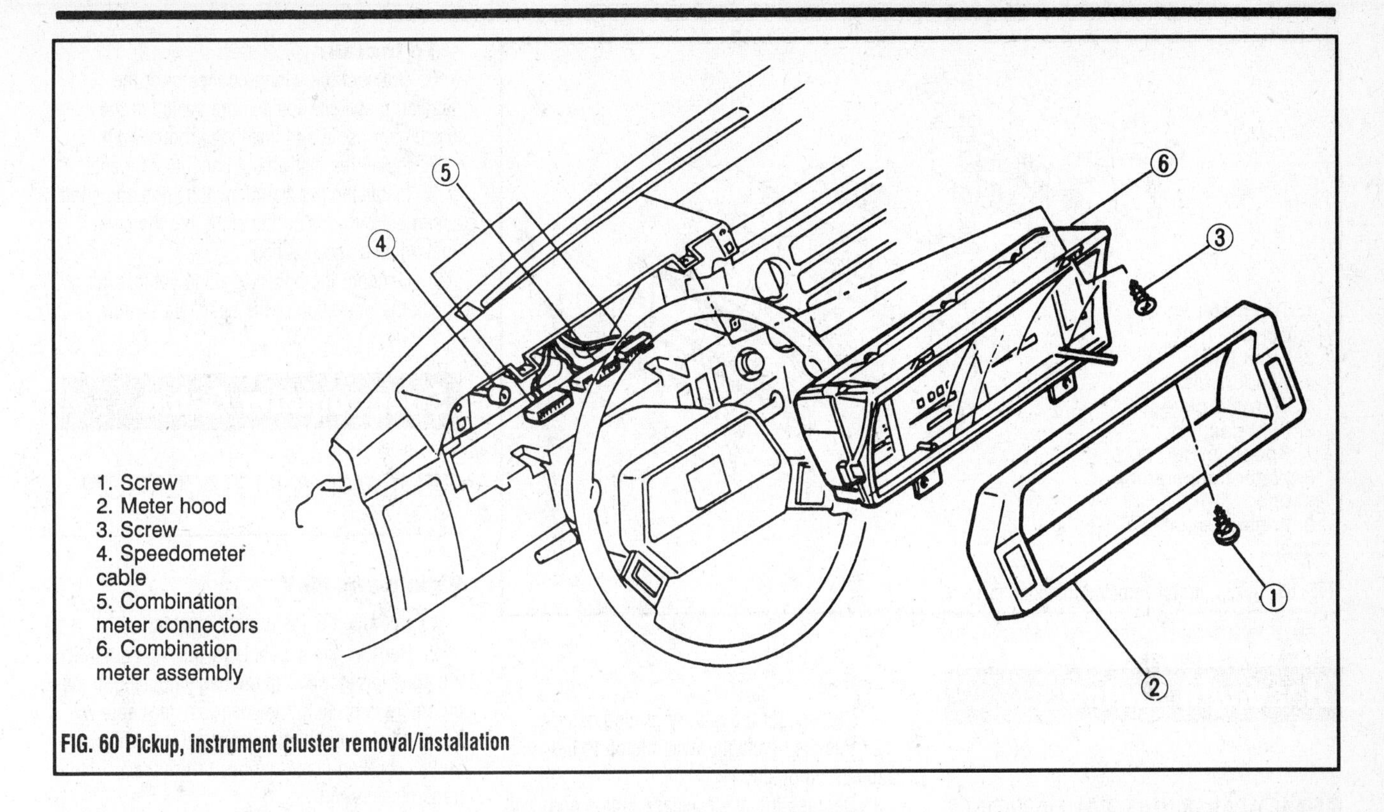

FIG. 60 Pickup, instrument cluster removal/installation

2. Remove all control knobs from the cluster hood.
3. Remove the 3 cluster hood screws. There are 2 on the bottom of the hood and 1 on the upper center hidden under a snap-off cover. Remove the hood.
4. Remove the 4 cluster assembly retaining screws and pull the cluster towards you slowly and carefully, until you can reach behind it and disconnect the electrical connectors and the speedometer cable.
5. Remove the cluster.
6. Installation is the reverse of removal.

Navajo

1. Disconnect the battery ground cable.
2. Remove the two steering column shroud-to-panel retaining screws and remove the shroud.
3. Remove the lower instrument panel trim.
4. Remove the cluster trim cover from the instrument panel by removing the eight screws.
5. Remove the four instrument cluster to panel retaining screws.
6. Position the cluster slightly away from the panel for access to the back of the cluster to disconnect the speedometer.

➡ If there is not sufficient access to disengage the speedometer cable from the speedometer, it may be necessary to remove the speedometer cable at the transmission and pull cable through cowl, to allow room to reach the speedometer quick disconnect.

7. Disconnect the wiring harness connector from the printed circuit, and any bulb-and-socket assemblies from the wiring harness to the cluster assembly and remove the cluster assembly from the instrument panel.

To install:

8. Apply approximately 1/8 in. diameter ball of D7AZ-19A331–A Silicone Dielectric compound or equivalent in the drive hole of the speedometer head.
9. Position the cluster near its opening in the instrument panel.
10. Connect the wiring harness connector to the printed circuit, and any bulb-and-socket assemblies from the wiring harness to the cluster assembly.
11. Position the cluster to the instrument panel and install the four cluster to panel retaining screws.
13. Install the panel trim covers and the steering column shroud.
14. Connect the battery ground cable.
15. Check operation of all gauges, lamps and signals.

Fuel, Oil Pressure, Voltage and Coolant Temperature Gauges

Each of the gauges can be removed in the same manner, once the instrument cluster is removed.

1. Disconnect the negative battery cable.
2. Remove the instrument cluster assembly.
3. Remove the lens from the instrument cluster.
4. Pull the gauge from the cluster.
5. Install the gauge, by pushing it firmly into position.
6. Install the cluster lens and install the cluster into the instrument panel.

Windshield Wiper Switch

REMOVAL & INSTALLATION

The windshield wiper switch is part of the multi-function switch mounted in the steering column. For service procedures, see Section 8.

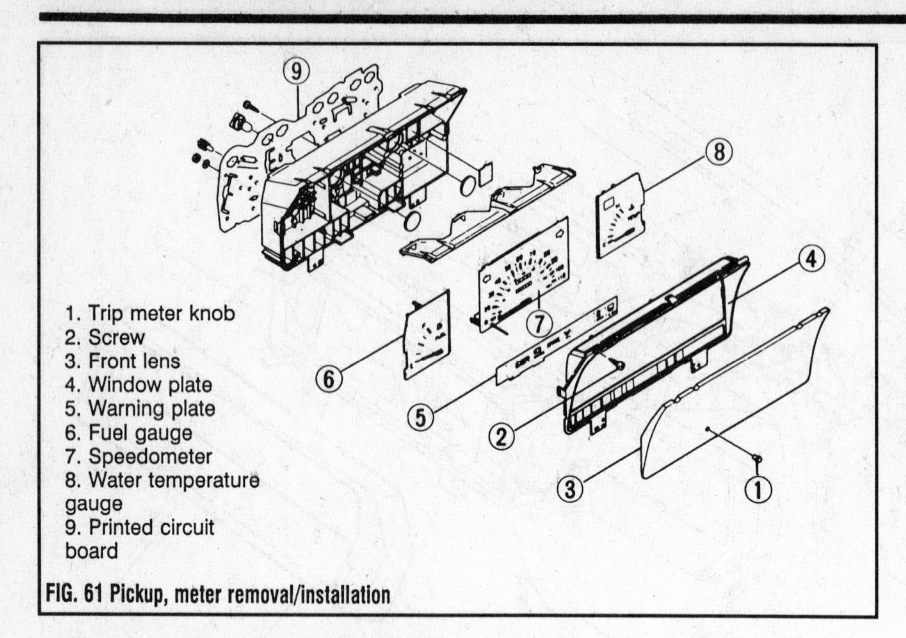

FIG. 61 Pickup, meter removal/installation

Headlight Switch

REMOVAL & INSTALLATION

Pickup and MPV

The switch is part of the multi-function switch mounted in the steering column. For service procedures, see Section 8.

Navajo

1. Disconnect the battery ground cable.
2. Pull the headlight switch knob to the headlight on position.
3. Depress the shaft release button and remove the knob and shaft assembly.
4. Remove the instrument panel finish panel.
5. Unscrew the mounting nut and remove the switch from the instrument panel, then remove the wiring connector from the switch.

To install:

6. Connect the wiring connector to the headlamp switch, position the switch in the instrument panel and install the mounting nut.
7. Install the instrument panel finish panel.
8. Install the headlamp switch knob and shaft assembly by pushing the shaft into the switch until it locks into position.
9. Connect the battery ground cable, and check the operation of the headlight switch.

Speedometer Cable

REMOVAL & INSTALLATION

Pickup and MPV

1. Remove the instrument cluster.
2. Remove the old cable by pulling it out from the speedometer end of the cable housing. If the old cable is broken, the speedometer cable will have to be disconnected from the transmission and the broken piece removed from the transmission end.
3. Lubricate the lower $3/4$ of the new cable with speedometer cable lubricant, and feed the cable into the housing.
4. Connect the speedometer cable to the speedometer, and to the transmission if disconnected there.
5. Replace the instrument cluster.

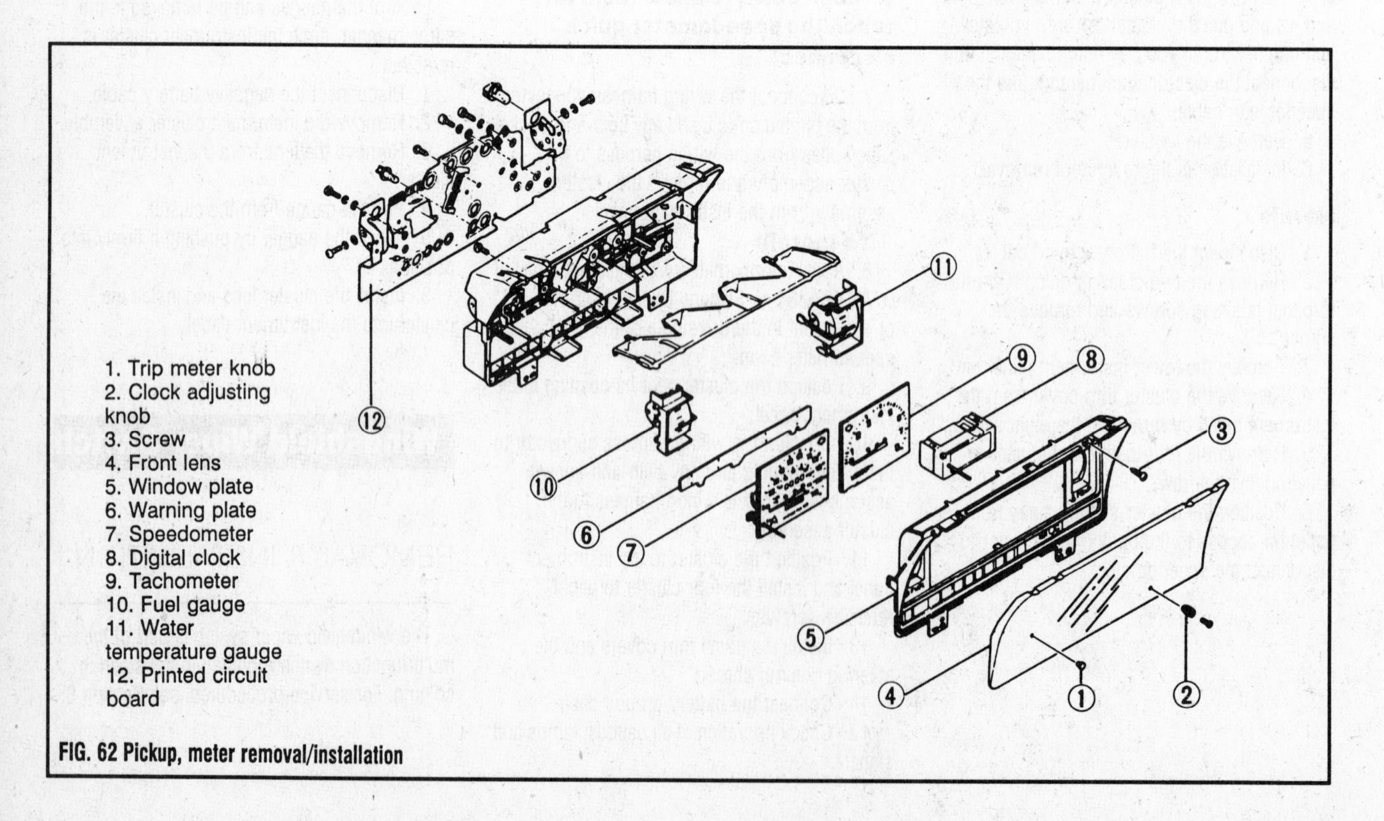

FIG. 62 Pickup, meter removal/installation

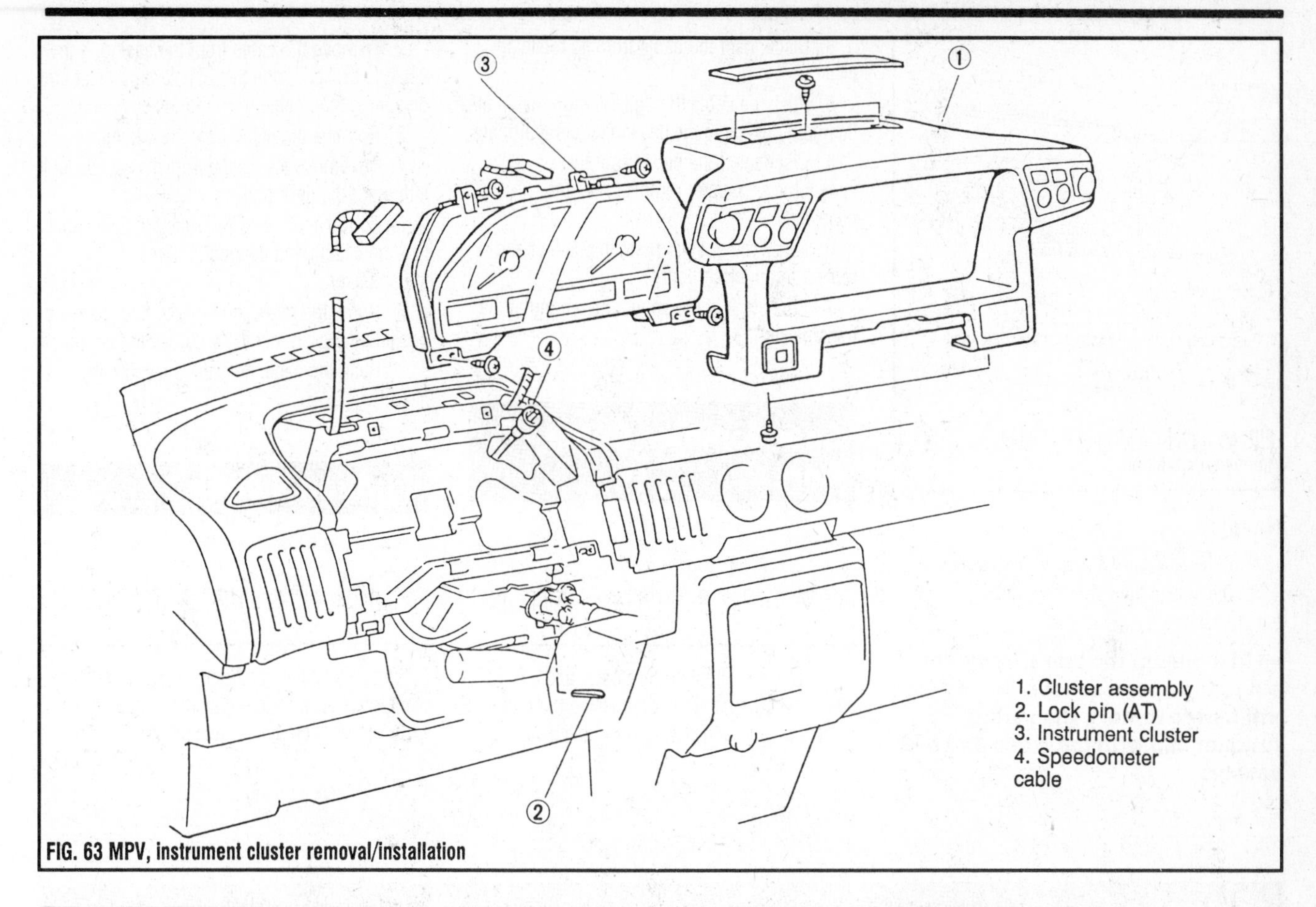

FIG. 63 MPV, instrument cluster removal/installation

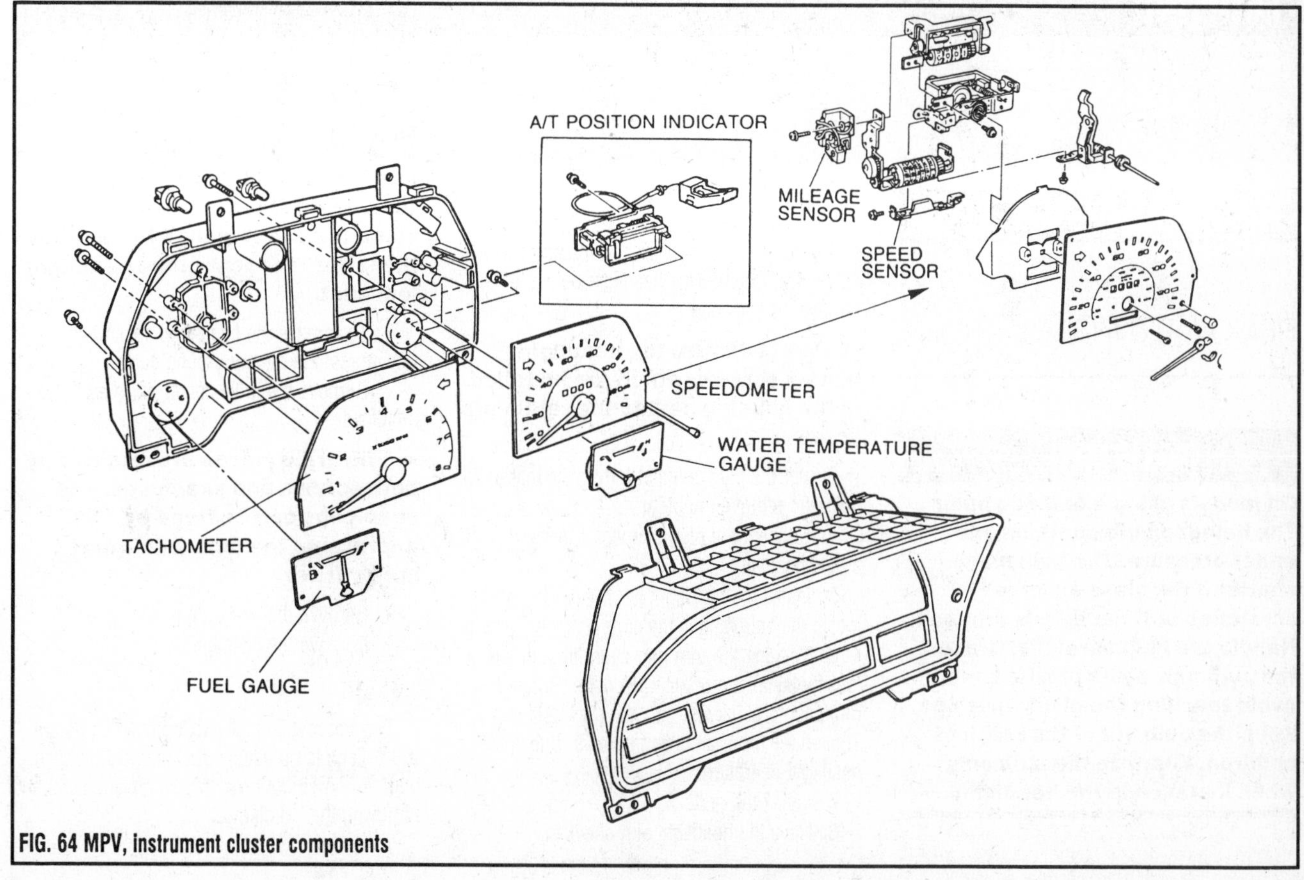

FIG. 64 MPV, instrument cluster components

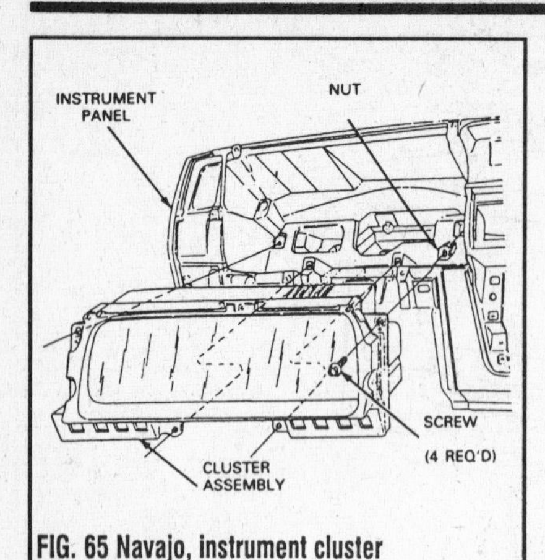

FIG. 65 Navajo, instrument cluster removal/installation

Navajo

1. Raise and safely support the vehicle.
2. Disengage the cable from the transmission.

➡ **Disconnect the cable by pulling it out of the speed sensor. Do not attempt to remove the spring retainer clip with the cable and the sensor.**

3. Disconnect the cable from its retaining clips.
4. Push the cable through the grommet in the floor and pull it into the passenger compartment.
5. Disconnect the cable from the speedometer, cluster removal may be necessary.
6. Install the speedometer in position and route it through the floor.
7. Connect it at the speedometer and at the transmission.

Speedometer Cable Core

REMOVAL & INSTALLATION

1. Reach up behind the cluster and disconnect the cable by depressing the quick disconnect tab and pulling the cable away.
2. Remove the cable from the casing. If the cable is broken, raise the vehicle on a hoist and disconnect the cable from the transmission.
3. Remove the cable from the casing.
4. To remove the casing from the vehicle, pull it through the floor pan.
5. To replace the cable, slide the new cable into the casing and connect it at the transmission.
6. Route the cable through the floor pan and position the grommet in its groove in the floor.
7. Push the cable onto the speedometer head.

Ignition Switch

REMOVAL & INSTALLATION

Ignition switches and ignition locks on these models are located in the steering column. For service procedures, see Section 8.

LIGHTING

➧ SEE FIGS. 66-80

Headlights

REMOVAL & INSTALLATION

❊❊ CAUTION

On models using a halogen bulb: The halogen bulb contains gas under pressure. The bulb may shatter if the glass envelope is scratched or if the bulb is dropped. Handle the bulb carefully. Grasp the bulb only by its plastic base. Avoid touching the glass envelope. Keep the bulb out of the reach of children. Energize the bulb only when installed in the headlamp.

Pickups

1. Remove the radiator grille attaching screws and remove the grille.
2. Remove the headlight bulb trim ring, by removing the three screws and rotating the ring clockwise. Support the headlight bulb and remove the trim ring.

➡ **Do not disturb the headlight aiming screws, which are installed in the housing next to the retaining screws.**

3. Pull the plug connector from the rear of the bulb and remove the bulb.
4. Connect the plug connector to the rear of a new headlight.
5. Install the headlight in the housing, and locate the bulb tabs in the slots and the housing.
6. Position the trim ring over the bulb and loosely install the retaining screws. Rotate the ring counterclockwise to lock it in position. Tighten the three attaching screws. Check the headlight operation.
7. Install the grille.
8. Have the headlight aim checked.

MPV

➡ **These headlights have replaceable bulb elements. These elements are replaced by removing them from the rear of the headlight lens unit.**

1. To remove the headlamp assembly: Disconnect the battery ground cable.
2. Remove the grille center piece and side moldings.

➡ **The grille pieces are retained by both screws and snap-clips. The snap-clips can be freed by depressing the tabs with a small screwdriver.**

3. Remove the headlight trim ring.
4. Remove the headlight.

Navajo

Two aerodynamically styled headlamps are used. Each lamp uses a dual filament halogen bulb. A burned out bulb may be replaced without removing the headlamp.

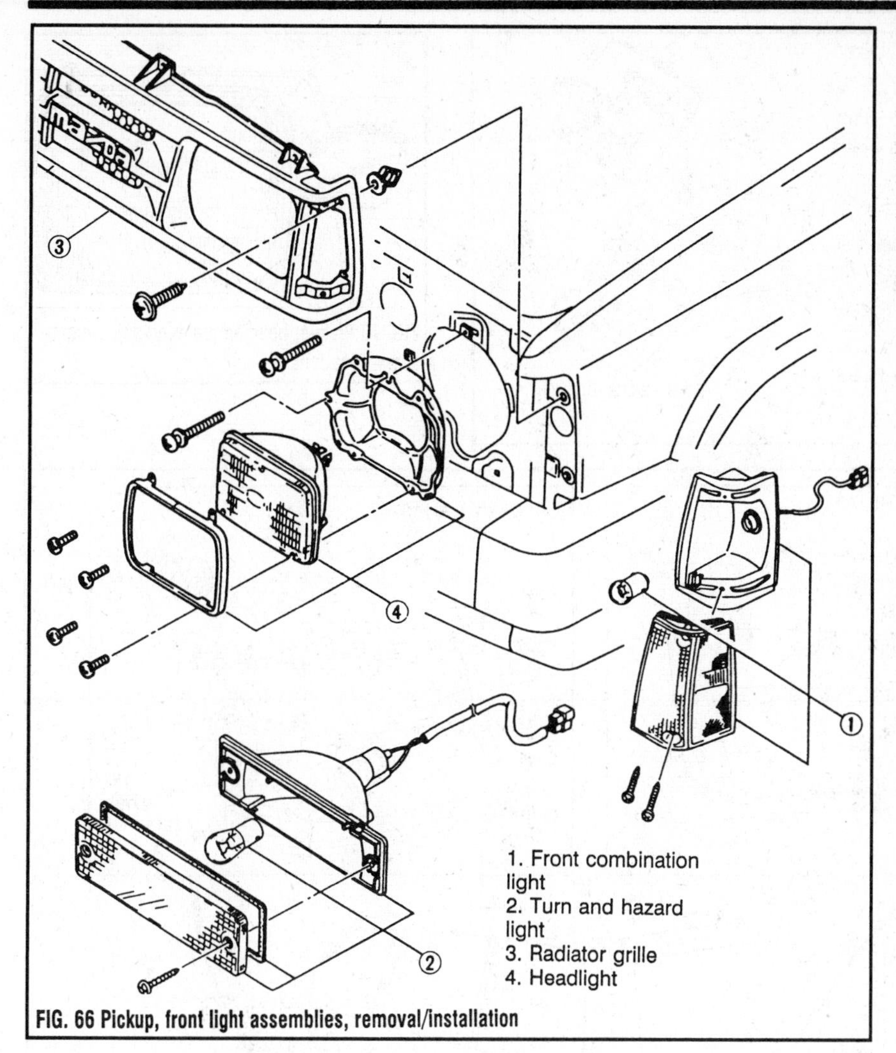

FIG. 66 Pickup, front light assemblies, removal/installation

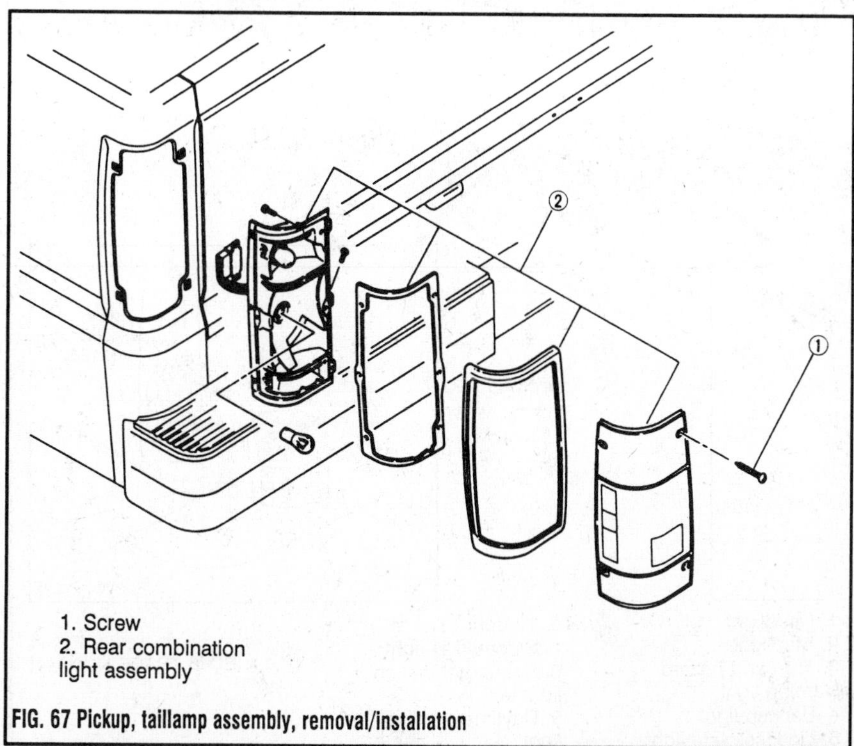

FIG. 67 Pickup, taillamp assembly, removal/installation

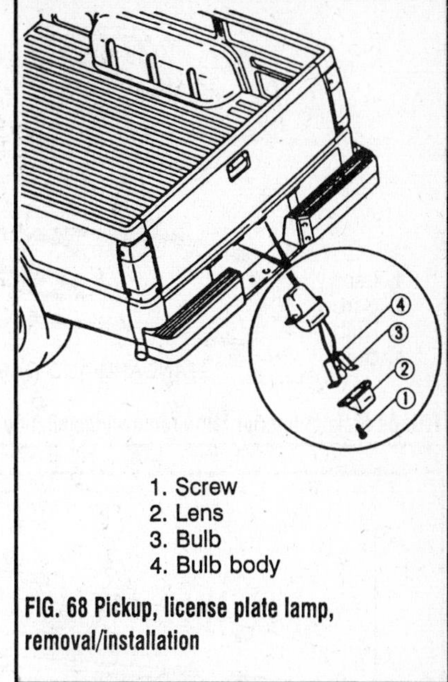

FIG. 68 Pickup, license plate lamp, removal/installation

1. Check that the headlamp switch is turned OFF. Lift the hood and locate the bulb installed in the rear of the headlamp body.

2. Remove the electrical connector from the bulb by squeezing the connector tabs firmly and snapping the connector rearward.

3. Remove the bulb retaining ring by rotating counterclockwise. Slide the ring off the plastic base. Keep the ring for reinstallation.

4. Carefully remove the headlamp bulb from the socket by gently pulling straight backward out of the socket. Do not rotate the bulb during removal.

5. With the flat side of the bulb facing upward, insert the glass envelope of the bulb into the socket. Turn the base slightly, if necessary, to align the grooves in the forward part of the plastic base with the corresponding locating tabs inside the socket. When the grooves are aligned, push the bulb into the socket until the mounting flange contacts the rear face of the socket.

6. Install the plastic lock ring and connect the wiring. Turn the headlamps on and check for proper operation.

➡ A properly aimed headlamp need not be realmed after installation of the bulb.

7. To remove the headlamp assembly: Disconnect the headlamp bulb connector. Remove the screw retaining the side marker assembly to the vehicle and remove the assembly.

8. Remove the fasteners retaining the grille to the grille reinforcement and remove the grille. Remove the spring clips retaining the headlamp assembly to the grille reinforcement and remove the assembly. Install in reverse order.

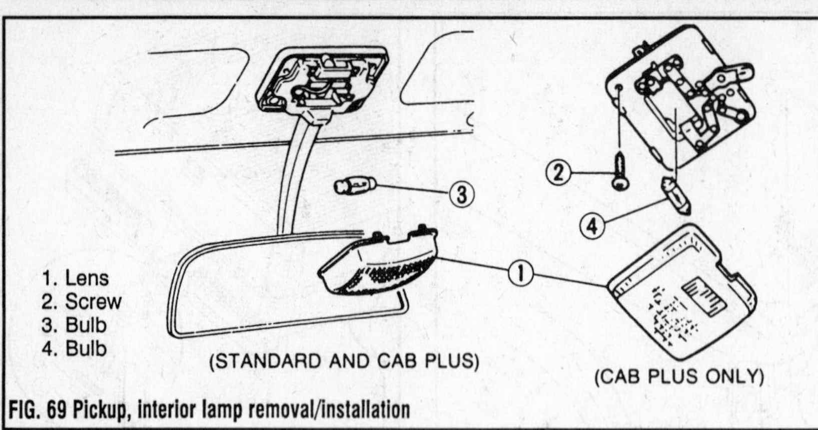

FIG. 69 Pickup, interior lamp removal/installation

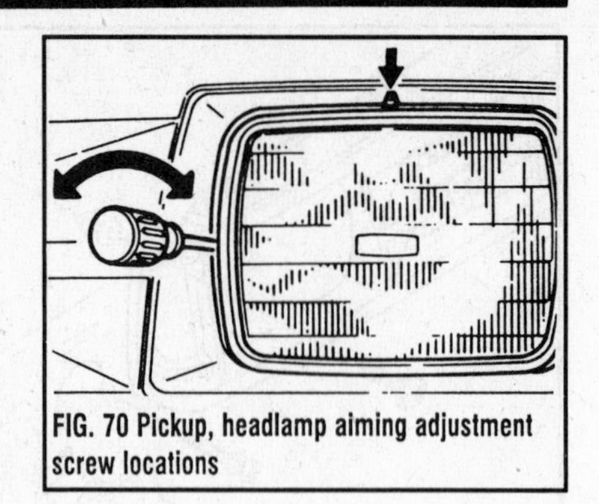

FIG. 70 Pickup, headlamp aiming adjustment screw locations

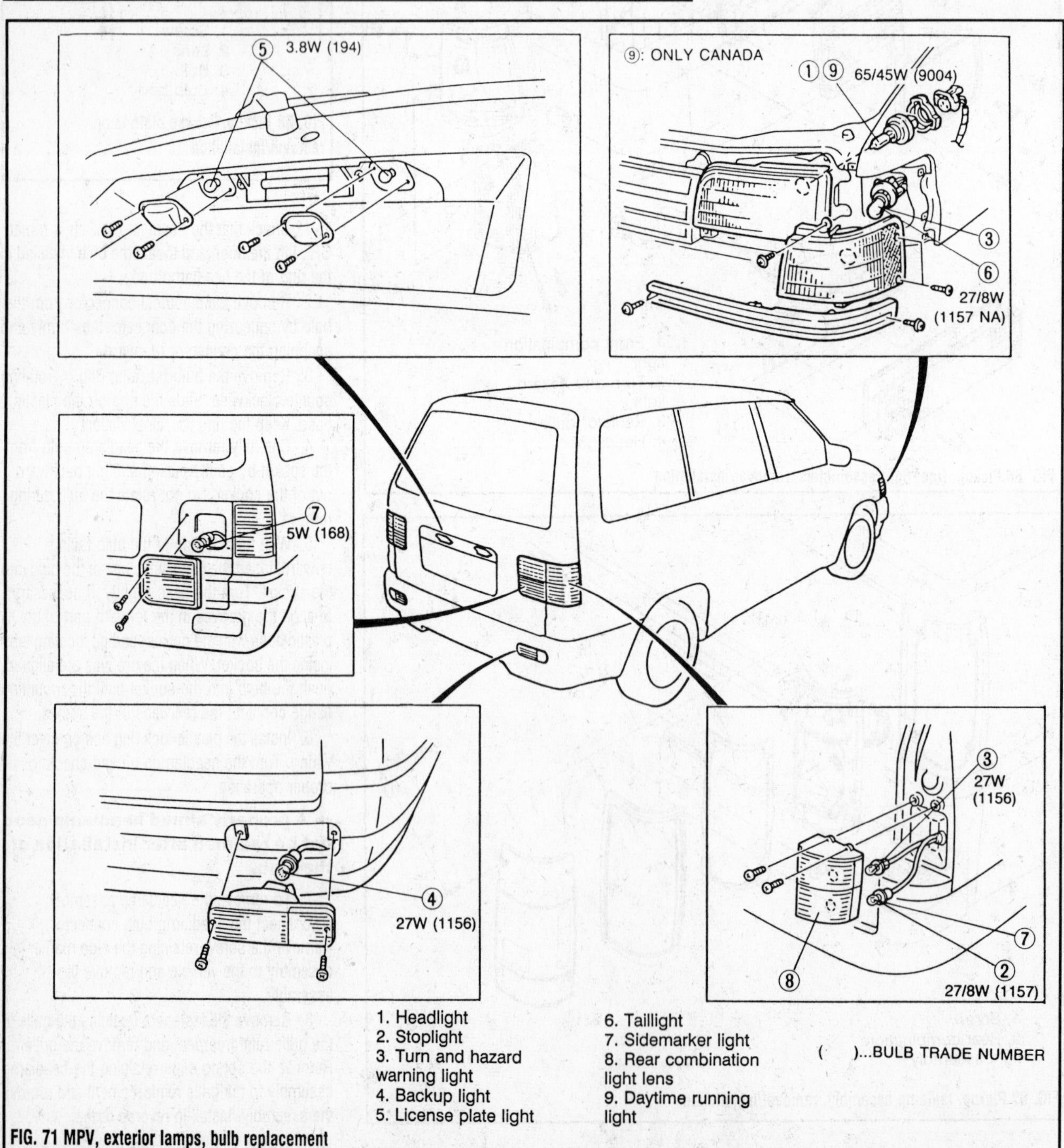

FIG. 71 MPV, exterior lamps, bulb replacement

Front Combination Lights

REMOVAL & INSTALLATION

Pickups

1. Remove the grille.
2. Remove the lens mounting screws and pull off the lens.
3. Carefully push in on the bulb and twist it counterclockwise to remove it.
4. Installation is the reverse of removal.

MPV

1. Disconnect the battery ground cable.
2. Remove the grille center piece and side moldings.

➡ The grille pieces are retained by both screws and snap-clips. The snap-clips can be freed by depressing the tabs with a small screwdriver.

3. Remove the lens mounting screws and pull off the lens.
4. Carefully push in on the bulb and twist it counterclockwise to remove it.
5. Installation is the reverse of removal.

Front Turn Signal Lights

REMOVAL & INSTALLATION

Pickups

1. Remove the lens mounting screws and pull off the lens.
2. Carefully push in on the bulb and twist it counterclockwise to remove it.
3. Installation is the reverse of removal.

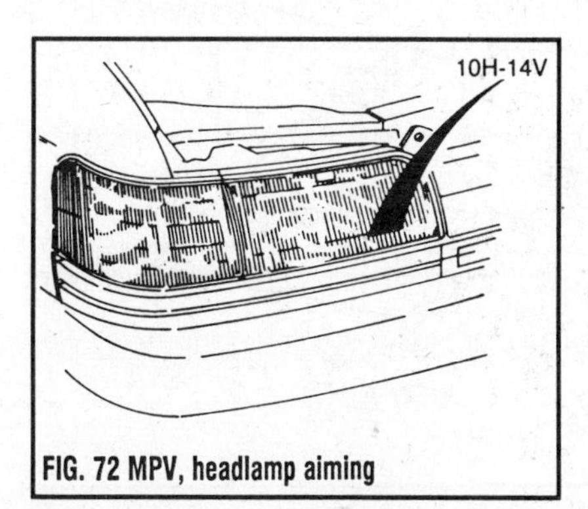

FIG. 72 MPV, headlamp aiming

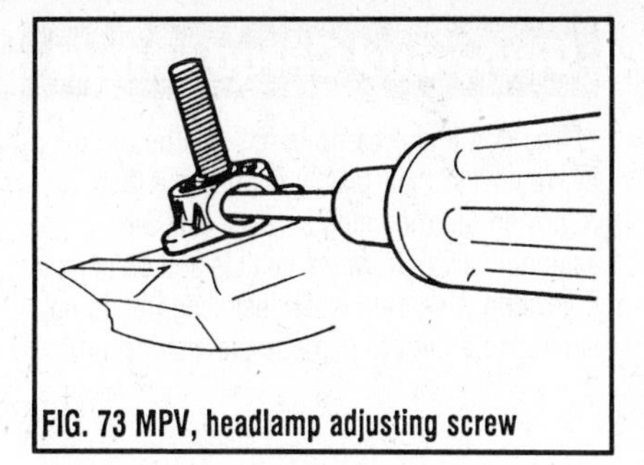

FIG. 73 MPV, headlamp adjusting screw

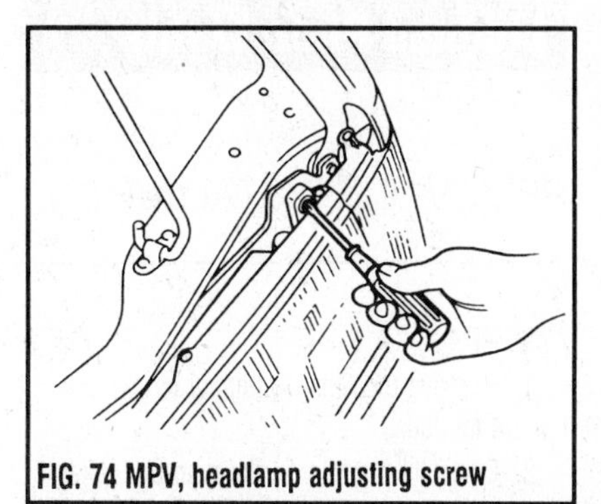

FIG. 74 MPV, headlamp adjusting screw

Front Marker and Turn Signal

REMOVAL & INSTALLATION

Navajo

1. Remove the grille.
2. Carefully rotate the headlight door away from the vehicle, rotating the inboard side away from the vehicle.
3. Remove the side marker, parking and turn signal bulbs and sockets from the headlamp door assembly. They can be removed by turning them.
4. Remove the retaining screws for the lens to be changed and remove it from the headlight door.
5. Install the removed lens assembly and install the bulbs and sockets.
6. Install the headlight door assembly.
7. Check the operation of the lights.

Rear Combination Lights

REMOVAL & INSTALLATION

Pickups

1. Remove the lens mounting screws and pull off the lens.
2. Carefully push in on the bulb and twist it counterclockwise to remove it.
3. Installation is the reverse of removal.

MPV

1. Remove the lens mounting screws and pull off the lens.
2. Carefully push in on the bulb and twist it counterclockwise to remove it.
3. Installation is the reverse of removal.

Navajo

1. Remove the 4 screws retaining the lamp assembly to the vehicle.
2. Remove the lamp assembly from the vehicle by pulling it outward. Make sure the 2 retainers at the bottom of the assembly release.
3. Remove the bulbs and sockets.
4. Install the lamp assembly in position, making sure the bottom of the assembly seats properly.

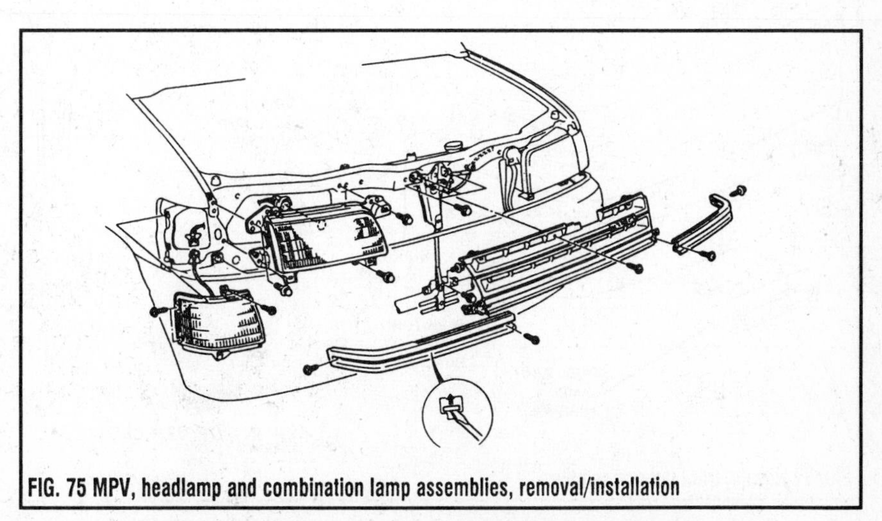

FIG. 75 MPV, headlamp and combination lamp assemblies, removal/installation

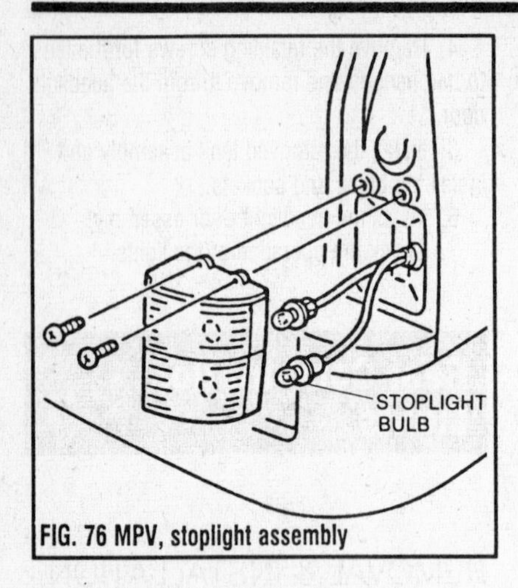

FIG. 76 MPV, stoplight assembly

High Mount Brake Light

REMOVAL & INSTALLATION

1. Remove the screws retaining the lamp to the tailgate.
2. Pull the lamp away from the vehicle and disconnect the wiring connector.
3. Install the lamp assembly back into position, making sure it is seated properly.

Dome and Cargo Lamps

The dome and cargo lamps can be removed by, removing their plastic covers and then removing the mounting screws. Pull the assembly away from the vehicle and disconnect the wiring. Use care when installing the dome lamps, so as not to damage the interior trim.

License Plate Lights

REMOVAL & INSTALLATION

Pickups

1. Remove the lens mounting screws and pull off the lens.
2. Carefully push in on the bulb and twist it counterclockwise to remove it.
3. Installation is the reverse of removal.

MPV

1. Remove the lens mounting screws and pull off the lens.
2. Carefully push in on the bulb and twist it counterclockwise to remove it.
3. Installation is the reverse of removal.

FIG. 78 Halogen lamp replacement, Navajo shown

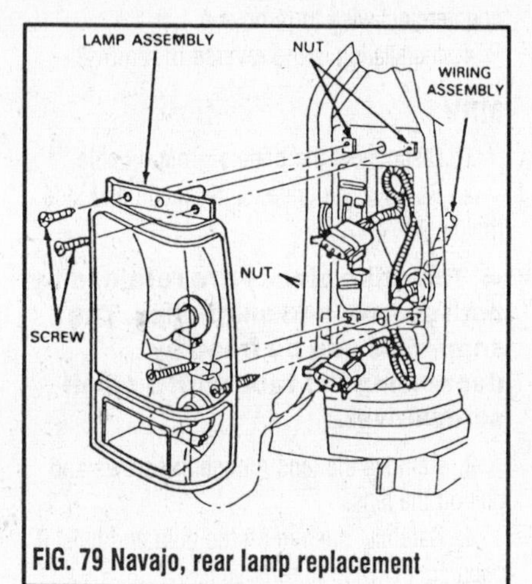

FIG. 79 Navajo, rear lamp replacement

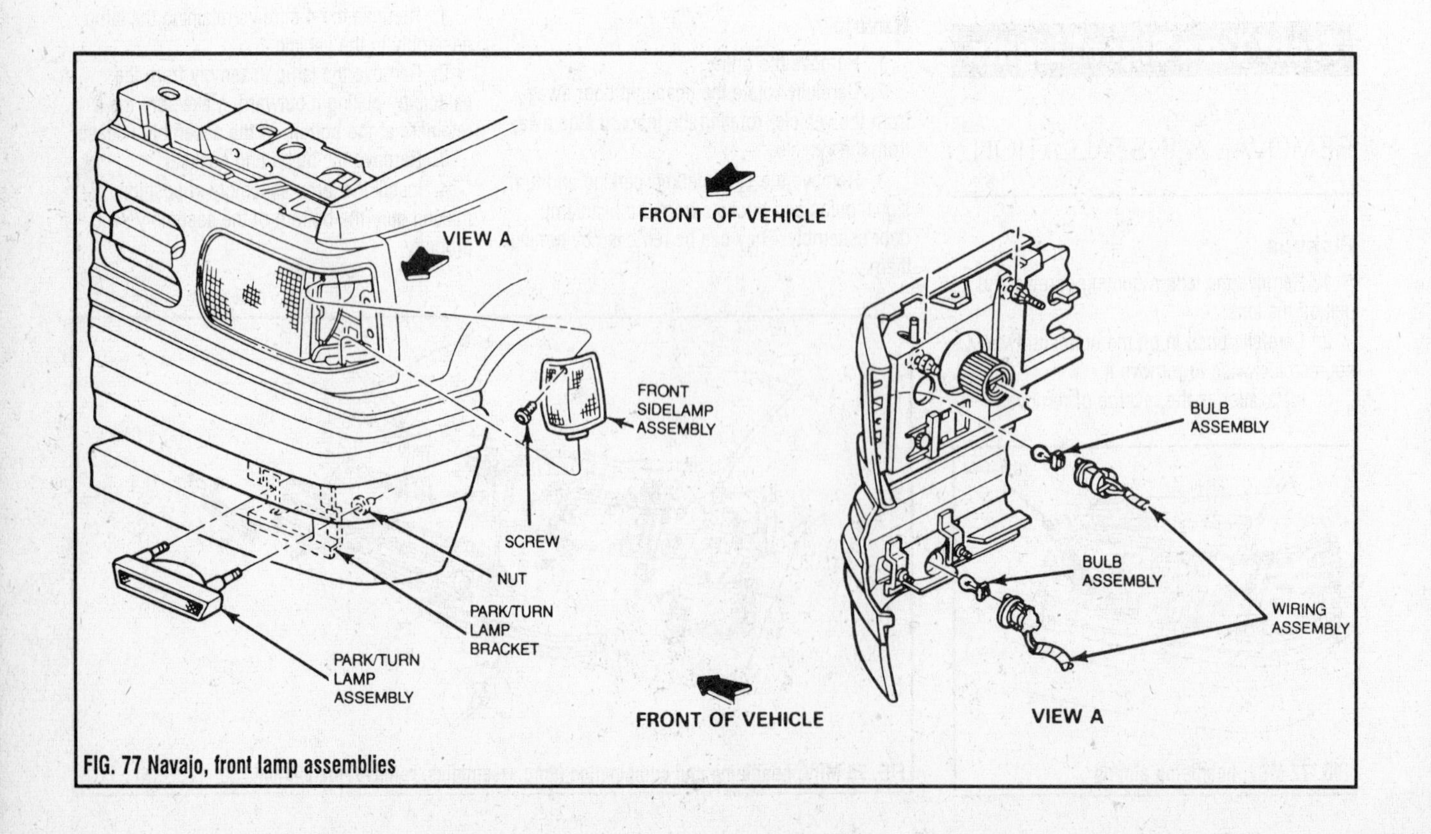

FIG. 77 Navajo, front lamp assemblies

Navajo

1. Using a thin bladed tool, apply pressure to the lamp assembly locking tab. While applying pressure, use another thin bladed tool to carefully pry the lamp assembly from the bumper.
2. Replace the bulb or assembly as required. Install in reverse order.

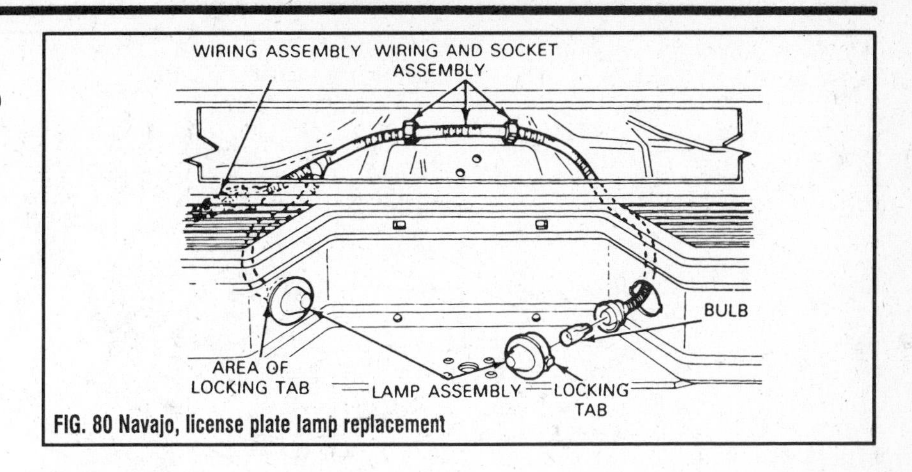

FIG. 80 Navajo, license plate lamp replacement

TRAILER WIRING

Wiring the truck for towing is fairly easy. There are a number of good wiring kits available and these should be used, rather than trying to design your own. All trailers will need brake lights and turn signals as well as tail lights and side marker lights. Most states require extra marker lights for overly wide trailers. Also, most states have recently required back-up lights for trailers, and most trailer manufacturers have been building trailers with back-up lights for several years.

Additionally, some Class I, most Class II and just about all Class III trailers will have electric brakes.

Add to this number an accessories wire, to operate trailer internal equipment or to charge the trailer's battery, and you can have as many as seven wires in the harness.

Determine the equipment on your trailer and buy the wiring kit necessary. The kit will contain all the wires needed, plus a plug adapter set which included the female plug, mounted on the bumper or hitch, and the male plug, wired into, or plugged into the trailer harness.

When installing the kit, follow the manufacturer's instructions. The color coding of the wires is standard throughout the industry.

One point to note, some domestic vehicles, and most imported vehicles, have separate turn signals. On most domestic vehicles, the brake lights and rear turn signals operate with the same bulb. For those vehicles with separate turn signals, you can purchase an isolation unit so that the brake lights won't blink whenever the turn signals are operated, or, you can go to your local electronics supply house and buy four diodes to wire in series with the brake and turn signal bulbs. Diodes will isolate the brake and turn signals. The choice is yours. The isolation units are simple and quick to install, but far more expensive than the diodes. The diodes, however, require more work to install properly, since they require the cutting of each bulb's wire and soldering in place of the diode.

One final point, the best kits are those with a spring loaded cover on the vehicle mounted socket. This cover prevents dirt and moisture from corroding the terminals. Never let the vehicle socket hang loosely. Always mount it securely to the bumper or hitch.

CIRCUIT PROTECTION

➧ SEE FIGS. 81-90

Fuses

Pickup

The pickup's fuse box is located under the instrument panel, on the left of the driver.

These trucks have an master fuse block located under a protective cover on the right fender apron just behind the battery on the B2200, or, on the left fender apron on B2600 models. This fuse block contains a 30 amp and an 80 amp fuse. The 30 amp fuse can be removed without disturbing the fuse block by simply pulling it out and pushing a new one in. To remove the 80 amp fuse, you'll have to remove the fuse block, remove the cover, unscrew the wiring terminal and pull out the fuse.

The master fuse(s) protects the entire electrical system; all systems will be dead if it has blown.

When a fuse blows out, inspect the electrical system for shorts or other faults. Fuses of specified capacity should be installed in their respective positions. Oversize fuses will allow excessive current to flow and should not be used.

Spare fuses should be kept in a vinyl bag in the glove compartment.

MPV

The MPV has 2 fuse boxes. A main fuse box is located in the engine compartment on the right fender liner. This fuse box contains all the high

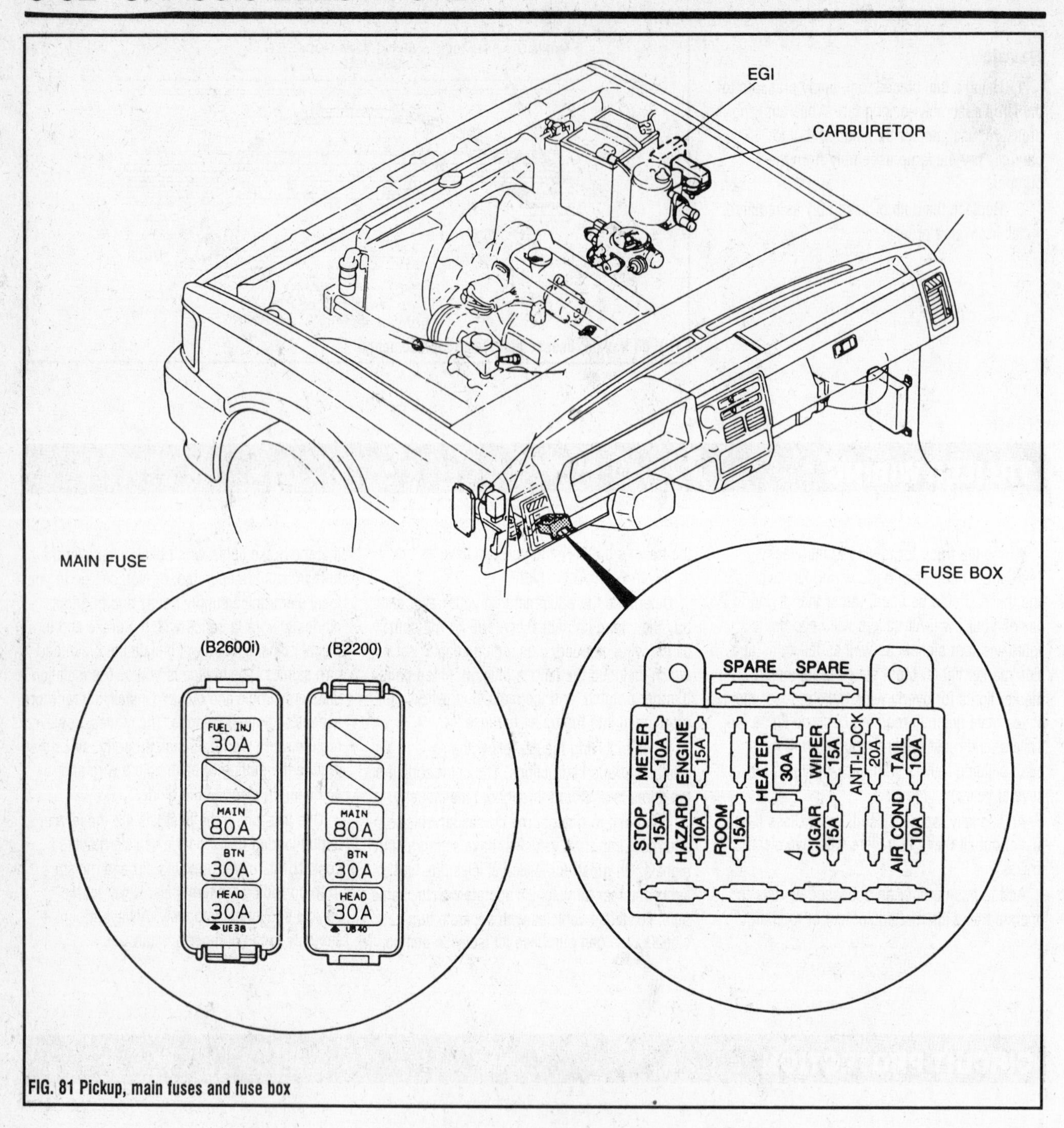

FIG. 81 Pickup, main fuses and fuse box

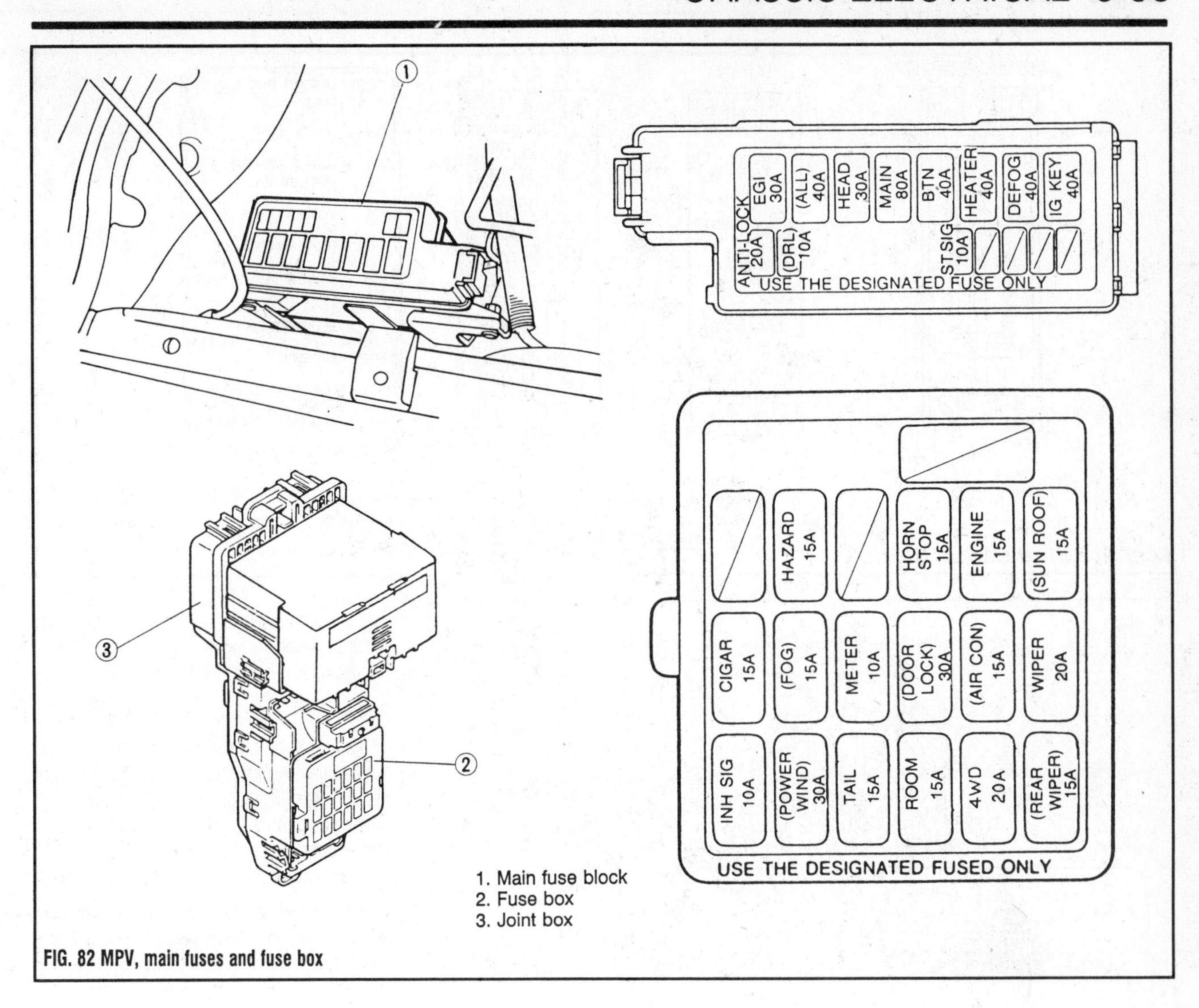

FIG. 82 MPV, main fuses and fuse box

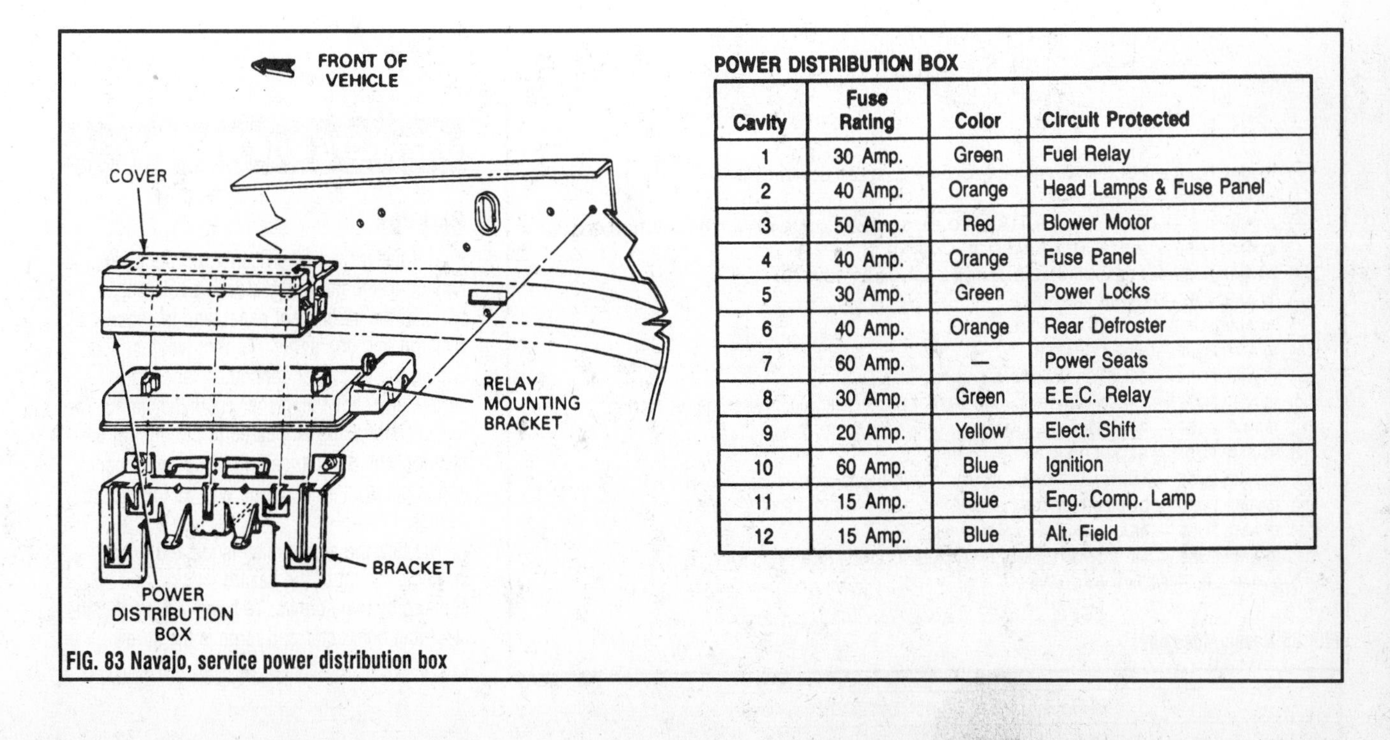

POWER DISTRIBUTION BOX

Cavity	Fuse Rating	Color	Circuit Protected
1	30 Amp.	Green	Fuel Relay
2	40 Amp.	Orange	Head Lamps & Fuse Panel
3	50 Amp.	Red	Blower Motor
4	40 Amp.	Orange	Fuse Panel
5	30 Amp.	Green	Power Locks
6	40 Amp.	Orange	Rear Defroster
7	60 Amp.	—	Power Seats
8	30 Amp.	Green	E.E.C. Relay
9	20 Amp.	Yellow	Elect. Shift
10	60 Amp.	Blue	Ignition
11	15 Amp.	Blue	Eng. Comp. Lamp
12	15 Amp.	Blue	Alt. Field

FIG. 83 Navajo, service power distribution box

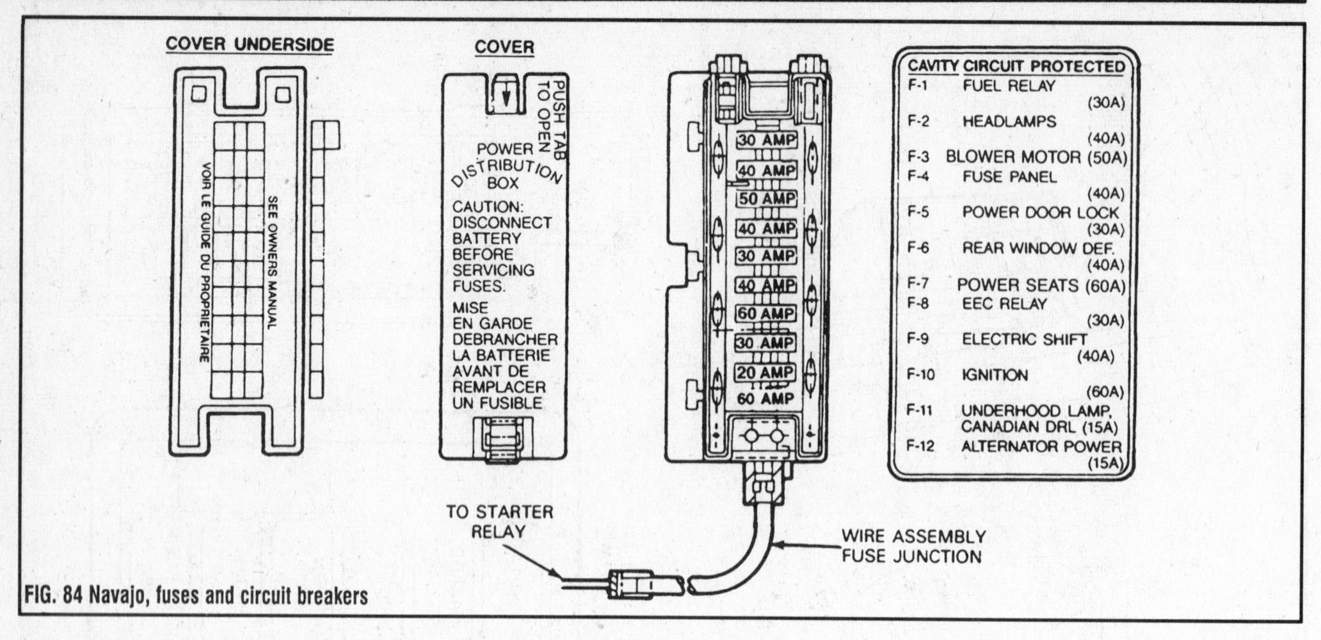

FIG. 84 Navajo, fuses and circuit breakers

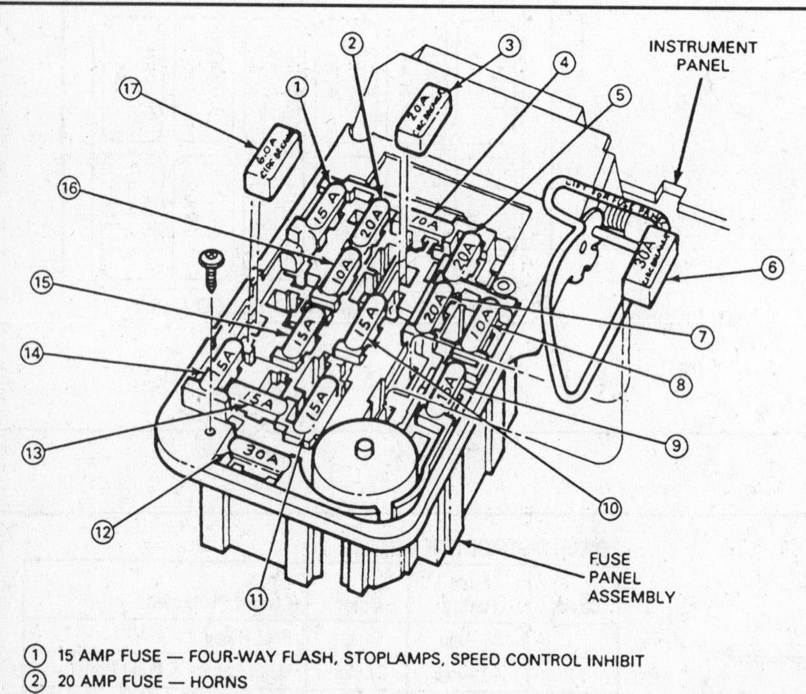

① 15 AMP FUSE — FOUR-WAY FLASH, STOPLAMPS, SPEED CONTROL INHIBIT
② 20 AMP FUSE — HORNS
③ 20 AMP C.B. — CIGAR LIGHTER, FLASH TO PASS, POWER LUMBAR, MULTI-FUNCTION SWITCH
④ 10 AMP FUSE — INSTRUMENT PANEL ILLUMINATION
⑤ 20 AMP FUSE — PREMIUM RADIO AMPLIFIER, TRAILER TOW
⑥ 30 AMP C.B. — POWER WINDOWS
⑦ 20 AMP FUSE — R.A.B.S. MODULE
⑧ 10 AMP FUSE — HEGO HEATER
⑨ 15 AMP FUSE — CLUSTER WARNING LAMPS
⑩ 15 AMP FUSE — SPEED CONTROL AMPLIFIER, ELECTRONIC ALL WHEEL DRIVE, RADIO
⑪ 15 AMP FUSE — PARK/LICENSE LAMPS
⑫ 30 AMP FUSE — BLOWER MOTOR
⑬ 15 AMP FUSE — TURN LAMPS, B/U LAMPS, TURN INDICATOR, R. DEF. CONTROL
⑭ 15 AMP FUSE — DOME/COURTESY LAMP
⑮ 15 AMP FUSE — REAR WINDOW WASH/WIPE
⑯ 10 AMP FUSE — AIR CONDITIONING SWITCHES, CLUTCH COIL
⑰ 6 AMP C.B. — FRONT WASH/WIPE

FIG. 85 Navajo, fuse box

amp fuses, including an 80 amp main fuse. The second fuse box is located above the driver's side kick panel inside the van.

Navajo

The fuse panel is located under the instrument panel to the left of the steering column. There is also a power distribution box located in the engine compartment on the right inner fender, next to the starter relay, which contains mostly high-current fuses.

➡ All circuit breakers on Navajo are located in the fuse panel except for a 4.5 amp circuit breaker for the rear wiper/washer and a 22 amp circuit breaker for the high beams which is integral with the headlight switch.

Flashers and Relays

Pickups

The hazard warning flasher, on the pickup, is located to the left of the steering column, beneath the instrument panel, and is secured by a clamp and one screw. To remove it, simply unplug the electrical connector, loosen the screw, and slide the flasher out of the clamp. The turn signal flasher is located to the right of the steering column, beneath the instrument panel, and is secured in the same way as the hazard flasher.

The turn the signal relay is located to the immediate right of the hazard flasher, and is secured by two screws. To remove it, unplug the electrical connector and remove the screws.

MPV

The relays and flashers are located under the dash, near the fusebox.

Navajo

Both the turn signal flasher and the hazard warning flasher are mounted on the fuse panel on the truck. To gain access to the fuse panel,remove the cover from the lower edge of the instrument panel below the steering column. First remove the two fasteners from the lower edge of the cover. Then pull the cover downward until the spring clips disengage from the instrument panel.

The turn signal flasher unit is mounted on the front of the fuse panel, and the hazard warning flasher is mounted on the rear of the fuse panel.

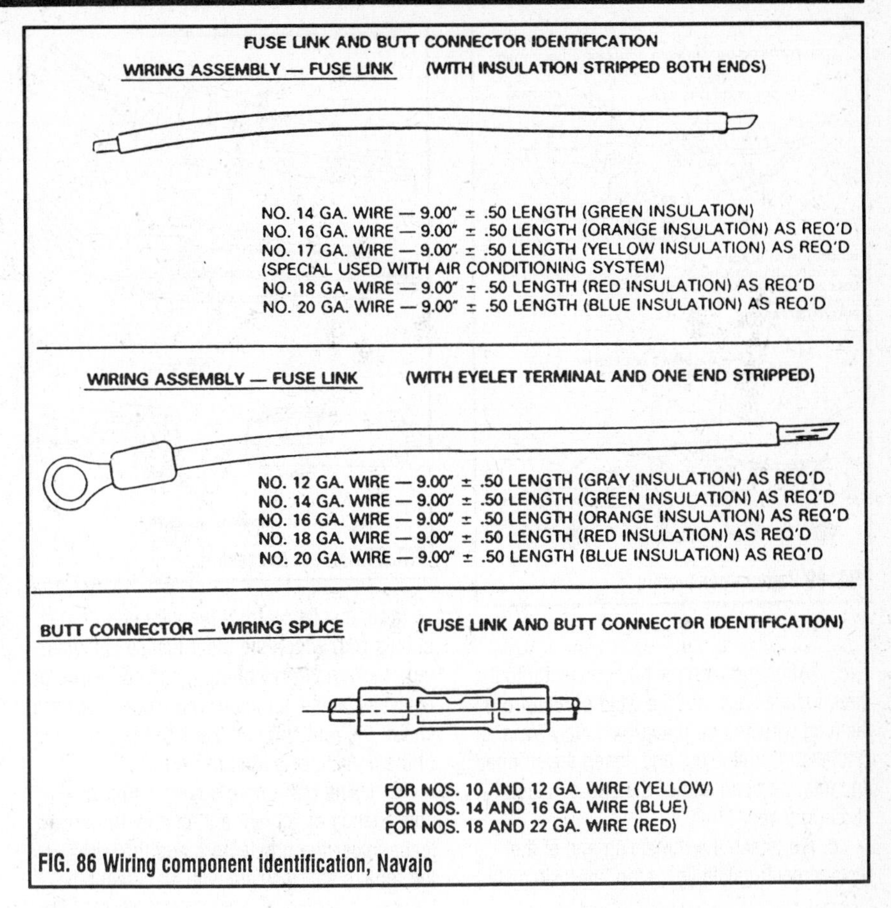

FIG. 86 Wiring component identification, Navajo

Fusible Links

The fusible link is a short length of special, Hypalon (high temperature) insulated wire, integral with the engine compartment wiring harness and should not be confused with standard wire. It is several wire gauges smaller than the circuit which it protects. Under no circumstances should a fuse link replacement repair be made using a length of standard wire cut from bulk stock or from another wiring harness.

REPLACEMENT

To repair any blown fusible link use the following procedure:

1. Determine which circuit is damaged, its location and the cause of the open fusible link. If the damaged fuse link is one of three fed by a common No. 10 or l2 gauge feed wire, determine the specific affected circuit.
2. Disconnect the negative battery cable.
3. Cut the damaged fusible link from the wiring harness and discard it. If the fusible link is one of three circuits fed by a single feed wire, cut it out of the harness at each splice end and discard it.
4. Identify and procure the proper fusible link and butt connectors for attaching the fusible link to the harness.
5. To repair any fusible link in a 3–link group with one feed:
   a. After cutting the open link out of the harness, cut each of the remaining undamaged fusible links close to the feed wire weld.

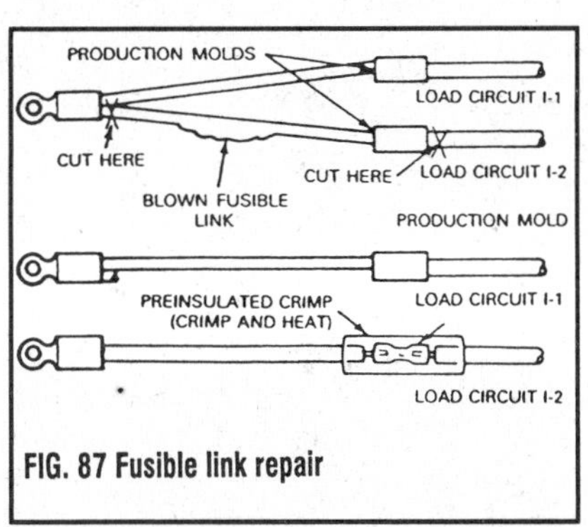

FIG. 87 Fusible link repair

   b. Strip approximately 1/2 in. of insulation from the detached ends of the two good fusible links. Then insert two wire ends into one end of a butt connector and carefully push one stripped end of the replacement fuse link into the same end of the butt connector and crimp all three firmly together.

➡ Care must be taken when fitting the three fusible links into the butt connector as the internal diameter is a snug fit for three wires. Make sure to use a proper crimping tool. Pliers, side cutters, etc. will not apply the proper crimp to retain the wires and withstand a pull test.

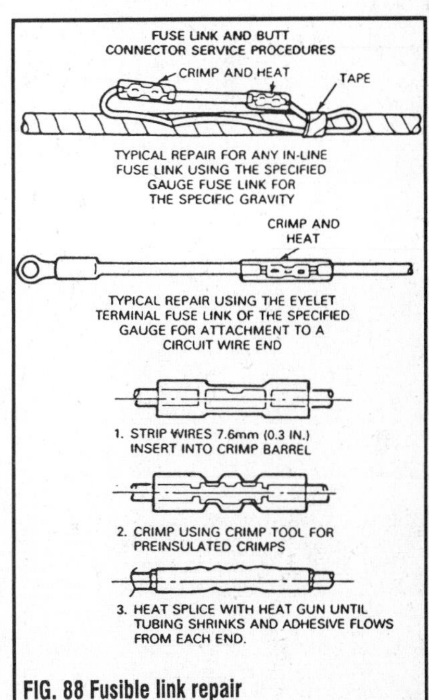

FIG. 88 Fusible link repair

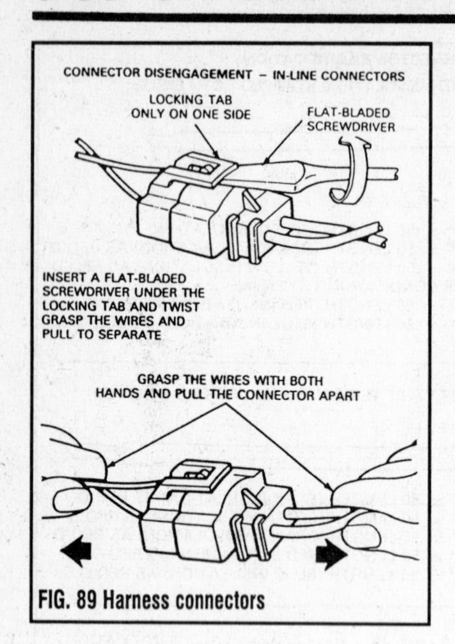

FIG. 89 Harness connectors

c. After crimping the butt connector to the three fusible links, cut the weld portion from the feed wire and strip approximately 1/2 in. of insulation from the cut end. Insert the stripped end into the open end of the butt connector and crimp very firmly.

d. To attach the remaining end of the replacement fusible link, strip approximately

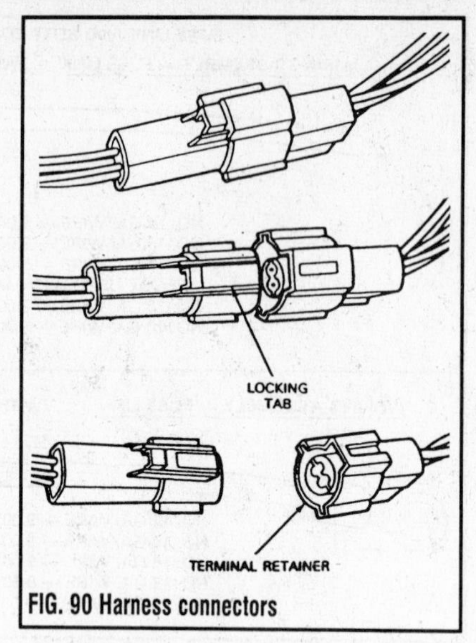

FIG. 90 Harness connectors

1/2 in. of insulation from the wire end of the circuit from which the blow fusible link was removed, and firmly crimp a butt connector or equivalent to the stripped wire. Then, insert the end of the replacement link into the other end of the connector and crimp firmly.

e. Using rosin core solder with a consistency of 60 percent tin and 40 percent lead, solder the connectors and the wires at the repairs and insulate with electrical tape.

7. To repair any fusible link which has an eyelet terminal on one end such as the charging circuit, cut off the open fusible link behind the weld, strip approximately 1/2 in. of insulation from the cut end and attach the appropriate new eyelet fusible link to the cut stripped wire with an appropriate size butt connector. Solder the connectors and wires at the repair and insulate with tape.

8. Connect the negative battery cable to the battery and test the system for proper operation.

➡ **Do not mistake a resistor wire for a fusible link. The resistor wire is generally longer and has print stating, "Resistor–don't cut or splice". When attaching a single No. 16, 17, 18 or 20 gauge fusible link to a heavy gauge wire, always double the stripped wire end of the fusible link before inserting and crimping it into the butt connector for positive wire retention.**

WIRING DIAGRAMS

Harness symbols

DESCRIPTION HARNESS	COLOR	SYMBOL	DESCRIPTION HARNESS	SYMBOL
FRONT HARNESS		(F)	INJECTION HARNESS	(INJ)
INSTRUMENT PANEL HARNESS		(I)	INTERIOR LAMP HARNESS	(IN)
REAR HARNESS		(R)	FLOOR HARNESS	(FR)
ENGINE HARNESS		(E)	AIR CONDITIONER HARNESS NO.1	(AC1)
EMISSION HARNESS		(EM)	AIR CONDITIONER HARNESS NO.2	(AC2)

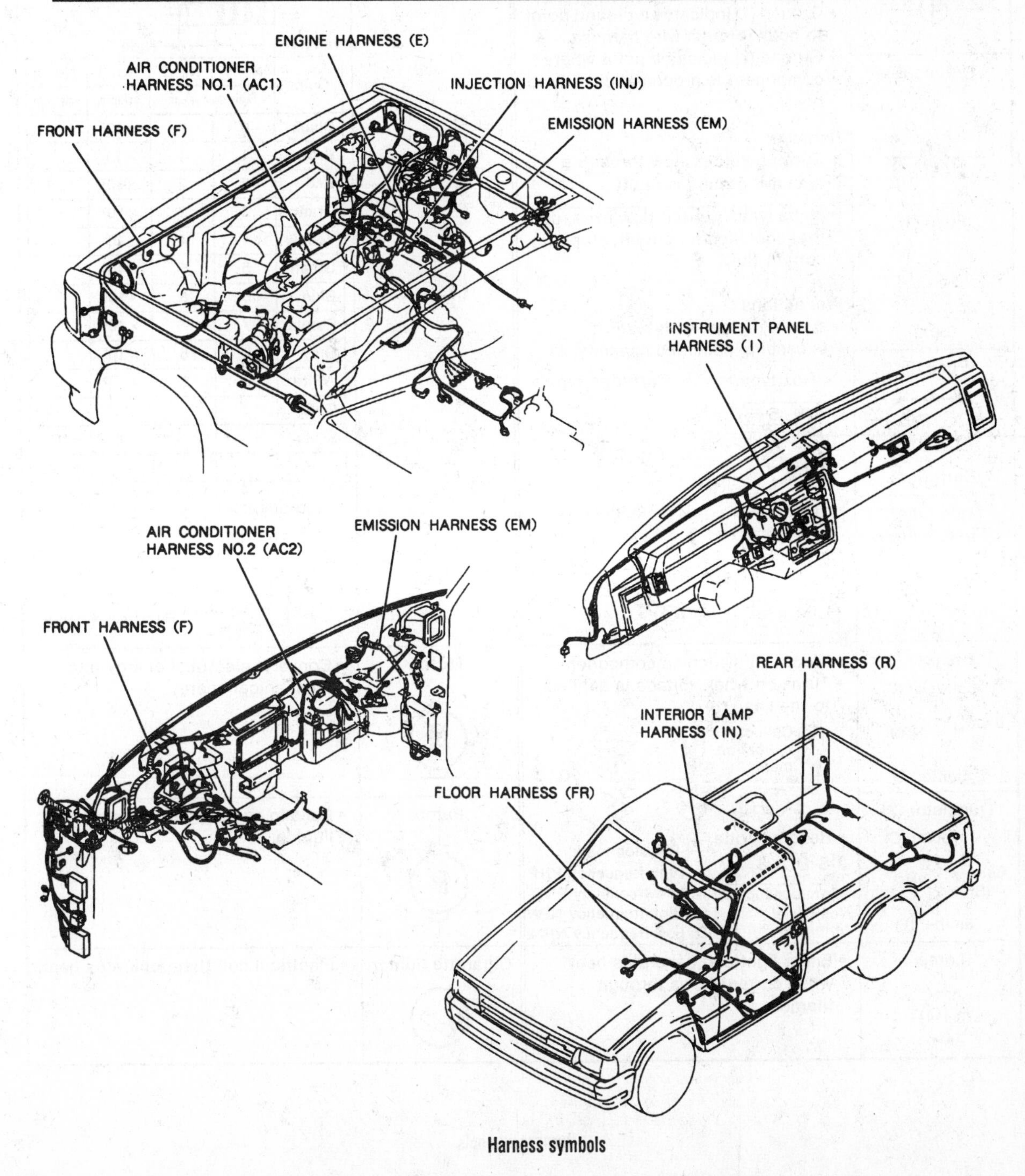

Harness symbols

Symbols

Symbol	Meaning
Battery 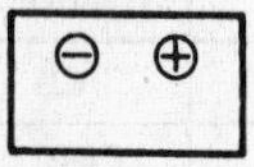 ⊖ ⊕	• Generates electricity through chemical reaction. • Supplies direct current to circuits.
Ground (1) (1) 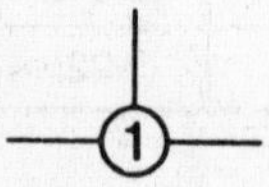	• Connecting point to vehicle body or other ground wire where current flows from positive to negative terminal of battery. • Ground (1) indicates a ground point to body through wire harness. • Ground (2) indicates point where component is grounded directly to body. Remarks • Current will not flow through a circuit if ground is faulty.
Ground (2) 	
Fuse (1)  (box)	• Melts when current flow exceeds that specified for circuit, stopping current flow. Precautions • Do not replace with fuses exceeding specified capacity. <Box type> 15 <Cartridge type>
Fuse (2) 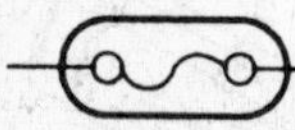 (Cartridge)	 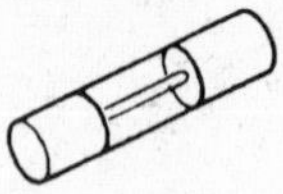
Main fuse/ Fusible link 	<Main fuse>  <Fusible link> 
Transistor (1) 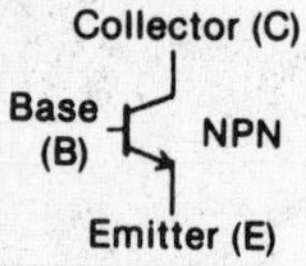 Collector (C) Base (B) NPN Emitter (E)	• Electrical switching component. • Turns on when voltage is applied to the base (B). 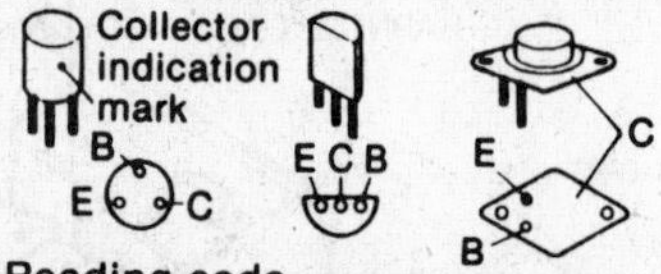 Collector indication mark B E C E C B E C B • Reading code. 2 S C 828 A Number of terminals Semiconductor Revision mark A: High-frequency PNP B: Low-frequency PNP C: High-frequency NPN D: Low-frequency NPN
Transistor (2) Collector (C) Base (B) PNP Emitter (E) 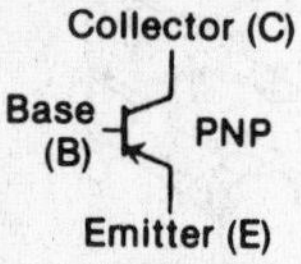	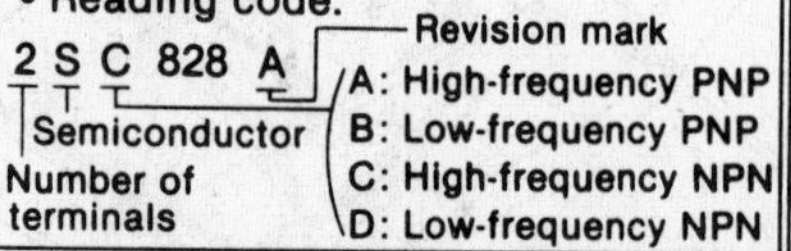
Lamp 3.4W 	• Emits light and generates heat when current flows through filament.

Symbol	Meaning
Resistance 	• A resistor with a constant value. • Mainly used to protect electrical components in circuits by maintaining rated voltage. • Reading resistance values. <Colored> 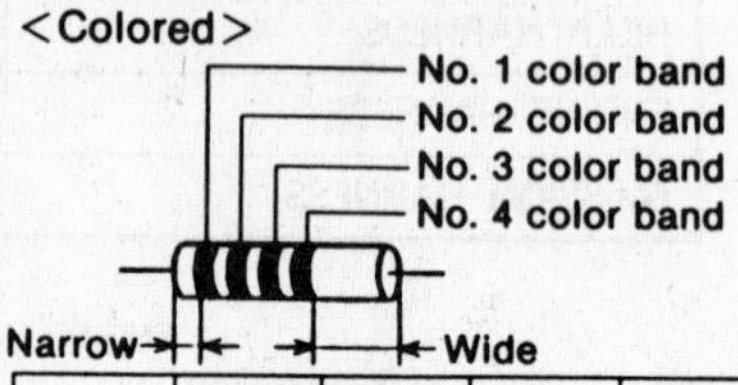 No. 1 color band No. 2 color band No. 3 color band No. 4 color band Narrow / Wide
Motor M 	• Converts electrical energy into mechanical energy.
Pump  P	• Pulls in and expels gases and liquids.
Cigarette lighter 	• Electrical coil that generates heat.

Color	No. 1	No. 2	No. 3	No. 4
	Resistance values		Multiplier	Tolerance
Black	0	0	$\times 10^0$	
Brown	1	1	$\times 10^1$	
Red	2	2	$\times 10^2$	
Orange	3	3	$\times 10^3$	
Yellow	4	4	$\times 10^4$	
Green	5	5	$\times 10^5$	
Blue	6	6	$\times 10^6$	
Purple	7	7	$\times 10^7$	
Grey	8	8	$\times 10^8$	
White	9	9	$\times 10^9$	
Gold			$\times 10^{-1}$	±5%
Silver			$\times 10^{-2}$	±10%
—				±20%

<Numerical>

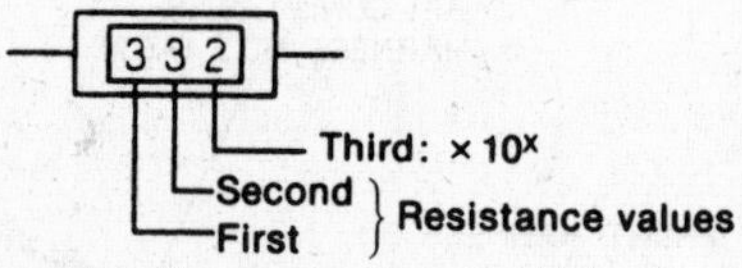

3 3 2

Third: $\times 10^x$

Second, First: Resistance values

Harness symbols

Symbol	Meaning
Horn	• Generates sound when current flows.
Speaker	
Heater	• Generates heat when current flows.
Speed sensor	• Movement of magnet in speedometer turns contact within sensor on and off.
Ignition switch (ST, OFF, ACC)	• Turning ignition key operates switch contacts to complete various circuits.
Relay (1) Normally open (NO)	• Current flowing through coil produces electromagnetic force causing contact to open or close.
Relay (2) Normally closed (NC)	
Sensor (variable)	• Resistor whose resistance changes with operation of other components.
Sensor (thermistor)	• Resistor whose resistance changes with temperature.
Capacitor	• Component that temporarily stores electrical charge.
Solenoid	• Current flowing through coil generates electromagnetic force to operate plungers.

	Open	Closed
Normally open relay (NO)	No flow	Closed
Normally closed relay (NC)	Flow	No flow

Symbol	Meaning
Switch (1) Normally open (NO)	• Allows or breaks current flow by opening and closing circuits.
Switch (2) Normally closed (NC)	
Harness (Not connected)	• Unconnected intersecting harness.
(Connected)	• Connected intersecting harness.
Diode	• Known as a semiconductor rectifier, the diode allows current flow in one direction only. Cathode (K) Anode (A) ← Flow of electric current; K A K A K A
Light-emitting diode (LED)	• A diode that lights when current flows. • Unlike ordinary light bulbs, the diode does not generate heat when lit. Cathode (K) Anode (A); Cathode (K); Anode (A); Flow of electric current
Reference diode (Zener diode)	• Allows current to flow in one direction up to a certain voltage; allows current to flow in the other direction once that voltage is exceeded.

Harness symbols

Logic symbols

Types of logic symbols	Operation	Expressing output	Simple relay circuits
OR	Input to A or B will produce output at C.	Low electrical potential (L) at A and B→no output (L) at C High electrical potential (H) at A or B→output (H) at C	
AND	Input to A and B will produce output at C.	High electrical potential (H) at A and B→output (H) at C Low electrical potential (L) at A or B→no output (L) at C	
INV	No input to A will produce an output at B. An input to A will not produce an output at B.	Low electrical potential (L) at A→no ground (H) B High electrical potential (H) at A→grounds (L) B	
PROCESS	Simplified representation of complex functions within circuit describes main function. 1. Signal detector for emission control unit, cooling unit, and tachometer. 2. Signal converter for turn and hazard flasher unit and breakerless transistor igniter unit.		(Examples) Breakerless transistor igniters Signal converter Coil signal converted to ON/OFF signal

Abbreviations used in this booklet

A Ampere
AAS Autoadjusting Suspension
ABS Antilock Brake System
ACV Air Control Valve
AE Acoustic Equilibration
AIS Air Injection System
ALL Automatic Load Leveling
AS Autostop
ASV Air Supply Valve
A/C Air Conditioner
A/F Air Fuel
A/R Auto Reverse
A/T Automatic Transmission
ACC Accessory
ACCEL Accelerator
ADD Additional
ALT Alternator
AM Amplitude Modulation
AMP Amplifier
ANT Antenna
ATP Atmospheric Pressure
ATX Automatic Transaxle
B Battery
BAC Bypass Air Control Valve
B/L Bilevel
CPU Central Processing Unit
CSD Cold Start Device
CARB Carburetor
CCT Circuit
CIGAR Cigarette
COMBI Combination
CON Conditioner
CONT Control
DOHC Double-Overhead Camshaft
DEF Defroster
EC-AT Electronic Controlled Automatic Transmission
Electrically Control Automatic Transaxle
ECPS Electronically Controlled Power Steering
ECU Engine Control Unit
EGI Electronic Gasoline Injection
EGR Exhaust Gas Recirculation
ELR Emergency Locking Retractor
ELEC Electric
ETR Electronic Tuner
EXH Exhaust
F Front
FICB Fast-Idle Cam Breaker
FL Front Left
FR Front Right
F/B Feedback
F/I Fuel Injector
FM Frequency Modulation
GEN Generator
HEI High-Energy Ignition
H/D Heater/Defroster
HEAT Heater
HI High
ISC Idle-Speed Control
IG Ignition
ILLUMI Illumination
INT Intermittent
JB Joint Box
LH Left Hand
LCD Liquid Crystal Display
LO Low
LW Low Wave
M Motor
MIL Malfunction Indicator Lamp
MTR Mechanical Tuning Radio
M/T Manual Transmission
MID Middle
MIN Minute
MIX Mixture
MPX Multiplex
MTX Manual Transaxle
MW Middle Wave
NC Normally Closed
NO Normally Open
OD Overdrive
OFF Switch Off
ON Switch On
P Power
PRCV Pressure Regulator Control Solenoid Valve
PTC Positive Temperature Coefficient Heater
P/S Power Steering
PRG Purge Solenoid Valve
QSS Quick-Start System
R Rear
RH Right Hand
RL Rear Left
RPM Revolutions Per Minute
RR Rear Right
REC Recirculation
SOL Solenoid
ST Start
SW Short Wave
SW Switch
TCV Twin Scroll Turbocharger Solenoid Valve
TICS Triple Induction Control System
TEMP Temperature
TR Transistor
TWS Total Wiring System
V Volt
VRIS Variable Resonance Induction System
VENT Ventilation
VOL Volume
W Watt (s)

Precautions to take when servicing an electrical system

- Note the following items when servicing the electrical system.
- Do not alter the wiring or electrical equipment in any way; this may damage the vehicle or cause a fire from short-circuiting a circuit or overloading it.

- Always disconnect the negative (−) battery cable first and reconnect it last when disconnecting the battery.

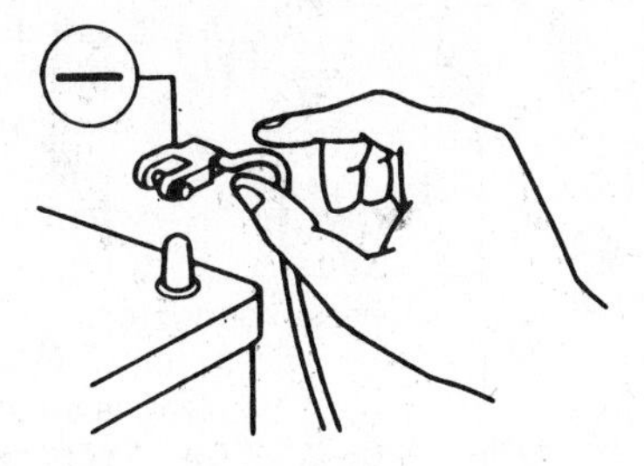

Caution
- Be sure that the ignition and other switches are off before disconnecting or connecting the battery terminals.
  Failure to do so may damage the semiconductor components.

- Replace blown fuses with ones having the same designated capacity.

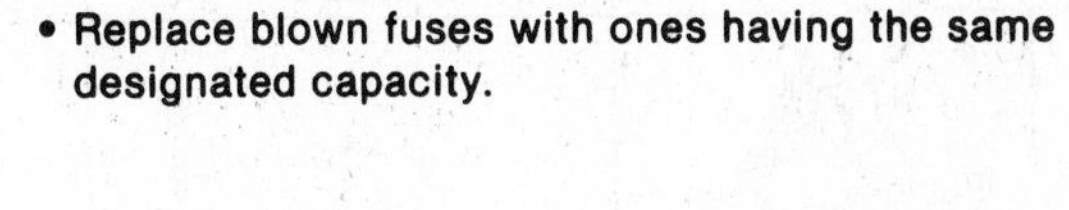

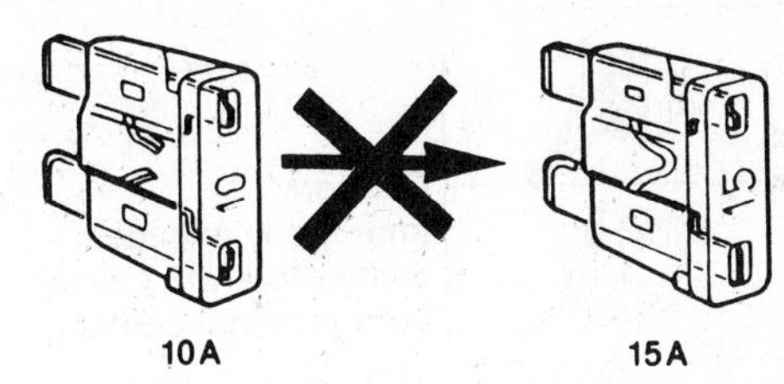

Caution
- Replacing a fuse with one of a larger capacity than designated may damage components or cause a fire.

- Secure harnesses with provided clamps to take up slack.

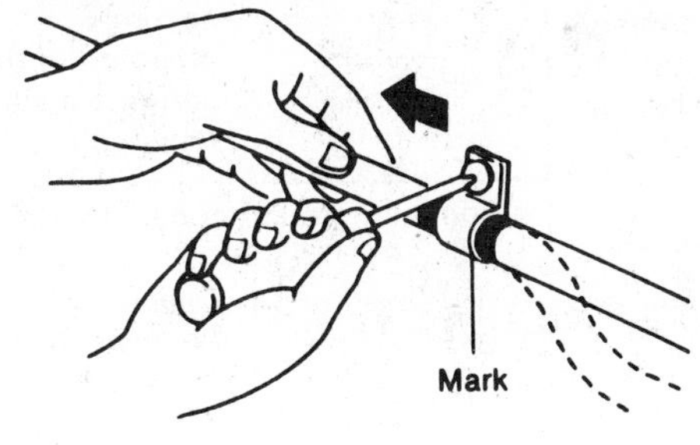

Caution
- Clamp all harnesses near vibrating components (for example, the engine) to remove slack and to prevent contact resulting from vibration.

- Tape areas of the harness that may rub or bump against sharp edges to protect it from damage.
- When mounting components, be sure the harness is not caught or damaged.

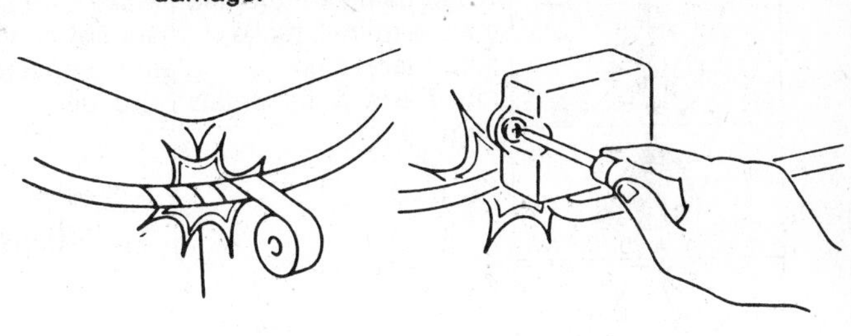

- Do not handle electrical components roughly or drop them.

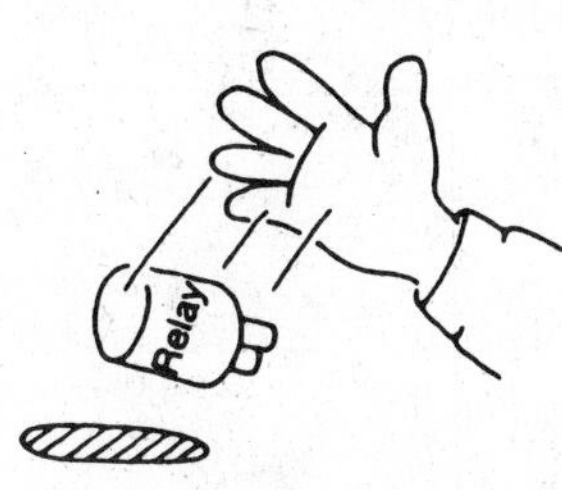

- Disconnect heat-sensitive parts (for example, relays and ECUs) when performing maintenance (such as welding) where temperatures may exceed 80°C (176°F).

- Make sure that the connectors are securely connected when installed.

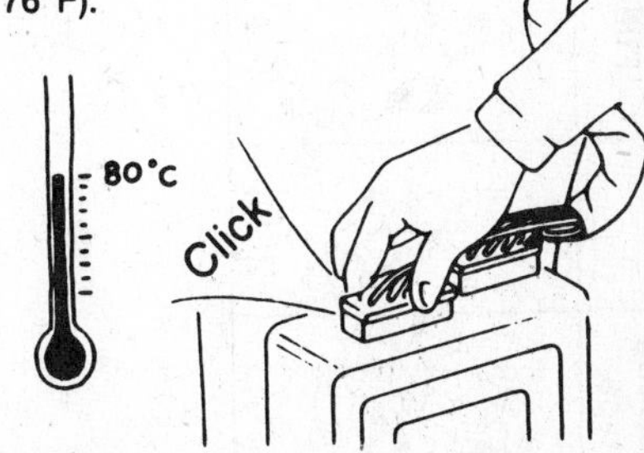

Precautions to take when servicing an electrical system

Handling connectors

Caution

- Be sure to grasp the connectors, not the wires, when disconnecting them.

Connector removal	Checking connector contacts	Checking for loose terminals	Repairing terminal
Push type Remove Pull-up type Spring type	Caution Improperly engaged connectors will cause poor terminal contact. When using a matching male terminal, make sure there is no looseness in the female terminal.	Caution A loose terminal will cause poor terminal contact. Make sure the terminals are not pushed out of the connector when engaged. Lightly pull each wire to make sure the terminal does not pull out of the connector.	<CPU connector> 1. Open the rear cover. 2. Lift the tab with a small screwdriver and remove the terminal. <General connector> Lift the tab with a small screwdriver and remove the terminal. <Round connectors> 1. Open the cover. 2. Lift the terminal to remove it. 3. Make sure the terminal is securely mounted in the connector when reinstalling. <Common ground connectors> 1. Open the cover. 2. Remove A. 3. Lift the tab with a small screwdriver and remove the terminal. A

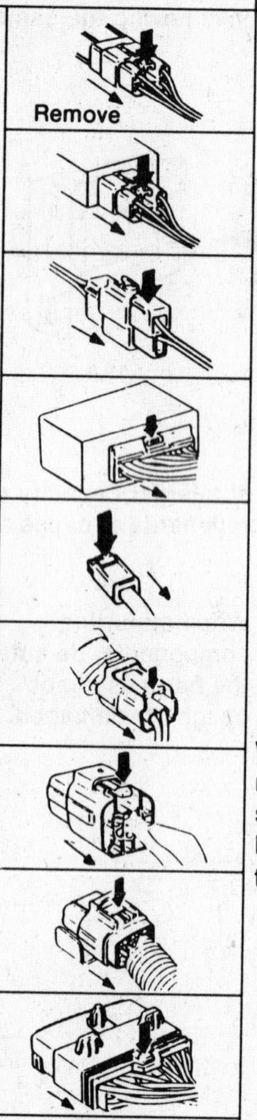

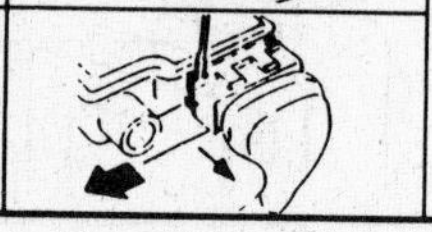

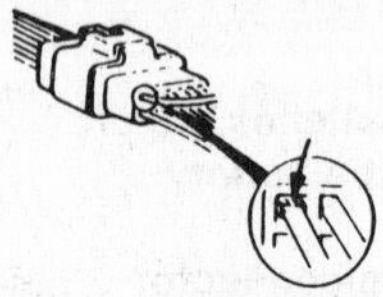

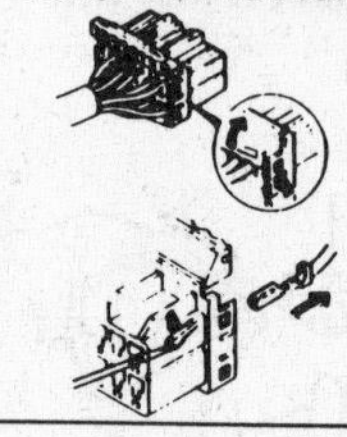

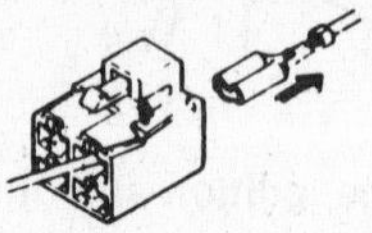

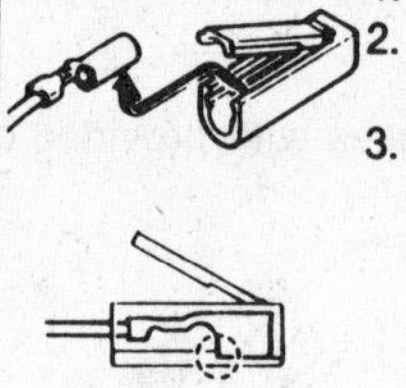

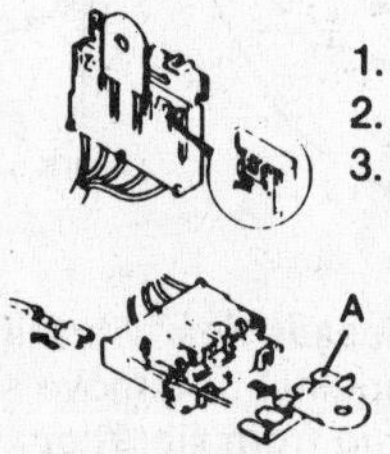

Handling connectors

Using electrical measuring equipment

Equipment	Use	Operation	Handling precautions
Test lamp	Test to find open or shorted circuits.	• Connect the test lamp between the circuit being measured and a ground. • The lamp will light if the circuit is energized to the point tested.	• Test lamps use 12V 1.4W or 3.4W bulbs or light-emitting diodes (LEDs). Using a large-capacity bulb may damage the CPU.
Jumper wire	Used to create a temporary circuit.	• Connect the jumper wire between the terminals of a circuit to bypass a switch.	• Do not connect the power side directly to a ground; this may burn the harness or damage electrical components.
Voltmeter	Used for measuring the voltage of a circuit to locate possible opens or shorts.	• Connect the positive (+) lead to where voltage is to be measured and the negative (−) lead to a ground.	• Connect the voltmeter in parallel with the circuit. • Set the range to the desired voltage. • Use the service hole when measuring the voltage at the diagnosis connector. • Tie a thin wire to the positive (+) lead to access narrow terminals.
Ohmmeter	Used to find opens and shorts in the circuit, to confirm continuity of switches, and to check sensor resistance.	• Zero the ohmmeter. • Verify that current is not flowing through the circuit. • Touch the leads to the check points.	• Zero the meter after switching to the measuring range. • Before using the ohmmeter, make sure the ignition switch is off or the negative (−) battery cable is disconnected to prevent burning the ohmmeter.
Ammeter	Used to check alternator output, current supplied to the starter, and dark current within a circuit. Note Dark current is the current flowing through the circuit when the ignition switch is OFF.	• Connect the ammeter in series with the circuit by touching the positive (+) lead to the power-side terminal and the negative (−) lead to the ground-side terminal.	• Set the range to the desired amperage. • Connect the ammeter in series with the circuit. The ammeter may be burned if it is connected in parallel.

Using electrical measuring equipment

Measuring voltage

Checks

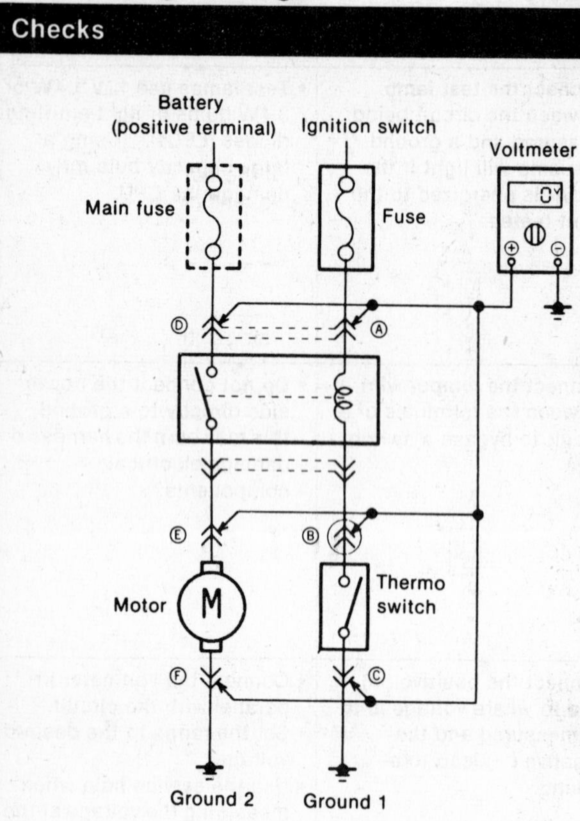

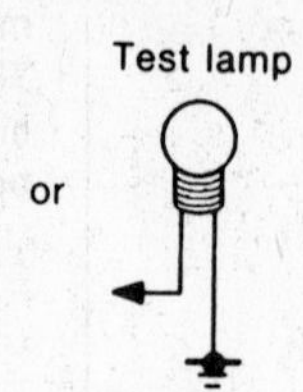

1. Use a voltmeter or test lamp to ascertain voltage at the measuring points.

Measuring points	Circuit operation					
	Ignition switch: OFF		Ignition switch: ON			
			Thermo switch: OFF		Thermo switch: ON	
Ⓐ	0V	×	12V	☼	12V	☼
Ⓑ	0V	×	12V	☼	0V	×
Ⓒ	0V	×	0V	×	0V	×
Ⓓ	12V	☼	12V	☼	12V	☼
Ⓔ	0V	×	0V	×	12V	☼
Ⓕ	0V	×	0V	×	0V	×

☼ : Test lamp ON
× : Test lamp OFF

Precautions during checks

Measuring voltage of connectors

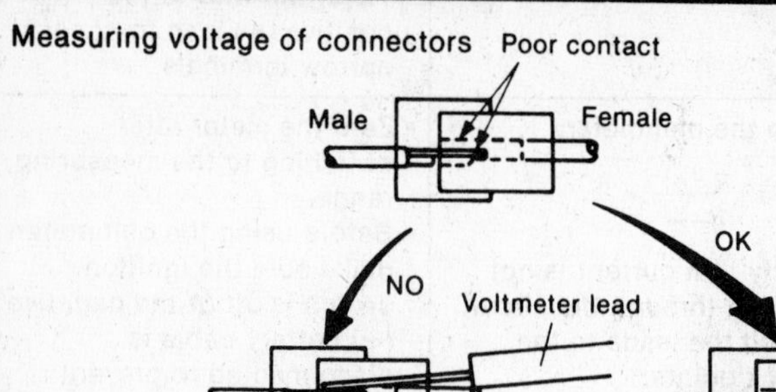

A voltmeter lead may momentarily connect a terminal when inserted into the connector and give an erroneous reading when checking for improperly engaged connectors, poor terminal contacts, or loose terminals.

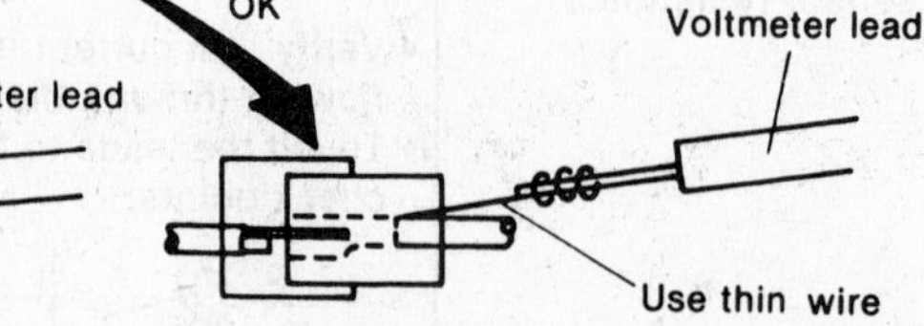

Measuring voltage of ground unit

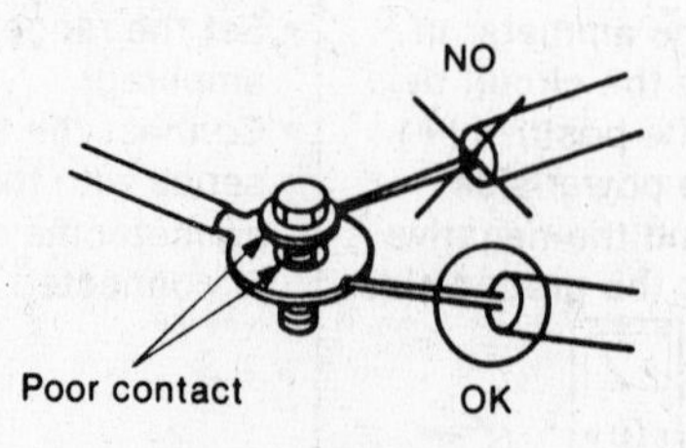

Touch the voltmeter lead to the ground wire when checking the ground circuit.

Measuring continuity/resistance

Checking switches

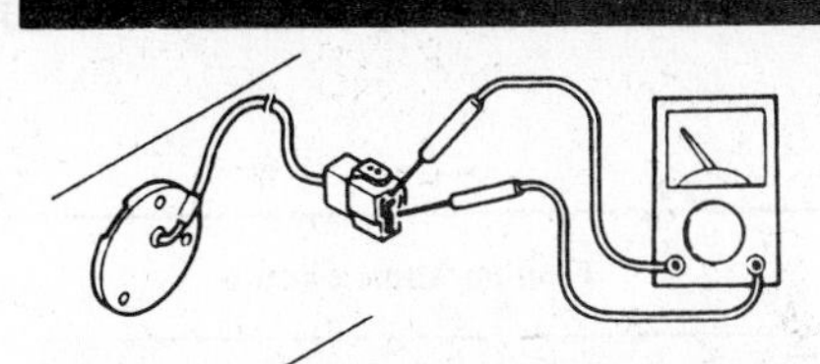

Touch the ohmmeter leads to the switch terminals to check continuity.

Caution
Verify the operating state of the switch before checking continuity because readings vary accordingly.

Checking diodes

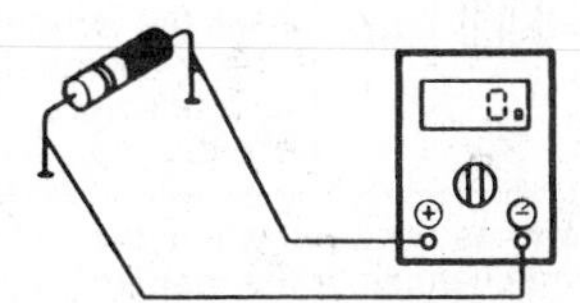

Remark
The negative (−) lead of the ohmmeter is connected to the positive terminal of the internal ohmmeter battery, the positive (+) lead to the negative terminal of the battery.

Continuity is checked according to the direction of the positive (+) and negative (−) leads of the ohmmeter in the circuit containing the diode.

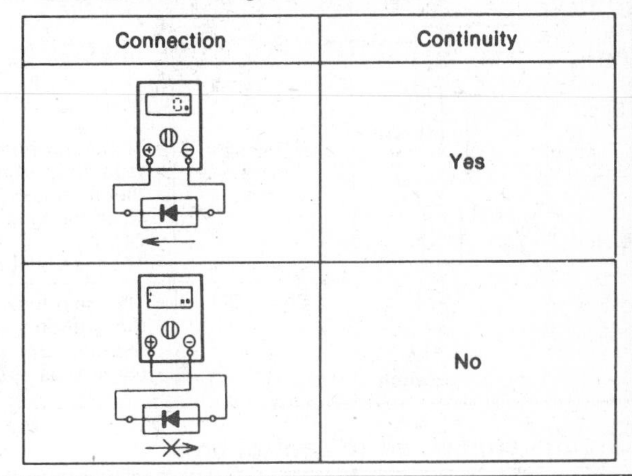

Connection	Continuity
	Yes
	No

Checking sensors and solenoid valves

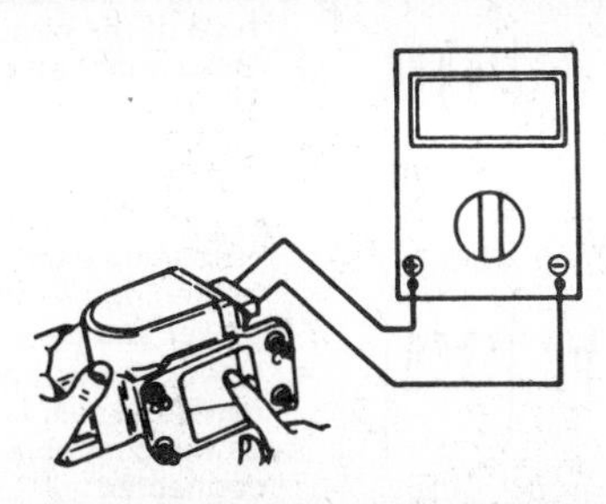

Connect the ohmmeter leads to the sensor or solenoid valve terminals to check resistance.

Caution
Verify the operating state of the sensor before checking resistance because readings vary accordingly.

Checking condensers

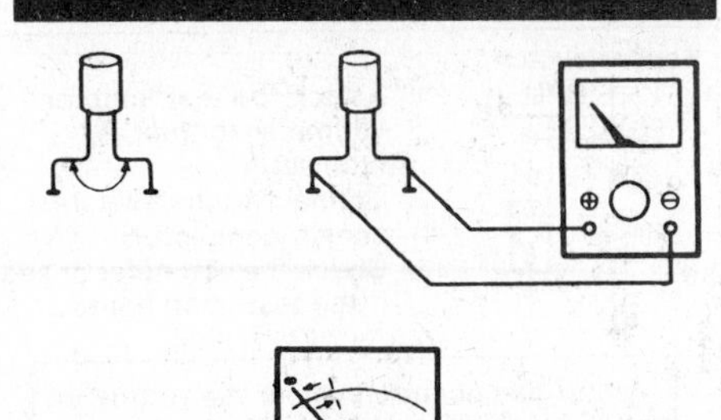

1. Short between the terminals with a jumper wire to discharge the capacitor.
2. Set the ohmmeter range to × 10kΩ and connect it to the capacitor terminals.
3. The capacitor is good if the needle of the ohmmeter swings once and returns to its original position.

Finding short circuits

Shorts occur between the power (positive) and ground (negative) sides of a circuit. Therefore, finding a short circuit requires determining how the circuit is routed.

Circuits not connected to control unit

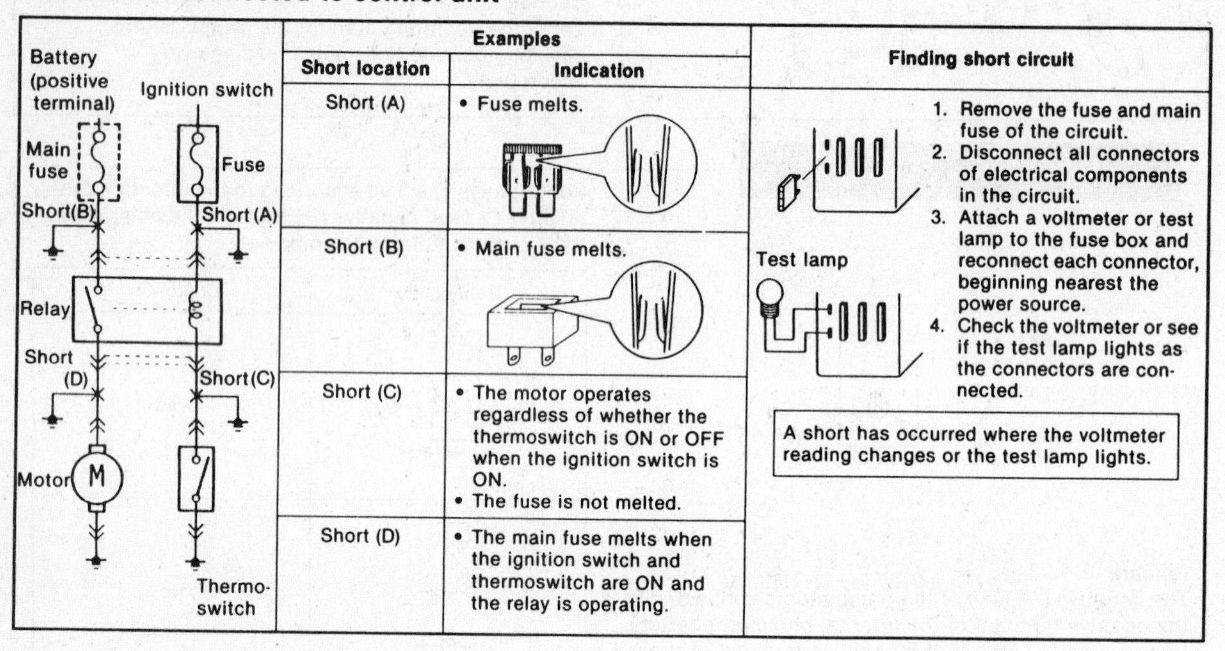

Examples: Short location	Examples: Indication	Finding short circuit
Short (A)	• Fuse melts.	1. Remove the fuse and main fuse of the circuit. 2. Disconnect all connectors of electrical components in the circuit. 3. Attach a voltmeter or test lamp to the fuse box and reconnect each connector, beginning nearest the power source. 4. Check the voltmeter or see if the test lamp lights as the connectors are connected. A short has occurred where the voltmeter reading changes or the test lamp lights.
Short (B)	• Main fuse melts.	
Short (C)	• The motor operates regardless of whether the thermoswitch is ON or OFF when the ignition switch is ON. • The fuse is not melted.	
Short (D)	• The main fuse melts when the ignition switch and thermoswitch are ON and the relay is operating.	

Circuits connected to control unit

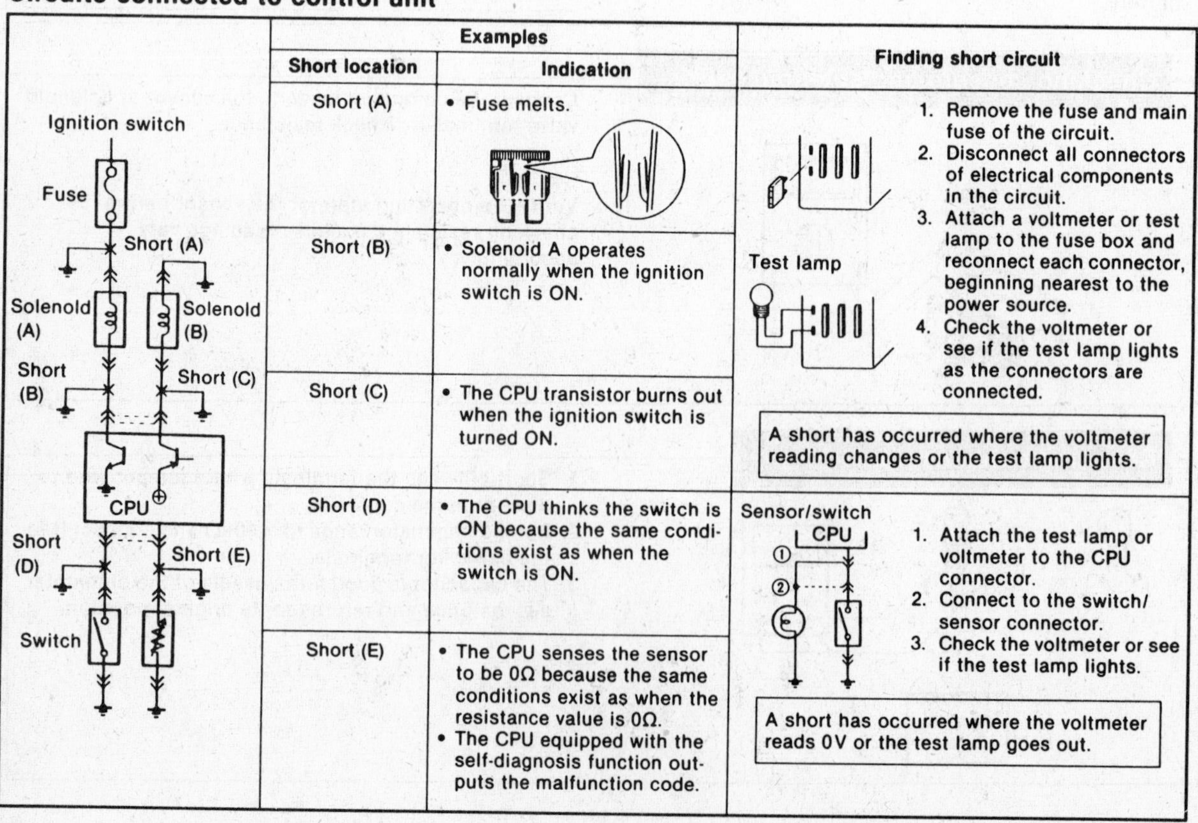

Examples: Short location	Examples: Indication	Finding short circuit
Short (A)	• Fuse melts.	1. Remove the fuse and main fuse of the circuit. 2. Disconnect all connectors of electrical components in the circuit. 3. Attach a voltmeter or test lamp to the fuse box and reconnect each connector, beginning nearest to the power source. 4. Check the voltmeter or see if the test lamp lights as the connectors are connected. A short has occurred where the voltmeter reading changes or the test lamp lights.
Short (B)	• Solenoid A operates normally when the ignition switch is ON.	
Short (C)	• The CPU transistor burns out when the ignition switch is turned ON.	
Short (D)	• The CPU thinks the switch is ON because the same conditions exist as when the switch is ON.	1. Attach the test lamp or voltmeter to the CPU connector. 2. Connect to the switch/sensor connector. 3. Check the voltmeter or see if the test lamp lights. A short has occurred where the voltmeter reads 0V or the test lamp goes out.
Short (E)	• The CPU senses the sensor to be 0Ω because the same conditions exist as when the resistance value is 0Ω. • The CPU equipped with the self-diagnosis function outputs the malfunction code.	

Finding short circuits

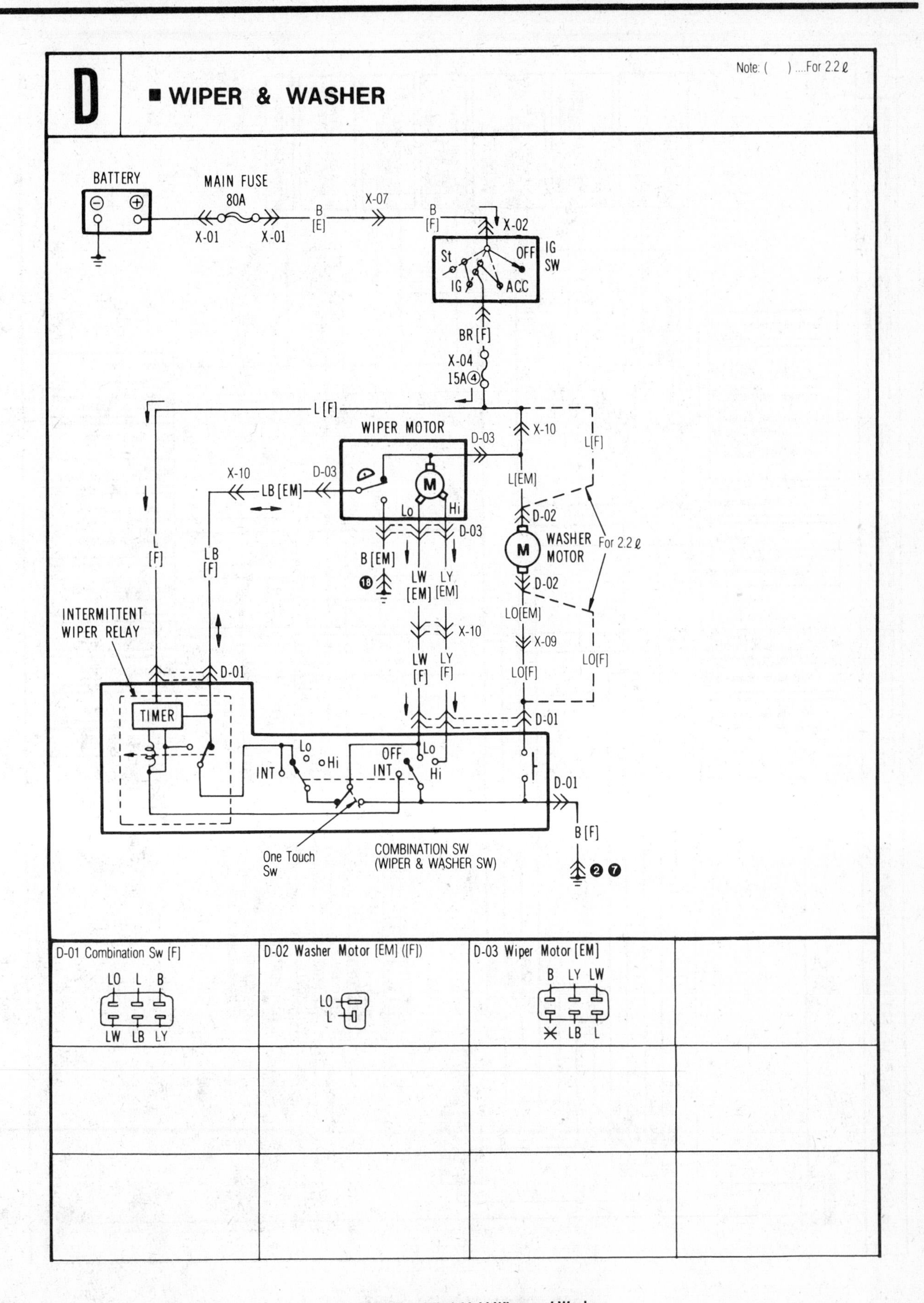
D
WIPER & WASHER
Note: ( ) ....For 2.2 ℓ
BATTERY
MAIN FUSE
80A
X-01
X-01
B [E]
X-07
B [F]
X-02
St
OFF
IG
ACC
IG SW
BR [F]
X-04
15A④
L [F]
WIPER MOTOR
D-03
X-10
L[F]
L[EM]
X-10
D-03
LB [EM]
Lo
Hi
D-02
WASHER MOTOR
For 2.2 ℓ
D-03
B [EM]
LW [EM]
LY [EM]
D-02
L [F]
LB [F]
LO[EM]
INTERMITTENT WIPER RELAY
X-10
X-09
LW [F]
LY [F]
LO[F]
LO[F]
D-01
D-01
TIMER
Lo
Hi
INT
OFF
Lo
INT
Hi
D-01
B [F]
One Touch Sw
COMBINATION SW (WIPER & WASHER SW)
D-01 Combination Sw [F]
LO L B
LW LB LY
D-02 Washer Motor [EM] ([F])
LO
L
D-03 Wiper Motor [EM]
B LY LW
LB L

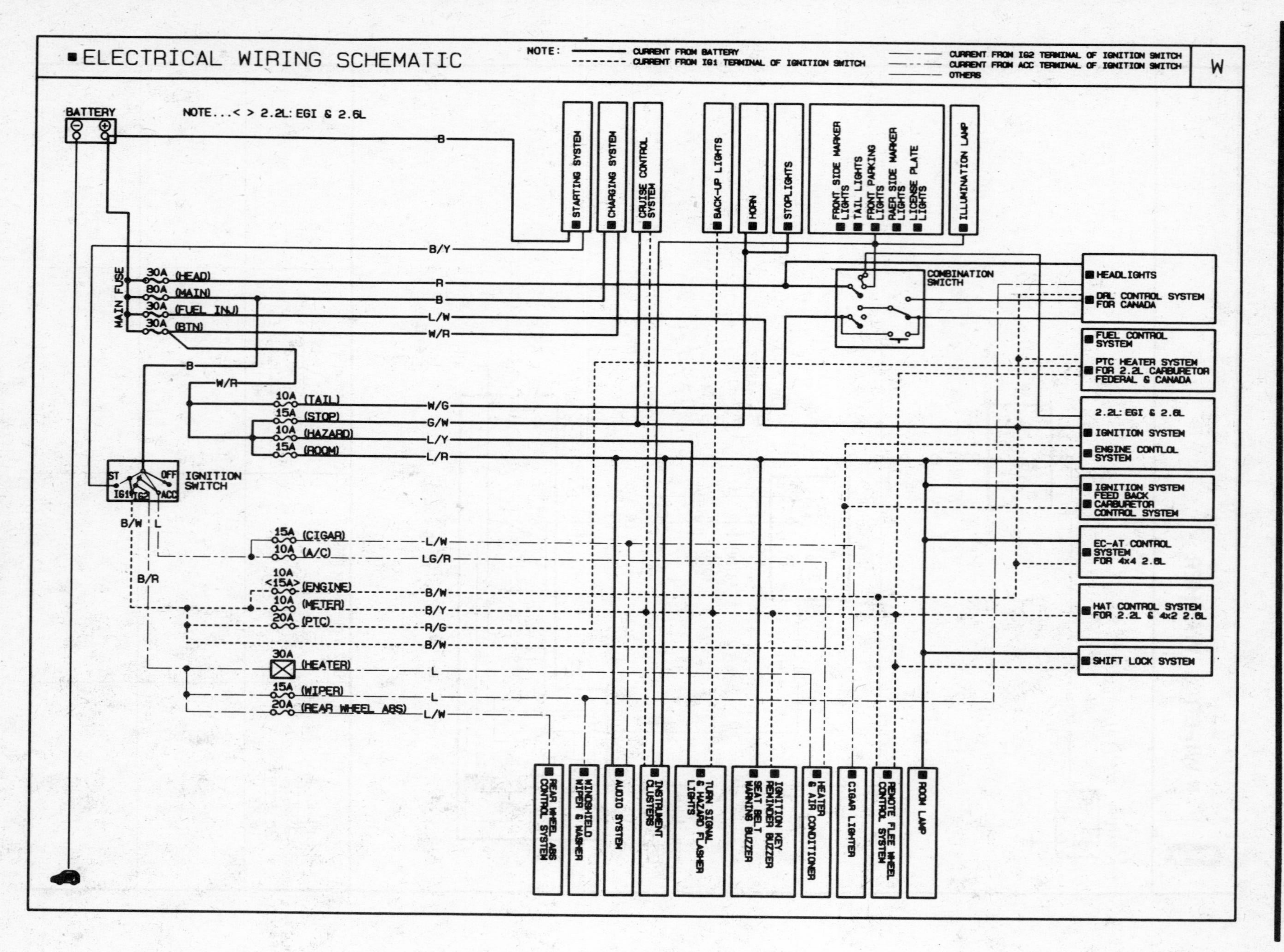

1989-92 Pickup, Wiring Schematic

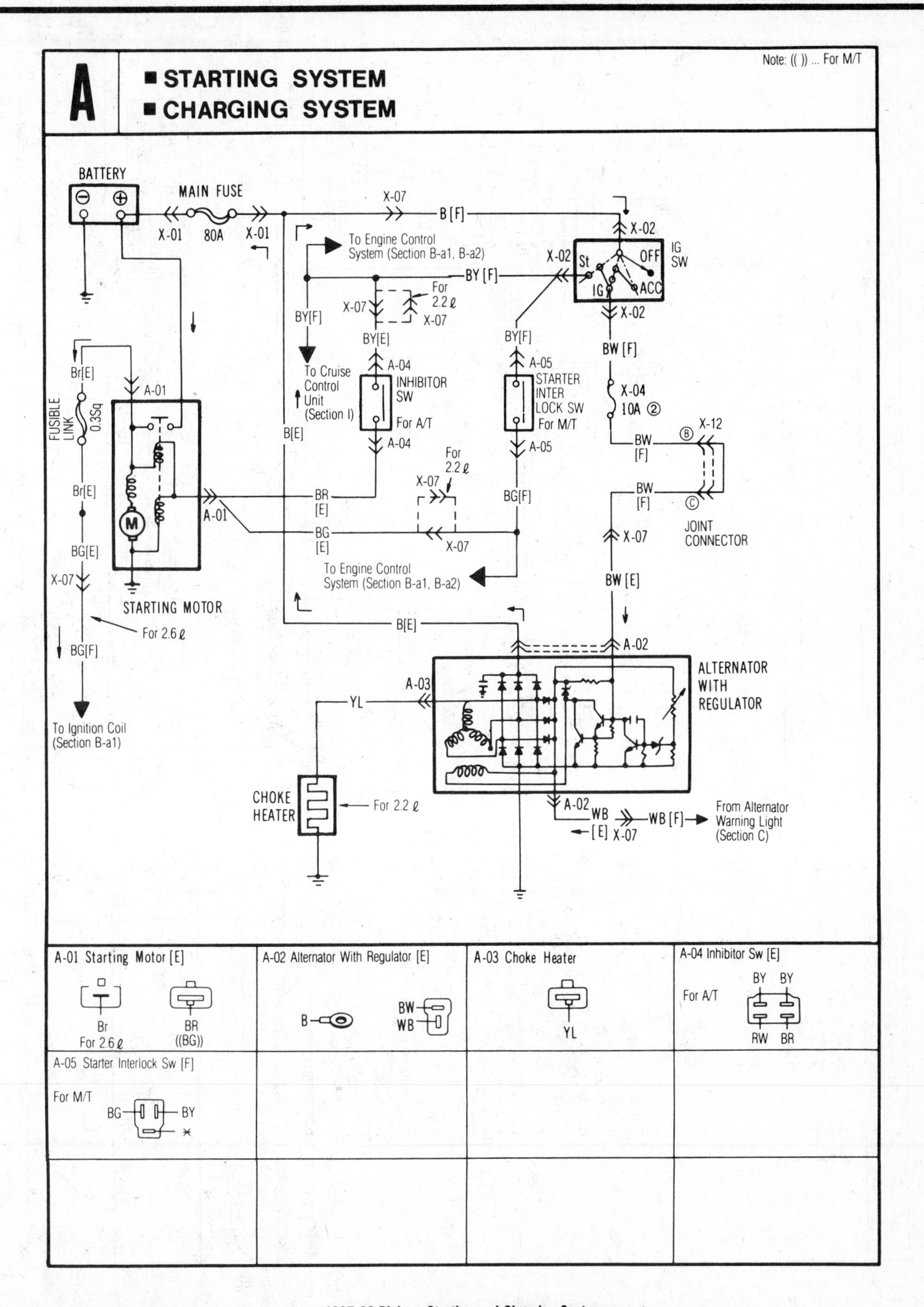
A
STARTING SYSTEM
CHARGING SYSTEM
Note: (( )) ... For M/T
BATTERY
MAIN FUSE
X-01
80A
X-01
X-07
B [F]
X-02
To Engine Control
System (Section B-a1, B-a2)
IG
SW
St
OFF
IG
ACC
BY [F]
For
2.2 ℓ
X-07
BY[F]
BY[E]
BY[F]
BW [F]
To Cruise
Control
Unit
(Section I)
A-04
INHIBITOR
SW
For A/T
A-05
STARTER
INTER
LOCK SW
For M/T
X-04
10A ②
X-12
BW
[F]
Br[E]
A-01
FUSIBLE
LINK
0.3Sq
B[E]
BR
[E]
BG
[E]
BG[F]
JOINT
CONNECTOR
BG[E]
X-07
To Engine Control
System (Section B-a1, B-a2)
BW [E]
STARTING MOTOR
For 2.6 ℓ
B[E]
A-02
ALTERNATOR
WITH
REGULATOR
A-03
YL
To Ignition Coil
(Section B-a1)
CHOKE
HEATER
For 2.2 ℓ
WB
WB [F]
[E]
From Alternator
Warning Light
(Section C)
A-01 Starting Motor [E]
Br
For 2.6 ℓ
BR
((BG))
A-02 Alternator With Regulator [E]
B
BW
WB
A-03 Choke Heater
YL
A-04 Inhibitor Sw [E]
For A/T
BY BY
RW BR
A-05 Starter Interlock Sw [F]
For M/T
BG
BY
*

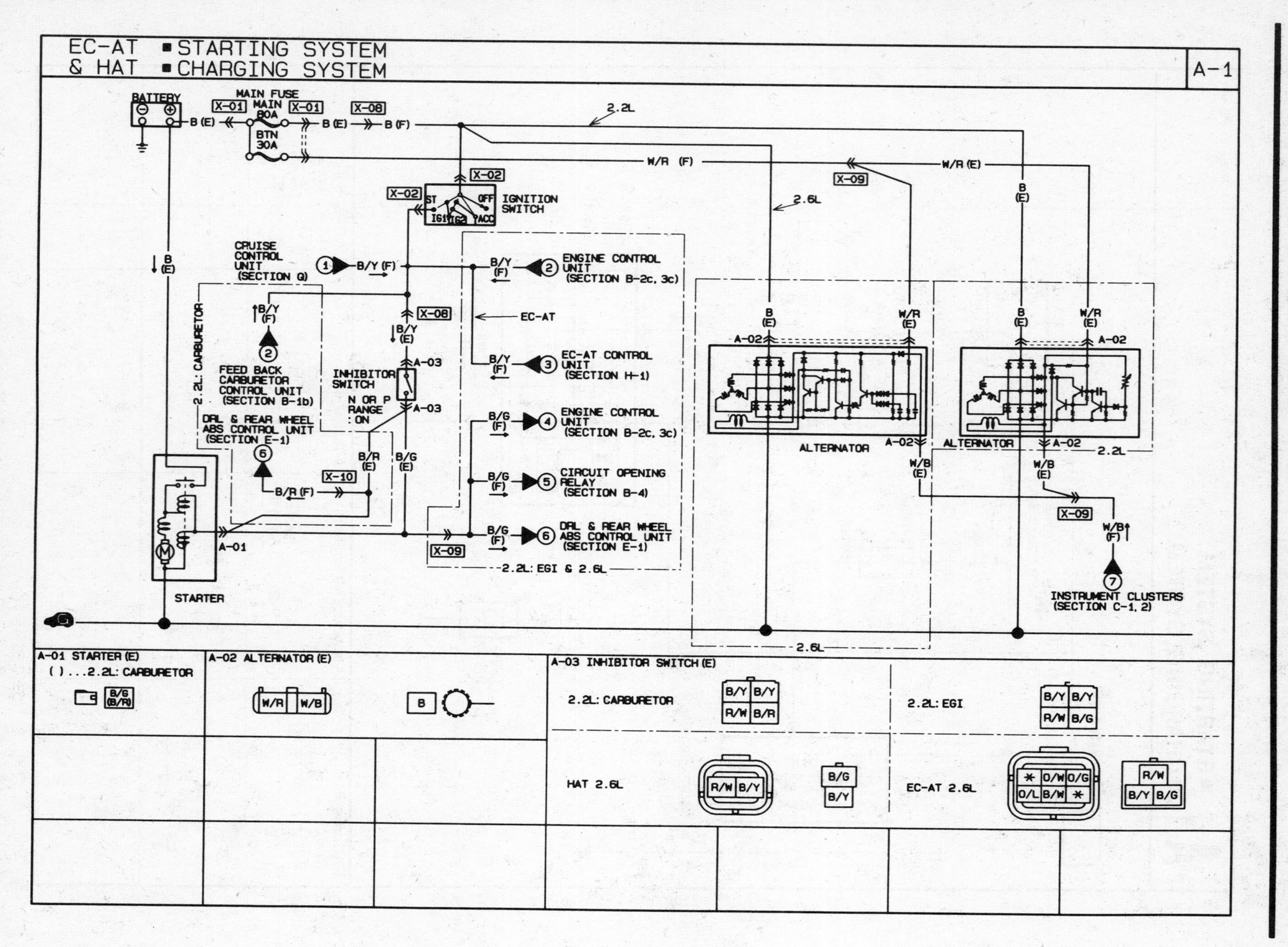

1989-92 Pickup, Starting and Charging Systems w/AT

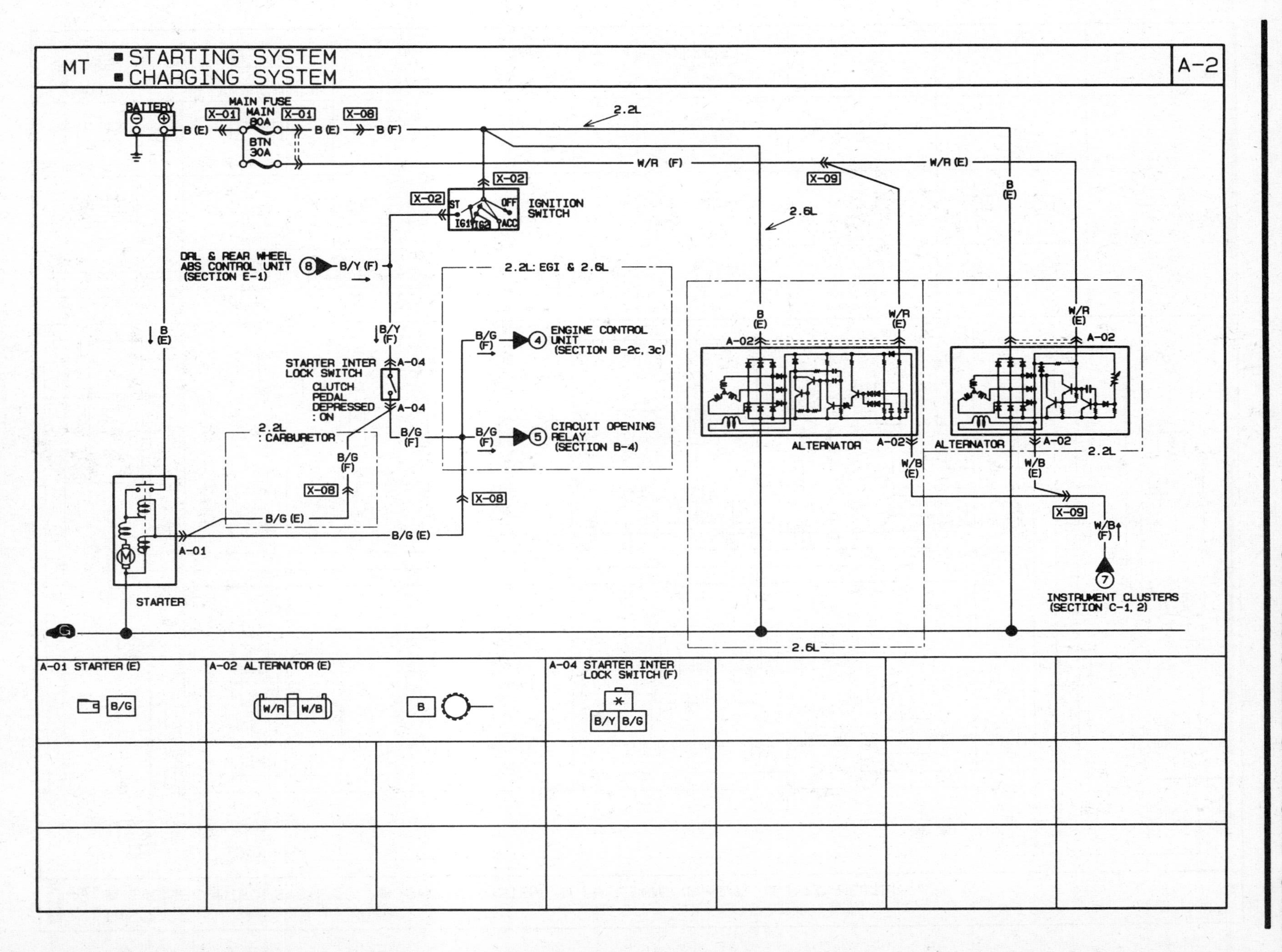

1989-92 Pickup, Starting and Charging Systems w/MT

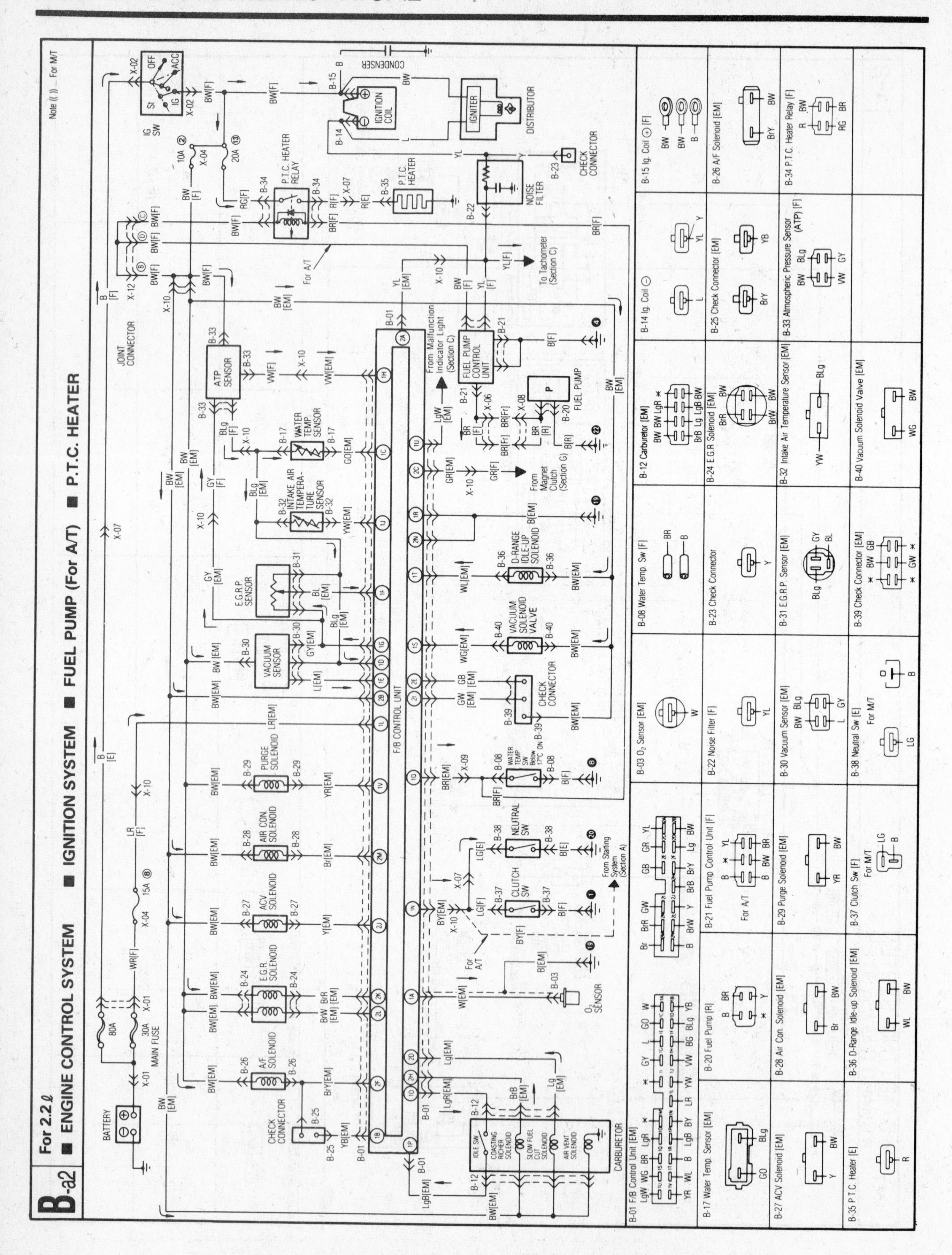

1987-88 Pickup 2.2L, Engine Control System, Ignition System, Fuel Pump (w/AT)

Z WIRING DIAGRAM

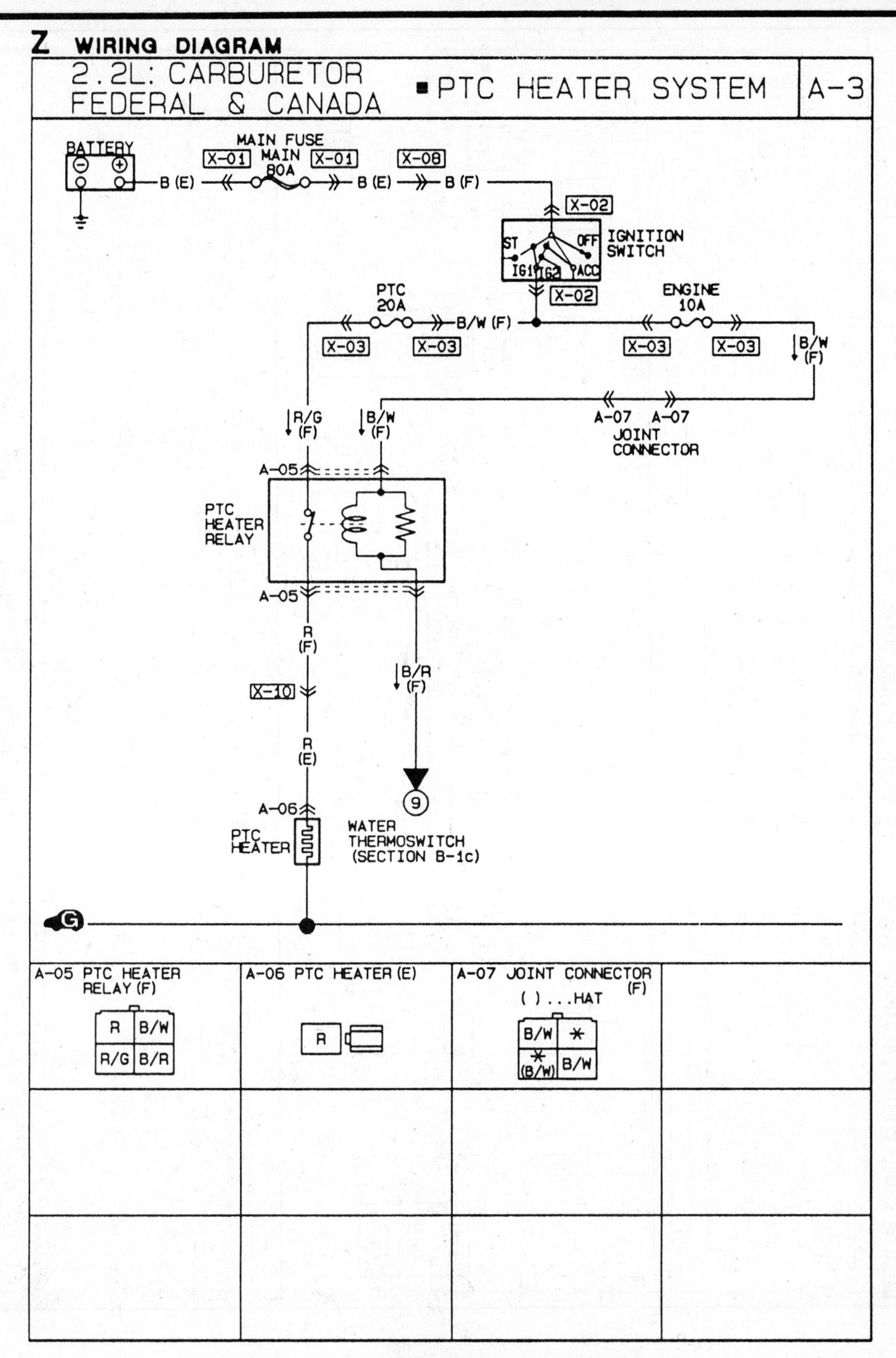

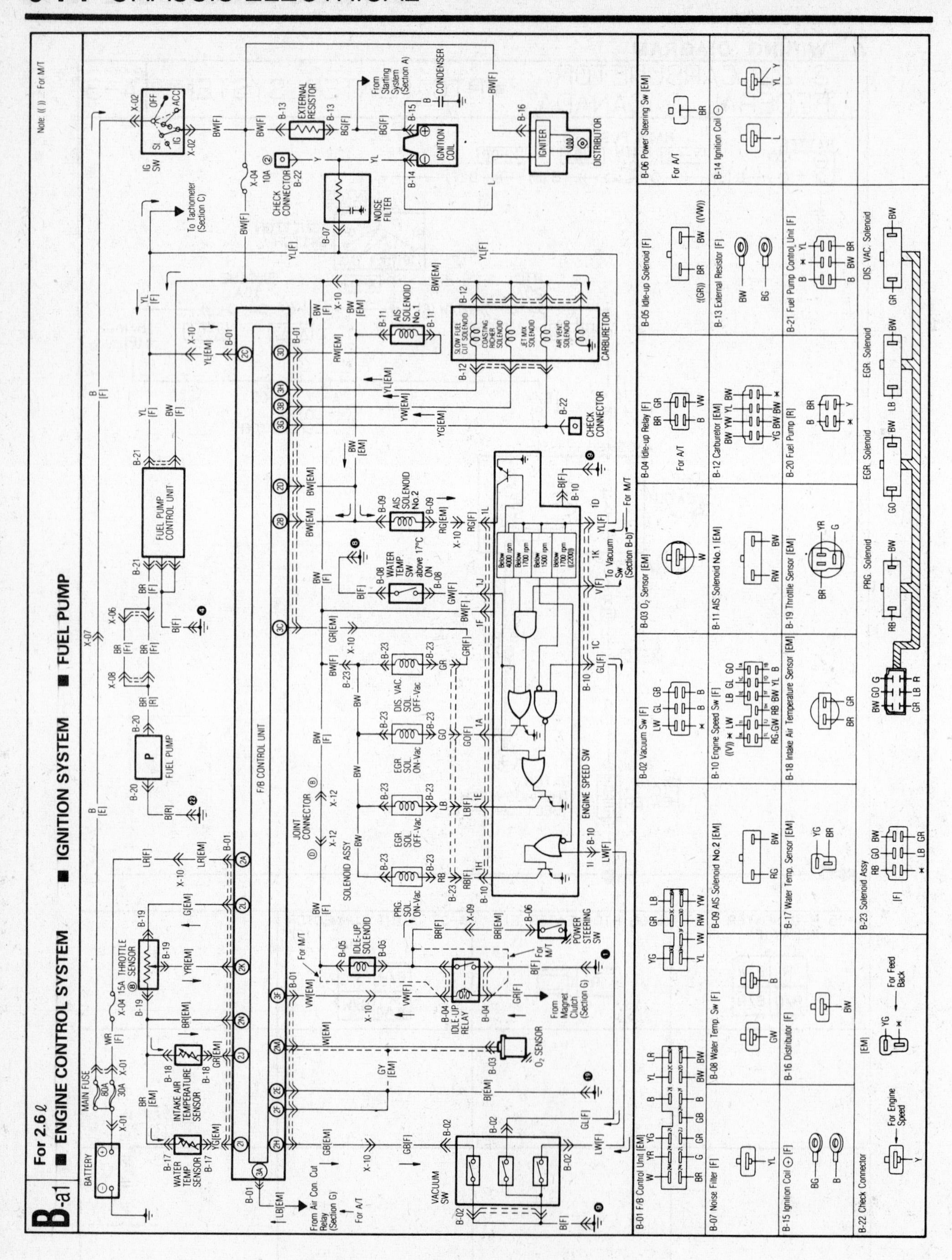

1987-88 Pickup 2.6L, Engine Control System, Ignition System

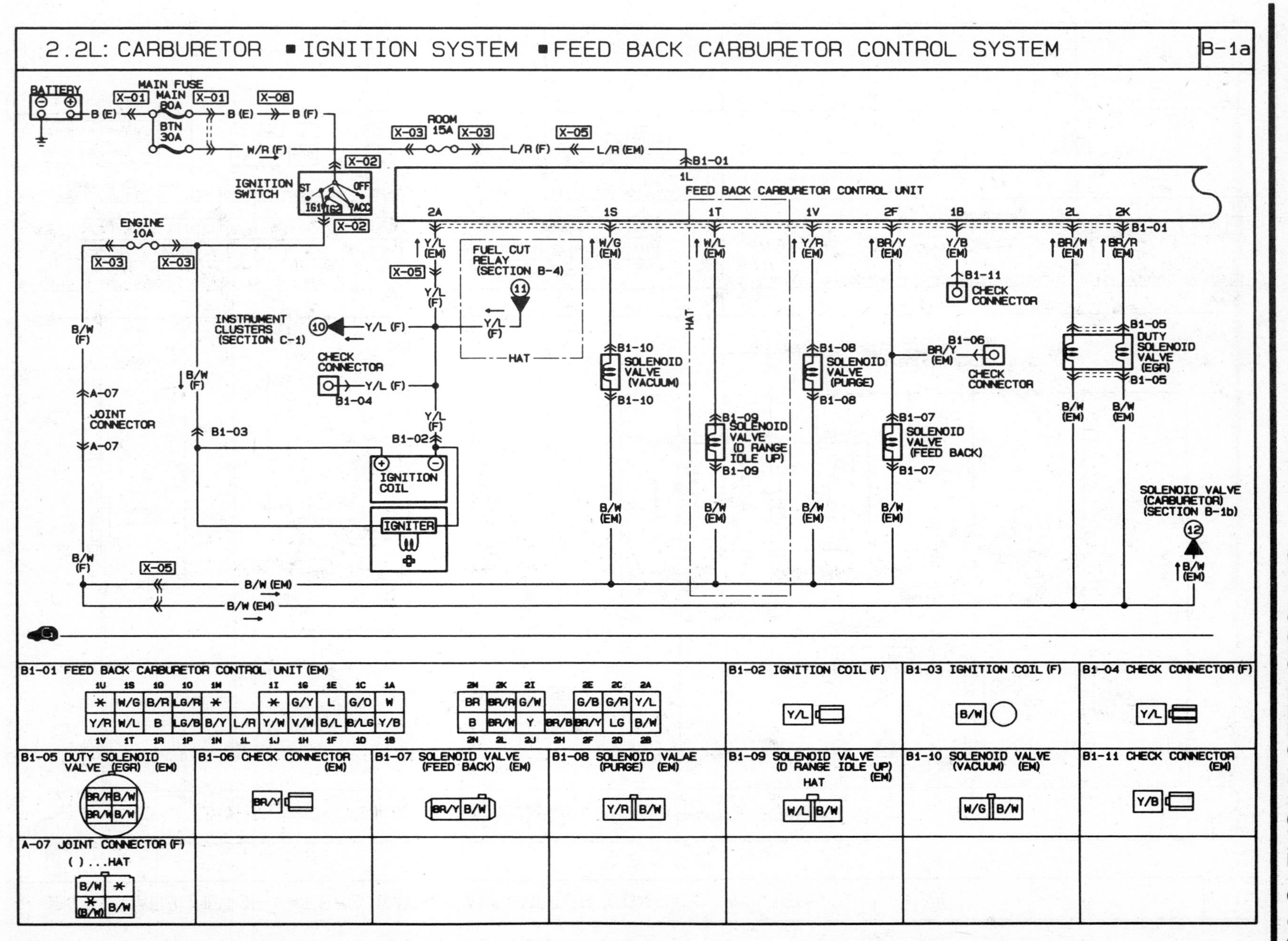

1989-92 Pickup 2.2L Carburetor, Ignition System, Feedback Carburetor Control System

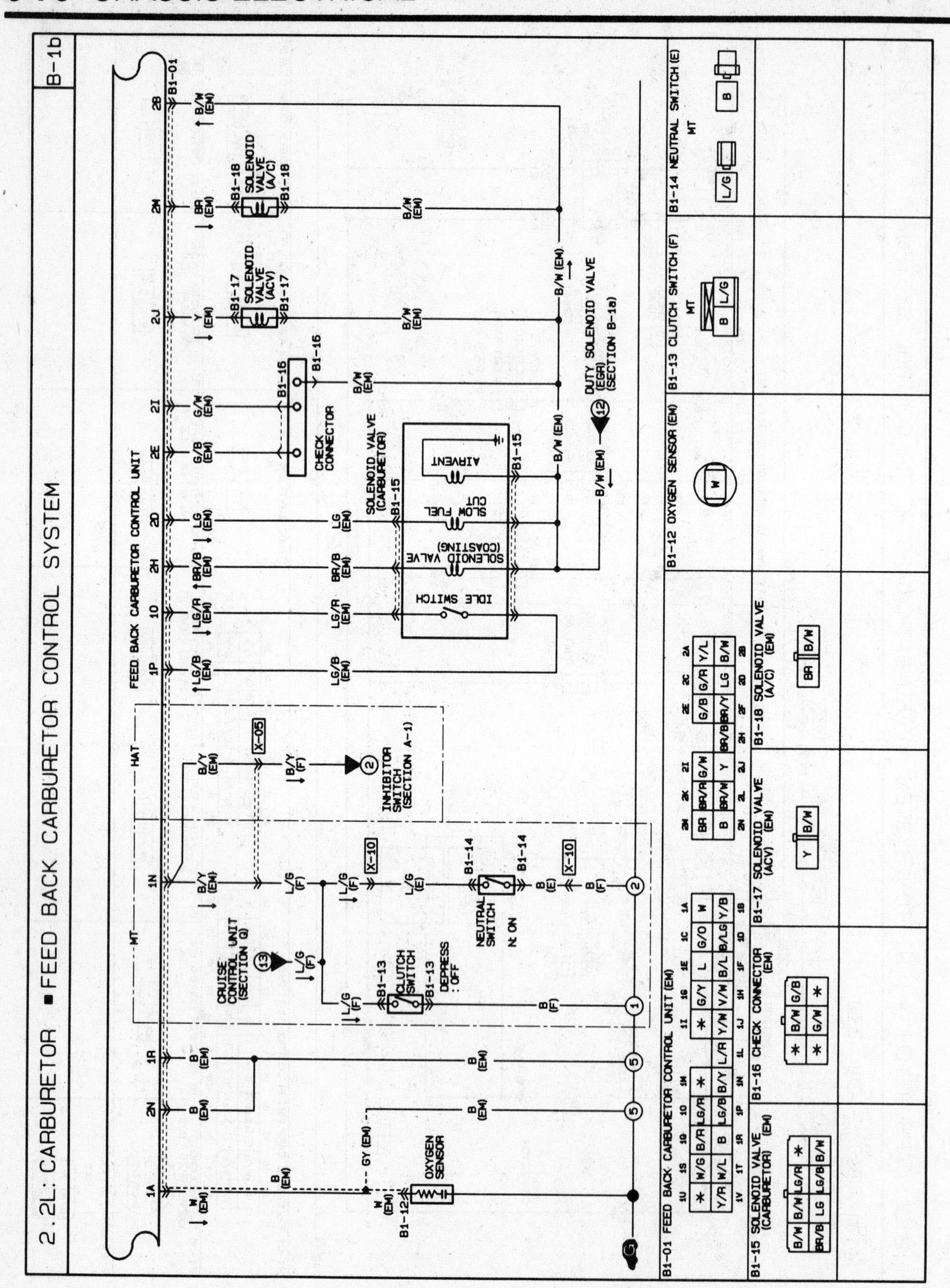

1989-92 Pickup 2.2L Carburetor, Feedback Carburetor Control System

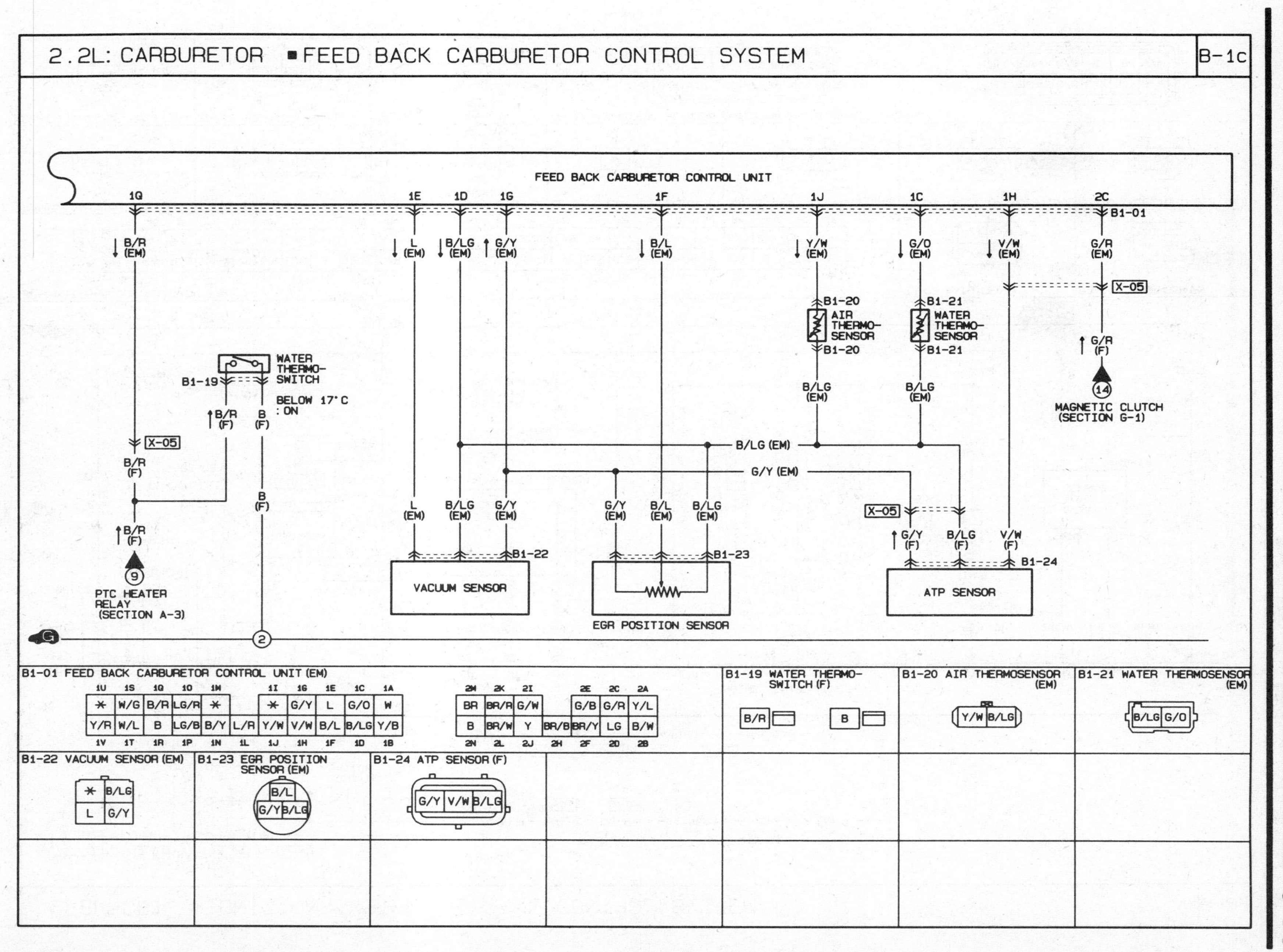

1989-92 Pickup 2.2L Carburetor, Feedback Carburetor Control System

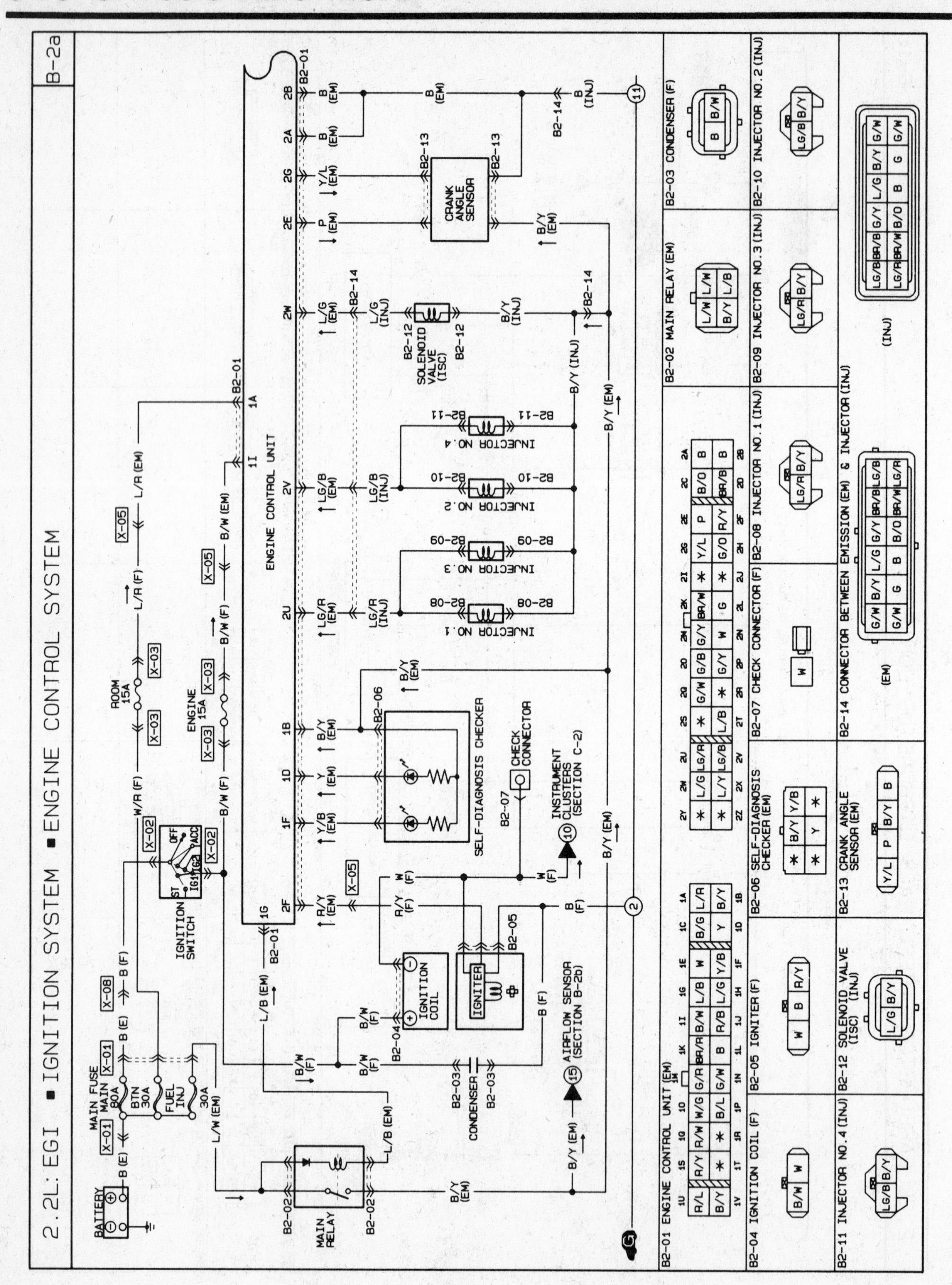

1989-92 Pickup 2.2 Injected, Ignition System, Engine Control System

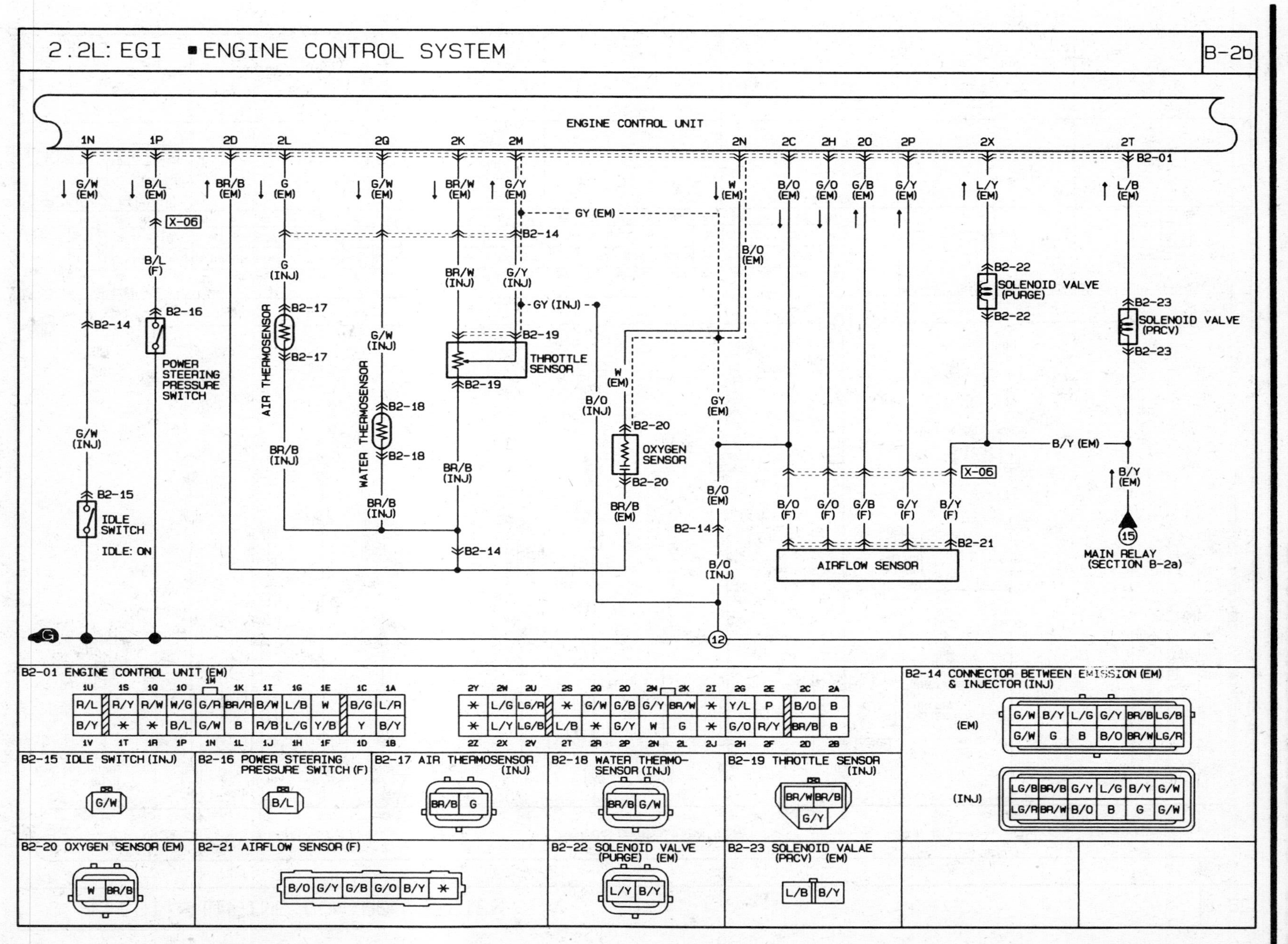

1989-92 Pickup 2.2L Injected, Engine Control System

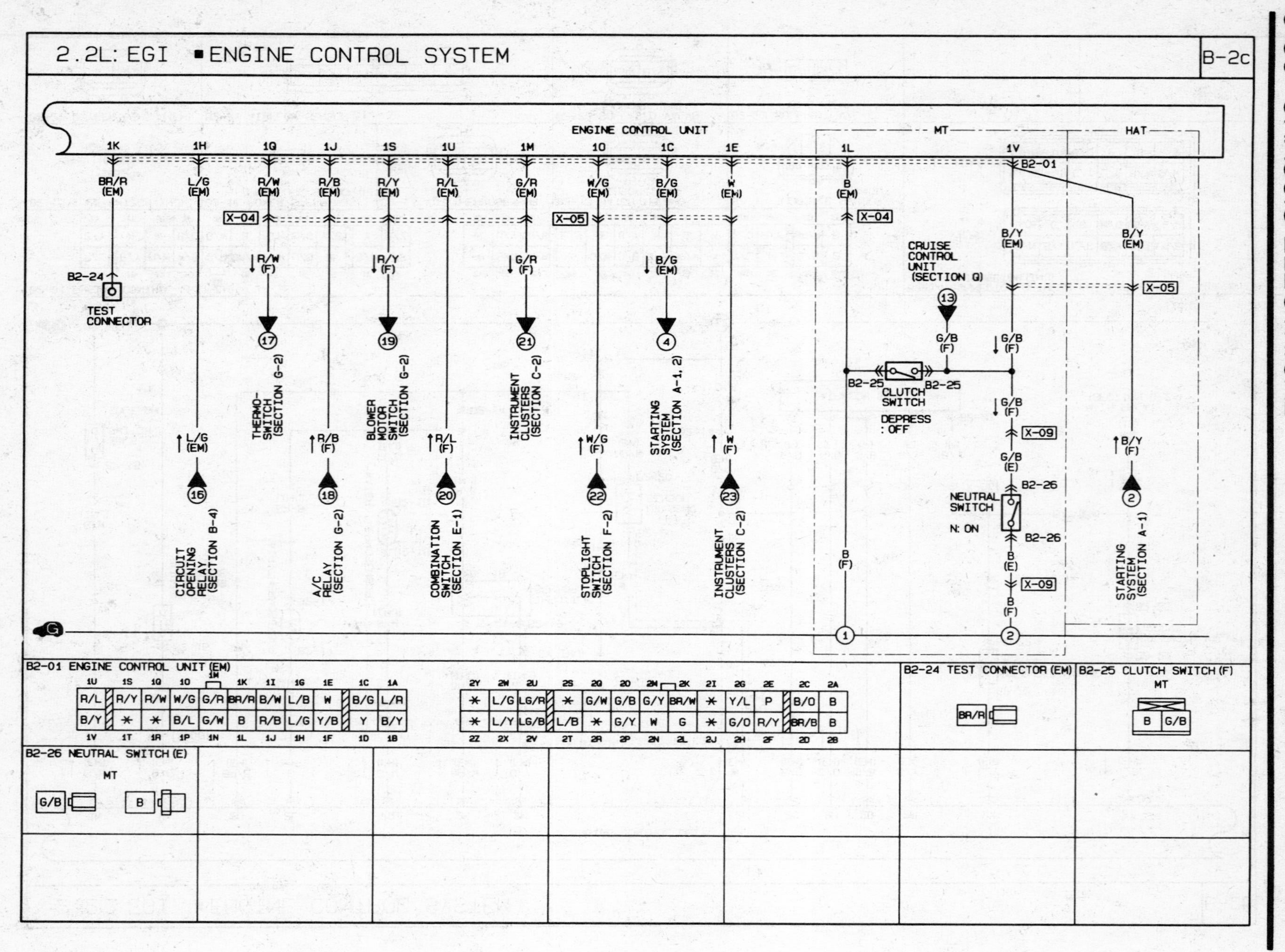

1989-92 Pickup 2.2L Injected, Engine Control System

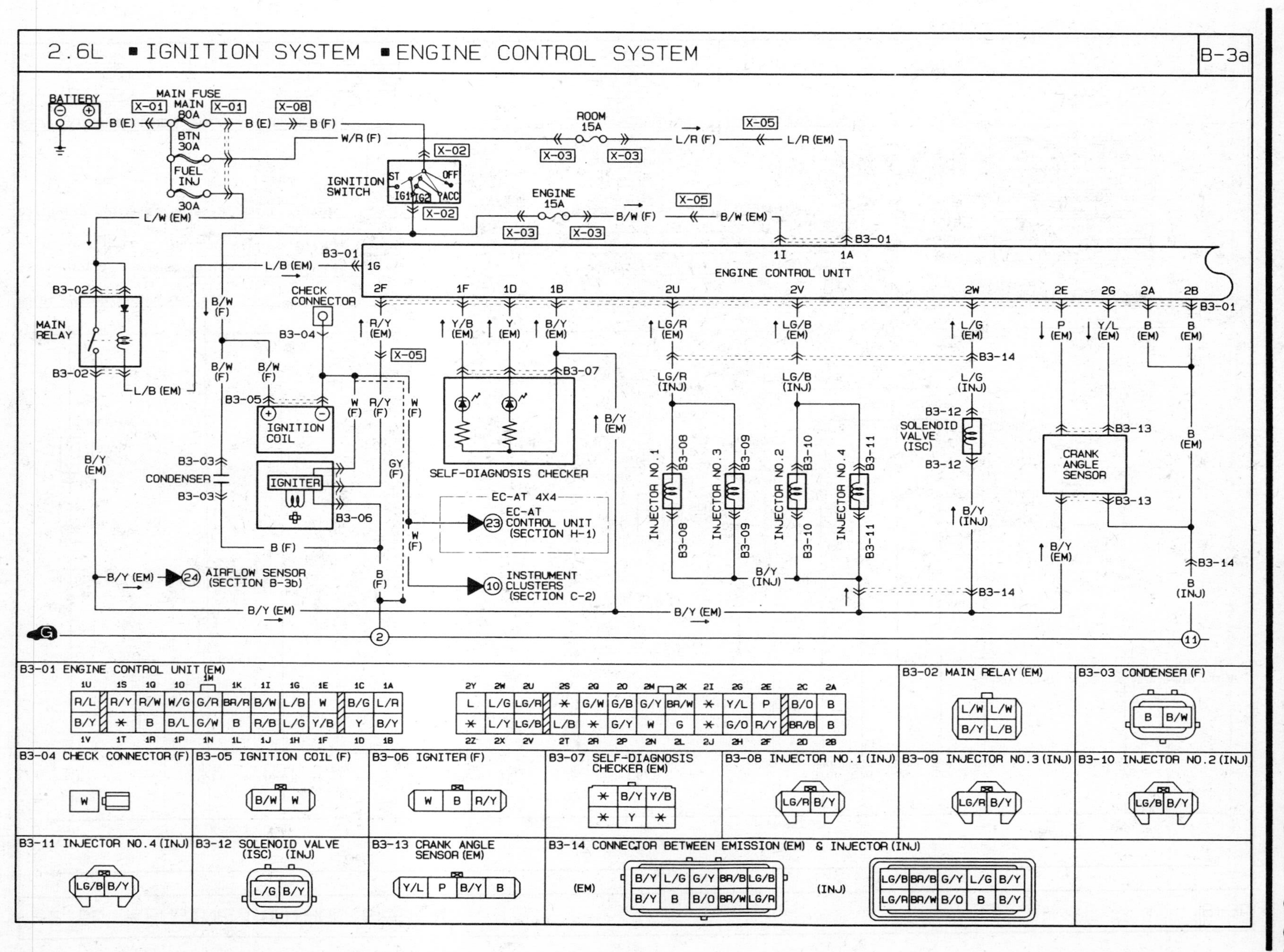

1989-92 Pickup 2.6L, Ignition System, Engine Control System

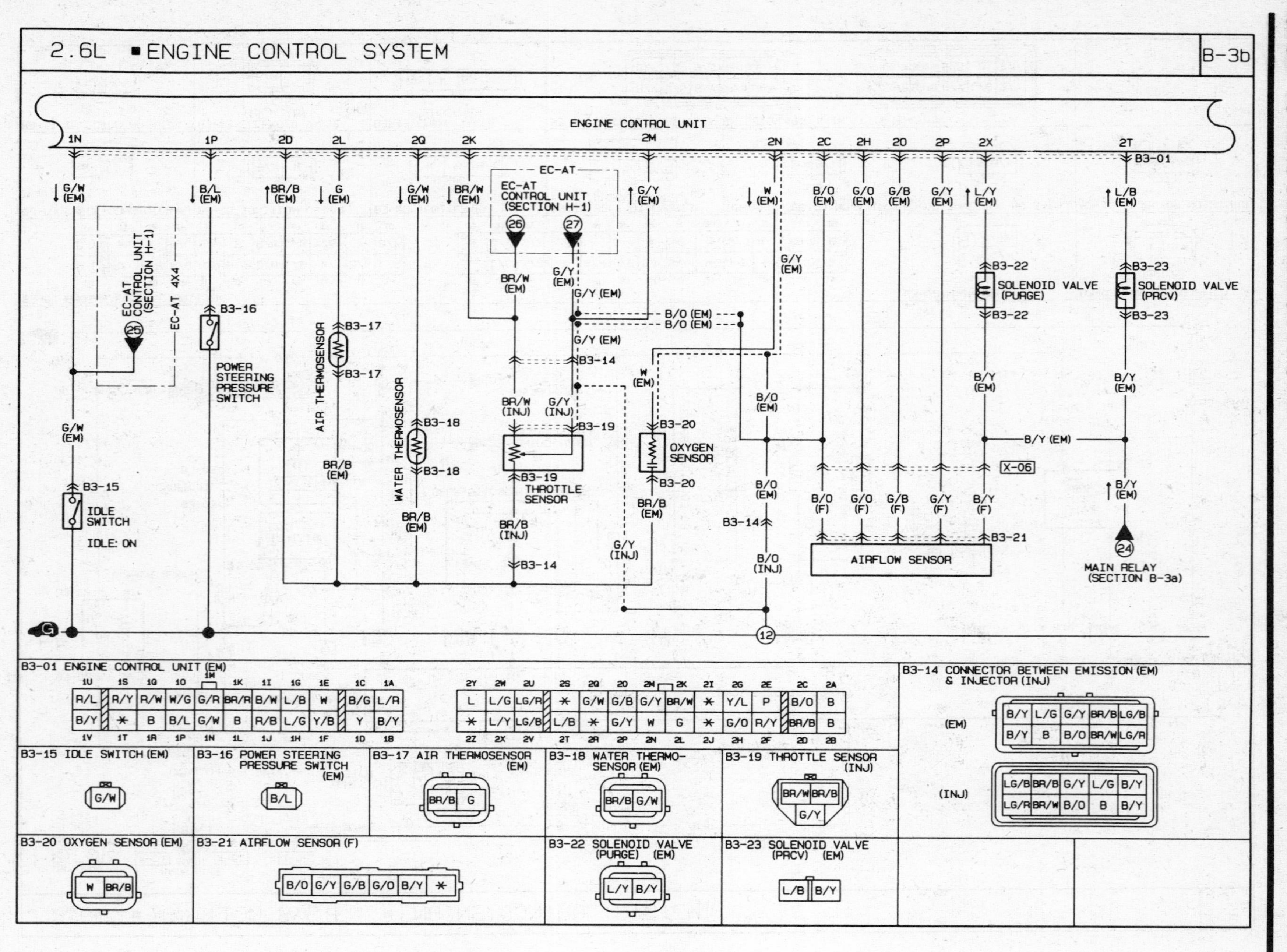

1989-92 Pickup 2.6L, Engine Control System

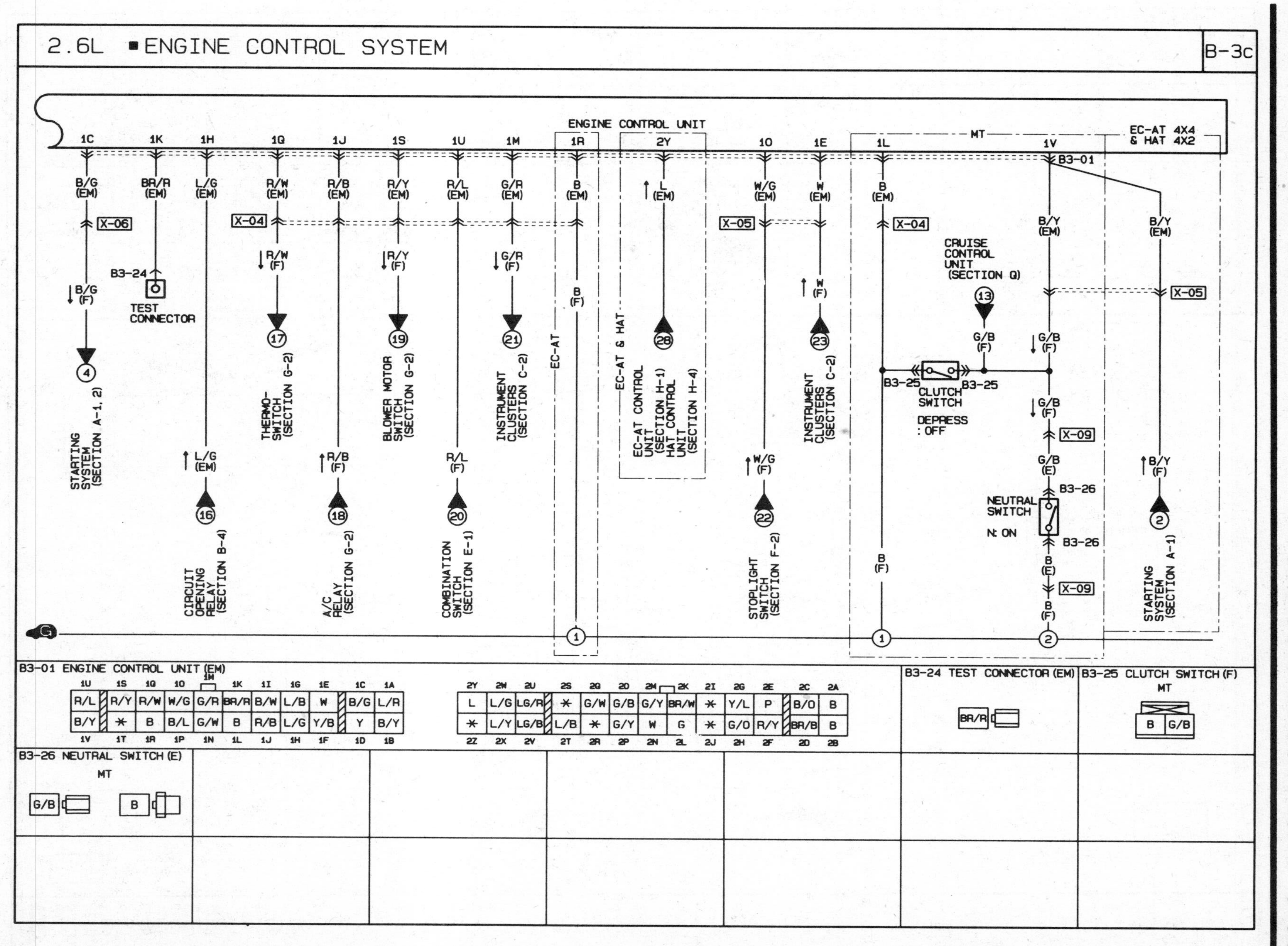

1989-92 Pickup 2.6L, Engine Control System

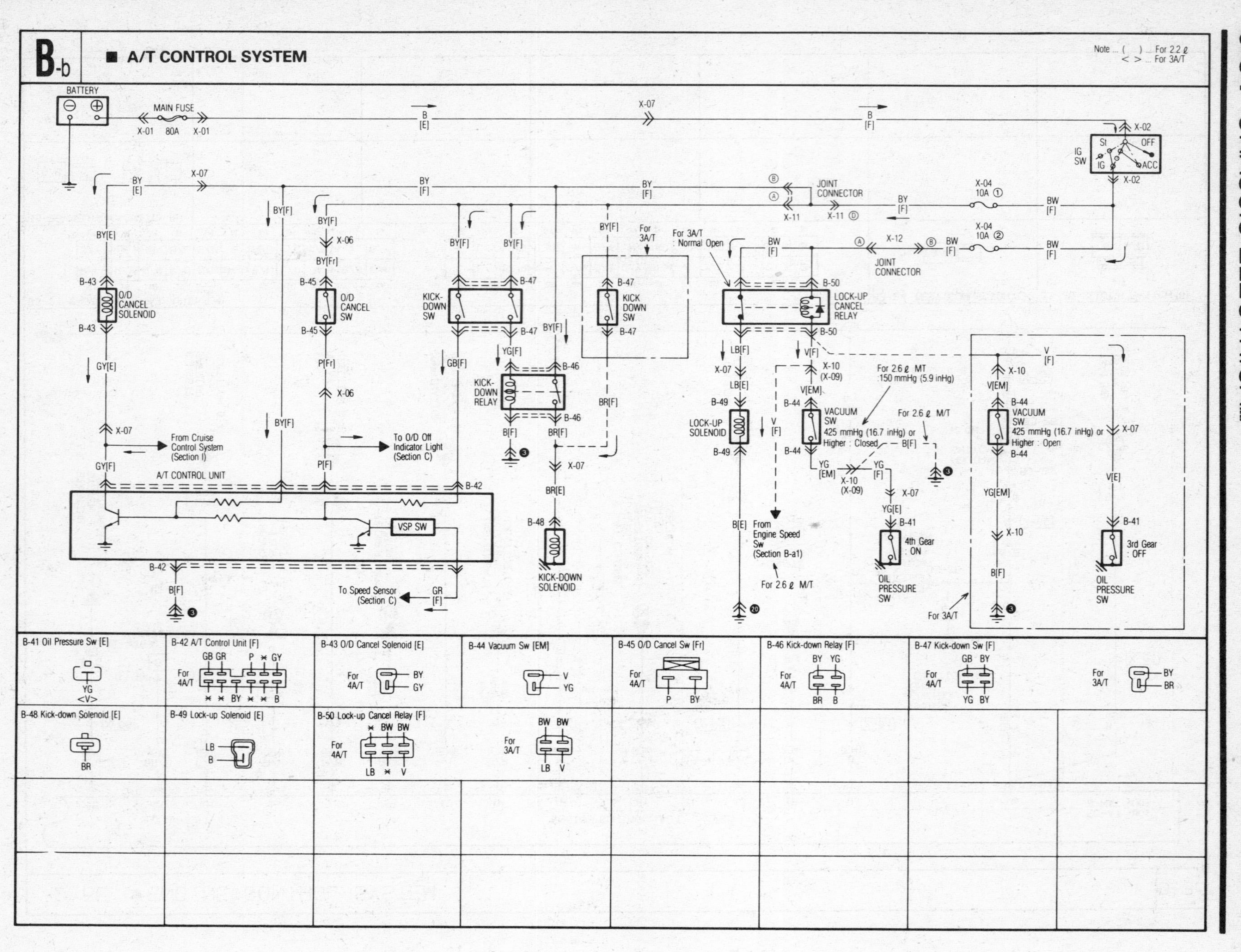
B-b
A/T CONTROL SYSTEM
Note ... ( ) ... For 2.2 ℓ
< > ... For 3A/T
BATTERY
MAIN FUSE
80A
IG SW
JOINT CONNECTOR
LOCK-UP CANCEL RELAY
VACUUM SW
425 mmHg (16.7 inHg) or Higher : Open
For 2.6 ℓ MT
150 mmHg (5.9 inHg)
For 2.6 ℓ M/T
425 mmHg (16.7 inHg) or Higher : Closed
OIL PRESSURE SW
3rd Gear : OFF
4th Gear : ON
For 3A/T
For 3A/T : Normal Open
From Engine Speed Sw (Section B-a1)
LOCK-UP SOLENOID
KICK DOWN SW
KICK-DOWN RELAY
KICK-DOWN SOLENOID
O/D CANCEL SW
O/D CANCEL SOLENOID
To O/D Off Indicator Light (Section C)
To Speed Sensor (Section C)
VSP SW
From Cruise Control System (Section I)
A/T CONTROL UNIT
B-41 Oil Pressure Sw [E]
B-42 A/T Control Unit [F]
B-43 O/D Cancel Solenoid [E]
B-44 Vacuum Sw [EM]
B-45 O/D Cancel Sw [F]
B-46 Kick-down Relay [F]
B-47 Kick-down Sw [F]
B-48 Kick-down Solenoid [E]
B-49 Lock-up Solenoid [E]
B-50 Lock-up Cancel Relay [F]
For 4A/T
For 3A/T

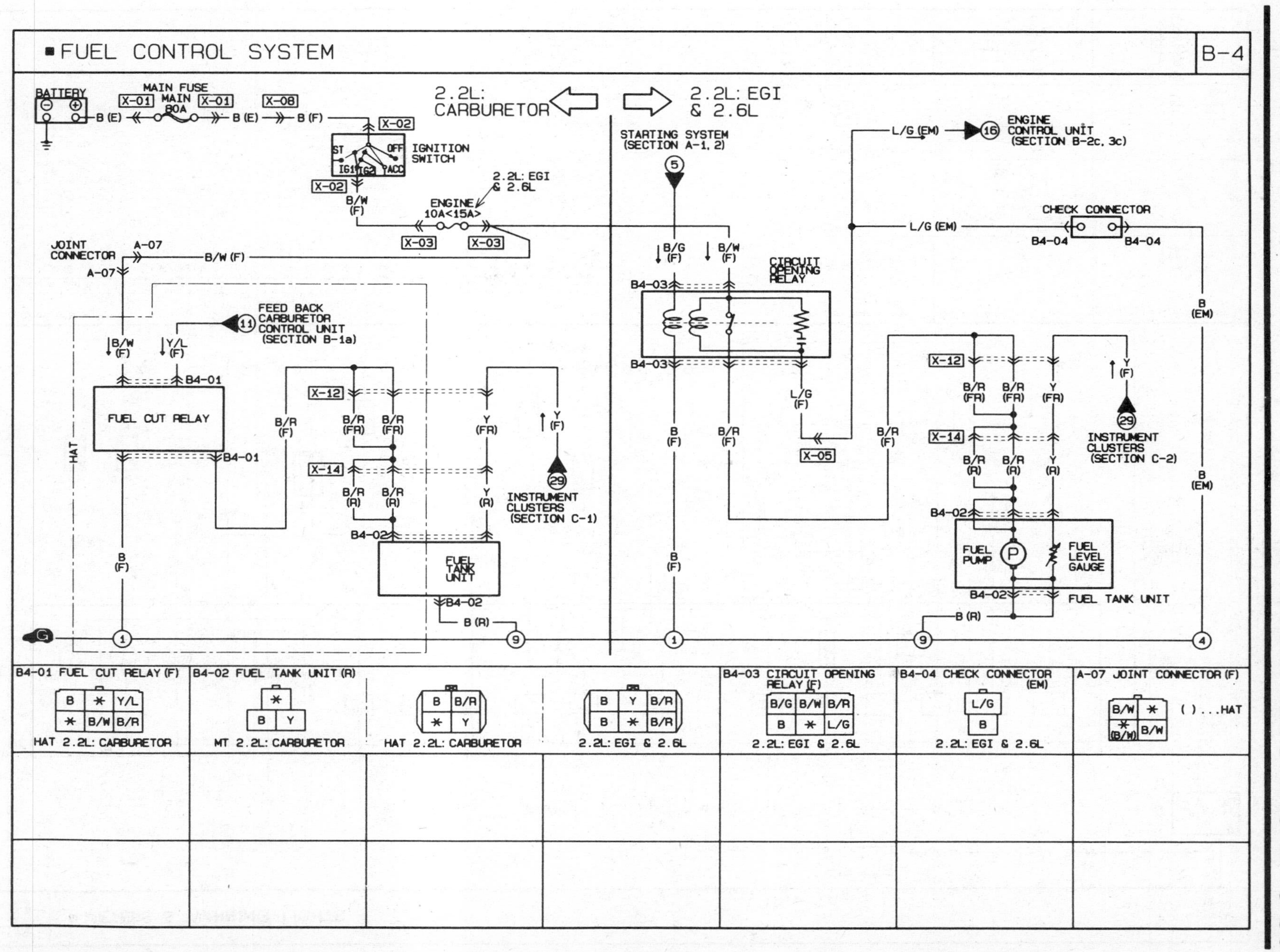

1989-92 Pickup, Fuel Control System

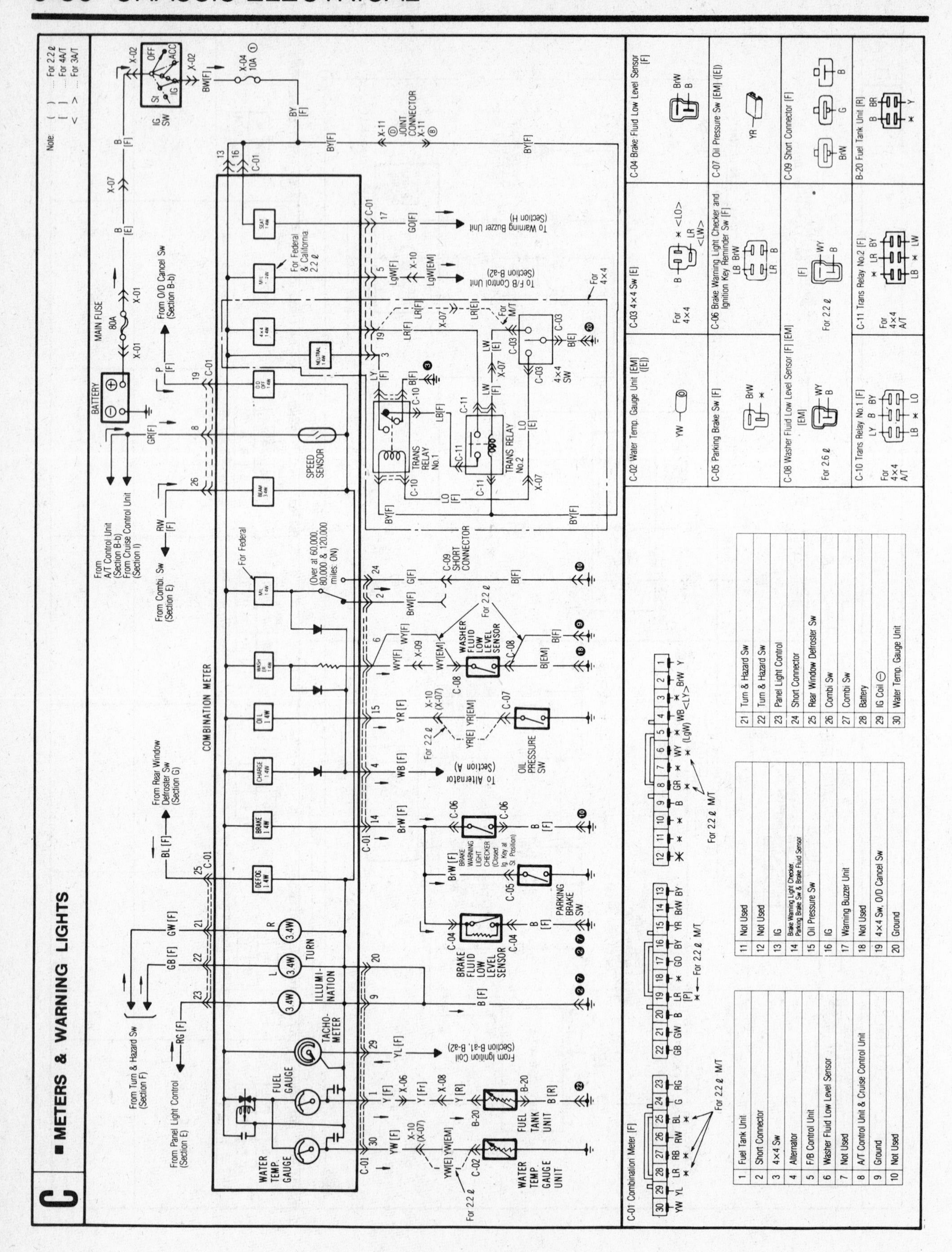

1987-88 Pickup, Meters and Warning Lights

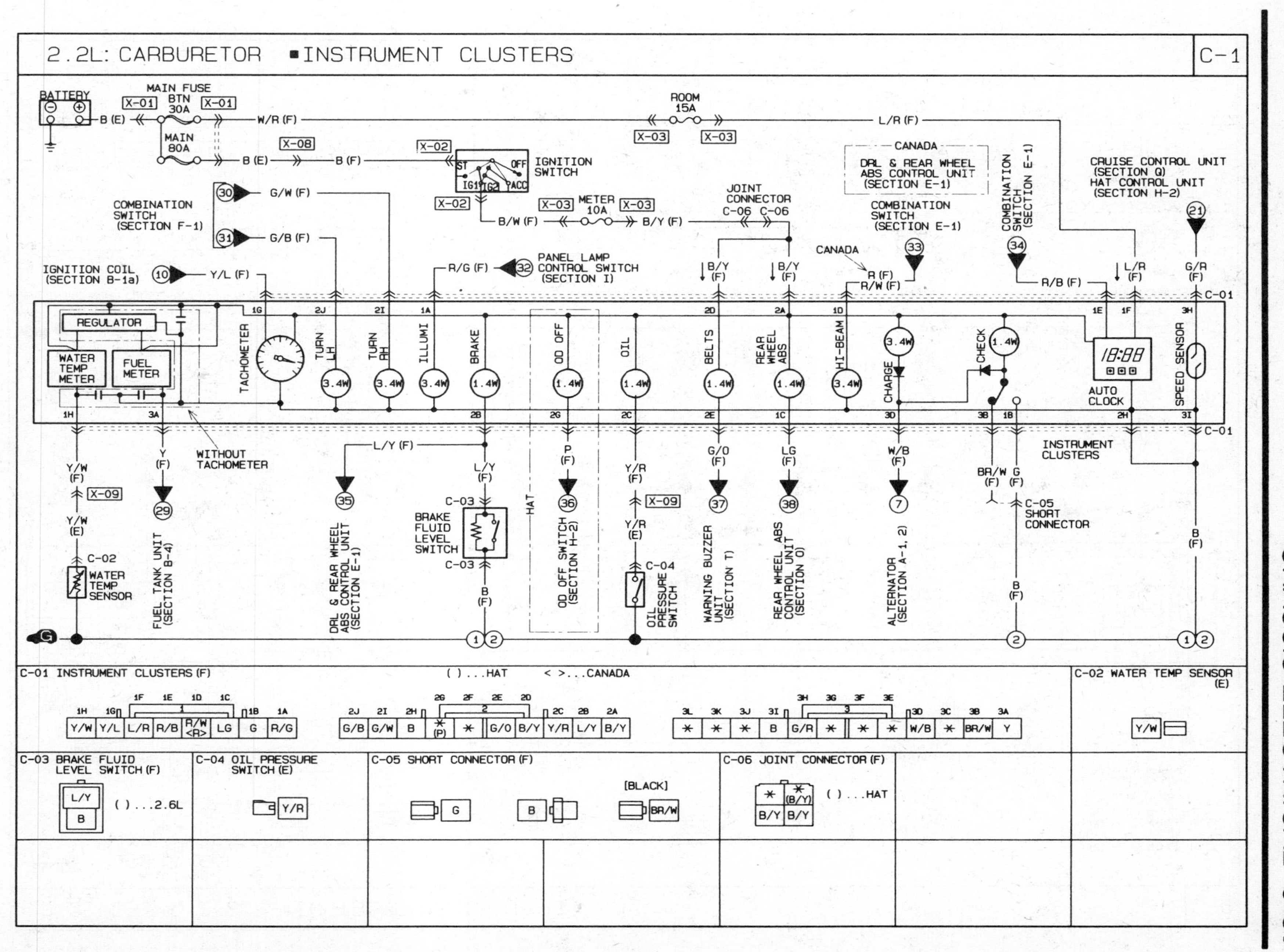

1989-92 Pickup 2.2L Carburetor, Instrument Clusters

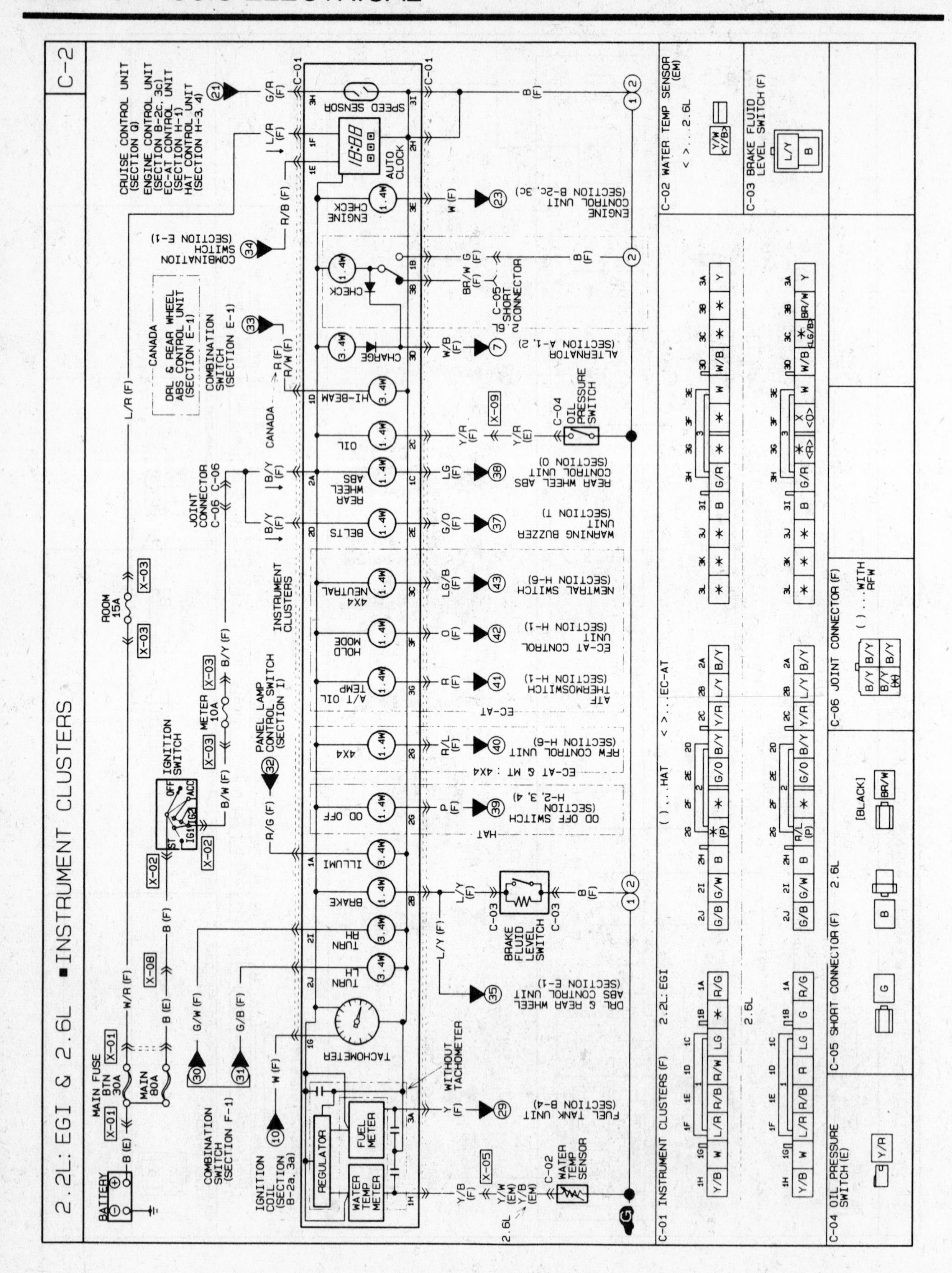

1989-92 Pickup Injected, Instrument Clusters

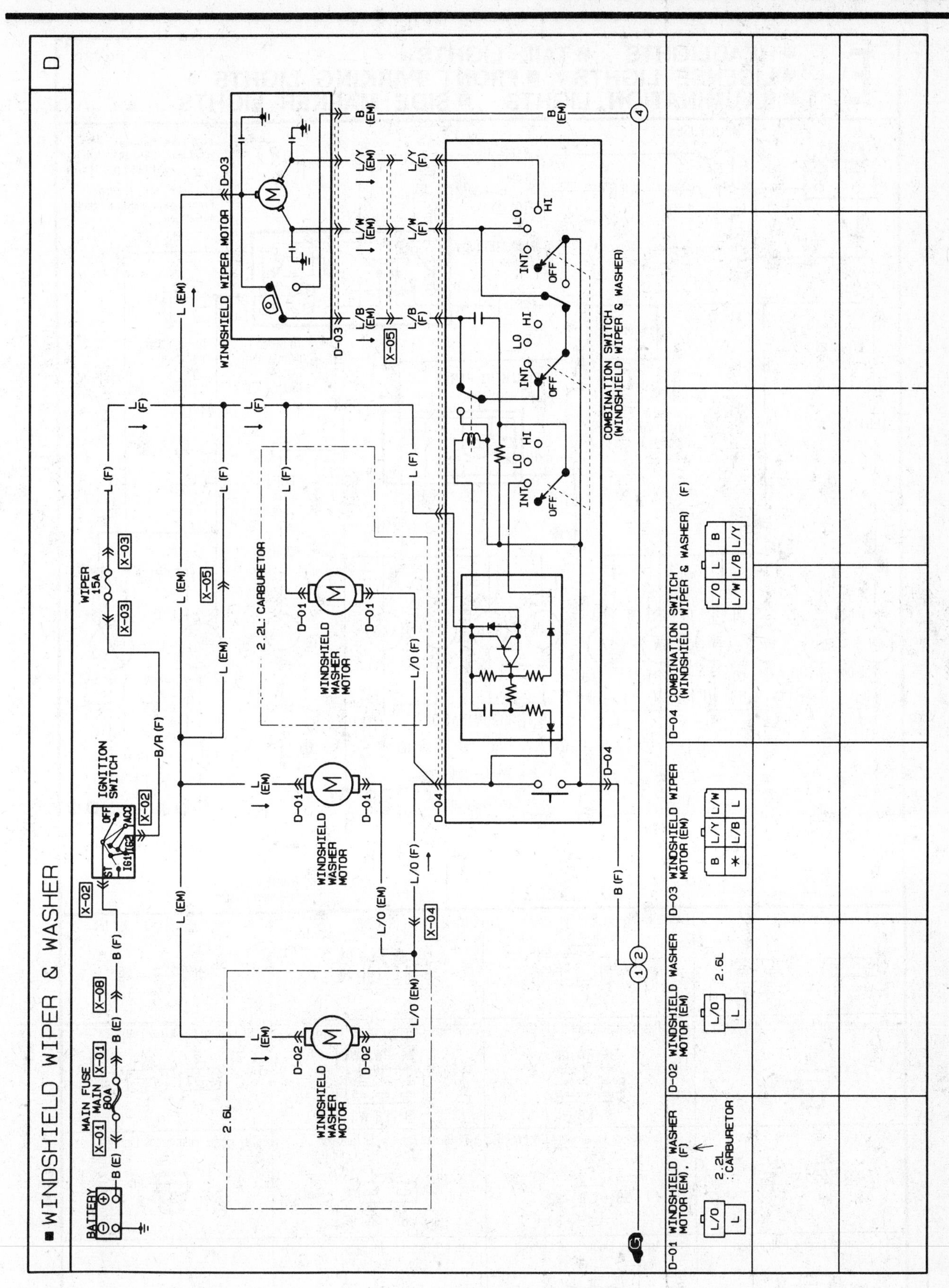

1989-92 Pickup, Windshield Wiper and Washers

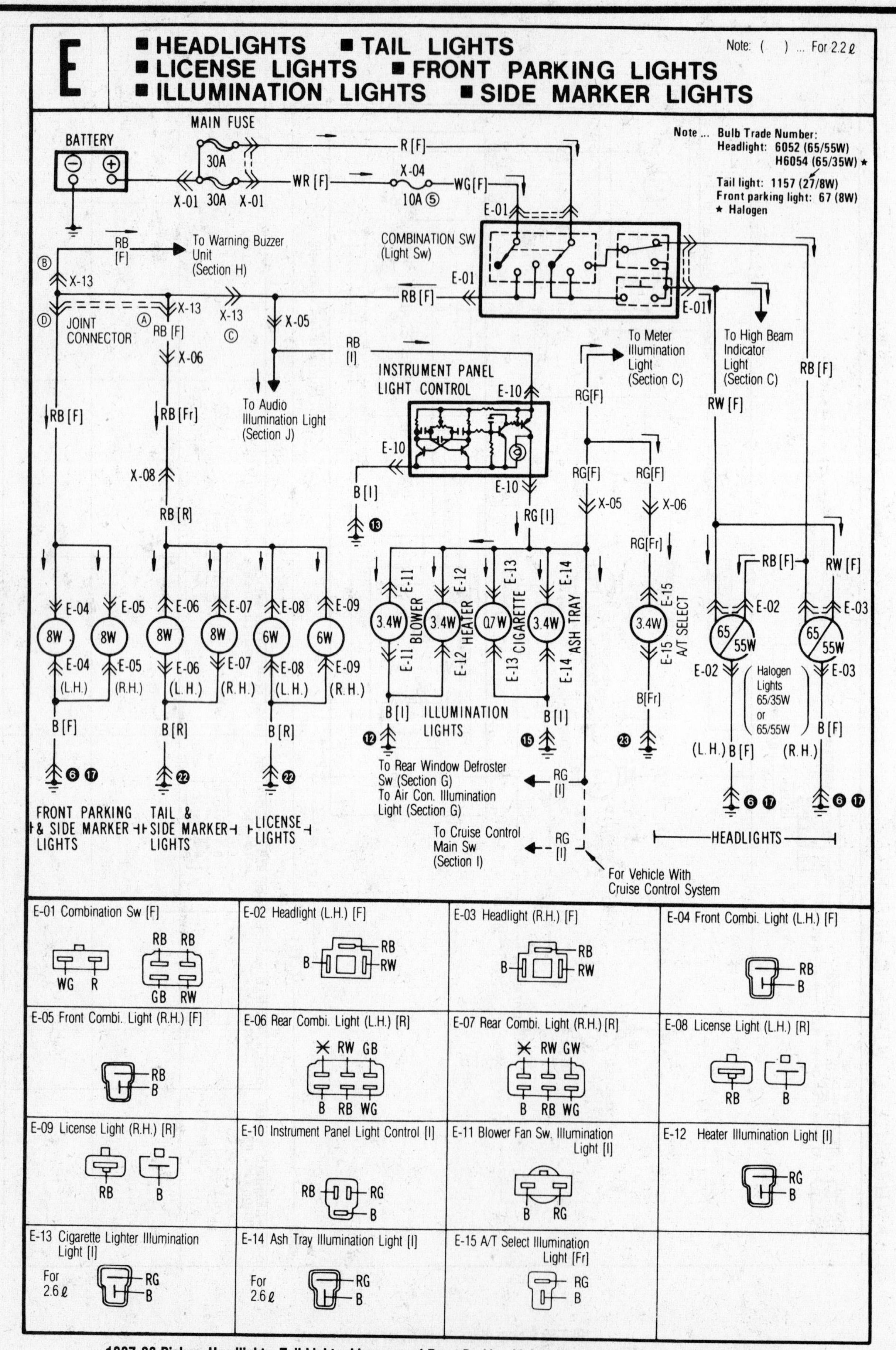

1987-88 Pickup, Headlights, Tail Lights, License and Front Parking Lights, Illumination Lights, Side Marker Lights

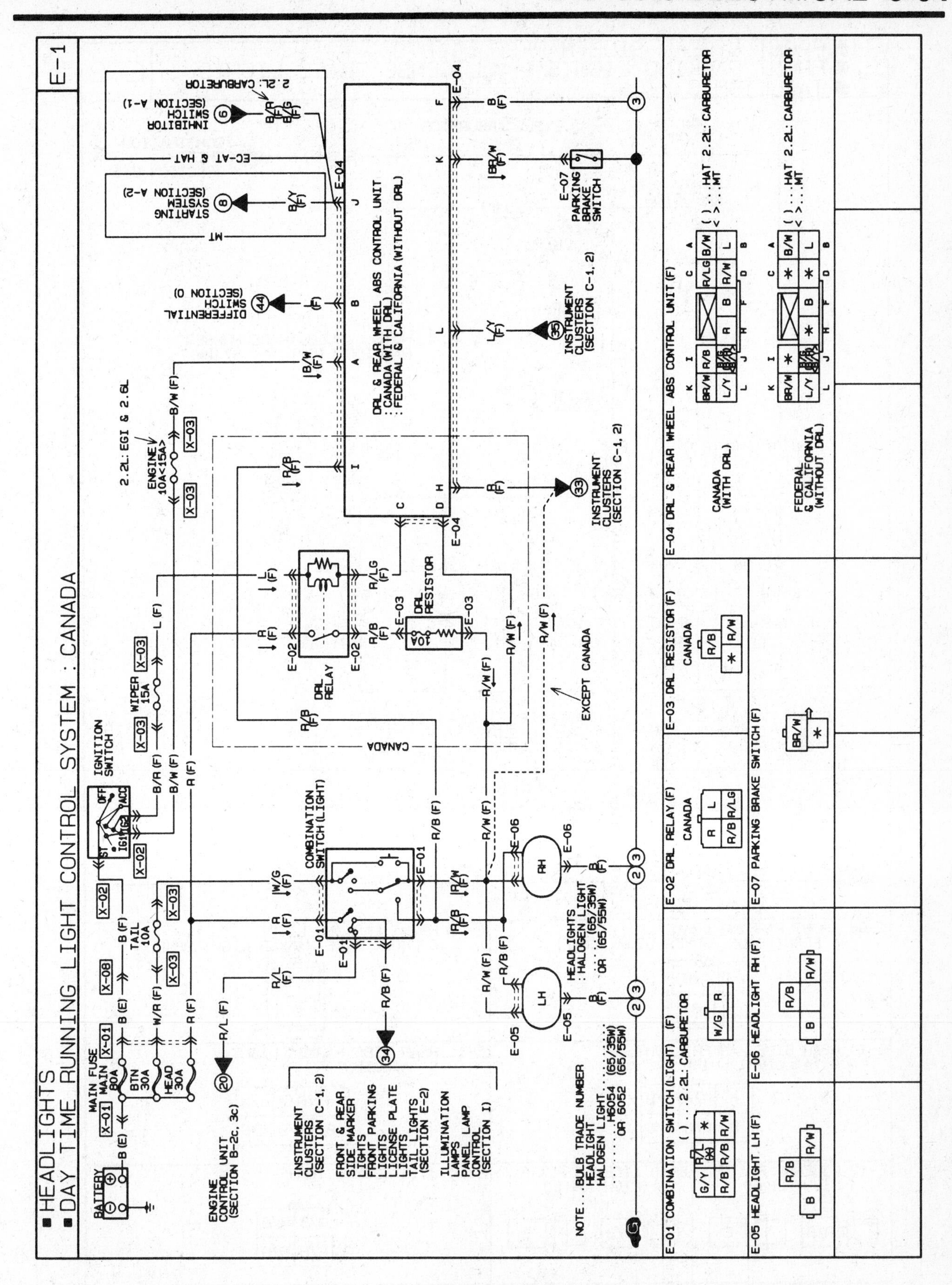

1989-92 Pickup Canada, Lights

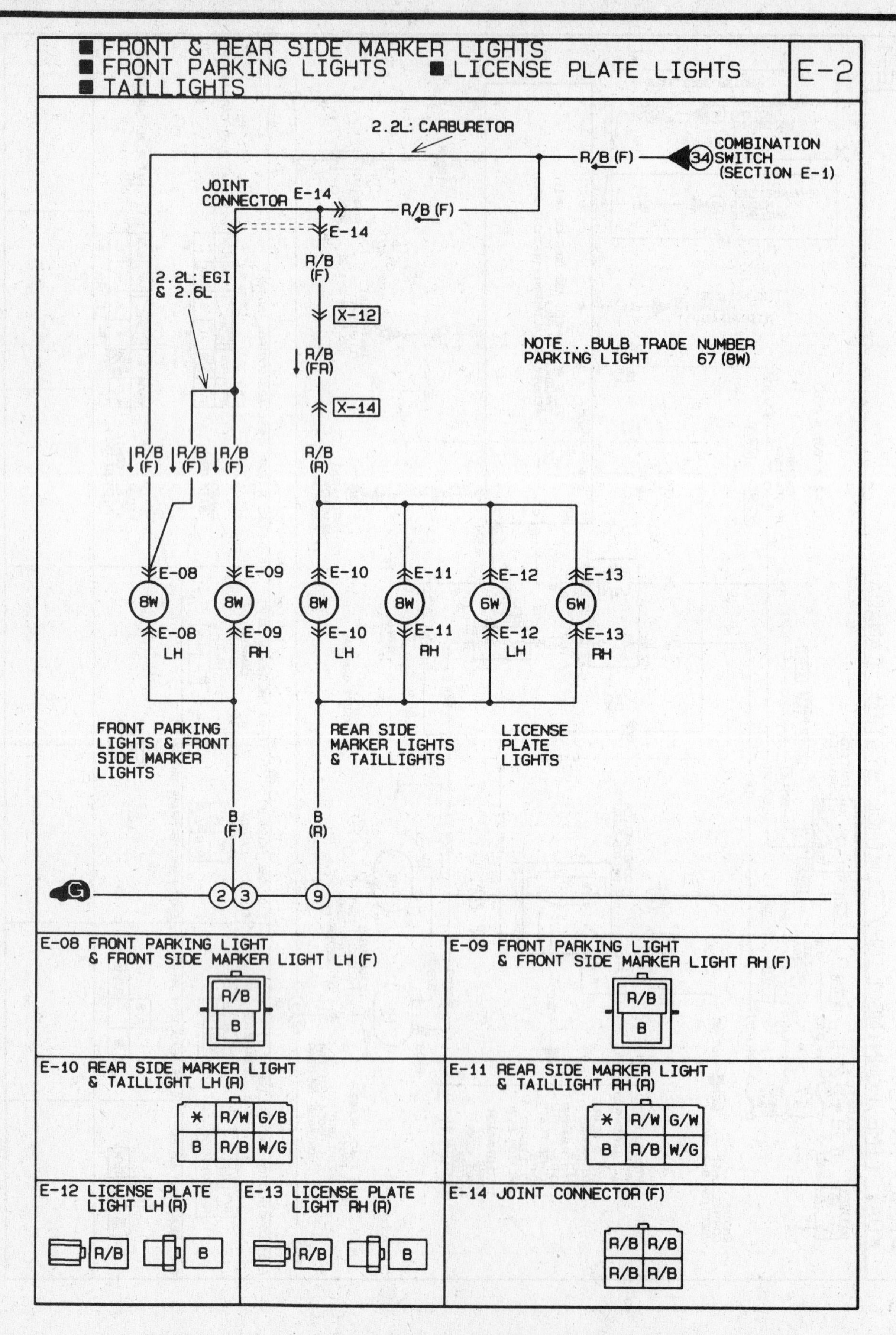

1989-92 Pickup, Front & Rear Side Marker Lights, Front Parking Lights, License Plate Lights, Taillights

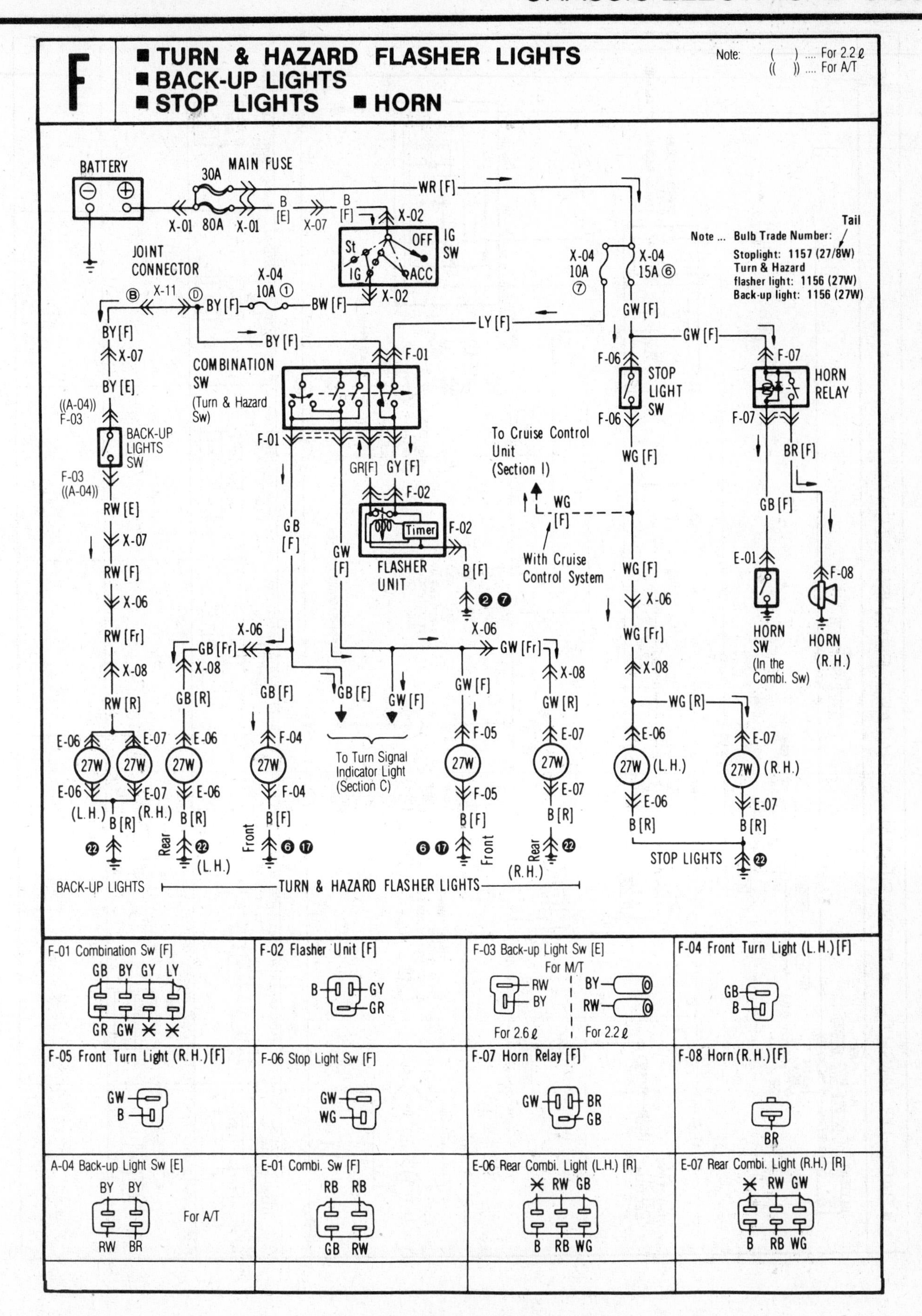

1987-88 Pickup, Turn & Hazard Flasher Lights, Back-up Lights, Stop Lights, Horn

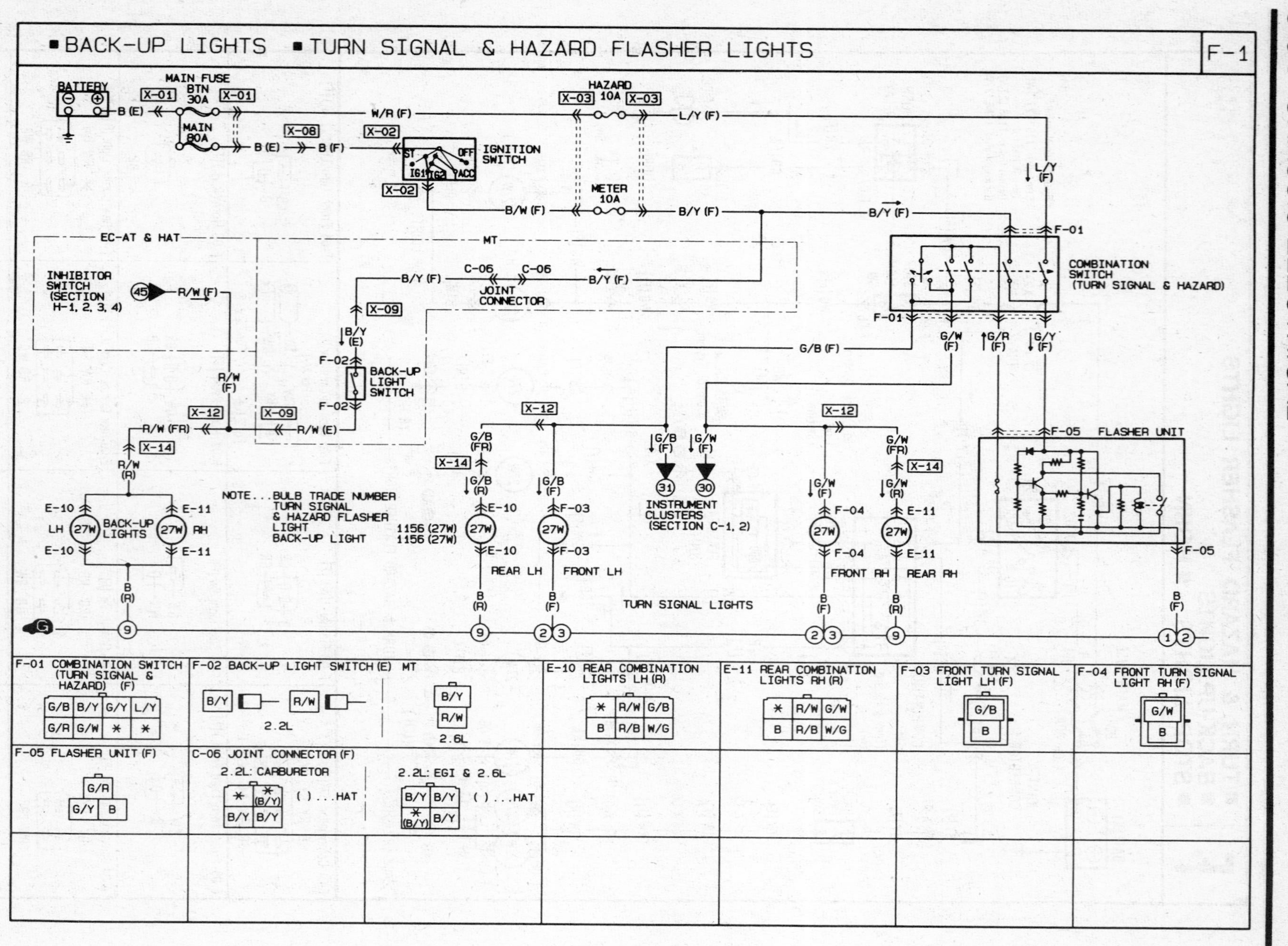

1989-92 Pickup, Back-up Lights, Turn Signal & Hazard Lights

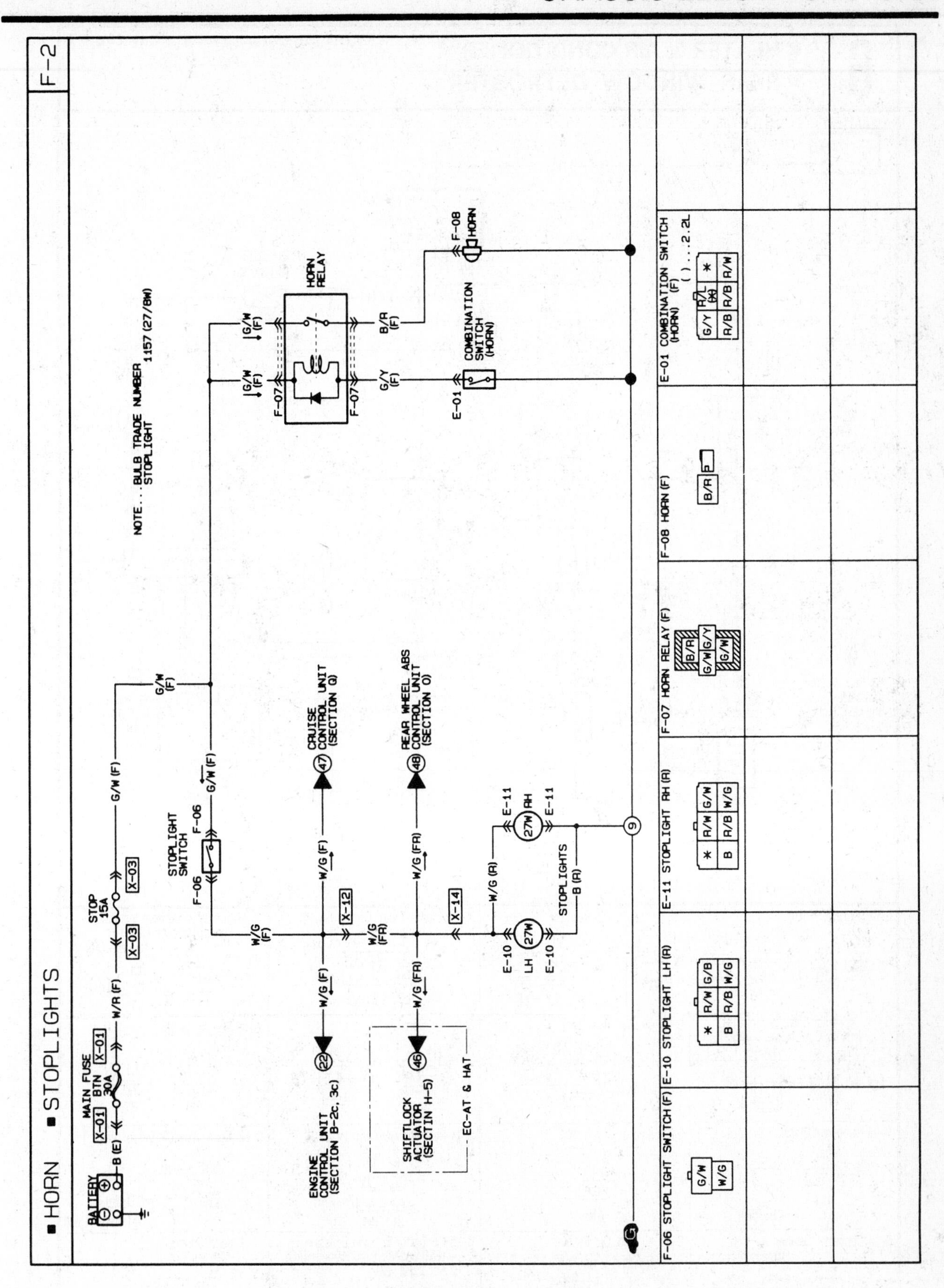
F-2
■ HORN ■ STOPLIGHTS
NOTE...BULB TRADE NUMBER
STOPLIGHT 1157 (27/8W)
BATTERY
MAIN FUSE BTN 30A
STOP 15A
STOPLIGHT SWITCH
HORN RELAY
COMBINATION SWITCH (HORN)
HORN
ENGINE CONTROL UNIT (SECTION B-2c, 3c)
CRUISE CONTROL UNIT (SECTION Q)
REAR WHEEL ABS CONTROL UNIT (SECTION O)
SHIFTLOCK ACTUATOR (SECTIN H-5)
EC-AT & HAT
STOPLIGHTS
LH
RH
F-06 STOPLIGHT SWITCH (F)
E-10 STOPLIGHT LH (R)
E-11 STOPLIGHT RH (R)
F-07 HORN RELAY (F)
F-08 HORN (F)
E-01 COMBINATION SWITCH (HORN) (F)
( )...2.2L

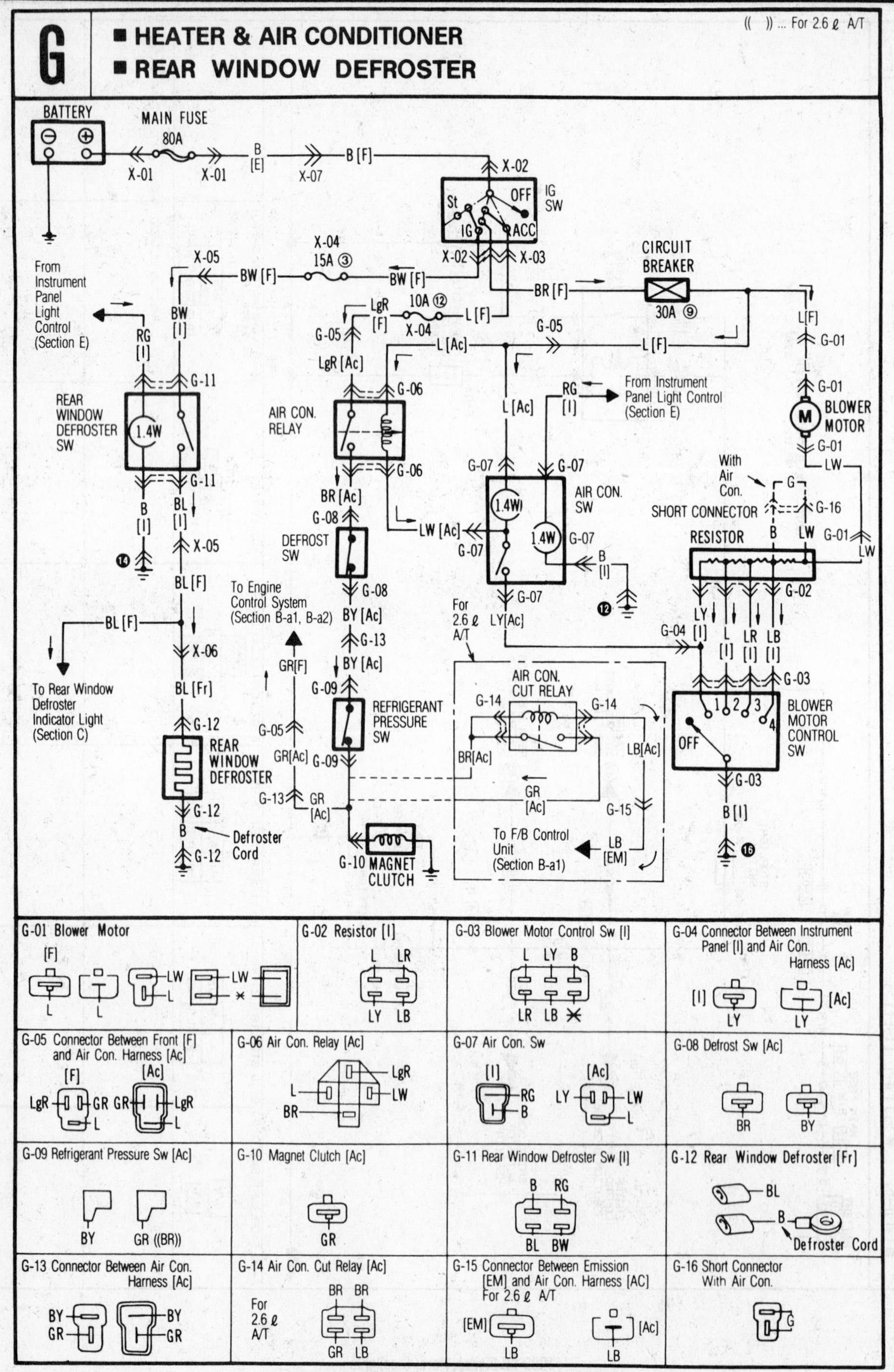

1987-88 Pickup. Heater & A/C, Rear Window Defroster

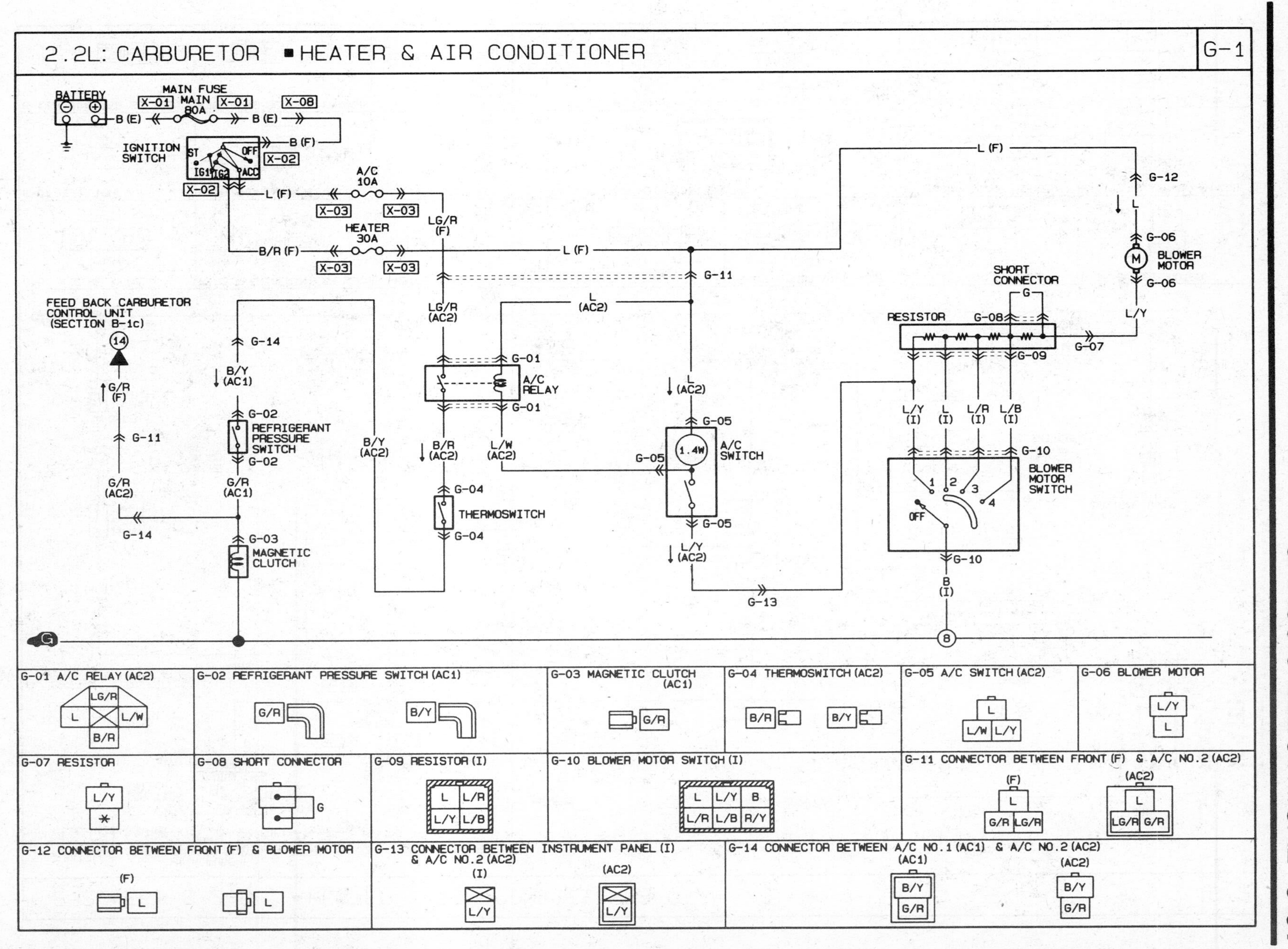

1989-92 Pickup 2.2L Carburetor Equipped, Heater & A/C

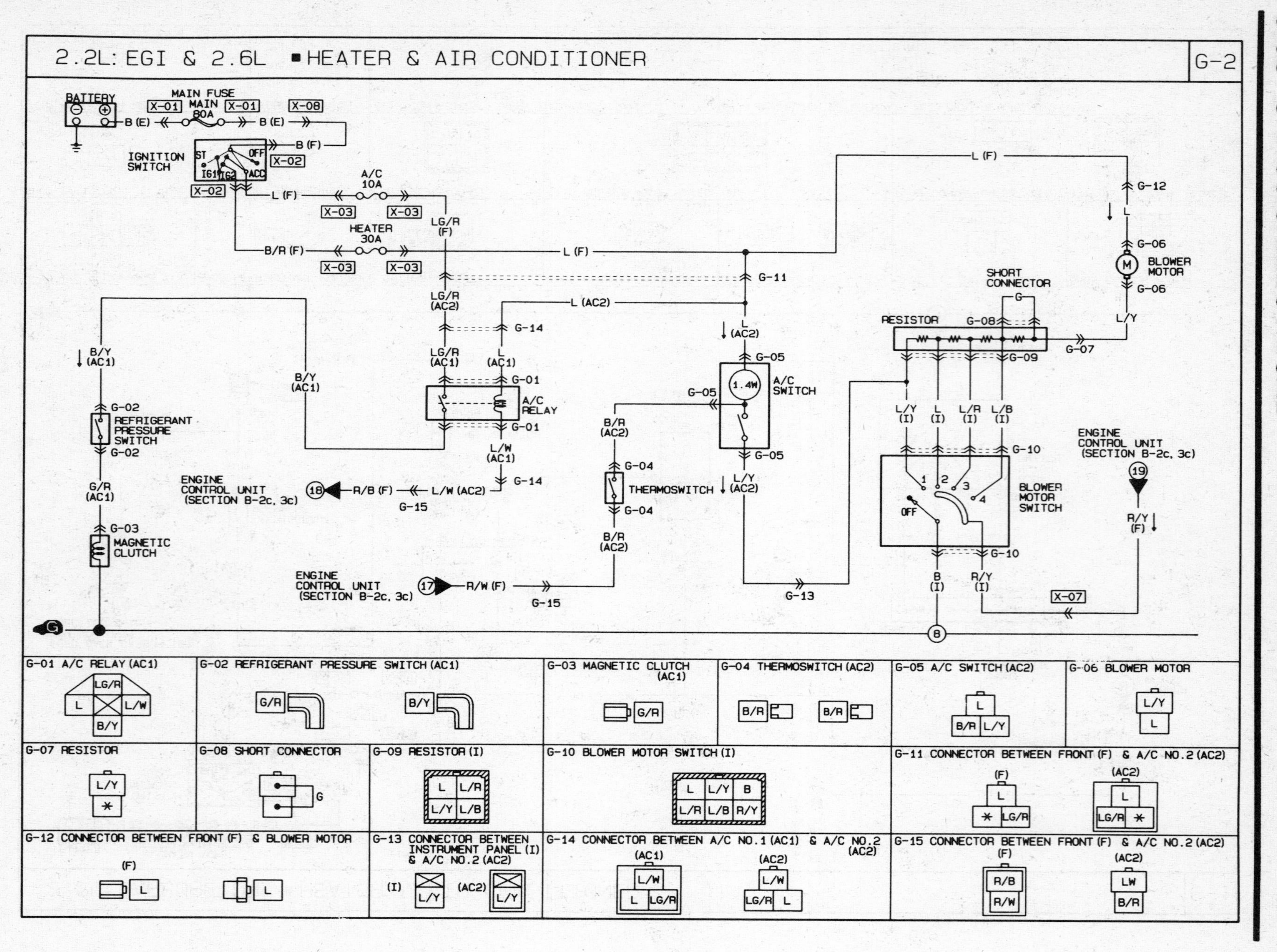

1989-92 Pickup Injected, Heater & A/C

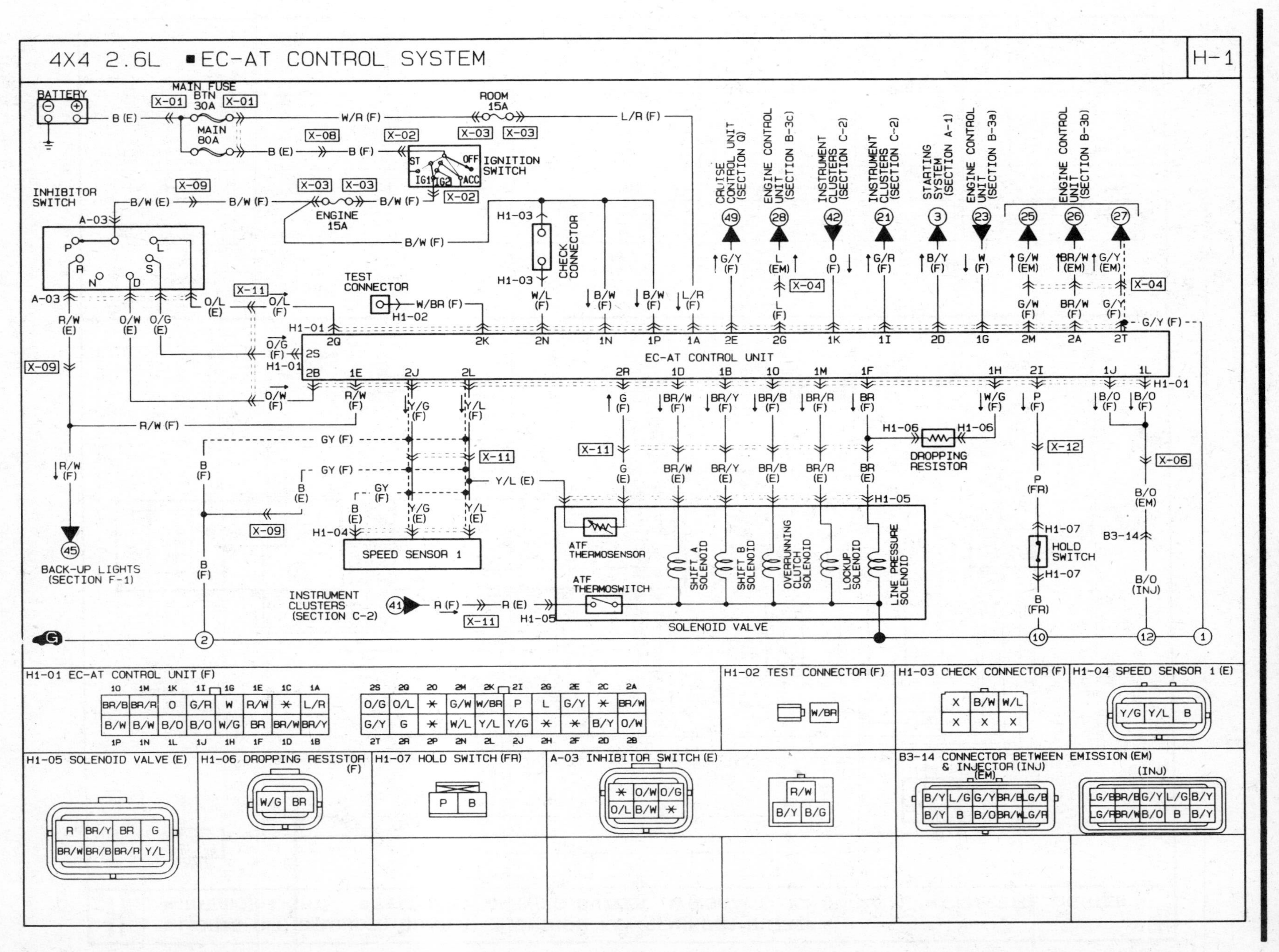

1989-92 Pickup 4x4 2.6L, EC-AT Control System

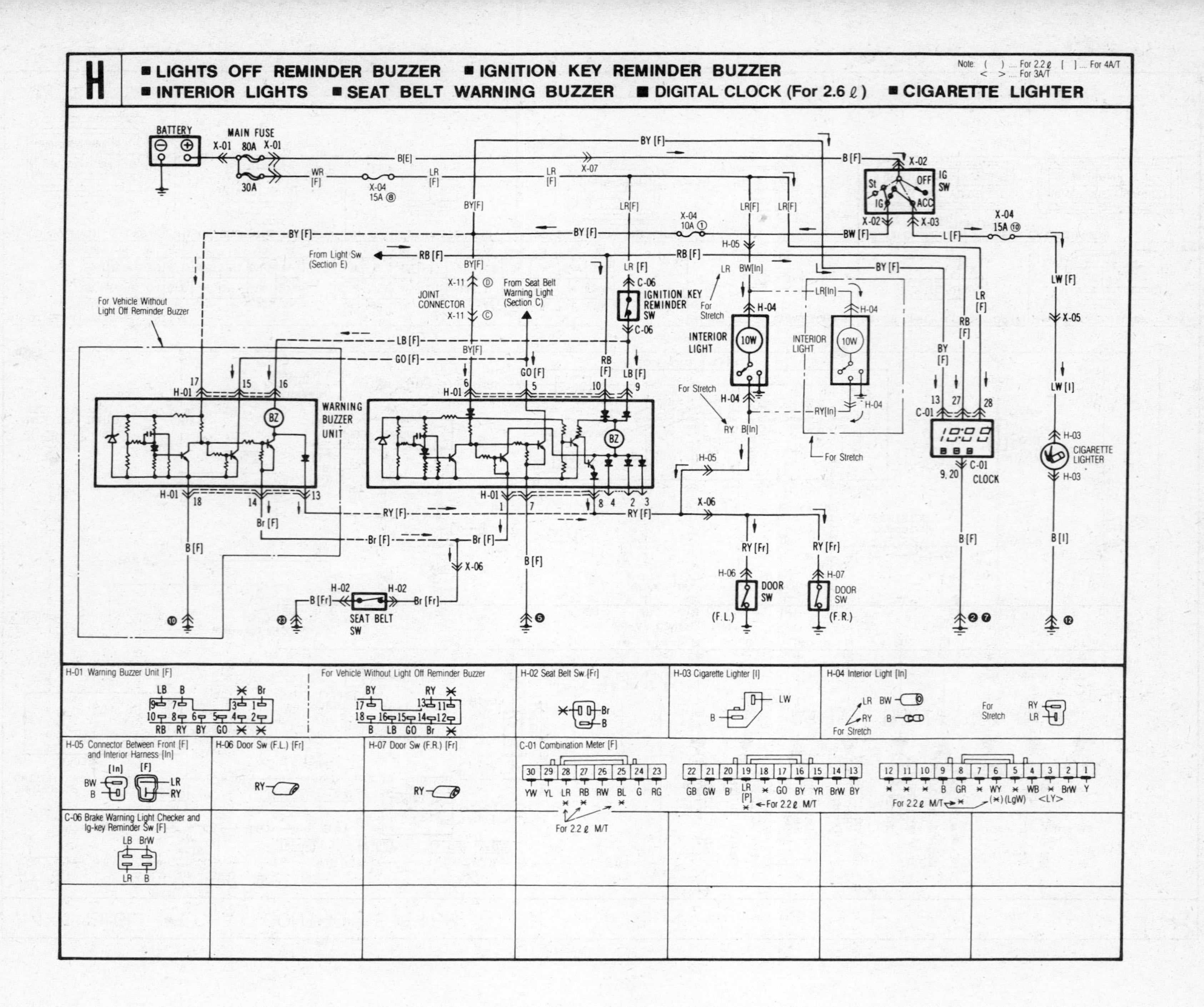

1987-88 Pickup, Buzzers, Clock, Cigarette Lighter

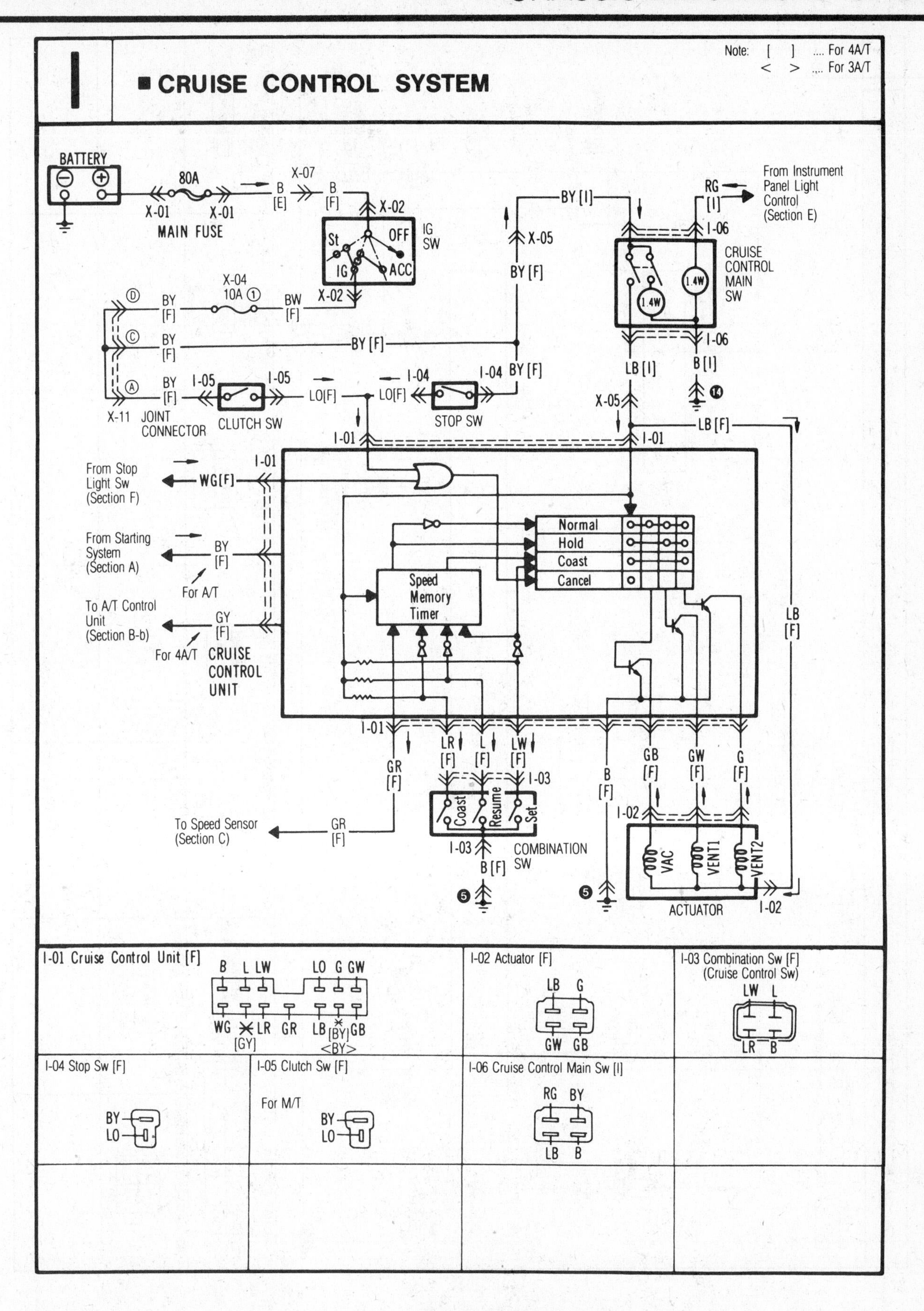

1987-88 Pickup, Cruise Control System

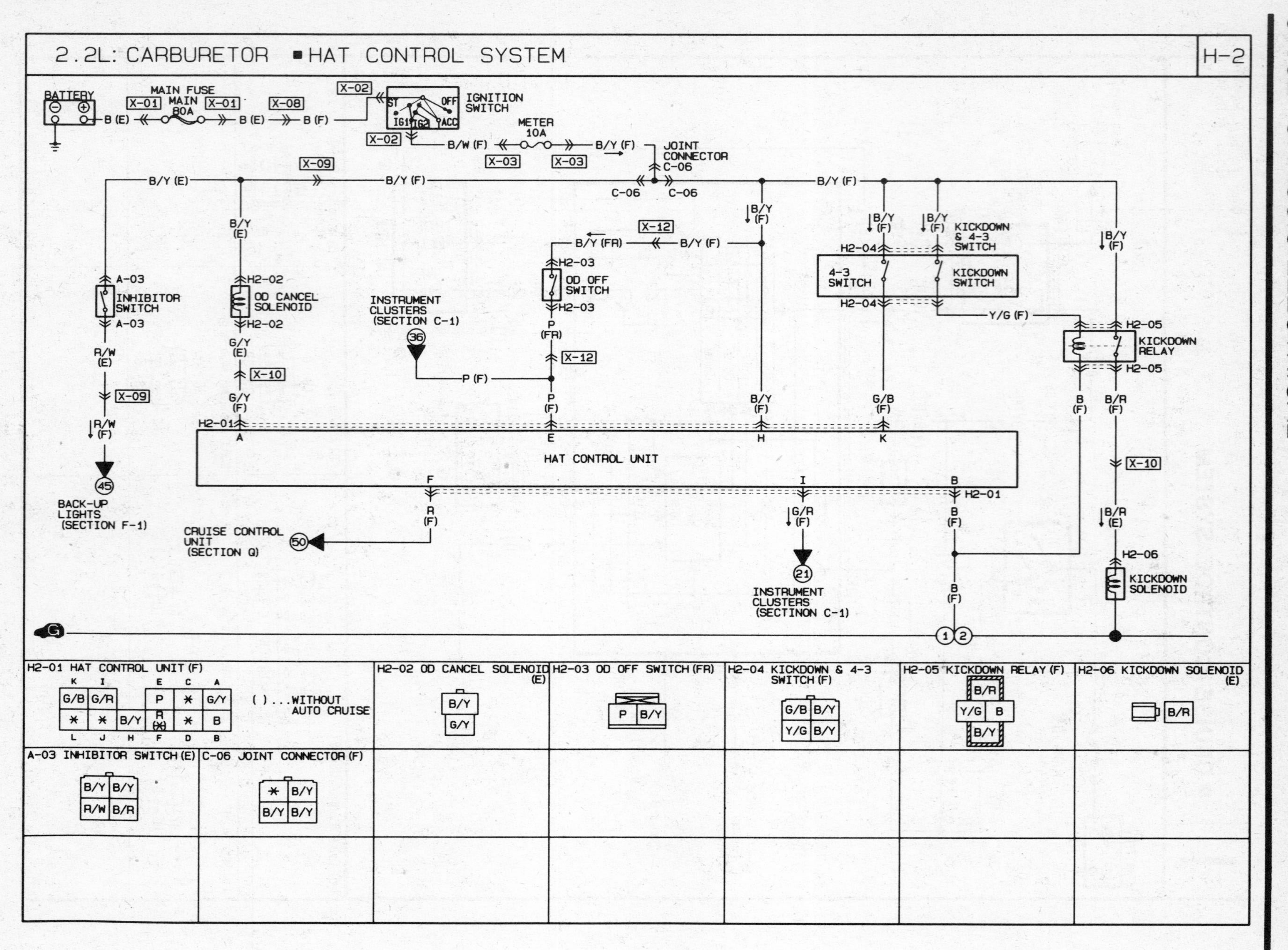

1989-92 Pickup 2.2L Carburetor Equipped, AT Control System

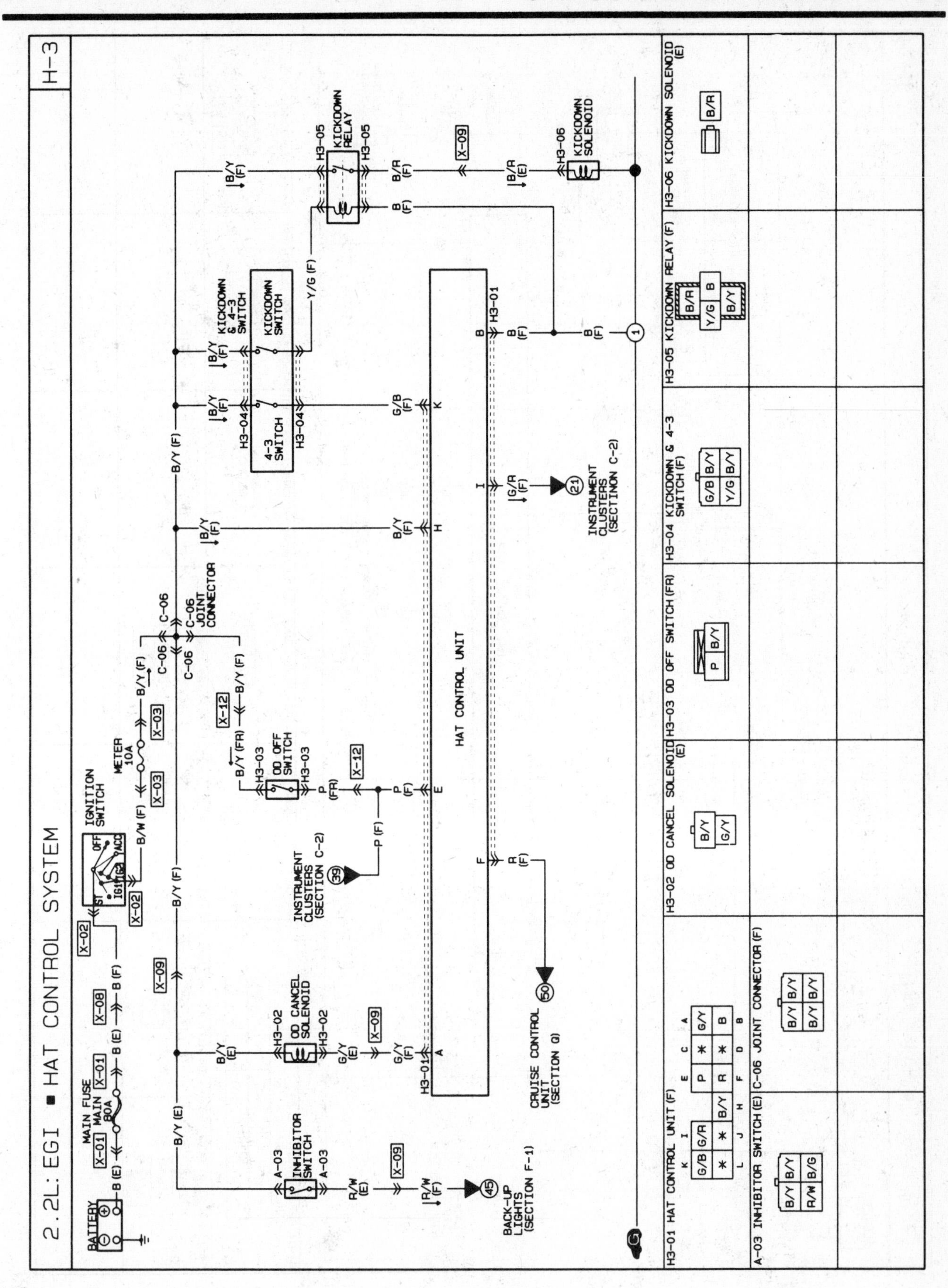

1989-92 Pickup 2.2L Injected, AT Control System

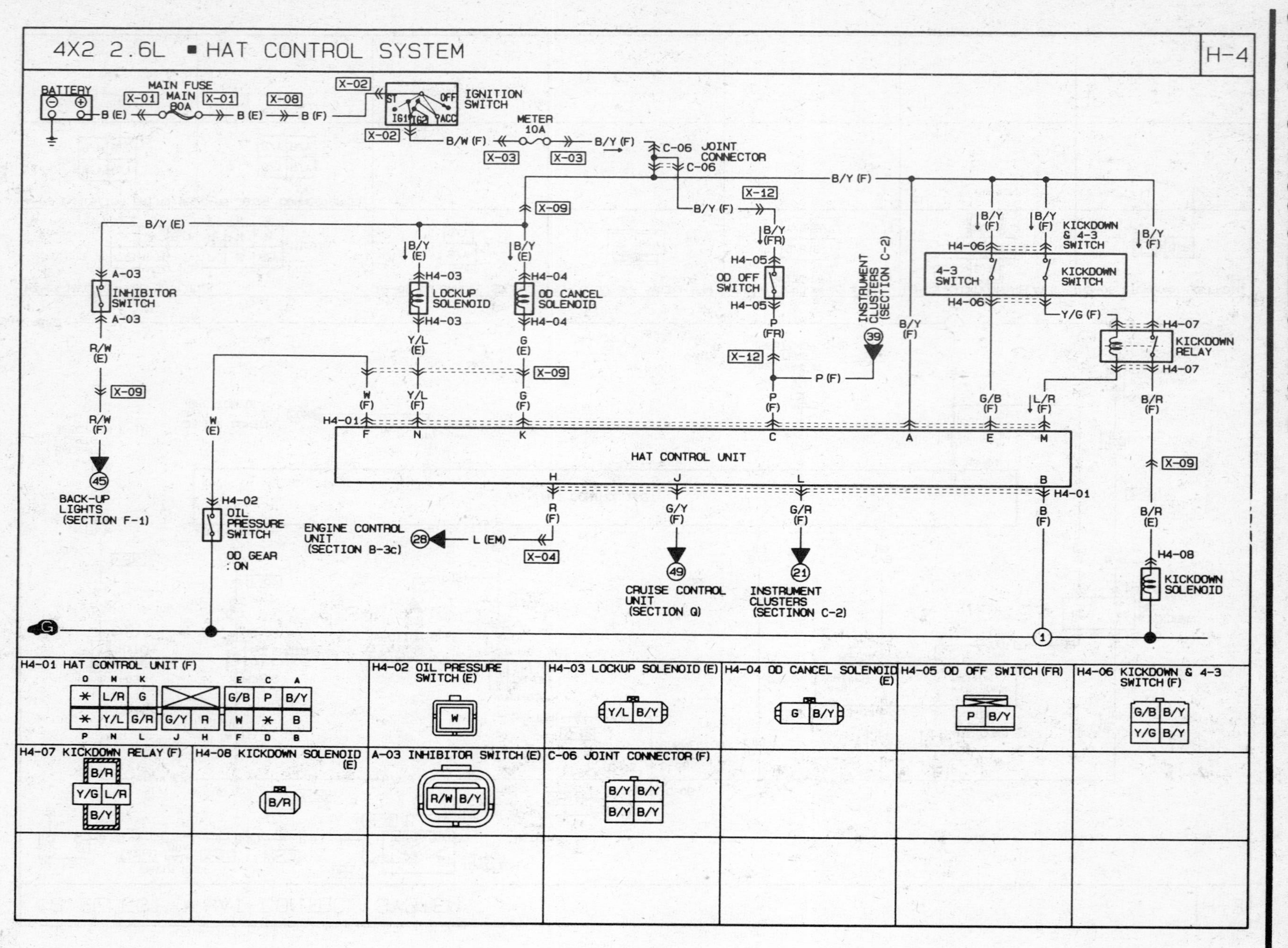

1989-92 Pickup 4x2 2.6L, ST Control System

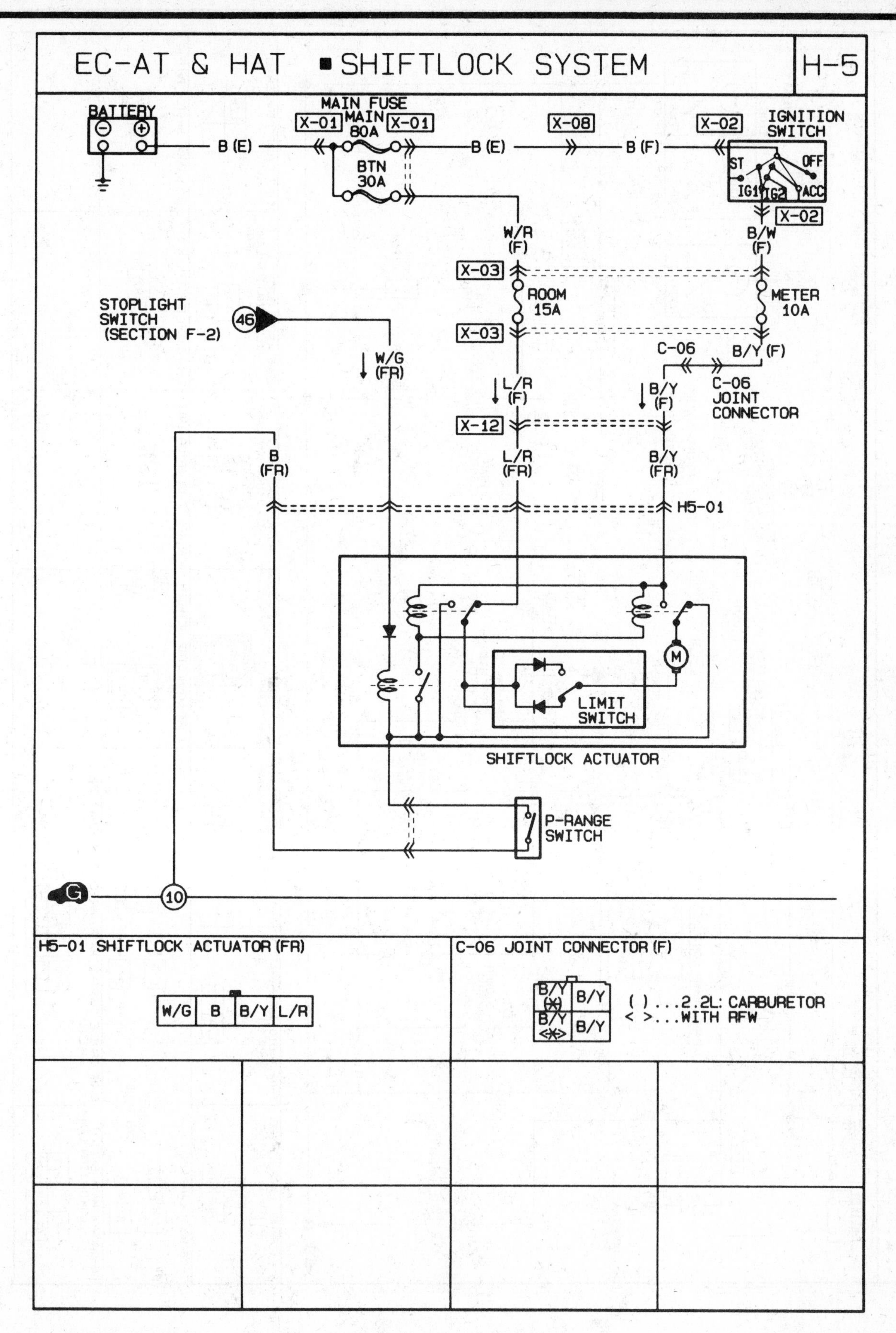

1989-92 Pickup, AT Shift Lock System

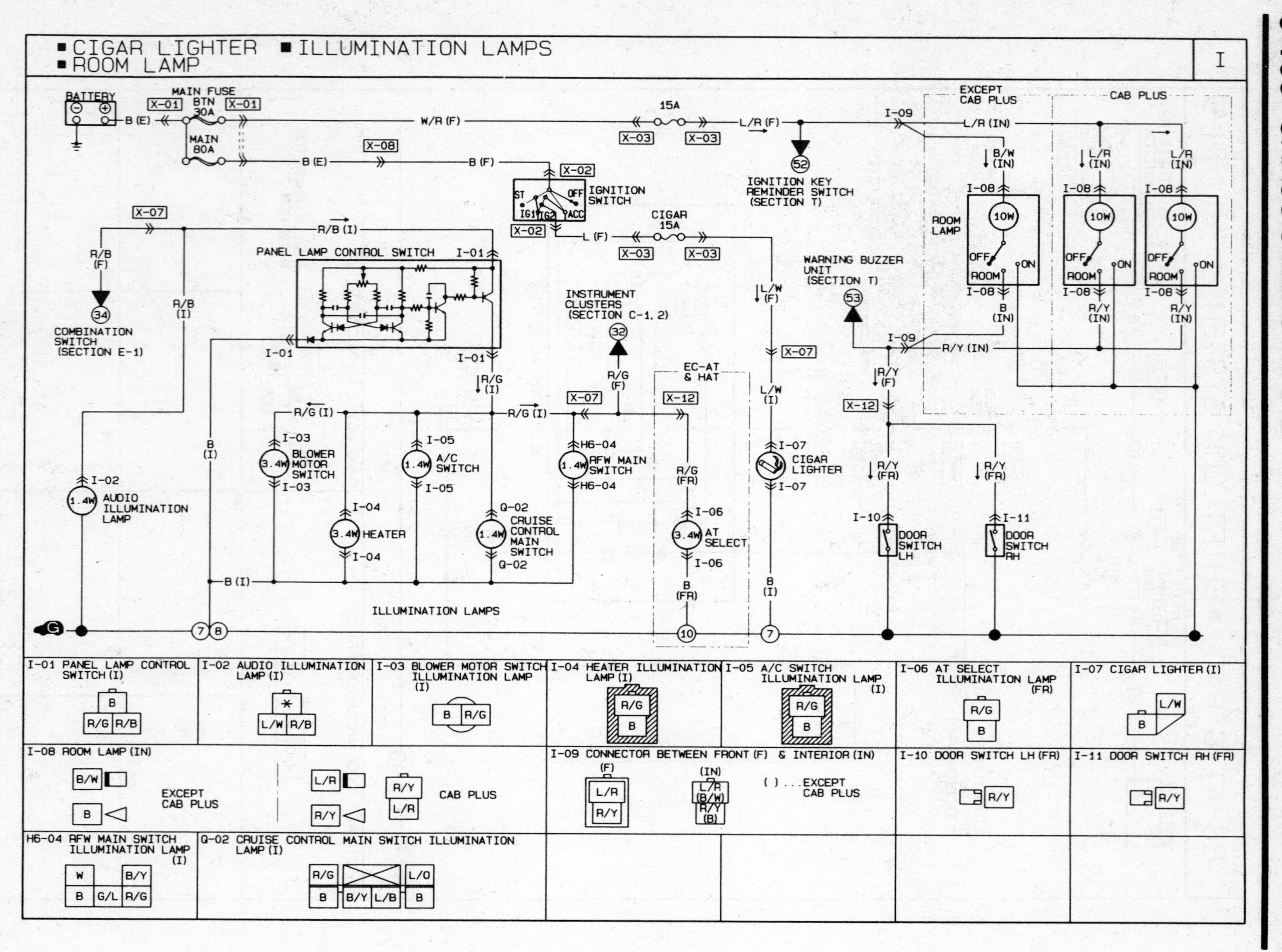

1989-92 Pickup, Cigar Lighter, Illumination Lamps, Room Lamp

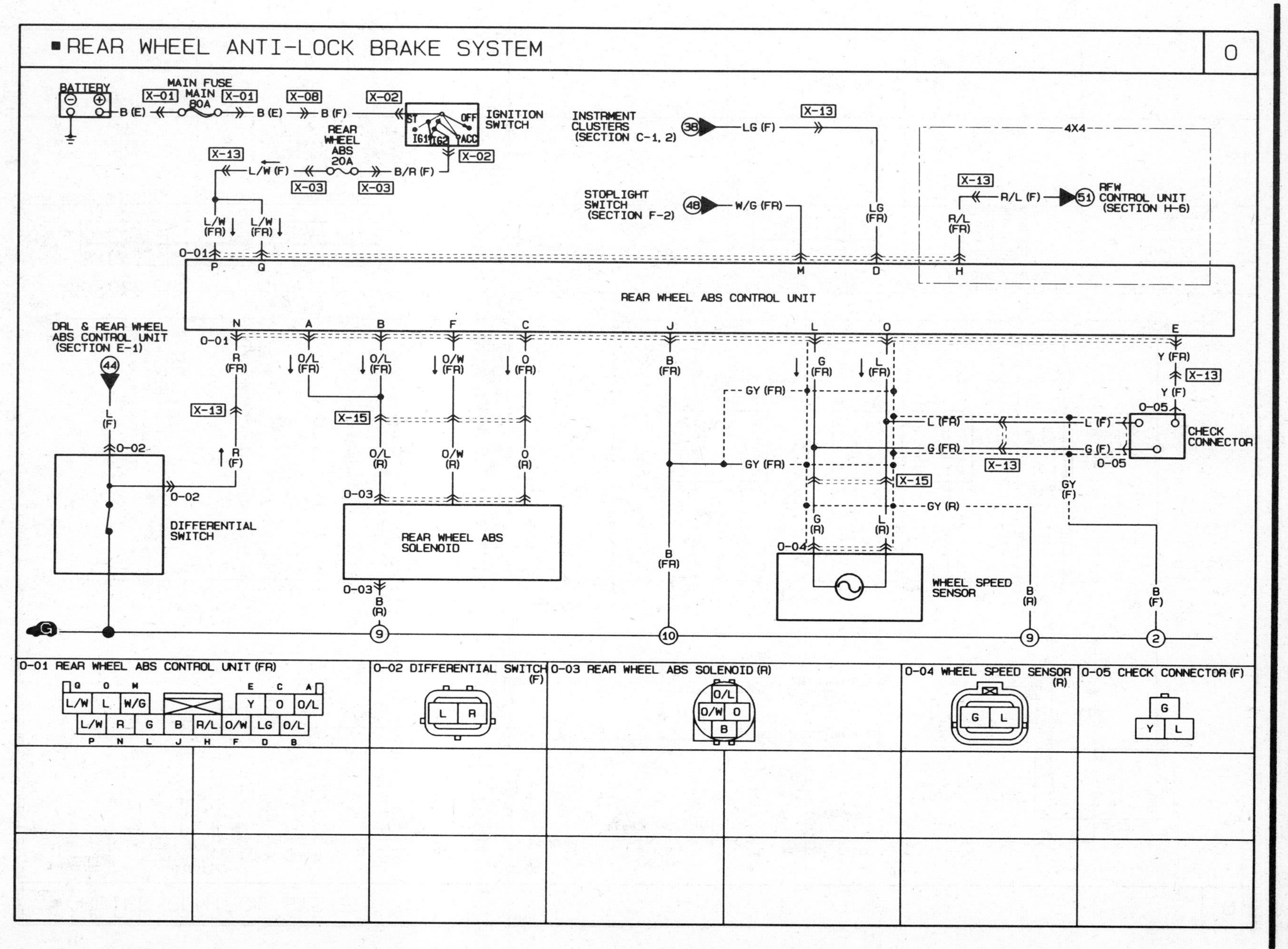

1989-92 Pickup, Rear Wheel Anti-Lock Brake System

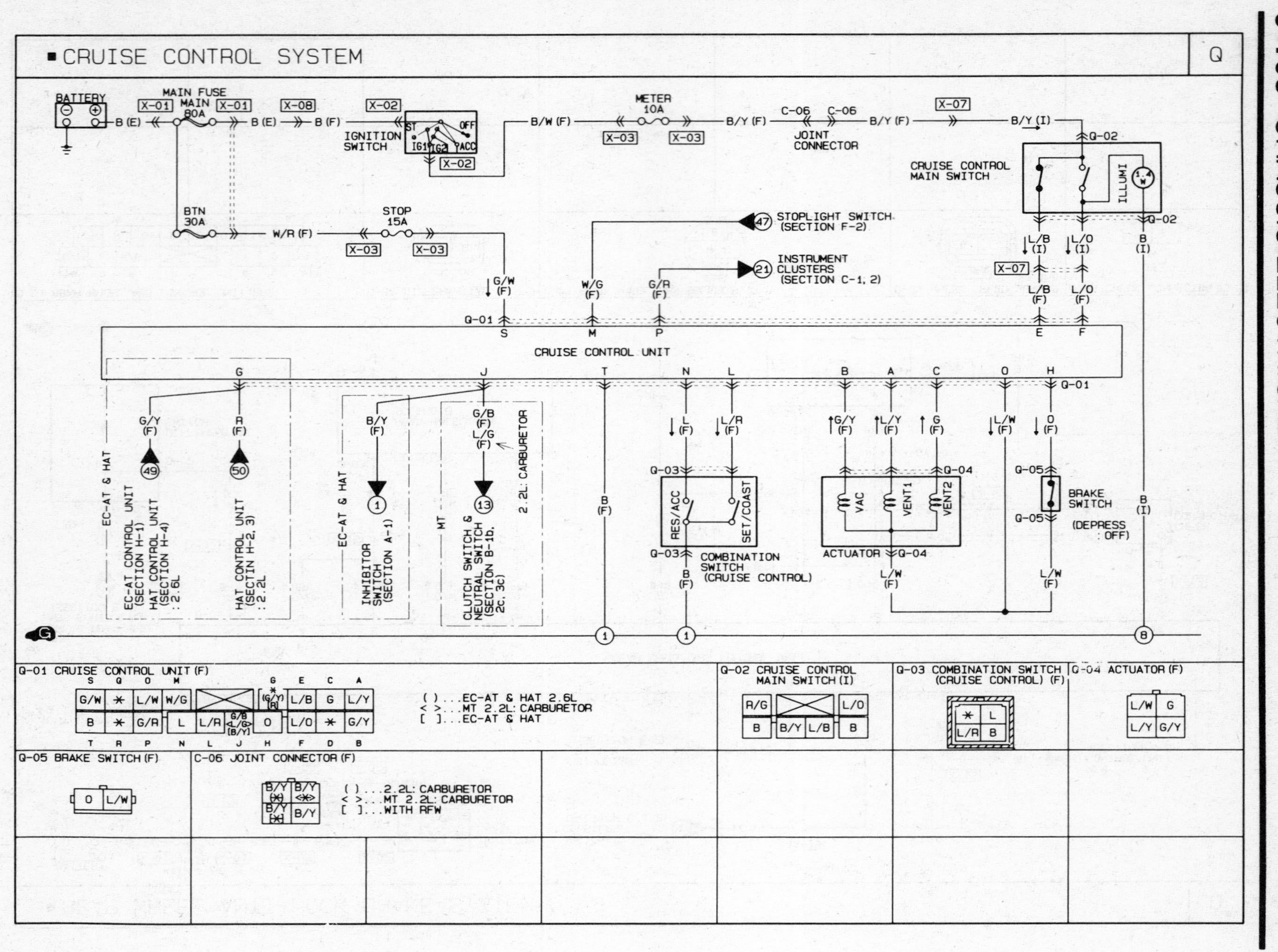

1989-92 Pickup, Cruise Control System

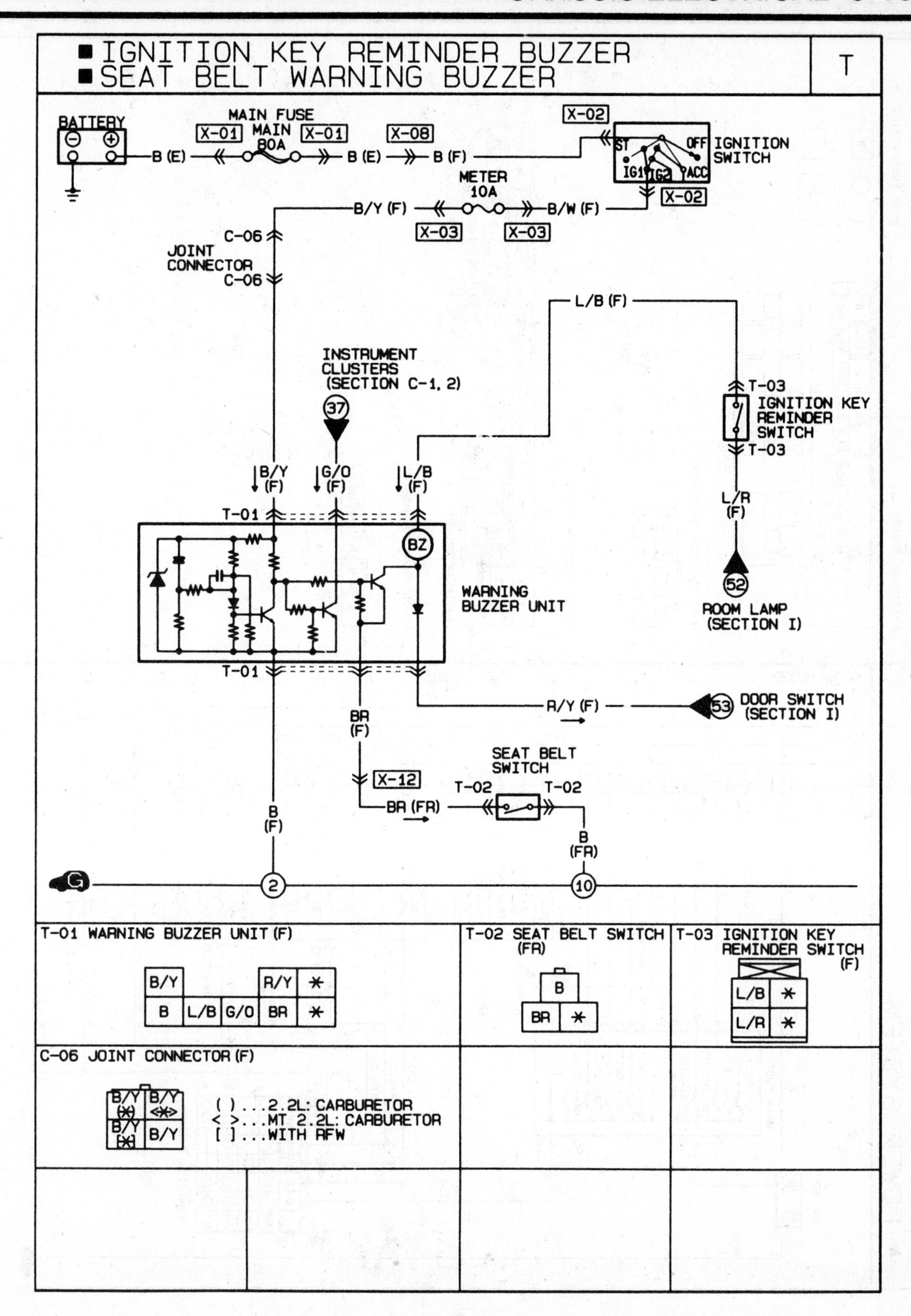

1989-92 Pickup, Ignition Key Remainder Buzzer, Seat Belt Warning Buzzer

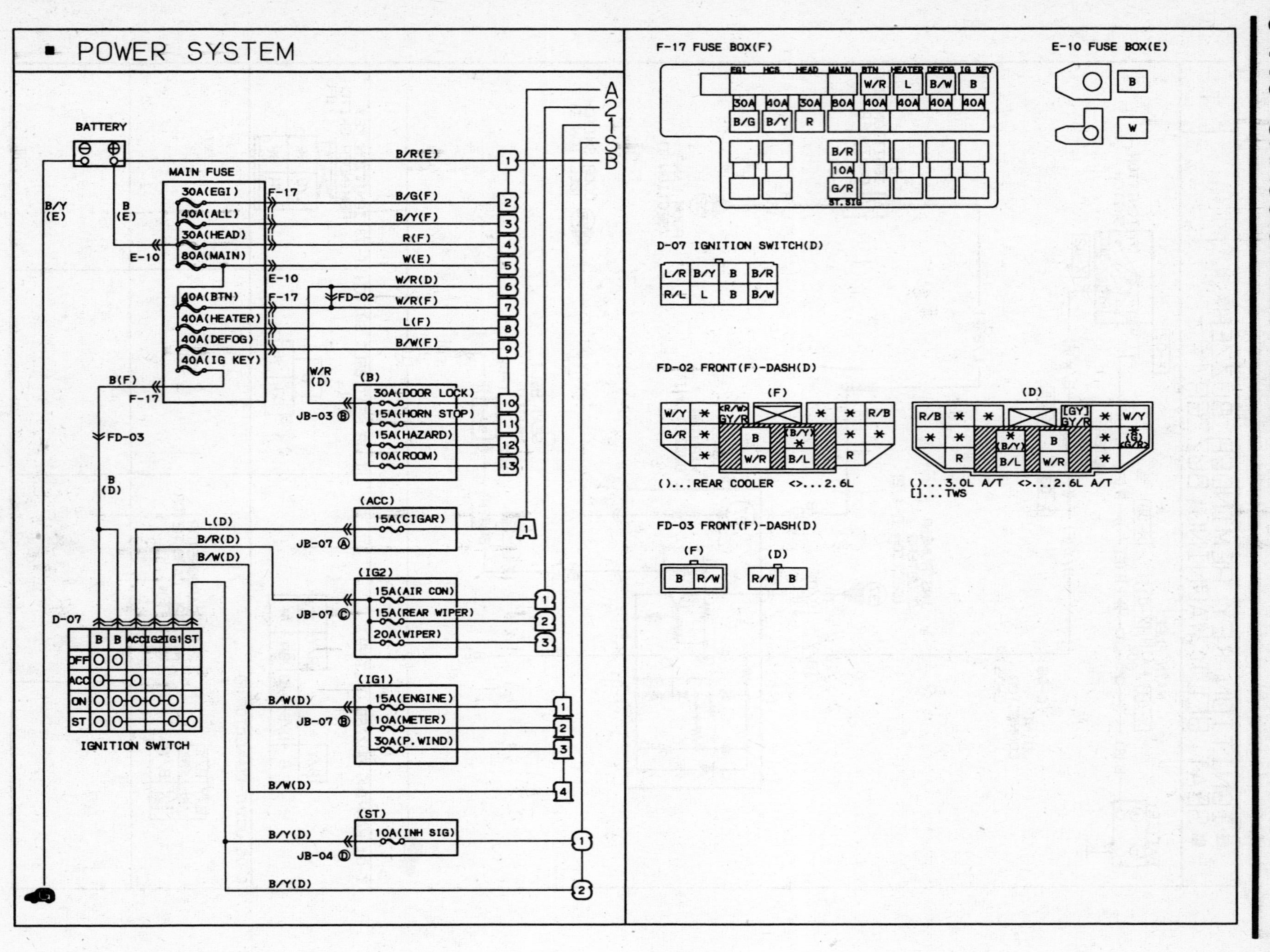

1989 MPV power system

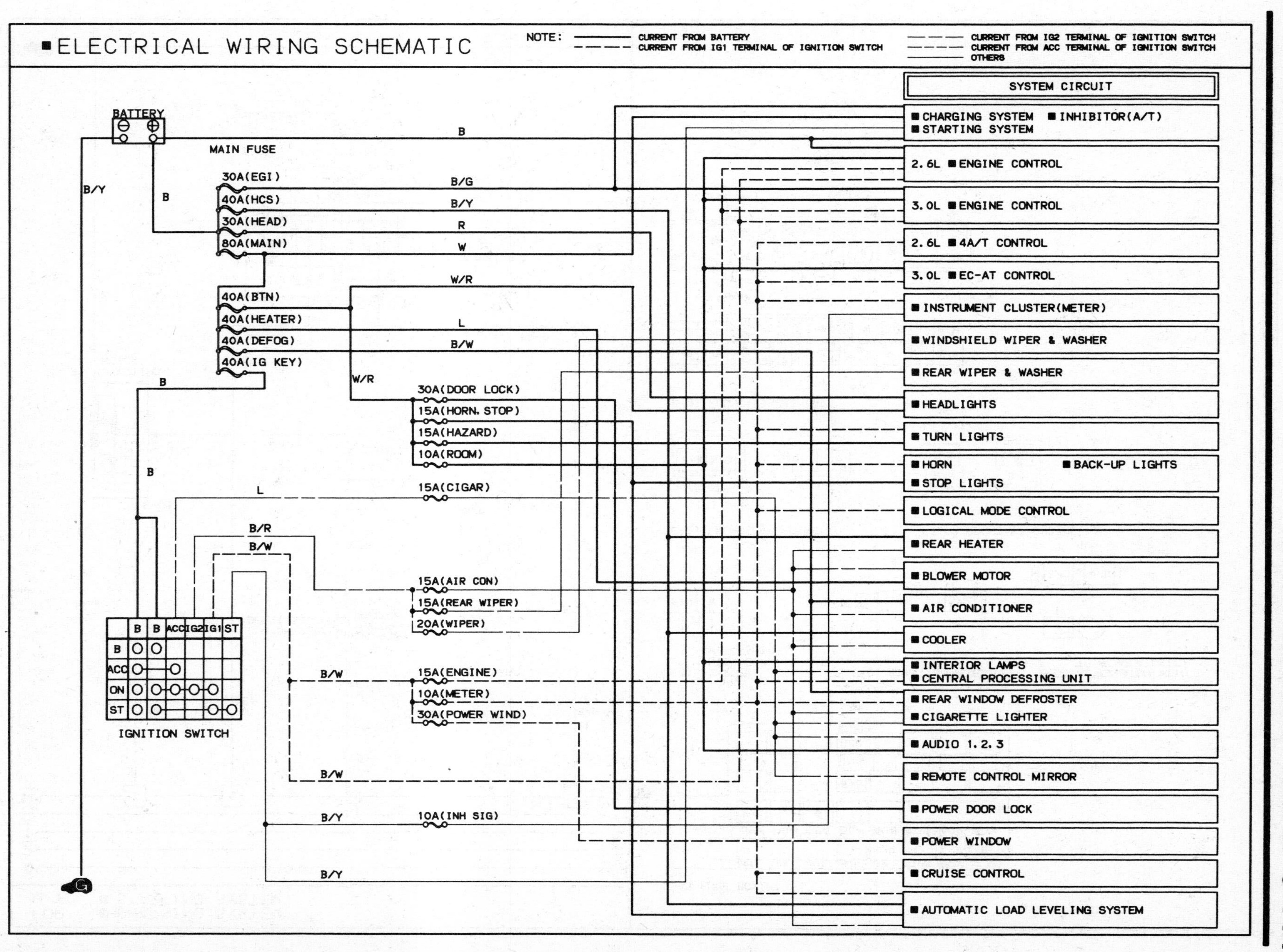
ELECTRICAL WIRING SCHEMATIC
NOTE:
CURRENT FROM BATTERY
CURRENT FROM IG1 TERMINAL OF IGNITION SWITCH
CURRENT FROM IG2 TERMINAL OF IGNITION SWITCH
CURRENT FROM ACC TERMINAL OF IGNITION SWITCH
OTHERS
SYSTEM CIRCUIT
CHARGING SYSTEM
STARTING SYSTEM
INHIBITOR(A/T)
2.6L ENGINE CONTROL
3.0L ENGINE CONTROL
2.6L 4A/T CONTROL
3.0L EC-AT CONTROL
INSTRUMENT CLUSTER(METER)
WINDSHIELD WIPER & WASHER
REAR WIPER & WASHER
HEADLIGHTS
TURN LIGHTS
HORN
BACK-UP LIGHTS
STOP LIGHTS
LOGICAL MODE CONTROL
REAR HEATER
BLOWER MOTOR
AIR CONDITIONER
COOLER
INTERIOR LAMPS
CENTRAL PROCESSING UNIT
REAR WINDOW DEFROSTER
CIGARETTE LIGHTER
AUDIO 1.2.3
REMOTE CONTROL MIRROR
POWER DOOR LOCK
POWER WINDOW
CRUISE CONTROL
AUTOMATIC LOAD LEVELING SYSTEM
BATTERY
MAIN FUSE
30A(EGI)
40A(HCS)
30A(HEAD)
80A(MAIN)
40A(BTN)
40A(HEATER)
40A(DEFOG)
40A(IG KEY)
30A(DOOR LOCK)
15A(HORN, STOP)
15A(HAZARD)
10A(ROOM)
15A(CIGAR)
15A(AIR CON)
15A(REAR WIPER)
20A(WIPER)
15A(ENGINE)
10A(METER)
30A(POWER WIND)
10A(INH SIG)
IGNITION SWITCH
B
ACC
IG2
IG1
ST
ON
B/Y
B/G
R
W
W/R
L
B/W
B/R

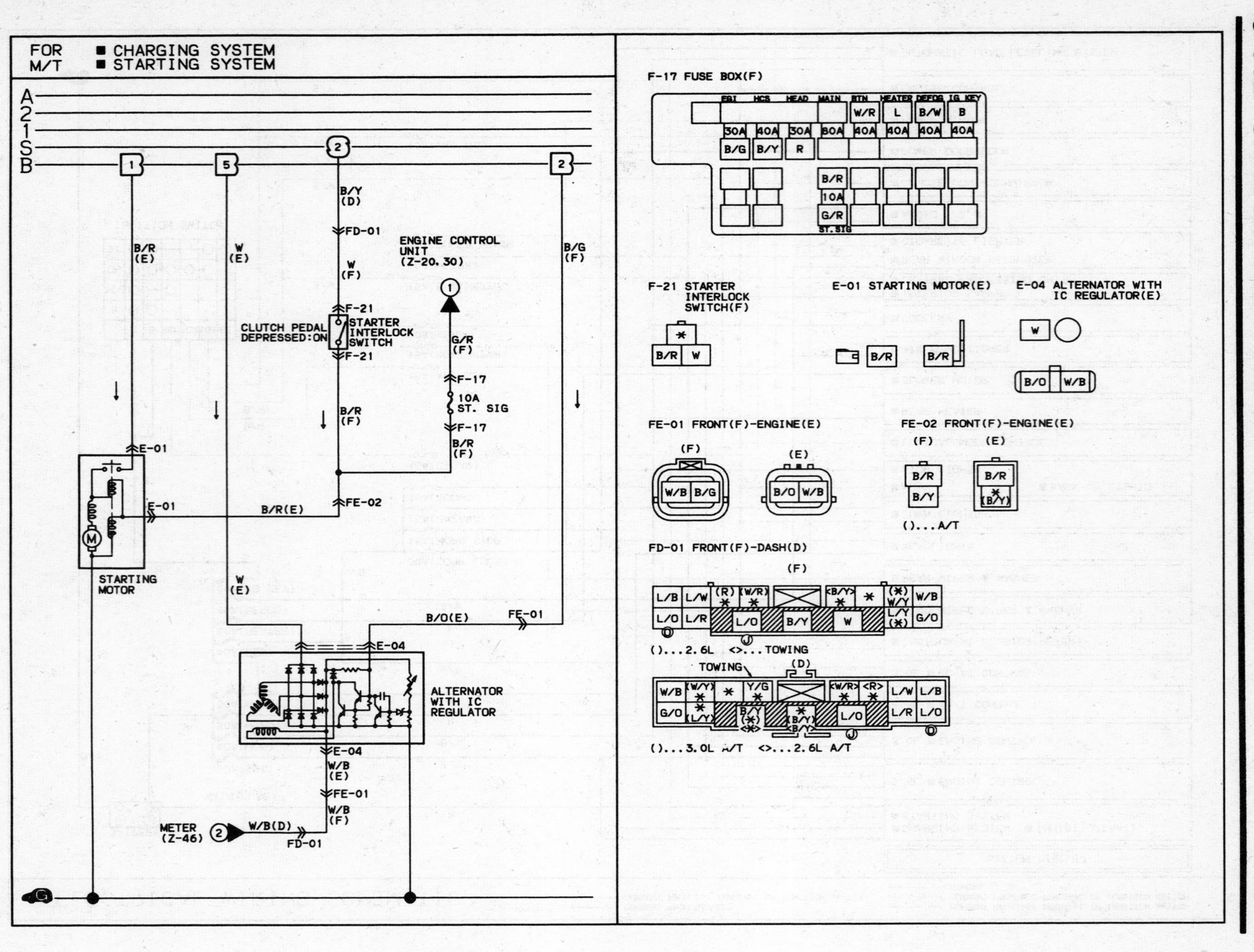

1989 MPV charging/starting system

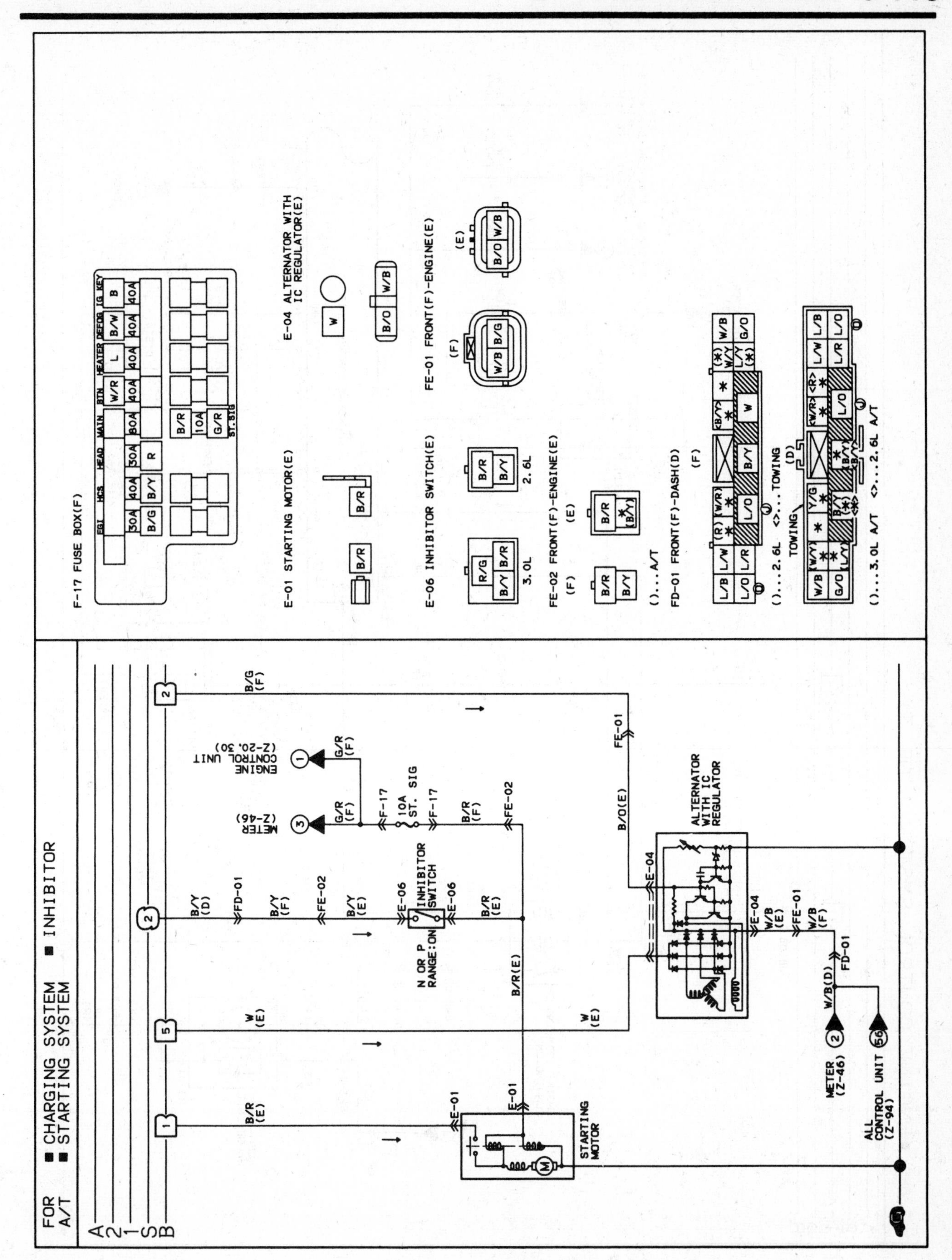

1989 MPV charging/starting system

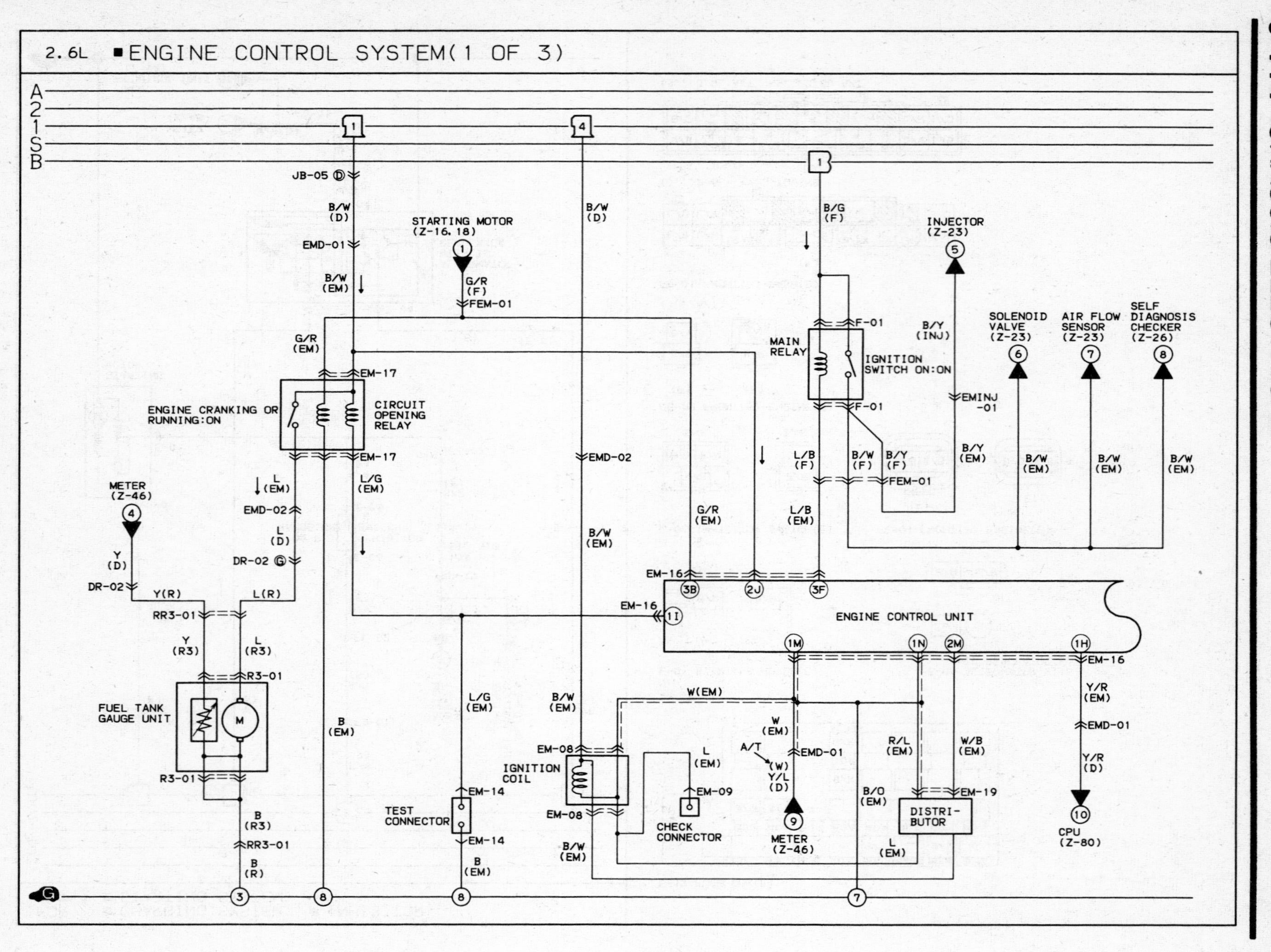

1989 MPV 2.6L engine control system

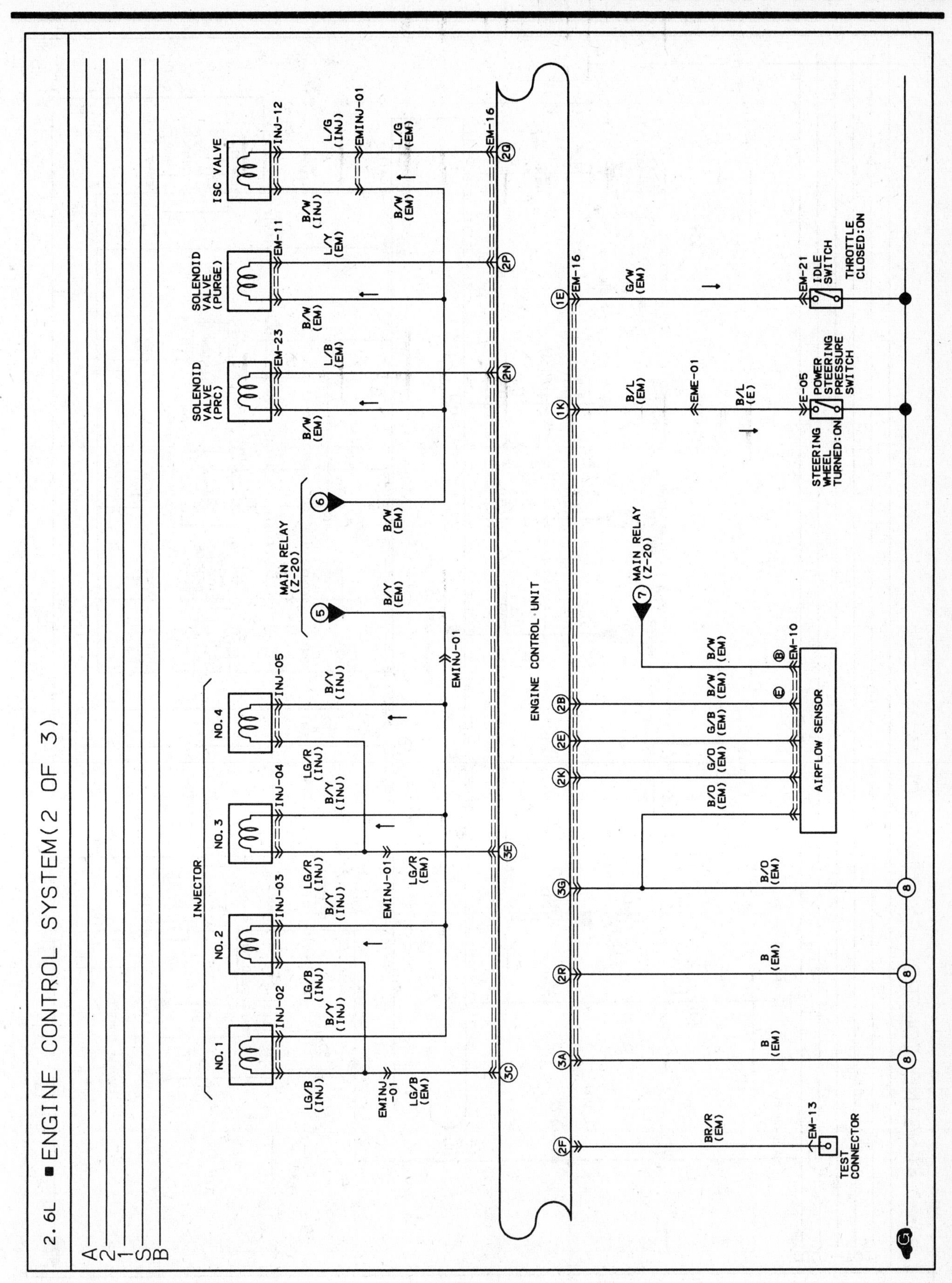

1989 MPV 2.6L engine control system

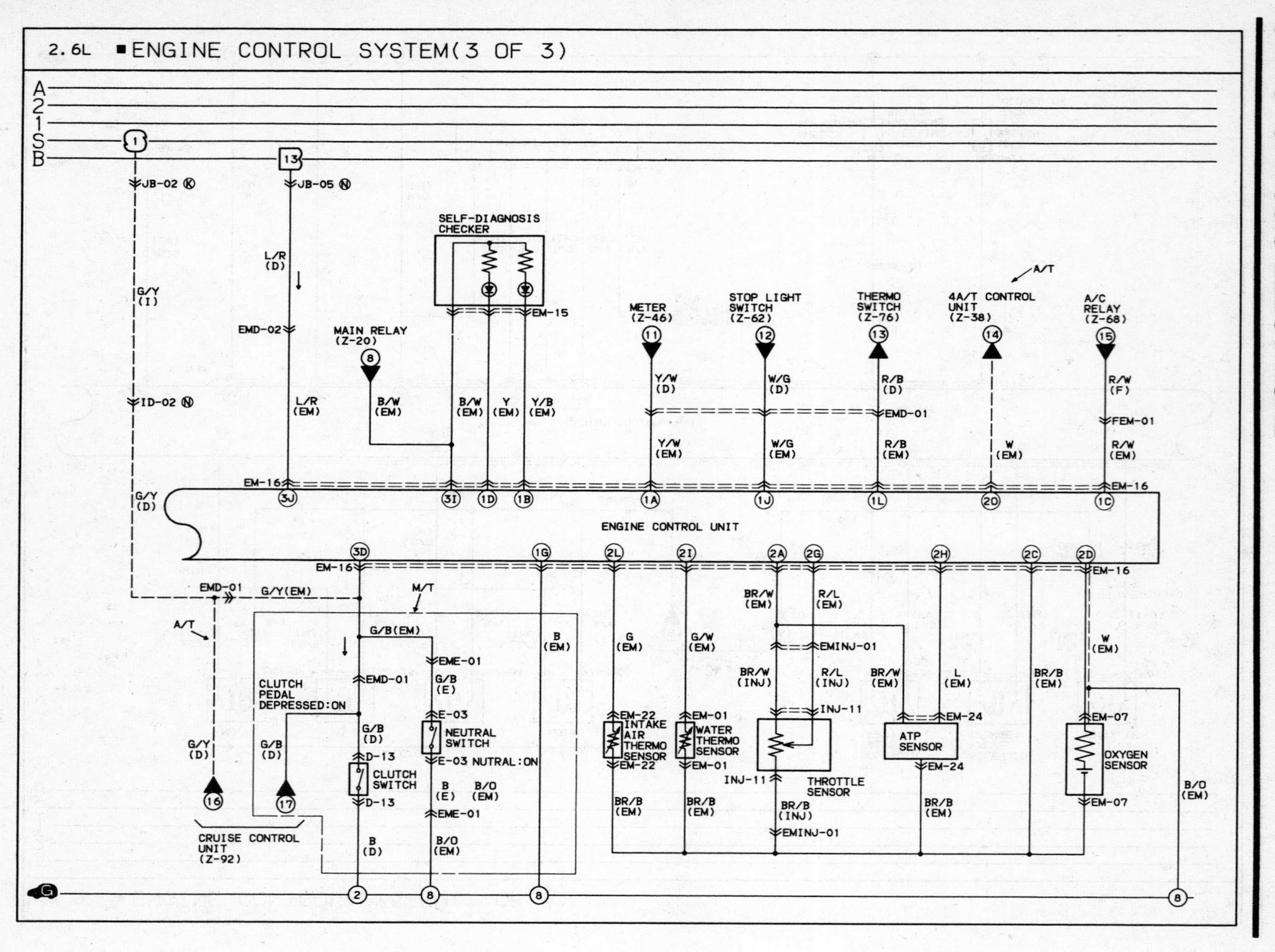

1989 MPV 2.6L engine control system

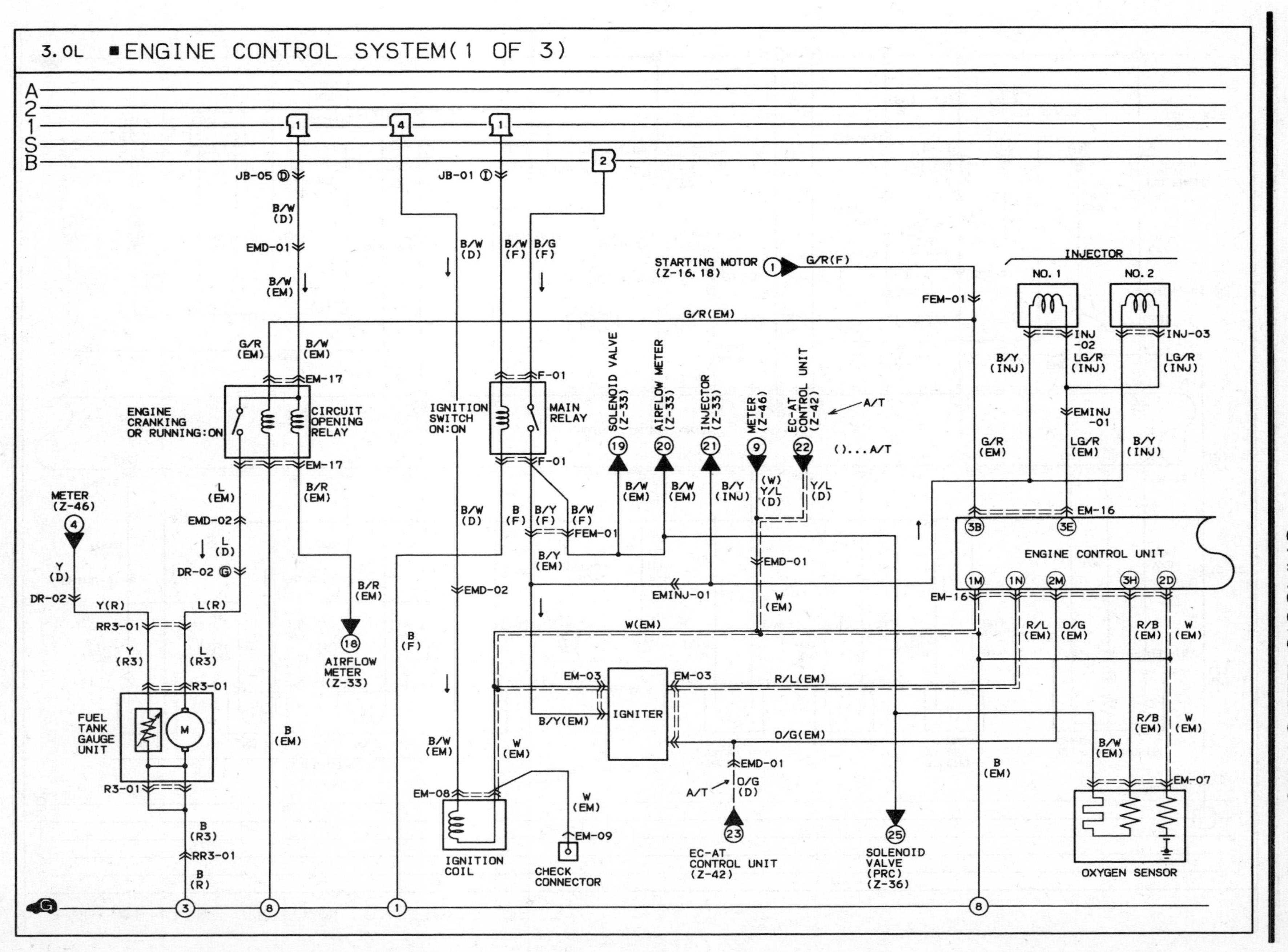

1989 MPV 3.0L engine control system

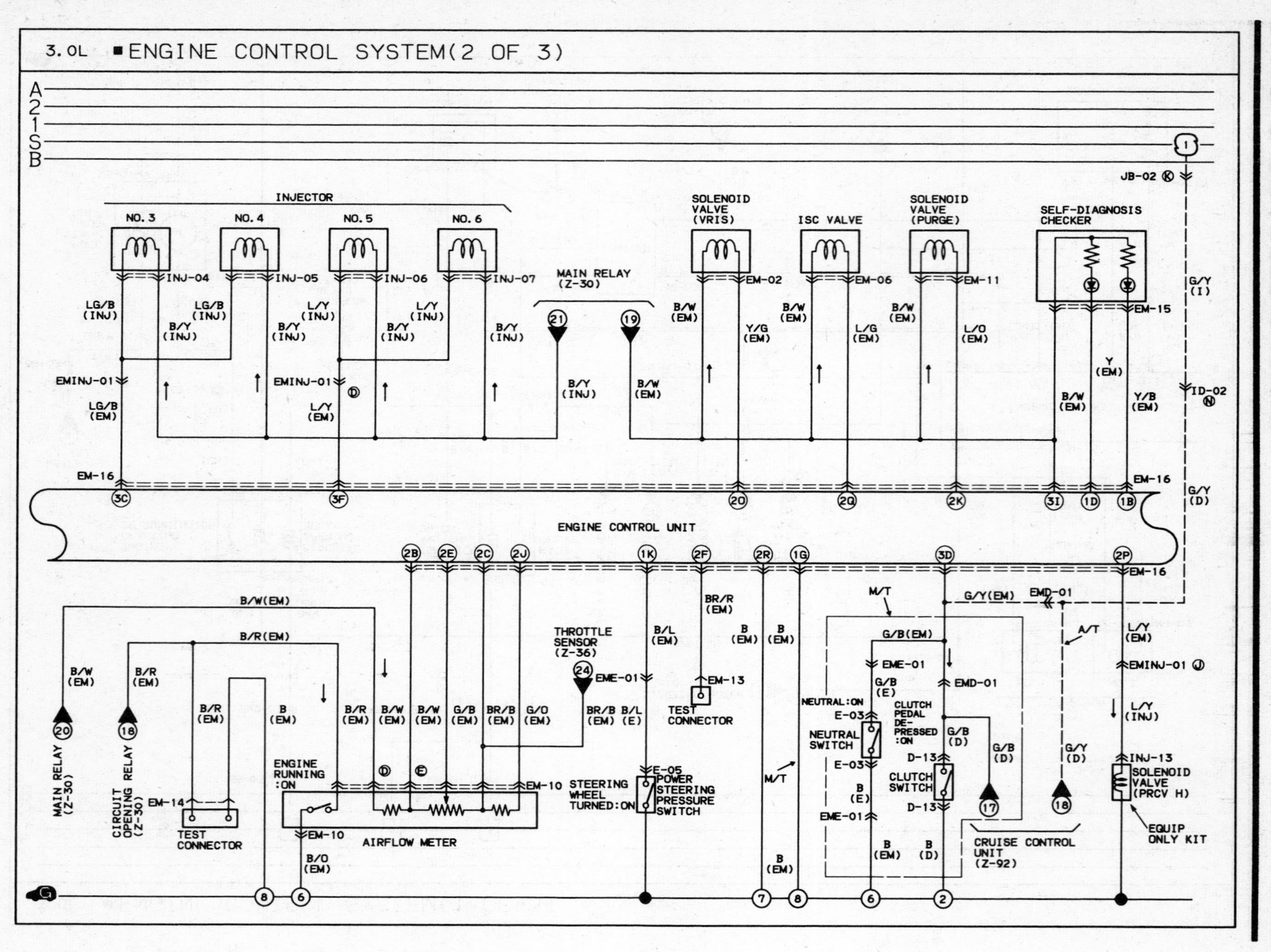

1989 MPV 3.0L engine control system

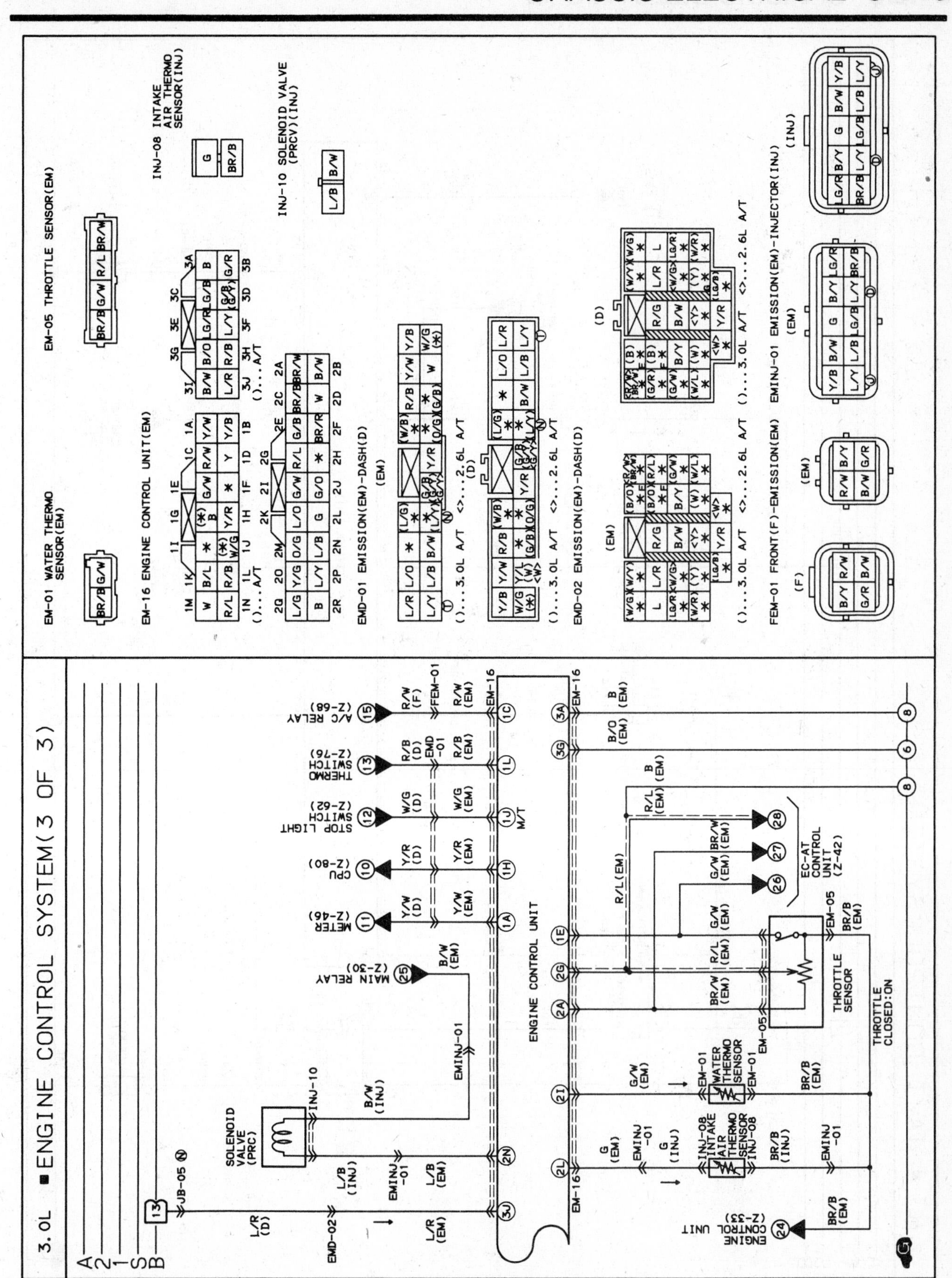

1989 MPV 3.0L engine control systems

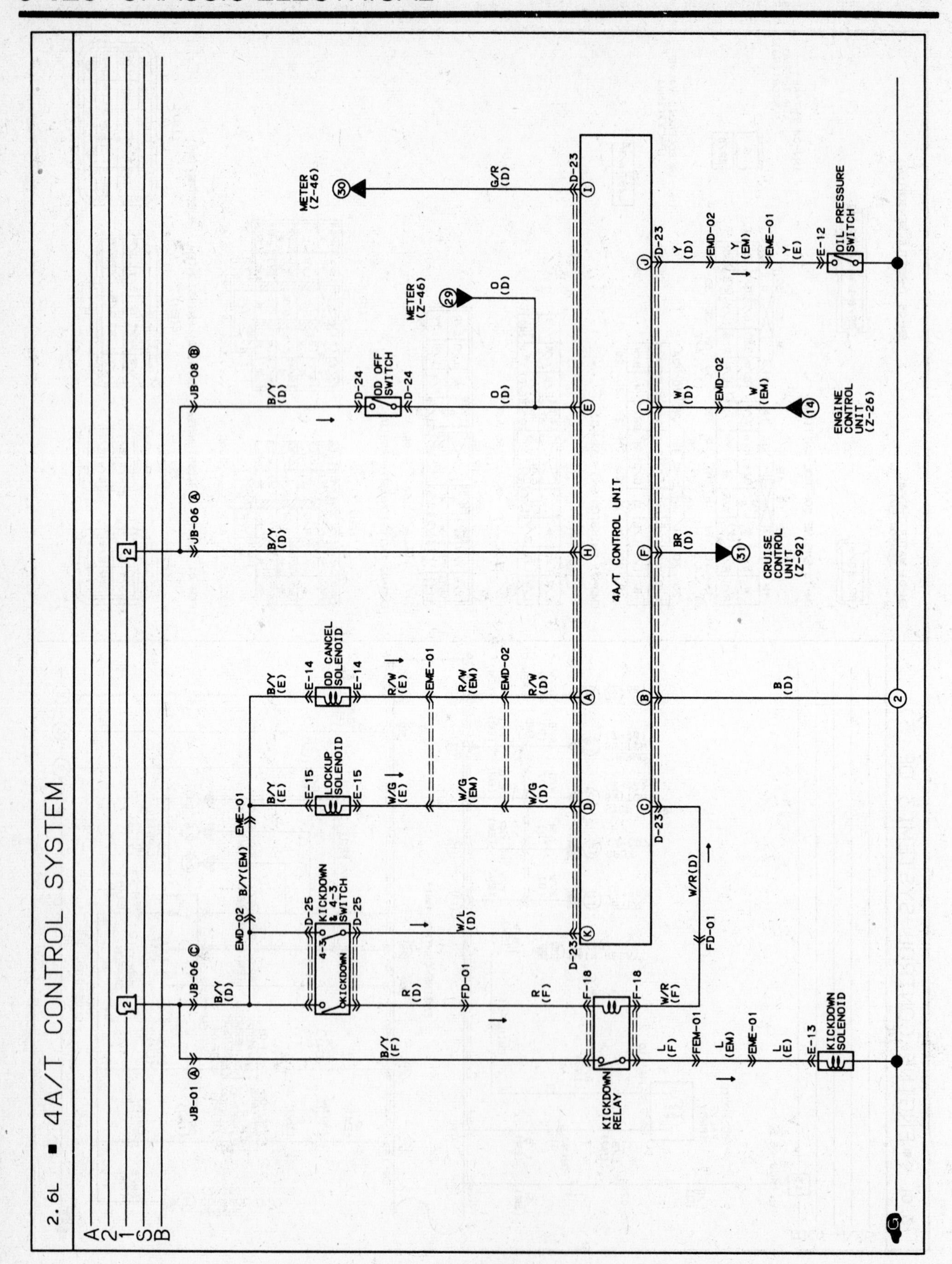

1989 MPV 2.6L 4 AT control system

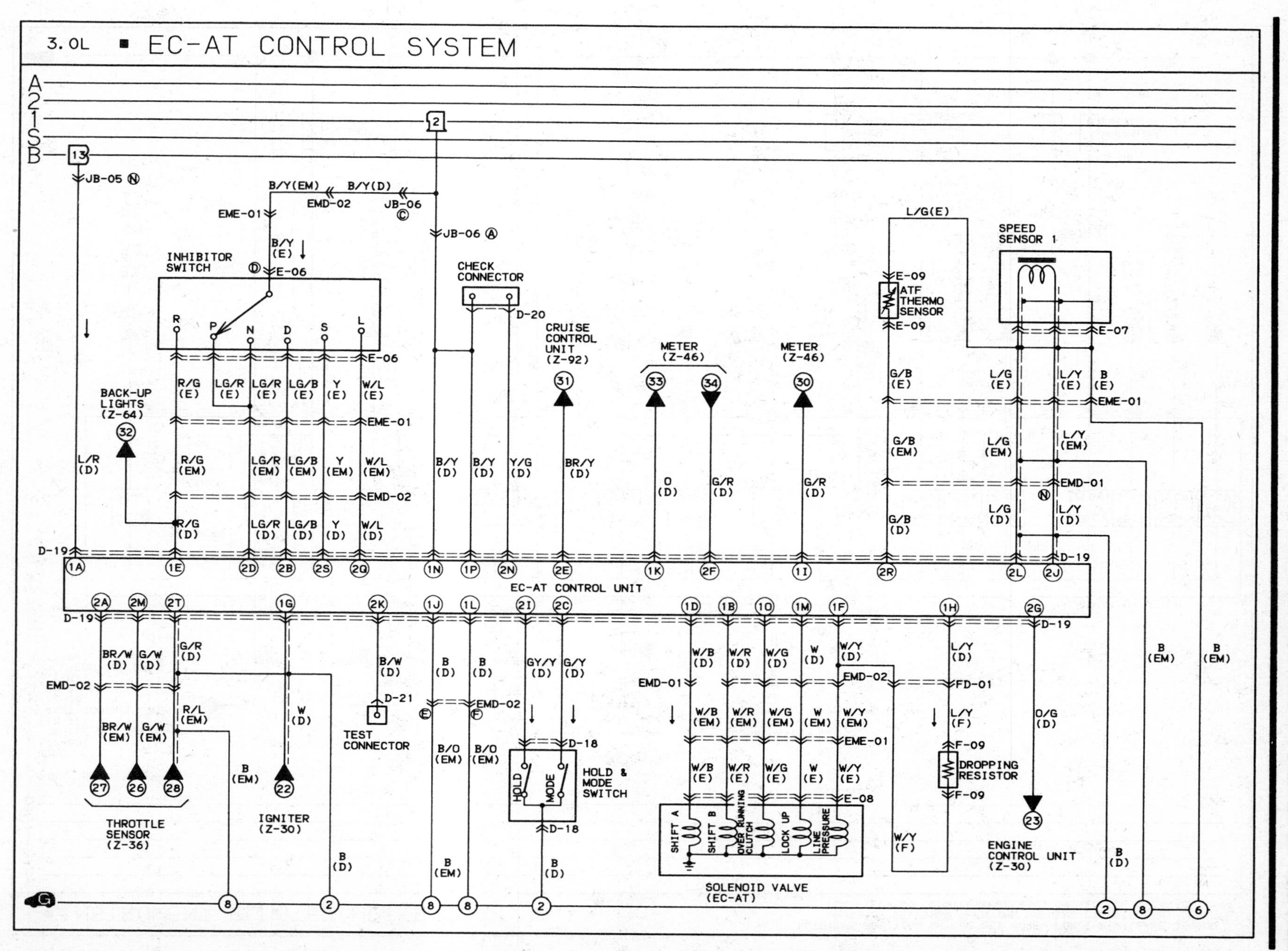

1989 MPV 3.0L EC-AT control system

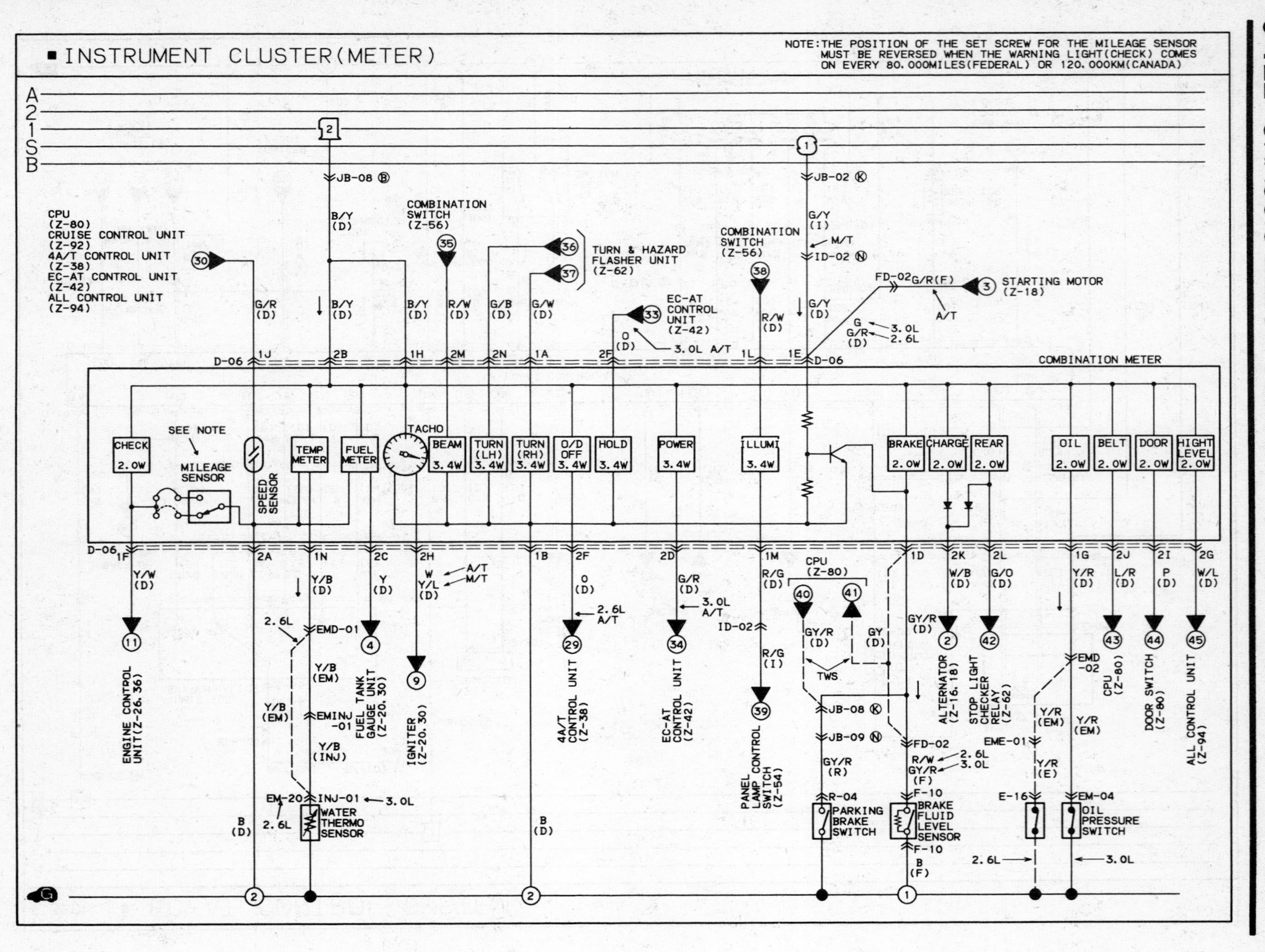

1989 MPV instrument cluster

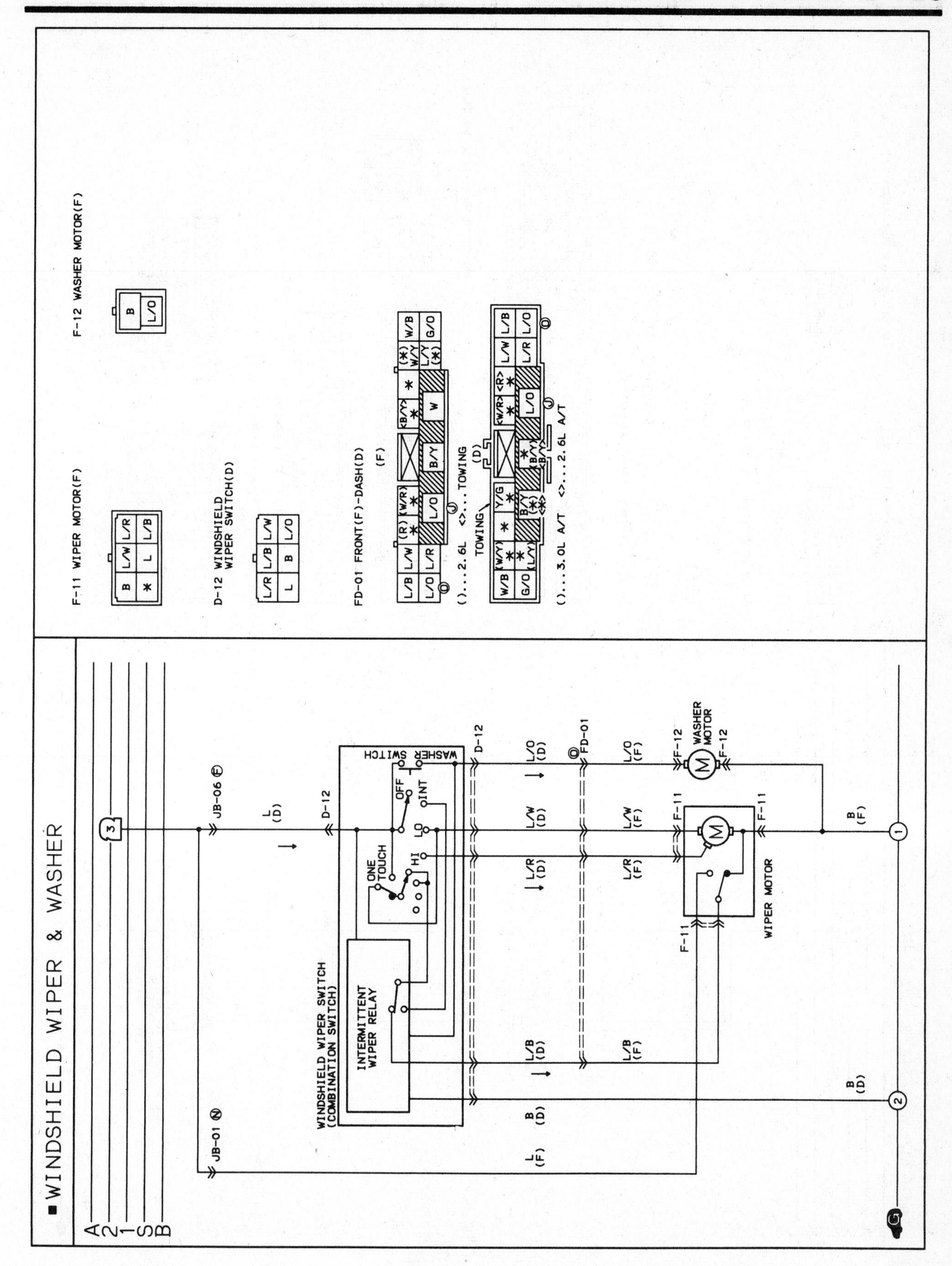

1989 MPV windshield wiper and washer

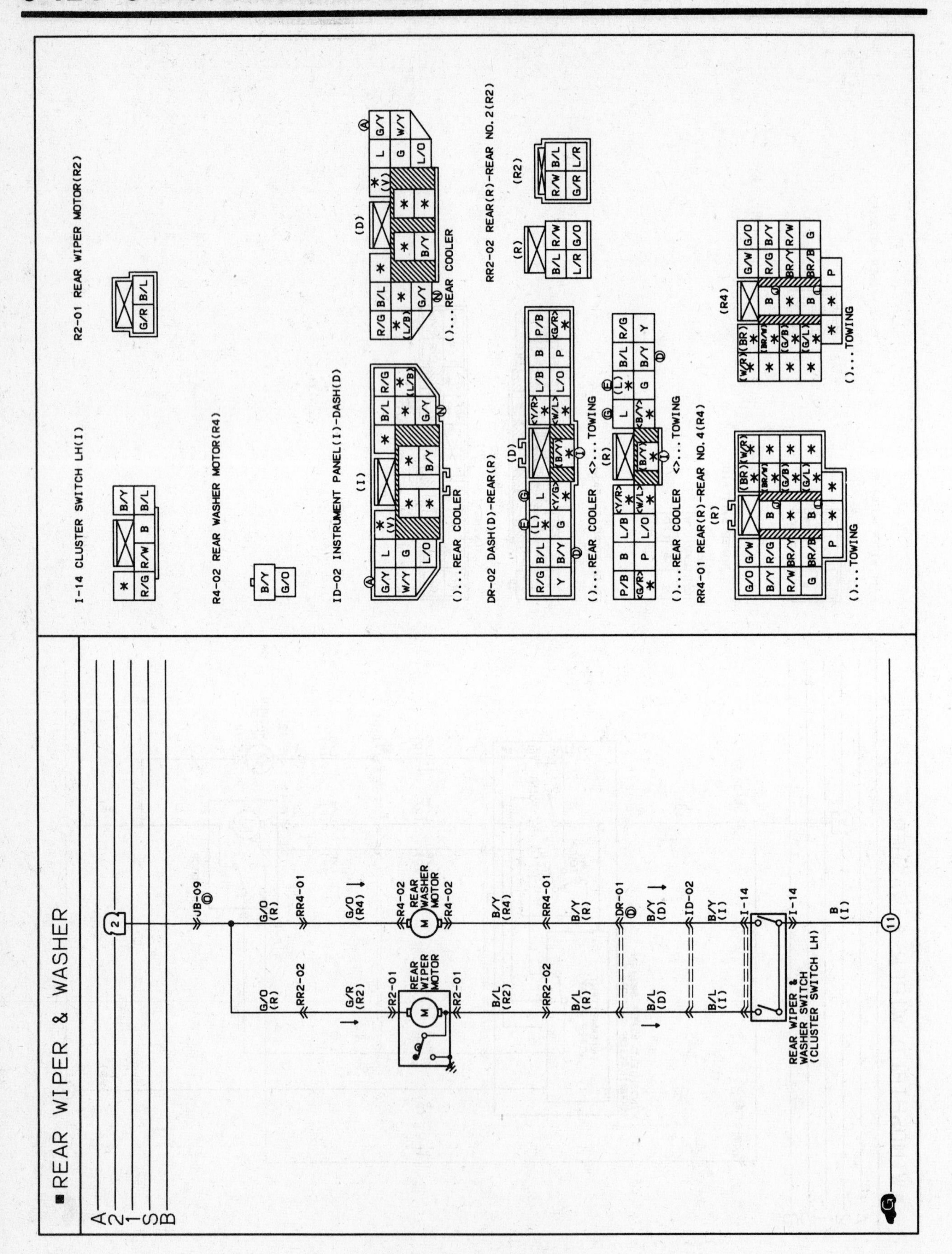

1989 MPV rear wiper and washer

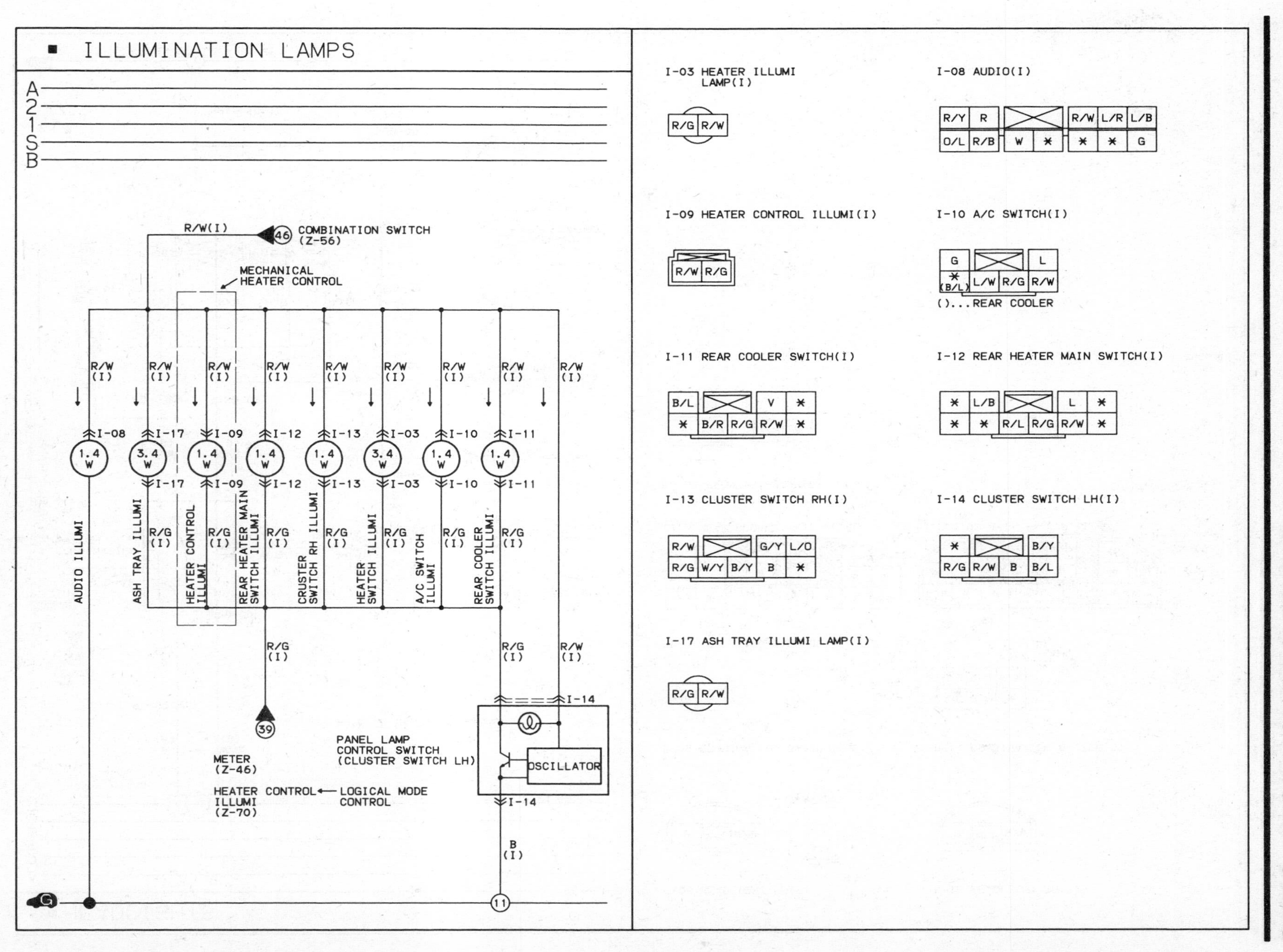

1989 MPV illumination lamps

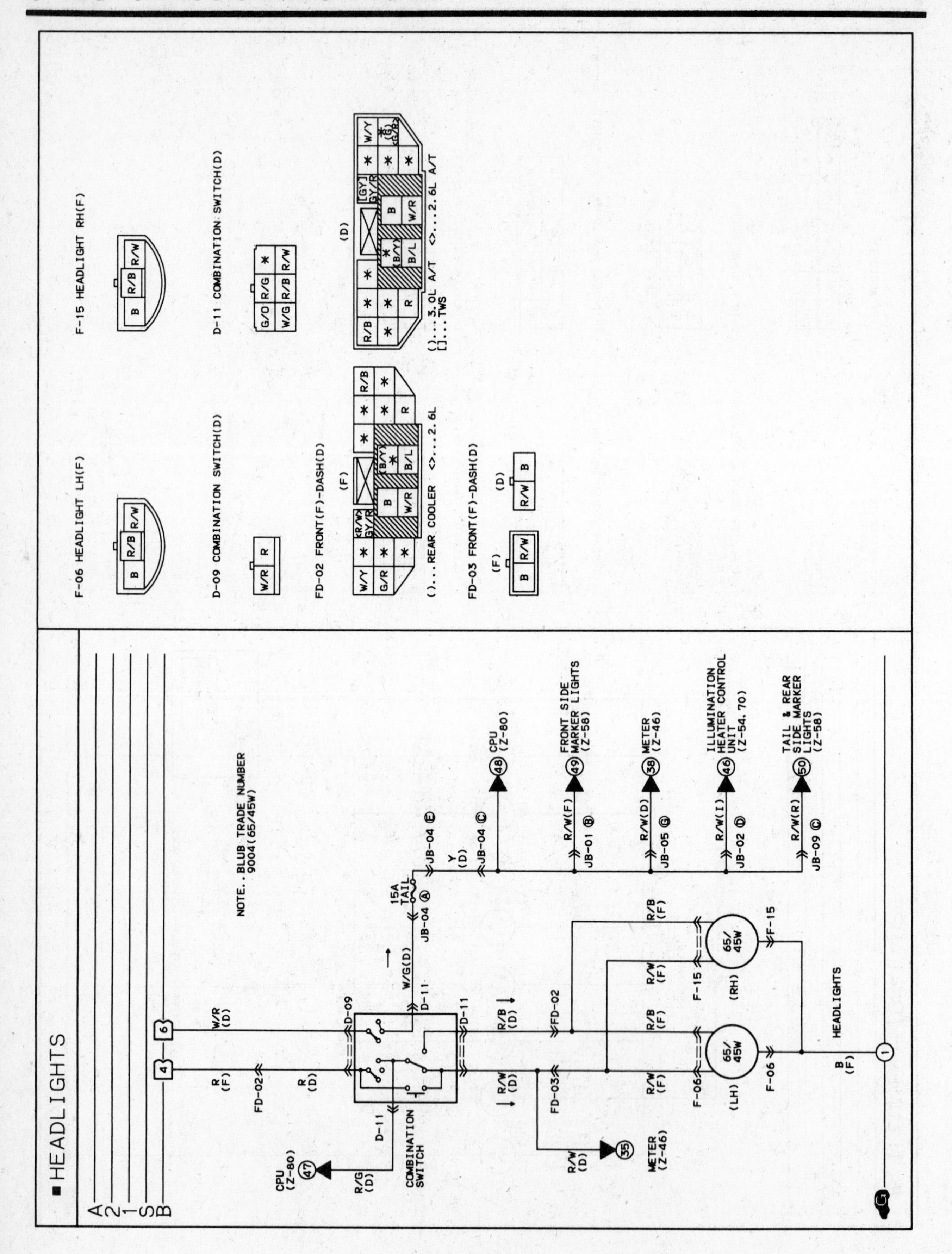

1989 MPV headlights

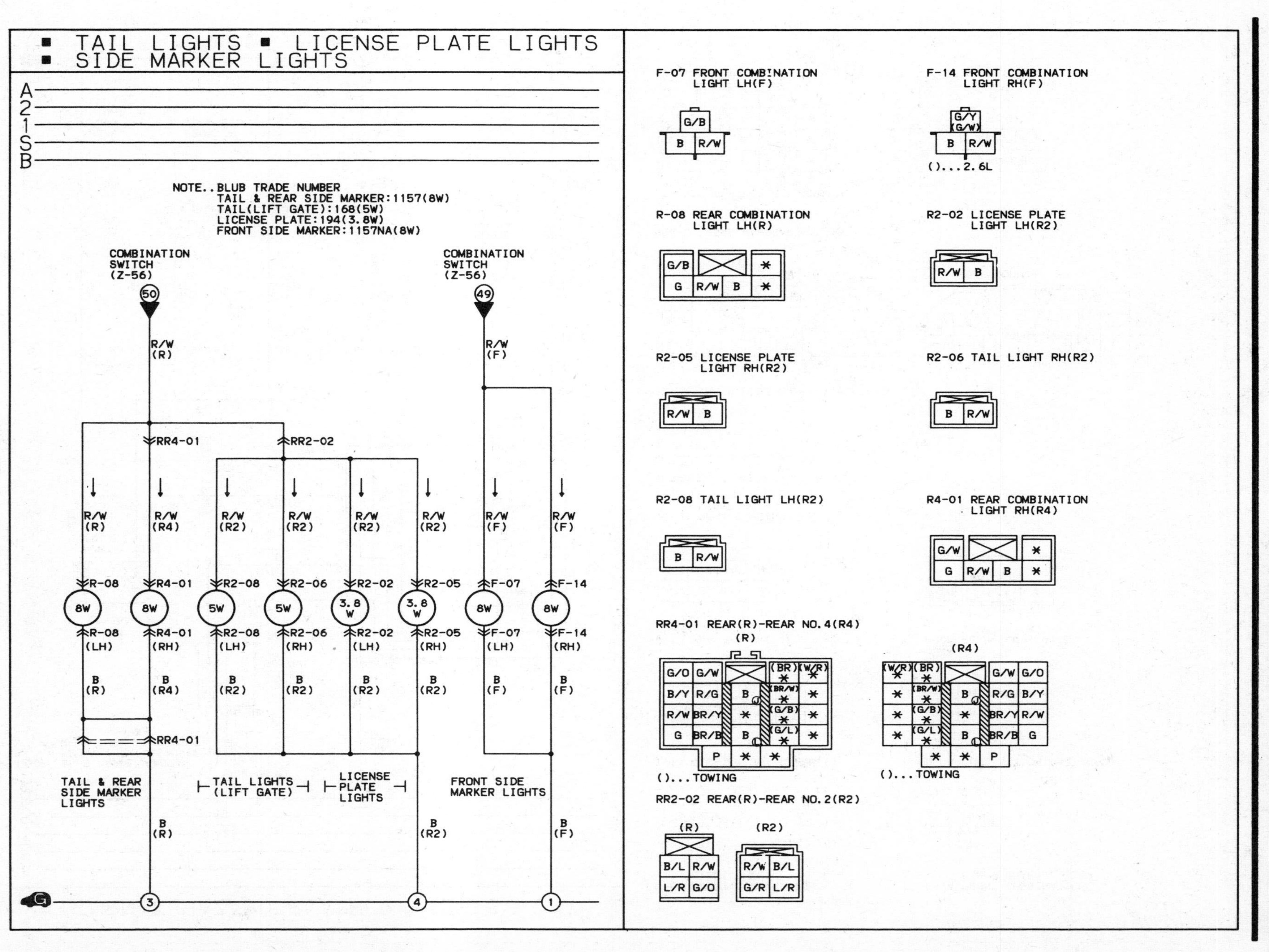

1989 MPV exterior lights

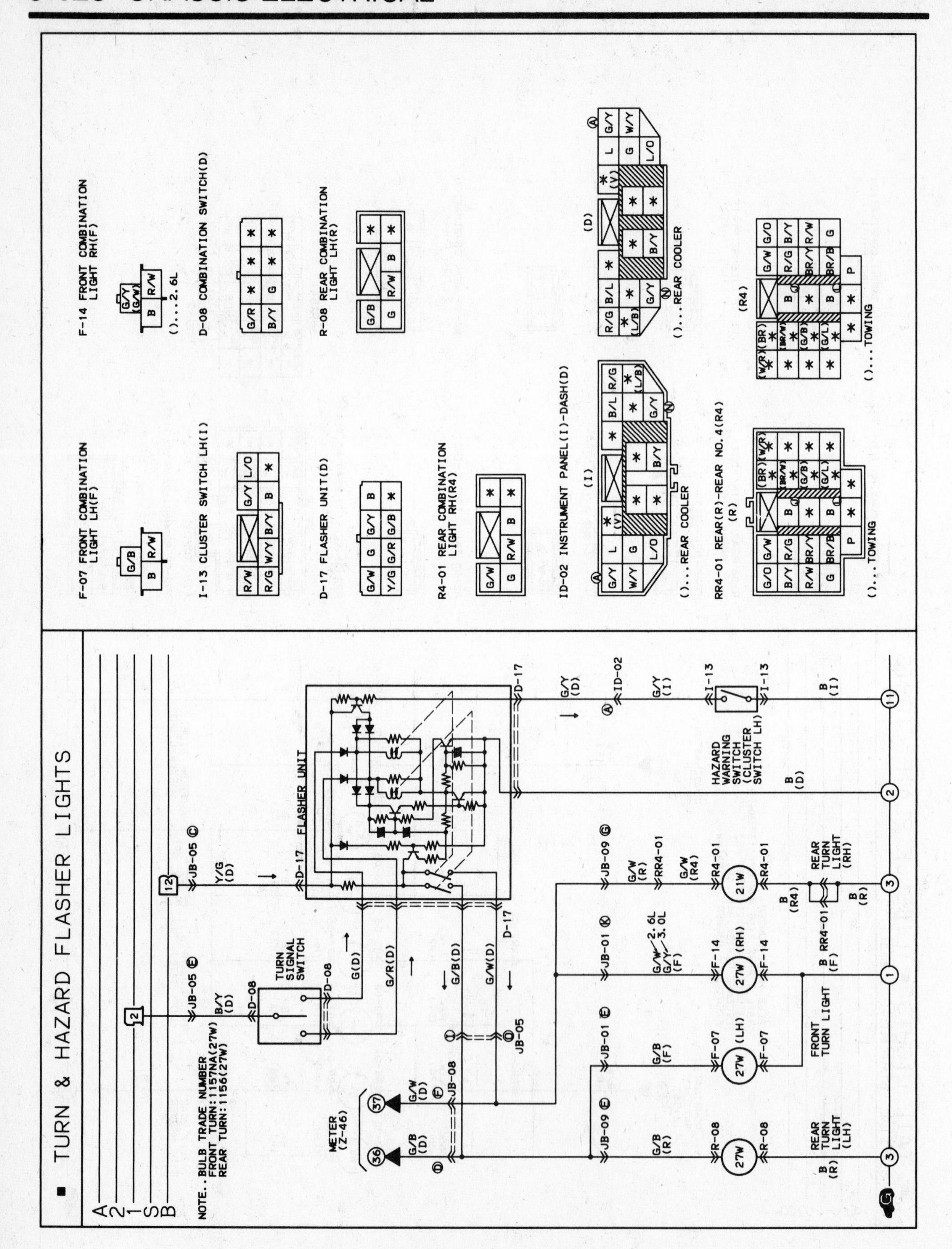

1989 MPV turn and hazard flasher lights

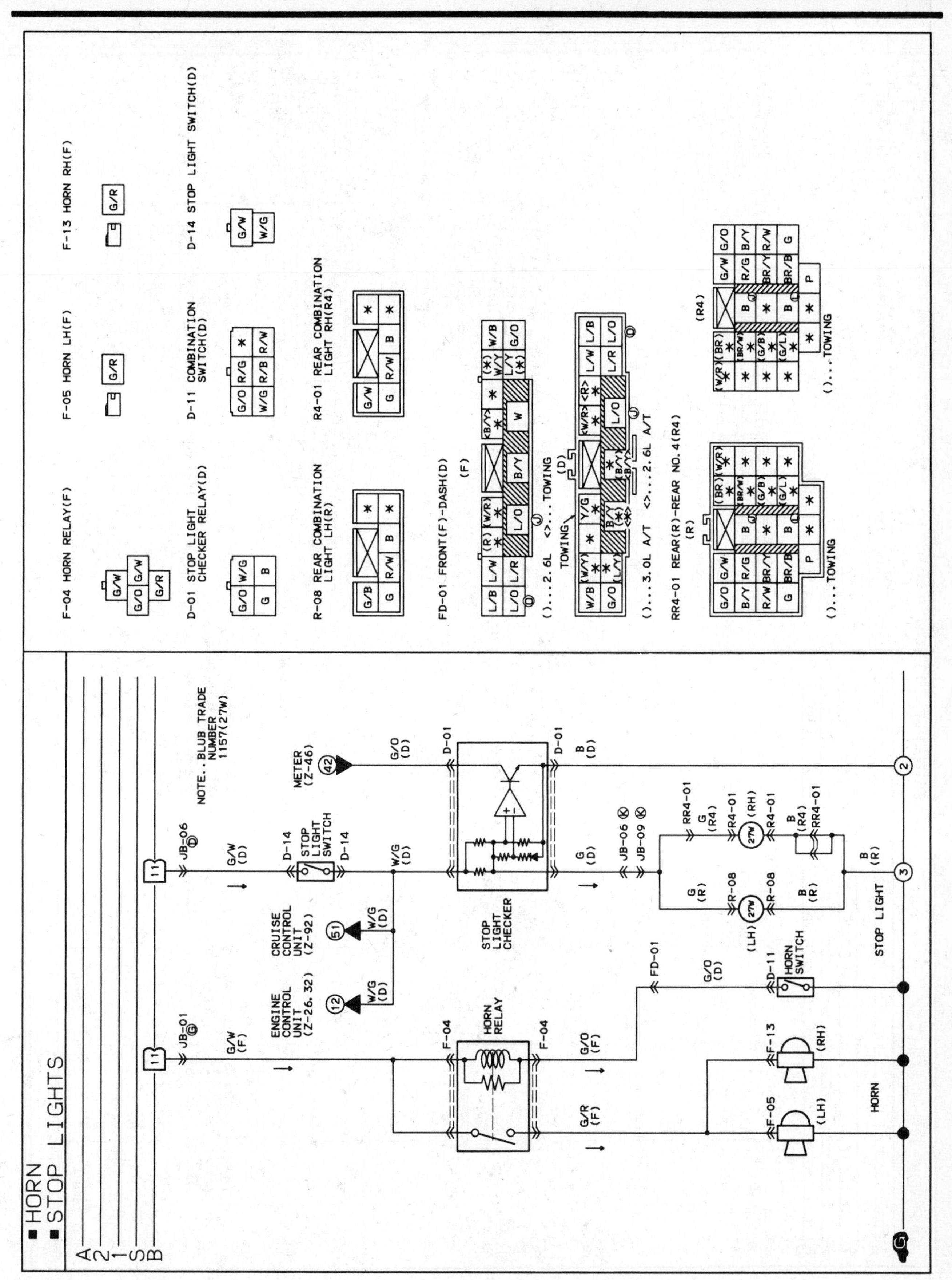

1989 MPV horn, stoplights

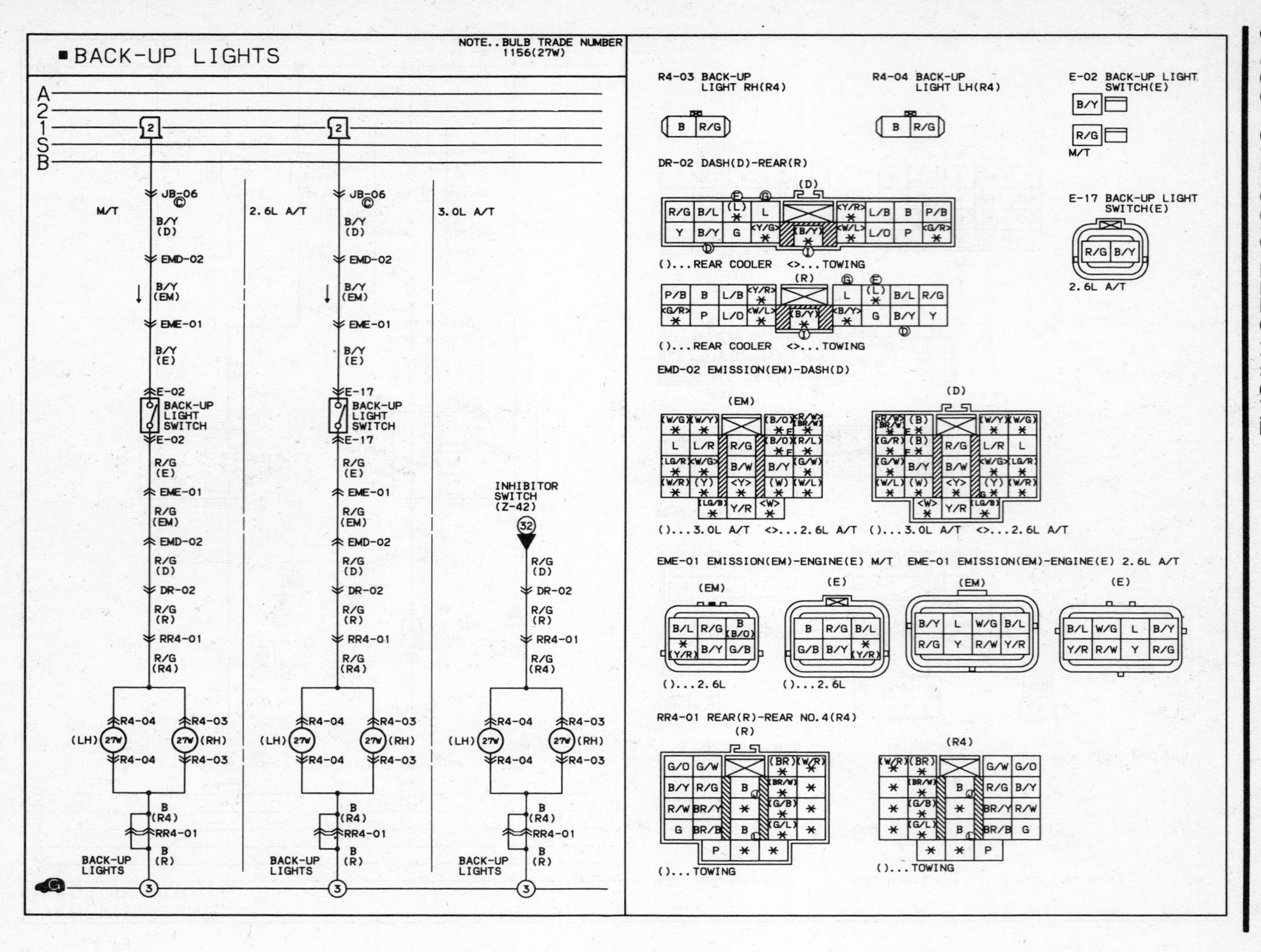

1989 MPV backup lights

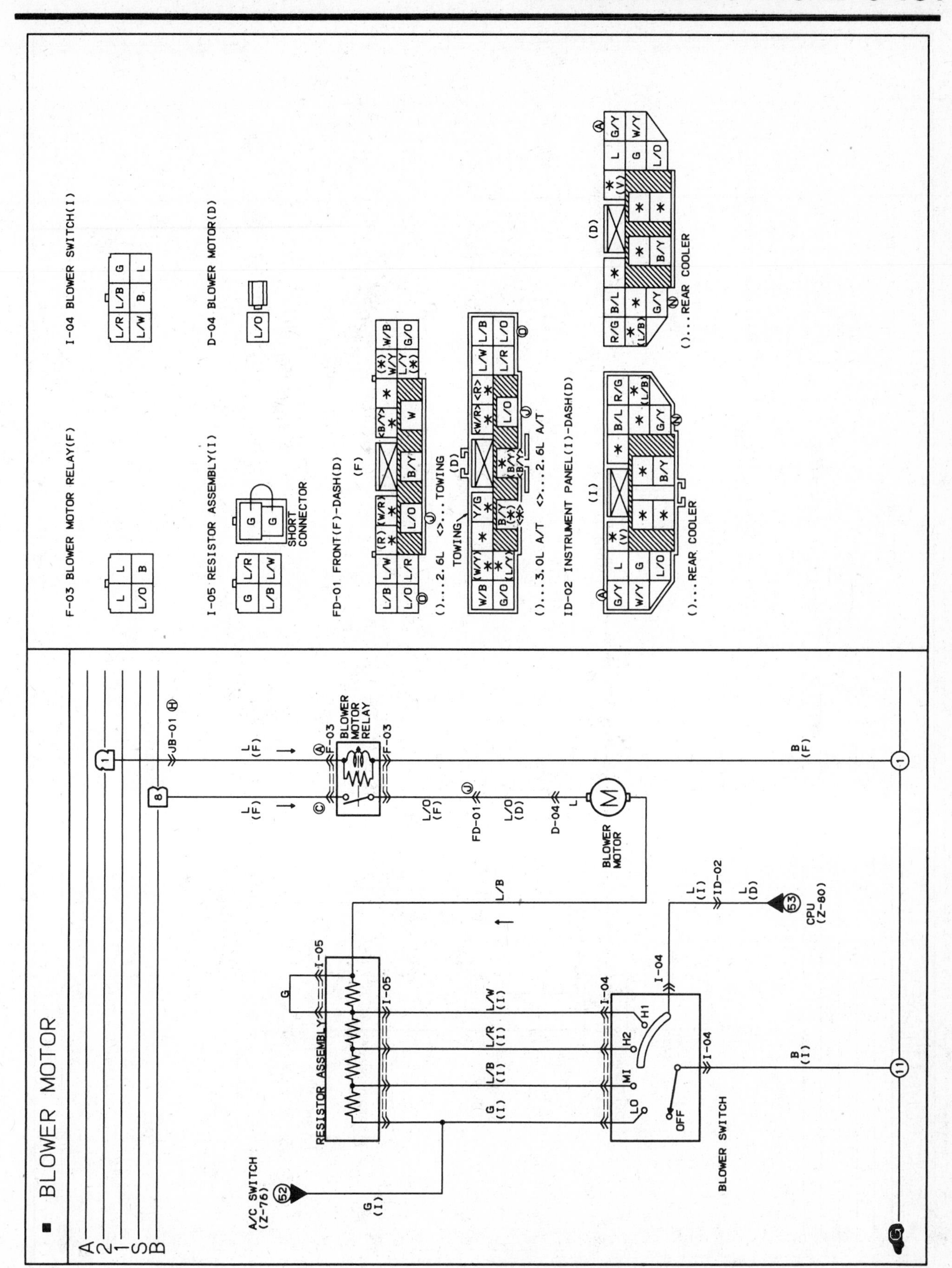

1989 MPV blower motor

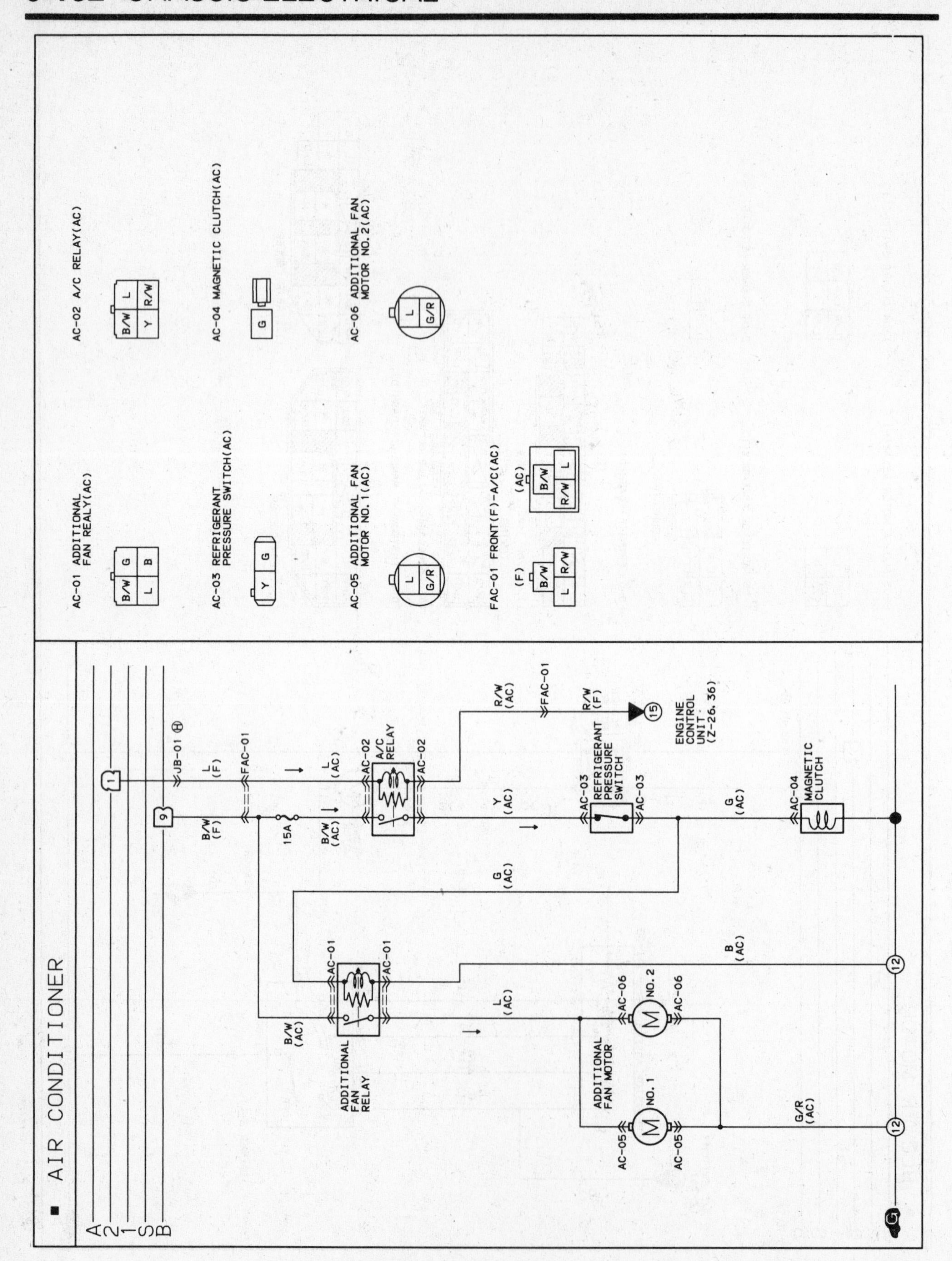

1989 MPV air conditioner

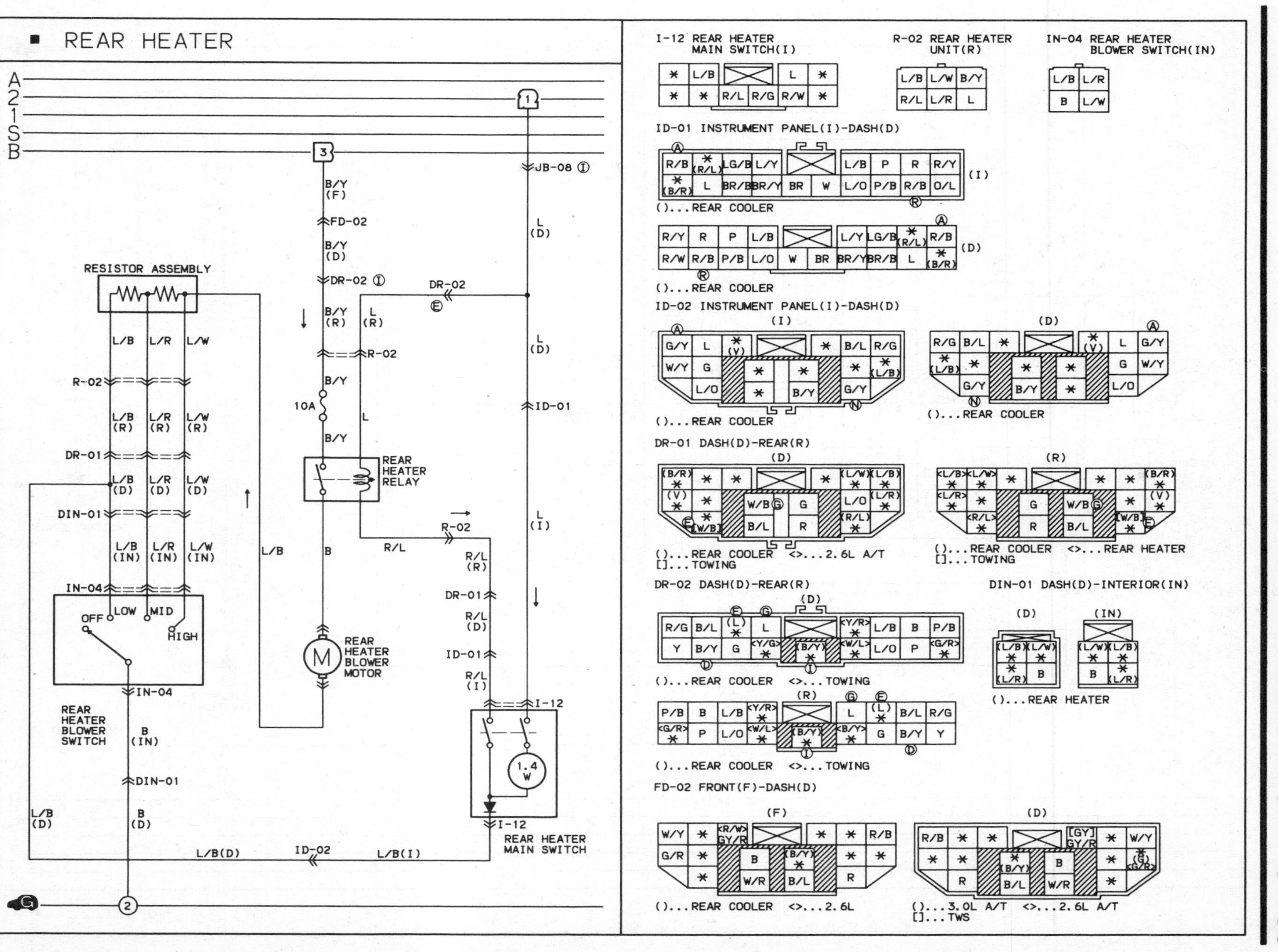

1989 MPV rear heater

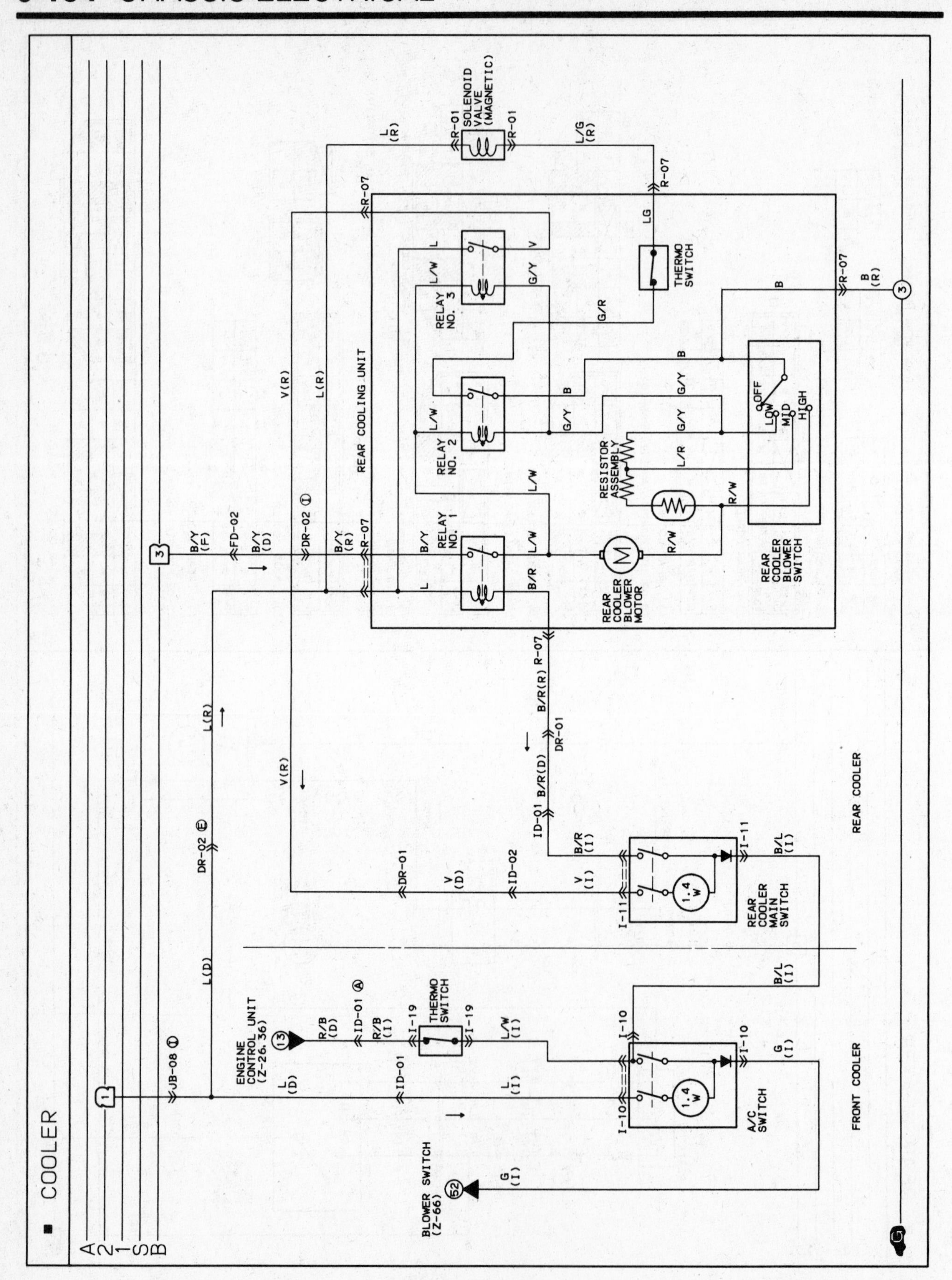

1989 MPV coolers

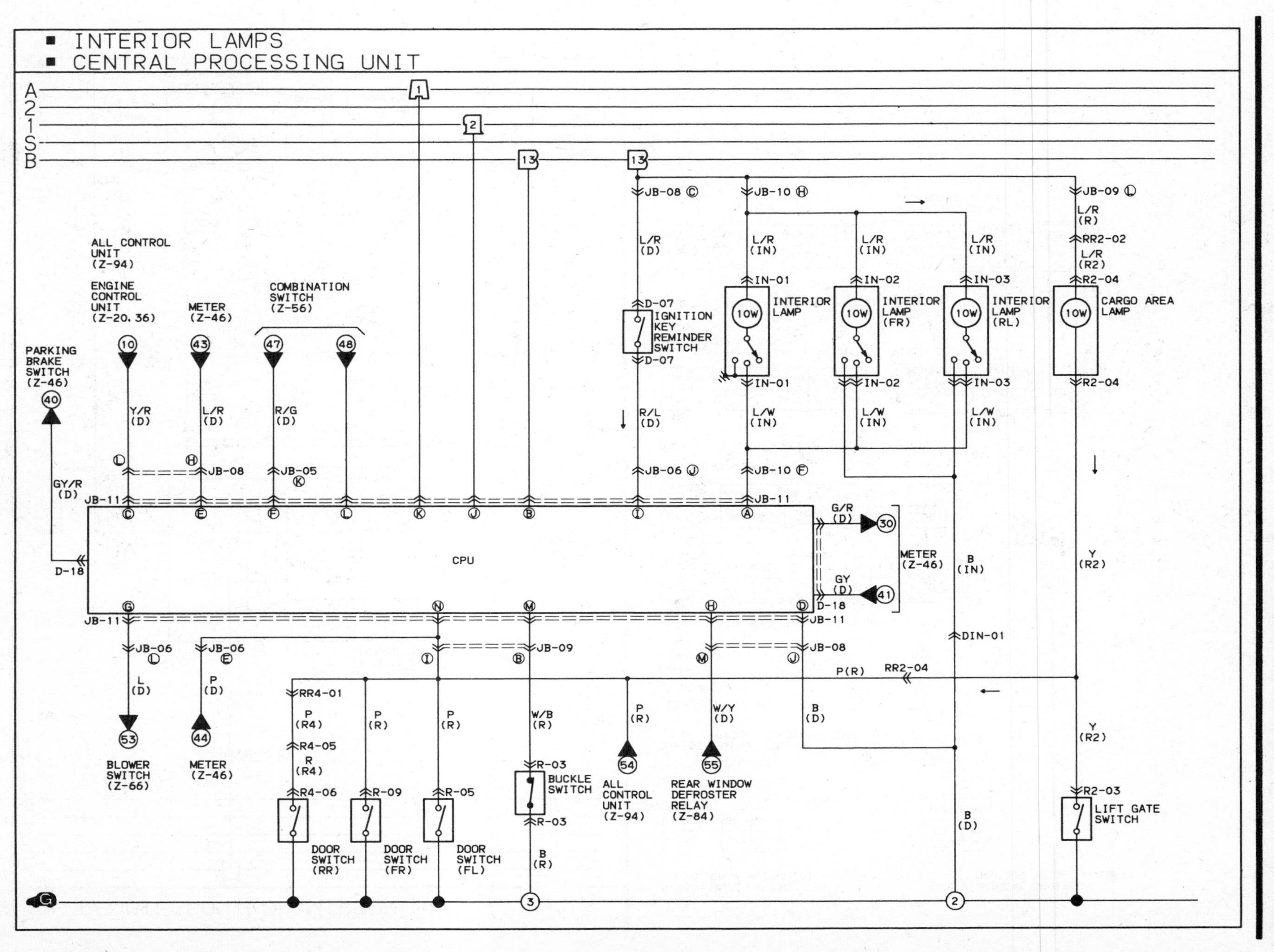

1989 MPV interior lamps, central processing unit

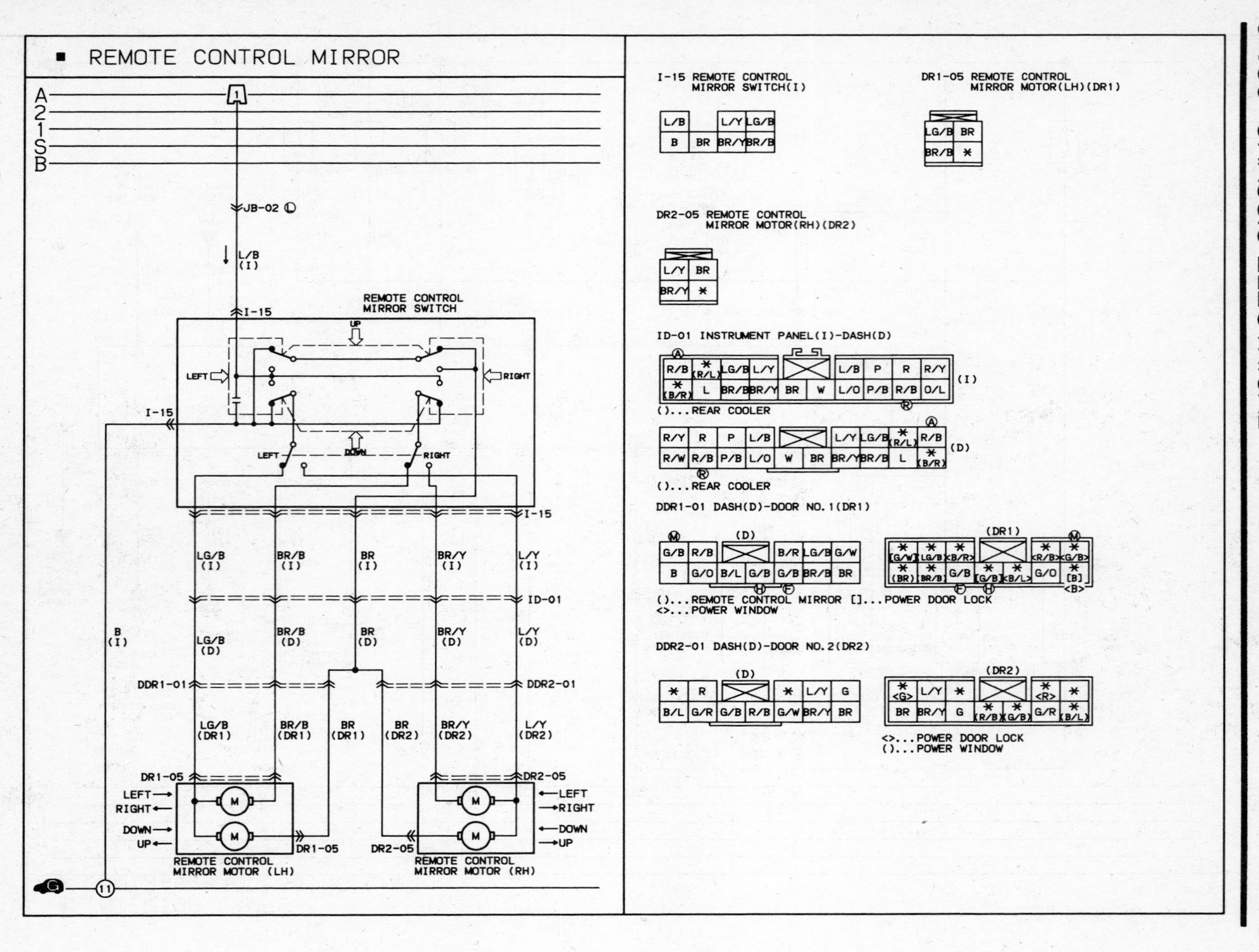

1989 MPV remote control mirror

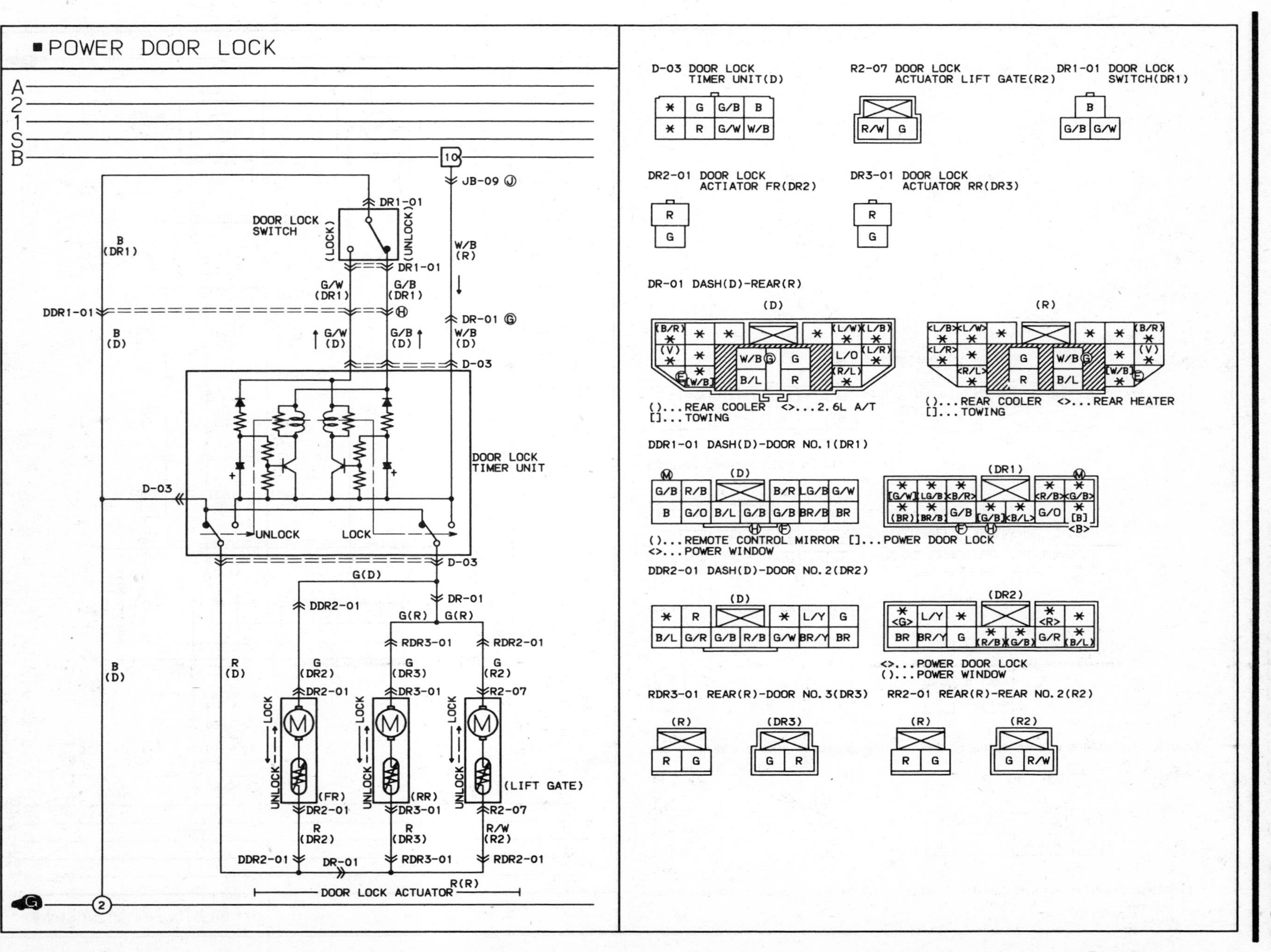

1989 MPV power door lock

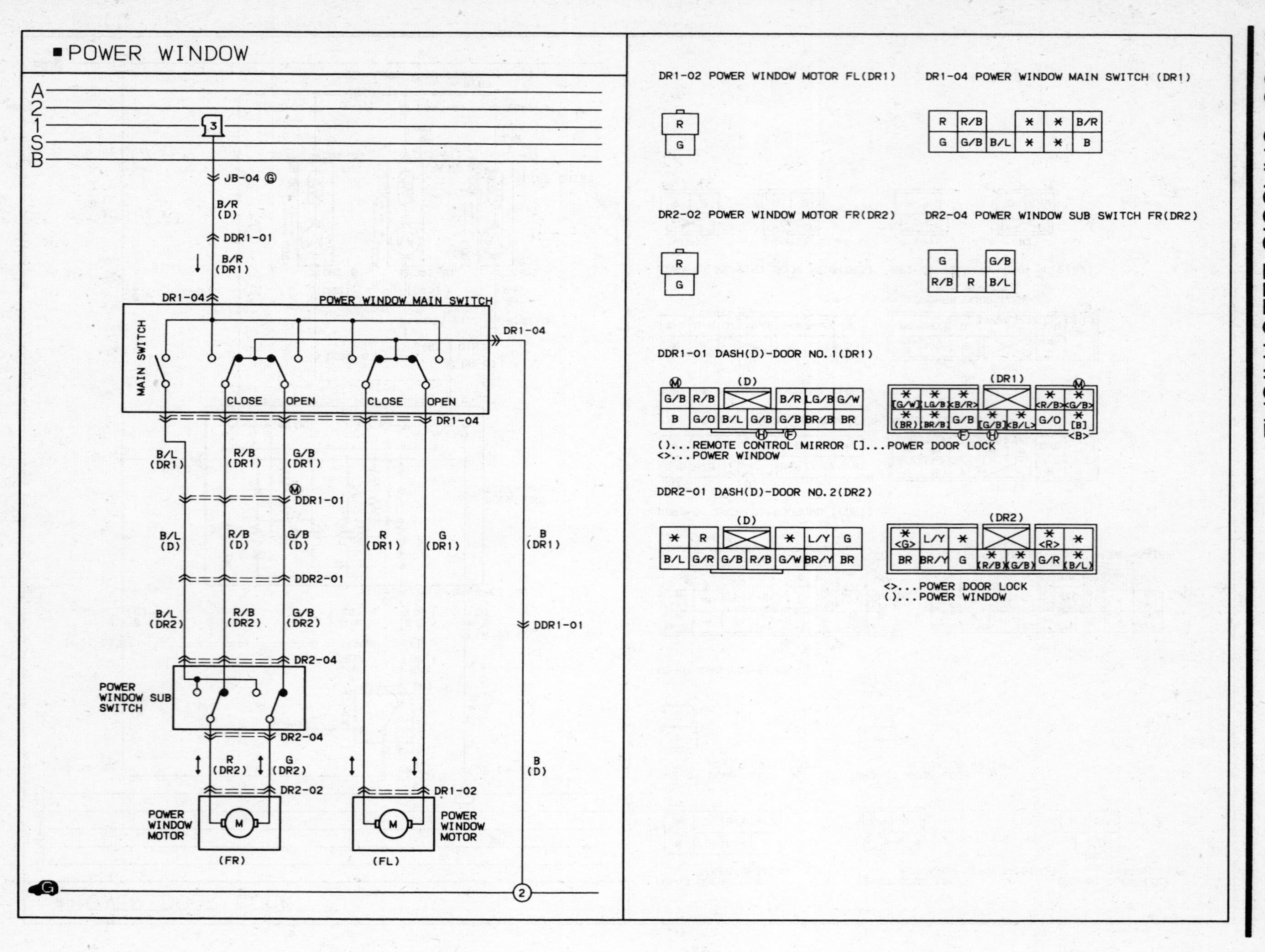

1989 MPV power window

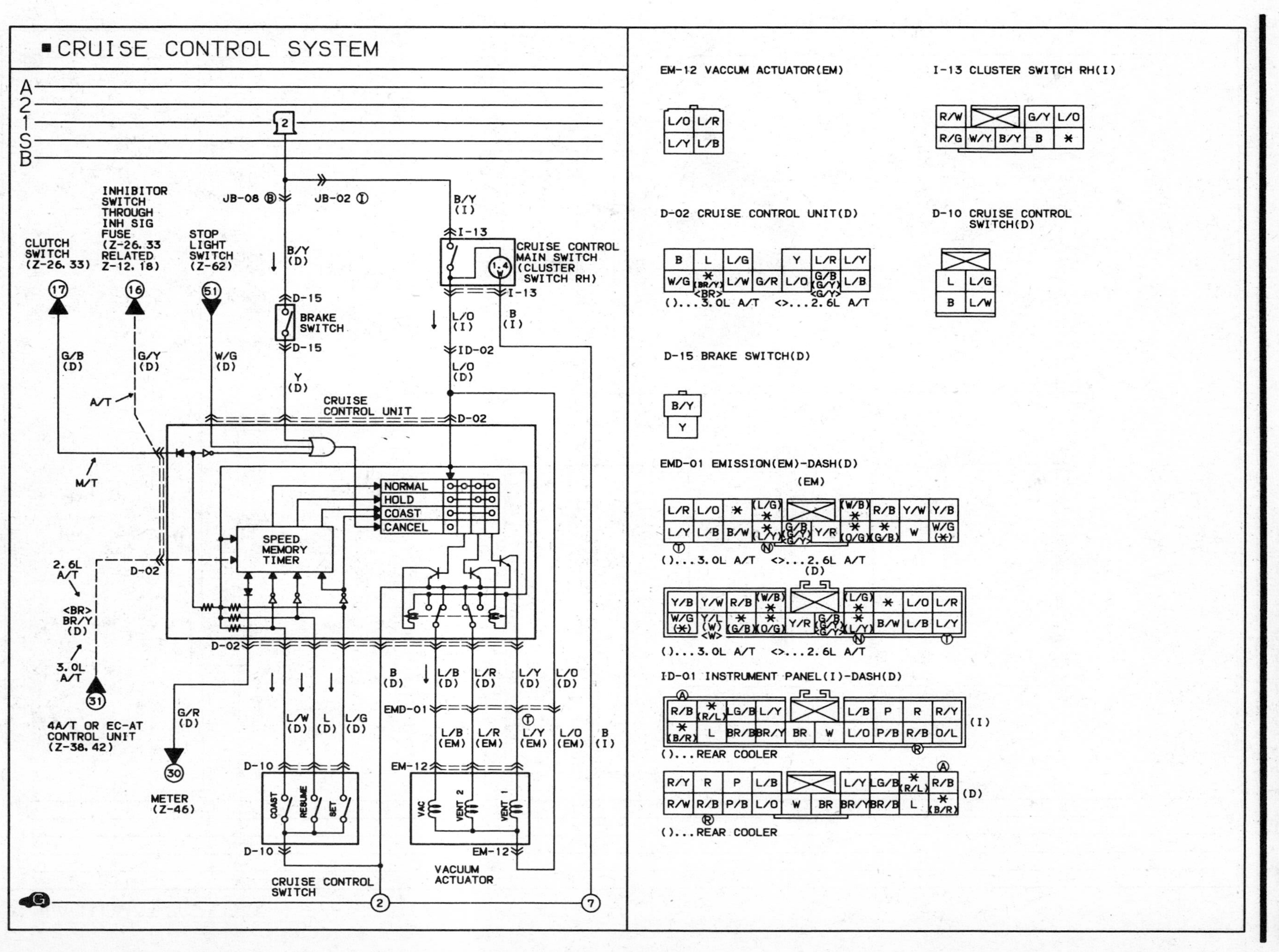

1989 MPV cruise control system

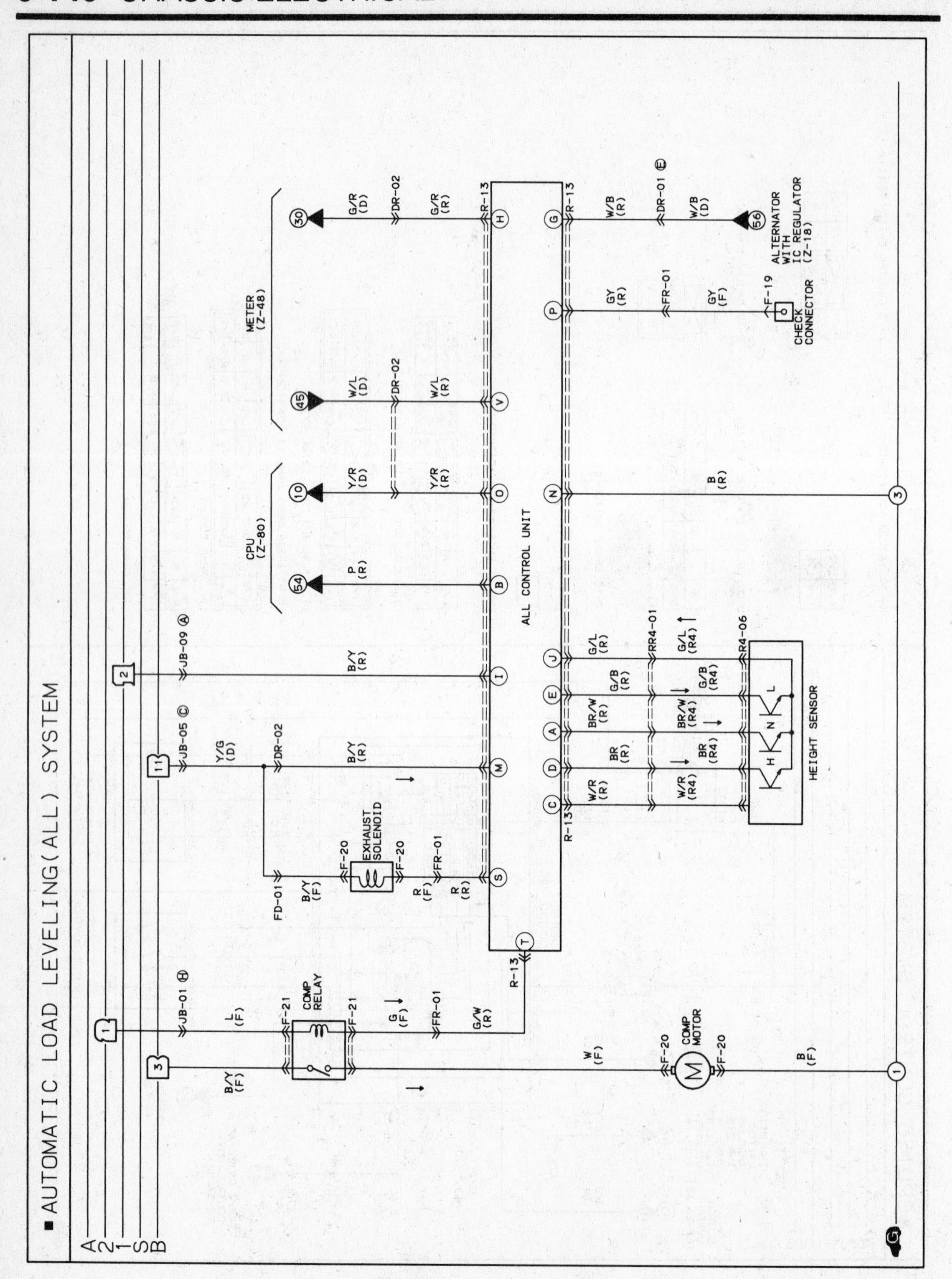

1989 MPV automatic load leveling system

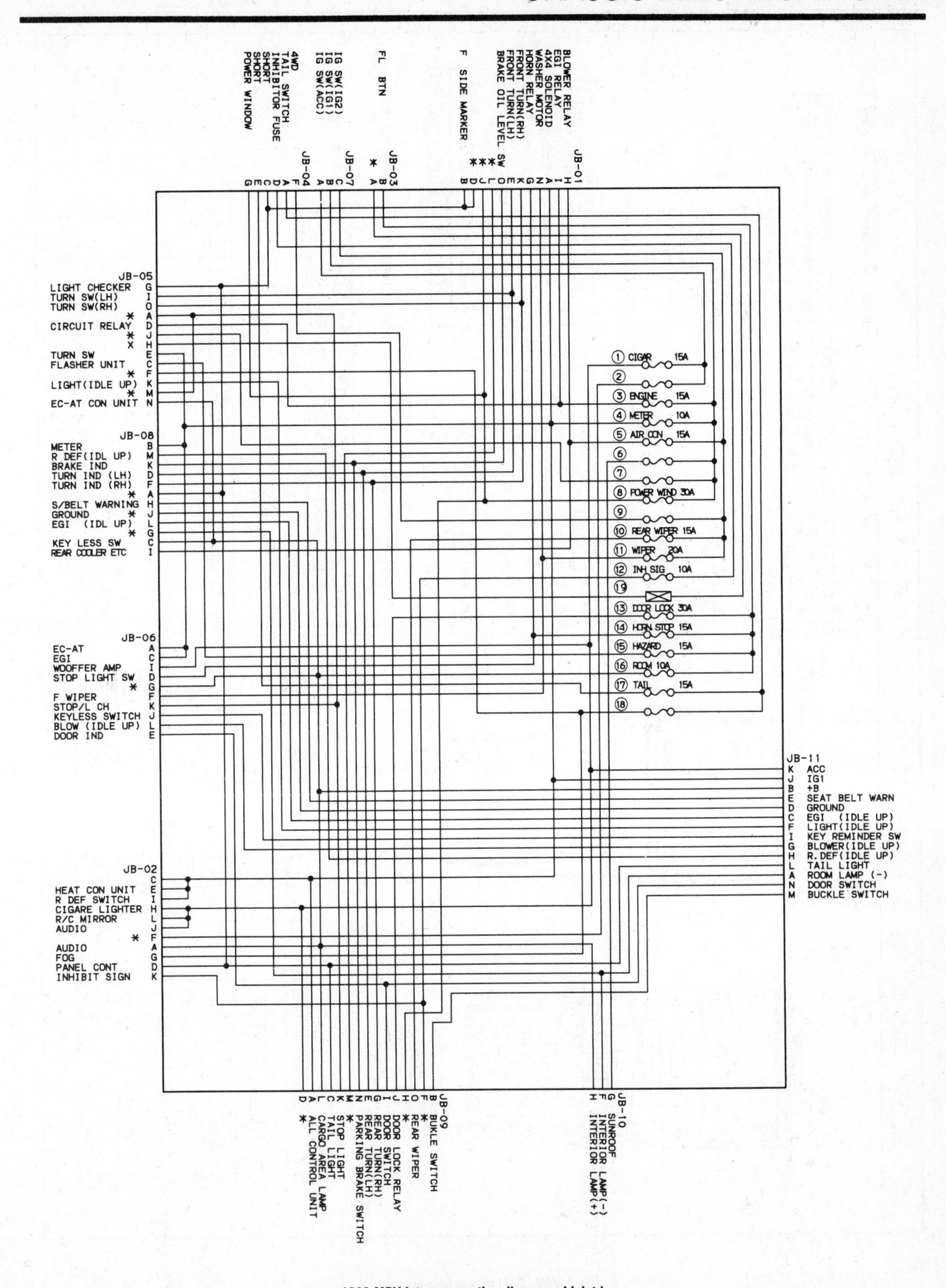

1989 MPV inter connecting diagram of joint box

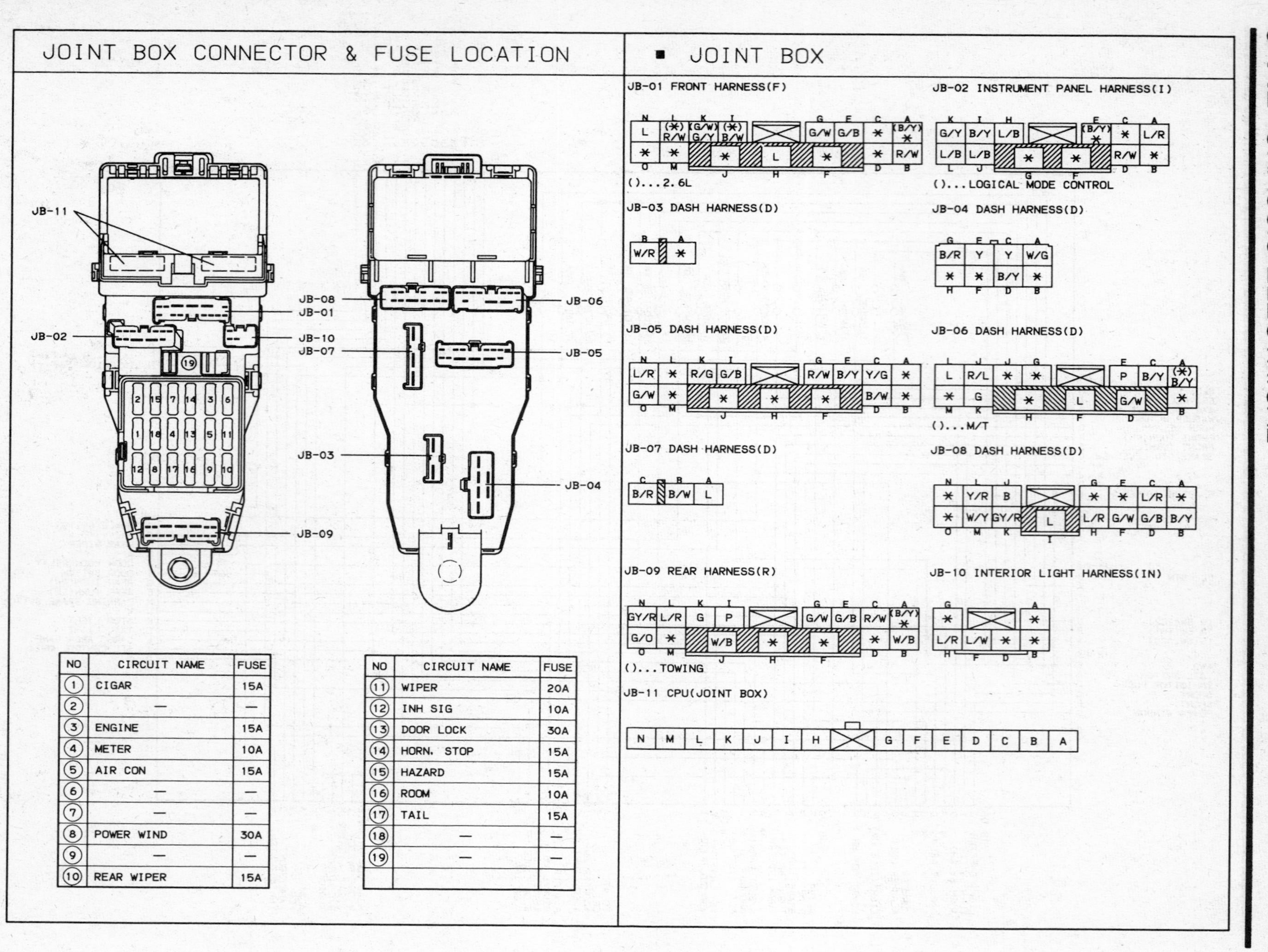

NO	CIRCUIT NAME	FUSE
1	CIGAR	15A
2	—	—
3	ENGINE	15A
4	METER	10A
5	AIR CON	15A
6	—	—
7	—	—
8	POWER WIND	30A
9	—	—
10	REAR WIPER	15A

NO	CIRCUIT NAME	FUSE
11	WIPER	20A
12	INH SIG	10A
13	DOOR LOCK	30A
14	HORN, STOP	15A
15	HAZARD	15A
16	ROOM	10A
17	TAIL	15A
18	—	—
19	—	—

1989 MPV joint box and fuse location

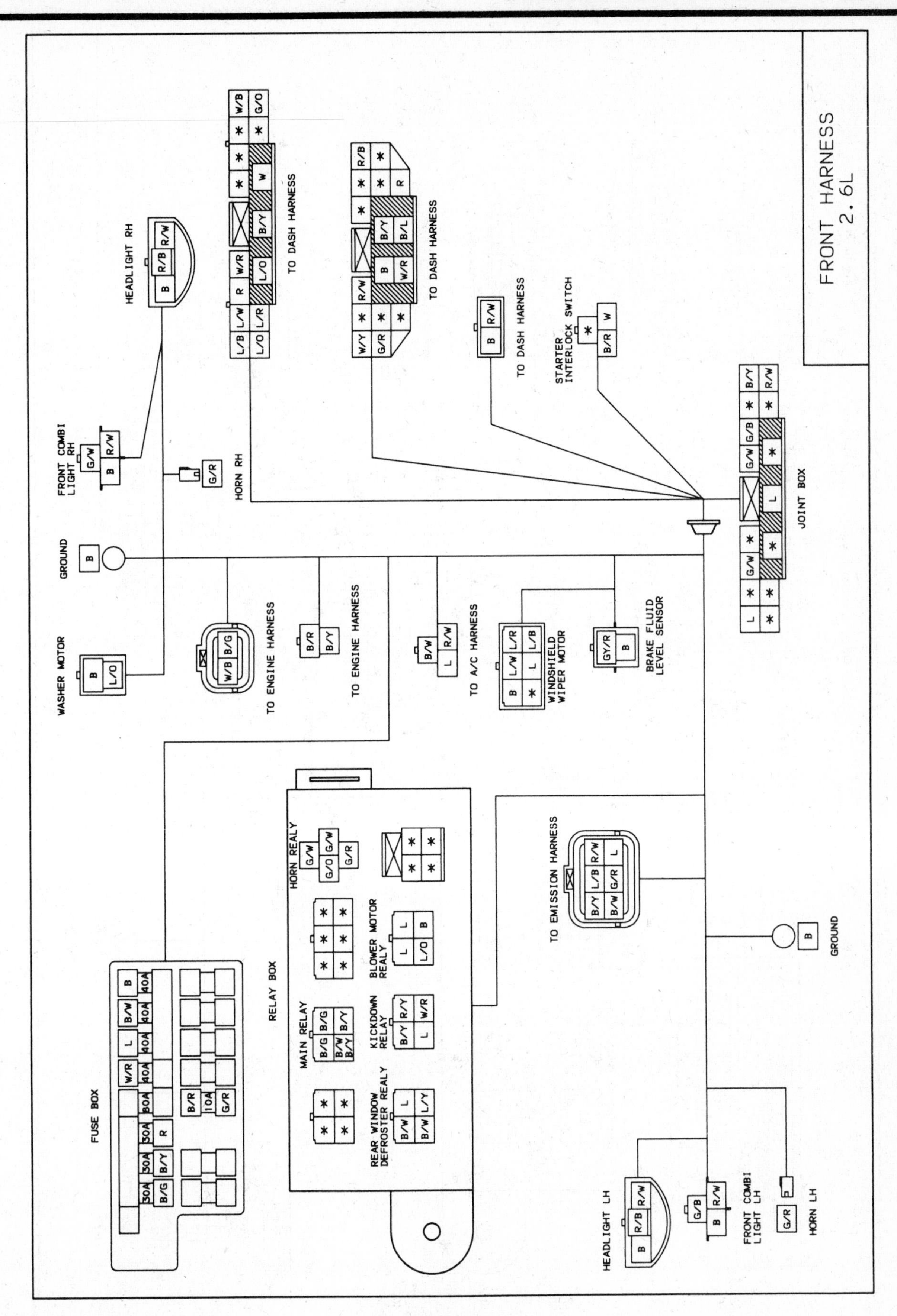

1989 MPV 2.6L front harness

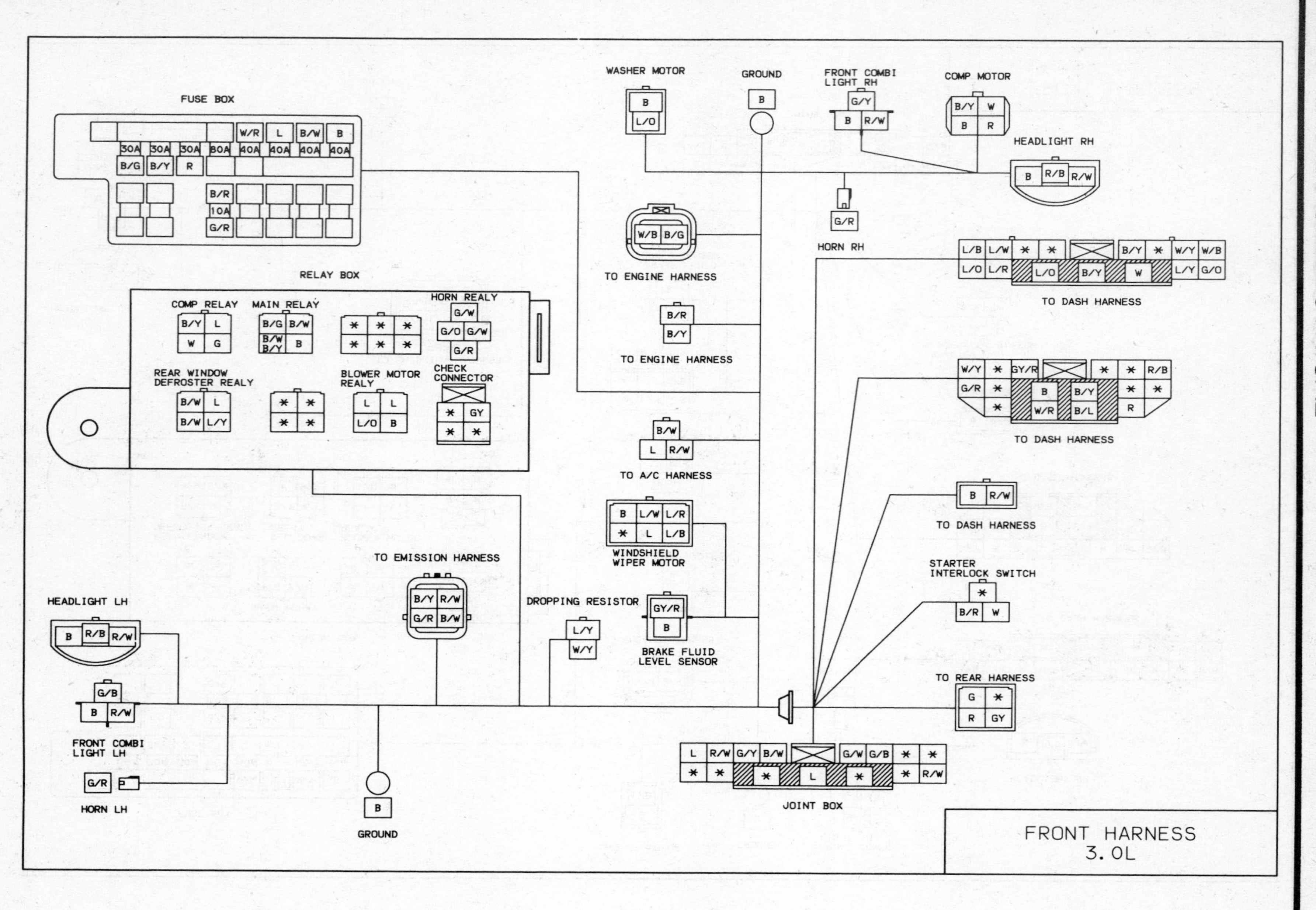

1989 MPV 3.0L front harness

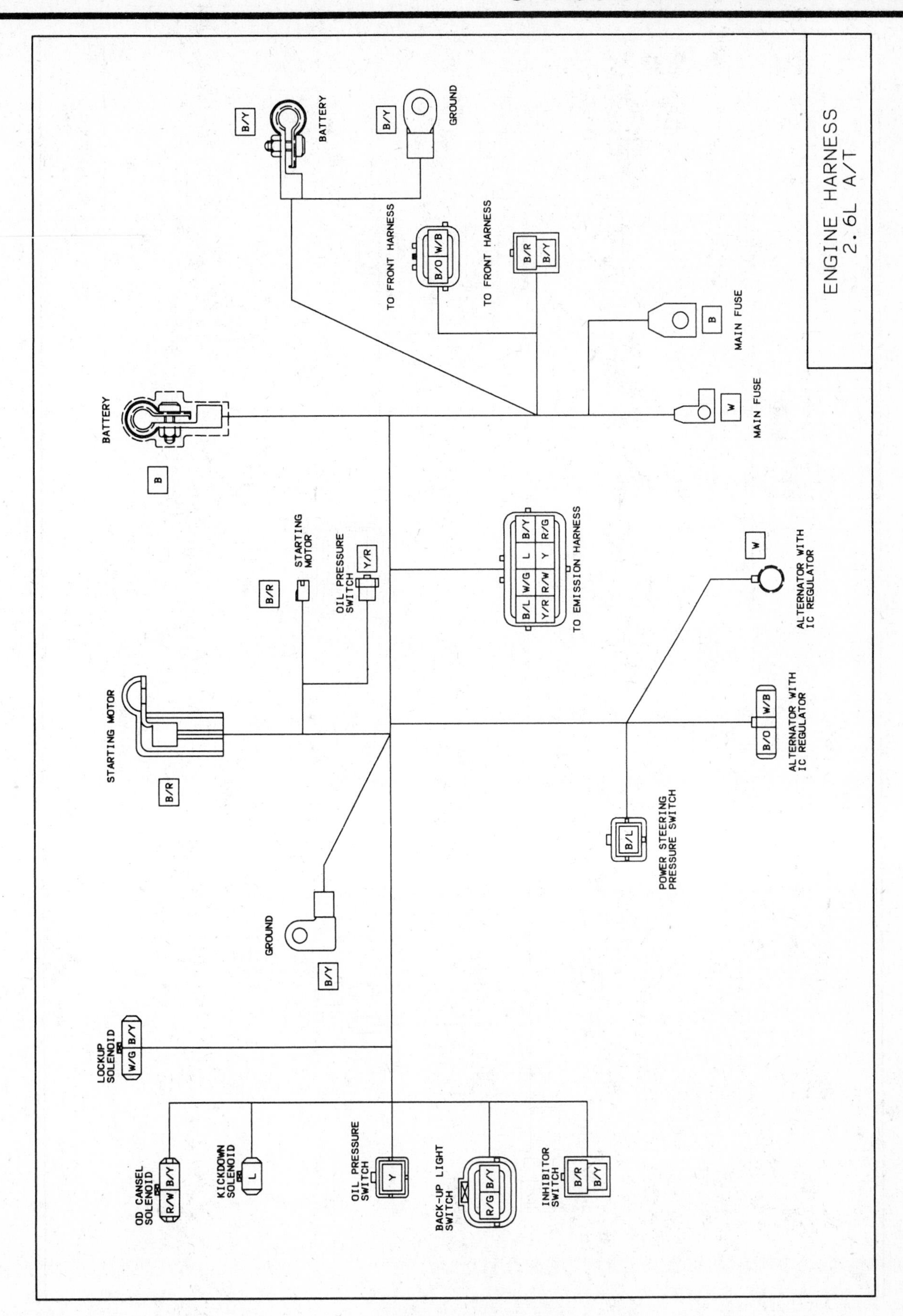

1989 MPV 2.6L AT engine harness

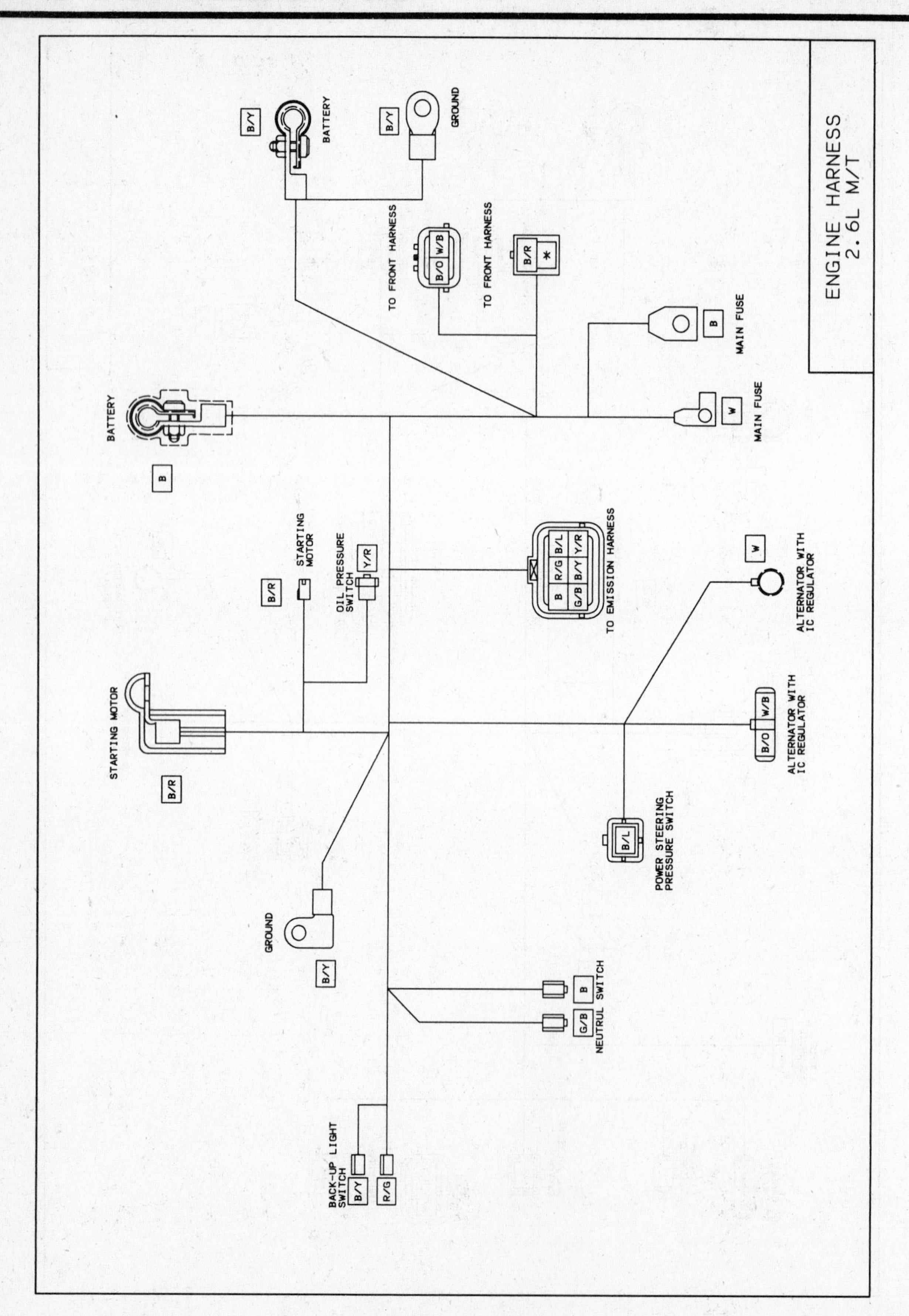

1989 MPV 2.6L MT engine harness

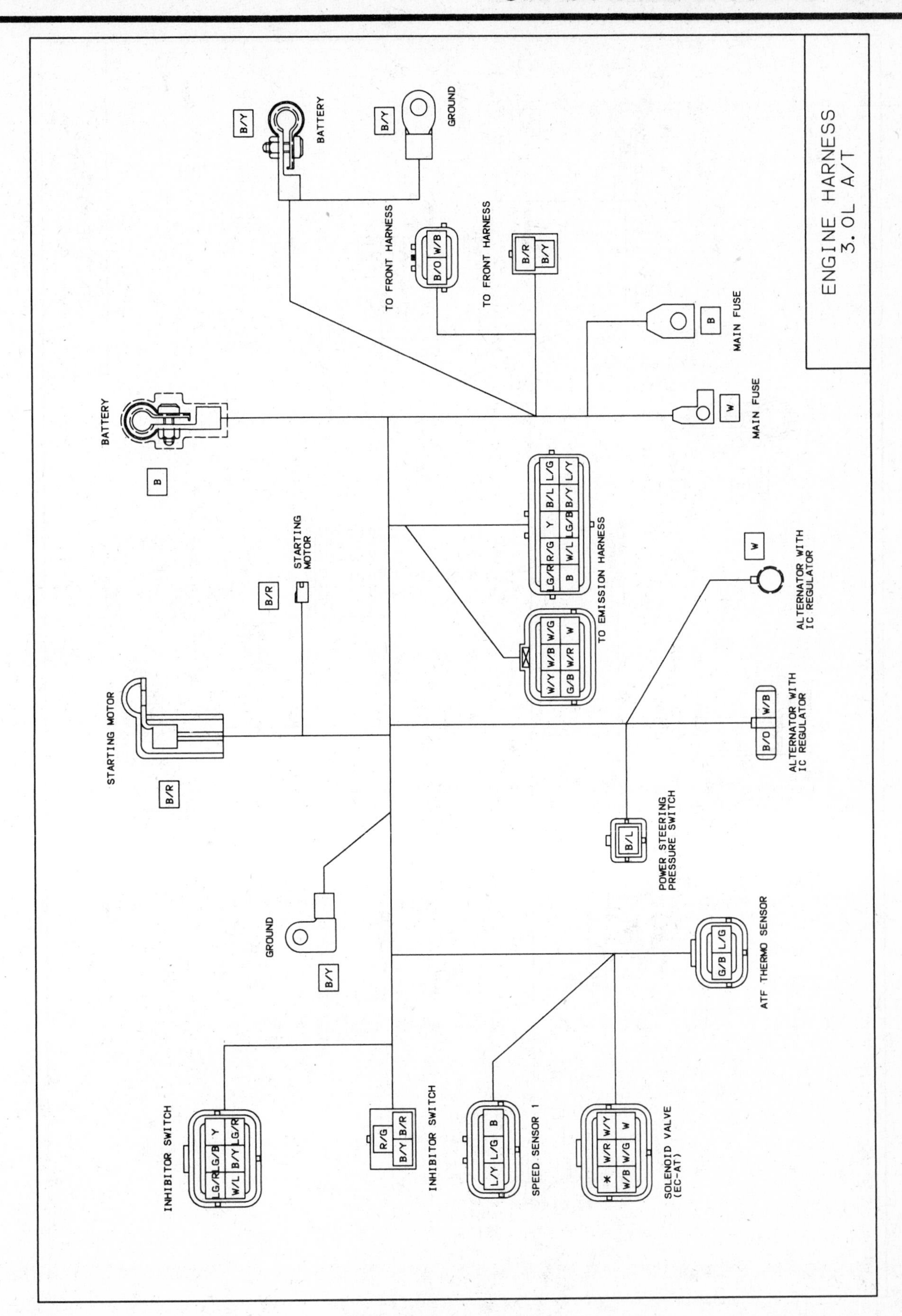

1989 MPV 3.0L AT engine harness

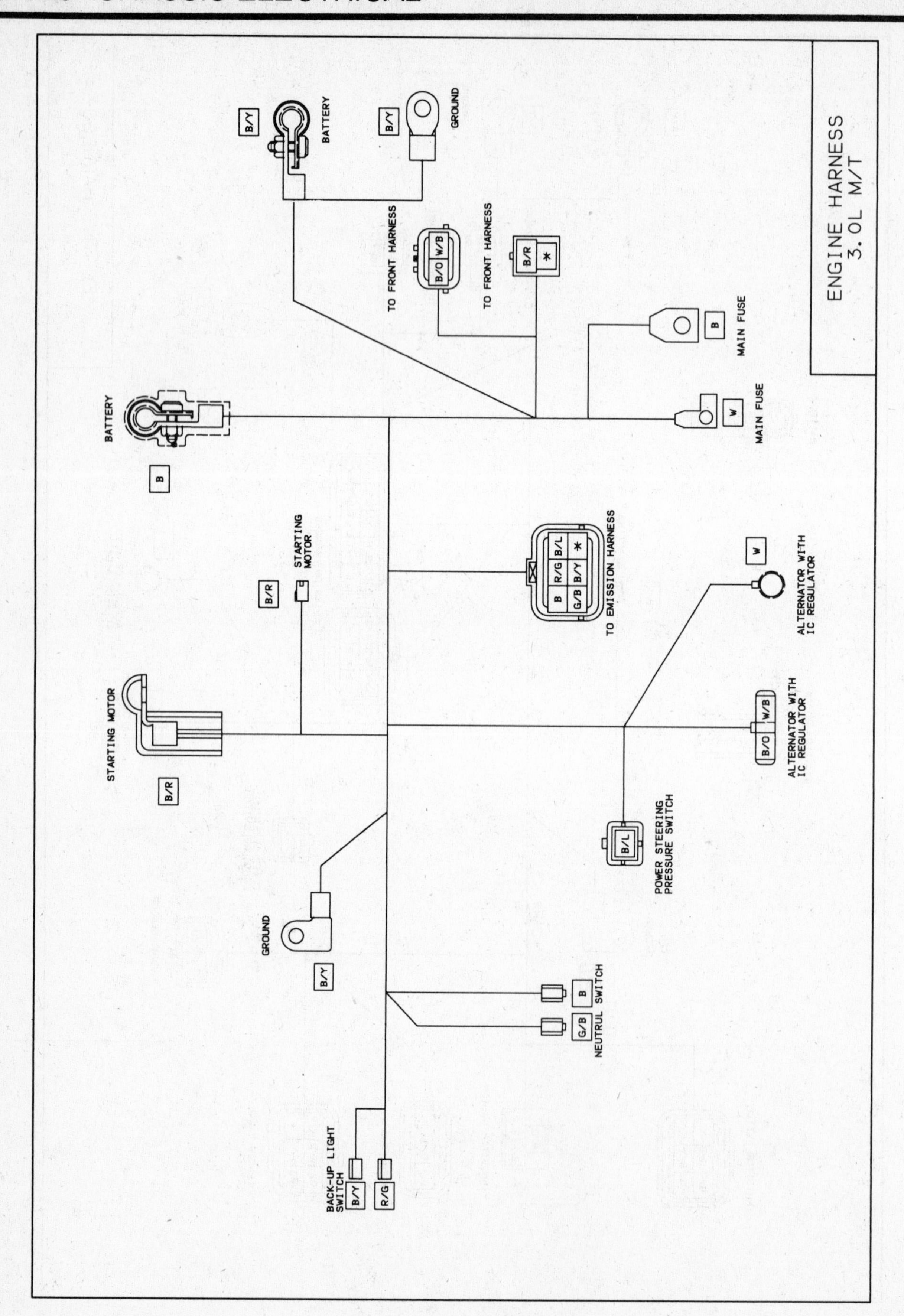

1989 MPV 3.0L MT engine harness

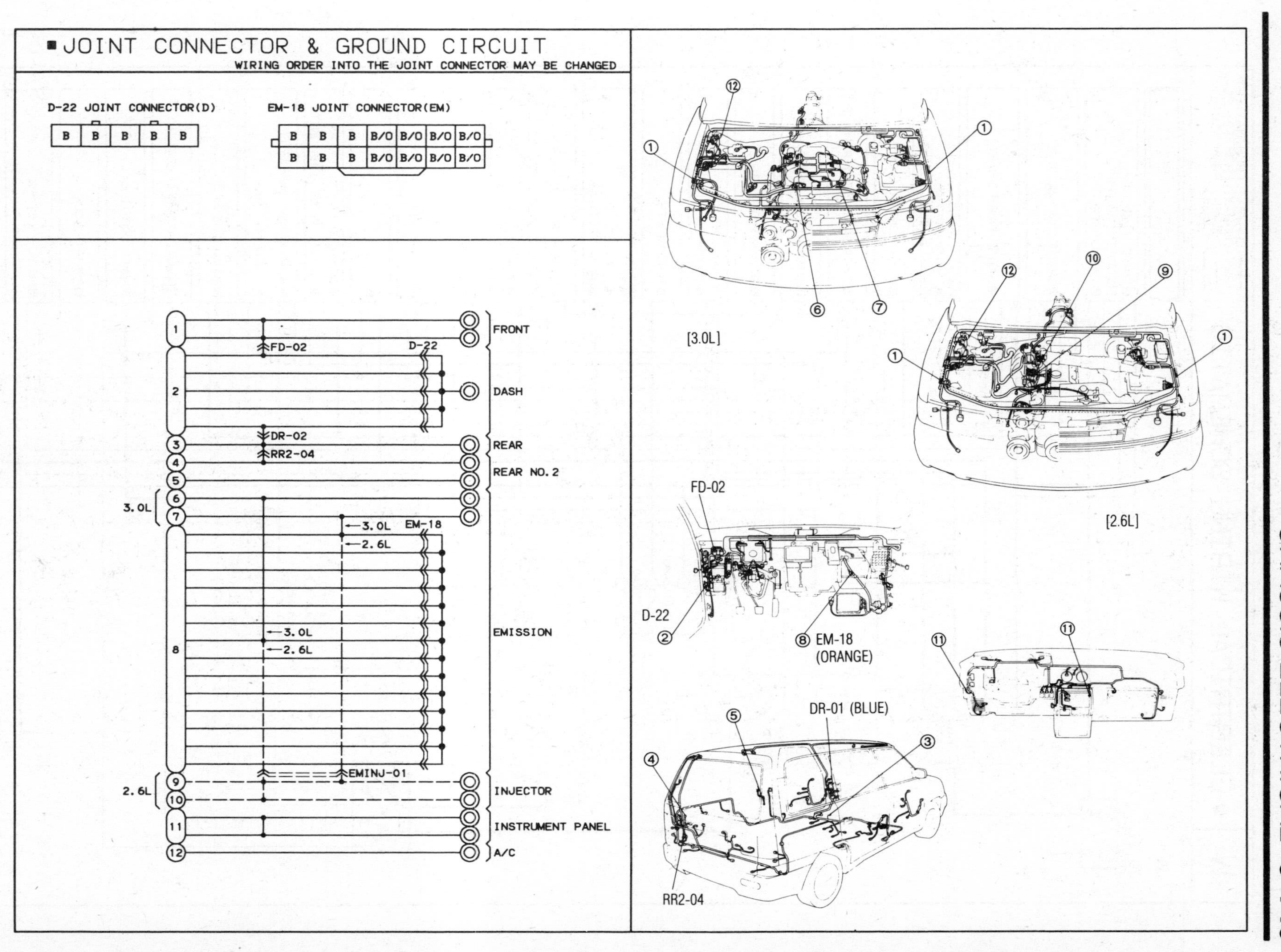

1989 MPV joint connector and ground circuit

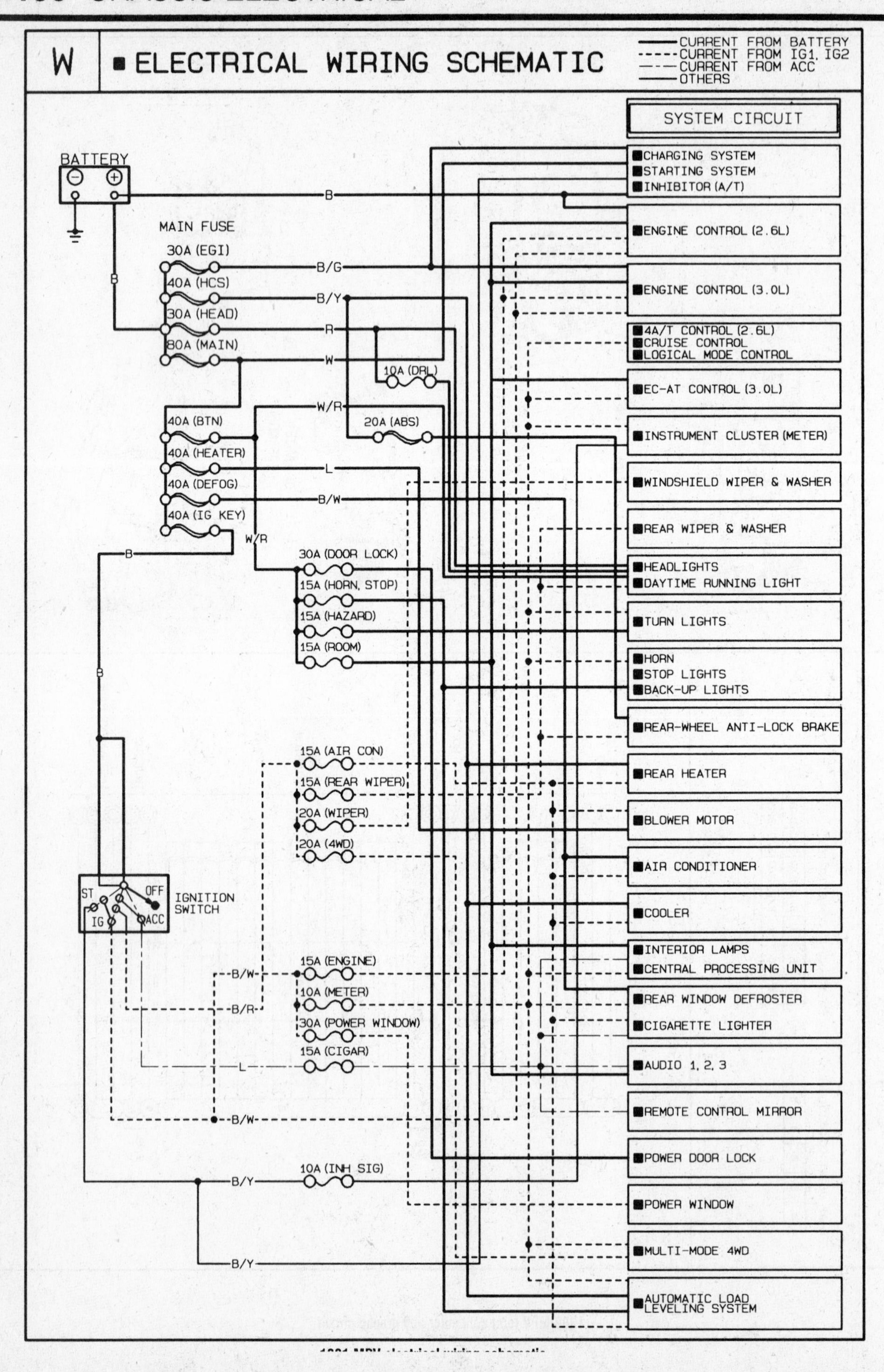

1991 MPV electrical wiring schematic

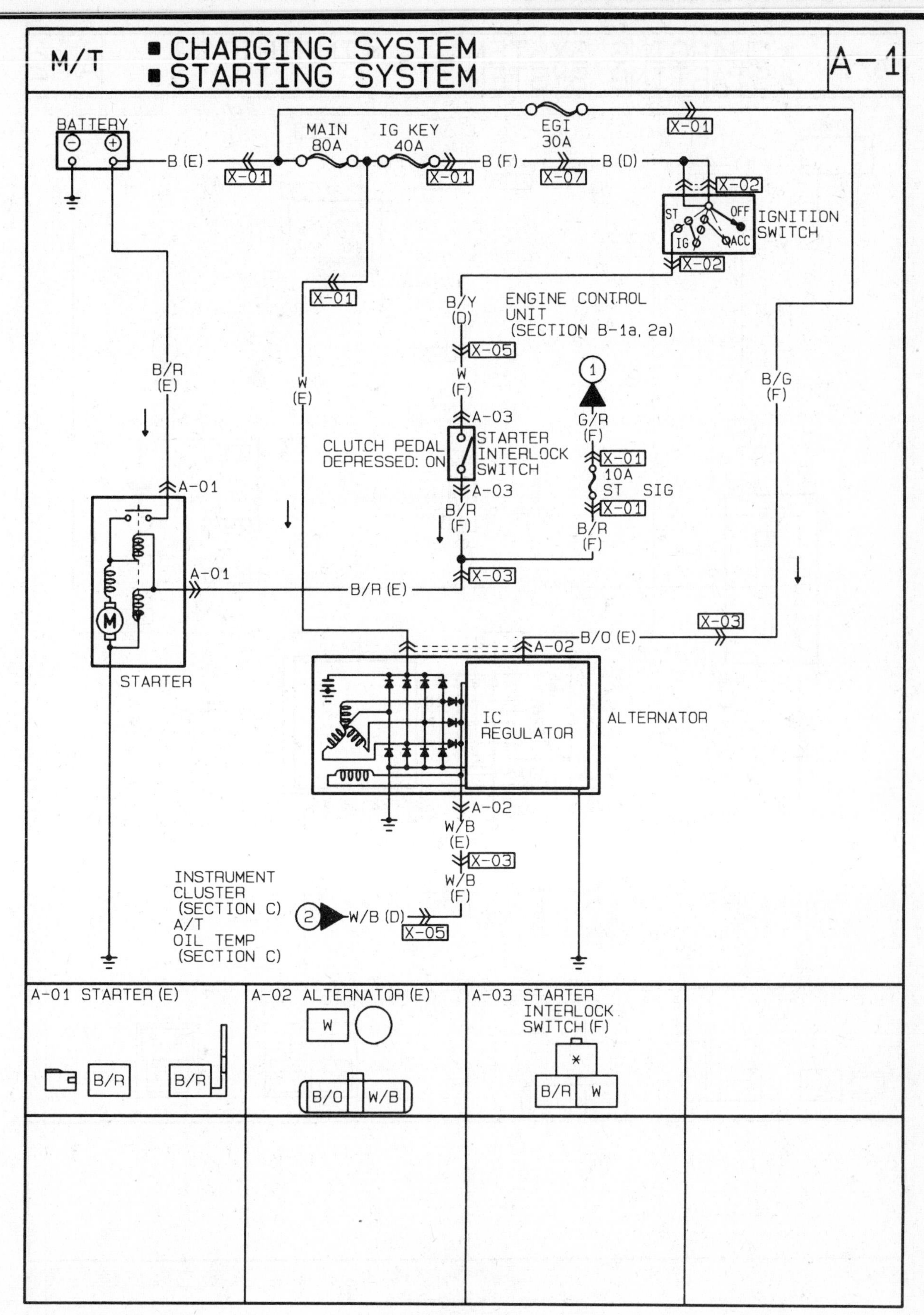

1991 MPV MT charging/starting systems

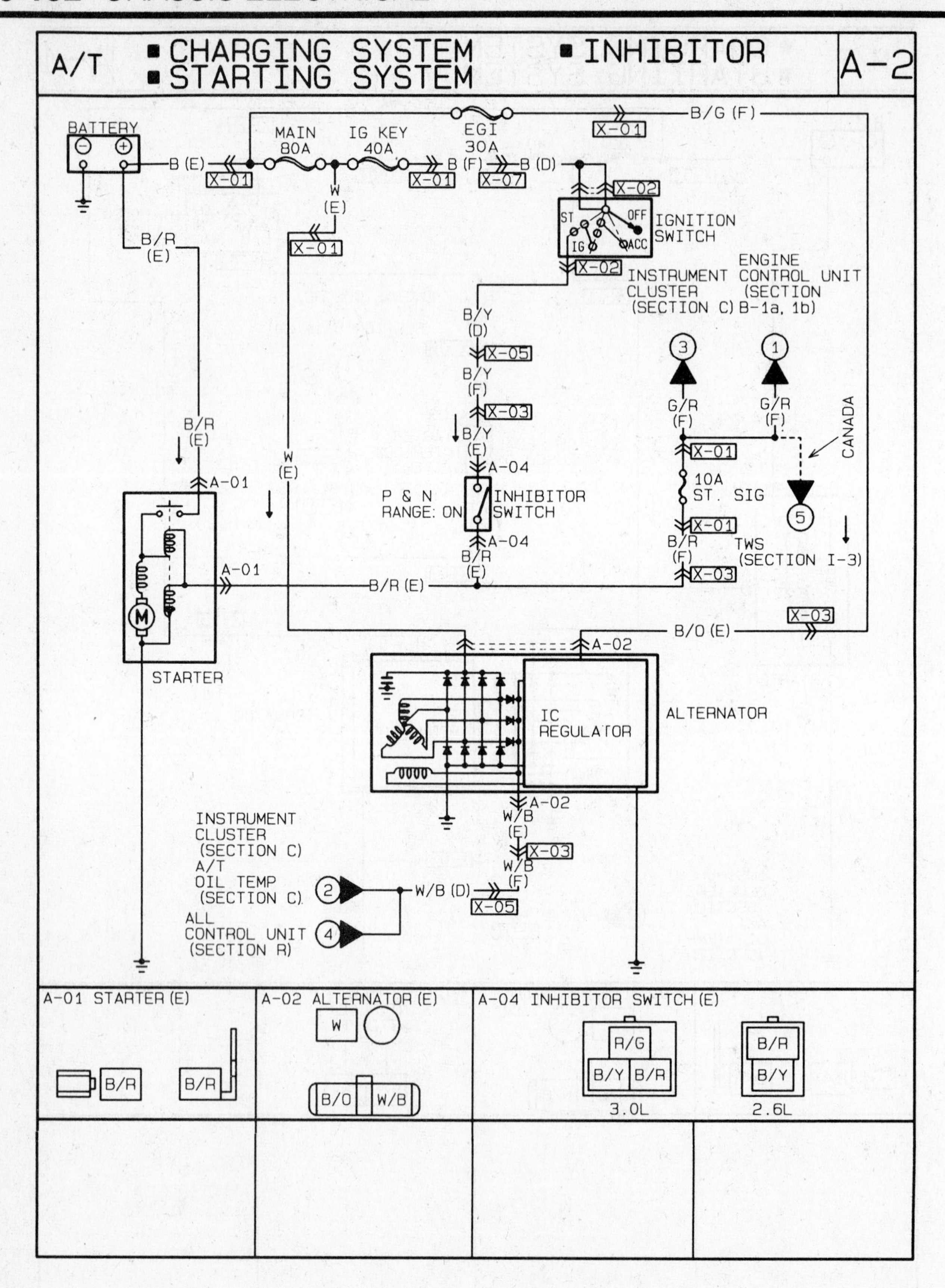

1991 MPV AT charging/starting systems

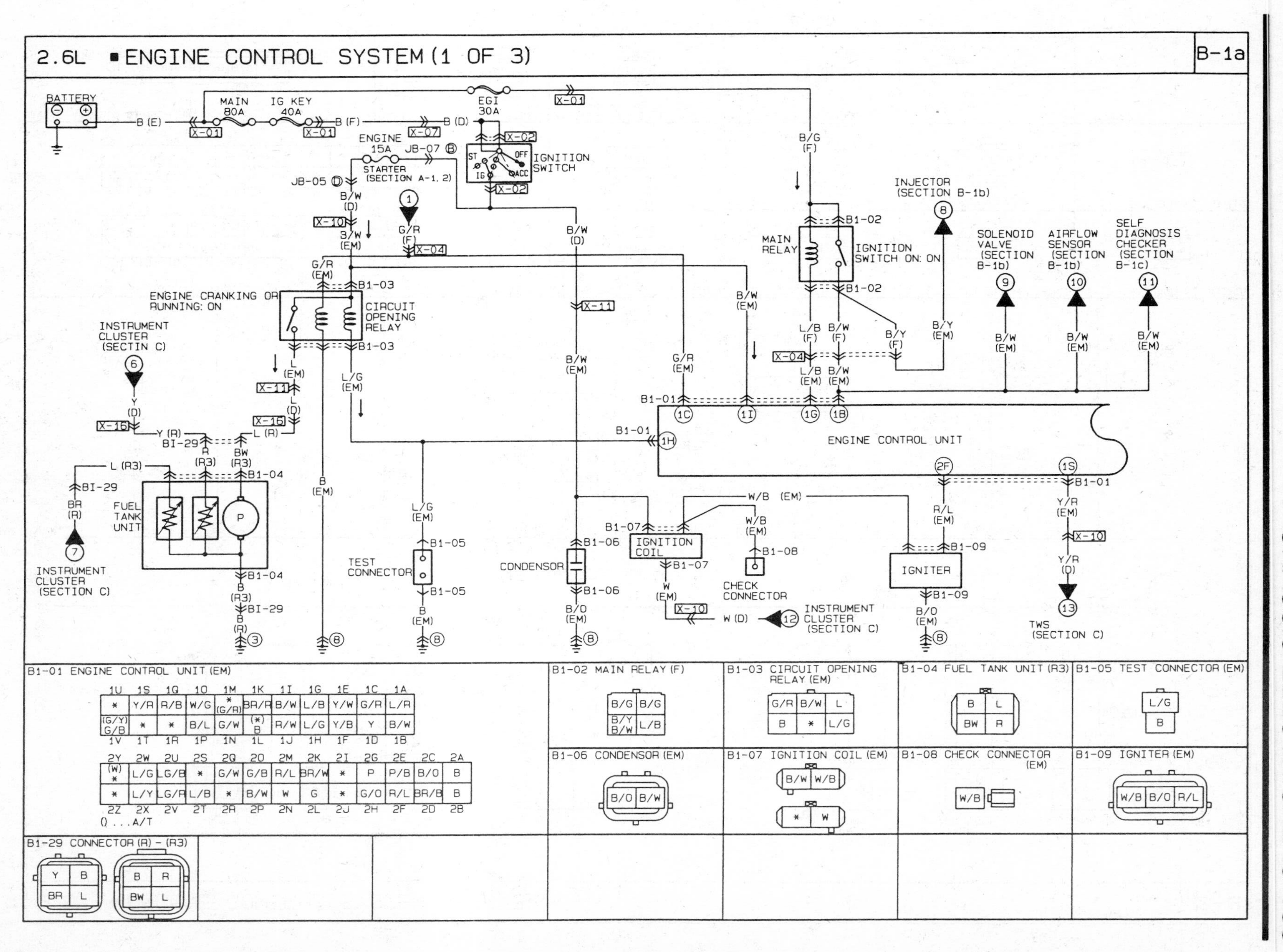

1991 MPV 2.6L engine control system

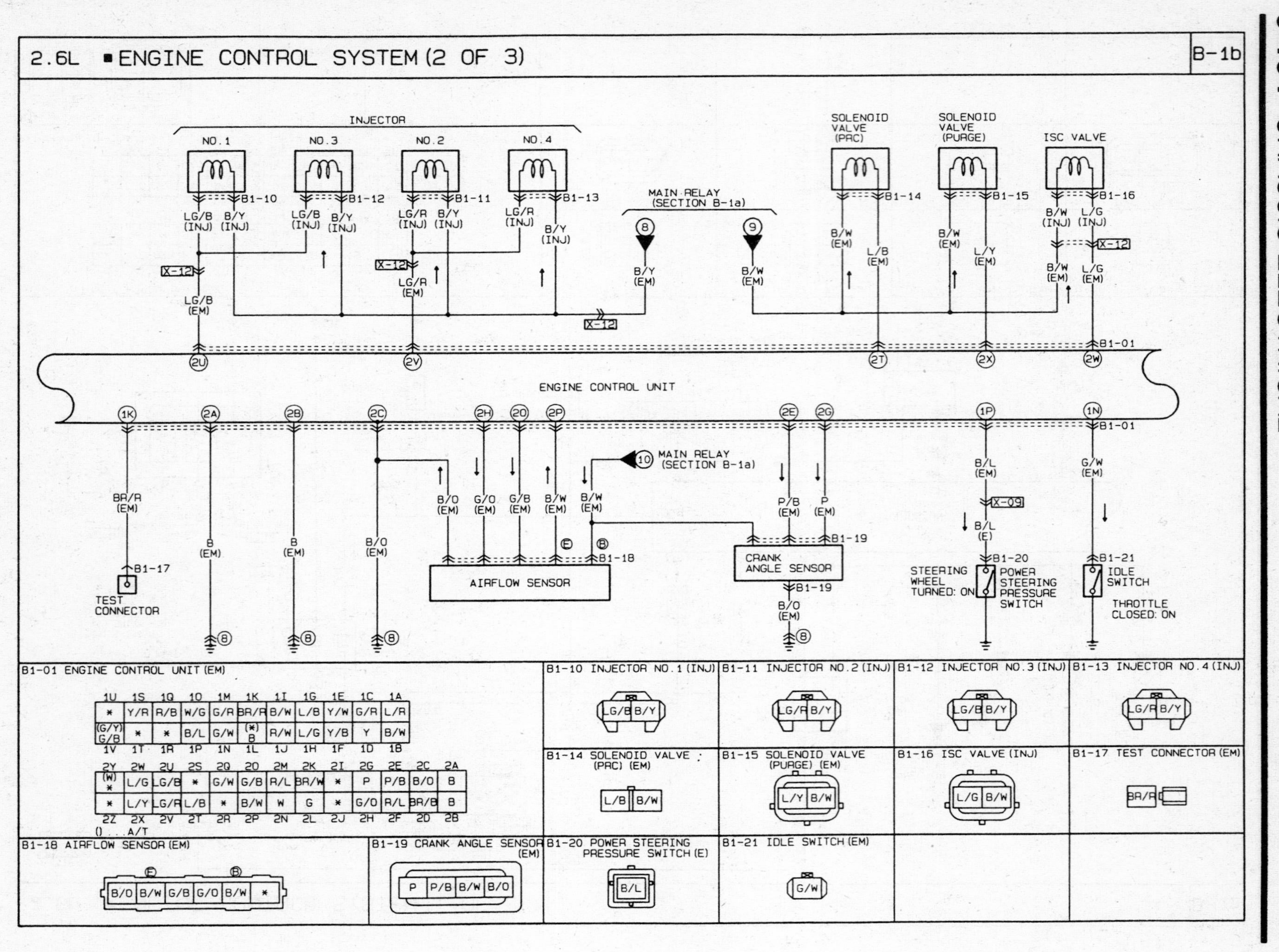

1991 MPV 2.6L engine control system

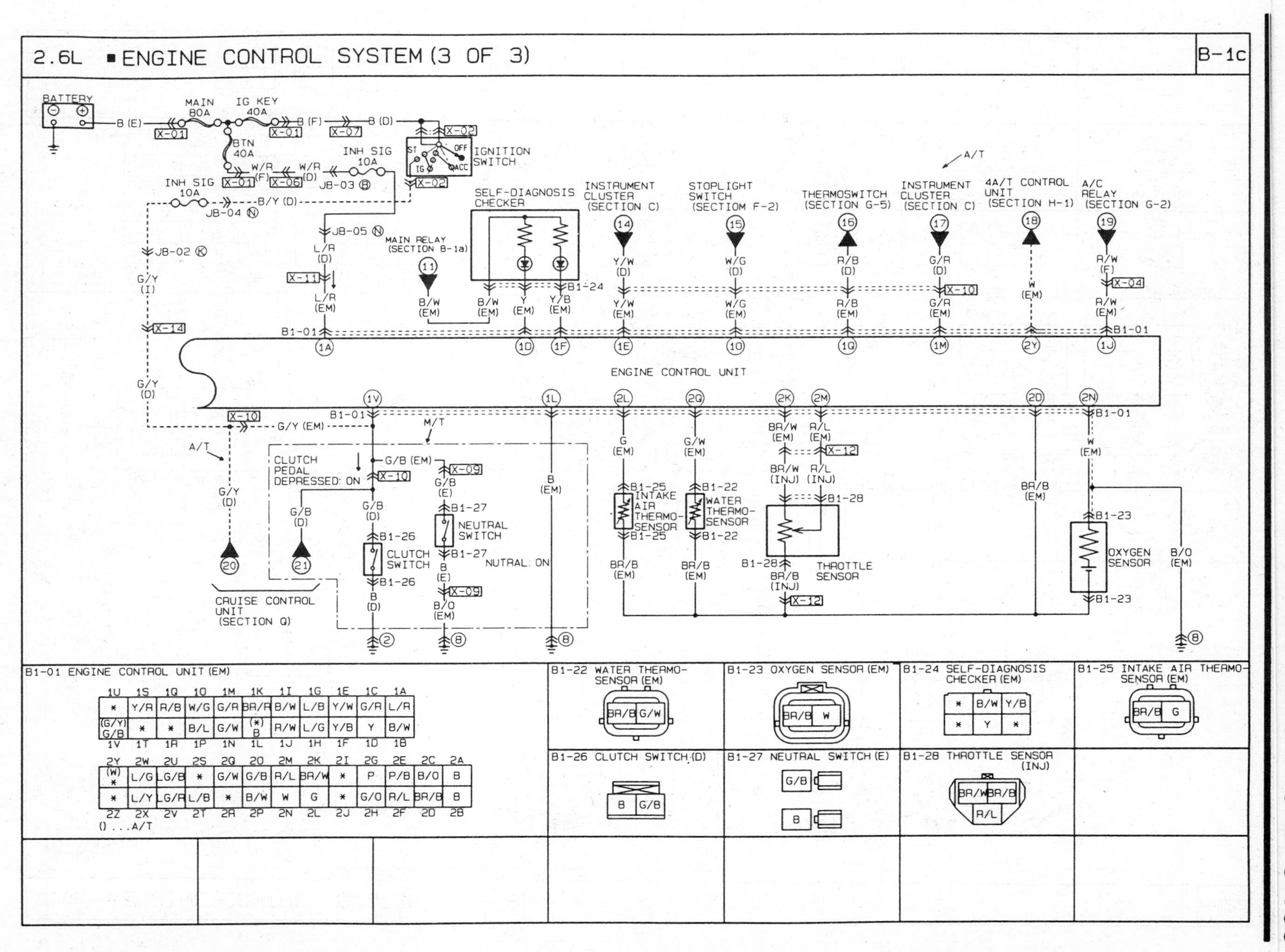

1991 MPV 2.6L engine control system

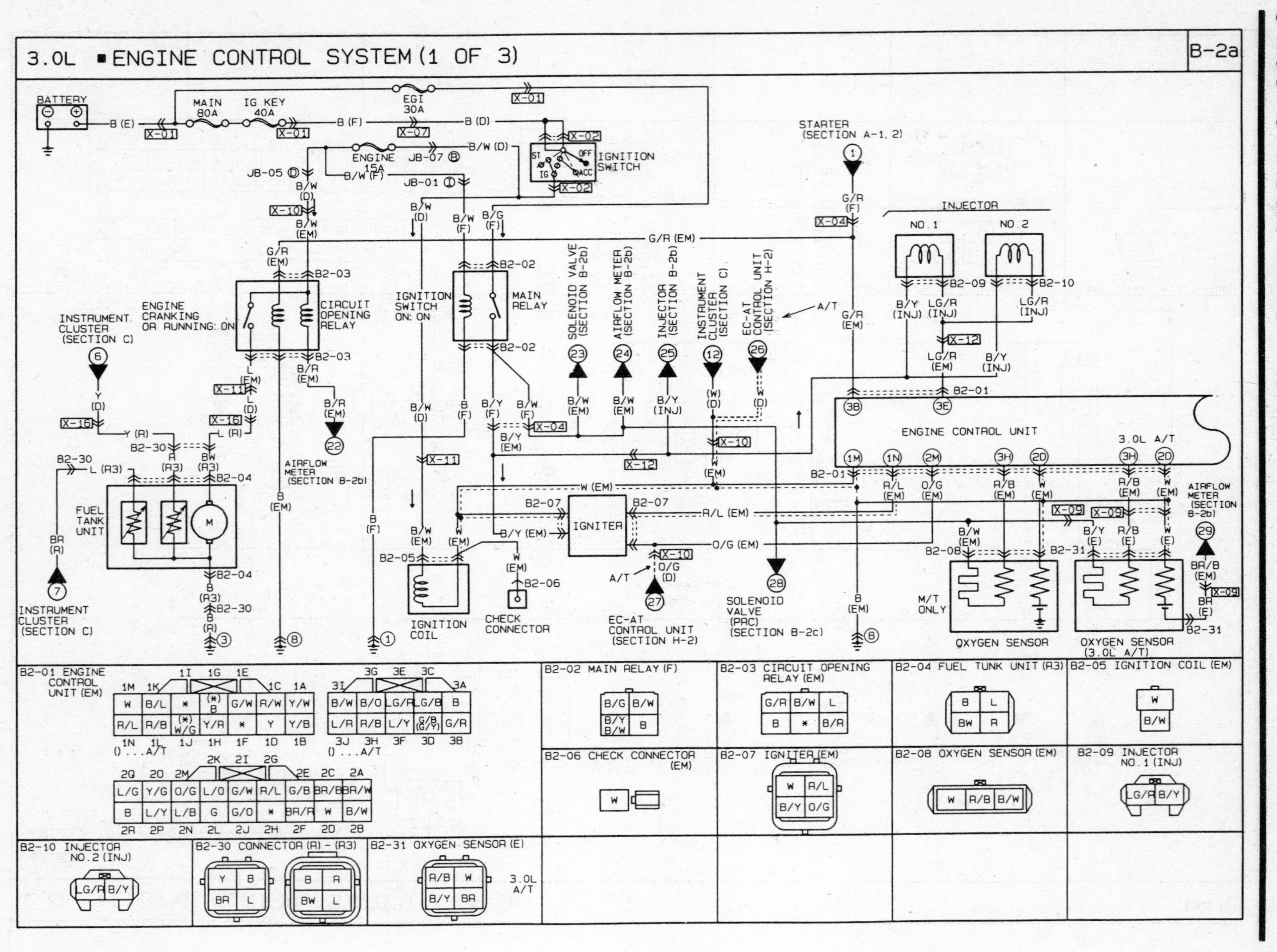

1991 3.0L engine control system

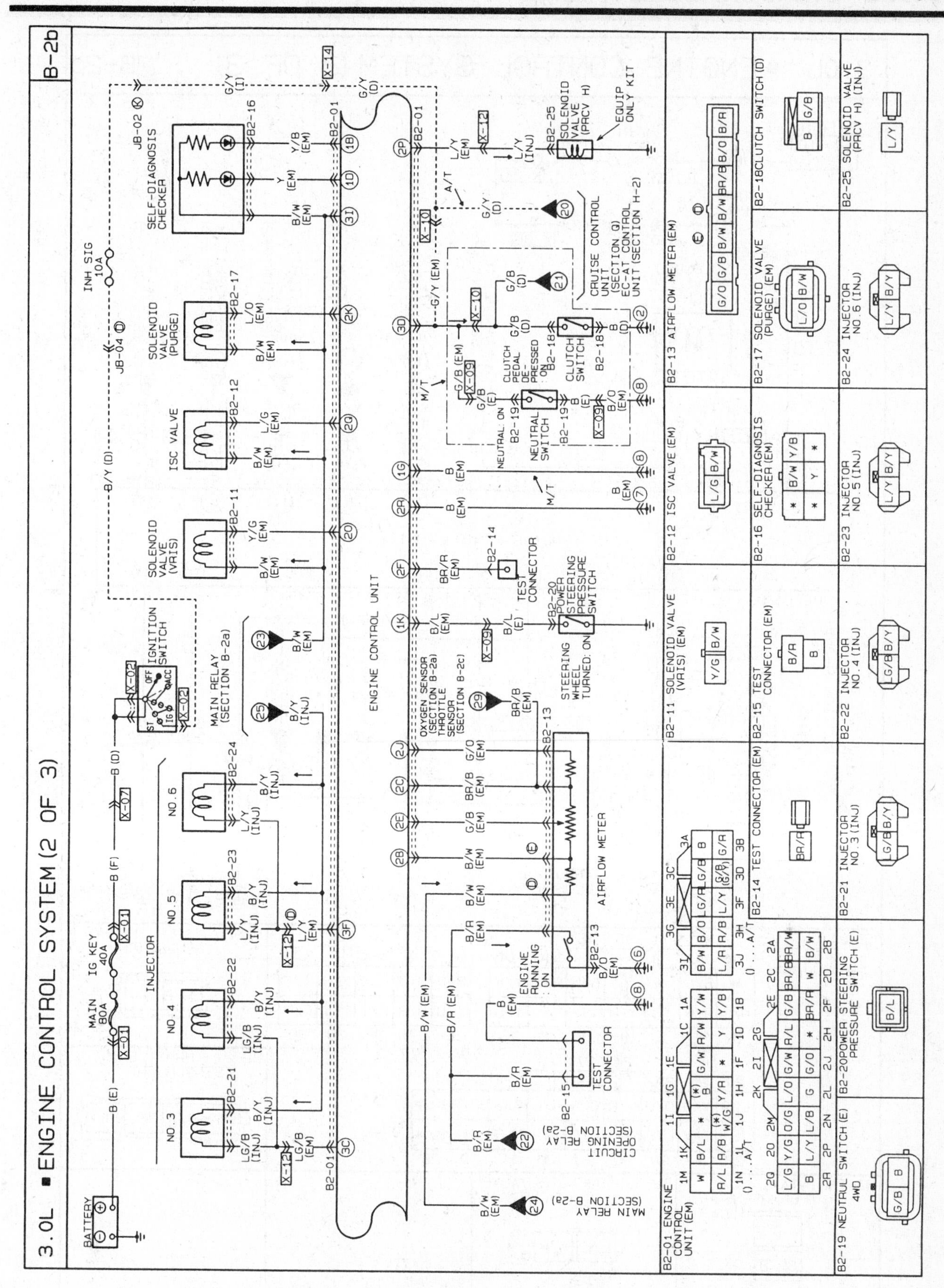

1991 3.0L engine control system

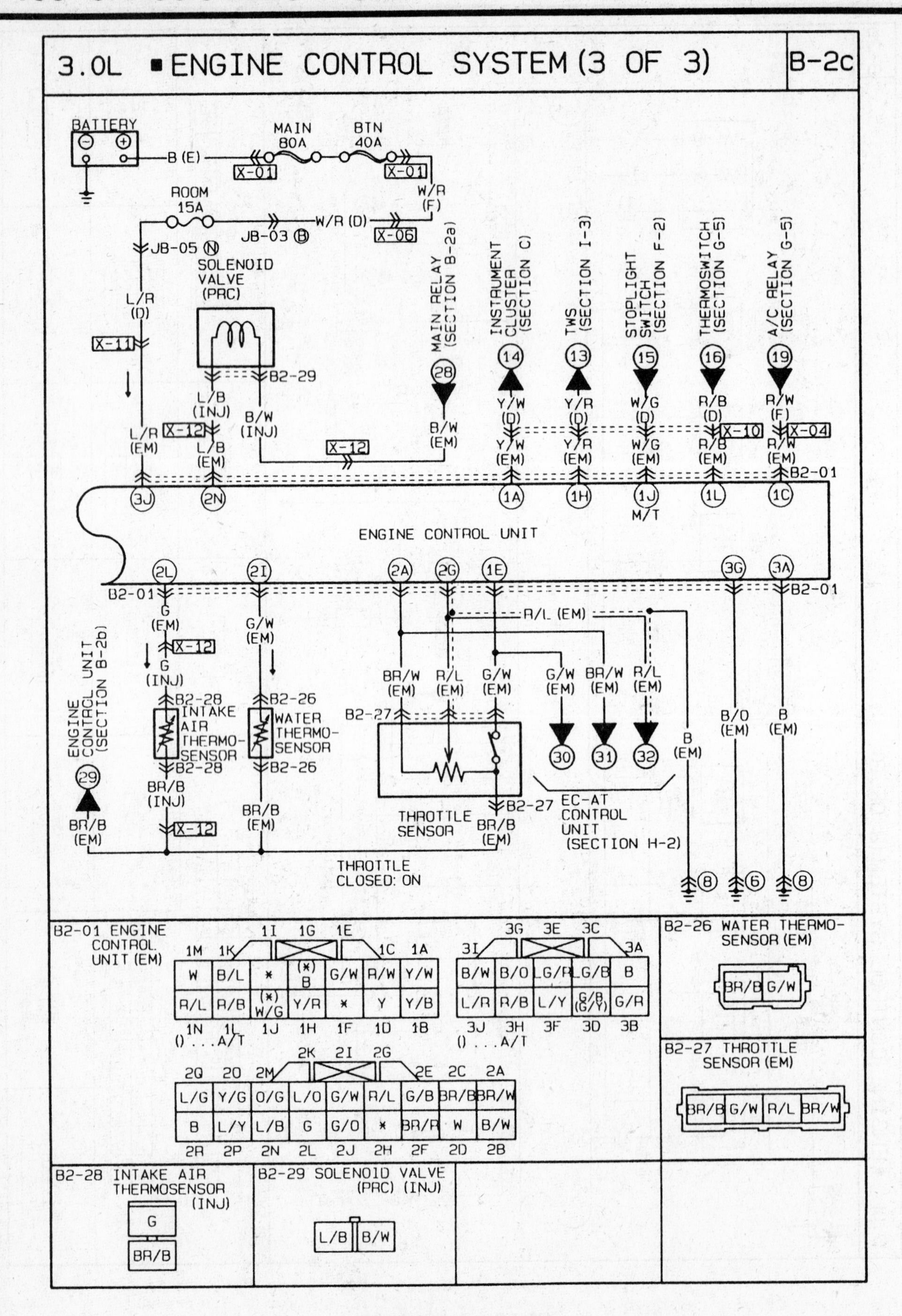

1991 3.0L engine control system

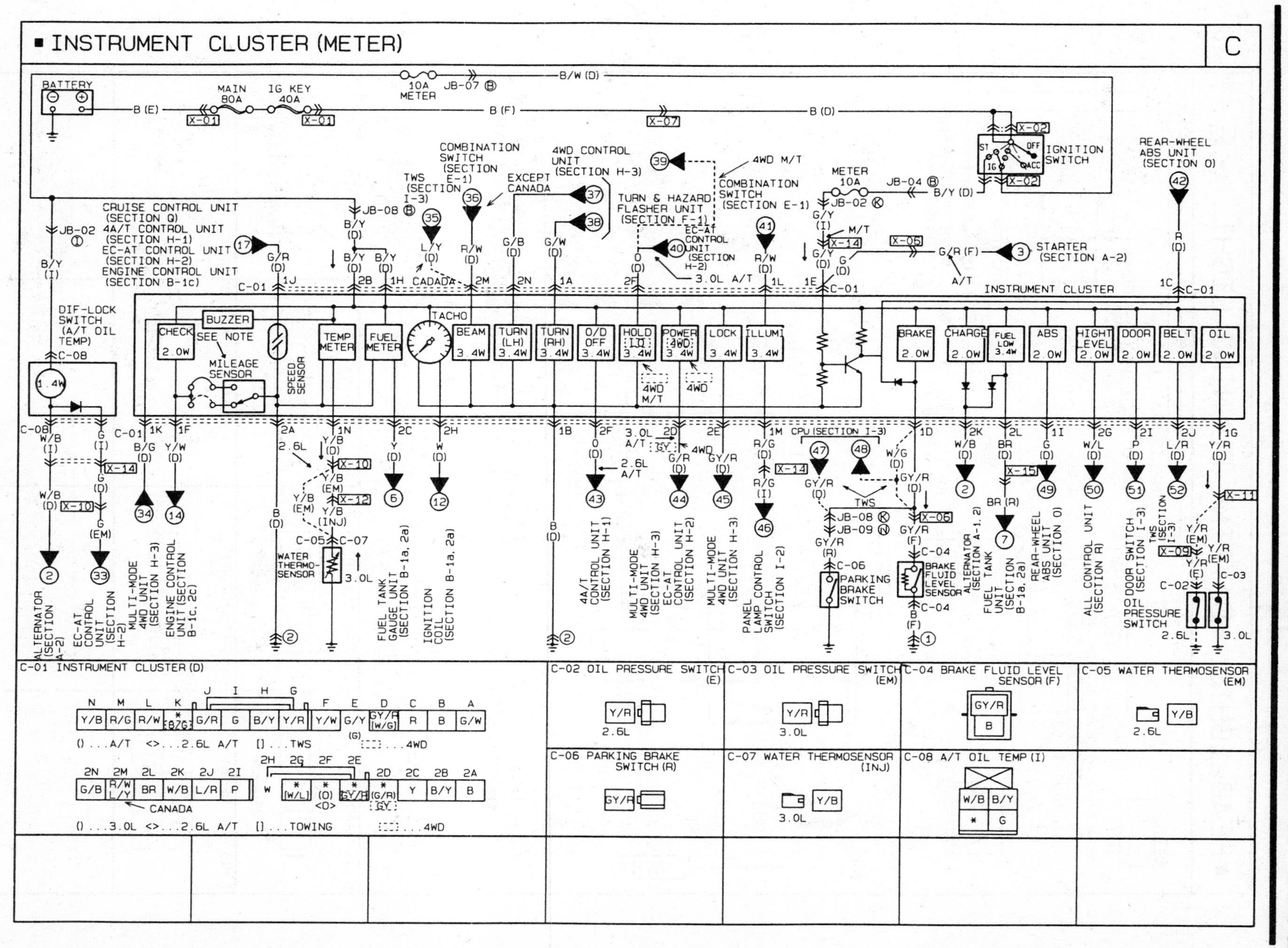

1991 MPV instrument cluster

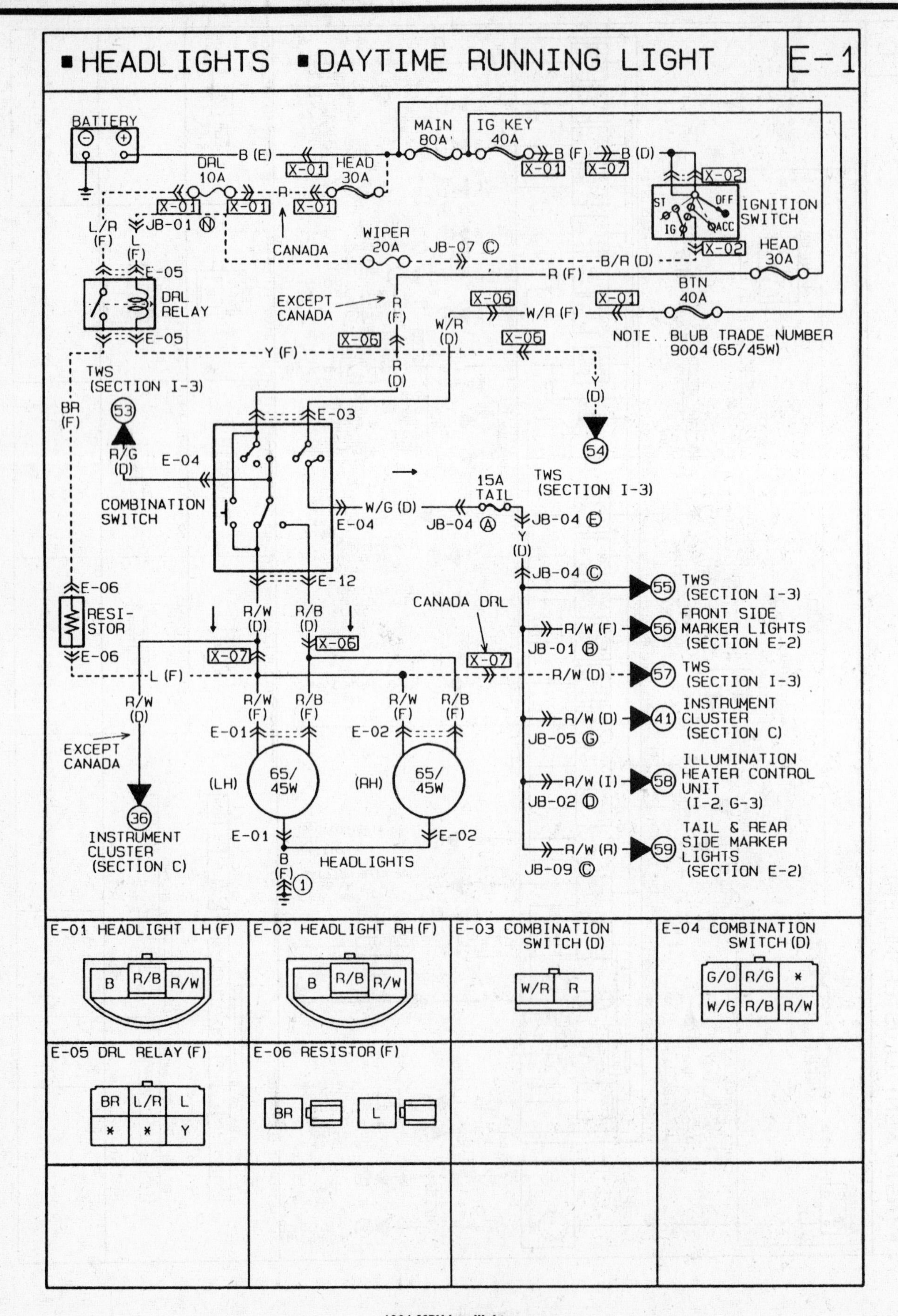

1991 MPV headlights

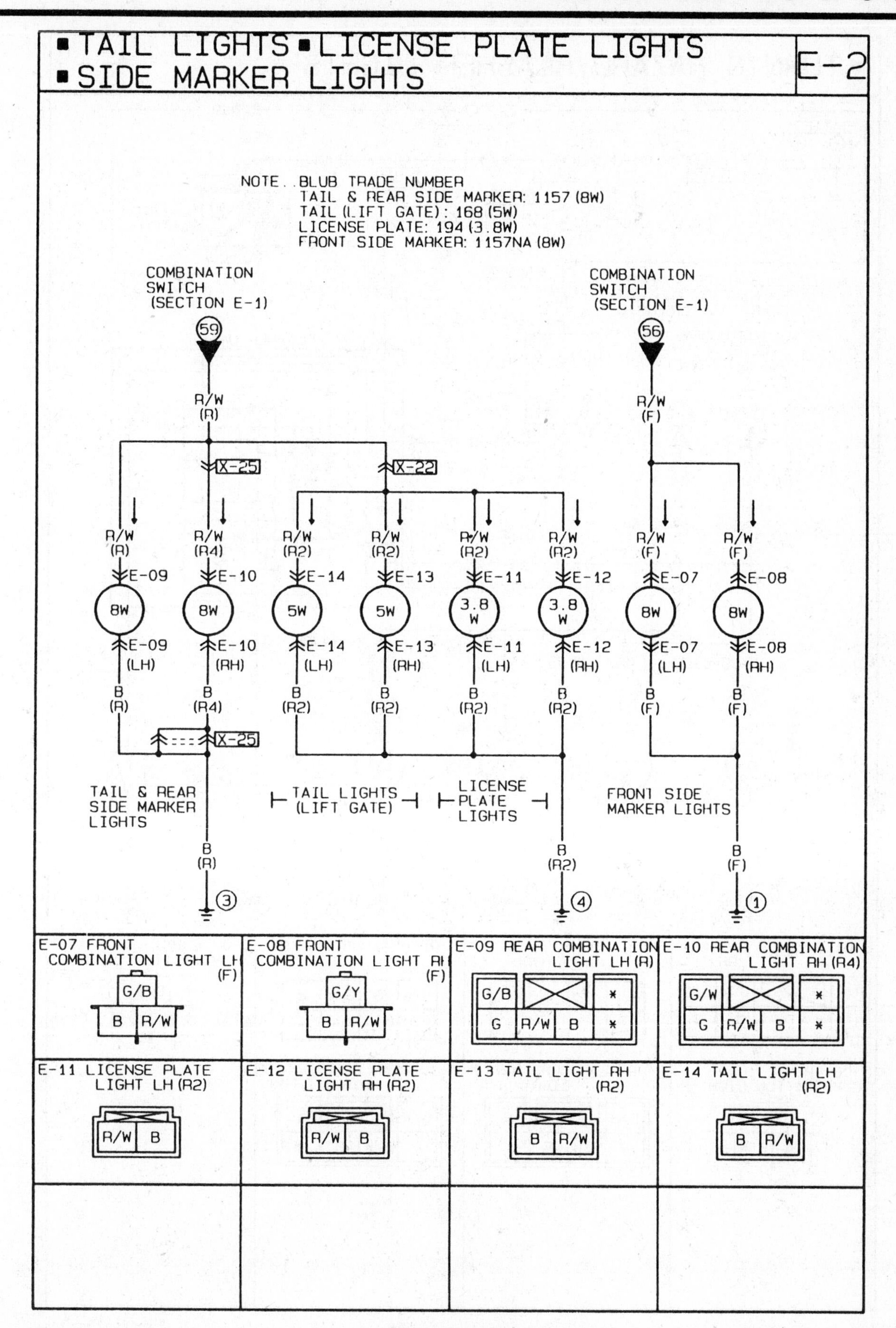

1991 MPV exterior lights

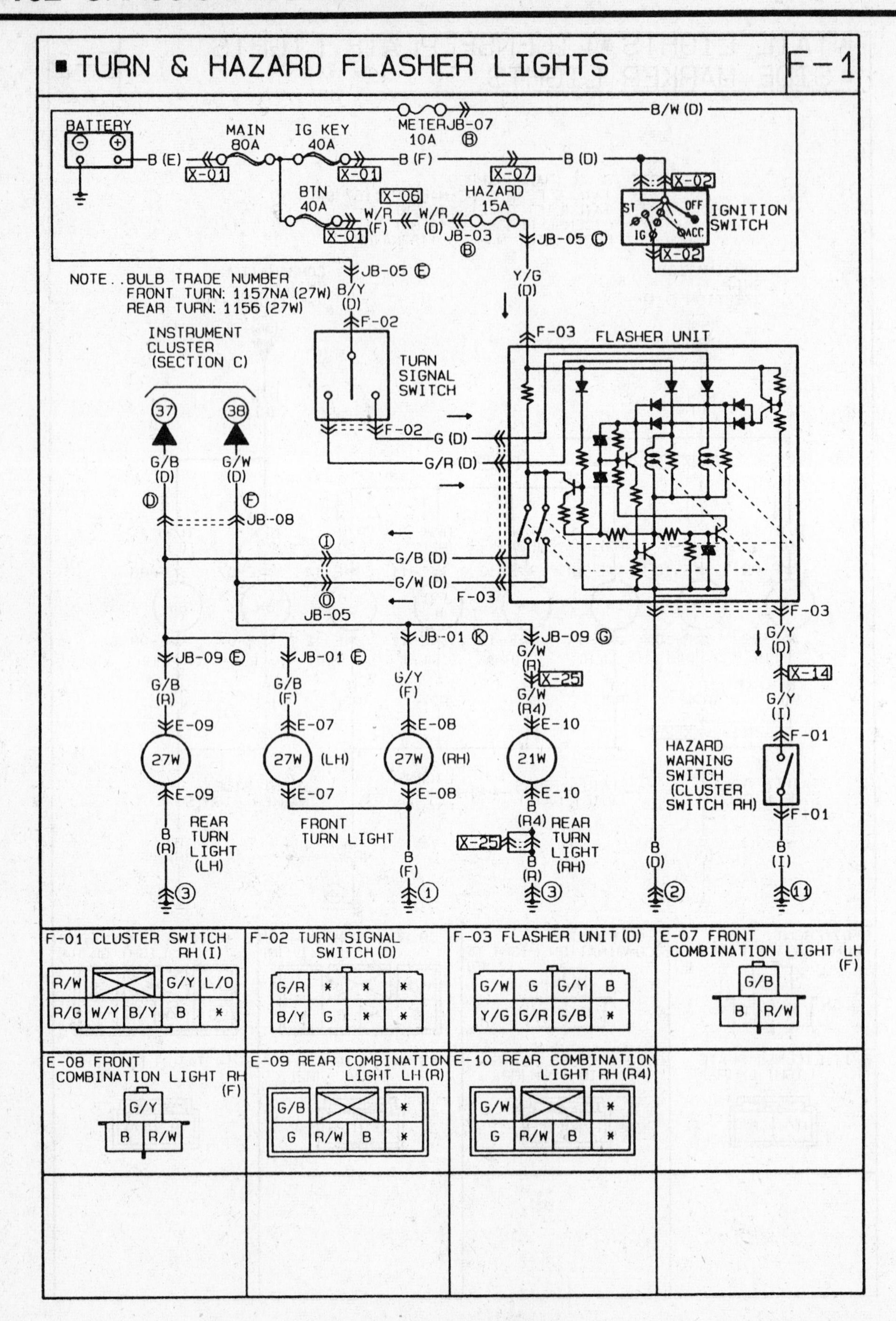

1991 MPV turn and hazard flasher lights

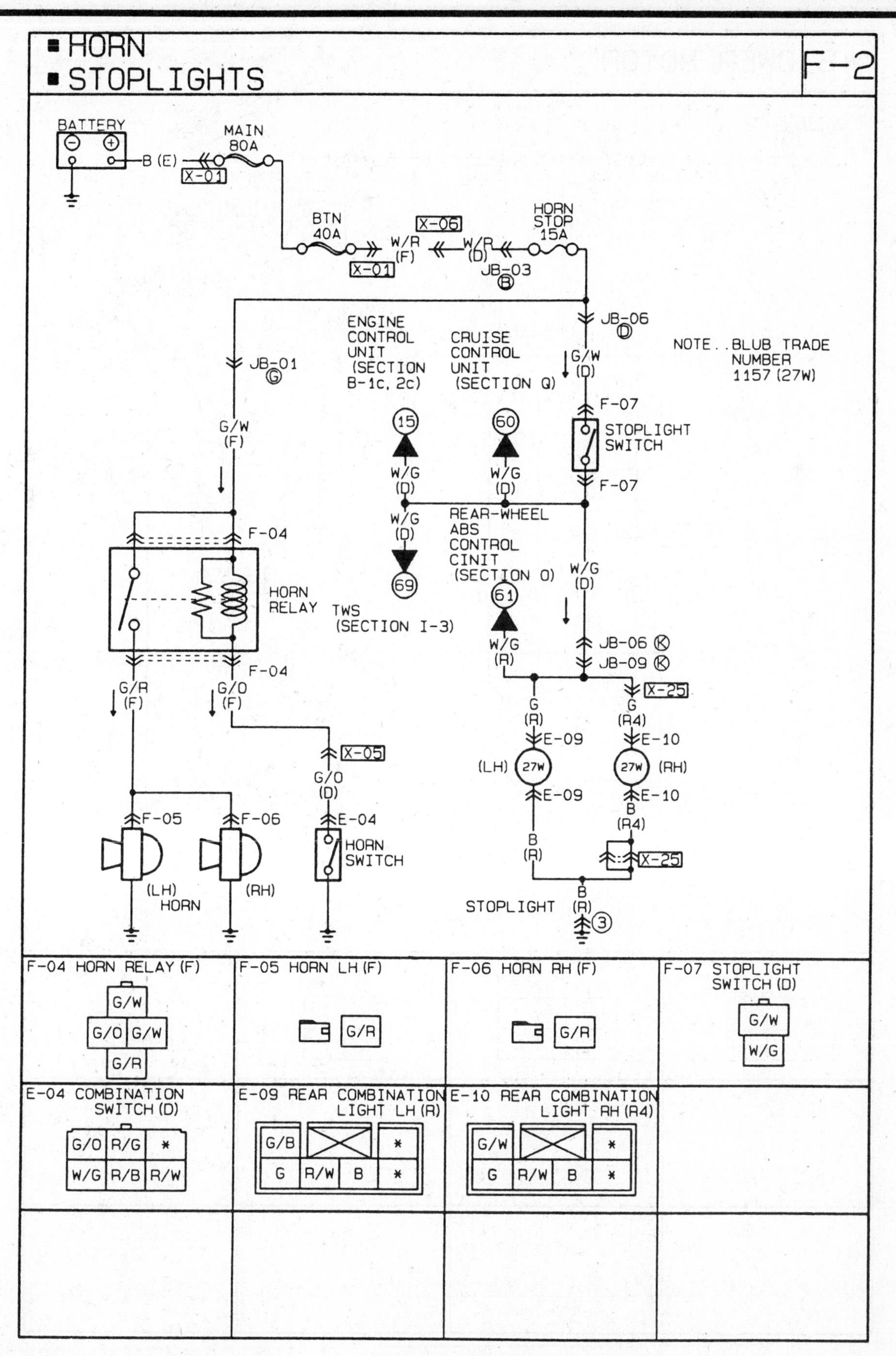

1991 MPV horn, stoplights

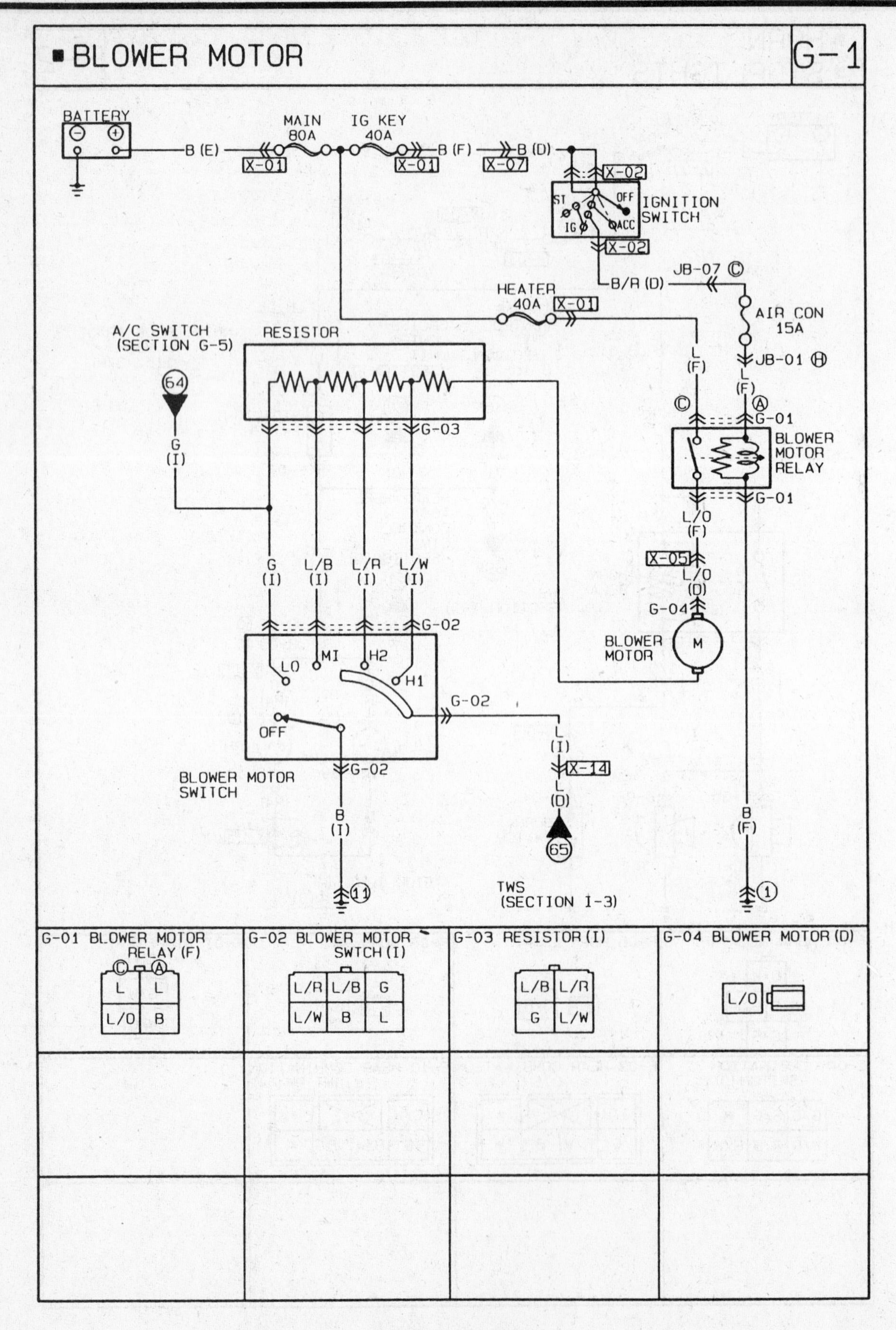

1991 MPV blower motor

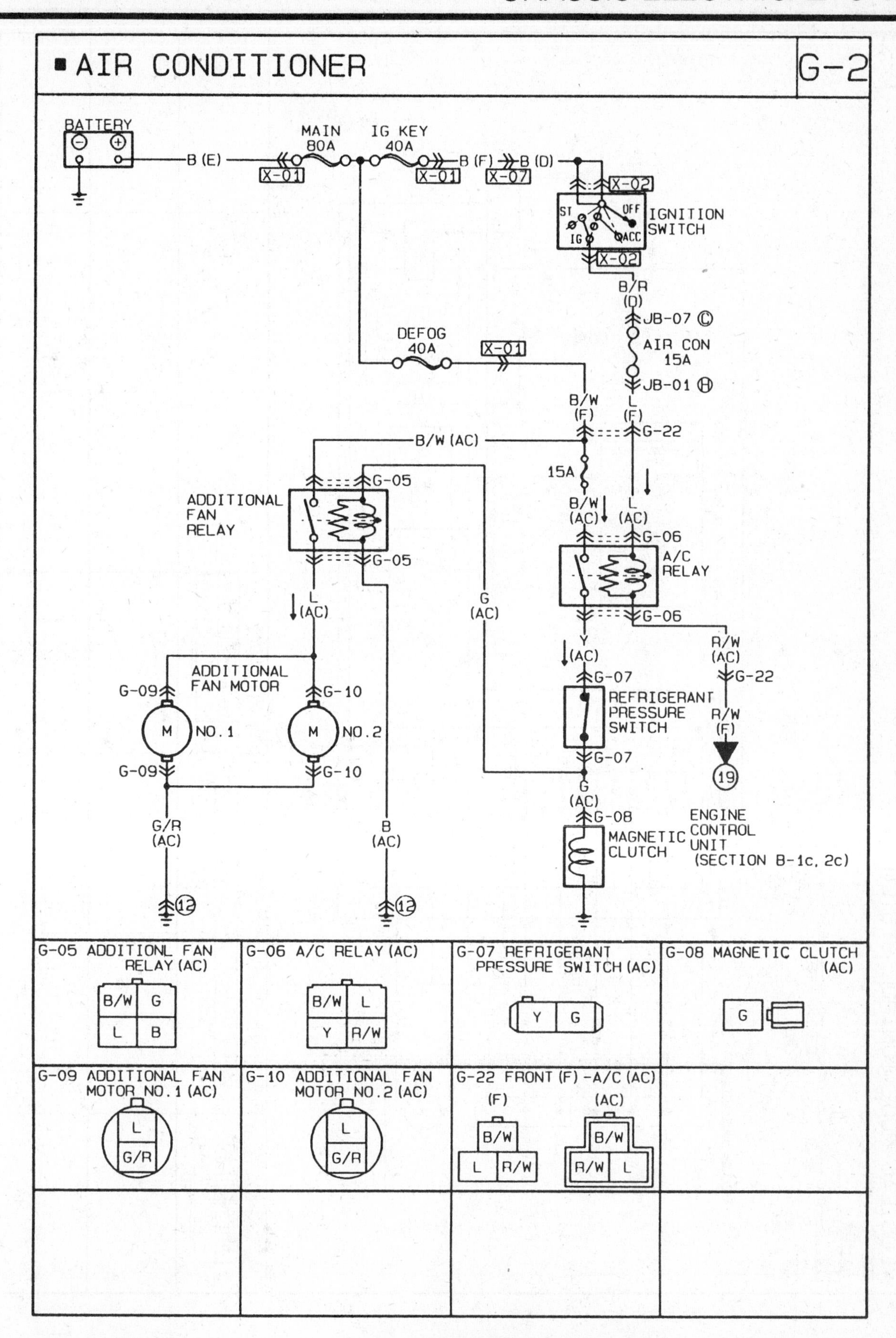

1991 MPV air conditioner

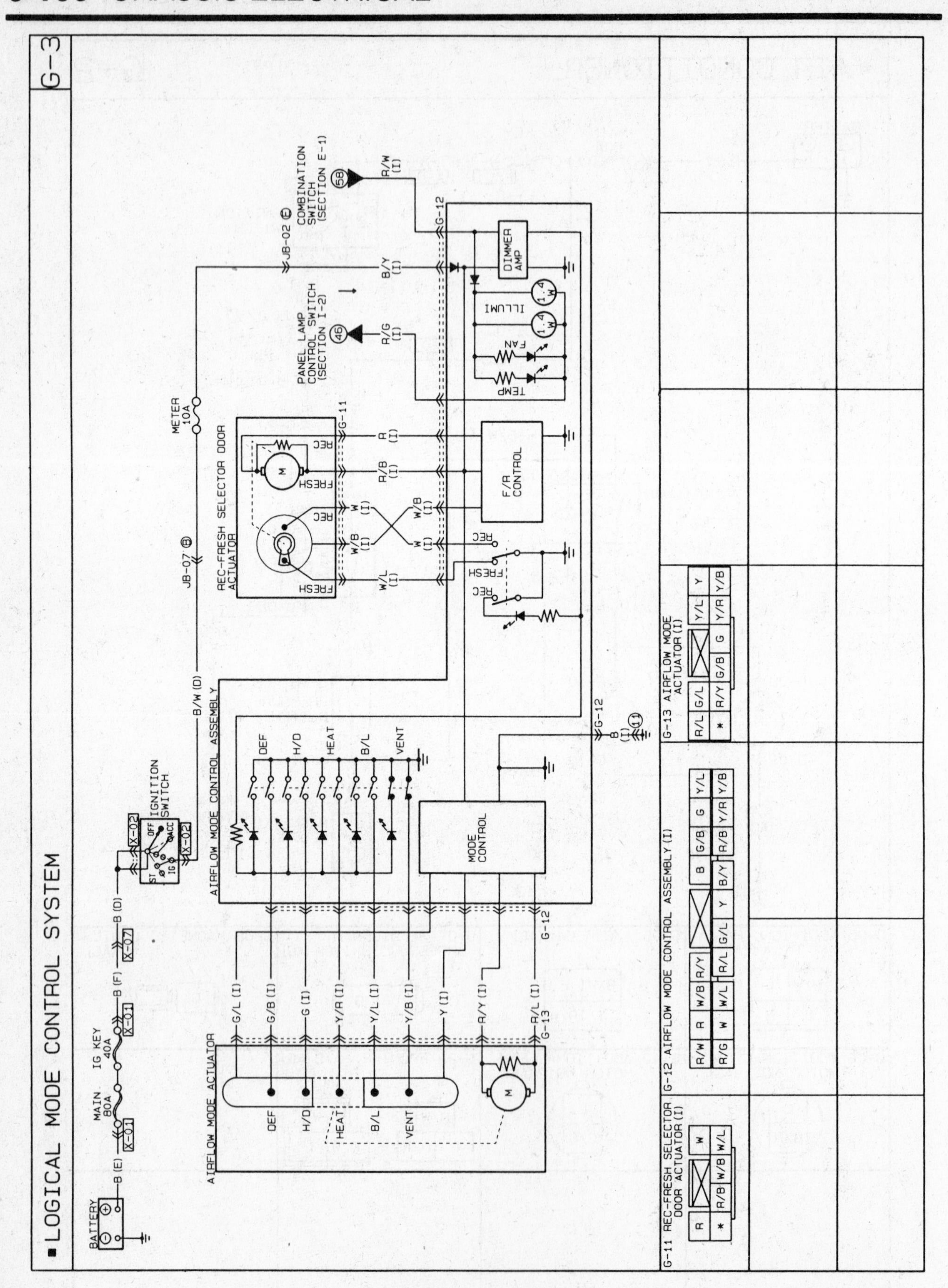

1991 MPV climate logical mode control system

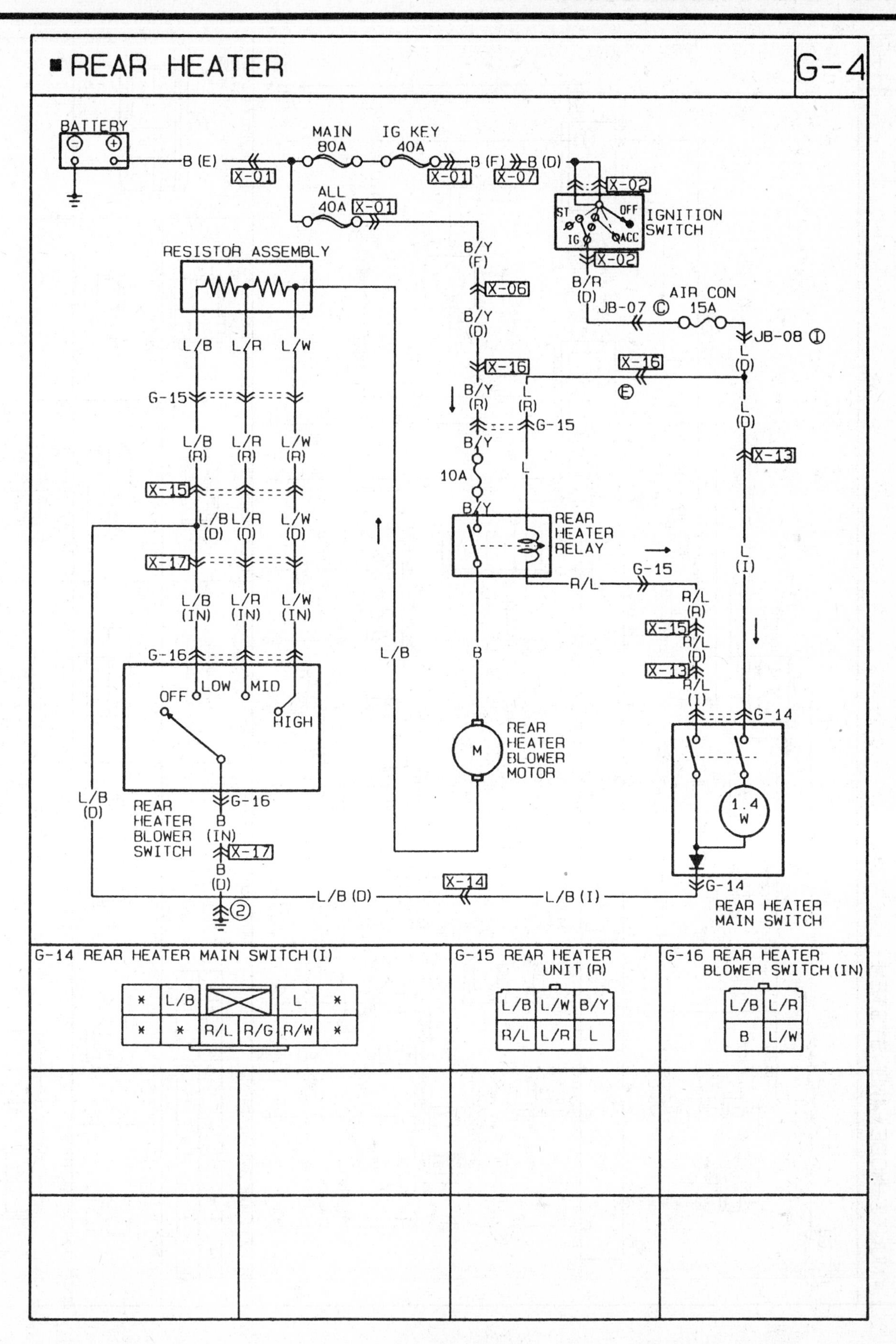

*	L/B		L	*
*	*	R/L R/G	R/W	*

L/B	L/W	B/Y
R/L	L/R	L

L/B	L/R
B	L/W

1991 MPV rear heater

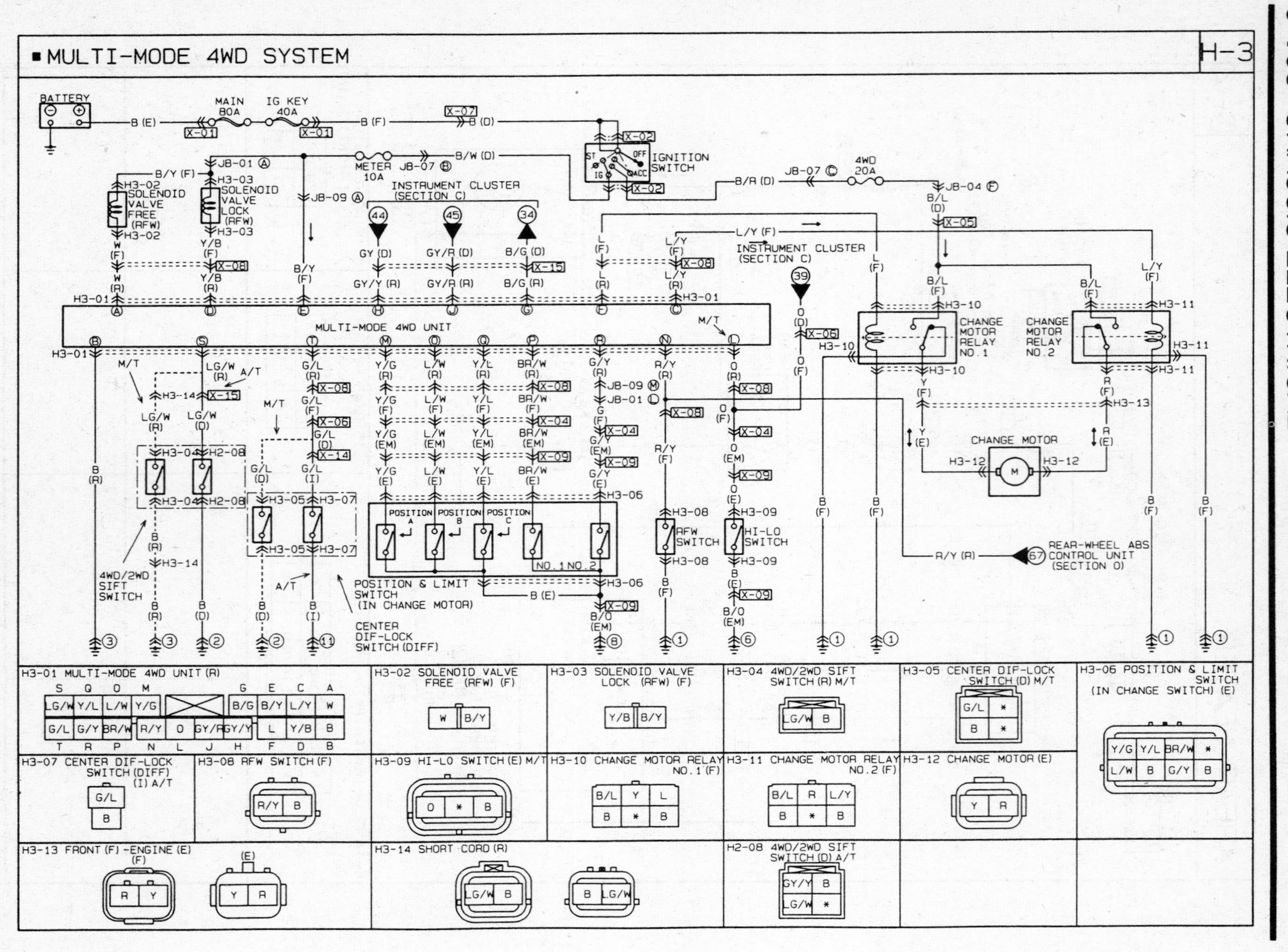

1991 MPV multi-mode 4WD system

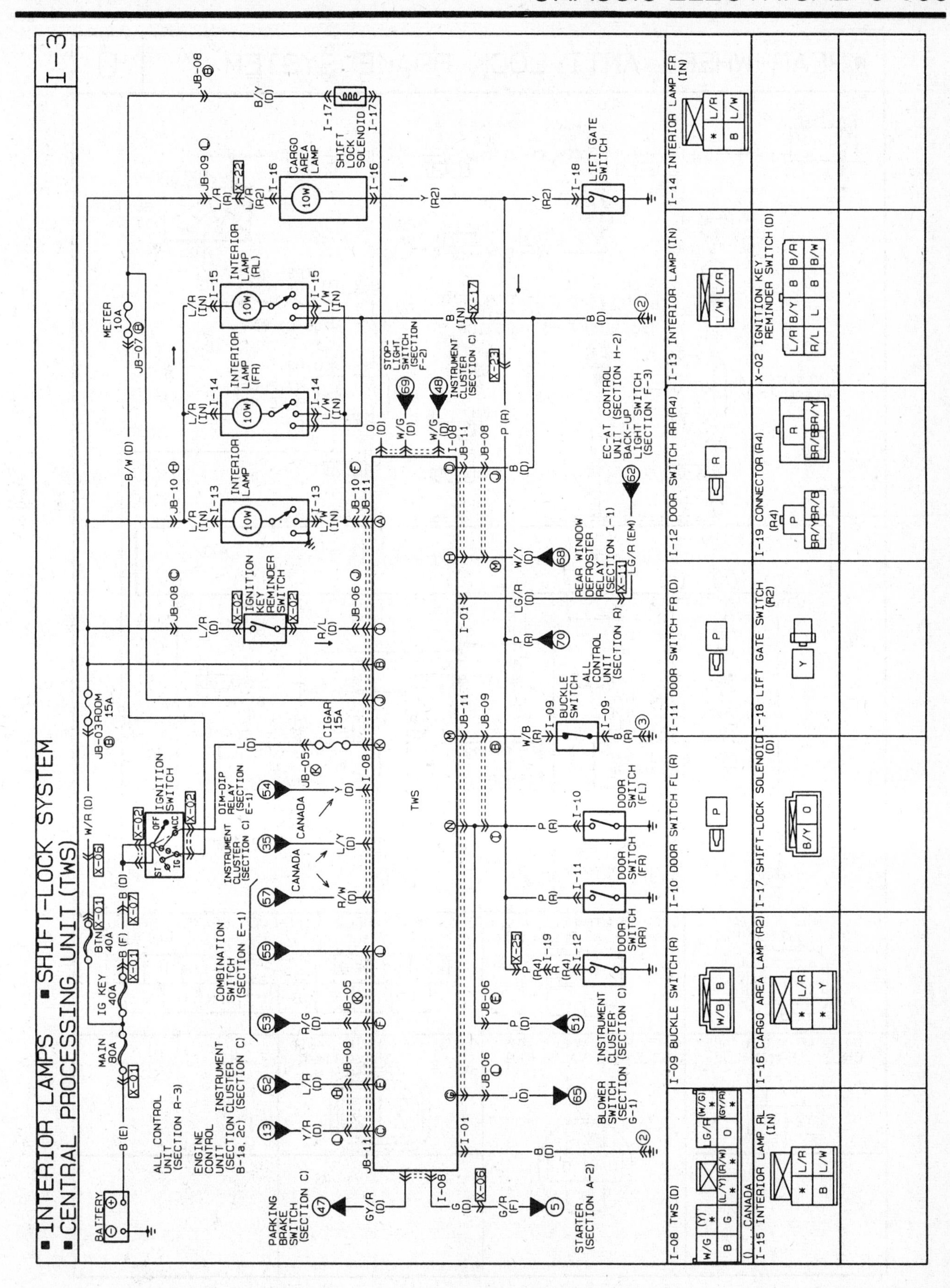

1991 MPV interior lamps, shift-lock system, central processing unit

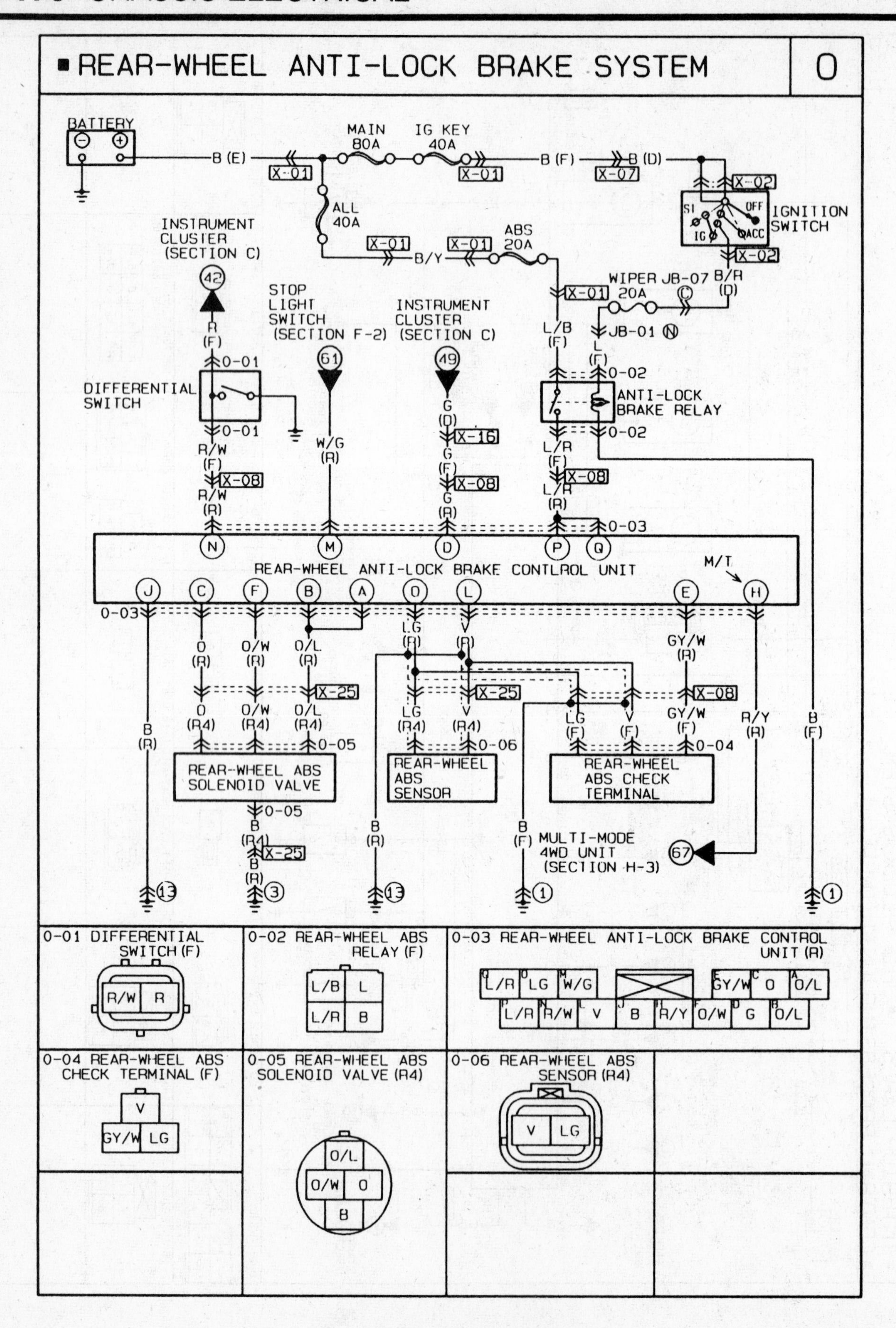

1991 MPV rear wheel anti-lock brake system

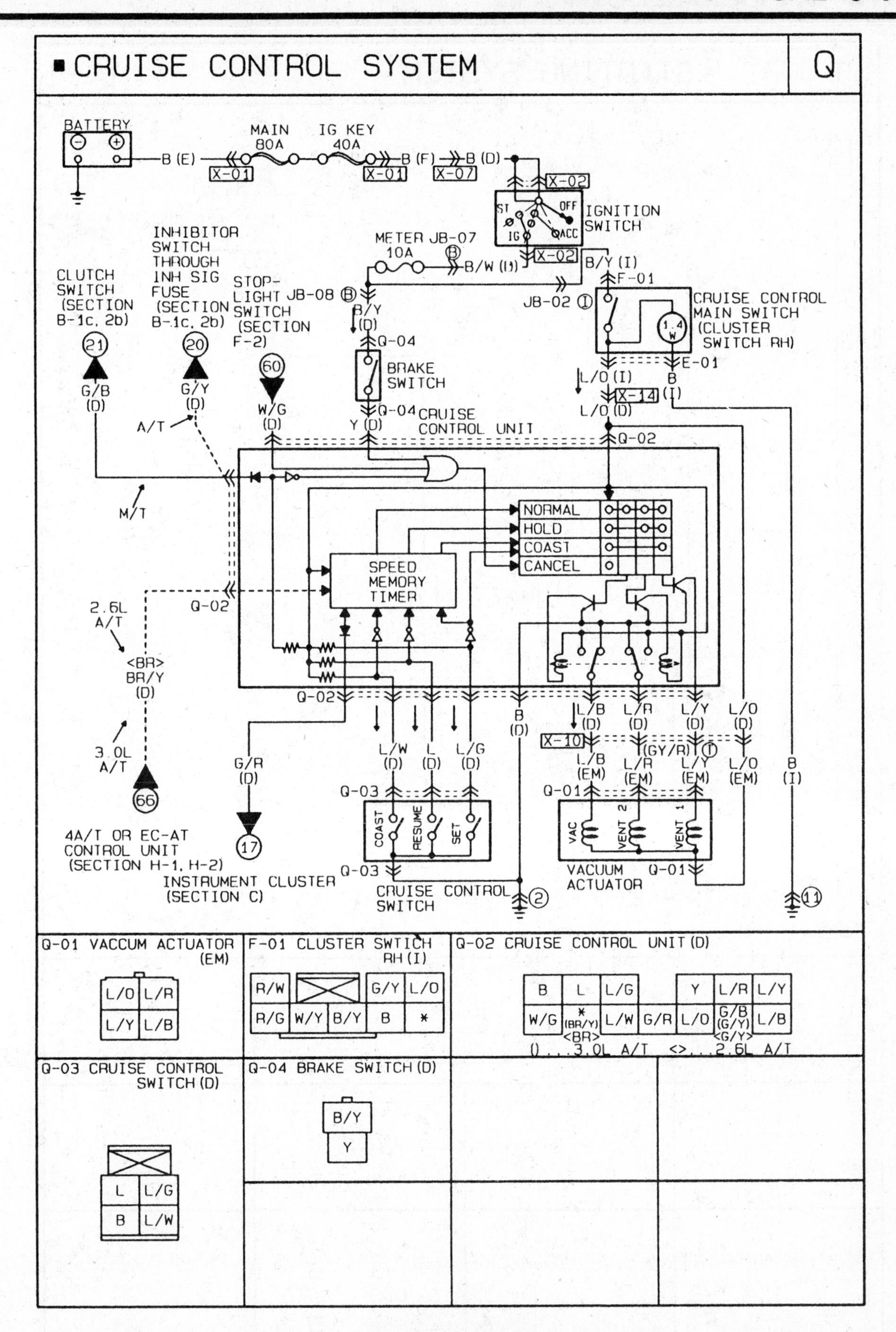

1991 MPV cruise control system

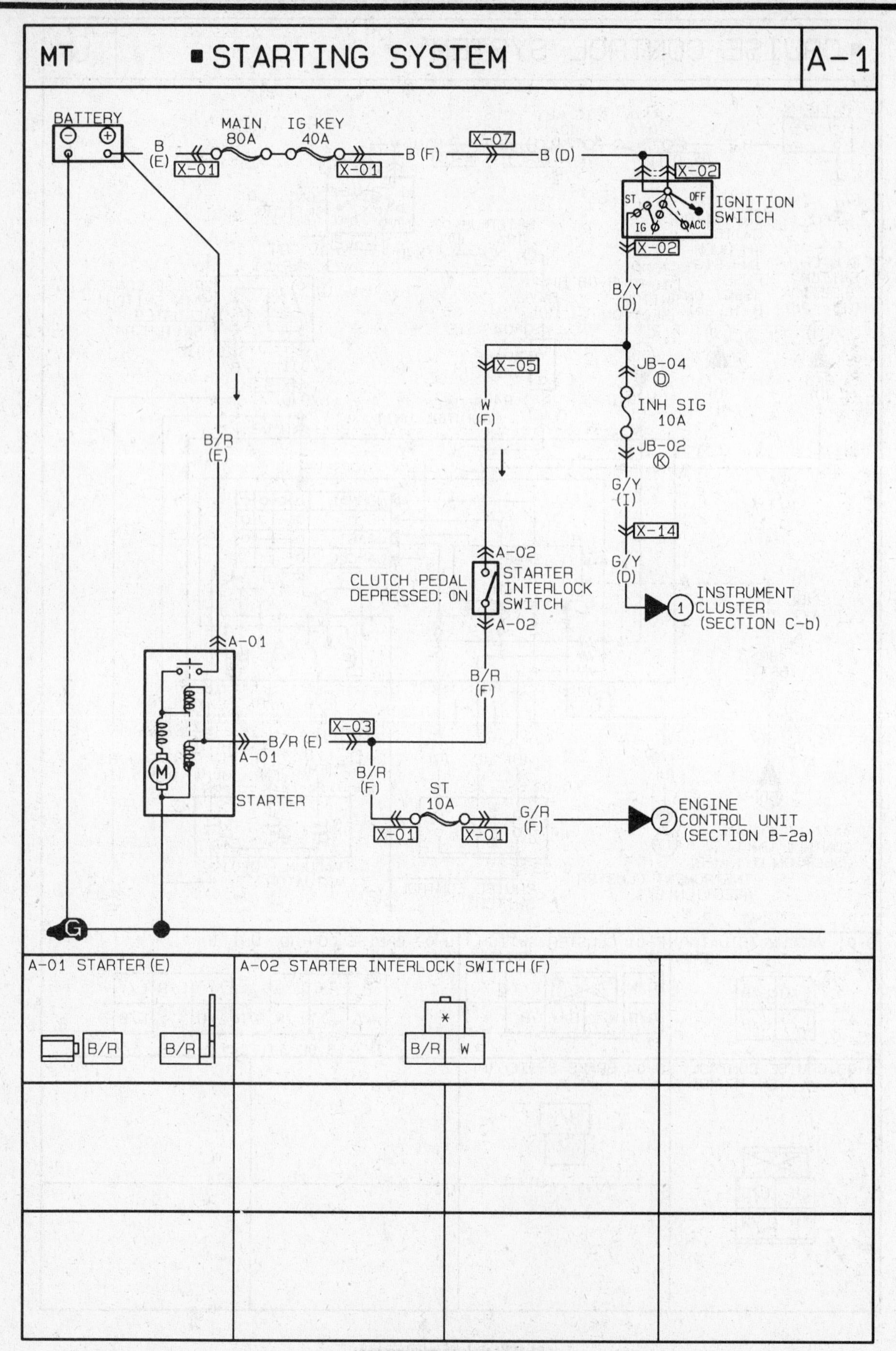

1992 MPV MT starting system

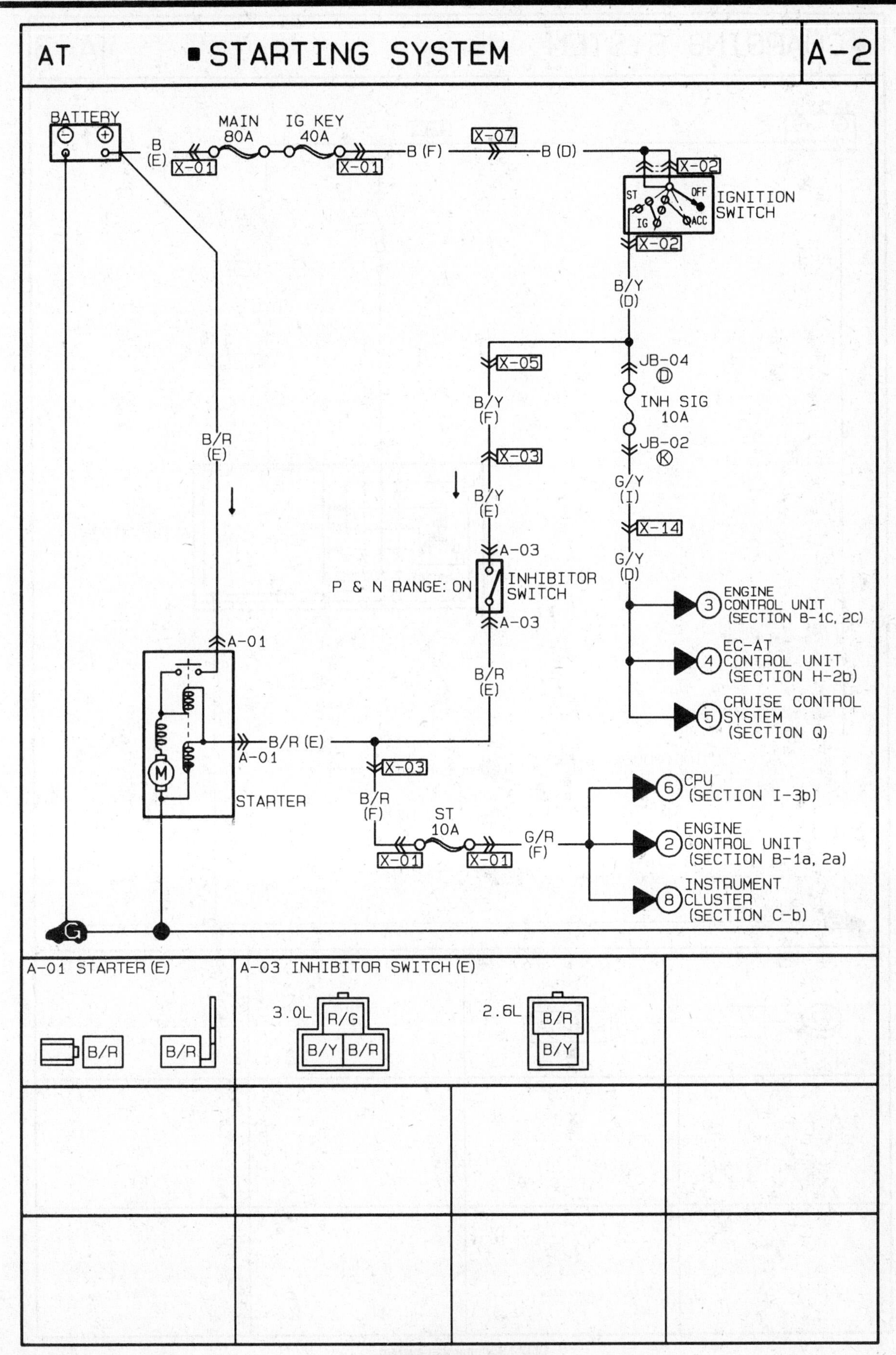

1992 MPV AT starting system

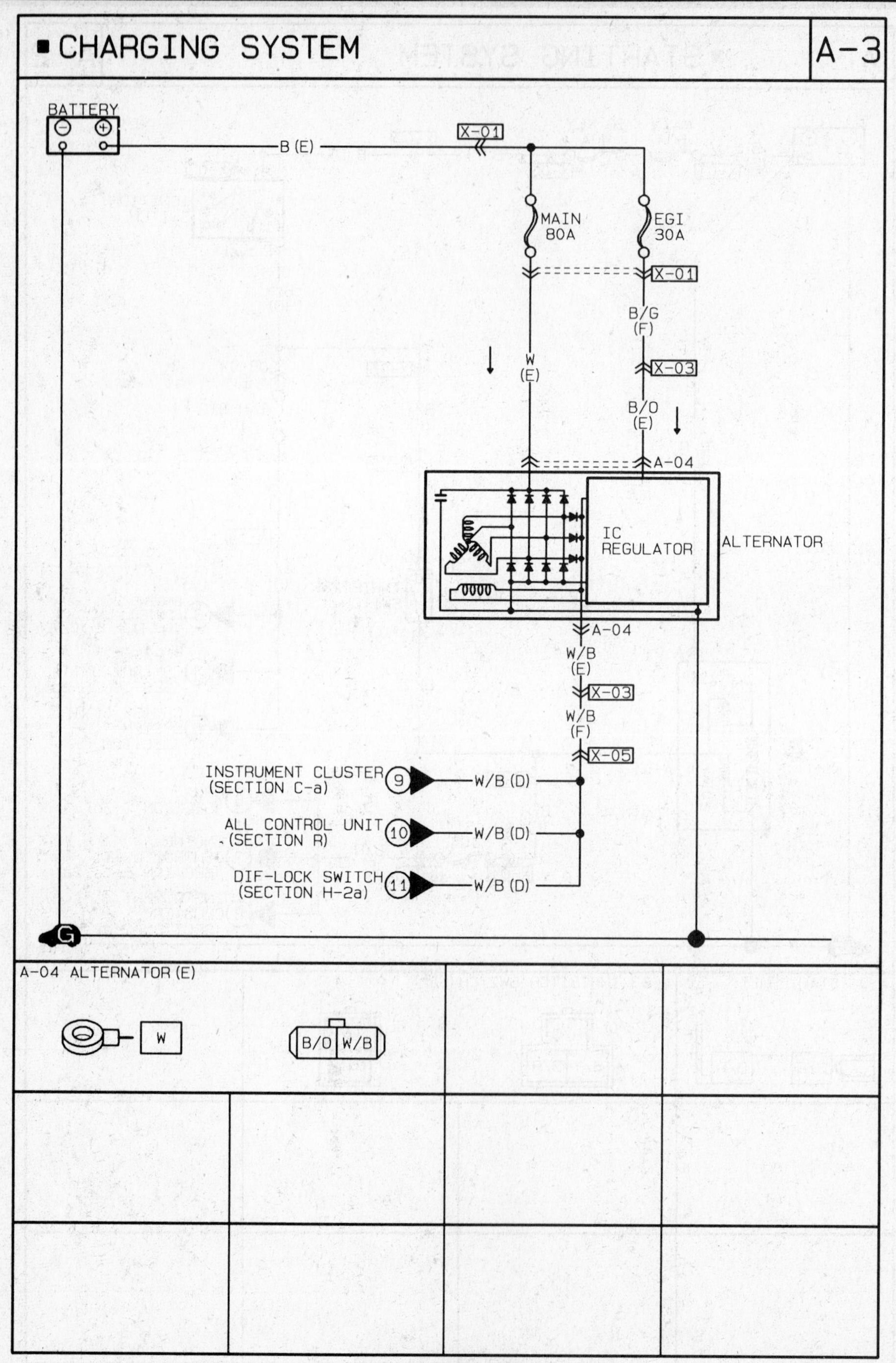

1992 MPV charging system

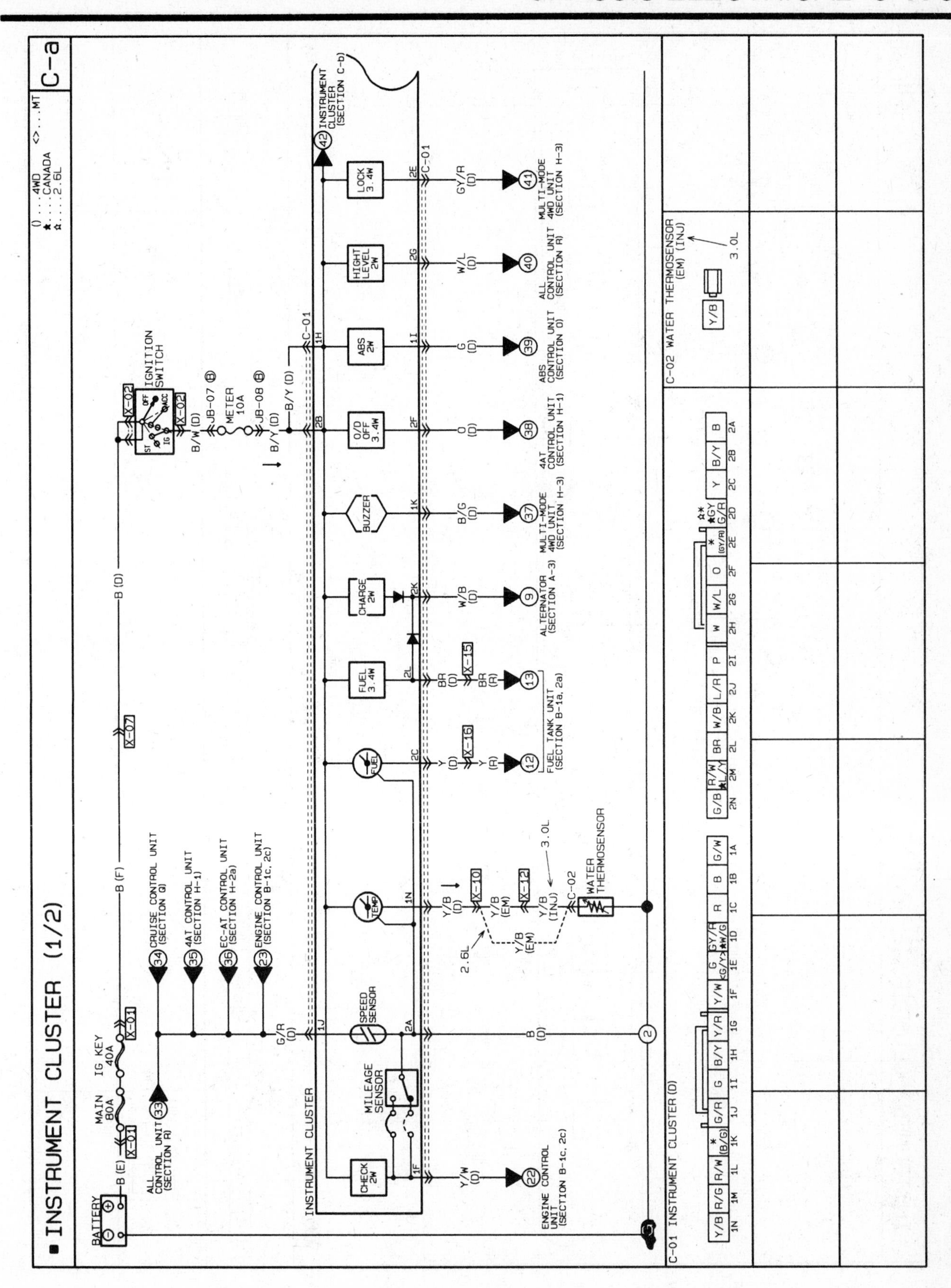

1992 MPV instrument cluster

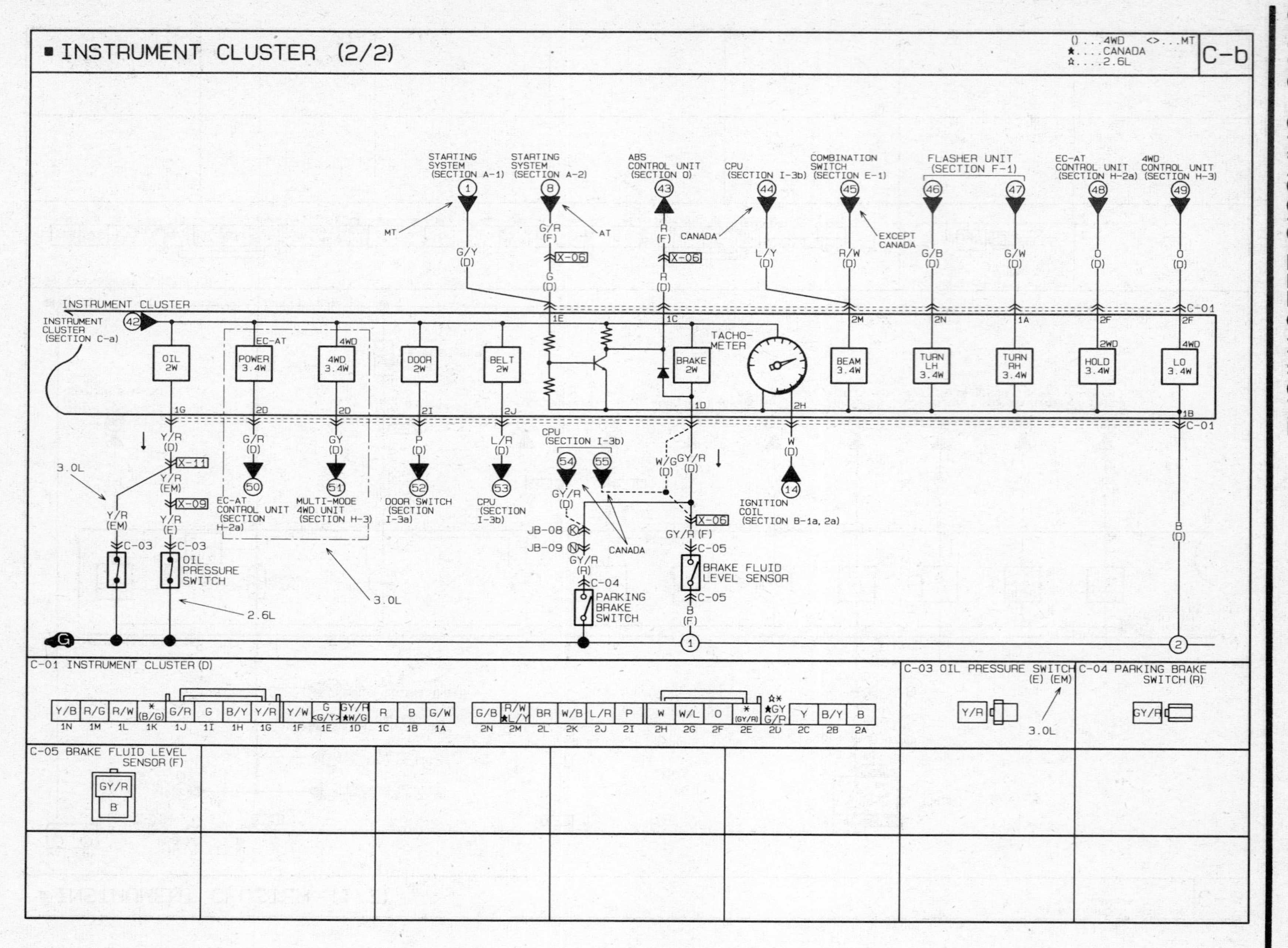

1992 MPV instrument panel

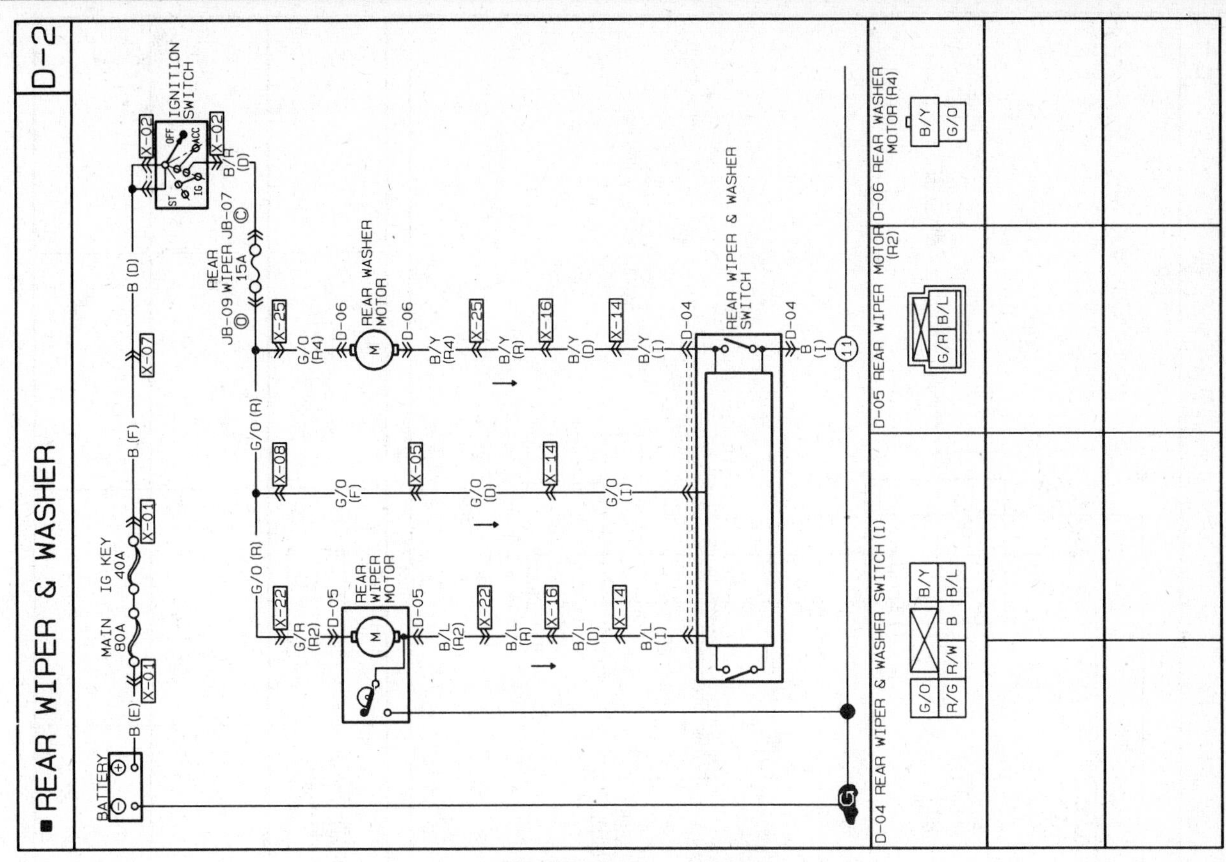

1992 MPV rear wiper and washer

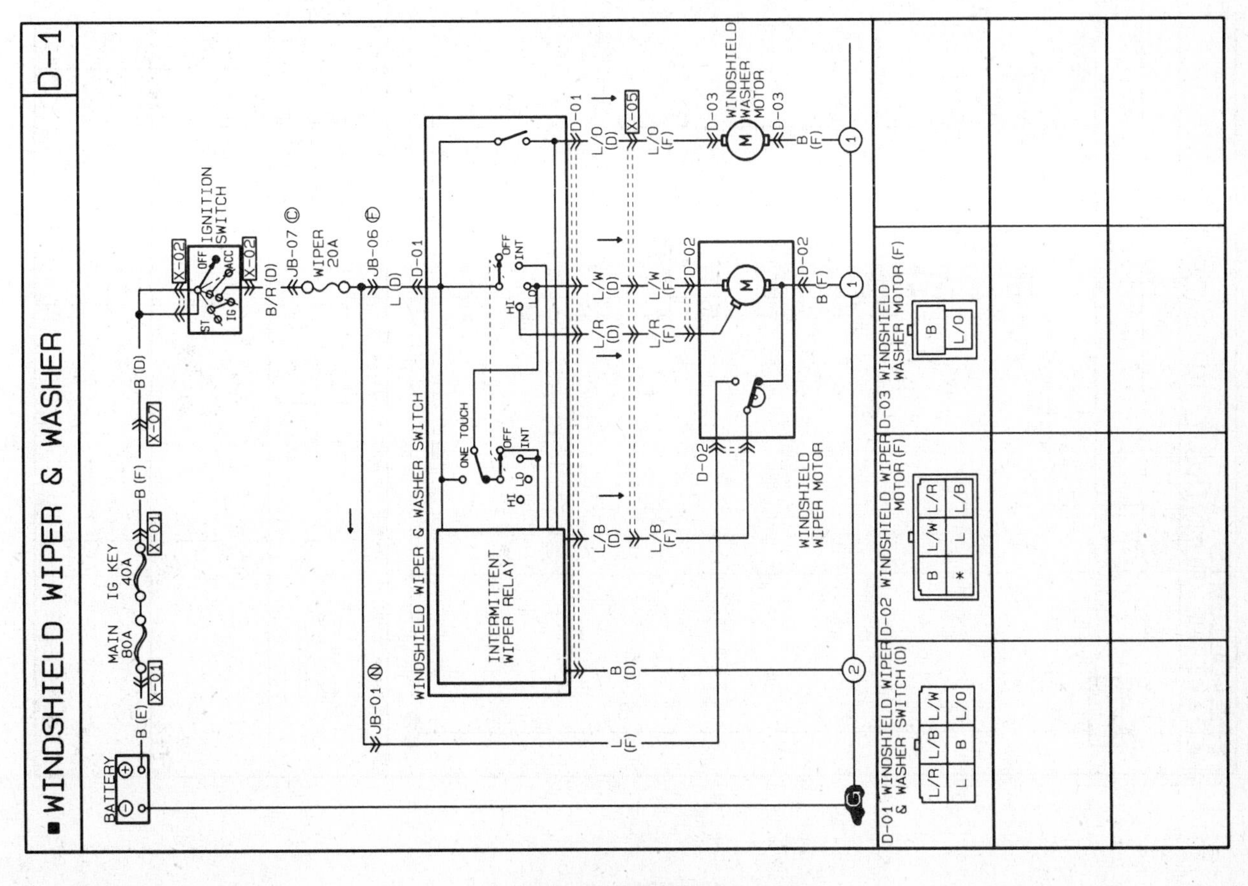

1992 MPV windshield wiper and washer

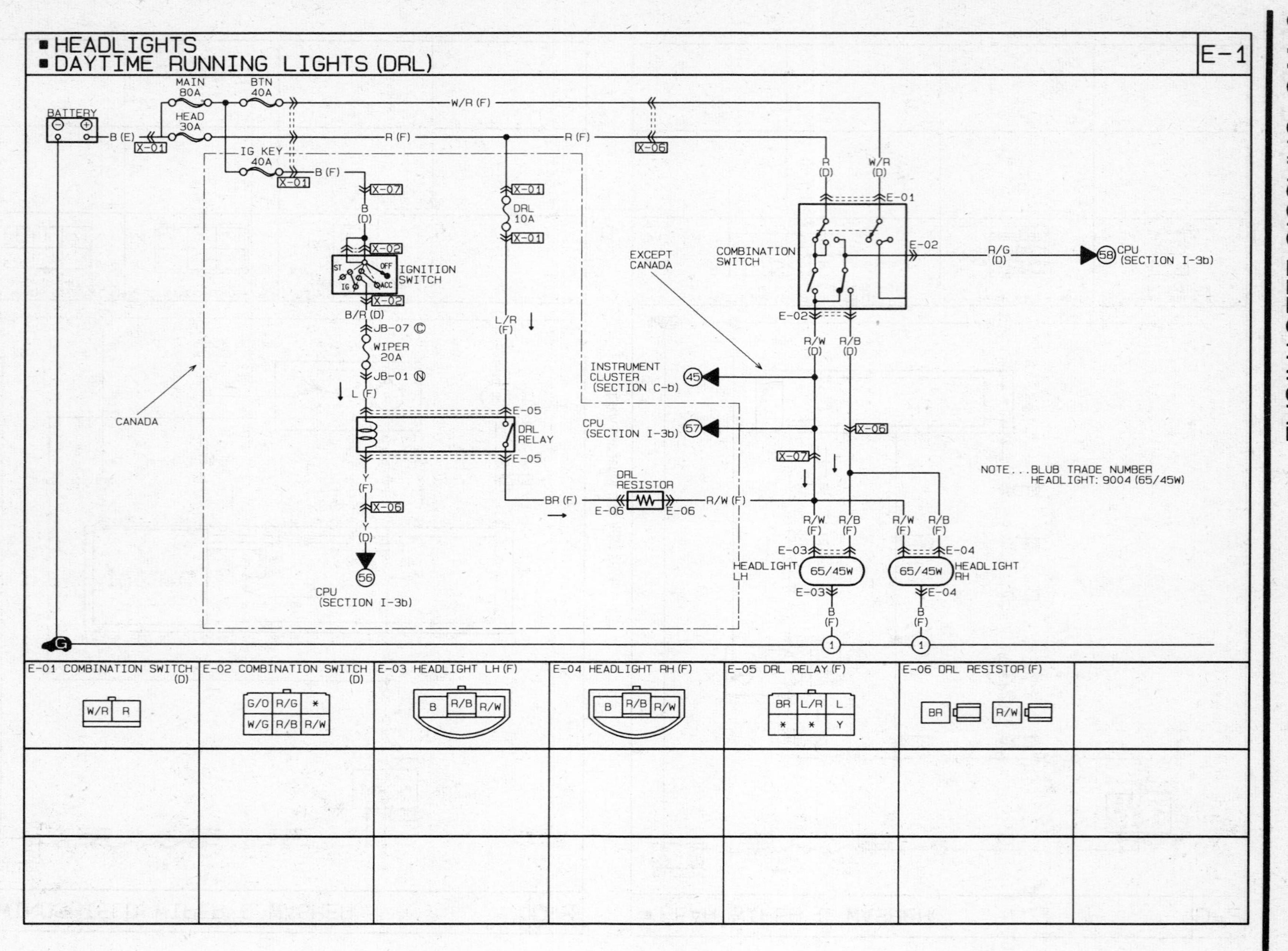

1992 MPV headlights

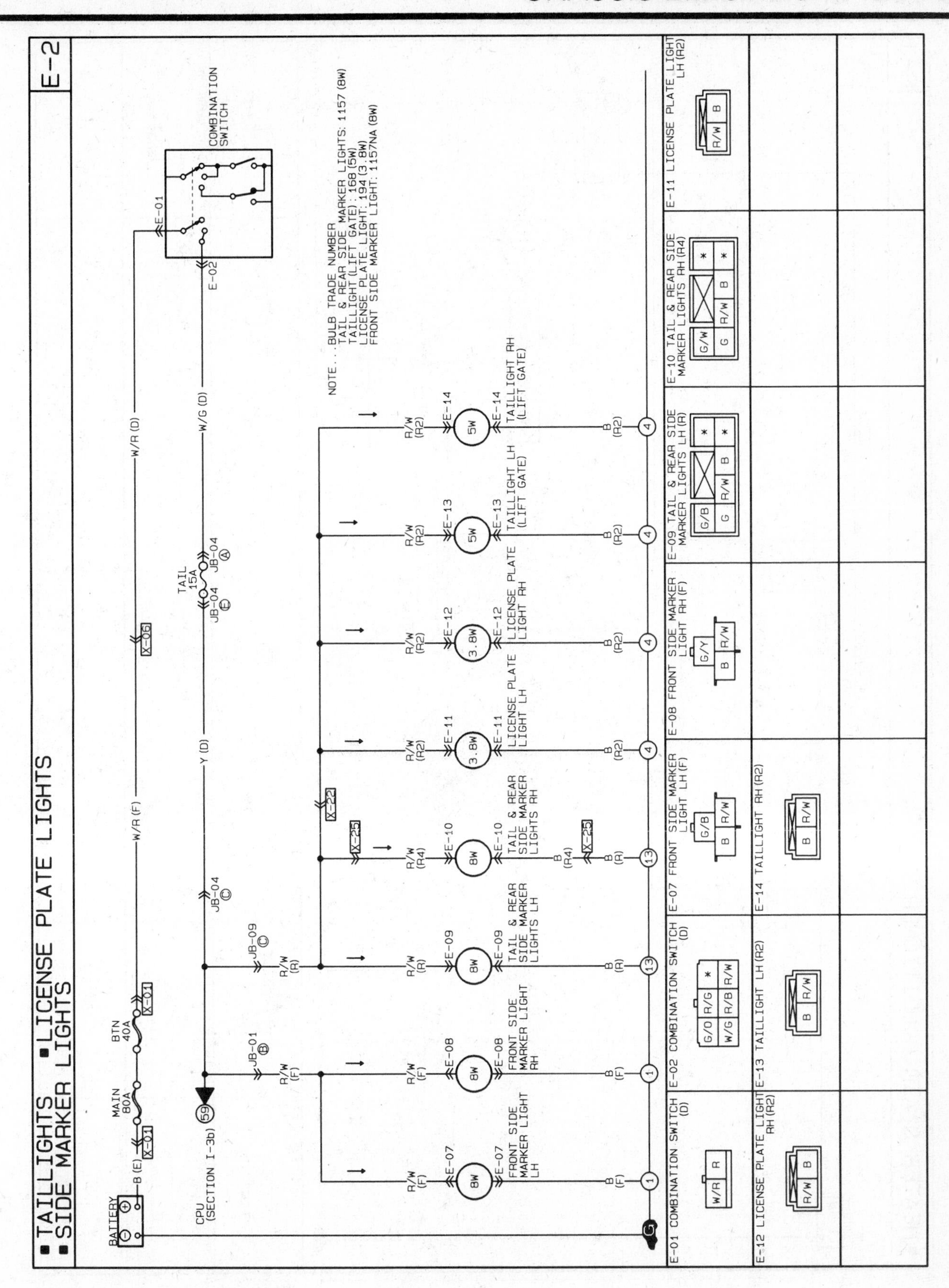

1992 MPV exterior lights

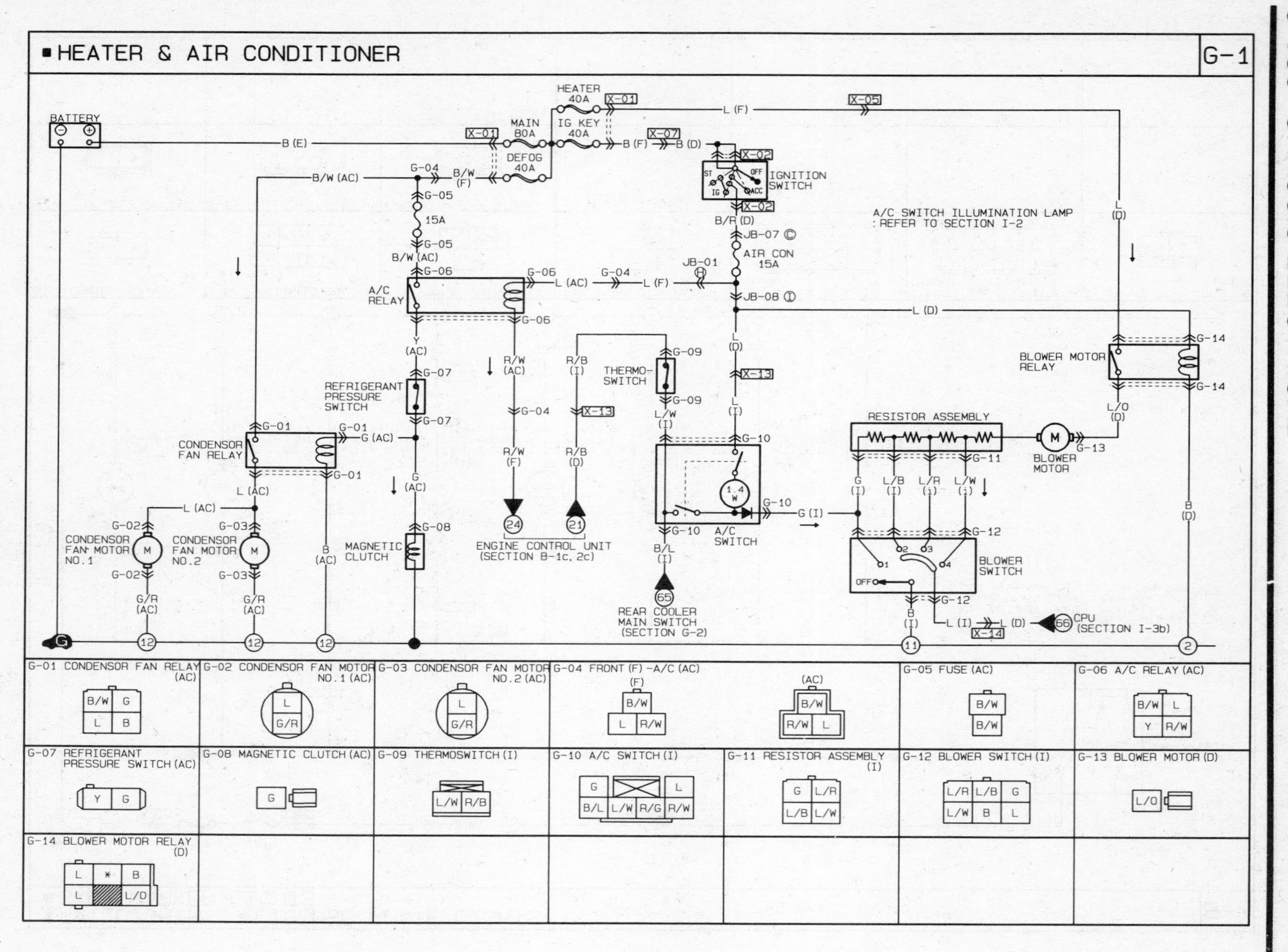

1992 MPV heater and air conditioner

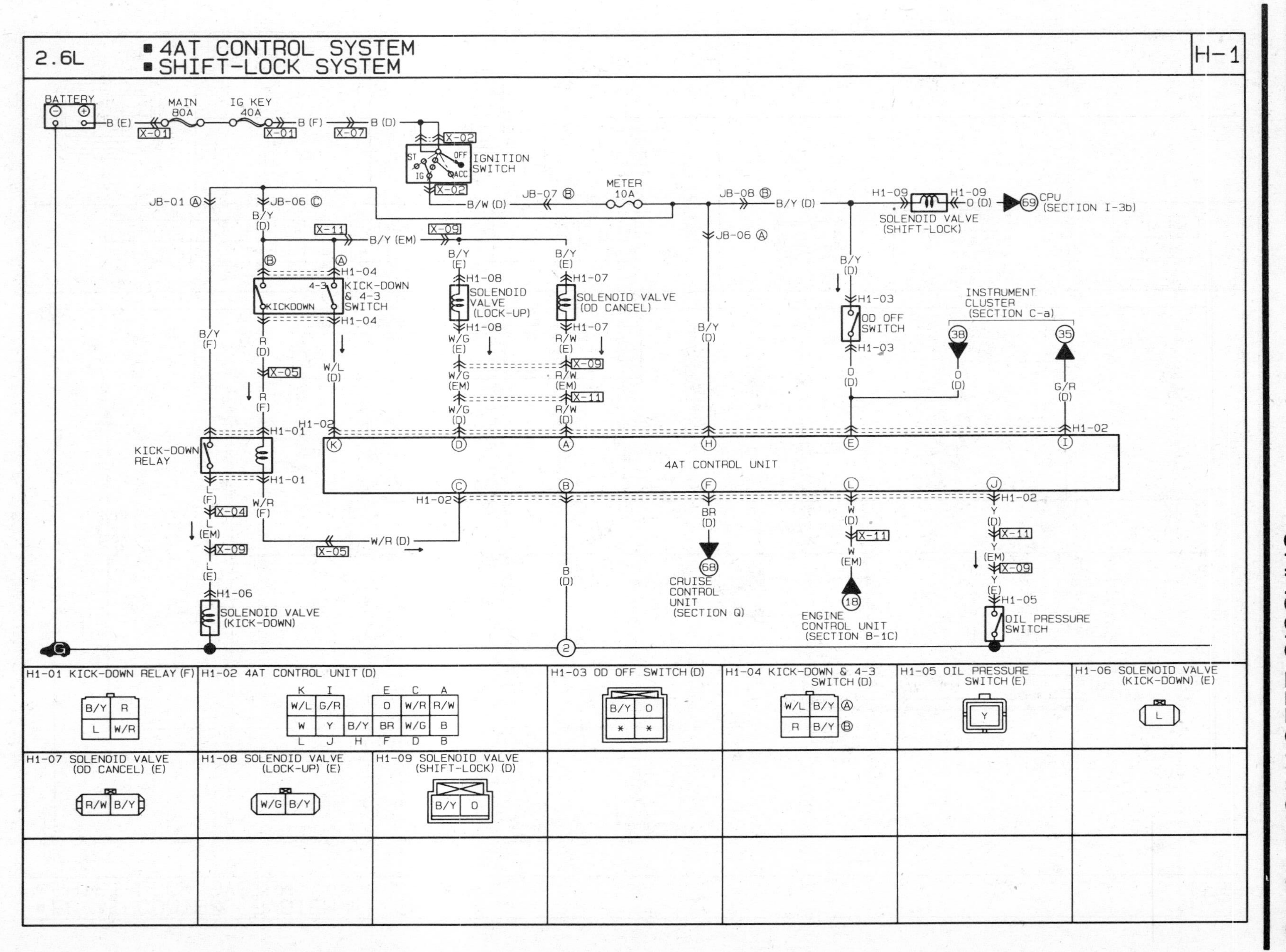

1992 MPV 4AT control system, shift lock system

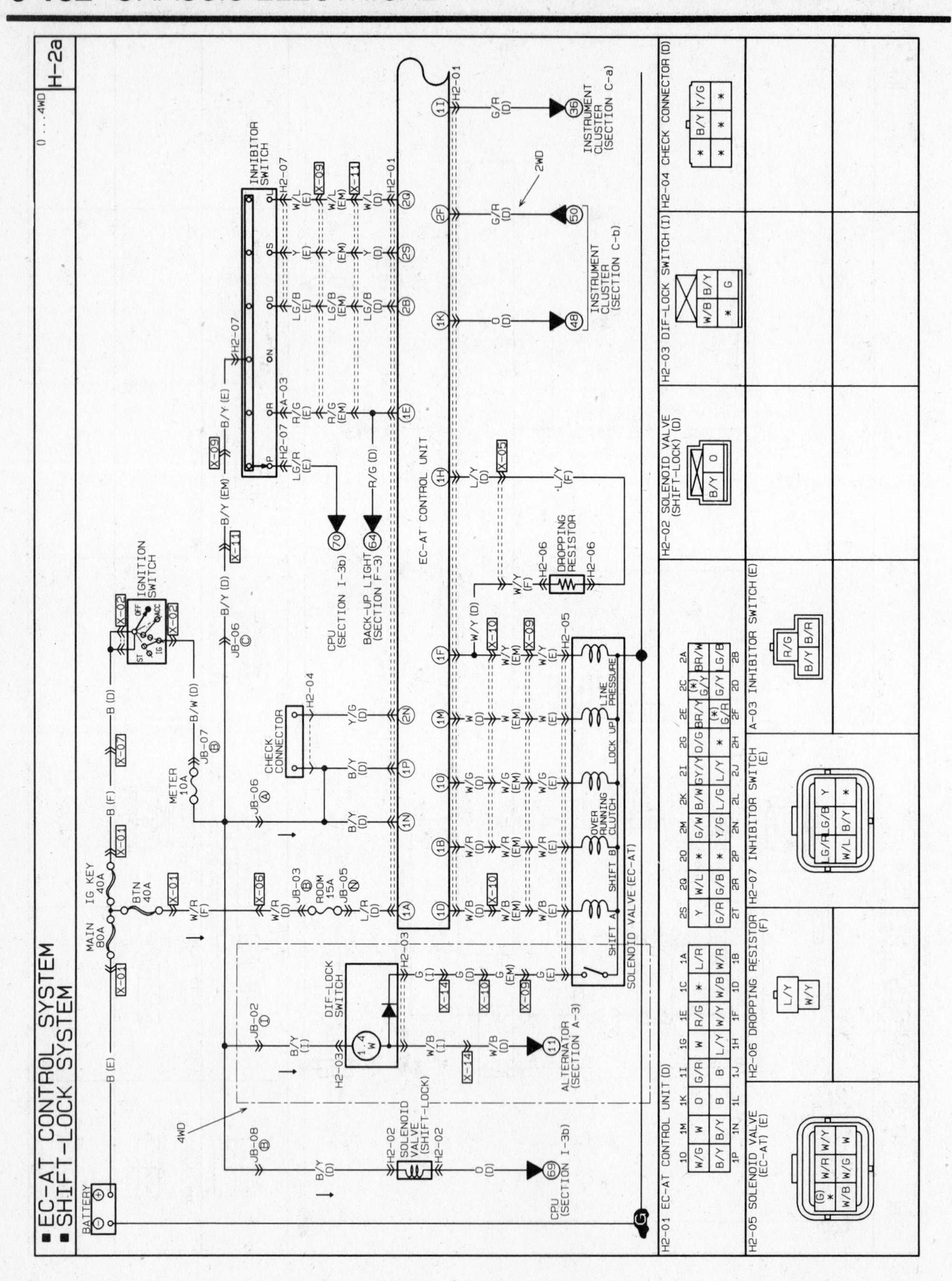

1992 MPV EC-AT control system, shift lock system

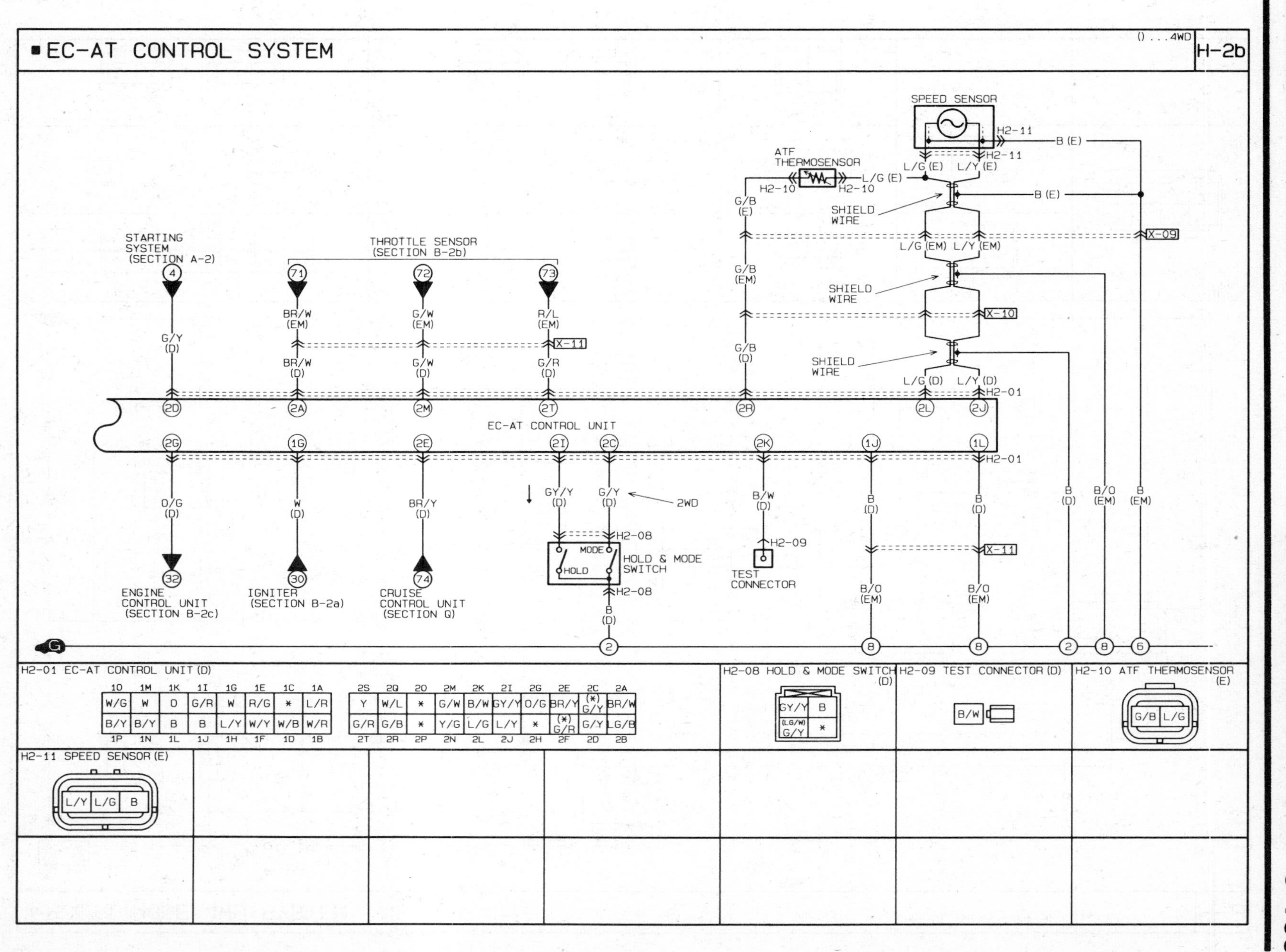

1992 MPV EC-AT control system

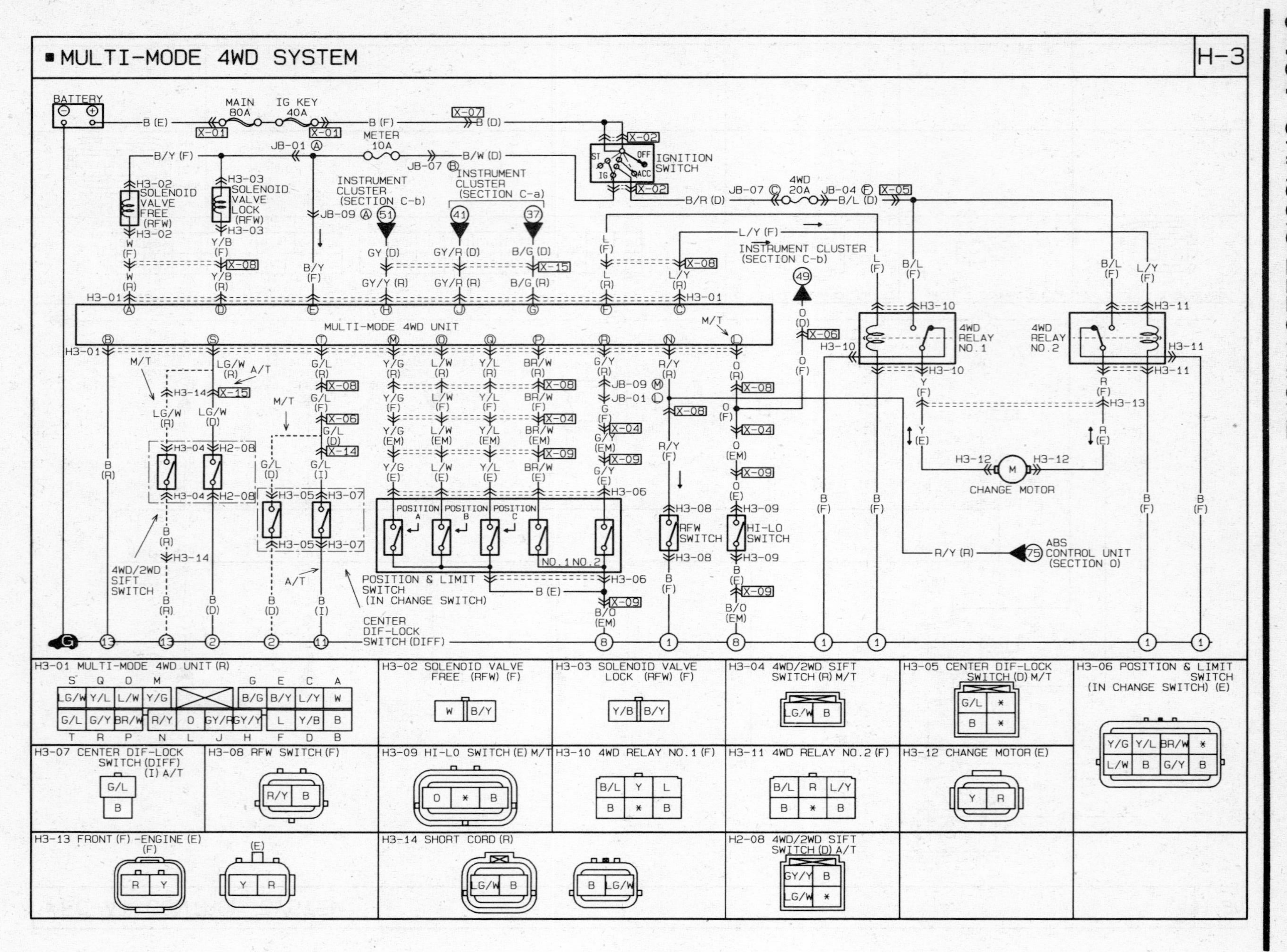

1992 MPV multi-mode 4WD system

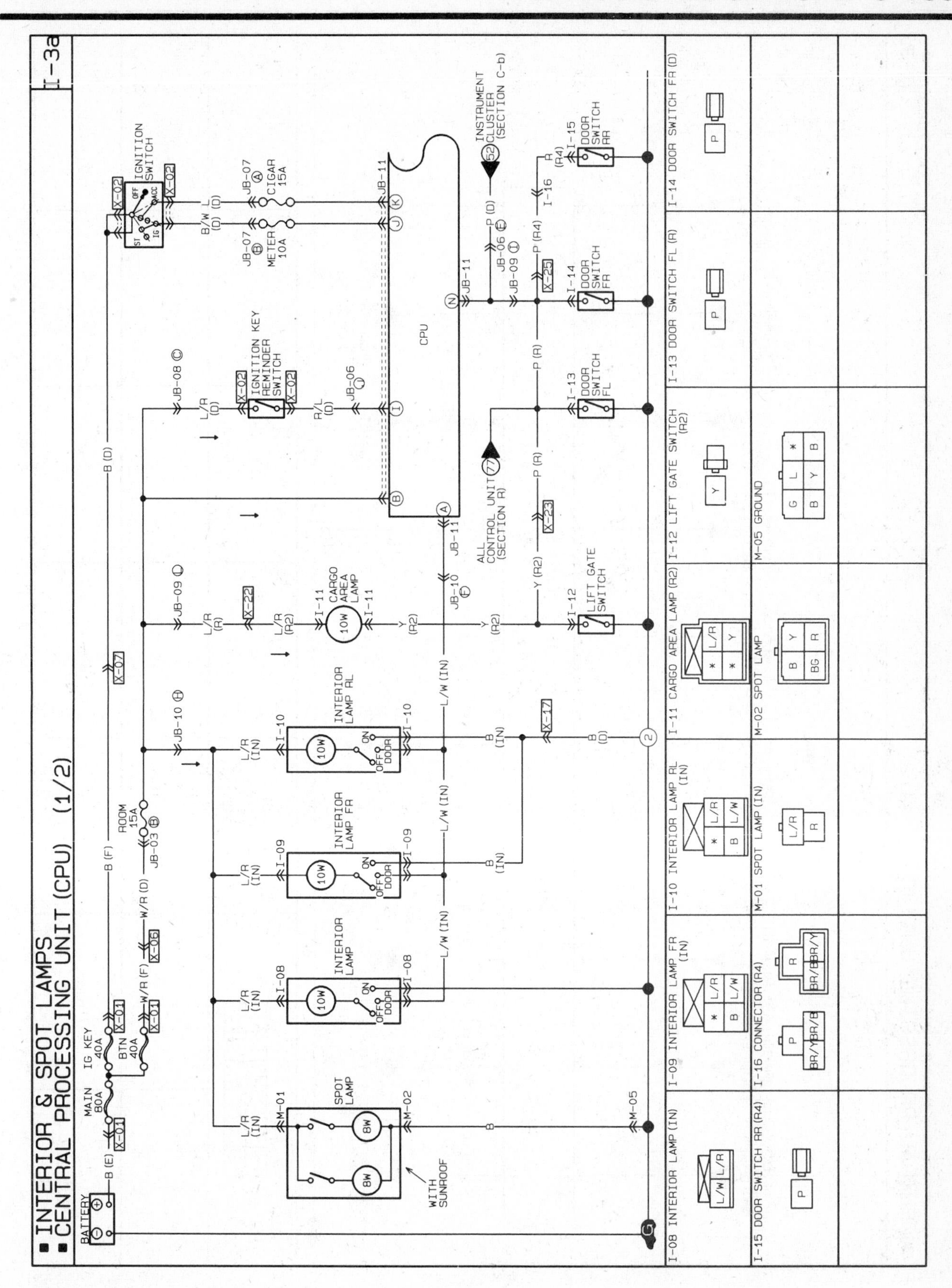

1992 MPV interior lamps, central processing unit

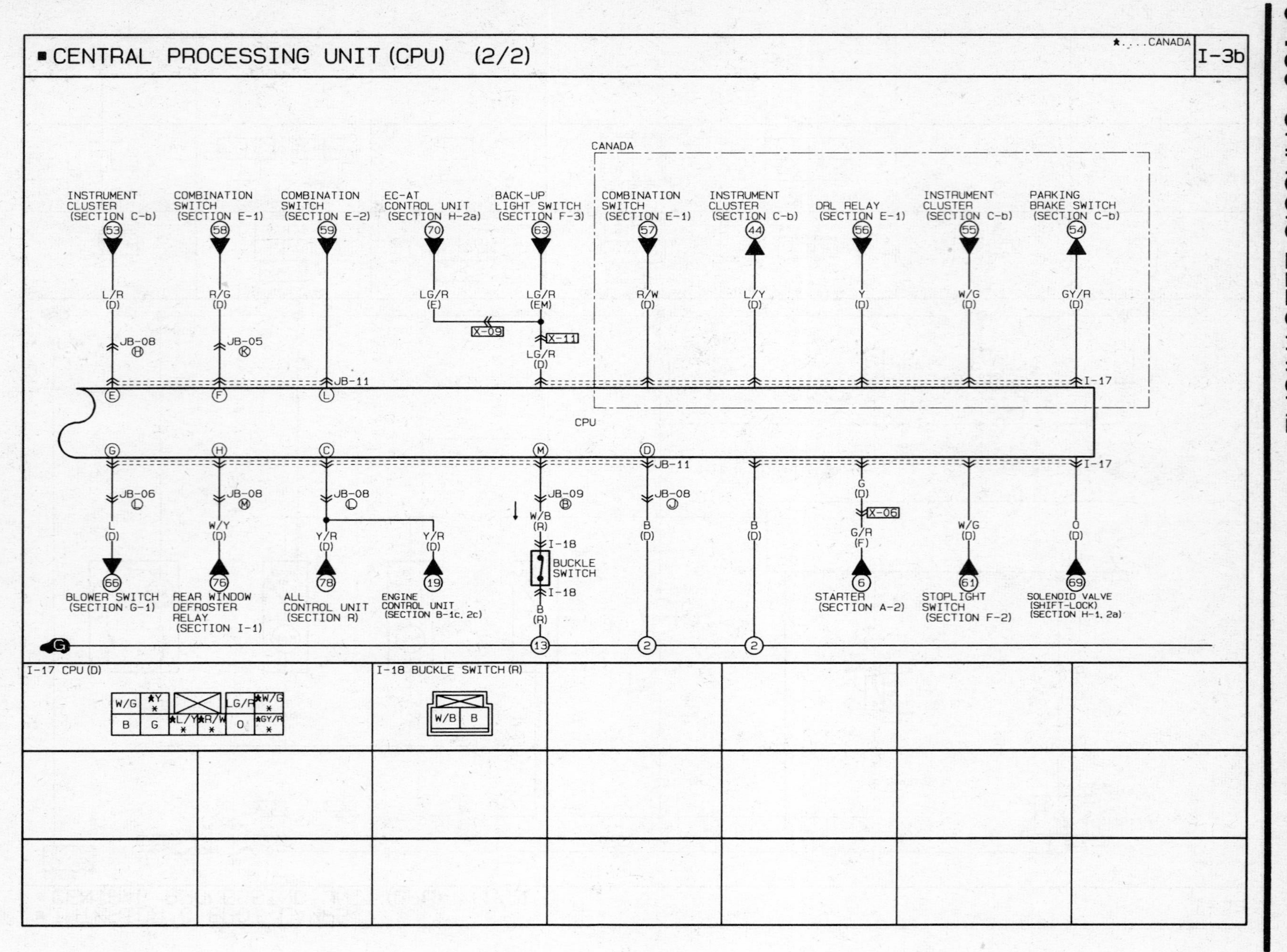

1992 MPV central processing unit

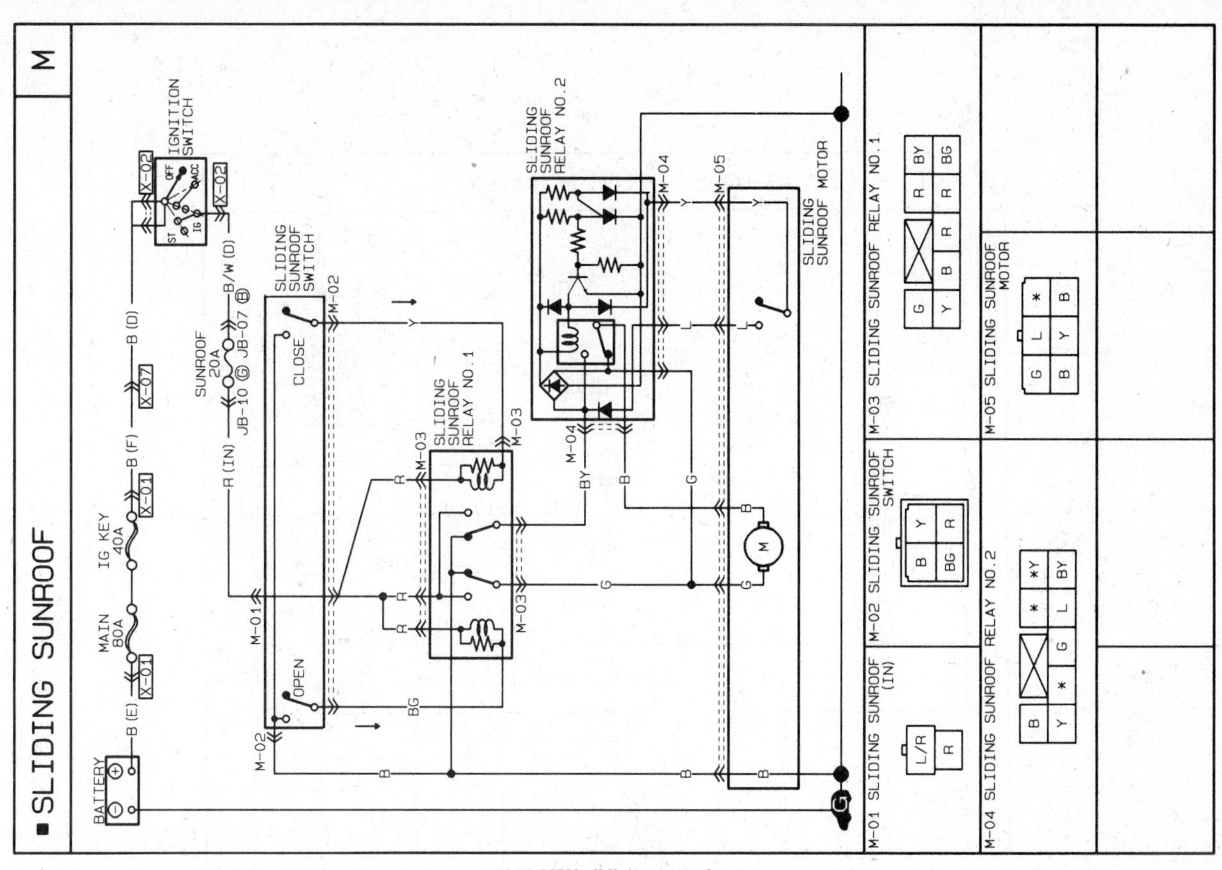

1992 MPV sliding sun roof

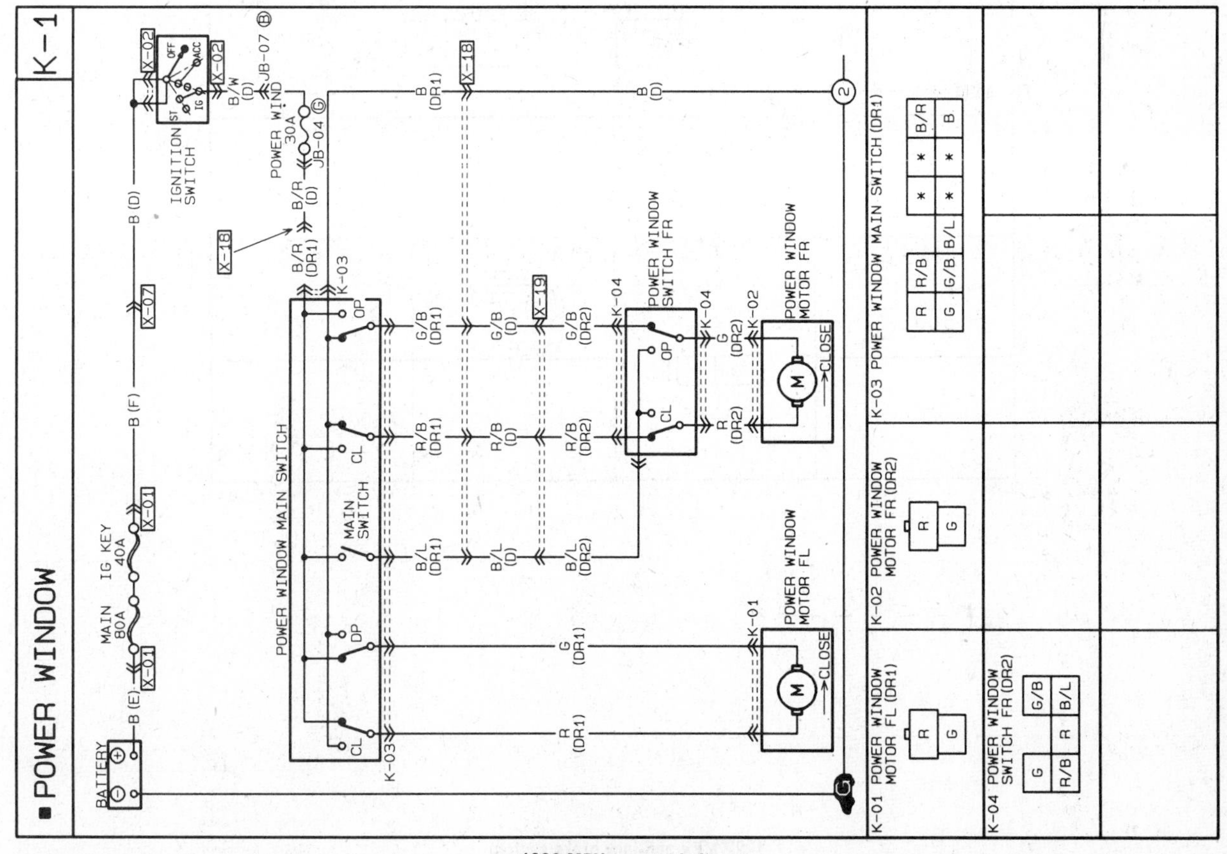

1992 MPV power window

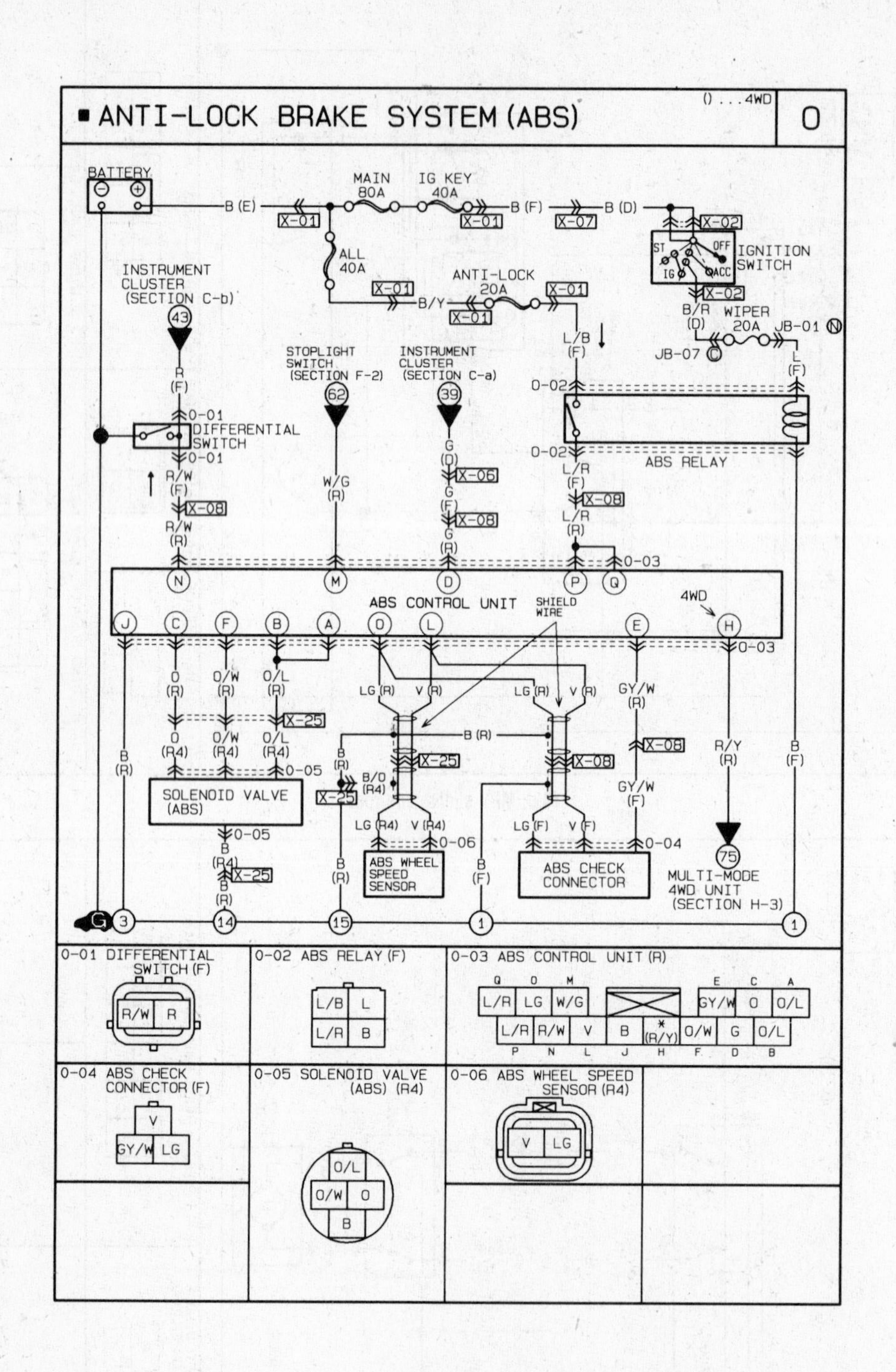

1992 MPV anti-lock brake system

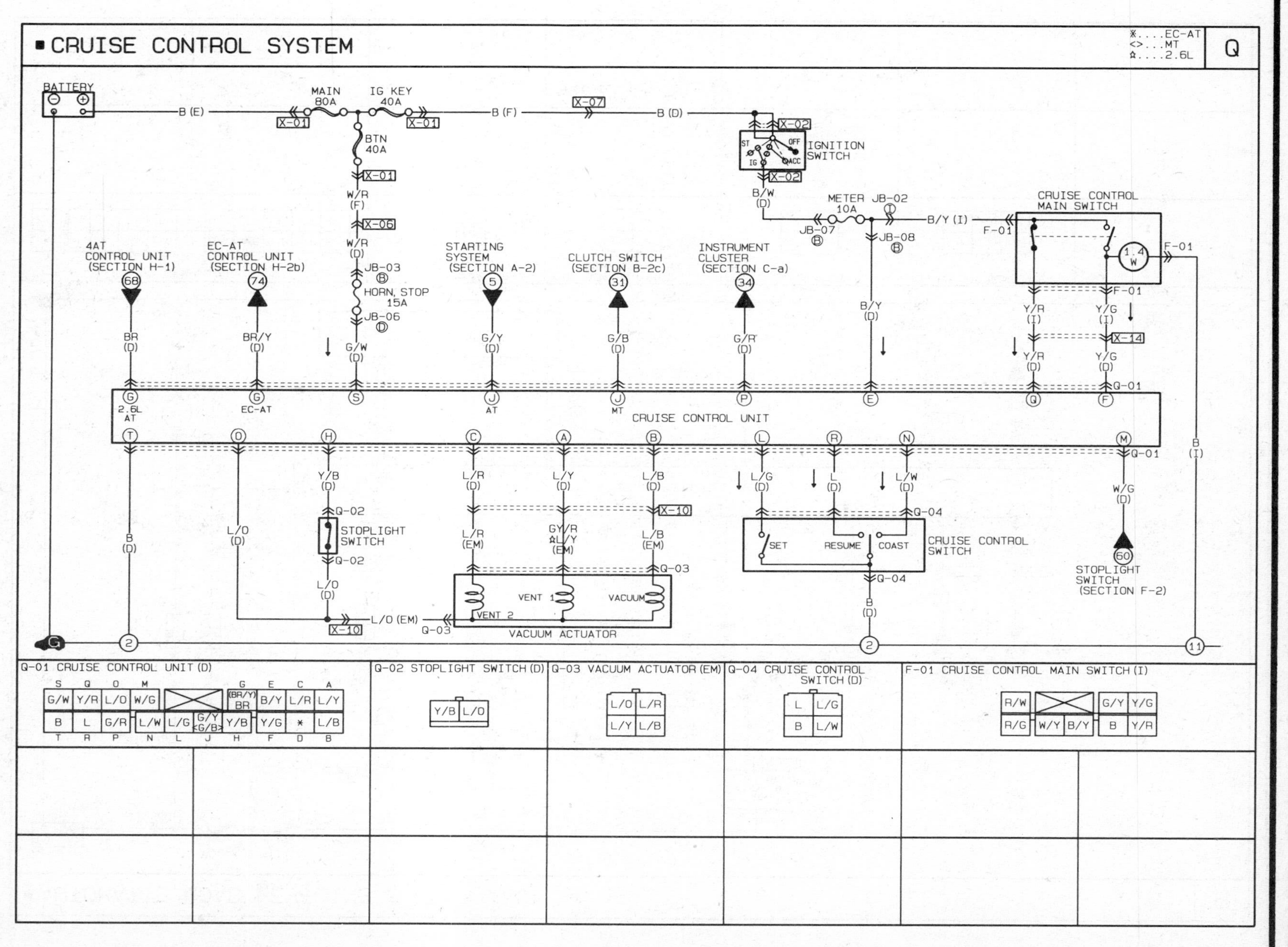

1992 MPV cruise control system

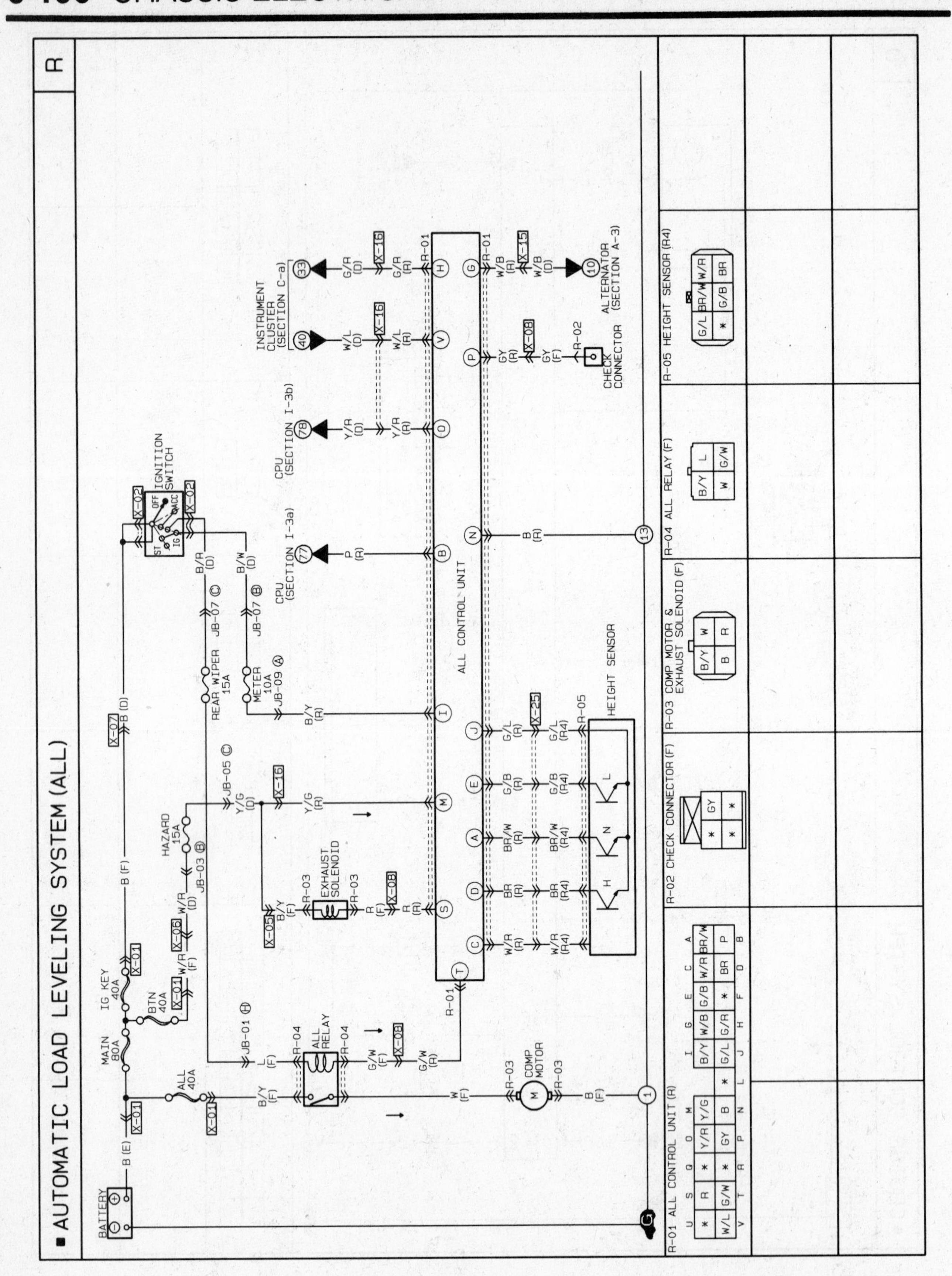

1992 MPV automatic load leveling system

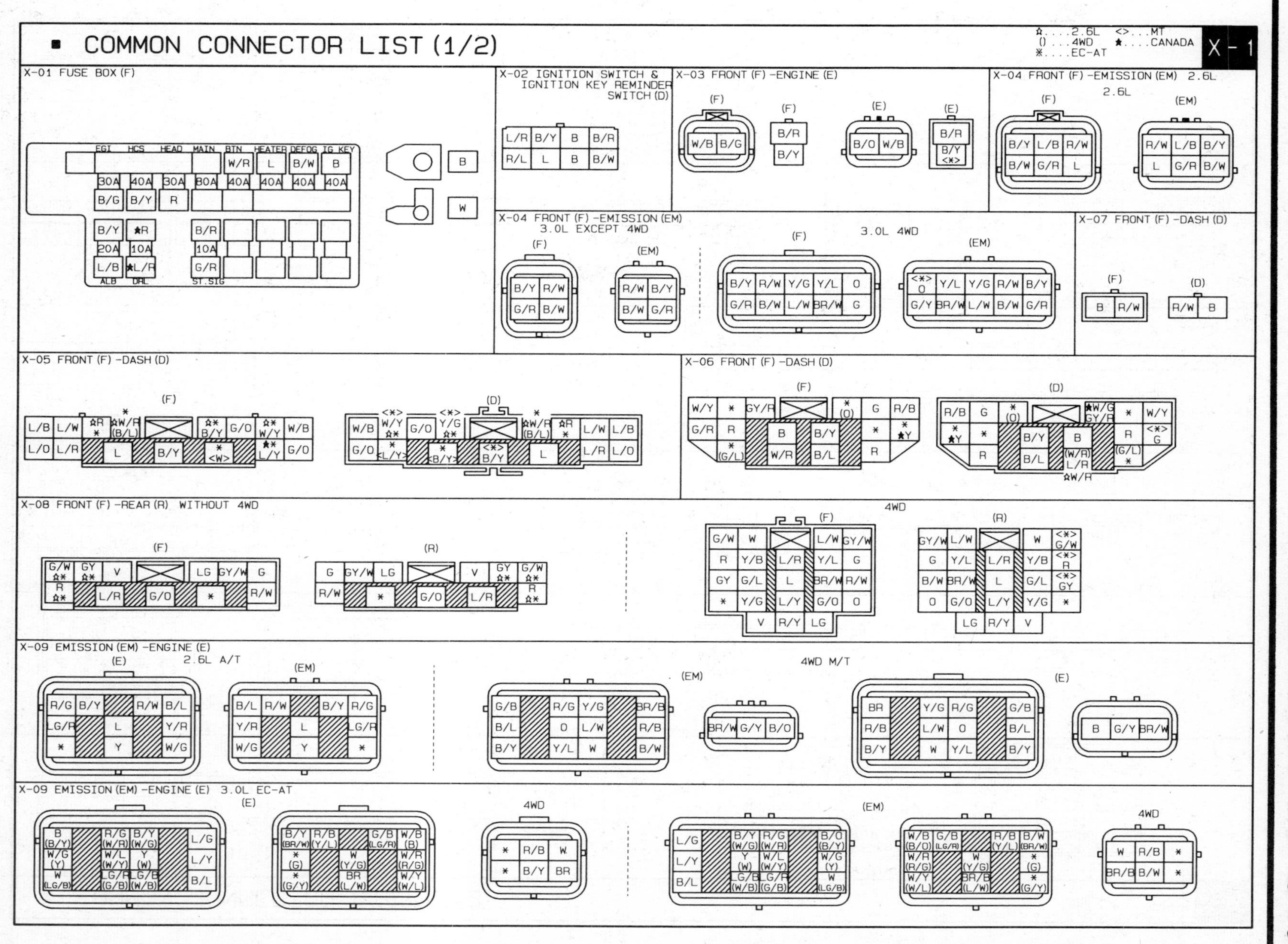

1992 MPV common connector list

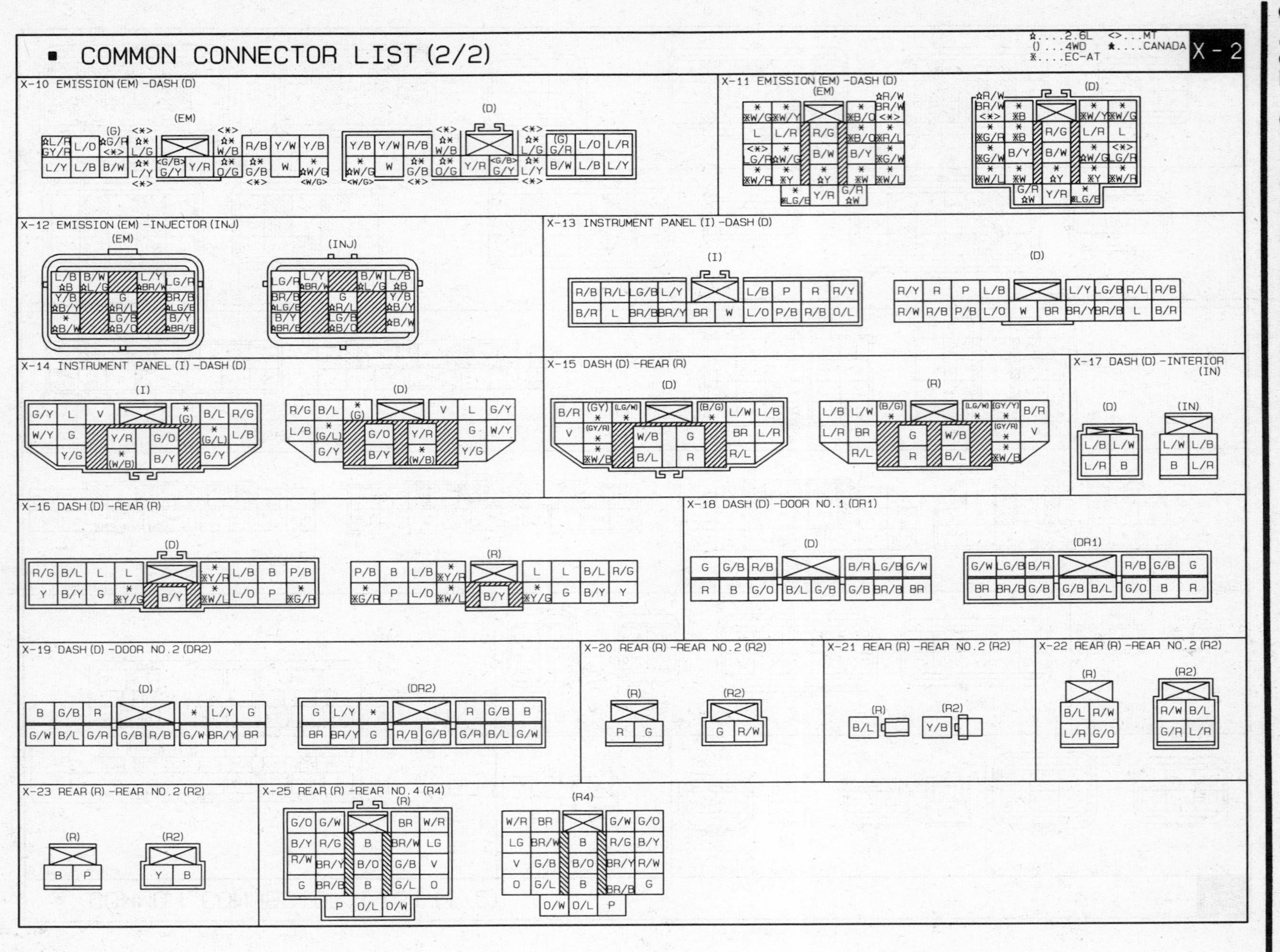

1992 MPV common connector list

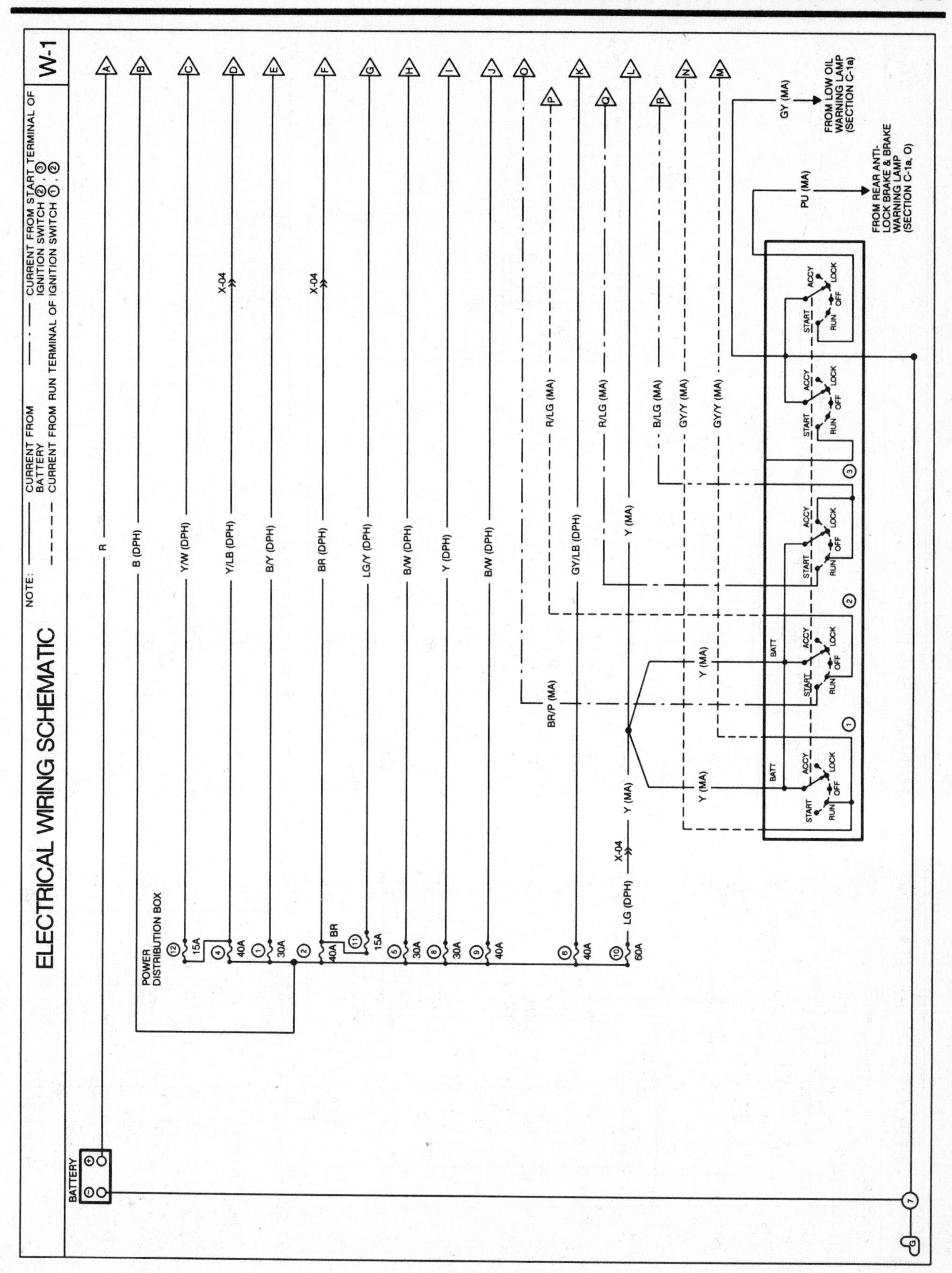

Navajo electrical wiring schematic (1991 shown)

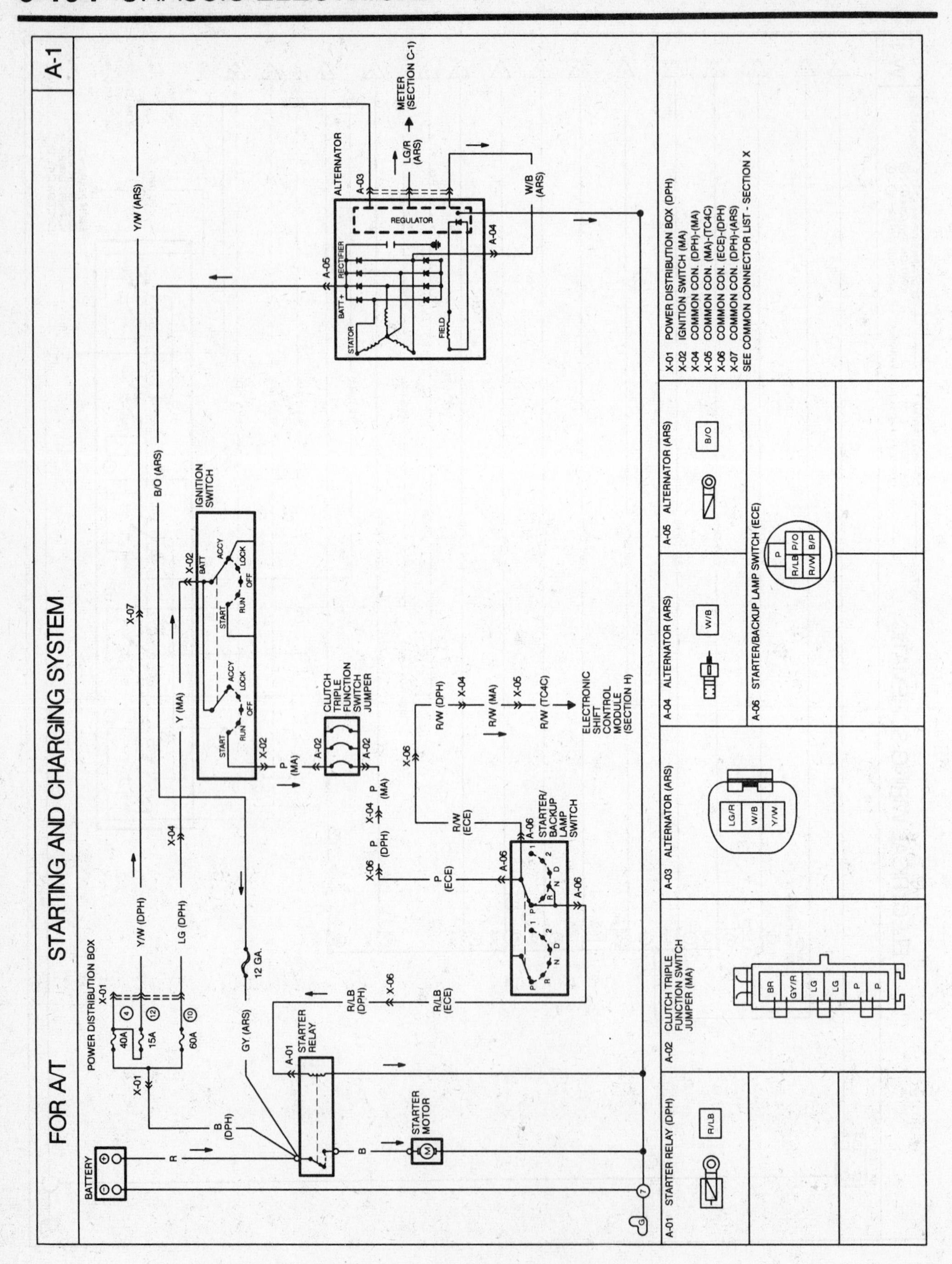

Navajo AT starting and charging systems (1991 shown)

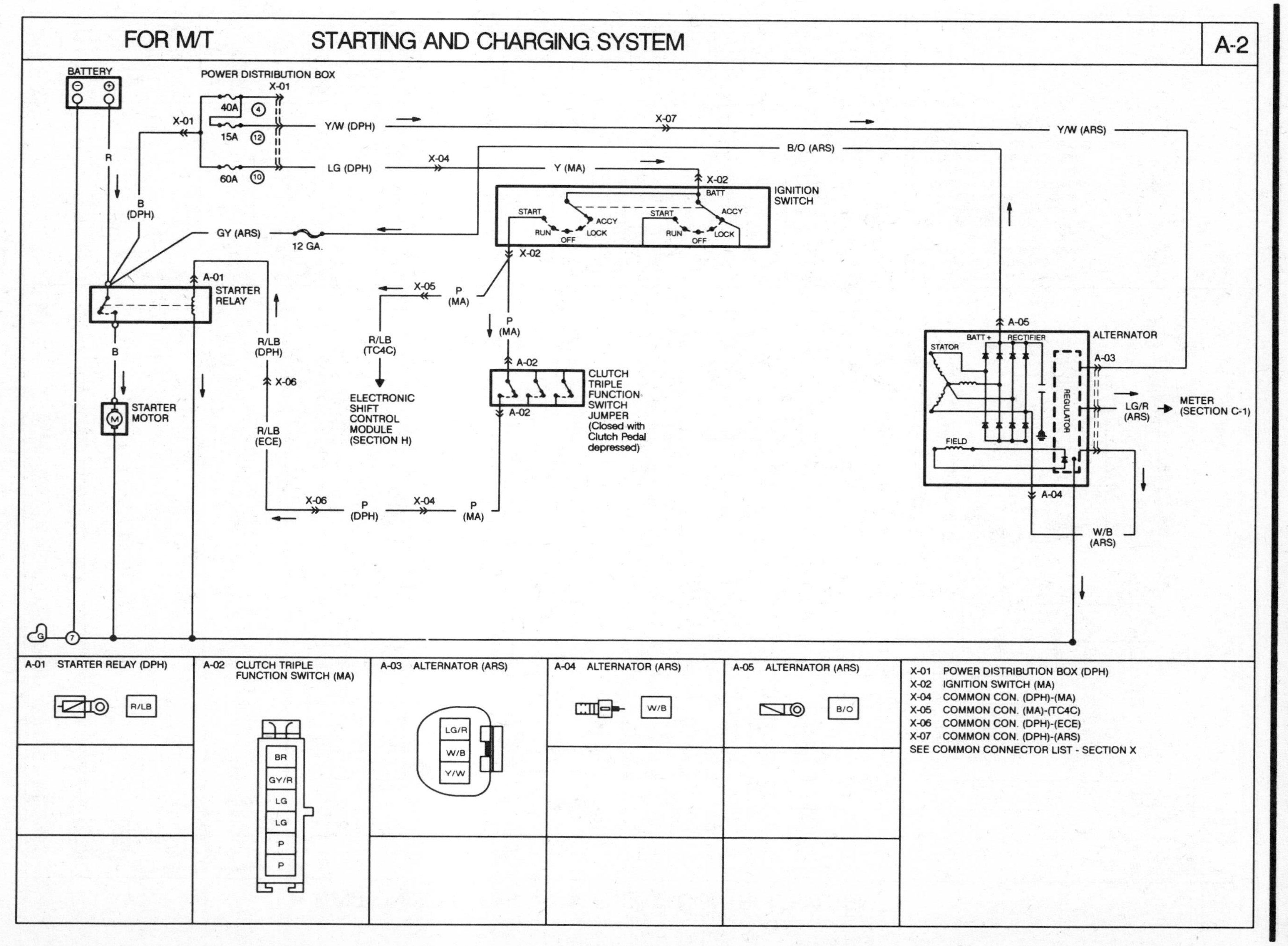

Navajo MT starting and charging system (1991 shown)

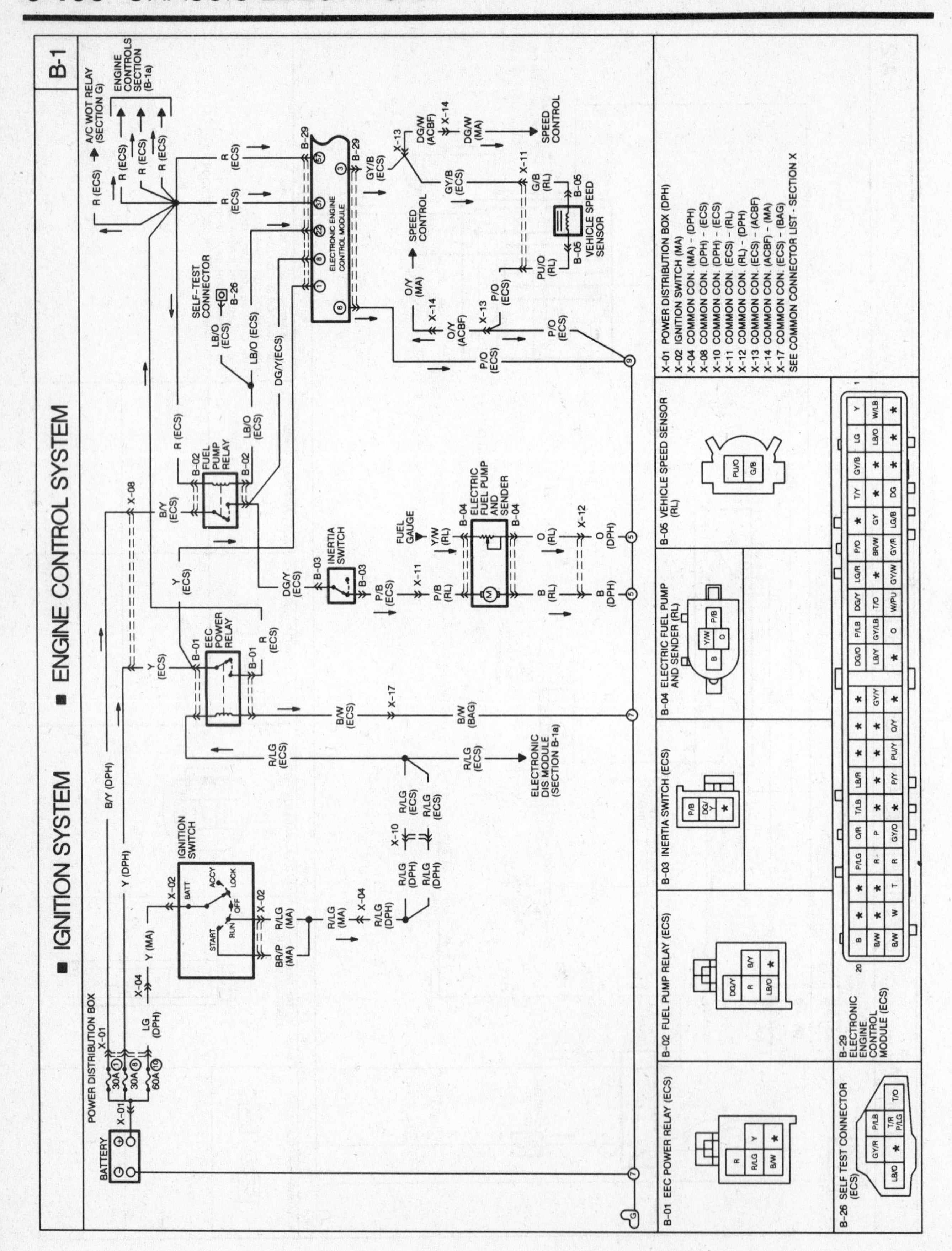

Navajo ignition and engine control system (1991 shown)

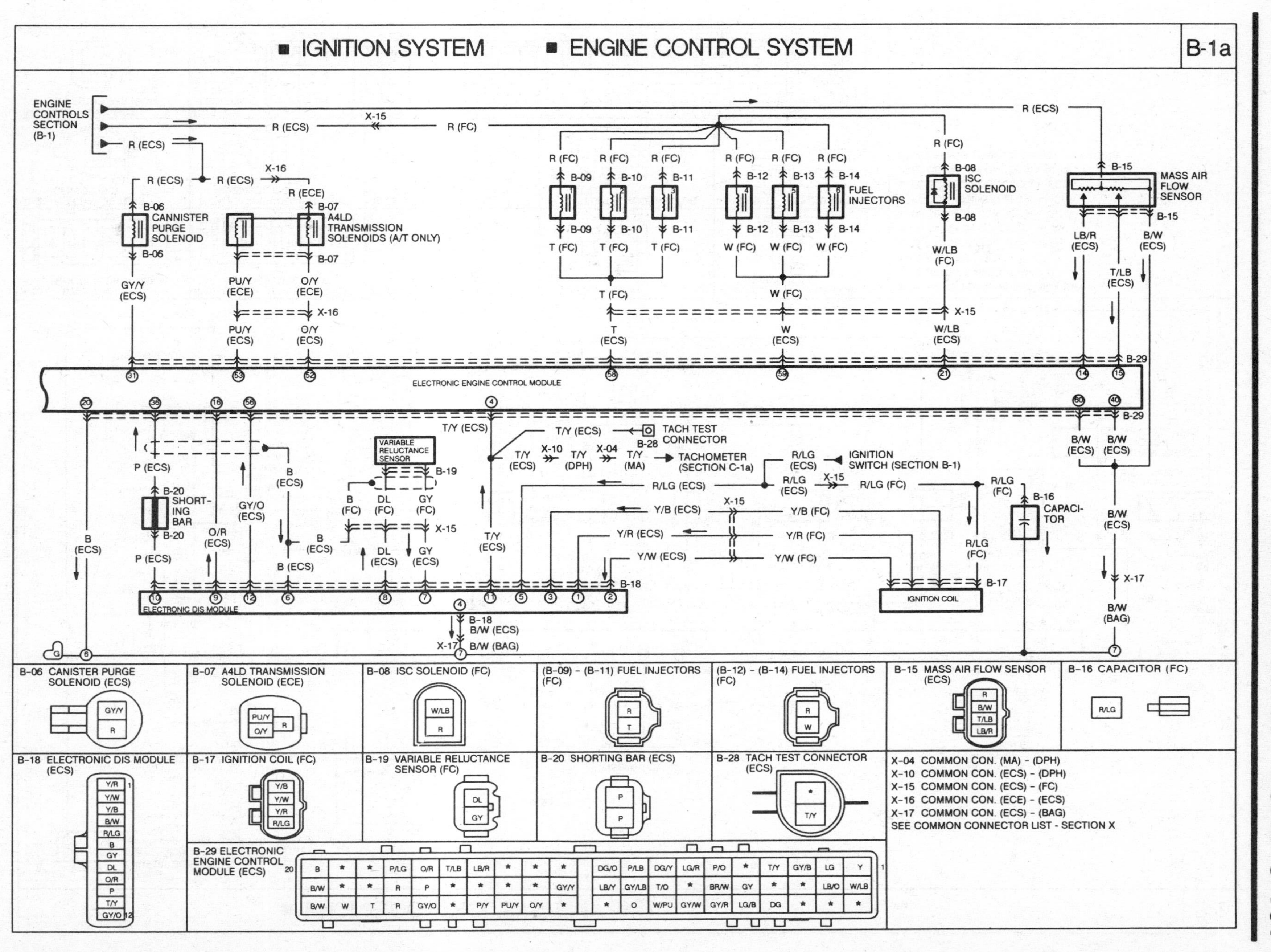

Navajo ignition and engine control system (1991 shown)

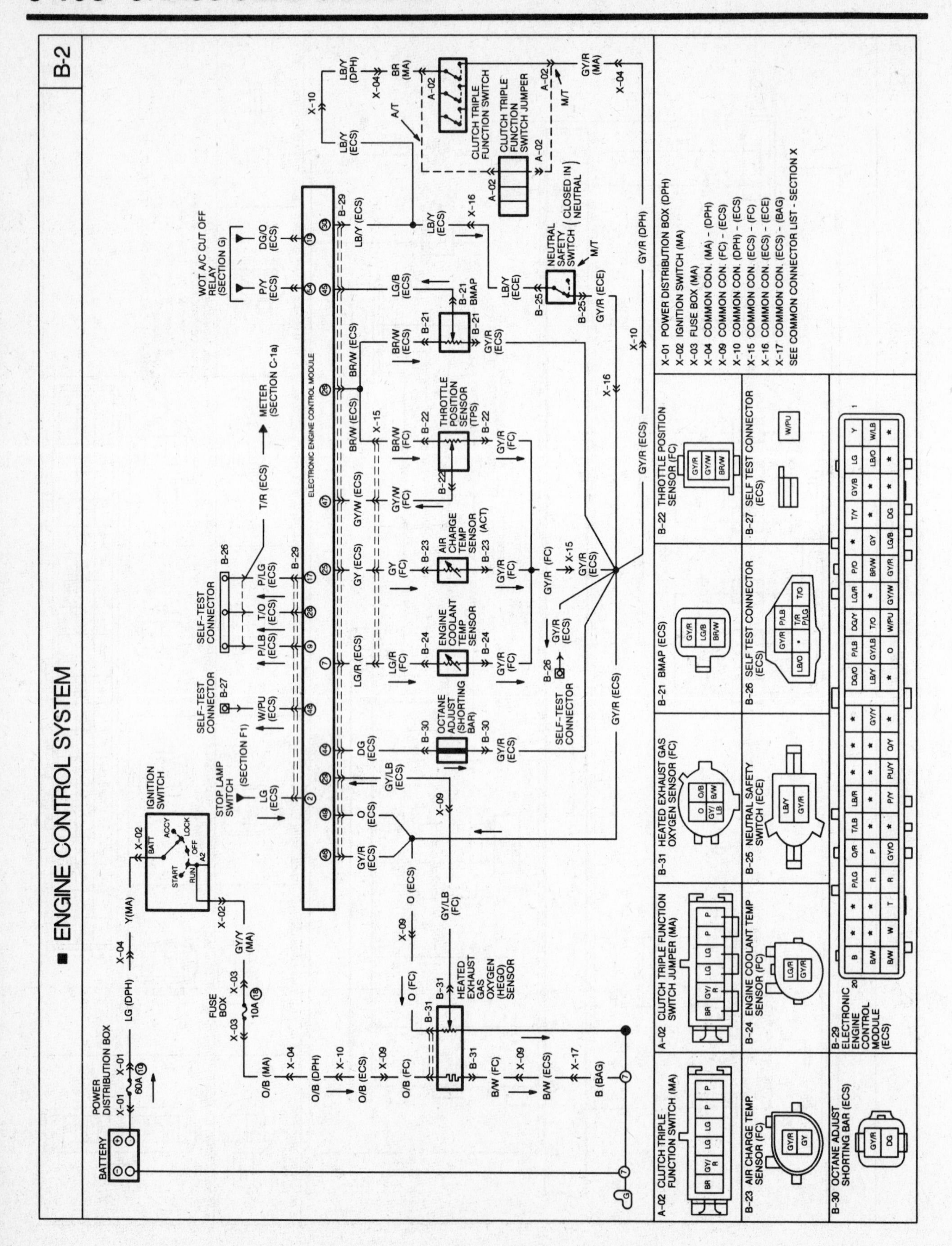

Navajo engine control system (1991 shown)

■ ELECTRONIC ENGINE CONTROL MODULE TERMINAL (UNIT SIDE)

B-3

ECM

20																			1
B	*	*	P/LG	O/R	T/LB	LB/R	*	*	*	DG/O	P/LB	DG/Y	LG/R	P/O	*	T/Y	GY/B	LG	Y
B/W	*	*	R	P	*	*	*	*	GY/Y	LB/Y	GY/LB	T/O	*	BR/W	GY	*	*	LB/O	W/LB
B/W	W	T	R	GY/O	*	P/Y	PU/Y	O/Y	*	*	O	W/PU	GY/W	GY/R	LG/B	DG	*	*	*

SENSORS/ INPUTS	Signal Pin #	KOEO	Units	HOT IDLE	30 MPH	55 MPH	Units
OCTADJ	44	0	DCV	0	0	0	DCV
MAF	14	0	DCV	.6	1.3–1.4	1.7–2.0	DCV
TP	47	1.0	DCV	1.0	1.2–1.3	1.4–1.6	DCV
ECT	7	.6	DCV	.6	.6	.6	DCV
ACT	25	2.2	DCV	2.6	2.7	2.9	DCV
BP	45	158	Hz	158	158	158	Hz
IDM	4	0	RPM	750–850	1500–1700	1800–2000	RPM
PIP	56	0	RPM	750–850	1500–1700	1800–2000	RPM
HEGO	29	0	DCV	switching	switching	switching	DCV
BOO	2	0	DCV	0/VBAT①	0	0	DCV
FPM	8	0	DCV	VBAT	VBAT	VBAT	DCV
ACCS	10	0	DCV	0/VBAT②	0	0	DCV
VSS+	3	0	MPH	0	30	55	MPH
NDS	30	0	DCV	0	5.0	5.0	DCV
STI	48	5.0	DCV	5.0	5.0	5.0	DCV
ACTUATORS/ OUTPUTS							
INJ Bank 2	59	VBAT③	DCV	3.0–3.2	3.9–4.4	5.0–7.0	mS
INJ Bank 1	58	VBAT③	DCV	3.0–3.2	3.8–4.4	5.0–7.0	mS
SS 3/4 (A/T)	52	VBAT	DCV	VBAT	VBAT	0	DCV
STO/MIL	17	.6	DCV	VBAT	VBAT	VBAT	DCV
CANP	31	VBAT	DCV	VBAT	7.0–9.0	.2	DCV
WAC	54	0	DCV	0/VBAT②	0	0	DCV
ISC-BPA	21	VBAT	DCV	8.0–12.0	7.3–8.4	5.5–6.8	DCV
FP	22	VBAT	DCV	.1	.1	.1	DCV
SAW	36	0	RPM	750–850	1500–1700	1800–2000	RPM
CCO (A/T)	53	VBAT	DCV	VBAT	VBAT	0	DCV
OTHER							
IGN TIMING	TIMING			10	10	10	DEG

NOTES: ① – Brake pedal depressed.
② – A/C on.
③ – Monitor in DCV manual mode.
HEGO in 'switching' mode ranges from .2 to .9 DCV.
Reference values shown may vary ±20% depending on operating conditions and other factors.
RPM values are axle and tire dependent.

Navajo electronic engine control module terminal & values (1991 shown)

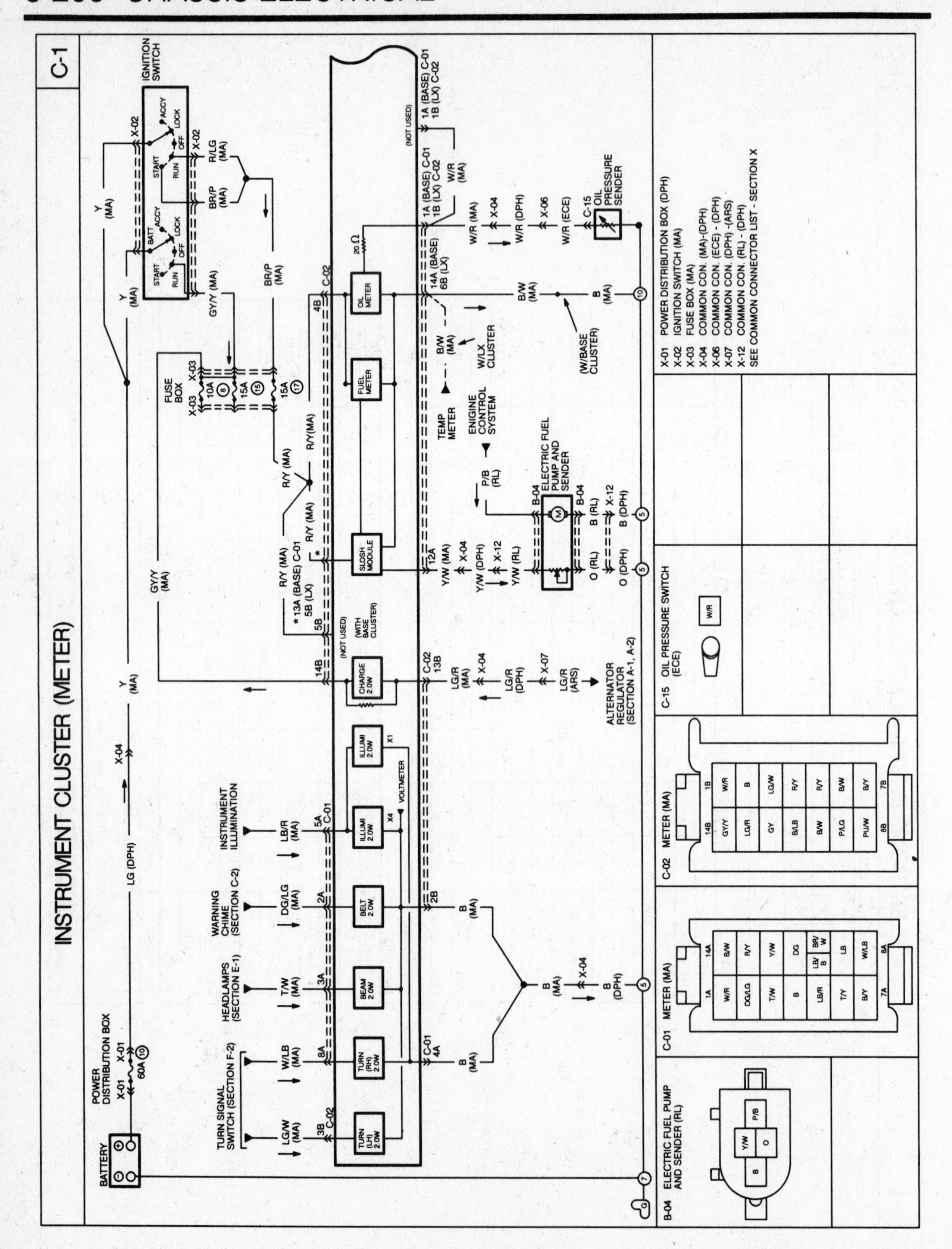

Navajo instrument cluster (1991 shown)

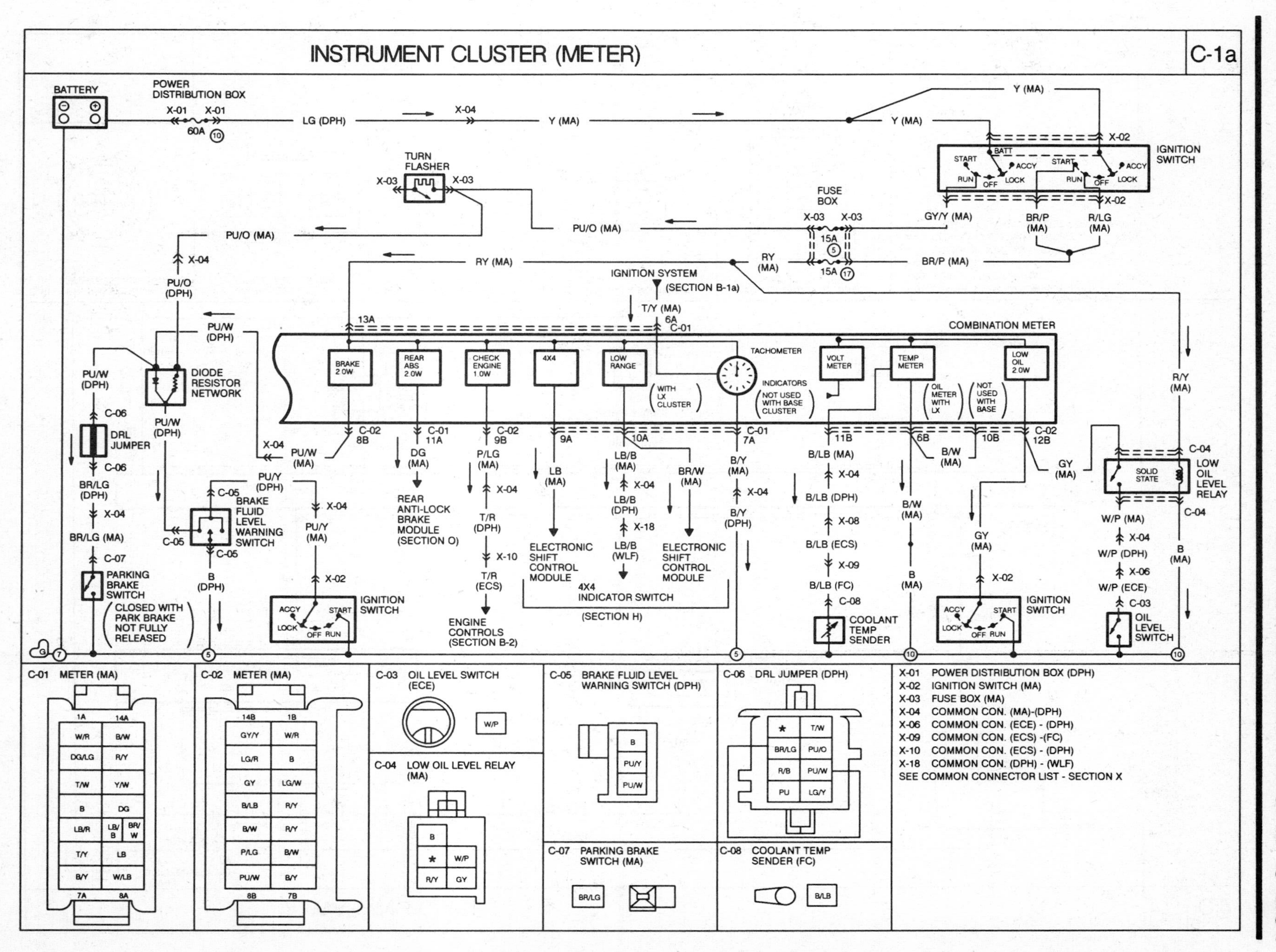

Navajo instrument cluster (1991 shown)

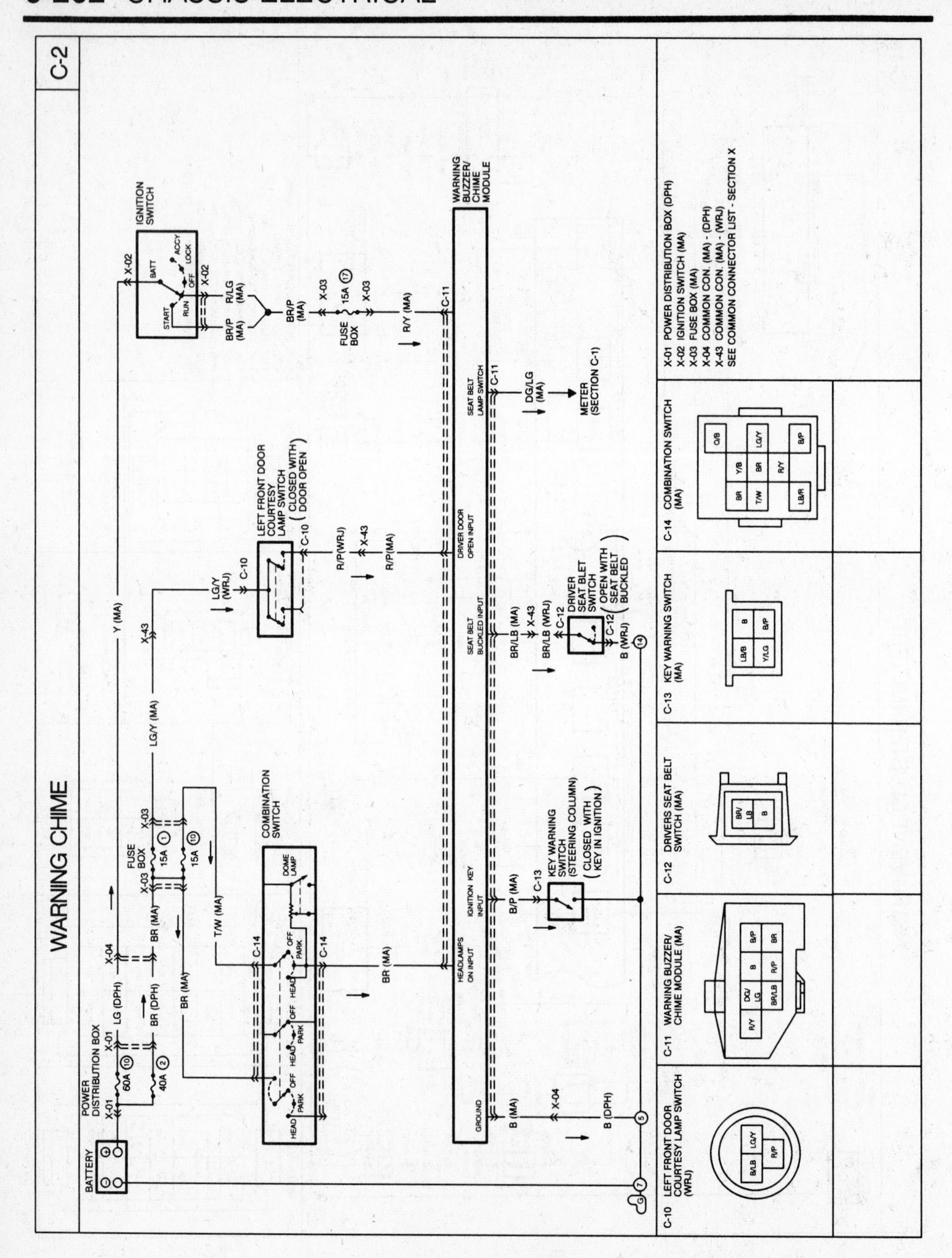

Navajo warning chime (1991 shown)

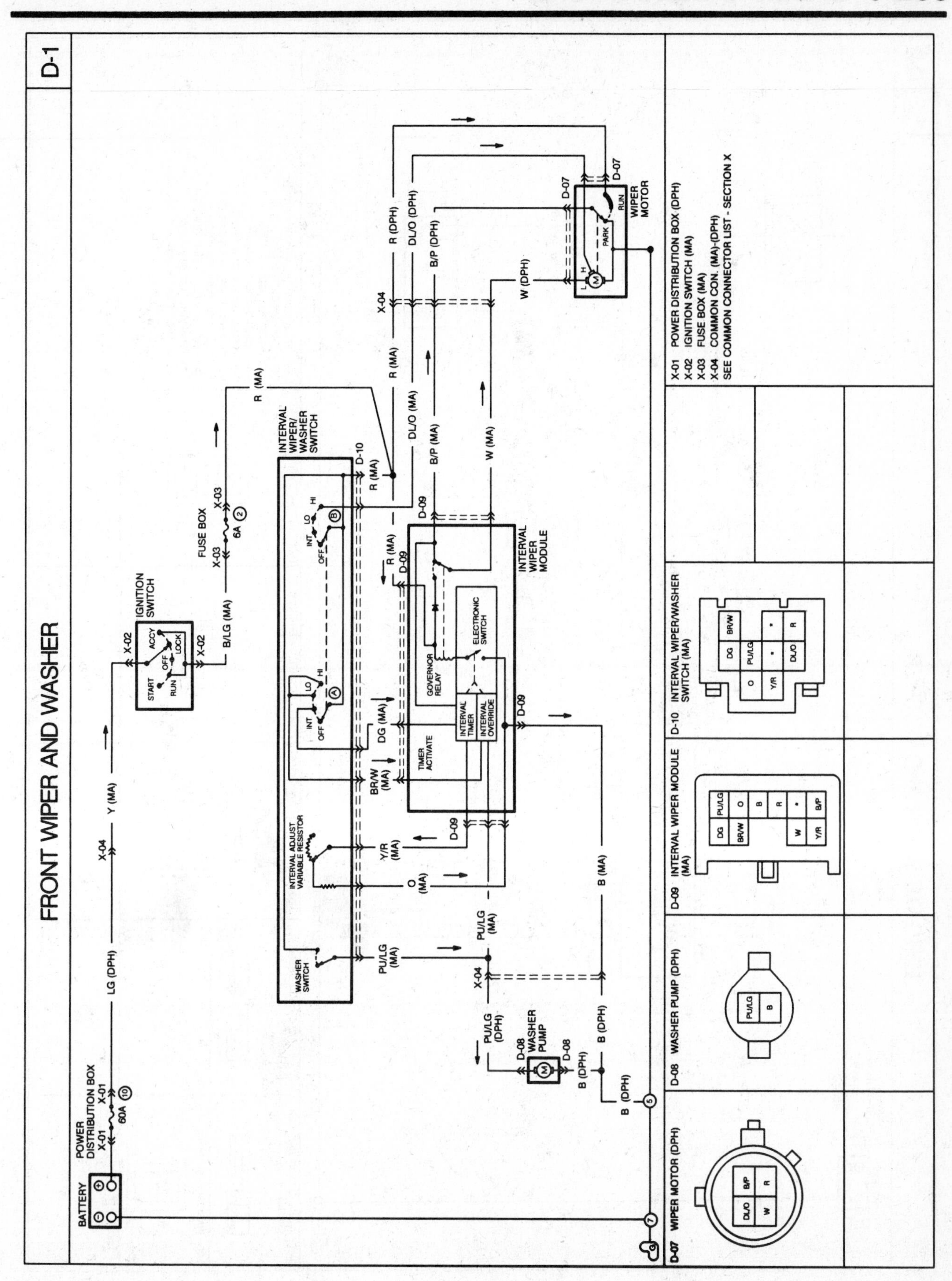

Navajo front wiper and washer (1991 shown)

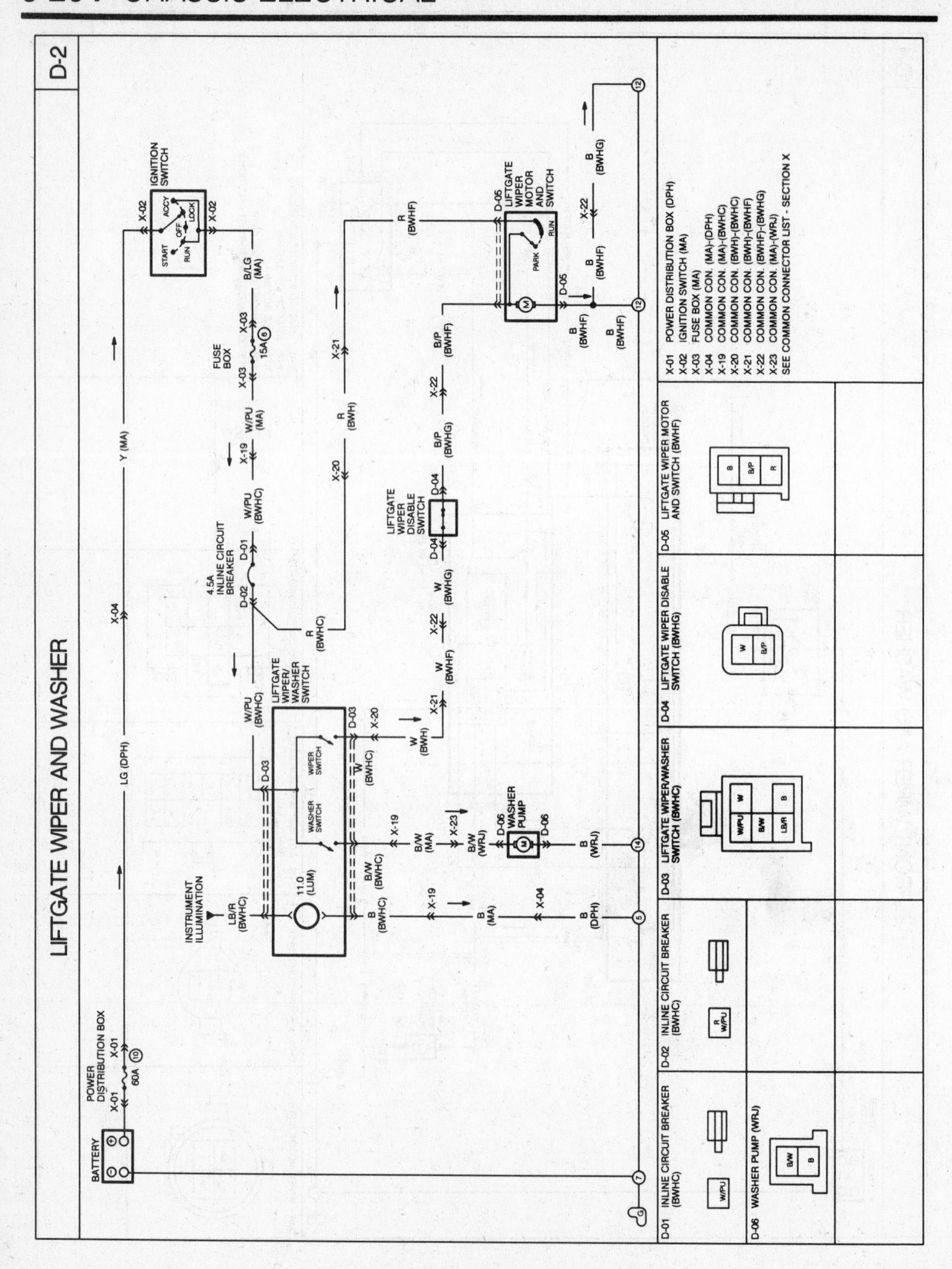

Navajo liftgate wiper and washer (1991 shown)

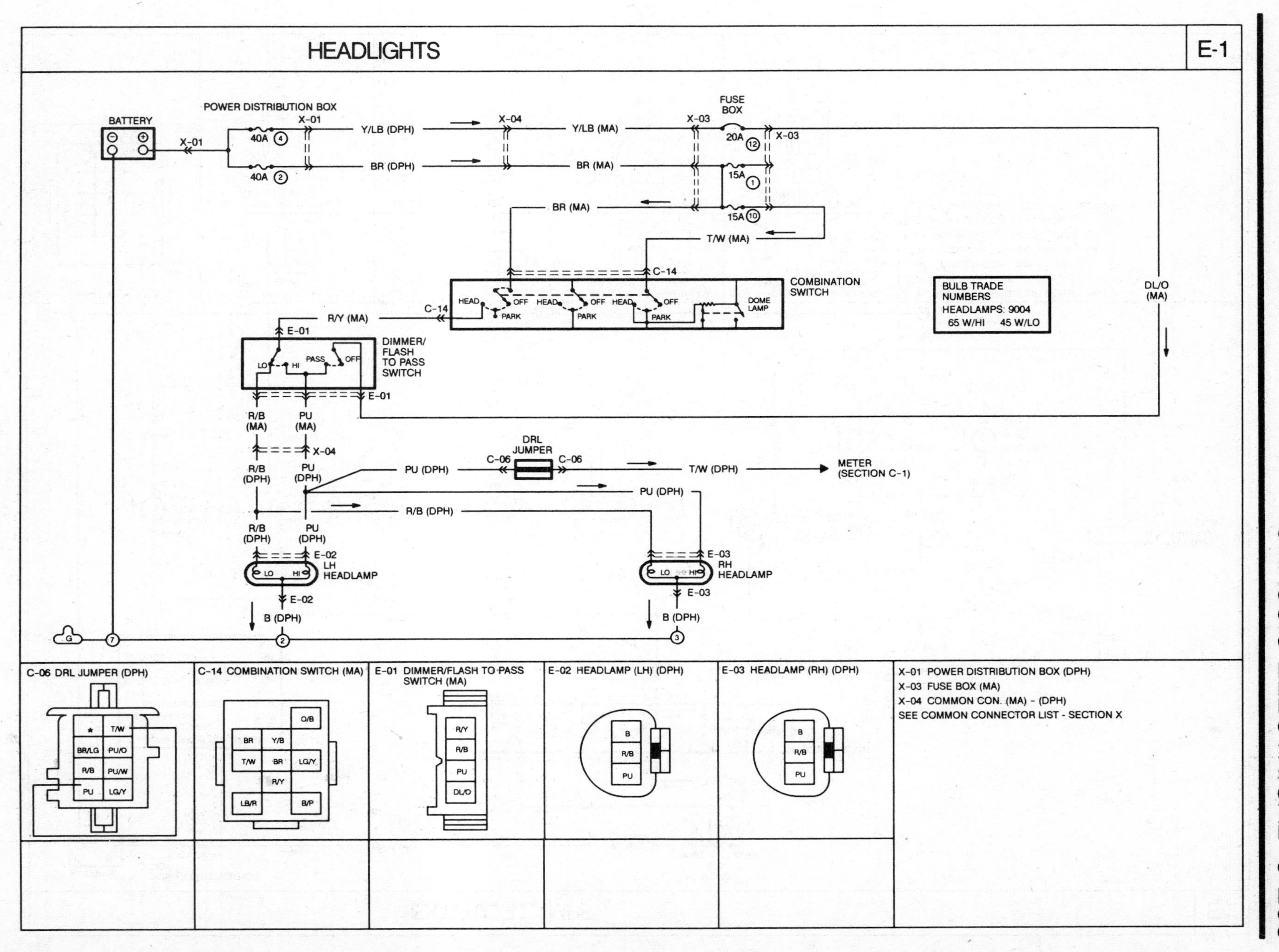

Navajo headlights (1991 shown)

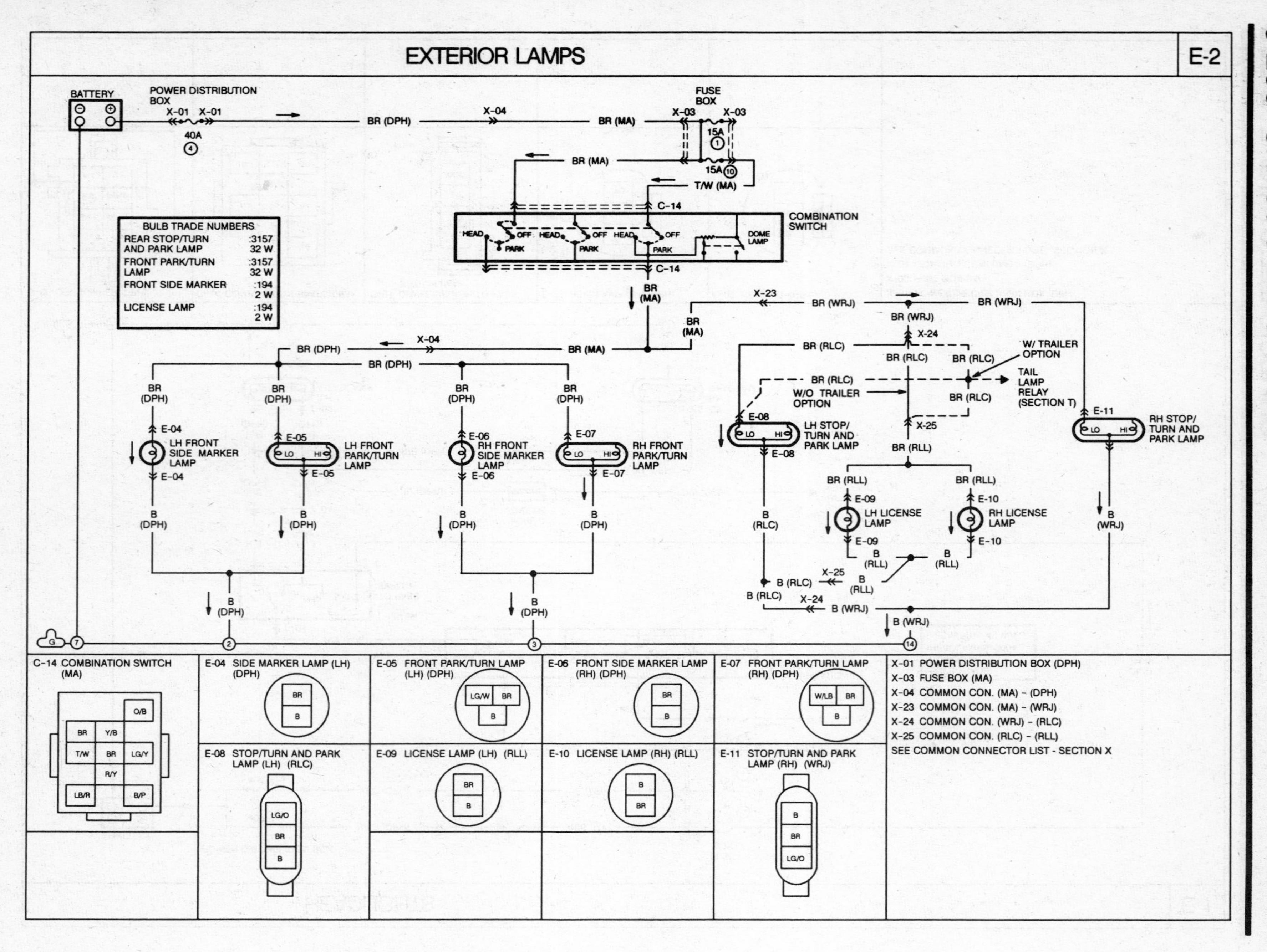

Navajo exterior lamps (1991 shown)

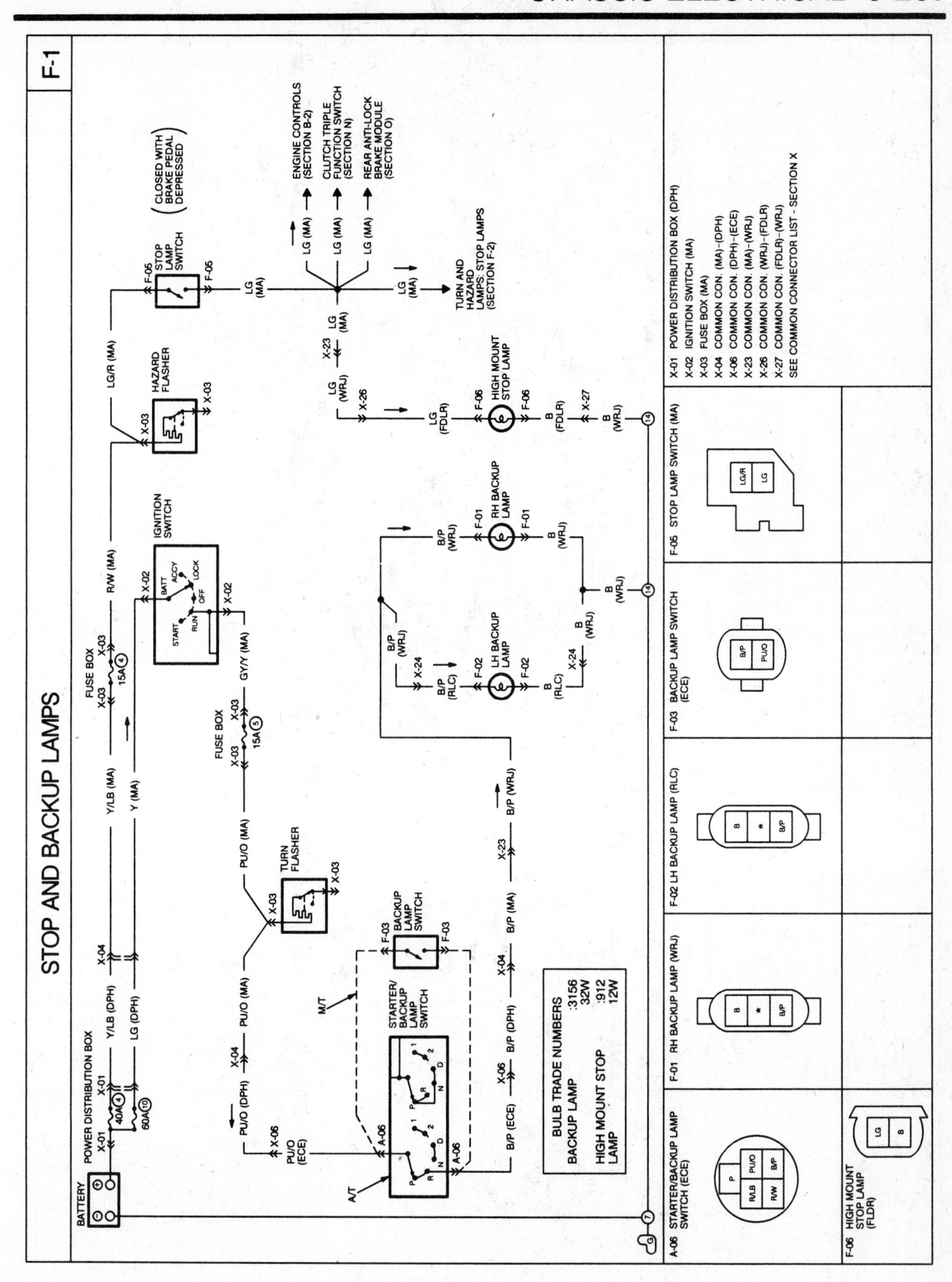

Navajo stop and backup lamps (1991 shown)

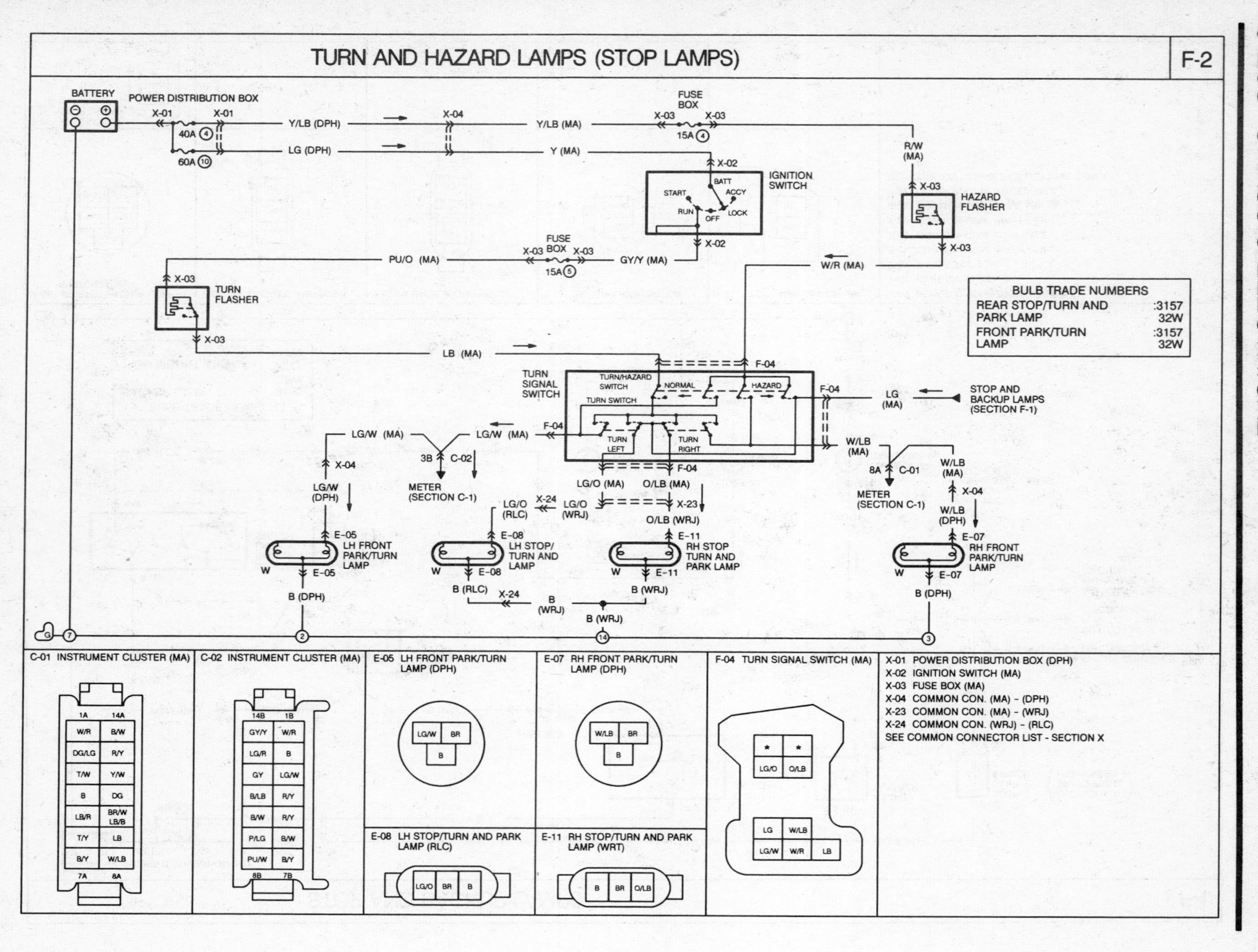

Navajo turn and hazard lamps (1991 shown)

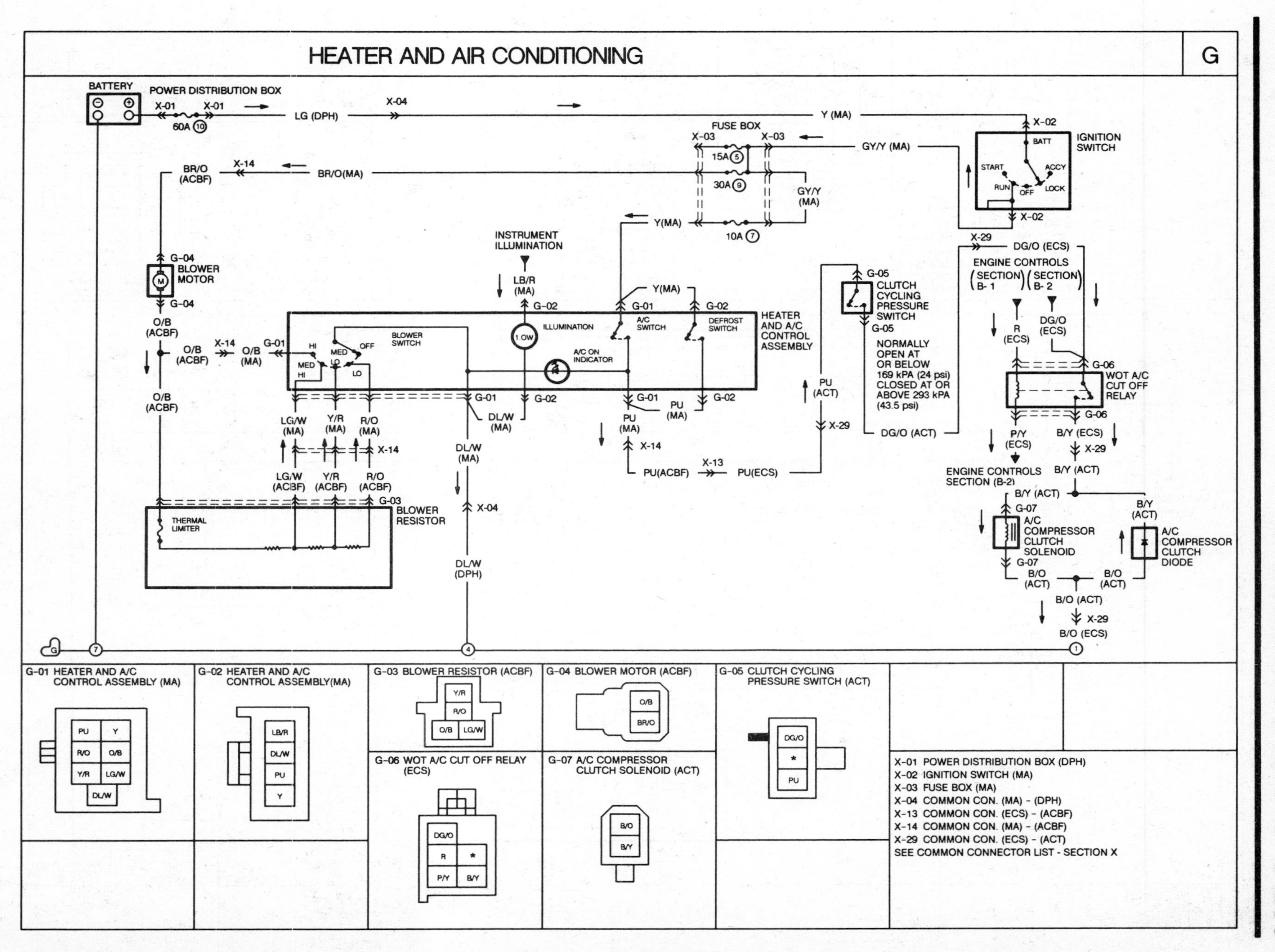

Navajo heater and air conditioning (1991 shown)

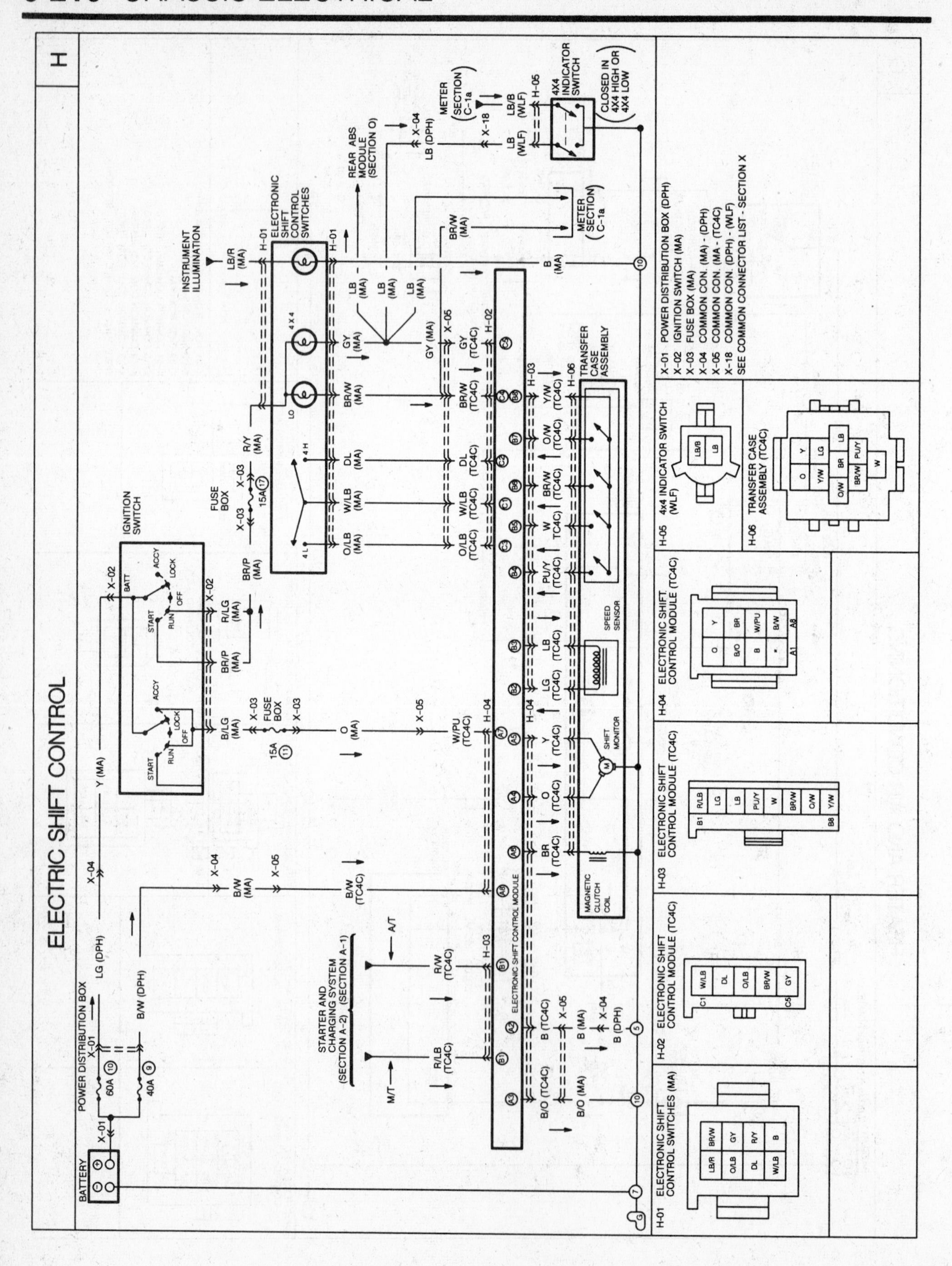

Navajo electric shift control (1991 shown)

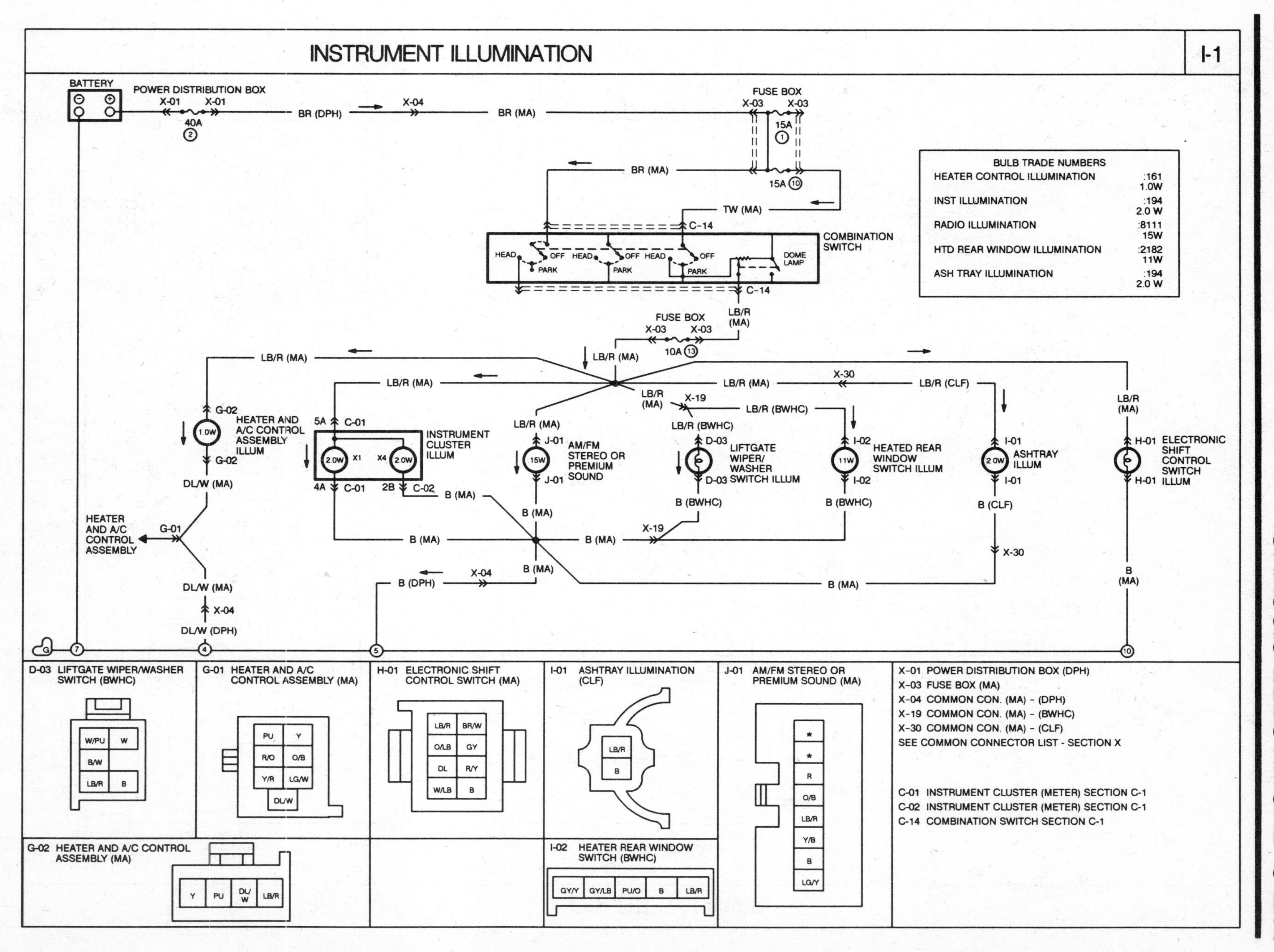

Navajo instrument illumination (1991 shown)

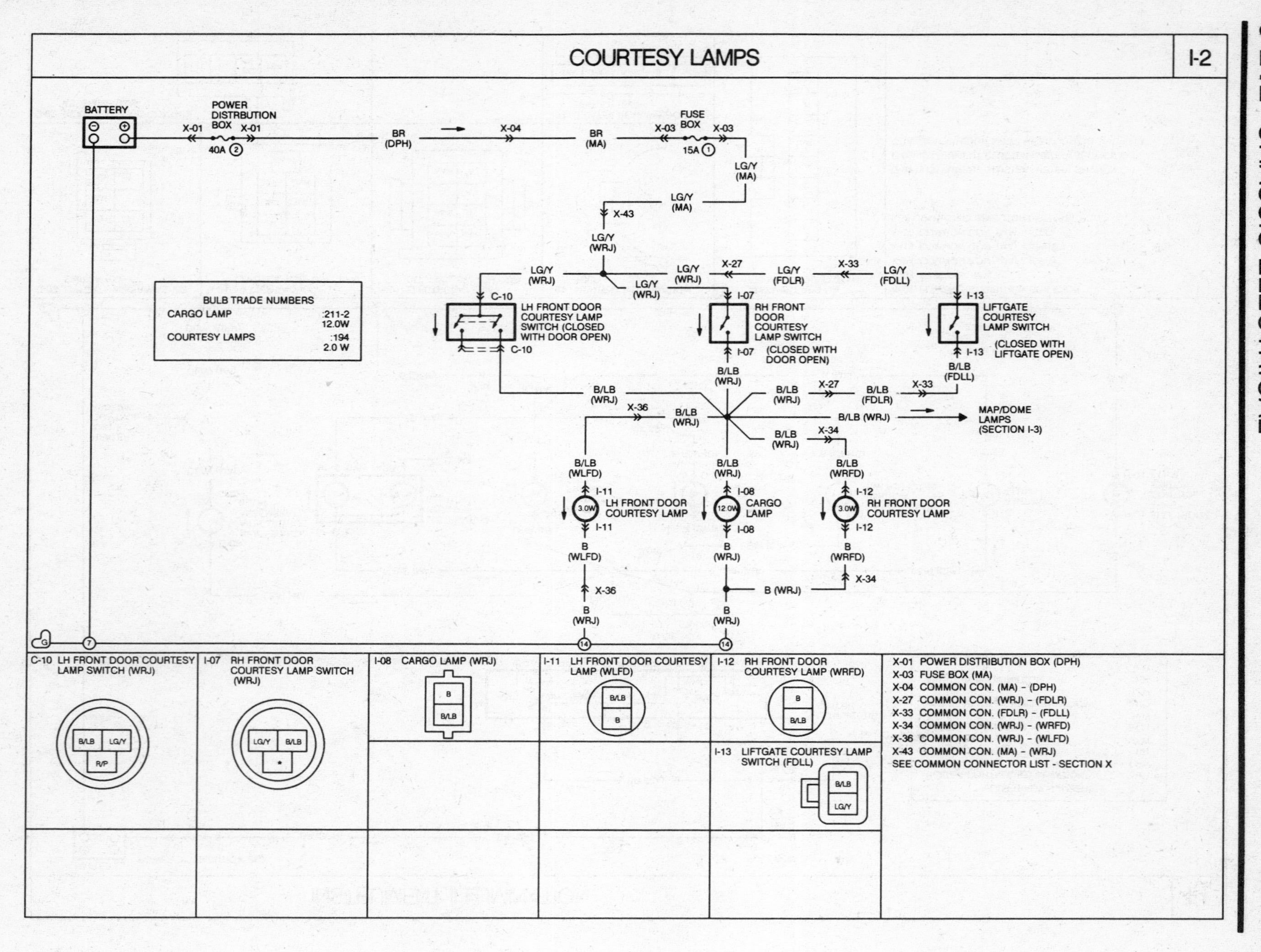

Navajo courtesy lamps (1991 shown)

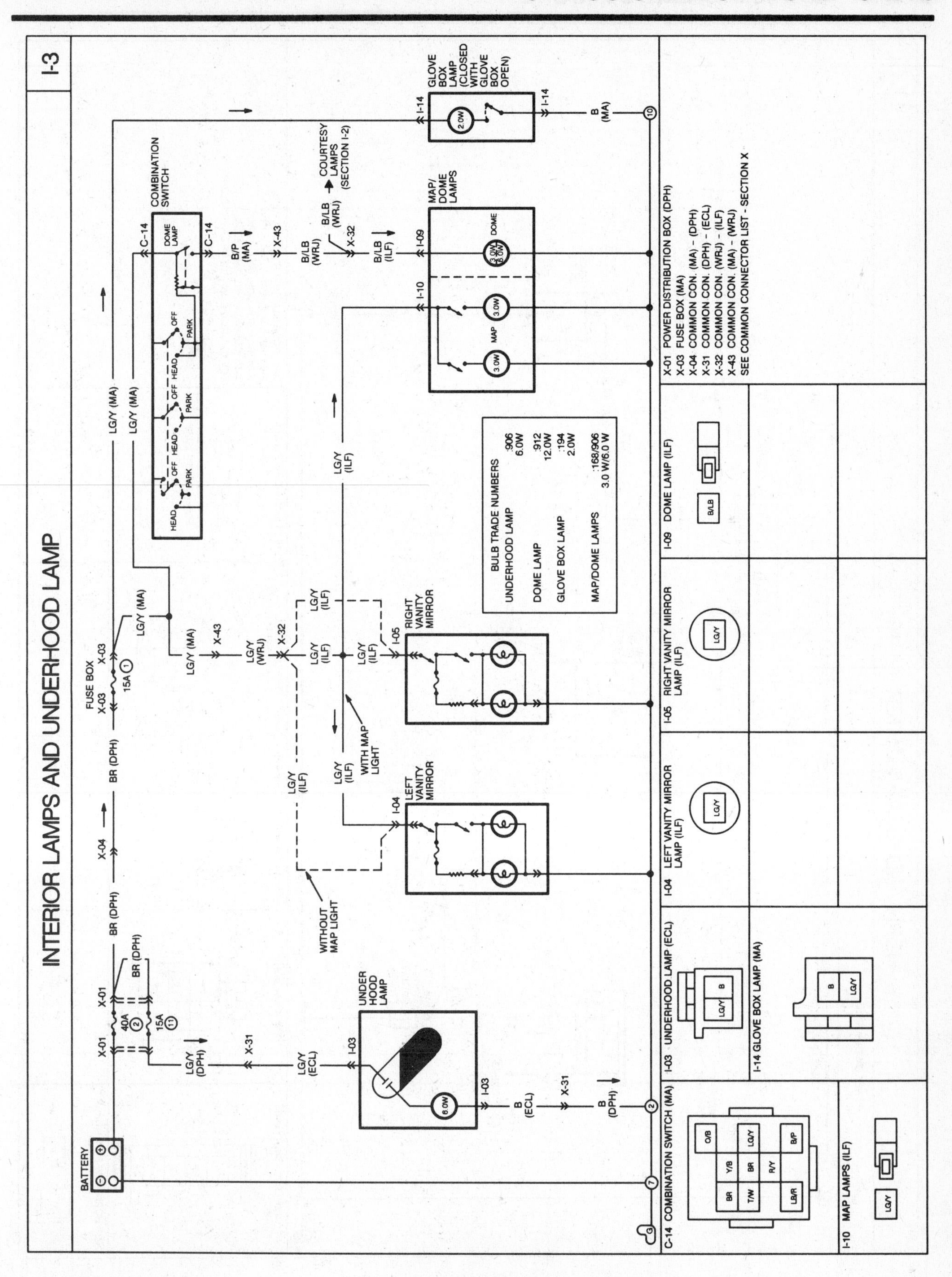

Navajo interior lamps and underhood lamp (1991 shown)

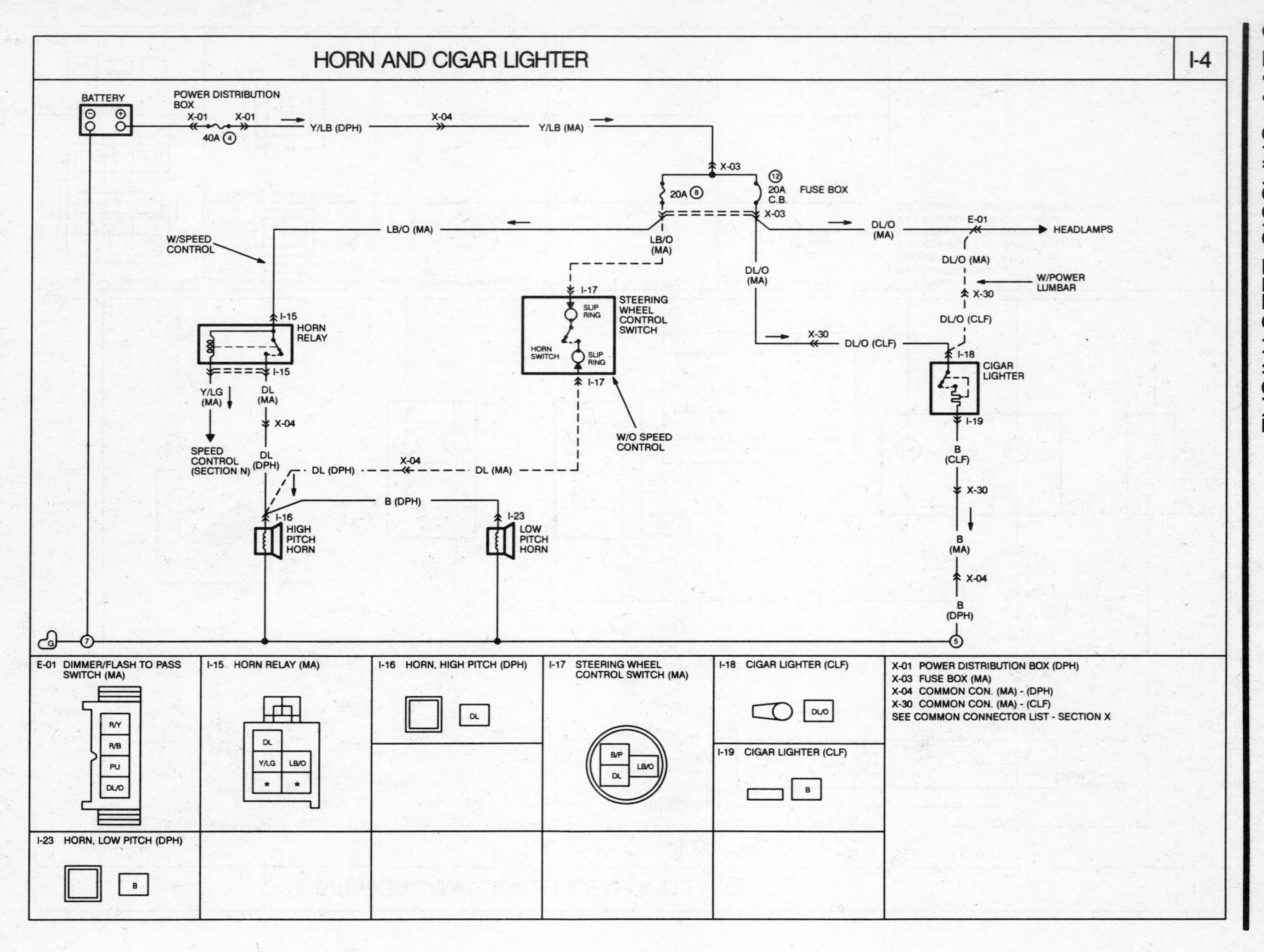

Navajo horn and cigar lighter (1991 shown)

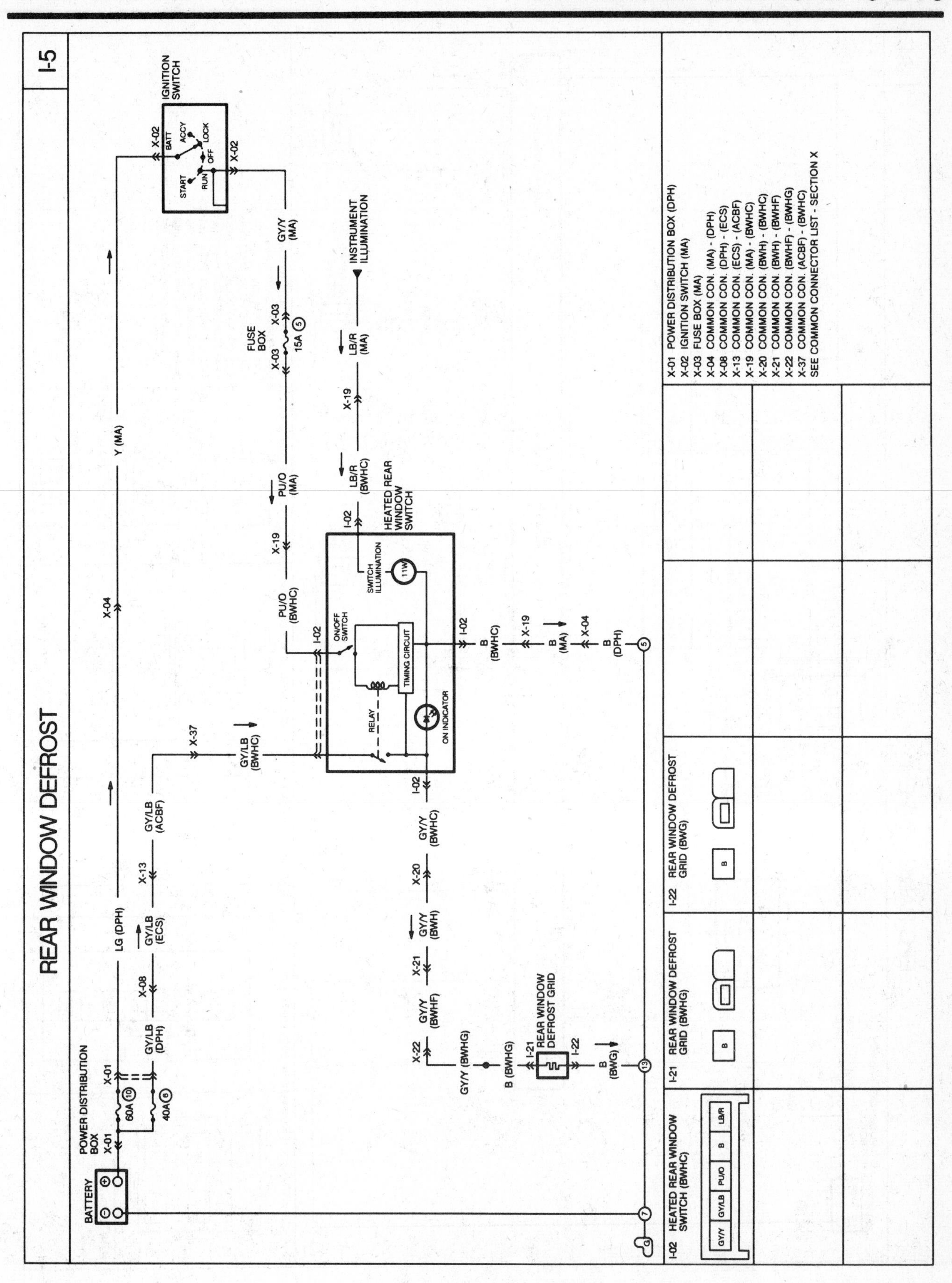

Navajo rear window defrost (1991 shown)

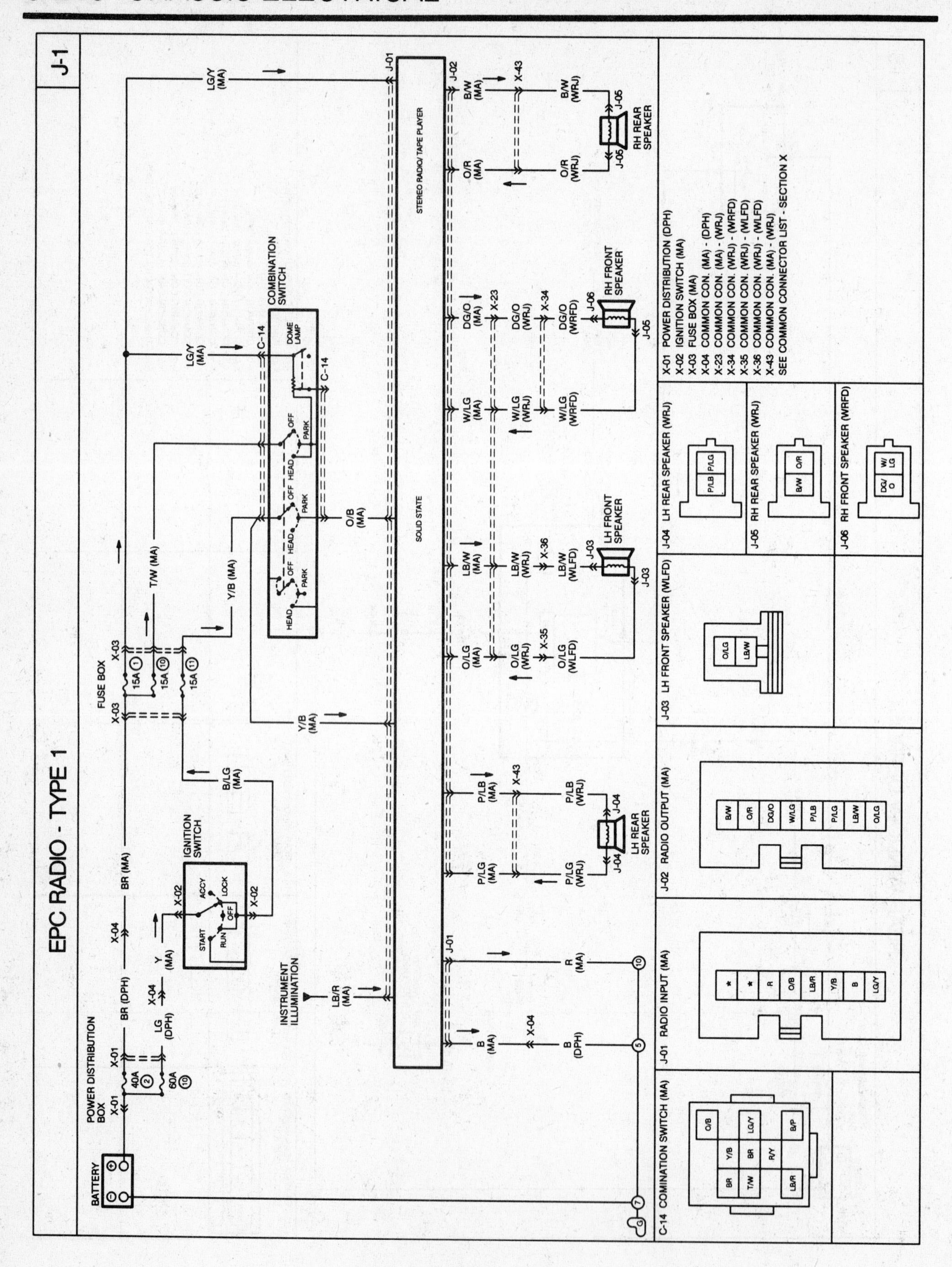

Navajo EPC radio type 1 (1991 shown)

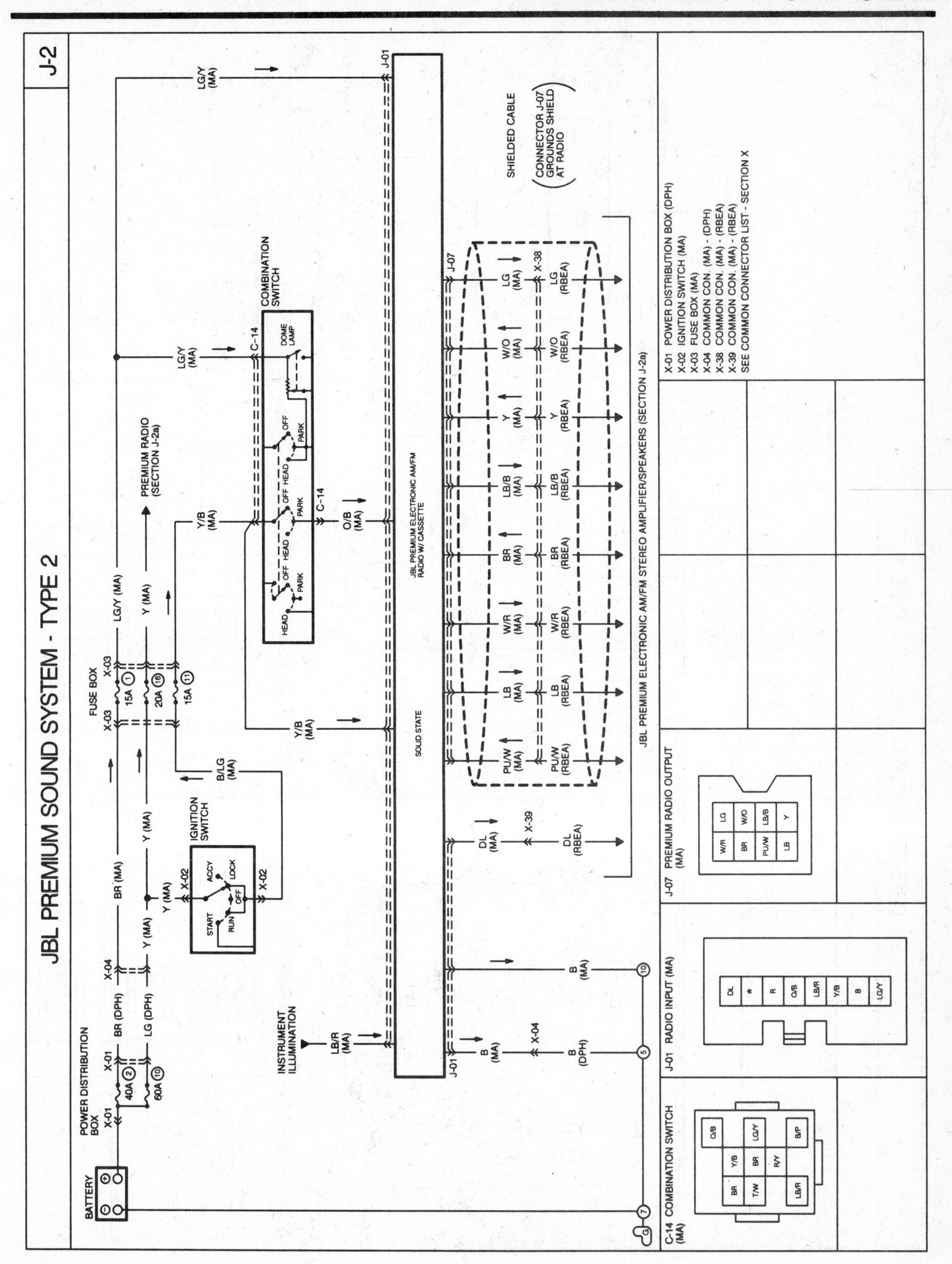

Navajo JBL premium sound system type 2 (1991 shown)

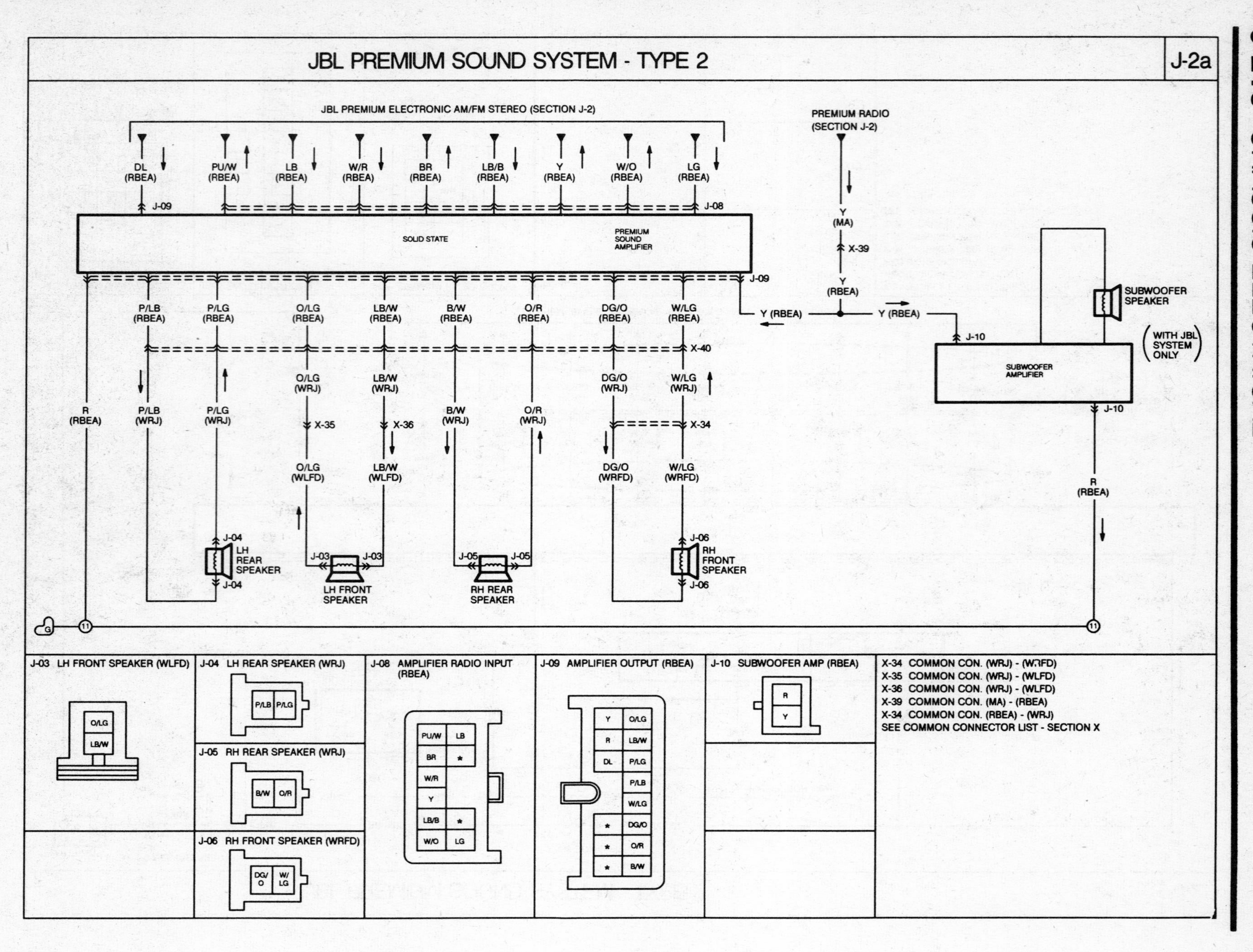

Navajo JBL premium sound system type 2 (1991 shown)

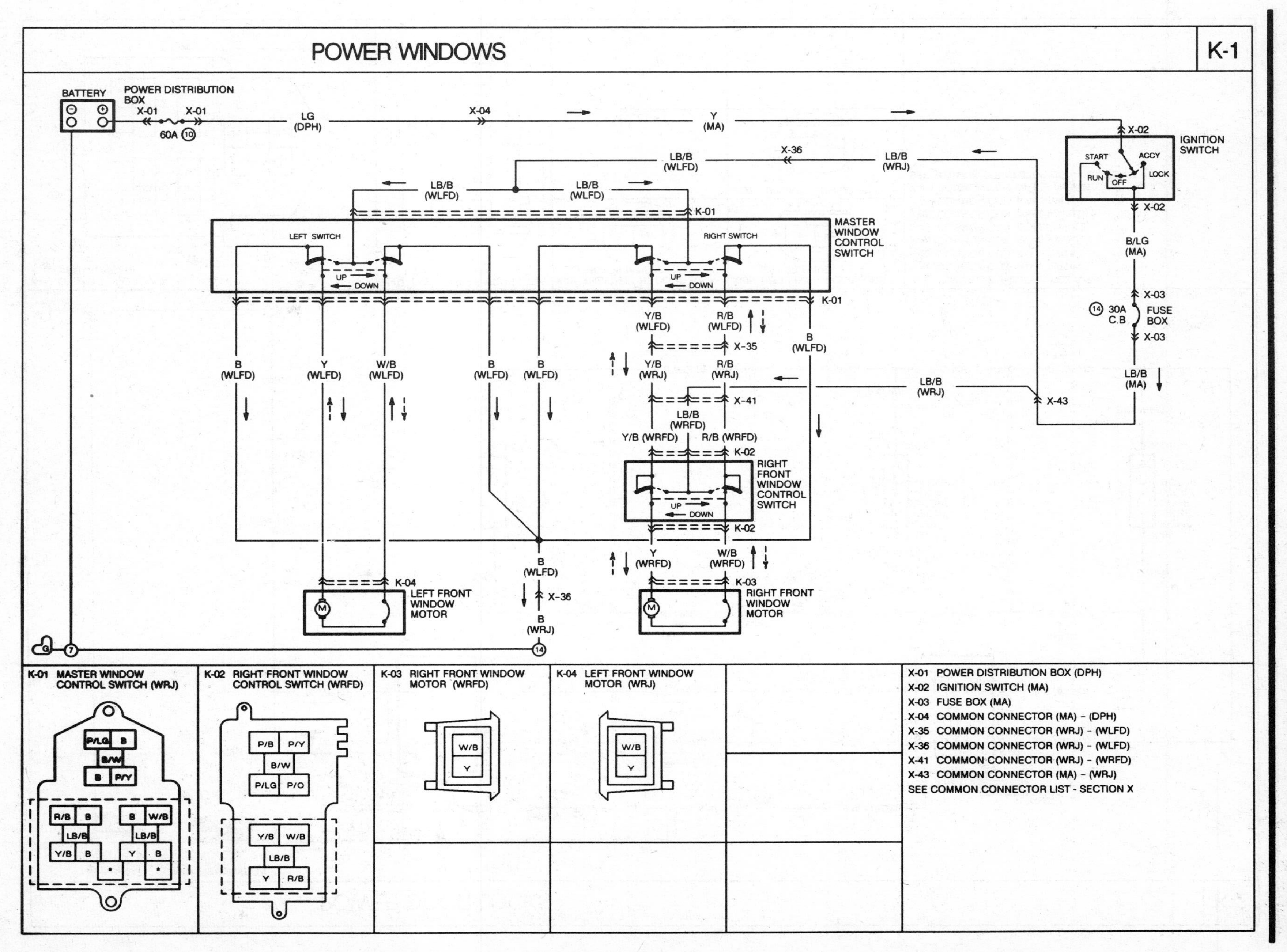

Navajo power windows (1991 shown)

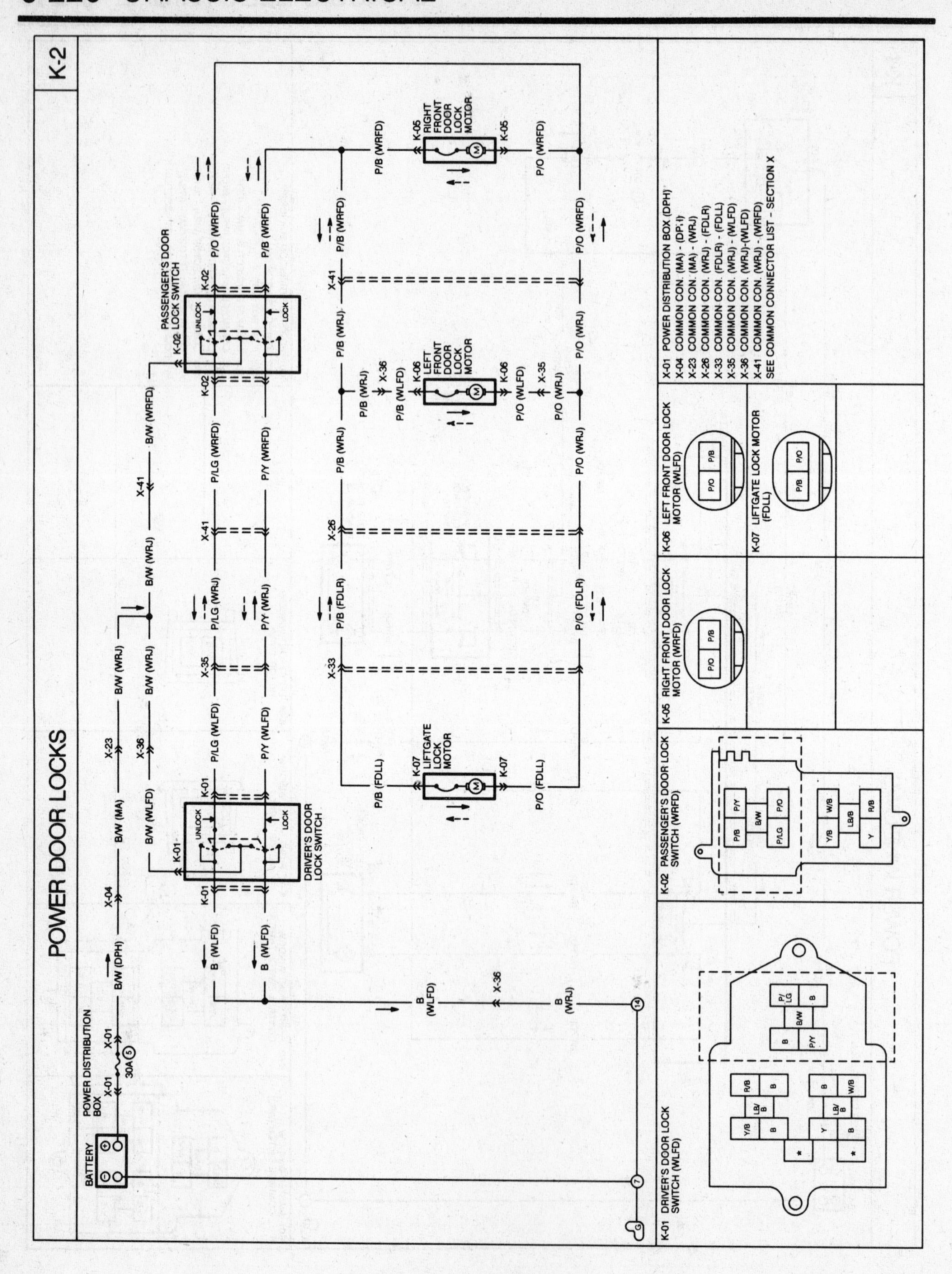

Navajo power door locks (1991 shown)

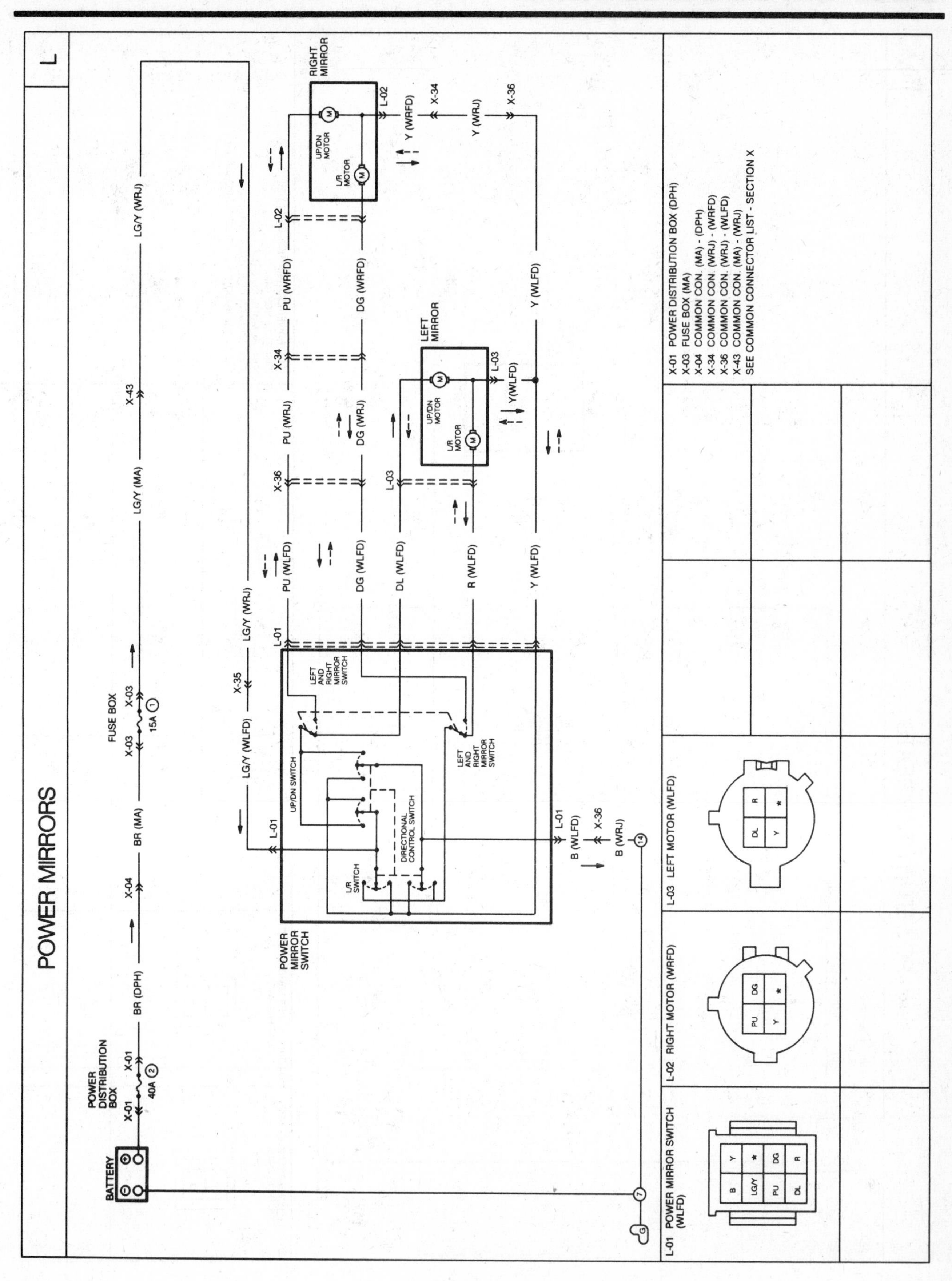

Navajo power mirrors (1991 shown)

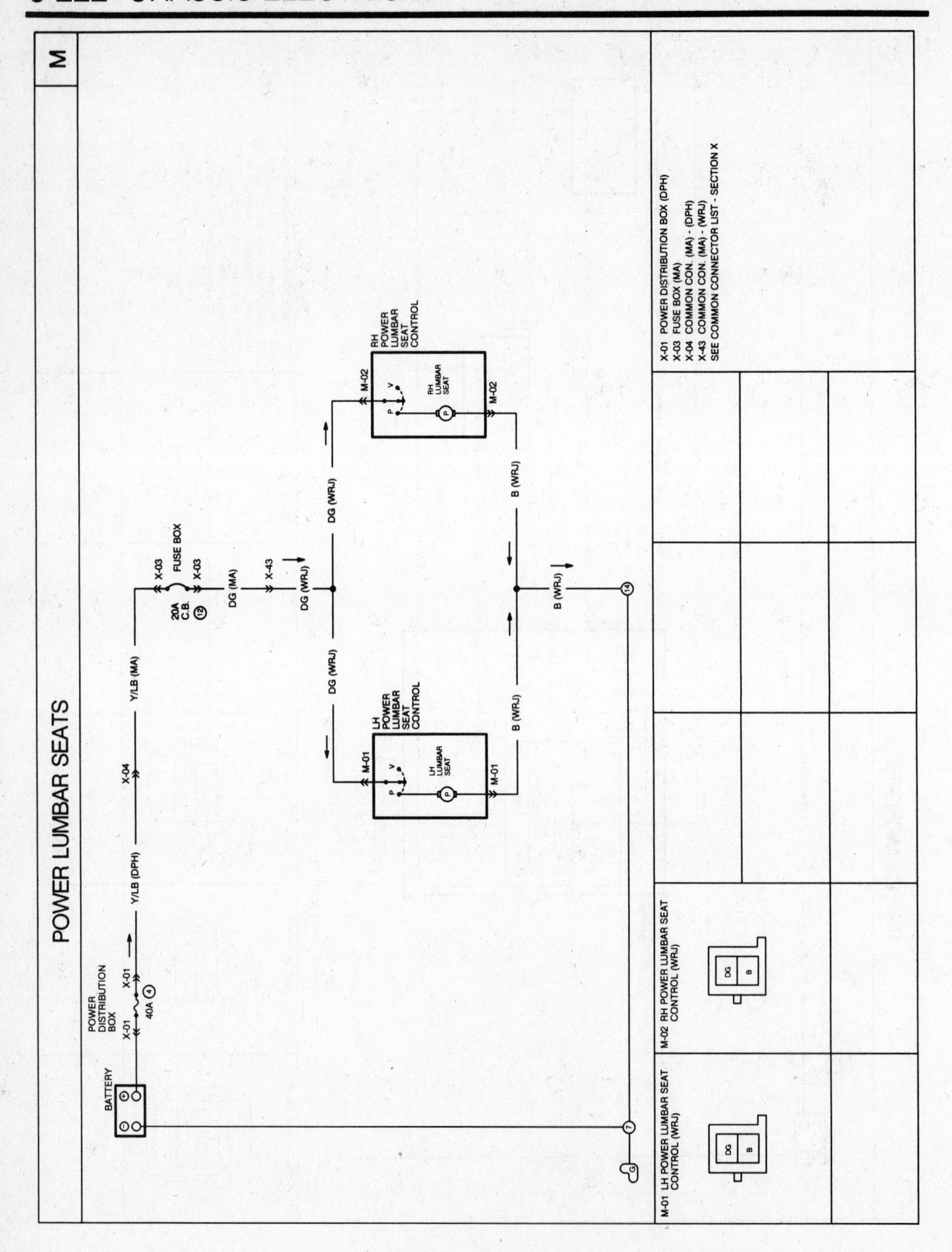

Navajo power lumbar seats (1991 shown)

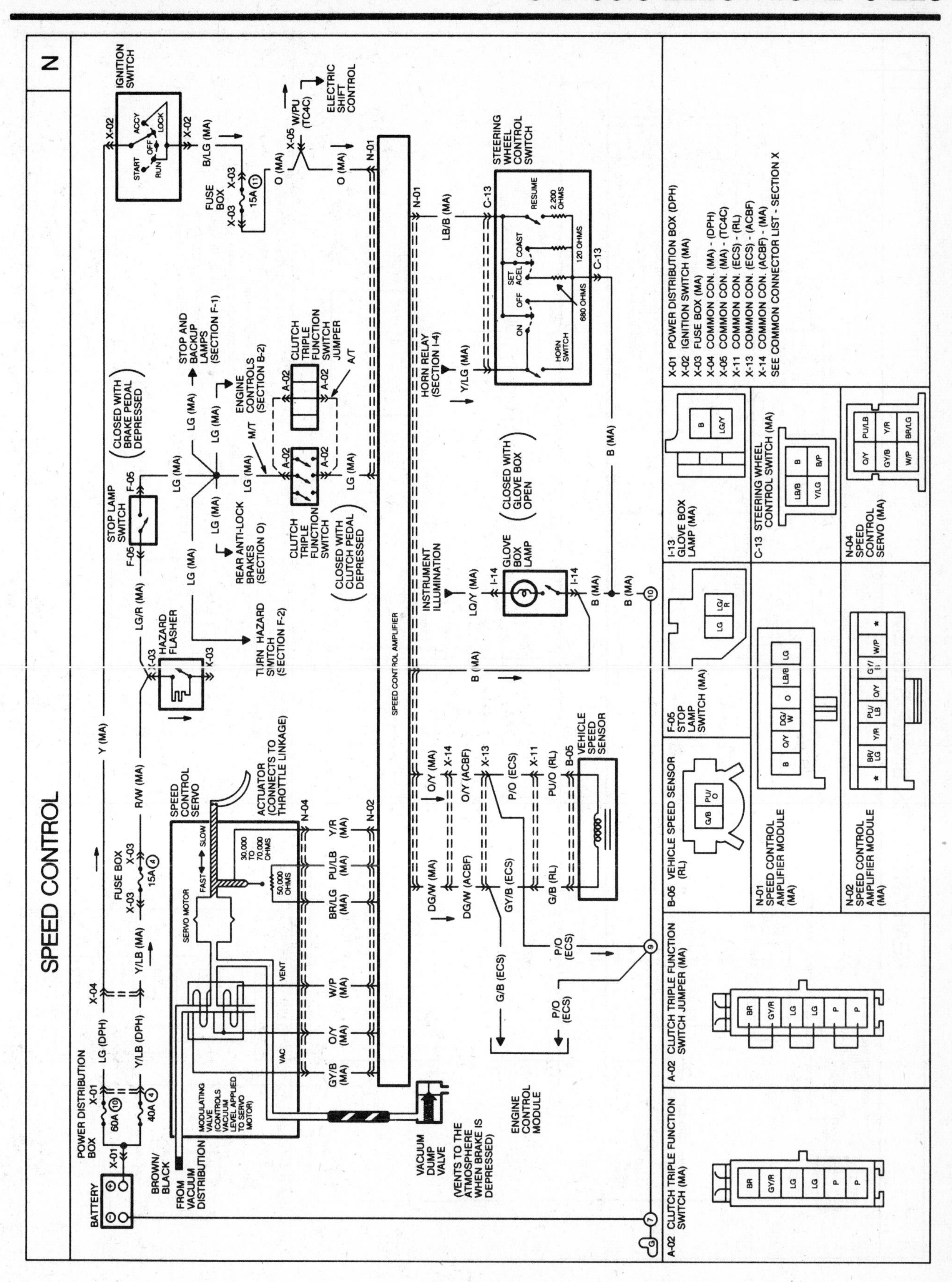

Navajo speed control (1991 shown)

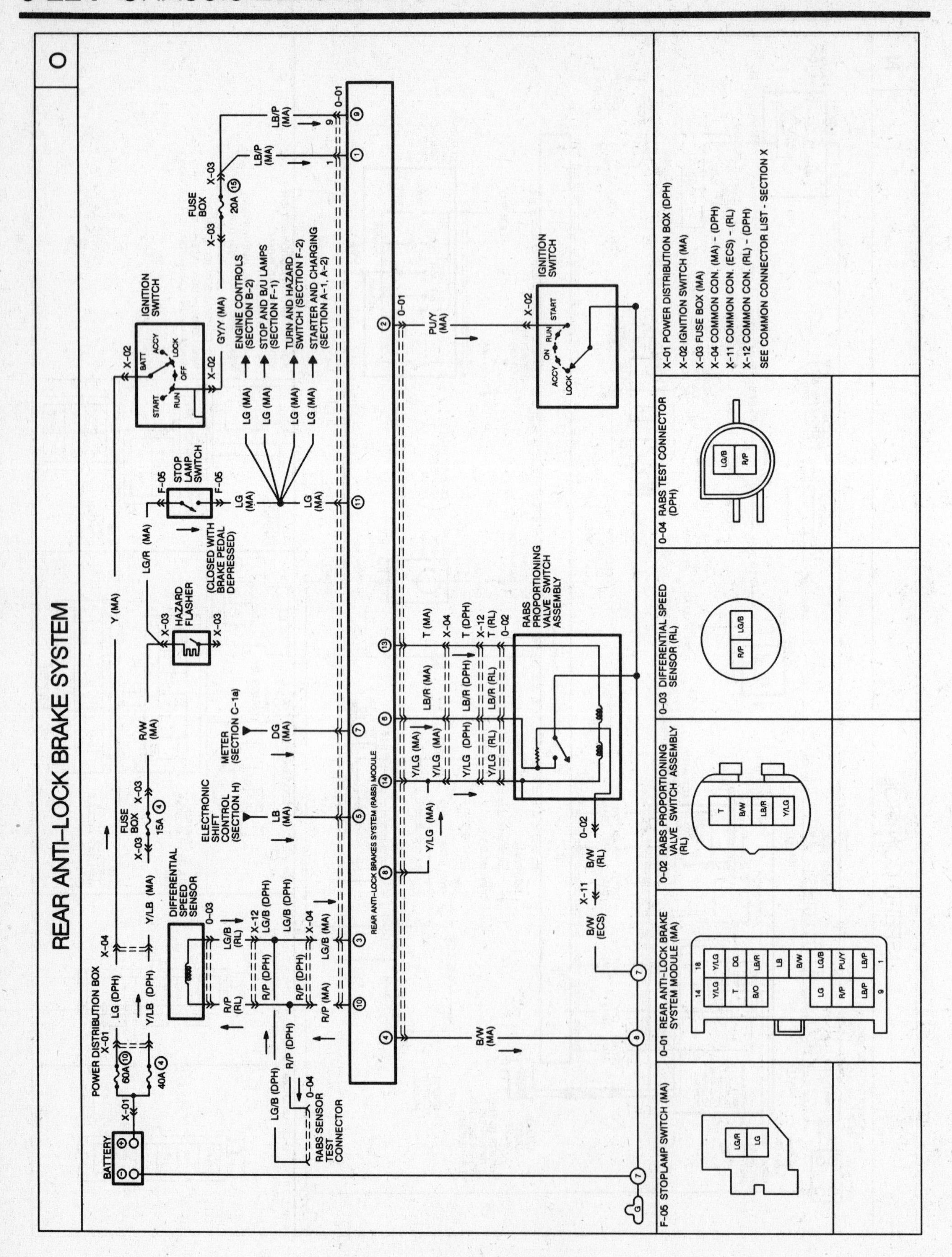

Navajo rear anti-lock brake system (1991 shown)

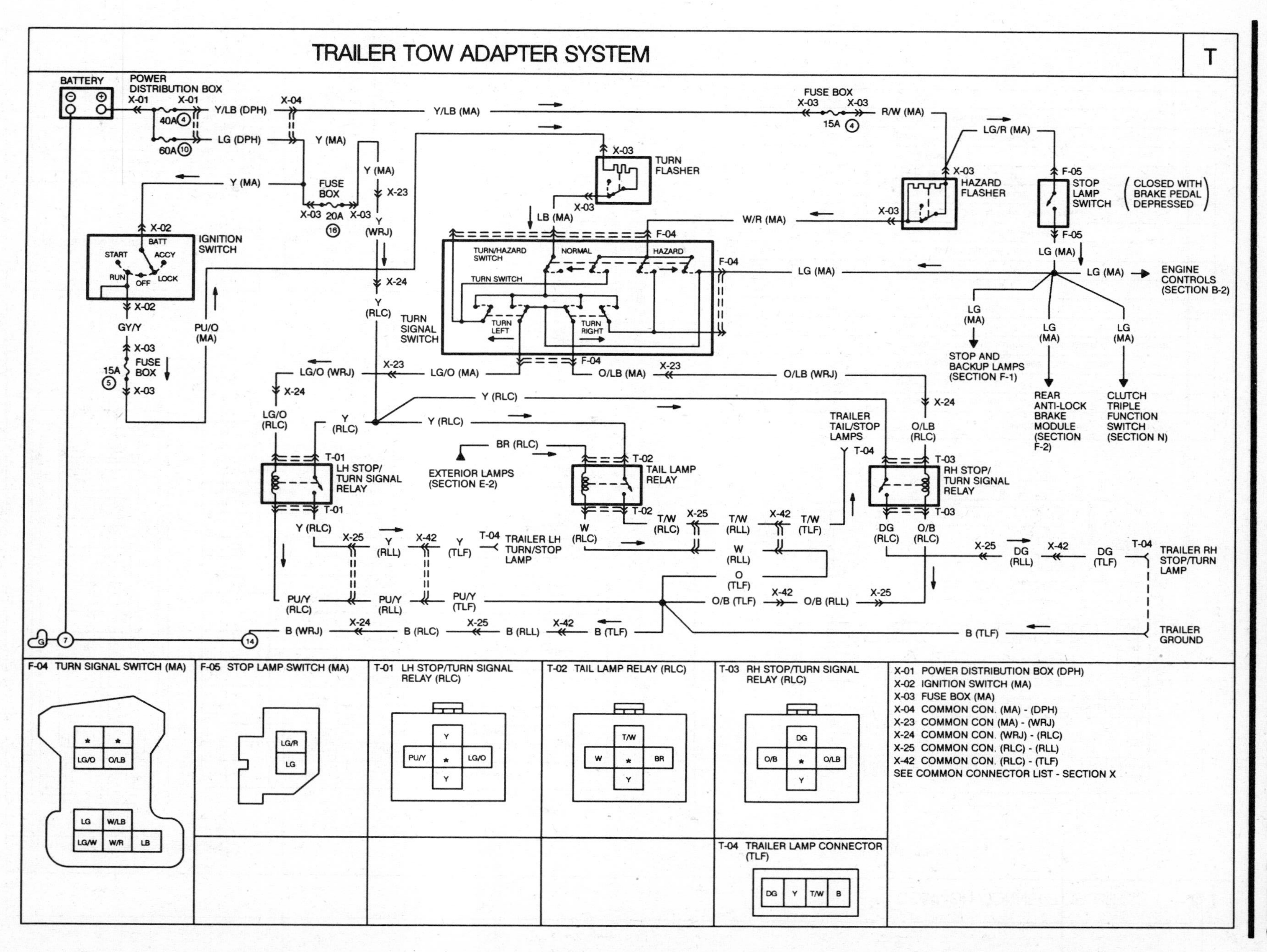

Navajo trailer tow adapter system (1991 shown)

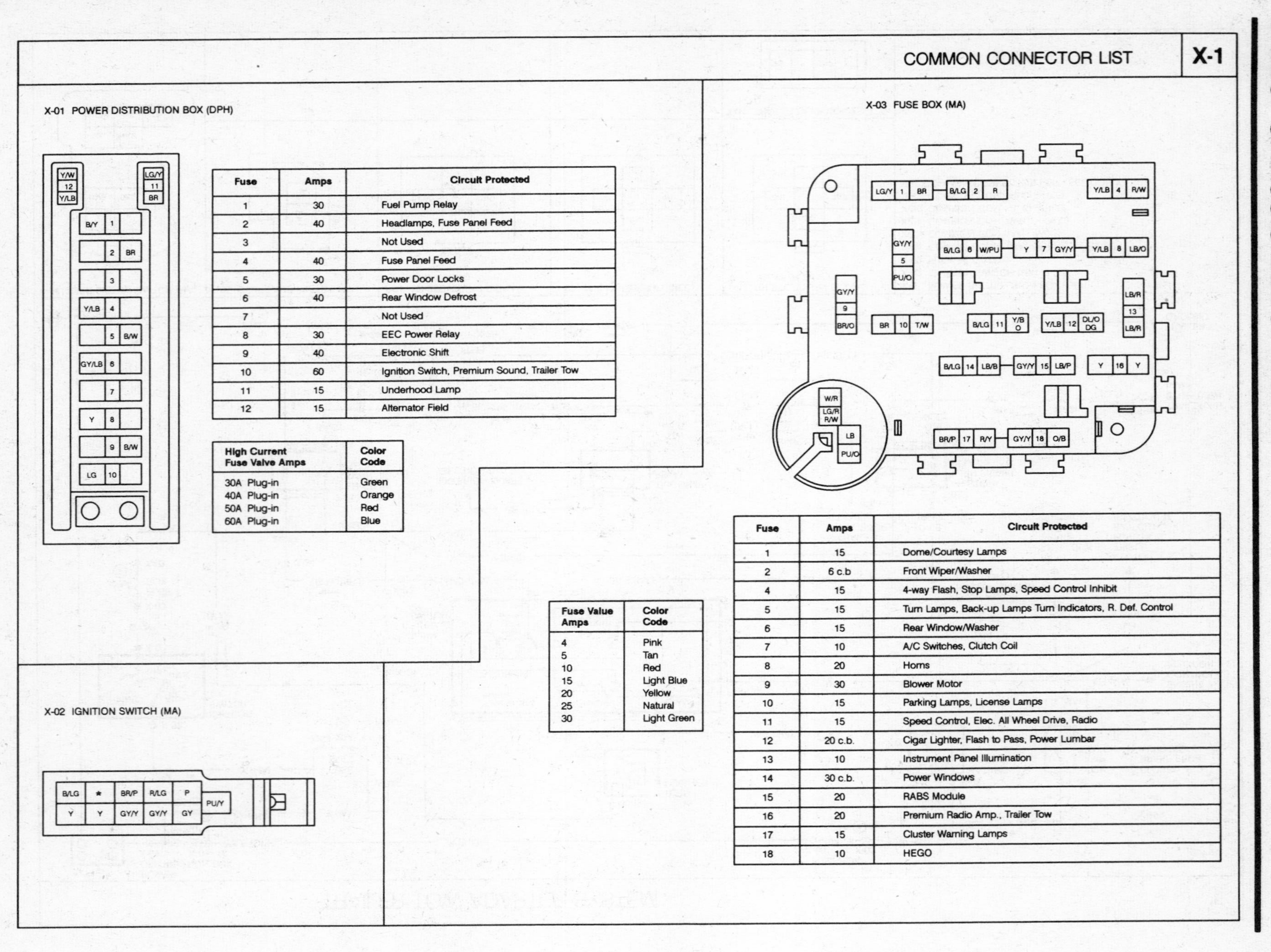

X-01 POWER DISTRIBUTION BOX (DPH)

Fuse	Amps	Circuit Protected
1	30	Fuel Pump Relay
2	40	Headlamps, Fuse Panel Feed
3		Not Used
4	40	Fuse Panel Feed
5	30	Power Door Locks
6	40	Rear Window Defrost
7		Not Used
8	30	EEC Power Relay
9	40	Electronic Shift
10	60	Ignition Switch, Premium Sound, Trailer Tow
11	15	Underhood Lamp
12	15	Alternator Field

High Current Fuse Valve Amps	Color Code
30A Plug-in	Green
40A Plug-in	Orange
50A Plug-in	Red
60A Plug-in	Blue

X-03 FUSE BOX (MA)

Fuse	Amps	Circuit Protected
1	15	Dome/Courtesy Lamps
2	6 c.b	Front Wiper/Washer
4	15	4-way Flash, Stop Lamps, Speed Control Inhibit
5	15	Turn Lamps, Back-up Lamps Turn Indicators, R. Def. Control
6	15	Rear Window/Washer
7	10	A/C Switches, Clutch Coil
8	20	Horns
9	30	Blower Motor
10	15	Parking Lamps, License Lamps
11	15	Speed Control, Elec. All Wheel Drive, Radio
12	20 c.b.	Cigar Lighter, Flash to Pass, Power Lumbar
13	10	Instrument Panel Illumination
14	30 c.b.	Power Windows
15	20	RABS Module
16	20	Premium Radio Amp., Trailer Tow
17	15	Cluster Warning Lamps
18	10	HEGO

Fuse Value Amps	Color Code
4	Pink
5	Tan
10	Red
15	Light Blue
20	Yellow
25	Natural
30	Light Green

Navajo common connector list (1991 shown)

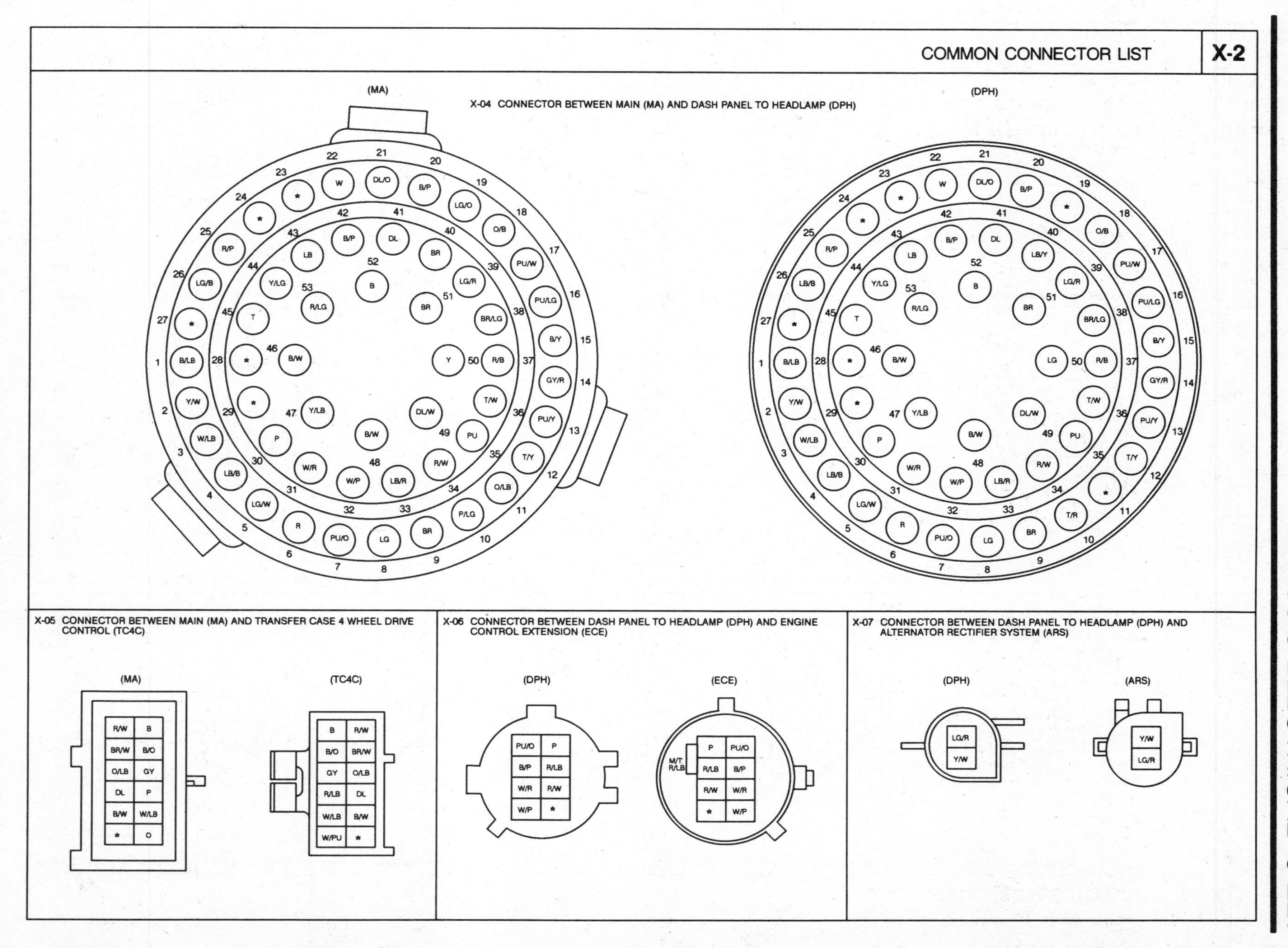

Navajo common connector list (1991 shown)

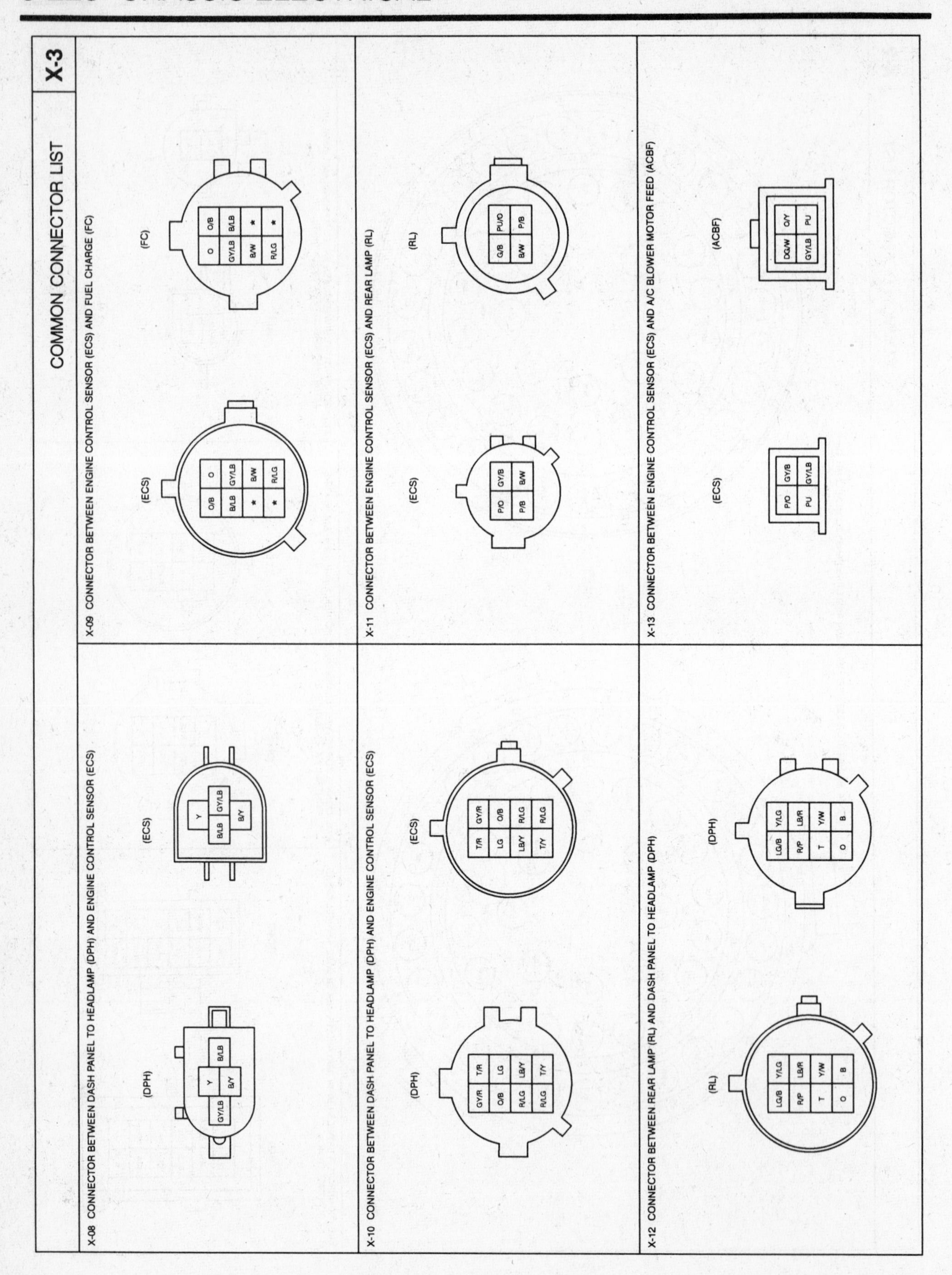
COMMON CONNECTOR LIST
X-3
X-08 CONNECTOR BETWEEN DASH PANEL TO HEADLAMP (DPH) AND ENGINE CONTROL SENSOR (ECS)
(DPH)
(ECS)
X-09 CONNECTOR BETWEEN ENGINE CONTROL SENSOR (ECS) AND FUEL CHARGE (FC)
(ECS)
(FC)
X-10 CONNECTOR BETWEEN DASH PANEL TO HEADLAMP (DPH) AND ENGINE CONTROL SENSOR (ECS)
(DPH)
(ECS)
X-11 CONNECTOR BETWEEN ENGINE CONTROL SENSOR (ECS) AND REAR LAMP (RL)
(ECS)
(RL)
X-12 CONNECTOR BETWEEN REAR LAMP (RL) AND DASH PANEL TO HEADLAMP (DPH)
(RL)
(DPH)
X-13 CONNECTOR BETWEEN ENGINE CONTROL SENSOR (ECS) AND A/C BLOWER MOTOR FEED (ACBF)
(ECS)
(ACBF)

Navajo common connector list (1991 shown)

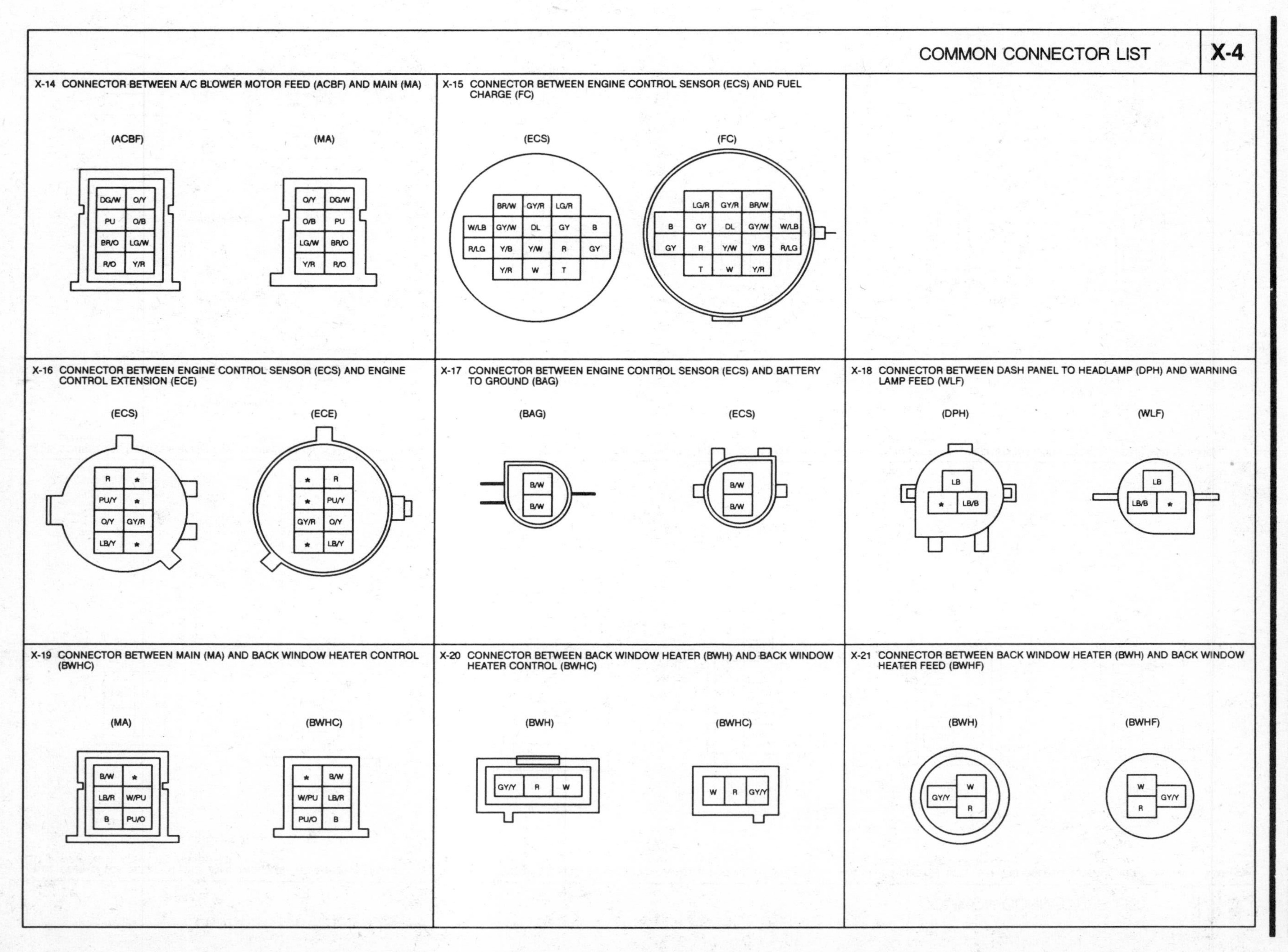
COMMON CONNECTOR LIST
X-4
X-14 CONNECTOR BETWEEN A/C BLOWER MOTOR FEED (ACBF) AND MAIN (MA)
(ACBF)
(MA)
X-15 CONNECTOR BETWEEN ENGINE CONTROL SENSOR (ECS) AND FUEL CHARGE (FC)
(ECS)
(FC)
X-16 CONNECTOR BETWEEN ENGINE CONTROL SENSOR (ECS) AND ENGINE CONTROL EXTENSION (ECE)
(ECS)
(ECE)
X-17 CONNECTOR BETWEEN ENGINE CONTROL SENSOR (ECS) AND BATTERY TO GROUND (BAG)
(BAG)
(ECS)
X-18 CONNECTOR BETWEEN DASH PANEL TO HEADLAMP (DPH) AND WARNING LAMP FEED (WLF)
(DPH)
(WLF)
X-19 CONNECTOR BETWEEN MAIN (MA) AND BACK WINDOW HEATER CONTROL (BWHC)
(MA)
(BWHC)
X-20 CONNECTOR BETWEEN BACK WINDOW HEATER (BWH) AND BACK WINDOW HEATER CONTROL (BWHC)
(BWH)
(BWHC)
X-21 CONNECTOR BETWEEN BACK WINDOW HEATER (BWH) AND BACK WINDOW HEATER FEED (BWHF)
(BWH)
(BWHF)

Navajo common connector list (1991 shown)

COMMON CONNECTOR LIST X-5

X-22 CONNECTOR BETWEEN BACK WINDOW HEATER FEED (BWHF) AND BACK WINDOW HEATER GROUND (BWHG)

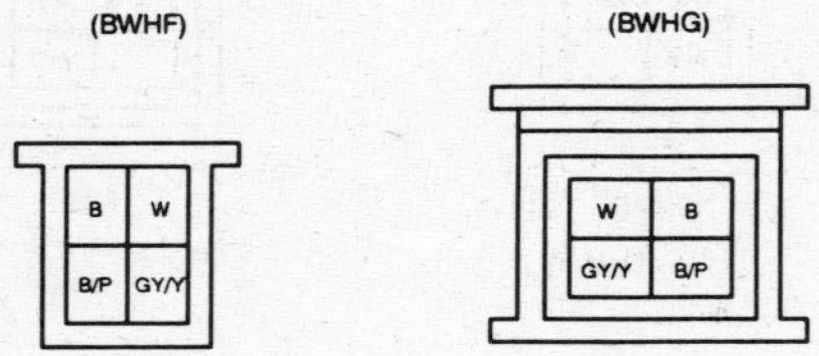

(BWHF)

B	W
B/P	GY/Y

(BWHG)

W	B
GY/Y	B/P

X-23 CONNECTOR BETWEEN MAIN (MA) AND WINDOW REGULATOR JUMPER (WRJ)

(MA)

B/W	LG
LB/W	O/LG
DG/O	W/LG
B/W	Y
O/LB	B/P
LG/O	BR

(WRJ)

LG	B/W
O/LG	LB/W
W/LG	DG/O
Y	B/W
B/P	O/LB
BR	LG/O

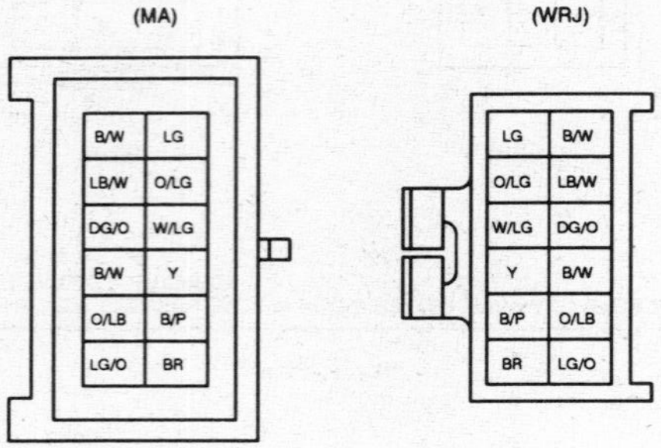

X-24 CONNECTOR BETWEEN WINDOW REGULATOR JUMPER (WRJ) AND REAR LAMP CONNECTOR (RLC)

(WRJ)

O/LB	B/P
LG/O	Y
BR	B
*	*

(RLC)

B/P	O/LB
Y	LG/O
B	BR
*	*

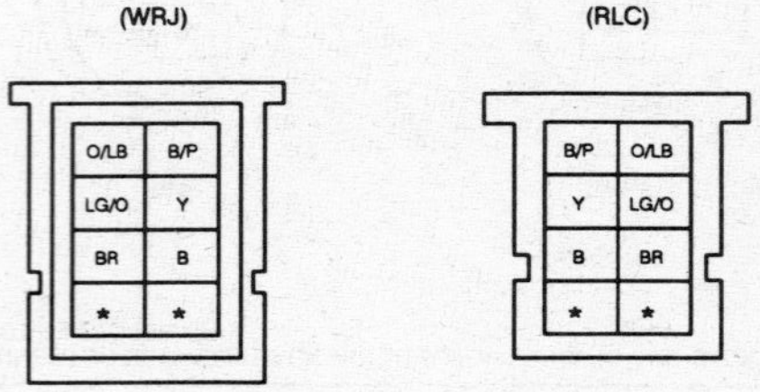

X-25 CONNECTOR BETWEEN REAR LAMP CONNECTOR (RLC) AND REAR LICENSE LAMP (RLL)

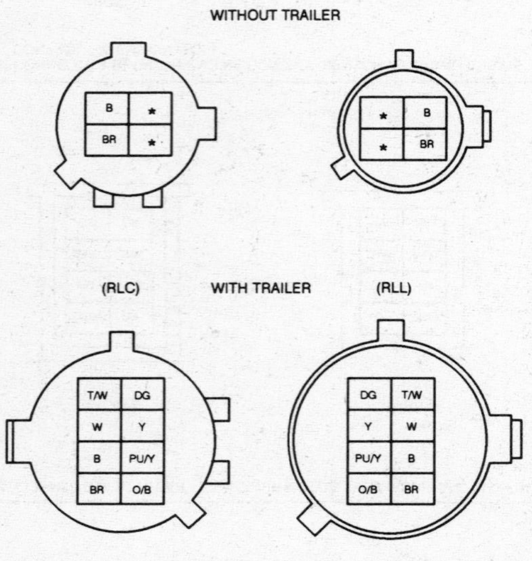

WITHOUT TRAILER

B	*
BR	*

*	B
*	BR

WITH TRAILER

(RLC)

T/W	DG
W	Y
B	PU/Y
BR	O/B

(RLL)

DG	T/W
Y	W
PU/Y	B
O/B	BR

X-26 CONNECTOR BETWEEN WINDOW REGULATOR JUMPER (WRJ) AND FRONT DOOR LOCK RH (FDLR)

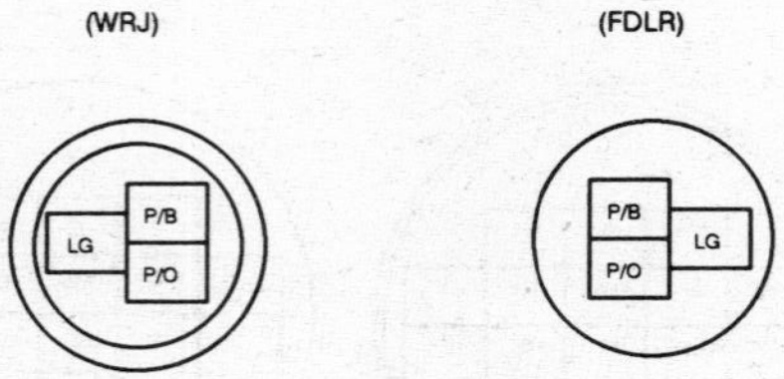

(WRJ)

LG, P/B, P/O

(FDLR)

P/B, P/O, LG

X-27 CONNECTOR BETWEEN FRONT DOOR LOCK RH (FDLR) AND WINDOW REGULATOR JUMPER

(WRJ)

B/LB
LG/Y
B

(FDLR)

B/LB
LG/Y
B

Navajo common connector list (1991 shown)

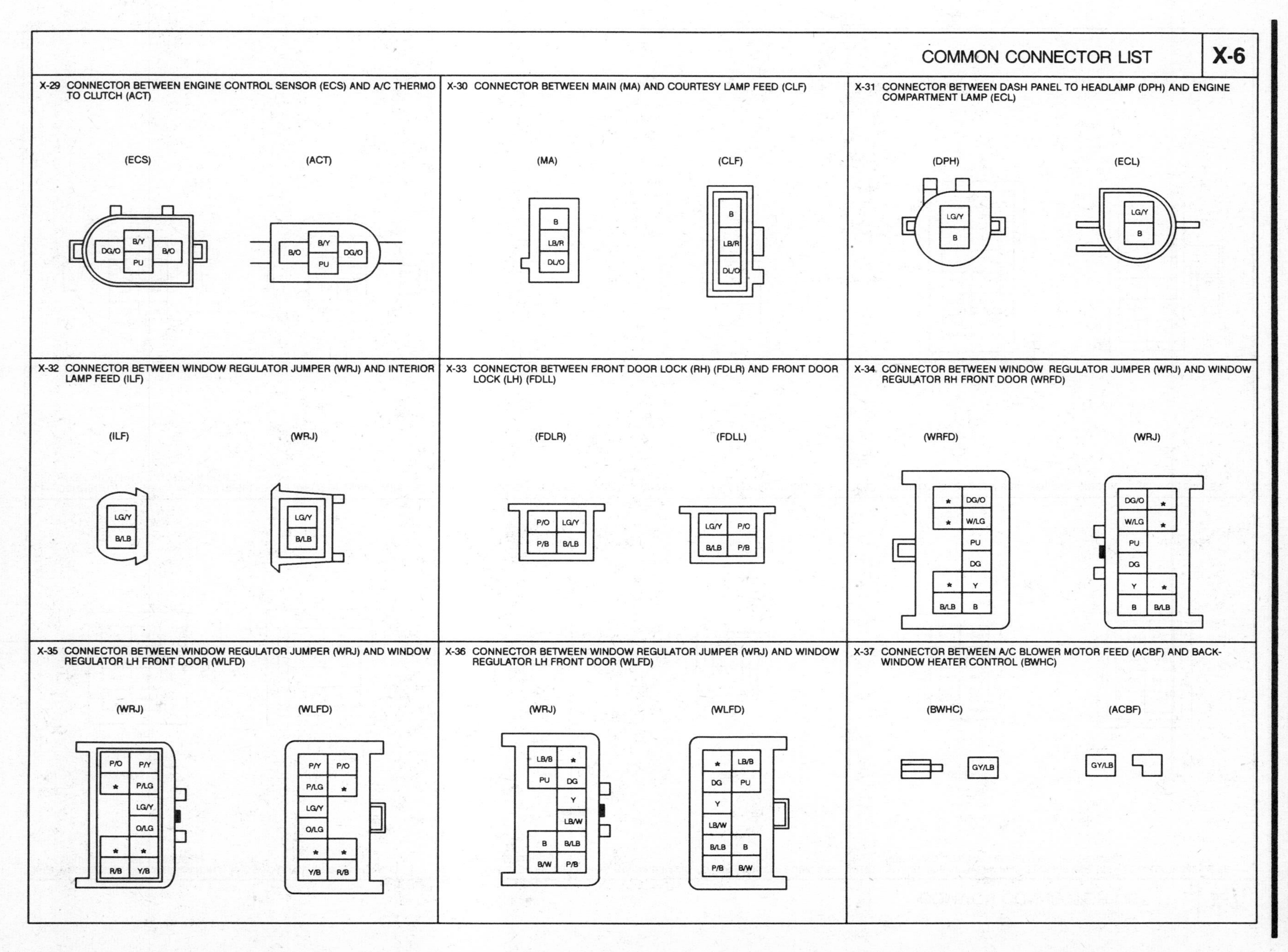
COMMON CONNECTOR LIST
X-6
X-29 CONNECTOR BETWEEN ENGINE CONTROL SENSOR (ECS) AND A/C THERMO TO CLUTCH (ACT)
(ECS)
(ACT)
X-30 CONNECTOR BETWEEN MAIN (MA) AND COURTESY LAMP FEED (CLF)
(MA)
(CLF)
X-31 CONNECTOR BETWEEN DASH PANEL TO HEADLAMP (DPH) AND ENGINE COMPARTMENT LAMP (ECL)
(DPH)
(ECL)
X-32 CONNECTOR BETWEEN WINDOW REGULATOR JUMPER (WRJ) AND INTERIOR LAMP FEED (ILF)
(ILF)
(WRJ)
X-33 CONNECTOR BETWEEN FRONT DOOR LOCK (RH) (FDLR) AND FRONT DOOR LOCK (LH) (FDLL)
(FDLR)
(FDLL)
X-34 CONNECTOR BETWEEN WINDOW REGULATOR JUMPER (WRJ) AND WINDOW REGULATOR RH FRONT DOOR (WRFD)
(WRFD)
(WRJ)
X-35 CONNECTOR BETWEEN WINDOW REGULATOR JUMPER (WRJ) AND WINDOW REGULATOR LH FRONT DOOR (WLFD)
(WRJ)
(WLFD)
X-36 CONNECTOR BETWEEN WINDOW REGULATOR JUMPER (WRJ) AND WINDOW REGULATOR LH FRONT DOOR (WLFD)
(WRJ)
(WLFD)
X-37 CONNECTOR BETWEEN A/C BLOWER MOTOR FEED (ACBF) AND BACK-WINDOW HEATER CONTROL (BWHC)
(BWHC)
(ACBF)

Navajo common connector list (1991 shown)

COMMON CONNECTOR LIST X-7

X-38 CONNECTOR BETWEEN MAIN (MA) AND RADIO POWER BOOSTER AND EQUALIZER AMPLIFIER (RBEA)

(MA)

LG	W/R
W/O	BR
LB/B	PU/W
Y	LB

(RBEA)

W/R	LG
BR	W/O
PU/W	LB/B
LB	Y

X-39 CONNECTOR BETWEEN MAIN (MA) AND RADIO POWER BOOSTER EQUALIZER AMPLIFIER (RBEA)

(MA)

Y
DL

(RBEA)

Y
DL

X-40 CONNECTOR BETWEEN RADIO POWER BOOSTER EQUALIZER AMPLIFIER (RBEA) AND WINDOW REGULATOR JUMPER (WRJ)

(RBEA)

DG/O	O/R
W/LG	B/W
P/LB	O/LG
P/LG	LB/W

(WRJ)

O/R	DG/O
B/W	W/LG
O/LG	P/LB
LB/W	P/LG

X-41 CONNECTOR BETWEEN WINDOW REGULATOR JUMPER (WRJ) AND WINDOW REGULATOR RH FRONT DOOR (WRFD)

(WRJ)

Y/B	B/W
R/B	LB/B
P/B	P/LG
P/O	P/Y

(WRFD)

B/W	Y/B
LB/B	R/B
P/LG	P/B
P/Y	P/O

X-42 CONNECTOR BETWEEN TRAILER LAMP FEED (TLF) AND REAR LICENSE LAMP (RLL)

(TLF)

O/B	*
PU/Y	O
DG	B
Y	T/W

(RLL)

*	O/B
O	PU/Y
B	DG
T/W	Y

X-43 CONNECTOR BETWEEN MAIN (MA) AND WINDOW REGULATOR JUMPER (WRJ)

(MA)

O/R	P/LG
B/W	P/LB
R/P	*
*	LB/B
LG/Y	BR/LB
DG	B/P

(WRJ)

P/LG	O/R
P/LB	B/W
*	R/P
LB/B	*
BR/LB	LG/Y
B/LB	DG

Navajo common connector list (1991 shown)

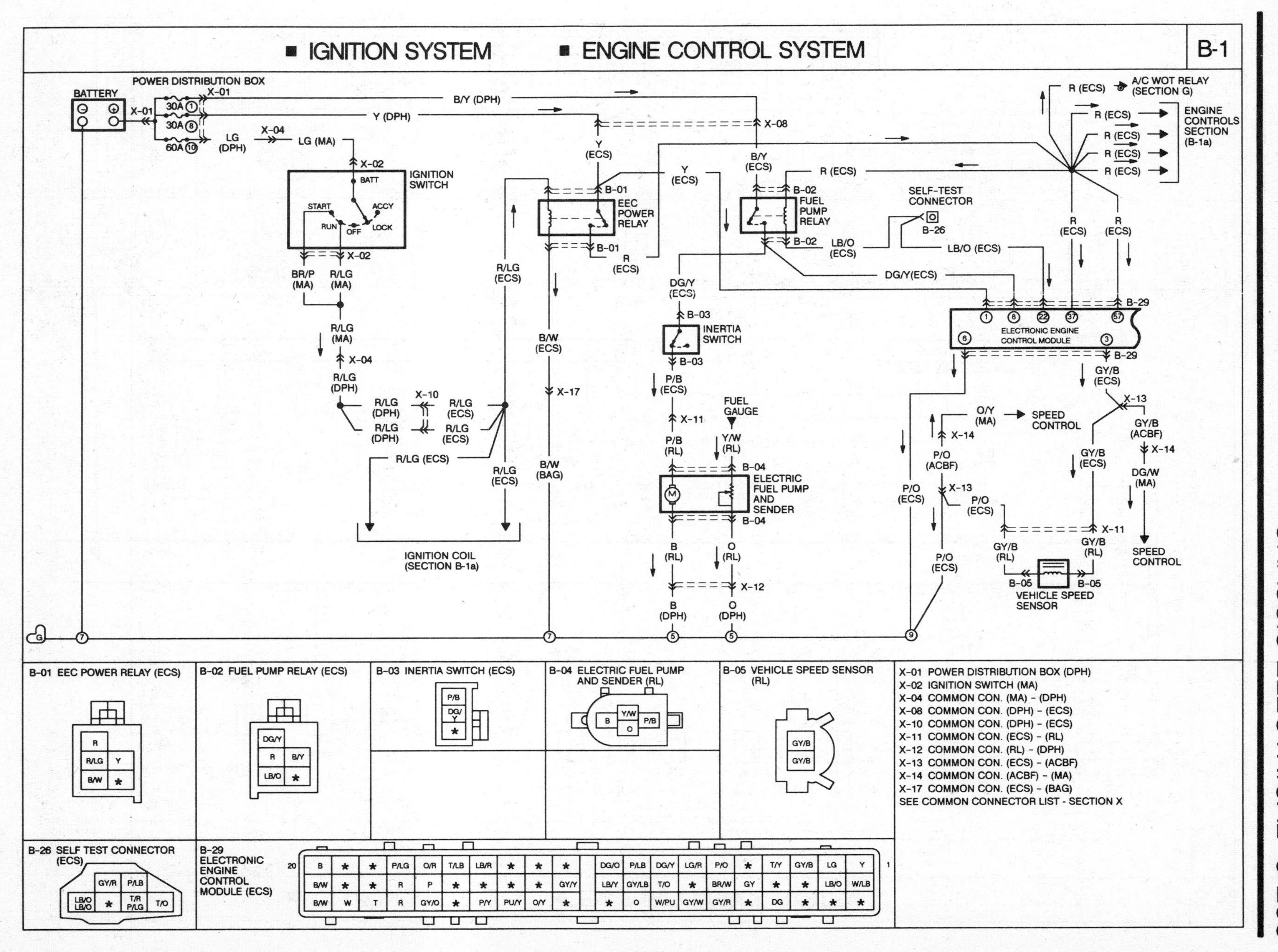

Navajo ignition and engine control system (1992 shown)

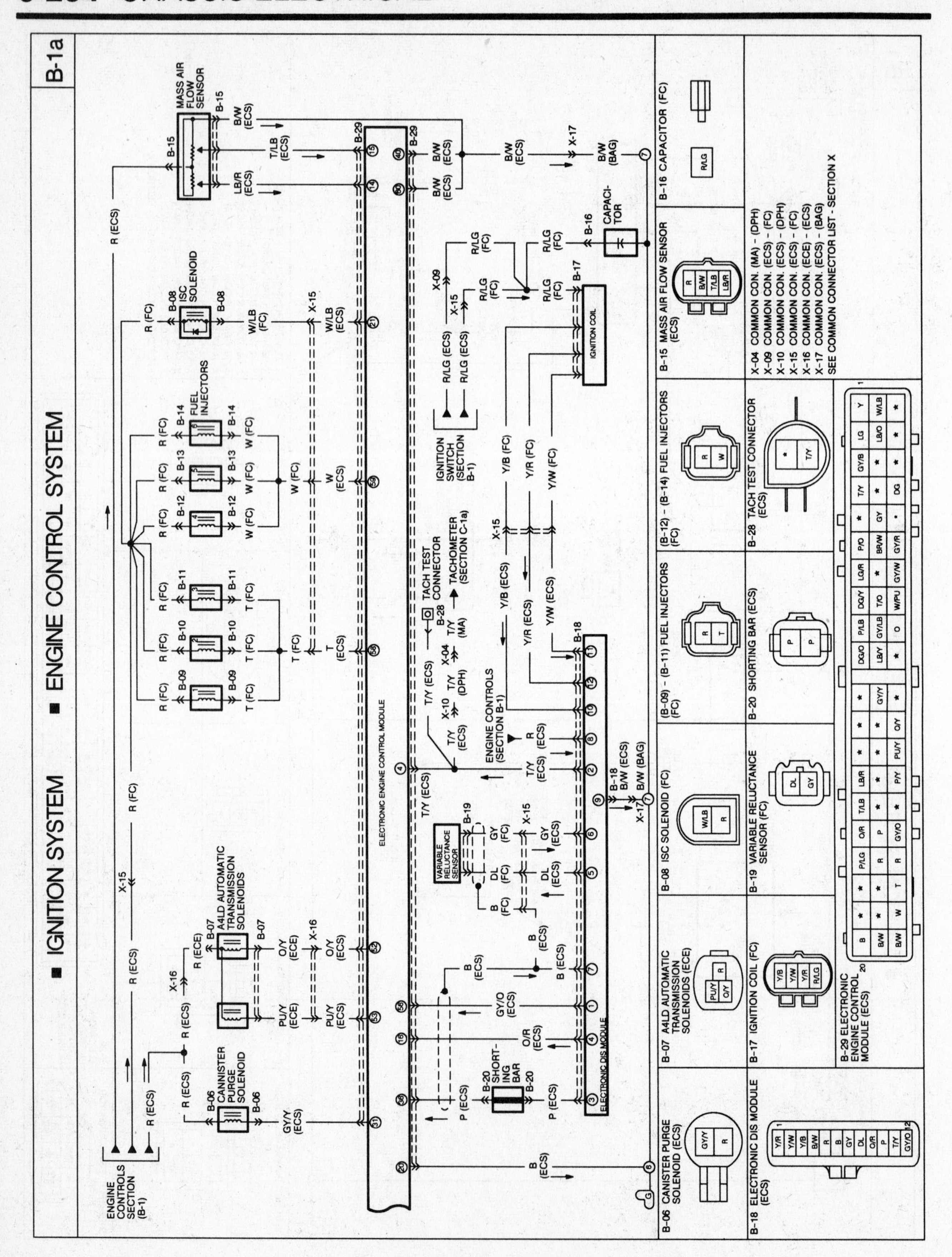

Navajo ignition and engine control system (1992 shown)

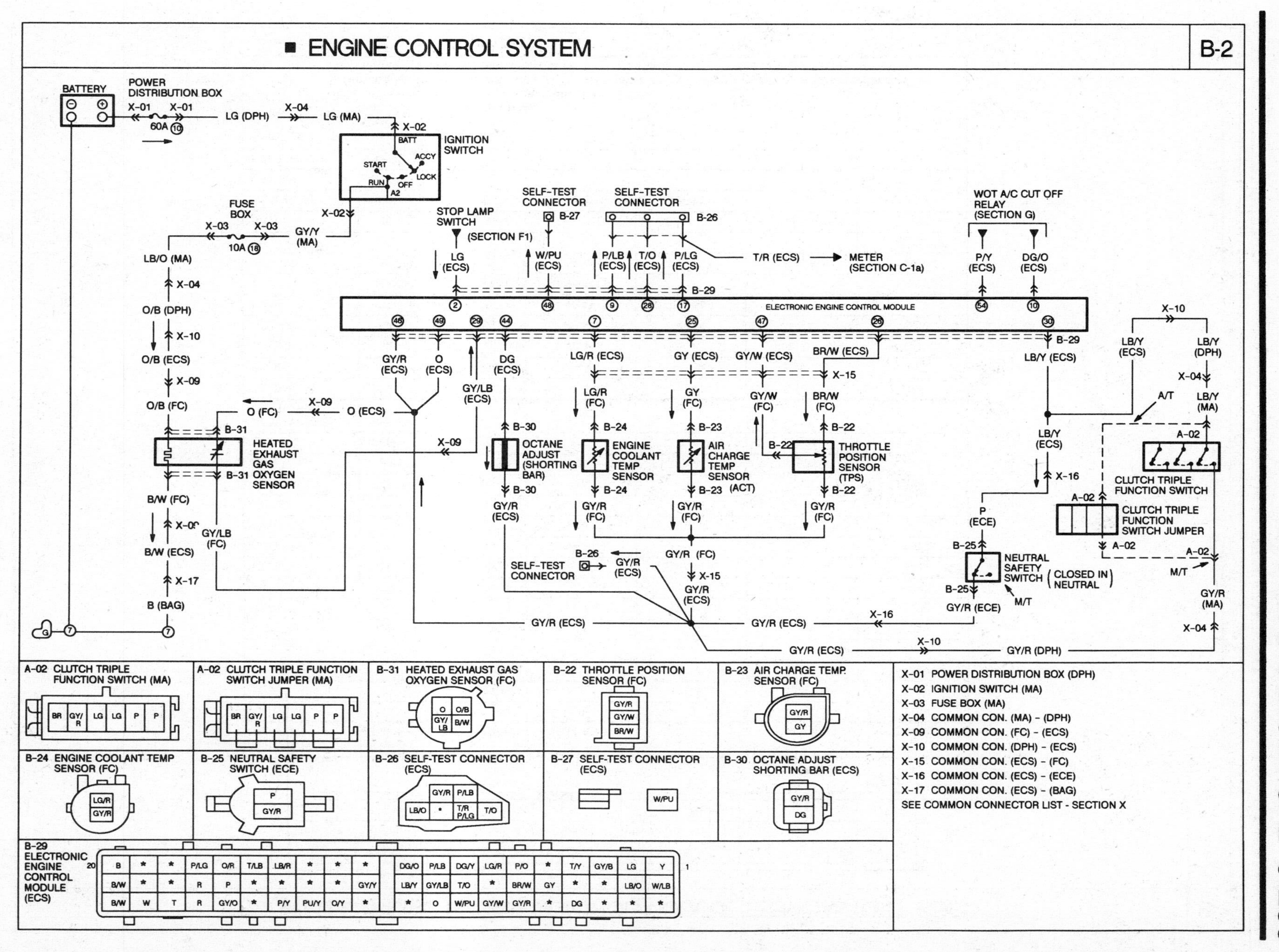

Navajo engine control system (1992 shown)

■ ELECTRONIC ENGINE CONTROL MODULE TERMINAL (UNIT SIDE)

B-3

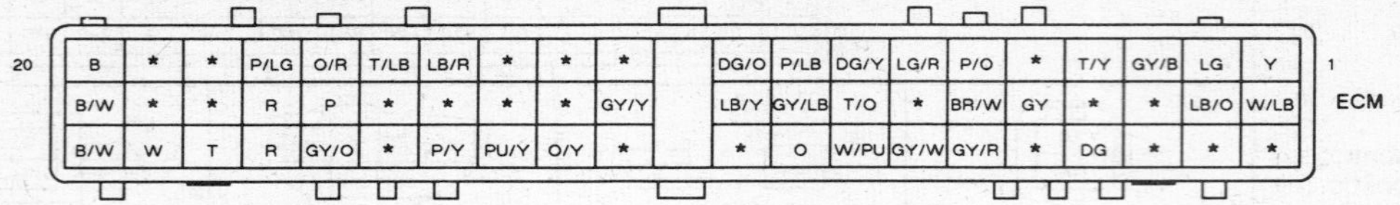

20																				1
B	*	*	P/LG	O/R	T/LB	LB/R	*	*	*	DG/O	P/LB	DG/Y	LG/R	P/O	*	T/Y	GY/B	LG	Y
B/W	*	*	R	P	*	*	*	*	GY/Y	LB/Y	GY/LB	T/O	*	BR/W	GY	*	*	LB/O	W/LB	ECM
B/W	W	T	R	GY/O	*	P/Y	PU/Y	O/Y	*	*	O	W/PU	GY/W	GY/R	*	DG	*	*	*

SENSORS/ INPUTS	Signal Pin #	KOEO	Units	HOT IDLE	30 MPH	55 MPH	Units
OCTADJ	44	0	DCV	0	0	0	DCV
MAF	14	0	DCV	.6	1.3–1.4	1.7–2.0	DCV
TP	47	1.0	DCV	1.0	1.2–1.3	1.4–1.6	DCV
ECT	7	.6	DCV	.6	.6	.6	DCV
ACT	25	2.2	DCV	2.6	2.7	2.9	DCV
IDM	4	0	RPM	750–850	1500–1700	1800–2000	RPM
PIP	56	0	RPM	750–850	1500–1700	1800–2000	RPM
HEGO	29	0	DCV	switching	switching	switching	DCV
BOO	2	0	DCV	0/VBAT	0	0	DCV
FPM	8	0	DCV	VBAT ①	VBAT	VBAT	DCV
ACCS	10	0	DCV	0/VBAT	0	0	DCV
VSS+	3	0	MPH	0 ②	30	55	MPH
NDS	30	0	DCV	0	5.0	5.0	DCV
STI	48	5.0	DCV	5.0	5.0	5.0	DCV
ACTUATORS/ OUTPUTS							
INJ Bank 2	59	VBAT ③	DCV	3.0–3.2	3.9–4.4	5.0–7.0	mS
INJ Bank 1	58	VBAT ③	DCV	3.0–3.2	3.8–4.4	5.0–7.0	mS
SS 3/4 (A/T)	52	VBAT	DCV	VBAT	VBAT	0	DCV
STO/MIL	17	.6	DCV	VBAT	VBAT	VBAT	DCV
CANP	31	VBAT	DCV	VBAT	7.0–9.0	.2	DCV
WAC	54	0	DCV	0/VBAT ②	0	0	DCV
ISC-BPA	21	VBAT	DCV	8.0–12.0	7.3–8.4	5.5–6.8	DCV
FP	22	VBAT	DCV	.1	.1	.1	DCV
SAW	36	0	RPM	750–850	1500–1700	1800–2000	RPM
CCO (A/T)	53	VBAT	DCV	VBAT	VBAT	0	DCV
OTHER							
IGN TIMING	TIMING			10	10	10	DEG

NOTES: ① – Brake pedal depressed.
② – A/C on.
③ – Monitor in DCV manual mode.
HEGO in 'switching' mode ranges from .2 to .9 DCV.
Reference values shown may vary ±20% depending on operating conditions and other factors.
RPM values are axle and tire dependent.

Navajo electronic engine control module terminal & values (1992 shown)

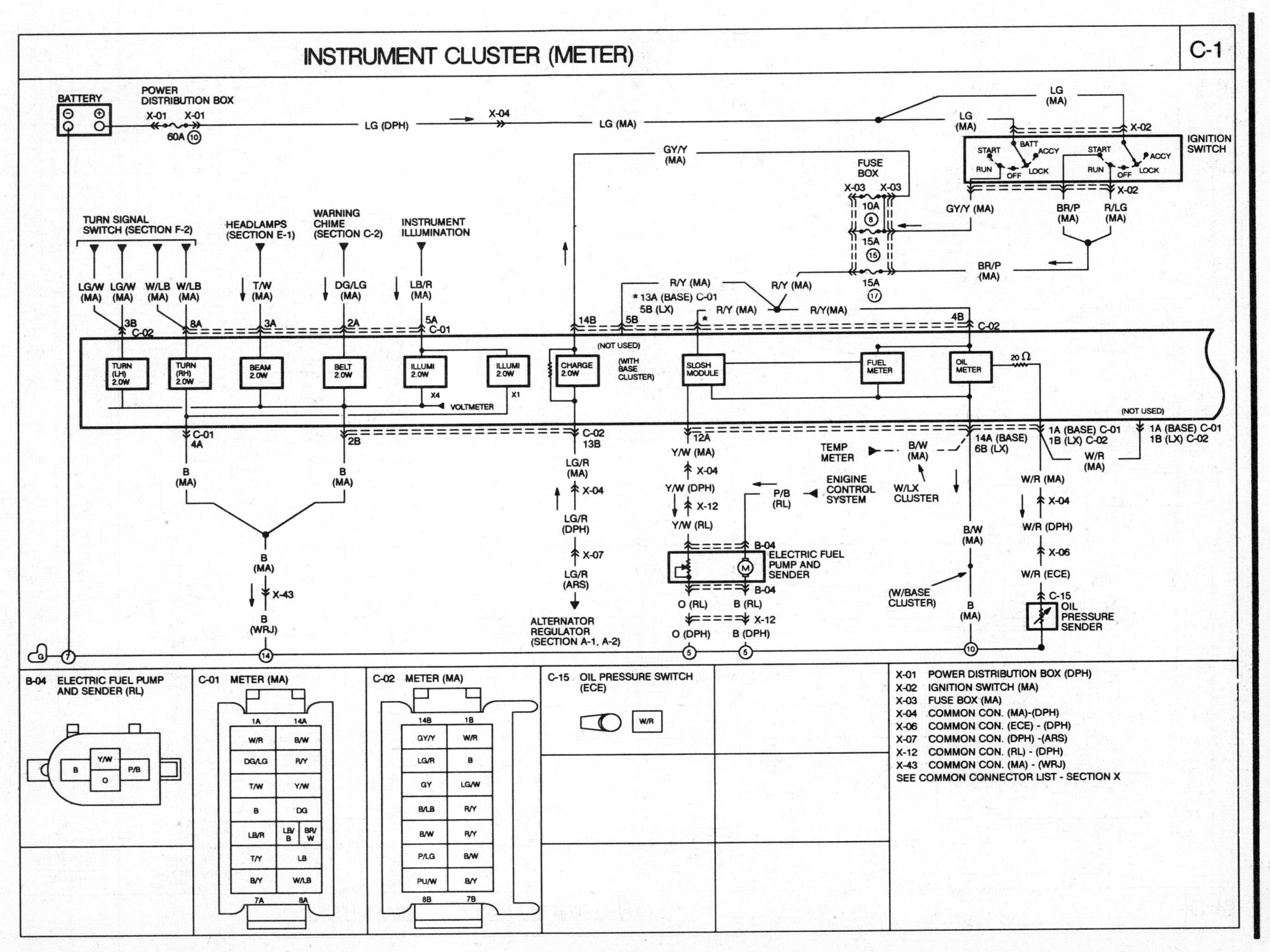

Navajo instrument cluster (1992 shown)

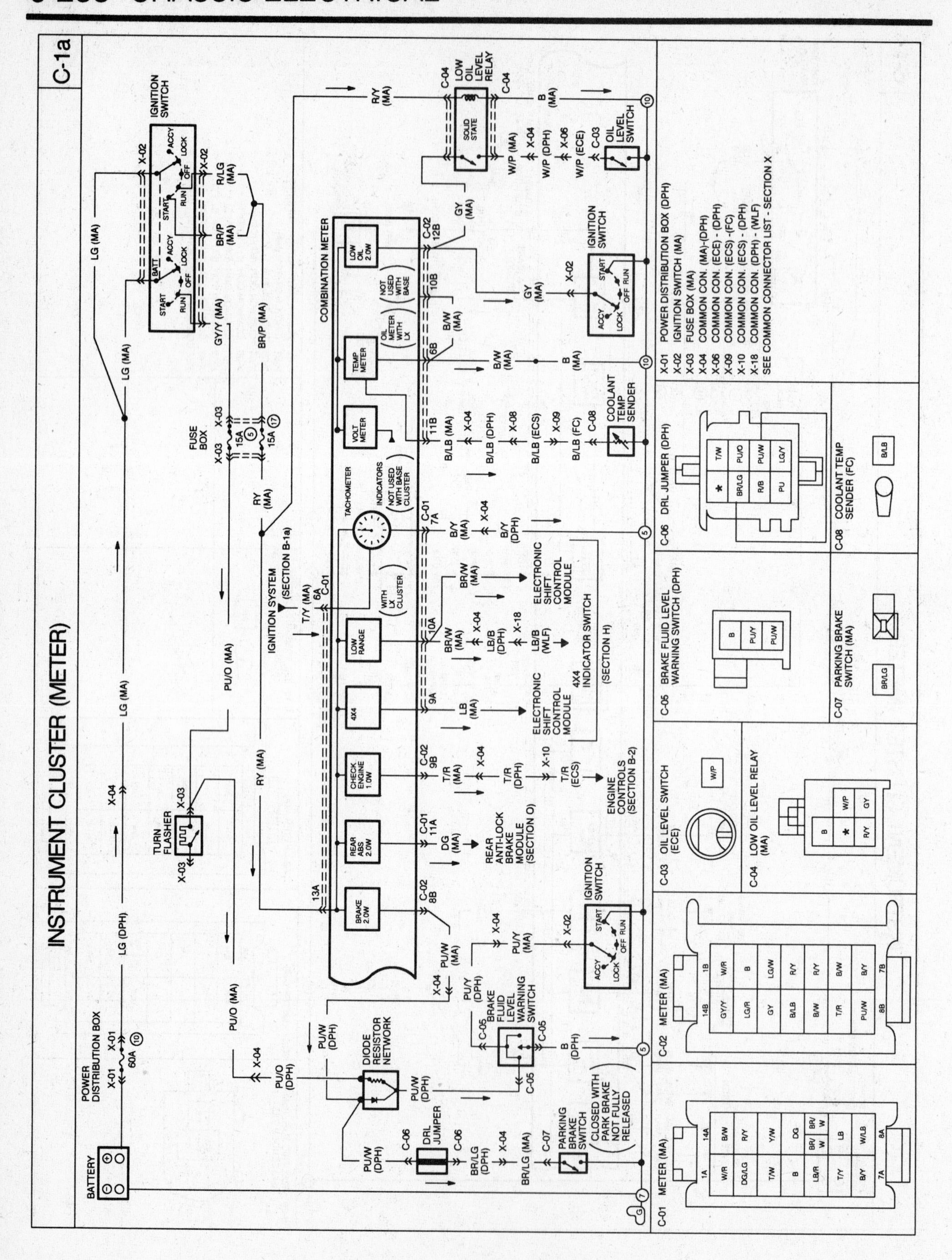

Navajo instrument cluster (1992 shown)

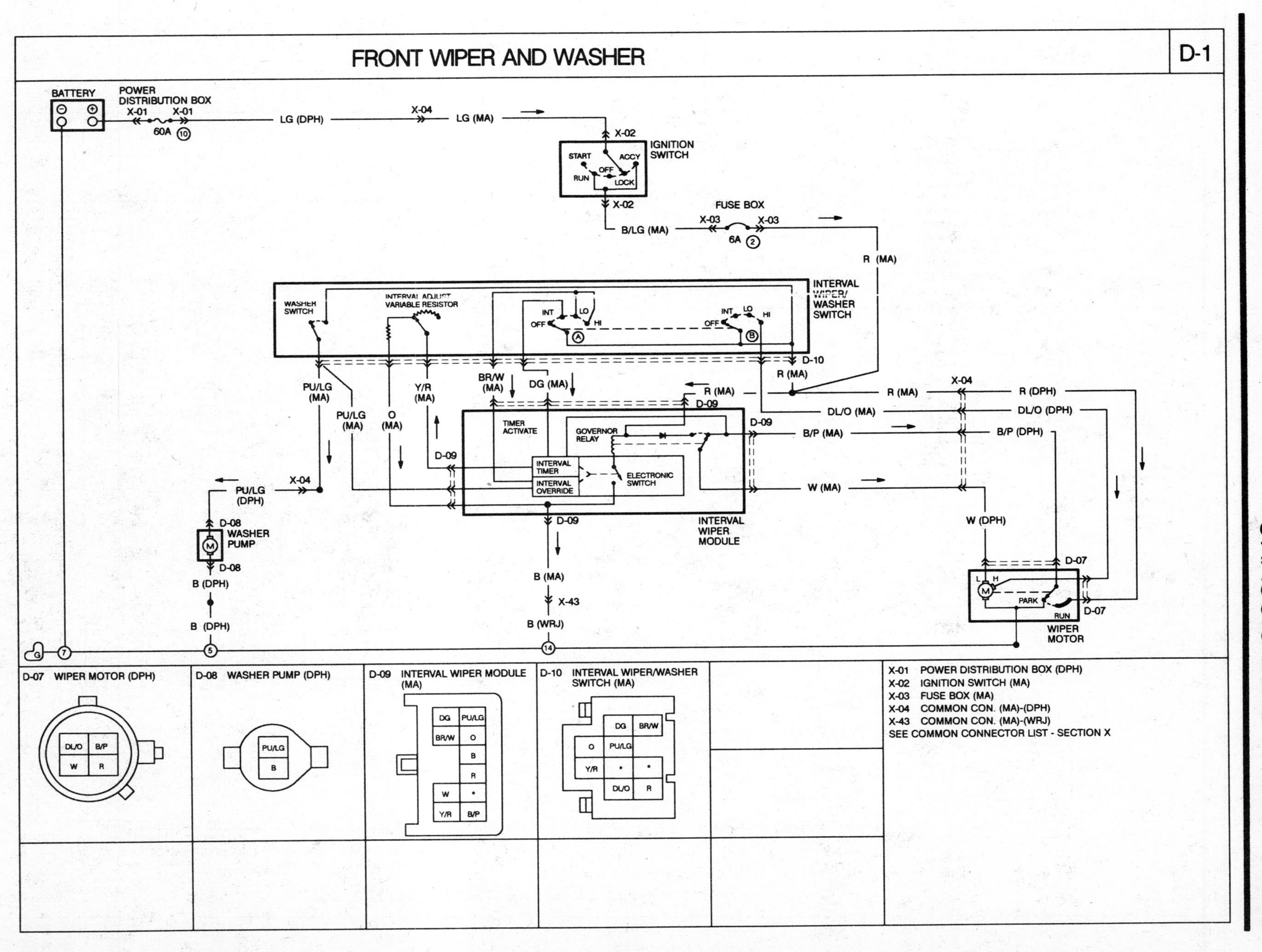

Navajo front wiper and washer (1992 shown)

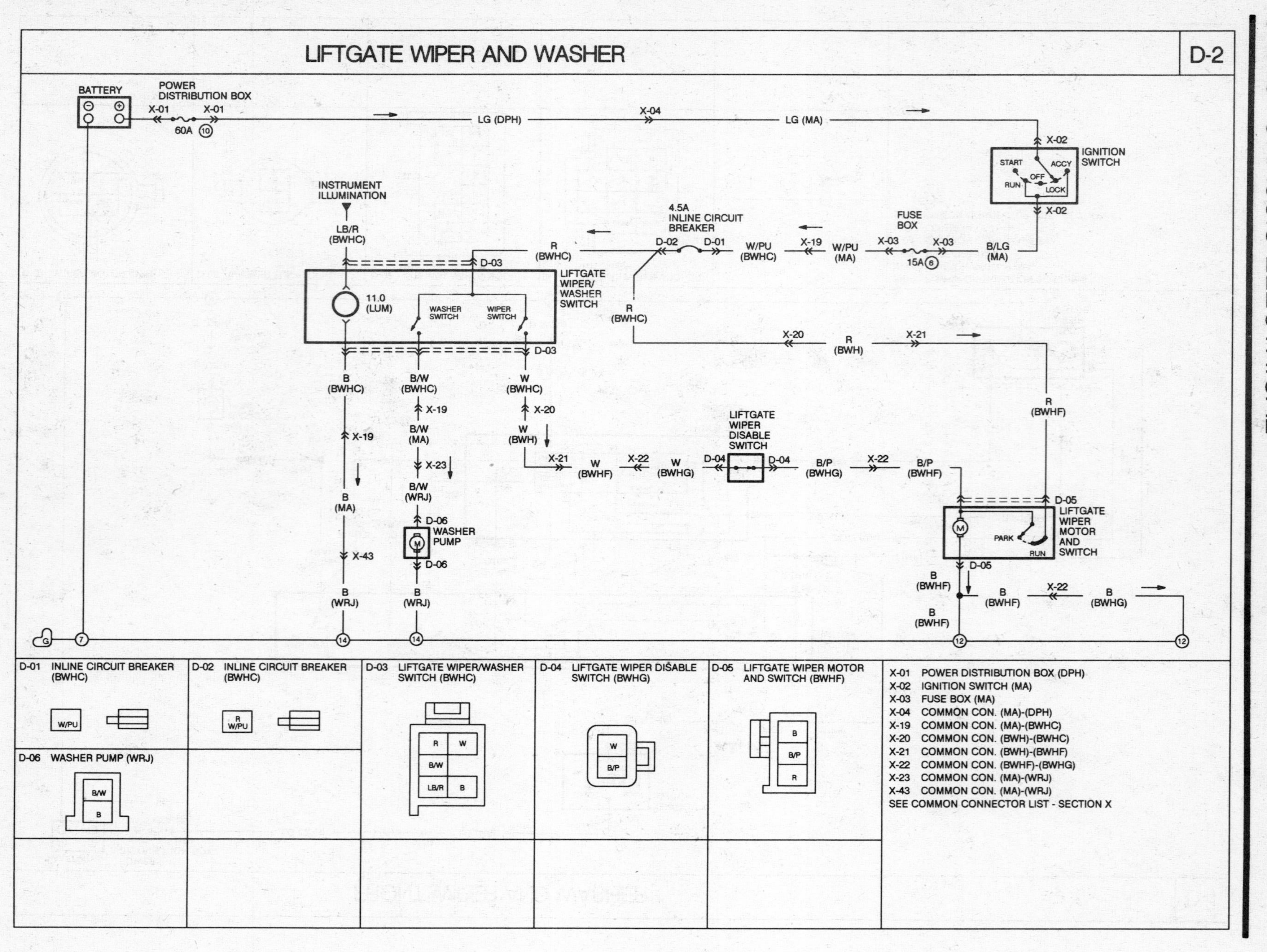

Navajo liftgate wiper and washer (1992 shown)

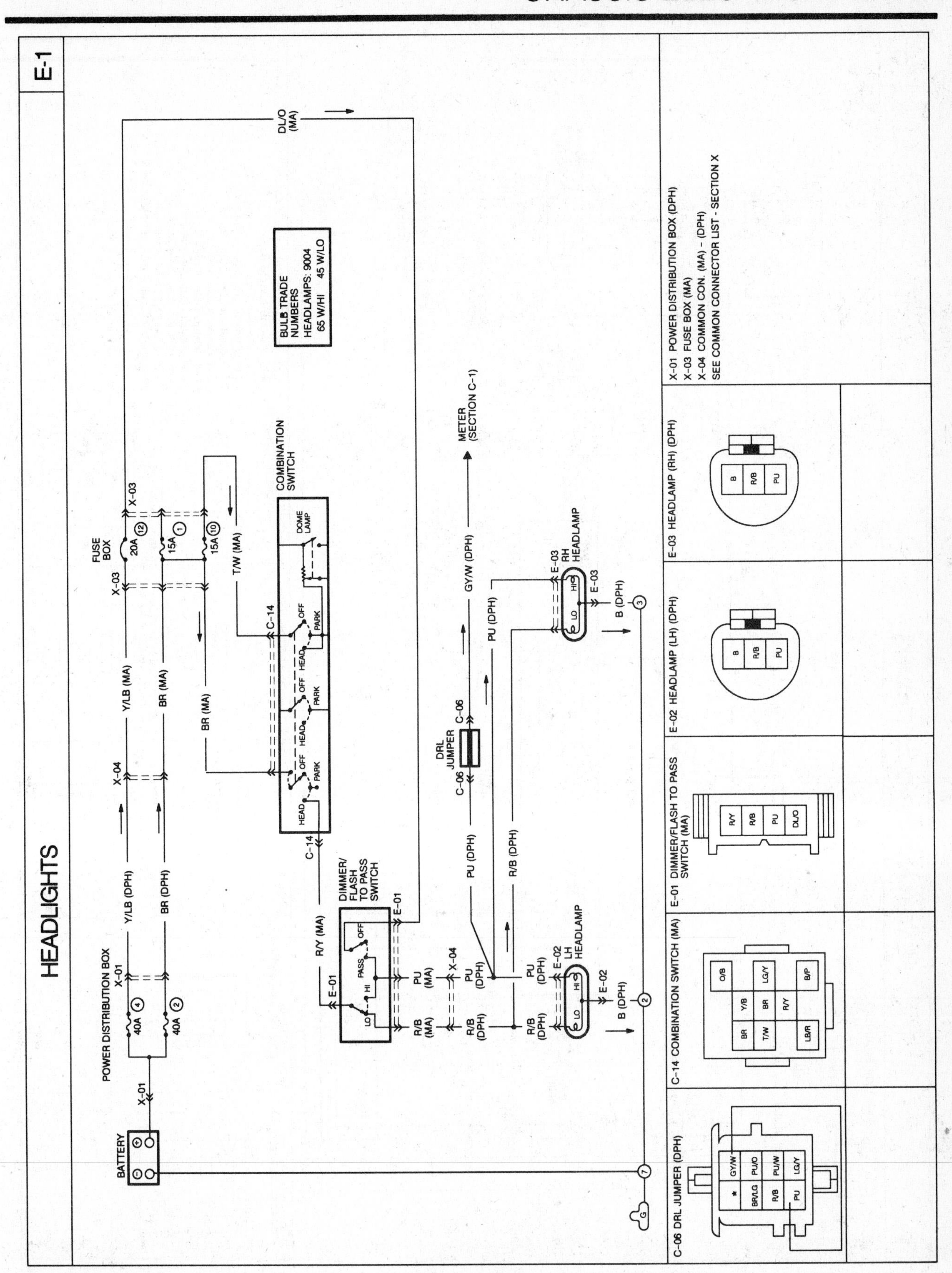

Navajo headlights (1992 shown)

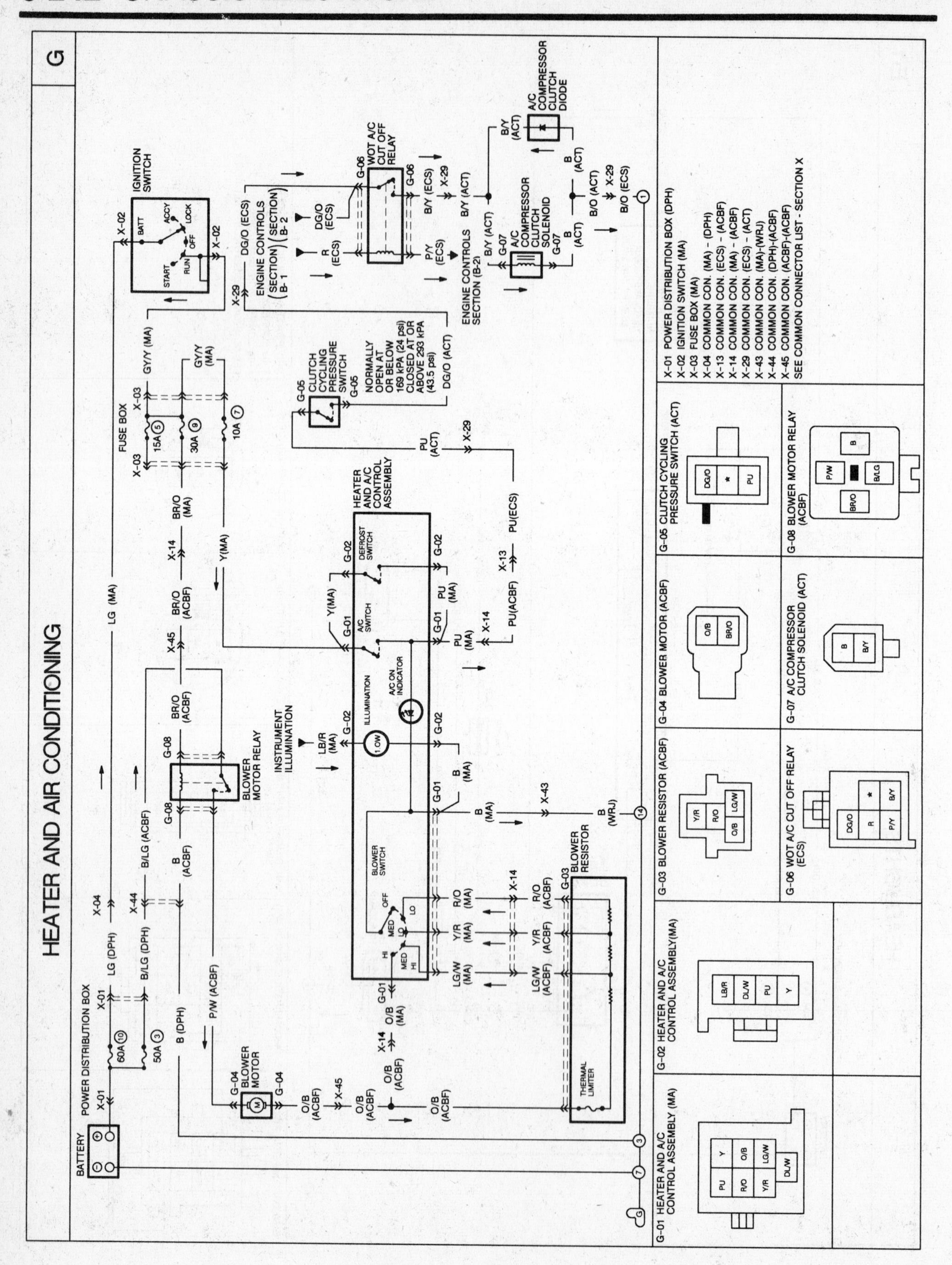

Navajo heater and air conditioning (1992 shown)

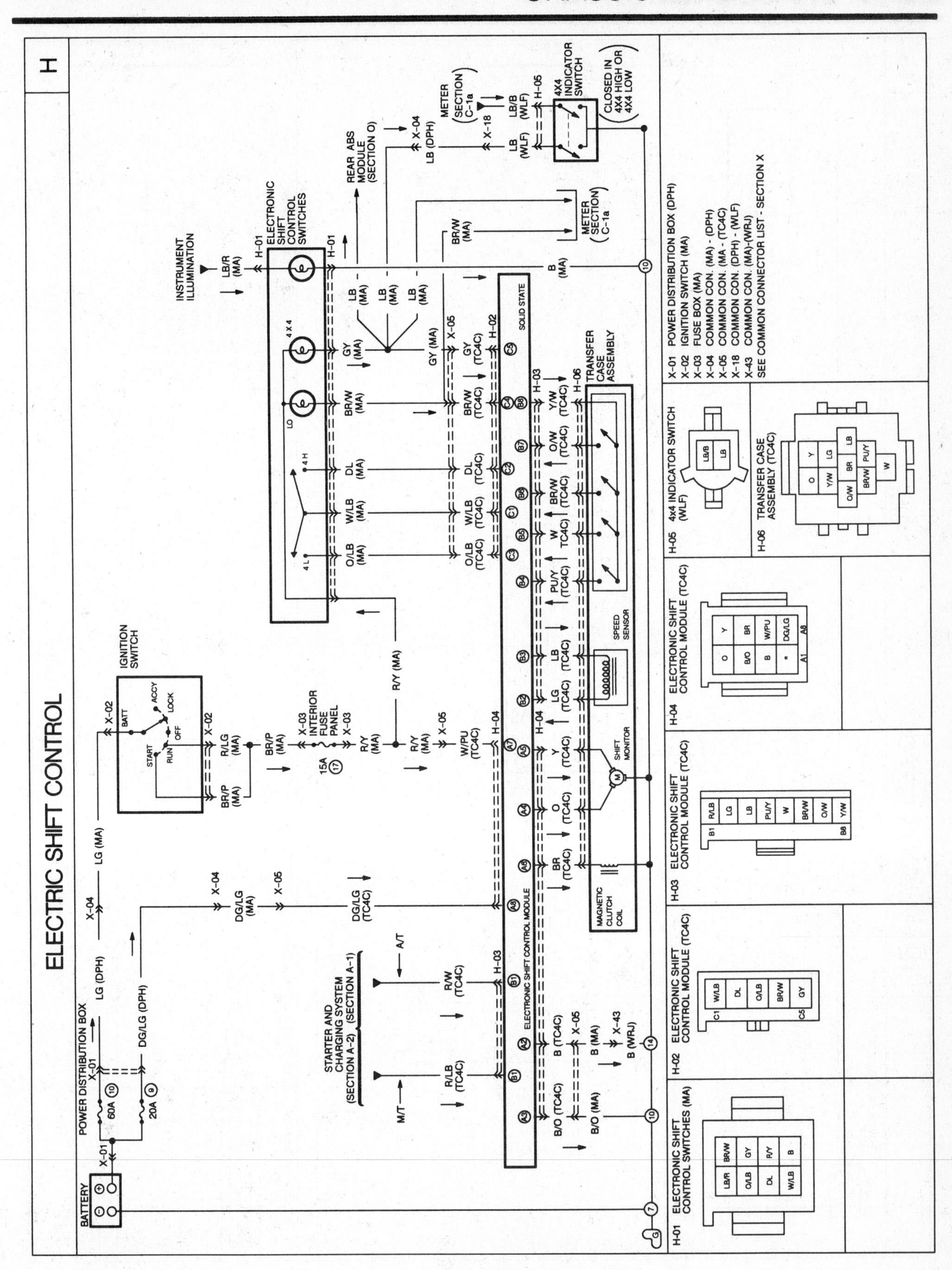

Navajo electric shift control (1992 shown)

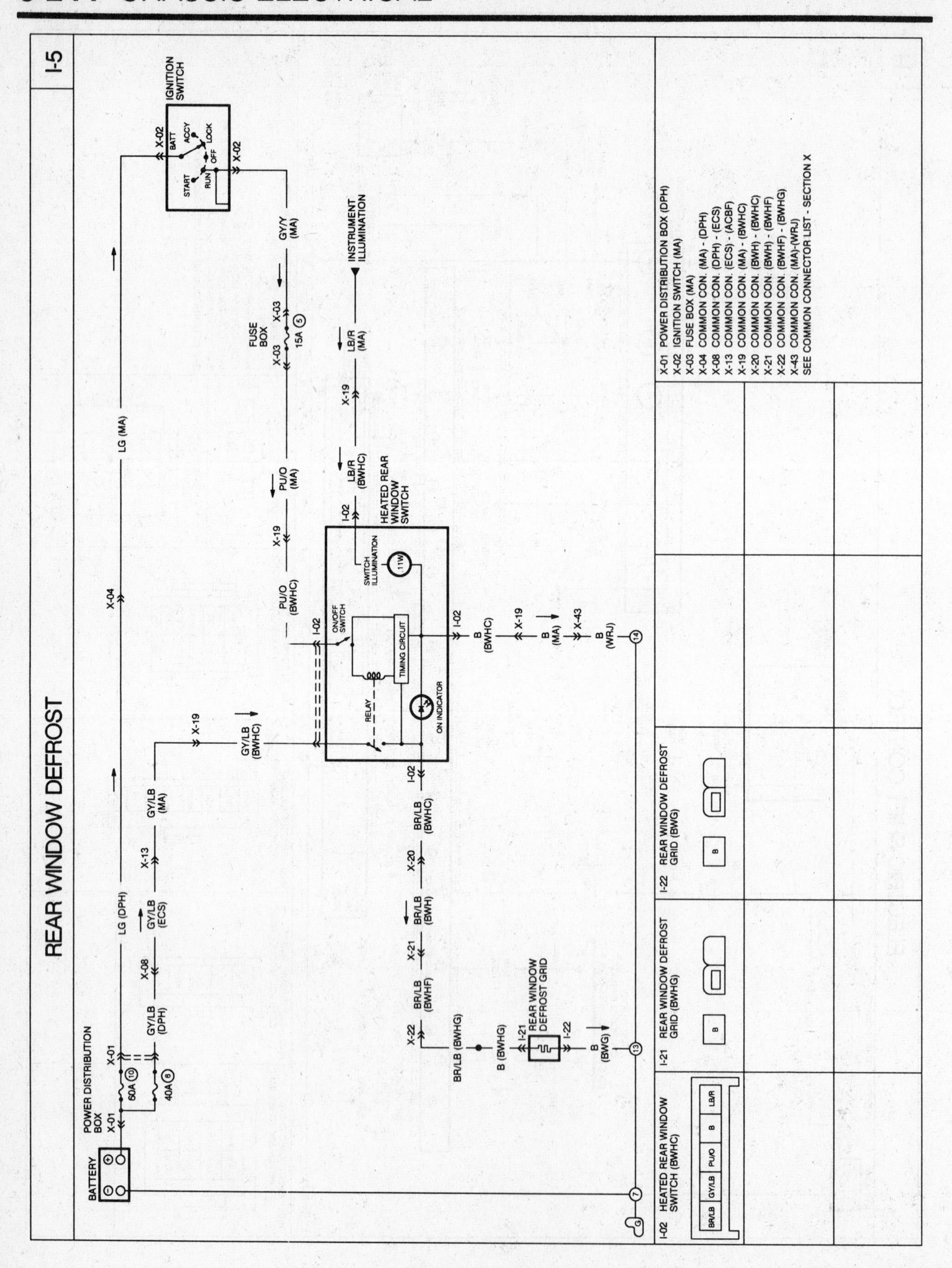

Navajo rear window defrost (1992 shown)

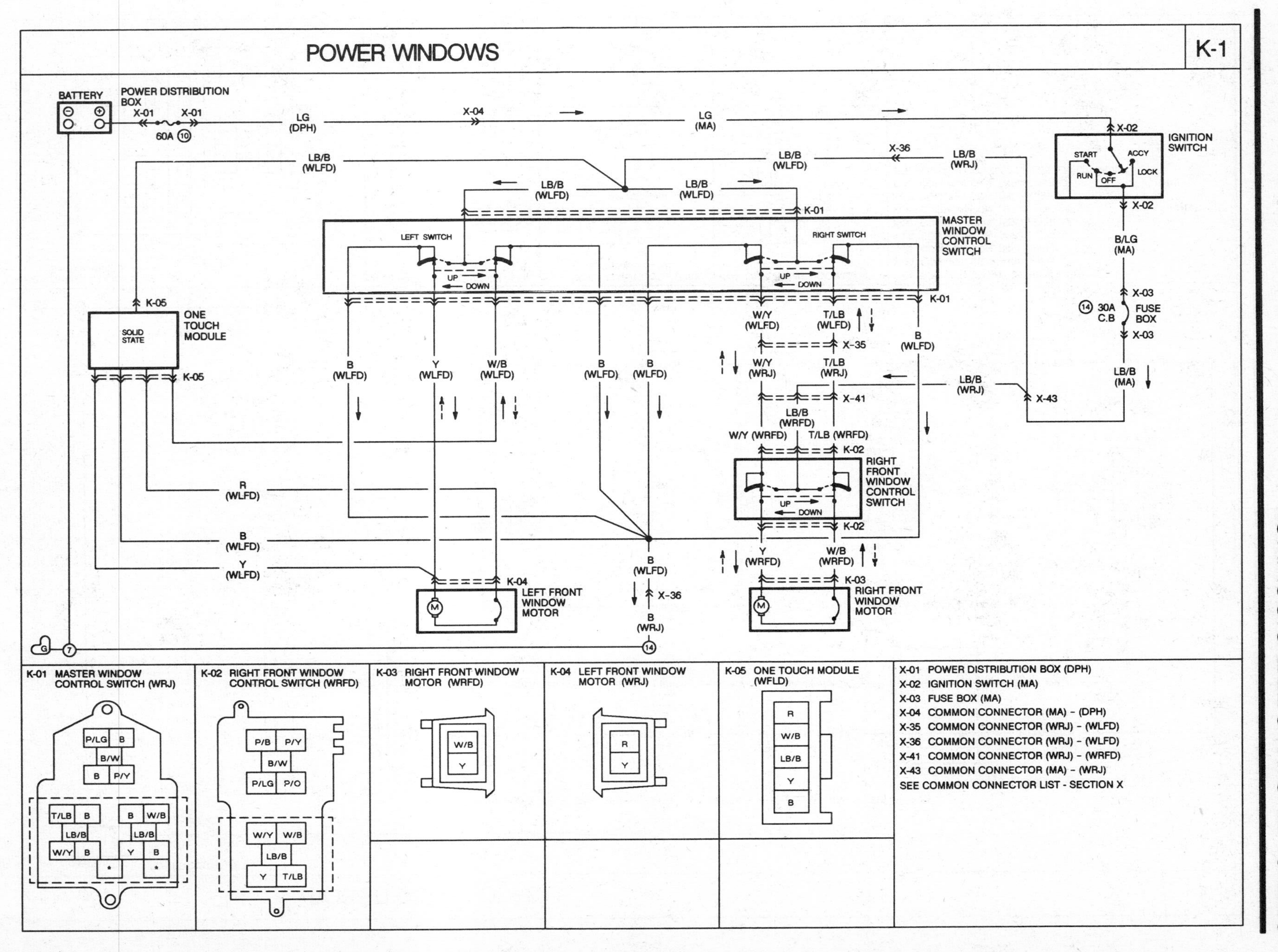

Navajo power windows (1992 shown)

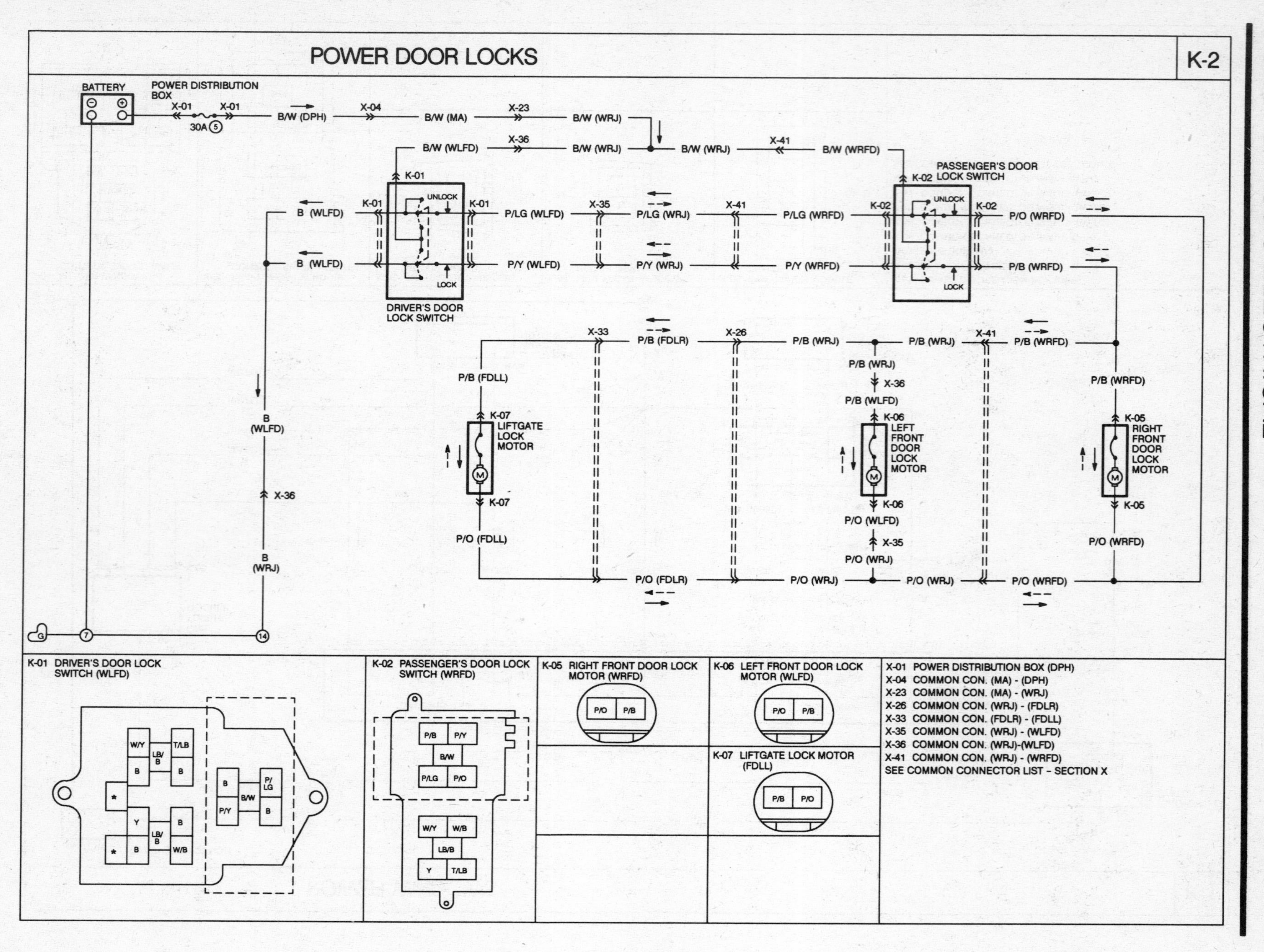

Navajo power door locks (1992 shown)

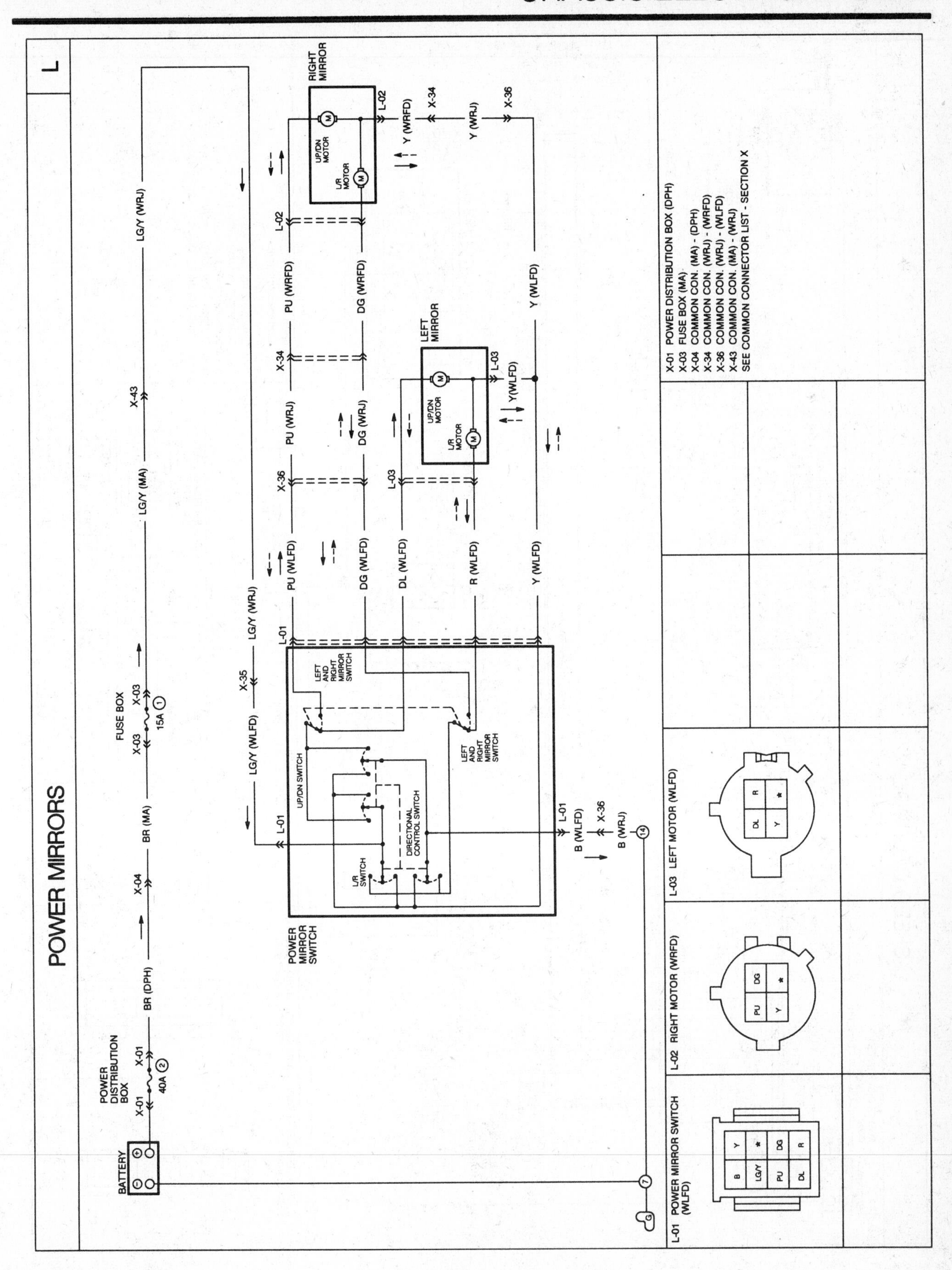

Navajo power mirrors (1992 shown)

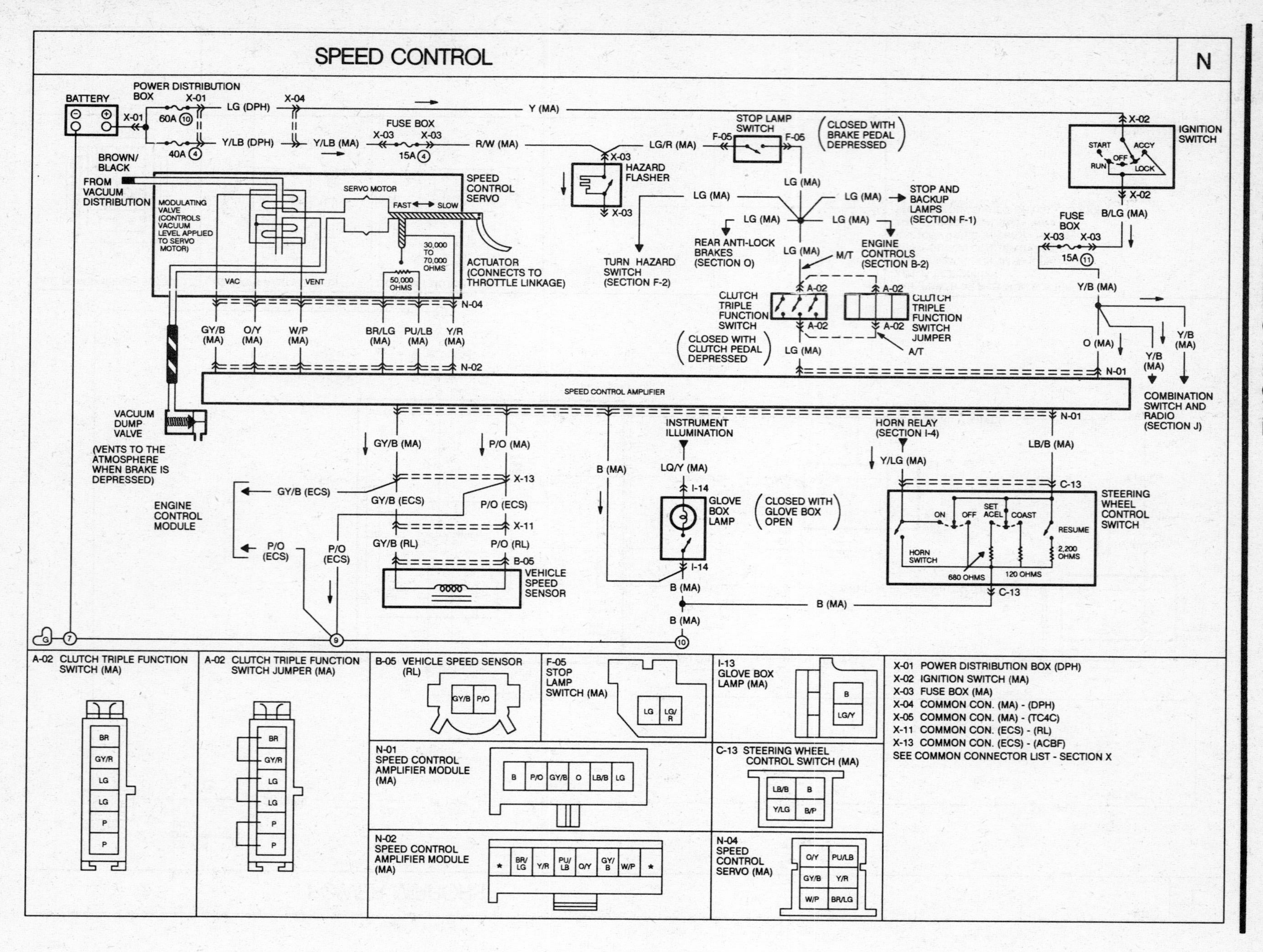

Navajo speed control (1992 shown)

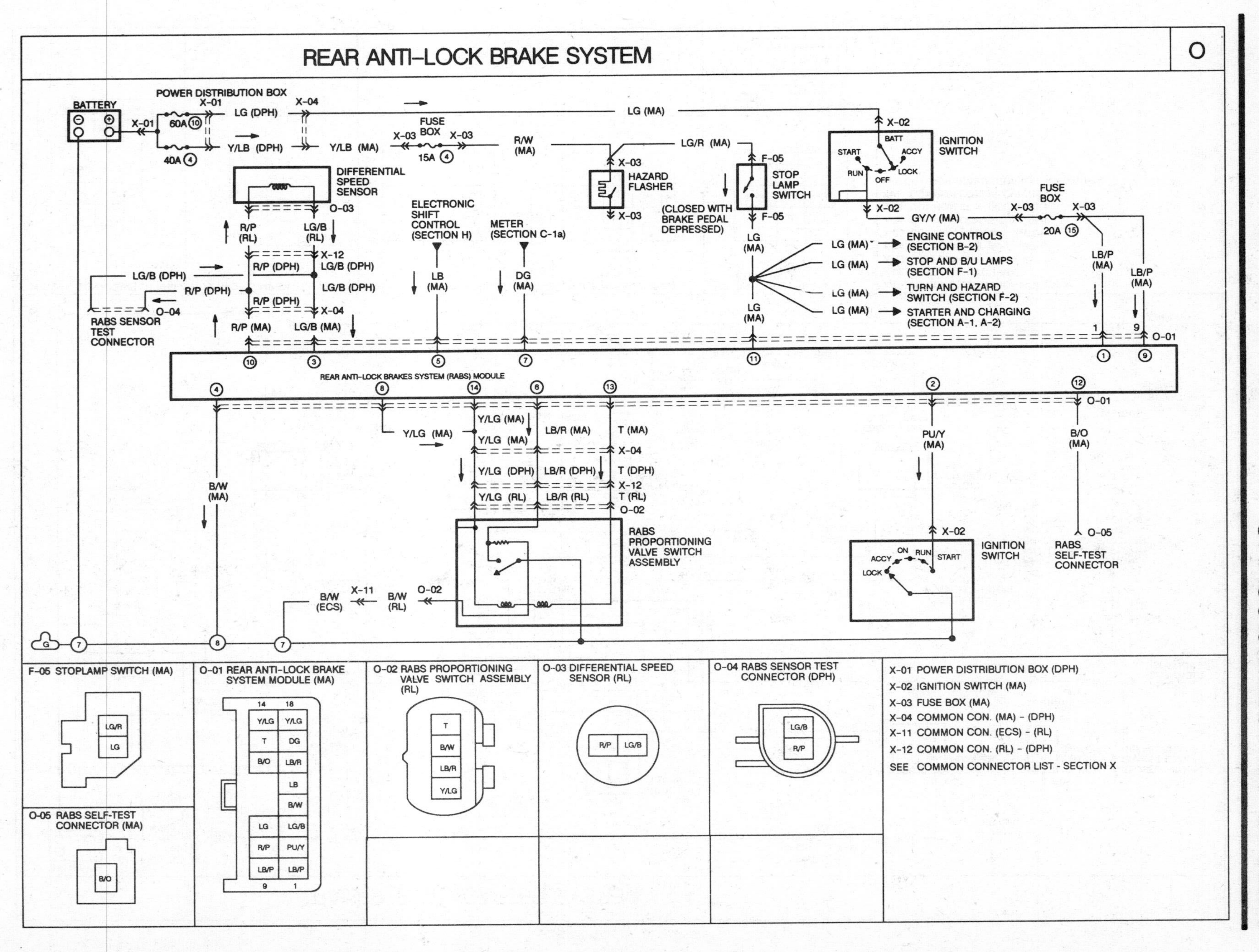

Navajo rear anti-lock brake system (1992 shown)

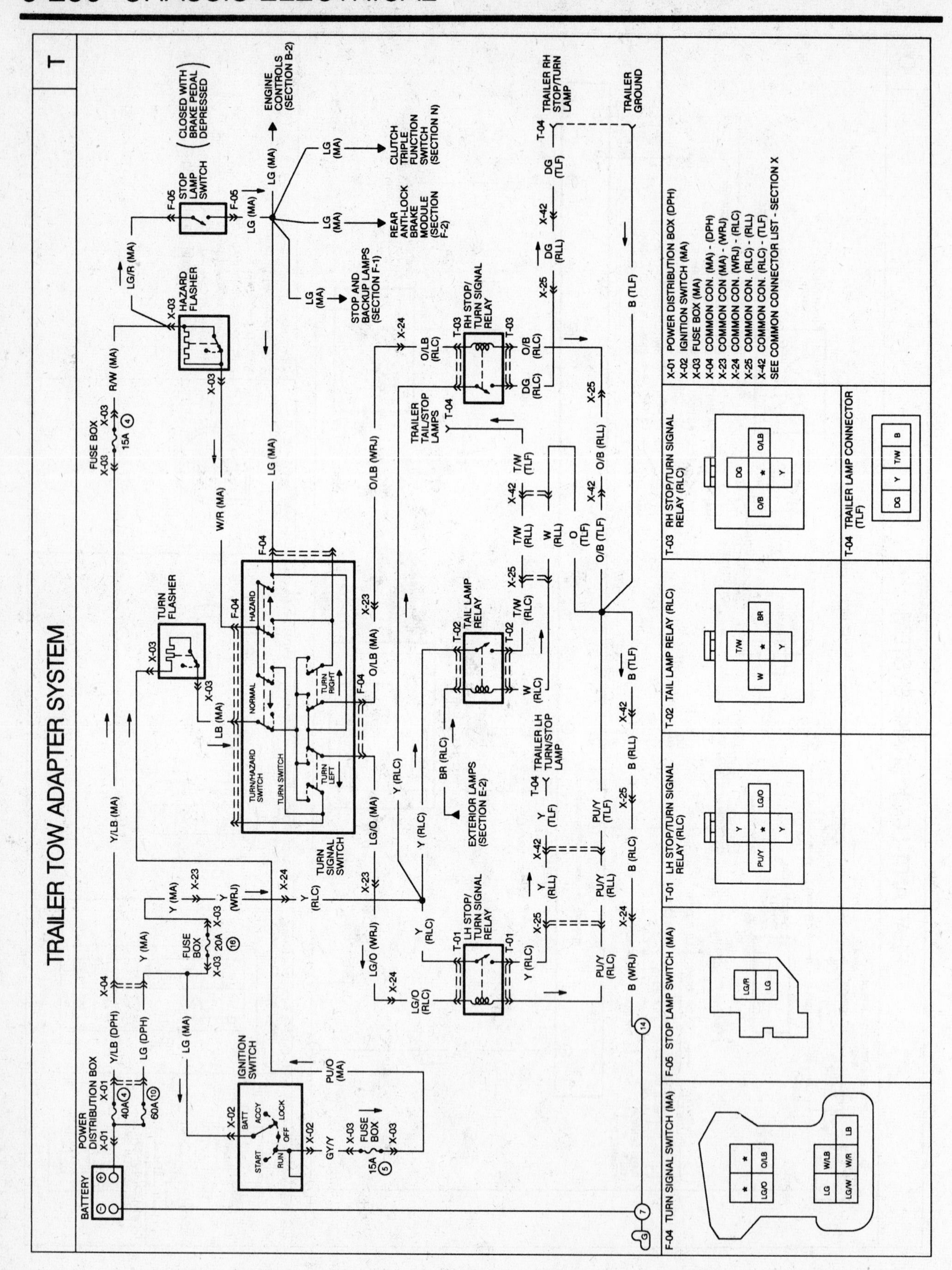

Navajo trailer tow adapter system (1992 shown)

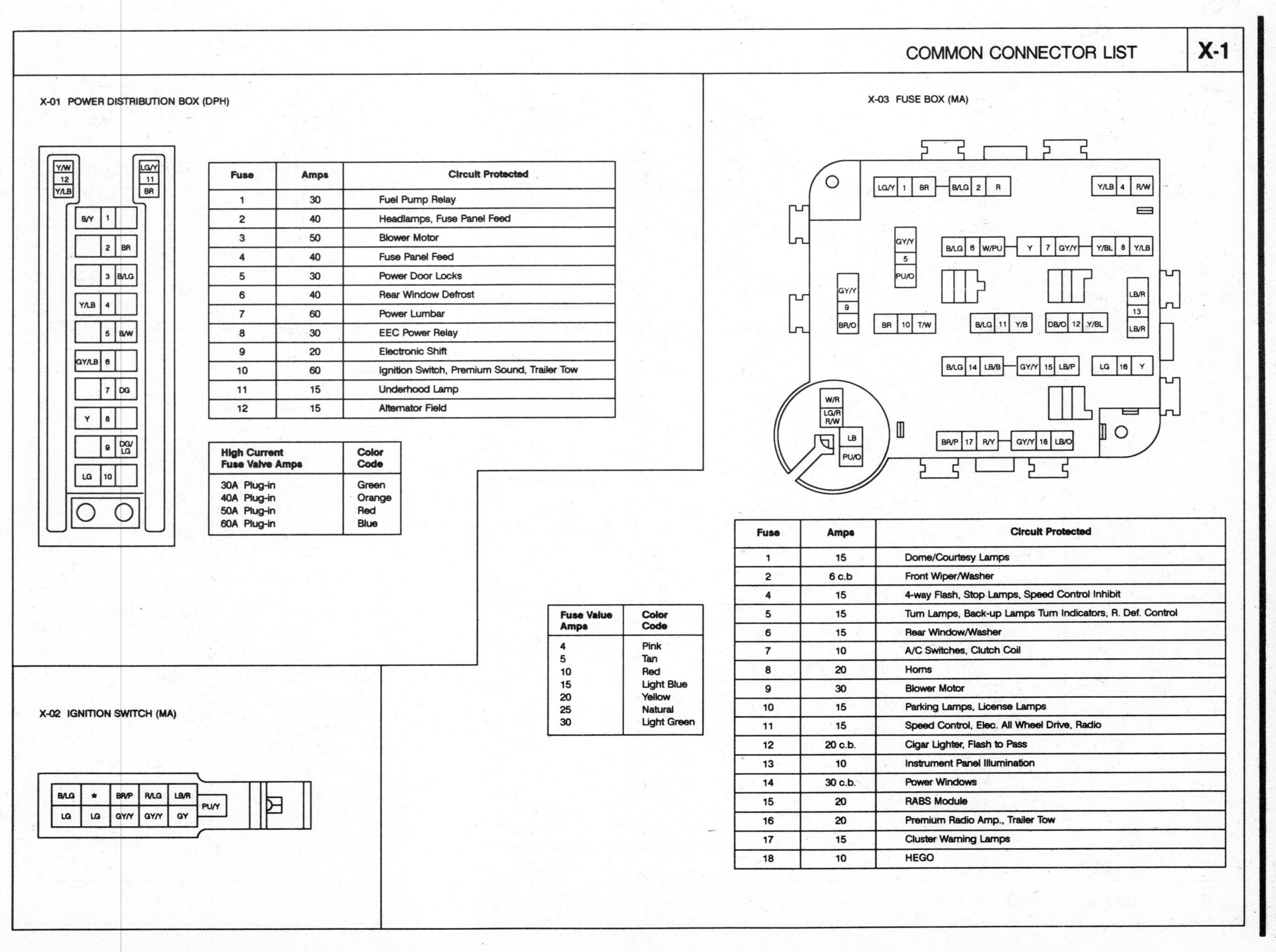

Fuse	Amps	Circuit Protected
1	30	Fuel Pump Relay
2	40	Headlamps, Fuse Panel Feed
3	50	Blower Motor
4	40	Fuse Panel Feed
5	30	Power Door Locks
6	40	Rear Window Defrost
7	60	Power Lumbar
8	30	EEC Power Relay
9	20	Electronic Shift
10	60	Ignition Switch, Premium Sound, Trailer Tow
11	15	Underhood Lamp
12	15	Alternator Field

High Current Fuse Valve Amps	Color Code
30A Plug-in	Green
40A Plug-in	Orange
50A Plug-in	Red
60A Plug-in	Blue

Fuse	Amps	Circuit Protected
1	15	Dome/Courtesy Lamps
2	6 c.b	Front Wiper/Washer
4	15	4-way Flash, Stop Lamps, Speed Control Inhibit
5	15	Turn Lamps, Back-up Lamps Turn Indicators, R. Def. Control
6	15	Rear Window/Washer
7	10	A/C Switches, Clutch Coil
8	20	Horns
9	30	Blower Motor
10	15	Parking Lamps, License Lamps
11	15	Speed Control, Elec. All Wheel Drive, Radio
12	20 c.b.	Cigar Lighter, Flash to Pass
13	10	Instrument Panel Illumination
14	30 c.b.	Power Windows
15	20	RABS Module
16	20	Premium Radio Amp., Trailer Tow
17	15	Cluster Warning Lamps
18	10	HEGO

Fuse Value Amps	Color Code
4	Pink
5	Tan
10	Red
15	Light Blue
20	Yellow
25	Natural
30	Light Green

Navajo common connector list (1992 shown)

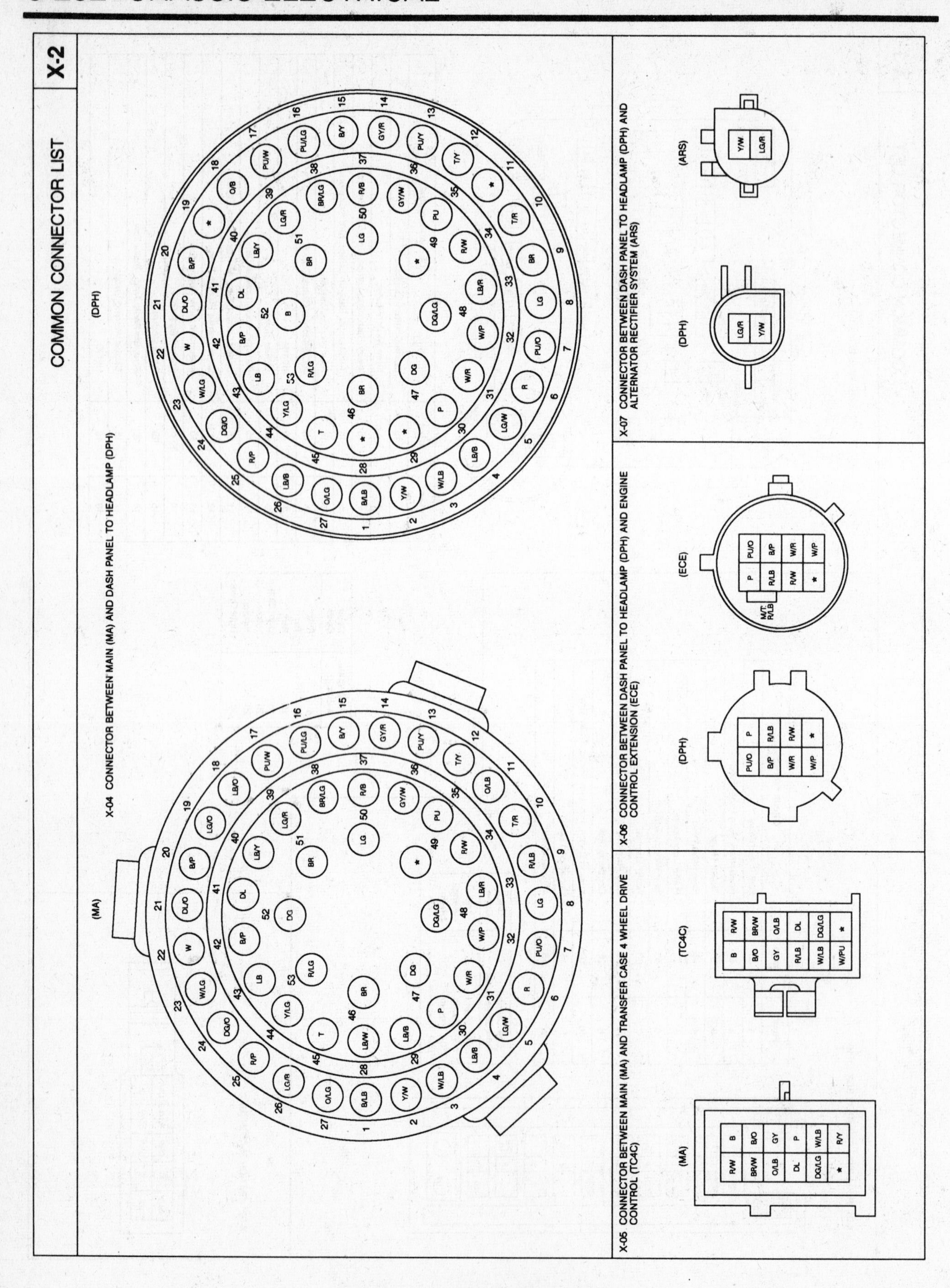

Navajo common connector list (1992 shown)

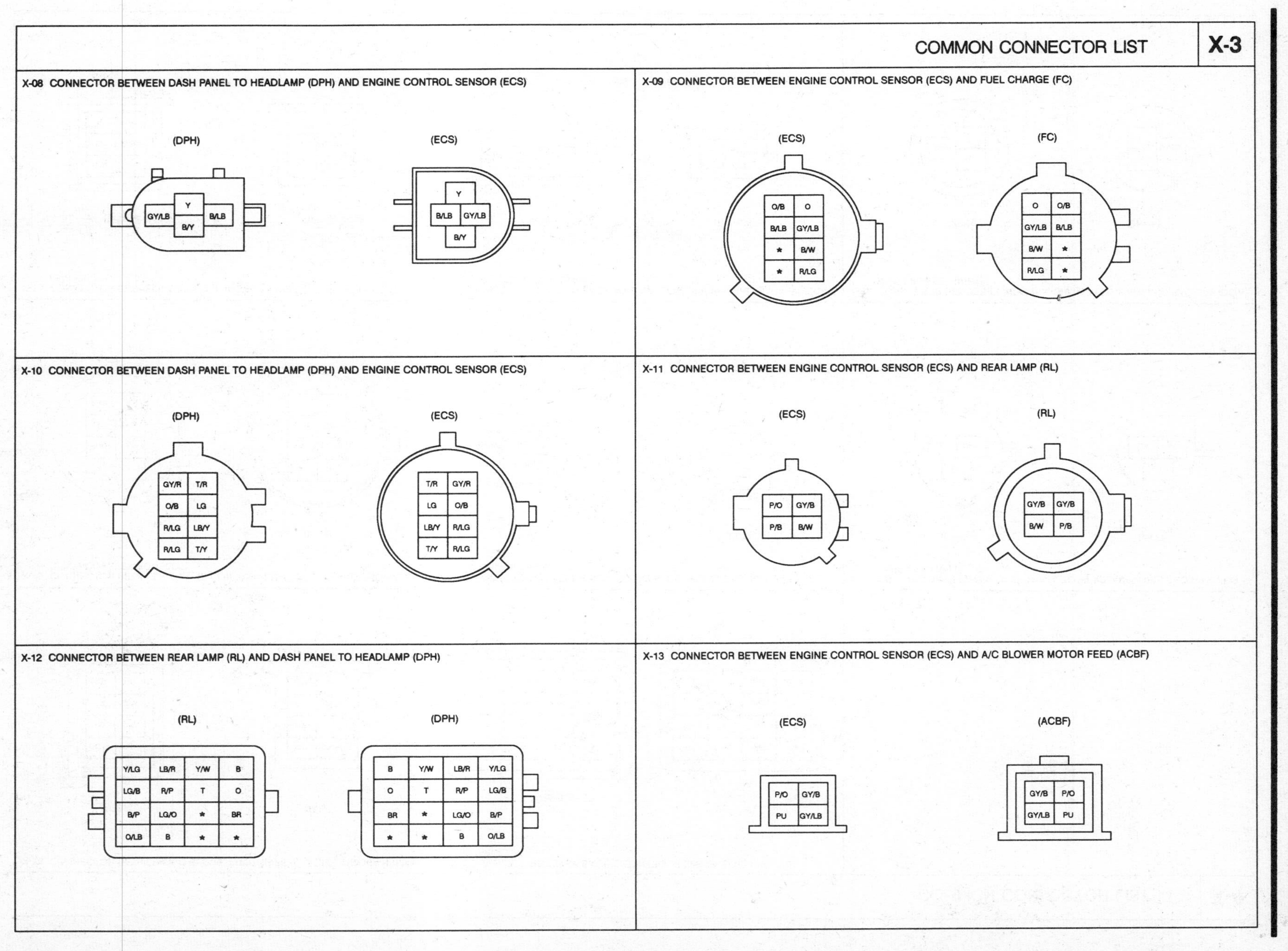

Navajo common connector list (1992 shown)

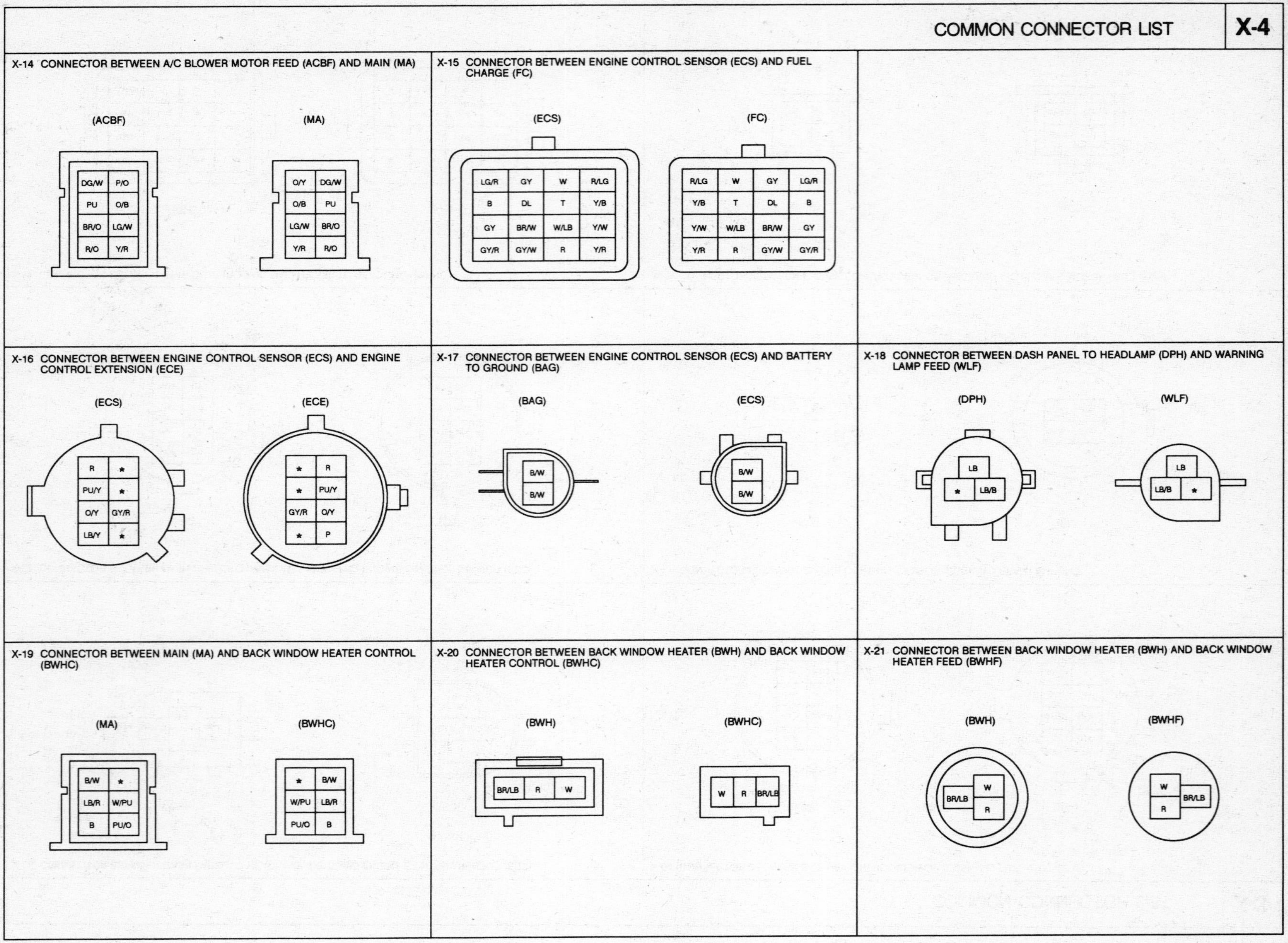

COMMON CONNECTOR LIST X-4

X-14 CONNECTOR BETWEEN A/C BLOWER MOTOR FEED (ACBF) AND MAIN (MA)

(ACBF)
DG/W P/O
PU O/B
BR/O LG/W
R/O Y/R

(MA)
O/Y DG/W
O/B PU
LG/W BR/O
Y/R R/O

X-15 CONNECTOR BETWEEN ENGINE CONTROL SENSOR (ECS) AND FUEL CHARGE (FC)

(ECS)
LG/R GY W R/LG
B DL T Y/B
GY BR/W W/LB Y/W
GY/R GY/W R Y/R

(FC)
R/LG W GY LG/R
Y/B T DL B
Y/W W/LB BR/W GY
Y/R R GY/W GY/R

X-16 CONNECTOR BETWEEN ENGINE CONTROL SENSOR (ECS) AND ENGINE CONTROL EXTENSION (ECE)

(ECS)
R *
PU/Y *
O/Y GY/R
LB/Y *

(ECE)
* R
* PU/Y
GY/R O/Y
* P

X-17 CONNECTOR BETWEEN ENGINE CONTROL SENSOR (ECS) AND BATTERY TO GROUND (BAG)

(BAG)
B/W
B/W

(ECS)
B/W
B/W

X-18 CONNECTOR BETWEEN DASH PANEL TO HEADLAMP (DPH) AND WARNING LAMP FEED (WLF)

(DPH)
LB
* LB/B

(WLF)
LB
LB/B *

X-19 CONNECTOR BETWEEN MAIN (MA) AND BACK WINDOW HEATER CONTROL (BWHC)

(MA)
B/W *
LB/R W/PU
B PU/O

(BWHC)
* B/W
W/PU LB/R
PU/O B

X-20 CONNECTOR BETWEEN BACK WINDOW HEATER (BWH) AND BACK WINDOW HEATER CONTROL (BWHC)

(BWH)
BR/LB R W

(BWHC)
W R BR/LB

X-21 CONNECTOR BETWEEN BACK WINDOW HEATER (BWH) AND BACK WINDOW HEATER FEED (BWHF)

(BWH)
BR/LB W
R

(BWHF)
W BR/LB
R

Navajo common connector list (1992 shown)

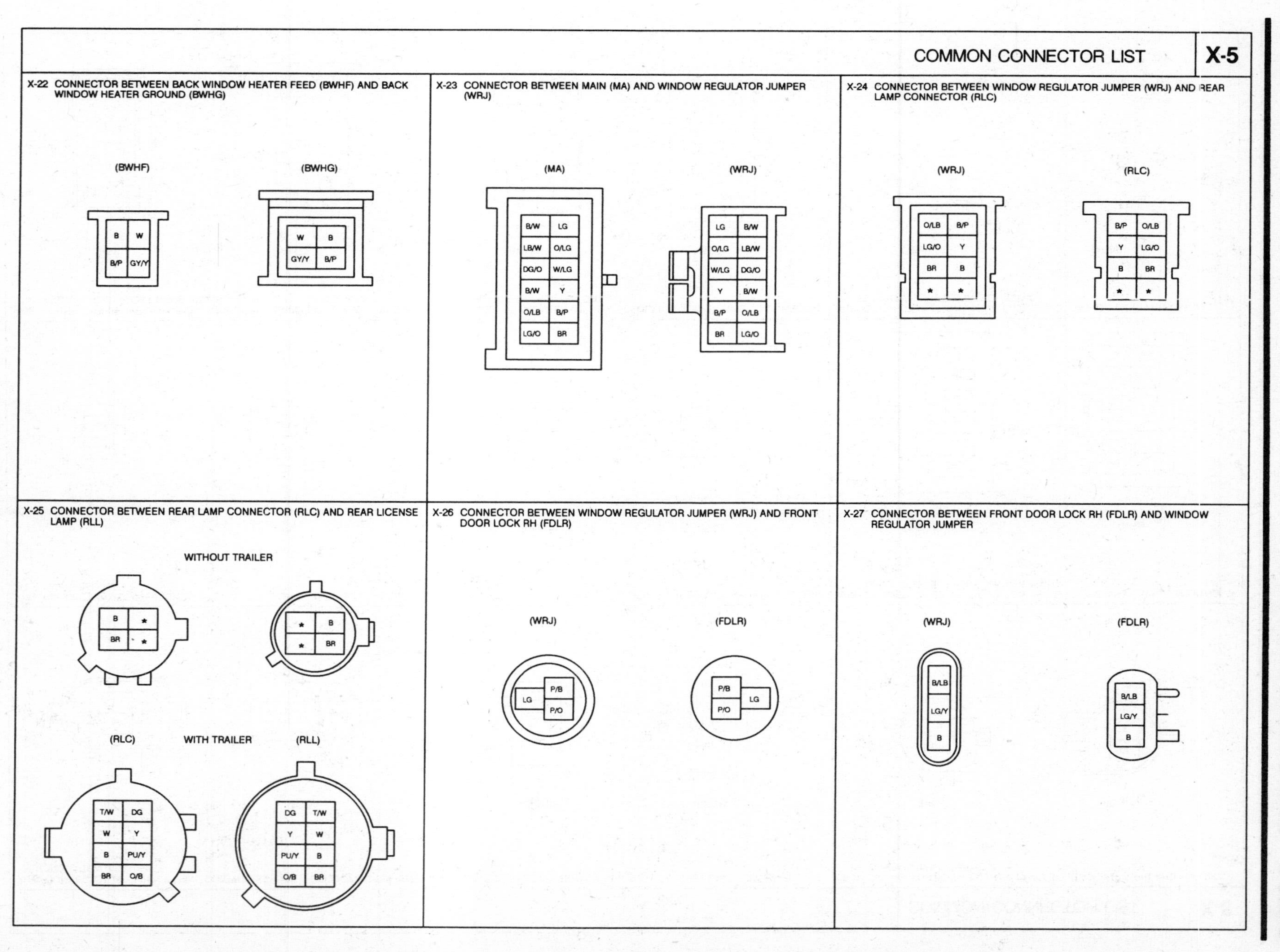
COMMON CONNECTOR LIST
X-5
X-22 CONNECTOR BETWEEN BACK WINDOW HEATER FEED (BWHF) AND BACK WINDOW HEATER GROUND (BWHG)
(BWHF)
(BWHG)
X-23 CONNECTOR BETWEEN MAIN (MA) AND WINDOW REGULATOR JUMPER (WRJ)
(MA)
(WRJ)
X-24 CONNECTOR BETWEEN WINDOW REGULATOR JUMPER (WRJ) AND REAR LAMP CONNECTOR (RLC)
(WRJ)
(RLC)
X-25 CONNECTOR BETWEEN REAR LAMP CONNECTOR (RLC) AND REAR LICENSE LAMP (RLL)
WITHOUT TRAILER
(RLC)
WITH TRAILER
(RLL)
X-26 CONNECTOR BETWEEN WINDOW REGULATOR JUMPER (WRJ) AND FRONT DOOR LOCK RH (FDLR)
(WRJ)
(FDLR)
X-27 CONNECTOR BETWEEN FRONT DOOR LOCK RH (FDLR) AND WINDOW REGULATOR JUMPER
(WRJ)
(FDLR)

Navajo common connector list (1992 shown)

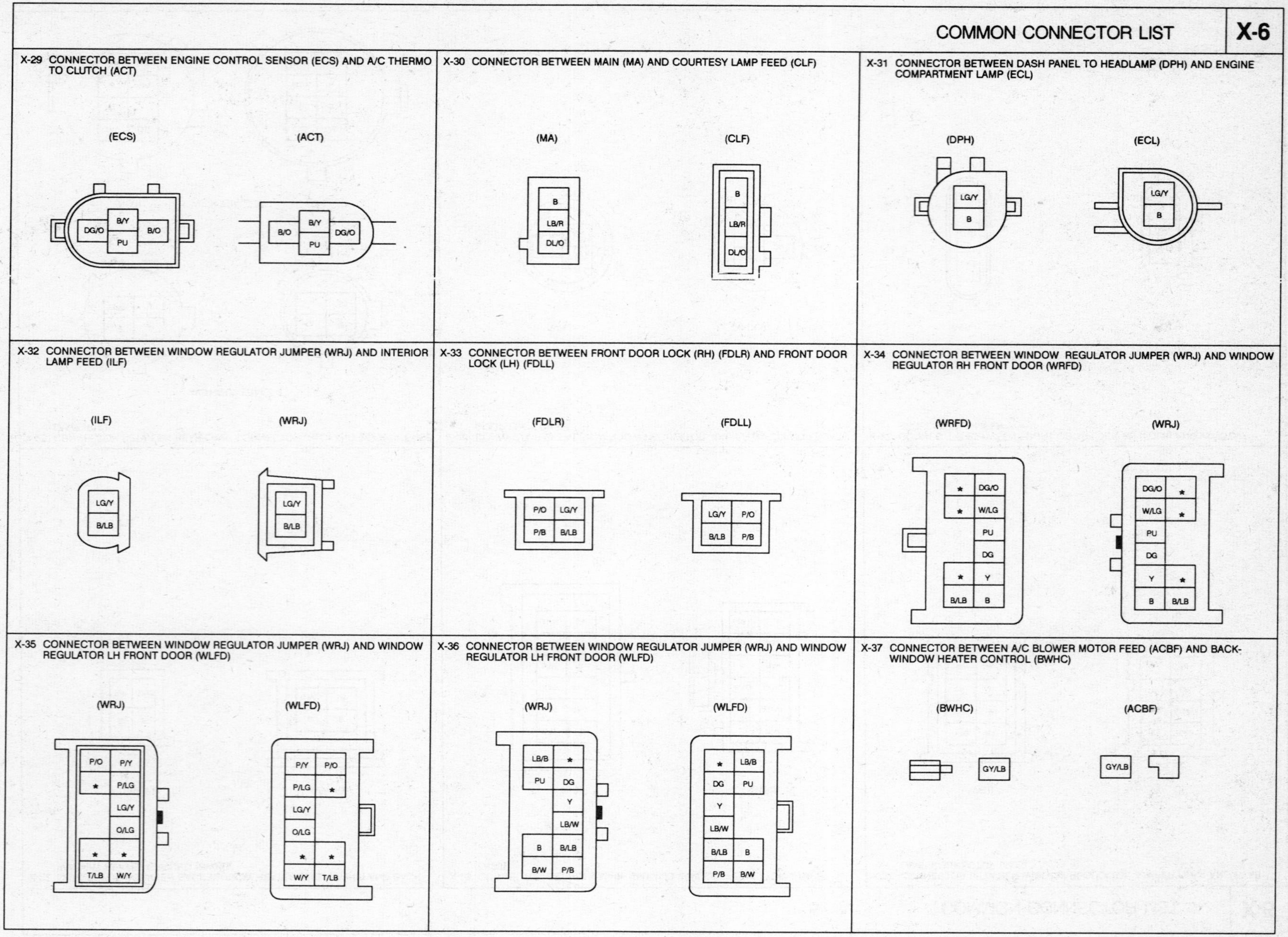

COMMON CONNECTOR LIST — X-6

X-29 CONNECTOR BETWEEN ENGINE CONTROL SENSOR (ECS) AND A/C THERMO TO CLUTCH (ACT)

(ECS) DG/O B/Y PU B/O

(ACT) B/O B/Y PU DG/O

X-30 CONNECTOR BETWEEN MAIN (MA) AND COURTESY LAMP FEED (CLF)

(MA) B LB/R DL/O

(CLF) B LB/R DL/O

X-31 CONNECTOR BETWEEN DASH PANEL TO HEADLAMP (DPH) AND ENGINE COMPARTMENT LAMP (ECL)

(DPH) LG/Y B

(ECL) LG/Y B

X-32 CONNECTOR BETWEEN WINDOW REGULATOR JUMPER (WRJ) AND INTERIOR LAMP FEED (ILF)

(ILF) LG/Y B/LB

(WRJ) LG/Y B/LB

X-33 CONNECTOR BETWEEN FRONT DOOR LOCK (RH) (FDLR) AND FRONT DOOR LOCK (LH) (FDLL)

(FDLR) P/O LG/Y P/B B/LB

(FDLL) LG/Y P/O B/LB P/B

X-34 CONNECTOR BETWEEN WINDOW REGULATOR JUMPER (WRJ) AND WINDOW REGULATOR RH FRONT DOOR (WRFD)

(WRFD) * DG/O * W/LG PU DG * Y B/LB B

(WRJ) DG/O * W/LG * PU DG Y * B B/LB

X-35 CONNECTOR BETWEEN WINDOW REGULATOR JUMPER (WRJ) AND WINDOW REGULATOR LH FRONT DOOR (WLFD)

(WRJ) P/O P/Y * P/LG LG/Y O/LG * * T/LB W/Y

(WLFD) P/Y P/O P/LG * LG/Y O/LG * * W/Y T/LB

X-36 CONNECTOR BETWEEN WINDOW REGULATOR JUMPER (WRJ) AND WINDOW REGULATOR LH FRONT DOOR (WLFD)

(WRJ) LB/B * PU DG Y LB/W B B/LB B/W P/B

(WLFD) * LB/B DG PU Y LB/W B/LB B P/B B/W

X-37 CONNECTOR BETWEEN A/C BLOWER MOTOR FEED (ACBF) AND BACK-WINDOW HEATER CONTROL (BWHC)

(BWHC) GY/LB

(ACBF) GY/LB

Navajo common connector list (1992 shown)

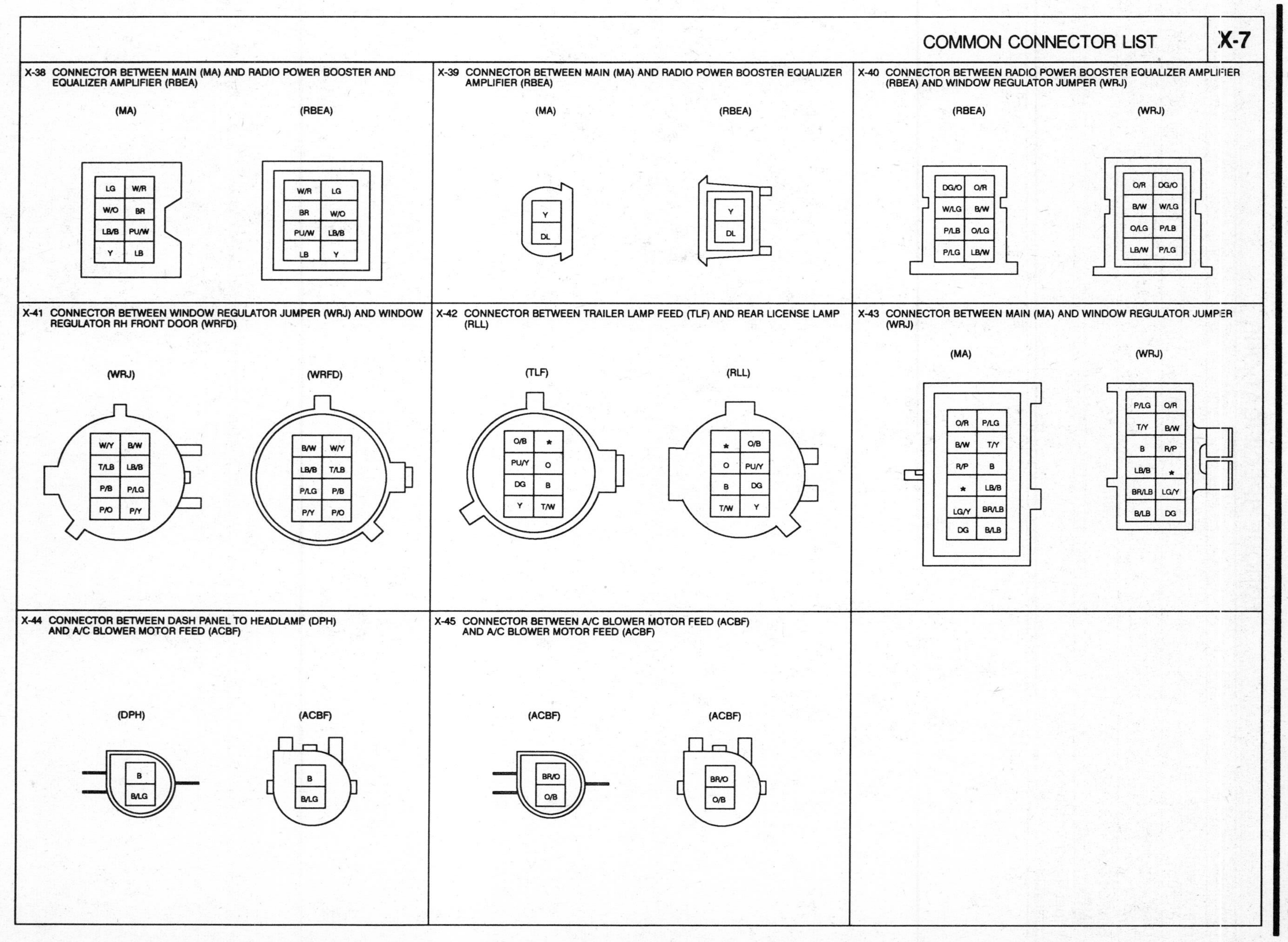
COMMON CONNECTOR LIST
X-7
X-38 CONNECTOR BETWEEN MAIN (MA) AND RADIO POWER BOOSTER AND EQUALIZER AMPLIFIER (RBEA)
(MA)
(RBEA)
X-39 CONNECTOR BETWEEN MAIN (MA) AND RADIO POWER BOOSTER EQUALIZER AMPLIFIER (RBEA)
(MA)
(RBEA)
X-40 CONNECTOR BETWEEN RADIO POWER BOOSTER EQUALIZER AMPLIFIER (RBEA) AND WINDOW REGULATOR JUMPER (WRJ)
(RBEA)
(WRJ)
X-41 CONNECTOR BETWEEN WINDOW REGULATOR JUMPER (WRJ) AND WINDOW REGULATOR RH FRONT DOOR (WRFD)
(WRJ)
(WRFD)
X-42 CONNECTOR BETWEEN TRAILER LAMP FEED (TLF) AND REAR LICENSE LAMP (RLL)
(TLF)
(RLL)
X-43 CONNECTOR BETWEEN MAIN (MA) AND WINDOW REGULATOR JUMPER (WRJ)
(MA)
(WRJ)
X-44 CONNECTOR BETWEEN DASH PANEL TO HEADLAMP (DPH) AND A/C BLOWER MOTOR FEED (ACBF)
(DPH)
(ACBF)
X-45 CONNECTOR BETWEEN A/C BLOWER MOTOR FEED (ACBF) AND A/C BLOWER MOTOR FEED (ACBF)
(ACBF)
(ACBF)

Navajo common connector list (1992 shown)

TORQUE SPECIFICATIONS

Component	U.S.	Metric
Arm retaining nuts		
Pickups	8-10 ft. lbs.	10.88-13.6 Nm
Discharge lines		
MPV	10 ft. lbs.	13.6 Nm
Suction line		
MPV	25 ft. lbs.	34 Nm
Wiper motor attaching screws		
Navajo	60-65 inch lbs.	6.72-7.28 Nm

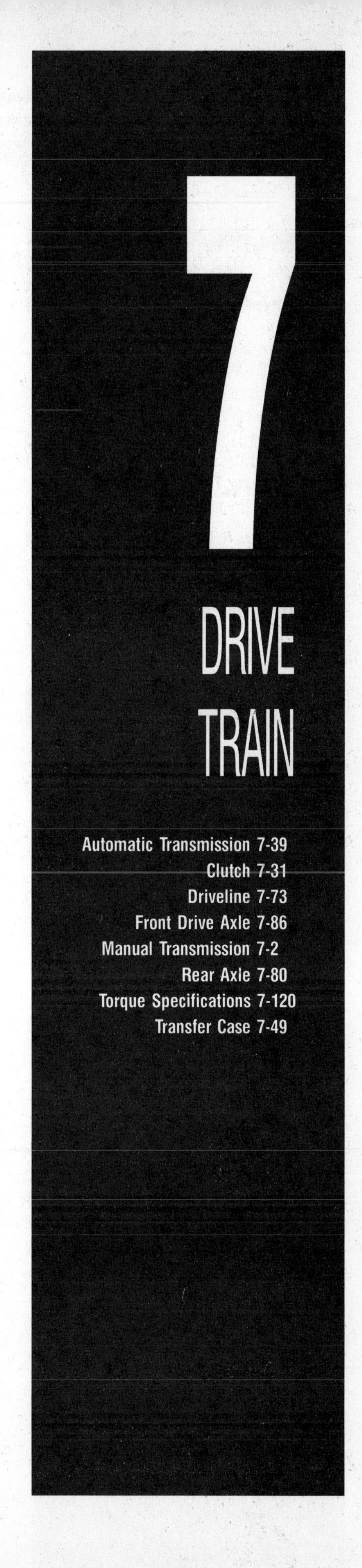

7 DRIVE TRAIN

MANUAL TRANSMISSION

Transmission Application

M4M-D 4-speed and M5M-D 5-speed transmissions are used on the B2200 Pickup. The R5M-D is used on 2-wheel drive, while a variation, the R5MX-D is used on 4-wheel drive models of the B2600 and MPV. On 4-wheel drive models, a transfer case is mounted on the rear of the transmission. The Navajo uses a M5OD 5-speed transmission.

➡ The Navajo is made by Ford Motor Co. Therefore, in procedures relating to the Navajo, special tools will be listed by their Ford part number.

Shift Handle

REMOVAL & INSTALLATION

Pickups and MPV

1. Disconnect the negative battery cable.
2. Shift the transmission into Neutral. Remove the gearshift lever knob and transfer case selector lever knob (if equipped). The knob unscrews from the shift lever.
3. Remove the console or boot retainer mounting screws. Remove the console and/or boot assembly. Slide it up and over the shift lever. If the shift lever is equipped with a 4WD indicator, disconnect the wiring connector after raising the boot assembly to gain working room.
4. Make sure the shift lever is in Neutral, remove the shift lever to transmission mounting bolts and lift the assembly up and away from the transmission.
5. Install the shift lever and secure the mounting bolts to:
   - B2200 — 69–95 inch lbs. (7.8–11.0Nm)
   - B2600 — 25–37 ft. lbs. (34–50Nm.)

➡ The gear shift linkage, on these transmissions, is internally mounted and requires no adjustment.

Navajo (M5OD)

1. Disconnect the negative battery cable.

➡ Do not remove the shift ball, unless the shift ball or boot is to be replaced. Otherwise, remove the shift ball, boot and lever as an assembly.

2. Remove the plastic shift pattern insert from the shift ball.
3. Heat the shift ball to 140–180°F (60–82°C), using a heat gun.
4. Position a block of wood beneath the shift ball and carefully hammer the ball from the lever. Be careful not to damage the finish on the shift lever.
5. Place the gearshift lever in **N** position.
6. Remove the rubber boot retainer screws.
7. Remove the shift lever-to-extension housing/transfer case adapter housing retaining bolts. Pull the gearshift lever straight up and away from the gearshift lever retainer.

To install:

8. Prior to installing the shift lever, lubricate the shift lever ball stud, using C1AZ-19590-B (ESA-M1C75-B) or equivalent.
9. Fit the shift lever into place and install the retaining bolts. Tighten and torque the retaining bolts 20–27 ft. lbs. (28–36 Nm).
10. Install the rubber boot and retaining screws.
11. If the shift ball was removed, heat the shift ball to 140°–180°F (60°–82°C), using a heat gun. Tap the ball onto the shift lever, using a suitable size (11mm will work) socket and mallet.
12. Place the shift lever in **N** position. Then, align the shift pattern plastic insert with the vehicle centerline and install it to the shift ball.

Neutral Sensing Switch

All Navajo manual transmission vehicles are equipped with a neutral sensing switch. The neutral sensing switch signals the vehicle on-board computer, which allows the vehicle to start only when the transmission is in **N**.

REMOVAL & INSTALLATION

1. Disconnect the negative battery cable.
2. Raise and support the vehicle safely.
3. Place the transmission in any position other than **N**.
4. Clean the area around the switch, then remove the switch.

To install:

5. Install the switch and tighten 8–12 ft. lbs (11–16Nm).
6. Reconnect the harness connector to the switch.
7. Lower the vehicle.
8. Reconnect the negative battery cable.

Back-Up Light Switch

REMOVAL & INSTALLATION

Pickup and MPV

The switch is located on the upper left rear of the transmission case. To replace it, disconnect the wiring and unscrew the switch from the case. Don't lose the washer.

Navajo

1. Disconnect the negative battery cable.
2. Raise and support the vehicle safely.
3. Place the transmission in any position other than **R** or **N**.
4. Clean the area around the switch, then remove the switch.

To install:

5. Install the switch and tighten 8–12 ft. lbs (11–16Nm).
6. Reconnect the harness connector to the switch.
7. Lower the vehicle.
8. Reconnect the negative battery cable.

Extension Housing Seal

REMOVAL & INSTALLATION

M5OD 5-Speed Transmission

1. Disconnect the negative battery cable.
2. Raise and support the vehicle safely.
3. Place a suitable drain pan beneath the extension housing. Clean the area around the transfer extension housing seal.

4. Matchmark the driveshaft to the rear axle flange. Disconnect the driveshaft and pull it rearward from the unit.
5. Remove the extension housing seal using tool T74P–77248–A or equivalent, remove the extension housing seal.

To Install:

6. Lubricate the inside diameter of the oil seal and install the seal into the extension housing using tool T61L–7657–A. Check to ensure that the oil seal drain hole faces downward.
7. Install the driveshaft to the extension housing. Connect the driveshaft to the rear axle flange. Make sure the marks made during removal are in alignment. Fit the attaching washer, lockwasher and nuts.
8. Check and adjust the transmission fluid level, using Ford manual transmission lube D8DZ–19C547–A (ESP–M2C83–C) or equivalent.
9. Lower the vehicle.
10. Reconnect the negative battery cable.

Transmission

➧ SEE FIGS. 1-4

REMOVAL & INSTALLATION

B2200

1. Disconnect the negative battery cable.
2. Remove the gearshift knob and shift console attaching screws. Remove the console.
3. Remove the shift lever to extension housing attaching bolts and remove the shift lever.
4. Raise and support the vehicle safely.
5. Drain the transmission oil.
6. Matchmark and remove the driveshaft.
7. Disconnect the speedometer cable from the transmission.
8. Remove the starter motor.
9. Disconnect and the back-up light switch wiring at the transmission.
10. Disconnect the parking brake return spring and parking brake cables.
11. Disconnect the clutch slave cylinder from the transmission.
12. Remove the transmission-to-engine gusset plate.
13. Disconnect the exhaust pipe at the transmission and manifold.
14. Support the transmission and engine separately with jacks.
15. Remove the transmission crossmember.
16. Lower the transmission to gain access to the top bolts and remove the transmission-to-engine bolts.
17. Pull the transmission straight back, away from the engine and remove transmission from the vehicle.

To Install:

18. Raise the transmission into position. Install the transmission-to-engine bolts and tighten to 51–65 ft. lbs. (69–88 Nm).
19. Install the transmission crossmember and tighten the crossmember-to-chassis bolts to 23–34 ft. lbs. (31–46 Nm).
20. Lower the transmission onto the crossmember and remove the jacks. Install the crossmember-to-mount bolts to 12–17 ft. lbs. (16–23 Nm).
21. Connect the exhaust pipe to the manifold and transmission bracket. Tighten the exhaust pipe-to-manifold nuts to 30–41 ft. lbs. (40–55 Nm) and the exhaust pipe-to-transmission bracket bolt to 13–20 ft. lbs. (18–26 Nm).
22. Install the gusset plate and tighten the bolts to 27–38 ft. lbs. (37–52 Nm).
23. Install the clutch slave cylinder and tighten the bolts to 12–17 ft. lbs. (16–23 Nm).
24. Install the parking brake cables and the return spring.
25. Connect the back-up light switch wiring connector and connect the speedometer cable.
26. Install the driveshaft, aligning the marks that were made during removal.
27. Install the starter. Fill the transmission with the proper type and quantity of engine oil.
28. Lower the vehicle. Install the shift lever and tighten the attaching bolts to 69–95 inch lbs. (7.8–11.0 Nm).
29. Install the console and the shift knob.
30. Connect the negative battery cable. Check the transmission for leaks and proper operation.

B2600

➡ On 4WD vehicles, the transmission and transfer case are removed as a unit.

1. Disconnect the negative battery cable.
2. Remove the knobs from the transfer case, if equipped and transmission shifters.
3. Remove the console box, if equipped.
4. Remove the insulator plate and shifter boot.
5. Remove the attaching bolts and the shift lever(s).
6. Raise and support the vehicle safely. Drain the transfer case, if equipped and transmission oil.
7. Remove the transmission and transfer case, if equipped, splash shields. Remove the starter.
8. Disconnect and remove the front exhaust pipe.
9. Matchmark and remove the driveshaft(s).
10. Disconnect the speedometer cable, 4WD switch, if equipped and backup light switch wires from the transmission or transmission/transfer case.
11. Remove the slave cylinder without disconnecting the fluid line. Support the slave cylinder aside.
12. Remove the transmission gusset plates and clutch housing cover. Support the transmission and engine with jacks.
13. Raise the transmission or transmission/transfer case and remove the crossmember.
14. Remove the transmission or transmission/transfer case.

To Install:

15. Raise the transmission or transmission/transfer case assembly into position. Install the transmission-to-engine bolts and tighten to 51–65 ft. lbs. (69–88 Nm).
16. Install the crossmember and tighten the crossmember-to-chassis bolts to 23–34 ft. lbs. (31–46 Nm).
17. Lower the transmission or transmission/transfer case assembly and remove the jacks. Install the crossmember-to-transmission mount nuts and tighten to 23–34 ft. lbs. (31–46 Nm).
18. Install the gusset plates and clutch housing cover. Install the slave cylinder.
19. Connect the backup light and, if equipped, 4WD switch electrical connectors and the speedometer cable.
20. Install the driveshaft(s), aligning the marks that were made during removal.
21. Install the front exhaust pipe and the starter. Install the splash shields.
22. Fill the transmission and, if equipped, transfer case with the proper type and quantity of fluid. Lower the vehicle.
23. Install the shift lever(s) and tighten the mounting bolts to 25–37 ft. lbs. (34–50 Nm).
24. Install the shifter boot and insulator plate. Tighten the mounting bolts to 25–37 ft. lbs. (34–50 Nm).
25. Install the console box and the shifter knob(s).
26. Connect the negative battery cable. Check the transmission for leaks and proper operation.

MPV

➡ On 4WD vehicles, the transmission and transfer case are removed as a unit.

1. Disconnect the negative battery cable.
2. Remove the shift lever knob and boot.
3. Shift the transmission into **N** and unbolt and remove the shift lever.
4. Raise and safely support the vehicle.
5. Drain the transmission and, if equipped, transfer case fluid.

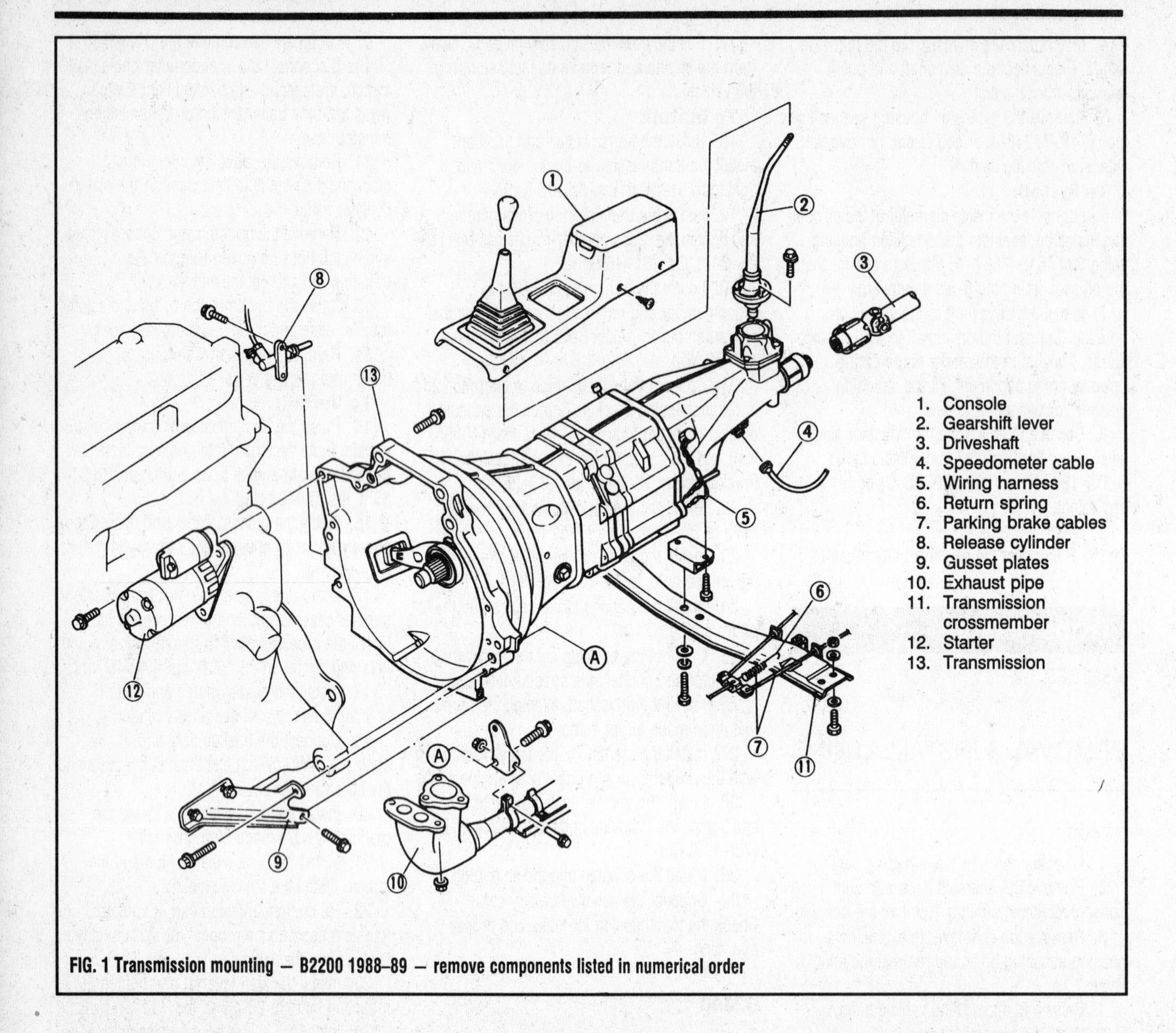

FIG. 1 Transmission mounting — B2200 1988–89 — remove components listed in numerical order

6. Disconnect the speedometer cable and, if equipped, the Hi-Lo shift cable.
7. Disconnect the electrical connectors at the transmission.
8. Matchmark and remove the driveshaft(s). Stuff a rag in the double offset joint to prevent damage to the boot from the driveshaft.
9. On the 2.6L engine, unbolt the support bracket from the transmission, if equipped.
10. Remove the starter.
11. Remove the clutch slave cylinder and hydraulic line bracket. It is not necessary to disconnect the hydraulic line. Remove the bellhousing inspection plate.
12. Remove the front exhaust pipe and heat shield.
13. Remove the gusset plates and support the transmission and engine with jacks.
14. Remove the transmission-to-crossmember bolts. Remove the crossmember.
15. Remove the transmission-to-engine bolts.
16. Pull the transmission straight back on the jack until the mainshaft clears the clutch. Lower the transmission and pull it out from under the vehicle.

To install:

17. Raise the transmission into position.
18. Push the transmission straight forward on the jack until the mainshaft enters the clutch and the transmission engages the locating dowels on the engine.
19. Install the transmission-to-engine bolts and tighten to 27–38 ft. lbs. (37–52 Nm) on 3.0L engine or 51–65 ft. lbs. (69–88 Nm) on 2.6L engine.
20. Install the starter. Install the crossmember and tighten the crossmember-to-chassis bolts to 32–45 ft. lbs. (43–61 Nm).
21. Lower the transmission and remove the jacks. Install the transmission-to-crossmember bolts and tighten the nuts to 23–34 ft. lbs. (31–46 Nm) or bolts/nuts to 32–45 ft. lbs. (43–61 Nm).
22. Install the front exhaust pipe and heat shield.
23. Install the transmission gusset plates. Install the clutch release cylinder and bracket.
24. Connect the speedometer cable and, if equipped, Hi-Lo shift cable. Connect the electrical wiring.
25. Install the driveshaft(s), aligning the marks that were made during removal. Install the bellhousing inspection plate.

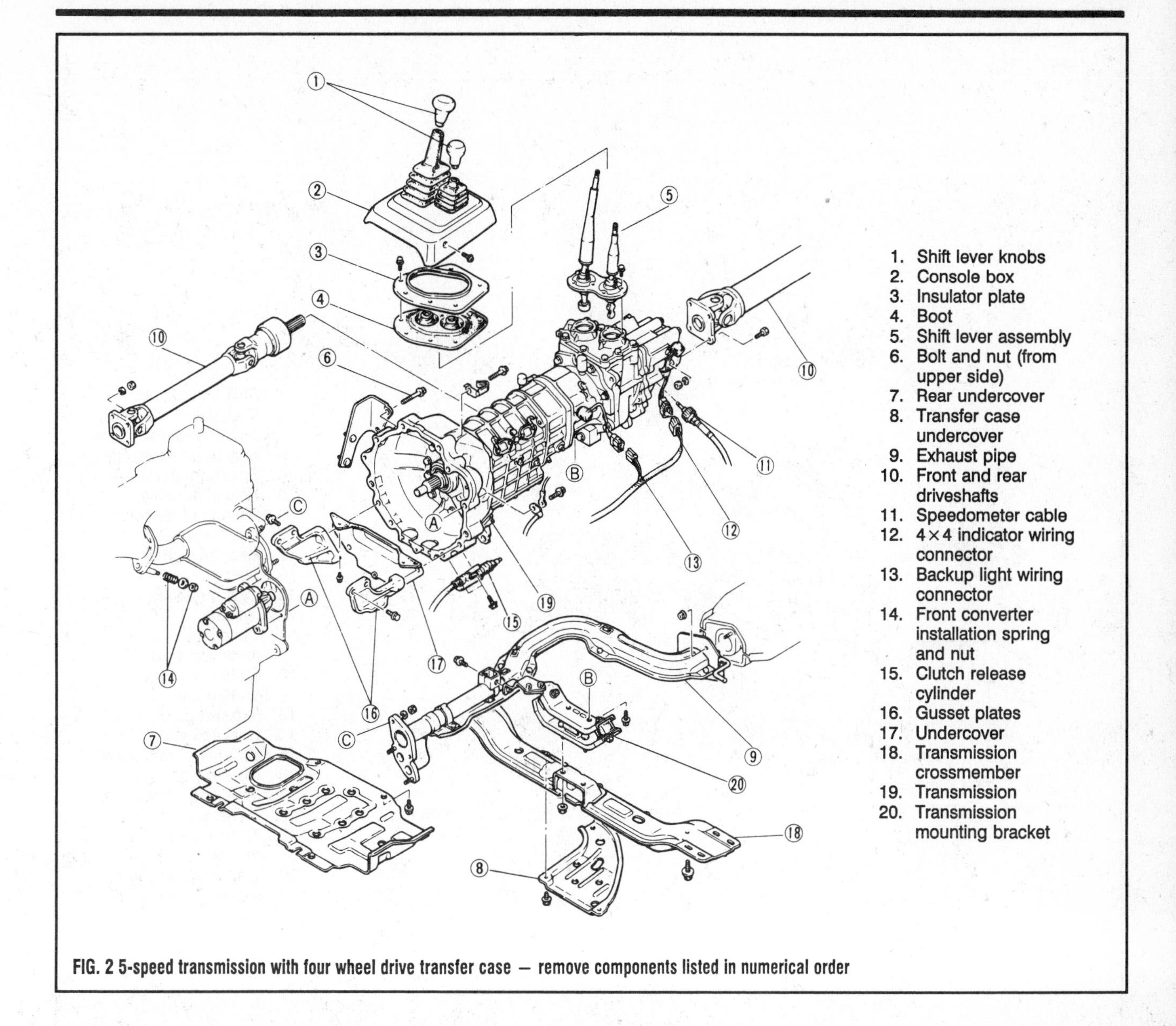

FIG. 2 5-speed transmission with four wheel drive transfer case — remove components listed in numerical order

26. Fill the transmission and, if equipped, transfer case with the proper type and quantity of fluid. Lower the vehicle.
27. Install the shift lever.
28. Install the shifter knob and boot.
29. Connect the negative battery cable. Check the transmission for leaks and proper operation.

Navajo

1. Disconnect the negative battery cable.
2. Remove the gearshift lever assembly from the control housing.
3. Cover the opening in the control housing with a cloth to prevent dirt from falling into the unit.
4. Raise the vehicle and support it safely.
5. Matchmark the driveshaft to the rear axle flange. Pull the driveshaft rearward and disconnect it from the transmission.
6. Disconnect the clutch hydraulic line at the clutch housing. Plug the lines.
7. Disconnect the speedometer from the transfer case/extension housing.
8. Disconnect the starter motor and back-up lamp switch harness connector.
9. Place a wood block on a service jack and position the jack under the engine oil pan.
10. Remove the transfer case from the vehicle.
11. Remove the starter motor.
12. Position a transmission jack, under the transmission.
13. Remove the transmission-to-engine retaining bolts and washers.
14. Remove the nuts and bolts attaching the transmission mount and damper to the crossmember.
15. Remove the nuts and bolts attaching the crossmember to the frame side rails and remove the crossmember.
16. Lower the engine jack. Work the clutch housing off the locating dowels and slide the clutch housing and the transmission rearward until the input shaft clears the clutch disc.
17. Remove the transmission from the vehicle.

To Install:

18. Check that the mating surfaces of the clutch housing, engine rear and dowel holes are free of burrs, dirt and paint.
19. Place the transmission on the transmission jack. Position the transmission under the vehicle, then raise it into position. Align the input shaft splines with the clutch disc splines and work the transmission forward into the locating dowels.

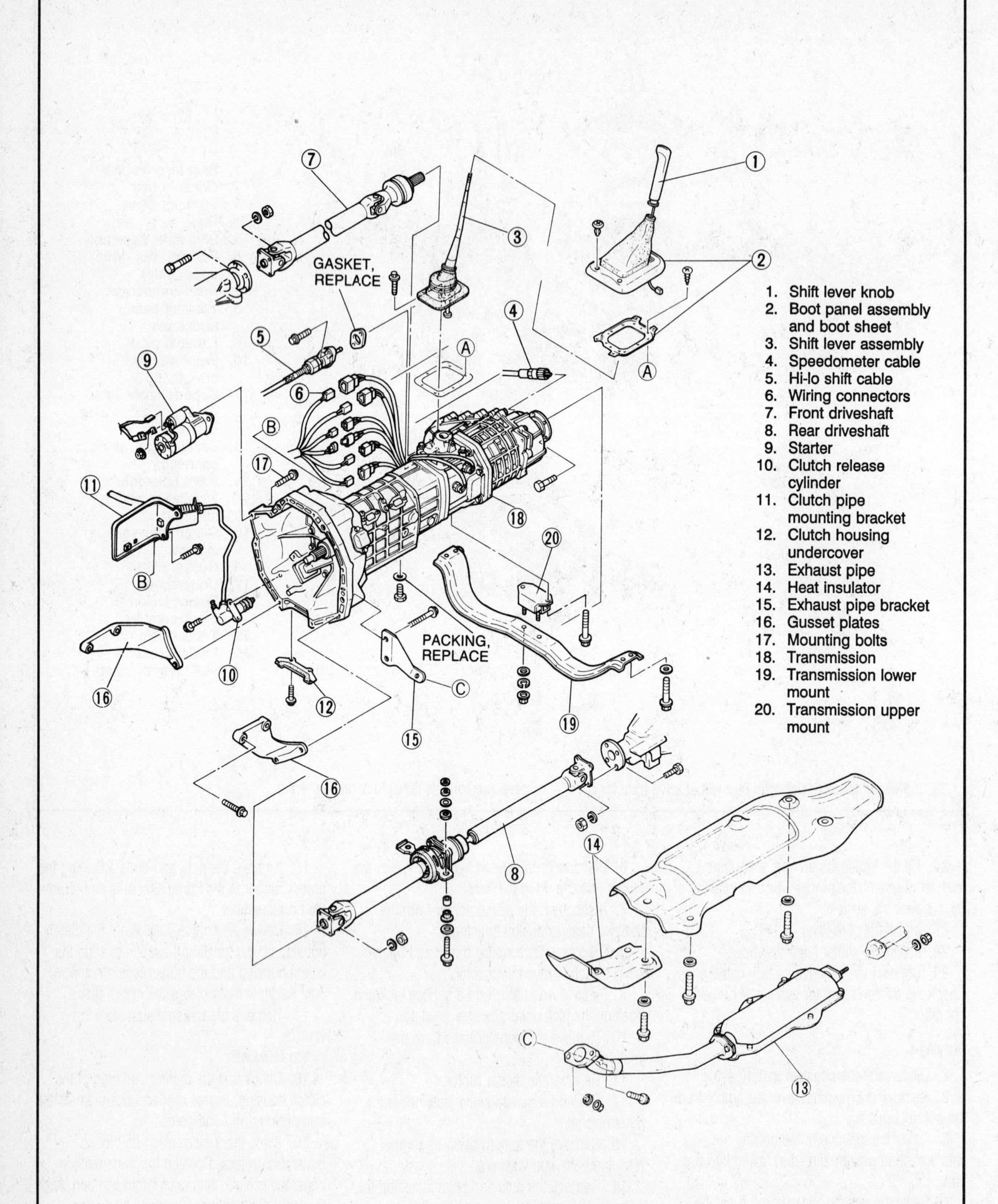

FIG. 3 5-speed R5MX-D transmission MPV — remove components listed in numerical order

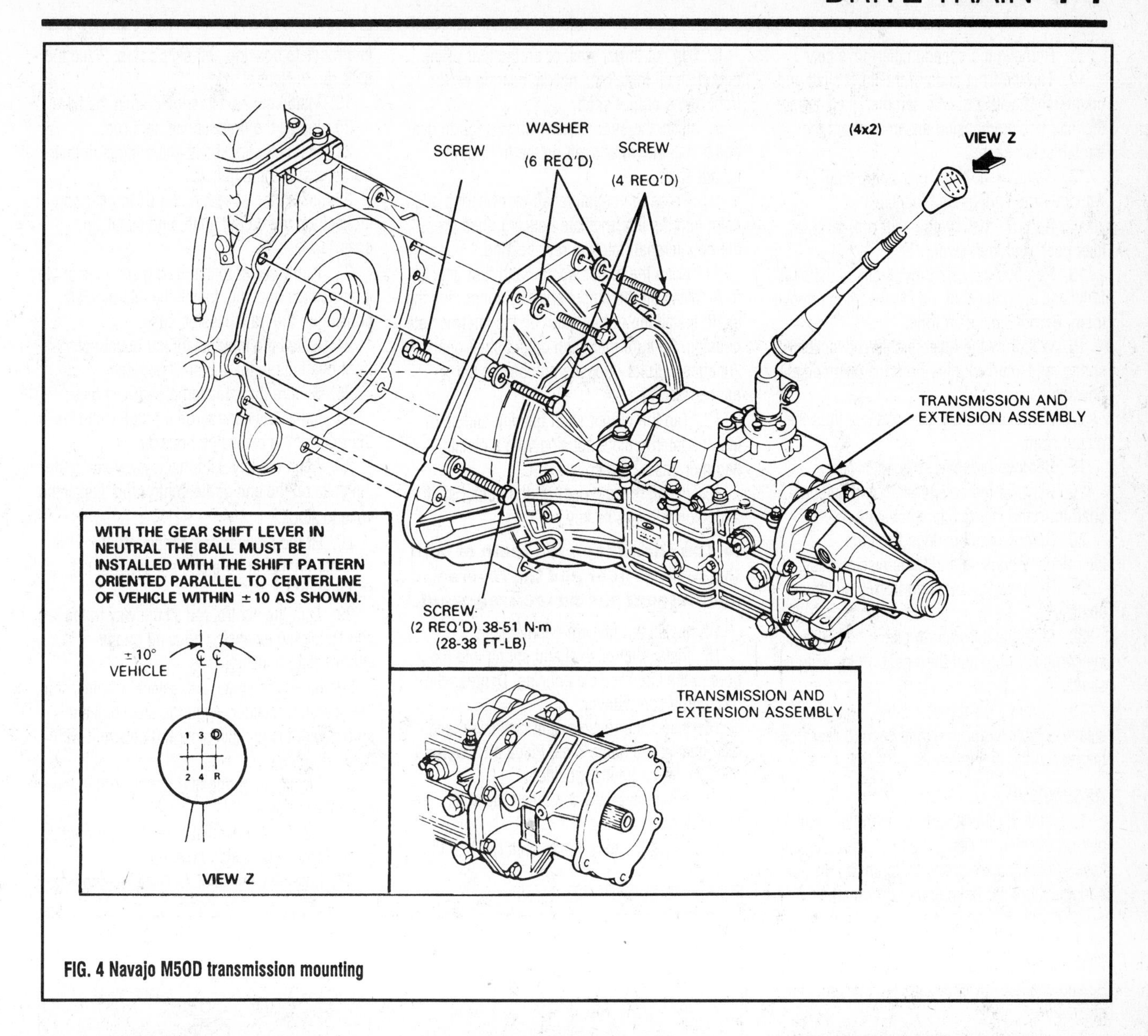

FIG. 4 Navajo M50D transmission mounting

20. Install the transmission-to-engine retaining bolts and washers. Tighten and torque the retaining bolts 28–38 ft. lbs. (38–52Nm). Remove the transmission jack.
21. Install the starter motor. Tighten the attaching nuts to 15–20 ft. lbs. (21–27 Nm).
22. Raise the engine and install the rear crossmember, insulator and damper and attaching nuts and bolts. Tighten and torque the bolts to specification.
23. Install the transfer case.
24. Insert the driveshaft into the transmission extension housing and install the center bearing attaching nuts, washers and lockwashers.
25. Connect the driveshaft to the rear axle drive flange.
26. Connect the starter motor and back-up lamp switch connectors.
27. Connect the hydraulic clutch line and bleed the system.
28. Install the speedometer cable.
29. Check and adjust the fluid level.
30. Lower the vehicle.
33. Install the gearshift lever assembly. Install the boot cover and bolts.
34. Reconnect the negative battery cable.
35. Check for proper shifting and operation of the transmission.

OVERHAUL

M4M-D 4-Speed

➧ SEE FIGS. 5-13

DISASSEMBLY

1. Remove the throwout bearing return spring, throwout bearing, and the release fork.
2. Remove the bearing housing.
3. Remove the input shaft and countershaft snaprings.
4. Remove the floorshift lever retainer, complete with gasket.
5. Unfasten the cap bolt and withdraw the spring, steel ball, select lock pin and spring from the retainer.
6. Remove the extension housing. Turn the control lever as far left as it will go and slide the extension housing off the output shaft.
7. Remove the spring seat and spring from the end of the shift control lever.
8. Loosen the spring cap and withdraw the spring and plunger from their bore.
9. Remove the control rod and boss from the extension housing.
10. Remove the speedometer driven gear. Remove the back-up light switch.

11. Remove the speedometer drive gear.
12. Tap the front ends of the input shaft and countershaft with a plastic hammer, then remove the intermediate housing assembly from the transmission case.
13. Remove the three cap bolts, then withdraw the springs and lockballs.
14. Remove the reverse shift rod, reverse idler gear, and shift lever.
15. Remove the setscrews from all the shift forks and push the shift rods rearward to remove them. Remove the shift forks.
16. Withdraw the reverse shift rod lockball, spring, and interlock pins from the intermediate housing.
17. Remove reverse gear and key from the output shaft.
18. Remove the reverse counter gear.
19. Remove the countershaft and output shaft from the intermediate housing.
20. Remove the bearings from the intermediate housing and transmission case.
21. Remove the snapring from the output shaft.
22. Slide the third/fourth clutch hub, sleeve, synchronizer ring, and third gear off the output shaft.
23. Remove the thrust washer, first gear, sleeve, synchronizer ring, and second gear from the rear of the output shaft.

ASSEMBLY

1. Install the third/fourth synchronizer clutch hub on the sleeve. Place the three synchronizer keys in the clutch hub key slots. Install the key springs with their open ends 120° apart.
2. Install third gear and the synchronizer ring on the front of the output shaft. Install the third/fourth clutch hub assembly on the output shaft. Be sure that the larger boss faces the front of the shaft.
3. Secure the gear and synchronizer with the snapring.
4. Perform Step 1 to the first/second synchronizer assembly.
5. Position the synchronizer ring on second gear. Slide second gear on the output shaft so that the synchronizer ring faces the rear of the shaft.
6. Install the first/second clutch hub assembly on the output shaft so that its oil grooves face the front of the shaft. Engage the keys in the notches on the second gear synchronizer ring.
7. Slide the first gear sleeve onto the output shaft. Position the synchronizer ring on first gear. Install the first gear on the output shaft so that the synchronizer ring faces frontward. Rotate the first gear as required to engage the notches in the synchronizer ring with the keys in the clutch hub.
8. Slip the thrust washer on the rear of the output shaft. Install the needle bearing on the front of the output shaft.
9. Install the synchronizer ring on fourth gear and install the input shaft on the front of the output shaft.
10. Press the countershaft rear bearing and shim into the intermediate housing, then press the countershaft into the rear bearing.
11. Keep the thrust washer and first gear from falling off the output shaft by supporting the shaft. Install the output shaft on the intermediate housing. Be sure that each output shaft gear engages with its opposite number on the countershaft.
12. Tap the output shaft bearing and shim into the intermediate housing with a plastic hammer. Install the cover.
13. Install reverse gear on the output shaft and secure it with its key.

➡ The chamfer on the teeth of both the reverse gear and the reverse countergear should face rearward.

14. Install the reverse countergear.
15. Install the lockball and spring into the bore in the intermediate housing. Depress the ball with a screwdriver.
16. Install the reverse shift rod, lever, and idler gear at the same time. Place the reverse shift rod in the neutral position.
17. Align the bores and insert the shift interlock pin.
18. Install the third/fourth shift rod into the intermediate housing and shift bores. Place the shift rod in Neutral.
19. Install the next interlock pin in the bore.
20. Install the first/second shift rod.
21. Install the lockballs and springs in their bores. Install the cap bolt.
22. Install the speedometer drive gear and lockball on the output shaft, and install its snapring.
23. Apply sealer to the mating surfaces of the intermediate housing. Install the intermediate housing in the transmission case.
24. Install the input shaft and countershaft front bearings in the transmission case.
25. Secure the speedometer driven gear.
26. Install the control rod through the holes in the front of the extension housing.
27. Align the key with the keyway and install the yoke on the end of the control rod. Install the yoke lockbolt.
28. Fit the plunger and spring into the extension housing bore and secure with the spring cap.
29. Turn the control rod all the way to the left and install the extension housing on the intermediate housing.
30. Insert the spring and select lockpin inside the gearshift retainer. Align the steel ball and spring with the lockpin slot, and secure it with the spring cap.
31. Install the spring and spring seat in the control rod yoke.
32. Install the gearshift lever retainer over its gasket on the extension housing.
33. Lubricate the lip of the front bearing cover

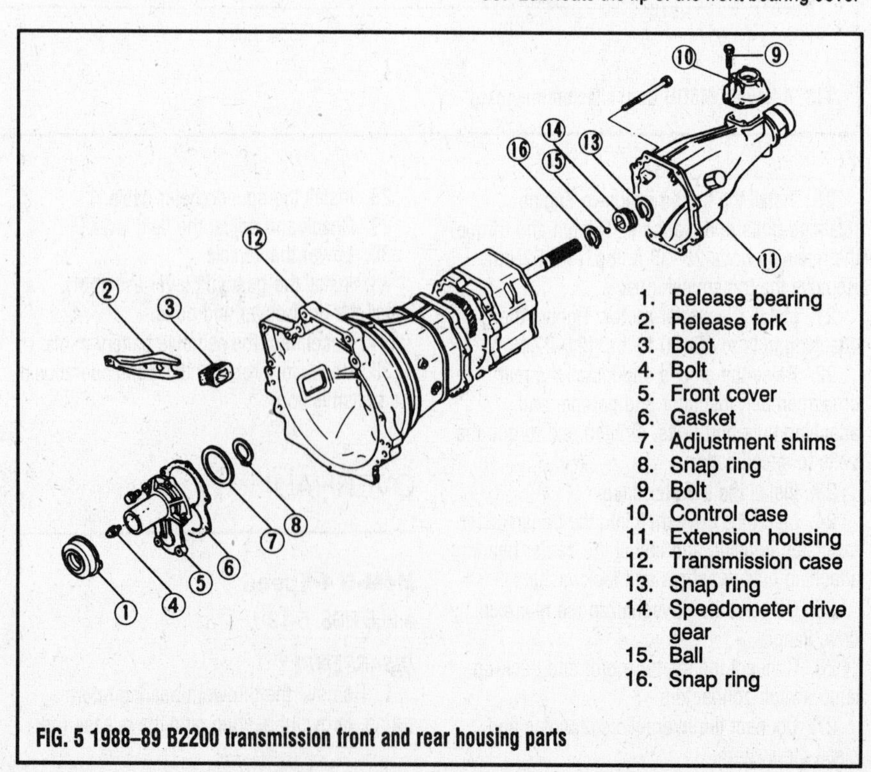

FIG. 5 1988–89 B2200 transmission front and rear housing parts

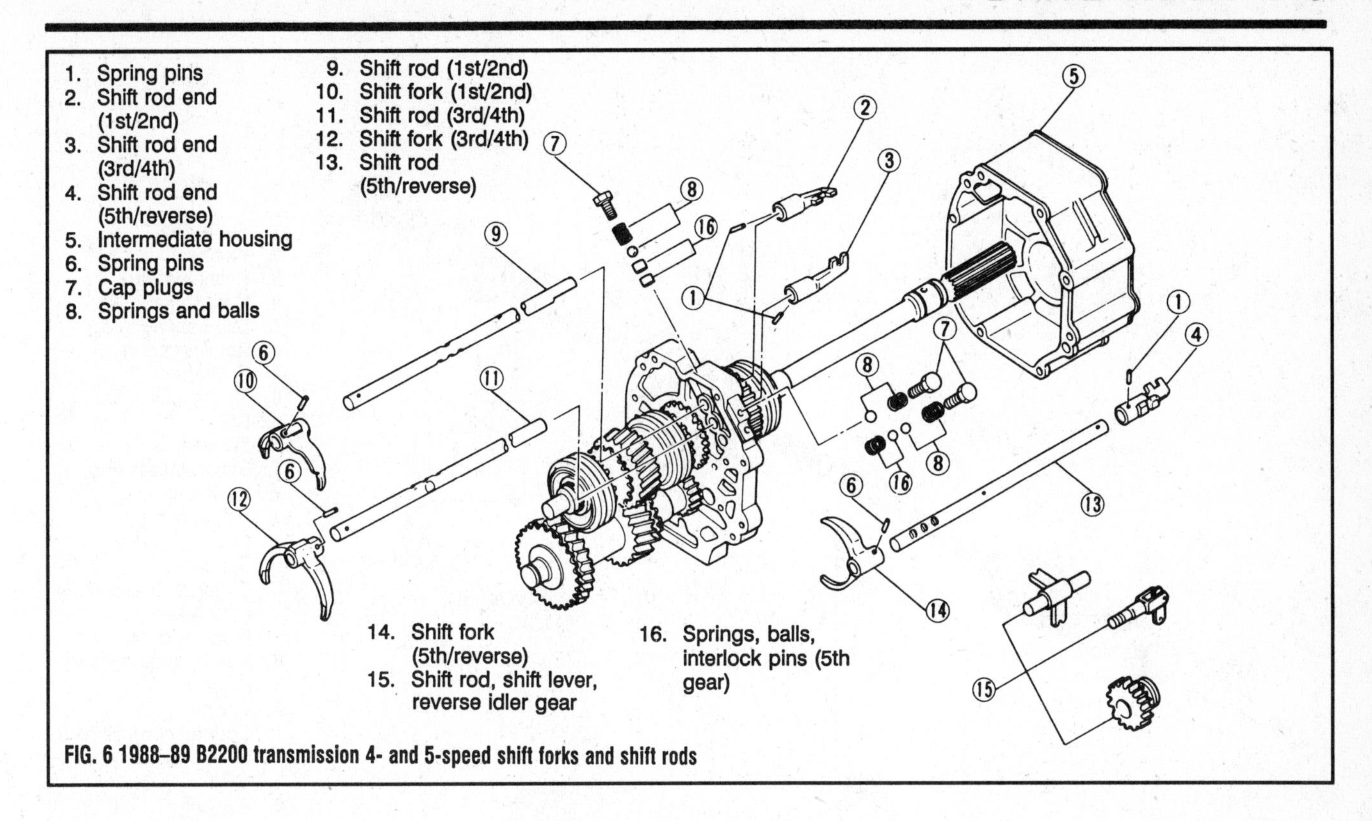

FIG. 6 1988–89 B2200 transmission 4- and 5-speed shift forks and shift rods

oil seal and secure the cover on the transmission case.

34. Check the clearance between the front bearing cover and bearing. It should be less than 0.15mm (0.0059 in.). If it is not within specifications insert additional adjusting shims. The shims are available in 0.15mm or 0.30mm sizes.

35. Install the throwout bearing, return spring and release fork.

M5M-D 5-Speed

DISASSEMBLY

1. Remove the throwout bearing return spring, throwout bearing, and the release fork.
2. Remove the bearing housing.
3. Remove the input shaft and countershaft snaprings.
4. Remove the floorshift lever retainer, complete with gasket.
5. Unfasten the cap bolt and withdraw the spring, steel ball, select lock pin and spring from the retainer.
6. Remove the extension housing. Turn the control lever as far left as it will go and slide the extension housing off the output shaft.
7. Remove the spring seat and spring from the end of the shift control lever.
8. Loosen the spring cap and withdraw the spring and plunger from their bore.
9. Remove the control rod and boss from the extension housing.
10. Remove the speedometer driven gear. Remove the back-up light switch.
11. Remove the speedometer drive gear.
12. Tap the front ends of the input shaft and countershaft with a plastic hammer, then remove the intermediate housing assembly from the transmission case.
13. Remove the three cap bolts, then withdraw the springs and lockballs.
14. Remove the reverse shift rod, reverse idler gear, and shift lever.
15. Remove the setscrews from all the shift forks and push the shift rods rearward to remove them. Remove the shift forks.
16. Withdraw the reverse shift rod lockball, spring, and interlock pins from the intermediate housing.
17. Remove reverse gear and key from the output shaft.
18. Remove the reverse countergear.
19. Remove the countershaft and output shaft from the intermediate housing.
20. Remove the bearings from the intermediate housing and transmission case.
21. Remove the snapring from the output shaft.
22. Slide the third/fourth clutch hub, sleeve, synchronizer ring, and third gear off the output shaft.
23. Remove the thrust washer, first gear, sleeve, synchronizer ring, and second gear from the rear of the output shaft.

ASSEMBLY

1. Install the third/fourth synchronizer clutch hub on the sleeve. Place the three synchronizer keys in the clutch hub key slots. Install the key springs with their open ends 120° apart.
2. Install third gear and the synchronizer ring on the front of the output shaft. Install the third/fourth clutch hub assembly on the output shaft. Be sure that the larger boss faces the front of the shaft.
3. Secure the gear and synchronizer with the snapring.
4. Perform Step 1 to the first/second synchronizer assembly.
5. Position the synchronizer ring on second gear. Slide second gear on the output shaft so that the synchronizer ring faces the rear of the shaft.
6. Install the first/second clutch hub assembly on the output shaft so that its oil grooves face the front of the shaft. Engage the keys in the notches on the second gear synchronizer ring.
7. Slide the first gear sleeve onto the output shaft. Position the synchronizer ring on first gear. Install the first gear on the output shaft so that the synchronizer ring faces frontward. Rotate the first gear as required to engage the notches in the synchronizer ring with the keys in the clutch hub.
8. Slip the thrust washer on the rear of the output shaft. Install the needle bearing on the front of the output shaft.
9. Install the synchronizer ring on fourth gear and install the input shaft on the front of the output shaft.

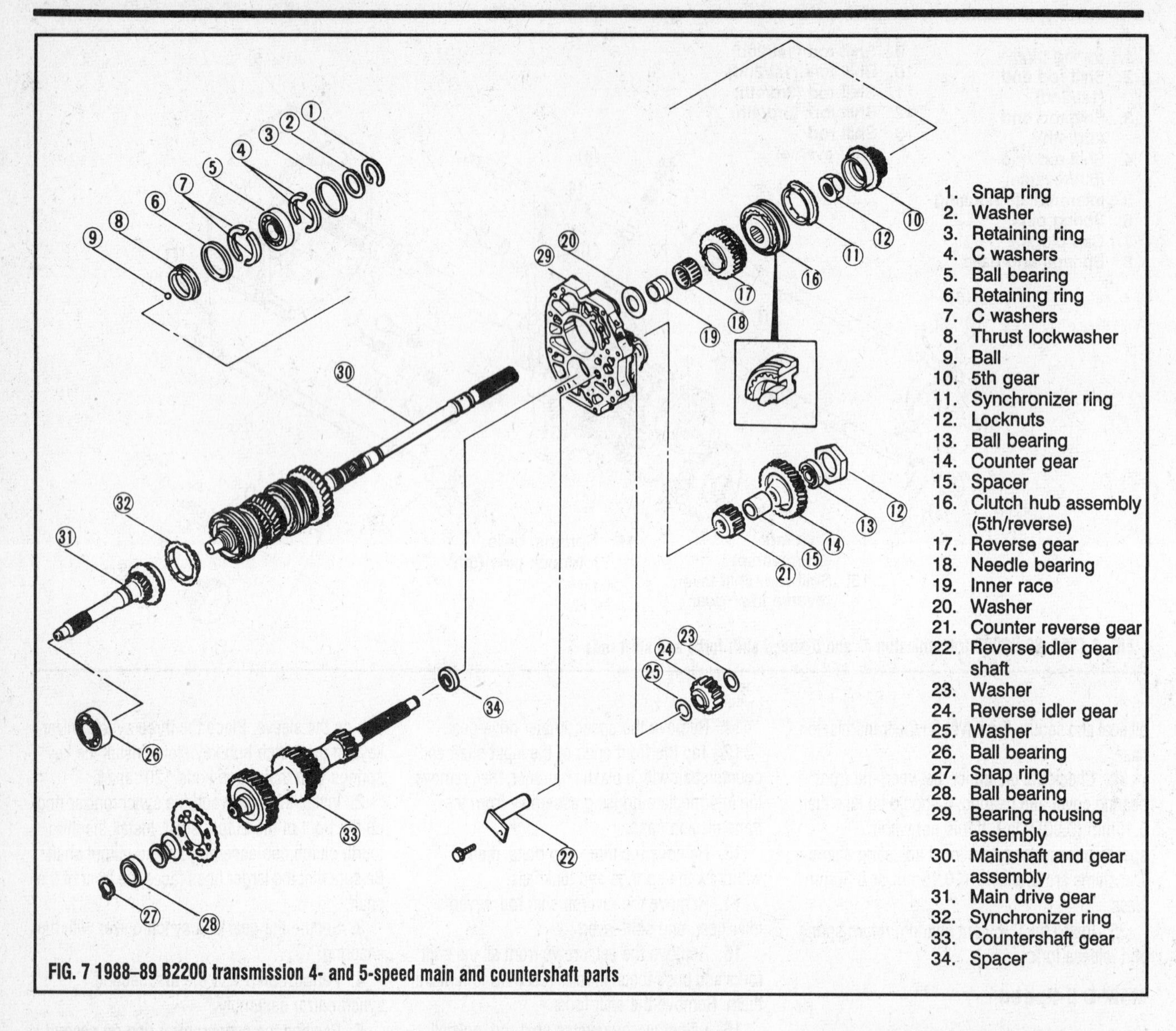

FIG. 7 1988–89 B2200 transmission 4- and 5-speed main and countershaft parts

10. Press the countershaft rear bearing and shim into the intermediate housing, then press the countershaft into the rear bearing.
11. Keep the thrust washer and first gear from falling off the output shaft by supporting the shaft. Install the output shaft on the intermediate housing. Be sure that each output shaft gear engages with its opposite number on the countershaft.
12. Tap the output shaft bearing and shim into the intermediate housing with a plastic hammer. Install the cover.
13. Install reverse gear on the output shaft and secure it with its key.

➡ The chamfer on the teeth of both the reverse gear and the reverse countergear should face rearward.

14. Install the reverse countergear.
15. Install the lockball and spring into the bore in the intermediate housing. Depress the ball with a screwdriver.
16. Install the reverse shift rod, lever, and idler gear at the same time. Place the reverse shift rod in the neutral position.
17. Align the bores and insert the shift interlock pin.
18. Install the third/fourth shift rod into the intermediate housing and shift bores. Place the shift rod in Neutral.
19. Install the next interlock pin in the bore.
20. Install the first/second shift rod.
21. Install the lockballs and springs in their bores. Install the cap bolt.
22. Install the speedometer drive gear and lockball on the output shaft, and install its snapring.
23. Apply sealer to the mating surfaces of the intermediate housing. Install the intermediate housing in the transmission case.
24. Install the input shaft and countershaft front bearings in the transmission case.
25. Secure the speedometer driven gear.
26. Install the control rod through the holes in the front of the extension housing.
27. Align the key with the keyway and install the yoke on the end of the control rod. Install the yoke lockbolt.
28. Fit the plunger and spring into the extension housing bore and secure with the spring cap.
29. Turn the control rod all the way to the left and install the extension housing on the intermediate housing.
30. Insert the spring and select lockpin inside the gearshift retainer. Align the steel ball and spring with the lockpin slot, and secure it with the spring cap.
31. Install the spring and spring seat in the control rod yoke.
32. Install the gearshift lever retainer over its gasket on the extension housing.

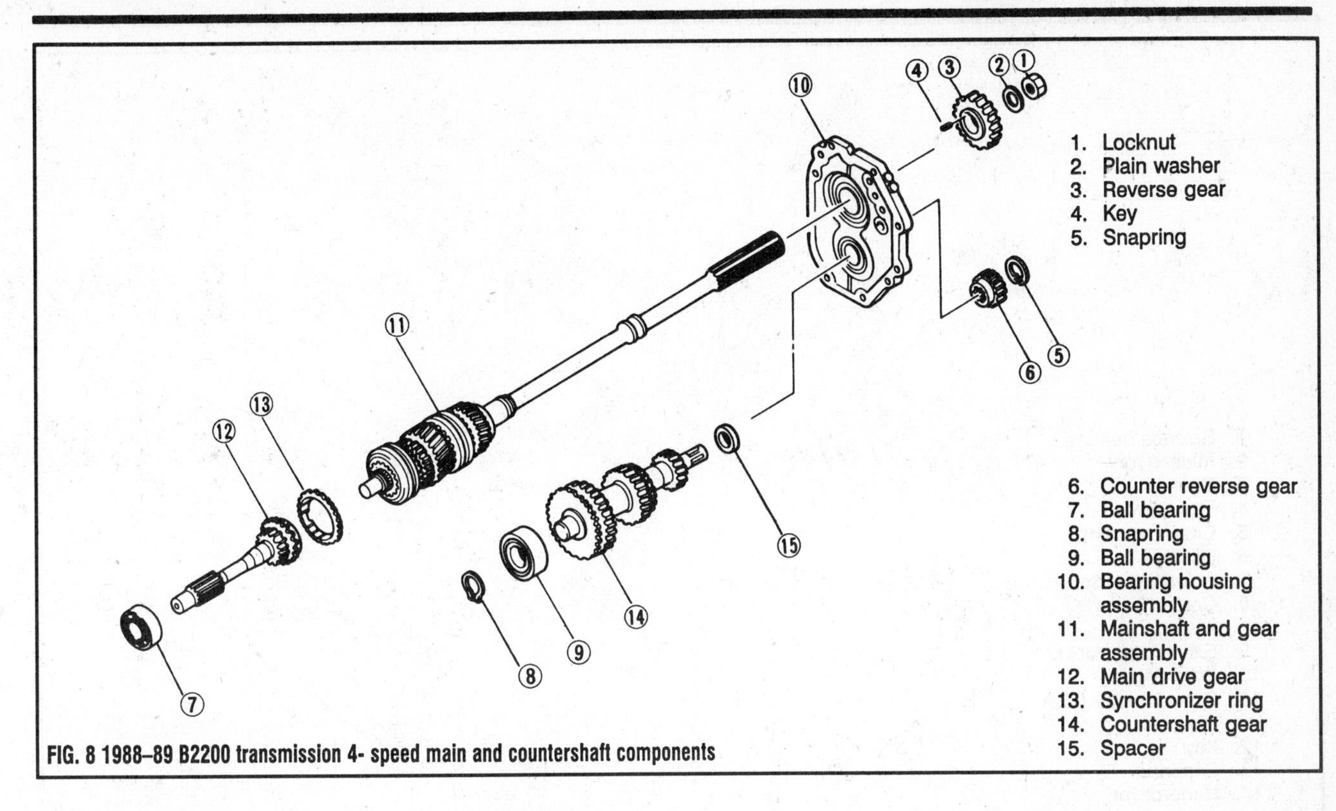

FIG. 8 1988–89 B2200 transmission 4- speed main and countershaft components

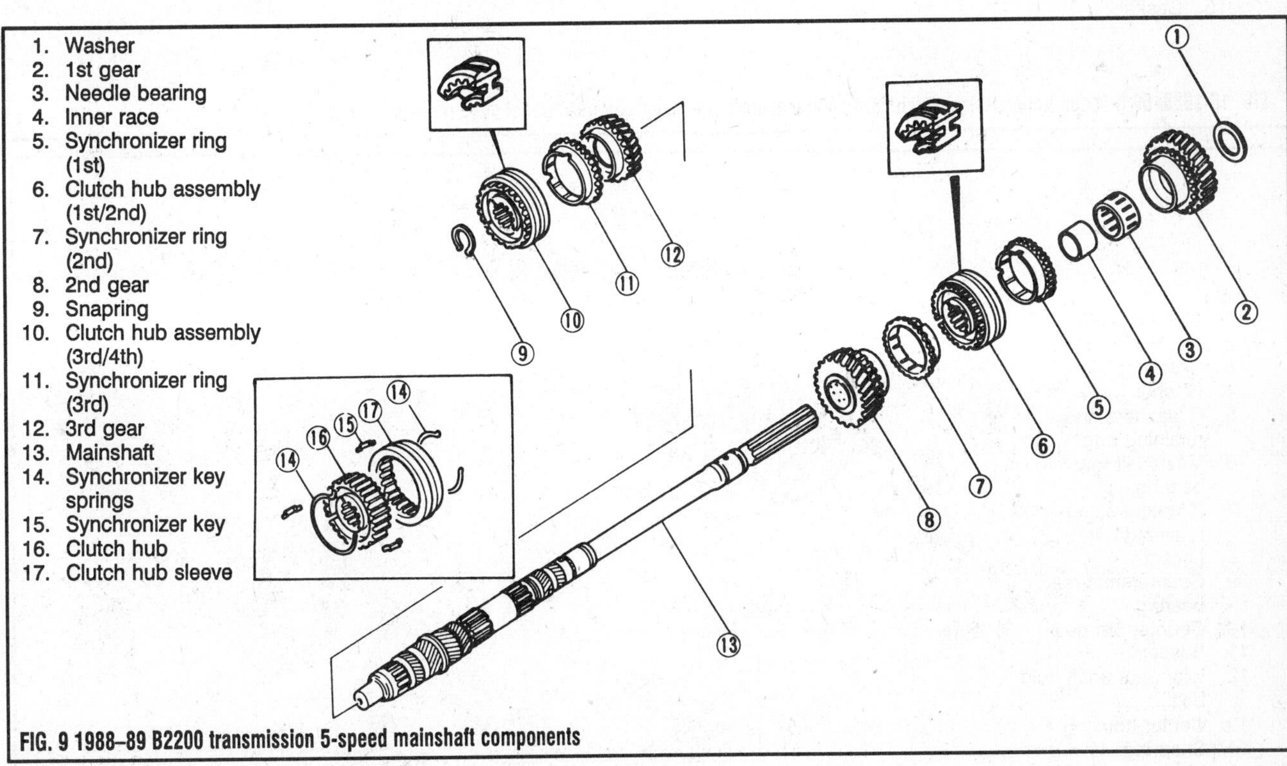

FIG. 9 1988–89 B2200 transmission 5-speed mainshaft components

33. Lubricate the lip of the front bearing cover oil seal and secure the cover on the transmission case.

34. Check the clearance between the front bearing cover and bearing. It should be less than 0.15mm (0.0059 in.). If it is not within specifications insert additional adjusting shims. The shims are available in 0.15mm or 0.30mm sizes.

35. Install the throwout bearing, return spring and release fork.

36. The 5th gear housing can be removed by taking out the retaining bolts. The housing will have to be lightly tapped with a soft-faced hammer. The removal of the housing exposes the 5th/reverse synchronizer assembly, the reverse countergear, the countershaft and mainshaft bearings. The bearings are pulled from the shafts and then the gears can be removed. Assembly is the reverse of disassembly.

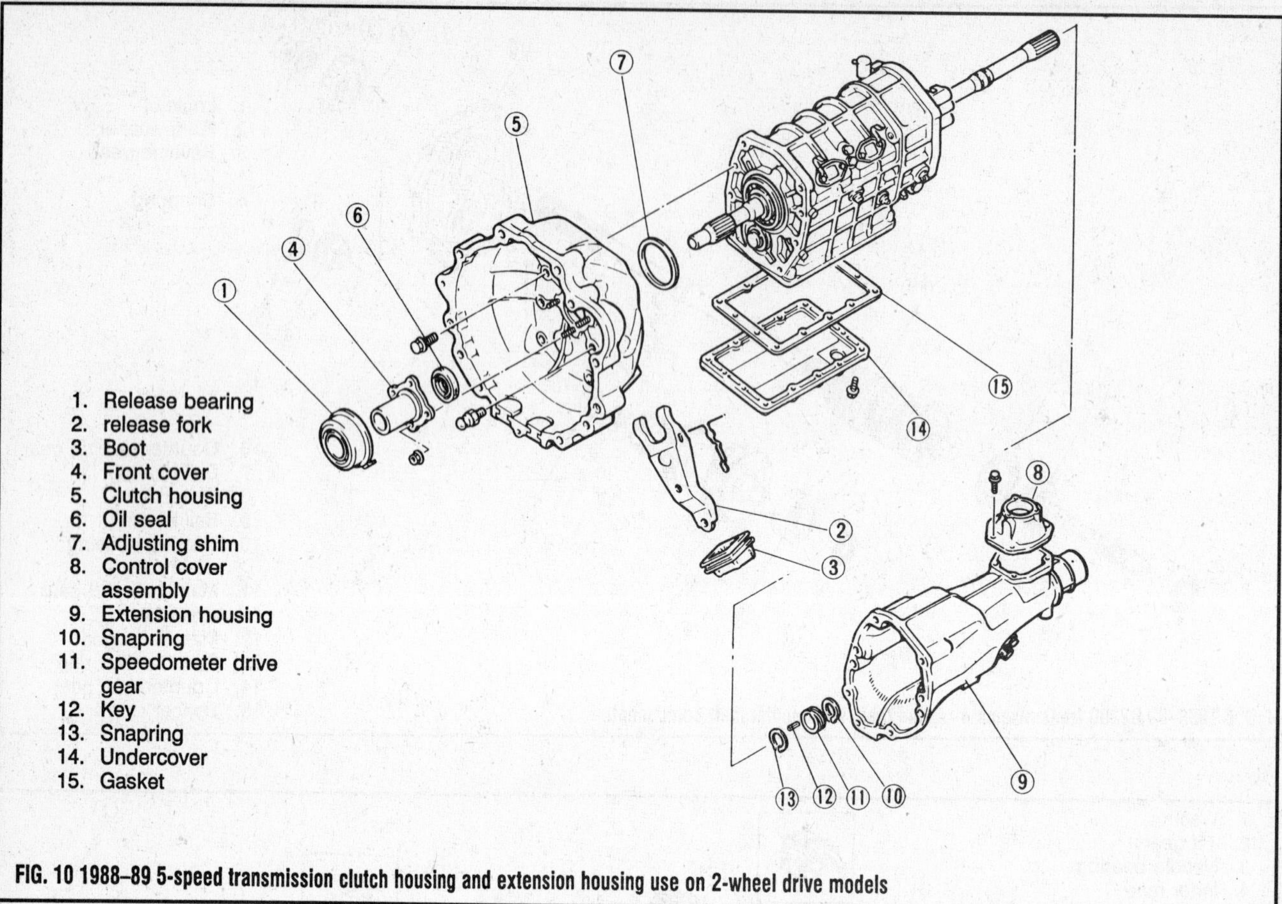

FIG. 10 1988–89 5-speed transmission clutch housing and extension housing use on 2-wheel drive models

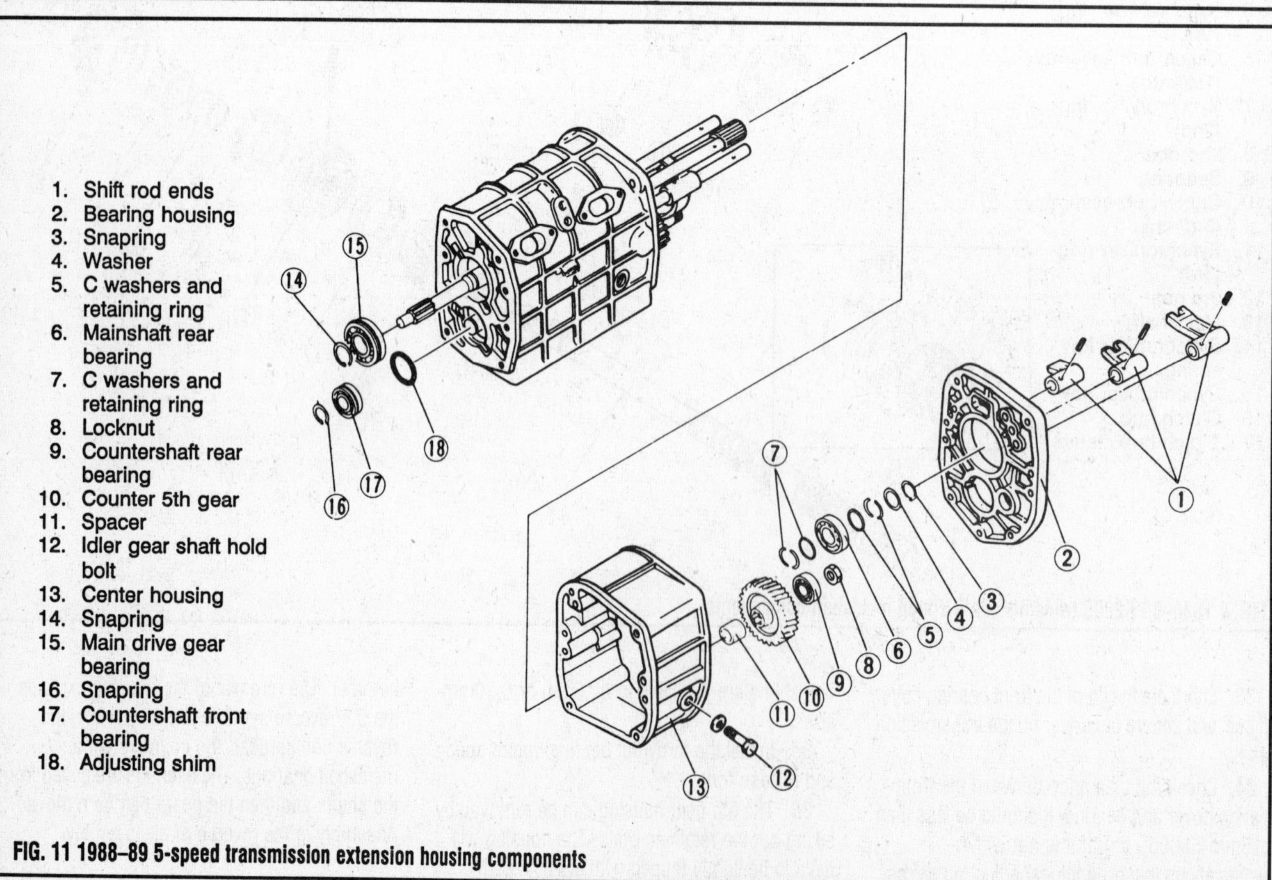

FIG. 11 1988–89 5-speed transmission extension housing components

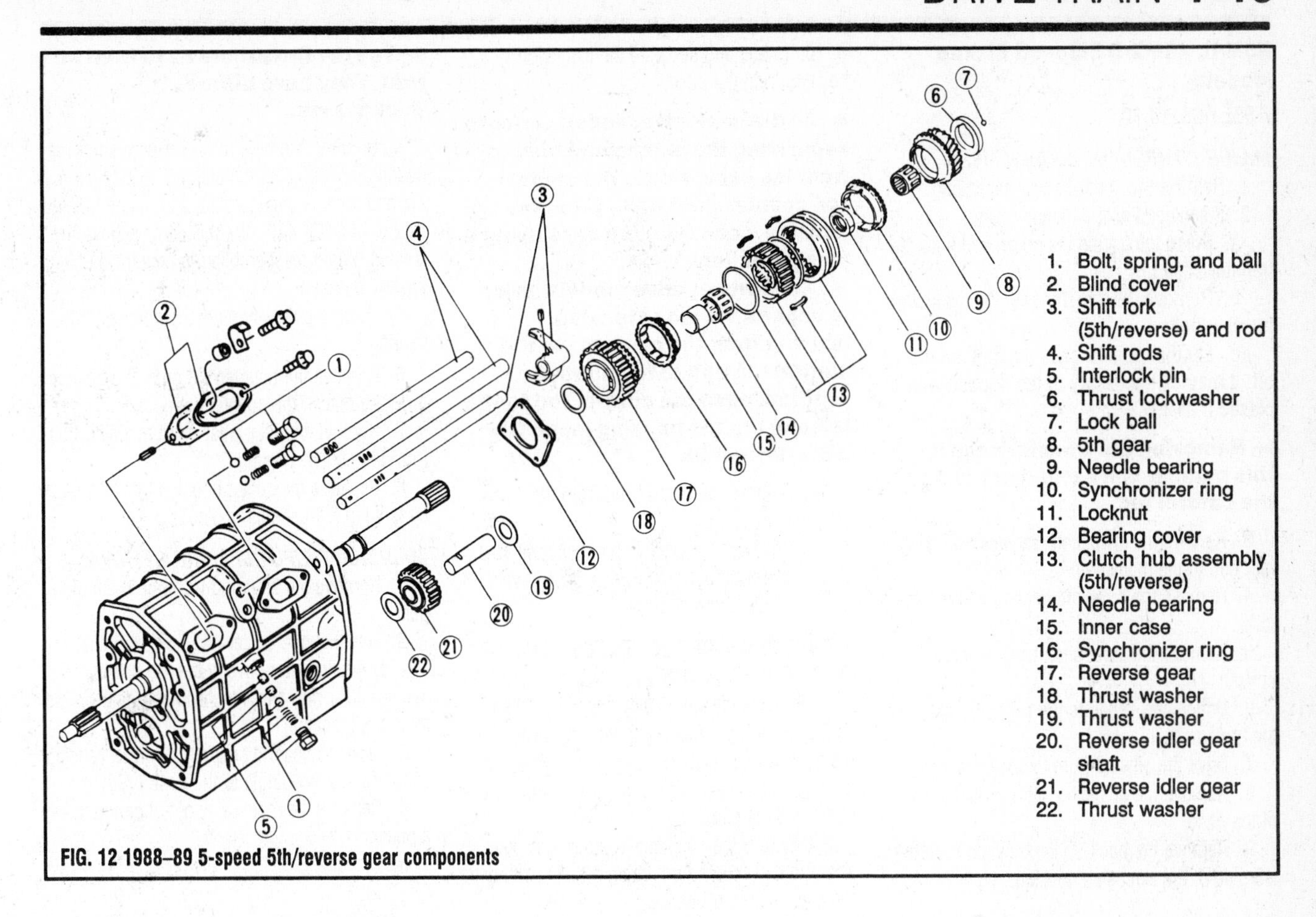

FIG. 12 1988–89 5-speed 5th/reverse gear components

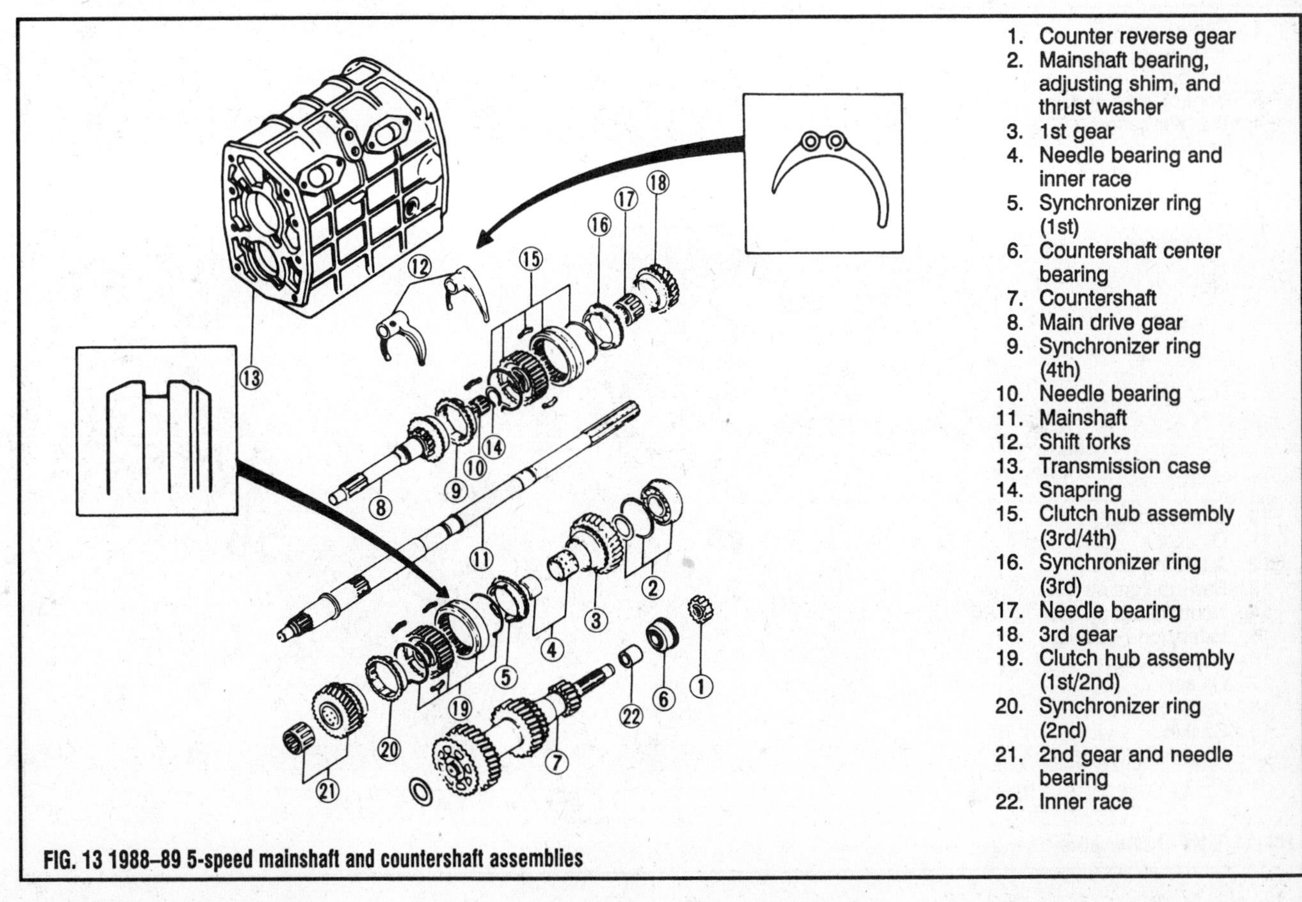

FIG. 13 1988–89 5-speed mainshaft and countershaft assemblies

R5M-D, R5MX-D 5-Speed Pickup Models

➧ SEE FIGS. 14-20

MAJOR COMPONENT DISASSEMBLY

1. Remove the control cover assembly.
2. If equipped with a transfer case:
   a. Stand the transmission on end with the transfer case up.
   b. Remove the transfer case-to-extension housing bolts.
   c. Lift the transfer case straight up and off. It may be necessary to tap it loose with a plastic mallet.

➡ Removing the transfer case in this manner will avoid damage to the control rod.

3. Remove the mainshaft rear sleeve from the rear end of the mainshaft.
4. Remove the throwout bearing and release fork.
5. Remove the input shaft front bearing cover.
6. Unbolt and separate the bellhousing from the transmission case.
7. Drive the oil seal from the bellhousing.
8. Remove the adjusting shim from the front of the case.
9. Remove the back-up light switch from the left side of the extension housing.
10. Unbolt and separate the extension housing from the case.

➡ On 4-wheel drive models, prior to separating the extension housing from the case, rotate the control rod counterclockwise, then, tap the housing loose from the case using a plastic mallet.

On 2-wheel drive models, prior to separating the extension housing from the case, move the control rod end to the neutral position, push the control rod to the left and tap the housing loose with a plastic mallet.

11. Remove the control rod from the extension housing.
12. Drive out the extension housing oil seal.
13. Remove the transmission case lower cover and discard the gasket.

DISASSEMBLY OF THE CENTER HOUSING AND RELATED PARTS

1. Remove the spring pins and shift rod ends.
2. Gently pry the bearing housing away from the transmission case. Be careful to avoid damage to the case. When the housing is loose, slide it off the shafts.
3. Remove the snapring, washer, retaining ring and C-washers and, using a puller, remove the mainshaft rear bearing.

➡ Tag the C-washers as to front and rear. They have different thicknesses.

4. Uncrimp the tabs on the countershaft rear bearing locknut, shift the clutch hub sleeves to 1st and reverse engagement, and, using holding fixture 49 S120 440, or equivalent, remove the locknut. When reassembling, a new locknut **must** be used.
5. Using a puller, remove the countershaft bearing.
6. Remove the counter 5th gear and spacer from the rear of the countershaft.
7. Remove the idler gear shaft retaining bolt from the center housing.
8. Separate the center housing from the case by tapping it loose with a plastic mallet.

MAINSHAFT INPUT BEARING REMOVAL

1. Remove the snapring from the main drive gear.
2. Install synchronizer ring holder 49 F017 101, or equivalent, between the 4th speed synchronizer ring and synchromesh gear on the main drive gear.
3. Turn the bearing snaprings so that the ring ends are at a 90° angle to the case grooves.
4. Remove the main drive gear bearing using a puller.

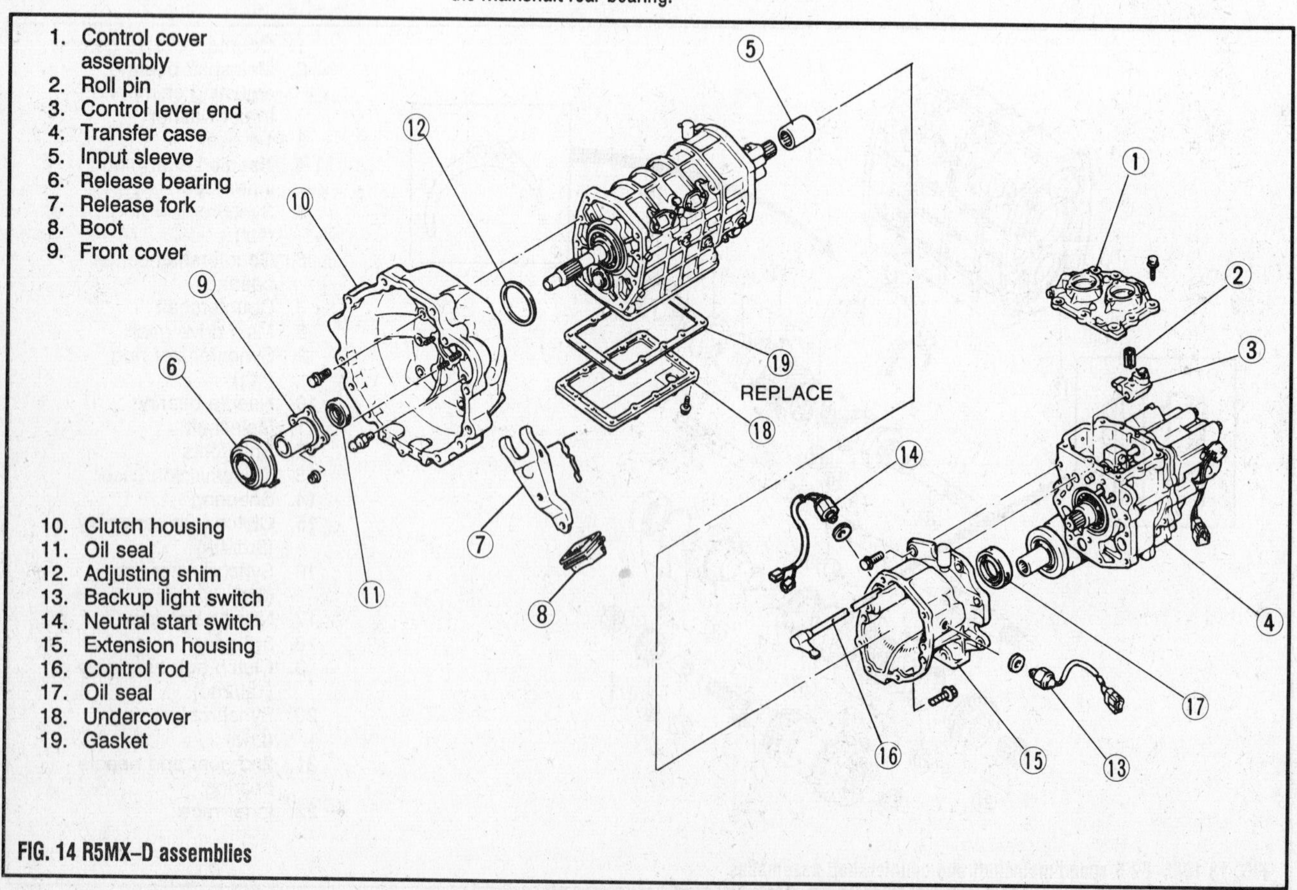

FIG. 14 R5MX–D assemblies

COUNTERSHAFT FRONT BEARING REMOVAL

1. Remove the snapring from the front of the countershaft.
2. Using a puller, remove the countershaft.

5th/Reverse Gear and Related Parts Removal

1. Remove the 3 shift rod spring bolts, then remove the balls and springs.
2. Drive the spring pin from the 5th/reverse shift fork. Slide the 5th/reverse shift rod out of the case.
3. Remove the 2 access covers and gaskets.
4. Drive the spring pin from the 3rd/4th shift fork.
5. Slide the 3rd/4th shift rod out from the rear of the case.
6. Drive the spring pin from the 1st/2nd shift fork and slide the 1st/2nd shift rod out the rear of the case.
7. Remove both interlock pins.
8. Remove the thrust lockwasher, lock ball, needle bearings, 5th gear and synchronizer ring from the rear of the mainshaft.
9. Uncrimp the tabs on the 5th/reverse clutch hub locknut.
10. Lock the mainshaft by engaging 1st and reverse gears.
11. Remove the locknut by using tool 49 1243 465A, or equivalent. Discard the locknut. A new locknut **must** be used.
12. Remove the bearing cover bolts.
13. Remove the bearing cover assembly with a puller. From the cover disassemble the following parts:
    - 5th/reverse clutch hub
    - Synchronizer ring
    - Needle bearing
    - Inner race
    - Reverse gear
    - Thrust washer
14. Remove the thrust washers, reverse idler gear shaft and reverse idler gear.

MAINSHAFT DISASSEMBLY

1. Using a puller, remove the mainshaft bearing.
2. Remove 1st gear.
3. Remove the countershaft center bearing with a puller.
4. Remove the countershaft.
5. Remove the main drive gear and needle bearing.
6. Remove the mainshaft and gear assembly.
7. Remove the snapring from the front of the mainshaft.
8. Position tool 49 0636 145, or equivalent, between 2nd and 3rd gears.
9. Using a press, drive the mainshaft out of 3rd gear and the 3rd/4th clutch hub assembly.
10. Press the 1st/2nd clutch hub assembly and 1st gear sleeve from the mainshaft.
11. Remove the countershaft center bearing inner race using a puller.

COMPONENT INSPECTION

1. Check all parts for signs of wear or damage. Replace any suspected part.
2. Using a dial indicator, check the mainshaft runout. Total runout must not exceed 0.2mm (0.0079 in.).
3. Check reverse idler gear-to-shaft clearance. Clearance must not exceed 0.15mm (0.0059 in.).
4. Check the clearance between each synchronizer and its gear. Clearance should not exceed 0.8mm (0.0315 in.).
5. Check clutch hub sleeve-to-shift fork clearance. Clearance must not exceed 0.5mm (0.0197 in.).
6. Check control lever-to-shift rod gate clearance. Clearance must not exceed 0.8mm (0.0315 in.).

COMPONENT ASSEMBLY

All the synchronizers have the same basic shape. To tell the difference:

- 5th and reverse are the smallest
- 5th has 2 notches in the teeth
- 4th and 3rd are the next size up and are identical
- 2nd and 1st are the largest and are identical

There are 2 types of synchronizer keys. They are differentiated by size.

- 1st and reverse are 18mm × 5.45mm × 6mm
- 3rd, 4th, 5th and reverse are 17mm × 4.25mm × 5mm

Check, before any assembly to make sure the parts are facing in the right direction

1. Place the 2nd gear, with its needle bearing, and the 1st/2nd clutch hub assembly, on a press and press the mainshaft into them.
2. Place the 3rd gear, needle bearing and 3rd/4th clutch hub assembly into position and press the 3rd/4th clutch hub assembly onto the mainshaft.
3. Install the snapring on the front of the mainshaft.
4. Install the inner race, needle bearing, 1st gear and thrust washer.
5. Press the countershaft center bearing inner race onto the countershaft.
6. Measure the depth of the mainshaft bearing bore in the case.
7. Measure the mainshaft bearing snapring height. The difference between the two figures is the required thickness of the adjusting shim. Standard thrust play should be 0-0.1mm (0-0.0039 in.). The adjusting shim thickness should be 0.1-0.3mm (0.0039-0.0118 in.).
8. Measure the depth of the countershaft front bearing bore in the case.
9. Measure the countershaft front bearing snapring height. Choose an adjusting shim that will allow the difference between the two figures to equal the standard bearing height. Standard bearing height should be 0.9-1.0mm (0.0354-0.0394 in.).
10. Position the 1st/2nd shift fork and 3rd/4th shift fork into the groove of the clutch hub and sleeve assembly.
11. Slide the needle bearing and main drive gear onto the front of the mainshaft.
12. Position the countershaft in the case, making sure that it engages each gear on the mainshaft.
13. Using a suitable length of pipe, drive on the countershaft center bearing.
14. Install the correctly predetermined shim on the mainshaft bearing.
15. Using a suitable length of pipe, drive on the mainshaft bearing.
16. Install the bearing cover and tighten the bolts to 20 ft. lbs.
17. Install the synchronizer ring holder tool between the 4th synchronizer ring and the synchromesh gear on the main drive gear.
18. Using a driver, drive in the main gear bearing.
19. Install the main gear bearing snapring.
20. Place the correctly predetermined shim in the countershaft front bearing.
21. Drive the countershaft front bearing on using a bearing driver.
22. Install the snapring.

➡ The countershaft bearing snapring is smaller than the mainshaft bearing snapring.

23. Install the reverse idler gear and shaft with a spacer on each side of the gear.
24. Install the counter reverse gear and spacer, with the chamfer on the gear forward.
25. Install the thrust washer, reverse gear, inner race, needle bearing and clutch hub assembly.
26. Engage 1st and reverse gears to lock the mainshaft.
27. Install a new locknut on the mainshaft and torque it to 174 ft. lbs. using tool 49 1243 465A, or equivalent.
28. Check the clearance between the synchronizer key and the exposed edge of the synchronizer ring. The clearance must not exceed 2.0mm (0.0787 in.). If it does, adjust it by added or deleting thrust washers at the mainshaft bearing front and rear.

➡ Total combined thickness of the front and rear thrust washers should not exceed 6mm (0.2362 in.).

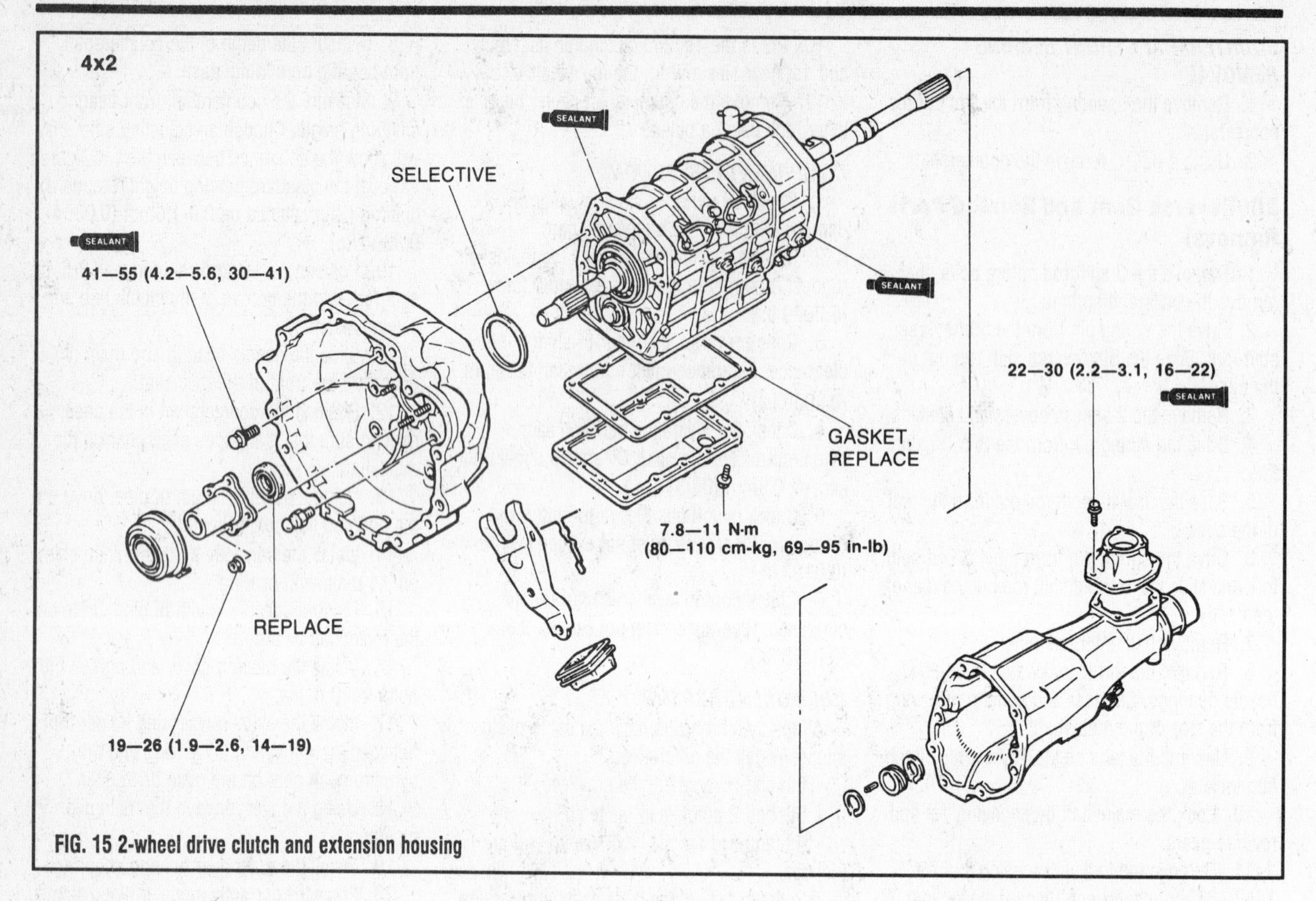

FIG. 15 2-wheel drive clutch and extension housing

29. Stake the locknut onto the shaft.

30. Install the synchronizer ring, 5th gear and needle bearing.

31. Install the 5th gear lock ball and thrust lockwasher.

32. Install the 5th gear 3mm thick C-washers and retaining ring.

33. Measure the clearance between the C-washers and the thrust lockwasher. Clearance should not exceed 0.2mm (0.0079 in.). Adjust by installing thrust washers of differing thicknesses.

➡ **When installing the shift rods, you can tell them apart by noting that the 3rd/4th rod is the longest; the 5th/reverse rod has a hole for the shift fork at the rear of the rod.**

34. Slide the 1st/2nd shift rod into the case.

35. Secure the 1st/2nd shift fork to the rod with the spring pin.

➡ **The spring pin should be installed with the groove as shown.**

36. Slide the 2 shift for assembly guides, 49 0862 350, into the case and install the first interlock pin.

37. Remove the 3rd/4th shift fork guide from the case.

38. Slide the 3rd/4th shift rod into the case.

39. Secure the 3rd/4th shift rod to the fork with the spring pin.

40. Insert the remaining interlock pin and remove the shift fork guide.

41. Install the 5th/reverse shift fork onto the clutch hub and slide the reverse/5th rod into the case.

42. Secure the 5th/reverse fork to the rod with the spring pin.

43. Install the 2 covers and gaskets.

44. Install the detent balls springs and bolts. Torque the 2 upper bolts to 43 ft. lbs.; the lower bolt to 19 ft. lbs.

45. Coat the mating surface of the transmission case with RTV gasket material and install the center housing.

46. Align the reverse idler gear shaft boss with the holding bolt hole and install the bolt and gasket. Torque the bolt to 122 inch lbs.

47. Install the spacer and counter 5th gear.

48. Drive on the countershaft rear bearing using a bearing driver.

49. Install the mainshaft holder.

50. Engage 1st and reverse gears to lock the countershaft.

51. Install the countershaft locknut and torque the nut to 145 ft. lbs. Stake the nut.

52. Drive on the mainshaft rear bearing.

53. Install the C-washers and hold them in place with the retaining ring.

54. Measure the clearance between the C-washers and the groove. Clearance should be 0-0.1mm (0-0.0039 in.). If not, change the thickness of the C-washers.

55. Coat the contact surfaces of the center housing and bearing housing with RTV gasket material and install the bearing housing on the center housing.

56. Engage the shift rod ends and shift rods and install the spring pins.

57. Measure the depth of the main drive gear bearing bore in the clutch housing.

58. Measure the main drive gear bearing height. The difference between the two is the required thickness of the adjusting shim. The adjusting shim thickness should be 0.1-0.3mm.

59. Apply oil to the seal lip and drive it into the bellhousing with a seal driver.

60. Coat the mating surfaces of the bellhousing and transmission case with RTV gasket material and install the bellhousing. Torque the bolts to 34 ft. lbs.

61. Install the input shaft bearing cover in the clutch housing. Torque the bolts to 95 inch lbs.

62. Install the bottom cover and gasket. Torque the bolts to 95 inch lbs.

63. Apply a coat of molybdenum disulfide grease to the contact surfaces of the clutch release arm and install the throwout bearing and release arm.

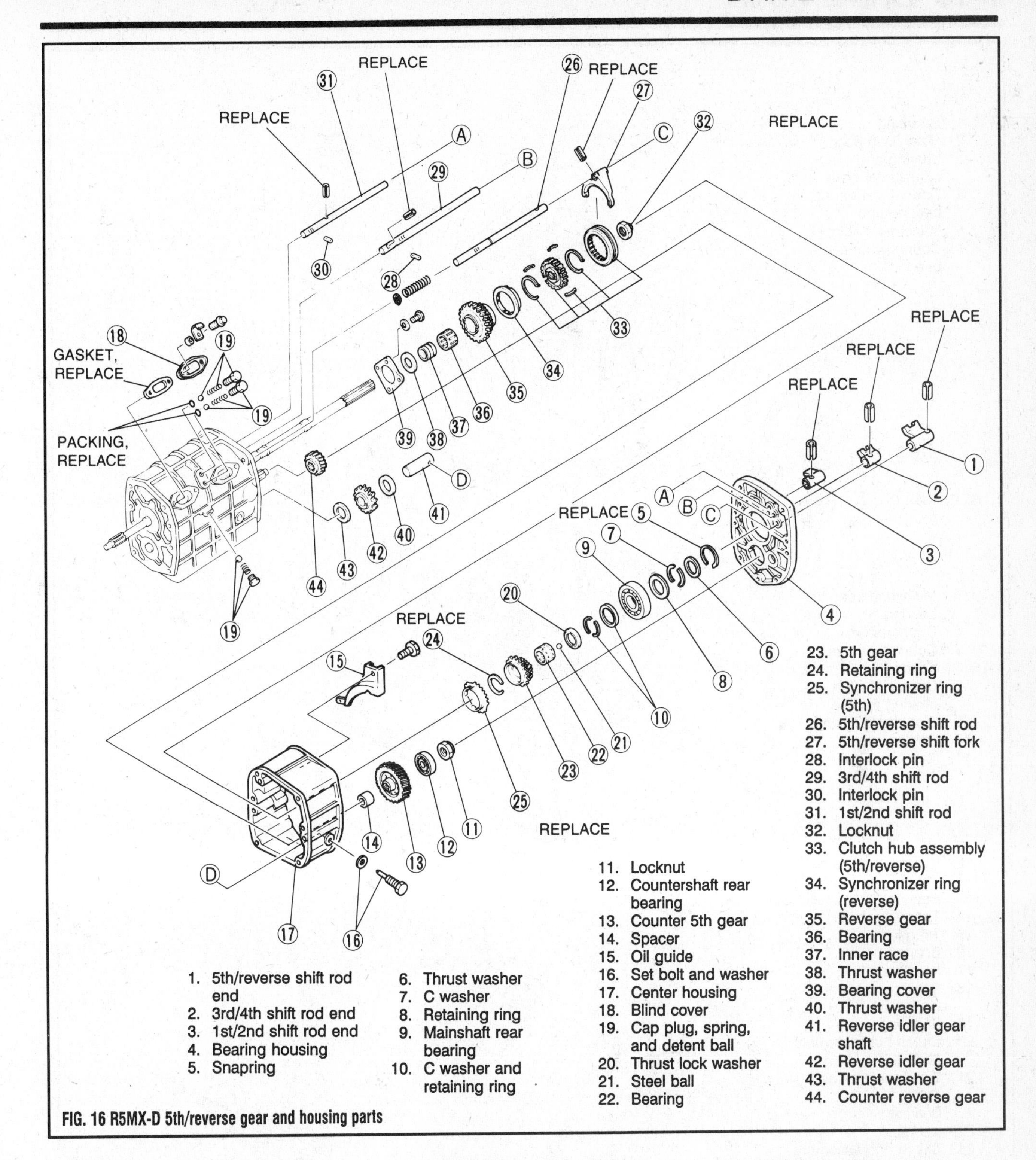

FIG. 16 R5MX-D 5th/reverse gear and housing parts

64. On trucks with 4-wheel drive:

a. Apply oil to the oil seal lip and install it in the extension housing using a seal driver.

b. Install the control rod in the extension housing.

c. Coat the mating surfaces of the extension housing and bearing housing with RTV gasket material.

d. Install the extension housing on the bearing housing. Torque the bolts to 34 ft. lbs.

e. Install the back-up light switch. Torque the switch to 40 ft. lbs.

f. Install the mainshaft rear sleeve.

g. Stand the transmission on end with the rear up.

h. Coat the mating surfaces of the transfer case and extension housing with RTV gasket material.

i. Install the transfer case on the extension housing, indexing the control lever end.

j. Apply RTV gasket material to the bolt threads and torque them to 35 ft. lbs.

k. Secure the control lever end with a spring pin.

l. Coat the mating surfaces of the shift control lever case and transfer case with RTV gasket material and install the shift control

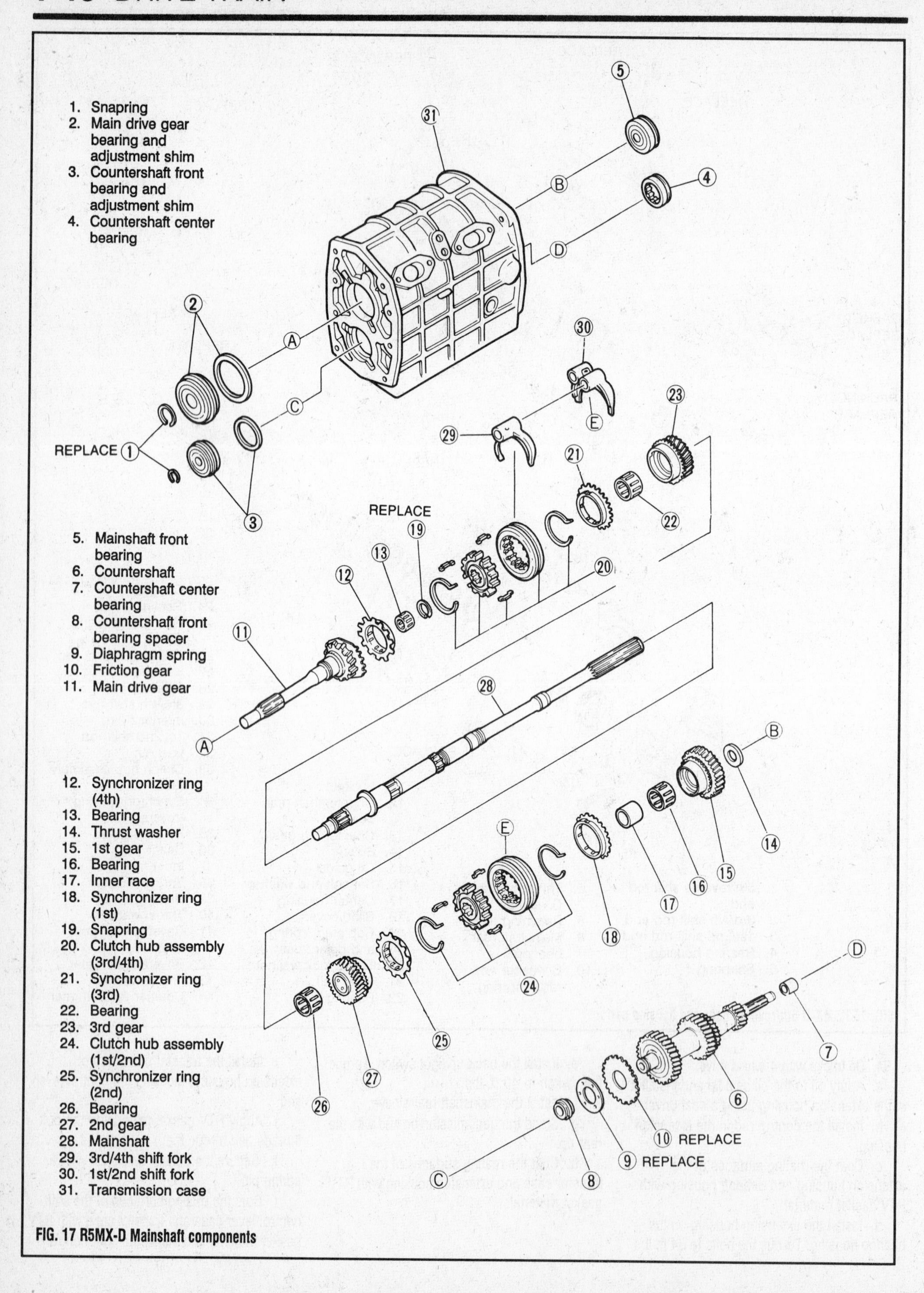
1. Snapring
2. Main drive gear bearing and adjustment shim
3. Countershaft front bearing and adjustment shim
4. Countershaft center bearing
5. Mainshaft front bearing
6. Countershaft
7. Countershaft center bearing
8. Countershaft front bearing spacer
9. Diaphragm spring
10. Friction gear
11. Main drive gear
12. Synchronizer ring (4th)
13. Bearing
14. Thrust washer
15. 1st gear
16. Bearing
17. Inner race
18. Synchronizer ring (1st)
19. Snapring
20. Clutch hub assembly (3rd/4th)
21. Synchronizer ring (3rd)
22. Bearing
23. 3rd gear
24. Clutch hub assembly (1st/2nd)
25. Synchronizer ring (2nd)
26. Bearing
27. 2nd gear
28. Mainshaft
29. 3rd/4th shift fork
30. 1st/2nd shift fork
31. Transmission case
REPLACE
REPLACE
REPLACE
REPLACE

FIG. 17 R5MX-D Mainshaft components

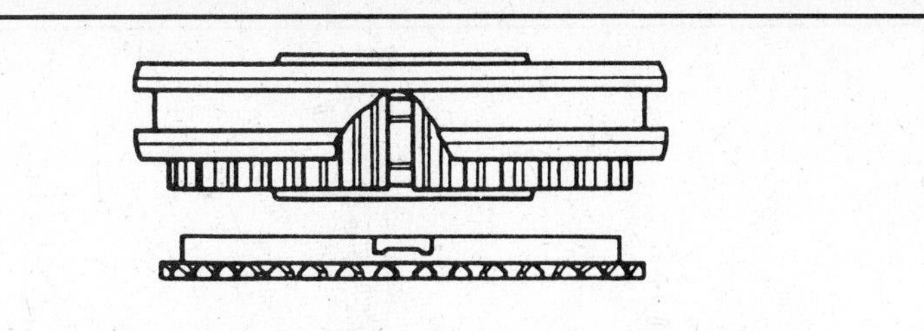
FIG. 18 Align the synchronizer ring grooves with the clutch hub keys during installation

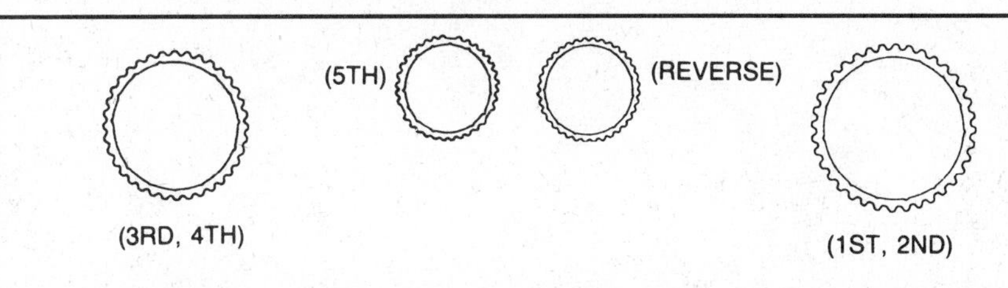

FIG. 19 The synchronizer rings all have the same basic shape. Carefully note these distinguishing features. 5th and reverse synchronizer rings are the smallest. 5th has notches in the teeth. 4th and 3rd are the next larger in size and are exactly the same. 2nd and 1st are the biggest and are exactly the same. The wider synchronizer keys are used on the 1st and 2nd rings

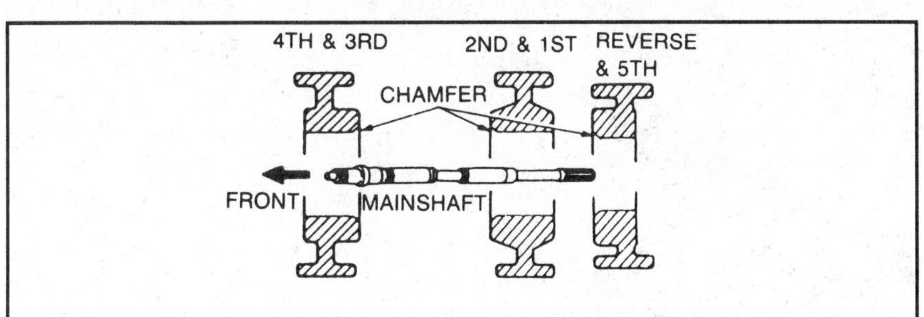

FIG. 20 Press each clutch hub assembly onto the mainshaft in the proper direction. Install the clutch hubs with the chamfers of the inner gear teeth as shown

case. Apply RTV to the bolts and tighten them to 22 ft. lbs.

65. On 2-wheel drive models:

a. Install the speedometer gear snapring and key.

b. Install the speedometer drive gear and snapring.

c. Coat the contact surfaces of the extension housing and bearing housing with RTV gasket material.

d. Turn the control rod counterclockwise and install the extension housing. Torque the bolts to 34 ft. lbs.

e. Coat the mating surfaces of the shift control lever case and transfer case with RTV gasket material and install the shift control case. Apply RTV to the bolts and tighten them to 22 ft. lbs.

R5M-D, R5MX-D 5-Speed MPV Models

SEE FIGS. 21-24

MAJOR COMPONENT DISASSEMBLY

1. Remove the throwout bearing and release fork.
2. Remove the input shaft front bearing cover.
3. Remove the speedometer gear from the right side of the extension housing.
4. Remove the back-up light switch from the left side of the extension housing.
5. Remove the control cover assembly.
6. Remove the shift gate assembly.
7. Unbolt the extension housing, rotate if clockwise and pull it from the case.
8. Remove the snapring from the output shaft, then the speedometer drive gear, snapring and key.
9. Unbolt and separate the bellhousing from the transmission case.
10. Drive the oil seal from the bellhousing.
11. Remove the transmission case lower cover and discard the gasket.
12. Remove the control rod from the extension housing.
13. Remove the control lever end and selector.
14. Remove the oil passage assembly.
15. Drive out the extension housing oil seal.

DISASSEMBLY OF THE CENTER HOUSING AND RELATED PARTS

1. Remove the 5th/reverse shift rod end.
2. Remove the 3rd/4th shift rod end.
3. Remove the 1st/2nd shift rod end.
4. Remove the retaining ring, spring retainer, spring, pin and retaining ring from the 1st/2nd shift rod end.
5. Gently pry the bearing housing away from the transmission case. Be careful to avoid damage to the case. When the housing is loose, slide it off the shafts.
6. Remove the snapring, washer, retaining ring and C-washers and, using a puller, remove the mainshaft rear bearing.

Tag the C-washers as to front and rear. They have different thicknesses.

7. Uncrimp the tabs on the countershaft rear bearing locknut, shift the clutch hub sleeves to 1st and reverse engagement, and, using holding fixture 49 S120 440, or equivalent, remove the locknut. When reassembling, a new locknut **must** be used.
8. Using a puller, remove the countershaft bearing.
9. Remove the counter 5th gear and spacer from the rear of the countershaft.
10. Remove the idler gear shaft retaining bolt from the center housing.
11. Remove the oil guide.
12. Separate the center housing from the case by tapping it loose with a plastic mallet.

5TH/REVERSE GEAR AND RELATED PARTS REMOVAL

1. Remove the 3 shift rod spring bolts, then remove the balls and springs.
2. Drive the spring pin from the 5th/reverse shift fork. Slide the 5th/reverse shift rod out of the case.
3. Remove the 2 access covers and gaskets.
4. Drive the spring pin from the 3rd/4th shift fork.
5. Slide the 3rd/4th shift rod out from the rear of the case.
6. Drive the spring pin from the 1st/2nd shift fork and slide the 1st/2nd shift rod out the rear of the case.

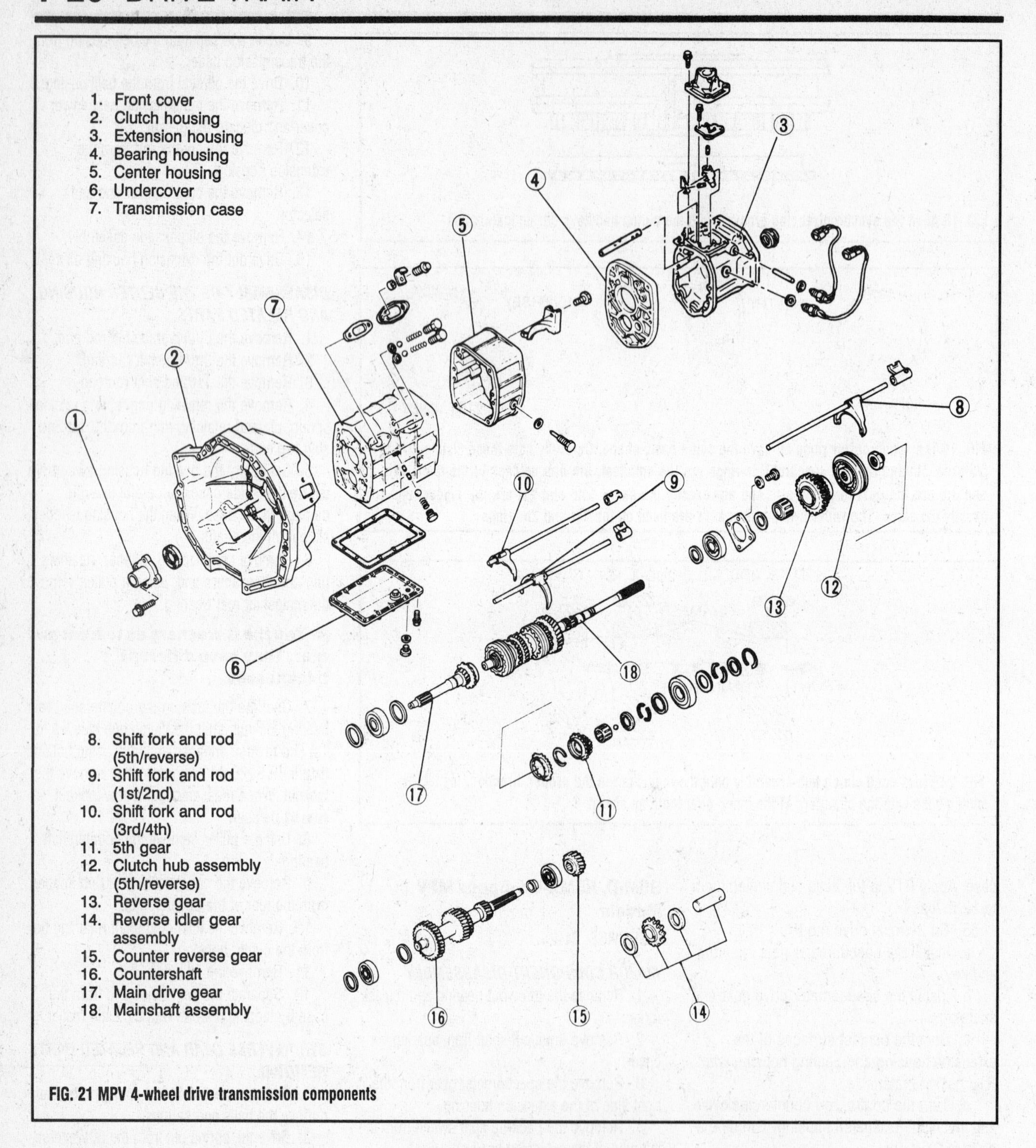

FIG. 21 MPV 4-wheel drive transmission components

7. Remove both interlock pins.

8. Remove the thrust lockwasher, lock ball, needle bearings, 5th gear and synchronizer ring from the rear of the mainshaft.

9. Uncrimp the tabs on the 5th/reverse clutch hub locknut.

10. Lock the mainshaft by engaging 1st and reverse gears.

11. Remove the locknut by using tool 49 1243 465A, or equivalent. Discard the locknut. A new locknut **must** be used.

12. Remove the bearing cover bolts.

13. Remove the bearing cover assembly with a puller. From the cover disassemble the following parts:

- 5th/reverse clutch hub
- Synchronizer ring
- Needle bearing
- Inner race
- Reverse gear
- Thrust washer

14. Remove the thrust washers, reverse idler gear shaft and reverse idler gear.

MAINSHAFT INPUT BEARING REMOVAL

1. Remove the snapring from the main drive gear.

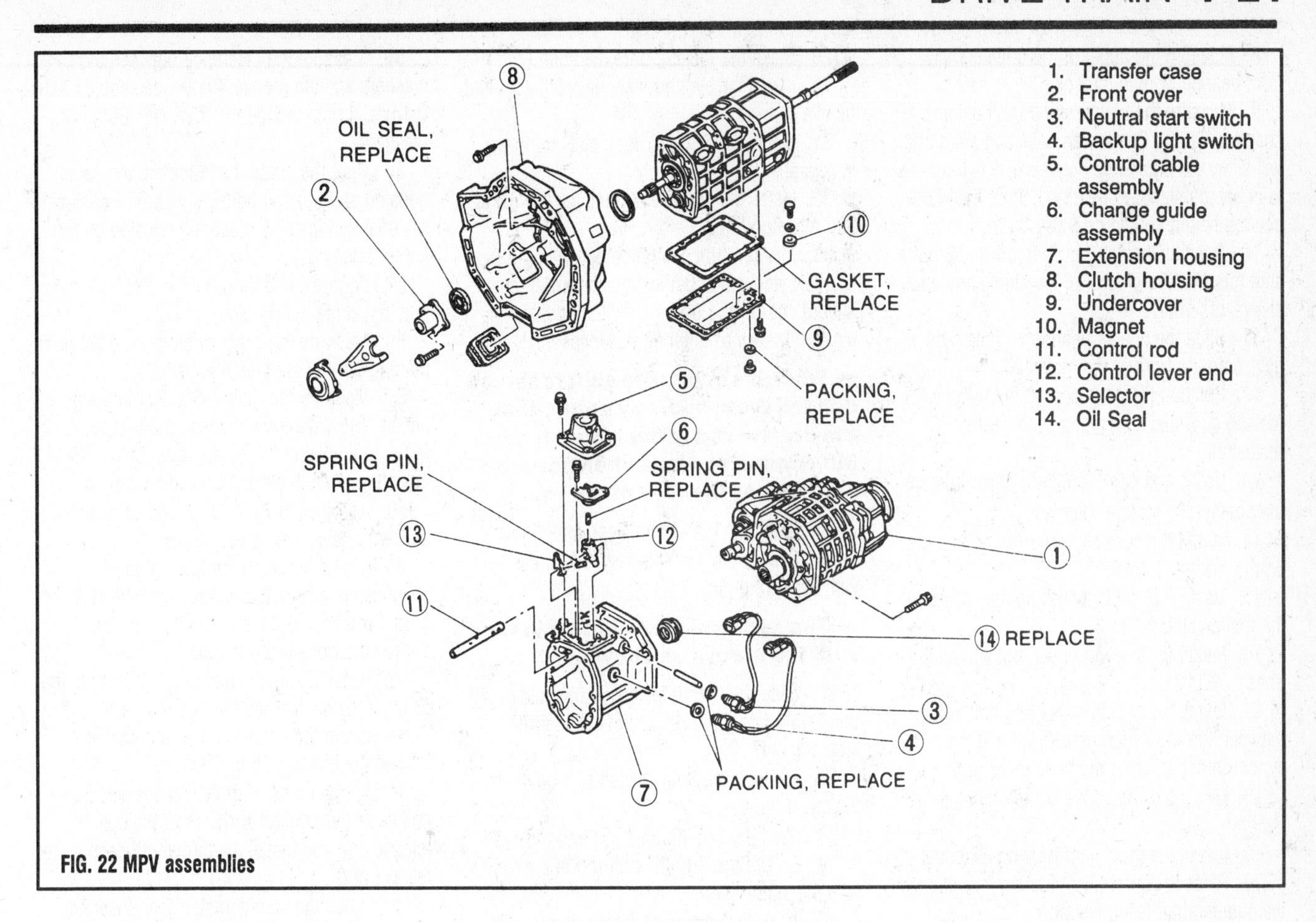

FIG. 22 MPV assemblies

2. Install synchronizer ring holder 49 F017 101, or equivalent, between the 4th speed synchronizer ring and synchromesh gear on the main drive gear.

3. Turn the bearing snaprings so that the ring ends are at a 90° angle to the case grooves.

4. Remove the main drive gear bearing using a puller.

COUNTERSHAFT FRONT BEARING REMOVAL

1. Remove the snapring from the front of the countershaft.

2. Using a puller, remove the countershaft.

MAINSHAFT DISASSEMBLY

1. Using a puller, remove the mainshaft bearing.

2. Remove 1st gear.

3. Remove the countershaft center bearing with a puller.

4. Remove the countershaft.

5. Remove the main drive gear and needle bearing.

6. Remove the mainshaft and gear assembly.

7. Remove the snapring from the front of the mainshaft.

8. Position tool 49 0636 145, or equivalent, between 2nd and 3rd gears.

9. Using a press, drive the mainshaft out of 3rd gear and the 3rd/4th clutch hub assembly.

10. Press the 1st/2nd clutch hub assembly and 1st gear sleeve from the mainshaft.

11. Remove the countershaft center bearing inner race using a puller.

COMPONENT INSPECTION

1. Check all parts for signs of wear or damage. Replace any suspected part.

2. Using a dial indicator, check the mainshaft runout. Total runout must not exceed 0.03mm.

3. Check reverse idler gear-to-shaft clearance. Clearance must not exceed 0.15mm.

4. Check the clearance between each synchronizer and its gear. Clearance should not exceed 0.8mm.

5. Check clutch hub sleeve-to-shift fork clearance. Clearance must not exceed 0.5mm.

6. Check control lever-to-shift rod gate clearance. Clearance must not exceed 0.8mm.

7. Measure the free length of the springs.

- Detent ball spring: 22.5mm
- 1st/2nd shift rod end spring: 32mm

COMPONENT ASSEMBLY

All the synchronizers have the same basic shape. To tell the difference:

- 5th and reverse are the smallest
- 5th has 2 notches in the teeth
- 4th and 3rd are the next size up and are identical
- 2nd and 1st are the largest and are identical

There are 2 types of synchronizer keys. They are differentiated by size.

- 1st and reverse are 18mm × 5.45mm × 6mm
- 3rd, 4th, 5th and reverse are 17mm × 4.25mm × 5mm

Make sure the parts are facing in the right direction

1. Place the 2nd gear, with its needle bearing, and the 1st/2nd clutch hub assembly, on a press and press the mainshaft into them.

2. Place the 3rd gear, needle bearing and 3rd/4th clutch hub assembly into position and press the 3rd/4th clutch hub assembly onto the mainshaft.

3. Install the snapring on the front of the mainshaft.

4. Install the inner race, needle bearing, 1st gear and thrust washer.

5. Press the countershaft center bearing inner race onto the countershaft.

6. Measure the depth of the mainshaft bearing bore in the case.

7. Measure the mainshaft bearing snapring height. The difference between the two figures is the required thickness of the adjusting shim. Standard thrust play should be 0-0.1mm. The adjusting shim thickness should be 0.1-0.3mm.

8. Measure the depth of the countershaft front bearing bore in the case.

9. Measure the countershaft front bearing snapring height. Choose an adjusting shim that will allow the difference between the two figures to equal the standard bearing height. Standard bearing height should be 0.9-1.0mm.

10. Position the 1st/2nd shift fork and 3rd/4th shift fork into the groove of the clutch hub and sleeve assembly.

11. Slide the needle bearing and main drive gear onto the front of the mainshaft.

12. Position the countershaft in the case, making sure that it engages each gear on the mainshaft.

13. Using a suitable length of pipe, drive on the countershaft center bearing.

14. Install the correctly predetermined shim on the mainshaft bearing.

15. Using a suitable length of pipe, drive on the mainshaft bearing.

16. Install the bearing cover and tighten the bolts to 20 ft. lbs.

17. Install the synchronizer ring holder tool between the 4th synchronizer ring and the synchromesh gear on the main drive gear.

18. Using a driver, drive in the main gear bearing.

19. Install the main gear bearing snapring.

20. Place the correctly predetermined shim in the countershaft front bearing.

21. Drive the countershaft front bearing on using a bearing driver.

22. Install the snapring.

➡ The countershaft bearing snapring is smaller than the mainshaft bearing snapring.

23. Install the reverse idler gear and shaft with a spacer on each side of the gear.

24. Install the counter reverse gear and spacer, with the chamfer on the gear forward.

25. Install the thrust washer, reverse gear, inner race, needle bearing and clutch hub assembly.

26. Engage 1st and reverse gears to lock the mainshaft.

27. Install a new locknut on the mainshaft and torque it to 174 ft. lbs. using tool 49 1243 465A, or equivalent.

28. Check the clearance between the synchronizer key and the exposed edge of the synchronizer ring. The clearance must not exceed 2.0mm. If it does, adjust it by added or deleting thrust washers at the mainshaft bearing front and rear.

➡ Total combined thickness of the front and rear thrust washers should not exceed 6mm.

29. Stake the locknut onto the shaft.

30. Install the synchronizer ring, 5th gear and needle bearing.

31. Install the 5th gear lock ball and thrust lockwasher.

32. Install the 5th gear 3mm thick C-washers and retaining ring.

33. Measure the clearance between the C-washers and the thrust lockwasher. Clearance should not exceed 0.2mm. Adjust by installing thrust washers of differing thicknesses.

➡ When installing the shift rods, you can tell them apart by noting that the 3rd/4th rod is the longest; the 5th/reverse rod has a hole for the shift fork at the rear of the rod.

34. Slide the 1st/2nd shift rod into the case.

35. Secure the 1st/2nd shift fork to the rod with the spring pin.

➡ The spring pin should be installed with the groove as shown.

36. Slide the 2 shift for assembly guides, 49 0862 350, into the case and install the first interlock pin.

37. Remove the 3rd/4th shift fork guide from the case.

38. Slide the 3rd/4th shift rod into the case.

39. Secure the 3rd/4th shift rod to the fork with the spring pin.

40. Insert the remaining interlock pin and remove the shift fork guide.

41. Install the 5th/reverse shift fork onto the clutch hub and slide the reverse/5th rod into the case.

42. Secure the 5th/reverse fork to the rod with the spring pin.

43. Install the 2 covers and gaskets.

44. Install the detent balls springs and bolts. Torque the 2 upper bolts to 43 ft. lbs.; the lower bolt to 19 ft. lbs.

45. Coat the mating surface of the transmission case with RTV gasket material and install the center housing.

46. Install the oil guide. Torque it to 95 inch lbs.

47. Install the spacer and counter 5th gear.

48. Align the reverse idler gear shaft boss with the holding bolt hole and install the bolt and gasket. Torque the bolt to 122 inch lbs.

49. Drive on the countershaft rear bearing using a bearing driver.

50. Install the mainshaft holder.

51. Engage 1st and reverse gears to lock the countershaft.

52. Install the countershaft locknut and torque the nut to 145 ft. lbs. Stake the nut.

53. Drive on the mainshaft rear bearing.

54. Install the C-washers and hold them in place with the retaining ring.

55. Measure the clearance between the C-washers and the groove. Clearance should be 0-0.1mm. If not, change the thickness of the C-washers.

56. Coat the contact surfaces of the center housing and bearing housing with RTV gasket material and install the bearing housing on the center housing.

57. Engage the shift rod ends and shift rods and install the spring pins.

58. Measure the depth of the main drive gear bearing bore in the clutch housing.

59. Measure the main drive gear bearing height. The difference between the two is the required thickness of the adjusting shim. The adjusting shim thickness should be 0-0.1mm.

60. Apply oil to the seal lip and drive it into the bellhousing with a seal driver.

61. Coat the mating surfaces of the bellhousing and transmission case with RTV gasket material and install the bellhousing. Torque the bolts to 34 ft. lbs.

62. Install the input shaft bearing cover in the clutch housing. Torque the bolts to 19 ft. lbs.

63. Install the bottom cover and gasket. Torque the bolts to 95 inch lbs.

64. Apply a coat of molybdenum disulfide grease to the contact surfaces of the clutch release arm and install the throwout bearing and release arm.

65. Install the speedometer gear snapring and key.

66. Install the speedometer drive gear and snapring.

67. Install the oil passage in the extension housing. Torque it to 95 inch lbs.

68. Install the control rod, control lever end and selector.

69. Install the roll pins as shown in the accompanying illustration.

➡ Make sure that the inner shift lever and shift rod end are aligned.

70. Coat the contact surfaces of the extension housing and bearing housing with RTV gasket material.

71. Apply RTV sealant to the bolt threads and install the extension housing. Torque the bolts to 35 ft. lbs.

72. Coat the mating surfaces of the shift control lever case and transfer case with RTV gasket material and install the shift control case. Apply RTV to the bolts and tighten them to 22 ft. lbs.

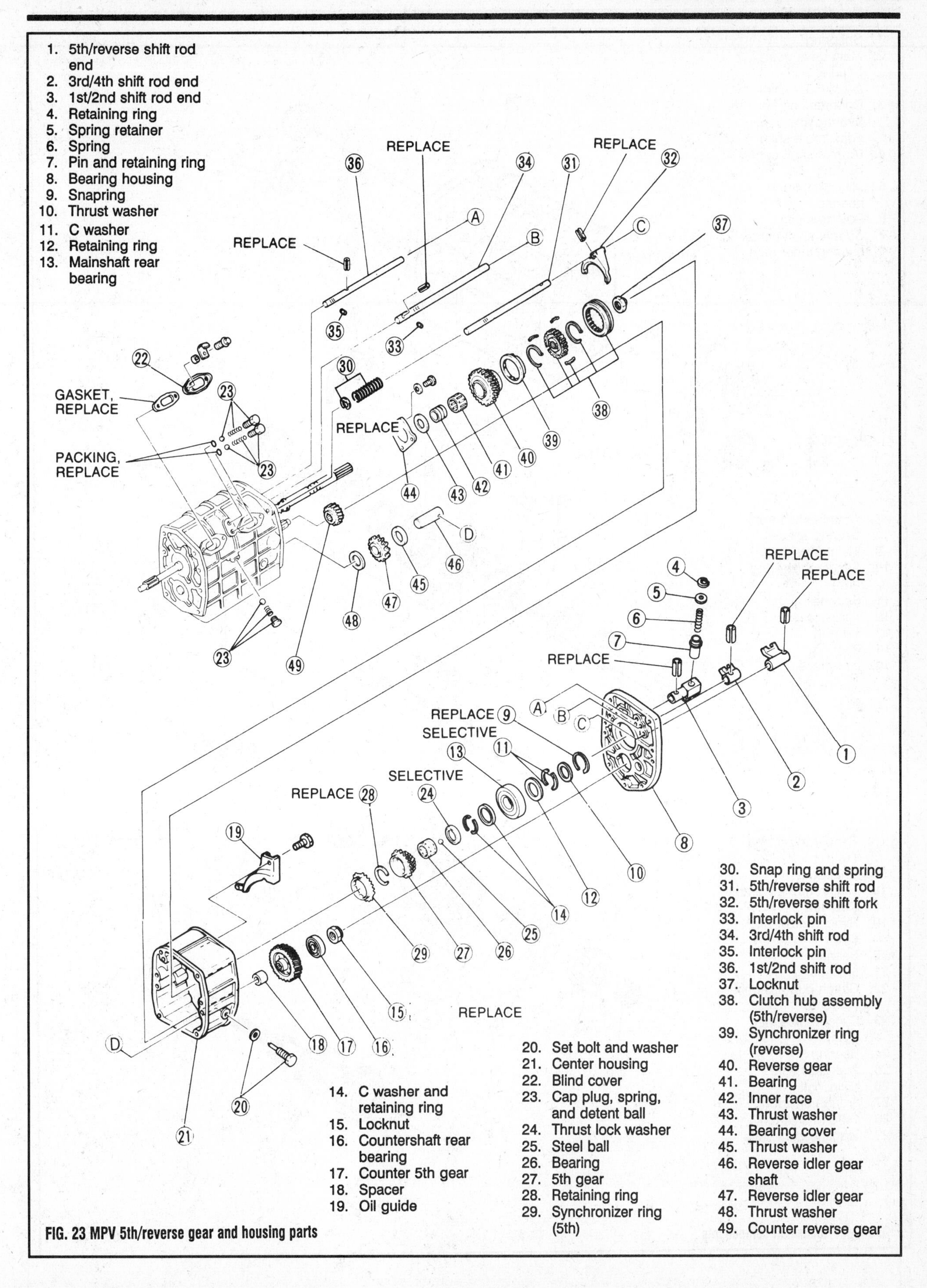
1. 5th/reverse shift rod end
2. 3rd/4th shift rod end
3. 1st/2nd shift rod end
4. Retaining ring
5. Spring retainer
6. Spring
7. Pin and retaining ring
8. Bearing housing
9. Snapring
10. Thrust washer
11. C washer
12. Retaining ring
13. Mainshaft rear bearing
14. C washer and retaining ring
15. Locknut
16. Countershaft rear bearing
17. Counter 5th gear
18. Spacer
19. Oil guide
20. Set bolt and washer
21. Center housing
22. Blind cover
23. Cap plug, spring, and detent ball
24. Thrust lock washer
25. Steel ball
26. Bearing
27. 5th gear
28. Retaining ring
29. Synchronizer ring (5th)
30. Snap ring and spring
31. 5th/reverse shift rod
32. 5th/reverse shift fork
33. Interlock pin
34. 3rd/4th shift rod
35. Interlock pin
36. 1st/2nd shift rod
37. Locknut
38. Clutch hub assembly (5th/reverse)
39. Synchronizer ring (reverse)
40. Reverse gear
41. Bearing
42. Inner race
43. Thrust washer
44. Bearing cover
45. Thrust washer
46. Reverse idler gear shaft
47. Reverse idler gear
48. Thrust washer
49. Counter reverse gear
REPLACE
GASKET, REPLACE
PACKING, REPLACE
SELECTIVE
A
B
C
D

FIG. 23 MPV 5th/reverse gear and housing parts

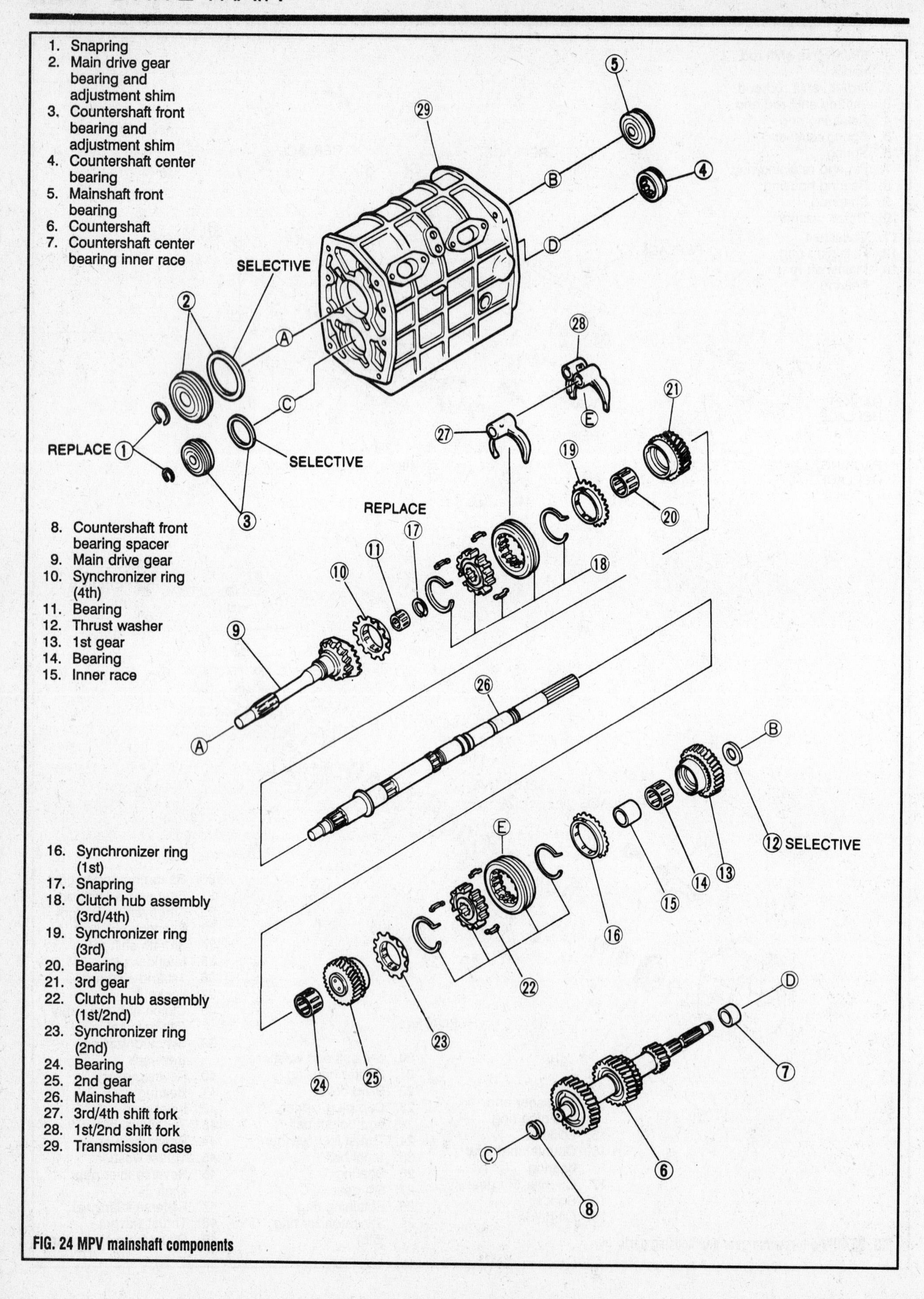
1. Snapring
2. Main drive gear bearing and adjustment shim
3. Countershaft front bearing and adjustment shim
4. Countershaft center bearing
5. Mainshaft front bearing
6. Countershaft
7. Countershaft center bearing inner race
8. Countershaft front bearing spacer
9. Main drive gear
10. Synchronizer ring (4th)
11. Bearing
12. Thrust washer
13. 1st gear
14. Bearing
15. Inner race
16. Synchronizer ring (1st)
17. Snapring
18. Clutch hub assembly (3rd/4th)
19. Synchronizer ring (3rd)
20. Bearing
21. 3rd gear
22. Clutch hub assembly (1st/2nd)
23. Synchronizer ring (2nd)
24. Bearing
25. 2nd gear
26. Mainshaft
27. 3rd/4th shift fork
28. 1st/2nd shift fork
29. Transmission case
SELECTIVE
REPLACE
SELECTIVE
REPLACE
SELECTIVE

FIG. 24 MPV mainshaft components

Navajo M5OD 5-Speed

➧ SEE FIGS. 25-28

TRANSMISSION DISASSEMBLY

1. Remove the transmission drain plug and drain the transmission fluid into a suitable drain pan.
2. Remove the shift lever and dust boot is necessary. Remove the 10 top cover assembly retaining bolts. Remove the top cover assembly.
3. Remove the 9 extension housing retaining bolts. Pry gently at the locations provided on the extension housing and transmission case. Remove the extension housing from the case.
4. Lock the transmission into 1st/3rd gears. Using countershaft locknut staking tool T–77J–7025–F or equivalent, release the staked areas securing the output shaft and countershaft locknut. The staked areas of locknuts must be fully released or damage to shaft threads will result.
5. Remove and discard the countershaft rear bearing locknut. Remove the countershaft bearing and thrust washer.
6. Using the mainshaft locknut wrench tool 49 UN01 011 and remover tube tool 49 1243 465A or equivalents, remove and discard output shaft locknut. Remove the reverse idler shaft fixing bolt. Remove the reverse idler gear assembly by grasping and pulling rearward.
7. Remove the output shaft rear bearing from the output shaft using Bearing Puller set 49 0839 425C and Hook 49 0839 425C or equivalents.
8. Using a suitable brass drift and hammer, drive the reverse gear from the output shaft. Remove the sleeve from the output shaft. Remove the counter reverse gear with the 2 needle bearings and reverse synchronizer ring.
9. Remove the thrust washer and split washer from the countershaft. Remove the 5th/reverse shift rod fixing bolt.
10. Remove the 5th/reverse synchronizer hub and sleeve as an assembly. Remove the 5th/reverse shift fork and rod. Do not separate the steel ball and spring (remove from the shift fork groove) unless necessary.
11. Remove the 5th gear synchronizer ring. Remove the 5th/reverse counter lever lockplate retaining bolt and inner circlip. Remove the counter lever assembly from the transmission case. Do not remove the Torx® nut retaining the counter lever pin at this time.
12. Remove the 5th gear (counter) with needle bearing. Remove the 5th gear from the output shaft.
13. Remove the 5th gear sleeve and position ball.
14. Remove the 6 center bearing cover retaining bolts. Remove the center bearing cover. For reference during assembly, observe that the reference arrow in the middle of the center bearing cover points upward. Observe the flanged side of the center bearing cover faces inward.
15. Remove the 6 front bearing cover attaching bolts. Remove the front bearing cover by threading 2 of the originally installed retaining bolts into the front bearing cover service bolt locations (9 o'clock and 3 o'clock). Alternately tighten bolts until the front bearing cover can be lifted away by hand. Remove and discard the front bearing cover oil baffle. The bolt threaded into the service bolt locations will bottom out and lift the front bearing cover away from the transmission case. Do not remove the plastic scoop ring from the input shaft at this time.
16. Remove the oil trough retaining bolt and oil trough from the upper transmission case. Pull the input shaft forward and remove the input bearing outer race. Pull the output shaft rearward.
17. Pull input shaft forward and separate it from the output shaft. Incline output shaft upward and lift it from the transmission case. Remove the input shaft from the transmission case.
18. Remove the countershaft bearing outer races (front and center) by moving the countershaft forward and rearward. Pull the countershaft rearward enough to permit the tool clearance behind the front countershaft bearing. Using bearing race puller tool T88T–7120–A and slide hammer tool T50T–100–A or equivalents, remove the front countershaft bearing. Tap the bearing gently during removal. A forceful blow can cause damage to the bearing or transmission case.

CLEANING

During overhaul, all components of the transmission (except bearing assemblies) should be thoroughly cleaned with solvent and dried with air pressure prior to inspection and reassembly.

1. Clean the bearing assemblies as follows:

➡ Proper cleaning of bearings is of utmost importance. Bearings should always be cleaned separately from other parts.

a. Soak all bearing assemblies in clean solvent or fuel oil. Bearings should never be cleaned in a hot solution tank.

b. Slush bearings in solvent until all old lubricant is loosened. Hold races so that bearings will not rotate, then clean bearings with a soft bristled brush until all dirt has been removed. Remove loose particles of dirt by tapping bearing flat against a block of wood.

c. Rinse bearings in clean solvent, then blow bearings dry with air pressure.

➡ Do not spin bearings while drying.

d. After drying, rotate each bearing slowly while examining balls or rollers for roughness, damage, or excessive wear. Replace all bearings that are not in first class condition.

➡ After cleaning and inspecting bearings, lubricate generously with recommended lubricant, then wrap each bearing in clean paper until ready for reassembly.

2. Remove all portions of old gaskets from parts, using a stiff brush or scraper.

INSPECTION

1. Inspect all parts for discoloration or warpage.
2. Examine all gears and splines for chipped, worn, broken or nicked teeth. Small nicks or burrs may be removed with a fine abrasive stone.
3. Inspect the breather assembly to make sure that it is open and not damaged.
4. Check all threaded parts for damaged, stripped, or crossed threads.
5. Replace all gaskets, oil seals and snaprings.
6. Inspect housings, retainers and covers for cracks or other damage. Replace the damaged parts.
7. Inspect keys and keyways for condition and fit.
8. Inspect shift forks for wear, distortion or any other damage.
9. Check detent ball springs for free length, compressed length, distortion or collapsed coils.
10. Check bearing fit on their respective shafts and in their bores or cups. Inspect bearings, shafts and cups for wear.

➡ If either bearings or cups are worn or damaged, it is advisable to replace both parts.

11. Inspect all bearing rollers or balls for pitting or galling.
12. Examine detent balls for corrosion or brinneling. If shift bar detents show wear, replace them.
13. Inspect the synchronizer ring for wear. To check the wear of the synchronizer ring, fit the synchronizer ring evenly to the gear cone. Measure the clearance between the side faces of the synchronizer ring and gear with a feeler gauge. If the clearance is less than 0.031 in. (0.8mm), replace the synchronizer ring or gear.
14. Check the contact surfaces of the shift fork and clutch hub sleeve for evidence of wear or damage. Measure from the shift fork to the clutch hub sleeve. If the clearance exceeds 0.031 in. (0.8mm), replace the shift fork/clutch hub sleeve.

a. The standard clearance for the 1st/2nd and 3rd/4th shift fork/clutch hub sleeves is 0.003–0.014 in. (0.1–0.358mm). The maximum is 0.314 in. (0.8mm).

b. The standard clearance for the 5th/reverse shift fork/clutch hub sleeves is 0.003–0.015 in. (0.1–0.37mm). The maximum is 0.314 in. (0.8mm).

15. Replace all worn or damaged parts. When assembling the transmission, coat all moving parts with recommended lubricant.

INPUT SHAFT DISASSEMBLY

1. Remove and discard the plastic scoop ring.
2. Press the tappered roller bearing from the input shaft using bearing cone remover tool T71P–4621–B or equivalent.

INSPECTION

1. Clean and inspect the input shaft and gear assemblies.
2. Replace any and all worn or damaged components, as necessary.

INPUT SHAFT ASSEMBLY

1. Install the input shaft tappered roller bearing onto the input shaft using a suitable press and bearing cone replacer tool T88T–7025–B or equivalent.
2. Install a plastic scoop ring onto the input shaft. Manually rotate the ring clockwise to ensure that the input oil holes properly engage the scoop ring. A click should be heard as the scoop ring notches align with the input shaft oil holes.

OUTPUT SHAFT DISASSEMBLY

1. Pull back and separate the 3rd gear and the 2nd gear from the output shaft flange.
2. Remove the pilot bearing (needle roller), snapring, needle bearing and spacer from the front (short side of the flange) of the output shaft.
3. Position the front (short side of the flange) of the output shaft so that it faces upward. Lift off the following components as an assembly.
   a. Clutch hub and sleeve assembly (3rd/4th).
   b. Synchronizer ring (3rd).
   c. 3rd gear.
   d. Needle bearing.
4. Position the output shaft with the rear end (long side of the flange) facing upward. Position the output shaft into the press with the press cradle contacting the lower part of 2nd gear.

➡ Ensure that the output shaft flange does not contact or ride up onto the press cradle. Improper positioning of the output shaft can cause component damage.

5. Press off the following components as a unit, center bearing, 1st gear sleeve, 1st gear needle bearing, 1st/2nd clutch hub and sleeve assembly, 1st/2nd synchronizer rings, 2nd gear and the needle bearing using bearing replacer tool T53T–4621–B and bearing cone replacer tool T88T–7025–B or equivalents.

INSPECTION

1. Clean and inspect the output shaft and gear assemblies.
2. Replace any and all worn or damaged components as necessary.
3. Check the output shaft for run-out by mounting the shaft between V-blocks and applying a dial indicator tool to several places along the shaft.
4. The standard reading of the dial indicator for the run-out should be less than 0.002 in. (0.05mm). If the run-out exceeds the specifications, replace the mainshaft.
5. Replace the input shaft if the splines are damaged. If the needle bearing surface in the bore of the bearing is worn or rough, or if the cone surface is damaged, replace the shaft.

OUTPUT SHAFT ASSEMBLY

During assembly apply the recommended transmission fluid to all rotating or sliding parts.

1. Position the output shaft so that the rear end (long side of the flange) faces upward. Install the following components in the order listed as follows:
   a. 2nd gear needle bearing.
   b. 2nd gear.
   c. 2nd gear synchronizer rings.
   d. 1st/2nd clutch hub and sleeve assembly.
   e. 1st gear synchronizer rings.
   f. 1st gear needle bearing.
   g. 1st gear.
   h. 1st gear sleeve.
   i. Center bearing (inner).

➡ To install the components onto the output shaft, press the components into position using bearing replacer tool T53T–4621–B and bearing plate tool T75L–1165–B or equivalents.

2. Ensure that the center bearing race is installed into the transmission case.
3. When installing the 1st/2nd clutch hub and sleeve, ensure that the smaller width of the sleeve faces 2nd gear (front) side. Ensure that the reference marks face the rear of the transmission, they reference the synchronizer key installation position.
4. Install the center bearing to the output shaft.
5. Position the output flange so that the front (short side) of the output shaft flange faces upward. Install the 3rd gear needle bearing, 3rd gear and 3rd gear synchronizer ring.
6. Install the 3rd/4th clutch hub and sleeve as follows:
   a. Mate the clutch hub synchronizer key groove with reference mark on the clutch hub sleeve. The mark should face rearward.
   b. Install the longer flange on the clutch hub sleeve toward 3rd gear (rear) side.

➡ The front and rear sides of the clutch hub are the same except for the reference mark on one side.

7. Install the spacer, needle bearing (install the rollers upward), retaining ring and pilot bearing (roller). Install the original retaining ring. Check the clutch hub endplay using a feeler gauge.
8. If necessary, adjust the 3rd/4th clutch hub endplay to 0.00–0.0019 in. (0.00–0.05mm) by selecting a required retaining ring.

COUNTERSHAFT DISASSEMBLY

1. Using a suitable press and bearing cone remover tool T71P–4621–B or equivalent, remove the countershaft center bearing inner race.
2. Using a press and bearing splitter tool D84L–1123–A or equivalent, remove the countershaft front bearing inner race.

INSPECTION

1. Clean and inspect the output shaft and gear assemblies.
2. Replace any and all worn or damaged components, as necessary.

COUNTERSHAFT ASSEMBLY

1. Using a suitable press, a press plate and bearing replacer tool T53T–4621–B or equivalent, install the center bearing inner race.
2. Using a suitable press, a press plate and bearing replacer tool T53T–4621–B or equivalent, install the countershaft front bearing inner race.

REVERSE IDLER GEAR DISASSEMBLY

Remove the retaining ring, spacer, idler gear, needle bearing and thrust washer from the reverse idler gear shaft.

INSPECTION

1. Clean and inspect the reverse idler gear shaft and gear assemblies.
2. Replace any and all worn or damaged components, as necessary.

REVERSE IDLER GEAR ASSEMBLY

1. Install the thrust washer onto the reverse idler gear shaft. Ensure that the tab on the thrust washer mates with the groove on the reverse idler shaft to prevent rotation of the thrust washer.

2. Install the needle bearing, idler gear and spacer.

3. Install the original retaining ring onto the reverse idler gear shaft. Insert a feeler gauge between the retaining ring and reverse idler gear to measure the reverse idler gear endplay.

4. Using the proper size retaining rings, adjust the endplay to 0.0039–0.0078 in. (0.1–0.2mm).

TOP COVER DISASSEMBLY

1. If necessary, remove the dust boot and shift lever from the top cover. Remove the 3 dust cover screws and remove the dust cover.

➡ For reference during assembly, notice that the grooves in the bushing align with the slots in the lower shift lever pivot ball. Notice that the notch in the lower shift lever faces toward the front of the transmission.

2. Position the top cover assembly into a suitable holding fixture.

3. Remove the backup lamp switch from the top cover. Remove the backup lamp switch pin from the groove in the top cover. There is only 1 type of backup lamp pin used.

4. Use a drift pin to remove the spring pins retaining the shift forks to the shift rail. Discard the original spring pins.

5. Ensure that the 5th/reverse shift rail is in the fully forward position. Remove the spring pin from the end of the 5th/reverse rail.

6. Remove the 3 rubber plugs blocking the shift rod service bores.

➡ Perform the following shift rail removal procedures with great care. Cover the lock ball bores and friction device and spring seats with a clean cloth held firmly in place during shift rail removal. Failure to firmly cover the lock ball bores and friction device can result in component loss when the ball/friction device and spring forcefully leave their installed positions. Be sure to wear safety goggles while performing the shift rail removal procedure.

7. Remove the 1st/2nd shift rail from the top cover through the service bore. If necessary, insert a drift pin punch through the spring pin bore and gently rock the shift rail from side to side while maintaining rearward pressure.

8. Remove the 3rd/4th shift rail from the top cover through the service bore. If necessary, insert a drift pin punch through the spring pin bore and gently rock the shift rail from side to side while maintaining rearward pressure.

9. Remove the 5th/reverse cam lockout plate retaining bolts and remove the 5th/reverse cam lockout plate.

INSPECTION

1. Clean and inspect the shift rail and shift fork assemblies.

2. Replace any and all worn or damaged components, as necessary.

TOP COVER ASSEMBLY

1. With the top cover in a suitable holding fixture. Position the 5th/reverse cam lockout plate to the top cover. Install the 5th/reverse cam lockout plate retaining bolts and torque them to 6–7 ft. lbs. (8–10mm).

2. Position the 3rd/4th shift rail into the top cover through the service bore. If necessary, insert a drift pin punch through the spring bore and gently rock the shift rail from side to side while maintaining forward pressure. Position the detent ball and spring into the top cover spring seats.

3. Compress the detent ball and spring assembly using a suitable tool and push the shift rail into position over the detent ball. Position the friction device and spring into the top cover seats. Compress the fiction device and spring assembly using a suitable tool and push the shift rail into position over the friction device. Install the spring pins, retaining the shift rail to top cover. Install the spring retaining 3rd/4th shift fork to the shift rail.

4. Position the 1st/2nd shift rail into the top cover through the service bore. If necessary, insert a drift pin punch through the spring bore and gently rock the shift rail from side to side while maintaining forward pressure. Position the detent ball and spring into the top cover spring seats.

5. Compress the detent ball and spring assembly using a suitable tool and push the shift rail into position over the detent ball. Position the friction device and spring into the top cover seats. Compress the fiction device and spring assembly using a suitable tool and push the shift rail into position over the friction device. Install the spring pins, retaining the shift rail to top cover. Install the spring retaining 1st/2nd shift fork to the shift rail.

6. Position the 5th/reverse shift rail into the top cover through the service bore. If necessary, insert a drift pin punch through the spring bore and gently rock the shift rail from side to side while maintaining forward pressure. Position the detent ball and spring into the top cover spring seats. Compress the detent ball and spring assembly using a suitable tool and push the shift rail into position over the detent ball. Position the friction device and spring into the top cover seats.

7. Compress the fiction device and spring assembly using a suitable tool and push the shift rail into position over the friction device. Install the spring pins, retaining the shift rail to top cover. Install the spring retaining 5th/reverse shift fork to the shift rail.

8. Install the rubber plugs into the service bores. Install the interlock pins into the 1st/2nd and 3rd/4th shift rails. Ensure that the large and small interlock pins are installed into their original positions.

➡ Improper installation of the interlock pins will prevent activation of the backup lamp switch.

9. Apply a sealant to the backup lamp switch. Install the switch to the top cover and torque the switch to 18–26 ft. lbs. (25–35 Nm).

10. Position the lower shift lever and dust cover assembly to the top cover. Install and tighten the 3 retaining screws.

TRANSMISSION ASSEMBLY

1. Position the countershaft into the transmission case through the top opening.

2. Position the input shaft into the transmission case through the top opening. Be sure that the needle roller bearing is installed into the input shaft.

3. Position the output shaft assembly into the transmission case. Mate the input shaft and output shaft assemblies by positioning them at an upward angle and setting them together. Be sure that 4th gear synchronizer ring is installed at this time.

4. Install the output shaft center bearing outer race using a brass drift. Seat the center bearing outer races.

5. Install the countershaft center bearing. Be sure that the center bearing outer races are squarely position in their bores.

6. Position the center bearing cover to the transmission case with reference arrow pointing upward. Install and tighten the center bearing cover retaining bolts and torque them to 14–19 ft. lbs. Be sure that all center bearing cover retaining bolt heads are marked with an 8.

7. Position the transmission vertically (input shaft and clutch housing facing upward). Be sure that the input shaft front bearing outer race is squarely position in the bore. If removed install the front cover oil seal using front cover seal installer tool T77J–7025–G or equivalent.

8. Install the countershaft front bearing by hand.

➡ **If any related parts (such as output shaft, bearing, etc.) have been replaced, measure the dimensions of the height of the input shaft bearing outer race above the transmission front bearing cover mating surface. Depth of the front cover outer race bore (input shaft). Depth of the countershaft front bearing race (transmission case to the front cover mating surface). Depth of the front cover outer race bore (countershaft). After measuring all dimensions, select bearing shim to maintain the endplay within specified limits.**

9. Remove any sealant residue remaining on the mating surfaces of the transmission and front cover. To prevent damage to the oil seal lip during assembly, tape the input shaft splines along their entire length.

10. Apply a thin coat of oil to the front cover oil seal lip. Position the bearing shim and baffle plate into the front cover (install the shim with groove showing). Install the spacer to transmission case countershaft front bearing bore. If necessary apply a sufficient quantity of petroleum jelly to the shim, bearing cover and oil baffle to retain them in position during assembly.

11. Apply a 1/8 in. (3mm) bead of RTV sealant to the front cover and front cover retaining bolt threads. Install the front bearing cover to the transmission case. Install and torque the front bearing cover retaining bolts to 9–17 ft. lbs. (12–22mm). Be sure the front bearing cover retaining bolt heads are marked with a 6.

12. Position the transmission horizontally in a holding fixture. Assemble the following parts in the following order, 5th gear sleeve positioning ball, 5th gear sleeve, output shaft locknut, countershaft locknut, countershaft rear bearing, thrust washer, reverse idler gear fixing bolt, reverse idle gear assembly, output shaft rear bearing, output shaft reverse gear, output shaft sleeve, countershaft reverse gear and needle bearing.

13. Install the reverse synchronizer ring, thrust washer, split washer, shift rod fixing bolt, shift rail/fork/hub/sleeve assembly, steel lock ball, shift rail, shift rail spring, 5th gear synchronizer ring, 5th gear output shaft, 5th gear countershaft, 5th gear needle bearing, 5th gear sleeve, ball, center bearing cover, 5th/reverse counter lever lockplate retaining bolt.

➡ **Install the 5th gear sleeve using nut, shaft adapter replacing tool T75L-7025-L, adapter tool T88T-7025-J2, and remove and replacer tube tool T75L-7025-B or equivalents.**

14. Install the 5th gear needle bearing onto the 5th gear (countershaft).

15. Install the 5th gear onto the output shaft, by hand, or use gear installing spacer tool T88T-7025-F, gear installation spacer tool T88T-

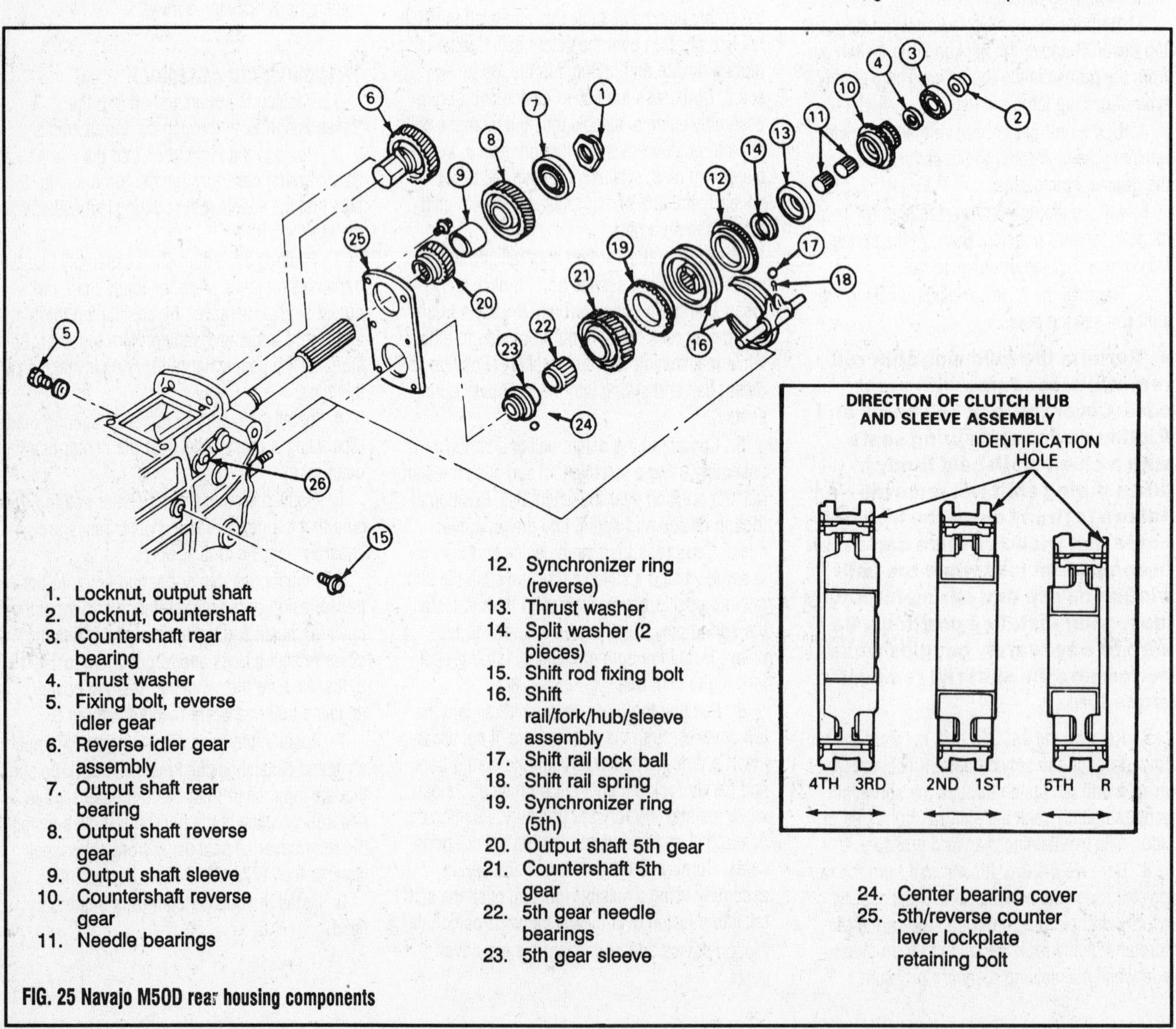

FIG. 25 Navajo M50D rear housing components

7025–G, shaft adapter tool T75L–7025–P, shaft adapter screw tool T75L–7025–K, remover/replacer tube tool T85T–7025–A, nut and washer or equivalents. Be sure that the long flange on the 5th gear faces forward.

16. Position the counter lever assembly to the transmission and install the thrust washer and retaining ring. Apply sealant to the counter lever fixing bolt threads. Install the counter lever fixing bolt and torque it to 6–7 ft. lbs. (8–10 Nm).

17. If removed, position the 5th/reverse shift fork and shift rail to the top cover. Insert the 5th/reverse shift rail through the top cover bore and 5th/reverse shift fork. Install the spring and detent ball to lower part of the rod.

18. Assemble the 5th/reverse synchronizer hub, sleeve and 5th gear synchronizer ring to the 5th/reverse shift fork and rod assembly. Be sure to install the longer flange (on the 5th/reverse hub, sleeve and synchronizer assembly) toward the front of the transmission. The reference mark on the synchronizer sleeve must be installed toward the reverse gear side.

19. Install the 5th/reverse shift fork and shift rail assembly (including 5th/reverse synchronizer hub, sleeve and 5th gear synchronizer ring) to countershaft. Mate the shift fork gate to the 5th/reverse counter lever end. Install the 5th/reverse fork and shift rail assembly with threaded fixing bolt bores (in rail and transmission case) aligned with each other.

➡ For ease of assembly, position the 5th/reverse shift fork into the rear most threaded bore of the 3 detent positions. Return the shift fork to the neutral gear position after installation.

20. Apply a suitable sealant to the 5th/reverse shift rail fixing bolt threads. Install the 5th/reverse shift rail fixing bolt to the transmission case and torque it to 16–22 ft. lbs. (20–30 Nm).

21. Apply a suitable sealant to the oil passage retaining bolt. Position the oil passage to transmission case and install the retaining bolt. Torque the oil passage retaining bolt to 6–7 ft. lbs. (8–9 Nm).

22. Install the split washer and thrust washer onto the countershaft.

➡ If the clutch hub and or counter reverse gear have been replaced, new split washers must be selected to maintain endplay within specified limits. Measure the endplay using a feeler gauge. Be sure the split washers are a matched set of identical thickness.

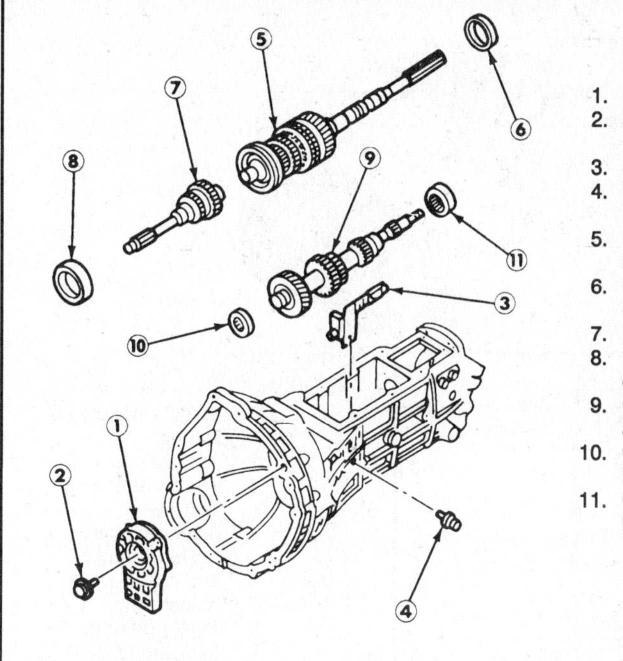

FIG. 26 Navajo M50D main case components

23. Install the reverse synchronizer ring and needle bearings onto the counter reverse gear. Install the counter reverse gear and needle bearing onto the countershaft as an assembly. Install the thrust washer to the countershaft.

24. Press the thrust washer forward against the shoulder on the countershaft. Maintain forward pressure against the thrust washer and insert a feeler gauge between the thrust washer and counter reverse gear. Using the proper size thrust washer, bring the counter reverse gear endplay into specifications. The counter reverse gear endplay should be 0.009–0.013 in. (0.25–0.35mm).

25. Temporarily install a suitable spacer (inner bore larger than 21mm, outer bore smaller than 36mm, 15–20mm over all length) in place of the countershaft bearing. Loosely install the countershaft locknut to retain the components.

➡ The installation of a suitable spacer prevents the thrust washers from slipping off the shaft and avoids interference with the reverse idler gears.

26. Install the reverse idler gear assembly. Apply a suitable sealant to the threads of the reverse idler gear fixing bolt. Torque the bolt to 58–86 ft. lbs. (79–116 Nm).

27. Drive the sleeve and reverse gear assembly onto the output shaft using gear installing spacer tool T88T–7025–G, shaft adapter tool T75L–7025–P, shaft adapter screw tool T75L–7025–K, remover/replacer tube tool T85T–7025–A, nut and washer or equivalents. Install the reverse gear with the longer flange facing rearward.

28. Install the output shaft rear bearing using gear installing spacer T88T–7025–G, shaft adapter tool T75L–7025–P, shaft adapter screw tool T75L–7025–K, remover/replacer tube tool T85T–7025–A, nut and washer or equivalents. Remove the temporary spacer from the countershaft.

29. Install the countershaft rear bearing by hand. Tightening the shaft locknuts without fully seating the bearing can cause damage to the output shaft threads.

30. Lock the transmission into 1st/3rd gears. Install a new output and countershaft locknuts. Torque the output shaft locknut to 160–200 ft. lbs. (216–274 Nm) and the countershaft locknut to 94–144 ft. lbs. (128–196 Nm).

➡ Always install new output and countershaft locknuts when assembling the transmission. Locknuts unstaked during disassembly cannot be reused.

31. Stake the locknuts to the bottom shaft groove using countershaft locknut staking tool T77J–7025–F or equivalent.

32. Install the speedometer drive gear and steel ball to the output shaft.

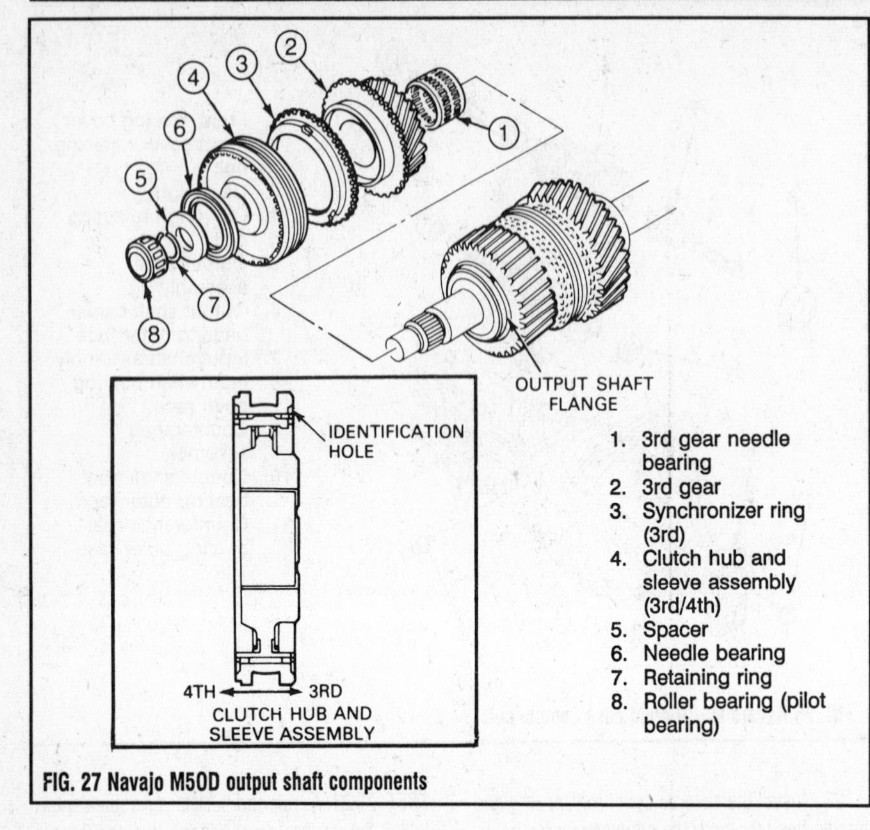

FIG. 27 Navajo M50D output shaft components

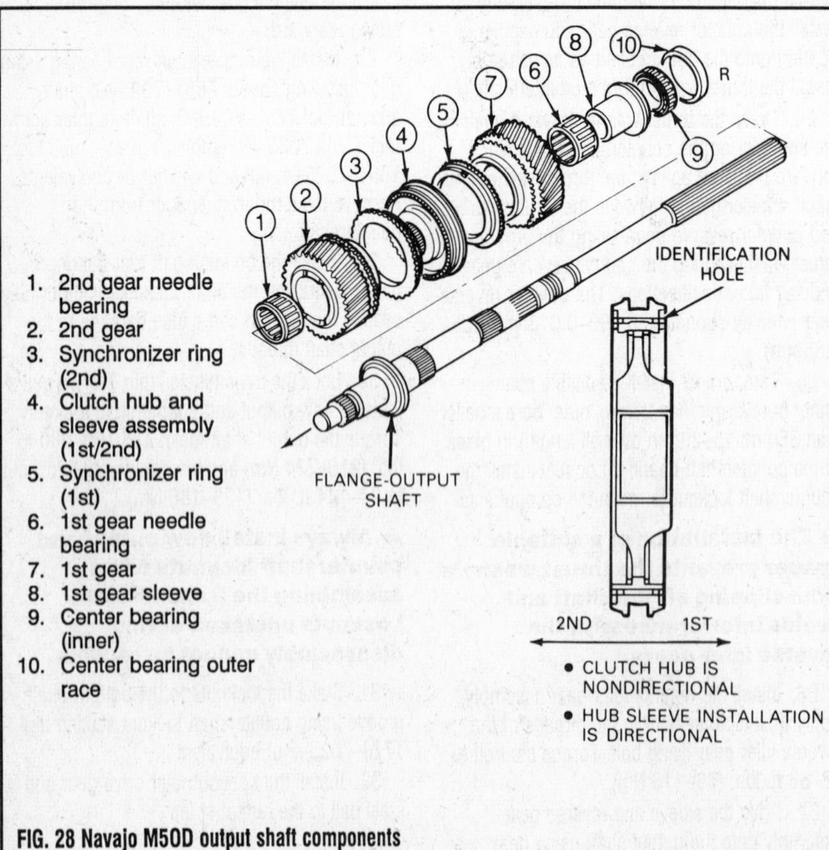

FIG. 28 Navajo M50D output shaft components

➡ **The speedometer drive gear contains 3 detents into which the steel drive ball can be installed. The steel drive ball can be installed into any of the 3 detents. For reference during assembly, observe and record speedometer drive gear color. Depending upon application, 1 or 2 different speedometer drive gear may be installed. It will be color coded either green or white. Speedometer drive gear colors and corresponding part numbers are as follows, white E8TZ-17285-B and green E8TZ-17285-C.**

33. Remove any sealant residue from the mating surfaces of the transmission case and extension housing. Apply a 1/8 in. (3mm) bead of RTV sealant or equivalent to the transmission case.

➡ **The extension housing bushing cannot be serviced. If the bushing requires service, the extension housing must be replaced as a unit.**

34. Position the extension housing to the transmission case and install the extension housing retaining bolts. Torque the bolts to 24–34 ft. lbs. (32–46 Nm). Place the synchronizers into the neutral gear position. Be sure that the shift forks on the top cover assembly are in the neutral position.

35. Position the top cover on the transmission case. Carefully engage the shift forks with the synchronizers.

36. Apply a suitable sealant to the 2 rear most top cover retaining bolts and install them into the top cover rear retaining bolt locations. Install the remaining top cover retaining bolts (no sealant) and torque them to 12–16 ft. lbs. (16–22 Nm).

➡ **Do not apply sealant to the top cover or transmission mating surfaces. If necessary, apply a small quantity of grease to the sealing gasket to retain the gasket in position during assembly.**

37. If removed, install the rear oil seal into the extension housing using extension housing seal replacer tool T61L-7657-A or equivalent. Be sure that the oil seal drain hole faces downward.

38. Install the transmission drain plug and torque it to 29–43 ft. lbs. (40–58 Nm).

CLUTCH

Application

The clutch is a dry single disc type, consisting of a clutch disc, clutch cover and pressure plate and a clutch release mechanism. It is hydraulically operated by a firewall mounted master cylinder and a clutch release slave cylinder mounted on the clutch housing.

** CAUTION

The clutch driven disc contains asbestos, which has been determined to be a cancer causing agent. Never clean clutch surfaces with compressed air! Avoid inhaling any dust from any clutch surface! When cleaning clutch surfaces, use a commercially available brake cleaning fluid.

Adjustments

PEDAL HEIGHT/FREE-PLAY

➧ SEE FIG. 29-30

Except Navajo

1. Measure the distance from the top of the clutch pedal pad to the carpet. The distance should be as follows:

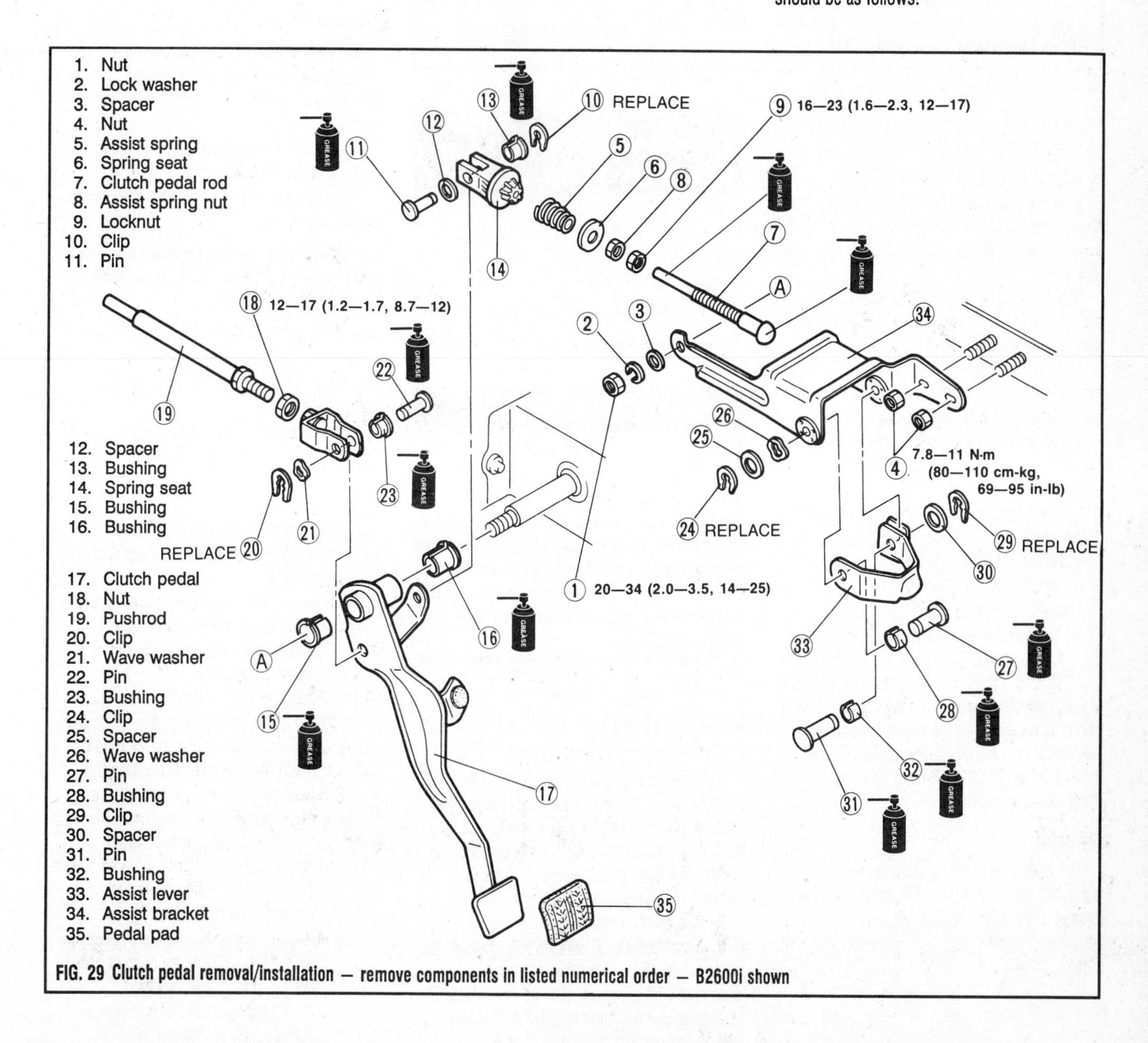

FIG. 29 Clutch pedal removal/installation — remove components in listed numerical order — B2600i shown

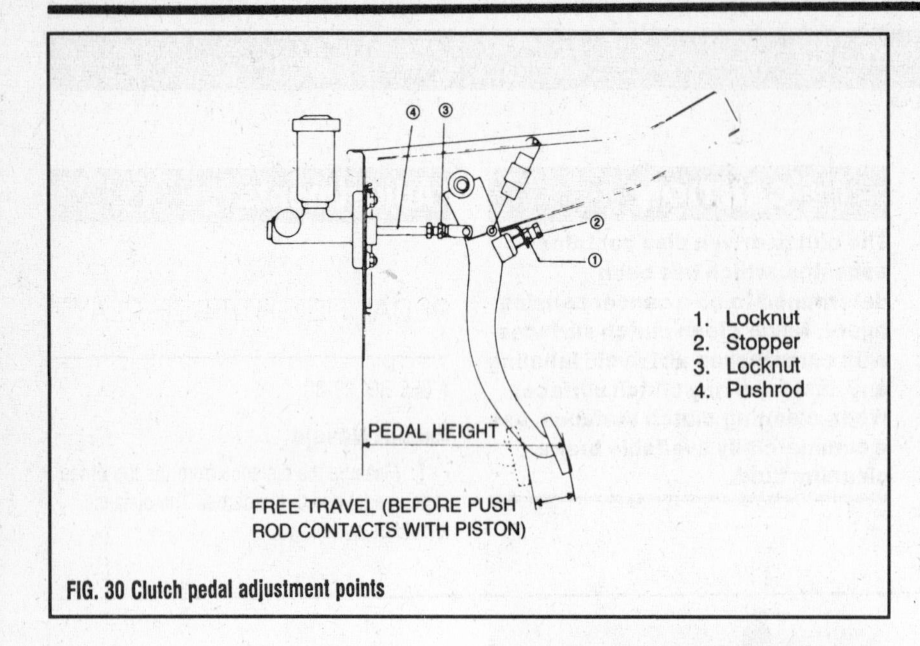

FIG. 30 Clutch pedal adjustment points

- B2200: 7.13–7.52 in. (181–191mm)
- B2600: 7.52–7.91 in. (191–201mm)
- MPV: 8.19–8.58 in. (208–218mm)

2. If the distance is not within specification, loosen the clutch switch locknut and turn the switch until the distance is correct. Tighten the lock nut.

3. Check the free-play by pressing the pedal by hand until clutch resistance is felt. The free-play should be 0.02–0.12 in. (0.6–3.0mm).

4. If the free-play is not within specification, loosen the locknut on the actuator rod and turn the actuator rod until the free-play is correct.

5. Check that the disengagement height from the upper surface of the pedal height to the carpet is correct when the pedal is fully depressed. The disengagement height should be as follows:

- B2200: 2.60 in. (66mm)
- B2600: 2.80 in. (71mm)
- MPV: 1.38 in. (35mm)

6. Tighten the actuator rod locknut to 8.7–12.0 ft. lbs. (12–17 Nm).

7. Recheck the pedal height. Certain models are equipped with a clutch assist spring. The spring is mounted on the clutch linkage, and is adjustable. The correct length should be between 1.33–1.37 in. (33.8-34.8mm). Adjust by turning the locknut.

Navajo

The hydraulic clutch system provides automatic adjustment. No adjustment of clutch linkage or pedal position is required.

Driven Disc and Pressure Plate

SEE FIGS. 31-32

REMOVAL & INSTALLATION

CAUTION

The clutch driven disc contains asbestos, which has been determined to be a cancer causing agent. Never clean clutch surfaces with compressed air! Avoid inhaling any dust from any clutch surface! When cleaning clutch surfaces, use a commercially available brake cleaning fluid.

Pickup and MPV

1. Remove the transmission.

2. Remove the four attaching and two pilot bolts holding the clutch cover to the flywheel. Loosen the bolts evenly and a turn or two at a time. If the clutch cover is to be reinstalled, mark the flywheel and clutch cover to show the location of the two pilot holes.

3. Remove the clutch disc.

4. Install the clutch disc on the flywheel. Do not touch the facing or allow the facing to come in contact with grease or oil. The clutch disc can be aligned using a tool made for that purpose, or with an old mainshaft.

5. Install the clutch cover on the flywheel and install the four standard bolts and the two pilot bolts.

6. To avoid distorting the pressure plate, tighten the bolts evenly a few turns at a time until they are all tight.

7. Torque the bolts to 13-20 ft.lbs. using a crossing pattern.

8. Remove the aligning tool.

9. Apply a light film of lubricant to the release bearing, release lever contact area on the release bearing hub and to the input shaft bearing retainer.

10. Install the transmission.

11. Check the operation of the clutch and if necessary, adjust the pedal free-play and the release lever.

Navajo

1. Disconnect the negative battery cable.

2. Disconnect the clutch hydraulic system master cylinder from the clutch pedal and remove.

3. Raise the vehicle and support it safely.

4. Remove the starter.

5. Disconnect the hydraulic coupling at the transmission.

➡ **Clean the area around the hose and slave cylinder to prevent fluid contamination.**

6. Remove the transmission from the vehicle.

7. Mark the assembled position of the pressure plate and cover the flywheel, to aid during re-assembly.

8. Loosen the pressure plate and cover attaching bolts evenly until the pressure plate springs are expanded, and remove the bolts.

9. Remove the pressure plate and cover assembly and the clutch disc from the flywheel. Remove the pilot bearing only for replacement.

To install:

10. Position the clutch disc on the flywheel so that the Clutch Alignment Shaft Tool T74P-7137-K or equivalent can enter the clutch pilot bearing and align the disc.

11. When reinstalling the original pressure plate and cover assembly, align the assembly and flywheel according to the marks made during the removal operations. Position the pressure plate and cover assembly on the flywheel, align the pressure plate and disc, and install the retaining bolts that fasten the assembly to the flywheel. Tighten the bolts to 15–25 ft.lbs. (21–35 Nm) in the proper sequence. Remove the clutch disc pilot tool.

12. Install the transmission into the vehicle.

13. Connect the coupling by pushing the male coupling into the slave cylinder.

14. Connect the hydraulic clutch master cylinder pushrod to the clutch pedal.

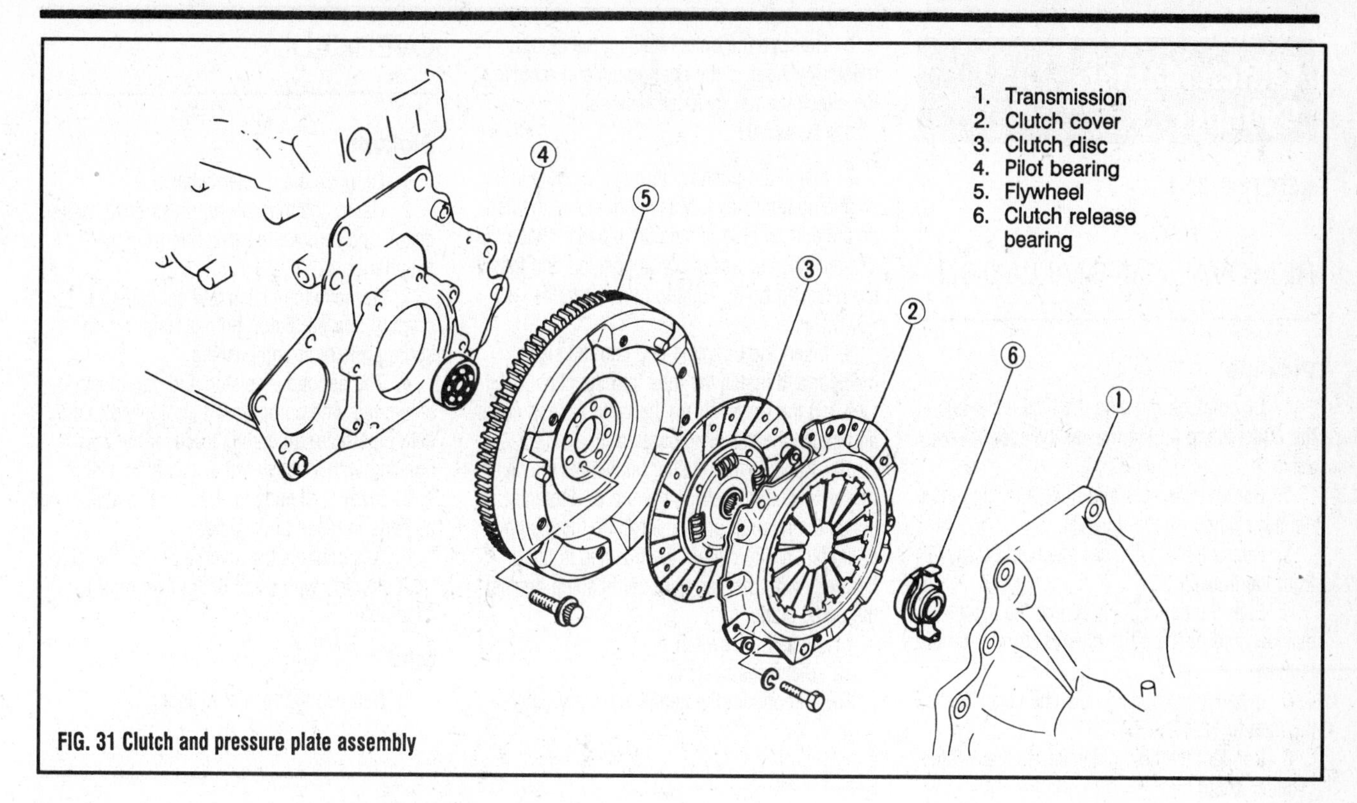

FIG. 31 Clutch and pressure plate assembly

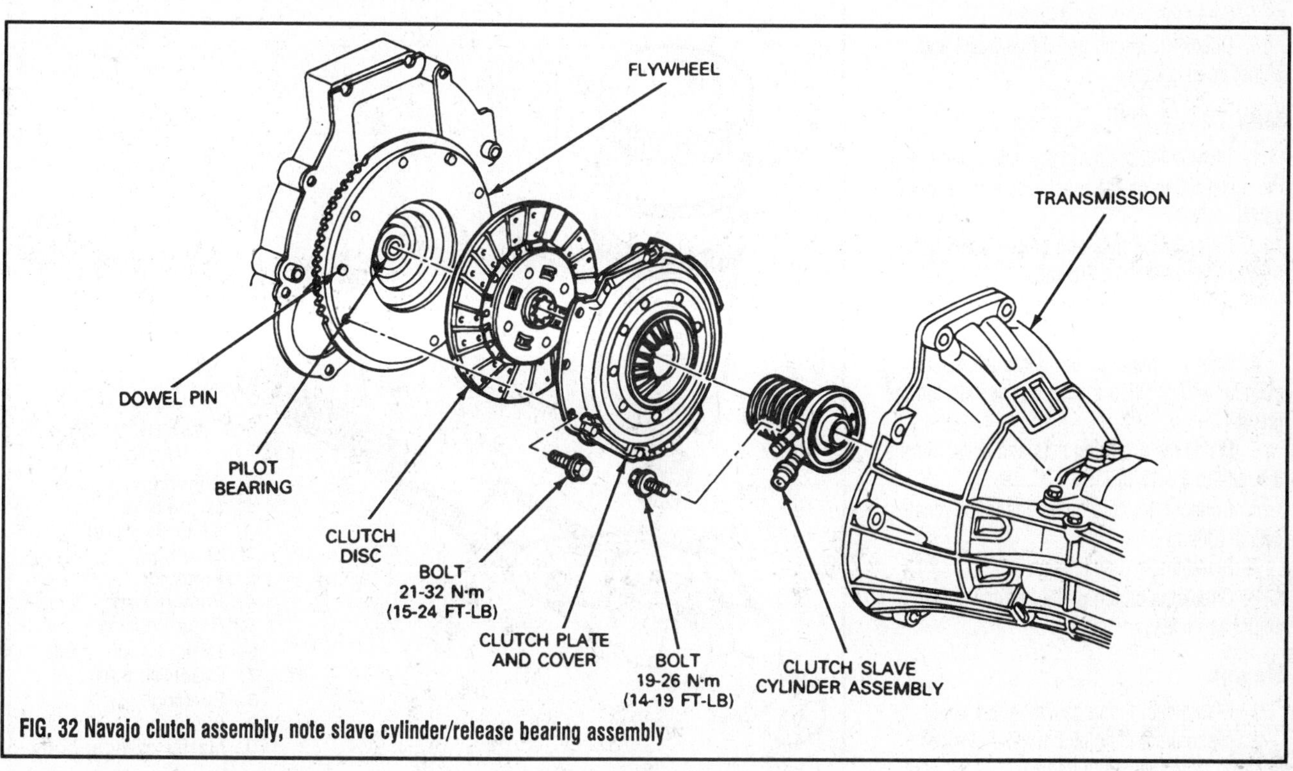

FIG. 32 Navajo clutch assembly, note slave cylinder/release bearing assembly

Clutch Master Cylinder

➧ SEE FIGS. 33-41

REMOVAL & INSTALLATION

Pickups

1. Disconnect and plug the fluid outlet line at the outlet fitting on the master cylinder one-way valve.
2. Remove the nuts and bolts attaching the master cylinder to the firewall.
3. Remove the cylinder straight out away from the firewall.
4. Start the pedal pushrod into the master cylinder and position the master cylinder on the firewall.
5. Install the attaching nuts and bolts. Torque the nuts to 12-17 ft. lbs.
6. Connect the fluid outlet line to the master cylinder fitting.
7. Bleed the hydraulic system.
8. Check the clutch pedal free-travel and adjust as necessary.

MPV

1. Disconnect and plug the fluid outlet line at the outlet fitting on the master cylinder one-way valve.
2. Remove the nuts and bolts attaching the master cylinder to the firewall.
3. Remove the cylinder straight out away from the firewall.
4. Start the pedal pushrod into the master cylinder and position the master cylinder on the firewall.
5. Install the attaching nuts and bolts. Torque the nuts to 12-17 ft. lbs.
6. Connect the fluid outlet line to the master cylinder fitting.
7. Bleed the hydraulic system.
8. Check the clutch pedal free-travel and adjust as necessary.

Navajo

1. Disconnect the negative battery cable.
2. Disconnect the clutch master cylinder pushrod from the clutch pedal.
3. Remove the switch from the master cylinder assembly, if equipped.
4. Remove the screw retaining the fluid reservoir to the cowl access cover.
5. Disconnect the tube from the slave cylinder and plug both openings.
6. Remove the bolts retaining the clutch master cylinder to the dash panel and remove the clutch master cylinder assembly.

To install:

7. Install the pushrod through the hole in the engine compartment. Make certain it is located on the correct side of the clutch pedal. Place the master cylinder assembly in position and install the retaining bolts. Tighten to 8–12 ft. lbs. (11–16Nm).
8. Insert the coupling end into the slave cylinder and install the tube into the clips.
9. Fit the reservoir on the cowl access cover and install the retaining screws.
10. Replace the retainer bushing in the clutch master cylinder pushrod if worn or damaged. Install the retainer and pushrod on the clutch pedal pin. Make certain the bushing is fitted correctly with the flange of the bushing against the pedal blade.
11. Install the switch.
12. Bleed the system.
13. Reconnect the negative battery cable.

OVERHAUL

Pickups

1. Remove the master cylinder.
2. Using snapring pliers, press down on the piston and remove the snapring from the cylinder bore.
3. Remove the piston and secondary cup, primary cup protector, primary cup, return spring, reservoir and bushing.
4. The secondary piston and cup must be blown out with compressed air applied to the fluid pipe hole. Be careful to cover the bore opening with a heavy rag to catch the piston.
5. Inspect all parts for wear or damage. Clean all parts in clean brake fluid.
6. Assembly is the reverse of disassembly. Coat all parts with clean brake fluid prior to assembly.

MPV

1. Remove the master cylinder.

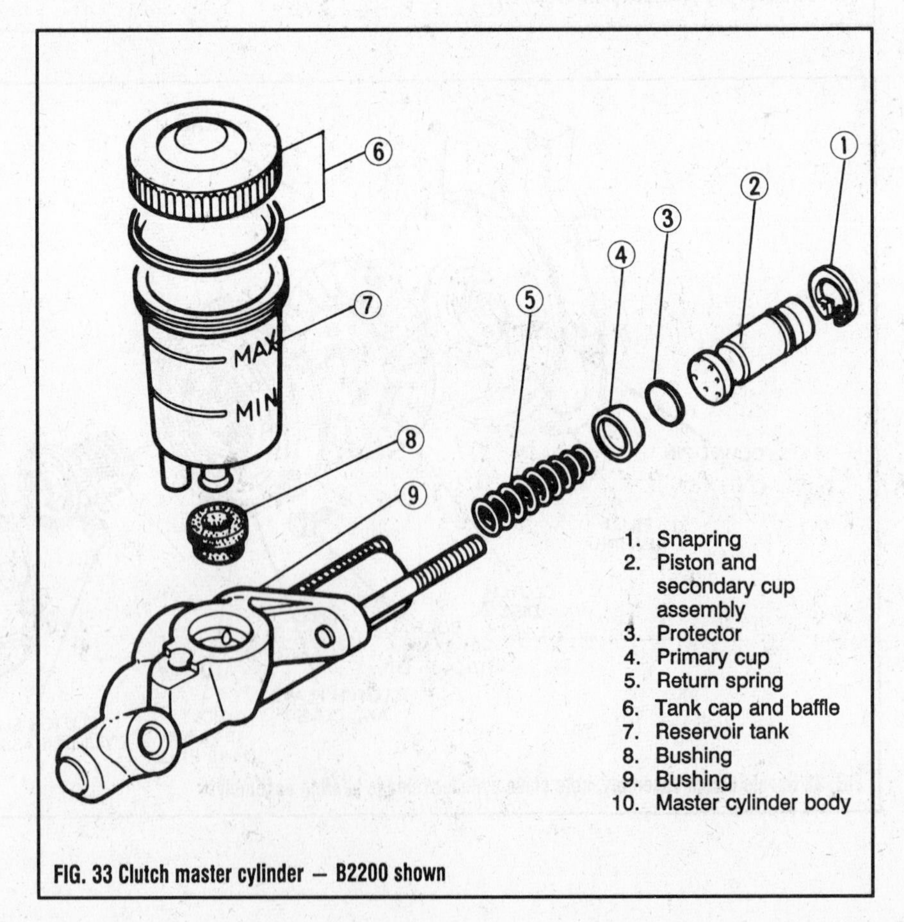

FIG. 33 Clutch master cylinder — B2200 shown

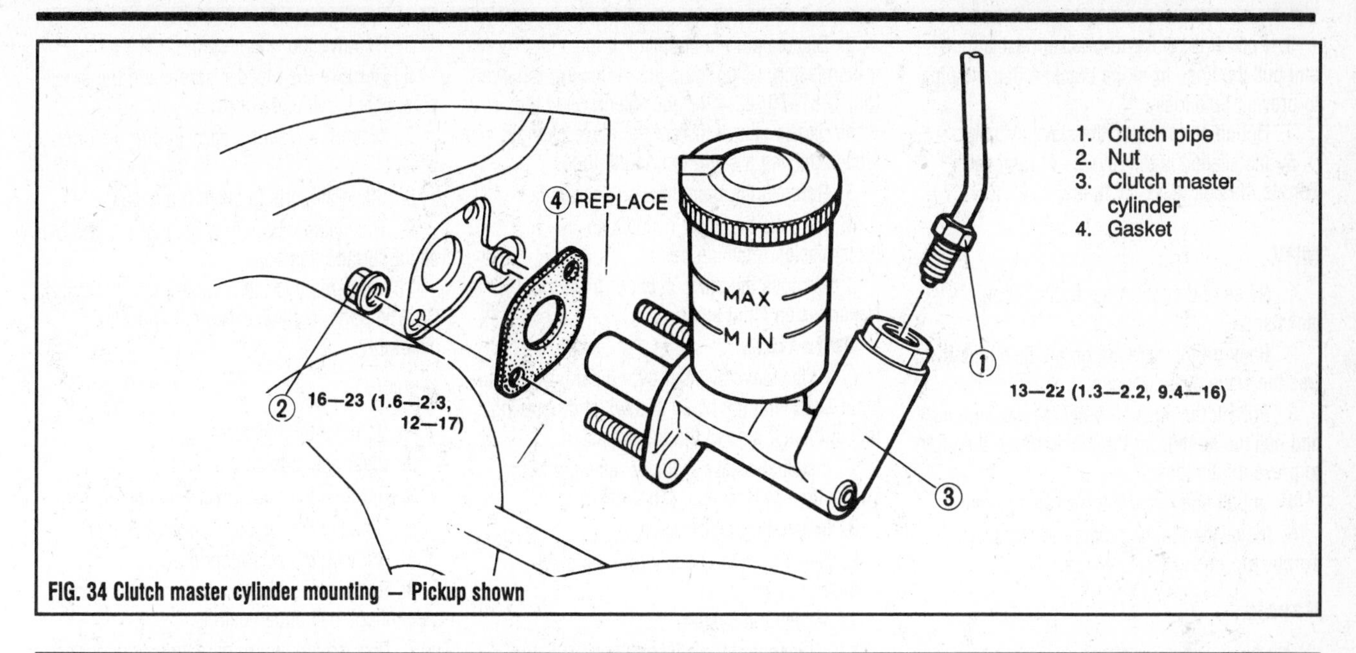

FIG. 34 Clutch master cylinder mounting — Pickup shown

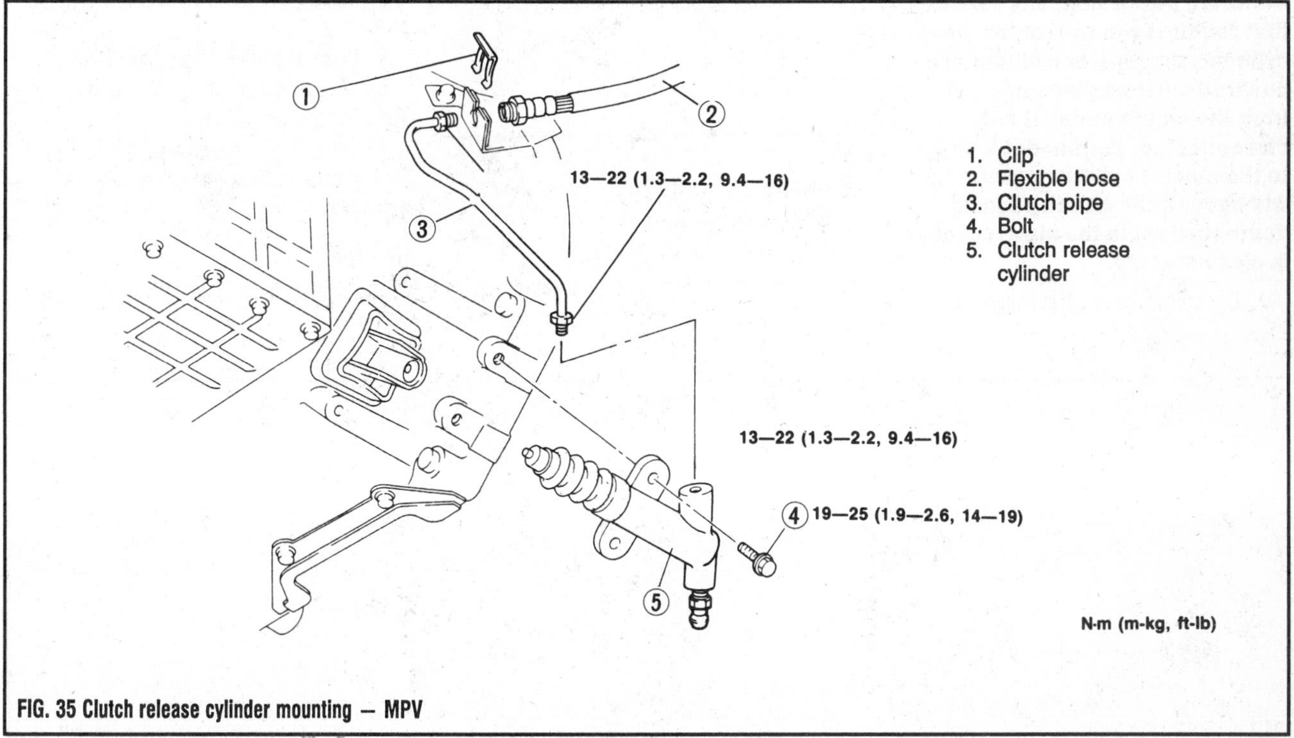

FIG. 35 Clutch release cylinder mounting — MPV

2. Using snapring pliers, press down on the piston and remove the snapring from the cylinder bore.

3. Remove the piston and secondary cup, primary cup protector, primary cup, return spring, reservoir and bushing.

4. The secondary piston and cup must be blown out with compressed air applied to the fluid pipe hole. Be careful to cover the bore opening with a heavy rag to catch the piston.

5. Inspect all parts for wear or damage. Clean all parts in clean brake fluid.

6. Assembly is the reverse of disassembly. Coat all parts with clean brake fluid prior to assembly.

ONE-WAY VALVE REMOVAL AND INSTALLATION

1. Remove the cap from the side of the master cylinder.

2. Remove the washer, one-way valve, and the spring.

3. Installation is the reverse.

Navajo

The master cylinder is not rebuildable.

Clutch Slave Cylinder

REMOVAL & INSTALLATION

Pickups

1. Raise and support the front end on jackstands.

2. Back off the flare nut on the fluid pipe to free the slave cylinder hose.

3. Pull off the hose-to-bracket retaining clip and pull the hose from the bracket. Cap the pipe to prevent fluid loss.
4. Unbolt and remove the slave cylinder.
5. Installation is the reverse of removal. Torque the bolt to 12-17 ft. lbs.

MPV

1. Raise and support the front end on jackstands.
2. Back off the flare nut on the fluid pipe to free the slave cylinder hose.
3. Pull off the hose-to-bracket retaining clip and pull the hose from the bracket. Cap the pipe to prevent fluid loss.
4. Unbolt and remove the slave cylinder.
5. Installation is the reverse of removal. Torque the bolt to 12-17 ft. lbs.

Navajo

➡ **Before performing any service that requires removal of the slave cylinder, the master cylinder and pushrod must be disconnected from the clutch pedal. If not disconnected, permanent damage to the master cylinder assembly will occur if the clutch pedal is depressed while the slave cylinder is disconnected.**

1. Disconnect the negative battery cable.
2. Disconnect the coupling at the transmission, using the clutch coupling removal tool T88T–70522–A or equivalent. Slide the white plastic sleeve toward the slave cylinder while applying a slight tug on the tube.
3. Remove the transmission assembly.
4. Remove the slave cylinder-to-transmission retaining bolts.
5. Remove the slave cylinder from the transmission input shaft.

To install:

6. Fit the slave cylinder over the transmission input shaft with the bleed screws and coupling facing the left side of the transmission.
7. Install the slave cylinder retaining bolts. Torque to 13–19 ft. lbs. (18–26Nm).
8. Install the transmission.
9. Reconnect the coupling to the slave cylinder.
10. Bleed the system.
11. Reconnect the negative battery cable.

OVERHAUL

Pickups

1. Remove the cylinder.
2. Clean the outside thoroughly.
3. Remove the dust cover and release rod.
4. Remove the piston from the cylinder.
5. Remove the return spring.
6. Remove the bleeder screw and the small steel check ball underneath it.
7. Discard any worn, damaged or distorted parts.
8. Clean all parts in clean brake fluid.
9. The cylinder bore may be honed to remove slight surface damage.
10. Assembly is the reverse of disassembly. Coat all parts in clean brake fluid prior to assembly.

MPV

1. Remove the cylinder.
2. Clean the outside thoroughly.
3. Remove the dust cover and release rod.
4. Remove the piston from the cylinder.
5. Remove the return spring.
6. Remove the bleeder screw and the small steel check ball underneath it.
7. Discard any worn, damaged or distorted parts.
8. Clean all parts in clean brake fluid.
9. The cylinder bore may be honed to remove slight surface damage.
10. Assembly is the reverse of disassembly. Coat all parts in clean brake fluid prior to assembly.

Navajo

The slave cylinder is not rebuildable.

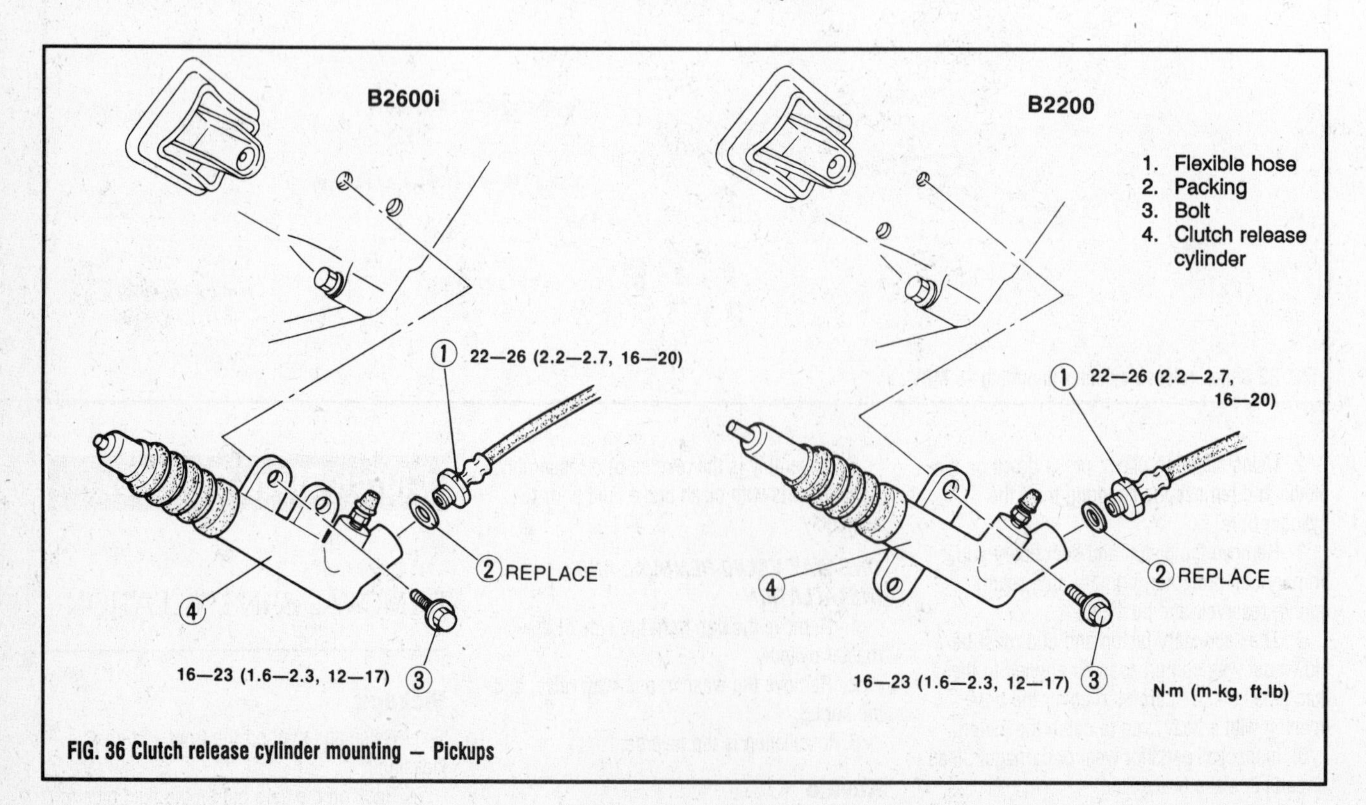

FIG. 36 Clutch release cylinder mounting — Pickups

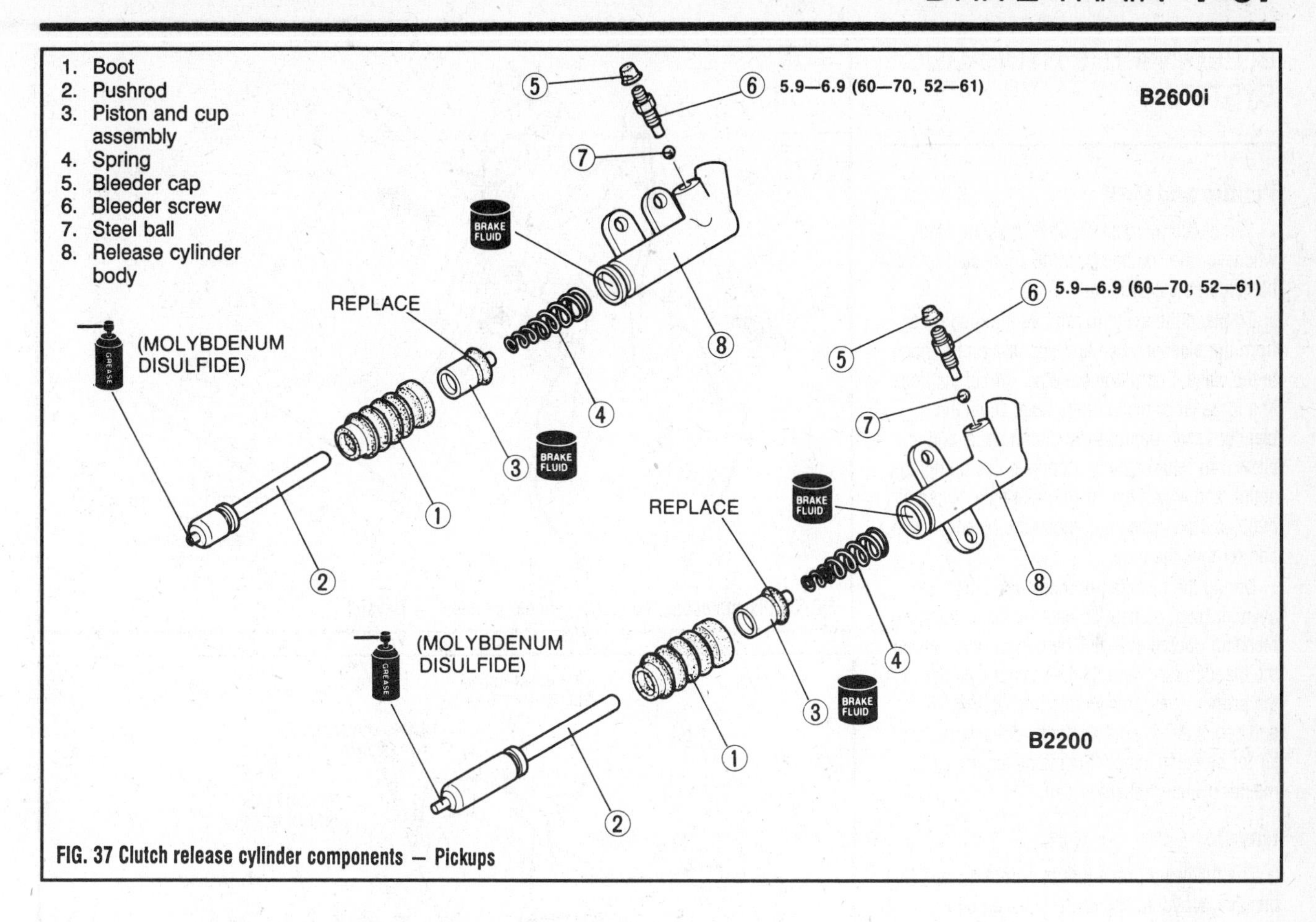

FIG. 37 Clutch release cylinder components — Pickups

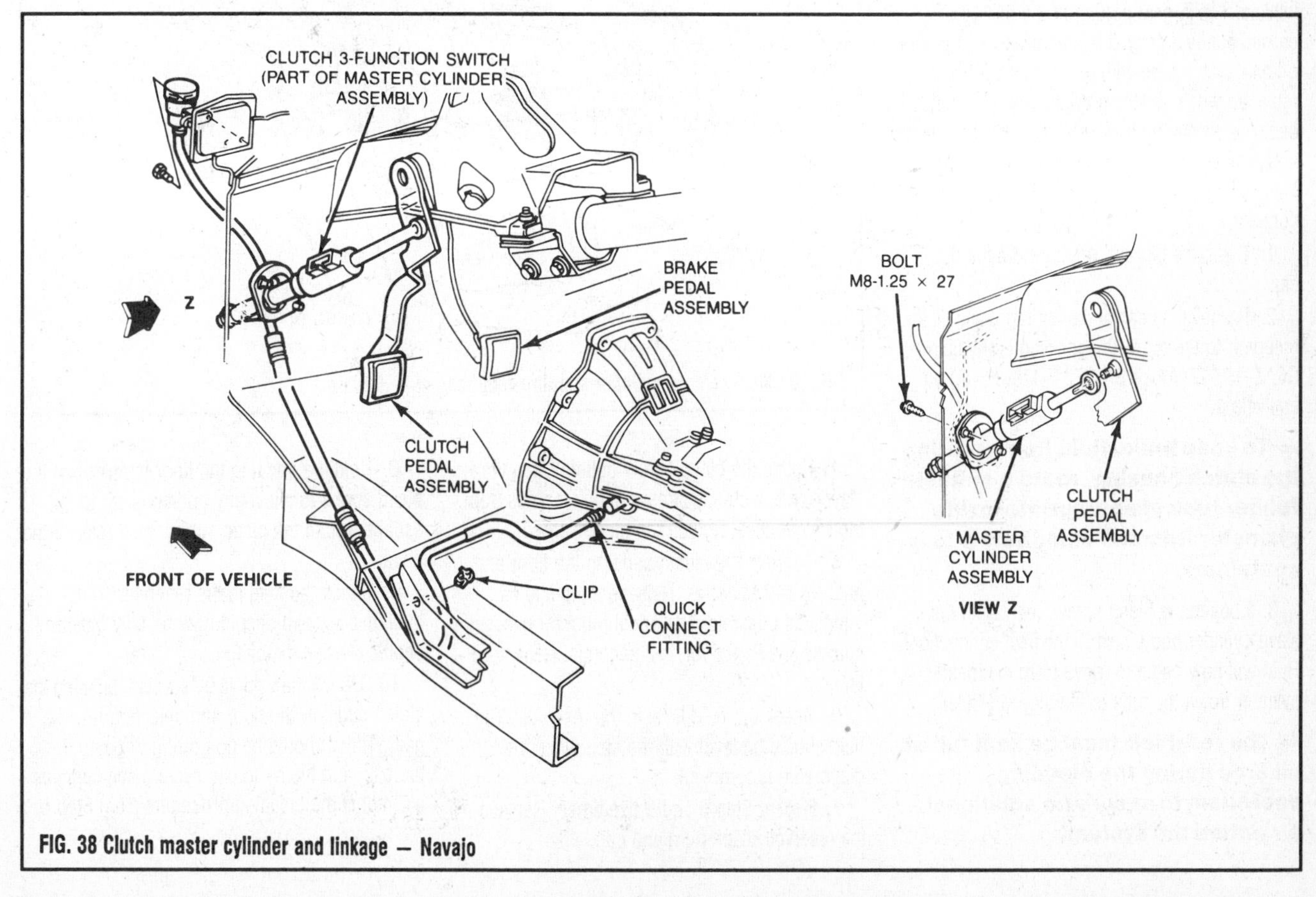

FIG. 38 Clutch master cylinder and linkage — Navajo

BLEEDING THE HYDRAULIC SYSTEM

Pickup and MPV

The clutch hydraulic system must be bled whenever the line has been disconnected or air has entered the system.

To bleed the system, remove the rubber cap from the bleeder valve and attach a rubber hose to the valve. Submerge the other end of the hose in a large jar of clean brake fluid. Open the bleeder valve. Depress the clutch pedal and allow it to return slowly. Continue this pumping action and watch the jar of brake fluid. When air bubbles stop appearing, close the bleeder valve and remove the tube.

During the bleeding process, the master cylinder must be kept at least 3/4 full. After the bleeding operation is finished, install the cap on the bleeder valve and fill the master cylinder to the proper level. Always use fresh brake fluid, and above all, do not use the fluid that was in the jar for bleeding, since it contains air. Install the master cylinder reservoir cap.

Navajo

The following procedure is recommended for bleeding a hydraulic system installed on the vehicle. The largest portion of the filling is carried out by gravity. It is recommended that the original clutch tube with quick connect be replaced when servicing the hydraulic system because air can be trapped in the quick connect and prevent complete bleeding of the system. The replacement tube does not include a quick connect.

1. Clean the dirt and grease from the dust cap.
2. Remove the cap and diaphragm and fill the reservoir to the top with approved brake fluid C6AZ–19542–AA or BA, (ESA–M6C25–A) or equivalent.

➡ To keep brake fluid from entering the clutch housing, route a suitable rubber tube of appropriate inside diameter from the bleed screw to a container.

3. Loosen the bleed screw, located in the slave cylinder body, next to the inlet connection. Fluid will now begin to move from the master cylinder down the tube to the slave cylinder.

➡ The reservoir must be kept full at all time during the bleeding operation, to ensure no additional air enters the system.

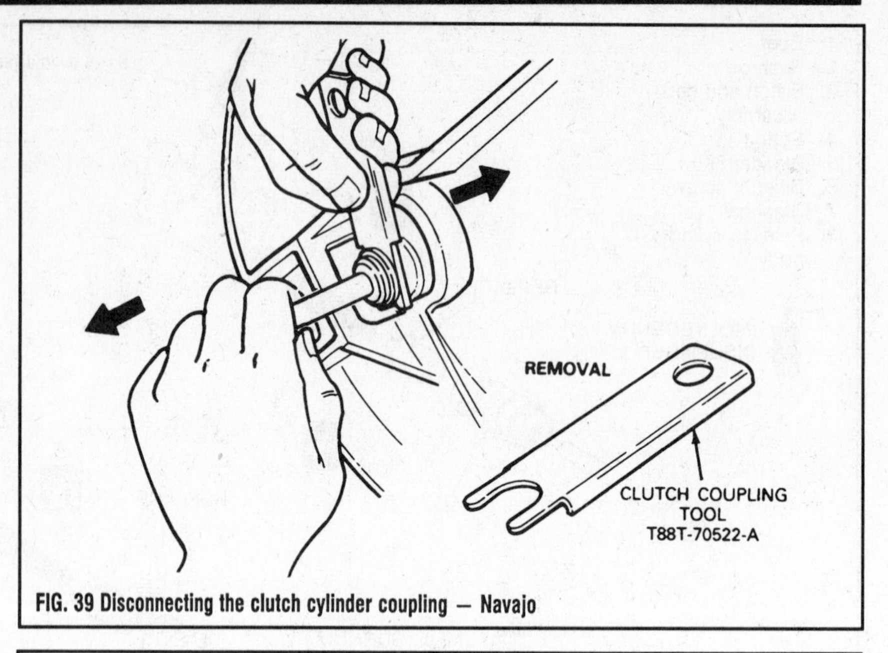

FIG. 39 Disconnecting the clutch cylinder coupling — Navajo

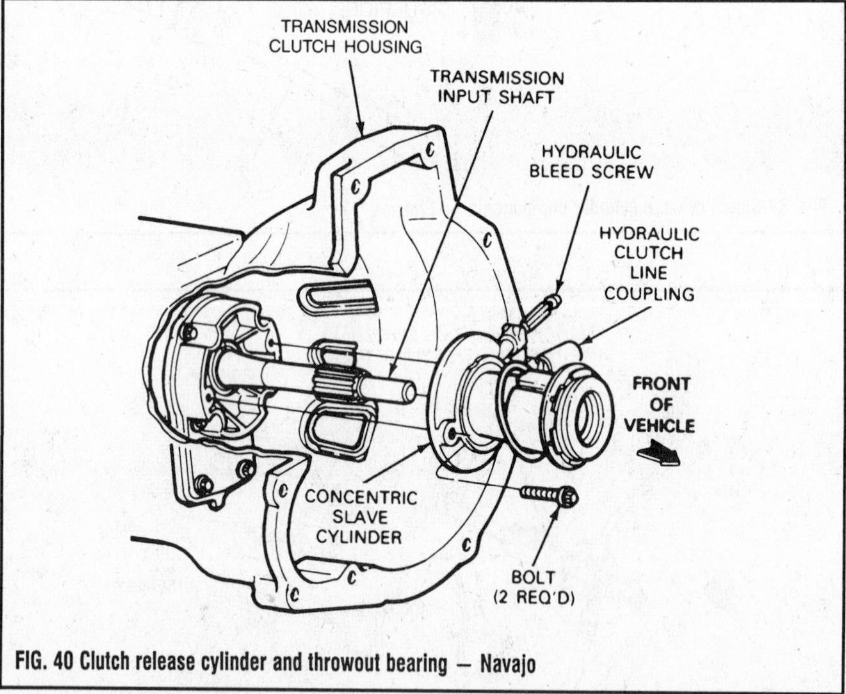

FIG. 40 Clutch release cylinder and throwout bearing — Navajo

4. Notice the bleed screw outlet. When the slave is full, a steady stream of fluid comes from the slave outlet. Tighten the bleed screw.
5. Depress the clutch pedal to the floor and hold for 1–2 seconds. Release the pedal as rapidly as possible. The pedal must be released completely. Pause for 1–2 seconds. Repeat 10 times.
6. Check the fluid level in the reservoir. The fluid should be level with the step when the diaphragm is removed.
7. Repeat Step 5 and 6 five times. Replace the reservoir diaphragm and cap.
8. Hold the pedal to the floor, crack open the bleed screw to allow any additional air to escape. Close the bleed screw, then release the pedal.
9. Check the fluid in the reservoir. The hydraulic system should now be fully bled and should release the clutch.
10. Check the vehicle by starting, pushing the clutch pedal to the floor and selecting reverse gear. There should be no grating of gears. If there is, and the hydraulic system still contains air, repeat the bleeding procedure from Step 5.

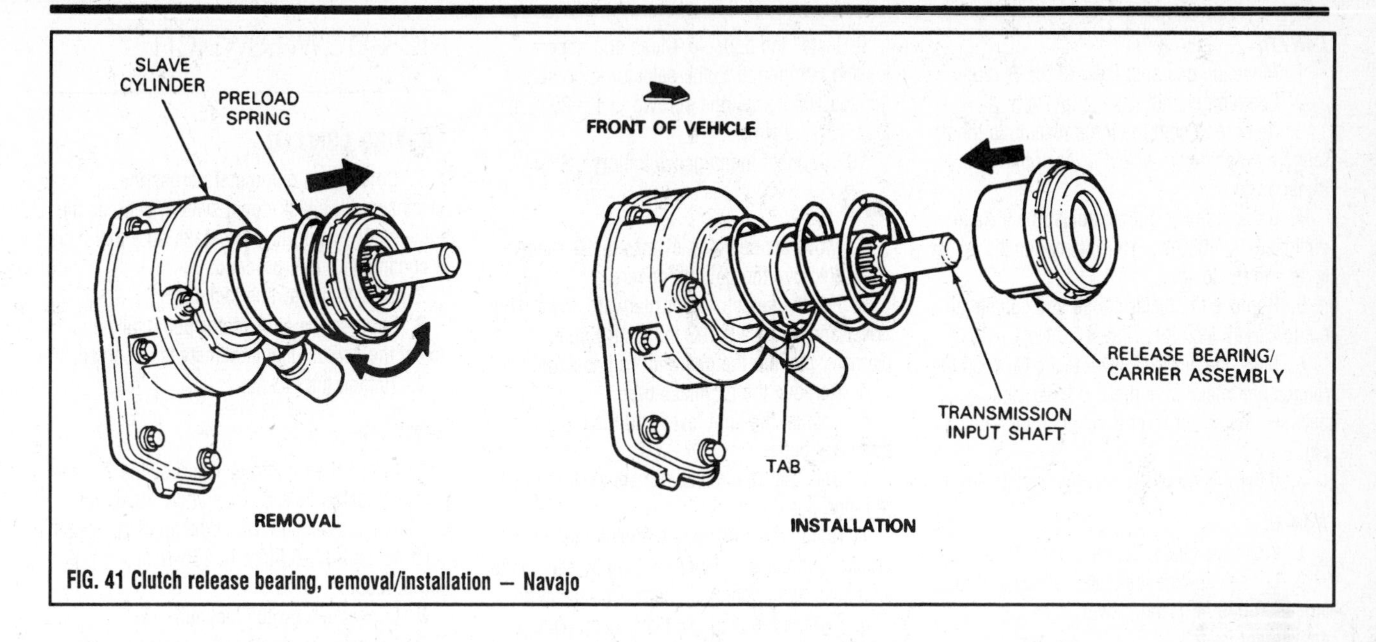

FIG. 41 Clutch release bearing, removal/installation — Navajo

AUTOMATIC TRANSMISSION

Application

Pickups

In 1987, a 3-speed lock-up torque converter transmission was introduced. Its designation is L3N71B. It was offered only on the B2200. There are no band adjustments. This unit continued on the B2200 through 1988.

Also in 1987 a 4-speed unit was offered as an option on the B2200 and as standard on the B2600. It is designated L4N71B. This unit continues through 1988.

In 1989, only the L4N71B is offered on pickups.

For 1990-92 the N4A-HL 4-speed is used on all 4-cylinder pickups and 2WD 6-cylinder pickups. 4WD 6-cylinder pickups use the electronically controlled R4AX-EL 4-speed.

MPV

The MPV uses a 4-speed overdrive transmission called the N4A-HL. This unit is a conventional, hydraulically controlled transmission.

As an option, there is an electronically controlled 4-speed automatic designated R4A-EL. The transmission is computer controlled and has no owner serviceable or adjustable components other than the neutral start switch.

4-Wheel Drive MPVs use the R4AX-EL, which is essentially the same unit as the R4A-EL.

Navajo

The Navajo uses a Ford A4LD 4-speed transmission. Special tools will be listed by their Ford part number.

➡ **The following adjustments should be performed in the order given. Be sure that the idle speed is set before performing any adjustments.**

Fluid Usage

All transmissions use Dexron®II ATF.

Transmission Fluid Pan

REMOVAL & INSTALLATION

1. Disconnect the negative battery cable.
2. Raise and support the vehicle safely.
3. Loosen the transmission pan attaching bolts to drain the fluid from the transmission.
4. When all the fluid has drained from the transmission, remove and thoroughly clean the pan and screen. Discard the pan gasket.

To Install:

5. Place a new gasket on the pan, and install the pan on the transmission.
6. Add 3 quarts of fluid to the transmission through the filler tuber.
7. Check the fluid level. Adjust, if required.

Adjustments

SHIFT LINKAGE

Pickups

L3N71B

1. Move the gearshift lever to the **P** range.
2. Loosen shift linkage locknuts.
3. Be sure to shift the transmission to the **P** range by moving the select lever of the transmission.
4. Push and hold the gearshift lever forward with a force of approximately 22 lbs.
5. Tighten linkage locknuts.

L4N71B

1. Move the gearshift lever to the **P** range.
2. Loosen the shift linkage locknuts.
3. Be sure to shift the transmission to the **P** range by moving the select lever of the transmission.
4. Using a feeler gauge, adjust the linkage until there is 0.039 in. (1mm) between the adjust lever and the locknut.
5. Remove the feeler gauge and tighten jam nut to 69–95 inch lbs. (7.8–11.0 Nm).
6. Move the gearshift lever to the **N**, **D** and **P** ranges and make sure there is clearance between the select lever bracket and the guide pin.
7. If there is no clearance, readjust the lever..

N4A-HL

1. Move the gearshift lever to the **P** range.
2. Loosen linkage locknuts so they are both at least 0.039 in. (1mm) away from the adjustment lever.
3. Shift the transmission to the **P** range by moving the manual shaft of the transmission.
4. With the link at 90 degrees to the lever, adjust the clearance using a feeler gauge to 0.039 in. (1mm) between the adjustment lever and the locknut.
5. Remove the feeler gauge and tighten the jam nut to 69–95 inch lbs. (8–11 Nm).
6. Measure the clearance between the guide plate and the guide pin in the **P** range. There should be 0.039 in. (1mm) clearance in front of the pin and 0.020 in. (0.5mm) clearance behind the pin.
7. Move the gearshift lever to the **N** and **D** ranges and check that the clearance between the guide plate and guide pin is the same in both ranges. If not, readjust.

R4AX-EL

1. Disconnect the negative battery cable to deactivate the shift-lock.
2. Remove the selector knob and console.
3. Loosen linkage locknuts and lock bolt.
4. Shift the transmission manual shaft to the **P** range.
5. Push and hold the selector lever forward with a force of approximately 22 lbs., then tighten the lock bolt to 67–95 inch lbs. (8–11 Nm).
6. Turn the locknut by hand until it just touches the spacer, then tighten the jam nut to 67–95 inch lbs. (8–11 Nm).
7. Check the lever so the clearance between the guide plate and the guide pin in the **P** range with the pushrod lightly depressed is as specified.
8. Move the selector lever to the **N** and **D** ranges and make sure there is the same clearance between the guide plate and guide pin. If not, readjust the lever.
9. Install the console. Clean and apply locking compound to the selector knob screw threads and tighten the screws to 13–26 inch lbs. (1.5–2.9 Nm).
10. Connect the negative battery cable.

MPV

1. Move the selector lever to the **P** range.
2. Remove the column covers.
3. Pull the selector lever rearward, toward the driver and insert a 0.197 in. (5mm) outer diameter pin into the gearshift rod assembly.
4. Remove the air intake tube.
5. Loosen the shift lever and the top lever mounting bolts.
6. Shift the transmission manual shaft to the **P** range position.
7. Adjust the clearance between the lower bracket and the shift lever bushing by sliding the shift lever assembly until there is no clearance.
8. Tighten the shift lever mounting bolts to 12–17 ft. lbs. (16–23 Nm).
9. Make sure the detent ball is positioned in the center of the **P** range detent. If not, loosen the linkage bolts and turn the bracket to adjust the position, then retighten the bolts to 61–87 inch lbs. (6.9–9.8 Nm).
10. Adjust the clearance between the lower bracket and the shift lever bushing by turning the top lever until there is no clearance. Tighten the top lever mounting bolt, then retighten the remaining bolt to 12–17 ft. lbs. (16–23 Nm).
11. Remove the pin from the gear shift rod assembly and install the column covers. Check selector lever operation.

Navajo

1. Raise and safely support the vehicle, as necessary. From inside the vehicle, place the column shift selector lever in the **OD** position. Hang an 8 lb. weight on the selector lever.
2. From below the vehicle, pull down the lock tab on the shift cable and remove the fitting from the transmission manual control lever ball stud.
3. Position the transmission manual control lever in the **OD** position by moving the lever all the way rearward and then moving it 3 detents forward.
4. Connect the cable end fitting to the transmission manual control lever. Push up on the lock tab to lock the cable in the correctly adjusted position.
5. Remove the 8 lb. weight from the column shift selector.
6. After adjustment, check for **P** engagement. Check the column shift selector lever in all detent positions with the engine running to ensure correct adjustment.

KICK-DOWN SWITCH

1987-89 L3N71B

1. Connect an ohmmeter across the terminals of the kick-down switch, depress the accelerator pedal fully and make sure that there is continuity. If not, proceed:
2. Loosen the switch locknut.
3. Depress the accelerator pedal fully and adjust the switch until continuity is observed.
4. Tighten the locknut.

L4N71B

1. Connect an ohmmeter across the 2 lower terminals of the kick-down switch. Make sure that there is continuity when the tip of the switch is depressed 6.0-6.5mm (0.236-0.256 in.). If not, proceed:
2. Loosen the switch locknut.
3. Depress the accelerator pedal fully and adjust the switch until continuity is observed when the tip of the switch is depressed 6.0-6.5mm (0.236-0.256 in.).
4. Tighten the locknut.

N4A-HL

1. Connect an ohmmeter across the 2 lower terminals of the kick-down switch. Make sure that there is continuity when the tip of the switch is depressed 6.0-6.5mm. If not, proceed:
2. Disconnect the wiring.
3. Loosen the switch locknut and back the switch out fully.
4. Depress the accelerator pedal fully and hold it.
5. With the pedal held down, turn the kick-down switch clockwise until a click is heard, then, turn it 1/4 turn further.
6. Tighten the locknut.
7. Release the pedal and reconnect the wiring.
8. Apply 12 volts to the kick-down solenoid and observe that a click is heard. If not, replace the solenoid.

KICKDOWN CABLE

A4LD transmission

The kickdown cable is self-adjusting over a tolerance range of 1 in. (25mm). If the cable requires readjustment, reset the by depressing the semi-circular metal tab on the self-adjuster mechanism and pulling the cable forward (toward the front of the vehicle) to the "Zero" position setting. The cable will then automatically readjust to the proper length when kicked down.

MANUAL LINKAGE

L3N71B

1. Place the shift lever in **P**.
2. Loosen the 3 locknuts on the linkage trunion.
3. Move the transmission lever to the **P** range.
4. Apply a forward force of about 20 lbs. to the shift handle and tighten the locknuts to 95 inch lbs.
5. Move the shift handle to **N**, **P**, and **D** ranges. Make sure that there is clearance between the select lever bracket and guide pin. If there is no clearance, adjust the lever by adjusting the locknuts.

L4N71B

1. Place the shift lever in **P**.
2. Remove the shifter boot.
3. Loosen the 2 locknuts on the cable at the base of the shifter.
4. Raise and support the truck on jackstands.
5. Move the transmission lever to the **P** range.
6. Using a feeler gauge, turn the locknuts until there is 1mm (0.039 in.) clearance between the forward locknut and the adjust lever.
7. Tighten the rear locknut.
8. Move the shift handle to **N**, **P**, and **D** ranges. Make sure that there is clearance between the select lever bracket and guide pin. If there is no clearance, adjust the lever by adjusting the locknuts.

A4LD

Before the linkage is adjusted, be sure the engine idle speed and anti-stall dashpot are properly adjusted.

1. Position the transmission selector control lever in **D** position and loosen the trunion bolt.

➡ Make sure that the shift lever detent pawl is held against the rearward Drive detent stop during the linkage adjustment procedure.

2. Position the transmission manual lever in the **D** position, by moving the bellcrank lever all the way rearward, then forward 3 detents.
3. With the transmission selector lever/manual lever in the **D** position, apply light forward pressure to the shifter control tower arm while tightening the trunion bolt to 12–23 ft. lbs. Forward pressure on the shifter lower arm will ensure correct positioning within the **D** detent as noted in Step 1.

After adjustment, check for Park engagement. The control lever must move to the right when engaged in Park. Check the transmission control lever in all detent positions with the engine running to ensure correct detent transmission action. Readjust if necessary.

NEUTRAL SAFETY/BACK-UP LIGHT SWITCH

L3N71B
L4N71B

The switch is located on the right side of the transmission case.

1. Adjust the manual linkage.
2. Place the shift lever in Neutral.
3. Loosen the switch attaching bolts. Remove the screw from the alignment pin hole at the bottom of the switch.
4. Rotate the switch and insert an alignment pin, 2mm (0.0787 in.) diameter into the alignment pin hole and internal rotor.
5. Tighten the two switch attaching bolts and remove the alignment pin.
6. Reinstall the alignment pin hole screw in the switch body.
7. Check the operation of the switch. The engine should start, only with the transmission selector lever in Neutral or Park. The back-up lights should come on, only with the lever in Reverse.
8. If the switch is defective, replace it by simply removing the attaching screws and disconnecting the wiring.

MPV w/N4A-HL

The switch is located on the right side of the transmission case.

1. Adjust the manual linkage.
2. Place the shift lever in Neutral.
3. Loosen the switch attaching bolts. Remove the screw from the alignment pin hole at the bottom of the switch.
4. Rotate the switch and insert an alignment pin, 2mm diameter into the alignment pin hole and internal rotor.
5. Tighten the two switch attaching bolts and remove the alignment pin.
6. Reinstall the alignment pin hole screw in the switch body.
7. Check the operation of the switch. The engine should start, only with the transmission selector lever in Neutral or Park. The back-up lights should come on, only with the lever in Reverse.
8. If the switch is defective, replace it by simply removing the attaching screws and disconnecting the wiring.

MPV w/R4A-EL

1. Place the shift lever in Neutral.
2. Loosen the switch attaching bolts.
3. Rotate the switch and insert an alignment pin, 4mm diameter, into the alignment pin hole and lever.
4. Tighten the two switch attaching bolts and remove the alignment pin.
5. Check the operation of the switch. The engine should start, only with the transmission selector lever in Neutral or Park. The back-up lights should come on, only with the lever in Reverse.
6. If the switch is defective, replace it by simply removing the attaching screws and disconnecting the wiring.

A4LD

The switch is not adjustable. If it is defective, replace by:

1. Disconnect the negative battery cable.
2. Raise and support the vehicle safely.
3. Disconnect the harness connector from the neutral start switch.
4. Clean the area around the switch. Remove the switch and O-ring, using a thin wall socket (tool T74P–77247–A or equivalent).

To Install:

5. Fit a new O-ring to the switch. Install the switch.
6. Reconnect the harness connector to the switch.
7. Lower the vehicle.
8. Reconnect the negative battery cable.
9. Check the operation of the switch, with the parking brake engaged. The engine should only start in **N** or **P**. The back-up lamps should come ON only in **R**.

Vacuum Diaphragm

REMOVAL & INSTALLATION

A4LD Transmission

1. Disconnect the negative battery cable.
2. Raise and support the vehicle safely.
3. Disconnect the hose from the vacuum diaphragm.
4. Remove the vacuum diaphragm retaining clamp bolt and clamp. Do not pry on the clamp.
5. Pull the vacuum diaphragm from the transmission case and remove the vacuum diaphragm control rod from the transmission case.

To Install:

6. Install the vacuum diaphragm control rod from the transmission case.
7. Push the vacuum diaphragm into the case and secure it with the clamp and bolt. Tighten to 80–106 inch lbs. (9–12Nm).

8. Fit the vacuum hose to the diaphragm.
9. Lower the vehicle.
10. Reconnect the negative battery cable.

Extension Housing Seal

REMOVAL & INSTALLATION

A4LD

1. Disconnect the negative battery cable.
2. Raise and support the vehicle safely.
3. Matchmark the driveshaft end yoke and rear axle companion flange to assure proper positioning during assembly. Remove the driveshaft.
4. Remove the oil seal from the extension housing, using seal remover T71P–7657–A or equivalent.

To install:

Before install the replacement seal, inspect the sealing surface of the universal joint yoke for scores. If scoring is found, replace the yoke.

5. Install the new seal, using seal installer T74P–77052–A or equivalent. Coat the inside diameter at the end of the rubber boot portion of the seal with long-life lubricant (C1AZ–19590–BA or equivalent).
6. Align the matchmarks and install the driveshaft.
7. Lower the vehicle.
8. Reconnect the negative battery cable.

Transmission

➧ SEE FIGS. 42-45

REMOVAL & INSTALLATION

Pickup w/L3N71B

1. Disconnect the negative cable from the battery.
2. Raise and support the truck.
3. Drain the transmission fluid but do not remove the pan. After the fluid has drained, install a few bolts to hold the pan in place, temporarily.
4. Remove the exhaust pipe bracket bolt from the right side of the converter housing.
5. Remove the splash shield and skid plate.
6. Remove the exhaust pipe flange bolts from the rear of the resonator or catalytic converter, and disconnect the pipe.
7. Matchmark and disconnect the front and or rear the driveshaft(s).
8. Disconnect the speedometer cable.
9. Disconnect the shift rod from the manual lever.
10. Remove the shift knob.
11. Remove the console.
12. On 4-wheel drive trucks, remove the 4-wheel drive shift lever plate and transfer case lever.
13. On 4-wheel drive trucks, disconnect the 4-wheel drive indicator wiring.
14. Remove the vacuum hose from the diaphragm. Disconnect the electrical connectors from the downshift solenoid and inhibitor switch, and remove their wires from the clip.
15. Disconnect and plug the cooler lines from the radiator at the transmission. Use a flare nut wrench if one is available.
16. Remove the side support plates.
17. Remove the access cover from the lower front of the converter housing.
18. Matchmark the drive plate (flywheel) and torque converter for reassembly. Remove the four bolts holding the torque converter to the drive plate.
19. Remove the bolts connecting the crossmember to the transmission.
20. Support the transmission with a jack. Remove the crossmember-to-frame bolts, and remove the crossmember.
21. Make sure that the transmission is securely supported. Secure it to the jack with a safety chain, if necessary.
22. Lower the transmission to provide working clearance, and remove the starter.
23. Remove the converter housing-to-engine bolts.
24. Remove the fluid filler tube.
25. With a pry bar, exert light pressure between the converter and the drive plate to prevent the converter from disengaging from the transmission as it is removed.
26. Lower the transmission and converter as an assembly. Be careful not to let the converter fall out.

To install:

27. Place the transmission on the jack. Be sure that the converter is properly installed.
28. Raise the transmission into place. Install the converter housing-to-engine bolts, and torque in two stages to 23-34 ft. lbs.
29. Lower the transmission on the jack and install the starter.
30. Install the fluid filler tube with a new O-ring.
31. Raise the transmission slightly, and install the crossmember to the frame. Tighten the bolts to 23-34 ft. lbs.
32. Lower the transmission and install the transmission-to-crossmember bolts. Tighten to 23-34 ft. lbs.
33. Align the matchmarks made earlier on the torque converter and drive plate. Install the four attaching bolts and torque to 25-36 ft. lbs. in three stages.
34. Install the side support plates.
35. Install the access cover. Remove the jack.
36. Connect the cooler lines.
37. On 4-wheel drive trucks, install the 4-wheel drive shift lever plate and transfer case lever.
38. On 4-wheel drive trucks, connect the 4-wheel drive indicator wiring.
39. Install the electrical connectors to the switch and solenoid, and replace the wires in the clip. Install the diaphragm vacuum hose.
40. connect the shift rod to the lever.
41. Reconnect the speedometer cable.
42. Insert the driveshaft into the transmission. Install the center bearing support. Bolt the driveshaft to the rear of the axle flange.
43. Connect the exhaust pipe to the resonator or catalytic converter, using a new gasket. Reinstall the exhaust pipe clamp onto the converter housing, and torque the bolt to 10-15 ft. lbs.
44. Install a new pan gasket and the fluid pan, if this has not already been done.
45. Install the shift knob.
46. Install the console.
47. Lower the truck. Connect the battery cable. Fill the transmission through the dipstick tube with the specified fluid, being careful not to overfill, and check for leaks.

Pickup w/L4N71B

1. Disconnect the negative cable from the battery.
2. Raise and support the truck.
3. Drain the transmission fluid but do not remove the pan. After the fluid has drained, install a few bolts to hold the pan in place, temporarily.
4. Remove the exhaust pipe.
5. Remove the splash shield.
6. Matchmark and disconnect the driveshaft.
7. Disconnect the speedometer cable.
8. Disconnect the shift rod from the manual lever.
9. Disconnect and plug the cooler lines from the radiator at the transmission. Use a flare nut wrench if one is available.
10. Remove the side support plates.
11. Remove the access cover from the lower front of the converter housing.

12. Matchmark the drive plate (flywheel) and torque converter for reassembly. Remove the four bolts holding the torque converter to the drive plate.

13. Remove the bolts connecting the crossmember to the transmission.

14. Support the transmission with a jack. Remove the crossmember-to-frame bolts, and remove the crossmember.

15. Make sure that the transmission is securely supported. Secure it to the jack with a safety chain, if necessary.

16. Lower the transmission to provide working clearance, and remove the starter.

17. Remove the converter housing-to-engine bolts.

18. Remove the fluid filler tube.

19. With a pry bar, exert light pressure between the converter and the drive plate to prevent the converter from disengaging from the transmission as it is removed.

20. Lower the transmission and converter as an assembly. Be careful not to let the converter fall out.

To Install:

21. Place the transmission on the jack. Be sure that the converter is properly installed.

22. Raise the transmission into place. Install the converter housing-to-engine bolts, and torque in two stages to 23-34 ft. lbs.

23. Lower the transmission on the jack and install the starter.

24. Install the fluid filler tube with a new O-ring.

25. Raise the transmission slightly, and install the crossmember to the frame. Tighten the bolts to 23-34 ft. lbs.

26. Lower the transmission and install the transmission-to-crossmember bolts. Tighten to 23-34 ft. lbs.

27. Align the matchmarks made earlier on the torque converter and drive plate. Install the four attaching bolts and torque to 25-36 ft. lbs. in three stages.

28. Install the side support plates.

29. Install the access cover. Remove the jack.

30. Connect the cooler lines.

31. Install the electrical connectors to the switch and solenoid, and replace the wires in the clip. Install the diaphragm vacuum hose.

32. Connect the shift rod to the lever.

33. Reconnect the speedometer cable.

34. Insert the driveshaft into the transmission. Install the center bearing support. Bolt the driveshaft to the rear of the axle flange.

35. Connect the exhaust pipe to the resonator or catalytic converter, using a new gasket. Reinstall the exhaust pipe clamp onto the converter housing, and torque the bolt to 10-15 ft. lbs.

36. Install a new pan gasket and the fluid pan, if this has not already been done.

37. Lower the truck. Connect the battery cable. Fill the transmission through the dipstick tube with the specified fluid, being careful not to overfill, and check for leaks.

Pickup w/N4A-HL 2WD

1. Disconnect the negative battery cable. Raise and safely support the vehicle.

2. Drain the transmission fluid.

3. Mark the position of the driveshaft on the axle flange and remove the driveshaft.

4. Disconnect the speedometer cable, vacuum hose and shift lever. Remove the vacuum line bracket from the transmission.

5. Remove the gusset plates and bellhousing cover.

6. Remove the torque converter attaching bolts from the flywheel.

7. Support the transmission and engine with jacks.

8. Remove the transmission mount and mount bracket.

9. Tag and disconnect the electrical connectors from the neutral safety switch, kickdown solenoid and overdrive cancel solenoid.

10. Remove the transmission fluid dipstick and tube.

11. Disconnect and plug the transmission fluid lines.

12. Remove the transmission.

To Install:

13. Raise the transmission into position. Install the transmission-to-engine bolts and tighten to 27–38 ft. lbs. (37–52 Nm).

14. Unplug and connect the transmission fluid lines. Tighten the banjo bolts to 17–26 ft. lbs. (24–35 Nm).

15. Install the transmission fluid dipstick and tube.

16. Connect the electrical connectors.

17. Install the transmission mount and tighten the bolts to 7.2–17 ft. lbs. (9.8–23 Nm). Install the mount bracket to the crossmember and tighten the bolts to 23–34 ft. lbs. (31–46 Nm). Install the mount-to-mount bracket bolts to 23–34 ft. lbs. (31–46 Nm).

18. Remove the support jacks.

19. Install the torque converter attaching bolts and tighten to 25–36 ft. lbs. (34–49 Nm).

20. Install the gusset plates and bellhousing cover. Tighten the gusset plate bolts to 27–38 ft. lbs. (37–52 Nm).

21. Connect the shift lever, vacuum hose and speedometer cable. Attach the vacuum line bracket.

22. Install the driveshaft and lower the vehicle.

23. Connect the negative battery cable. Fill the transmission with the proper type and quantity of fluid.

24. Check the transmission for leaks and proper operation.

Pickup w/R4AX-EL 4WD

1. Disconnect the negative battery cable.

2. Remove the shifter knob and the console box.

3. Remove the insulator plate and boot. Remove the 4WD shift lever.

4. Raise and safely support the vehicle. Remove the splash shields and drain the transmission fluid.

5. Disconnect and remove the front exhaust pipe.

6. Mark the position of the driveshaft on the flanges and remove the driveshafts.

7. Disconnect the speedometer cable and the 4WD indicator switch connector, if equipped.

8. Disconnect the shift cable and vacuum hose, if equipped.

9. Remove the gusset plate, if equipped.

10. On 1990–92 vehicles, loosen the front differential mounting bolts and remove the No. 2 crossmember.

11. Remove the torque converter attaching bolts.

12. Support the transmission and engine with jacks. Remove the transmission-to-engine bolts.

13. Disconnect and plug the transmission fluid lines at the transmission. Remove the bracket from the transmission.

14. Remove the rear transmission crossmember.

15. Tag and disconnect the electrical connectors at the transmission.

16. Remove the transmission dipstick and tube.

17. Lower the transmission from the vehicle.

To Install:

18. Raise the transmission into position and install the transmission-to-engine bolts. Tighten to 27–38 ft. lbs. (37–52 Nm).

19. Install the dipstick and tube.

20. Connect the electrical connectors.

21. Install the rear transmission crossmember and tighten the transmission-to-chassis bolts to 23–34 ft. lbs. (31–46 Nm).

22. Lower the transmission to the crossmember and install the mount-to-crossmember nuts. Tighten to 23–34 ft. lbs. (31–46 Nm). Remove the jacks.

23. Connect the transmission fluid lines to the transmission and tighten the banjo bolts to 17–26 ft. lbs. (24–35 Nm). Attach the fluid line bracket.

24. Install the torque converter attaching bolts and tighten to 27–40 ft. lbs. (36–54 Nm). Install the bellhousing cover.
25. Install the No. 2 crossmember.
26. Install the gusset plates, if equipped.
27. Connect the shifter cable and the bracket, if equipped. Connect the speedometer cable.
28. Install the driveshafts, aligning the marks that were made during removal.
29. Install the front exhaust pipe and the splash shields. Lower the vehicle.
30. Install the 4WD shift lever and the insulator plate and boot.
31. Install the console box and the shifter knob.
32. Connect the negative battery cable. Fill the transmission with the proper type and quantity of fluid.
33. Check the transmission for leaks and proper operation.

MPV w/N4A-HL

1. Disconnect the negative cable from the battery.
2. Raise and support the van.
3. Drain the transmission fluid but do not remove the pan. After the fluid has drained, install a few bolts to hold the pan in place, temporarily.
4. Disconnect the speedometer cable.
5. Disconnect all electrical wiring at the transmission.
6. Remove the splash shield.
7. Matchmark and disconnect the driveshaft.
8. Remove the linkage.
9. Remove the filler tube.
10. Remove the heat shield.
11. Remove the exhaust pipe.
12. Disconnect and plug the cooler lines from the radiator at the transmission. Use a flare nut wrench if one is available.
13. Remove the side support plates.
14. Remove the access cover from the lower front of the converter housing.
15. Matchmark the drive plate (flywheel) and torque converter for reassembly. Remove the four bolts holding the torque converter to the drive plate.
16. Remove the starter.
17. Remove the vacuum pipe.
18. Remove the bolts connecting the crossmember to the transmission.
19. Support the transmission with a jack. Remove the crossmember-to-frame bolts, and remove the crossmember.
20. Make sure that the transmission is securely supported. Secure it to the jack with a safety chain, if necessary.
21. Remove the converter housing-to-engine bolts.

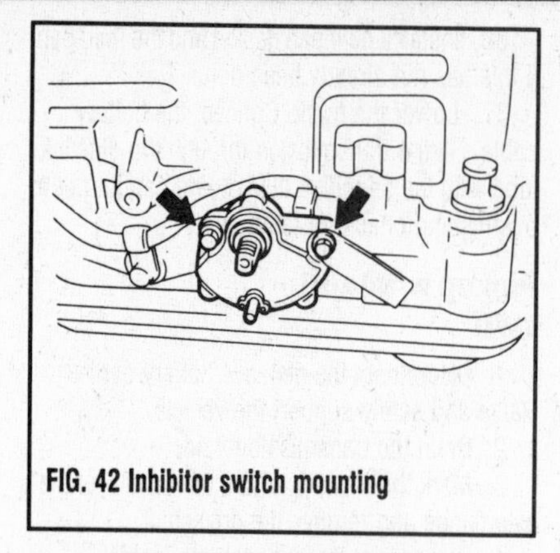

FIG. 42 Inhibitor switch mounting

22. With a pry bar, exert light pressure between the converter and the drive plate to prevent the converter from disengaging from the transmission as it is removed.
23. Lower the transmission and converter as an assembly. Be careful not to let the converter fall out.

To install:

24. Place the transmission on the jack. Be sure that the converter is properly installed.
25. Raise the transmission into place. Install the converter housing-to-engine bolts, and torque in two stages to 23-34 ft. lbs.
26. Lower the transmission on the jack and install the starter.
27. Install the fluid filler tube with a new O-ring.
28. Raise the transmission slightly, and install the crossmember to the frame. Tighten the bolts to 23-34 ft. lbs.
29. Lower the transmission and install the transmission-to-crossmember bolts. Tighten to 23-34 ft. lbs.
30. Align the matchmarks made earlier on the torque converter and drive plate. Install the four attaching bolts and torque to 25-36 ft. lbs. in three stages.
31. Install the side support plates.
32. Install the access cover. Remove the jack.
33. Connect the cooler lines.
34. Install the electrical connectors, and replace the wires in the clip. Install the vacuum hose.
35. Connect the shift rod to the lever.
36. Reconnect the speedometer cable.
37. Insert the driveshaft into the transmission. Install the center bearing support. Bolt the driveshaft to the rear of the axle flange.
38. Connect the exhaust pipe to the resonator or catalytic converter, using a new gasket. Reinstall the exhaust pipe clamp onto the converter housing, and torque the bolt to 10-15 ft. lbs.
39. Install a new pan gasket and the fluid pan, if this has not already been done.
40. Lower the truck. Connect the battery cable. Fill the transmission through the dipstick tube with the specified fluid, being careful not to overfill, and check for leaks.

MPV w/R4A-EL

1. Disconnect the negative cable from the battery.
2. Raise and support the van.
3. Drain the transmission fluid but do not remove the pan. After the fluid has drained, install a few bolts to hold the pan in place, temporarily.
4. Disconnect the speedometer cable.
5. Label for identification and location and then disconnect all electrical wiring at the transmission.
6. Remove the splash shield.
7. Matchmark and disconnect the driveshaft.
8. Remove the linkage.
9. Remove the filler tube.
10. Remove the heat shield.
11. Remove the exhaust pipe.
12. Disconnect and plug the cooler lines from the radiator at the transmission. Use a flare nut wrench if one is available.
13. Remove the side support plates.
14. Remove the access cover from the lower front of the converter housing.
15. Matchmark the drive plate (flywheel) and torque converter for reassembly. Remove the four bolts holding the torque converter to the drive plate.
16. Remove the starter.
17. Remove the vacuum pipe.
18. Remove the bolts connecting the crossmember to the transmission.
19. Support the transmission with a jack. Remove the crossmember-to-frame bolts, and remove the crossmember.
20. Make sure that the transmission is securely supported. Secure it to the jack with a safety chain, if necessary.
21. Remove the converter housing-to-engine bolts.
22. With a pry bar, exert light pressure between the converter and the drive plate to prevent the converter from disengaging from the transmission as it is removed.
23. Lower the transmission and converter as an assembly. Be careful not to let the converter fall out.

To install:

24. Place the transmission on the jack. Be sure that the converter is properly installed.
25. Raise the transmission into place. Install the converter housing-to-engine bolts, and torque in two stages to 23-34 ft. lbs.
26. Lower the transmission on the jack and install the starter.

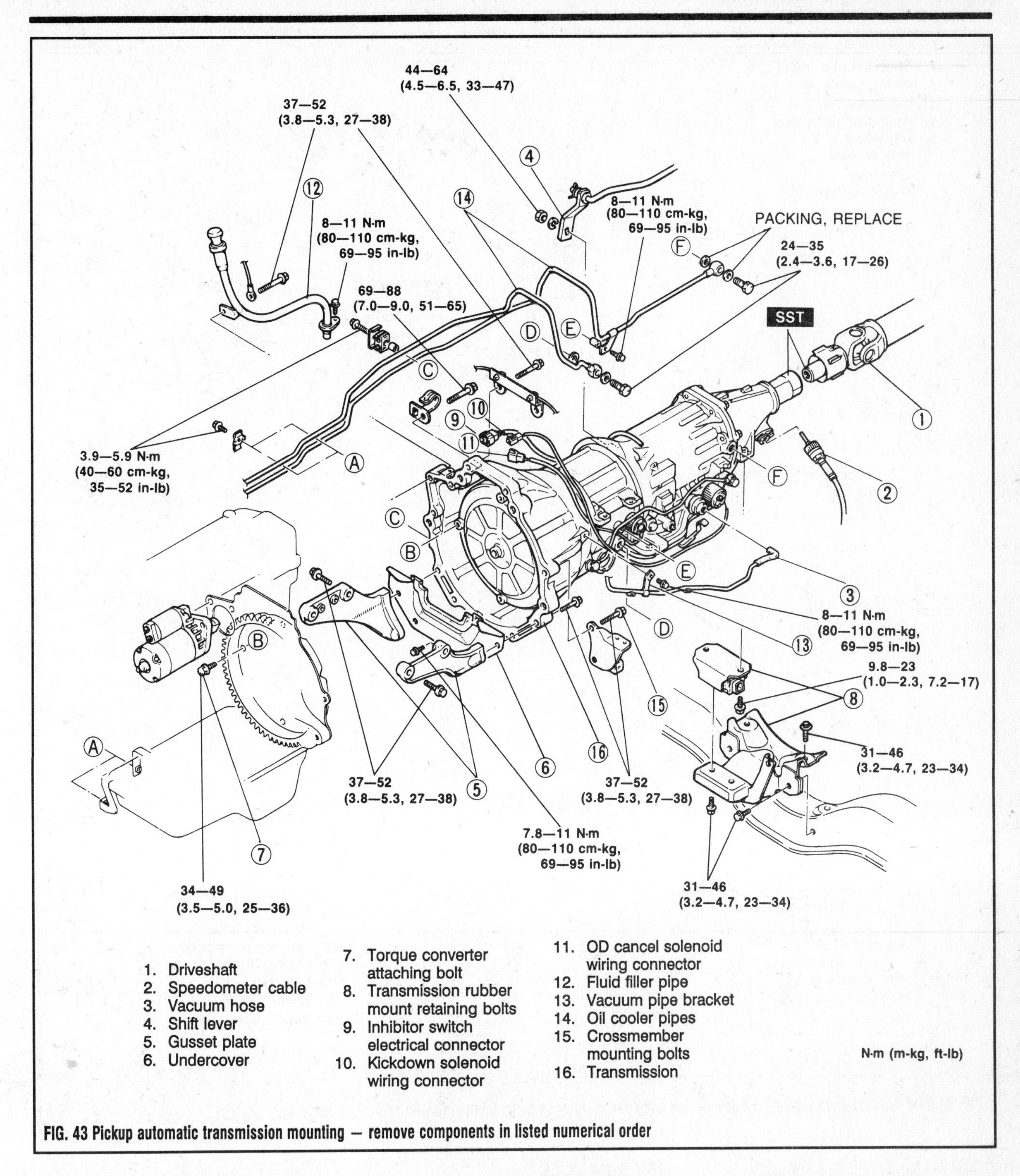

FIG. 43 Pickup automatic transmission mounting — remove components in listed numerical order

27. Install the fluid filler tube with a new O-ring.

28. Raise the transmission slightly, and install the crossmember to the frame. Tighten the bolts to 23-34 ft. lbs.

29. Lower the transmission and install the transmission-to-crossmember bolts. Tighten to 23-34 ft. lbs.

30. Align the matchmarks made earlier on the torque converter and drive plate. Install the four attaching bolts and torque to 25-36 ft. lbs. in three stages.

31. Install the side support plates.

32. Install the access cover. Remove the jack.

33. Connect the cooler lines.

34. Install the electrical connectors, and replace the wires in the clip. Install the vacuum hose.

35. Connect the shift rod to the lever.

36. Reconnect the speedometer cable.

37. Insert the driveshaft into the transmission. Install the center bearing support. Bolt the driveshaft to the rear of the axle flange.

38. Connect the exhaust pipe to the resonator

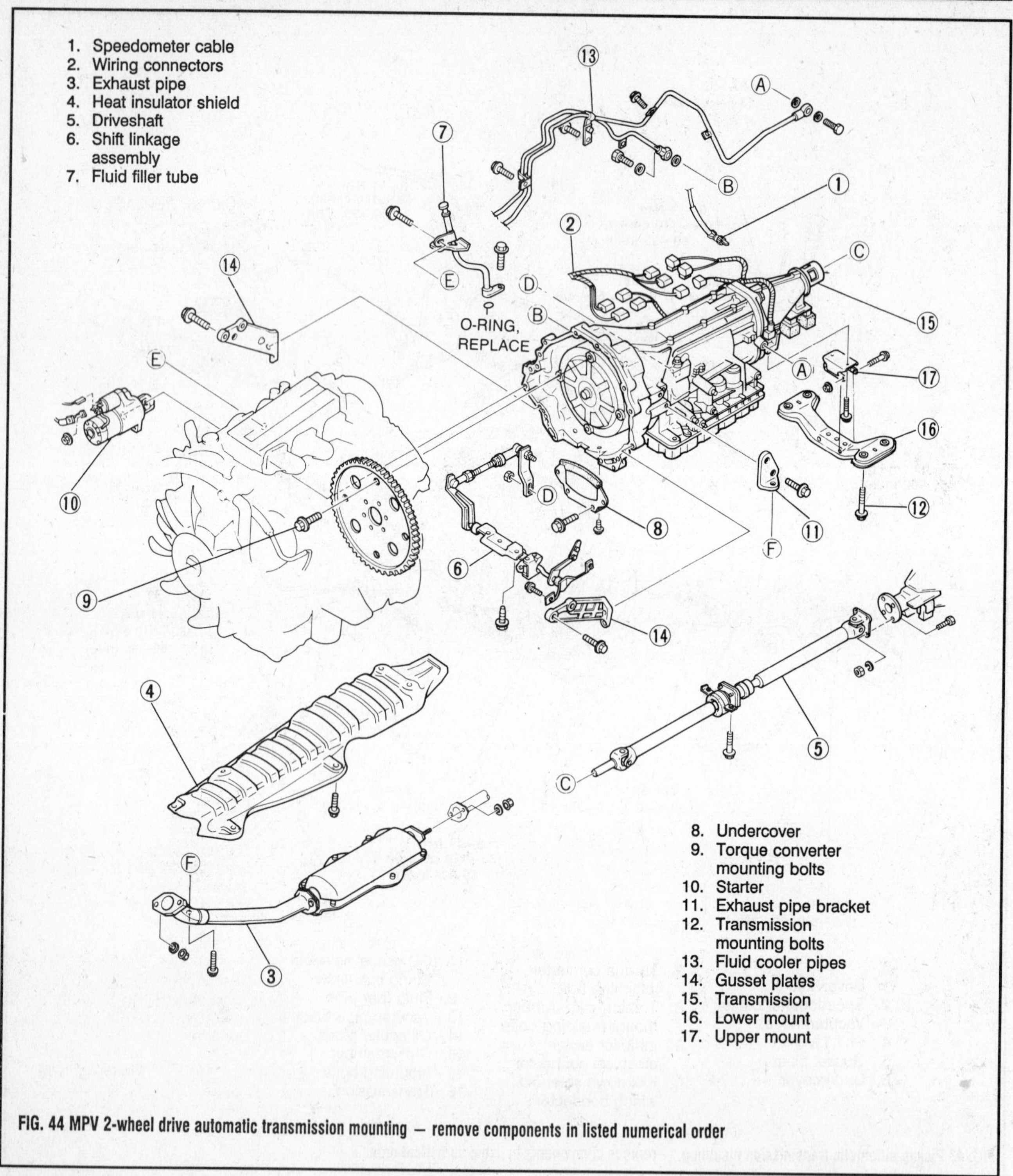

FIG. 44 MPV 2-wheel drive automatic transmission mounting — remove components in listed numerical order

or catalytic converter, using a new gasket. Reinstall the exhaust pipe clamp onto the converter housing, and torque the bolt to 10-15 ft. lbs.

39. Install a new pan gasket and the fluid pan, if this has not already been done.

40. Lower the truck. Connect the battery cable. Fill the transmission through the dipstick tube with the specified fluid, being careful not to overfill, and check for leaks.

MPV w/R4AX-EL

1. Disconnect the negative battery cable. Raise and safely support the vehicle.

2. Drain the transmission fluid.

3. Disconnect the speedometer cable. Label and disconnect all wiring connectors at the transmission.

4. Remove the front exhaust pipe and heat shields.

5. Scribe mating marks on the front and rear driveshaft yoke and companion flanges for reinstallation reference.

6. Push a rag into the double off-set joint to prevent damage to the boot by the driveshaft. Remove the rear driveshaft, and then the front driveshaft.

7. Remove the shifting mechanism that runs under the front of the transmission. Remove the filler tube.

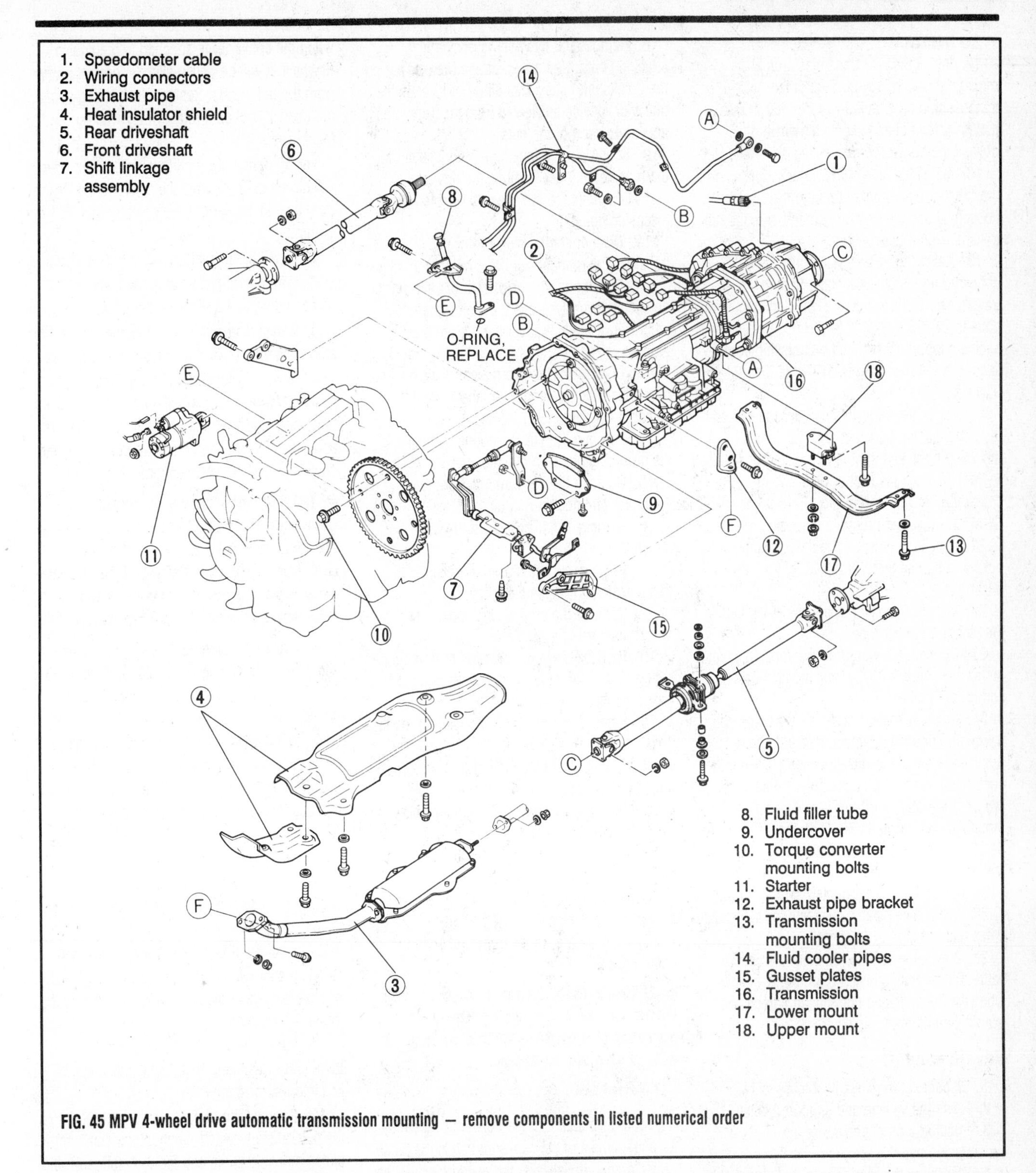

FIG. 45 MPV 4-wheel drive automatic transmission mounting — remove components in listed numerical order

8. Remove the bell housing access cover plate.

9. Remove the torque converter mounting bolts.

10. Remove the starter motor. Remove the exhaust pipe mounting bracket.

11. Remove the bolts connecting the crossmember to the transmission.

12. Support the engine. Support the transmission with a jack. Remove the crossmember-to-frame bolts, and remove the crossmember.

13. Make sure that the transmission is securely mounted on the jack. Secure it to the jack with a safety chain, if necessary.

14. Disconnect the oil cooler tubes from the transmission. Remove the side support gusset plates. Remove the converter housing-to-engine bolts.

15. With a pry bar, exert light pressure between the converter and the drive plate to prevent the converter from disengaging from the transmission as it is removed.

16. Lower the transmission and converter as an assembly. Be careful not to let the converter fall out.

To Install:

17. Install the rear transmission rubber mount if it was removed. Secure the transmission on a jack. Keep the rear of the transmission pointed slightly downward to prevent the converter from falling off of the front.

18. Install the side support gusset plates and the exhaust pipe bracket to the transmission. Loosely attach the rear crossmember to the rear transmission rubber mount.

19. Raise the transmission, align the converter and engine flexplate. Secure the transmission to the engine. Tighten the mounting bolts to 27–38 ft. lbs. (37–52Nm.). Remove the engine support. Install the transmission cooler lines. Tighten the fitting to 17–26 ft. lbs. (24–35Nm.).

20. Align the rear crossmember mount, raise the transmission if necessary. Install the mounting bolts and tighten to 32-45 ft. lbs. (43-61Nm.). Tighten the rubber mount to crossmember bolt and nut to 32-45 ft. lbs. (43-61 Nm.). Lower and remove the jack.

21. Install the converter to flexplate mounting bolts and tighten them to 27-40 ft. lbs. (36-54Nm.).

22. Install the converter access plate. Install the starter and filler tube.

23. Connect the wiring connectors. Connect the speedometer cable. Install the heat shields and exhaust pipe.

24. Align the mating marks on the companion flange and driveshaft yokes. Install the front driveshaft. Install the rear driveshaft. Secure the center support bearing assembly. Remove the rag from the double off-set joint. Driveshaft mounting bolt torque is 36-43 ft. lbs. (49-59Nm.). Center bearing mounting bolt torque is 27-39 ft. lbs. (36-53Nm.).

25. Install the front mounted shifting linkage.

26. Install a new pan gasket and the fluid pan, if this has not already been done.

27. Lower the vehicle. Connect the battery cable. Fill the transmission through the dipstick tube with the specified fluid, being careful not to overfill, and check for leaks.

Navajo w/A4LD

1. Disconnect the negative battery cable.
2. Raise the vehicle and support it safely.
3. Position a drain pan under the transmission pan.
4. Starting at the rear, loosen, but do not remove the pan bolts.
5. Loosen the pan from the transmission and allow the fluid to drain gradually.
6. Remove all of the pan bolts except 2 at the front or rear and allow the fluid to continue draining.
7. Remove the access cover and adapter plate bolts from the lower left side of the converter housing.
8. Remove the flywheel to converter attaching nuts. Use a socket and breaker bar on the crankshaft pulley attaching bolt. Rotate the pulley clockwise as viewed from the front to gain access to each of the nuts.
9. Scribe a mark indexing the driveshaft to the rear axle flange. Remove the driveshaft.
10. Remove the speedometer cable from the extension housing.
11. Disconnect the shift rod or cable at the transmission manual lever and retainer bracket.
12. Disconnect the downshift cable from the downshift lever. Depress the tab on the retainer and remove the kickdown cable from the bracket.
13. Disconnect the neutral start switch wires, converter clutch solenoid and the 3–4 shift solenoid connector.
14. Remove the starter mounting bolts and the ground cable. Remove the starter.
15. Remove the vacuum line from the transmission vacuum modulator.
16. Remove the filler tube from the transmission.
17. Position a transmission jack under the transmission and raise it slightly.
18. Remove the engine rear support to crossmember bolts.
19. Remove the crossmember to frame side support attaching nuts and bolts. Remove the crossmember.
20. Remove the converter housing to engine bolts.
21. Slightly lower the jack to gain access to the oil cooler lines. Disconnect the oil cooler lines at the transmission. Plug all openings to keep dirt and contamination out.
22. Move the transmission to the rear so it disengages from the dowel pins and the converter is disengaged from the flywheel. Lower the transmission from the vehicle.
23. Remove the torque converter from the transmission.

➡ **If the transmission is to be removed for a period of time, support the engine with a safety stand and wood block.**

To Install:

Proper installation of the converter requires full engagement of the converter hub in the pump gear. To accomplish this, the converter must be pushed and at the same time rotated through what feels like 2 notches or bumps. When fully installed, rotation of the converter will usually result in a clicking noise heard, caused by the converter surface touching the housing to case bolts.

This should not be a concern, but an indication of proper converter installation since, when the converter is attached to the engine flywheel, it will be pulled slightly forward away from the bolt heads. Besides the clicking sound, the converter should rotate freely with no binding.

For reference, a properly installed converter will have a distance from the converter pilot nose from face to converter housing outer face of 11–14mm.

1. Install the converter on the transmission.
2. With the converter properly installed, position the transmission on the jack.
3. Rotate the converter so that the drive studs are in alignment with the holes in the flywheel.
4. Move the converter and transmission assembly forward into position, being careful not to damage the flywheel and converter pilot. The converter housing is piloted into position by the dowels in the rear of the engine block.

➡ **During this move, to avoid damage, do not allow the transmission to get into a nose down position as this will cause the converter to move forward and disengage from the pump gear.**

5. Install the converter housing to engine attaching bolts and tighten to 28–38 ft. lbs. (38–51 Nm). The 2 longer bolts are located at the dowel holes.
6. Remove the jack supporting the engine.
7. Raise the transmission. Position the crossmember to the frame side supports. Install the attaching bolts and tighten to 20–30 ft. lbs. (27–41 Nm).
8. Lower the transmission and install the rear engine to crossmember nut and tighten to 60–80 ft. lbs. (82–108 Nm). Remove the transmission jack.
9. Install the filler tube in the transmission.
10. Install the oil cooler lines in the retaining clip at the cylinder block. Connect the lines to the transmission case.
11. Install the vacuum hose on the transmission vacuum unit. Install the vacuum line into the retaining clip.
12. Connect the neutral start switch plug to the neutral start switch. Connect the converter clutch solenoid wires and the 3–4 shift solenoid wires.
13. Install the starter and tighten the bolts to 15–20 ft. lbs. (20–27 Nm).
14. Install the flywheel to converter attaching nuts and tighten to 20–34 ft. lbs. (27–46 Nm).
15. Connect the muffler inlet pipe to the exhaust manifold.
16. Connect the transmission shift rod or cable to the manual lever.

17. Connect the downshift cable to the downshift lever.

18. Install the speedometer cable or sensor.

19. Install the driveshaft making sure to line up the scribe marks made during removal on the driveshaft and axle flange. Tighten the companion flange U-bolt attaching nuts to 70–95 ft. lbs. (95–130 Nm).

20. Adjust the manual and downshift linkages.

21. Lower the vehicle. Connect the negative battery cable.

22. Fill the transmission to the proper level with the specified fluid.

23. Check the transmission, converter and oil cooler lines for leaks.

TRANSFER CASE

Adjustments

Manual Shift Borg-Warner 13-54

The following procedure should be used, if a partial or incomplete engagement of the transfer case shift lever detent is experienced or if the control assembly requires removal.

1. Disconnect the negative battery cable.
2. Raise the shift boot to expose the top surface of the cam plates.
3. Loosen the 1 large and 1 small bolt, approximately 1 turn. Move the transfer case shift lever to the **4L** position (lever down).
4. Move the cam plate rearward until the bottom chamfered corner of the neutral lug just contacts the forward right edge of the shift lever.
5. Hold the cam plate in this position and torque the larger bolt first to 70–90 ft. lbs. (95–122 Nm) and torque the smaller bolt to 31–42 ft. lbs. (42–57 Nm).
6. Move the transfer case in cab shift lever to all shift positions to check for positive engagement. There should be a clearance between the shift lever and the cam plate in the **2H** front and **4H** rear (clearance not to exceed 3.3mm) and **4L** shift positions.
7. Install the shift boot assembly.
8. Reconnect the negative battery cable.

Rear Output Shaft Oil Seal

REMOVAL & INSTALLATION

1. Raise and safely support the vehicle.
2. Remove the driveshaft after match-marking the flange and shaft for installation reference. On models with a double offset joint, push a rag into the joint to keep the shaft straight so boot damage will not occur.
3. Hold the companion flange with a suitable tool, and remove the mounting nut. Remove the flange. It may be necessary to use a puller, on some models, to remove the flange.
4. Pry out the old seal. Clean the mounting surface. Apply oil to the lips of the seal and install the seal using the appropriate driver. Install the flange and the driveshaft.

Front Output Shaft Oil Seal

REMOVAL & INSTALLATION

1. Raise and safely support the vehicle.
2. Remove the skid plate, if equipped. Mark the driveshaft to flange for installation reference.
3. Drain the fluid from the transfer case if the support angle suggests an oil spill when the flange is removed from the transfer case. Remove the driveshaft.
4. Remove the retaining nut, washer, etc. Remove the companion flange.
5. Pry the seal from the housing. Clean the seal mounting surfaces.
6. Oil the seal lips. Install the seal using the proper driver. Install the flange and the driveshaft.

REMOVAL & INSTALLATION

Pickups w/Manual Transmission

1. Disconnect the battery ground cable.
2. Raise and support the truck on jackstands.
3. Drain the transmission.
4. Remove the shift knobs and boots.
5. Remove the console.
6. Remove the insulator plate.
7. Remove the shift grommet.
8. Remove the shift levers.
9. Remove the upper right side transmission support plate.
10. Remove the transmission splash shield.
11. Remove the transfer case splash shield.
12. Remove the exhaust pipe.
13. Matchmark and remove the front and rear driveshafts.
14. Disconnect the speedometer cable.
15. Disconnect the 4-wheel drive indicator connector.
16. Disconnect the back-up light switch.
17. Remove the front converter spring and nut.
18. Remove the clutch release cylinder.
19. Remove the transmission side support plates.
20. Remove the bellhousing inspection cover.
21. Support the transmission/transfer case with a transmission jack.
22. Remove the crossmember.
23. Lower the transmission assembly until all the transmission-to-engine bolts are available.
24. Support the engine with a jackstand.
25. Remove the transmission-to-engine bolts.
26. Pull the unit backward until the mainshaft clears the clutch.
27. Lower the unit and remove it from under the truck.
28. Stand the transmission on end with the transfer case up.
29. Remove the transfer case-to-extension housing bolts.
30. Lift the transfer case straight up and off. It may be necessary to tap it loose with a plastic mallet.

➡ **Removing the transfer case in this manner will avoid damage to the control rod.**

To Install:

31. Stand the transmission on end with the rear up.
32. Coat the mating surfaces of the transfer case and extension housing with RTV gasket material.
33. Install the transfer case on the extension housing, indexing the control lever end.
34. Apply RTV gasket material to the bolt threads and torque them to 35 ft. lbs.
35. Secure the control lever end with a spring pin.
36. Coat the mating surfaces of the shift control lever case and transfer case with RTV gasket material and install the shift control case. Apply RTV to the bolts and tighten them to 22 ft. lbs.
37. Raise the unit into position.
38. Push the unit forward until the mainshaft enters the clutch. and the locating lugs engage the bellhousing.
39. Install the transmission-to-engine bolts. Torque the bolts to 45 ft. lbs.
40. Install the crossmember. Torque the crossmember bolts to 50 ft. lbs.; the crossmember-to-transmission bolts to 40 ft. lbs.
41. Remove the engine jackstand.
42. Remove the transmission/transfer case transmission jack.
43. Install the bellhousing inspection cover.
44. Install the transmission side support plates.
45. Install the clutch release cylinder.
46. Install the front converter spring and nut.
47. Connect the back-up light switch.
48. Connect the 4-wheel drive indicator connector.
49. Connect the speedometer cable.
50. Install the front and rear driveshafts.
51. Install the exhaust pipe.
52. Install the transmission splash shield.
53. Install the transfer case splash shield.
54. Install the upper right side transmission support plate.
55. Install the shift levers.
56. Install the shift grommet.
57. Install the insulator plate.
58. Install the console.
59. Install the shift knobs and boots.
60. Fill the transmission.
61. Lower the truck.
62. Connect the battery ground cable.

Pickups w/Automatic Transmission

1. Disconnect the negative cable from the battery.
2. Raise and support the truck.
3. Drain the transmission fluid but do not remove the pan. After the fluid has drained, install a few bolts to hold the pan in place, temporarily.
4. Remove the exhaust pipe bracket bolt from the right side of the converter housing.
5. Remove the splash shield and skid plate.
6. Remove the exhaust pipe flange bolts from the rear of the resonator or catalytic converter, and disconnect the pipe.
7. Matchmark and disconnect the front and or rear the driveshaft(s).
8. Disconnect the speedometer cable.
9. Disconnect the shift rod from the manual lever.
10. Remove the shift knob.
11. Remove the console.
12. Remove the 4-wheel drive shift lever plate and transfer case lever.
13. Disconnect the 4-wheel drive indicator wiring.
14. Remove the vacuum hose from the diaphragm. Disconnect the electrical connectors from the downshift solenoid and inhibitor switch, and remove their wires from the clip.
15. Disconnect and plug the cooler lines from the radiator at the transmission. Use a flare nut wrench if one is available.
16. Remove the side support plates.
17. Remove the access cover from the lower front of the converter housing.
18. Matchmark the drive plate (flywheel) and torque converter for reassembly. Remove the four bolts holding the torque converter to the drive plate.
19. Remove the bolts connecting the crossmember to the transmission.
20. Support the transmission with a jack. Remove the crossmember-to-frame bolts, and remove the crossmember.
21. Make sure that the transmission is securely supported. Secure it to the jack with a safety chain, if necessary.
22. Lower the transmission to provide working clearance, and remove the starter.
23. Remove the converter housing-to-engine bolts.
24. Remove the fluid filler tube.
25. With a pry bar, exert light pressure between the converter and the drive plate to prevent the converter from disengaging from the transmission as it is removed.
26. Lower the transmission and converter as an assembly. Be careful not to let the converter fall out.
27. Stand the transmission on end with the transfer case up.
28. Remove the transfer case-to-extension housing bolts.
29. Lift the transfer case straight up and off. It may be necessary to tap it loose with a plastic mallet.

➡ **Removing the transfer case in this manner will avoid damage to the control rod.**

To Install:

30. Stand the transmission on end with the rear up.
31. Coat the mating surfaces of the transfer case and extension housing with RTV gasket material.
32. Install the transfer case on the extension housing, indexing the control lever end.
33. Apply RTV gasket material to the bolt threads and torque them to 35 ft. lbs.
34. Secure the control lever end with a spring pin.
35. Coat the mating surfaces of the shift control lever case and transfer case with RTV gasket material and install the shift control case. Apply RTV to the bolts and tighten them to 22 ft. lbs.
36. Place the transmission on the jack. Be sure that the converter is properly installed.
37. Raise the transmission into place. Install the converter housing-to-engine bolts, and torque in two stages to 23-34 ft. lbs.
38. Lower the transmission on the jack and install the starter.
39. Install the fluid filler tube with a new O-ring.
40. Raise the transmission slightly, and install the crossmember to the frame. Tighten the bolts to 23-34 ft. lbs.
41. Lower the transmission and install the transmission-to-crossmember bolts. Tighten to 23-34 ft. lbs.
42. Align the matchmarks made earlier on the torque converter and drive plate. Install the four attaching bolts and torque to 25-36 ft. lbs. in three stages.
43. Install the side support plates.
44. Install the access cover. Remove the jack.
45. Connect the cooler lines.
46. Install the 4-wheel drive shift lever plate and transfer case lever.
47. Connect the 4-wheel drive indicator wiring.
48. Install the electrical connectors to the switch and solenoid, and replace the wires in the clip. Install the diaphragm vacuum hose.
49. connect the shift rod to the lever.
50. Reconnect the speedometer cable.
51. Insert the driveshaft into the transmission. Install the center bearing support. Bolt the driveshaft to the rear of the axle flange.
52. Connect the exhaust pipe to the resonator or catalytic converter, using a new gasket. Reinstall the exhaust pipe clamp onto the converter housing, and torque the bolt to 10-15 ft. lbs.
53. Install a new pan gasket and the fluid pan, if this has not already been done.
54. Install the shift knob.
55. Install the console.

56. Lower the truck. Connect the battery cable. Fill the transmission through the dipstick tube with the specified fluid, being careful not to overfill, and check for leaks.

MPV

1. Disconnect the negative battery cable. Raise and safely support the vehicle. Drain the transfer case.
2. Mark the position of the driveshafts on the flanges and remove the driveshafts. Push a rag into the double-offset joint to hold the rear driveshaft straight to prevent damaging the boot.
3. Support the transmission with a jack and remove the transmission lower mount. Remove the upper mount.
4. Remove the front exhaust pipe and heat insulator.
5. Disconnect the speedometer and transfer case shift cable. Tag and disconnect the electrical connectors.
6. Support the transfer case with a jack and remove the transfer case attaching bolts. Remove the transfer case.

To install:

7. Apply silicone sealant to the transfer case flange.
8. Support the transfer case with a jack and install the transfer case. Apply sealant to the bolt threads and tighten to 27–40 ft. lbs. (36–54 Nm).
9. Connect the electrical connectors, transfer case shift cable and speedometer cable. Adjust the transfer case shift cable.
10. Install the exhaust pipe and heat insulator.
11. Install the upper transmission mount.
12. Install the lower transmission mount. Loosely install the center washers and nuts and tighten the outer bolts to 32–45 ft. lbs. (43–61 Nm), then tighten the center nuts to 23–34 ft. lbs. (31–46 Nm).
13. Remove the support jacks.
14. Install the driveshafts, aligning the marks that were made during removal. Remove the rag from the double-offset joint and check the boot for damage.
15. Fill the transfer case with the proper type and quantity of fluid.
16. Lower the vehicle and connect the negative battery cable. Check the transfer case for leaks and proper operation.

Navajo

MECHANICAL SHIFT TYPE

1. Disconnect the negative battery cable. Raise and safely support the vehicle.
2. If equipped, remove the skid plate from the frame. Remove the damper from the transfer case, if equipped.
3. Place a drain pan under the transfer case, remove the drain plug and drain the fluid. Disconnect the 4WD indicator switch wire connector at the transfer case.
4. Disconnect the front driveshaft from the transfer case output shaft yoke and wire the driveshaft out of the way.
5. Disconnect the rear driveshaft from the transfer case output shaft flange and wire the driveshaft out of the way.
6. Disconnect the speedometer driven gear from the transfer case rear cover. Disconnect the vent hose from the control lever.
7. Disconnect the nut from the shift lever and remove the shift lever.
8. Remove the large and small bolts retaining the shifter to the extension housing. Remove the lever assembly and bushing.
9. Support the transfer case with a transmission jack. Remove the 5 bolts retaining the transfer case to the transmission and extension housing.
10. Slide the transfer case rearward off the transmission output shaft and lower the transfer case from the vehicle. Remove the gasket from between the transfer case and extension housing.

To install:

11. Install a new gasket on the front mounting face of the transfer case assembly.
12. Raise the transfer case with the transmission jack so the transmission output shaft aligns with the transfer case input shaft. Slide the transfer case forward onto the transmission output shaft and onto the dowel pin. Install the 5 retaining bolts and tighten, in sequence, to 25–43 ft. lbs. (34–58 Nm).
13. Remove the transmission jack.
14. Install and adjust the shifter. Always tighten the large bolt retaining the shifter to the extension housing before tightening the small bolt.
15. Install the vent assembly so the white marking on the hose is in position in the notch in the shifter. The upper end of the vent hose should be 3/4 in. (19mm) above the top of the shifter and positioned just below the floor pan.
16. Connect the speedometer driven gear to the transfer case rear cover. Tighten the screw to 20–25 inch lbs. (2.3–2.8 Nm).
17. Connect the rear driveshaft to the transfer case output shaft flange. Tighten the bolts to 61–87 ft. lbs. (83–118 Nm).
18. Connect the front driveshaft to the transfer case output shaft yoke. Tighten the bolts to 12–16 ft. lbs. (16–22 Nm).
19. Connect the 4WD indicator switch wire connector at the transfer case.
20. Install the drain plug and tighten to 14–22 ft. lbs. (19–30 Nm). Remove the fill plug and fill the transfer case with the proper type of fluid to the bottom of the fill hole. Install the fill plug and tighten to 14–22 ft. lbs. (19–30 Nm).
21. Install the damper to the transfer case, if equipped. Using new damper bolts, tighten to 25–35 ft. lbs. (34–48 Nm).
22. Install the skid plate, if equipped. Tighten the nuts and bolts to 15–20 ft. lbs. (20–27 Nm).
23. Lower the vehicle and connect the negative battery cable.

ELECTRONIC SHIFT TYPE

1. Disconnect the negative battery cable. Raise and safely support the vehicle.
2. If equipped, remove the nuts, bolts and skid plate from the frame. Remove the damper from the transfer case, if equipped.
3. Place a drain pan under the transfer case, remove the drain plug and drain the fluid.
4. Remove the wire connector from the feed wire harness at the rear of the transfer case. First squeeze the locking tabs, then pull the connectors apart.

➡ Do not pull directly on the wires or pull outwardly on the locking tabs.

5. Remove the connector for the transfer case motor from the mounting bracket.
6. Disconnect the front driveshaft from the transfer case output shaft yoke and wire the driveshaft out of the way.
7. Disconnect the rear driveshaft from the transfer case output shaft flange and wire the driveshaft out of the way.
8. Disconnect the speedometer driven gear from the transfer case rear cover. Disconnect the vent hose from the mounting bracket.
9. Support the transfer case with a transmission jack. Remove the 5 bolts retaining the transfer case to the transmission and extension housing.
10. Slide the transfer case rearward off the transmission output shaft and lower the transfer case from the vehicle. Remove the gasket from between the transfer case and extension housing.

To install:

11. Install a new gasket on the front mounting face of the transfer case assembly.
12. Raise the transfer case with the transmission jack so the transmission output shaft aligns with the transfer case input shaft. Slide the transfer case forward onto the transmission output shaft and onto the dowel pin. Install the 5 retaining bolts and tighten, in sequence, to 25–43 ft. lbs. (34–58 Nm).
13. Remove the transmission jack.
14. Install the vent hose so the white marking on the hose aligns with the notch in the mounting bracket.
15. Connect the speedometer driven gear to the transfer case rear cover. Tighten the screw to 20–25 inch lbs. (2.3–2.8 Nm).
16. Connect the rear driveshaft to the transfer

case output shaft flange. Tighten the bolts to 61–87 ft. lbs. (83–118 Nm).

17. Connect the front driveshaft to the transfer case output shaft yoke. Tighten the bolts to 12–16 ft. lbs. (16–22 Nm).

18. Attach the connector for the transfer case motor to the mounting bracket.

19. Connect the wire connectors on the rear of the transfer case, making sure the retaining tabs lock.

20. Install the drain plug and tighten to 14–22 ft. lbs. (19–30 Nm). Remove the fill plug and fill the transfer case with the proper type of fluid to the bottom of the fill hole. Install the fill plug and tighten to 14–22 ft. lbs. (19–30 Nm).

21. Install the damper to the transfer case, if equipped. Using new damper bolts, tighten to 25–35 ft. lbs. (34–48 Nm).

22. Install the skid plate, if equipped. Tighten the nuts and bolts to 15–20 ft. lbs. (20–27 Nm).

23. Lower the vehicle and connect the negative battery cable.

Overhaul Pickups and MPV

➧ SEE FIGS. 46-128

DISASSEMBLY & INSPECTION

➡ The transfer case has been removed from the transmission for the following procedure.

1. Remove the two stopper pins.
2. Hold the companion flange with special tool 49 S120 710 "coupling flange holder" and remove the companion flange nut.
3. Remove the companion flange by lightly tapping the backside with a plastic hammer.
4. Remove the 4×4 indicator switch, pin, plugs, detent springs and balls.
5. Remove the speedometer drive gear.
6. Remove the snap ring from the end of the input shaft.
7. Using special tool, 49 0839 425C or equivalent, remove the outer bearing.
8. Position the flat section of the input shaft gear toward the countershaft gear, then, remove the input shaft gear and bearing.
9. Using a plastic hammer, separate the chain cover from the transfer case and remove the chain cover.

➡ Lift the chain cover vertically to prevent damaging the shift rods.

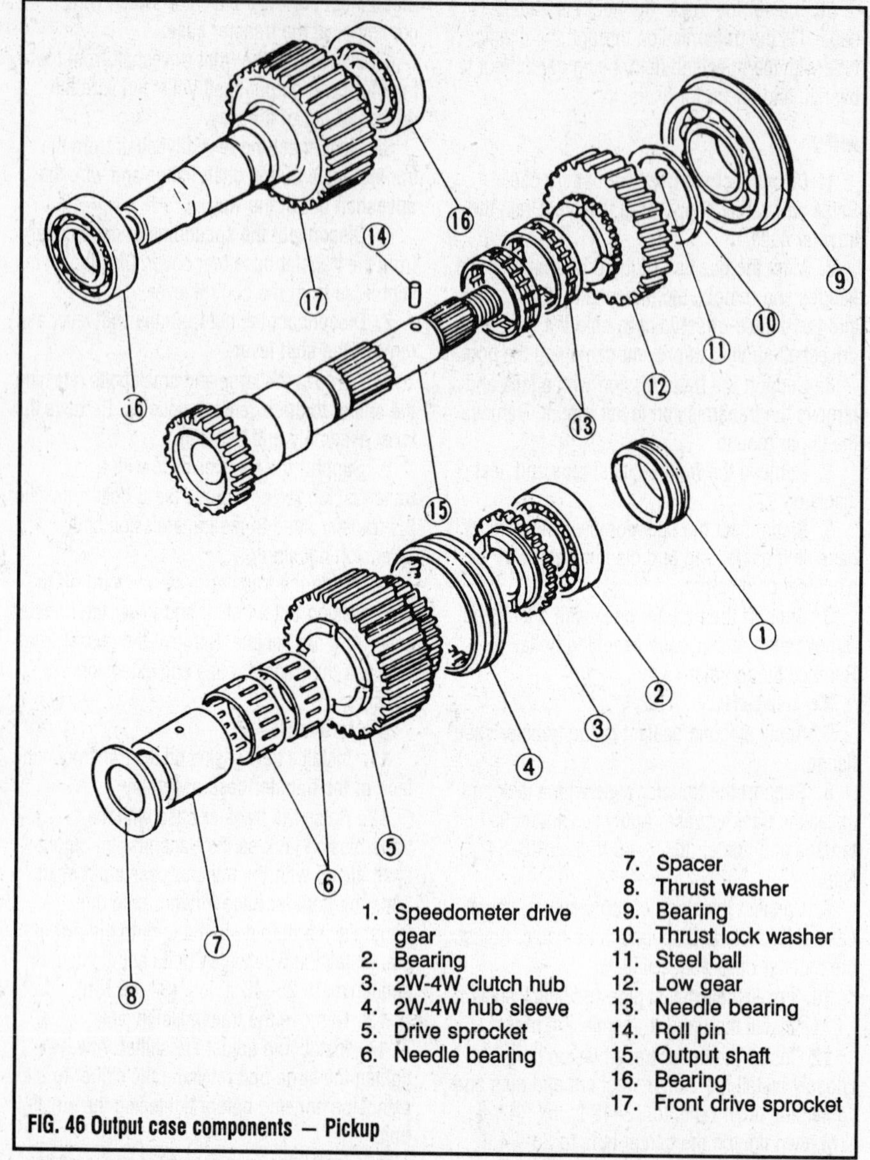

FIG. 46 Output case components — Pickup

10. Remove the speedometer drive gear from the output shaft, then, remove the knock pin and bearing.
11. Remove the oil passage by lightly tapping with a plastic hammer.
12. Tap out the spring pin and remove the High/Low shift rod, spacer and shift fork.
13. Tap out the spring pin and remove the 2W-4W shift rod assembly, spacer and 2W-4W shift end.
14. Tap out the spring pins and remove the retainers, 2W-4W shift fork, spring and spacer. Remove the pin for the 4×4 indicator switch from the rod.
15. Using a magnet, remove the pin and interlock pin from the chain cover.
16. Set the input gear on the output shaft.
17. Remove the output shaft and the front drive sprocket from the transfer case housing by lightly tapping on the input shaft gear and the front drive sprocket with a plastic hammer.
18. Remove the input shaft gear from the transfer case housing.
19. Remove the lock plate.
20. Tap out the countershaft gear support using a punch and hammer.
21. Re move the counter gear and thrust washers.
22. Remove the needle bearings and spacer from the countershaft gear.
23. Remove the O-ring from the countershaft.
24. Using a press and special tool 49 G030 370, press the output shaft assembly apart.
25. Remove the parts from the output shaft in the sequence shown below.
26. Using bearing puller set 49 0839 425C or equivalent, remove the bearings from both sides of the front drive sprocket.
27. Remove the oil seals.
28. Remove the snap ring.
29. Using special tool 49 F401 331 or

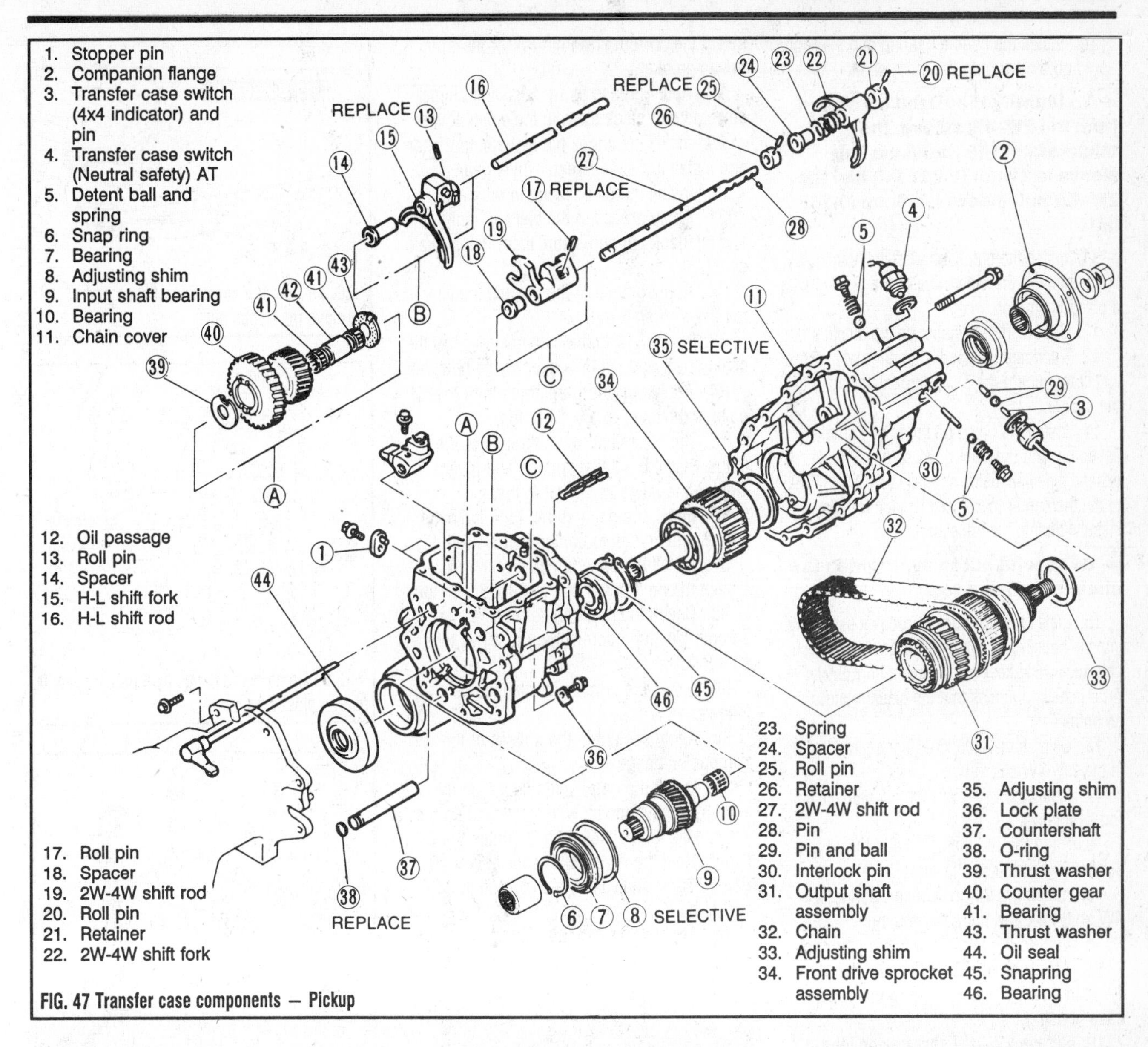

FIG. 47 Transfer case components — Pickup

equivalent, press the front sprocket bearing out of the housing.

ASSEMBLY

1. Using tool 49 0727 415 or equivalent, press the front drive sprocket bearing into the transfer case housing. Install the snap ring and secure the bearing.
2. Apply oil to the lip of the oil seal and install the seal into the transfer case housing, using tool 49 0727 415 or equivalent.
3. Apply oil to the lip of the oil seal and install the seal into the chain cover, using tool 49 0727 415 or equivalent.
4. Using tool 49 0727 415 or equivalent, press the bearings on both sides of the front drive sprocket. Press the bearings until they stop.
5. Install the lower gear on the output shaft. Lubricate the needle bearing assembly with oil and set it on the shaft.
6. Set the steel ball in the shaft, and install the thrust lock washer.
7. Using special tool 49 0727 415 or equivalent, press the bearing on the output shaft.
8. Install the counter gear as follows:
   a. While lubricating the contact surface of the thrust washer and the housing, install the washer so that the dished (convex) part of the washer sets down into the housing.
   b. Lubricate the needle bearings with oil, then install them and the spacer in the counter gear.
   c. Install the counter gear in the housing.
   d. Lubricate a new O-ring with oil and install it on the countershaft.
   e. Center the inside needle bearing and slide the counter shaft into the case.
   f. Install the lock plate and tighten the bolt to 14–19 ft. lbs.
9. Install the input shaft as follows:
   a. Measure the bearing bore depth **A** of the housing with vernier calipers.
   b. Measure the height **B** of the bearing clip with vernier calipers and a surface plate.
   c. Calculate the difference between measurement **A** and **B** to determine the clearance. The formula looks like this: **Difference (Clearance) A - B**.
   d. Select and install the proper shim to obtain a clearance of 0–0.1mm (0-0.0039 in.).
   e. Using tool 49 0727 415 or equivalent, press the bearing onto the input shaft gear. Install the snap ring.
   f. Install the input shaft assembly in the housing by lightly tapping the outer race of the bearing with a plastic hammer.

10. Install the needle bearing and the High/Low hub sleeve onto the input shaft.

➡ To identify the High/Low sleeve from the 2W-4W sleeve, the thickness of the High/Low hub sleeve is 21mm (0.827 in.) and the 2W-4W hub sleeve is 18mm (0.709 in.).

11. Install the output shaft in the housing by lightly tapping the outer race of the bearing with a plastic hammer.

12. Set the thrust washer on the output shaft.

13. Lubricate the needle bearings with oil and install them onto the drive sprocket along with the spacer.

14. Install the chain on the drive sprocket assembly and the front drive sprocket, and expand the chain using special tool 49 S231 395 to set the center to center distance for easy installation into the housing.

➡ Be careful not to overtighten the chain expansion tool.

15. Install the front drive sprocket assembly into the housing by lightly tapping it with a plastic hammer, while keeping the chain horizontal. After installing, check that the chain rotates smoothly.

16. Using tool 49 0500 330 or equivalent, tap in the 2W-4W clutch hub.

17. Install the 2W-4W shift fork onto the shift rod as follows:

a. Slide the retainer on the shift rod and secure it with the spring pin.

b. Install the 20mm spacer, spring, 2W-4W shift fork and the other retainer.

c. Secure the retainer with the spring pin.

18. Assemble the 2W-4W hub sleeve to the shift fork and insert them to the transfer case housing.

19. Set the 2W-4W shift fork and the 20mm spacer into the case and slide the shift rod assembly through it.

20. Secure the 2W-4W shift end to the rod with the spring pin.

21. Install the High/Low shift fork, 37mm spacer, and the rod in the transfer case housing.

22. Secure the High/Low shift fork with the spring pin.

23. Install the bearing on the output shaft.

24. Measure the bearing height and the bearing bore depth for the output shaft using the shim selector gauge set tool 49 U017 3A0.

25. Put the two pieces of the gauge set together and measure the clearance.

26. Select the proper adjusting shim to adjust the clearance to 0-0.1mm (0-0.0039 in.).

27. Repeat the procedures above and select the correct size shim(s) for the front drive sprocket.

28. Apply grease to the adjusting shims selected and place them in the chain cover.

29. Install the knock pin in the output shaft and install the speedometer drive gear.

30. Install the oil passage in the case.

31. Apply grease to the ball (A/T only), pin and interlock pin and install them in the chain cover.

32. Apply grease to the pin and install it in the 2W-4W shift rod.

33. Apply RTV to the mating surface of the chain cover and set the cover on the housing.

34. Apply sealant to the threads of the bolts and tighten to 14-19 ft. lbs.

35. Apply sealant to the threads of the plugs. Install the balls, springs and plugs. Tighten the plugs to 14-19 ft. lbs.

36. Install the pin and the 4×4 indicator switch and tighten to tighten to 18-25 ft. lbs.

37. Install the speedometer gear and tighten the hold down bolt to 69-95 inch lbs.

38. Check that the transfer case shifts smoothly using a screwdriver to move the shift forks.

39. Install the companion flanges as follows:

a. Apply sealant to the splines of the companion flange.

b. Install the companion flange on the shaft by lightly tapping with a plastic hammer.

c. Use a new locknut and tighten the flange. Hold the flange with special tool 49 S120 710 or equivalent, then torque to 94-130 ft lbs.

40. Apply sealant to the contact surfaces of the stopper pins and install them with new O-rings.

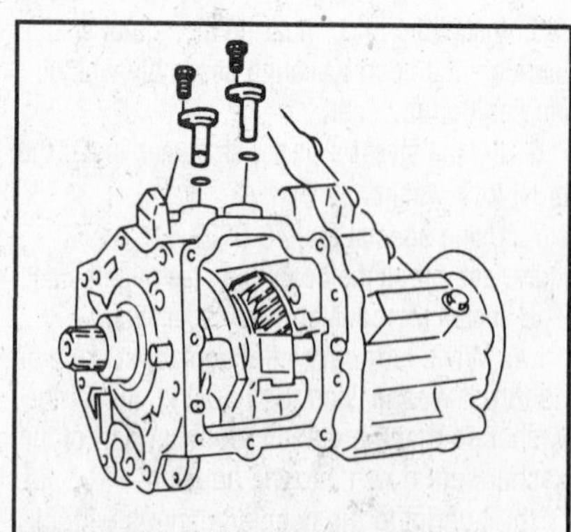

FIG. 48 Remove the stopper pins

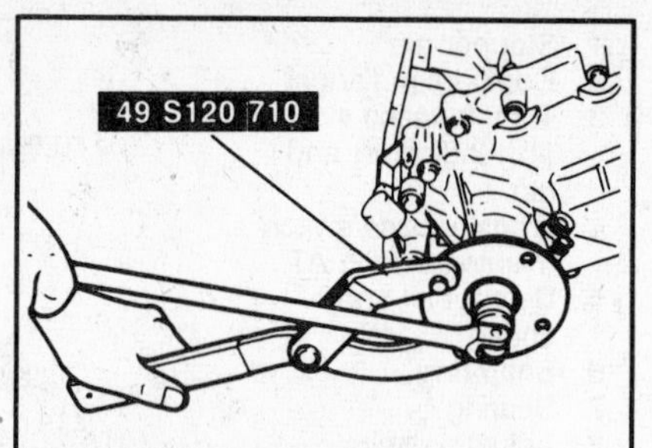

FIG. 49 Hold the companion flange and remove the flange nut

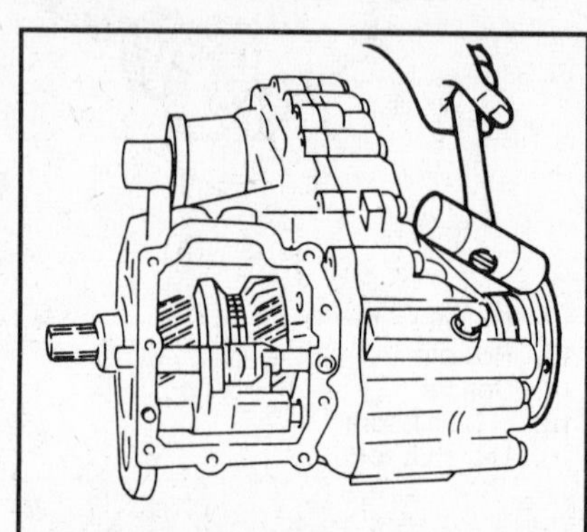

FIG. 50 Remove the flange by lightly tapping it with a plastic hammer

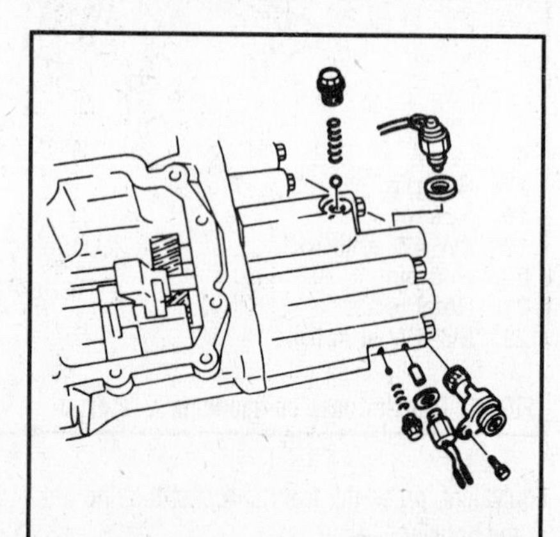

FIG. 51 Remove the four wheel drive indicator switch, pin, neutral switch (AT), plugs, detent spring, and balls. Remove the speedometer driven gear

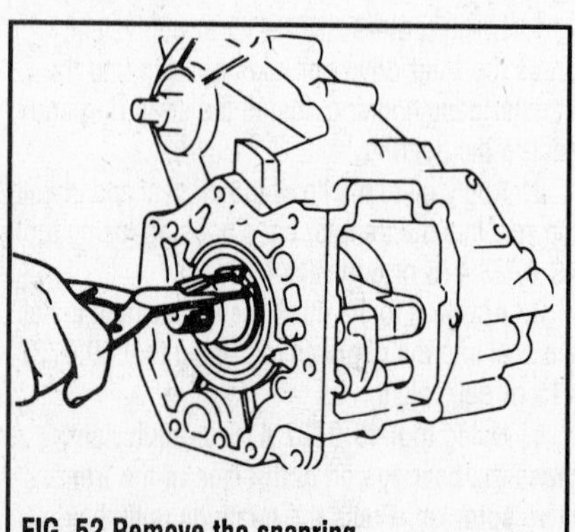

FIG. 52 Remove the snapring

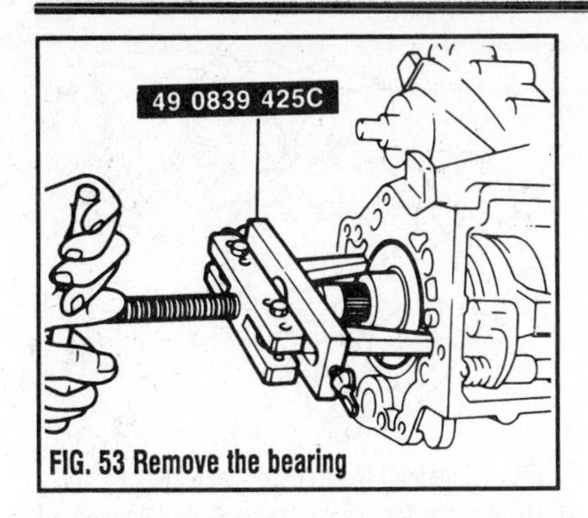

FIG. 53 Remove the bearing

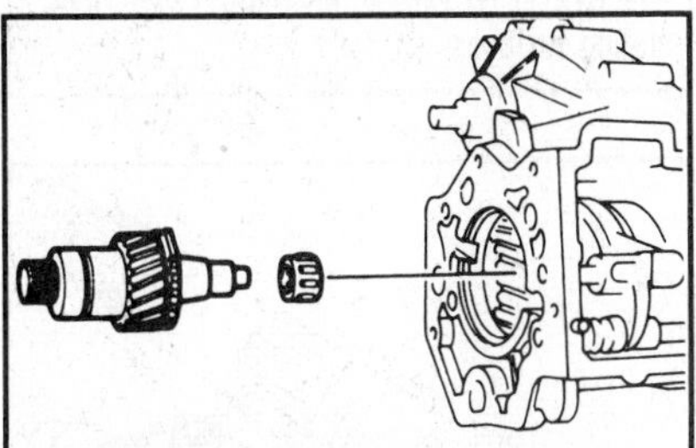
FIG. 54 Remove the input gear and bearing. For removal, position the flat section of the gear toward the countershaft gear

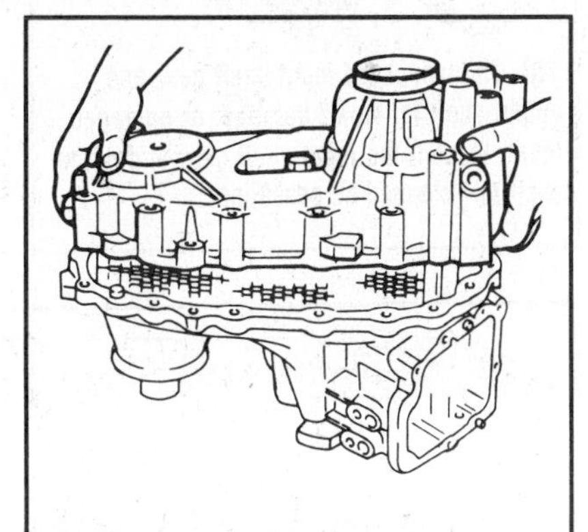
FIG. 55 Use a plastic hammer and separate the chain cover from the transfer case. Lift the chain cover vertically to prevent damaging the shift rods

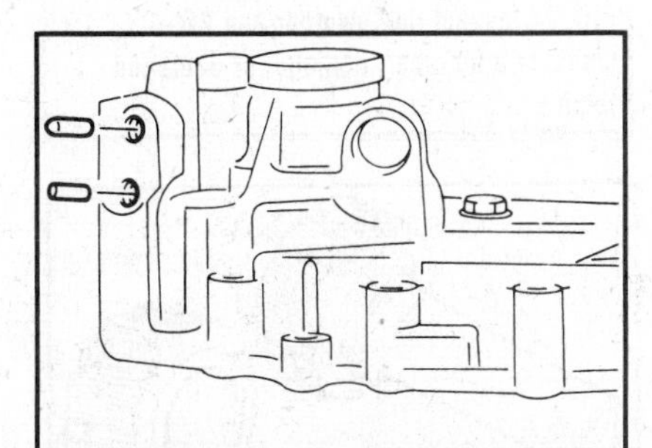
FIG. 56 Remove the pin and interlock pin from the chain cover with a magnet

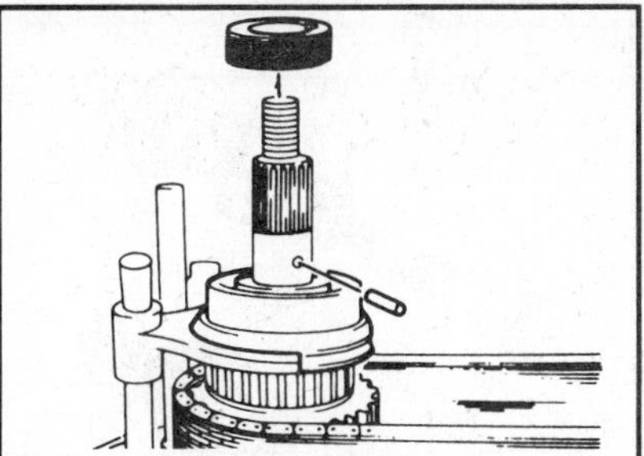
FIG. 57 Remove the speedometer drive gear. Remove the knock pin and bearing

FIG. 58 Remove the oil passage by lightly tapping it with a plastic hammer

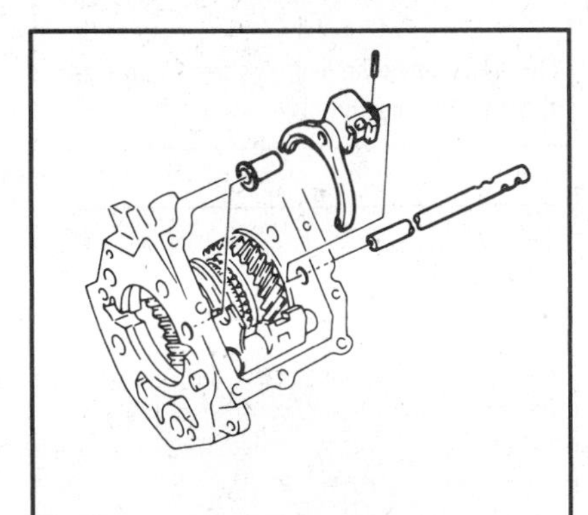
FIG. 59 Tap out the roll pin and remove the Hi, Low shift rod, spacer and shift fork

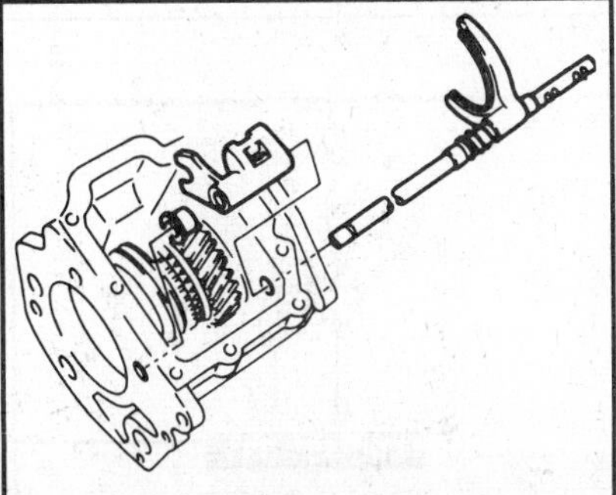
FIG. 60 Tap out the roll pin and remove the 2W-4W shift rod assembly, spacer, and 2W-4W shift end

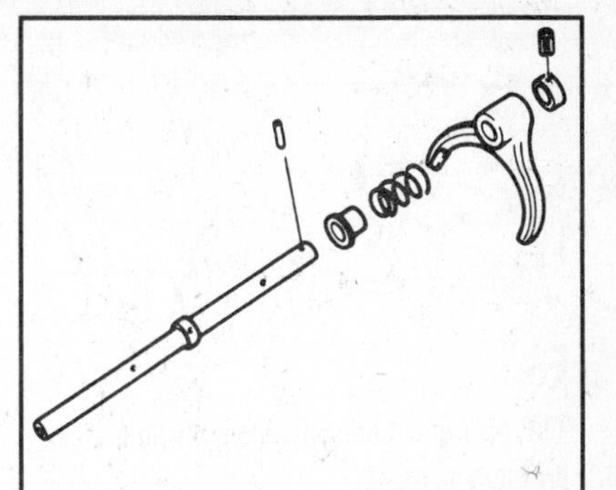
FIG. 61 Tap out the roll pins and remove the retainers, 2W-4W shift fork, spring and spacer. Remove the pin for the 4 × 4 indicator switch from the rod

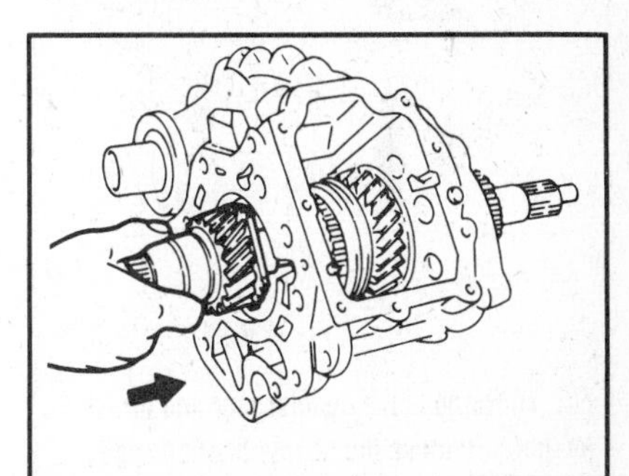
FIG. 62 Set the input shaft on the output shaft

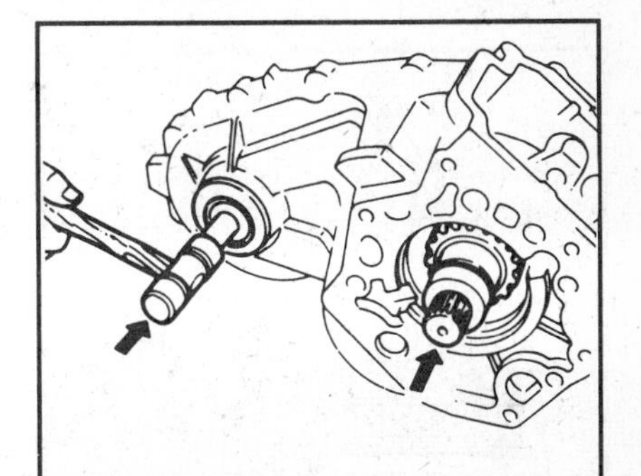
FIG. 63 Remove the output shaft and the front drive sprocket from the transfer case housing by lightly tapping the input shaft gear and the front drive sprocket with a plastic hammer

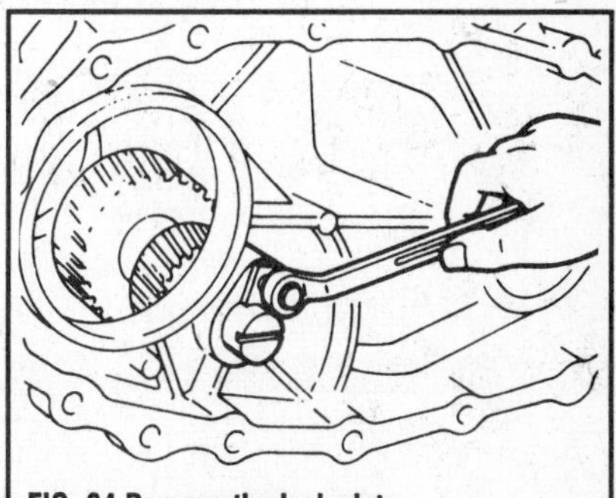
FIG. 64 Remove the lock plate

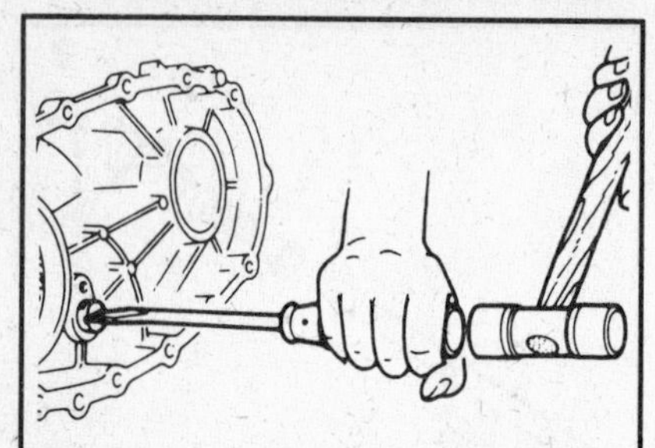
FIG. 65 Tap out the countershaft with a brass drift and hammer

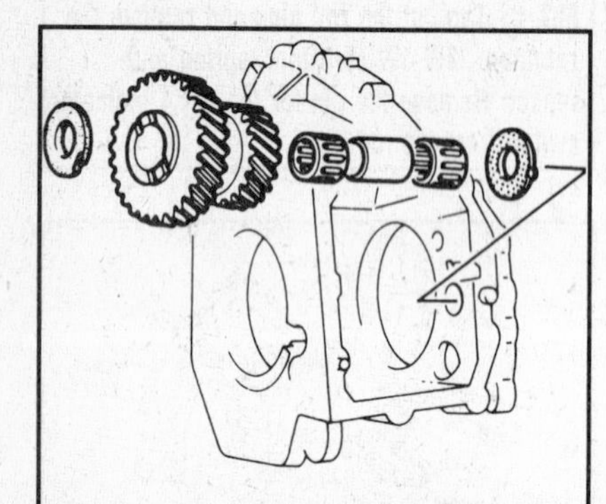
FIG. 66 Remove the countergear and thrust washers. Remove the needle bearings and spacer from the counter gear. Remove the O-ring from the countershaft

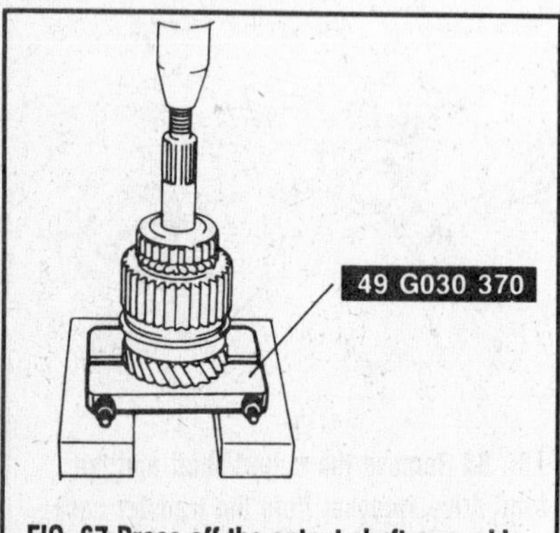

FIG. 67 Press off the output shaft assembly components

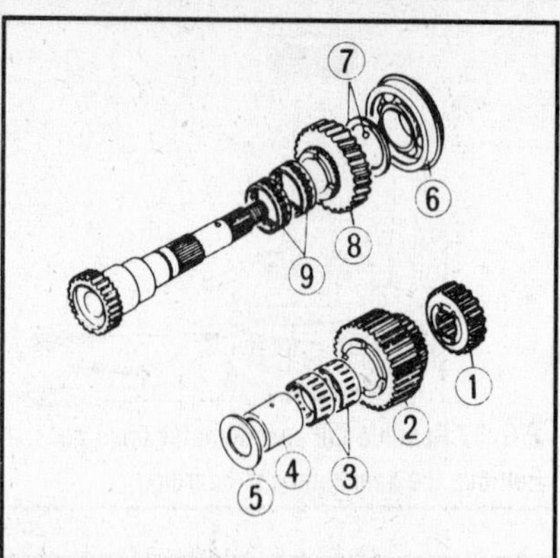

FIG. 68 Remove the parts from the output shaft in the order shown — 2W-4W clutch hub, drive sprocket, needle bearings, spacer, thrust washer, bearing, thrust lock washer and steel ball, low gear, needle bearings

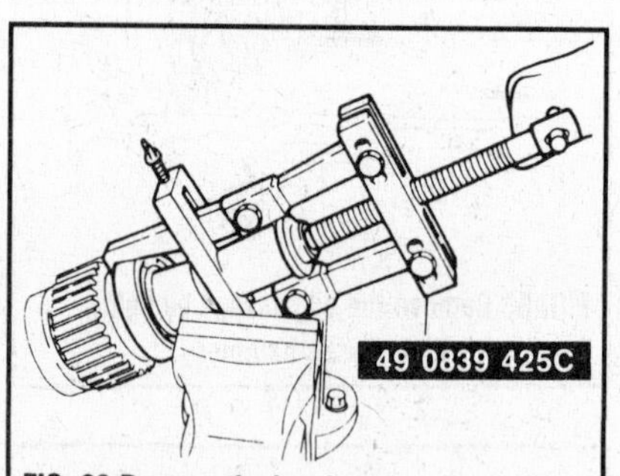

FIG. 69 Remove the bearings from both sides of the front drive sprocket

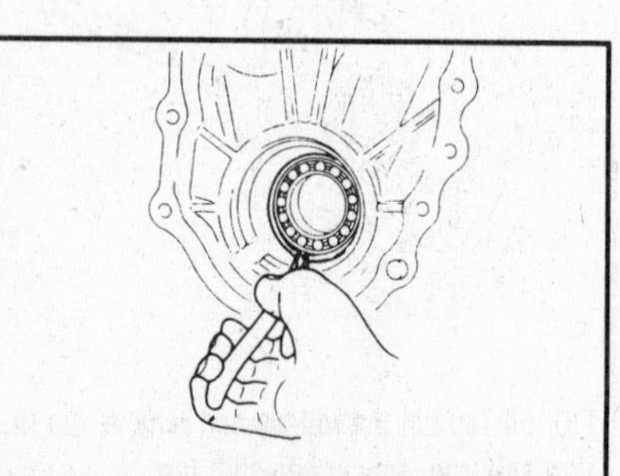
FIG. 70 Remove the oil seals. Remove the snapring

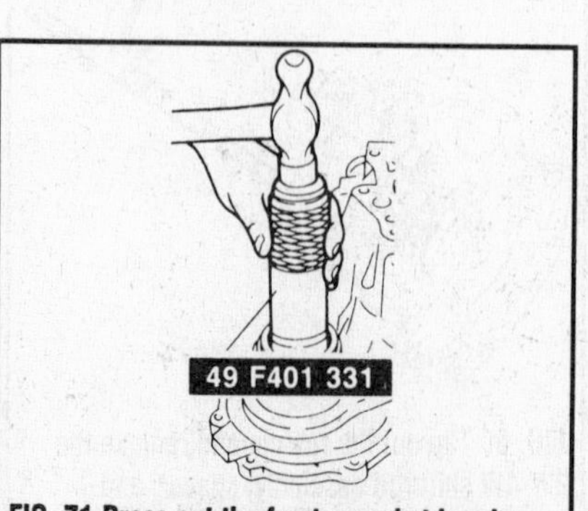

FIG. 71 Press out the front sprocket bearing

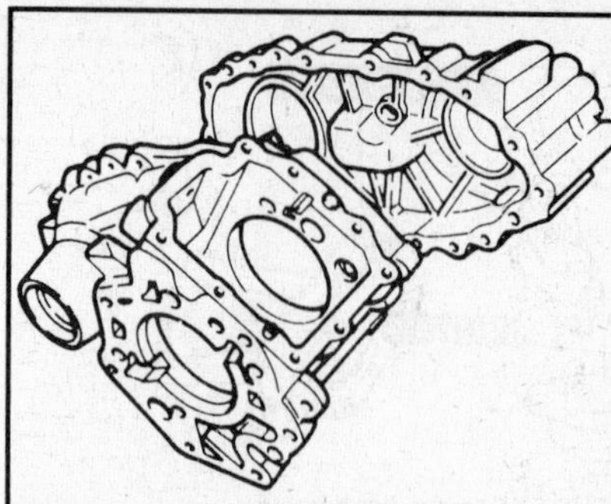
FIG. 72 Inspect the transfer case housing and chain cover for cracks, damage or damaged mating surfaces

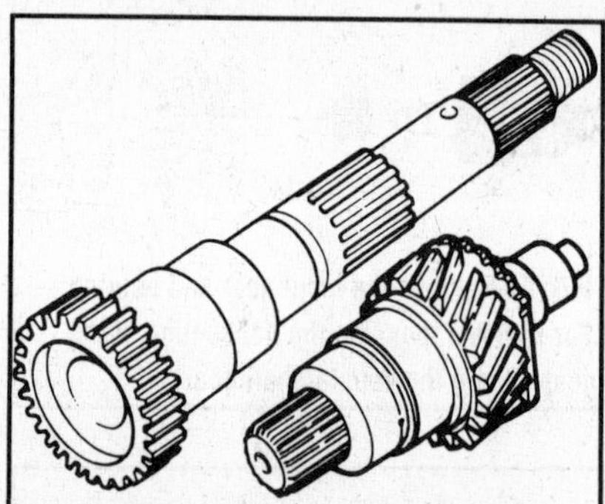
FIG. 73 Inspect the input shaft gear and output shaft for wear, damage, or damaged teeth. Inspect the input shaft gear and output shaft for clogged oil passages

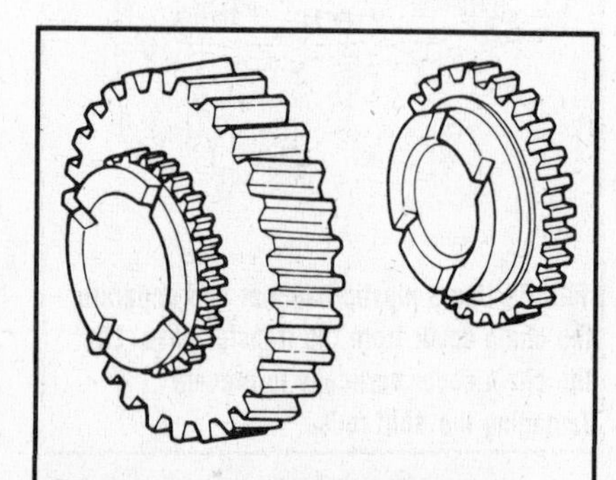
FIG. 74 Inspect the low gear and 2W-4W clutch hub for wear, damage, or damaged teeth

FIG. 75 Inspect the drive sprocket and front drive sprocket for wear, damage, or damaged teeth

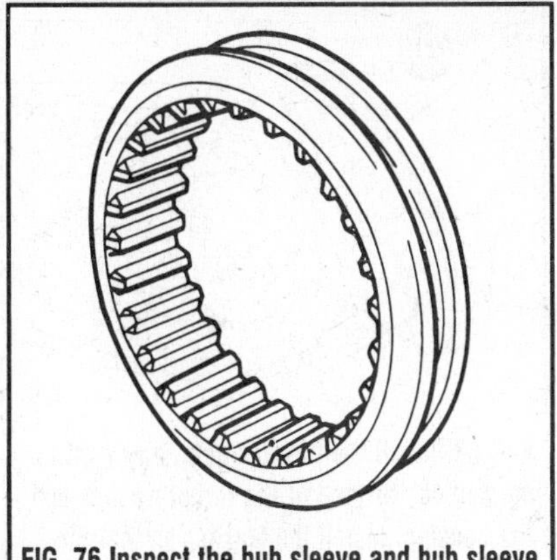
FIG. 76 Inspect the hub sleeve and hub sleeve groove for wear or damage

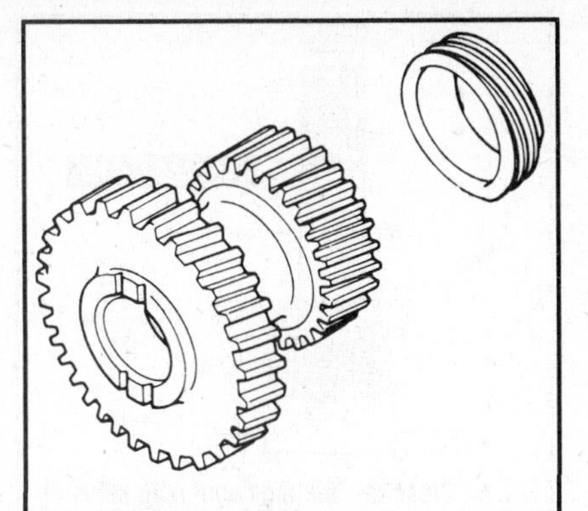
FIG. 77 Inspect the counter gear, countershaft, and speedometer drive gear for wear or damaged teeth

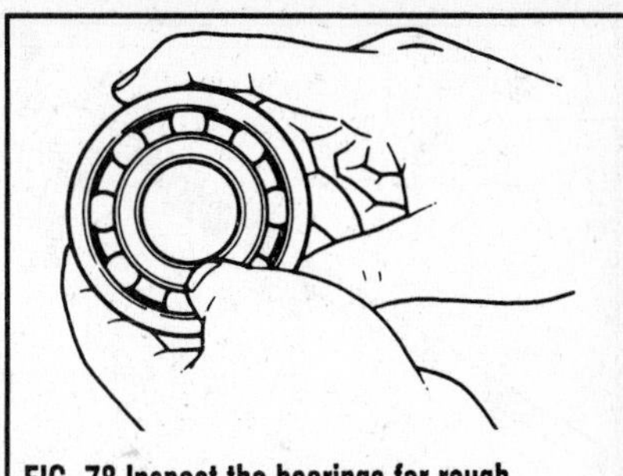
FIG. 78 Inspect the bearings for rough operation or noise while turning

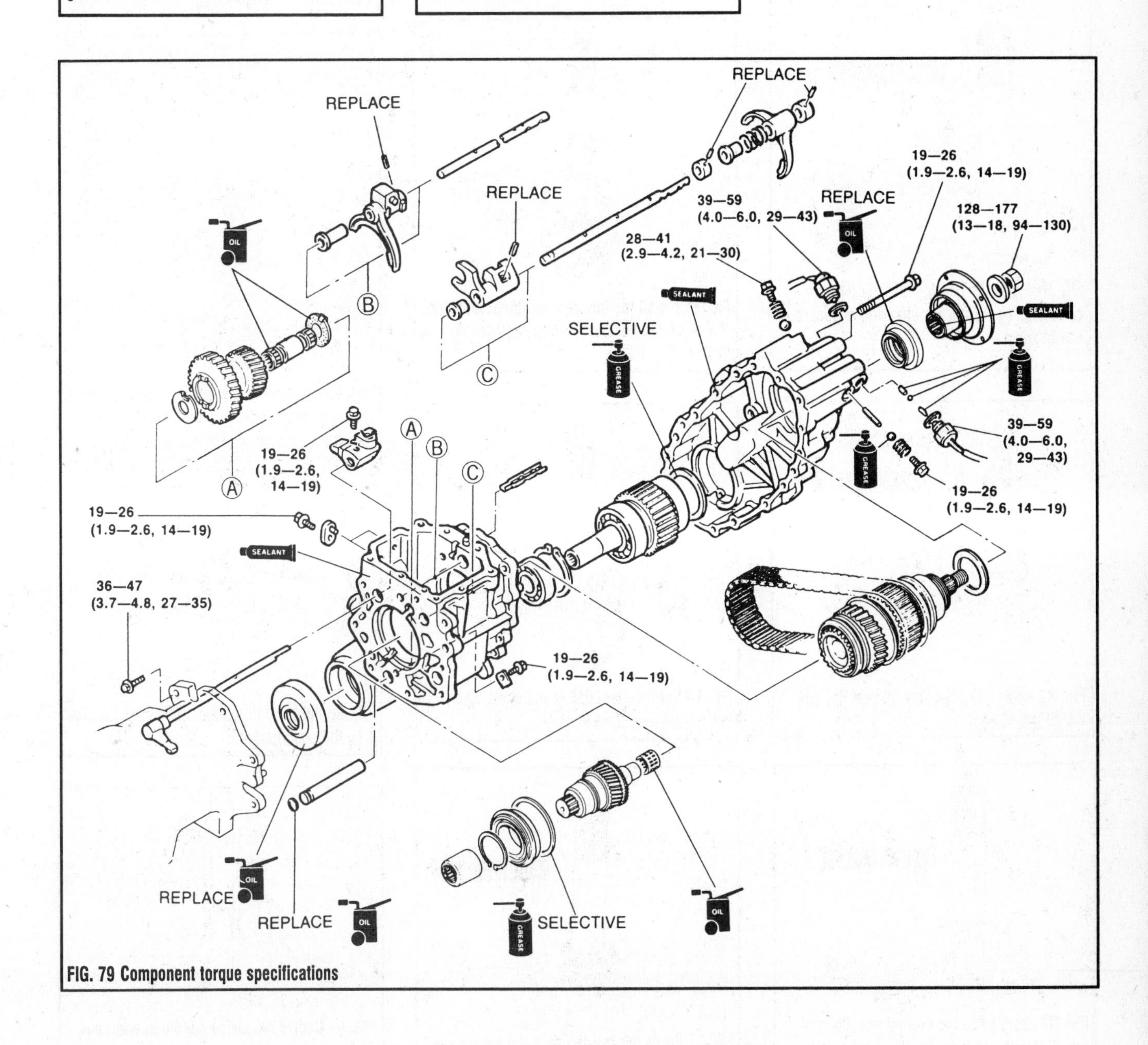

FIG. 79 Component torque specifications

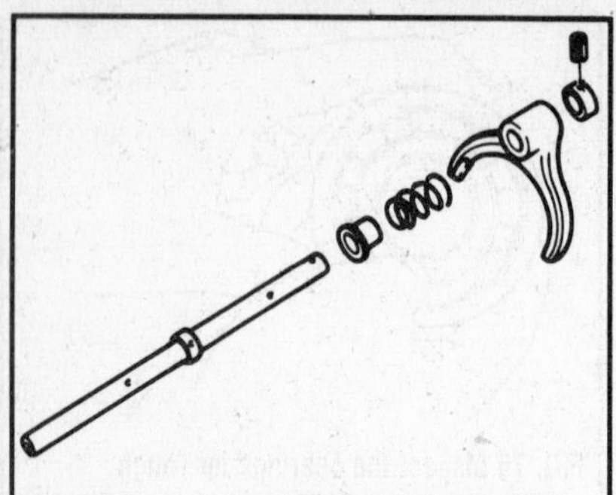
FIG. 80 Inspect the shift fork or shift rod for wear or damage. Check the shift spring for tension

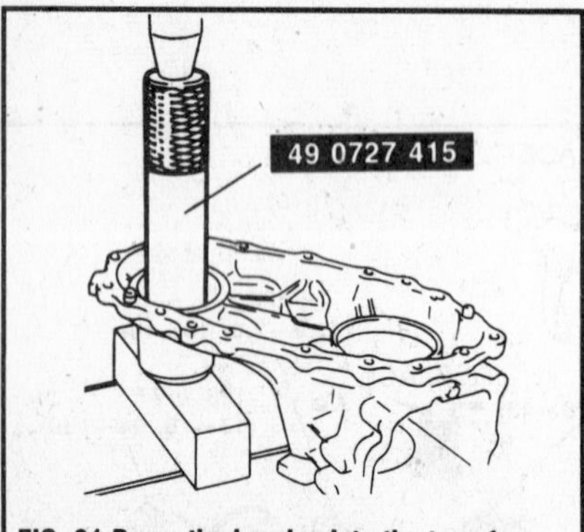

FIG. 81 Press the bearing into the transfer case housing. Install the snapring to secure the bearing

FIG. 82 Apply oil to the new oil seal lip, and install the oil seal

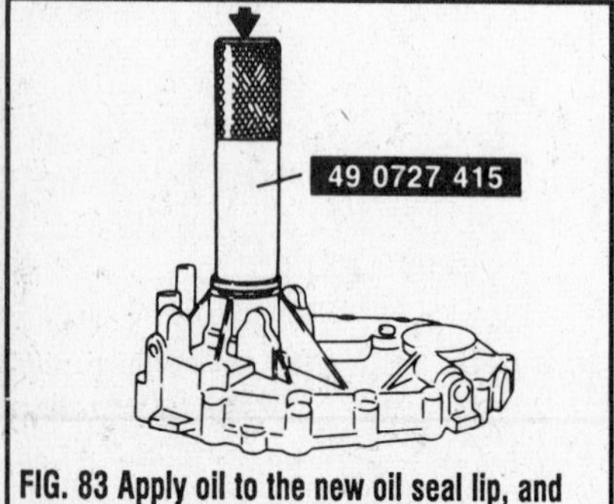

FIG. 83 Apply oil to the new oil seal lip, and install the oil seal into the chain cover

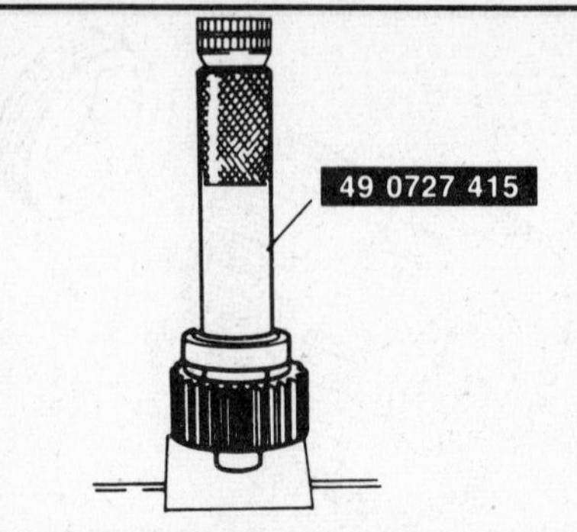

FIG. 84 Press the bearings onto both sides of the front drive sprocket. Press on the bearings until the stop

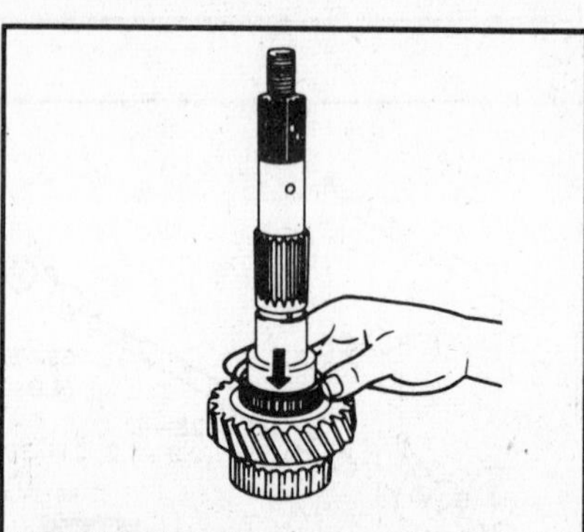
FIG. 85 Install the low gear on the output shaft. Put oil on the needle bearings, and set the gear on the shaft

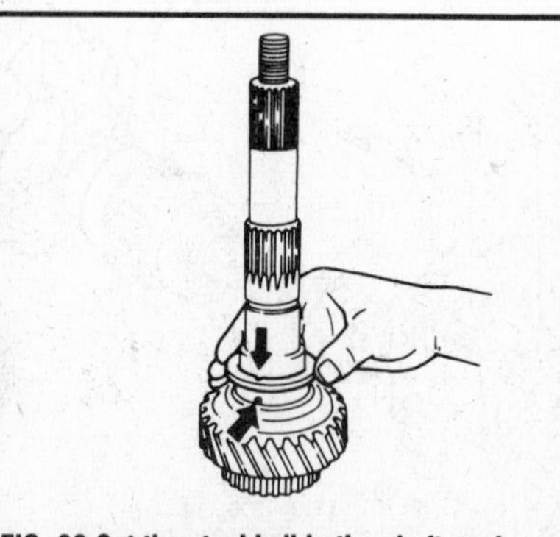
FIG. 86 Set the steel ball in the shaft, and install the thrust lock washer

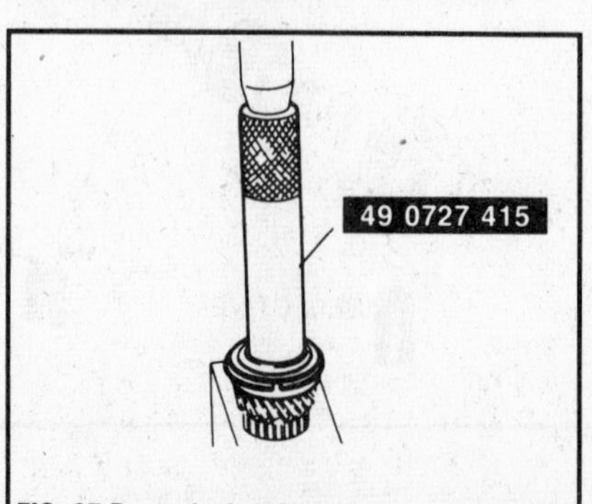

FIG. 87 Press the bearing onto the output shaft

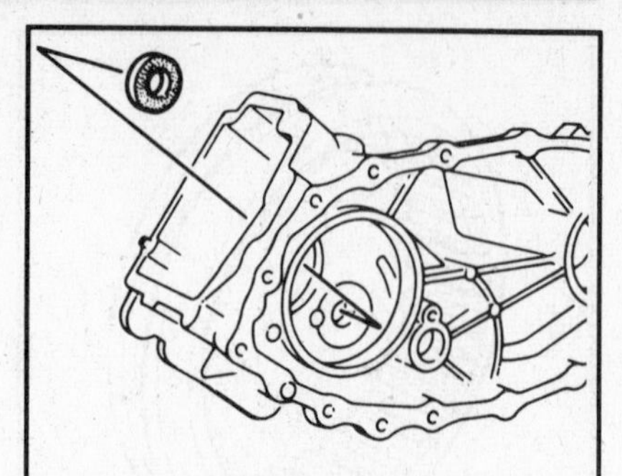
FIG. 88 Install the counter gear, apply oil to the contact surface of the thrust washer and the housing. Install the washer so that the dished (convex) part of the washer sets down into the housing

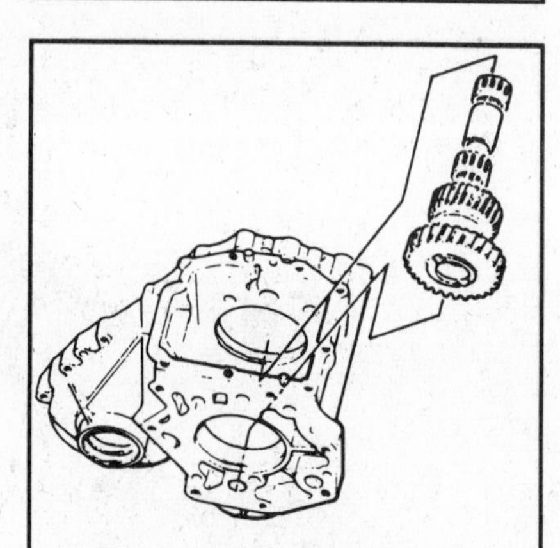
FIG. 89 Apply oil to the needle bearings, install them and the spacer into the counter gear. Install the counter gear into the housing

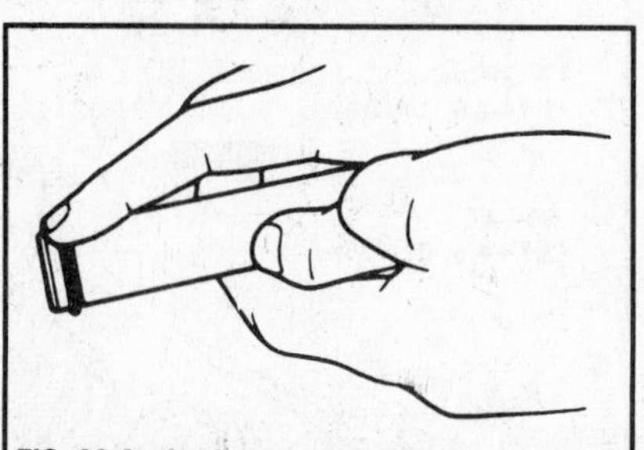
FIG. 90 Apply oil to the new O-ring, and install it on the countershaft

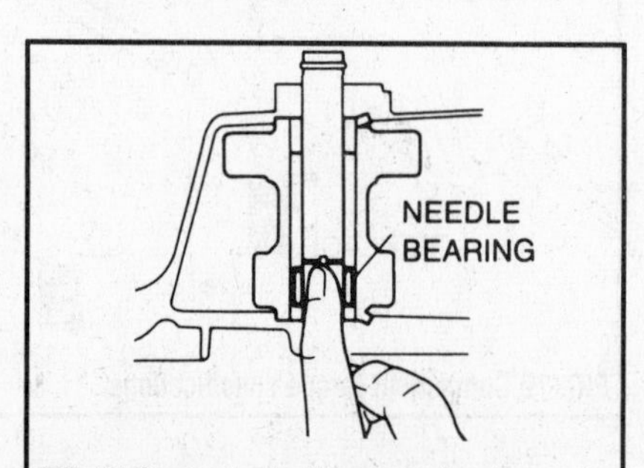

FIG. 91 Center the inside needle bearing and slide the countershaft into the case

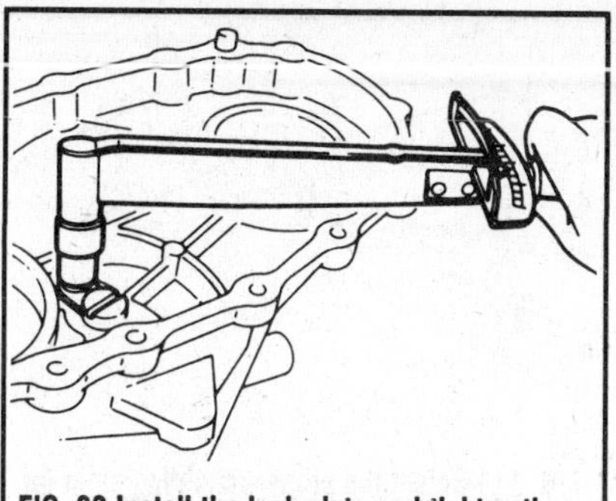
FIG. 92 Install the lock plate and tighten the bolt to 14–1Q9 ft. lbs. (19–26Nm)

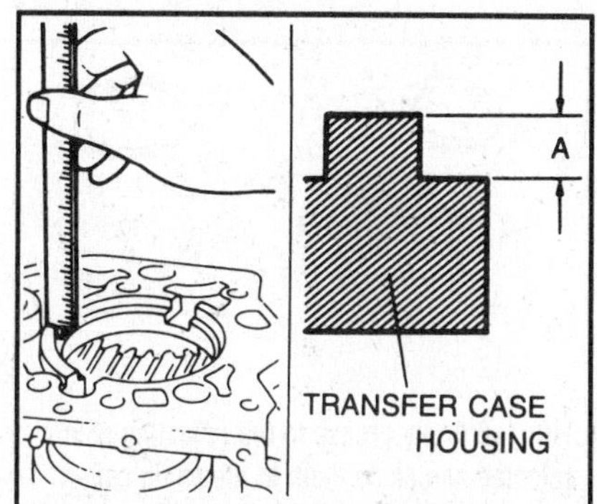

FIG. 93 Install the input shaft as follows – measure the bearing bore depth (A) of the housing

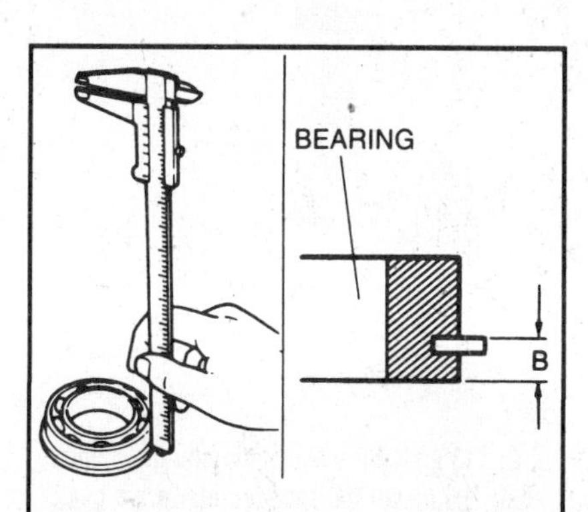

FIG. 94 Measure the height (B) of the bearing clip. Calculate the difference between (A) and (B) to determine the clearance

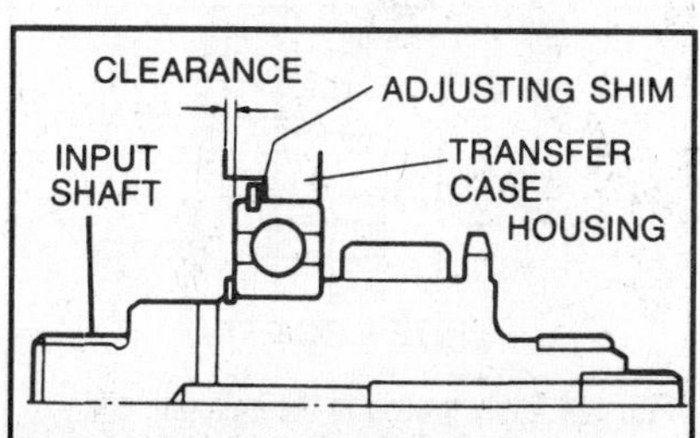

FIG. 95 Select and install the proper shim to obtain the standard clearance of 0–0.004 in. (0-0.10mm)

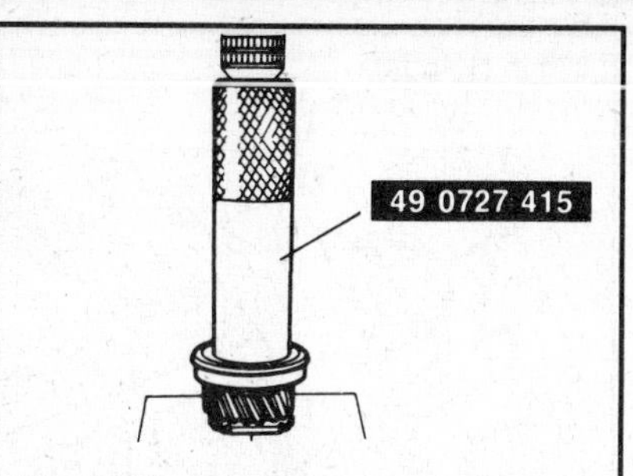

FIG. 96 Press the bearing onto the input shaft gear

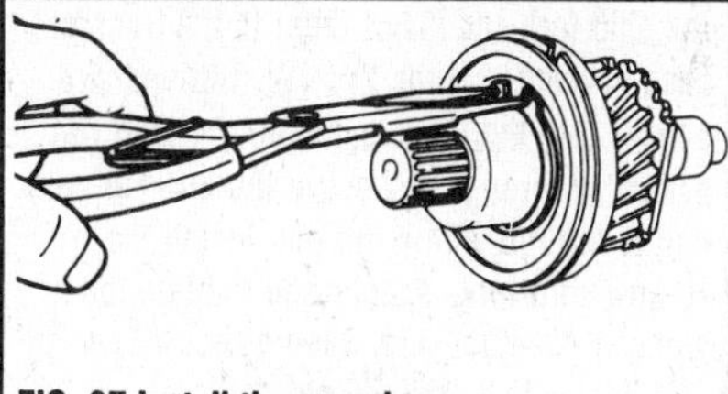
FIG. 97 Install the snapring

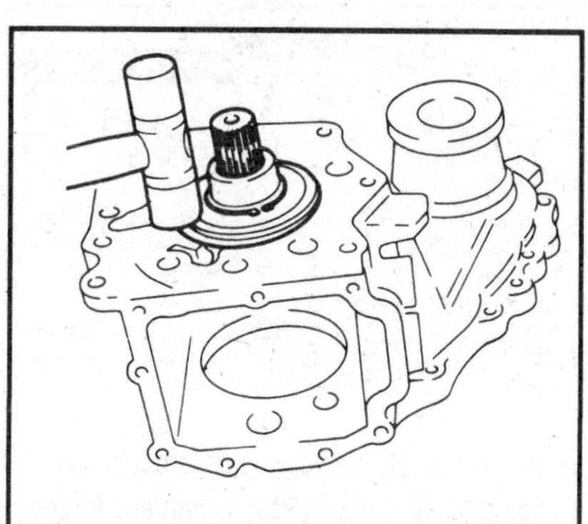
FIG. 98 Install the input shaft assembly into the housing by lightly tapping the outer race of the bearing with a plastic hammer

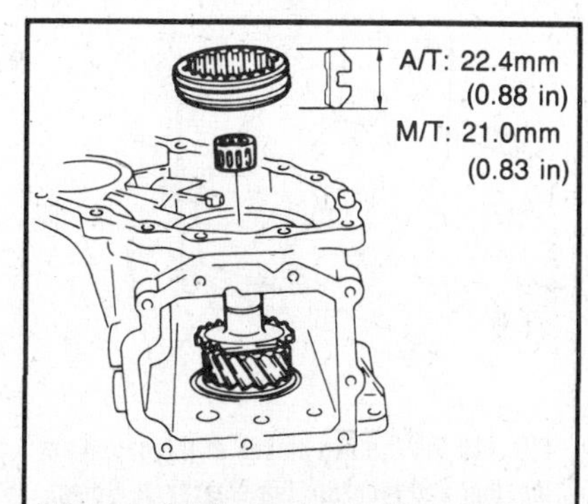

FIG. 99 Install the needle bearing and Hi-Low hub sleeve onto the input shaft

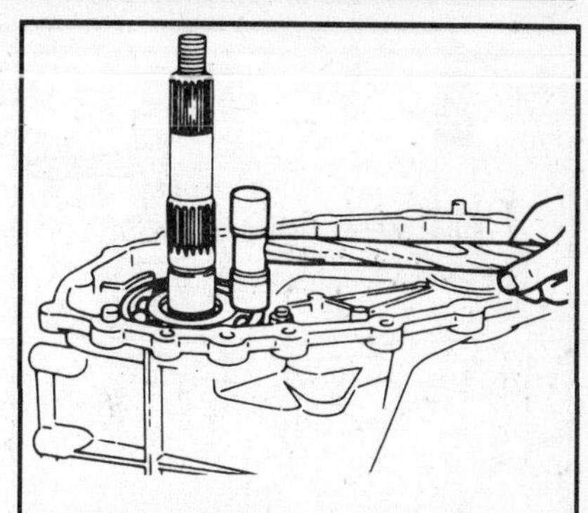
FIG. 100 Install the output shaft into the housing by lightly tapping the outer race of the bearing with a plastic hammer

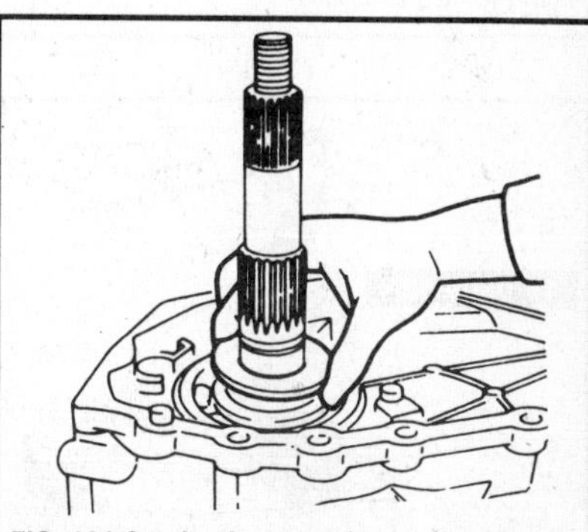
FIG. 101 Set the thrust washer on the output shaft

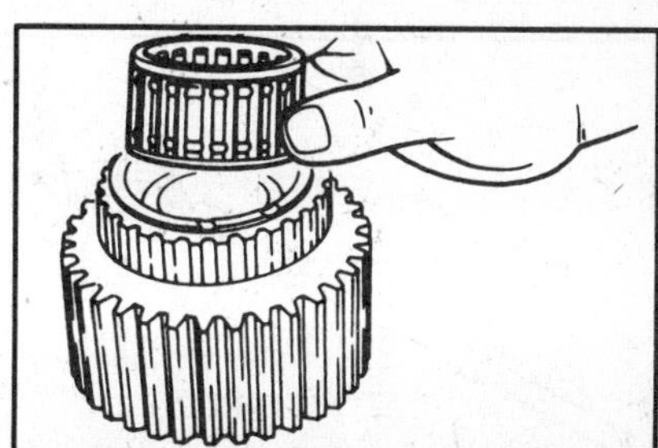
FIG. 102 Apply oil to the needle bearings and install them onto the drive sprocket along with the spacer

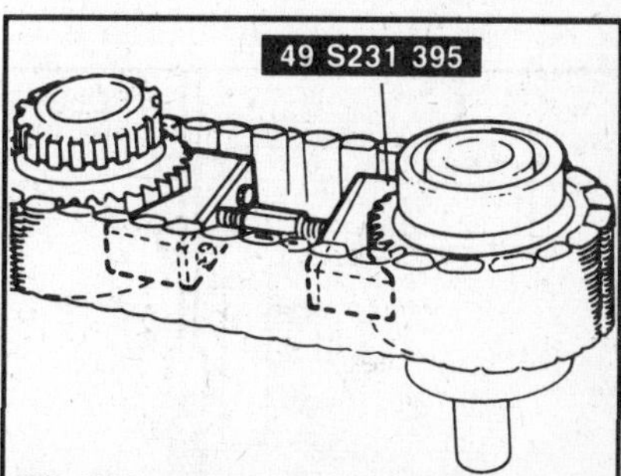

FIG. 103 Install the chain on the drive sprocket assembly and the front drive sprocket. Expand the chain with a suitable tool to set the center-to-center distance for easy installation into the housing. Do not overtighten the expansion tool

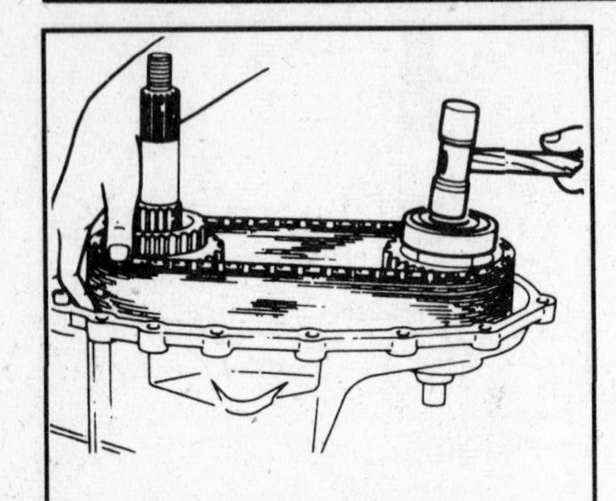

FIG. 104 Install the front drive sprocket assembly into the housing by lightly tapping it with a plastic hammer keeping the chain horizontal. After installation, verify that the chain rotates smoothly

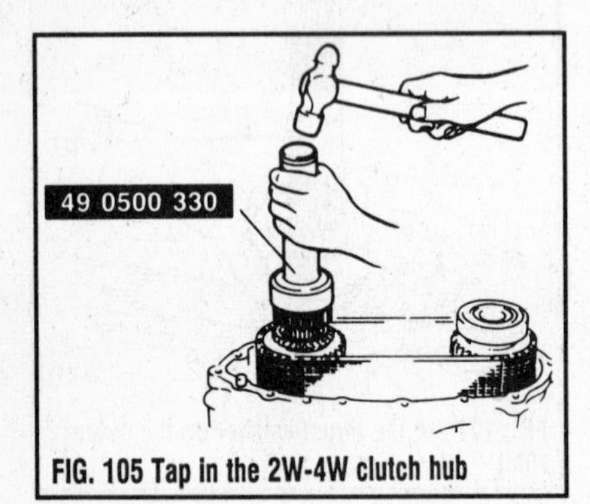

FIG. 105 Tap in the 2W-4W clutch hub

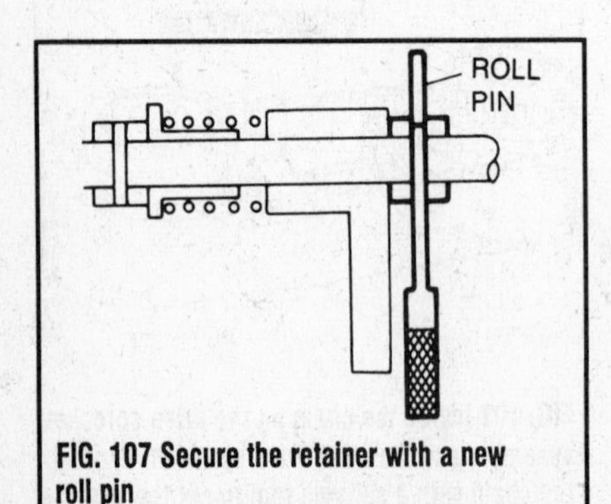

FIG. 106 Install the 2W-4W shift fork onto the shaft

FIG. 107 Secure the retainer with a new roll pin

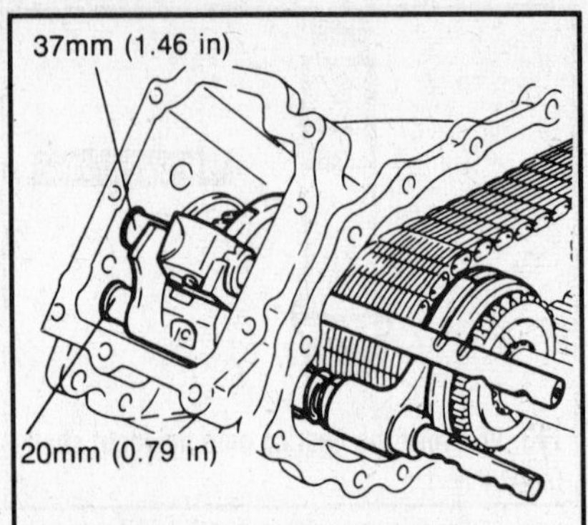

FIG. 108 Assemble the 2W-4W hub sleeve to the shift fork and insert them to the transfer case housing. Set the 2W-4W shift end and spacer into the case and slide the shift rod assembly through it. Secure the 2W-4W shift end to the rod with a roll pin. Install the Hi-Low shift fork, spacer and rod into the transfer case housing. Secure the Hi-Low shift fork with a new roll pin

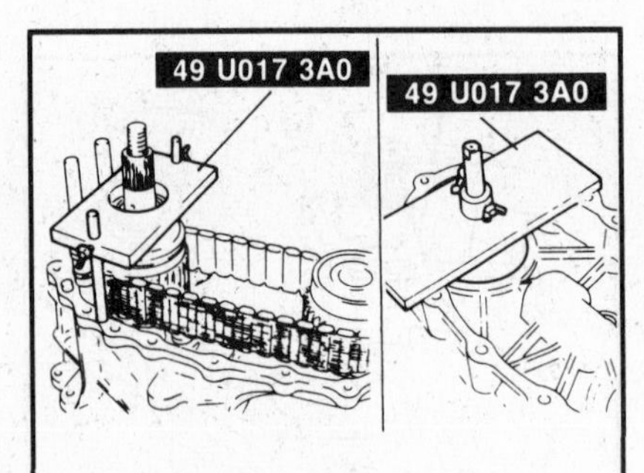

FIG. 109 Install the bearing onto the output shaft. Measure the bearing height and bearing bore depth for the output shaft

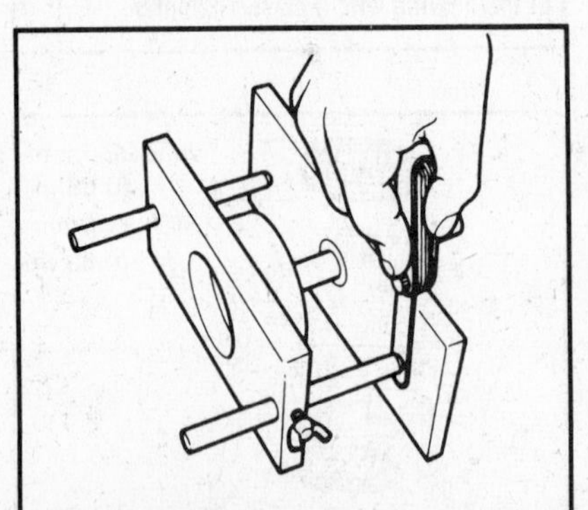

FIG. 110 Put the two pieces of the gauge set together and measure the clearance. Select the proper adjusting shim to adjust the clearance. Standard clearance is 0–0.004 in (0-0.10mm)

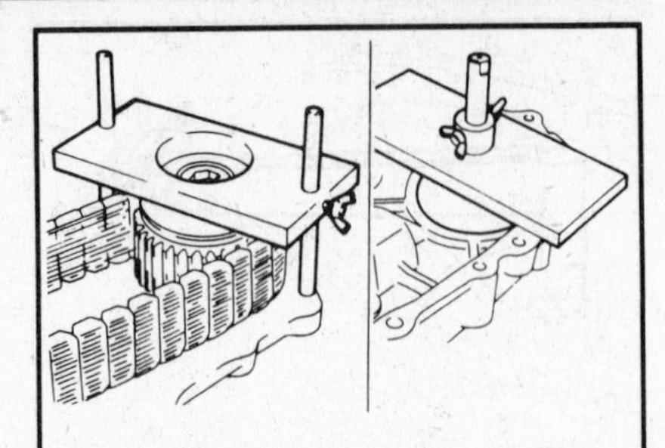

FIG. 111 Select the proper adjusting shim for the front drive sprocket bearing in the same way as the output shaft side

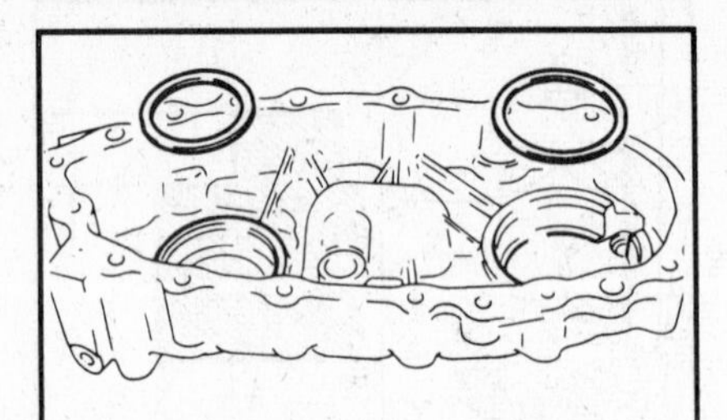

FIG. 112 Apply grease to the adjusting shims selected and place them in the chain cover

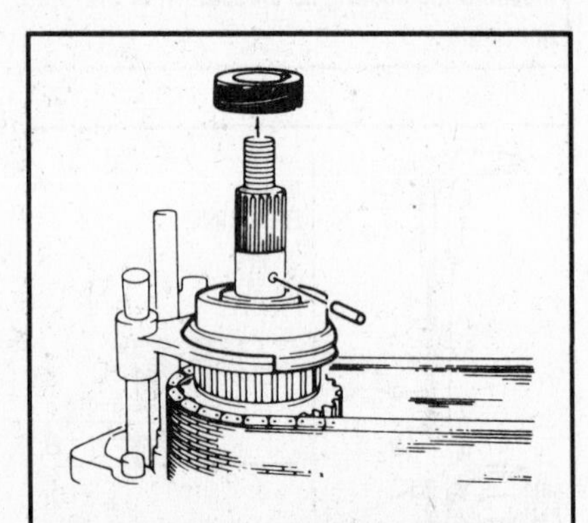

FIG. 113 Install the knock pin into the output shaft and install the speedometer drive gear. Install the oil passage into the case

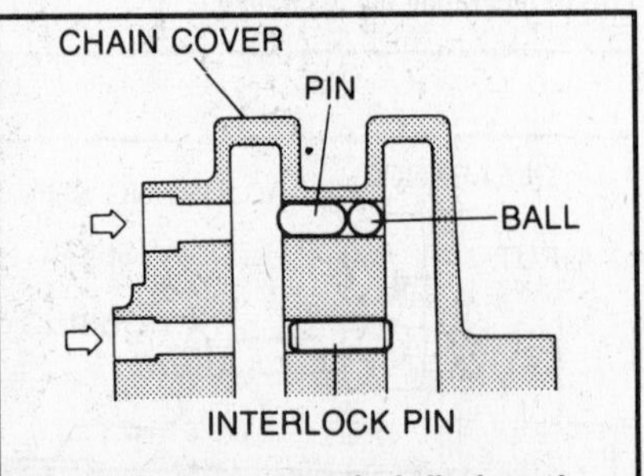

FIG. 114 Apply grease to the ball, pin, and interlock pin. Install them into the chain cover

1. Protector plate
2. Change motor
3. O-ring
4. Companion flange
5. Speedometer driven gear
6. Rear cover
7. Adjustment shims
8. Speedometer drive gear
9. Key
10. Rear chain cover
11. Adjustment shim
12. Clutch gear
13. Needle bearing
14. Magnet
15. Rear oil pipe
16. O-ring
17. Thrust washer
18. Change drum
19. Thrust washer
20. 2-4 shift rod
21. 2-4 shift fork
22. Drive gear and chain assembly
23. Thrust washer
24. Needle bearings
25. Center differential and output shaft assembly
26. Needle bearing
27. Snapring
28. Outer clutch gear
29. Control cover assembly
30. Detent spring
31. Detent ball
32. Spring pin
33. Hi-Lo shift rod
34. Hi-Lo hub sleeve
35. Inner clutch gear
36. Hi-Lo shift fork
37. Pump cover
38. Outer pump rotor
39. Inner pump rotor
40. Key
41. Pump housing
42. Adjustment shims
43. Front oil pipe
44. O-rings
45. Rear oil pipe
46. O-rings
47. Retaining ring
48. Input gear
49. Baffle plate
50. Rear oil pipe
51. O-ring
52. Transfer case
53. Oil seal
54. Bearing, input shaft side
55. Oil seal
56. Bearing, output shaft side
57. Oil seal

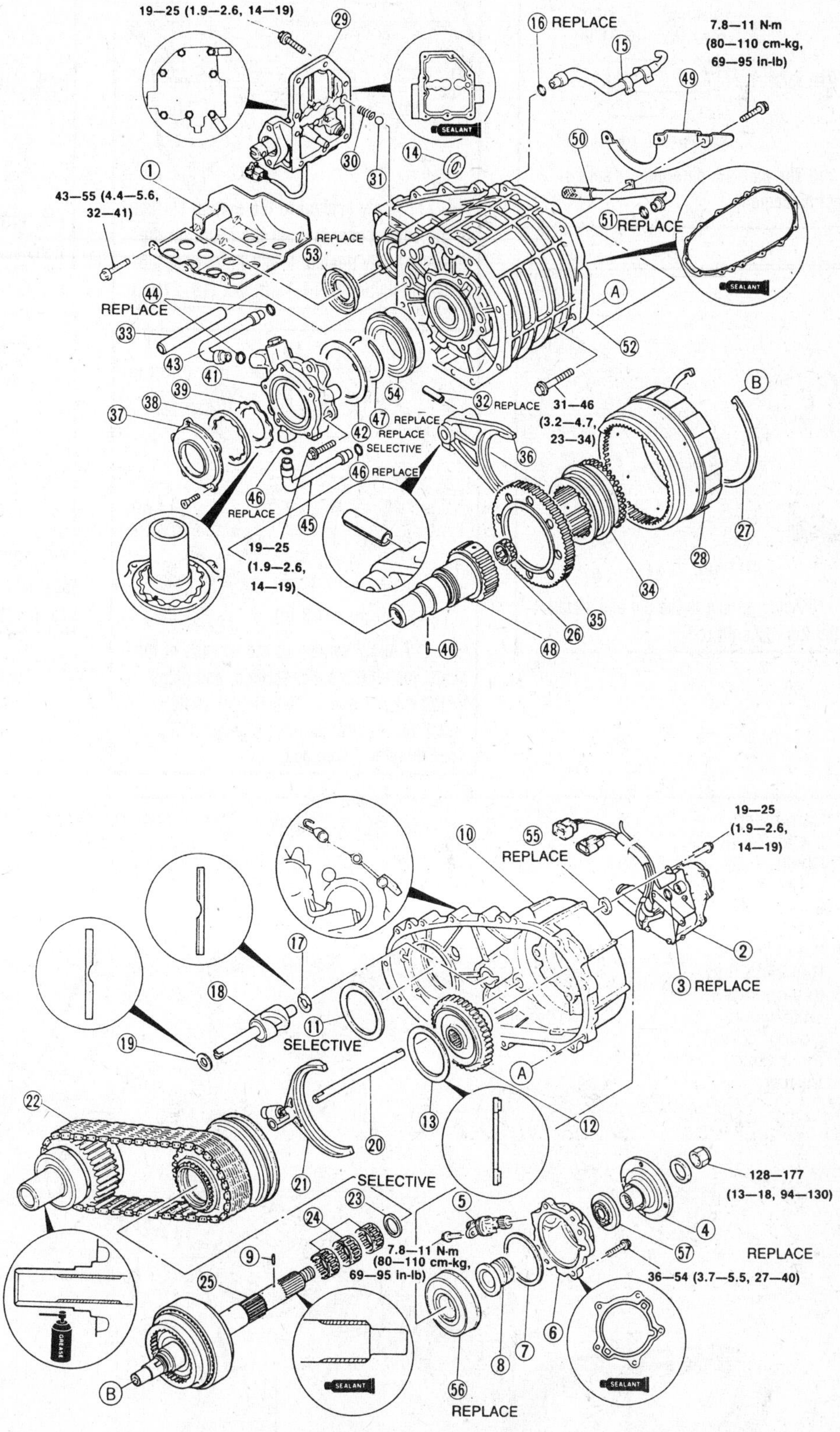

FIG. 121 / 122 MPV with manual transmission transfer case components

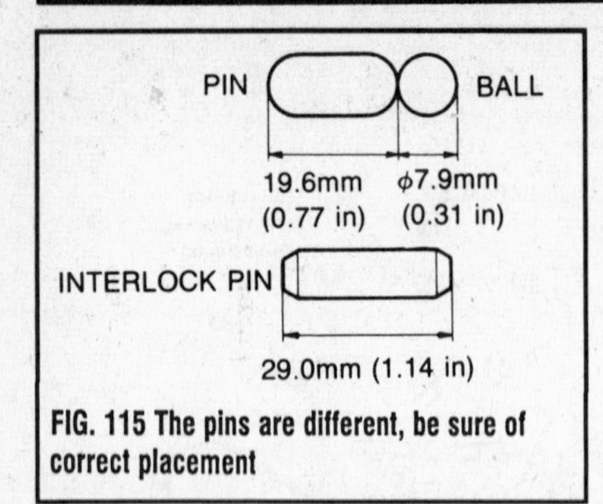

FIG. 115 The pins are different, be sure of correct placement

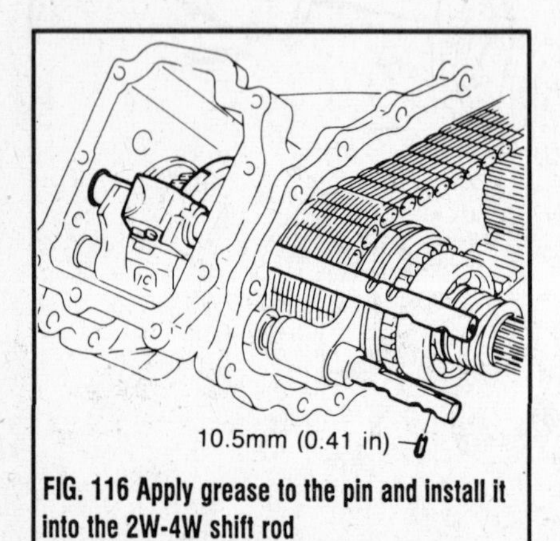

FIG. 116 Apply grease to the pin and install it into the 2W-4W shift rod

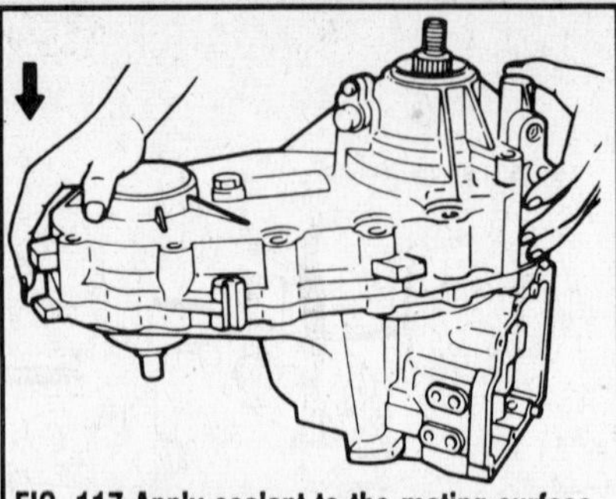

FIG. 117 Apply sealant to the mating surface of the chain cover and set the cover on the housing. Apply sealant to the threads of the bolts and tighten to 14–19 ft. lbs. (19–27Nm)

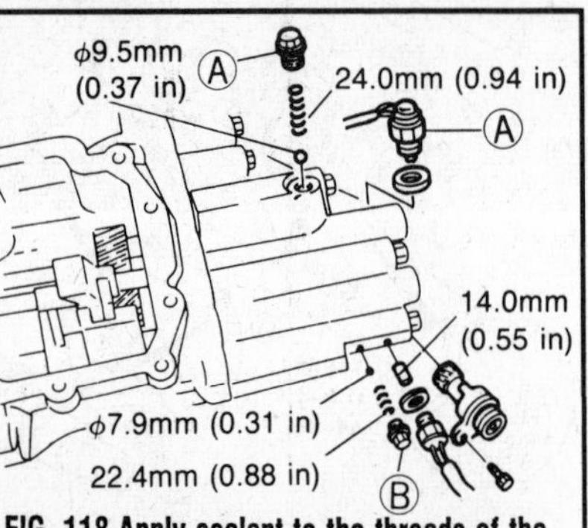

FIG. 118 Apply sealant to the threads of the plugs. Install the balls, springs, and plugs. Install the pin and 4×4 indicator switch. Install the neutral switch (AT). Install the speedometer driven gear

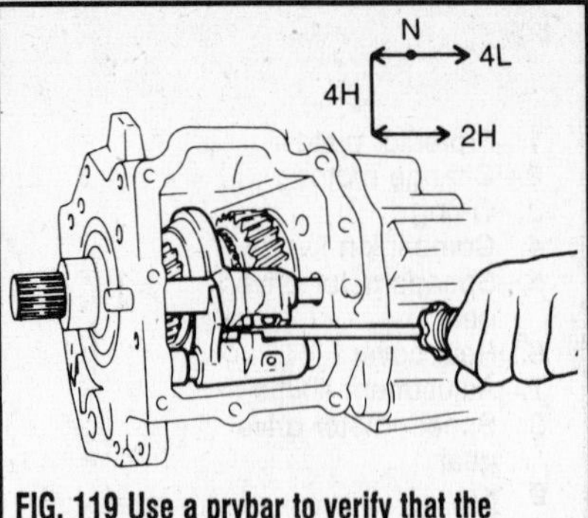

FIG. 119 Use a prybar to verify that the transfer case shifts smoothly

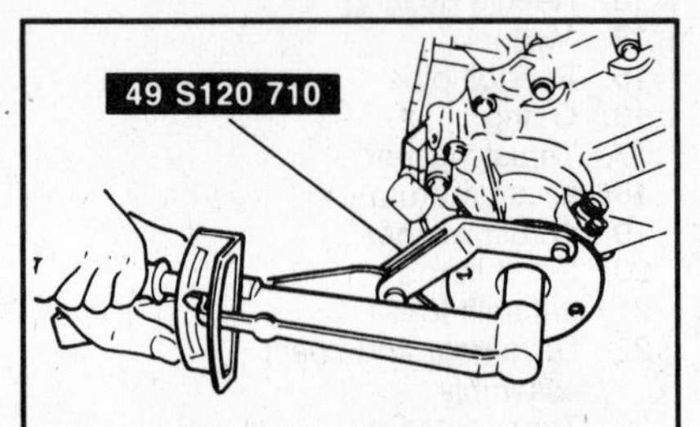

FIG. 120 Apply transmission oil to a new oil seal and install it. Install the companion flange. Torque the nut to 94–130 ft. lbs. (128–177Nm)

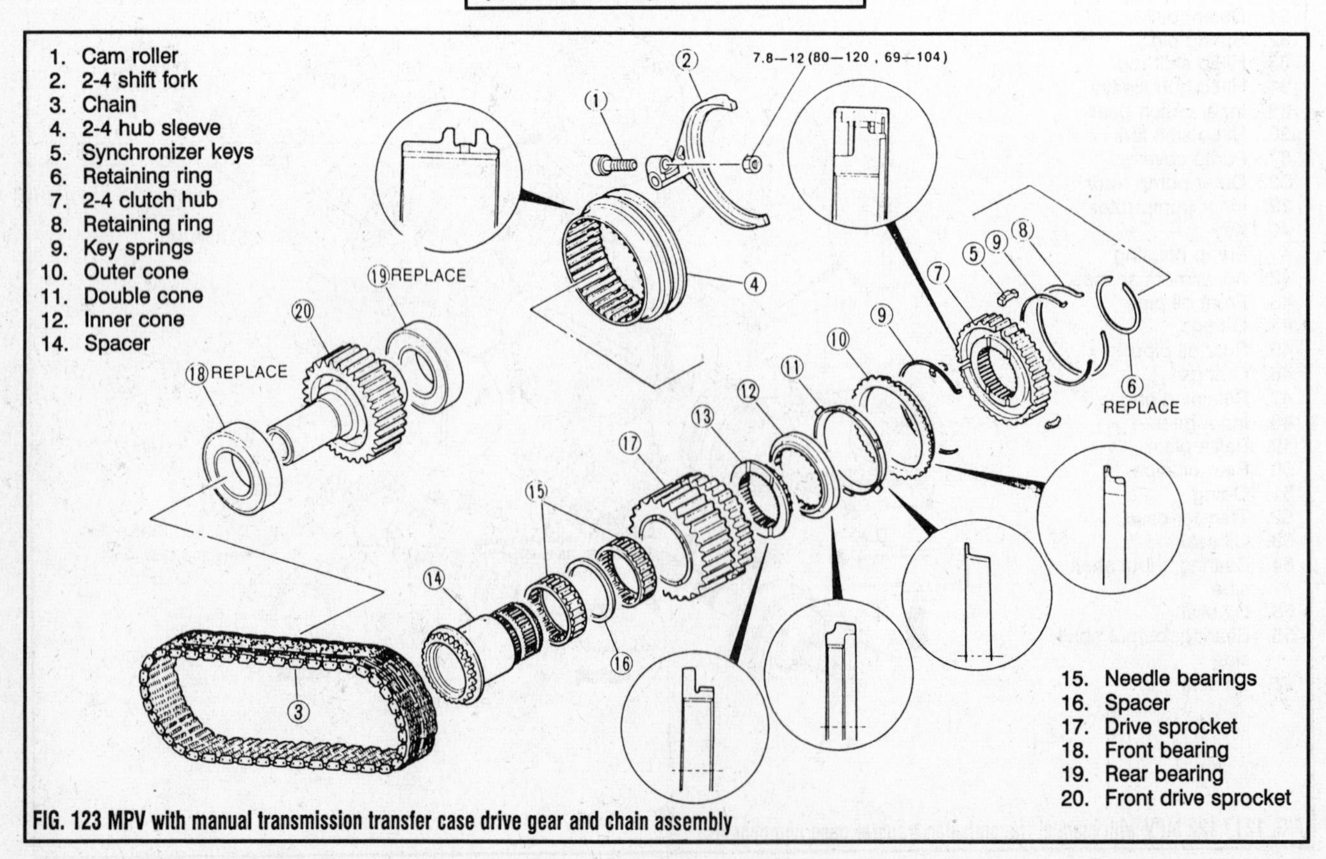

FIG. 123 MPV with manual transmission transfer case drive gear and chain assembly

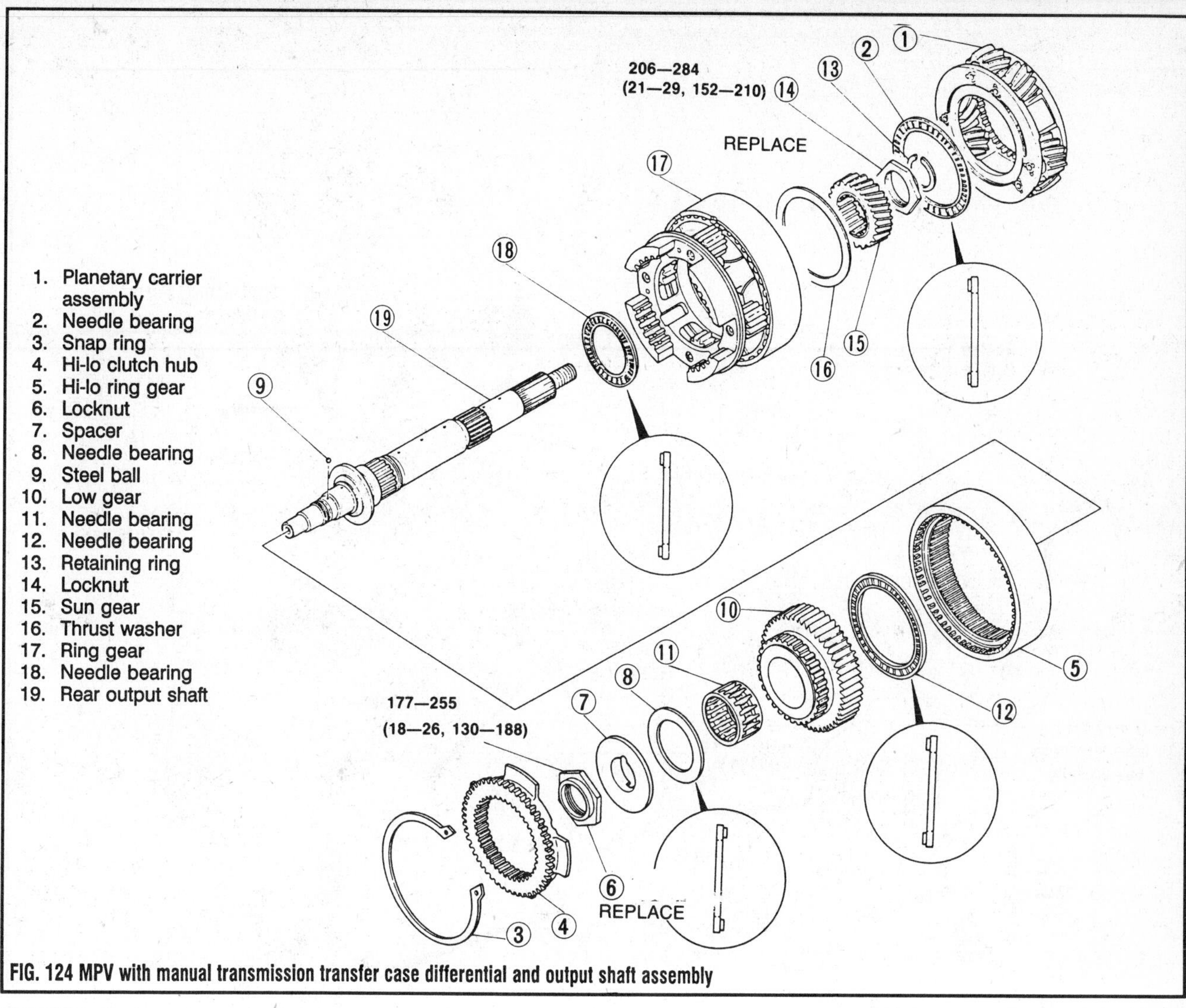

FIG. 124 MPV with manual transmission transfer case differential and output shaft assembly

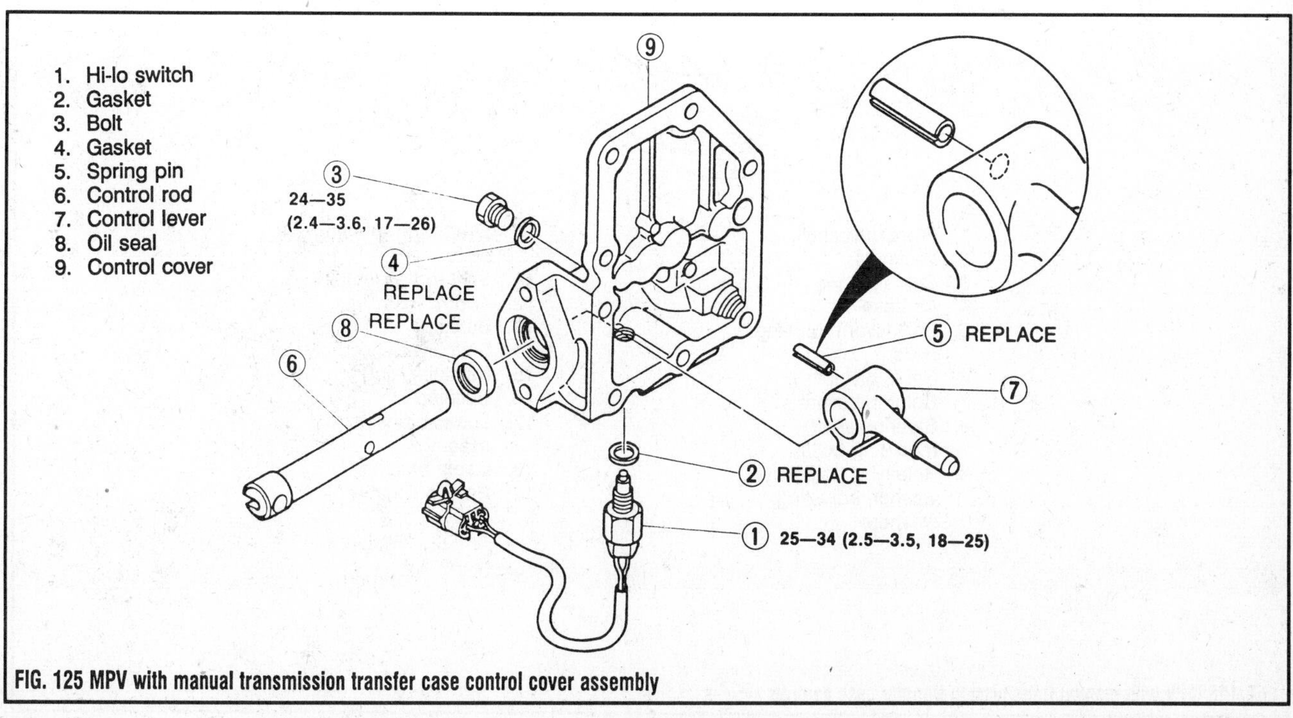

FIG. 125 MPV with manual transmission transfer case control cover assembly

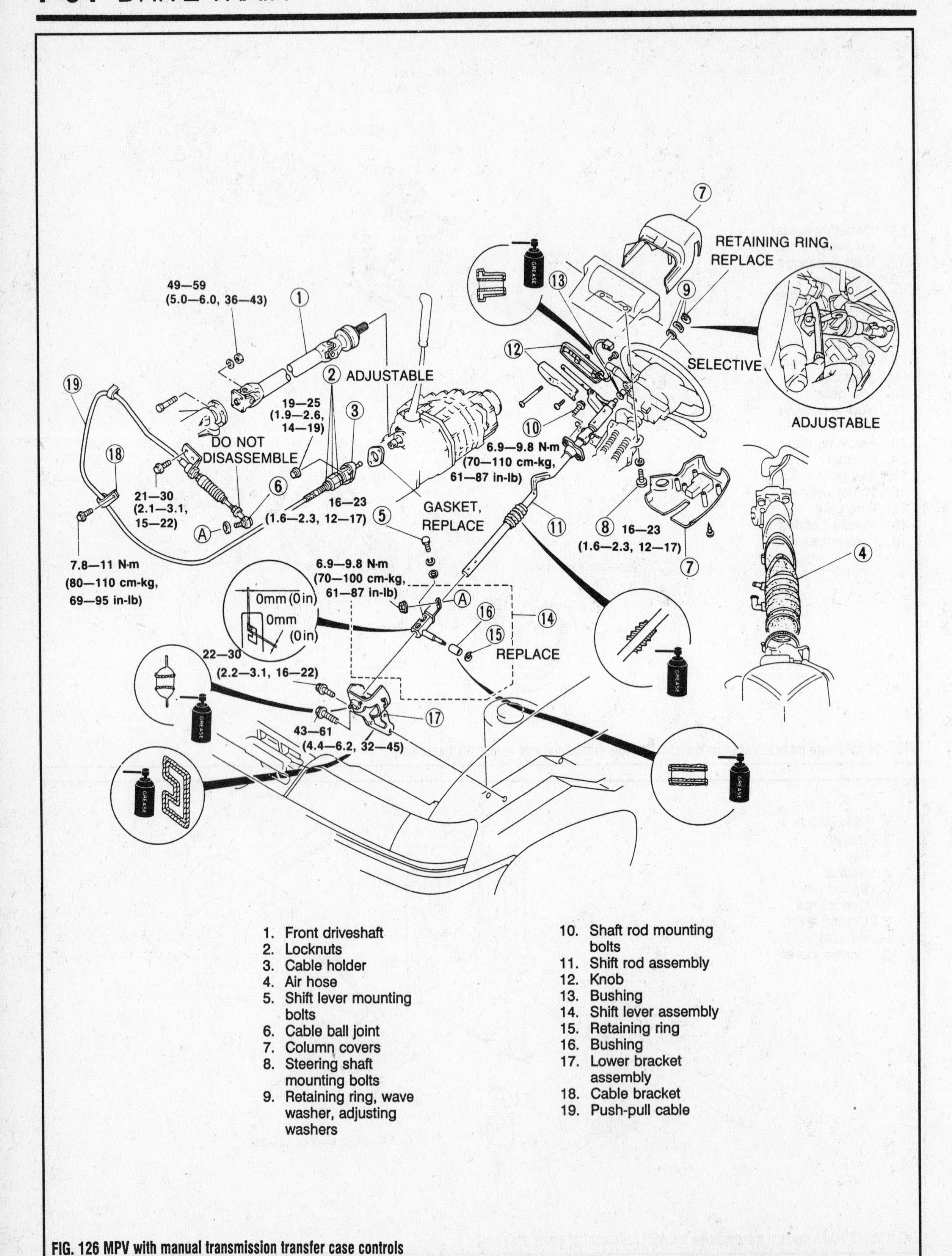

1. Front driveshaft
2. Locknuts
3. Cable holder
4. Air hose
5. Shift lever mounting bolts
6. Cable ball joint
7. Column covers
8. Steering shaft mounting bolts
9. Retaining ring, wave washer, adjusting washers
10. Shaft rod mounting bolts
11. Shift rod assembly
12. Knob
13. Bushing
14. Shift lever assembly
15. Retaining ring
16. Bushing
17. Lower bracket assembly
18. Cable bracket
19. Push-pull cable

FIG. 126 MPV with manual transmission transfer case controls

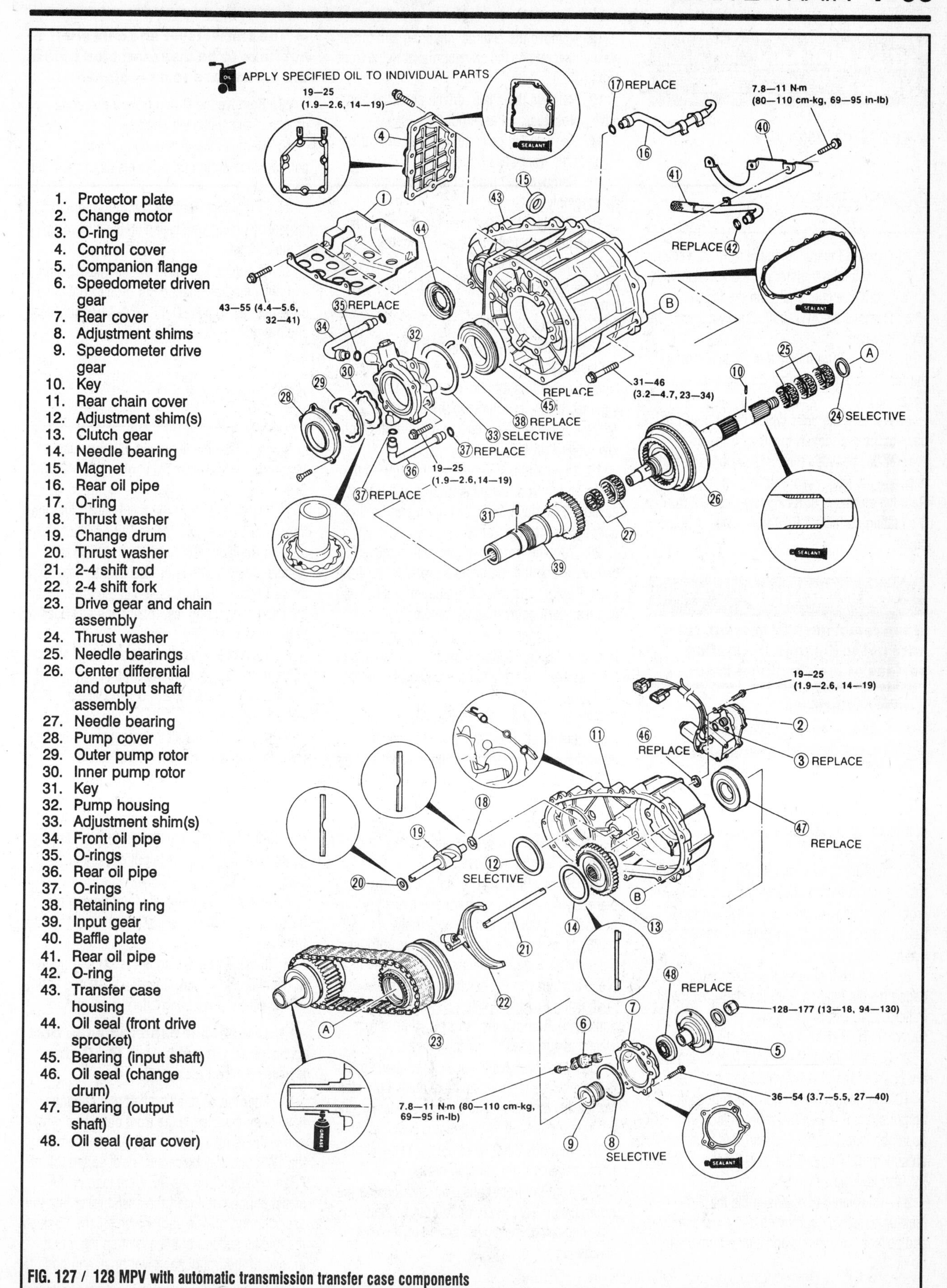
APPLY SPECIFIED OIL TO INDIVIDUAL PARTS
1. Protector plate
2. Change motor
3. O-ring
4. Control cover
5. Companion flange
6. Speedometer driven gear
7. Rear cover
8. Adjustment shims
9. Speedometer drive gear
10. Key
11. Rear chain cover
12. Adjustment shim(s)
13. Clutch gear
14. Needle bearing
15. Magnet
16. Rear oil pipe
17. O-ring
18. Thrust washer
19. Change drum
20. Thrust washer
21. 2-4 shift rod
22. 2-4 shift fork
23. Drive gear and chain assembly
24. Thrust washer
25. Needle bearings
26. Center differential and output shaft assembly
27. Needle bearing
28. Pump cover
29. Outer pump rotor
30. Inner pump rotor
31. Key
32. Pump housing
33. Adjustment shim(s)
34. Front oil pipe
35. O-rings
36. Rear oil pipe
37. O-rings
38. Retaining ring
39. Input gear
40. Baffle plate
41. Rear oil pipe
42. O-ring
43. Transfer case housing
44. Oil seal (front drive sprocket)
45. Bearing (input shaft)
46. Oil seal (change drum)
47. Bearing (output shaft)
48. Oil seal (rear cover)
19—25 (1.9—2.6, 14—19)
17 REPLACE
7.8—11 N·m (80—110 cm-kg, 69—95 in-lb)
SEALANT
REPLACE 42
43—55 (4.4—5.6, 32—41)
35 REPLACE
31—46 (3.2—4.7, 23—34)
REPLACE 45
38 REPLACE
33 SELECTIVE
37 REPLACE
24 SELECTIVE
19—25 (1.9—2.6, 14—19)
37 REPLACE
19—25 (1.9—2.6, 14—19)
46 REPLACE
3 REPLACE
47 REPLACE
12 SELECTIVE
48 REPLACE
128—177 (13—18, 94—130)
36—54 (3.7—5.5, 27—40)
7.8—11 N·m (80—110 cm-kg, 69—95 in-lb)
8 SELECTIVE
GREASE

FIG. 127 / 128 MPV with automatic transmission transfer case components

13-54 Overhaul Navajo

➧ SEE FIGS. 129, 130-130j

DISASSEMBLY

1. Remove the transfer case from the vehicle.
2. Remove the transfer case drain plug with a 3/8 in. drive ratchet and drain the fluid.
3. Remove the 4WD indicator switch and the breather vent.
4. Using a 30mm thin wall socket, remove the rear output nut, washer, rubber seal and yoke.
5. Remove the bolts which retain the front case to the rear cover. Insert a 1/2 in. drive breaker bar between the three pry bosses and separate the front case from the rear cover. Remove all traces of RTV gasket sealant from the mating surfaces of the front case and rear cover.

WARNING

When removing RTV sealant, take care not to damage the mating surface of the aluminum case!

6. If the speedometer drive gear or ball bearing assembly is to be replaced, first, drive out the output shaft oil seal from either the inside of the rear cover with a brass drift and hammer or from the outside by bending and pulling on the curved-up lip of the oil seal. Remove and discard the oil seal.
7. Remove the internal snapring that retains the rear output shaft ball bearing in the bore. From the outside of the case, drive out the ball bearing using D80L-630-A, step plate with a suitable drift.
8. If required, remove the front output shaft caged needle bearing from the rear cover with Puller Collet, D80L-100-S and Impact Slide Hammer, T50T-100-A or equivalent.
9. Remove the 2W-4W shift fork spring from the boss on the 2W-4W shift fork.
10. Remove the shift collar hub from the output shaft. Remove the 2W-4W lock-up assembly and the 2W-4W shift fork together as an assembly. Remove the 2W-4W fork from the 2W-4W lock-up assembly.
11. If required to disassemble the 2W-4W lock-up assembly, remove the internal snapring and pull the lock-up hub and spring from the lock-up collar.
12. Remove the external snapring and thrust washer that retains the drive sprocket to the front output shaft.
13. Remove the chain, driven sprocket and drive sprocket as an assembly.
14. Remove the collector magnet from the notch in the front case bottom.
15. Remove the output shaft and oil pump as an assembly.
16. If required to disassemble the oil pump , remove the bolts from the body. Note the position and markings of the front cover , body, pins, spring, rear cover, and pump retainer as removed.
17. Pull out the shift rail.
18. Slip the high-low range shift fork out of the inside track of the shift cam and remove the high-low shift fork and high-low shift collar together. If required, remove the pin, roller retainer assembly by pressing it out of the high-low range shift fork.
19. Push and pull out the anchor end of the assist spring from the locking post in the front case half. Remove the assist spring and roller out of the shift cam.
20. Turn the front case over and remove the bolts retaining the mounting adapter to the front case. Remove the mounting adapter, input shaft and planetary gearset as an assembly.
21. If required, remove the ring gear from the front case using a press. Note the relationship of the serrations to the chamfered pilot diameter during removal.
22. Expand the tangs of the large snapring in the mounting adapter. With the input shaft against a bench, push the adapter down and slide the adapter off the ball bearing. Lift the input shaft and planetary gearset from the adapter.
23. If required, remove the oil from the mounting adapter by prying and pulling on the curved-up lip of the oil seal.
24. Remove the internal snapring from the planetary carrier and separate the planetary gearset from the input shaft assembly.
25. Remove the external snapring from the input shaft. Place the input shaft assembly in a press and remove the ball bearing from the input shaft using Bearing Splitter, D79L-4621-A or equivalent. Remove the thrust washer, thrust plate and sun gear off the input shaft.
26. Move the shift lever by hand down to the 4L position, then up 2 detents to the 4H position. Mark a line on the outside of the front case using the side of the shift lever and a grease pencil.
27. Remove the 2 head set screws from the front case and from the shift cam.
28. Turn the front case over and remove the external clip. Pry the shift shaft out of the front case and shift cam. Do not pound on the external clip during removal.

➡ The shifter lever and cam shaft do not have to be disassembled unless the parks have to be replaced.

29. Remove the O-ring from the second groove in the shift lever shaft.
30. Remove the detent plunger and compression spring from the inside of the front case.
31. If required, remove the front output shaft oil seal by prying and pulling on the curved-up lip of the oil seal.
32. If required, remove the internal snapring and drive the ball bearing out of the front case bore, using step plate D80L-630-A or equivalent, and a drift.

ASSEMBLY

Before assembly, lubricate all parts with Motorcraft® Automatic Transmission Fluid, XT2-QDX or equivalent.

1. If removed, drive the ball bearing into the front output case bore, using Output Shaft Bearing Replacer, T83T-7025-B and Driver Handle, T80T-4000-W or equivalent. Make sure the ball bearing is not cocked in the bore. Install the internal snapring that retains the ball bearing to the front case.
2. If removed, install the front output oil seal in the front case bore, using Output Shaft Seal Installer, T83T-7025-B and Driver Handle, T80T-4000-W or equivalent.
3. If removed, install the ring gear in the front case. Align the serrations on the outside diameter of the ring gear to the serrations previously cut in the front case bore. Using press, start the piloted chamfered end of the ring gear first and press in until it is fully seated. Make sure the ring gear is not cocked in the bore.
4. Install the compression spring and the detent plunger into the bore from the inside of the front case.
5. Install a new O-ring in the second groove of the shift lever shaft. Coat the shaft and O-ring with Multi-Purpose Long-Life Lubricant.

➡ Use a rubber band to fill the first groove so as not to cut the O-ring. Discard the rubber band.

6. After the cam, shift shaft and snapring have been installed in the front case assembly and with the shift shaft assembly positioned in the 4WH position, place the assist spring roll into "Park-Position" on the 90° bent tang of the assist spring and insert the assist roller into the assist spring/roller slot of the shift cam. Position the middle section of the assist spring into the groove of the front case pivot boss and push to

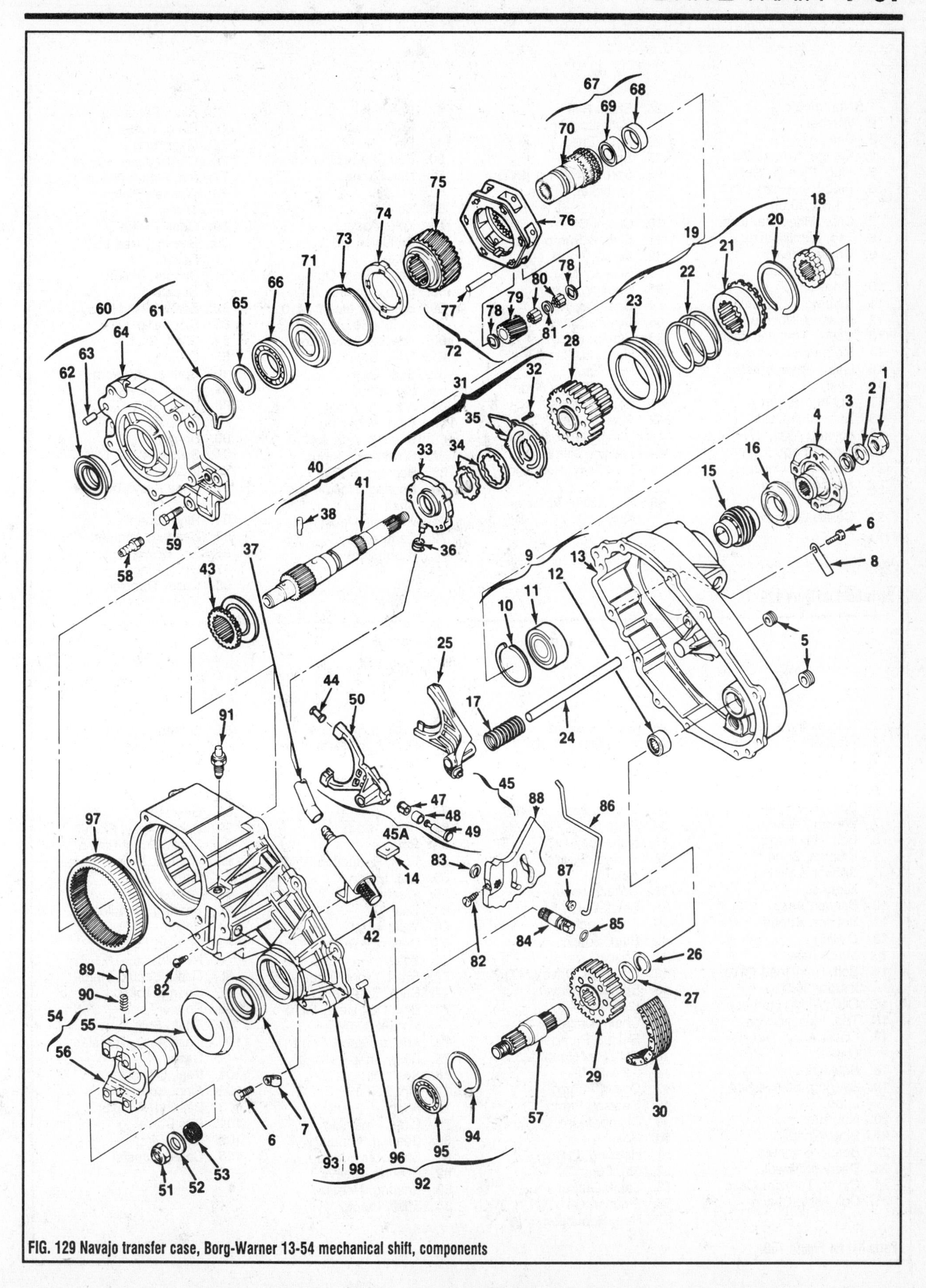

FIG. 129 Navajo transfer case, Borg-Warner 13-54 mechanical shift, components

1. Nut, metric
2. Washer
3. Seal, oil
4. Flange, Companion
5. Plug, Pipe (1/2-14)
6. Bolt, Hex Head (M10 x 1.5 x 30.0)
7. Clip, Wiring Harness
8. Tag, Identification
9. Cover, Assay, Transfer Case
10. Ring, Snap
11. Bearing, Annular
12. Bearing, Needle
13. Cover, Transfer Case
14. Magnet
15. Gear, Speedometer
16. Seal, Oil
17. Spring, Return
18. Hub, Shift Collar
19. Lockup Assy, 2W-4W
20. Ring, Snap
21. Hub, Shift Collar
22. Spring, Sleeve Return
23. Collar, Lockup
24. Shaft, Rail
25. Fork, Lockup
26. Ring, Snap
27. Spacer
28. Sprocket, Drive (24T)
29. Sprocket, Driven (24T)
30. Chain, Drive
31. Shaft & Pump Assy
32. Screw, Torx® T-20 Recess (M5)
33. Housing, Pump
34. Gear Set, Pump
35. Cover, Pump
36. Clamp, Hose
37. Housing, Pump
38. Pin, Pump
40. Cover, Pump (Front)
41. Shaft, Output
42. Strainer, Oil
43. Hub, Reduction
44. Facing, Shift Fork
45. Fork Assy, Reduction Shift
46. Rin, Roller, Retainer Assy
47. Retainer
48. Roller, Cam
49. Pin
50. Fork, Reduction Shift
51. Nut, Metric
52. Washer
53. Seal, Oil
54. Yoke Assy
55. Deflector, Dust
56. Yoke
57. Shaft, Front Output
58. Barb, Breather
59. Bolt, Hex Head (M10 x 1.5 x 30.0)
60. Adapter Assy, Front
61. Ring, Snap
62. Seal, Oil
63. Pin, Spiral
64. Adapter, Front
65. Ring, Retaining
66. Bearing, Annular
67. Shaft Assy, Input
68. Bearing, Sleeve
69. Bearing, Needle
70. Shaft, Input
71. Washer, Thrust
72. Carrier Assy, (Complete)
73. Ring, Retaining
74. Plate, Thrust
75. Gear, Sun
76. Carrier Assy, Planet
77. Pin, Planet Pinion
78. Washer, Pinion Thrust
79. Gear, Pinion
80. Bearing, Needle Roller
81. Spacer, Pinion Needle
82. Screw, Pan Head
83. Ring, Clip
84. Shaft, Shift
85. O-Ring
86. Spring, 4L Assist
87. Roller, 4L Assist
88. Cam, Shift
89. Poppet
90. Spring
91. Switch, 4WD Indicator
92. Case Assy, Transfer
93. Seal, Oil
94. Ring, Snap
95. Bearing, Annular
96. Pin, Dowel
97. Gear, Ring
98. Case, Transfer

Parts list for Figure 129

---

1. Nut, Metric
2. Washer
3. Seal, Oil
4. Flange, Companion
5. Plug, Pipe (1/2-14)
6. Bolt, Hex Head
7. Washer, Flat
8. Bolt, Hex Head
9. Bracket, Speed Sensor & Wiring Harness
10. Sensor, Assy
11. Sensor, Speed
12. O-Ring
13. Motor Assy
14. Bolt, Hex Head (M10 x 1.5 x 30.0)
15. Clip, Wiring Harness
16. Tag, Identification
17. Cover Assy, Transfer Case
18. Seal, Oil
19. Bearing, Sleeve-Self Lube
20. Nut, Hex
21. Ring, Snap
22. Bearing, Annular
23. Bearing, Needle
24. Cover, Transfer Case
25. Coil Assy, Clutch
26. Gear, Speedo
27. Seal, Oil
28. Spring, Return
29. Magnet
31. Housing, Clutch
33. Lockup Assy 2W-4W
34. Ring, Snap
35. Hub, Lockup
36. Spring, Sleeve Return
37. Collar, Lockup
38. Shaft, Rail
39. Fork, Lockup
40. Ring, Snap
41. Spacer
42. Sprocket, Drive (24T)
43. Sprocket, Driven (24T)
44. Chain, Drive
45. Shaft & Pump Assy
46. Bolt, Hex Head (M5 x 0.8 x 20.0)
47. Cover, Pump
48. Gearset, Pump
49. Clamp, Hose
50. Hose
51. Housing, Pump
52. Pin, Pump
55. Shaft, Output
56. Strainer, Oil
57. Hub, Reduction
58. Facing, Shift Fork
59. Fork Assy, Reduction Shift
60. Pin, Roller Retainer Assy
61. Pin
62. Roller, Cam
63. Retainer
64. Fork, Reduction Shift
65. Nut, Metric
66. Washer
67. Seal, Oil
68. Yoke Assy
69. Deflector Dust
70. Yoke
71. Shaft, Front Output
72. Barb, Breather
73. Bolt, Hex Head (M10 x 1.5 x 30.0)
74. Adapter Assy, Front
75. Ring, Snap
76. Seal, Oil
77. Pin, Spiral
78. Adapter, Front
79. Ring, Retaining
80. Bearing, Annular
81. Shaft Assy, Input
82. Bearing, Sleeve
83. Bearing, Needle
84. Shaft, Input
85. Washer, Thrust
86. Carrier Assy, (Complete)
87. Ring, Retaining
88. Plater, Thrust
89. Gear, Sun
90. Carrier Assy, Planet
91. Shaft, Planet Pinion
92. Washer, Pinion Thrust
93. Gear, Pinion
94. Bearing, Needle Roller
95. Spacer, Pinion Needle
96. Cam, Electric Shift
97. Spring, Torsion
98. Spacer
99. Shaft, Shift
100. Case Assy, Transfer Case
101. Seal, Oil
102. Ring, Snap
103. Bearing, Annular
104. Pin, Dowel
105. Gear, Ring
106. Case, Transfer

Parts list for Figure 130

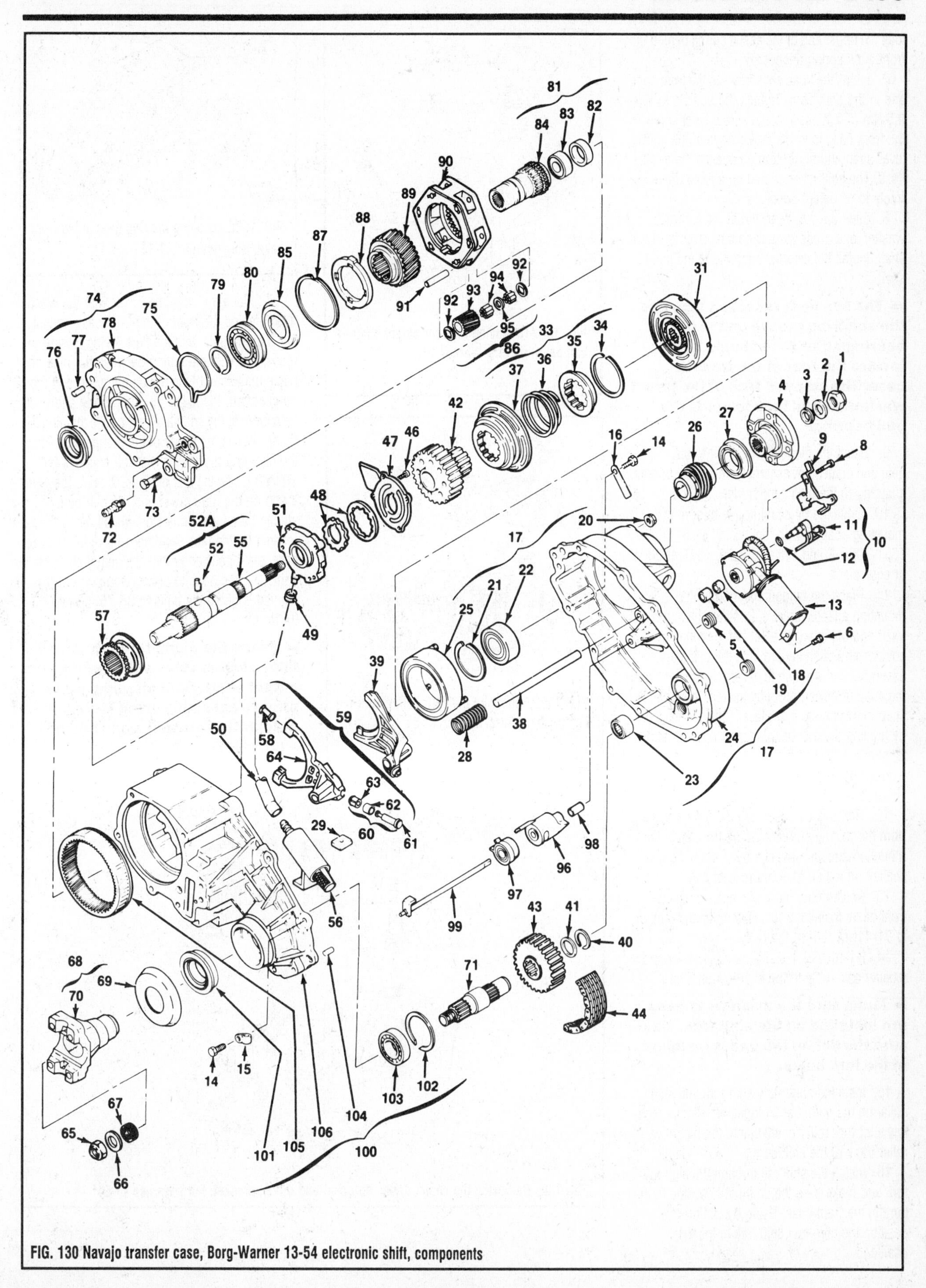

FIG. 130 Navajo transfer case, Borg-Warner 13-54 electronic shift, components

lock the upper end of the assist spring behind the front case spring anchor tab.

7. Install the head set screws in the front case and in the shift cam. Tighten the screws to 6.8-9.5 Nm (5-7 ft. lbs.). Make sure the set screw in the front case is in the first groove of the shift lever shaft and not bottomed against the shaft itself. The shift lever should be able to move freely to all detent positions.

8. Slide the sun gear, thrust plate, thrust washer, and press the ball bearing over the input shaft. Install the external snapring to the input shaft.

➡ The sun gear recessed face and the snapring groove on the ball bearing outer race should be toward the rear of the transfer case. The stepped face of the thrust washer should face towards the ball bearing.

9. Install the planetary gear set to the sun gear and input shaft assembly. Install the internal snapring to the planetary carrier.

10. Drive the oil seal into the bore of the mounting adapter with Input Shaft Seal Installer, T83T-7065-A and Driver Handle, T80T-4000-W or equivalent.

11. Place the tanged snapring in the mounting adapter groove. Position the input shaft and planetary gearset in the mounting adapter and push inward until the planetary assembly and input shaft assembly are seated in the adapter. When properly seated, the tanged snapring will snap into place. Check installation by holding the mounting adapter by hand and tapping the face of the input shaft against a wooden block to ensure that the snapring is engaged.

12. Remove all traces of RTV gasket sealant from the mating surfaces of the front case and mounting adapter. Install a bead of RTV gasket sealant on the surface of the front case.

13. Position the mounting adapter on the front case. Install the retaining bolts and tighten to 31-41NM (25-30 ft. lbs.).

14. If removed, install a new pin, roller and retainer assembly to the high-low shift fork.

➡ Make sure the nylon wear pads are installed on the shift fork. Make sure the dot on the pad is installed in the fork holes.

15. Install the high-low shift fork and shift collar on the output shaft together. Slip the high-low shift fork roller bushing into the high-low roller track of the shift cam.

16. Install the shift rail through the high-low fork and make sure the shift rail is seated in the bore in the front case. Using the shift lever, position the high-low shift fork in the 4H position.

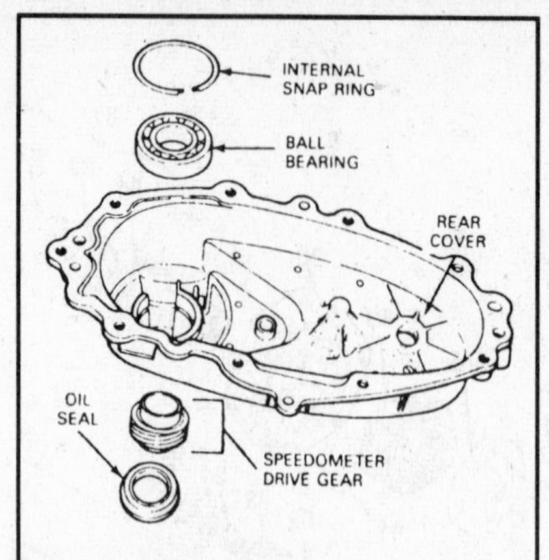

FIG. 130a Removing the rear output shaft ball bearing, Borg-Warner 13-54

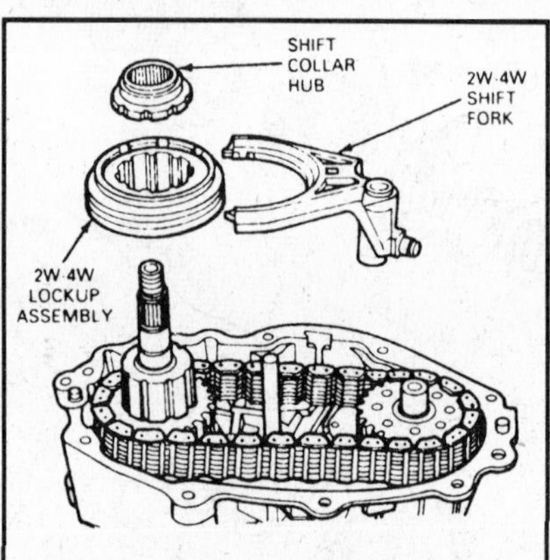

FIG. 130b Removing the shift collar from the output shaft, Borg-Warner 13-54

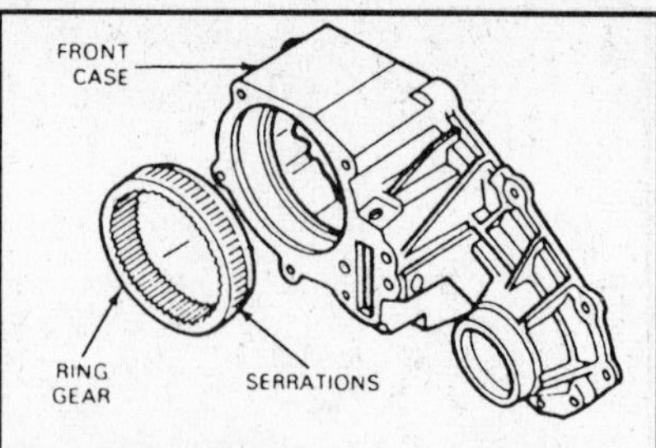

FIG. 130d Installing the ring gear in the front case, Borg-Warner 13-54

17. Place the oil pump cover with the word **TOP** facing the front of the front case. Install the 2 pump pins with the flats facing toward the rear cover with the spring between the pins and place the assembly in the oil pump bore in the output shaft. Place the oil pump body and pick-up tube over the shaft and make sure the pins are riding against the inside of the pump body. Place the oil pump rear cover with the words **TOP REAR** facing the rear of the front case. The word **TOP** on the front cover and the rear cover should be on the same side. Install the pump retainer so the tabs face the front of the transfer case, the 4 bolts and rotate the output shaft while tightening the bolts to prevent the pump from binding. Tighten the bolts to 35-75 ft. lbs. (4.3-9.2Nm).

➡ Prime the pump through the oil filler pick-up tube while turning the output shaft. Coat all pump parts prior to assembly using Mercon® Automatic Transmission Fluid or equivalent.

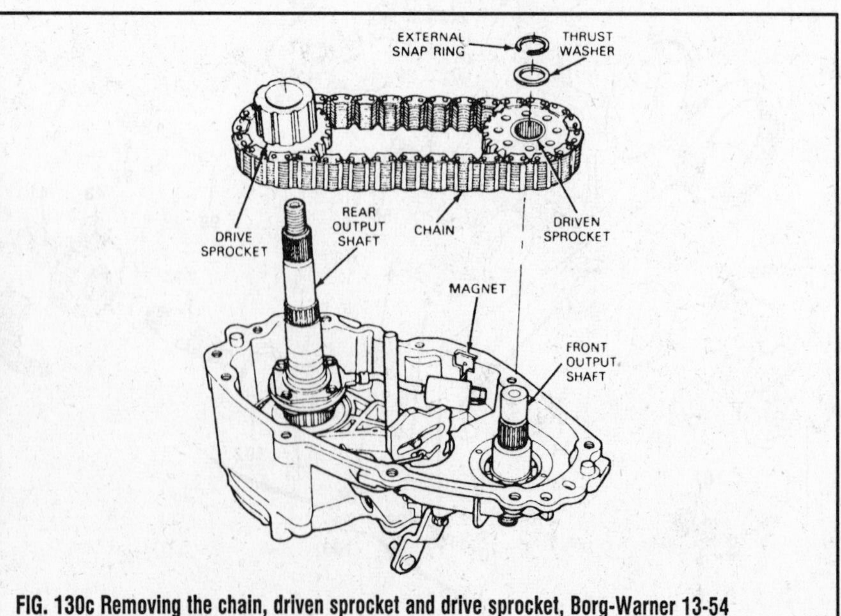

FIG. 130c Removing the chain, driven sprocket and drive sprocket, Borg-Warner 13-54

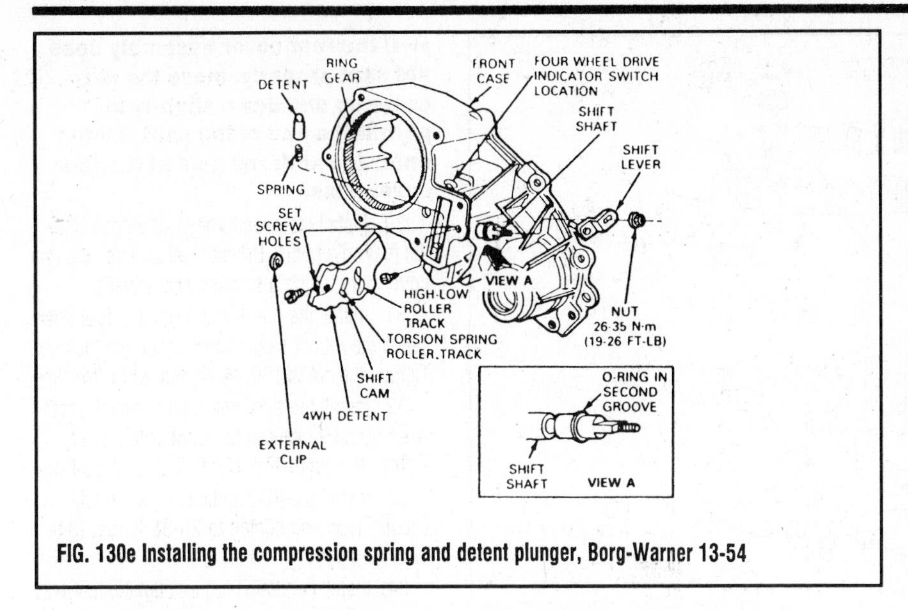

FIG. 130e Installing the compression spring and detent plunger, Borg-Warner 13-54

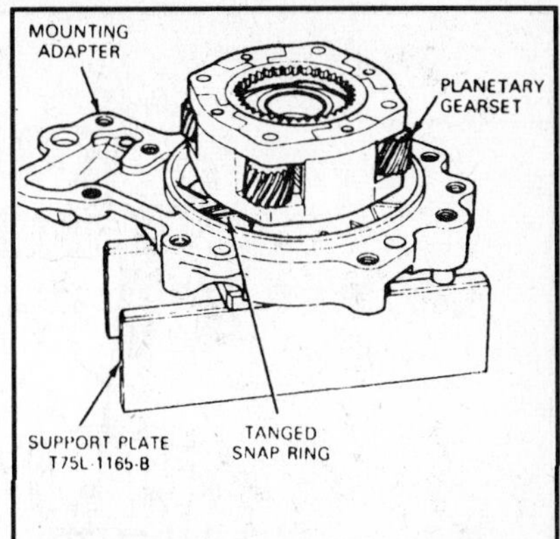

FIG. 130g Installing the planetary assembly and input shaft assembly in the adapter, Borg-Warner 13-54

18. Install the output shaft and oil pump assembly in the input shaft. Make certain the external splines of the output shaft engage the internal splines of the high-low shift collar. Make certain the oil pump retainer and the oil filter leg are in the groove and notch of the front case.

WARNING

The output shaft must turn freely within the oil pump. If binding occurs, loosen the 4 bolts and retighten again.

19. Install the collector magnet in the notch in the front case.

20. Install the chain, drive sprocket and driven sprocket as an assembly over the shaft. Install the thrust washer on the front output shaft and install a new external snapring over the thrust washer to retain the driven sprocket

21. If disassembled, assemble the 2W-4W shift fork to the 2W-4W lock up assembly. Install the spring in the lock up collar. Place the lock up hub over the spring and engage the lock up hub in the notches in the lock up collar. Retain the lock up hub to the lock up collar with an internal snapring.

22. Install the 2W-4W shift fork and lock-up assembly on the output shaft and onto the shift rail.

23. Install the shift collar hub to the output shaft.

24. If removed, drive the caged needle bearing into the rear cover bore with the needle bearing replacer tool T83T-7127-A and drive handle T80T-4000-W or equivalent.

25. If removed, install the ball bearing in the rear cover bore. Drive the bearing into the rear cover bore with output shaft bearing replacer tool T83T-7025-B and driver handle T80-4000-W or equivalent. Make sure the ball bearing is not cocked in the bore. Install the internal

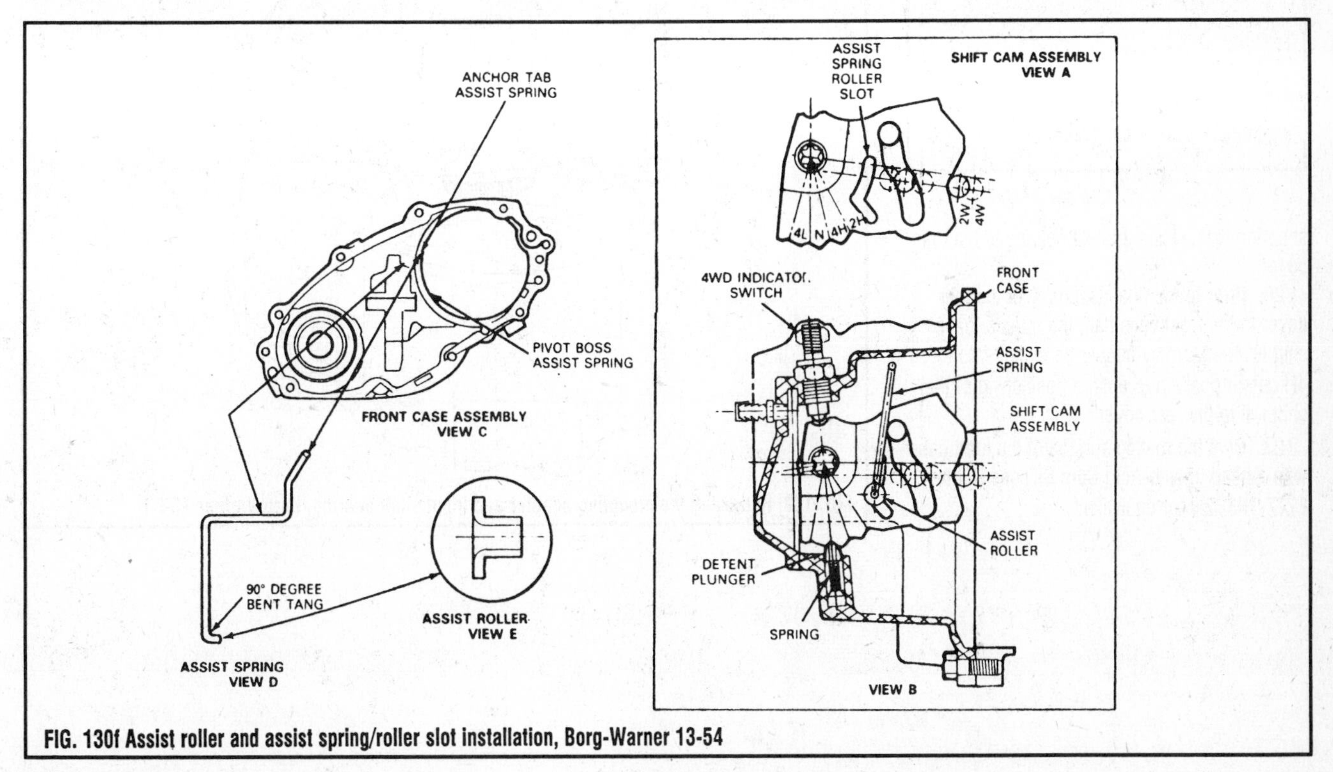

FIG. 130f Assist roller and assist spring/roller slot installation, Borg-Warner 13-54

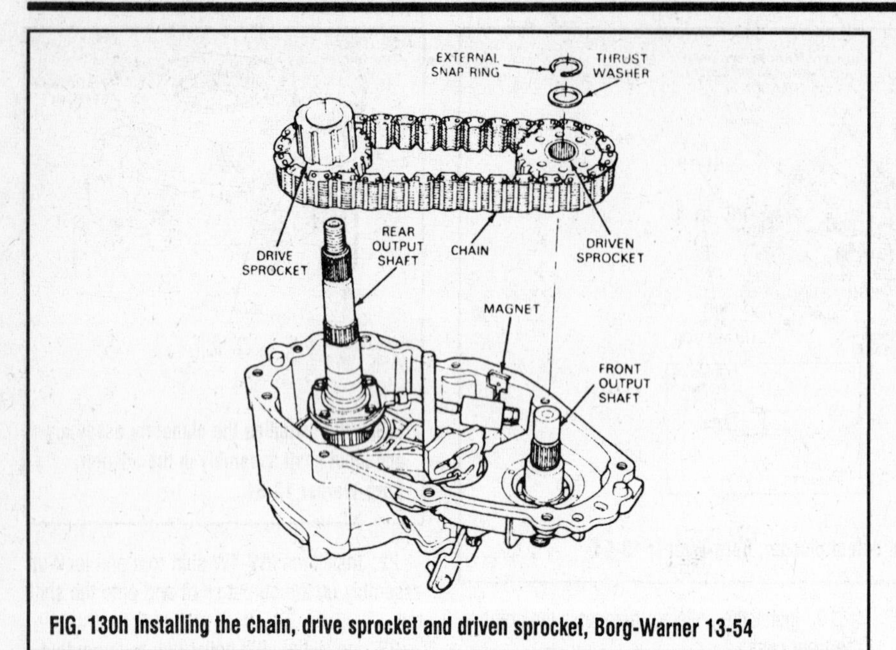

FIG. 130h Installing the chain, drive sprocket and driven sprocket, Borg-Warner 13-54

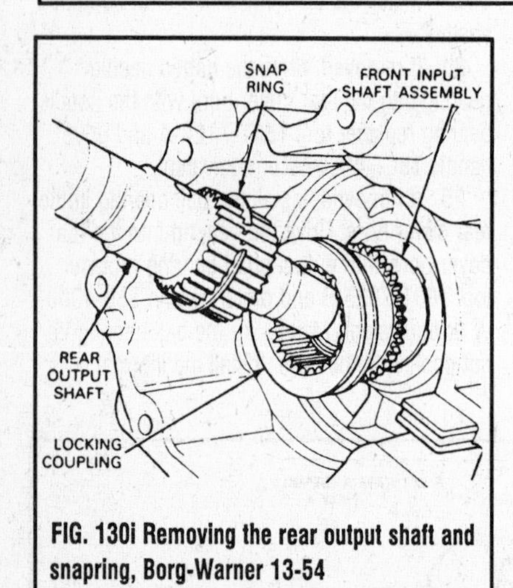

FIG. 130i Removing the rear output shaft and snapring, Borg-Warner 13-54

snapring that retains the ball bearing to the rear cover.

26. Prior to the final assembly of the rear cover to the front case half, the transfer case shift lever assembly should be shifted into the 4H detent position to assure positioning of the shift rail to the rear cover.

27. Coat the mating surface of the front case with a bead of Non-Acid Cure Silicone Rubber E7TZ-19562-A or equivalent.

28. Install the 2W-4W shift fork spring to the shift rail and shift fork with spring mounted in a vertical position.

29. Position the rear cover so that the spring boss engages the 2W-4W shift fork spring and shift rail. Install the nine bolts, starting with the bolts on the rear cover and torque the bolts to 23-30 ft. lbs. (31-41Nm).

➡ **If the rear cover assembly does not seat properly, move the rear cover up and down slightly to permit the end of the shift rail to enter the shift rail hole in the rear cover boss.**

30. Install the speedometer drive gear into the rear cover bore. Drive the oil seal into the rear cover bore, using a suitable seal installer.

31. Install the rear flange on the output shaft. Install the rubber seal, steel washer and lock nut. Tighten the nut to 150-180 ft. lbs. (203-244Nm).

32. Install the front yoke, rubber seal, steel washer and locknut to the front output shaft. Tighten the nut to 150-180 ft. lbs. (203-244Nm).

33. Install the 4WD indicator switch with Teflon® tape and tighten to 25-35 ft. lbs. (34-47Nm).

34. Install the drain plug and tighten to 14-22 ft. lbs. (19-30Nm).

35. Remove the fill plug. Refill the transfer case with 2½ pints (1.2L) of Motorcraft Mercon® Automatic Transmission fluid or equivalent. Torque the level plug and the drain plugs to 14-22 ft. lbs. Torque the fill plug to 14-22 ft. lbs.

36. Install the transfer case.

37. Start the engine and check the transfer case for correct operation. Stop the engine and check the fluid level, add as necessary.

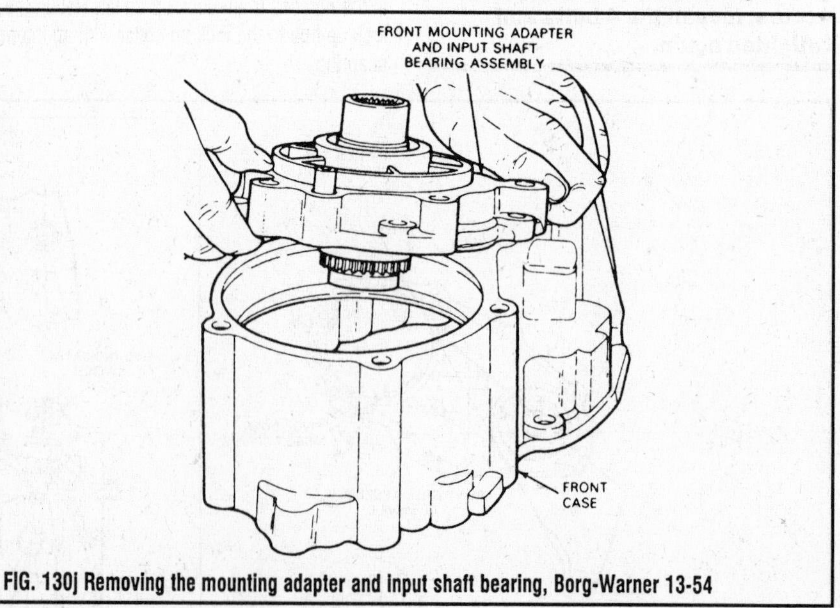

FIG. 130j Removing the mounting adapter and input shaft bearing, Borg-Warner 13-54

DRIVESHAFT AND U-JOINTS

General Description

The driveshaft is a steel tubular or aluminum shaft which is used to transfer the torque from the engine, through the transmission output shaft, to the differential in the axle, which in turn transmits torque to the wheels.

The splined slip yoke and transmission output shaft permit the driveshaft to move forward and rearward as the axle moves up and down. This provides smooth performance during vehicle operation.

The front driveshaft connects the power flow from the transfer case to the front drive axle.

Some vehicles may be equipped with a Double Cardan type driveshaft. This driveshaft incorporates 2 U-joints, a centering socket yoke and a center slip at the transfer case end of each shaft. A single U-joint is used at the axle end of the shaft.

The Constant Velocity (CV) type U-joint allows the driveline angel to be adjusted according to the up-and-down movement of the vehicle without disturbing the power flow. The CV U-joint is composed of an outer bearing retainer and flange, spring, cap, circlip, inner bearing assembly and wire ring. The inner bearing assembly is composed of a bearing cage, 6 ball bearings and an inner race.

The driveshafts may be 1 of 3 types. They are as follows:

- Front and rear driveshaft — Single Cardan type U-joint
- Front and rear driveshaft — Double Cardan type U-joint
- Rear driveshaft — CV (Constant Velocity) type U-joint

Front Driveshaft

SEE FIGS. 131-155

REMOVAL & INSTALLATION

1. Disconnect the negative battery cable.
2. Raise and support the vehicle safely.

The driveshaft is a balanced unit. Before removing the drive shaft, matchmark the driveshaft in relationship to the end yoke so that it may be installed in its original position.

3. Using a shop cloth or gloves, pull back on the dust slinger to remove the boot from the transfer case slip yoke.
4. Remove the bolts and straps that retains the driveshaft to the front driving axle yoke. Remove the U-joint assembly from the front driving axle yoke.
5. Slide the splined yoke assembly out of the transfer case and remove the driveshaft assembly.
6. Inspect the boot for rips or tears. Inspect the stud yoke splines for wear or damage. Replace any damage parts.

To install:

7. Apply a light coating of Multi-purpose Long-Life lubricant C1AZ-19490-B or equivalent, to the yoke splines and the edge of the inner diameter of the rubber boot.
8. Slide the driveshaft into the transfer case front output yoke assembly. Make certain the wide tooth splines on the slip yoke are indexed to the output yoke in the transfer case.
9. Position the U-joint assembly in the front drive axle yoke in its original position. Install the retaining bolts and straps. Tighten the bolts to 10–15 ft. lbs. (14–20Nm).
10. Firmly press the dust slinger until the boot is felt to engage the output yoke in the transfer case.
11. Lower the vehicle.
12. Connect the negative battery cable.

If replacement of the dust slinger/boot is necessary. Use the following procedure.

DUST SLINGER/BOOT REPLACEMENT

1. Remove the boot clamp using cutter pliers and discard the clamp. Remove the boot from the stud yoke.
2. Install a new dust slinger/boot on the stud yoke making certain the boot is seated in the groove in the yoke.
3. Install a new clamp on the boot. Position the clamp tabs in the slots so each tab fits into a slot. Then, crimp the clamp securely using a pair of clamp pliers T63P-9171-A or equivalent. Do not crimp to the point where the clamp damage the boot.

Rear Driveshaft

REMOVAL & INSTALLATION

2WD Pickups

1. Matchmark the rear U-joint with the rear companion flange. Remove the bolts attaching the driveshaft to the rear companion flange.
2. On 2-piece units, remove the center support bearing bracket from the underbody.
3. Pull the driveshaft rearward and out of the transmission. Plug the rear seal opening.
4. Installation is the reverse of removal. Make sure that you align the matchmarks. Torque the rear companion flange bolts to 39-47 ft. lbs.; the center bearing bracket nuts to 27-38 ft. lbs.

MPV

1. Matchmark the rear U-joint with the rear companion flange. Remove the bolts attaching the driveshaft to the rear companion flange.
2. Remove the center support bearing bracket from the underbody.
3. Pull the driveshaft rearward and out of the transmission. Plug the rear seal opening.
4. Installation is the reverse of removal. Make sure that you align the matchmarks. Torque the rear companion flange bolts to 39-47 ft. lbs.; the center bearing bracket nuts to 27-38 ft. lbs.

Navajo

1. Disconnect the negative battery cable.
2. Raise and support the vehicle safely.

The driveshaft is a balanced unit. Before removing the driveshaft, matchmark the driveshaft yoke in relationship to the axle flange so that it may be installed in its original position.

3. Remove the retaining bolts and disconnect the driveshaft from the axle companion flange.
4. Remove the retaining bolts that retains the driveshaft to the rear of the transfer case.
5. Remove the driveshaft.

To install:

6. Install the driveshaft into the rear of the transfer case. Make certain that the driveshaft is positioned with the slip yoke toward the front of the vehicle. Install the bolts and tighten to 41–55 ft. lbs. (55–74Nm).
7. Install the driveshaft so the index mark on the rear yoke is in line with the index mark on the axle companion flange.

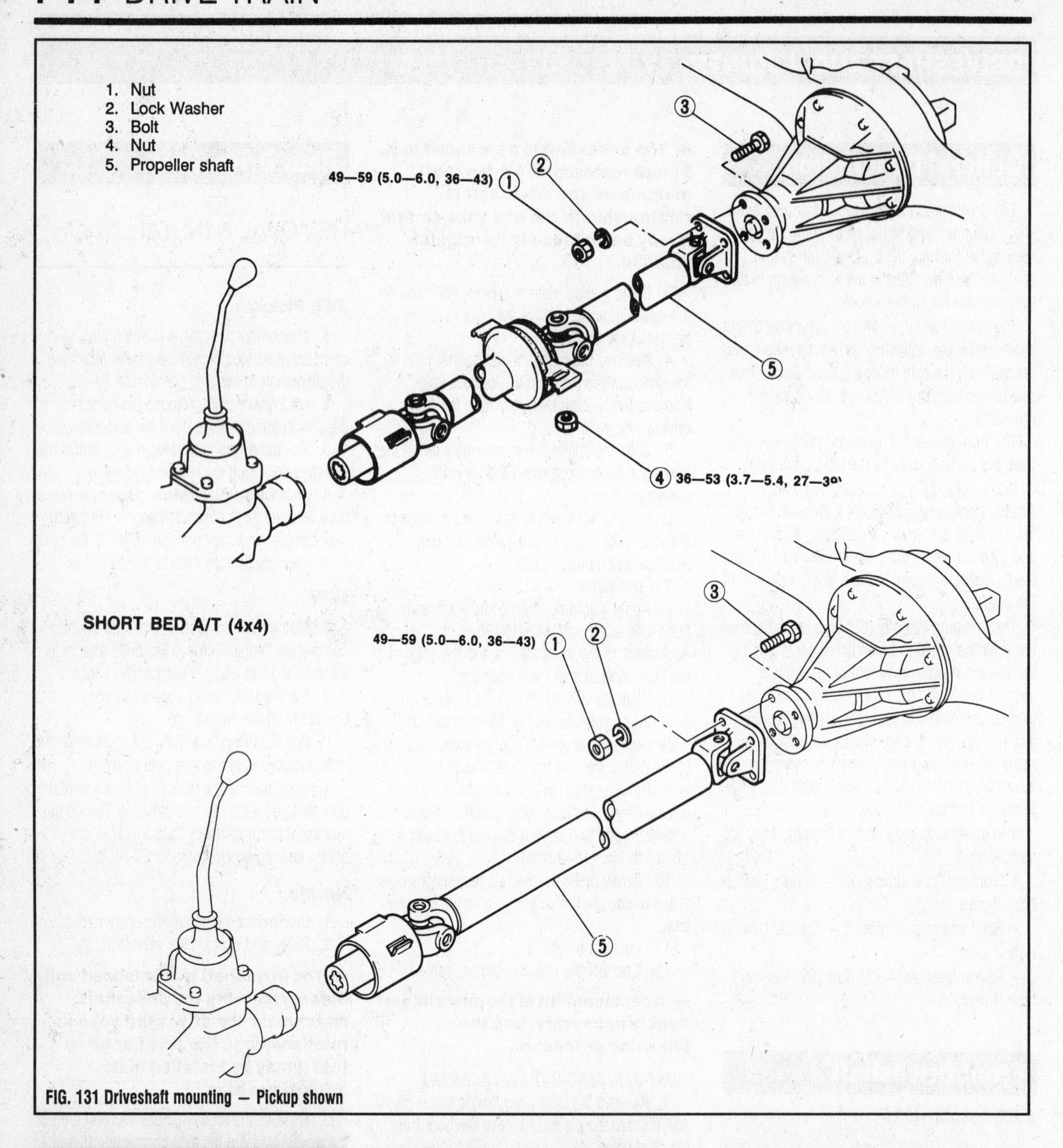

FIG. 131 Driveshaft mounting — Pickup shown

Single Cardan U-Joint

OVERHAUL

1. Remove the driveshaft.
2. If the front yoke is to be disassembled, matchmark the driveshaft and sliding splined yoke (transmission yoke) so that driveline balance is preserved upon reassembly. Remove the snaprings which retain the bearing caps.
3. Select two sockets, one small enough to pass through the yoke holes for the bearing caps, the other large enough to receive the bearing cap.
4. Using a vise or a press, position the small and large sockets on either side of the U-joint. Press in on the smaller socket so that it presses the opposite bearing cap out of the yoke and into the larger socket. If the cap does not come all the way out, grasp it with a pair of pliers and work it out.
5. Reverse the position of the sockets so that the smaller socket presses on the cross. Press the other bearing cap out of the yoke.
6. Repeat the procedure on the other bearings.
7. To install, grease the bearing caps and needles thoroughly if they are not pregreased. Start a new bearing cap into one side of the yoke. Position the cross in the yoke.

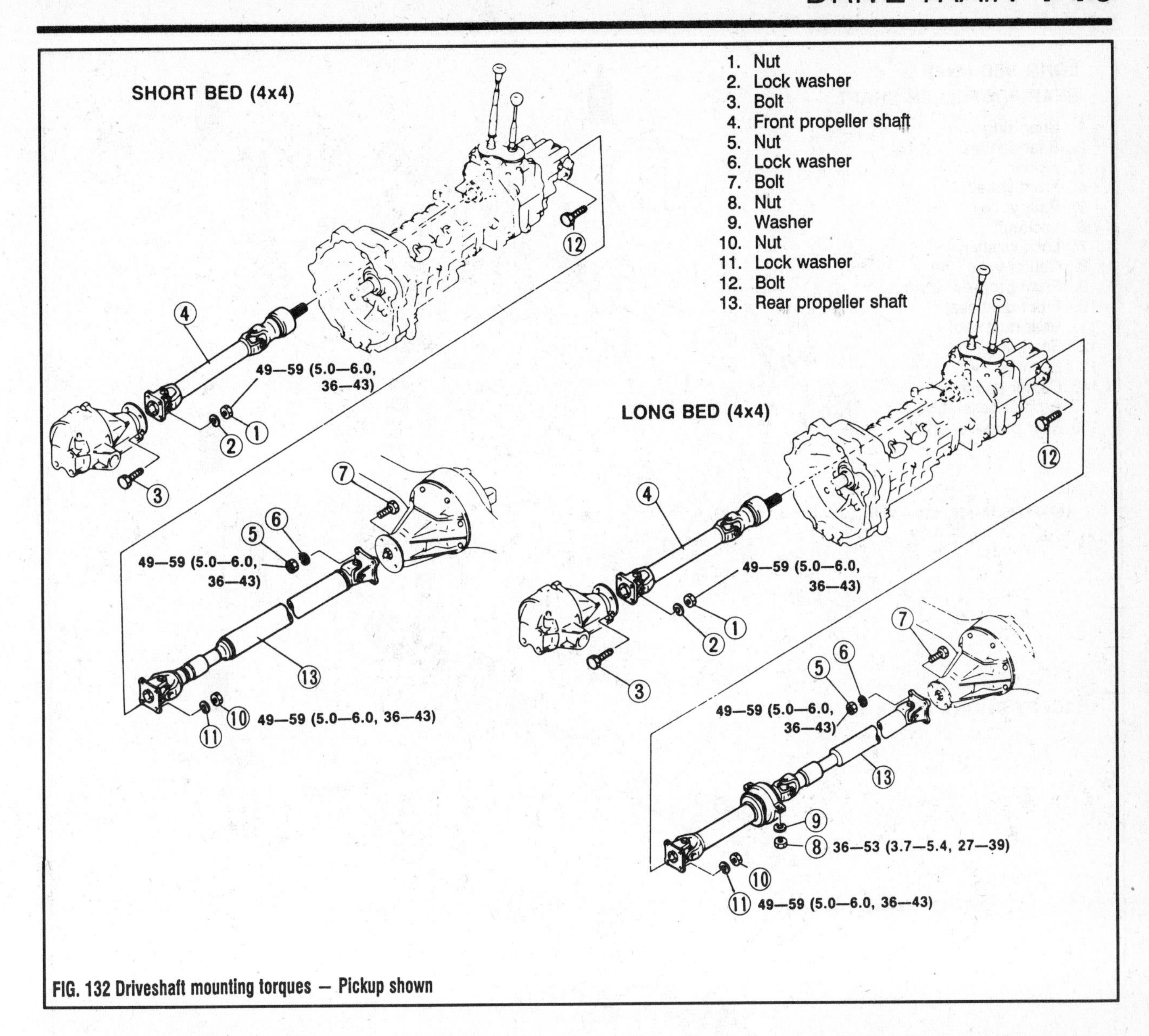

FIG. 132 Driveshaft mounting torques — Pickup shown

8. Select two sockets small enough to pass through the yoke holes. Put the sockets against the cross and the cap, and press the bearing cap 1/4 in. (6mm) below the surface of the yoke. If there is a sudden increase in the force needed to press the cap into place, or if the cross starts to bind, the bearings are cocked, They must be removed and restarted in the yoke. Failure to do so will greatly reduce the life of the bearing.

9. Install a new snapring.

10. Start a new bearing into the opposite side. Place a socket on it and press in until the opposite bearing contacts the snapring.

11. Install a new snapring. It may be necessary to grind the facing surface of the snapring slightly to permit easier installation.

12. Install the other bearings in the same manner.

13. Check the joint for free movement. If binding exists, smack the yoke ears with a brass or plastic faced hammer to seat the bearing needles. Do not strike the bearings, and support the shaft firmly. Do not install the driveshaft until free movement exists at all joints.

14. The nut attaching the yoke and bearing to the front coupling is torqued to 115-130 ft. lbs.

Double Cardan Type U-Joint

REMOVAL & INSTALLATION

1. Disconnect the negative battery cable.
2. Raise and support the vehicle safely.

➡ The driveshaft is a balanced unit. Before removing the drive shaft, matchmark the driveshaft in relationship to the axle flange so that it may be installed in its original position.

3. Remove the bolts retaining the flange to the transfer case. Disconnect the U-joint from the flange at the transfer case.
4. Remove the bolts retaining the flange to the rear axle. Disconnect the U-joint from the flange at the rear axle.
5. Remove the driveshaft.

To Install:

6. Position the single U-joint end of the driveshaft to the rear axle and install the retaining bolts. Tighten the bolts to 61–87 ft. lbs. (83–118Nm).
7. Position the double Cardan U-joint to the

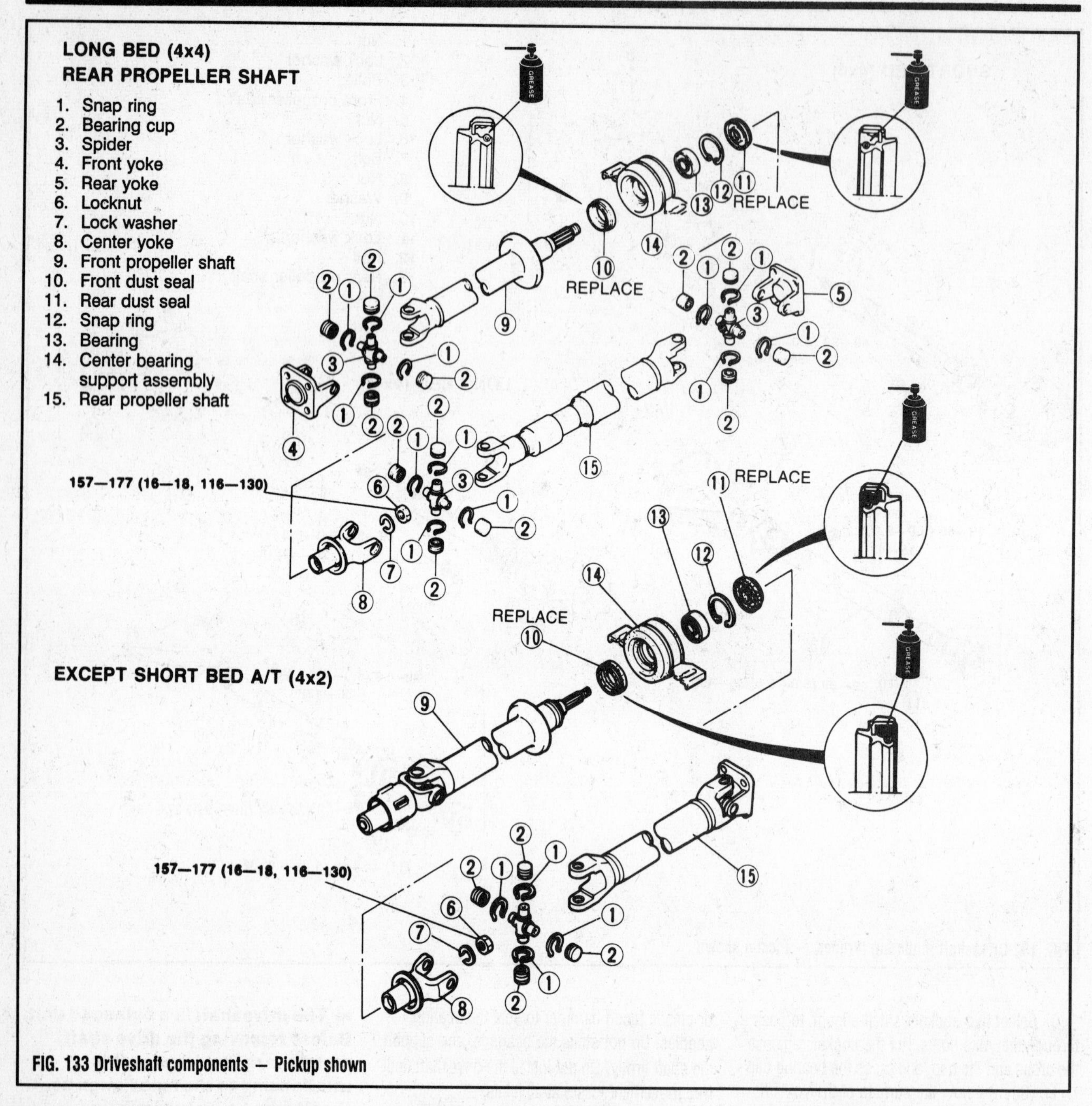

FIG. 133 Driveshaft components — Pickup shown

transfer case and install the retaining bolts. Tighten the bolts to 12–16 ft. lbs. (17–22Nm).

8. Lower the vehicle.
9. Reconnect the negative battery cable.

DISASSEMBLY AND ASSEMBLY

1. Place the driveshaft on a suitable workbench.
2. Matchmark the positions of the spiders, the center yoke and the centering socket yoke as related to the stud yoke which is welded to the front of the driveshaft tube.

➡ **The spiders must be assembled with the bosses in their original position to provide proper clearance.**

3. Remove the snaprings that secure the bearings in the front of the center yoke.
4. Position the U-joint tool, T74P–4635–C or equivalent, on the center yoke. Thread the tool clockwise until the bearing protrudes approximately 3/8 in. (10mm) out of the yoke.
5. Position the bearing in a vice and tap on the center yoke to free it from the bearing. Lift the 2 bearing cups from the spider.
6. Re-position the tool on the yoke and move the remaining bearing in the opposite direction so that it protrudes approximately 3/8 in. (10mm) out of the yoke.
7. Position the bearing in a vice. Tap on the center yoke to free it from the bearing. Remove the spider from the center yoke.
8. Pull the centering socket yoke off the center stud. Remove the rubber seal from the centering ball stud.
9. Remove the snaprings from the center yoke and from the driveshaft yoke.
10. Position the tool on the driveshaft yoke and press the bearing outward until the inside of the center yoke almost contacts the slinger ring at the front of the driveshaft yoke. Pressing beyond this point can distort the slinger ring interference point.

11. Clamp the exposed end of the bearing in a vice and drive on the center yoke with a soft-faced hammer to free it from the bearing.

12. Reposition the tool and press on the spider to remove the opposite bearing.

13. Remove the center yoke from the spider. Remove the spider form the driveshaft yoke.

14. Clean all serviceable parts in cleaning solvent. If using a repair kit, install all of the parts supplied in the kit.

15. Remove the clamps on the driveshaft boot seal. Discard the clamps.

16. Note the orientation of the slip yoke to the driveshaft tube for installation during assembly. Mark the position of the slip yoke to the driveshaft tube.

17. Carefully pull the slip yoke from the driveshaft. Be careful not to damage the boot seal.

18. Clean and inspect the spline area of the driveshaft.

To assemble:

19. Lubricate the driveshaft slip splines with Multi-purpose Long-Life lubricant C1AZ–19490–B or equivalent.

20. With the boot loosely installed on the driveshaft tube, install the slip yoke into the driveshaft splines in their original orientation.

21. Using new clamps, install the driveshaft boot in its original position.

22. To assemble the double Cardan joint, position the spider in the driveshaft yoke. Make certain the spider bosses (or lubrication plugs on kits) will be in the same position as originally installed. Press in the bearing using the U-joint tool. Then, install the snaprings.

23. Pack the socket relief and the ball with Multi-purpose Long-Life lubricant C1AZ–19490–B or equivalent, then position the center yoke over the spider ends and press in the bearing. Install the snaprings.

24. Install a new seal on the centering ball stud. Position the centering socket yoke on the stud.

25. Place the front spider in the center yoke. Make certain the spider bosses (or lubrication plugs on kits) are properly positioned.

26. With the spider loosely positioned on the center stop, seat the first pair of bearings into the centering socket yoke. Then, press the second pair into the centering yoke. Install the snaprings.

27. Apply pressure on the centering socket yoke and install the remaining bearing cup.

28. If a kit was used, lubricate the U-joint through the grease fitting, using Multi-purpose Long-Life lubricant C1AZ–19490–B or equivalent.

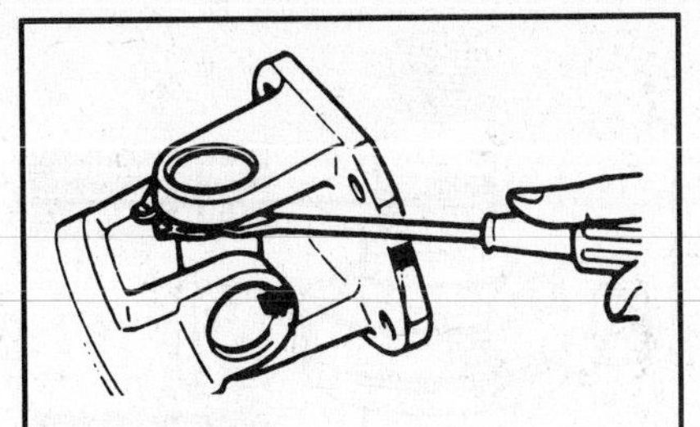
FIG. 134 Remove all snaprings with a flat bladed tool

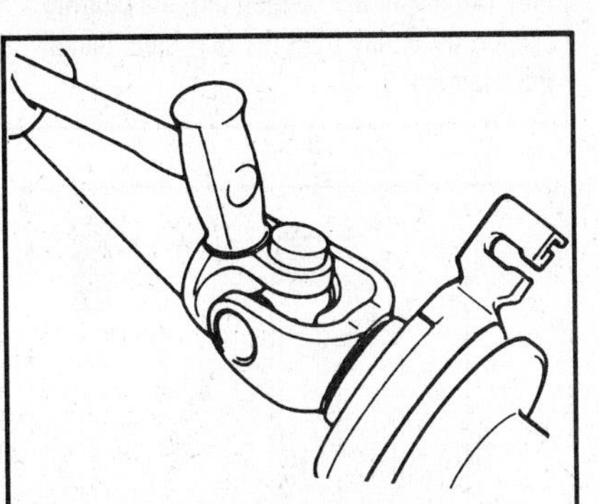
FIG. 135 Remove the bearings on the driveshaft side by lightly tapping with a hammer. Remove the bearings and spider by lightly tapping the spider

FIG. 136 Remove the bearing and the spider

FIG. 137 Remove the locknut

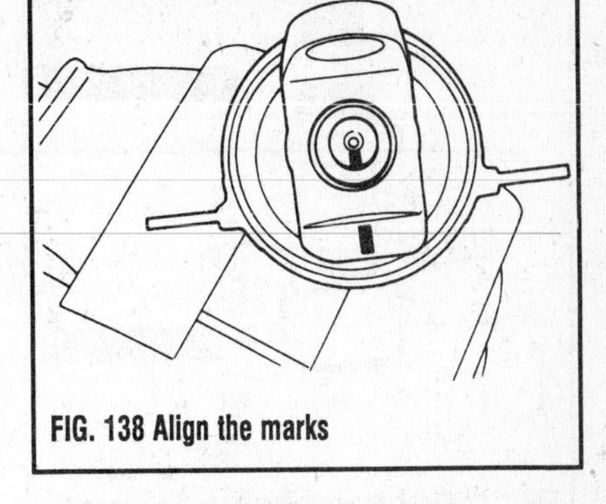
FIG. 138 Align the marks

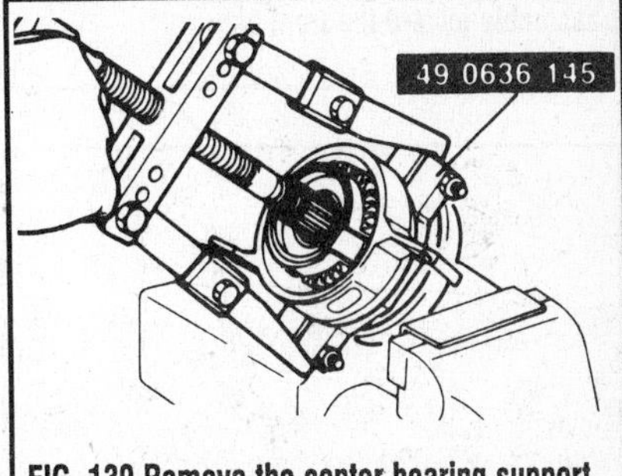

FIG. 139 Remove the center bearing support assembly with a puller set

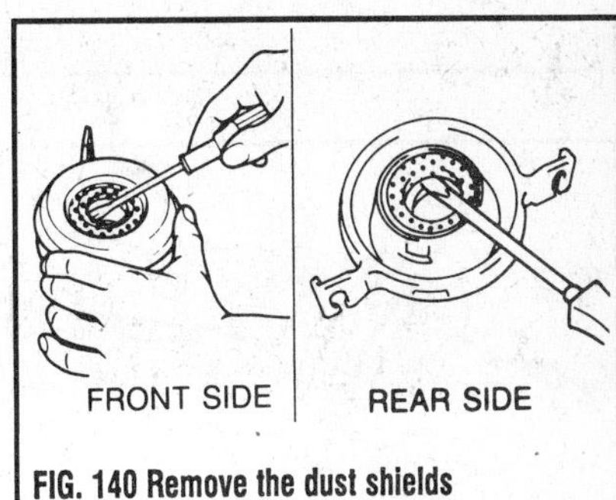

FIG. 140 Remove the dust shields

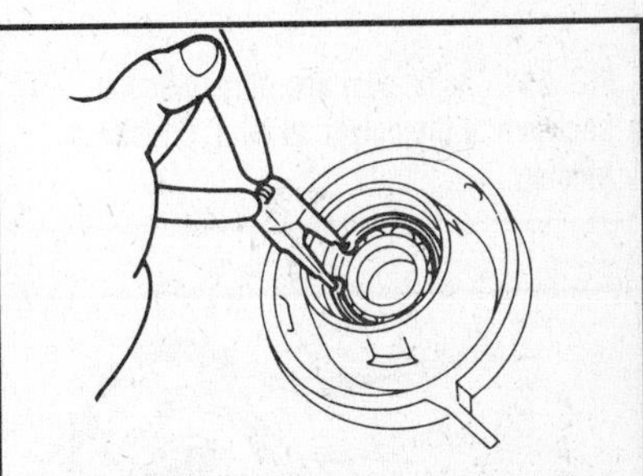
FIG. 141 Remove the snapring with snapring pliers

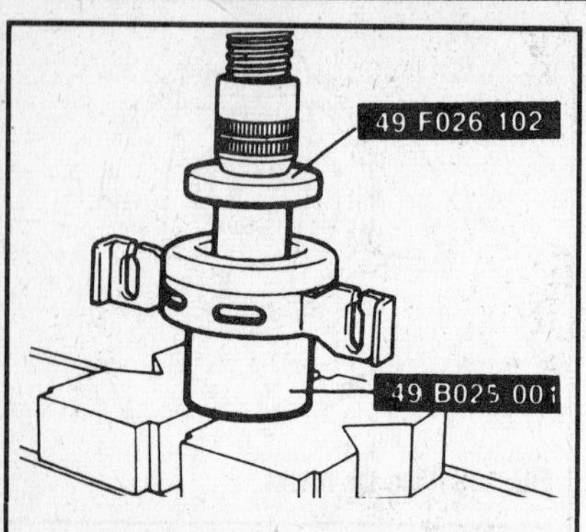

FIG. 142 Press the bearing from the support assembly toward the front side

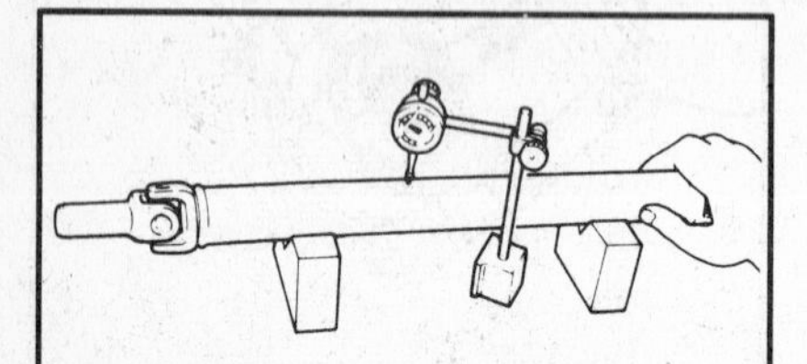
FIG. 143 Measure the front and rear shaft runout, replace if runout is excessive

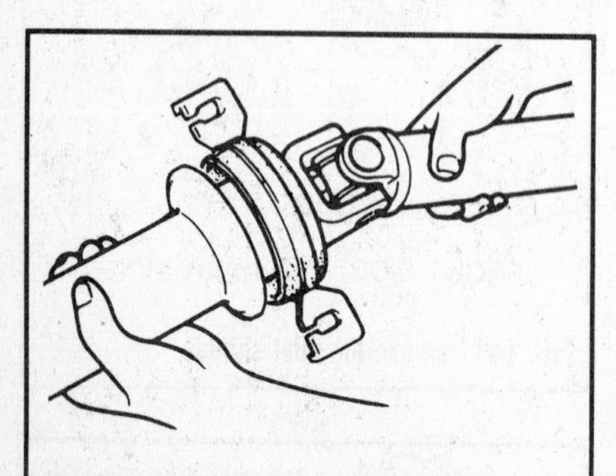
FIG. 144 Check axial and perpendicular backlash of the universal joint. Check for binding

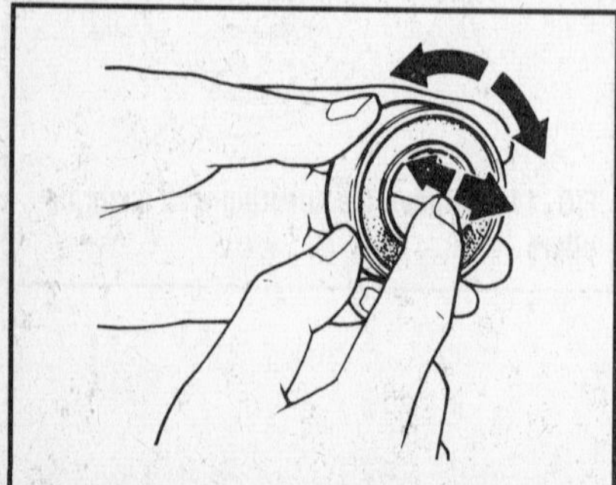
FIG. 145 Turn the bearing while applying force in the axial direction. If the bearing sticks or has excessive resistance, replace it

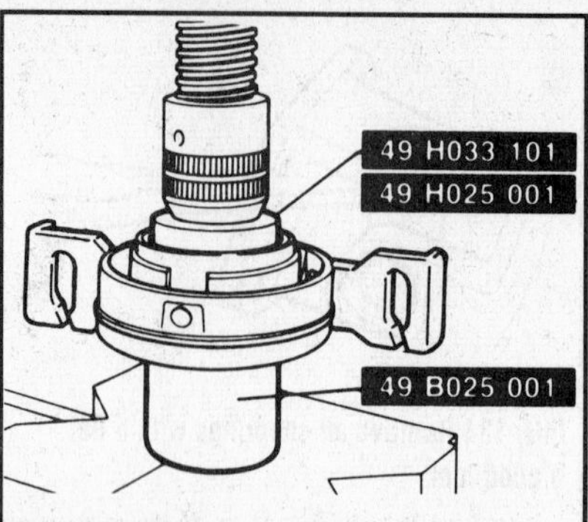

FIG. 146 Install the bearing into the bearing support assembly from the rear side. Install the snapring

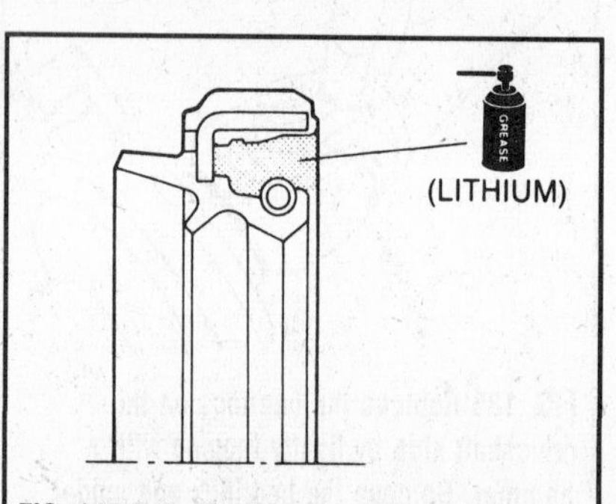

FIG. 147 Before installing a new dust seal, apply lithium based grease in the seal groove

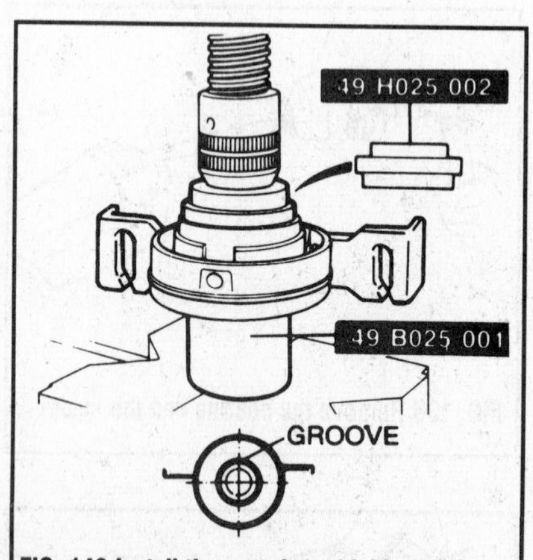

FIG. 148 Install the rear dust shield onto the support assembly from the rear side using a seal driver

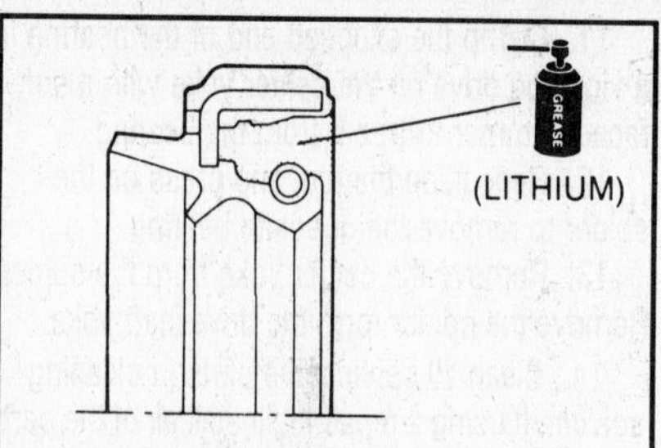

FIG. 149 Before installing the front seal apply lithium grease behind the seal lip

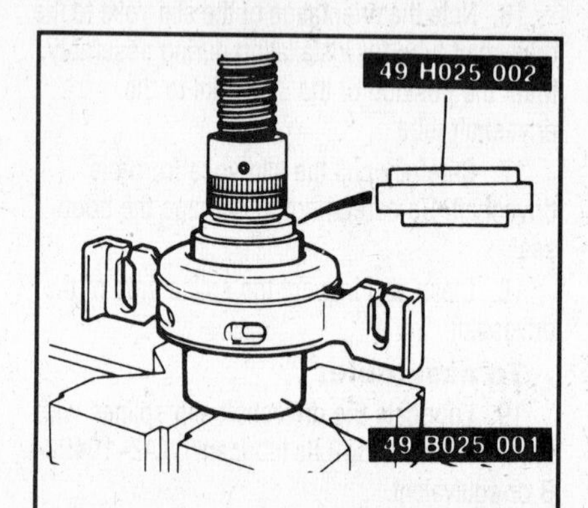

FIG. 150 Install the front grease seal into the support assembly from the front side

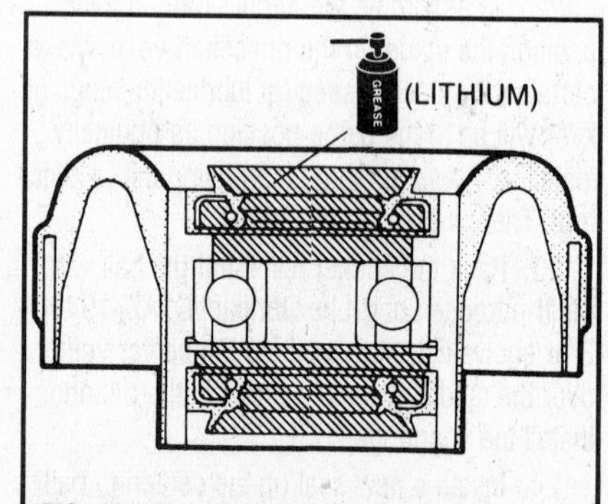

FIG. 151 Apply lithium grease to the area indicated

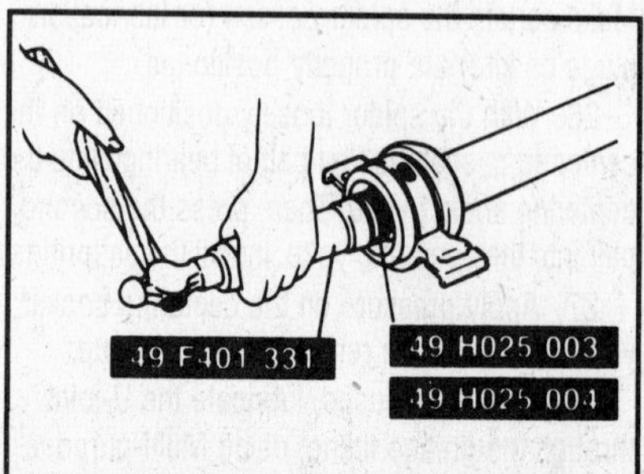

FIG. 152 Install the center bearing assembly

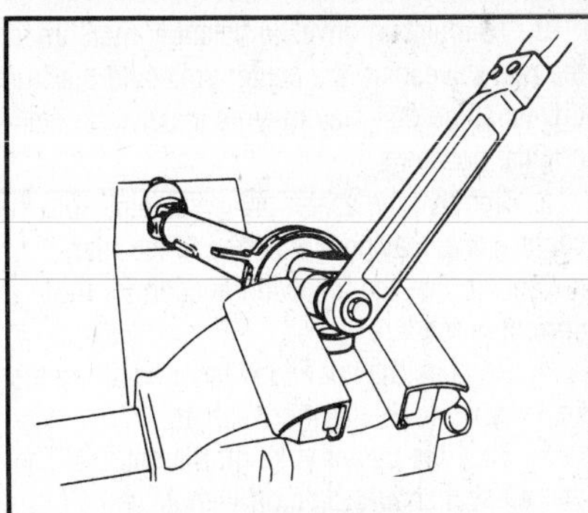
FIG. 153 Align the matchmarks on the yoke and shaft. Install the center yoke

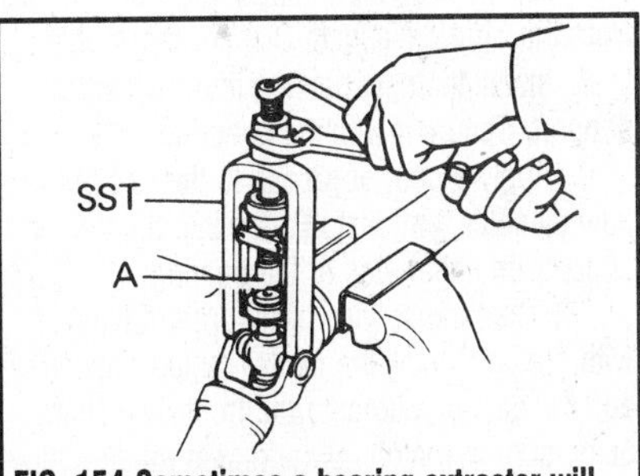

FIG. 154 Sometimes a bearing extractor will make joint removal easier

Constant Velocity (CV) Type U-joint

REMOVAL & INSTALLATION

1. Disconnect the negative battery cable.
2. Raise and support the vehicle safely.

➡ **The driveshaft is a balanced unit. Before removing the drive shaft, matchmark the driveshaft in relationship to the flange on the transfer case and the flange on the rear axle so that it may be installed in its original position.**

3. Remove the bolts retaining the driveshaft to the transfer case.
4. Remove the bolts retaining the driveshaft to the rear axle flange.
5. Remove the driveshaft.

To install:

6. Position the driveshaft to the rear axle flange so that the marks made previously are line up. Install and tighten the retaining bolts to 61–87 ft. lbs. (83–118Nm).
7. Position the driveshaft to the transfer case flange so that the marks made previously are line up. Install and tighten the retaining bolts to 61–87 ft. lbs. (83–118Nm).
8. Lower the vehicle.
9. Reconnect the negative battery cable.

DISASSEMBLY AND ASSEMBLY

1. Place the driveshaft on a suitable workbench.

➡ **The CV joint components are matched. Extreme care should be take not to mix or substitute components.**

2. Remove the clamp retaining the shroud to the outer bearing race and flange assembly.
3. Carefully tap the shroud lightly with a blunt tool and remove the shroud. Be careful not to damage the shroud, dust boot or outer bearing race and flange assembly.
4. Peel the boot upward and away from the outer bearing race and flange assembly.
5. Remove the wire ring that retains the inner race to the outer race.

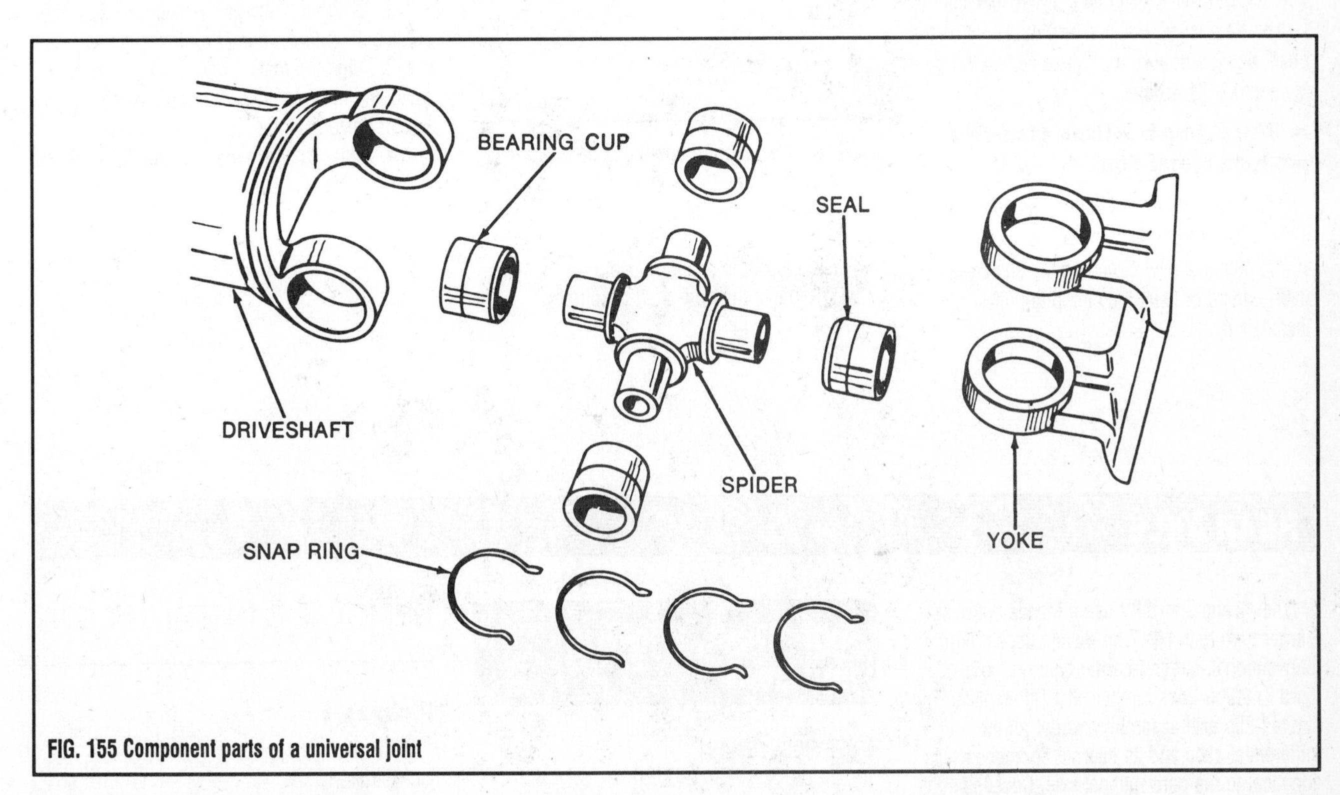

FIG. 155 Component parts of a universal joint

6. Remove the inner race and shaft assembly from the outer race and flange assembly. Remove the cap and spring from inside the outer retainer.

7. Remove the circlip retaining the inner race assembly to the shaft, using snapring pliers. Discard the clip and remove the inner race assembly.

8. If required, remove the clamp retaining the boot to the shaft and remove the boot.

9. Carefully pry the ball bearings from the cage. Be careful not to scratch or damage the cage, race or ball bearings.

10. Rotate the inner race to align with the cage windows and remove the inner race through the wider end of the cage.

To assemble: 12. Install the inner bearing race in the bearing cage. Install the race through the large end of the cage with the counterbore facing the large end of the cage.

13. Push the race to the top of the cage and rotate the race until all the ball slots are aligned with the windows. This will lock the race to the top of the cage.

14. With the bearing cage and inner race properly aligned, install the ball bearings. The bearings can be pressed through the bearing cage with the heel of the hand. Repeat this step until the remaining ball bearings are installed.

15. If removed, install a new dust boot on the shaft, using a new clamp. Make certain the boot is seated in its groove.

➡ The clamp is a fixed diameter push-on metal ring.

16. Install the inner bearing assembly on the shaft. Make certain the circlip is exposed.

17. Install a new circlip on the shaft. Do not over-expand or twist the circlip during installation.

18. Install the spring and cap in the outer bearing retainer and flange.

19. Fill the outer bearing retainer with 3 oz. of Constant Velocity Joint Grease, D8RZ-19590-A or equivalent.

20. Insert the inner race and shaft assembly in the outer bearing retainer and flange.

21. Push the inner race down until the wire spring groove is visible and install the wire ring.

22. Fill the top of the outer bearing retainer with Constant Velocity Joint Grease, D8RZ-19590-A or equivalent. Remove all excess grease from the external surfaces.

23. Pull the dust boot over the retainer. Make certain the boot is seated in the groove and that any air pressure which may have built up in the boot is relieved.

➡ Insert a dulled screwdriver blade between the boot and outer bearing retainer and allow the trapped air to escape from the boot.

24. Install the shroud over the boot and retainer and install the clamp.

Center Bearing

REPLACEMENT

The center support bearing is a sealed unit which requires no periodic maintenance. The following procedure should be used if it becomes necessary to replace the bearing. You will need a pair of snapring pliers for this job.

1. Remove the driveshaft assembly.

2. To maintain driveline balance, matchmark the rear driveshaft, the center yoke and the front driveshaft so that they may be installed in their original positions.

3. Remove the center universal joint from the center yoke, leaving it attached to the rear driveshaft. See the following section for the correct procedure.

4. Remove the nut and washer securing the center yoke to the front driveshaft.

5. Slide the center yoke off the splines. The rear oil seal should slide off with it.

6. If the oil has remained on top of the snapring, remove and discard the seal. Remove the snapring from its groove. Remove the bearing.

7. Slide the center support and front oil seal from the front driveshaft. Discard the seal.

8. Install the new bearing into the center support. Secure it with the snapring.

9. Apply a coat of grease to the lips of the new oil seals, and install them into the center support on either side of the bearing.

10. Coat the splines of the front driveshaft with grease. Install the center support assembly and the center yoke onto the front driveshaft, being sure to match up the marks made during disassembly.

11. Install the washer and nut. Torque the nut to 116-130 ft. lbs.

12. Check that the center support assembly rotates smoothly around the driveshaft.

13. Align the mating marks on the center yoke and the rear driveshaft, and assemble the center universal joint.

14. Install the driveshaft. Be sure that the rear yoke and the axle flange re aligned properly.

REAR AXLE

The pickup and MPV use a Mazda removable carrier type rear axle. The Navajo uses a Ford conventional, integral-carrier type rear axle or Ford Traction-Lock Limited Slip Differential. The limited-slip axle assembly, except for the differential case and its internal components, is identical to the conventional axle. Consequently, part numbers and tool numbers listed in the Navajo procedures will be Ford numbers.

Axle Shaft, Bearing and Seal

➧ SEE FIGS. 156-161

REMOVAL & INSTALLATION

Pickups

1. Raise and support the rear end on jackstands.

2. Remove the wheel and brake drum.

3. Remove the brake shoes.

4. Remove the parking brake cable retainer.

5. Disconnect and cap the brake lines at the wheel cylinders.

6. Remove the bolts securing the backing plate and bearing housing.

7. Slide the axle shaft from the axle housing. Be careful to avoid damaging the oil seal with the shaft.

8. If the seal in the axle housing is damaged in any way, it must be replaced. The seal can be removed using a slide hammer and adapter.

9. Remove two of the backing plate bolts, diagonally from each other.

10. Using a grinding wheel, grind down the bearing retaining collar in one spot, until about 5mm (0.197 in.) remains before you get to the axle shaft. Place a chisel at this point and break the collar. Be careful to avoid damaging the shaft.

CAUTION

Wear some kind of protective goggles when grinding the collar and breaking the collar from the shaft!

11. Using a press or puller, remove the hub and bearing assembly from the shaft. Remove the spacer from the shaft.

12. Remove the bearing and seal from the hub.

13. Using a drift, tap the race from the hub.

14. Check all parts for wear or damage. If either race is to be replaced, both must be replaced. The race in the axle housing can be removed with a slide hammer and adapter. It's a good idea to replace the bearing and races as a set. It's also a good idea to replace the seals, regardless of what other service is being performed.

15. The outer race must be installed using an arbor press. The inner race can be driven into place in the axle housing.

16. Pack the hub with lithium based wheel bearing grease.

17. Tap a new oil seal into the axle housing until it is flush with the end of the housing. Coat the seal lip with wheel bearing grease.

18. Install a new spacer on the shaft with the larger flat surface up.

19. Install a new seal in the hub.

20. Thoroughly pack the bearing with clean, lithium based, wheel bearing grease. If one is available, use a grease gun adapter meant for packing bearings. These are available at all auto parts stores.

21. Place the bearing in the hub, and, using a press, press the hub and bearing assembly onto the shaft.

22. Press the new collar onto the shaft. The press pressure for the collar is critical. Press pressures should be 9,240-13,420 lb. (4,200-6100 kg).

23. Install one shaft in the housing being very careful to avoid damaging the inner seal.

24. If only on shaft was being serviced, the other must now be removed to check bearing play on the serviced axle. If both shafts were removed, leave the other one out for now.

25. Tighten the backing plate bolts on the one installed axle to 80 ft. lbs.

26. Mount a dial indicator on the backing plate, with the pointer resting on the axle shaft flange. Check the axial play. Standard bearing play should be 0.65-0.95mm (0.0256-0.0374 in.).

27. If play is not within specifications, shims are available for correcting it.

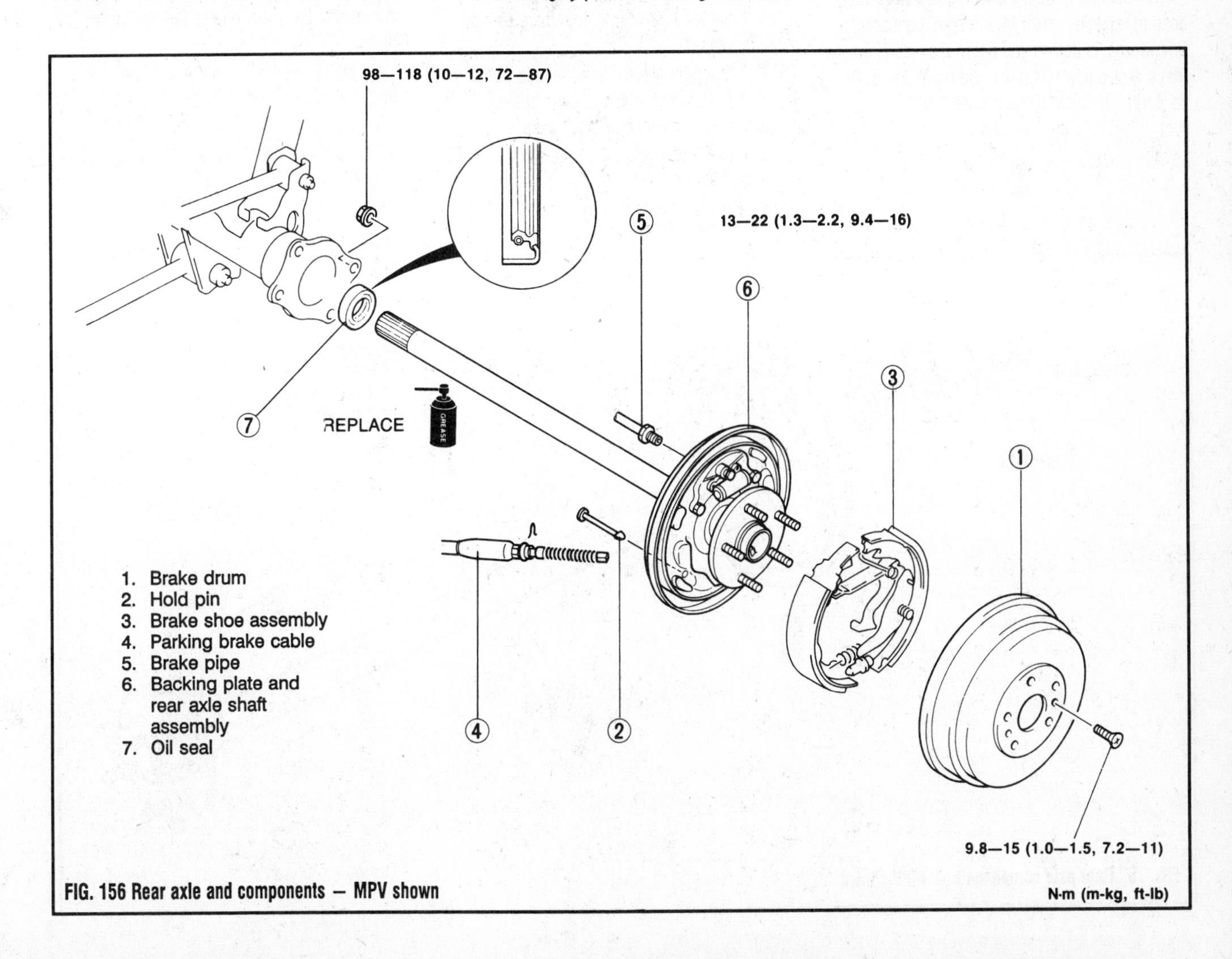

FIG. 156 Rear axle and components — MPV shown

28. Install the other shaft and torque the backing plate bolts. Check the play as on the first shaft. Play should be 0.05-0.25mm (0.0019-0.0098 in.). If not, correct it with shims.

29. Install the brake drums and wheels. Bleed the brake system.

MPV

1. Raise and support the rear end on jackstands.
2. Remove the wheel and brake drum.
3. Remove the brake shoes.
4. Remove the parking brake cable retainer.
5. Disconnect and cap the brake lines at the wheel cylinders.
6. Remove the bolts securing the backing plate and bearing housing.
7. Slide the axle shaft from the axle housing. Be careful to avoid damaging the oil seal with the shaft.
8. If the seal in the axle housing is damaged in any way, it must be replaced. The seal can be removed using a slide hammer and adapter.
9. Remove two of the backing plate bolts, diagonally from each other.
10. Using a grinding wheel, grind down the bearing retaining collar in one spot, until about 5mm remains before you get to the axle shaft. Place a chisel at this point and break the collar. Be careful to avoid damaging the shaft.

CAUTION

Wear some kind of protective goggles when grinding the collar and breaking the collar from the shaft!

11. Using a press or puller, remove the hub and bearing assembly from the shaft. Remove the spacer from the shaft.
12. Remove the bearing and seal from the hub.
13. Using a drift, tap the race from the hub.
14. Check all parts for wear or damage. If either race is to be replaced, both must be replaced. The race in the axle housing can be removed with a slide hammer and adapter. It's a good idea to replace the bearing and races as a set. It's also a good idea to replace the seals, regardless of what other service is being performed.
15. The outer race must be installed using an arbor press. The inner race can be driven into place in the axle housing.
16. Pack the hub with lithium based wheel bearing grease.
17. Tap a new oil seal into the axle housing until it is flush with the end of the housing. Coat the seal lip with wheel bearing grease.
18. Install a new spacer on the shaft with the larger flat surface up.
19. Install a new seal in the hub.
20. Thoroughly pack the bearing with clean, lithium based, wheel bearing grease. If one is available, use a grease gun adapter meant for packing bearings. These are available at all auto parts stores.
21. Place the bearing in the hub, and, using a press, press the hub and bearing assembly onto the shaft.
22. Press the new collar onto the shaft. The press pressure for the collar is critical. Press pressures should be 9,240-13,420 lb. (4,200-6,100 kg).
23. Install one shaft in the housing being very careful to avoid damaging the inner seal.
24. If only on shaft was being serviced, the other must now be removed to check bearing play on the serviced axle. If both shafts were removed, leave the other one out for now.
25. Tighten the backing plate bolts on the one installed axle to 80 ft. lbs.
26. Mount a dial indicator on the backing plate, with the pointer resting on the axle shaft flange. Check the axial play. Standard bearing play should be 0.57mm.
27. If play is not within specifications, shims are available for correcting it. See the table below:
28. Install the other shaft and torque the backing plate bolts. Check the play as on the first shaft.
29. Install the brake drums and wheels. Bleed the brake system.

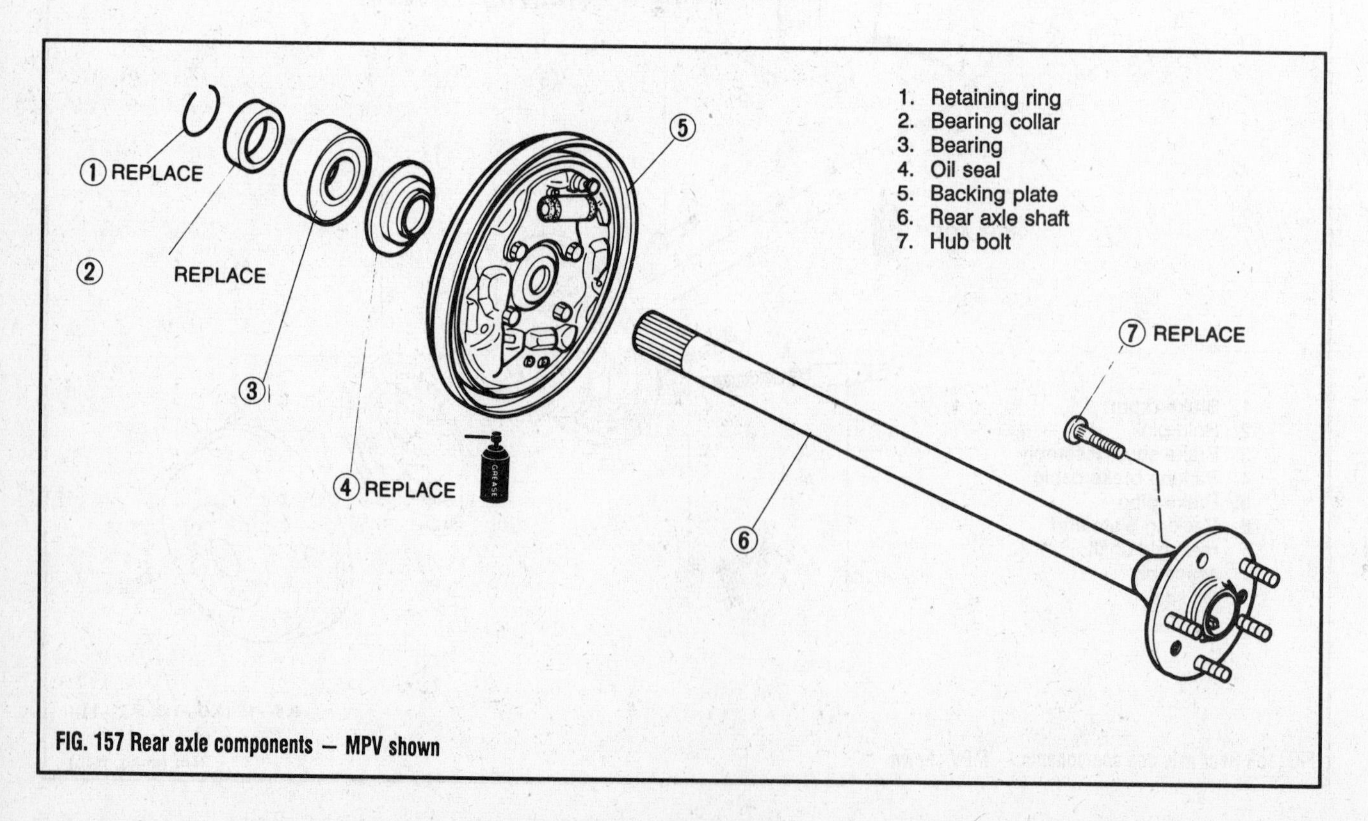

FIG. 157 Rear axle components — MPV shown

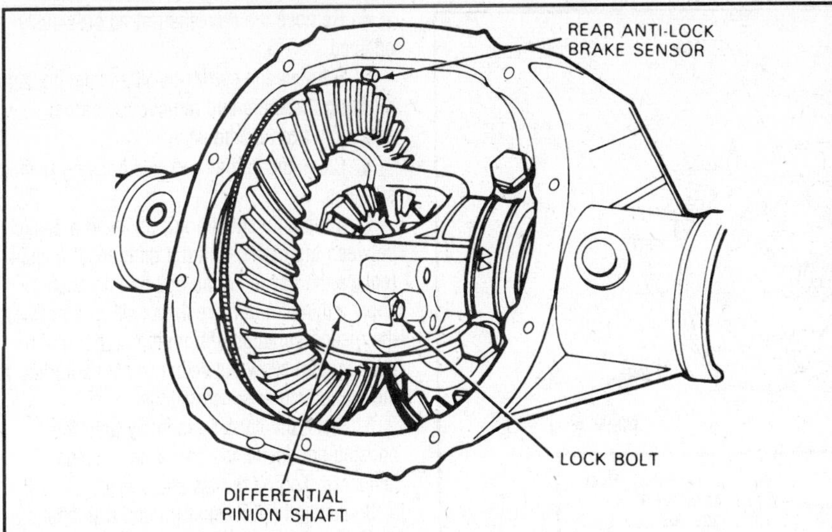

FIG. 158 Clean the differential rear cover. Remove the cover and drain the lube. Remove the pinion shaft lock bolt and push out the shaft — Navajo

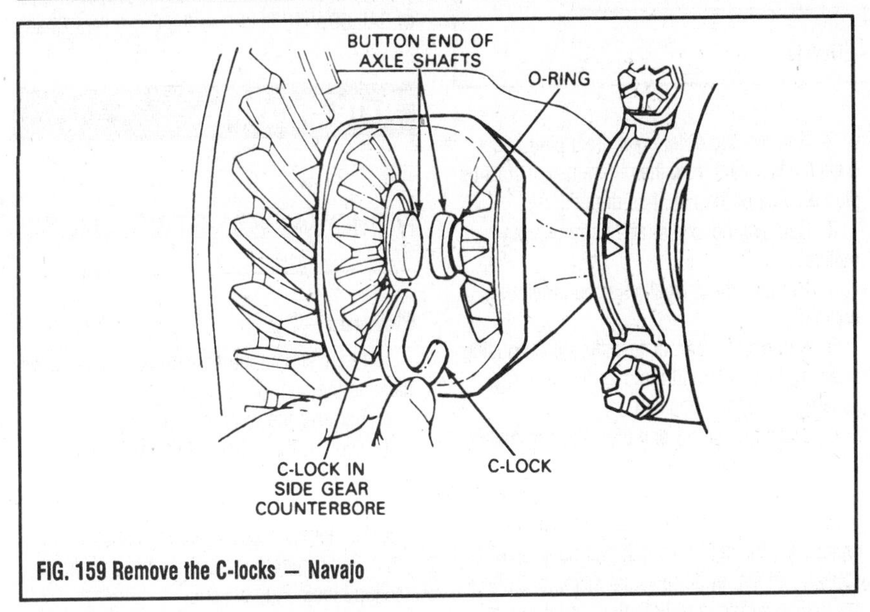

FIG. 159 Remove the C-locks — Navajo

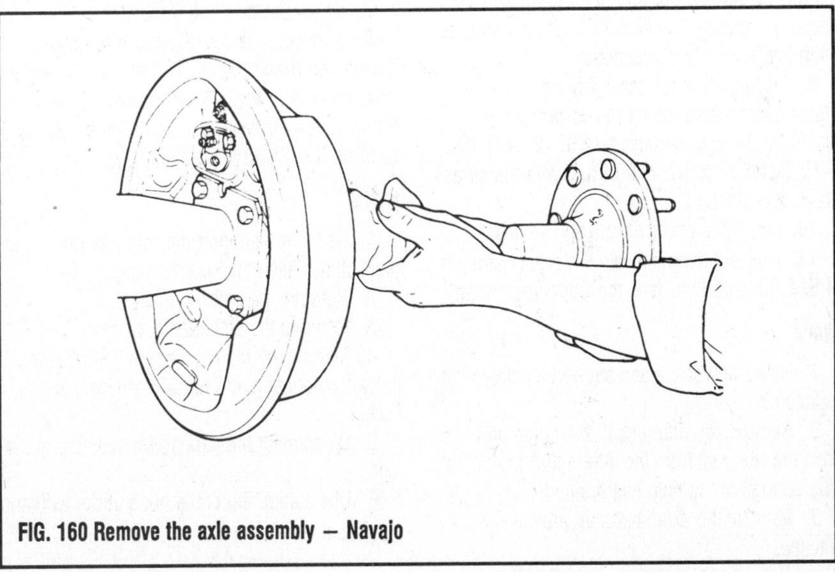
FIG. 160 Remove the axle assembly — Navajo

Navajo

1. Disconnect the negative battery cable.
2. Raise and support the vehicle safely.
3. Remove the rear wheels and brake drums.
4. Drain the rear axle lubricant.
5. For all axles except 3.73:1 and 4.10:1 ratio.
   a. Remove the differential pinion shaft lock bolt and differential pinion shaft.

➡ The pinion gears may be left in place. Once the axle shafts are removed, reinstall the pinion shaft and lock bolt.

   b. Push the flanged end of the axle shafts toward the center of the vehicle and remove the C-lockwasher from the end of the axle shaft.
   c. Remove the axle shafts from the housing. If the seals and/or bearing are not being replaced, be careful not to damage the seals with the axle shaft splines upon removal.
6. For 3.73:1 and 4.10:1 ratio axles.
   a. Remove the pinion shaft lock bolt. Place a hand behind the differential case and push out the pinion shaft until the step contacts the ring gear.
   b. Remove the C-lockwasher from the axle shafts.
   c. Remove the axle shafts from the housing. If the seals and/or bearing are not being replaced, be careful not to damage the seals with the axle shaft splines upon removal.
7. Insert the wheel bearing and seal remover, T85L–1225–AH or equivalent, and a slide hammer into the axle bore and position it behind the bearing so the tanks on the tool engage the bearing outer race. Remove the bearing and seal as a unit.

To Install:

8. If removed, lubricate the new bearing with rear axle lubricant and install the bearing into the housing bore. Use axle tube bearing replacer, T78P–1225–A or equivalent.
9. Apply Multi-Purpose Long-Life Lubricant, C1AZ–19590–B or equivalent, between the lips of the axle shaft seal.
10. Install a new axle shaft seal using axle tube seal replacer T78P–1177–A or equivalent.

➡ To permit axle shaft installation on 3.73:1 and 4.10:1 ratio axles, make sure the differential pinion shaft contacts the ring gear before performing Step 11.

11. Carefully slide the axle shaft into the axle housing, making sure not to damage the oil seal. Start the splines into the side gear and push firmly until the button end of the axle shaft can be seen in the differential case.

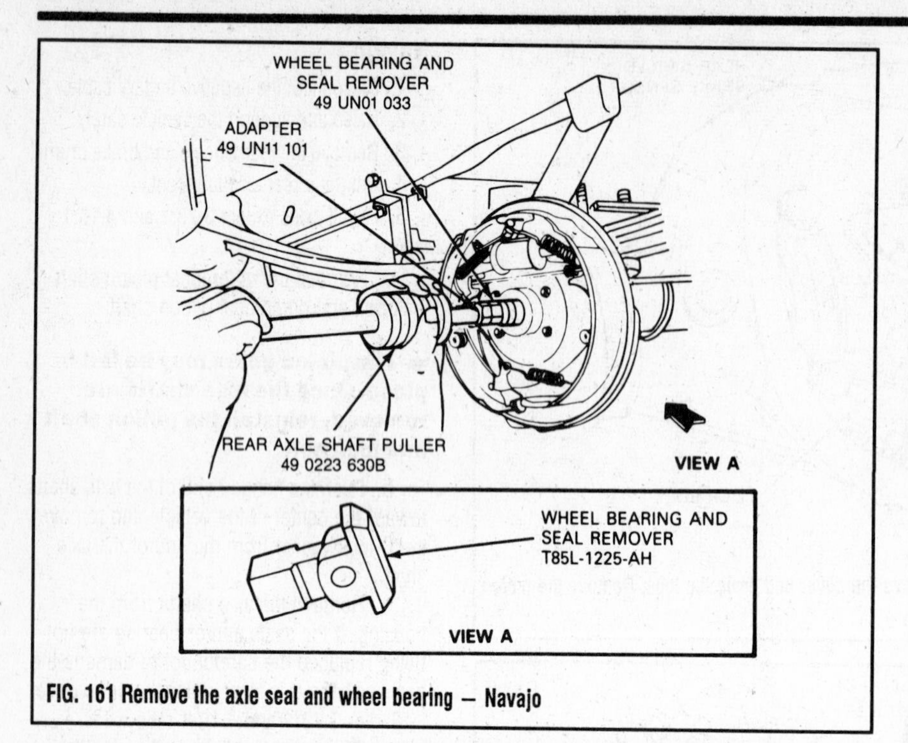

FIG. 161 Remove the axle seal and wheel bearing — Navajo

12. Install the C-lockwasher on the end of the axle shaft splines, then pull the shaft outboard until the shaft splines engage the C-lockwasher seats in the counterbore of the differential side gear.
13. Position the differential pinion shaft through the case and pinion gears, aligning the hole in the shaft with the lock screw hole. Install the lock bolt and tighten to 15–22 ft. lbs. (21–29Nm).
14. Clean the gasket mounting surface on the rear axle housing and cover. Apply a continuous bead of Silicone Rubber Sealant ESE-M4G195-A or equivalent to the carrier casting face.
15. Install the cover and tighten the retaining bolts to 25–35 ft. lbs. (20–34Nm).

➡ **The cover assembly must be installed within 15 minutes of application of the silicone sealant.**

16. Add lubricant until it is 1/4 in. (6mm) below the bottom of the filler hole in the running position. Install the filler plug and tighten to 15–30 ft. lbs. (20–41Nm).

Differential Carrier

REMOVAL & INSTALLATION

Pickups

1. Raise the vehicle and support it safely with jackstands.
2. Remove the differential drain plug and drain the lubricant from the differential. Install the plug after all of the fluid has drained.
3. Remove the axle shafts as previously outlined.
4. Remove the driveshaft(s) as previously outlined.
5. Remove the carrier-to-differential housing retaining fasteners and remove the carrier assembly from the housing.
6. Clean the carrier and axle housing mating surfaces.
7. If the differential originally used a gasket between the carrier and the differential housing, replace the gasket. If the unit had no gasket, apply a thin film of oil-resistant silicone sealer to the mating surfaces of both the carrier and the housing and allow the sealer to set according to the manufacturer's instructions.
8. Place the carrier assembly onto the housing and install the carrier-to-housing fasteners. Torque the fasteners to 12-17 ft. lbs.
9. Install the driveshaft(s) and axle shafts as previously outlined.
10. Install the brake drums and wheels.
11. Fill the differential with the proper amount of SAE 80W-90 fluid (see the Capacities Chart).

MPV

1. Raise the vehicle and support it safely with jackstands.
2. Remove the differential drain plug and drain the lubricant from the differential. Install the plug after all of the fluid has drained.
3. Remove the axle shafts as previously outlined.
4. Remove the driveshaft(s) as previously outlined.
5. Remove the carrier-to-differential housing retaining fasteners and remove the carrier assembly from the housing.
6. Clean the carrier and axle housing mating surfaces.
7. If the differential originally used a gasket between the carrier and the differential housing, replace the gasket. If the unit had no gasket, apply a thin film of oil-resistant silicone sealer to the mating surfaces of both the carrier and the housing and allow the sealer to set according to the manufacturer's instructions.
8. Place the carrier assembly onto the housing and install the carrier-to-housing fasteners. Torque the fasteners to 12-17 ft. lbs.
9. Install the driveshaft(s) and axle shafts as previously outlined.
10. Install the brake drums and wheels.
11. Fill the differential with the proper amount of SAE 80W-90 fluid (see the Capacities Chart).

Axle Housing

REMOVAL & INSTALLATION

Pickups

1. Raise and support the truck on jackstands, allowing the rear axle to hang freely.
2. Remove the wheels.
3. Support the weight of the axle with a floor jack.
4. Disconnect the shock absorbers.
5. Remove the axle-to-spring U-bolts.
6. Disconnect the brake line hose at the junction block. Plug the line.
7. Lower the axle and remove it.
8. Installation is the reverse of removal. Torque the U-bolt nuts to 100 ft. lbs. on 4-wheel drive models; 58 ft. lbs. on 2-wheel drive models. Torque the shock absorber lower bolts to 58 ft. lbs. Bleed the brakes.

MPV

1. Raise and support the rear end on jackstands. Allow the axle to hang freely.
2. Remove the splash shield.
3. Remove the stabilizer bar.
4. Matchmark the height sensing adjusting link and mounting and remove the connecting bolt.
5. Disconnect the parking brake cable at the axle.
6. Disconnect the brake hose at the axle and plug the line.

7. Support the weight of the axle with a floor jack.
8. Disconnect the shock absorbers.
9. Remove the lateral rod.
10. Remove the upper links.
11. Remove the lower links.
12. Lower the axle slowly and remove the coil springs.
13. Remove the axle.

To install:

14. Position the axle under the truck.
15. Position the coil springs on the axle with the larger end downward.
16. Raise the axle slowly into position.
17. Install the lower links. Hand tighten the bolts.
18. Install the upper links. Hand tighten the bolts.
19. Install the lateral rod. Hand tighten the bolts.
20. Connect the shock absorbers. Hand tighten the bolts.
21. Support the weight of the axle with a floor jack.
22. Connect the brake hose at the axle.
23. Connect the parking brake cable at the axle.
24. Install the height sensor connecting bolt. Torque it to 19 ft. lbs on standard models; 104 inch lbs. on models with a towing package.
25. Install the stabilizer bar. Tighten the clamp bolts to 38 ft. lbs. Tighten the end link bolts so that 7mm of thread is exposed above the nut.
26. Lower the truck to the ground. Observe the following torques:
   - Shock absorber: 56 ft. lbs.
   - Upper links: 127 ft. lbs.
   - Lower links: 127 ft. lbs.
   - Lateral rod: 127 ft. lbs.
27. Install the splash shield.

Navajo

1. Disconnect the negative battery cable.
2. Raise and support the vehicle safely.
3. Matchmark and disconnect the driveshaft at the axle.
4. Remove the wheels and brake drums.
5. Disengage the brake line from the clips that retain the line to the housing.
6. Disconnect the vent tube from the housing.
7. Remove the axle shafts.
8. Remove the brake backing plate from the housing and support them with wire. Do not disconnect the brake line.
9. Disconnect each rear shock absorber from the mounting bracket stud on the housing.
10. Lower the axle slightly to reduce some of the spring tension. At each rear spring, remove the spring clip (U-bolt) nuts, spring clips and spring seat caps.
11. Remove the housing from under the vehicle.

To Install:

12. Position the axle housing under the rear springs. Install the spring clips (U-bolts), spring seat clamps and nuts. Tighten the spring clamps evenly to 115 ft. lbs.
13. If a new axle housing is being installed, remove the bolts that attach the brake backing plate and bearing retainer from the old housing flanges. Position the bolts in the new housing flanges to hold the brake backing plates in position. Torque the bolts to 40 ft. lbs.
14. Install the axle shafts.
15. Connect the vent tube to the housing.
16. Position the brake line to the housing and secure it with the retaining clips.
17. Raise the axle housing and springs enough to allow connecting the rear shock absorbers to the mounting bracket studs on the housing. Torque the nuts to 60 ft. lbs.
18. Connect the driveshaft to the axle. Torque the nuts to 8–15 ft. lbs.
19. Install the brake drums and wheels.
20. Lower the vehicle.
21. Reconnect the negative battery cable.

Pinion Seal

REMOVAL & INSTALLATION

Pickups and MPV

1. Raise and support the front end on jackstands.
2. Matchmark and remove the driveshaft.
3. Remove the wheels and brake calipers.
4. Using an inch lbs. torque wrench on the companion flange nut, measure the rotational torque of the differential and note the reading.
5. Hold the companion flange from turning and remove the locknut.
6. Using a puller, remove the companion flange.
7. Using a center punch to deform the seal and pry it out of the bore.
8. Coat the outer edge of the new seal with sealer and drive it into place with a seal driver.
9. Coat the seal lip with clean gear oil.
10. Coat the companion flange with chassis lube and install it.
11. Install the nut and tighten it until the previously noted rotational torque is achieved. Torque on the nut should not exceed 130 ft. lbs.
12. Install the driveshaft.
13. Replace any lost gear oil.

Navajo

1. Disconnect the negative battery cable.
2. Raise and support the vehicle safely. Allow the axle to drop to rebound position for working clearance.
3. Remove the rear wheels and brake drums. No drag must be present on the axle.
4. Mark the companion flanges and U-joints for correct reinstallation position.
5. Remove the driveshaft.
6. Using an inch pound torque wrench and socket on the pinion yoke nut measure the amount of torque needed to maintain differential rotation through several clockwise revolutions. Record the measurement.
7. Use a suitable tool to hold the companion flange. Remove the pinion nut.
8. Place a drain pan under the differential. Clean the area around the seal and mark the yoke-to-pinion relation.
9. Use a 2-jawed puller to remove the companion flange.
10. Remove the seal with a small prybar.

To Install:

11. Thoroughly clean the oil seal bore.

➡ **If you are not absolutely certain of the proper seal installation depth, the proper seal driver must be used. If the seal is misaligned or damaged during installation, it must be removed and a new seal installed.**

12. Drive the new seal into place with a seal driver such as T83T–4676–A. Coat the seal lip with clean, waterproof wheel bearing grease.
13. Coat the splines with a small amount of wheel bearing grease and install the yoke, aligning the matchmarks. Never hammer the yoke onto the pinion!
14. Install a new nut on the pinion.
15. Hold the yoke with a holding tool. Tighten the pinion nut, taking frequent turning torque readings until the original preload reading is attained. If the original preload reading, that you noted before disassembly, is lower than the specified reading of 8–14 inch lbs. for used bearings; 16–29 inch lbs. for new bearings, keep tightening the pinion nut until the specified reading is reached. If the original preload reading is higher than the specified values, torque the nut just until the original reading is reached.

WARNING

Under no circumstances should the nut be backed off to reduce the preload reading! If the preload is exceeded, the yoke and bearing must be removed and a new collapsible spacer must be installed. The entire process of preload adjustment must be repeated.

15. Install the driveshaft using the matchmarks. Torque the nuts to 15 ft. lbs.
16. Lower the vehicle.
17. Reconnect the negative battery cable.

FRONT DRIVE AXLE

The Navajo employs a Ford/Dana 35 integral carrier drive axle. Consequently, tool numbers and part numbers listed in the procedures for that axle will be Ford numbers.

Manual Locking Hubs

SEE FIGS. 162-164

REMOVAL & INSTALLATION

B Series Pickup

1. Raise and safely support the vehicle. Remove the wheel and tire assembly.
2. Set the locking hub in the **FREE** position.
3. Remove the locking hub mounting bolts and remove the locking hub.
4. With the hub removed, install 2 bolts and nuts opposite each other to hold the hub together.
5. Check for smooth turning of the control handle.
6. Check for smooth rotation of the inner hub with the control lever in the **FREE** position.
7. Check for no rotation of the inner hub with the control lever in the **LOCK** position.

To install:

8. Coat the surface of the hub with sealant.
9. Place the control lever in the **FREE** position.
10. Install the hub on the vehicle and tighten the bolts to 22–25 ft. lbs. (29–34 Nm).
11. Install the wheel and tire assembly and check the operation of the hub. Lower the vehicle.

Navajo

1. Raise and support the vehicle safely.
2. Remove the lug nuts and remove the wheel and tire assembly.
3. Remove the retainer washers from the lug nut studs and remove the manual locking hub assembly. To remove the internal hub lock assembly from the outer body assembly, remove the outer lock ring seated in the hub body groove. The internal assembly, spring and clutch gear will now slide out of the hub body. Do not remove the screw from the plastic dial.
4. Rebuild the hub assembly in the reverse order of disassembly.
5. Adjust the wheel bearing if necessary. Install the manual locking hub assembly over the spindle and place the retainer washers on the lug nut studs.
6. Install the wheel and tire assembly and lower the vehicle.

ADJUSTMENT

Navajo

1. Raise and safely support the vehicle. Remove the wheel and tire assembly.
2. Remove the retainer washers from the lug nut studs and remove the manual locking hub assembly from the spindle.
3. Remove the snapring from the end of the spindle shaft.
4. Remove the axle shaft spacer.
5. Remove the outer wheel bearing locknut from the spindle using locknut wrench 49 UN01 042 or equivalent. Make sure the tabs on the tool engage the slots in the locknut.
6. Remove the locknut washer from the spindle.
7. Loosen the inner wheel bearing locknut using the locknut wrench. Make sure the tabs on the tool engage the slots in the locknut and the slot in the tool is centered over the locknut pin.
8. Tighten the inner locknut to 35 ft. lbs. (47 Nm) to seat the bearings.
9. Spin the rotor and back off the inner locknut 1/4 turn. Retighten the inner locknut to 16 inch lbs. (1.8 Nm). Install the lockwasher on the spindle. It may be necessary to tighten the inner locknut slightly so the pin on the locknut aligns with the closest hole in the lockwasher.
10. Install the outer wheel bearing locknut using the locknut wrench. Tighten the locknut to 150 ft. lbs. (203 Nm).
11. Install the axle shaft spacer.
12. Clip the snapring onto the end of the spindle. Install the manual hub assembly over the spindle and install the retainer washers.
13. Install the wheel and tire assembly. Check the endplay of the wheel and tire assembly on the spindle. Final endplay should be 0–0.003 in. (0–0.08mm). The maximum torque to rotate the hub should be 25 inch lbs. (2.8 Nm).
14. Lower the vehicle.

Automatic Locking Hubs

REMOVAL & INSTALLATION

Navajo

1. Raise and support the vehicle safely. Remove the wheel lug nuts and remove the wheel and tire assembly.
2. Remove the retainer washers from the lug nut studs and remove the automatic locking hub assembly from the spindle.
3. Remove the snapring from the end of the spindle shaft.
4. Remove the axle shaft spacer.
5. Being careful not to damage the plastic moving cam or thrust spacers, pull the cam assembly off the wheel bearing adjusting nut. Remove the 2 plastic thrust spacers from the adjusting nut.
6. Using a magnet, remove the locking key. It may be necessary to rotate the adjusting nut slightly to relieve the pressure against the locking key, before the key can be removed.

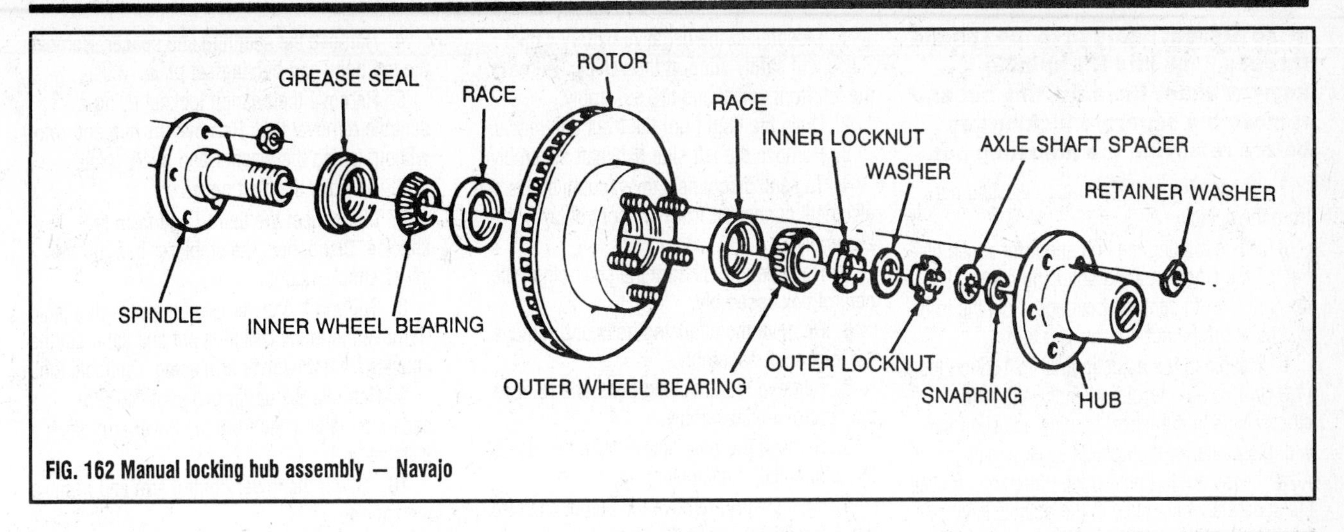

FIG. 162 Manual locking hub assembly — Navajo

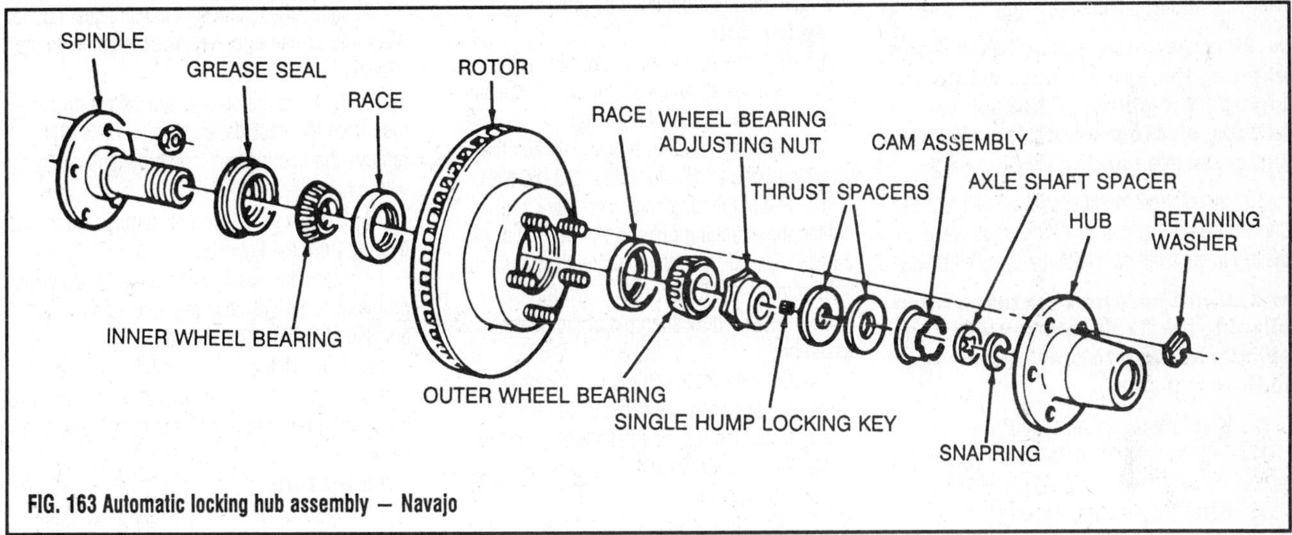

FIG. 163 Automatic locking hub assembly — Navajo

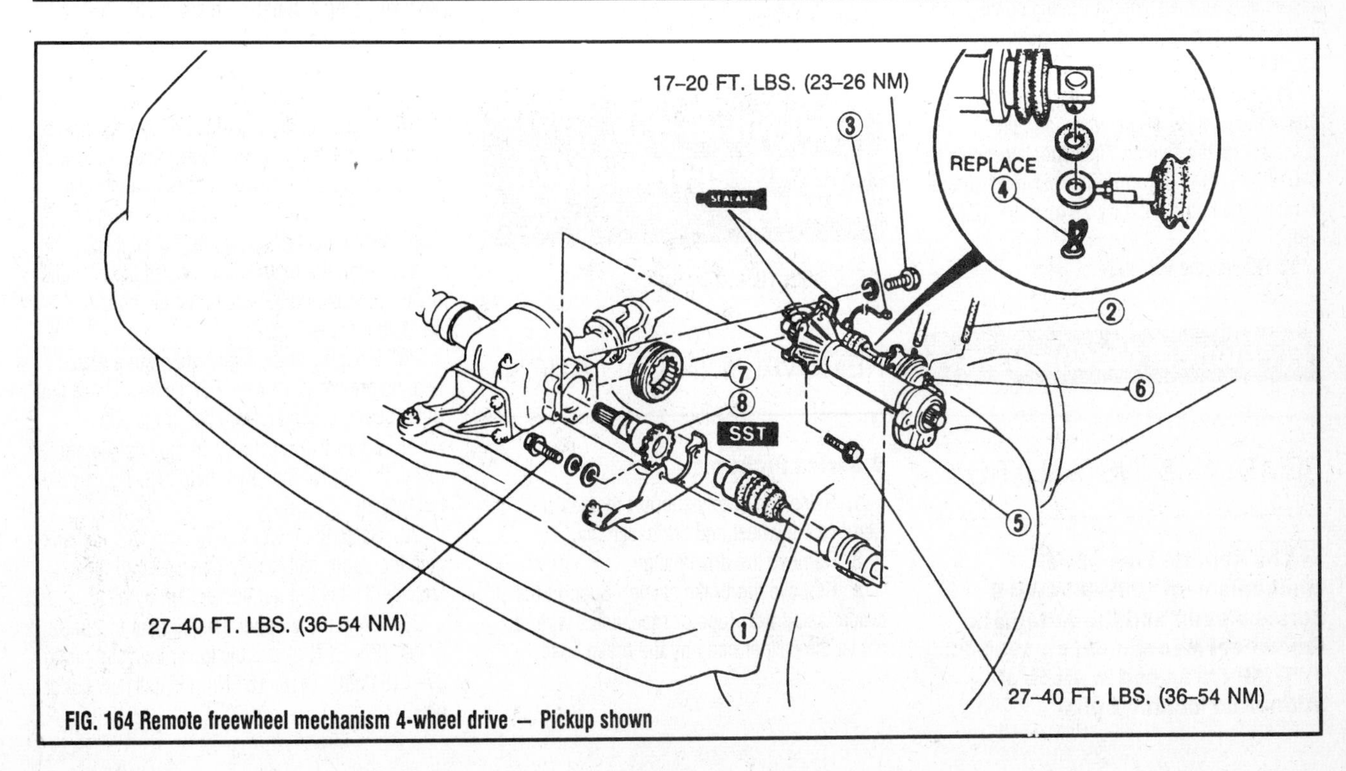

FIG. 164 Remote freewheel mechanism 4-wheel drive — Pickup shown

➡ To prevent damage to the spindle threads, look into the spindle keyway under the adjusting nut and remove the separate locking key before removing the adjusting nut.

7. Loosen the wheel bearing adjusting nut from the spindle.
8. While rotating the hub and rotor assembly, tighten the wheel bearing adjusting nut to 35 ft. lbs. (47 Nm) to seat the bearings. Spin the rotor and back off the nut one-quarter turn.
9. Retighten the adjusting nut to 16 inch lbs. (1.8 Nm) using a torque wrench. Align the closest hole in the wheel bearing adjusting nut with the center of the spindle keyway slot. Advance the nut to the next lug if required. Install the separate locking key in the spindle keyway under the adjusting nut.

➡ Extreme care must be taken when aligning the spindle nut adjustment lug with the center of the spindle keyway slot to prevent damage to the separate locking key.

10. Install the 2 thrust spacers. Push or press the cam assembly onto the locknut by lining up the key in the fixed cam with the spindle keyway.

➡ Extreme care must be taken when aligning the fixed cam key with the spindle keyway to prevent damage to the fixed cam.

11. Install the axle shaft spacer.
12. Clip the snapring onto the end of the spindle.
13. Install the automatic locking hub assembly over the spindle by lining up the 3 legs in the hub assembly with the 3 pockets in the cam assembly. Install the retainer washers.
14. Install the wheel and tire assembly. Check the endplay of the wheel and tire assembly on the spindle. Final endplay should be 0–0.003 in. (0–0.08mm). The maximum torque to rotate the hub should be 25 inch lbs. (2.8 Nm).
15. Lower the vehicle.

Freewheel Mechanism

REMOVAL & INSTALLATION

➡ The Remote Freewheel Mechanism on 1989–92 4WD B Series pickup and the Automatic Freewheel Mechanism on 1990–92 4WD MPV are used in place of automatic locking hubs.

1. Disconnect the negative battery cable. Raise and safely support the vehicle. Remove the left front wheel and tire assembly.
2. Drain the fluid from the front differential.
3. Remove the left side halfshaft assembly.
4. Tag and disconnect the vacuum hoses and electrical connector from the control box assembly.
5. Remove and discard the snap pin at the control box assembly.
6. Remove the attaching bolts and remove the joint shaft assembly.
7. Remove the attaching bolts and remove the control box assembly.
8. Remove the gear sleeve from the side of the differential, if necessary.
9. If necessary, remove the output shaft from the differential using a slide hammer.

To Install:

10. If removed, install a new clip on the end of the output shaft and install in the differential. Install the gear sleeve, if removed.
11. Install the control box and tighten the attaching bolts to 17–20 ft. lbs. (23–26 Nm).
12. Install the joint shaft assembly and tighten the attaching bolts to 27–40 ft. lbs. (36–54 Nm). On MPV, install the attaching nut and tighten to 49–72 ft. lbs. (67–97 Nm).
13. Install a new snap pin at the control box assembly.
14. Connect the electrical connector and vacuum hoses at the control box assembly.
15. Install the left side halfshaft assembly.
16. Fill the differential with the proper type and quantity of fluid.
17. Install the wheel and tire assembly and lower the vehicle.

Front Wheel Hub, Knuckle/Spindle and Bearings

➧ SEE FIGS. 165-167

REMOVAL & INSTALLATION

B Series Pickups

1. Raise and safely support the vehicle. Remove the wheel and tire assembly.
2. Remove the drive flange.
3. Remove the brake caliper. Support the caliper aside with rope or mechanics wire; do not let the caliper hang by the brake hose.
4. Remove the snapring and spacer. Remove the set bolts and bearing set plate.
5. Remove the bearing locknut using a suitable removal tool. Remove the hub and rotor without letting the washer and bearing fall.
6. Remove the dust cover.
7. Disconnect the tie rod end from the knuckle. Disconnect the stabilizer bar and the lower shock mount.
8. Support the lower control arm with a jack. Remove the lower ball joint nut and separate the knuckle from the lower arm using a suitable tool.
9. Remove the upper ball joint nut and separate the knuckle from the lower arm using a suitable tool.
10. Lower the lower control arm and remove the knuckle.
11. Inspect the knuckle, hub and bearings for wear and or damage. Replace components, as necessary.
12. Remove the oil seal and the bearing inner race from the knuckle. Using a suitable drift, remove the bearing outer race by tapping lightly with a hammer.
13. Using a slide hammer, remove the needle bearing from the knuckle.
14. Mark the position of the disc brake rotor on the hub, then remove the bolts and disassemble the rotor and hub.
15. Remove the oil seal and the bearing inner race from the hub. Using a suitable drift, remove the bearing outer race by tapping lightly with a hammer.

To Install:

16. Press a new needle bearing into the knuckle using a suitable driver.
17. After installing the inner bearing into the knuckle, press in a new oil seal. Apply wheel bearing grease to the oil seal lip.
18. Press fit the outer side bearing outer race, then the inner side bearing outer race, into the hub using suitable drivers. Press in a new oil seal until it is flush with the hub end surface. Apply wheel bearing grease to the seal lip.
19. Align the matching marks of the hub and brake rotor and tighten the mounting bolts to 40–51 ft. lbs. (54–69 Nm).
20. Liberally apply high temperature wheel bearing grease to the inside of the hub. Install the outer bearing race and washer in the hub.
21. Insert the halfshaft into the knuckle and install the nut for the lower ball joint. Tighten the nut by hand.
22. Raise the lower control arm with the jack until the upper ball joint is connected to the knuckle. Install the nut and tighten by hand.
23. Tighten the upper ball joint nut to 22–38 ft. lbs. (29–51 Nm) and the lower ball joint nut to 87–116 ft. lbs. (118–157 Nm). Install new cotter pins.

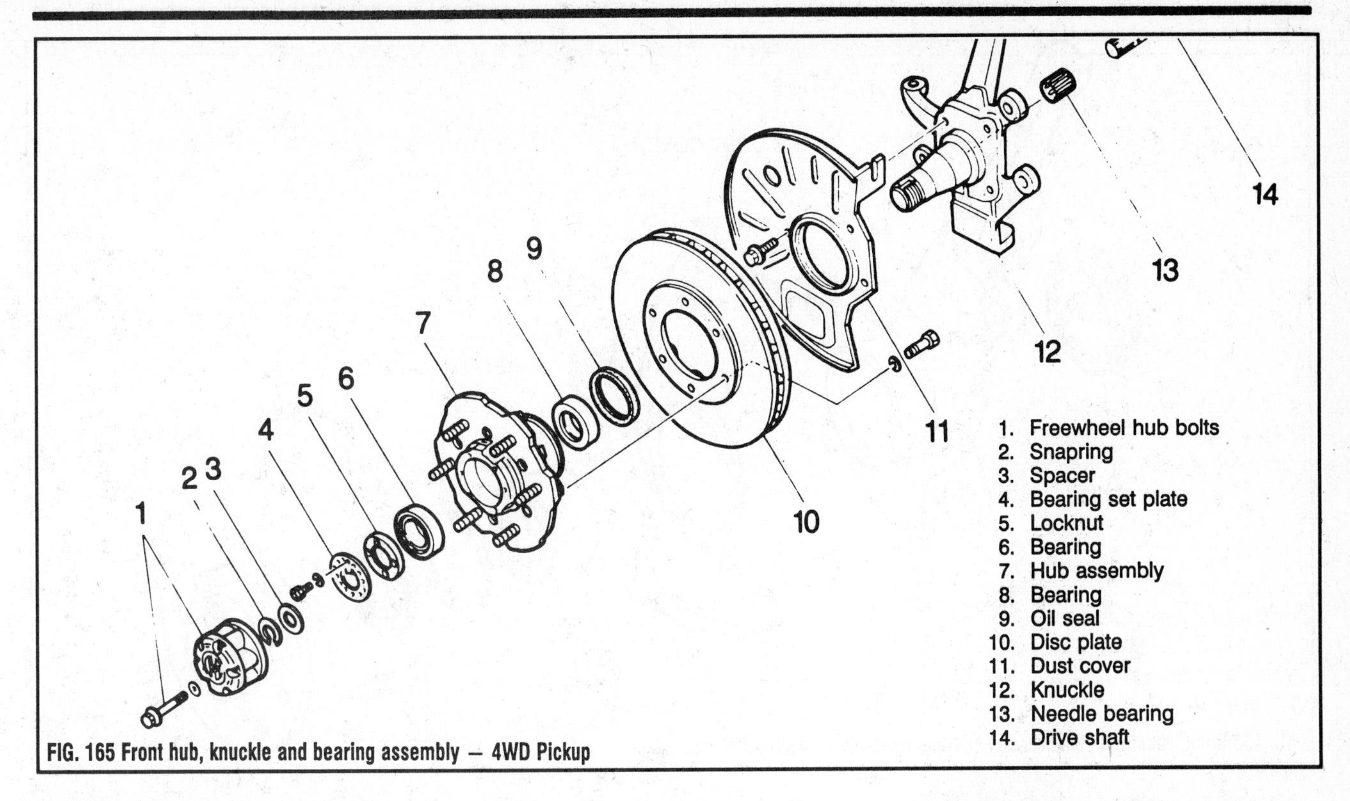

FIG. 165 Front hub, knuckle and bearing assembly — 4WD Pickup

24. Connect the tie rod end to the knuckle, tighten the nut to 23–43 ft. lbs. (44–59 Nm) and install a new cotter pin.
25. Install the dust cover to the knuckle and tighten to 14–19 ft. lbs. (19–26 Nm).
26. After loosely installing the lower shock absorber mount, install the stabilizer bar.
27. Install the hub and rotor assembly, then adjust the bearing preload as follows:
a. Tighten the locknut, then turn the hub and rotor 2–3 times to seat the bearing.
b. Loosen the locknut so they can be turned by hand.
c. Attach a suitable pull scale to a wheel lug bolt and measure the frictional forces. The preload is the frictional force plus 1.3–2.6 lbs.
d. Tighten the locknut until the preload is as specified.
e. Install the bearing set plate using 2 bolts. Tighten the bolts to 43–61 inch lbs. (5–7 Nm).
f. Coat the spacer with grease and install it. Install a new snapring.
28. Install the caliper, wheel and tire assembly and drive flange. Lower the vehicle.
29. Tighten the lower shock mount to 41–59 ft. lbs. (55–80 Nm) with the vehicle unloaded.
30. Check the front end alignment.

MPV

1. Raise and safely support the vehicle. Remove the wheel and tire assembly.
2. Remove and discard the locknut from the end of the halfshaft.
3. Remove the brake caliper and disc brake rotor. Support the caliper aside with rope or mechanics wire; do not let the caliper hang by the brake hose.
4. Remove the cotter pin and nut and, using a suitable tool, disconnect the tie rod end from the knuckle.
5. Remove the cotter pin and loosen the lower ball joint nut. Separate the lower arm from the knuckle using a suitable tool.
6. Remove the knuckle-to-strut bolts and nuts and remove the knuckle/hub assembly from the vehicle.
7. Pry out the inner oil seal from the knuckle.
8. Position the knuckle/hub assembly in a press and, using a suitable driver, press the hub from the knuckle.

➡ If the inner bearing race remains on the hub, position the hub in a vise, secured by the flange. Move the race away from the hub using a hammer and chisel, then position the hub in a press and press the race off of the hub.

9. Pry out the outer oil seal from the knuckle.
10. Remove the retaining ring and position the knuckle in a press. Using a suitable driver, press the wheel bearing from the knuckle.
11. If necessary, mark the position of the dust shield on the knuckle and remove the dust shield, using a hammer and chisel. Do not reuse the dust cover, if removed.

To Install:

12. If the dust cover was removed, mark the new cover in the same place as the old was marked during removal. Align the cover and knuckle marks and press the cover onto the knuckle.
13. Press a new wheel bearing into the knuckle, using a suitable driver. Install the retaining ring and a new outer seal. Apply grease to the seal lip.
14. Press the hub into the knuckle, using a suitable driver. Install a new inner seal and lubricate the seal lip with grease.
15. Install the knuckle/hub assembly onto the strut, install the bolts and nuts and tighten to 69–86 ft. lbs. (93–117 Nm).
16. Install the lower ball joint into the knuckle and tighten the nut to 115–137 ft. lbs. (157–187 Nm). Install a new cotter pin.
17. Connect the tie rod to the knuckle and install the nut. Tighten to 43–58 ft. lbs. (59–78 Nm) and install a new cotter pin.
18. Install the brake rotor and caliper.
19. Install a new locknut on the end of the halfshaft and tighten to 174–231 ft. lbs. (235–314 Nm). After tightening, stake the nut with a blunt chisel.
20. Install the wheel and tire assembly and lower the vehicle. Check the front end alignment.

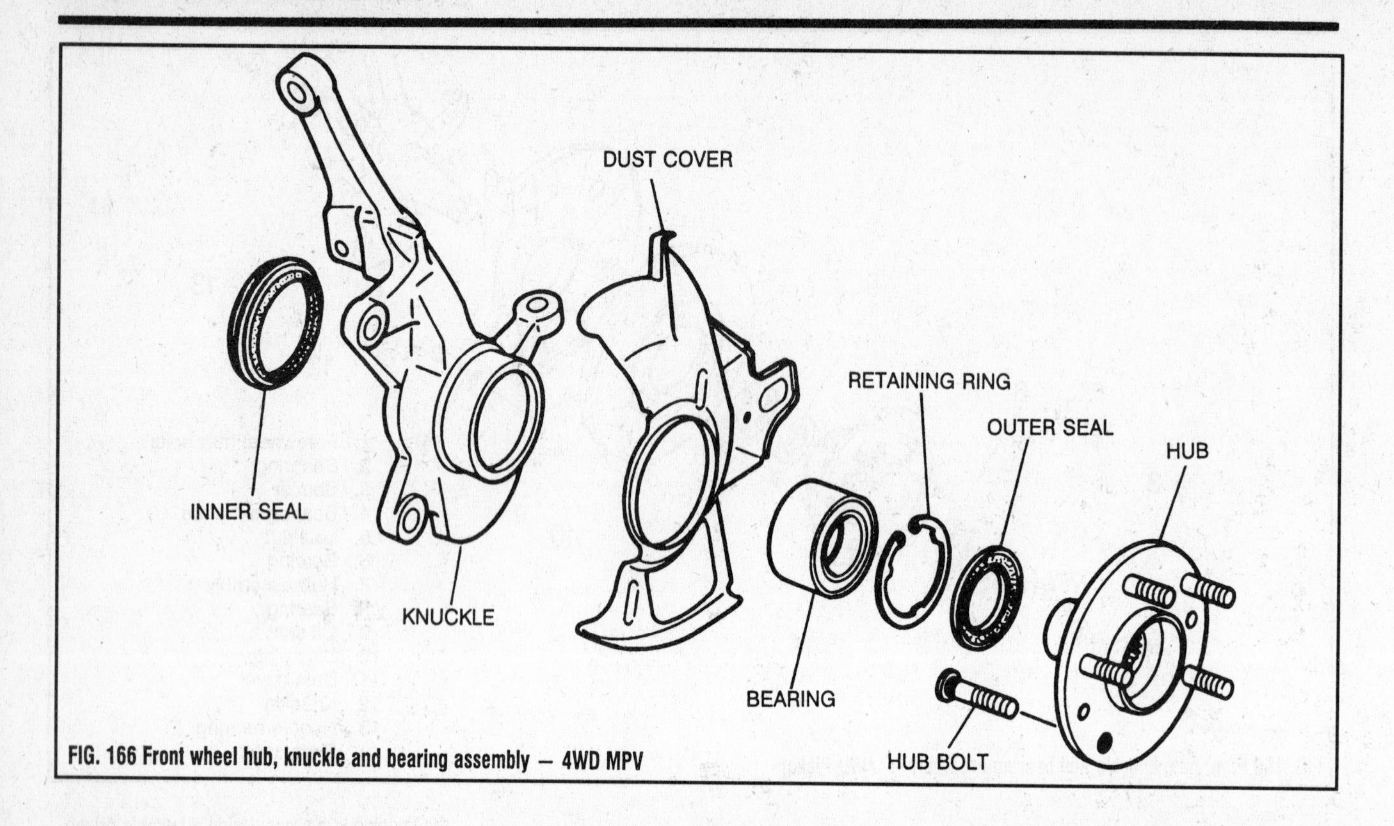

FIG. 166 Front wheel hub, knuckle and bearing assembly — 4WD MPV

Navajo

1. Raise and safely support the vehicle. Remove the front wheel and tire assemblies.
2. Remove the disc brake caliper and wire it to the frame. Do not let the caliper hang by the brake hose.
3. Remove the hub locks, wheel bearings and locknuts.
4. Remove the hub, rotor and outer wheel bearing.
5. Remove the grease seal from the rotor with a seal removal tool. Remove the inner wheel bearing.
6. If the wheel bearings are to be replaced, remove the inner and outer bearing races with a suitable puller or a hammer and brass drift.
7. Remove the nuts retaining the spindle to the steering knuckle. Tap the spindle with a plastic hammer to jar the spindle from the knuckle. Remove the splash shield.
8. On the left side of the vehicle, remove the shaft and joint assembly by pulling the assembly out of the carrier. On the right side of the carrier, remove and discard the clamp from the shaft and joint assembly and the stub shaft. Pull the shaft and joint assembly from the splines of the stub shaft.
9. Place the spindle in a vise on the second step of the spindle. Wrap a shop towel around the spindle or use a brass-jawed vise to protect the spindle.
10. Remove the oil seal and needle bearing from the spindle with a slide hammer and seal remover TOOL–1175–AC or equivalent. If necessary, remove the slinger from the shaft by driving off with a hammer.
11. Remove the cotter pin from the tie rod nut and then remove the nut. Tap on the tie rod stud to free it from the steering arm.
12. Remove the upper ball joint snapring and remove the upper ball joint pinch bolt. Loosen the lower ball joint nut to the end of the stud.
13. Strike the inside of the knuckle near the upper and lower ball joints to break the knuckle loose from the ball joint studs.
14. Remove the camber adjuster sleeve. Note the position of the slot in the camber adjuster so it can be reinstalled in the same position during assembly.
15. Remove the lower ball joint nut. Place the knuckle in a vise and remove the snapring from the bottom ball joint socket, if equipped.
16. Assemble C-frame T74P–4635–C and ball joint remover T83T–3050–A or equivalents on the lower ball joint. Turn the forcing screw clockwise until the lower ball joint is removed from the steering knuckle.
17. Assemble the C-frame and ball joint remover on the upper ball joint and remove in the same manner.

➡ Always remove the lower ball joint first.

To Install:

18. Clean the steering knuckle bore and insert the lower ball joint in the knuckle as straight as possible.
19. Assemble C-frame T74P–4635–C, ball joint installer T83T–3050–A and receiver cup T80T–3010–A3 or equivalents to install the lower ball joint. Turn the forcing screw clockwise until the lower ball joint is firmly seated. Install the snapring on the lower ball joint.

➡ The lower ball joint must always be installed first.

20. Assemble the C-frame, ball joint installer and receiver cup to install the upper ball joint. Turn the forcing screw clockwise until the ball joint is firmly seated.
21. Install the camber adjuster into the support arm, making sure the slot is in the original position.

➡ The torque sequence in Steps 22 and 23 must be followed exactly when securing the knuckle. Excessive knuckle turning effort may result in reduced steering returnability if this procedure is not followed.

22. Install a new nut on the bottom ball joint stud. Tighten the nut to 90 ft. lbs. (122 Nm) minimum, then tighten to align the next slot in the nut with the hole in the stud. Install a new cotter pin.
23. Install the snapring on the upper ball joint stud. Install the upper ball joint pinch bolt and tighten to 48–65 ft. lbs. (65–88 Nm).

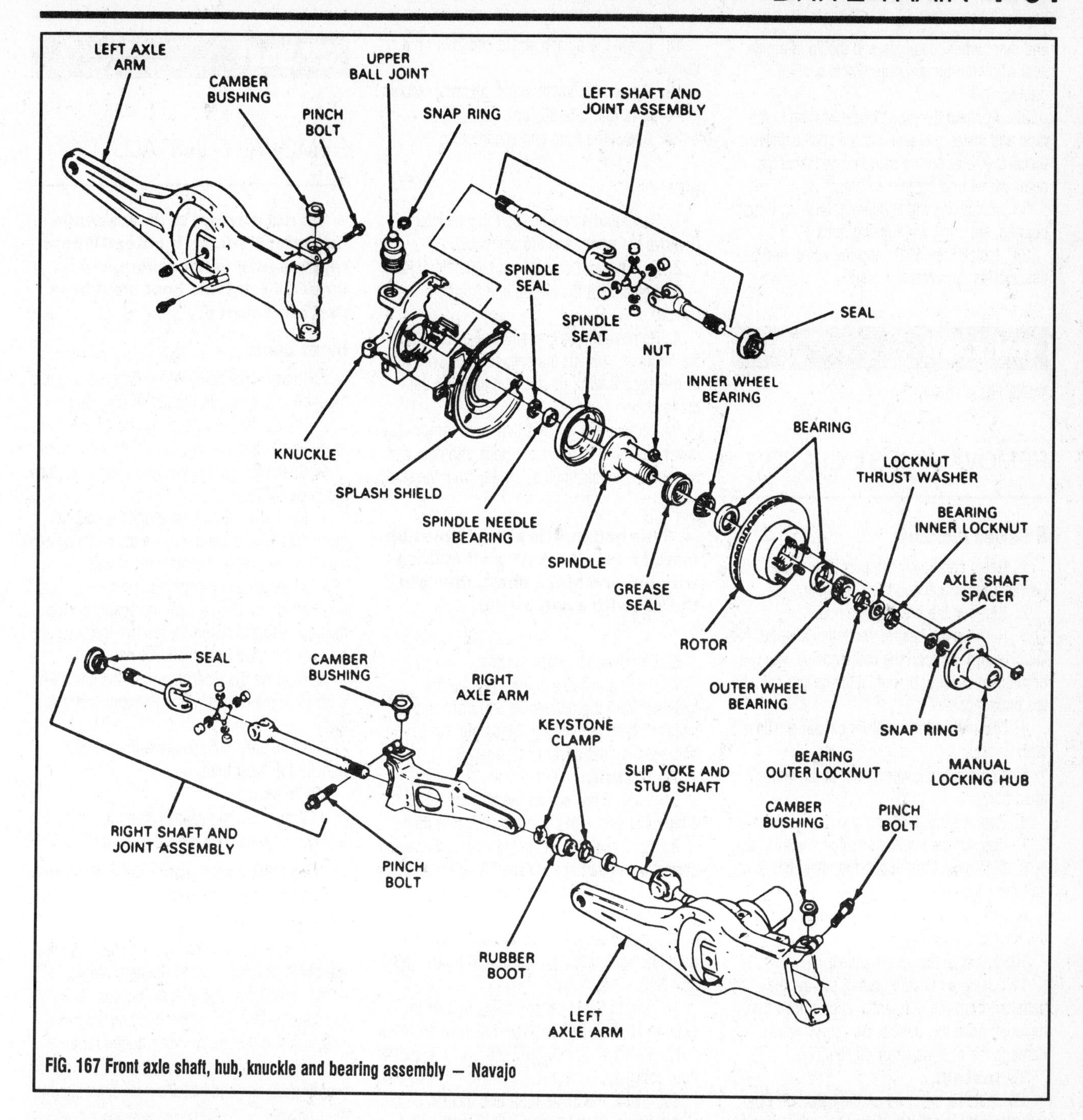

FIG. 167 Front axle shaft, hub, knuckle and bearing assembly — Navajo

➡ The camber adjuster will seat itself into the knuckle at a predetermined position during the tightening sequence. Do not attempt to adjust this position.

24. Clean all dirt and grease from the spindle bearing bore. The bearing bores must be free from nicks and burrs.

25. Place the bearing in the bore with the manufacturers identification facing outward. Drive the bearing into the bore using spindle bearing replacer T80T–4000–S and driver handle T80T–4000–W or equivalents.

26. Install the grease seal in the bearing bore with the lip side of the seal facing towards the tool. Drive the seal in the bore using the same tools as in Step 25. Coat the bearing seal lip with high-temperature lubricant.

27. If removed, press on a new shaft slinger.

28. On the right side of the carrier, install the rubber boot and new keystone clamps on the stub shaft slip yoke. Slide the right shaft and joint assembly into the slip yoke making sure the splines are fully engaged. Slide the boot over the assembly and crimp the keystone clamp using suitable pliers.

➡ The Dana model 35 axle does not have a blind spline, therefore pay special attention to make sure the yoke ears are in phase (in line) during assembly.

29. On the left side of the carrier, slide the shaft and joint assembly through the knuckle and engage the splines on the shaft in the carrier.

30. Install the splash shield and spindle onto the steering knuckle. Install and tighten the spindle nuts to 45 ft. lbs. (61 Nm).

31. If removed, drive the bearing races into the rotor using a suitable driver. Pack the inner

and outer wheel bearings and the lip of a new seal with high-temperature wheel bearing grease.

32. Position the inner wheel bearing in the race and install the seal using a seal installer. Install the rotor on the spindle and install the outer wheel bearing in the race.

33. Install the wheel bearing, locknut, thrust bearing, snapring and locking hubs.

34. Install the caliper and the wheel and tire assemblies. Lower the vehicle.

Halfshaft

➧ SEE FIGS. 168-187

REMOVAL & INSTALLATION

B Series Pickup

1. Raise and safely support the vehicle. Remove the wheel and tire assembly.
2. Remove the drive flange hub.
3. Remove the caliper, mounting support and knuckle arm. Support the caliper aside with rope or mechanics wire; do not let the caliper hang by the brake hose.
4. Disconnect the stabilizer bar and the tie rod end.
5. Remove the lower mount of the shock absorber.
6. Remove the snapring and spacer.
7. Support the lower control arm with a jack.
8. Disconnect the upper and lower ball joints and the knuckle.
9. Lower the lower control arm and remove the knuckle assembly.
10. Remove the splash shield.
11. Using a suitable prybar, pry out the halfshaft from the differential and remove the halfshaft from the vehicle. Be careful not to damage the dust cover or oil seal.

To install:

12. Install a new clip on the halfshaft. Coat the differential seal with clean transmission fluid.
13. Install the halfshaft in the differential, being careful not to damage the seal. After installation, attempt to pull the halfshaft outward to make sure it does not come out.
14. Install the knuckle and hub to the halfshaft and ball joints. Install the spacer and a new snapring.
15. Install the lower mount of the shock absorber and loosely tighten the bolt.
16. Connect the stabilizer bar and tie rod end.
17. Install the caliper assembly, knuckle arm and wheel and tire assembly. Apply sealant to the drive flange and install it.
18. Install the splash shield and lower the vehicle.
19. Tighten the lower shock absorber mount to 41–59 ft. lbs. (55–80 Nm).
20. Check the front end alignment.

MPV

1. Raise and safely support the vehicle. Remove the wheel and tire assembly.
2. Remove and discard the halfshaft locknut.
3. Disconnect the tie rod end from the knuckle.
4. Remove the caliper and brake rotor from the knuckle. Support the caliper aside with rope or mechanics wire; do not let it hang by the brake hose.
5. Remove the nut and bolts and remove the lower ball joint. Remove the bolts and nuts and remove the knuckle/hub assembly from the strut.

➡ **If the halfshaft is stuck to the hub, install a used locknut so it is flush with the end of the shaft, then tap the nut with a soft mallet.**

6. Remove the splash shield.
7. Using a suitable prybar, pry out the halfshaft from the differential and remove the halfshaft from the vehicle. Be careful not to damage the dust cover or oil seal.

To install:

8. Install a new clip on the halfshaft. Coat the differential seal with clean transmission fluid.
9. Install the halfshaft in the differential, being careful not to damage the seal. After installation, attempt to pull the halfshaft outward to make sure it does not come out.
10. Install the knuckle/hub assembly to the strut and tighten the nuts to 69–86 ft. lbs. (93–117 Nm).
11. Install the lower ball joint. Tighten the bolts to 75–101 ft. lbs. (102–137 Nm) and the nut to 115–137 ft. lbs. (157–187 Nm). Install a new cotter pin.
12. Install the brake rotor and caliper.
13. Connect the tie rod end to the knuckle.
14. Install a new locknut and tighten to 174–231 ft. lbs. (235–314 Nm). After tightening, stake the locknut using a blunt chisel.
15. Install the splash shield. Install the wheel and tire assembly and lower the vehicle.
16. Check the front end alignment.

CV-Boot

REMOVAL & INSTALLATION

➡ **Do not attempt to disassemble the outer CV-joint. If outer CV-boot replacement is necessary, the inner CV-joint and boot must be first be removed.**

Inner Boot

1. Remove the halfshaft from the vehicle and mount it in a vise with protective jaw caps.
2. Pry up the boot band locking clips with a small prybar and remove the bands with pliers.
3. Slide the boot back on the shaft to expose the inner CV-joint.
4. Mark the CV-joint housing and cage for proper reassembly and remove the retaining clip with a small prybar. Remove the housing.
5. Mark the shaft, cage, balls and inner ring for reassembly and remove the snapring. Turn the cage about 30 degrees, remove the balls and remove the cage from the inner ring.
6. Remove the inner ring from the shaft with a press or drive it off with a hammer and brass drift.
7. Wrap the shaft splines with tape and remove the inner boot.

To install:

8. Wrap the shaft splines with tape and slide a new boot onto the shaft. Remove the tape.

➡ **The inner and outer CV-boots are different and cannot be interchanged.**

9. Install the inner ring on the shaft, aligning the marks that were made during removal.
10. Install the cage with the big end facing the snapring groove. Install the cage on the inner ring, aligning the marks made during removal and turn it 30 degrees. Install the balls into their proper positions and install a new snapring into the groove.
11. Fill the CV-joint housing with the proper quantity and type of CV-joint grease and apply the grease thoroughly to the cage, inner ring and ball assembly.
12. Align the marks and install the CV-joint housing on the shaft and install a new retaining clip.
13. Apply about 120 grams (4.2 oz.) of CV-joint grease to the inside of the inner boot and slide the boot over the CV-joint. Carefully lift up the small end of the boot to release any trapped air.

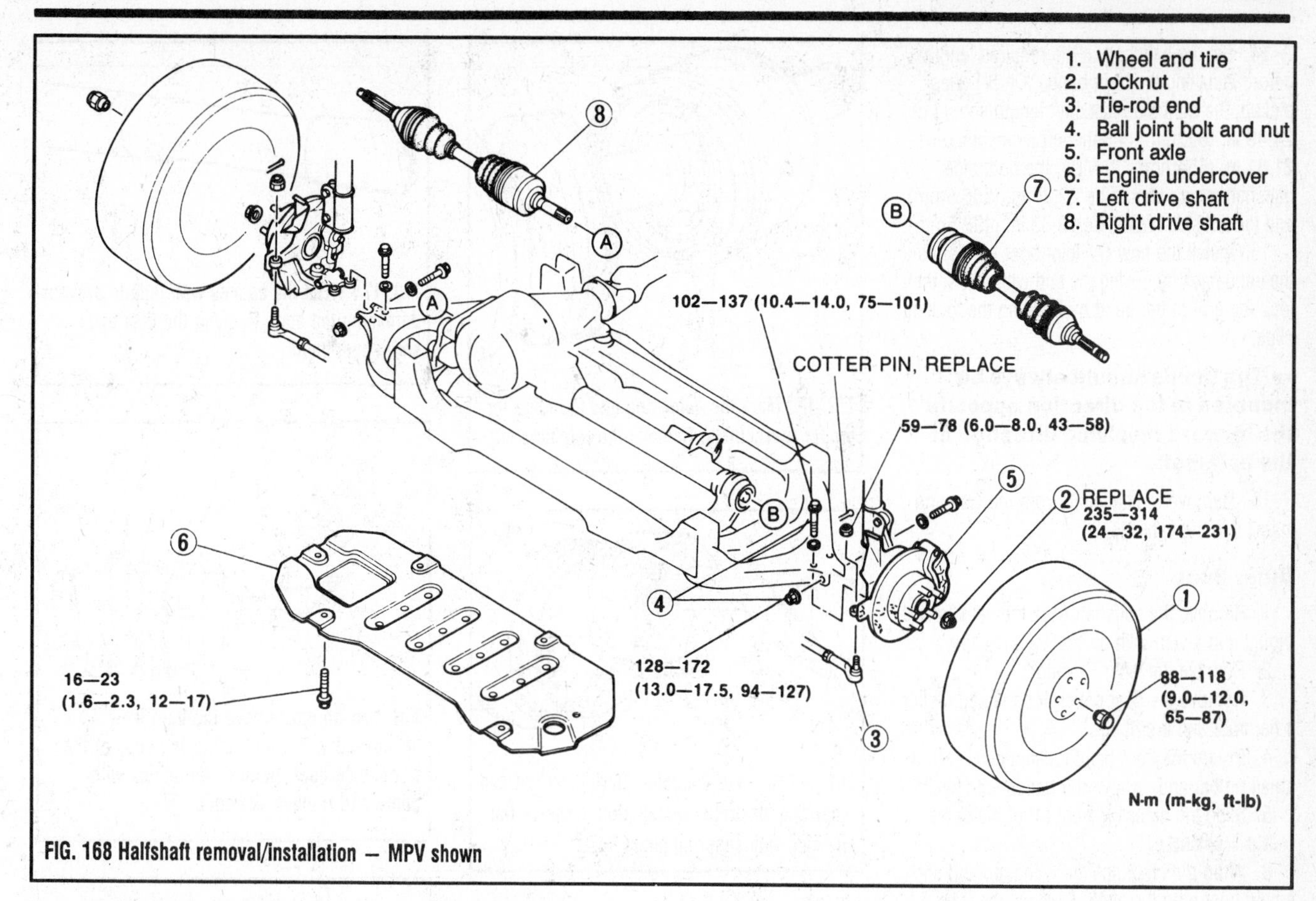

FIG. 168 Halfshaft removal/installation — MPV shown

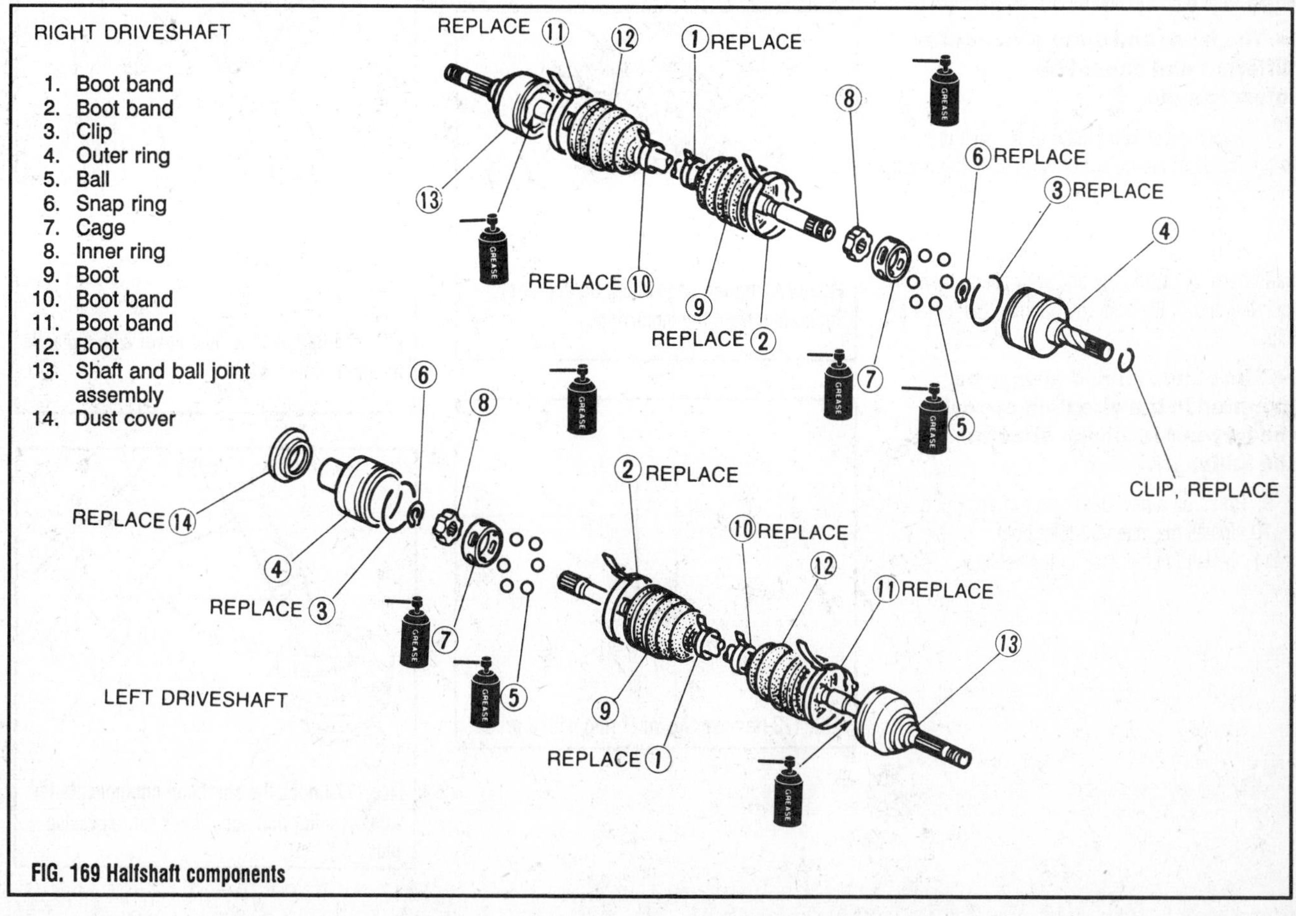

FIG. 169 Halfshaft components

14. Set the halfshaft to the required length before installing the boot bands. On B Series pickup, the right side halfshaft length should be 24.49 in. (622mm) and the left side should be 21.81 in. (554mm). On MPV, the right side halfshaft length should be 22.30 in. (566.5mm) and the left side should be 19.63 in. (498.5mm).

15. Install the new CV-joint boot bands. Fold the band back by pulling the end with pliers, then lock the end of the band by bending the locking clips.

➡ The bands should always be mounted in the direction opposite the forward revolving direction of the halfshaft.

16. Remove the halfshaft from the vise and install it in the vehicle.

Outer Boot

1. Remove the halfshaft from the vehicle and mount it in a vise with protective jaw caps.
2. Remove the inner CV-boot.
3. Remove the dust cover, if equipped, using a hammer and a drift.
4. Pry up the boot band locking clips with a small prybar and remove the bands with pliers.
5. Slide the outer CV-boot off of the shaft.

To Install:

6. Wrap the shaft splines with tape and slide a new boot onto the shaft. Remove the tape.

➡ The inner and outer CV-boots are different and cannot be interchanged.

7. Apply about 120 grams of CV-joint grease to the inside of the outer boot and slide the boot over the CV-joint. Carefully lift up the small end of the boot to release any trapped air.
8. Install new CV-joint boot bands. Fold the band back by pulling the end with pliers, then lock the end of the band by bending the locking clips.

➡ The bands should always be mounted in the direction opposite the forward revolving direction of the halfshaft.

9. Press on a new dust cover, if equipped.
10. Install the inner CV-joint boot.
11. Install the halfshaft in the vehicle.

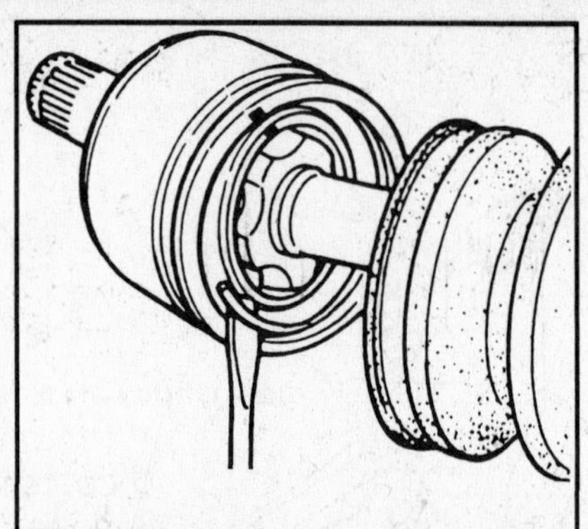

FIG. 170 Mark the outer ring and the cage for proper reassembly. Remove the retaining clip

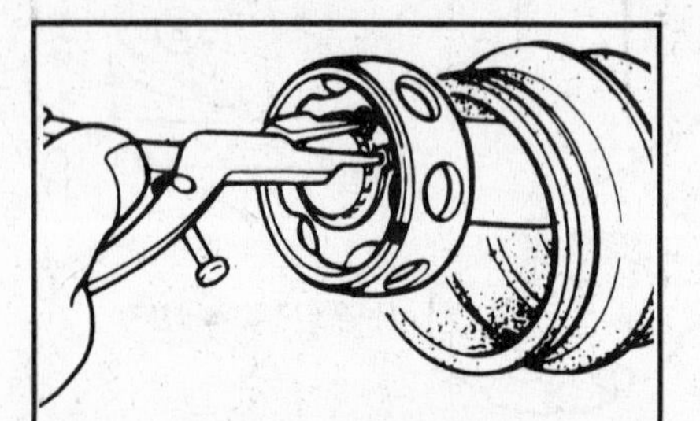

FIG. 171 Remove the balls. Mark the shaft and inner ring for proper installation. Remove the snapring with snapring pliers

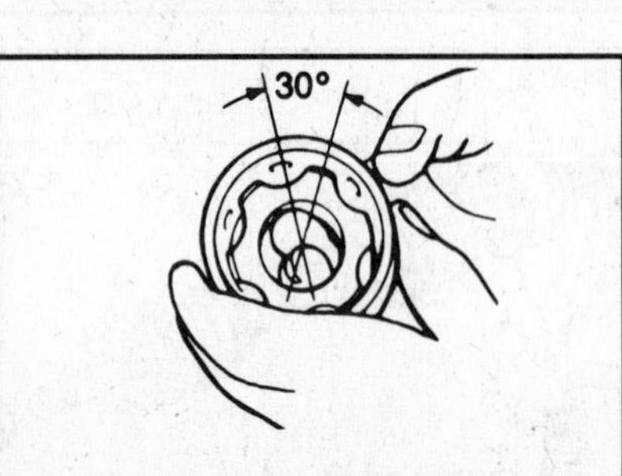

FIG. 172 Turn the cage about 30 degrees, Separate it from the inner ring

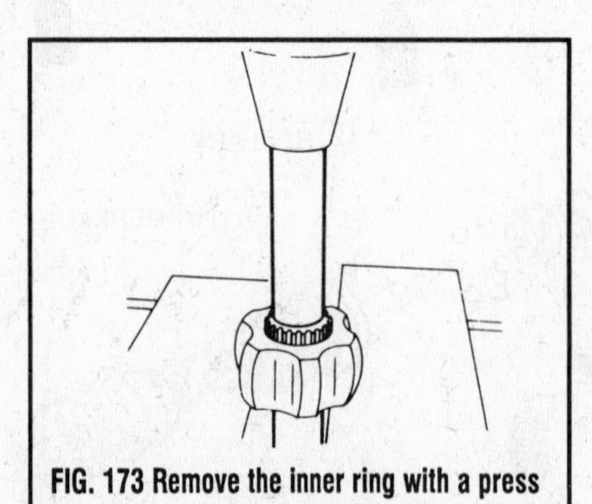

FIG. 173 Remove the inner ring with a press

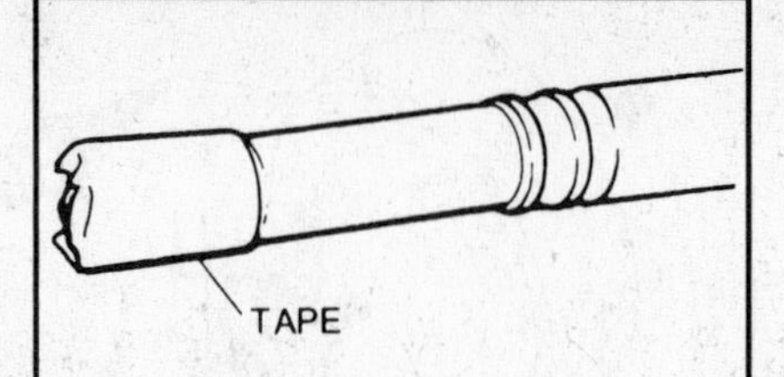

FIG. 174 Wrap the splines with tape to prevent damaging the boot. Remove the boot and small boot band

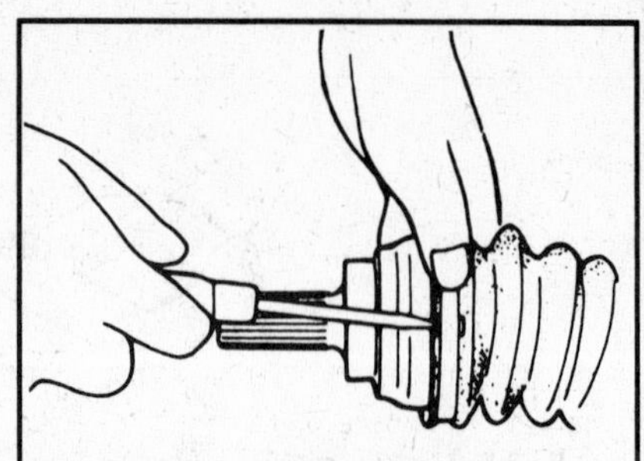

FIG. 175 Do not remove the boot if unnecessary. Pry up the locking clips of the wheel side boot. Remove the bands with pliers and remove the boot

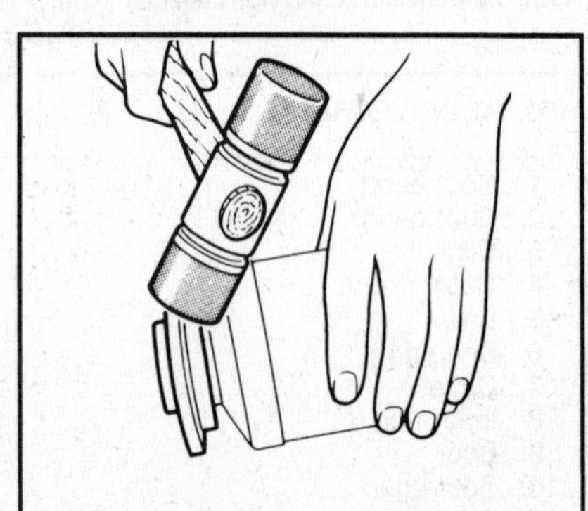

FIG. 176 Remove the dust cover with a plastic hammer, if necessary

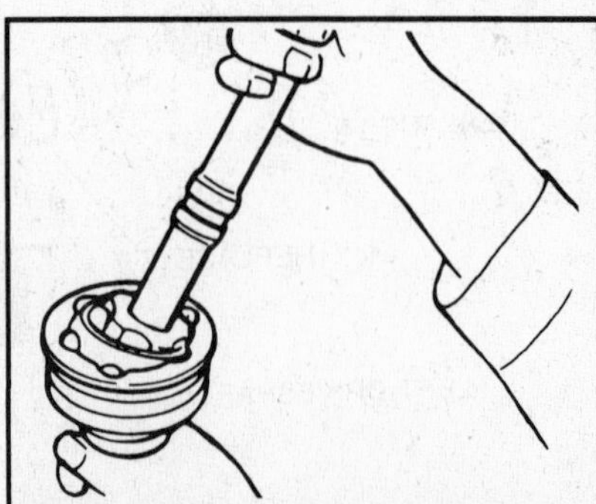

FIG. 177 Check the shaft and components for wear or other damage. Check for excessive play

FIG. 178 Install a new dust cover if removed

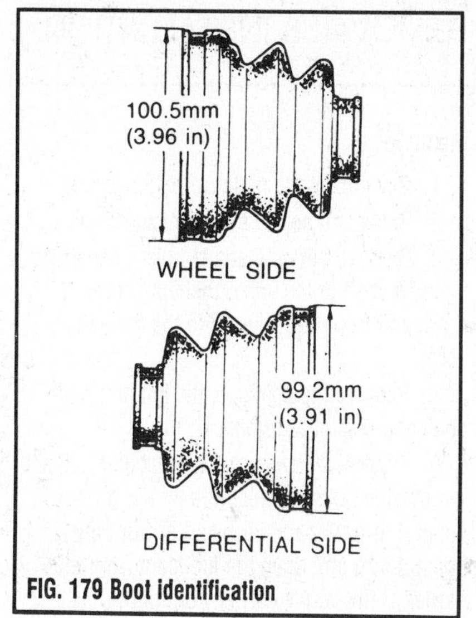

FIG. 179 Boot identification

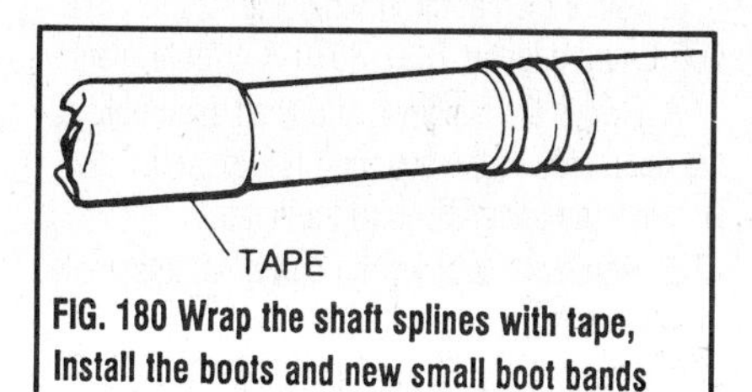

FIG. 180 Wrap the shaft splines with tape, Install the boots and new small boot bands

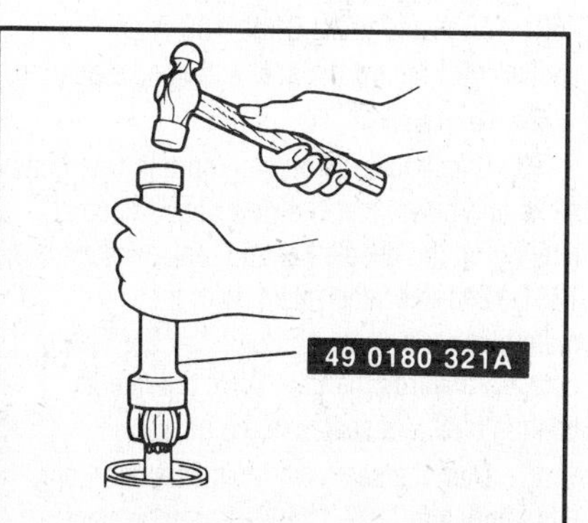

FIG. 181 Slide the cage over the shaft. Install the cage with the larger diameter facing the snapring groove. If installed incorrectly, the driveshaft may become disengaged. Align the marks and install the inner ring on the shaft with the driver tool

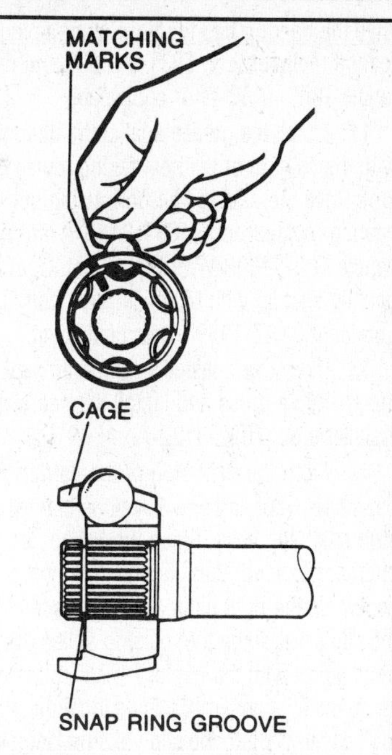

FIG. 182 Align the marks and install the balls to the inner ring. Install the cage, inner ring, and ball assembly to the driveshaft in the direction shown. Fit a new snapring into the groove in the shaft

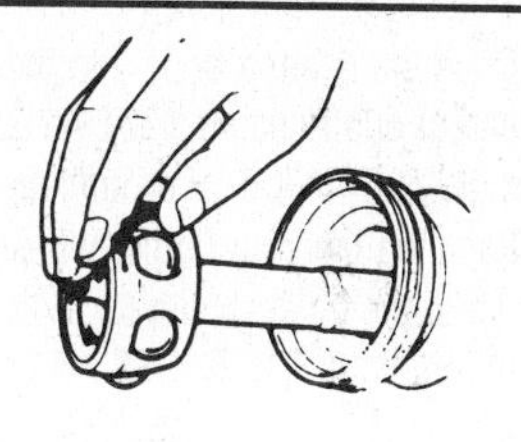
FIG. 183 Install the cage on the inner ring, and turn the cage about thirty degrees with respect to the inner ring. Fit the balls through the cage into the ball grooves of the inner ring. Apply the yellow type joint grease to the cage, inner ring and balls

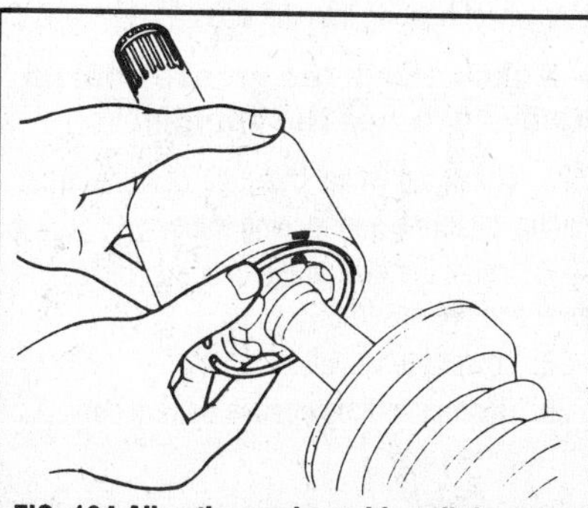
FIG. 184 Align the marks and install the outer ring on the shaft. Install a new clip onto the outer ring

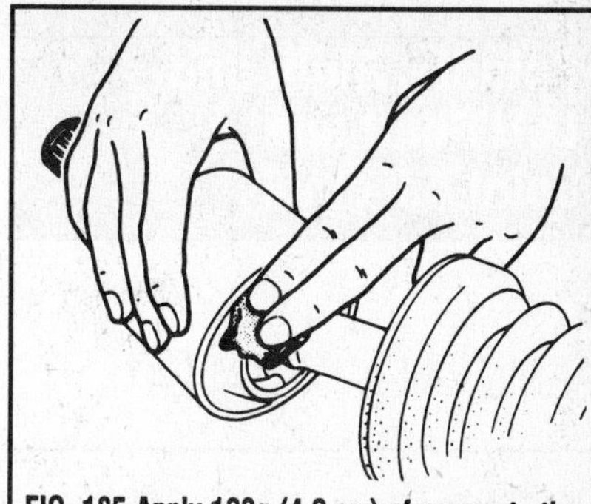
FIG. 185 Apply 120g (4.2 oz.) of grease to the differential boot and joint. If the wheel side joint was removed, apply grease to it

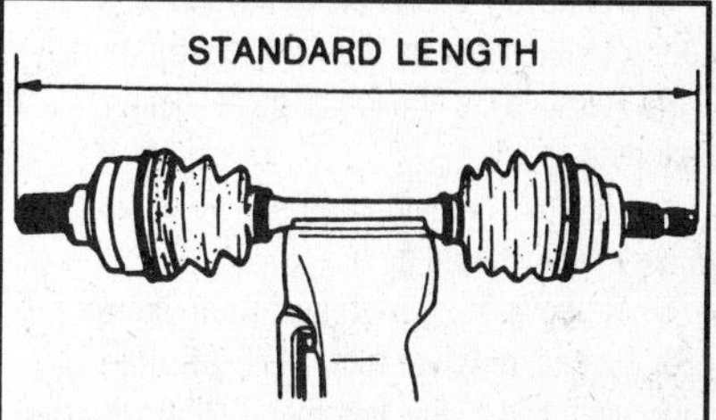

FIG. 186 Be sure the boot is not dented or twisted. Carefully lift up the small end of the boot to release any trapped air. Install the boot. Measure shaft length. Right side should be 22.30 in. (566.5mm), Left side should be 19.63 in. (498.5mm)

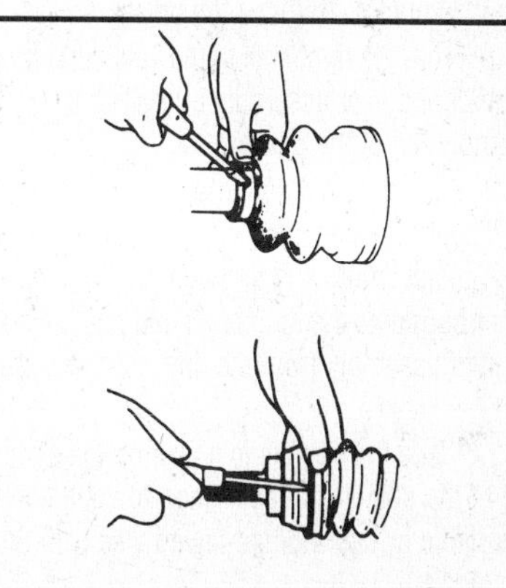
FIG. 187 Always use new bands. The bands should be mounted in the direction opposite the forward revolving direction of the shaft. Fold the band back by pulling the end of it with pliers. Lock the end of the band by bending the locking clips

Spindle, Right and Left Shaft and Joint Assembly

REMOVAL & INSTALLATION

Navajo

1. Disconnect the negative battery cable.
2. Raise and support the vehicle safely. Remove the wheel and tire assembly.
3. Remove the disc brake calipers and support the caliper on the vehicle's frame rail.
4. Remove the hub locks, wheel bearings and lock nuts.
5. Remove the hub and rotor. Remove the outer wheel bearing cone.
6. Remove the grease seal from the rotor with the seal remover tool, 1175-AC or equivalent, and a slide hammer. Discard the seal.
7. Remove the inner wheel bearing.
8. Remove the inner and outer bearing cups from the rotor with bearing cup puller tool, D78P-1225-B or equivalent.
9. Remove the nuts retaining the spindle to the steering knuckle. Tap the spindle with a plastic or rawhide hammer to jar the spindle from the knuckle. Remove the splash shield.
10. From the right side of the vehicle, remove the shaft and joint assembly by pulling the assembly out of the carrier.
11. From the right side of the carrier, remove and discard the keystone clamp from the shaft and joint assembly and the stub shaft. Slide the rubber boot onto the stub shaft and pull the shaft and joint assembly from the splines of the stub shaft.
12. Place the spindle in a vise on the second step of the spindle. Wrap a shop towel around the spindle or use a brass-jawed vise to protect the spindle.
13. Remove the oil seal and needle bearing from the spindle with a slide hammer and seal remover tool, 1175-AC or equivalent.
14. If required, remove the seal from the shaft, by driving off with a hammer.

To Install:

15. Clean all dirt and grease from the spindle bearing bore. Bearing bore must be free from nicks and burrs.
16. Place the bearing in the bore with the manufacturer's identification facing outward. Drive the bearing into the bore using spindle bearing replacer tool, T83T-3123-A and drive handle T80T-4000-W or equivalent.
17. Install the grease seal in the bearing bore with the lip side of the seal facing towards the tool. Drive the seal in t he bore using spindle bearing replacer tool, T83T-3123-A and drive handle T80T-4000-W or equivalent. Coat the bearing seal lip with Multi-Purpose Long Life Lubricant C1AZ-19590-B or equivalent.
18. If removed, install a new shaft seal. Place the shaft in a press and install the seal with seal installer took, T83T-3132-A.
19. From the right side of the carrier, install the rubber boot and new keystone clamps on the stub shaft slip yoke. Since the splines on the shaft are phased, there is only 1 way to assemble the right shaft and joint assembly into the slip yoke. Align the missing spline in the slip yoke barrel with the gapless male spline on the shaft and joint assembly. Slide the right shaft and joint assembly into the slip yoke making sure the splines are fully engaged. Slide the boot over the assembly and crimp the keystone clamp.
20. From the left side of the carrier, slide the shaft and joint assembly through the knuckly and engage the splines on the shaft in the carrier.
21. Install the splash shield and spindle onto the steering knuckle. Install and tighten the spindle nuts to 35-45 ft. lbs. (47-61Nm).
22. Drive the bearing cups into the rotor, using bearing cup replacer T73T-4222-B and drive handle T80T-4000-W or equivalent.
23. Pack the inner and outer wheel bearings and the lip of the oil seal with Multi-Purpose Long Life Lubricant C1AZ-19590-B or equivalent.
24. Place the inner wheel bearing in the inner cup. Drive the grease seal into the bore with hub seal replacer tool, T83T-1175-B and drive handle T80T-4000-W or equivalent. Coat the bearing seal lip with Multi-Purpose Long Life Lubricant C1AZ-19590-B or equivalent.
25. Install the rotor on the spindle. Install the outer wheel bearing into the cup.

➡ **Make certain the grease seal lip totally encircles the spindle.**

26. Install the wheel bearing, locknut, thrust bearing, snapring and locking hubs.
27. Install the disc brake calipers. Install the wheel and tire assembly.
28. Lower the vehicle.
29. Reconnect the negative battery cable.

Right Hand Slip Yoke and Stub Shaft Assembly, Carrier, Carrier Oil Seal and Bearing

REMOVAL & INSTALLATION

Navajo

1. Disconnect the negative battery cable.
2. Raise and support the vehicle safely.
3. Remove the nuts and U-bolts connecting the driveshaft to the yoke. Disconnect the driveshaft from the yoke. Wire the driveshaft aside.
4. Remove the spindles, the left and right shaft and U-joint assemblies.
5. Support the carrier with a suitable jack and remove the bolts retaining the carrier to the support arm. Separate the carrier from the support arm and drain the lubricant from the carrier. Remove the carrier from the vehicle.
6. Place the carrier in a holding fixture T57L-500-B and adapter T83T-3010-A or equivalent.
7. Rotate the slip yoke and shaft assembly so the open side of the snapring is exposed. Remove the snapring from the shaft.
8. Remove the slip yoke and shaft assembly from the carrier.
9. Remove the oil seal and caged needle bearings at the same time, using slide hammer T50T-100-A and collet D80L-100-A or equivalent. Discard the seal and needle bearing.

To Install:

10. Check that the bearing bore is free from nicks and burrs. Install a new caged needle bearing on the needle bearing replacer tool, T83T-1244-A or equivalent, with the manufacturer's name and part number facing outward towards the tool. Drive the needle bearing until it is seated in the bore.
11. Coat the seal with Multi-Purpose Long Life Lubricant C1AZ-19590-B or equivalent. Drive the seal into the carrier using needle bearing replacer tool, T83T-1244-A or equivalent.
12. Install the slip yoke and shaft assembly into the carrier so the grooves in the shaft are visible in the differential case.

13. Install the snapring in the groove in the shaft. Force the snapring into position. Do not tap the center of the snapring. This may damage the snapring.

14. Clean all traces of gasket sealant from the surfaces of the carrier and support arm and make sure the surfaces are free from dirt and oil.

15. Apply a bead of RTV sealant to the surface of the carrier. Position the carrier on a suitable jack and install it into position on the support arm, using guide pine to align. Install the retaining bolts and hand tighten. Then, tighten the bolts in a clockwise or counterclockwise pattern to 40-50 ft. lbs. (54-68Nm).

16. Install the shear bolt retaining the carrier to the axle arm and tighten to 75-95 ft. lbs (102-129Nm).

17. Install both spindles, the left and right shaft and joint assemblies.

18. Connect the driveshaft to the yoke. Install the nuts and U-bolts and tighten to 8-15ft. lbs. (11-20Nm).

19. Lower the vehicle.

20. Reconnect the negative battery cable.

Pinion Seal

REMOVAL & INSTALLATION

➡ This service procedure disturbs the pinion bearing preload and this preload must be carefully reset when assembling.

1. Raise the vehicle and support it safely.

2. Remove the wheels and the brake drums.

3. Mark the driveshaft and the axle companion flange so the driveshaft can be reinstalled in the same position. Remove the driveshaft.

4. Using an inch pound torque wrench on the pinion nut, record the torque required to maintain rotation of the pinion through several revolutions.

5. While holding the companion flange with a suitable tool, remove the pinion nut. Mark the companion flange in relation to the pinion shaft so the flange can be reinstalled in the same position.

6. Using a suitable puller, remove the rear axle companion flange. Use a small prybar to remove the seal from the carrier.

To Install:

7. Make sure the splines of the pinion shaft are free of burrs.

8. Apply grease to the lips of the pinion seal and install, using a seal installer.

9. Check the seal surface of the companion flange for scratches, nicks or a groove. Replace the companion flange, as necessary. Apply a small amount of lubricant to the splines. Align the mark on the flange with the mark on the pinion shaft and install the companion flange.

➡ The companion flange must never be hammered on or installed with power tools.

10. Install a new nut on the pinion shaft. Hold the companion flange with a suitable tool while tightening the nut.

11. Tighten the pinion nut, rotating the pinion occasionally to ensure proper bearing seating. Take frequent pinion bearing torque preload readings until the original recorded preload reading is obtained.

➡ Under no circumstances should the pinion nut be backed off to reduce preload. If reduced preload is required, a new collapsible pinion spacer and pinion nut must be installed.

12. Install the driveshaft and check the fluid level in the carrier. Lower the vehicle.

Differential Carrier

REMOVAL & INSTALLATION

B Series Pickup

➡ On 1989–92 vehicles, the differential is removed as a unit with the freewheel mechanism. After removal, the differential can then be separated from the freewheel mechanism, if necessary.

1. Raise and safely support the vehicle. Remove the wheel and tire assemblies.

2. Remove the splash shield and drain the differential fluid.

3. Remove the halfshafts.

4. Mark the position of the driveshaft on the axle flange and remove the driveshaft.

5. On 1989–92 vehicles, tag and disconnect the vacuum hoses and electrical connector from the freewheel mechanism control box.

6. Support the differential with a jack.

7. Remove the crossmember bolts adjacent to the lower control arm. Lower the differential/crossmembers assembly from the vehicle.

8. Remove the crossmembers from the differential, if necessary. On 1989–92 vehicles, remove the freewheel mechanism from the differential, if necessary.

To Install:

9. If removed, install the freewheel mechanism.

10. If removed, install the differential to the crossmembers.

11. Raise the differential/crossmembers assembly into position. Install the crossmember mounting bolts and tighten to 69–85 ft. lbs. (93–116 Nm). Remove the jack.

12. Install the remaining components in the reverse order of their removal. Fill the differential with the proper type and quantity of fluid.

MPV

➡ The differential is removed as a unit with the freewheel mechanism. After removal, the differential can then be separated from the freewheel mechanism, if necessary.

1. Raise and safely support the vehicle. Remove the wheel and tire assemblies.

2. Remove the splash shield and drain the differential fluid.

3. Remove the halfshafts.

4. Mark the position of the driveshaft on the axle flange and remove the driveshaft.

5. Tag and disconnect the vacuum hoses and electrical connector from the freewheel mechanism control box.

6. Support the differential with a jack.

7. Remove the bolts/nuts attaching the differential/freewheel mechanism assembly in 3 places and lower the assembly from the vehicle.

8. If necessary, separate the freewheel mechanism from the differential.

To Install:

9. If removed, install the freewheel mechanism.

10. Raise the differential/freewheel mechanism assembly into position and install the attaching bolts/nuts. Tighten to 49–72 ft. lbs. (67–97 Nm). Remove the jack.

11. Install the remaining components in the reverse order of their removal. Fill the differential with the proper type and quantity of fluid.

Axle Housing

REMOVAL & INSTALLATION

Navajo

1. Raise and safely support the vehicle.

Remove the front axle shaft and spindle assemblies.

2. Mark the front axle yoke and the driveshaft so they can be reassembled in the same position. Disconnect the driveshaft from the front axle yoke.

3. Remove the cotter pin and nut retaining the steering linkage to the knuckle. Disconnect the linkage from the knuckle.

4. Remove the left stabilizer bar link lower bolt and remove the link from the radius arm bracket.

5. Position a jack under the left axle arm and slightly compress the coil spring. Remove the shock absorber lower nut and disconnect the shock absorber from the radius arm bracket.

6. Remove the nut that retains the lower part of the spring to the axle arm. Slowly lower the jack and remove the coil spring, spacer, seat and stud.

7. Remove the stud and bolts that connect the radius arm bracket and radius arm to the axle arm. Remove the bracket and radius arm.

8. Position another jack under the differential housing. Remove the bolt that connects the left axle arm to the axle pivot bracket. Lower the jacks and remove the left axle arm assembly.

To install:

9. Position a jack under the left support arm and raise the arm into position in the pivot bracket. Install the nut and bolt and tighten to 120–150 ft. lbs. (163–203 Nm). Do not remove the jack from under the differential housing at this time.

10. Position the radius arm and front bracket on the left axle arm. Install a new stud and nut on the top of the axle and radius arm assembly and tighten to 190–230 ft. lbs. (258–311 Nm). Install the bolts in the front of the bracket and tighten to 27–37 ft. lbs. (37–50 Nm).

11. Install the seat, spacer retainer and coil spring on the stud and nut. Raise the jack to compress the coil spring. Install the nut and tighten to 70–100 ft. lbs. (95–135 Nm).

12. Connect the shock absorber to the radius arm. Install the nut and tighten to 42–72 ft. lbs. (57–97 Nm).

13. Connect the tie rod ball joint to the knuckle. Install the nut and tighten to 50–75 ft. lbs. (68–101 Nm). Install the stabilizer bar mounting bracket and tighten to 203–240 ft. lbs. (275–325 Nm).

14. Connect the front driveshaft to the front axle yoke, aligning the marks that were made during removal. Install the U-bolts and tighten the nuts to 8–15 ft. lbs. (11–20 Nm).

15. Install the spindle and axle shaft assemblies. Lower the vehicle.

DIFFERENTIAL OVERHAUL

➡ This service repair requires special tools,great deal of mechanical ability and automotive experience. Use this service procedure as guide for this repair.

Since the differentials used in the Navajo are Ford or Ford/Dana units, part numbers and tool numbers listed in those procedures will be Ford numbers.

Front and Rear Drive Axles Pickup and MPV

➧ SEE FIGS. 188-192

DISASSEMBLY AND ASSEMBLY

1. Position the removed differential carrier assembly in a suitable holding fixture.

2. Apply identification punch marks on the carrier, the differential bearing cap and adjusters for correct reassembly.

3. Remove the adjuster lock plates.

4. Loosen the bolts securing the bearing cap and slowly back off the adjuster slightly to relieve the preload.

5. Remove the nuts, bearing caps and adjusters. Keep each bearing cap with its own adjuster.

6. Lift out the differential assembly and keep each bearing outer race with its own bearing.

7. If the differential bearings are to be replaced, mark for correct installation and remove using a suitable puller.

8. Remove the bolts (in diagonal pattern) and washers retaining the ring gear to the case.

9. Remove the ring gear. On conventional differential, position the assembly in a vise or equivalent and remove the lock pin (tap out toward the ring gear side) with a 4mm punch.

10. On conventional differential, remove the pinion shaft and the thrust block. Rotate the differential pinion gears 90 degrees and remove. Remove the differential side gears and thrust washers.

11. On limited slip differential move the limited slip differential carrier assembly.

12. Using a holding tool, steady the companion flange and remove the nut.

13. Remove the companion flange using suitable puller.

14. Remove the front bearing, drive pinion and rear bearing from the carrier, which may require tapping with a plastic mallet or equivalent. Guide the pinion assembly to avoid damage to any component.

15. Remove the oil seal and the front bearing.

16. The pinion bearing outer races (cups) can be removed (mark for correct installation) from the carrier by tapping out using a drift in the slots provided.

17. Remove the rear bearing from the pinion (support the pinion during removal) using suitable press and separator plate.

18. Check the drive pinion for damaged or worn teeth, damaged bearing journals or splines. Inspect the ring gear again for worn or chipped teeth. If any of the above conditions are found, replace both drive pinion and ring gear as a set.

19. Inspect bearing cones and cups and replace and showing wear, flaking or damage. Replace only in sets. Do not use an old cup with a new bearing or an old bearing with a new cup.

20. Check companion flange carefully for cracks or worn splines. If either exist, the part should be replaced. Check for rough or scratched oil seal contact surface. If only slight scratches appear, it may be possible to repair with crocus cloth. Otherwise, replace it. Be sure to use a new oil seal when reassembling the carrier.

21. On conventional differential assemble the side gears, thrust washers, thrust block, pinion gears, pinion shaft, and lock pin. After installing

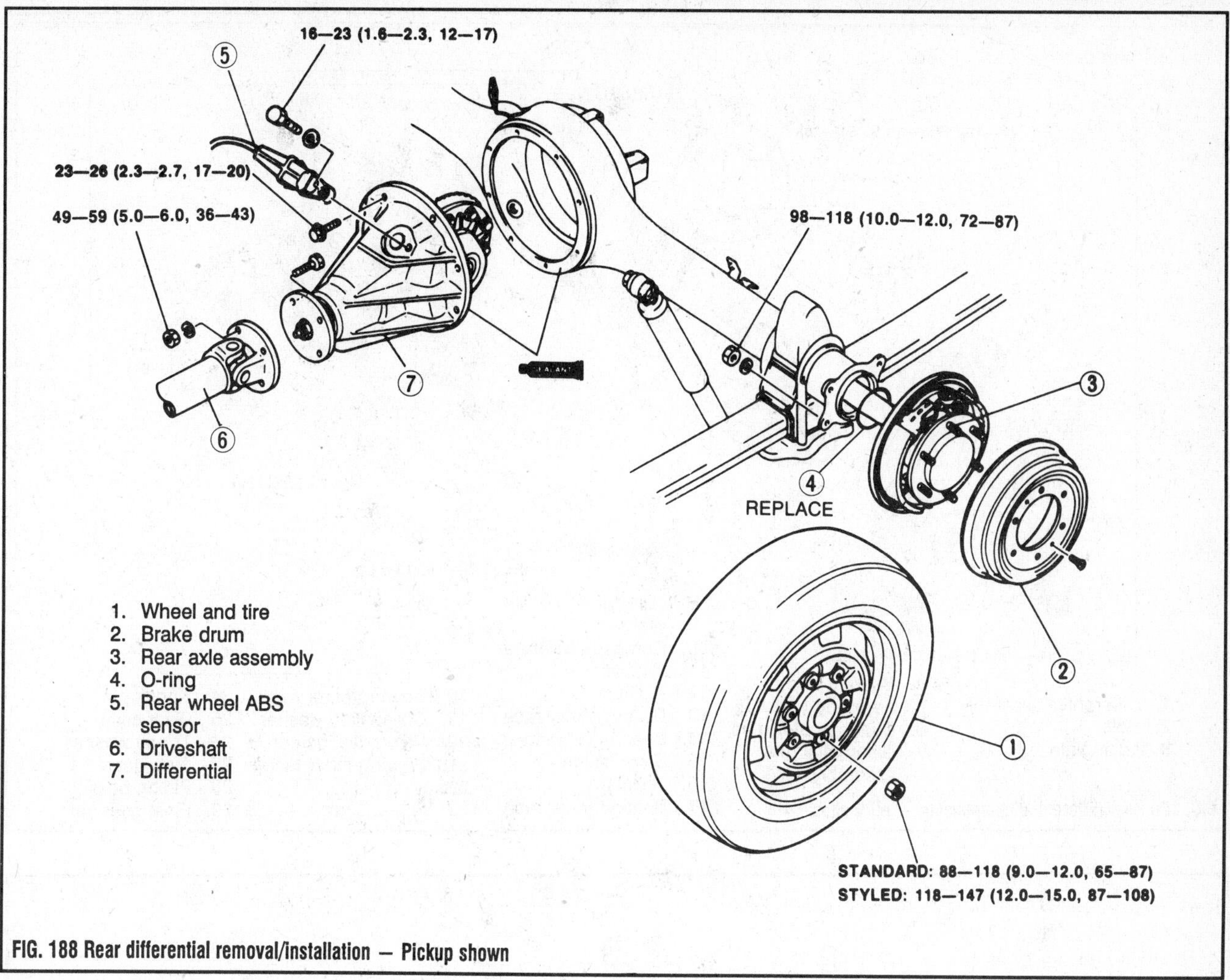

FIG. 188 Rear differential removal/installation — Pickup shown

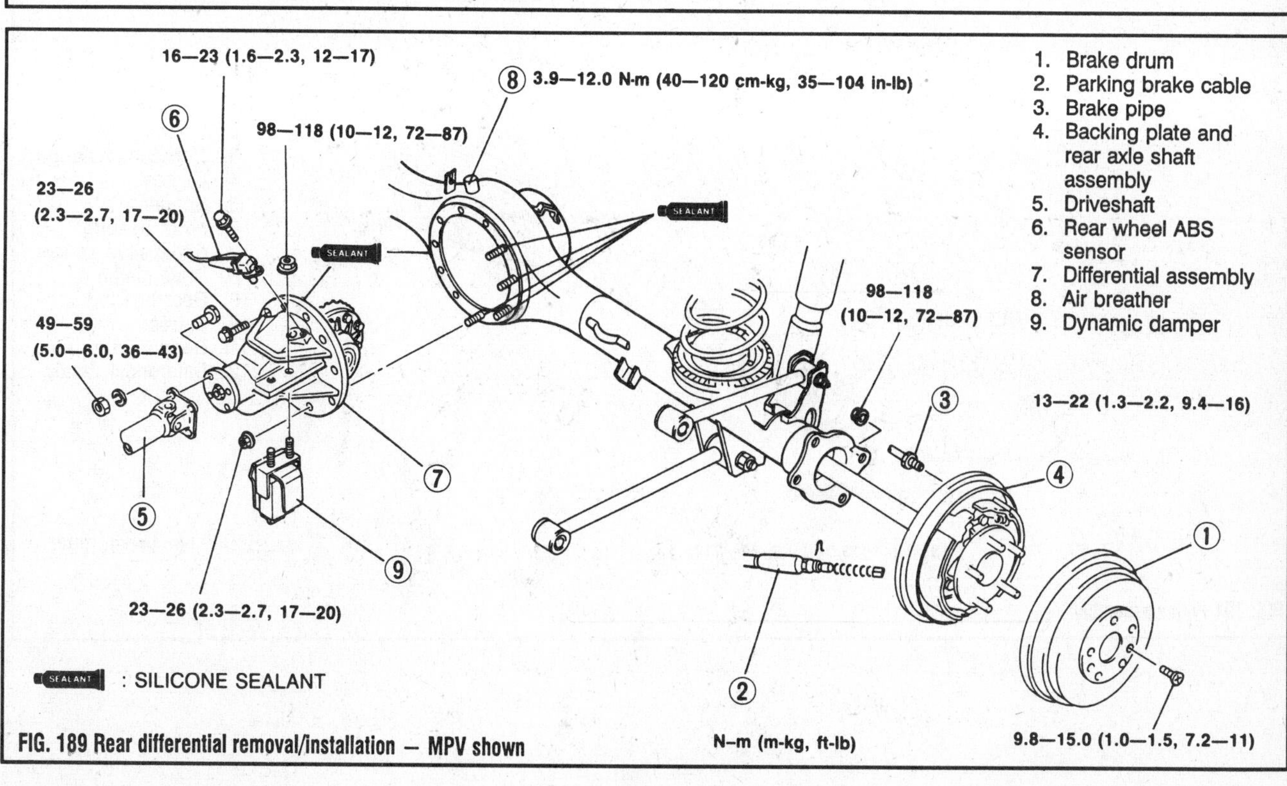

FIG. 189 Rear differential removal/installation — MPV shown

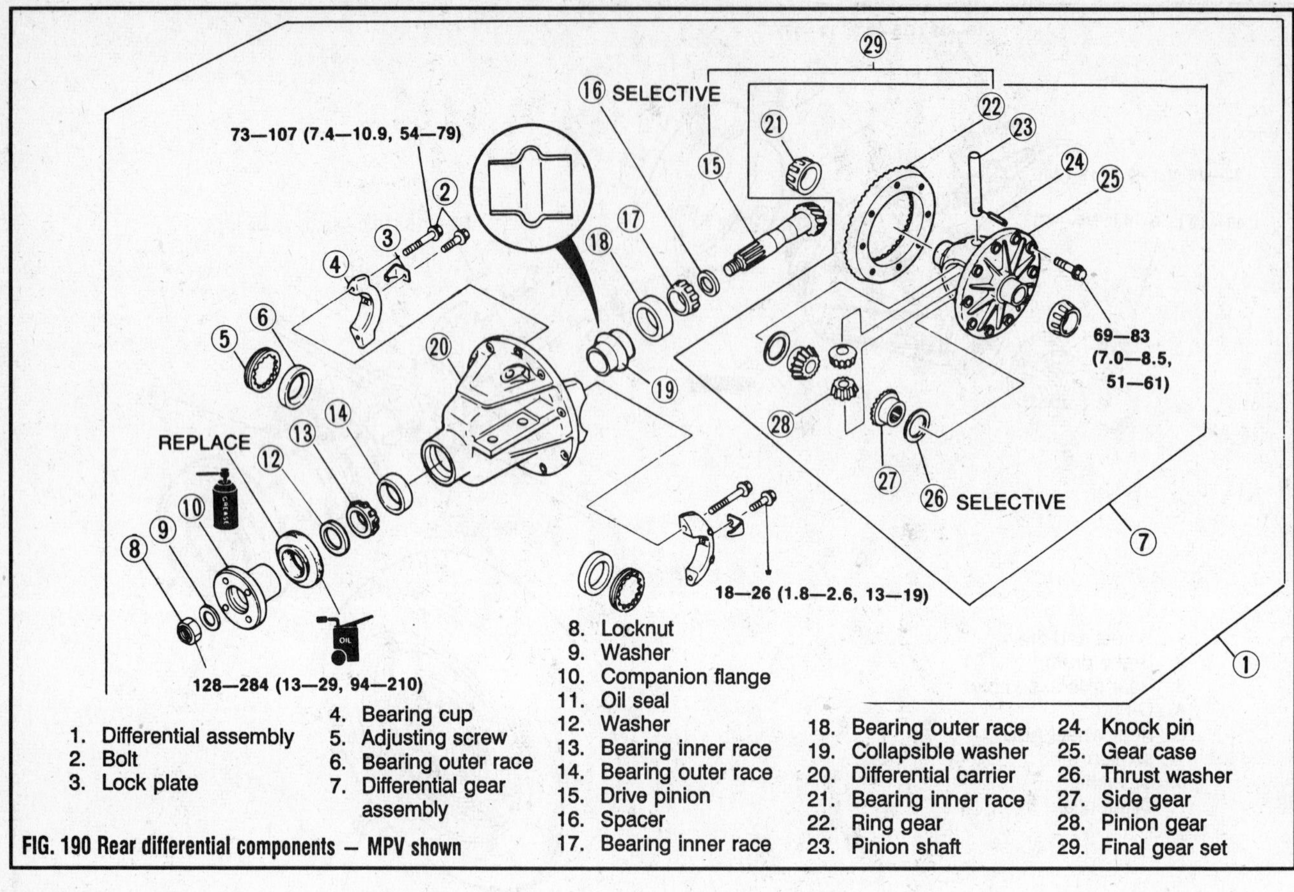

16 SELECTIVE
73—107 (7.4—10.9, 54—79)
69—83 (7.0—8.5, 51—61)
REPLACE
GREASE
OIL
26 SELECTIVE
18—26 (1.8—2.6, 13—19)
128—284 (13—29, 94—210)
1. Differential assembly
2. Bolt
3. Lock plate
4. Bearing cup
5. Adjusting screw
6. Bearing outer race
7. Differential gear assembly
8. Locknut
9. Washer
10. Companion flange
11. Oil seal
12. Washer
13. Bearing inner race
14. Bearing outer race
15. Drive pinion
16. Spacer
17. Bearing inner race
18. Bearing outer race
19. Collapsible washer
20. Differential carrier
21. Bearing inner race
22. Ring gear
23. Pinion shaft
24. Knock pin
25. Gear case
26. Thrust washer
27. Side gear
28. Pinion gear
29. Final gear set

FIG. 190 Rear differential components – MPV shown

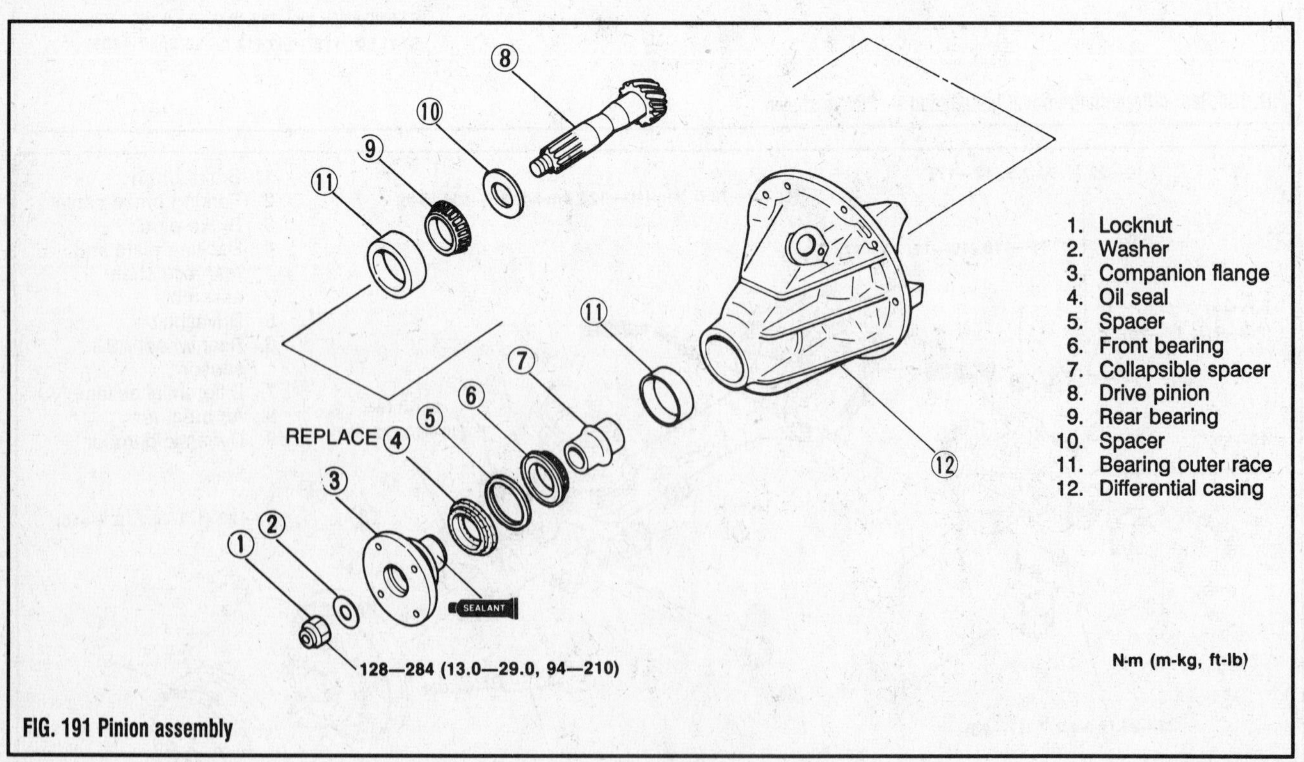

REPLACE
SEALANT
128—284 (13.0—29.0, 94—210)
N·m (m-kg, ft-lb)
1. Locknut
2. Washer
3. Companion flange
4. Oil seal
5. Spacer
6. Front bearing
7. Collapsible spacer
8. Drive pinion
9. Rear bearing
10. Spacer
11. Bearing outer race
12. Differential casing

FIG. 191 Pinion assembly

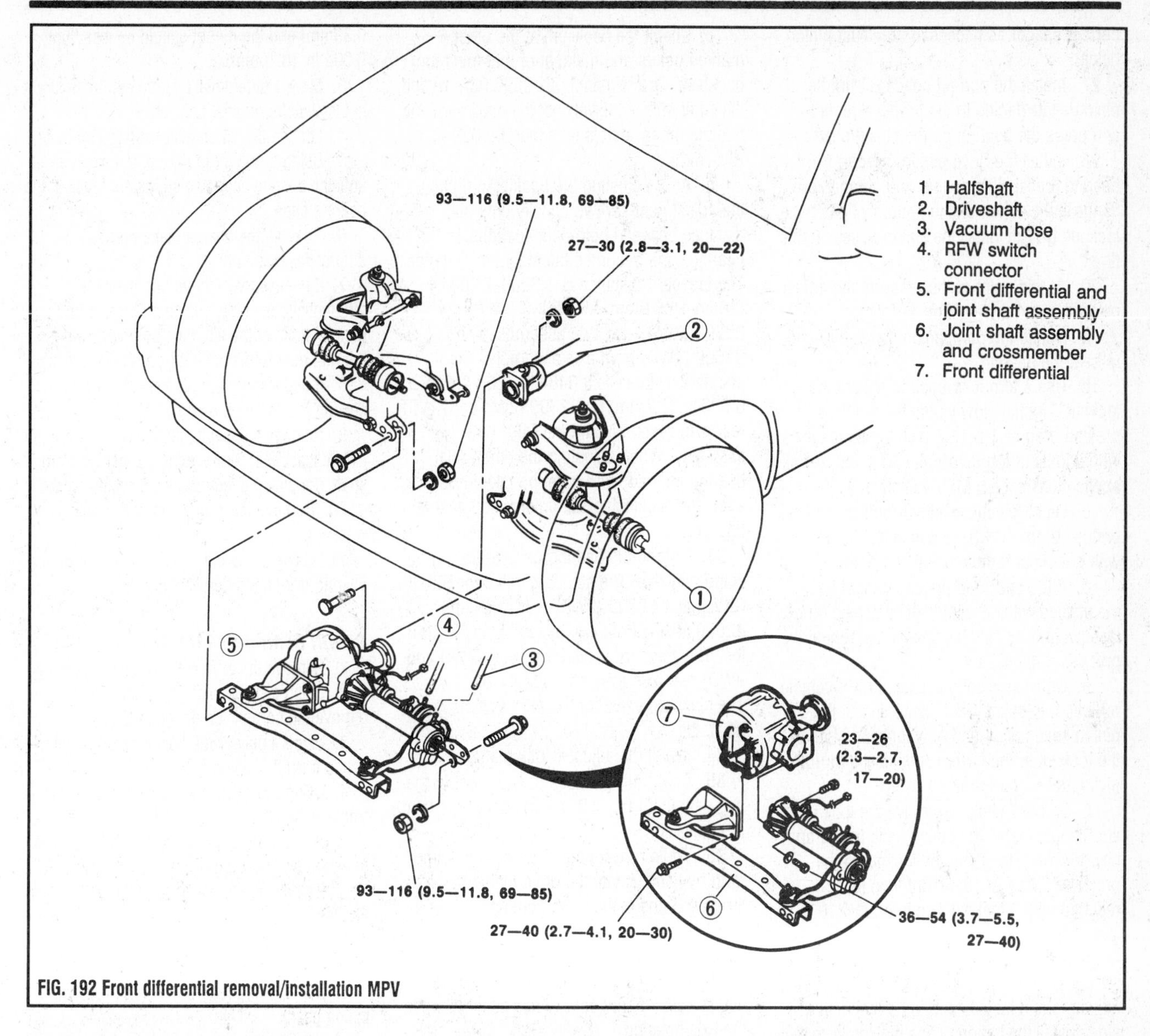

FIG. 192 Front differential removal/installation MPV

lock pin stake pin so pin cannot come out of gear case.

22. On conventional differential assemble press the side bearings (correct location) onto the gear case using suitable tools. Adjust the backlash of the side gears and pinion gear as follows:

a. Position a dial indicator against the pinion gear. Secure one of the side gears.

b. Move the pinion gear and measure the backlash at the end of the pinion gear.

c. The standard valve for backlash is 0-0.004 in. (0-0.10mm) on all vehicles. If backlash exceeds the standard valve use suitable thrust washer to adjust.

23. On conventional and limited slip differential carriers apply thread locking compound install ring gear to differential assembly. Torque the retaining bolts to 51-61 ft. lbs. all vehicles in diagonal pattern.

24. Press fit the companion flange side bearing outer races using bearing installer set.

25. Press fit the ring gear side bearing outer races using bearing installer set.

➡ **Special tools are required to check and adjust the pinion height, these include a drive pinion model tool 498531565, a pinion height adjustment gauge body tool 490727570 and a gauge block tool 400305555.**

26. At this point of the reassembly, adjust the pinion height as follows:

a. Fit the spacer, rear bearing and collar onto the drive pinion model. Secure the collar with an O-ring and install in the assembly in the carrier.

b. Attach the front bearing, collar, companion flange, washer and nut to the drive pinion model. Use the same spacer and nut which were removed at disassembly. Be careful to install collars in their correct position facing in the correct direction.

c. Tighten the nut until the drive pinion model can be turned by hand without and apparent play.

d. Install a dial indicator on the pinion height adjustment gauge body. Place the gauge block on top of the drive pinion model and then set the pinion height adjustment gauge body on top of the gauge block.

e. Place the measuring probe of the dial indicator so that it contacts the location where the side bearing is installed in the carrier. Zero and set up the indicator to measure the lowest point. Measure both the left and right sides. Add the 2 valves (right and left side readings) and divide the total by 2. The standard valve of this specification is **0** on all vehicles. Install correct spacer as necessary to adjust pinion height.

27. Install the correct spacer(s) on the pinion shaft (facing in the proper direction) and press the bearing on the pinion shaft.

28. Install the drive pinion, spacer, front bearing, collapsible spacer and companion flange in the carrier and temporarily tighten the locknut. Do Not install the pinion oil seal at this time.

29. At this point of the reassembly, adjust preload of the drive pinion as follows:

a. Rotate the companion flange by hand to seat the bearing.

b. Use a torque wrench to tighten the locknut. Tighten slowly until the required preload drag of 7.8-12.2 inch lbs. is reached with a locknut torque of 94-130 ft. lbs. for all applications except MPV vehicle.

c. On MPV vehicle, slowly tighten until the preload drag of 11.3-15.6 inch lbs. is reached with a locknut torque of 94-210 ft. lbs.

d. If the specified preload cannot be maintained within the locknut tightening range, install a new collapsible spacer and repeat the process if necessary.

e. On all applications except MPV vehicle remove the locknut and flange. Install the pinion seal, flange and new locknut. Tighten the locknut to the ft. lbs. specification torque giving the correct preload.

f. On MPV vehicle, remove the locknut and flange. Install the pinion seal, flange and new locknut. Retighten the locknut to the preloaded drag of 13.9-18.2 inch lbs. is reached with a locknut torque of 94-210 ft. lbs.

30. Install the differential gear assembly in the carrier. Note the identification marks on the adjusters and install each to its respective side. Install the bearing caps making sure that the identification marks on the caps correspond with those on the carrier and install the bolts.

31. Loosely tighten the bearing cap mounting bolts and completely tighten the adjustment screws by hand. Then, while turning the ring gear, alternately tighten the left and right adjustment screws using a suitable tool.

32. At this point of the reassembly, adjust the drive pinion and ring gear backlash and side bearing preload as follows:

a. Mark the ring gear at 4 points at approximately 90 degree intervals and mount a dial indicator to the carrier flange so that the feeler comes in contact at right angles with one of the ring gear teeth.

b. Turn both bearing adjusters equally until backlash becomes (standard valve for all vehicles) 0.0035-0.0043 in. (0.09-0.11mm).

c. Check the backlash at the other 3 marked points and make sure that minimum backlash is more than 0.002 in. (0.05mm) and the difference in the valve of the maximum and minimum backlash is less than 0.0028 in. (0.07mm).

d. After adjusting the backlash, tighten the adjustment screws equally until the distance between both pilot sections on the bearing caps becomes the standard distance. The standard distance is 7.3004-7.3031 in. (185.4-1.85.5mm) for B2000 (2WD) and B2200 (2WD) rear axle assemblies and B2600 (4WD) front axle assembly. The standard distance is 8.0484 in. (204.4mm) ± 0.028 in. (0.7mm) for B2600 (2WD and 4WD) rear axle assembly and the MPV rear axle assembly. When adjusting the differential bearing preload, care must be taken not to affect the backlash of the drive pinion gear and ring gear.

33. Tighten the bearing caps to the standard valve. The standard valve for B2000 (2WD) and B2200 (2WD) rear axles and B2600 (4WD) front axle assembly is 27-38 ft. lbs. The standard valve for B2600 (2WD and 4WD) rear axle assemblies is 41-59 ft. lbs. The standard valve for the MPV vehicle is 51-61 ft. lbs.

34. Install the adjuster lock plates.

35. Coat both surfaces of 6-8 teeth of the ring gear uniformly with a thin coat of red lead or equivalent.

36. While moving the ring gear back and forth by hand, rotate the drive pinion several times and check the tooth contact.

37. If pattern is not correct readjust the pinion height then the backlash.

38. Apply gear oil to all moving parts and use sealant and or gasket when assembling to the axle housing.

Navajo 8.8 Inch Rear Axle Conventional Carrier

➧ SEE FIGS. 193-202

DIFFERENTIAL CARRIER DISASSEMBLY

1. Remove the cover and clean the lubricant from the internal parts.

2. Using a dial indicator, measure and record the ring gear backlash and the runout; the backlash should be 0.008-0.015 in. (0.20-0.38mm) and the runout should be less than 0.004 in. (0.10mm).

3. Mark 1 differential bearing cap to ensure it is installed its original position.

4. Loosen the differential bearing cap bolts.

5. Using a prybar, pry the differential carrier until the bearing caps and shims are loose in the bearing caps.

6. Remove the bearing caps and the differential assembly.

7. If necessary, remove ring gear-to-differential case bolts. Using a hammer and a punch, strike at the alternate bolt holes around the ring gear to dislodge it from the differential.

8. If necessary, remove the excitor ring by striking it with a soft hammer.

9. Remove the pinion shaft lock bolt from the differential case. Remove the differential pinion shaft, the pinion gears and the thrust washers.

10. Remove the side gears and thrust washers.

11. Using a bearing puller tool, press the bearing from the differential carrier.

PINION GEAR DISASSEMBLY

1. Remove the differential carrier assembly.

2. Using a companion flange holding tool, remove the companion flange nut.

3. Using a puller tool, press the companion flange form the pinion gear.

4. Using a soft hammer, drive the pinion gear from the housing.

5. Using a prybar, remove the pinion gear oil seal from the housing.

6. Remove the oil slinger and the front pinion bearing.

7. Using a shop press, press the bearing cone from the pinion gear.

8. Remove and record the shim from the pinion gear.

INSPECTION

1. Clean the differential components in solvent and use compressed air to dry them; do not use compressed air on the bearings, only shop towels.

2. Check the components for wear or damage; replace them, if necessary.

3. Inspect the bearing cups for wear, cracks, or scoring; replace them if necessary.

4. Inspect the side and pinion gears for wear, cracks or scoring; replace them, if necessary.

5. Inspect the ring and pinion gears for wear and/or damage; replace them, if necessary.

6. Inspect the differential case for cracks or damage; replace it, if necessary.

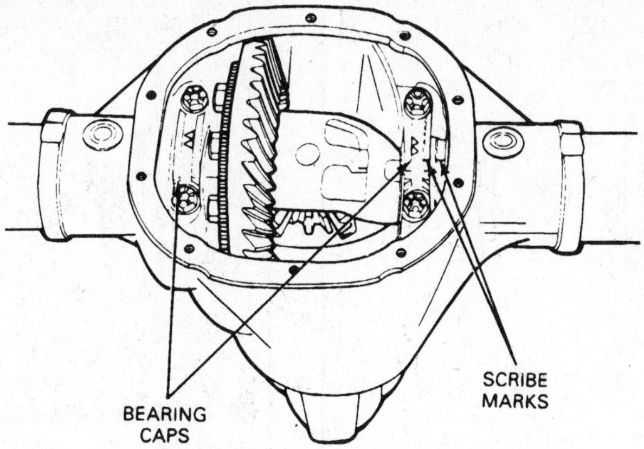

FIG. 193 Mark the differential caps — Navajo rear 8.8 in. (223.5mm) differential

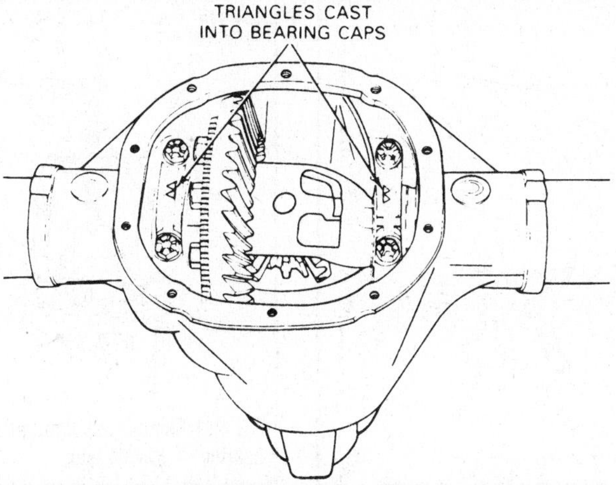

FIG. 194 Loosen the bearing caps. The direction and location of the triangles on the bearing caps must be noted. They must be pointing the same way at installation — Navajo

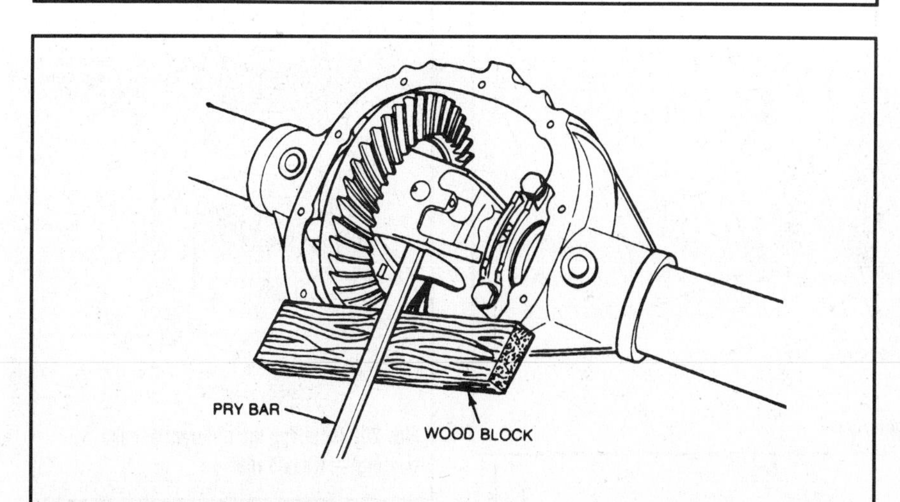

FIG. 195 Pry the differential case, bearing cups and shims out until they are loose in the bearing caps. Remove the bearing caps and remove the differential assembly from the carrier — Navajo

PINION GEAR ASSEMBLY

➡ When replacing the ring and pinion gear, the correct shim thickness for the new gear set to be installed is determined by following procedure using a pinion depth gauge tool set.

1. Assemble the appropriate aligning adapter, the gauge disc and the gauge block to the screw.
2. Place the rear pinion bearing over the aligning tool and insert it into the rear portion of the bearing cup of the carrier. Place the front bearing into the front bearing cup and assemble the tool handle into the screw. Roll the assemble back and forth a few times to seat the bearings while tightening the tool handle, by hand, to 20 ft. lbs. (27 Nm).

➡ The gauge block must be offset 45 degrees to obtain an accurate reading.

3. Center the gauge tube into the differential bearing bore. Install the bearing caps and tighten the bolts to 70-85 ft. lbs. (96-115 Nm); be sure to install the caps with the triangles pointing outward.
4. Place the selected shim(s) on the pinion and press the pinion bearing cone and roller assembly until it is firmly seated on the shaft, using the pinion bearing cone replacer and the axle bearing/seal plate.
5. Place the collapsible spacer on the pinion stem against the pinion stem shoulder.
6. Install the front pinion bearing and oil slinger in the housing bore and install the pinion seal on the pinion seal replacer. Using a hammer, install the seal until it seats.

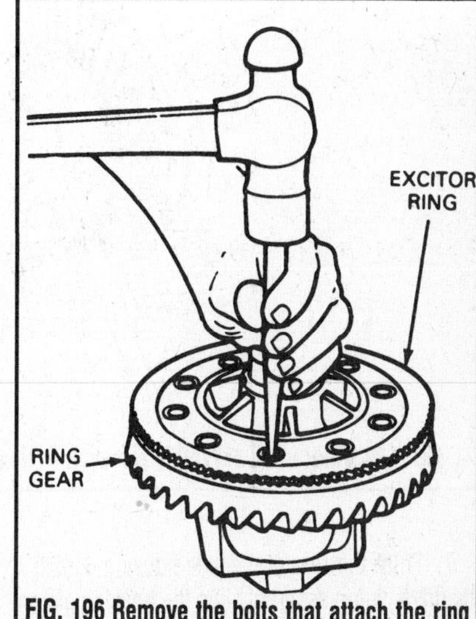

FIG. 196 Remove the bolts that attach the ring gear to the carrier. Remove the ring gear from the case by striking at alternate holes around the gear — Navajo

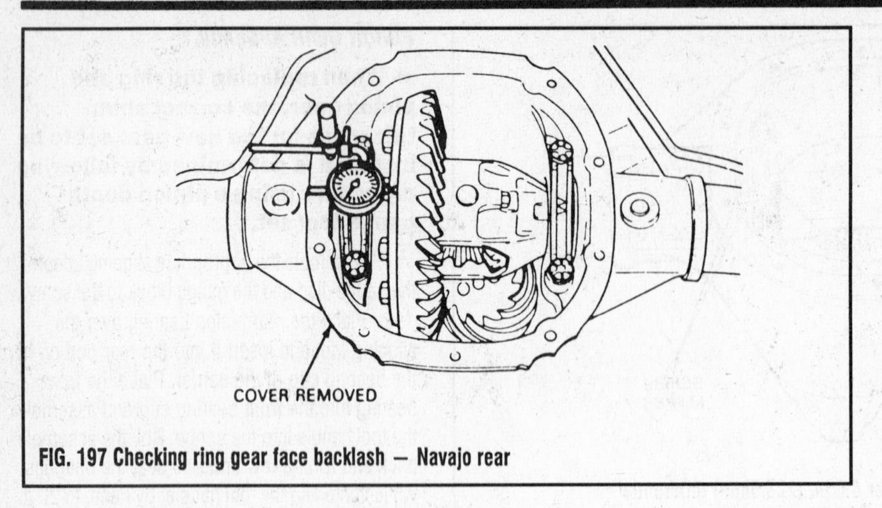

FIG. 197 Checking ring gear face backlash — Navajo rear

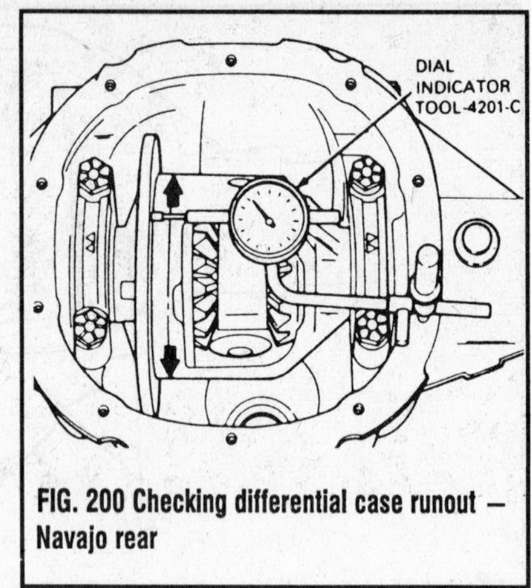

FIG. 200 Checking differential case runout — Navajo rear

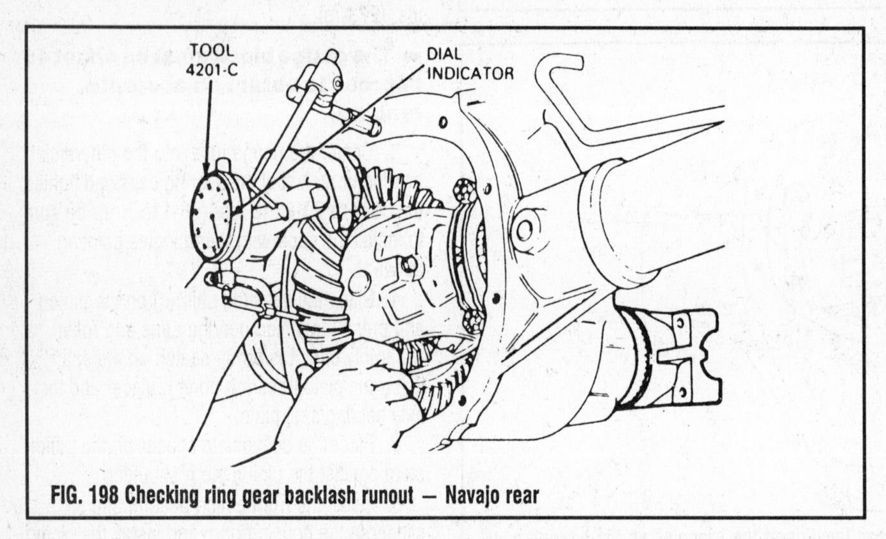

FIG. 198 Checking ring gear backlash runout — Navajo rear

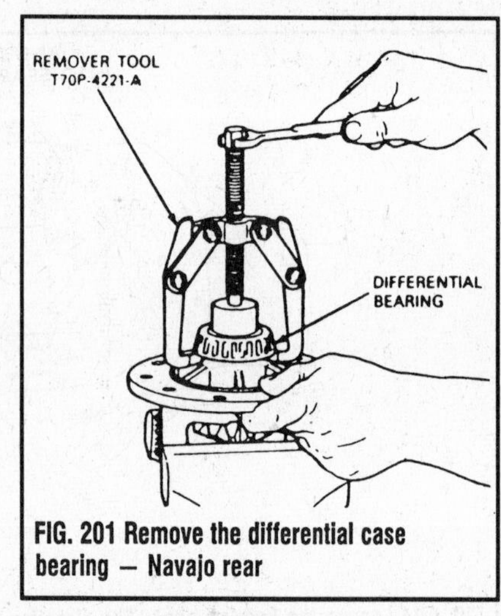

FIG. 201 Remove the differential case bearing — Navajo rear

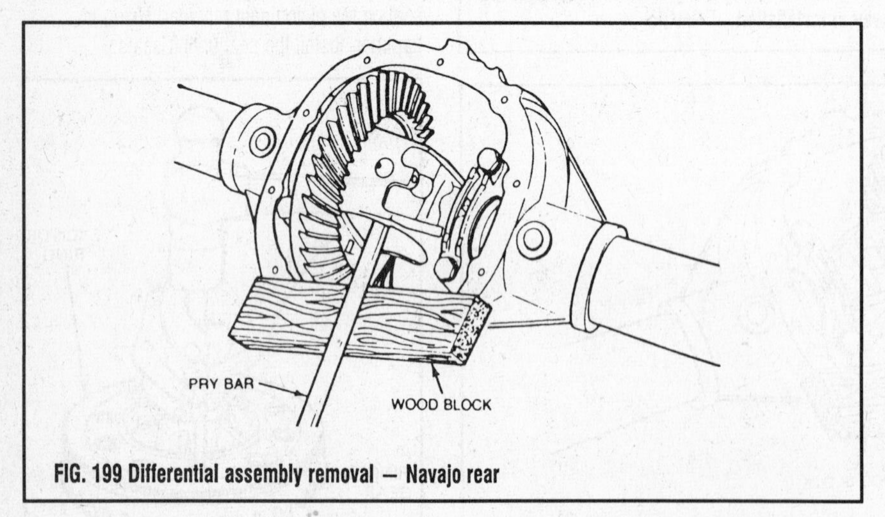

FIG. 199 Differential assembly removal — Navajo rear

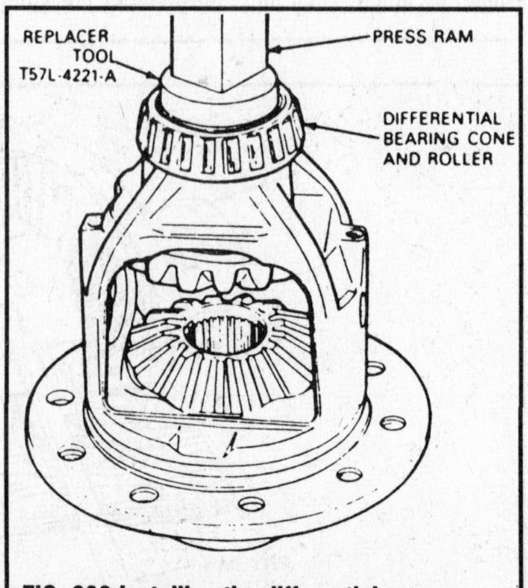

FIG. 202 Installing the differential case bearing — Navajo rear

7. From the rear of the axle housing, install the drive pinion assembly into the housing pinion shaft bore.

8. Lubricate the pinion shaft splines and install the companion flange.

9. Using a companion flange holder tool, torque the pinion nut to 160 ft. lbs. (217 Nm); rotate the pinion gear, occasionally, to ensure proper bearing seating.

10. Using an inch pound torque wrench, measure the pinion bearing preload; it should be 9-14 inch lbs. for used bearings or 16-29 inch lbs. for new bearings.

➡ **If the preload is higher than the specification, tighten to the original reading as recorded; never back off the pinion nut.**

CARRIER ASSEMBLY

1. If the bearings were removed, use a shop press to press them onto the differential case.
2. Install the side gears and thrust washers. Install the pinion gears, the thrust washer, the pinion shaft and the pinion shaft lock bolt.
3. Using a shop press, align the excitor ring tab with the differential case slot and press the ring gear and excitor ring onto the differential case. Install the ring gear-to-differential case bolts and torque them to 100-120 ft. lbs. (135-162 Nm).
4. Place the differential case with the bearing cups into the housing.
5. On the left side, install a 0.265 in. (6.7mm) shim. Install the bearing cap and tighten the bolts finger tight.
6. On the right side, install progressively larger shims until the largest can be install by hand. Install the bearing cap.
7. Torque the bearing cap-to-housing bolts to 70-85 ft. lbs. (95-115Nm).
8. Rotate the assembly to ensure free rotation.
9. Adjust the ring gear backlash.

BACKLASH ADJUSTMENT

1. Using a dial indicator, measure the ring gear and pinion backlash; it should be 0.008-0.015 in. (0.20-0.38mm). If the backlash is 0.001-0.007 in. (0.025-0.178mm) or greater than 0.015 in. (0.38mm) proceed to step 3. If the backlash is **0**, proceed to step 2.
2. If the backlash is zero, add 0.020 in. (0.5mm) shim(s) to the right side and subtract a 0.020 in. (0.5mm) shim(s) from the left side.
3. If the backlash is within specification, go to step 7. In the backlash is 0.001-0.007 in. (0.025-0.178mm) or greater than 0.015 in. (0.38mm), increase the thickness of a shim on 1 side and decrease the same thickness of another shim on the other side, until the backlash comes within range.
4. Install and torque the bearing cap bolts to 80-95 ft. lbs. (109-128 Nm).
5. Rotate the assembly several times to ensure proper seating.
6. Recheck the backlash, if it is not within specification, go to step 7.
7. Remove the bearing caps. Increase the shim sizes, on both sides by 0.006 in. (0.15mm); make sure the shims are fully seated and the assembly turns freely. Use a shim driver to install the shims.
8. Install the bearing caps and torque the bearing caps to 80-95 ft. lbs. (109-128 Nm). Recheck the backlash; if not to specification, repeat this entire procedure.

Navajo 8.8 In. Rear Axle Traction-Lok Differential

➧ SEE FIGS. 203-217

OPERATIONAL CHECK

A limited-slip differential can be checked for proper operation without removing the differential from the axle housing as follows:

1. Disconnect the negative battery cable.
2. Place the transmission in N Position.
3. Raise 1 rear wheel and remove the wheel cover.
4. Install torque tool T59L-4204-A or equivalent on the axle shaft flange studs.
5. Using torque wrench, (torque wrench with a capacity of at least 200 ft. lbs.), rotate the axle shaft. The break-away torque required to start rotation should be at least 20 ft. lbs. (27Nm). The initial break-away torque may be higher than the continuous turning torque, but this is normal. The axle shaft should turn with even pressure throughout the check without slipping or binding. If the torque reading is less than specified, check the differential for proper adjustment.

➡ A vehicle equipped with a limited-slip differential will always have one wheel driving. If only 1 wheel is raised off the floor and the rear axle is driven by the engine, the wheel on the floor could drive the vehicle off the stand or jack.

Adjustment

1. Disconnect the negative battery cable.
2. Raise and support the vehicle safely.
3. Remove the rear wheels and brake drums.
4. Remove the cover from the carrier casting face and drain the lubricant.
5. Perform an inspection before removing the differential case.
6. Working through the cover opening, remove the pinion shaft lock bolt and remove the pinion shaft.
7. Push the axle shafts inward until the C-locks at the end of the shafts are clear of the side gear recess.
8. Remove the C-locks and pull the axle shafts completely out of the housing.

➡ Care should be taken not to damage the axle seals when removing the axle shafts from the housing.

9. Drive the S-shaped preload spring half-way out of the differential case, using a suitable drift. Rotate the case 180°.
10. Hold the S-shaped preload spring with a pair of pliers and tap the spring until it is removed from the differential.

➡ Be careful when removing the S-Shaped spring, due to the spring tension.

11. Rotate the pinion gears until the gears can be removed from the differential.
12. Remove and tag the gears, clutch pack and shims from both sides. Inspect the clutch pack for wear. Replace, if necessary.

➡ Do not use cleaning solvents on the clutch plate friction surfaces. Wipe them clean only.

13. Install tool T84P-4946-A or equivalent on each of the side gear clutch packs without the shim. Tighten to 60 ft. lbs. (6.7Nm). Using a feeler blade, select the thickest blade that will enter between the tool and the clutch pack. This reading will be the thickness of the new shim.

➡ Be sure to lubricate friction plates with the proper hypoid gear lubricant prior to reassembly.

To Install:

14. Install the clutch pack and new shim into the cavity in the differential case. Repeat this step for both sides.
15. Place the pinion gears and thrust washers 180° apart on the side gears. Rotate the tool until the pinion gears are aligned with the pinion shaft holes.
16. Hold the S-shaped preload spring up to the differential case window and with a soft-faced mallet, hammer the spring into position.
17. Install the axle shafts and C-locks into positions and push the axle shaft outboard as far as possible.
18. Install the pinion shaft and pinion shaft lock bolt. Tighten the bolt to 15-30 ft. lbs. (20-40Nm).
19. Install the rear brake drums and wheels. Perform the traction-lock operational check to insure that the unit is within specification.
20. Apply silicone sealant, D6AZ-19562-B or equivalent, to the rear cover. Install the cover. Tighten the retaining bolts 25-35 ft. lbs. (34-47Nm).
21. Fill the unit to the bottom of the fill hole with the axle in the running position. Use 5.0 pints (2.6L) of Hypoid Gear Lubricant (E0AZ-19580-A) or equivalent.

Differential Case

DISASSEMBLY

1. Remove and discard the ring gear-to-differential case retaining bolts.

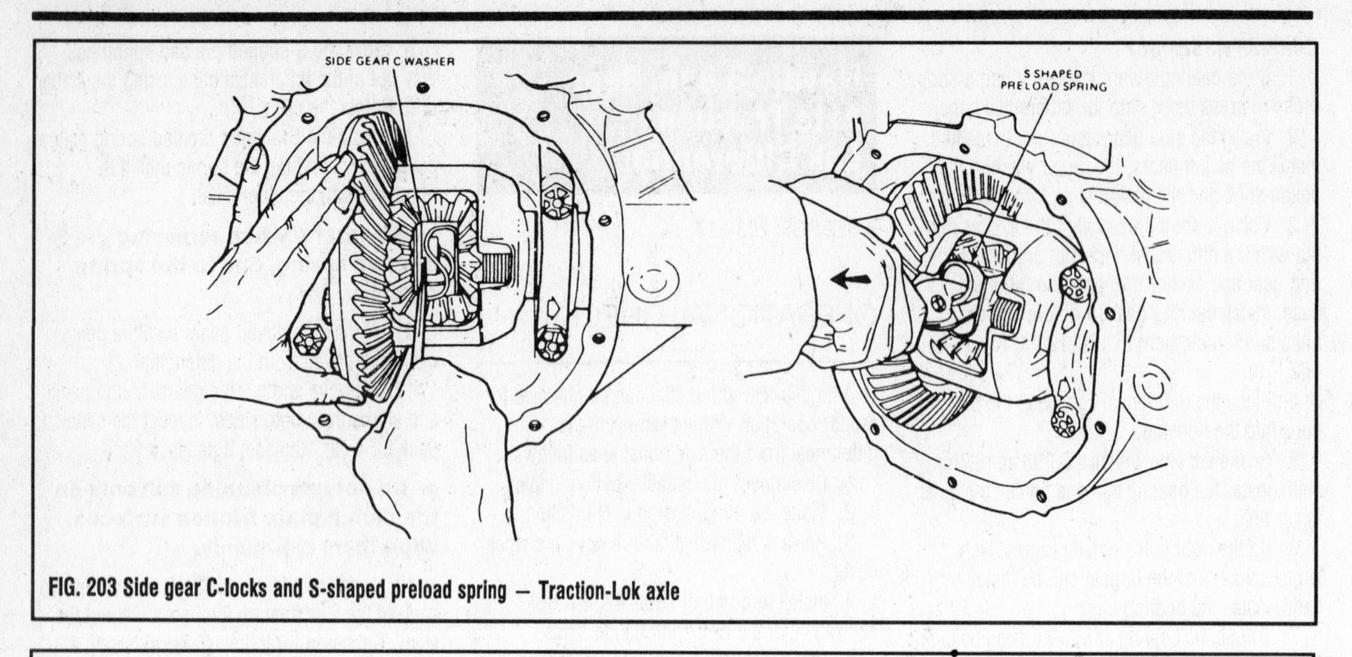

FIG. 203 Side gear C-locks and S-shaped preload spring — Traction-Lok axle

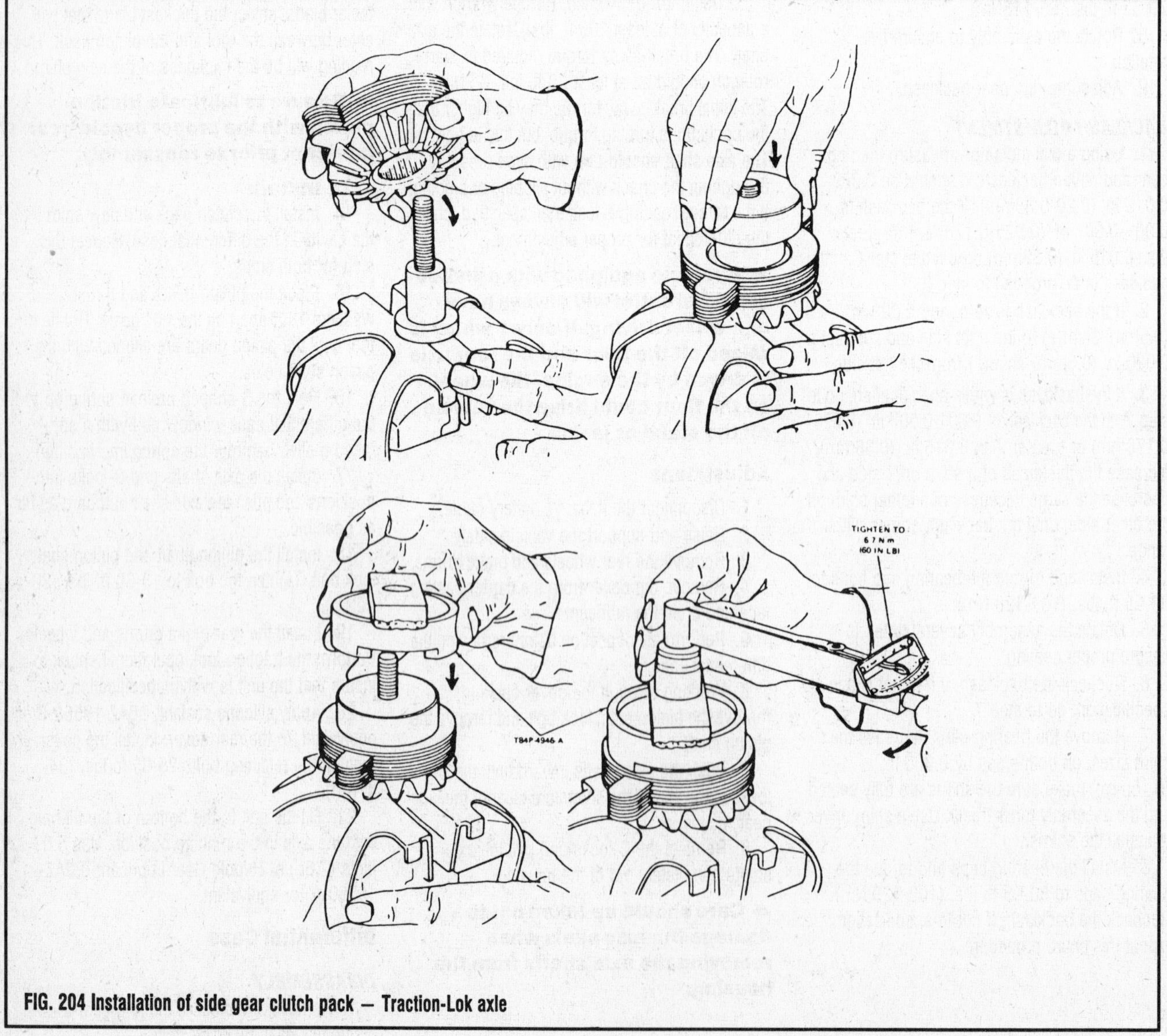

FIG. 204 Installation of side gear clutch pack — Traction-Lok axle

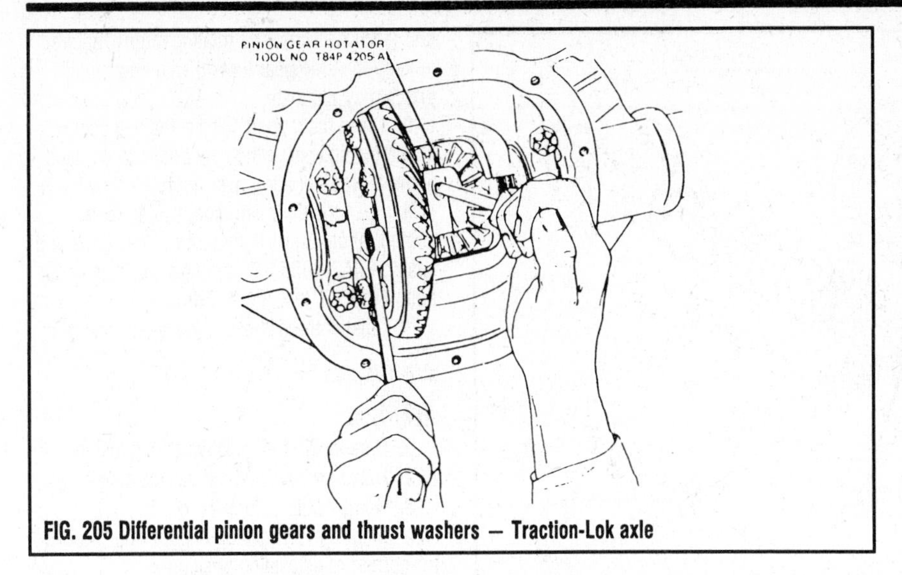

FIG. 205 Differential pinion gears and thrust washers — Traction-Lok axle

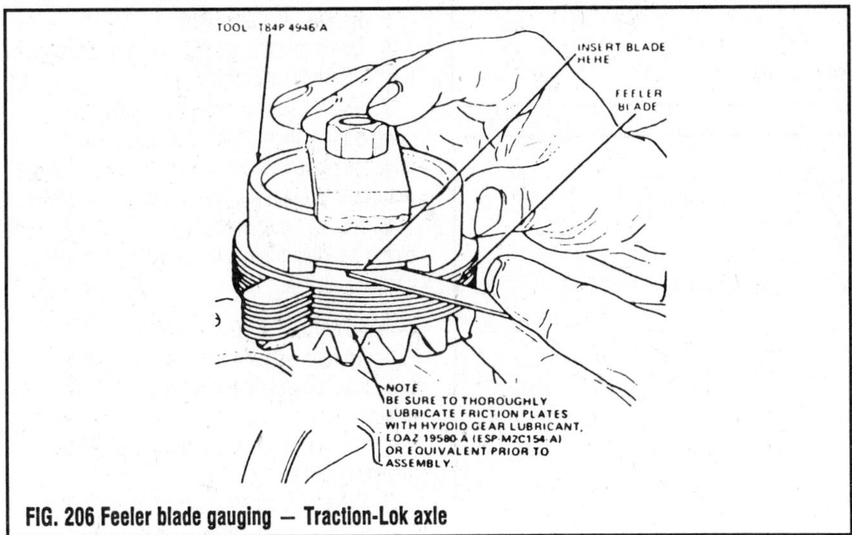

FIG. 206 Feeler blade gauging — Traction-Lok axle

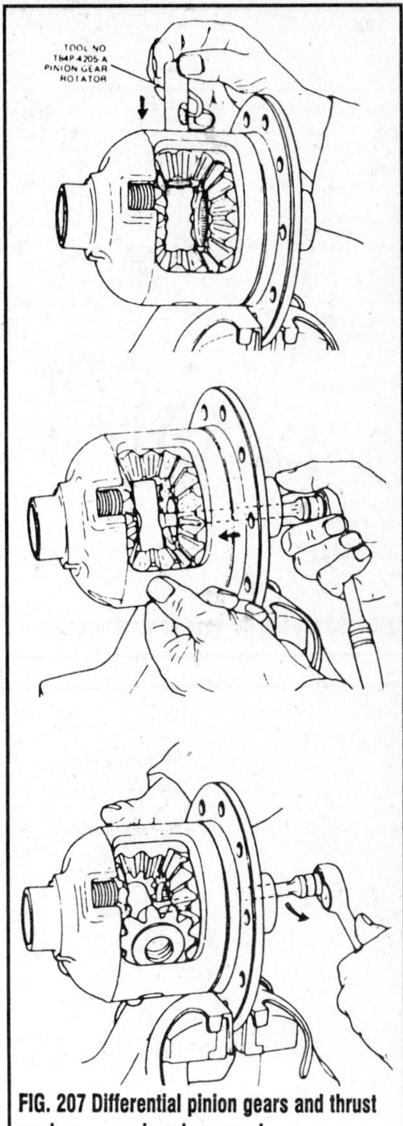

FIG. 207 Differential pinion gears and thrust washers — on-bench removal — Traction-Lok axle

2. Lightly tap the ring gear to remove it from the differential case.
3. Remove the differential pinion shaft lock bolt and remove the pinion shaft.
4. Drive out the S-shaped preload spring, using a suitable drift.

➡ Be careful when removing the S-shaped spring, due to the spring tension.

5. Rotate the pinion gears until the gears and thrust washers can be removed.
6. Remove and tag the gears, clutch pack and shims from both sides. Inspect the clutch pack for wear. Replace, if necessary.

➡ Do not use cleaning solvents on the clutch plate friction surfaces. Wipe them clean only.

Clutch Pack Shim Selection

1. Assemble the clutch pack on t he side gear. No shim is required at this point. However, all plates must be thoroughly prelubricated with Hypoid Gear Lubricant (E0AZ-19580-A) or equivalent.
2. Assemble tool T84P-4946-A or equivalent on the side gear clutch pack.
3. Using a feeler gauge took, select the thickest feeler blade that will enter between the tool and the clutch pack. This reading will be the shim required for that clutch pack.

➡ Do not mix the clutches or shims.

4. Repeat Steps 1-3 for the opposite clutch pack.

ASSEMBLY

1. Prior to assembly, lubricate all parts with Hypoid Gear Lubricant (E0AZ-19580-A) or equivalent in the differential case.
2. Mount the differential case in a soft jawed vise and place the clutch packs and side gears in their proper cavities in the differential case.
3. Place the pinion gears and thrust washers on the side gears. Install tool T84P-4946-A, or equivalent, in the case.
4. Rotate the pinion gears until the bores in the gears are aligned with the pinion shaft holes in the differential case. Remove the tool from the differential case.
5. Hold the S-shaped preload spring up to the differential case window and with a soft-faced mallet, hammer the spring into position.
6. Install the pinion shaft and lock bolt. Do not tighten the lock bolt at this point.
7. Prior to installation of the locking differential into a vehicle, a bench torque check must be made. With the locker tools T59L-4204-A or equivalent, check the torque required to rotate 1 side gear while the other is held stationery.
8. The initial breakaway torque, if original clutch plates are used, should be no less than 20 ft. lbs. (27Nm). If new clutch plates are used, the break-away torque should be from 150-250 ft.

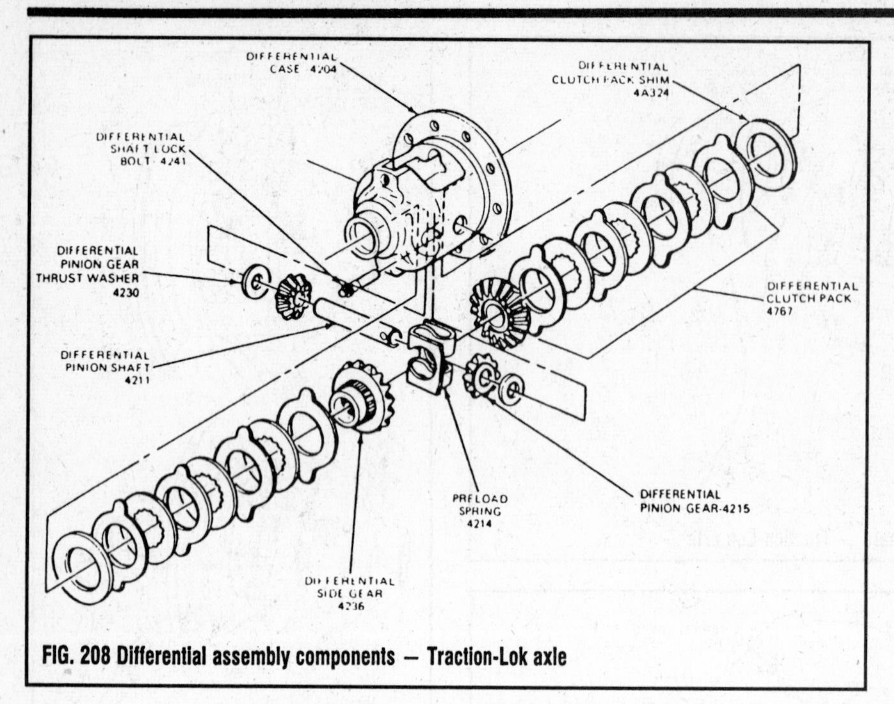

FIG. 208 Differential assembly components — Traction-Lok axle

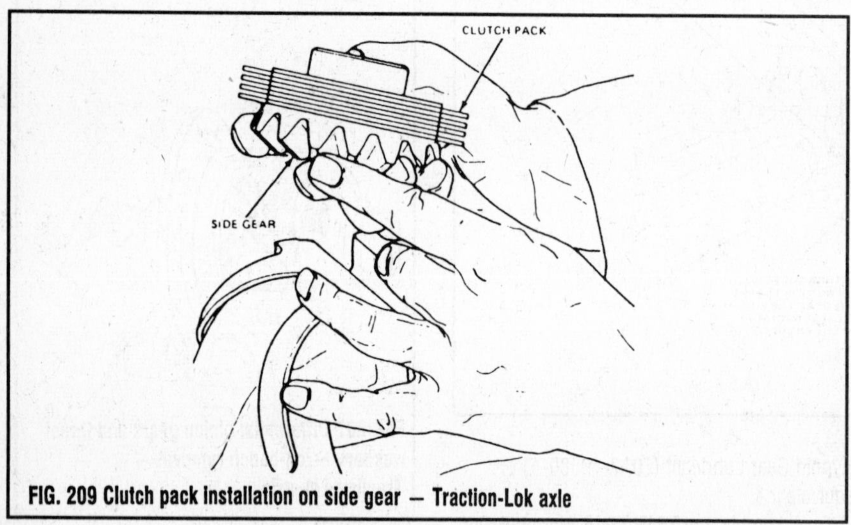

FIG. 209 Clutch pack installation on side gear — Traction-Lok axle

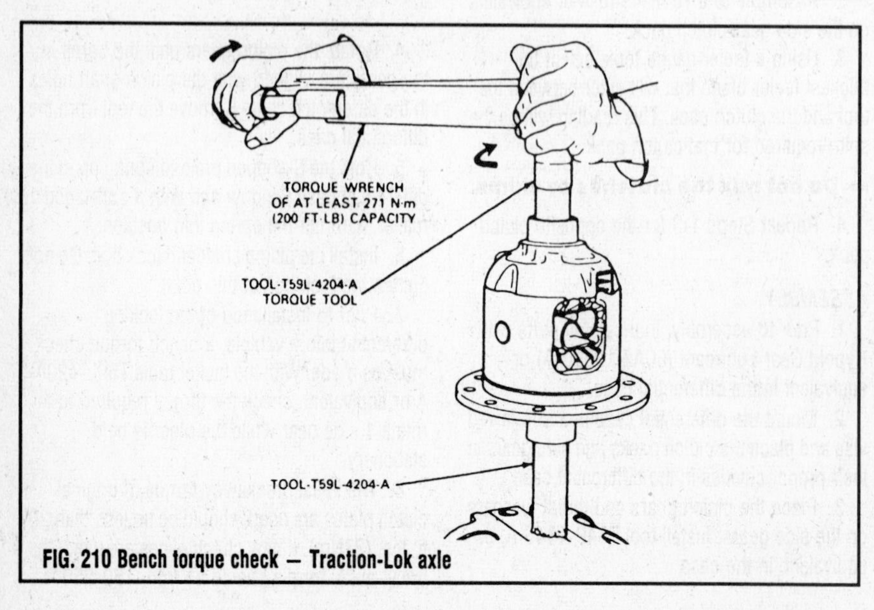

FIG. 210 Bench torque check — Traction-Lok axle

lbs. (135-338Nm). The rotating torque required to keep the side gear turning with new clutch plates may fluctuate.

9. Clean the tapped holes in the ring gear with a suitable solvent. If the new boolts to be used show a green coating over approximately 1/2 in. (13mm) of the threaded area, use as is. If not coated, apply a small amount of threadlock and sealer, E0AZ-19554-B or equivalent. Tighten the bolts 70-85 ft. lbs. (95-115Nm).

10. Install the differential case and ring gear.

Drive Pinion

REMOVAL

1. Disconnect the negative battery cable.
2. Raise and support the vehicle safely.
3. Remove the differential case.
4. Mark the companion flanges and U-joints for correct reinstallation position.
5. Remove the driveshaft.
6. Use a suitable tool to hold the companion flange. Remove the pinion nut.
7. Use a 2-jawed puller to remove the companion flange. With a soft-faced hammer, drive the pinion out of the front bearing cone and remove it through the rear of the carrier casting.
8. Remove the drive pinion oil seal, front pinion bearing cone, roller and slinger from the carrier.

DISASSEMBLY AND ASSEMBLY

1. To remove the pinion rear bearing cone, use pinion bearing cone replacer, T719-4621-B or equivalent. Measure the shim found under the bearing cone with a micrometer. Record the thickness of the shim.
2. Determine the drive pinion depth following the procedure preceding the heading "Drive Pinion Depth Adjustment".
3. Place the selected shim(s) on the pinion shaft and press the pinion bearing until firmly seated on the shaft.

DRIVE PINION DEPTH ADJUSTMENT

Individual differences in machining the carrier casting and the gear set and variation in bearing widths requires a shim between the pinion rear bearing and pinion head, in order to locate the pinion for correct tooth contact with the ring gear. When replacing a ring and pinion gear, the correct shim thickness for the new gear set to be installed is determined by the following procedure using tool T79P-4020-A or equivalent.

1. Place the rear pinion bearing over the aligning disc and insert it into the pinion bearing cup of the carrier. Place the front bearing into the front bearing cup and assemble the tool handle into the screw and tighten to 20 ft. lbs. (27Nm).

➡ The gauge block must be offset to obtain an accurate reading.

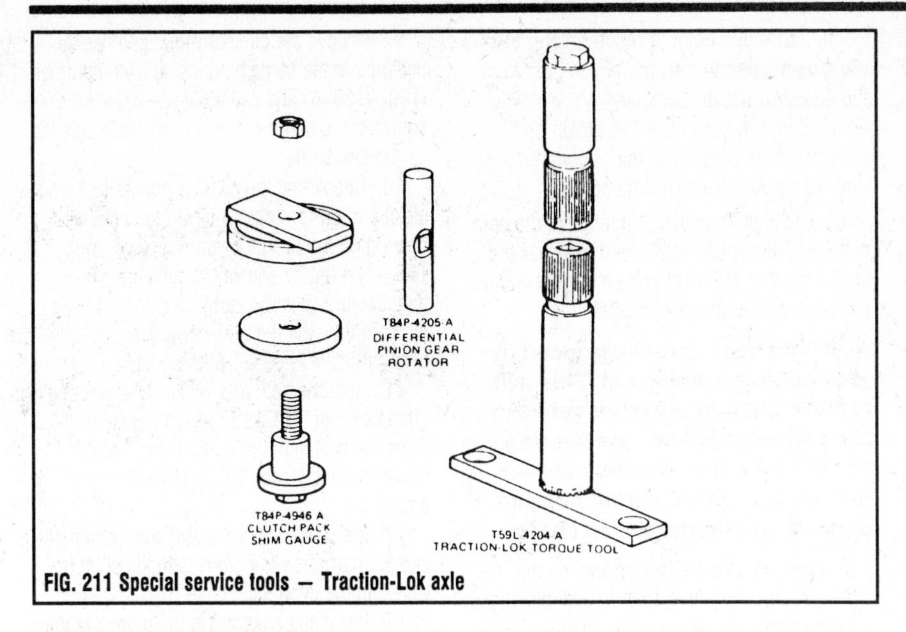

FIG. 211 Special service tools — Traction-Lok axle

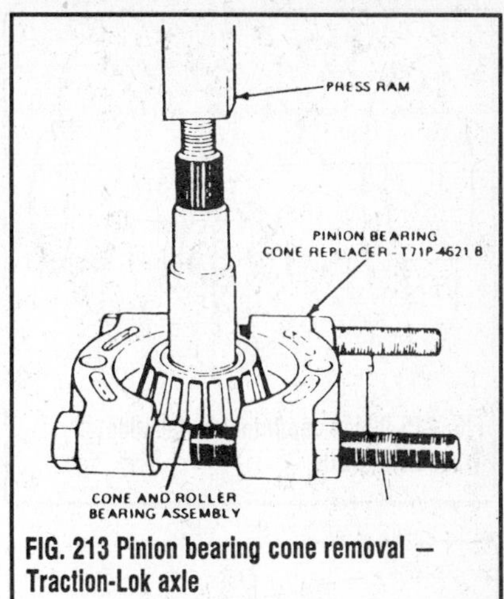

FIG. 213 Pinion bearing cone removal — Traction-Lok axle

2. Center the gauge tube into the differential bearing bore. Install the bearing caps and tighten the bolts to 70-85 ft. lbs. (95-115Nm).

3. Make sure that the gauge handle adapter screw, sligning adapter, gauge disc and gauge block assembly are securely mounted between the front and rear bearing. Recheck tool handle torque prior to gauging to ensure that the bearings are properly seated. This can affect final shim selection when improperly assembled. Clean the bearing cups and differential pedestal surfaces thoroughly. Apply only light oil film on the bearing assemblies prior to gauging.

4. Gauge block should then be rotated several half turns to ensure rollers are properly seated in the bearings cups. Rotational torque on the gauge assembly should be 20 inch lbs. with new bearings. Final position should be approximately 45° in line with gauge tube high point. This area should be utilized for pinion shim selection. Selection of pinion shim with gauge block not lined up with tube high point will cause improper shim selection and may result in axle noise.

Special Service Tools

Utilize pinion shims as the gauge for shim selection. This will minimize errors in attempting to stack feeler gauge stock together or simple addition errors in calculating correct shim thickness. Shims must be flat. Do not use dirty, bent, nicked or mutilated shims as a gauge.

It is important to utilize a light drag on the shim for the correct selection. Do not attempt to force the shim between the gauge block and the gauge tube. This will minimize selection to a shim thicker than required which results in a deep tooth contact in final assembly for integral axles.

If the pinion has a plus + marking, subtract this amount from the feeler gauge measurement. If the pinion has a minus - marking, add this amount to the feeler gauge measurement.

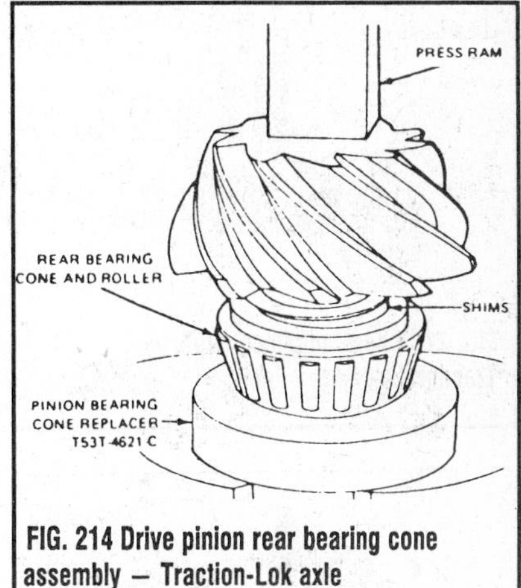

FIG. 214 Drive pinion rear bearing cone assembly — Traction-Lok axle

INSTALLATION

1. Install the pinion front bearing and slinger.
2. Apply Multi-Purpose Long-Life Lubricant, C1AZ-19590-B or equivalent, between the lips of the pinion seal and install the pinion seal.
3. Install the companion flange into the seal and hold it firmly against the pinion front bearing cone. From the rear of the carrier casting, insert

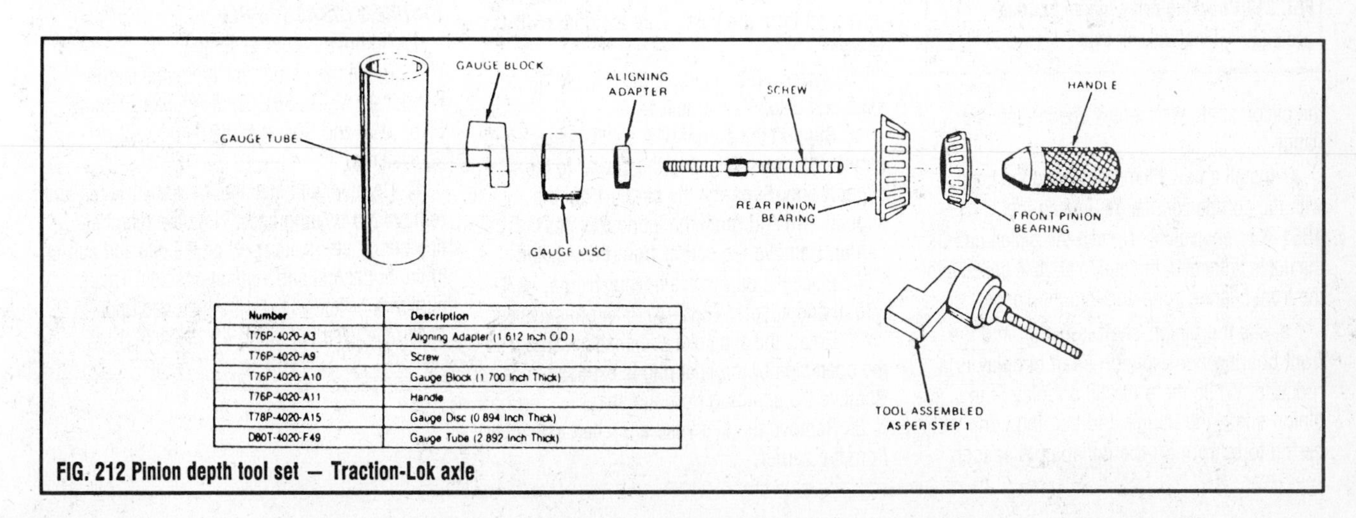

Number	Description
T76P-4020-A3	Aligning Adapter (1 612 Inch O D)
T76P-4020-A9	Screw
T76P-4020-A10	Gauge Block (1 700 Inch Thick)
T76P-4020-A11	Handle
T78P-4020-A15	Gauge Disc (0 894 Inch Thick)
D80T-4020-F49	Gauge Tube (2 892 Inch Thick)

FIG. 212 Pinion depth tool set — Traction-Lok axle

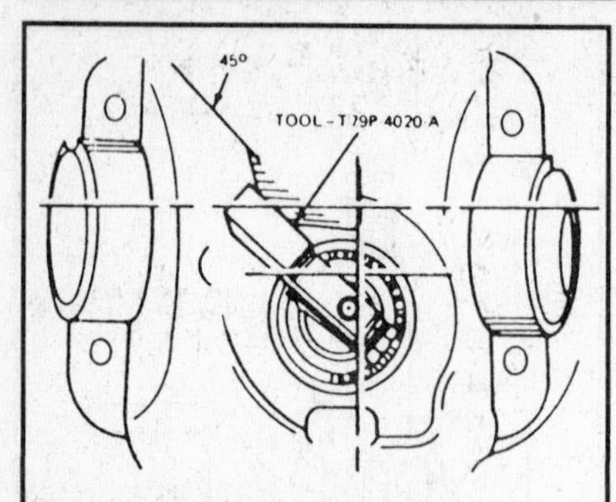

FIG. 215 Pinion depth tool installation — Traction-Lok axle

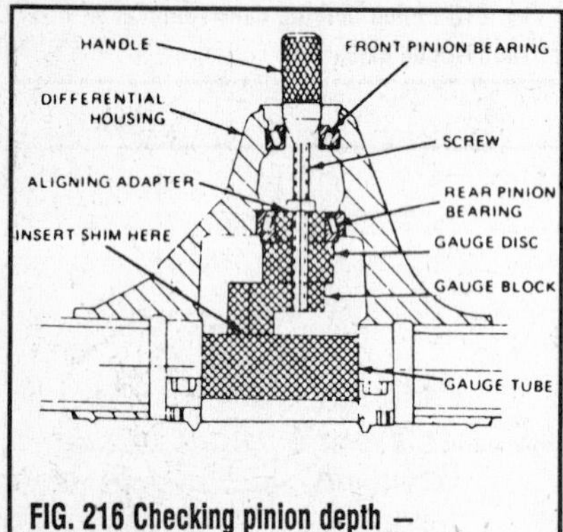

FIG. 216 Checking pinion depth — Traction-Lok axle

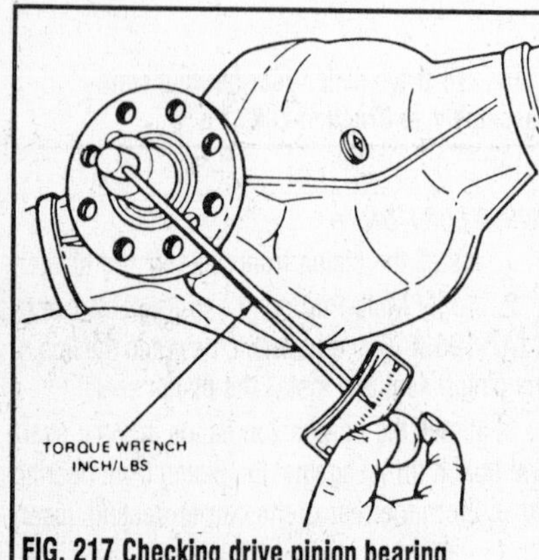

FIG. 217 Checking drive pinion bearing preload — Traction-Lok axle

the pinion shaft, with a new spacer, into the flange.

4. Install a new pinion nut. Hold the flange with the companion flange holding tool, T78P-4851-A or equivalent. Tighten the pinion nut. As the nut is tightened, the pinion shaft is pulled into the front bearing cone and into the flange.

a. As the pinion shaft is pulled into the front bearing cone, pinion shaft endplay is reduced. While there is still endplay in the pinion shaft, the flange and bearing cone will be felt to bottom on the collapsible spacer.

b. From this point, a much greater torque must be applied to turn the pinion nut, since the spacer must be collapsed. Very slowly, tighten the nut, but check the pinion shaft endplay often to see that the pinion bearing preload does not exceed the limits.

c. If the pinion nut is tightened to the point that the pinion bearing preload exceeds the limits, the pinion shaft must be removed and a new collapsible spacer installed.

➡ Do not decrease the preload by loosening the pinion nut. This will remove the compression between the pinion front and rear bearing cones and the collapsible spacer. It may also permit the front bearing cone to turn on the pinion shaft.

5. As soon as there is a preload on the bearings, turn the pinion shaft in both directions several times to set the bearing rollers.

6. Adjust the bearing preload to 8-14 inch lbs. (for original bearings) or 16-29 inch lbs. (for new bearings). Measure the preload with an inch-pound torque wrench.

Navajo Front Differential

➧ SEE FIGS. 218-238

Right Hand Slip Yoke and Stub Shaft Assembly, Carrier, Carrier Oil Seal and Bearing

REMOVAL & INSTALLATION

1. Disconnect the negative battery cable.
2. Raise and support the vehicle safely.
3. Remove the nuts and U-bolts connecting the driveshaft to the yoke. Disconnect the driveshaft from the yoke. Wire the driveshaft aside.
4. Remove the spindles, the left and right shaft and U-joint assemblies.
5. Support the carrier with a suitable jack and remove the bolts retaining the carrier to the support arm. Separate the carrier from the support arm and drain the lubricant from the carrier. Remove the carrier from the vehicle.
6. Place the carrier in a holding fixture, T57L-500-B and adapter T83T-3010-A or equivalent.
7. Rotate the slip yoke and shaft assembly so the open side of the snapring is exposed. Remove the snapring from the shaft.
8. Remove the slip yoke and shaft assembly from the carrier.
9. Remove the oil seal and caged needle bearings at the same time, using slide hammer (T50T-100-A) and collet (D80L-100-A) or equivalent. Discard the seal and needle bearing.

To Install:

10. Check that the bearing bore is free from nicks and burrs. Install a new caged needle bearing on the needle bearing replacer tool, T83T-1244-A or equivalent, with the manufacturer's name and part number facing outward towards the tool. Drive the needle bearing until it is seated in the bore.
11. Coat the seal with Multi-Purpose Long Life Lubricant C1AZ-19590-B or equivalent. Drive the seal into the carrier using needle bearing replacer tool, T83T-1244-A or equivalent.
12. Install the slip yoke and shaft assembly into the carrier so the grooves in the shaft is visible in the differential case.
13. Install the snapring in the groove in the shaft. Force the snapring into position. Do not tap the center of the snapring. This may damage the snapring.
14. Clean all traces of gasket sealant from the surfaces of the carrier and support arm and make sure the surfaces are free from dirt and oil.
15. Apply a bead of RTV sealant to the surface of the carrier. Position the carrier on a suitable jack and install it into position on the support arm, using guide pins to align. Install the retaining bolts and hand tighten. Then, tighten the bolts in a clockwise or counterclockwise pattern to 40-50 ft. lbs. (54-68Nm).
16. Install the shear bolt retaining the carrier to the axle arm and tighten to 75-95 ft. lbs. (102-129Nm).
17. Install both spindles, the left and right shaft and joint assemblies.
18. Connect the driveshaft to the yoke. Install the nuts and U-bolts and tighten to 8-15 ft. lbs. (11-20Nm).
19. Lower the vehicle.
20. Reconnect the negative battery cable.

CARRIER DISASSEMBLY

1. Remove carrier assembly.
2. Place the carrier in Differential Carrier Hanger 49 M001 561 using Adapter Plate 49 UN01 027 and Spacers T80T-4000-B2 or equivalents.
3. Remove and clean all gasket surfaces and remove the bearing caps. Note the matched number or letters stamped on the cap and carrier in the horizontal and vertical position. These numbers or letters must be matched upon assembly. Use spreader, 49 UN01 026.

✻✻ CAUTION

Do not spread carrier more than 0.25mm (0.010 inch)!

4. Remove the differential case from the carrier. It may be necessary to pry the case from the carrier with pry bars. Use caution to avoid damaging any machined surfaces. Remove and tag bearing cups to indicate from which side they were removed. Remove the spreader tool. Note the differential bearing outboard selective shims located on each side of the differential bearing bore. Remove and tag which side they were removed from (ring gear or opposite side). They will be reused during assembly, unless damaged or worn.

➡ Check outboard selective shims for damage (bent or deep grooves caused by worn bearings). If damaged, they should be replaced with new ones at time of reassembly.

5. Turn the nose of the carrier up. Hold the end yoke with End Yoke Tool 49 S120 710 or equivalent and remove the pinion nut and washers form the pinion shaft.

6. Remove the end yoke with Companion Flange Remover, T77F-4220-B1 (or equivalent). If the yoke shows any sign of wear in the area of seal contact, replace the yoke.

7. Remove the drive pinion by tapping on the drive pinion shaft with a rawhide or plastic hammer. Catch the pinion to prevent damage to the pinion teeth.

✻✻ CAUTION

Gear teeth may have sharp edges. When handling gear, use care to avoid personal injury.

8. Remove the drive pinion oil seal from the carrier bore by using Seal Puller, TOOL-1175-AC, Slide Hammer 49 0223 630 B and adapter 49 UN01 101 or equivalents. Replace the oil seal with a new seal during assembly.

9. Remove the outer pinion bearing cone, oil slinger and collapsible spacer from the carrier. Discard the collapsible spacer and replace with a new one upon assembly.

10. To remove the inner pinion bearing cup, pass Pinion Bearing Cup Remover T867-4628-BH and Drive Handle, 49 F027 003 through the outer pinion bearing cup and against the inner bearing cup. Drive out the inner bearing cup. Remove the oil baffle from the inner bearing cup bore.

➡ An oil baffle is located between the inner bearing cup and carrier bore. Replace with a baffle of equal thickness. If a baffle of the same thickness cannot be obtained, select adjustment shims, located behind the head of the pinion, to compensate for the difference.

11. To remove the outer pinion bearing cup, pass the Pinion Bearing Cup Remover, T86T-4628-BH and Handle, 49 F027 003 or equivalents through the inner bearing cup. Drive the outer pinion bearing cup out with a hammer.

12. Remove the differential case bearings from the case. Place Step Plate, D80L-630-4 under bearing to protect the bearing. Install Universal Bearing Remover, 49 UN01 029 or equivalent and remove the bearing. Turn the case over and remove the other bearing.

13. Wire the shims, bearing cup and cone together and identify from which side of the differential case they were removed.

➡ It is recommended that bearings be replaced.

14. Place a few shop towels over the vise to prevent the ring gear teeth from being nicked, after it is free from the case. Place the case in a vise. Remove the ring gear bolts. Tap the ring gear with a rawhide hammer to free it from the case. Remove the case and ring gear from the vise.

➡ Whenever removing the ring gear bolts, discard the bolts and replace with new bolts upon assembly.

15. Remove the inner pinion bearing cone and oil slinger from the drive pinion with Universal Bearing Remover, 49 UN01 029 or equivalent.

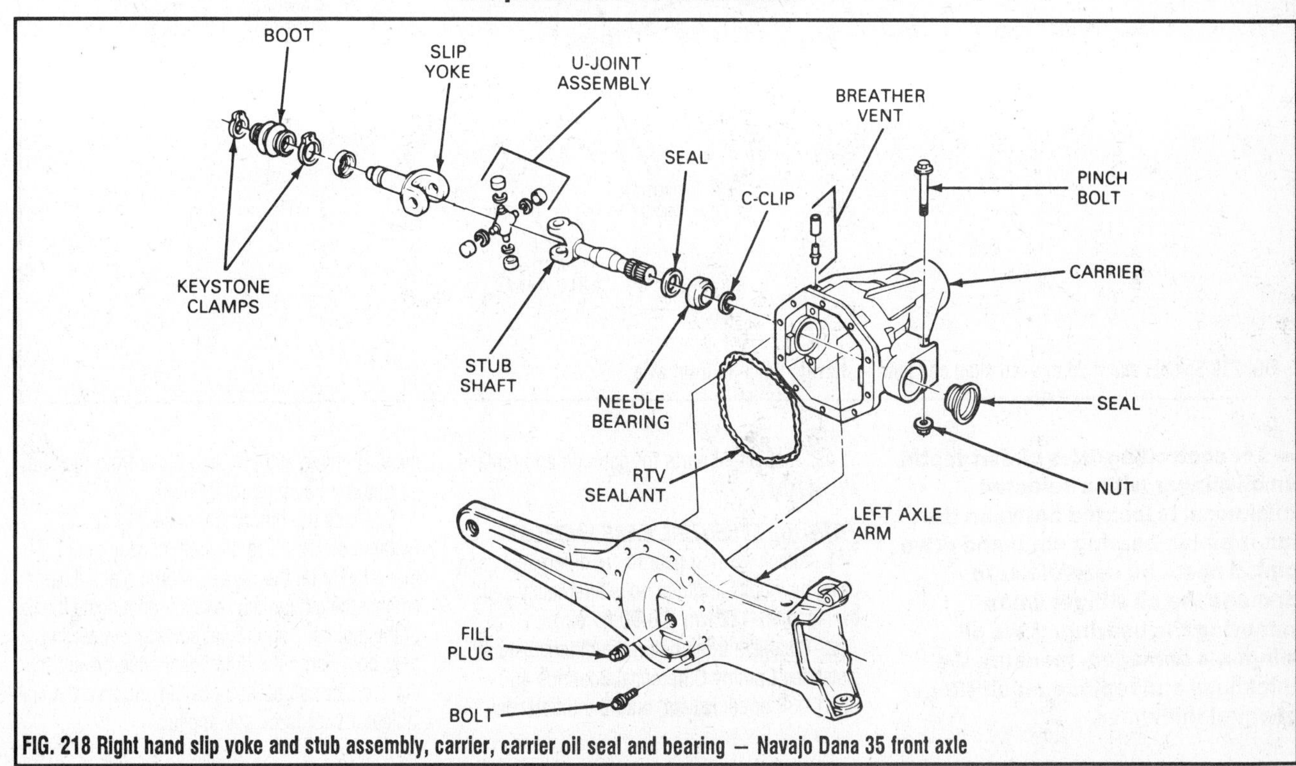

FIG. 218 Right hand slip yoke and stub assembly, carrier, carrier oil seal and bearing — Navajo Dana 35 front axle

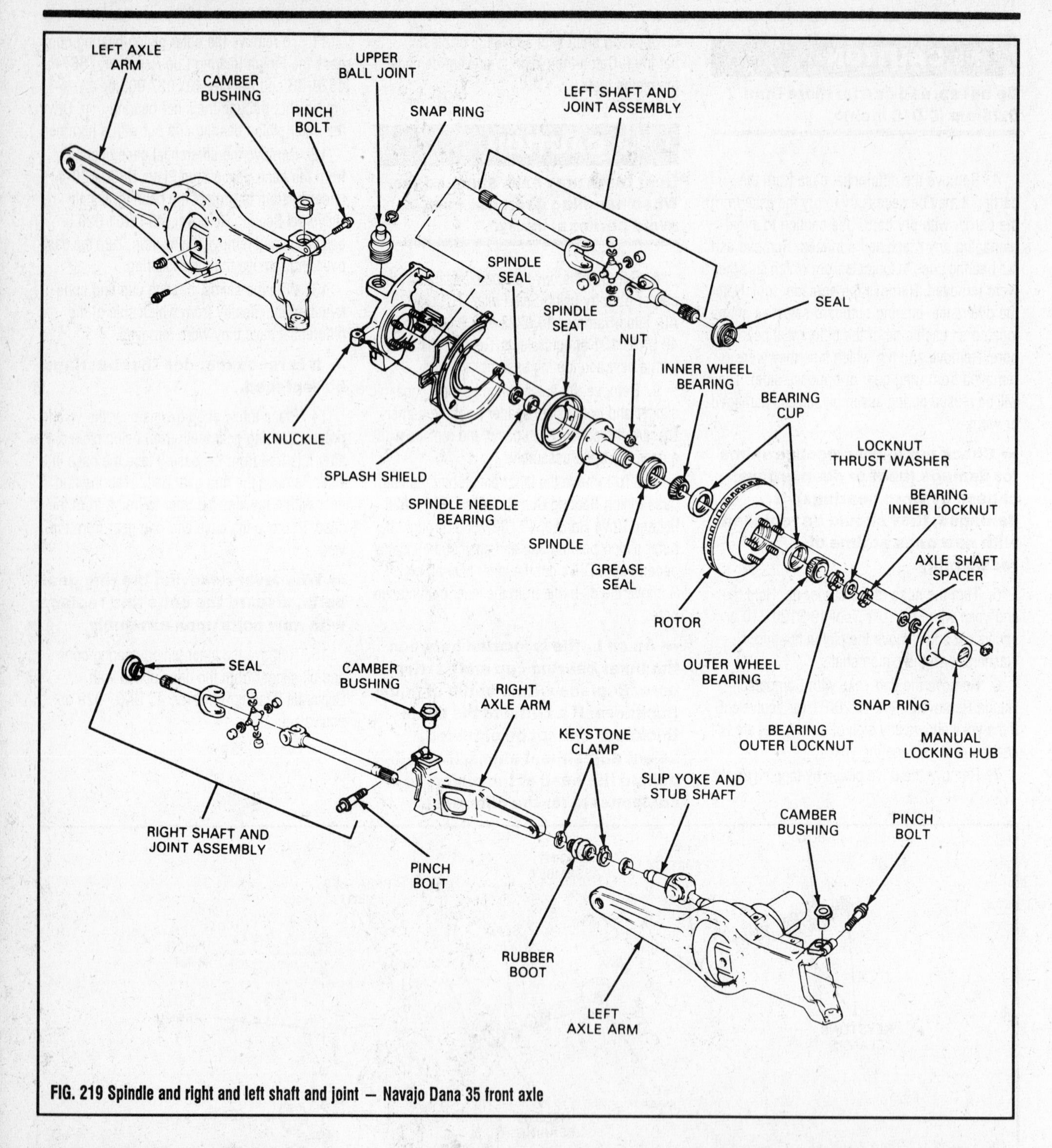

FIG. 219 Spindle and right and left shaft and joint — Navajo Dana 35 front axle

➡ For controlling drive pinion depth, an oil slinger with a selected thickness, is located between the inner pinion bearing cone and drive pinion head. Be careful not to damage the oil slinger when removing the bearing. If the oil slinger is damaged, measure the thickness and replace an oil slinger of equal thickness.

16. Inspect all parts for damage and replace as required.

TOTAL DIFFERENTIAL CASE ENDPLAY

1. Attach the ring gear to the differential case using new bolts. Tighten bolts alternately and evenly to 95-122 Nm (70-90 ft. lbs.).

2. Clean the trunions on the differential and install the Dummy Differential Bearings 459 UN01 030 or equivalent, onto the differential case. Remove all burrs and nicks from the hubs so dummy bearings rotate freely.

3. Place the differential case into carrier (without pinion). The differential case could move freely on the carrier. Mount dial indicator against the differential case flange. Locate the tip of the indicator on the flat surface of one ring gear bolt. Force the differential case toward the dial indicator as far as possible and zero the dial indicator with force still applied.

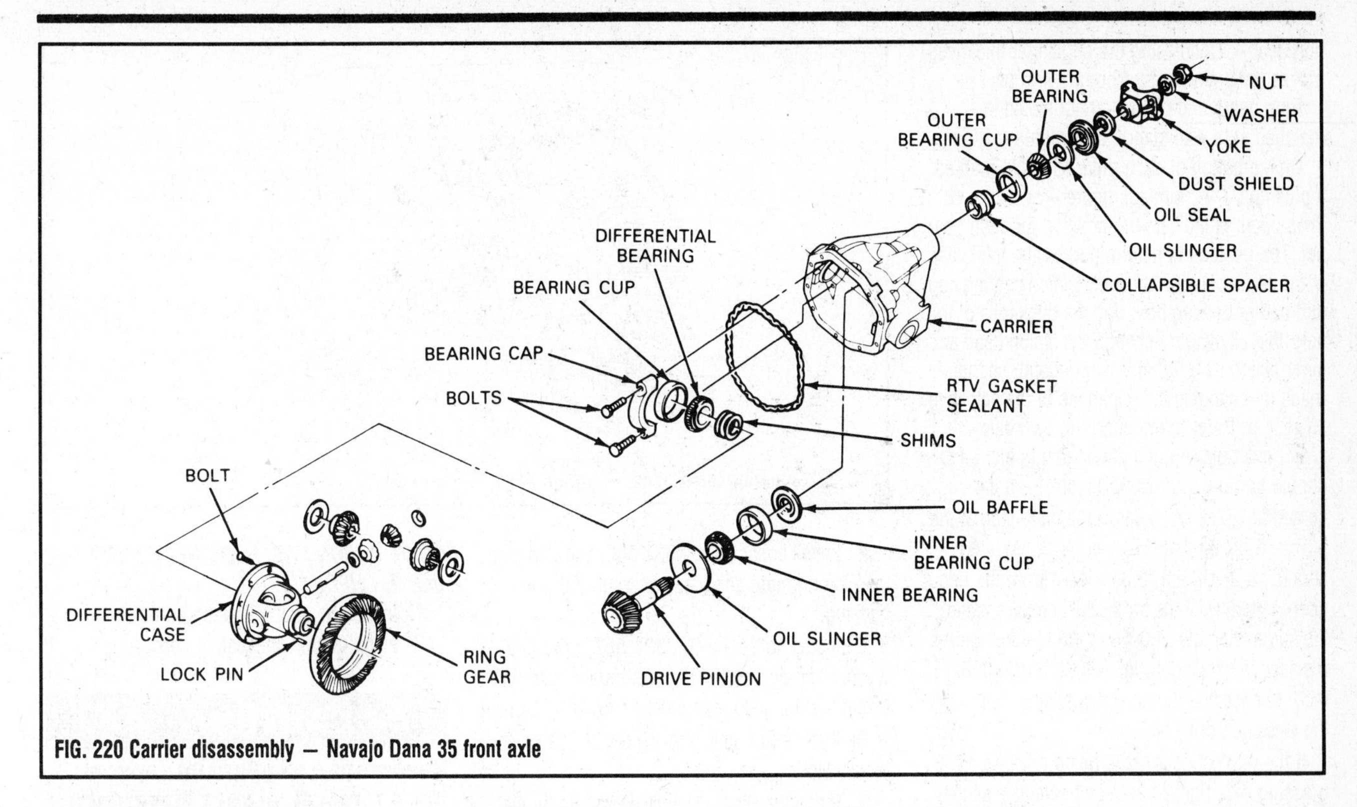

FIG. 220 Carrier disassembly — Navajo Dana 35 front axle

➡ Dial indicator should have minimum travel capability of 8.89mm (0.350 in.)

4. Force the differential case away from the dial indicator as far as it will go. Repeat this procedure until the same reading is obtained. Record the dial indicator reading as measurement **A** on the worksheet for calculating ring gear backlash and differential bearing preload shims. This reading indicates the amount of shims needed behind the differential side bearings to take up total clearance between the differential bearing cup and carrier. The reading will be used under Pinion and Ring Gear Backlash.

5. Remove the differential case from the carrier. Do not remove the master differential bearings at this time.

DRIVE PINION INSTALLATION

Two separate adjustments affect contact between the ring gear and the drive pinion: Pinion Depth and Pinion to Ring Gear Backlash.

Pinion Depth is controlled by an oil slinger (with a selective thickness) located between drive pinion head and inner pinion bearing cone and an oil baffle located between the inner bearing cup and carrier bore.

Pinion to Ring Gear Backlash is controlled by a selective preload spacer located between the differential bearing cup and the carrier.

In the Pinion Depth Adjustment, the size of the selected thickness oil slinger and the oil baffle controls the pinion position. Increasing the oil slinger thickness moves the pinion toward the

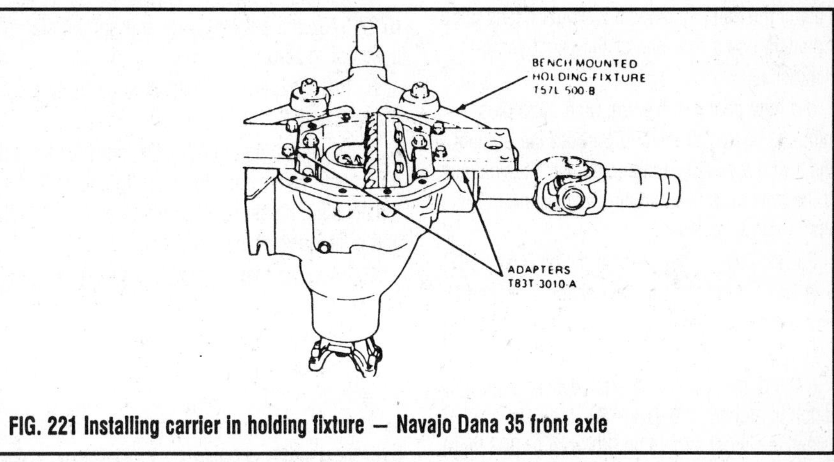

FIG. 221 Installing carrier in holding fixture — Navajo Dana 35 front axle

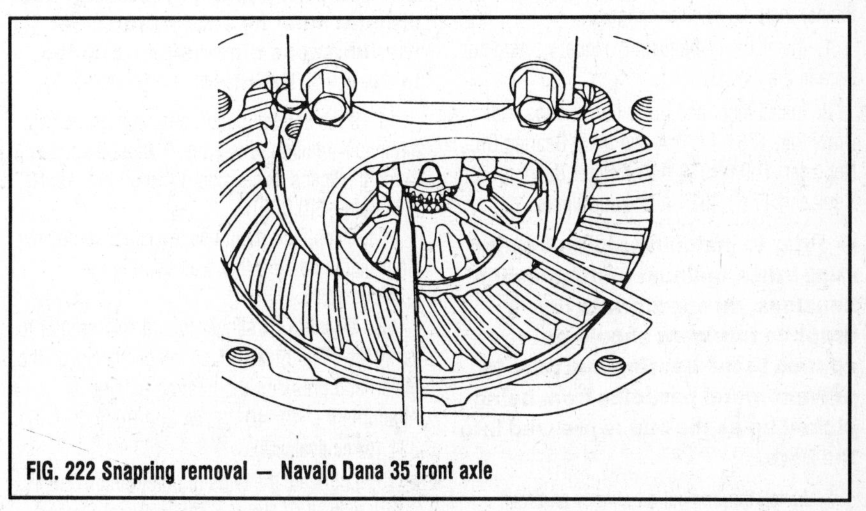

FIG. 222 Snapring removal — Navajo Dana 35 front axle

ring gear –. Decreasing the oil slinger thickness moves the pinion away from the ring gear +.

Ring gears and pinions are supplied in matched sets with standard or metric markings.

On the button of each drive pinion is marked a plus figure +, a minus figure – or a zero **O**. These figures indicate the position for each gear set. The position is determined by the thickness of the baffle between the inner pinion bearing cup and carrier bearing bore and the thickness of the selective oil slinger between the pinion head and inner pinion bearing. Any pinion depth change is made by changing the thickness of the selective oil slinger. Refer to the charts shown below.

For example: A drive pinion that is etched **O** should be 96.85mm (3.813 inch) from the centerline of the ring gear to the back face of the pinion. A pinion that is etched **+3 (m+8)** should be 96.93mm (3.816 inch) from the ring gear centerline. If the baffle thickness remains the same, then the **+3 (m+8)** pinion requires a selective oil slinger that is 0.08mm (0.003 inch) thinner that the selective slinger used with the **O** etched drive pinion.

If the original gear set is being re-used, measure the original baffle and selective slinger. If either the baffle or selective slinger needs to be replaced, use a new one of the exact same thickness.

If a new gear set is used, notice the plus +, minus -, or zero **O** etching on both the original and the new drive pinion and adjust the thickness of the new selective oil linger according to the charts shown below.

For example: If the original pinion is etched **+4 (m+10)** and the new pinion is etched **O**, then the new selective slinger is 0.08mm (0.004 inch) thicker that the original selective oil slinger.

If the original pinion is etched **O** and the new pinion is etched **+3 (m+8)**, the new selective slinger should be 0.08mm (0.003 inch) thinner than the original slinger.

1. Install the oil baffle in the inner nearing cup bore in the carrier.
2. Install inner and outer pinion cups with Draw Bar, T75T-1176-A and Inner Bearing Cup Replacer, T60K-4616-A and Outer Bearing Cap Replacer, T71P-4616-A or equivalents.

➡ Prior to installing pinion bearing cups into aluminum or magnesium housings, an appropriate dry graphite lubricant should be applied to the bearing cup bore to prevent metal particles from being picked up as the cup is pressed into the bore.

3. Install the original oil slinger and rear bearing to Pinion Model, 49 8531 565.

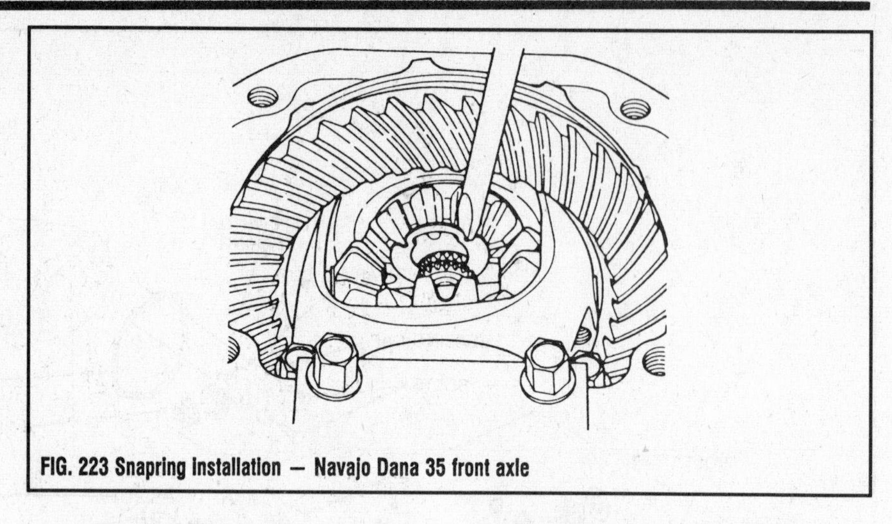

FIG. 223 Snapring installation — Navajo Dana 35 front axle

4. Install collar B, 49 8531 568, and O-ring to the Pinion Model and insert them to the axle housing.
5. Install collar, A, 49 8531 567, yoke, and washer and tighten the Pinion Model Nut to the extent that the yoke can still be turned by hand.
6. Put the Gauge Block, 49 UN27 001 on the Pinion Model.
7. Place the Pinion Height Gauge Body, 49 0727 570 on a surface plate and set the dial indicator to zero.
8. Place the Pinion Height Gauge Body atop of the Gauge Block.
9. Place the feeler of the dial indicator so that it contacts where the side bearing is installed in the housing. Measure the lowest point on the left and right sides of the housing.
10. Add the two (left and right) values obtained, and divide the total by 2. 11. If not within specification, adjust the pinion height by using a selective oil slinger.

➡ If the service pinion gear is marked with a plus (+) reading, this amount must be subtracted from the thickness dimension obtained in Step 10 (Example: +2[+0.002]).

11. If the service pinion gear is marked with a minus – reading, this amount must be added to the thickness dimension obtained in Step 10 (Example: -2[0.002]).

In addition, you must use the exact same new inner pinion bearing that was used in the previous steps.

12. Measure oil slinger with a micrometer to verify the slinger size. Place the oil slinger on the pinion and press on the bearing using Attachment C 49 f401 337A and Body 49 F401 331 (or equivalents).
13. Lubricate the ends of outer pinion bearing rollers with NLGI No. 2 (Lithium Base) Grease.

DRIVE PINION PRELOAD CHECK AND FINAL DEPTH CHECK

1. Install the pinion into the carrier.
2. Install a new collapsible spacer.

CAUTION

Never reuse a collapsible spacer. Upon removal, always discard the old spacer and install the new spacer for assembly.

3. Assemble the outer pinion bearing cone and thrust washer.
4. Coat the oil seal with API GL-5 90 lubricant. Install the drive pinion oil seal with Pinion Oil Seal Replacer T79P-4676-A, or equivalent. After installation, make sure the garter spring did not pop off. If the garter spring pops off, remove and replace the seal.
5. Install the yoke with Companion Flange Replacer T85T-4851-AH, or equivalent. Install the washer and nut and tighten the nut to 271 Nm (200 ft. lbs.). Check torque required to rotate the pinion which should be 1.7-2.8 Nm (15-25 inch lbs.). If torque required to rotate pinion is low, tighten nut further in small increments until proper torque to rotate pinion is obtained.
6. If the reading is more than 2.8 Nm (25 inch lbs.), the collapsible spacer must be replaced.

CAUTION

Never tighten the pinion nut more than 475 Nm (350 ft. lbs.), or the collapsible spacer will be compressed too far.

DIFFERENTIAL CASE DISASSEMBLY

1. Remove retainer bolts and remove ring gear from carrier.

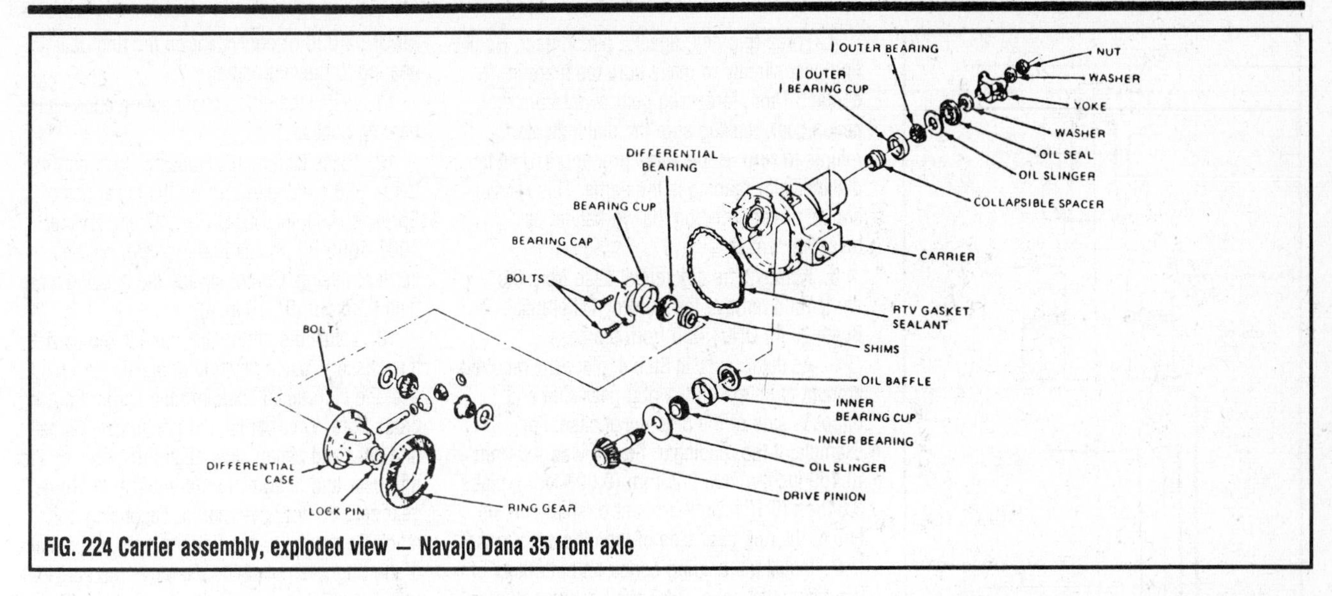

FIG. 224 Carrier assembly, exploded view — Navajo Dana 35 front axle

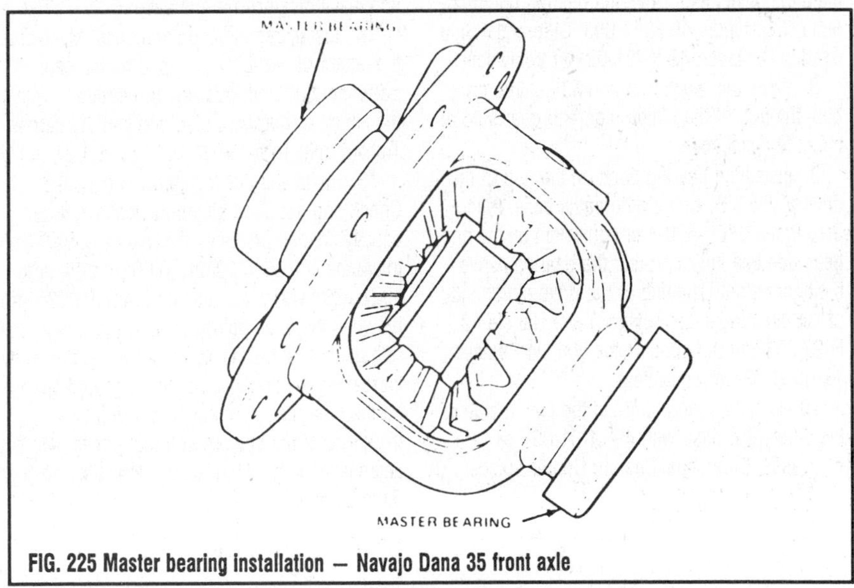

FIG. 225 Master bearing installation — Navajo Dana 35 front axle

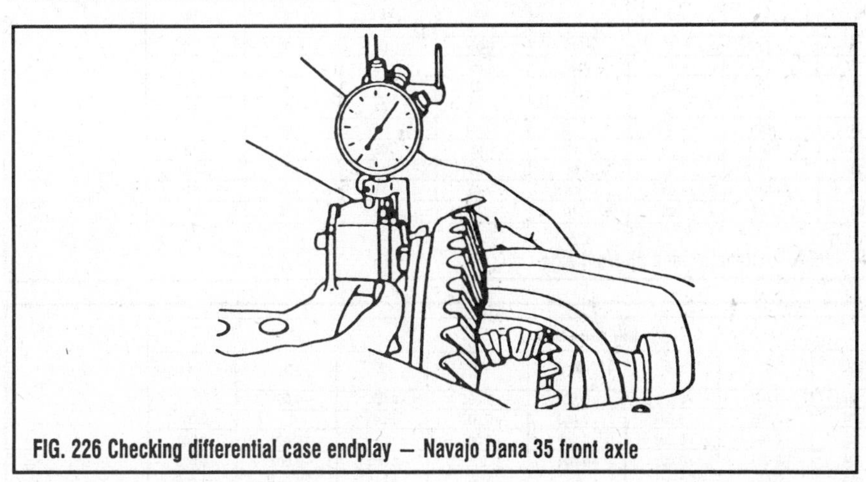
FIG. 226 Checking differential case endplay — Navajo Dana 35 front axle

2. Place differential case in vise and drive out lock pin that retains the pinion mate shaft to case.

3. Remove pinion mate shaft with a drift.

4. Rotate the pinion mate gears and side gears until the pinion mate gears turn to the windows of the case. Remove pinion mate gears and spherical washers.

5. Lift side gears and thrust washers from case.

ASSEMBLY

1. Inspect components for wear and replace as required.

➡ Always replace gears as a complete set. Do not mix new gears with old gears, as this may cause uneven wear and short gear life.

2. Apply API GL-5 90 lubricant to side gear thrust washers, hub and thrust face of side gears. Lubricate pinion mate gears and spherical washer with API GL-5 90 lubricant.

3. Hold side gears on place in case with one hand and install pinion mate gears and spherical washers with other hand. Rotate the side gears and pinion mate gears until the holes in the washers and pinion mate gears line up exactly with the holes in the case.

4. Insert the pinion mate shift in the case. Make sure that lock pin hole in the shaft lines up with the lock pin holes in the case.

5. Insert lock pin. Peen some metal of the case over the pin to lock it in place.

6. Install the ring gear and retainer bolts. Tighten to 95-122 Nm (70-90 ft. lbs.).

DIFFERENTIAL CASE ASSEMBLY TO CARRIER

1. Assemble ring gear to differential case. Use new bolts and tighten alternately and evenly to 93-122 Nm (70-90 ft. lbs.).

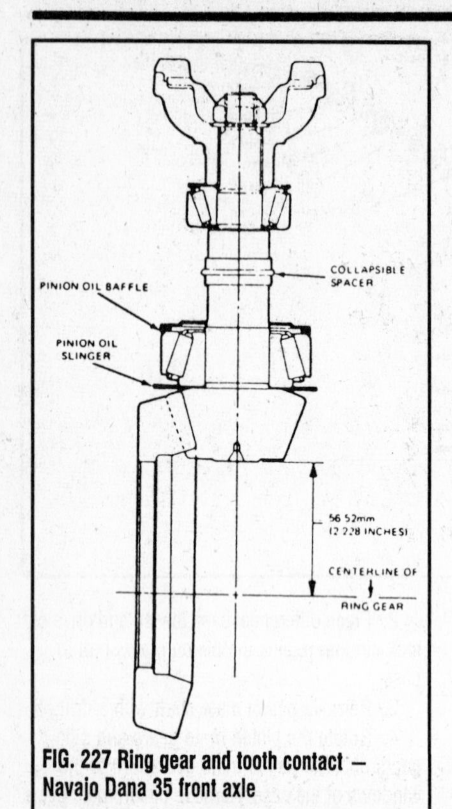

FIG. 227 Ring gear and tooth contact — Navajo Dana 35 front axle

2. Place the differential case into position in the carrier. (Dummy Differential Bearings 49 UN01 030 or equivalent should be installed.)

3. Force the differential case away from the drive pinion gear, until it is completely seated against the cross bore face of the carrier. Position a dial indicator so the indicator tip rests on a ring gear bolt head, or a flat machined surface. Zero the dial indicator.

4. Force ring gear against pinion gear. Rock ring gear slightly to make sure teeth are in contact. Then, force ring gear away from drive pinion gear, making sure the dial indicator returns to zero. Repeat this procedure, until the dial indicator reading is the same. This reading should be recorded on the worksheet as measurement **B**.

5. Remove the differential case from the carrier and remove the Dummy Differential Bearings 49 UN01 030 from the case.

6. As determined in Step 4, place the required amount of shims on the ring gear side and opposite side of the differential case. For example: If the reading in Step 4 was 4.04mm (0.159 inch) minus 0.20mm (0.008 inch), place 3.84mm (0.151 inch) amount of shims on the hub of the ring gear side of the differential case.

7. Install the bearing cones on both hubs of the differential case. Drive the bearing onto the hub using Handle 49 F027 003, Differential Side Bearing Replacer, 49 UN01 031 or equivalent.

8. Place the required amount of shims on both the hub of the pinion side and gear side of the differential case.

9. Install the bearing cone on the hub of the drive pinion side of the differential case. Place Step Plate, D80L-630-4 or equivalent on the ring gear side bearing to protect the bearing. Drive the bearing onto the hub of the drive pinion side of the differential case using Driver Handle 49 F027 003 and Differential Side Bearing Replacer, 49 UN01 031 or equivalent.

10. Install bearing cone on the pinion side of the differential case with 49 UN01 031 or equivalent, Differential Bearing Cone Replacer, 49 UN01 036 or equivalent on the ring gear nearing to prevent damage.

11. Install the differential bearing cups on the bearing cones.

12. Place Differential Housing Spreader, 49 UN01 026 (or equivalent) on the case, using Spreader Adapters 49 UN01 027 and Spacer T80T-4000-B2. Install Dial Indicator on the carrier housing. Do not spread the housing more than 0.25mm (0.010 inch).

13. Install the differential case in the carrier. If necessary, use a rawhide or plastic hammer to seat the differential case into the carrier housing cross bore. With partial and nonhunting/partial ring gear and pinion sets, align the marks on the ring gear and drive pinion (if applicable. Some gear sets do not have marks, depending upon ratio). Be careful to not nick the teeth of the teeth of the ring gear or pinion. Remove the spreader and dial indicator from the case.

14. Install bearing caps and bolts. Make sure the letters or numbers stamped on the caps correspond in both position and direction with the letters or numbers stamped into the carrier. Tighten bolts to 64-91 Nm (47-67 ft. lbs.)

15. Install the dial indicator on the case. Check ring gear and pinion backlash at three equally spaced points on the ring gear. Backlash tolerance is 0.13-0.20mm (0.005-0.008 inch) and cannot vary more than 0.08mm (0.003 inch) between the three points. If backlash is high, the ring gear must be moved closer to the pinion by increasing the thickness of the outboard spacer on the ring gear side and decreasing the thickness of the spacer on the opposite side by an equal amount. If backlash is low, the ring gear must be moved away from the pinion by

Old Pinion Marking	New Pinion Marking								
	-10	-8	-5	-3	0	+3	+5	+8	+10
+10	+.20	+.18	+.15	+.13	+.10	+.08	+.05	+.03	0
+8	+.18	+.15	+.13	+.10	+.08	+.05	+.03	0	-.03
+5	+.15	+.13	+.10	+.08	+.05	+.03	0	-.03	-.05
+3	+.13	+.10	+.08	+.05	+.03	0	-.03	-.05	-.08
0	+.10	+.08	+.05	+.03	0	-.03	-.05	-.08	-.10
-3	+.08	+.05	+.03	0	-.03	-.05	-.08	-.10	-.13
-5	+.05	+.03	0	-.03	-.05	-.08	-.10	-.13	-.15
-8	+.03	0	-.03	-.05	-.08	-.10	-.13	-.15	-.18
-10	0	-.03	-.05	-.08	-.10	-.13	-.15	-.18	-.20

FIG. 228 Shim adjustment for pinion replacement — metric — Navajo Dana 35 front axle

Old Pinion Marking	New Pinion Marking								
	-4	-3	-2	-1	0	+1	+2	+3	+4
+4	+0.008	+0.007	+0.006	+0.005	+0.004	+0.003	+0.002	+0.001	0
+3	+0.007	+0.006	+0.005	+0.004	+0.003	+0.002	+0.001	0	-0.001
+2	+0.006	+0.005	+0.004	+0.003	+0.002	+0.001	0	-0.001	-0.002
+1	+0.005	+0.004	+0.003	+0.002	+0.001	0	-0.001	-0.002	-0.003
0	+0.004	+0.003	+0.002	+0.001	0	-0.001	-0.002	-0.003	-0.004
-1	+0.003	+0.002	+0.001	0	-0.001	-0.002	-0.003	-0.004	-0.005
-2	+0.002	+0.001	0	-0.001	-0.002	-0.003	-0.004	-0.005	-0.006
-3	+0.001	0	-0.001	-0.002	-0.003	-0.004	-0.005	-0.006	-0.007
-4	0	-0.001	-0.002	-0.003	-0.004	-0.005	-0.006	-0.007	-0.008

FIG. 229 Shim adjustment for pinion replacement — U.S. — Navajo Dana 35 front axle

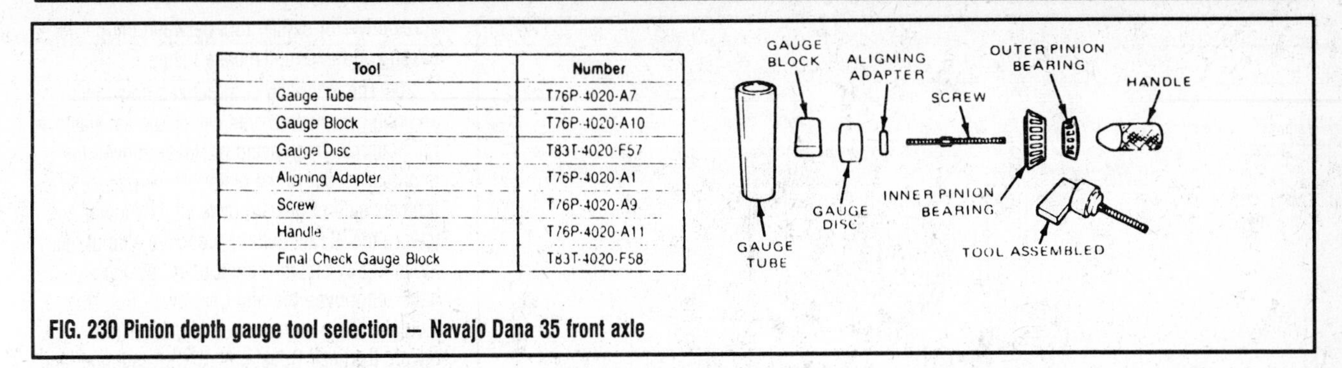

Tool	Number
Gauge Tube	T76P-4020-A7
Gauge Block	T76P-4020-A10
Gauge Disc	T83T-4020-F57
Aligning Adapter	T76P-4020-A1
Screw	T76P-4020-A9
Handle	T76P-4020-A11
Final Check Gauge Block	T83T-4020-F58

FIG. 230 Pinion depth gauge tool selection — Navajo Dana 35 front axle

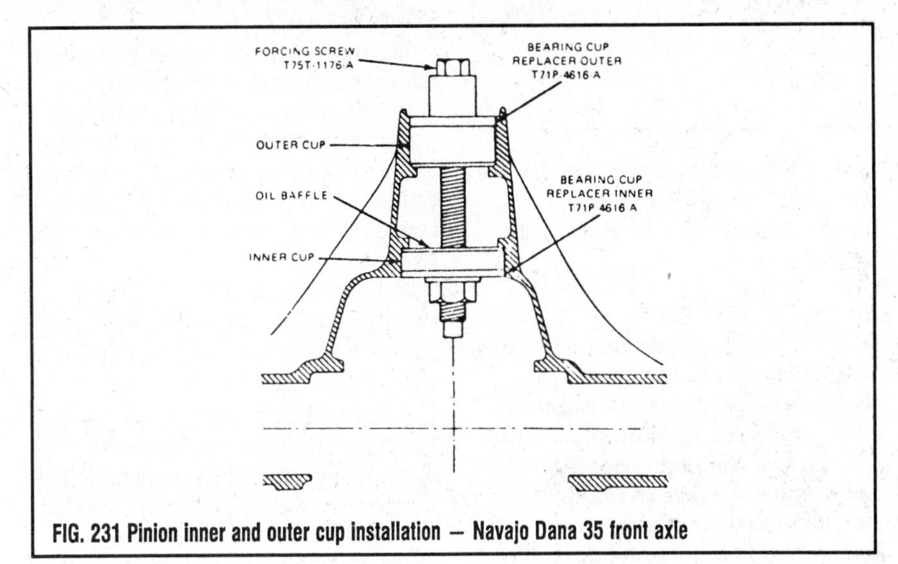

FIG. 231 Pinion inner and outer cup installation — Navajo Dana 35 front axle

decreasing the thickness of the outboard spacer on the ring gear side and decreasing the thickness of the spacer on the opposite side by an equal amount.

16. Ring gear and pinion tooth pattern interpretation follows.

17. The final pinion position will be verified by using the GEAR CONTACT PATTERN METHOD described as follows.

18. The TOE of the gear tooth is the portion of the tooth surface at the end towards the center. The HEEL of the gear tooth is the portion of the tooth surface at the outer end. The TOP LAND of a gear tooth is the surface for the top of the tooth. Every gear has a characteristic pattern. The illustrations show typical pattern only, and explains how patterns shift as gear location is changed. When making pinion position changes,

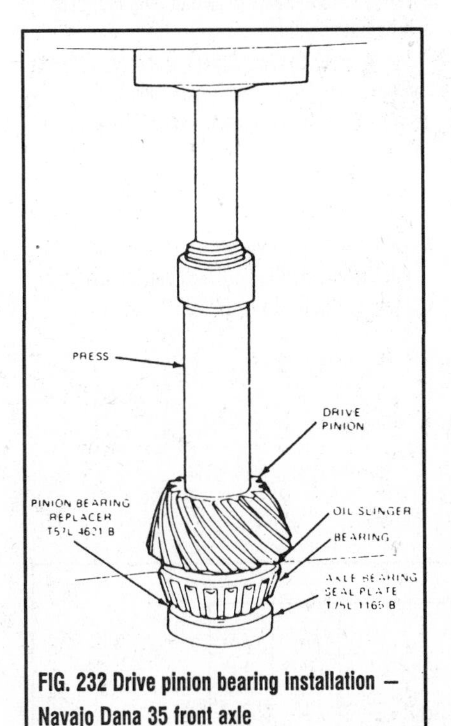

FIG. 232 Drive pinion bearing installation — Navajo Dana 35 front axle

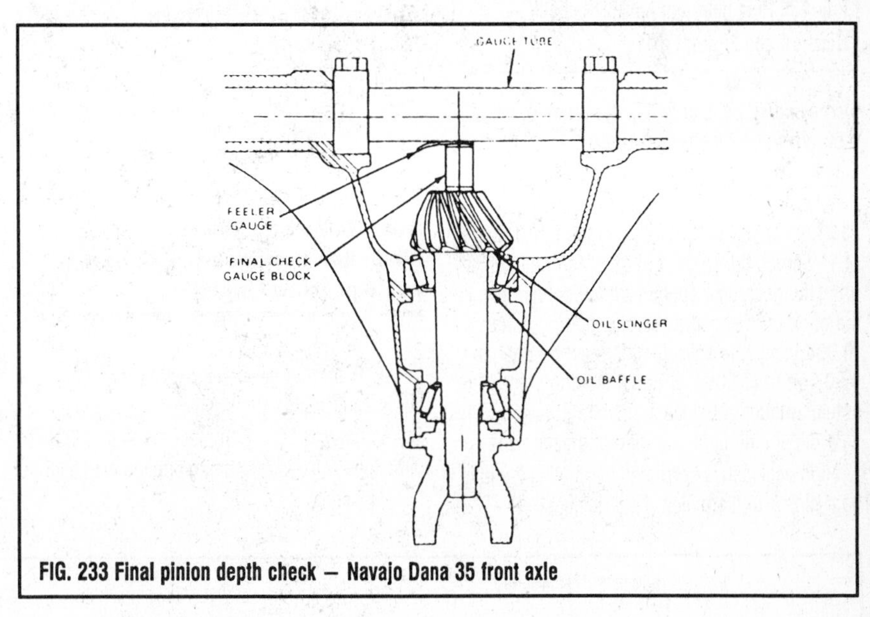

FIG. 233 Final pinion depth check — Navajo Dana 35 front axle

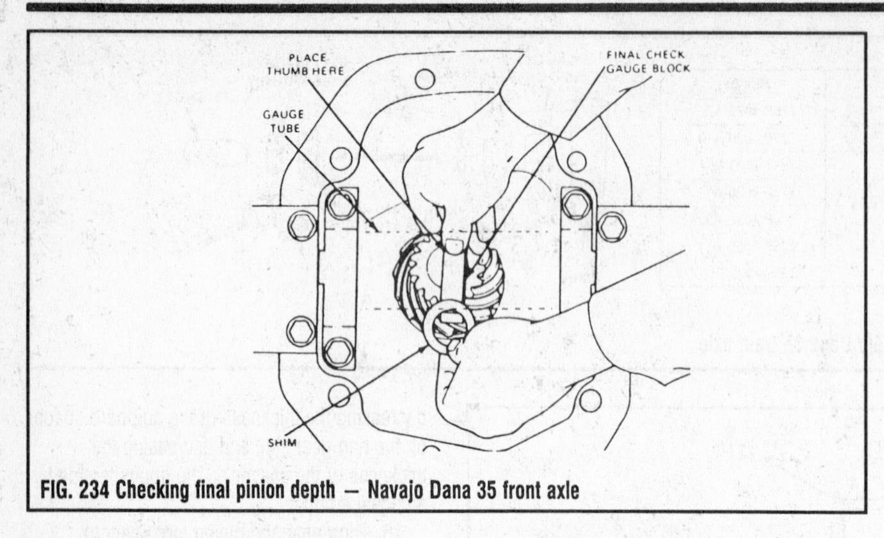

FIG. 234 Checking final pinion depth — Navajo Dana 35 front axle

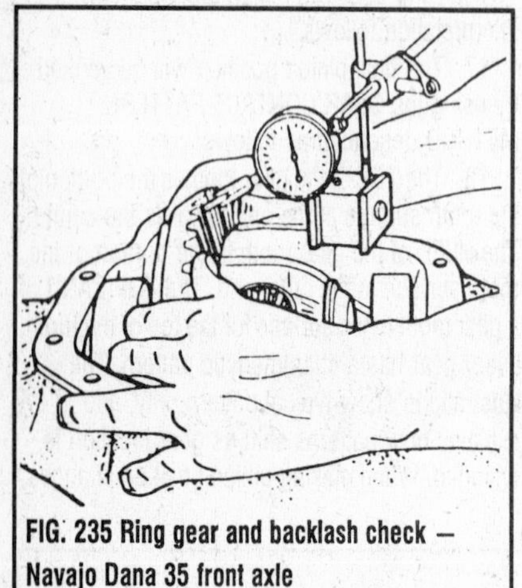
FIG. 235 Ring gear and backlash check — Navajo Dana 35 front axle

shims should be changed in the range of 0.05mm (0.002 inch) to 0.10mm (0.004 inch) until correct pattern has been obtained.

When a change in backlash is required, backlash shims should be changed in the range of 1½ times the amount of backlash required to bring the gears into specification. For example, if the backlash needed to be changed by 0.10mm (0.004 inch), the shim pack should be changed by 0.15mm (0.006 inch) as a starting point. The actual amount of backlash change obtained will vary depending upon the ratio and gear size.

High backlash is corrected by moving the ring gear closer to the pinion. Low backlash is corrected by moving the ring gear away from the pinion. These corrections are made by increasing or decreasing the thickness of the outboard spacers.

➡ When making changes, note that two variables are involved. Example: If you have the backlash set correctly to specifications and you change the pinion position shim, you may have to readjust the backlash to the correct specification before checking the pattern. Refer to pattern interpretation.

CAUTION

Gear teeth may have sharp edges. When handling gears, use care to avoid personal injury!

19. Paint ring gear teeth with a marking compound to both the drive and coast side. Rotate ring gear one complete revolution in both directions while load is being applied with a large screwdriver or similar tool between the carrier casting and differential case flange.

20. The following summarizes how pinion and ring gear movements will obtain satisfactory roll patterns: Decreasing backlash moves the ring gear closer to the pinion. Drive pattern (convex side of gear) moves slightly lower and toward toe. Coast pattern (concave side of gear) movers lower toward the toe. Increasing backlash moves the ring gear away from the pinion. Drive pattern moves slightly higher toward the heel. Coast pattern moves higher and towards the heel.

Thicker pinion position shim with the backlash constant moves the pinion closer to the ring gear. Drive pattern moves deeper on the tooth (flank contact) and slightly toward the toe. Coast pattern moves deeper on the tooth and toward the heel. Thinner pinion position shim with the backlash constant moves the pinion further from the ring gear.

Drive pattern moves toward the top of the tooth (face contact) and toward the heel. Coast pattern moves toward the top of the tooth and slightly toward the toe.

21. Apply a bead 3-6mm (⅛-¼ in.) high and 3-6mm (¼-½ in.) wide of an appropriate silicone rubber sealant on the mating surfaces of the carrier mounting face support arm. Allow one hour curing time after the axle carrier is assembled to the axle before adding lubricant and operating vehicle.

22. Mount the differential assembly to the left hand axle arm, using two guide pins being careful not to smear gasket sealant. Install and tighten bolts to 54-68 Nm (40-50 ft. lbs.) Tighten one bolt and then tighten the bolt directly opposite it. Tighten the rest of the bolts in either a clockwise or counterclockwise direction.

23. Assemble the carrier shear bolt and nut. Tighten to 102-129 Nm (75-95 ft. lbs.).

TORQUE SPECIFICATIONS

Description	Torque		Description	Torque	
	N-m	Ft-Lbs		N-m	Ft-Lbs
Axle Pivot Bolt	163-203	120-150	Carrier Shear Bolt	102-129	75-95
Axle Pivot Bracket to Frame Nut	95-124	70-92	Front Driveshaft U-Bolt Nuts	11-20	8-15
Axle Stud	211-277	155-205	Lower Shock Absorber to Radius Arm Nut	57-97	42-72
Ball Joint Nut — Lower	109	80	Lower Spring Seat Nut	95-135	70-100
Ball Joint Nut — Upper	150	110	Radius Arm Bracket Front Bolt	37-50	27-37
Bearing Cap Bolts	48-54	35-40	Radius Arm Bracket Lower Bolt	217-298	160-220
Carrier to Axle Arm Bolts	54-68	40-50	Ring Gear Bolts	68-81	50-60

SPECIAL SERVICE TOOLS

Number	Description	Number	Description
D80L-100-A	Blind Hole Puller Set	T80T-4000-W	Driver Handle
T50T-100-A	Impact Slide Hammer	TOOL-4000-E	Differential Housing Spreader
T57L-500-B	B nch Mounted Holding Fixture	T76P-4020-A1	Pinion Depth Gauge Aligning Adapter
D80L-630-5	Step Plate Adapter	T76P-4020-A10	Gauge Block
T77F-1102-A	Bearing Cup Puller	T76P-4020-A11	Handle
T75L-1165-B	Axle Bearing/Seal Plate	T76P-4020-A7	Gauge Tube 2.563 O.D.
T83T-1175-B	Hub Seal Replacer	T76P-4020-A9	Screw
TOOL-1175-AC	Seal Remover	T83T-4020-F57	Pinion Depth Gauge Disc
T75T-1176-A	Threaded Drawbar	T83T-4020-F58	Final Check Gauge Block
D84T-1197-A	Four-Prong Spindle Nut Spanner Wrench	D78P-4201-B	Dial Indicator Magnetic Base
D78P-1225-B	Two Jaw Bearing Cup Puller	TOOL-4201-C	Dial Indicator with Bracketry
T83T-1244-A	Needle Bearing Replacer	D81L-4220-A	Universal Bearing Puller
T82T-3006-A1	Bushing Replacer	T73T-4222-B	Differential Bearing Cone Replacer
T83T-3006-A	Bushing Shell Flaring Tool	T83T-4222-A	Dummy Bearings
D79T-3010-BE	Forcing Screw (Part of D79T-3010-A)	T71P-4616-A	Pinion Bearing Cups Replacer
T71T-3010-R	Pinion Seal Replacer	T53T-4621-C	Pinion Bearing Cone Replacer
T80T-3010-A	Part of 4WD Ball Joint Set	T57L-4621-B	Pinion Bearing Cone Replacer
T80T-3010-A3	Part of 4WS Ball Joint Set	T83T-4628-A	Pinion Bearing Cup Driver
T83T-3010-A	Bench Mount/Housing Spreader Adapter	T74P-4635-C	C-Frame
T83T-3050-A	Ball Joint Tool Adapter	T65L-4851-B	Companion Flange Remover
T83T-3123-A	Spindle Bearing Seal Replacer	T78P-4851-A	Companion Flange Holder
T83T-3132-A	Spindle/Axle Seal Replacer	T83T-4851-A	Companion Flange Replacer
T64P-3590-F	Pitman Arm Remover	T78P-5638-A1	Forcing Screw
T80T-4000-B	Differential Spreader Adapters	T78P-5638-A4	Receiving Cup
T80T-4000-G	Companion Flange Replacer	T80T-5638-A2	Pivot Bushing Remover
T80T-4000-J	Differential Bearing Cone Replacer	T63P-9171-A	Keystone Clamp Pliers

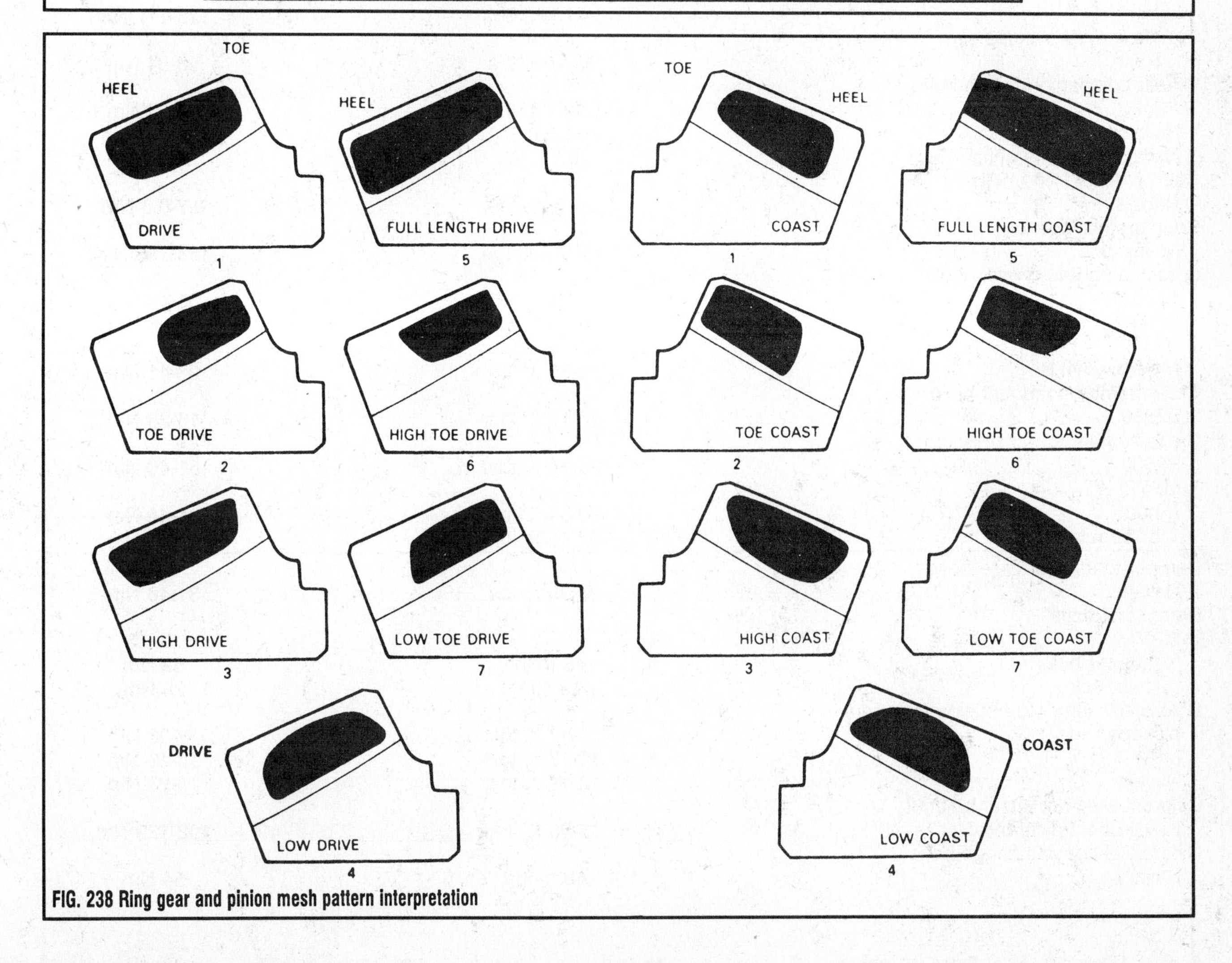

FIG. 238 Ring gear and pinion mesh pattern interpretation

TORQUE SPECIFICATIONS

Component	U.S.	Metric
Actuator rod locknut		
Pickup & MPV	8.7-12 ft. lbs.	12-16 Nm
Backup lamp switch bolt		
Navajo	18-26 ft. lbs.	25-35 Nm
Bearing cover bolts		
pickups	20 ft. lbs.	27 Nm
MPV	20 ft. lbs.	27 Nm
Bottom cover bolts		
MPV	95 inch lbs.	11 Nm
Cam plate bolts		
manual shift Borg-Wagner		
larger bolt	70-90 ft. lbs.	95-122 Nm
smaller bolt	31-42 ft. lbs.	42-57 Nm
Center bearing mount bolt	27-39 ft. lbs.	37-53 Nm
Center bearing support assembly nuts		
Navajo & 4WD pickups	116-130 ft. lbs.	158-177 Nm
Center bearing cover bolts		
Navajo	14-19 ft. lbs.	19-26 Nm
Clutch pressure plate		
pickups & MPV	13-20 ft. lbs.	18-27 Nm
Navajo	15-25 ft. lbs.	20-34 Nm
Clutch slave cylinder bolts		
B2200	12-17 ft. lbs.	16-23 Nm
Companion flange nuts		
4WD pickups		
front	94-130 ft. lbs.	128-177 Nm
2WD & 4WD pickups		
Rear	39-47 ft. lbs.	53-64 Nm
Rear companion flange bolts		
MPV	39-47 ft. lbs.	53-64 Nm
Navajo rear differential	70-95 ft. lbs.	95-129 Nm
Navajo front differential	200 ft. lbs.	272 Nm
Counter lever fixing bolts		
Navajo	6-7 inch lbs.	0.7-0.8 Nm
Countershaft locknut		
Navajo	94-144 ft. lbs.	128-196 Nm
Crossmember-to-chassis bolts		
B2200	23-34 ft. lbs.	31-46 Nm
B2600	23-34 ft. lbs.	31-46 Nm
MPV	32-45 ft. lbs.	44-61 Nm
Navajo w/A4LD	20-30 ft. lbs.	27-41 Nm
Crossmember-to-mount bolts		
B2200	12-17 ft. lbs.	16-23 Nm
Crossmember-to-transmission		
B2600	23-34 ft. lbs.	31-46 Nm
MPV		
nuts	23-34 ft. lbs.	31-46 Nm
bolts/nuts	32-45 ft. lbs.	44-61 Nm
Damper-to-transfer case bolts		
Navajo	25-35 ft. lbs.	31-46 Nm
Detent ball bolts		
MPV		
2 upper bolts	43 ft. lbs.	58 Nm
lower bolt	19 ft.lbs.	26 Nm
Differential carrier-to-housing fasteners		
pickups	12-17 ft. lbs.	16-23 Nm
MPV	12-17 ft. lbs.	16-23 Nm
Navajo	12-17 ft. lbs.	16-23 Nm
Differential carrier shear bolt/nut		
Navajo front differential	75-95 ft. lbs.	102-129 Nm
Differential housing flange bolts		
Navajo	40 ft. lbs.	54 Nm

TORQUE SPECIFICATIONS

Component	U.S.	Metric
Differential assembly mounting bolts		
Navajo front differential	40-50 ft. lbs.	54-68 Nm
Differential pinion shaft bolts		
Navajo	15-22 ft. lbs.	20-30 Nm
Differential side bearing caps		
2WD B2200, 4WD B2600 front axle	27-38 ft. lbs.	37-52 Nm
2WD & 4WD B2600 rear axle	41-59 ft. lbs.	56-80 Nm
MPV	51-61 ft. lbs.	69-83 Nm
Navajo		
Rear	70-85 ft. lbs.	95-116 Nm
Front	47-67 ft. lbs.	64-91 Nm
Driveshaft mounting bolt		
MPV w/R4AX-EL	36-43 ft. lbs.	49-58 Nm
Exhaust pipe-to-manifold nuts		
B2200	30-41 ft. lbs.	41-56 Nm
Exhaust pipe-to-transmission bracket bolt		
B2200	13-20 ft. lbs.	18-27 Nm
Extension housing bolts		
pickups w/2WD	34 ft. lbs.	46 Nm
MPV	35 ft. lbs.	47 Nm
Navajo	24-34 ft. lbs.	33-46 Nm
5th/reverse cam lockout plate bolts		
Navajo	6-7 ft. lbs.	8-10 Nm
5th/reverse shift rail fixing bolt		
Navajo	16-22 ft. lbs.	22-30 Nm
Front drive shaft-to-front output shaft yoke bolts		
Navajo	8-15 ft. lbs.	11-20 Nm
Front driveshaft-to-transfer case output shaft yoke bolt		
Navajo	12-16 ft. lbs.	16-22 Nm
Gusset plate bolts		
B2200	27-38 ft. lbs.	37-52 Nm
Height sensor connecting bolt		
MPV		
standard models	19 ft. lbs.	26 Nm
w/towing package	104 inch lbs.	12 Nm
Hub-to-axle bolts		
Navajo	25 ft. lbs.	34 Nm
Inner locknut-to-seat front axle bearings		
Navajo	35 ft. lbs.	48 Nm
Inner adjusting nut		
Navajo front axle bearings	35 ft. lbs.	48 Nm
Input shaft bearing cover bolts		
MPV	19 ft. lbs.	26 Nm
Lock plate bolts		
pickups	14-19 ft. lbs.	19-26 Nm
Mainshaft locknut		
pickups	174 ft. lbs.	237 Nm
MPV	174 ft. lbs.	237 Nm
Master cylinder bolts/nuts		
pickups	12-17 ft. lbs.	16-23 Nm
MPV	12-17 ft. lbs.	17-23 Nm
Navajo	8-12 ft. lbs.	11-17 Nm
Oil guide bolts		
MPV	95 inch lbs.	11 Nm
Oil passage		
MPV	95 inch lbs.	11 Nm
Navajo	6-7 ft. lbs.	8-10 Nm
Output shaft locknut		
Navajo	160-200 ft. lbs.	218-272 Nm

TORQUE SPECIFICATIONS

Component	U.S.	Metric
Pinion bearing preload		
Navajo rear axle		
new bearings	9-14 inch lbs.	12-19 Nm
old bearings	16-29 inch lbs.	22-39 Nm
Pinion locknut		
MPV	94-210 ft. lbs.	128-286 Nm
Navajo	160 ft. lbs.	218 Nm
Rear axle cover bolts		
Navajo	25-35 ft. lbs.	34-48 Nm
Rear driveshaft-to-rear output shaft yoke bolts		
Navajo	20-28 ft. lbs.	27-38 Nm
Rear driveshaft-to-transfer case output shaft yoke bolt		
Navajo	61-87 ft. lbs.	83-118 Nm
Rear side frame bolts		
Navajo	85 ft. lbs.	116 Nm
Reverse idler gear shaft boss bolt		
MPV	122 inch lbs.	14 Nm
Reverse idler gear fixing bolt		
Navajo	58-86 ft. lbs.	79-117 Nm
Ring gear-to-differential assembly bolts		
pickups and MPV	51-61 ft. lbs.	69-83 Nm
Navajo rear axle	100-120 ft. lbs.	136-163 Nm
Navajo front differential	70-90 ft. lbs.	95-122 Nm
Shifter boot & insulator plate bolts		
B2600	25-37 ft. lbs.	34-50 Nm
Shift control case bolts		
pickups	22 ft. lbs.	30 Nm
Shift control lever-to-transfer case bolts		
MPV	22 ft. lbs.	30 Nm
Shift lever bolts		
B2200	69-95 inch lbs.	8-11 Nm
B2600	25-37 ft. lbs.	34-50 Nm
Navajo	20-27 ft. lbs.	27-34 Nm
Shift handle locknuts		
Navajo	95 inch lbs.	11 Nm
Skid plate bolts/nuts		
Navajo	15-20 ft. lbs.	20-27 Nm
Slave cylinder bolts		
pickups	12-17 ft. lbs.	16-23 Nm
MPV	12-17 ft. lbs.	16-23 Nm
Navajo	13-19 ft. lbs.	18-26 Nm
Speedometer drive gear bolt		
Navajo	20-25 ft. lbs.	27-34 Nm
pickups	69-95 inch lbs.	8-11 Nm
Starter motor nuts		
Navajo	15-20 ft. lbs.	20-27 Nm
Subframe bolts		
Navajo		
A	76 ft. lbs.	103 Nm
B	59 ft. lbs.	80 Nm
Top cover retaining bolts		
Navajo	12-16 ft. lbs.	16-22 Nm
Torque converter & drive plate bolts		
pickups	25-36 ft. lbs.	34-49 Nm
MPV w/R4AX-EL	27-40 ft. lbs.	37-54 Nm
Navajo w/A4LD	20-34 ft. lbs.	27-46 Nm
Transfer case bolts		
pickups	22 ft. lbs.	30 Nm
MPV	27-40 ft. lbs.	37-54 Nm
Navajo	26-43 ft. lbs.	35-58 Nm

TORQUE SPECIFICATIONS

Component	U.S.	Metric
Transfer case chain cover bolts		
pickups	14-19 ft. lbs.	19-26 Nm
Transfer case drain plug		
Navajo	14-22 ft. lbs.	19-30 Nm
Transfer case fill plug		
Navajo	14-22 ft. lbs.	19-30 Nm
Transmission cooler lines bolts		
MPV w/R4AX-EL	17-26 ft. lbs.	23-35 Nm
Transmission drain plug		
Navajo	29-43 ft. lbs.	39-58 Nm
Transmission-to-engine bolts		
B2200, B2600		
w/MT	51-65 ft. lbs.	69-88 Nm
2WD w/AT, exc. N4A-HL	23-34 ft. lbs.	31-46 Nm
4WD pickup w/R4AX-EL	27-38 ft. lbs.	37-52 Nm
N4A-HL	27-38 ft. lbs.	37-52 Nm
MPV w/3.0L	27-38 ft. lbs.	37-52 Nm
MPV w/2.6L	51-65 ft. lbs.	69-88 Nm
MPV w/N4A-HL	23-34 ft. lbs.	31-46 Nm
Navajo	28-38 ft. lbs.	38-52 Nm
Transmission-to-chassis bolts		
4WD pickup w/R4AX-EL	23-34 ft. lbs.	31-46 Nm
Transmission mount bolts		
2WD pickups w/N4A-HL	7.2-17 ft. lbs.	10-23 Nm
MPV w/R4AX-EL	27-38 ft. lbs.	37-52 Nm
Transmission mount bracket bolt		
2WD pickup w/N4A-HL	23-34 ft. lbs.	31-46 Nm
Transmission rear crossmember mount bolts		
MPV w/R4AX-EL	32-45 ft. lbs.	44-61 Nm
Navajo w/A4LD	60-80 ft. lbs.	82-109 Nm
Trunion bolt		
Navajo	12-23 ft. lbs.	16-31 Nm
U-joint assembly bolts		
pickups & Navajo	10-15 ft. lbs.	14-20 Nm
Double cardan U-joint bolts		
Navajo & 4WD pickups	12-16 ft. lbs.	16-22 Nm
U-joint end of driveshaft-to-rear axle		
Navajo & 4WD pickups	61-87 ft. lbs.	83-118 Nm
Vacuum diaphragm bolt		
Navajo A4LD transmission	80-106 inch lbs.	9-12 Nm

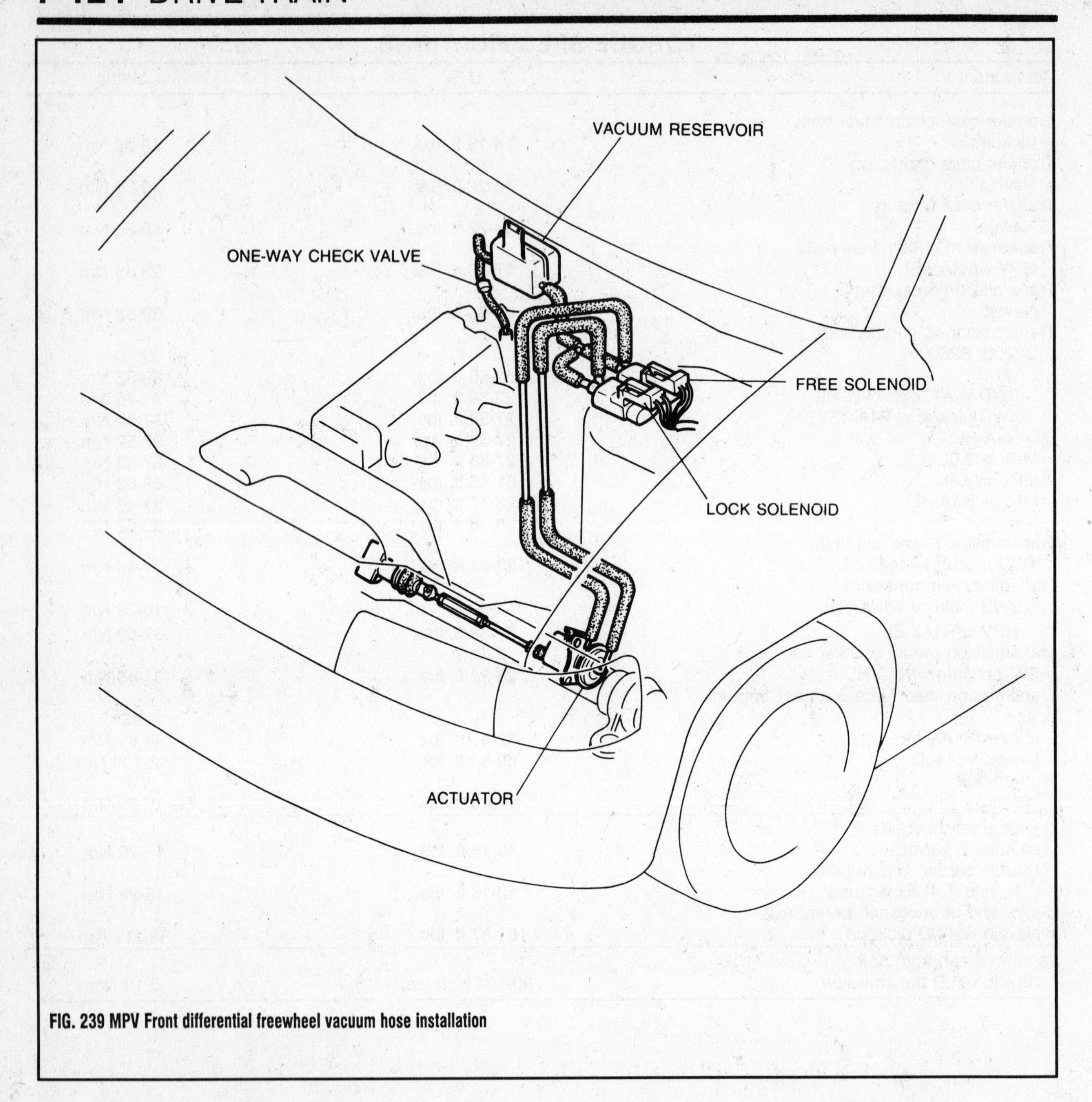

FIG. 239 MPV Front differential freewheel vacuum hose installation

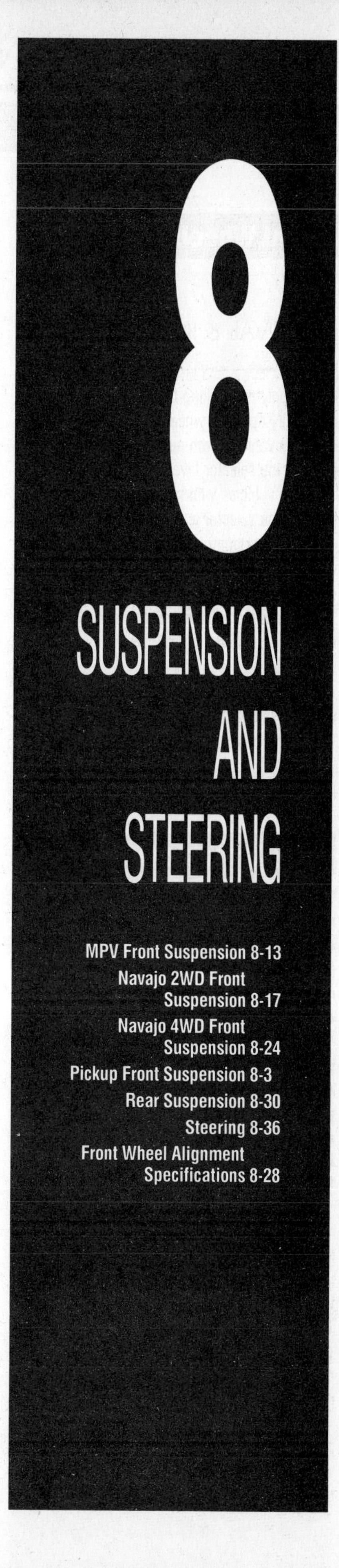

8 SUSPENSION AND STEERING

WHEELS

Front Wheels

REMOVAL & INSTALLATION

1. Apply the parking brake. Block the diagonally opposite wheel.
2. On vehicles with automatic transmission position the selector lever in **PARK**.
3. On vehicles with manual transmission position the selector lever in **NEUTRAL**.
4. As necessary, remove the hubcap or wheel cover. Loosen the lug nuts, but do not remove them.
5. Raise the vehicle until the wheel and tire assembly clears the floor. Properly support the vehicle.
6. Remove the lug nuts. Remove the tire and wheel assembly from its mounting.

To install:

7. Position the wheel and tire assembly on its mounting.

**** CAUTION**

Whenever a wheel is installed be sure to remove any corrosion, dirt or foreign material that may be present on the mounting surfaces of the hub, drum or rotor that contacts the wheel.

Installing wheels without proper metal to metal contact at the wheel mounting surfaces can cause the wheel lug nuts to loosen and could allow the wheel to come off while the vehicle is in motion!

8. Install the lug nuts. Be sure that the cone end of the lug nut faces inward.
9. With the lug nuts loosely installed, turn the wheel until one nut is at the top of the bolt circle. Tighten the lug nut until snug.
10. In a criss cross manner tighten the remaining lug nuts until snug in order to minimize runout.
11. Lower the vehicle. Torque the lug nuts to: Pickups, non-styled wheels 65-87 ft. lbs. Styled wheels 87-108 ft. lbs. MPV, 65-87 ft. lbs. Navajo, 100 ft. lbs., in the proper sequence

**** CAUTION**

Tighten the wheel lug nuts to specification after about 500 miles of driving. Failure to do this could result in the wheel coming off while the vehicle is in motion possibly causing loss of vehicle control or collision.

INSPECTION

Replace wheels if they are bent, cracked, leaking air or heavily rusted or if the lug nuts often become loose. Do not use bent wheels that have been straightened or do not use inner tubes in leaking wheels. Do not replace wheels with used wheels. Wheels that have been straightened or are leaking air or are used may have structural damage and could fail without warning.

Front Wheel Lug Nut Studs

REMOVAL & INSTALLATION

1. Raise and support the vehicle safely.
2. Remove the tire and wheel assembly.
3. Remove the disc brake rotor. Be sure to properly support the brake caliper to avoid damage to the brake line hose.
4. Position the disc brake rotor in a press so that press ram pressure is not directly exerted on the disc brake rotor surface.
5. Using the proper press stock, press the lug stud from the disc brake rotor. Discard the lug stud. Remove the disc brake rotor from its mounting in the press.

To install:

6. Position a new lug stud in the disc brake rotor hole. Align the serrations of the new stud with the serration marks from the old lug stud.
7. Using a hammer tap the lug stud until the serrations on the stud are started in the hole. Be sure that the lug stud is not installed in an off centered position.
8. Reposition the disc brake rotor in the press so that the rotor is supported on the wheel mounting flange. Be sure to allow enough clearance for the stud to pass through the hole.
9. Do not apply ram pressure directly to the rotor surface. Using the proper press stock, press the lug stud in position until the stud is flush against the inner surface of the disc brake rotor hub.
10. Install the disc brake rotor. Reposition the brake caliper. Install the tire and wheel assembly. Lower the vehicle.

**** CAUTION**

Tighten the wheel lug nuts to specification after about 500 miles of driving. Failure to do this could result in the wheel coming off while the vehicle is in motion possibly causing loss of vehicle control or collision.

Rear Wheels

REMOVAL & INSTALLATION

1. Apply the parking brake. Block the diagonally opposite wheel.
2. On vehicles with automatic transmission position the selector lever in **PARK**.
3. On vehicles with manual transmission position the selector lever in **NEUTRAL**.
4. As necessary, remove the hubcap or wheel cover. Loosen the lug nuts, but do not remove them.
5. Raise the vehicle until the wheel and tire assembly clears the floor. Properly support the vehicle.
6. Remove the lug nuts. Remove the tire and wheel assembly from its mounting.

To install:

7. Position the wheel and tire assembly on its mounting.

✻✻ CAUTION

Whenever a wheel is installed be sure to remove any corrosion, dirt or foreign material that may be present on the mounting surfaces of the hub, drum or rotor that contacts the wheel. Installing wheels without proper metal to metal contact at the wheel mounting surfaces can cause the wheel lug nuts to loosen and could allow the wheel to come off while the vehicle is in motion.

8. Install the lug nuts. Be sure that the cone end of the lug nut faces inward.
9. With the lug nuts loosely installed, turn the wheel until one nut is at the top of the bolt circle. Tighten the lug nut until snug.
10. In a criss cross manner tighten the remaining lug nuts until snug in order to minimize runout.
11. Lower the vehicle. Torque the lug nuts to proper tightness, in the proper sequence

✻✻ CAUTION

Tighten the wheel lug nuts to specification after about 500 miles of driving. Failure to do this could result in the wheel coming off while the vehicle is in motion possibly causing loss of vehicle control or collision.

INSPECTION

Replace wheels if they are bent, cracked, leaking air or heavily rusted or if the lug nuts often become loose. Do not use bent wheels that have been straightened or do not use inner tubes in leaking wheels. Do not replace wheels with used wheels. Wheels that have been straightened or are leaking air or are used may have structural damage and could fail without warning.

Rear Wheel Lug Nut Studs

REMOVAL & INSTALLATION

1. Raise and support the vehicle safely.
2. Remove the tire and wheel assembly.
3. Remove the brake drum.
4. Using wheel stud removal tool, press the lug stud from its seat in the hub.

✻✻ WARNING

Never use a hammer to remove the lug stud, as damage to the hub or bearing may result.

To install:

5. Insert the new lug stud in the hole in the hub. Rotate the stud slowly to assure the serrations are aligned with those made by the old lug nut stud.
6. Place 4 flat washers over the outside end of the lug nut stud and thread the wheel lug nut with the flat washer side against the washers.
7. Tighten the wheel nut until the stud head seats against the back side of the hub. Do not use air tools as the serrations may be stripped from the stud.
8. Remove the wheel lug nut and washers. Install the brake drum. Install the tire and wheel assembly. Lower the vehicle.

✻✻ CAUTION

Tighten the wheel lug nuts to specification after about 500 miles of driving. Failure to do this could result in the wheel coming off while the vehicle is in motion possibly causing loss of vehicle control or collision.

FRONT SUSPENSION
B SERIES PICKUPS

➧SEE FIGS. 1-18

Pickups use a torsion bar type front suspension, with upper and lower control arms. The lower control arm is further located by tension rods extending to the frame forward of the axle. Conventional, double-acting shock absorbers are employed to dampen motion. A stabilizer bar is standard equipment.

Shock Absorber

TEST

The easiest way to check the performance of your shocks is to go to one corner of the truck and start it bouncing up and down. Get it going as much as you can and then release it. It should stop bouncing in less than two full bounces.

REMOVAL & INSTALLATION

1. Raise and safely support the vehicle. Remove the wheel and tire assembly.
2. Remove the upper shock absorber nuts, retainer and bushing.
3. Remove the lower shock absorber-to-lower control arm mounting bolt, nut and washer.
4. Slightly compress the shock absorber and remove it from the vehicle. Remove the remaining retainers and bushing from the upper shock absorber stud.

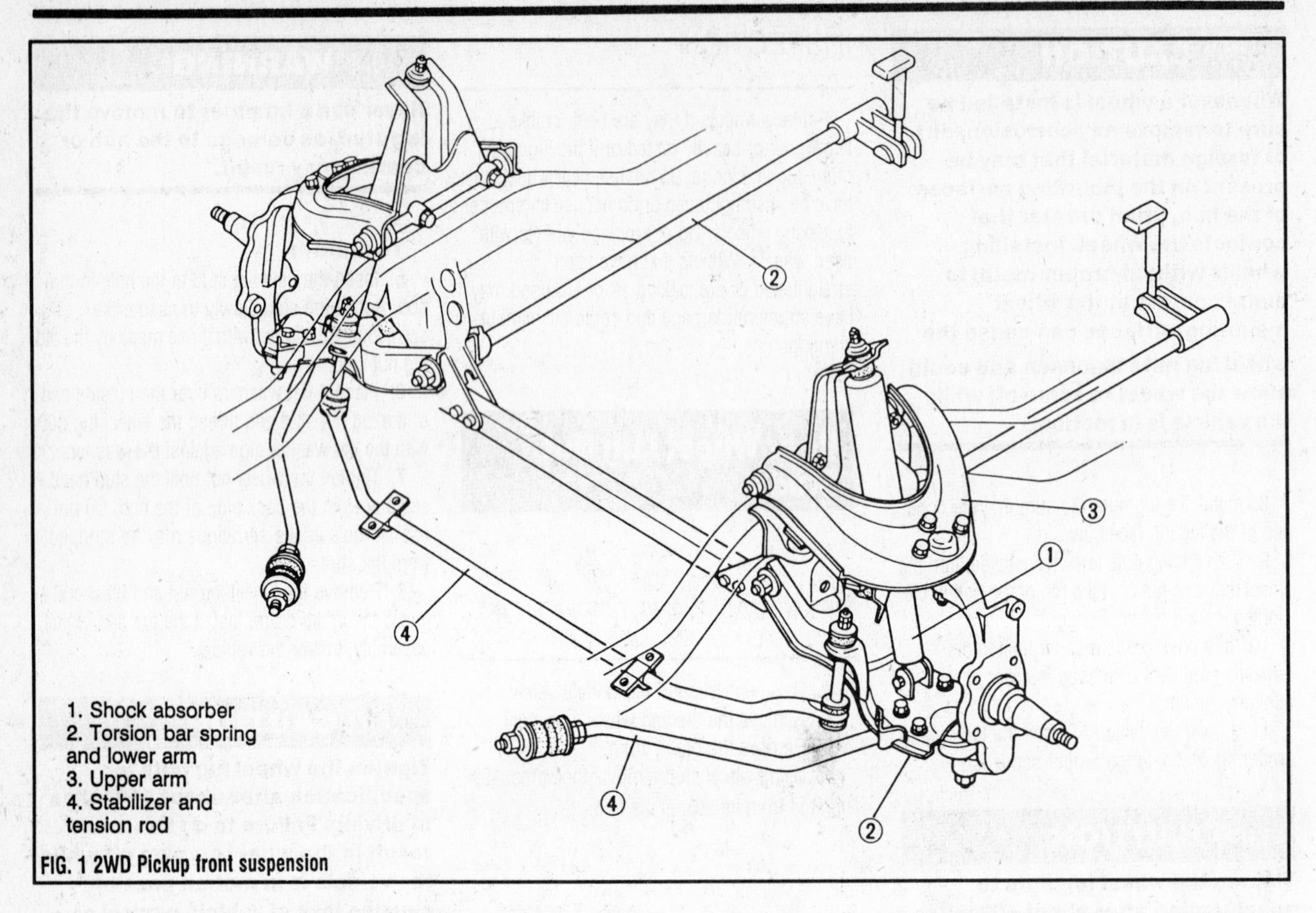

FIG. 1 2WD Pickup front suspension

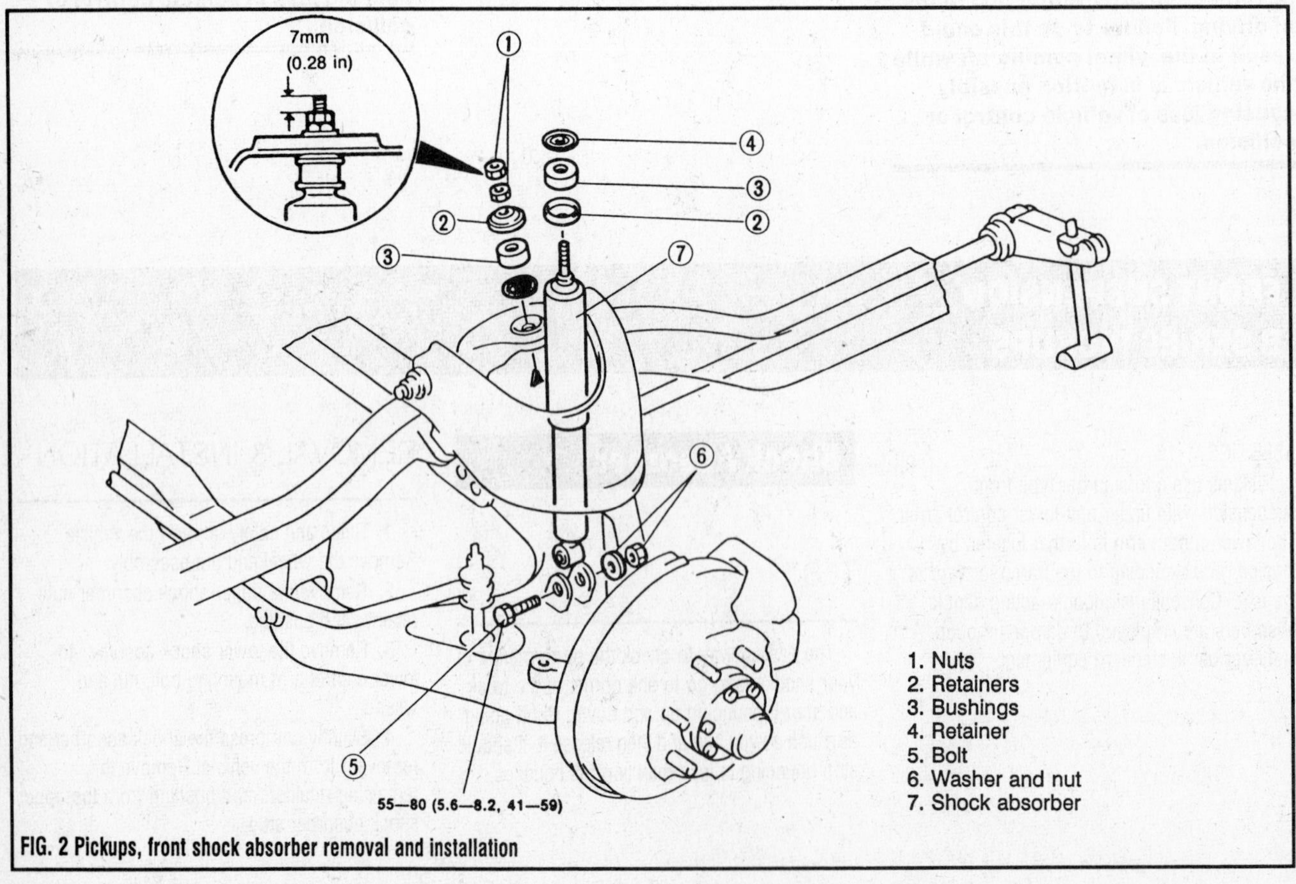

FIG. 2 Pickups, front shock absorber removal and installation

To install:

5. Install the shock absorber and install the mounting bolts, nuts, washers and bushings. Do not tighten at this time.

6. Install the wheel and tire assembly and lower the vehicle.

7. With the vehicle unladen, tighten the upper shock absorber mounting nuts until the stud protrudes 0.28 in. (7mm) above the upper nut. Tighten the lower mounting bolt and nut to 41–59 ft. lbs. (55–80 Nm).

8. Check the front end alignment.

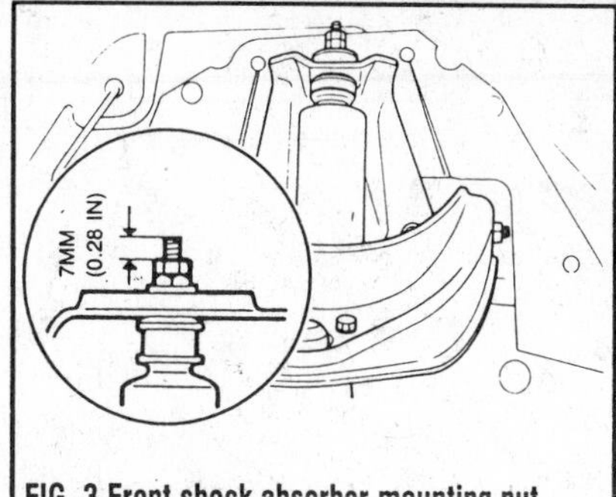

FIG. 3 Front shock absorber mounting nut tightening on Pickups

Torsion Bar

REMOVAL & INSTALLATION

1. Raise and safely support the vehicle. Remove the wheel and tire assembly.

2. Support the lower control arm with a jack.

3. Remove the cotter pin and nut from the lower ball joint stud. Separate the ball joint from the knuckle using tool 49 0727 575 or equivalent.

4. Remove the bolt, washer and nut attaching the shock absorber to the lower control arm.

5. Mark the position of the anchor bolt and swivel for reference during reassembly and remove the anchor bolt and swivel.

6. Mark the position of the torsion bar on the anchor arm and remove the anchor arm.

7. Mark the position of the torsion bar on the torque plate and remove the torsion bar. If removing the torsion bar from both sides of the vehicle, mark their positions as the torsion bars are not interchangeable.

8. Remove the attaching bolts and remove the torque plate.

9. Check the torsion bar for bending or for looseness between the serrations of the torsion bar and anchor arm and/or torque plate, replace as necessary.

To install:

10. Install the torque plate and tighten the attaching bolts to 55–69 ft. lbs. (75–93 Nm).

11. Coat the serrations of the torsion bar with grease and install in the torque plate, aligning the marks made during the removal procedure. If both torsion bars were removed, make sure the correct torsion bar is being installed.

12. Coat the serrations on the other end of the torsion bar with grease and install the anchor arm onto the torsion bar, aligning the marks made during the removal procedure.

13. Install the anchor bolt and swivel. Tighten the anchor bolt until the marks made during removal are aligned.

14. Connect the shock absorber to the lower control arm and loosely tighten the nut and bolt. Connect the lower ball joint to the knuckle; install the nut and tighten to 87–116 ft. lbs. (118–157 Nm). Install a new cotter pin.

15. Install the wheel and tire assembly and lower the vehicle. With the vehicle unladen, tighten the shock absorber-to-lower control arm bolt and nut to 41–59 ft. lbs. (55–80 Nm).

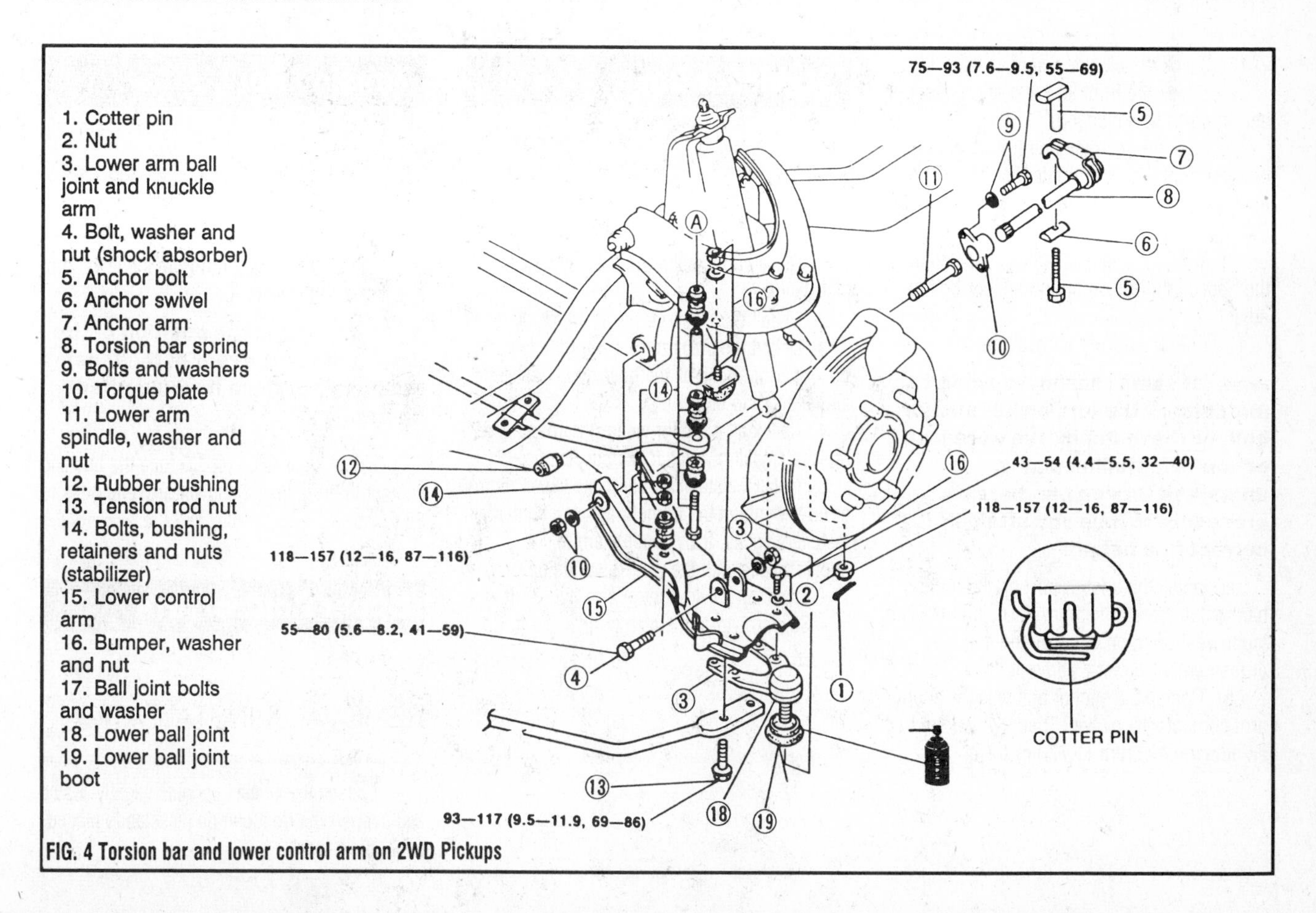

FIG. 4 Torsion bar and lower control arm on 2WD Pickups

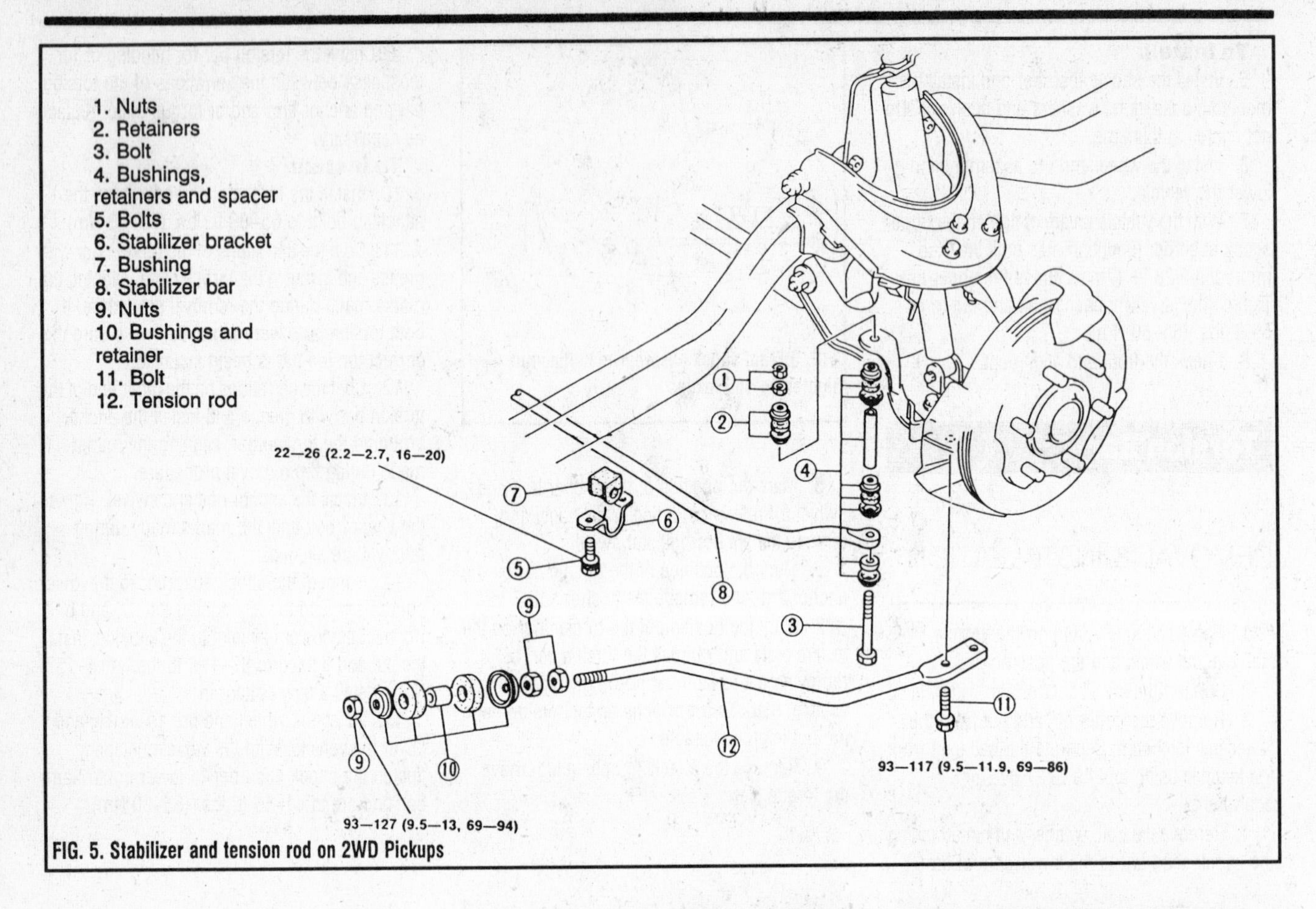

FIG. 5. Stabilizer and tension rod on 2WD Pickups

16. Check vehicle ride height as follows:
   a. Check the front and rear tire pressures and bring to specification.
   b. Measure the distance from the center of each front wheel to the fender brim. The difference must not be greater than 0.39 in. (10mm).
   c. If the difference is not as specified, turn the necessary torsion spring anchor bolt to adjust.
17. Check the front end alignment.

➡ If, for some reason, you didn't matchmark the torsion bar anchor bolt, or the matchmarks were lost, or you're installing a new, unmarked torsion bar, here's a procedure to help you attain the correct ride height:

   a. Install the anchor arm on the torsion bar so that there is 125mm (4.92 in.) between the lowest point on the arm and the crossmember directly above it.
   b. Tighten the anchor bolt until the anchor arm contacts the swivel. Then, tighten the bolt an additional 45mm (1.77 in.) travel.

Stabilizer Bar

REMOVAL & INSTALLATION

1. Raise and support the front end on jackstands.
2. Unbolt the stabilizer bar-to-frame clamps.
3. Unbolt the stabilizer bar from the lower control arms. Keep all the bushings, washers and spacers in order.
4. Check all parts for wear or damage and replace anything which looks suspicious.
5. Install the stabilizer bar to the lower control arms and mount the frame brackets. Tighten all fasteners lightly, then torque them to specifications with the wheels on the ground.
   - Stabilizer bar-to-control arm nut: 34 ft. lbs.
   - Stabilizer-to-frame clamp bolts: 19 ft. lbs.

Tension Rod

REMOVAL & INSTALLATION

1. Unbolt the tension rod from the lower arm and frame and remove it.

➡ Don't change the position of the double nut at the rear of the tension rod bushing, since it would affect caster.

2. Install the tension rod. Torque the bushing end nut to 90 ft. lbs.; the lower arm end bolts to 85 ft. lbs.

Upper Control Arm

REMOVAL & INSTALLATION

1. Loosen the wheel lugs nuts slightly. Raise and support the front end on jackstands placed under the frame.

2. Remove the wheels. Support the lower arm with a floor jack.
3. Remove the cotter pin and nut from the upper ball joint and separate the ball joint from the upper arm using a ball joint separator tool.
4. Remove the nuts and bolts that retain the upper arm shaft to the support bracket. Note the number and location of the shims under the nuts. These must be installed in their exact locations for proper wheel alignment. Check all parts for wear or damage. Replace any suspect parts.
5. Place the control arm assembly in position. Install the mounting bolts and nuts with the alignment shims in correct positions. Torque the upper arm shaft mounting bolts to: 2WD 60-68 ft. lbs. 4WD 69-85 ft. lbs. Tighten the ball joint nut to 30-37 ft. lbs. and install a new cotter pin.

Lower Control Arms

REMOVAL & INSTALLATION

1. Raise and safely support the vehicle. Remove the wheel and tire assembly.
2. Support the lower control arm with a jack.
3. Remove the cotter pin and nut from the lower ball joint stud. Separate the ball joint from the knuckle using tool 49 0727 575 or equivalent.
4. Remove the bolt, washer and nut attaching the shock absorber to the lower control arm.
5. Remove the torsion bar, anchor arm and torque plate assembly.
6. Remove the bolt(s) and nut(s) attaching the lower control arm to the frame.
7. On 2WD vehicles, remove the bolts attaching the tension rod to the lower control arm.
8. Remove the bolts, bushings, retainers, spacer and nuts connecting the stabilizer bar to the lower control arm.
9. Remove the lower control arm from the vehicle. Remove the lower ball joint, if necessary.

To Install:

10. Position the lower control arm to the frame and install the attaching bolt(s) and nut(s), but do not tighten at this time.
11. Install the torsion bar, anchor arm and torque plate assembly.
12. On 2WD vehicles, install the tension rod bolt and tighten to 69–86 ft. lbs. (93–117 Nm).
13. Attach the stabilizer bar to the control arm with the bolts, bushings, retainers, spacer and nuts. Tighten the nuts so 0.73 in. (18.5mm) of thread is exposed at the end of the bolt.

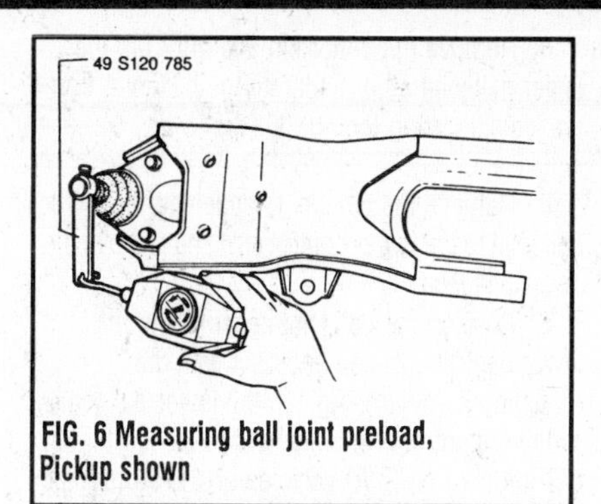

FIG. 6 Measuring ball joint preload, Pickup shown

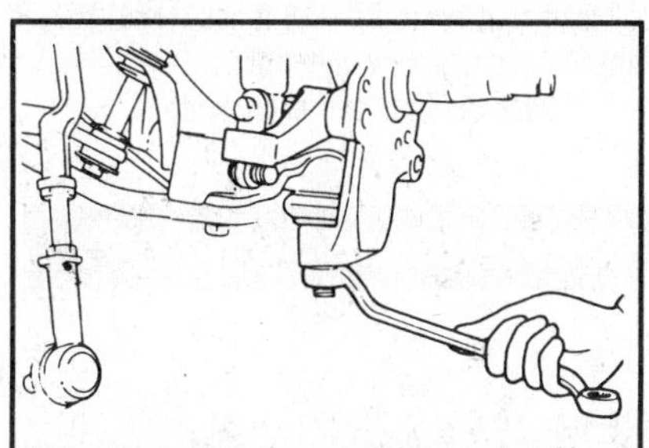
FIG. 7 Tighten the lower ball joint to knuckle mounting nut, Pickup shown

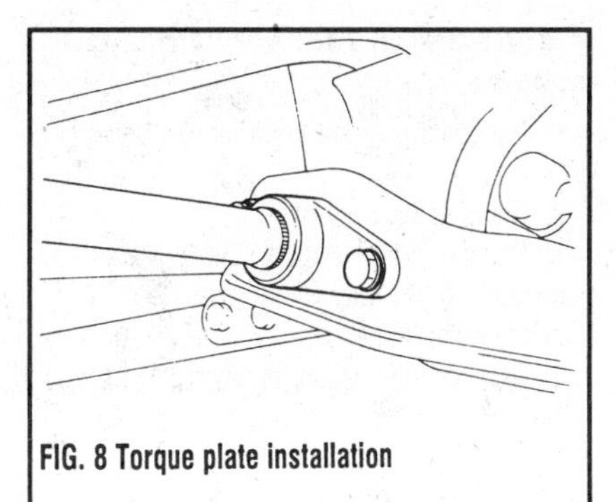
FIG. 8 Torque plate installation

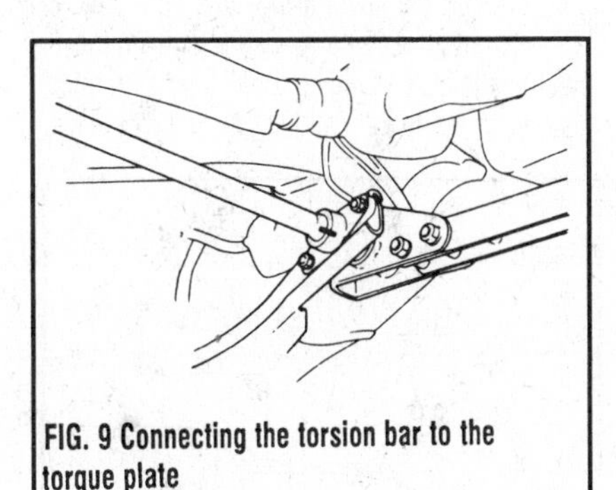
FIG. 9 Connecting the torsion bar to the torque plate

14. Install the shock absorber to the lower control arm and loosely tighten the mounting bolt and nut.
15. Install the wheel and tire assembly and lower the vehicle.
16. With the vehicle unladen, tighten the lower control arm-to-frame bolt and nut on 2WD vehicles and the front side lower control arm-to-frame bolt and nut on 4WD vehicles to 87–116 ft. lbs. (118–157 Nm). Tighten the rear side lower control arm-to-frame bolt and nut on 4WD vehicles to 116–145 ft. lbs. (157–196 Nm).
17. With the vehicle unladen, tighten the shock absorber-to-lower control arm bolt and nut to 41–59 ft. lbs. (55–80 Nm).
18. Check vehicle ride height as follows:
   a. Check the front and rear tire pressures and bring to specification.
   b. Measure the distance from the center of each front wheel to the fender brim. The difference must not be greater than 0.39 in. (10mm).
   c. If the difference is not as specified, turn the necessary torsion spring anchor bolt to adjust.
19. Check the front end alignment.

Upper Ball Joints

INSPECTION

1. Raise and safely support the vehicle. Remove the wheel and tire assembly.
2. Support the lower control arm with a jack.
3. Remove the clip attaching the brake hose to the upper control arm and disconnect the hose from the arm.
4. Remove the cotter pin and nut from the upper ball joint stud. Using tool 49 0727 575 or equivalent, separate the upper ball joint from the knuckle.
5. Install tool 49 0180 510B or equivalent to the ball joint stud and attach a suitable pull scale to the stud.
6. After rocking the ball joint stud back and forth 3–4 times, measure the pull scale reading while the ball joint stud is rotating. The pull scale reading should be 4.4–7.7 lbs.
7. If the pull scale reading is not as specified, replace the upper ball joint.

REMOVAL & INSTALLATION

1. Raise and safely support the vehicle. Remove the wheel and tire assembly.
2. Support the lower control arm with a jack.

3. Remove the clip attaching the brake hose to the upper control arm and disconnect the hose from the arm.
4. Remove the cotter pin and nut from the upper ball joint stud. Using tool 49 0727 575 or equivalent, separate the upper ball joint from the knuckle.
5. Remove the upper ball joint-to-upper control arm attaching bolts and remove the upper ball joint.
6. Position the ball joint assembly on the upper control arm and secure the mounting hardware. Tighten the upper ball joint-to-upper control arm attaching bolts to 18–25 ft. lbs. (25–33 Nm) and the upper ball joint stud nut to 22–38 ft. lbs. (29–51 Nm). Install a new cotter pin.
7. Check the front end alignment.

Lower Ball Joints

INSPECTION

1. Raise and safely support the vehicle. Remove the wheel and tire assembly.
2. Support the lower control arm with a jack.
3. Remove the cotter pin and nut from the lower ball joint stud. Separate the ball joint from the knuckle using tool 49 0727 575 or equivalent.
4. Install tool 49 0180 510B or equivalent to the ball joint stud and attach a suitable pull scale to the stud.
5. After rocking the ball joint stud back and forth 3–4 times, measure the pull scale reading while the ball joint stud is rotating. The pull scale reading should be 4.4–7.7 lbs.
6. If the pull scale reading is not as specified, replace the lower ball joint.

REMOVAL & INSTALLATION

1. Raise and safely support the vehicle. Remove the wheel and tire assembly.
2. Support the lower control arm with a jack.
3. On 2WD vehicles, remove the bolts attaching the tension rod to the lower control arm.
4. Remove the cotter pin and nut from the lower ball joint stud. Separate the ball joint from the knuckle using tool 49 0727 575 or equivalent.
5. Remove the bolts/nuts attaching the lower ball joint to the lower control arm and remove the lower ball joint.
6. Position the ball joint assembly to the lower control arm and secure it with the mounting hardware. Tighten the lower ball joint-to-lower control arm bolts/nuts to 32–40 ft. lbs. (43–54 Nm) on 2WD vehicles or 41–50 ft. lbs. (55–68 Nm) on 4WD vehicles. Tighten the lower ball joint stud nut to 87–116 ft. lbs. (118–157 Nm) and install a new cotter pin.
7. Check the front end alignment.

Knuckle and Spindle

REMOVAL & INSTALLATION

2WD Models

➡ See Section 7 for servicing 4WD models.

1. Raise and support the front end on jackstands.
2. Remove the wheels.
3. Remove brake calipers. Suspend the calipers out of the way with a wire. Don't disconnect the brake line.
4. Remove the brake rotor, hub and bearings.
5. Remove the tie rod-to-knuckle nut, and, using a ball joint separator, remove the tie rod end from the knuckle.
6. Support the lower arm with a floor jack.
7. Remove the cotter pin and nut from the lower ball joint, and, using a ball joint separator, disconnect the lower ball joint from the knuckle.

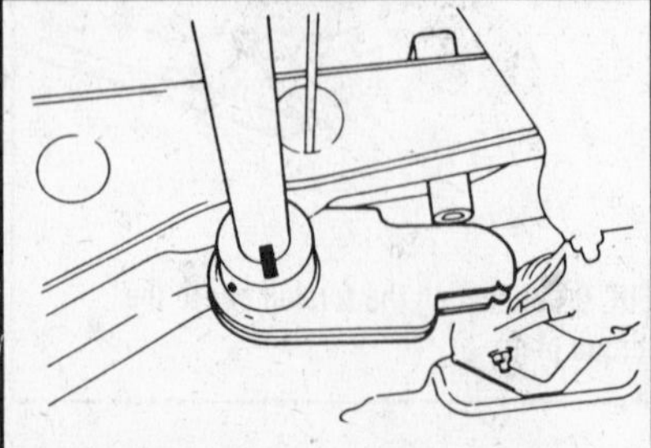
FIG. 10 Connecting the anchor arm to the torsion bar

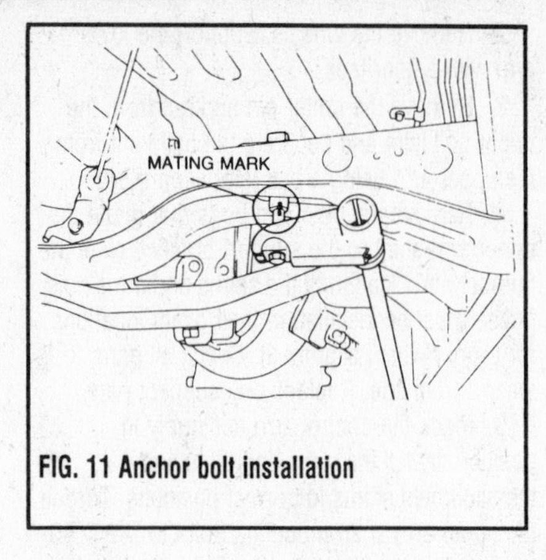

FIG. 11 Anchor bolt installation

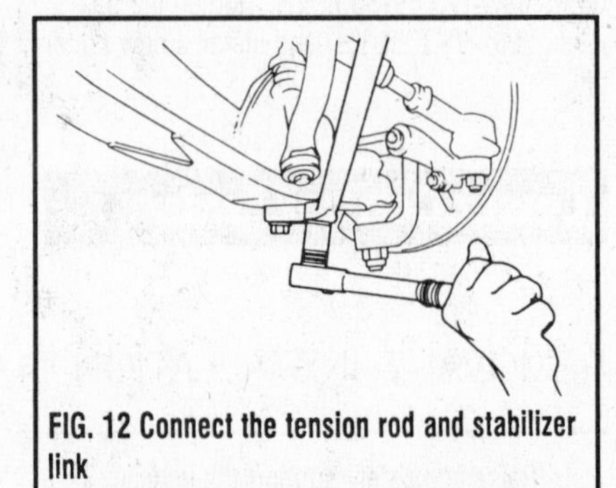
FIG. 12 Connect the tension rod and stabilizer link

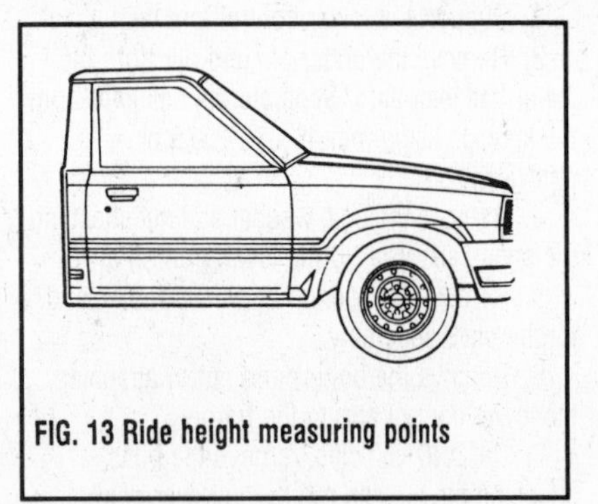
FIG. 13 Ride height measuring points

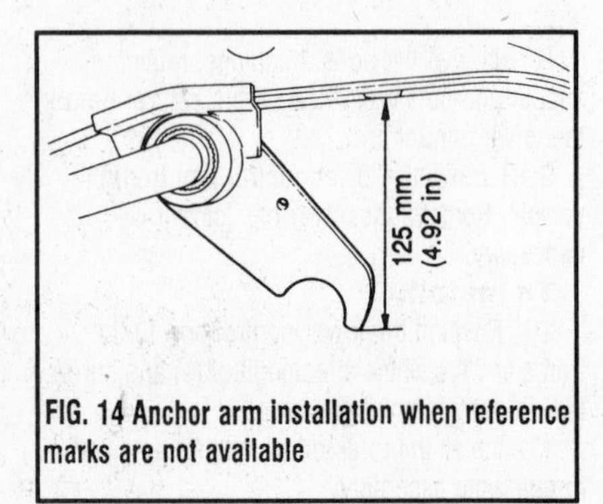

FIG. 14 Anchor arm installation when reference marks are not available

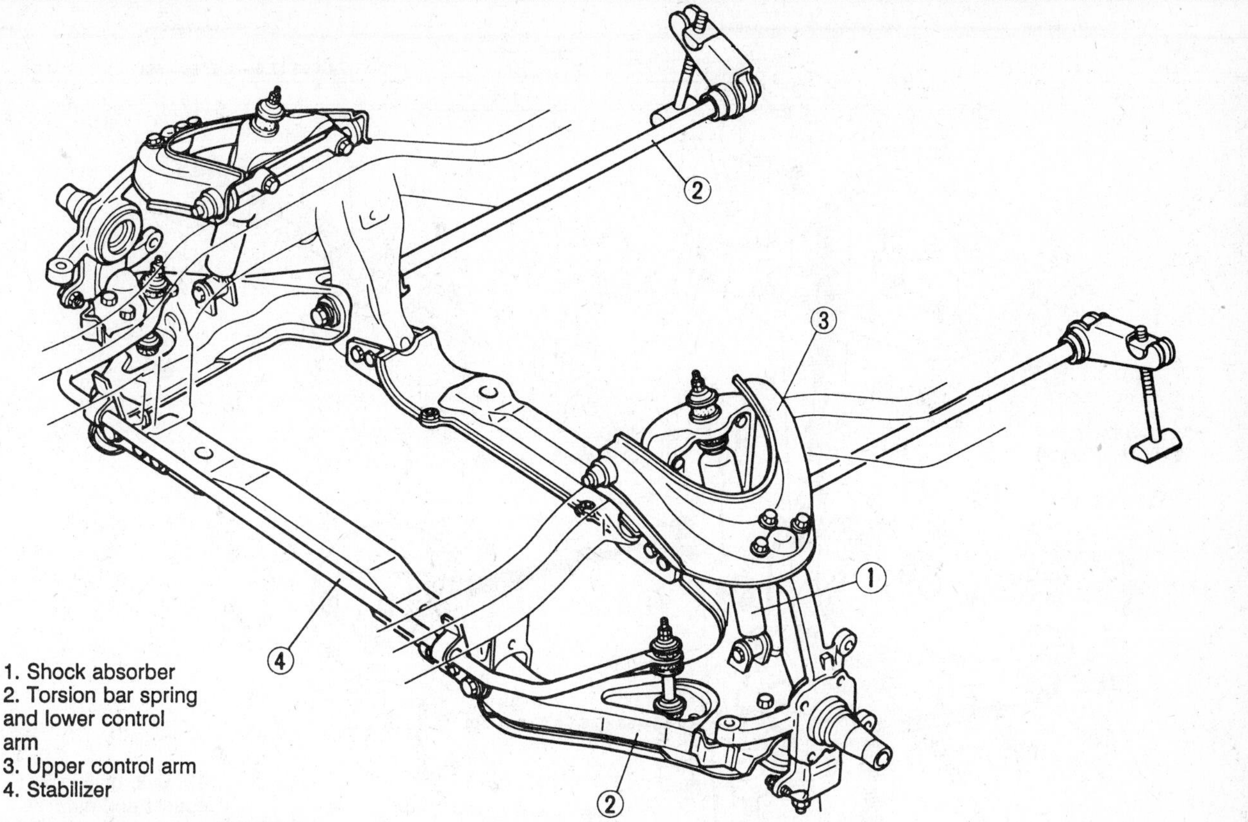

1. Shock absorber
2. Torsion bar spring and lower control arm
3. Upper control arm
4. Stabilizer

FIG. 15 Front suspension on 4WD Pickups

8. Remove the cotter pin and nut from the upper ball joint, and, using a ball joint separator, disconnect the upper ball joint from the knuckle.
9. Pull the knuckle and spindle assembly from the control arms.
10. The knuckle arm may now be removed.
11. Clean and inspect all parts for wear or damage. Replace parts as necessary.
12. Secure the knuckle in a vise and install the knuckle arm, if removed. Torque the bolts to 70-74 ft. lbs.
13. Install the knuckle assembly on the ball joints and secure the mounting nuts. Install the tie rod to knuckle arm, and install the remaining components. Observe the following torques.

- Upper ball joint-to-knuckle: 35-38 ft. lbs.
- Lower ball joint-to-knuckle: 116 ft. lbs.
- Tie rod end-to-knuckle: 22-29 ft. lbs.

Front Wheel Bearings 2WD Models

ADJUSTMENT

1. Raise and safely support the vehicle. Remove the wheel and tire assembly.
2. Remove the brake caliper and suspend it aside with rope or mechanics wire; do not let the caliper hang by the brake hose.
3. Remove the dust cap and cotter pin.
4. Tighten the locknut to 14–22 ft. lbs. (20–29 Nm) and turn the hub and rotor 2–3 times to seat the bearings.
5. Loosen the locknut until it can be turned by hand.
6. Attach a suitable pull scale to a wheel lug bolt and measure the frictional force.
7. Tighten the locknut until the pull scale reading, the initial turning torque, reaches the frictional force plus 1.3–2.4 lbs. Insert the retainer and secure with a new cotter pin.
8. Install the dust cap and the caliper. Install the wheel and tire assembly and lower the vehicle.
9. Before driving the vehicle, pump the brake pedal several times to restore normal brake travel.

REMOVAL & INSTALLATION

1. Raise and safely support the vehicle. Remove the wheel and tire assembly.
2. Remove the brake caliper and support it with mechanics wire. Do not let the caliper hang by the brake hose.
3. Remove the grease cap, cotter pin, retainer, adjusting nut and washer. Discard the cotter pin.
4. Remove the outer bearing and pull the hub and rotor off the spindle. Remove the grease seal using a seal removal tool. Discard the grease seal.

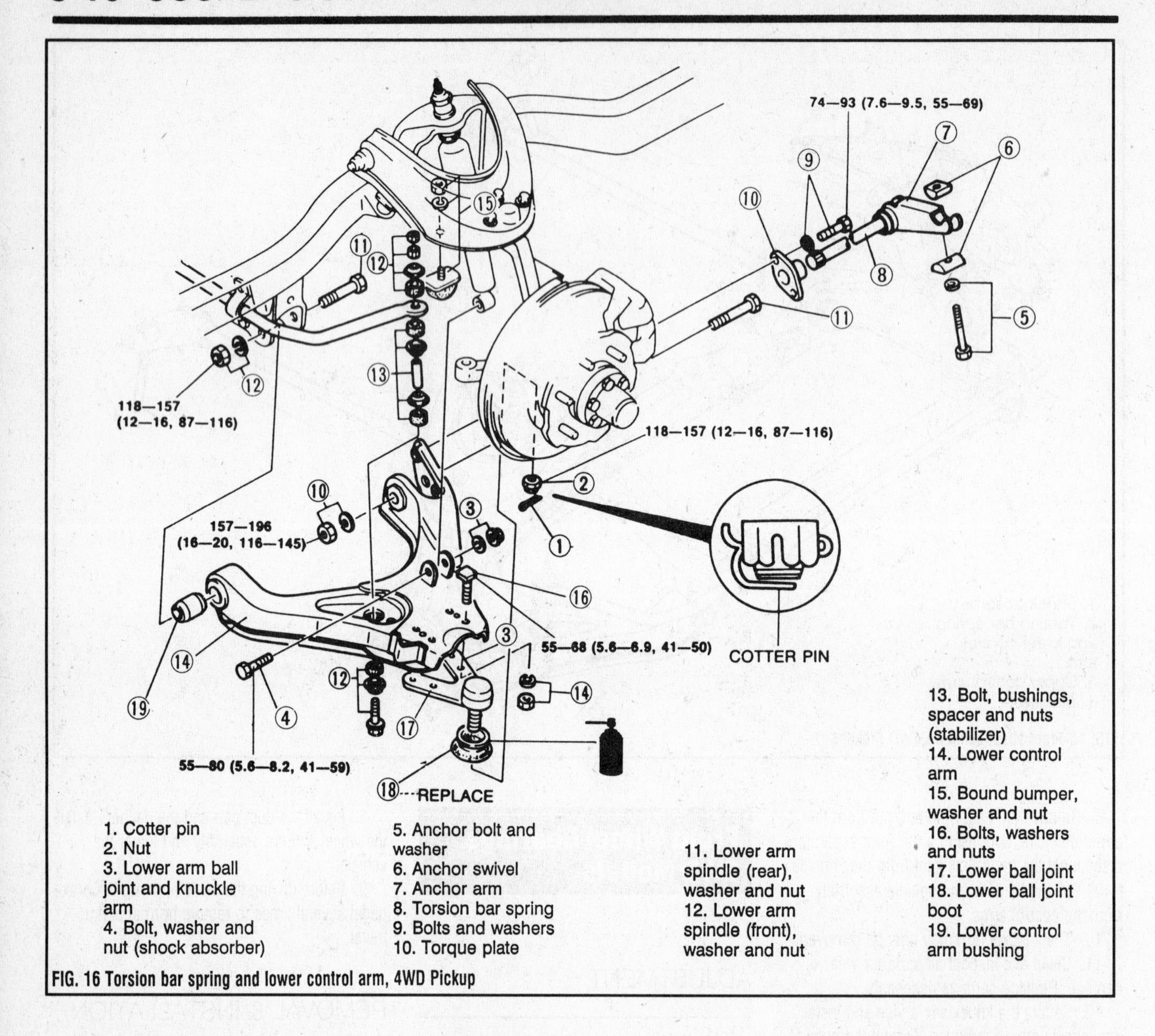

FIG. 16 Torsion bar spring and lower control arm, 4WD Pickup

5. Remove the inner bearing from the hub. Remove all traces of old lubricant from the bearings, hub and spindle with solvent and dry thoroughly.

6. Inspect the bearings and bearing races for scratches, pits or cracks. If the bearings and/or races are worn or damaged, remove the races with a brass drift.

To install:

7. If the bearing races were removed, install new races in the hub with suitable installation tools. Make sure the races are properly seated.

8. Using a bearing packer, pack the bearings with high-temperature wheel bearing grease. If a packer is not available, work as much grease as possible between the rollers and cages by hand.

9. Place a small amount of grease within the hub and grease the races. Install the inner bearing. Install a new wheel seal using a seal installer. Apply grease to the lips of the seal.

10. Install the hub and rotor assembly on the spindle. Install the outer bearing, washer and adjusting nut. Adjust the bearings.

11. Install the retainer, a new cotter pin and the grease cap.

12. Install the caliper and the wheel and tire assembly. Lower the vehicle.

13. Before driving the vehicle, pump the brake pedal several times to restore normal brake travel.

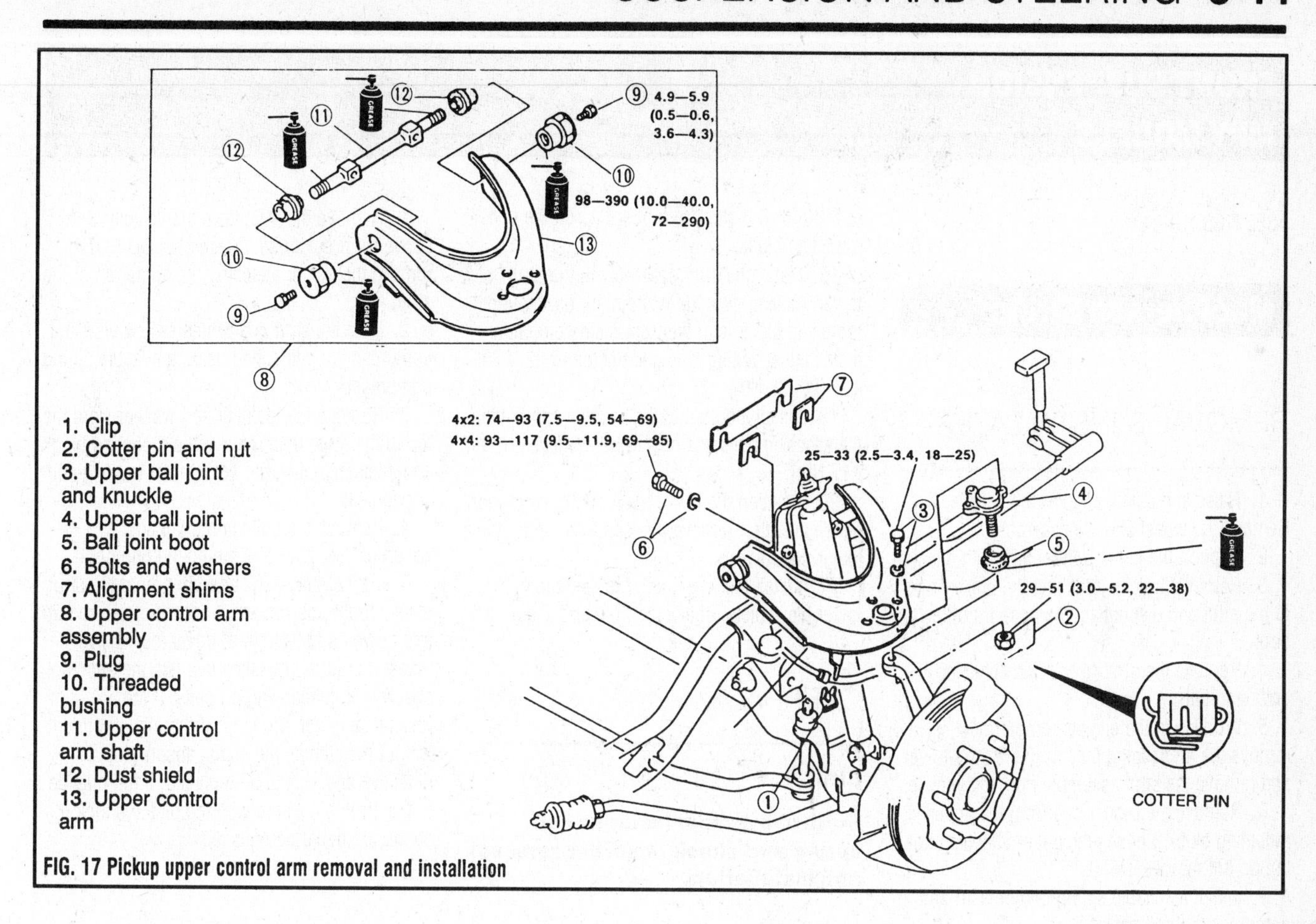

FIG. 17 Pickup upper control arm removal and installation

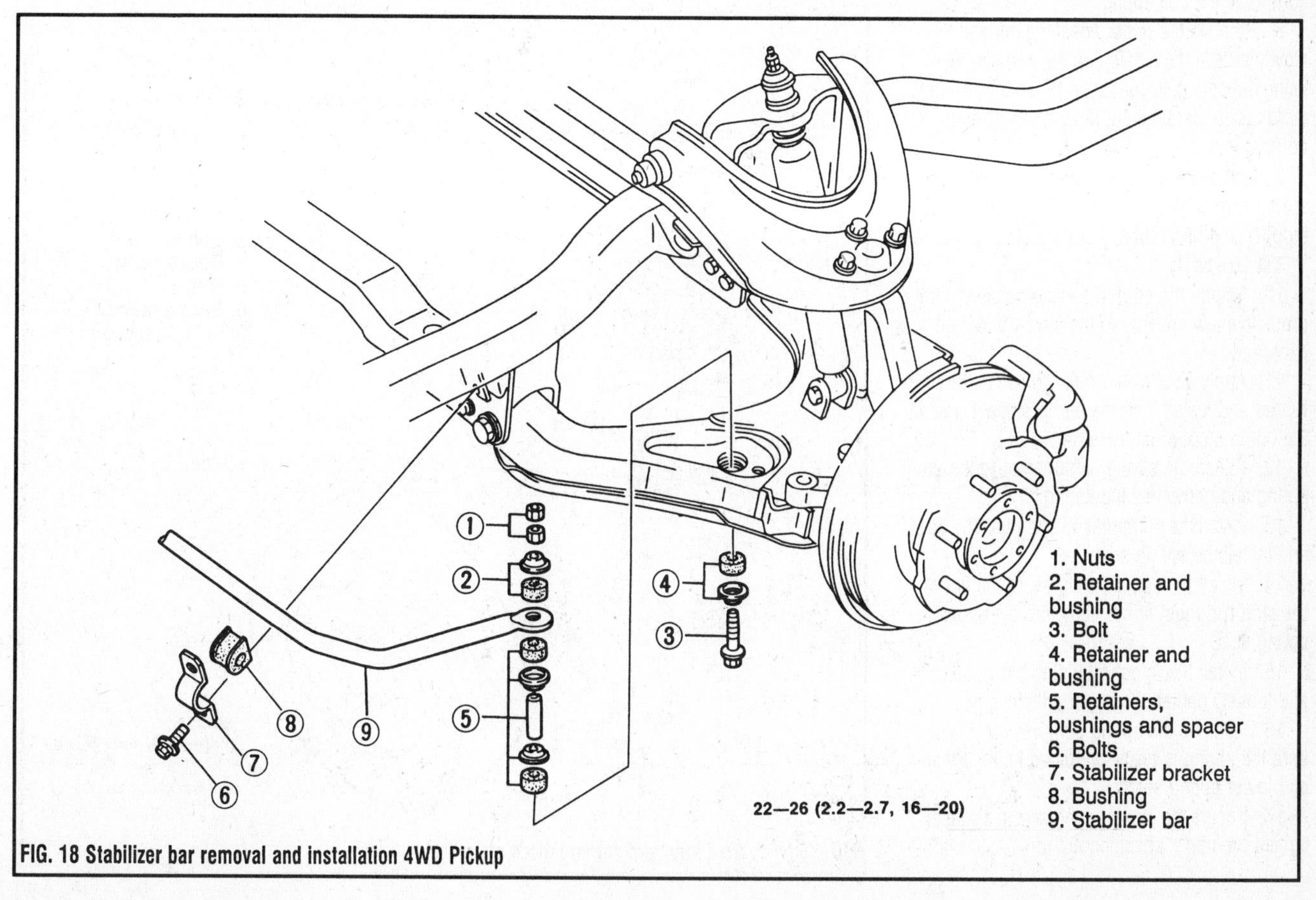

FIG. 18 Stabilizer bar removal and installation 4WD Pickup

FRONT SUSPENSION
MPV MODELS

SEE FIGS. 19-24

MacPherson Struts

REMOVAL & INSTALLATION

1. Raise and safely support the vehicle. Remove the wheel and tire assembly.
2. Support the lower control arm with a jack.
3. Remove the clip attaching the brake hose to the strut and disconnect the hose from the strut.
4. Remove the strut-to-knuckle attaching bolts and nuts.
5. Working in the engine compartment, remove the 4 attaching nuts from the strut tower and remove the strut assembly from the vehicle.
6. Remove the rubber cap from the upper mounting block. Loosen the upper attaching nut, but do not remove it.
7. Install a suitable spring compressor and compress the coil spring.
8. Remove the upper attaching nut and slowly relieve the tension on the coil spring, using the spring compressor. When the spring is no longer under tension, remove the spring compressor.
9. Remove the upper mounting block, upper spring seat, spring seat, coil spring, bump stopper and ring rubber from the strut.

To install:

10. Secure the strut in a vise equipped with protective jaw covers, so the strut will not be damaged.
11. Apply a suitable rubber grease to the ring rubber and install it on the bump stopper. Install the bump stopper on the strut.
12. Attach the spring compressor to the coil spring and compress the spring.
13. Install the compressed spring on the strut and install the spring seat.
14. Install the upper spring seat. The flat of the strut rod must fit correctly into the upper spring seat.
15. Install the upper mounting block. Install and loosely tighten the upper attaching nut.
16. Remove the spring compressor. Make sure the spring is properly seated in the upper and lower spring seats.
17. Secure the upper spring seat in a vise and tighten the upper attaching nut to 47–59 ft. lbs. (64–80 Nm). Install the rubber cap on the upper mounting block.
18. Install the strut assembly in the strut tower, making sure the white mark on the upper mounting block is in the front-inside direction. Install the attaching nuts and tighten to 22–27 ft. lbs. (29–36 Nm).
19. Install the strut to the knuckle and tighten the attaching bolts and nuts to 69–86 ft. lbs. (93–117 Nm).
20. Position the brake hose on the strut and install the clip. Remove the jack from under the lower control arm.
21. Install the wheel and tire assembly and lower the vehicle. Check the front end alignment.

OVERHAUL

Strut

➡ Strut overhaul includes coil spring and shock absorber removal and installation.

1. Remove the strut from the vehicle. See above for procedures. Loosen but DO NOT remove the center attaching nut at the top of the strut.
2. Hold the strut in a protected jaw vise and compress the coil spring using a suitable spring compressor.
3. Remove the lock nut and washer from the top of the strut, then remove the mounting block and adjusting plate, the seat, thrust bearing and spring seat.
4. Remove the coil spring, the shock absorber dust boot and the bound bumper.
5. To test the shock absorber, hold the strut in its upright position and work the piston rod up and down its full length of travel four or five times. If a strong resistance is felt, the shock absorber is functioning properly. If the resistance is not strong, or if there is a sudden lack of resistance, the shock absorber is defective and should be replaced. If the outside of the strut is covered with the oil the shock absorber should be replaced.

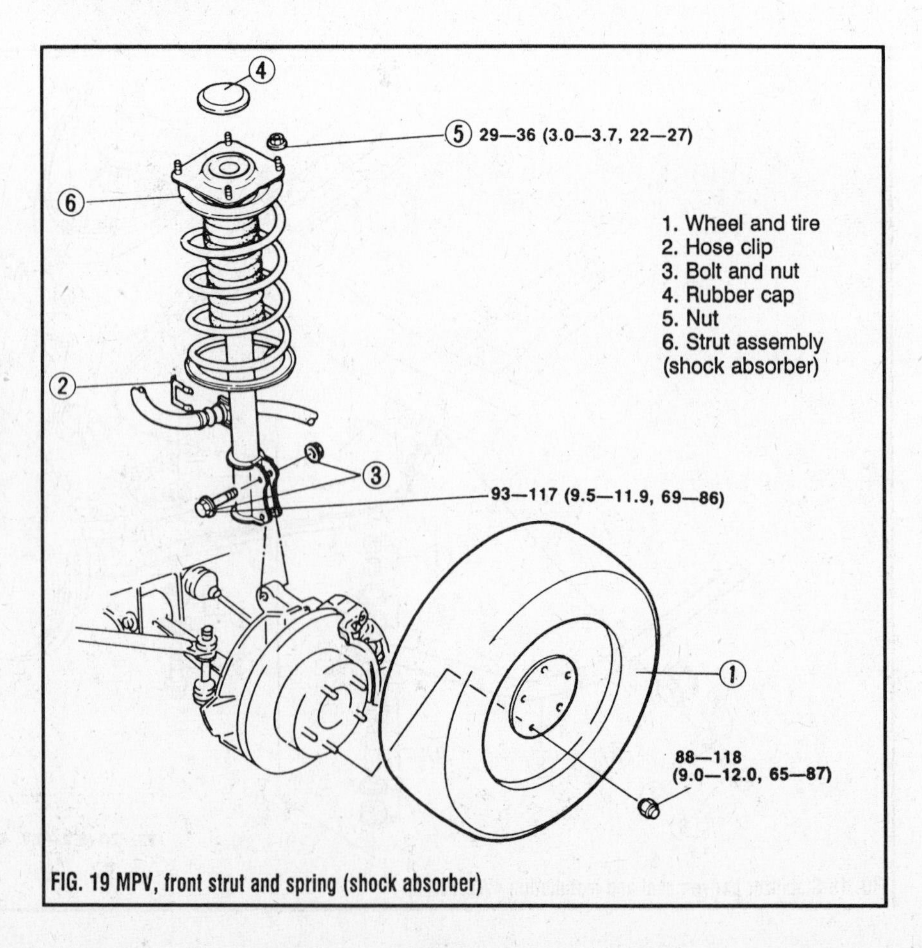

FIG. 19 MPV, front strut and spring (shock absorber)

6. Hold the strut body in a vise and remove the cap nut cover and the cap nut. Mazda makes a special socket (tool number 49–0259–700A) to remove the cap nut.

7. Remove the O-ring on the piston rod guide.

8. Remove the inner shock absorber assembly from the strut tube.

9. Check all strut components for wear, and check the coil spring for cracks. Check the shock absorber seal for damage. Drain and clean the strut.

10. Assembly is essentially the reverse of disassembly. Observe the following.

➡ Cartridge shock absorbers are available as replacements for the open oil type. If cartridge shock absorbers are installed, go to step 14.

11. If open oil type shock absorbers are used, install the shock piston and fill the reservoir with 225cc of fresh shock absorber fluid.

12. Install the special pilot (tool number 49–0370–590) or some other protector over the threads of the shock absorber plunger rod to protect the oil seal in the cap nut, grease the seal and install the cap nut carefully onto the strut.

13. Tighten the cap nut temporarily with the plunger rod extended as far as it will go. Make sure the rod is not binding.

14. Fully lower the piston rod and tighten the cap nut to 36–43 ft. lbs. with nut wrench (tool number 49 0259 700A).

15. On cartridge type shock absorbers, tighten the cap nut to 58–108 ft. lbs. with nut wrench tool number 49–0259–700A.

16. Apply rubber grease to the upper strut thrust bearing.

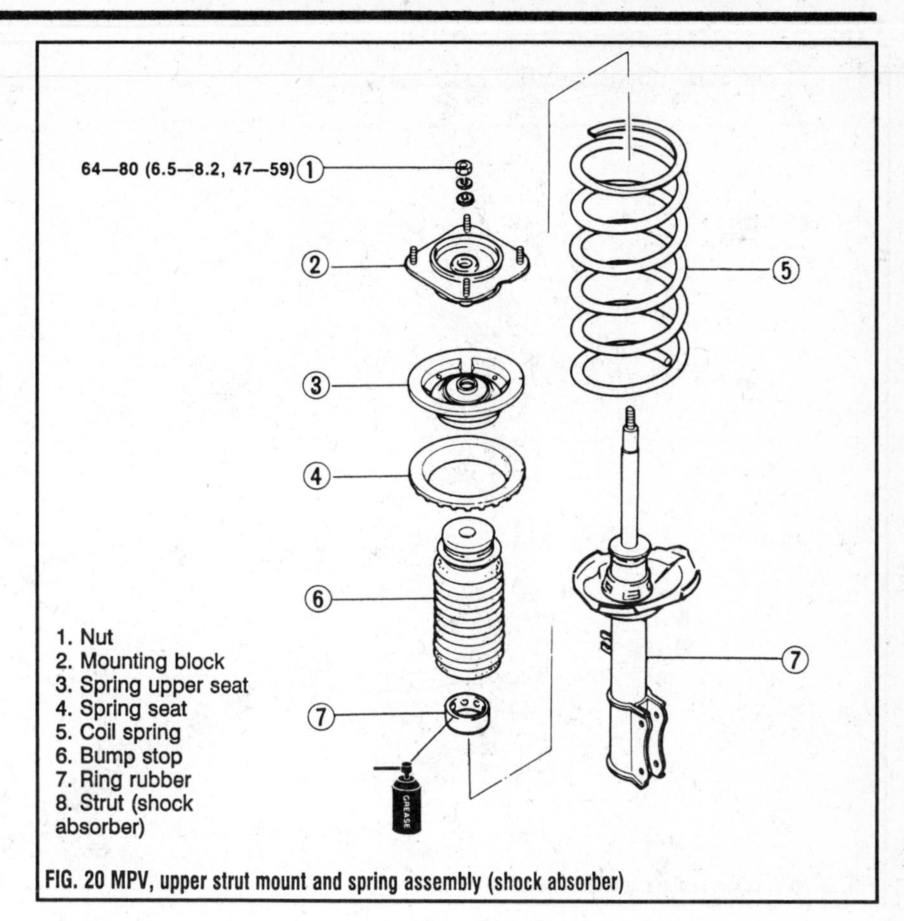

FIG. 20 MPV, upper strut mount and spring assembly (shock absorber)

Coil Spring and Shock Absorber

Coil spring and shock absorber removal and installation is covered in the strut overhaul section, above. Two types of shock absorbers are used; the sealed cartridge and the open oil type.

Shock Absorber Test

This test can be done without removing the shock absorber strut from the vehicle.

Visually inspect the strut for evidence of leakage from the shock absorber. If an excessive amount of oil is found, the shock is defective and must be replaced.

If there is no sign of excessive leakage (a small amount of weeping is normal) bounce the car at one corner by pressing up and down on the fender or bumper. When you have the car bouncing as much as possible, step back and count how many times the car bounces by itself until it stops. It should stop bouncing after the first rebound. If it continues to bounce past the center point of its up and down motion more than one, the shock absorbers are worn and should be replaced.

Compression Rods

REMOVAL & INSTALLATION

1. Raise and support the front end on jackstands.

2. Disconnect the stabilizer link at the compression rod.

3. Remove the compression rod-to-lower arm bolts.

4. Remove the compression rod end nut and washer.

➡ The end nut on the left compression rod is equipped with left handed threads.

5. Unbolt the compression rod fluid-filled bushing and remove the bushing and washers.

6. Check the bushing for signs of leakage. Replace it if leaking or damaged.

7. Install the compression rod and components in reverse order. Observe the following torques:

- Fluid-filled bushing bolts: 76 ft. lbs.
- Compression rod end nut: 127 ft. lbs.
- Compression rod-to-lower arm: 93 ft. lbs.

8. Tighten the stabilizer bar end link bolt until 13mm of thread is visible above the nut.

Lower Ball Joints

INSPECTION, REMOVAL & INSTALLATION

On 2WD models, the lower ball joints are pressed into the lower control arm. The ball joints cannot be removed from the lower control arms and in the event of the defective ball joint, the lower control arm and ball joint must be replaced as an assembly. Defective ball joints are determined by checking the rotational torque with a special preload attachment and spring scale. Ripped ball joint dust boots can be

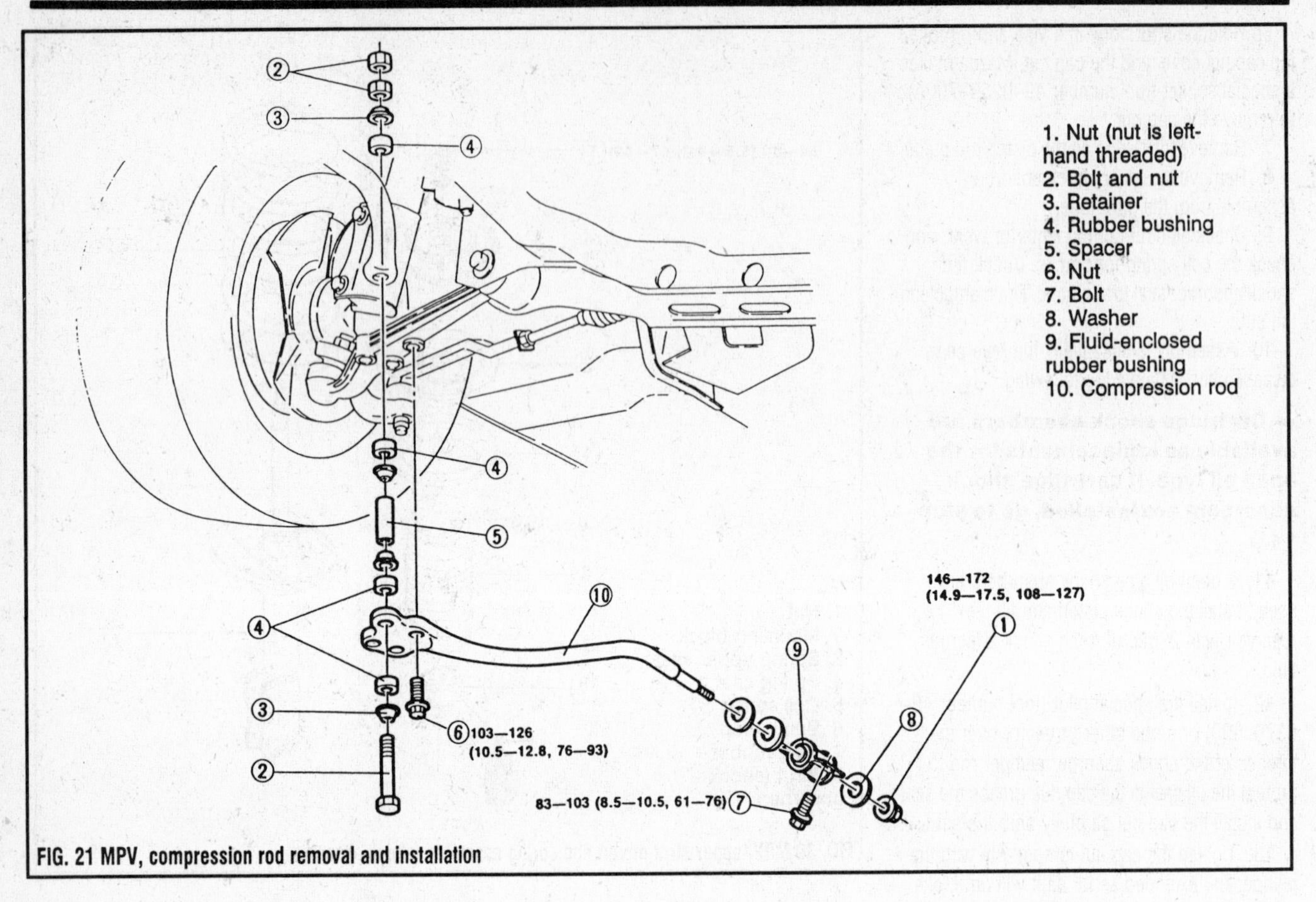

FIG. 21 MPV, compression rod removal and installation

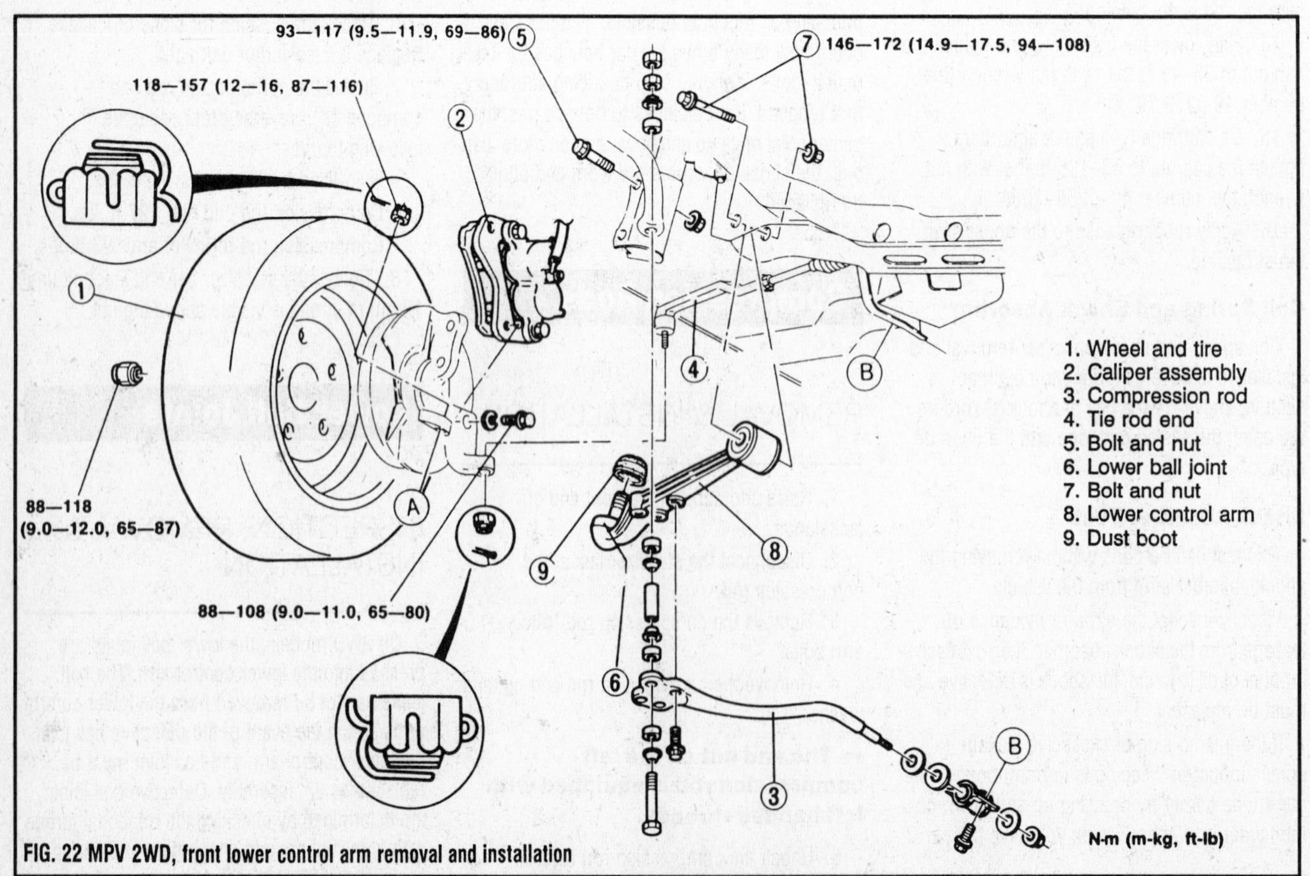

FIG. 22 MPV 2WD, front lower control arm removal and installation

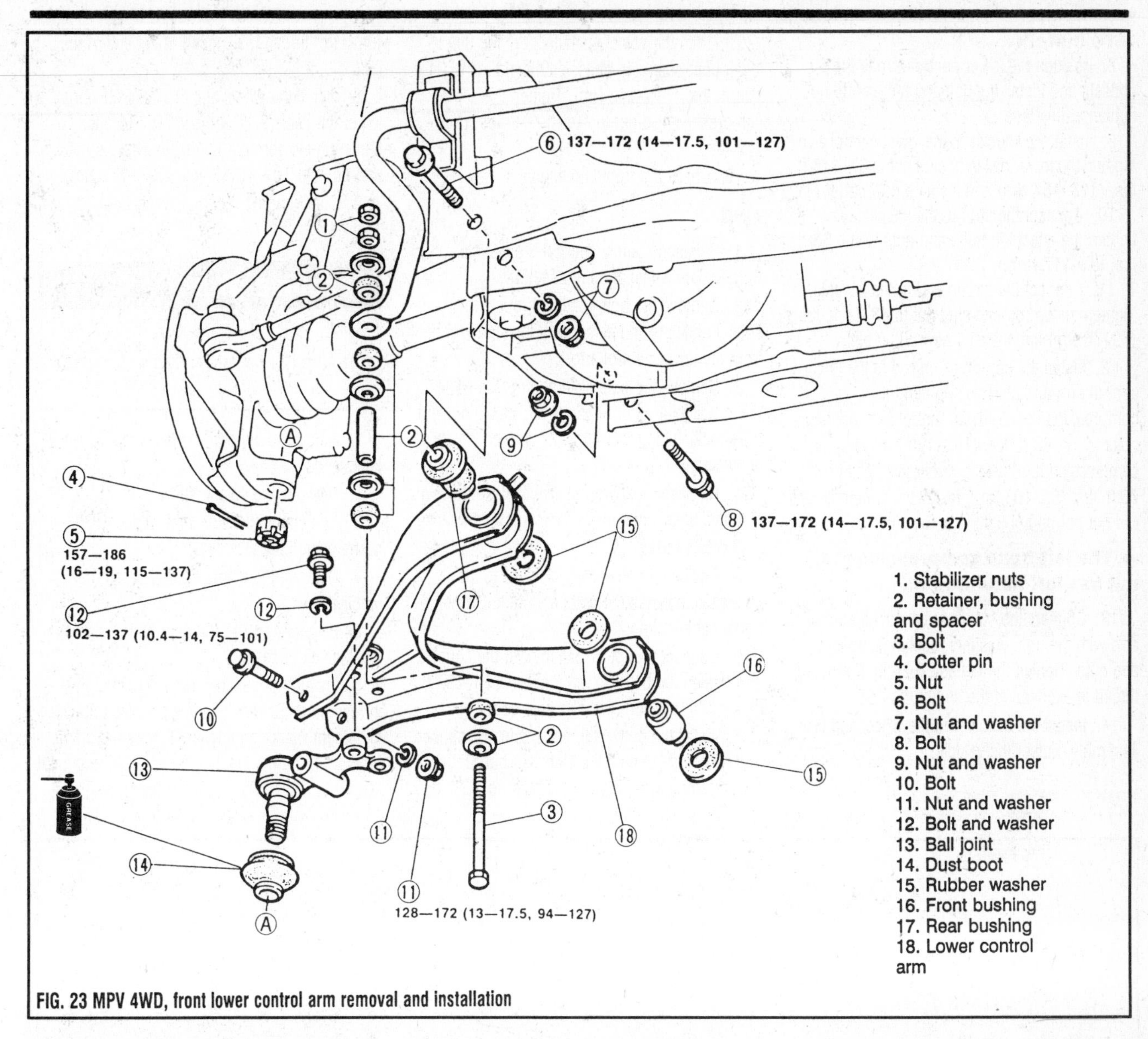

FIG. 23 MPV 4WD, front lower control arm removal and installation

replaced. Replacement of the ball joint dust boot is accomplished by removing the lower control arm from the vehicle and chiseling the off old boot. Coat the inside of the new dust boot with lithium grease and press it into the ball joint using the proper tool. Check the ball joint stud threads for damage and repair as necessary. Check the ball joint preload and install the lower control arm by reversing the removal procedure.

1. On 4WD models, raise and safely support the vehicle. Remove the wheel and tire assembly.
2. Disconnect the stabilizer bar from the lower control arm.
3. Remove the cotter pin and nut from the lower ball joint stud. Separate the ball joint from the knuckle using tool 49 0727 575 or equivalent.
4. Install tool 49 0180 510B or equivalent to the ball joint stud and attach a suitable pull scale to the stud.
5. After rocking the ball joint stud back and forth 3–4 times, measure the pull scale reading while the ball joint stud is rotating. The pull scale reading should be 4.4–7.7 lbs.
6. If the pull scale reading is not as specified, replace the lower ball joint. The ball joint assembly is bolted onto the lower control arm. Remove the two upper and one through bolt and remove the ball joint. Install in the reverse order.

Lower Control Arm

REMOVAL & INSTALLATION

2WD

1. Raise and safely support the vehicle. Remove the wheel and tire assembly.
2. Remove the brake caliper and support it aside with mechanics wire, do not let it hang by the brake hose.
3. Remove the nuts, bolts, spacer, washers and bushings and remove the compression rod from the lower control arm and chassis and disconnect the stabilizer bar from the lower control arm.
4. Remove the cotter pin and nut and, using tool 49 0118 850C or equivalent, separate the tie rod end from the knuckle.
5. Remove the bolts and nuts and disconnect the strut from the knuckle.
6. Remove the cotter pin and nut from the lower ball joint stud. Using tool 49 0727 575 or equivalent, separate the lower ball joint from the knuckle.
7. Remove the mounting bolt and nut and remove the lower control arm from the vehicle.

To install:

8. Position the lower control arm to the chassis and install the bolt and nut, but do not tighten at this time.

9. Install the knuckle to the lower control arm. Tighten the lower ball joint stud nut to 87–116 ft. lbs. (118–157 Nm) and install a new cotter pin.

10. Connect the strut to the knuckle and tighten the attaching bolts and nuts to 69–86 ft. lbs. (93–117 Nm).

11. Connect the tie rod end to the knuckle. Tighten the tie rod end stud nut to 43–58 ft. lbs. (59–78 Nm) and install a new cotter pin.

12. Install the compression rod to the lower control arm and chassis. Tighten the compression rod-to-lower control arm mounting bolts to 76–93 ft. lbs. (103–126 Nm) and the compression rod bushing-to-chassis bolts to 61–76 ft. lbs. (83–103 Nm). Install the compression rod nut but do not tighten at this time.

➡ **The left-hand compression rod nut has left-hand thread.**

13. Connect the stabilizer bar to the control arm with the bolt, washers, bushings, spacer and nuts. Tighten the nuts so 0.24 in. (6mm) of thread is exposed at the end of the bolt.

14. Install the caliper and the wheel and tire assembly. Lower the vehicle.

15. With the vehicle unladen, tighten the lower control arm-to-chassis bolt and nut to 94–108 ft. lbs. (146–172 Nm). Tighten the compression rod nut to 108–127 ft. lbs. (146–172 Nm).

16. Check the front end alignment.

4WD

1. Raise and safely support the vehicle. Remove the wheel and tire assembly.

2. Remove the bolt, retainers, bushings, spacer and nuts and disconnect the stabilizer bar from the lower control arm.

3. Remove the cotter pin and nut from the lower ball joint stud. Separate the ball joint from the knuckle using tool 49 0727 575 or equivalent.

4. Remove the lower control arm-to-chassis nuts and bolts and remove the lower control arm.

To install:

5. Position the lower control arm to the chassis and install the bolts and nuts. Do not tighten at this time.

6. Connect the lower ball joint to the knuckle and tighten the ball joint stud nut to 115–137 ft. lbs. (157–186 Nm). Install a new cotter pin.

7. Install the bolt, retainers, bushings, spacer and nuts and connect the stabilizer bar to the lower control arm. Tighten the nuts so 0.24 in. (6mm) of thread is exposed at the end of the bolt.

8. Install the wheel and tire assembly and lower the vehicle. With the vehicle unladen, tighten the lower control arm-to-chassis nuts and bolts to 101–127 ft. lbs. (137–172 Nm).

9. Check the front end alignment.

Stabilizer Bar

REMOVAL & INSTALLATION

1. Raise and support the front end on jackstands.

2. Remove the splash shield.

3. Disconnect the end links at the compression rods.

4. Remove the clamp bolts. Lift out the stabilizer bar.

5. Inspect all parts for wear and/or damage. Replace as necessary.

6. Install the Stabilizer Bar and components in reverse order. The end link bushings have alignment marks on the bar. Torque the clamp bolts to 45 ft. lbs. Tighten the end link bolts until 13mm ± 1mm of thread is visible above the nut.

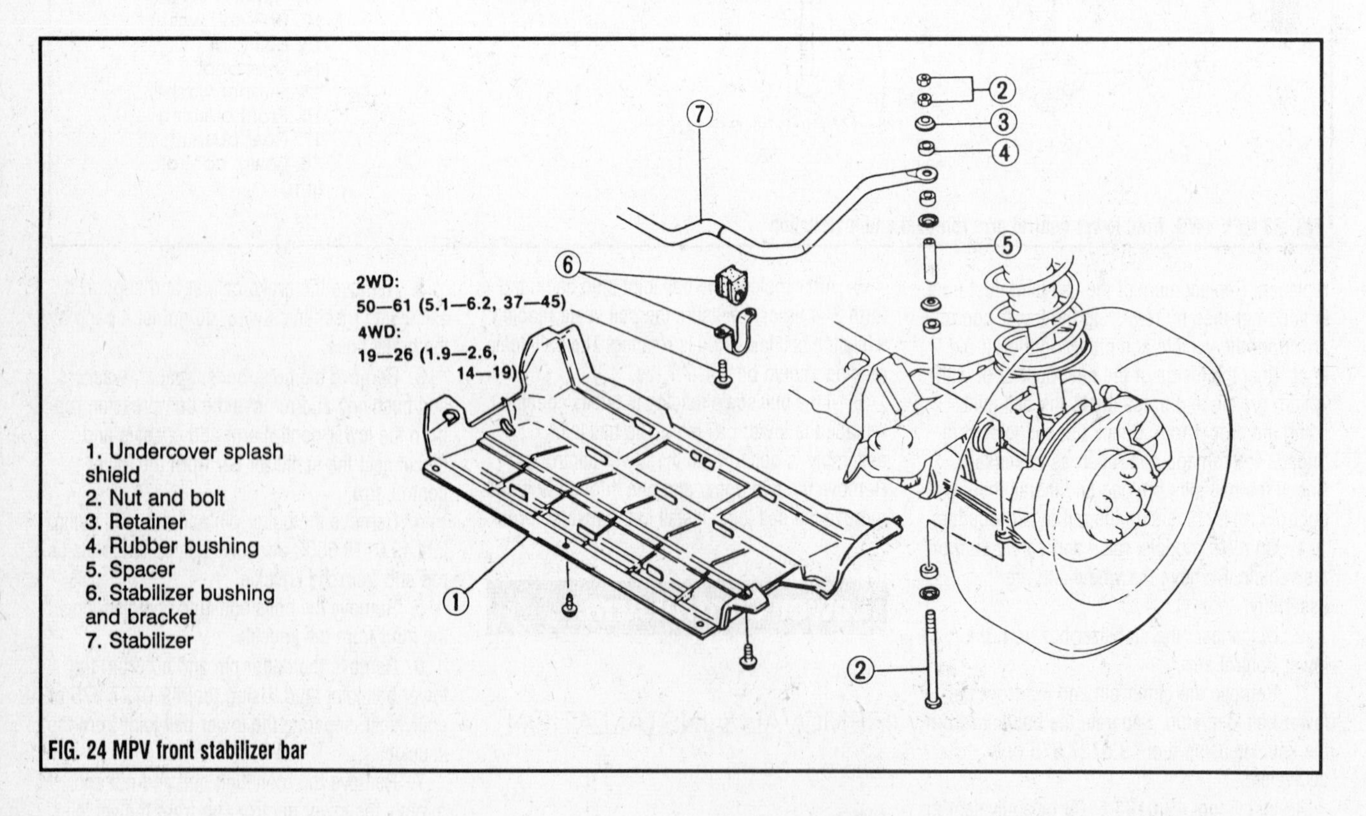

FIG. 24 MPV front stabilizer bar

FRONT SUSPENSION
2WD NAVAJO MODELS

➧SEE FIGS. 25-37

Coil Springs

REMOVAL & INSTALLATION

1. Loosen the wheel lugs slightly. Raise the front of the vehicle and place jackstands under the frame and a jack under the axle. Remove the wheels.

⁂ WARNING

The axle must not be permitted to hang by the brake hose. If the length of the brake hoses is not sufficient to provide adequate clearance for removal and installation of the spring, the disc brake caliper must be removed from the spindle. A Strut Spring Compressor, T81P-5310-A or equivalent may be used to compress the spring sufficiently, so that the caliper does not have to be removed. After removal, the caliper must be placed on the frame or otherwise supported to prevent suspending the caliper from the caliper hose. These precautions are absolutely necessary to prevent serious damage to the tube portion of the caliper hose assembly!

2. Remove the nut attaching the shock absorber to radius arm and slide the shock absorber off of the mounting stud. Remove the nut securing the lower retainer to spring seat. Remove the lower retainer.
3. Lower the axle as far as it will go without stretching the brake hose and tube assembly. The axle should now be unsupported without hanging by the brake hose. If not, then either remove the caliper or use Strut Spring Compressor Tool, T81P-5310-A or equivalent. Remove the spring.
4. If there is a lot of slack in the brake hose assembly, a pry bar can be used to lift the spring over the bolt that passes through the lower spring seat.
5. Rotate the spring so the built-in retainer on the upper spring seat is cleared.
6. Remove the spring from the vehicle.

To install:

7. If removed, install the bolt in the axle arm and install the nut all the way down. Install the spring lower seat and lower insulator. Install the stabilizer bar mounting bracket and spring spacer.
8. With the axle in the lowest position, install the top of the spring in the upper seat. Rotate the spring into position.
9. Lift the lower end of the spring over the bolt.
10. Raise the axle slowly until the spring is seated in the lower spring upper seat. Install the lower retainer and nut. Tighten the nut to 70-100 ft. lbs. (95-136 Nm).
11. Install the shock absorber. Tighten the lower mounting nut to 39-53 ft. lbs. (53-72 Nm).
12. Install the front wheels. Remove the jack and jackstands and lower vehicle.

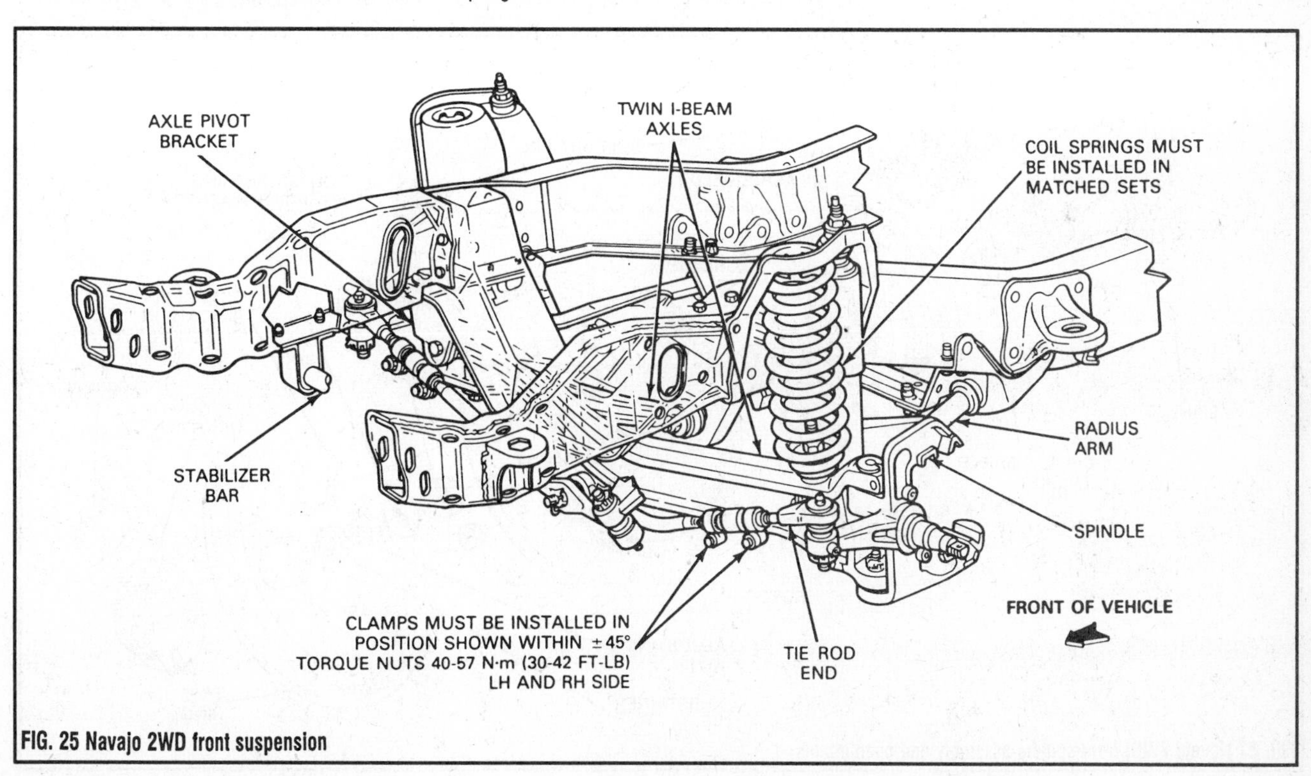

FIG. 25 Navajo 2WD front suspension

Shock Absorbers

REMOVAL & INSTALLATION

➡ Low pressure gas shocks are charged with Nitrogen gas. Do not attempt to open, puncture or apply heat to them. Prior to installing a new shock absorber, hold it upright and extend it fully. Invert it and fully compress and extend it at least 3 times. This will bleed trapped air.

1. Raise the vehicle, as required to provide additional access and remove the bolt and nut attaching the shock absorber to the lower bracket on the radius arm.
2. Remove the nut, washer and insulator from the shock absorber at the frame bracket and remove the shock absorber.
3. Position the washer and insulator on the shock absorber rod and position the shock absorber to the frame bracket.
4. Position the insulator and washer on the shock absorber rod and install the attaching nut loosely.
5. Position the shock absorber to the lower bracket and install the attaching bolt and nut loosely.
6. Tighten the lower mounting nut to 39-53 ft. lbs. (53-72 Nm) and the upper to 25-35 ft. lbs. (34-48 Nm).

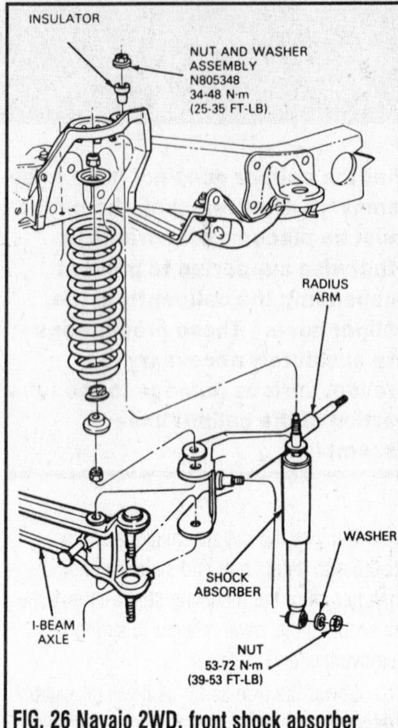

FIG. 26 Navajo 2WD, front shock absorber mounting

TESTING

1. Visually check the shock absorbers for the presence of fluid leakage. A thin film of fluid is acceptable. Anything more than that means that the shock absorber must be replaced.
2. Disconnect the lower end of the shock absorber. Compress and extend the shock fully as fast as possible. If the action is not smooth in both directions, or there is no pressure resistance, replace the shock absorber. Shock absorbers should be replaced in pairs. In the case of relatively new shock absorbers, where one has failed, that one, alone, may be replaced.

Upper Ball Joint

INSPECTION

1. Raise the vehicle and position a jackstand under the I-beam axle beneath the coil spring. Check and adjust the front wheel bearings.
2. Have a helper grasp the lower edge of the tire and move the wheel assembly in and out.
3. While the wheel is being moved, observe the upper spindle arm and the upper part of the axle jaw.
4. One thirty-second inch (0.8mm) or greater movement between the upper part of the axle jaw and the upper spindle arm indicates that the upper ball joint must be replaced.

REMOVAL & INSTALLATION

1. Raise and safely support the vehicle. Remove the wheel and tire assembly.

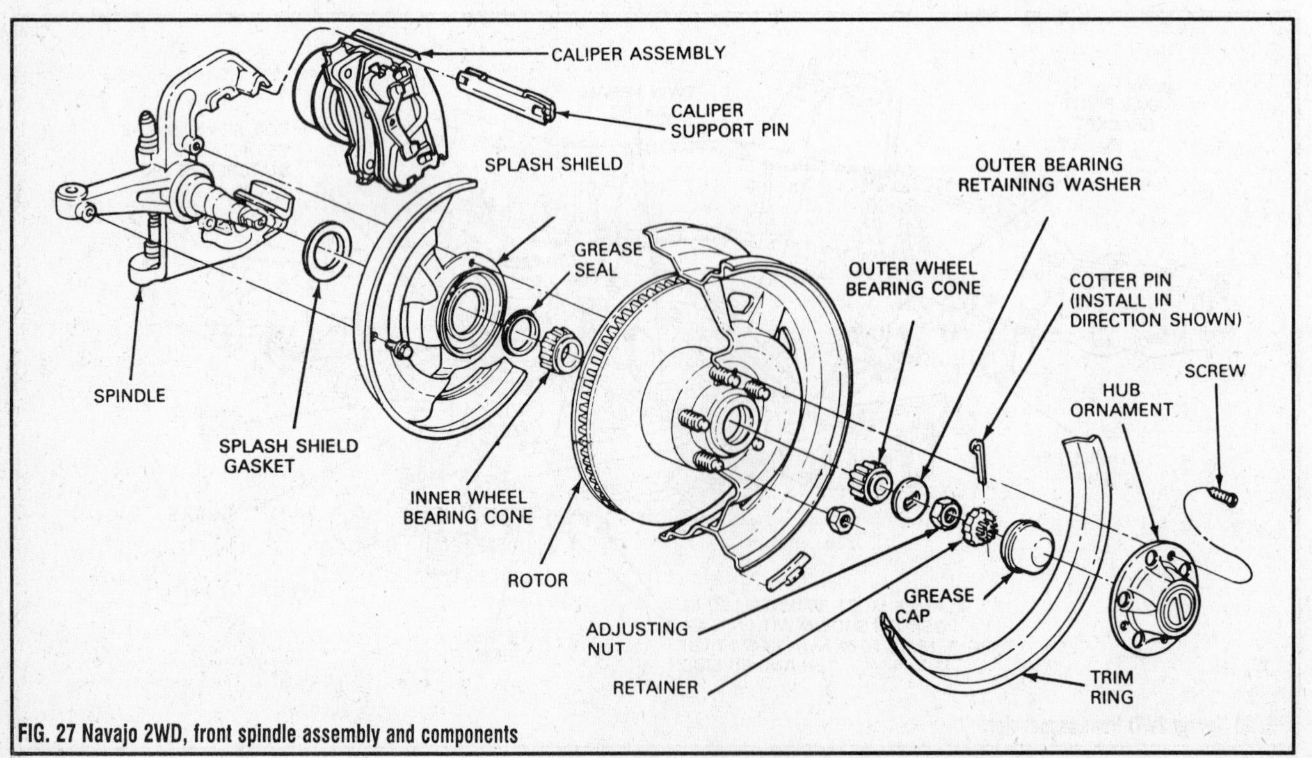

FIG. 27 Navajo 2WD, front spindle assembly and components

2. Remove the brake caliper and support it aside with mechanics wire. Do not let the caliper hang by the brake hose.

3. Remove the dust cap, cotter pin, nut retainer, washer and outer bearing and remove the brake rotor from the spindle. Remove the brake dust shield.

4. Disconnect the steering linkage from the spindle and spindle arm by removing the cotter pin and nut. Remove the tie rod end from the spindle arm.

5. Remove the cotter pin and nut from the lower ball joint stud. Remove the axle clamp bolt from the axle.

6. Remove the camber adjuster from the upper ball joint stud and axle beam.

7. Strike the inside area of the axle to pop the lower ball joint loose from the axle beam. Remove the spindle and ball joint assembly from the axle.

➡ **Do not use a pickle fork to separate the ball joint from the axle as this will damage the seal and ball joint socket.**

8. Install the spindle assembly in a vise and remove the snapring from the lower ball joint. Remove the lower ball joint from the spindle using C-frame T74P–4635–C or equivalent and a suitable receiver cup to press the ball joint from the spindle.

➡ **The lower ball joint must be removed first.**

9. Repeat the procedure in Step 8 to remove the upper ball joint.

➡ **Do not heat the ball joints or the spindle to aid in removal.**

To install:

10. Assemble the C-frame and receiver cup and press in the upper ball joint.

11. Repeat the procedure in Step 10 to install the lower ball joint.

➡ **Do not heat the ball joints or axle to aid in installation.**

12. Install the snapring onto the ball joint.

13. Place the spindle and ball joints into the axle. Install the camber adjuster in the upper spindle over the ball joint stud making sure it is properly aligned.

14. Tighten the lower ball joint stud nut to 104–146 ft. lbs. (141–198 Nm). Continue tightening the castellated nut until it lines up with the hole in the stud, then install the cotter pin.

15. Install the clamp bolt into the axle boss and tighten to 48–65 ft. lbs. (65–88 Nm).

16. Install the remaining components.

Lower Ball Joint

INSPECTION

1. Raise the vehicle and position a jackstand under the I-beam axle beneath the coil spring. Check and adjust the front wheel bearings.

2. Have a helper grasp the upper edge of the tire and move the wheel assembly in and out.

3. While the wheel is being moved, observe the lower spindle arm and the lower part of the axle jaw.

4. One thirty-second inch (0.8mm) or greater movement between the lower part of the axle jaw and the lower spindle arm indicates that the lower ball joint must be replaced.

REMOVAL & INSTALLATION

1. Raise and safely support the vehicle. Remove the wheel and tire assembly.

2. Remove the brake caliper and support it aside with mechanics wire. Do not let the caliper hang by the brake hose.

3. Remove the dust cap, cotter pin, nut retainer, washer and outer bearing and remove the brake rotor from the spindle. Remove the brake dust shield.

4. Disconnect the steering linkage from the spindle and spindle arm by removing the cotter pin and nut. Remove the tie rod end from the spindle arm.

5. Remove the cotter pin and nut from the lower ball joint stud. Remove the axle clamp bolt from the axle.

6. Remove the camber adjuster from the upper ball joint stud and axle beam.

7. Strike the inside area of the axle to pop the lower ball joint loose from the axle beam. Remove the spindle and ball joint assembly from the axle.

➡ **Do not use a pickle fork to separate the ball joint from the axle as this will damage the seal and ball joint socket.**

8. Install the spindle assembly in a vise and remove the snapring from the lower ball joint. Remove the lower ball joint from the spindle using C-frame T74P–4635–C or equivalent and a suitable receiver cup to press the ball joint from the spindle.

➡ **Do not heat the ball joint or the spindle to aid in removal.**

To install:

9. Assemble the C-frame and receiver cup and press in the lower ball joint.

➡ **Do not heat the ball joint or axle to aid in installation.**

10. Install the snapring onto the ball joint.

11. Place the spindle and ball joints into the axle. Install the camber adjuster in the upper spindle over the ball joint stud making sure it is properly aligned.

12. Tighten the lower ball joint stud nut to 104–146 ft. lbs. (141–198 Nm). Continue tightening the castellated nut until it lines up with the hole in the stud, then install the cotter pin.

13. Install the clamp bolt into the axle boss and tighten to 48–65 ft. lbs. (65–88 Nm).

14. Install the remaining components.

Spindle

REMOVAL & INSTALLATION

1. Raise the front of the vehicle and install jackstands.

2. Remove the wheel and tire assembly.

3. Remove the caliper assembly from the rotor and hold it out of the way with wire.

4. Remove the dust cap, cotter pin, nut, nut retainer, washer, and outer bearing, and remove the rotor from the spindle.

5. Remove inner bearing cone and seal. Discard the seal.

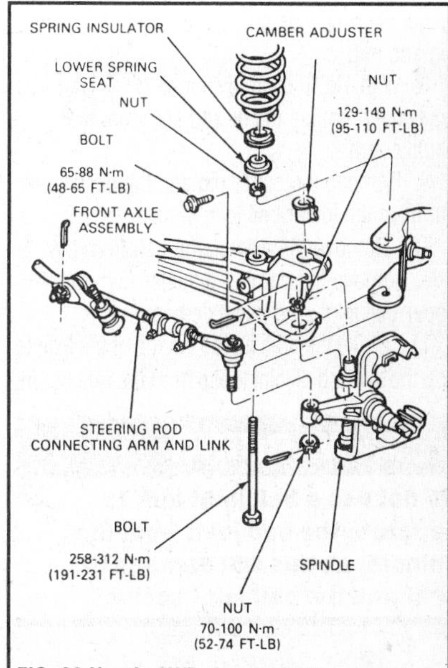

FIG. 28 Navajo 2WD, front spindle removal and installation

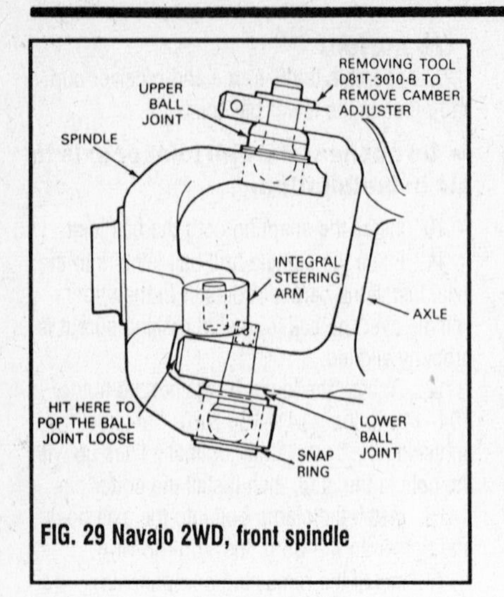

FIG. 29 Navajo 2WD, front spindle

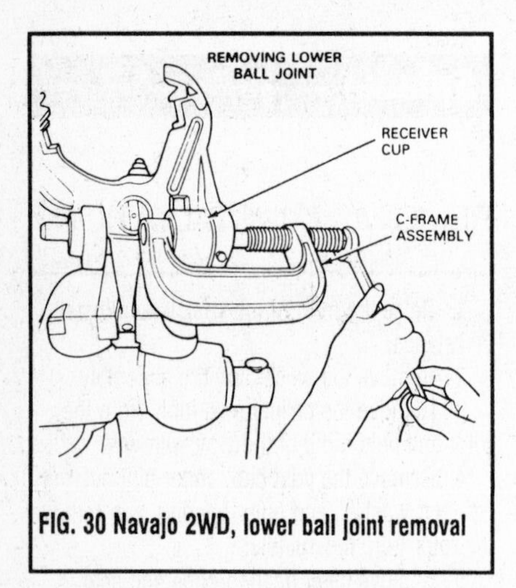

FIG. 30 Navajo 2WD, lower ball joint removal

6. Remove brake dust shield.

7. Disconnect the steering linkage from the spindle and spindle arm by removing the cotter pin and nut.

8. With Tie Rod removal tool 3290–D or equivalent remove the tie rod end from the spindle arm.

9. Remove the cotter pin and the castellated nut from the lower ball joint stud.

10. Remove the axle clamp bolt from the axle. Remove the camber adjuster from the upper ball joint stud and axle beam.

11. Strike the area inside the top of the axle to pop the lower ball joint loose from the axle beam.

WARNING

Do not use a ball joint fork to separate the ball joint from the spindle, as this will damage the seal and the ball joint socket!

12. Remove the spindle and the ball joint assembly from the axle.

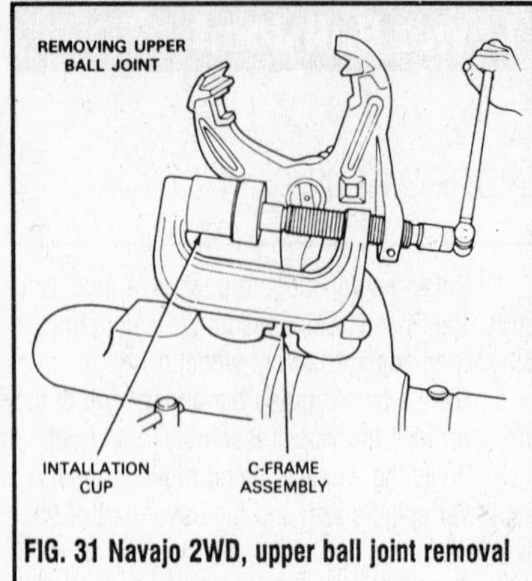

FIG. 31 Navajo 2WD, upper ball joint removal

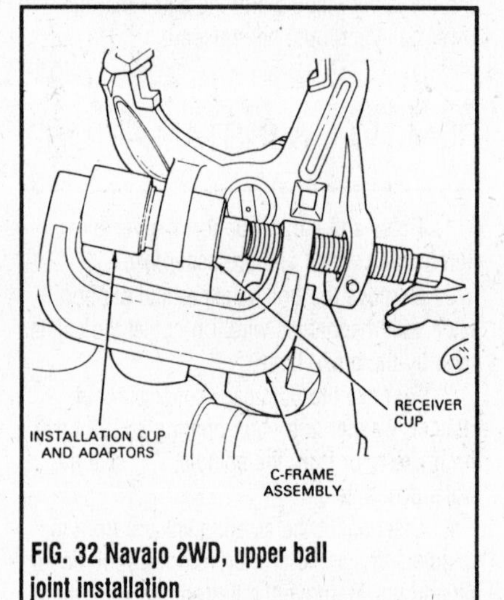

FIG. 32 Navajo 2WD, upper ball joint installation

To install:

➡ A 3 step sequence for tightening ball joint stud nuts must be followed to avoid excessive turning effort of spindle about axle.

13. Prior to assembly of the spindle, make sure the upper and lower ball joints seals are in place.

14. Place the spindle and the ball joint assembly into the axle.

15. Install the camber adjuster in the upper over the upper ball joint. If camber adjustment is necessary, special adapters must be installed.

16. Tighten the lower ball joint stud to 95–110 ft. lbs. Continue tightening the castellated nut until it lines up with the hole in the ball joint stud. Install the cotter pin. Install the dust shield.

17. Pack the inner and outer bearing cones with high temperature wheel bearing grease. Use a bearing packer. If a bearing packer is unavailable, pack the bearing cone by hand working the grease through the cage behind the rollers.

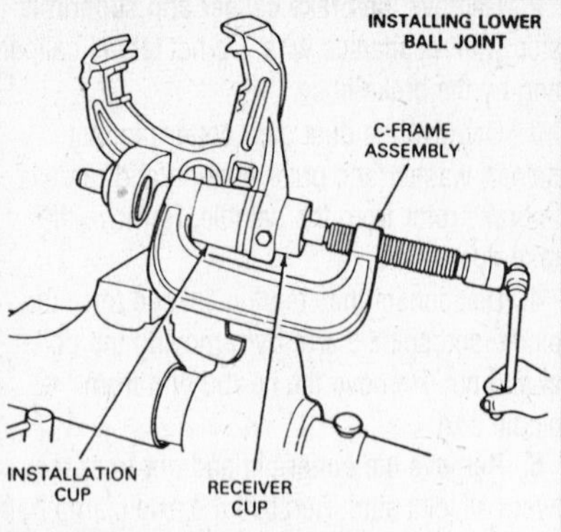

FIG. 33 Navajo 2WD, lower ball joint installation

18. Install the inner bearing cone and seal. Install the hub and rotor on the spindle.

19. Install the outer bearing cone, washer, and nut. Adjust bearing endplay and install the cotter pin and dust cap.

20. Install the caliper.

21. Connect the steering linkage to the spindle. Tighten the nut to 52–74 ft. lbs. and advance the nut as required for installation of the cotter pin.

22. Install the wheel and tire assembly. Lower the vehicle. Check, and if necessary, adjust the toe setting.

Radius Arm

REMOVAL & INSTALLATION

1. Raise the front of the vehicle, place jackstands under the frame. Place a jack under the axle.

WARNING

The axle must be supported on the jack throughout spring removal and installation, and must not be permitted to hang by the brake hose. If the length of the brake hose is not sufficient to provide adequate clearance for removal and installation of the spring, the disc brake caliper must be removed from the spindle. After removal, the caliper must be placed on the frame or otherwise supported to prevent suspending the caliper from the caliper hose. These

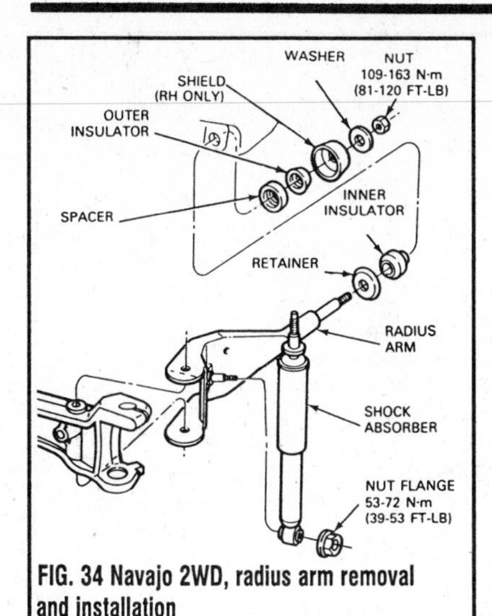

FIG. 34 Navajo 2WD, radius arm removal and installation

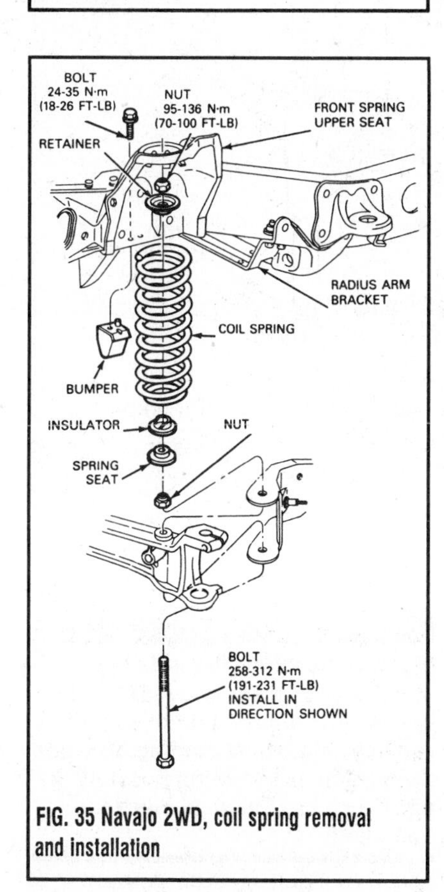

FIG. 35 Navajo 2WD, coil spring removal and installation

precautions are absolutely necessary to prevent serious damage to the tube portion of the caliper hose assembly.

2. Disconnect the lower end of the shock absorber from the shock lower bracket (bolt and nut).
3. Remove the front spring. Loosen the axle pivot bolt.
4. Remove the spring lower seat from the radius arm, and then remove the bolt and nut that attaches the radius arm to the axle and front bracket.
5. Remove the nut, rear washer and insulator from the rear side of the radius arm rear bracket.
6. Remove the radius arm from the vehicle, and remove the inner insulator and retainer from the radius arm stud.

To install:

7. Position the front end of the radius arm to the axle. Install the attaching bolt from underneath, and install the nut finger tight.
8. Install the retainer and inner insulator on the radius arm stud and insert the stud through the radius arm rear bracket.
9. Install the rear washer, insulator and nut on the arm stud at the rear side of the arm rear bracket. Tighten the nut to 81–120 ft. lbs.
10. Tighten the nut on the radius arm-to-axle bolt to 160–220 ft. lbs.
11. Install the spring lower seat and spring insulator on the radius arm so that the hole in the seat goes over the arm-to-axle bolt.
12. Install the front spring.
13. On 1990–91 vehicles connect the lower end of the shock absorber to the stud on the radius arm with the retaining nut. Torque the nut to 40–63 ft. lbs.

Stabilizer Bar

REMOVAL & INSTALLATION

1. As required, raise and support the vehicle safely.
2. Remove the nuts and washer and disconnect the stabilizer link assembly from the front I-beam axle.
3. Remove the mounting bolts and remove the stabilizer bar retainers from the stabilizer bar assembly.
4. Remove the stabilizer bar from the vehicle.

To install:

5. Place stabilizer bar in position on the frame mounting brackets.
6. Install retainers and tighten retainer bolt to 30–50 ft. lbs. If removed, install the stabilizer bar link assembly to the stabilizer bar. Install the nut and washer and tighten to 30–40 ft. lbs.
7. Position the stabilizer bar link in the I-beam mounting bracket. Install the bolt and tighten to 30–44 ft. lbs.

I-Beam Axle

REMOVAL & INSTALLATION

1. Raise and safely support the vehicle. Remove the front wheel spindle. Remove the front spring. Remove the front stabilizer bar, if equipped.
2. Remove the spring lower seat from the radius arm, and then remove the bolt and nut that attaches the stabilizer bar bracket, and the radius arm to the (I-Beam) front axle.
3. Remove the axle-to-frame pivot bracket bolt and nut.

To install:

4. Position the axle to the frame pivot bracket and install the bolt and nut finger tight.
5. Position the opposite end of the axle to the radius arm, install the attaching bolt from underneath through the bracket, the radius arm,, and the axle. Install the nut and tighten to 191-220 ft. lbs.
6. Install the spring lower seat on the radius arm so that the hole in the seat indexes over the arm-to-axle bolt.
7. Install the front spring.

➡ Lower the vehicle on its wheels or properly support the vehicle at the front springs before tightening the axle pivot bolt and nut.

8. Tighten the axle-to-frame pivot bracket bolt to 120–150 ft. lbs.
9. Install the front wheel spindle.

Front Wheel Bearings

REPLACEMENT

1. Raise and support the vehicle safely. Remove the tire and wheel assembly from the hub and rotor.
2. Remove the caliper from its mounting and position it to the side with mechanics wire in order to prevent damage to the brake line hose.
3. Remove the grease cap from the hub. Remove the cotter pin, retainer, adjusting nut and flatwasher from the spindle.
4. Remove the outer bearing cone and roller assembly from the hub. Remove the hub and rotor from the spindle.
5. Using seal removal tool 1175–AC or equivalent remove and discard the grease seal. Remove the inner bearing cone and roller assembly from the hub.

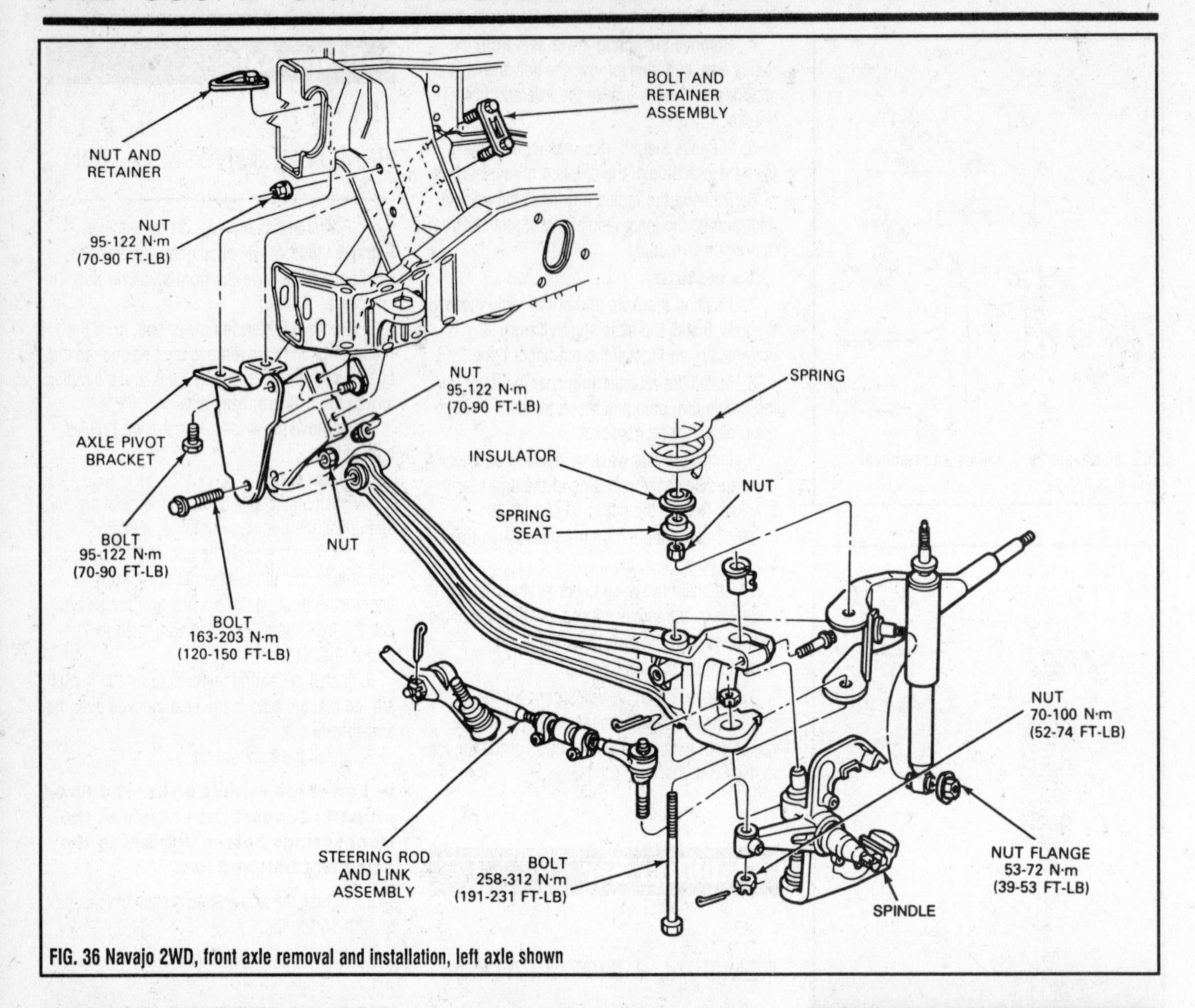

FIG. 36 Navajo 2WD, front axle removal and installation, left axle shown

6. Clean the inner and outer bearing assemblies in solvent. Inspect the bearings and the cones for wear and damage. Replace defective parts, as required.

7. If the cups are worn or damaged, remove them with front hub remover tool T81P–1104–C and tool T77F–1102–A or equivalent.

8. Wipe the old grease from the spindle. Check the spindle for excessive wear or damage. Replace defective parts, as required.

To install:

9. If the inner and outer cups were removed, use bearing driver handle tool T80–4000–W or equivalent and replace the cups. Be sure to seat the cups properly in the hub.

10. Use a bearing packer tool and properly repack the wheel bearings with the proper grade and type grease. If a bearing packer is not available work as much of the grease as possible between the rollers and cages. Also, grease the cone surfaces.

11. Position the inner bearing cone and roller assembly in the inner cup. A light film of grease should be included between the lips of the new grease retainer (seal).

12. Install the retainer using the proper installer tool. Be sure that the retainer is properly seated.

13. Install the hub and rotor assembly onto the spindle. Keep the hub centered on the spindle to prevent damage to the spindle and the retainer.

14. Install the outer bearing cone and roller assembly and flatwasher on the spindle. Install the adjusting nut. Adjust the wheel bearings.

15. Install the retainer, a new cotter pin and the grease cap. Install the caliper.

16. Lower the vehicle and tighten the lug nuts to 100 ft. lbs. Before driving the vehicle pump the brake pedal several times to restore normal brake pedal travel.

**** CAUTION**

Tighten the wheel lug nuts to specification after about 500 miles of driving. Failure to do this could result in the wheel coming off while the vehicle is in motion possibly causing loss of vehicle control or collision.

ADJUSTMENT

1. Raise and support the vehicle safely. Remove the wheel cover. Remove the grease cap from the hub.

2. Wipe the excess grease from the end of the spindle. Remove the cotter pin and retainer. Discard the cotter pin.

3. Loosen the adjusting nut 3 turns.

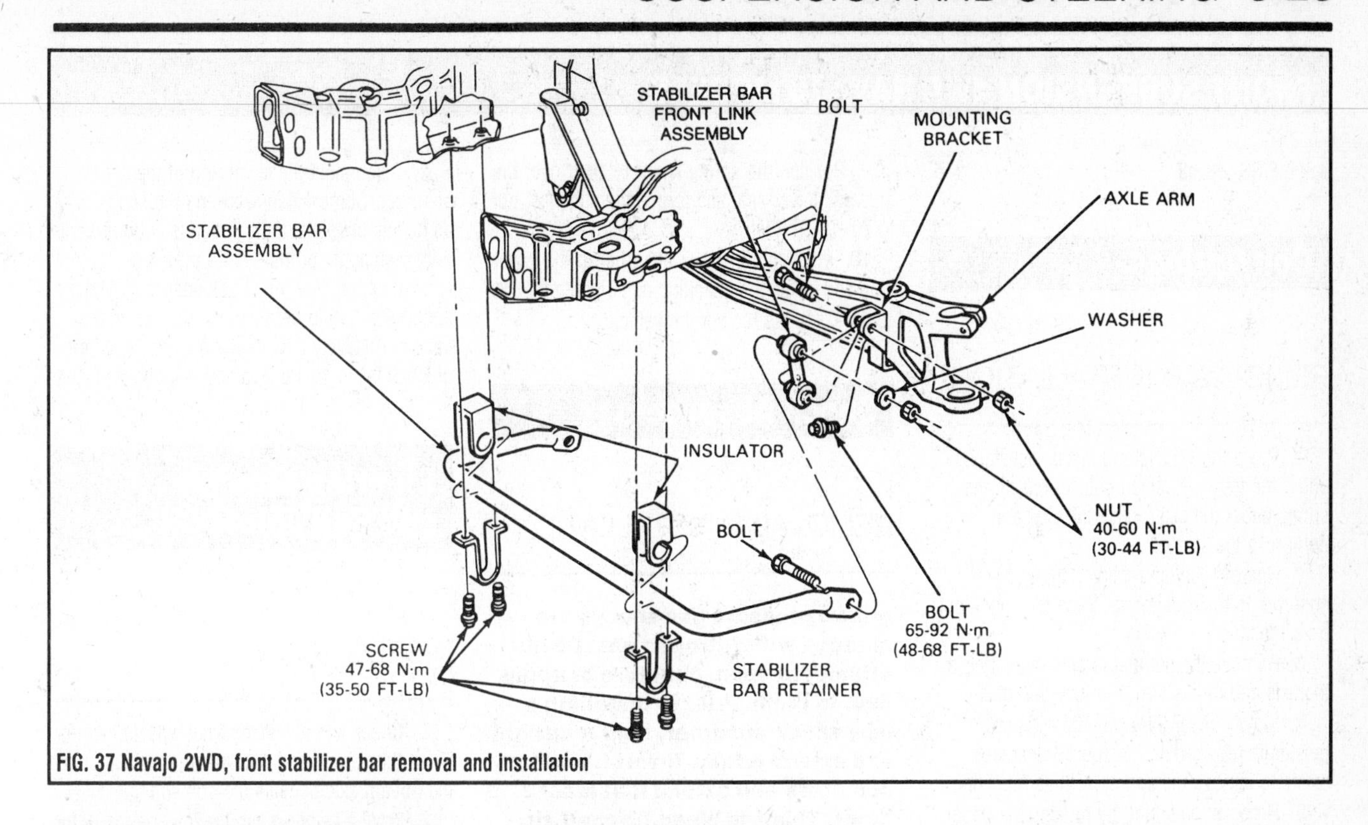

FIG. 37 Navajo 2WD, front stabilizer bar removal and installation

CAUTION

Obtain running clearance between the disc brake rotor surface and shoe linings by rocking the entire wheel assembly in and out several times in order to push the caliper and brake pads away from the rotor. An alternate method to obtain proper running clearance is to tap lightly on the caliper housing. Be sure not to tap on any other area that may damage the disc brake rotor or the brake lining surfaces. Do not pry on the phenolic caliper piston. The running clearance must be maintained throughout the adjustment procedure. If proper clearance cannot be maintained, the caliper must be removed from its mounting.

4. While rotating the wheel assembly, tighten the adjusting nut to 17–25 ft. lbs. in order to seat the bearings. Loosen the adjusting nut a half turn. Tighten the adjusting nut 18–20 inch lbs.

5. Place the retainer on the adjusting nut. The castellations on the retainer must be in alignment with the cotter pin holes in the spindle. Once this is accomplished install a new cotter pin and bend the ends to insure its being locked in place.

6. Check for proper wheel rotation. If correct, install the grease cap and wheel cover. If rotation is noisy or rough recheck your work and correct as required.

7. Lower the vehicle and tighten the lug nuts to 100 ft. lbs., if the wheel was removed. Before driving the vehicle pump the brake pedal several times to restore normal brake pedal travel.

CAUTION

If the wheel was removed, tighten the wheel lug nuts to specification after about 500 miles of driving. Failure to do this could result in the wheel coming off while the vehicle is in motion possibly causing loss of vehicle control or collision.

FRONT SUSPENSION 4WD NAVAJO MODELS

➧SEE FIGS. 38-43

Coil Springs

REMOVAL & INSTALLATION

1. Raise the vehicle and install jackstands under the frame. Position a jack beneath the spring under the axle. Raise the jack and compress the spring.
2. Remove the nut retaining the shock absorber to the radius arm. Slide the shock out from the stud.
3. Remove the nut that retains the spring to the axle and radius arm. Remove the retainer.
4. Slowly lower the axle until all spring tension is released and adequate clearance exists to remove the spring from its mounting.
5. Remove the spring by rotating the upper coil out of the tabs in the upper spring seat. Remove the spacer and the seat.

**** WARNING**

The axle must be supported on the jack throughout spring removal and installation, and must not be permitted to hang by the brake hose. If the length of the brake hose is not sufficient to provide adequate clearance for removal and installation of the spring, the disc brake caliper must be removed from the spindle. After removal, the caliper must be placed on the frame or otherwise supported to prevent suspending the caliper from the brake line hose. These precautions are absolutely necessary to prevent serious damage to the tube portion of the caliper hose assembly!

6. If required, remove the stud from the axle assembly.

To install:

7. If removed, install the stud on the axle and torque to 190–230 ft. lbs. Install the lower seat and spacer over the stud.
8. Place the spring in position and slowly raise the front axle. Ensure springs are positioned correctly in the upper spring seats.
9. Position the spring lower retainer over the stud and lower seat and torque the attaching nut to 70–100 ft. lbs.
10. Position the shock absorber to the lower stud and install the attaching nut. Tighten the nut to 41–63 ft. lbs. Lower the vehicle.

Shock Absorbers

REMOVAL & INSTALLATION

➡ **Low pressure gas shocks are charged with Nitrogen gas. Do not attempt to open, puncture or apply heat to them. Prior to installing a new shock absorber, hold it upright and extend it fully. Invert it and fully compress and extend it at least 3 times. This will bleed trapped air.**

1. Raise the vehicle, as required to provide additional access and remove the bolt and nut attaching the shock absorber to the lower bracket on the radius arm.
2. Remove the nut, washer and insulator from the shock absorber at the frame bracket and remove the shock absorber.

To install:

3. Position the washer and insulator on the shock absorber rod and position the shock absorber to the frame bracket.
4. Position the insulator and washer on the shock absorber rod and install the attaching nut loosely.
5. Position the shock absorber to the lower bracket and install the attaching bolt and nut loosely.
6. Tighten the lower attaching bolts to 39–53 ft. lbs., and the upper attaching bolts to 25–35 ft. lbs.

TESTING

1. Visually check the shock absorbers for the presence of fluid leakage. A thin film of fluid is acceptable. Anything more than that means that the shock absorber must be replaced.
2. Disconnect the lower end of the shock absorber. Compress and extend the shock fully as fast as possible. If the action is not smooth in both directions, or there is no pressure resistance, replace the shock absorber. Shock absorbers should be replaced in pairs. In the case of relatively new shock absorbers, where one has failed, that one, alone, may be replaced.

Steering Knuckle and Ball Joints

INSPECTION

1. Check and adjust the front wheel bearings. Raise the vehicle and position a jackstand under the I-beam axle beneath the coil spring.
2. Have a helper grasp the lower edge of the tire and move the wheel assembly in and out.
3. While the wheel is being moved, observe the lower spindle arm and the lower part of the axle jaw.
4. One thirty second inch (0.8mm) or greater movement between the lower part of the axle jaw and the lower spindle arm indicates that the lower ball joint must be replaced
5. To check the upper ball joints, while the wheel is being moved, observe the upper spindle arm and the upper part of the axle jaw.

REMOVAL & INSTALLATION

1. Raise the vehicle and support on jackstands.
2. Remove the wheel and tire assembly.
3. Remove the caliper.
4. Remove hub locks, wheel bearings, and locknuts.
5. Remove the hub and rotor. Remove the outer wheel bearing cone.
6. Remove the grease seal from the rotor with seal remover tool 1175–AC and slide hammer 750T–100–A or equivalent. Discard seal and replace with a new one upon assembly.
7. Remove the inner wheel bearing.
8. Remove the inner and outer bearing cups from the rotor with a bearing cup puller.

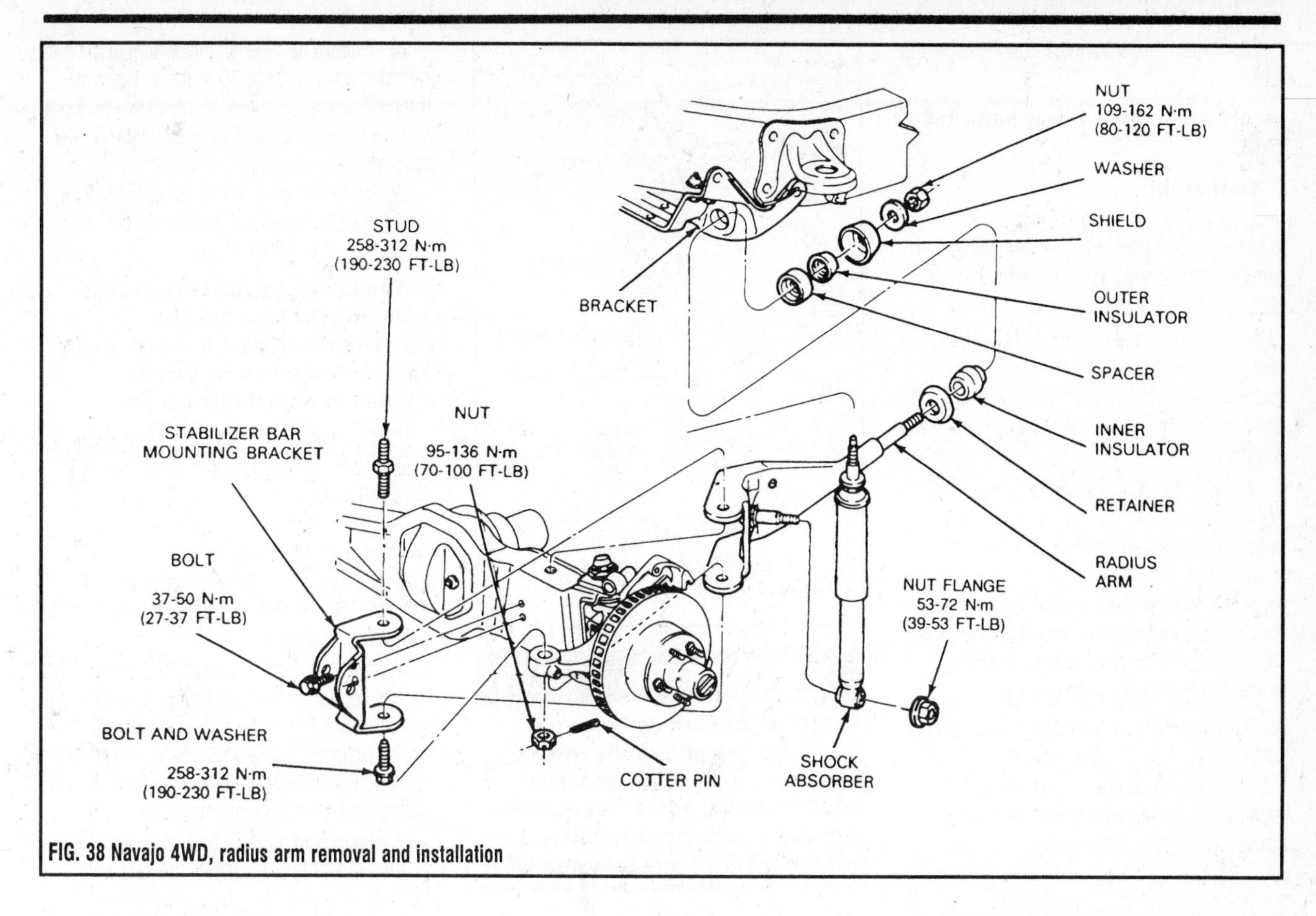

FIG. 38 Navajo 4WD, radius arm removal and installation

9. Remove the nuts retaining the spindle to the steering knuckle. Tap the spindle with a plastic or rawhide hammer to jar the spindle from the knuckle. Remove the splash shield.

10. On the left side of the vehicle remove the shaft and joint assembly by pulling the assembly out of the carrier.

11. On the right side of the carrier, remove and discard the keystone clamp from the shaft and joint assembly and the stub shaft. Slide the rubber boot onto the stub shaft and pull the shaft and joint assembly from the splines of the stub shaft.

12. Place the spindle in a vise on the second step of the spindle. Wrap a shop towel around the spindle or use a brass-jawed vise to protect the spindle.

13. Remove the oil seal and needle bearing from the spindle with slide hammer T50T-100-A and seal remover tool 1175-A-C or equivalent.

14. If required, remove the seal from the shaft, by driving off with a hammer.

15. If the tie rod has not been removed, then remove cotter pin from the tie rod nut and then remove nut. Tap on the tie rod stud to free it from the steering arm.

16. Remove the upper ball joint cotter pin and nut. Loosen the lower ball joint nut to the end of the stud.

17. Strike the inside of the spindle near the upper and lower ball joints to break the spindle loose from the ball joint studs.

18. Remove the camber adjuster sleeve. If required, use pitman arm puller, T64P-3590-F or equivalent to remove the adjuster out of the spindle. Remove the lower ball joint nut.

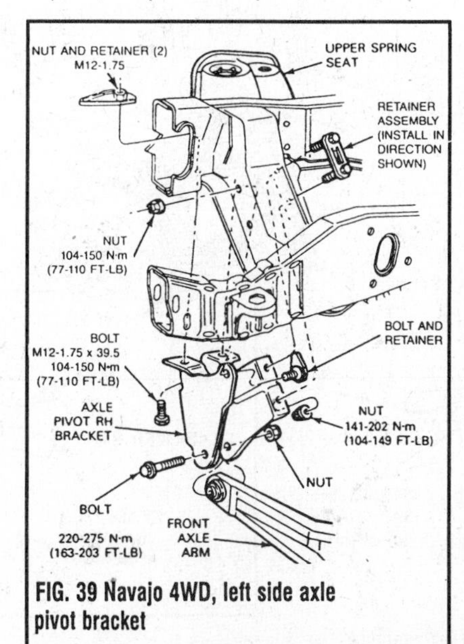

FIG. 39 Navajo 4WD, left side axle pivot bracket

19. Place knuckle in vise and remove snapring from bottom ball joint socket if so equipped.

20. Assemble the C-frame, T74P-4635-C, forcing screw, D79T-3010-AE and ball joint remover T83T-3050-A or equivalent on the lower ball joint.

21. Turn forcing screw clockwise until the lower ball joint is removed from the steering knuckle.

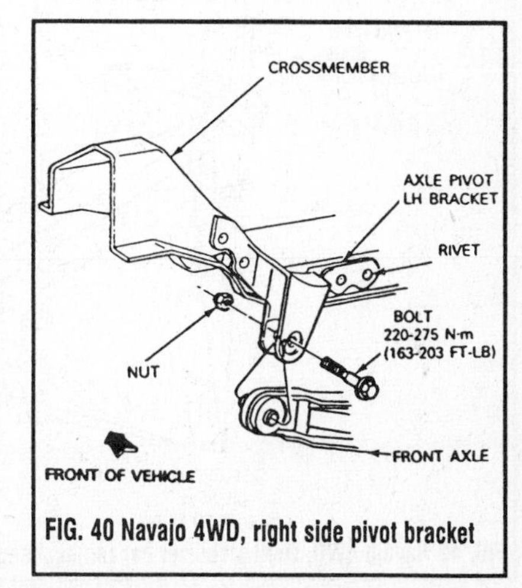

FIG. 40 Navajo 4WD, right side pivot bracket

22. Repeat Steps 20 and 21 for the upper ball joint.

➡ **Always remove lower ball joint first.**

To install:

23. Clean the steering knuckle bore and insert lower ball joint in knuckle as straight as possible. The lower ball joint doesn't have a cotter pin hole in the stud.

24. Assemble the C-frame, T74P–4635–C, forcing screw, D790T–3010–AE, ball joint installer, T83T–3050–A and receiver cup T80T–3010–A3 or equivalent tools, to install the lower ball joint.

25. Turn the forcing screw clockwise until the lower ball joint is firmly seated. Install the snapring on the lower ball joint.

➡ **If the ball joint cannot be installed to the proper depth, realignment of the receiver cup and ball joint installer will be necessary.**

26. Repeat Steps 24 and 25 for the upper ball joint.

27. Install the camber adjuster into the support arm. Position the slot in its original position.

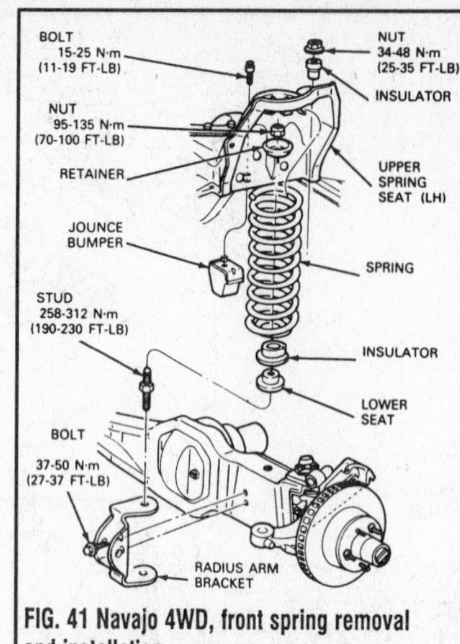

FIG. 41 Navajo 4WD, front spring removal and installation

CAUTION

The following torque sequence must be followed exactly when securing the spindle. Excessive spindle turning effort may result in reduced steering returnability if this procedure is not followed.

28. Install a new nut on the bottom of the ball joint stud and torque to 90 ft. lbs. (minimum). Tighten to align the nut to the next slot in the nut with the hole in the ball joint stud. Install a new cotter pin.

29. Install the snapring on the upper ball joint stud. Install the upper ball joint pinch bolt and torque the nut to 48–65 ft. lbs.

➡ **The camber adjuster will seat itself into the knuckle at a predetermined position during the tightening sequence. Do not attempt to adjust this position.**

30. Clean all dirt and grease from the spindle bearing bore. Bearing bores must be free from nicks and burrs.

31. Place the bearing in the fore with the manufacturer's identification facing outward. Drive the bearing into the bore using spindle replacer, T80T–4000S and driver handle T80T–4000–W or equivalent.

32. Install the grease seal in the bearing bore with the lip side of the seal facing towards the tool. Drive the seal in the bore with spindle bearing replacer, T83T–3123–A and driver handle T80–4000–W or equivalent. Coat the bearing seal lip with Lubriplate®.

33. If removed, install a new shaft seal. Place the shaft in a press, and install the seal with

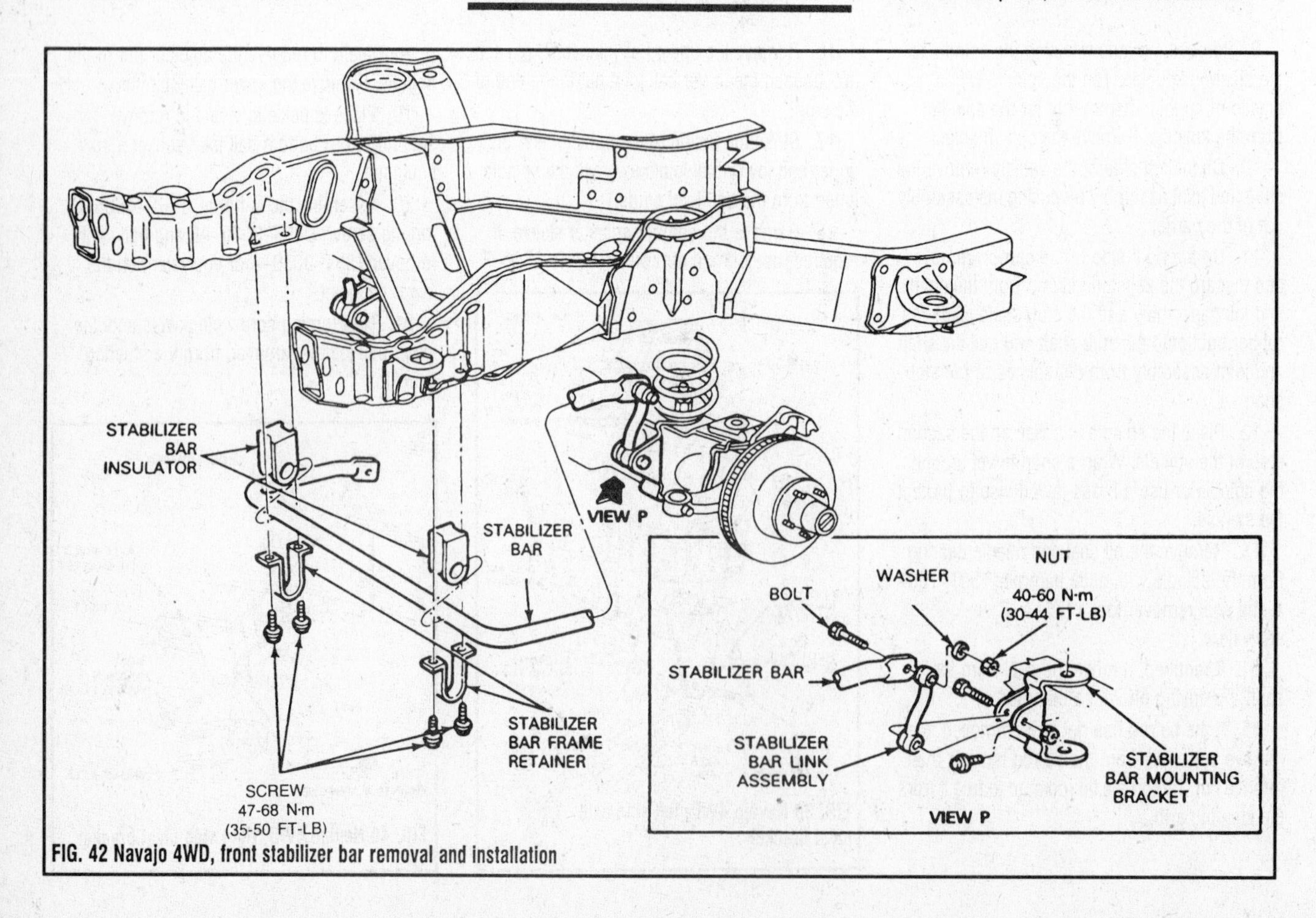

FIG. 42 Navajo 4WD, front stabilizer bar removal and installation

spindle/axle seal installer, T83T–3132–A, or equivalent.

34. On the right side of the carrier, install the rubber boot and new keystone clamps on the stub slip yoke.

➡ **This axle does not have a blind spline. Therefore, special attention should be made to assure that the yoke ears are in line during assembly.**

35. Slide the boot over the assembly and crimp the keystone clamp using keystone clamp pliers, T63P–9171–A or equivalent.

36. On the left side of the carrier slide the shaft and joint assembly through the knuckle and engage the splines on the shaft in the carrier.

37. Install the splash shield and spindle onto the steering knuckle. Install and tighten the spindle nuts to 40–50 ft. lbs.

38. Drive the bearing cups into the rotor using bearing cup replacer T73T–4222–B and driver handle, T80T–4000–W or equivalent.

39. Pack the inner and outer wheel bearings and the lip of the oil seal with Multi–Purpose Long-Life Lubricant, C1AZ–19590–B or equivalent.

40. Place the inner wheel bearing in the inner cup. Drive the grease seal into the bore with hub seal replacer, T80T–4000–T and driver handle, T80T–4000–W or equivalent. Coat the bearing seal lip with multipurpose long life lubricant, C1AZ–19590–B or equivalent.

41. Install the rotor on the spindle. Install the outer wheel bearing into cup.

➡ **Verify that the grease seal lip totally encircles the spindle.**

42. Install the wheel bearing, locknut, thrust bearing, snapring, and locking hubs.

Radius Arm

REMOVAL & INSTALLATION

1. Raise the front of the vehicle, place jackstands under the frame. Place a jack under the axle.

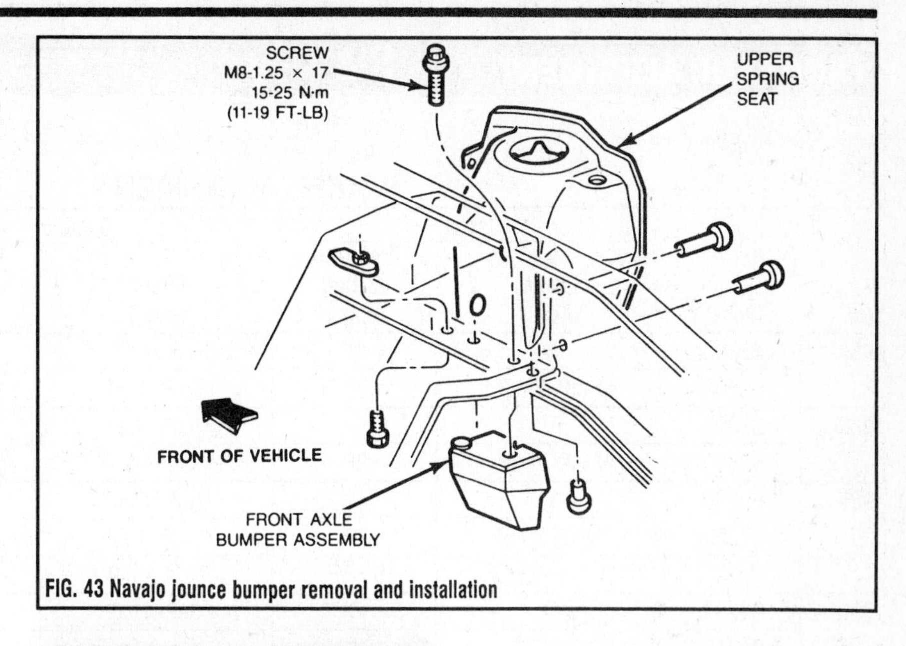

FIG. 43 Navajo jounce bumper removal and installation

✲✲ WARNING

The axle must be supported on the jack throughout spring removal and installation, and must not be permitted to hang by the brake hose. If the length of the brake hose is not sufficient to provide adequate clearance for removal and installation of the spring, the disc brake caliper must be removed from the spindle. After removal, the caliper must be placed on the frame or otherwise supported to prevent suspending the caliper from the caliper hose.

These precautions are absolutely necessary to prevent serious damage to the tube portion of the caliper hose assembly.

2. Disconnect the lower end of the shock absorber from the lower stud. Remove the front spring from the vehicle.

3. Remove the spring lower seat and stud from the radius arm. Remove the bolts that attach the radius arm to the axle and front bracket.

4. Remove the nut, rear washer and insulator from the rear side of the radius arm rear bracket.

5. Remove the radius arm from the vehicle. Remove the inner insulator and retainer from the radius arm stud.

To install:

6. Position the front end of the radius arm from bracket to axle. Install the retaining bolts and stud in the bracket finger tight.

7. Install the retainer and inner insulator on the radius arm stud and insert the stud through the radius arm rear bracket.

8. Install the rear washer, insulator and nut on the arm stud at the rear side of the arm rear bracket. Tighten the nut to 80–120 ft. lbs.

9. Tighten the stud to 190–230 ft. lbs. Tighten the front bracket to axle bolts to 37–50 ft. lbs. and the lower bolt and washer to 190–230 ft. lbs.

10. Install the spring lower seat and spring insulator on the radius arm so that the hole in the seat goes over the arm to axle bolt. Tighten the axle pivot bolt to 120–150 ft. lbs.

11. Install the front spring. Connect the lower end of the shock absorber to the stud of the radius arm and torque the retaining nut to 39–53 ft. lbs.

Stabilizer Bar

REMOVAL & INSTALLATION

1. As required, raise and support the vehicle safely. Remove the bolts and the retainers from the center and right hand end of the stabilizer bar.

2. Remove the nut, bolt and washer retaining the stabilizer bar to the stabilizer link.

3. Remove the stabilizer bar and bushings from the vehicle.

4. Installation is the reverse of the removal procedure. Tighten the retainer bolts to 35–50 ft. lbs. Tighten the stabilizer bar to link nut to 30–44 ft. lbs.

FRONT END ALIGNMENT

WHEEL ALIGNMENT

Year	Model	Caster Range (deg.)	Caster Preferred Setting (deg.)	Camber Range (deg.)	Camber Preferred Setting (deg.)	Toe-in (in.)	Steering Axis Inclination (deg.)
1987	B2200	①	②	7/16P-1 1/4P	3/4P	1/8	8 1/4
	B2600	1 1/4P-2 2/3P	2P	11/16P-1 1/2P	1P	1/8	10 5/16
1988	B2200	①	②	7/16P-1 1/4P	3/4P	1/8	8 1/4
	B2600	1 1/4P-2 2/3P	2P	11/16P-1 1/2P	1P	1/8	10 5/16
1989	B2200	①	②	7/16P-1 1/4P	3/4P	1/8	8 1/4
	B2600i	1 1/4P-2 2/3P	2P	11/16P-1 1/2P	1P	1/8	10 5/16
	MPV	4 11/16P-6 3/16P	5 7/16P	3/8N-1 1/8P	3/8P	5/32	12 15/16
1990	B2200	①	②	7/16P-1 1/4P	3/4P	1/8	8 1/4
	B2600i	①	②	③	④	1/8	⑤
	MPV	⑥	⑦	⑧	⑨	5/32	⑩
1991	B2200	①	②	7/16P-1 1/4P	3/4P	1/8	8 1/4
	B2600i	①	②	③	④	1/8	⑤
	MPV	⑥	⑦	⑧	⑨	5/32	⑩
	Navajo	2 1/2P-6P	NA	3/4N-1 1/4P	NA	0	NA
1992	B2200	①	②	7/16P-1 1/4P	3/4P	1/8	8 1/4
	B2600i	①	②	③	④	1/8	⑤
	MPV	⑥	⑦	⑧	⑨	5/32	⑩
	Navajo	2 1/2P-6P	NA	3/4N-1 1/4P	NA	0	NA

NA—Not available

① 2WD
With manual steering: 1/10P-1 9/16P
With power steering: 1/16P-2 9/16P
4WD
1 1/4P-2 3/4P

② 2WD
With manual steering: 13/16P
With power steering: 1 13/16P
4WD
2P

③ 2WD: 7/16P-1 1/4P
4WD: 11/16P-1 1/2P

④ 2WD: 3/4P
4WD: 1P

⑤ 2WD: 8 1/4
4WD: 10 5/16

⑥ 2WD: 4 11/16P-6 3/16P
4WD: 4 3/4P-6 1/4P

⑦ 2WD: 5 7/16P
4WD: 5 1/2P

⑧ 2WD: 3/8P-1 1/8P
4WD: 5/16N-11/16P

⑨ 2WD: 3/8P
4WD: 3/16P

⑩ 2WD: 12 15/16
4WD: 11 13/16

Navajo – 2WD Models

CASTER AND CAMBER

If you should start to notice abnormal tire wear patterns and handling (steering wheel is hard to return to straight ahead position after negotiating a turn on pavement), and misalignment of caster and camber are suspected, make the following checks:

1. Check the air pressure in all the tires. Make sure that the pressures agree with those specified for the tires and vehicle being checked.
2. Raise the front of the vehicle off the ground and support it safely. Grasp each front tire at the front and rear, and push the wheel inward and outward. If any free-play is noticed, adjust the wheel bearings.

➡ There is supposed to be a very, very small amount of free-play present where the wheel bearings are concerned. Replace the bearings if they are worn or damaged.

3. Check all steering linkage for wear or maladjustment. Adjust and/or replace all worn parts.
4. Check the steering gear mounting bolts and tighten if necessary.
5. Rotate each front wheel slowly, and observe the amount of lateral or side runout. If the wheel runout exceeds 1/8 in. (3mm), replace the wheel or install the wheel on the rear.
6. Inspect the radius arms to be sure they are not bent or damaged. Inspect the bushings at the radius arm-to-axle attachment and radius arm-to-frame attachment points for wear or looseness. Repair or replace parts as required.

Caster is the number of degrees of backward (positive) or forward (negative) tilt of the spindle or the line connecting the ball joint centers. Camber is the number of degrees the top of the wheel tilts outward (positive) or inward (negative) from a vertical plane.

Before checking caster or camber, perform the toe alignment check. Using alignment equipment known to be accurate and following the equipment manufacturer's instructions, measure and record the caster angle and the camber angle of both front wheels.

If the caster and camber measurements exceed the maximum variances, inspect for damaged front suspension components. Replace as required.

➡ Twin-I-Beam axles are not to be bent or twisted to correct caster or camber readings.

Both caster and camber adjustments are possible with service adjusters. These service adjusters are available in 1/2, 1 and 1 1/2 degree increments. On of these adjusters is used to adjust both caster and camber.

Navajo – 4WD Models

CASTER AND CAMBER

If you should start to notice abnormal tire wear patterns and handling (steering wheel is hard to return to straight ahead position after negotiating a turn on pavement), and misalignment of caster and camber are suspected, make the following checks:

1. Check the air pressure in all the tires. Make sure that the pressures agree with those specified for the tires and vehicle being checked.
2. Raise the front of the vehicle off the ground and support it safely. Grasp each front tire at the front and rear, and push the wheel inward and outward. If any free-play is noticed, adjust the wheel bearings.

➡ There is supposed to be a very, very small amount of free-play present where the wheel bearings are concerned. Replace the bearings if they are worn or damaged.

3. Check all steering linkage for wear or maladjustment. Adjust and/or replace all worn parts.
4. Check the steering gear mounting bolts and tighten if necessary.
5. Rotate each front wheel slowly, and observe the amount of lateral or side runout. If the wheel runout exceeds 1/8 in. (3mm), replace the wheel or install the wheel on the rear.
6. Inspect the radius arms to be sure they are not bent or damaged. Inspect the bushings at the radius arm-to-axle attachment and radius arm-to-frame attachment points for wear or looseness. Repair or replace parts as required.

Caster is the number of degrees of backward (positive) or forward (negative) tilt of the spindle or the line connecting the ball joint centers. Camber is the number of degrees the top of the wheel tilts outward (positive) or inward (negative) from a vertical plane.

Before checking caster or camber, perform the toe alignment check. Using alignment equipment known to be accurate and following the equipment manufacturer's instructions, measure and record the caster angle and the camber angle of both front wheels.

If the caster and camber measurements exceed the maximum variances, inspect for damaged front suspension components. Replace as required.

Both caster and camber adjustments are possible with service adjusters. These service adjusters are available in 1/2, 1 and 1 1/2 degree increments. On of these adjusters is used to adjust both caster and camber.

B Series Pickups and MPV Models

CASTER

Pickups

Caster is adjusted by changing the shims between the upper arm shaft and the frame, or, by turning the shaft until the correct angle is obtained.

MPV

Caster is adjusted by changing the position of the upper strut mounting block.

CAMBER

Camber is the outward or inward tilting of the wheels at the top.

Pickups

Camber is adjusted by adding or subtracting the shims between the upper arm shaft and the frame. Shims are available in thicknesses of 1.0mm, 1.5mm, 2.0mm, and 3.0mm.

MPV

Camber is adjusted by changing the position of the upper strut mounting block.

TOE-IN

Toe-in is the amount, measured in fractions of an inch, that the wheels are closer together in the front than the rear.

Toe-in can be changed by changing the length of the tie rods. Threaded sleeves on the rods are provided for this purpose.

TURNING ANGLE

Turning stop screws are located at the steering knuckle. If necessary, the screws can be adjusted.

REAR SUSPENSION

Leaf Springs

REMOVAL & INSTALLATION

Pickups

SEE FIGS. 44-45

1. Raise and support the rear of the truck on jackstands under the frame.

CAUTION

The rear leaf springs are under considerable tension. Be very careful when removing and installing them, they can exert enough force to cause serious injuries.

2. Place a floor jack under the rear axle to take up its weight.
3. Disconnect the lower end of the shock absorbers.
4. Remove the spring U-bolts and plate.
5. Remove the spring front bolt.
6. Remove the rear shackle nuts and the shackle.
7. Lift the spring from the truck.
8. Place the leaf spring in position and install the rear shackle and front mount bolt. Install the spring U bolts. Secure all fasteners snugly and lower the truck. When the truck is on its wheels, torque the nuts and bolts. Observe the following torques:
   - Spring rear shackle nuts: 58 ft. lbs.
   - 2-wheel drive U-bolt nuts: 58 ft. lbs.
   - 4-wheel drive U-bolt nuts: 101 ft. lbs.

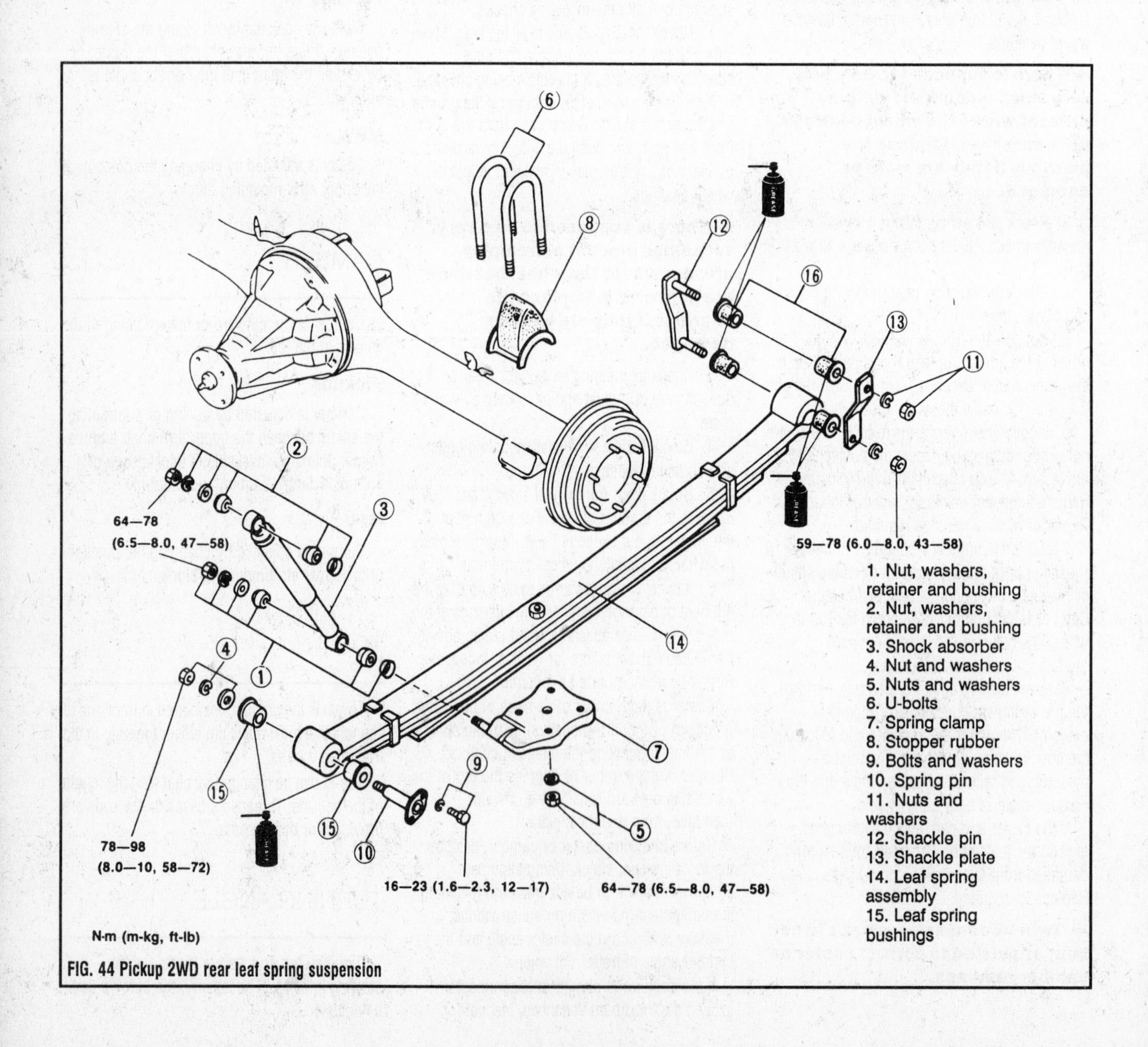

FIG. 44 Pickup 2WD rear leaf spring suspension

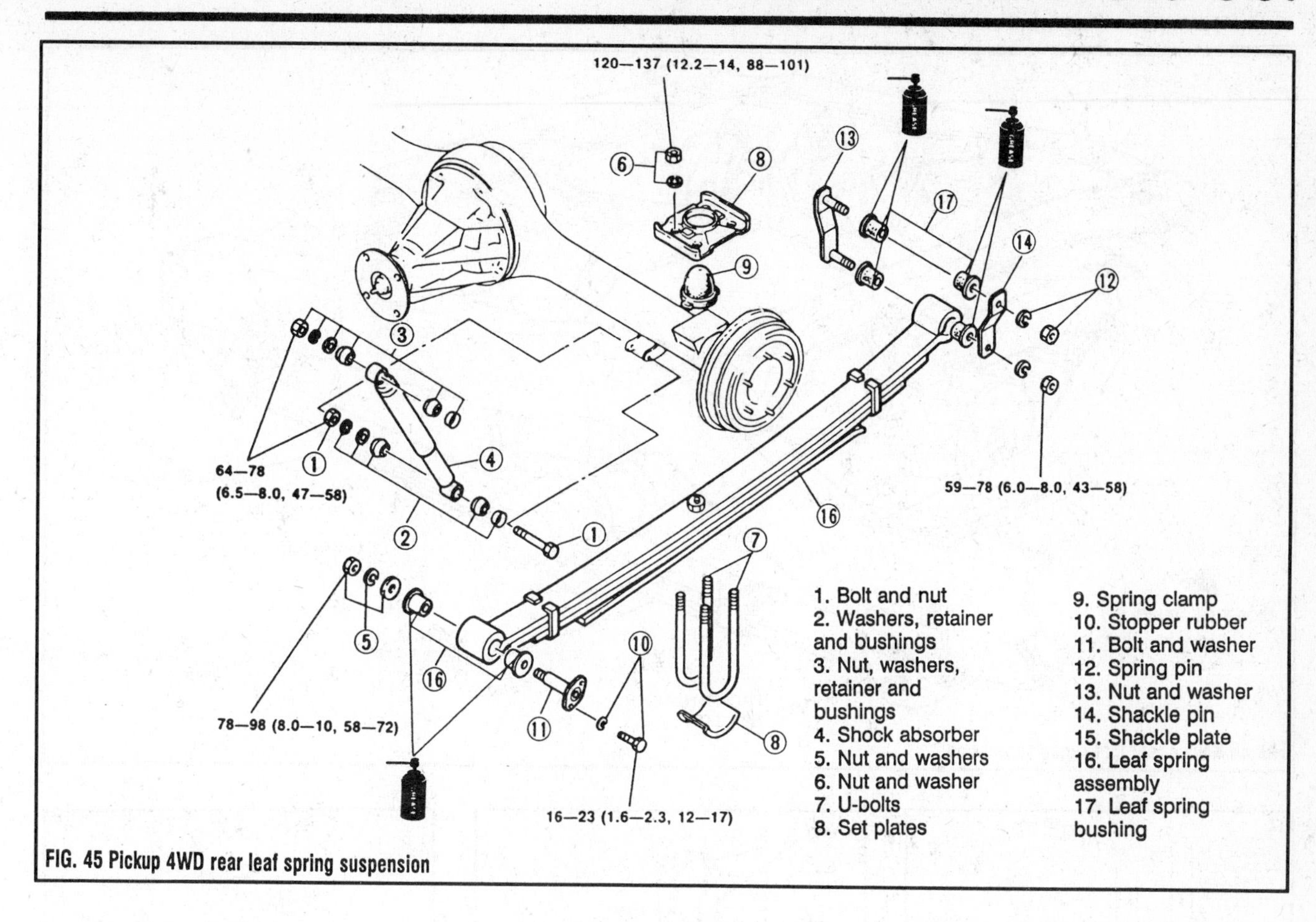

FIG. 45 Pickup 4WD rear leaf spring suspension

- Front spring pin nut: 72 ft. lbs.
- Shock absorber: 58 ft. lbs.

Navajo

SEE FIGS. 46-51

1. Raise the vehicle and install jackstands under the frame. The vehicle must be supported in such a way that the rear axle hangs free with the tires still touching the ground.
2. Remove the nuts from the spring U-bolts and drive the U-bolts from the U-bolt plate.
3. Remove the spring to bracket nut and bolt at the front of the spring.
4. Remove the shackle upper and lower nuts and bolts at the rear of the spring.
5. Remove the spring and shackle assembly from the rear shackle bracket.

To install:

6. Position the spring in the shackle. Install the upper shackle spring bolt and nut with the bolt head facing outward.
7. Position the front end of the spring in the bracket and install the bolt and nut.
8. Position the shackle in the rear bracket and install the nut and bolt.
9. Position the spring on top of the axle with the spring tie bolt centered in the hole provided in the seat.
10. Lower the vehicle to the floor. Torque the spring U-bolt nuts to 65–75 ft. lbs. Torque the front spring bolt to 75–115 ft. lbs. Torque the rear shackle nuts and bolts to 75–115 ft. lbs.

Coil Springs

REMOVAL & INSTALLATION

MPV

SEE FIGS. 52-54

1. Raise and safely support the vehicle. Remove the splash shield.
2. Remove the stabilizer bar.
3. Remove the nut and disconnect the height sensor from the rear axle.
4. Remove the bolt attaching the parking brake cable bracket.
5. Support the rear axle housing with a jack. Raise the jack slightly to take the load off the shock absorbers.
6. Remove the attaching bolts and nuts and disconnect the shock absorbers from the lower axle housing.
7. Slowly lower the axle housing until the spring tension is relieved. Remove the coil springs.
8. Remove the spring seats and bump stopper, if equipped.

To install:

9. Install the upper and lower spring seats and the bump stopper, if removed.
10. Install the coil springs, making sure the larger diameter coil is toward the axle housing.
11. Raise the axle housing enough to connect the shock absorbers. Install the attaching bolts and nuts and tighten to 56–76 ft. lbs. (76–103 Nm). Remove the jack.
12. Install the bolt attaching the parking brake cable bracket and the nut attaching the height sensor.
13. Install the stabilizer bar. Tighten the link bolt nut until 0.28 in. (7mm) of thread is exposed at the top of the link bolt. Do not tighten the stabilizer bar bushing bracket bolts at this time.
14. Lower the vehicle. With the vehicle unladen, tighten the stabilizer bar bushing bracket bolts to 23–38 ft. lbs. (34–51 Nm).
15. Install the splash shield.

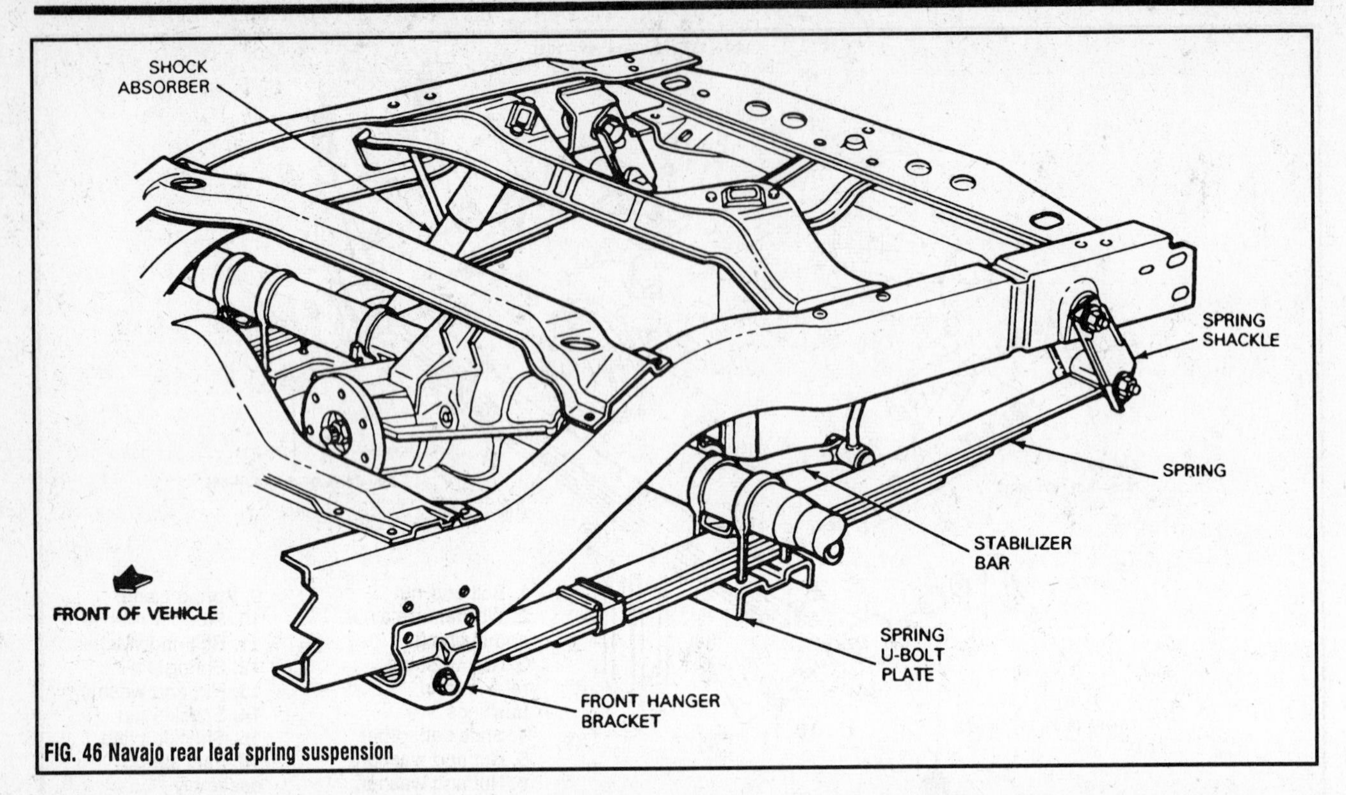

FIG. 46 Navajo rear leaf spring suspension

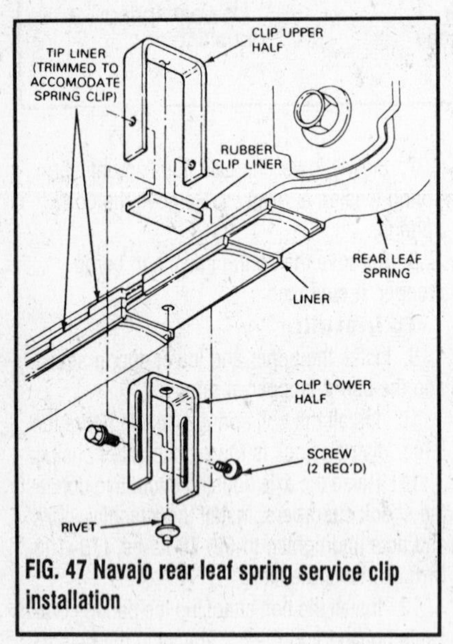

FIG. 47 Navajo rear leaf spring service clip installation

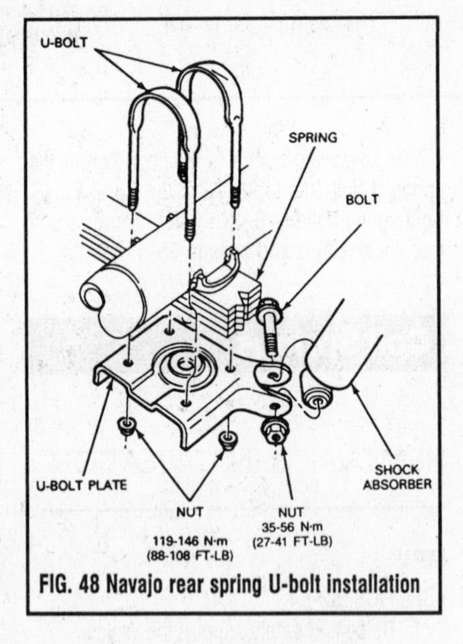

FIG. 48 Navajo rear spring U-bolt installation

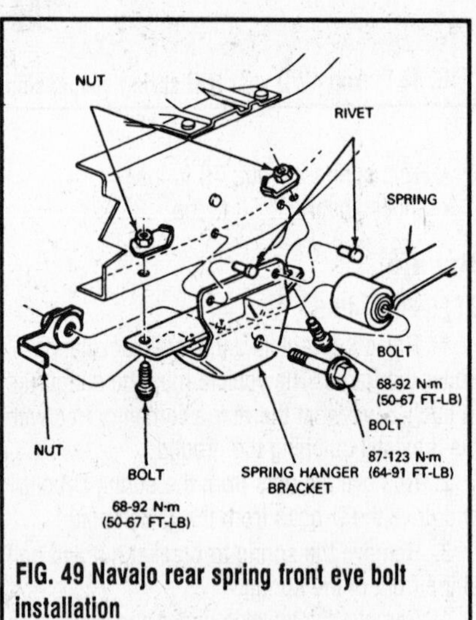

FIG. 49 Navajo rear spring front eye bolt installation

Shock Absorbers

CHECKING

See the procedure for front shocks.

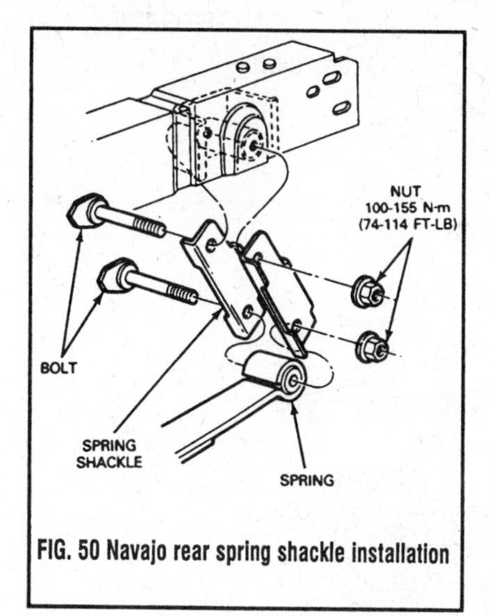

FIG. 50 Navajo rear spring shackle installation

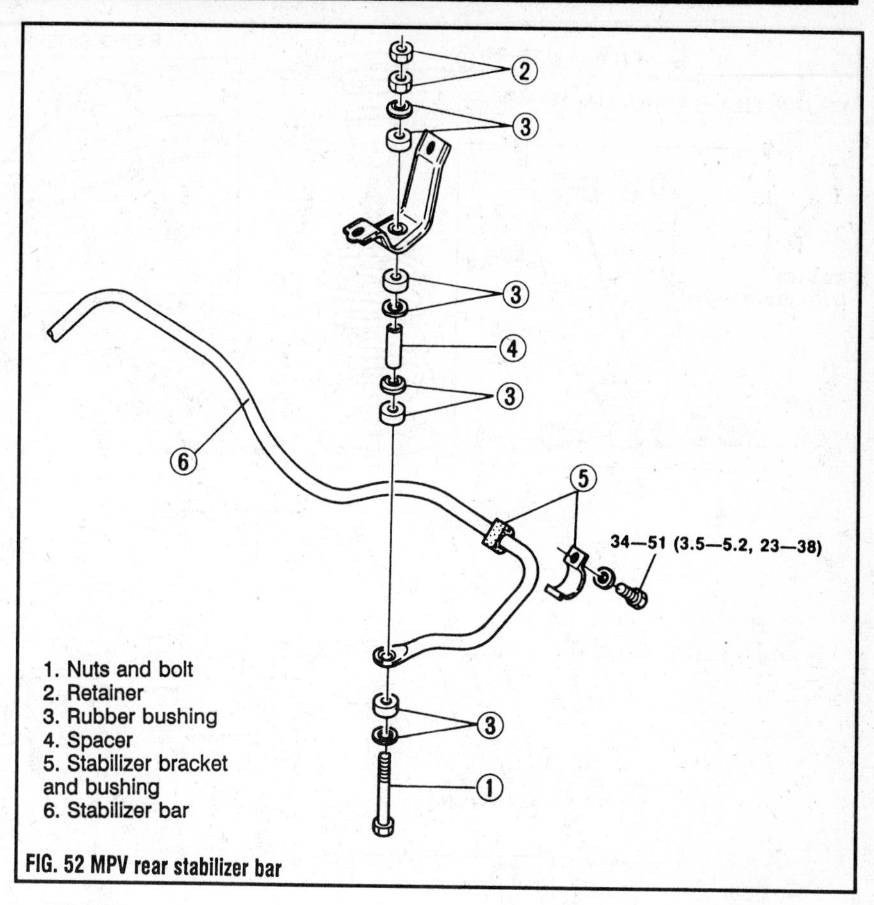

FIG. 52 MPV rear stabilizer bar

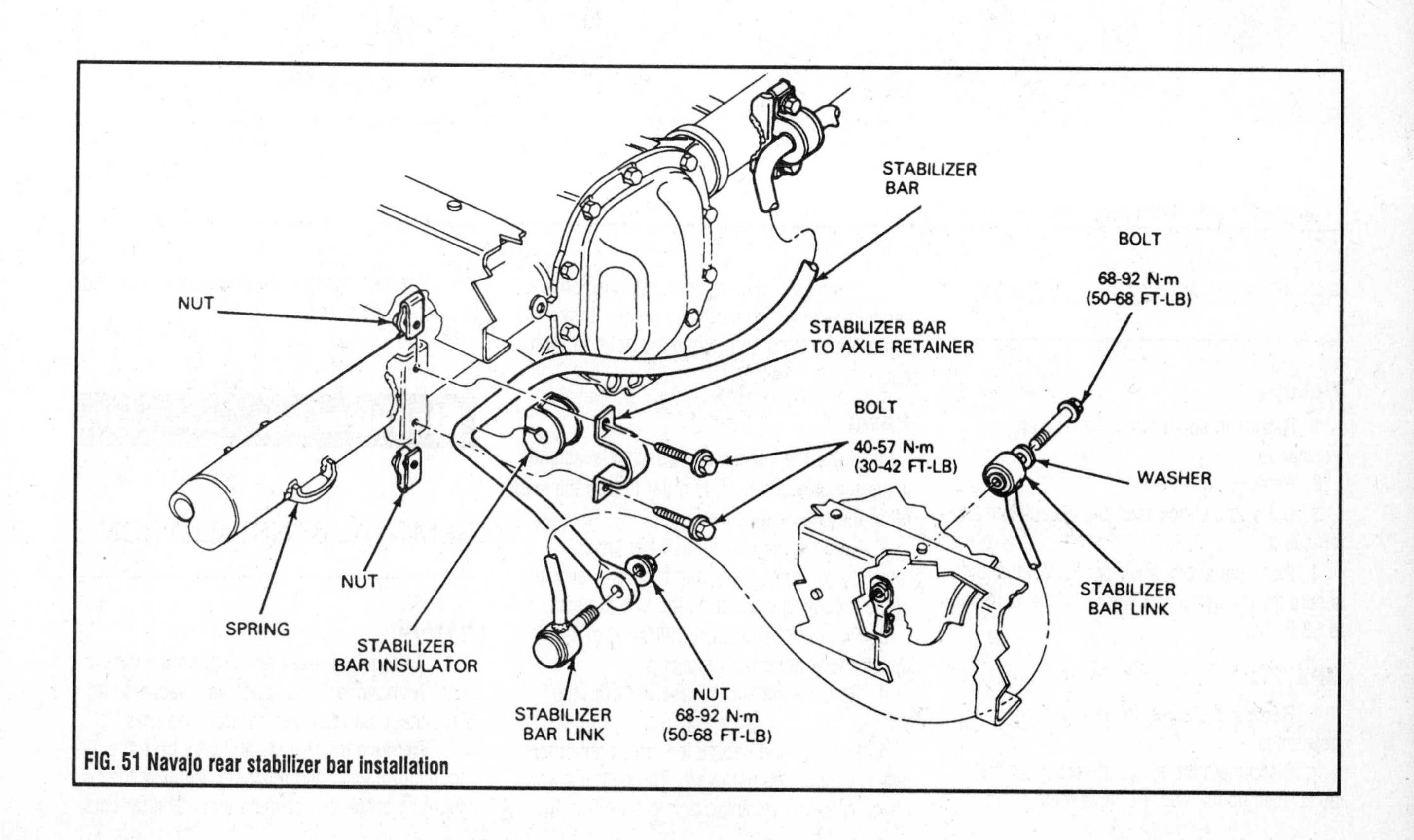

FIG. 51 Navajo rear stabilizer bar installation

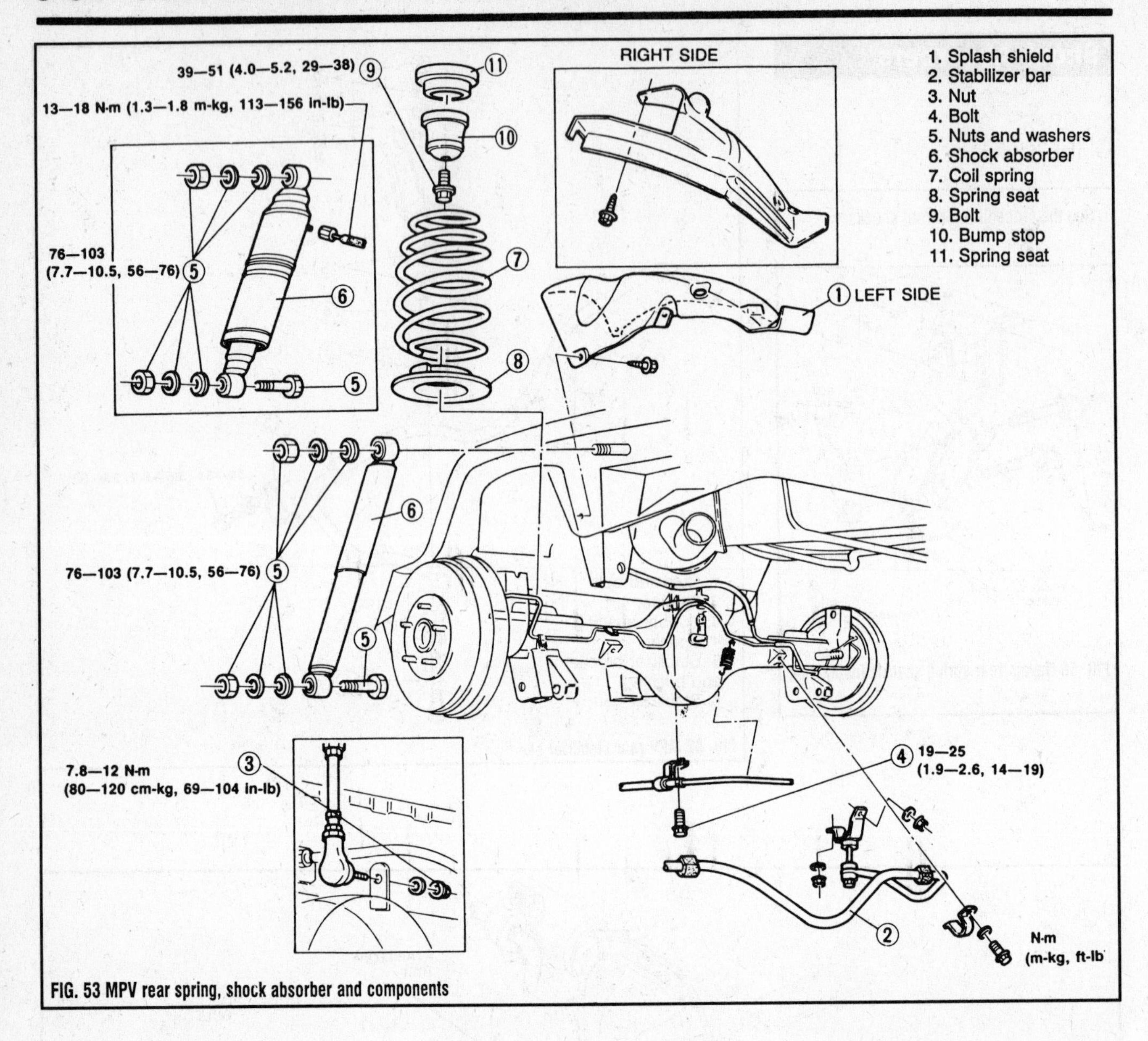

FIG. 53 MPV rear spring, shock absorber and components

REMOVAL & INSTALLATION

Pickups

1. Raise and support the rear end on jackstands.
2. Remove the wheels.
3. Unbolt the shock absorber at each end and remove it.
4. Place the shock absorber in position and secure the mounting hardware. Torque each bolt to 58 ft. lbs.

MPV

1. Raise and support the rear end on jackstands.
2. Disconnect the shock absorbers at the lower, then upper, end. Remove them.
3. Place the shock absorber in position and secure the mounting hardware snugly. Lower the van to the ground and torque the bolts to 76 ft. lbs.

Navajo

1. Raise the vehicle and position jackstands under the axle or wheel, in order to take the load off of the shock absorber.
2. Remove the shock absorber lower retaining nut and bolt. Swing the lower end free of the mounting bracket on the axle housing.
3. Remove the retaining nut(s) from the upper shock absorber mounting
4. Remove the shock absorber from the vehicle.
5. Position and secure the shock absorber with the mounting hardware. Torque the lower shock absorber retaining bolt to 39–53 ft. lbs.
6. Torque the upper shock absorber retaining nuts to 15–21 ft. lbs.

Stabilizer Bar

REMOVAL & INSTALLATION

Navajo

1. As required, raise and support the vehicle.
2. Remove the nuts, bolts and washers and disconnect the stabilizer bar from the links.
3. Remove the U-bolts and nuts from the mounting bracket and retainers. Remove the mounting brackets, retainers and stabilizer bars.

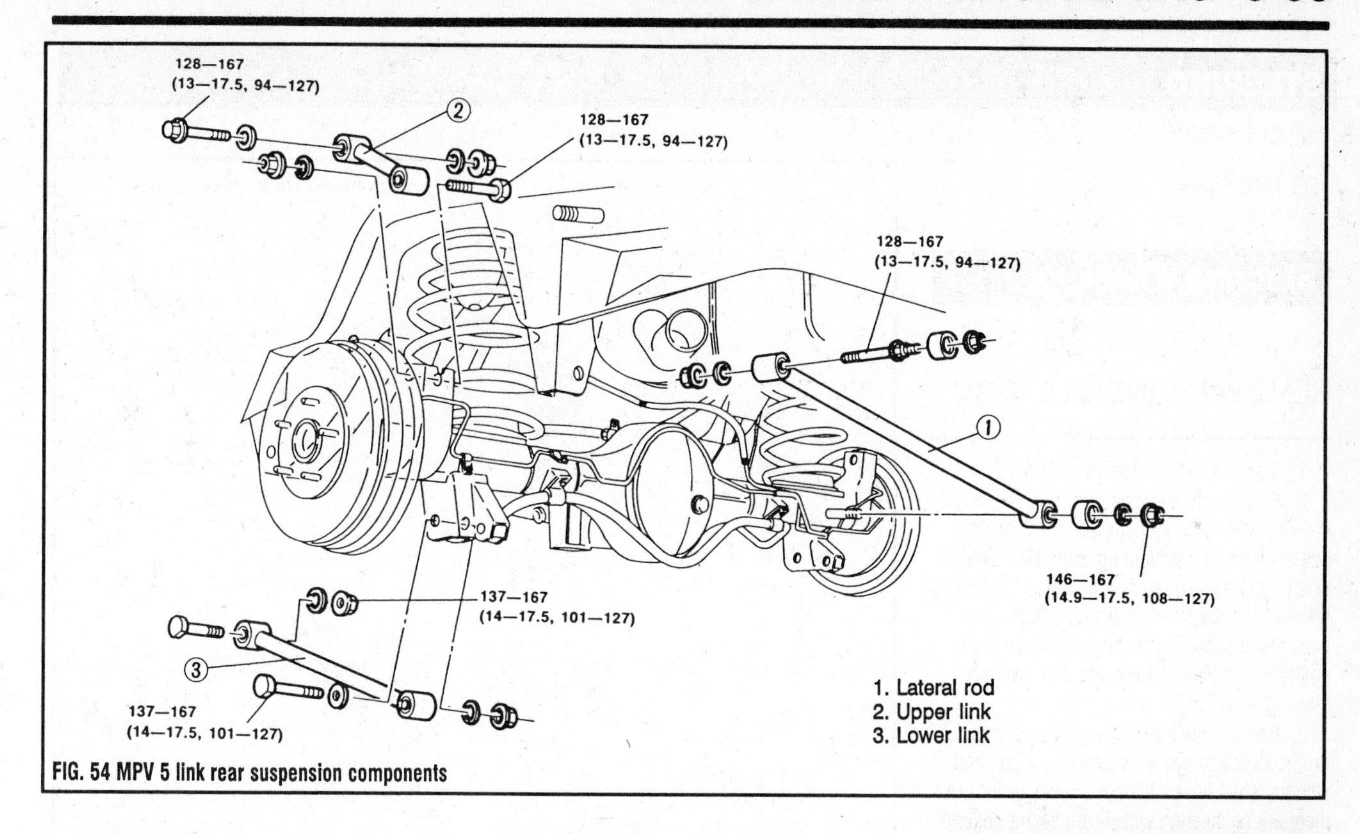

FIG. 54 MPV 5 link rear suspension components

To Install:

4. Position the U-bolts and mounting brackets on the axle with the brackets having the **UP** marking in the proper position.
5. Install the stabilizer bar and retainers on the mounting brackets with the retainers having the **UP** marking in the proper position.
6. Connect the stabilizer bar to the rear links. Install the nuts, bolts, and washers and tighten.
7. Tighten the mounting bracket U-bolt nuts to 30–42 ft. lbs.

Rear Control Arms

REMOVAL & INSTALLATION

MPV

LATERAL ROD

1. Raise and safely support the vehicle.
2. Support the axle housing with a jack.
3. Remove the lateral rod-to-chassis stud bolt and nut and the lateral rod-to-axle housing nut.
4. Remove the lateral rod.
5. Place the lateral rod in position and secure it with the mounting hardware. Make sure the lateral rod is installed with the identification mark toward the body.
6. Tighten the lateral rod-to-axle housing nut to 108–127 ft. lbs. (146–167 Nm). Tighten the lateral rod-to-chassis stud bolt and nuts to 94–127 ft. lbs. (128–167 Nm).

UPPER CONTROL ARMS

1. Raise and safely support the vehicle.
2. Support the axle housing with a jack.
3. Remove the upper control arm-to-chassis bolt and nut and the upper control arm-to-axle housing bolt and nut.
4. Remove the upper control arm.
5. Place the control arm in position and secure it with the mounting bolts. Tighten the upper control arm attaching bolts and nuts to 94–127 ft. lbs. (128–167 Nm).

LOWER CONTROL ARMS

1. Raise and safely support the vehicle.
2. Support the axle housing with a jack.
3. Remove the lower control arm-to-chassis bolt and nut and the lower control arm-to-axle housing bolt and nut.
4. Remove the lower control arm.
5. Position the lower control arm and install the mounting bolts. Tighten the upper control arm attaching bolts and nuts to 101–127 ft. lbs. (137–167 Nm).

Height Sensor

REMOVAL & INSTALLATION

MPV

The height sensor is found on models equipped with a towing package and automatic leveling.

1. Raise and support the rear end on jackstands.
2. Lower the spare tire about 300mm (12 in.).
3. Disconnect the wiring.
4. Remove the bolts and remove the sensor.
5. Place the sensor in position and secure with the mounting bolts. Torque the bolts to 20 ft. lbs.

ADJUSTMENT

The height sensor is attached to the rear axle housing by an adjustable rod and bracket. The length of the rod, between the two end connectors should be: 2WD models 59.5-60.5mm (2.34-2.38 in.) and on 4WD 99.5-100.5mm (3.92-3.96 in.)

1. Measure the length of the height sensor between the 2 nuts.
2. If adjustment is required, loosen the 2 nuts and turn the center section (turn buckle nut) to adjust the length.

STEERING

➧SEE FIGS. 55-93

Steering Wheel

REMOVAL & INSTALLATION

1. Disconnect the negative battery cable.
2. Remove the steering wheel pad from the steering wheel. On Pickups and MPV models, pull the horn pad straight up from the steering wheel. On Navajos, remove the mounting screws from behind the steering wheel. Pull the pad back and disconnect the horn switch and, if equipped, cruise control wires. Remove the steering wheel pad.
3. Remove the steering wheel attaching bolt or nut. Check to see if the steering wheel and steering shaft have alignment marks or flats. If there are no steering wheel-to-steering column shaft alignment marks or flats, matchmark the steering wheel and column shaft so they can be reassembled in the same position.
4. Using a suitable puller, remove the steering wheel from the steering column shaft.

➡ Do not hammer on the steering wheel or steering shaft or use a knock-off type steering wheel puller, as either will damage the steering column.

To install:

5. Install the steering wheel on the steering column shaft, aligning the marks or flats on the steering wheel with the marks or flats on the steering shaft.
6. On all except Navajo, install the steering wheel attaching nut and tighten to 29–36 ft. lbs. (39–49 Nm). On Navajo, install the steering wheel attaching bolt and tighten to 23–33 ft. lbs. (31–45 Nm).
7. Connect the horn switch and, if equipped, cruise control wires and install the steering wheel pad.
8. Connect the negative battery and check the steering column for proper operation.

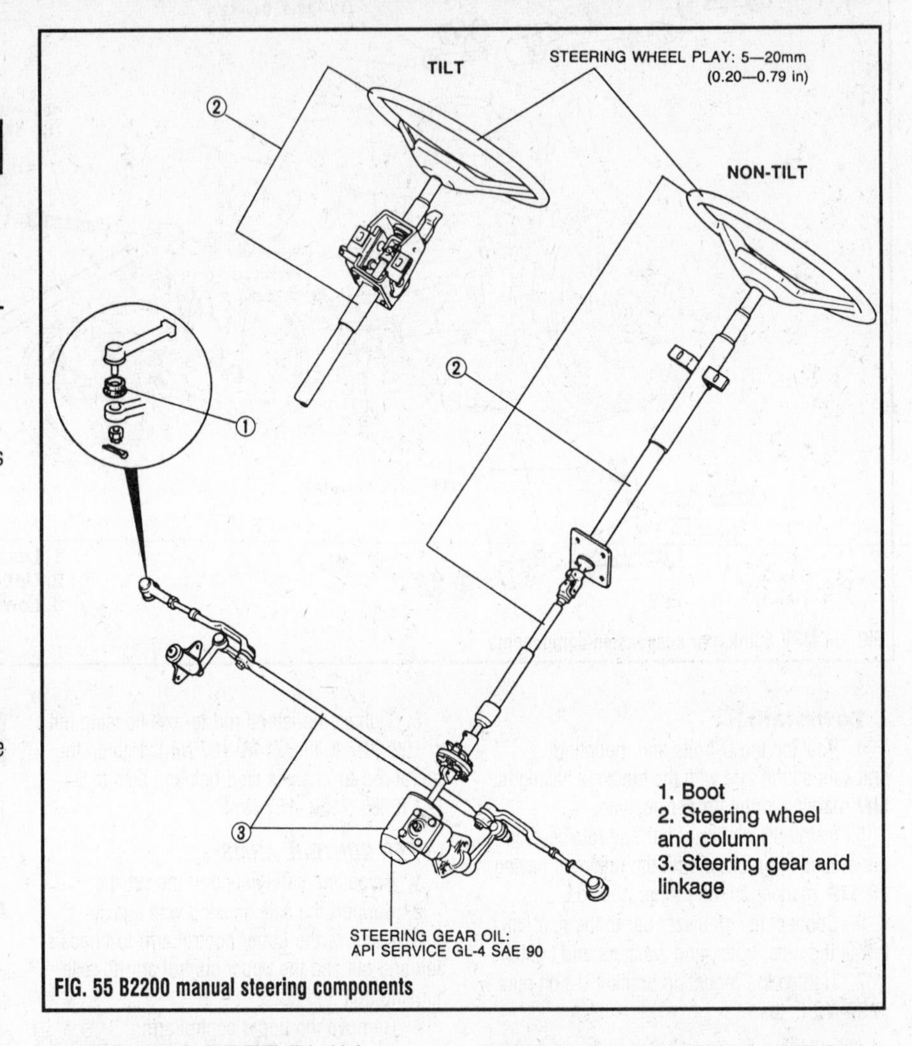

FIG. 55 B2200 manual steering components

CHECKING FREE PLAY

Steering wheel free play is measured from any point on the outer circumference of the wheel. Free play in either direction must not exceed 6-19mm (0.236-0.748 in.). If it does, check for:

a. worn ball joints
b. worn idler arm bushings
c. loose wheel bearings
d. worn or out-of-adjustment steering gear

Combination Switch

The combination turn signal, windshield wiper, and headlight switch is mounted on the steering column, and must be replaced as an assembly.

REMOVAL & INSTALLATION

Pickups

1. Disconnect the negative battery cable.
2. Remove the steering wheel.
3. Remove the "Lights-Hazard" Indicator and the steering column shroud.
4. Unplug the electrical multiple connectors at the base of the steering column.
5. Pull the headlight knob from its shaft.
6. Remove the snapring, which retains the switch, from the steering shaft. Pull the turn indicator canceling cam from the shaft.
7. Remove the single retaining bolt near the bottom of the switch. Remove the complete switch from the column.

8. Place the switch in position and secure it. Install the turn indicator cam and snapring. Install the remaining components. Check the operation of the switch before installing the steering wheel.

MPV

1. Disconnect the battery. Remove the horn cover cap.
2. Remove the steering wheel attaching nut, and pull off the wheel with a puller.
3. Remove the attaching screws, and remove the right and left steering column covers.
4. Disconnect the connector for the combination switch or, if the ignition switch is being replaced, disconnect connectors for both that and the combination switch.
5. Remove the retaining ring from the steering column.
6. Remove the combination retaining screw, and remove the switch.
7. Install the combination switch and secure with the retaining screw.
8. Install the steering column retaining ring (if so equipped).
9. Connect all combination or ignition switch connectors at this time.
10. Install the steering column covers with retaining screws.
11. Install the steering wheel and horn cap. Connect the negative battery cable and check all the functions of the combination switch for proper operation.

Navajo

1. Disconnect the negative battery cable. Remove the steering wheel.
2. On vehicles equipped with tilt wheel, remove the tilt lever.
3. On vehicles equipped with tilt wheel, remove the steering column collar by pressing on the collar from the top and bottom while removing the collar.
4. Remove the instrument panel trim cover retaining screws. Remove the trim cover.
5. Remove the 2 screws from the bottom of the steering column shroud. Remove the bottom half of the shroud by pulling the shroud down and toward the rear of the vehicle.
6. If the vehicle is equipped with automatic transmission, move the shift lever as required to aid in removal of the shroud. Lift the top half of the shroud from the column.
7. If the vehicle is equipped with automatic transmission, disconnect the selector indicator actuation cable by removing the screw from the column casting and the plastic plug at the end of the cable.

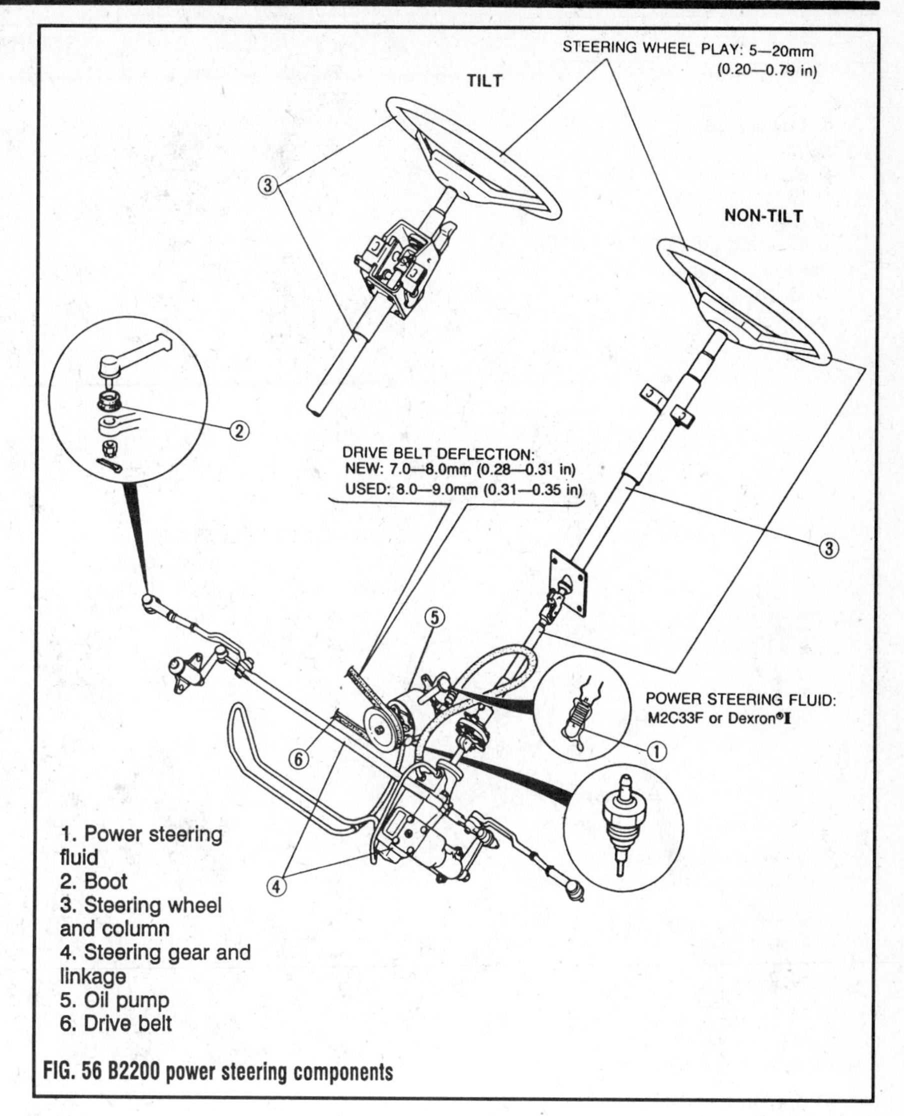

FIG. 56 B2200 power steering components

8. To remove the plastic plug from the shift lever socket casting push on the nose of the plug until the head clears the casting and pull the plug from the casting.
9. Remove the plastic clip that retains the combination switch wiring to the steering column bracket.
10. Remove the 2 self taping screws that retain the combination switch to the steering column casting. Disengage the switch from the casting.
11. Disconnect the 3 electrical connectors, using caution not to damage the locking tabs. Be sure not to damage the PNDRL cable.
12. Installation is the reverse of the removal procedure. Torque the combination switch retaining screws to 18–27 inch lbs.

Ignition Switch

REMOVAL & INSTALLATION

Pickups and MPV

1. Disconnect the battery ground cable.
2. Remove the steering column covers.
3. Disconnect the wiring harness connector at the switch.
4. Remove the attaching screw and lift out the switch.
5. Installation is the reverse of removal.

Navajo

1. Disconnect the negative battery cable.
2. Remove the steering wheel.
3. As necessary, remove all under dash panels in order to gain access to the ignition switch.

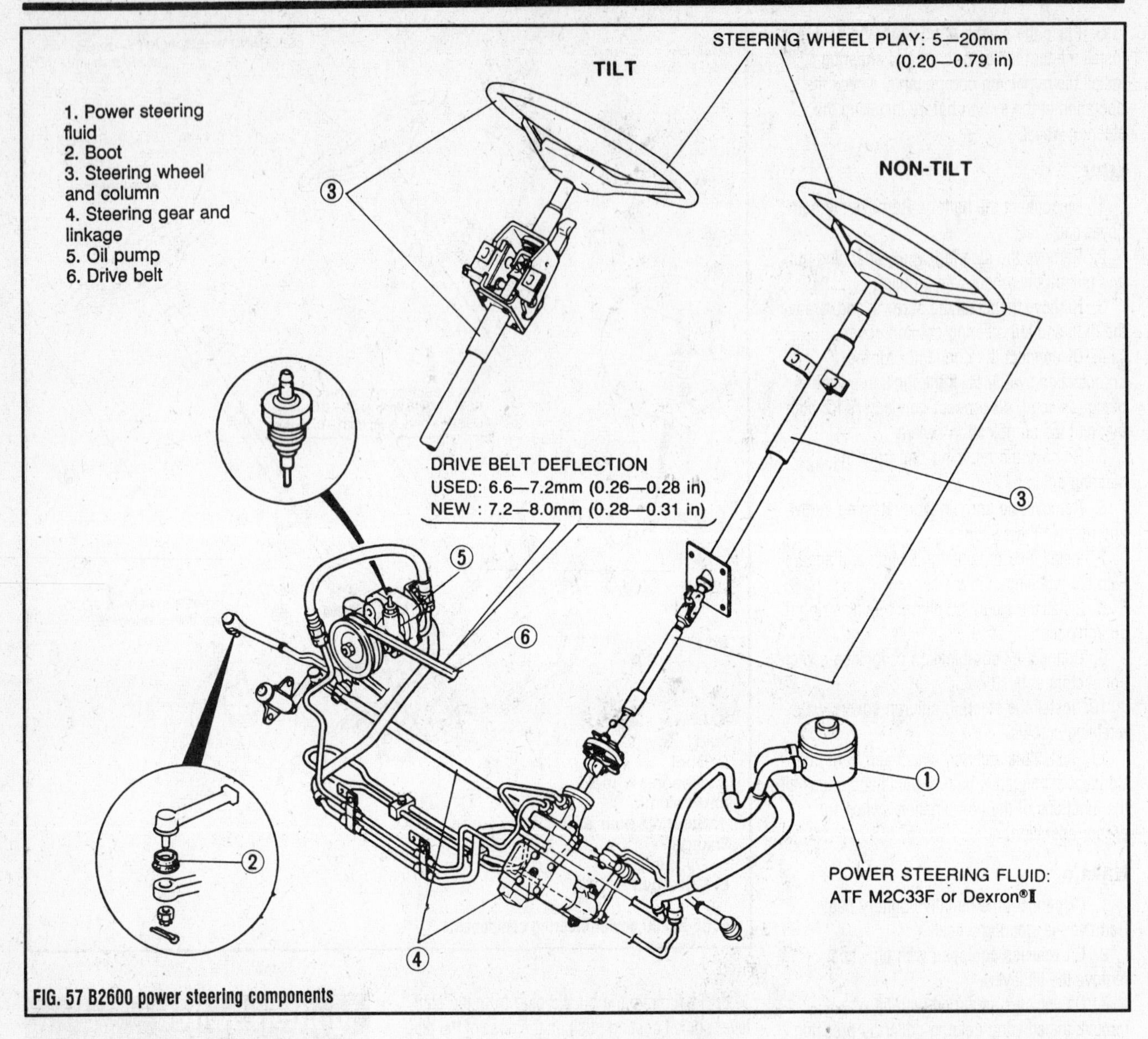

FIG. 57 B2600 power steering components

4. As necessary, lower the steering column to gain working clearance.

5. Disconnect the ignition switch electrical connectors.

6. Remove the ignition switch retaining screws from the studs. Disengage the ignition switch from switch rod. Remove the switch from the vehicle.

To install:

7. Position the lock cylinder in the **LOCK** position.

8. To set the switch, position a wire in the opening in the outer surface of the switch through its positions until the wire drops down into the slot.

➡ The slot is in the bottom of the switch where the rod must be inserted to allow full movement through the switch positions.

9. Position the ignition switch on the column studs and over the actuating rod. Torque the retaining nuts to 3.3–5.3 ft. lbs.

10. Remove the wire from the slot in the housing. Continue the installation in the reverse order of the removal procedure.

Ignition Lock

REMOVAL & INSTALLATION

Pickups and MPV

1. Disconnect the negative battery terminal.
2. Remove the steering wheel.
3. Remove the steering column shroud.
4. Disconnect the multiple connectors at the base of the combination switch.
5. Remove the switch retaining snap ring. Pull the turn signal indicator canceling cam off the shaft.
6. Remove the switch retaining bolt and remove the complete switch from the column.

➡ Make a groove on the head of the bolts attaching the steering lock body to the column shaft using a saw. A screwdriver can be used to loosen the screws.

7. Remove the steering lock attaching bolts. Remove the steering lock.
8. Installation is the reverse of removal. During installation position a new steering lock on the column shaft. Tighten the bolts until the heads break off.

Navajo

1. Disconnect the negative battery cable. Remove the steering wheel.
2. On vehicles equipped with tilt wheel, remove the tilt lever.
3. On vehicles equipped with tilt wheel, remove the steering column collar by pressing on the collar from the top and bottom while removing the collar.
4. Remove the instrument panel trim cover retaining screws. Remove the trim cover.
5. Remove the 2 screws from the bottom of the steering column shroud. Remove the bottom half of the shroud by pulling the shroud down and toward the rear of the vehicle.
6. If the vehicle is equipped with automatic transmission, move the shift lever as required to aid in removal of the shroud. Lift the top half of the shroud from the column.
7. Turn the lock cylinder with the ignition key in it to the **ON** position. On vehicles equipped with automatic transmission be sure that the selector lever is in the **PARK** position.
8. Push down on the lock cylinder retaining pin with a 1/8 in. (3mm) diameter wire pin or small punch. Pull the lock cylinder from the column housing. Disconnect the lock cylinder wiring plug from the horn brush wiring connector.

To install:

9. Prior to installation of the lock cylinder, lubricate the cylinder cavity, including the drive gear, with Lubriplate® or equivalent.
10. To install the lock cylinder, turn the lock cylinder to the **ON** position, depress the retaining pin. Insert the lock cylinder housing into its housing in the flange casting. Be sure that the tab at the end of the cylinder aligns with the slot in the ignition drive gear.
11. Turn the key to the **OFF** position. This action will permit the cylinder retaining pin to extend into the cylinder casting housing hole.
12. Using the ignition key rotate the lock cylinder to ensure correct mechanical operation in all positions. Connect the key warning wire plug.
13. Install the steering column lower shroud. Install the steering wheel.
14. Check for proper vehicle operation in **PARK** and **NEUTRAL**. Also be sure that the start circuit cannot be actuated in **DRIVE** or **REVERSE**.

Steering Column

REMOVAL & INSTALLATION

Pickups and MPV Models

1. Disconnect the negative battery cable. Place the front wheels in the straight ahead position.
2. Remove the steering wheel.
3. Remove the steering column covers and remove the combination switch.
4. Remove the necessary dash panels from under the steering column.
5. Disconnect the automatic transmission interlock cable, if equipped. Tag and disconnect the necessary electrical connectors.
6. Disconnect the steering column from the steering linkage by removing the bolt at the intermediate shaft universal joint. Mark the position of the intermediate shaft on the column shaft before disconnecting so they can be reassembled in the same position.
7. Remove the nuts attaching the column at the firewall.
8. Support the steering column and remove the bolts attaching the column to the underside of the dash. Remove the steering column.
9. Align the marks that were made on the intermediate shaft and steering column shaft during removal. Position the column assembly and secure it. Install the components. Tighten the intermediate shaft universal joint bolt to 13–18 ft. lbs. (18–25 Nm). Tighten the bolts attaching the steering column to the underside of the dash to 12–17 ft. lbs. (16–23 Nm).Tighten the nuts attaching the column at the firewall to 14–19 ft. lbs. (19–26 Nm) on B Series pickup or 12–17 ft. lbs. (16–23 Nm) on MPV.

Navajo

1. Disconnect the negative battery cable and apply the parking brake. Place automatic transmission in **N**.
2. Remove the bolt that holds the intermediate shaft to the steering column shaft. Using a prybar, compress the intermediate shaft until it is clear of the steering column shaft.
3. If equipped with automatic transmission, remove the nuts from the studs and remove the shift cable bracket from the steering column bracket. Disconnect the shift cable from the column lever.
4. Remove the steering wheel. If equipped with tilt column, make sure the steering wheel is in the full up position before removal.
5. If equipped with tilt column, remove the tilt lever and remove the column collar by pressing on the collar from the top and bottom while removing the collar.
6. Remove the retaining screws and remove the panel trim cover.
7. Remove the 2 screws from the bottom of the column shroud. Remove the bottom half of the shroud by pulling the shroud down and toward the rear of the vehicle. If equipped with automatic transmission, move the shift lever as required to ease shroud removal. Lift the top half of the shroud from the column.
8. If equipped with automatic transmission, disconnect the selector indicator cable by removing the screw from the column casting and the plastic plug at the end of the cable. To remove the plastic plug from the shift lever socket casting, push on the nose of the plug until the head clears the casting, then pull the plug from the casting.
9. Remove the plastic clip that holds the combination switch wiring to the steering column bracket. Remove the 2 screws from the combination switch and remove the switch from the column, leaving the wiring connectors attached to the switch. Position the switch and wiring aside.
10. Disconnect the key warning buzzer wire from the horn brush wire. Remove the screw that holds the horn brush connector to the column and remove the connector.
11. Remove the 5 screws that hold the toe plate to the dash panel and loosen the toe plate clamp bolt.
12. Support the column and remove the bolts that hold the breakaway bracket to the pedal support bracket. Pry apart the locking tabs and disconnect the ignition switch wiring harness.
13. Carefully remove the column from the vehicle.

To install:

14. Carefully position the column in the hole in the vehicle floor. Connect the ignition switch wiring harness to the column connector.
15. Install the bolts that hold the breakaway bracket to the pedal support bracket, but do not tighten at this time.
16. Tighten the bolts that hold the toe plate to the floor to 8 ft. lbs. (11 Nm), then tighten the breakaway bracket-to-pedal support bracket bolts to 19–27 ft. lbs. (25–36 Nm). Tighten the toe plate clamp to 6–13 ft. lbs. (8–18 Nm).
17. Install the horn brush connector to the column and tighten the retaining screw to 21–29 inch lbs. (2.3–3.3 Nm). Attach the key warning buzzer wire connector to the horn brush wire. Route the wiring to prevent contact with moving parts.

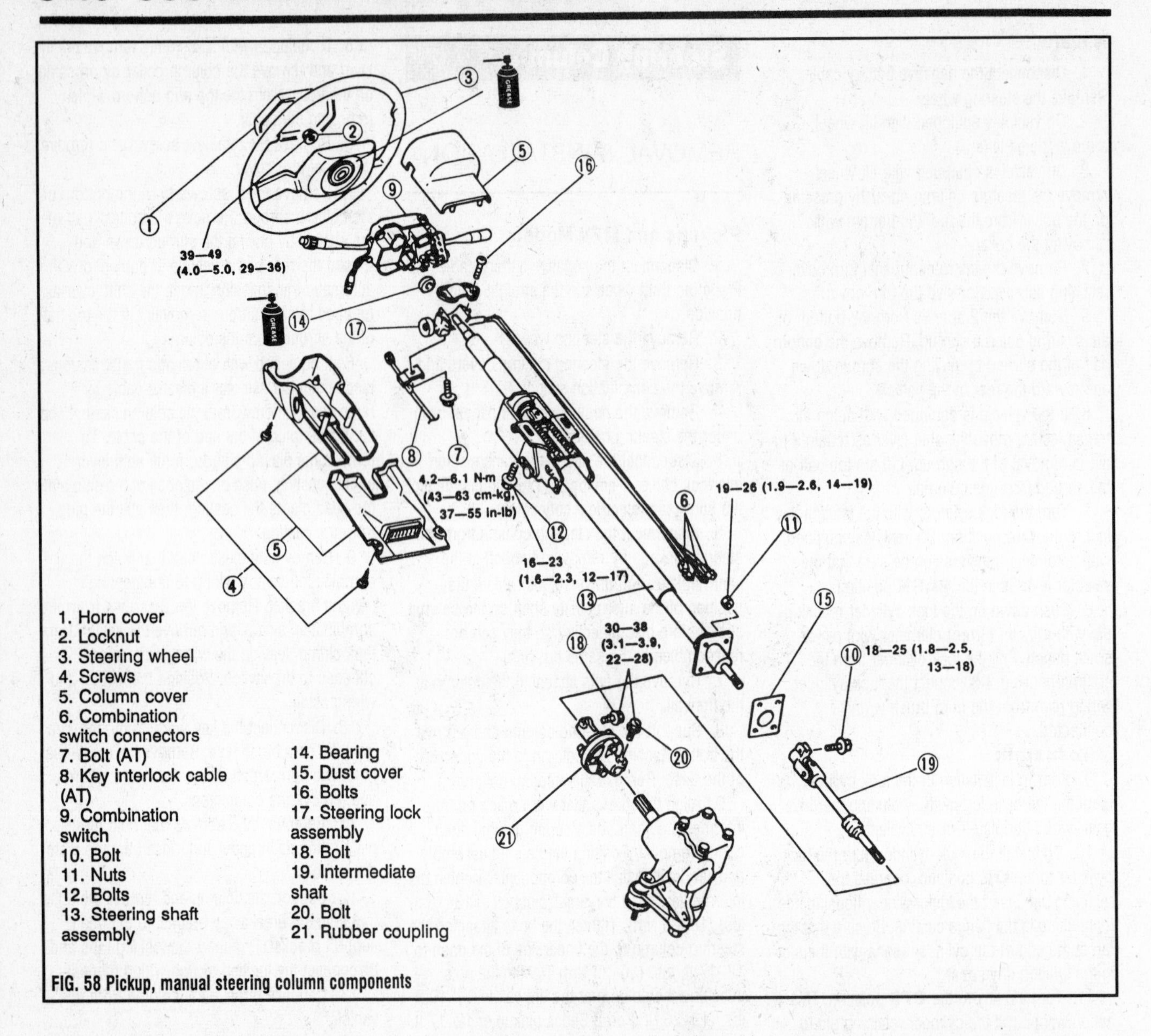

FIG. 58 Pickup, manual steering column components

18. Position the combination switch on the column with the attaching screws. Tighten to 18–26 inch lbs. (2–3 Nm). Install the plastic clip that holds the switch wiring to the steering column breakaway bracket.

19. If equipped with automatic transmission, connect the selector indicator cable by pushing the plastic plug at the end of the cable into the shift lever socket casting. When installed, the nose of the plug should be facing the steering wheel and the head of the plug away from the wheel. Install the cable retaining screw in the column and adjust the cable. If the shift lever was removed, install it at this time.

20. Position the top half of the shroud on the column so the screw moldings on the shroud seat in the mounting bores in the column. Place the automatic transmission shift lever in the lowest position to aid assembly.

21. Install the bottom half of the shroud by sliding the guides in the shroud bottom half into the tabs in the shroud top half. Install the shroud retaining screws and tighten to 6–10 inch lbs. (0.7–1.1 Nm).

22. If equipped with tilt column, install the column collar by pressing on the collar from the top and bottom while installing the collar on the column. Install the tilt lever and tighten to 2.2–3.6 ft. lbs. (3–5 Nm).

23. If equipped, place the automatic transmission selector lever in **N**. Install the steering wheel and the lower trim cover panel.

24. If equipped with automatic transmission, install the nuts on the studs and install the shift cable bracket on the steering column bracket. Connect the shift cable to the column lever.

25. Connect the column shaft to the intermediate shaft U-joint and tighten the pinch bolt to 25–35 ft. lbs. (34–47 Nm). The intermediate shaft must be in collapsed state to align, both shafts have a flat side, and then pulled up the column shaft until the bolt holes align. Make sure the intermediate shaft does not contact the plastic retainer at the base of the column. If it does, pull the lower shaft of the column slightly out of the column.

26. Connect the negative battery cable and check the adjustment of the selector indicator cable. Pull the shift lever toward the steering wheel until the **OD** detent in the transmission is felt. Release the shift lever, it should be against the detent wall in the column.

27. Release the parking brake lever and test drive the vehicle.

Steering Linkage

REMOVAL & INSTALLATION

Idler Arm

PICKUPS

1. Raise and support the front end on jackstands.
2. Remove the idler arm-to-center link nut and cotter pin. Disconnect the center link from the idler arm using a ball joint separator.
3. Unbolt and remove the idler arm.
4. Install and secure the idler arm. Connect the center link. Always install new cotter pins. Torque the center link nut to 43 ft. lbs.; the frame mounting bolts to 69 ft. lbs.

Pitman Arm

PICKUPS

1. Raise and support the front end on jackstands.
2. Remove the cotter pin and nut attaching the center link to the pitman arm.
3. Disconnect the center link from the pitman arm with a ball joint separator.
4. Matchmark the pitman arm and sector shaft.
5. Remove the pitman arm-to-sector shaft nut and remove the pitman arm. It may be necessary to use a puller.
6. Install and attach the pitman arm and components. Make sure you align the matchmarks. Tighten the pitman arm-to-sector shaft nut to 130 ft. lbs.; the pitman arm-to-center link nut to 43 ft. lbs. If the cotter pin does not align, tighten the nut to make it line up, never loosen it!

NAVAJO

1. As required, raise and safely support the vehicle using jackstands.
2. Remove the cotter pin and nut from the drag link ball stud at the pitman arm.
3. Remove the drag link ball stud from the pitman arm using pitman arm removal tool T64P–3590–F or equivalent.
4. Remove the pitman arm retaining nut and washer. Remove the pitman arm from the steering gear sector shaft using tool T64P–3590–F or equivalent.
5. Install and secure the pitman arm and components. Torque the pitman arm attaching washer and nut to 170–230 ft. lbs. Torque the drag link ball stud nut to 50–70 ft. lbs. and install a new cotter pin.
6. Check and adjust front end alignment, as required.

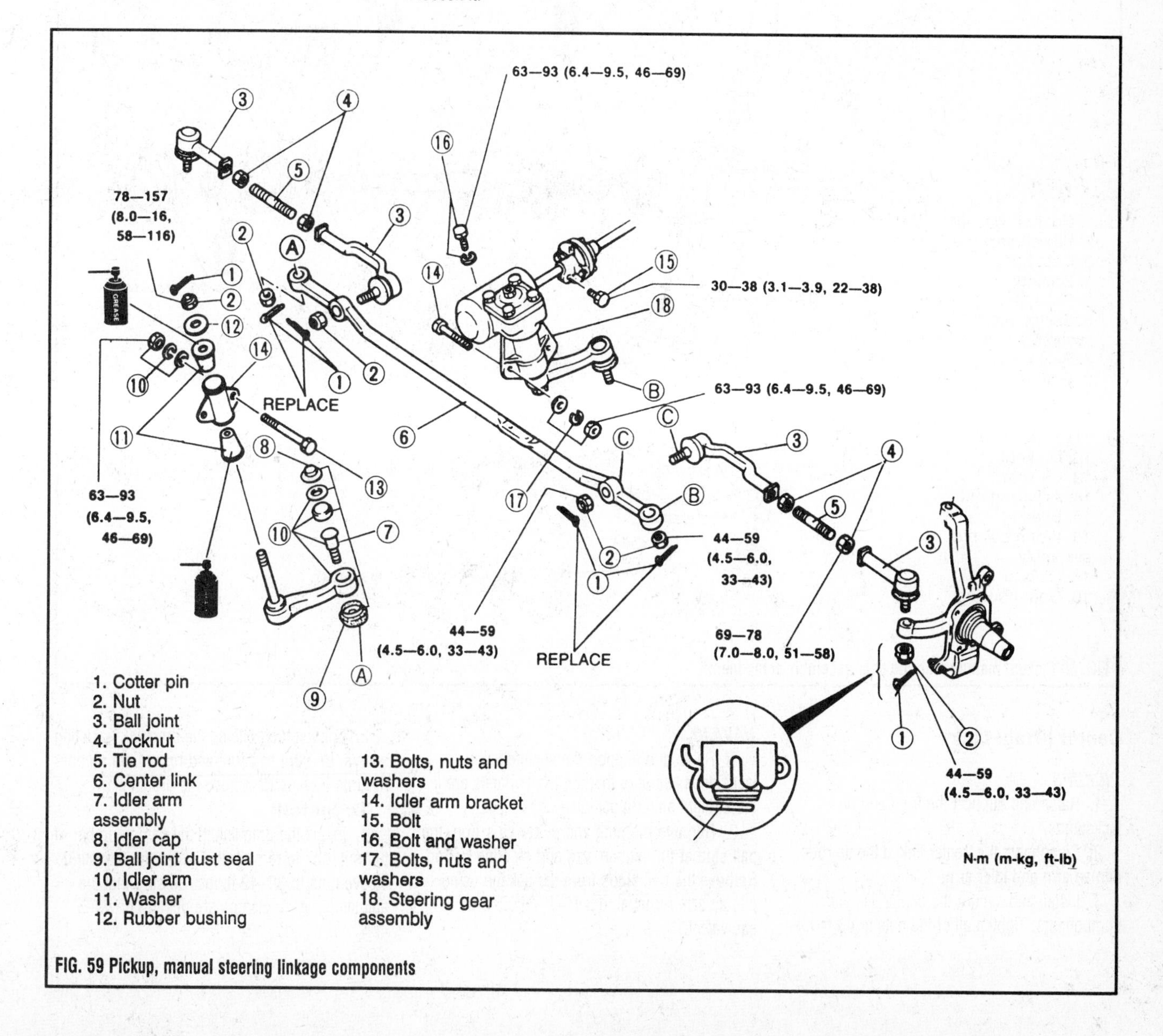

FIG. 59 Pickup, manual steering linkage components

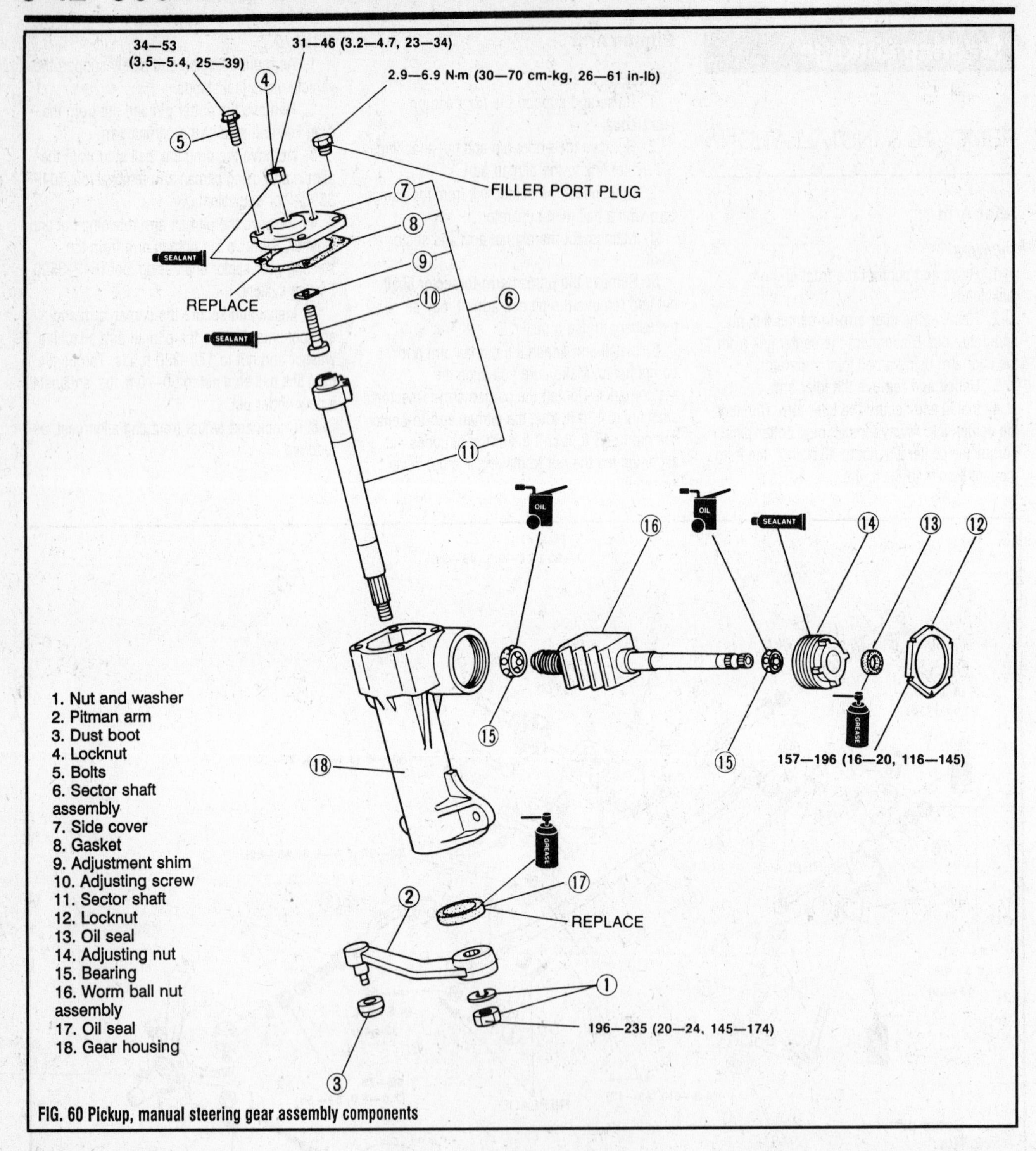

FIG. 60 Pickup, manual steering gear assembly components

Center (Drag) Link

PICKUPS

1. Raise and support the front end on jackstands.
2. Disconnect the center link at the tie rods, pitman arm and idler arm.
3. Install and secure the center link and components. Tighten all of the nuts to 43 ft. lbs.

NAVAJO

1. Raise and support the vehicle using jackstands. Be sure that the front wheels are in the straight ahead position.
2. Remove the nuts and cotter pins from the ball stud at the pitman arm and steering tie rod. Remove the ball studs from the linkage using pitman arm removal tool T64P–3590–F or equivalent.
3. Loosen the bolts on the drag link adjusting sleeve. Be sure to count and record the number of turns it takes to remove the drag link.

To Install:

4. Install the drag link in the same number of turns it took to remove it. Tighten the adjusting sleeve nuts to 30–42 ft. lbs. Be sure that the adjusting sleeve clamps are pointed down ± 45°.

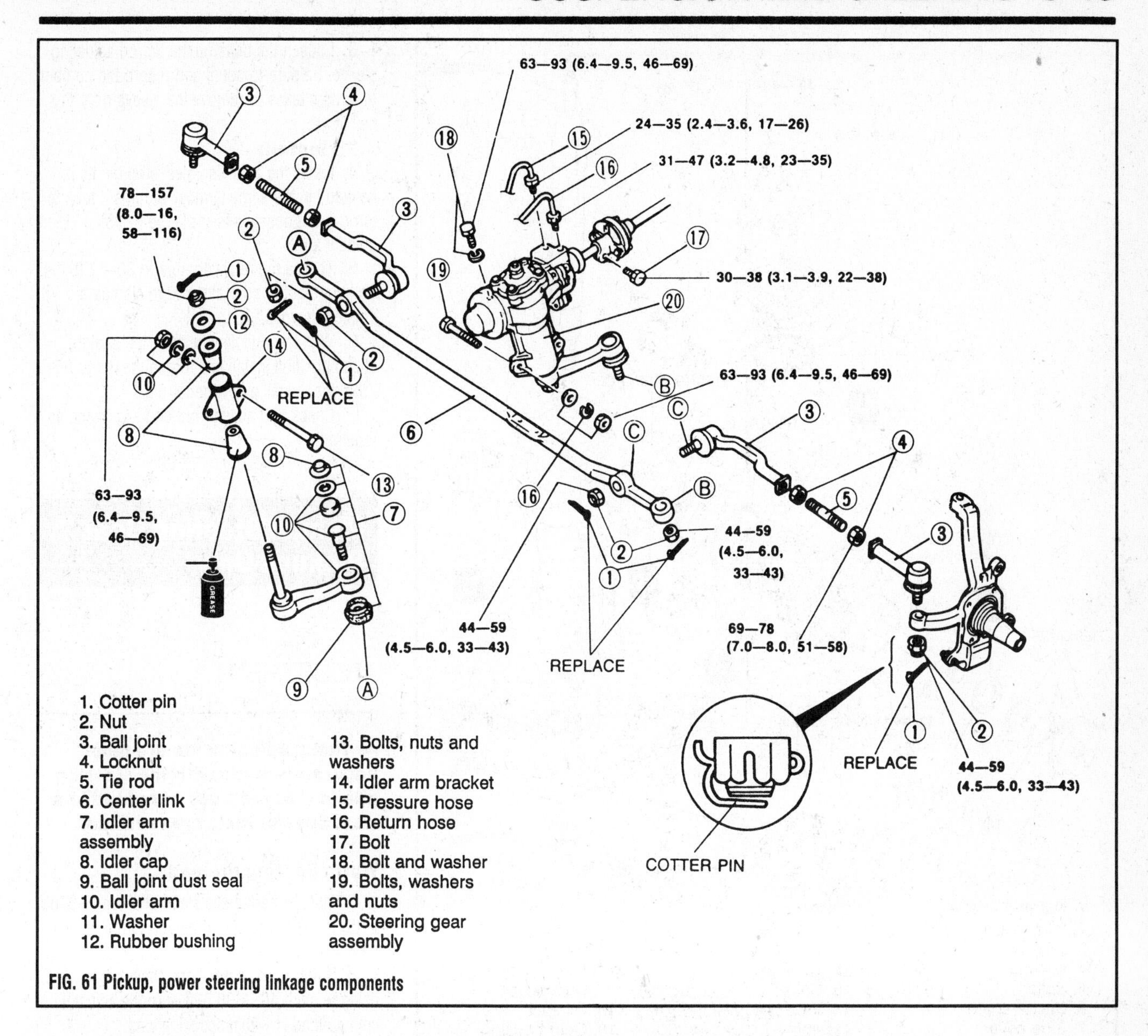

FIG. 61 Pickup, power steering linkage components

5. Position the drag link ball stud in the pitman arm. Position the steering tie rod ball stud in the drag link. With the vehicle wheels in the straight ahead position install and torque the nuts to 50–75 ft. lbs. Install a new cotter pin.

6. Check and adjust front end alignment, as required.

Tie Rod

NAVAJO

1. Raise and support the vehicle using jackstands. Be sure that the front wheels are in the straight ahead position.

2. Remove the nut and cotter pin from the ball stud on the drag link. Remove the ball stud from the drag link using pitman arm removal tool T64P–3590–F or equivalent.

3. Loosen the bolts on the tie rod adjusting sleeve. Be sure to count and record the number of turns it takes to remove the tie rod from the tie rod adjusting sleeve. Remove the tie rod from the vehicle.

To install:

4. Install the tie rod in the tie rod sleeve in the same number of turns it took to remove it. Torque the tie rod adjusting sleeve nuts to 30–42 ft. lbs.

5. Be sure that the adjusting sleeve clamps are pointed down ± 45°. Tighten the tie rod ball stud to drag link retaining bolt to 50–75 ft. lbs. Install a new cotter pin.

6. Check and adjust front end alignment, as required.

Tie Rod Ends

PICKUPS

1. Loosen the tie rod jam nuts.

2. Remove and discard the cotter pin from the ball socket end, and remove the nut.

3. Use a ball joint puller to loosen the ball socket stud from the center link. Remove the stud from the kingpin steering arm in the same way.

4. Unscrew the tie rod end from the threaded sleeve, counting the number of threads until it's off. The threads may be left or right hand threads. Tighten the jam nuts to 58 ft. lbs.

5. To install, lightly coat the threads with grease, and turn the new end in as many turns as were required to remove it. This will give the approximate correct toe-in.

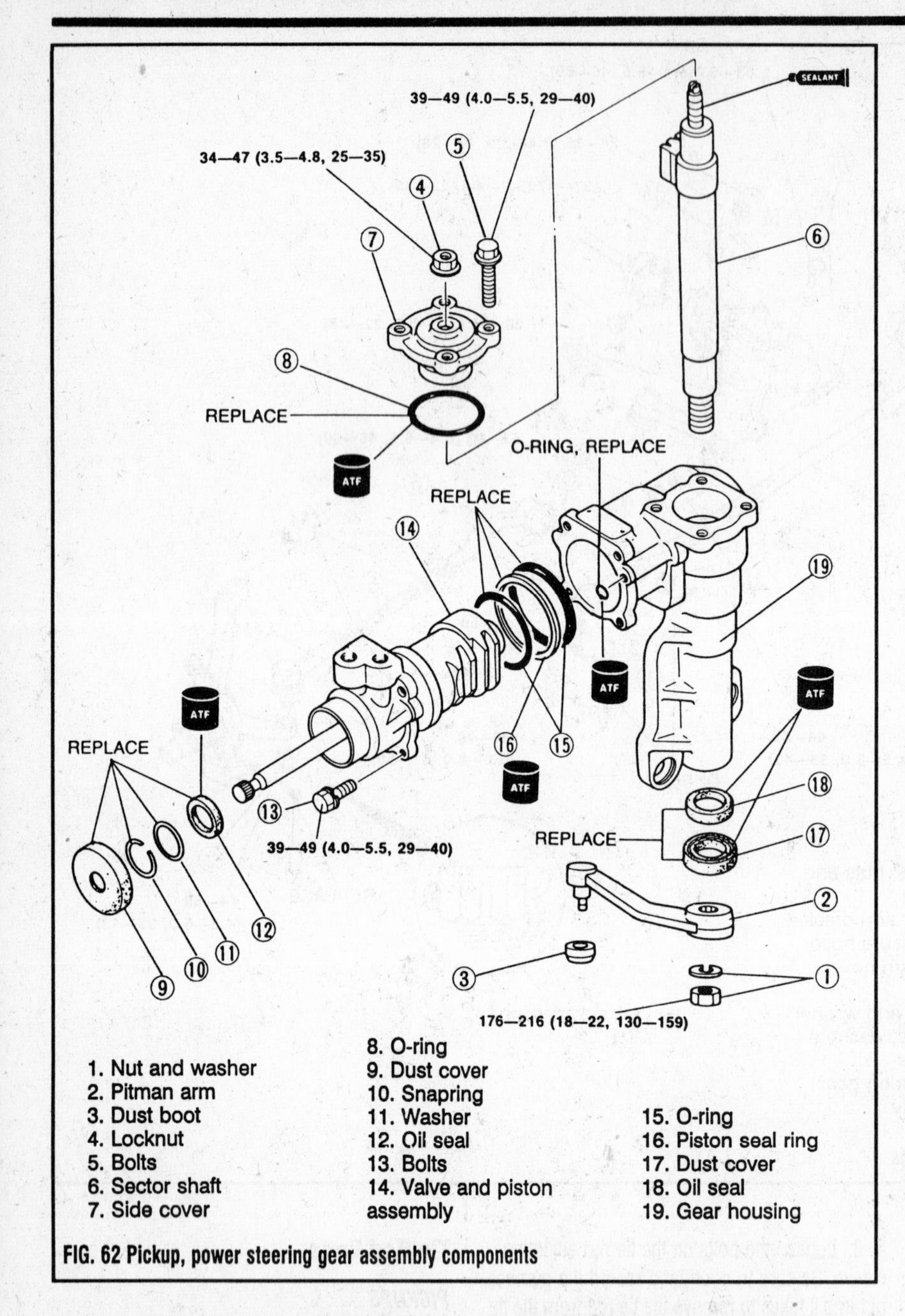

FIG. 62 Pickup, power steering gear assembly components

6. Install the ball socket studs into center link and kingpin steering arm. Tighten the nuts to 43 ft. lbs. Install a new cotter pin. You may tighten the nut to fit the cotter pin, but don't loosen it.

7. Check and adjust the toe-in, and tighten the tie rod clamps or jam nuts.

MPV

1. Raise and support the front end on jackstands.

2. Remove the wheels.

3. Loosen the tie rod end ball stud nut and separate the tie rod end from the knuckle arm with a separator tool.

4. Matchmark the tie rod end and tie rod and loosen the locknut.

5. Unscrew the tie rod end, counting the number of turns until it's off, for installation purposes.

6. Installation is the reverse of removal. Tighten the locknut to 58 ft. lbs.; the ball stud nut to 58 ft. lbs. Always use a new cotter pin on the ball stud nut. Always advance the nut to align the cotter pin hole. Never back it off!

NAVAJO

1. Raise and support the vehicle using jackstands. Be sure that the front wheels are in the straight ahead position.

2. Remove the nut and cotter pin from the ball stud on the drag link. Remove the ball stud from the drag link using pitman arm removal tool T64P–3590–F or equivalent.

3. Loosen the bolts on the tie rod adjusting sleeve. Be sure to count and record the number of turns it takes to remove the sleeve from the ball stud.

To install:

4. Install the adjusting sleeve on the tie rod ball stud in the same number of turns it took to remove it. Loosely assemble the ball stud in the spindle arm.

5. Torque the retaining nuts to 30–42 ft. lbs. Be sure that the adjusting sleeve clamps are pointed down $\pm$ 45°.

6. With the vehicle wheels in the straight ahead position install and torque the nut to 50–75 ft. lbs. Install a new cotter pin.

7. Check and adjust front end alignment, as required.

Manual Steering Gear Pickups Only

ADJUSTMENT

➡ These adjustments are most accurately made with the steering gear out of the truck, mounted in a vise. Special tools are required.

Worm Bearing Preload

1. Install a spring scale and adapter 49 0180 510B to the wormshaft. Rotating torque should be 3/4-1.3 lb.

2. If not, Loosen the wormshaft locknut and, using wrench 49 UB39 585, turn the adjuster until preload is within specifications.

3. Using wrench 49 1391 580, or equivalent, tighten the locknut to 140 ft. lbs.

Backlash

1. Mount a dial indicator next to the vise, with the pointer on the end of the pitman arm. With the gear in what would be the straight ahead position, backlash should be 0.

2. If not, adjust it using the adjusting screw on top of the gear. Hold the screw with a screwdriver and loosen the locknut. Turn the screw until backlash is correct. Make sure that the pitman arm is in the position it would be with the wheels straight ahead.

3. When backlash is correct, hold the screw and tighten the locknut.

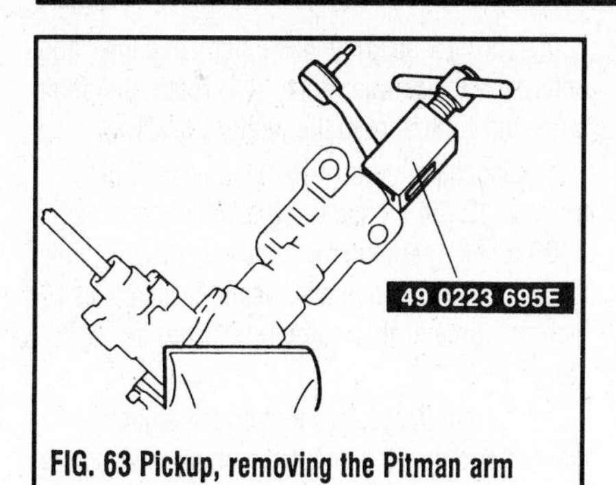

FIG. 63 Pickup, removing the Pitman arm

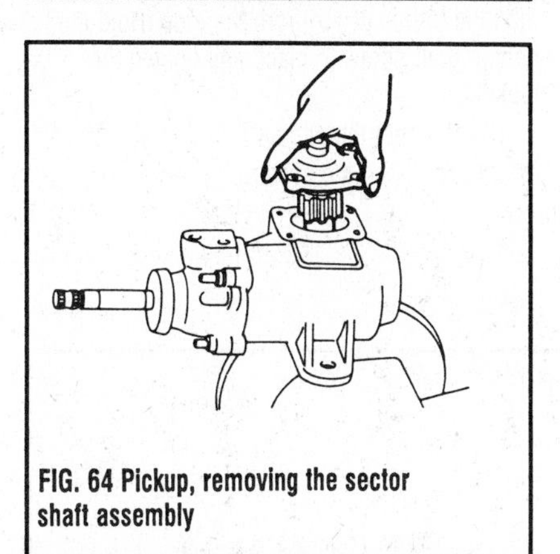
FIG. 64 Pickup, removing the sector shaft assembly

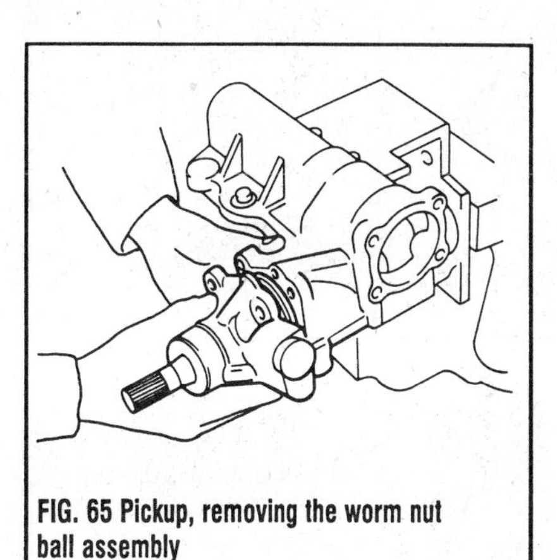
FIG. 65 Pickup, removing the worm nut ball assembly

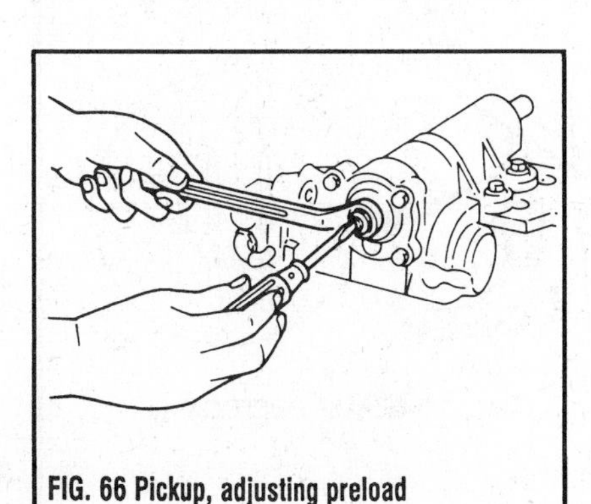
FIG. 66 Pickup, adjusting preload

REMOVAL & INSTALLATION

1. Raise and support the front end on jackstands.
2. Remove the pinch bolt securing the wormshaft to the steering shaft coupling.
3. Remove the cotter pin and nut securing the pitman arm to the center link and separate the pitman arm from the link with a ball joint tool.
4. Unbolt the steering gear from the frame.
5. If the pitman arm is to be removed from the sector shaft, first matchmark their positions, relative to each other.
6. Install the steering gear and connect the center link. Observe the following torques:
   - Steering gear-to-frame: 69 ft. lbs.
   - Wormshaft-to-steering shaft yoke: 38 ft. lbs.
   - Pitman arm-to-sector shaft: 130 ft. lbs.
   - Pitman arm-to-center link: 43 ft. lbs.

OVERHAUL

1. Remove the steering box from the vehicle. Remove the oil filler plug from the sector shaft cover and drain the oil into a suitable container. Install the filler plug. Secure the steering box in a soft jawed vise.
2. Remove the pitman arm using a puller.
3. Position the steering gear assembly in the vise with the sector shaft cover (the cover the filler plug screws into) facing upward. Center the sector shaft. Remove the bolts that mount the sector shaft cover assembly to the steering gear housing.
4. Tap the sector shaft (pitman arm end) with a plastic hammer to loosen the shaft. Lift the sector shaft cover and sector shaft assembly from the steering gear housing.
5. Position the steering gear housing in the vise with the worm ball nut assembly shaft facing upward.
6. Remove the large retaining flange locknut with a suitable spanner wrench, special tool 49 1391 580, or equivalent. Remove the adjusting nut with the spanner wrench.
7. Remove the worm ball nut assembly. Loosen the vise and carefully remove the housing. Remove the bearings and seals mounted in the housing. Remove the adjusting nut oil seal.
8. Clean and inspect all components. Check the bearings for sticking, abnormal noise or galling. Replace as necessary. Check the gear housing for damage or deformation. Check the worm ball nut assembly for poor rotation or play caused by wear in the axial direction. Check the sector shaft for damage or deformation. Replace worn parts as required.
9. Assemble and install the worm nut ball assembly after install new bearings and seals into the gear housing, adjusting nut and shafts. Install the adjusting nut and tighten enough to produce the required preload. Install and tighten the locknut.
10. Check the worm shaft preload with a pull scale before installing the sector shaft. The pull scale reading should be 0.7-1.3 lbs.(3-6N). Loosen the locknut and loosen or tighten the adjusting nut as required. After the proper preload is obtained, tighten the locknut to 116-145 ft. lbs. (157-196Nm).
11. Check the sector shaft adjustment screw for clearance. Set the adjusting screw and the adjustment screw in the T groove. Measure the clearance in the axial direction. If clearance exceeds specification, adjust it with the required shim. Shims are available in an adjusting shim kit. Clearance required is 0-0.004 in. (0-0.1mm).
12. After the desired clearance is obtained, install the sector shaft assembly into the gear assembly with the sector shaft and ball nut centered.
13. Secure the sector cover. Install the pitman arm. Check and adjust the steering gear backlash. Adjust the backlash with the steering gear in the center position, otherwise the gears could be damaged. Backlash is 0mm.
14. Install the gear assembly on the truck and fill with required lube.

Power Steering Gear

ADJUSTMENT

Wormshaft Preload

PICKUPS

1. With the steering gear mounted in a vise, and the pitman are positioned in a "wheels straight ahead" position, attach a spring scale and adapter 49 0180 510B to the wormshaft.
2. Check the rotating torque of the wormshaft. Rotating torque should be 1.3-2.2 lbs., but at least 1/2 to 1 lb higher than what the rotating torque is at a point 360° from straight ahead.
3. If preload is not correct, hold the adjusting screw on top of the gear with a screwdriver and loosen the locknut. Turn the adjusting screw to obtain the correct preload.

4. When preload is correct, hold the adjusting screw and tighten the locknut to 35 ft. lbs. Make sure that the adjusting screw does not move while the locknut is being tightened.

Meshload

NAVAJO

1. As required, raise and support the vehicle using jackstands.
2. Disconnect the pitman arm from the sector shaft using tool T64P–3590–F or equivalent.
3. Disconnect and cap the fluid return line at the reservoir return line pipe.
4. Place the end of the return line in a clean container and turn the steering wheel from stop to stop several times to discharge the fluid from the gear. Discard the used fluid.
5. Turn the steering gear 45° from the right stop.

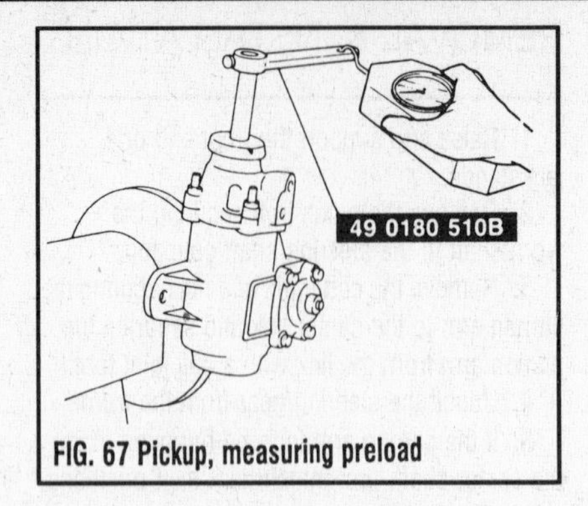

FIG. 67 Pickup, measuring preload

6. Remove the steering wheel hub cover. Attach an inch lb. torque wrench to the steering wheel nut and determine the torque required to rotate the shaft slowly about 1/8 turn from the 45° position toward center.
7. Turn the steering wheel back to center and determine the torque required to rotate the shaft back and forth across the center position.
8. Specification for vehicles under 5000 miles is 12–24 inch lbs. If the vehicle has over 5000 miles, reset the meshload measured while rocking the input shaft over center is less than 10 inch lbs. greater than torque 45° from the right stop.
9. If reset is required loosen the adjuster locknut and turn the sector shaft adjuster screw until the reading is the specified value greater than the torque at 45° from the stop. Hold the sector shaft screw in place and tighten the locknut.
10. Connect the pitman arm. Connect the return line. Bleed the system.

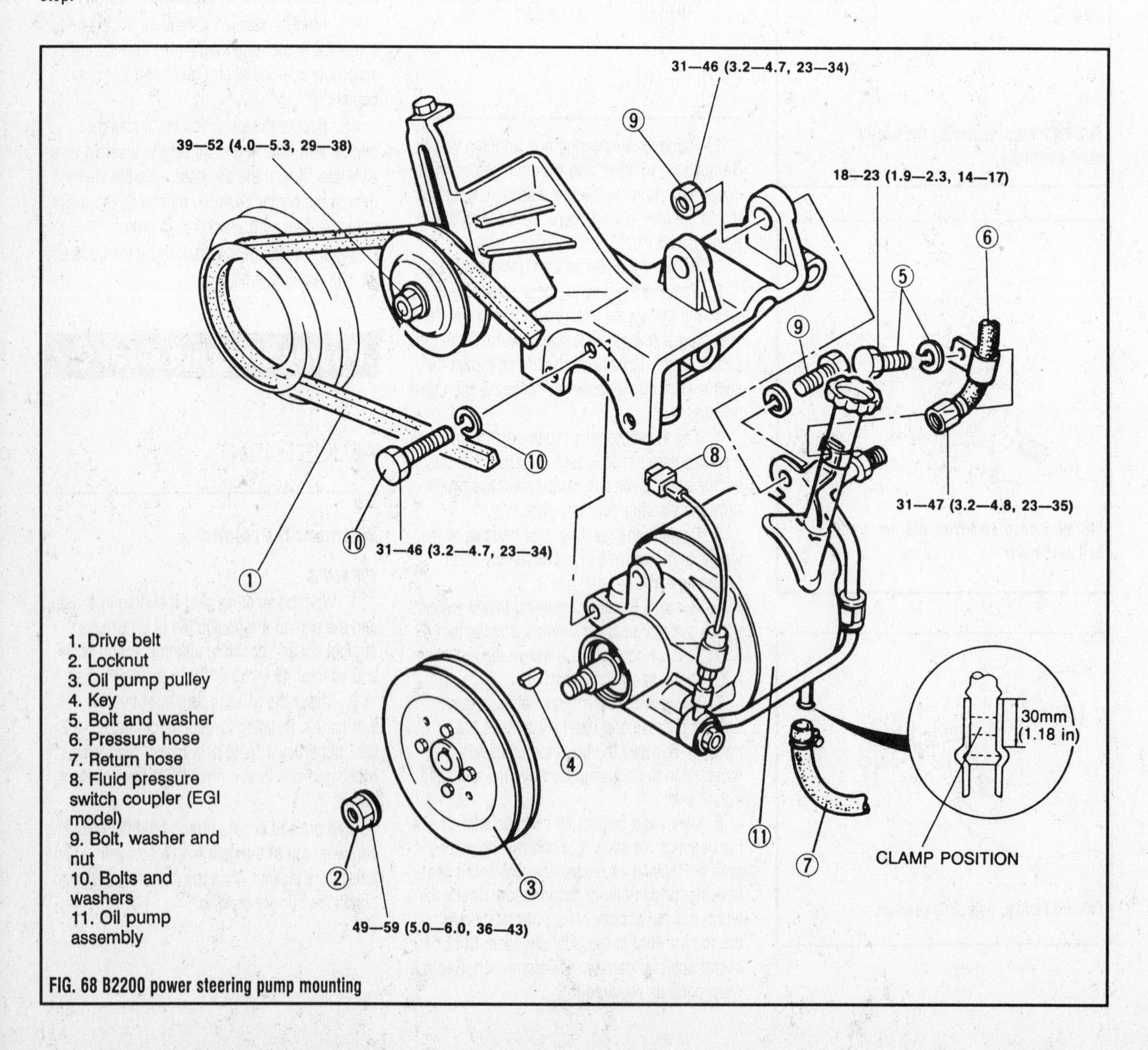

FIG. 68 B2200 power steering pump mounting

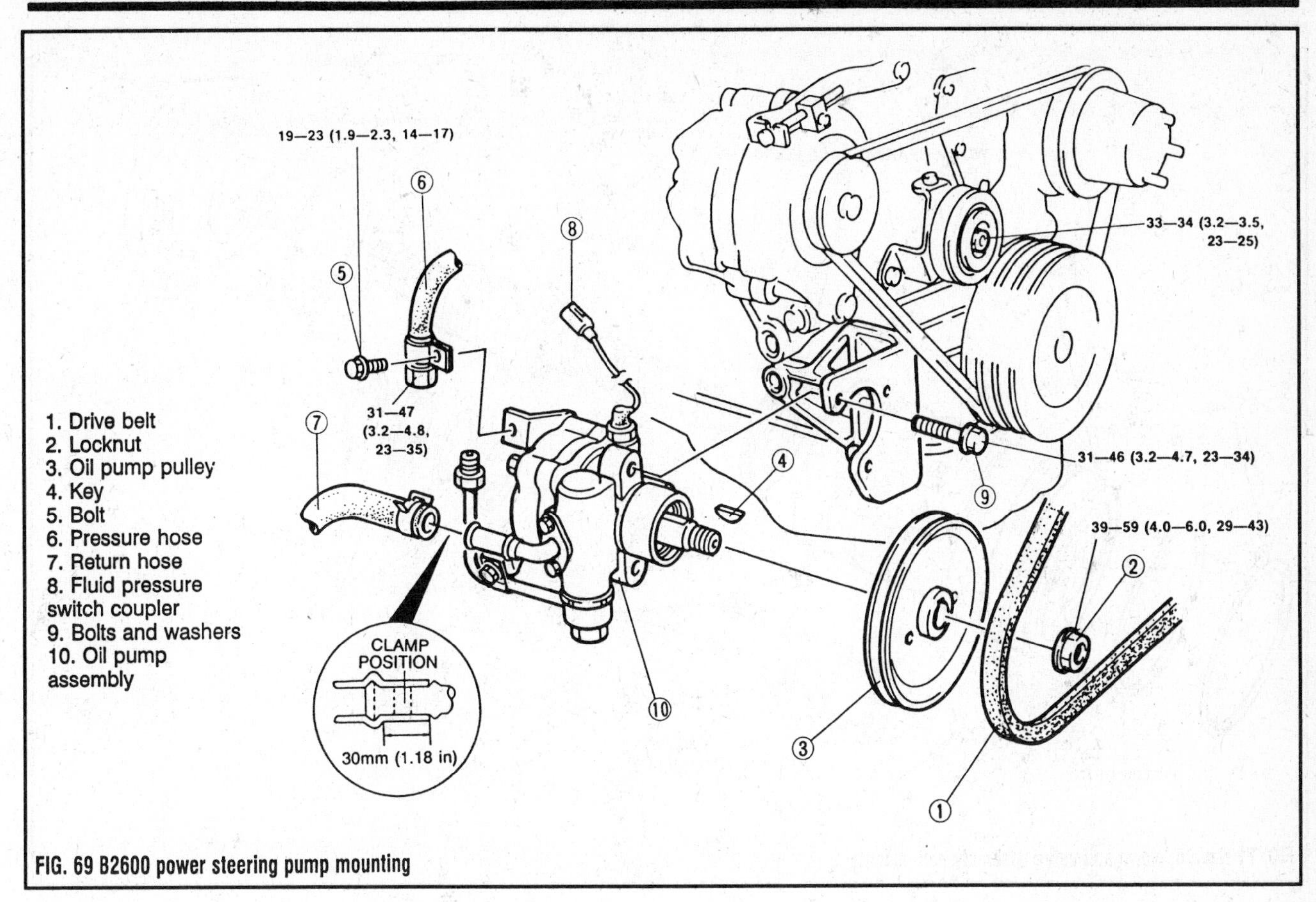

FIG. 69 B2600 power steering pump mounting

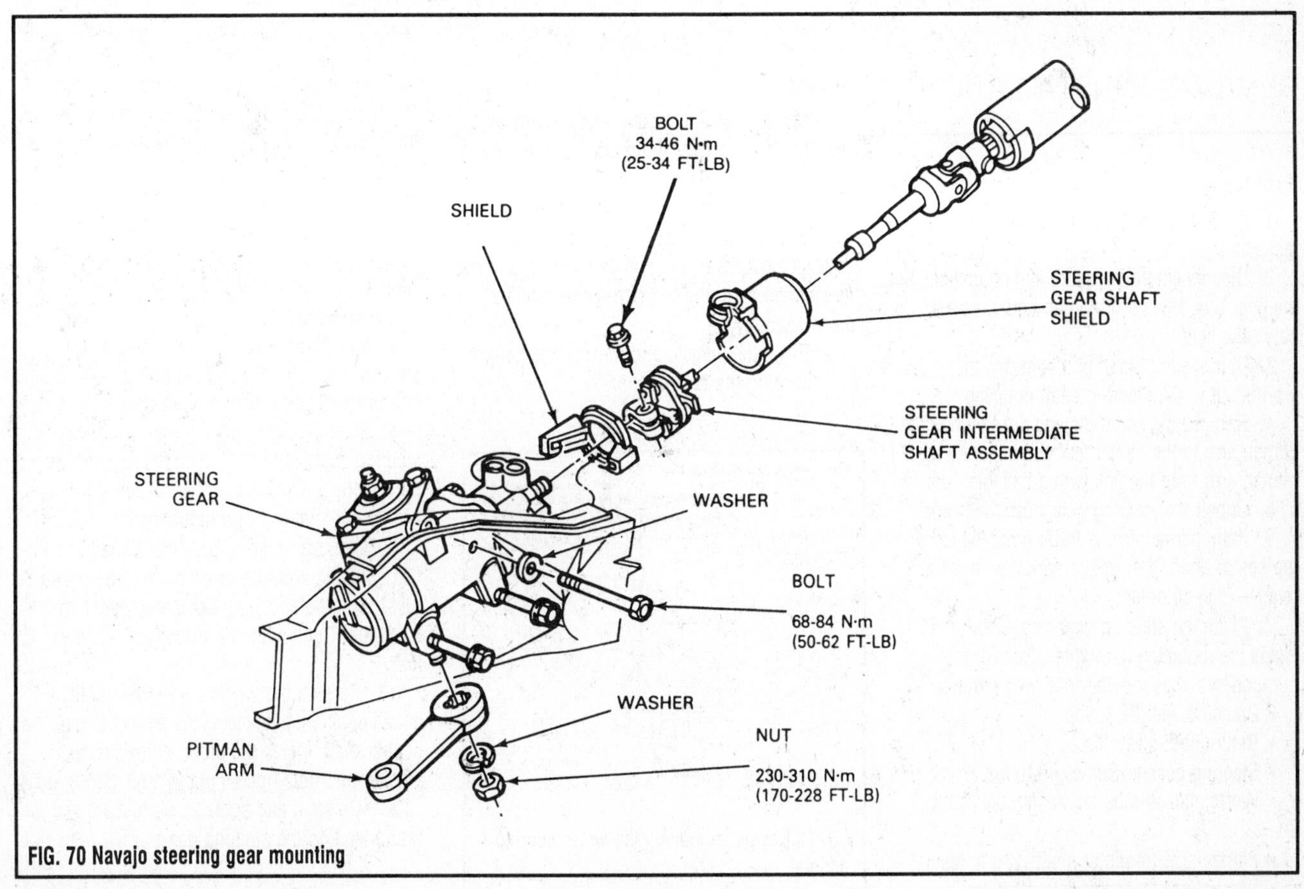

FIG. 70 Navajo steering gear mounting

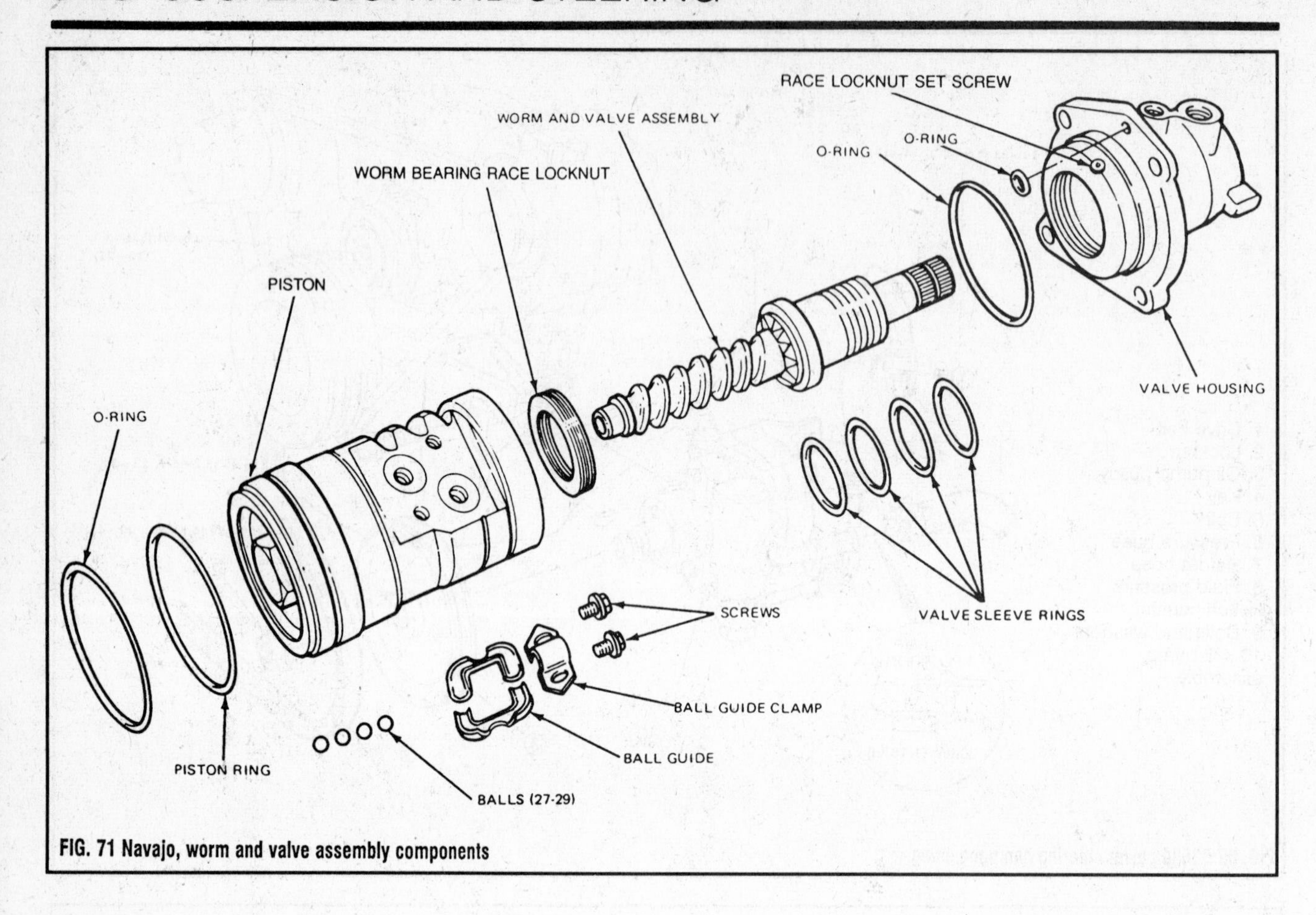

FIG. 71 Navajo, worm and valve assembly components

REMOVAL & INSTALLATION

Pickups

1. Raise and support the front end on jackstands.
2. Disconnect the pressure and return lines at the gear box. Have a drain pan underneath to catch the fluid.
3. Remove the pinch bolt securing the wormshaft to the steering shaft coupling.
4. Remove the cotter pin and nut securing the pitman arm to the center link and separate the pitman arm from the link with a ball joint tool.
5. Unbolt the steering gear from the frame.
6. If the pitman arm is to be removed from the sector shaft, first matchmark their positions, relative to each other.
7. Place the steering gear in position and install the mounting hardware. Connect the components. Observe the following torques:
- Pressure line: 26 ft. lbs.
- Return line: 35 ft. lbs.
- Steering gear-to-frame: 69 ft. lbs.
- Wormshaft-to-steering shaft yoke: 38 ft. lbs.
- Pitman arm-to-sector shaft: 130 ft. lbs.
- Pitman arm-to-center link: 43 ft. lbs.

Navajo

1. Disconnect the pressure and return lines from the steering gear. Plug the lines and the ports in the gear to prevent entry of dirt.
2. Remove the upper and lower steering gear shaft U-joint shield from the flex coupling. Remove the bolts that secure the flex coupling to the steering gear and to the column steering shaft assembly.
3. Raise the vehicle and remove the pitman arm attaching nut and washer.

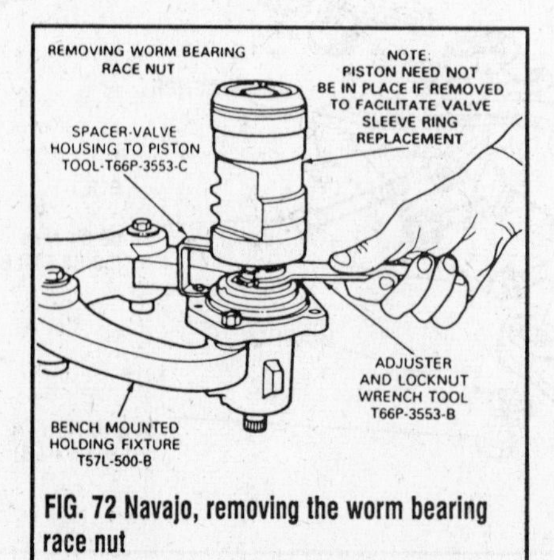

FIG. 72 Navajo, removing the worm bearing race nut

4. Remove the pitman arm from the sector shaft using tool T64P–3590–F. Remove the tool from the pitman arm. Do not damage the seals.
5. Support the steering gear, and remove the steering gear attaching bolts.
6. Work the steering gear free of the flex coupling. Remove the steering gear from the vehicle.

To install:

7. Install the lower U–joint shield onto the steering gear lugs. Slide the upper U-joint shield into place on the steering shaft assembly.
8. Slide the flex coupling into place on the steering shaft assembly. Turn the steering wheel so that the spokes are in the horizontal position. Center the steering gear input shaft.
9. Slide the steering gear input shaft into the flex coupling and into place on the frame side rail. Install the attaching bolts and tighten to 50–62 ft. lbs. Tighten the flex coupling bolt 26–34 ft. lbs.
10. Be sure the wheels are in the straight ahead position, then install the pitman arm on the sector shaft. Install the pitman arm attaching washer and nut. Tighten nut to 170–230 ft. lbs.
11. Connect and tighten the pressure and the return lines to the steering gear.

12. Disconnect the coil wire. Fill the reservoir. Turn on the ignition and turn the steering wheel from left to right to distribute the fluid.

13. Recheck fluid level and add fluid, if necessary. Connect the coil wire, start the engine and turn the steering wheel from side to side. Inspect for fluid leaks.

OVERHAUL

Pickups

1. Remove the steering gear assembly from the truck. Place the gear box in a soft jawed vise with the pitman arm facing at and angle that allows arm removal. Remove the pitman arm using a suitable puller.

2. Position the steering gear assembly in the vise with the sector shaft cover facing upward. Loosen the locknut. Remove the side cover mounting bolts.

3. Set the sector shaft in the center position. Tap the end of the sector shaft with a plastic hammer to loosen the shaft. Lift the sector shaft assembly up and out of the gear housing.

4. Position the gear housing in the vise and remove the valve and piston assembly mounting bolts. Carefully pull the valve and piston assembly from the housing.

5. Remove all oil seals, O rings and sealing rings. Clean and inspect all components and gear housing for damage or deformation. Replace any damage components.

6. Install new O rings, sealing rings and oil seals. Lubricate them with automatic transmission fluid.

7. Position the gear housing in the vise so that the valve and piston assembly can be installed. Insert the valve and piston assembly into the housing. Be careful not to scratch the piston seal ring and the new O ring against the housing. Insert the piston while slightly turning it to the left and right to prevent damage to the new O ring and the new seal ring. Secure the assembly with the mounting bolts.

8. Center the valve and piston assembly. Center and install the sector shaft. Secure the sector shaft cover mounting bolts. Set the sector shaft adjusting screw so that the preload is 1.3-2.0 lbs. (5.9-8.8N). Use a pull scale to check the preload. The preload at the centered position must be 0.4-0.9 lbs. higher than when the worm shaft is turned 360 degrees to the left and right.

9. If the specified preload is not obtained, once again disassemble the steering box and check the gears for dirt and foreign material. Check the installation of the oil seals. Once again assemble the steering box and check preload. After preload is correct, tighten the adjusting screw locknut to 25-35 ft. lbs. (34-47 Nm).

Navajo

1. Remove the steering gear for the vehicle. Hold the assembly upside down over a drain pan and allow the fluid to drain from the housing. Cycle the input shaft several times to help in draining the fluid. Clean as much dirt as possible from the outside of the housing assembly.

2. Secure the steering gear in a soft jawed vise. Turn the input shaft to either stop, then turn it back two turns to center the gear. The indexed flat on the input shaft spline should be facing downward.

3. Remove the sector shaft cover attaching bolts. Tap the lower end of the sector shaft with a plastic hammer to loosen it. Lift the cover and shaft assembly from the housing as an assembly. Discard the O ring.

4. If the sector shaft is to be removed from the sector assembly, remove the nut from the sector shaft adjusting screw. Turn the sector shaft cover counterclockwise and remove it from the sector shaft adjusting screw. It may be necessary to hold the screw with a screwdriver.

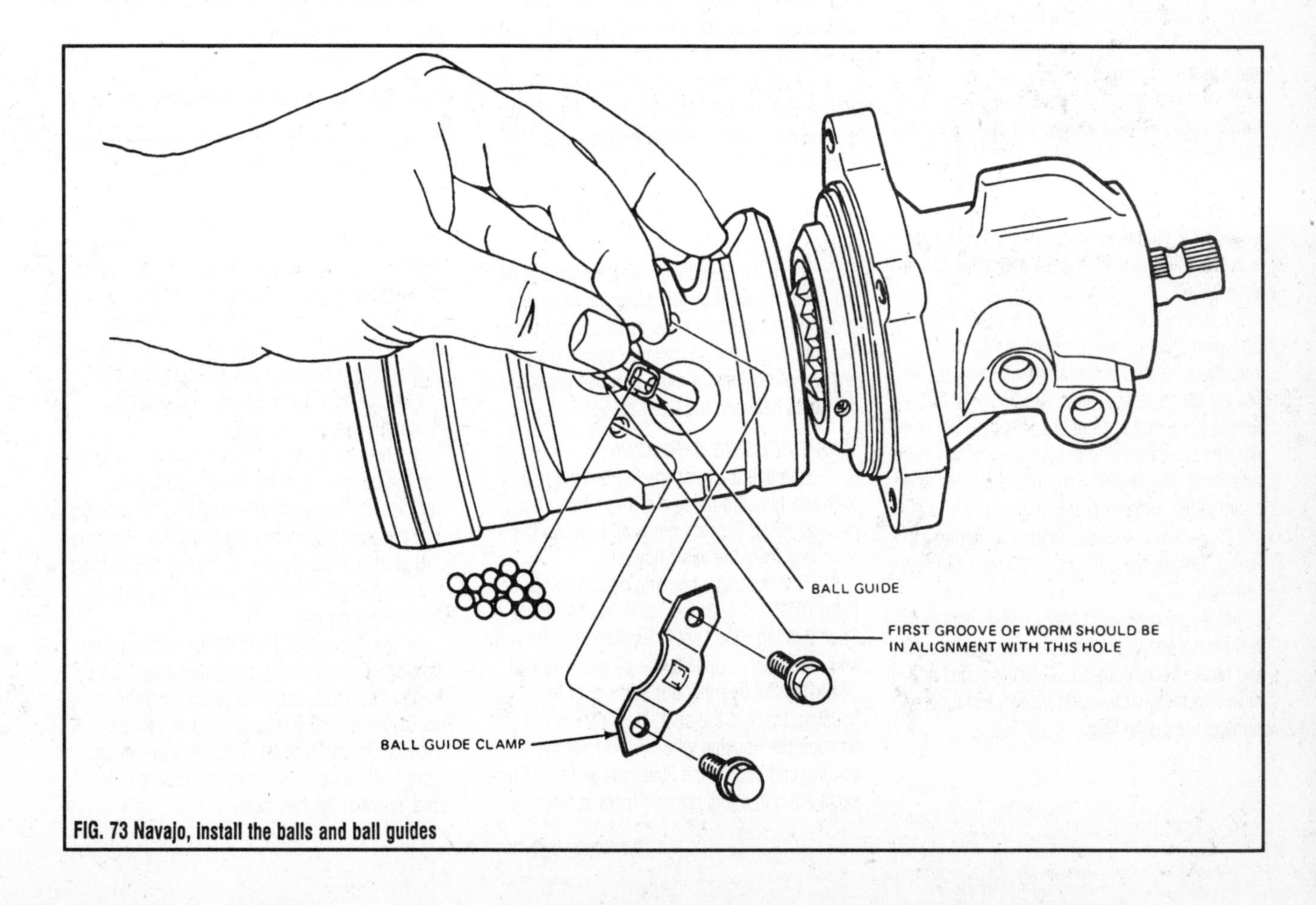

FIG. 73 Navajo, install the balls and ball guides

5. Remove the valve housing attaching bolts and ID tag. Lift the housing off of the steering gear housing. Remove the valve and piston assembly and the control valve assembly and gasket. Discard the gasket.

6. If the valve sleeve rings need replacing, the balls need to be removed. With the piston held so that the ball guide faces up, remove the ball guide clamp screws and ball guide clamp. With a finger over the opening in the ball guide, turn the piston so that the ball guide faces down over a clean container. Let the guide tubes drop into the container.

7. Rotate the input shaft from stop to stop until all balls fall from the piston into the container. The valve assembly can be removed from the piston. Inspect the piston bore to insure all balls have been removed.

8. If the valve housing or the valve sleeve seals are to be replaced, mount the valve body assembly into a suitable holding device and loosen the Allen head race nut screw from the valve housing. Remove the worm bearing race nut. Slide the input shaft, worm and valve assembly carefully out of the valve housing.

9. To assemble: After cleaning, inspecting and replacing as required, mount the valve housing in a suitable holding fixture with the flanged end up. Apply a light coat of ATF fluid to the rings on the valve sleeve. Carefully install the worm shaft and valve in the housing.

10. Install the worm bearing race nut in the housing and tighten to 55-90 ft. lbs. (75-122Nm). Install the Allen head race nut set screw through the valve housing and tighten to 12-25 inch lbs. (1.7-2.8Nm).

11. Place the power cylinder on the bench with the ball guide holes facing up. Insert the worm shaft into the piston so that the first groove is in line with the hole nearest the center of the piston.

12. Place the ball guides in the piston. Turn the worm shaft counterclockwise as viewed from the input end of the shaft, place the balls into the guide plate. During assembly 27 to 29 balls are required. If all of the balls have not been inserted upon reaching the left stop, rotate the input shaft in one direction, then the other while inserting the remaining balls.

13. Secure the guides in the ball nut with the clamp. Tighten the bolts to 42-70 inch lbs. (4.8-7.9Nm).

14. Apply petroleum jelly or equivalent to the seal on the piston. Place a new control valve O ring on the valve housing. Slide the piston and valve into the gear housing being careful not to damage the piston ring.

15. Align the oil passage in the valve housing with the passage in the gear housing. Place a new O ring onto the oil passage hole of the gear housing. Place the ID tag in position on the housing under the upper right valve housing bolt. Install, but do not tighten, the attaching bolts.

16. Rotate the piston so that the teeth are in the same plane as the sector teeth. Tighten the valve housing attaching bolts to 30-45 ft. lbs. (41-62 Nm).

17. Position the sector cover O ring into the steering gear housing. Turn the input shaft to center the piston.

18. Apply petroleum jelly or equivalent to the sector shaft journal. Position the sector shaft and cover assembly into the gear housing. Tighten the cover mounting bolts to 55-70 ft. lbs. (75-94Nm).

19. Adjust the meshload as described previously.

STEERING GEAR HOUSING SERVICING

1. Remove the snapring from the lower end of the housing. Remove the dust shield using a suitable slide hammer and internal jawed puller. Remove the pressure oil seal with the puller.

2. Using an appropriate seal installing tool and the following procedures must be used to prevent damage to the seals during assembly.

3. Lubricate the new pressure seal and dust seal with NLGI No. 2 (Lithium Base) multi-purpose grease. Apply the multi-purpose grease to the sector shaft seal bore.

4. Place the dust seal on the Sector Shaft Replacement Tool T77L 3576A, or equivalent, so that the raised lip of the seal is toward the tool. Place the pressure seal on the tool with the seal lip away from the tool. The flat back side of the pressure seal should be against the flat side of the dust seal.

5. Insert the seal driver into the bore and drive the seals in until they just clear the snap ring groove. Do not bottom the seals against the bearing. Install the snap ring. Apply a generous amount of the lithium multi-purpose grease to the areas between the two seal lips.

VALVE HOUSING SERVICING

1. Remove the dust shield from the rear of the valve housing using a slide hammer and internal puller. Discard the seal. Remove the snap ring from the valve housing.

2. Turn the valve housing over. Insert special tools T65P 3524A2 and T65P 3524A3 Input Shaft Bearing/Seal Tool or equivalent in the valve body assembly opposite the oil seal end and gently tap the bearing and seal out of the housing. Discard the seal. Take care not to damage the housing when driving out the bearing and seal. If the fluid inlet and outlet tube seats are damaged, remove them at this time.

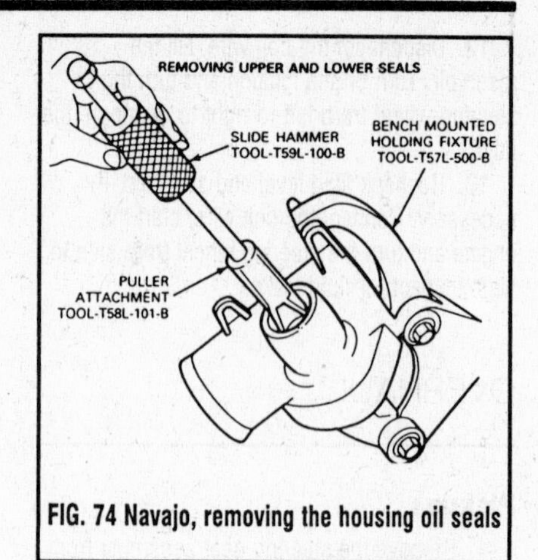

FIG. 74 Navajo, removing the housing oil seals

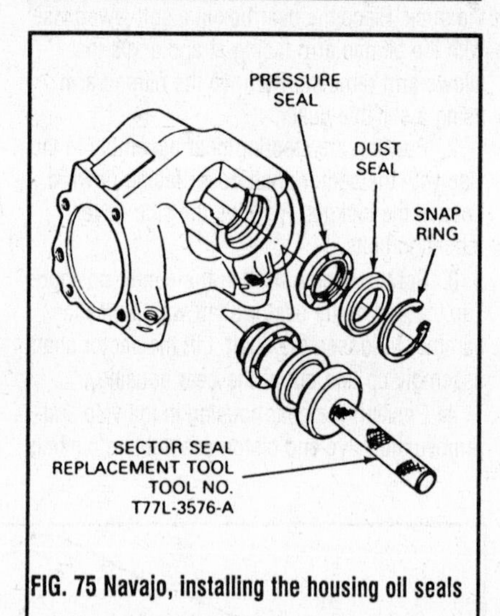

FIG. 75 Navajo, installing the housing oil seals

3. To assemble: Coat the inlet and outlet tube seats with petroleum jelly or equivalent. Install them into the housing using tool T74P 3504M or equivalent. Coat the bearing and seal surface of the housing with petroleum jelly or equivalent.

4. Install the bearing with the metal side covering the rollers facing outward. Seat the bearing into the valve housing using tool T65P 3524A1 or equivalent. Be sure the bearing rotates freely.

5. Dip a new oil seal in ATF fluid and place it into the housing with the metal side facing outward. Carefully drive the seal into the housing until the outer edge dose not quite clear the snap ring groove. Place the snap ring into the housing and drive in the snap ring until it seats in the mounting groove.

6. Place the dust seal into the housing with the dished side (rubber side) facing out. Drive the dust seal into position. When properly installed, the seal will be located behind the undercut in the input shaft. Apply a generous amount of lithium multi-purpose grease to the area between the two seals.

WORM AND VALVE SLEEVE SERVICING

1. Remove the valve sleeve rings from the sleeve by inserting a small pocket knife blade under them and cutting them off.
2. A Seal Installation Set such as TOOL T75L 3517A, or equivalent is required to prevent damage to the seals during installation.
3. Mount the worm end of the worm and valve assembly into a soft jawed vise. Install Mandrel Tool T75L 3517A1, or equivalent, over the sleeve. Slide one sleeve ring over the tool. Slide the Pusher Tool T75L 3517A2 over the mandrel. Rapidly push down on the pusher tool forcing the ring down the ramp and into the fourth groove of the valve sleeve. Repeat the procedure to install each of the three remaining seals. Install a spacer T75L 3517A3 under mandrel tool before installing each ring. The mandrel will line up with the next groove of the valve sleeve after each spacer is added.
4. After the four sleeve rings are installed, apply a light coat of ATF fluid to the sleeve and rings.
5. Insert one spacer, T75L 3517A3 or equivalent, over the input shaft for installing the sizing tube. Slowly install the sizing tube Tool T75L 3517A4 over the sleeve valve end of the worm shaft onto the valve seal rings. Make sure that the rings are not being bent over as the tube is slid over them. Allow the sizing tube to sit over the rings for five minutes. Remove the sizing tube and check the condition of the rings. Make sure that the rings turn freely in the grooves. No further service or disassembly of the worm valve assembly is possible. Valve centering will be destroyed if disassembly is attempted.

PISTON SERVICING

1. Remove the piston ring and O-ring from the piston and ball nut. Discard both rings.
2. Dip a new O-ring in ATF fluid and install it on the piston and ball nut. Install a new piston ring on the piston and ball nut. Take care not to stretch the ring more than necessary for installation.

Power Steering Rack and Pinion

REMOVAL & INSTALLATION

MPV – 2WD

1. Place the front wheels in the straight ahead position. Raise and safely support the vehicle.

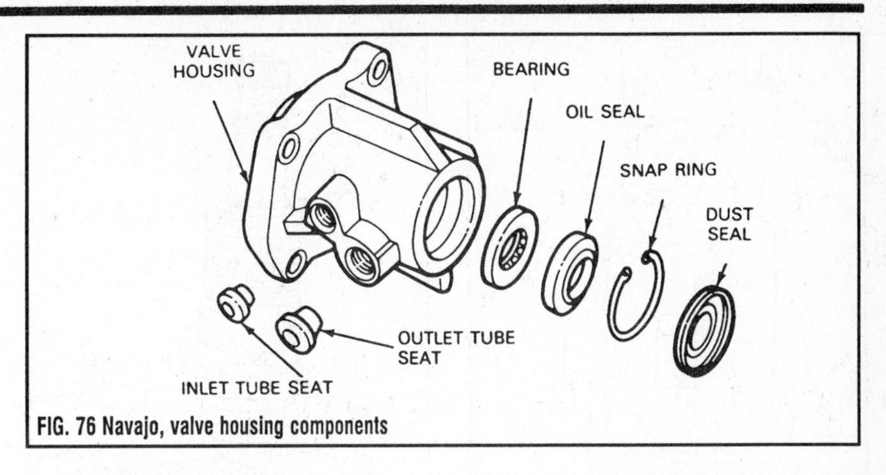

FIG. 76 Navajo, valve housing components

2. Remove the wheel and tire assemblies. Remove the splash shield.
3. Remove the cotter pins and nuts from both tie rod end studs. Use separator tool 49 0727 575 or equivalent, to separate the tie rod ends from the knuckles.
4. Remove the pinch bolt from the intermediate shaft-to-pinion shaft coupling.
5. Disconnect and plug the pressure line from the rack and pinion assembly. Loosen the clamp and disconnect the return line from the rack and pinion assembly. Plug the line.
6. If equipped with automatic transmission, remove the change counter assembly to remove the protector plate mounting bolt.
7. Remove the steering bracket mounting bolts and remove the rack and pinion assembly and brackets.
8. If necessary, remove the brackets.

To install:

9. If removed, install the brackets and tighten the mounting bolts, in sequence, to 54–69 ft. lbs. (74–93 Nm).
10. Install the rack and pinion assembly and brackets in the vehicle. Tighten the bracket-to-chassis bolts to 46–69 ft. lbs. (63–93 Nm).
11. If equipped with automatic transmission, install the change counter assembly.
12. Connect the return line and tighten the clamp. Connect the pressure line and tighten the nut to 23–35 ft. lbs. (31–47 Nm).
13. Install the pinch bolt in the intermediate shaft-to-pinion shaft coupling and tighten to 13–20 ft. lbs. (18–26 Nm).
14. Position the tie rod end studs in the knuckles and install the nuts. Tighten the nuts to 43–58 ft. lbs. (59–78 Nm) and install new cotter pins.
15. Install the splash shield and the wheel and tire assemblies. Lower the vehicle and bleed the power steering system.

MPV – 4WD

1. Place the front wheels in the straight ahead position. Raise and safely support the vehicle.

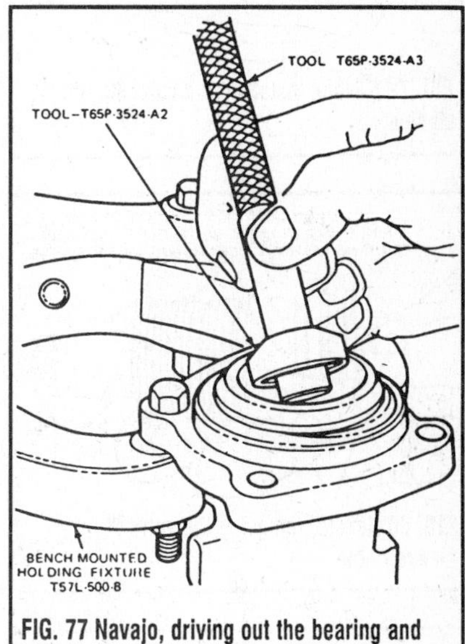

FIG. 77 Navajo, driving out the bearing and oil seal

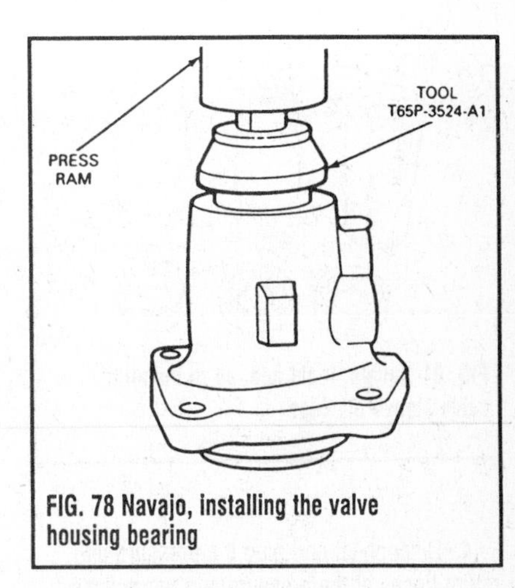

FIG. 78 Navajo, installing the valve housing bearing

2. Remove the wheel and tire assemblies. Remove the splash shield.
3. Remove the cotter pins and nuts from both tie rod end studs. Use separator tool 49 0727 575 or equivalent, to separate the tie rod ends from the knuckles.

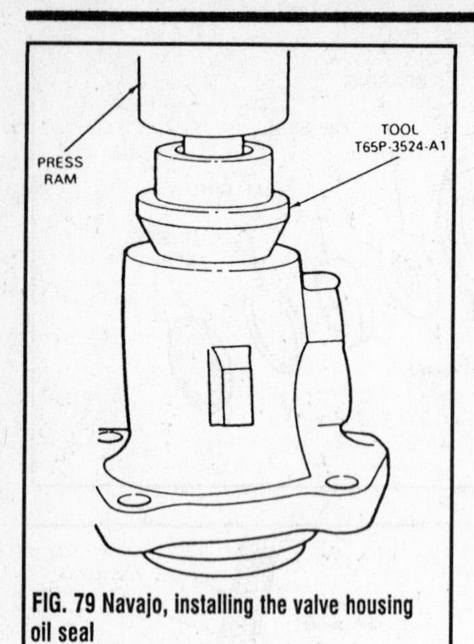

FIG. 79 Navajo, installing the valve housing oil seal

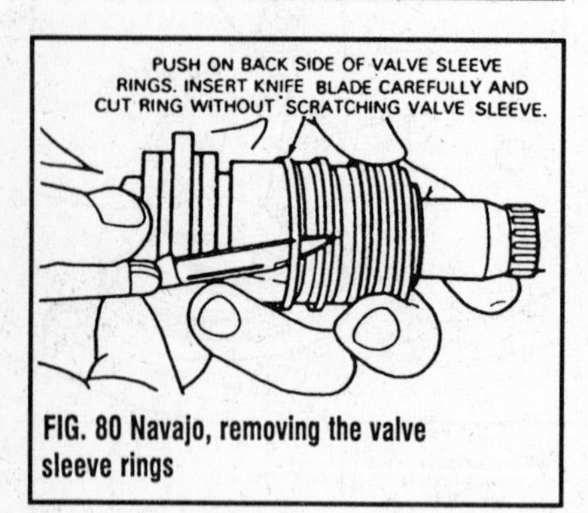

PUSH ON BACK SIDE OF VALVE SLEEVE RINGS. INSERT KNIFE BLADE CAREFULLY AND CUT RING WITHOUT SCRATCHING VALVE SLEEVE.

FIG. 80 Navajo, removing the valve sleeve rings

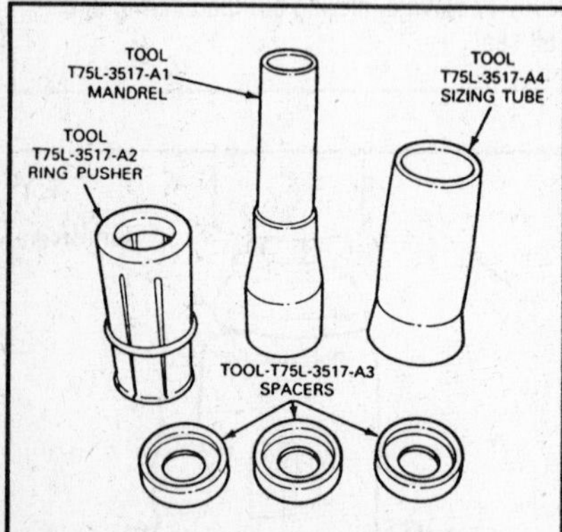

FIG. 81 Navajo, tools needed to install the valve sleeve oil rings

4. Disconnect and plug the pressure and return hoses at the pressure and return lines.

5. Remove the pressure and return lines from the rack and pinion assembly.

6. Remove the pinch bolt from the intermediate shaft-to-pinion shaft coupling.

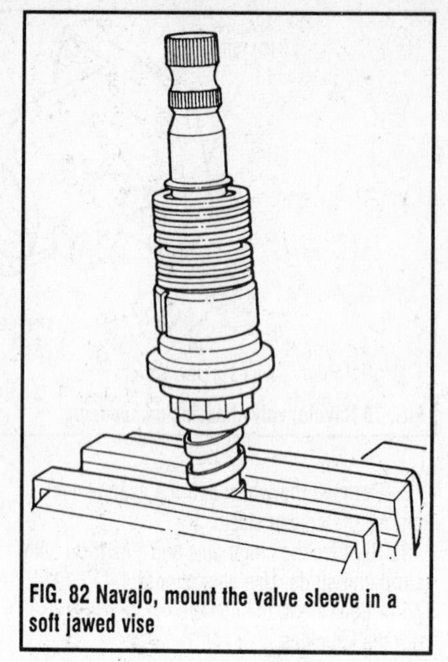
FIG. 82 Navajo, mount the valve sleeve in a soft jawed vise

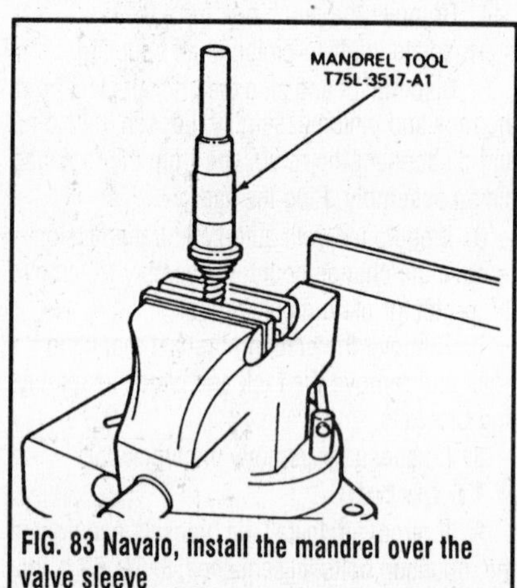

FIG. 83 Navajo, install the mandrel over the valve sleeve

7. Working inside the vehicle, remove the lower panel and column cover from under the steering column. Remove the steering column mounting bolts and nuts and pull the column and intermediate shaft rearward to separate the intermediate shaft from the pinion shaft.

8. Mark the position of the front driveshaft on the axle flange and remove the front driveshaft.

9. Remove the rack and pinion assembly mounting bracket bolts and the front differential/joint shaft assembly mounting bolts.

10. Slide the differential/joint shaft assembly rearward. Slide the rack and pinion assembly rearward and turn it 90 degrees, then remove it from the left side of the vehicle.

To install:

11. Install the rack and pinion assembly from the left side of the vehicle, turn it 90 degrees and move it forward into position. Install the mounting bolts and tighten, in sequence, to 54–69 ft. lbs. (74–93 Nm).

12. Move the differential/joint shaft assembly forward, install the mounting bolts and tighten to 49–72 ft. lbs. (67–97 Nm).

13. Install the driveshaft, aligning the marks made during removal.

14. Working inside the vehicle, move the steering column and intermediate shaft forward to engage the intermediate shaft with the pinion shaft. Install and tighten the steering column nuts and bolts to 12–17 ft. lbs. (16–23 Nm). Install the lower panel and column cover.

15. Install the pinch bolt in the intermediate shaft-to-pinion shaft coupling and tighten to 13–20 ft. lbs. (18–26 Nm).

16. Install the pressure and return lines on the rack and pinion assembly. Connect the pressure and return hoses to the lines.

17. Position the tie rod end studs in the knuckles and install the nuts. Tighten the nuts to 43–58 ft. lbs. (59–78 Nm) and install new cotter pins.

18. Install the splash shield and the wheel and tire assemblies. Lower the vehicle and bleed the power steering system.

Power Steering Pump

REMOVAL & INSTALLATION

B2200

1. Raise and support the front end on jackstands.

2. Loosen the idler pulley bolt and remove the drive belt.

3. Remove the pump pulley nut.

4. Using a puller, remove the pulley from the pump.

5. Disconnect the return hose from the pump. Have a drain pan ready to catch the fluid.

6. Remove the pressure hose bracket bolt and unscrew the pressure hose from the pump. Always use a back-up wrench.

7. Support the pump and remove the front and rear pump-to-bracket bolts. Remove the pump.

8. Place the pump in position and install the mounting bolts. Connect the pressure and return lines. Install the drive pulley and belt. Adjust the drive belt to the proper tension. Fill and bleed the system. Observe the following torques:

- Pump pulley: 43 ft. lbs.
- Pressure line connection: 35 ft. lbs.
- Pressure line bracket: 17 ft. lbs.
- Pump-to-bracket: 34 ft. lbs.

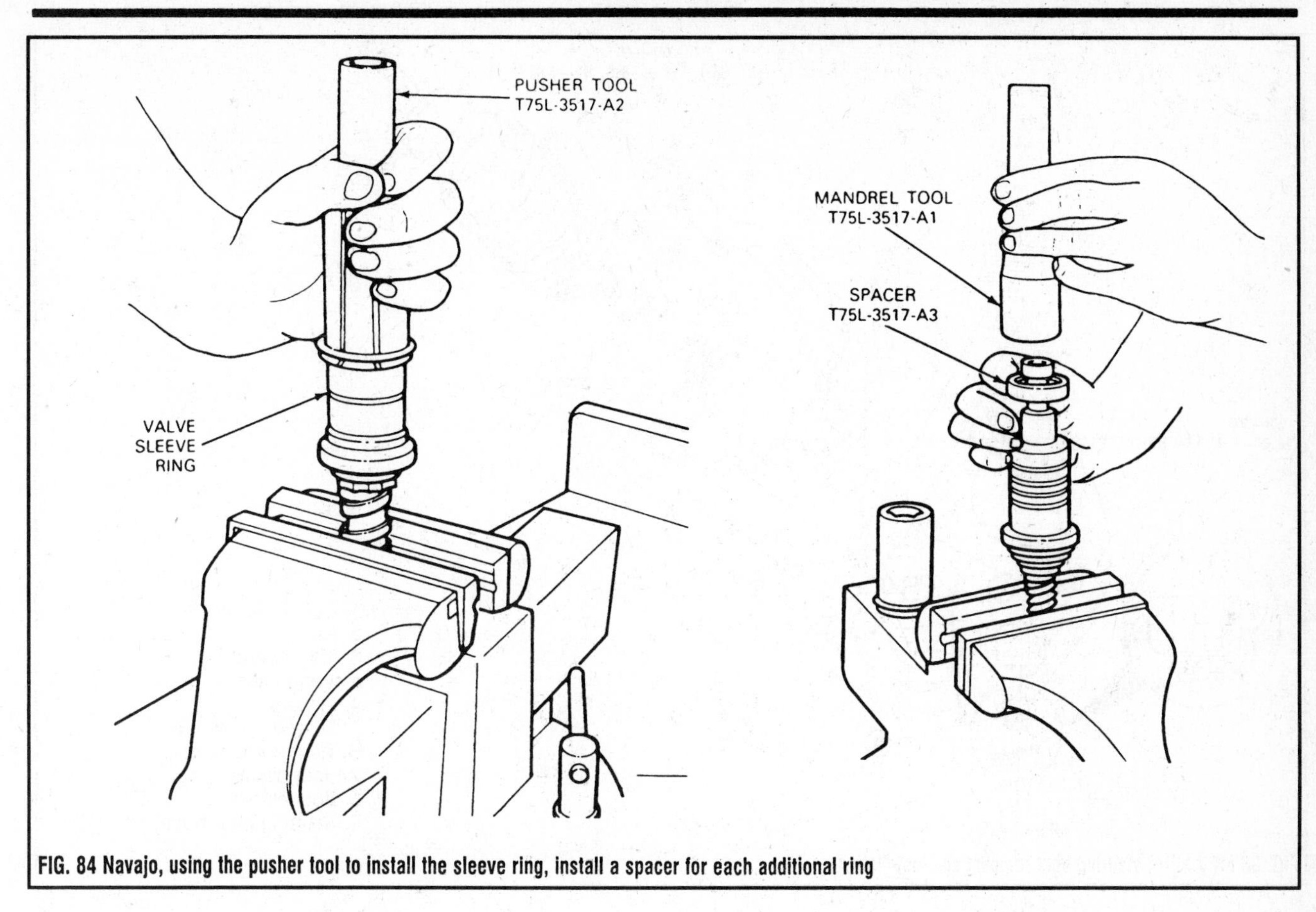

FIG. 84 Navajo, using the pusher tool to install the sleeve ring, install a spacer for each additional ring

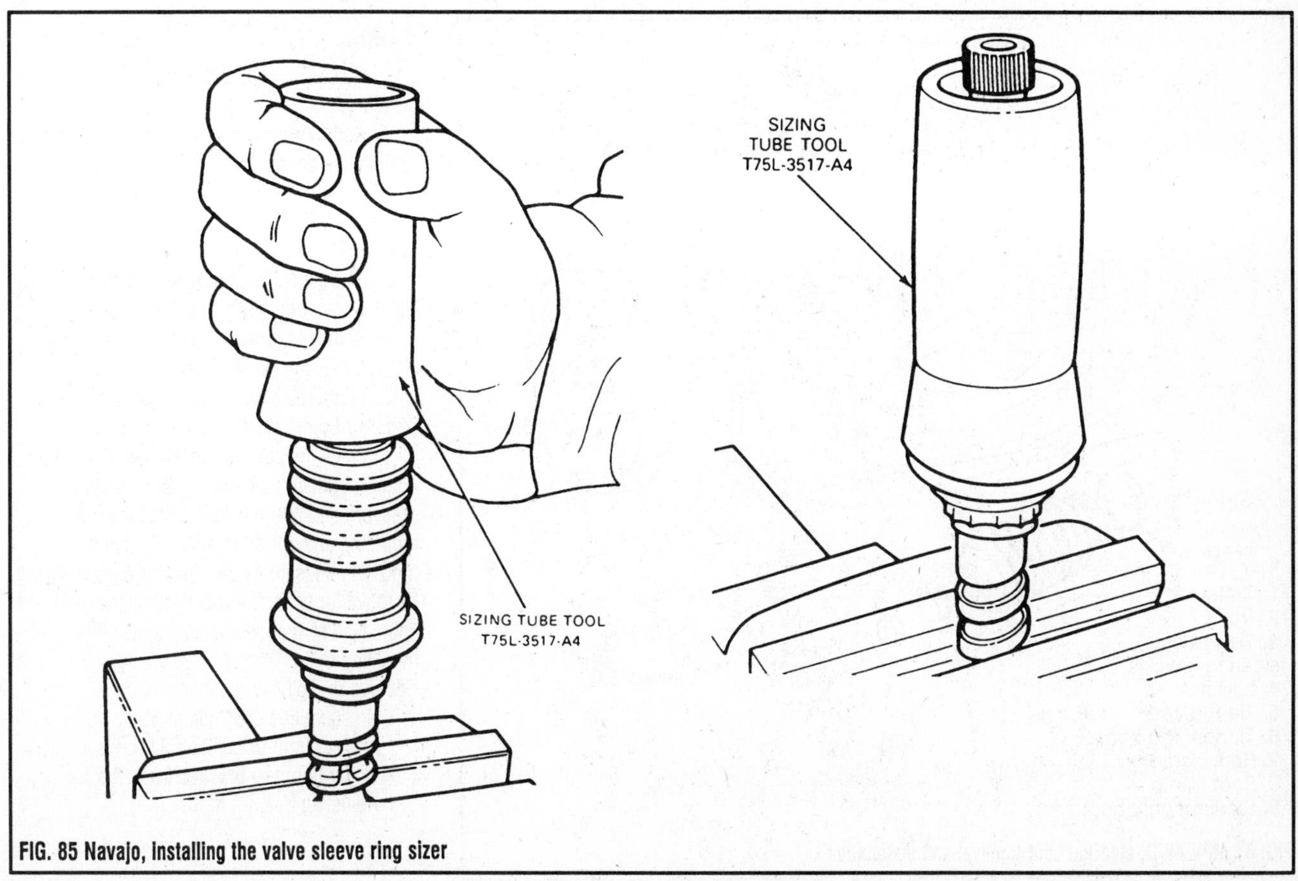

FIG. 85 Navajo, installing the valve sleeve ring sizer

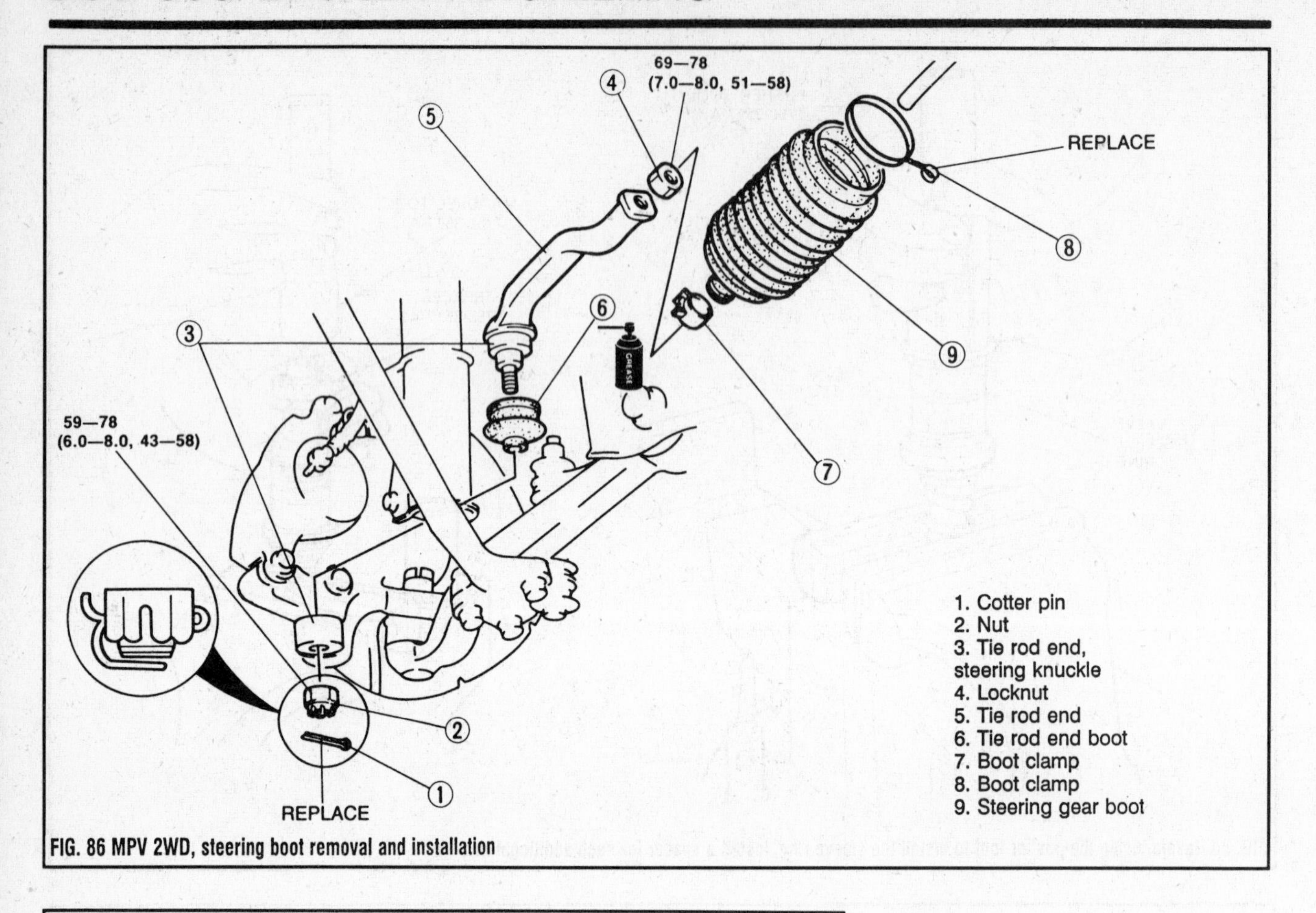

FIG. 86 MPV 2WD, steering boot removal and installation

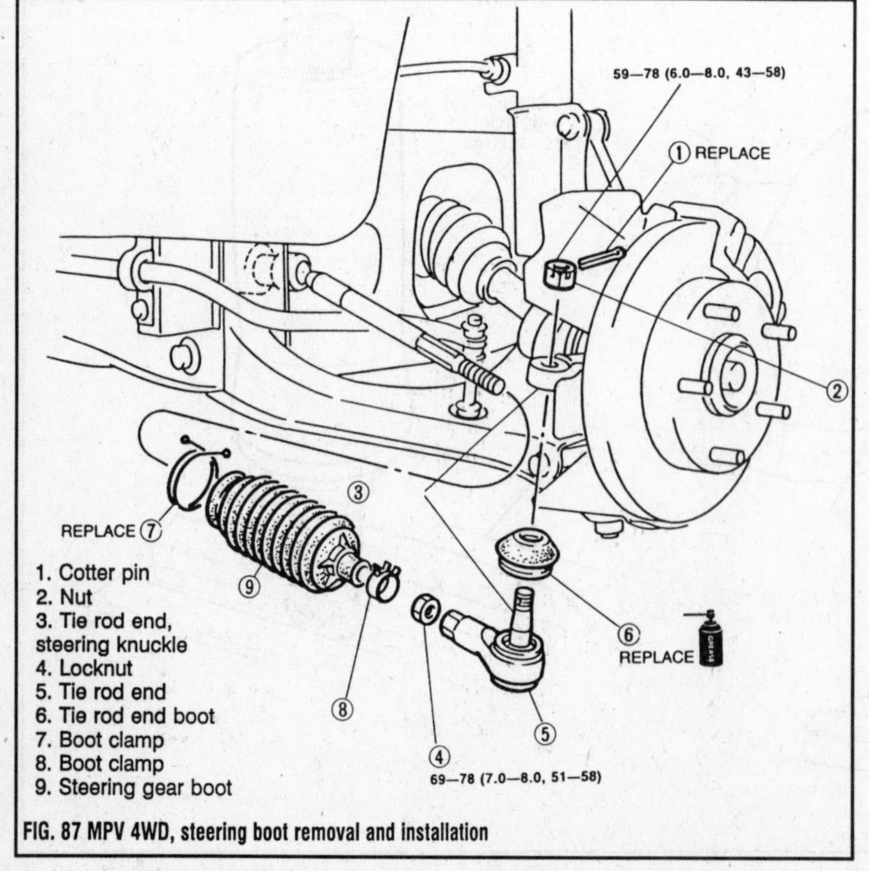

FIG. 87 MPV 4WD, steering boot removal and installation

B2600

1. Raise and support the front end on jackstands.
2. Remove the pump adjusting bolt and remove the drive belt.
3. Remove the lower pump-to-bracket through-bolt and spacer.
4. Rotate the pump to get to the hoses.
5. Disconnect the return hose from the pump. Have a drain pan ready to catch the fluid.
6. Remove the pressure hose from the pump. Always use a back-up wrench.
7. Support the pump and remove the upper pump-to-bracket bolt. Remove the pump.
8. Place the pump in position and install the upper mounting bolt loosely. Connect the pressure and return hoses. Install the lower mounting and adjusting bolts. Tighten the mounting bolts enough so that the pump can still be move for belt adjustment. Install the drive belt and adjust to proper tension. Tighten the mounting bolts. Fill and bleed the system. Observe the following torques:
   - Pressure line connection: 35 ft. lbs.
   - Lower pump-to-bracket: 34 ft. lbs.
   - Upper pump-to-bracket: 20 ft. lbs.
   - Adjusting bolt: 34 ft. lbs.

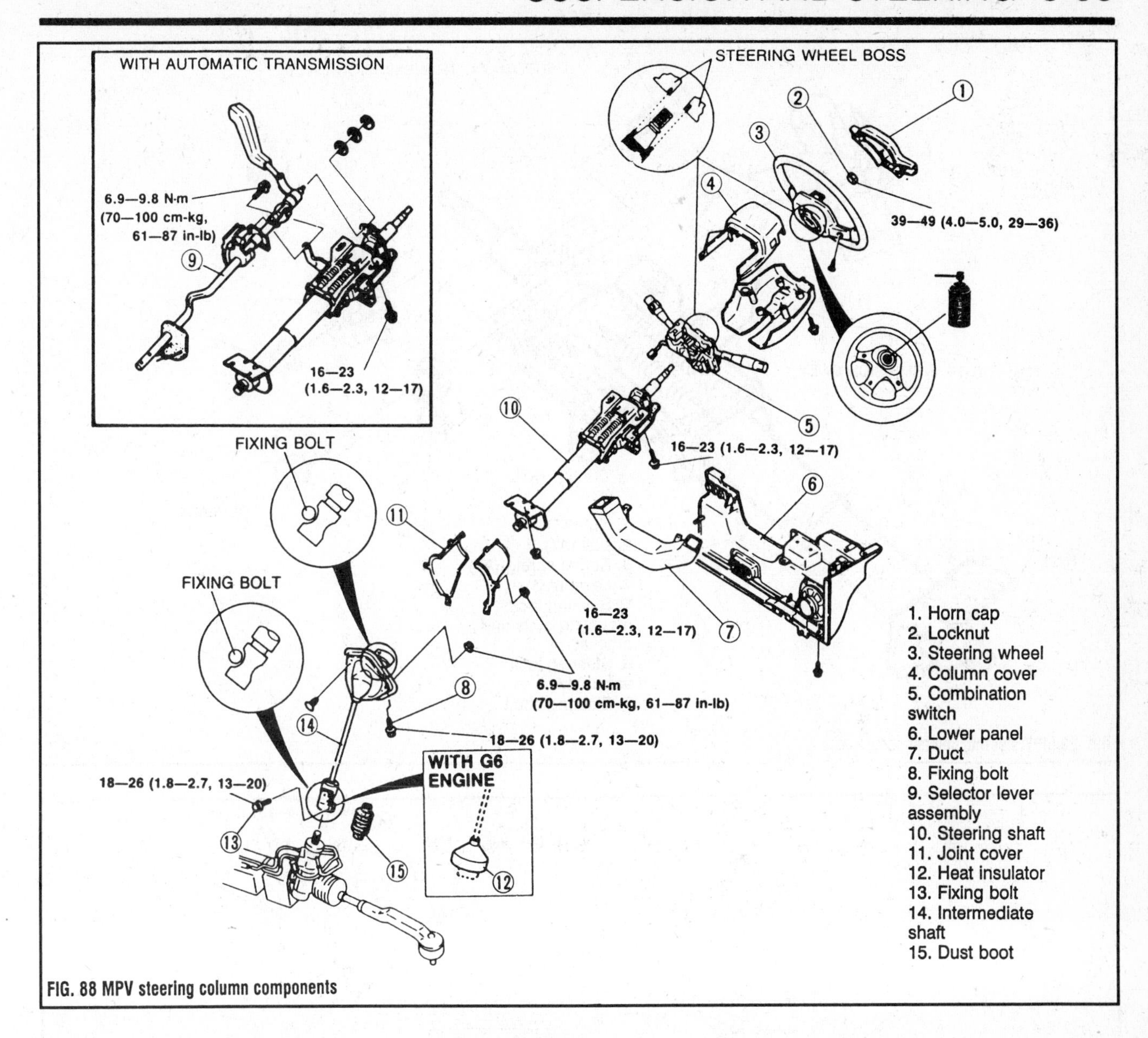

FIG. 88 MPV steering column components

MPV w/6-Cylinder Engine

1. Loosen the idler pulley locknut.
2. Loosen the pump adjusting bolt.
3. Remove the drive belt.
4. Remove the pump pulley nut.
5. Using a puller, remove the pulley.
6. Disconnect the pressure switch wiring connector.
7. Place a drain pan under the pump.
8. Matchmark the pressure line connection and disconnect it.
9. Remove the pressure line bracket bolt.
10. Disconnect the return line.
11. Remove the pump-to-bracket bolts and lift out the pump.
12. Place the pump in position and install the mounting bolts. Connect the return and pressure. Install the drive pulley and belt. Adjust the drive belt to the proper tension. Fill and bleed the system. Observe the following torques:
   - mounting bolts to 34 ft. lbs.
   - pressure line connection to 35 ft. lbs.
   - pressure line bracket bolt: 17 ft. lbs.
   - pulley bolt: 43 ft. lbs.
   - adjusting bolt: 35 ft. lbs.
   - idler pulley locknut: 38 ft. lbs.

MPV w/4-Cylinder Engine

1. Place a drain pan under the pump.
2. Loosen the idler pulley locknut and the pump adjusting bolt and remove the pump drive belt.
3. Remove the pump pulley nut.
4. Remove the pulley.
5. Unplug the pressure switch coupler.
6. Matchmark the high pressure line coupling and disconnect the line.
7. Remove the return hose.
8. Remove the pump-to-bracket bolts and lift out the pump.
9. Place the pump in position and install and tighten the mounting bolts. Connect the return and pressure hoses. Install the drive pulley. Install and adjust the drive belt. Fill and bleed the system. Tighten the high pressure coupling to 23-35 ft. lbs., aligning the high pressure coupling matchmarks. Tighten the pump mounting bolts to 23-34 ft. lbs. Tighten the pulley nut to 29-43 ft. lbs. Tighten the idler pulley locknut to 27-38 ft. lbs.

Navajo

1. Disconnect the negative battery cable.

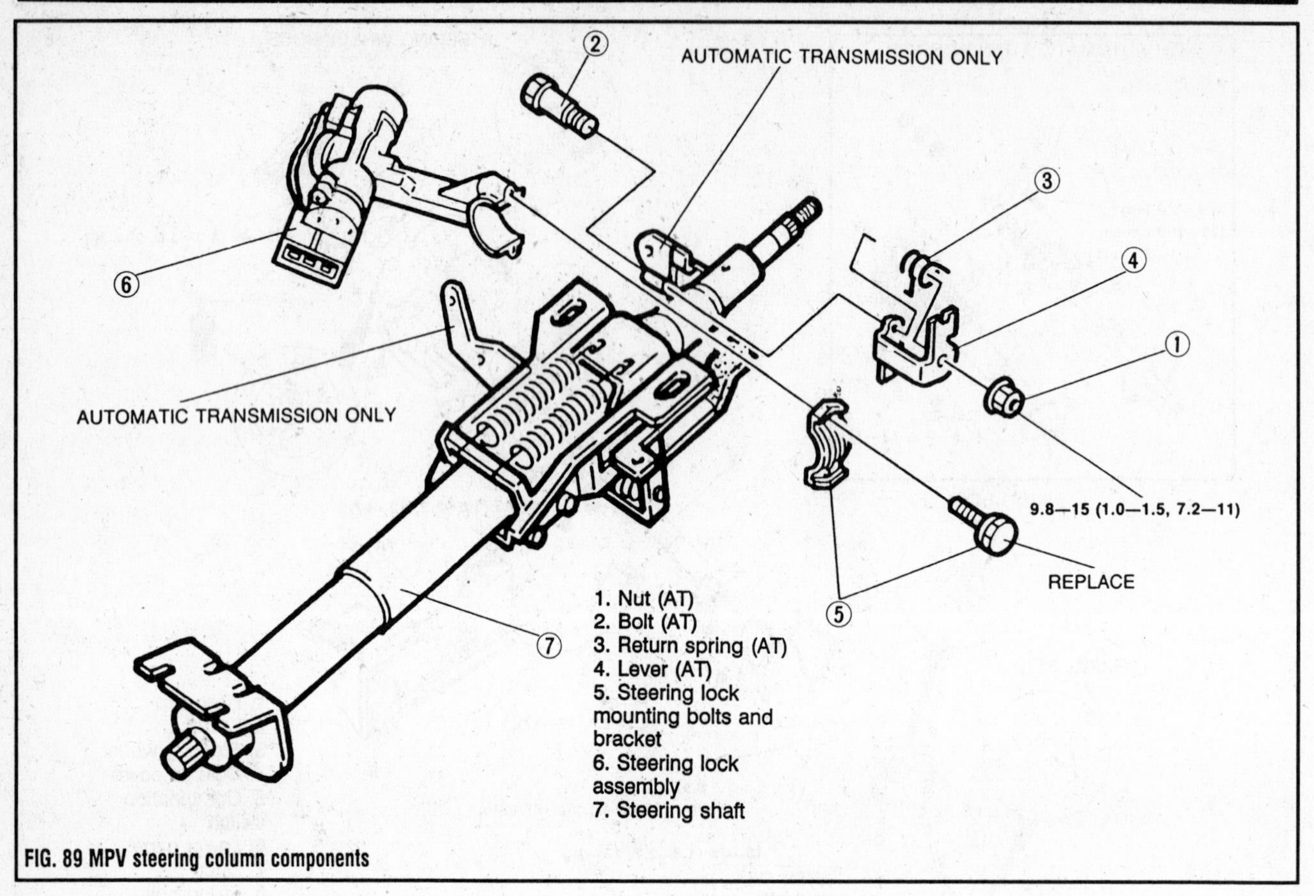

FIG. 89 MPV steering column components

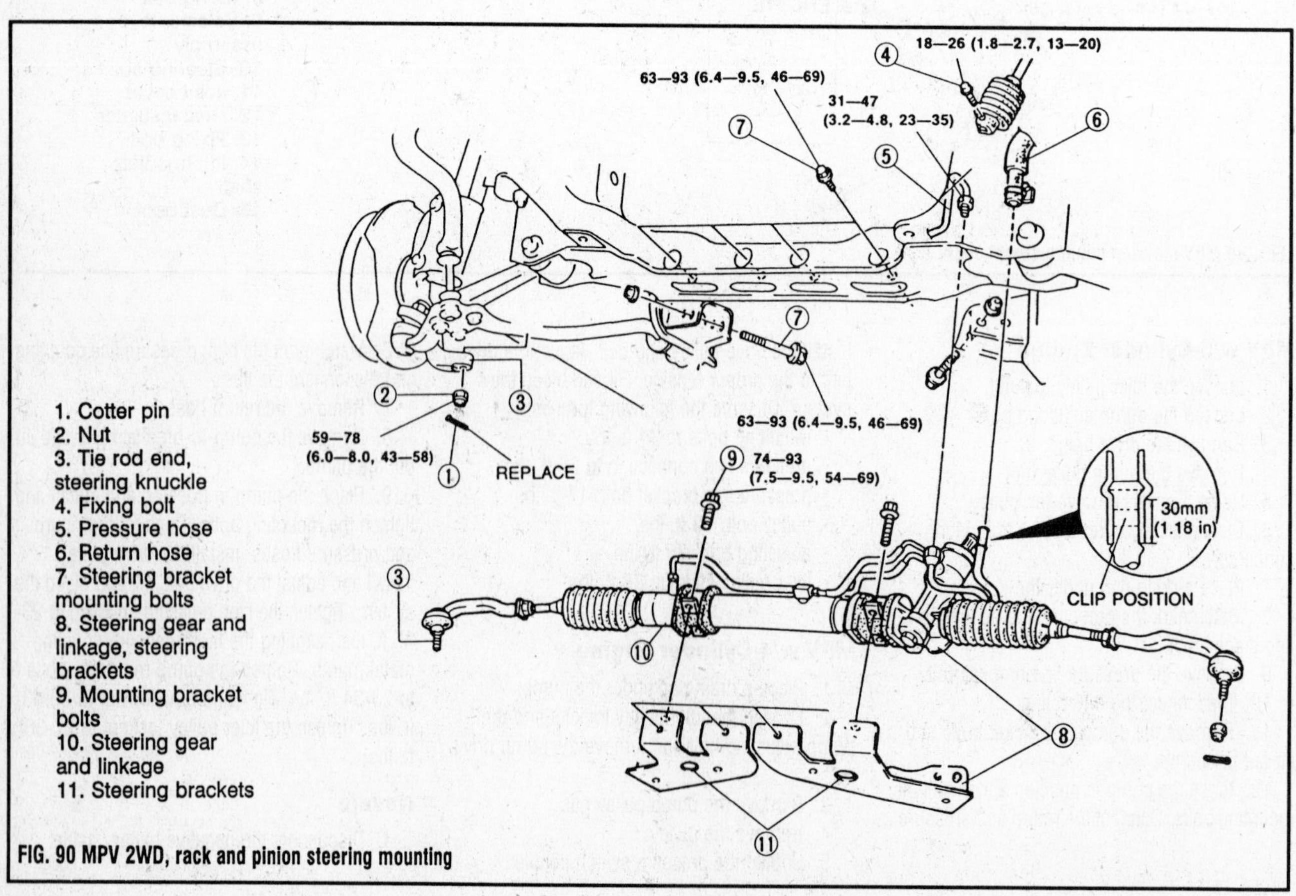

FIG. 90 MPV 2WD, rack and pinion steering mounting

2. Remove some power steering fluid from the reservoir by disconnecting the fluid return line hose at the reservoir. Drain the fluid into a container and discard it.

3. Remove the pressure hose from the pump. If equipped, disconnect the power steering pump pressure switch.

4. Slacken belt tension by lifting the tensioner pulley in a clockwise direction. Remove the drive belt from under the tensioner pulley and slowly lower the pulley to its stop.

5. Remove the drive belt from the pulley. If necessary, remove the oil dipstick tube.

6. If equipped, remove the power steering pump bracket support brace.

7. Install power steering pump pulley removal tool T69L–10300–B or equivalent. Hold the pump and rotate the tool counterclockwise to remove the pulley. Do not apply in and out pressure to the pump shaft, as internal pump damage will occur.

8. Remove the power steering retaining bolts. Remove the power steering pump from the vehicle.

To install:

9. Position the pump on the bracket. Install and tighten the retaining bolts.

10. Install the pulley removal tool and install the power steering pump pulley to the power steering pump.

➡ Fore and aft location of the pulley on the power steering pump shaft is critical. Incorrect belt alignment may cause belt squeal or chirp. Be sure that the pull off groove on the pulley is facing front and flush with the end of the shaft ± 0.010 in. (0.25mm).

11. Continue the installation in the reverse order of the removal procedure. Adjust the belt tension to specification.

12. While lifting the tensioner pulley in a clockwise direction, slide the belt under the tensioner pulley and lower the pulley to the belt.

BLEEDING THE SYSTEM

Pickups and MPV

1. Raise and support the front end on jackstands.

2. Check the fluid level and fill it, if necessary.

3. Start the engine and let it idle. Turn the steering wheel lock-to-lock, several times. Recheck the fluid level.

4. Lower the truck to the ground.

5. With the engine idling, turn the wheel lock-to-lock several times again. If noise is heard in the fluid lines, air is present.

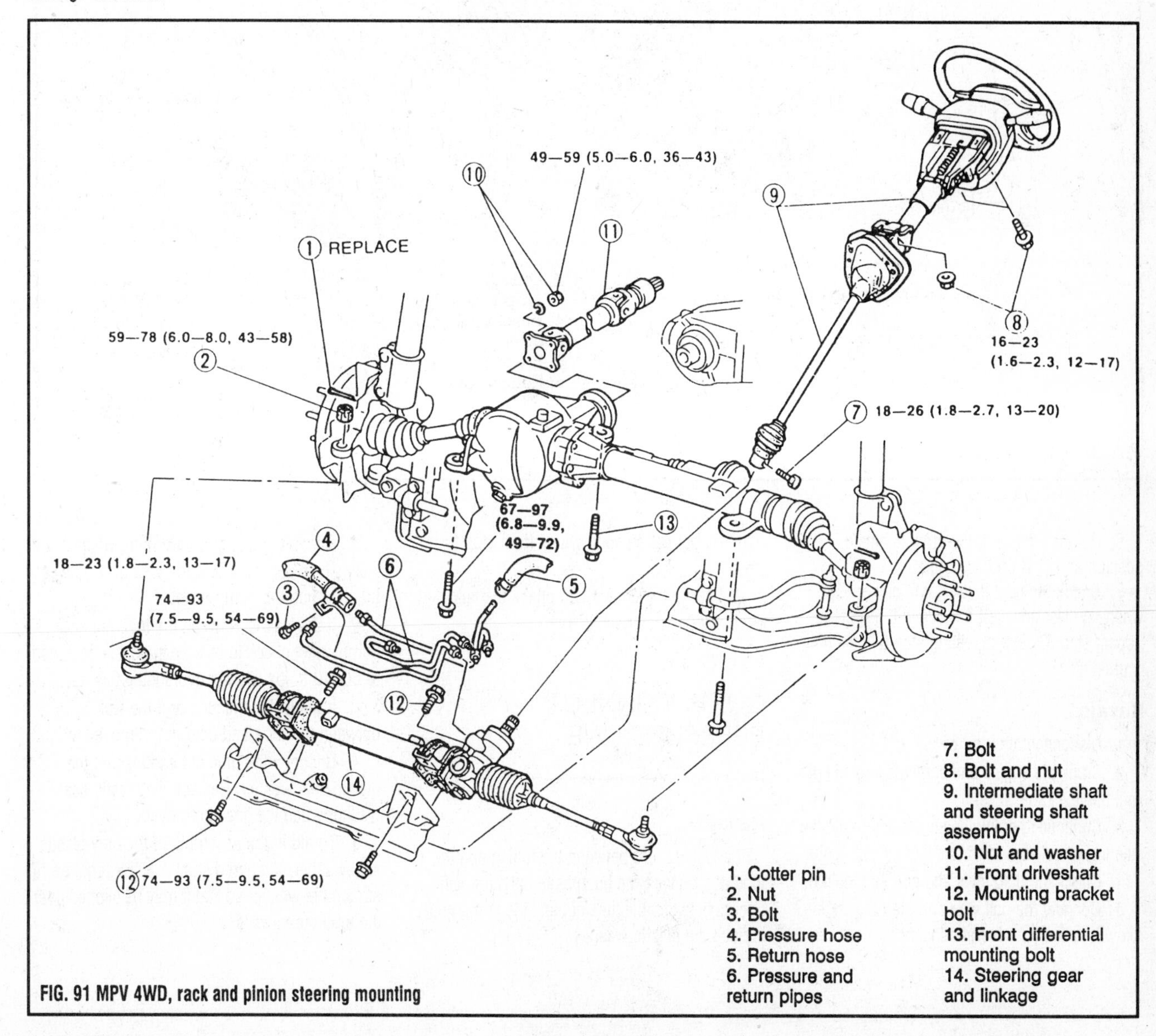

FIG. 91 MPV 4WD, rack and pinion steering mounting

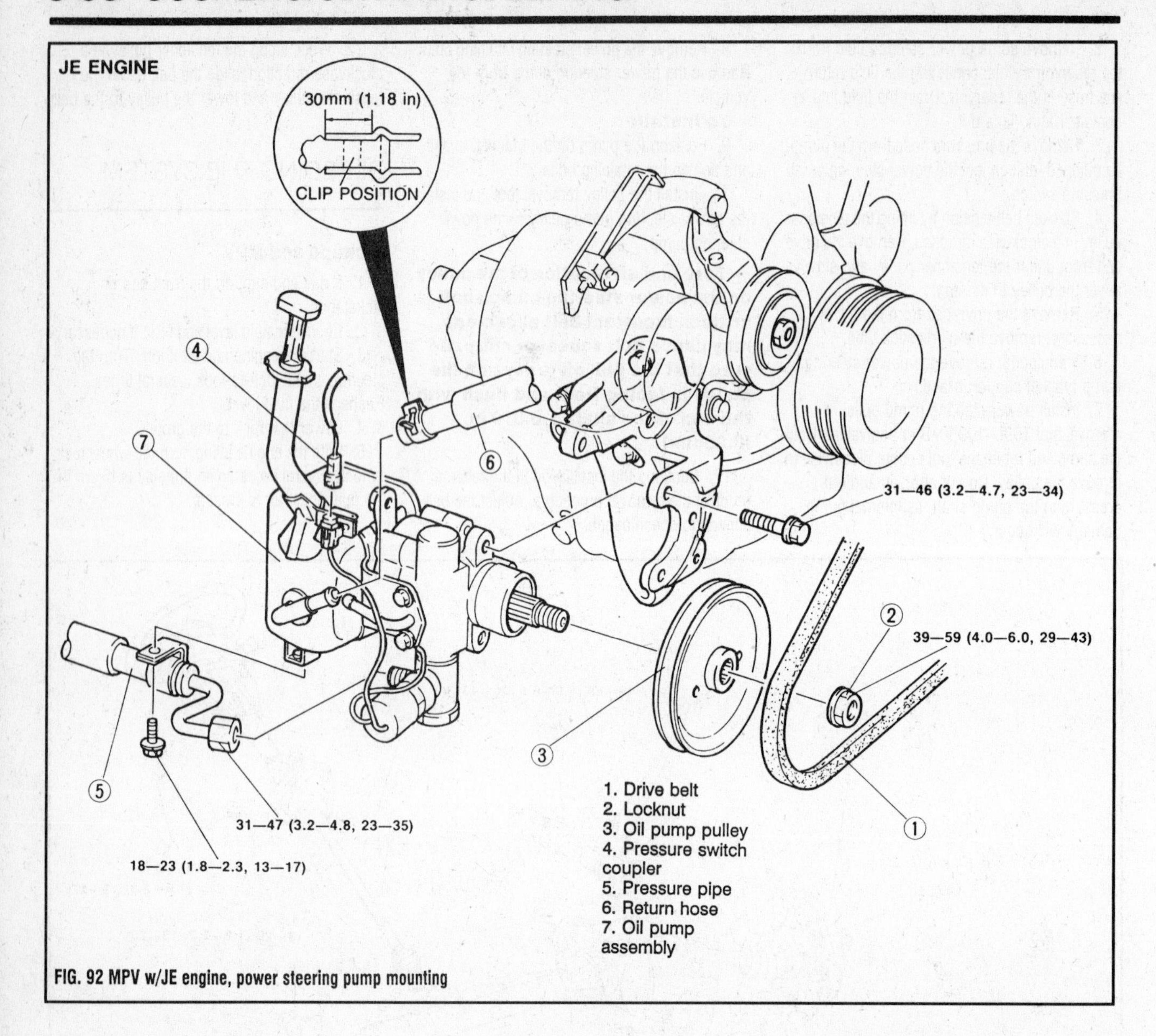

FIG. 92 MPV w/JE engine, power steering pump mounting

6. Put the wheels in the straight ahead position and shut off the engine.
7. Check the fluid level. If it is higher than when you last checked it, air is in the system. Repeat step 5. Keep repeating step 5 until no air is present.

Navajo

1. Disconnect the coil wire.
2. Crank the engine and continue adding fluid until the level stabilizes.
3. Continue to crank the engine and rotate the steering wheel about 30° to either side of center.
4. Check the fluid level and add as required.
5. Connect the coil wire and start the engine. Allow it to run for several minutes.
6. Rotate the steering wheel from stop to stop.
7. Shut of the engine and check the fluid level. Add fluid as necessary.

QUICK-CONNECT PRESSURE LINE

Navajo

If a leak occurs between the tubing and the tube nut, replace the hose assembly. If a leak occurs between the tube nut and the pump outlet replace the plastic washer.

1. Check the fitting to determine whether the leak is between the tube and tube nut or between the tube nut and pump outlet.
2. If the leak is between the tube nut and pump outlet check to be sure the nut is tightened to 30–40 ft. lbs. Do not overtighten this nut.
3. If the leak continues or if the leak is between the tube and tube nut, remove the line.
4. Unscrew the tube nut and inspect the plastic seal washer. Replace the plastic seal washer when the line is removed.
5. To aid in the assembly of the new plastic seal washer, a tapered shaft may be required to stretch the washer so that it may be slipped over the tube nut threads.

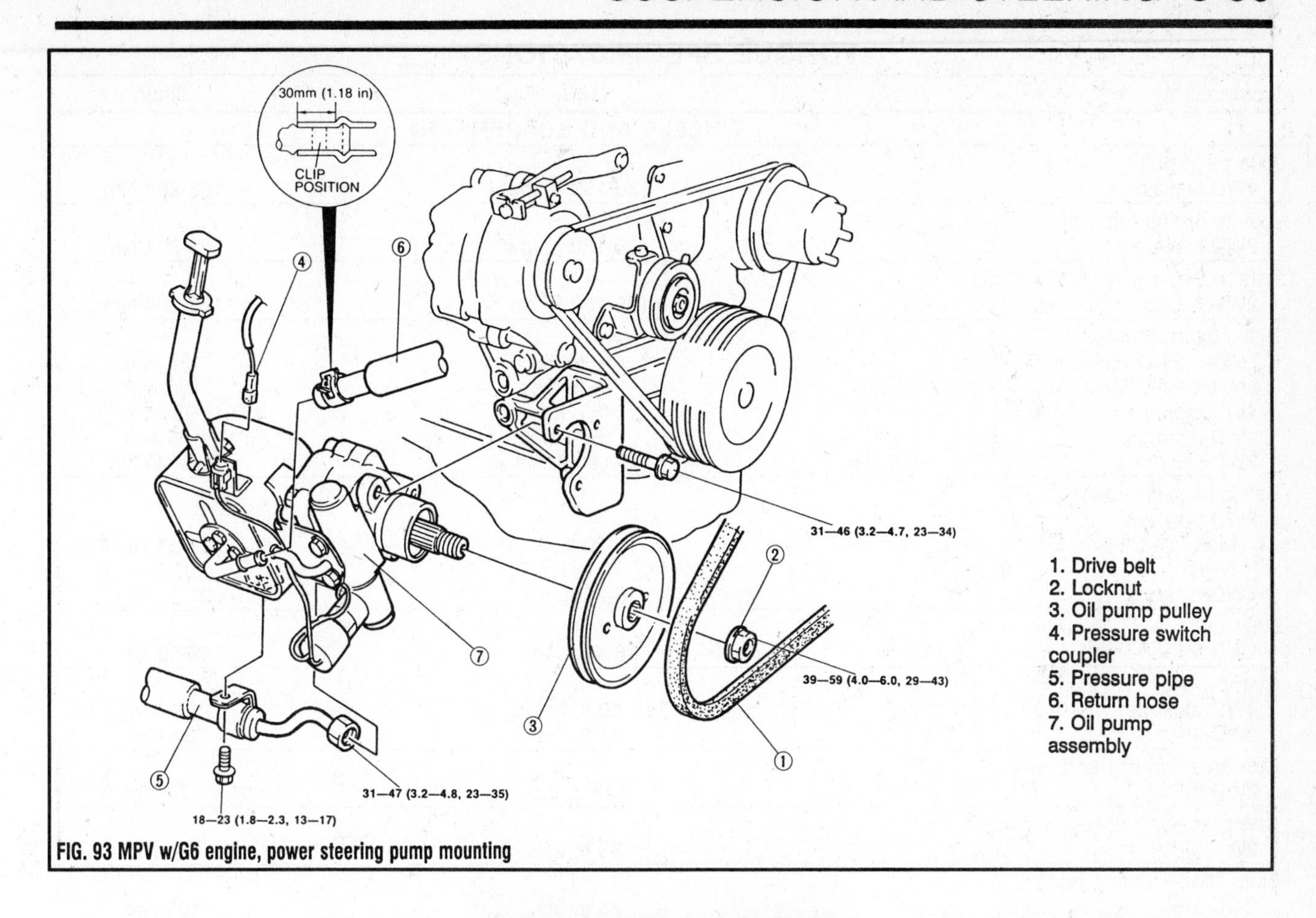

FIG. 93 MPV w/G6 engine, power steering pump mounting

6. If the rubber O-ring is damaged it cannot be serviced and the hose assembly will have to be replaced.

7.Connect the tube nut and torque to 30–40 ft. lbs.

CAUTION

The quick connect fitting may disengage if not fully assembled, if the snapring is missing or if the tube nut or hose end is not machined properly. If the fitting disengages, replace the hose assembly. The fitting is fully engaged when the hose will not pull out. To test for positive engagement, the system should be properly filled, the engine started and the steering wheel turned from stop to stop.

TORQUE SPECIFICATIONS

Component	U.S.	Metric
WHEELS AND SUSPENSION		
Axle pivot bolt		
4WD Navajo	120-150 ft. lbs.	163-204 Nm
Axle-to-radius arm nut		
2WD Navajo	120-150 ft. lbs.	163-204 Nm
Axle-to-frame pivot bracket bolt		
2WD Navajo	120-150 ft. lbs.	163-204 Nm
Ball joint stud nut		
Lower, 2WD pickups	116 ft. lbs.	158 Nm
Lower, 2WD MPV	116 ft. lbs.	158 Nm
4WD pickups	70 ft. lbs.	95 Nm
4WD pickups	115 ft. lbs.	156 Nm
2WD Navajo	85-110 ft. lbs.	116-149 Nm
Ball joint-to-arm bolts		
2WD pickups		
old	15-20 ft. lbs.	21-27 Nm
New	70 ft. lbs.	95 Nm
4WD pickups	15-20 ft. lbs.	21-27 Nm
Cap nut		
2WD MPV	36-43 ft. lbs.	49-58 Nm
Clamp bolts		
4WD pickups	19 ft. lbs.	26 Nm
2WD MPV	45 ft. lbs.	61 Nm
Compression rod end nuts		
2WD MPV	127 ft. lbs.	173 Nm
Compression rod-to-lower arm		
2WD MPV	93 ft. lbs.	126 Nm
Fluid-filled bushing bolts		
2WD MPV	76 ft. lbs.	103 Nm
Front bracket-to-axle bolts		
4WD Navajo	37-50 ft. lbs.	50-68 Nm
Height sensor link		
MPV	104 inch lbs.	12 Nm
Height sensor bolts		
MPV	20 ft. lbs.	27 Nm
Insulator-to-arm stud nut		
4WD Navajo	80-120 ft. lbs.	109-163 Nm
Knuckle arm bolts		
2WD pickups	70-74 ft. lbs.	95-100 Nm
Lateral rod bolts		
MPV	127 ft. lbs.	173 Nm
Lower arm-to-frame nut		
2WD pickups	115 ft. lbs.	156 Nm
4WD pickups	115 ft. lbs.	156 Nm
2WD MPV	108 ft. lbs.	147 Nm
Lower arm end bolts		
2WD pickups	85 ft. lbs.	116 Nm
4WD pickups	85 ft. lbs.	116 Nm
Lower link bolts		
MPV	127 ft. lbs.	173 Nm
Lower strut bolts		
2WD MPV	86 ft. lbs.	117 Nm
Lug nuts		
Pickups		
non-styled wheels	65-87 ft. lbs.	89-118 Nm
styled wheels	87-108 ft. lbs.	119-146 Nm
MPV	65-87 ft. lbs.	89-118 Nm
Navajo	100 ft. lbs.	136 Nm

TORQUE SPECIFICATIONS

Component	U.S.	Metric
WHEELS AND SUSPENSION		
Mounting block		
Lower Bolts		
2WD MPV	85 ft. lbs.	116 Nm
Upper Nuts		
2WD MPV	25 ft. lbs.	34 Nm
Parking brake cable clamp		
MPV	19 ft. lbs.	26 Nm
Radius arm-to-axle bolt/nut		
2WD Navajo	160-220 ft. lbs.	218-299 Nm
Radius rod bushing end nut	90 ft. lbs.	122 Nm
Rebound spring bracket		
MPV	19 ft. lbs.	26 Nm
Shock absorber		
Pickups	55-59 ft. lbs.	75-80 Nm
Navajo		
lower	40-63 ft. lbs.	55-85 Nm
upper	25-35 ft. lbs.	34-47 Nm
MPV	76 ft. lbs.	103 Nm
Springs		
Front Shackle Bolt		
Navajo	75-115 ft. lbs.	102-156 Nm
Front Spring Pin Nut		
Pickups	72 ft. lbs.	98 Nm
Lever Retainer Nut		
4WD Navajo	35-105 ft. lbs.	95-136 Nm
Rear Shackle Nuts		
Pickups	58 ft. lbs.	79 Nm
Navajo	75-115 ft. lbs.	102-156 Nm
U-Bolt Nuts		
Navajo	65-75 ft. lbs.	89-102 Nm
2-Wheel Drive Pickups	58 ft. lbs.	79 Nm
4-wheel Drive Pickups	101 ft. lbs.	137 Nm
Stabilizer bar bolt		
2WD pickups	19 ft. lbs.	26 Nm
4WD pickups	19 ft. lbs.	26 Nm
Stablilzer bar-to-control arm nut		
2WD pickups	34 ft. lbs.	46 Nm
Stabilizer-to-frame clamp bolts		
2WD pickups	16 ft. lbs.	22 Nm
Stabilizer bar clamp		
MPV	38 ft. lbs.	52 Nm
Stabilizer bar link-to-stabilizer bar		
2WD Navajo	30-40 ft. lbs.	41-54 Nm
Stabilizer bar link-to-mounting bracket		
2WD Navajo	30-44 ft. lbs.	41-59 Nm
Stabilizer bar-to-link nut		
4WD Navajo	30-44 ft. lbs.	41-59 Nm
Steering linkage-to-spindle nut		
2WD Navajo	52-74 ft. lbs.	71-100 Nm
Tie rod end-to-knuckle bolt		
2WD pickups	22-29 ft. lbs.	30-39 Nm
Tie rod end nut		
2WD MPV	58 ft. lbs.	79 Nm
Torque plate bolts		
2WD pickups	68 ft. lbs.	92 Nm
4WD pickups	68 ft. lbs.	92 Nm

TORQUE SPECIFICATIONS

Component	U.S.	Metric
WHEELS AND SUSPENSION		
Upper control arm shaft mounting bolts		
2WD pickups	60-68 ft. lbs.	82-92 Nm
Upper ball joint-to-knuckle bolt		
2WD pickups	35-38 ft. lbs.	48-52 Nm
Upper arm shaft mounting bolts		
4WD pickups	60-68 ft. lbs.	82-92 Nm
Upper ball joint pinch bolt nut		
4WD Navajo	48-65 ft. lbs.	65-88 Nm
Upper link bolts		
MPV	127 ft. lbs.	173 Nm
STEERING		
Ball socket stud nuts		
Pickups	45 ft. lbs.	61 Nm
Ball stud nut		
MPV	58 ft. lbs.	79 Nm
Navajo	30-42 ft. lbs.	41-57 Nm
Center link nut		
Pickups	43 ft. lbs.	58 Nm
Combination switch retaining screws		
Navajo	18-27 in. lbs.	2-3 Nm
Drag link		
Navajo	50-70 ft. lbs.	68-95 Nm
Pickups	43 ft. lbs.	58 Nm
Ignition switch nuts		
Navajo	3.3-5.3 ft. lbs.	5-7 Nm
Pitman arm nut		
Navajo	170-230 ft. lbs.	231-313 Nm
Pickups	130 ft. lbs.	177 Nm
Pitman arm-to-center link nut		
Pickups	43 ft. lbs.	58 Nm
Power steering pump pulley		
B2200	43 ft. lbs.	58 Nm
MPV	29-43 ft. lbs.	40-58 Nm
Power steering pump pressure line connection		
B2200	35 ft. lbs.	48 Nm
B2600	35 ft. lbs.	48 Nm
MPV	35 ft. lbs.	48 Nm
Power steering pump pressure line bracket		
B2200	17 ft. lbs.	23 Nm
MPV	17 ft. lbs.	23 Nm
Power steering return Line		
Pickups	35 ft. lbs.	48 Nm
Power steering pump mounting bolts		
B2200	34 ft. lbs.	46 Nm
B2600	34 ft. lbs.	46 Nm
MPV	34 ft. lbs.	46 Nm

TORQUE SPECIFICATIONS

Component	U.S.	Metric
Power steering pump adjusting bolt	34 ft. lbs.	46 Nm
Power steering pump pulley bolt		
MPV	43 ft. lbs.	58 Nm
Power steering pump belt idler pulley locknut		
MPV	38 ft. lbs.	52 Nm
Steering column bracket		
Pickups	16 ft. lbs.	22 Nm
Steering gear input shaft bolts		
Navajo	50-62 ft. lbs.	68-84 Nm
Steering gear-to-frame mounting bolts		
Pickups	69 ft. lbs.	94 Nm
MPV	69 ft. lbs.	94 Nm
Steering gear-to-lower bracket clamp bolts		
MPV	69 ft. lbs.	94 Nm
Steering shaft coupling bolt		
Pickups	18 ft. lbs.	24 Nm
Navajo	26-34 ft. lbs.	35-46 Nm
Steering wheel attaching nut		
Pickups & MPV	35 ft. lbs.	48 Nm
Steering wheel lock bolt		
Navajo	23-33 ft. lbs.	31-45 Nm
Tie rod ball stud nuts		
Navajo	50-75 ft. lbs.	68-102 Nm
MPV	58 ft. lbs.	79 Nm
Tie rod adjusting sleeve nuts		
Navajo	30-42 ft. lbs.	41-57 Nm
Tie rod end jam nuts		
Pickups	58 ft. lbs.	79 Nm
MPV	58 ft. lbs.	79 Nm
Wormshaft locknut		
Pickups w/manual steering	140 ft. lbs.	191 Nm
Wormshaft-to-steering shaft yoke		
Pickups w/manual steering	38 ft. lbs.	52 Nm

Troubleshooting the Manual Steering Gear

Problem	Cause	Solution
Vehicle leads to one side	· Improper tire pressures	· Inflate tires to recommended pressures
	· Front tires with uneven tread depth, wear pattern, or different cord design (i.e., one bias ply and one belted or radial tire on front wheels)	· Install tires of same cord construction and reasonably even tread depth, design, and wear pattern
	· Incorrect front wheel alignment	· Align incorrect angles
	· Brakes dragging	· Adjust or repair brakes
	· Pulling due to uneven tire construction	· Replace faulty tire

Troubleshooting the Manual Steering Gear

Problem	Cause	Solution
Hard or erratic steering	• Incorrect tire pressure	• Inflate tires to recommended pressures
	• Insufficient or incorrect lubrication	• Lubricate as required (refer to Maintenance Section)
	• Suspension, or steering linkage parts damaged or misaligned	• Repair or replace parts as necessary
	• Improper front wheel alignment	• Adjust incorrect wheel alignment angles
	• Incorrect steering gear adjustment	• Adjust steering gear
	• Sagging springs	• Replace springs
Play or looseness in steering	• Steering wheel loose	• Inspect shaft spines and repair as necessary. Tighten attaching nut and stake in place.
	• Steering linkage or attaching parts loose or worn	• Tighten, adjust, or replace faulty components
	• Pitman arm loose	• Inspect shaft splines and repair as necessary. Tighten attaching nut and stake in place
	• Steering gear attaching bolts loose	• Tighten bolts
	• Loose or worn wheel bearings	• Adjust or replace bearings
	• Steering gear adjustment incorrect or parts badly worn	• Adjust gear or replace defective parts
Wheel shimmy or tramp	• Improper tire pressure	• Inflate tires to recommended pressures
	• Wheels, tires, or brake rotors out-of-balance or out-of-round	• Inspect and replace or balance parts
	• Inoperative, worn, or loose shock absorbers or mounting parts	• Repair or replace shocks or mountings
	• Loose or worn steering or suspension parts	• Tighten or replace as necessary
	• Loose or worn wheel bearings	• Adjust or replace bearings
	• Incorrect steering gear adjustments	• Adjust steering gear
	• Incorrect front wheel alignment	• Correct front wheel alignment
Tire wear	• Improper tire pressure	• Inflate tires to recommended pressures
	• Failure to rotate tires	• Rotate tires
	• Brakes grabbing	• Adjust or repair brakes
	• Incorrect front wheel alignment	• Align incorrect angles
	• Broken or damaged steering and suspension parts	• Repair or replace defective parts
	• Wheel runout	• Replace faulty wheel
	• Excessive speed on turns	• Make driver aware of conditions

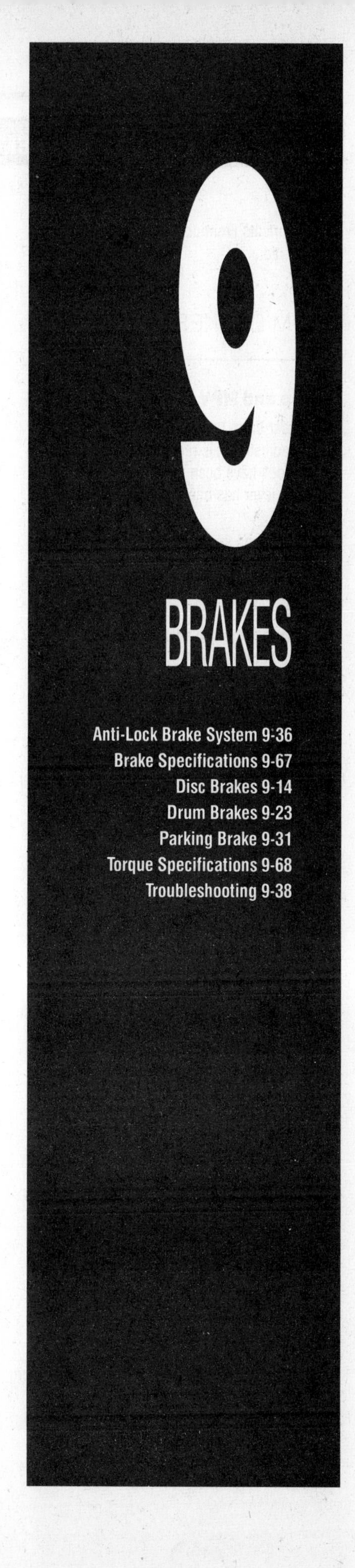

9 BRAKES

BRAKE OPERATING SYSTEM

Adjustments Front disc brake adjustment is not required.

DRUM BRAKES

Pickup and MPV

The rear drum brakes are self-adjusting. Manual adjustment is required only when the brake shoes have been replaced, or when the operating lever has been removed for some reason.

1. Raise and support the rear of the truck. The wheels must be free to turn.
2. Make sure the parking brake is fully released.
3. Remove the two adjusting hole plugs from the brake backing plate.
4. An arrow stamped on the backing plate indicates the direction to turn the adjuster starwheel to expand the shoes. Insert a brake spoon through the adjuster hole and turn the starwheel until the brakes are locked.
5. Insert a drift through the other adjuster hole. Use the drift to push the lever of the self-adjuster away from the starwheel. Back off the starwheel until the wheel rotates freely (no drag).
6. Repeat the adjustment on the other wheel. Make sure the adjustment is exactly the same. Install the adjuster hole rubber plug covers. Remove the jackstands and lower the vehicle. Road test for equal brake action and readjust as necessary.

Navajo

The drum brakes are self-adjusting and require a manual adjustment only after the brake shoes have been replaced.

To adjust the rear brakes with drums installed, follow the procedure given below:

1. Raise the vehicle and support it with safety stands.
2. Remove the rubber plug from the adjusting slot on the backing plate.
3. Turn the starwheel adjuster using a brake shoe adjustment spoon, inserted through the backing plate adjustment slot, to expand the brake shoes until they drag against the brake drum and lock the drum.
4. Insert a small drift into the adjusting slot and push the automatic adjusting lever out and free of the starwheel on the adjusting screw and hold it there.
5. Engage the topmost tooth possible on the starwheel with the brake adjusting spoon. Move the end of the adjusting spoon upward to back the shoes away from the brake drum. Back off the adjusting screw starwheel until the wheel spins FREELY with a minimum of drag, about 10 to 12 notches. Keep track of the number of turns that the starwheel is backed off, or the number of strokes taken with the brake adjusting spoon.
6. Repeat this operation for the other side. When backing off the brakes on the other side, the starwheel adjuster must be backed off the same number of turns to prevent side-to-side brake pull.
7. After both sides, remove the safety stands and lower the vehicle and make several stops while backing the vehicle, to equalize the brakes.
8. Road test the vehicle. PERFORM THE ROAD TEST ONLY WHEN THE BRAKES WILL APPLY AND THE VEHICLE CAN BE STOPPED SAFELY!

BRAKE PEDAL

➧SEE FIGS. 1-3

No pedal adjustments are possible on the Navajo. On trucks with power brakes, depress the pedal a few times to dispel all vacuum from the booster.

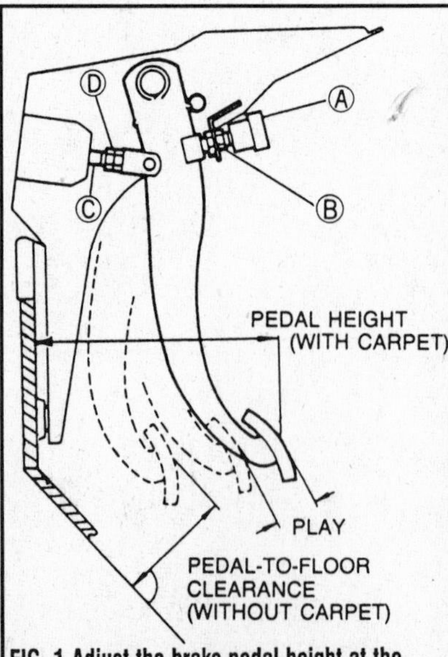

FIG. 1 Adjust the brake pedal height at the stoplight switch. A: switch, B: locknut, C: adjusting rod, D: locknut

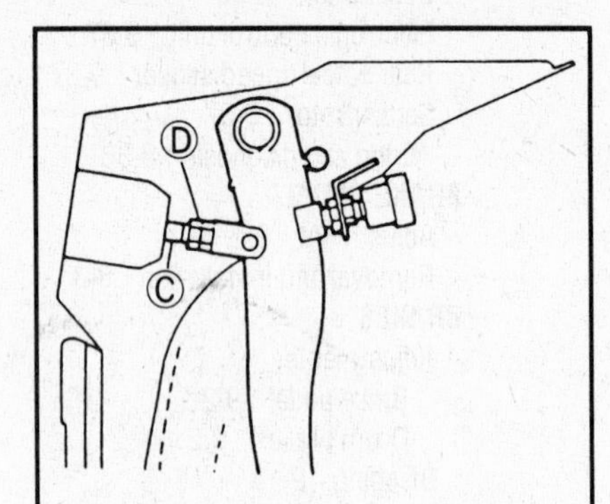

FIG. 2 Brake pedal height adjustment; loosen locknut D, turn operating rod C, to gain correct adjustment

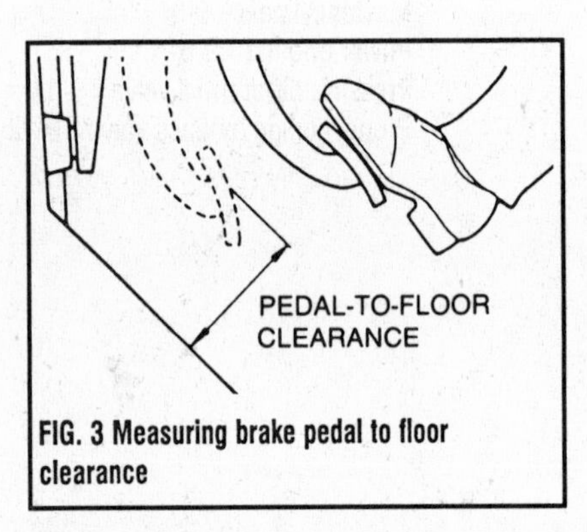

FIG. 3 Measuring brake pedal to floor clearance

Pedal Freeplay

Using the top of the pedal pad as a reference point, there should be 4.0-7.0mm (0.157-0.276 in.) on pickups with power brakes and MPV, and, a little less than 3mm (0.118 in.) free-play before the pushrod contacts the master cylinder piston on models with non-power brakes.

1. Loosen the locknut on the master cylinder pushrod at the clevis.
2. Turn the pushrod to obtain the proper free-play, then tighten the nut.

Brake Pedal Height

No pedal adjustments are possible on the Navajo.

Pedal height is measured from the center of the pedal pad surface, horizontally to the firewall. Pedal height should be 209-214mm (8.23-8.43 in.) for 1987-88 pickups; 180-185mm (7.09-7.28 in.) 1989 and later pickups; 191-201mm (7.52-7.91 in.) for MPV models.

If not, loosen the stop light switch locknut and turn the switch until the proper height is obtained. Tighten the locknut.

Brake Light Switch

REMOVAL & INSTALLATION

Pickups and MPV

The switch is located at the top of the brake pedal.

1. Disconnect the wiring from the switch.
2. Loosen the locknut and adjusting nut and unscrew the switch from the bracket.
3. Install the new switch. Adjust the brake pedal. Tighten the locknut.

Navajo

1. Lift the locking tab on the switch connector and disconnect the wiring.
2. Remove the hairpin retainer, slide the stoplamp switch, pushrod and nylon washer off of the pedal. Remove the washer, then the switch by sliding it up or down.

➡ **On some vehicles equipped with speed control, the spacer washer is replaced by the dump valve adapter washer.**

3. To install the switch, position it so that the U-shaped side is nearest the pedal and directly over/under the pin.
4. Slide the switch up or down, trapping the master cylinder pushrod and bushing between the switch side plates.
5. Push the switch and pushrod assembly firmly towards the brake pedal arm. Assemble the outside white plastic washer to the pin and install the hairpin retainer.

➡ **Don't substitute any other type of retainer. Use only the specified hairpin retainer.**

6. Assemble the connector on the switch.
7. Check stoplamp operation.

➡ **Make sure that the stoplamp switch wiring has sufficient travel during a full pedal stroke.**

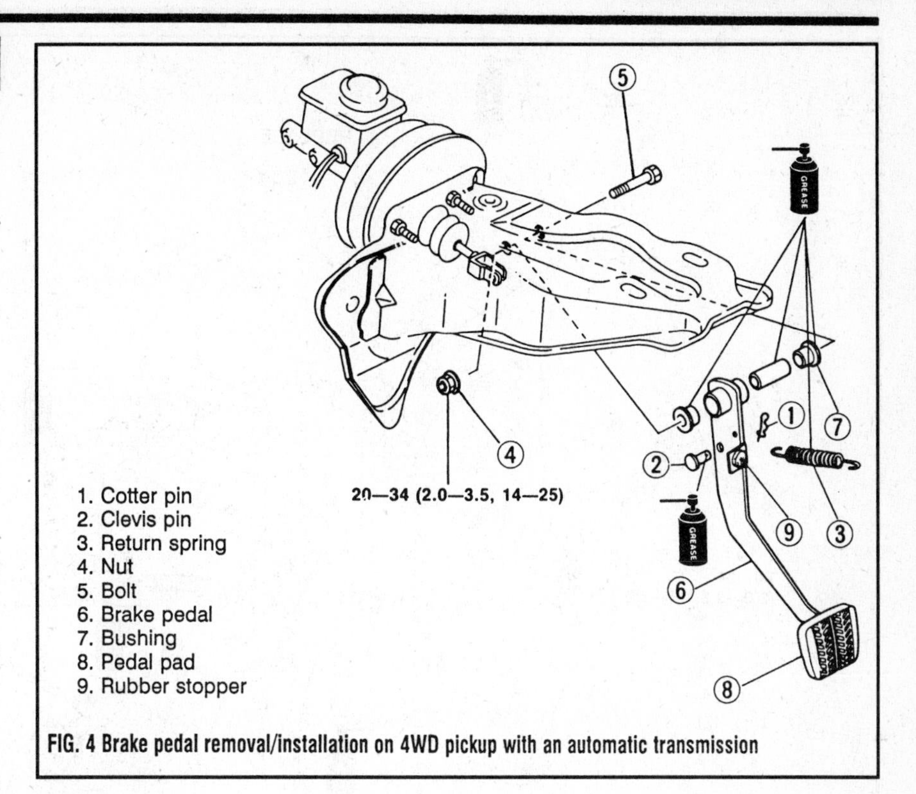

FIG. 4 Brake pedal removal/installation on 4WD pickup with an automatic transmission

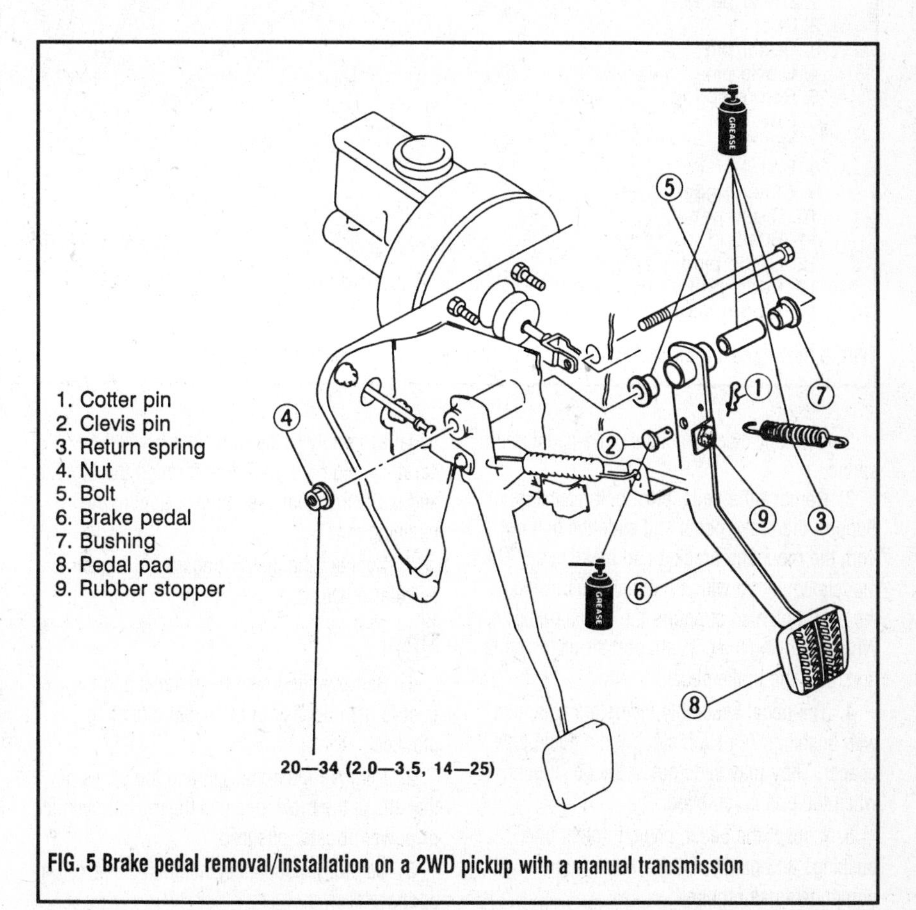

FIG. 5 Brake pedal removal/installation on a 2WD pickup with a manual transmission

Brake Pedal

➧SEE FIGS. 4-6

REMOVAL & INSTALLATION

Pickup

1. Remove the cotter pin and the clevis pin that attach the brake pedal to the master cylinder or power booster pushrod.

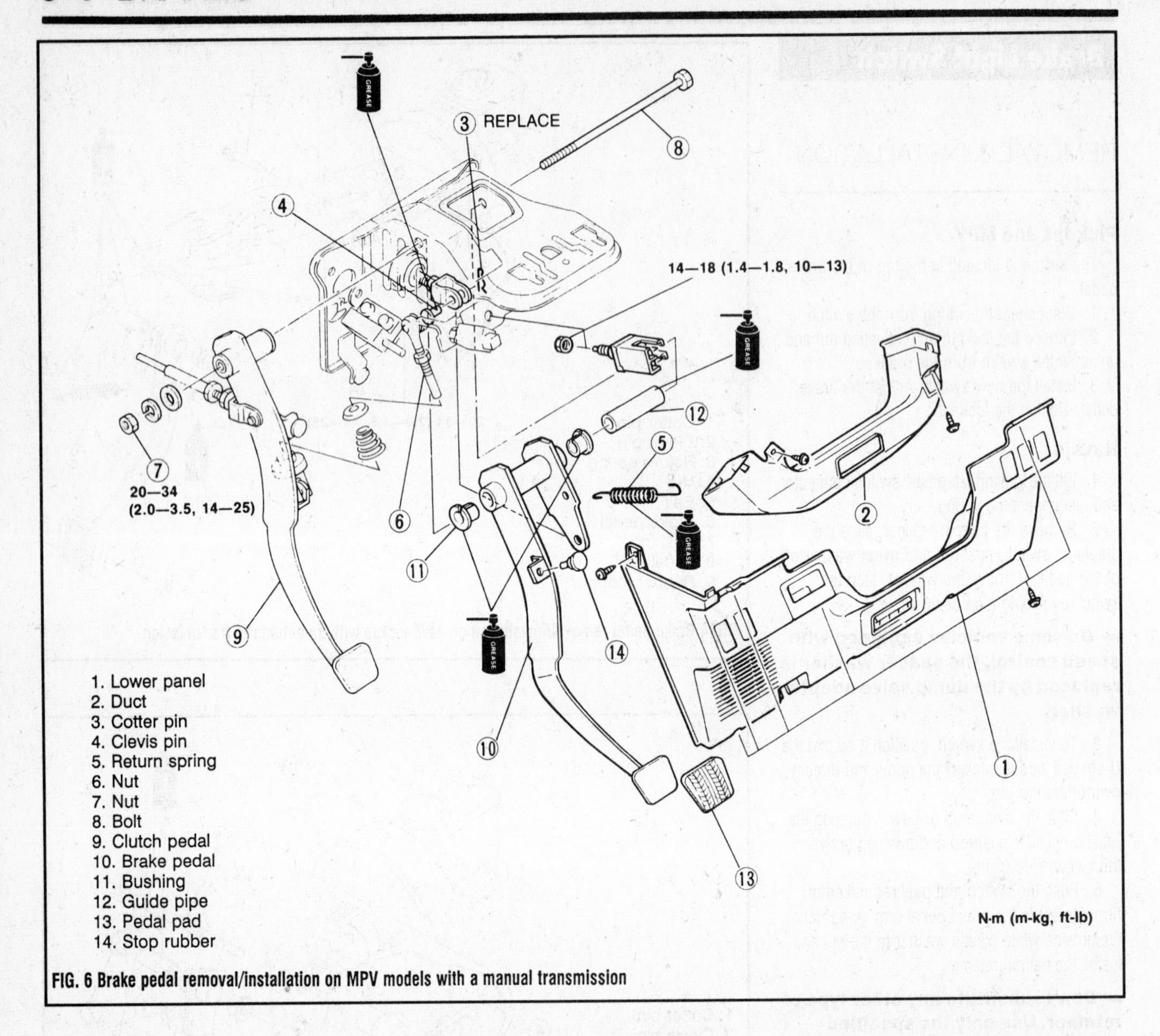

FIG. 6 Brake pedal removal/installation on MPV models with a manual transmission

2. Carefully disconnect the brake pedal return spring.

3. Remove the pedal pivot bolt retaining nut. Support the brake pedal and slide the bolt out from the mounting bracket and brake pedal. On models equipped with a manual transmission, the pivot bolt also supports the clutch pedal. When removing the bolt, support the clutch pedal first, than the brake pedal.

4. The pedal assembly pivots are equipped with bushings (on each side) and a guide pipe spacer. They may slide out of the pedal pivot when the bolt is removed.

5. Inspect the pedal, pivot, through bolt, bushings and guide pipe for wear. Replace components as required.

6. Lubricate the inner surfaces of the bushings and guide pipe. Assemble the bushings and guide pipe to the pedal pivot. Position the pedal assembly in the mounting bracket and carefully slide the pivot bolt through the bracket and pedal or pedal assemblies. Secure the retaining nut.

7. Connect the power booster or master cylinder pushrod.

MPV

1. Remove the lower dash panel and the air duct to gain access to the pedal mounting bracket.

2. Remove the cotter pin and the clevis pin that attach the brake pedal to the master cylinder or power booster pushrod.

3. Carefully disconnect the brake pedal return spring.

4. Remove the pedal pivot bolt retaining nut. Support the brake pedal and slide the bolt out from the mounting bracket and brake pedal. On models equipped with a manual transmission, the pivot bolt also supports the clutch pedal. When removing the bolt, support the clutch pedal first, than the brake pedal.

5. The pedal assembly pivots are equipped with bushings (on each side) and a guide pipe spacer. They may slide out of the pedal pivot when the bolt is removed.

6. Inspect the pedal, pivot, through bolt, bushings and guide pipe for wear. Replace components as required.

7. Lubricate the inner surfaces of the bushings and guide pipe. Assemble the bushings and guide pipe to the pedal pivot. Position the pedal assembly in the mounting bracket and carefully slide the pivot bolt through the bracket

and pedal or pedal assemblies. Secure the retaining nut.

8. Connect the power booster or master cylinder pushrod. Install the duct and lower dash panel.

Navajo

1. Models with a manual transmission.
2. Disconnect the stoplight switch and booster pushrod from the brake pedal. Disconnect the clutch/starter interlock switch from the clutch pedal.
3. Remove the retaining nut from the mounting shaft. The shaft is secured to the clutch pedal assembly, the retaining nut is on the brake pedal side.
4. Slide the clutch pedal and shaft away from the pivot support. Remove the clutch pedal and brake pedal.
5. Remove the spring washer and inner bushings from the brake pedal. Remove the bushings from the support bracket.
6. Inspect all components. Replace as required.
7. Lubricate the pivot and pedal bushings. Install the bushings into the support bracket. Place the brake pedal, inner bushings and spring washer in position inside the support bracket. Install the clutch pedal and shaft through the support bracket and brake pedal assembly. Install and tighten the retaining nut.
8. Connect the clutch/starter interlock switch on the clutch pedal. Install the stoplight switch and booster pushrod to the brake pedal. Check for operation.

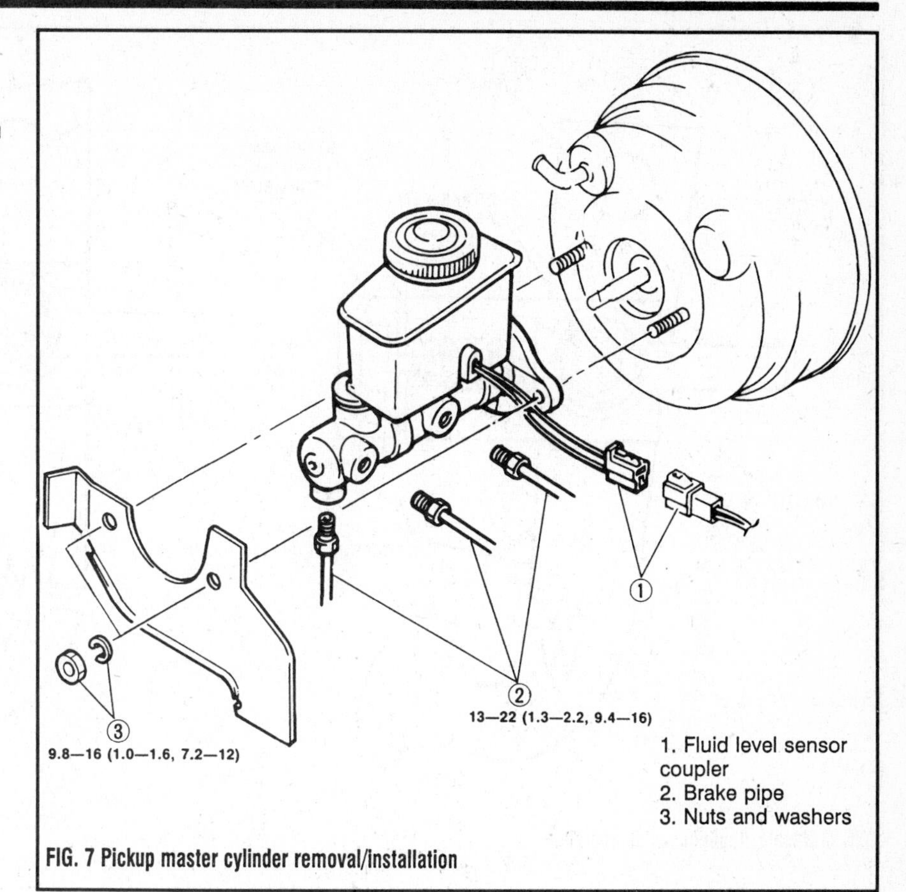

FIG. 7 Pickup master cylinder removal/installation

Master Cylinder

SEE FIGS. 7-9

REMOVAL & INSTALLATION

➡ Be careful not to spill brake fluid on the painted surfaces, it will harm the painted finish. If the reservoir is removed for any reason, install new mounting grommets. If the fluid has been emptied from the cylinder it is probably easier to bench bleed the cylinder prior to installation. See bleeding. Before installation the clearance between the power booster pushrod and the piston of the master cylinder should be check. Refer to the following booster procedures.

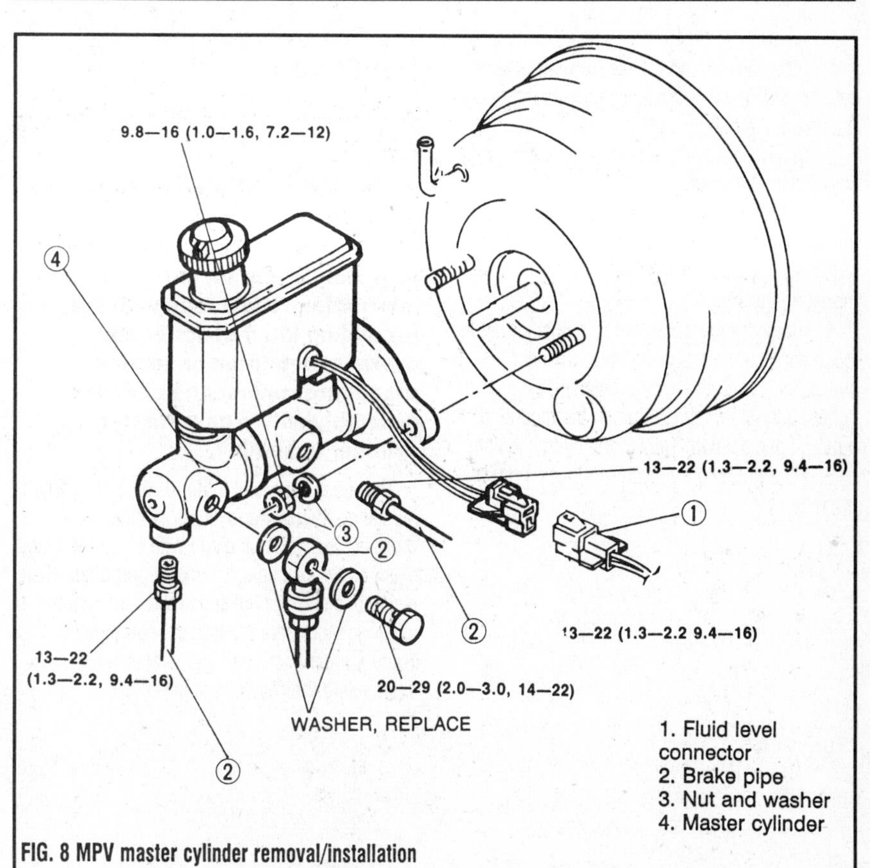

FIG. 8 MPV master cylinder removal/installation

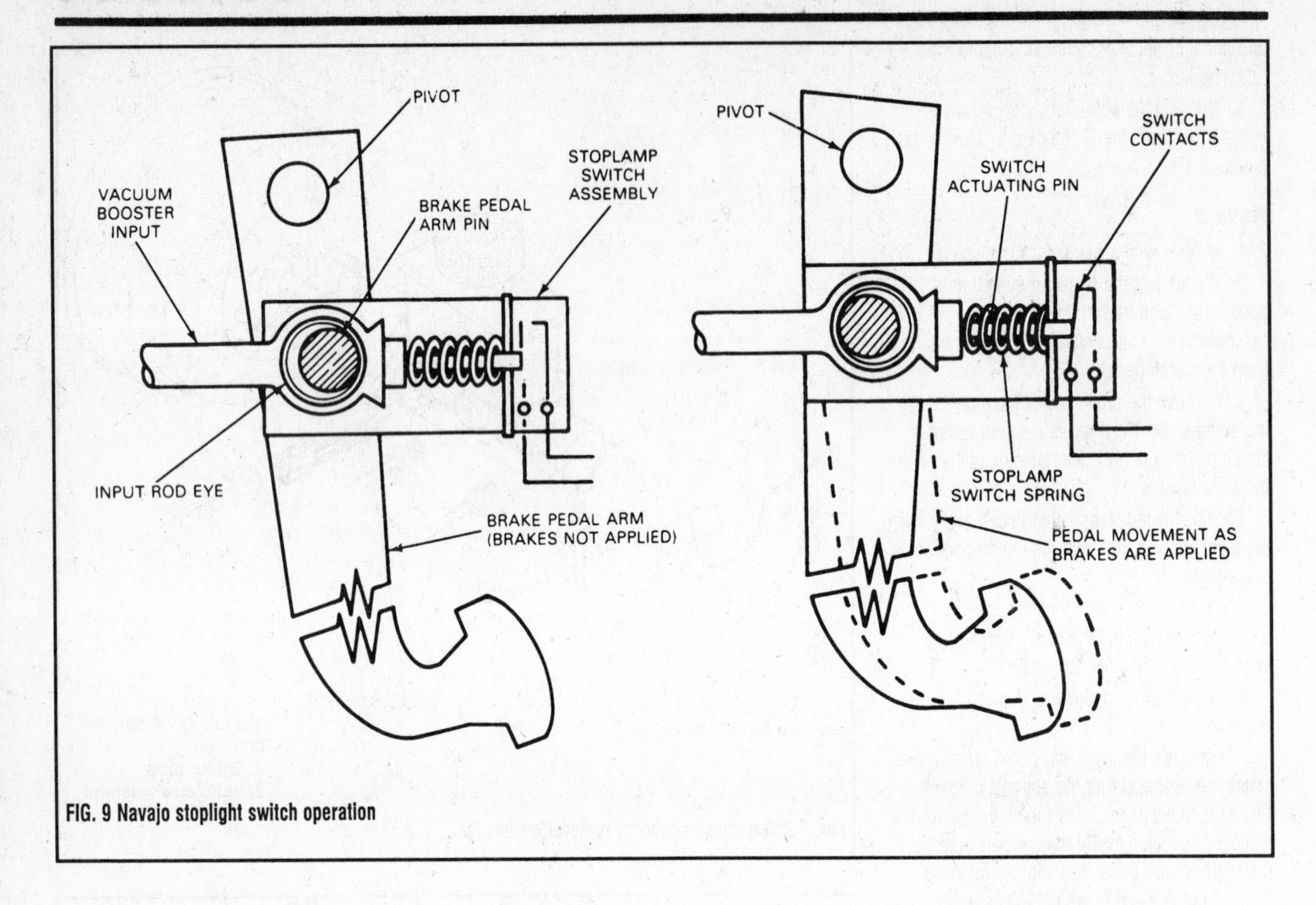

FIG. 9 Navajo stoplight switch operation

1. Clean all dirt and grease from the master cylinder and lines. Disconnect and cap the brake lines from the master cylinder.
2. Disconnect the fluid level sensor coupling, on models equipped.
3. Unbolt and remove the master cylinder from the firewall or power booster. Service as required. Replace the cylinder to booster mounting gasket.
4. Place the master cylinder in position and loosely install the mounting nuts. Connect the hydraulic lines to the master cylinder, but do not tighten fully at this time. Tighten the mounting nuts to specification. Tighten the hydraulic lines.
5. Fill and bleed the system. Check system operation.

OVERHAUL

➧SEE FIGS. 10-12

➡ Use this service procedure and exploded view diagrams as a guide for overhaul of the master cylinder assembly. Refer to, and follow any instructions that come with the rebuilding kit. If in doubt about overhaul condition or service procedure replace the complete assembly with a new master cylinder assembly.

The most important thing to remember when rebuilding the master cylinder is cleanliness. Work in clean surroundings with clean tools and clean cloths or paper for drying purposes. Have plenty of clean alcohol and brake fluid on hand to clean and lubricate the internal components. There are service repair kits available for overhauling the master cylinder.

Pickups and MPV

1. Rock the reservoir from side-to-side to remove it from the master cylinder.
2. Remove the reservoir grommets.
3. Remove the piston stopper screw from the bottom of the master cylinder.
4. Depress the piston and remove the snap ring.
5. Remove the primary piston assembly.
6. Remove the secondary piston assembly. Compressed air applied to the rear most fluid port (cover the other port) may be necessary to remove the secondary piston. If so, place a heavy rag over the cylinder bore to catch the piston.
7. Clean all parts in clean brake fluid.
8. Inspect all parts for wear or damage. Replace any worn, discolored, misshapen or suspect part. If the cylinder bore is etched, pitted, scored or damaged, replace the master cylinder.

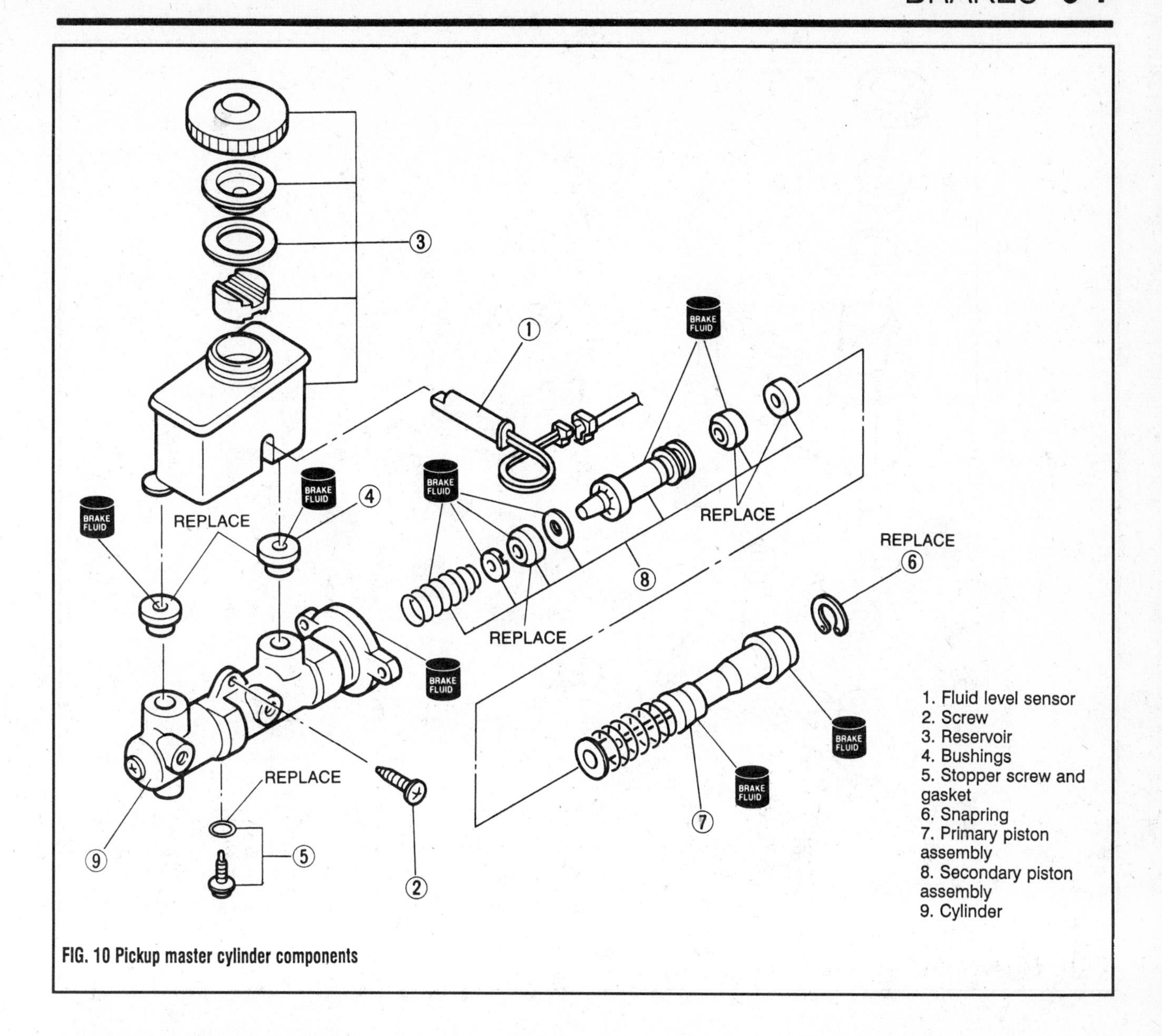

FIG. 10 Pickup master cylinder components

Master cylinder assembly is performed in the following order:

1. Dip all of the components, except for the cylinder, in clean brake fluid.
2. Insert the return spring and the valve components into the cylinder bore.
3. Fit the secondary cup and the primary cup over the secondary piston. The flat side of the cups should face the piston.
4. Place the secondary piston components into the cylinder bore.
5. Using a Phillips head screwdriver, depress the secondary piston as far as it will go into the cylinder bore. Screw the stopper screw (with new O-ring) into the hole. The stopper screw requires only 17–22 inch lbs. of torque. Push and release the piston to verify that it is held by the stopper screw.
6. Place the primary cups on the primary piston with the flat side of the cups facing the piston.
7. Insert the return spring and the primary piston into the bore.
8. Depress the primary piston, then install the stop washer and snapring. Install the reservoir using new mounting grommets. Bench bleed the cylinder.

Navajo

1. Clean the outside of the master cylinder and remove the filler cap and gasket (diaphragm). Pour out any fluid that remains in the cylinder reservoir. Do not use any fluids other than brake fluid or alcohol to clean the master cylinder.
2. Depress the primary piston and remove the snapring retaining the primary and secondary piston assemblies within the cylinder body.
3. Remove the primary piston assembly from the master cylinder. Discard the piston assembly.
4. Apply air pressure to the rear brake outlet port of the cylinder body (cover the other port) and carefully blow the secondary piston out of the cylinder body. Place a shop rag over the cylinder bore to prevent the piston assembly from popping out with force.
5. Remove the secondary piston assembly and discard.
6. Clean the master cylinder using isopropyl alcohol and inspect the cylinder bore. If the bore is etched, pitted, scored or damaged, replace the master cylinder.

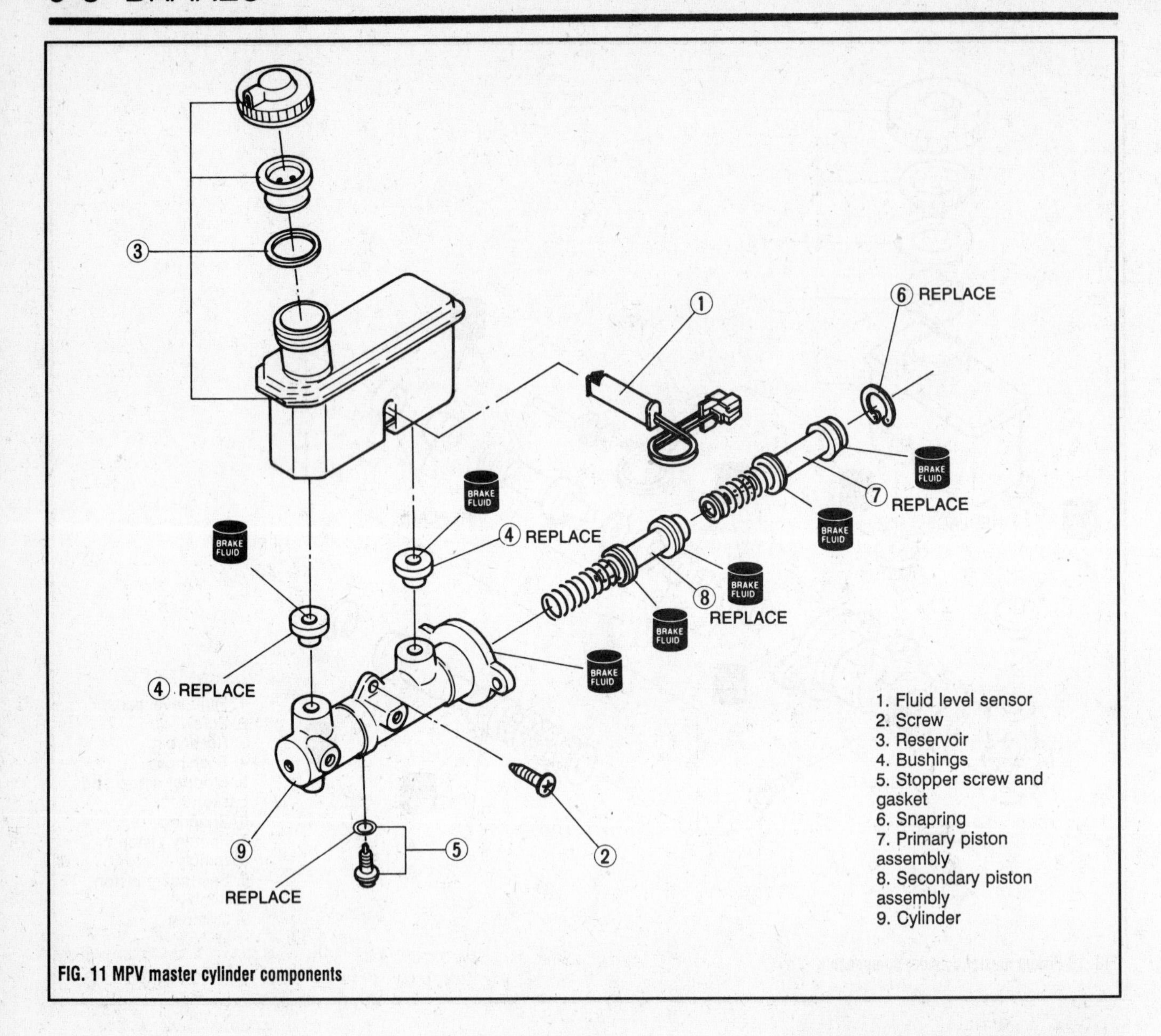

FIG. 11 MPV master cylinder components

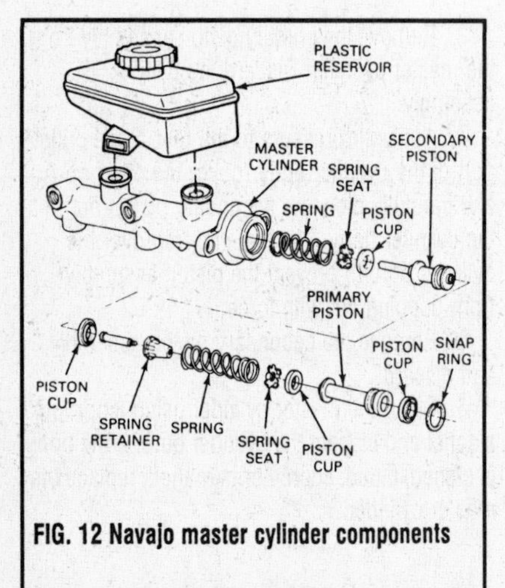

FIG. 12 Navajo master cylinder components

7. Install the secondary piston assembly into the master cylinder after dipping it in clean brake fluid. Dip the primary piston assembly in clean brake fluid. Install the primary piston assembly into the master cylinder. Depress the piston assemblies and install the snapring.

8. Install the reservoir using new mounting grommets.

9. Fill the reservoir with brake fluid and bench bleed the cylinder.

Power Booster

➧SEE FIGS. 13-15

REMOVAL & INSTALLATION

Pickups

1. Remove the master cylinder and proportioning bypass valve bracket (if equipped).
2. Disconnect the vacuum line at the booster.
3. Disconnect the pushrod at the brake pedal.
4. Unbolt and remove the power booster from the firewall (under the dash).

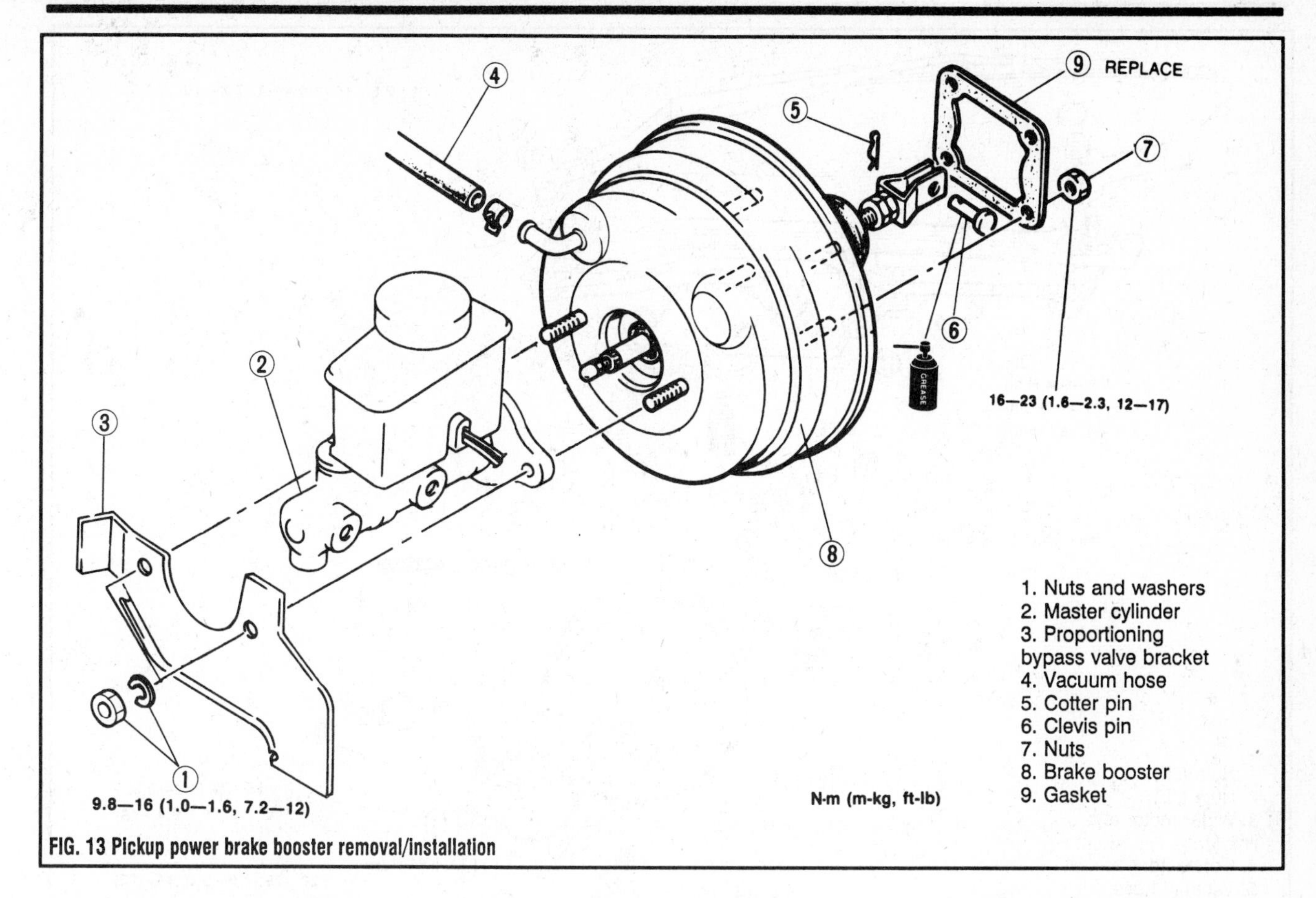

FIG. 13 Pickup power brake booster removal/installation

5. Installation is the reverse of removal. Check the clearance between the master cylinder piston and the power booster pushrod. Clearance should be 0. If not, adjust it at the pushrod. Torque the mounting nuts to 17 ft. lbs.

MPV w/6-Cylinder Engine

1. Remove the wiper arms.
2. Remove the drive link nuts from the top of the cowl.
3. Working under the hood, disconnect the battery ground cable.
4. Remove the wiper motor and linkage mounting bolts and lift out the assembly.
5. Remove the master cylinder.
6. Disconnect the pushrod at the pedal.
7. Disconnect the vacuum line at the booster.
8. Unbolt and remove the power booster from the firewall.

To install:

9. Check the clearance between the master cylinder piston and the power booster pushrod. Clearance should be 0, but the piston should not depress the pushrod. Adjust the clearance at the pushrod.
10. Position a new mounting gasket, coated with sealant, on the firewall.
11. Position the vacuum unit on the firewall and install the nuts. Torque the mounting nuts to 19 ft. lbs.
12. Connect the pushrod at the pedal.
13. Connect the vacuum line.
14. Install the master cylinder.
15. Install the wiper motor and linkage. When installing the wiper arms, make sure that the at-rest position gives a gap of 30mm between the blade tips and the lower windshield molding.
16. Bleed the brakes.

MPV w/4-Cylinder Engine

1. Disconnect the fluid sensor line.
2. Remove the master cylinder.
3. Disconnect the pushrod at the pedal.
4. Disconnect the vacuum line at the booster.
5. Unbolt and remove the power booster from the firewall.

To install:

6. Check the clearance between the master cylinder piston and the power booster pushrod. Clearance should be 0, but the piston should not depress the pushrod. Adjust the clearance at the pushrod.
7. Position a new mounting gasket, coated with sealant, on the firewall.
8. Position the vacuum unit on the firewall and install the nuts. Torque the mounting nuts to 19 ft. lbs.
9. Connect the pushrod at the pedal.
10. Connect the vacuum line.
11. Install the master cylinder.
12. Bleed the brakes.

Navajo

➡ **Make sure that the booster rubber reaction disc is properly installed if the master cylinder push rod is removed or accidentally pulled out. A dislodged disc may cause excessive pedal travel and extreme operation sensitivity. The disc is black compared to the silver colored valve plunger that will be exposed after the push rod and front seal is removed. The booster unit is serviced as an assembly and must be replaced if the reaction disc cannot be properly installed and aligned, or if it cannot be located within the unit itself.**

1. Disconnect the stop lamp switch wiring to prevent running the battery down.
2. Support the master cylinder from the underside with a prop.

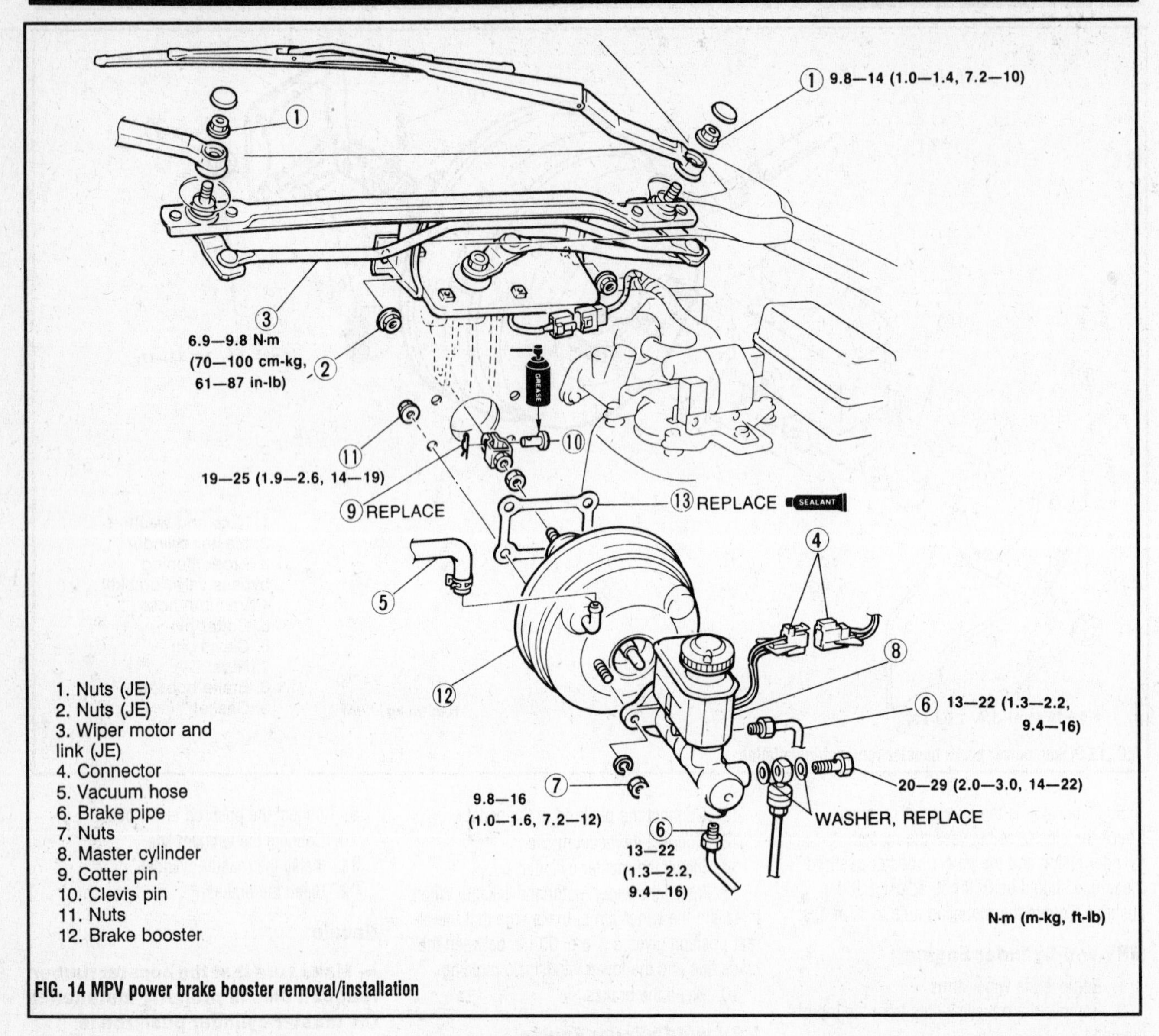

FIG. 14 MPV power brake booster removal/installation

3. Remove the master cylinder-to-booster retaining nuts.

4. Loosen the clamp that secures the manifold vacuum hose to the booster check valve, and remove the hose. Remove the booster check valve.

5. Pull the master cylinder off the booster and leave it supported by the prop, far enough away to allow removal of the booster assembly.

6. From inside the cab on vehicles equipped with push rod mounted stop lamp switch, remove the retaining pin and slide the stop lamp switch, push rod, spacers and bushing off the brake pedal arm.

7. From the engine compartment remove the bolts that attach the booster to the dash panel.

To install:

8. Mount the booster assembly on the engine side of the dash panel by sliding the bracket mounting bolts and valve operating rod in through the holes in the dash panel.

➡ **Make certain that the booster push rod is positioned on the correct side of the master cylinder to install onto the push pin prior to tightening the booster assembly to the dash.**

9. From inside the cab, install the booster mounting bracket-to-dash panel retaining nuts.

10. Position the master cylinder on the booster assembly, install the retaining nuts, and remove the prop from underneath the master cylinder.

11. Install the booster check valve. Connect the manifold vacuum hose to the booster check valve and secure with the clamp.

12. From inside the cab on vehicles equipped with push rod mounted stop lamp switch, install the bushing and position the switch on the end of the push rod. Then install the switch and rod on the pedal arm, along with spacers on each side, and secure with the retaining pin.

13. Connect the stop lamp switch wiring.

14. Start the engine and check brake operation.

PUSHROD CLEARANCE

1. On all except Navajo, adjust the power brake booster pushrod clearance as follows: Install clearance adjusting tool 49 F043 001 or equivalent on the rear of the master cylinder.

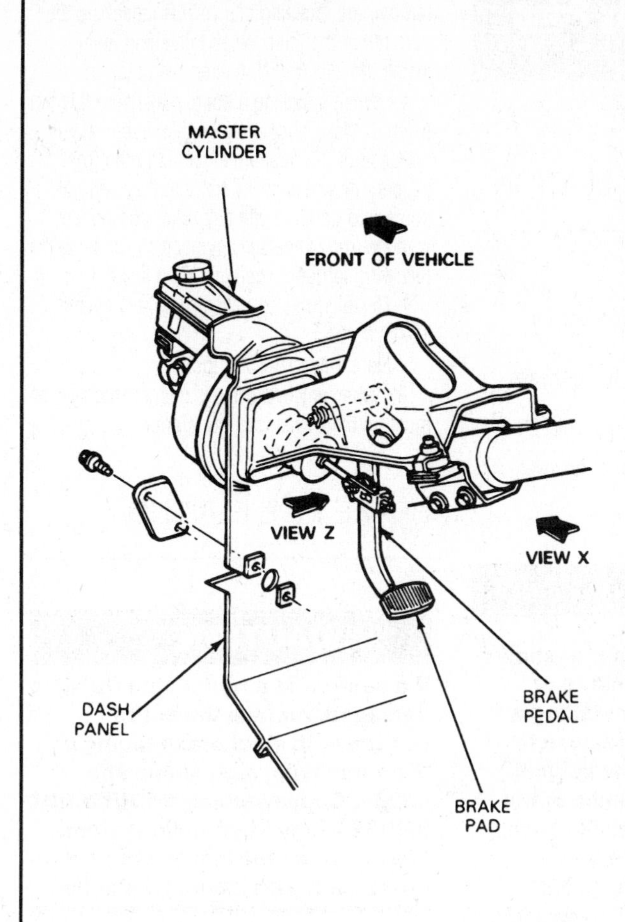

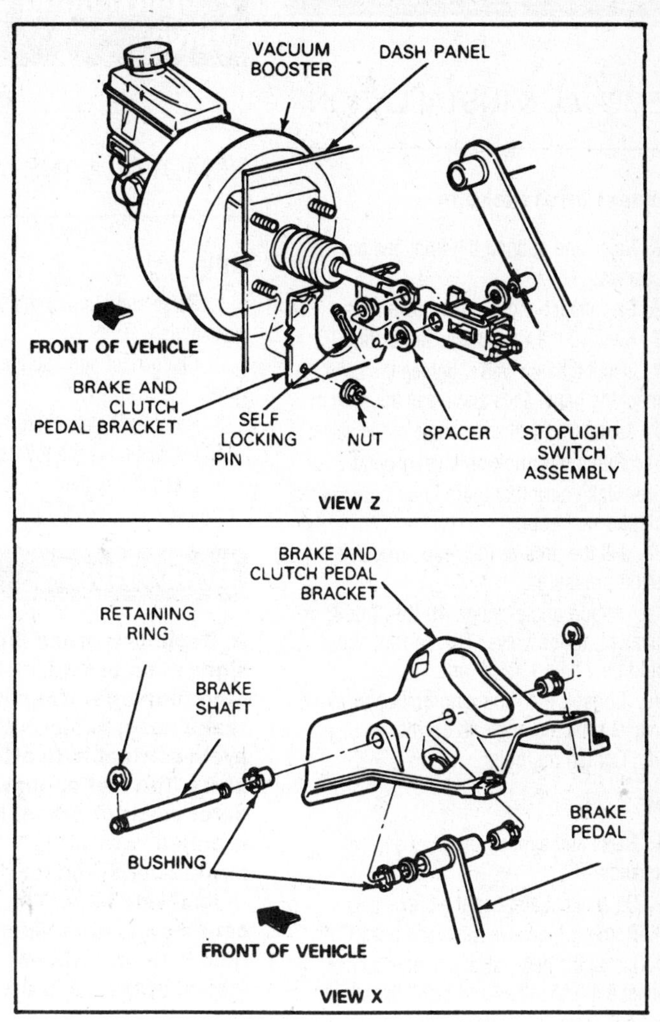

FIG. 15 Navajo power brake booster removal/installation

Turn the adjusting bolt until it bottoms in the pushrod hole in the piston. Apply 19.7 in.Hg vacuum to the power brake booster with a vacuum pump. Invert the clearance adjusting tool and place it on the power brake booster. Turn the pushrod locknut until there is no clearance between the tool and the pushrod.

2. On the Navajo, measure the distance between the outer end of the booster pushrod and the front face of the booster assembly. The distance should be 25.3mm (0.995 in.). Turn the pushrod adjusting screw in or out until the distance is as specified.

Pressure Differential Valve 2-Wheel Drive Pickups

REMOVAL & INSTALLATION

1. Disconnect the brake warning light switch connector, at the switch.
2. Disconnect the brake lines at the valve, and plug the lines.
3. Unbolt and remove the valve.
4. Installation is the reverse of removal. Bleed the system.

CENTRALIZING THE PRESSURE DIFFERENTIAL VALVE

After the brake system has been opened for repairs, or bled, the brake light may remain on. The pressure differential valve must be centered to make the light go off.

1. Turn the ignition switch ON, but don't start the engine.
2. Make sure that the master cylinder reservoirs are filled.
3. Slowly depress the brake pedal. The valve should center itself and the light go off. If not, bleed the brakes again and repeat the above procedure.

Load Sensing G-Valve

REMOVAL & INSTALLATION

4-Wheel Drive Pickups

1. Raise and support the front end on jackstands.
2. Disconnect and cap the brake lines.
3. Remove the valve mounting bolts.
4. Install the new valve, tighten the bolts, connect the brake lines and bleed the system.
5. Adjust the inclination angle of the valve:
   a. Place the truck on level ground.
   b. Make sure that there is no cargo in the truck and no people.
   c. Fill the tires to the recommended inflation pressure.
   d. Attach angle gauge 49 U043 003, or equivalent, to the valve. The correct angle should be 7° ± 1$^1/_2$°. If not:
   e. Loosen the mounting bolts and move the valve until the angle is correct.
   f. Tighten the bolts.

MPV

1. Raise and support the front end on jackstands.
2. Disconnect and cap the brake lines.
3. Remove the valve mounting bolts.
4. Install the new valve, tighten the bolts, connect the brake lines and bleed the system.
5. Adjust the inclination angle of the valve:
   a. Place the van on level ground.
   b. Make sure that there is no cargo in the van and no people.
   c. Fill the tires to the recommended inflation pressure.
   d. Attach angle gauge 49 U043 003, or equivalent, to the valve. The correct angle should be 8$^1/_2$° ± 1°. If not:
   e. Loosen the mounting bolts and move the valve until the angle is correct.
   f. Tighten the bolts.

Proportioning By-Pass Valve

REMOVAL & INSTALLATION

MPV

1. Raise and support the front end on jackstands.
2. Disconnect and cap the brake lines at the valve.
3. Remove the attaching bolts.
4. Installation is the reverse of removal.
5. Bleed the system.

Brake Hoses

➡ Replace a brake line that shows signs of softening, cracking or other damage. When installing a brake hose, position the hose to avoid contact with other vehicle parts. The wet appearance of the outer cover of rubber brake hoses is called "sweating". This is a normal condition for neoprene rayon braid hose. The "sweating" condition is not evidence of a brake fluid leak and will not result in a loss of pressure in the system.

INSPECTION AND REPLACEMENT

1. Clean the brake hose thoroughly before inspecting it.
2. Check all flexible hoses for any signs of swelling, cracking or brittleness. Replace any hose that shows any of these symptoms.
3. Check the hoses for any sign that they are rubbing against any other component. If shiny marks or scuffing is found. Determine what the hose is rubbing against and correct the problem. If scuffing has removed **any** material from the hose, replace it.
4. Check brake pipes for corrosion or dents. Replace any damaged pipe.
5. Check all connections for signs of leakage. Check threads for damage.
6. When disconnecting hoses and pipes, remove the retaining clip AFTER loosening the flare nut at the joint. When tightening fittings, install the clip, THEN, tighten the flare nut.
7. When installing a hose, make sure it is not twisted. Make absolutely certain, especially in the case of the hoses connected to the front calipers or wheel cylinders, that they will not come into contact with any other component with the front wheels in any position. Observe the following torques when installing lines:
   - Flexible hose-to-caliper or wheel cylinder: 16-19 ft. lbs.
   - Flare nuts: 10-15 ft. lbs.
8. When any brake line is opened, the system must be bled when the job is done.

BRAKE PIPE FLARING

⁂ CAUTION

If a section of a brake pipe (tube) is damaged, replace the entire section with steel brake tubing of the same type, size, shape and length. Copper tubing SHOULD NOT BE USED in the hydraulic system. Always clean the inside of a new brake tube with isopropyl alcohol.

Auto parts stores sell various lengths and diameters of steel brake line. If, however, you must make your own line, the ends must be either double flared, or ISO flared. Either method requires the use of a special flaring tool and adapters. The most common flaring tool is a split-die type. The following procedure for line flaring describes the method using a split-die tool to make a double flare. Always follow the instructions packed with the flaring tool.

1. The following procedures are for making a double flare end. Adapters and methods for making an ISO flare differ, follow the tool manufacturer's instructions: Cut off and straighten the required length of line. A tubing cutter will simplify making a clean and square cut.
2. Square off the ends of the line with a file, and chamfer the end of the line to be flared.
3. Place the fitting on the tube, threaded side toward the end of the tube being flared. Select the split die for the size line to be used and insert the die into the tapered hole in the body. Push the tube through the die until the end is even with the face of the die. Lock the tube in this position by tightening the die clamp wing nut.

4. Take the correct punch (usually marked 1) and slide the first operation punch into the hole in the center of the threaded body. Tighten the screw securely to form the single flare.

5. Loosen the screw and replace the first punch with the second (usually marked 2). Again, tighten the screw to form the double flare.

6. Loosen the screw and remove the tool. Open the die and remove the tube. Inspect the flare for cracks or poor flare form. If the flare is not correct, cut it off and square the end. Flare.

Brake Bleeding

The hydraulic brake system must be free of air to operate properly. Air can enter the system when hydraulic parts are disconnected for servicing or replacement, or when the fluid level in the master cylinder reservoirs is very low. Air in the system will give the brake pedal a spongy feeling upon application.

The quickest and easiest of the two ways for system bleeding is the pressure method, but special equipment is needed to externally pressurize the hydraulic system. The other, more commonly used method of brake bleeding is done manually.

BLEEDING SEQUENCE

1. Master cylinder. If the cylinder is not equipped with bleeder screws, open the brake line(s) to the wheels slightly while pressure is applied to the brake pedal. Be sure to tighten the line before the brake pedal is released. The procedure for bench bleeding the master cylinder is covered below.
2. Pressure Differential Valve: If equipped with a bleeder screw.
3. Front/Back Split Systems: Start with the wheel farthest away from the master cylinder, usually the right rear wheel. Bleed the other rear wheel then the right front and left front.

CAUTION

Do not allow brake fluid to spill on the truck's finish, it will remove the paint. Flush the area with water.

➡ If the vehicle is equipped with anti-lock brakes, the electro-hydraulic valve must also be bled. It is not necessary to energize the valve to bleed it.

MANUAL BLEEDING

1. Clean the bleed screw at each wheel.
2. Start with the wheel farthest from the master cylinder (right rear), or the left rear if the right side wheel cylinder is not equipped with a bleeder..
3. Attach a small rubber hose to the bleed screw and place the end in a container of clear brake fluid.
4. Fill the master cylinder with brake fluid. (Check often during bleeding). Have an assistant slowly pump up the brake pedal and hold pressure.
5. Open the bleed screw about one-quarter turn, press the brake pedal to the floor, close the bleed screw and slowly release the pedal. Continue until no more air bubbles are forced from the cylinder on application of the brake pedal.
6. Repeat procedure on remaining wheel cylinders and calipers, still working from cylinder/caliper farthest from the master cylinder.

Master cylinders equipped with bleed screws may be bled independently. When bleeding the Bendix-type dual master cylinder it is necessary to solidly cap one reservoir section while bleeding the other to prevent pressure loss through the cap vent hole.

CAUTION

The bleeder valves must be closed at the end of each stroke, and before the brake pedal is released, to insure that no air can enter the system. It is also important that the brake pedal be returned to the full up position so the piston in the master cylinder moves back enough to clear the bypass outlets.

PRESSURE BLEEDING DISC BRAKES

CAUTION

Special adapters are required when pressure bleeding cylinders with plastic reservoirs.

Pressure bleeding equipment should be diaphragm type, placing a diaphragm between the pressurized air supply and the brake fluid. This prevents moisture and other contaminants from entering the hydraulic system.

➡ Some front disc/rear drum equipped vehicles use a metering valve which closes off pressure to the front brakes under certain conditions. These systems contain manual release actuators, which must be engaged to pressure bleed the front brakes.

1. Connect the tank hydraulic hose and adapter to the master cylinder.
2. Close hydraulic valve on the bleeder equipment.
3. Apply air pressure to the bleeder equipment

CAUTION

Follow equipment manufacturer's recommendations for correct air pressure.

4. Open the valve to bleed air out of the pressure hose to the master cylinder.

➡ Never bleed this system using the secondary piston stopscrew on the bottom of many master cylinders.

5. Open the hydraulic valve and bleed each wheel cylinder and caliper. Bleed rear brake system first when bleeding both front and rear systems.

FLUSHING HYDRAULIC BRAKE SYSTEMS

Hydraulic brake systems must be totally flushed if the fluid becomes contaminated with water, dirt or other corrosive chemicals. To flush, simply bleed the entire system until all fluid has been replaced with the correct type of new fluid.

BENCH BLEEDING MASTER CYLINDER

Bench bleeding the master cylinder before installing it on the truck reduces the possibility of getting air into the lines.

1. Connect two short pieces of brake line to the outlet fittings, bend them until the free end is below the fluid level in the master cylinder reservoirs.

2. Fill the reservoirs with fresh brake fluid. Pump the piston until no more air bubbles appear in the reservoir(s).

3. Disconnect the two short lines, refill the master cylinder and securely install the cylinder cap(s).

4. Install the master cylinder on the truck. Attach the lines but do not completely tighten them. Force any air that might have been trapped in the connection by slowly depressing the brake pedal. Tighten the lines before releasing the brake pedal.

FRONT DISC BRAKES

CAUTION

Brake shoes contain asbestos, which has been determined to be a cancer causing agent. Never clean the brake surfaces with compressed air! Avoid inhaling any dust from any brake surface! When cleaning brake surfaces, use a commercially available brake cleaning fluid.

Brake Pads

SEE FIGS. 16-25

INSPECTION

The brake pads can be visually inspected after the front wheels have been removed. A cut out in the top of the caliper is provided. Check the lining thickness of both the outboard and inboard pads. If the lining is worn within 3mm (1/8 in.) of its metal backing (check local inspection requirements) replace all of the brake pads.

REMOVAL & INSTALLATION

CAUTION

Brake pads contain asbestos, which has been determined to be a cancer causing agent. Never clean the brake surfaces with compressed air! Avoid inhaling any dust from any brake surface! When cleaning brake surfaces, use a commercially available brake cleaning fluid.

Pickups

1. Raise and support the front end on jackstands.
2. Remove the wheels.
3. Remove the lower lock pin bolt from the caliper.
4. Rotate the caliper upward and remove the brake pads and shims.
5. Remove the master cylinder reservoir cap and remove about half of the fluid from the reservoir.
6. Using a large C-clamp, depress the caliper piston until it bottoms in its bore.
7. Install the shims and new pads.
8. Reposition the caliper and install the lock pin bolt. Torque the bolt to 30 ft. lbs.
9. Install the wheels, lower the truck, refill the master cylinder and depress the brake pedal a few times to restore pressure. Bleed the system if required.

MPV

1. Raise and support the front end on jackstands.
2. Remove the wheels.
3. Remove the lower lock pin bolt from the caliper.
4. Rotate the caliper upward and remove the brake pads and shims.
5. Remove the master cylinder reservoir cap and remove about half of the fluid from the reservoir.
6. Using a large C-clamp and suitable piece of wood, depress the caliper pistons until they bottom in their bores.
7. Install the shims and new pads.
8. Reposition the caliper and install the lock pin bolt. Torque the bolt to 69 ft. lbs.
9. Install the wheels, lower the vehicle, refill the master cylinder and depress the brake pedal a few times to restore pressure. Bleed the system if required.

Navajo

1. To avoid fluid overflow when the caliper piston is pressed into the cylinder bore, siphon part of the brake fluid out of the master cylinder reservoir. Discard the removed fluid.
2. Raise the vehicle and install jackstands. Remove a front wheel and tire assembly.
3. Place an 203mm (8 in.) C-clamp on the caliper and tighten the clamp to move the piston into the cylinder bore about 3mm (1/8 in.). Avoid clamp contact with the outer pad spring clip. Place the screw end of the clamp below the spring clip. Avoid pad displacement beyond locking tab engagement. Remove the clamp.

➡ Do not use a screwdriver or similar tool to pry piston away from the rotor.

4. Clean excess dirt from the areas around the pin tabs.
5. Using a 1/4 in. drive socket, 3/8 in. deep and a light hammer, tap the upper caliper pin towards the outboard side until the pin tabs pass the spindle face.
6. Place one end of a 11mm (7/16 in.) diameter punch against the end of the caliper pin and tap the pin out of the caliper slide groove.
7. Repeat Steps 5 and 6 to remove the lower pin.
8. Remove the caliper and hang in out of the way with mechanic's wire. Do not allow the caliper to hang by the brake hose.
9. Compress the anti-rattle clip and remove the inner brake pad from the caliper. Press each ear of the outer pad away from the caliper and slide the torque buttons out of the retaining notches. Remove the brake pad.

FIG. 16 Cleaning the front brake assembly

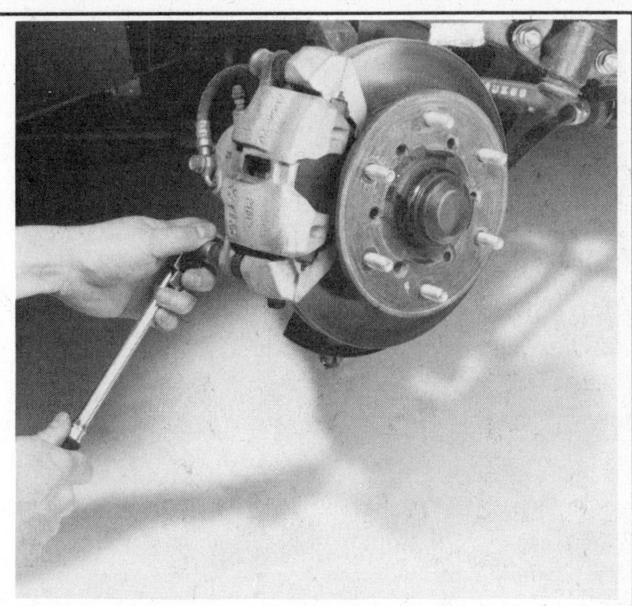

FIG. 18 Removing the lower caliper mounting pin, Pickup shown

FIG. 17 Bleeding the caliper

FIG. 19 The lower caliper mounting pin, Pickup shown

To install:

10. Bottom the caliper piston using the C-clamp. Place a piece of wood or the worn out brake pad on the piston before tightening the clamp. Do not attempt to bottom the piston with the outer pad installed. Place a new anti-rattle clip on the lower end of the inner pad. Be sure the tabs on the clip are positioned properly and the clip is fully seated.

11. Position the inner pads and anti-rattle clip in the abutment with the anti-rattle clip tab against the pad abutment and the loop-type spring away from the rotor. Compress the anti-rattle clip and slide the upper end of the pad in position.

12. Install the outer pad, making sure the torque buttons on the pad spring clip are seated solidly in the matching holes in the caliper.

13. Install the caliper, using new pins, make sure the mounting surfaces are free of dirt and lubricate the caliper grooves with Disc Brake Caliper Grease. From the outboard side, position the upper pin between the caliper and spindle grooves. The pin must be positioned so the tabs will be installed against the spindle outer face. Tap the pin, on the outboard end with a soft hammer until the retention tabs on the sides of the pin contact the spindle face. Repeat the procedure for the lower pin.

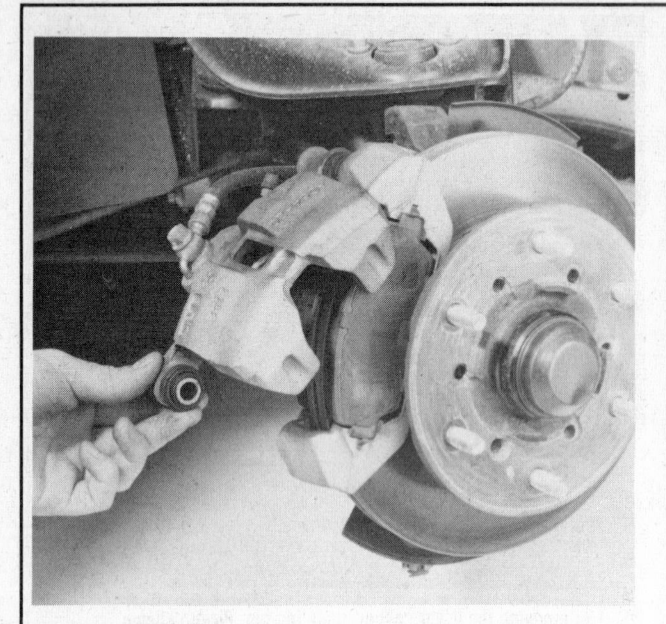

FIG. 20 Pivot the caliper upward

FIG. 22 Compressing the caliper piston

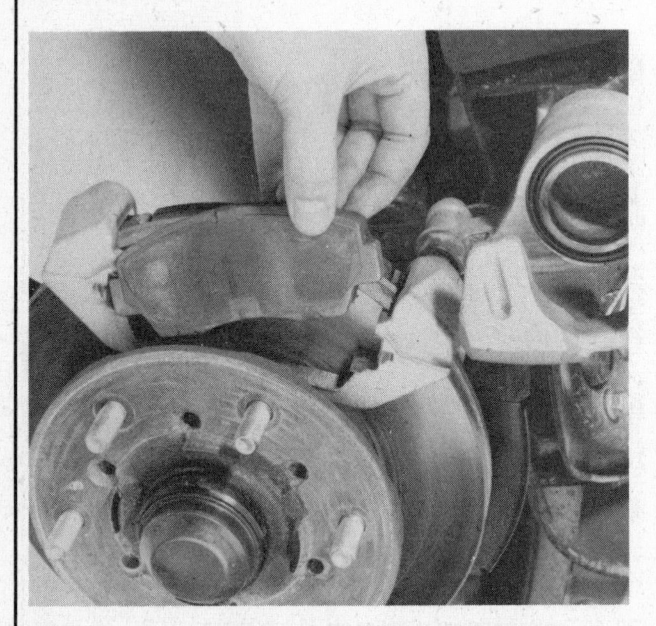

FIG. 21 Removing/installing the outboard brake pad, Pickup shown

FIG. 23 Master cylinder mounting, Pickup shown

WARNING

Never reuse caliper pins. Always install new pins whenever a caliper is removed.

14. Pump the brake pedal several times to position the pads to the rotor. Fill the master cylinder.

15. Bleed the brake system if required.

16. Install the wheel and tire assembly. Torque the lug nuts to 85–115 ft. lbs.

17. Remove the jackstands and lower the vehicle. Check the brake fluid level and fill as necessary. Check the brakes for proper operation.

Caliper

REMOVAL & INSTALLATION

CAUTION

Brake pads contain asbestos, which has been determined to be a cancer causing agent. Never clean the brake surfaces with

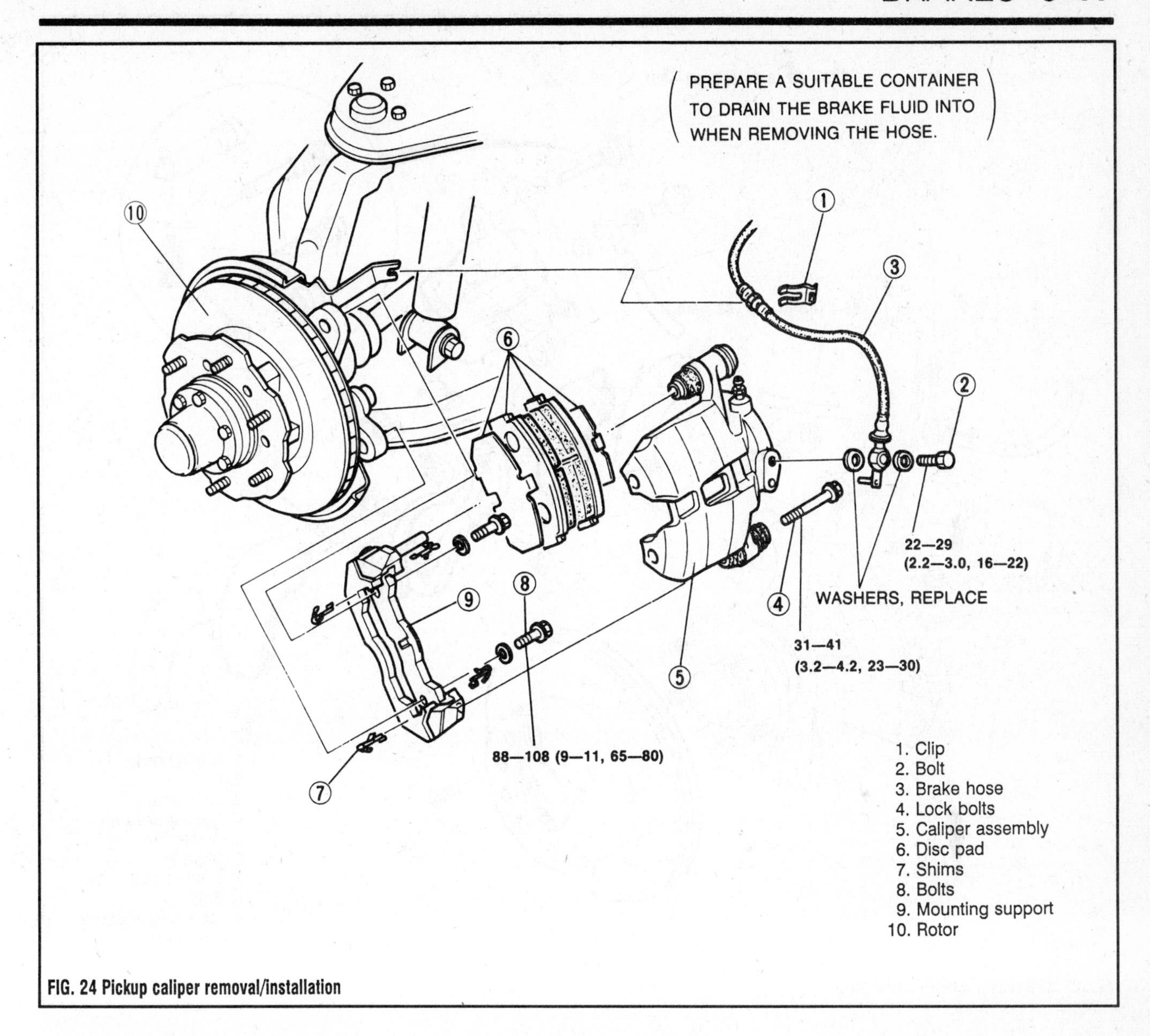

FIG. 24 Pickup caliper removal/installation

compressed air! Avoid inhaling any dust from any brake surface! When cleaning brake surfaces, use a commercially available brake cleaning fluid.

Pickups and MPV

1. Raise and safely support the vehicle. Remove the wheel and tire assembly.
2. Remove the banjo bolt and disconnect the brake hose from the caliper. Plug the hose to prevent fluid leakage.
3. On pickups, remove the caliper mounting bolt and pivot the caliper about the mounting pin and off of the brake rotor. Remove the caliper from the pin.
4. On MPV, remove the caliper mounting bolts and remove the caliper.
5. To install, place the caliper in position and secure the mounting bolts following the reverse order of removal. Lubricate the caliper mounting bolts or bolt and pin prior to installation.
6. Tighten the caliper mounting bolt(s) to 23–30 ft. lbs. (31–41 Nm) on pickups; 61–69 ft. lbs. (83–93 Nm) on MPV. Bleed the brake system.

Navajo

1. Siphon part of the brake fluid out of the master cylinder to avoid overflow when the caliper piston is pressed into the caliper bore.
2. Raise the vehicle and support it safely. Remove the wheel and tire assembly.
3. Position an 203mm (8 in.) C-clamp on the caliper and tighten the clamp to move the caliper piston into the bore approximately 3mm ($^1/_8$ in.). Avoid clamp contact with the outer shoe spring clip. Remove the clamp.

➡ Do not pry the piston away from the rotor.

4. Clean excess dirt from the pin tab area.
5. Using a $^1/_4$ in. drive socket, $^3/_8$ in. deep and a light hammer, tap the upper caliper pin towards the outboard side until the pin tabs pass the spindle face.
6. Place one end of a 11mm ($^7/_{16}$ in.) diameter punch against the end of the caliper pin and tap the pin out of the caliper slide groove.

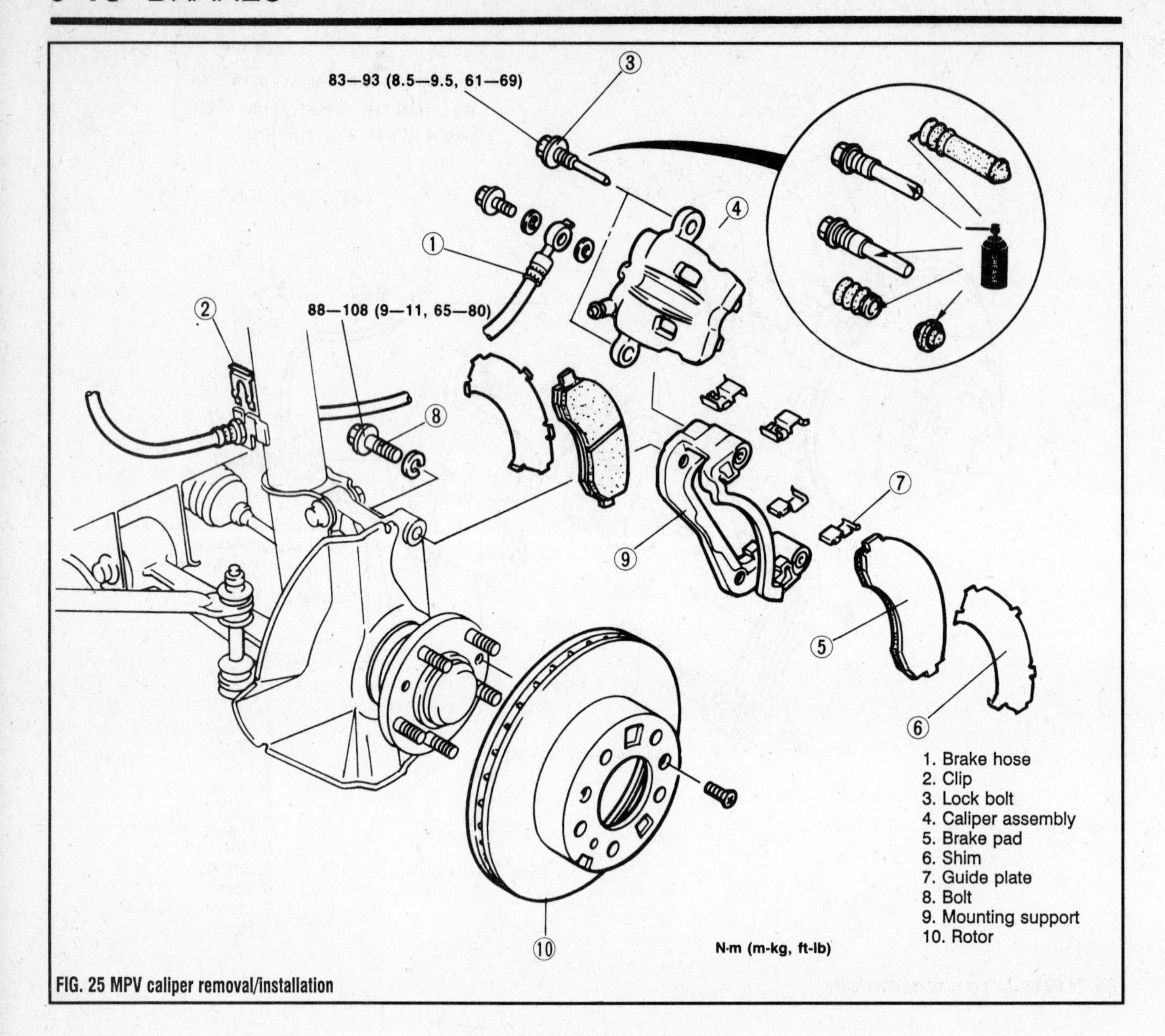

FIG. 25 MPV caliper removal/installation

7. Repeat the procedure to remove the lower caliper pin.

8. Disconnect and plug the brake hose at the caliper. Remove the caliper from the rotor.

To install:

9. Make sure the caliper mounting surfaces are free of dirt. Lubricate the caliper grooves with disc brake caliper grease and install the caliper.

10. From the caliper outboard side, position the pin between the caliper and spindle grooves. The pin must be positioned so the tabs will be installed against the spindle outer face.

11. Tap the pin on the outboard end with a hammer until the retention tabs on the sides of the pin contact the spindle face.

12. Repeat the procedure to install the lower pin.

➡ During installation, do not allow the tabs of the caliper pin to be tapped too far into the spindle groove. If this happens, it will be necessary to tap the other end of the caliper pin until the tabs snap in place. The tabs on each end of the pin must be free to catch on the spindle face.

13. Connect the brake hose to the caliper. Bleed the brake system.

14. Install the wheel and tire assembly and lower the vehicle. Check the brake fluid level and check the brakes for proper operation.

OVERHAUL

➧SEE FIGS. 26-38

CAUTION

Brake pads contain asbestos, which has been determined to be a cancer causing agent. Never clean the brake surfaces with compressed air! Avoid inhaling any dust from any brake surface! When cleaning brake surfaces, use a commercially available brake cleaning fluid.

1. Piston
2. Dust seal
3. Piston seal
4. Bleeder screw and cap
5. Pin boot
6. Pin
7. Bushing

GREASE
REPLACE
GREASE
REPLACE

FIG. 26 Caliper components, Pickup shown

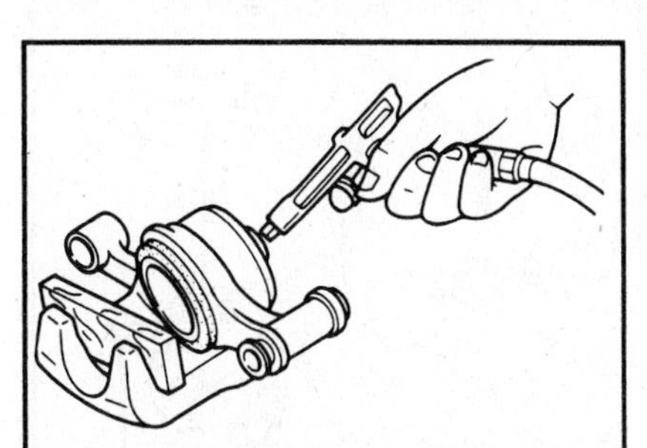

FIG. 27 Place a piece of wood in the caliper, then blow compressed air through the hole to force the piston out of the caliper. Covering the caliper and wood with a rag will help avoid fluid splatter

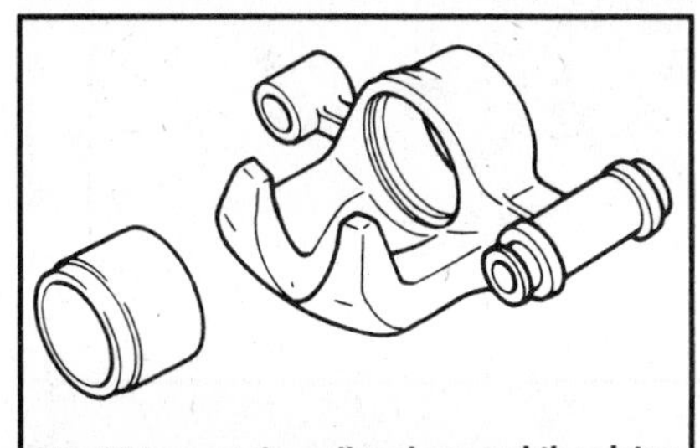

FIG. 28 Inspect the caliper bore and the piston for excess wear, rust or pitting

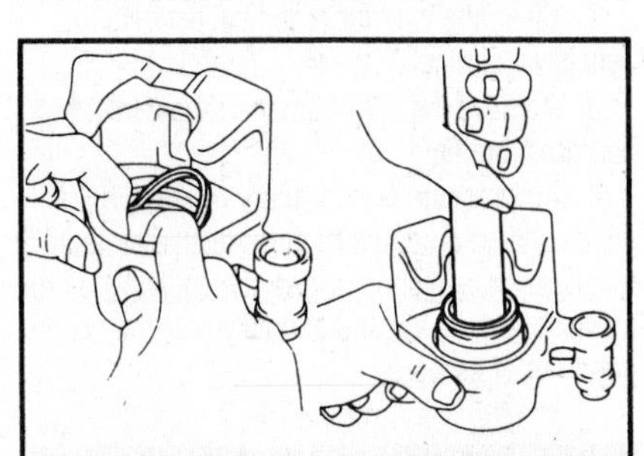

FIG. 29 Coat the piston seal with the lubricant supplied with the rebuilding kit (or brake fluid if not lube was supplied). Install the seal, coat the piston with brake fluid and install it squarely into the caliper bore

Pickups

1. Remove the caliper.
2. Place a thin piece of wood in the caliper, in front of the piston. Apply enough compressed air through the brake line inlet hole to force the piston out of the caliper. Don't try to catch the piston with your fingers. A set of mashed fingers will result. It's also a good idea to wear safety glasses, as a spray of brake fluid will often result. If the piston is seized, try tapping around the caliper while applying pressure. If that doesn't work, fill the caliper with a rust dissolving agent such as Liquid Wrench® or WD-40® and let it stand for a while.
3. Discard all rubber parts.
4. Remove the bleeder screw.
5. Clean all parts in clean brake fluid. Inspect the piston and bore for any signs of wear, damage or heat discoloration. Minor damage can be corrected with light polishing using a crocus cloth.
6. Rebuilding kits are equipped with two kinds of grease, color coded orange and red. See the illustration for application details. Install a new seal, lubricated with clean brake fluid, on the piston. Be sure that the seal is not twisted!
7. Lubricate the piston and bore with clean brake fluid and insert the piston in the bore.
8. Install a new dust boot and retainer.
9. Install the bleeder screw.
10. Install the caliper and bleed the brake system.

MPV

1. Thoroughly clean the outside of the caliper.
2. Remove the dust boot retainer and the boot.
3. Place a piece of hardwood in front of the pistons.
4. Gradually apply compressed air through the hydraulic line fitting and withdraw the piston.

➡ **If the pistons are frozen and cannot be removed from the caliper, tap lightly around them, while air pressure is being applied.**

5. Withdraw the piston and seal from the caliper bore.
6. If necessary, remove the bleeder screw.
7. Wash all of the parts in clean brake fluid. Dry them off with compressed air.

**** CAUTION**

Do not wash the parts in kerosene or gasoline.

8. Examine the caliper bores and pistons for scores, scratches, or rust. Replace either part, as required. Minor scratches or scoring can be corrected by dressing with crocus cloth.

➡ **Discard the old piston seal and dust boot. Replace them with new ones. Apply clean brake fluid to the piston and bore. Assemble the caliper in the reverse order of disassembly.**

9. Install the dust seal onto the piston and then install the assembly into the caliper. Apply the red grease packed in the seal kit to the piston seal. Apply the orange grease to the dust seal. Also apply the orange grease to the pin outer circumference, the inner surface of the bushing, and the dust boot. Install the caliper and bleed the brake system.

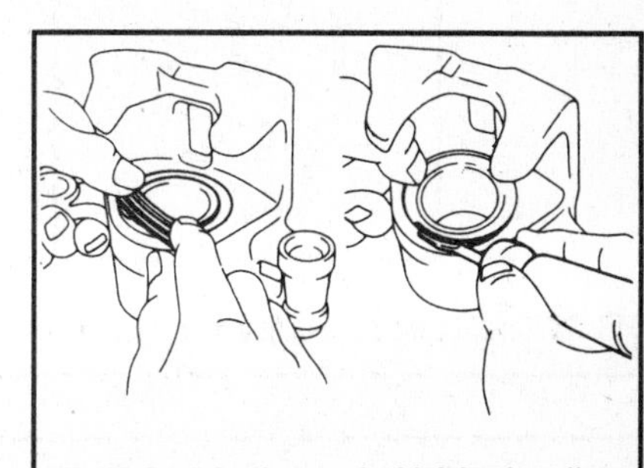

FIG. 30 Coat the dust seal with lube, install on the piston lip and caliper

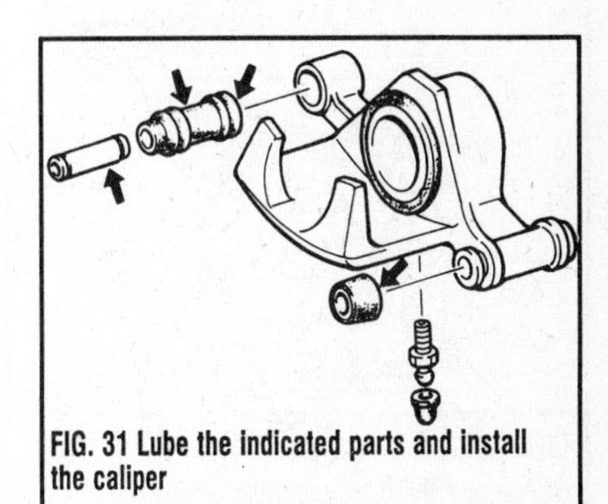

FIG. 31 Lube the indicated parts and install the caliper

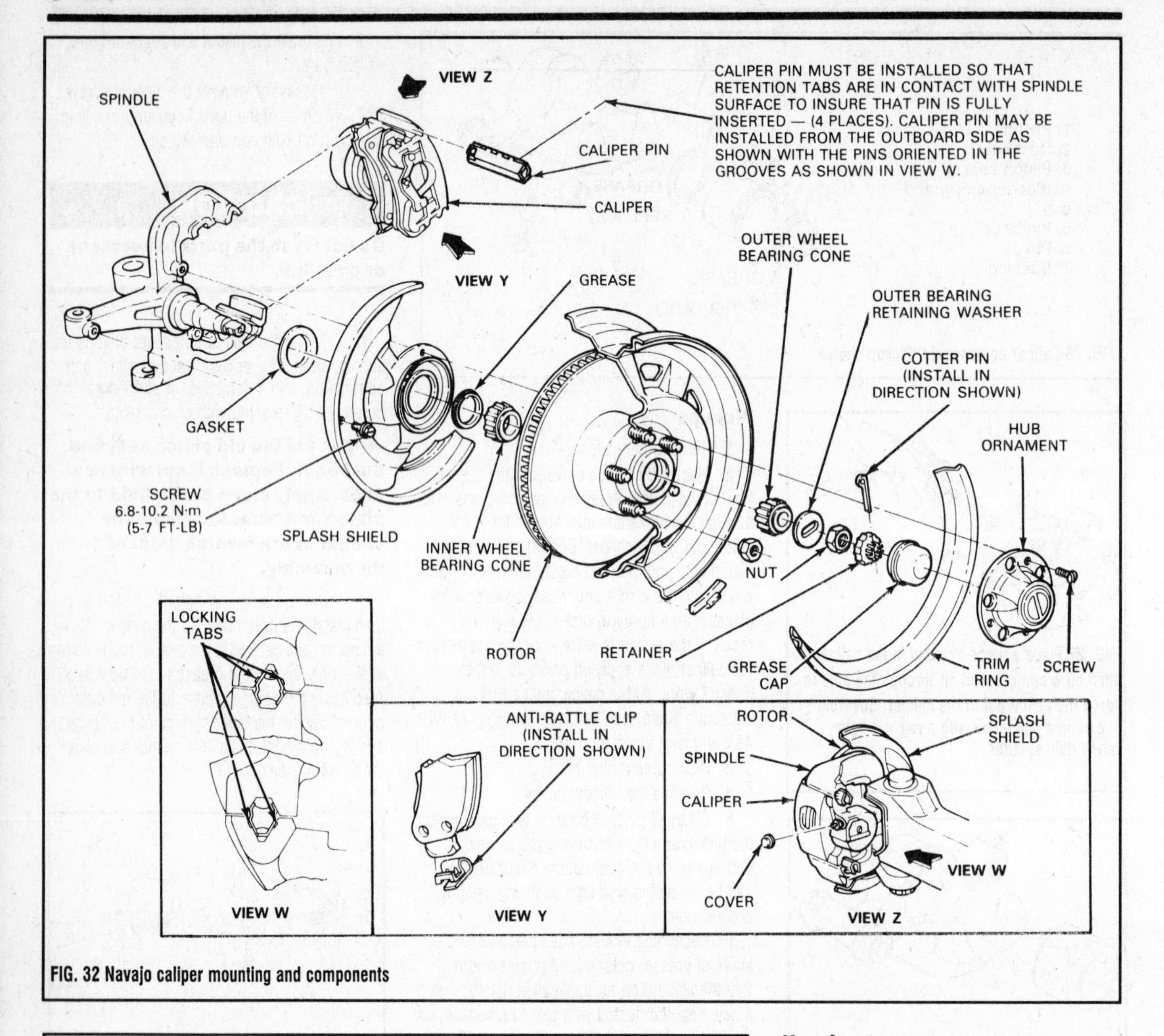

FIG. 32 Navajo caliper mounting and components

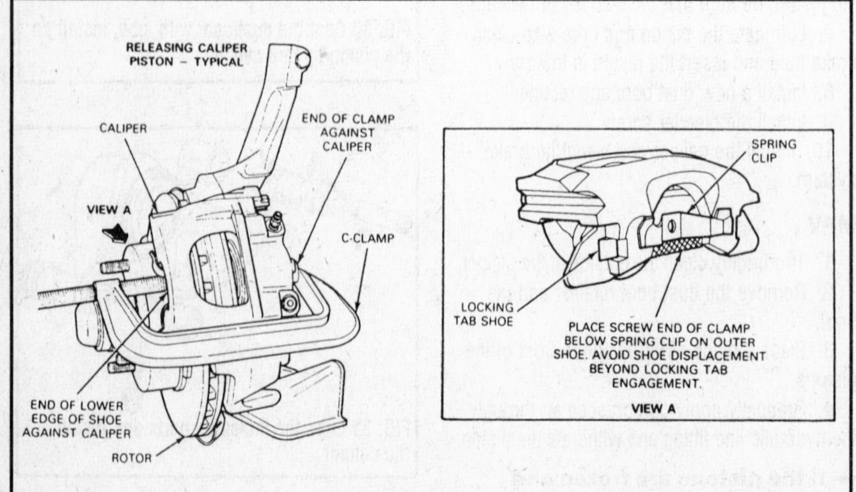

FIG. 33 Use a C-clamp to push the caliper piston back into the bore slightly before removing the caliper on Navajo models

Navajo

1. Disconnect the brake hose and the caliper from the vehicle.
2. Clean the exterior of the caliper with denatured alcohol.
3. Remove the plug from the caliper inlet port and drain the fluid.
4. Air pressure is necessary to remove the piston. When a source of compressed air is found, such as a shop or gas station, apply air to the inlet port slowly and carefully until the piston pops out of its bore.

CAUTION

If high pressure air is applied, the piston will pop out with considerable force and cause damage or injury.

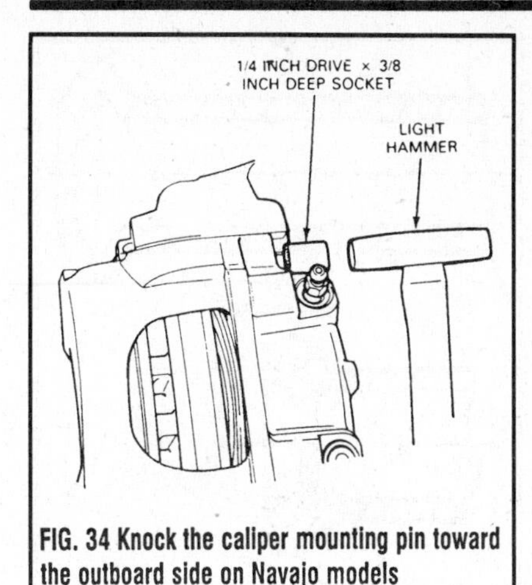

FIG. 34 Knock the caliper mounting pin toward the outboard side on Navajo models

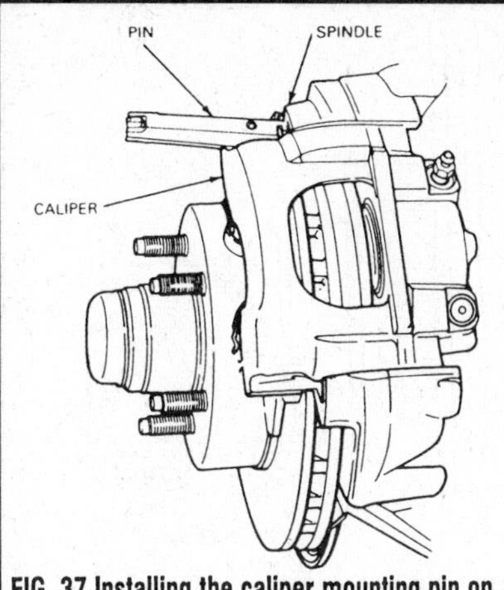

FIG. 37 Installing the caliper mounting pin on Navajo models

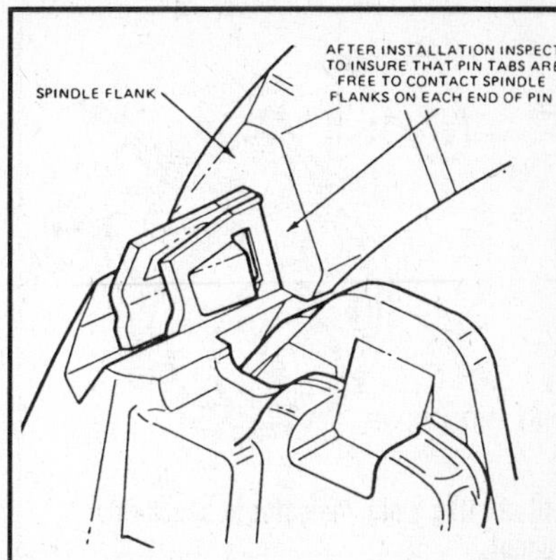

FIG. 38 Tap the mounting pin on the outboard end until the retention tabs on the side of the pin contact the spindle face

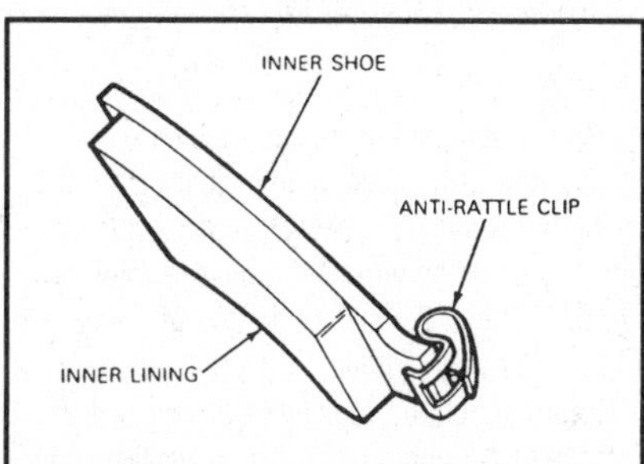

FIG. 35 Anti rattle clip installation on Navajo brake pads

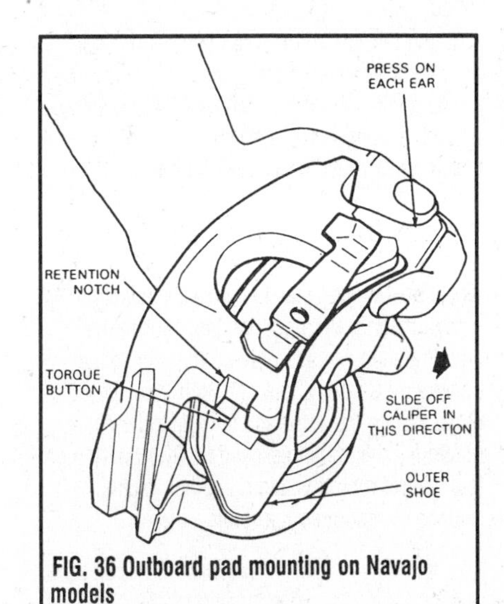

FIG. 36 Outboard pad mounting on Navajo models

5. If the piston jams, release the air pressure and tap sharply on the piston end with a soft hammer. Reapply air pressure.

6. When the piston is out, remove the boot from the piston and the seal from the bore.

7. Clean the housing and piston with denatured alcohol. Dry with compressed air.

8. Lubricate the new piston seal, boot and piston with clean brake fluid, and assemble them in the caliper.

9. The dust boot can be worked in with the fingers and the piston should be pressed straight in until it bottoms. Be careful to avoid cocking the piston in the bore.

10. A C-clamp may be necessary to bottom the piston.

11. Install the caliper and bleed the brake system.

Brake Rotor

CAUTION

Brake pads contain asbestos, which has been determined to be a cancer causing agent. Never clean the brake surfaces with compressed air! Avoid inhaling any dust from any brake surface! When cleaning brake surfaces, use a commercially available brake cleaning fluid.

REMOVAL & INSTALLATION

1. Raise and safely support the vehicle. Remove the wheel and tire assembly.

2. Remove the caliper and support it aside with mechanic's wire; do not let the caliper hang by the brake hose. On all except Navajo, remove the disc brake pads and mounting support.

3. On 2WD Pickups and Navajo, remove the dust cap, cotter pin, nut, washer and outer bearing and remove the rotor from the spindle.

4. On 4WD Pickups, remove the locking hub or drive flange, snapring and spacer, set bolts and bearing set plate. Remove the bearing locknut using a suitable puller and remove the hub and rotor assembly, being careful not to let the washer and bearing fall.

5. On 4WD Navajo, remove the locking hub and remove the brake rotor.

6. On MPV models, remove the attaching screw and remove the rotor.

7. Inspect the rotor for scoring, wear and runout. Machine or replace as necessary.

8. If rotor replacement is necessary on pickup models, remove the attaching bolts and separate the rotor from the hub.

9. Install the rotor. On B Series pickup, tighten the rotor-to-hub bolts to 40–51 ft. lbs. (54–69 Nm). Adjust the wheel bearings.

INSPECTION

SEE FIGS. 39-45

Brake roughness is a shudder, vibration or pedal pulsation occurring during braking operation. It may be caused by a foreign materiall build-up on the rotor braking surfaces or by excessive rotor variation or distortion.

If there is a foreign material build-up or contamination found on the rotor or lining surfaces, hand sand both the linings and rotor braking surfaces. Brake squeal or squeak is a higher frequency vibration which can result from foreign material build-up or glazing of the lining and rotor surfaces. Hand sanding the rotor and linings may correct the condition.

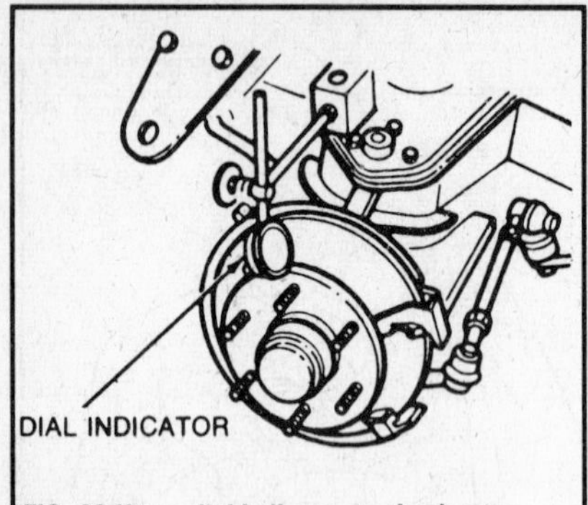

FIG. 39 Use a dial indicator to check rotor runout

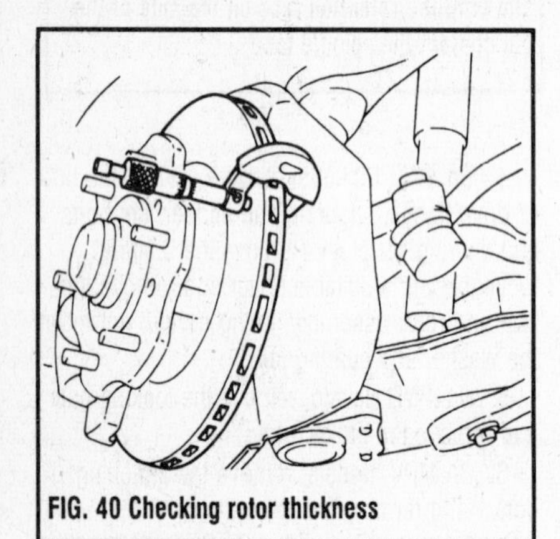

FIG. 40 Checking rotor thickness

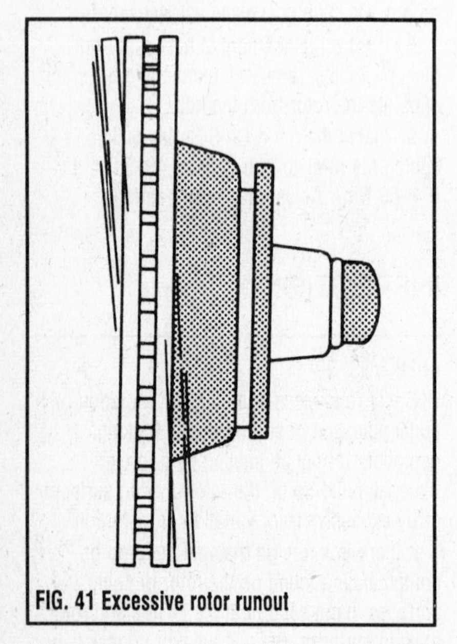

FIG. 41 Excessive rotor runout

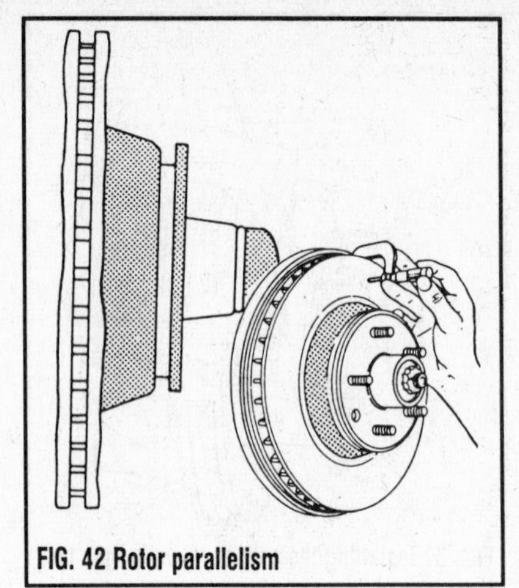

FIG. 42 Rotor parallelism

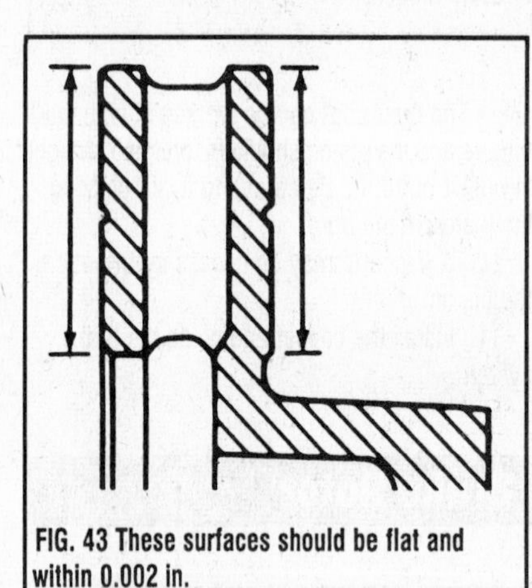

FIG. 43 These surfaces should be flat and within 0.002 in.

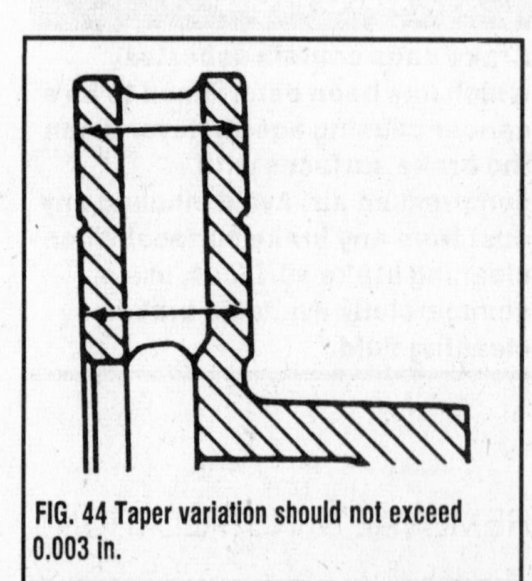

FIG. 44 Taper variation should not exceed 0.003 in.

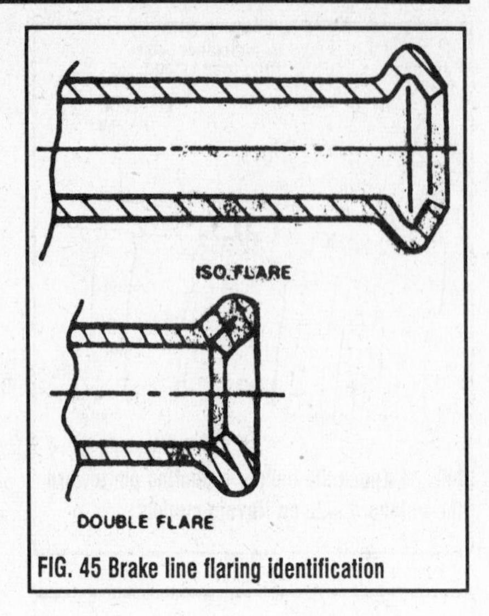

FIG. 45 Brake line flaring identification

Always replace the linings if they are excessively worn. Check the caliper piston for roll back release. A sticking caliper piston can cause rapid lining wear and possible rotor damage. Check the sliding motion of the caliper on the mounting pinrails. Service as necessary.

Rotors should be replaced for structural damage to the hub casting, for excessive rotor wear when the minimum rotor thickness is below spec, and for heavy scoring or excessive runout.

Lathe turn the rotor to remove minor rotor scoring or scratching that cannot be removed by hand sanding. Deep scoring usually occurs when the lining is worn down to the point where the rivets or metal pad backing contacts the rotor.

Minor rotor runout may be corrected by lathe turning. To check rotor runout, first eliminate wheel bearing end play by correctly adjusting the wheel bearing. Clamp a dial indicator to the steering knuckle assembly so that the stylus contacts the rotor about one inch from the outer edge. Rotate the rotor and take an indicator reading. If the reading exceeds 0.008-0.010 inch total lateral runout within a six-inch radius, replace or resurface the rotor.

REAR DRUM BRAKES

➧SEE FIGS. 46-60

✻✻ CAUTION

Brake shoes contain asbestos, which has been determined to be a cancer causing agent. Never clean the brake surfaces with compressed air! Avoid inhaling any dust from any brake surface! When cleaning brake surfaces, use a commercially available brake cleaning fluid.

Brake Drums

REMOVAL & INSTALLATION

Pickups and MPV

1. Raise and support the rear end on jackstands.
2. Remove the wheels.
3. Remove the drum attaching screws and insert them in the threaded holes in the drum. Turn the screws inward, evenly, to force the rum off the hub.
4. Thoroughly inspect the drum. Discard a cracked drum. If the drum is suspected of being out of round, or shows signs of wear or has a ridged or rough surface, have it turned on a lathe at a machine shop. The maximum oversize is stamped into the drum.
5. Installation is the reverse of removal. Make sure that the holes are aligned for the attaching screws. Tighten the screws evenly to install the drum.

Navajo

1. Raise the vehicle so that the wheel to be worked on is clear of the floor and install jackstands under the vehicle.
2. Remove the hub cap and the wheel/tire assembly. Remove the 3 retaining nuts and remove the brake drum. It may be necessary to back off the brake shoe adjustment in order to remove the brake drum. This is because the drum might be grooved or worn from being in service for an extended period of time.
3. Before installing a new brake drum, be sure and remove any protective coating with carburetor degreaser.
4. Install the brake drum in the reverse order of removal and adjusts the brakes.

INSPECTION

After the brake drum has been removed from the vehicle, it should be inspected for runout, severe scoring cracks, and the proper inside diameter.

Minor scores on a brake drum can be removed with fine emery cloth, provided that all grit is removed from the drum before it is installed on the vehicle.

A badly scored, rough, or out-of-round (runout) drum can be ground or turned on a brake drum lathe. Do not remove any more material from the drum than is necessary to provide a smooth surface for the brake shoe to contact. The maximum diameter of the braking surface is shown on the inside of each brake drum. Brake drums that exceed the maximum braking surface diameter shown on the brake drum, either through wear or refinishing, must be replaced. This is because after the outside wall of the brake drum reaches a certain thickness (thinner than the original thickness) the drum loses its ability to dissipate the heat created by the friction between the brake drum and the brake shoes, when the brakes are applied. Also the brake drum will have more tendency to warp and/or crack.

The maximum braking surface diameter specification, which is shown on each drum, allows for a 1.5mm (0.060 in.) machining cut over the original nominal drum diameter plus 0.76mm (0.030 in.) additional wear before reaching the diameter where the drum must be discarded. Use a brake drum micrometer to measure the inside diameter of the brake drums.

Brake Shoes

✻✻ CAUTION

Brake shoes contain asbestos, which has been determined to be a cancer causing agent. Never clean the brake surfaces with compressed air! Avoid inhaling any dust from any brake surface! When cleaning brake surfaces, use a commercially available brake cleaning fluid.

INSPECTION

After wheel and brake drum removal, visually inspect the brake shoe lining for wear. Replace the brake shoe set if the lining is worn to 0.8mm ($\frac{1}{32}$ in.) above the rivet head or the shoes metal webbing (check local inspection requirements).

REMOVAL & INSTALLATION

2-Wheel Drive Pickups

1. Raise and support the rear end on jackstands.
2. Remove the drums.
3. Remove the retracting springs.
4. Remove the holddown springs and guide pins by turning the collars 90° with a pliers, or spring tool, releasing the springs.
5. Remove the parking brake link and disconnect the parking brake cable from the lever.
6. Remove the adjusting pawl and spring.
7. Remove the shoes, noting in which place the shoe with the longer lining is installed.
8. Inspect the shoes for cracks, heat checking or contamination by oil or grease. Minimum lining thickness is 1.00mm (0.039 in.). If heat checking or discoloration is noted, the wheel cylinders are probably at fault and will have to be rebuilt or replaced.

FIG. 46 Loosen the rear drum mounting screws. An impact driver may be used if the screw is stubborn

FIG. 47 Install and tighten the retaining screws evenly in the holes provided to remove the brake drum

FIG. 48 Rear drum brake installation, Pickup shown

FIG. 49 Removing the brake shoe holddown clips, Pickup shown

➡ Never replace the shoes on one side of the truck, only! Always replace shoes on both sides!

9. Clean the backing plate with an approved cleaning fluid.
10. Lubricated the threads of the starwheel with lithium based or silicone based grease. Apply a small dab of lithium or silicone based grease to the pads on which the brake shoes ride.

To install:

11. Transfer the parking brake lever to the new shoe.
12. Position the shoes on the backing plate.
13. Connect the parking brake cable to the lever.
14. Install the holddown springs and guide pins.
15. Install the adjusting pawl and spring.
16. Install the adjusting screw assembly.
17. Install the retracting springs.
18. Install the drums.
19. Working through the 2 holes in the backing plate, reach through the hole in the center with a brake adjusting spoon and turn the star-wheel screw until the wheel is locked, that is, it can't be turned by hand.
20. Reach through the outside hole with a small bar and hold off the adjusting pawl while backing off the star-wheel about 6-7 clicks, or until the wheel is free to rotate.

➡ The adjustment should be the same on both wheels.

21. Adjust the parking brake.
22. Operate the brake pedal a few times. If the brakes feel at all spongy, bleed the system.

4-Wheel Drive Pickups

1. Raise and support the rear end on jackstands.
2. Remove the wheels.
3. Remove the brake drum.
4. Disconnect the parking brake cable.
5. Remove the holddown spring assemblies.
6. Remove the self-adjusting lever.
7. Remove the lever link.
8. Remove the pull-off spring.
9. Remove the lower shoe-to-shoe spring.
10. Remove the 2 upper return springs.
11. Remove the star-wheel adjuster.
12. Remove the brake shoes and strut.
13. Remove the parking brake cable lever.
14. Inspect the shoes for cracks, heat checking or contamination by oil or grease.

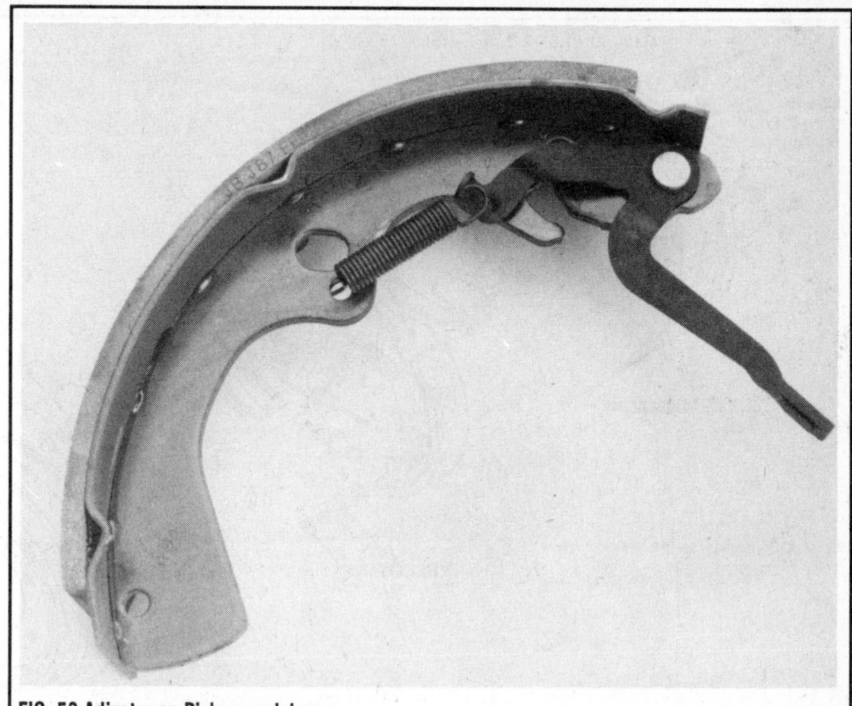

FIG. 50 Adjuster on Pickup models

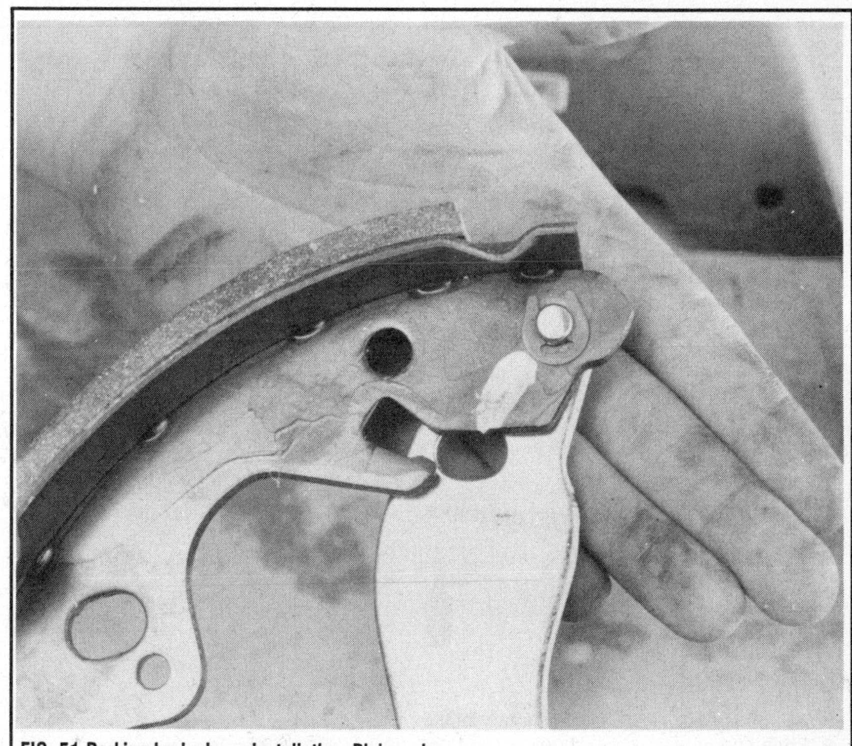

FIG. 51 Parking brake lever installation, Pickup shown

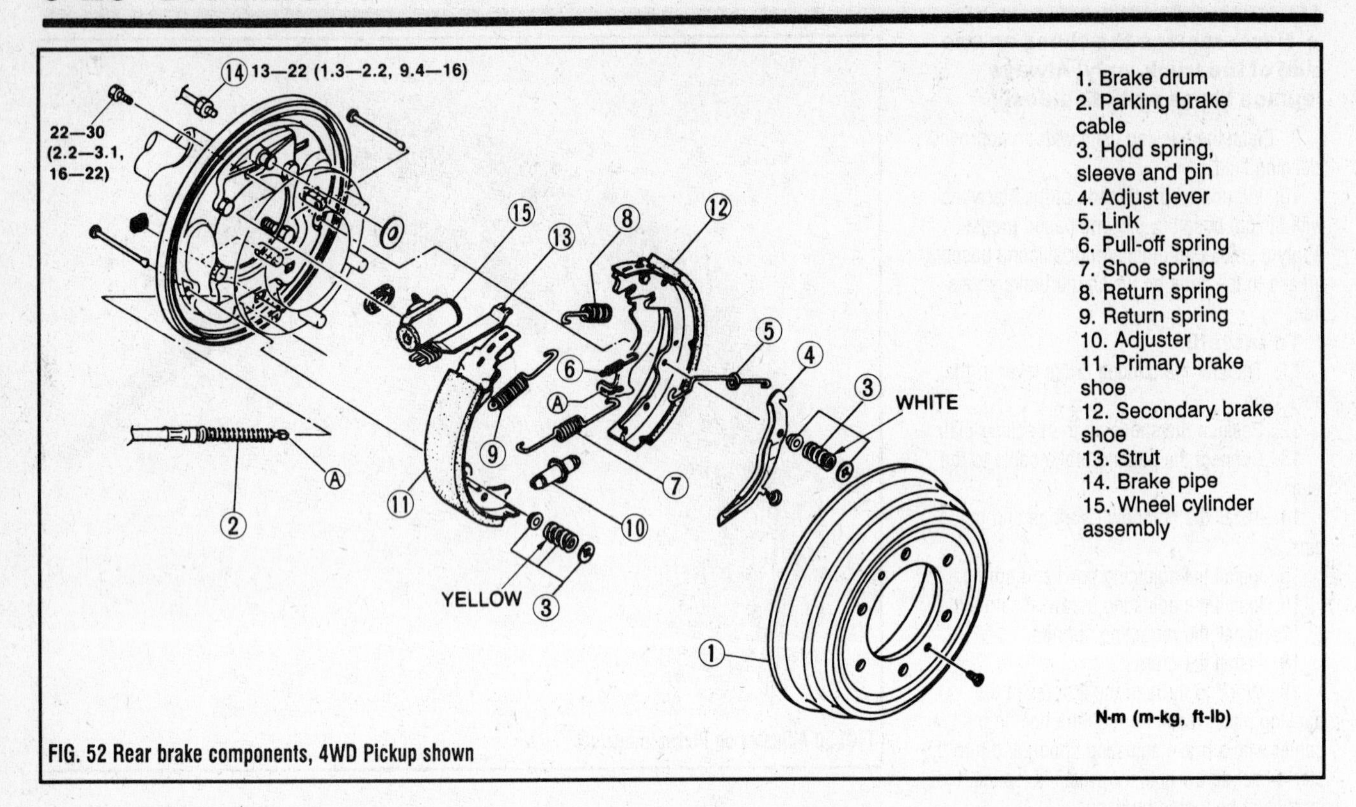

FIG. 52 Rear brake components, 4WD Pickup shown

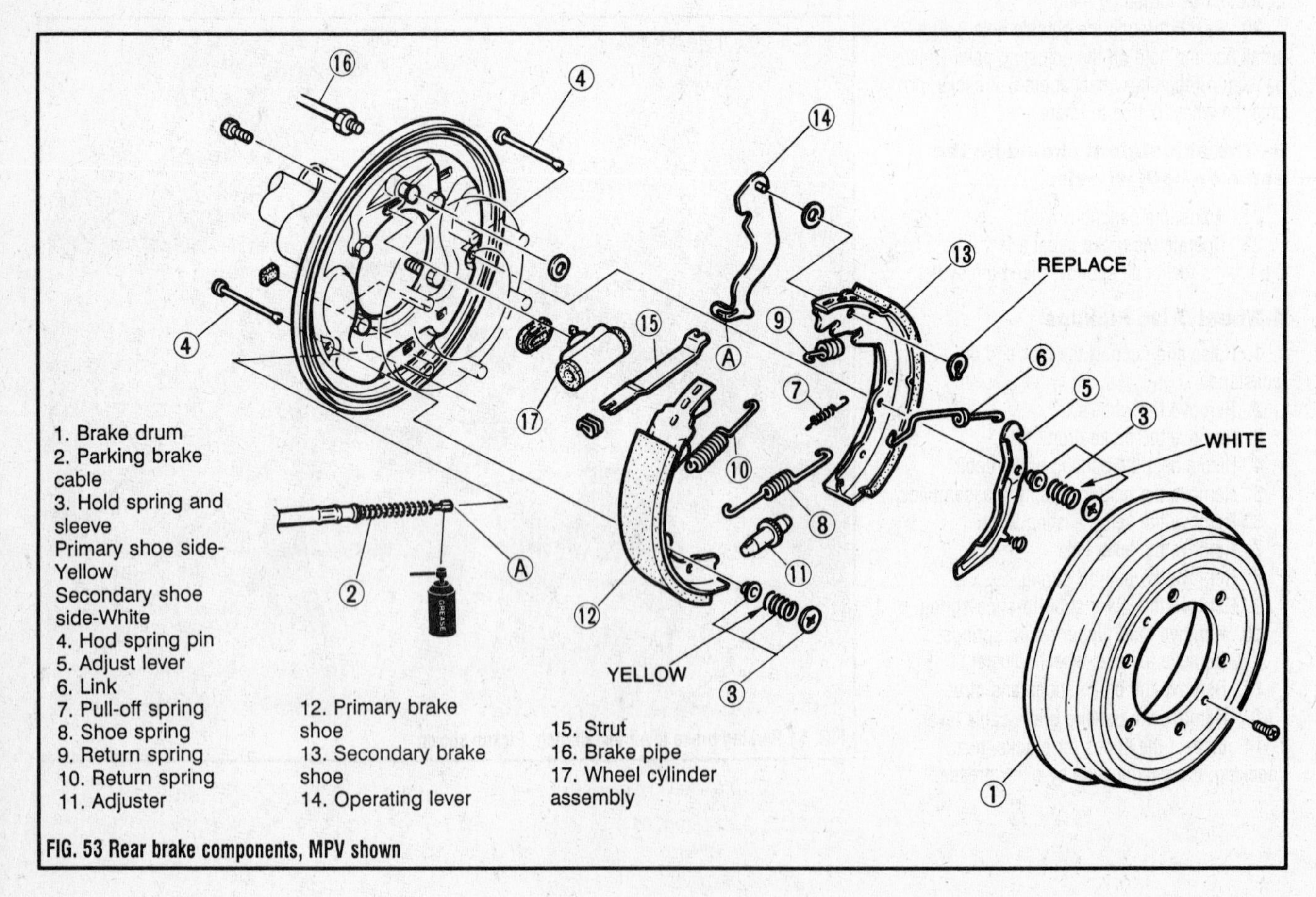

FIG. 53 Rear brake components, MPV shown

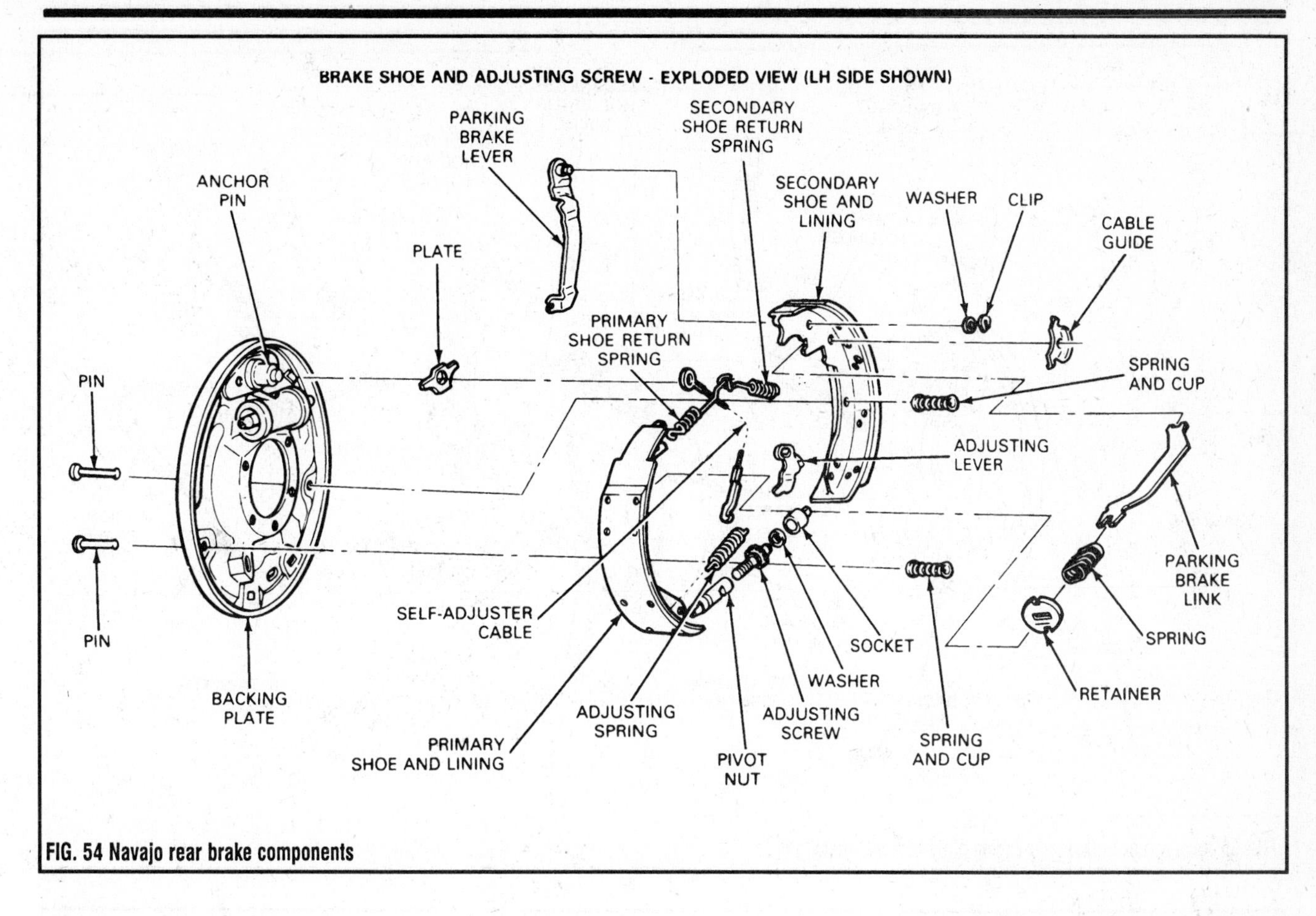

FIG. 54 Navajo rear brake components

Minimum lining thickness is 1.00mm (0.039 in.). If heat checking or discoloration is noted, the wheel cylinders are probably at fault and will have to be rebuilt or replaced.

CAUTION

Never replace the shoes on one side of the truck, only! Always replace shoes on both sides!

15. Clean the backing plate with an approved cleaning fluid.
16. Lubricated the threads of the starwheel with lithium based or silicone based grease. Apply a small dab of lithium or silicone based grease to the pads on which the brake shoes ride.

To install:

17. Position the brake shoes on the backing plate.
18. Connect the parking brake.
19. Install the holddown spring assemblies.
20. Install the strut and star-wheel adjuster.
21. Install the 2 upper return springs.
22. Install the lower spring.
23. Install the pull-off spring.
24. Install the lever link and self-adjusting lever.
25. Install the brake drum.
26. Working through the hole in the backing plate, turn the star-wheel screw with a brake adjusting spoon until the wheel is locked, that is, it can't be turned by hand.
27. Back off the adjuster about 8-10 clicks, or until the wheel is free to rotate.

➡ The adjustment should be the same on both wheels.

28. Adjust the parking brake.
29. Operate the brake pedal a few times. If the brakes feel at all spongy, bleed the system.

MPV

1. Raise and support the rear end on jackstands.
2. Remove the wheels.
3. Remove the brake drum.
4. Disconnect the parking brake cable.
5. Remove the holddown spring assemblies.
6. Remove the self-adjusting lever.
7. Remove the lever link.
8. Remove the pull-off spring.
9. Remove the lower shoe-to-shoe spring.
10. Remove the 2 upper return springs.
11. Remove the star-wheel adjuster.
12. Remove the brake shoes and strut.
13. Remove the parking brake cable lever.
14. Inspect the shoes for cracks, heat checking or contamination by oil or grease. Minimum lining thickness is 1.00mm. If heat checking or discoloration is noted, the wheel cylinders are probably at fault and will have to be rebuilt or replaced.

CAUTION

Never replace the shoes on one side of the truck, only! Always replace shoes on both sides!

15. Clean the backing plate with an approved cleaning fluid.
16. Lubricated the threads of the starwheel with lithium based or silicone based grease. Apply a small dab of lithium or silicone based grease to the pads on which the brake shoes ride.

To install:

17. Position the brake shoes on the backing plate.
18. Connect the parking brake.
19. Install the holddown spring assemblies.
20. Install the strut and star-wheel adjuster.

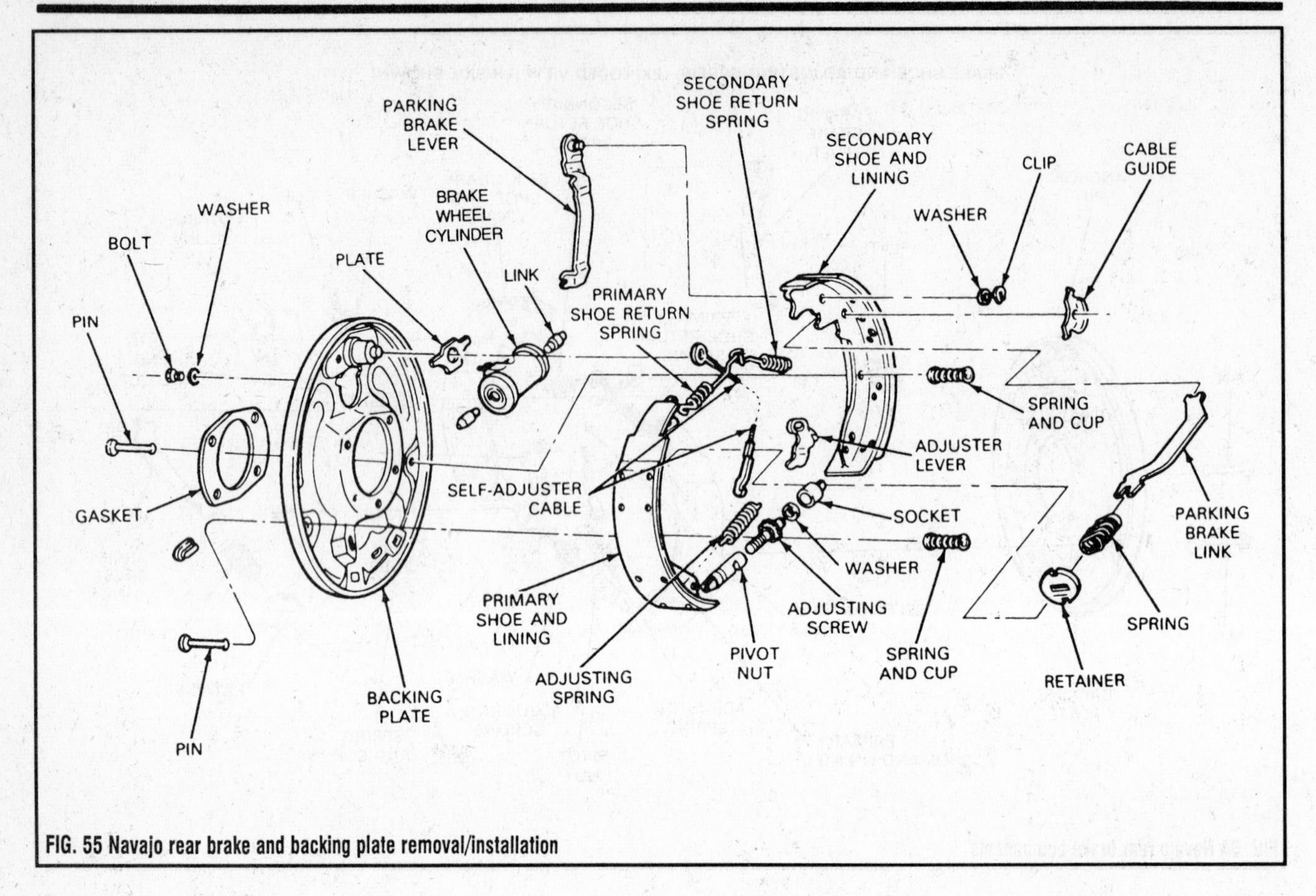

FIG. 55 Navajo rear brake and backing plate removal/installation

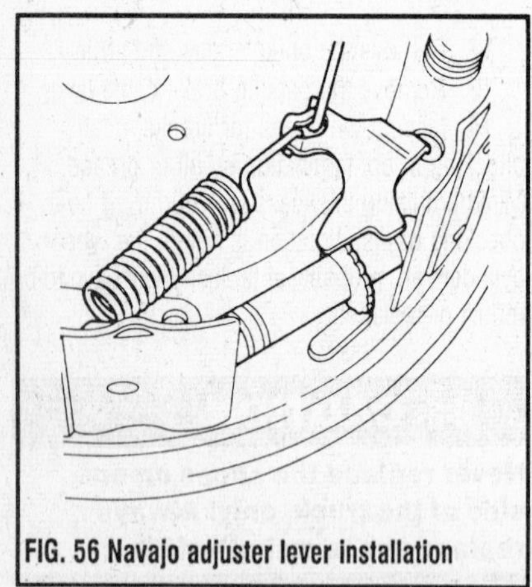
FIG. 56 Navajo adjuster lever installation

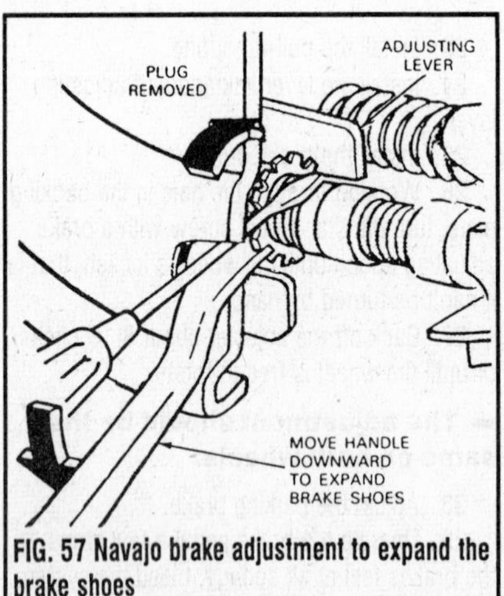

FIG. 57 Navajo brake adjustment to expand the brake shoes

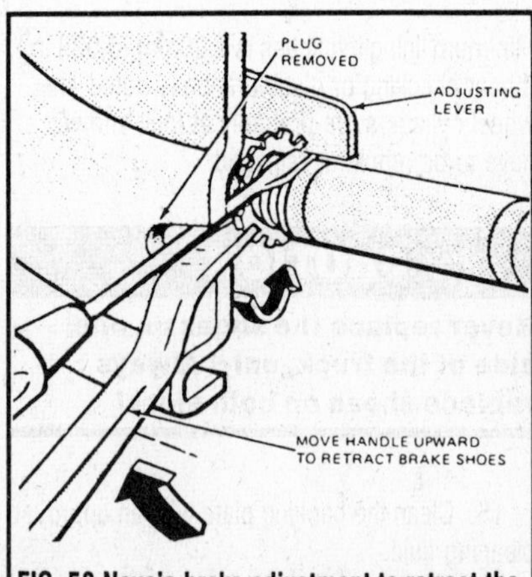

FIG. 58 Navajo brake adjustment to retract the brake shoes

21. Install the 2 upper return springs.
22. Install the lower spring.
23. Install the pull-off spring.
24. Install the lever link and self-adjusting lever.
25. Install the brake drum.
26. Working through the hole in the backing plate, turn the star-wheel screw with a brake adjusting spoon until the wheel is locked, that is, it can't be turned by hand.
27. Back off the adjuster about 8-10 clicks, or until the wheel is free to rotate.

➡ **The adjustment should be the same on both wheels.**

28. Adjust the parking brake.
29. Operate the brake pedal a few times. If the brakes feel at all spongy, bleed the system.

Navajo

1. Raise and safely support the vehicle. Remove the wheel and tire assembly and the brake drum.
2. Pull backward on the adjusting lever cable to disengage the adjusting lever from the adjusting screw. Move the outboard side of the adjusting screw upward and back off the pivot nut as far as it will go.
3. Pull the adjusting lever, cable and automatic adjuster spring down and toward the rear to unhook the pivot hook from the large hole in the secondary shoe web. Do not pry the pivot hook from the hole.
4. Remove the automatic adjuster spring and adjusting lever.

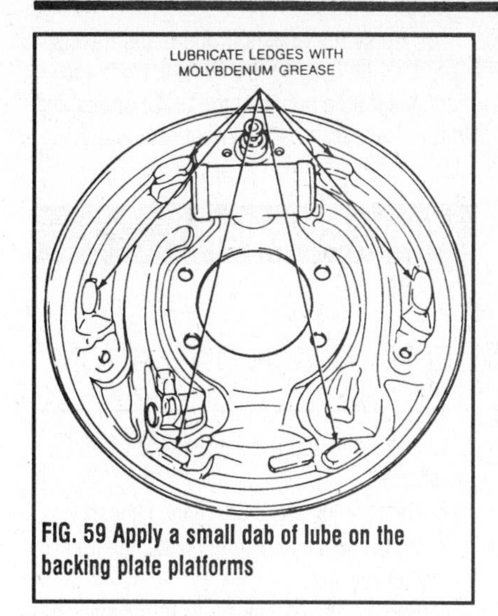

FIG. 59 Apply a small dab of lube on the backing plate platforms

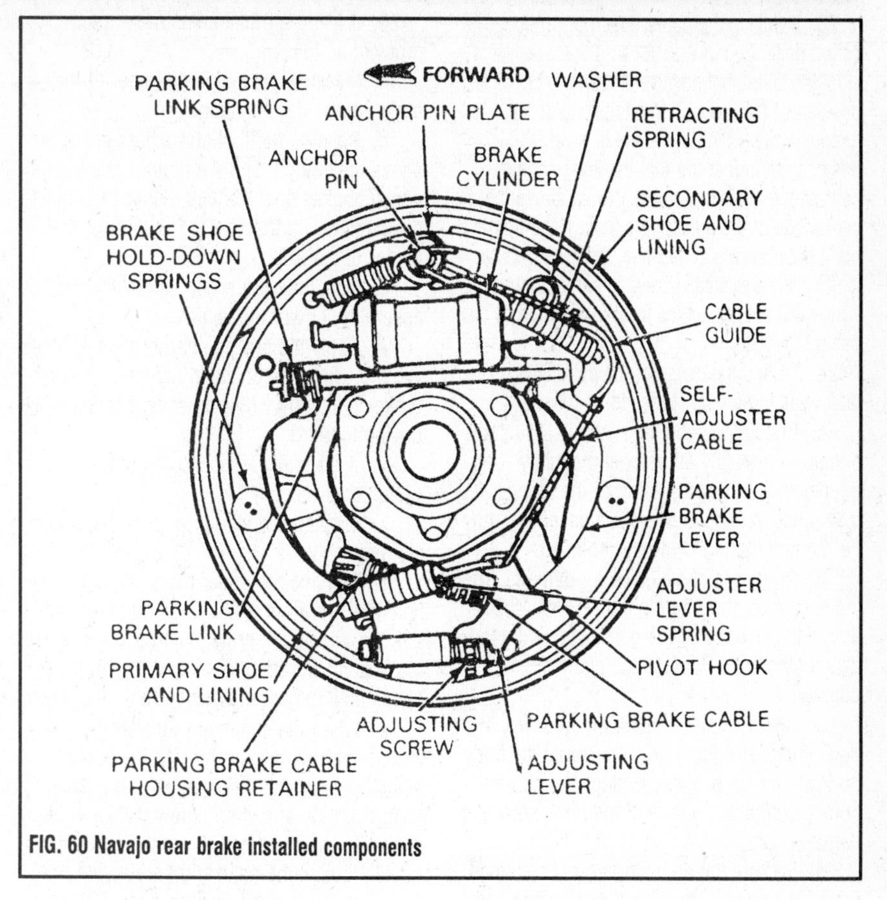

FIG. 60 Navajo rear brake installed components

5. Remove the secondary shoe-to-anchor spring using a suitable brake spring removal/installation tool. Using the tool, remove the primary shoe-to-anchor spring and unhook the cable anchor. Remove the anchor pin plate, if equipped.

6. Remove the cable guide from the secondary shoe.

7. Remove the shoe hold-down springs, shoes, adjusting screw, pivot nut and socket. Note the color and position of each hold-down spring so they can be reassembled in the same position.

8. Remove the parking brake link and spring. Disconnect the parking brake cable from the parking brake lever.

9. Remove the secondary brake shoe. Remove the retainer clip and spring washer and remove the parking brake lever.

To install:

10. Clean the backing plate ledge pads and sand lightly. Apply a light coating of high temperature lithium grease to the points where the brake shoes touch the backing plate.

11. Install the parking brake lever on the secondary shoe and secure with the spring washer and retaining clip.

12. Position the brake shoes on the backing plate and install the hold-down spring pins, springs and cups. Install the parking brake link, spring and washer. Connect the parking brake cable to the parking brake lever.

13. Install the anchor pin plate, if equipped, and place the cable anchor over the anchor pin with the crimped side toward the backing plate.

14. Install the primary shoe-to-anchor spring using the brake spring removal/installation tool.

15. Install the cable guide on the secondary shoe with the flanged hole fitted into the hole in the secondary shoe. Thread the cable around the cable guide groove.

➡ Make sure the cable is positioned in the groove and not between the guide and shoe web.

16. Install the secondary shoe-to-anchor (long) spring.

➡ Make sure the cable end is not cocked or binding on the anchor pin when installed. All parts should be flat on the anchor pin.

17. Apply high temperature lithium grease to the threads and the socket end of the adjusting screw. Turn the adjusting screw into the adjusting pivot nut to the end of the threads and then loosen, 1/2 turn.

18. Place the adjusting socket on the screw and install the assembly between the shoe ends with the adjusting screw nearest the secondary shoe.

➡ Be sure to install the adjusting screw on the same side of the vehicle from which it came. To prevent incorrect installation, the socket end of each adjusting screw is stamped with R or L, to indicate installation on the right or left side of the vehicle. The adjusting pivot nuts have lines machined around the body of the nut, 2 lines indicating the right side nut and 1 line indicating the left side nut.

19. Hook the cable hook into the hole in the adjusting lever from the outboard plate side. The adjusting levers are also stamped with an **R** or **L** to indicate right or left side installation.

20. Place the hooked end of the adjuster spring in the large hole in the primary shoe web and connect the loop end of the spring to the adjuster lever hole.

21. Pull the adjuster lever, cable and automatic adjuster spring down toward the rear to engage the pivot hook in the large hole in the secondary shoe web.

22. After installation, check the action of the adjuster by pulling the section of the cable between the cable guide and the adjusting lever toward the secondary shoe web far enough to lift the lever past a tooth on the adjusting screw wheel. The lever should snap into position behind the next tooth and releasing the cable should cause the adjuster spring to return the lever to its original position. This return action will turn the adjusting screw 1 tooth.

23. If pulling the cable does not produce the action described in Step 22 or if lever action is sluggish instead of positive and sharp, check the position of the lever on the adjusting screw toothed wheel. With the brake in a vertical position, anchor at the top, the lever should contact the adjusting wheel 1 tooth above the center line of the adjusting screw. If the contact point is below the center line, the lever will not lock on the adjusting screw wheel teeth and the screw will not turn as the lever is actuated by the cable.

24. To find the cause of the condition described in Step 23, proceed as follows:

a. Check the cable and fittings. The cable should completely fill or extend slightly beyond the crimped section of the fittings. If this does not happen, the cable assembly may be damaged and should be replaced.

b. Check the cable guide for damage. The cable groove should be parallel to the shoe web and the body of the guide should lie flat against the web. Replace the guide if it shows damage.

c. Check the pivot hook on the lever. The hook surfaces should be square with the body on the lever for proper pivoting. Repair the hook or replace the lever if the hook shows damage.

d. Be sure the adjusting screw socket is properly seated in the notch in the shoe web.

25. Adjust the brake shoes using either a brake adjustment gauge or manually with the drums installed.

26. If using a brake adjustment gauge, proceed as follows:

a. Measure the inside diameter of the brake drum with the gauge.

b. Reverse the tool and adjust the brake shoes until they touch the gauge. The gauge contact points on the shoes must be parallel to the vehicle with the center line through the center of the axle.

c. Install the drum and wheel and tire assembly. Lower the vehicle.

d. Apply the brakes sharply several times while driving the vehicle in reverse. Check brake operation by making several stops while driving forward.

27. If manually adjusting the brakes, proceed as follows:

a. Install the brake drum and wheel and tire assembly.

b. Remove the cover from the adjusting hole at the bottom of the backing plate and turn the adjusting screw, using a suitable brake adjusting tool, to expand the brake shoes until they drag against the brake drum.

c. When the shoes are against the drum, insert a narrow prybar through the brake adjusting hole and disengage the adjusting lever from the adjusting screw. While holding the adjusting lever away from the adjusting screw, loosen the adjusting screw with the brake adjusting tool, until the drum rotates freely without drag.

d. Install the adjusting hole cover and lower the vehicle.

e. Apply the brakes. If the pedal travels more than halfway to the floor, there is too much clearance between the brake shoes and drums. Repeat the adjustment procedure.

Wheel Cylinder

REMOVAL & INSTALLATION

1. Raise and support the rear end on jackstands.
2. Remove the brake drum and shoes.
3. Disconnect and plug the brake line(s) at the wheel cylinder.
4. Remove the attaching nuts from behind the backing plate and remove the wheel cylinder.
5. Installation is the reverse of removal.

OVERHAUL

➧SEE FIG. 61

Wheel cylinder rebuilding kits are available for reconditioning wheel cylinders. The kits usually contain new cup springs, cylinder cups, and in some, new boots. The most important factor to keep in mind when rebuilding wheel cylinders is cleanliness. Keep all dirt away from the wheel cylinders when you are reassembling them.

1. Remove the wheel cylinder.

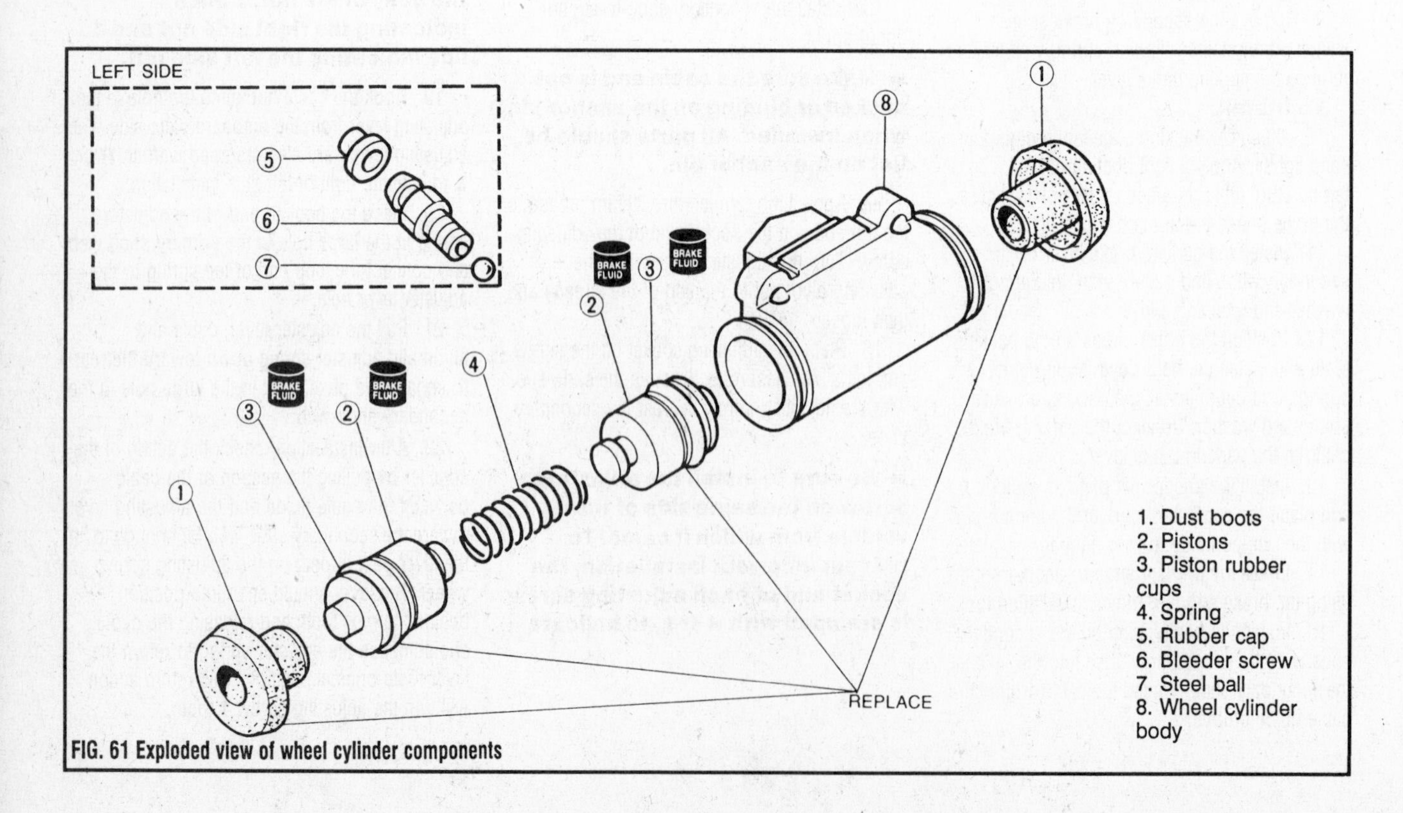

FIG. 61 Exploded view of wheel cylinder components

2. Remove the piston and adjusting screw, then remove the boot and adjuster.
3. Using compressed air in the inlet port, blow out the piston cup, expander and spring.
4. Clean all parts in clean brake fluid.
5. Inspect all parts for wear or damage. Replace any worn, discolored, misshapen or suspect part. The cylinder bore may be honed to remove light scoring, pitting or discoloration. If honing cannot polish the interior, discard the cylinder. Check the piston-to-bore clearance. If the clearance exceeds 0.15mm (0.0059 in.), replace the cylinder.
6. Assembly is the reverse of disassembly. Coat all parts in clean brake fluid before assembly.
7. Install the wheel cylinder and all other parts. Bleed the system.

Brake Backing Plate

Refer to the Rear Wheel Bearing procedures in Section 7 for reference. Backing plate replacement is necessary when grooves are worn into the raised platform surfaces the brake shoes slid on, or other damage occurs. The grooves will prevent proper brake shoe release causing rapid lining and drum wear. The platform surfaces should always be lubricated with a dab of white grease when the brake shoes are replaced, or other services requiring shoe removal is performed.

Follow the procedures for drum and shoe removal and installation. Disconnect the brake line(s) to the rear cylinder. Remove the retaining bolts/nuts securing the backing plate to the rear axle. Remove the backing plate. Always replace the mounting gasket, if equipped, when installing the backing plate.

PARKING BRAKE

➧SEE FIGS. 62-66

Cables

REMOVAL & INSTALLATION

Front

PICKUPS AND MPV

1. Make sure the parking brake is fully released. Remove the parking brake lever adjusting nut from the forward end of the front cable.
2. Remove the seat(s) and roll back the front format, as required. On MPV, remove the cable cover. Raise and safely support the vehicle, as necessary.
3. Disengage the rear cables from the equalizer and remove the spring. Disconnect the front cable from the equalizer.
4. Remove the bolts from the cable retaining straps and remove the cable.
5. Install in reverse order. Adjust the parking brake.

NAVAJO

1. Raise and safely support the vehicle.
2. Back off the equalizer nut and remove the cable end of the intermediate cable from the tension limiter.
3. Remove the intermediate cable from the bracket and disconnect the intermediate cable from the front cable.
4. Lower the vehicle. Remove the forward ball end of the parking brake cable from the control assembly clevis.
5. Remove the cable from the control assembly.
6. Using a cord attached to the control lever end of the cable, remove the cable from the vehicle pulling it up into the passenger compartment.

To install:

7. Transfer the cord to the new cable. Position the cable in the vehicle, routing the cable through the dash panel. Remove the cord and secure the cable to the control.
8. Connect the forward ball end of the brake cable to the clevis of the control assembly. Raise and safely support the vehicle.
9. Route the cable through the bracket. Connect the front cable to the intermediate cable.
10. Connect the slug of the front or intermediate cable to the tension limiter connector. Adjust the parking brake cable at the equalizer using initial adjustment or field adjustment, as necessary.
11. Rotate both wheels to make sure the parking brakes are not dragging.

Rear

PICKUPS AND MPV

1. Make sure the parking brake is fully released. Loosen the parking brake lever adjusting nut.
2. Remove the seat(s) and roll back the front format, as required. On MPV, remove the cable cover.
3. Raise and safely support the vehicle. Disconnect the rear cable from the equalizer.
4. Remove the rear wheel and tire assembly, brake drum and brake shoes. Disconnect the cable from the backing plate.
5. Remove the bolts from the cable retaining straps and disconnect the spring from the cable. Remove the cable.
6. Install in reverse order. Adjust the parking brake.

NAVAJO

1. Release the parking brake control.
2. Raise and safely support the vehicle. Remove the wheel and tire assembly, brake drum and brake shoes.
3. Remove the locknut on the threaded rod at the equalizer. Disconnect the rear parking brake cable from the equalizer.
4. Compress the prongs that retain the cable housing to the frame bracket or crossmember and pull out the cable and housing.
5. Working on the wheel side of the backing plate, compress the prongs on the cable retainer so they can pass through the hole in the brake backing plate.
6. Lift the cable out of the slot in the parking brake lever, attached to the secondary brake shoe, and remove the cable through the brake backing plate hole.

To install:

7. Route the cable through the hole in the backing plate. Insert the cable anchor behind the slot in the parking brake lever. Make sure the cable is securely engaged in the parking brake lever so the cable return spring is holding the cable in the parking brake lever.
8. Push the retainer through the hole in the backing plate so the retainer prongs engage the backing plate.
9. Properly route the cable and insert the front of the cable through the frame bracket or crossmember until the prongs expand. Connect the rear cables to the equalizer.

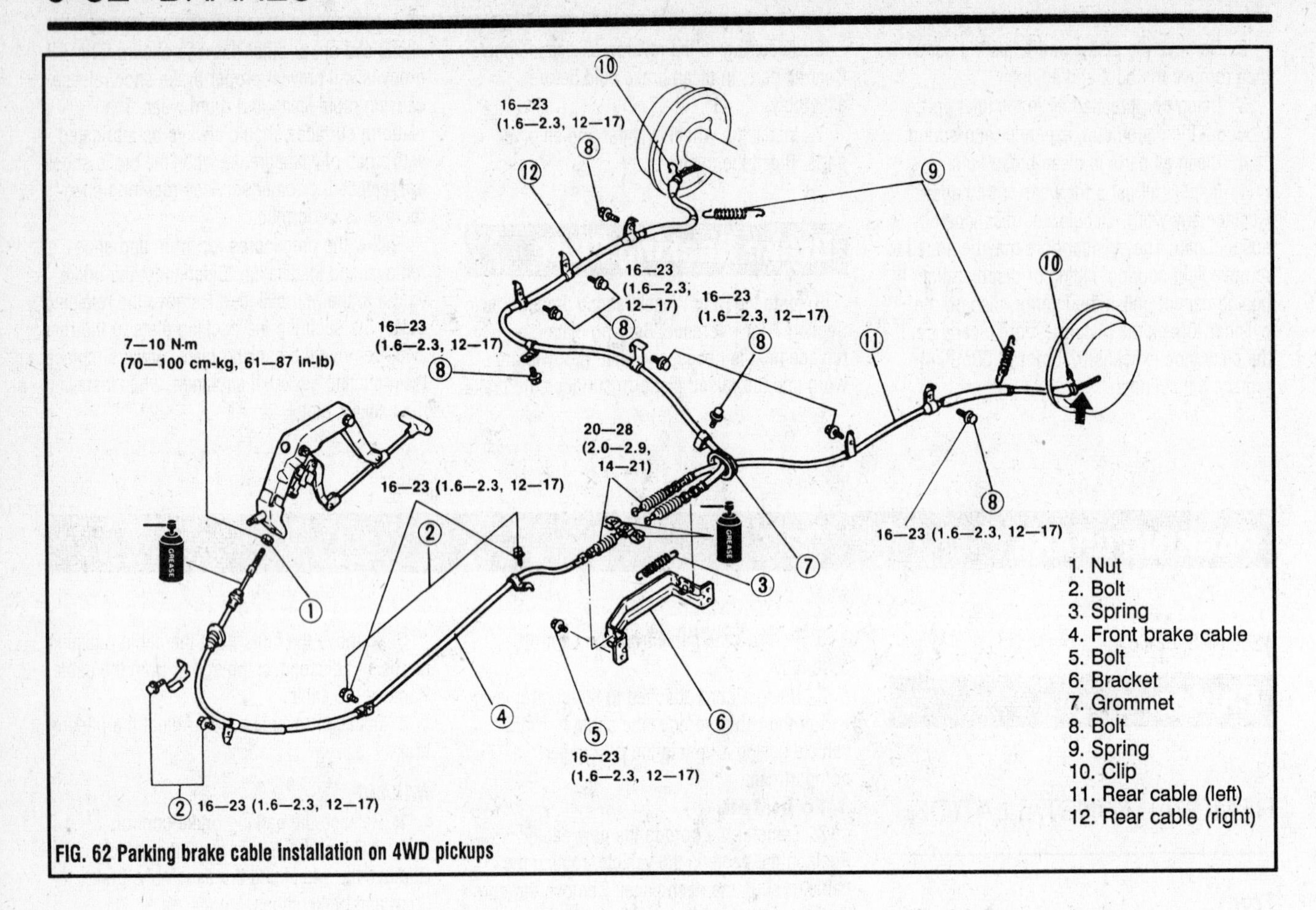

FIG. 62 Parking brake cable installation on 4WD pickups

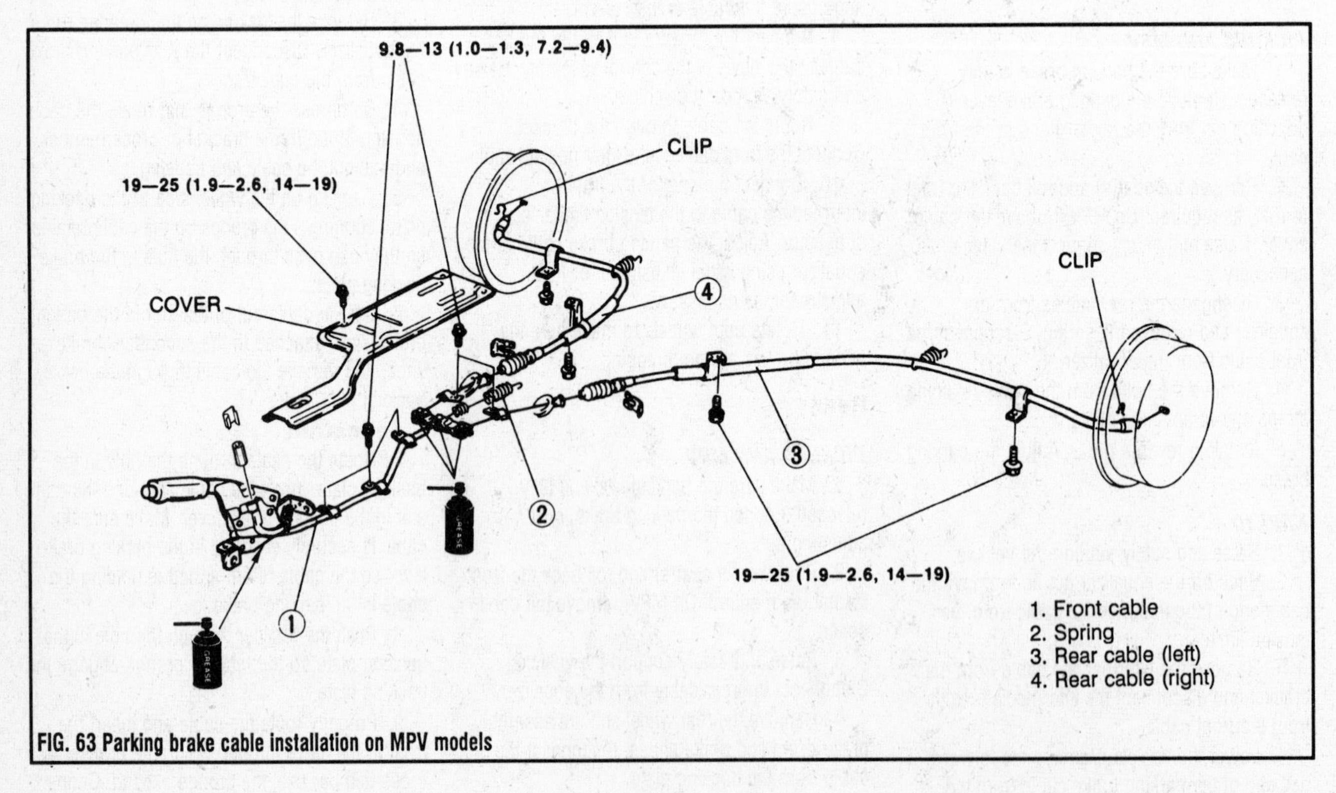

FIG. 63 Parking brake cable installation on MPV models

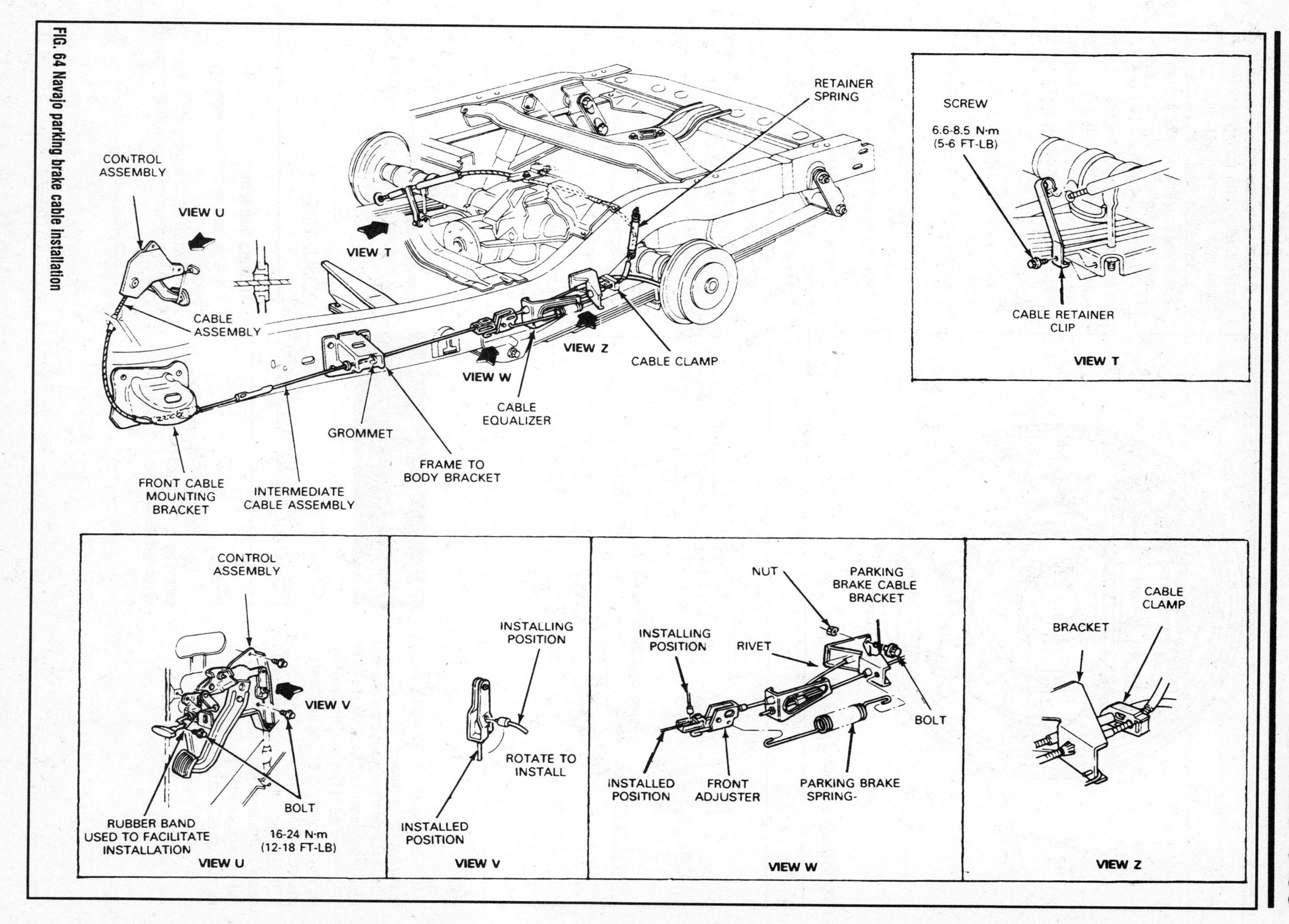
CONTROL
ASSEMBLY
VIEW U
VIEW T
RETAINER
SPRING
CABLE
ASSEMBLY
VIEW Z
CABLE CLAMP
VIEW W
CABLE
EQUALIZER
GROMMET
FRAME TO
BODY BRACKET
FRONT CABLE
MOUNTING
BRACKET
INTERMEDIATE
CABLE ASSEMBLY
SCREW
6.6-8.5 N·m
(5-6 FT-LB)
CABLE RETAINER
CLIP
VIEW T
CONTROL
ASSEMBLY
VIEW V
BOLT
RUBBER BAND
USED TO FACILITATE
INSTALLATION
16-24 N·m
(12-18 FT-LB)
VIEW U
INSTALLING
POSITION
ROTATE TO
INSTALL
INSTALLED
POSITION
VIEW V
NUT
PARKING
BRAKE CABLE
BRACKET
INSTALLING
POSITION
RIVET
BOLT
INSTALLED
POSITION
FRONT
ADJUSTER
PARKING BRAKE
SPRING-
VIEW W
CABLE
CLAMP
BRACKET
VIEW Z

FIG. 64 Navajo parking brake cable installation

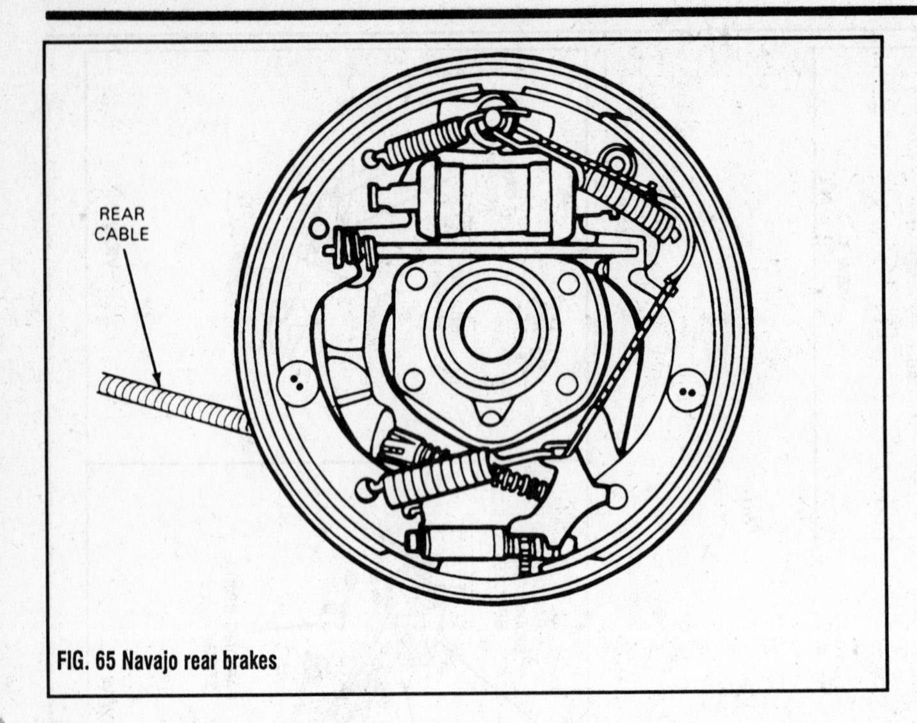

FIG. 65 Navajo rear brakes

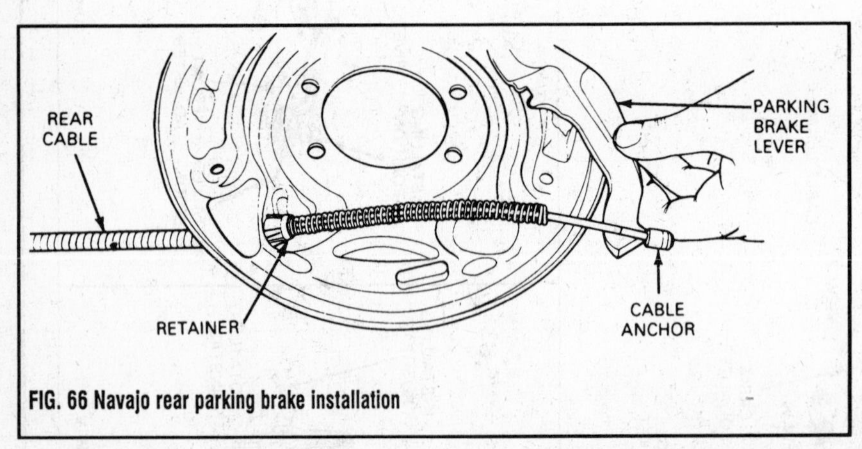

FIG. 66 Navajo rear parking brake installation

10. Rotate the equalizer 90° and recouple the threaded rod to the equalizer.
11. Install the brake shoes, brake drum and wheel and tire assembly. Adjust the rear brakes.
12. Adjust the parking brake tension using the initial adjustment or the field adjustment procedure, as necessary.
13. Apply and release the parking brake control several times. Rotate both wheels to make sure the parking brakes are applied and released and not dragging.

Parking Brake Control

SEE FIGS. 67-68

REMOVAL & INSTALLATION

Pickup

1. Block the wheels firmly and release the parking brake. Disconnect the cable from the operating lever. Disconnect the parking brake switch.
2. Remove the operating lever support bracket mounting bolts and brace bracket mounting bolts. Remove the assembly.
3. Service as required. Place the assembly in position and secure the mounting brackets. Connect and adjust the parking brake cable.
4. Install the parking brake switch so that it contacts the parking brake lever when the lever is fully released. Turn the ignition switch ON and check that the warning lamp switch comes on when the lever is pulled out one notch.

MPV

1. Block the wheels firmly and release the parking brake.
2. Remove the parking brake lever assembly cover.
3. Disconnect the apply warning switch.
4. Disconnect the parking brake cable. Remove the assembly mounting bolts and remove the assembly. Service as required.
5. Place the assembly in position and secure the mounting bolts. Install and adjust the parking brake cable. Install and adjust the parking brake apply warning switch.
6. Install the parking brake switch so that it contacts the parking brake lever when the lever is fully released. Turn the ignition switch ON and check that the warning lamp switch comes on when the lever is pulled out one notch.

Navajo

1. Loosen the adjusting nut at the parking brake equalizer.
2. From under the instrument panel, remove the bolts attaching the control assembly to the body side panel.
3. Disconnect the parking brake cable from the control assembly and remove the assembly. Service as required.
4. Connect the parking brake cable to the control assembly. Place the control in position against the side panel and secure it with the mounting bolts. Tighten the bolts to 12-18 ft. lbs.
5. Adjust the parking brake.

ADJUSTMENT

Pickups and MPV

1. Make sure the rear brake shoes are properly adjusted.
2. Start the engine and depress the brake pedal several times while the vehicle is moving in reverse.
3. Stop the engine.

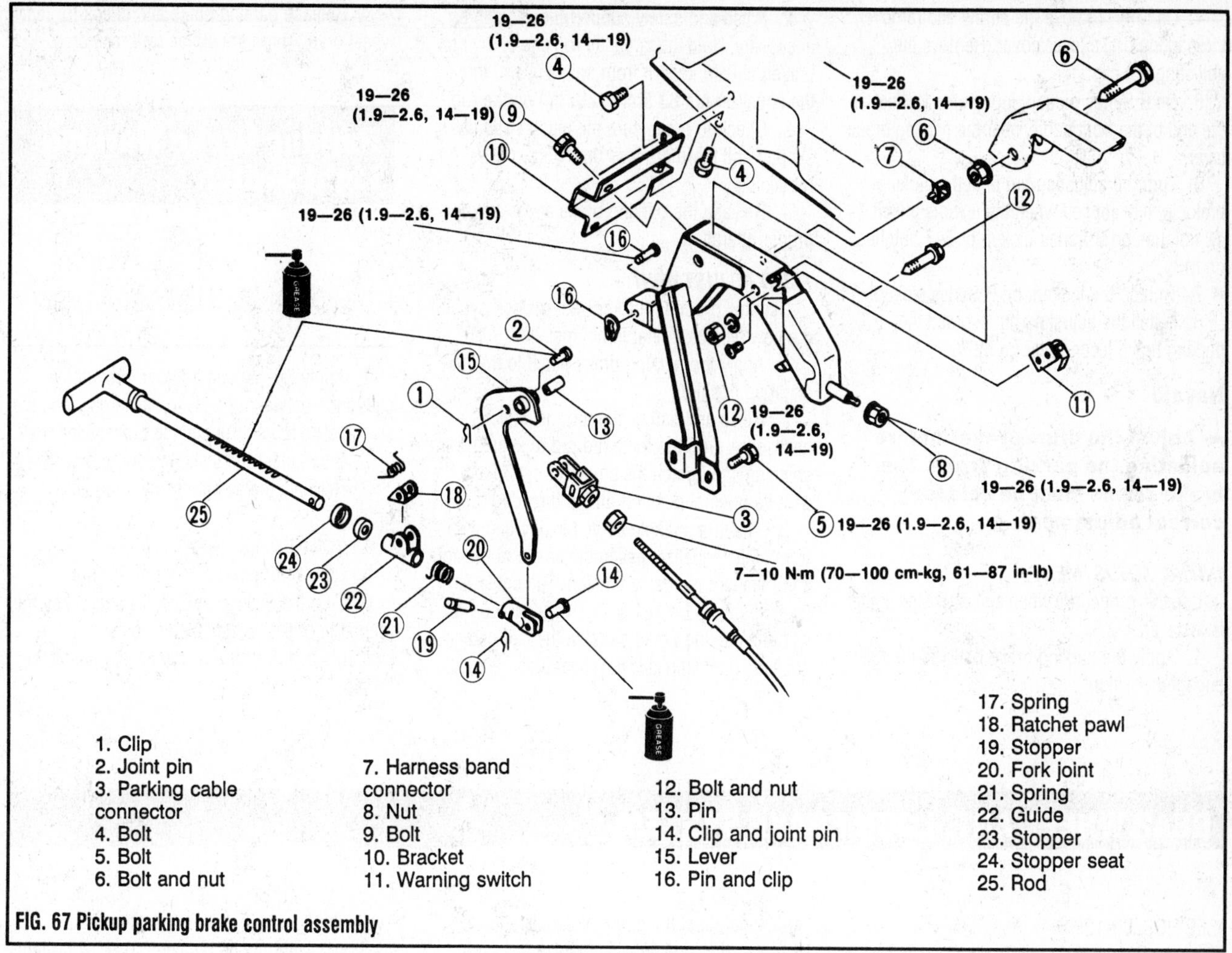

FIG. 67 Pickup parking brake control assembly

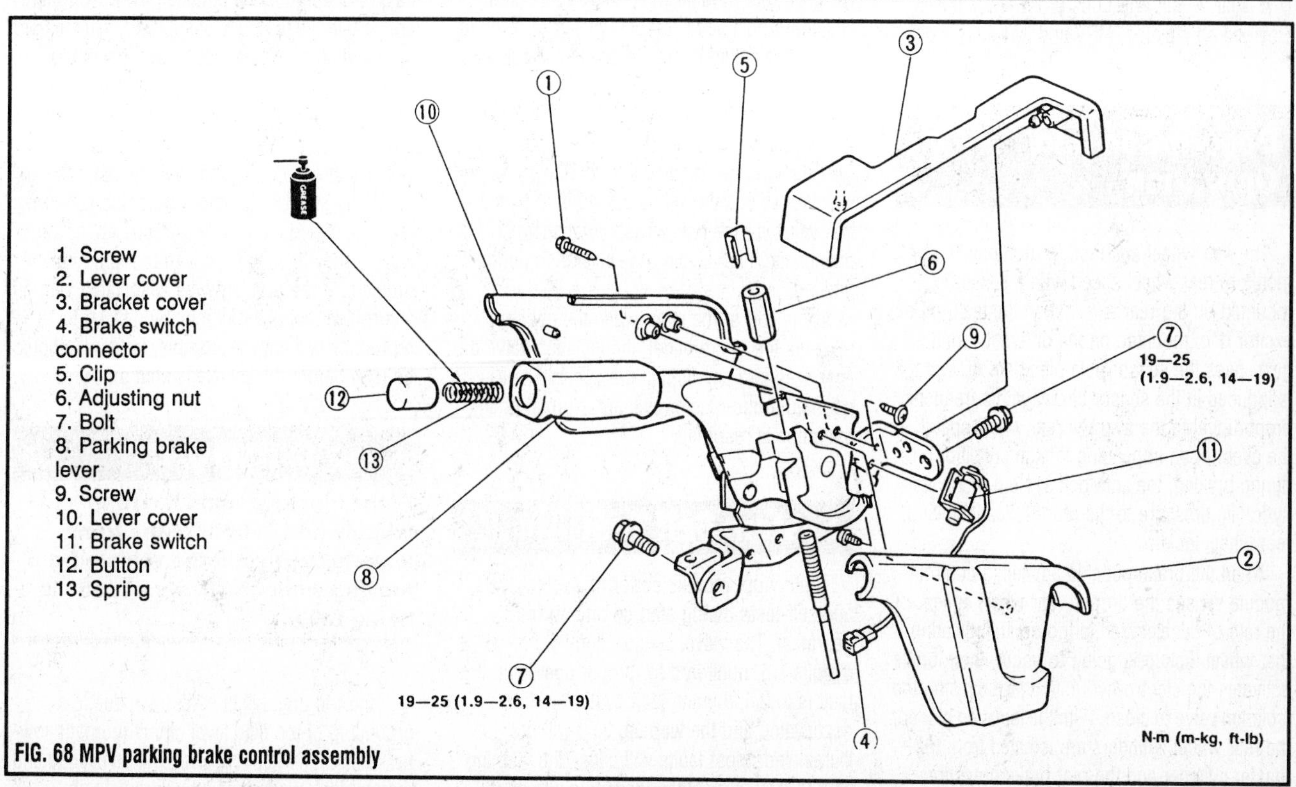

FIG. 68 MPV parking brake control assembly

4. On MPV, remove the screw and remove the parking brake lever cover. Remove the adjusting nut clip.
5. On B Series pickup, loosen the locknut at the end of the front cable, near the parking brake lever.
6. Turn the adjusting nut until the parking brake is fully applied when the lever is pulled 7–12 notches on B Series pickup or 5–7 notches on MPV.
7. Tighten the locknut on B Series pickup.
8. Install the adjusting nut clip and the parking brake lever cover on MPV.

Navajo

➡ **Adjust the drum brakes before adjusting the parking brake. The brake drums must be cold for correct adjustment.**

INITIAL ADJUSTMENT

Use this procedure when a new tension limiter is installed.

1. Apply the parking brake pedal to the fully engaged position.
2. Raise and safely support the vehicle, as necessary. Hold the threaded rod end of the right brake cable to keep it from spinning and thread the equalizer nut 63.5mm ($2^1/_2$ in.) up the rod.
3. Check to make sure the cinch strap has slipped and there are less than 35mm ($1^3/_8$ in.) remaining.
4. Release the parking brake and check for proper operation.

FIELD ADJUSTMENT

Use this procedure to correct a slack system if a new tension limiter is not installed.

1. Apply the parking brake pedal to the fully engaged position.
2. Raise and safely support the vehicle, as necessary. Grip the threaded rod to keep it from spinning and tighten the equalizer nut 6 full turns past its original position on the threaded rod.
3. Attach a suitable cable tension gauge in front of the equalizer assembly on the front cable and measure the cable tension. The cable tension should be 181.5-272 kg (400–600 lbs.) with the parking brake pedal in the last detent position. If tension is low, repeat Steps 2 and 3.
4. Release parking brake and check for rear wheel drag. There should be no brake drag.

Parking Brake Warning Light Switch

REMOVAL & INSTALLATION

1. Apply the parking brake to provide clearance between the switch assembly and the switch stop tab on the parking brake lever shaft.
2. Disconnect the switch wiring connector.
3. Remove the switch from its mounting bracket.
4. Install the attaching screws.
5. Connect the switch wire connector.
6. Turn the ignition switch ON and check the operation of the switch. No adjustment to the switch is possible. If it is defective, replace the switch.

REAR WHEEL ANTI-LOCK BRAKE SYSTEM

➧SEE FIGS. 69-129

A Rear Wheel Anti-Lock Brake System is provided on pickups, MPV and Navajo models.

Description and Operation

The rear wheel anti-lock system continually monitors rear wheel speed with a sensor mounted on the rear axle. When the teeth on an excitor ring, mounted on the differential ring gear, pass the sensor pole piece, an AC voltage is induced in the sensor circuit with a frequency proportional to the average rear wheel speed. In the event of an impending lockup condition during braking, the anti-lock system modulates hydraulic pressure to the rear brakes inhibiting rear wheel lockup.

When the brake pedal is applied, a control module senses the drop in rear wheel speed. If the rate of deceleration is too great, indicating that wheel lockup is going to occur, the module activates the electro-hydraulic valve causing the isolation valve to close. With the isolation closed, the rear wheel cylinders are isolated from the master cylinder and the rear brake pressure cannot increase. If the rate of deceleration is still too great, the module will energize the dump solenoid with a series of rapid pulses to bleed off rear cylinder fluid into an accumulator built into the electro-hydraulic valve. This will reduce the rear wheel cylinder pressure and allow the rear wheels to spin back to the vehicle speed. Continuing under module control, the dump and isolation solenoids will be pulsed in a manner that will keep the rear wheels rotating while still maintaining high levels of deceleration during braking.

At the end of the stop, when the operator releases the brake pedal, the isolation valve de-energizes and any fluid in the accumulator is returned to the master cylinder. Normal brake operation is resumed.

System Self Test

The control module performs system tests and self-tests during start up and normal operation. The valve, sensor, and fluid level circuits are monitored for proper operation. If a fault is found, the anti-lock system will be deactivated and the warning light will be illuminated. Most faults will cause the warning light to stay on until the ignition is turned off. While the light is illuminated a diagnostic flashout code may be obtained. However, there are certain faults (those associated with the fluid level switch or loss of power to the module), which cause the system to be deactivated and the warning light to be illuminated, but will not provide a diagnostic flashout code.

In most cases, the code will be lost if the vehicle is shut off. In other cases, the code may reappear when the vehicle is restarted, or the vehicle may have to be driven to reproduce the problem. If the problem was associated with an intermittent condition, it may be difficult to reproduce. Whenever possible, the code should be read before the vehicle is shut off.

CAUTION

Place blocks behind the rear wheels and in front of the front wheels to prevent the vehicle from moving while the flashout code is being taken.

If the red brake light is also on, due to a grounding of the fluid level circuit (perhaps low brake fluid), no flashout code will be flashed and the anti-lock warning lamp will remain on steadily. If there is more than one system fault, only the first recognized code may be obtained.

A flashout code may be obtained only when the anti-lock warning light is on. No code will be flashed when the system is OK.

To check the anti-lock warning light for normal operation, insert the key in the ignition lock and turn it to the ON or START positions. The light should perform a self-check, glowing for about two seconds.

To obtain the flashout code, keep the ignition key in the **ON** position.

⁂ CAUTION

Place blocks behind the rear wheels and in front of the front wheels to prevent the vehicle from moving while the flashout code is being taken.

1. Locate the diagnostic connector. On pickups and MPVs, the blue three pin connector is located in the left of the engine compartment. See the illustration for Navajo connector, which is located on the main wire bundle inside of cab under the dash, slightly rearward driver side.
2. Attach a jumper wire to the terminal C. On pickups, the yellow wire; on MPVs, the gray/white wire.
3. On Navajo models, attach a jumper wire to the connector with the black/orange wire.
4. Momentarily ground the jumper to the chassis. When the ground is made and broken, the anti-lock warning lamp should begin to flash.

➡ A flashing pattern consists of short flashes and ends with a long flash. Count the short flashes and include the long flash in the count. A same flashing pattern repeats until the ignition switch is turned OFF. Count the flash sequence several times to verify the number of flashes.

Precautions

Use caution when disassembling any hydraulic components as the system will contain residual pressure. Cover the area around the component to be removed with a shop cloth to catch any brake fluid spray. Do not allow brake fluid to come in contact with painted surfaces.

Electronic Control Unit

REMOVAL & INSTALLATION

1. Disconnect the negative battery cable.
2. On B Series pickup, remove the driver's seat. On MPV, remove the inside trim panel from the left rear of the vehicle. The control unit is located under the dash on Navajo.
3. Disconnect the electrical connector from the control unit.
4. Remove the attaching screws and remove the control unit.
5. Installation is the reverse of the removal procedure. Check the system for proper operation.

Electro-Hydraulic Valve

REMOVAL & INSTALLATION

1. Disconnect the negative battery cable.
2. Disconnect and plug the 2 brake lines connected to the valve.
3. Disconnect the wiring harness from the valve harness.
4. Remove the screw(s) retaining the valve and remove the valve.
5. Installation is the reverse of the removal procedure. Tighten the valve retaining screw(s) to 14–19 ft. lbs. (19–25 Nm) on all except Navajo where the torque is 11–14 ft. lbs. (15–20 Nm). Bleed the brake system.

Speed Sensor

REMOVAL & INSTALLATION

Except Navajo

1. Disconnect the negative battery cable.
2. Pull the wiring harness connector off.
3. Remove the sensor hold-down bolt and remove the sensor from the axle housing.

To install:

4. Clean the axle mounting surface. Use care to prevent dirt from entering the axle housing.
5. Inspect the sensor O-ring for damage and replace, if necessary.
6. Check the sensor-to-sensor rotor clearance as follows:
    a. Measure the distance between the sensor attaching surface and the sensor rotor teeth.
    b. Measure the distance between the sensor attaching surface and the sensor pole piece.
    c. Subtract the distance recorded in Step B from the distance recorded in Step a.
    d. The clearance should be 0.5–1.0mm (0.020–0.039 in.) on B2200 or 0.5–1.2mm (0.020–0.047 in.) on B2600 and MPV.
7. If the clearance is less than specified, increase it using adjusting shim P049 27 155 or equivalent, during sensor installation. If the clearance is more than specified, replace the speed sensor.
8. Lubricate the speed sensor with clean engine oil and install the speed sensor. Tighten the attaching bolt to 12–17 ft. lbs. (16–23 Nm).

Navajo

1. Disconnect the negative battery cable.
2. Pull the wiring harness connector off.
3. Remove the sensor hold-down bolt and remove the sensor from the axle housing.
4. Clean the axle mounting surface. Use care to prevent dirt from entering the axle housing.
5. Inspect and clean the magnetized sensor pole piece to ensure that it is free from loose metal particles which could cause erratic system operation. Inspect the sensor O-ring for damage and replace, if necessary.
6. Lightly lubricate the sensor O-ring with motor oil, align the sensor bolt hole and install. Do not apply force to the plastic sensor connector. The sensor flange should slide to the mounting surface. This will insure the air gap setting is between 0.127–1.14mm (0.005–0.045 in.).
7. Install the hold down bolt and tighten to 25–30 ft. lbs. (34–40 Nm).
8. Inspect the blue sensor connector seal and replace if missing or damaged. Push the connector on the sensor.
9. Connect the negative battery cable.

Sensor Rotor

INSPECTION

1. Remove the speed sensor.
2. View the sensor rotor teeth through the sensor hole. Rotate the rear axle and check the sensor rotor teeth for damage or breakage. Dented or broken teeth could cause the rear anti-lock brake system to function when not required.

REMOVAL & INSTALLATION

To service the sensor rotor, the differential case must be removed from the axle housing and the sensor rotor pressed off the case.

➡ Upon removal, the sensor rotor is to be discarded. It is not to be reused.

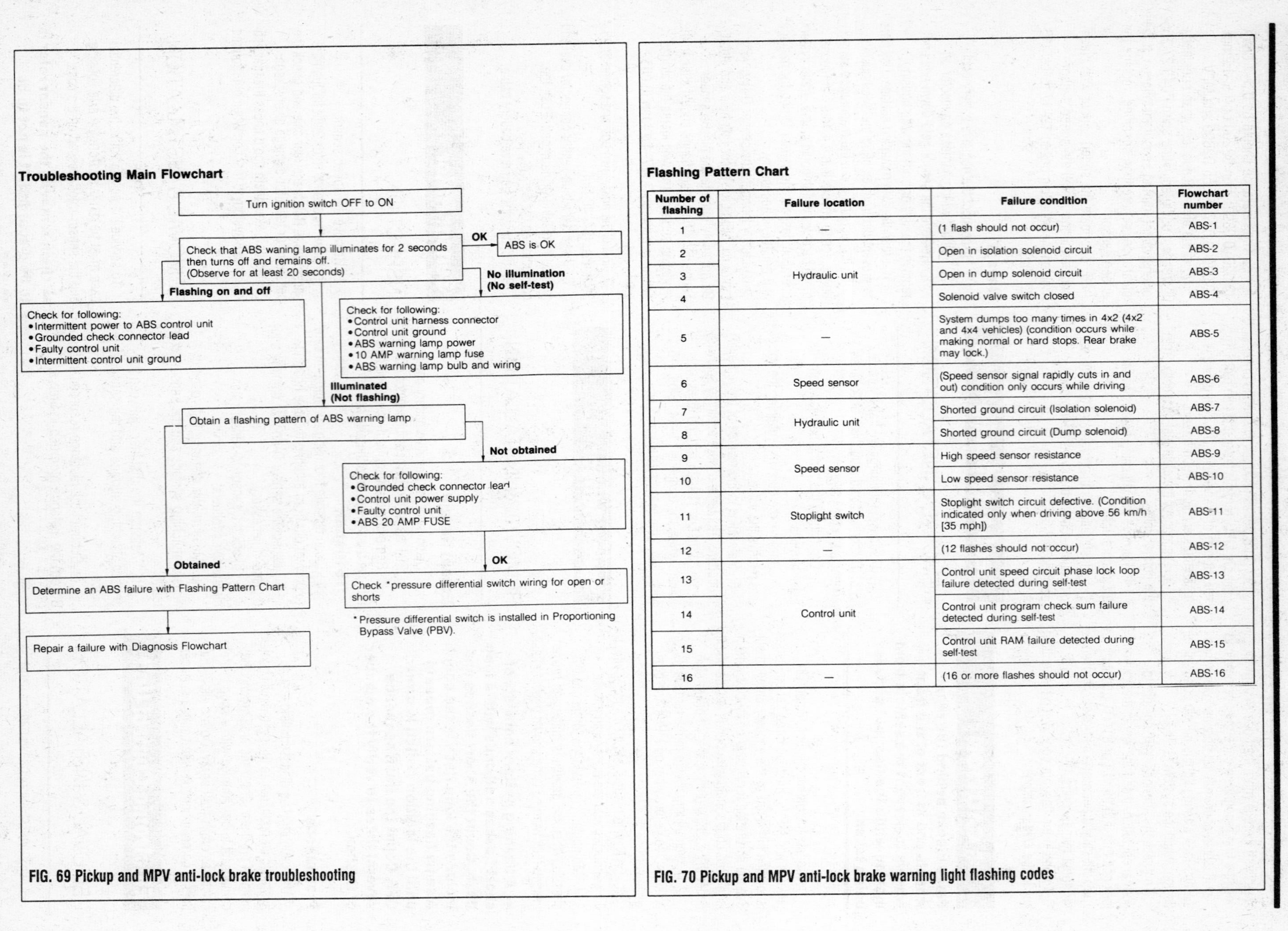
Troubleshooting Main Flowchart
Turn ignition switch OFF to ON
Check that ABS waning lamp illuminates for 2 seconds then turns off and remains off. (Observe for at least 20 seconds)
OK
ABS is OK
Flashing on and off
Check for following:
•Intermittent power to ABS control unit
•Grounded check connector lead
•Faulty control unit
•Intermittent control unit ground
No illumination (No self-test)
Check for following:
•Control unit harness connector
•Control unit ground
•ABS warning lamp power
•10 AMP warning lamp fuse
•ABS warning lamp bulb and wiring
Illuminated (Not flashing)
Obtain a flashing pattern of ABS warning lamp
Not obtained
Check for following:
•Grounded check connector lead
•Control unit power supply
•Faulty control unit
•ABS 20 AMP FUSE
Obtained
OK
Determine an ABS failure with Flashing Pattern Chart
Check *pressure differential switch wiring for open or shorts
*Pressure differential switch is installed in Proportioning Bypass Valve (PBV).
Repair a failure with Diagnosis Flowchart

FIG. 69 Pickup and MPV anti-lock brake troubleshooting

Flashing Pattern Chart

Number of flashing	Failure location	Failure condition	Flowchart number
1	—	(1 flash should not occur)	ABS-1
2	Hydraulic unit	Open in isolation solenoid circuit	ABS-2
3		Open in dump solenoid circuit	ABS-3
4		Solenoid valve switch closed	ABS-4
5	—	System dumps too many times in 4x2 (4x2 and 4x4 vehicles) (condition occurs while making normal or hard stops. Rear brake may lock.)	ABS-5
6	Speed sensor	(Speed sensor signal rapidly cuts in and out) condition only occurs while driving	ABS-6
7	Hydraulic unit	Shorted ground circuit (Isolation solenoid)	ABS-7
8		Shorted ground circuit (Dump solenoid)	ABS-8
9	Speed sensor	High speed sensor resistance	ABS-9
10		Low speed sensor resistance	ABS-10
11	Stoplight switch	Stoplight switch circuit defective. (Condition indicated only when driving above 56 km/h [35 mph])	ABS-11
12	—	(12 flashes should not occur)	ABS-12
13	Control unit	Control unit speed circuit phase lock loop failure detected during self-test	ABS-13
14		Control unit program check sum failure detected during self-test	ABS-14
15		Control unit RAM failure detected during self-test	ABS-15
16	—	(16 or more flashes should not occur)	ABS-16

FIG. 70 Pickup and MPV anti-lock brake warning light flashing codes

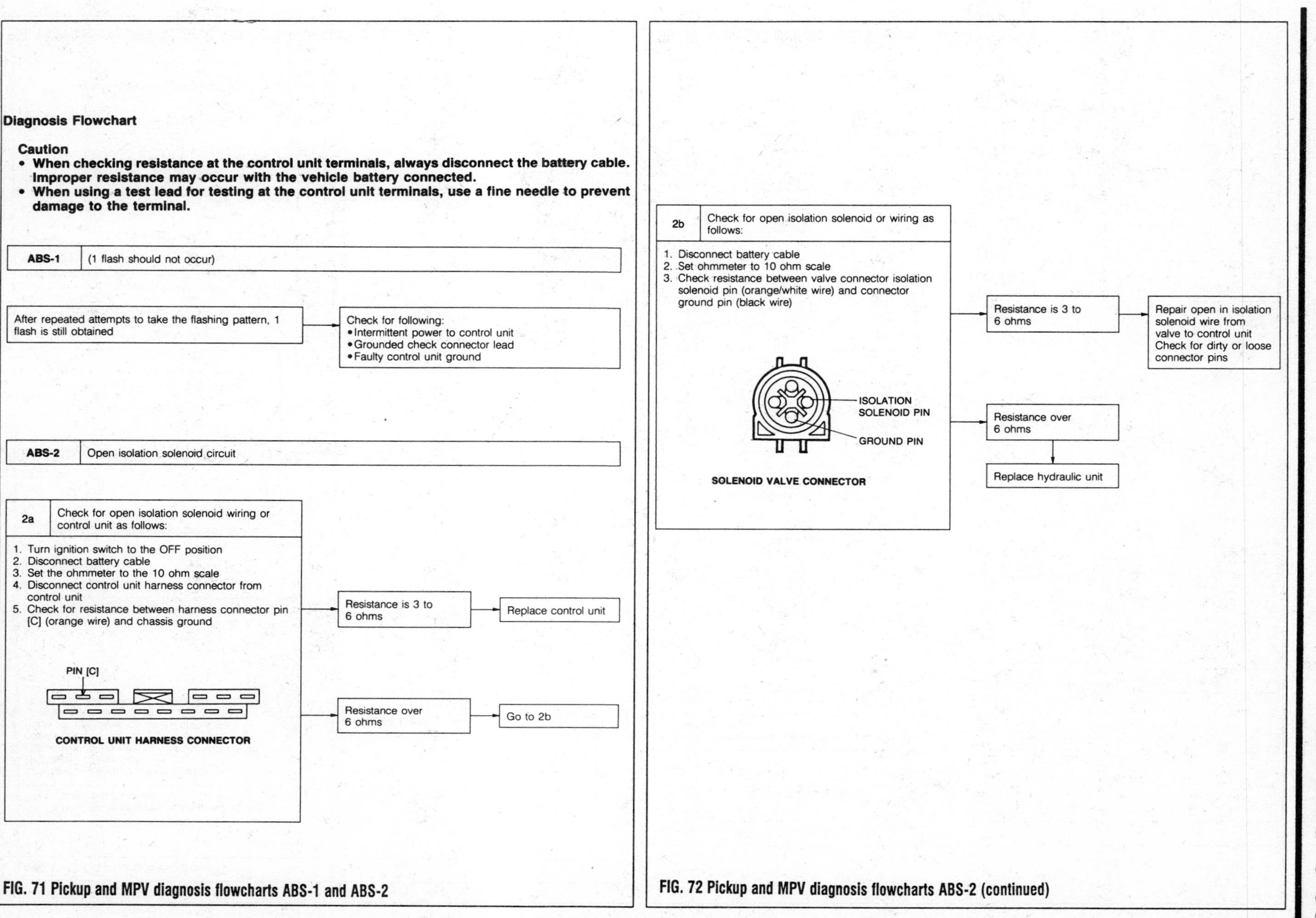

• When using a test lead for testing at the control unit terminals, use a fine needle to prevent damage to the terminal.

Check for following:

• Grounded check connector lead

FIG. 71 Pickup and MPV diagnosis flowcharts ABS-1 and ABS-2

2b
Check for open isolation solenoid or wiring as follows:
1. Disconnect battery cable
2. Set ohmmeter to 10 ohm scale
3. Check resistance between valve connector isolation solenoid pin (orange/white wire) and connector ground pin (black wire)
ISOLATION SOLENOID PIN
GROUND PIN
SOLENOID VALVE CONNECTOR
Resistance is 3 to 6 ohms
Repair open in isolation solenoid wire from valve to control unit Check for dirty or loose connector pins
Resistance over 6 ohms
Replace hydraulic unit

FIG. 72 Pickup and MPV diagnosis flowcharts ABS-2 (continued)

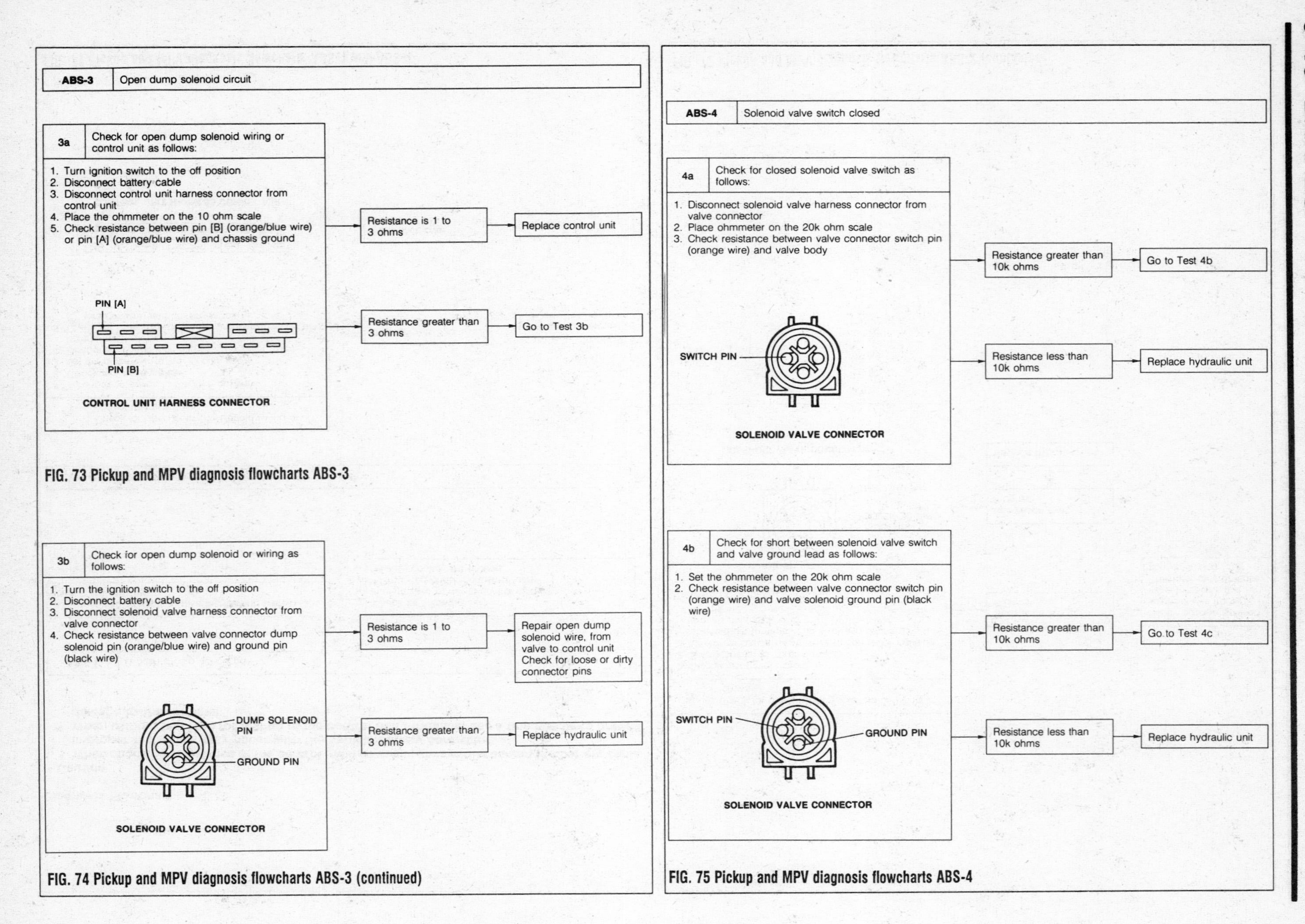

ABS-3
Open dump solenoid circuit
3a
Check for open dump solenoid wiring or control unit as follows:
1. Turn ignition switch to the off position
2. Disconnect battery cable
3. Disconnect control unit harness connector from control unit
4. Place the ohmmeter on the 10 ohm scale
5. Check resistance between pin [B] (orange/blue wire) or pin [A] (orange/blue wire) and chassis ground
PIN [A]
PIN [B]
CONTROL UNIT HARNESS CONNECTOR
Resistance is 1 to 3 ohms
Replace control unit
Resistance greater than 3 ohms
Go to Test 3b
3b
Check for open dump solenoid or wiring as follows:
1. Turn the ignition switch to the off position
2. Disconnect battery cable
3. Disconnect solenoid valve harness connector from valve connector
4. Check resistance between valve connector dump solenoid pin (orange/blue wire) and ground pin (black wire)
DUMP SOLENOID PIN
GROUND PIN
SOLENOID VALVE CONNECTOR
Resistance is 1 to 3 ohms
Repair open dump solenoid wire, from valve to control unit Check for loose or dirty connector pins
Resistance greater than 3 ohms
Replace hydraulic unit
ABS-4
Solenoid valve switch closed
4a
Check for closed solenoid valve switch as follows:
1. Disconnect solenoid valve harness connector from valve connector
2. Place ohmmeter on the 20k ohm scale
3. Check resistance between valve connector switch pin (orange wire) and valve body
SWITCH PIN
SOLENOID VALVE CONNECTOR
Resistance greater than 10k ohms
Go to Test 4b
Resistance less than 10k ohms
Replace hydraulic unit
4b
Check for short between solenoid valve switch and valve ground lead as follows:
1. Set the ohmmeter on the 20k ohm scale
2. Check resistance between valve connector switch pin (orange wire) and valve solenoid ground pin (black wire)
SWITCH PIN
GROUND PIN
SOLENOID VALVE CONNECTOR
Resistance greater than 10k ohms
Go to Test 4c
Resistance less than 10k ohms
Replace hydraulic unit

FIG. 73 Pickup and MPV diagnosis flowcharts ABS-3

FIG. 74 Pickup and MPV diagnosis flowcharts ABS-3 (continued)

FIG. 75 Pickup and MPV diagnosis flowcharts ABS-4

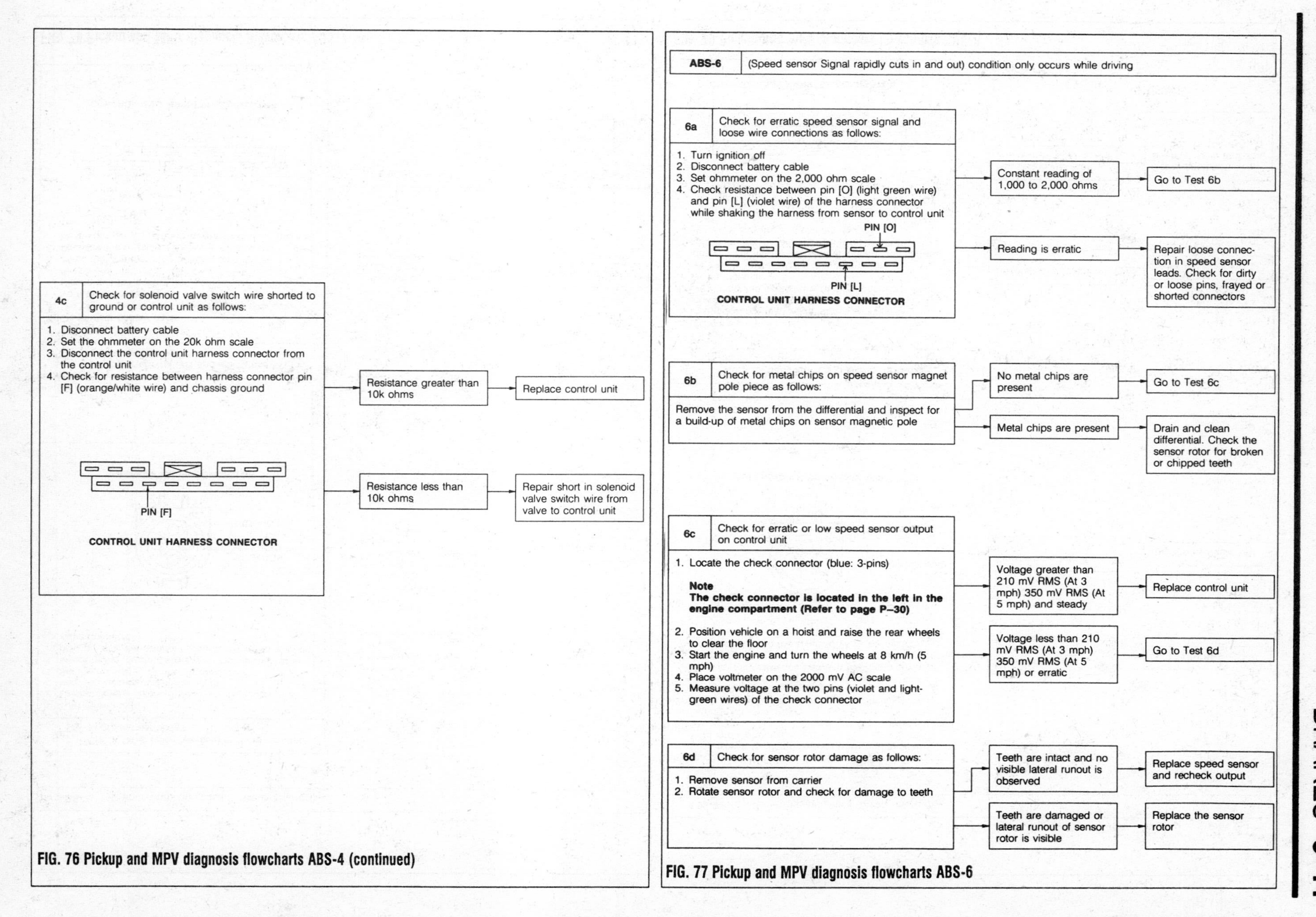
4c
Check for solenoid valve switch wire shorted to ground or control unit as follows:
1. Disconnect battery cable
2. Set the ohmmeter on the 20k ohm scale
3. Disconnect the control unit harness connector from the control unit
4. Check for resistance between harness connector pin [F] (orange/white wire) and chassis ground
PIN [F]
CONTROL UNIT HARNESS CONNECTOR
Resistance greater than 10k ohms
Replace control unit
Resistance less than 10k ohms
Repair short in solenoid valve switch wire from valve to control unit
ABS-6
(Speed sensor Signal rapidly cuts in and out) condition only occurs while driving
6a
Check for erratic speed sensor signal and loose wire connections as follows:
1. Turn ignition off
2. Disconnect battery cable
3. Set ohmmeter on the 2,000 ohm scale
4. Check resistance between pin [O] (light green wire) and pin [L] (violet wire) of the harness connector while shaking the harness from sensor to control unit
PIN [O]
PIN [L]
CONTROL UNIT HARNESS CONNECTOR
Constant reading of 1,000 to 2,000 ohms
Go to Test 6b
Reading is erratic
Repair loose connection in speed sensor leads. Check for dirty or loose pins, frayed or shorted connectors
6b
Check for metal chips on speed sensor magnet pole piece as follows:
Remove the sensor from the differential and inspect for a build-up of metal chips on sensor magnetic pole
No metal chips are present
Go to Test 6c
Metal chips are present
Drain and clean differential. Check the sensor rotor for broken or chipped teeth
6c
Check for erratic or low speed sensor output on control unit
1. Locate the check connector (blue: 3-pins)
Note
The check connector is located in the left in the engine compartment (Refer to page P–30)
2. Position vehicle on a hoist and raise the rear wheels to clear the floor
3. Start the engine and turn the wheels at 8 km/h (5 mph)
4. Place voltmeter on the 2000 mV AC scale
5. Measure voltage at the two pins (violet and light-green wires) of the check connector
Voltage greater than 210 mV RMS (At 3 mph) 350 mV RMS (At 5 mph) and steady
Replace control unit
Voltage less than 210 mV RMS (At 3 mph) 350 mV RMS (At 5 mph) or erratic
Go to Test 6d
6d
Check for sensor rotor damage as follows:
1. Remove sensor from carrier
2. Rotate sensor rotor and check for damage to teeth
Teeth are intact and no visible lateral runout is observed
Replace speed sensor and recheck output
Teeth are damaged or lateral runout of sensor rotor is visible
Replace the sensor rotor

FIG. 76 Pickup and MPV diagnosis flowcharts ABS-4 (continued)

FIG. 77 Pickup and MPV diagnosis flowcharts ABS-6

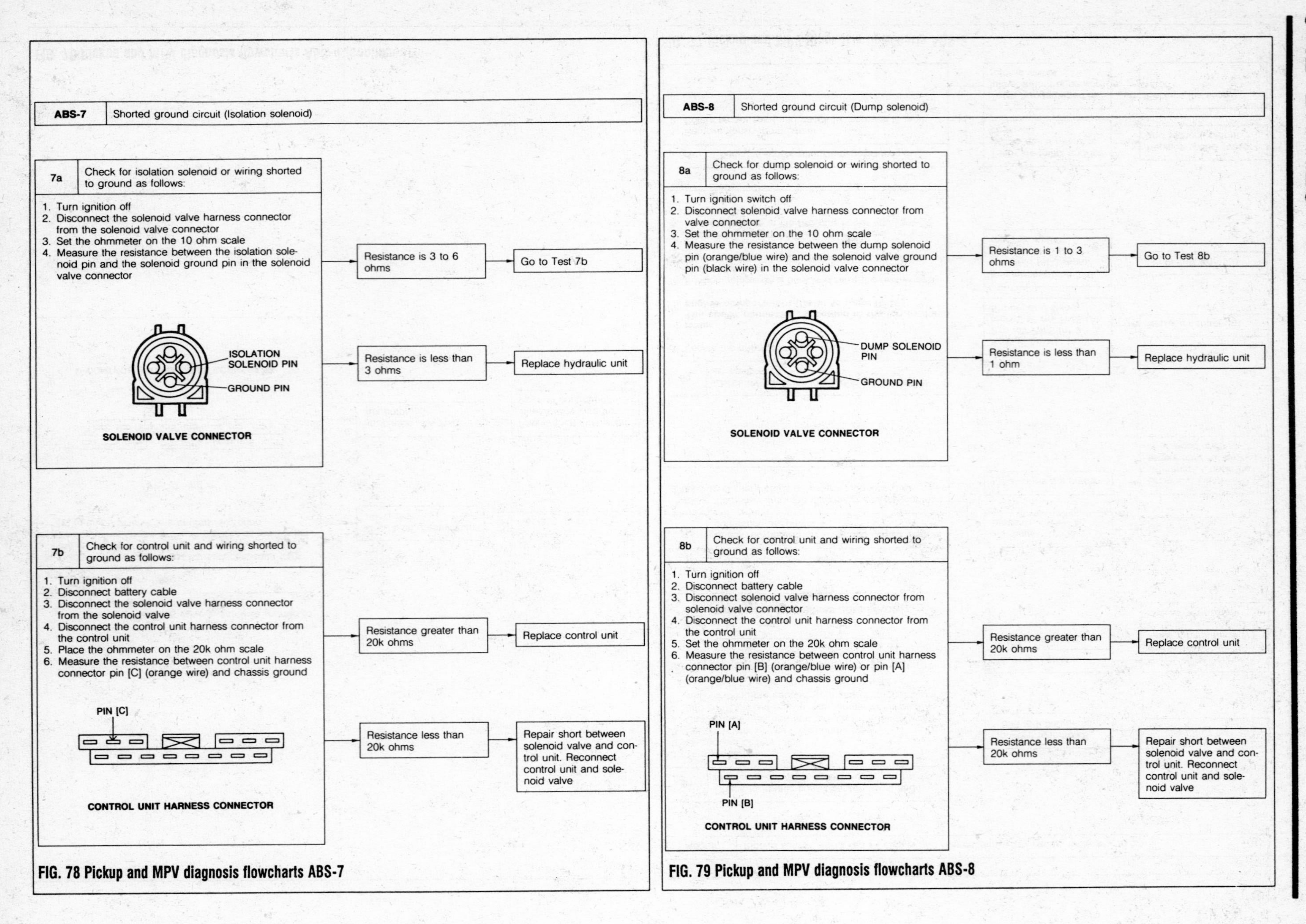

FIG. 78 Pickup and MPV diagnosis flowcharts ABS-7

ABS-8
Shorted ground circuit (Dump solenoid)
8a
Check for dump solenoid or wiring shorted to ground as follows:
1. Turn ignition switch off
2. Disconnect solenoid valve harness connector from valve connector
3. Set the ohmmeter on the 10 ohm scale
4. Measure the resistance between the dump solenoid pin (orange/blue wire) and the solenoid valve ground pin (black wire) in the solenoid valve connector
DUMP SOLENOID PIN
GROUND PIN
SOLENOID VALVE CONNECTOR
Resistance is 1 to 3 ohms
Go to Test 8b
Resistance is less than 1 ohm
Replace hydraulic unit
8b
Check for control unit and wiring shorted to ground as follows:
1. Turn ignition off
2. Disconnect battery cable
3. Disconnect solenoid valve harness connector from solenoid valve connector
4. Disconnect the control unit harness connector from the control unit
5. Set the ohmmeter on the 20k ohm scale
6. Measure the resistance between control unit harness connector pin [B] (orange/blue wire) or pin [A] (orange/blue wire) and chassis ground
PIN [A]
PIN [B]
CONTROL UNIT HARNESS CONNECTOR
Resistance greater than 20k ohms
Replace control unit
Resistance less than 20k ohms
Repair short between solenoid valve and control unit. Reconnect control unit and solenoid valve

FIG. 79 Pickup and MPV diagnosis flowcharts ABS-8

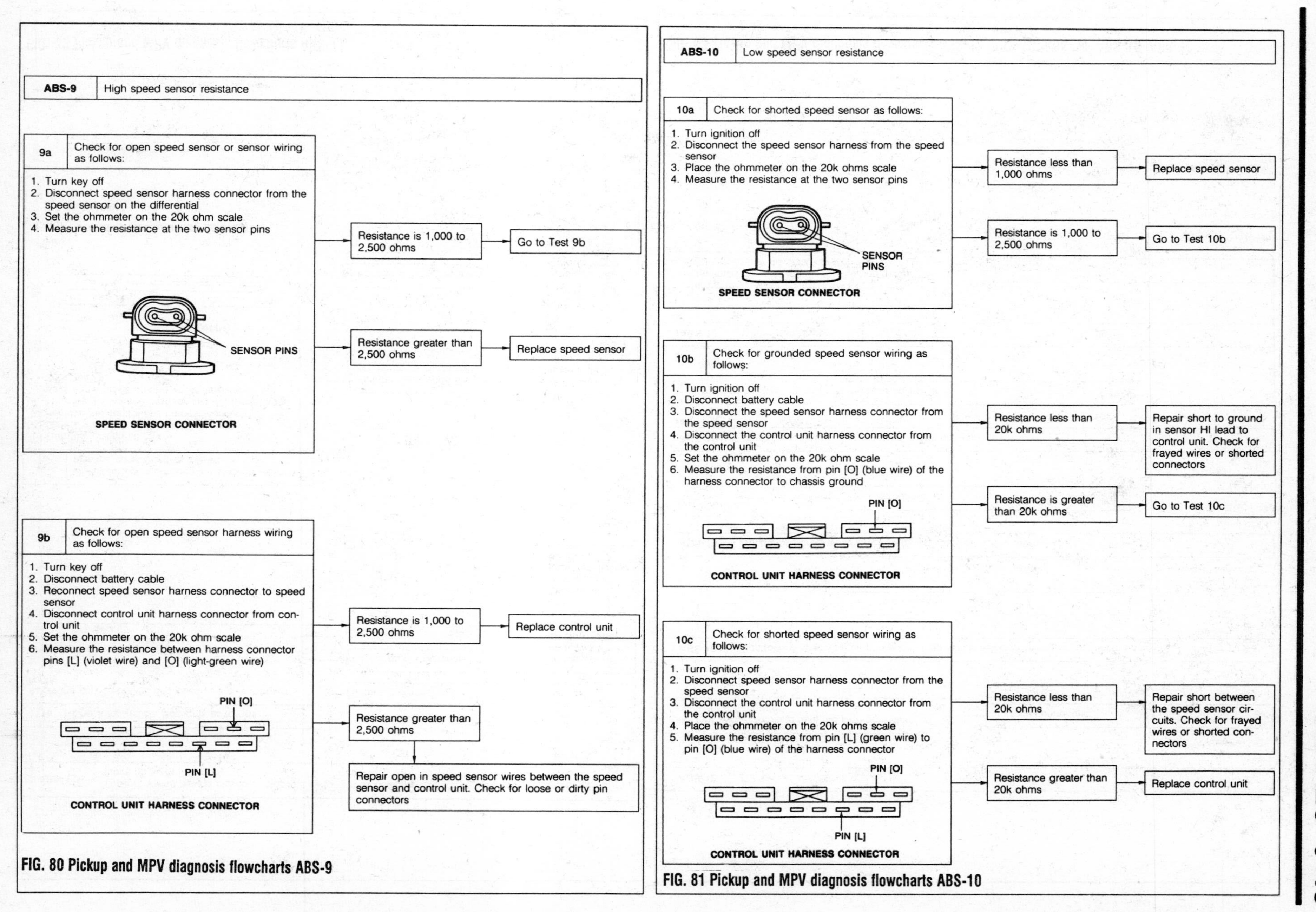

ABS-9
High speed sensor resistance
9a
Check for open speed sensor or sensor wiring as follows:
1. Turn key off
2. Disconnect speed sensor harness connector from the speed sensor on the differential
3. Set the ohmmeter on the 20k ohm scale
4. Measure the resistance at the two sensor pins
SENSOR PINS
SPEED SENSOR CONNECTOR
Resistance is 1,000 to 2,500 ohms
Go to Test 9b
Resistance greater than 2,500 ohms
Replace speed sensor
9b
Check for open speed sensor harness wiring as follows:
1. Turn key off
2. Disconnect battery cable
3. Reconnect speed sensor harness connector to speed sensor
4. Disconnect control unit harness connector from control unit
5. Set the ohmmeter on the 20k ohm scale
6. Measure the resistance between harness connector pins [L] (violet wire) and [O] (light-green wire)
PIN [O]
PIN [L]
CONTROL UNIT HARNESS CONNECTOR
Resistance is 1,000 to 2,500 ohms
Replace control unit
Resistance greater than 2,500 ohms
Repair open in speed sensor wires between the speed sensor and control unit. Check for loose or dirty pin connectors
ABS-10
Low speed sensor resistance
10a
Check for shorted speed sensor as follows:
1. Turn ignition off
2. Disconnect the speed sensor harness from the speed sensor
3. Place the ohmmeter on the 20k ohms scale
4. Measure the resistance at the two sensor pins
SENSOR PINS
SPEED SENSOR CONNECTOR
Resistance less than 1,000 ohms
Replace speed sensor
Resistance is 1,000 to 2,500 ohms
Go to Test 10b
10b
Check for grounded speed sensor wiring as follows:
1. Turn ignition off
2. Disconnect battery cable
3. Disconnect the speed sensor harness connector from the speed sensor
4. Disconnect the control unit harness connector from the control unit
5. Set the ohmmeter on the 20k ohm scale
6. Measure the resistance from pin [O] (blue wire) of the harness connector to chassis ground
PIN [O]
CONTROL UNIT HARNESS CONNECTOR
Resistance less than 20k ohms
Repair short to ground in sensor HI lead to control unit. Check for frayed wires or shorted connectors
Resistance is greater than 20k ohms
Go to Test 10c
10c
Check for shorted speed sensor wiring as follows:
1. Turn ignition off
2. Disconnect speed sensor harness connector from the speed sensor
3. Disconnect the control unit harness connector from the control unit
4. Place the ohmmeter on the 20k ohms scale
5. Measure the resistance from pin [L] (green wire) to pin [O] (blue wire) of the harness connector
PIN [O]
PIN [L]
CONTROL UNIT HARNESS CONNECTOR
Resistance less than 20k ohms
Repair short between the speed sensor circuits. Check for frayed wires or shorted connectors
Resistance greater than 20k ohms
Replace control unit

FIG. 80 Pickup and MPV diagnosis flowcharts ABS-9

FIG. 81 Pickup and MPV diagnosis flowcharts ABS-10

ABS-11 — Stoplight switch always closed or stoplight switch circuit defective. (Condition indicated only when driving above 56 km/h [35 mph])

11a — Check for vehicle stoplights as follows:

Apply the service brakes and observe the rear brake lights

- Lights illuminate → Go to Test 11b
- Lights do not illuminate → Repair or replace vehicle stoplight switch. Check for blown stoplight switch fuse. Investigate reason for blown fuse. Check for open stoplight switch wiring or blown stoplights. Repair as needed

11b — Check for open between the stoplight switch and the control unit as follows:

1. Turn the ignition off
2. Set the voltmeter on the 20 VDC scale
3. Remove the control unit harness connector
4. Measure the voltage between pin [M] (white/green wire) and chassis ground while stepping on the brake pedal

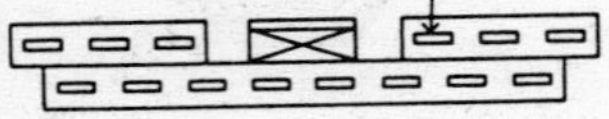

PIN [M]

CONTROL UNIT HARNESS CONNECTOR

- Voltage is less than 9V → Repair the open between stoplight switch and control unit circuit
- Voltage is 9V or more → Check 4 way flasher and directional wiring. This condition could create feedback through the stoplight circuit

FIG. 82 Pickup and MPV diagnosis flowcharts ABS-11

ABS-12 — (12 flashes should not occur)

After repeated attempts to take the flashing pattern, 12 flashes are still obtained → Replace control unit

ABS-13 — Control unit speed circuit phase lock loop failure detected during control unit self-test

→ Replace control unit

ABS-14 — Control unit program check sum failure detected during self-test

→ Replace control unit

ABS-15 — Control unit RAM failure detected during self-test

→ Replace control unit

ABS-16 — (16 or more flashes should not occur)

After repeated attempts to take the flashing pattern, 16 or more flashes are still obtained → Replace control unit

FIG. 83 Pickup and MPV diagnosis flowcharts ABS-12, ABS-13, ABS-14, ABS-15, ABS-16

Vв: Battery voltage

Tester connection ( ) indicates wire color	Measured item	Remark	Resistance (Battery cable off)	Voltage (IG switch ON)
L (V) – 0 (LG)	Speed sensor	—	Approx. 1.4 kΩ	—
P (L/R) – Ground	Battery	—	∞	Vв
N (R/W) – Ground	Pressure differential switch (PBV)	—	—	Vв
L (V) – Ground	Speed sensor	—	∞	—
H (R/Y) – Ground	Automatic freewheel (AFW) switch (4WD only)	2WD mode	∞	—
		4WD mode	0Ω	
F (O/W) – Ground	Pressure switch (Hydraulic unit)	—	∞	—
D (G) –Ground	Warning lamp	—	Approx. 23Ω	Vв
B (O/L) – Ground	Dump solenoid	—	1—3Ω	0V
Q (L/R) – Ground	Battery	—	∞	Vв
O (LG) – Ground	Speed sensor	—	∞	—
M (W/G) – Ground	Stoplight switch	Switch ON	Approx. 1.0Ω	Vв
		Switch OFF		0V
E (GY/W) – Ground	Check connector	—	∞	0V
C (O) – Ground	Isolation solenoid	—	3—6Ω	0V
A (O/L) – Ground	Dump solenoid	—	1—3Ω	0V
J (B) – Ground	Ground	—	Continuity	—

FIG. 84 Pickup and MPV control unit testing chart: Remove cover disconnect the harness from the control unit and check the harness connector terminals for voltage or resistance

A C E M O Q

B D F H J L N P

FIG. 85 Control unit harness connector terminal identification: When checking resistance at the control terminals always disconnect the negative battery cable. Improper resistance may occur with the battery connected. Use a fine needle test lead to prevent terminal damage

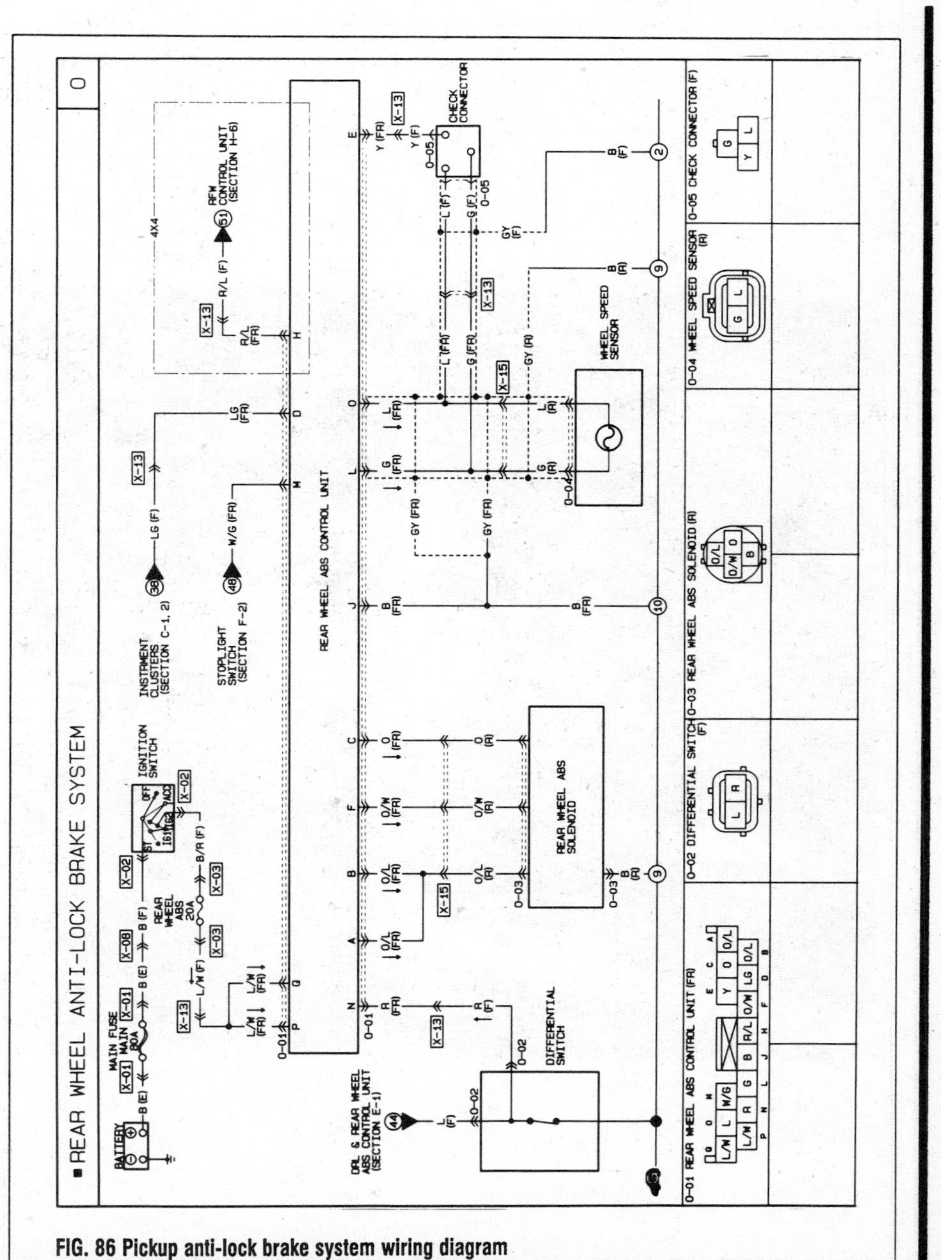

FIG. 86 Pickup anti-lock brake system wiring diagram

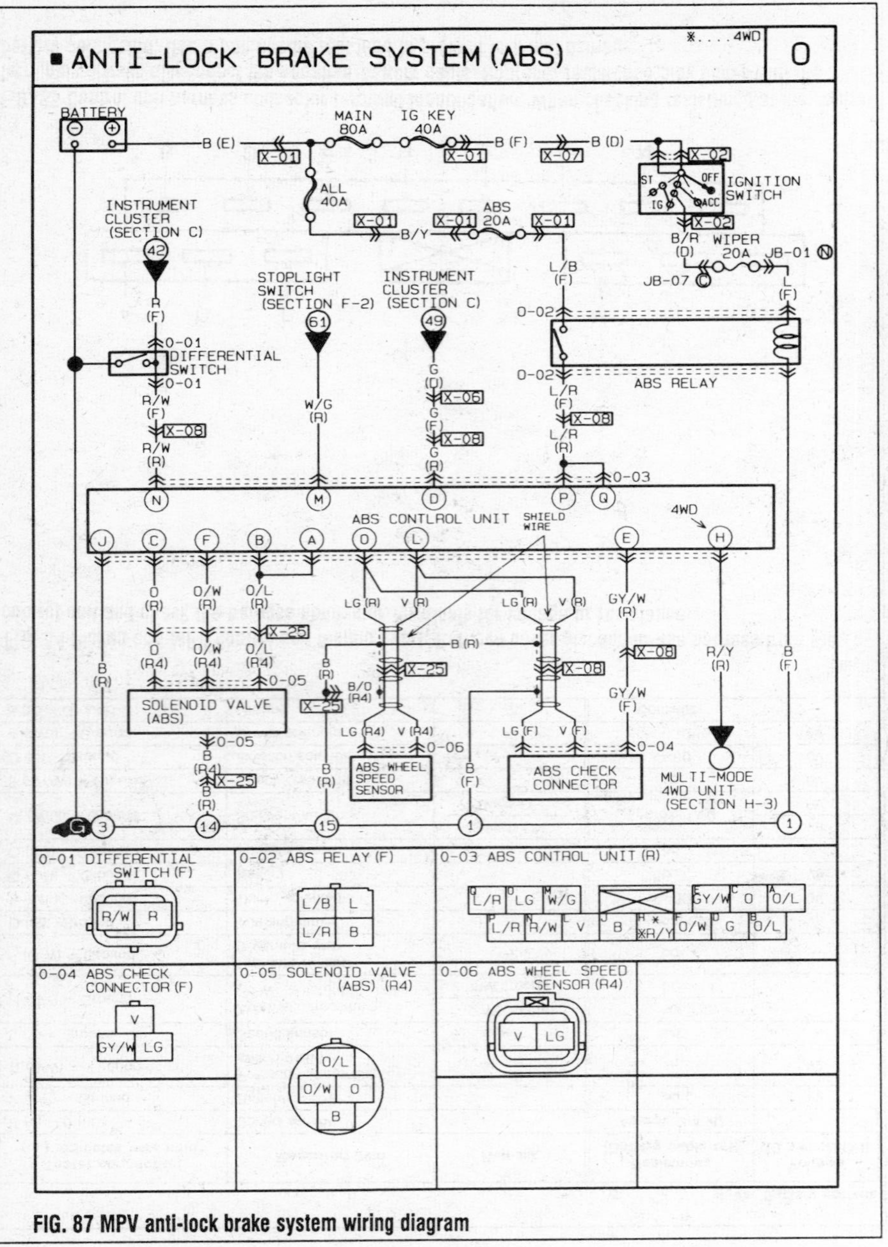

FIG. 87 MPV anti-lock brake system wiring diagram

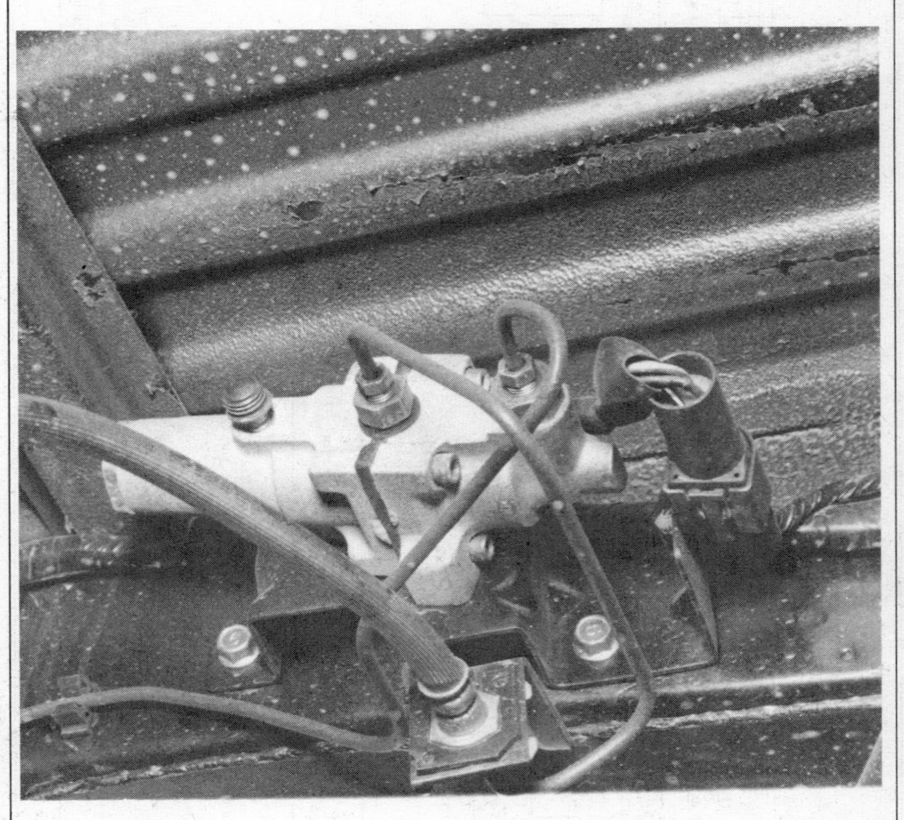

FIG. 88 Anti-lock brake hydraulic unit, Pickup shown

RABS Component Location

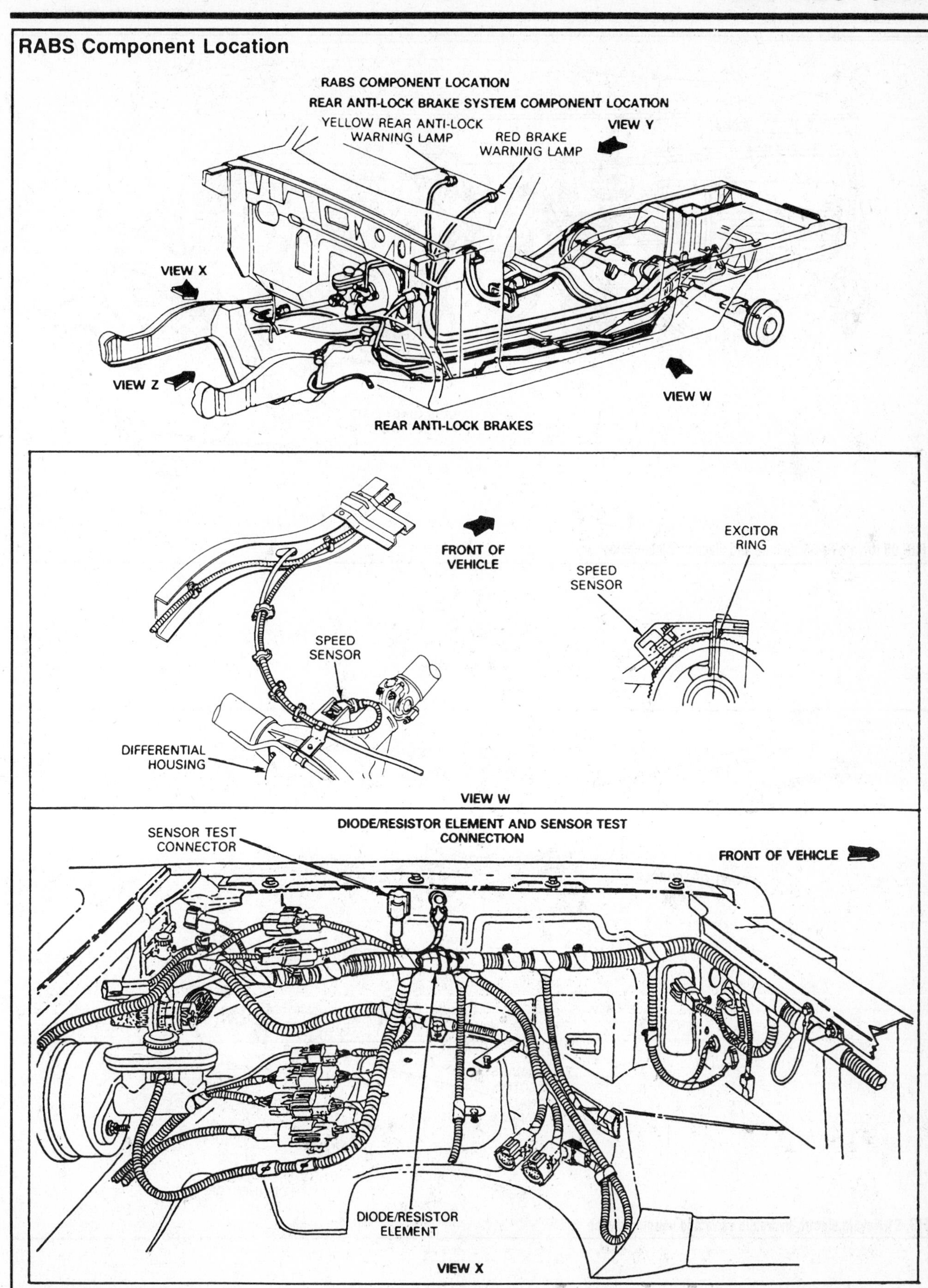

FIG. 89 Navajo RABS component location

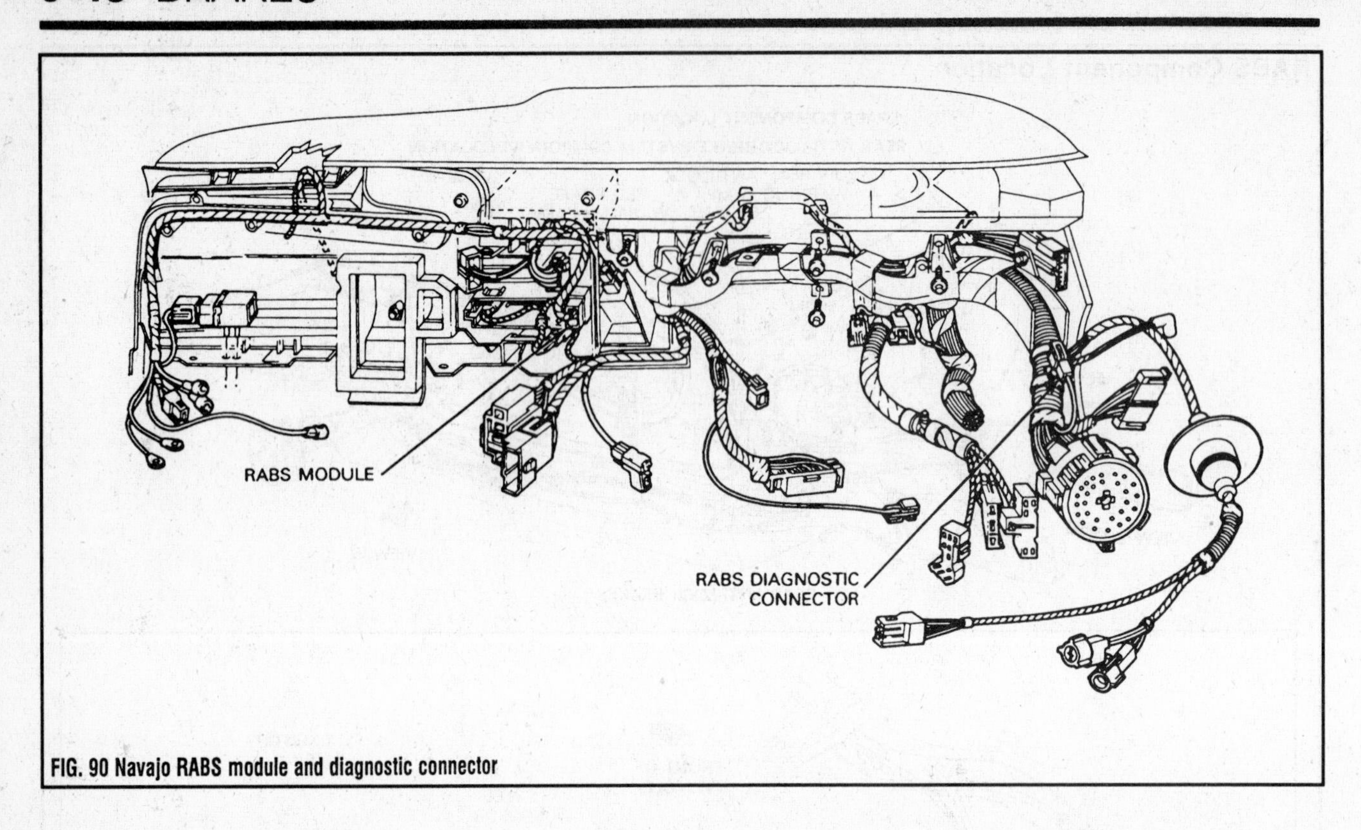

FIG. 90 Navajo RABS module and diagnostic connector

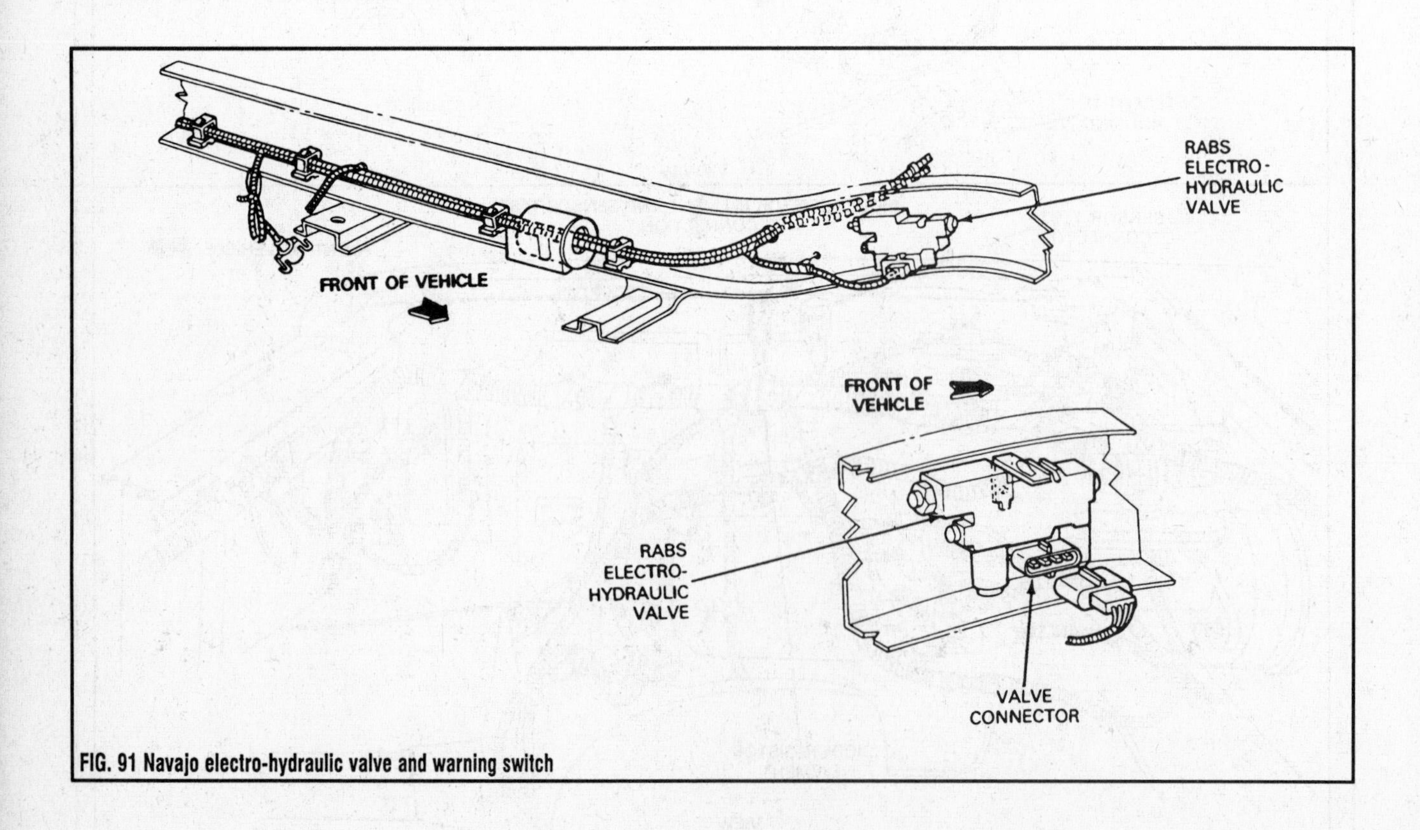

FIG. 91 Navajo electro-hydraulic valve and warning switch

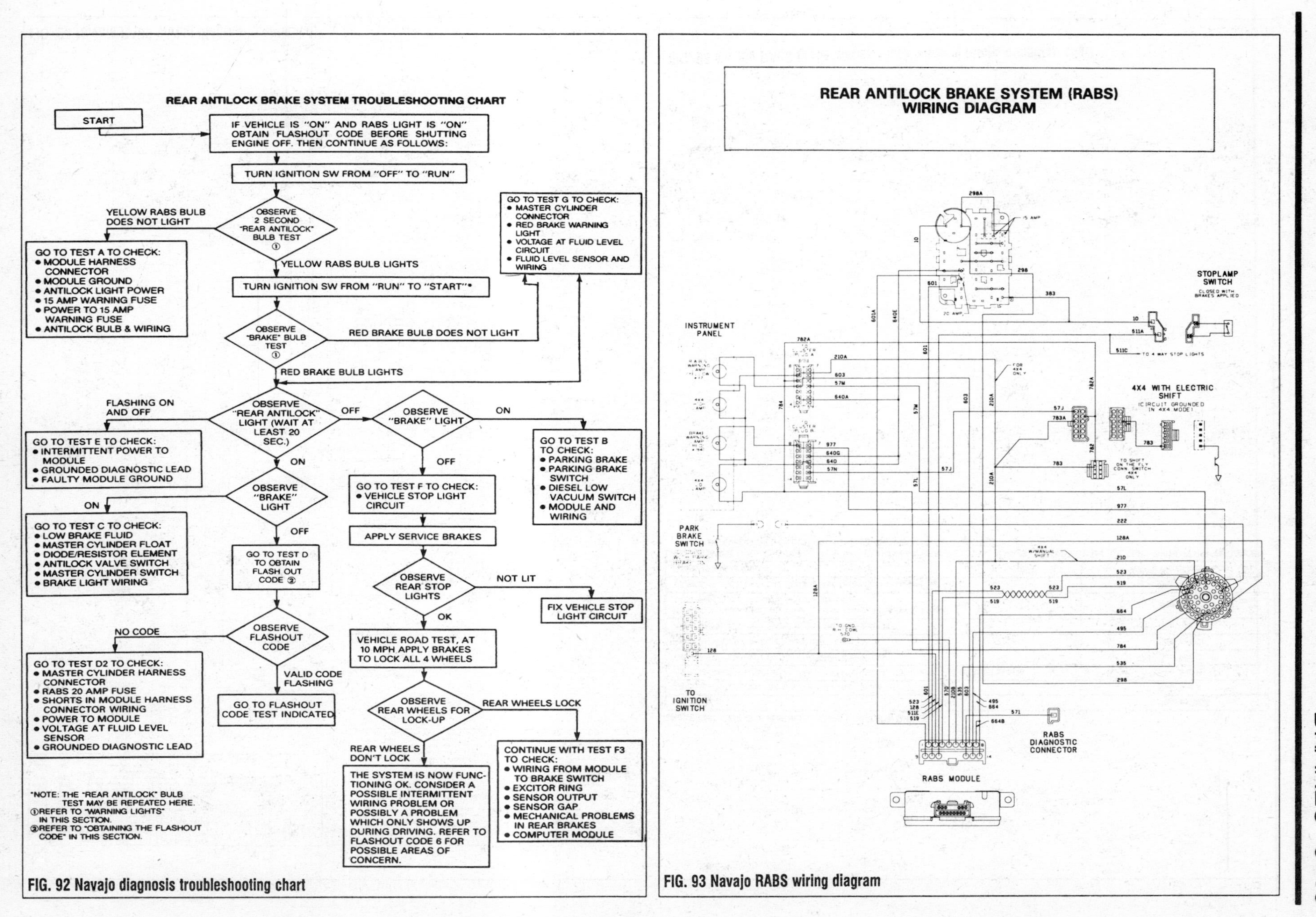

FIG. 92 Navajo diagnosis troubleshooting chart

FIG. 93 Navajo RABS wiring diagram

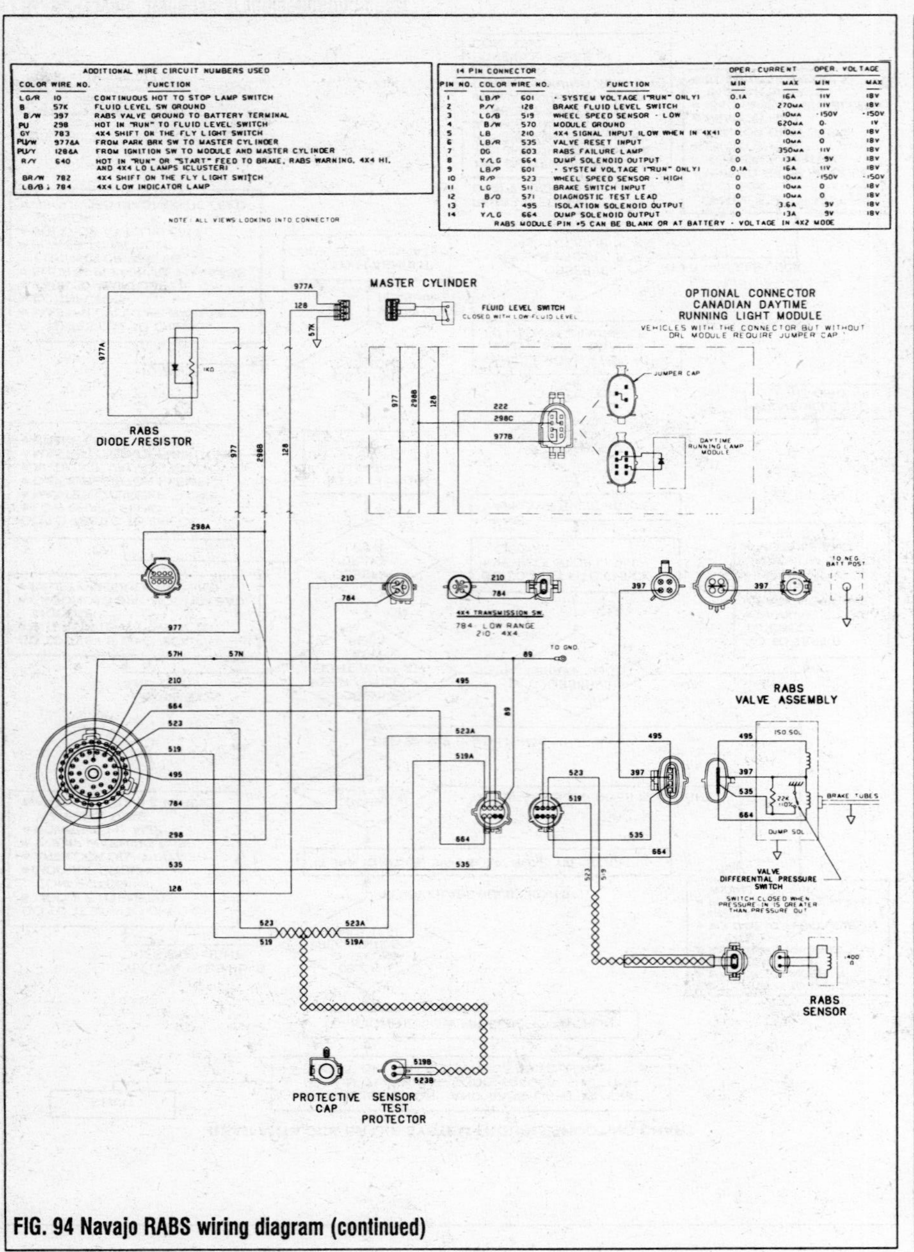

ADDITIONAL WIRE CIRCUIT NUMBERS USED

COLOR	WIRE NO.	FUNCTION
LG/R	10	CONTINUOUS HOT TO STOP LAMP SWITCH
B	57K	FLUID LEVEL SW GROUND
B/W	397	RABS VALVE GROUND TO BATTERY TERMINAL
PU	298	HOT IN "RUN" TO FLUID LEVEL SWITCH
GY	783	4X4 SHIFT ON THE FLY LIGHT SWITCH
PU/W	977&A	FROM PARK BRK SW TO MASTER CYLINDER
PU/Y	128&A	FROM IGNITION SW TO MODULE AND MASTER CYLINDER
R/Y	640	HOT IN "RUN" OR "START" FEED TO BRAKE, RABS WARNING, 4X4 HI, AND 4X4 LO LAMPS (CLUSTER)
BR/W	782	4X4 SHIFT ON THE FLY LIGHT SWITCH
LB/B	784	4X4 LOW INDICATOR LAMP

14 PIN CONNECTOR

PIN NO.	COLOR	WIRE NO.	FUNCTION	OPER. CURRENT MIN	OPER. CURRENT MAX	OPER. VOLTAGE MIN	OPER. VOLTAGE MAX
1	LB/P	601	• SYSTEM VOLTAGE ("RUN" ONLY)	0.1A	16A	11V	18V
2	P/Y	128	BRAKE FLUID LEVEL SWITCH	0	270MA	11V	18V
3	LG/B	519	WHEEL SPEED SENSOR - LOW	0	10MA	-150V	-150V
4	B/W	570	MODULE GROUND	0	620MA	0	1V
5	LB	210	4X4 SIGNAL INPUT (LOW WHEN IN 4X4)	0	10MA	0	18V
6	LB/R	535	VALVE RESET INPUT	0	10MA	0	18V
7	DG	603	RABS FAILURE LAMP	0	350MA	11V	18V
8	Y/LG	664	DUMP SOLENOID OUTPUT	0	13A	9V	18V
9	LB/P	601	• SYSTEM VOLTAGE ("RUN" ONLY)	0.1A	16A	11V	18V
10	R/P	523	WHEEL SPEED SENSOR - HIGH	0	10MA	-150V	-150V
11	LG	511	BRAKE SWITCH INPUT	0	10MA	0	18V
12	B/O	571	DIAGNOSTIC TEST LEAD	0	10MA	0	18V
13	T	495	ISOLATION SOLENOID OUTPUT	0	3.6A	9V	18V
14	Y/LG	664	DUMP SOLENOID OUTPUT	0	13A	9V	18V

RABS MODULE PIN #5 CAN BE BLANK OR AT BATTERY - VOLTAGE IN 4X2 MODE

FIG. 94 Navajo RABS wiring diagram (continued)

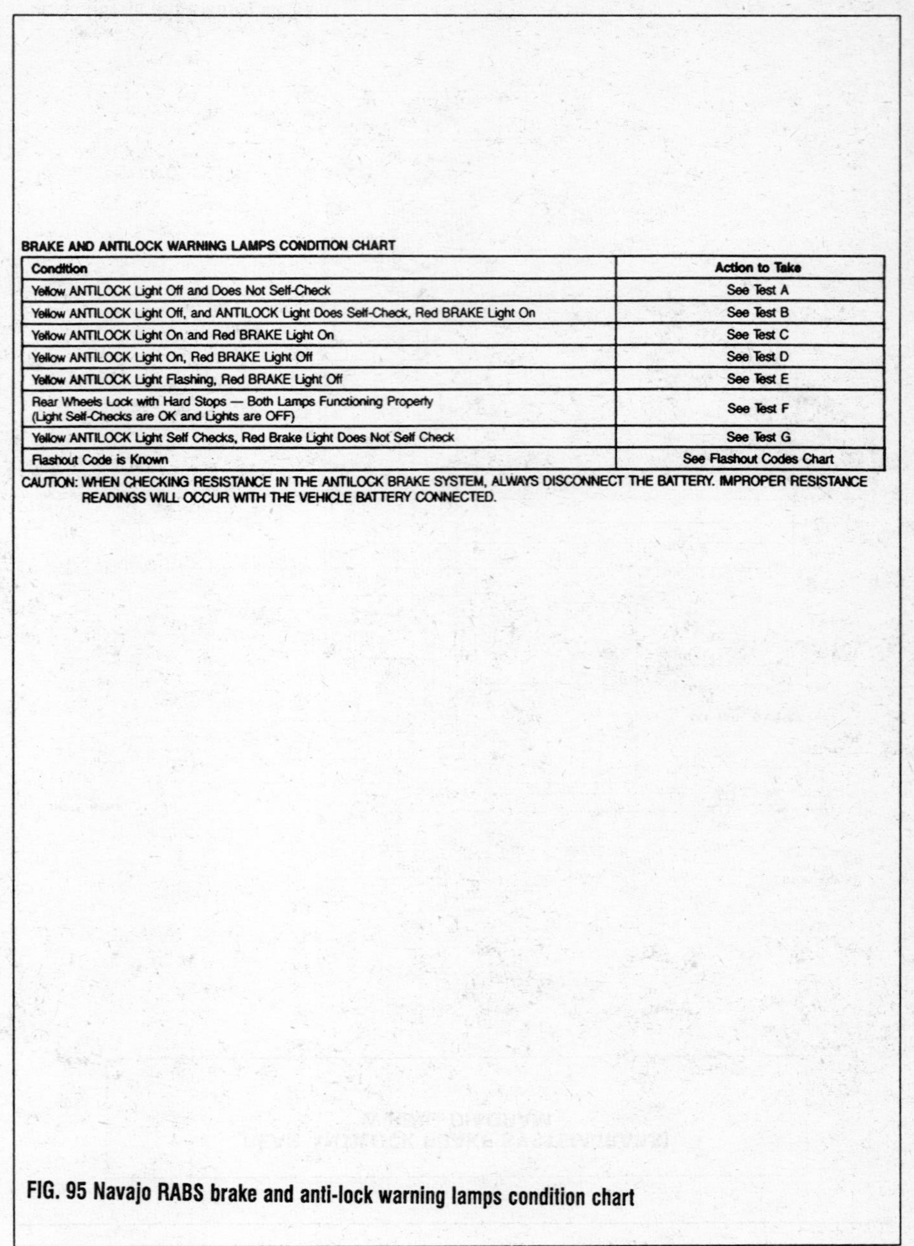

BRAKE AND ANTILOCK WARNING LAMPS CONDITION CHART

Condition	Action to Take
Yellow ANTILOCK Light Off and Does Not Self-Check	See Test A
Yellow ANTILOCK Light Off, and ANTILOCK Light Does Self-Check, Red BRAKE Light On	See Test B
Yellow ANTILOCK Light On and Red BRAKE Light On	See Test C
Yellow ANTILOCK Light On, Red BRAKE Light Off	See Test D
Yellow ANTILOCK Light Flashing, Red BRAKE Light Off	See Test E
Rear Wheels Lock with Hard Stops — Both Lamps Functioning Properly (Light Self-Checks are OK and Lights are OFF)	See Test F
Yellow ANTILOCK Light Self Checks, Red Brake Light Does Not Self Check	See Test G
Flashout Code is Known	See Flashout Codes Chart

CAUTION: WHEN CHECKING RESISTANCE IN THE ANTILOCK BRAKE SYSTEM, ALWAYS DISCONNECT THE BATTERY. IMPROPER RESISTANCE READINGS WILL OCCUR WITH THE VEHICLE BATTERY CONNECTED.

FIG. 95 Navajo RABS brake and anti-lock warning lamps condition chart

Yellow ANTILOCK Light Off and Does Not Self-Check — Test A

TEST STEP	RESULT ▶	ACTION TO TAKE
A1 MODULE HARNESS CONNECTOR		
• Check to make sure module harness is fully plugged into computer module.	Harness is fully plugged in ▶	GO to Test **A2**.
	Harness is not fully plugged in ▶	CONNECT harness to module.
A2 COMPUTER MODULE GROUND		
• Check for good computer module ground: 1. Disconnect Battery 2. Remove harness connector from module. 3. Set ohmmeter on the 200 ohm scale. 4. Check for resistance between harness connector pin 4 and chassis ground PIN NO. 4 14 13 12 / 11 10 9 / 8 7 6 5 4 3 2 1 MODULE HARNESS CONNECTOR — PIN VIEW	Resistance less than 1 ohm ▶	GO to Test **A3**.
	Resistance 1 ohm or greater ▶	CHECK for open in module ground wire. CHECK for loose, dirty or broken connector pins.
CAUTION: WHEN CHECKING RESISTANCE IN THE ANTILOCK SYSTEM, ALWAYS DISCONNECT THE BATTERY. IMPROPER RESISTANCE MAY OCCUR WITH THE VEHICLE BATTERY CONNECTED.		
A3 ANTILOCK LIGHT POWER		
• Check for voltage to ANTILOCK light: 1. Reconnect the battery. 2. Set voltmeter on 20 VDC scale position. 3. Turn ignition to the on position. 4. Check voltage between harness connector pin 7 and a known good chassis ground. 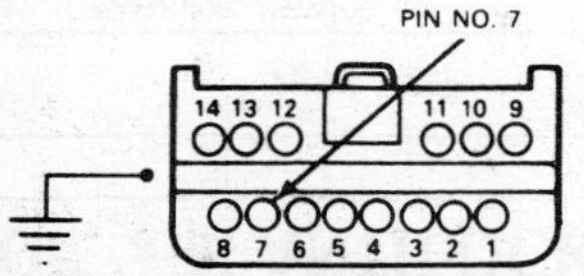 PIN NO. 7 14 13 12 / 11 10 9 / 8 7 6 5 4 3 2 1 MODULE HARNESS CONNECTOR — PIN VIEW	Voltage greater than 9V ▶	REPLACE Module.
	Voltage less than 9V ▶	GO to Test **A4**

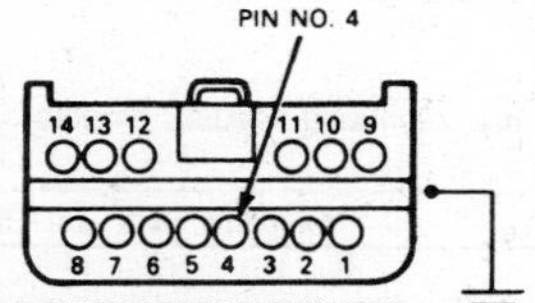

FIG. 96 Navajo: RABS condition chart: TEST A

Yellow ANTILOCK Light Off and Does Not Self-Check (Cont'd) — Test A

TEST STEP	RESULT ▶	ACTION TO TAKE
A4 RABS 15 AMP LIGHT FUSE		
• Remove and inspect RABS 15 amp light fuse.	Fuse is OK ▶	REPLACE fuse and GO to Test **A5**.
	Fuse is blown ▶	CHECK for short to ground between fuse panel and warning lamps. REPAIR short and replace 15 amp fuse.
A5 POWER TO RABS LIGHT FUSE		
• Check for voltage to fuse. 1. Set voltmeter to 20 VDC scale. 2. Turn ignition to the on position. 3. Check voltage between panel fuse connector and known good chassis ground.	Voltage greater than 9V ▶	GO to Test **A6**.
	Voltage less than 9V ▶	REPAIR fuse panel or vehicle electrical system.
A6 RABS LIGHT BULB		
• Check RABS light bulb.	Bulb is OK ▶	REPAIR open between RABS light fuse and pin 7 of the module wiring harness connector.
	Bulb is not OK ▶	REPLACE bulb.

FIG. 97 Navajo: RABS condition chart: TEST A (continued)

Red BRAKE Light On, Yellow ANTILOCK Light Off, and ANTILOCK Light Does Self-Check — Test B

TEST STEP	RESULT ►	ACTION TO TAKE
B1 PARKING BRAKE		
• Check parking brake application: 1. Turn ignition key to the on position. 2. Check the parking brake pedal and release if applied.	BRAKE light goes off ►	PERFORM road test. If lockup occurs GO to Test **B2**.
	BRAKE light stays on ►	GO to Test **B2**.
B2 PARKING BRAKE SWITCH		
• Check parking brake switch: 1. Disconnect the parking brake switch connector.	BRAKE light goes off ►	ADJUST parking brake or REPLACE parking brake switch.
	BRAKE light remains on ►	GO to Test **B3**.
B3 MODULE AND WIRING		
• Remove module harness connector from module.	BRAKE light goes off ►	REPLACE the computer module.
	If BRAKE light remains on ►	CHECK for short to ground in wiring from BRAKE light to the RABS diode/resistor.

FIG. 98 Navajo: RABS condition chart: TEST B

Yellow ANTILOCK Light On and Red BRAKE Light On — Test C

TEST STEP	RESULT ►	ACTION TO TAKE
C1 LOW BRAKE FLUID		
• Check the brake fluid level at the master cylinder reservoir.	Brake fluid level OK ►	GO to Test **C2**.
	Brake fluid level low ►	CHECK for fluid leaks in vehicle brake system and repair as required. Fill master cylinder to required level.
C2 MASTER CYLINDER FLOAT		
• Check master cylinder float for buoyancy: 1. Remove cap from master cylinder reservoir. 2. Using a clean steel implement, push down on float in reservoir.	Float moves down ►	GO to Test **C3**.
	Float does not move down (sits at the bottom of the reservoir) ►	REPLACE master cylinder reservoir.
C3 DIODE/RESISTOR ELEMENT		
• Check for proper functioning of the diode/resistor element. 1. Turn ignition key to the on position. 2. Check parking brake and release if applied.	Both the ANTILOCK and BRAKE warning lamps go off ►	REPLACE RABS diode/resistor element.
	Both the ANTILOCK and BRAKE warning lamps stay on ►	GO to Test **C4**.
C4 DIODE/RESISTOR ELEMENT CONTINUED		
• Continue to check for proper functioning of the diode/resistor element. 1. Remove the parking brake switch and the diesel low vacuum switch, if so equipped.	Both the ANTILOCK and BRAKE warning lamps go off ►	REPLACE RABS diode/resistor element.
	Both the ANTILOCK and BRAKE warning lamps stay on ►	GO to Test **C5**.

FIG. 99 Navajo: RABS condition chart: TEST C

Yellow ANTILOCK Light On and Red BRAKE Light On — Cont'd — Test C

TEST STEP	RESULT ▶	ACTION TO TAKE
C5 ANTILOCK VALVE SWITCH		
• Obtain the flashout code as described in Diagnosis and Testing in this Section.	Flashout code is obtained ▶	REFER to Flashout Codes Charts in this Section.
	ANTILOCK and BRAKE warning lamps stay on steady ▶	GO to Test **C6**.
C6 MASTER CYLINDER SWITCH		
• Check for proper functioning of the master cylinder fluid level indicator switch: 1. Remove the connector from the master cylinder. 2. Connect a jumper wire between the purple/yellow wire, and the purple/white wire. 3. Turn the ignition key to the on position.	ANTILOCK and BRAKE warning lamps stay on ▶	GO to Test **C7**.
	ANTILOCK and BRAKE warning lamps go off ▶	REPLACE the master cylinder reservoir.
C7 BRAKE LIGHT WIRING		
• Check for shorts in brake light wiring. 1. Disconnect module harness connector from module. 2. Turn ignition key to the on position.	ANTILOCK light goes off and BRAKE light stays on ▶	CHECK for short to ground in the PU/W and PU/Y circuit connected to the fluid level switch. REFER to wiring diagram in this Section.
	Both ANTILOCK and BRAKE warning lamps go off ▶	REPLACE module.

FIG. 100 Navajo: RABS condition chart: TEST C (continued)

Yellow ANTILOCK Light On, Red BRAKE Light Off — Test D

TEST STEP	RESULT ▶	ACTION TO TAKE
D1 OBTAIN THE FLASHOUT CODE		
• Obtain the flashout code as described in Diagnosis and Testing in this Section.  RABS DIAGNOSTIC CONNECTOR — PIN VIEW	Flashout code cannot be obtained ▶	GO to Test **D2**.
	Flashout code is obtained ▶	Refer to the Flashout Code Charts in this Section.
D2 MASTER CYLINDER CONNECTOR		
• Make sure master cylinder connector is fully plugged in.	Master cylinder connector is not fully plugged in ▶	PLUG in the master cylinder connector.
	Master cylinder connector is plugged in ▶	GO to Test **D3**.
D3 RABS 20 AMP FUSE		
• Remove and inspect the RABS 20 amp fuse.	Fuse is OK ▶	REPLACE Fuse. GO to Test **D4**.
	Fuse is blown ▶	Short to ground between the fuse panel and the module wiring harness connector. REPAIR short in the two LB/P wires between RABS module and fuse and REPLACE the 20 amp. fuse.
D4 SHORTS IN MODULE HARNESS CONNECTOR WIRING		
• Check wiring for short to ground: 1. Turn ignition switch to the on position. 2. Remove the module harness connector from the module. 3. Observe the REAR ANTILOCK light.	Light goes off ▶	GO to Test **D5**.
	Light remains on ▶	CHECK for a short to ground in the DG wire.

FIG. 101 Navajo: RABS condition chart: TEST D

Yellow ANTILOCK Light On, Red BRAKE Light Off (Cont'd) — Test D

TEST STEP	RESULT ▶	ACTION TO TAKE
D5 POWER TO THE MODULE		
• Check for an open in the circuit supplying power to the module: 1. Set the voltmeter on the 20 VDC scale. 2. Turn the ignition switch to the on position. 3. Measure the voltage between pin 1 (or pin 9) and chassis ground. (MODULE HARNESS CONNECTOR — PIN VIEW; PIN NO. 9; PIN NO. 1)	Voltage less than 9V. ▶	REPAIR the open in the two LB/P wires or power to the fuse panel.
	Voltage greater than 9V. ▶	GO to Test **D6**.
D6 VOLTAGE AT THE FLUID LEVEL CIRCUIT		
• Check the voltage from the fluid level switch circuit: 1. Set the voltmeter on the 20 VDC Scale. 2. Turn the ignition switch to the on position. 3. Measure the voltage between pin 2 and chassis ground. (MODULE HARNESS CONNECTOR — PIN VIEW; PIN NO. 2)	Voltage less than 8V. ▶	GO to Test **D7**.
	Voltage greater than 8V. ▶	GO to Test **D8**.
D7 FLUID LEVEL SENSOR AND WIRING		
• Check for voltage at the fluid level sensor: 1. Set voltmeter on the 20 VDC scale. 2. Turn the ignition switch to the on position. 3. Measure the voltage at the purple/white wire, and at the purple/yellow wire at the back of the master cylinder fluid level switch connector without disconnecting the connector. (BLACK WIRE; PURPLE/YELLOW WIRE; PURPLE/WHITE WIRE; MASTER CYLINDER FLUID LEVEL SWITCH CONNECTOR)	Voltage greater than 8V at both wires. ▶	CHECK for open in 128 PU/W and PU/Y circuits.
	Voltage less than 8V at both wires. ▶	REPLACE diode resistor element or open in R/Y wire between the instrument panel and fuse panel including 15A fuse (cluster warning lamps).
	Voltage greater than 8V at one wire and less than 8V at the other wire. ▶	CHANGE the master cylinder reservoir.

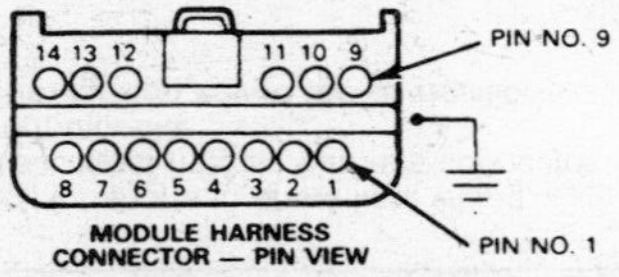

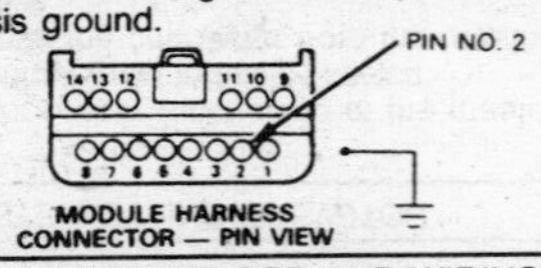

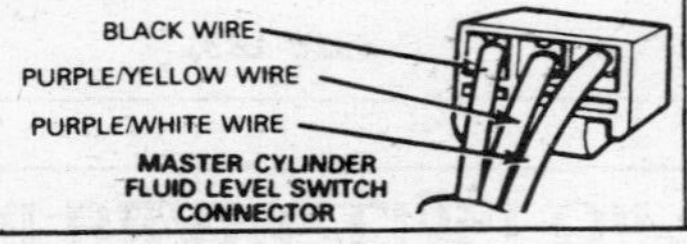

FIG. 102 Navajo: RABS condition chart: TEST D (continued)

Yellow ANTILOCK Light On, Red BRAKE Light Off (Cont'd) — Test D

TEST STEP	RESULT ▶	ACTION TO TAKE
D8 GROUNDED DIAGNOSTIC LEAD		
• Check the voltage at the diagnostic lead. 1. Reconnect the module harness connector. 2. Set the voltmeter on the 20 VDC scale. 3. Turn the ignition to the on position. 4. Measure the voltage between the diagnostic lead and chassis ground. (RABS DIAGNOSTIC CONNECTOR PIN VIEW)	Voltage is less than 1V ▶	CHECK for a short in the B/O diagnostic circuit. If no short is found, GO to Test **D9**.
	Voltage is greater than 1V ▶	GO to Test **D9**.
 **D9 COMPUTER MODULE**		
• Replace computer module and retest.		

FIG. 103 Navajo: RABS condition chart: TEST D (continued)

YELLOW ANTILOCK LIGHT FLASHING, RED BRAKE LIGHT OFF — TEST E

TEST STEP	RESULT	ACTION TO TAKE
E1 INTERMITTENT POWER TO MODULE		
• Check for intermittent open in the two LB/P circuits, power to module. 1. Remove the module harness connector from the module. 2. Set the voltmeter on the 20 VDC scale. 3. Turn the ignition to the ON position. 4. Shake the instrument panel harness. Check for battery voltage between pin 1 (and pin 9) and chassis ground.	Voltage is steady and greater than 9V ▶	GO to Test **E2**.
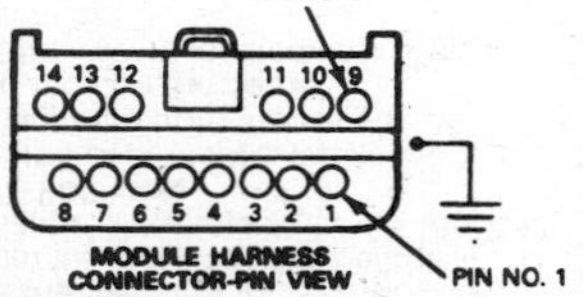 PIN NO. 9 / PIN NO. 1 / MODULE HARNESS CONNECTOR-PIN VIEW	Voltage is intermittent or less than 9V ▶	REPAIR break in the two LB/P circuits.
E2 GROUNDED DIAGNOSTIC LEAD		
• Check for an intermittent ground to chassis in the diagnostic lead circuit: 1. Turn the ignition switch off. 2. Disconnect the battery. 3. Set the ohmmeter on the 200K ohm scale. 4. Shake the module harness and check the resistance between pin 12 and chassis ground.	Resistance is steady and greater than 100K ohms ▶	GO to Test **E3**.
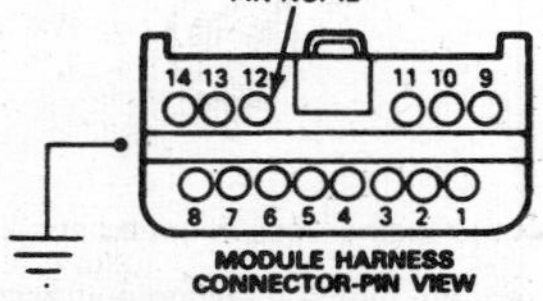 PIN NO. 12 / MODULE HARNESS CONNECTOR-PIN VIEW	Resistance is below 100K ohms or fluctuates ▶	REPAIR short in the B/O circuit.
E3 FAULTY MODULE GROUND		
• Check for intermittent or poor module ground: 1. Disconnect the battery. 2. Set the voltmeter on the 200 ohm scale. 3. Shake the module harness and check the resistance between pin 4 of the module harness connector and chassis ground.	Resistance is less than 1 ohm and steady ▶	REPLACE module.
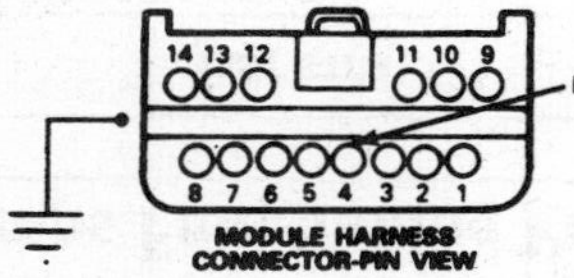 PIN NO. 4 / MODULE HARNESS CONNECTOR-PIN VIEW	Resistance is greater than 1 ohm or fluctuates ▶	REPAIR poor ground in the B/W circuit.

FIG. 104 Navajo: RABS condition chart: TEST E

Rear Wheels Lock with Hard Stops — Both Lamps Functioning Properly

Test F

TEST STEP	RESULT	ACTION TO TAKE
F1 STOPLAMPS		
• Check for stoplamp operation: 1. Apply the service brakes and observe the rear brakelamps.	Rear stoplamps not illuminated ▶	REPAIR the stoplamp circuit.
	Rear stoplamps OK ▶	GO to Test **F2**.
F2 VEHICLE ROAD TEST		
• Perform a low speed vehicle road test: 1. At approximately 10 mph apply the service brakes in an attempt to lock all four wheels while observing the left rear wheel in the side mirror.	Rear wheels lock ▶	GO to Test **F3**.
	Rear wheels do not lock ▶	The system is now functioning OK. Consider a possible intermittent wiring problem or possibly a problem which only shows up during driving. REFER to Flashout Code 6.
F3 WIRING FROM MODULE TO BRAKE SWITCH		
• Check for an open between the brake switch and the module: 1. Turn the ignition off. 2. Set the voltmeter on the 20 VDC scale. 3. Remove the module harness connector. 4. Measure the voltage between pin 11 and chassis ground while stepping on the brake pedal.	Voltage is less than 9V ▶	REPAIR the open in the 511 circuit.
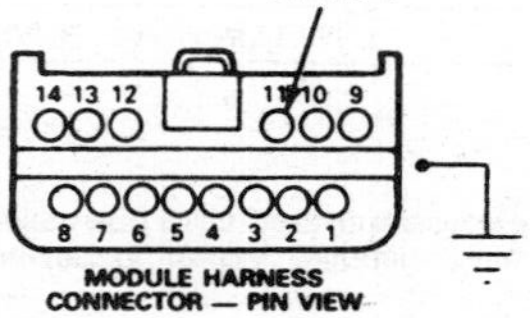 PIN NO. 11 / MODULE HARNESS CONNECTOR — PIN VIEW	Voltage is 9V or more ▶	GO to Test **F4**.
F4 EXCITOR RING INSPECTION		
• Remove sensor from carrier and check for: 1. Presence of the excitor ring 2. Condition of the teeth.	Ring is present with the teeth intact ▶	REINSTALL the sensor and GO to Test **F5**.
	Ring is not present or the teeth are damaged ▶	REPAIR axle.

FIG. 105 Navajo: RABS condition chart: TEST F

Rear Wheels Lock with Hard Stops — Both Lamps Functioning Properly (Continued) — Test F

TEST STEP	RESULT ▶	ACTION TO TAKE
F5 SENSOR OUTPUT		
• Check for low sensor signal output: 1. Set the voltmeter on the 2000 mV AC scale. 2. Position the vehicle on the hoist and raise the rear wheels off the ground. 3. Remove the cap from the sensor test connector and connect the voltmeter across the connector leads. 4. Start the engine and turn the rear wheels at 5 mph. 5. Measure the voltage output of the sensor. CONNECTOR PINS SENSOR TEST CONNECTOR – PIN VIEW	Voltage is 650 mV (RMS) or greater ▶	REINSTALL the sensor test connector cap and GO to Test **F7**.
	Voltage is less than 650 mV (RMS) ▶	REPLACE the sensor, RETEST, and REINSTALL the sensor test connector cap. If the voltage is still low, GO to Test **F6**.
F6 SENSOR GAP		
• Determine the sensor gap: 1. Remove the sensor from the carrier. 2. Measure the height of the sensor pole piece from the mounting face of the sensor flange. Pole should be 27.18-27.43 mm (1.07-1.08 inch). 3. Measure the depth to the top of the excitor ring teeth from the sensor mounting face on the carrier. 4. Subtract the two measurements. This is the sensor gap.	Gap is less than 1.27 mm (0.050 inches) ▶	GO to Test **F7**.
	Gap is greater than 0.050 inches ▶	The gap is too large. CHECK for defective sensor or carrier housing.
F7 MECHANICAL PROBLEMS IN REAR BRAKES		
• Check the rear brakes for mechanical problems such as grabbing, locking or pulling.	Rear Brakes OK ▶	GO to Test **F8**.
	Rear brakes lock, grab or pull ▶	REPAIR and RETEST.
F8 COMPUTER MODULE		
• Replace computer module and retest.		

FIG. 106 Navajo: RABS condition chart: TEST F (continued)

Yellow Anti-Lock Light Self Checks, Red Brake Light Does Not Self Check — Test G

TEST STEP	RESULT ▶	ACTION TO TAKE
G1 MASTER CYLINDER CONNECTORS		
• Check connectors on master cylinder, brake fluid level switch and delta pressure switch if equipped.	Connectors are fully plugged in ▶	GO to Test **G2**.
	Connector is not fully plugged in ▶	CONNECT connector to master cylinder.
G2 RED BRAKE WARNING LIGHT		
• Apply parking brake to see if red brake warning light lights.	Red warning light lights ▶	GO to Test **D6**.
	Red warning light does not light ▶	REPAIR warning lamp circuit. CHECK for open bulb.

FIG. 107 Navajo: RABS condition chart: TEST G

FLASHOUT CODES CHART

CONDITION	ACTION TO TAKE
No Flashout Code	See Flashout Code 0
Yellow REAR ANTILOCK Light Flashes 1 Time This Code Should Not Occur	See Flashout Code 1
Yellow REAR ANTILOCK Light Flashes 2 Times Open Isolate Circuit	See Flashout Code 2
Yellow REAR ANTILOCK Light Flashes 3 Times Open Dump Circuit	See Flashout Code 3
Yellow REAR ANTILOCK Light Flashes 4 Times Red Brake Warning Light Illuminated RABS Valve Switch Closed or Open Dump Valve	See Flashout Code 4
Yellow REAR ANTILOCK Light Flashes 5 Times System Dumps Too Many Times in 2WD Condition Occurs While Making Normal or Hard Stops. Rear Brake May Lock	See Flashout Code 5
Yellow REAR ANTILOCK Light Flashes 6 Times (Sensor Signal Rapidly Cuts In and Out) Condition Only Occurs While Driving	See Flashout Code 6
Yellow REAR ANTILOCK Light Flashes 7 Times No Isolate Valve Self Test	See Flashout Code 7
Yellow REAR ANTILOCK Light Flashes 8 Times No Dump Valve Self Test	See Flashout Code 8
Yellow REAR ANTILOCK Light Flashes 9 Times High Sensor Resistance	See Flashout Code 9
Yellow REAR ANTILOCK Light Flashes 10 Times Low Sensor Resistance	See Flashout Code 10
Yellow REAR ANTILOCK Light Flashes 11 Times Stop Lamp Switch Circuit Defective. Condition Indicated Only When Driving Above 35 mph	See Flashout Code 11
Yellow REAR ANTILOCK Light Flashes 12 Times Low Brake Fluid Level Detected During Antilock Stop	See Flashout Code 12
Yellow REAR ANTILOCK Light Flashes 13 Times Speed Processor Check	See Flashout Code 13
Yellow REAR ANTILOCK Light Flashes 14 Times Program Check	See Flashout Code 14
Yellow REAR ANTILOCK Light Flashes 15 Times Memory Failure	See Flashout Code 15
Yellow REAR ANTILOCK Light Flashes 16 Times or More 16 or More Flashes Should Not Occur	See Flashout Code 16

NOTE: Refer to Obtaining the Flashout Code in this Section for procedure to obtain flashout code.

CAUTION: WHEN CHECKING RESISTANCE IN THE RABS SYSTEM, ALWAYS DISCONNECT THE BATTERY. IMPROPER RESISTANCE READINGS MAY OCCUR WITH THE VEHICLE BATTERY CONNECTED.

FIG. 108 Navajo flashout codes chart

No Flashout Code

Flashout Code 0

TEST STEP	RESULT ▶	ACTION TO TAKE
0a NO FLASHOUT CODE BUT RABS LIGHT IS ILLUMINATED		
• There are some faults that illuminate the REAR ANTILOCK light but will not provide a Flashout Code. Refer to Obtaining the Flashout Code in this Section for procedure. Also, be sure to make a good, momentary ground from the diagnostic lead.	No Flashout Code ▶	GO to Test **D2**.

FIG. 109 Navajo: FLASHOUT CODE 0

Yellow REAR ANTILOCK Light Flashes 1 Time — This Code Should Not Occur

Flashout Code 1

TEST STEP	RESULT ▶	ACTION TO TAKE
1a NO TEST		
• This code should not occur. Refer to Obtaining the Flashout Code in this Section for procedures involved in getting the code.	Flashout Code is 1 ▶	If after repeated attempts to take the Flashout Code, Code 1 is still obtained GO to Test **E**.

FIG. 110 Navajo: FLASHOUT CODE 1

Yellow REAR ANTILOCK Light Flashes 2 Times (Open Isolate Circuit)

Flashout Code 2

TEST STEP	RESULT ▶	ACTION TO TAKE
2a CHECK FOR OPEN RABS VALVE ISOLATION SOLENOID WIRING OR MODULE		
1. Turn ignition switch to the OFF position. 2. Disconnect battery. 3. Set the ohmmeter to the 200 ohm scale. 4. Disconnect module harness connector from module. 5. Check for resistance between harness connector Pin 13 and chassis ground.	Resistance less than 6 ohms ▶	REPLACE RABS module.
	Resistance over 6 ohms ▶	GO to **2b**.
PIN NO. 13 14 13 12 11 10 9 8 7 6 5 4 3 2 1 MODULE HARNESS CONNECTOR — PIN VIEW		
2b CHECK FOR OPEN RABS VALVE ISOLATION SOLENOID OR WIRING		
1. Disconnect battery. 2. Set ohmmeter to 200 ohm scale. 3. Check resistance between valve connector isolation solenoid pin and connector ground pin.	Resistance less than 6 ohms ▶	REPAIR open in tan wire, isolation solenoid wire from valve to computer module. CHECK for dirty, loose or bent connector pins.
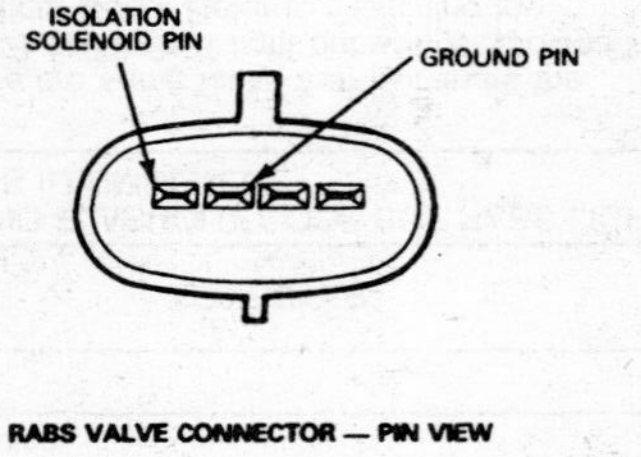 ISOLATION SOLENOID PIN GROUND PIN RABS VALVE CONNECTOR — PIN VIEW	Resistance over 6 ohms ▶	REPLACE RABS valve.

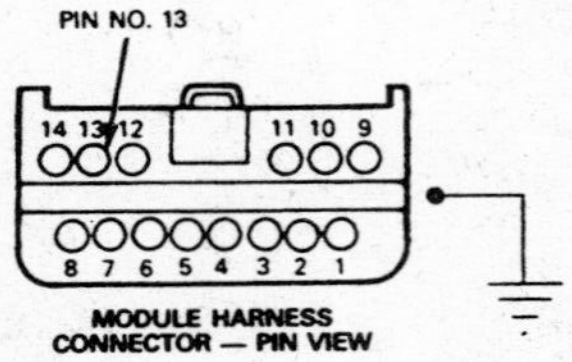

FIG. 111 Navajo: FLASHOUT CODE 2

Yellow REAR ANTILOCK Light Flashes 3 Times (Open Dump Circuit)

Flashout Code 3

TEST STEP	RESULT	ACTION TO TAKE
3a CHECK FOR OPEN RABS VALVE DUMP SOLENOID WIRING OR COMPUTER MODULE		
1. Turn ignition switch to the off position. 2. Disconnect the battery. 3. Disconnect module harness connector from module. 4. Place the ohmmeter on the 200 ohm scale. 5. Check resistance between pin 8 (or pin 14) and chassis ground. PIN NO. 14 14 13 12 11 10 9 8 7 6 5 4 3 2 1 PIN NO. 8 MODULE HARNESS CONNECTOR — PIN VIEW	Resistance less than 3 ohms ▶	REPLACE computer module.
	Resistance greater than 3 ohms ▶	GO to Test **3b**.
3b CHECK FOR OPEN RABS VALVE DUMP SOLENOID OR WIRING		
1. Turn the ignition switch to the off position. 2. Disconnect the battery. 3. Disconnect RABS valve harness connector from valve connector. 4. Check resistance between valve connector dump solenoid pin and ground pin. DUMP SOLENOID PIN GROUND PIN RABS VALVE CONNECTOR — PIN VIEW	Resistance less than 3 ohms ▶	REPAIR open in Y/LG circuit, dump solenoid wire, from valve to module. CHECK for loose, dirty or bent connector pins.
	Resistance greater than 3 ohms ▶	REPLACE RABS valve.

FIG. 112 Navajo: FLASHOUT CODE 3

Yellow REAR ANTILOCK Light Flashes 4 Times Red Brake Warning Light Illuminated RABS Valve Switch/Wiring or Open Dump Valve

Flashout Code 4

TEST STEP	RESULT	ACTION TO TAKE
4a CHECK FOR CLOSED RABS VALVE SWITCH		
1. Disconnect RABS valve harness connector from valve connector. 2. Place ohmmeter on the 20K scale. 3. Check resistance between valve connector switch pin and valve body. SWITCH PIN RABS VALVE BODY GROUND RABS VALVE CONNECTOR — PIN VIEW	Resistance greater than 10K ohms ▶	GO to Test **4B**.
	Resistance less than 10K ohms ▶	REPLACE RABS valve.
4b CHECK RESISTANCE BETWEEN VALVE SWITCH AND VALVE GROUND		
1. Set the ohmmeter on the 20K ohm scale. 2. Check resistance between valve connector switch pin and valve solenoid ground pin. VALVE SWITCH PIN GROUND PIN RABS VALVE CONNECTOR — PIN VIEW	Resistance 18-26K ohms ▶	GO to Test **4C**.
	Resistance higher than 26K or lower than 18K ▶	REPLACE RABS valve.

FIG. 113 Navajo: FLASHOUT CODE 4

Yellow REAR ANTILOCK Light Flashes 4 Times
Red Brake Warning Light Illuminated
RABS Valve Switch, Wiring or Open Dump (Continued)

Flashout Code 4

TEST STEP	RESULT ▶	ACTION TO TAKE
4c CHECK FOR HYDRAULIC LEAK IN DUMP SECTION OF VALVE		
1. Set the ohmmeter on the 200K scale. 2. Check resistance between valve connector switch pin and valve body with hydraulic pressure applied for at least 30 seconds.	Resistance greater than 10K ohms ▶	GO to Test **4d**.
	Resistance lower than 10K ohms ▶	REPLACE RABS valve.

SWITCH PIN
RABS VALVE BODY GROUND
VALVE CONNECTOR — PIN VIEW

FIG. 114 Navajo: FLASHOUT CODE 4 (continued)

Yellow REAR ANTILOCK Light Flashes 4 Times
Red Brake Warning Light Illuminated
RABS Valve Switch or Wiring (Continued)

Flashout Code 4

TEST STEP	RESULT ▶	ACTION TO TAKE
4d CHECK FOR OPEN RABS VALVE GROUND WIRE		
1. Set ohmmeter on 200 ohm scale. 2. Check for resistance between ground pin of harness connector and chassis ground.	Resistance less than 1 ohm ▶	GO to Test **4e**.
	Resistance 1 ohm or more ▶	REPAIR open in B/W circuit, isolation solenoid wire. CHECK for dirty or loose connector pins.
4e CHECK RESISTANCE IN RABS VALVE WIRING FROM THE MODULE CONNECTOR TO VALVE (OR MODULE)		
1. Install RABS valve connector into valve. 2. Disconnect battery 3. Disconnect the module harness connector from the module. 4. Set the ohmmeter on 200K scale. 5. Check resistance between pin 4 and pin 6 of module harness connector.	Resistance 18-26K ohms ▶	REPLACE computer module.
	Resistance higher than 26K or lower than 18K ▶	REPAIR open or short in LB/R circuit, valve switch wire from valve to computer module.

GROUND PIN
RABS VALVE HARNESS CONNECTOR — PIN VIEW

SWITCH PIN NO. 6
GROUND PIN NO. 4
14 13 12 11 10 9
8 7 6 5 4 3 2 1
MODULE HARNESS CONNECTOR — PIN VIEW

FIG. 115 Navajo: FLASHOUT CODE 4 (continued)

Yellow REAR ANTILOCK Light Flashes 5 Times System Dumps Too Many Times in 2WD Condition Occurs While Making Normal or Hard Stops. Rear Brakes May Lock

Flashout Code 5

TEST STEP	RESULT ▶	ACTION TO TAKE
5a		
The problem was initiated in 4x2 mode		GO to Step **5b**.
The problem was initiated in 4x4 mode only		GO to Step **5c**.
5b CHECK FOR MECHANICAL PROBLEMS IN REAR BRAKE SYSTEM		
1. Disconnect the RABS module harness connector from the module to deactivate the RABS. 2. Drive the vehicle (in 4x2 mode). 3. Make normal stops in a safe area to determine the condition of the rear brake system.	Rear brakes are grabby or tend to lock up easily ▶	REPAIR rear brake system and RETEST.
	Rear brakes are satisfactory for normal braking ▶	REPLACE RABS valve.
5c CHECK FOR MISSING SIGNAL FROM 4 WD SWITCH TO COMPUTER MODULE		
1. Disconnect the RABS module harness from the module. 2. Turn ignition switch on. 3. Shift into 4x4 mode. 4. Set voltmeter to 20 VDC scale. 5. Measure voltage between pin 5 and chassis ground.	Voltage is less than 1 volt ▶	REPLACE RABS valve.
	Voltage is greater than 1 volt ▶	REPAIR 4x4 indicator switch.

FIG. 116 Navajo: FLASHOUT CODE 5

Yellow REAR ANTILOCK Light Flashes 6 Times (Sensor Signal Rapidly Cuts In and Out) Condition Only Occurs While Driving

Flashout Code 6

TEST STEP	RESULT ▶	ACTION TO TAKE
6a CHECK FOR ERRATIC SENSOR SIGNAL AND LOOSE WIRE CONNECTIONS		
1. Turn ignition off. 2. Disconnect battery. 3. Set ohmmeter on the 2000 ohm scale. 4. Check resistance between Pin 10 and Pin 3 of the harness connector while shaking the harness from sensor to module.	Constant reading of 1000 to 2000 ohms ▶	GO to Step **6b**.
	Reading is erratic ▶	REPAIR loose connection in the LG/B or R/P circuits (sensor leads). CHECK for dirty or loose pins, frayed or shorted connectors.
6b CHECK FOR METAL CHIPS ON SENSOR MAGNET POLE PIECE		
• Remove the sensor from the differential and inspect for a build-up of metal chips on sensor magnetic pole.	No metal chips are present ▶	GO to Step **6c**.
	Metal chips are present ▶	DRAIN and CLEAN differential. CHECK the excitor ring for broken or chipped teeth.
6c CHECK FOR EXCITOR RING DAMAGE		
1. Remove sensor from carrier. 2. Rotate excitor ring and check for damage to teeth.	Teeth are intact and no visible lateral runout is observed ▶	REINSTALL sensor and GO to Test **6d**.
	Teeth are damaged or lateral runout of excitor ring is visible ▶	REPAIR axle.

FIG. 117 Navajo: FLASHOUT CODE 6

Yellow REAR ANTILOCK Light Flashes 6 Times (Sensor Signal Rapidly Cuts In and Out) Condition Only Occurs While Driving (Cont'd)

Flashout Code 6

TEST STEP	RESULT ▶	ACTION TO TAKE
6d CHECK FOR ERRATIC OR LOW SENSOR OUTPUT ON COMPUTER MODULE		
1. Locate the sensor test connector. 2. Position vehicle on a hoist and raise the rear wheels to clear the floor. 3. Start the engine and turn the wheels at 5 mph. 4. Place voltmeter on the 2000 mv AC scale. 5. Measure voltage at the two pins of the sensor test connector. CONNECTOR PINS SENSOR TEST CONNECTOR — PIN VIEW	Voltage greater than 650 mV RMS and steady ▶	REPLACE module.
	Voltage less than 650 mV RMS or erratic ▶	REPLACE sensor and recheck output and replace the sensor test connector cap.

FIG. 118 Navajo: FLASHOUT CODE 6 (continued)

Yellow REAR ANTILOCK Light Flashes 7 Times No Isolate Valve Self Test

Flashout Code 7

TEST STEP	RESULT ▶	ACTION TO TAKE
7a CHECK FOR RABS VALVE ISOLATION SOLENOID OR WIRING SHORTED TO GROUND		
1. Turn ignition off. 2. Disconnect the valve harness connector from the valve connector. 3. Set the ohmmeter on the 200 ohm scale. 4. Measure the resistance between the valve isolation solenoid pin and the valve ground pin in the valve connector. ISOLATION SOLENOID PIN GROUND PIN RABS VALVE CONNECTOR PIN VIEW	Resistance is greater than 3 ohms ▶	GO to Test **7B**.
	Resistance is less than 3 ohms ▶	REPLACE RABS valve.
7b CHECK FOR BLOWN INTERNAL FUSE IN THE MODULE		
1. Turn ignition off. 2. Disconnect the battery. 3. Disconnect the valve harness connector from the valve. 4. Disconnect the module harness connector from the module. 5. Place the ohmmeter on the 20K ohm scale. 6. Measure the resistance between module harness connector pin 13 and chassis ground. PIN NO. 13 14 13 12 11 10 9 8 7 6 5 4 3 2 1 MODULE HARNESS CONNECTOR — PIN VIEW	Resistance greater than 20K ohms ▶	REPLACE module.
	Resistance less than 20K ohms ▶	REPAIR short in tan wire circuit between RABS valve and module. RECONNECT module and valve.

FIG. 119 Navajo: FLASHOUT CODE 7

Yellow REAR ANTILOCK Light Flashes 8 Times No Dump Valve Self Test

Flashout Code 8

TEST STEP	RESULT ▶	ACTION TO TAKE
8a CHECK FOR RABS VALVE SOLENOID OR WIRING SHORTED TO GROUND		
1. Turn ignition switch off. 2. Disconnect valve harness connector from valve connector. 3. Set the ohmmeter on the 200 ohm scale. 4. Measure the resistance between the valve dump solenoid pin and the valve ground pin in the valve connector. GROUND PIN; DUMP SOLENOID PIN RABS VALVE CONNECTOR — PIN VIEW	Resistance greater than 1 ohm ▶	GO to Test **8b**.
	Resistance is less than 1 ohm ▶	REPLACE RABS valve.
8b CHECK COMPUTER MODULE		
1. Turn ignition off. 2. Disconnect battery. 3. Disconnect valve harness connector from valve connector. 4. Disconnect the module harness connector from the module. 5. Set the ohmmeter on the 20K ohm scale. 6. Measure the resistance between module harness connector pin 8 (or pin 14) and chassis ground. PIN NO. 14; 14 13 12; 11 10 9; 8 7 6 5 4 3 2 1; PIN NO. 8 MODULE HARNESS CONNECTOR — PIN VIEW	Resistance greater than 20K ohm ▶	REPLACE module.
	Resistance less than 20K ohm ▶	REPAIR short in Y/LG wires circuit between RABS valve and RABS module. RECONNECT module and valve.

FIG. 120 Navajo: FLASHOUT CODE 8

Yellow REAR ANTILOCK Light Flashes 9 Times High Sensor Resistance

Flashout Code 9

TEST STEP	RESULT ▶	ACTION TO TAKE
9a CHECK FOR OPEN SENSOR OR SENSOR WIRING		
1. Turn key off. 2. Disconnect sensor harness connector from the sensor on the differential. 3. Set the ohmmeter on the 20K ohm scale. 4. Measure the resistance at the two sensor pins. SENSOR PINS SENSOR — PIN VIEW	Resistance less than 2500 ohms ▶	GO to Test **9b**.
	Resistance greater than 2500 ohms ▶	REPLACE sensor.
9b CHECK FOR OPEN SENSOR HARNESS WIRING		
1. Turn key off. 2. Disconnect battery. 3. Reconnect sensor harness connector to sensor. 4. Disconnect module harness connector from module. 5. Set the ohmmeter on the 20K ohm scale. 6. Measure the resistance between harness connector pins 3 and 10. 14 13 12; 11 10 9; 8 7 6 5 4 3 2 1; PIN NO. 10; PIN NO. 3 MODULE HARNESS CONNECTOR — PIN VIEW	Resistance less than 2500 ohms ▶	REPLACE module.
	Resistance greater than 2500 ohms ▶	REPAIR open in circuits LG/B or R/P, sensor wires between the sensor and module. CHECK for loose or dirty pin connectors. If defect is found in wiring harness (from sensor to left frame rail), REPLACE with original equipment high flex wire. Splice connector must be used.

FIG. 121 Navajo: FLASHOUT CODE 9

Yellow REAR ANTILOCK Light Flashes 10 Times Low Sensor Resistance

Flashout Code 10

TEST STEP	RESULT	ACTION TO TAKE
10c CHECK FOR SHORTED SENSOR WIRING		
1. Turn ignition off. 2. Disconnect sensor harness connector from the sensor. 3. Disconnect the module harness connector from the module. 4. Place the ohmmeter on the 20K ohm scale. 5. Measure the resistance from pin 3 to pin 10 of the harness connector.	Resistance less than 20K ohms ▶	REPAIR short between the R/P and LG/B sensor circuits. CHECK for frayed wires or shorted connectors. If defect is found in the wiring harness (from sensor to left frame rail), REPLACE with original equipment high flex wire and SPLICE using Splice Connector.
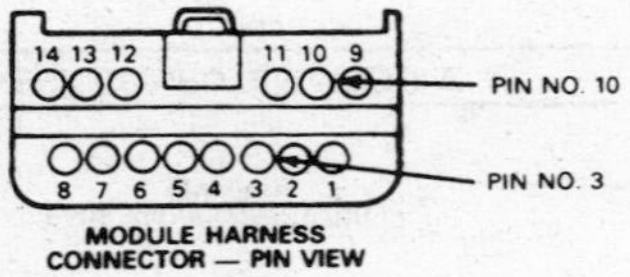	Resistance greater than 20K ohms ▶	REPLACE the RABS module.

FIG. 122 Navajo: FLASHOUT CODE 10

Yellow REAR ANTILOCK Light Flashes 10 Times Low Sensor Resistance

Flashout Code 10

TEST STEP	RESULT	ACTION TO TAKE
10a CHECK FOR SHORTED SENSOR		
1. Turn ignition off. 2. Disconnect the sensor harness from the sensor. 3. Place the ohmmeter on the 20K ohms scale. 4. Measure the resistance at the two sensor pins.	Resistance less than 1000 ohms ▶	REPLACE sensor.
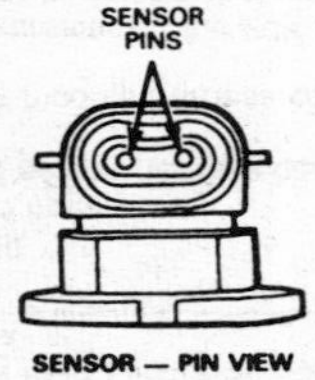	Resistance is greater than 1000 ohms ▶	GO to Test **10b**.
10b CHECKING FOR GROUNDED SENSOR WIRING		
1. Turn ignition off. 2. Disconnect the battery. 3. Disconnect the sensor harness connector from the sensor. 4. Disconnect the module harness connector from the module. 5. Set the ohmmeter on the 20K ohm scale. 6. Measure the resistance from pin 10 of the harness connector to chassis ground.	Resistance less than 20K ohms ▶	REPAIR short to ground in R/P circuit, sensor HI lead to module. CHECK for frayed wires or shorted connectors. If defect is found in the wiring harness (from sensor to left frame rail), REPLACE with original equipment high flex wire and splice using Splice Connector.
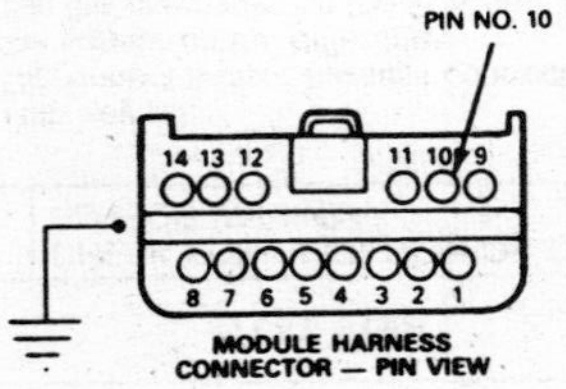	Resistance is greater than 20K ohms ▶	GO to Test **10c**.

FIG. 123 Navajo: FLASHOUT CODE 10 (continued)

Yellow REAR ANTILOCK Light Flashes 11 Times. Stop Lamp Switch Always Closed or Stop Lamp Switch Circuit Defective. Condition Indicated Only When Driving Above 35 mph.

Flashout Code 11

TEST STEP	RESULT ▶	ACTION TO TAKE
11a CHECK VEHICLE STOP LIGHTS		
• Apply the service brakes and observe the rear brake lamps.	Lamps illuminate ▶	GO to Test **11b**.
	Lamps do not illuminate ▶	REPAIR or REPLACE vehicle stop light switch. CHECK for blown stop light switch fuse. Investigate reason for blown fuse. CHECK for open stop light switch wiring or blown stop lamps. REPAIR as needed.
11b WIRING FROM MODULE TO BRAKE SWITCH		
• Check for an open between the brake switch and the module: 1. Turn the ignition off. 2. Set the voltmeter on the 20 VDC scale. 3. Remove the module harness connector. 4. Measure the voltage between pin 11 and chassis ground while stepping on the brake pedal.	Voltage is less than 9V ▶	REPAIR the open in the LG circuit.
	Voltage is 9V or more ▶	CHECK 4 way flasher and directional wiring. This condition could create feedback through the stop light circuit. Also, cruise controls may not operate correctly.

FIG. 124 Navajo: FLASHOUT CODE 11

Yellow REAR ANTILOCK Light Flashes 12 Times, Red Brake WARNING LIGHT Illuminated, Loss of Hydraulic Brake Fluid for One Second During Antilock Stop

Flashout Code 12

TEST STEP	RESULT ▶	ACTION TO TAKE
12a		
• Check the brake fluid level at the master cylinder reservoir.	Brake fluid level low ▶	Check for fluid leaks in vehicle brake system and repair as required. Fill master cylinder to required level.
	Brake fluid level OK ▶	GO to Test **12b**.
12b MASTER CYLINDER SWITCH		
• Check for proper functioning of the master cylinder fluid level indicator switch: 1. Remove the connector from the master cylinder. 2. Connect a jumper wire between the purple/yellow wire and the purple/white wire. 3. Turn the ignition key to the on position.	ANTILOCK and BRAKE warning lamps stay on ▶	GO to Test **12c**.
	ANTILOCK and BRAKE warning lamps go off ▶	REPLACE the master cylinder reservoir. REFER to Section 06.06 Hydraulic Brake Actuation for procedure.
12c BRAKE LIGHT WIRING		
• Check for shorts in brake light wiring. 1. Disconnect module harness connector from module. 2. Turn ignition key to the on position.	ANTILOCK light goes off and BRAKE light stays on ▶	CHECK for short to ground in the 977 and 128 circuit. REFER to wiring diagram in this Section.
	Both ANTILOCK and BRAKE warning lamps go off ▶	REPLACE module.

FIG. 125 Navajo: FLASHOUT CODE 12

Yellow REAR ANTILOCK Light Flashes 13 Times Speed Processor Check

Flashout Code 13

TEST STEP	RESULT ▶	ACTION TO TAKE
13a NO TEST		
• RABS module general failure detected during module self test.	13 flashes are present ▶	REPLACE RABS module.

FIG. 126 Navajo: FLASHOUT CODE 13

Yellow REAR ANTILOCK Light Flashes 14 Times Program Check

Flashout Code 14

TEST STEP	RESULT ▶	ACTION TO TAKE
14a NO TEST		
• RABS module program check sum failure detected during self test.	If 14 flashes are present ▶	REPLACE RABS module.

FIG. 128 Navajo: FLASHOUT CODE 15

Yellow REAR ANTILOCK Light Flashes 15 Times Memory Failure

Flashout Code 15

TEST STEP	RESULT ▶	ACTION TO TAKE
15a NO TEST		
• RABS module RAM failure detected during self test.	If 15 flashes are present ▶	REPLACE RABS module.

FIG. 127 Navajo: FLASHOUT CODE 14

Yellow REAR ANTILOCK Light Flashes 16 Times or More 16 or More Flashes Should Not Occur

Flashout Code 16

TEST STEP	RESULT ▶	ACTION TO TAKE
16a NO TEST		
• This code should not occur. Refer to obtaining the Flashout Code in this Section for procedures involved in getting the code.	Flashout Code is 16 ▶	If after repeated attempts to take the Flashout Code, Code 16 is still obtained, REPLACE RABS module.

FIG. 129 Navajo: FLASHOUT CODE 16

BRAKE SPECIFICATIONS

All measurements in inches unless noted.

Year	Model	Lug Nut Torque (ft. lbs.)	Master Cylinder Bore	Brake Disc Minimum Thickness	Brake Disc Maximum Runout	Standard Brake Drum Diameter	Minimum Lining Thickness Front	Minimum Lining Thickness Rear
1987	B2200	①	0.875	0.71	0.006	10.24	0.118	0.04
	B2600	①	0.875	0.79	0.006	10.24	0.118	0.04
1988	B2200	①	0.875	0.71	0.006	10.24	0.118	0.04
	B2600	①	0.875	0.79	0.006	10.24	0.118	0.04
1989	B2200	①	0.875	0.71	0.006	10.24	0.118	0.04
	B2600i	①	0.875	0.79	0.006	10.24	0.118	0.04
	MPV	65–87	0.940	0.87	0.004	10.24	0.080	0.04
1990	B2200	①	0.875	0.71	0.006	10.24	0.118	0.04
	B2600i	①	0.875	②	0.006	10.24	0.118	0.04
	MPV	65–87	0.940	0.87	0.004	10.24	0.080	0.04
1991	B2200	①	0.875	0.71	0.006	10.24	0.118	0.04
	B2600i	①	0.875	②	0.006	10.24	0.118	0.04
	MPV	65–87	0.940	③	0.004	10.24	0.080	0.04
	Navajo	100	0.937	0.81	0.003	10.00	0.120	0.03
1992	B2200	①	0.875	0.71	0.006	10.24	0.118	0.04
	B2600i	①	0.875	②	0.006	10.24	0.118	0.04
	MPV	65–87	0.940	③	0.004	10.24	0.080	0.04
	Navajo	100	0.937	0.81	0.003	10.00	0.120	0.03

① Design wheels 65–87 ft. lbs.
Styled wheels 87–108 ft. lbs.

② 2WD—0.71 in.
4WD—0.79 in.

③ 2WD—1.10 in.
4WD—1.02 in.

TORQUE SPECIFICATIONS

Component	U.S.	Metric
Brake line bolt	22 ft. lbs.	29.92 Nm
Brake pipes		
MPV without ABS	15 ft. lbs.	20.4 Nm
MPV w/ ABS	16-20 ft. lbs.	22.76-27.2 Nm
Caliper lock pin bolt		
MPV	69 ft. lbs.	93.84 Nm
Pickups	30 ft. lbs.	40.8 Nm
Caliper mounting bolts		
MPV	61-69 ft. lbs.	82.96-93.84 Nm
Pickups	23-30 ft. lbs.	31.28-40.8 Nm
Caliper support bolts		
Pickups & MPV	80 ft. lbs.	108.8 Nm
Flare nuts		
Navajo	10-15 ft. lbs.	13.6-20.4 Nm
Flexible hose-to-caliper fasteners		
Navajo	16-19 ft. lbs.	22.76-25.84 Nm
Hold down bolt		
Navajo w/ ABS	30 ft. lbs.	40.8 Nm
Lead tang to caliper nut		
Navajo	32-47 in. lbs.	3.584-5.264 Nm
Lower lock pin bolt		
Pickups & MPV	30 ft. lbs.	40.8 Nm
Lug nuts		
Navajo	85-115 ft. lbs.	115.6-156.4 Nm
Master cylinder bolts/nuts		
MPV	13-25 ft. lbs.	27.68-34 Nm
Pickups	15 ft. lbs.	20.4 Nm
Outer bearing hub nut		
2WD pickups	22 ft. lbs.	29.92 Nm
Power booster nuts		
Pickups	17 ft. lbs.	23.12 Nm
Rotor-to-hub bolts		
2WD pickups	40 ft. lbs.	54.4 Nm
4WD pickups	50 ft. lbs.	68 Nm
Speed sensor		
all except Navajo	12-17 ft. lbs.	16.32-23.12 Nm
Navajo	25-30 ft. lbs.	34-40.8 Nm
Stop bolt		
MPV	17-22 in. lbs.	23.12-29.92 Nm
Vacuum unit nuts		
MPV w/ 4-cylinder engine	19 ft. lbs.	25.84
MPV w/ 6-cylinder engine	19 ft. lbs.	25.84 Nm
Valve retaining screws		
all except Navajo	14-19 ft. lbs.	19.04-25.84 Nm
Navajo	11-14 ft. lbs.	14.96-19.04 Nm

10

BODY

EXTERIOR

Doors

➧ SEE FIGS. 1-5

REMOVAL & INSTALLATION

1. Matchmark the hinge-to-body and hinge-to-door locations. Support the door either on jackstands or have somebody help hold and support it for you.
2. On models with a door check bar, push in on the claw, remove the pin or unbolt the retainer.
3. Disconnect the wiring harnesses (after disconnecting the negative battery cable) on models having door mounted radio speakers or light harness.
4. Remove the lower hinge-to-door bolts.
5. Remove the upper hinge-to-door bolts and lift the door from the vehicle.
6. If the hinges are being replaced, remove them from the door pillar.
7. Install the door and hinges with the bolts finger tight.
8. Adjust the door and tighten the hinge bolts.

➡ If the door being removed is going to be replaced, and its internal components (glass and regulator, latch etc.) are to be used in the replacement door, it may be easier to remove the parts while the door is still mounted on the vehicle.

ALIGNMENT

When checking door alignment, look carefully at each seam between the door and body. The gap should be constant and even all the way

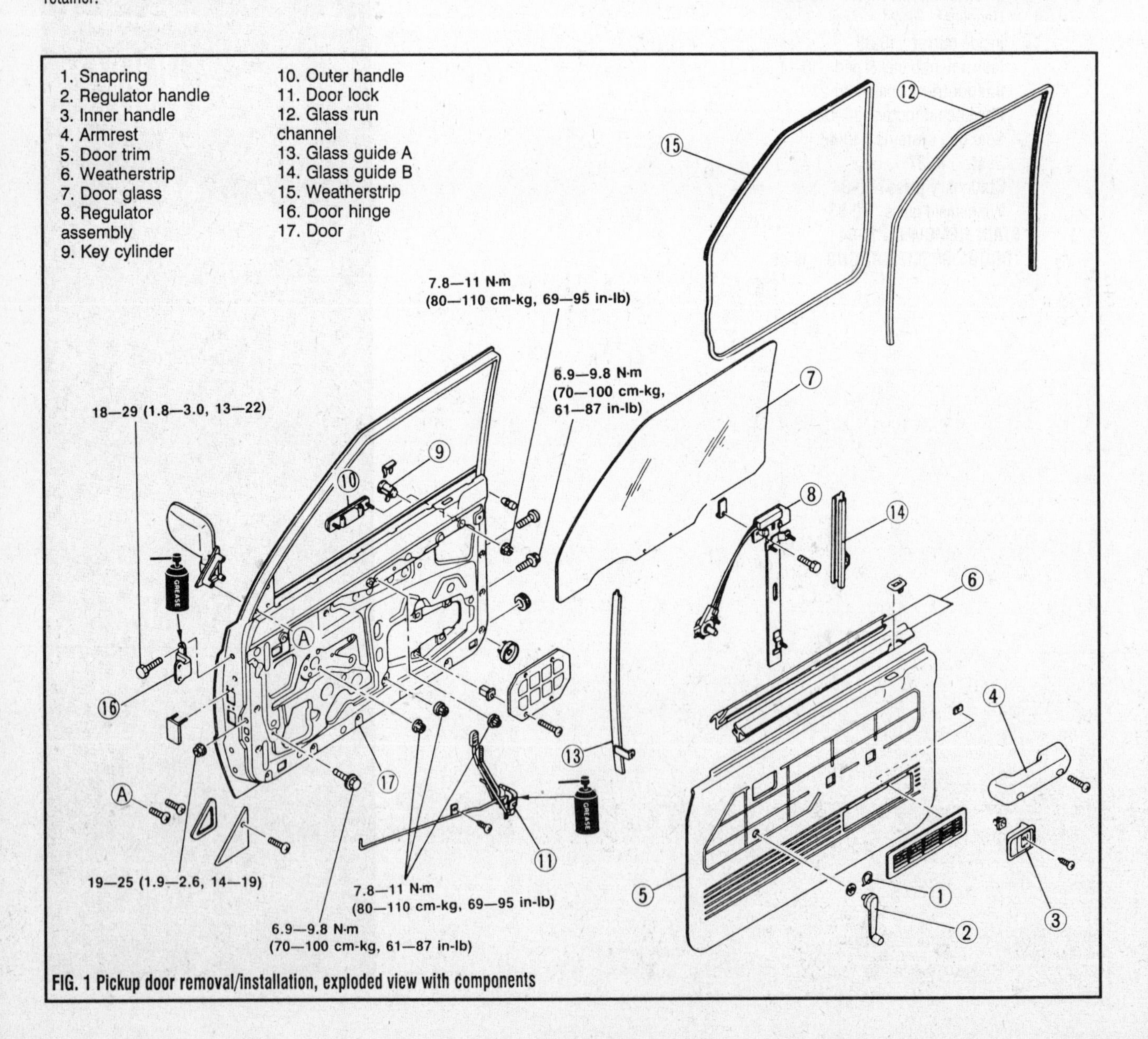

FIG. 1 Pickup door removal/installation, exploded view with components

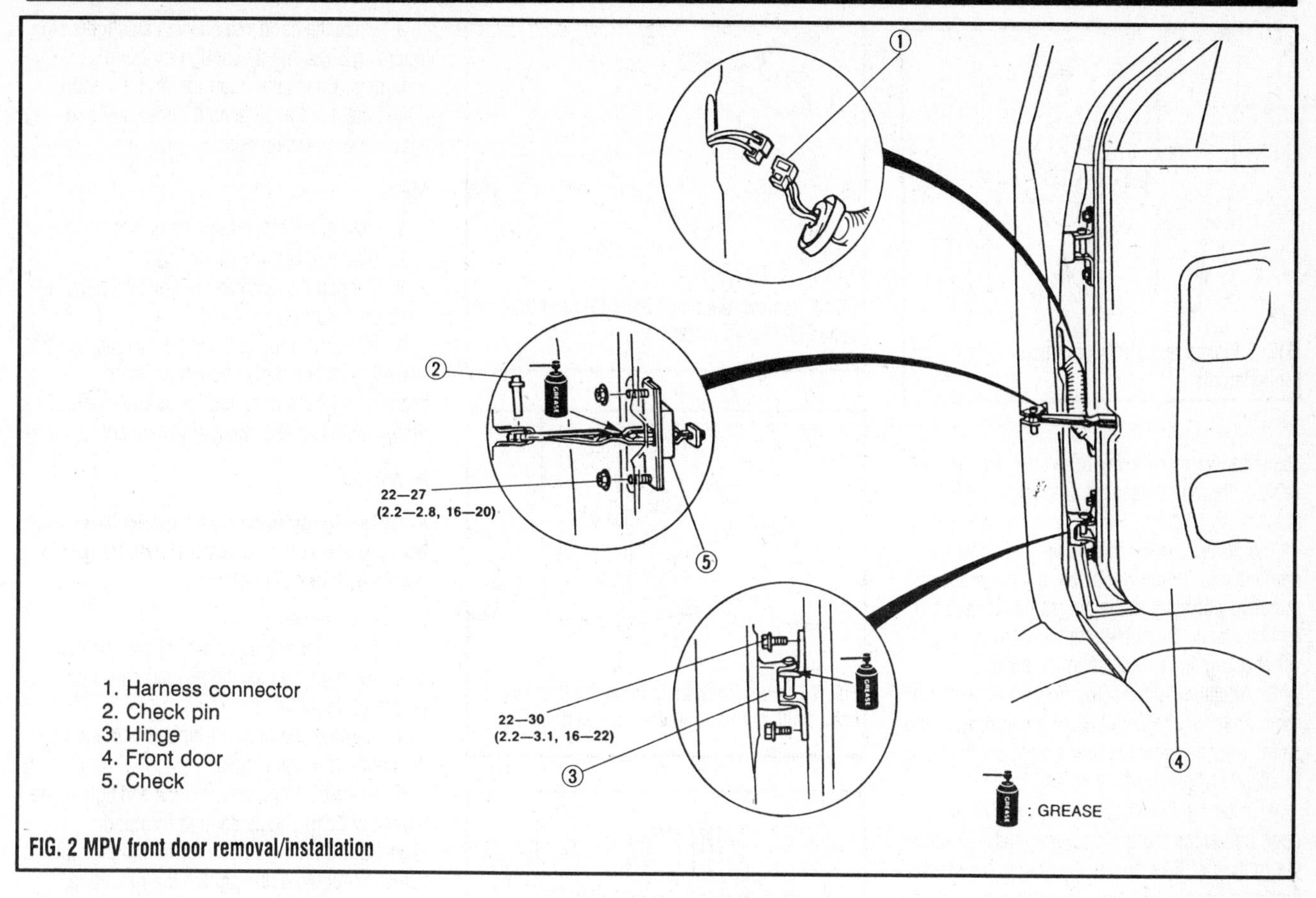

FIG. 2 MPV front door removal/installation

around the door. Pay particular attention to the door seams at the corner farthest from the hinges, this is the area where errors will be most evident. Additionally, the door should pull against the weatherstrip when latched to seal out wind and water. The contact should be even all the way around and the stripping should be about half compressed.

The position of the door can be adjusted in three dimensions: fore and aft, up and down, in and out. The primary adjusting points are the hinge-to-body bolts. Apply tape to the fender (or door pillar and quarter panel) and door edges to protect the paint. Two layers of common masking tape works well. Loosen the bolts just enough to allow the hinge to move. With the help of an assistant, position the door and tighten the bolts. Inspect the door seams carefully and repeat the adjustment until correctly aligned.

The in-out adjustment (how far the door "sticks out" from the body) is adjusted by loosening the hinge-to-door bolts. Again, loosen the bolts, move the door into place, tighten the bolts. The dimension affects both the amount of crush on the weatherstrip and the amount of "bite" on the striker.

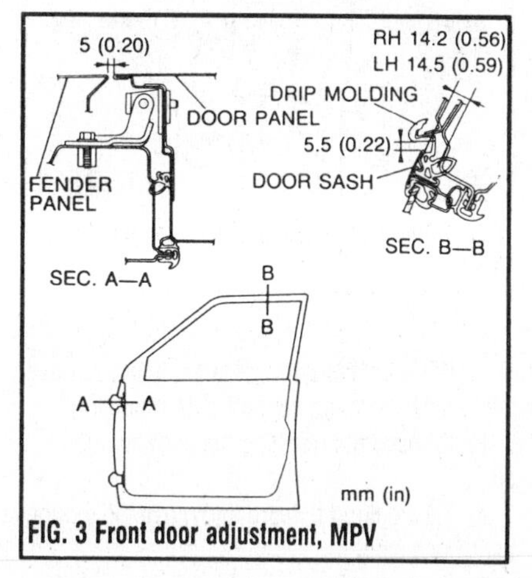

FIG. 3 Front door adjustment, MPV

Further adjustment for closed position and smoothness of latching is made at the latch plate or striker. This piece is located at the rear edge of the door and is attached to the body work; it is the piece the door latch engages when the door is closed.

1. To adjust the striker: Loosen the large cross-pointed screws mounting the striker to the body. The striker mounting screws are usually very tight; an impact screwdriver is a handy tool to have for this job. Make sure you are using the proper size bit. On models equipped with a screw in post striker, loosen the post slightly counterclockwise.

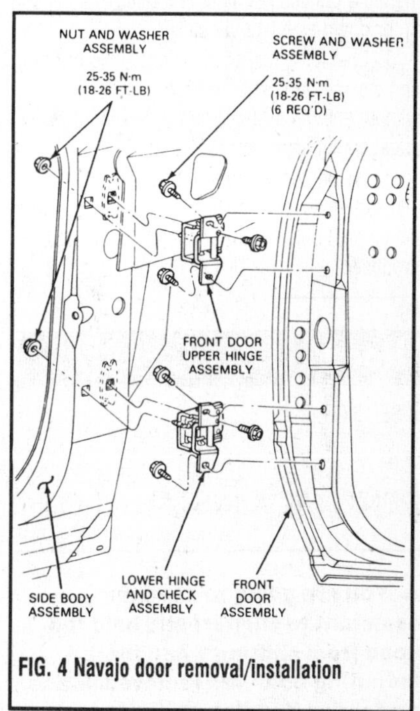

FIG. 4 Navajo door removal/installation

2. With bolts, or post just loose enough to allow the striker to move, hold the outer door handle in the released position and close the door. The striker should move into the correct location to match the door latch. Open the door and tighten the bolts or post. The striker may be

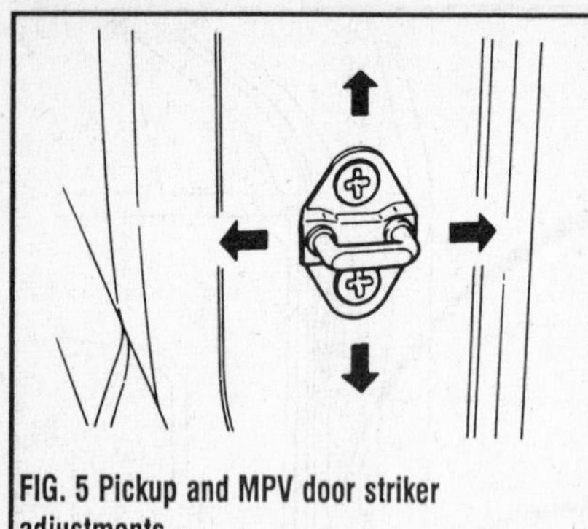
FIG. 5 Pickup and MPV door striker adjustments

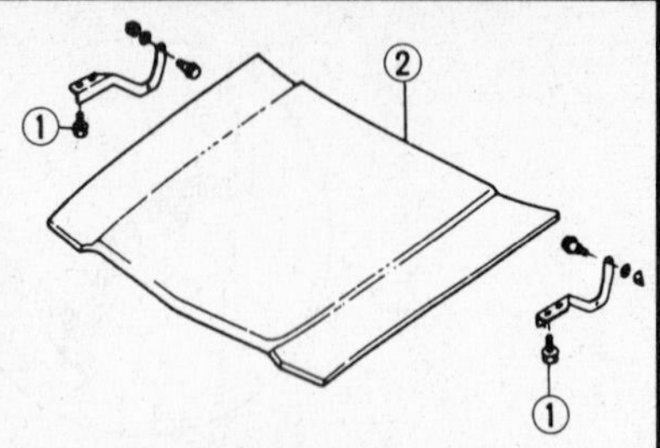

FIG. 6 Remove the hinge bolts (1), and the hood (2), Pickup models

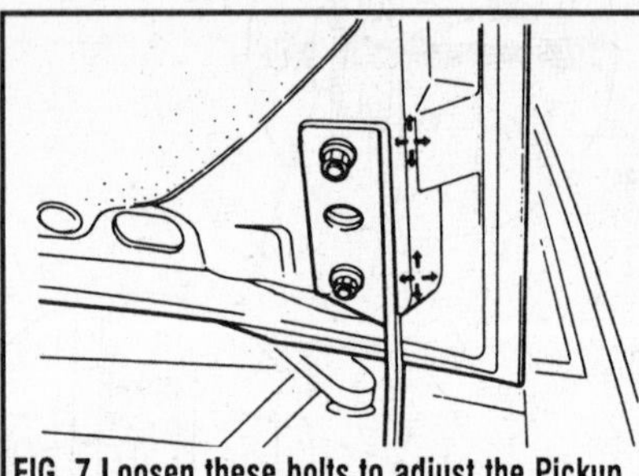
FIG. 7 Loosen these bolts to adjust the Pickup hood front and rear, side to side alignment

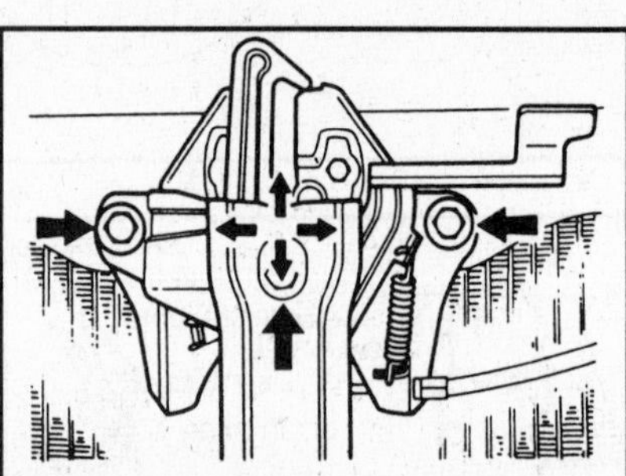
FIG. 8 Adjust the hood lock after the hood has been aligned, Pickup

aligned towards or away from the center of the vehicle, thereby tightening or loosening the door fit.

The striker can be moved up and down to compensate for door position, but if the door is mounted correctly at the hinges this should not be necessary. Do not attempt to correct height variations (sag) by adjusting the striker.

3. Additionally, some models may use one or more spacers or shims behind the striker. These shims may be removed or added in combination to adjust the reach of the striker.

4. After tightening the striker bolts or post, open and close the door several times. Observe the motion of the door as it engages the striker; it should continue straight-in motion and deflect up or down as it hits the striker.

5. Check the feel of the latch during opening and closing. It must be smooth and linear, without any trace of grinding or binding during engagement or release.

It may be necessary to repeat the striker adjustment several times (and possibly re-adjust the hinges) before correct door to body match is produced.

Hood

➧ SEE FIGS. 9-12

REMOVAL & INSTALLATION

➡ You are going to need an assistant to support and hold the hood from shifting when the mounting bolts are removed. Place protective padding on the fenders and cowl.

Pickups with Self-Supporting Hood

1. Open the hood and trace the outline of the hinges on the body.

2. While an assistant holds the hood, remove the retainer from the support strut mounting pin.

3. Remove the retaining pin and the hood stop.

4. Tilt the hood forward and move the torsion bar to one side.

5. Remove the hinge-to-body bolts and lift the hood off.

6. Place the hood into position and tighten the mounting bolts snugly enough for hood alignment. Align the outlines previously made. Check that the hood closes properly. Adjust hood alignment, if necessary and tighten the mounting bolts. Install the hood support strut.

Pickups with Hood Prop

1. Outline the hinge position on the hood.

2. Support the hood and remove the hinge-to-hood bolts. Lift off the hood.

3. Place the hood into position and tighten the mounting bolts snugly enough for hood alignment. Check the hood for fit and closure. Adjust the hood alignment, if necessary and tighten the mounting bolts.

MPV

1. Outline the hinge position on the hood.

2. Disconnect the washer hose.

3. Support the hood and remove the hinge-to-hood bolts. Lift off the hood.

4. Place the hood into position and tighten the mounting bolts snugly enough for hood alignment. Check the hood for fit and closure. Adjust the hood alignment, if necessary.

Navajo

➡ It is highly recommended that you have at least one assistant helping during this operation.

1. Open the hood.

2. Match mark the hood-to-hinge position.

3. Have you're assistant(s) support the weight of the hood.

4. Remove the hood-to-hinge bolts and lift the hood off of the hinges.

5. Place the hood into position and tighten the mounting bolts snugly enough for hood alignment. Check the hood for fit and closure, adjust as required and tighten the mounting bolts.

ALIGNMENT

Pickups and MPV

On self-supporting hoods, alignment can be adjusted front-to-rear or side-to-side by loosening the hood-to-hinge or hinge-to-body bolts. The front edge of the hood can be adjusted for closing height by adding or deleting shims under the hinges. The rear edge of the hood can be adjusted for closing height by raising or lowering the rear hood bumpers.

On hoods supported with a prop, alignment is accomplished by loosening the lock plate bolts and moving the lock plate up or down; side-to-side.

Navajo

1. Open the hood and match mark the hinge and latch positions.

2. Loosen the hinge-to-hood bolts just enough to allow movement of the hood.

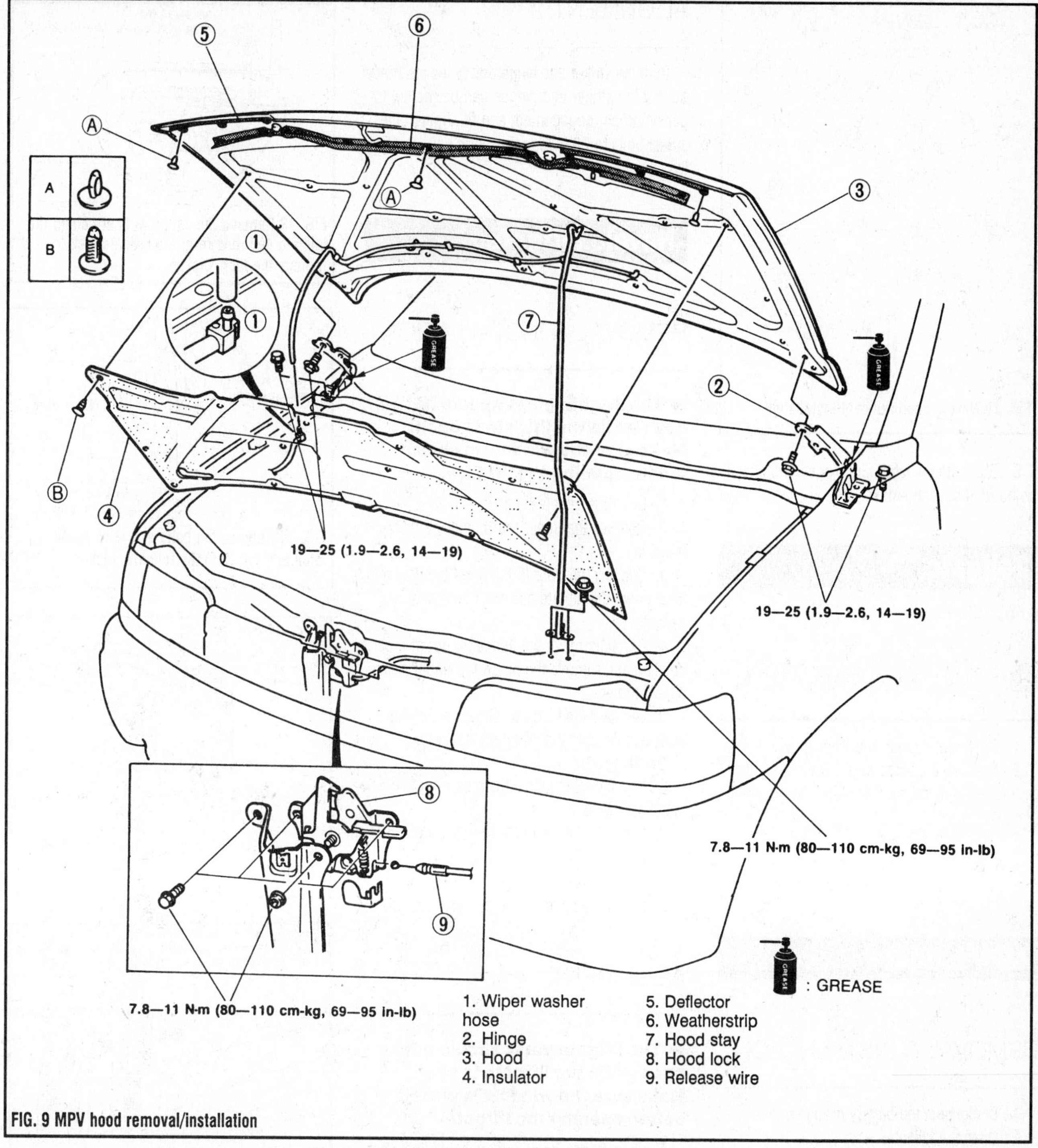

FIG. 9 MPV hood removal/installation

3. Move the hood as required to obtain the proper fit and alignment between the hood and all adjoining body panels. When satisfactorily aligned, tighten the mounting bolts. To raise or lower the hood, loosen the hinge to body attaching bolts and raise or lower the hood as required.

4. Loosen the latch attaching bolts.

5. Move the latch from side-to-side to align the latch with the striker. Tighten the latch bolts.

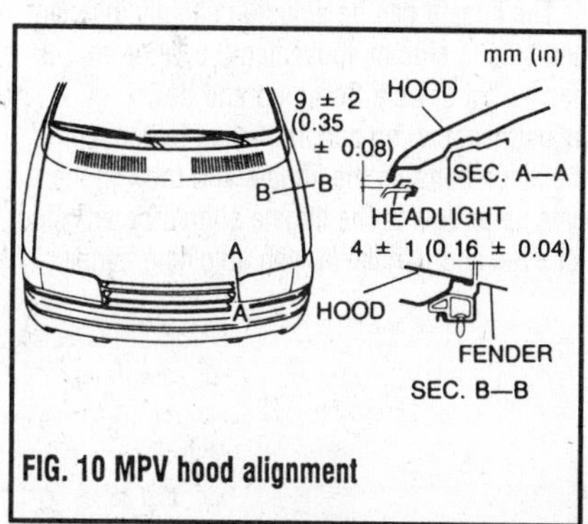

FIG. 10 MPV hood alignment

FIG. 11 Adjust the hood lock after the hood has been aligned, MPV

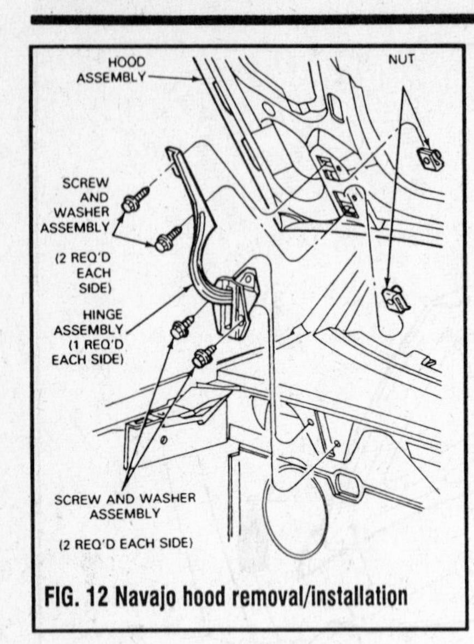

FIG. 12 Navajo hood removal/installation

6. Lubricate the latch and hinges and check the hood fit several times.

Tailgate

➧ SEE FIGS. 13-18

REMOVAL & INSTALLATION

1. Open and support the tailgate.
2. Remove the hinge pins by removing the cotter pins and washers, then driving the hinge pins out.
3. Lift off the tailgate.
4. Position the tailgate and install the mounting bolts.

MPV Liftgate

REMOVAL & INSTALLATION

1. Disconnect the battery ground cable.
2. Open the tailgate.
3. Disconnect the wiring connector.
4. Disconnect the washer hose.
5. Remove the strut-to-tailgate bolts.
6. Match mark the hinge position.
7. Support the tailgate and remove the hinge bolts. Lift off the tailgate.
8. Position the liftgate and install the mounting bolts. Torque the hinge-to-tailgate bolts to 10 ft. lbs.; the strut-to-tailgate bolts to 104 inch lbs.

ALIGNMENT

Both the striker and hinge bolt holes are made so that the striker and hinges can be moved to permit proper engagement and fit. Tighten the striker bolts to 20 ft. lbs.; the hinge bolts to 10 ft. lbs.

Navajo Liftgate

REMOVAL & INSTALLATION

➡ The liftgate glass should not be open while the liftgate is open. Make sure the window is closed before opening the liftgate.

1. Open the liftgate door.
2. Remove the upper rear center garnish molding.
3. Support the door in the open position and disconnect the liftgate gas cylinder assist rod assemblies.
4. Carefully move the headliner out of position and remove the hinge-to-header panel attaching nuts.
5. Remove the hinge-to-liftgate attaching bolts and remove the complete assembly.

To Install:

6. Install the hinge to liftgate door and tighten the attaching bolts.
7. Install the hinge to roof header panel and tighten the nut.
8. Adjust the liftgate hinge as necessary.
9. Install the header and garnish molding.

ALIGNMENT

➡ The liftgate glass should not be open while the liftgate is open. Make sure the window is closed before opening the liftgate.

The liftgate can be adjusted slightly in or out and side to side by loosening the hinge-to-header nut or bolt. Some up and down adjustment can be accomplished by loosening the hinge bolts on the liftgate and moving the gate up or down. The liftgate should be adjusted for even and parallel fit with adjoining panels.

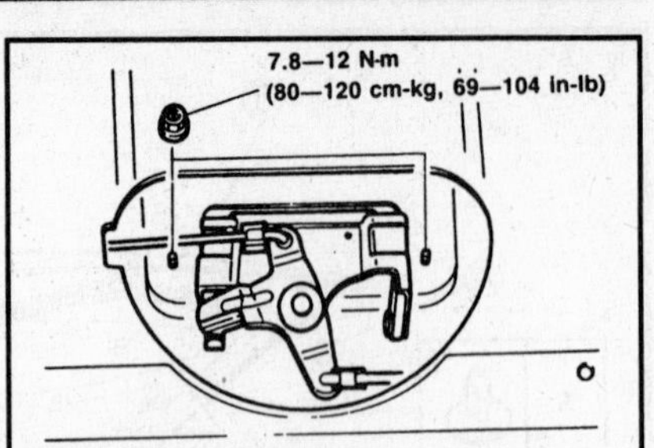

FIG. 13 Remove the cover, nuts attaching the tailgate and rods from the tailgate lock, remove the lock, Pickup

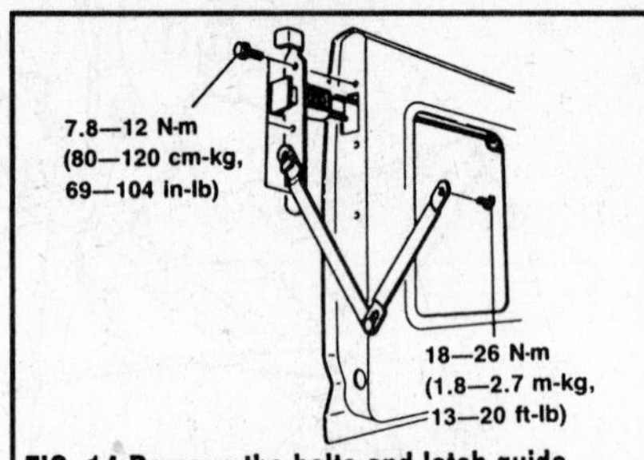

FIG. 14 Remove the bolts and latch guide, latch and rod from the tailgate, Pickup

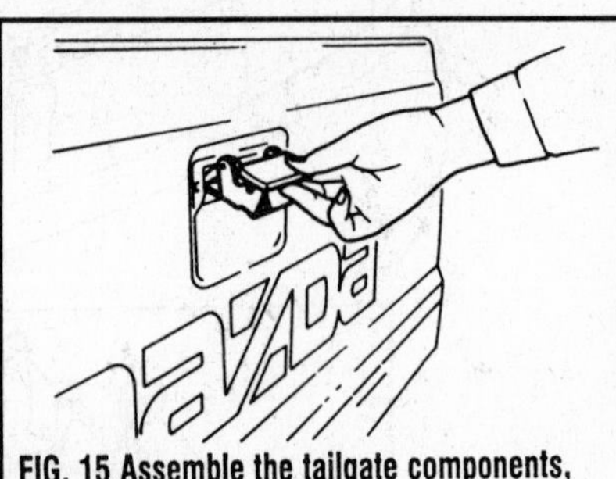

FIG. 15 Assemble the tailgate components, Pickup

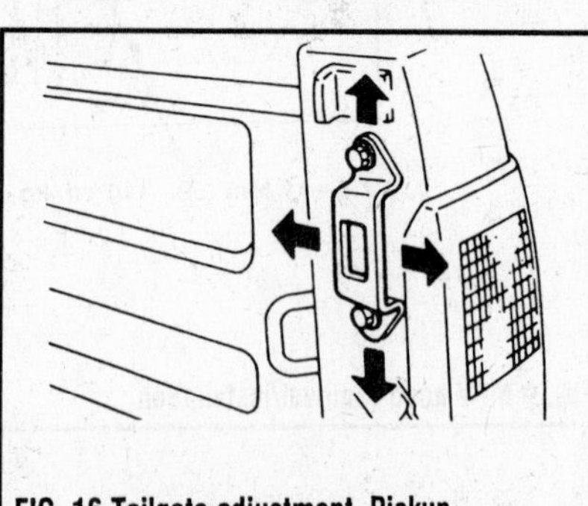

FIG. 16 Tailgate adjustment, Pickup

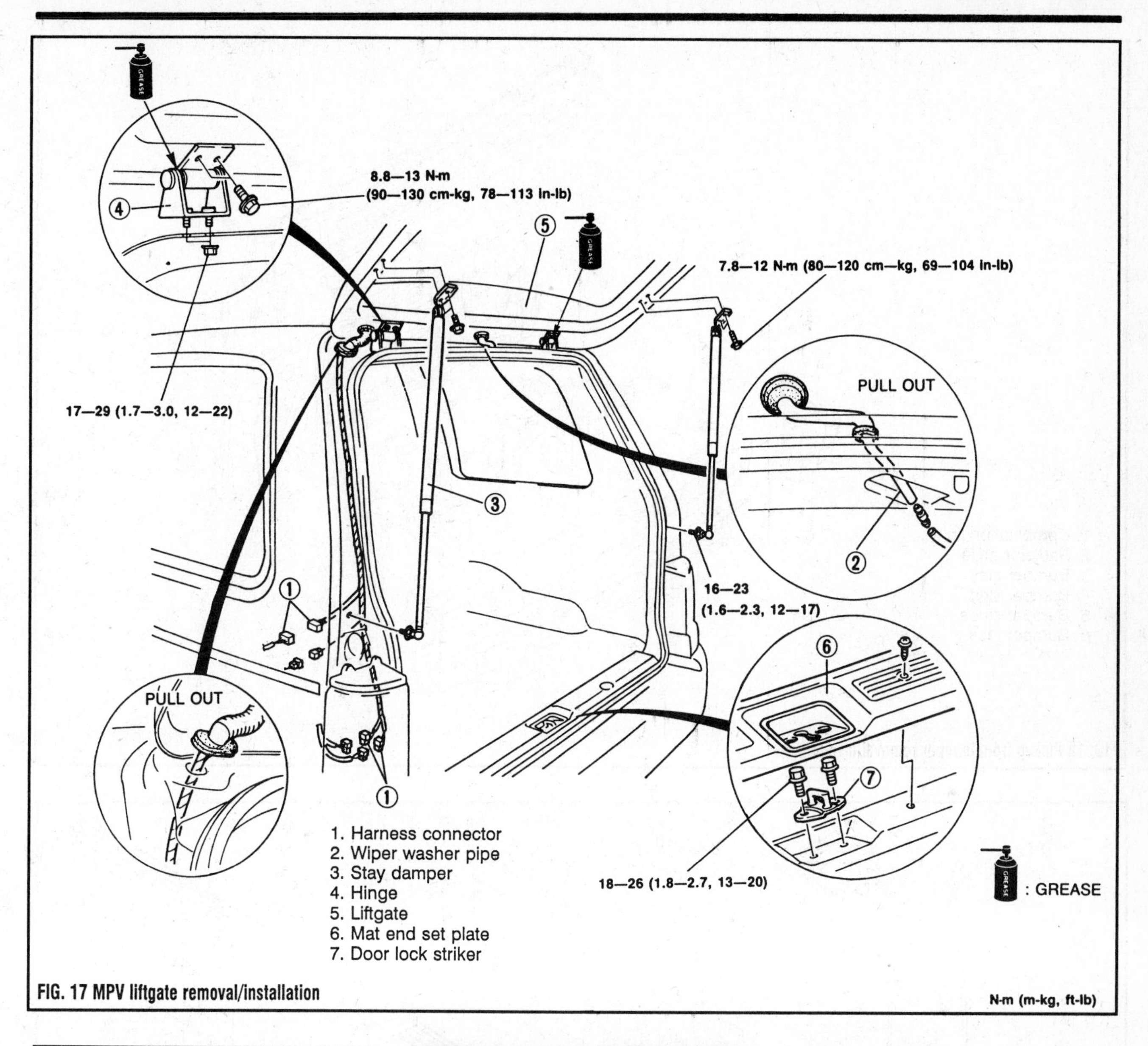

FIG. 17 MPV liftgate removal/installation

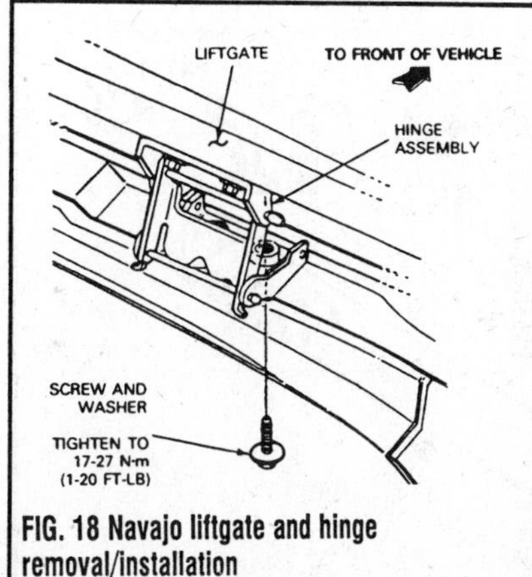

FIG. 18 Navajo liftgate and hinge removal/installation

Front Bumper

➧ SEE FIGS. 19-24

REMOVAL & INSTALLATION

Pickups

1. Remove the combination lamps from the grille.
2. Remove the grille.
3. Unplug the wiring from the lamps on the bumper skirt.
4. Remove the bumper skirt and end pieces.
5. Support the bumper.
6. Remove the bumper bracket-to-frame bolts.
7. Remove the bumper-to-bracket bolts.
8. Install in reverse order.

MPV

1. Remove the grille and side pieces (lower section).
2. Remove the lower under engine to bumper splash shield.
3. Remove the bumper upper end corners to body mounting bolts.
4. Support the bumper. In some cases it may be necessary to unbolt the bumper from the radiator support and body brackets instead of unbolting the bracket themselves. If not, remove the bumper stay to radiator support mounting bolts and the bumper bracket to body mounting bolts.

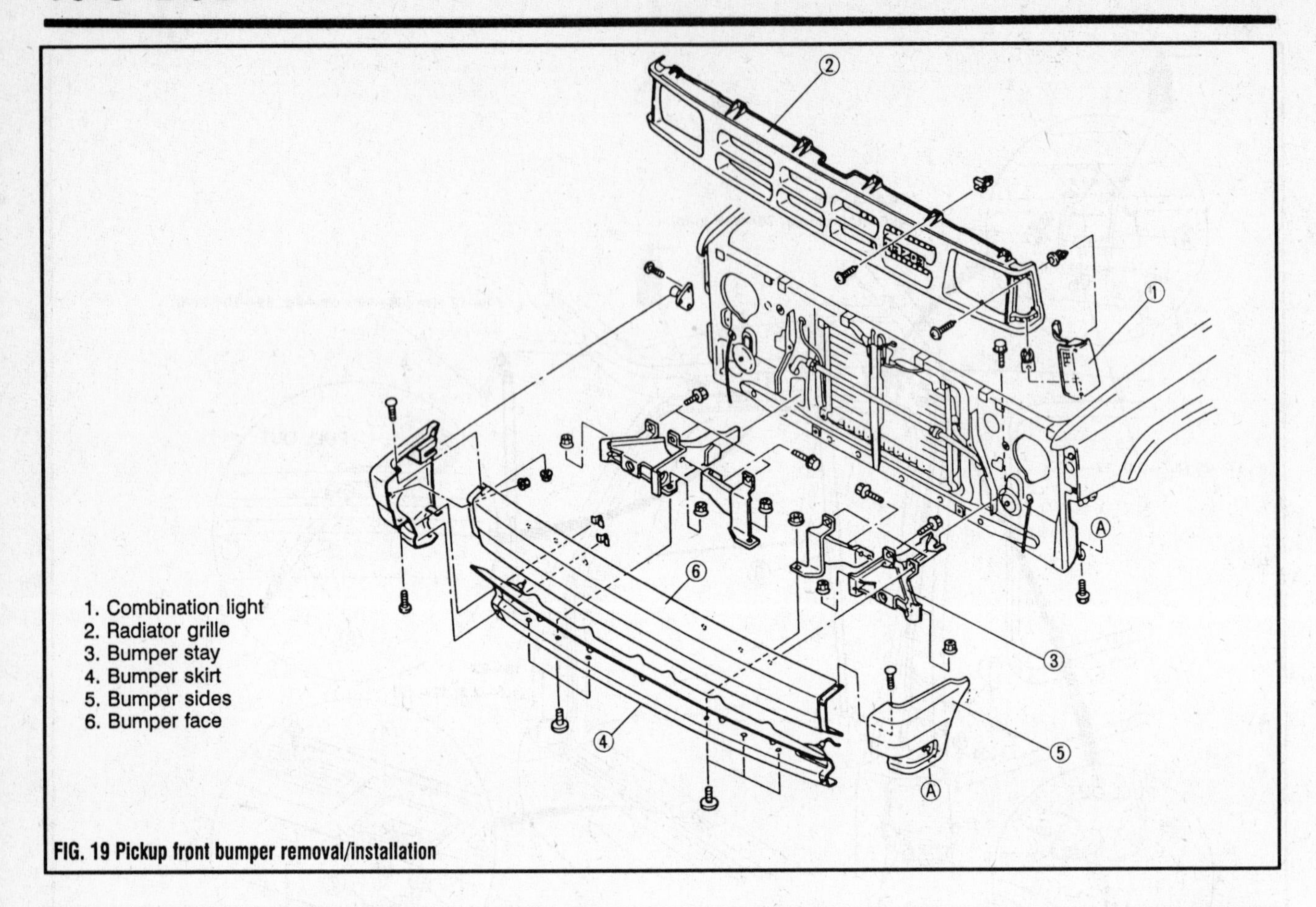

FIG. 19 Pickup front bumper removal/installation

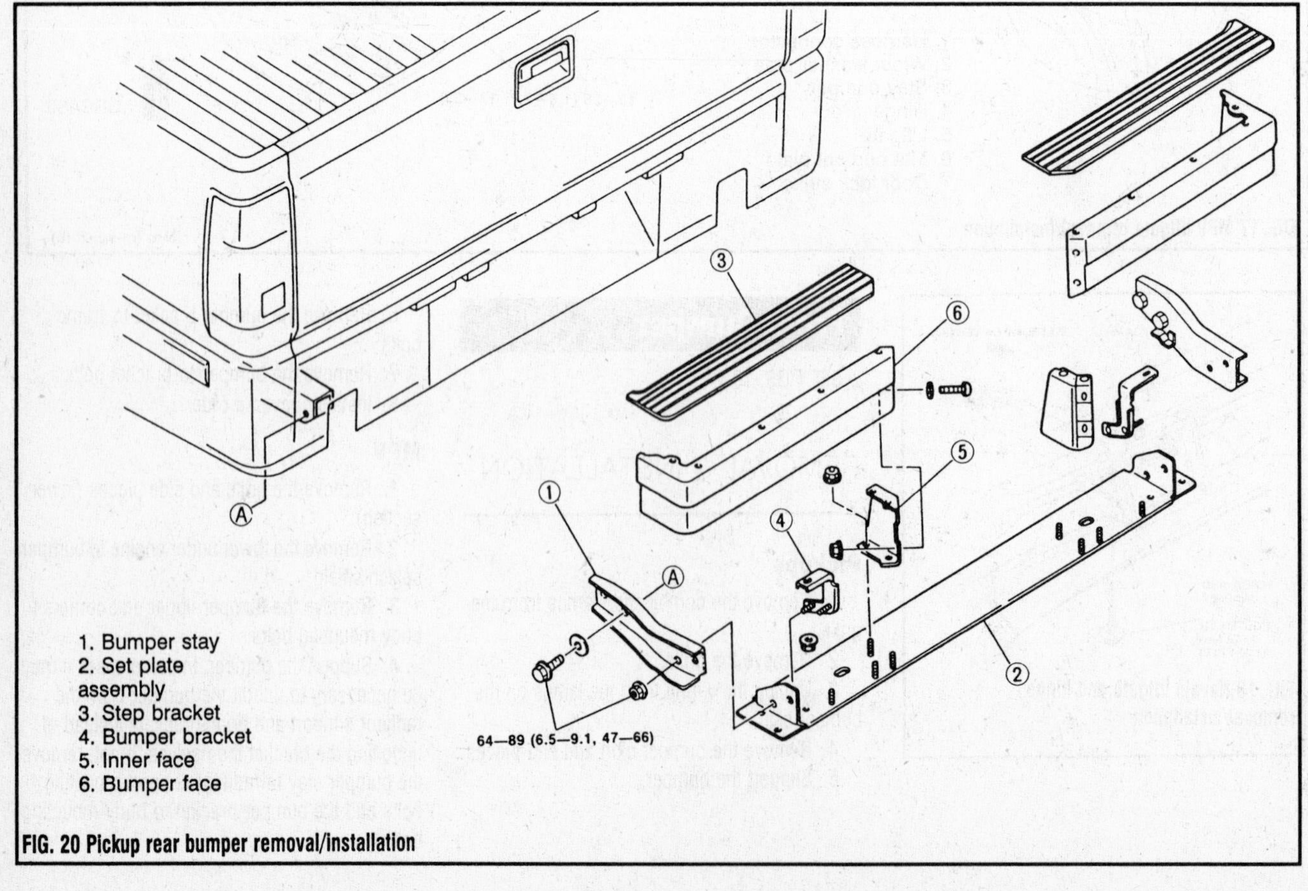

FIG. 20 Pickup rear bumper removal/installation

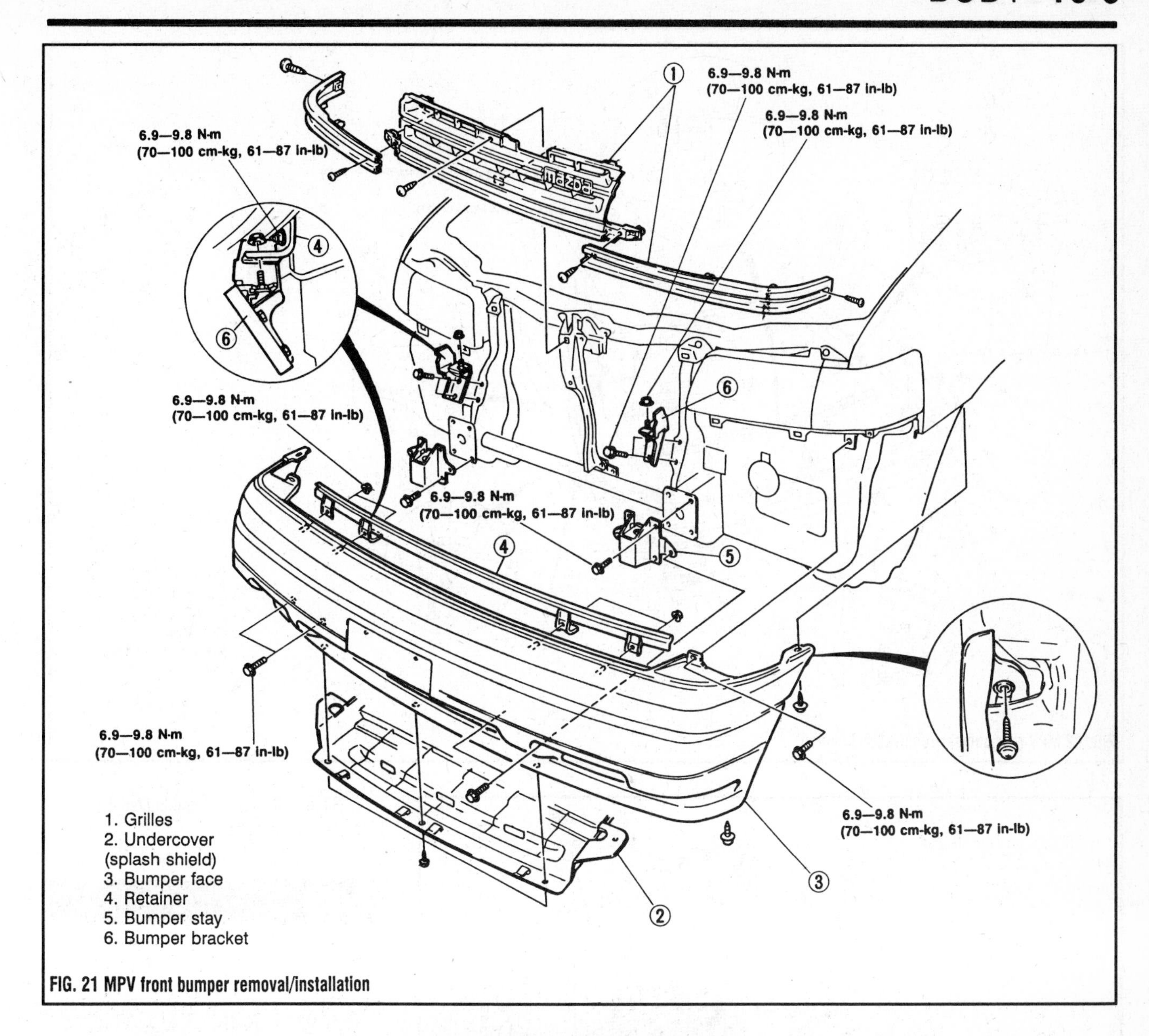

FIG. 21 MPV front bumper removal/installation

5. Remove the bumper.
6. Install in reverse order.

Navajo

1. Support the bumper. Disconnect electrical pigtails, if applicable.
2. Remove the nuts and bolts attaching the bumper brackets to the frame. Once the bumper is removed from the truck, remove the brackets from the bumper.
3. Remove the valance panel and rub strip from the bumper as required.
4. Install in reverse order. Use a leveling tool to ensure a level installation before tightening the bolts.
5. Support the bumper and tighten the bracket-to-frame bolts.

Rear Bumper

REMOVAL & INSTALLATION

Pickups

1. Support the bumper.
2. Remove the bumper bracket-to-frame bolts.
3. Remove the bumper-to-bracket bolts.
4. Install in reverse order.

MPV

1. Disconnect the negative battery cable.
2. Remove the back-up lamp assemblies.
3. Support the bumper. Remove the bolts mounting the bumper face to the body mounting brackets.
4. Remove the side bumper stays, the across body bumper retainer and the side reflectors.
5. Install in reverse order.

Navajo

1. Support the bumper. Disconnect electrical pigtails, if applicable.
2. Remove the nuts and bolts attaching the bumper brackets to the frame. Once the bumper is removed from the truck, remove the brackets from the bumper.
3. Remove the valance panel and rub strip from the bumper as required.
4. Install in reverse order. Use a leveling tool to ensure a level installation before tightening the bolts.

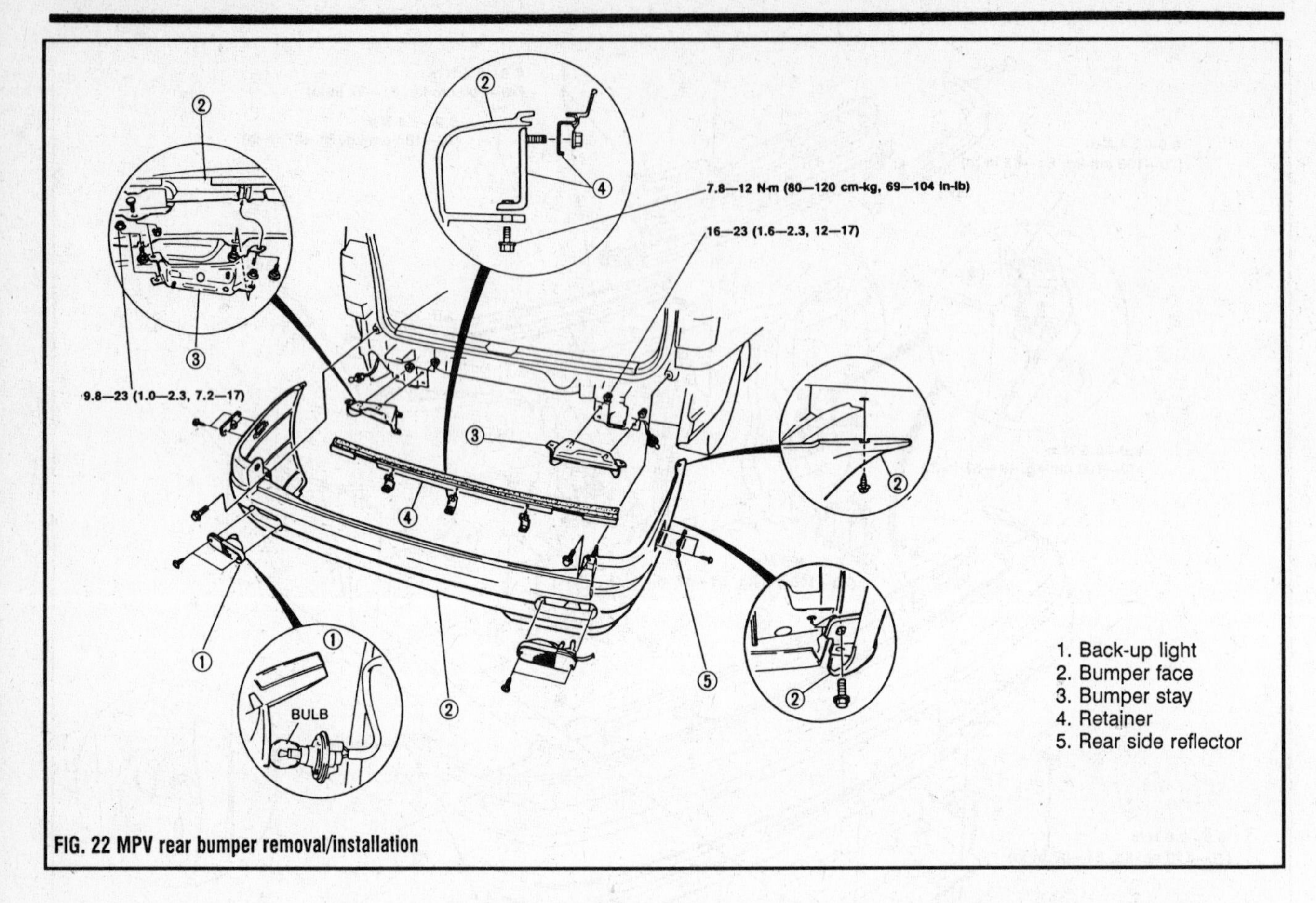

FIG. 22 MPV rear bumper removal/installation

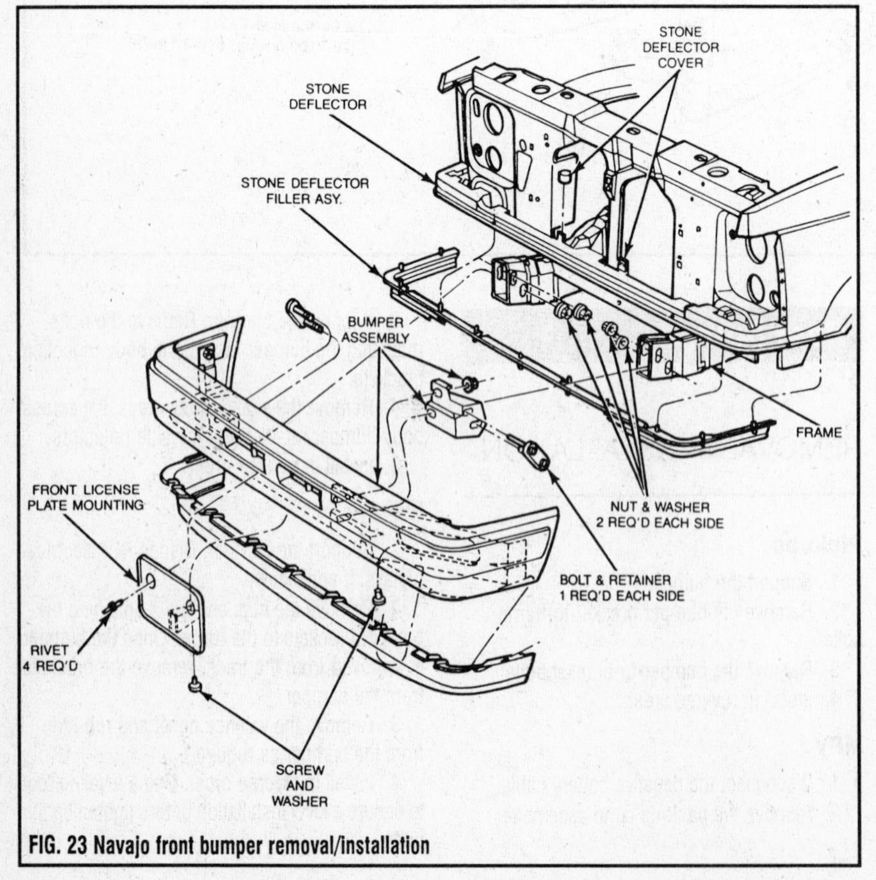

FIG. 23 Navajo front bumper removal/installation

5. Support the bumper and tighten the bracket-to-frame bolts.

Grille

➧ SEE FIG. 25

REMOVAL & INSTALLATION

Pickups

1. Open the hood.
2. Remove the combination lamps from the grille.
3. Remove the grille retaining screws and lift off the grille.
4. Install in reverse order.

MPV

The grille is in 3 pieces: 1 center piece and 2 side pieces. To remove any or all of these, remove the screws and disengage the retaining clips. To disengage the retaining clips, depress the tabs of the clip with a small screwdriver.

To install the clips, simply press them into place.

Navajo

1. Remove the plastic retainers attaching the grille to the air deflector.
2. Remove the screws attaching the grille to the radiator cross support. Depress the spring tabs at the lower outboard openings and detach the grille from the headlamp housings.
3. Remove the grille.
4. Install in reverse order.

Outside Mirrors

➧ SEE FIG. 26

REMOVAL & INSTALLATION

The mirrors can be removed from the door without disassembling the door liner or other components except on Navajo models. The mirrors may be manual, manual remote, or electric remote. If the mirror glass is broken, replacements may be available through your dealer or a glass shop. If the housing is cracked or damaged, the entire mirror must be replaced. To remove the mirror:

1. If the mirror is manual remote, check to see if the adjusting handle is retained by a hidden screw, usually under the endcap on the lever. Or if it is retained by a threaded trim nut. If so, remove the screw, nut or other remote assembly retainer.
2. Remove the plastic delta cover from the door window corner where the mirror is mounted. It can be removed with a blunt plastic or wooden tool. Don't use a screwdriver, the plastic will be marred.
3. Depending on the model and style mirror, there may be concealed plugs or other minor parts under the delta cover. If electrical connectors are present, disconnect them.
4. Support the mirror from the outside and remove the retaining screws or nuts. Remove the mirror.
5. Fit the mirror in position and secure it with the mounting screws or nuts. Connect any wiring. Pay particular attention to the placement and alignment of any gaskets or weatherstrips around the mirror; serious wind noises may result from careless work.

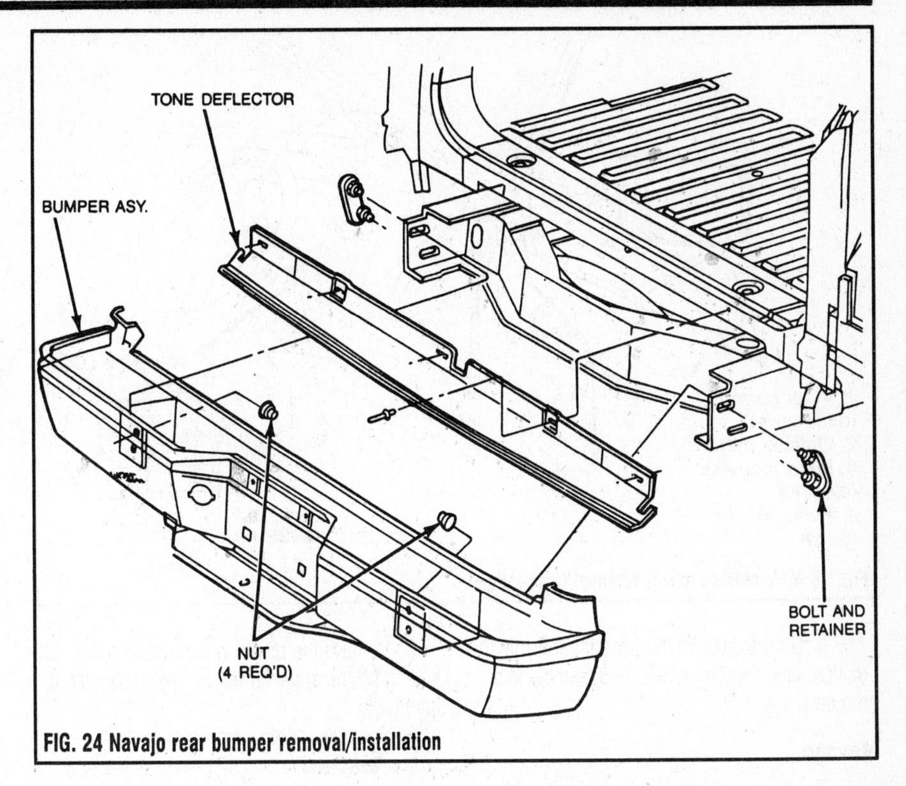

FIG. 24 Navajo rear bumper removal/installation

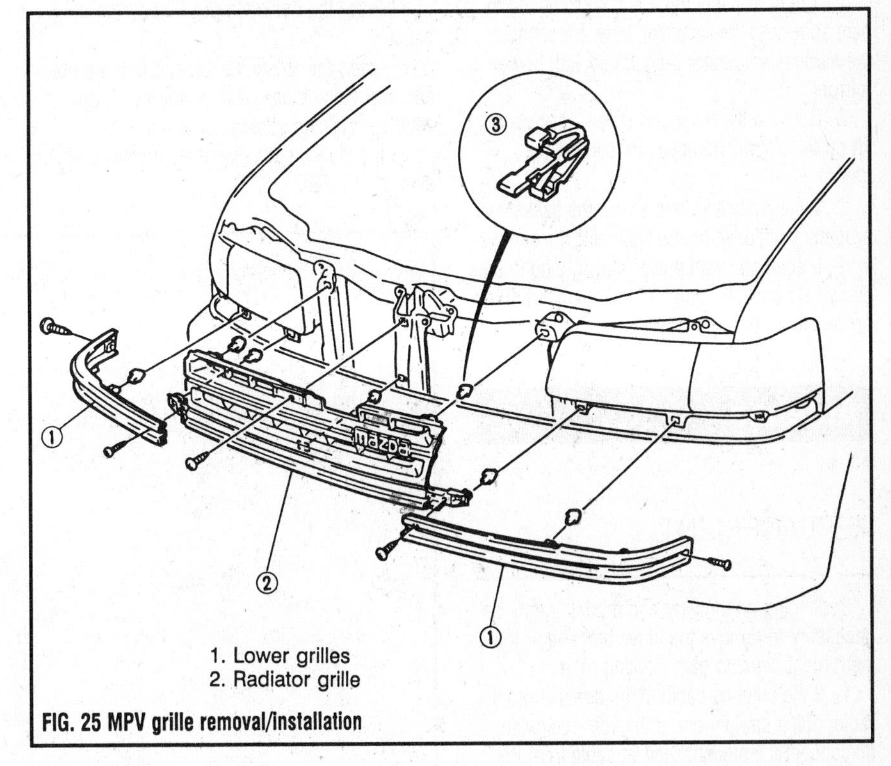

FIG. 25 MPV grille removal/installation

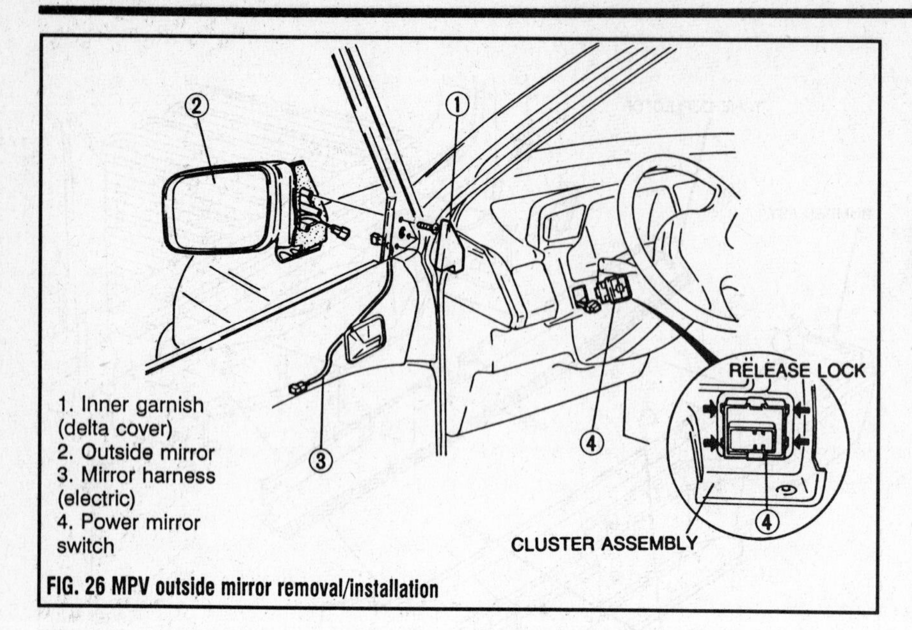

FIG. 26 MPV outside mirror removal/installation

6. Install the delta cover, pressing it firmly in position. Install the remote lever assembly and or knob.

Navajo

1. The door panel must first be removed to gain access to the mounting nuts. Disconnect the harness connector if equipped with power mirrors.
2. Remove the mounting screws or nuts and lift off the mirror. Remove and discard the gasket.
3. When installing, make sure the gasket is properly positioned before tightening the screws.
4. If equipped with power mirror, plug in the electrical connector and test the operation of the power mirror before installing the door panel.

Antenna

REPLACEMENT

Depending on the year and model, it may be necessary to remove the glove box and or the instrument panel to gain working room.

1. If the antenna cable plugs directly into the radio, pull it straight out of the set. Otherwise, disconnect the antenna lead-in cable from the cable assembly in-line connector above the glove box.
2. Working under the instrument panel, disengage the cable from its retainers.
3. Outside, unsnap the cap from the antenna base. Or, on some models, unscrew the mounting tower nut.
4. Remove the retaining screws, or tower nut and lift off the antenna, pulling the cable with it, carefully.
5. Remove and discard the gasket.

To install:

6. Place the gasket in position on the cowl panel.
7. Insert the antenna cable through the hole and seat the antenna base on the cowl. Secure with the retaining screws, or tower nut.
8. Position the cap over the antenna base and snap it into place.
9. Route the cable in exactly the same position as before removal behind the instrument panel.
10. Connect the cable to the radio or in-line connector.

Fenders

➧ SEE FIG. 27

REMOVAL & INSTALLATION

1. Clean all of the dirt from the fender mounting screws, bolts and nuts.
2. Remove the headlamp door, headlamp assembly, sidemarker lamp, or parking lamp assembly, depending on model.
3. Remove the bolt(s) attaching the rear of the front fender to the windshield cowl. This bolt is usually accessed from inside the vehicle with the door opened.
4. Remove the top bolts that mount the fender to the inter-body.
5. Loosen the wheel lugs slightly. Raise and safely support the vehicle. Remove the wheel and tire assembly.
6. Remove the bolts attaching the fender brace to the body. Remove the bolts attaching the fender to the radiator support, and remove the bolts attaching the fender to the fender apron (inner splash shield).

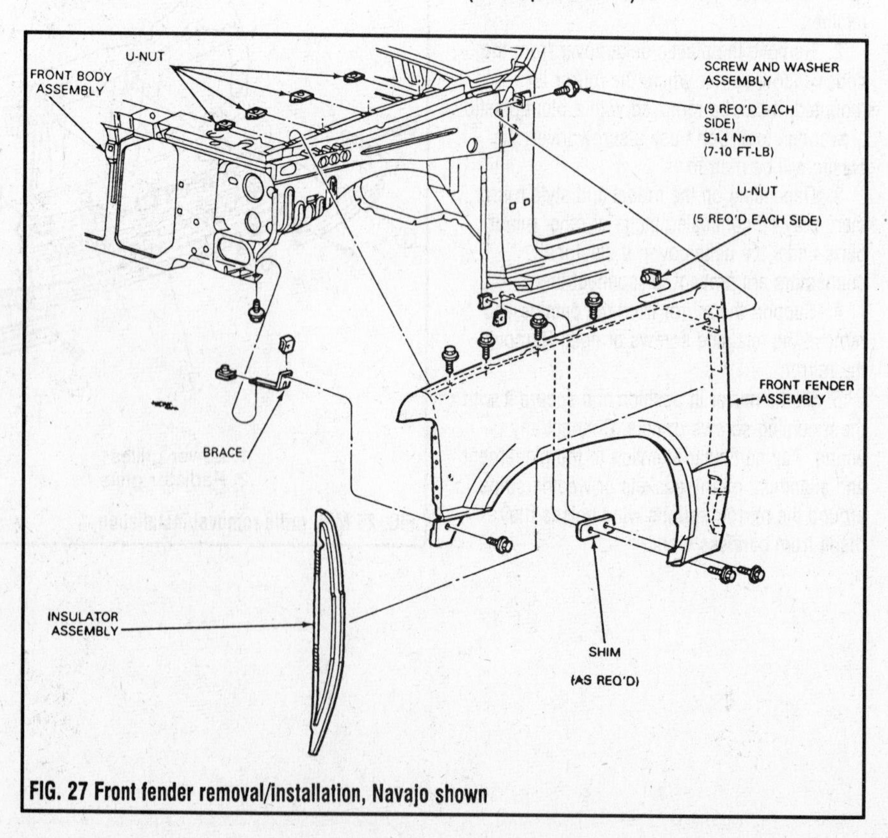

FIG. 27 Front fender removal/installation, Navajo shown

7. Remove the bolts mounting the fender to the lower rocker sill. Check for any other mounting bolts, remove them. Remove the fender.

8. Place the fender in position and install the mounting bolts loosely. Align the lower edge of the fender to the rocker sill and secure the bolts. Align the upper edge of the fender to the cowl and tighten the bolts.

9. Tighten the remaining mounting bolts. Install the lighting equipment.

Sliding Sunroof

➧ SEE FIGS. 26-37

REMOVAL & INSTALLATION

MPV

➡ **Service to the sunroof harness, sunroof relay, drive unit assembly, sunroof frame, sunshade and guide rail require headliner removal.**

1. Make sure the sunroof is fully closed, if possible. Disconnect the negative battery cable.

2. Slide the sunshade all the way to the rear. Fully close the sliding panel. Remove the decoration cover mounting screws from the right and left decoration covers and remove the covers.

3. Remove the retaining nuts from the sliding panel and bracket. Remove the sliding panel by pushing it upward from inside the vehicle. Take care to remove the shims between the sliding panel and brackets before removing the sliding panel.

4. Remove the front guide assembly.

5. Remove the air deflector. Remove the E-ring at the rear of the deflector link, and remove the pin. Remove the screws and the deflector. Take care not to damage the deflector link or connector.

6. Remove the guide rail cover.

7. Remove the sliding roof unit. Remove the mounting nuts securing the drive unit and sliding roof unit to the body. With an assistant to help you, remove the unit.

8. Remove the sunshade from the guide rail. Remove the set plate. Remove the guide rail mounting screws. Lift up the rear end of the guide rail and pull out the rear guide assembly. Remove the guide rail from the sliding roof frame, lifting up the rear end of the guide rail.

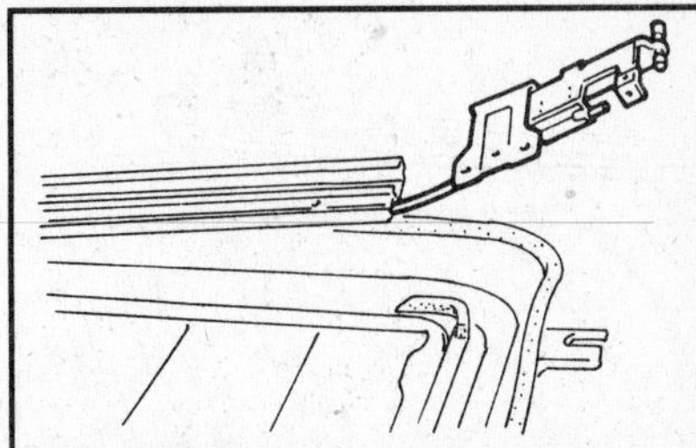

FIG. 29 MPV, remove the guide mounting screws, lift the guide rail up and pull the rear guide assembly backward

9. Remove the sliding roof harness, sliding roof relay, drive unit assembly and the sliding roof frame.

To Install:

10. Place the roof frame, drive unit, relay and harness in position.

11. Put the guide rail on the sliding roof frame after applying sealant to the underside of the guide rail.

12. Set the guide rail to the sliding roof frame and install bolts to the second screw holes.

13. Install the set plate to the guise rail. Lift up the rear end of the rail and insert the rear guide assembly until it reaches the set plate. Be sure to assemble the bracket and drive cable before insertion.

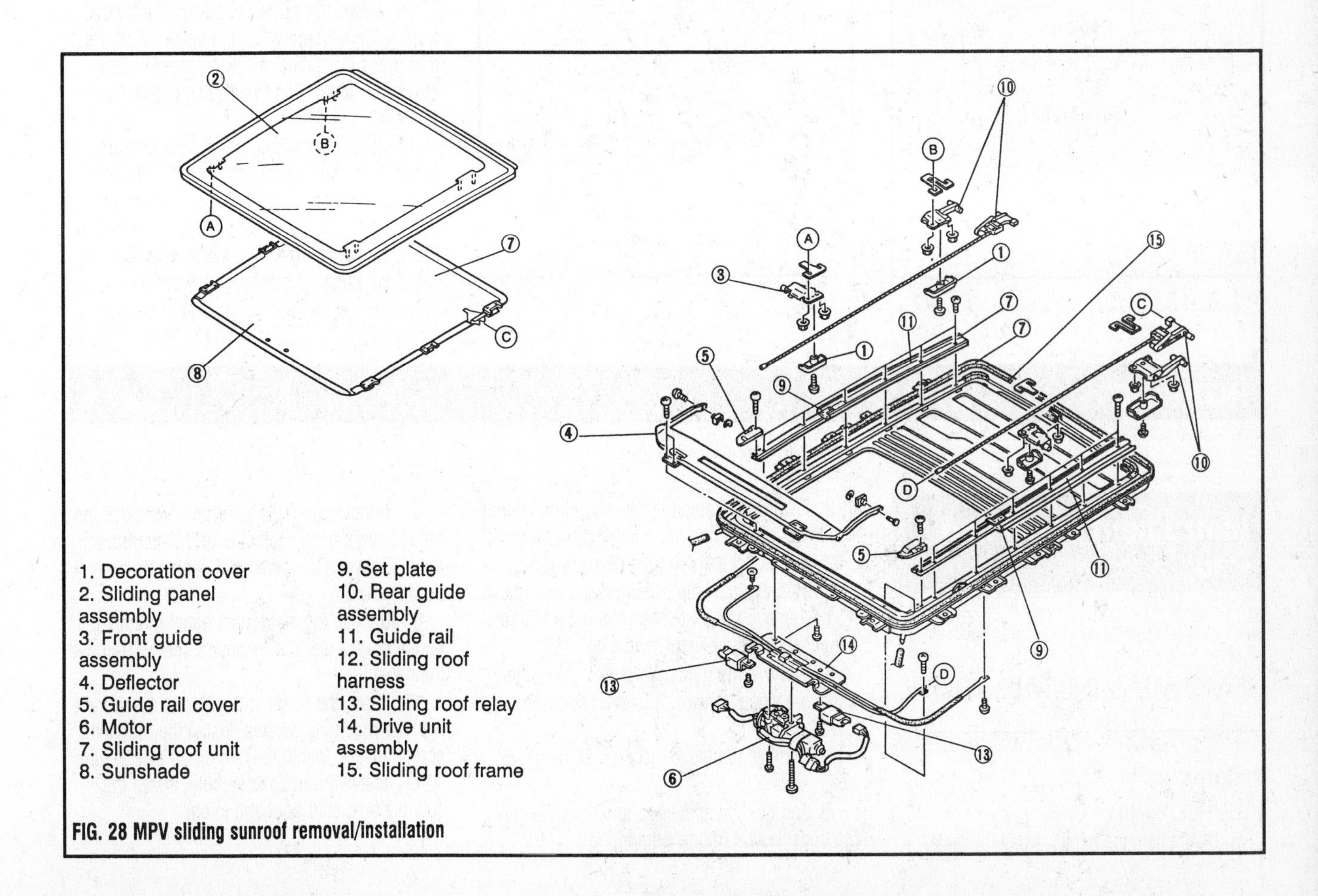

FIG. 28 MPV sliding sunroof removal/installation

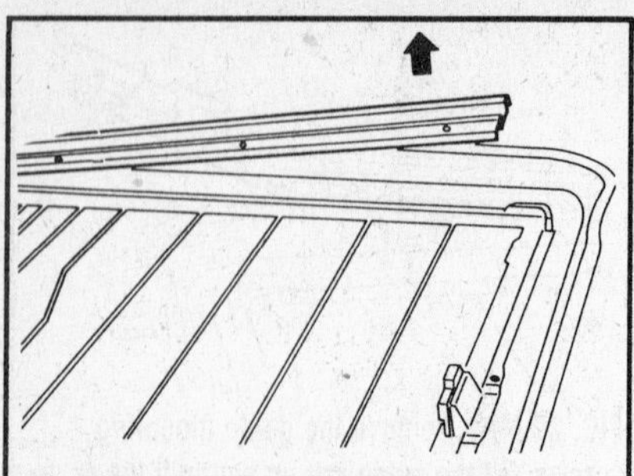
FIG. 30 MPV, remove the guide rail from the sliding roof frame, lifting up the rear end of the guide rail

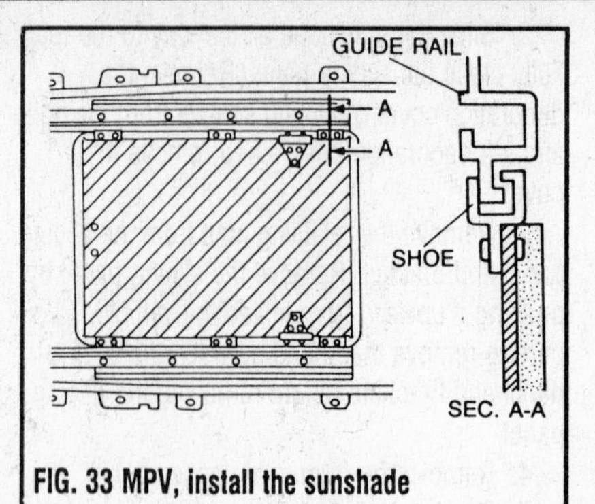

FIG. 33 MPV, install the sunshade

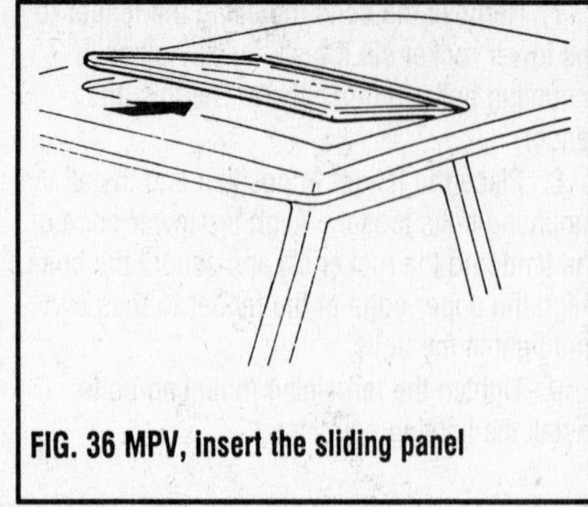
FIG. 36 MPV, insert the sliding panel

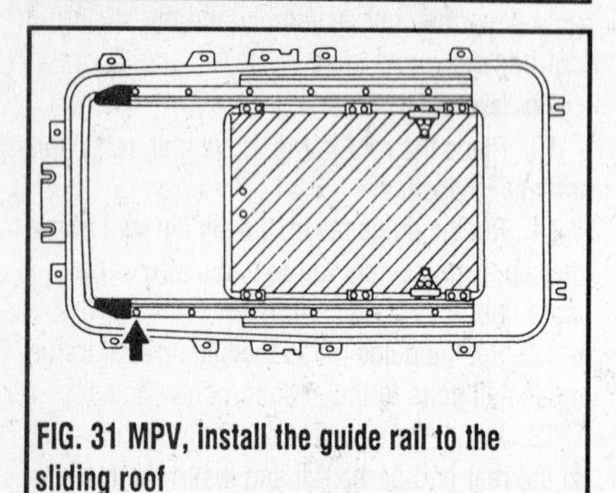
FIG. 31 MPV, install the guide rail to the sliding roof

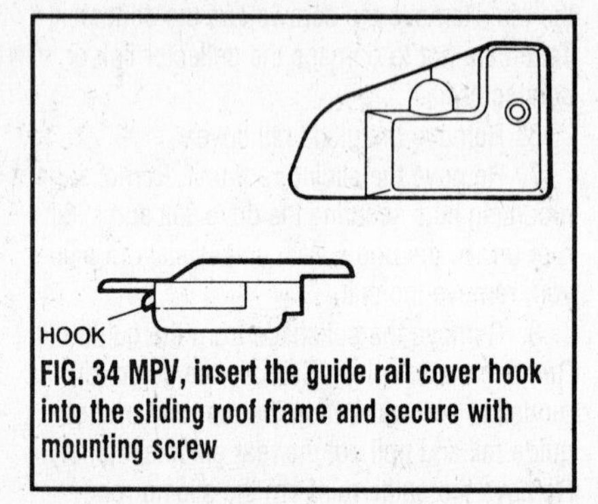

FIG. 34 MPV, insert the guide rail cover hook into the sliding roof frame and secure with mounting screw

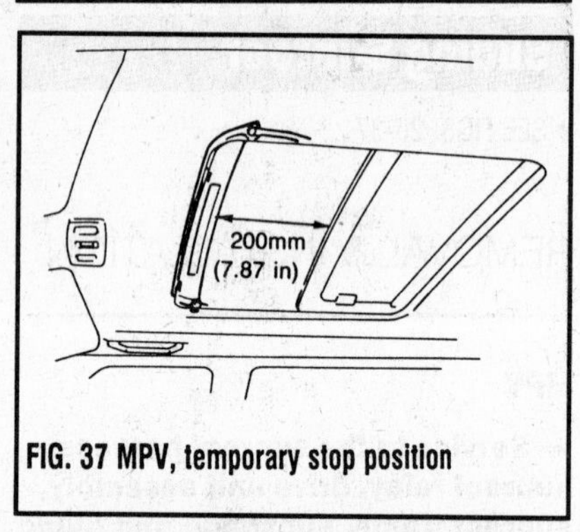

FIG. 37 MPV, temporary stop position

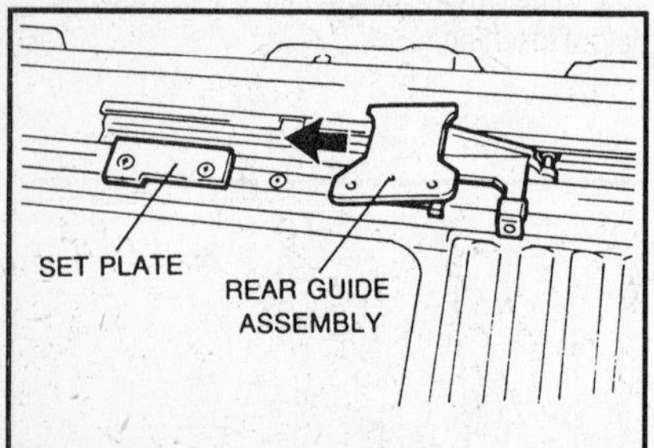

FIG. 32 MPV, install the set plate to the guide rail

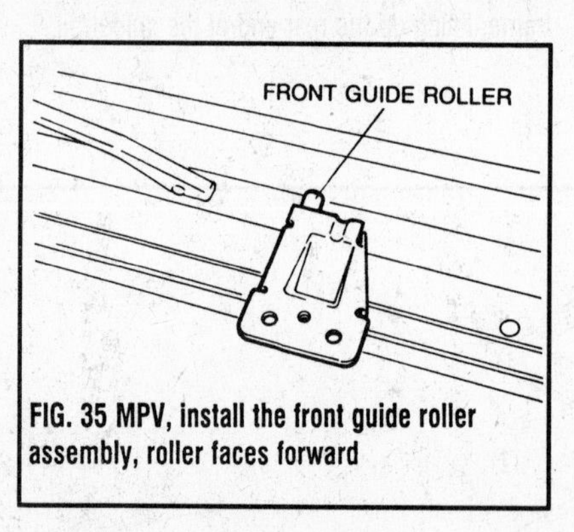

FIG. 35 MPV, install the front guide roller assembly, roller faces forward

14. Lift up on the guide rail and install the sunshade sliding shoes into the guide rail. Secure the guide rail to the sliding roof frame. Secure the sliding roof unit to the body roof.
15. Install the guide rail covers. Insert the front guide assembly into the guide rail and set it to press the deflector link (sunroof in fully closed position). The front guide rollers face forward.
16. Install the sliding panel, rear end first. Insert the sliding panel bolts into the bracket holes of the front and rear guide assemblies, tighten the nuts. Be sure to install the shims in the same position from which they were removed. Install the direction covers.

INTERIOR

Instrument Panel and Pad

REMOVAL & INSTALLATION

Pickups

SEE FIGS. 38-40

1. Disconnect the negative battery cable.
2. Remove the steering wheel. Column upper and lower covers and the combination switch.
3. Remove the instrument cluster meter hood. Remove the instrument cluster assembly.
4. Remove the switch knob and the left side panel (next to the cluster mounting.
5. Remove the trim covers over the center panel mounting screws. Remove the center cover.
6. Remove the glove box lid and the glove box.
7. Remove the shift knob and boot. Remove the console box (models equipped).
8. Remove the radio assembly. Remove the small covers from each side of the instrument panel. Between the panel and each side body door frame.
9. Remove the instrument panel mounting screw covers and the mounting screw. Remove the panel.
10. Place the panel in position and secure it with the mounting screws. Install the mounting screw covers. Install the two small side covers.
11. Install the radio assembly. Install the console box, shift boot and knob.

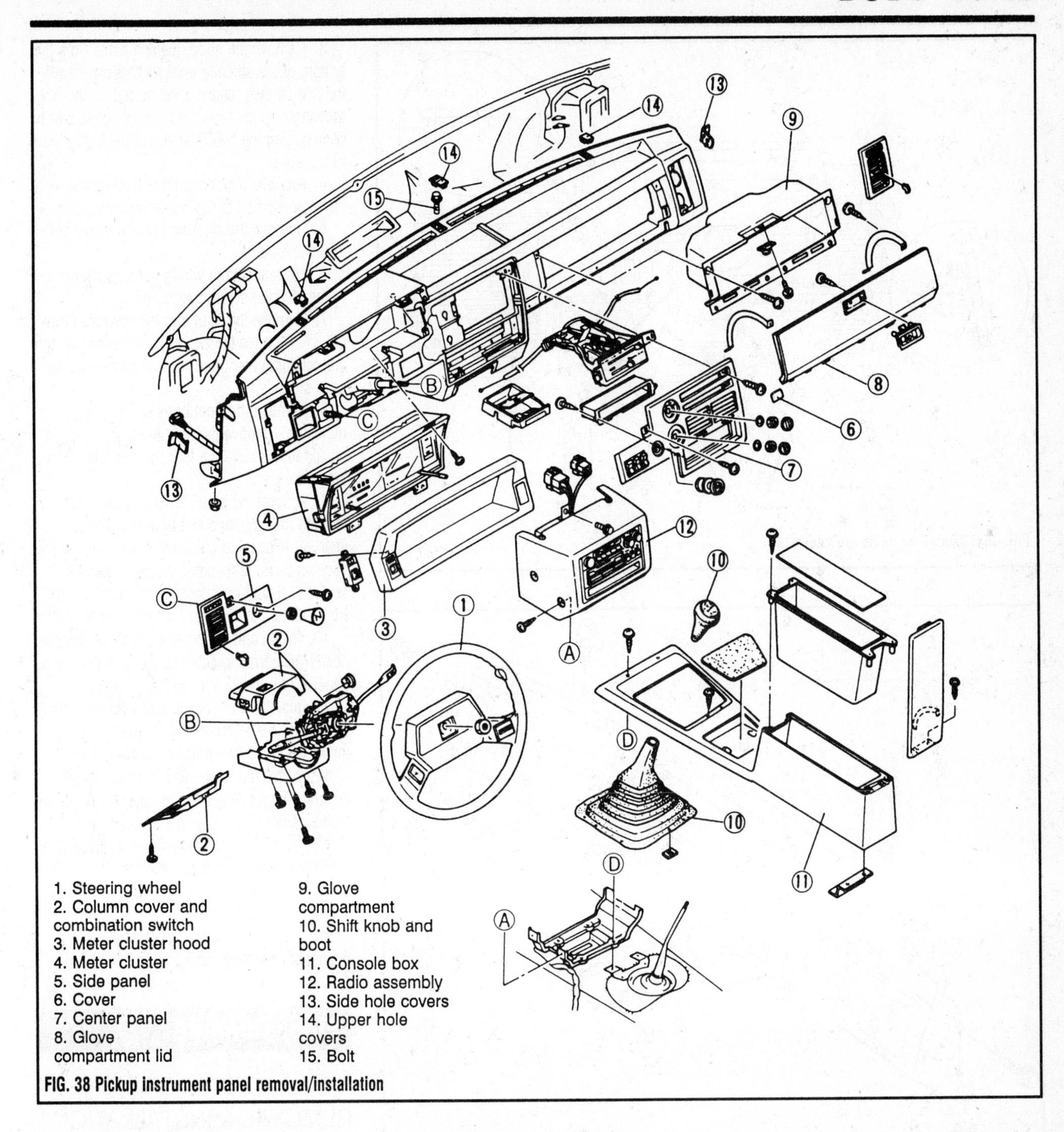

FIG. 38 Pickup instrument panel removal/installation

12. Install the glove box and glove box lid.
13. Install the center panel and screw covers. Install the left side panel, instrument cluster and hood.
14. Install the combination switch and column covers. Install the steering wheel. Connect the negative battery cable.

MPV

➧ SEE FIGS. 41-46

1. Disconnect the negative battery cable.
2. Remove the hood release knob, steering wheel and column cover.
3. Remove the combination switch.
4. Remove the instrument cluster assembly and meter set. Remove the side cover.
5. Remove the right side undercover pad (vehicles equipped). Remove the right and left side lower panel assemblies.
6. Remove the left side duct, ashtray and audio panel assembly.
7. Remove the audio unit. Remove the lower center panel.
8. Remove the switch knobs and the upper switch panel. Remove the temperature control, blower control and airflow mode control.
9. Remove the upper garnish and the dash panel.
10. Position and secure the dash panel. Install the upper garnish. Install the airflow mode control, blower control and temperature control.
11. Install the upper switch panel and switch knobs.
12. Install the lower center panel. Install the audio unit, audio panel, ashtray and left side duct.
13. Install the left and right side lower panel assemblies. If equipped, install the right side undercover pad.

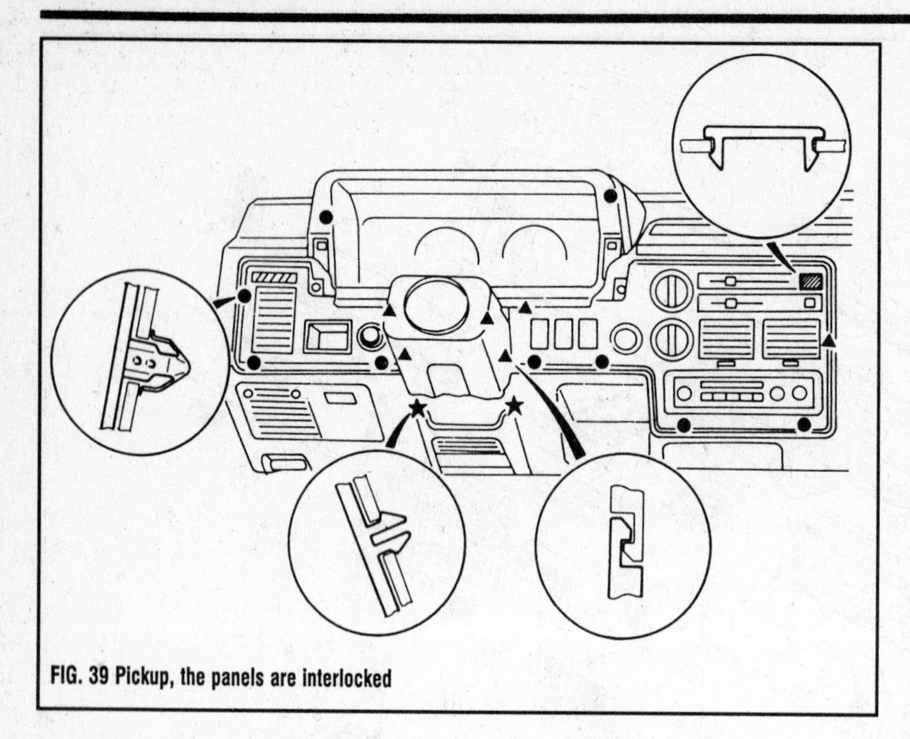

FIG. 39 Pickup, the panels are interlocked

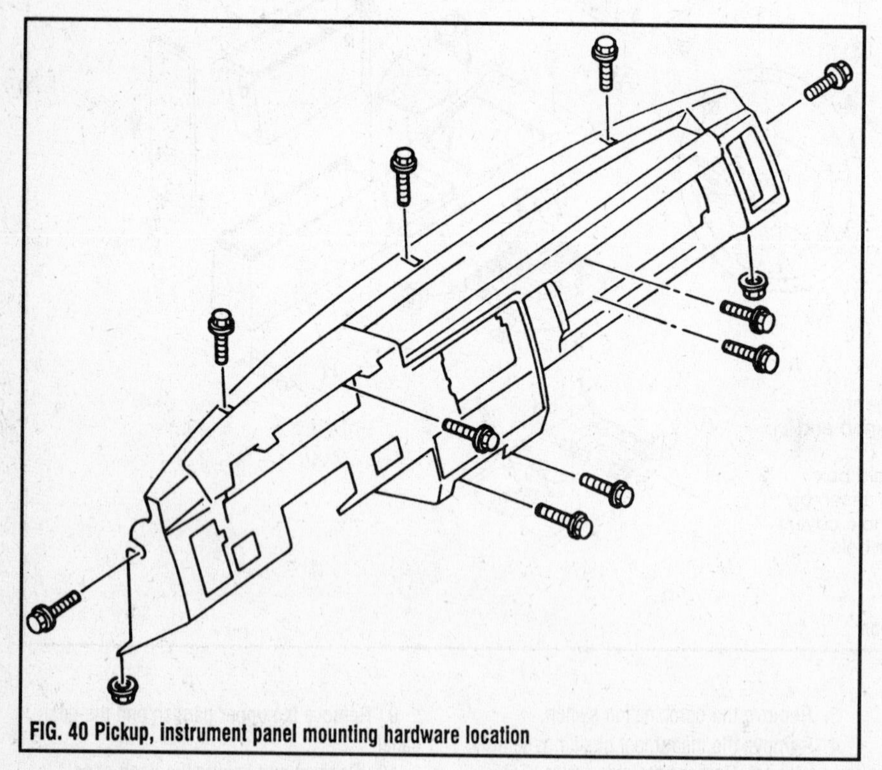

FIG. 40 Pickup, instrument panel mounting hardware location

14. Install the side cover, meter set and cluster assembly. Install the combination switch and steering column cover.

15. Install the steering wheel. Install the hood release knob. Connect the negative battery cable.

Navajo

➧ SEE FIGS. 47-49

1. Disconnect the negative battery cable.

2. Remove the ashtray and retainer assembly. Remove the instrument cluster finish panel by unsnapping the seven snap-in retainers. Remove the cluster retaining screws. Pull the cluster forward and disconnect the speedometer and electrical connectors. Remove the cluster.

3. Remove the hood opening cable from the bottom of the steering column cover. Remove the two screws retaining the bottom of the steering column cover and remove the cover by disengaging the two retainers at the top corners of the cover.

4. Remove the screw that attaches the instrument panel to the brake/clutch support.

5. Remove the steering column upper and lower shrouds.

6. Disconnect the wiring harness connectors to the steering column switches.

7. Remove the right and left cowl side trim covers. Remove the two bolts retaining the right and left instrument panel lower corners to the cowl side.

8. Remove the front body inside pillar moldings. Remove the right lower insulator, if equipped. Remove the four screws retaining the top of the panel.

9. Support the panel assembly and reach through the openings and underneath the instrument panel to disconnect the panel wiring, vacuum lines, radio antenna and heater/AC controls. (Label for reinstallation identification). Remove the panel mounting bolts and the panel.

10. Install and secure the panel. Connect the heater/AC controls, antenna, vacuum lines and panel wiring.

11. Install the top cover, and right insulator (if equipped). Install the two side pillar moldings. Install the two lower corner mounting bolts.

12. Install the right and left cowl side trim covers. Connect the steering column switches. Install the steering column shrouds.

13. Install the mounting screw at the clutch/brake pedal support. Install the steering column cover. Secure the hood release cable. Install the instrument cluster and finish panel.

14. Install the retainer and ashtray. Connect the negative battery cable.

Floor Console

REMOVAL & INSTALLATION

Navajo

1. Remove the arm rest mounting access covers. Unscrew the arm rest mounting bolts and remove the armrest.

2. Remove the screws in the utility tray assembly and panel console. Remove the console.

3. Install the console in the reverse order.

DASHPANEL

1. Hood release knob
2. Steering wheel
3. Steering column cover
4. Combination switch
5. Cluster assembly
6. Meter set
7. Side cover
8. Undercover (right)
9. Right lower panel
10. Left lower panel
11. Left duct
12. Ashtray
13. Audio panel assy.
14. Audio unit
15. Center lower panel assy.
16. Knob
17. Switch panel assy.
18. Temperature control
19. Blower control
20. Air mode control
21. Upper garnish
22. Dashpanel

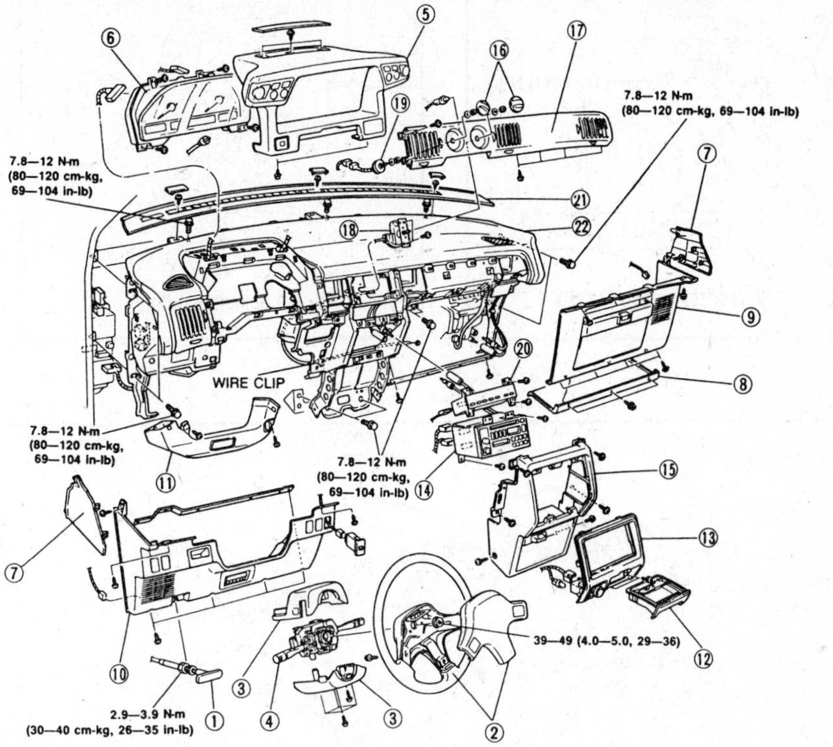

7.8—12 N·m (80—120 cm-kg, 69—104 in-lb)

WIRE CLIP

39—49 (4.0—5.0, 29—36)

2.9—3.9 N·m (30—40 cm-kg, 26—35 in-lb)

FIG. 41 MPV, instrument panel removal/installation

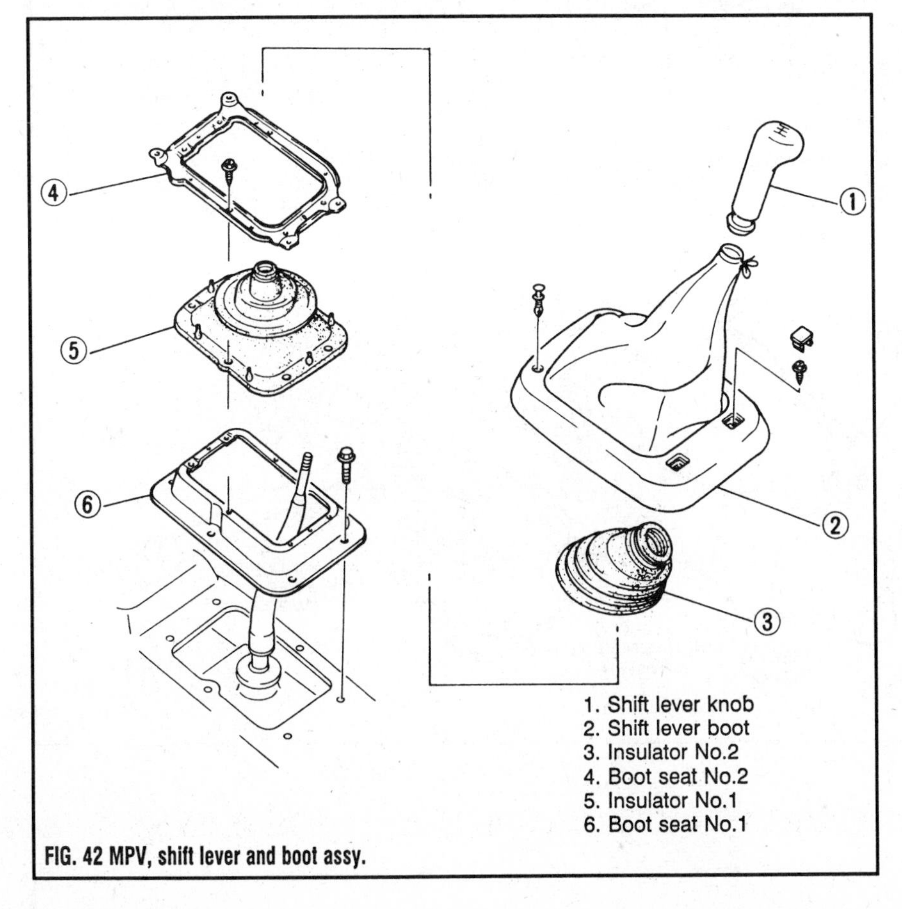

FIG. 42 MPV, shift lever and boot assy.

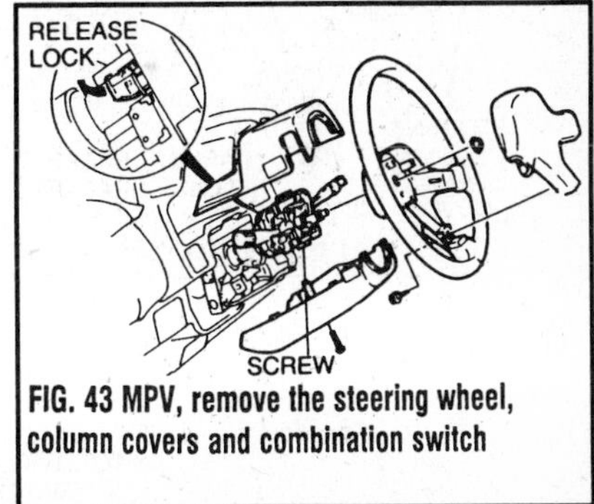

FIG. 43 MPV, remove the steering wheel, column covers and combination switch

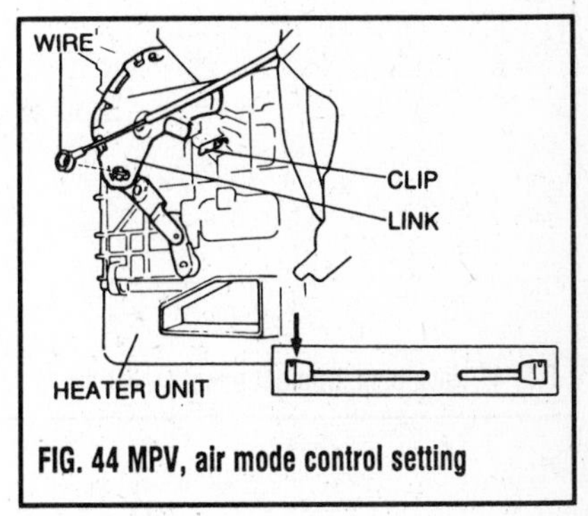

FIG. 44 MPV, air mode control setting

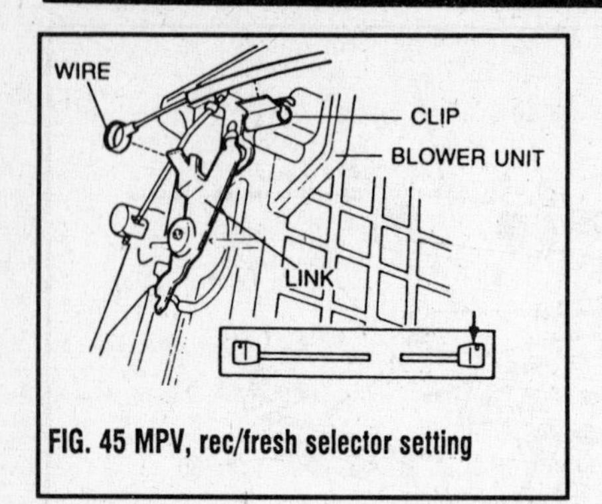

FIG. 45 MPV, rec/fresh selector setting

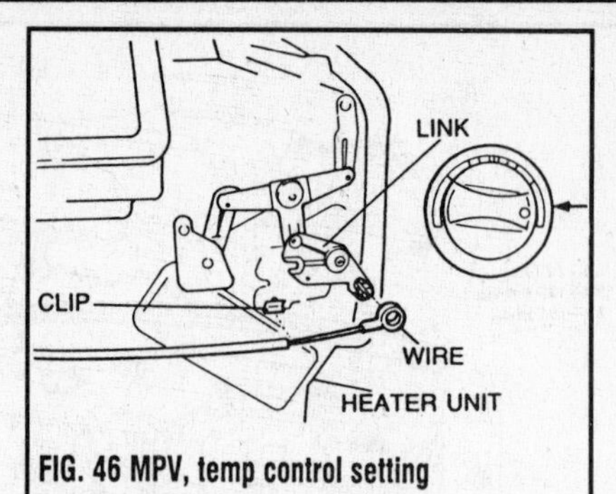

FIG. 46 MPV, temp control setting

Door Panels

➧ SEE FIGS. 50-52

➡ Refer to the illustrations in this section for door assemblies on the various models that show door panel and other component mounting.

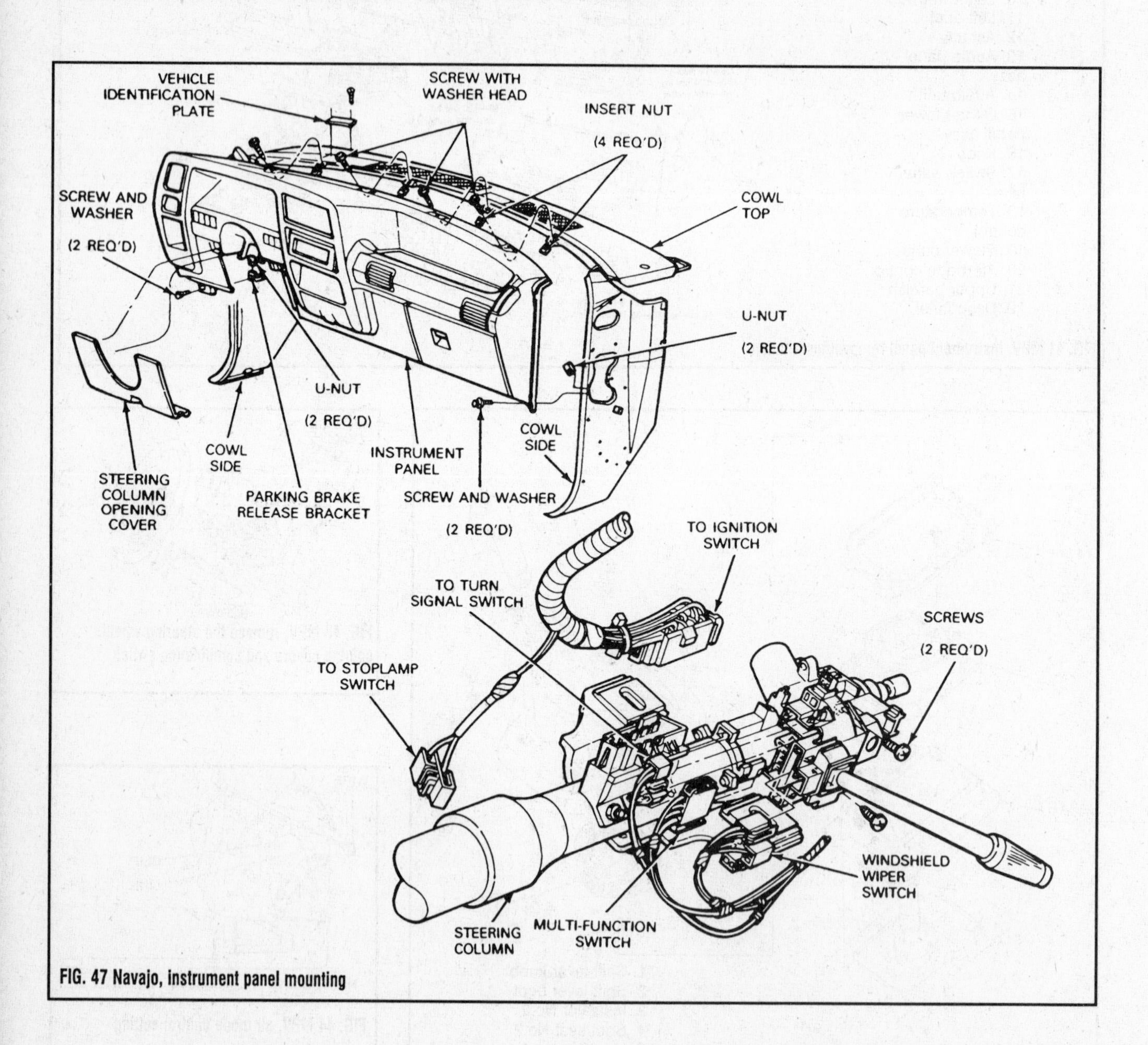

FIG. 47 Navajo, instrument panel mounting

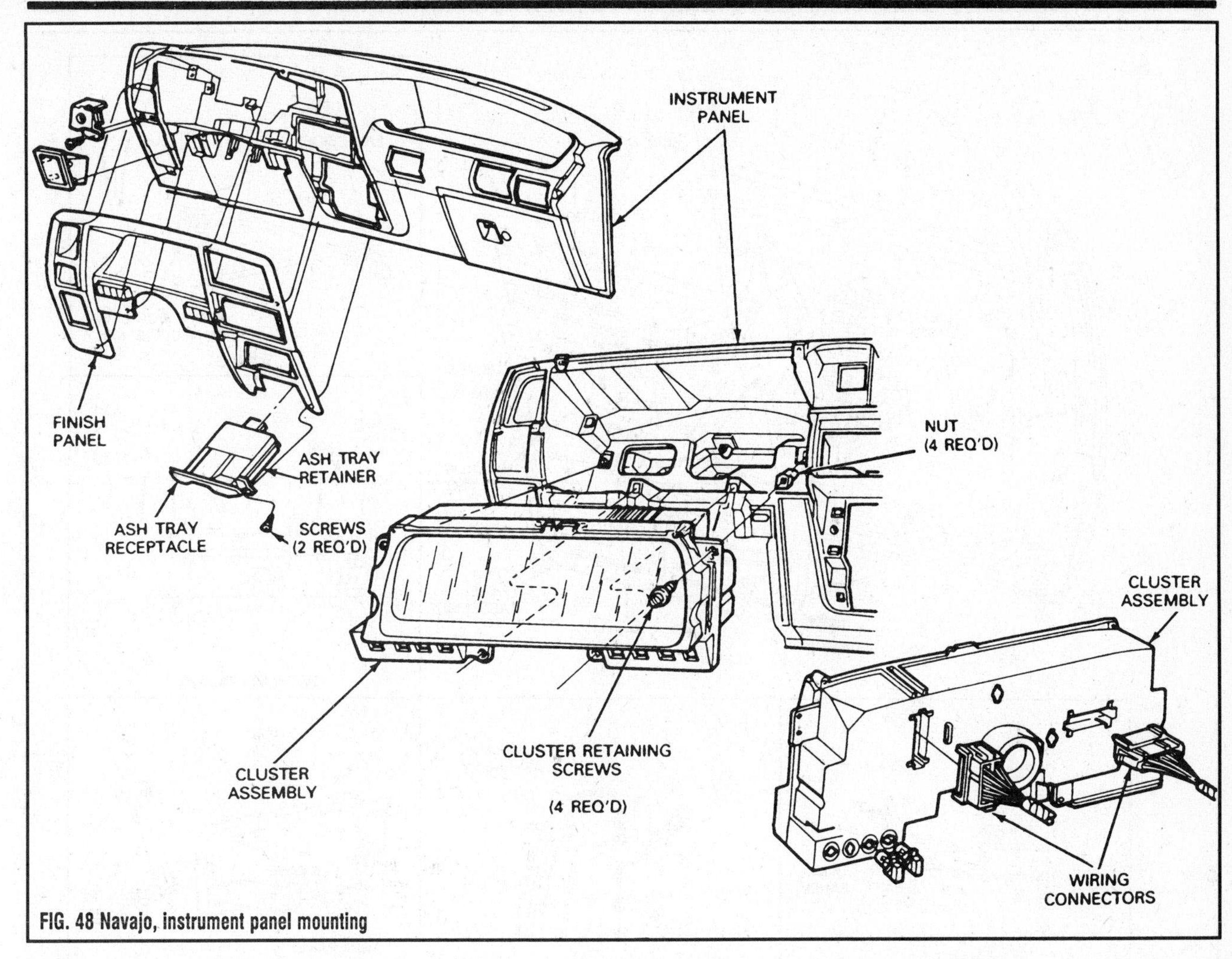

FIG. 48 Navajo, instrument panel mounting

REMOVAL & INSTALLATION

Pickups

1. Remove the attaching screw and door handle.
2. Remove the armrest.
3. Push in on the door panel, slightly, at the window handle and pry off the snapring retaining the handle to the regulator stem. Remove the handle.
4. Carefully slip a thin prying instrument behind the door panel and slide it along until you hit one of the retaining clips. Pry as close as possible to the clip to snap the clip from the door. Be very careful to avoid tearing the clip from the panel.
5. Pry out each clip, in turn, and lift off the door panel.
6. Installation is the reverse of removal. When snapping the clips into place, make sure that they are squarely over the holes to avoid bending them.

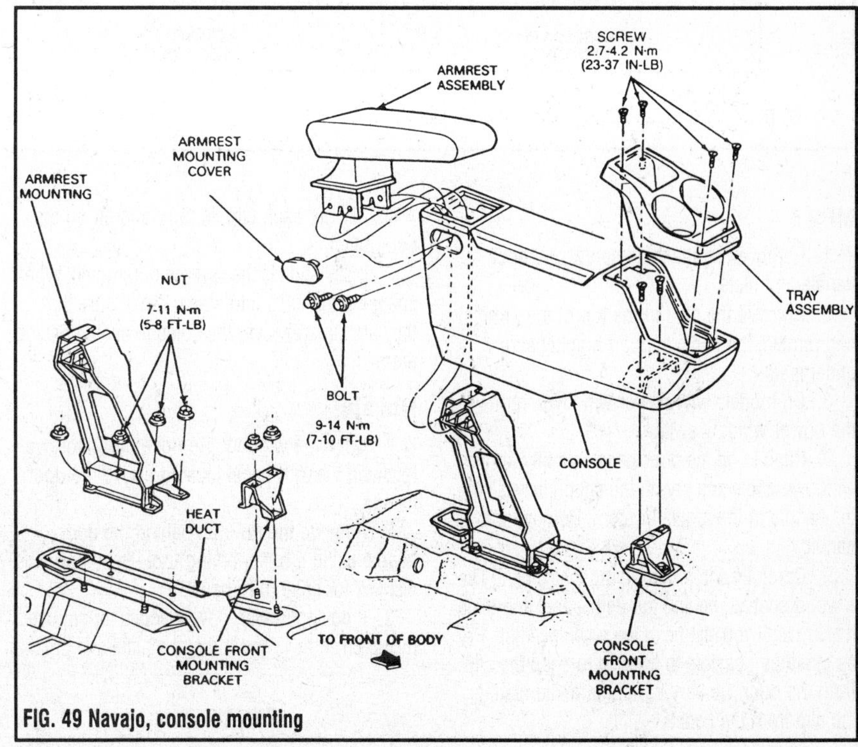

FIG. 49 Navajo, console mounting

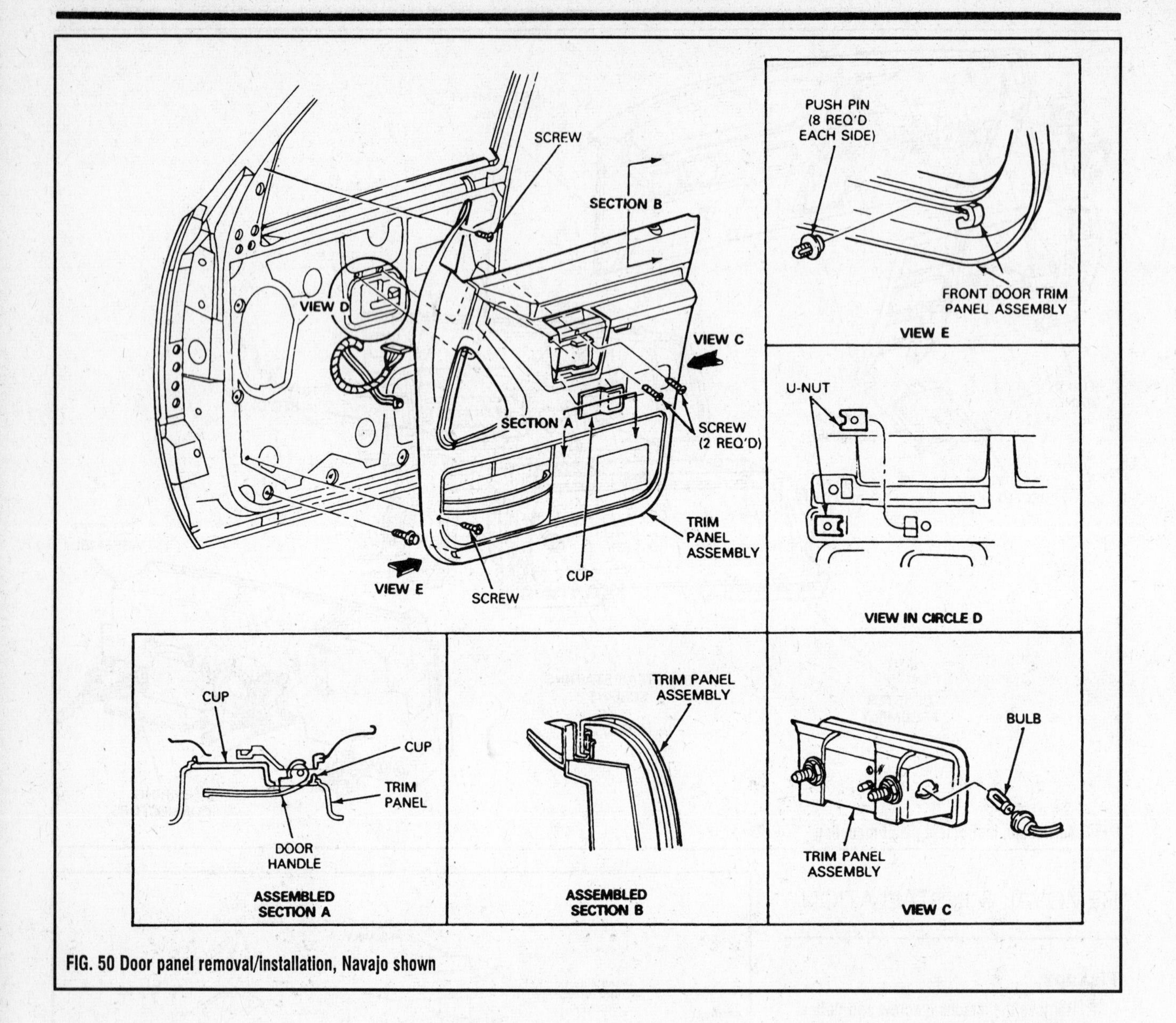

FIG. 50 Door panel removal/installation, Navajo shown

MPV

1. Remove the attaching screw and door handle and plate.
2. Remove the plug in the top of the armrest and remove the panel support bracket screw underneath.
3. On models with power windows, remove the power window switch.
4. Push in on the door panel, slightly, at the window handle and pry off the snapring retaining the handle to the regulator stem. Remove the handle.
5. Carefully slip a thin prying instrument, like a wood spatula, behind the door panel and slide it along until you hit one of the retaining clips. Pry as close as possible to the clip to snap the clip from the door. Be very careful to avoid tearing the clip from the panel.
6. Pry out each clip, in turn, and lift off the door panel.
7. Installation is the reverse of removal. When snapping the clips into place, make sure that they are squarely over the holes to avoid bending them.

Navajo

1. Open the window. Remove the 2 screws retaining the trim panel located above the door handle.
2. Remove the rim cup behind the door handle using a small prying tool. Retention nibs will flex for ease of removal.
3. If equipped with power accessories, use the notch at the lower end of the plate and pry the plate off. Remove the plate from the trim panel and pull the wiring harness from behind the panel. Disconnect the harness from the switches.
4. Using a flat wood spatula, insert it carefully behind the panel and slide it along to find the push-pins. When you encounter a pin, pry the pin outward. Do this until all the pins are out. NEVER PULL ON THE PANEL TO REMOVE THE PINS!
5. Lift slightly to disengage the panel from the flange at the top of the door.
6. Disconnect the door courtesy lamp and remove the panel completely. Replace any damaged or bent attaching clips.
7. Installation is the reverse of removal.

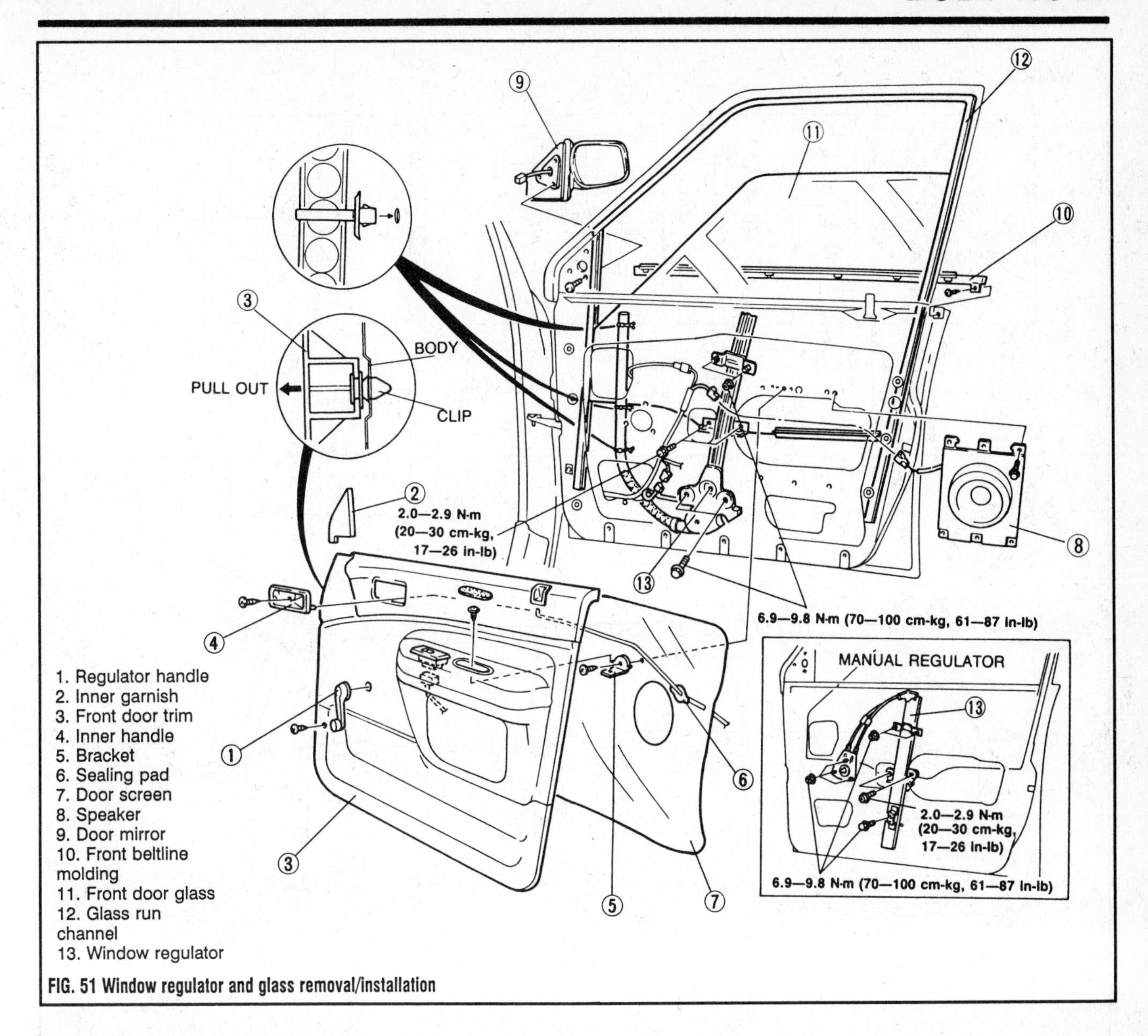

FIG. 51 Window regulator and glass removal/installation

Interior Trim Panels

➧ SEE FIGS. 53-59

REMOVAL & INSTALLATION

MPV and Navajo

Refer to the illustrations provided. Seat assemblies, seat belt anchors, trim molding or scuff plate removal may be required, depending on which trim panel requires attention.

Headliner

REMOVAL & INSTALLATION

Pickup

➧ SEE FIGS. 60-69

1. Remove the back window, the rear view mirror, sun visors and assist handle (if equipped).

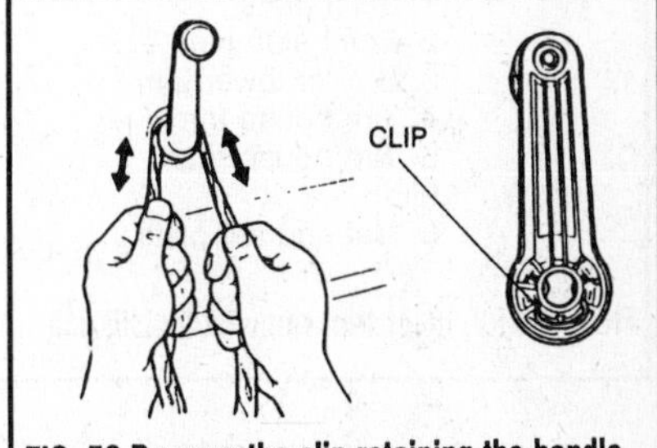

FIG. 52 Remove the clip retaining the handle using a rag as shown

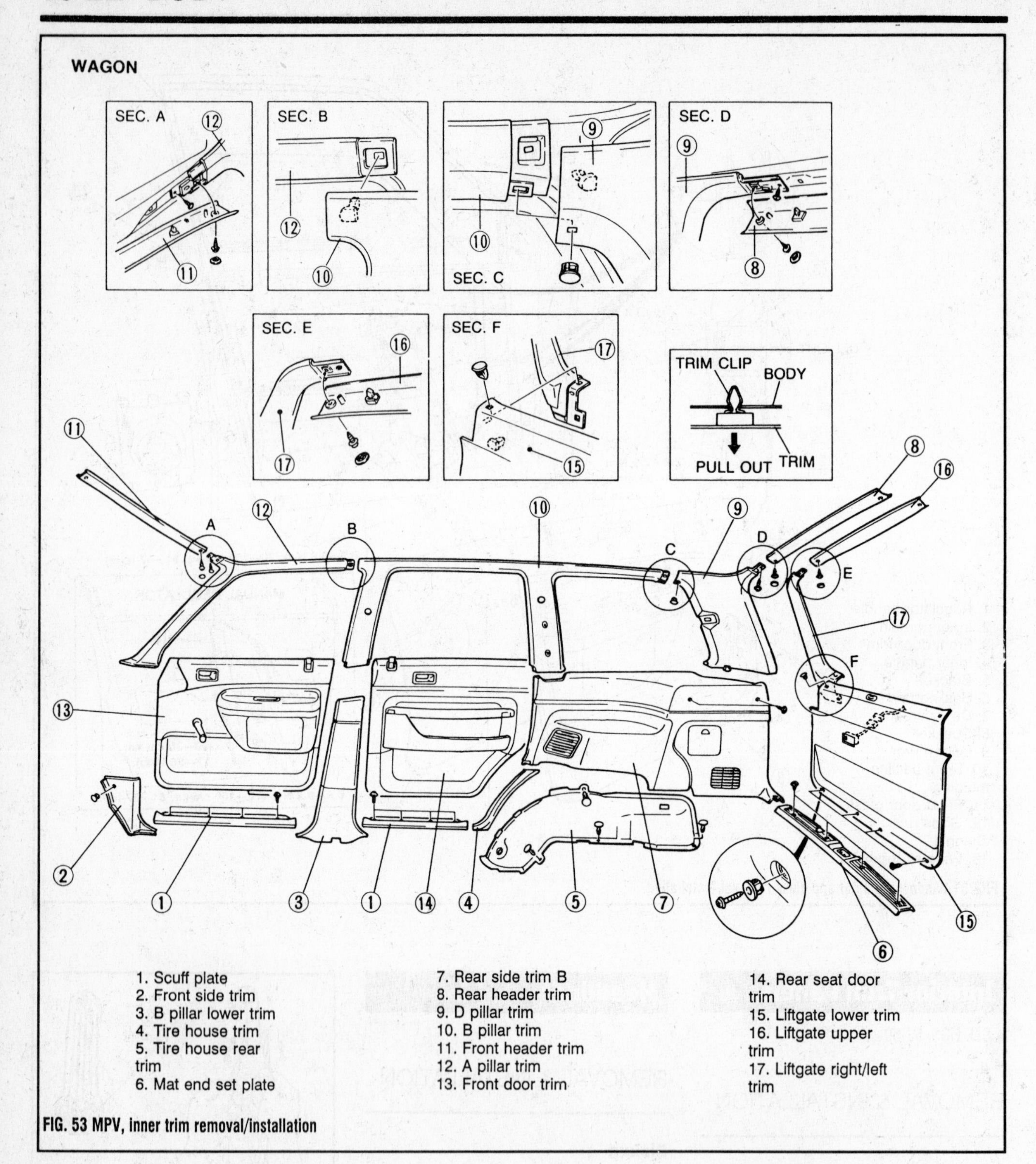

1. Scuff plate
2. Front side trim
3. B pillar lower trim
4. Tire house trim
5. Tire house rear trim
6. Mat end set plate
7. Rear side trim B
8. Rear header trim
9. D pillar trim
10. B pillar trim
11. Front header trim
12. A pillar trim
13. Front door trim
14. Rear seat door trim
15. Liftgate lower trim
16. Liftgate upper trim
17. Liftgate right/left trim

FIG. 53 MPV, inner trim removal/installation

WAGON

WITH REAR COOLER

Caution

- **Remove bolt Ⓐ, being careful not to let it fall into the duct.**

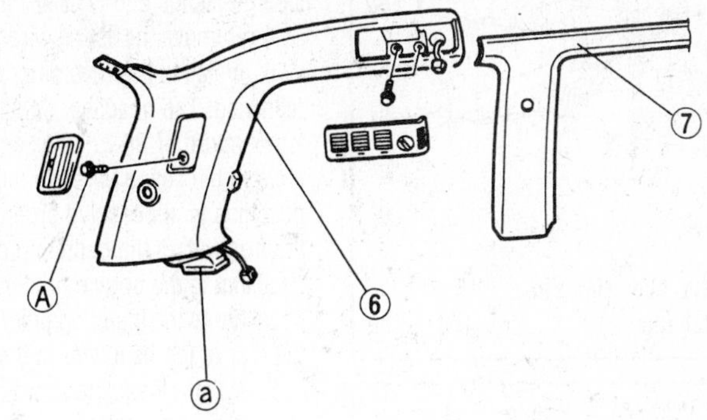

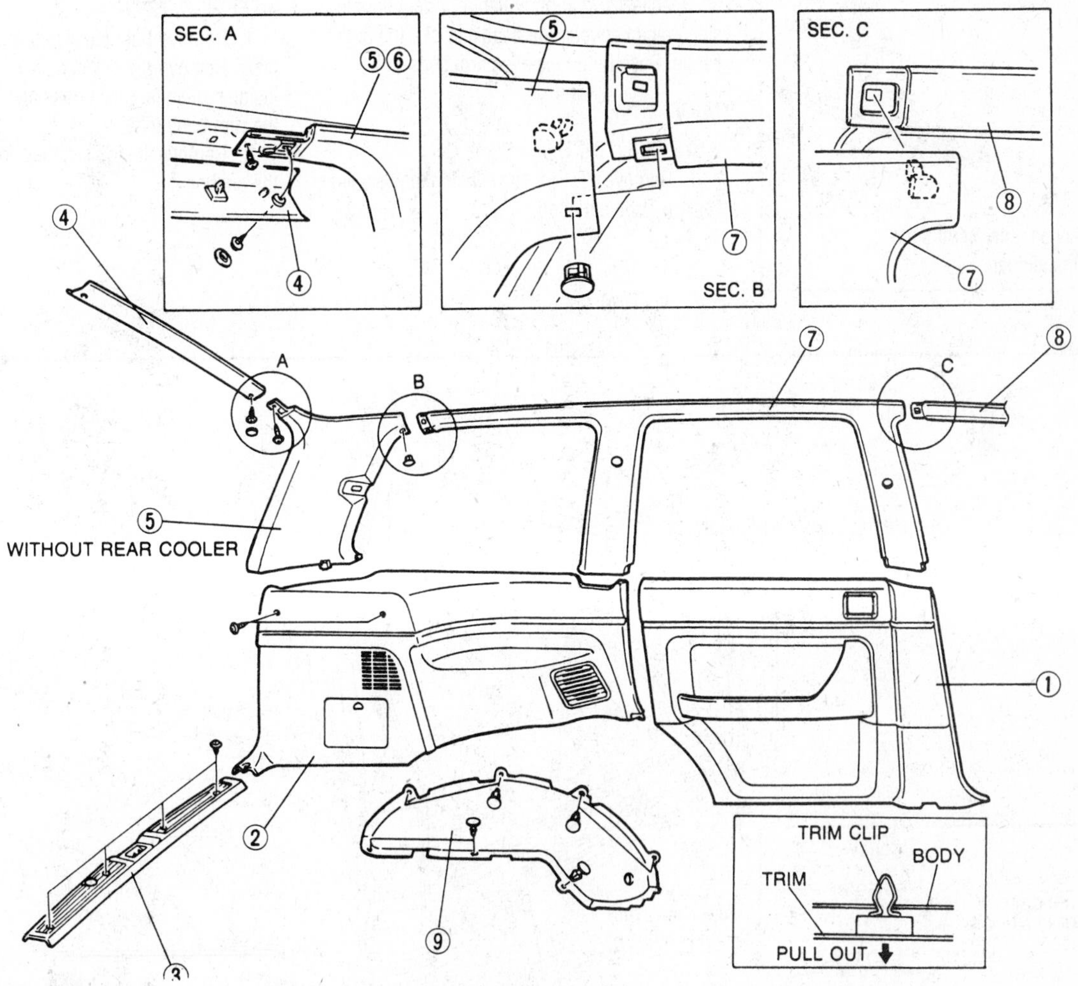

1. Rear side trim A
2. Rear side trim B
3. Mat end set plate
4. Rear header trim
5. D pillar trim
6. Rear cooler trim
7. B pillar trim
8. A pillar trim
9. Tire house trim

FIG. 54 MPV, inner trim removal/installation

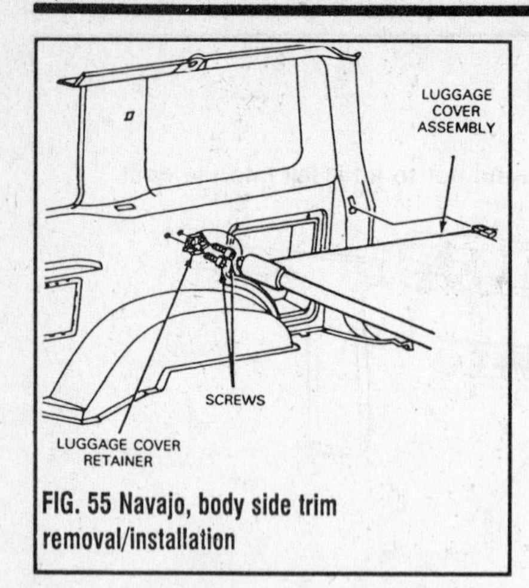

FIG. 55 Navajo, body side trim removal/installation

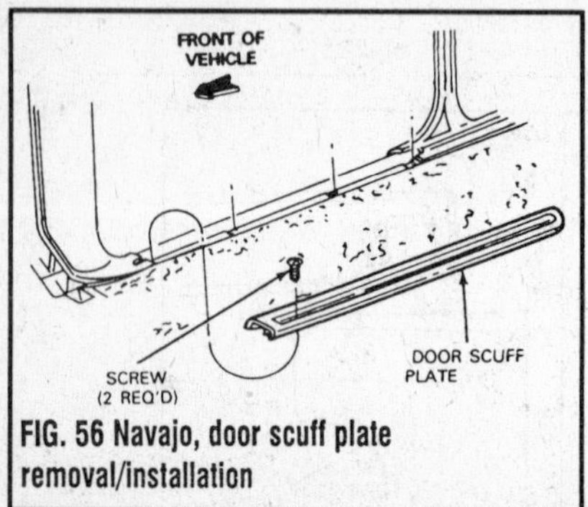

FIG. 56 Navajo, door scuff plate removal/installation

2. Remove the interior lamp attaching screws, disconnect the wiring connector and remove the lamp.
3. Remove the seat belt anchors, upper part of the seaming welt, front side pillar trims, top side garnishes and B pillar trims.
4. Remove the listing wires and the headliner.
5. Install in the reverse order. Note the following: The headliner should be at a temperature of 86 to 122 degrees F. Insert both ends of the listing wires to their respective positions in successive order, beginning from the front. Align the centering mark on the headliner to the body mark. Insert the front of the headliner to the inserting point of the body. Insert the rear of the headliner to the body flange.
6. Pull the headliner from both sides to remove any looseness and insert both sides of the headliner to the body flange. Apply double-sided tape between the headliner and the body flange. Push in the expansion buttons.

MPV

SEE FIGS. 70-71

1. Remove the trim surrounding the headliner section to be serviced.
2. Front top ceiling: Remove the interior lamp, assist handle, coat hanger, sunvisors, rearview mirror (with interior lamp), the front top headliner section and the insulator pad.
3. Rear top ceiling: Remove the interior lamp, coat hanger, rear top headliner section and the insulator pad.
4. Models equipped with a sunroof, front top ceiling: Remove the interior lamp (middle), assist handle, coat hanger, sunvisors, rearview mirror (with interior lamp), overhead console, front top ceiling headliner and the insulator pad.
5. Models equipped with a sunroof, rear top ceiling: Remove the interior lamp, coat hanger, rear top ceiling headliner and insulator pad.
6. Install in reverse order.

Navajo

SEE FIGS. 72-75

1. Remove both sunvisors and visor arm clips. Remove the assist handles, front pillar inside moldings, coat hooks and the pushpins at the roof centerline.
2. Remove the top seat belt anchor cover and the anchor.

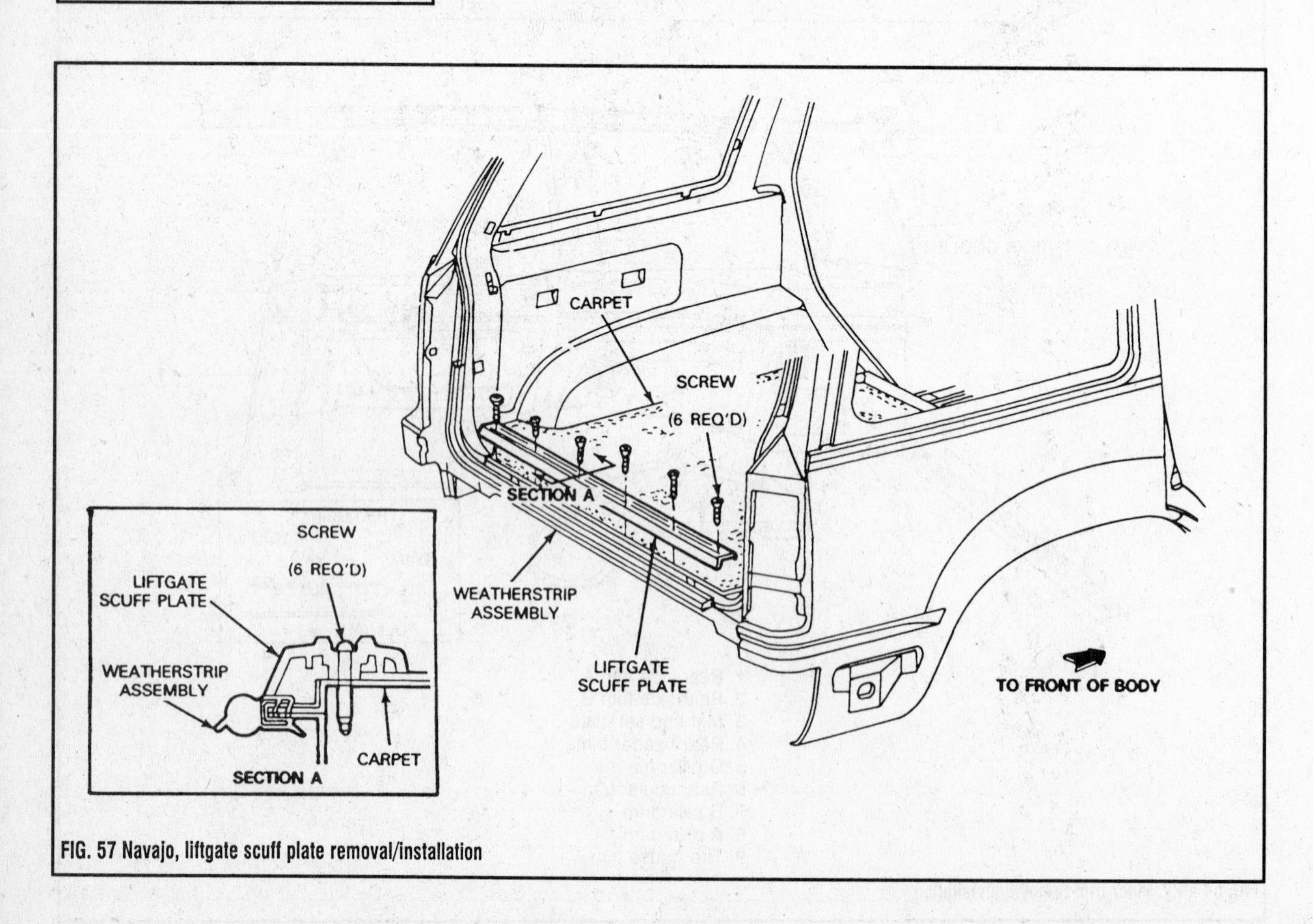

FIG. 57 Navajo, liftgate scuff plate removal/installation

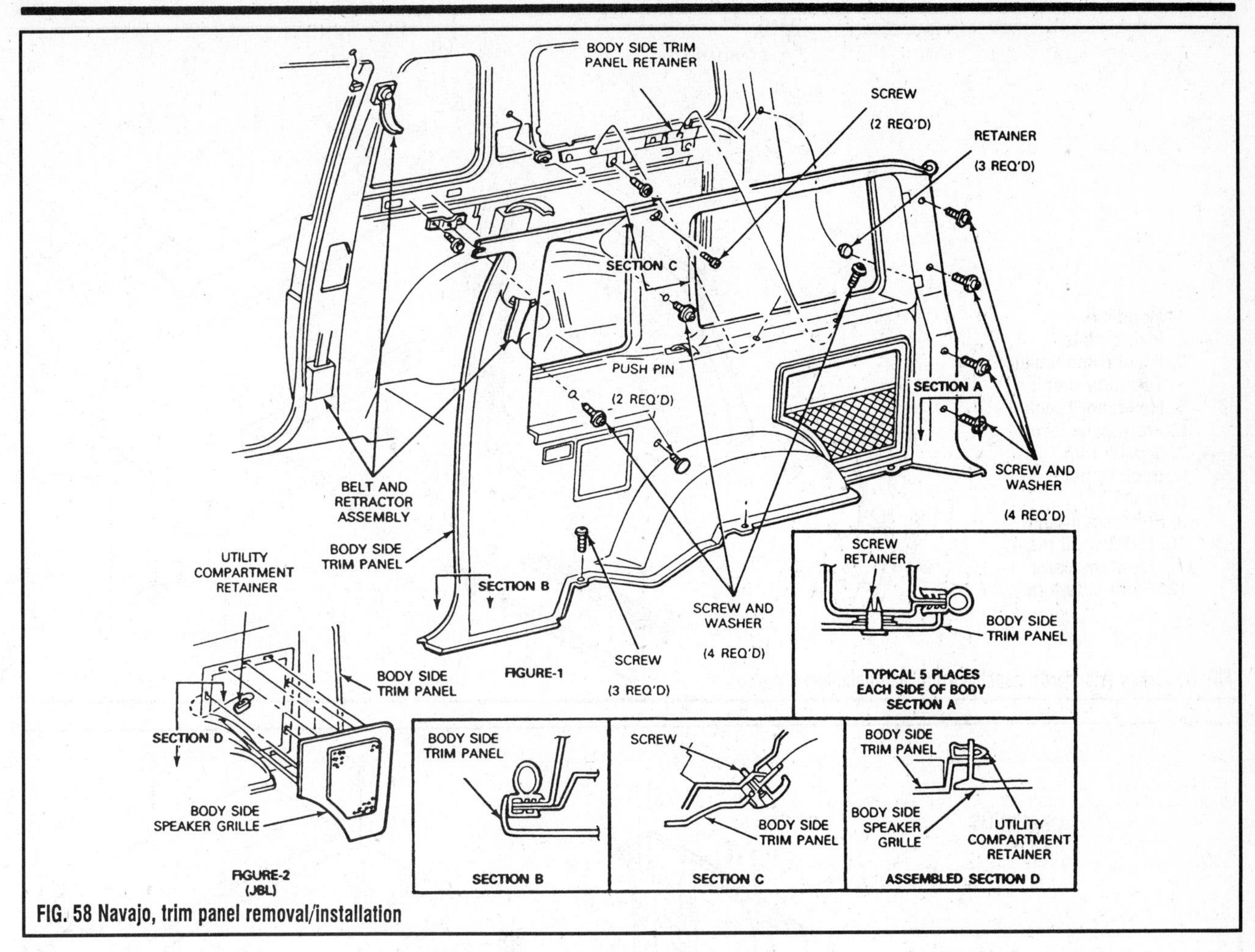

FIG. 58 Navajo, trim panel removal/installation

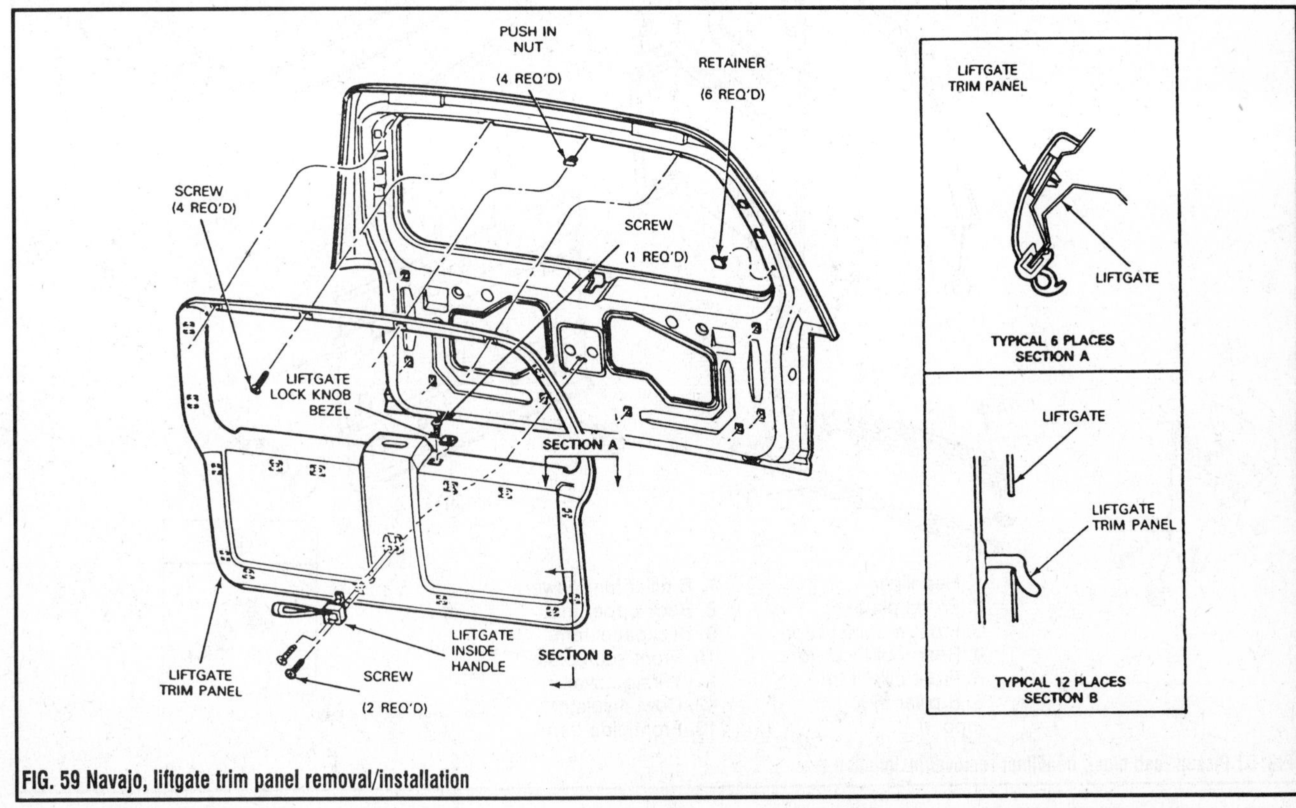

FIG. 59 Navajo, liftgate trim panel removal/installation

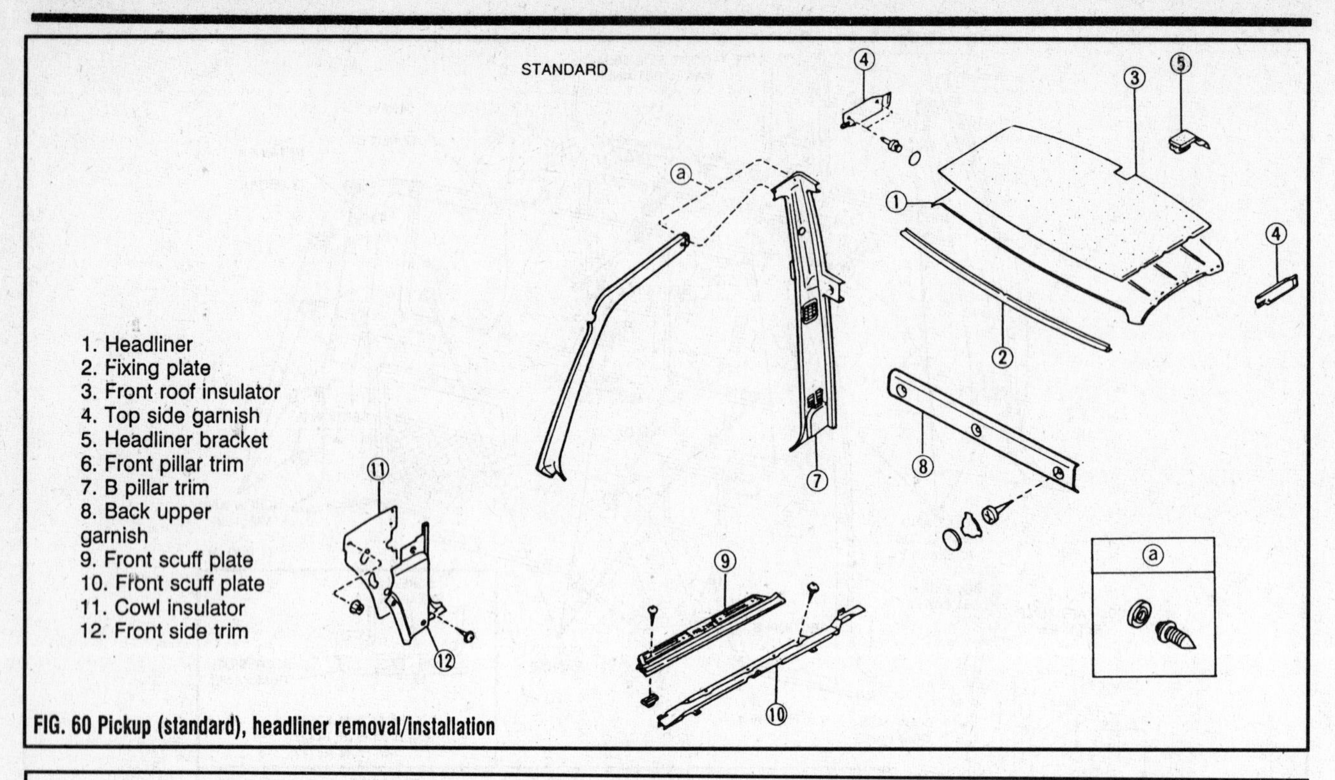

FIG. 60 Pickup (standard), headliner removal/installation

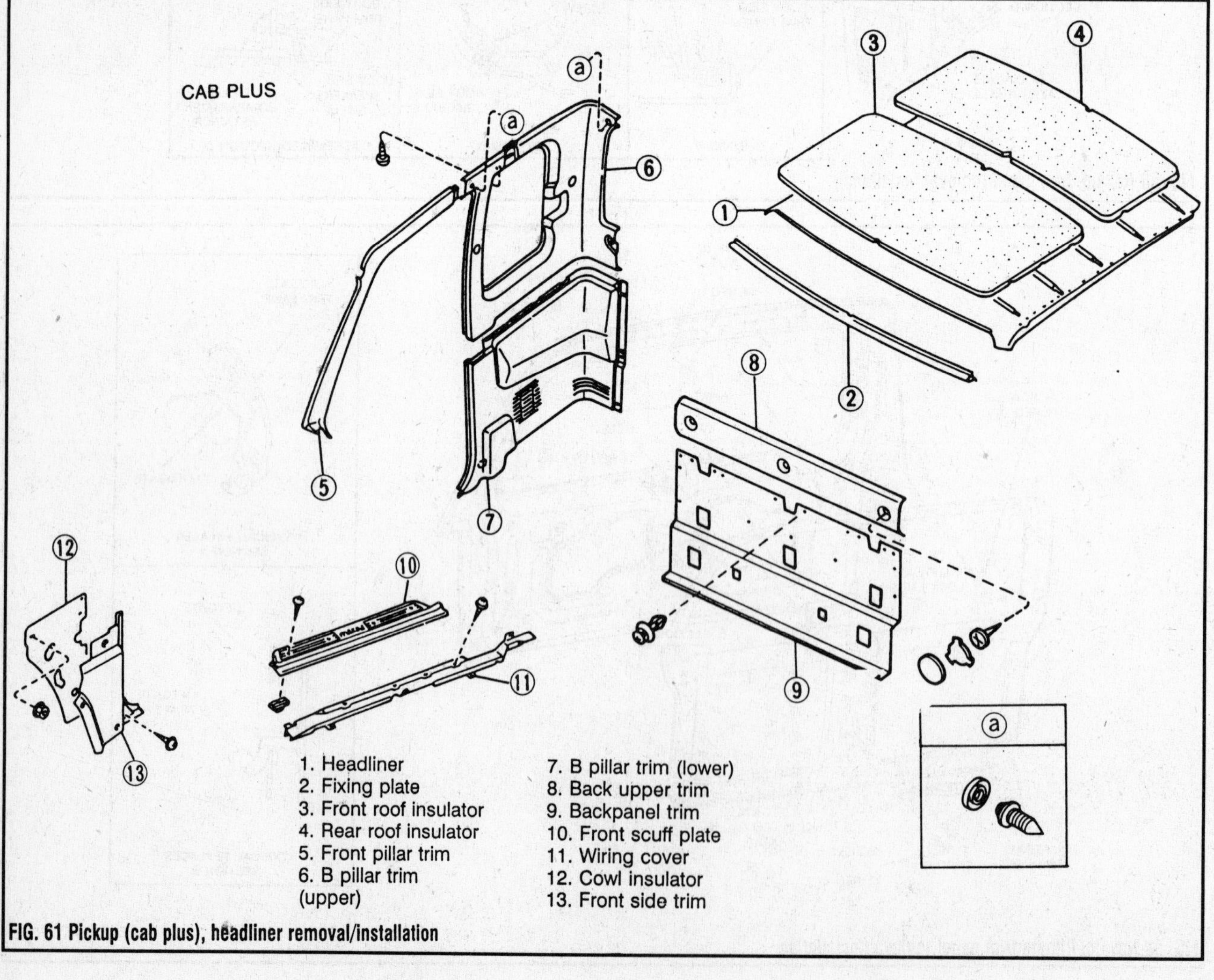

FIG. 61 Pickup (cab plus), headliner removal/installation

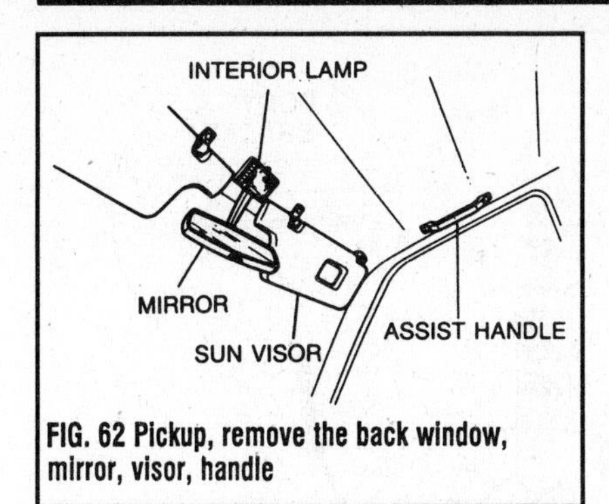

FIG. 62 Pickup, remove the back window, mirror, visor, handle

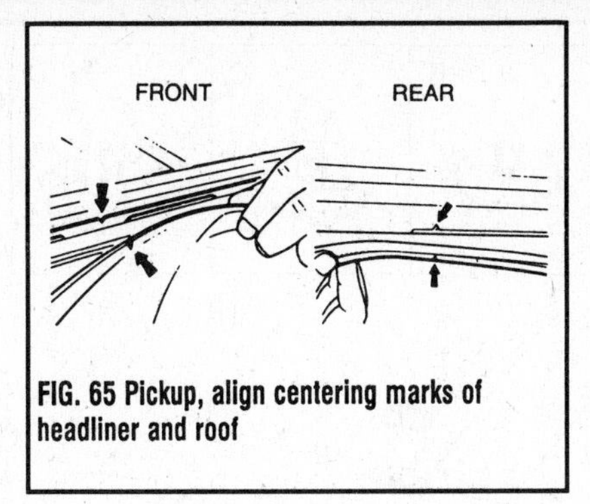

FIG. 65 Pickup, align centering marks of headliner and roof

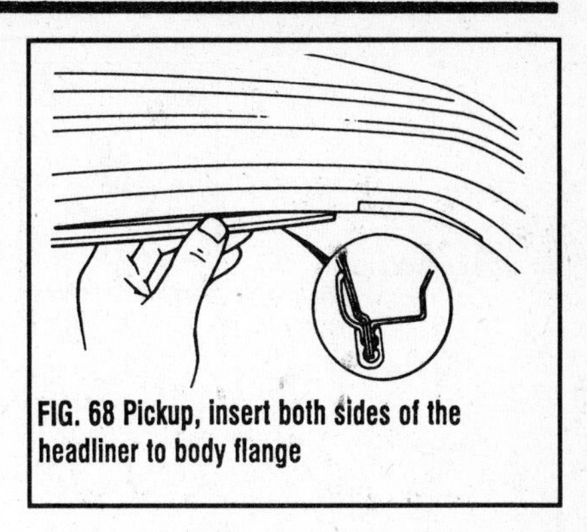
FIG. 68 Pickup, insert both sides of the headliner to body flange

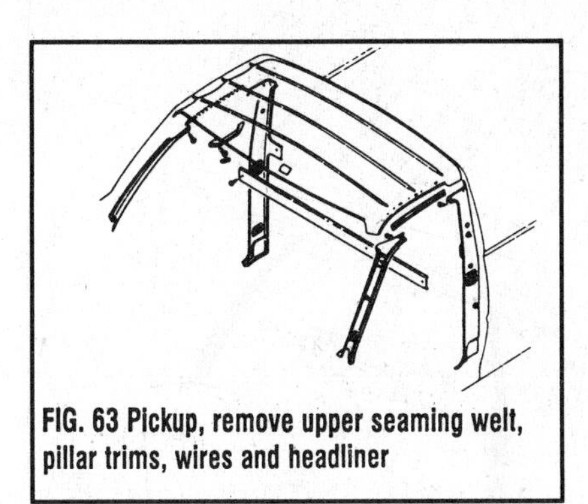
FIG. 63 Pickup, remove upper seaming welt, pillar trims, wires and headliner

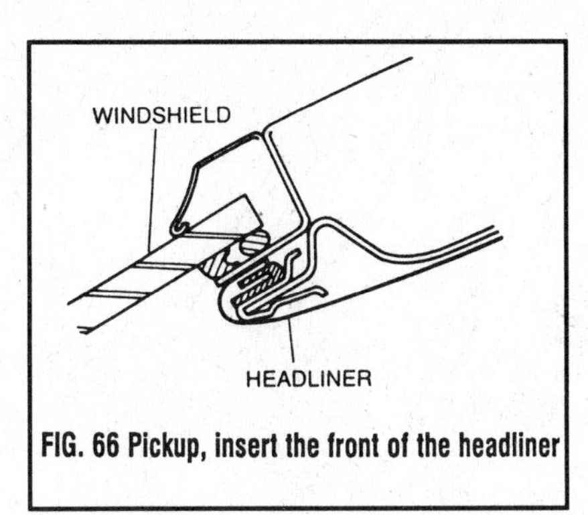

FIG. 66 Pickup, insert the front of the headliner

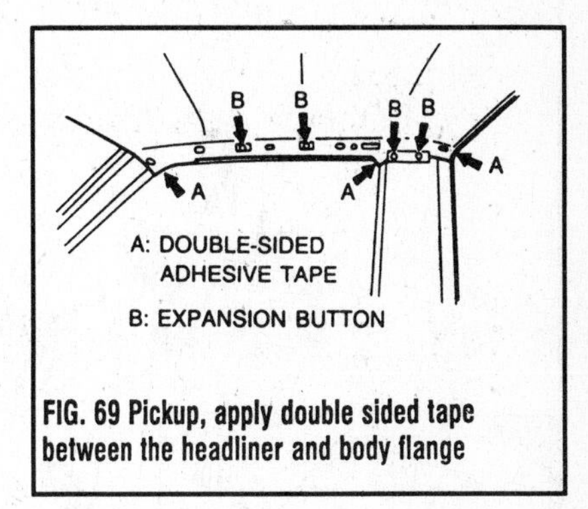

FIG. 69 Pickup, apply double sided tape between the headliner and body flange

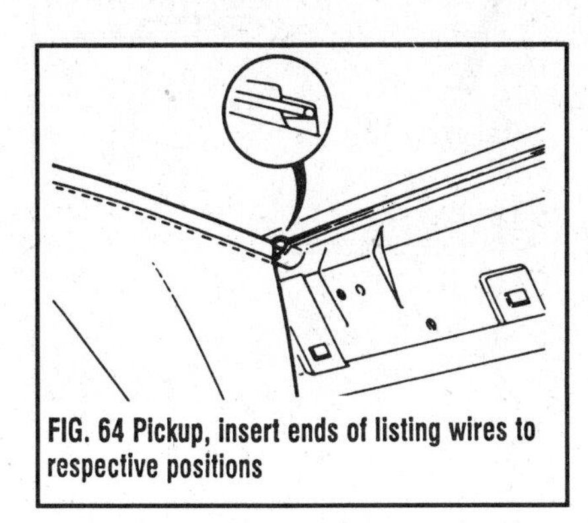
FIG. 64 Pickup, insert ends of listing wires to respective positions

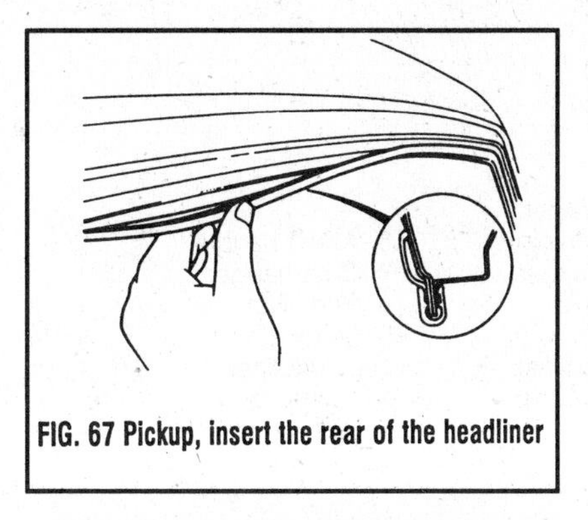
FIG. 67 Pickup, insert the rear of the headliner

3. Remove the body side trim panel assembly, dome lamp assembly and cargo lamp.

4. Remove the push pin retainers above the front doors, rear edge and mid-vehicle. If the headliner is being removed for reason either than replacement, install "U" channel reinforcements along the outer edges to prevent damage to the headliner. Remove the headliner.

5. When install a new headliner, leave the "U" channel reinforcements in place until the headliner is secured with the push pins. Install the headliner in reverse order of removal.

Door and Liftgate Locks

➧ SEE FIGS. 76-77

REMOVAL & INSTALLATION

➡ **A key code is stamped on the lock cylinder to aid in replacing lost keys.**

Pickups and MPV

1. Remove the door trim panel.

2. Pull the weathersheet, gently, away from the door lock access holes.

3. Using a screwdriver, push the lock cylinder retaining clip upward, noting the position of the lock cylinder.

4. Remove the lock cylinder from the door.

5. Install the lock cylinder in reverse of removal. It's a good idea to open the window before checking the lock operation, just in case it doesn't work properly.

Navajo

1. Remove the trim panel and watershield.

2. Disconnect the actuating rod from the lock control link clip.

3. Slide the retainer away from the lock cylinder.

4. Remove the cylinder from the door.

5. Use a new gasket when installing to ensure a watertight fit.

6. Lubricate the cylinder with suitable oil recommended for this application.

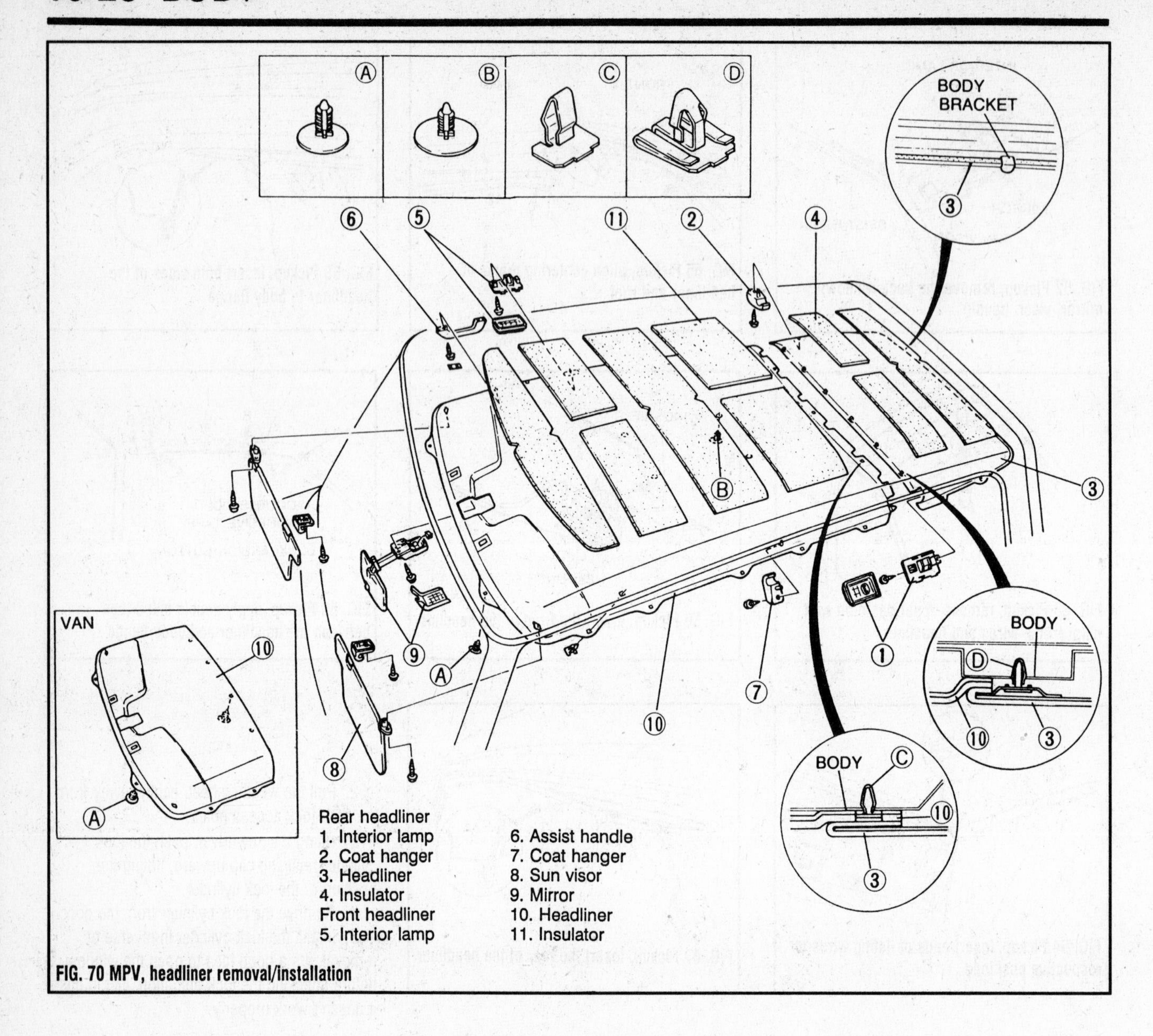

FIG. 70 MPV, headliner removal/installation

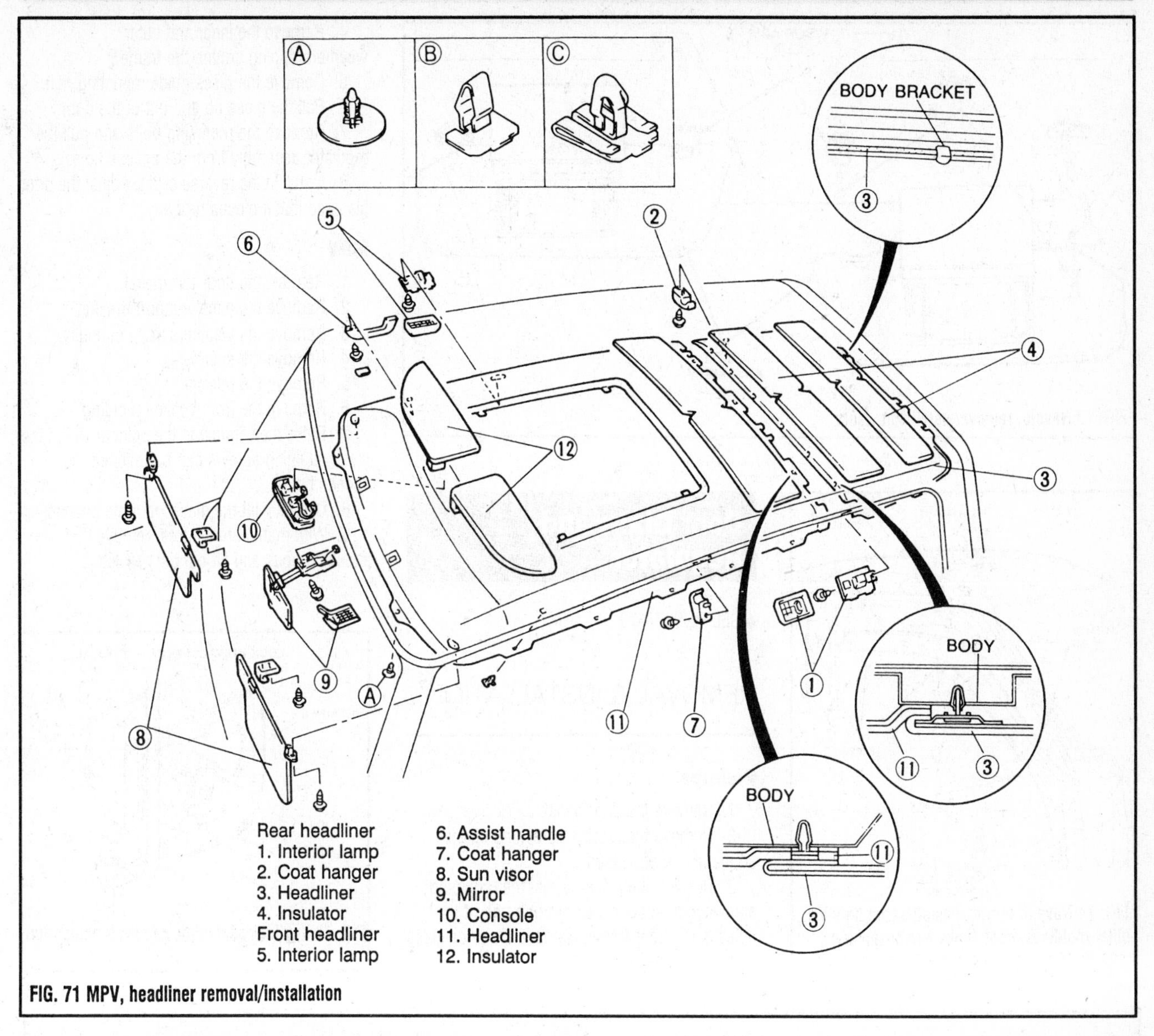

FIG. 71 MPV, headliner removal/installation

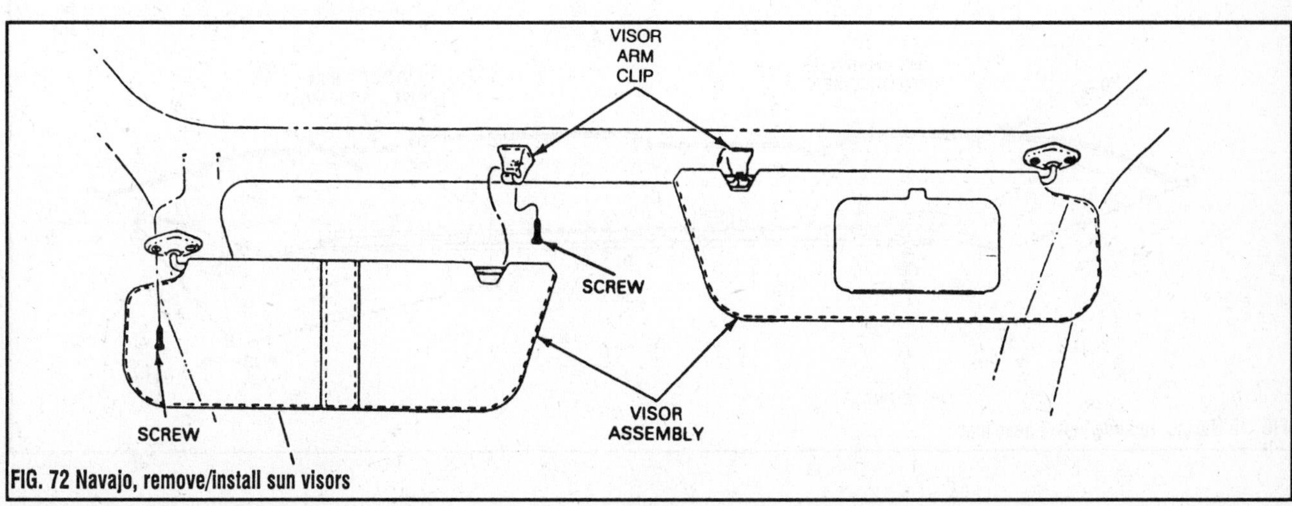

FIG. 72 Navajo, remove/install sun visors

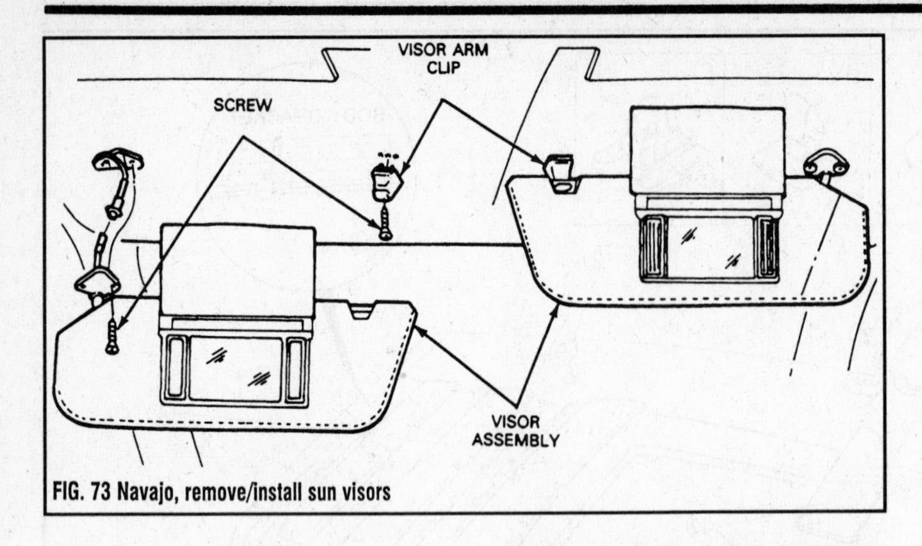

FIG. 73 Navajo, remove/install sun visors

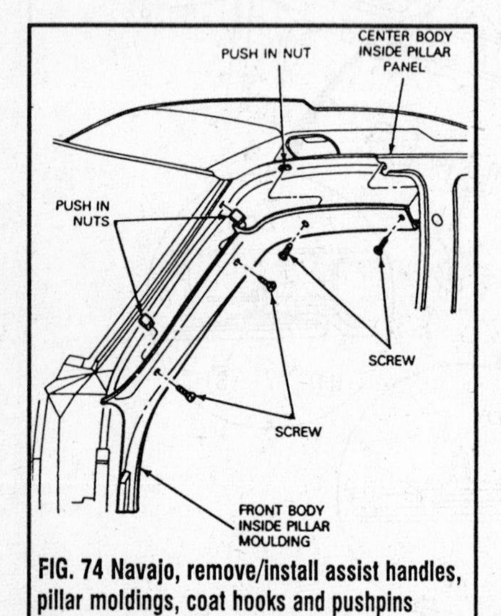

FIG. 74 Navajo, remove/install assist handles, pillar moldings, coat hooks and pushpins

Door Glass and Regulator

➧ SEE FIGS. 78-79

REMOVAL & INSTALLATION

Pickups

1. Remove the door panel.
2. Remove the weatherscreening carefully, so that it can be reused.
3. Position the glass so that the mounting screws can be accessed through one of the holes in the door frame. Remove the door glass mounting screws.
4. Remove the inner and outer weatherstripping around the frame.
5. Remove the glass guide mounting bolt.
6. Pull the glass up and out of the door.
7. Remove the mounting bolts and pull the regulator assembly from the access hole.
8. Install in the reverse order. Adjust the door glass so that it closes properly.

MPV

1. Remove the door trim panel.
2. Remove the panel support bracket.
3. Remove the weatherscreen carefully.
4. Remove the speaker.
5. Remove the mirror.
6. Remove the front beltline molding.
7. Raise the window to the point at which the glass retaining screws can be reached the access holes.
8. Carefully lift the glass from the channel.
9. With manual regulators, remove the attaching bolts and lift out the regulator.

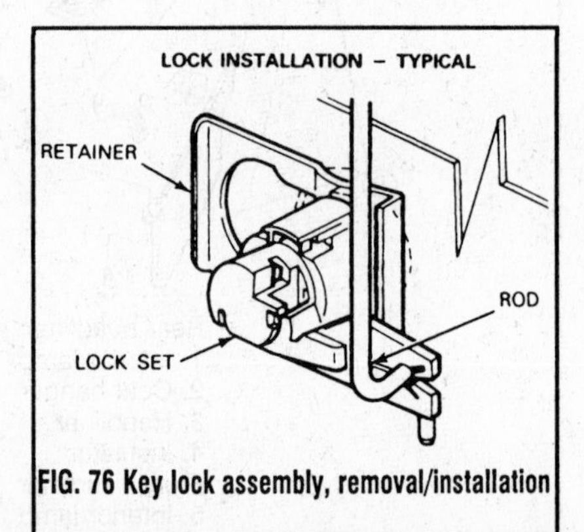

FIG. 76 Key lock assembly, removal/installation

"U" CHANNEL REINFORCEMENT
ROOF TRIM PANEL ASSEMBLY
PUSH PIN
DRIVE PIN

FIG. 75 Navajo, remove/install headliner

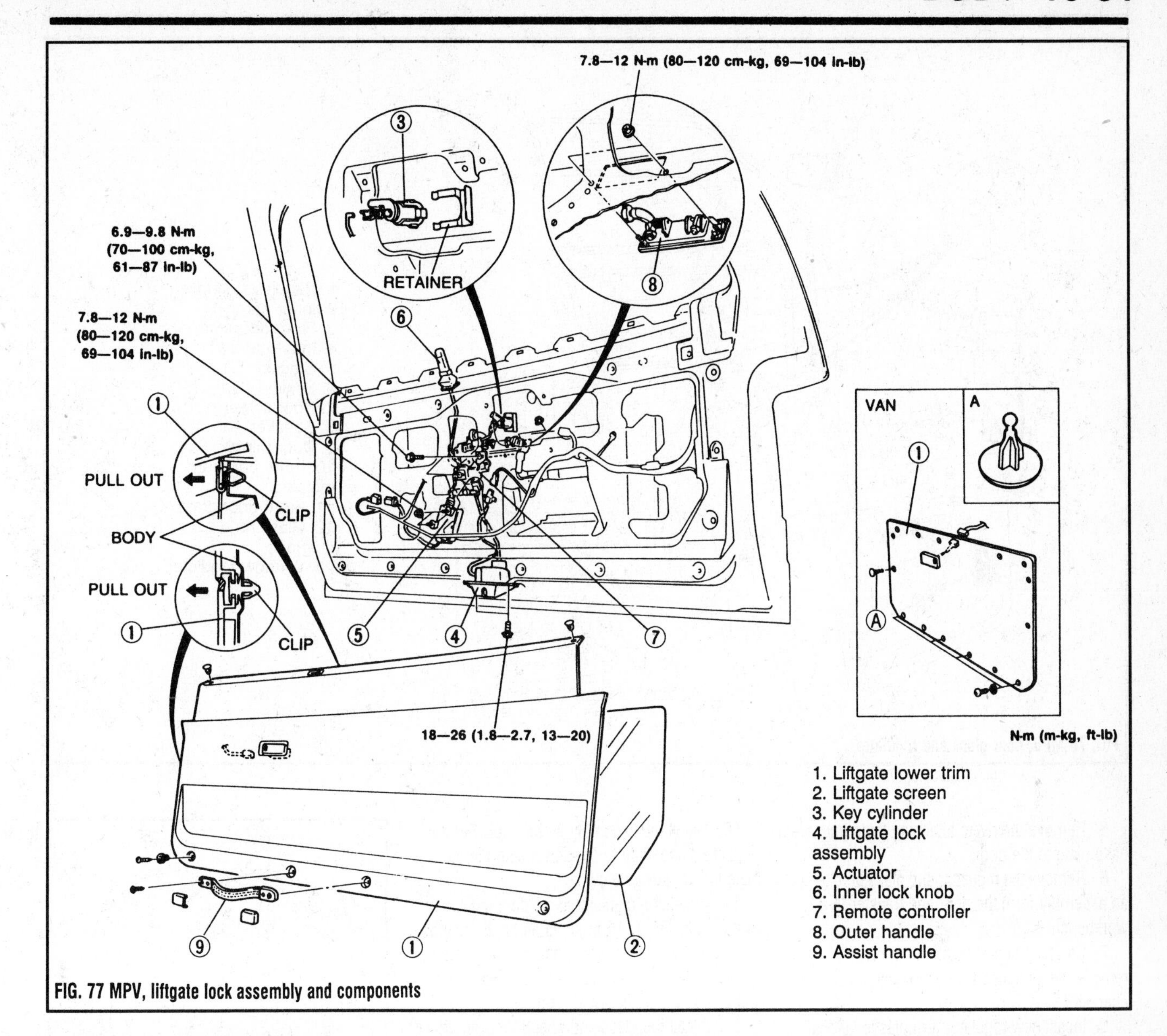

FIG. 77 MPV, liftgate lock assembly and components

10. With power regulators, remove the attaching bolts and drill out the rivets. Lift out the regulator.

11. Place the regulator in position and secure. Install then components in reverse order. Use new rivets on power regulators.

Navajo

GLASS

1. Remove the door trim panel and speaker if applicable.

2. Remove the screw from the division bar. Remove the inside belt weaterstrip(s) if equipped.

3. Remove the 2 vent window attaching screws from the front edge of the door.

4. Lower the glass and pull the glass out of the run retainer near the vent window division bar, just enough to allow the removal of the vent window, if equipped.

5. Push the front edge of the glass downward and remove the rear glass run retainer from the door.

6. If equipped with retaining rivets, remove them carefully. Otherwise, remove the glass from the channel using Glass and Channel Removal Tool 2900, made by the Sommer and Mala Glass Machine Co. of Chicago, ILL., or its equivalent. Remove the glass through the belt opening if possible.

To Install:

7. Install the glass spacer and retainer into the retention holes.

8. Install the glass into the door, position on the bracket and align the retaining holes.

9. Carefully install the retaining rivets or equivalent.

10. Raise the glass to the full closed position.

11. Install the rear glass run retainer and glass run. Install the inside belt weatherstrip(s).

12. Check for smooth operation before installing the trim panel.

REGULATOR

1. Remove the door trim panel and watershield.

2. Remove the inside door belt weatherstrip and glass stabilizer.

3. Remove the door glass.

4. Remove the 2 nuts attaching the equalizer bracket.

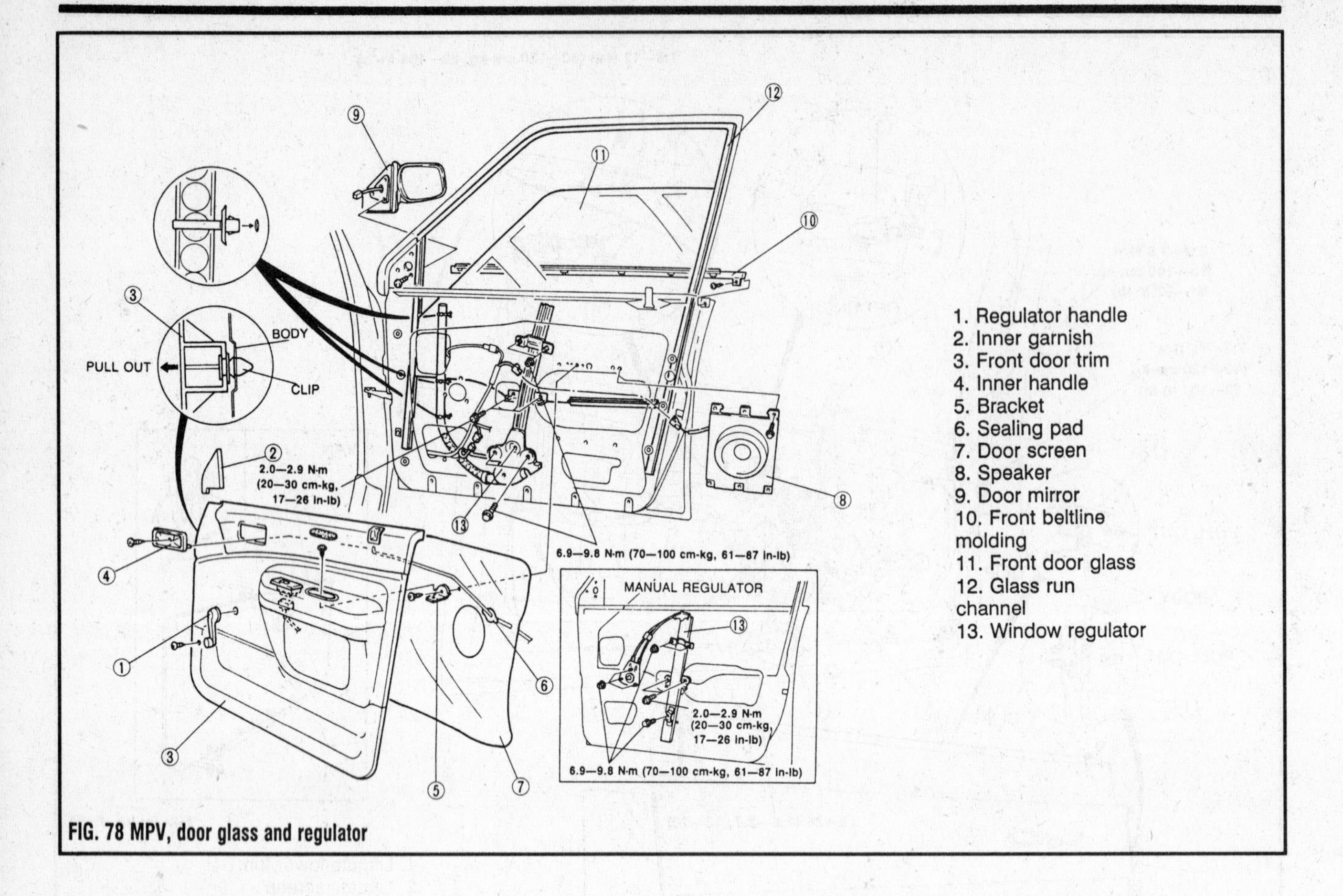

FIG. 78 MPV, door glass and regulator

5. Remove the rivets attaching the regulator base plate to the door.

6. Remove the regulator and glass bracket as an assembly from the door and transfer to a workbench.

7. Carefully bend the tab flat in order to remove the air slides from the glass bracket C-channel.

8. Install new regulator arm plastic guides into the C-channel and bend the tab back 90°. If the tab is broken or cracked, replace the glass bracket assembly. Make sure the rubber bumper is installed properly on the new glass bracket, if applicable.

CAUTION

If the regulator counterbalance spring is to be removed, make sure the regulator arms are in a fixed position prior to removal. This will prevent possible injury when the C-spring unwinds.

To install:

9. Assemble the glass bracket and regulator assembly.

10. Install the assembly in the door. Set the regulator base plate to the door using the base plate locator tab as a guide.

11. Attach the regulator to the door using new rivets. $^1/_4$ in.-20 × $^1/_2$ in. bolts and nuts may be used in place of the rivets to attach the regulator.

12. Install the equalizer bracket, door belt weatherstrip and glass stabilizer.

13. Install the glass and check for smooth operation before installing the door trim panel.

Electric Window Motor

REMOVAL & INSTALLATION

Navajo

1. Raise the window fully if possible. If not, you will have to support the window during this procedure. Disconnect the battery ground.

2. Remove the door trim panel.

3. Disconnect the window motor wiring harness.

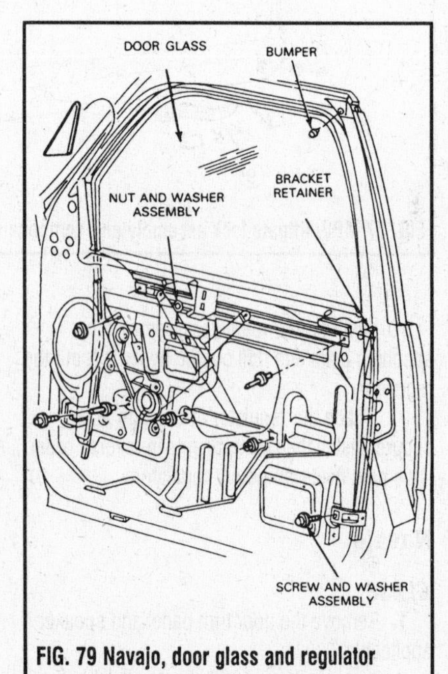

FIG. 79 Navajo, door glass and regulator

4. There may be a drill dimple in the door panel, opposite the concealed motor retaining bolt. Drill out the dimple to gain access to the bolt. Be careful to avoid damage to the wires.

5. Remove the motor mounting bolts (front door) or rivets(rear door).

6. Push the motor towards the outside of the door to disengage it from the gears. You'll have to support the window glass once the motor is disengaged.
7. Remove the motor from the door.
8. Installation is the reverse of removal. To avoid rusting in the drilled areas, prime and paint the exposed metal, or, cover the holes with waterproof body tape. Make sure that the motor works properly before installing the trim panel.

Windshield

SEE FIGS. 80-90

REMOVAL & INSTALLATION

You'll need an assistant for this job. A special kit, Mazda #49 0305 870A, is available for replacing glass. The references to adhesives and bonding agents contained in this procedure are taking for granted that this kit is being used. Aftermarket kits are also available which contain all the necessary equipment.

1. Remove the wiper arms.
2. Remove the rear view mirror and front pillar trim molding.
3. Cover the sheet metal around the windshield with masking tape to protect it from scratches.
4. Remove the windshield trim molding. It's best to use a tool made for that purpose, although it can be pried off. If a special tool is not used, it's very easy to damage the molding, so be careful!
5. Drill a small hole through the rubber weatherstripping at its base. Pass a length of piano wire through the hole. Wrap each end of the wire around a wood dowel. Grip one dowel in each hand, or have your assistant take one dowel, and, using a sawing motion, pass the wire all the way around the perimeter of the weatherstripping to cut through the sealer.
6. Remove the glass.
7. Using a sharp knife, cut away the old sealer so that a 1-2mm (0.039-0.079 in.) thickness of old sealer remains around the circumference of the frame. If the old sealer comes completely off in any spot, rebuild that spot to the 1-2mm (0.039-0.079 in.) thickness with new sealer.
8. Secure a new windshield trim dam to the glass with a glass cement. The new dam should be positioned so that its outer edge is 7mm (0.276 in.) from the edge of the glass, with the lip facing outward.
9. Apply a thin coat of primer to the bonding areas of the frame and glass. Allow the primer to dry for 30 minutes. Do not allow any dirt or dust to contact the primer while it's drying. If primer gets on your hands, wash it off immediately.
10. Cement the spacers to the frame.

The upper and lower spacers are different. Don't get them mixed up.

11. Install the molding clips. If any are defective, replace them.
12. Cut the nozzle of the sealer tube as illustrated, so that it will run along the edge of the glass.
13. Apply sealer around the whole circumference so that it will fill the gap between the dam and the edge of the glass, with a bead of sealer about 8mm (0.315 in.) high. Keep the bead smooth and even, shaping it with the spatula where necessary.
14. Open the door windows. Position the glass in the frame, pushing inward lightly to compress the sealer.

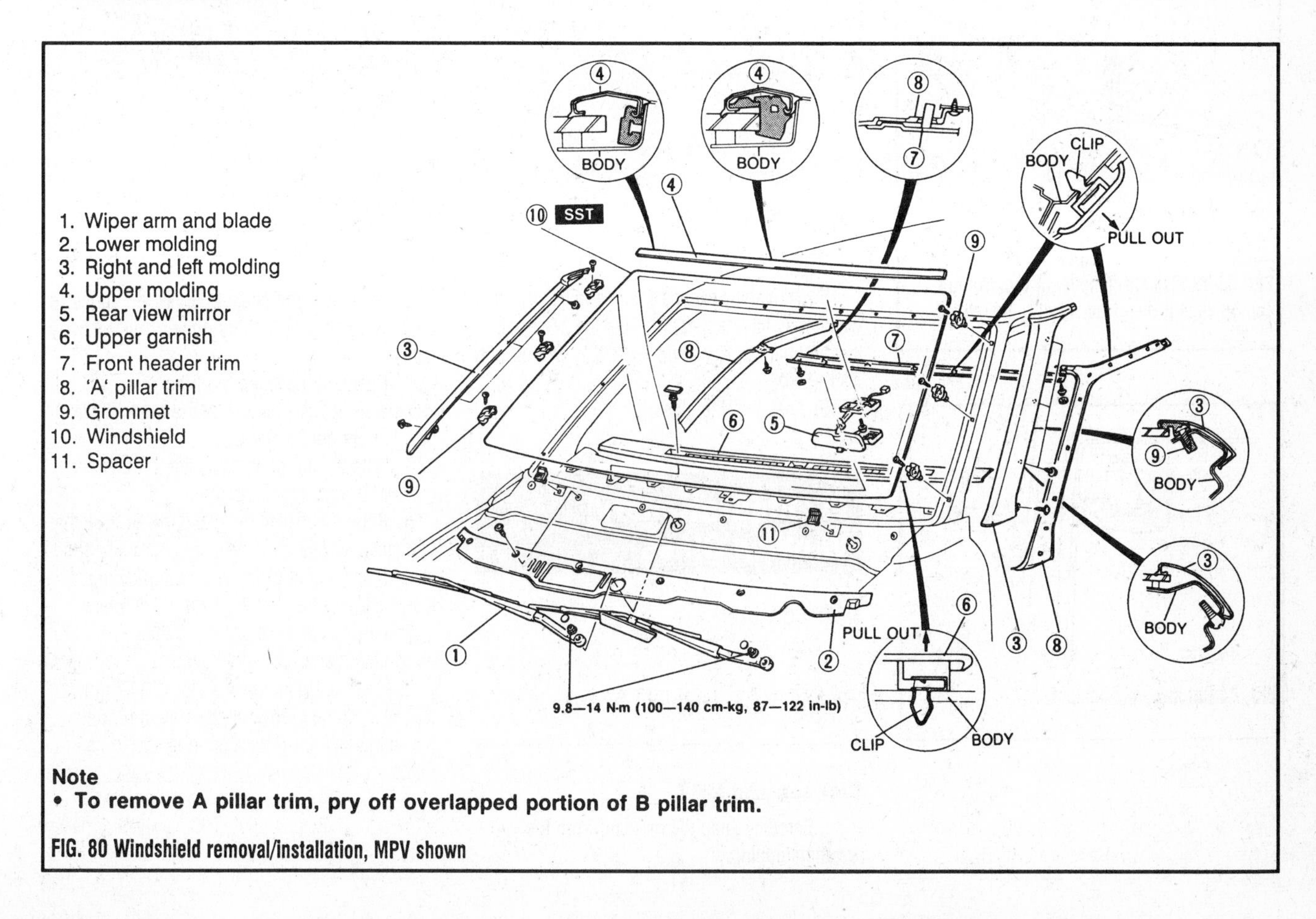

FIG. 80 Windshield removal/installation, MPV shown

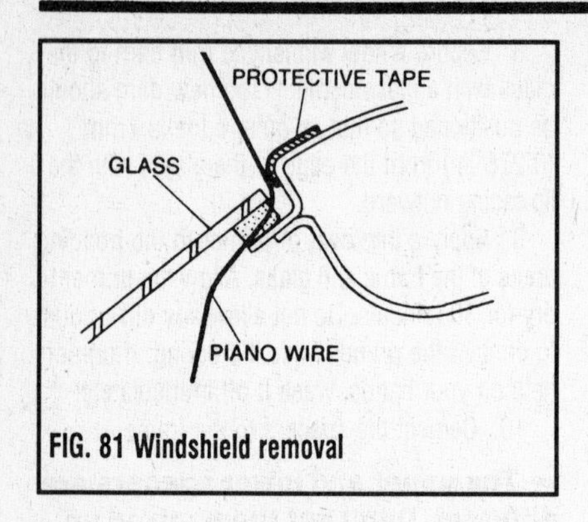

FIG. 81 Windshield removal

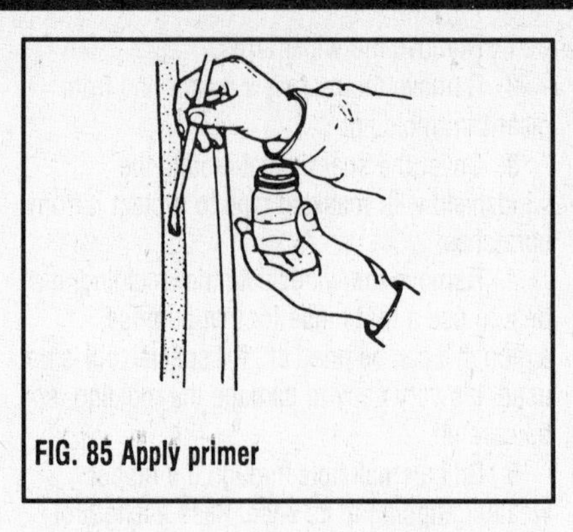
FIG. 85 Apply primer

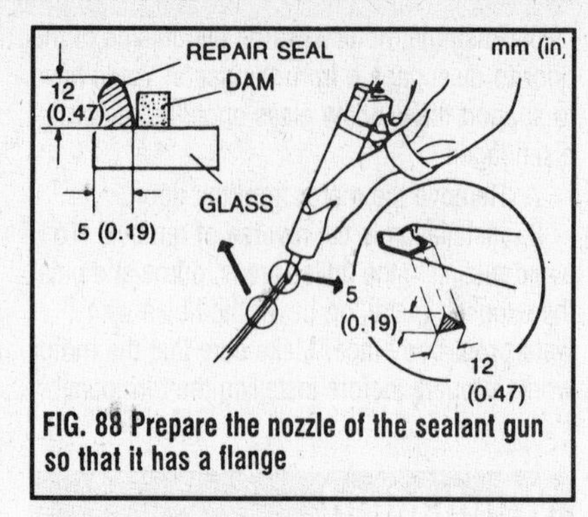

FIG. 88 Prepare the nozzle of the sealant gun so that it has a flange

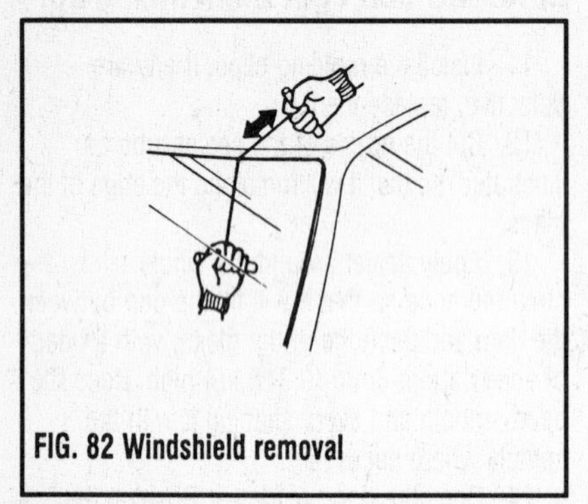
FIG. 82 Windshield removal

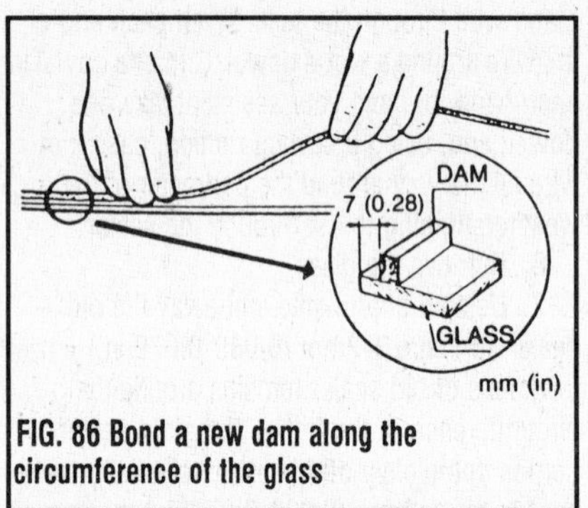

FIG. 86 Bond a new dam along the circumference of the glass

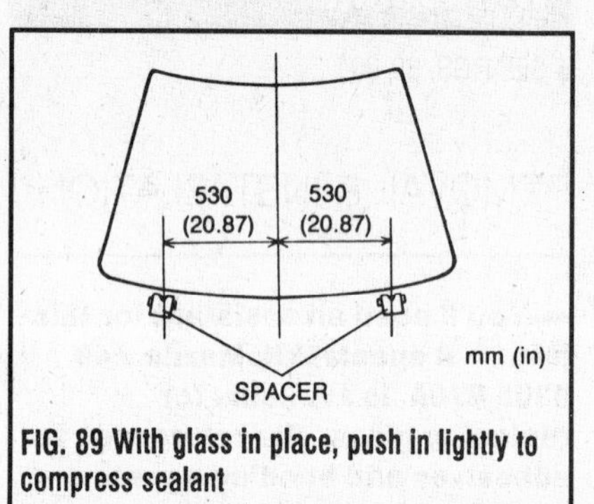

FIG. 89 With glass in place, push in lightly to compress sealant

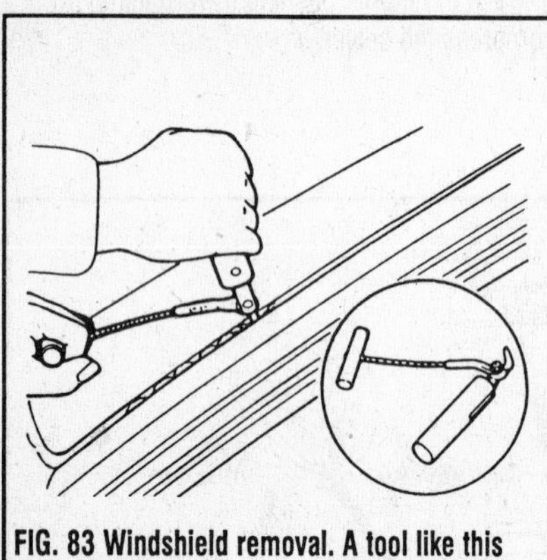
FIG. 83 Windshield removal. A tool like this can be used if the glass is not to be reused

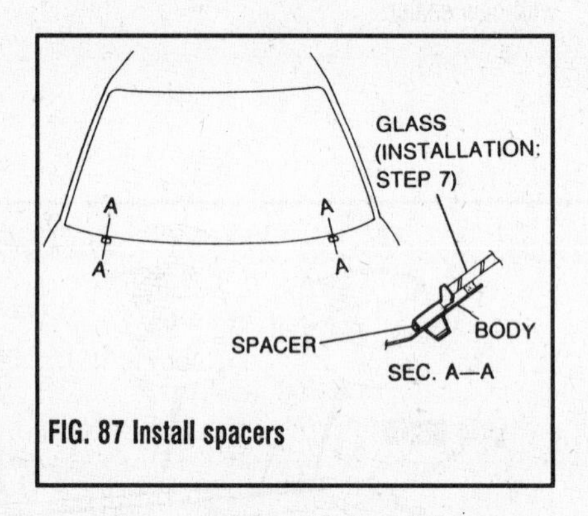

FIG. 87 Install spacers

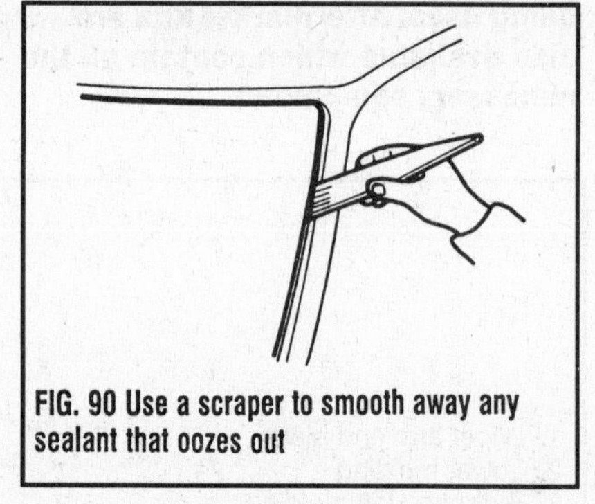
FIG. 90 Use a scraper to smooth away any sealant that oozes out

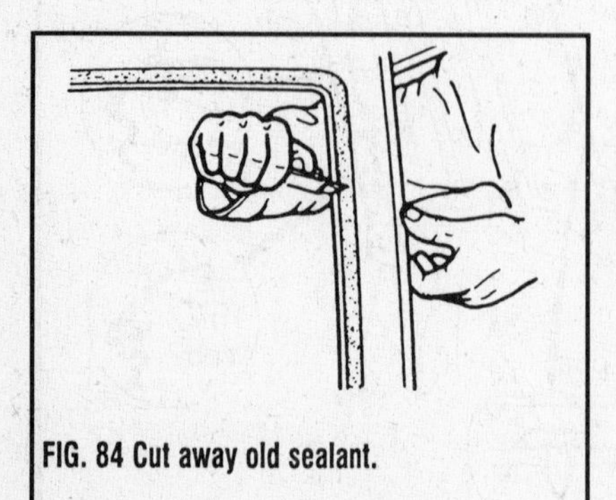
FIG. 84 Cut away old sealant.

15. Trim away excess sealer and fill any gaps which may have appeared. Give the sealer at least 5 hours to dry at 68°F (20°C); 24 hours at 41°F (5°C).

16. Leak test the glass.

Fixed (Stationary) Window Glass

➧ SEE FIGS. 91-93

REMOVAL & INSTALLATION

Pickups and MPV

1. Carefully snap the molding from the weatherstripping.

2. Using a wood spatula, break the adhesive bond between the weatherstripping and the body flange.

3. Push out the inner lip of the weatherstripping, from inside the truck, while pushing out on the glass.

4. With the aid of an assistant, remove the glass and weatherstripping.

5. Before installing the glass, make sure that you clean all of the old adhesive from all parts.

6. Place a coat of primer in the molding. Install the weatherstripping around the glass.

7. Liberally wet the groove in the weatherstripping with liquid soap.

8. Place a string, about 4mm (0.157 in.) in diameter, in the groove all the way around the weatherstripping. Allow a good length to hang free.

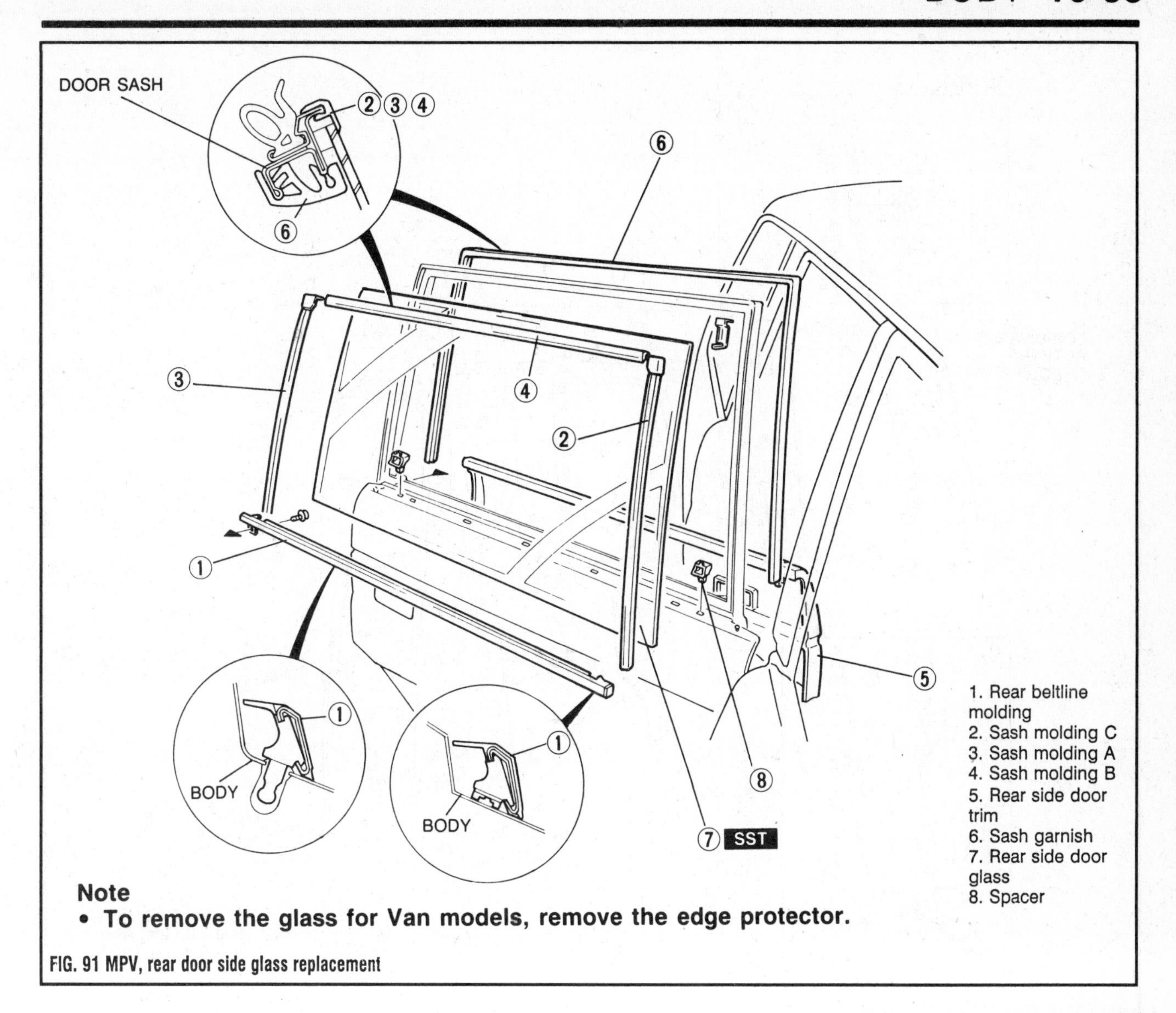

FIG. 91 MPV, rear door side glass replacement

9. Place the glass into position in the frame, with the free end of the string hanging inside the truck. Pull the string while pushing inward on the glass, to properly position the inner lip of the weatherstripping.

10. Go around the inner and outer sides of the weatherstripping with a thin tool to make sure that the weatherstripping is flat against the frame.

11. Using a thin coat of rubber sealer, seal the outer edge of the weatherstripping against the frame.

12. Snap the molding into place.

Navajo Fixed Side Window

1. Remove the interior trim around the window.

2. Remove the nuts from inside window assembly and remove the molding.

3. Remove the glass by pushing on it with enough force to separate the butyl seal.

4. Clean all traces of the original seal from the window opening and repair the sheet metal as required.

To install:

5. If the replacement window is not complete with sealer tape, then apply a continuous strip of Foam Core Butyl Tape, or equivalent, to the back of the window. The ends must meet at the bottom and overlap 1–2 in. (25–50mm).

6. Press the window in place with just enough force to seat the window firmly into the sealing material.

7. Install the retaining nuts.

8. Leak test the installation. If it is satisfactory, install the interior trim.

Inside Rear View Mirror

The mirror is held in place with a single setscrew. Loosen the screw and lift the mirror off. Don't forget to unplug the electrical connector if the truck has an electric Day/Night mirror.

Repair kits for damaged mirrors are available and most auto parts stores. The most important part of the repair is the beginning. Mark the outside of the windshield to locate the pad, then scrape the old adhesive off with a razor blade. Clean the remaining adhesive off with chlorine-based window cleaner (not petroleum-based solvent) as thoroughly as possible. Follow the manufacturers instructions exactly to complete the repair..

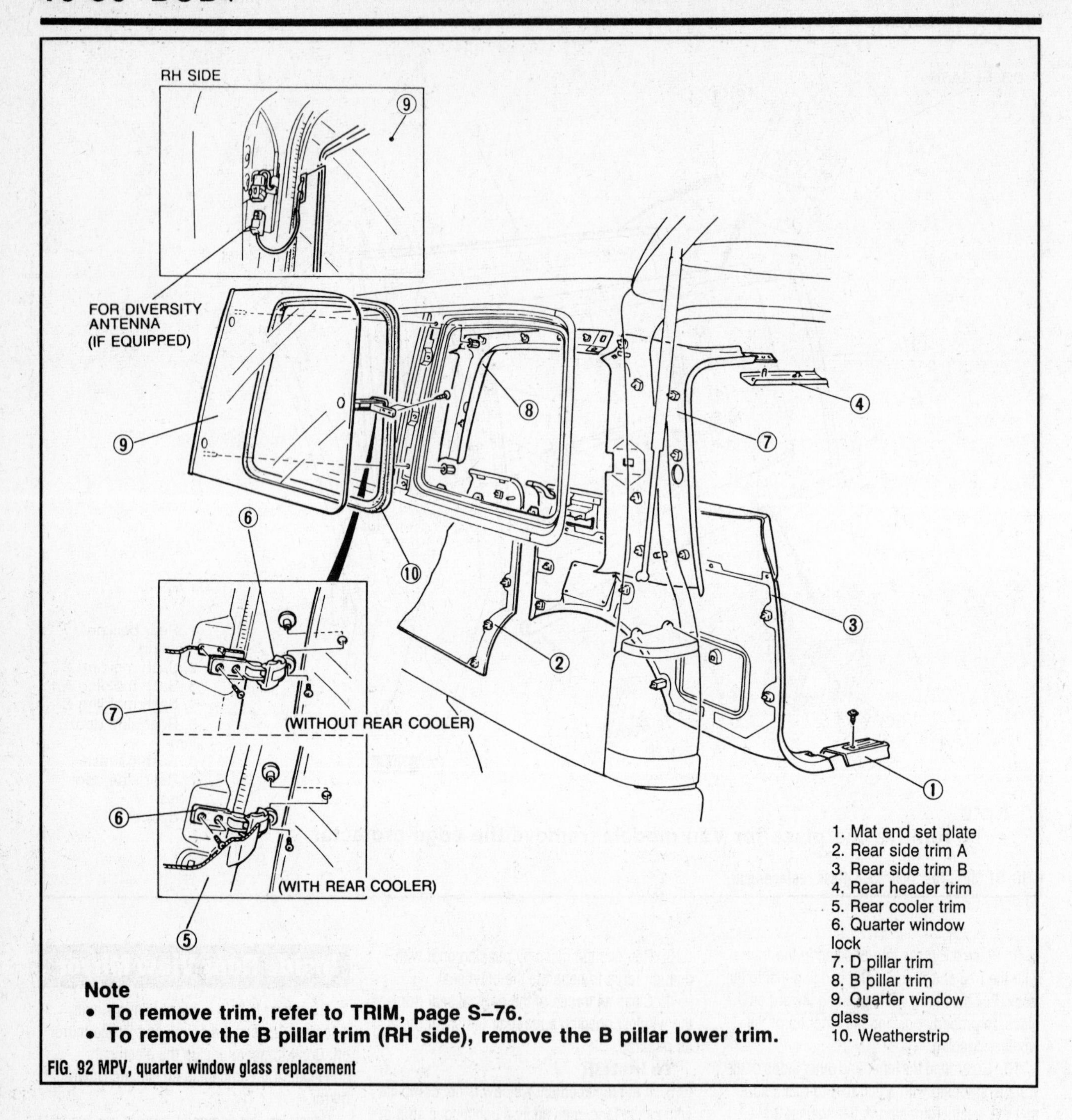

FIG. 92 MPV, quarter window glass replacement

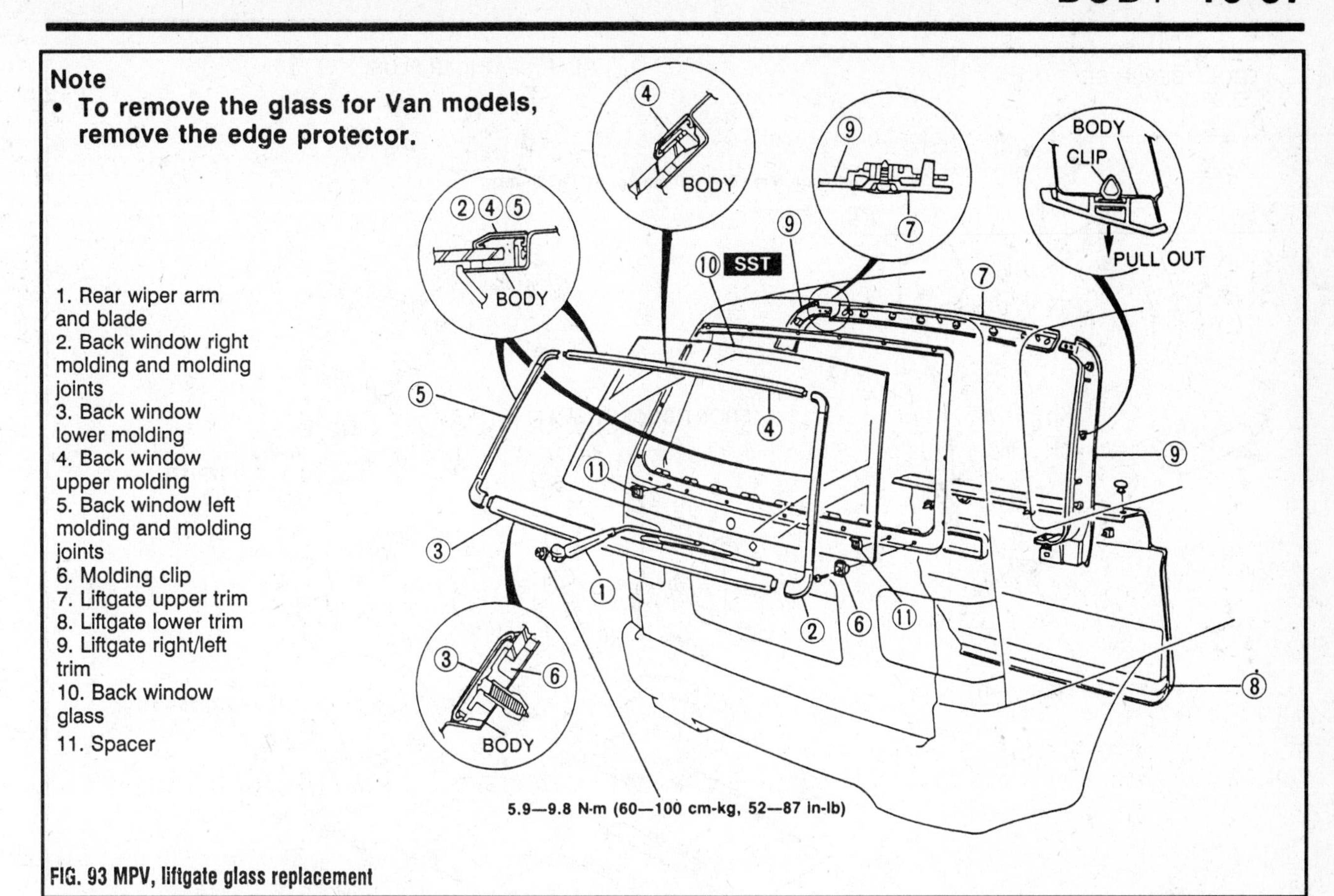

FIG. 93 MPV, liftgate glass replacement

Seats

➧ SEE FIGS. 94-105

REMOVAL & INSTALLATION

Pickups

1. Remove the seat anchor bolts.
2. Lift out the seat.
3. Installation is the reverse of removal.

MPV Driver's Seat

1. Remove the fuel filler lid opener.
2. Remove the parking brake lever.
3. Remove the seat bracket covers.
4. Remove the seat leg covers.
5. Remove the seat bracket-to-floor bolts and lift out the seat.
6. Installation is the reverse of removal. Torque the bracket-to-floor bolts to 38 ft. lbs.

MPV Front Right Seat

1. Remove the jack cover.
2. Remove the jack and jack handle.
3. Remove the seat bracket covers.
4. Remove the seat leg covers.
5. Remove the seat bracket-to-floor bolts and lift out the seat.
6. Installation is the reverse of removal. Torque the bracket-to-floor bolts to 38 ft. lbs.

MPV No.1 Rear Seat

The seat is removed by simply unlatching the release levers on the seat legs.

MPV No.2 Rear Seat

1. Remove the seat bracket cover.
2. Remove the folding link bolts.
3. Remove the rear hinge bolts.
4. Remove the front hinge bolts.
5. Lift out the seat.
6. Installation is the reverse of removal. Torque all bolts to 22 ft. lbs.

Navajo Bucket or 60/40 Seats

1. Remove the 4 seat track-to-floorpan screws (2 each side) and lift the seat and track assembly from the vehicle.
2. To remove the seat tracks from the seat cushion, position the seat upside down on a clean bench.
3. Disconnect the latch tie rod assembly and assist spring from the tracks.
4. Remove 4 track-to-seat cushion screws (2 each side) from the track assemblies. Remove the tracks from seat cushion.

To install:

5. Position the tracks to the seat cushion. Install the 4 track-to-seat cushion screws (2 each side) and tighten.
6. Connect the latch tie rod assembly and assist spring to the tracks.
7. Position the seat and track assembly in the vehicle.
8. Install 4 track-to-floorpan screws and tighten to specification.

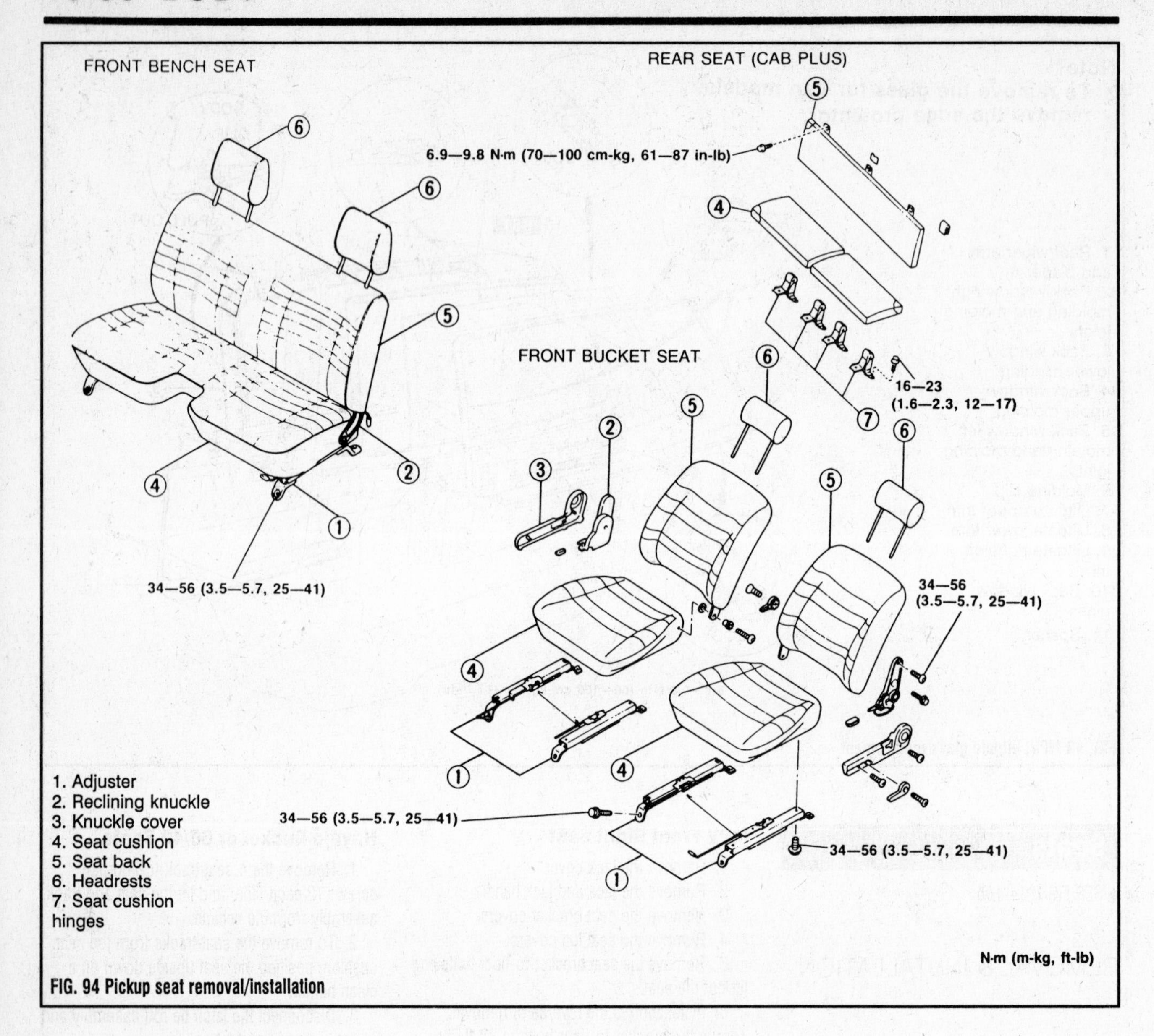

FIG. 94 Pickup seat removal/installation

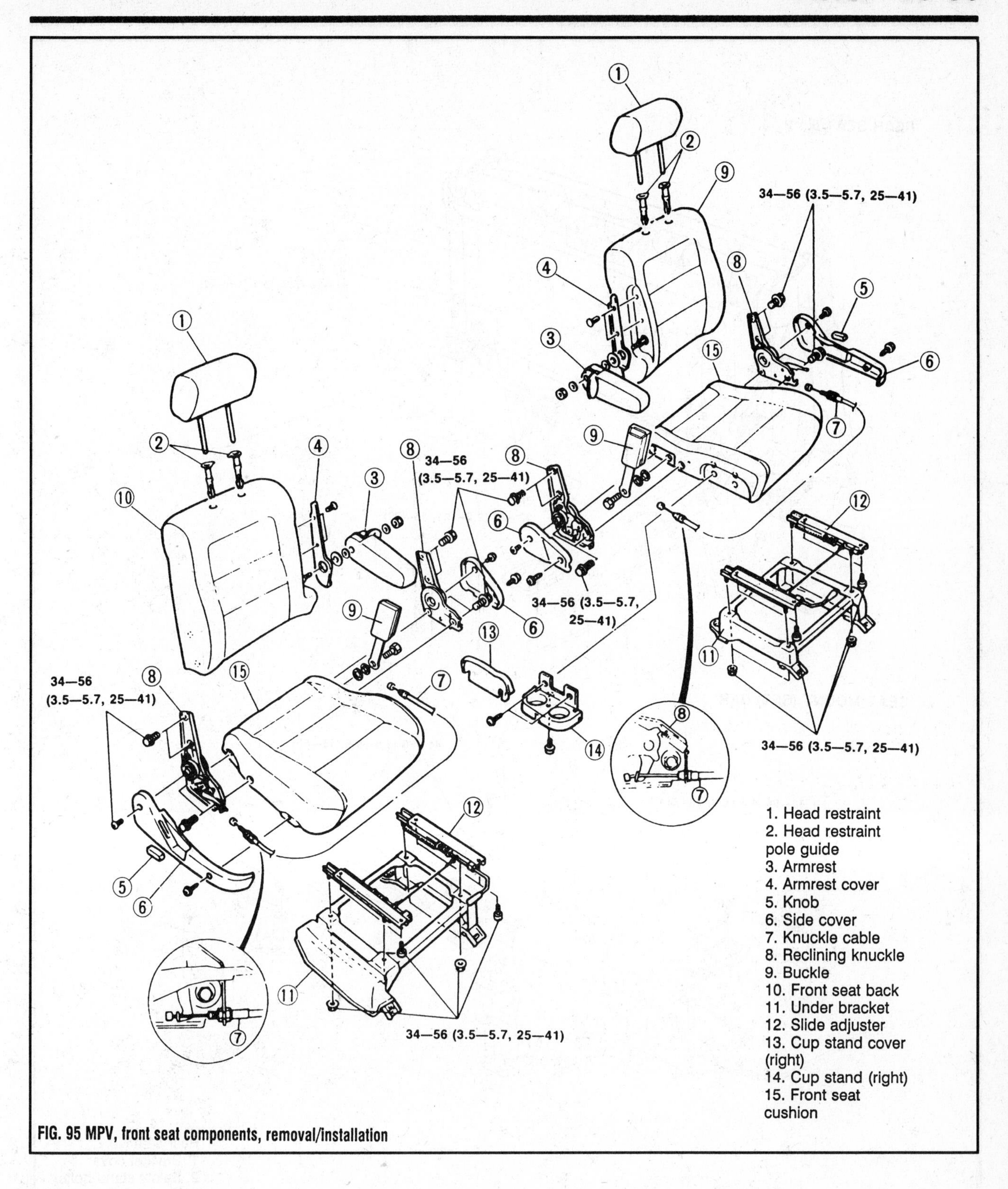

FIG. 95 MPV, front seat components, removal/installation

REAR SEAT No.2

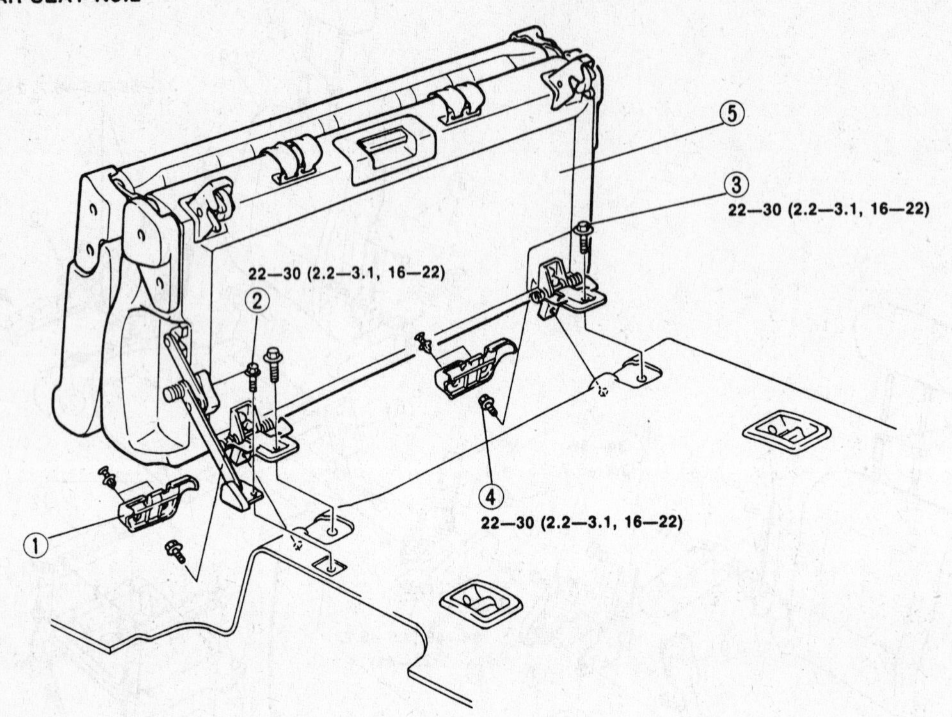

SEAT MOUNT (SET) BAR

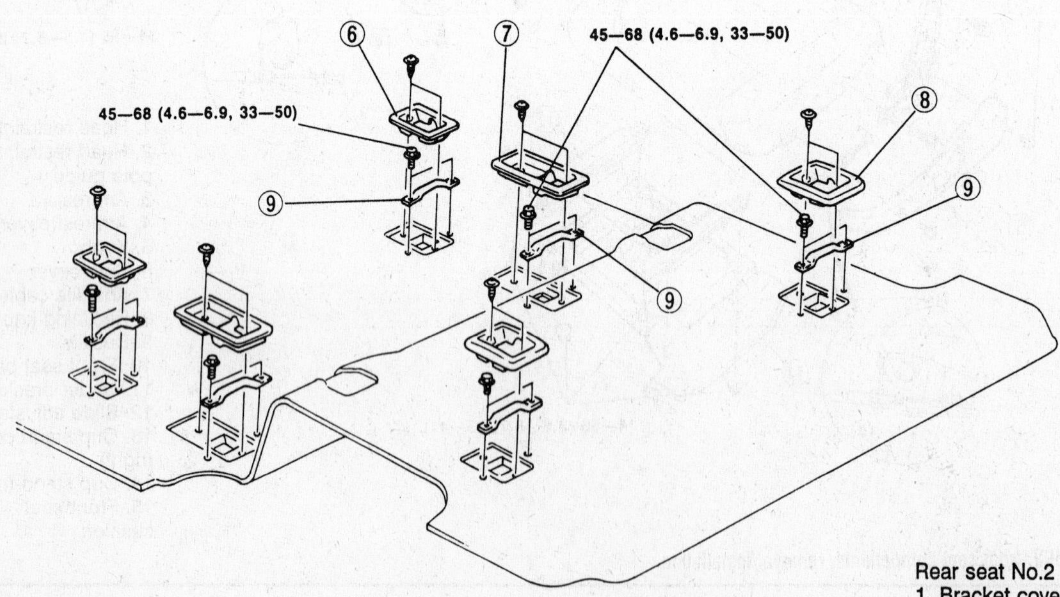

Rear seat No.2
1. Bracket cover
2. Safety stand bolts
3. Rear hinge bolts
4. Front hinge bolts
5. Rear seat No.2

Seat mount
6. Mat cover No.1
7. Mat cover No.2
8. Mat cover No.4
9. Seat mount bar

FIG. 96 MPV, rear seat No.2 and seat mount, removal/installation

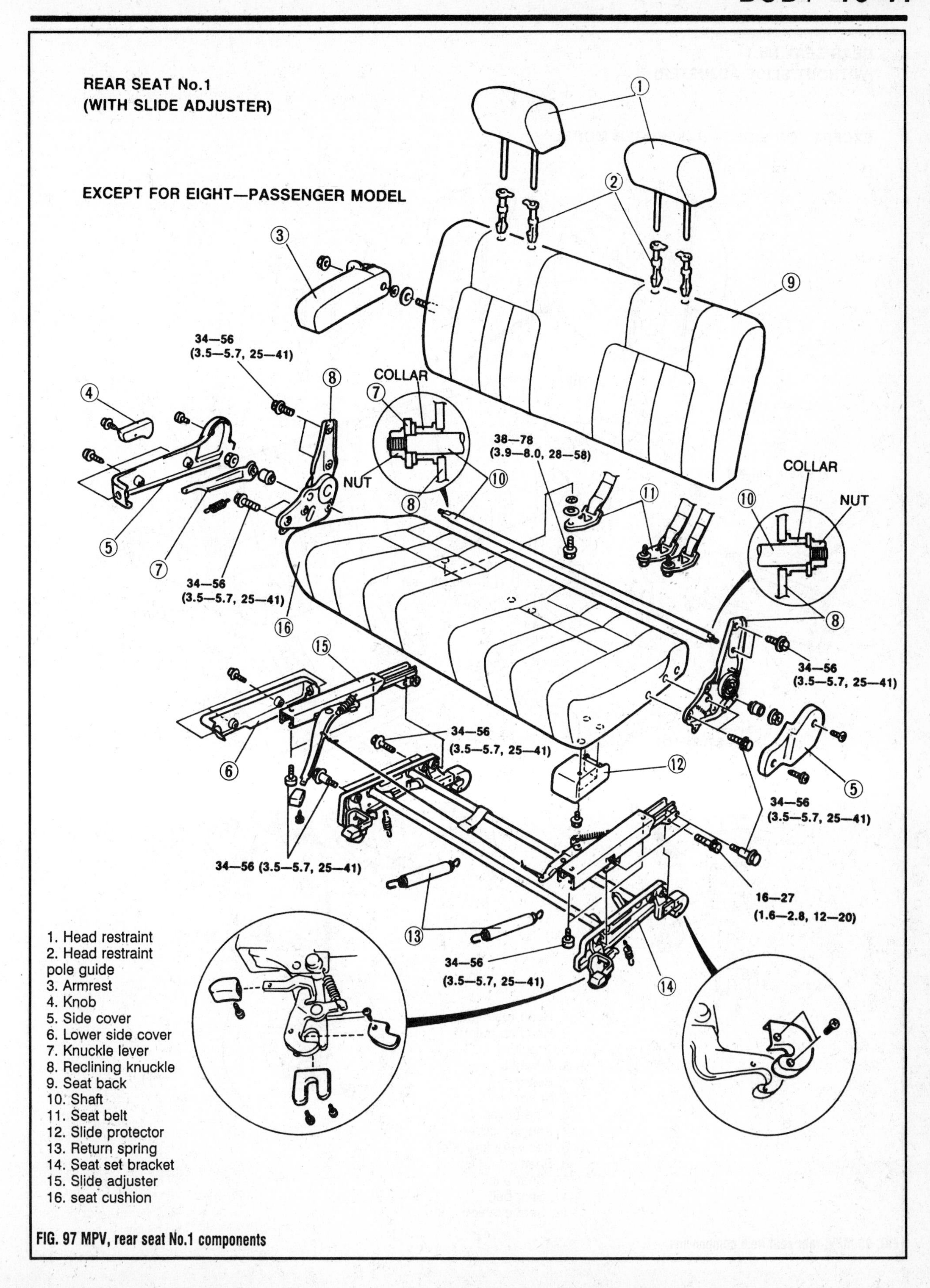
REAR SEAT No.1
(WITH SLIDE ADJUSTER)
EXCEPT FOR EIGHT—PASSENGER MODEL
34—56
(3.5—5.7, 25—41)
COLLAR
NUT
38—78
(3.9—8.0, 28—58)
COLLAR
NUT
34—56
(3.5—5.7, 25—41)
34—56
(3.5—5.7, 25—41)
34—56
(3.5—5.7, 25—41)
34—56
(3.5—5.7, 25—41)
34—56 (3.5—5.7, 25—41)
16—27
(1.6—2.8, 12—20)
34—56
(3.5—5.7, 25—41)
1. Head restraint
2. Head restraint pole guide
3. Armrest
4. Knob
5. Side cover
6. Lower side cover
7. Knuckle lever
8. Reclining knuckle
9. Seat back
10. Shaft
11. Seat belt
12. Slide protector
13. Return spring
14. Seat set bracket
15. Slide adjuster
16. seat cushion

FIG. 97 MPV, rear seat No.1 components

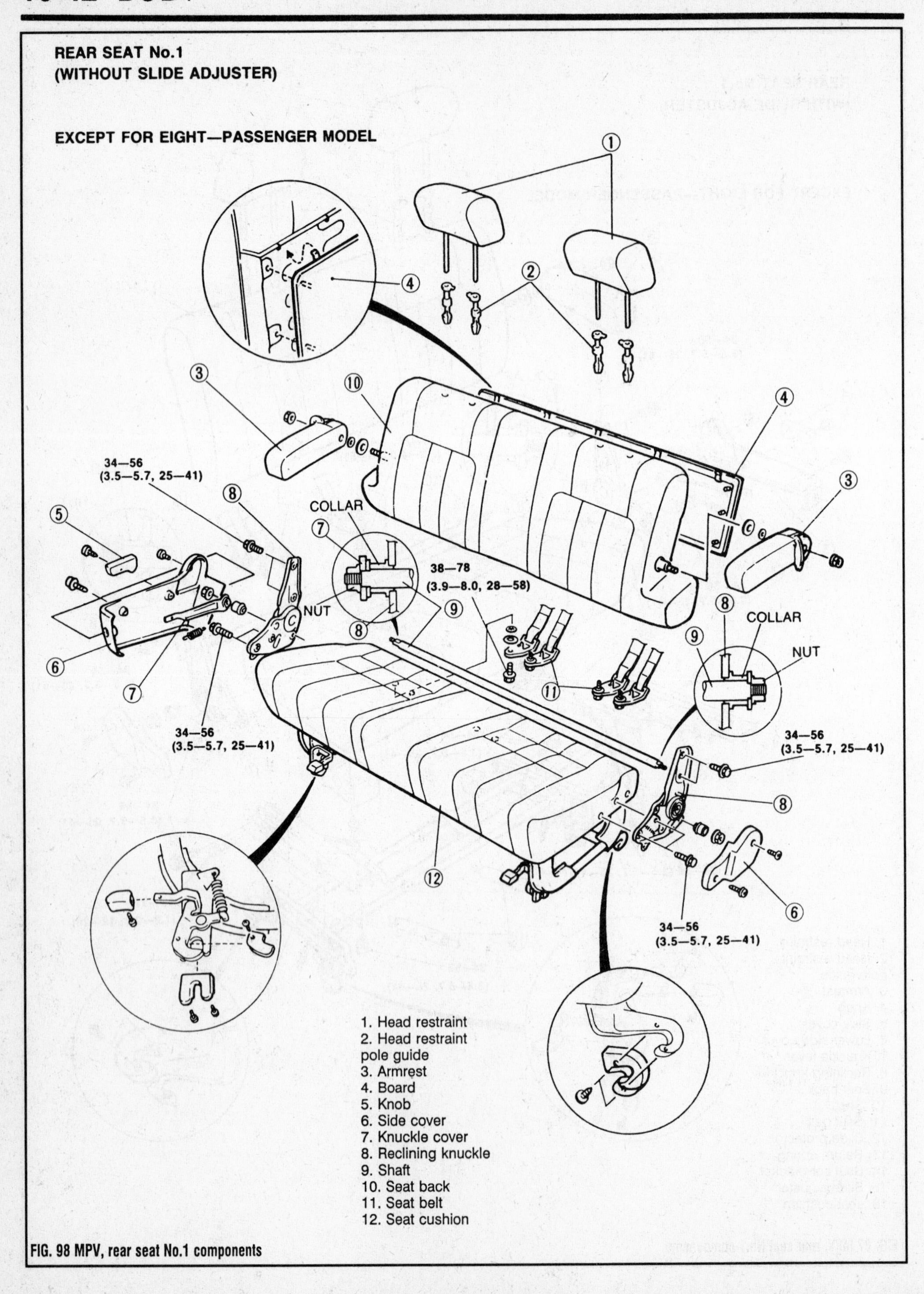
REAR SEAT No.1
(WITHOUT SLIDE ADJUSTER)
EXCEPT FOR EIGHT—PASSENGER MODEL
34—56
(3.5—5.7, 25—41)
COLLAR
38—78
(3.9—8.0, 28—58)
NUT
34—56
(3.5—5.7, 25—41)
COLLAR
NUT
34—56
(3.5—5.7, 25—41)
34—56
(3.5—5.7, 25—41)
1. Head restraint
2. Head restraint
pole guide
3. Armrest
4. Board
5. Knob
6. Side cover
7. Knuckle cover
8. Reclining knuckle
9. Shaft
10. Seat back
11. Seat belt
12. Seat cushion

FIG. 98 MPV, rear seat No.1 components

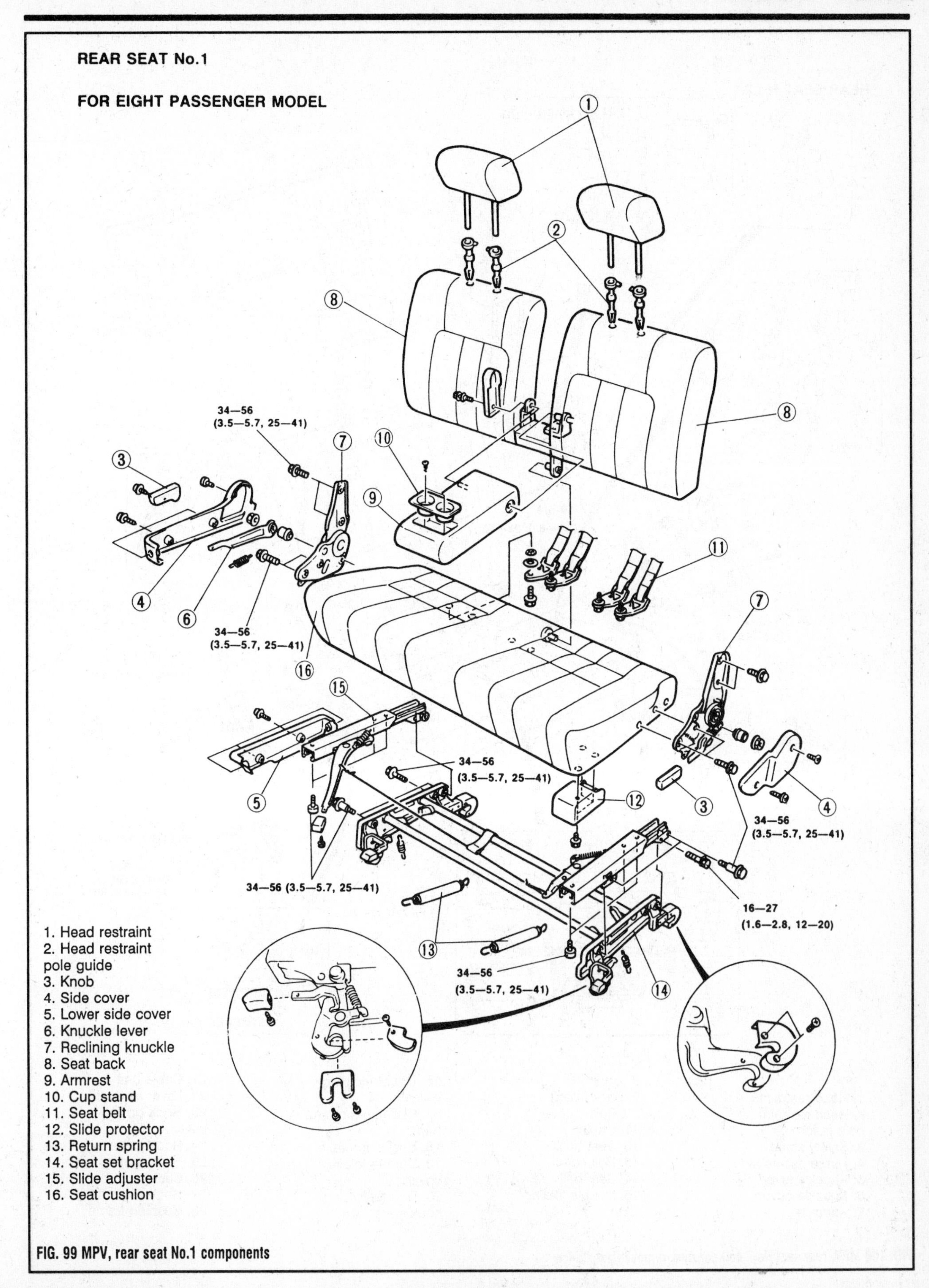
REAR SEAT No.1
FOR EIGHT PASSENGER MODEL
34—56
(3.5—5.7, 25—41)
34—56
(3.5—5.7, 25—41)
34—56
(3.5—5.7, 25—41)
34—56
(3.5—5.7, 25—41)
34—56 (3.5—5.7, 25—41)
16—27
(1.6—2.8, 12—20)
34—56
(3.5—5.7, 25—41)
1. Head restraint
2. Head restraint pole guide
3. Knob
4. Side cover
5. Lower side cover
6. Knuckle lever
7. Reclining knuckle
8. Seat back
9. Armrest
10. Cup stand
11. Seat belt
12. Slide protector
13. Return spring
14. Seat set bracket
15. Slide adjuster
16. Seat cushion

FIG. 99 MPV, rear seat No.1 components

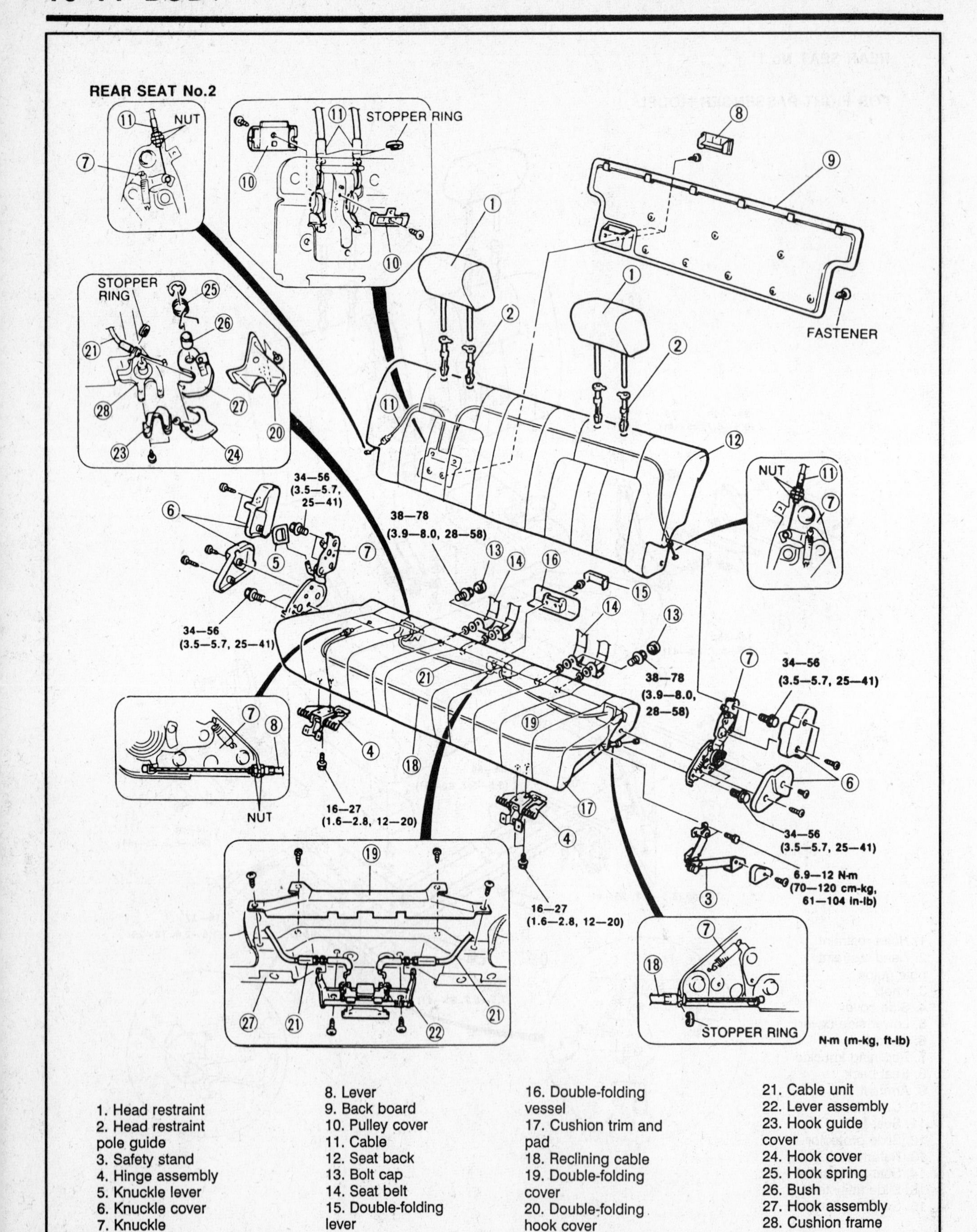
REAR SEAT No.2
NUT
STOPPER RING
FASTENER
STOPPER RING
34—56 (3.5—5.7, 25—41)
38—78 (3.9—8.0, 28—58)
34—56 (3.5—5.7, 25—41)
38—78 (3.9—8.0, 28—58)
34—56 (3.5—5.7, 25—41)
NUT
16—27 (1.6—2.8, 12—20)
NUT
34—56 (3.5—5.7, 25—41)
6.9—12 N·m (70—120 cm-kg, 61—104 in-lb)
16—27 (1.6—2.8, 12—20)
STOPPER RING
N·m (m-kg, ft-lb)
1. Head restraint
2. Head restraint pole guide
3. Safety stand
4. Hinge assembly
5. Knuckle lever
6. Knuckle cover
7. Knuckle
8. Lever
9. Back board
10. Pulley cover
11. Cable
12. Seat back
13. Bolt cap
14. Seat belt
15. Double-folding lever
16. Double-folding vessel
17. Cushion trim and pad
18. Reclining cable
19. Double-folding cover
20. Double-folding hook cover
21. Cable unit
22. Lever assembly
23. Hook guide cover
24. Hook cover
25. Hook spring
26. Bush
27. Hook assembly
28. Cushion frame

FIG. 100 MPV, rear seat No.2 components, removal/installation

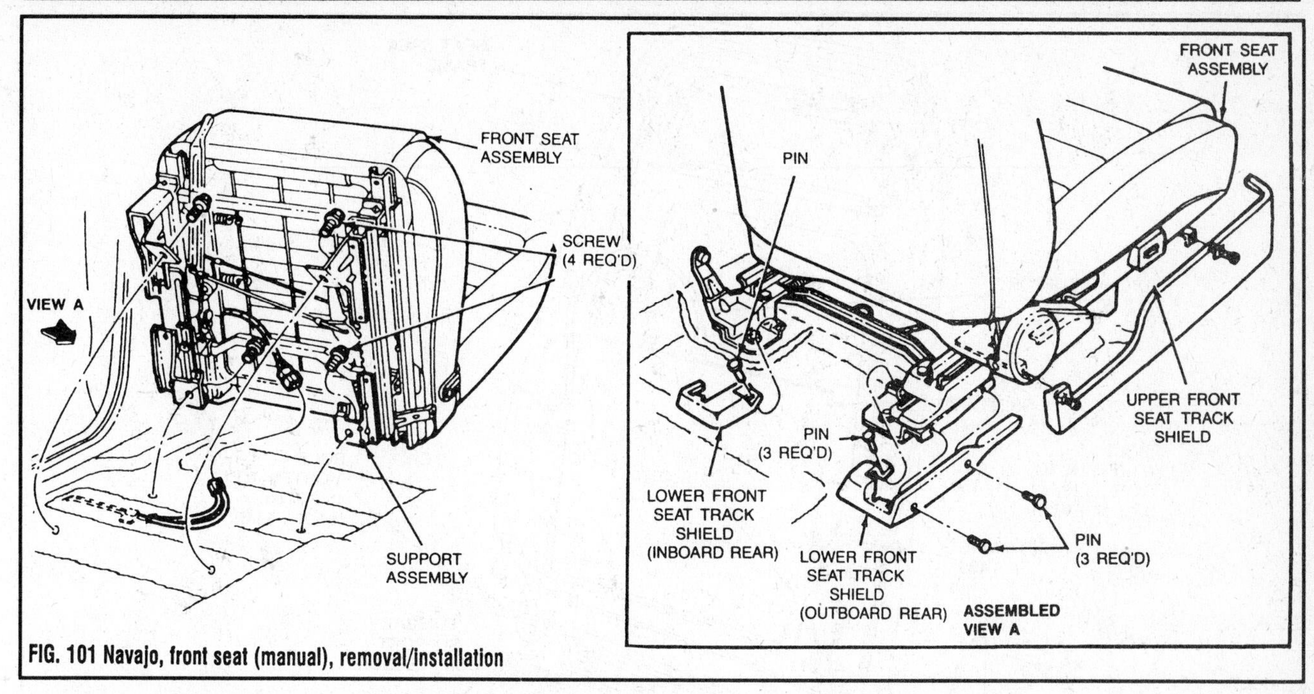

FIG. 101 Navajo, front seat (manual), removal/installation

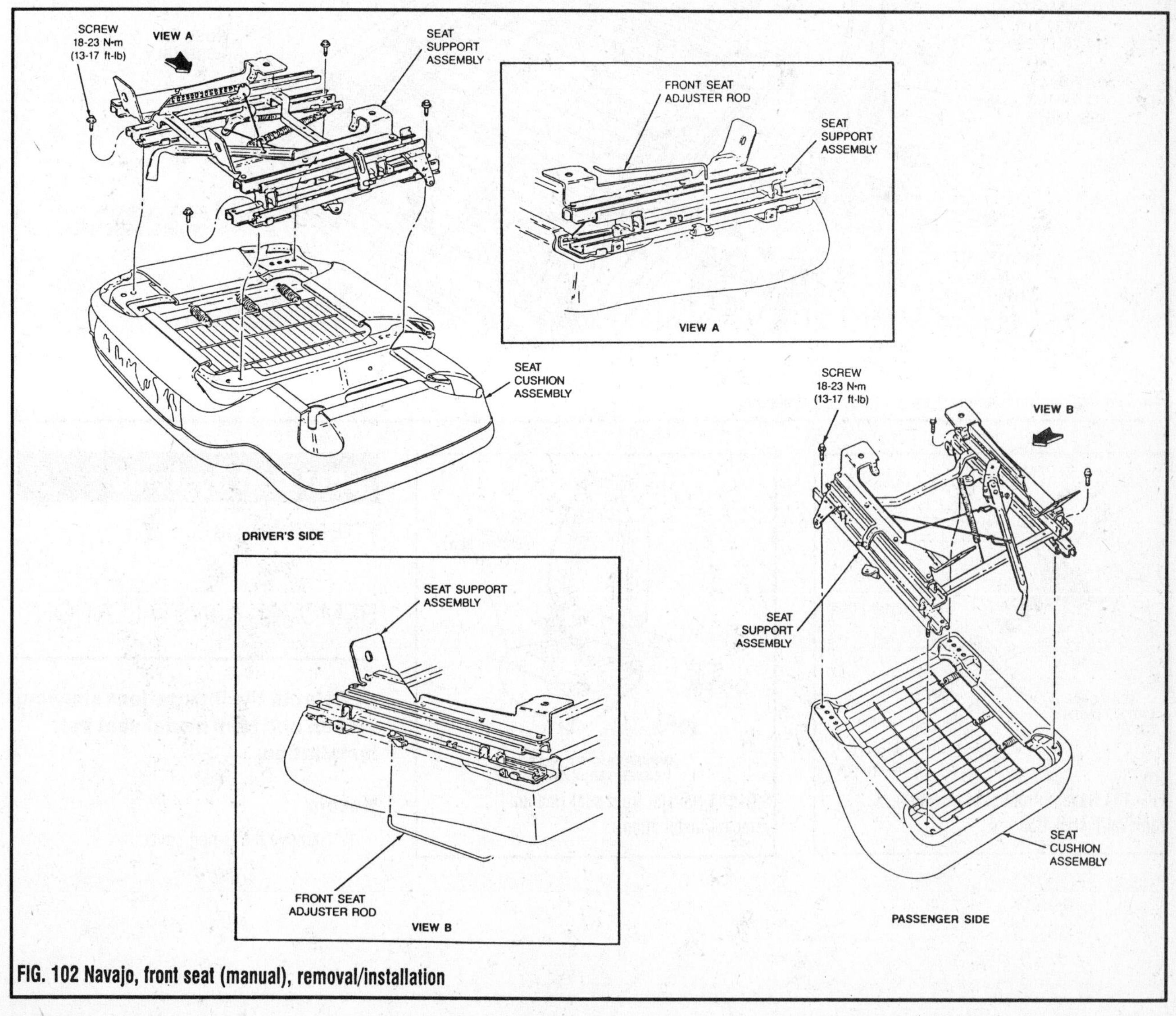

FIG. 102 Navajo, front seat (manual), removal/installation

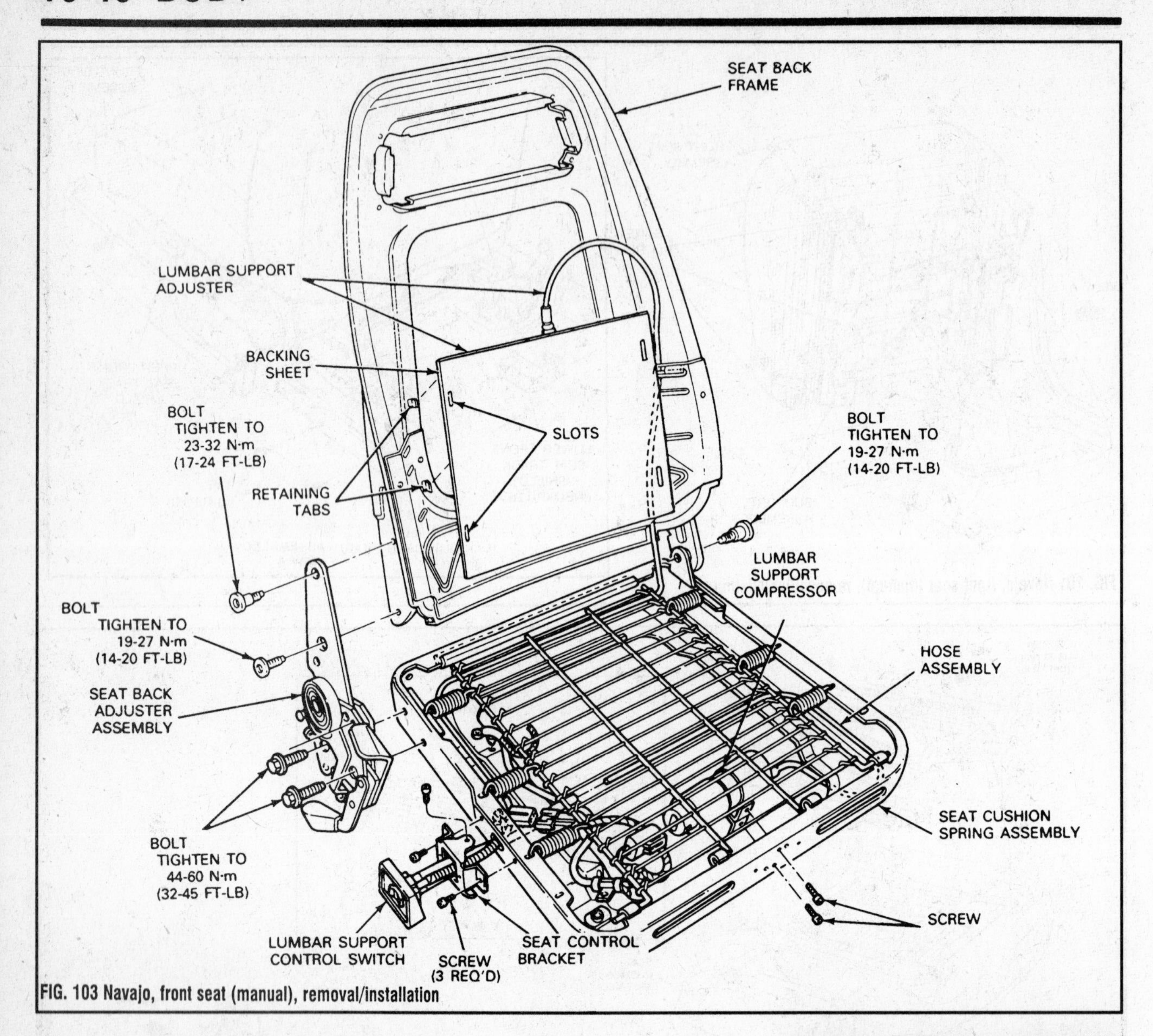

FIG. 103 Navajo, front seat (manual), removal/installation

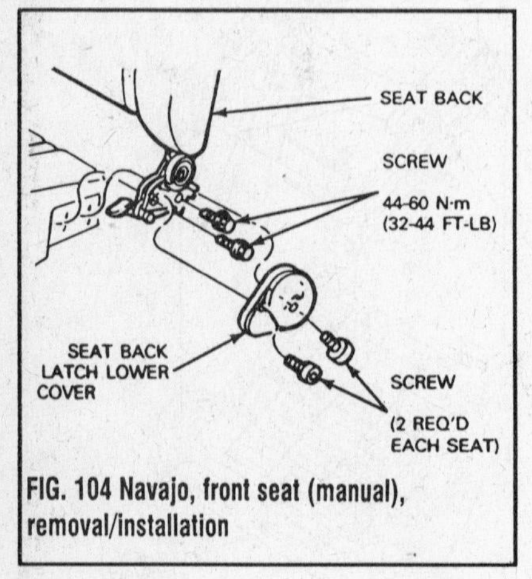

FIG. 104 Navajo, front seat (manual), removal/installation

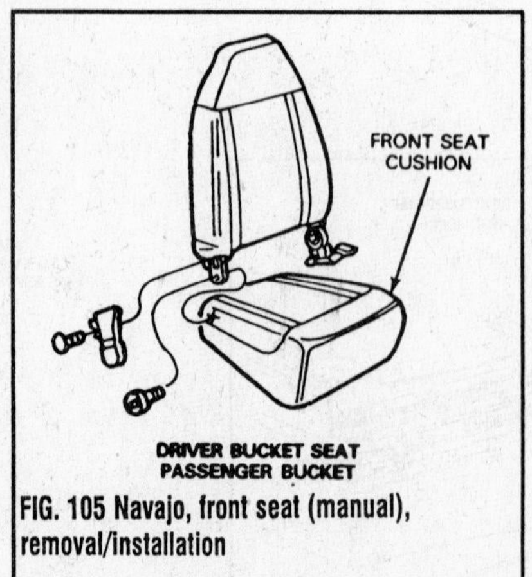

FIG. 105 Navajo, front seat (manual), removal/installation

Seat Belt Systems

SEE FIGS. 106-110

REMOVAL & INSTALLATION

Refer to the illustrations showing Pickup and MPV model seat belt installation.

Navajo

1. Remove the D-ring cover.

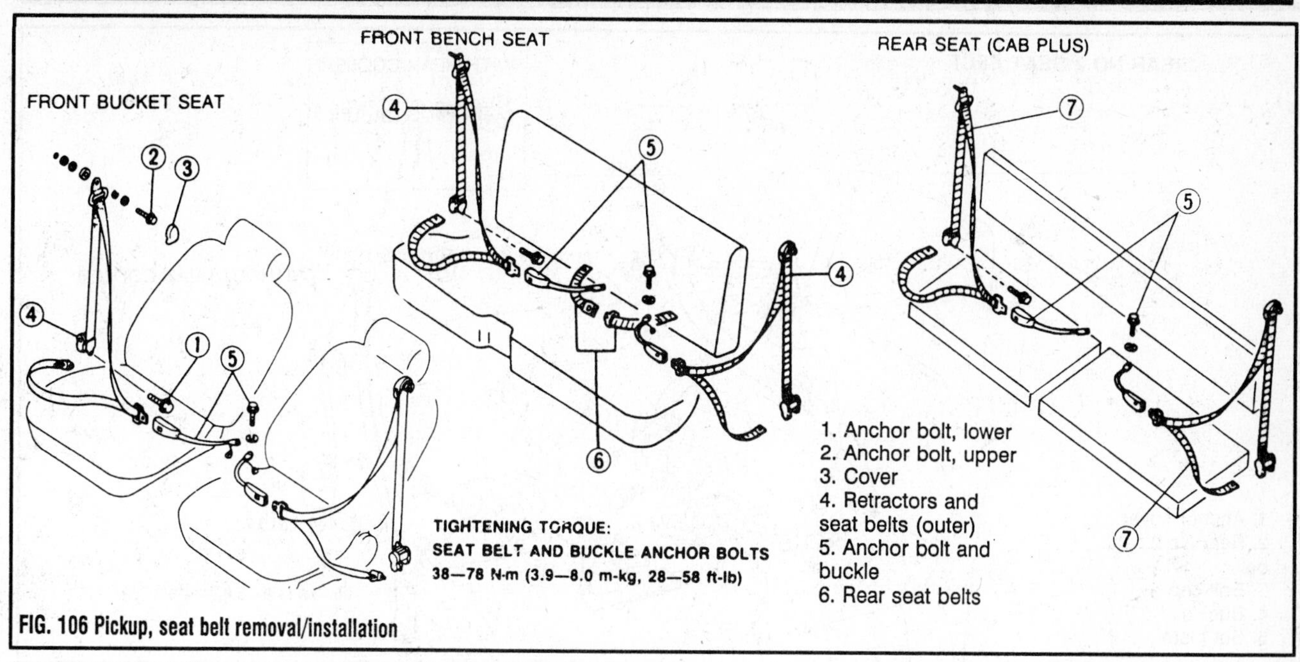

FIG. 106 Pickup, seat belt removal/installation

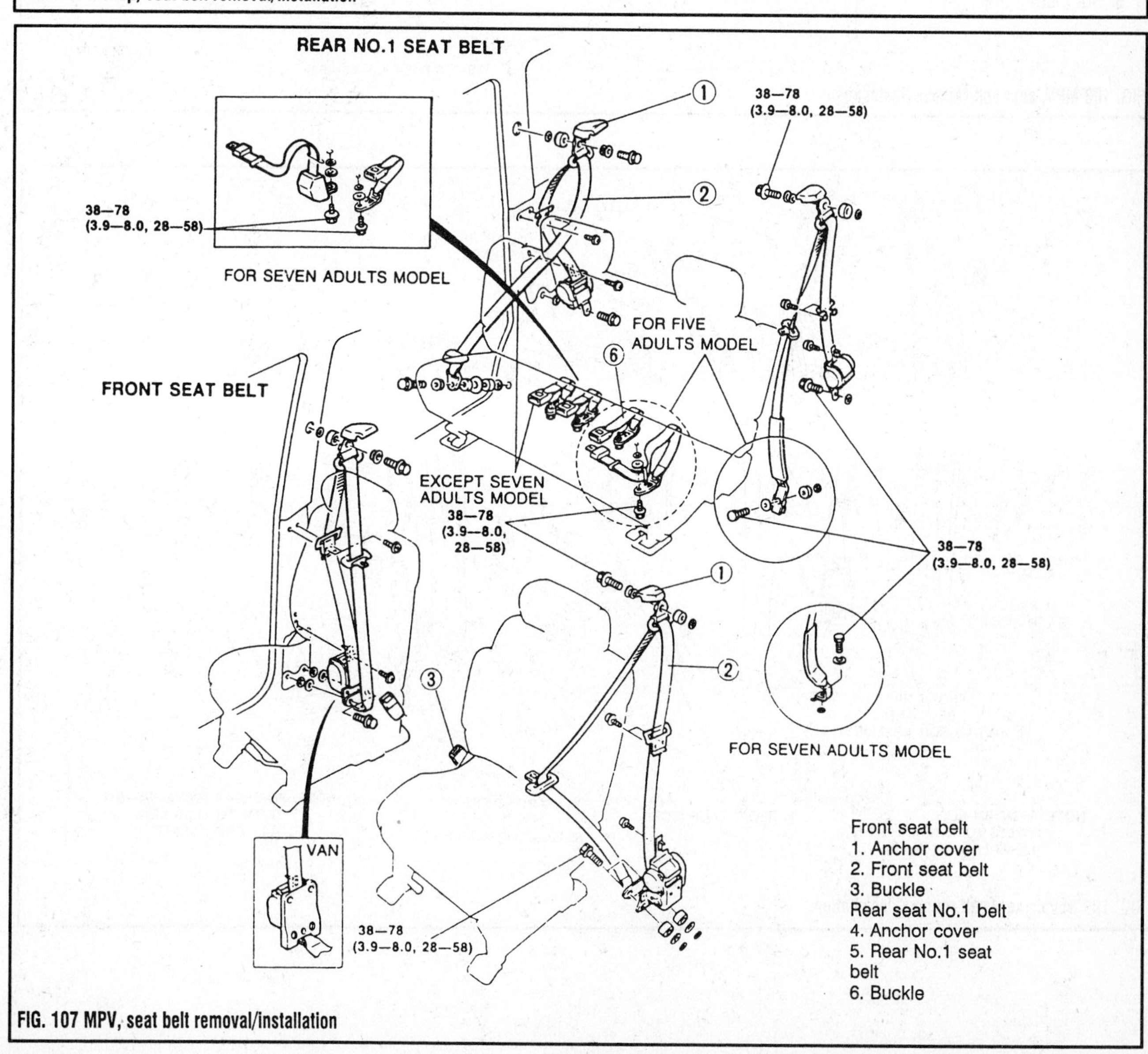

FIG. 107 MPV, seat belt removal/installation

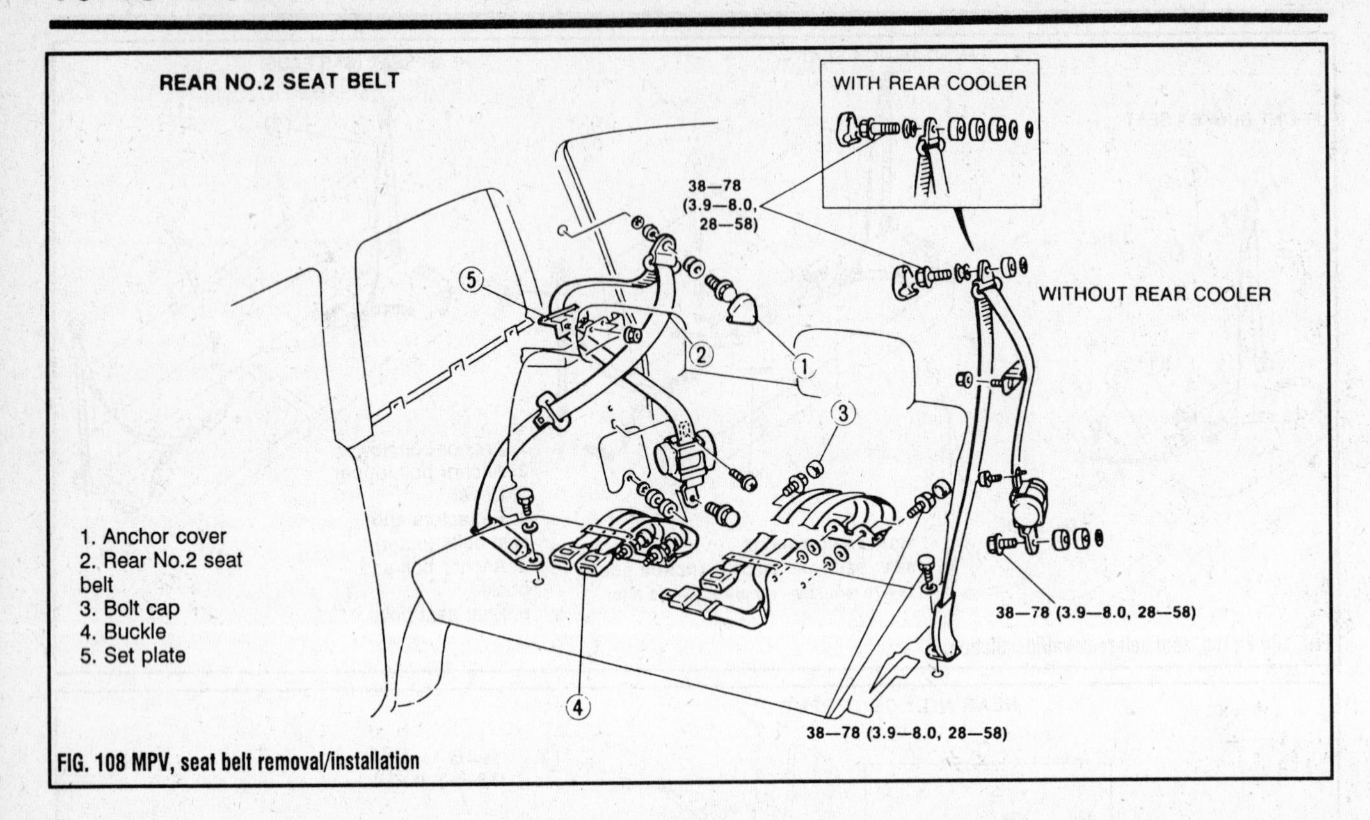

FIG. 108 MPV, seat belt removal/installation

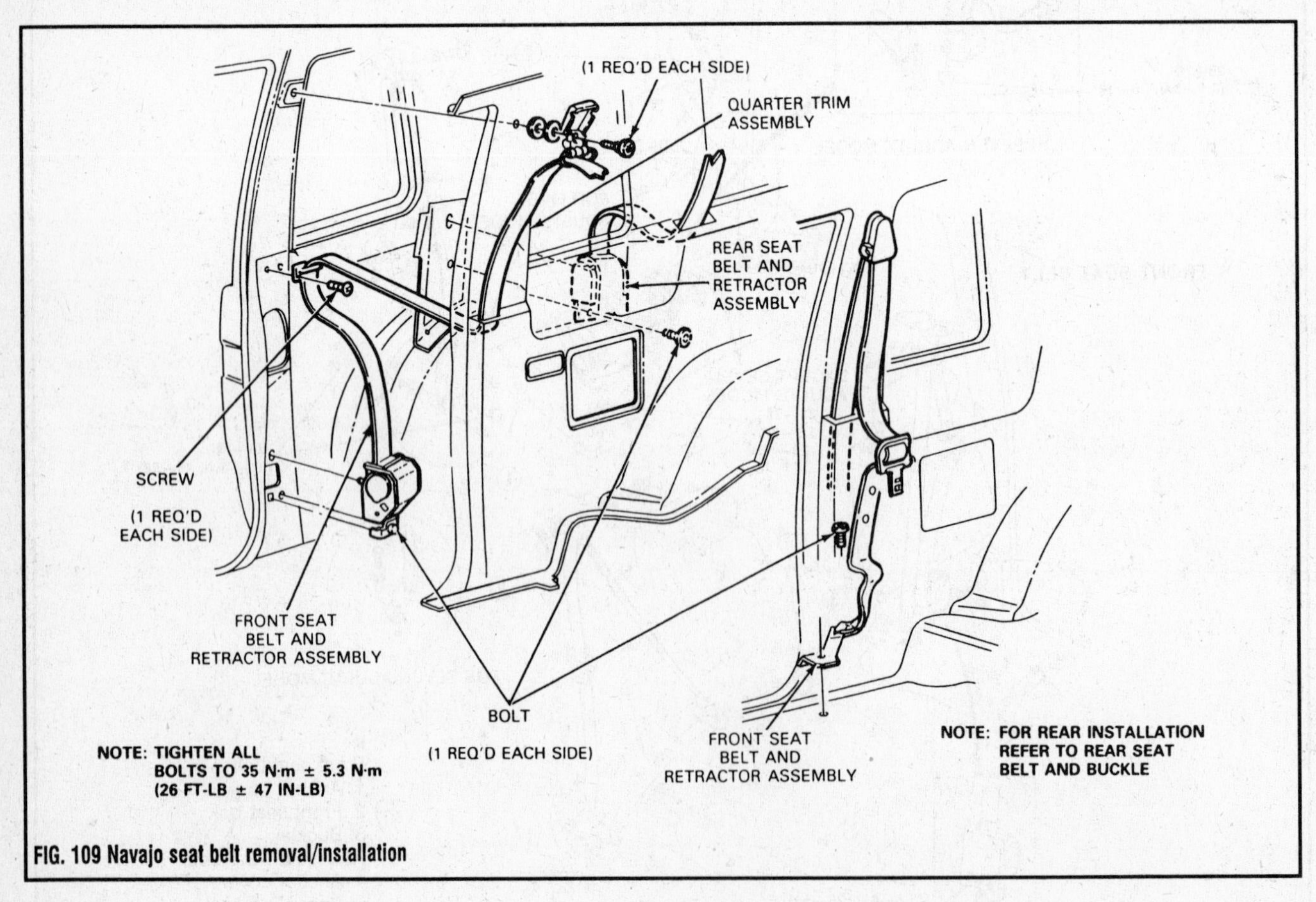

FIG. 109 Navajo seat belt removal/installation

2. Gain access to the bolt retaining the floor anchor end of the belt assembly to the floor pan by lifting up the carpet or mat. Remove the bolt.

3. Remove the quarter trim panel. Remove the screw retaining the belt loop to the sheet metal. Remove the bolt retaining the retractor assembly. Remove the belt assembly.

4. Install the seat belt in the reverse order of removal.

5. To remove the rear seat belt and buckle, remove the bolts that secure the belt and buckle assemblies to the floorpan. Remove the assembly. Install in the reverse order.

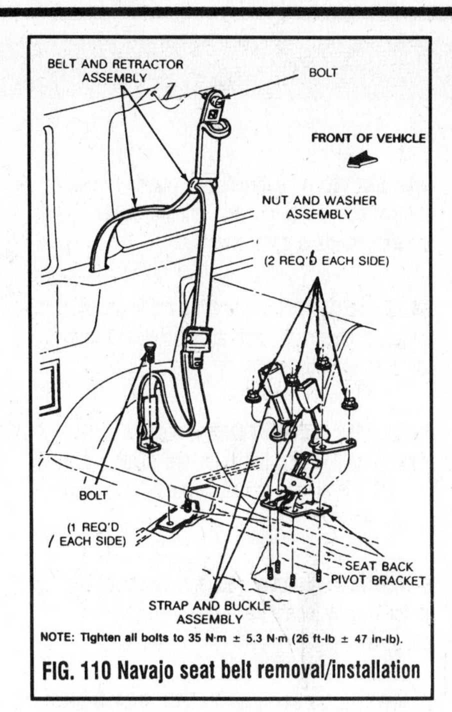

FIG. 110 Navajo seat belt removal/installation

Power Seat Motor

REMOVAL & INSTALLATION

The optional six-way power seat system on the Navajo uses a screw-type drive for seat adjustment.

The six-way power seat provides horizontal, vertical, and tilt adjustments. It consists of a reversible armature motor, switch and housing assembly, vertical screw, and horizontal screw drives.

The motor assembly, which contains three armatures, the flexible shafts, the screw drive and gear mechanism are not serviced individually and can be serviced only by replacing the complete track assembly.

TORQUE SPECIFICATIONS

Component	U.S.	Metric
Door hinge bolts		
MPV	10 ft. lbs.	13.6 Nm
Door striker bolts		
MPV	20 ft. lbs.	27.2 Nm
Seat bracket-to-floor bolts		
MPV front seats	38 ft. lbs.	51.68 Nm
MPV no.2 rear seat bolts	22 ft. lbs.	29.92 Nm
Strut-to-tailgate bolts		
MPV	104 inch lbs.	11.648 Nm
Tailgate hinge-to-tailgate bolts		
MPV	10 ft. lbs.	13.6 Nm

GLOSSARY

AIR/FUEL RATIO: The ratio of air to gasoline by weight in the fuel mixture drawn into the engine.

AIR INJECTION: One method of reducing harmful exhaust emissions by injecting air into each of the exhaust ports of an engine. The fresh air entering the hot exhaust manifold causes any remaining fuel to be burned before it can exit the tailpipe.

ALTERNATOR: A device used for converting mechanical energy into electrical energy.

AMMETER: An instrument, calibrated in amperes, used to measure the flow of an electrical current in a circuit. Ammeters are always connected in series with the circuit being tested.

AMPERE: The rate of flow of electrical current present when one volt of electrical pressure is applied against one ohm of electrical resistance.

ANALOG COMPUTER: Any microprocessor that uses similar (analogous) electrical signals to make its calculations.

ARMATURE: A laminated, soft iron core wrapped by a wire that converts electrical energy to mechanical energy as in a motor or relay. When rotated in a magnetic field, it changes mechanical energy into electrical energy as in a generator.

ATMOSPHERIC PRESSURE: The pressure on the Earth's surface caused by the weight of the air in the atmosphere. At sea level, this pressure is 14.7 psi at 32°F (101 kPa at 0°C).

ATOMIZATION: The breaking down of a liquid into a fine mist that can be suspended in air.

AXIAL PLAY: Movement parallel to a shaft or bearing bore.

BACKFIRE: The sudden combustion of gases in the intake or exhaust system that results in a loud explosion.

BACKLASH: The clearance or play between two parts, such as meshed gears.

BACKPRESSURE: Restrictions in the exhaust system that slow the exit of exhaust gases from the combustion chamber.

BAKELITE: A heat resistant, plastic insulator material commonly used in printed circuit boards and transistorized components.

BALL BEARING: A bearing made up of hardened inner and outer races between which hardened steel balls roll.

BALLAST RESISTOR: A resistor in the primary ignition circuit that lowers voltage after the engine is started to reduce wear on ignition components.

BEARING: A friction reducing, supportive device usually located between a stationary part and a moving part.

BIMETAL TEMPERATURE SENSOR: Any sensor or switch made of two dissimilar types of metal that bend when heated or cooled due to the different expansion rates of the alloys. These types of sensors usually function as an on/off switch.

BLOWBY: Combustion gases, composed of water vapor and unburned fuel, that leak past the piston rings into the crankcase during normal engine operation. These gases are removed by the PCV system to prevent the buildup of harmful acids in the crankcase.

BRAKE PAD: A brake shoe and lining assembly used with disc brakes.

BRAKE SHOE: The backing for the brake lining. The term is, however, usually applied to the assembly of the brake backing and lining.

BUSHING: A liner, usually removable, for a bearing; an anti-friction liner used in place of a bearing.

BYPASS: System used to bypass ballast resistor during engine cranking to increase voltage supplied to the coil.

CALIPER: A hydraulically activated device in a disc brake system, which is mounted straddling the brake rotor (disc). The caliper contains at least one piston and two brake pads. Hydraulic pressure on the piston(s) forces the pads against the rotor.

CAMSHAFT: A shaft in the engine on which are the lobes (cams) which operate the valves. The camshaft is driven by the crankshaft, via a belt, chain or gears, at one half the crankshaft speed.

CAPACITOR: A device which stores an electrical charge.

CARBON MONOXIDE (CO): A colorless, odorless gas given off as a normal byproduct of combustion. It is poisonous and extremely dangerous in confined areas, building up slowly to toxic levels without warning if adequate ventilation is not available.

CARBURETOR: A device, usually mounted on the intake manifold of an engine, which mixes the air and fuel in the proper proportion to allow even combustion.

CATALYTIC CONVERTER: A device installed in the exhaust system, like a muffler, that converts harmful byproducts of combustion into carbon dioxide and water vapor by means of a heat-producing chemical reaction.

CENTRIFUGAL ADVANCE: A mechanical method of advancing the spark timing by using fly weights in the distributor that react to centrifugal force generated by the distributor shaft rotation.

CHECK VALVE: Any one-way valve installed to permit the flow of air, fuel or vacuum in one direction only.

CHOKE: A device, usually a movable valve, placed in the intake path of a carburetor to restrict the flow of air.

CIRCUIT: Any unbroken path through which an electrical current can flow. Also used to describe fuel flow in some instances.

CIRCUIT BREAKER: A switch which protects an electrical circuit from overload by opening the circuit when the current flow exceeds a predetermined level. Some circuit breakers must be reset manually, while most reset automatically

COIL (IGNITION): A transformer in the ignition circuit which steps up the voltage provided to the spark plugs.

COMBINATION MANIFOLD: An assembly which includes both the intake and exhaust manifolds in one casting.

COMBINATION VALVE: A device used in some fuel systems that routes fuel vapors to a charcoal storage canister instead of venting them into the atmosphere. The valve relieves fuel tank pressure and allows fresh air into the tank as the fuel level drops to prevent a vapor lock situation.

COMPRESSION RATIO: The comparison of the total volume of the cylinder and combustion chamber with the piston at BDC and the piston at TDC.

CONDENSER: 1. An electrical device which acts to store an electrical charge, preventing voltage surges.
2. A radiator-like device in the air conditioning system in which refrigerant gas condenses into a liquid, giving off heat.

CONDUCTOR: Any material through which an electrical current can be transmitted easily.

CONTINUITY: Continuous or complete circuit. Can be checked with an ohmmeter.

COUNTERSHAFT: An intermediate shaft which is rotated by a mainshaft and transmits, in turn, that rotation to a working part.

CRANKCASE: The lower part of an engine in which the crankshaft and related parts operate.

CRANKSHAFT: The main driving shaft of an engine which receives reciprocating motion from the pistons and converts it to rotary motion.

CYLINDER: In an engine, the round hole in the engine block in which the piston(s) ride.

CYLINDER BLOCK: The main structural member of an engine in which is found the cylinders, crankshaft and other principal parts.

CYLINDER HEAD: The detachable portion of the engine, fastened, usually, to the top of the cylinder block, containing all or most of the combustion chambers. On overhead valve engines, it contains the valves and their operating parts. On overhead cam engines, it contains the camshaft as well.

DEAD CENTER: The extreme top or bottom of the piston stroke.

DETONATION: An unwanted explosion of the air/fuel mixture in the combustion chamber caused by excess heat and compression, advanced timing, or an overly lean mixture. Also referred to as "ping".

DIAPHRAGM: A thin, flexible wall separating two cavities, such as in a vacuum advance unit.

DIESELING: A condition in which hot spots in the combustion chamber cause the engine to run on after the key is turned off.

DIFFERENTIAL: A geared assembly which allows the transmission of motion between drive axles, giving one axle the ability to turn faster than the other.

DIODE: An electrical device that will allow current to flow in one direction only.

DISC BRAKE: A hydraulic braking assembly consisting of a brake disc, or rotor, mounted on an axle, and a caliper assembly containing, usually two brake pads which are activated by hydraulic pressure. The pads are forced against the sides of the disc, creating friction which slows the vehicle.

DISTRIBUTOR: A mechanically driven device on an engine which is responsible for electrically firing the spark plug at a predetermined point of the piston stroke.

DOWEL PIN: A pin, inserted in mating holes in two different parts allowing those parts to maintain a fixed relationship.

DRUM BRAKE: A braking system which consists of two brake shoes and one or two wheel cylinders, mounted on a fixed backing plate, and a brake drum, mounted on an axle, which revolves around the assembly. Hydraulic action applied to the wheel cylinders forces the shoes outward against the drum, creating friction, slowing the vehicle.

DWELL: The rate, measured in degrees of shaft rotation, at which an electrical circuit cycles on and off.

ELECTRONIC CONTROL UNIT (ECU): Ignition module, amplifier or igniter. See Module for definition.

ELECTRONIC IGNITION: A system in which the timing and firing of the spark plugs is controlled by an electronic control unit, usually called a module. These systems have no points or condenser.

ENDPLAY: The measured amount of axial movement in a shaft.

ENGINE: A device that converts heat into mechanical energy.

EXHAUST MANIFOLD: A set of cast passages or pipes which conduct exhaust gases from the engine.

FEELER GAUGE: A blade, usually metal, of precisely predetermined thickness, used to measure the clearance between two parts. These blades usually are available in sets of assorted thicknesses.

F-HEAD: An engine configuration in which the intake valves are in the cylinder head, while the camshaft and exhaust valves are located in the cylinder block. The camshaft operates the intake valves via lifters and pushrods, while it operates the exhaust valves directly.

FIRING ORDER: The order in which combustion occurs in the cylinders of an engine. Also the order in which spark is distributed to the plugs by the distributor.

FLATHEAD: An engine configuration in which the camshaft and all the valves are located in the cylinder block.

FLOODING: The presence of too much fuel in the intake manifold and combustion chamber which prevents the air/fuel mixture from firing, thereby causing a no-start situation.

FLYWHEEL: A disc shaped part bolted to the rear end of the crankshaft. Around the outer perimeter is affixed the ring gear. The starter drive engages the ring gear, turning the flywheel, which rotates the crankshaft, imparting the initial starting motion to the engine.

FOOT POUND (ft.lb. or sometimes, ft. lbs.): The amount of energy or work needed to raise an item weighing one pound, a distance of one foot.

FUSE: A protective device in a circuit which prevents circuit overload by breaking the circuit when a specific amperage is present. The device is constructed around a strip or wire of a lower amperage rating than the circuit it is designed to protect. When an amperage higher than that stamped on the fuse is present in the circuit, the strip or wire melts, opening the circuit.

GEAR RATIO: The ratio between the number of teeth on meshing gears.

GENERATOR: A device which converts mechanical energy into electrical energy.

HEAT RANGE: The measure of a spark plug's ability to dissipate heat from its firing end. The higher the heat range, the hotter the plug fires.

HUB: The center part of a wheel or gear.

HYDROCARBON (HC): Any chemical compound made up of hydrogen and carbon. A major pollutant formed by the engine as a byproduct of combustion.

HYDROMETER: An instrument used to measure the specific gravity of a solution.

INCH POUND (In.lb. or sometimes, In. lbs.): One twelfth of a foot pound.

INDUCTION: A means of transferring electrical energy in the form of a magnetic field. Principle used in the ignition coil to increase voltage.

INJECTION PUMP: A device, usually mechanically operated, which meters and delivers fuel under pressure to the fuel injector.

INJECTOR: A device which receives metered fuel under relatively low pressure and is activated to inject the fuel into the engine under relatively high pressure at a predetermined time.

INPUT SHAFT: The shaft to which torque is applied, usually carrying the driving gear or gears.

INTAKE MANIFOLD: A casting of passages or pipes used to conduct air or a fuel/air mixture to the cylinders.

JOURNAL: The bearing surface within which a shaft operates.

KEY: A small block usually fitted in a notch between a shaft and a hub to prevent slippage of the two parts.

MANIFOLD: A casting of passages or set of pipes which connect the cylinders to an inlet or outlet source.

MANIFOLD VACUUM: Low pressure in an engine intake manifold formed just below the throttle plates. Manifold vacuum is highest at idle and drops under acceleration.

MASTER CYLINDER: The primary fluid pressurizing device in a hydraulic system. In automotive use, it is found in brake and hydraulic clutch systems and is pedal activated, either directly or, in a power brake system, through the power booster.

MODULE: Electronic control unit, amplifier or igniter of solid state or integrated design which controls the current flow in the ignition primary circuit based on input from the pick- up coil. When the module opens the primary circuit, the high secondary voltage is induced in the coil.

NEEDLE BEARING: A bearing which consists of a number (usually a large number) of long, thin rollers.

OHM:(Ω) The unit used to measure the resistance of conductor to electrical flow. One ohm is the amount of resistance that limits current flow to one ampere in a circuit with one volt of pressure.

OHMMETER: An instrument used for measuring the resistance, in ohms, in an electrical circuit.

OUTPUT SHAFT: The shaft which transmits torque from a device, such as a transmission.

OVERDRIVE: A gear assembly which produces more shaft revolutions than that transmitted to it.

OVERHEAD CAMSHAFT (OHC): An engine configuration in which the camshaft is mounted on top of the cylinder head and operates the valves either directly or by means of rocker arms.

OVERHEAD VALVE (OHV): An engine configuration in which all of the valves are located in the cylinder head and the camshaft is located in the cylinder block. The camshaft operates the valves via lifters and pushrods.

OXIDES OF NITROGEN (NOx): Chemical compounds of nitrogen produced as a byproduct of combustion. They combine with hydrocarbons to produce smog.

OXYGEN SENSOR: Used with the feedback system to sense the presence of oxygen in the exhaust gas and signal the computer which can reference the voltage signal to an air/fuel ratio.

PINION: The smaller of two meshing gears.

PISTON RING: An open ended ring which fits into a groove on the outer diameter of the piston. Its chief function is to form a seal between the piston and cylinder wall. Most automotive pistons have three rings: two for compression sealing; one for oil sealing.

PRELOAD: A predetermined load placed on a bearing during assembly or by adjustment.

PRIMARY CIRCUIT: Is the low voltage side of the ignition system which consists of the ignition switch, ballast resistor or resistance wire, bypass, coil, electronic control unit and pick-up coil as well as the connecting wires and harnesses.

PRESS FIT: The mating of two parts under pressure, due to the inner diameter of one being smaller than the outer diameter of the other, or vice versa; an interference fit.

RACE: The surface on the inner or outer ring of a bearing on which the balls, needles or rollers move.

REGULATOR: A device which maintains the amperage and/or voltage levels of a circuit at predetermined values.

RELAY: A switch which automatically opens and/or closes a circuit.

RESISTANCE: The opposition to the flow of current through a circuit or electrical device, and is measured in ohms. Resistance is equal to the voltage divided by the amperage.

RESISTOR: A device, usually made of wire, which offers a preset amount of resistance in an electrical circuit.

RING GEAR: The name given to a ring-shaped gear attached to a differential case,or affixed to a flywheel or as part a planetary gear set.

ROLLER BEARING: A bearing made up of hardened inner and outer races between which hardened steel rollers move.

ROTOR: 1. The disc-shaped part of a disc brake assembly, upon which the brake pads bear; also called, brake disc.
2. The device mounted atop the distributor shaft, which passes current to the distributor cap tower contacts.

SECONDARY CIRCUIT: The high voltage side of the ignition system, usually above 20,000 volts. The secondary includes the ignition coil, coil wire, distributor cap and rotor, spark plug wires and spark plugs.

SENDING UNIT: A mechanical, electrical, hydraulic or electromagnetic device which transmits information to a gauge.

SENSOR: Any device designed to measure engine operating conditions or ambient pressures and temperatures. Usually electronic in nature and designed to send a voltage signal to an on-board computer, some sensors may operate as a simple on/off switch or they may provide a variable voltage signal (like a potentiometer) as conditions or measured parameters change.

SHIM: Spacers of precise, predetermined thickness used between parts to establish a proper working relationship.

SLAVE CYLINDER: In automotive use, a device in the hydraulic clutch system which is activated by hydraulic force, disengaging the clutch.

SOLENOID: A coil used to produce a magnetic field, the effect of which is to produce work.

SPARK PLUG: A device screwed into the combustion chamber of a spark ignition engine. The basic construction is a conductive core inside of a ceramic insulator, mounted in an outer conductive base. An electrical charge from the spark plug wire travels along the conductive core and jumps a preset air gap to a grounding point or points at the end of the conductive base. The resultant spark ignites the fuel/air mixture in the combustion chamber.

SPLINES: Ridges machined or cast onto the outer diameter of a shaft or inner diameter of a bore to enable parts to mate without rotation.

TACHOMETER: A device used to measure the rotary speed of an engine, shaft, gear, etc., usually in rotations per minute.

THERMOSTAT: A valve, located in the cooling system of an engine, which is closed when cold and opens gradually in response to engine heating, controlling the temperature of the coolant and rate of coolant flow.

TOP DEAD CENTER (TDC): The point at which the piston reaches the top of its travel on the compression stroke.

TORQUE: The twisting force applied to an object.

TORQUE CONVERTER: A turbine used to transmit power from a driving member to a driven member via hydraulic action, providing changes in drive ratio and torque. In automotive use, it links the driveplate at the rear of the engine to the automatic transmission.

TRANSDUCER: A device used to change a force into an electrical signal.

TRANSISTOR: A semi-conductor component which can be actuated by a small voltage to perform an electrical switching function.

TUNE-UP: A regular maintenance function, usually associated with the replacement and adjustment of parts and components in the electrical and fuel systems of a vehicle for the purpose of attaining optimum performance.

TURBOCHARGER: An exhaust driven pump which compresses intake air and forces it into the combustion chambers at higher than atmospheric pressures. The increased air pressure allows more fuel to be burned and results in increased horsepower being produced.

VACUUM ADVANCE: A device which advances the ignition timing in response to increased engine vacuum.

VACUUM GAUGE: An instrument used to measure the presence of vacuum in a chamber.

VALVE: A device which control the pressure, direction of flow or rate of flow of a liquid or gas.

VALVE CLEARANCE: The measured gap between the end of the valve stem and the rocker arm, cam lobe or follower that activates the valve.

VISCOSITY: The rating of a liquid's internal resistance to flow.

VOLTMETER: An instrument used for measuring electrical force in units called volts. Voltmeters are always connected parallel with the circuit being tested.

WHEEL CYLINDER: Found in the automotive drum brake assembly, it is a device, actuated by hydraulic pressure, which, through internal pistons, pushes the brake shoes outward against the drums.

How to Remove Stains from Fabric Interior

For best results, spots and stains should be removed as soon as possible. Never use gasoline, lacquer thinner, acetone, nail polish remover or bleach. Use a 3′ x 3″ piece of cheesecloth. Squeeze most of the liquid from the fabric and wipe the stained fabric from the outside of the stain toward the center with a lifting motion. Turn the cheesecloth as soon as one side becomes soiled. When using water to remove a stain, be sure to wash the entire section after the spot has been removed to avoid water stains. Encrusted spots can be broken up with a dull knife and vacuumed before removing the stain.

Type of Stain	How to Remove It
Surface spots	Brush the spots out with a small hand brush or use a commercial preparation such as K2R to lift the stain.
Mildew	Clean around the mildew with warm suds. Rinse in cold water and soak the mildew area in a solution of 1 part table salt and 2 parts water. Wash with upholstery cleaner.
Water stains	Water stains in fabric materials can be removed with a solution made from 1 cup of table salt dissolved in 1 quart of water. Vigorously scrub the solution into the stain and rinse with clear water. Water stains in nylon or other synthetic fabrics should be removed with a commercial type spot remover.
Chewing gum, tar, crayons, shoe polish (greasy stains)	Do not use a cleaner that will soften gum or tar. Harden the deposit with an ice cube and scrape away as much as possible with a dull knife. Moisten the remainder with cleaning fluid and scrub clean.
Ice cream, candy	Most candy has a sugar base and can be removed with a cloth wrung out in warm water. Oily candy, after cleaning with warm water, should be cleaned with upholstery cleaner. Rinse with warm water and clean the remainder with cleaning fluid.
Wine, alcohol, egg, milk, soft drink (non-greasy stains)	Do not use soap. Scrub the stain with a cloth wrung out in warm water. Remove the remainder with cleaning fluid.
Grease, oil, lipstick, butter and related stains	Use a spot remover to avoid leaving a ring. Work from the outside of the stain to the center and dry with a clean cloth when the spot is gone.
Headliners (cloth)	Mix a solution of warm water and foam upholstery cleaner to give thick suds. Use only foam—liquid may streak or spot. Clean the entire headliner in one operation using a circular motion with a natural sponge.
Headliner (vinyl)	Use a vinyl cleaner with a sponge and wipe clean with a dry cloth.
Seats and door panels	Mix 1 pint upholstery cleaner in 1 gallon of water. Do not soak the fabric around the buttons.
Leather or vinyl fabric	Use a multi-purpose cleaner full strength and a stiff brush. Let stand 2 minutes and scrub thoroughly. Wipe with a clean, soft rag.
Nylon or synthetic fabrics	For normal stains, use the same procedures you would for washing cloth upholstery. If the fabric is extremely dirty, use a multi-purpose cleaner full strength with a stiff scrub brush. Scrub thoroughly in all directions and wipe with a cotton towel or soft rag.

MASTER
INDEX